11-05-07 Sadd

D0797029

TEXAS ALMANAC
2006-2007

17.00

SESQUICENTENNIAL EDITION 1857-2007

Published by

The Dallas Morning News

Elizabeth Cruce Alvarez, Editor

Robert Plocheck, Associate Editor

Brian Morren, Art Director

Cover image is of San Francisco de la Espada Mission in San Antonio by John Collier; pastel.

John Collier's artwork has won many awards and recognitions, and his work has been exhibited widely in the United States and abroad, most recently at the Smithsonian Museum, Christie's Auction House, and the New York Historical Society. In addition to pastel and oil paintings, his artistic vision also encompasses sculpture, and many institutions nationwide commission his large figures in bronze. He recently completed four bronze sculptures for the World Trade Center Memorial at St. Peter's Catholic Church in New York. He and his wife, Shirley, live in Dallas.

ISBN (hardcover) 0-914511-37-8
ISBN (softcover) 0-914511-38-6

Library of Congress Control Number: 2005904131

www.texasalmanac.com

Distributed by Texas A&M University Press Consortium
4354 TAMUS, College Station, Texas 77843-4354

To order online, log on to www.texasalmanac.com
To order by telephone, call 1-800-826-8911

The *Texas Almanac* also publishes a companion Teacher's Guide (ISBN 0-914511-39-4), a 130-page supplement containing lessons, activities, maps and puzzles that make use of the factually dense *Texas Almanac*. The Teacher's Guide was developed by a team of veteran social studies teachers and curriculum writers, and each lesson is coded to indicate how it helps fulfill TEKS requirements and TAKS objectives.

Printed in the United States of America

THE SOURCE FOR ALL THINGS TEXAN SINCE 1857

PREFACE

*T*he first edition of the *Texas Almanac* was published in January 1857, only 21 years after Texas won its independence from Mexico and 12 years after it became a state.

One hundred and fifty years later, with the *Texas Almanac 2006–2007*, we celebrate this historic book's sesquicentennial. To mark this occasion, the *Texas Almanac* has undergone a major renovation. Most noticeably, for you regular Almanac readers, the book has been printed in full color, an enhancement that shows off the photographs of the beautiful and varied Texas landscape. There's nothing like looking at a field of bluebonnets — especially when they are blue, rather than gray.

Color also inspired us to re-create all of the Almanac's maps. The *Texas Almanac* has traditionally been a place to go to find maps of the state and each of its 254 counties. Our county maps are unique because we continually update them using many sources. Our new county maps are tremendous because they make use of color and relief, showing the rise from sea level at the Gulf Coast to the 8,749 feet of the West Texas mountains.

The county maps were painstakingly worked on for more than a year, and they show cities and towns, roadways, rivers, lakes, highest elevations, railroads, airports, parks, recreation areas and historic sites. Each county map is accompanied by a locator map, pinpointing where that county is in Texas, and a detailed profile of the county.

All of our state maps, which appear in such sections as Environment, Weather, Recreation, and Business, also were updated and rendered in color. In addition, we included a foldout map of Texas, located between pages 192 and 193, showing the counties and interstate highways, perfect for travelers wanting to enrich their journeys through Texas. We would like to thank map artist Carol Zuber-Mallison for all of the beautiful and informative maps she created for this edition.

This *Texas Almanac* begins with several fascinating articles about the Lone Star State. Associate Editor Robert Plocheck writes about the history of the Spanish Mission system in Texas. Mission buildings and sites, which can be found from San Antonio and Goliad to El Paso, represent a unique part of this state's history. The San Antonio missions comprise the most extensive concentration of mission architecture in the United States. Mr. Plocheck also traveled the state, literally from one end to the other, shooting photos of myriad places, many off the beaten path.

Award-winning Western author Elmer Kelton of San Angelo writes about ranching, still a major part of the Texas economy and a cherished way of life for many Texans. Mr. Kelton, a longtime farm and ranch writer and editor, tells of the history of ranching and how time and technology have changed this enterprise and the face of the land.

Mary Ramos, *Texas Almanac* editor emerita, writes about the mesquite trees that grow over nearly two-thirds of the state and about the many mineral-water springs that occur in almost every Texas county and the spas that sprang up near them beginning in the late 1800s. Mrs. Ramos also researched the hundreds of Rosenwald Schools that were built in Texas, which served to educate black children in the early 20th century.

This Sesquicentennial Edition of the *Texas Almanac* also includes all of the traditional sections that our readers have come to know and use. They have all been updated with the latest information available to us from the thousands of sources who graciously fill out our surveys and supply us with the most current facts and figures available to them.

In 1857, Willard Richardson, the first *Texas Almanac* editor, apologized in his preface for not being able to include everything he wanted to in that edition. One hundred and fifty years later, I must do the same. Texas is vast and varied, and although we try to fill the *Texas Almanac* with the information that is the most important and most useful to our readers, there is always something else we wish we could have added. We hope you enjoy all of the articles and information that we have included and that you use this Almanac to enrich your travels through the state and to learn more about this beautiful and fascinating place that is Texas.

Elizabeth Cruce Alvarez
Editor, 2005

TABLE OF CONTENTS

INDEX OF MAPS

INDEX OF TABLES

Texas

The Lone Star State

On this and the following page we present a demographic and geographic profile of the second-largest, second-most-populous state in the United States. Look in the index to find more-detailed information on each subject.

The Government

Capital: Austin
Government: Bicameral Legislature
28th State to enter the Union: Dec. 29, 1845
Present Constitution adopted: 1876

State motto: Friendship (1930)
State symbols:
　　Flower: Bluebonnet (1901)
　　Bird: Mockingbird (1927)
　　Tree: Pecan (1919)
　　Song: "Texas, Our Texas" (1929)

Origin of name: Texas, or Tejas, was the Spanish pronunciation of a Caddo Indian word meaning "friends" or "allies."

Nickname: Texas is called the Lone Star State because of the design of the state flag: a broad vertical blue stripe at left centered by a single white star, and at right, horizontal bars of white (top) and red.

The People

Population (Jan. 2004 State Data Center estimate) 22,490,022
Population (July 2002 U.S. Bureau of the Census estimate) 21,779,893
Population, 2000 U.S. Census count 20,851,820
Population, 1990 U.S. Census count 16,986,510
Population increase, 1990–2000 . . . . 22.8%
Population increase, 2000–2004 . . . . 7.9%

Ethnicity, 2000 (for explanation of categories, see **page 167**):

	Number	Percent
Anglo	11,074,716	53.11%
Hispanic	6,669,666	31.99%
Black	2,421,653	11.61%
Other	685,785	3.29%

Population density (2003) . . . . 84.5 per sq. mi.
Voting-age population (2004) 16,071,153
(Statistical Abstract of the United States 2004–2005)

On an Average Day in Texas in 2002:

There were **1,020** resident live **births**.
There were **426** resident **deaths**.
There were **594** more births than deaths.
There were **499** marriages.
There were **234** divorces.
(2003 Texas Vital Statistics, Texas Dept. of Health)

Ten largest cities:

Houston (Harris Co.)	2,033,400
San Antonio (Bexar Co.)	1,228,512
Dallas (Dallas Co.)	1,211,437
Austin (Travis Co.)	681,437
Fort Worth (Tarrant Co.)	592,836
El Paso (El Paso Co.)	588,452
Arlington (Tarrant Co.)	361,717
Corpus Christi (Nueces Co.)	278,708
Plano (Collin Co.)	252,368
Garland (Dallas Co.)	219,070

(January 2004 State Data Center estimate)

Number of counties 254
Number of incorporated cities 1,210
Number of cities of 100,000 pop. or more 25
Number of cities of 50,000 pop. or more 58
Number of cities of 10,000 pop. or more 221

The Natural Environment

Area (total) . . . . 268,581 sq. miles
　　(171,891,840 acres)
Land area . . . . 261,797 sq. miles
　　(167,550,080 acres)
Water area . . . . 6,784 sq. miles
　　(4,341,760 acres)

Geographic center: About 15 miles northeast of Brady in northern McCulloch County.
Highest point: Guadalupe Peak (8,749 ft.) in Culberson County in far West Texas.
Lowest point: Gulf of Mexico (sea level).

Normal average annual precipitation range:
　　From 60.57 inches at Jasper County in far East Texas, to 9.43 inches at El Paso, in far West Texas.

Record highest temperature:
　　Seymour, August 12, 1936 . . . . .120°F
　　Monahans, June 28, 1994 . . . . .120°F

Record lowest temperature:
　　Tulia, Feb. 12, 1899 . . . .−23°F
　　Seminole, Feb. 8, 1933 . . . .−23°F

Business

Gross State Product (2003) . . . . $806.2 billion
Per Capita Personal Income (2003) $29,074
Civilian Labor Force (January 2005) 9,443,600
(GSP: Texas Comptroller of Public Accounts and U.S. Bureau of Economic Analysis; per capita income: U.S. Bureau of Economic Analysis; civilian labor force: Texas Workforce Commission.)

Principal products:

Manufactures: Chemicals and allied products, petroleum and coal products, food and kindred products, transportation equipment.

Farm products: Cattle, cotton, vegetables, fruits, nursery and greenhouse, dairy products.

Minerals: Petroleum, natural gas, natural gas liquids.

Finance (as of 12/31/2004):
　　Number of banks 639
　　Total deposits. $122,928,270,000
　　Number of savings and loan associations 20
　　Total assets $51,000,806,000
　　Number of savings banks 22
　　Total assets $12,981,650,000
(Banks: Federal Reserve Bank of Dallas; savings and loans and savings banks: Texas Savings and Loan Dept.)

Agriculture:
　　Total farm marketings, 2002 . . . .$14,664 million
　　Number of farms, 2002 229,000
　　Land in farms (acres, 2002). . . . . 129.9 million
　　Cropland (acres, 2000) 26,938,000
　　Pastureland (acres, 2000) 15,914,000
　　Rangeland (acres, 2000). 95,745,000
(2004–2005 Statistical Abstract of the United States)

Texas' Rank Among the United States

Texas' rank among the United States in selected categories are given below. Others categories are covered in other sections in the Texas Almanac, such as, Agriculture, Business and Transportation, Science and Health.

Source (unless otherwise noted): Statistical Abstract of the United States, 2002 and 2004–2005, U.S. Census. Bureau: **www.census.gov/statab/www/**

Ten Most Populous States, 2003

Rank	Population 2000	%Change 2000–2003
1.	California 35,484,000	. . . . 4.8
2.	**Texas. 22,119,000**	**. 6.1**
3.	New York 19,190,000	. . . . 1.1
4.	Florida 17,019,000	. . . . 6.5
5.	Illinois. 12,654,000	. . . . 1.9
6.	Pennsylvania 12,365,000	. . . . 0.7
7.	Ohio 11,436,000	. . . . 0.7
8.	Michigan 10,080,000	. . . . 1.4
9.	Georgia 8,685,000	. . . . 6.1
10.	New Jersey 8,638,000	. . . . 2.7

(United States, ... 290,810,000 . . . . 3.3)

Ten Fastest Growing States, 2003

Rank	State	Population Change 2000–2003
1.	Nevada. 12.2%
2.	Arizona. 8.8%
3.	Florida 6.5%
4.	**Texas. 6.1%**
5.	Georgia 6.1%
6.	Colorado. 5.8%
7.	Idaho 5.6%
8.	Utah 5.3%
9.	California 4.8%
10.	North Carolina 4.5%

States with Highest Immigration, 2002

Rank	State	Immigrants
1.	California 219,216
2.	New York 114,827
3.	Florida 90,819
4.	**Texas. 88,365**
5.	New Jersey 57,721
6.	Illinois 47,235
7.	Massachusetts. 31,615
8.	Washington 25,704
9.	Virginia. 25,411
10.	Maryland 23,751

(United States. . . . . 1,063,732)

States with Most Live Births, 2002

Rank	State	Births
1.	California. 529,357
2.	**Texas 372,450**
3.	New York 251,415
4.	Florida 205,579
5.	Illinois 180,622
6.	Ohio. 148,720

(United States . . . . 4,021,726)

States with Highest Birth Rates, 2002

Rank	State	Births per 1,000 Pop.
1.	Utah. 21.2
2.	**Texas 17.1**
3.	Arizona 16.1
4.	Georgia 15.6
5.	Idaho 15.6
6.	Colorado 15.2

(United States . . . . 13.9)

States with Most Farms, 2002

Rank	State	No. of Farms
1.	**Texas 229,000**
2.	Missouri 107,000
3.	Iowa 91,000
4.	Tennessee. 88,000
5.	Kentucky 87,000
6.	Oklahoma 83,000

States with Most Land in Farms, 2002

Rank	State	Farm Acreage
1.	**Texas. 129,900,000**
2.	Montana. 59,600,000
3.	Kansas. 47,200,000
4.	Nebraska. 45,900,000
5.	New Mexico 44,800,000
6.	South Dakota. 44,800,000

State Flags and Symbols

Our thanks to Charles A. Spain, Jr., of Houston for his advice in updating this section of the Texas Almanac.

United States, 1845–1861; 1865–Present

Republic, 1836–1845; State, 1845–Present

Spain
1519–1685
1690–1821

Mexico
1821–1836

France
1685–1690

Confederate
States of
America
1861–1865

Texas often is called the **Lone Star State** because of its state flag with a single star. The state flag was also the **flag of the Republic of Texas**. The following information about historic Texas flags, the current flag and other Texas symbols may be supplemented by information available from the **Texas State Library** in Austin. (On the Web: **www.texasalmanac.com/flags.htm** and **www.tsl.state.tx.us/ref/abouttx/index.html#flags**)

Six Flags of Texas

Six different flags have flown over Texas during eight changes of sovereignty. The accepted sequence of these flags follows:

Spanish — 1519–1685
French — 1685–1690
Spanish — 1690–1821
Mexican — 1821–1836
Republic of Texas — 1836–1845
United States — 1845–1861
Confederate States of America — 1861–1865
United States — 1865 to the present.

Evolution of the Lone Star Flag

The Convention at Washington-on-the-Brazos in March 1836 allegedly adopted a flag for the Republic that was designed by Lorenzo de Zavala. The design of de Zavala's flag is unknown, but the convention journals state that a "Rainbow and star of five points above the western horizon; and a star of six points sinking below" was added to de Zavala's flag.

There was a suggestion that the letters "T E X A S" be placed around the star in the flag, but there is no evidence that the Convention ever approved a final flag design. Probably because of the hasty dispersion of the Convention and loss of part of the Convention notes, nothing further was done with the Convention's proposals for a national flag. A **so-called "Zavala flag"** is sometimes flown in Texas today that consists of a blue field with a white five-pointed star in the center and letters "T E X A S" between the star points, but there is no historical evidence to support this flag's design.

The **first official flag of the Republic,** known as the **National Standard of Texas** or **David G. Burnet's flag,** was adopted by the Texas Congress and approved by President Sam Houston on Dec. 10, 1836. The design "shall be an azure ground with a large golden star central."

The Lone Star Flag

On Jan. 25, 1839, President Mirabeau B. Lamar approved the adoption by Congress of a new national flag. This flag consisted of "a blue perpendicular stripe of the width of one third of the whole length of the flag, with a white star of five points in the centre thereof, and two horizontal stripes of equal breadth, the upper stripe white, the lower red, of the length of two thirds of length of the whole flag." This is the **Lone Star Flag,** which later became the state flag.

Although Senator William H. Wharton proposed the adoption of the Lone Star Flag in 1838, no one knows who actually designed the flag. The legislature in 1879 inadvertently repealed the law establishing the state flag, but the legislature adopted a new law in 1933 that legally re-established the flag's design.

The red, white and blue of the state flag stand, respectively, for bravery, purity and loyalty. The proper finial for use with the state flag is either a star or a spearhead. Texas is one of only two states that has a flag that formerly served as the flag of an independent nation. The other is Hawaii.

Rules for Display of the State Flag

The Texas Flag Code was first adopted in 1933 and completely revised in 1993. Laws governing display of the state flag are found in sections 3100.051 through 3100.072 of the Texas Government Code. (On the Web: **www.tsl.state.tx.us/ref/abouttx/flagcode.html**). A summary of those rules follows:

The Texas flag should be displayed on state and national holidays and on special occasions of historical significance, and it should be displayed at every school on regular school days. **When flown out-of-doors,** the Texas flag should not be flown earlier than sunrise nor later than sunset unless properly illuminated. It should not be left out in inclement weather unless a weatherproof flag is used. It should be flown with the white stripe uppermost except in case of distress.

No flag other than the **United States flag** should be placed above or, if on the same level, to the state flag's right (observer's left). The state flag should be underneath the national flag when the two are flown from the same halyard. **When flown from adjacent flagpoles,** the national flag and the state flag should be of approximately the same size and on flagpoles of equal height; the national flag should be on the flag's own right (observer's left).

If the state flag is displayed with the flag of another U.S. state, a nation other than the U.S., or an international organization, the state flag should be, from an observer's perspective, to the left of the other flag on a separate flagpole or flagstaff, and the state flag should not be above the other flag on the same flagpole or flagstaff or on a taller flagpole or flagstaff. If the state flag and the U.S. flag are displayed from crossed flagstaffs, the state flag should be, from an observer's perspective, to the right of the U.S. flag and the state flag's flagstaff should be behind the U.S. flag's flagstaff.

When the flag is displayed horizontally, the white stripe should be above the red stripe and, from an observer's perspective, to the right of the blue stripe. **When the flag is displayed vertically,** the blue stripe should be uppermost and the white stripe should be to the state flag's right (observer's left).

If the state and national flags are both **carried in a procession,** the national flag should be on the marching right and state flag should be on the national flag's left (observer's right).

On Memorial Day, the state flag should be displayed at half-staff until noon and at that time raised to the peak of the flagpole. **On Peace Officers Memorial Day** (May 15), the state flag should be displayed at half-staff all day, unless that day is also Armed Forces Day.

The state flag should not touch anything beneath it or be dipped to any person or things except the U.S. flag. Advertising should not be fastened to a flagpole, flagstaff or halyard on which the state flag is displayed. If a state flag is no longer used or useful as an emblem for display, it should be destroyed, preferably by burning. A **flag retirement ceremony** is set out in the Texas Gov-

The Texas quarter began circulating in 2004. File photo.

ernment Code at the Texas State Library Web site mentioned above.

Pledge to the Texas Flag

A pledge to the Texas flag was adopted by the 43rd Legislature. It contained a phrase, "Flag of 1836," which inadvertently referred to the David G. Burnet flag instead of the Lone Star Flag adopted in 1839. In 1965, the 59th Legislature changed the pledge to its current form:

"Honor the Texas flag;
I pledge allegiance to thee,
Texas, one and indivisible."

A person reciting the pledge to the state flag should face the flag, place the right hand over the heart and remove any easily removable hat.

The pledge to the Texas flag may be recited at all public and private meetings at which the pledge of allegiance to the national flag is recited and at state historical events and celebrations. The pledge to the Texas flag should be recited after the pledge of allegiance to the United States flag if both are recited.

State Song

The state song of Texas is **"Texas, Our Texas."** The music was written by the late William J. Marsh (who died Feb. 1, 1971, in Fort Worth at age 90), and the words by Marsh and Gladys Yoakum Wright, also of Fort Worth. It was the winner of a state song contest sponsored by the legislature and was adopted in 1929. The wording has been changed once: Shortly after Alaska became a state in Jan. 1959, the word "Largest" in the third line was changed by Mr. Marsh to "Boldest." The text follows:

Texas, Our Texas

Texas, our Texas! All hail the mighty State!
Texas, our Texas! So wonderful, so great!
Boldest and grandest, Withstanding ev'ry test;
O Empire wide and glorious, You stand supremely blest.
Chorus
God bless you Texas!
And keep you brave and strong,
That you may grow in power and worth,
Thro'out the ages long.

Refrain

Texas, O Texas! Your freeborn single star,
Sends out its radiance to nations near and far.
Emblem of freedom! It sets our hearts aglow,
With thoughts of San Jacinto and glorious Alamo.

Texas, dear Texas! From tyrant grip now free,
Shines forth in splendor your star of destiny!
Mother of heroes! We come your children true,
Proclaiming our allegiance, our faith, our love for you.

State Motto

The state motto is **"Friendship."** The word Texas, or Tejas, was the Spanish pronunciation of a Caddo Indian word meaning "friends" or "allies." (41st Legislature in 1930.)

State Citizenship Designation

The people of Texas usually call themselves **Texans.** However, **Texian** was generally used in the early period of the state's history.

State Seal

The design of the **obverse (front)** of the State Seal consists of "a star of five points encircled by olive and live oak branches, and the words, 'The State of Texas'." (State Constitution, Art. IV, Sec. 19.) This design is a slight modification of the Great Seal of the Republic of Texas, adopted by the Congress of the Republic, Dec. 10, 1836, and readopted with modifications in 1839.

An official design for the **reverse (back)** of the seal was adopted by the 57th Legislature in 1961, but there were discrepancies between the written description and the artistic rendering that was adopted at the same time. To resolve the problems, the 72nd Legislature in 1991 adopted an official design.

The 73rd Legislature in 1993 finally adopted the reverse by law. The current description is in the Texas Government Code, section 3101.001:

"(b) The reverse side of the state seal contains a shield displaying a depiction of: (1) the Alamo; (2) the cannon of the Battle of Gonzales; and (3) Vince's Bridge. (c) The shield on the reverse side of the state seal is encircled by: (1) live oak and olive branches; and (2) the unfurled flags of: (A) the Kingdom of France; (B) the Kingdom of Spain; (C) the United Mexican States: (D) the Republic of Texas; (E) the Confederate States of America; and (F) the United States of America. (d) Above the shield is emblazoned the motto, "REMEMBER THE ALAMO," and beneath the shield are the words, "TEXAS ONE AND INDIVISIBLE." (e) A white five-pointed star hangs over the shield, centered between the flags."

State Symbols

State Bird — The **mockingbird** (*Mimus polyglottos*) is the state bird of Texas, adopted by the 40th Legislature of 1927 at the request of the Texas Federation of Women's Clubs.

State Flower — The state flower of Texas is the **bluebonnet,** also called **buffalo clover, wolf flower** and *el conejo* (the rabbit). The bluebonnet was adopted as the state flower, on request of the Society of Colonial Dames in Texas, by the 27th Legislature in 1901. The original resolution designated *Lupinus subcarnosus* as

State Seal of Texas

the state flower, but a resolution by the 62nd Legislature in 1971 provided legal status as the state flower of Texas for "*Lupinus Texensis* and any other variety of bluebonnet."

State Tree — The **pecan** is the state tree of Texas. The sentiment that led to its official adoption probably grew out of the request of Gov. James Stephen Hogg that a pecan tree be planted at his grave. The 36th Legislature in 1919 adopted the pecan tree.

Other Symbols

(In 2001, the legislature placed restrictions on the adoption of future symbols by requiring that a joint resolution to designate a symbol must specify the item's historical or cultural significance to the state.)

State Air Force — The **Confederate Air Force**, based in Midland at the Midland International Airport, was proclaimed the state air force of Texas by the 71st Legislature in 1989.

State Dinosaur — The **Brachiosaur Sauropod, Pleurocoelus**, was designated the state dinosaur by the 75th Legislature in 1997.

State Dish — **Chili** was proclaimed the Texas state dish by the 65th Legislature in 1977.

State Fiber and Fabric — **Cotton** was designated the state fiber and fabric by the 75th Legislature in 1997.

State Fish — The **Guadalupe bass,** a member of the genus *Micropterus* within the sunfish family, was named the state fish of Texas by the 71st Legislature in 1989. It is one of a group of fish collectively known as black bass.

State Folk Dance — The **square dance** was designated the state folk dance by the 72nd Legislature in 1991.

State Fruit — The **Texas red grapefruit** was designated the state fruit by the 73rd Legislature in 1993.

State Gem — **Texas blue topaz,** the state gem of Texas, is found in the Llano uplift area, especially west to northwest of Mason. It was designated by the 61st Legislature in 1969.

State Grass — **Sideoats grama** (*Bouteloua curtipendula*), a native grass found on many different soils, was designated by the 62nd Legislature as the state grass of Texas in 1971.

State Insect — The **Monarch butterfly** (*Danaus plexippus*) was designated the state insect by the 74th Legislature in 1995.

State Mammals — The **armadillo** was designated the state **small mammal**; the **longhorn** was designated the state **large mammal**; and the **Mexican free-tailed bat** was designated the state **flying mammal** by the 74th Legislature in 1995.

State Musical Instrument — The **guitar** was named the state musical instrument of Texas by the 75th Legislature in 1997.

State Native Pepper — The **chiltepin** was named the state native pepper of Texas by the 75th Legislature in 1997.

State Pepper — The **jalapeño pepper** was designated the state pepper by the 74th Legislature in 1995.

State Plant — The **prickly pear cactus** was designated the state plant by the 74th Legislature in 1995.

State Reptile — The **Texas horned lizard** was named the state reptile by the 73rd Legislature in 1993.

State Seashell — The **lightning whelk** *(Busycon perversum pulleyi)* was named as the official state seashell by the 70th Legislature in 1987. One of the few shells that open on the left side, the lightning whelk is named for its colored stripes. It is found only on the Gulf Coast.

State Ship — The battleship **Texas** was designated the state ship by the 74th Legislature in 1995.

State Shrub — The **crape myrtle** *(Lagerstroemia indica)* was designated the official state shrub by the 75th Legislature in 1997.

The bluebonnet was adopted as the state flower by the 27th Legislature in 1901.

The mockingbird was adopted as the state bird by the 40th Legislature in 1927.

State Sport — **Rodeo** was named the state sport of Texas by the 75th Legislature in 1997.

State Stone — **Petrified palmwood**, found in Texas principally in counties near the Texas Gulf Coast, was designated the state stone by the 61st Legislature in 1969.

State Tartan — The Texas Bluebonnet Tartan was named the official state tartan by the 71st Texas Legislature in 1989.

State Vegetable — The **Texas sweet onion** was designated the state vegetable by the 75th Legislature in 1997. ☆

The Spanish Missions of Texas
Cooperation and Conflict Color Life for Indians, Friars and Soldiers
By Robert Plocheck

*T*he Spanish royal administration closely coordinated all missionary activity in the New World. The intermingling of church and state was a legacy of Spain's own long struggle to push Islam out of the Iberian Peninsula and to re-establish a homogeneous Christian faith and culture there. This experience of reconquest set the Spanish nation on a crusade for most of the rest of its history, combining all civil and religious activity into one.

In Texas, this meant that only rarely did missionaries venture into hinterlands without official authorization and without soldiers being stationed at nearby presidios for protection. This process of approving a new mission could be lengthy, sometimes beginning in Spain, but often determined by the viceroy in Mexico. The friars were almost always eager, but politics and financial restraints often created delays by the civil authorities. The establishment of the Texas missions, which were to total some 35, came in spurts, following the rhythm of the fortunes of Spain.

The Order of Friars Minor, known as the Franciscans, was founded by St. Francis of Assisi in the 13th century. It was the Franciscans who were given responsibility for all the Texas missions. The first missionary journeys into Texas came from the west, where the Franciscans had begun evangelizing the Indian pueblos around Santa Fe soon after it was made the capital of New Mexico in 1610.

These earliest missions at San Angelo, El Paso and Presidio were directed from New Mexico, but later most of the Texas missions were directed from two conventos or colegios (colleges) of Franciscans in Mexico. These two units of the order that had custody of the Texas missions were the College of Santa Cruz at Querétero and the College of Nuestra Señora de Guadalupe at Zacatecas. Later, there were three missionaries from the College of San Fernando in Mexico City who served at the Apache missions on the San Saba River and the upper Nueces River.

This division of custody between the colleges of Querétero and Zacatecas was reflected in various decisions throughout the Texas mission history. For example, when the civil authorities removed the Presidio de los Dolores from East Texas (Nacogdoches County) in 1729, the Querétero Franciscans decided to remove their three missions from the area and eventually relocate them to San Antonio, while the nearby Zacatecas missions in Nacogdoches and San Augustine remained.

Besides providing protection for the Spanish missions and nearby settlements, the soldiers who lived at the presidios often became the source of trouble with the Indians and were often in conflict with the friars. Thus, there was a constant dilemma over whether to place the presidio close enough to the mission to provide quick

Mission San José is one of several 18th century missions along a nine-mile stretch in south San Antonio that make up the San Antonio Missions National Historical Park. It is the most extensive concentration of mission architecture in the United States. Texas Almanac photo.

response during attack or far enough away to keep the soldiers from harassing and aggravating the mission Indians.

The general purpose of the missions was to "reduce" or congregate the often nomadic tribes into a settlement, convert them to Christianity, and teach them crafts and agricultural techniques. Once these goals were met, the mission was to be "secularized"; that is, the church was to be turned over to the local bishop and administered by "secular" clergy (local priests not belonging to a religious order). The land was to be turned over to the Christianized Indians.

The Spanish civil authorities saw the missions and presidios as financial drains and were often the early proponents of shutting down the mission activities. Almost without exception, the decision to secularize was opposed by the friars. They felt the Indians were not sufficiently educated and would be taken advantage of by the authorities and the Spanish settlers. Thus, not until 1830 were the last missions in Texas secularized.

Early morning worshippers leave Ysleta Mission, above, in south El Paso. Renovation work was conducted on Socorro Mission, below, in 2004. These missions, along with the Chapel of San Elizario, are part of the El Paso Mission Trail. Texas Almanac photos.

Early Evangelizing

The first mission in Texas was established in 1632 near present-day San Angelo. It was a follow-up effort to an initial 1629 missionary trip to the area at the request of the Jumano Indians, which was the first journey into Texas specifically for Christian evangelization. The Spanish Franciscans spent only a short time there in 1629 but promised to return. The 1632 mission existed for six months before it was abandoned because of its remoteness from the Franciscan home base in New Mexico (see "Franciscan Missionaries to Texas before 1690," *Texas Almanac 2004–2005*).

This mission is believed to have been located near the confluence of the Concho River and the Colorado River, which was known as the Río San Clemente at that time. (Later, in 1684, another San Clemente mission was located in the same general area; see San Clemente section, below). Today, there is a small commemorative monument along the Concho River in the city of San Angelo.

El Paso Missions

In 1680, the Indians at Santa Fe in northern New Mexico revolted, causing the Spanish settlers there to flee and take refuge in the El Paso area. Along with the Spanish came friendly Indian tribes who settled along the Rio Grande. Here, the Franciscans began the missions of Corpus Christi de la Isleta (Ysleta), Nuestra Señora de la Limpia Concepción del Socorro and San

Antonio de Senecú.

Ysleta exists today as a parish, although in 1881 the church name was changed to Our Lady of Mount Carmel. The present mission church, which dates to an 1851 reconstruction, required major renovation after a 1907 fire. However, some of the walls and bells date to the 1744 church.

Socorro also exists today as a parish, La Purísima, with a church built in 1843 and renovated in the 1980s. It is currently undergoing another renovation.

There is a state historical marker two miles north of Ysleta marking the approximate site of the Senecú mission.

The first missionary efforts in the whole area of El Paso del Norte were on the Mexican side of the Rio Grande in the 1630s. After failed attempts, a temporary church was built in 1656 and a successful mission was founded in 1659. There were subsequent missions in the area, and some sources say the Senecú mission was established soon after 1659 and before the refugees arrived from New Mexico in 1680.

Other sources list a fourth church after 1680, San

Lorenzo, on the Texas side, but this appears to have been primarily a settlement of the Spanish refugees and was not a mission for Indians. But historian Robert S. Weddle says San Lorenzo later became a mission in 1726. Historian Carlos Castañeda says the settlement, Real de San Lorenzo, was first located at present-day San Elizario. In 1684, San Lorenzo was moved upriver to be closer to the protection of the presidio. In 1936, a state historical marker was placed in south El Paso commemorating San Lorenzo.

Included on El Paso's Mission Trail today is the Chapel of San Elizario (Elceario). It was not a mission but served the presidio that was moved there from across the river in 1789. The present chapel was built in 1877 after floods destroyed the original, and the chapel interior has been redone since a fire damaged it in 1935.

La Junta Missions

In the area of present-day Presidio, in the Big Bend region, the Rio Grande is joined from the south by the Río Conchos of Mexico. Called La Junta (the junction), this area was on the principal route used by the Spanish to travel from the settled areas of northern New Spain (Mexico) to New Mexico. The first missionary efforts at La Junta began as early as 1670.

In 1683 and 1684, the Franciscan friars at El Paso were petitioned by the La Junta pueblos to establish missions at the ancient site. The area is considered the oldest continuously cultivated farmland in Texas. Corn farmers of the Cochise culture settled there around 1500 B.C.

In is not clear which missions were in Texas and which were on the Mexican side, although today most sources agree that El Apóstol Santiago was on Alamito Creek between Presidio and Redford. Also on the Texas side, about four miles to the north along the Rio Grande, was El Navidad de las Cruces. These missions were abandoned in 1688.

State historical markers have been erected for El Apóstol Santiago four miles east of Presidio and for San Francisco de los Julimes 10 miles north of Presidio, although most sources now believe San Francisco de los Julimes was one of the La Junta missions on the Mexican side of the Rio Grande.

San Clemente Mission

In 1684, a second mission in the area of San Angelo existed from March to May. Its location was near the juncture of the Colorado (San Clemente) River and the Concho River of Texas (then called the Nueces), most sources say.

Others have placed the mission farther east, on the South Llano River and the San Saba River. Because it is not known exactly where the San Clemente mission was located, several markers in the area commemorate the site. A state historical marker erected in 1968 is about six miles south of Ballinger on US 83 in Runnels County. It states, "The building was probably constructed of logs, its lower story serving as a chapel and its upper story as a lookout post."

There was another state historical marker erected in 1936, about 12 miles north of Millersview on FM 2134 in Concho County. The Texas Department of Transportation has placed a sign in Millersview, and there is a commemorative plaque there at the Church of Our

Lady of Guadalupe.

Records show that thousands of Indians were baptized at San Clemente, but hostile Apache tribes forced the Franciscans to abandon the mission. The missionaries wanted to return to the area, but with the arrival of the La Salle Expedition on the Texas coast in 1685, the Spanish government decided to concentrate its energies on East Texas.

East Texas Missions

Efforts were turned to East Texas in 1690. The missionaries traveled along El Camino Real, the highway through Central Texas, toward Louisiana. Deep into the Piney Woods, just west of the Neches River, they founded San Francisco de los Tejas. Recent research places the site on San Pedro Creek, east of present-day Augusta, and a few miles west of Mission Tejas State Park, which is near Weches in Houston County. The park has a representation of a log chapel that was built in 1934.

A few months after San Francisco de los Tejas was started, Santísima Nombre de María was established closer to the Neches River. There is a historical marker in Houston County four miles east of Weches on Texas 21. In 1692, a flood destroyed Santísma Nombre de María and the friars returned to San Francisco de los Tejas, which, in turn, was abandoned in 1693 because of sickness and hostile Indians.

More Missions at La Junta

From 1700 until 1713, the War of Spanish Succession created turmoil in Spain and frustrated developments in Mexico, but—after the Bourbon king won the struggle with the Hapsburgs—in 1715, more missions were established around Presidio. San Cristóbal was located near the present-day town of Redford, and Santa María de la Redonda de los Cíbolos was located near what is now Shafter in Presidio County. The missions were partially abandoned during periods of Indian hostilities and then re-established. Cíbolos Mission finally was abandoned around 1726 and San Cristóbal around 1775, and both fell into ruin.

These two missions are mentioned in a state historical marker at the site of Fort Leaton, one mile southeast of Presidio. Also mentioned are other missions at La Junta, including San Antonio de los Puliques (sometimes referred to as San José de los Puliques) and San Pedro Alcantara. Whether these missions were east or west of the Rio Grande is not known for sure. In any case, all the missions on the Texas side had ceased to function by 1795.

Return to East Texas

Nuestro Padre San Francisco de los Tejas was re-established on the west bank of the Neches River in 1716 as the successor to the Mission Tejas, the mission that had been abandoned in 1693. In 1721, the mission was moved to the east bank of the river in what is now Cherokee County and renamed San Francisco de los Neches. The site was about seven miles west of the present-day town of Alto. There is a state historical marker on Texas 21.

Also in 1716, three missions were founded in Nacogdoches County: Nuestra Señora de Guadalupe de los Nacogdoches, Nuestra Señora de la Purísima

Texas Missions

▲ 1600s

1. San Clemente, 1632, 1684
2. Corpus Christi de la Isleta, 1680
3. Nuestra Señora de la Limpia Concepción del Socorro, 1680
4. San Antonio de Senecú, 1680
5. La Navidad de los Cruces, 1683
6. El Apóstol Santiago, 1684
7. San Francisco de los Tejas, 1690
8. Santísimo Nombre de María, 1690

◆ early 1700s

9. San Cristóbal, 1715
10. Santa María de la Redonda de los Cíbolos, 1715
11. San Francisco de los Neches, 1716 (originally Nuestro Padre San Francisco de los Tejas)

● mid, late 1700s

24. Nuestra Señora de los Dolores del Río de San Xavier, 1745
25. San Francisco Xavier de Horcasitas, 1748
26. San Ildefonso, 1748
27. Nuestra Señora de la Candaleria, 1749
28. Nuestra Señora del Rosario, 1754
29. San Xavier (San Marcos), 1755
30. San Francisco Xavier on Guadalupe (New Braunfels), 1756
31. Nuestra Señora de la Luz del Orcoquisac, 1756
32. Santa Cruz de San Sabá, 1757
33. San Lorenzo de la Santa Cruz, 1762
34. Nuestra Señora de la Candelaria del Cañon, 1762
35. Nuestra Señora del Refugio, 1793

12. Nuestra Señora de Guadalupe de los Nacogdoches, 1716
13. Nuestra Señora de la Purísima Concepción de los Hasinai, 1716
14. San José de los Nazonis, 1716
15. Nuestra Señora de Dolores de los Ais, 1717
16. San Antonio de Valero (Alamo), 1718
17. San José y San Miguel de Aguayo, 1720
18. Nuestra Señora de la Bahía del Espíritu Santo de Zúñiga, 1722 (relocated inland to site 18c, 1749)
19. San Francisco Xavier de Nájara, 1722
20. Three East Texas missions moved to Colorado River (Austin), 1730
21. Nuestra Señora de la Purísima Concepión de Acuña, 1731
22. San Juan Capistrano, 1731
23. San Francisco de la Espada, 1731

■ visitas, ranchos

A. Tonkawa Bank, 1726
B. Rancho de las Cabras, 1731
C. Nuestra Señora de los Dolores, 1750
D. La Purísima Concepción (Mier), 1750s
E. San Agustín de Laredo, (Camargo) 1750s
F. San Joaquín del Monte, (Reynosa) 1750s
G. San Francisco Solano de Ampuero (Revilla), 1750s

Concepción de los Hasinai and San José de los Nazonis. In San Augustine County in January 1717, the Franciscans founded Nuestra Señora de Dolores de los Ais.

Mission Concepción de los Hasinai was located near Douglass, and there is a state historical marker about seven miles south of the town off FM 225. San José de los Nazonis was in northwest Nacogdoches County. The Texas Department of Transportation has placed a marker about two miles north of the town of Cushing.

In 1719, French incursions from Louisiana caused all the East Texas missions to be temporarily vacated, but they were restored in 1721. While the three missions operated by the Querétero Franciscan college (San Francisco, Concepión, and San José) were removed to

Dating to 1755, Mission Concepción is the oldest structure among the San Antonio missions to survive without major renovation. Texas Almanac photo.

Austin in 1730 (see below), Missions Dolores and Guadalupe remained in East Texas until they were abandoned in 1773. Today, there are state historical markers in Nacogdoches and San Augustine commemorating the two missions.

The Alamo

San Antonio de Valero Mission was established May 1, 1718, as the Spanish created the Presidio of San Antonio de Béxar and the attached civil settlement, which is present-day San Antonio. The community was to be a way-station on the journey from the Rio Grande to the East Texas missions.

After three moves from its original location west of San Pedro Creek, the San Antonio mission was placed at its present site in 1724. The earliest buildings do not survive. The parts that exist today were begun in 1727 when the stone convento was built. The existing chapel, the Alamo Shrine, was begun during the 1750s.

Protecting walls were constructed around the mission because it had to provide for its own defense, since the Spanish administration never completed the presidio. The mission was secularized in 1793, meaning it ceased to be a mission and its services passed to the parish of San Fernando de Béxar, just across the San Antonio River.

In 1803, the old mission buildings housed a company of Spanish soldiers from Álamo de Parras, Coahuila, Mexico, and, from that association, it may have acquired the name, Alamo. Other sources say the name comes from a grove of cottonwoods (álamo in Spanish) growing near the site.

San José

San José y San Miguel de Aguayo was established in San Antonio in 1720. Father Antonio Margil de Jesús, president of the Zacatecas Francisican college, initiated the plans in 1719 after the French incursion had caused the East Texas missions to be temporarily vacated. Like so many missions, San José was at various sites: first, on the east side of the San Antonio River, and finally, in 1739, at its present site on the west side of the river.

The friary was begun in the 1740s. Construction on the present church structure began in 1768, about the same time that the mission was enclosed in protective walls because of hostile Apaches.

The mission was secularized in 1824 and placed under the care of San Fernando Church. Through the following years, the mission buildings deteriorated, including the collapse of the roof, dome and bell tower. In 1933, major restoration began as a collaboration between local church and civic preservationists and the federal Work Projects Administration (WPA) and Civil Works Administration. Since 1978, Mission San José has been part of the San Antonio National Historical Park.

A few miles upriver, San Francisco Xavier de Nájara was established in 1722. This mission lasted only four years before it was merged with San Antonio de Valero.

Goliad

Nuestra Señora de la Bahía del Espíritu Santo de Zúñiga was founded in 1722 on the Bay of the Holy Spirit (La Bahía del Espíritu Santo), now called

Matagorda Bay and Lavaca Bay. The site was across Garcitas Creek from the ruins of La Salle's Fort St. Louis. Although retaining its common name, La Bahía, the mission moved inland, away from the bay, in 1726 to a site near present-day Mission Valley on the Guadalupe River.

Then, in 1749, Espíritu Santo was moved to the north bank of the San Antonio River near Goliad. Despite repeated orders to turn the church over to secular (diocesan) priests, there were still two Franciscan priests taking care of the settlers in Goliad in 1830, when Mission Espíritu Santo became one of the last missions to be secularized.

Deterioration of the physical building occurred over time, until restoration began in the 1930s with Civilian Conservation Corps labor. More reconstruction occurred in the 1960s, so that today the replica mission looks much as it did in 1749. Across the San Antonio River, within sight of the mission, is Presidio La Bahía. The presidio chapel has been virtually intact since 1749.

The earlier locations of La Bahía are noted by state historical markers. The first site is mentioned in the marker at FM 444 and US 59 in Victoria County, which says, "Thirteen miles southeast of Inez is located the site of Fort St. Louis . . . [and] Nuestra Señora del Espíritu Santo."

San Juan Capistrano was the least developed of the San Antonio missions. Its buildings date to 1756 and include the chapel, friary and granary. Texas Almanac photo.

Also, some 10 miles north of Victoria off Lower Mission Valley Road is a marker for the second location of the mission. In Victoria's Riverside City Park, there is a state historical marker for a ranch of the mission called Tonkawa Bank.

Austin

The Spanish authorities decided in 1729 to abolish the presidio, Nuestra Señora de los Dolores de los Tejas, which protected the East Texas missions. The presidio near present-day Douglass was unnecessary, the government said, because of the peaceful demeanor of the Indians. Also influencing the decision was the need for the royal administration to cut expenses. The missionaries of the Franciscan college of Querétero protested the decision, but to no avail.

As a result, the friars decided in July 1730 to remove their three missions, La Purísima Concepción, San Francisco de los Neches and San José de los Nazonis, to a site on the Colorado River, near Barton Springs in present-day Austin.

This site had been suggested by viceregal authorities, but the friars found it undesirable, and within months they petitioned to remove the three missions

once again, this time to the San Antonio River. A state historical maker at Barton Springs briefly mentions the experiment; "During 1730–1731, Spanish friars located three missions here."

San Antonio Relocations

By spring of 1731, the three Querétero missions were relocated to San Antonio, with name changes.

La Purísima Concepción de los Hasiani was situated near what had been San Francisco Xavier de Nájara and became La Purísima Concepción de Acuña, commonly referred to simply as Mission Concepción.

San Francisco de los Neches, a legacy of the original 1690 San Francisco de los Tejas, was relocated at a site farther south along the San Antonio River and renamed San Francisco de la Espada.

Situated between this new Mission Espada and the older Mission San José (y San Miguel), the East Texas mission San José de los Nazonis became San Juan Capistrano.

Today, along a nine-mile stretch in south San Antonio, these three missions, along with Mission San José and the Alamo Shrine, provide the most extensive concentration of mission architecture in the United States.

Mission Concepción's stone church was completed in 1755 and remains much as it was then. The mission was merged with San José in 1815, and by 1819, church services were no longer held there. In 1835, during the Texas Revolution, some of the buildings were damaged in the Battle of Concepción.

In the 1850s, the Marianist religious order acquired title to the mission, and after repairs, the church was reopened for services in 1861. The Marianists deeded the mission back to the bishop of San Antonio in 1911. Today, the virtually unrestored church survives, along with some other buildings.

The small chapel at Mission Espada (shown on the cover) was completed in 1756, but—after the roof collapsed—by 1777 only the façade and the rear wall remained standing. Although officially secularized in 1794, the Franciscans did not give up the mission until 1824. Beginning in 1858, the chapel was rebuilt by the pastor, Francis Bouchu, a diocesan priest who had been a bricklayer and stonemason. He also restored the convent, which served as his residence. The Indian quarters and granary remain as they were built in 1745.

Irrigation ditches and this aqueduct near Mission Espada were built by Spanish missionaries in the 1740s. Today they continue to provide irrigation to farmland. Texas Almanac photo.

San Juan Capistrano was the least developed of the missions in San Antonio and the large church was never completed. The mission was secularized in 1794. What survives today are 1756 buildings, which were also restored by Father Bouchu, including the chapel, friary and granary. In the 1930s and 1960s, further repairs were conducted.

In 1978, all three missions became part of San Antonio Missions National Historical Park, along with Mission San José. Operation of the park began after a 1982 legal opinion by the U.S. Department of Justice that allows the National Park Service to manage the park, while the Archdiocese of San Antonio continues to use the missions as churches.

In addition to the buildings, the elaborate system of dams and acequias (irrigation ditches) built by the Spanish missionaries in the 1740s are preserved and still provide irrigation to farmlands in the area. The system includes an aqueduct, shown above, over Piedras Creek.

In 1995, a ranch outpost of Mission Espada, called Rancho de las Cabras, was added to the national historical park. It is in Wilson County off Texas 97 near Floresville.

San Xavier Missions

Milam County was the site of three missions along the San Gabriel River. The river originally had been named the San Xavier in 1716. (One source says that on his 1828 map, Stephen F. Austin mistakenly labeled the river "San Javriel," a name that evolved into the present one.)

In 1745, a group of Indians approached the missionaries in San Antonio to ask that missions be established in their area. The immediate result was the temporary mission of Nuestra Señora de los Dolores del Río de San Xavier, which was served by one missionary friar.

In February 1748, it was succeeded by the first official mission, San Francisco Xavier de Horcasitas, located on the south bank of the river. This was followed late in that year by the establishment of San Ildefonso, and, early in 1749, the mission Nuestra Señora de la Candelaria. All three were clustered near a presidio, San Francisco Xavier de Gigedo.

Conflict between the missionaries and the military authorities, especially over the soldiers' mistreatment of the Indians, caused the missionary work to suffer, and, at one time, the entire presidio garrison was excommunicated by the missionary chaplain. The continual harassment of the Indians caused the atmosphere to become hostile, such that in 1752, one missionary and a civilian were killed by unknown assailants. Finally, in 1755, the three missions were removed to the San Marcos River.

Various ceramics and glass objects, as well as indications of adobe walls have been discovered in the San Xavier Mission Complex Archeological District. Here, eight miles west of Rockdale on FM 908, there is also a state historical marker for San Francisco Xavier.

On the north side of the river, six miles east of San Gabriel on FM 487, there is a marker for San Ildefonso. Closer to San Gabriel, also on FM 487, is a state historical marker for Candelaria Mission.

San Marcos, New Braunfels

In August 1755, the San Xavier missions were relocated to the San Marcos River near the present-day city of San Marcos. In the year spent there, some 1,000 Apaches joined the missions. However, by 1756, plans were made to establish a mission farther west in Central Texas to reach more of the Apaches. The Indians of San Xavier were transferred to the San Antonio missions, and the property was earmarked for the planned Central Texas mission, Santa Cruz de San Sabá.

One tribe of Indians, the Mayeyes, persuaded the Franciscans to keep a mission in the New Braunfels area. So San Francisco Xavier mission was re-established on the Guadalupe River in late 1756 at present-day New Braunfels. Some accounts say it was renamed Nuestra Señora de Guadalupe. The mission was abandoned in March 1758.

A state historical marker at San Marcos Springs commemorates the San Xavier mission there, and another in New Braunfels marks the site of the Guadalupe mission.

Second Goliad Mission

Disputes between the various Karankawa tribes and the other Indians at Mission Espíritu Santo necessitated the creation of another mission in 1754. Nuestra Señora del Rosario was established in November of that year on the San Antonio River four miles west of Goliad.

There were periods when the mission was abandoned, only to be reopened. By 1789 the mission had developed a ranch with 50,000 head of cattle. Rosario was combined with the mission in Refugio in 1807 and was finally secularized in 1831.

There is a 1936 state historical marker off US 59. Various artifacts have been found among the ruins at the site, which is not open to the public. Among the items found was a mural that is on display at Goliad State Park.

Southeast Texas

To counter the influence of the French in southeast Texas, the Spanish authorities established Nuestra Señora de la Luz del Orcoquisac mission in 1756 on the Trinity River in Chambers County.

This mission and its accompanying presidio, San Agustín de Ahumada, have been described as "two of the most misfortune-ridden outposts of Spain in Texas." Illness, insects and conflict between the missionaries and soldiers plagued the effort. When Spain acquired Louisiana in 1763, ending the French threat, the Spanish administration no longer was interested in the area. In addition, supplies were hard to get because the site was so isolated from the settled parts of Texas. In 1771, most of the garrison left. One missionary stayed at the request of the Orcoquisacs, but he too left a few months later.

In 1936, a state historical marker was placed on the west bank of the Trinity River, but excavations in the 1960s established the site instead on the east bank of the Trinity, near Lake Miller. Outside the post office in Wallisville is a 1970 state marker commemorating the mission.

San Saba River

The Apaches, who had long been hostile to the missions, became the focus of a new evangelizing effort into west-central Texas in 1757. The Franciscans had been interested in such an effort since 1725 and finally received government support following reports of mineral deposits in the area

The remnants of the San Xavier missions, which had existed first in Milam County, were now pooled to establish Santa Cruz de San Sabá Mission on the San Saba River in present-day Menard County.

The Apaches never congregated at the mission. A group of 3,000 camped briefly near the mission in June 1757 but moved on to hunting grounds, leaving only two members of their tribe. They were the only Apaches at the mission when 2,000 members of other tribes, including Comanches and Wichitas, attacked the mission on March 16, 1758. (See "Fate of Spanish Mission Changed Face of West Texas," *Texas Almanac 1996–1997*.)

The garrison of Presidio de San Luis de las Amarillas was four miles away across the river, not close enough to be of immediate help. When soldiers did arrive at the smoldering mission ruins the next day, they found two priests and six others massacred.

The presidio was rebuilt of stone in 1761 and held on for another decade of bloody conflict. It was abandoned in 1770 and officially closed in 1772.

The chapel of Presidio La Bahía has been virtually intact since 1749. It lies across the San Antonio River from Espíritu Santo (La Bahía) Mission, part of Mission Espíritu State Historic Site located within Goliad State Park. Texas Almanac photo.

In 1993, the site of Santa Cruz de San Sabá mission was discovered on private property about three miles east of Menard. There is a 1936 state historical marker on FM 2092 commemorating the mission. Also in 1936, there was an attempt to rebuild the presidio, just west of Menard.

Nueces River

After the destruction of Santa Cruz de San Sabá mission, other sites for evangelizing the eastern Apaches were selected to the south. These missions were to be under the protection of the Presidio de San Luis de las Amarillas, or Presidio de San Sabá, as it came to be called.

In January 1762, San Lorenzo de la Santa Cruz was established on the upper Nueces River. About 12 miles down the river, another mission, Nuestra Señora de la Candelaria del Cañon, was begun in the following month. It took its name from its predecessor that had been among the San Xavier missions.

Again, the Apaches showed they were not interested in settling in the missions, which were not where the viceregal authorities had wanted them located anyway. They wanted new missions to the west of the presidio as way-stations between Texas and New Mexico. Because the two missions were never very successful in converting the area tribes, they were essentially abandoned by 1767, although formal closure did not come until 1771.

The site of San Lorenzo de la Santa Cruz has been excavated on the north edge of Camp Wood in Real County. There is a state historical marker commemorating Nuestra Señora de la Candelaria in the town of Montell in northwestern Uvalde County.

Refugio

The last mission to be established in Texas was Nuestra Señora del Refugio on Feb. 4, 1793. The Karankawa Indians had deserted the two missions in the Goliad area but said they would come to a mission closer to their home area on the coast.

The Indians helped choose the site of the new mission in an area known as El Paraje del Refugio, "Place of Refuge," on Goff Bayou in present-day Calhoun County. However, Indian attacks caused the mission to be moved in 1794 farther inland to Mosquitos Creek. In 1795, the mission moved to its final site at the present-day town of Refugio. After frequent attacks from non-mission Indians and ongoing internal conflicts, the mission was gradually abandoned until, in January 1830, it was officially closed.

In the early 1830s, when Irish colonists arrived, the town was named for the mission and the settlers occupied some of the old buildings. From March 12–15, 1836, the mission church served as a fortress for the Texans at the Battle of Refugio.

By 1859, the mission ruins were described as still the most distinguishing feature of the town. Today, only traces of the foundation of the mission can be found under the present parish church of Our Lady of Refuge. There are no visible remains at the two earlier sites.

Lower Rio Grande Valley

In 1749, in a major colonizing effort along the Rio Grande, four towns were founded on the south bank of the river in Mexico: Reynosa, Camargo, Mier and Revilla (now Guerrero). Some time later, the missions in these settlements all established outposts on the Texas side when some of the settlers began to move across the river. These outposts were visitas and took their names from those missions. A visita was a kind of country chapel that was visited by the priests for Mass or to administer sacraments.

One of these visitas was in Zapata County. It was an outpost of the Mission San Francisco Solano de Ampuero that was in the Mexican town of Revilla. Called Mission Revilla a Visita, it is commemorated with a state historical marker in the present-day city of Zapata at the courthouse plaza.

Also in Zapata County was the ranch settlement of Nuestra Señora de los Dolores, established in 1750, about 11 miles north of San Ygnacio. Today, the site is referred to as Dolores Hacienda. Although a state historical marker put up by the Texas Centennial Commission in 1936 says there was a mission there, later research indicates there was only a small chapel for religious services provided by priests from Revilla.

In 1755, another ranch settlement was founded on the east bank of the river at Laredo. Until 1760, when it received its first resident secular priest, Franciscan friars from the Revilla mission visited Laredo on occasion to minister to the settlers.

The Mexican city of Mier was the site of the mission La Purísima Concepción, and across the river in present-day Starr County was Mission Mier a Visita, begun sometime in the mid-1750s. There is a state historical marker on US 83, 3.5 miles west of Roma. At the same time, another visita was established from San Agustin de Laredo mission in Camargo, Mexico. There is a state historical marker 2.5 miles west of Rio Grande City on US 83.

Farther south in Hidalgo County a visita was established in the mid-1750s from the mission San Joaquín del Monte in Reynosa. A marker in McAllen Park in Hidalgo commemorates the visita.

Robert Plocheck *is associate editor of the Texas Almanac.*

Sources

Ashford, Gerald. *Spanish Texas: Yesterday and Today,* Jenkins Publishing Co., Austin and New York, 1971.

Bannon, John Francis. *The Spanish Borderlands Frontier 1513–1821,* University of New Mexico Press, Albuquerque, 1974.

Castañeda, Carlos E. *Our Catholic Heritage in Texas 1519–1936,* Von Boeckmann-Jones Company, Austin, 1936.

Chipman, Donald E. *Spanish Texas 1519–1821,* University of Texas Press, Austin, 1992.

Habig, Marion A. O.F.M. *Spanish Texas Pilgrimage: The Old Franciscan Missions and Other Spanish Settlements of Texas 1632–1821,* Franciscan Herald Press, Chicago, 1990.

Hickerson, Nancy Parrott. *The Jumanos: Hunters and Traders of the South Plains,* University of Texas Press, Austin, 1994.

Simons, Helen and Cathryn A. Hoyt, eds. *Hispanic Texas: A Historical Guide,* University of Texas Press, 1992. "The Spanish Missions in Texas" by Robert S. Weddle.

Sonnichsen, C.L. *Pass of the North I-II,* Texas Western Press, El Paso, 1968.

Stephens, A. Ray and William Holmes, *Historical Atlas of Texas,* University of Oklahoma Press, 1989. "Spanish Missions."

New Handbook of Texas, Texas State Historical Association, 1996, various: "La Junta de los Ríos," by María Eva Flores C.D.P. and Julia Cauble Smith. "Fort Leaton State Historic Site," by Julia Cauble Smith. "La Isla," and "El Paso Del Norte," by W.H. Timmons. "Nuestra Señora de la Candelaria del Cañón," "San Lorenzo de la Santa Cruz," "San Francisco Xavier Mission on the Guadalupe River," "Antonio Margil de Jesús," by Donald E. Chipman.

"Franciscans," by Marion A. Habig O.F.M. "Catholic Church," and "Spanish Missions," by Robert E. Wright O.M.I. "Juan de Salas," "Nuestra Señora de Guadalupe de los Nacogdoches," by Robert Bruce Blake. "Posalime Indians," by Thomas N. Campbell. "San Francisco de la Junta Pueblo," by Rosalind Z. Rock. "San Clemente Mission," by Mary M. Standifer. "San Antonio de Senecú," by John H. McNeely.

"Catholic Diocese of El Paso," by Okla A. McKee. "San Elizario, Texas," "San Lorenzo, Texas," by Martin Donell Kohout. "Corpus Christi de la Isleta Mission," by Rick Hendricks. "Nuestra Señora de la Limpia Concepción de Socorro Mission," by Ernest J. Burrus S.J. "Santa Cruz de San Sabá," "San Francisco de los Tejas Mission," "Santísimo Nombre de María Mission," by Robert S. Weddle. "San Luis de las Amarillas Presidio," "Nuestra Señora del Rosario Mission," "San Ildefonso Mission," "San Francisco Xavier de Horcasitas Mission," "Nuestra Señora de la Candelaria Mission," by Kathleen Kirk Gilmore. "Nuestra Señora de los Dolores Hacienda," by John Hazelton.

"Hidalgo County," by Alicia A. Garcia. "Zapata County," by Alicia A. Garcia and Christopher Long. "Rancho de las Cabras State Historica Site," by Christopher Long. "Laredo, Texas," by Carlos E. Cuéllar. "La Bahía," "Nuestra Señora del Espíritu Santo de Zúñiga Mission," "Nuestra Señora de Loreto Presidio," "Battle of Refugio," by Craig H. Roell. "Amon Butler King," by Hobart Huson and Craig H. Roell. "Nuestra Señora de la Luz Mission," by Robert Wooster. "Refugio, Texas," "Refugio County," by John Leffler. "Nuestra Señora del Refugio Mission," by June Melby Benowitz.

"San Xavier Missions," by Joan E. Supplee. "San Gabriel River," by Art Leatherwood. "Comal County," by Daniel P. Greene. "San Antonio de Valero," by Susan Prendergast Schoelwer. "Alamo," by Amelia W. Williams. "Nuestra Señora de la Purísima Concepción de Acuña Mission," "José Antonio Díaz de León," by Aníbal A. González. "San Francisco de la Espada Mission," by Clint E. Davis. "Francis Bouchu," by James T. Escobedo Jr. "San José y San Miguel de Aguayo Mission," "San Antonio Missions National Historical Park," by Gilberto R. Cruz. "San José de los Nazonis Mission," by Winifred W. Vigness.

"Nuestra Señora de los Dolores de los Ais Mission," by James E. Corbin. "Travis County," by Vivian Elizabeth Smyrl. "Socorro, Texas." "San Francisco Xavier de Náxara Mission." "San Juan Capistrano Mission." "College of Nuestra Señora de Guadalupe de Zacatecs." "College of Santa Cruz de Querétaro." "Nuestro Padre San Francisco de los Tejas Mission." "San Francisco de los Neches Mission." "Nuestra Señora de los Dolores de los Tejas Presidio."

Journal of Texas Catholic History and Culture, Texas Catholic Historical Society, 1992. "The Legacy of Columbus: Spanish Mission Policy in Texas" by Félix D. Almaráz Jr. "Before They Crossed the Great River: Cultural Background of the Spanish Franciscans in Texas" by Kieran McCarty O.F.M.

Archdiocese of San Antonio, 75th Anniversary.

Diocese of El Paso, online.

San Antonio Convention and Visitors Bureau, online.

Mission Trail Association, El Paso, online.

National Park Service, Washington, D.C., online.

Texas Historical Commission, Austin, online.

Texas Parks & Wildlife, Austin, online. ☆

Visiting the Texas Missions

SAN ANTONIO Missions

The four missions of the San Antonio Missions National Historical Park are open all year. The park visitors center is at San José Mission and is open from 9 a.m. to 5 p.m. every day except Thanksgiving, Christmas and New Year's Day. The missions are on the south side of the city on the Mission Trail that runs parallel and just west of Interstate 37.

Concepción Mission — Closest to downtown San Antonio, the church was completed in1755 and is the oldest structure of the park's missions to have survived without major renovation.

San José Mission — (Full name Mission San José and San Miguel) has the large visitors center that serves the entire historical park.

San Juan Capistrano Mission — Between San José and this mission begins the system of dams and acequias. The church was never built here. What remains today is the small chapel.

San Francisco de la Espada Mission — This southernmost San Antonio mission (depicted on the cover) is just south of Loop 410. Nearby are more of the acequias, the Espada Dam and the aqueduct that make up the irrigation system still in use.

Rancho de las Cabras — The mission livestock ranch is 30 miles south of Espada in Wilson County. Although the site is currently undeveloped, park rangers lead one-hour tours on the first Saturday of each month. It is south of Texas 97, southwest of Floresville.

The Alamo — The shrine of Texas independence from Mexico (originally the mission San Antonio de Valero) is open to the public year-round. This is not part of the national historical park but is maintained by the Daughters of the Republic of Texas.

El PASO Missions

Three mission churches in El Paso are still in operation as places of worship, although the buildings are more recent than the 1680 foundation dates. The El Paso Mission Trail Association works toward preservation of the missions, which are open to the public. The Mission Heritage Association, the Texas Historical Commission, city and county governments, and the Catholic Diocese of El Paso have also helped to preserve the buildings.

Ysleta Mission — Founded as Corpus Christi de la Ysleta, the church is now called Our Lady of Mount Carmel and is a parish of the El Paso diocese. It is located at 131 South Zaragoza near the intersection of Texas 20 and FM 258. The church was severely damaged by fire in 1907 and has been renovated a few times since then. However, some of the walls date to 1744.

Socorro Mission — Nuestra Señora de la Limpia Concepcíon is now called La Purísima, a synonymous abbreviation. The church dates to 1843, with several renovations since, and still serves as a parish. It is located at 328 South Nevarez, a street that runs between Texas 20 and FM 258. (In 2005, the church was undergoing major renovation.)

San Elizario Chapel — The old chapel to the Spanish presidio is the largest existing church on the Mission Trail, which runs south of El Paso. The structure dates to 1877 and Masses still are regularly celebrated there. It is located at 1556 San Elizario Road near the intersection of FM 258 and FM 1110.

Old stone arches connect the convento to the church at San José Mission in the San Antonio Missions National Historical Park. Texas Almanac photo.

GOLIAD Missions

Within the Goliad State Park is the Mission Espíritu State Historic Site. The park, a quarter-mile south of Goliad on US 183, is open seven days a week year-round.

Espíritu Santo (La Bahía) Mission — Reconstructed on the original foundations in the 1930s, the mission today includes interpretive exhibits in the church and adjacent granary.

Presidio La Bahía Chapel — Less than a mile farther south on US 183, this chapel has been virtually intact since 1749, making it the oldest surviving structure in Texas of the Spanish missions and related presidios. The Catholic Diocese of Victoria operates the site, which serves as a community church. The chapel is open to visitors year-round except Thanksgiving, Christmas, New Year's Day and Easter.

Rosario Mission — Contains largely undisturbed remains, mostly foundations. Visitation is by appointment only.

OTHER Missions

All that remains of most of the other mission sites in Texas are state historical markers, which are noted in the accompanying story. Exceptions include:

San Lorenzo Mission — Excavations revealing the mission foundations are on the northern edge of Camp Wood on Texas 55 in Real County.

Mission Tejas State Park — This East Texas park contains only a log structure representing the mission. It is on Texas 21 in Houston County.

Presidio de San Sabá — Partial rebuilding on the ruins of the old presidio are located just west of Menard on US 190. ☆

Ranching in a Changing Land
Landowners Adjust as Time and Technology Alter the Landscape
By Elmer Kelton

*I*t has been said that ranchers and farmers are the original environmentalists. They are directly and forcefully affected every day by their natural environment. Typically, the first thing they do when they step outside early in the morning is to look for sign of a rain cloud. Rainfall or the lack of it, the weather cold or hot, the availability of water are concerns with which they must deal day by day, year by year.

To whatever extent technology has allowed, they have tried to influence their environment to their benefit. Some of the results have been favorable. Others have fallen victim to the unwritten law of unintended consequences, trading one set of problems for another.

Beginning at sunup each day, ranchers deal with the environment. From left, cowboy Ignacio Santillan, neighbor Mike Williams, rancher Mary Joe Reynolds and ranch foreman Clay Furlong prepare for an early morning roundup on Reynolds' West Texas ranch. File photo.

A pristine environment prevailed for the first Texas ranches that began in the late 1600s and early 1700s with Spanish land grants along the Rio Grande. These were stocked by herds from Mexico, where a vast cattle empire already flourished. Like the Indians who had been there first, those Texas rancheros had to accept the land as they found it, for they could do little to enhance it. Their cattle watered at the river or from whatever creeks and springs nature had provided.

Livestock survived or languished on the native vegetation, for it was technically impossible to provide supplemental feed in any significant way. Stock raising expanded as pioneering padres established Catholic missions to the north. Each mission had herds and flocks intended to feed priests and Indian converts. Early Spanish settlements north of the Rio Grande included San Antonio de Bexar, La Bahía (later, better known as Goliad) and Nacogdoches. Herds began to increase around these.

Pressure from hostile Indians forced abandonment of many early land grants. As harried owners and workers retreated south of the Rio Grande, they left cattle behind. In addition, animals straying from loosely tended mission herds added to the numbers propagating in the wild. Few people felt a strong incentive to gather or control them, for they were difficult to handle and had little monetary value.

The Roots of Ranching

For a time, ranching came to be dominated by the missions. Where private operators managed to survive, they followed in general the old Spanish mesta regulatory system, which set standards aimed at establishing individual owners' rights and obligations and minimizing territorial disputes.

Many ranching customs taken for granted today had

their origins in Spain, including branding and ear-marking to denote ownership. Texas ranching derived many of its working procedures from Spanish and Mexican cattle-handling methods. Even much of the ranching vocabulary has been handed down from Spanish, though many of the terms have been Anglicized almost beyond recognition. *La reata* became lariat. *Chaparejos* became chaps. The word *remuda* still denotes a band of horses. The Spanish term *vaquero* became buckaroo in English.

Legal American immigration into Texas began with Stephen F. Austin's Old Three Hundred in 1821, though illegal immigrants had imposed an elusive American presence on the eastern Texas redlands many years earlier. The first Anglo settlers brought with them small herds of English-type cattle, primarily from the southeastern states. These began mixing with the abundant Spanish stock already here. For the most part, early American Texans were farmers to whom cattle were a secondary consideration. They were slow to take hold of the Spanish-Mexican concept of ranching on a large scale.

Most saw the undeveloped native environment as an obstacle to be conquered. They agreed with Austin's declaration that nature was not to be accepted as it was but tamed for the benefit of man. Like their European forebears, they set about to change it by plowing up the land and hacking away at the forests and dense thickets so prevalent in eastern Texas at the time. A clean field and a cleared forest were seen as signs of a progressive civilization.

In Mexican colonial Texas, the 10 years of the Republic, and the early years of statehood, wild cattle were so plentiful that beef had but little value. If a settler wanted meat, he could venture out and kill an unbranded Longhorn. A cattle owner found little outside market because Texas was too far from Eastern states where there might have been a demand. The only paying market for cattle was along the Gulf Coast. There, they were slaughtered for their hides and tallow to be shipped by boat to the Eastern seaboard. Most of the meat went to waste.

Trail Drives Begin

By the 1850s, some limited trail driving had begun, moving cattle afoot to such markets as New Orleans, St. Louis and, in at least one recorded instance, all the way to New York. Though these early experiments had but small economic impact on the state, they set the stage and trained cadres for the legendary drives that would begin after the Civil War. They demonstrated that it was feasible to push sizeable herds for long distances while they lived off the land through which they passed.

The war and Union blockades along the Mississippi stopped most of this traffic, though Texans continued to drive cattle as far as New Orleans to help supply Confederate troops.

During the war years, the numbers of unbranded cattle running free in the southern part of the state mushroomed because of neglect. Many working-age men went into Confederate military service, leaving home, ranches and stock farms tended poorly, if at all.

The state suffered little physical damage during the war. Union troops barely touched Texas soil except on a bit of the Gulf Coast and along the Rio Grande from its mouth up to about Laredo. However, when the guns fell silent, the state was financially drained. Cotton was its only major cash crop capable of finding an outside market and bringing in hard currency. That was not enough.

The surplus of near-worthless free-roaming cattle took on a new significance. Demand for beef was strong in the North and East. Intrepid cattlemen, remembering the pre-war drives to distant markets, realized that animals worth no more than a dollar or two on their home range might fetch twenty dollars if they could be delivered to a suitable market. Jobless men home from the war were happy to become drovers at a dollar a day or less. The cattle could subsist on grass along the way and, if handled properly, might even gain weight on the trail.

Early drives took Texas cattle to Sedalia, Missouri. As railroads pushed westward, drovers switched destinations to such Kansas towns as Newton, Ellsworth, Abilene and Dodge City, each in its own turn. A typical trail herd numbered from 1,000 to 2,000 or 2,500 head, handled by 10 to a dozen cowboys, along with a horse wrangler, wagon cook and perhaps a cook's helper. Drives began with rising of the grass in the spring, typically took two to three months and ended late in the fall. Usually the best prices were paid early in the season, so there was a rush to be among the first arrivals at the shipping points. Those drovers who came late in the fall usually found the market tired and oversupplied.

Moreover, the early herds had the best grass. As each season wore on, plodding hooves left the original trail badly beaten out. Drovers moved their herds to one side or the other, seeking fresh grass. By fall, the hard-used trail was far wider than before. This deepening scar was considered to be of little importance. It was taken for granted that it would heal by next year in time for resumption of the drives. Anyway, there was still lots of land.

Though it eventually became common to speak of "old trail drivers" because later generations knew them as aging men, most of the drovers were young. Many were little more than boys, their first time away from home. It was not unusual for a trail boss to be no more than 21 or 22 years old. As has been said of war, trail driving consisted of long periods of boredom punctuated by occasional moments of sheer terror. Though stampedes and Indian attacks have been the subject of much trail-drive fiction, far and away the greatest hazard was river crossings. The average cowboy could not swim. Many a grave was dug on the banks of a swollen river.

Most drovers turned to other work after one or two trips up the trail. A few, however, stayed with it until the

A cowboy helps drive a herd of Longhorns on Big Bend State Ranch in Brewster County. File photo.

Janell Kleberg surveys the King Ranch in South Texas, where ranching got its start in the state. Janell's husband Stephen "Tio" Kleberg ran the family ranch for many years. The King Ranch marked its 150th year in operation in 2003. File photo.

trails closed for the last time. J. Frank Dobie cited the case of a Hispanic trail boss who had made many journeys to the railroad but finally had to send his son to tell the cattle owner he could not captain the next drive. He apologized that he was ill and "had to stay home and die."

The trail drives helped establish cattle raising as a viable business in Texas by giving the animals a real value. Ranching boomed for a few years. From its beginnings in South Texas with such large operations as the King Ranch, it spread northward into Central and North Texas and eventually into the Panhandle in the wake of the great buffalo slaughter and Indian removal that freed up hundreds of thousands of acres of grazing land. Millions of dollars of European capital flowed into Texas in the quest for the "beef bonanza." Texas cow herds were drifted north into the mountain states to establish ranches on old Indian hunting grounds. Money flowed freely, for a time. And if grass was getting short on the heavily stocked ranges, few felt any great concern. A good rain would bring it back, most believed.

Overgrazing, Drought Take Their Toll

Reality came like a clap of thunder, bursting the speculative bubble. Overgrazing and droughts took a toll on the grass. Severe blizzards of the mid to late 1880s caused catastrophic death losses that staggered cattlemen large and small. A major break in cattle prices added to the financial misery, triggering bankruptcies that reverberated all the way to the counting rooms of New York, England and Scotland.

Those cattlemen who survived became better businessmen and, as a class, more careful, methodical operators. As small settlers took up more and more land that had been regarded as free range, ranchmen began seeing the need to own the land on which their cattle grazed. They started fencing their property with barbed wire to keep their animals in and others out. By isolating their herds, they were able to take advantage of better bulls and upgrade their native Longhorns. They imported such European breeds as Herefords, Shorthorns and Aberdeen-Angus to produce meatier if less hardy off-spring.

Opposition to barbed-wire fences spurred violence in some areas, but free-range advocates lost out to changing times and passage of strict Texas fencing laws.

As an industry, ranching never stood still for long. It was in a constant state of change, adapting to new technology as it appeared. Along with fencing came drilling of wells and erection of windmills to produce water from underground where it did not exist on the surface. This allowed grazing of ranges once regarded as useless because they were too far from water.

Once ranchers had fenced their perimeters, they began cross-fencing into smaller pastures more easily managed with less labor. This made it easier to breed cattle selectively, mating the best bulls with the best cows for quicker progress.

This progress created problems, however. Fencing led to herd concentration and yearlong grazing, which in turn led to deterioration of the range at a rate so gradual that it went largely unnoticed at the time. Most early ranchers had come from elsewhere, usually areas accustomed to greater rainfall. Basing decisions on their previous experience, they tended to overestimate the land's carrying capacity and concentrate more livestock on it than it could safely accommodate, especially in dry country west of the 98th meridian.

Buffalo, the previous dominant grazers, had moved freely across the open range, migrating by seasons. Though in their great numbers they might graze off the grass and trample the ground into powder, they moved on and left the land to rest and recover for months, even years, before they returned. Domestic cattle, by contrast, were confined to a limited space. A cow might live out a long lifetime without moving more than a few miles from where she was born.

The long-range result was loss of the more productive forage and an increase in less desirable grass species and weeds. Invasive woody plants such as mesquite, cedar and whitebrush took hold where there had been little or none before.

An aerial photograph taken some 60 years ago plainly showed the old Chisholm Trail, a line of mesquite brush marking the path the South Texas cattle had followed, scattering seed in their droppings as they moved along. Away from the trail the land remained relatively free of brush. A photograph made there today would show brush covering the entire range. It would be difficult to discern the trail, for the land is all heavily infested.

A Midland-area rancher recalled that when he was a boy early in the 20th century, most of the Midland range was open grassland. Wood was scarce. He recalled chuckwagon cooks traveling miles out of their way to find wood for their fires. In recent decades, millions of dollars have been spent in the same area in an effort to control mesquite.

Various forms of cactus, particularly prickly pear, also spread as a result of constant grazing. Untold amounts of money have been invested in seeking efficient chemical and mechanical methods of fighting this invasion at an affordable cost. In past years, conservationists spoke hopefully of eventual brush eradication. Today the best they hope for is a measure of control.

Conservationists may argue about the various methods of meeting the problem, but it is generally agreed that heavy brush infestation has come at a sizeable cost to the state's water supply. Mesquite, cedar and other such invading plants are of little or no economic value but consume horrendous amounts of water, as well as displacing the original vegetation. They reduce or eliminate water flow into creeks and rivers. They dry up springs and seeps that formerly ran the year around.

The water-improving benefit of brush elimination

This replica of Colonel Charles Goodnight's dugout can be seen at Palo Duro Canyon State Park near Canyon. Texas Almanac photo.

was demonstrated some 30 years ago on Rocky Creek, northwest of San Angelo. Historically Rocky had flowed constantly until the 1920s, when it gradually ceased except after a rain. Old-timers agreed that this decrease in flow was accompanied by a large increase in brush infestation over the watershed. Ranchers along the creek joined hands in an ambitious brush-clearing project. With the brush removed, old springs and seeps once again came to life. Rocky Creek began flowing the year around. It still does, though gradual brush reinfestation has again reduced the flow, proving the old-timers' point.

Brush control for water enhancement is part of the long-range Texas statewide water plan, though the state has done little of it so far.

Financially Hazardous Way of Life

Ranching has always been financially hazardous. Cattle prices have long been cyclical, each high point followed by a sharp slide, then a painfully slow climb back from the bottom. These movements have almost always reflected overall cattle numbers. When they are low, prices move up. When cattle raisers respond to higher prices by increasing their herds, prices break and cause a selloff that further escalates the downtrend.

Though at this writing cattle prices are at an all-time high, they have not been there long, and history indicates that present levels will not long endure. One of the industry's most destructive downturns came in the fall of 1973, when prices plunged precipitously. Over the next three decades, many ranches that had been in family

Cowhands sit near the chuckwagon during a roundup on the JA Ranch at Palo Duro Canyon in 1898. Goodnight started the ranch in 1876, and he is credited with the invention of the chuckwagon. The cowboys' remuda of horses can be seen in the upper right. The JA Ranch is still a working ranch. Photo courtesy of the Panhandle-Plains Historical Museum.

hands for several generations slid into bankruptcy. Cattle ranching—and sheep and goat ranching along with it—went through one of the longest periods of economic stress its participants could remember.

Though predatory animals have been of relatively minor importance to the cattle industry, coyotes will sometimes take down small calves and even attack a cow or heifer while she is giving birth. Predators have had a far greater impact on sheep and goat ranching, to a point that they have driven hundreds of operators out of that business and have caused major shrinkage in the outside perimeter of the sheep-and-goat producing area. Political pressures by animal-rights groups have made it increasingly difficult for stockmen to protect themselves against these predators.

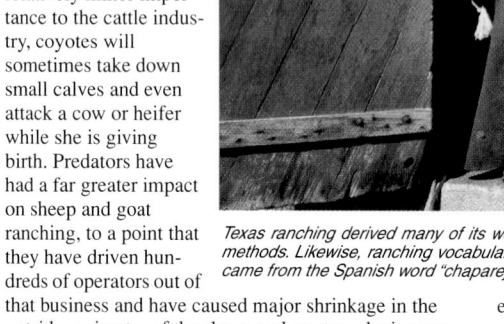

Texas ranching derived many of its working procedures from Spanish and Mexican cattle-handling methods. Likewise, ranching vocabulary evolved from the Spanish, such as the word "chaps," which came from the Spanish word "chaparejos." File photo.

Eradication of the Screwworm

The Texas livestock industry has experienced one great boon in recent times: eradication of the screwworm. This pest, spread by a specific type of blowfly, caused hundreds of thousands of livestock deaths each year and an incalculable toll on wildlife. Through the efforts of agricultural scientists, a method was developed to control them by sterilizing laboratory-raised screwworm flies in the pupae stage through exposure to nuclear radiation, then distributing them in numbers that overwhelmed the native population.

Ranchers accustomed to the old-fashioned way of neutering animals were highly skeptical about doing it to millions upon millions of flies. Despite their doubts, enough of them voluntarily took a gamble on this far-fetched proposition to raise funds for a pilot project that proved the process workable. Texas is screwworm-free for the first time ever. The screwworm was gradually eradicated from Mexico, and a constant barrier is maintained at the Isthmus of Tehuantepec to prevent its return.

Beyond its positive effect on the livestock industry, the elimination of the screwworm caused a boom in wildlife numbers. A high percentage of the Texas fawn crop each year used to die of screwworm infestation. Survival rates have skyrocketed in recent years, at times leading to a serious overpopulation and occasional die-offs through starvation.

Economic necessity has brought many changes to the livestock industry as ranchers have sought ways to supplement their lagging livestock income. A major development has been an increasing emphasis on recreation, especially hunting. Though landowners in the Hill Country had sold hunting leases for many years, ranchers in most other parts of the state took their wildlife for granted. They did not recognize it as an economic resource.

Because of landowner efforts and screwworm eradication, deer are more numerous today over much of the state than when the Indians held the land. On many ranches, particularly in the Hill Country and South Texas, income from hunting of deer, turkey, quail and other wildlife exceeds the income from livestock. Ranchers have catered to hunters by providing special amenities, even to the point of building permanent hunting camps and landing strips, allowing their guests to rough it in comfort. Here and there, some ranchers have abandoned their cattle, sheep and goat operations and devoted all their attention to enhancing their wildlife and hunting potential.

Because Texas hunting seasons restrict native whitetail and blacktail deer harvest to late fall and early winter, exotic wildlife from other parts of the world, particularly Africa and Asia, have been introduced over much of the Hill Country to provide year-around hunting income. By law, native deer are considered property of the state until they are brought down. Exotics, however, belong to the landowner.

Exotics have not been without their problems. Some are highly competitive with native deer and can starve them out if not controlled. This has caused second thoughts among some ranchmen who have experienced a decline in native populations as their exotics increased. Today a trophy whitetail buck will bring a higher premium from hunters than most exotics.

The law of unintended consequences sometimes comes into play. In the 1920s a landowner near San Antonio imported Russian boars for sport hunting. Some escaped, and today these wild hogs have become a menace to calves, lambs and kid goats in many Hill Country counties. Exotic wildlife do not necessarily remain where their owners put them. Many ranchers who originally invested significant sums to acquire them have seen them migrate to neighboring ranches whether they are wanted there or not.

Double-high fences have been built in an effort to contain these exotics, as well as to allow at least some selection in the breeding of native whitetails to produce better antlers and greater body size. However, an undesirable side effect can be intensified grazing and browsing competition by the exotics to the detriment of fenced-in natives.

On many ranches, water for livestock comes from relatively shallow wells, mostly serviced by windmills or small submergible pumps. Their drain on groundwater supplies is minimal. File photo.

Wind and Water

It has been said, with more than a little justification, that the cowboy's life changed relatively little from early ranching days after the Civil War to the outbreak of World War II. He no longer worked on the open range, of course, but within the perimeters of a ranch's fences, and he might go to town in a car instead of on horseback. But on larger ranches he still spent a major part of the year out with a chuckwagon, sleeping on the ground, taking his meals from a line of Dutch ovens after a cook prepared them over hot coals or an open fire. Though the boss in town might have electric lights, the ranch probably did not. The cowboy's method of working cattle was inherited from his open-range grandfather, who in turn had probably learned it from Mexican vaqueros. His wages had not improved much since trail-driving days.

World War II and its manpower shortages forced drastic changes upon the ranching scene. Much of the workforce went into military service. Ranchers had to streamline operations for efficiency, automating wherever possible, cutting pasture sizes, substituting machinery for manual labor, pickup trucks for horses. Most of these changes became permanent, for much of the pre-war manpower never returned. Former cowboys found higher paying jobs in the oilfields and in town.

Many innovations appeared in the first decades after the war: crossbreeding, artificial insemination and computerization being only a few.

A seven-year drought in the 1950s drove home severe lessons in range management, bringing a greater awareness of proper stocking rates, encouraging rotation grazing, grass reseeding, new methods of brush control. Ranchers today tend to know more about conservation than their forebears, calling upon the accumulated experience of past generations as well as their own.

Water is by all odds Texas' greatest long-range problem. Ranching has far less impact upon the state's water supply than do irrigation farming and many types of heavy industry. By and large, livestock's water needs are met by relatively shallow wells, mostly serviced by windmills or small submergible pumps. Their drain on groundwater supplies is minimal. However, ranchers can be affected by both surface and underground pollution, usually coming from outside sources such as oilfields, mining or chemical runoff from cultivated fields.

The condition of the range affects both quality and quantity of runoff water that finds its way into rivers, streams and reservoirs.

A relatively new development in certain areas is landowner sale of water rights to towns, cities and industry, which critics see as having a potential to drain underground reservoirs and leave future generations without sufficient water. They point to experience with the great Ogallala aquifer, which underlies much of the Panhandle. It has been reduced markedly over the last 50 years, largely by irrigation and municipal pumping at levels far exceeding the modest natural recharge rate. Further shrinking of the water table could force irrigation farmers back to dryland operations and leave ranchers without water for their livestock.

Wind has been a constant part of the Texas environment, especially in the western part of the state including the Panhandle. Early plains cattleman Charles Goodnight once remarked that wind became such a part of daily life that he noticed it only when it stopped.

A few ranch owners have found a way to cash in on the wind in today's search for alternative sources of energy. Vast windmill "farms" have sprung up on rangelands in such wind-swept locales as Rankin, McCamey and Big Spring, generating electricity from this one element of the Texas environment that seems inexhaustible.

From an economic standpoint, ranching is no longer as large a segment of the state's economy as it once was. Texas today is regarded as being urban. In terms of population, that is true. Most Texans today live in one of several major urban areas. Yet, all of those areas if lumped together in a single mass would barely cover Presidio County in the Big Bend. The rest of this vast state remains rural, a major part of it privately owned rangeland.

The future of the Texas environment will be influenced heavily by what happens on that land.

Elmer Kelton of San Angelo is an award-winning Western author, who grew up on a ranch in Crane County and worked for many years as a farm and ranch writer and editor.

Suggested Reading

Dary, David, *Cowboy Culture, a Saga of Five Centuries,* Alfred A. Knopf, New York, 1981.

Dobie, J. Frank, *Cow People,* Little Brown & Co., Boston, 1964.

Dobie, J. Frank, *The Longhorns,* Little Brown & Co., Boston, 1941.

Haley, J. Evetts, *Charles Goodnight, Cowman and Plainsman,* University of Oklahoma Press, Norman, 1936.

Jackson, Jack, *Los Mesteños, Spanish Ranching in Texas, 1721–1821,* Texas A&M University Press, College Station, 1986.

Lea, Tom, *The King Ranch, The Hundred Year Story of the Greatest Ranch in the World,* Little Brown & Co., Boston, 1957.

Wellman, Paul I., *The Trampling Herd, The Story of the Cattle Range in America,* Doubleday, New York, 1939.

Wilhelm, Steve, *Cavalcade of Hooves and Horns,* The Naylor Co., San Antonio, 1958. ☆

The Ubiquitous Mesquite

Cursed by Some, Hailed by Others, This Tough Tree Flourishes in Texas

By Mary G. Ramos

"I could ask for no better monument over my grave than a good mesquite tree, its roots down deep like those of people who belong to the soil, its hardy branches, leaves and fruit holding memories of the soil. . . ."
— *J. Frank Dobie, Texas writer*

[Mesquite is] "the devil with roots. It scabs my cows, spooks my horses, and gives little shade."
— *W.T. Waggoner,*
pioneer northwest Texas rancher

*O*pinions of 21st-century Texans on the subject of mesquite are as divided as the two 20th-century views quoted above:

• Ranchers consider it a noxious weed, whose thorns injure cattle, horses and cowhands. Worst of all, its extensive root system uses more than its fair share of water, which otherwise could grow cattle-nourishing grasses.

• Botanists know mesquite (genus Prosopis), a member of the legume family, as a nitrogen-fixing plant. Rather than depleting the soil of nitrogen, as do most plants, mesquites enrich soil by returning nitrogen to it.

• Most gardeners wouldn't consider using the misshapen mesquite in their landscapes.

• Cooks value mesquite chips and charcoal for the luscious flavor they impart to grilled meats and fish.

• Some artisans and furniture makers prize mesquite for its deep colors, rich patina and interesting irregularities.

The ubiquitous mesquite grows—nay, flourishes—on at least one-third of the land area of the state; that is, on more than 56 million of Texas' 167.5 million acres of land, from the Rio Grande to the Panhandle, across Central and North-Central Texas, and into much of West Texas. Mesquite grows in all regions of the state except the East Texas Piney Woods. Of all the mesquite in the United States, 76 percent grows in Texas.

Of the more than 40 species of mesquite found worldwide, at least 90 percent grows in Latin America,

These mesquite logs show the beautiful heartwood. Photo by Mary G. Ramos.

principally Argentina and Chile. Mesquite also thrives in arid and semi-arid regions of North America, Africa, the Middle East, Tunisia, Algeria, India, Pakistan, Afghanistan, Myanmar (Burma), Russia, Hawaii, West Indies, Puerto Rico and Australia.

Seven varieties of mesquite grow in Texas. The most widely distributed is *Prosopis glandulosa* var. *glandulosa*, also called honey mesquite, found in all regions of Texas except deep East Texas. In this article, unless noted otherwise, that is the variety being discussed.

Mesquite trees vary tremendously in size, depending on growing conditions. Where water is plentiful, and if the seedlings are not injured by weather or animals, trees may grow 40 to 50 feet tall, with a spread of 40 feet or more. The trunk forks only a few feet above the ground. If a new shoot is disturbed, the plant develops into a sprawling multi-trunked shrub.

The leaves are delicate and feathery. Sharp, tough-as-nails thorns, up to two inches long, emerge from the base of the leaf stems. The fluffy, creamy-white flowers, which often have a greenish or yellowish cast, appear from May to September. The beans, which mature between August and September, develop in a pod between four and nine inches long. When ripe, the beans are covered by a sweetish coating, which has a sugar content as high as 30 percent. This author can personally

Mesquite Varieties Native to Texas

Scientific name	Common name(s)	Where found
P. glandulosa var. *glandulosa*	Honey mesquite, algarrobo, ironwood	All regions except extreme East Texas
P. glandulosa var. *prostrata*	Running mesquite	Same regions as above
P. glandulosa var. *torreyana*	Torrey mesquite	Trans-Pecos and Southwest Texas high plains
P. pubescens	Screwbean or screwpod mesquite, tornillo	Trans-Pecos
P. reptans var. *cinerascens*	Creeping or dwarf screwbean mesquite	Lower Rio Grande Valley
P. laevigata var. *laevigata*	Mezquite or algarrobo	Nueces County only
P. velutina	Velvet mesquite	Far West Texas
In the above table, "P." before the name is the abbreviation for the genus name Prosopis.		

The National Champion Honey Mesquite grows on a ranch in Real County in South-Central Texas. It is listed on the Texas Forest Service's Big Tree Registry as measuring 172 inches in circumference and 55 feet high, with an 89-foot crown spread. Photo by Susan M. Sander, Texas Forest Service.

attest that they are delicious to chew (you chew the coating off the beans, not the beans themselves) as a substitute for the candy your parents won't let you have.

Mesquite beans furnish food for livestock when grass is scarce. The trees also provide shade, such as it is, for the animals. In the 1840s, a traveler in Texas said that "to find shade under a mesquite tree is like dipping water with a sieve." But in much of Texas, it's often the only shade around.

Mesquites supply food and cover for wildlife including quail, dove, raven, turkey, mallard duck, white-tail and mule deer, wood rat, kangaroo rat, chipmunk, pocket mouse, rock squirrel, ground squirrel, prairie dog, porcupine, cottontail, jackrabbit, skunk, peccary (javelina), coyote and Mexican raccoon.

Mesquite Survival Tactics

Mesquite has several characteristics that help it survive.

• It adapts to almost any soil that is not soggy.

• Mesquite beans can lie dormant for many years—some say up to 40 years—waiting for the right conditions for sprouting.

• Taproots of mesquites are legendary, growing seemingly as deep as needed to reach the water table—often 25 to 65 feet in length. In Texas Highways magazine in 1979, Steve Wilson, then director of the Museum of the Great Plains in Lawton, Oklahoma, reported some mesquite taproots a phenomenal 175 feet long. By contrast, the taproots of most large Texas hardwoods, such as oaks and hickories, reach a maximum of three to seven feet. The longleaf pine, an exceptionally long-rooted tree, has a taproot of only 12 to 15 feet. The mesquite's lateral roots may fan out up to 50 feet in all directions.

• Most of Texas' deciduous trees produce new leaves in late March or early April, putting them at risk of being nipped by a late freeze. The mesquite is one of the last trees to leaf out, usually in May, and therefore is rarely hurt by spring cold snaps. Texas farmers in the 19th and early 20th centuries often waited for mesquites to green up each spring before planting cotton or setting out tomato plants, believing that their crops would therefore be safe from freezing.

History of Mesquites in Texas

The Aztecs called it mizquitl, which the Spaniards Hispanicized into mesquite. Early Anglo-Texans spelled the word in a variety of ways: mesquit, mezquit, muskeet and musquit.

Historians once believed that mesquite was originally limited to extreme South Texas and spread north only after the Civil War when cattle drives became frequent. Cattle eat mesquite beans when grass is not plentiful. The bean's husks are so hard that about 50 percent of them travel through cattle's digestive systems unscathed, to be deposited on the ground with a large helping of natural fertilizer. The historians figured that cattle distributed seeds along the trails as they went north.

But well before the heyday of cattle drives, mesquite was growing in the same areas where it is found today. Mesquite trees were part of Texas' landscape long before Spanish explorers, in the early 1500s, first recorded finding

These utensils made of mesquite were created by Nancy Lou Webster of Elgin. The art of making wooden utensils is called "treen," and Webster sells her treenware at her shop in historic downtown Elgin and on the Internet at www.treenbynancylou.com. Photo by Mary G. Ramos.

them, mainly along Texas' rivers, creeks and draws, but also completely covering some prairies. What has increased since then is not the range, but the density.

The primary reasons for the density increase seem to be the actions of the ranchers themselves:

Control of prairie fires: When unchecked, naturally occurring prairie fires kept mesquite in check. Control of fires as settlers populated the prairies allowed mesquites to grow at will.

Overgrazing: Whether done by cattle, sheep or goats, overgrazing strips native grasses from the land, leaving it bare and open to mesquite invasion.

Eradication of prairie dogs: Range specialists believe that prairie dogs inhibit the spread of mesquite by eating beans, pods and tender new shoots. In 1905, an estimated 800 million prairie dogs inhabited an area of about 90,000 square miles in Texas. But because they competed with cattle for grasses, ranchers, aided by the U.S. Department of Agriculture, poisoned almost all wild prairie dogs in Texas beginning in the early 1900s. Recent estimates put the Texas prairie-dog population at about 2.2 million.

Today's ranchers are still waging the long-running "Great Mesquite Wars" using a formidable array of weapons: diesel oil, bulldozers dragging heavy chains, chemical sprays, prescribed burns and root plowing. Some win occasional costly battles. Overall, though, the mesquite is still winning the war.

Early Uses of Mesquite

As Plains Indians used all parts of the bison, Southwestern Indians used all parts of the tree: beans, bean pods, leaves, roots, trunk, limbs, bark and gum.

Perhaps the first written description of mesquite's uses among Texas Indians was by Spanish explorer Alvar Nuñez Cabeza de Vaca. Shipwrecked and cast up on the Texas Gulf Coast in 1528, Cabeza de Vaca and several companions lived a nomadic life for six years, much of it as Indian captives, before escaping to a Spanish outpost in Mexico. In his journal, he recorded that the natives pounded mesquite-bean pods with a wooden pestle in a dirt hole, mixed the resulting meal with some of the dirt and added water to make a kind of mush.

Later European explorers and Anglo settlers reported Southwestern Indians using mesquite in these ways:

Drink

A drink called atole was made from a decoction of ground beans and water. Fermenting it produced a mildly intoxicating drink—bean beer, so to speak.

Shelter

Trunks and limbs were used for shelters and fencing.

Medicines

Aztecs made a lotion to soothe sore eyes from ground mesquite leaves mixed with water. Yuma Indians treated venereal disease with an infusion of leaves, and Comanches relieved toothaches by chewing the leaves. Yaquis treated headaches with a poultice made from mashing leaves to a pulp, mixing them with water and binding the mixture to the forehead.

Gum, or sap, that oozed from mesquite bark was mixed with water to treat sore throats and diarrhea, aid digestion, and help wounds heal. The Yavapai rubbed a mixture of mud and mesquite gum into their hair to simultaneously kill lice and dye their hair.

Fuel

Roots provided a reliable source of fuel in the generally treeless desert Southwest.

Dye and Glue

The light-amber colored gum that oozes from mesquite bark in the fall was used as a glue to mend pottery. Indian women made cuts in the bark to gather a darker gum, full of tannins, to use as hair dye or to decorate bark clothing.

Clothing

Indian women pounded bark into flat sheets of fiber for clothing.

Recreational Equipment

Papago Indians used a ball made of mesquite wood or gum about the size of a croquet ball in a footrace game. Pimas used mesquite sticks and Maricopas used a mesquite ball in games similar to field hockey.

Other Tools and Equipment

Southwestern Indians used mesquite wood or root fiber to fashion harpoons, harpoon cords, bowstrings, cradles, and agricultural tools including weed cutters and planters. Mesquite gum glued arrow points and feathers onto arrow shafts, and it waterproofed the insides and outsides of basket-jars for carrying water.

Mexicans fattened cattle and hogs on mesquite beans and pods. Rural Mexican women whitened their clothes by boiling mesquite leaves along with clothing in their wash pots.

Mesquite Uses by Settlers

Early settlers in Texas favored mesquite wood for fences because not only was it plentiful, but it also resisted rotting. Before commercial barbed wire came to Texas in the mid-1870s, ranchers built sturdy corrals from mesquite-log picket fences. Travelers fashioned hubs and spokes for wagon wheels from mesquite, as well as ribs for small boats. Railroad crews used mesquite logs and roots as boiler fuel.

During the Civil War when coffee was scarce, Texans made ersatz coffee from roasted and ground mesquite beans, in addition to okra seeds, wheat, corn or acorns. They boiled dried mesquite leaves to make tea. Honey made from mesquite-flower pollen was especially prized.

In the absence of pins, settlers often substituted mesquite thorns.

The *1870 Texas Almanac* included an article by Dr. John E. Park of Seguin, asserting that "mesquit" made a "superior tanning material." During the Civil War, Texans had to manufacture many of the goods that they normally bought elsewhere, including leather. Dr. Park tested the barks of various Texas trees; mesquite was the richest in tannic acid, a substance used to tan leather. He extracted the tannins by chopping the wood and boiling

Robert Hensarling of Uvalde uses mesquite to make furniture, such as his *Texas Classic Rocker.* The mesquite wood used in his furniture is chosen for its unique grain pattern; www.mesquiterocker.com. Photo courtesy of Robert Hensarling.

it in water.

Dr. Park reported that not only was the quality of mesquite-tanned leather superior to that of leather tanned with other concoctions, but mesquite tannin also penetrated the leather exceptionally fast. More commonly used tanning agents worked so slowly that the center of a hide might rot before the tannin could penetrate it, especially in Texas' hot summers. Mesquite tannins worked fast enough that leather was seldom lost to decomposition, and tanning operations were not limited to winter months.

The U.S. Patent Office granted Dr. Park U.S. Patent No. 51,407 on Dec. 5, 1865, for his tanning method using mesquite.

In 1872, the United States Dispensatory reported that confectioners in the eastern United States bought 24,000 pounds of Texas mesquite gum to use in the manufacture of gumdrops.

In the late 1880s, the first streets to be paved in San Antonio—Alamo Plaza and surrounding streets—were surfaced with hexagonal creosote-treated mesquite blocks. When soaked with rain, the blocks swelled

The rich tones of mesquite warm the lobby and mezzanine of the Hilton Palacio del Rio in San Antonio. Photo courtesy of Hilton Palacio del Rio.

enough to push some of them up above the surface of the street, making for a rough ride. Even so, the city council in late 1891 voted to pave streets around Military Plaza—including parts of Market, St. Mary's, Treviño, Flores, Dolorosa and West Commerce—in a similar manner.

Current Uses

Although ranchers are still trying to annihilate mesquite, a dedicated group of about 250 Texans can't get enough of it. They are mostly artisans who value mesquite for its beauty, the ease with which it can be worked and the high sheen of finished pieces. Some even prize its irregularities.

Mesquite has a swirling grain, radial cracks, mineral deposits in the bark, and often many insect holes, which make working it a challenge. Finding a large, intact piece is almost impossible. But mesquite is dimensionally stable: As most hardwoods dry, they shrink more in one direction than they do in the other. Mesquite shrinks the same percentage in both directions. It has a surface hardness of 2,336 pounds per square inch, equal to that of hickory and almost twice that of oak and maple, and a density of 45 pounds per foot, greater than oak, maple, pecan and hickory.

Artisans use mesquite today for furniture, flooring, "turned" (on a lathe) and carved decorative items, and an array of other articles from golf clubs to jewelry. Companies produce chips and chunks that restaurant chefs and home cooks across the country use to flavor grilled meats.

Turnings and Carvings

Some mesquite crafters use lathes or their own carving skills to create everything from heirloom rocking horses to guitars, plus smaller decorative items: jewelry boxes, desk sets, vases, bowls and kitchen utensils.

Furniture

Finding mesquite pieces large enough to make into furniture is difficult—less so if you prefer rustic furniture and don't mind having the imperfections on view. However, artisans creating fine furniture sometimes go through many cords of mesquite to find enough usable wood to make a chair, a desk or a table.

Flooring

Mesquite's deep, rich, red-brown wood makes exquisite floors, using either planks, as in a standard hardwood floor, or cross-grain blocks. The cross-grain pieces are more than 50 percent harder than flat-sawn planks, with swirls and radial cracks that make each one unique. The lobby and mezzanine of the Hilton Palacio del Rio in San Antonio are floored with mesquite.

Is it a furniture, flooring, and artisan's treasure or is it a noxious weed? Whether you swear by mesquite, or swear at it, there is no doubt that it is here to stay.

Mary G. Ramos, a Dallas freelance writer, is editor emerita of the Texas Almanac.

Bibliography:

Dobie, J. Frank, "My Texas: Mesquite" (page 12-IV, Feb. 9, 1941) and "My Texas: More About the Mesquite" (page 8-I, Feb. 16, 1941). *The Dallas Morning News*, Dallas, Texas, 1941.

Jordan, Terry G., *Environment and Environmental Perceptions in Texas*. American Press, Boston, 1981.

"MESQUITE." The Handbook of Texas Online. http://www.tsha.utexas.edu/handbook/online/articles/view/MM/tpm1.html. [Accessed Wed Oct 13 11:27:22 US/Central 2004].

Richardson, Willard, ed., *Texas Almanac for 1870*, "Mesquit a Superior Tanning Material." Galveston News, Galveston, 1870.

Rogers, Ken E., *The Magnificent Mesquite*. University of Texas Press, Austin, 2000.

Texas A&M University, Native Plants Database (http://aggie-horticulture.tamu.edu/ornamentals/natives/).

Texas Big Tree Registry, Texas Forest Service, The Texas A&M University System (http://texasforestservice.tamu.edu/shared/article.asp?DocumentID=476&mc=forest). Click on "Big Tree Registry."

USDA, NRCS. 2004. The PLANTS Database, Version 3.5 (http://plants.usda.gov). National Plant Data Center, Baton Rouge, LA 70874-4490 USA.

Vines, Robert A., *Trees, Shrubs, and Woody Vines of the Southwest*. University of Texas Press, Austin, 1960. ☆

Texans 'Take the Waters'
Mineral-Water Spas Saw Commercial Boom a Century Ago
By Mary G. Ramos

*T*exas' many sources of fresh, sweet water have sustained human life for many thousands of years. Ancient Indian artifacts—metates and manos (stones for grinding grain), arrowheads and hand axes, flint quarries and rock paintings—are clustered around freshwater springs in every region of the state and give mute evidence of camp sites used long before Anglo settlers arrived.

Similar artifacts reveal that ancient inhabitants also gathered around springs that produce heavily mineralized water. (All non-distilled water contains some amount of dissolved minerals, also called "salts." Water with a combined mineral content greater than 500 milligrams per liter is called mineral water.)

The predominant mineral in Texas' mineral waters is often sulfur, hydrogen sulphide or iron. Among the many other minerals found in Texas waters, a few are radioactive: radon gas, radium or uranium.

Many of these minerals give the water a strong flavor and odor. Instead of shunning these foul-smelling and -tasting waters, American Indians and the settlers who followed bathed in and/or drank the mineral waters, believing them to have medicinal benefits. For example, Indians carved crude bathtubs out of rocks at Boquillas Hot Springs in what is now Big Bend National Park so they could bathe in the hot mineral water. In 1909, J.O. Langford incorporated the aboriginal bathing facilities into the earliest version of his commercial spa at the site.

No one knows just when America's Indians first began using mineral waters for bathing and drinking, but as early as the Roman Empire, Europeans indulged in hot mineral baths. The elaborate network of hot mineral-water bathing facilities built by first-century Romans at Bath, England, is one of those early spas.

Texas' Mineral Waters

In the *Texas Almanac for 1868,* Texas naturalist Gideon Lincecum extolled the "medicated waters of Texas." The widely respected Lincecum stated that ". . . nearly every county in Texas has its mineral springs," and today's geologists agree.

Mineral water can be broadly categorized by source or temperature:

Spring or Well?

Mineral springs bubble up out of the ground or down from rocks. Underground mineral waters usually are discovered by well-drillers seeking fresh water for drinking or irrigation.

Cool or Hot?

Although most mineral waters are cool, others emerge from the earth at temperatures well above average body temperature. Geologists say that, generally, the deeper the source of the water, the hotter the water is. Each spring in a cluster may have a unique temperature and concentration of minerals because each may originate from a different depth. The seven springs that make up Hudspeth County's Hot Springs, for example, vary in water temperature from 81degrees F to 117 degrees F.

SECTION OF MINERAL WELLS, TEXAS, SHOWING BAKER HOTEL IN CENTER

PHOTO BY TEXAS NATIONAL GUARD   6A-H505

When the Baker Hotel opened in Mineral Wells in 1929, it was the destination for many people—including such celebrities as Will Rogers and Judy Garland—who wanted to partake of the mineral waters abundant in the area. This 1940s postcard is from the collections of the Texas/Dallas History and Archives Division of the Dallas Public Library.

Commercial Mineral-Spa Development

Not all of Texas' mineral-water sources were commercially exploited. Residents near many of the smaller or more remote mineral springs used the water as a home remedy before modern medicines were developed.

The owners of a few of Texas' mineral springs opened them to the public during the 1840s and 1850s; serious commercial development began about 1860. The facilities around Sour Lake in Hardin County, though, were still relatively crude when Sam Houston spent a month there in 1863 taking mineral baths.

The popularity of "taking the waters"—visiting mineral-water spas—peaked in the 1890s. During that decade, nearly 100 Texas spas, most in the eastern half of the state, welcomed thousands of guests annually. Their use began declining in the 1900s and decreased rapidly during the following 30 years. That experience was repeated across the country. In 1945, physician Richard Kovacs noted that of the 425 spas active in the United States in 1927, only 34 were in business in 1943.

The simplest operations offered little more than access to the spring or well, a place to fill bottles with water, bathhouses and perhaps a camping area, simple cottages or rustic barracks. The more sophisticated establishments often advertised rigorous schedules of treatments supervised by physicians. A few were full-blown luxury spas, with elegant hotels that featured orchestras and other entertainments amid lavishly landscaped grounds, with "taking the waters" just one choice on a long list of activities.

Spas promoted treatments for an exhaustive list of ailments, including, but not limited to, alcoholism, arthritis, baldness, Bright's disease, cancer, catarrh, chapped hands, constipation, diabetes, diarrhea, "female complaints," flux, gout, hectic fever, high and low blood pressure, indigestion, insomnia, jake leg (a neurological malady caused by drinking moonshine whiskey containing tri-ortho-cresyl phosphate, an industrial chemical), malaria, milk leg, neuralgia, opium addiction, piles, pneumonia, rheumatism, ringworm, scurvy, sour stomach, St. Vitus' dance, toothache, ulcers, and venereal diseases, plus various other unspecified skin, eye, stomach, bladder, liver, spleen and kidney problems.

Promotional literature for most spas featured a chemical analysis of the water plus testimonials from people who claimed to have been successfully treated. Some included physicians' statements as to the efficacy of the water in curing specific medical problems, but hardly any scientific studies were done. With no documented medical diagnosis before treatment and no follow-up, confirmations of cures were virtually nil.

For those unable to spend three weeks at a spa for the usual regimen of treatment, some companies bottled their water and sold it by mail order. In 1910 alone, Mineral Wells establishments shipped more than 3 million bottles of water, and in 1914, 15 Texas companies were sending mineral water to distant markets. Some companies distilled the water and sold the resulting solids as mineral salts or crystals, to be reconstituted by the buyer with tap water.

Below are brief sketches of a representative sample of Texas' most successful mineral-water spas:

Lampasas

The first Anglo to make medicinal use of the mineral springs of Lampasas was probably Moses Hughes, who brought his ailing wife there in the 1850s. When her liver problem was "cured" after 21 days of drinking the water, the Hughes moved permanently to Lampasas. As news of the healing waters spread, others joined the Hughes family, and the town was established.

Lampasas' Hancock Springs contained enough sulfur that, according to an 1889 account, "Fumes can be smelled fifty yards or more, and are so strong as to tarnish gold coins, to the color of copper, in fifteen minutes, if exposed to the open air near the springs." Nearby were the not-so-stinky Hanna Springs.

Most visitors during the 1870s camped out around the springs in tents. They created their own simple diversions, shared their treatment experiences, and attended an occasional singing or camp meeting.

After the arrival of the Gulf, Colorado and Santa Fe Railroad (GC&SF) in 1882, a group of Galveston railroad men developed the reeking springs into the "Saratoga Springs of the Southwest," equating it with the famed New York mineral-springs spa that attracted a wealthy Eastern clientele.

Near Hancock Springs, they built the grand 200-room Park Hotel, with a large dining room, ballrooms, and 19th-century luxuries such as carpeted hallways and electric lights throughout. An orchestra provided year-round entertainment. In 1883, the Park Hotel was the most elegant resort in Central Texas. The Hanna Springs Company built a handsome pavilion over its springs, with lodging and a large entertainment hall upstairs and a bathhouse downstairs.

Unlike the campers, hotel guests came more for social diversion than for the mineral water. Lampasas flourished, but its popularity began declining after the GC&SF extended its tracks to Ballinger in 1886. Although business was waning, Hanna Springs alone recorded 6,000 baths taken during 1888. But by 1891, the Park Hotel's business was in the red. For several years, the Keely Institute operated a treatment center for alcoholics in the building. In 1894, Centenary College moved in; in 1895, the main building was destroyed by fire. A few visitors continued to camp out at the springs through the early 1900s.

Mineral Wells

When J.A. Lynch drilled a well in Palo Pinto County in 1880, the water he found was smelly. But Mrs. Lynch drank it, and it seemed to cure her rheumatism. The following year, Billy Wiggins drilled nearby what came to be called the "Crazy Well." The origin of the name is vague, but the water from it and several other area wells contains significant quantities of lithium, a substance used today to treat bipolar disorder (manic-depression).

Believing in its curative power, people piled into Mineral Wells to drink the water. Some returned home; others settled in and drilled their own wells. An 1893 article reported that "40-plus" wells were operating commercially in the city. By 1909, Mineral Wells had 46 hotels or boarding houses, and published reports said that by 1910, some 150,000 people a year were visiting the wells.

Of course, visitors did not drink water all day. Entertainments ranged from games of dominoes and viewing the area's scenic vistas to riding donkeys to the top of East Mountain, attending shows at the 1905 Chautauqua Theater, or riding a streetcar to Elmhurst Park, a 100-acre amusement park with a bandstand, cafés, merry-go-

Hot mineral water was discovered at Marlin in Falls County in 1891. By 1900, the town had several bathhouses and sanitariums. The popularity of mineral-water treatments even lured the New York Giants, who trained in Marlin from 1908–1919. This postcard from the early 1900s is from the collections of the Texas/Dallas History and Archives Division of the Dallas Public Library.

round, lake, and a casino.

When the Crazy Well Hotel, built in 1915, burned 10 years later, brothers Hal and Carr P. Collins bought the site. In 1927, they opened the renamed 200-room, seven-story Crazy Water Hotel as a posh resort hotel. The Crazy Water Hotel boasted such amenities as barber and beauty shops, dress shop, drugstore, doctors' office, curio shop, florist and valet service.

The Crazy Water Hotel was dwarfed in 1929 by the opening, 35 days after the Oct. 29 stock-market crash, of the opulent 14-story, 450-room Baker Hotel, complete with gymnasium, 18,500-square-foot drinking pavilion, drugstore, dress shop and bowling alley, all topped by a roof garden and dance floor. The Baker attracted such celebrities as Will Rogers, Judy Garland, Tom Mix, Gen. John J. Pershing, Marlene Dietrich, Jean Harlow, Sam Goldwyn, Jack Dempsey, Clark Gable, Helen Keller, Roy Rogers, and even the Three Stooges.

The Crazy Water Hotel began bleeding red ink until the Collins brothers began selling Crazy Water Crystals, the dehydrated minerals from Crazy Well water. The Crazy Water Crystals radio show promoted the product to the entire nation on the NBC network from the lobby of the Crazy Water Hotel. It featured a lineup of popular country musicians and comedians, plus earnest endorsements of the benefits of using the product. Even in the midst of the Depression, the Crazy Water Company made as much as $3 million per year from mineral-crystal sales.

Today the Crazy Water Hotel is a retirement residence, and the Baker stands silent and empty.

Marlin

While digging to find a water supply for the city of Marlin's 2,500 residents in 1891, city engineers struck sulfur-laden water that gushed out of the ground at 147 degrees F. Several physicians interested in the curative properties of Marlin's water established clinics, bathhouses and sanitariums. More wells were drilled, hotels and boarding houses opened their doors, and by 1900, Marlin was a popular spa emphasizing medical water treatments.

So well-regarded was Marlin's water that the New York Giants baseball team trained there from 1908 to 1919. Perhaps it was mere coincidence that the Giants won the National League pennant in 1911, 1912 and 1913.

In the 1920s, the Marlin Hot Wells Foundation for Crippled Children established a hospital to treat young polio victims.

By the 1930s, up to 100,000 health-seekers visited Marlin annually. Although Marlin's mineral-water business survived the Depression, principally because Marlin's doctors shifted their emphasis from baths alone to using baths as part of a therapy regimen, interest subsequently diminished. Despite sporadic attempts to revive them, Marlin's mineral-water establishments were pretty much gone by the 1960s.

Mineral Water in the Alamo City

Although the San Antonio area had at least three popular mineral-water spas, neither of the others achieved the reputation for luxury of the Hot Wells Hotel and Bath House, which opened in 1900 near San José Mission.

Among the multitude of bathing facilities were three swimming pools, 45 private bathing areas and 200 individual dressing rooms, plus six different kinds of baths. "Taking the waters" was almost an afterthought in the three-story pleasure palace, which quickly became the place to be among San Antonio's social set.

Besides dances, bowling, swimming, concerts,

Texas' Commercial Mineral-Water Spas

This table lists a selection of Texas' commercial mineral-water spas. It is not intended to be complete but lists 72 spas that seem to have been the most commercially active. In parentheses after the spa names are alternate names by which they were known. If the spa name is not the name of the town where it was located, the town the spa was in or near is preceded by "I/N". The years of operation represent approximate active commercial life of the spa, although the waters may have been used by local residents or had sporadic commercial use earlier or later than the time periods listed. These regional abbreviations are used: CE, Central; GC, Gulf Coast; EN, East-Northeast; NC, North-Central; PP, Panhandle-Plains; SO, South; TP, Trans-Pecos; WC, West-Central.

No.	Region	County	Name (alternate names)	Dates
1	CE	Bell	Salado (Key's Wells)	1900s
2	CE	Brazos	Manganic Wells (I/N Bryan)	1880s–1890s
3	CE	Caldwell	Burdette's (Burditt's) Wells (I/N Lockhart)	1870s–1910s
4	CE	Caldwell	Rogers' Springs (Cardwell Springs; Texas Sour Wells) (I/N Lockhart)	1870s–1890s
5	CE	Colorado	Kessler Springs (I/N Columbus)	1870–1888
6	CE	Falls	Marlin	1892–1942
7	CE	Lampasas	Hancock Springs (Sulphur or Great Boiling Springs) (I/N Lampasas)	1850s–1890s
8	CE	Lampasas	Hanna Springs (I/N Lampasas)	1870s–1910s
9	CE	Lampasas	Hughes Spring (Gooch Spring) (I/N Lampasas)	1850s–1870s
10	CE	Limestone	Kennedy Sulphur Spring (I/N Groesbeck)	1890s–1910s
11	CE	McLennan	Waco Hot Artesian Wells	1886–1920s
12	CE	Robertson	Franklin/Overall	1890s–1920s
13	CE	Robertson	Wootan Wells (Wooten Wells) (I/N Bremond)	1878–1910s
14	CE	Travis	Santa Monica Springs (I/N Austin)	1890s
15	CE	Williamson	Georgetown Mineral Wells (White Sulphur Springs)	1880s–1910s
16	EN	Anderson	Elkhart Mineral Wells	1880s–1890s
17	EN	Bowie	Dalby Springs (Pirkey Spring; Farrier Spring)	1840s–1910s
18	EN	Cass	Hughes Springs (Chalybeate* Springs)	1878–1920
19	EN	Cherokee	Chalybeate* City (I/N Rusk)	1870s–1890s
20	EN	Cherokee	Seven Sisters Springs (I/N New Birmingham)	1870s–1890s
21	EN	Grimes	Kellum's White Sulphur Springs (I/N Anderson)	1830s–1880s
22	EN	Grimes	Piedmont Sulphur Springs	1840s–1870s
23	EN	Harrison	Hynson Springs (Marshall or Iron Springs, Noonday Camp) (I/N Marshall)	1851–1905
24	EN	Harrison	Montvale Springs (I/N Harleton)	1890s–1900s
25	EN	Harrison	Rosborough (Roseborough Springs) (I/N Marshall)	1880s–1930s
26	EN	Hopkins	Sulphur Springs (Crabtree's Sour Wells)	1870s–1900s
27	EN	Hunt	Campbell Mineral Wells	1900s–1920s
28	EN	Lamar	Blossom (Beauchamp Wells; Bell's Mineral Wells; Carlsbad)	1880s–1910s
29	EN	Lamar	Bloy's Well (I/N Paris)	1880s–1930s
30	EN	Panola	Midyett (Breckenridge Springs)	1870s–1910s
31	EN	Rusk	Welch Springs (I/N Brachfield)	1880s–1890s
32	EN	Smith	Headache Springs (Brown's Sulphur Springs) (I/N Tyler)	1850s–1870s
33	EN	Titus	Red Mineral Springs (Dellwood Hotel; Indian Springs) (I/N Mount Pleasant)	1890s–1912
34	EN	Tyler	Sulphur Springs (I/N Mt. Hope)	1870s–1890s
35	EN	Upshur	Phillips Springs (I/N Union Grove)	1877–1900
36	EN	Van Zandt	Myrtle Springs (Holden Springs)	1890s
37	EN	Walker	Sulphur Springs (I/N Bidias Creek)	1850s–1860s
38	EN	Walker	Tuscaloosa (Wyser's Bluff)	1850s–1890s
39	EN	Wood	Mineola	1880s–1924
40	EN	Wood	Musgrove Springs (Chalybeate* Springs) (I/N Winnsboro)	1880s–1895
41	GC	Galveston	High Island (Sea View; White Doe; Smith's Well)	1890s–1910s
42	GC	Hardin	Saratoga (Saratoga Springs; New Sour Lake)	1870s–1890s
43	GC	Hardin	Sour Lake (Sour Springs)	1850s–1902
44	GC	Harris	Cypress (Houston Hot Well)	1914–1950
45	NC	Callahan	Putnam Mineral Wells	1800s–1910s
46	NC	Dallas	Gill Well (I/N Oak Lawn area, Dallas)	1903–1930s
47	NC	Eastland	Mangum	1902–1910s
48	NC	Erath	Duffau Wells	1882–1910s
49	NC	Grayson	Tioga (Tioga Springs)	1880s–1970s
50	NC	Hill	Hubbard Hot Well	1900s–1920s
51	NC	Hood	Thorp Spring	1870s–1890s
52	NC	Jack	Wizard Wells (Vineyard)	1882–1968
53	NC	Palo Pinto	Mineral Wells	1885–1960s
54	NC	Palo Pinto	Oran	1908–1920s
55	NC	Somervell	Glen Rose	1880s–1940s
56	NC	Tarrant	Arlington Mineral Wells	1892–1951
57	NC	Young	Stovall Hot Wells (I/N South Bend)	1930s–1994
58	PP	Nolan	Grogan Mineral Wells (Daniel Mineral Wells) (I/N Sweetwater)	1905–1920s
59	SO	Bee	Mineral (Mineral City)(I/N Beeville)	1877–1889
60	SO	Bexar	Dullnig Wells (I/N San Antonio)	1890s–1925
61	SO	Bexar	Harlandale Hot Sulphur Well (I/N San Antonio)	1910s–1920
62	SO	Bexar	Hot Wells (Hot Wells Hotel) (I/N San Antonio)	1892–1923
63	SO	Bexar	Terrell Wells (I/N San Antonio)	1890s–1940s
64	SO	Karnes	Kenedy Hot Wells	1910s–1950s
65	SO	Uvalde	Reagan Wells (I/N Uvalde)	1880–1945
66	SO	Wilson	Sutherland Springs	1840s–1920s
67	TP	Brewster	Hot Springs (Boquillas Hot Springs) (I/N Big Bend Nat'l Park)	1927–1952
68	TP	Hudspeth	Hot Wells	1900s–1920s
69	TP	Hudspeth	Indian Hot Springs (Ojos Calientes de los Indios)	1925–1940; 1967–1974
70	TP	Presidio	Ruidosa Hot Springs (Kingston or Chinati Hot Springs)	1930s–present
71	WC	Tom Green	Carlsbad	1900s–1910s
72	WC	Tom Green	Christoval Mineral Wells	1915–1980s

Texas Mineral Spas

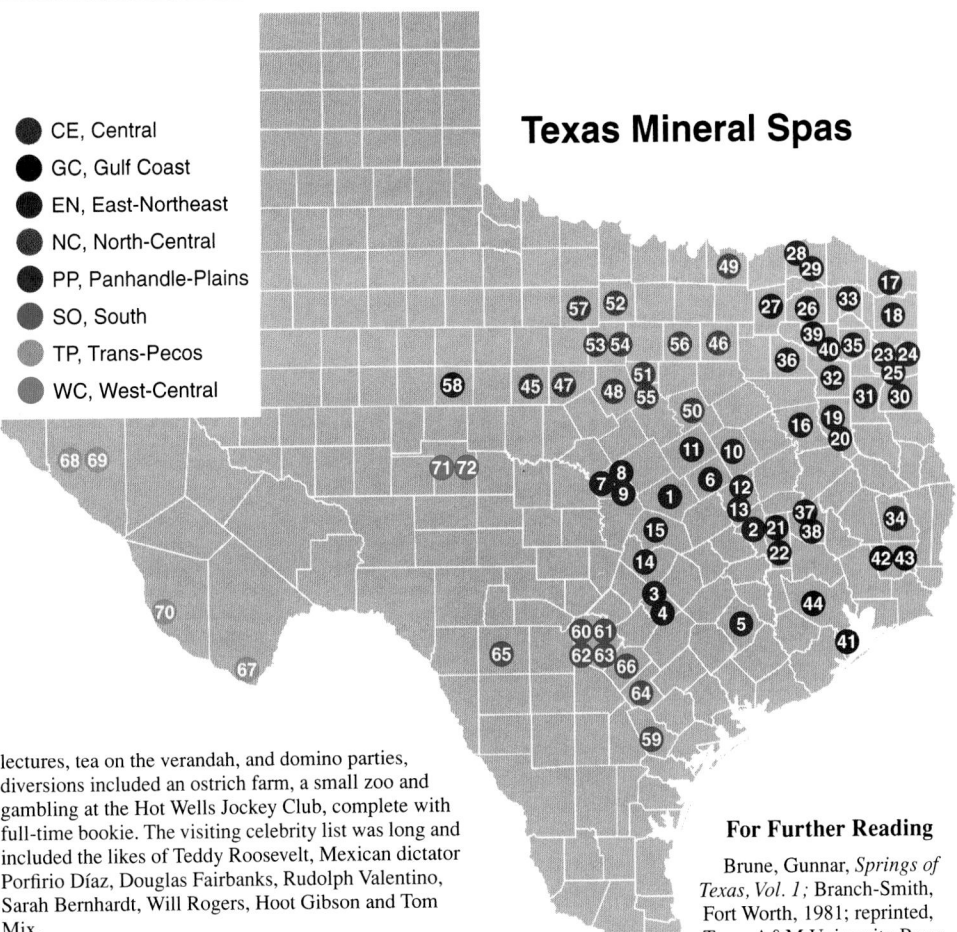

- ● CE, Central
- ● GC, Gulf Coast
- ● EN, East-Northeast
- ● NC, North-Central
- ● PP, Panhandle-Plains
- ● SO, South
- ● TP, Trans-Pecos
- ● WC, West-Central

lectures, tea on the verandah, and domino parties, diversions included an ostrich farm, a small zoo and gambling at the Hot Wells Jockey Club, complete with full-time bookie. The visiting celebrity list was long and included the likes of Teddy Roosevelt, Mexican dictator Porfirio Díaz, Douglas Fairbanks, Rudolph Valentino, Sarah Bernhardt, Will Rogers, Hoot Gibson and Tom Mix.

The Hot Wells' popularity died off by the early 1920s. The burned ruins of the grand resort still can be seen in southeast San Antonio.

The Era Ends

Several factors contributed to the demise of mineral-water spas.
- Some lost their buildings to fires and could not afford to rebuild;
- Many modern medicines appeared in the 1930s, such as antibiotics, beginning with the discovery of penicillin in the late 1920s, as well as vaccines and other medications;
- The economic hardships of the Great Depression;
- The U.S. Food and Drug Administration's 1930s campaign for pure foods and medicines. The FDA seized shipments of some bottled mineral water and packages of salts and crystals, claiming either that the products were contaminated or that the labels contained fraudulent claims, or both.

Most mineral-water spas were shuttered by 1940. A few, such as Stovall Hot Wells and Chinati Hot Springs, for example, continue to offer hot mineral-water baths to the public.

Mary G. Ramos, a Dallas freelance writer, is editor emerita of the Texas Almanac.

For Further Reading

Brune, Gunnar, *Springs of Texas, Vol. 1;* Branch-Smith, Fort Worth, 1981; reprinted, Texas A&M University Press, College Station, 2002.

Fowler, Gene, *Crazy Water: The Story of Mineral Wells and Other Texas Health Resorts;* Texas Christian University Press, Fort Worth, 1991.

Handbook of Texas Online (http://www.tsha.utexas.edu/handbook/online/), s.v. Collins, Carr P.; Cypress, TX; Dalby Springs; Hardin County; Hot Springs, TX; Hubbard, TX; Hughes Springs, TX; Hynson Springs, TX; Indian Hot Springs; Kenedy, TX; Kingston Hot Springs; Lampasas, TX; Mangum, TX; Marlin, TX; Mineral, TX; Mineral-water Springs and Wells; Mineral Wells, TX; Oran, TX; Piedmont Springs; Putnam, TX; Rosborough Springs, TX; Saratoga, TX; Sour Lake, TX; South Bend, TX; Sutherland Springs, TX; Terrell Wells, TX; Thorp Spring, TX; Tioga, TX.

Lampasas, Texas: Its Mineral Springs; Poole Bros., Chicago; reproduced 1972 for Lampasas' First Spring-Ho Festival.

Lincecum, Gideon, "Medicated Waters of Texas," *Texas Almanac for 1868; Galveston News,* Galveston, 1867.

Valenza, Janet Mace, *Taking the Waters in Texas: Springs, Spas, and Fountains of Youth;* University of Texas Press, Austin, 2000. ☆

Rosenwald Schools

A Boost for Black Education in the Early 20th Century

By Mary G. Ramos

*J*ulius Rosenwald was an unlikely fairy godfather. But Rosenwald, child of German-Jewish immigrants and a high-school dropout, was just that for more than half a million poor, mostly rural, Southern black children in the 1920s, including more than 50,000 in Texas. Rosenwald made it possible for them to receive an education in decent, attractive surroundings.

In the early 1900s, most black schoolchildren in the rural South, including many in Texas, attended classes in dilapidated buildings with discarded furniture and equipment and out-of-date textbooks—cast-offs from white schools. In some cases, the white local school-district officials did not

A teacher, center, and his students proudly stand in front of the Sandy Grove School during the 1923–1924 school year. Located in Burleson County, this school is an example of a one-room, one-teacher Rosenwald design. There were 92 one-teacher Rosenwald schools constructed in Texas. They were phased out by 1930 in favor of multiple-teacher designs. Photo courtesy of Karen Riles.

provide a building at all, leaving black educators and parents to seek classroom space in churches and lodge halls.

Born in Springfield, Illinois, in 1862, Rosenwald started working in the clothing business at age 17. In 1897, he joined the four-year-old Sears, Roebuck and Company in Chicago when the company's mail-order catalogs were becoming fixtures in millions of American households. By 1909, he was president and chief operating officer of the company, which had grown into the world's largest retailer.

Rosenwald believed that America could not prosper "if any large segment of its people were left behind," so, as his wealth grew, he began donating money to a number of organizations that helped the less fortunate. One of the schools benefiting from the philanthropist's generosity was Tuskegee Normal and Industrial Institute in Tuskegee, Alabama, now Tuskegee University.

Booker T. Washington, eminent black leader and educator, was the founder and principal of Tuskegee, which emphasized industrial education, such as carpentry, farming and mechanics. A number of other black leaders, among them W.E.B. Du Bois, believed that industrial training relegated black people to dead-end trades rather than giving them the opportunity, through college educations focusing on academics, to be groomed for leadership and advancement. Washington, however, thought that solving basic educational and economic needs were the first steps toward integration and equal rights.

Rosenwald gave Tuskegee $25,000 for a black

teacher-training program in 1912. Washington persuaded Rosenwald to let him use a small portion of it for a pilot program to build six school buildings in rural Alabama. Two years later, Rosenwald made a $30,000 gift to construct 100 rural schools, followed by later gifts for another 200 schools.

In 1917, Rosenwald formed the Julius Rosenwald Fund to make and oversee the grants, with Tuskegee managing the construction projects and dealing with the school boards. The program quickly overwhelmed the Tuskegee managers, and in 1919, the Rosenwald Fund staff assumed responsibility for the entire building project.

How the Grants Worked

The Rosenwald grants, which varied based on the number of teachers to be employed at the school, ranged from $500 for a one-teacher plan to $2,100 for a school with a capacity of 10 or more teachers. They were matching grants: The black communities where the schools were built had to contribute cash and in-kind donations of material and labor to match the grant.

These donations were usually great sacrifices, but the communities pitched in, organizing committees to find and buy the school site, cut lumber, haul building materials, and help construct the building. Church congregations and fraternal lodges held fundraisers; farmers donated the proceeds from an acre of cotton or from selling a number of chickens.

Additional funds came from white donors, but the largest source of funding was tax money. Each county school board—at that time made up of only whites—had to be persuaded to accept the idea of a new, state-of-the-art, schoolbuilding for black students. The school district was also required to take ownership of the property and maintain it as part of the public-school system.

The Rosenwald Fund administrators set specific minimum standards for site size and length of school term. School boards were required to provide new blackboards and desks for each classroom, as well as two sanitary privies.

Orderly, Clean and Bright

The school plans, designed by architects who specialized in school design, used banks of large, double-hung sash windows to maximize natural lighting, essential in rural areas without electric service. They also included provisions for good ventilation and sanitation. Designers specified room sizes, blackboard and desk placement, and colors of paint. The buildings' exteriors were simple and functional. The interiors were orderly, clean and bright.

Sliding doors and removable blackboards in the smaller schools allowed the space to be opened up for community gatherings. Some larger schools had separate meeting rooms, auditoriums or gymnasiums for gatherings, allowing the schools to become community centers as well as educational centers.

Some communities had no provision for housing teachers. In those, grants and plans for "teacherages"—teachers' houses—were provided. In some cases, a room for teaching shop class was part of the basic school building. For some larger schools, a separate grant provided for a detached shop building.

The Rosenwald Fund expanded to include other grant opportunities:

• Grants to county boards of education to finance term extensions allowed black students to attend school for a full scholastic year and black teachers to earn a decent salary by working a longer term.

• Low-cost school libraries—sets of carefully chosen books—were offered to Rosenwald schools and to rural white schools, as well.

• Transportation grants, inaugurated in 1929, paid for buses to transport students to consolidated schools.

Rosenwald Schools by the Numbers

	Texas	United States
Schools	464	4,977
Homes	31	217
Shops	32	163
Total Buildings	527	5,357
Student Capacity	57,330	663,615
Teacher Capacity	1,274	14,747
Black Contrib.	$392,851	$4,725,891
White Contrib.	$60,495	$1,211,975
Tax Funds	$1,623,800	$18,105,805
Rosenwald Fund	$419,376	$4,364,869
Total Cost	$2,496,521	$28,408,520

Source: National Trust for Historic Preservation's Rosenwald Schools Web site, accessed Feb. 21, 2005. (www.rosenwaldschools.com/history.html).

The Rosenwald Fund made their building plans available to any school that wanted to use them. More than 15,000 white schools across the South with no other connection to the Rosenwald project were built using Rosenwald plans.

By the time the last nail was hammered home in 1932, there were 663,615 black schoolchildren in 15 states attending classes in Rosenwald schools. Julius Rosenwald had inspired, guided and partially funded the construction of 5,357 educational buildings across the South: 4,977 schools, serving an estimated one-third of the region's rural black schoolchildren, 217 teachers' homes and 163 shops.

Texas received 527 buildings in 52 counties, most of them in the eastern half of the state: 464 schools with a 57,330-student capacity, 31 teachers' homes and 32 shops.

A 1934 report, "The Development and Present Status of Negro Education in East Texas," was quoted in a

Students and teachers of Washington School at Center Point in Nacogdoches County gathered for a group photo during the 1951–1952 school year. At far left is teacher Lorene Watson, who taught grades 4–6, and next to her is Mamie Rogers Hodge, who taught grades 1–3. J.W. Wilson, far right, was principal and taught grades 7–8. Their three-teacher Rosenwald school was constructed during the 1926–1927 school year. Photo courtesy of Karen Riles.

Texas Council for the Humanities article as stating, "Every Negro school visited, . . . except the Rosenwald schools, was housed in crude unpainted box shacks, with no foundation, . . . no desks, blackboard, no window shades, no library and no equipment."

Where Are They Now?

As important as they were at the time they were built, a great many of the Rosenwald buildings have disappeared. Many of the tiny communities where schools were located no longer exist, having been abandoned in the general movement of people from farms to cities beginning with World War II. Other schools, left vacant when white schools were desegregated in the 1960s, decayed from neglect.

A few Rosenwald buildings were put to other uses by school districts or churches. The Hopewell School in Round Rock, closed in 1966 because of desegregation, was used for a time by the Round Rock Independent School District as a transportation facility. By 1999, it had been sold and was threatened with demolition. Round Rock's black community protested, proposing a plan to relocate and rehabilitate the building. With volunteer labor, donated materials and funds, and with the Round Rock ISD picking up costs for moving the building to its headquarters, the old five-teacher Rosenwald school was turned into a district teacher-training and meeting facility.

A Baptist church near the Sweet Home Vocational and Agricultural High School in the Seguin vicinity is currently using a former Rosenwald building as a fellowship hall and nutritional center.

The Rosenwald Initiative, a project of the National Trust for Historic Preservation in concert with state historic preservation offices, is coordinating the effort to find and document the remaining Rosenwald school buildings. Fisk University in Nashville, Tennessee, is partnering with the National Trust to conserve and digitize the Rosenwald Fund records.

The National Trust has established a Web site for the Rosenwald project: http://www.rosenwaldschools.com/. In addition to the history of the school-building project and updates on the organization's research and recognition efforts, the site will eventually feature access to Fisk University's database of Rosenwald schools information.

Of the 527 buildings in Texas partially funded by the Jewish fairy godfather from Chicago, about 30 still-existing structures had been identified as of early spring 2005. Four of those have been listed on the National Register of Historic Places; they are: the Sweet Home Vocational and Agricultural High School south of Seguin; the Lockhart Vocational/Carver High School; the Garland Community School Teacherage, a five-teacher house near DeKalb in far northeast Texas; and the Pleasant Hill School near Linden in Cass County. The nomination of the Hopewell School in Bastrop County is awaiting final approval.

The Texas Historical Commission is participating in the National Trust's project to find Rosenwald buildings, and its search for the historical buildings is ongoing.

Mary G. Ramos, a Dallas freelance writer, is editor emerita of the Texas Almanac.

For Further Reading

Ascoli, Peter M., JR: *A Biography of Julius Rosenwald;* Indiana University Press, Bloomington, IN, fall 2006.

Hoffschwelle, Mary S., *Preserving Rosenwald Schools;* National Trust for Historic Preservation, Washington, D.C., 2003.

Hoffschwelle, Mary S., *The Rosenwald Schools of the American South;* University Press of Florida, Gainesville, FL, 2005.

Johnson, D'Ann, "Preserving History with Time Running Out"; *Texas Co-op Power,* February 2004.

National Trust for Historic Preservation Rosenwald Initiative Web site, accessed November 2, 2004. (www.rosenwaldschools.com/; www.rosenwaldschools.com/history.html)

Riles, Karen D., "Historic and Architectural Resources Associated with the Rosenwald School Building Program: The Rosenwald School Building Program in Texas, 1920–1932"; National Register of Historic Places Multiple Property Documentation Form, National Park Service, U.S. Department of the Interior, July 1997–October 1998. (www.nr.nps.gov/multiples/64500652.pdf). ☆

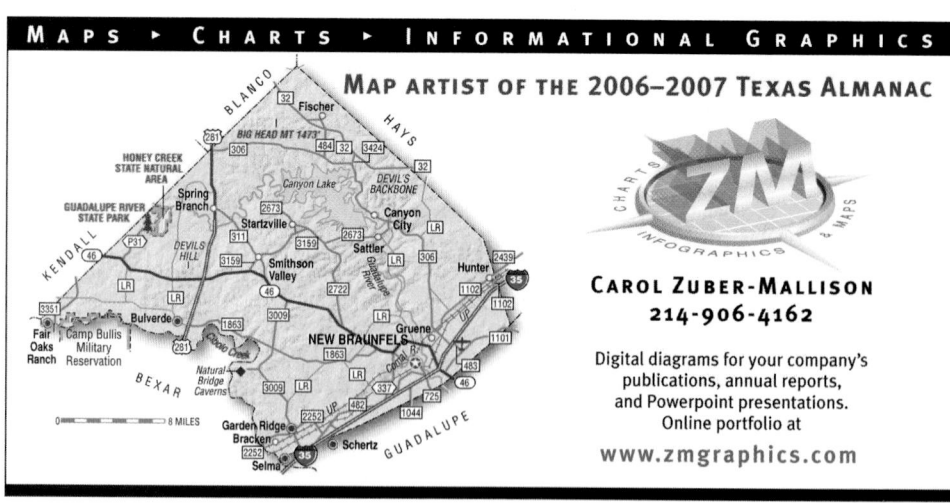

A Brief Sketch of Texas History

This two-part sketch of Texas' past, from prehistoric times to 1980, is based on "A Concise History of Texas" by former Texas Almanac editor Mike Kingston. Mr. Kingston's history was published in the 1986–1987 edition of the Texas Almanac, which marked Texas' sesquicentennial. Robert Plocheck, associate editor of the Texas Almanac, edited and expanded Mr. Kingston's history.

Prehistory to Annexation

Prehistoric Texas

Early Texans are believed to have been descendants of Asian groups that migrated across the Bering Strait during the Ice Ages of the past 50,000 years.

At intermittent periods, enough water accumulated in massive glaciers worldwide to lower the sea level several hundred feet. During these periods, the Bering Strait became a 1,300-mile-wide land bridge between North America and Asia.

These early adventurers worked their way southward for thousands of years, eventually getting as far as Tierra del Fuego in South America about 10,000 years ago.

Biologically they were completely modern homo sapiens. No evidence has been found to indicate that any evolutionary change occurred in the New World.

Four basic stages reflecting cultural advancement of early inhabitants are used by archaeologists in classifying evidence. These stages are the Paleo-Indian (20,000 to 7,000 years ago), Archaic (7,000 years ago to about the time of Christ), Woodland (time of Christ to 800–1,000 years ago), and Neo-American or Late Prehistoric (800–1,000 years ago until European contact).

Not all early people advanced through all these stages in Texas. Much cultural change occurred in adaptation to changes in climate. The Caddo tribes of East Texas, for example, reached the Neo-American stage before the Spanish and French explorers made contact in the 1500s and 1600s.

Others, such as the Karankawas of the Gulf Coast, advanced no further than the Archaic stage of civilization at the same time. Still others advanced and then regressed in the face of a changing climate.

The earliest confirmed evidence indicates that humans were in Texas between 10,000 and 13,000 years ago.

Paleo-Indians were successful big-game hunters. Artifacts from this period are found across the state but not in great number, indicating that they were a small, nomadic population.

As Texas' climate changed at the end of the Ice Age about 7,000 years ago, inhabitants adapted. Apparently the state experienced an extended period of warming and drying, and the population during the **Archaic** period increased.

These Texans began to harvest fruits and nuts and, to exploit rivers for food, as indicated by the fresh-water mussel shells in ancient garbage heaps.

The **Woodland** stage is distinguished by the development of settled societies, with crops and local wild plants providing much of their diet. The bow and arrow came into use, and the first pottery is associated with this period.

Pre-Caddoan tribes in East Texas had formed villages and were building distinctive mounds for burials and for ritual.

The **Neo-American** period is best exemplified by the highly civilized Caddoes, who had a complex culture with well-defined social stratification. They were fully agricultural and participated in trade over a wide area of North America.

Steps lead to the top of an ancient burial mound at Caddoan Mounds State Historical Site near Crockett in East Texas. The mound is one of several built by early Caddo Indians about 1,000 years ago. File photo.

The Spanish Explorations

Spain's exploration of North America was one of the first acts of a vigorous nation that was emerging from centuries of campaigns to oust the Islamic Moors from the Iberian Peninsula.

In early **1492**, the Spanish forces retook the province of Granada, completing the *reconquista* or reconquest. Later in the year, the Catholic royals of the united country, Ferdinand and Isabella, took a major stride toward shaping world history by commissioning Christopher Columbus for the voyage that was to bring Europeans to America.

As early as **1519, Capt. Alonso Alvarez de Pineda**, in the service of the governor of Jamaica, mapped the coast of Texas.

The **first recorded exploration of today's Texas** was made in the 1530s by **Alvar Núñez Cabeza de Vaca**, along with two other Spaniards and a Moorish slave named Estevanico. They were members of an expedition commanded by Panfilo de Narváez that left Cuba in 1528 to explore what is now the southeastern United States. Ill-fated from the beginning, many members of the expedition lost their lives, and others, including Cabeza de Vaca, were shipwrecked on the Texas coast. Eventually the band wandered into Mexico in 1536.

In **1540**, Francisco Vázquez de Coronado was commissioned to lead an exploration of the American Southwest. The quest took him to the land of the Pueblo Indians in what is now New Mexico. Native Americans, who had learned it was best to keep Europeans away from their homes, would suggest vast riches could be found in other areas. So Coronado pursued a fruitless search for gold and silver across the **High Plains of Texas**, Oklahoma and Kansas.

While Coronado was investigating Texas from the west, Luis de Moscoso Alvarado approached from the east. He assumed leadership of Hernando de Soto's expedition when the commander died on the banks of the Mississippi River. In **1542**, Moscoso's group ventured as far west as **Central Texas** before returning to the Mississippi.

Forty years passed after the Coronado and Moscoso expeditions before Fray Agustín Rodríguez, a Franciscan missionary, and Francisco Sánchez Chamuscado, a soldier, led an expedition into Texas and New Mexico.

Following the Río Conchos in Mexico to its confluence with the Rio Grande near present-day **Presidio**, and then turning northwestward up the great river's valley, **the** explorers passed through the El Paso area in **1581**.

Juan de Oñate was granted the right to develop this area populated by Pueblo Indians in 1598. He blazed a trail across the desert from Santa Barbara, Chihuahua, to intersect the Rio Grande at the Pass of the North. For the next 200 years, this was the supply route from the interior of Mexico that served the northern colonies.

Texas was attractive to the Spanish in the 1600s. Small expeditions found trade possibilities, and missionaries ventured into the territory. Frays Juan de Salas and Diego López responded to a request by the Jumano Indians for religious instruction in **1629**, and for a brief time priests lived with the Indians near present-day **San Angelo**.

The first permanent settlement in Texas was established in **1681–82** after New Mexico's Indians rebelled and drove Spanish settlers southward. The colonists retreated to the **El Paso** area, where the missions of Corpus Christi de la Isleta and Nuestra Señora del Socorro — each named for a community in New Mexico — were established. Ysleta pueblo originally was located on the south side of the Rio Grande, but as the river changed course, it ended up on the north bank. Now part of El Paso, the community is considered the oldest European settlement in Texas.

French Exploration

In 1682, **René Robert Cavelier, Sieur de La Salle**, explored the Mississippi River to its mouth at the Gulf of Mexico. La Salle claimed the vast territory drained by the river for France.

Two years later, La Salle returned to the New World with four ships and enough colonists to establish his country's claim. Guided by erroneous maps, this second expedition overshot the mouth of the Mississippi by 400 miles and ended up on the Texas coast. Though short of supplies because of the loss of two of the ships, the French colonists established Fort Saint Louis on Garcitas Creek several miles inland from Lavaca Bay.

In 1687, La Salle and a group of soldiers began an overland trip to find French outposts on the Mississippi. Somewhere west of the Trinity River, the explorer was murdered by some of his men. His grave has never been found. (A more detailed account of La Salle's expedition can be found in the *Texas Almanac 1998–1999* and on the Texas Almanac Web site.)

In 1689, Spanish authorities sent **Capt. Alonso de León**, governor of Coahuila (which at various times included Texas in its jurisdiction), into Texas to confront the French. He headed eastward from present-day **Eagle Pass** and found the tattered remnants of Fort Saint Louis.

Indians had destroyed the settlement and killed many colonists. León continued tracking survivors of the ill-fated colony into East Texas.

Spanish Rule

Father **Damián Massanet** accompanied León on this journey. The priest was fascinated with tales about the "Tejas" Indians of the region.

Tejas meant *friendly*, but at the time the term was considered a tribal name. Actually these Indians were members of the Caddo Confederacy that controlled parts of four present states: Texas, Louisiana, Arkansas and Oklahoma.

The Caddo religion acknowledged one supreme god, and when a Tejas chief asked Father Massanet to stay and instruct his people in his faith, the Spaniards promised to return and establish a mission.

The pledge was redeemed in **1690** when the mission San Francisco de los Tejas was founded near present-day Weches in Houston County.

Twin disasters struck this missionary effort. Spanish government officials quickly lost interest when the French threat at colonization diminished. And as was the case with many New World Indians who had no resistance to European diseases, the Tejas soon were felled by an epidemic. The Indians blamed the new religion and resisted conversion. The mission languished, and it was hard to supply from other Spanish outposts in northern Mexico. In 1693, the Spanish officials closed the mission effort in **East Texas**. *(See page 16 for an account of early Spanish missionaries in Texas.)*

Although Spain had not made a determined effort to settle Texas, great changes were coming to the territory. Spain introduced horses into the Southwest. By the late 1600s, Comanches were using the horses to expand their range southward across the plains, displacing the Apaches.

In the **1720s**, the **Apaches** moved onto the lower Texas Plains, usurping the traditional hunting grounds of the Jumanos and others. The nomadic Coahuiltecan bands were particularly hard hit.

In 1709, Fray Antonio de San Buenaventura y Olivares had made an initial request to establish a mission at San Pedro Springs (today's San Antonio) to minister to the Coahuiltecans. The request was denied. However, new fears of French movement into East Texas changed that.

Another Franciscan, **Father Francisco Hidalgo**, who had earlier served at the missions in East

Horse armor and stirrups offer a glimpse of Spanish explorers in Texas. These artifacts reside at the Bob Bullock Texas State History Museum in Austin. File photo.

Texas, returned to them when he and **Father Antonio Margil de Jesús** accompanied **Capt. Diego Ramón** on an expedition to the area in 1716. In that year, the mission of San Francisco de los Neches was established near the site of the old San Francisco de los Tejas mission. Nuestra Señora de Guadalupe was located at the present-day site of Nacogdoches, and Nuestra Señora de los Dolores was placed near present-day San Augustine.

The East Texas missions did little better on the second try, and supplying the frontier missions remained difficult. It became apparent that a way station between northern Mexico and East Texas was needed.

In **1718**, Spanish officials consented to Fray Olivares' request to found a mission at San Pedro Springs. That mission, called **San Antonio de Valero**, was later to be known as the **Alamo**. Because the Indians of the region often did not get along with each other, other missions were established to serve each group.

These missions flourished and each became an early ranching center. But the large herds of cattle and horses attracted trouble. The San Antonio missions began to face the wrath of the Apaches. The mission system, which attempted to convert the Indians to Christianity and to "civilize" them, was partially successful in subduing minor tribes but not larger tribes like the Apaches.

The Spanish realized that more stable colonization efforts must be made. Indians from Mexico, such as the Tlascalans who fought with Cortés against the Aztecs, were brought into Texas to serve as examples of "good" Indians for the wayward natives.

In **1731**, Spanish colonists from the **Canary Islands** were brought to Texas and founded the **Villa of San Fernando de Béxar**, the first civil jurisdiction in the province and today's **San Antonio.**

In the late 1730s, Spanish officials became concerned over the vulnerability of the large area between the Sierra Madre Oriental and the Gulf Coast in northern Mexico. The area was unsettled, a haven for runaway Indian slaves and marauders, and it was a wide-open pathway for the English or French from the Gulf to the rich silver mines in Durango.

For seven years the search for the right colonizer went on before **José de Escandón** was selected in 1746. A professional military man and successful administrator, Escandón earned a high reputation by subduing Indians in central Mexico. On receiving the assignment, he launched a broad land survey of the area running from the mountains to the Gulf and from the Río Pánuco in Tamaulipas, Mexico, to the Nueces River in Texas.

In 1747, he began placing colonists in settlements throughout the area. **Tomás Sánchez** received a land grant on the Rio Grande in **1755** from which **Laredo** developed. And other small Texas communities along the river sprang up as a result of Escandón's well-executed plan. Many old Hispanic families in Texas hold title of their land based on grants in this period.

In the following decades, a few other Spanish colonists settled around the old missions and frontier forts. **Antonio Gil Ybarbo** led one group that settled **Nacogdoches** in the **1760s and 1770s.**

The Demise of Spain

Spain's final 60 years of control of the province of Texas were marked with a few successes and a multitude of failures, all of which could be attributed to a breakdown in the administrative system.

Charles III, the fourth of the Bourbon line of kings, took the Spanish throne in 1759. He launched a series of reforms in the New World. The king's choice of administrators was excellent. In 1765, José de Gálvez was dispatched to New Spain (an area that then included all of modern Mexico and much of today's American West) with instructions to improve both the economy and the defense.

Gálvez initially toured parts of the vast region, gaining first-hand insight into the practical problems of the colony. There were many that could be traced to Spain's basic concepts of colonial government. Texas, in particular, suffered from the mercantilist economic system that attempted to funnel all colonial trade through ports in Mexico.

But administrative reforms by Gálvez and his nephew, Bernardo Gálvez, namesake of Galveston, were to be followed by ill-advised policies by successors.

Problems with the Comanches, Apaches and "Norteños," as the Spanish called some tribes, continued to plague the province, too.

About the same time, Spain undertook the administration of Louisiana Territory. One of the terms of the cession by France was that the region would enjoy certain trading privileges denied to other Spanish dependencies. So although Texas and Louisiana were neighbors, trade between the two provinces was banned.

The crown further complicated matters by placing the administration of Louisiana under authorities in Cuba, while Texas remained under the authorities in Mexico City.

The death of Charles III in 1788 and the beginning of the French Revolution a year later weakened Spain's hold on the New World dominions. Charles IV was not as good a sovereign as his predecessor, and his choice of ministers was poor. The quality of frontier administrators declined, and relations with Indians soured further.

Charles IV's major blunder, however, was to side with French royalty during the revolution, earning Spain the enmity of Napoleon Bonaparte. Spain also allied with England in an effort to thwart Napoleon, and in this losing cause, the Spanish were forced to cede Louisiana back to France.

In 1803, Napoleon broke a promise to retain the territory and sold it to the United States. Spain's problems in the New World thereby took on an altogether different dimension. Now, Anglo-Americans cast longing eyes on the vast undeveloped territory of Texas.

With certain exceptions for royalists who left the American colonies during the revolution, Spain had maintained a strict prohibition against Anglo or other non-Spanish settlers in their New World territories. But they were unprepared to police the eastern border of Texas after removing the presidios in the 1760s. What had been a provincial line became virtually overnight an international boundary, and an ill-defined one at that.

American Immigrants

Around **1800, Anglo-Americans** began to probe the Spanish frontier. Some settled in East Texas and others crossed the Red River and were tolerated by authorities.

Others, however, were thought to have nefarious designs. Philip Nolan was the first of the American filibusters to test Spanish resolve. Several times he entered Texas to capture wild horses to sell in the United States. But in 1801, the Spanish perceived an attempted insurrection by Nolan and his followers. He was killed

in a battle near present-day Waco, and his company was taken captive to work in the mines in northern Mexico.

Spanish officials were beginning to realize that the economic potential of Texas must be developed if the Anglo-Americans were to be neutralized. But Spain's centuries-long role in the history of Texas was almost over.

Resistance to Spanish rule had developed in the New World colonies. Liberal ideas from the American and French revolutions had grown popular, despite the crown's attempts to prevent their dissemination.

In Spain, three sovereigns — Charles IV, Napoleon's brother Joseph Bonaparte, and Ferdinand VII — claimed the throne, often issuing different edicts simultaneously. Since the time of Philip II, Spain had been a tightly centralized monarchy with the crown making most decisions. Now, chaos reigned in the colonies.

As Spain's grip on the New World slipped between 1790 and 1820, Texas was almost forgotten, an internal province of little importance. Colonization was ignored; the Spanish government had larger problems in Europe and in Mexico.

Spain's mercantile economic policy penalized colonists in the area, charging them high prices for trade goods and paying low prices for products sent to markets in the interior of New Spain. As a result, settlers from central Mexico had no incentives to come to Texas. Indeed, men of ambition in the province often prospered by turning to illegal trade with Louisiana or to smuggling. On the positive side, however, Indians of the province had been mollified through annual gifts and by developing a dependence on Spain for trade goods.

Ranching flourished. In **1795,** a census found **69 families** living on 45 ranches in the **San Antonio** area. A census in **1803** indicated that there were **100,000 head of cattle** in Texas. But aside from a few additional families in Nacogdoches and La Bahía (near present-day Goliad), the province was thinly populated.

The largest group of early immigrants from the United States was not Anglo, but Indian.

As early as **1818, Cherokees** of the southeastern United States came to Texas, settling north of Nacogdoches on lands between the Trinity and Sabine rivers. The Cherokees had been among the first U.S. Indians to accept the federal government's offers of resettlement. As American pioneers entered the newly acquired lands of Georgia, Alabama and other areas of the Southeast, the Indians were systematically removed, through legal means or otherwise.

Some of the displaced groups settled on land provided in Arkansas Territory, but others, such as the Cherokees, came to Texas. These Cherokees were among the "Five Civilized Tribes" that had adopted agriculture and many Anglo customs in an unsuccessful attempt to get along with their new neighbors. Alabama and Coushatta tribes had exercised squatters' rights in present Sabine County in the early 1800s, and soon after the Cherokees arrived, groups of Shawnee, Delaware and Kickapoo Indians came from the United States.

A **second wave of Anglo** immigrants began to arrive in Texas, larger than the first and of a different character. These Anglos were not so interested in agricultural opportunities as in other schemes to quickly recoup their fortunes.

Spain recognized the danger represented by the

unregulated colonization by Americans. The Spanish Cortes' colonization law of 1813 attempted to build a buffer between the eastern frontier and northern Mexico. Special permission was required for Americans to settle within 52 miles of the international boundary, although this prohibition often was ignored.

As initially envisioned, Americans would be allowed to settle the interior of Texas. Colonists from Europe and Mexico would be placed along the eastern frontier to limit contact between the Americans and the United States. Spanish officials felt that the Americans already in Texas illegally would be stable if given a stake in the province through land ownership.

Moses Austin, a former Spanish subject in the vast Louisiana Territory, applied for the first empresario grant from the Spanish government. With the intercession of Baron de Bastrop, a friend of Austin's from Missouri Territory, the request was approved in January **1821.**

Austin agreed to settle **300 families** on land bounded by the Brazos and Colorado rivers on the east and west, by El Camino Real (the old military road running from San Antonio to Nacogdoches) on the north and by the Gulf Coast.

Col-lee, chief of a band of the Cherokees. As early as 1818, Cherokees settled in Texas north of Nacogdoches on lands between the Trinity and Sabine rivers. Photo from the Smithsonian Institution.

But Austin died in June 1821, leaving the work to his son, **Stephen F. Austin**. Problems began as soon as the first authorized colonists arrived in Texas the following December when it was learned that Mexico had gained independence from Spain.

Mexico, 1821–1836

Mexico's war for independence, 1810–1821, was savage and bloody in the interior provinces, and Texas suffered as well.

In early 1812, Mexican revolutionary José Bernardo Gutiérrez de Lara traveled to Natchitoches, La., where, with the help of U.S. agents, an expedition was organized. **Augustus W. Magee**, a West Point graduate, commanded the troop, which entered Texas in August 1812. This "Republican Army of the North" easily took Nacogdoches, where it gathered recruits.

After withstanding a siege at La Bahía, the army took San Antonio and proclaimed the First Republic of Texas in April 1813. A few months later, the republican forces were bloodily subdued at the Battle of Medina River.

Royalist Gen. Joaquín de Arredondo executed a staggering number of more than 300 republicans, including some Americans, at San Antonio, and a young lieutenant, **Antonio López de Santa Anna**, was recognized for valor under fire.

When the war finally ended in Mexico in 1821, little more had been achieved than separation from Spain.

Sensing that liberal reforms in Spain would reduce the authority of royalists in the New World, Mexican conservatives had led the revolt against the mother country. They also achieved early victories in the debate over the form of government the newly independent Mexico should adopt.

An independent Mexico was torn between advocates of centralist and federalist forms of government.

The former royalists won the opening debates, settling Emperor Agustín de Iturbide on the new Mexican throne. But he was overthrown and the Constitution of 1824, a federalist document, was adopted.

The Mexican election of 1828 was a turning point in the history of the country when the legally elected administration of Manuel Gómez Pedraza was overthrown by supporters of Vicente Guerrero, who in turn was ousted by his own vice president Anastasio Bustamante. Mexico's most chaotic political period followed. Between 1833 and 1855, the Mexican presidency changed hands 36 times.

Texas, 1821–1833

Mexico's **land policy**, like Spain's, differed from the U.S. approach. Whereas the United States sold land directly to settlers or to speculators who dealt with the pioneers, the Mexicans retained tight control of the property transfer until predetermined agreements for development were fulfilled.

But a 4,428-acre *sitio* — a square league — and a 177-acre *labor* could be obtained for only surveying costs and administrative fees as low as $50. The empresario was rewarded with grants of large tracts of land, but only when he fulfilled his quota of families to be brought to the colonies.

Considering the prices the U.S. government charged, Texas' land was indeed a bargain and a major attraction to those Americans looking for a new start.

More than 25 empresarios were commissioned to settle colonists. Empresarios included **Green DeWitt** and **Martín de León**, who in 1824 founded the city of Guadalupe Victoria (present-day Victoria).

By 1830, Texas boasted an estimated population of 15,000, with Anglo-Americans outnumbering Hispanics by a margin of four to one.

Stephen F. Austin was easily the most successful empresario. After his initial success, Austin was authorized in 1825 to bring 900 more families to Texas, and in 1831, he and his partner, **Samuel Williams**, received another concession to bring 800 Mexican and European families.

Through Austin's efforts, 1,540 land titles were issued to settlers.

In the early years of colonization, the settlers busied themselves clearing land, planting crops, building homes and fending off Indian attacks. Many were successful in establishing a subsistence economy.

One weakness of the Mexican colonial policy was that it did not provide the factors for a market economy. Although towns were established, credit, banks and good roads were not provided by the government.

Ports were established at Galveston and Matagorda bays after Mexican independence, but the colonists felt they needed more, particularly one at the mouth of the Brazos. And foreign ships were barred from coastwise trade, which posed a particular hardship since Mexico had few merchant ships.

To settle in Texas, pioneers had to become Mexican citizens and to embrace Roman Catholicism. Most of the Americans were Protestants, if they adhered to any religion, and they were fiercely defensive of the right to **religious freedom** enjoyed in the United States.

Although no more than one-fourth of the Americans ever swore allegiance to the Catholic Church, the requirement was a long-standing irritation.

Slavery, too, was a point of contention. Mexico prohibited the introduction of slavery after December 1827. Nevertheless, several efforts were made to evade the government policy. Austin got the state Legislature to recognize labor contracts under which slaves were technically free but bound themselves to their masters for life. Often entire families were covered by a single contract. While many early Anglo colonists were not slaveholders, they were Southerners, and the ownership of slaves was a cultural institution that they supported. The problem was never settled during the colonial period despite the tensions it generated.

Most of the early Anglo-American colonists in Texas intended to fulfill their pledge to become good Mexican citizens. But the political turmoil following the 1828 presidential election raised doubts in the Americans' minds about the ability of Mexico to make representative government function properly.

On a tour of Texas in 1827 and 1828, Gen. Manuel Mier y Terán noted that the Texans "carried their constitutions in their pockets." And he feared the Americans' desire for more rights and liberties than the government was prepared to offer would lead to rebellion.

Unrest increased in Texas when Gen. Mier y Terán began reinforcing existing garrisons and establishing new ones.

But a major factor in the discontent of Americans came with the **decree of April 6, 1830**, when the Mexican government in essence banned further American immigration into Texas and tried to control slavery. *(For a related account on how Texans opposed this decree at Fort Anahuac, see page 27.)*

Austin protested that the prohibition against American immigration would not stop the flow of Anglos into Texas; it would stop only the stable, prosperous Americans from coming.

Austin's predictions were fulfilled. Illegal immigrants continued to come. By 1836, the estimated number of people in Texas had reached 35,000.

Prelude to Revolution

In the midst of all the turmoil, Texas was prospering. By 1834, some 7,000 bales of cotton with a value of $315,000 were shipped to New Orleans. In the middle of the decade, Texas exports, including cotton and beaver, otter and deer skins, amounted to $500,000.

Trade ratios were out of balance, however, because $630,000 in manufactured goods were imported. And, there was little currency in Texas. Ninety percent of the business transactions were conducted in barter or credit.

In 1833 and 1834, the **Coahuila y Texas** legislature was diligently trying to respond to the complaints of the Texas colonists. The English language was recognized for official purposes. Religious toleration was approved. The court system was revised, providing Texas with an appellate court and trial by jury.

In Mexico City, however, a different scenario was developing. **Santa Anna** assumed supreme authority in April 1834 and began dismantling the federalist government. Among the most offensive changes dictated by Santa Anna was the reduction of the state militias to one man per each 500 population. The intent was to eliminate possible armed opposition to the emerging centralist government.

But liberals in the state of Zacatecas in central Mexico rebelled. Santa Anna's response was particularly brutal, as he tried to make an example of the rebels. Troops were allowed to sack the state capital after the victory over the insurgents.

Trouble also was brewing closer to the Texans.

In March 1833, the Coahuila y Texas legislature moved the state capital from Saltillo to Monclova. The Monclova legislature in 1834 gave the governor authority to sell 400 sitios — or 1.77 million acres of land — to finance the government and to provide for protection. A year later the lawmakers criticized Santa Anna's reputation on federalism. Seeing a chance to regain lost prestige, Saltillo declared for Santa Anna and set up an opposition government. In the spring of 1835, Santa Anna sent his brother-in-law, Martín Perfecto de Cos, to break up the state government at Monclova.

Texans were appalled by the breakdown in state government, coming on the heels of so many assurances that the political situation was to improve.

Texas politics were polarizing. A "war party" advocated breaking away from Mexico altogether, while a "peace party" urged calm and riding out the political storm. Most of the settlers, however, aligned with neither group.

In January 1835, Santa Anna sent a detachment of soldiers to Anahuac to reinforce the customs office, but duties were being charged irregularly at various ports on the coast. William B. Travis, in an act not supported by all colonists, led a contingent of armed colonists against the Mexican soldiers, who withdrew without a fight.

Although some members of the peace party wrote Mexican Gen. **Martín Perfecto de Cos**, stationed at Matamoros, apologizing for the action, he was not compromising. Cos demanded that the group be arrested and turned over to him. The Texans refused.

The committees of correspondence, organized at the Convention of 1832 (which had asked that Texas be separated from Coahuila), began organizing another meeting. Because the term "convention" aroused visions of revolution in the eyes of Mexican officials, the gathering at Washington-on-the-Brazos in October 1835 was called a "consultation." But with the breakdown of the state government and with Santa Anna's repeal of the Constitution of 1824, the American settlers felt well within their rights to provide a new framework with which to govern Texas.

Fresh from brutally putting down the rebellion in Zacatecas, Santa Anna turned his attention to Texas. Gen. Cos was determined to regarrison the state, and the settlers were equally determined to keep soldiers out.

Col. **Domingo de Ugartechea**, headquartered at San Antonio, became concerned about armed rebellion when he heard of the incident at Anahuac. He recalled a six-pound cannon that had been given DeWitt colonists to fight Indians.

Ugartechea ordered Cpl. Casimira de León with five men to Gonzales to retrieve the weapon. No problems were expected, but officials at Gonzales refused to surrender the weapon. When the Mexicans reinforced Cpl. León's men, a call was sent out for volunteers to help the Gonzales officials. Dozens responded.

Oct. 2, 1835, the Texans challenged the Mexicans with a **"come-and-take-it" flag** over the cannon. After a brief skirmish, the Mexicans withdrew, but the first rounds in the Texas Revolution had been fired.

Winning Independence

As 1836 opened, Texans felt in control of their destiny and secure in their land and their liberties. The Mexican army had been driven from their soil.

But tragedy loomed. Easy victories over government forces at Anahuac, Nacogdoches, Goliad, Gonzales and San Antonio in the fall of 1835 had given them a false sense of security. That independent mood was their undoing, for no government worthy of the name coordinated the defense of Texas. Consequently, as the Mexican counterattack developed, no one was in charge. Sam Houston was titular commander-in-chief of the Texas forces, but he had little authority.

Some even thought the Mexicans would not try to re-enter Texas. Few Texans counted on the energy and determination of Santa Anna, the dictator of Mexico.

The status of the strongholds along the San Antonio River was of concern to Houston. In mid-January, Houston sent **James Bowie** to San Antonio to determine if the Alamo was defensible. If not, Bowie had orders to destroy it and withdraw the men and artillery to Gonzales and Copano.

On Feb. 8, David Crockett of Tennessee, bringing 12 men with him, arrived to aid the revolutionaries.

On Feb. 12, 1836, Santa Anna's main force crossed the Rio Grande headed for San Antonio. The Mexican battle plan had been debated. But Mexico's national pride was bruised by the series of defeats the nation's army had suffered in 1835, capped by Gen. Cos's ouster from San Antonio in December.

On Feb. 11, the Consultation's "governor of the government" **Henry Smith**, sent **William B. Travis** to San Antonio. Immediately a split in command at the **Alamo** garrison arose. Most were American volunteers who looked to the Houston-appointed Bowie as their leader. Travis had only a handful of Texas army regulars. Bowie and Travis agreed to share the command of 150 men.

Arriving at the Alamo on Feb. 23, Santa Anna left no doubt regarding his attitude toward the defenders. He hoisted a blood-red flag, the traditional Mexican symbol of no quarter, no surrender, no mercy. Travis and Bowie defiantly answered the display with a cannon shot.

Immediately the Mexicans began surrounding the Alamo and bombarding it. Throughout the first night and nights to come, Santa Anna kept up a continual din to destroy the defenders' morale.

On Feb. 24, Bowie became ill and relinquished his share of command to Travis. Although the Mexican bombardment of the Alamo continued, none of the defenders was killed. In fact, they conducted several successful forays outside the fortress to burn buildings that were providing cover for the Mexican gunners and to gather firewood.

Messengers also successfully moved through the Mexican lines at will, and 32 reinforcements from Gonzales made it into the Alamo without a loss on March 1.

Historians disagree over which flag flew over the defenders of the Alamo.

Mexican sources have said that Santa Anna was outraged when he saw flying over the fortress a Mexican tricolor, identical to the ones carried by his troops except with the numbers "1 8 2 4" emblazoned upon it. Some Texas historians have accepted this version because the defenders of the Alamo could not have known that Texas' independence had been declared on March 2. To the knowledge of the Alamo's defenders, the last official position taken by Texas was in support of the Constitution of 1824, which the flag symbolized. But the only flag found after the battle, according to historian Walter Lord, was one flown by the **New Orleans Greys**.

By March 5, Santa Anna had 4,000 men in camp, a force he felt sufficient to subdue the Alamo.

Historians disagree on the date, but the story goes that on March 3 or 5, Travis called his command together and explained the bleak outlook. He then asked those willing to die for freedom to stay and fight; those not willing could try to get through enemy lines to safety. Even the sick Jim Bowie vowed to stay. Only Louis (Moses) Rose, a veteran of Napoleon's retreat from Moscow slipped out of the Alamo that night.

At dawn March 6, Santa Anna's forces attacked. When the fighting stopped between 8:30 and 9 a.m., all the defenders were dead. Only a few women, children and black slaves survived the assault. **Davy Crockett**'s fate is still debated. Mexican officer Enrique de la Peña held that Crockett was captured with a few other defenders and was executed by Santa Anna.

Santa Anna's victory came at the cost of almost one-third his forces killed or wounded. Their deaths in such number set back Santa Anna's timetable. The fall of the Alamo also brutally shook Texans out of their lethargy.

Sam Houston, finally given command of the entire Texas army, left the convention at **Washington-on-the-Brazos** on the day of the fall of the Alamo.

On March 11, he arrived at Gonzales to begin organizing the troops. Two days later, **Susanna Dickinson**, the wife of one of the victims of the Alamo, and two slaves arrived at Houston's position at Gonzales with the news of the fall of the San Antonio fortress.

Houston then ordered **James Fannin** to abandon the old presidio **La Bahía** at Goliad and to retreat to Victoria. Fannin had arrived at the fort in late January with more than 400 men. As a former West Pointer, he had a background in military planning, but Fannin had refused Travis' pleas for help, and after receiving Houston's orders, Fannin waited for scouting parties to return.

Finally, on March 19, he left, but too late. Forward elements of Gen. José de Urrea's troops caught Fannin's command on an open prairie. After a brief skirmish Fannin surrendered.

Santa Anna was furious when Gen. Urrea appealed for clemency for the captives. The Mexican leader issued orders for their execution. On March 27, a Palm Sunday, most of the prisoners were divided into groups and marched out of Goliad, thinking they were being transferred to other facilities. When the executions began, many escaped. But about 350 were killed.

On March 17, Houston reached the Colorado near the present city of La Grange and began receiving reinforcements. Within a week, the small force of several hundred had become almost respectable, with 1,200-1,400 men in camp.

At the time Houston reached the Colorado, the convention at Washington-on-the-Brazos was completing work. **David Burnet**, a New Jersey native, was named interim president of the new Texas government, and **Lorenzo de Zavala**, a Yucatán native, was named vice president.

On March 27, Houston moved his men to San Felipe on the Brazos. The Texas army was impatient for a fight, and there was talk in the ranks that, if action did not develop soon, a new commander should be elected.

As the army marched farther back toward the San Jacinto River, two Mexican couriers were captured and gave Houston the information he hoped for. Santa Anna in his haste had led the small Mexican force in front of Houston. Now the Texans had an opportunity to win the war.

Throughout the revolt, Houston's intelligence system had operated efficiently. Scouts, commanded by **Erastus "Deaf" Smith**, kept the Texans informed of Mexican troop movements. **Hendrick Arnold**, a free black, was a valuable spy, posing as a runaway slave to enter Mexican camps to gain information.

Early on April 21, Gen. Cos reinforced Santa Anna's troops with more than 500 men. The new arrivals, who had marched all night, disrupted the camp's routine for a time, but soon all the soldiers and officers settled down for a midday rest.

About 3 p.m., Houston ordered his men to parade and the battle was launched at 4:30 p.m.

A company of Mexican-Texans, commanded by **Juan Seguín**, had served as the rear guard for Houston's army through much of the retreat across Texas and had fought many skirmishes with the Mexican army in the process.

Perhaps fearing the Mexican-Texans would be mistaken for Santa Anna's soldiers, Houston had assigned the company to guard duty as the battle approached. But after the men protested, they fought in the battle of San Jacinto.

Historians disagree widely on the number of troops on each side. Houston probably had about 900 while Santa Anna had between 1,100 and 1,300.

But the Texans had the decided psychological advantage. Two thirds of the fledgling Republic's army were "old Texans" who had family and land to defend. They had an investment of years of toil in building their homes. And they were eager to avenge the massacre of men at the Alamo and Goliad.

In less than 20 minutes they set the Mexican army to rout. More than 600 Mexicans were killed and hundreds more wounded or captured. Only nine of the Texans died in the fight.

It was not until the following day that Santa Anna was captured. One Texan noticed that a grubby soldier his patrol found in the high grass had a silk shirt under his filthy jacket. Although denying he was an officer, he was taken back to camp, where he was acknowledged with cries of "El Presidente" by other prisoners. Santa Anna introduced himself when taken to the wounded Houston.

President Burnet took charge of Santa Anna, and on May 14 the dictator signed **two treaties at Velasco**, a public document and a secret one. The public agreement declared that hostilities would cease, that the Mexican army would withdraw to south of the Rio Grande, that prisoners would be released and that Santa Anna would be shipped to Veracruz as soon as possible.

In the secret treaty, Santa Anna agreed to recognize Texas' independence, to give diplomatic recognition, to negotiate a commercial treaty and to set the **Rio Grande** as the new Republic's boundary.

Republic of Texas, 1836–1845

Sam Houston was easily the most dominant figure through the nearly 10-year history of the Republic of Texas. While he was roundly criticized for the retreat across Texas during the revolution, the victory at San Jacinto endeared him to most of the new nation's inhabitants.

Houston handily defeated Henry Smith and Stephen F. Austin in the election called in September 1836 by the interim government, and he was inaugurated as president on Oct. 22.

In the same September election, voters overwhelmingly approved a proposal to request annexation to the United States.

The first cabinet appointed by the new president represented an attempt to heal old political wounds. Austin was named secretary of state and Smith was secretary of the treasury. But Texas suffered a major tragedy in late December 1836 when Austin, the acknowledged **"Father of Texas,"** died of pneumonia.

A host of problems faced the new government. Santa Anna was still in custody, and public opinion favored his execution. Texas' leadership wisely kept Santa Anna alive, first to keep from giving the Mexicans an emotional rallying point for launching another invasion. Second, the Texas leaders hoped that the dictator would keep his promise to work for recognition of Texas.

Santa Anna was released in November 1836 and made his way to Washington, D.C. Houston hoped the dictator could persuade U.S. President **Andrew Jackson** to recognize Texas.

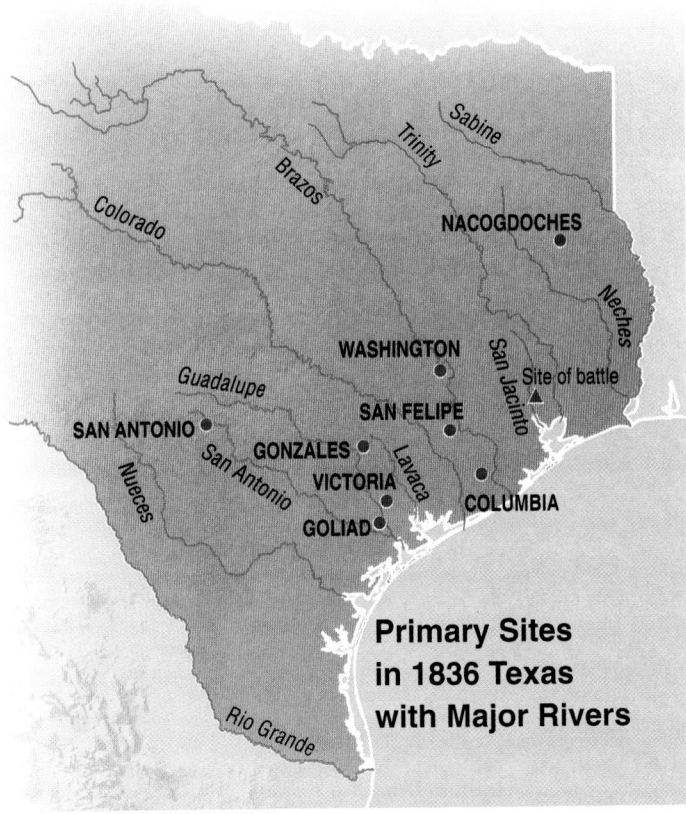

Primary Sites in 1836 Texas with Major Rivers

Jackson refused to see Santa Anna, who returned to Mexico, where he had fallen from power.

Another major challenge was the Texas army. The new commander, Felix Huston, favored an invasion of Mexico, and the troops, made up now mostly of American volunteers who came to Texas after the battle of San Jacinto, were rebellious and ready to fight.

President Houston tried to replace Felix Huston with **Albert Sidney Johnston**, but Huston seriously wounded Johnston in a duel. In May 1837, Huston was asked to the capital in Columbia to discuss the invasion. While Huston was away from the troops, Houston sent **Thomas J. Rusk**, the secretary of war, to furlough the army without pay — but with generous land grants. Only 600 men were retained in the army.

The Republic's other problems were less tractable. The economy needed attention, Indians still were a threat, Mexico remained warlike, foreign relations had to be developed, and relations with the United States had to be solidified.

The greatest disappointment in Houston's first term was the failure to have the Republic annexed to the United States. Henry Morfit, President Jackson's agent, toured the new Republic in the summer of 1836. Although impressed, Morfit reported that Texas' best chance at continued independence lay in the "stupidity of the rulers of Mexico and the financial embarrassment

of the Mexican government." He recommended that annexation be delayed.

Houston's foreign policy achieved initial success when **J. Pinckney Henderson** negotiated a trade treaty with Great Britain. Although the agreement was short of outright diplomatic recognition, it was progress. In the next few years, France, Belgium, The Netherlands and some German states recognized the new Republic.

Under the constitution, Houston's first term lasted only two years, and he could not succeed himself. His successor, **Mirabeau B. Lamar,** had grand visions and was a spendthrift. Houston's first term cost Texas only about $500,000, while President Lamar and the Congress spent $5 million in the next three years.

Early in 1839, Lamar gained recognition as the "Father of Education" in Texas when the Congress granted each of the existing 23 counties three leagues of land to be used for education. Fifty leagues of land were set aside for a university.

Despite the lip service paid to education, the government did not have the money for several years to set up a school system. Most education during the Republic was provided by private schools and churches.

Lamar's Indian policies differed greatly from those under Houston. Houston had lived with Cherokees as a youth, was adopted as a member of a tribe and advocated Indian rights long before coming to Texas. Lamar reflected more the frontier attitude toward American

A replica of the first capitol of the Republic of Texas stands in West Columbia in Brazoria County. In 1836, when it was the capital, the town was called simply Columbia. File photo.

Indians. His first experience in public life was as secretary to Gov. George Troup of Georgia, who successfully opposed the federal government's policy of assimilation of Indians at the time. Indians were simply removed from Georgia.

Texans first tried to negotiate the Cherokees' removal from the region, but in July 1839, the Indians were forcibly ejected from Texas at the **Battle of the Neches River** in Van Zandt County. Houston's close friend, the aging Cherokee chief **Philip Bowles**, was killed in the battle while Houston was visiting former President Jackson in Tennessee. The Cherokees moved on to Arkansas and Indian Territory.

Houston was returned to the presidency of the Republic in 1841. His second administration was even more frugal than his first; soon income almost matched expenditures.

Houston re-entered negotiations with the Indians in Central Texas in an attempt to quell the raids on settlements. A number of trading posts were opened along the frontier to pacify the Indians.

War fever reached a high pitch in Texas in 1842, and Houston grew increasingly unpopular because he would not launch an offensive war against Mexico.

In March 1842, Gen. **Rafael Vásquez** staged guerrilla raids on San Antonio, Victoria and Goliad, but quickly left the Republic.

A force of 3,500 Texas volunteers gathered at San Antonio demanding that Mexico be punished. Houston urged calm, but the clamor increased when Mexican **Gen. Adrian Woll** captured San Antonio in September. He raised the Mexican flag and declared the reconquest of Texas.

Ranger Capt. **Jack Hays** was camped nearby. Within days 600 volunteers had joined him, eager to drive the Mexican invaders from Texas soil. Gen. Woll withdrew after the **Battle of Salado**.

Alexander Somervell was ordered by Houston to follow with 700 troops and harass the Mexican army. He reached Laredo in December and found no Mexican troops. Somervell crossed the Rio Grande to find military targets. A few days later, the commander returned home, but 300 soldiers decided to continue the raid under the command of William S. Fisher. On Christmas day, this group attacked the village of **Mier**, only to be defeated by a Mexican force that outnumbered them 10-to-1.

After attempting mass escape, the survivors of the Mier expedition were marched to Mexico City where Santa Anna, again in political power, ordered their execution. When officers refused to carry out the order, it was amended to require execution of one of every 10 Texans. The prisoners drew beans to determine who would be shot; bearers of **black beans** were executed. Texans again were outraged by the treatment of prisoners, but the war fever soon subsided.

As Houston completed his second term, the United States was becoming more interested in annexation. Texas had seriously flirted with Great Britain and France, and the Americans did not want a rival republic with close foreign ties on the North American continent. Houston orchestrated the early stages of the final steps toward annexation. It was left to his successor, **Anson Jones**, to complete the process.

The Republic of Texas' main claim to fame is simply endurance. Its settlers, unlike other Americans who had military help, had cleared a large region of Indians by themselves, had established farms and communities and had persevered through extreme economic hardship.

Adroit political leadership had gained the Republic recognition from many foreign countries. Although dreams of empire may have dimmed, Texans had established an identity on a major portion of the North American continent. The frontier had been pushed to a line running from Corpus Christi through San Antonio and Austin to the Red River.

The U.S. presidential campaign of 1844 was to make Texas a part of the Union. ☆

Annexation to 1978

Annexation

Annexation to the United States was far from automatic for Texas once independence from Mexico was gained in 1836. Sam Houston noted that Texas "was more coy than forward" as negotiations reached a climax in 1845.

William H. Wharton was Texas' first representative in Washington. His instructions were to gain diplomatic recognition of the new Republic's independence.

After some squabbles, the U.S. Congress appropriated funds for a minister to Texas, and President Andrew Jackson recognized the new country in one of his last acts in office in March 1837.

Texas President **Mirabeau B. Lamar** (1838–41) opposed annexation. He held visions of empire in which Texas would rival the United States for supremacy on the North American continent.

During his administration, Great Britain began a close relationship with Texas and made strenuous efforts to get Mexico to recognize the Republic. This relationship between Great Britain and Texas raised fears in the United States that Britain might attempt to make Texas part of its empire.

Southerners feared for the future of slavery in Texas, which had renounced the importation of slaves as a concession to get a trade treaty with Great Britain, and American newspapers noted that trade with Texas had suffered after the Republic received recognition from European countries.

In Houston's second term in the Texas presidency, he instructed **Isaac Van Zandt**, his minister in Washington, to renew the annexation negotiations. Although U.S. President **John Tyler** and his cabinet were eager to annex Texas, they were worried about ratification in the U.S. Senate. The annexation question was put off.

In January 1844, Houston again gave Van Zandt instructions to propose annexation talks. This time the United States agreed to Houston's standing stipulation that, for serious negotiations to take place, the United States must provide military protection to Texas. U.S. naval forces were ordered to the Gulf of Mexico and U.S. troops were positioned on the southwest border close to Texas.

On April 11, 1844, Texas and the United States signed a treaty for annexation. Texas would enter the Union as a territory, not a state, under terms of the treaty. The United States would assume Texas' debt up to $10 million and would negotiate Texas' southwestern boundary with Mexico.

On June 8, 1844, the U.S. Senate rejected the treaty with a vote of 35-16, with much of the opposition coming from the slavery abolition wing of the Whig Party.

But **westward expansion** became a major issue in the U.S. presidential election that year. James K. Polk, the Democratic nominee, was a supporter of expansion, and the party's platform called for adding Oregon and Texas to the Union.

After Polk won the election in November, President Tyler declared that the people had spoken on the issue of annexation, and he resubmitted the matter to Congress.

Several bills were introduced in the U.S. House of Representatives containing various proposals.

In **February 1845**, the U.S. Congress approved a resolution that would bring Texas into the Union as a state. Texas would cede its public property, such as forts and custom houses, to the United States, but it could keep its public lands and must retain its public debt. The region could be divided into four new states in addition to the original Texas. And the United States would negotiate the Rio Grande boundary claim.

British officials asked the Texas government to delay consideration of the U.S. offer for 90 days to attempt to get Mexico to recognize the Republic. The delay did no good: Texans' minds were made up.

President Anson Jones, who succeeded Houston in 1844, called a convention to write a **state constitution** in Austin on July 4, 1845.

Mexico finally recognized Texas' independence, but the recognition was rejected. **Texas voters overwhelmingly accepted the U.S. proposal** and approved the new constitution in a referendum.

On **Dec. 29, 1845**, the U.S. Congress accepted the state constitution, and Texas became the 28th state in the Union. The first meeting of the Texas Legislature took place on Feb. 16, 1846.

1845–1860

The entry of Texas into the Union touched off the **War with Mexico**, a war that some historians now think was planned by President James K. Polk to obtain the vast American Southwest.

Gen. **Zachary Taylor** was sent to Corpus Christi, just above the Nueces River, in July 1845. In February 1846, right after Texas formally entered the Union, the general was ordered to move troops into the disputed area south of the Nueces to the mouth of the Rio Grande. Mexican officials protested the move, claiming the status of the territory was under negotiation.

After Gen. Taylor refused to leave, Mexican President **Mariano Paredes** declared the opening of a defensive war against the United States on April 24, 1846.

After initial encounters at **Palo Alto** and **Resaca de la Palma**, both a few miles north of today's **Brownsville**, the war was fought south of the Rio Grande.

President Polk devised a plan to raise 50,000 volunteers from every section of the United States to fight the war. About 5,000 Texans saw action in Mexico.

Steamboats provided an important supply link for U.S. forces along the Rio Grande. Historical figures such as **Richard King**, founder of the legendary King Ranch, and **Mifflin Kenedy**, another rancher and businessman, first came to the **Lower Rio Grande Valley** as steamboat operators during the war.

Much farther up the Rio Grande, the war was hardly noticed. U.S. forces moved south from Santa Fe, which had been secured in December 1846. After a minor skirmish with Mexican forces north of El Paso, the U.S. military established American jurisdiction in this part of Texas.

Gen. **Winfield Scott** brought the war to a close in March 1847 with the capture of Mexico City.

When the **Treaty of Guadalupe Hidalgo** was signed on Feb. 2, 1848, the United States had acquired

Log cabins, such as the Himes Log House at Heritage Park in Euless, were built by early settlers in Texas. The Himes Log House was a one-room cabin with a loft that was built in the 1850s. It is the oldest structure in Euless. Texas Almanac photo.

the American Southwest for development. And in Texas, the Rio Grande became an international boundary.

Europeans, of whom the vast majority were **German**, rather than Anglos, were the first whites to push the Texas frontier into west Central Texas after annexation. **John O. Meusebach** became leader of the German immigration movement in Texas, and he led a wagon train of some 120 settlers to the site of **Fredericksburg** in May 1846.

Germans also migrated to the major cities, such as San Antonio and Galveston, and by 1850 there were more people of German birth or parentage in Texas than there were Mexican-Texans.

The estimated population of 150,000 at annexation grew to 212,592, including 58,161 slaves, in the first U.S. census count in Texas in 1850.

As the state's population grew, the regions developed distinct population characteristics. The southeast and eastern sections attracted immigrants from the Lower South, the principal slaveholding states. Major plantations developed in these areas.

North Texas got more Upper Southerners and Midwesterners. These immigrants were mostly small farmers and few owned slaves.

Mexican-Texans had difficulty with Anglo immigrants. The **"cart war"** broke out in 1857. Mexican teamsters controlled the transportation of goods from the Gulf coast to San Antonio and could charge lower rates than their competition.

A campaign of terror was launched by Anglo haulers, especially around Goliad, in an attempt to drive the Mexican-Texans out of business. Intervention by the U.S. and Mexican governments finally brought the situation under control, but it stands as an example of the attitudes held by Anglo-Texans toward Mexican-Texans.

Cotton was by far the state's largest money crop, but corn, sweet potatoes, wheat and sugar also were produced. **Saw milling** and grain milling became the major industries, employing 40 percent of the manufacturing workers.

Land disputes and the public-debt issue were settled with the **Compromise of 1850**. Texas gave up claims to territory extending to Santa Fe and beyond in exchange for $10 million from the federal government. That sum was used to pay off the debt of the Republic.

Personalities, especially Sam Houston, dominated elections during early statehood, but, for most Texans, politics were unimportant. Voter turnouts were low in the 1850s until the movement toward secession gained strength.

Secession

Texas' population almost tripled in the decade between 1850 and 1860, when 604,215 people were counted, including 182,921 slaves.

Many of these new settlers came from the Lower South, a region familiar with slavery. Although three-quarters of the Texas population and two-thirds of the farmers did not own slaves, slaveowners controlled 60 to

70 percent of the wealth of the state and dominated the politics.

In 1850, 41 percent of the state's officeholders were from the slaveholding class; a decade later, more than 50 percent of the officeholders had slaves.

In addition to the political power of the slaveholders, they also provided role models for new immigrants to the state. After these newcomers got their first land, they saw slave ownership as another step up the economic ladder, whether they owned slaves or not. Slave ownership was an economic goal.

This attitude prevailed even in areas of Texas where slaveholding was not widespread or even practical.

These factors were the wind that fanned the flames of the secessionist movement throughout the late 1850s.

The appearance of the **Know-Nothing Party**, which based its platform on a pro-American, anti-immigrant foundation, began to move Texas toward party politics. Because of the large number of foreign-born settlers, the party attracted many Anglo voters.

In 1854, the Know-Nothings elected candidates to city offices in San Antonio, and a year later, the mayor of Galveston was elected with the party's backing. Also in 1855, the Know-Nothings elected 20 representatives and five senators to the Legislature.

The successes spurred the **Democrats** to serious party organization for the first time. In 1857, **Hardin Runnels** was nominated for governor at the Democratic convention held in Waco.

Sam Houston sought the governorship as an independent, but he also got Know-Nothing backing. Democrats were organized, however, and Houston was dealt the only election defeat in his political career.

Runnels was a strong states'-rights Democrat who irritated many Texans during his administration by advocating reopening the slave trade. His popularity on the frontier also dropped when Indian raids became more severe.

Most Texans still were ambivalent about secession. The Union was seen as a protector of physical and economic stability. No threats to person or property were perceived in remaining attached to the United States.

In 1859, Houston again challenged Runnels, basing his campaign on Unionism. Combined with Houston's personal popularity, his position on the secession issue apparently satisfied most voters, for they gave him a solid victory over the more radical Runnels. In addition, Unionists **A.J. Hamilton** and **John H. Reagan** won the state's two congressional seats. Texans gave the states'-rights Democrats a sound whipping at the polls.

Within a few months, however, events were to change radically the political atmosphere of the state. On the frontier, the army could not control Indian raids, and with the later refusal of a Republican-controlled Congress to provide essential aid in fighting Indians, the federal government fell into disrepute.

Secessionists played on the growing distrust. Then in the summer of 1860, a series of fires in the cities

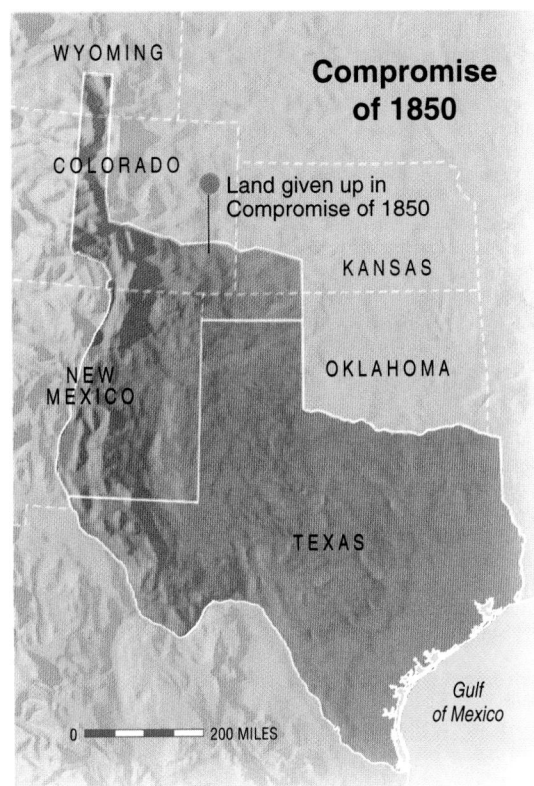

Compromise of 1850

Land given up in Compromise of 1850

WYOMING

COLORADO

KANSAS

NEW MEXICO

OKLAHOMA

TEXAS

Gulf of Mexico

0 ▬▬▬ 200 MILES

around the state aroused fears that an abolitionist plot was afoot and that a slave uprising might be at hand — a traditional concern in a slaveholding society.

Vigilantes lynched blacks and Northerners across Texas, and a siege mentality developed.

When **Abraham Lincoln** was elected president (he was not on the ballot in Texas), secessionists went to work in earnest.

Pleas were made to Gov. Houston to call the Legislature into session to consider secession. Houston refused, hoping the passions would cool. They did not. Finally, **Oran M. Roberts** and other secessionist leaders issued a call to the counties to hold elections and send delegates to a convention in Austin. Ninety-two of 122 counties responded, and on Jan. 28, 1861, the meeting convened.

Only eight delegates voted against secession, while 166 supported it. An election was called for Feb. 23, 1861, and the ensuing campaign was marked by intolerance and violence. Opponents of secession were often intimidated — except the governor, who courageously stumped the state opposing withdrawal from the Union. Houston also argued that if Texas did secede it should revert to its status as an independent republic and not join the Confederacy.

Only one-fourth of the state's population had been in Texas during the days of independence, and the argument carried no weight. On election day, 76 percent of 61,000 voters favored secession.

President Lincoln, who took office within a couple of weeks, reportedly sent the Texas governor a letter offering 50,000 federal troops to keep Texas in the Union. But after a meeting with other Unionists, Houston declined the offer. "I love Texas too well to bring strife and bloodshed upon her," the governor declared.

On March 16, Houston refused to take an oath of loyalty to the Confederacy and was replaced in office by Lt. Gov. **Edward Clark**.

See page 410 for the results of the Referendum on Ordinance of Secession of 1861.

Civil War

Texas did not suffer the devastation of its Southern colleagues in the Civil War. On but a few occasions did Union troops occupy territory in Texas, except in the El Paso area.

An early version of the American flag waves in the breeze during a demonstration by the Sons of the Confederate Veterans at the Texas History Alive festival in Farmers Branch. File photo.

The state's cotton was important to the Confederate war effort because it could be transported from Gulf ports when other Southern shipping lanes were blockaded.

Some goods became difficult to buy, but unlike other states of the Confederacy, Texas still received consumer goods because of the trade that was carried on through Mexico during the war.

Although accurate figures are not available, historians estimate that between 70,000 and 90,000 Texans fought for the South, and between 2,000 and 3,000, including some former slaves, saw service in the Union army.

Texans became disenchanted with the Confederate government early in the war. State taxes were levied for the first time since the Compromise of 1850, and by war's end, the Confederacy had collected more than $37 million from the state.

But most of the complaints about the government centered on Brig. Gen. **Paul O. Hebert**, the Confederate commander of the Department of Texas.

In April 1862, Gen. Hebert declared martial law without notifying state officials. Opposition to the South's new conscription law, which exempted persons owning more than 15 slaves among other categories of exemptions, prompted the action.

In November 1862, the commander prohibited the export of cotton except under government control, and this proved a disastrous policy.

The final blow came when Gen. Hebert failed to defend **Galveston** and it fell into Union hands in the fall of 1862.

Maj. Gen. **John B. Magruder**, who replaced Hebert, was much more popular. The new commander's first actions were to combat the Union offensive against Texas ports. Sabine Pass had been closed in September 1862 by the Union blockade, and Galveston was in Northern hands.

On Jan. 1, 1863, Magruder retook Galveston with the help of two steamboats lined with cotton bales. Sharpshooters aboard proved devastating in battles against the Union fleet. Three weeks later, Magruder used two other cotton-clad steamboats to break the Union blockade of Sabine Pass, and two of the state's major ports were reopened.

Late in 1863, the Union launched a major offensive against the Texas coast that was partly successful. On Sept. 8, however, Lt. **Dick Dowling** and 42 men fought off a 1,500-man Union invasion force at **Sabine Pass**. In a brief battle, Dowling's command sank two Union gunboats and put the other invasion ships to flight.

Federal forces were more successful at the mouth of the Rio Grande. On Nov. 1, 1863, 7,000 Union troops landed at **Brazos Santiago**, and five days later, Union forces entered Brownsville.

Texas Unionists led by **E.J. Davis** were active in the Valley, moving as far upriver as Rio Grande City. Confederate Col. **John S. "Rip" Ford**, commanding state troops, finally pushed the Union soldiers out of Brownsville in July 1864, reopening the important port for the Confederacy.

Most Texans never saw a Union soldier during the war. The only ones they might have seen were in the **prisoner-of-war camps**. The largest, **Camp Ford**, near Tyler, housed 5,000 prisoners. Others operated in Kerr County and at Hempstead.

As the war dragged on, the mood of Texans changed. Those on the homefront began to feel they were sacrificing loved ones and suffering hardship so cotton speculators could profit.

Public order broke down as refugees flocked to Texas. And slaves from other states were sent to Texas for safekeeping. When the war ended, there were an estimated 400,000 slaves in Texas, more than double the number counted in the 1860 census.

Morale was low in Texas in early 1865. Soldiers at Galveston and Houston began to mutiny. At Austin, Confederate soldiers raided the state treasury in March and found only $5,000 in specie. Units began breaking up, and the army was beginning to dissolve before Gen. **Robert E. Lee** surrendered at **Appomattox** in April 1865. He surrendered the Army of Northern Virginia, and while this assured Union victory, the surrender of other Confederate units was to follow until the last unit gave up in Oklahoma at the end of June.

The last land battle of the Civil War was fought at **Palmito Ranch** near Brownsville on May 13, 1865. After the Confederate's victory, they learned the governors of the Western Rebel states had authorized the disbanding of armies, and, a few days later, they accepted a truce with the Union forces.

Reconstruction

On June 19, 1865, **Gen. Gordon Granger**, under the command of Gen. Philip M. Sheridan, arrived in Galveston with 1,800 federal troops to begin the Union occupation of Texas. Gen. Granger proclaimed the emancipation of the slaves.

A.J. Hamilton, a Unionist and former congressman from Texas, was named provisional governor by President Andrew Johnson.

Texas was in turmoil. Thousands of the state's men had died in the conflict. Indian raids had caused as much damage as the skirmishes with the Union army, causing the frontier to recede up to 100 miles eastward in some areas.

Even worse, confusion reigned. No one knew what to expect from the conquering forces.

Gen. Granger dispatched troops to the population centers of the state to restore civil authority. But only a handful of the 50,000 federal troops that came to Texas was stationed in the interior. Most were sent to the Rio Grande as a show of force against the French forces in Mexico, and clandestine aid was supplied to Mexican President Benito Juarez in his fight against the French and Mexican royalists.

The **frontier forts**, most of which were built during the early 1850s by the federal government to protect western settlements, had been abandoned by the U.S. Army after secession. These were not remanned, and a prohibition against a militia denied settlers a means of self-defense against Indian raids. *(For an overview of the frontier forts, see Texas Almanac 2004–2005.)*

Thousands of freed black slaves migrated to the cities, where they felt the federal soldiers would provide protection. Still others traveled the countryside, seeking family members and loved ones from whom they had been separated during the war.

The **Freedman's Bureau**, authorized by Congress in March 1865, began operation in September 1865 under Gen. E.M. Gregory. It had the responsibility to provide education, relief aid, labor supervision and judicial protection for the newly freed slaves.

The bureau was most successful in opening schools for blacks. Education was a priority because 95 percent of the freed slaves were illiterate.

The agency also was partially successful in getting blacks back to work on plantations under reasonable labor contracts.

Some plantation owners harbored hopes that they would be paid for their property loss when the slaves were freed. In some cases, the slaves were not released from plantations for up to a year.

To add to the confusion, some former slaves had the false notion that the federal government was going to parcel out the plantation lands to them. These blacks simply bided their time, waiting for the division of land.

Under pressure from President Johnson, Gov.

Hamilton called for an election of delegates to a **constitutional convention** in January 1866. Hamilton told the gathering what was expected: Former slaves were to be given civil rights; the secession ordinance had to be repealed; Civil War debt had to be repudiated; and slavery was to be abolished with ratification of the Thirteenth Amendment.

Many delegates to the convention were former secessionists, and there was little support for compromise.

J.W. Throckmorton, a Unionist and one of eight men who had opposed secession in the convention of 1861, was elected chairman of the convention. But a coalition of conservative Unionists and Democrats controlled the meeting. As a consequence, Texas took limited steps toward appeasing the victorious North.

Slavery was abolished, and blacks were given some civil rights. But they still could not vote and were barred from testifying in trials against whites.

No action was taken on the Thirteenth Amendment because, the argument went, the amendment already had been ratified.

Otherwise, the constitution that was written followed closely the constitution of 1845. President Johnson in August 1866 accepted the new constitution and declared insurrection over in Texas, the last of the states of the Confederacy so accepted under **Presidential Reconstruction**.

Throckmorton was elected governor in June, along with other state and local officials. However, Texans had not learned a lesson from the war.

When the Legislature met, a series of laws limiting the rights of blacks were passed. In labor disputes, for example, the employers were to be the final arbitrators. The codes also bound an entire family's labor, not just the head of the household, to an employer.

Funding for black education would be limited to what could be provided by black taxpayers. Since few blacks owned land or had jobs, that provision effectively denied education to black children. However, the thrust of the laws and the attitude of the legislators was clear: Blacks simply were not to be considered full citizens.

Many of the laws later were overturned by the Freedman's Bureau or military authorities when, in March 1867, Congress began a **Reconstruction plan** of its own. The Southern states were declared to have no legal government and the former Confederacy was divided into districts to be administered by the military until satisfactory Reconstruction was effected. Texas and Louisiana made up the Fifth Military District under the command of Gen. Philip H. Sheridan.

Gov. Throckmorton clashed often with Gen. Sheridan. The governor thought the state had gone far enough in establishing rights for the newly freed slaves and other matters. Finally in August 1867, Throckmorton and other state officials were removed from office by Sheridan because they were considered an "impediment to the reconstruction." **E.M. Pease**, the former two-term governor and a Unionist, was named provisional governor by the military authorities.

A **new constitutional convention** was called by Gen. Winfield S. Hancock, who replaced Sheridan in November 1867. For the first time, blacks were allowed to participate in the elections that selected delegates. A total of 59,633 whites and 49,497 blacks registered. The elected delegates met on June 1, 1868. Deliberations got bogged down on partisan political matters, however, and the convention spent $200,000, an astronomical sum for the time.

This constitution of 1869, as it came to be known, granted full rights of citizenship to blacks, created a system of education, delegated broad powers to the governor and generally reflected the views of the state's Unionists.

Gov. Pease, disgusted with the convention and with military authorities, resigned in September 1869. Texas had no chief executive until January 1870, when the newly elected **E.J. Davis** took office.

Meeting in February 1870, the Legislature created a **state militia** under the governor's control; created a **state police force**, also controlled by the governor; postponed the 1870 general election to 1872; enabled the governor to appoint more than 8,500 local officeholders; and granted subsidized **bonds for railroad construction** at a rate of $10,000 a mile.

For the first time, a **system of public education** was created. The law required compulsory attendance at school for four months a year, set aside one-quarter of the state's annual revenue for education and levied a poll tax to support education. Schools also were to be integrated, which enraged many white Texans.

The Davis administration was the most unpopular in Texas' history. In fairness, historians have noted that Davis did not feel that whites could be trusted to assure the rights of the newly freed blacks.

Violence was rampant in Texas. One study found that between the close of the Civil War and mid-1868, 1,035 people were murdered in Texas, including 486 blacks, mostly victims of white violence.

Gov. Davis argued that he needed broad police powers to restore order. Despite their unpopularity, the state police and militia — blacks made up 40 percent of the police and a majority of the militia — brought the lawlessness under control in many areas.

Democrats, aided by moderate Republicans, regained control of the Legislature in the 1872 elections, and, in 1873, the lawmakers set about stripping the governor of many of his powers.

The political turmoil ended with the gubernatorial election of 1873, when **Richard Coke** easily defeated Davis. Davis tried to get federal authorities to keep him in office, but President Grant refused to intervene.

In January of 1874, Democrats were in control of state government again. The end of Reconstruction concluded the turbulent Civil War era, although the attitudes that developed during the period lasted well into the 20th century.

Capital and Labor

A **constitutional convention** was called in 1875 to rewrite the 1869 constitution, a hated vestige of Radical Republican rule.

Every avenue to cutting spending at any level of government was explored. Salaries of public officials were slashed. The number of offices was reduced. Judgeships, along with most other offices, were made elective rather than appointive.

The state road program was curtailed, and the immigration bureau was eliminated.

Perhaps the worst change was the destruction of the statewide school system. The new charter created a "community system" without a power of taxation, and schools were segregated by race.

Despite the basic reactionary character, the new constitution also was visionary. Following the lead of several other states, the Democrats declared railroads to be common carriers and subject to regulation.

To meet the dual challenge of lawlessness and Indian insurrection, Gov. Coke in 1874 re-established the **Texas Rangers**.

While cowboys and cattle drives are romantic subjects for movies on the Texas of this period, the fact is that the simple cotton farmer was the backbone of the state's economy.

But neither the farmer nor the cattleman prospered throughout the last quarter of the 19th century. At the root of their problems was federal monetary policy and the lingering effects of the Civil War.

Although the issuance of paper money had brought about a business boom in the Union during the war, inflation also increased. Silver was demonetized in 1873. Congress passed the Specie Resumption Act in 1875 that returned the nation to the gold standard in 1879.

Almost immediately a contraction in currency began. Between 1873 and 1891, the amount of national bank notes in circulation declined from $339 million to $168 million.

The reduction in the money supply was devastating in the defeated South. Land values plummeted. In 1870, Texas land was valued at an average of $2.62 an acre, compared with the national average of $18.26 an acre.

With the money supply declining and the national economy growing, farm prices dropped. In 1870, a bushel of wheat brought $1. In the 1890s, wheat was 60 cents a bushel. Except for a brief spurt in the early 1880s, cattle prices followed those of crops.

Between 1880 and 1890, the number of farms in Texas doubled, but the number of tenants tripled. By 1900, almost half the state's farmers were tenants.

The much-criticized crop-lien system was developed following the war to meet credit needs of the small farmers. Merchants would extend credit to farmers through the year in exchange for liens on their crops. But the result of the crop-lien system, particularly when small farmers did not have enough acreage to operate efficiently, was a state of continual debt and despair.

The work ethic held that a man would benefit from his toil. When this apparently failed, farmers looked to the monetary system and the railroads as the causes. Their discontent hence became the source of the agrarian revolt that developed in the 1880s and 1890s.

The entry of the Texas & Pacific and the Missouri-Kansas-Texas **railroads** from the northeast changed trade patterns in the state.

Since the days of the Republic, trade generally had flowed to Gulf ports, primarily Galveston. Jefferson in Northeast Texas served as a gateway to the Mississippi River, but it never carried the volume of trade that was common at Galveston.

The earliest railroad systems in the state also were centered around Houston and Galveston, again directing trade southward. With the T&P and Katy lines, North Texas had direct access to markets in St. Louis and the East.

Problems developed with the railroads, however. In 1882, Jay Gould and Collis P. Huntington, owner of the Southern Pacific, entered into a secret agreement that amounted to creation of a monopoly of rail service in Texas. They agreed to stop competitive track extensions; to divide under a pooling arrangement freight moving from New Orleans and El Paso; to purchase all competing railroads in Texas; and to share the track between Sierra Blanca and El Paso.

The Legislature made weak attempts to regulate railroads, as provided by the state constitution. Gould thwarted an attempt to create a commission to regulate the railroads in 1881 with a visit to the state during the Legislature's debate.

The railroad tycoon subdued the lawmakers' interest with thinly disguised threats that capital would abandon Texas if the state interfered with railroad business.

As the 19th century closed, Texas remained an agricultural state. But the industrial base was growing. Between 1870 and 1900, the per capita value of manufactured goods in the United States rose from $109 to $171. In Texas, these per capita values increased from $14 to $39, but manufacturing values in Texas industry still were only one-half of annual agricultural values.

In 1886, a new breed of Texas politician appeared. **James Stephen Hogg** was not a Confederate veteran, and he was not tied to party policies of the past.

As a reform-minded attorney general, Hogg had actively enforced the state's few railroad regulatory laws. With farmers' support, Hogg was elected governor in 1890, and at the same time, a debate on the constitutionality of a **railroad commission** was settled when voters amended the constitution to provide for one.

The reform mood of the state was evident. Voters returned only 22 of the 106 members of the Texas House in 1890.

Despite his reputation as a reformer, Hogg accepted the growing use of **Jim Crow laws** to limit blacks' access to public services. In 1891, the Legislature responded to public demands and required railroads to provide separate accommodations for blacks and whites.

The stage was being set for one of the major political campaigns in Texas history, however. Farmers did not think that Hogg had gone far enough in his reform program, and they were distressed that Hogg had not appointed a farmer to the railroad commission. Many began to look elsewhere for the solutions to their problems. The **People's Party** in Texas was formed in August 1891.

The 1892 general election was one of the most spirited in the state's history. Gov. Hogg's supporters shut conservative Democrats out of the convention in Houston, so the conservatives bolted and nominated railroad attorney George Clark for governor.

The People's Party, or **Populists**, for the first time had a presidential candidate, James Weaver, and a gubernatorial candidate, T.L. Nugent.

Texas Republicans also broke ranks. The party's strength centered in the black vote. After the death of former Gov. E.J. Davis in 1883, **Norris Wright Cuney**, a black, was party leader. Cuney was considered one of the most astute politicians of the period, and he controlled federal patronage.

White Republicans revolted against the black leadership, and these "Lily-whites" nominated **Andrew Jackson Houston**, son of Sam Houston, for governor.

Black Republicans recognized that alone their strength was limited, and throughout the latter part of the 19th century, they practiced fusion politics, backing candidates of third parties when they deemed it appropriate. Cuney led the Republicans into a coalition with the conservative Democrats in 1892, backing George Clark.

The election also marked the first time major Democratic candidates courted the black vote. Gov. Hogg's supporters organized black voter clubs, and the governor got about half of the black vote.

Black farmers were in a quandary. Their financial problems were the same as those small farmers who backed the Populists.

White Populists varied in their sympathy with the racial concerns of blacks. On the local level, some whites showed sympathy with black concerns about education, voting and law enforcement. Black farmers also were reluctant to abandon the Republican Party because it was their only political base in Texas.

Hogg was re-elected in 1892 with a 43 percent plurality in a field of five candidates.

Populists continued to run well in state races until 1898. Historians have placed the beginning of the party's demise in the 1896 presidential election in which national Populists fused with the Democrats and supported **William Jennings Bryan**.

Although the Populist philosophy lived on, the party declined in importance after 1898. Farmers remained active in politics, but most returned to the Democratic Party, which usurped many of the Populists' issues.

Oil

Seldom can a people's history be profoundly changed by a single event on a single day. But Texas' entrance into the industrial age can be linked directly to the discovery of oil at **Spindletop**, three miles from **Beaumont**, on Jan. 10, 1901.

From that day, Texas' progress from a rural, agricultural state to a modern industrial giant was steady.

1900–1920

One of the greatest natural disasters ever to strike the state occurred on Sept. 8, 1900, when a **hurricane devastated Galveston**, killing 6,000 people. (For a more detailed account, see "After the Great Storm" in the 1998-1999 *Texas Almanac*). In rebuilding from that disaster, Galveston's civic leaders fashioned the **commission form of municipal government**.

Amarillo later refined the system into the **council-manager organization** that is widely used today.

The great Galveston storm also reinforced arguments by Houston's leadership that an inland port should be built for protection against such tragedies and disruptions of trade. The **Houston Ship Channel** was soon a reality.

The reform spirit in government was not dead after the departure of Jim Hogg. In 1901, the Legislature prohibited the issuing of railroad passes to public officials. More than 270,000 passes were issued to officials that year, and farmers claimed that the free rides increased their freight rates and influenced public policy as well.

In 1903, state Sen. **A.W. Terrell** got a major **election-reform law** approved, a measure that was further modified two years later. A **primary system** was established to replace a hodgepodge of practices for nominating candidates that had led to charges of irregularities after each election.

Also in the reform spirit, the Legislature in 1903 prohibited abuse of **child labor** and set minimum ages at which children could work in certain industries. The action preceded federal child-labor laws by 13 years.

However, the state, for the first time, imposed the **poll tax** as a requirement for voting. Historians differ on whether the levy was designed to keep blacks or poor whites — or both — from voting. Certainly the poll tax cut election turnouts. Black voter participation dropped from about 100,000 in the 1890s to an estimated 5,000 in 1906.

The Democratic State Executive Committee also recommended that county committees limit participation in primaries to whites only, and most accepted the suggestion.

The election of **Thomas M. Campbell** as governor in 1906 marked the start of a progressive period in Texas politics. Interest revived in controlling corporate influence.

Under Campbell, the state's **antitrust laws** were strengthened and a **pure food and drug bill** was passed. Life insurance companies were required to invest in Texas 75 percent of their reserves on policies in the state. Less than one percent of the reserves had been invested prior to the law.

Some companies left Texas. But the law was beneficial in the capital-starved economy. In 1904, voters amended the constitution to allow the state to charter **banks** for the first time, and this eased some of the farmers' credit problems. In 1909, the Legislature approved a bank-deposit insurance plan that predated the federal program.

With corporate influence under acceptable control, attention turned to the issue of prohibition of alcohol. Progressives and prohibitionists joined forces against the conservative establishment to exert a major influence in state government for the next two decades.

Prohibitionists had long been active in Texas. They had the **local-option clause** written into the Constitution of 1876, which allowed counties or their subdivisions to be voted dry. But in 1887, a prohibition amendment to the state constitution had been defeated by a two-to-one margin, and public attention had turned to other problems.

In the early 20th century, the prohibition movement gathered strength. Most of Texas already was dry because of local option. When voters rejected a prohibition amendment by a slim margin in 1911, the state had 167 dry counties and 82 wet or partially wet counties. The heavily populated counties, however, were wet. Prohibition continued to be a major issue.

Problems along the U.S.-Mexico border escalated in 1911 as the decade-long **Mexican Revolution** broke out. Soon the revolutionaries controlled some northern Mexican states, including Chihuahua. Juarez and El Paso were major contact points. El Paso residents could stand on rooftops to observe the fighting between revolutionaries and government troops. Some Americans were killed.

After pleas to the federal government got no action,

The Santa Rita #1 was the first oil well to blow in on University of Texas lands on May 18, 1923. File photo.

Gov. Oscar Colquitt sent state militia and Texas Rangers into the Valley in 1913 to protect Texans after Matamoros fell to the rebels. Unfortunately, the Rangers killed many innocent Mexican-Texans during the operation. In addition to problems caused by the fighting and raids, thousands of Mexican refugees flooded Texas border towns to escape the violence of the revolution.

In 1914, **James E. Ferguson** entered Texas politics and for the next three decades, "Farmer Jim" was one of the most dominating and colorful figures on the political stage. Ferguson, a banker from Temple, skirted the prohibition issue by pledging to veto any legislation pertaining to alcoholic beverages.

His strength was among farmers, however. Sixty-two percent of Texas' farmers were tenants, and Ferguson pledged to back legislation to limit tenant rents. Ferguson also was a dynamic orator. He easily won the primary and beat out three opponents in the general election.

Ferguson's first administration was successful. The Legislature passed the law limiting tenants' rents, although it was poorly enforced, and aid to rural schools was improved.

In 1915, the border problems heated up. A Mexican national was arrested in the Lower Rio Grande Valley carrying a document outlining plans for Mexican-Americans, Indians, Japanese and blacks in Texas and the Southwest to eliminate all Anglo males over age 16 and create a new republic. The document, whose author was never determined, started a bloodbath in the Valley. Mexican soldiers participated in raids across the Rio Grande, and Gov. Ferguson sent in the Texas Rangers.

Historians differ on the number of people who were

killed, but a safe assessment would be hundreds. Gov. Ferguson and Mexican President Venustiano Carranza met at Nuevo Laredo in November 1915 in an attempt to improve relations. The raids continued.

Pancho Villa raided Columbus, N.M., in early 1916; two small Texas villages in the Big Bend, Glenn Springs and Boquillas, also were attacked. In July, President **Woodrow Wilson** determined that the hostilities were critical and activated the National Guard.

Soon 100,000 U.S. troops were stationed along the border. **Fort Bliss** in El Paso housed 60,000 men, and **Fort Duncan** near Eagle Pass was home to 16,000 more.

With the exception of Gen. John J. Pershing's pursuit of Villa into Northern Mexico, few U.S. troops crossed into Mexico. But the service along the border gave soldiers basic training that was put to use when the United States entered World War I in 1917.

Ferguson was easily re-elected in 1916, and he worked well with the Legislature the following year. But after the Legislature adjourned, the governor got into a dispute with the board of regents of the **University of Texas**. The disagreement culminated in the governor's vetoing all appropriations for the school.

As the controversy swirled, the Travis County grand jury indicted Ferguson for misappropriation of funds and for embezzlement. In July 1917, Speaker of the Texas House F.O. Fuller called a special session of the Legislature to consider **impeachment** of the governor.

The Texas House voted 21 articles of impeachment, and the Senate in August 1917 convicted Ferguson on 10 of the charges. The Senate's judgment not only removed Ferguson from office, but also barred him from seeking office again. Ferguson resigned the day before the Senate rendered the decision in an attempt to avoid the prohibition against seeking further office.

Texas participated actively in **World War I**. Almost 200,000 young Texans, including 31,000 blacks, volunteered for military service, and 450 Texas women served in the nurses' corps. Five thousand lost their lives overseas, either fighting or in the **influenza pandemic** that swept the globe.

Texas also was a major training ground during the conflict, with 250,000 soldiers getting basic training in the state.

On the negative side, the war frenzy opened a period of intolerance and nativism in the state. German-Texans were suspect because of their ancestry. A law was passed to prohibit speaking against the war effort. Persons who failed to participate in patriotic activities often were punished. Gov. William P. Hobby even vetoed the appropriation for the German department at the University of Texas.

Ferguson's removal from office was a devastating blow to the anti-prohibitionists. Word that the former governor had received a $156,000 loan from members of the brewers' association while in office provided ammunition for the progressives.

In February 1918, a special session of the Legislature prohibited saloons within a 10-mile radius of military posts and ratified the national prohibition amendment, which had been introduced in Congress by Texas Sen. **Morris Sheppard**.

Women also were given the **right to vote in state primaries** at the same session.

Although national prohibition was to become effective in early 1920, the Legislature presented a prohibition amendment to voters in May 1919, and it was approved, bringing prohibition to Texas earlier than to the rest of the nation. At the same time, a woman suffrage amendment, which would have granted women the right to vote in all elections, was defeated.

Although World War I ended in November 1918, it brought many changes to Texas. Rising prices during the war had increased the militancy of labor unions.

Blacks also became more militant after the war. Discrimination against black soldiers led in 1917 to a riot in Houston in which several people were killed.

With the election of Mexican President Alvaro Obregón in 1920, the fighting along the border subsided.

In 1919, state Rep. J.T. Canales of Brownsville initiated an investigation of the **Texas Rangers'** role in the border problems. As a result of the study, the Rangers' manpower was reduced from 1,000 members to 76, and stringent limitations were placed on the agency's activities. Standards for members of the force also were upgraded.

By 1920, although still a rural state, the face of Texas was changing. Nearly one-third of the population was in the cities.

Pat M. Neff won the gubernatorial election of 1920, beating Sen. Joseph W. Bailey in the primary. As a former prosecuting attorney in McLennan County, Neff made law and order the major thrust of his administration. During his tenure the state took full responsibility for developing a **highway system**, a **gasoline tax** was imposed, and a state **park board** was established.

In 1921, a group of West Texans threatened to form a new state because Neff vetoed the creation of a new college in their area. Two years later, **Texas Technological College** (now Texas Tech University) was authorized in Lubbock and opened its doors in 1925.

Although still predominantly a rural state, Texas cities were growing. In 1900, only 17 percent of the population lived in urban areas; by 1920, that figure had almost doubled to 32 percent. A discontent developed with the growth of the cities. Rural Texans had long seen cities as hotbeds of vice and immorality. Simple rural values were cherished, and it seemed that those values were threatened in a changing world. After World War I, this transition accelerated.

KKK and Minorities

In addition, "foreigners" in the state became suspect; nativism reasserted itself. German-Texans were associated with the enemy in the war, and Mexican-Texans were mostly Roman Catholics and likened to the troublemakers along the border. Texas was a fertile ground for the new **Ku Klux Klan** that entered the state in late 1920. The Klan's philosophy was a mixture of patriotism, law-and-order, nativism, white supremacy and Victorian morals. Its influence spread quickly across the state, and reports of Klan violence and murder were rampant.

Prohibition had brought a widespread disrespect for law. Peace officers and other officials often ignored speakeasies and gambling. The Klan seemed to many Texans to be an appropriate instrument for restoring law and order and for maintaining morality in towns and cities. By 1922, many of the state's large communities were under direct Klan influence, and a Klan-backed candidate, Earle Mayfield, was elected to the U.S. Senate, giving Texas the reputation as the most powerful Klan bastion in the Union. Hiram Wesley Evans of Dallas also was elected imperial wizard of the national Klan in that year.

The Klan became more directly involved in politics and planned to elect the next governor in 1924. Judge Felix Robertson of Dallas got the organization's backing in the Democratic primary. Former governor Jim Ferguson filed to run for the office, but the Texas Supreme Court ruled that he could not because of his impeachment conviction. So Ferguson placed his wife, **Miriam A. Ferguson**, on the ballot. Several other prominent Democrats also entered the race.

The Fergusons made no secret that Jim would have a big influence on his wife's administration. One campaign slogan was, "Two governors for the price of one." Mrs. Ferguson easily won the runoff against Robertson when many Texans decided that "Fergusonism" was preferable to the Klan in the governor's office.

Minorities began organizing in Texas to seek their civil rights. The National Association for the Advancement of Colored People (**NAACP**) opened a Texas chapter in 1912, and by 1919, there were chapters in 31 Texas communities. Similarly, Mexican-Texans formed Orden Hijos de America in 1921, and in 1929, the **League of United Latin American Citizens** (LULAC) was organized in Corpus Christi.

The Klan dominated the Legislature in 1923, passing a law barring blacks from participation in the Democratic primary. Although blacks had in fact been barred from voting in primaries for years, this law gave **Dr. Lawrence A. Nixon**, a black dentist from El Paso, the opportunity to go to court to fight the all-white primary. IIn 1927, the U.S. Supreme Court overturned the statute, but that was only the beginning of several court battles, which were not resolved until 1944.

Disgruntled Democrats and Klansmen tried to beat Mrs. Ferguson in the general election in 1924, but she was too strong. Voters also sent 91 new members to the Texas House, purging it of many of the Klan-backed representatives. After that election, the Klan's power ebbed rapidly in Texas.

Mrs. Ferguson named Emma Grigsby Meharg as Texas' first woman secretary of state in 1925. The governors Ferguson administration was stormy. Jim was accused of cronyism in awarding highway contracts and in other matters. And "Ma" returned to her husband's practice of liberal clemency for prisoners. In two years, Mrs. Ferguson extended clemency to 3,595 inmates.

Although Jim Ferguson was at his bombastic best in the 1926 Democratic primary, young Attorney General **Dan Moody** had little trouble winning the nomination and the general election.

At age 33, Moody was the youngest person ever to become governor of Texas. Like many governors during this period, he was more progressive than the Legislature, and much of his program did not pass. Moody was successful in some government reorganization. He also cleaned up the highway department, which had been criticized under the Fergusons, and abandoned the liberal clemency policy for prisoners. And Moody worked

at changing Texas' image as an anti-business state. "The day of the political trust-buster is gone," he told one Eastern journalist.

Progressives and prohibitionists still had a major influence on the Democratic Party, and 1928 was a watershed year for them. Moody easily won renomination and re-election. But the state party was drifting away from the direction of national Democrats. When **Al Smith**, a wet and a Roman Catholic, won the presidential nomination at the national Democratic convention in Houston, Texans were hard-pressed to remain faithful to the "party of the fathers." Moody, who had been considered a potential national figure, ruined his political career trying to straddle the fence, angering both wets and drys, Catholics and Protestants. Former governor O.B. Colquitt led an exodus of so-called **"Hoovercrats"** from the state Democratic convention in 1928, and for the first time in its history, Texas gave its electoral votes to a Republican, Herbert Hoover, in the general election.

Through the 1920s, oil continued to increase in importance in Texas' economy. New discoveries were made at Mexia in 1920, Luling in 1922, Big Lake in Reagan Conty in 1923, in the Wortham Field in 1924 and in Borger in 1926. But oil still did not dominate the state's economic life.

As late as **1929**, meat packing, cottonseed processing and various milling operations exceeded the added value of petroleum refining. And as the 1920s ended, lumbering and food processing shared major economic roles with the petroleum industry. During the decade, Texas grew between 35 and 42 percent of U.S. cotton and 20-30 percent of the world crop. Irrigation and mechanization opened the South Plains to cotton growing. Eight years later, more than 1.1 million bales were grown in the region, mostly around Lubbock.

But Texas, with the rest of the nation, was on the threshhold of a major economic disaster that would have irreversible consequences. The **Great Depression** was at hand.

Depression Years

Historians have noted that the state's economic collapse was not as severe as that which struck the industrialized states. Texas' economy had sputtered through the decade of the 1920s, primarily because of the fluctuation of the price of cotton and other agricultural products. But agricultural prices were improving toward the end of the decade.

The Fergusons attempted a political comeback in the gubernatorial election of 1930. But Texans elected **Ross S. Sterling**, the founder of Humble Oil Co. Early in the Depression, Texans remained optimistic that the economic problems were temporary, another of the cyclical downturns the nation experienced periodically. Indeed, some Texans even felt that the hardships would be beneficial, ridding the economy of speculators and poor businessmen. Those attitudes gave way to increasing concern as the poor business conditions dragged on.

A piece of good luck turned into a near economic disaster for the state in late 1930. **C.M. "Dad" Joiner** struck oil near Kilgore, and soon the **East Texas oil boom** was in full swing. Millions of barrrels of new oil flooded the market, making producers and small landowners wealthy. Soon the glut of new oil drove market prices down from $1.10 a barrel in 1930 to 10 cents in

1931. Many wells had to be shut in around the state because they could not produce oil profitably at the low prices.

The Texas Railroad Commission attempted in the spring of 1931 to control production through proration, which assigned production quotas to each well (called the allowable). The first proration order limited each well to about 1,000 barrels a day of production. **Proration** had two goals: to protect reserves through conservation and to maintain prices by limiting production. But, on July 28, a federal court ruled that proration was an illegal attempt to fix prices.

In August 1931, Gov. Sterling placed four counties of the East Texas field under martial law and briefly shut down oil production there altogether. A federal court later ruled the governor's actions illegal. Gov. Sterling was roundly criticized for sending troops. Opponents said the action was taken to aid the major oil companies to the disadvantage of independent producers.

In 1932, Gov. Sterling appointed **Ernest O. Thompson** to a vacancy on the railroad commission. Thompson, who had led a coalition in favor of output regulation, is credited with fashioning a compromise between independents and major oil companies. In April 1933, the railroad commission prorated production on the basis, in part, of bottom-hole pressure in each well, and the courts upheld this approach. But enforcement remained a problem.

Finally in 1935, Texas' Sen. **Tom Connally** authored the Hot Oil Act, which involved the federal government in regulation by prohibiting oil produced in violation of state law from being sold in interstate commerce. Thereafter, Texas' producers accepted the concept of proration. Since Texas was the nation's largest oil producer, the railroad commission could set the national price of oil through proration for several decades thereafter.

Despite these problems, the oil boom helped East Texas weather the Depression better than other parts of the state. Farmers were hit particularly hard in 1931. Bumper crops had produced the familiar reduction in prices. Cotton dropped from 18 cents per pound in 1928 to six cents in 1931. That year Louisiana Gov. **Huey Long** proposed a ban on growing cotton in 1932 to eliminate the surplus. The Louisiana legislature enacted the ban, but Texas was the key state to the plan since it led the nation in cotton production. Gov. Sterling was cool to the idea, but responded to public support of it by calling a special session of the Legislature. The lawmakers passed a **cotton acreage limitation** bill in 1931, but the law was declared unconstitutional the following year.

One feature of the Depression had become the number of transients drifting from city to city looking for work. Local governments and private agencies tried to provide relief for the unemployed, but the effort was soon overwhelmed by the number of persons needing help. In Houston, blacks and Mexican-Texans were warned not to apply for relief because there was not enough money to take care of whites, and many Mexicans returned to Mexico voluntarily and otherwise.

To relieve the local governments, Gov. Sterling proposed a bond program to repay counties for highways they had built and to start a public-works program. Texans' long-held faith in self-reliance and rugged individualism was put to a severe test.

By **1932**, many were looking to the federal government to provide relief from the effects of the Depression.

U.S. Speaker of the House **John Nance Garner** of Texas was a presidential candidate when the Democrats held their national convention. To avoid a deadlocked convention, Garner maneuvered the Texans to change strategy. On the fourth ballot, the Texas delegation voted for the eventual nominee, New York Gov. **Franklin D. Roosevelt**. Garner got the second place on the ticket that swept into office in the general election.

In Texas, **Miriam Ferguson** was successful in unseating Gov. Sterling in the Democratic primary, winning by about 4,000 votes. Her second administration was less turbulent than the first. State government costs were reduced, and voters approved $20 million in so-called "bread bonds" to help provide relief. In 1933, **horse racing** came to the state, authorized through a rider on an appropriations bill legalizing pari-mutuel betting. The law was repealed in 1937. Prohibition also was repealed in 1933, although much of Texas remained dry under the **local-option** laws and the prohibition against open saloons.

State government faced a series of financial problems during Mrs. Ferguson's second term. The annual deficit climbed to $14 million, and the state had to default on the interest payments on some bonds. Voters aggravated the situation by approving a $3,000 **homestead exemption**. Many property owners were losing their homes because they could not pay taxes. And while the exemption saved their homesteads, it worsened the state's financial problems.

Many Texas banks failed during the Depression, as did banks nationally. One of Roosevelt's first actions was to declare a national bank holiday in 1933. Gov. Ferguson closed state banks at the same time, although she had to "assume" authority that was not in the law.

The New Deal

In Washington, Texans played an important role in shaping Roosevelt's **New Deal**. As vice president, Garner presided over the Senate and maneuvered legislation through the upper house. **Texans** also chaired major committees in the House: **Sam Rayburn**, Interstate and Foreign Commerce; **Hatton W. Sumners**, Judiciary; **Fritz G. Lanham**, Public Buildings and Grounds; **J.J. Mansfield**, Rivers and Harbors; and **James P. Buchanan**, Appropriations. With this influence, the Texas delegation supported the president's early social programs. In addition, **Jesse Jones** of Houston served as director of the Reconstruction Finance Corporation, the Federal Loan Administration and as Secretary of Commerce. Jones was one of the most influential men in Washington and second only to Roosevelt in wielding financial power to effect recovery.

Poor conservation practices had left many of the state's farmlands open to erosion. During the **Dust Bowl** days of the early and mid-1930s, for example, the weather bureau in Amarillo reported 192 dust storms within a three-year period. Cooperation between state and federal agencies helped improve farmers' conservation efforts and reduced the erosion problem by the end of the decade.

Mrs. Ferguson did not seek re-election in 1934, and Attorney General **James V. Allred** was elected. Under his administration, several social-welfare programs were initiated, including old-age pensions, teachers' retirement and worker's compensation. Allred was re-elected in 1936.

Some of the New Deal's luster dimmed when the nation was struck by another recession in 1937.

Although Texas' economic condition improved toward the end of the decade, a full recovery was not realized until the beginning of World War II — when the state went through another industrial revolution.

Tragedy struck the small East Texas town of **New London** in Rusk County on March 18, 1937. At 3:05 p.m., natural gas, which had seeped undetected into an enclosed area beneath a school building from a faulty pipe connection, exploded when a shop teacher turned on a sander. Approximately 298 of the 540 students and teachers in the school died, and all but 130 of the survivors were injured. The disaster prompted the Legislature to pass a law requiring that a malodorant be added to gas so leaks could be detected by smell.

In 1938, voters elected one of the most colorful figures in the state's political history to the governor's office. **W. Lee "Pappy" O'Daniel**, a flour salesman and leader of a radio hillbilly band, came from nowhere to defeat a field of much better known candidates in the Democratic primary and to easily win the general election. When re-elected two years later, O'Daniel became the first candidate to poll more than one million votes in a Texas election.

But O'Daniel's skills of state did not equal his campaigning ability, and throughout his administration, the governor and the Legislature were in conflict. In early **1941**, long-time U.S. Senator Morris Sheppard died, and O'Daniel wanted the office. He appointed Andrew Jackson Houston, Sam Houston's aged son, to fill the vacancy. Houston died after only 24 days in office. O'Daniel won the special election for the post in a close race with a young congressman, **Lyndon B. Johnson**.

Lt. Gov. **Coke R. Stevenson** succeeded O'Daniel as governor and brought a broad knowledge of government to the office. Stevenson was elected to two full terms. Thanks to frugal management and greatly increasing revenues during the war years, he left the state treasury with a surplus in 1947. Voters also solved the continuing deficit problem by approving a pay-as-you-go amendment to the constitution in 1942. It requires the state comptroller to certify that tax revenues will be available to support appropriations. Otherwise the money cannot be spent.

World War II

As in every war after Texas entered the Union, young Texans flocked to military service when the United States entered World War II. More than 750,000 served, including 12,000 women in the auxiliary services. In December 1942, U.S. Secretary of the Navy Frank Knox said Texas contributed the largest percentage of its male population to the armed forces of any state. Thirty Texans won Congressional Medals of Honor in the fighting. **Audie Murphy**, a young farm boy from Farmersville, became one of the most decorated soldiers of the war. Dallas-born **Sam Dealey** was the most-decorated Navy man.

Important contributions also were made at home. Texas was the site of 15 training posts, at which more than a quarter million men were trained, and of several prisoner-of-war camps.

World War II irrevocably changed the face of Texas. During the decade of the 1940s, the state's population switched from predominantly rural to 60 percent **urban**. The number of **manufacturing** workers almost doubled. And as had been the dream of Texas leaders for more than a century, the state began to attract new industries.

Conservatives vs. Liberals

The state's politics became increasingly controlled by conservative Democrats after Gov. Allred left office. In 1946, **Beauford H. Jester**, a member of the railroad commission, gained the governorship. Under Jester in 1947, the Legislature passed the state's **right-to-work** law, prohibiting mandatory union membership, and reorganized public education with passage of the **Gilmer-Aikin Act**.

During the Jester administration several major constitutional amendments were adopted. Also, one of Texas' greatest tragedies occurred on April 16, 1947, when the French ship *SS Grandcamp*, carrying a load of ammonium nitrate, exploded at **Texas City**. More than 500 died and 4,000 sustained injuries. Property damage exceeded $200 million.

In **1948**, Sen. W. Lee O'Daniel did not seek re-election. Congressman Lyndon Johnson and former Gov. Coke Stevenson vied for the Democratic nomination. In the runoff, Johnson won by a mere **87 votes** in the closest — and most hotly disputed — statewide election in Texas' history. Johnson quickly rose to a leadership position in the U.S. Senate, and, with House Speaker Sam Rayburn, gave Texas substantial influence in national political affairs.

Although re-elected in 1948, Jester died in July 1949, the only Texas governor to die in office, and Lt. Gov. **Allan Shivers** succeeded him. During Shivers' administration, state spending more than doubled, reaching $805.7 million in 1956, as the governor increased appropriations for public-health institutions, school salaries, retirement benefits, highways and old-age pensions.

Shivers broke with tradition, successfully winning three full terms as governor after completing Jester's unexpired term. Shivers also led a revolt by Texas Democrats against the national party in **1952**. The governor, who gained both the Democratic and Republican nominations for the office under the law that allowed cross-filing that year, supported Republican Dwight Eisenhower for the presidency. Many Texas Democrats broke with the national party over the so-called "**Tidelands issue**." Texas claimed land 12 miles out into the Gulf as state lands. The issue was important because revenue from oil and natural gas production from the area supported public education in the state.

Major oil companies also backed Texas' position because state royalties on minerals produced from the land were much lower than federal royalties. President Harry S. Truman vetoed legislation that would have given Texas title to the land. Democratic presidential nominee Adlai Stevenson was no more sympathetic to the issue, and Texas gave its electoral votes to Republican Dwight Eisenhower in an election that attracted a two million-vote turnout for the first time in Texas. President Eisenhower signed a measure into law guaranteeing Texas' tidelands.

Scandal struck state government in 1954 when irregularities were discovered in the handling of funds in the veterans' land program in the General Land Office. Land Commissioner Bascom Giles was convicted of several charges and sent to prison. Several insurance companies also went bankrupt in the mid-1950s, prompting a reorganization of the State Board of Insurance in 1957.

In 1954, the U.S. Supreme Court ruled unconstitutional the segregation of schools, and for the next quarter-century, **school integration** became a major political issue. By the late 1960s, most institutions were integrated, but the state's major cities continued to wage court battles against forced busing of students to attain racial balance. Blacks and Mexican-Texans also made gains in voting rights during the 1950s.

President John F. Kennedy (left) was assassinated in downtown Dallas on Nov. 22, 1963, while riding in a motorcade. Texas Gov. John B. Connally (in front of Kennedy) was seriously wounded in the attack. File photo.

Shivers had easily defeated **Ralph W. Yarborough** in the Democratic primary in 1952, but the divisions between the party's loyalists and those who bolted ranks to join Republicans in presidential races were growing. Shivers barely led the first 1954 primary over Yarborough and won the nomination with 53 percent of the vote in the runoff. Yarborough ran an equally close race against **Price Daniel**, a U.S. Senator who sought the governorship in 1956. Upon election as governor, Daniel left the Senate, and Yarborough won a special election to fill the vacancy in 1957. Yarborough won re-election in 1964 before losing to **Lloyd Bentsen** in 1970 in the Democratic primary. Although a liberal, Yarborough proved to be unusually durable in Texas' conservative political climate.

The state budget topped $1 billion for the first time in 1958. The Legislature met for 205 days in regular and special sessions in 1961–62 and levied, over Gov. Daniel's opposition, the state's first broad-based **sales tax in 1962**.

Technological Growth

Through the 1950s and 1960s, Texas' industrial base had expanded and diversified. Petroleum production and refining remained the cornerstones, but other industries grew. Attracted by cheap electricity, the aluminum industry came to Texas. Starting from the base developed during World War II, defense industries and associated high-tech firms, specializing in electronics and computers, centered on the Dallas–Fort Worth area and Houston. One of the most important scientific breakthroughs of the century came in 1958 in Dallas. **Jack Kilby**, an engineer at **Texas Instruments**, developed and patented the integrated circuit that became the central part of computers.

Sen. Lyndon Johnson unsuccessfully sought the Democratic presidential nomination in 1960, and **John F. Kennedy** subsequently selected the Texan as his running mate. Johnson is credited with keeping several Southern states, including Texas, in the Democratic column in the close election. Kennedy was a Roman Catholic and a liberal, a combination normally rejected by the Southern states. When Johnson left the Senate to assume his new office in 1961, **John Tower** won a special election that attracted more than 70 candidates. Tower became the first Republican since Reconstruction to serve as a Texas senator.

During the early 1960s, Harris County was chosen as the site for the National Aeronautics and Space Administration's manned spacecraft center. The acquisition of **NASA** further diversified Texas' industrial base.

In 1962, **John B. Connally**, a former aide to LBJ and Secretary of the Navy under Kennedy, returned to Texas to seek the governorship. Gov. Daniel sought an unprecedented fourth term and was defeated in the Democratic primary. Connally won a close Democratic runoff over liberal **Don Yarborough** and was elected easily. As governor, Connally concentrated on improving **public education, state services** and **water development**. He was re-elected in 1964 and 1966.

The Assassination

One of the major tragedies in the nation's history occurred in Dallas on **Nov. 22, 1963**, when President Kennedy was assassinated while riding in a motorcade. Gov. Connally also was seriously wounded. Lyndon Johnson was administered the oath of the presidency by Federal Judge Sarah T. Hughes of Dallas aboard Air Force One at Love Field. Lee Harvey Oswald was arrested for the murder of the president on the afternoon of the assassination, but Oswald was killed by Dallas nightclub operator Jack Ruby two days later.

An extensive investigation into the assassination of President Kennedy was conducted by the Warren Commission. The panel concluded that Oswald was the killer and that he acted alone. Ruby, who was convicted of killing Oswald, died of cancer in the Dallas County jail in 1967 while the case was being appealed.

The assassination damaged the Republican Party in Texas, however. Building strength in Texas' conservative political atmosphere in 1962, eight Republicans, the most in decades, had been elected to the Texas House. And two Republicans — Ed Foreman of Odessa and Bruce Alger of Dallas — served in Congress. All were defeated in the 1964 general election.

In the emotional aftermath of the tragedy, Johnson, who won the presidency outright in a **landslide election in 1964**, persuaded the Congress to pass a series of civil-rights and social-welfare programs that changed the face of the nation. Texas was particularly affected by the civil-rights legislation and a series of lawsuits challenging election practices. During the 1960s, the state constitutional limitation of urban representation in the Legislature was overturned. The poll tax was declared unconstitutional, and the practice of electing officials from at-large districts fell to the so-called "one-man, one-vote" ruling. As a result, more Republican, minority and liberal officials were elected, particularly from urban areas. In 1966, **Curtis Graves** and **Barbara Jordan** of Houston and **Joe Lockridge** of Dallas became the first blacks to serve in the Texas Legislature since 1898.

Lyndon Johnson did not seek re-election in 1968. The nation had become involved in an unpopular war in Vietnam, and Johnson bowed out of the race in the interest of national unity.

Sharpstown Scandal

Democrats, however, stayed firmly in control of state government. **Preston Smith** was elected governor, and **Ben Barnes** gained the lieutenant governorship. Both also were re-elected in 1970. Although state spending continued to increase, particularly on education, the Legislature otherwise was quiet. A minimum-wage law was approved, and public kindergartens were authorized in 1969.

At a special session, the **Sharpstown scandal**, one of the state's major scandals developed. Gov. Smith allowed the lawmakers to consider special banking legislation supported by Houston banker Frank Sharp. Several public officials were implicated in receiving favors from the banker for seeing that the legislation passed. Texas House Speaker Gus Mutscher and Rep. Tommy Shannon were convicted of conspiracy to accept bribes in a trial held in Abilene.

Voters in **1972** demanded a new leadership in the state capital. Smith and Barnes were defeated in the Democratic primary, and **Dolph Briscoe** was elected governor. In the fall, Texans gave presidential candidate Richard Nixon the state's electoral votes. Nixon carried 246 counties over Democrat George McGovern and received more than 65 percent of the popular vote.

The Legislature in 1973 was dominated by a reform atmosphere in the wake of the Sharpstown scandal. Price Daniel Jr., son of the former governor, was selected speaker of the House, and several laws concerning ethics and disclosure of campaign donations and spending were passed. Open meetings and open records statutes also were approved.

By 1970, Texas had become an even more urban state. The census found almost 11.2 million people in the state, ranking it sixth nationally. Three Texas cities, Houston, Dallas and San Antonio, were among the 10 largest in the nation.

Through the first half of the 1970s, several major changes were made in state policy. **Liquor-by-the-drink** became legal and the **age of majority** was lowered from 20 to 18, giving young people the right to vote. Also, the state's first **Public Utilities Commission** was created, hearing its initial case in September 1976.

Prosperity

Texas entered a period of unparalleled prosperity in 1973 when the Organization of Petroleum Exporting Countries (OPEC) boycotted the U.S. market. Severe energy shortages resulted, and the price of oil and natural gas skyrocketed. The federal government had allowed foreign oil to be imported through the 1960s, severely reducing the incentives to find and produce domestic oil. Consequently, domestic producers could not compensate for the loss in foreign oil as a result of the boycott. The Texas Railroad Commission had long complained about the importation of foreign oil, and in 1972, the panel had removed proration controls from wells in the state, allowing 100 percent production. For the rest of the decade, domestic producers mounted a major exploration effort, drilling thousands of wells. Nevertheless, **Texas' oil and gas production peaked in 1970** and has been declining since. Newly discovered oil and gas have not replaced the declining reserves. While Texans suffered from the inflation that followed, the state prospered. Tax revenues at all levels of government increased, and state revenues, basically derived from oil and gas taxes, spiraled, as did the state budget.

With the new revenue from inflation and petroleum taxes, state spending rose from $2.95 billion in 1970 to $8.6 billion in 1979, and education led the advance, moving from 42 percent of the budget to 51.5 percent. But there was no increase in state tax rates.

It was no surprise that **education** was one of the major beneficiaries of increased state spending. After World War II, more emphasis was placed on education across the state. **Community colleges** sprang up in many cities, and a total of 109 colleges were established between the end of the war and 1980. Quantity did not assure quality, however, and Texas' public and higher education seldom were ranked among national leaders.

In 1972, voters approved an amendment authorizing the Legislature to sit as a **constitutional convention** to rewrite the 1876 charter. The lawmakers met for several months and spent $5 million, but they failed to propose anything to be considered by voters. The public was outraged, and in 1975, the Legislature presented the work of the convention to voters in the form of eight constitutional amendments. All were defeated in a special election in November 1975.

Texas voters participated in their **first presidential primary in 1976**. Jimmy Carter of Georgia won the Democratic primary, and eventually the presidency. Ronald Reagan carried the state's Republicans, but lost the party's nomination to President Gerald Ford.

The state proved politically volatile in **1978**. First, Attorney General **John Hill** defeated Gov. Dolph Briscoe in the Democratic primary. A political newcomer, Dallas businessman **William P. Clements**, upset Hill in the general election, giving Texas its first Republican governor since Reconstruction. Also for the first time since Reconstruction, state officials were elected to **four-year terms**. ☆

Environment

Extending from sea level at the Gulf of Mexico to over 8,000 feet in the Guadalupe Mountains of far West Texas and from the semitropical Lower Rio Grande Valley to the High Plains of the Panhandle, Texas has a natural environment of remarkable variety. This section discusses the physical features, geology, soils, water, vegetation, and wildlife that are found in the Lone Star State.

The Physical State of Texas

Area of Texas

Texas occupies about 7 percent of the total water and land area of the United States. **Second in size** among the states, Texas has a land and water area of 268,580 square miles as compared with Alaska's 663,267 square miles, according to the United States Bureau of the Census. California, the third largest state, has 163,696 square miles. Texas is as large as all of New England, New York, Pennsylvania, Ohio and North Carolina combined.

The **state's total area** consists of 261,797 square miles of land and 6,783 square miles of water.

Length and Breadth

The **longest straight-line distance** in a general north-south direction is 801 miles from the northwest corner of the Panhandle to the extreme southern tip of Texas on the Rio Grande below Brownsville. The greatest east-west distance is 773 miles from the extreme eastward bend in the Sabine River in Newton County to the extreme western bulge of the Rio Grande just above El Paso.

The **geographic center** of Texas is southwest of Mercury in northern McCulloch County at approximately 99° 20' West longitude and 31° 08' North latitude.

Texas' Boundary Lines

The boundary of Texas by segments, including only larger river bends and only the great arc of the coastline, is as follows:

Boundary	Miles
Rio Grande	889.0
Coastline	367.0
Sabine River, Lake and Pass	180.0
*Sabine River to Red River	106.5
† Red River	480.0
*East Panhandle line	133.6
*North Panhandle line	167.0
*West Panhandle line	310.2
*Along 32nd parallel	209.0
Total	**2,842.3**

Following the smaller meanderings of the rivers and the tidewater coastline, the following are the boundary measurements:

Rio Grande	1,254
Coastline (tidewater)	624
Sabine River, Lake and Pass	292
† Red River	726
*The five unchanged line segments above	926
Total (including segments marked *)	**3,822**

*† A history of the **Red River boundary dispute** between Texas and Oklahoma can be found in the 2002–2003 Texas Almanac.*

Latitude and Longitude

The extremes of latitude and longitude are as follows: From 25° 50' North latitude at the extreme southern turn of the Rio Grande on the south line of Cameron County to 36° 30' North latitude along the north line of the Panhandle, and from 93° 31' West longitude at the extreme eastern point on the Sabine River on the east line of Newton County to 106° 38' West longitude on the extreme westward point on the Rio Grande above El Paso.

Texas' Highs and Lows

The highest point in the state is **Guadalupe Peak** at **8,749 feet** above sea level. Its twin, **El Capitan**, stands at **8,085 feet** and also is located in Culberson County near the New Mexico state line. Both are in the Guadalupe Mountains National Park, which includes scenic McKittrick Canyon. These elevations and the others in this article have been determined by the U.S. Geological Survey, unless otherwise noted.

The named peaks above 8,000 feet and the counties in which they are located are listed below. These elevations may differ from those in earlier editions of the Almanac because of the more accurate measuring methods currently being used by the USGS.

Named Peaks in Texas Above 8,000 Feet

Name, County	Elevation
Guadalupe Peak, Culberson	8,749
Bush Mountain, Culberson	8,631
Shumard Peak, Culberson	8,615
Bartlett Peak, Culberson	8,508
Mount Livermore (Baldy Peak), Jeff Davis	8,378
Hunter Peak (Pine Top Mtn.), Culberson	8,368
El Capitan, Culberson	8,085

Fort Davis in Jeff Davis County is the **highest town** of any size in Texas at 5,050 feet above sea level, and the county has the **highest average elevation**. The **highest state highway point** also is in Jeff Davis County at **McDonald Observatory** on **Mount Locke** where the road reaches 6,781 feet above sea level, as determined by the Texas Department of Transportation.

The **highest railway point** is Paisano Pass, at 5,074 above sea level, 14 miles east of Marfa in Presidio County.

Sea level is the **lowest elevation** determined in Texas, and it can be found in all the coastal counties. No point in the state has been found by the geological survey to be below sea level. ☆

Physical Regions

This section was reviewed by Dr. David R. Butler, professor of geography at Texas State University–San Marcos.

The principal physical regions of Texas are usually listed as follows (see also **Vegetational Areas** and **Soils**):

The Gulf Coastal Plains

Texas' Gulf Coastal Plains are the western extension of the coastal plain extending from the Atlantic to beyond the Rio Grande. Its characteristic rolling to hilly surface covered with a heavy growth of pine and hardwoods extends into East Texas. In the increasingly arid west, however, its forests become secondary in nature, consisting largely of post oaks and, farther west, prairies and brushlands.

The interior limit of the Gulf Coastal Plains in Texas is the line of the **Balcones Fault and Escarpment.** This geologic fault or shearing of underground strata extends eastward from a point on the Rio Grande near Del Rio. It extends to the northwestern part of Bexar County where it turns northeastward and extends through Comal, Hays and Travis counties, intersecting the Colorado River immediately above Austin. The fault line is a single, definite geologic feature, accompanied by a line of southward- and eastward-facing hills.

The resemblance of the hills to balconies when viewed from the plain below accounts for the Spanish name for this area: *balcones.*

North of Waco, features of the fault zone are sufficiently inconspicuous that the interior boundary of the Coastal Plain follows the traditional geologic contact between upper and lower Cretaceous rocks. This contact is along the western edge of the **Eastern Cross Timbers.**

This fault line is usually accepted as the boundary between lowland and upland Texas. Below the fault line the surface is characteristically coastal plains. Above the Balcones Fault the surface is characteristically interior rolling plains.

Pine Belt or "Piney Woods"

The Pine Belt, called the "Piney Woods," extends into Texas from the east 75 to 125 miles. From north to south it extends from the Red River to within about 25 miles of the Gulf Coast. Interspersed among the pines are some hardwood timbers, usually in valleys of rivers and creeks. This area is the source of practically all of Texas' commercial timber production **(see Texas Forest Resources, page 97).** It was settled early in Texas' history and is an older farming area of the state.

This area's soils and climate are adaptable to production of a variety of fruit and vegetable crops. Cattle raising is widespread, accompanied by the development of pastures planted to improved grasses. Lumber production is the principal industry. There is a large iron-and-steel industry near Daingerfield in Morris County based on nearby iron deposits. Iron deposits are also worked in Rusk and one or two other counties.

A great oil field discovered in Gregg, Rusk and Smith counties in 1931 has done more than anything else to contribute to the economic growth of the area. This area has a variety of clays, lignite and other minerals as potentials for development.

Post Oak Belt

The main Post Oak Belt of Texas is wedged between the Pine Belt on the east, Blacklands on the west, and the Coastal Prairies on the south, covering a considerable area in East Central Texas. The principal industry is diversified farming and livestock raising. Throughout, it is spotty in character, with some insular areas of blackland soil and some that closely resemble those of the Pine Belt. There is a small isolated area of loblolly pines in Bastrop County known as the **"Lost Pines,"** the westernmost southern pines in the United States. The Post Oak Belt has lignite, commercial clays and some other minerals.

The Piney Woods extend from the Red River to within about 25 miles of the Gulf Coast. This area is the source of most of Texas' commercial timber production. File photo.

Blackland Belt

The Blackland Belt stretches from the Rio Grande to the Red River, lying just below the line of the **Balcones Fault,** and varying in width from 15 to 70 miles. It is narrowest below the segment of the Balcones Fault from the Rio Grande to Bexar County and gradually widens as it runs northeast to the Red River. Its rolling prairie, easily turned by the plow, developed rapidly as a farming area until the 1930s and was the principal cotton-producing area of Texas. Now, however, other Texas irrigated, mechanized areas lead in farming. Because of the early growth, the Blackland Belt is still the most thickly populated area in the state and contains within it and along its border more of the state's large and middle-sized cities than any other area. Primarily because of this concentration of population, this belt has the most diversified manufacturing industry in the state.

Coastal Prairies

The Texas Coastal Prairies extend westward along the coast from the Sabine River, reaching inland 30 to 60 miles. Between the Sabine and Galveston Bay, the line of demarcation between the prairies and the Pine Belt forests to the north is very distinct. The Coastal Prairie extends along the Gulf from the Sabine to the Lower Rio Grande Valley. The eastern half is covered with a heavy growth of grass; the western half, which is more arid, is covered with short grass and, in some places, with small timber and brush. The soil is heavy clay. Grass supports the densest cattle population in Texas, and cattle ranching is the principal agricultural industry. Rice is a major crop, grown under irrigation from wells and rivers. Cotton, grain sorghum and truck crops are grown.

Coastal Prairie areas have seen the greatest industrial development in Texas history since World War II. Chief concentration has been from Orange and Beaumont to Houston, and much of the development has been in petrochemicals and the aerospace industry.

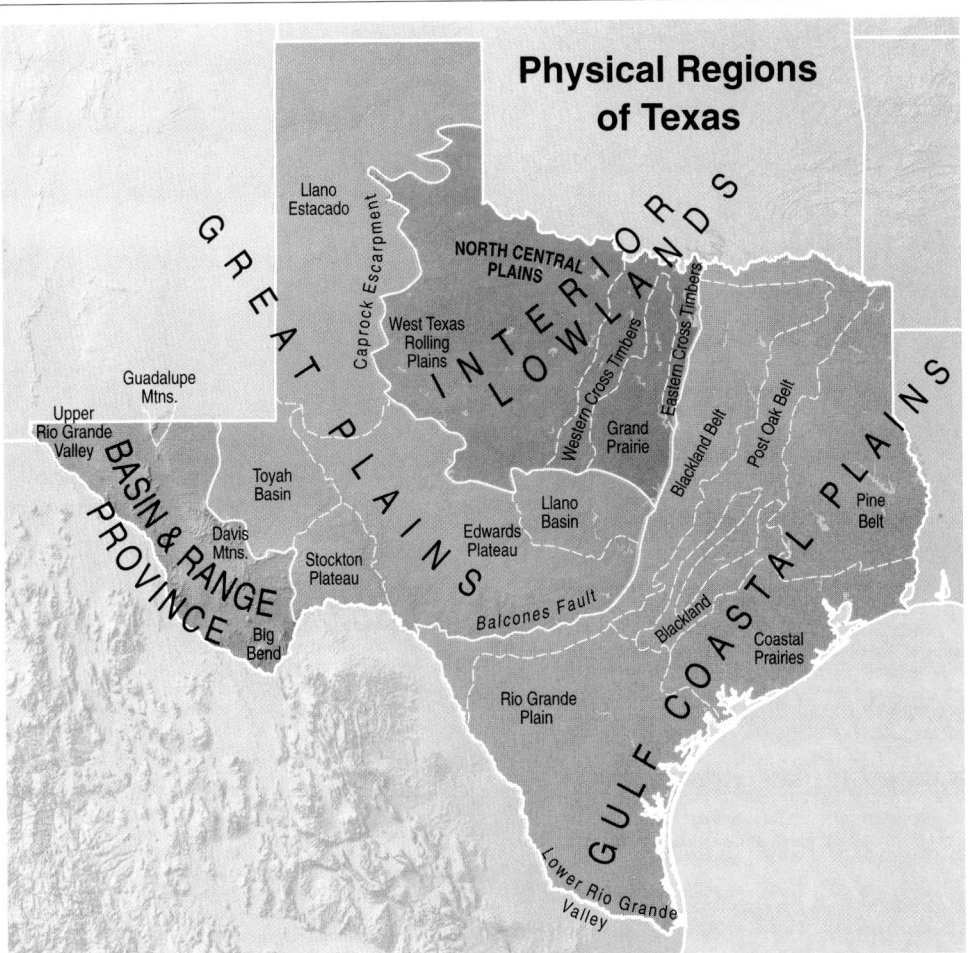

Physical Regions of Texas

Llano Estacado

NORTH CENTRAL PLAINS

Caprock Escarpment

GREAT

West Texas Rolling Plains

Guadalupe Mtns.

Upper Rio Grande Valley

BASIN & RANGE PROVINCE

Toyah Basin

Davis Mtns.

Stockton Plateau

Big Bend

PLAINS

Western Cross Timbers

Eastern Cross Timbers

INTERIOR LOWLANDS

Grand Prairie

Blackland Belt

Post Oak Belt

Llano Basin

Edwards Plateau

Balcones Fault

Blackland

Pine Belt

Rio Grande Plain

GULF COASTAL PLAINS

Coastal Prairies

Lower Rio Grande Valley

Corpus Christi, in the Coastal Bend, and Brownsville, in the Lower Rio Grande Valley, have seaports and agricultural and industrial sections. Cotton, grain, vegetables and citrus fruits are the principal crops. Cattle production is significant, with the famed King Ranch and other large ranches located here.

Lower Rio Grande Valley

The deep alluvial soils and distinctive economy cause the Lower Rio Grande Valley to be classified as a subregion of the Gulf Coastal Plain. The Lower Valley, as it is called locally, is Texas' greatest citrus-winter vegetable area because of the normal absence of freezing weather and the rich delta soils of the Rio Grande. Despite occasional damaging freezes, as in 1951 and 1961, the Lower Valley ranks high among the nation's fruit-and-truck regions. Much of the acreage is irrigated, although dry-land farming also is practiced.

Rio Grande Plain

This may be roughly defined as lying south of San Antonio between the Rio Grande and the Gulf Coast. The Rio Grande Plain shows characteristics of both the Texas Gulf Coastal Plain and the North Mexico Plains because there is similarity of topography, climate and plant life all the way from the Balcones Escarpment in Texas to the Sierra Madre Oriental in Mexico, which runs past Monterrey about 160 miles south of Laredo.

The Rio Grande Plain is partly prairie, but much of it is covered with a dense growth of **prickly pear, cactus, mes-** **quite, dwarf oak, catclaw, guajillo, huisache, black-** **brush, cenizo** and other wild shrubs. This country is devoted primarily to raising cattle, sheep and goats. The Texas Angora goat and mohair industry centers in this area and on the **Edwards Plateau**, which borders it on the north. San Antonio and Laredo are its chief commercial centers, with San Antonio dominating trade.

There is some farming, and the **Winter Garden**, centering in Dimmit and Zavala counties north of Laredo, is irrigated from wells and streams to produce vegetables in late winter and early spring. Primarily, however, the central and western part of the Rio Grande Plain is devoted to livestock raising. The rainfall is less than 25 inches annually and the hot summers bring heavy evaporation, so that cultivation without irrigation is limited. Over a large area in the central and western parts of the Rio Grande Plain, the growth of **small oaks, mesquite, prickly pear (Opuntia) cactus** and a variety of wild shrubs is very dense and it is often called the **Brush Country**. It is also referred to as the **chaparral** and the **monte**. (Monte is a Spanish word, one meaning of which is dense brush.)

Interior Lowlands

North Central Plains

The North Central Plains of Texas are a southwestern extension into Texas of the interior, or central, lowlands that extend northward to the Canadian border, paralleling the Great Plains to the West. The North Central Plains of Texas

Jimmy Dreiss, owner of Flat Rock Creek Ranch, rides through a herd of Angora goats on his 1,300-acre ranch in Central Texas. The Edwards Plateau is the United States' leading Angora goat and mohair producing region. File photo.

extend from the Blackland Belt on the east to the Caprock Escarpment on the west. From north to south they extend from the Red River to the Colorado.

West Texas Rolling Plains

The West Texas Rolling Plains, approximately the western two-thirds of the North Central Plains in Texas, rise from east to west in altitude from about 750 feet to 2,000 feet at the base of the **Caprock Escarpment**. Annual rainfall ranges from about 30 inches on the east to 20 on the west. In general, as one progresses westward in Texas the precipitation not only declines but also becomes more variable from year to year. Temperature varies rather widely between summer's heat and winter's cold.

This area still has a large cattle-raising industry with many of the state's largest ranches. However, there is much level, cultivable land.

Grand Prairie

Near the eastern edge of the North Central Plains is the Grand Prairie, extending south from the Red River in an irregular band through Cooke, Montague, Wise, Denton, Tarrant, Parker, Hood, Johnson, Bosque, Coryell and some adjacent counties. It is a limestone-based area, usually treeless except along the numerous streams, and adapted primarily to livestock raising and staple-crop growing. Sometimes called the Fort Worth Prairie, it has an agricultural economy and largely rural population, with no large cities except Fort Worth on its eastern boundary.

Eastern and Western Cross Timbers

Hanging over the top of the Grand Prairie and dropping down on each side are the Eastern and Western Cross Timbers. The two southward-extending bands are connected by a narrow strip along the Red River. The Eastern Cross Timbers extend southward from the Red River through eastern Denton County and along the Dallas-Tarrant County boundary, then through Johnson County to the Brazos River and into Hill County. The much larger Western Cross Timbers extend from the Red River south through Clay, Montague, Jack, Wise, Parker, Palo Pinto, Hood, Erath, Eastland, Comanche, Brown and Mills counties to the Colorado River, where they meet the Edwards Plateau. Their soils are adapted to fruit and vegetable crops, which reach considerable commercial production in some areas in Parker, Erath, Eastland and Comanche counties.

Great Plains

High Plains

The Great Plains which lie to the east of the base of the Rocky Mountains extend into Northwest Texas. This area,

commonly known as the **High Plains**, is a vast, flat, high plain covered with thick layers of alluvial material. It is also known as the **Staked Plains** or the Spanish equivalent, **Llano Estacado**.

Historians differ as to the origin of this name. Some think that it came from the fact that the Coronado expedition, crossing the trackless sea of grass, staked its route so that it would be guided on its return trip. Others think that the "estacado" refers to the palisaded appearance of the Caprock in many places, especially the west-facing escarpment in New Mexico.

The **Caprock Escarpment** is the dividing line between the High Plains and the Lower Rolling Plains of West Texas. Like the Balcones Escarpment, the Caprock Escarpment is a striking physical feature, rising abruptly 200, 500 and in some places almost 1,000 feet above the plains. Unlike the **Balcones Escarpment**, the Caprock was caused by surface erosion. Where rivers issue from the eastern face of the Caprock, there frequently are notable canyons, such as the **Palo Duro Canyon** on the **Prairie Dog Town Fork (main channel) of the Red River** and the breaks along the Canadian as it crosses the Panhandle north of Amarillo.

Along the eastern edge of the Panhandle there is a gradual descent of the earth's surface from high to low plains, but at the Red River the Caprock Escarpment becomes a striking surface feature. It continues as an east-facing wall south through Briscoe, Floyd, Motley, Dickens, Crosby, Garza and Borden counties, gradually decreasing in elevation. South of Borden County the escarpment is less obvious, and the boundary between the High Plains and the Edwards Plateau occurs where the alluvial cover of the High Plains disappears.

Stretching over the largest level plain of its kind in the United States, the High Plains rise gradually from about 2,700 feet on the east to more than 4,000 in spots along the New Mexico border.

Chiefly because of climate and the resultant agriculture, subdivisions are called the North Plains and South Plains. The North Plains, from Hale County north, has primarily wheat and grain sorghum farming, but with significant ranching and petroleum developments. Amarillo is the largest city, with Plainview on the south and Borger on the north as important commercial centers.

The South Plains, also a leading grain sorghum region, leads Texas in cotton production. Lubbock is the principal city, and Lubbock County is one of the state's largest cotton producers. Irrigation from underground reservoirs, centered around Lubbock and Plainview, waters much of the crop acreage.

Edwards Plateau

Geographers usually consider that the Great Plains at the foot of the Rocky Mountains actually continue southward from the High Plains of Northwest Texas to the Rio Grande and the Balcones Escarpment. This southern and lower extension of the Great Plains in Texas is known as the Edwards Plateau.

It lies between the Rio Grande and the Colorado River. Its southeastern border is the **Balcones Escarpment** from the Rio Grande at Del Rio eastward to San Antonio and thence to Austin on the Colorado. Its upper boundary is the Pecos River, though the **Stockton Plateau** is geologically and topographically classed with the Edwards Plateau. The Edwards Plateau varies from about 750 feet high at its southern and eastern borders to about 2,700 feet in places. Almost the entire surface is a thin, limestone-based soil covered with a medium to thick growth of **cedar, small oak** and **mesquite** with a varying growth of **prickly pear.** Grass for cattle, weeds for sheep and tree foliage for the browsing goats support three industries — cattle, goat and sheep raising — upon which the area's economy depends. It is the **nation's leading Angora goat and mohair producing region** and one of the nation's leading sheep and wool areas. A few crops are grown.

The Hill Country

The Hill Country is a popular name for an area of hills and spring-fed streams along the edge of the **Balcones Escarpment** in the southeast portion of the Edwards Plateau south of the Llano Basin. Notable large springs include **Barton Springs** at Austin, **San Marcos Springs** at San Marcos, **Comal Springs** at New Braunfels, several springs at San Antonio, and a number of others. The Hill Country is characterized by rugged hills with relatively steep slopes and thin soils overlying limestone bedrock. High gradient streams combine with these steep hillslopes and occasionally heavy precipitation to produce an area with a significant flash-flood hazard.

Toyah Basin

To the northwest of the Edwards and Stockton plateaus is the Toyah Basin, a broad, flat remnant of an old sea floor that occupied the region as recently as Quaternary time. Located in the Pecos River Valley, this region, in relatively recent time, has become important for many agricultural products as a result of irrigation. Additional economic activity is afforded by local oil fields.

The Llano Basin

The Llano Basin lies at the junction of the Colorado and Llano rivers in Burnet and Llano counties. Earlier this was known as the "Central Mineral Region," because of the evidence there of a large number of minerals.

On the Colorado River in this area, a succession of dams impounds two large and five small reservoirs. Uppermost is **Lake Buchanan,** one of the large reservoirs, between Burnet and Llano counties. Below it in the western part of Travis County is **Lake Travis.** Between these two large reservoirs are three smaller ones, **Inks, L. B. Johnson** (formerly Granite Shoals) and **Marble Falls** reservoirs, used primarily for maintaining heads to produce electric power from the overflow from Lake Buchanan. **Lake Austin** is just above the city of Austin. Still another small lake, **Town Lake,** is formed by a low-water dam in Austin. The recreational area around these lakes is called the **Highland Lakes Country.** This is an interesting area with Precambrian and Paleozoic rocks found on the surface. Granitic domes, exemplified by Enchanted Rock north of Fredericksburg, form the core of this area of ancient rocks.

Basin and Range Province

The Basin and Range province, with its center in Nevada, surrounds the Colorado Plateau on the west and south and enters far West Texas from southern New Mexico. It consists of broad interior drainage basins interspersed with scattered fault-block mountain ranges. Although this is the only part of Texas regarded as mountainous, these should not be confused with the Rockies. Of all the indepen-

Cotton is grown across much of Texas, but the High Plains is the state's top cotton-producing region. File photo.

dent ranges in West Texas, only the Davis Mountains resemble the Rockies, and there is much debate about this.

Texas west of the Edwards Plateau, bounded on the north by New Mexico and on the south by the Rio Grande, is distinctive in its physical and economic conditions. Traversed from north to south by fault-block mountains, it contains all of Texas' true mountains and also is very interesting geologically.

Highest of the Trans-Pecos Mountains is the **Guadalupe Range,** which enters the state from New Mexico. It comes to an abrupt end about 20 miles south of the boundary line, where **Guadalupe Peak,** (8,749 feet, highest in Texas) and **El Capitan** (8,085 feet) are situated. El Capitan, because of perspective, appears to the observer on the plain below to be higher than Guadalupe. Lying just west of the Guadalupe range and extending to the **Hueco Mountains** a short distance east of El Paso is the **Diablo Plateau** or basin. It has no drainage outlet to the sea. The runoff from the scant rain that falls on its surface drains into a series of salt lakes that lie just west of the Guadalupe Mountains. These lakes are dry during periods of low rainfall, exposing bottoms of solid salt, and for years they were a source of **commercial salt.**

Davis Mountains

The Davis Mountains are principally in Jeff Davis County. The highest peak, **Mount Livermore** (8,378 feet), is **one of the highest in Texas;** there are several others more than 7,000 feet high. These mountains intercept the moisture-bearing winds and receive more precipitation than elsewhere in the Trans-Pecos, so they have more vegetation than the other Trans-Pecos mountains. Noteworthy are the **San Solomon Springs** at the northern base of these mountains.

Big Bend

South of the Davis Mountains lies the Big Bend country, so called because it is encompassed on three sides by a great southward swing of the Rio Grande. It is a mountainous country of scant rainfall and sparse population. Its principal mountains, the **Chisos,** rise to 7,825 feet in **Mount Emory.** Along the Rio Grande are the **Santa Elena, Mariscal** and **Boquillas canyons** with rim elevations of 3,500 to 3,775 feet. They are among the noteworthy canyons of the North American continent. Because of its remarkable topography and plant and animal life, the southern part of this region along the Rio Grande is home to the **Big Bend National Park,** with headquarters in a deep valley in the Chisos Mountains. It is a favorite recreation area.

Upper Rio Grande Valley

The Upper Rio Grande (El Paso) Valley is a narrow strip of irrigated land running down the river from El Paso for a distance of 75 miles or more. In this area are the historic towns and missions of **Ysleta, Socorro and San Elizario, oldest in Texas.** Cotton is the chief product of the valley, much of it the long-staple variety. This limited area has a dense urban and rural population, in marked contrast to the territory surrounding it. ☆

Geology of Texas

Source: Bureau of Economic Geology, The University of Texas at Austin; www.beg.utexas.edu/

History in the Rocks

Mountains, seas, coastal plains, rocky plateaus, high plains, forests — all this physiographic variety in Texas is controlled by the varied rocks and structures that underlie and crop out across the state. The fascinating geologic history of Texas is recorded in the rocks — both those exposed at the surface and those penetrated by holes drilled in search of oil and natural gas.

The rocks reveal a dynamic, ever-changing earth — ancient mountains, seas, volcanoes, earthquake belts, rivers, hurricanes and winds. Today, the volcanoes and great earthquake belts are no longer active, but rivers and streams, wind and rain, and the slow, inexorable alterations of rocks at or near the surface continue to change the face of Texas. The geologic history of Texas, as documented by the rocks, began more than a billion years ago. Its legacy is the mineral wealth and varied land forms of modern Texas.

A geologist examines rock in Santa Elena Canyon in Big Bend National Park. The canyon's limestone walls rise to a height of 1,500 feet above the Rio Grande, which separates Mexico on the left from the United States. File photo.

Geologic Time Travel

The story preserved in rocks requires an understanding of the origin of strata and how they have been deformed. **Stratigraphy** is the study of the composition, sequence and origin of rocks: what rocks are made of, how they were formed and the order in which the layers were formed. Structural geology reveals the architecture of rocks: the locations of the mountains, volcanoes, sedimentary basins and earthquake belts. The map on the following page shows where rocks of various geologic ages are visible on the surface of Texas today. History concerns events through time, but geologic time is such a grandiose concept, most find it difficult to comprehend. So geologists have named the various chapters of earth history.

Precambrian Eon

Precambrian rocks, more than 600 million years old, are exposed at the surface in the **Llano Uplift** of Central Texas and in scattered outcrops in **West Texas,** around and north of Van Horn and near El Paso. These rocks, some more than a billion years old, include complexly deformed rocks that were originally formed by cooling from a liquid state as well as rocks that were altered from preexisting rocks.

Precambrian rocks, often called the "basement complex," are thought to form the foundation of continental masses. They underlie all of Texas. The outcrop in Central Texas is only the exposed part of the **Texas Craton,** which is primarily buried by younger rocks. (A craton is a stable, almost immovable portion of the earth's crust that forms the nuclear mass of a continent.)

Paleozoic Era

During the early part of the Paleozoic Era (approximately 600 million to 350 million years ago), broad, relatively shallow seas repeatedly inundated the Texas Craton and much of North and West Texas. The evidence for these events is found exposed around the Llano Uplift and in far West Texas near Van Horn and El Paso, and also in the subsurface throughout most of West and North Texas. The evidence includes early Paleozoic rocks — sandstones, shales and limestones, similar to sediments that form in seas today — and the fossils of animals, similar to modern crustaceans — the brachiopods, clams, snails and related organisms that live in modern marine environments.

By **late Paleozoic** (approximately 350 million to 240 million years ago), the Texas Craton was bordered on the east and south by a long, deep marine basin called the **Ouachita Trough.** Sediments slowly accumulated in this trough until late in the Paleozoic Era. Plate-tectonic theory postulates that the collision of the North American Plate (upon which the Texas Craton is located) with the European and African–South American plates uplifted the thick sediments that had accumulated in the trough to form the Ouachita Mountains. At that time, the Ouachitas extended across Texas. Today, the Texas portion of the old mountain range is entirely buried by younger rocks, and all that remains at the surface of the once-majestic Ouachita Mountain chain is exposed only in southeastern Oklahoma and southwestern Arkansas.

During the **Pennsylvanian Period,** however, the Ouachita Mountains bordered the eastern margin of shallow inland seas that covered most of West Texas. Rivers flowed westward from the mountains to the seas bringing sediment to form deltas along an ever-changing coastline. The sediments were then reworked by the waves and currents of the inland sea. Today, these fluvial, delta and shallow marine deposits compose the late Paleozoic rocks that crop out and underlie the surface of North-Central Texas.

Broad marine shelves divided the West Texas seas into several sub-basins, or deeper areas, that received more sediments than accumulated on the limestone shelves. Limestone reefs rimmed the deeper basins. Today, these reef limestones are important **oil reservoirs in West Texas.** These seas gradually withdrew from Texas, and by the late **Permian Period,** all that was left in West Texas were shallow basins and wide tidal flats in which salt, gypsum and red muds accumulated in a hot, arid

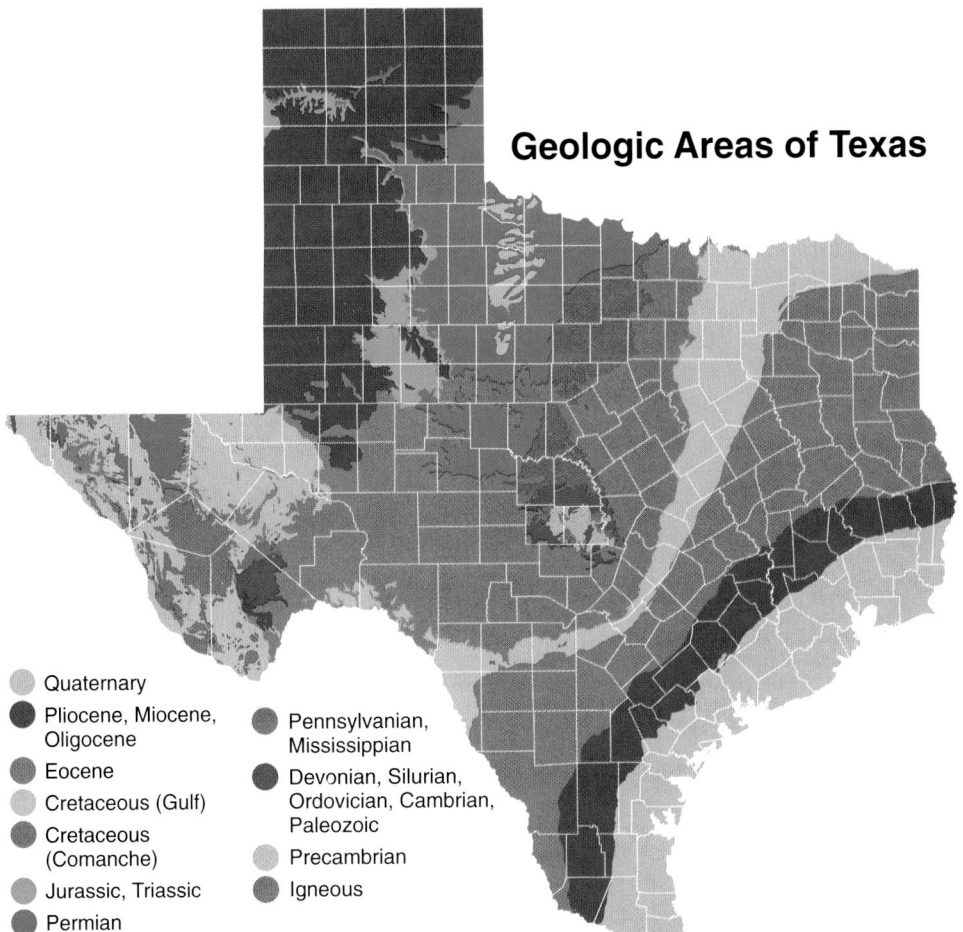

Geologic Areas of Texas

- Quaternary
- Pliocene, Miocene, Oligocene
- Eocene
- Cretaceous (Gulf)
- Cretaceous (Comanche)
- Jurassic, Triassic
- Permian
- Pennsylvanian, Mississippian
- Devonian, Silurian, Ordovician, Cambrian, Paleozoic
- Precambrian
- Igneous

land. Strata deposited during the Permian Period are exposed today along the edge of the Panhandle, as far east as Wichita Falls and south to Concho County, and in the Trans-Pecos.

Mesozoic Era

Approximately 240 million years ago, the major geologic events in Texas shifted from West Texas to East and Southeast Texas. The European and African–South American plates, which had collided with the North American plate to form the Ouachita Mountains, began to separate from North America. A series of faulted basins, or rifts, extending from Mexico to Nova Scotia were formed. These rifted basins received sediments from adjacent uplifts. As Europe and the southern continents continued to drift away from North America, the Texas basins were eventually buried beneath thick deposits of marine salt within the newly formed East Texas and Gulf Coast basins.

Jurassic and **Cretaceous** rocks in East and Southeast Texas document a sequence of broad limestone shelves at the edge of the developing Gulf of Mexico. From time to time, the shelves were buried beneath deltaic sandstones and shales, which built the northwestern margin of the widening Gulf of Mexico to the south and southeast. As the underlying salt was buried more deeply by dense sediments, the salt became unstable and moved toward areas of least pressure. As the salt moved, it arched or pierced overlying sediments forming, in some cases, columns known as "**salt domes**." In some cases, these salt domes moved to the surface; others remain beneath a sedimentary overburden. This mobile salt formed numerous structures that would later serve to trap oil and natural gas.

By the early **Cretaceous** (approximately 140 million years ago), the shallow **Mesozoic seas** covered a large part of Texas, eventually extending west to the Trans-Pecos area and north almost to present-day state boundaries. Today, the limestone deposited in those seas are exposed in the walls of the magnificent **canyons of the Rio Grande** in the Big Bend National Park area and in the canyons and headwaters of streams that drain the Edwards Plateau, as well as in Central Texas from San Antonio to Dallas.

Animals of many types lived in the shallow Mesozoic seas, tidal pools and coastal swamps. Today these lower Cretaceous rocks are some of the most fossiliferous in the state. Tracks of **dinosaurs** occur in several places, and remains of **terrestrial, aquatic** and **flying reptiles** have been collected from Cretaceous rocks in many areas.

During most of the late Cretaceous, much of Texas lay beneath **marine waters** that were deeper than those of the early Cretaceous seas, except where rivers, deltas and shallow marine shelves existed. River delta and strandline sandstones are the reservoir rocks for the most

Visitors hike on Enchanted Rock, a giant pink granite batholith (an underground rock formation uncovered by erosion) that covers 640 acres in Enchanted Rock State Natural Area. It is the second-largest batholith in the United States. File photo.

prolific oil field in Texas. When discovered in 1930, this East Texas oil field contained recoverable reserves estimated at 5.6 billion barrels. The chalky rock that we now call the **"Austin Chalk"** was deposited when the Texas seas became deeper.

Today, the chalk (and other Upper Cretaceous rocks) crops out in a wide band that extends from near Eagle Pass on the Rio Grande, east to San Antonio, north to Dallas and east to the Texarkana area. The Austin Chalk and other upper Cretaceous rocks dip southeastward beneath the East Texas and Gulf Coast basins. The late Cretaceous was the time of the last major seaway across Texas, because mountains were forming in the western United States that influenced areas as far away as Texas.

A **chain of volcanoes** formed beneath the late Cretaceous seas in an area roughly parallel to and south and east of the old, buried Ouachita Mountains. The eruptions of these volcanoes were primarily on the sea floor and great clouds of steam and ash likely accompanied them. Between eruptions, invertebrate marine animals built reefs on the shallow volcanic cones. **Pilot Knob**, located southeast of Austin, is one of these old volcanoes that is now exposed at the surface.

Cenozoic Era

At the dawn of the Cenozoic Era, approximately 65 million years ago, deltas fed by rivers were in the northern and northwestern margins of the East Texas Basin. These streams flowed eastward, draining areas to the north and west. Although there were minor incursions of the seas, the Cenozoic rocks principally document extensive seaward building by broad deltas, marshy lagoons, sandy barrier islands and embayments. Thick vegetation covered the levees and areas between the streams. Coastal plains were taking shape under the same processes still at work today.

The Mesozoic marine salt became buried by thick sediments in the coastal plain area. The salt began to form ridges and domes in the Houston and Rio Grande areas. The heavy load of sand, silt and mud deposited by the deltas eventually caused some areas of the coast to subside and form large fault systems, essentially parallel to the coast. Many of these coastal faults moved slowly and probably generated little earthquake activity. However, movement along the Balcones and Luling-Mexia-Talco zones, a **complex system of faults** along the western and northern edge of the basins, likely generated large earthquakes millions of years ago.

Predecessors of modern animals roamed the Texas Cenozoic coastal plains and woodlands. Bones and teeth of **horses, camels, sloths, giant armadillos, mam-moths, mastodons, bats, rats, large cats** and other modern or extinct mammals have been excavated from coastal plain deposits. Vegetation in the area included varieties of plants and trees both similar and dissimilar to modern ones. **Fossil palmwood**, the Texas **"state stone,"** is found in sediments of early Cenozoic age.

The Cenozoic Era in Trans-Pecos Texas was entirely different. There, **extensive volcanic eruptions** formed great calderas and produced copious lava flows. These eruptions ejected great clouds of volcanic ash and rock particles into the air — many times the amount of material ejected by the 1980 eruption of Mount St. Helens. Ash from the eruptions drifted eastward and is found in many of the sand-and-siltstones of the Gulf Coastal Plains. **Lava** flowed over older Paleozoic and Mesozoic rocks, and igneous intrusions melted their way upward into crustal rocks. These volcanic and intrusive igneous rocks are well exposed in arid areas of the Trans-Pecos today.

In the Texas Panhandle, streams originating in the recently elevated southern Rocky Mountains brought floods of gravel and sand into Texas. As the braided streams crisscrossed the area, they formed great **alluvial fans**. These fans, which were deposited on the older **Paleozoic** and **Mesozoic** rocks, occur from northwestern Texas into Nebraska. Between 1 million and 2 million years ago, the streams of the Panhandle were isolated from their Rocky Mountain source, and the eastern edge of this sheet of alluvial material began to retreat westward, forming the **Caprock** of the modern High Plains.

Late in the Cenozoic Era, a great **Ice Age** descended on the northern North American continent. For more than 2 million years, there were successive advances and retreats of the thick sheets of glacial ice. Four periods of extensive glaciation were separated by warmer interglacial periods. Although the glaciers never reached as far south as Texas, the state's climate and sea level underwent major changes with each period of glacial advance and retreat.

Sea level during times of glacial advance was 300 to 450 feet lower than during the warmer interglacial periods because so much sea water was captured in the ice sheets. The climate was both more humid and cooler than today, and the major Texas rivers carried more water and more sand and gravel to the sea. These deposits underlie the outer 50 miles or more of the Gulf Coastal Plain.

Approximately 3,000 years ago, sea level reached its modern position. The rivers, deltas, lagoons, beaches and barrier islands that we know as coastal Texas today have formed since that time. ☆

Oil and natural gas, as well as nonfuel minerals, are important to the Texas economy. For a more detailed discussion, see pages 602–619.

Soils of Texas

Source: Natural Resources Conservation Service, U. S. Department of Agriculture, Temple, Texas; www.tx.nrcs.usda.gov/

Soil is one of Texas' most important natural resources. The soils of Texas are complex because of the wide diversity of climate, vegetation, geology and landscape. **More than 1,300 different kinds of soil** are recognized in Texas. Each has a specific set of properties that affect its use.

The location of each soil and information about use are in soil survey reports available for most counties. Contact the **Natural Resources Conservation Service** for more information: 101 S. Main St., Temple 76501-7602; phone: 254-742-9850. On the Web: **www.-tx.nrcs.-usda.gov**; click on "Information About: Soils."

The vast expanse of Texas soils encouraged wasteful use of soil and water throughout much of the state's history. About 21 percent of all land area in Texas has been classified as "prime farmland."

Settlers, attracted to these rich soils and the abundant water of the eastern half of the region, used them to build an agriculture and agribusiness of vast proportions, and then found their abuse had created critical problems.

Soil Conservation

In the 1930s, interest in soil and water conservation began to mount. In 1935, the Soil Conservation Service, now called the **Natural Resources Conservation Service,** was created in the U.S. Department of Agriculture. In 1939, the **Texas Soil Conservation Law** made it possible for landowners to organize local soil and water conservation districts.

As of July 2003, Texas had **216 conservation districts,** which manage conservation functions within the district. A subdivision of state government, each district is governed by a board of five elected landowners. Technical assistance in planning and applying conservation work is provided through the USDA, Natural Resources Conservation Service. State funds for districts are administered through the **Texas State Soil and Water Conservation Board.**

The 1997 National Resources Inventory showed that **land use** in Texas consisted of about 57 percent rangeland, 16 percent cropland, 9 percent pastureland, 6 percent forestland, 5 percent developed land, 2 percent federal land, 2 percent land in the conservation reserve program (CRP), 1 percent miscellaneous land and 2 percent water.

Soil Subdivisions

Texas can be divided into 21 major subdivisions, called **Major Land Resource Areas,** that have similar or related soils, vegetation, topography, climate and land uses. Brief descriptions of these subdivisions follow.

Trans-Pecos Soils

The 18.7 million acres of the Trans-Pecos, mostly west of the Pecos River, are diverse plains and valleys intermixed with mountains. Surface drainage is slow to rapid. This arid region is used mainly as rangeland. A small amount of irrigated cropland is on the more fertile soils along the Rio Grande and the Pecos River. Vineyards are a more recent use of these soils, as is the disposal of large volumes of municipal wastes.

Upland soils are mostly well-drained, light reddish-brown to brown clay loams, clays and sands (some have a large amount of gypsum or other salts). Many areas have shallow soils and rock outcrops, and sizable areas have deep sands. Bottomland soils are deep, well-drained, dark grayish-brown to reddish-brown silt loams, loams, clay loams and clays. Lack of soil moisture and wind erosion are the major soil-management problems. Only irrigated crops can be grown on these soils, and most areas lack an adequate source of good water.

Upper Pecos, Canadian Valleys and Plains Soils

The Upper Pecos and Canadian Valleys and Plains area occupies a little over a half-million acres and is in the northwest part of Texas near the Texas-New Mexico border. It is characterized by broad rolling plains and tablelands broken by drainageways and tributaries of the Canadian River. It includes the Canadian Breaks, which are rough, steep lands below the adjacent High Plains. The average annual precipitation is about 15 inches, but it fluctuates widely from year to year. Surface drainage is slow to rapid.

The soils are well drained and alkaline. The mostly reddish-brown clay loams and sandy loams were formed mostly in material weathered from sandstone and shale. Depths range from shallow to very deep.

The area is used mainly as rangeland and wildlife habitat. Native vegetation is mid- to short-grass prairie species, such as hairy grama, sideoats grama, little bluestem, alkali sacaton, vine-mesquite, and galleta in the plains and tablelands. Juniper and mesquite grow on the relatively higher breaks. Soil management problems include low soil moisture and brush control.

High Plains Soils

The High Plains area comprises a vast high plateau of more than 19.4 million acres in northwestern Texas. It lies in the southern part of the Great Plains province that includes large similar areas in Oklahoma and New Mexico. The flat, nearly level treeless plain has few streams to cause local relief. However, several major rivers originate in the High Plains or cross the area. The largest is the Canadian River, which has cut a deep valley across the Panhandle section.

Playas, small intermittent lakes scattered through the area, lie up to 20 feet below the surrounding plains. A 1965 survey counted more than 19,000 playas in 44 counties occupying some 340,000 acres. Most runoff from rainfall is collected in the playas, but only 10 to 40 percent of this water percolates back to the Ogallala Aquifer. The aquifer is virtually the exclusive water source in this area.

Upland soils are mostly well-drained, deep, neutral to alkaline clay loams and sandy loams in shades of brown or red. Sandy soils are in the southern part. Many soils have large amounts of lime at various depths and some are shallow over caliche. Soils of bottomlands are minor in extent.

The area is used mostly for cropland, but significant areas of rangeland are in the southwestern and extreme northern parts. Millions of cattle populate the many large feedlots in the area. The soils are moderately productive, and the flat surface encourages irrigation and mechanization. Limited soil moisture, constant danger of wind erosion and irrigation water management are the major soil-management problems, but the region is Texas' leading producer of three important crops: cotton, grain sorghums and wheat.

Rolling Plains Soils

The Rolling Plains include 21.7 million acres east of the High Plains in northwestern Texas. The area lies west of the North Central Prairies and extends from the edge of the Edwards Plateau in Tom Green County northward into

The Madera Canyon area of the Davis Mountains is within the 18.7 million acres of the Trans-Pecos. Shallow soils and rock outcrops occur in many areas of this region. Photo courtesy of The Nature Conservancy.

Oklahoma. The landscape is nearly level to strongly rolling, and surface drainage is moderate to rapid. Outcrops of red beds, geologic materials and associated reddish soils led to use of the name **"Red Plains"** by some. Limestone underlies the soils in the southeastern part. The eastern part contains large areas of badlands.

Upland soils are mostly deep, pale-brown through reddish-brown to dark grayish-brown, neutral to alkaline sandy loams, clay loams and clays; some are deep sands. Many soils have a large amount of lime in the lower part, and a few others are saline; some are shallow and stony. Bottomland soils are mostly reddish-brown and sandy to clayey; some are saline.

This area is used mostly for rangeland, but cotton, grain sorghums and wheat are important crops. The major soil-management problems are brush control, wind erosion, low fertility and lack of soil mosture. Salt spots are a concern in some areas.

North Central Prairie Soils

The North Central Prairie occupies about 7 million acres in North Central Texas. Adjacent to this area on the north is the rather small (less than 1 million acres) Rolling Red Prairies area, which extends into Oklahoma and is included here because the soils and land use are similar. This area lies between the Western Cross Timbers and the Rolling Plains. It is dominantly grassland intermixed with small wooded areas. The landscape is undulating with slow to rapid surface drainage.

Upland soils are mostly deep, well-drained, brown or reddish-brown, slightly acid loams over neutral to alkaline, clayey subsoils. Some soils are shallow or moderately deep to shale. Bottomland soils are mostly well-drained, dark-brown or gray loams and clays.

This area is used mostly as rangeland, but wheat, grain sorghums and other crops are grown on the better soils. Brush control, wind and water erosion and limited soil moisture are the major soil-management concerns.

Edwards Plateau Soils

The 22.7 million acres of the Edwards Plateau are in southwest Texas east of the Trans-Pecos and west of the Blackland Prairie. Uplands are nearly level to undulating except near large stream valleys where the landscape is hilly with deep canyons and steep slopes. Surface drainage is rapid.

Upland soils are mostly shallow, stony or gravelly, dark alkaline clays and clay loams underlain by limestone. Lighter-colored soils are on steep sideslopes and deep, less-stony soils are in the valleys. Bottomland soils are mostly deep, dark-gray or brown, alkaline loams and clays.

Raising beef cattle is the main enterprise in this region, but it is also the center of Texas' and the nation's mohair and wool production. The area is a major deer habitat; hunting leases produce income. Cropland is mostly in the valleys on the deeper soils and is used mainly for growing forage crops and hay. The major soil-management concerns are brush control, large stones, low fertility, excess lime and limited soil moisture.

Central Basin Soils

The Central Basin, also known as the **Llano Basin**, occupies a relatively small area in Central Texas. It includes parts or all of Llano, Mason, Gillespie and adjoining counties. The total area is about 1.6 million acres of undulating to hilly landscape.

Upland soils are mostly shallow, reddish-brown to brown, mostly gravelly and stony, neutral to slightly acid sandy loams over granite, limestone, gneiss and schist bedrock. Large boulders are on the soil surface in some areas. Deeper, less stony sandy-loam soils are in the valleys. Bottomland soils are minor areas of deep, dark-gray or brown loams and clays.

Ranching is the main enterprise, with some farms producing peaches, grain sorghum and wheat. The area provides excellent deer habitat, and hunting leases are a major source of income. Brush control, large stones and limited soil moisture are soil-management concerns.

Northern Rio Grande Plain Soils

The Northern Rio Grande Plain comprises about 6.3 million acres in Southern Texas extending from Uvalde to Beeville. The landscape is nearly level to rolling, mostly brush-covered plains with slow to rapid surface drainage.

The major upland soils are deep, reddish-brown or dark grayish-brown, neutral to alkaline loams and clays. Bottomland soils are mostly dark-colored loams.

The area is mostly rangeland with significant areas of cropland. Grain sorghums, cotton, corn and small grains are the major crops. Crops are irrigated in the western part, especially in the Winter Garden area, where vegetables such as spinach, carrots and cabbage are grown. Much of the area is good deer and dove habitat; hunting leases are a major source of income. Brush control, soil fertility, and irrigation-water management are the major soil-management concerns.

Western Rio Grande Plain Soils

The Western Rio Grande Plain comprises about 5.3 million acres in an area of southwestern Texas from Del Rio to Rio Grande City. The landscape is nearly level to undulating except near the Rio Grande where it is hilly. Surface drainage is slow to rapid.

The major soils are mostly deep, brown or gray alkaline clays and loams. Some are saline.

Most of the soils are used for rangeland. Irrigated grain sorghums and vegetables are grown along the Rio Grande. Hunting leases are a major source of income. Brush control and limited soil moisture are the major soil-management problems.

Central Rio Grande Plain Soils

The Central Rio Grande Plain comprises about 5.9 million acres in an area of Southern Texas from Live Oak County to Hidalgo County. It Includes the South Texas Sand Sheet, an area of deep, sandy soils and active sand dunes. The landscape is nearly level to gently undulating. Surface drainage is slow to rapid.

Upland soils are mostly deep, light-colored, neutral to alkaline sands and loams. Many are saline or sodic. Bottomland soils are of minor extent.

Most of the area is used for raising beef cattle. A few areas, mostly in the northeast part, are used for growing grain sorghums, cotton and small grains. Hunting leases are a major source of income. Brush control is the major soil-management problem on rangeland; wind erosion and limited soil moisture are major concerns on cropland.

Lower Rio Grande Valley Soils

The Lower Rio Grande Valley comprises about 2.1 million acres in extreme southern Texas. The landscape is level to gently sloping with slow surface drainage.

Upland soils are mostly deep, grayish-brown, neutral to alkaline loams; coastal areas are mostly gray, silty clay loam and silty clay; some are saline. Bottomland soils are minor in extent.

Most of the soils are used for growing irrigated vegetables and citrus, along with cotton, grain sorghums and sugar cane. Some areas are used for growing beef cattle. Irrigation water management and wind erosion are the major soil-management problems on cropland; brush control is the major problem on rangeland.

Western Cross Timbers Soils

The Western Cross Timbers area comprises about 2.6 million acres. It includes the wooded section west of the Grand Prairie and extends from the Red River southward to the north edge of Brown County. The landscape is undulating and is dissected by many drainageways including the Brazos and Red rivers. Surface drainage is rapid.

Upland soils are mostly deep, grayish-brown, slightly acid loams with loamy and clayey subsoils. Bottomland soils along the major rivers are deep, reddish-brown, neutral to alkaline silt loams and clays.

The area is used mostly for grazing beef and dairy cattle on native range and improved pastures. Crops are peanuts, grain sorghums, small grains, peaches, pecans and vegetables. The major soil-management problem on grazing lands is brush control. Waste management on dairy farms is a more recent concern. Wind and water erosion are the major problems on cropland.

Eastern Cross Timbers Soils

The Eastern Cross Timbers area comprises about 1 million acres in a long narrow strip of wooded land that separates the northern parts of the Blackland Prairie and Grand Prairie and extends from the Red River southward to the Hill County. The landscape is gently undulating to rolling and is dissected by many streams, including the Red and Trinity rivers. Sandstone-capped hills are prominent in some areas. Surface runoff is moderate to rapid.

The upland soils are mostly deep, light-colored, slightly acid sandy loams and loamy sands with reddish loamy or clayey subsoils. Bottomland soils are reddish-brown to dark gray, slightly acid to alkaline loams or gray clays.

Grassland consisting of native range and improved pastures is the major land use. Peanuts, grain sorghums, small grains, peaches, pecans and vegetables are grown in some areas. Brush control, water erosion and low fertility are the major concerns in soil management.

Grand Prairie Soils

The Grand Prairie comprises about 6.3 million acres in North Central Texas. It extends from the Red River to about the Colorado River. It lies between the Eastern and Western Cross Timbers in the northern part and just west of the Blackland Prairie in the southern part. The landscape is undulating to hilly and is dissected by many streams including the Red, Trinity and Brazos rivers. Surface drainage is rapid.

Upland soils are mostly dark-gray, alkaline clays; some are shallow over limestone and some are stony. Some areas have light-colored loamy soils over chalky limestone. Bottomland soils along the Red and Brazos rivers are reddish silt loams and clays. Other bottomlands have dark-gray loams and clays.

Land use is a mixture of rangeland, pastureland and cropland. The area is mainly used for growing beef cattle. Some small grain, grain sorghums, corn and hay are grown. Brush control and water erosion are the major management concerns.

Blackland Prairie Soils

The Blackland Prairies consist of about 12.6 million acres of east-central Texas extending southwesterly from the Red River to Bexar County. There are smaller areas to the southeast. The landscape is undulating with few scattered wooded areas that are mostly in the bottomlands. Surface drainage is moderate to rapid.

Both upland and bottomland soils are deep, dark-gray to black alkaline clays. Some soils in the western part are shallow to moderately deep over chalk. Some soils on the eastern edge are neutral to slightly acid, grayish clays and loams over mottled clay subsoils (sometimes called graylands). Blackland soils are known as "cracking clays" because of the large, deep cracks that form in dry weather. This high shrink-swell property can cause serious damage to foundations, highways and other structures and is a safety hazard in pits and trenches.

Land use is divided about equally between cropland and grassland. Cotton, grain sorghums, corn, wheat, oats and hay are grown. Grassland is mostly improved pastures, with native range on the shallower and steeper soils. Water erosion, cotton root rot, soil tilth and brush control are the major management problems.

Claypan Area Soils

The Claypan Area consists of about 6.1 million acres in east-central Texas just east of the Blackland Prairie. The landscape is a gently undulating to rolling, moderately dissected woodland also known as the **Post Oak Belt** or **Post Oak Savannah**. Surface drainage is moderate.

Upland soils commonly have a thin, light-colored, acid sandy loam surface layer over dense, mottled red, yellow and gray claypan subsoils. Some deep, sandy soils with less clayey subsoils exist. Bottomlands are deep, highly fertile, reddish-brown to dark-gray loamy to clayey soils.

Land use is mainly rangeland. Some areas are in improved pastures. Most cropland is in bottomlands that are protected from flooding. Major crops are cotton, grain sorghums, corn, hay and forage crops, most of which are irrigated. Brush control on rangeland and irrigation water management on cropland are the major management problems. Water erosion is a serious problem on the highly erosive claypan soils, especially where they are overgrazed.

East Texas Timberland Soils

The East Texas Timberlands area comprises about 16.1 million acres of the forested eastern part of the state. The landscape is gently undulating to hilly and well dissected by many streams. Surface drainage is moderate to rapid.

The Coast Saline Prairies Soils extend over about 3.2 million acres along a narrow strip of wet lowlands adjacent to the Gulf Coast. At Galveston Island State Park, sea morning glories flourish in this soil. File photo.

This area has many kinds of upland soils but most are deep, light-colored, acid sands and loams over loamy and clayey subsoils. Deep sands are in scattered areas and red clays are in areas of "redlands." Bottomland soils are mostly brown to dark-gray, acid loams and some clays.

The land is used mostly for growing commercial pine timber and for woodland grazing. Improved pastures are scattered throughout and are used for grazing beef and dairy cattle and for hay production. Some commercial hardwoods are in the bottomlands. Woodland management problems include seedling survival, invasion of hardwoods in pine stands, effects of logging on water quality and control of the southern pine beetle. Lime and fertilizers are necessary for productive cropland and pastures.

Coast Prairie Soils

The Coast Prairie includes about 8.7 million acres near the Gulf Coast in southeast Texas. It ranges from 30 miles to 80 miles in width and parallels the coast from the Sabine River in Orange County to Baffin Bay in Kleberg County. The landscape is level to gently undulating with slow surface drainage.

Upland soils are mostly deep, dark-gray, neutral to slightly acid clay loams and clays. Lighter-colored and more-sandy soils are in a strip on the northwestern edge; some soils in the southern part are alkaline; some are saline and sodic. Bottomland soils are mostly deep, dark-colored clays and loams along small streams but are greatly varied along the rivers.

Land use is mainly grazing lands and cropland. Some hardwood timber is in the bottomlands. Many areas are also managed for wetland wildlife habitat. The nearly level topography and productive soils encourage farming. Rice, grain sorghums, cotton, corn and hay are the main crops. Brush management on grasslands and removal of excess water on cropland are the major management concerns.

Coast Saline Prairies Soils

The Coast Saline Prairies area includes about 3.2 million acres along a narrow strip of wet lowlands adjacent to the coast; it includes the barrier islands that extend from Mexico to Louisiana. The surface is at or only a few feet above sea level with many areas of salt-water marsh. Surface drainage is very slow. The soils are mostly deep, dark-colored clays and loams; many are saline and sodic. Light-colored sandy soils are on the barrier islands. The water table is at or near the surface of most soils.

Cattle grazing is the chief economic use of the various salt-tolerant cordgrasses and sedges. Many areas are managed for wetland wildlife. Recreation is popular on the barrier islands. Providing fresh water and access to grazing areas are the major management concerns.

Gulf Coast Marsh Soils

This 150,000-acre area lies in the extreme southeastern corner of Texas. The area can be subdivided into four parts: freshwater, intermediate, brackish, and saline (saltwater) marsh. The degree of salinity of this system grades landward from saltwater marshes along the coast to freshwater marshes inland. Surface drainage is very slow.

This area contains many lakes, bayous, tidal channels, and man-made canals. About one-half of the marsh is fresh, and one-half is salty. Most of the area is susceptible to flooding either by fresh water drained from lands adjacent to the marsh or by saltwater from the Gulf of Mexico.

Most of the soils are very poorly drained, continuously saturated, soft and can carry little weight. In general, the organic soils have a thick layer of dark gray, relatively undecomposed organic material over a gray, clayey subsoil. The mineral soils have a surface of dark gray, highly decomposed organic material over a gray, clayey subsoil.

Most of the almost treeless and uninhabited area is in marsh vegetation, such as grasses, sedges and rushes. It is used mainly for wildlife habitat. Part of the fertile and productive estuarine complex that supports marine life of the Gulf of Mexico, it provides wintering ground for waterfowl and habitat for many fur-bearing animals and alligators.

A significant acreage is firm enough to support livestock and is used for winter grazing of cattle. The major management problems are providing fresh water and access to grazing areas.

Flatwoods Soils

The Flatwoods area includes about 2.5 million acres of woodland in humid southeast Texas just north of the Coast Prairie and extending into Louisiana. The landscape is level to gently undulating. Surface drainage is slow.

Upland soils are mostly deep, light-colored, acid loams with gray, loamy or clayey subsoils. Bottomland soils are deep, dark-colored, acid clays and loams. The water table is near the surface at least part of the year.

The land is mainly used for forest, although cattle are grazed in some areas. Woodland management problems include seedling survival, invasion of hardwoods in pine stands, effects of logging on water quality and control of the southern pine beetle. ☆

Water Resources

Source: Texas Water Development Board; www.twdb.state.tx.us

Surface Water and Ground Water

In Texas, **water law has been historically different for surface water** and **ground water.** Surface water belongs to the state and, except for limited amounts of water for household and on-farm livestock use, requires permits for use.

In general, ground water is considered the property of the surface landowner by "right of capture," meaning the landowner may pump as much water from beneath his land as he can for any beneficial use. This right may be limited only through the creation of ground-water conservation districts, which may make rules to protect and conserve ground-water supplies within their boundaries.

The **Texas Commission on Environmental Quality** is responsible for permitting and adjudicating surface-water rights and uses. It is the primary regulator of surface water and polices contamination and pollution of both surface and ground water.

The **Texas Water Development Board** collects data on occurrence, availability and quality of water within the state; plans for future supply and use; and administers the state's funds for grants and loans to finance future water development and supply.

In January 2002, the Texas Water Development Board developed a comprehensive **statewide water plan,** which the 75th Texas Legislature in 1997 had required the board to do. The TWDB divided the state into 16 regional water-planning areas, and each area's Regional Water Planning Group is required to adopt a water plan that addresses conservation of water supplies, how to meet future water needs and how to respond to future droughts.

Ground-water Supplies and Use

Texas has historically relied on its wealth of fresh to slightly saline water that underlies more than 81 percent of the state. About 60 percent of the approximately 16 million acre-feet of water used yearly in Texas is derived from underground formations that make up 9 major and 21 minor aquifers.

Nearly 80 percent of the ground water produced in 2000 was used for irrigating crops, especially in the Panhandle region. Ground water also supplies about 36 percent of the state's municipal needs.

Major Aquifers

of Texas

Ogallala

The Ogallala aquifer extends under 46 counties of the Texas Panhandle and is the southernmost extension of the largest aquifer (High Plains aquifer) in North America. The Ogallala Formation of late Miocene to early Pliocene age consists of heterogeneous sequences of coarse-grained sand and gravel in the lower part, grading upward into clay, silt and fine sand. In Texas, the Panhandle is the most extensive region irrigated with ground water. About 96 percent of the water pumped from the Ogallala is used for irrigation.

Water-level declines are occurring in part of the region because of extensive pumping that far exceeds recharge. Water-conservation measures by agricultural and municipal users are being promoted. Computer models of the northern and southern portions of the Ogallala aquifer were completed by the TWDB and its contractor. Several agencies are investigating playa recharge and agricultural re-use projects over the aquifer.

Gulf Coast Aquifer

The Gulf Coast aquifer forms an irregularly shaped belt that parallels the Texas coastline and extends through 54 counties from the Rio Grande northeastward to the Louisiana border. The **aquifer system** is composed of the water-bearing units of the Catahoula, Oakville, Fleming, Goliad, Willis, Lissie, Bentley, Montgomery and Beaumont formations.

This system has been divided into three major water-producing components referred to as the **Chicot, Evangeline,** and **Jasper** aquifers. Municipal uses account for about 53 percent and irrigation accounts for about 35 percent of the total pumpage from the aquifer. Water quality is generally good northeast of the San Antonio River basin, but deteriorates to the southwest. Years of heavy pumpage have caused significant water-level declines in portions of the aquifer. Some of these declines have resulted in significant **land-surface subsidence,** particularly in the Houston-Galveston area. TWDB has developed computer models of the northern, central and southern portions of the aquifer.

Edwards (Balcones Fault Zone)

The Edwards (BFZ) aquifer forms a narrow belt extending through nine counties from a ground-water divide in Kinney County through the San Antonio area northeastward to the Leon River in Bell County. A poorly defined ground-water divide in Hays County hydrologically separates the aquifer into the San Antonio and Austin regions. Water in the aquifer occurs in fractures, honeycomb zones and solution channels in the Edwards and associated limestone formations of Cretaceous age.

More than 50 percent of aquifer pumpage is for municipal use, while irrigation is the principal use in the western segment. San Antonio is one of the largest cities in the world that relies solely on a single ground-water source for its municipal supply. The aquifer also feeds several well-known recreational springs and underlies some of the most environmentally sensitive areas in the state.

In 1993, the Edwards Aquifer Authority was created by the legislature to regulate aquifer pumpage to benefit all users from Uvalde County through a portion of Hays County. Barton Springs-Edwards Aquifer Conservation District provides aquifer management for the rest of Hays and southern Travis counties. The EAA has an active program to educate the public on water conservation and also operates several active groundwater recharge sites. The San Antonio River Authority also has a number of flood-control structures that effectively recharge the aquifer.

Conservation districts are promoting more-efficient irrigation techniques, and market-based, voluntary transfers of unused agricultural water rights to municipal uses are more common. The EAA has developed a computer model of the San Antonio segment of the Edwards aquifer.

Carrizo-Wilcox

Extending from the Rio Grande in South Texas northeastward into Arkansas and Louisiana, the Carrizo-Wilcox aquifer provides water to all or parts of 60 counties. The Wilcox Group and overlying Carrizo Sand form a hydrologically connected system of sand locally interbedded with clay, silt, lignite and gravel.

Throughout most of its extent in Texas, the aquifer yields fresh to slightly saline water, which is used primarily for irrigation in the **Winter Garden District** of South Texas and for public supply and industrial use in Central and Northeast Texas. Because of excessive pumping, the water level in the aquifer has been significantly lowered, particularly in the artesian portion of the Winter Garden District of Atascosa, Frio and Zavala counties and in municipal and industrial areas in Angelina and Smith counties. The TWDB has completed a computer model for much of the aquifer.

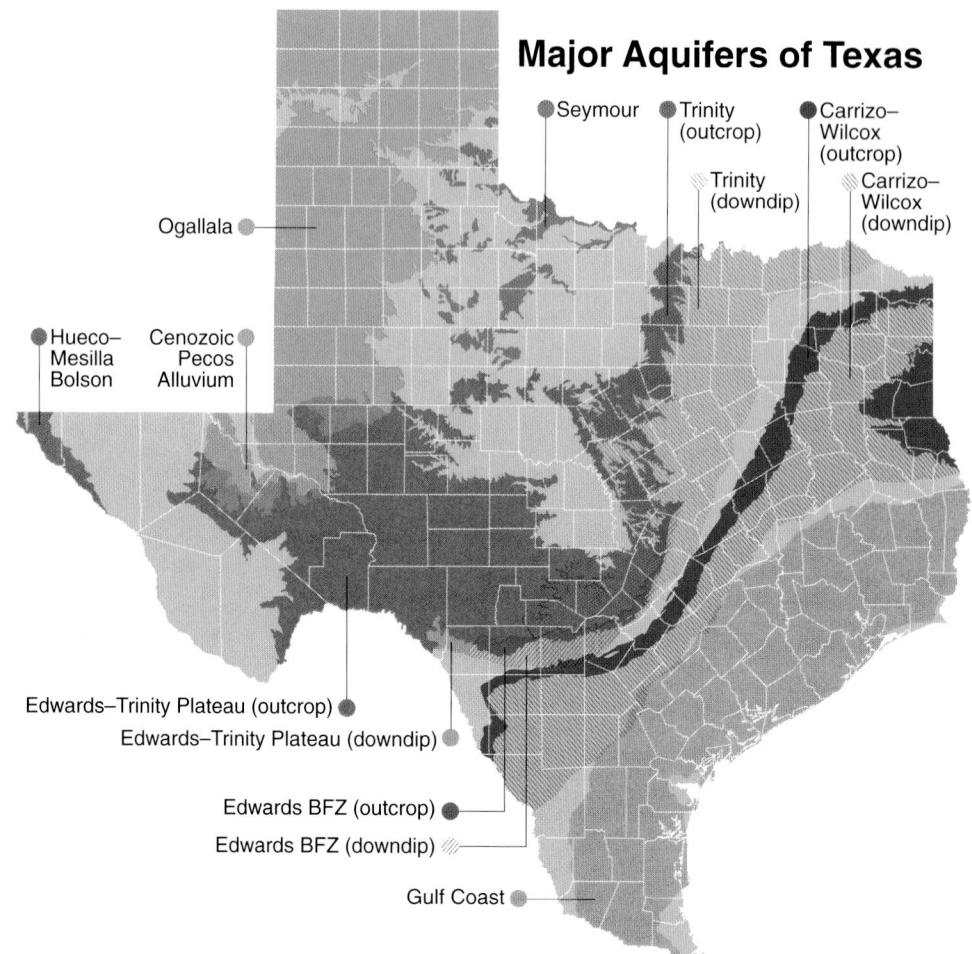

Major Aquifers of Texas

Seymour • Trinity (outcrop) • Carrizo–Wilcox (outcrop)

Trinity (downdip) • Carrizo–Wilcox (downdip)

Ogallala •

Hueco–Mesilla Bolson •   Cenozoic Pecos Alluvium •

Edwards–Trinity Plateau (outcrop) •
Edwards–Trinity Plateau (downdip) •

Edwards BFZ (outcrop) •
Edwards BFZ (downdip)

Gulf Coast •

Trinity

The Trinity aquifer consists of basal Cretaceous-age Trinity Group formations extending from the Red River in North Texas to the Hill Country of Central Texas. Formations comprising the aquifer include the **Twin Mountains, Glen Rose** and **Paluxy.** Where the Glen Rose thins or is absent, the Twin Mountains and Paluxy formations coalesce to form the **Antlers Formation.** In the south, the Trinity includes the Glen Rose and underlying **Travis Peak** formations. Water from the Antlers portion is used mainly for irrigation in the outcrop area of North and Central Texas.

Elsewhere, water from the Trinity aquifer is used primarily for municipal and domestic supply. Extensive development of the Trinity aquifer in the Dallas-Fort Worth and Waco areas has historically resulted in water-level declines of several hundred feet. TWBD has completed a computer model of the Hill Country area and the northern portion of the aquifer.

Edwards-Trinity (Plateau)

This aquifer underlies the **Edwards Plateau**, extending from the Hill Country of Central Texas westward to the Trans-Pecos region. It consists of sandstone and limestone formations of the Trinity formations, and limestones and dolomites of the Edwards and associated limestone formations. Ground-water movement is generally toward the southeast.

Near the plateau's edge, flow is toward the main streams, where the water issues from springs. Irrigation, mainly in the northwestern portion of the region, accounted for about 70 percent of total aquifer use in 2000 and has resulted in significant water-level declines in Glasscock and Reagan counties. Elsewhere, the aquifer supplies fresh but hard water for municipal, domestic and livestock use. The TWDB has developed a computer model of this aquifer.

Seymour

This aquifer consists of isolated areas of alluvium found in parts of 22 north-central and Panhandle counties in the upper Red River and Brazos River basins. Eastward-flowing streams during the Quaternary Period deposited discontinuous beds of poorly sorted gravel, sand, silt and clay that were later dissected by erosion, resulting in the isolated remnants of the formation. Individual accumulations vary greatly in thickness, but most of the Seymour is less than 100 feet.

The lower, more permeable part of the aquifer produces the greatest amount of ground water. Irrigation pumpage accounted for 93 percent of the total use from the aquifer in 1994. Water quality generally ranges from fresh to slightly saline. However, the salinity has increased in many heavily pumped areas to the point where the water has become unsuitable for domestic and municipal use. Natural salt pollution in the upper reaches of the Red and Brazos river basins precludes the full utilization of these water resources.

Hueco-Mesilla Bolson

These aquifers are located in El Paso and Hudspeth counties in far western Texas and occur in Quaternary basin-fill deposits that extend northward into New Mexico and westward into Mexico. The Hueco Bolson, located on the eastern side of the Franklin Mountains, consists of up to 9,000 feet of clay, silt, sand and gravel and is an important source of drinking water for both El Paso and Juarez, Mexico. Located west of the Franklin Mountains, the Mesilla Bolson reaches up to 2,000 feet in thickness and contains three separate water-producing zones. Ground-water depletion of the Hueco Bolson has become a serious problem.

Historical large-scale ground-water withdrawals, especially for the municipal uses of El Paso and Juarez, have caused major water-level declines and significantly changed the direction of flow, causing a deterioration in the chemical quality of the ground water in the aquifer. The USGS, along with El Paso Water Utilities, has developed a computer model of this aquifer.

Cenozoic Pecos Alluvium

Located in the upper Pecos River Valley of West Texas, this aquifer is the principal source of water for irrigation in Reeves and northwestern Pecos counties and for industrial uses, power supply and municipal use elsewhere. Consisting of up to 1,500 feet of alluvial fill, the aquifer occupies two hydrologically separate basins: the Pecos Trough in the west and the Monument Draw Trough in the east.

Water from the aquifer is generally hard and contains dissolved-solids concentrations ranging from less than 300 to more than 5,000 parts per million. Water-level declines in excess of 200 feet have historically occurred in Reeves and Pecos counties, but have moderated since the mid-1970s with the decrease in irrigation pumpage. TWDB has developed a computer model of the aquifer.

Major Rivers
of Texas

Some **11,247 named Texas streams** are identified in the **U.S. Geological Survey Geographic Names Information System.** Their combined length is about 80,000 miles, and they drain 263,513 square miles within Texas. **Thirteen major rivers** are described below, starting with the southernmost and moving northward:

Rio Grande

The Pueblo Indians called this river **P'osoge,** which means the "river of great water." In 1582, **Antonio de Espejo** of Nueva Vizcaya, Mexico, followed the course of the **Río Conchos** to its confluence with a great river, which he named **Río del Norte (River of the North).** The name **Rio Grande** was first given the stream apparently by the explorer **Juan de Oñate,** who arrived on its banks near present-day El Paso in 1598.

Thereafter the names were often consolidated, as **Río Grande del Norte.** It was shown also on early Spanish maps as **Río San Buenaventura** and **Río Ganapetuan.** In its lower course it early acquired the name **Río Bravo,** which is its name on most Mexican maps. At times it has also been known as **Río Turbio,** probably because of its muddy appearance during its frequent rises. Some people erroneously call this watercourse the **Rio Grande River.** From source to mouth, the Rio Grande drops 12,000 feet to sea level as a snow-fed mountain torrent, desert stream and meandering coastal river. Along its banks and in its valley Indian civilizations developed, and Europeans established some of their first North American settlements.

This river rises in Colorado, flows the north-south length of New Mexico and **forms the boundary of Texas and international U.S.-Mexican boundary for 889 to 1,254 river miles,** depending upon method of measurement. (See **Texas Boundary Line.**) The length of the Rio Grande, as of other rivers, depends on method of measurement and varies yearly as its course changes. The latest **International Boundary and Water Commission** figure is 1,896 miles, which is considerably below the 2,200-mile figure often used. Depending upon methods of measurement, the Rio Grande is the fourth- or fifth-longest North American river, exceeded only by the Missouri-Mississippi, McKenzie-Peace, St. Lawrence and possibly Yukon. Since all of these except the Missouri-Mississippi are partly in Canada, the Rio Grande is the **second-longest river entirely within or bordering the United States.** It is **Texas' longest river.**

The snow-fed flow of the Rio Grande is used for **irrigation** in Colorado below the San Juan Mountains, where the river rises at the Continental Divide. Turning south, it flows through a canyon in northern New Mexico and again irrigates a broad valley of central New Mexico. This is the oldest irrigated area of the United States, where Spanish missionaries encouraged Indian irrigation in the 1600s.

Southern New Mexico impounds Rio Grande waters in Elephant Butte Reservoir for irrigation of 150 miles of valley above and below El Paso. Here is the **oldest irrigated area in Texas** and one of the oldest in the United States. Extensive irrigation practically exhausts the water supply. In this valley are situated **three of the oldest towns in Texas — Ysleta, Socorro** and **San Elizario.** At the lower end of the El Paso irrigated valley, the upper Rio Grande virtually ends except in seasons of above-normal flow.

It starts as a perennially flowing stream again where the Río Conchos of Mexico flows into it at Presidio-Ojinaga. Through the **Big Bend** the Rio Grande flows through three successive **canyons,** the **Santa Elena,** the **Mariscal** and the **Boquillas.** The Santa Elena has a river bed elevation of 2,145 feet and a canyon-rim elevation of 3,661. Corresponding figures for Mariscal are 1,925 and 3,625, and for Boquillas, 1,850 and 3,490. The river here flows around the base of the **Chisos Mountains.** For about 100 miles the river is the southern boundary of **Big Bend National Park.** Below the Big Bend, the Rio Grande gradually emerges from mountains onto the Coastal Plains. A 191.2-mile strip on the American shore from Big Bend National Park downstream to the Terrell-Val Verde County line, has federal designation as the **Rio Grande Wild and Scenic River.**

At the confluence of the Rio Grande and the Devils River, the United States and Mexico have built **Amistad Dam,** to impound 3,505,400 acre-feet of water, of which Texas' share is 56.2 percent. **Falcon Reservoir,** also an international project, impounds 2,767,400 acre-feet of water, of which Texas' share in Zapata and Starr counties is 58.6 percent. The Rio Grande, where it joins the Gulf of Mexico, has created a fertile delta called the **Lower Rio Grande Valley,** a major vegetable- and fruit-growing area. The Rio Grande drains 48,259 square miles of Texas. Principal tributaries flowing from the Texas side of the Rio Grande are the **Pecos** and **Devils** rivers. On the Mexican side are **Río Conchos, Río Salado** and **Río San Juan.** About three-fourths of the water running into the Rio Grande below El Paso comes from the Mexican side.

Pecos River

The Pecos, one of the major tributaries of the Rio Grande, rises on the western slope of the Santa Fe mountain range in New Mexico. In Texas the river flows southeast, entering Val Verde County at its northwestern corner and angles across that county to its mouth on the Rio Grande in the Amistad Reservoir, between Comstock and Langtry northwest of Del Rio.

According to the *Handbook of Texas* the origins of the river's several names began with Antonio de Espejo, who called the river the Río de las Vacas ("river of the cows") because of the number of buffalo in the vicinity. Gaspar Castaño de Sosa, who followed the Pecos northward, called it the Río Salado because of its salty taste, which caused it to be shunned by men and animals alike. It is believed that the name "Pecos" first appears in Juan de Oñate's reports concerning the Indian pueblo of Cicuye, now known as the Pecos Pueblo, and is of unknown origin. To Mexicans the river was long known as the Río Puerco ("dirty river").

Through most of its more than 900-mile-long course, the Pecos River parallels the Rio Grande. The total drainage area of the Pecos in New Mexico and Texas is about 44,000 square miles. Most of its tributaries flow from the west; these include the Delaware River, Toyah Creek, and Comanche Creek.

The topography of the river valley ranges

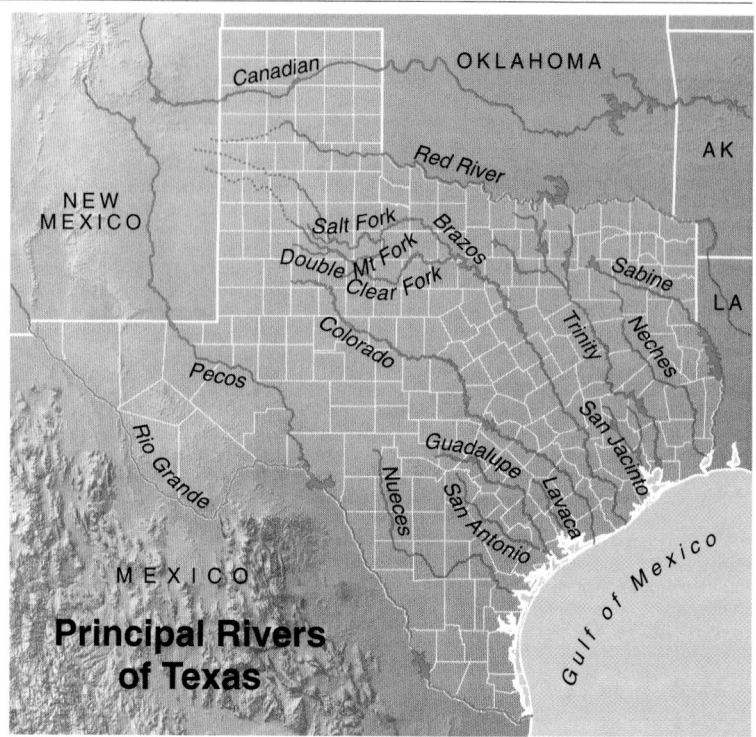

Principal Rivers of Texas

from mountain pastures in the north, with an elevation of more than 13,000 feet above sea level, to grasslands, semiarid irrigated farmlands, desert with sparse vegetation, and, in the lowermost reaches of the river, deep canyons.

Nueces River

The Nueces River rises in Edwards County and flows 315 miles to Nueces Bay on the Gulf near Corpus Christi. Draining 16,950 square miles, it is a beautiful, **spring-fed stream** flowing through **canyons** until it issues from the **Balcones Escarpment** onto the Coastal Plain in northern Uvalde County. **Alonso de León**, in 1689, gave it its name. (Nueces, plural of nuez, means nuts in Spanish.) Much earlier, Cabeza de Vaca had referred to a **Río de las Nueces** in this region, probably the same stream. Its original Indian name seems to have been **Chotilapacquen.** Crossing Texas in 1691, Terán de los Rios named the river **San Diego.** The Nueces was the boundary line between the Spanish provinces of Texas and Nuevo Santander.

After the Revolution of 1836, both Texas and Mexico claimed the territory between the Nueces and the Rio Grande, a dispute which was settled by the **Treaty of Guadalupe Hidalgo** in 1848, which fixed the international boundary at the Rio Grande. Average runoff of the Nueces is about 620,000 acre-feet a year in its lower course. Principal water conservation projects are **Lake Corpus Christi** and **Choke Canyon Reservoir.** Principal tributaries of the Nueces are the **Frio** and the **Atascosa.**

San Antonio River

The San Antonio River has its source in **large springs** within and near the city limits of San Antonio. It flows 180 miles across the Coastal Plain to a junction with the **Guadalupe** near the Gulf Coast. Its channel through San Antonio has been developed into a parkway known as the River Walk. Its principal tributaries are the **Medina River** and **Cibolo Creek**, both spring-fed streams and this, with its spring origin, gives it a remarkably steady flow of clear water. It was first named the **León** by Alonso de León in 1689; the name was not for himself, but he called it "lion" because its channel was filled with a rampaging flood.

Because of its limited and arid drainage area (4,180 square miles) the average runoff of the San Antonio River is relatively small, about 350,000 acre-feet annually near its mouth, but its flow, because of its springs, is one of the steadiest of Texas rivers.

Guadalupe River

The Guadalupe rises in its north and south prongs in the west-central part of Kerr County. A **spring-fed stream,** it flows eastward through the **Hill Country** until it issues from the **Balcones Escarpment** near New Braunfels. It then crosses the Coastal Plain to San Antonio Bay. Its total length is about 250 miles, and its drainage area is about 6,700 square miles. Its principal tributaries are the **San Marcos**, another spring-fed stream, which joins it in Gonzales County; the **San Antonio**, which joins it just above its mouth on San Antonio Bay; and the **Comal**, which joins it at New Braunfels.

The **Comal River** has its source in large springs within the city limits of New Braunfels and flows only about 2.5 miles to the Guadalupe. It is the **shortest river in Texas** and also the **shortest river in the United States** carrying an equivalent amount of water.

There has been power development on the Guadalupe near Gonzales and Cuero for many years, and there is also power generation at **Canyon Lake.** Because of its springs, and its considerable drainage area, the Guadalupe has an average annual runoff of more than 1 million acre-feet in its lower course. The name Guadalupe is derived from **Nuestra Señora de Guadalupe,** the name given the stream by Alonso de León.

Lavaca River

The Lavaca is considered a primary stream in the Texas Basin because it flows directly into the Gulf through Lavaca Bay. Without a spring-water source and with only a small watershed, including that of its principal tributary, the **Navidad,** its flow is intermittent. The Spanish called it the Lavaca (cow) River because of the numerous bison they found near it. It is the principal stream running to the Gulf between the Guadalupe and the Colorado, and drains

2,309 square miles. The principal lake on the **Navidad** is **Lake Texana.** Runoff averages about 600,000 acre-feet yearly into the Gulf.

Colorado River

Measured by length, the Colorado is the **largest river wholly in Texas.** (Its drainage basin extends into New Mexico, as does that of the Brazos River.) Rising in Dawson County, the Colorado flows about 600 miles to Matagorda Bay on the Gulf. Its drainage area is 39,893 square miles. Its average annual runoff reaches a volume of more than 2 million acre-feet near the Gulf. Its name is a Spanish word meaning **"reddish."** There is evidence that Spanish explorers originally named the muddy Brazos "Colorado," but Spanish mapmakers later transposed the two names.

The river flows through a rolling, mostly prairie terrain to the vicinity of San Saba County, where it enters the rugged **Hill Country** and **Burnet-Llano Basin.** It passes through a picturesque series of **canyons** until it issues from the **Balcones Escarpment** at Austin and flows across the Coastal Plain to the Gulf. In this area **the most remarkable series of reservoirs in Texas** has been built. The largest of these are **Lake Buchanan** in Burnet and Llano counties and **Lake Travis** in Travis County. Between the two in Burnet County are three smaller reservoirs: **Inks, Johnson** (formerly **Granite Shoals**) and **Marble Falls**, built to aid power production from water running over the Buchanan Lake spillway. Below Lake Travis is the older **Lake Austin,** largely filled with silt, whose dam is used to produce power from waters flowing down from the lakes above. **Town Lake** is in the city of Austin. This area is known as the **Highland Lakes Country.**

As early as the 1820s, Anglo-Americans settled on the banks of the lower Colorado, and in 1839 the **Capital Commission of the Republic of Texas** chose the picturesque area where the river flows from the **Balcones Escarpment** as the site of a new capital of the Republic — now **Austin,** capital of the state. The early colonists encouraged navigation along the lower channel with some success, and boats occasionally ventured as far upstream as Austin. However, a **natural log "raft"** in the channel near the Gulf blocked river traffic. Conservation and utilization of the waters of the Colorado are under jurisdiction of three agencies created by the state Legislature, the **Lower, Central** and **Upper Colorado River Authorities.**

The principal tributaries of the Colorado River are the several prongs of the **Concho River** on its upper course, **Pecan Bayou** (farthest west "bayou" in the United States) and the **Llano, San Saba** and **Pedernales** rivers. All except Pecan Bayou flow into the Colorado from the **Edwards Plateau** and are spring-fed, perennially flowing. In the numerous mussels found along these streams, **pearls** occasionally have been found. On early Spanish maps, the Middle Concho was called **Río de las Perlas.**

Brazos River

The Brazos is the largest river between the Rio Grande and the Red River and is **third in size** of all rivers in Texas. It rises in three upper forks, the **Double Mountain, Salt** and **Clear forks** of the Brazos. The Brazos River proper is considered as beginning where the Double Mountain and Salt Forks flow together in Stonewall County. The Clear Fork joins this main stream in Young County, just above **Possum Kingdom Lake.** The Brazos crosses most of the main physiographic regions of Texas — High Plains, West Texas Lower Rolling Plains, Western Cross Timbers, Grand Prairie and Gulf Coastal Plain.

The total length from the source of its longest upper prong, the Double Mountain Fork, to the mouth of the main stream at the Gulf, was reported to be 923.2 miles in a 1970 study by the Army Corps of Engineers. The drainage area is about 43,000 square miles. It flows directly into the Gulf near Freeport. Its average annual runoff at places along its lower channel exceeds 5 million acre-feet.

The original name of this river was **Brazos de Dios**, meaning "Arms of God." There are several legends as to why. One is that the Coronado expedition, wandering on the trackless **Llano Estacado,** exhausted its water and was threatened with death from thirst. Arriving at the bank of the river, they gave it the name "Brazos de Dios" in thankfulness. Another is that a ship exhausted its water supply and its crew was saved when they found the mouth of the Brazos. Still another story is that miners on the San Saba were forced by drought to seek water near present-day Waco and gratitude called it Brazos de Dios.

Much early Anglo-American colonization of Texas took place in the Brazos Valley. Along its channel were **San Felipe de Austin,** capital of Austin's colony; **Washington-on-the-Brazos,** where Texans declared independence; and other historic settlements. There was some **navigation of the lower channel** of the Brazos in this period. Near its mouth it intersects the **Gulf Intracoastal Waterway,** which provides connection with the commerce on the Mississippi.

Most of the Brazos Valley lies within the boundaries of the **Brazos River Authority,** which conducts a multipurpose program for development. A large reservoir on the Brazos is **Whitney Lake** (627,000 acre-feet capacity) on the main channel, where it is the boundary line between Hill and Bosque counties. Another large reservoir is **Possum Kingdom Lake** in Palo Pinto, Stephens, Young and Jack counties. **Waco Lake** on the Bosque and **Belton Lake** on the Leon are among the principal reservoirs on its tributaries. In addition to its three upper forks, other chief tributaries are the **Paluxy, Little** and **Navasota** rivers.

San Jacinto River

The San Jacinto is a short river with a drainage basin of 2,800 square miles and an average annual runoff of nearly 2 million acre-feet. It is formed by the junction of its East and West forks in the northeastern part of Harris County and runs directly to the Gulf through Galveston Bay. Its total length, including the East Fork, is about 85 miles.

Lake Conroe is on the **West Fork,** and **Lake Houston** is located at the junction of the West Fork and the **East Fork.** The **Houston Ship Channel** runs through the lower course of the San Jacinto and its tributary, **Buffalo Bayou,** connecting the Port of Houston with the Gulf.

There are two stories of the origin of its name. One is that when early explorers discovered it, its channel was choked with hyacinth ("jacinto" is the Spanish word for hyacinth). The other is that it was discovered on Aug. 17, St. Hyacinth's Day. The **Battle of San Jacinto** was fought on the shore of this river on April 21, 1836, when Texas won its independence from Mexico. **San Jacinto State Park and monument** commemorate the battle.

Trinity River

The Trinity rises in its East Fork, Elm Fork, West Fork and Clear Fork in Grayson, Montague, Archer and Parker counties, respectively. The main stream begins with the junction of the Elm and West forks at Dallas. Its length is 550 river miles, and its drainage area is 17,969 square miles. Because of moderate to heavy rainfall over its drainage area, it has a average annual flow of 5.8 million acre-feet near its mouth on the Gulf, exceeded only by the Neches, Red and Sabine river basins.

The Trinity derives its name from the Spanish **"Trinidad."** Alonso de León named it **La Santísima Trinidad** (the Most Holy Trinity).

Navigation was developed along its lower course with several riverport towns, such as **Sebastopol** in Trinity County. For many years there has been a basin-wide movement for navigation, conservation and utilization of its water. The **Trinity River Authority** is a state agency and the **Trinity Improvement Association** is a publicly supported nonprofit organization advocating its development.

The Trinity has in its valley **more large cities, greater population and more industrial development** than any other river basin in Texas. On the Lower Coastal Plain there is large use of its waters for **rice irrigation.** Largest reservoir on the Elm Fork is **Lewisville Lake** (formerly **Garza-Little Elm** and **Lake Dallas**). There are four reservoirs above Fort Worth: **Lake Worth, Eagle Mountain** and **Bridgeport** on the West Fork and **Benbrook Lake** on the Clear Fork.

Lavon Lake in southeast Collin County and **Lake Ray Hubbard** in Collin, Dallas, Kaufman and Rockwall counties are on the East Fork. **Livingston Lake** is in Polk, San Jacinto, Trinity and Walker counties.The three major reservoirs below the Dallas-Fort Worth area are **Cedar Creek Reservoir** and **Richland-Chambers Reservoir.**

Neches River

The Neches is in East Texas, with total length of about 416 miles and drainage area of 10,011 square miles. Abundant rainfall over its entire basin gives it an average annual flow near the Gulf of about 6 million acre-feet a year. The river takes its name from the **Neches Indians** that the early Spanish explorers found living along its banks. Principal tributary of the Neches, and comparable with the Neches in length and flow above their confluence, is the **Angelina River**, so named from **Angelina (Little Angel)**, a Hainai Indian girl who converted to Christianity and played an important role in the early development of this region.

Both the Neches and the Angelina run most of their courses in the **Piney Woods** and there was much settlement along them as early as the 1820s. **Sam Rayburn (McGee Bend) Reservoir**, near Jasper on the Angelina River, was completed and dedicated in 1965. Reservoirs located on the Neches River include **Lake Palestine** in the upper basin and **B. A. Steinhagen Lake** located at the junction of the Neches and the Angelina rivers.

Sabine River

The Sabine River is formed by three forks rising in Collin and Hunt counties. From its sources to its mouth on **Sabine Lake**, it flows approximately 360 miles and drains 7,426 square miles. Sabine comes from the **Spanish word for cypress**, as does the name of the **Sabinal River**, which flows into the Frio in Southwest Texas. The Sabine has the **largest average annual water discharge at its mouth of any Texas river:** 6.8 million acre-feet.

Throughout most of Texas history the lower Sabine has been the **eastern Texas boundary line,** though for a while there was doubt as to whether the Sabine or the Arroyo Hondo, east of the Sabine in Louisiana, was the boundary. For a number of years the outlaw-infested **neutral ground** lay between them. There was also a **boundary dispute** in which it was alleged that the Neches was really the Sabine and, therefore, the boundary.

Travelers over the part of the **Camino Real** known as the **Old San Antonio Road,** crossed the Sabine at the **Gaines Ferry,** and there were crossings for the **Atascosito Road** and other travel and trade routes of that day.

Two of Texas' largest man-made reservoirs have been created by dams on the Sabine River. The first of these is **Lake Tawakoni**, in Hunt, Rains and Van Zandt counties, with a capacity of 927,440 acre-feet. **Toledo Bend Reservoir** impounds 4,477,000 acre-feet of water on the Sabine in Newton, Panola, Sabine and Shelby counties. This is a joint project of Texas and Louisiana, through the **Sabine River Authority.**

Red River

The Red River (1,360 miles) is **exceeded in length only by the Rio Grande** among rivers associated with Texas. Its original source is water in Curry County, New Mexico, near the Texas boundary, forming a definite channel as it crosses Deaf Smith County, Texas, in tributaries that flow into **Prairie Dog Town Fork of the Red River.** These waters carve the spectacular **Palo Duro Canyon** of the High Plains before the Red River leaves the **Caprock Escarpment**, flowing eastward.

Where the Red River crosses the 100th meridian, the river becomes the **Texas-Oklahoma boundary** and is soon joined by the Salt Fork to form the main channel. Its length across the Panhandle is about 200 miles and, from the Panhandle east, it is the Texas-Oklahoma boundary line for 440 miles and thereafter the **Texas-Arkansas boundary**

for 40 miles before it flows into Arkansas, where it swings south to flow through Louisiana.

The Red River, which drains 24,463 square miles, is a part of the **Mississippi drainage basin,** and at one time it emptied all of its water into the Mississippi. In recent years, however, part of its water, especially at flood stage, has flowed to the Gulf via the **Atchafalaya.**

The Red River takes its name from the red color of the current. This caused every explorer who came to its banks to call it "red" regardless of the language he spoke — **Río Rojo** or **Río Roxo** in Spanish, **Rivière Rouge** in French and **Red River** in English.

The Spanish and French names were often found on maps until the mid-19th century when English came to be generally accepted. At an early date, the river became the axis for French advance from Louisiana northwestward as far as present-day Montague County. There was consistent **early navigation** of the river from its mouth on the Mississippi to Shreveport, above which navigation was blocked by a **natural log raft.**

A number of important gateways into Texas from the North were established along the stream such as **Pecan Point** and **Jonesborough** in Red River County, **Colbert's Ferry** and **Preston** in Grayson County and, later, **Doan's Store Crossing** in Wilbarger County.

The river was a menace to the early traveler because of both its variable current and its **quicksands**, which brought disaster to many a trail-herd cow as well as ox team and covered wagon.

The largest water conservation project on the Red River is **Texoma Lake**, which is the **largest lake** lying wholly or partly in Texas and the **tenth-largest reservoir (in capacity) in the United States.** Its capacity is 5,382,000 acre feet. Texas' share is 2,643,300.

Red River water's high content of salt and other minerals limits its usefulness along its upper reaches. Ten **salt springs** and tributaries in Texas and Oklahoma contribute most of these minerals.

The uppermost tributary of the Red River in Texas is **Tierra Blanca Creek**, which rises in Curry County, N.M., and flows easterly across Deaf Smith and Randall counties to become the **Prairie Dog Town Fork** a few miles east of Canyon. Other principal tributaries in Texas are the **Pease** and the **Wichita** in North Central Texas and the **Sulphur** in Northeast Texas, which flows into the Red River after it has crossed the boundary line into Arkansas.

The last major tributary in Northeast Texas is **Cypress Creek**, which flows into Louisiana before joining with the Red River. Major reservoirs on the Northeast Texas tributaries are **Wright Patman Lake, Lake O' the Pines** and **Caddo Lake**. From Oklahoma the principal tributary is the **Washita**. The **Ouachita,** a river with the same pronunciation of its name, though spelled differently, is the principal tributary to its lower course. The Red River boundary dispute, a long-standing feud between Oklahoma and Texas, was finally settled in 2000.

Canadian River

The Canadian River heads near **Raton Pass** in northern New Mexico near the Colorado boundary line and flows into Texas on the west line of Oldham County. It crosses the Texas Panhandle into Oklahoma and there flows into the Arkansas. It drains 12,700 square miles, and most of its course across the Panhandle is in a deep gorge.

A tributary dips into Texas' northern Panhandle and then flows to a confluence with the main channel in Oklahoma. One of several theories as to how the Canadian got its name is that some early explorers thought it flowed into Canada. **Lake Meredith**, formed by **Sanford Dam** on the Canadian, provides water for 11 Panhandle cities.

Because of the **deep gorge** and the **quicksand** at many places, the Canadian has been a particularly difficult stream to bridge. It is known especially in its lower course in Oklahoma as outstanding among the streams of the country for the great amount of quicksand in its channel. ☆

Artificial Lakes and Reservoirs

The large increase in the number of reservoirs in Texas during the past half-century has greatly improved water conservation and supplies.

As late as 1913, Texas had only eight major reservoirs with a total storage capacity of 376,000 acre-feet. Most of this capacity was in Medina Lake in southwest Texas, with 254,000 acre-feet* capacity, created by a dam completed in May 1913.

By January 2003, Texas had 204 major reservoirs (those with a normal capacity of 5,000 acre-feet or larger) existing or under construction, with a total conservation surface area of 1,678,708 acres and a conservation storage capacity of 40,947,816 acre-feet.

According to the U.S. Statistical Abstract of 2001, Texas has **4,959 square miles of inland water,** ranking it first in the 48 contiguous states, followed by Minnesota, with 4,780 sq. mi.; Florida, 4,683; and Louisiana, 4,153. There are about **6,736 reservoirs** in Texas with a normal storage capacity of 10 acre-feet or larger.

The following table lists reservoirs in Texas having **more than 5,000 acre-feet capacity.** With few exceptions, the listed reservoirs are those that were completed by Jan. 1, 2003. *Reservoirs that are normally dry are in italics.* Some industrial cooling reservoirs are not included.

Conservation storage capacity as of 2005 is used in the table below; the surface area used is that area at conservation elevation only. Because sediment deposition constantly reduces reservoir volumes over time, these are figures from the most recent surveys available. (Different methods of computing capacity area are used, and detailed information may be obtained from the **Texas Water Development Board,** Austin, from the **U.S. Army Corps of Engineers,** or from local sources.) It should be noted that boundary reservoir capacities include water designated for Texas use and non-Texas water, as well.

In the list below, information is in the following order: (1) Name of lake or reservoir; (2) year of first impounding of water; (3) county or counties in which located; (4) river or creek on which located; (5) location with respect to some city or town; (6) purpose of reservoir; (7) owner of reservoir.

Some of these items, when not listed, are not available. For the larger lakes and reservoirs, the dam impounding water to form the lake bears the same name, unless otherwise indicated.

Abbreviations in the list below are: L., lake; R., river; Co., county; Cr., creek; (C) conservation; (FC) flood control; (R) recreation; (P) power; (M) municipal; (D) domestic; (Ir.) irrigation; (In.) industry; (Mi.) mining, including oil production; (FH) fish hatchery; USAE, United States Army Corps of Engineers; WC&ID, Water Control and Improvement District; WID, Water Improvement District; USBR, United States Bureau of Reclamation; Auth., Authority; LCRA, Lower Colorado River Authority; USDA, United States Department of Agriculture; Imp., impounded. ☆

Natural Lakes

There are many natural lakes in Texas, though none is of great size. The largest designated natural lake touching the border of Texas is Sabine Lake, into which the Sabine and Neches rivers discharge. It is more properly a bay of the Gulf of Mexico. Also near the coast, in Calhoun County, is Green Lake, which at about 10,000 acre-feet is one of the state's largest natural freshwater lakes.

Caddo Lake, on the Texas-Louisiana border, was a natural lake originally, but its present capacity and surface area are largely due to dams built to raise the surface of the original body of water. Natural Dam Lake, in Howard County, has a similar history.

In East Texas are many small natural lakes formed by "horse-shoe" bends that have been eliminated from the main channel of a river. There are also a number of these "horse-shoe" lakes along the Rio Grande in the lower valley, where they are called *resacas.*

On the South Plains and west of San Angelo are lakes, such as Big Lake in Reagan County, that are usually dry.

An acre-foot is the amount of water necessary to cover an acre of surface area with water one foot deep.

*The **years** in the table below refer to first impounding of water.*

***Caddo Lake**— In November 1873, the U.S. Army used nitroglycerin charges to remove the last portion of the Red River raft, a natural logjam. This resulted in the gradual depletion of Caddo water. In 1914, a dam was completed near Mooringsport, La. In 1971, a larger replacement dam was completed.*

***Lake Austin** — In 1893, the first dam was completed. It broke in 1900. In 1915, a second dam was built but not completed. In 1939, the present Tom Miller Dam was completed.*

*Other **double years** refer to later, larger dams.*

SOURCES: U.S. Geological Survey, Texas Water Development Board, New Handbook of Texas, Texas Parks & Wildlife, U.S. Army Corps of Engineers, previous Texas Almanacs, various river basin authorities, Websites of owner of reservoirs.

Anglers at Lake Arrowhead State Park near Wichita Falls fish for crappie, white bass, black bass and catfish. Water in the 14,969-acre lake was first inpounded in 1966. Texas Parks & Wildlife photo.

Lakes and Reservoirs, Date of Origin	Surface Area (Acres)	Storage Capacity (Acre-Ft.)
Abilene, L. — (1919) Taylor Co.; Elm Cr.; 6 mi. NW Tuscola; (M-In.-R); City of Abilene	595	7,900
Addicks Reservoir — (1948) Harris Co.; South Mayde Cr.; 1 mi. E of Addicks; (FC only) USAE	*16,423*	*200,800*
Alan Henry, L. — (1993) Garza Co.; Double Mountain Fork Brazos River; 10 mi. E Justiceburg; (M-In.-Ir.); City of Lubbock	2,884	115,937
Alcoa L. — (1952) Milam Co.; Sandy Cr.; 7 mi. SW Rockdale; (In.-R); Alcoa Aluminum (also called Sandow L.)	914	15,650
Amistad Reservoir, International — (1969) Val Verde Co.; Rio Grande; an international project of the U.S. and Mexico; 12 mi. NW Del Rio; (C-R-Ir.-P-FC); International Boundary and Water Com. (Texas' share of conservation capacity is 56.2 percent.) (Formerly Diablo R.)	64,900	3,124,260
Amon G. Carter, L. — (1961) Montague Co.; Big Sandy Cr.; 6 mi. S Bowie; (M-In.); City of Bowie	1,540	20,050
Anahuac, L. — (1936, 1954) Chambers Co.; Turtle Bayou; near Anahuac; (Ir.-In.-Mi.); Chambers-Liberty Counties Navigation District. (also called Turtle Bayou Reservoir).	5,300	35,300
Anzalduas Channel Dam — Hidalgo Co.; Rio Grande; 11 mi. upstream from Hidalgo; (Ir.-FC); United States and Mexico	1,472	13,910
Aquilla L. — (1983) Hill Co.; Aquilla Cr.; 10.2 mi. W of Hillsboro; (FC-M-Ir.-In.-R); USAE-Brazos R. Auth	3,020	45,319
Arlington, L. — (1957) Tarrant Co.; Village Cr.; 7 mi. W Arlington, (M-In.); City of Arlington	1,939	38,785
Arrowhead, L. — (1966) Clay-Archer counties.; Little Wichita R.; 13 mi. SE Wichita Falls; (M); City of Wichita Falls	14,969	235,997
Athens, L. — (1962) Henderson Co.; 8 mi. E Athens; (M-FC-R); Athens Mun. Water Authority (formerly Flat Creek Reservoir)	1,799	29,475
Austin, L. — (1893, 1915, 1939) Travis Co.; Colorado R.; W Austin city limits; (M-In.-P); City of Austin, leased to LCRA (Imp. by Tom Miller Dam)	1,599	21,804
Ballinger/Moonen, L. — (1947) Runnels Co.; Valley Creek; 5 mi. W Ballinger; (M); City of Ballinger	500	6,850
Balmorhea, L. — (1917) Reeves Co.; Sandia Cr.; 3 mi. SE Balmorhea; (Ir.); Reeves Co. WID No. 1	573	6,350
Bardwell L. — (1965) Ellis Co.; Waxahachie Cr.; 3 mi. SE Bardwell; (FC-C-R); USAE	3,138	46,472
Barker Reservoir — (1945) Harris Co.; above Buffalo Bayou; (FC only) USAE.	*16,739*	*209,000*
Bastrop, L. — (1964) Bastrop Co.; Spicer Cr.; 3 mi. NE Bastrop; (In.); LCRA	906	16,590
Baylor Creek L. — (1950) Childress Co.; 10 mi. NW Childress; (M-R); City of Childress	610	9,220
Belton L. — (1954) Bell-Coryell counties; Leon R.; 3 mi. N. Belton; (M-FC-In.-Ir.); USAE-Brazos R. Auth.	12,385	434,500
Benbrook L. — (1952) Tarrant Co.; Clear Fk. Trinity R.; 10 mi. SW Fort Worth; (FC-R); USAE	3,635	85,648
Big Creek Reservoir — (1987) Delta Co.; Big Creek; 1 mi. N Cooper; (M); City of Cooper	512	4,890
Bivins L. — (1927) Randall Co.; Palo Duro Cr.; 8 mi. NW Canyon; (M); Amarillo; City of Amarillo (also called Amarillo City Lake).	379	5,120
Bob Sandlin, L. — (1977) Titus-Wood-Camp-Franklin counties; Big Cypress Cr.; 5 mi. SW Mount Pleasant; (In.-M-R); Titus Co. FWSD No. 1 (Imp. by Fort Sherman Dam).	9,004	204,678
Bonham, L. — (1969) Fannin Co.; Timber Cr.; 5 mi. NE Bonham; (M); Bonham Mun. Water Auth.	1,086	11,020
Brady Creek Reservoir — (1963) McCulloch Co.; Brady Cr.; 3 mi. W Brady; (M-In.); City of Brady	2,020	30,430
Brandy Branch Reservoir — (1983) Harrison Co.; Brandy Br.; 10 mi. SW Marshall; (In.); AEP-Southwestern Electric Power Co.	1,242	29,513
Braunig L., Victor — (1962) Bexar Co.; Arroyo Seco; 15 mi. SE San Antonio; (In.); Pub. Svc. Bd./San Antonio.	1,350	26,500
Brazoria Reservoir — (1954) Brazoria Co.; off-channel reservoir; 1 mi. NE Brazoria; (In.); Dow Chemical Co.	1,865	21,970
Bridgeport, L. — (1932) Wise-Jack counties; W. Fk. of Trinity R.; 4 mi. W Bridgeport; (M-In.-FC-R); Tarrant Regional Water Dist.	11,954	366,236
Brownwood, L. — (1933) Brown Co.; Pecan Bayou; 8 mi. N Brownwood; (M-In.-Ir.); Brown Co. WC&ID No. 1	6,490	128,196
Bryan L. — (1977) Brazos Co.; unnamed stream; 6 mi. NW Bryan; (R-In.); City of Bryan	829	15,227
Buchanan, L. — (1937) Burnet-Llano-San Saba counties; Colorado R.; 13 mi. W Burnet; (M-Ir.-Mi-P); LCRA	22,333	885,507
Buffalo Lake — (1938) Randall Co.; Tierra Blanca Cr.; 2 mi. S. Umbarger; (R); U.S. Fish and Wildlife Service; (Imp. by Umbarger Dam)	1,900	18,150
Caddo L. — (*1873,* 1914, 1971) Harrison-Marion counties, Texas and Caddo Parish, La. An original natural lake, whose surface and capacity were increased by construction of dams	26,700	128,675
Calaveras L. — (1969) Bexar Co.; Calaveras Cr.; 15 mi. SE San Antonio; (In.); Pub. Svc. Bd. of San Antonio.	3,624	63,200
Camp Creek L. — (1949) Robertson Co.; 13 mi. E Franklin; (R); Camp Creek Water Co.	750	7,000
Canyon L. — (1964) Comal Co.; Guadalupe R.; 12 mi. NW New Braunfels; (M-In.-P-FC); Guadalupe-Blanco R. Authority & USAE	8,308	378,852
Casa Blanca L. — (1951) Webb Co.; Chacon Cr.; 3 mi. NE Laredo; (R); Webb Co.; (Imp. by Country Club Dam)	1,680	20,000
Cedar Creek Reservoir — (1965) Henderson-Kaufman counties; Cedar Cr.; 3 mi. NE Trinidad; (M-R); Tarrant Regional Water Dist.; (also called Joe B. Hogsett, L.)	32,623	637,180
Champion Creek Reservoir — (1959) Mitchell Co.; 7 mi. S. Colorado City; (M-In.); City of Colorado City.	1,560	41,600
Cherokee, L. — (1948) Gregg-Rusk counties; Cherokee Bayou; 12 mi. SE Longview; (M-In.-R); Cherokee Water Co.	3,452	43,297
Choke Canyon Reservoir — (1982) Live Oak-McMullen counties; Frio R.; 4 mi. W Three Rivers; (M-In.-R-FC); City of Corpus Christi-USBR	25,989	695,271
Cisco, L. — (1923) Eastland Co.; Sandy Cr.; 4 mi. N. Cisco; (M); City of Cisco (Imp. by Williamson Dam).	1,050	26,000
Cleburne, L. Pat — (1964) Johnson Co.; Nolan R.; 4 mi. S. Cleburne; (M); City of Cleburne	1,558	25,730

Joe Pool Reservoir at Cedar Creek State Park is a popular spot for sailing at sunset. Joe Pool is 7,470 acres and was formerly called Lakeview Lake. File photo.

Lakes and Reservoirs, Date of Origin	Surface Area (Acres)	Storage Capacity (Acre-Ft.)
Clyde, L. — (1970) Callahan Co.; N. Prong Pecan Bayou; 6 mi. S. Clyde; (M); City of Clyde and USDA Soil Conservation Service	449	5,748
Coffee Mill L. — (1939) Fannin Co.; Coffee Mill Cr.; 12 mi. NW Honey Grove; (R); U.S. Forest Service . .	650	8,000
Coleman, L. — (1966) Coleman Co.; Jim Ned Cr.; 14 mi. N. Coleman; (M-In.); City of Coleman	2,000	38,846
Coleto Creek Reservoir — (1980) Goliad–Victoria counties; Coleto Cr.; 12 mi. SW Victoria; (In); Guadalupe–Blanco River Auth.	3,100	35,060
Colorado City, L. — (1949) Mitchell Co.; Morgan Cr.; 4 mi. SW Colorado City; (M-In.-P); TXU	1,612	30,800
Conroe, L. — (1973) Montgomery-Walker counties; W. Fk. San Jacinto R.; 7 mi. NW Conroe; (M-In.-Mi.); San Jacinto River Authority, City of Houston and Texas Water Dev. Bd.	20,118	416,228
Cooper, L./Olney— (1953) Archer Co.; Mesquite Crk; 8 mi. E Megargel; (W-R); City of Olney; (see L. Olney)	446	6,650
Cooper Lake— (1991) Delta-Hopkins counties; Sulphur R.; 3 mi.SE Cooper; (FC-M-R); USAE; (also called Jim Chapman Lake)	19,305	310,312
Corpus Christi, L. — (1930) Live Oak-San Patricio-Jim Wells counties; Nueces R.; 4 mi. SW Mathis; (P-M-In.-Ir.-Mi.-R.); Lower Nueces River WSD (Imp. by Wesley E. Seale Dam)	18,256	257,463
Cox Creek Reservoir — Calhoun Co.; Cox Creek; 2 mi. E Point Comfort; (In); Alcoa Alumninum; (Also called Raw Water Lake and Recycle Lake)	541	5,034
Crook, L. — (1923) Lamar Co.; Pine Cr.; 5 Mi. N. Paris; (M); City of Paris	1,060	9,210
Cypress Springs, L. — (1970) Franklin Co.; Big Cypress Cr.; 8 mi. SE Mount Vernon; (In-M); Franklin Co. WD and Texas Water Development Board (formerly Franklin Co. L.); (Imp. by Franklin Co. Dam) .	3,461	67,690
Daniel, L. — (1948) Stephens Co.; Gunsolus Cr.; 7 mi. S Breckenridge; (M-In.); City of Breckenridge; (Imp. by Gunsolus Creek Dam)	924	9,515
Davis, L. — Knox Co.; Double Dutchman Cr.; 5 mi. SE Benjamin; (Ir); League Ranch	585	5,454
Delta Lake Res. Units 1 and 2 — (1939) Hidalgo Co.; Rio Grande (off channel); 4 mi. N. Monte Alto; (Ir.); Hidalgo-Willacy counties WC&ID No. 1 (formerly Monte Alto Reservoir)	2,371	14,000
Diversion, L. — (1924) Archer-Baylor counties; Wichita R.; 14 mi. W Holliday; (M-In.); City of Wichita Falls and Wichita Co. WID No. 2.	3,133	33,420
Dunlap, L. — (1928) Guadalupe Co.; Guadalupe R.; 9 mi. NW Seguin; (P); Guadalupe-Blanco R. Auth.; (Imp. by TP-1 Dam)	410	5,900
Eagle L. — (1900) Colorado Co.; Colorado R. (off channel); in Eagle Lake; (Ir.); Lakeside Irrigation Co. .	1,200	9,600
Eagle Mountain Lake — (1934) Tarrant-Wise counties; W. Fk. Trinity R.; 14 mi. NW Fort Worth; (M-In.-Ir.); Tarrant Regional Water Dist.	8,738	182,583
Eagle Nest Lake — (1951) Brazoria Co.; off-channel Brazos R.; 12 mi. WNW Angleton; (Ir.); T.M. Smith, et al. (also called Manor Lake).	—	18,000
Eastman Lakes — 8 lakes; Harrison Co.; Sabine R. basin; NW of Longview; Texas Eastman Co.	—	8,135

Lakes and Reservoirs, Date of Origin	Surface Area (Acres)	Storage Capacity (Acre-Ft.)
Electra, L. — (1950) Wilbarger Co.; Camp Cr. and Beaver Cr.; 7 mi. SW Electra; (In.-M); City of Electra	731	5,626
Ellison Creek Reservoir — (1943) Morris Co.; Ellison Cr.; 8 mi. S. Daingerfield; (P-In.); Lone Star Steel	1,516	24,700
Fairfield L. — (1970) Freestone Co.; Big Brown Cr.; 11 mi. NE Fairfield; (In.); TXU; (formerly Big Brown Creek Reservoir).	2,159	44,169
Falcon Reservoir, International — (1954) Starr-Zapata counties; Rio Grande; (International—U.S.-Mexico); 3 mi. W Falcon Heights; (M-In.-Ir.-FC-P-R); International Boundary and Water Com.; (Texas' share of total conservation capacity is 58.6 per cent)	86,843	2,668,000
Fayette Co. Reservoir — (1958) Fayette Co.; Cedar Cr.; 8.5 mi. E. La Grange; (In.); LCRA (also called Cedar Creek Reservoir).	2,400	71,400
Forest Grove Reservoir — (1982) Henderson Co.; Caney Cr.; 7 mi. NW Athens; (In.); TXU, Agent	1,502	20,038
Fort Phantom Hill, Lake — (1938) Jones Co.; Elm Cr.; 5 mi. S. Nugent; (M-R); City of Abilene	4,213	70,036
Georgetown, L. — (1980) Williamson Co.; N. Fk. San Gabriel R.; 3.5 mi. W Georgetown; (FC-M-In.); USAE.	1,297	37,010
Gibbons Creek Reservoir — (1981) Grimes Co.; Gibbons Cr.; 9.5 mi NW Anderson; (In.); Texas Mun. Power Agency	2,770	32,084
Gilmer Reservoir — (2001) Upshur Co.; Kelsey Creek; 15 mi. N of Longview; 4 mi. W of Gilmer; (M); City of Gilmer	1,010	12,720
Gladewater, L. — (1952) Upshur Co.; Glade Cr.; in Gladewater; (M-R); City of Gladewater	481	4,738
Gonzales, Lake — (1931) Gonzales Co.; Guadalupe R.; 4.5 mi. SE Belmont; (P); Guadalupe-Blanco R. Auth. (also called H-4 Reservoir).	696	6,500
Graham, L. — (1929) Young Co.; Flint and Salt Creeks; 2 mi. NW Graham; (M-In.); City of Graham	2,444	45,302
Granbury, L. — (1969) Hood Co.; Brazos R.; 8 mi. SE Granbury; (M-In.-Ir.-P); Brazos River Authority (Imp. by DeCordova Bend Dam)	8,310	136,823
Granger L. — (1980) Williamson Co.; San Gabriel R.; 10 mi. NE Taylor; (FC-M-In.); USAE (formerly Laneport L.)	4,064	52,525
Grapevine L. — (1952) Tarrant-Denton counties; Denton Cr.; 2 mi. NE Grapevine; (M-FC-In.-R.); USAE	6,892	164,703
Greenbelt L. — (1967) Donley Co.; Salt Fk. Red R.; 5 mi. N Clarendon; (M-In.); Greenbelt M&I Water Auth.	2,025	58,200
Greenville City Lakes — 6 lakes; Hunt Co.; Conleech Fork, Sabine R.; 2 mi. Greenville; (M-Other); City of Greenville	—	6,864
Halbert, L. — (1921) Navarro Co.; Elm Cr.; 4 mi. SE Corsicana; (M-In.); City of Corsicana	603	6,033
Harris Reservoir, William — (1947) Brazoria Co.; off-channel between Brazos R. and Oyster Cr.; 8 mi. NW Angleton; (In.); Dow Chemical Co.	1,663	9,200
Hawkins, L. — (1962) Wood Co.; Little Sandy Cr.; 3 mi. NW Hawkins; (FC-R); Wood County; (Imp. by Wood Co. Dam No. 3)	800	11,890
Holbrook, L. — (1962) Wood Co.; Keys Cr.; 4 mi. NW Mineola; (FC-R); Wood County; (Imp. by Wood Co. Dam No. 2)	653	7,990
Hords Creek L. — (1948) Coleman Co.; Hords Cr.; 5 mi. NW Valera; (M-FC); City of Coleman and USAE	510	8,640
Houston, L. — (1954) Harris Co.; San Jacinto R.; 4 mi. N Sheldon; (M-In.-Ir.-Mi.-R); City of Houston	11,854	133,990
Houston County L. — (1966) Houston Co.; Little Elkhart Cr.; 10 mi. NW Crockett; (M-In.); Houston Co. WC&ID No. 1	1,330	17,665
Hubbard Creek Reservoir — (1962) Stephens Co.; 6 mi. NW Breckenridge; (M-In.-Mi.); West Central Texas Mun. Water Authority	14,992	324,983
Imperial Reservoir — (1912) Reeves-Pecos counties; Pecos R.; 35 mi. N Fort Stockton; (Ir.); Pecos County WC&ID No. 2	1,530	6,000
Inks L. — (1938) Burnet-Llano counties; Colorado R.; 12 mi. W Burnet; (M-Ir.-Mi.-P); LCRA	831	14,878
Jacksonville, L. — (1959) Cherokee Co.; Gum Cr.; 5 mi. SW Jacksonville; (M-R); City of Jacksonville; (Imp. by Buckner Dam)	1,320	30,500
J. B. Thomas, L. — (1952) Scurry-Borden counties; Colorado R.; 16 mi. SW Snyder; (M- In.-R); Colorado River Mun. Water Dist.; (Imp. by Colorado R. Dam).	7,282	200,604
J. D. Murphree Wildlife Management Area Impoundments — Jefferson Co.; off-channel reservoirs between Big Hill and Taylor bayous; at Port Acres; (FH-R); TP&WD (formerly Big Hill Reservoir).	6,881	32,000
Joe Pool Reservoir — (1986) Dallas-Tarrant-Ellis counties; Mountain Cr.; 14 mi. SW Dallas; (FC-M-R); USAE-Trinity River Auth. (formerly Lakeview Lake).	7,470	176,900
Johnson Creek Reservoir — (1961) Marion Co.; 13 mi. NW Jefferson; (In.); AEP-Southwestern Electric Power Co.	650	10,100
Kemp, L. — (1923) Baylor Co.; Wichita R.; 6 mi. N Mabelle; (M-P-Ir.); City of Wichita Falls; Wichita Co. WID 2	15,590	319,600
Kickapoo, L. — (1945) Archer Co.; N. Fk. Little Wichita R.; 10 mi. NW Archer City; (M); City of Wichita Falls	6,028	85,825
Kiowa, L. — (1967) Cooke Co.; Indian Cr.; 8 mi. SE Gainesville; (R); Lake Kiowa, Inc.	560	7,000
Kirby, L. — (1928) Taylor Co.; Cedar Cr.; 5 mi. S. Abilene; (M); City of Abilene	740	7,620
Kurth, L. — (1950) Angelina Co.; off-channel reservoir; 8 mi. N Lufkin; (In.); Abitibi Consolidated Industries.	726	14,769
Lake Creek L. — (1952) McLennan Co.; Manos Cr.; 4 mi. SW Riesel; (In.); TXU	550	8,400
Lake Fork Reservoir — (1980) Wood-Rains counties; Lake Fork Cr.; 5 mi. W Quitman; (M-In.); Sabine River Authority	27,264	636,133
Lake O' the Pines — (1959) Marion-Upshur-Morris counties; Cypress Cr.; 9 mi. W Jefferson; (FC-C-R-In.-M); USAE (Imp. by Ferrell's Bridge Dam).	16,919	241,081
Lavon, L. — (1953) Collin Co.; East Fk. Trinity R.; 2 mi. W Lavon; (M-FC-In.); USAE	21,400	443,800
Leon, Lake — (1954) Eastland Co.; Leon R.; 7 mi. S Ranger; (M-In.); Eastland Co. Water Supply Dist.	1,590	26,429
Lewis Creek Reservoir — Montgomery Co.; Lewis Cr.; 10 mi. NW Conroe; (In.); Gulf States Util. Co.	1,010	16,400
Lewisville L. — (1929, 1954) Denton Co.; Elm Fk. Trinity R.; 2 mi. NE Lewisville; (M-FC-In.-R); USAE; (also called Lake Dallas and Garza-Little Elm)	29,592	555,000
Limestone, L. — (1978) Leon-Limestone-Robertson cos.; Navasota R.; 7 mi. NW Marquez; (M-In.-Ir.); Brazos River Authority.	12,553	208,017

Fishing camps line the shore of Lake Balmorhea in Reeves County south of Pecos. The Barrilla Mountains rise in the background. The 573-acre lake was first impounded in 1917. Texas Almanac photo.

Lakes and Reservoirs, Date of Origin	Surface Area (Acres)	Storage Capacity (Acre-Ft.)
Livingston, L. — (1969) Polk-San Jacinto-Trinity-Walker counties; Trinity R.; 6 mi. SW Livingston; (M-In.-Ir.); City of Houston and Trinity River Authority	83,277	1,741,867
Loma Alta Lake — Cameron Co.; off-channel Rio Grande; 8 mi. NE Brownsville; (M-In.); Brownsville Navigation Dist.	2,490	26,500
Lost Creek Reservoir — (1990) Jack Co.; Lost Cr.; 4 mi. NE Jacksboro; (M); City of Jacksboro	368	11,961
Lyndon B. Johnson, L. — (1951) Burnet-Llano counties; Colorado R.; 5 mi. SW Marble Falls; (P); LCRA; (Imp. by Alvin Wirtz Dam); (formerly Granite Shoals L.)	6,534	134,353
Mackenzie Reservoir — (1974) Briscoe Co.; Tule Cr.; 9 mi. NW Silverton; (M); Mackenzie Mun. Water Auth.	896	46,450
Marble Falls, L. — (1951) Burnet Co.; Colorado R.; 1.25 mi. SE Marble Falls; (P); LCRA; (Imp. by Max Starcke Dam)	611	6,420
Martin Creek L. — (1974) Rusk-Panola counties; Martin Cr.; 17 mi. NE Henderson; (P); TXU.	4,981	75,116
Medina L. — (1913) Medina-Bandera counties; Medina R.; 8 mi. W Rio Medina; (Ir.); Bexar-Medina-Atascosa Co. WID No. 1	5,426	209,940
Meredith, L. — (1965) Moore-Potter-Hutchinson counties; Canadian R.; 10 mi. NW Borger; (M-In.-FC-R); cooperative project for municipal water supply by Amarillo, Lubbock and other High Plains cities. Canadian R. Municipal Water Authority-USBR; (Imp. by Sanford Dam)	16,411	817,970
Millers Creek Reservoir — (1990) Baylor-Throckmorton counties.; Millers Cr.; 9 mi. SE Goree; (M); North Central Texas Mun. Water Auth. and Texas Water Development Board	2,212	28,051
Mineral Wells, L. — (1920) Parker Co.; Rock Cr.; 4 mi. E Mineral Wells; (M); Palo Pinto Co. Mun. WD No. 1	440	7,065
Mitchell County Reservoir — (1993) Mitchell Co.; branch of Beals Creek; (Mi.-In.); Colorado River MWD	1,463	27,266
Monticello Reservoir — (1972) Titus Co.; Blundell Cr.; 2.5 mi. E. Monticello; (In.); TXU	2,001	34,740
Moss L., Hubert H. — (1960) Cooke Co.; Fish Cr.; 10 mi. NW Gainesville; (M-In.); City of Gainesville	1,140	24,155
Mountain Creek L. — (1937) Dallas Co.; Mountain Cr.; 4 mi. SE Grand Prairie; (In.); TXU.	2,170	22,840
Murvaul L. — (1958) Panola Co.; Murvaul Bayou; 10 mi. W Carthage; (M-In.-R); Panola Co. Fresh Water Supply Dist. No. 1.	3,397	37,260
Mustang Lake East/West — Brazoria Co.; Mustang Bayou; 6 mi. S Alvin; (Ir.-In.-R); Chocolate Bayou Land & Water Co.	—	6,451
Nacogdoches, L. — (1976) Nacogdoches Co.; Bayo Loco Cr.; 10 mi. W Nacogdoches; (M); City of Nacogdoches	2,212	39,523
Nasworthy, L. — (1930) Tom Green Co.; S Concho R.; 6 mi. SW San Angelo; (M-In.-Ir); City of San Angelo	1,380	10,108
Natural Dam L. — (1957, 1989) Howard Co.; Sulphur Springs Draw; 8 mi. W Big Spring; An original natural lake, whose surface and capacity were increased by construction of dams; (FC); Wilkinson Ranch & Colorado River MWD.	3,605	54,560
Navarro Mills L. — (1963) Navarro-Hill counties; Richland Cr.; 16 mi. SW Corsicana; (M-FC); USAE	5,070	55,810
Nocona, L. — (1960) Montague Co.; 8 mi. NE Nocona; (M-In.-Mi.); No. Montague County Water Supply District (also known as Farmers Creek Reservoir).	1,323	21,083
North Fk. Buffalo Creek Reservoir — (1964) Wichita Co.; 5 mi. NW Iowa Park; (M); Wichita Co. WC&ID No.3.	1,392	15,400

Lakes and Reservoirs, Date of Origin	Surface Area (Acres)	Storage Capacity (Acre-Ft.)
North L. — (1957) Dallas Co.; S. Fork Grapevine Cr.; 2 mi. SE Coppell; (In.); TXU	800	17,000
Oak Creek Reservoir — (1952) Coke Co.; 5 mi. SE Blackwell; (M-In.); City of Sweetwater	2,375	39,360
O. C. Fisher L. — (1952) Tom Green Co.; N. Concho R.; 3 mi. NW San Angelo; (M-FC-C- Ir.-R-In.-Mi); USAE —Upper Colo. River Auth. (formerly San Angelo L.)	5,440	119,200
O. H. Ivie Reservoir — (1990) Coleman-Concho-Runnels counties; 24 mi. SE Ballinger; (M-In.), Colorado R. Mun. Water Dist. (formerly Stacy Reservoir)	19,149	554,340
Olmos Reservoir — (1926) Bexar Co.; Olmos Cr.; in San Antonio; (FC only), City of San Antonio	*1,050*	*15,500*
Olney, L./Cooper— (1935) Archer Co.; Mesquite Crk; 8 mi. E Megargel; (W-R); City of Olney; (see L. Cooper)	446	6,650
Palestine, L. — (1962) Anderson-Cherokee-Henderson-Smith counties; Neches R.; 4 mi. E Frankston; (M-In.-R); Upper Neches R. MWA (Imp. by Blackburn Crossing Dam)	25,560	411,300
Palo Duro Reservoir — (1991) Hansford Co.; Palo Duro Cr.; 12 mi. N Spearman; (M-R); Palo Duro River Auth.	2,413	60,897
Palo Pinto, L. — (1964) Palo Pinto Co.; 15 mi. SW Mineral Wells; (M-In.); Palo Pinto Co. Muni. Water Dist. 1	2,498	27,650
Pat Mayse L. — (1967) Lamar Co.; Sanders Cr.; 2 mi. SW Arthur City; (M-In.-FC); USAE	5,940	118,110
Pinkston Reservoir — (1976) Shelby Co.; Sandy Cr.; 12.5 mi. SW Center; (M); City of Center; (formerly Sandy Creek Reservoir)	523	7,380
Possum Kingdom L. — (1941) Palo Pinto-Young-Stephens-Jack counties; Brazos R.; 11 mi. SW Graford; (M-In.-Ir.-Mi.-P-R); Brazos R. Authority; (Imp. by Morris Sheppard Dam)	17,624	556,220
Proctor L. — (1963) Comanche Co.; Leon R.; 9 mi. NE Comanche; (M-In.-Ir.-FC); USAE- Brazos River Auth.	4,537	55,457
Quitman, L. — (1962) Wood Co.; Dry Cr.; 4 mi. N Quitman; (FC-R); Wood County (Imp. by Wood Co. Dam No.1)	814	7,440
Randell L. — (1909) Grayson Co.; Shawnee Cr.; 4 mi. NW Denison; (M); City of Denison	280	6,290
Ray Hubbard, L. — (1968) Collin-Dallas-Kaufman-Rockwall counties; (formerly Forney Reservoir); E. Fk. Trinity R.; 15 mi. E Dallas; (M); City of Dallas	22,745	413,420
Ray Roberts, L. — (1987) Denton-Cooke-Grayson counties; Elm Fk. Trinity R.; 11 mi. NE Denton; (FC-M-D); City of Denton, Dallas, USAE; (also known as Aubrey Reservoir)	25,600	544,767
Red Bluff Reservoir — (1937) Loving-Reeves counties, Texas; and Eddy Co.; N.M.; Pecos R.; 5 mi. N Orla; (Ir.-P); Red Bluff Water Power Control District	11,193	289,670
Red Draw Reservoir — (1985) Howard Co.; Red Draw; 5 mi. E Bi Spring; (Mi.-In.); Colorado River MWD	374	8,538
Richland-Chambers Reservoir — (1987) Freestone-Navarro counties; Richland Cr.; 20 mi. SE Corsicana; (M); Tarrant Regional Water Dist.	41,356	1,136,600
Rita Blanca, L. — (1940) Hartley Co.; Rita Blanca Cr.; 2 mi. S Dalhart; (R) City of Dalhart	524	12,100
River Crest L. — (1953) Red River Co.; off-channel reservoir; 7 mi. SE Bogata; (In.); TXU	555	7,000
Sam Rayburn Reservoir — (1965) Jasper-Angelina-Sabine-Nacogdoches-San Augustine counties; Angelina R.; (FC-P-M-In.-Ir.-R); USAE; (formerly McGee Bend Reservoir)	114,500	2,876,300
San Bernard Reservoirs #1, #2, #3 — Brazoria Co.; Off-Channel San Bernard R.; 3 mi. N Sweeney; (In.); ConocoPhillips.	—	8,610
Santa Rosa L. — (1929) Wilbarger Co.; Beaver Cr.; 15 mi. S Vernon; (Mi.); W. T. Waggoner Estate	1,500	11,570
Sheldon Reservoir — (1943) Harris Co.; Carpenters Bayou; 2 mi. SW Sheldon; (R-FH); TP&WD	1,244	4,224
Smithers L. — (1957) Fort Bend Co.; Dry Creek; 10 mi. SE Richmond; (In.); Reliant Energy HL&P	2,480	18,700
Somerville L. — (1967) Burleson-Washington-Lee counties; Yegua Cr.; 2 mi. S Somerville; (M-In.-Ir.- FC); USAE-Brazos River Authority.	11,456	155,062
South Texas Project Reservoir — (1983) Matagorda Co.; off-channel Colorado R.; 16 mi. S Bay City; (In.); Reliant Energy HL&P.	7,000	202,600
Spence Reservoir, E. V. — (1969) Coke Co.; Colorado R.; 2 mi. W. Robert Lee; (M-In.-Mi); Colorado R. Mun. Water Dist.; (Imp. by Robert Lee Dam).	14,640	517,272
Squaw Creek Reservoir — (1983) Somervell-Hood counties; Squaw Cr.; 4.5 mi. N Glen Rose; (In.); TXU	3,297	151,418
Stamford, L. — (1953) Haskell Co.; Paint Cr.; 10 mi. SE Haskell; (M-In.); City of Stamford	5,124	51,573
Steinhagen L., B. A. — (1951) Tyler-Jasper counties; Neches R.; 1/2 mi. N Town Bluff; (FC-R-C); USAE (also called Town Bluff Reservoir and Dam B. Reservoir);(Imp. by Town Bluff Dam)	10,687	66,972
Stillhouse Hollow L. — (1968) Bell Co.; Lampasas R.; 5 mi. SW Belton; (M-In.-Ir.-FC); USAE- Brazos River Authority; (also called Lampasas Reservoir)	6,429	226,063
Striker Creek Reservoir — (1957) Rusk-Cherokee counties; Striker Cr.; 18 mi. SW Henderson; (M -In.); Angelina-Nacogdoches WC&ID No. 1.	1,863	20,977
Sulphur Springs, L. — (1950) Hopkins Co.; White Oak Cr.; 2 mi. N Sulphur Springs; (M); Sulphur Springs WD; (formerly called White Oak Creek Reservoir).	1,340	17,383
Sulphur Springs Draw Reservoir — (1992) Martin Co.; Sulphur Springs Draw; 12 mi. NE Stanton; (FC); Colorado River MWD.	—	7,997
Sweetwater, L. — (1930) Nolan Co.; Bitter Creek; 6 mi. SE Sweetwater (M-R); City of Sweetwater	630	11,900
Tawakoni, L. — (1960) Rains-Van Zandt-Hunt counties; Sabine R.; 9 mi. NW Wills Point; (M-In.-Ir-R); Sabine River Authority; (Imp. by Iron Bridge Dam).	37,879	888,137
Terrell City L. — (1955) Kaufman Co.; Muddy Cedar Cr.; 6 mi. E Terrell; (M-R); City of Terrell	849	8,594
Texana, L. — (1980) Jackson Co.; Navidad R. and Sandy Cr.; 6.8 mi. SE Edna; (M-Ir); USBR, Lavaca-Navidad R. Auth., Texas Water Dev. Bd.; (formerly Palmetto Bend Reservoir)	9,727	161,085
Texoma, L. — (1943) Grayson-Cooke cos., Texas; Bryan-Marshall-Love cos., Okla.; (Imp. by Denison Dam) on Red R. below confluence of Red and Washita rivers; (P-FC-C-R); USAE	74,686	2,516,232
Toledo Bend Reservoir — (1967) Newton-Panola-Sabine-Shelby counties; Sabine R.; 14 mi. NE Burkeville; (M-In.-Ir.-PR); Sabine River Authority (Texas' share of capacity is half amount shown)	181,600	4,472,900
Town Lake — (1960) Travis Co.; Colorado R.; within Austin city limits; (R); City of Austin	468	6,362

Lakes and Reservoirs, Date of Origin	Surface Area (Acres)	Storage Capacity (Acre-Ft.)
Tradinghouse Creek Reservoir — (1968) McLennan Co.; Tradinghouse Cr.; 9 mi. E Waco; (In.); TXU	2,010	37,800
Travis, L. — (1942) Travis-Burnet counties; Colorado R.; 13 mi. NW Austin; (M-In.-Ir.- Mi.-P-FC-R); LCRA; (Imp. by Mansfield Dam)	18,622	1,132,172
Trinidad L. — (1923) Henderson Co.; off-channel reservoir Trinity R.; 2 mi. S. Trinidad; (P); TXU.	740	6,200
Truscott Brine L. — (1987) Knox Co.; Bluff Cr.; 26 mi. NNW Knox City; (Chlorine Control); Red River Auth.	3,146	111,147
Twin Buttes Reservoir — (1963) Tom Green Co.; Concho R.; 8 mi. SW San Angelo; (M-In. -FC-Ir.-R.); City of San Angelo-USBR-Tom Green Co. WC&ID No. 1.	9,080	177,800
Twin Oaks Reservoir — (1982) Robertson Co.; Duck Cr.; 12 mi. N. Franklin; (In) TXU	2,330	30,319
Tyler, L./Lake Tyler East — (1949/1967) Smith Co.; Prairie and Mud Creeks.; 12 mi. SE Tyler; (M-In); City of Tyler; (Imp. by Whitehouse and Mud Creek dams)	4,737	80,198
Upper Nueces L. — (1926, 1948) Zavala Co.; Nueces R.; 6 mi. N Crystal City; (Ir.); Zavala-Dimmit Co. WID No. 1.	316	7,590
Valley Acres Reservoir — (1956) Hidalgo Co.; off-channel Rio Grande; 7 mi. N Mercedes; (Ir-M-FC); Valley Acres Water Dist.	325	1,950
Valley L. — (1961) Fannin-Grayson counties; 2.5 mi. N Savoy; (P); TXU; (formerly Brushy Creek Reservoir)	1,080	16,400
Waco, L. — (1929) McLennan Co.; Bosque R.; 2 mi. W Waco; (M-FC-C-R); City of Waco- USAE-Brazos River Authority	7,194	144,833
Walter E. Long, L. — (1967) Travis Co.; Decker Cr.; 9 mi. E Austin; (M-In.-R); City of Austin; (formerly Decker Lake)	1,269	33,940
Waxahachie, L. — (1956) Ellis Co.; S Prong Waxahachie Cr.; 4 mi. SE Waxahachie; (M-In); Ellis County WC&ID No. 1; (Imp. by S. Prong Dam)	656	11,386
Weatherford, L. — (1956) Parker Co.; Clear Fork Trinity River; 7 mi. E Weatherford; (M-In.); City of Weatherford.	1,158	18,714
Welsh Reservoir — (1976) Titus Co.; Swauano Cr.; 11 mi. SE Mount Pleasant; (R-In.); AEP-Southwestern Electric Power Co.; (formerly Swauano Creek Reservoir).	1,269	20,242
White River L. — (1963) Crosby Co.; 16 mi. SE Crosbyton; (M-In.-Mi.); White River Municipal Water Dist.	1,418	27,850
White Rock L. — (1911) Dallas Co.; White Rock Cr.; within NE Dallas city limits; (R); City of Dallas	1,088	9,004
Whitney, L. — (1951) Hill-Bosque-Johnson counties; Brazos R.; 5.5 mi. SW Whitney; (FC-P); USAE	23,560	622,800
Wichita, L. — (1901) Wichita Co.; Holliday Cr.; 6 mi. SW Wichita Falls; (M-P-R); City of Wichita Falls	2,200	14,000
Winnsboro, L. — (1962) Wood Co.; Big Sandy Cr.; 6 mi. SW Winnsboro; (FC-R); Wood County; (Imp. by Wood Co. Dam No. 4).	806	8,100
Winters, L. — (1983) Runnels Co.; Elm Cr.; 4.5 mi. E Winters; (M); City of Winters (also known as Elm Creek Lake and New Lake Winters).	643	8,374
Worth, L. — (1914) Tarrant Co.; W. Fk. Trinity R.; in NW Fort Worth; (M); City of Fort Worth	3,458	33,495
Wright Patman L. — (1957) Bowie-Cass-Morris-Titus-Red River counties; Sulphur R.; 8 mi. SW Texarkana; (FC-M); USAE; (formerly Texarkana Lake)	20,300	145,300

Sunrise reflects off Toledo Bend Reservoir in far East Texas. The huge reservoir borders Newton, Panola, Sabine and Shelby counties and separates Texas and Louisiana. It covers 181,600 acres and has a storage capacity of 4.47 million acre feet. File photo.

Texas Plant Life

This article was updated for the Texas Almanac by Stephan L. Hatch, Director, S.M. Tracy Herbarium and Professor, Dept. of Rangeland Ecology and Management, Texas A&M University.

Vegetational Diversity

Variations in amount and frequency of rainfall, in soils and in frost-free days, gives Texas a great variety of vegetation. From the forests of East Texas to the deserts of West Texas, from the grassy plains of North Texas to the semi-arid brushlands of South Texas, plant species change continuously.

More than 100 million acres of Texas are devoted to providing grazing for domestic and wild animals. This is the **largest single use for land in the state.** More than 80 percent of the acreage is devoted to range in the Edwards Plateau, Cross Timbers and Prairies, South Texas Plains and Trans-Pecos Mountains and Basins.

Sideoats grama, which occurs on more different soils in Texas than any other native grass, was officially designated as the **state grass of Texas** by the Texas Legislature in 1971.

The **10 principal plant life areas** of Texas, starting in the east, are:

1. Pineywoods

Most of this area of some 16 million acres ranges from about 50 to 700 feet above sea level and receives 40 to 56 inches of rain yearly. Many rivers, creeks and bayous drain the region. Nearly all of Texas' commercial timber comes from this area. There are three native species of pine, the principal timber: longleaf, shortleaf and loblolly. An introduced species, the **slash pine,** also is widely grown. Hardwoods include **oaks, elm, hickory, magnolia, sweet and black gum, tupelo** and others.

The area is interspersed with **native and improved grasslands.** Cattle are the primary grazing animals. **Deer** and **quail** are abundant in properly managed localities. Primary forage plants, under proper grazing management, include species of the **bluestems, rossettegrass, panicums, paspalums, blackseed needlegrass, Canada and Virginia wildryes, purpletop, broadleaf and spike woodoats, switchcane, lovegrasses, indiangrass** and numerous **legume** species.

Highly disturbed areas have understory and overstory of undesirable woody plants that suppress growth of pine and desirable grasses. The primary forage grasses have been reduced and the grasslands have been invaded by **threeawns, annual grasses, weeds, broomsedge bluestem, red lovegrass** and shrubby woody species.

2. Gulf Prairies and Marshes

The Gulf Prairies and Marshes cover approximately 10 million acres. There are two subunits: (a) The marsh and salt grasses immediately at tidewater, and (b) a little farther inland, a strip of bluestems and tall grasses, with some gramas in the western part. Many of these grasses make excellent grazing.

Oaks, elm and other hardwoods grow to some extent, especially along streams, and the area has some **post oak** and brushy extensions along its borders. Much of the Gulf Prairies is fertile farmland. The area is well suited for cattle.

Principal grasses of the Gulf Prairies are **tall bunchgrasses,** including **big bluestem, little bluestem, seacoast bluestem, indiangrass, eastern gamagrass, Texas wintergrass, switchgrass** and **gulf cordgrass. Saltgrass** occurs on moist saline sites.

Heavy grazing has changed the native vegetation in many cases so the predominant grasses are the less desirable **broomsedge bluestem, smutgrass, threeawns, tumblegrass** and many other inferior grasses. Other plants that have invaded the productive grasslands include **oak underbrush, Macartney rose, huisache, mesquite, prickly pear, ragweed, bitter sneezeweed, broomweed** and others.

Vegetation of the Gulf Marshes consists primarily of **sedges, bullrush, flat-sedges, beakrush** and other rushes, **smooth cordgrass, marshhay cordgrass, marsh millet** and **maidencane.** The marshes are grazed best during winter.

Wildflowers blanket a South Texas field on U.S. 181 between Floresville and San Antonio. Texas Almanac photo.

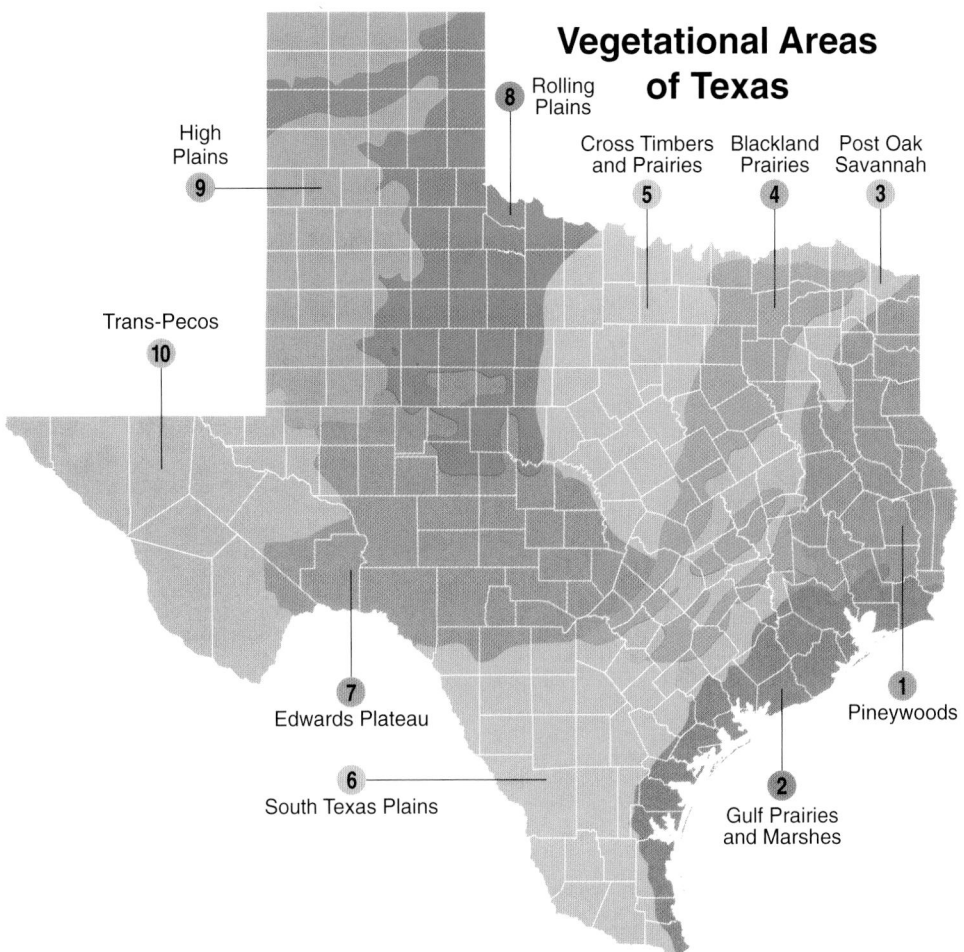

Vegetational Areas of Texas

Rolling Plains **8**

High Plains **9**

Cross Timbers and Prairies **5**

Blackland Prairies **4**

Post Oak Savannah **3**

Trans-Pecos **10**

Edwards Plateau **7**

South Texas Plains **6**

Pineywoods **1**

Gulf Prairies and Marshes **2**

3. Post Oak Savannah

This secondary forest area, also called the **Post Oak Belt**, covers some 7 million acres. It is immediately west of the primary forest region, with less annual rainfall and a little higher elevation. Principal trees are **post oak, blackjack oak** and **elm. Pecans, walnuts** and other kinds of water-demanding trees grow along streams. The southwestern extension of this belt is often poorly defined, with large areas of prairie.

The upland soils are **sandy and sandy loam**, while the bottomlands are **sandy loams and clays**.

The original vegetation consisted mainly of **little bluestem, big bluestem, indiangrass, switchgrass, purpletop, silver bluestem, Texas wintergrass, spike woodoats, longleaf woodoats, post oak** and **blackjack oak.** The area is still largely native or improved grasslands, with small farms located throughout. Intensive grazing has contributed to dense stands of a woody understory of **yaupon, greenbriar** and **oak** brush.

Mesquite has become a serious problem. Good forage plants have been replaced by such plants as **splitbeard bluestem, red lovegrass, broomsedge bluestem, broomweed, bullnettle** and **western ragweed.**

4. Blackland Prairies

This area of about 12 million acres, while called a "prairie," has much timber along the streams, including a variety of **oaks, pecan, elm, horse-apple (bois d'arc)** and **mesquite.** In its native state it was largely a grassy plain — the first native grassland in the westward extension of the Southern Forest Region.

Most of this fertile area has been cultivated, and only small acreages of grassland remain in original vegetation. In heavily grazed pastures, the tall bunchgrass has been replaced by **buffalograss, Texas grama** and other less productive grasses. **Mesquite, lotebush** and other woody plants have invaded the grasslands.

The original grass vegetation includes **big** and **little bluestem, indiangrass, switchgrass, sideoats grama, hairy grama, tall dropseed, Texas wintergrass** and **buffalograss.** Non-grass vegetation is largely legumes and composites.

5. Cross Timbers and Prairies

Approximately 15 million acres of alternating woodlands and prairies, often called the **Western Cross Timbers,** constitute this region. Sharp changes in the vegetational cover are associated with different soils and topography, but the grass composition is rather uniform.

The prairie grasses are **big bluestem, little bluestem, indiangrass, switchgrass, Canada wildrye, sideoats grama, hairy grama, tall grama, tall dropseed, Texas wintergrass, blue grama** and **buffalograss.**

On the Cross Timbers soils, the vegetation is composed of **big bluestem, little bluestem, hooded wind-**

Dogwoods bloom in Purtis Creek State Park, located about three miles north of Eustace in Henderson County. This county includes Piney Woods in the east, Post Oak Savannah in its center and Blackland Prairies in the west. Texas Parks & Wildlife photo.

millgrass, **sand lovegrass, indiangrass, switchgrass** with many species of legumes. The woody vegetation includes **shinnery, blackjack, post** and **live oaks**.

The entire area has been invaded heavily by woody brush plants of **oaks, mesquite, juniper** and other unpalatable plants that furnish little forage for livestock.

6. South Texas Plains

South of San Antonio, between the coast and the Rio Grande, are some 21 million acres of subtropical dryland vegetation, consisting of small trees, shrubs, cactus, weeds and grasses. The area is noteworthy for extensive brushlands, known as the **brush country**, or the Spanish equivalents of **chaparral** or **monte**. Principal plants are **mesquite, small live oak, post oak, prickly pear (Opuntia) cactus, catclaw, blackbrush, whitebrush, guajillo, huisache, cenizo** and others which often grow very densely.

The original vegetation was mainly perennial warm-season **bunchgrasses** in **post oak, live oak** and **mesquite savannahs**. Other brush species form dense thickets on the ridges and along streams. Long-continued grazing has contributed to the dense cover of brush. Most of the desirable grasses have only persisted under the protection of brush and cacti.

There are distinct differences in the original plant communities on various soils. Dominant grasses on the sandy loam soils are **seacoast bluestem, bristlegrass, paspalum, windmillgrass, silver bluestem, big sandbur** and **tanglehead**. Dominant grasses on the clay and clay loams are **silver bluestem, Arizona cottontop, buffalograss, common curlymesquite, bristlegrass, pap-**

pusgrass, gramas, plains lovegrass, Texas cupgrass, vinemesquite,** other **panicums** and **Texas wintergrass**.

Low saline areas are characterized by **gulf cordgrass, saltgrass, alkali sacaton and switchgrass**. In the post oak and live oak savannahs, the grasses are mainly **seacoast bluestem, indiangrass, switchgrass, crinkleawn, paspalums** and **panicums**. Today much of the area has been reseeded to **buffelgrass**.

7. Edwards Plateau

These 25 million acres are rolling to mountainous, with woodlands in the eastern part and grassy prairies in the west. There is a good deal of brushy growth in the central and eastern parts. The combination of grasses, weeds and small trees is ideal for **cattle, sheep, goats, deer and wild turkey**.

This limestone-based area is characterized by the large number of **springfed, perennially flowing streams** which originate in its interior and flow across the **Balcones Escarpment**, which bounds it on the south and east. The soils are shallow, ranging from sands to clays and are calcareous in reaction. This area is predominantly rangeland, with cultivation confined to the deeper soils.

In the east-central portion is the well-marked **Central Basin** centering in Mason, Llano and Burnet counties, with a mixture of granitic and sandy soils. The western portion of the area comprises the semi-arid **Stockton Plateau**. Noteworthy is the growth of **cypress** along the perennially flowing streams. Separated by many miles from cypress growth of the moist Southern Forest Belt, they constitute one of Texas' several **"islands" of vegetation**. These trees, which grow to stately proportions, were commercialized in the past.

The principal grasses of the clay soils are **cane bluestem, silver bluestem, little bluestem, sideoats grama, hairy grama, indiangrass, common curlymesquite, buffalograss, fall witchgrass, plains lovegrass, wildryes** and **Texas wintergrass.**

The rocky areas support tall or mid-grasses with an overstory of **live oak, shinnery oak, juniper and mesquite.** The heavy clay soils have a mixture of **tobosagrass, buffalograss, sideoats grama and mesquite.**

Throughout the Edwards Plateau, **live oak, shinnery oak, mesquite** and **juniper** dominate the woody vegetation. Woody plants have invaded to the degree that they should be controlled before range forage plants can re-establish.

8. Rolling Plains

This is a region of approximately 24 million acres of alternating woodlands and prairies. The area is half **mesquite woodland** and half **prairie.** Mesquite trees have steadily invaded and increased in the grasslands for many years, despite constant control efforts.

Soils range from coarse sands along outwash terraces adjacent to streams to tight or compact clays on redbed clays and shales. Rough broken lands on steep slopes are found in the western portion. About two-thirds of the area is rangeland, but cultivation is important in certain localities.

The original vegetation includes **big, little, sand and silver bluestems, Texas wintergrass, indiangrass, switchgrass, sideoats and blue gramas, wildryes, tobosagrass** and **buffalograss** on the clay soils. The sandy soils support **tall bunchgrasses, mainly sand bluestem. Sand shinnery oak, sand sagebrush** and **mesquite** are the dominant woody plants.

Continued heavy grazing contributes to the increase in woody plants, low-value grasses such as **red grama, red lovegrass, tumblegrass, gummy lovegrass, Texas grama, sand dropseed and sandbur, with western ragweed, croton** and many other weedy forbs. **Yucca** is a problem plant on certain rangelands.

9. High Plains

The High Plains, some 19 million treeless acres, are an extension of the Great Plains to the north. The level nature and porous soils prevent drainage over wide areas.

The relatively light rainfall flows into the numerous shallow **"playa" lakes** or sinks into the ground to feed the great **underground aquifer** that is the source of water for the countless wells that irrigate the surface of the plains. A large part of this area is under irrigated farming, but native grassland remains in about one-half of the High Plains.

Blue grama and **buffalograss** comprise the principal vegetation on the clay and clay loam "hardland" soils. Important grasses on the sandy loam "sandy land" soils are **little bluestem, western wheatgrass, indiangrass, switchgrass** and **sand reedgrass. Sand shinnery oak, sand sagebrush, mesquite** and **yucca** are conspicuous invading brushy plants.

10. Trans-Pecos, Mountains and Basins

With as little as eight inches of annual rainfall, long hot summers and usually cloudless skies to encourage evaporation, this 18-million-acre area produces only drought-resistant vegetation without irrigation. Grass is usually short and sparse.

The principal vegetation consists of **lechuguilla, ocotillo, yucca, cenizo, prickly pear** and other arid land plants. In the more arid areas, **gyp** and **chino grama,** and **tobosagrass** prevail. There is some **mesquite.** The vegetation includes **creosote-tarbush, desert shrub, grama grassland, yucca and juniper savannahs, pine oak forest and saline flats.**

The mountains are 3,000 to 8,751 feet in elevation and support **piñon pine, juniper** and some **ponderosa pine** and other forest vegetation on a few of the higher slopes. The grass vegetation, especially on the higher mountain slopes, includes many **southwestern and Rocky Mountain species** not present elsewhere in Texas. On the desert flats, **black grama, burrograss and fluffgrass** are frequent.

More productive sites have numerous species of **grama, muhly, Arizona cottontop, dropseed** and **perennial threeawn grasses.** At the higher elevations, **plains bristlegrass, little bluestem, Texas bluestem, sideoats grama, chino grama, blue grama, piñon ricegrass, wolftail** and several species of **needlegrass** are frequent.

The common invaders on all depleted ranges are **woody plants, burrograss, fluffgrass, hairy erioneuron, ear muhly, sand muhly, red grama, broom snakeweed, croton, cacti** and several poisonous plants. ☆

For Further Reading

Hatch, S.L., K.N. Gandhi and L.E. Brown, *Checklist of the Vascular Plants of Texas;* MP1655, Texas Agricultural Experiment Station, College Station, 1990.

Vegetation in the Trans-Pecos includes such drought-resistant plants as prickly pear and various desert shrubs. This 18.7-million-acre area receives as little as 8 inches of rain a year. Texas Almanac photo.

Texas Forest Resources

Source: Texas Forest Service, The Texas A&M University System, Tarrow Drive, Suite 364, College Station, TX 77840; http:// txforestservice.tamu.edu/

Texas' forest resources are abundant and diverse. Forest land covers roughly 13 percent of the state's land area. The 21.5 million acres of forests and woodlands in Texas is an area larger than the states of Massachusetts, Connecticut, New Hampshire, Rhode Island and Vermont combined.

The **six principal regions of forest and woodlands** are: the East Texas pine-hardwood region, often called the Piney Woods; the Post Oak Belt, which lies immediately west of the pine-hardwood forest; the Eastern and Western Cross Timbers areas of North-Central Texas; the Cedar Brakes of Central Texas; the Mountain Forests of West Texas; and the Coastal Forests of the southern Gulf Coast.

East Texas Piney Woods

Although Texas' forests and woodlands are extensive, detailed forest resource data is available for only the 43-county East Texas timber region. The Piney Woods, which form the western edge of the United States' southern pine region, extending from Bowie and Red River counties in Northeast Texas to Jefferson, Harris and Waller counties in southeast Texas, contain 11.9 million acres of timberland and produce nearly all of the state's commercial timber.

Following is a summary of the findings of the most recent Forest Inventory of East Texas, completed in 2003 by the Texas Forest Service in cooperation with the USDA Forest Service Southern Research Station.

Timberland Acreage and Ownership

Nearly all (11.9 million acres of 12.1 million acres) of the East Texas forest is classified as "timberland," which is suitable for producing timber products and not reserved as parks or wilderness areas. In contrast to the trends in several other Southern states, Texas timberland acreage increased by 0.9 percent between 1992 and 2002. Of the new timberland acres, 58.4 percent came from agricultural lands, such as idle farmland and pasture, which was either intentionally planted with trees or naturally reverted to forest.

Sixty-three percent of East Texas timberland is owned by approximately 210,000 private individuals, families, partnerships and non-wood-using corporations. Twenty-nine percent is owned by forest-products companies and investment groups, and 8 percent is owned by the government. The following table shows acreage of timberland by ownership:

Ownership Class	Thous. Acres
Non-industrial Private	7,534.4
Forest Industry/Corporate	3,396.7
Public:	
National Forest	685.7
Misc. Federal	112.5
State	103.9
County & Municipal	45.7
Total	**11,878.9**

There are distinct regional differences in ownership patterns. Most forest-industry land is found south of Nacogdoches County, and in some counties, such as Polk and Hardin, as much as 75 percent of timberland is owned by the forest-products industry. North of Nacog-doches, the non-industrial private landowner predominates, and industry owns a much smaller percent of timberland.

Forest Types

Six major forest types are found in the East Texas Piney Woods. Two pine-forest types are most common. The loblolly-shortleaf and longleaf-slash forest types are dominated by the four species of southern yellow pine. In these forests, pine trees make up at least 50 percent of the trees.

Oak-hickory is the second most common forest type. These are upland hardwood forests in which oaks or hickories make up at least 50 percent of the trees, and pine species are less than 25 percent. Oak-pine is a mixed-forest type in which more than 50 percent of the trees are hardwoods, but pines make up 25 to 49 percent of the trees.

Two forest types, oak-gum-cypress and elm-ash-cottonwood, are bottomland types which are commonly found along creeks, river bottoms, swamps and other wet areas. The oak-gum-cypress forests are typically made up of many species including blackgum, sweetgum, oaks and southern cypress. The elm-ash-cottonwood bottomland forests are dominated by those trees but also contain many other species, such as willows, sycamores and maples. The following table shows the breakdown in acreage by forest type:

Forest Type Group	Thous. Acres
Southern Pine:	
Loblolly-shortleaf	5,344.0
Longleaf-slash	216.2
Oak-pine	2,447.0
Oak-hickory	1,724.3
Bottomland Hardwood:	
Oak-gum-cypress	1,380.5
Elm-ash-cottonwood	554.7
Total	**11,666.7**

Southern pine plantations, established by tree planting and usually managed intensively to maximize timber production, are an increasingly important source of wood fiber. Texas forests include 2.8 million acres of pine plantations, 64 percent of which are on land owned by the forest industry, 32 percent on non-industrial private land, and 5 percent on public land. Plantation acreage increased 56 percent between 1992 and 2003. Genetically superior tree seedlings, produced at industry nurseries and Texas Forest Service nurseries, are usually planted to improve survival and growth.

Timber Volume and Number of Trees

Texas timberland contains 15.7 billion cubic feet of timber "growing-stock" volume. One billion cubic feet of growing stock produces roughly enough lumber to build a 2,000-square-foot home for one out of every three Texans. The inventory of softwood increased 15 percent from 8.1 billion cubic feet in 1992 to 9.2 billion cubic feet in 2003. The hardwood inventory increased 12 percent to 6.41 billion cubic feet between 1992 and 2003.

There are an estimated 7.5 billion live trees in East Texas, according to the 2003 survey, an increase of 0.6 billion from 1992. This includes 2.3 billion softwoods and 5.3 billion hardwoods. The predominant species are

The 2003 timber harvest in the 43-county East Texas timber region totaled 659.3 million cubic feet of growing stock, which includes both pine and hardwood. Although there are forests and woodlands throughout Texas, the East Texas timber region produces nearly all of the state's commercial timber. File photo.

loblolly and shortleaf pine; 2.2 billion pine trees are found in East Texas.

Timber Growth and Removals

Between 1992 and 2002, an annual average of 660.6 million cubic feet of growing stock timber was removed from the inventory either through harvest or land-use changes. Meanwhile, 744.1 million cubic feet of growing stock were added to the inventory through growth each year.

For pine, an average of 493.7 million cubic feet was removed during those years, while 526.8 million feet were added by growth. For hardwoods, 166.9 million feet were removed, while 217.3 million cubic feet were added by growth.

Other Tree Regions

Compared to commercially important East Texas, relatively little data are available for the other tree regions of Texas. However, these areas are environmentally important with benefits for wildlife habitat, improved water quality, recreation and aesthetics. A brief description of these areas — the Post Oak Belt, the Eastern and Western Cross Timbers, the Cedar Brakes, the Mountain Forests and the Coastal Forests — can be found in the descriptions of Texas' vegetation regions preceding this article.

The 2003 Timber Harvest

Total Removals

Total removal of growing stock in East Texas in 2003, including both pine and hardwood, was almost unchanged from the previous year. The total volume removed from the 43-county region was 659.3 million cubic feet in 2003, compared to 659.2 million cubic feet

in 2002. Included in the total removal was timber harvested for industrial use and an estimate of logging residue and other timber removals.

By species group, the total removal comprised 530.2 million cubic feet of pine and 129.1 million cubic feet of hardwood. Pine removal was down 0.6 percent while hardwood removal declined 2.1 percent from 2002.

Industrial roundwood harvest in Texas, the portion of the total removal that was subsequently used in manufacturing wood products, totaled 542.1 cubic feet for pine and 126.1 million cubic feet for hardwood. The pine industrial roundwood harvest was up 1.0 percent, and the hardwood roundwood harvest was down 3.4 percent from 2002. The combined harvest was up 0.1 percent to 668.3 million cubic feet. Note that the softwood roundwood harvest in 2003 was even bigger than the removal of softwood growing stock. That was because a part of the industrial roundwood harvest was from non-growing stock trees.

Jasper, Polk, Tyler, Angelina, Cass and Newton counties were the top producing counties in Texas. Jasper, Angelina, Tyler, San Augustine and Polk counties experienced the greatest relative timber harvesting intensity during 2003 in terms of cubic feet of harvest per acre of timberland.

Total Harvest Value

Stumpage value of the East Texas timber harvest decreased 13.2 percent in 2003 from its 2002 level to $412.3 million. The delivered value of timber was down 14.3 percent to $789.0 million. Pine timber accounted for 88.2 percent of the total stumpage value and 86.4 percent of the total delivered value.

The harvest of sawlogs for production of lumber was

up by 1.3 percent to 1.51 billion board feet, which accounted for 37 percent of the 2003 total timber harvest. The pine sawlog cut totaled 1.23 billion board feet, down 3.9 percent, while the hardwood sawlog harvest surged 36.7 percent to 288.1 million board feet. Cass, Jasper, Tyler, Polk and Angelina counties were the top producers of sawlogs.

Timber cut for the production of structural panels, including both plywood and OSB and hardwood veneer, totaled 179.0 million cubic feet. This represented 26.8 percent of the total timber harvest in 2003, a 6.2 percent decrease from 2002. This decrease was mostly caused by closures of plywood mills and production curtailment of the OSB mills in East Texas. Almost all of the veneer and panel roundwood were pine. Polk, Tyler, Harrison, Trinity, Panola and Angelina counties were the top producers of veneer and panel roundwood.

Harvest of timber for manufacture of pulp and paper products rose 3.6 percent from 2002 to 2.97 million cords in 2003. The roundwood pulpwood harvest accounted for 36 percent of the total timber harvest in 2003. Pine pulpwood made up 67.3 percent of the total pulpwood production in 2003. Jasper, Tyler, Polk and Newton counties were the top producers of pulpwood.

Other roundwood harvest included posts, poles and pilings and totaled 2.4 million cubic feet in 2001.

Import-Export Trends

Texas was a net importer of timber products in 2003. Net import of roundwood was 2.6 million cubic feet, or 0.4 percent of the total industrial wood production in Texas. Exports of roundwood from Texas were 67.5 million cubic feet, while imports totaled 70.1 million cubic feet in 2003. Texas mills consumed 89.9 percent of the timber harvested in the state in 2003. The remainder was mostly processed in Arkansas, Louisiana and Oklahoma.

Production of Forest Products
Lumber

Texas sawmills produced 1.75 billion board feet of lumber in 2003, an increase of 7.7 percent over 2002. Production of pine lumber rose 4.5 percent to 1.4 billion board feet in 2003, while hardwood lumber production soared 28.2 percent to 287.1 million board feet in 2003.

Texas Lumber Production, 1993–2003

Year	*Lumber Production	
	Pine	Hardwood
	(thousand board feet)	
1993	1,244,373	171,976
1994	1,340,882	195,693
1995	1,139,462	159,831
1996	1,248,627	175,570
1997	1,316,762	160,553
1998	1,293,432	191,165
1999	1,279,487	225,570
2000	1,410,999	184,172
2001	1,293,823	213,795
2002	1,425,613	223,932
2003	1,490,311	287,062

*Includes tie volumes.

Treated Wood

There was a 27-percent boost in the volume of wood processed by Texas wood treaters in 2003 over 2002.

The total volume treated in 2003 was 46.9 million cubic feet. Among major treated products, lumber accounted for 52.7 percent of total volume; crossties, 19.1 percent; switch ties, 9.8 percent; and utility poles, 7.5 percent.

Primary Mill Residue

Mill residue includes chips, sawdust, shavings and barks. Total mill residue in 2003 in primary mills, such as sawmills, panel mills and chip mills, was 9.54 million short tons, a slight decrease of 0.5 percent from 2002. Sixty-six percent of the residue was from pine species and 34 percent was from hardwood species. Barks accounted for 51.5 percent of mill residue, followed by chips (33.6 percent), sawdust (11.4 percent) and shavings (3.5 percent).

Structural Panel Products

Production of structural panels, including plywood and OSB, was down 3.4 percent to 2.72 billion square feet (3/8-inch basis) in 2003.

Texas Structural Panel Production, 1993–2003

Year	Pine (Thd. sq. ft.*)	Year	Pine (Thd. sq. ft.*)
1993	2,754,949	1999	3,260,055
1994	2,632,833	2000	3,265,644
1995	2,721,487	2001	2,732,940
1996	3,042,736	2002	2,818,356
1997	3,200,317	2003	2,723,225
1998	3,169,713	*3/8-inch basis	

Paper Products

Production of paper and paperboard totaled 2.43 million tons, an 11.2 percent decline from 2002. Paper production plummeted 53.7 percent to 0.26 million tons because of the closure of a major paper mill by the end of 2002. The output of paperboard decreased slightly by 0.4 percent to 2.17 million tons. There was no market pulp production in Texas in 2003.

Texas Pulp, Paper and Paperboard Production, 1993–2003

Year	Paper	Paperboard*	Total Paper Products
	(short tons)		
1993	1,182,826	2,059,091	3,241,917
1994	1,139,411	2,256,722	3,396,133
1995	1,159,677	2,317,212	3,476,889
1996	1,071,015	2,376,486	3,447,501
1997	1,116,018	2,052,153	3,168,171
1998	1,126,648	1,933,906	2,925,856
1999	1,079,397	1,979,592	3,058,989
2000	955,117	2,037,148	2,992,265
2001	599,902	2,083,326	2,683,228
2002	551,367	2,179,423	2,730,790
2003	255,462	2,170,185	2,425,647

*Includes fiberboard and miscellaneous products.

Reforestation

A total of 90,193 acres was planted during the winter 2002 and spring 2003 planting season, down 21.2 percent from the previous year. Industrial landowners planted 62,557 acres, a 22.2-percent drop from the previous year. The non-industrial private forest (NIPF) landowners planted 26,358 acres, down 20.5 percent. Public landowners only planted 1,278 acres in 2003. The NIPF landowners received $1,146,001 in cost-share assistance for reforestation through federal and industrial cost-share programs. Federal programs provided $907,098 in cost-share funds. The Texas Reforestation Foundation provided $238,903 cost-share funding.

Fire Protection

An abundance of rainfall contributed to very low wildfire activity across the state in 2004. Texas Forest Service fire crews took action on 583 wildfires that burned 17,190 acres of grass, brush and forest.

Texas faces a heightened risk of destructive wildfires in 2005 because of the heavy accumulations of vegetation produced by the rains of 2004. Should Texas experience a drought or significant dry spell, firefighters should expect any wildfires that arise to be more difficult and dangerous to control. Extreme care should be taken with all outdoor fire use, particularly with debris-burning because careless debris-burning remains the major cause of wildfires in Texas.

Forest Pests

The Texas Forest Service Forest Pest Management office, which has its headquarters in Lufkin, has a staff of trained forest health specialists (three entomologists and one pathologist) to assist the residents of Texas with tree pest problems. The southern pine beetle is the most destructive insect pest in the 12 million acres of commercial forests in East Texas. Typically, this bark beetle kills more timber annually than forest fires. Currently, this destructive insect is at very low levels in East Texas and has been for the past several years.

The Texas Forest Service coordinates all southern pine beetle control activity on state and private forestlands in Texas. These activities include detecting infestations from the air, checking infestations on the ground to evaluate the need for control, and notifying landowners and providing technical assistance when control is warranted.

Texas residents can get help with tree pest problems from the Texas Forest Service's Forest Pest Management office. Staff members monitor the destructive southern pine beetle, as well as oak wilt, cone and seed insects, regeneration insects and Texas leaf-cutting ants. File photo.

Although southern pine beetle populations currently are at low levels, other forest and tree pests are always present, and Forest Pest Management personnel monitor their activity.

Extensive mortality of live oaks in Central Texas (generally in about 60 counties between Dallas and San Antonio) is causing considerable public concern. A vascular wilt disease, called oak wilt, is the major cause of live oak mortality in Central Texas. A suppression project, administered by Texas Forest Service Forest Pest Management personnel, provides technical assistance and education for affected landowners.

Forest Pest Management personnel also administer the Western Gulf Forest Pest Management Cooperative. Through this coop, applied research and technical assistance are provided to members for a variety of forest pests including cone and seed insects, regeneration insects, pine bark beetles, and Texas leaf-cutting ants.

In addition, Forest Pest Management personnel coordinate and conduct an aerial photography program in East Texas. Color infrared aerial photographs are taken, scanned at 0.5-meter resolution, georectified, and placed in quarter quad format. These photographs can then be used with geographic information system computer software for forest management work, fire suppression activities, planning, forest health activities, among other uses.

Urban Forests

Texas is an urban state with three of the nations ten largest cities. In fact, just 15 of our 254 counties hold 64 percent, or 13 million, of our population. In addition,

Texas grew by more than 22 percent by adding about 3.9 million new residents between 1990 and 2000 — almost all to our cities. Because an estimated 86 percent of Texans now live in urban areas, urban trees and forests play an even more important role in the lives of Texans.

Trees reduce the urban heat island effect by shading and evaporative cooling. They also purify the air by absorbing pollutants, slowing the chemical reactions that produce harmful ozone, and filtering dust. Urban forests reduce storm water runoff and soil erosion and buffer against noise, glare and strong winds, while providing habitat for urban wildlife.

Environmental benefits from a single tree may be worth more than $275 each year. The value to real estate and the emotional and psychological benefits of urban trees raise the value of our urban trees even higher. ☆

Total Timber Production and Value by County in Texas, 2003

County	Pine	Hardwood	Total	Stumpage Value	Delivered Value
	Cubic feet			Thousand dollars	
Anderson	6,642,957	2,632,149	9,275,106	$ 6,187	$ 11,698
Angelina	31,423,886	3,706,293	35,130,179	21,432	41,806
Bowie	8,706,228	6,167,470	14,873,698	9,581	16,909
Camp	2,097,563	1,058,656	3,156,219	2,218	3,837
Cass	23,502,424	10,733,070	34,235,494	23,016	40,657
Chambers	1,423,866	89,139	1,513,005	837	1,696
Cherokee	13,858,758	6,490,709	20,349,467	13,974	26,327
Franklin	187,726	385,019	572,745	259	517
Gregg	2,860,268	1,509,670	4,369,938	3,167	5,887
Grimes	1,312,620	272,980	1,585,600	1,557	2,460
Hardin	23,874,061	3,588,587	27,462,648	14,433	29,748
Harris	4,413,180	1,649,385	6,062,565	5,015	8,251
Harrison	23,438,056	4,614,159	28,052,215	19,234	34,743
Henderson	1,335,715	1,084,758	2,420,473	1,687	3,305
Houston	15,115,429	3,530,222	18,645,651	11,784	22,007
Jasper	44,735,037	4,858,405	49,593,442	24,742	53,160
Jefferson	2,623,591	1,614,045	4,237,636	1,778	4,518
Leon	1,709,897	998,989	2,708,886	2,049	3,597
Liberty	10,599,618	3,917,983	14,517,601	7,926	15,772
Madison	6,927	19,360	26,287	12	21
Marion	11,652,079	4,428,524	16,080,603	11,273	19,934
Montgomery	10,693,529	1,804,541	12,498,070	10,823	17,872
Morris	2,692,448	1,095,477	3,787,925	3,156	5,249
Nacogdoches	23,436,921	4,110,527	27,547,448	17,968	34,071
Newton	29,185,213	3,673,796	32,859,009	17,795	36,611
Orange	4,058,266	1,016,521	5,074,787	1,892	4,575
Panola	19,408,940	5,324,072	24,733,012	14,721	27,818
Polk	44,789,740	3,718,292	48,508,032	31,334	59,093
Red River	3,567,822	5,222,402	8,790,224	4,446	8,377
Rusk	15,356,962	5,018,943	20,375,905	12,562	24,718
Sabine	16,725,690	1,573,322	18,299,012	8,644	18,907
San Augustine	24,555,566	1,771,714	26,327,280	16,601	31,524
San Jacinto	10,497,751	1,065,952	11,563,703	10,680	17,375
Shelby	18,450,201	3,097,264	21,547,465	11,198	23,014
Smith	7,519,073	2,933,343	10,452,416	7,494	13,724
Titus	615,228	1,769,028	2,384,256	983	1,959
Trinity	19,271,018	3,680,388	22,951,406	14,496	28,088
Tyler	38,811,872	9,435,908	48,247,780	25,753	54,535
Upshur	4,365,867	2,045,755	6,411,622	4,039	7,534
Van Zandt	240,149	759,876	1,000,025	488	922
Walker	11,612,776	648,853	12,261,629	11,078	18,208
Waller	274,255	4,846	279,101	308	474
Wood	2,569,936	1,092,057	3,661,993	1,971	3,850
Other Counties	1,926,929	1,906,303	3,833,232	1,701	3,664
Totals	**542,146,038**	**126,118,752**	**668,264,790**	**$412,292**	**$789,011**

National Forests and Grasslands in Texas

Source: U.S. Forest Service, Lufkin and Albuquerque, NM; www.fs.fed.us/r8/texas/

There are four national forests and all or part of five national grasslands in Texas. These federally owned lands are administered by the U.S. Department of Agriculture Forest Service and by district rangers. The national forests cover 637,472 acres in parts of 12 Texas counties. The national grasslands cover 117,394 acres in six Texas counties. Two of these grasslands extend into Oklahoma, as well.

Supervision of the East Texas forests and the two North Texas grasslands is by the Forest Supervisor of the division known as the National Forests and Grasslands in Texas (415 S. 1st St., Ste. 110, Lufkin 75901-3801; 936-639-8501).

The three West Texas grasslands (Black Kettle, McClellan Creek and Rita Blanca) are administered by the Forest Supervisor in Albuquerque, NM, as units of the Cibola National Forest. The following list gives the name of the forest or grassland, the administrative district(s) for each, the acreage in each county and the total acreage:

National Forests in Texas

Angelina National Forest — Angelina Ranger District (Zavalla); Angelina County, 58,520 acres; Jasper, 21,013; Nacogdoches, 9,238; San Augustine, 64,389. Total, 153,160 acres.

Davy Crockett National Forest — Davy Crockett District (Ratcliff); Houston County, 93,320 acres; Trinity, 67,323. Total, 160,643 acres.

Sabine National Forest — Sabine District (Hemphill); Jasper County, 64, acres; Newton, 1,781; Sabine, 95,456; San Augustine, 4,287; Shelby, 59,218. Total, 160,806 acres.

Sam Houston National Forest — Sam Houston District (New Waverly); Montgomery County, 47,801 acres; San Jacinto, 60,639; Walker, 54,597. Total, 163,037 acres.

National Grasslands in Texas
North Texas

Lyndon B. Johnson National Grassland and **Caddo National Grassland** — District Ranger at Decatur; Fannin County, 17,873 acres; Montague, 61; Wise, 20,252. Total, 38,186 acres.

West Texas

Black Kettle National Grassland — Lake Marvin District Ranger in Cheyenne, Okla.; Hemphill County, 576 acres; Roger Mills County, Okla., 30,724 acres. Total, 31,300 acres.

McClellan Creek National Grassland — District Ranger in Cheyenne, Okla.; Gray County, 1,449 acres. Total, 1,449 acres.

Rita Blanca National Grassland — District Ranger at Clayton, NM; Dallam County, 77,183 acres; Cimarron County, Okla., 15,639 acres. Total, 92,822 acres.

Establishment of National Forests and Grasslands

National forests in Texas were established by invitation of the Texas Legislature by an Act of 1933, autho-

LBJ and Caddo National Grasslands comprise 38,186 acres in Fannin and Montague counties in North Texas. The grasslands have a number of sites for camping and picnicking and many miles of horse trails. See page 159 for recreational opportunities at the National Forests and Grasslands in Texas. File photo.

rizing the purchase of lands in Texas for the establishment of national forests. President Franklin D. Roosevelt proclaimed these purchases on Oct. 15, 1936.

The national grasslands were originally submarginal Dust Bowl project lands, purchased by the federal government primarily under the Bankhead-Jones Farm Tenant Act (1937). Today they are well covered with grasses and native shrubs.

Uses of National Forests and Grasslands

The national forests are managed under the ecosystem management concept. Ecosystem management is a means to achieve sustainable conditions and provide wildlife and fish habitat, outdoor recreation, wilderness, water, wood, minerals and forage for public use while retaining the esthetic, historic and spiritual qualities of the land.

In 1960, the Multiple Use-Sustained Yield Act put into law what had been practiced on the National Forests in Texas for almost 30 years. This act emphasized that resources on public lands will be managed so that they are used in ways that best meet the needs of the people, that the benefits obtained will exist indefinitely, and that each natural resource will be managed in balance with other resources.

Forest management plans outline direction under ecosystem management, but even the most carefully planned system of management cannot foresee environmental or natural factors that can cause drastic changes in a forest. Fire, storms, insects and disease, for example, can prompt managers to deviate from land management plans and can alter the way a forest is managed.

Timber Production

About 486,000 acres of the national forests in Texas are suitable for timber production. Sales of sawtimber, pulpwood and other forest products are initiated to implement forest plans and objectives.

The estimated net growth is more than 200 million board feet per year and is valued at $40 million. A portion of this growth is normally removed by cutting.

Cattle Grazing

Permits to graze cattle on national grasslands are granted to the public for an annual fee. About 600 head of cattle are grazed on the Caddo-Lyndon B. Johnson National Grasslands annually.

On the Rita Blanca National Grasslands, 5,425 head of cattle are grazed each year, most of them in Texas.

Hunting and Fishing

State hunting and fishing laws and regulations apply to all national forest land. Game law enforcement is car-

Forests and Grasslands in Texas

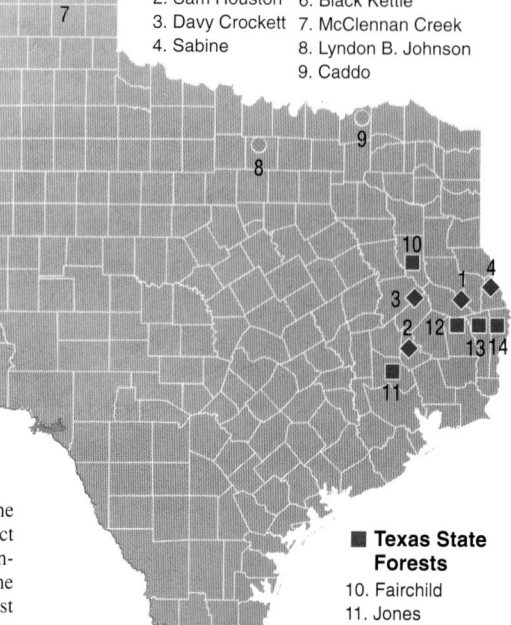

◆ **National Forests**
1. Angelina
2. Sam Houston
3. Davy Crockett
4. Sabine

● **National Grasslands**
5. Rita Blanca
6. Black Kettle
7. McClennan Creek
8. Lyndon B. Johnson
9. Caddo

■ **Texas State Forests**
10. Fairchild
11. Jones
12. Kirby
13. Masterson
14. Siecke

A giant eagle's nest (right) sits high up in a pine tree in Sam Houston National Forest. Sam Houston is 163,037 acres in Montgomery, San Jacinto and Walker counties. Texas has four national forests, five national grasslands and five state forests.

A couple fish at Cottonwood Lake in the LBJ National Grassland. The lake is about 40 acres and located 10 miles north of Decatur. A 4-mile trail connects this area with Black Creek Lake Recreation Area near Alvord. There are nearly 75 miles of multipurpose trails that run in the Cottonwood Lake area. File photo.

ried out by the Texas Parks and Wildlife.

A wide variety of fishing opportunities are available on the Angelina, Sabine, Neches and San Jacinto rivers; the Sam Rayburn and Toledo Bend reservoirs; Lake Conroe; and many small streams.

Hunting is not permitted on the McClellan Creek National Grassland nor at the Lake Marvin Unit of the Black Kettle National Grassland.

Recreational Facilities

An estimated 3 million people visit the recreational areas in the national forests and grasslands in Texas each year, primarily for picnicking, swimming, fishing, camping, boating and nature enjoyment.

The Sabine and Angelina National Forests are on the shores of Toledo Bend and Sam Rayburn Reservoirs, two large East Texas lakes featuring fishing and other water sports.

Lake Conroe and Lake Livingston offer water-related outdoor recreation opportunities on and near the Sam Houston National Forest. ☆

More recreational opportunities in the National Forests and Grasslands are listed on page 159 in the Recreation section.

Texas State Forests

Source: Texas Forest Service, College Station, Texas; http://txforestservice.tamu.edu/

Texas has **five state forests,** all of which are used primarily for demonstration and research. Recreational opportunities, such as camping, hiking, bird-watching, and picnicking, are available in all but the Masterson forest.

I.D. Fairchild State Forest — Texas' largest forest is located west of Rusk in Cherokee County. This forest was transferred from the state prison system in 1925. Additional land was obtained in 1963 from the Texas State Hospitals and Special Schools for a total acreage of 2,740.

W. Goodrich Jones State Forest — Located south of Conroe in Montgomery County, it comprises 1,733 acres. It was purchased in 1926 and named for the founder of the Texas Forestry Association.

John Henry Kirby State Forest — This 600-acre forest in Tyler County was donated by lumberman John Henry Kirby in 1929, as well as later donors. Revenue from this forest is given to the Association of Former Students of Texas A&M University for student-loan purposes.

Paul N. Masterson Memorial Forest — Mrs. Leonora O'Neal Masterson of Beaumont donated this 519 acres in Jasper County in 1984 in honor of her husband, who was a tree farmer and an active member of the Texas Forestry Association.

E.O. Siecke State Forest — The first state forest, it was purchased by the state in 1924. It contains 1,722 acres of pine land in Newton County. An additional 100 acres was obtained by a 99-year lease in 1946. ☆

Texas' Threatened and Endangered Species

Endangered species are those which the Texas Parks and Wildlife Department (TPWD) has named as being at risk of statewide extinction. Threatened species are those which are likely to become endangered in the future. The following species of Texas flora and fauna are either endangered or threatened as of July 15, 2005, according to the TPWD. This list varies slightly from the federal list. Any questions about protected species should be directed to the Endangered Resources Branch, Texas Parks and Wildlife, 4200 Smith School Road, Austin 78744; 1-800-792-1112; www.tpwd.state.tx.us/nature/endang/endang.htm

Endangered Species

Mammals
Bats: greater long-nosed and Mexican long-nosed bats. **Marine Mammals:** West Indian manatee; black right, blue, finback and sperm whales. **Carnivores:** black-footed ferret; jaguar; jaguarundi; ocelot; gray and red wolves.

Birds
Raptors: peregrine, American peregrine and northern aplomado falcons. **Shorebirds:** Eskimo curlew; interior least tern. **Upland Birds:** Attwater's greater prairie chicken. **Waterbirds:** Whooping crane; eastern brown pelican. **Woodpeckers:** ivory-billed and red-cockaded woodpeckers. **Songbirds:** southwestern willow flycatcher; black-capped vireo; Bachman's and golden-cheeked warblers.

The Kemp's ridley sea turtle, above, and the star cactus, below, are both endangered species in Texas. File photos.

Reptiles
Turtles: Atlantic hawksbill, leatherback and Kemp's ridley sea turtles.

Amphibians
Salamanders: Barton Springs and Texas blind salamanders. **Frogs & Toads:** Houston toad.

Fishes
Killifishes: Comanche Springs and Leon Springs pupfishes. **Livebearers:** Big Bend, Clear Creek, Pecos and San Marcos gambusias. **Minnows:** Rio Grande silvery minnow. **Perches:** Fountain darter.

Invertebrates
Crustaceans: Peck's cave amphipod. **Mollusks:** Ouachita rock pocketbook mussel.

Vascular Plants
Cacti: Black lace, Nellie Cory, Sneed pincushion, star and Tobusch fishhook cacti; Davis' green pitaya. **Grasses:** little aguja pondweed; Texas wild-rice. **Orchids:** Navasota ladies'-tresses. **Trees, Shrubs & Sub-shrubs:** Texas ayenia; Johnston's frankenia; Walker's manioc; Texas snowbells. **Wildflowers:** South Texas ambrosia; Zapata and white bladderpod; Terlingua Creek cat's-eye; ashy dogweed; Texas trailing phlox; Texas poppy-mallow; Texas prairie dawn; slender rush-pea; large-fruited sand verbena.

Threatened Species

Mammals
Bats: Rafinesque's big-eared, southern yellow, and spotted bats. **Carnivores:** black and Louisiana black bears; white-nosed coati; margay. **Marine Mammals:** Atlantic spotted and rough-toothed dolphins; dwarf sperm, false killer, Gervais' beaked, goose-beaked, killer, pygmy killer, pygmy sperm and short-finned pilot whales. **Rodents:** Palo Duro mouse; Coues' rice and Texas kangaroo rats.

Birds
Raptors: bald eagle; Arctic peregrine falcon; common black, gray, white-tailed and zone-tailed hawks; swallow-tailed kite; Mexican spotted owl; cactus ferruginous pygmy-owl. **Shorebirds:** piping plover; sooty tern. **Songbirds:** rose-throated becard; tropical parula; Bachman's, Texas Botteri's and Arizona Botteri's sparrows; northern beardless tyrannulet. **Waterbirds:** reddish egret; white-faced ibis; wood stork.

Reptiles
Lizards: reticulated gecko; mountain short-horned, reticulate collared and Texas horned lizards. **Snakes:** speckled racer; black-striped, Brazos water, Chihuahuan desert lyre, indigo, Louisiana pine, northern cat-eyed, smooth green, scarlet and Trans-Pecos black-headed snakes; timber (canebrake) rattlesnake. **Turtles:** loggerhead and green sea turtles; Texas tortoise; alligator snapping, Cagle's map and Chihuahuan mud turtles.

Amphibians
Salamanders: black-spotted newt; Blanco blind, Cascade Caverns, Comal blind and San Marcos salamanders; South Texas siren (large form). **Frogs & Toads:** sheep and white-lipped frogs; Mexican treefrog; Mexican burrowing toad.

Fishes
Catfishes: toothless blindcat and widemouth blindcat. **Coastal Fishes:** opossum pipefish; river and blackfin goby. **Large River Fish:** paddlefish and shovelnose sturgeon. **Livebearers:** blotched gambusia. **Killifishes:** Conchos and Pecos pupfishes. **Minnows:** Rio Grande chub; Devils River minnow; Arkansas River, bluehead, bluntnose, Chihuahua and proserpine shiners; Mexican stoneroller. **Perches:** blackside and Rio Grande darters. **Suckers:** blue sucker and creek chubsucker.

Vascular Plants
Cacti: Bunched cory, Chisos Mountains hedgehog and Lloyd's mariposa cacti. **Trees, Shrubs & Sub-shrubs:** Hinckley's oak. **Wildflowers:** Pecos Puzzle sunflower, tinytim. ☆

Texas Wildlife

Source: Texas Parks and Wildlife, Austin

Texas has many native animals and birds, as well as introduced species. More than **540 species of birds** — about three fourths of all different species found in the United States — have been identified in Texas.

Some **142 species of animals,** including some that today are extremely rare, are found in Texas. A list of plant and animal species designated as threatened or endangered by state wildlife officials is found elsewhere in this chapter.

A few of the leading land mammals of Texas are described here. Those marked by an asterisk (*) are non-native species. Information was provided by the **Nongame and Urban Program**, Texas Parks and Wildlife, and updated using the online version of *The Mammals of Texas* by William B. Davis and David J. Schmidly: **www.nsrl.ttu.edu/tmot1/contents.htm**; the print version was published by Texas Parks and Wildlife Press, Austin, 1994. For additional wildlife information on the Web: **www.tpwd.state.tx.us/nature/wild/wild.htm**.

Mammals

Armadillo — The **nine-banded armadillo** *(Dasypus novemcinctus)* is one of Texas' most interesting mammals. It is found in most of the state except the western Trans-Pecos. It is now common as far north and east as Oklahoma and Mississippi.

Badger — The **badger** *(Taxidea taxus)* is found throughout the state, except the extreme eastern parts. It is a fierce fighter, and it is valuable in helping control the rodent population.

Bat — Thirty-two species of these winged mammals have been found in Texas, more than in any other state in the United States. Of these, 27 species are known residents, though they are seldom seen by the casual observer. The **Mexican,** or **Brazilian, free-tailed bat** *(Tadarida brasiliensis)* and the **cave myotis** *(Myotis velifer)* constitute most of the cave-dwelling bats of Southwest and West Texas. They have some economic value for their

deposits of nitrogen-rich **guano.** Some commercial guano has been produced from **James River Bat Cave**, Mason County; **Beaver Creek Cavern**, Burnet County; and from large deposits in other caves including **Devil's Sinkhole** in Edwards County, **Blowout Cave** in Blanco County and **Bandera Bat Cave**, Bandera County. The largest concentration of bats in the world is found at **Bracken Cave** in Comal County, thought to hold between 20 and 40 million bats. The **big brown bat** *(Eptesicus fuscus),* the **red bat** *(Lasiurus borealis)* and the **evening bat** *(Nycticeius humeralis)* are found in East and Southeast Texas. The evening and big brown bats are forest and woodland dwelling mammals.

Most of the rarer species of Texas bats have been found along the Rio Grande and in the Trans-Pecos. Bats can be observed at dusk near a water source, and many species may also be found foraging on insects attracted to street lights. Everywhere bats occur, they are the main predators of night-flying insects, including mosquitoes and many crop pests. On the Web: **www.batcon.org/**

Bear — The **black bear** *(Ursus americanus),* formerly common throughout most of the state, is now surviving in remnant populations in portions of the Trans-Pecos.

Beaver — The **American beaver** *(Castor canadensis)* is found over most of the state except for the Llano Estacado and parts of the Trans-Pecos.

Bighorn — (See **Sheep.**)

Bison — The largest of native terrestrial wild mammals of North America, the **American bison** *(Bos bison),* commonly called **buffalo,** was formerly found in the western two-thirds of the state. Today it is extirpated or confined on ranches. Deliberate slaughter of this majestic animal for hides and to eliminate the Plains Indians' main food source reached a peak about 1877-78, and the bison was almost eradicated by 1885. Estimates of the number of buffalo killed vary, but as many as 200,000 hides were sold in Fort Worth at a single two-day sale. Except for the

Deer forage in Palo Duro Canyon State Park. The white-tailed deer is found throughout Texas, while the mule deer is found principally in the Trans-Pecos and the Panhandle. Texas Almanac photo.

interest of the late **Col. Charles Goodnight** and a few other foresighted men, the bison might be extinct.

Cat — The **jaguar** *(Felis onca)* is probably now extinct in Texas and, along with the **ocelot, jaguarundi** and **margay,** is listed as rare and endangered by both federal and state wildlife agencies. The **mountain lion** *(Felis concolor),* also known as **cougar** and **puma,** was once found statewide. It is now found in the mountainous areas of the trans-Pecos and the dense Rio Grande Plain brushland. The **ocelot** *(Felis pardalis),* also known as the **leopard cat,** is found usually along the border. The **red-and-gray cat,** or **jaguarundi** *(Felis yagouaroundi Geoffroy)* is found, rarely, in extreme South Texas. The **margay** *(Felis wiedii)* was reported in the 1850s near Eagle Pass. The **bobcat** *(Lynx rufus)* is found over the state in large numbers.

Chipmunk — The **gray-footed chipmunk** *(Tamias canipes)* is found at high altitudes in the Guadalupe and Sierra Diablo ranges of the Trans-Pecos (see also **Ground Squirrel,** with which it is often confused in public reference).

Coati — The **white-nosed coati** *(Nasua narica),* a relative of the raccoon, is occasionally found in southern Texas from Brownsville to the Big Bend. It inhabits woodland areas and feeds both on the ground and in trees. The coati, which is on the list of threatened species, is also found occasionally in Big Bend National Park.

Coyote — The **coyote** *(Canis latrans),* great in number, is the most destructive Texas predator of livestock. On the other hand, it is probably the most valuable predator in the balance of nature. It is a protection to crops and range lands by its control of rodents and rabbits. It is found throughout the state, but is most numerous in the brush country of southwest Texas. It is the second-most important fur-bearing animal in the state.

Deer — The **white-tailed deer** *(Odocoileus virginianus),* found throughout the state in brushy or wooded areas, is the most important Texas game animal. Its numbers in Texas are estimated at more than 3 million. The **mule deer** *(Odocoileus heminous)* is found principally in the Trans-Pecos and Panhandle areas. It has increased in number in recent years. The little **Del Carmen deer** (white-tailed subspecies) is found in limited numbers in the high valleys of the Chisos Mountains in the Big Bend. The only native **elk** in Texas *(Cervus merriami),* found in the southern Guadalupe Mountains, became extinct about the turn of the 20th century. The **wapiti** or **elk** *(Cervus elaphus),* was introduced into the same area about 1928. There are currently several herds totalling several hundred individuals.

A number of exotic deer species have been introduced, mostly for hunting purposes. The **axis deer*** *(Cervus axix).* is the most numerous of the exotics. Native to India, It is found mostly in central and southern Texas, both free-ranging and confined on ranches. **Blackbuck*** *(Antilope cervicapra),* also native to India, is the second-most numerous exotic deer in the state and is found on ranches in 86 counties. **Fallow deer*** *(Cervus dama),* native to the Mediterranean, has been introduced to 93 counties, while the **nilgai*** *(Boselaphus tragocamelus),* native of India and Pakistan, is found mostly on ranches in Kenedy and Willacy counties. The **sika deer*** *(Cervus nippon),* native of southern Siberia, Japan and China, has been introduced in 77 counties in central and southern Texas.

Ferret — The **black-footed ferret** *(Mustela nigripes)* was formerly found widely ranging through the West Texas country of the prairie dog on which it preyed. It is now considered extinct in Texas. It is of the same genus as the weasel and the mink.

Fox — The **common gray fox** *(Urocyon cinereoargenteus)* is found throughout most of the state, primarily in the woods of East Texas, in broken parts of the Edwards Plateau, and in the rough country at the foot of the Staked Plains. The **kit** or **Swift fox** *(Vulpes velox)* is found in the

western one-third of the state. A second species of **kit fox** *(Vulpes macrotis)* is found in the Trans-Pecos and is fairly numerous in some localities. The **red fox*** *(Vulpes vulpes),* which ranges across Central Texas, was introduced for sport.

Gopher — Nine species of pocket gopher occur in Texas. The **Botta's pocket gopher** *(Thomomys bottae)* is found from the Trans-Pecos eastward across the Edwards Plateau. The **plains pocket gopher** *(Geomys bursarius)* is found from Midland and Tom Green counties east and north to McLennan, Dallas and Grayson counties. The **desert pocket gopher** *(Geomys arenarius)* is found only in the Trans-Pecos, while the **yellow-faced pocket gopher** *(Cratogeomys castanops)* is found in the western one-third of the state, with occasional sightings along the Rio Grande in Maverick and Cameron counties. The **Texas pocket gopher** *(Geomys personatus)* is found in South Texas from San Patricio County to Val Verde County. **Attwater's pocket gopher** *(Geomys attwateri)* and **Baird's pocket gopher** *(Geomys breviceps)* are both found generally in East Texas from the Brazos River to the San Antonio River and south to Matagorda and San Patricio counties. **Jones' pocket gopher** *(Geomys knoxjonesi)* is found only in far West Texas, while the **Llano pocket gopher** *(Geomys texensis)* is found only in two isolated areas of the Hill Country.

Ground Squirrel — Five or more species of ground squirrel live in Texas, mostly in the western part of the state. The **rock squirrel** *(Spermophilus variegatus)* is found throughout the Edwards Plateau and Trans-Pecos. The **Mexican ground squirrel** *(Spermophilus mexicanus)* is found in southern and western Texas. The **spotted ground squirrel** *(Spermophilus spilosoma)* is found generally in the western half of the state. The **thirteen-lined ground squirrel** *(Spermophilus tridecemlineatus)* is found in a narrow strip from Dallas and Tarrant counties to the Gulf. The **Texas antelope squirrel** *(Ammospermophilus interpres)* is found along the Rio Grande from El Paso to Val Verde County.

Hog, Feral — (see Pig, Feral)

Javelina — The **javelina** or **collared peccary** *(Tayassu tajacu)* is found in brushy semidesert where prickly pear, a favorite food, is found. The javelina was hunted commercially for its hide until 1939. They are harmless to livestock and to people, though they can defend themselves ferociously when attacked by hunting dogs.

Mink — The **mink** *(Mustela vison)* is found in the eastern half of the state, always near streams, lakes or other water sources. Although it is an economically important fur-bearing animal in the eastern United States, it ranked only 13th in numbers and 9th in economic value to trappers in Texas in 1988-89, according to a Texas Parks and Wildlife Department survey.

Mole — The **eastern mole** *(Scalopus aquaticus)* is found in the eastern two-thirds of the state.

Muskrat — The **common muskrat** *(Ondatra zibethica),* occurs in aquatic habitats in the northern, southeastern and southwestern parts of the state. Although the muskrat was once economically valuable for its fur, its numbers have declined, mostly because of the loss of habitat.

Nutria* — This introduced species *(Myocastor coypus),* native to South America, is found in the eastern two-thirds of the state. The fur is not highly valued and, since nutria are in competition with muskrats, their spread is discouraged. They have been used widely in Texas as a cure-all for ponds choked with vegetation, with spotty results.

Opossum — A **marsupial,** the **Virginia opossum** *(Didelphis virginiana)* is found in nearly all parts of the state. The opossum has economic value for its pelt, and its meat is considered a delicacy by some. It is one of the chief contributors to the Texas fur crop.

Otter — A few **river otter** *(Lutra canadensis)* are found in the eastern quarter of the state. It has probably been extirpated from the Panhandle, north-central and southern Texas.

Pig, Feral — Feral pigs, found in areas of the Rio Grande and coastal plains as well as the woods of East Texas, are descendants of escaped domestic hogs or of European wild hogs that were imported for sport.

Porcupine — The yellow-haired porcupine *(Erethizon dorsatum)* is found from the western half of the state east to Bosque County.

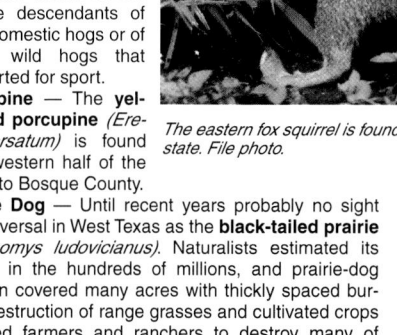

The eastern fox squirrel is found in the eastern two-thirds of the state. File photo.

Prairie Dog — Until recent years probably no sight was so universal in West Texas as the **black-tailed prairie dog** *(Cynomys ludovicianus)*. Naturalists estimated its population in the hundreds of millions, and prairie-dog towns often covered many acres with thickly spaced burrows. Its destruction of range grasses and cultivated crops has caused farmers and ranchers to destroy many of them, and it is extirpated from much of its former range. It is being propagated in several public zoos, notably in the **prairie dog town in Mackenzie Park** at Lubbock. It has been honored in Texas by the naming of the **Prairie Dog Town Fork** of the Red River, along one segment of which is located the beautiful **Palo Duro Canyon**.

Pronghorn — The **Pronghorn** *(Antilocapra americana)* formerly was found in the western two-thirds of the state. It is currently found only in limited areas from the Panhandle to the Trans-Pecos. Despite management efforts, its numbers have been decreasing in recent years.

Rabbit — The **black-tailed jack rabbit** *(Lepus californicus)* is found throughout Texas except in the Big Thicket area of East Texas. It breeds rapidly, and its long hind legs make it one of the world's faster-running animals. The **Eastern cottontail** *(Sylvilagus floridanus)* is found mostly in the eastern three-quarters of the state. The **desert cottontail** *(Sylvilagus auduboni)* is found in the western half of the state, usually on the open range. The **swamp rabbit** *(Sylvilagus aquaticus)* is found in East Texas and the coastal area.

Raccoon — The **raccoon** *(Procyon lotor)* is found throughout Texas, especially along streams and in urban settings. It is the most important fur-bearing animal in the state.

Rats and Mice — There are 40 to 50 species of rats and mice in Texas of varying characteristics, habitats and economic destructiveness. The **Norway rat*** *(Rattus norvegicus)* and the **roof rat*** *(Rattus rattus)*, both non-native species, are probably the most common and the most destructive. They also are instrumental in the transmission of several dread diseases, including bubonic plague and typhus. The **common house mouse*** *(Mus musculis)* is estimated in the hundreds of millions annually. The **Mexican vole** *(Microtus mexicanus guadalupensis)*, also called the **Guadalupe Mountain vole,** is found only in the higher elevations of the Guadalupe Mountains National Park and just over the border into New Mexico.

Ringtail — The **ringtail** *(Bassariscus astutus)* is found statewide but is rare in the Lower Valley and the Coastal Plains.

Sheep — The **mountain sheep** *(Ovis canadensis)*, also called **desert bighorn,** formerly was found in isolated areas of the mountainous Trans-Pecos, but the last native sheep were seen in 1959. They have been recently introduced into the same areas. The **barbary sheep***

(Ammotragus lervia), or **aoudad,** first introduced to the Palo Duro Canyon area in 1957–1958, has become firmly established. Private introductions have brought it into the Edwards Plateau, Trans-Pecos, South Texas, Rolling Plains and Post Oak Savannah regions.

Shrew — Four species are found in Texas: the **southern short-tailed shrew** *(Blarina Carolinensis)*, found in the eastern one-fourth of the state; the **least shrew** *(Cryptotis parva)*, in the eastern and central parts of the state; the **Elliot's short-tailed shrew** *(Blarina hylophaga)*, known only in Aransas, Montague and Bastrop counties); and the **desert shrew** *(Notiosorex crawfordi)*, found in the western two-thirds of the state.

Skunk — There are six species of skunk in Texas. The **Eastern spotted skunk** *(Spilogale putorius)* is found in the eastern half of the state and across north-central Texas to the Panhandle. A small skunk, it is often erroneously called civet cat. This skunk also is found in East Texas and the Gulf area. The **Western spotted skunk** *(Spilogale gracilis)* is found in the southwestern part of the state north to Garza and Howard counties and east to Bexar and Duval counties. The **striped skunk** *(Mephitis mephitis)* is found statewide, mostly in brush or wooded areas. The **hooded skunk** *(Mephitis macroura)* is found in limited numbers in the Big Bend and adjacent parts of the Trans-Pecos. The **eastern hog-nosed skunk** *(Conepatus leuconotus)*, found in the Gulf coastal plains, ranges southward into Mexico. The **common hog-nosed skunk** *(Conepatus mesoleucus)* is found in southwestern, central and southern Texas, north to Collin and Lubbock counties.

Squirrel — The **eastern fox squirrel** *(Sciurus niger)* is found in the eastern two-thirds of the state. The **eastern gray squirrel** *(Sciurus carolinensis)* is found generally in the eastern third of the state. The **flying squirrel** *(Glaucomys volans)* is found in wooded areas of East Texas.

Weasel — The **long-tailed weasel** *(Mustela frenata)*, akin to the mink, is found statewide, but is scarce in West Texas.

Wolf — The **red wolf** *(Canis rufus)* was once found throughout the eastern half of the state. It has now been extirpated from the wild, with the only known remnants of the population now in captive propagation. The **gray wolf** *(Canis lupus)* once had a wide range over the western two-thirds of the state. It is now considered extinct in Texas. The **red wolf** and **gray wolf** are on the federal and state rare and endangered species lists.

Reptiles and Arachnids

Most of the more than **100 species and subspecies of snakes** found in Texas are beneficial, as also are other reptiles. There are **16 poisonous species and subspecies**.

Poisonous reptiles include **three species of copperheads** (southern, broad-banded and Trans-Pecos); **one kind of cottonmouth** (western); **11 kinds of rattlesnakes** (canebrake, western massasauga, desert massasauga, western pigmy, western diamondback, timber, banded rock, mottled rock, northern blacktailed, Mojave and prairie); and the **Texas coral snake**.

Also noteworthy are the **horned lizard,** also called **horned toad,** which is on the list of **threatened species**; the **vinegarone,** a type of whip scorpion; **tarantula,** a hairy spider; and **alligator.** ☆

National Wildlife Refuges

Source: U.S. Fish and Wildlife Service, U.S. Department of the Interior.

Texas has more than 470,000 acres in **17 national wildlife refuges**. Their descriptions, with date of acquisition in parentheses, follow. Included in this acreage are two conservation easement refuges, which may be visited at different times of the year for bird watching and wildlife viewing, as well as hunting and fishing. Write or call before visiting to check on facilities and days and hours of operation. On the Web: **http://southwest.fws.gov/refuges/index.html**.

Anahuac (1963): The more than 34,000 acres of this refuge are located along the upper Gulf Coast in Chambers County. **Fresh and saltwater marshes** and miles of beautiful, sweeping **coastal prairie** provide wintering habitat for large flocks of waterfowl, including **geese, 27 species of ducks and six species of rails**. Roseate **spoonbills and white ibis** are among the other birds frequenting the refuge. Other species include **alligator, muskrat** and **bobcat**. Fishing, bird watching, auto tours and hunting are available. Office: Box 278, Anahuac 77514; 409-267-3337.

Aransas (1937): This refuge comprises 70,504 acres on Blackjack Peninsula and three satellite units in Aransas and Refugio counties. The three mainland units consist of **oak woodlands, fresh and saltwater marshes** and **coastal grasslands**. Besides providing wintering grounds for the endangered **whooping crane,** the refuge is home to many species of waterfowl and other migratory birds — more than 390 different bird species in all. Refuge is open daily, sunrise to sunset. Interpretive center is open daily, 8:30 a.m. to 4:30 p.m. Other facilities include a 40-foot observation tower, paved auto-tour loop and walking trails. Office: Box 100, Austwell 77950; 361-286-3559.

Attwater Prairie Chicken (1972): Established in 1972 in Colorado County to preserve habitat for the endangered **Attwater's prairie chicken,** the refuge comprises more than 10,000 acres of **native tallgrass prairie,** potholes, sandy knolls and some wooded areas. An auto-tour route is available year-round, and 350 acres of marsh are accessible for watching the more than 250 species of birds that visit the refuge. Refuge open sunrise to sunset. Office: Box 519, Eagle Lake 77434; 979-234-3021.

Balcones Canyonlands (1992): This 25,000-acre refuge was dedicated in 1992. Located in Burnet, Travis and Williamson counties northwest of Austin, it was established to protect the nesting habitat of two endangered birds: **black-capped vireo** and **golden-cheeked warbler.** Eventually, the refuge will encompass 30,500 acres of **oak-juniper woodlands** and other habitats. An observation deck can be used for birdwatching. Hunting available. Office: 24518 FM-1431, Box 1, Marble Falls, 78654; 512-339-9432.

Big Boggy (1983): This refuge occupies 5,000 acres of **coastal prairie** and **salt marsh** along East Matagorda Bay for the benefit of wintering **waterfowl. The refuge is generally closed,** and visitors are encouraged to visit nearby **San Bernard or Brazoria refuges.** Waterfowl hunting is permitted in season. Office: 1212 N. Velasco, #200, Angleton 77515; 979-849-6062.

Brazoria (1966): The 43,388 acres of this refuge, located along the Gulf Coast in Brazoria County, serve as haven for wintering waterfowl and a wide variety of other

A great white heron takes flight at Hagerman National Wildlife Refuge near Lake Texoma in Grayson County. File photo.

migratory birds. The refuge also supports many **marsh** and **water birds**, from **roseate spoonbills** and **great blue herons** to **white ibis** and **sandhill cranes**. Brazoria Refuge is within the **Freeport Christmas Bird Count** circle, which frequently achieves the highest number of species seen in a 24-hour period. Open daily sunrise to sunset. Hunting and fishing also available. Call for details. Office: 1212 N. Velasco, #200, Angleton 77515; 979-849-6062.

Buffalo Lake (1958): Comprising 7,664 acres in the **Central Flyway** in Randall County in the Panhandle, this refuge contains some of the best remaining **shortgrass prairie** in the United States. Buffalo Lake is now dry; a **marsh area** is artificially maintained for the numerous birds, reptiles and mammals. Available activities include picnicking, auto tour, birding, photography and hiking. Office: Box 179, Umbarger 79091; 806-499-3382.

A family of whooping cranes, an endangered species, gather on an island near the Aransas National Wildlife Refuge. The refuge comprises 75,504 acres and provides wintering grounds for the cranes and many other migratory birds. File photo.

Hagerman (1946): Hagerman National Wildlife Refuge lies on the Big Mineral arm of Texoma Lake in Grayson County. The 3,000 acres of **marsh** and water and 8,000 acres of **upland and farmland** provide a feeding and resting place for migrating **waterfowl**. Bird watching, fishing and hunting are available. Office: 6465 Refuge Road, Sherman 75092-5817; 903-786-2826.

Laguna Atascosa: Established in 1946 as southernmost waterfowl refuge in the **Central Flyway**, this refuge contains more than 45,000 acres fronting on the **Laguna Madre** in the Lower Rio Grande Valley in Cameron and Willacy counties. Open **lagoons, coastal prairies, salt flats and brushlands** support a wide diversity of wildlife. The United States' largest concentration of **redhead ducks** winters here, along with many other species of **waterfowl** and **shorebirds**. White-tailed deer, javelina and armadillo can be found, along with endangered **ocelot**. Bird watching and nature study are popular; auto-tour roads and nature trails are available. Camping and fishing are permitted within Adolph Thomae Jr. County Park. Hunting also available. Office: Box 450, Rio Hondo 78583; 956-748-3607.

Lower Rio Grande Valley (1979): The U.S. Fish and Wildlife Service has acquired about half the planned acreage in the Lower Rio Grande Valley for this refuge, which will eventually include 132,500 acres within Cameron, Hidalgo, Starr and Willacy counties. The refuge will include 11 different habitat types, including **sabal palm forest, tidal flats, coastal brushland, mid-delta thorn forest, woodland potholes and basins, upland thorn scrub, flood forest, barretal, riparian woodland** and **Chihuahuan thorn forest.** Nearly 500 species of birds and over 300 butterfly species have been found there, as well as four of the five cats that occur within the United States: **jaguarundi, ocelot, bobcat** and **mountain lion**. Office: Santa Ana/Lower Rio Grande Valley National Wildlife Refuges, Rt. 2, Box 202A, Alamo 78516; 956-784-2500.

Matagorda Island: Matagorda Island is **jointly owned and managed by the U.S. Fish and Wildlife Service and the State of Texas** under an agreement reached in 1983. Please check table of **Texas Wildlife Management Areas** on next page for facilities.

McFaddin (1980): Purchased in 1980, this refuge's 55,000 acres, in Jefferson and Chambers counties, are of great importance to wintering populations of **migratory waterfowl.** One of the densest populations of **alligators** in Texas is found here. Activities on the refuge include wildlife observation, hunting, fishing and crabbing. Access best by boat; limited roadways. Office: Box 609, Sabine Pass 77655; 409-971-2909.

Muleshoe (1935): Oldest of national refuges in Texas, Muleshoe provides winter habitat for **waterfowl** and the continent's largest wintering population of **sandhill cranes**. Comprising 5,809 acres in the High Plains of Bailey County, the refuge contains three **playa lakes, marsh areas, caliche outcroppings** and **native grasslands**. A nature trail, campground and picnic area are available. Office: Box 549, Muleshoe 79347; 806-946-3341.

San Bernard (1968): Located in Brazoria and Matagorda counties on the Gulf Coast near Freeport, this refuge's 27,414 acres attract **migrating waterfowl,** including thousands of **white-fronted and Canada geese and several duck species,** which spend the winter on the refuge. Habitats, consisting of **coastal prairies, salt/mud flats and saltwater and freshwater ponds and potholes,** also attract **yellow rails, roseate spoonbills, reddish egrets** and **American bitterns.** Visitors enjoy auto and hiking trails, photography, bird watching, fishing, and waterfowl hunting in season. Office: 1212 N. Velasco, #200, Angleton, 77515; 979-849-6062.

Santa Ana (1943): Santa Ana is located on the north bank of the Rio Grande in Hidalgo County. Santa Ana's 2,088 acres of **subtropical forest** and **native brushland** are at an **ecological crossroads** of subtropical, Gulf Coast, Great Plains and Chihuahuan desert habitats. Santa Ana attracts birders from across the United States who can view many species of **Mexican birds** as they reach the northern edge of their ranges in South Texas. Also found at Santa Ana are **ocelot** and **jaguarundi,** endangered members of the cat family. Visitors enjoy a tram or auto drive, bicycling and hiking trails. Office: Rt. 2, Box 202A, Alamo 78516; 956-784-7500.

Texas Point (1980): Texas Point's 8,900 acres are located in Jefferson County on the Upper Gulf Coast, 12 miles east of McFaddin NWR, where they serve a large wintering population of **waterfowl** as well as migratory birds. The endangered **southern bald eagle** and **peregrine falcon** may occasionally be seen during peak fall and spring migrations. **Alligators** are commonly observed during the spring, summer and fall months. Activities include wildlife observation, hunting, fishing and crabbing. Access to the refuge is by boat and on foot only. Office: Box 609, Sabine Pass 77655; 409-971-2909.

Trinity River (1994): Established to protect remnant **bottomland hardwood forests** and associated **wetlands,** this refuge, located in northern Liberty County off State Highway 787 approximately 15 miles east of Cleveland, provides habitat for **wintering, migrating** and **breeding waterfowl** and a variety of other wetland-dependent wildlife. Approximately 18,300 acres of the proposed 20,000-acre refuge have been purchased. Office: Box 10015, Liberty 77575; 936-336-9786. ☆

Texas Wildlife Management Areas

Source: Texas Parks and Wildlife Department; www.tpwd.state.tx.us/wma/index.htm.

Texas Parks and Wildlife Department is currently responsible for managing 51 wildlife management areas (WMAs) totaling approximately three quarters of a million acres. Of these, 32 WMAs are owned in fee title, while 19 are managed under license agreements with other agencies.

Wildlife management areas are used principally for hunting, but many are also used for research, fishing, wildlife viewing, hiking, camping, bicycling and horseback riding, when those activities are compatible with the primary goals for which the WMA was established.

Access to WMAs at times designated for public use is provided by various permits, depending on the activity performed.

Hunting permits include Special ($50 or $100), Regular daily ($10), or Annual ($40).

A Limited Public Use Permit ($10) allows access for such activities as birdwatching, hiking, camping or picnicking and on some WMAs under the Texas Conservation Passport (Gold $50, Silver $25). The Gold Passport also allows entry to state parks.

On most WMAs, restrooms and drinking water are not provided; check with the TPWD at the contacts above before you go.

For further information, write to Texas Parks and Wildlife Department, 4200 Smith School Rd., Austin 78744; 1-800-792-1112, menu #5, selection #1. ☆

Texas Wildlife Management Areas

1. Candy Cain Abshier
2. Alabama Creek
3. Alazan Bayou
4. Angelina-Neches/Dam B
5. Aquilla
6. Atkinson Island
7. Bannister
8. Big Lake Bottom
9. Black Gap
10. Walter Buck
11. Caddo Lake State Park
12. Caddo National Grasslands
13. Cedar Creek Islands
14. Chaparral
15. Cooper
16. James E. Daughtrey
17. Elephant Mountain
18. Gus Engeling
19. Granger
20. Guadalupe Delta
21. Tony Houseman
22. Sam Houston National Forest

Gene Howe
  23. Gene Howe Unit
  24. W.A. Pat Murphy Unit
25. Keechi Creek
26. Kerr
Las Palomas
  27. Lower Rio Grande Valley Units
  28. Ocotillo Unit
29. Lower Neches
30. Mad Island

31. Mason Mountain
32. Matador
33. Matagorda Island
34. Pat Mayse
35. Moore Plantation
36. J.D. Murphree
37. The Nature Center
38. M.O. Neasloney
39. North Toledo Bend
40. Old Sabine Bottom
41. Old Tunnel
42. Peach Point

Playa Lakes
  43. Taylor Lakes Unit
  44. Dimmitt and Armstong Units
45. Redhead Pond
46. Richland Creek
47. Ray Roberts
48. Sierra Diablo
49. Somerville
50. Tawakoni
51. Welder Flats
52. White Oak Creek
53. D.R. Wintermann

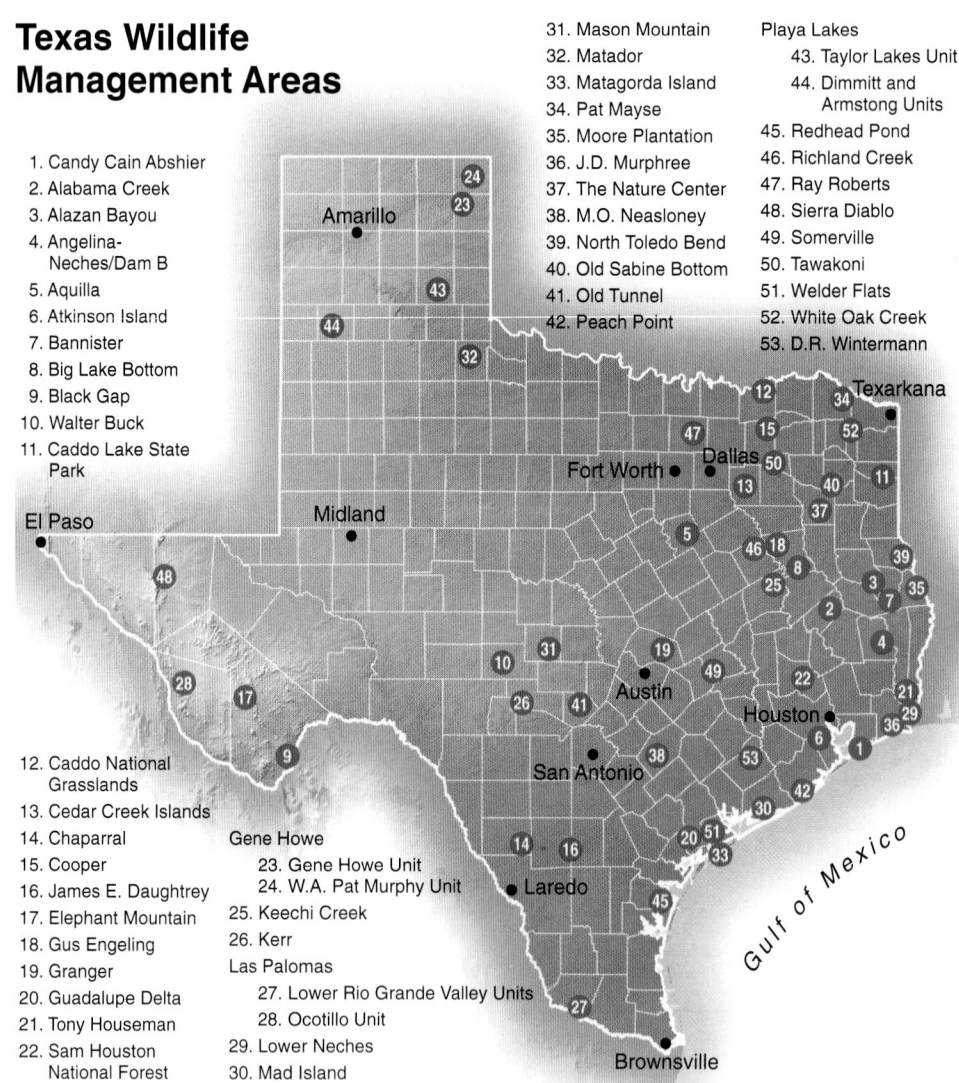

Texas Wildlife Management Areas (Acreage)	County	Day Use Only	Hunting	Fishing	Camping	Wildlife Viewing	Hiking	Interpretive Trail	Auto Tour	Bicycling	Horseback Riding	Comments
Candy Abshier (207)	CHAMBERS	★				★						Excellent birding spring and fall
Alabama Creek (14,561)	TRINITY		★	★	★	★	★		★	★	★	In Davy Crockett Nat. Forest
Alazan Bayou (2,063)	NACOGDOCHES		★	★	★	★					★	
Angelina-Neches/Dam B (12,636)	JASPER/TYLER		★	★	★	★	★		★			
Aquila (9,826)	HILL	★	★	★		★	★		★			
Atkinson Island (150)	CHAMBERS/HARRIS	★		★		★						Boat access only
Bannister (25,695)	SAN AUGUSTINE		★	★	★	★	★			★	★	In Angelina National Forest
Big Lake Bottom (4,071)	ANDERSON	★	★	★		★						2,870 acres available to public
Black Gap (119,000)	BREWSTER		★	★	★	★	★		★	★	★	NW of Big Bend National Park
Walter Buck (2,155)	KIMBLE	★	★			★	★			★		Camping at adjacent state park
Caddo Lake State Park & WMA (8,129)	MARION/HARRISON		★	★	★	★	★			★	★	
Caddo National Grasslands (16,150)	FANNIN	★	★	★	★	★					★	
Cedar Creek Islands (160)	HENDERSON	★		★		★						Access by boat only
Chaparral (15,200)	LA SALLE/DIMMIT		★		★	★	★		★	★		
Cooper (14,160)	DELTA/HOPKINS	★	★	★		★	★					Camping at nearby state park
James E. Daughtrey (4,400)	LIVE OAK/MCMULLEN	★	★			★	★					Primitive camping for hunters
Elephant Mountain (23,147)	BREWSTER		★		★	★	★		★			Primitive camping only
Gus Engling (10,958)	ANDERSON		★	★	★	★	★		★	★	★	
Granger (11,116)	WILLIAMSON		★	★	★	★	★			★		Primitive camping only
Guadalupe Delta (6,594)	CALHOUN/REFUGIO	★	★	★		★	★			★		Freshwater marsh
Tony Houseman (3,313)	ORANGE		★	★	★	★	★					
Sam Houston Natl Forest (161,508)	SAN JACINTO/WALKER		★	★	★	★	★		★	★	★	Also Montgomery County
Gene Howe (5,882)	HEMPHILL		★	★	★	★	★		★	★	★	Riding March–August only
Keechi Creek (1,500)	LEON		★									
Kerr (6,493)	KERR		★	★		★			★	★	★	On Guadalupe River
Las Palomas:												
Anacua Unit (222)	CAMERON		★			★						
Lower Rio Grande Valley Units (3,314)	CAMERON/HIDALGO	★	★			★	★					Also Starr & Willacy counties
Ocotillo Unit (2,082)	PRESIDIO		★	★	★	★	★					
Lower Neches (7,998)	ORANGE	★	★	★		★	★					Coastal marsh
Mad Island (7,200)	MATAGORDA	★	★			★						Coastal wetlands
Mason Mountain (5,301)	MASON	★	★									Restricted access
Matador (28,183)	COTTLE		★	★	★	★	★	★	★	★	★	Primitive camping
Matagorda Island (43,900)	CALHOUN		★	★	★	★	★			★		Access by boat only
Pat Mayse (8,925)	LAMAR		★	★	★	★	★			★	★	
Moore Plantation (26,519)	SABINE/JASPER		★	★	★	★	★		★	★	★	In Sabine National Forest
J.D. Murphree (24,250)	JEFFERSON	★	★	★		★						Access by boat only
The Nature Center (82)	SMITH	★				★		★				Primarily for school groups
M.O. Neasloney (100)	LULING/GONZALES	★				★	★	★				Primarily for school groups
North Toldeo Bend (3,650)	SHELBY		★	★	★	★	★				★	Limited use of horses
Old Sabine Bottom (5,158)	SMITH		★	★	★	★	★			★	★	Canoeing
Old Tunnel (16)	KENDALL	★				★	★	★				Bat-viewing April–October
Peach Point (10,311)	BRAZORIA	★	★			★	★	★		★		On Texas Coastal Birding Trail
Playa Lakes (1,492 in 3 units)	CASTRO/DONLEY	★	★			★	★					Hunting only on Donley Co. unit
Redhead Pond (37)	NUECES	★				★						Freshwater wetland
Richland Creek (13,796)	FREESTONE/NAVARRO		★	★	★	★	★		★	★	★	Primitive camping only
Ray Roberts (40,920)	COOKE/DENTON	★	★	★		★	★					Also Grayson Co.
Sierra Diablo (11,625)	HUDSPETH/CULBERSON		★									Restricted access
Somerville (3,180)	BURLESON/LEE	★	★	★		★	★			★		Camping at nearby state park
Tawakoni (2,335)	HUNT/VAN ZANDT		★	★	★	★	★			★		
Welder Flats (1,480)	CALHOUN	★		★		★						Boat access only
White Oak Creek (25,777)	BOWIE/CASS/MORRIS	★	★	★		★	★				★	Also Titus Co.
D.R. Wintermann (246)	WHARTON					★						Restricted access; bird refuge

Weather

Source: Unless otherwise noted, this information is provided by John W. Nielsen-Gammon, Texas State Climatologist; graduate assistant Andrew Odins; and undergraduate assistants Brent McRoberts and Michael Hammer, Texas A&M University, College Station.

Weather Highlights 2003

Feb. 24–26: A severe cold front brought freezing rain, sleet and snow to the North-Central region. Snow accumulations were as high as 5 inches, resulting in $15 million in damages. Most schools and businesses were closed for this period.

April 8: A severe thunderstorm caused one of the most destructive hail events in the history of Brownsville. Hail exceeded 2.75 inches in diameter and caused $50 million in damages to the city. At least 5 injuries were reported.

June 2: The outflow boundary from several severe storms led to 11 high-wind reports in southern Texas. Wind speeds topped out at 90 mph in Laredo, and more than $53 million in damages were reported. Most of the damage occurred at Laredo International Airport where 25 aircraft were damaged and a parked Boeing 737 was blown off a runway.

July 14–16: Hurricane Claudette made landfall near Port O'Connor in the late morning hours on the 14th. At landfall, wind speeds were more than 90 mph and moved westward toward Big Bend and northern Mexico. The system caused 1 death and 2 injuries, and total damages were estimated at more than $100 million.

September: Flooding was persistent during the month. The remnants of Tropical Storm Grace caused flash flooding along the Upper Coast region near Galveston at the beginning of September. Rainfall estimates in Matagorda County were 6 to 12 inches. During the second half of the month, deep south Texas was hit by a deluge of rain caused by a tropical wave combined with approaching cold fronts. Monthly rainfall totals ranged from 7 to 15 inches throughout the deep south, and damages were more than $2 million.

December: Lubbock ended 2003 with a total of 8.83 inches of precipitation for the year, the second-driest year on record. Year-end agricultural reports showed the effects of the 2003 drought, with total crop damage estimated at $240 million. It was reported that around 800,000 bales of cotton in the South Plains were lost and that the greatest damage occurred in July and August.

Climatic Data Regions of Texas

High Plains
Low Rolling Plains
Trans-Pecos
North Central
East Texas
Edwards Plateau
South Central
Southern
Upper Coast
Lower Valley

2003 Weather Extremes

Lowest Temp.: Lipscomb, Lipscomb Co., Feb. 25 . –2° F
Highest Temp.: Heath Canyon, Brewster Co., May 19 . . . . .116°F
24-hour Precip: LaPryor, Zavala Co., July 6 . . . . . .8.32"
Monthly Precip.: Freeport, Brazoria Co., Sept. . . .17.11"
Least Annual Precip.: El Paso, Hudspeth Co. . . . .4.21"
Greatest Annual Precip.: Beaumont, Jefferson Co. . . . . .64.45"

Monthly Summaries 2003

January was considerably dry across Texas as all first-order stations received below-normal precipitation. El

Average Temperatures 2003

	High Plains	Low Plains	North Central	East Texas	Trans-Pecos	Edwards Plateau	South Central	Upper Coast	South Texas	Lower Valley
Jan.	40.6	41.8	43.6	44.8	48.6	46.7	49.8	50.9	52.5	57.7
Feb.	39.6	43.2	45.8	47.9	50.6	48.5	53.0	54.7	56.5	60.9
Mar.	50.2	53.5	55.1	56.3	57.5	58.7	60.6	61.5	63.9	67.8
April	59.9	64.7	65.8	66.1	66.8	67.7	70.2	69.8	72.9	74.8
May	68.6	73.1	74.8	75.3	76.2	78.0	79.9	79.7	83.2	83.6
June	72.2	76.1	77.8	78.5	80.3	78.9	81.7	82.1	84.8	85.5
July	80.6	84.0	84.1	82.4	81.3	80.9	82.2	82.4	83.7	85.2
Aug.	80.1	84.1	84.5	83.6	81.7	82.7	84.0	83.9	85.8	86.0
Sep.	68.6	72.7	73.8	74.8	74.8	73.9	77.1	77.8	78.8	81.4
Oct.	62.4	66.2	67.6	67.8	66.4	66.9	71.0	71.6	72.1	75.6
Nov.	48.7	53.6	57.7	60.2	56.4	57.2	64.4	66.0	65.4	70.7
Dec.	41.6	46.4	48.7	48.6	46.9	48.8	54.3	54.4	56.1	61.3
Ann.	59.4	63.3	64.9	65.5	65.6	65.7	69.0	69.6	71.3	74.2

Precipitation 2003
(Inches)

	High Plains	Low Plains	North Central	East Texas	Trans-Pecos	Edwards Plateau	South Central	Upper Coast	South Texas	Lower Valley
Jan.	0.02	0.11	0.48	0.69	0.11	0.46	1.68	2.47	0.97	0.89
Feb.	0.26	0.67	3.33	6.91	1.08	1.82	3.31	3.42	2.41	1.13
Mar.	0.67	0.75	1.17	1.99	0.38	1.19	1.66	1.64	1.38	1.27
April	0.59	1.50	1.33	1.54	0.08	0.22	0.34	0.88	0.52	1.44
May	1.40	1.97	2.82	2.05	0.66	2.23	0.43	0.04	0.33	0.40
June	5.07	6.52	5.42	6.11	1.89	3.96	3.77	6.07	3.38	2.10
July	0.31	0.12	0.76	3.16	2.00	2.92	5.16	6.58	5.46	2.04
Aug.	1.47	1.98	2.52	2.82	1.51	2.39	1.71	4.26	1.08	2.61
Sep.	1.62	1.47	3.70	4.15	0.95	3.95	7.54	9.58	8.00	9.76
Oct.	0.85	1.31	2.52	2.61	2.41	3.54	2.57	5.02	5.72	6.77
Nov.	0.44	1.04	1.94	3.90	0.25	0.81	1.52	4.04	1.07	1.29
Dec.	0.07	0.02	0.71	2.70	0.00	0.07	0.90	3.42	0.24	0.10
Ann.	12.77	17.46	26.70	38.63	11.32	23.56	30.59	47.42	30.56	29.80

Paso, Wichita Falls and Amarillo received only a trace of precipitation. Temperatures fluctuated often during the month, as well. Several arctic air masses moved over Texas, cooling the state for a few days before moderating once again with the eastward shift in high pressure. Half of the first-order stations reached a maximum of 80 degrees, and only Brownsville failed to drop below freezing during the month.

February was very cold, and all stations received below-normal temperatures. The largest deviation was in Austin, where the temperature was 5.9 degrees below normal. Several frontal systems kept temperatures fluctuating from normal levels to below normal throughout the month.

An arctic frontal system brought heavy rains to Central Texas on the 20th, and College Station set a new 24-hour record for February with 4.20 inches of precipitation on that day. Both El Paso and College Station received over 300 percent of their normal monthly precipitation. Another cold front Feb. 24–26 brought snow and ice to the Dallas-Fort Worth Metroplex, causing around $15 million in damage.

Cool, dry weather characterized **March.** Austin had the most extreme departure from normal for the second consecutive month, this time at 5.7 degrees below normal. Amarillo, Del Rio, Lubbock, Midland, Port Arthur and San Angelo were the exceptions with temperatures slightly above normal for the month. Precipitation also was sparse around the state, and San Angelo was the only station with above-normal precipitation for the month.

There was a dramatic change in temperature in **April,** as all state weather stations had above-normal temperatures coupled with below-normal precipitation. Despite all stations failing to reach 2 inches of precipitation for the month, there was an abundance of severe weather.

Because of several cold fronts, tornadoes and large hail were reported on April 5, 6, 15, 23 and 29, including six tornadoes in the Panhandle on the 15th. Temperatures were extremely warm with 13 stations topping 90 degrees, and monthly averages were at least 0.5 degrees above normal.

The warming trend continued in **May,** and most of Texas was under moderate drought conditions, according to the U.S. Drought Monitor. Del Rio, Midland and Wichita Falls had above-normal precipitation for May, but all other stations were significantly below normal, including Corpus Christi, El Paso, Galveston, Houston, Port Arthur and Victoria, which had less than 0.10 inches of rain for the month. Severe weather also continued with large hail, high wind or tornado reports occurring on 19 out of 31 days. On the 15th, there were 18 tornadoes reported across the state.

June was much cooler than previous months, and the dry conditions ended as only five weather stations failed to reach normal precipitation for the month. Only three stations (El Paso, Lubbock and Midland) topped 100 degrees, and all stations north of the line from Houston to Del Rio had significantly below-normal temperatures.

July was divided as stations to the north received warm, extremely dry conditions while stations in the south had below-normal temperatures and heavy rainfall. Five stations (Abilene, Amarillo, Dallas, Lubbock and Wichita

Beach-goers continue to have fun in the surf as Tropical Storm Erika reaches the South Texas Coast on Friday, Aug. 15, 2003. File photo.

Falls) received less than 0.10 inches of rain, and they all had temperatures at least 1 degree above normal.

Stations in Central and South Texas ranged from 0.5 degrees to 2.8 degrees below normal. The story of the month was the landfall of Hurricane Claudette on the 15th. There were unofficial reports of winds as high as 100 mph, and Corpus Christi, Victoria, Del Rio and San Antonio received copious amounts of rain. San Antonio received the most, with 8.12 inches of rain (400 percent of its normal for the month).

In **August,** most of Texas saw typical summer weather with warm temperatures and little rainfall. The exceptions were stations in Central Texas, which had cooler temperatures and wet conditions because of thunderstorms and the remnants of Tropical Storm Grace.

September featured much cooler, wet conditions because of several cold fronts. The Trans-Pecos and High Plains regions were still very dry, but 13 of the 19 first-order stations received above-normal precipitation. As the cold fronts passed over the state bringing rain and cooler temperatures to the north, they stalled out and became stationary over the southern and coastal regions. Brownsville and Corpus Christi topped 10 inches of rain during the month, while Port Arthur and San Antonio each received 9 inches.

October began with warm temperatures and an abundance of severe weather. All but three weather stations reported above-normal temperatures. During the first 10 days of the month, two stationary fronts caused much severe weather.

Tornadoes were reported across the state every day between the Oct. 5 and 10, with several reports of large hail and high wind. The storms caused heavy rainfall in Brownsville, College Station, Del Rio and Port Arthur, and all four weather stations recorded between 160 percent

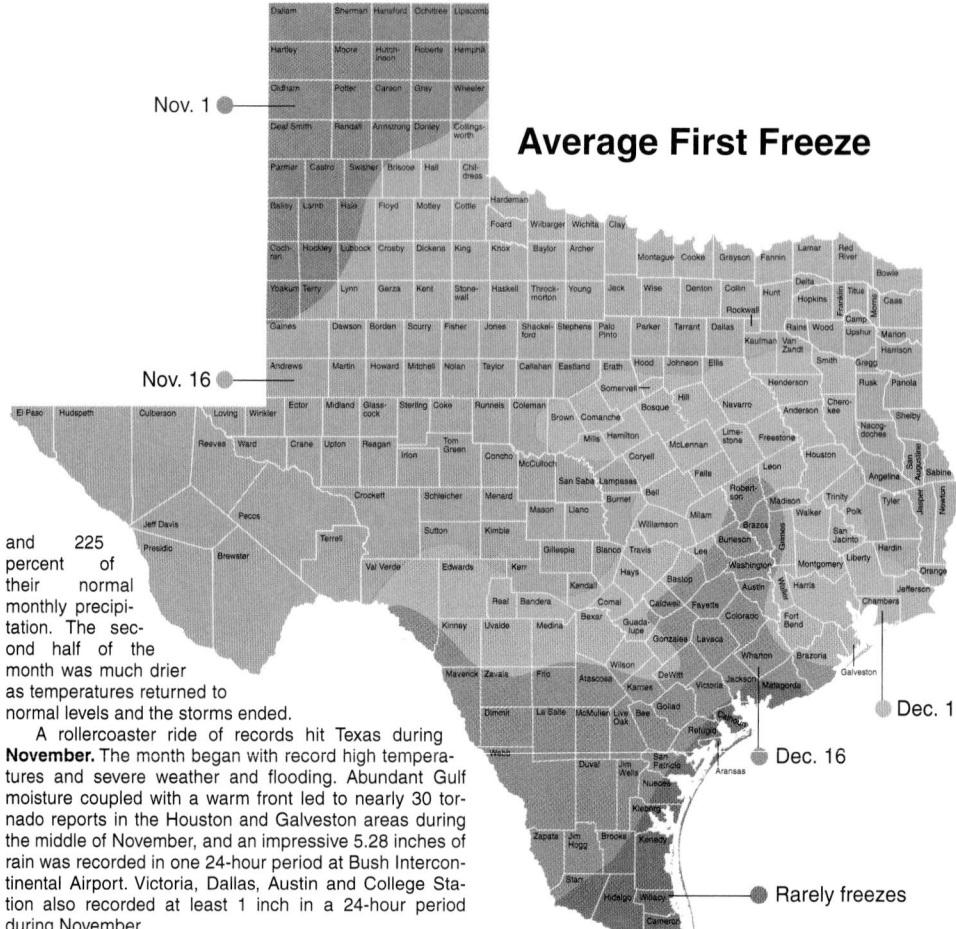

Average First Freeze

Nov. 1

Nov. 16

Dec. 1

Dec. 16

Rarely freezes

and 225 percent of their normal monthly precipitation. The second half of the month was much drier as temperatures returned to normal levels and the storms ended.

A rollercoaster ride of records hit Texas during **November.** The month began with record high temperatures and severe weather and flooding. Abundant Gulf moisture coupled with a warm front led to nearly 30 tornado reports in the Houston and Galveston areas during the middle of November, and an impressive 5.28 inches of rain was recorded in one 24-hour period at Bush Intercontinental Airport. Victoria, Dallas, Austin and College Station also recorded at least 1 inch in a 24-hour period during November.

Outside of these stations, however, most of the state experienced much drier than normal conditions. With the exception of Dallas, all first-order stations had above-normal temperatures despite a strong cold front at the end of the month, when 16 stations dropped below freezing.

December ended 2003 with above-normal temperatures and very little precipitation. With the exception of the Gulf Coast, temperatures ranged from 1 degree to 5 degrees above normal for December. Only Galveston recorded above-normal precipitation in the month, and five stations (Abilene, El Paso, Lubbock, Midland and San Angelo) had less than 1 percent of their average rainfall for the month. Lubbock ended 2003 with 8.83 inches of precipitation for the year, the second-driest year on record.

Weather Highlights 2004

June 1–9: Flash flooding because of an upper air disturbance and associated cold front caused damage to more than 1,000 homes across North-Central Texas. This was the first of many days in which heavy rains fell throughout the state. Estimated damages were more than $7.5 million.

June 21: Severe weather kicked up just ahead of a frontal boundary causing much damage to Amarillo and the surrounding area. Eight tornadoes were reported throughout the Panhandle, and there were many reports of hail topping out at 4.25 inches in diameter in Potter County. Thousands of homes were damaged, and the total damage was estimated at more than $150 million.

July 28–29: A stationary front lead to torrential rainfall

in Dallas and Waco. Hundreds of homes were damaged by flash flooding as 24-hour rainfall totals for the two cities neared 5 inches. Outlying areas of the cities reported as much as 7 inches of rain in a 12-hour period on the 29th. Damage estimates topped $20 million.

Sept. 14: A lightning strike during football practice at Grapeland High School caused injuries to 40 players and coaches. One player died the following day as a result of his injuries.

Dec. 24–26: Large portions of Southeast Texas saw their first white Christmas in recorded history. A cold front past over the state a few days prior to Christmas Eve dropping temperatures below freezing. Another cold front brought snow to the area, and it accumulated throughout Christmas Eve night and into Christmas day. Galveston and Houston recorded 4 inches of snow, while areas farther south, such as Victoria, had 12 inches.

2004 Weather Extremes

Lowest Temp.: Lipscomb, Lipscomb Co., Jan. 6 . . −6° F
Highest Temp.: Heath Canyon, Brewster Co.,
June 3 . . . . .114°F
24-hour Precip: Joe Pool Lake, Dallas Co., July 29
. . . . .12.05"
Monthly Precip.: El Campo, Wharton Co., Nov. . .25.43"
Least Annual Precip.: El Paso, El Paso Co. . . . . .11.73"
Greatest Annual Precip.: Houston Heights, Harris Co.
. . . . .81.13"

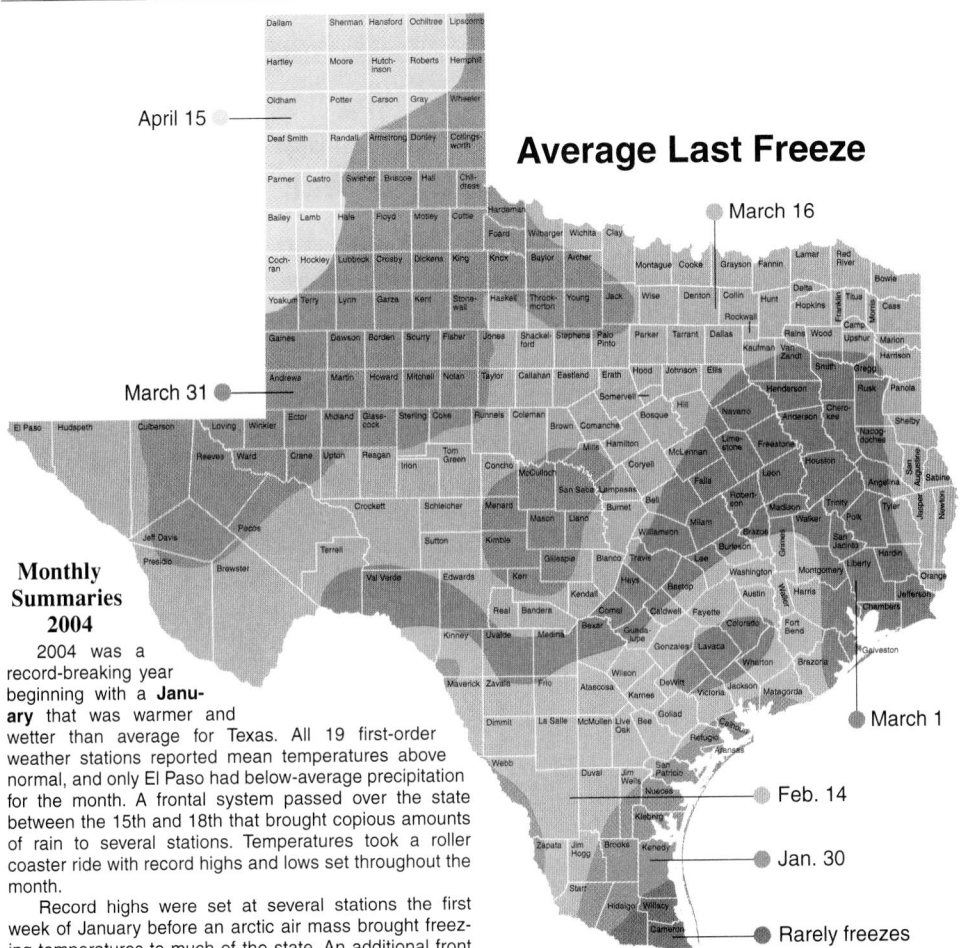

Average Last Freeze

April 15

March 31

March 16

March 1

Feb. 14

Jan. 30

Rarely freezes

Monthly Summaries 2004

2004 was a record-breaking year beginning with a **January** that was warmer and wetter than average for Texas. All 19 first-order weather stations reported mean temperatures above normal, and only El Paso had below-average precipitation for the month. A frontal system passed over the state between the 15th and 18th that brought copious amounts of rain to several stations. Temperatures took a roller coaster ride with record highs and lows set throughout the month.

Record highs were set at several stations the first week of January before an arctic air mass brought freezing temperatures to much of the state. An additional front at the end of the month brought colder temperatures to most of the state as well as more precipitation in the Eastern and Upper Coastal regions. College Station, Houston, Galveston and Port Arthur all received more than 1.5 inches of rain from this system. January concluded with below-average temperatures around most of the state, although monthly averages were 1–5 degrees above normal.

February was characterized by cold and wet weather. Nine first-order stations received more than 10 days of

measurable precipitation, and only Brownsville, Del Rio, El Paso and San Antonio had below-normal precipitation for the month. The month began with a series of cold fronts that soaked south and east Texas. They were followed by an arctic air mass that blanketed the Panhandle and West Texas regions on the 12th.

During the next week of February, temperatures across the state dropped into the 10s, 20s and 30s while

Average Temperatures 2004

	High Plains	Low Plains	North Central	East Texas	Trans-Pecos	Edwards Plateau	South Central	Upper Coast	South Texas	Lower Valley
Jan.	40.1	44.3	48.0	48.8	47.8	49.1	54.8	55.1	56.5	61.3
Feb.	39.1	42.6	44.6	46.2	47.7	47.4	52.6	53.4	56.3	61.0
Mar.	53.6	58.1	61.0	62.3	60.5	61.8	66.8	66.6	68.6	71.9
April	57.2	62.3	64.9	65.9	64.1	63.8	68.1	68.8	69.8	73.4
May	70.1	73.4	73.2	74.1	74.9	73.6	75.3	75.6	77.1	78.4
June	74.9	77.3	77.9	78.4	80.2	79.1	80.3	80.7	83.1	84.1
July	76.6	80.7	81.2	81.3	80.7	80.6	82.3	83.0	84.1	85.6
Aug.	74.3	78.3	79.3	80.2	78.3	79.6	82.6	82.4	84.7	86.0
Sep.	69.5	74.2	76.0	77.0	72.9	74.7	79.6	80.5	80.1	81.8
Oct.	59.7	65.5	70.2	72.9	66.3	70.2	76.6	76.8	78.5	80.6
Nov.	45.2	51.5	56.3	58.4	51.2	55.7	62.7	63.6	65.0	70.6
Dec.	41.1	45.9	48.5	51.1	45.3	50.5	53.2	56.7	56.2	61.4
Ann.	58.5	62.8	65.1	66.4	64.2	65.5	69.6	70.3	71.7	74.7

Precipitation 2004

(Inches)

	High Plains	Low Plains	North Central	East Texas	Trans-Pecos	Edwards Plateau	South Central	Upper Coast	South Texas	Lower Valley
Jan.	1.11	1.73	2.41	3.93	1.03	1.86	3.16	5.03	1.58	1.40
Feb.	1.66	2.63	4.49	6.71	0.49	1.87	2.99	5.28	1.65	0.86
Mar.	1.97	2.45	1.85	3.37	1.83	2.89	2.15	2.02	2.40	2.48
April	3.01	3.11	4.82	4.42	1.80	4.61	6.20	4.55	5.06	3.40
May	0.36	0.77	2.59	6.11	0.57	1.53	4.32	8.70	2.44	2.22
June	4.60	5.77	8.84	9.29	1.93	5.92	9.01	12.25	5.76	5.18
July	2.78	3.63	3.32	1.83	2.91	1.47	1.90	2.56	1.28	0.43
Aug.	3.34	3.59	3.20	3.36	3.12	3.97	2.29	2.21	3.03	1.97
Sep.	4.71	1.23	0.90	1.53	3.63	2.22	2.44	2.00	3.25	4.60
Oct.	3.07	4.22	5.47	5.36	1.96	5.09	4.89	5.17	2.05	1.96
Nov.	4.93	6.69	7.63	9.22	3.07	6.36	8.54	12.55	3.58	1.24
Dec.	0.28	0.55	0.63	1.98	0.22	0.51	0.18	1.56	0.17	1.11
Ann.	31.82	36.37	46.15	57.11	22.56	38.30	48.07	63.88	32.25	26.85

In inches:

- Under 14
- 14–18
- 18–22
- 22–26
- 26–30
- 30–34
- 34–38
- 38–42
- 42–46
- 46–50
- 50–54
- Above 54

Average Annual Precipitation

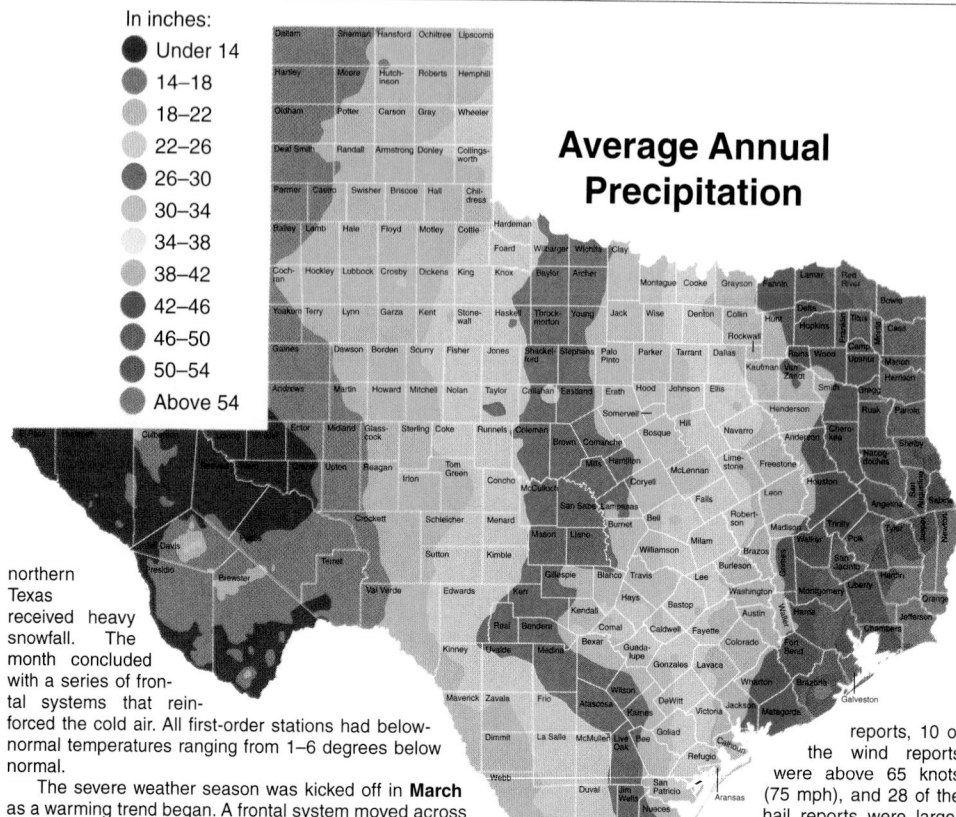

northern Texas received heavy snowfall. The month concluded with a series of frontal systems that reinforced the cold air. All first-order stations had below-normal temperatures ranging from 1–6 degrees below normal.

The severe weather season was kicked off in **March** as a warming trend began. A frontal system moved across the state and caused severe weather. There were 20 tornadoes, 24 large-hail occurrences, and more than 100 high-wind reports in Texas during the first week. Winds reached speeds of 91 mph in Wichita Falls and 80 mph south of Dallas-Fort Worth. A cloudy, warm week followed the outbreak of severe weather as the passage of two more cold fronts brought much needed rain to many stations. Thunderstorms developed late in the week along a boundary in West Texas leading to eight reports of large hail in the Trans-Pecos region.

More severe weather popped up across the northern part of the state during the third week. The month concluded with clear skies and warm temperatures. All first-order stations had mean temperatures over 2 degrees above normal. West and South Texas benefited from the heavy rainfall as Brownsville, El Paso, Midland and Del Rio had over 300 percent of their average precipitation.

April was a very wet month. Temperatures in West Texas were about a degree below normal, while temperatures in most of East Texas were a little above normal. Precipitation was above normal for 15 of the 19 first-order stations, with impressive totals in Corpus Christi and El Paso, which both received over 400 percent of their average April rainfall. Severe weather was very prominent across the state, as well.

During the first two weeks, low-pressure systems slowly made their way across the state, dropping large hail throughout Texas and causing several tornadoes in the south. A high-pressure system in the middle of the month brought the first 90-degree temperatures of the year. A low-pressure system brought heavy rainfall to the state during the third week, and Corpus Christi shattered a record with 6.18 inches of rain on the 25th.

For the entire month of April, there were 17 tornadoes reported, 46 wind reports and 290 hail reports. Of those reports, 10 of the wind reports were above 65 knots (75 mph), and 28 of the hail reports were larger than 2 inches in diameter.

May was warm and dry in the northern half of Texas, while the southern portion was rather wet and had below-normal temperatures. The first week was warm and dry, with average temperatures across the state. Beginning on the 8th, scattered showers brought some rain, which cooled temperatures throughout the southern, Upper Coast and eastern regions.

On the 13th, heavy rains fell, and flooding occurred in many parts of the state. The city of Hearne in Robertson County saw 17.5 inches of rain fall in a 9-hour period, and two dams within the county broke. Seven of the first-order stations had their first 100-degree weather for the year. A weak cold front passed over the state at the end of May, but temperatures remained in the 90s for most of the state.

Texas saw record-breaking rainfall in **June.** During the first week, the tail-end of a slow-moving frontal boundary brought heavy rain to much of the state, and an upper-level disturbance caused flooding problems throughout East and Central Texas on the 8th through the 10th. There were also many reports of large hail, and several tornadoes were spotted in southern Texas.

A low-pressure system moved onshore over Louisiana on the June 13, adding to already large rainfall totals. In one week, Houston received 7.23 inches, and several other stations were hit hard, as well. A series of frontal boundaries brought severe weather to the Panhandle in the second half of June. Hail as large as 4.25 inches in diameter was reported, and damage estimates soared over $100 million.

During the last week of June, a subtropical jet brought

more moist air to the state causing flooding and heavy rain. The already high rainfall totals surged higher, breaking many records for June precipitation. Victoria set a new June record for monthly precipitation (13.50 inches), and there were several near-records for monthly rainfall totals including: Austin (4th wettest June), College Station (2nd), Dallas-Fort Worth (2nd), Galveston (8th), Houston (2nd), San Antonio (3rd) and Waco (5th).

Austin, College Station, Dallas-Fort Worth, Galveston, Houston and Victoria all recorded more than 10 inches of rain and had over 250 percent of their normal June precipitation. Several stations were within 3 inches of their annual normal rainfall at the year's midpoint. Excess precipitation cooled temperatures throughout much of the state. The Panhandle and most of Central and East Texas were well below their average daily temperatures for June.

Texas was split during **July** as the Gulf Coast experienced warm, dry weather, and the remainder of the state was wet and colder than normal. The first week of the month saw a series of frontal systems that brought rain and severe weather to Texas. A high-pressure system followed, and temperatures soared as a result. The stretch of dry, warm weather continued until the end of the third week, when a shortwave trough moved across the northern part of the state. Temperatures dropped as a cold front slowly trekked eastward.

A stationary front over North-Central Texas at the end of July produced heavy rains in many counties. Dallas (4.14 inches) and Waco (4.94 inches) nearly doubled their normal monthly precipitation on the 28th and 29th. For the month, all but four first-order stations had below-normal temperatures, with the coldest averages in the north and central portions of the state. South, East and South-Central Texas all experienced a very dry July, with the exception of Victoria.

August 2004 was much cooler than normal, while precipitation varied from extremely dry at some stations to well above normal at others. The month began extremely warm as a high-pressure system sat over the state. A few cold fronts passed over Texas bringing several reports of severe weather to the Panhandle and West Texas. The middle of August was very cool and dry until a shortwave trough triggered heavy storms across large parts of Texas, followed by another cold front that trekked across the state bringing severe storms with it.

August ended with another cold front that brought heavy rain to North Texas. For the month, all first-order stations except for Brownsville and Corpus Christi had below-normal mean temperatures. The majority of the state had below-normal precipitation, but those that were above normal were well above. San Angelo, Wichita Falls and Dallas received 200 percent of their average August precipitation. The Upper Coast was extremely dry and well below August normals, such as in Port Arthur (29 percent), Galveston (18 percent) and Corpus Christi (5 percent).

Texas experienced an abnormal **September** in many ways. The month began with a continuation of the cool, dry weather that characterized August. A high-pressure system settled over the state after the first week of the month, and the weather was warm and dry for more than a week. A few scattered showers appeared during the end of the second week of September, but little else occurred until the third week. Showers began to soak most of West Texas beginning on the 20th due to a low-pressure system in the southwestern United States.

A frontal system that began to move over the state on the Sept. 22 became stationary and dropped copious amounts of rain in the Panhandle. In addition, an event with little precedence occurred — the remnants of Hurricane Ivan curved back into the Gulf and intensified back to tropical-storm strength. The storm hit land again just east of Port Arthur and moved parallel to the coast bringing rain to Port Arthur and Corpus Christi. For the month, the western half of Texas was wet and cool, while the eastern half received little rainfall and hot temperatures. Five stations

Meteorological Data

Source: Updated as of July 2005 by the National Climatic Data Center. Additional data for these locations are listed by county in the table of Texas temperature, freeze, growing season and precipitation records.

City	Temperature						Precipitation							Relative Humidity		Wind			Sun
	Record High	Month & Year	Record Low	Month & Year	No. Days Max. 90° and Above	No. Days Min. 32° and Below	Maximum in 24 Hours	Month & Year	Snowfall (Mean Annual)	Max. Snowfall in 24 Hours	Month & Year	6:00 a.m., CST	Noon, CST	Speed, MPH (Mean Annual)	Highest MPH	Month & Year	Percent Possible Sunshine
Abilene	110	7/1978	-9	1/1947	96	50	6.70	9/1961	4.6	9.3	4/1996	74	52	11.9	55	4/1998	70
Amarillo	108	6/1990	-14	2/1951	64	111	6.75	5/1951	16.2	20.6	3/1934	73	48	13.5	60	6/1994	74
Austin	112	9/2000	-2	1/1949	108	19	15.00	9/1921	0.9	9.7	11/1937	83	59	9.0	52	9/1987	60
Brownsville	106	3/1984	16	12/1989	121	2	12.19	9/1967	**	0.0		89	63	11.3	59	5/1999	59
Corpus Christi	109	9/2000	13	12/1989	106	5	8.92	8/1980	**	1.1	2/1973	89	65	12.0	56	5/1999	60
Dallas-Fort Worth	113	6/1980	-1	12/1989	97	37	5.91	10/1959	3.2	12.1	1/1964	81	58	10.7	73	8/1959	61
Del Rio	112	6/1988	10	12/1989	129	16	11.87	8/1998	0.9	8.6	1/1985	77	58	9.7	60	8/1970	84
El Paso	114	7/1994	-8	1/1962	108	60	2.63	7/1968	5.4	22.4	12/1987	56	28	8.8	64	1/1996	84
Galveston	104	9/2000	8	2/1999	12	3	14.35	7/2000	0.2	15.4	2/1895	83	72	11.0	*100	9/1900	59
†Houston	109	9/2000	7	12/1989	99	18	11.02	6/2001	0.4	2.0	1/1973	90	63	7.7	51	8/1983	72
Lubbock	114	6/1994	-16	1/1963	81	92	5.82	10/1983	10.1	16.3	1/1983	73	48	12.4	70	3/1952	72
Midland-Odessa	116	6/1994	-11	2/1985	100	63	5.99	7/1961	4.5	9.8	12/1998	73	45	11.1	67	2/1960	74
Prt. Arthur-Beaumont	108	8/2000	12	12/1989	83	14	17.76	7/1943	0.3	4.4	2/1960	91	66	9.6	65	6/1986	60
San Angelo	111	‡7/1960	-4	12/1989	109	52	6.25	9/1980	3.1	7.4	1/1978	77	52	10.3	75	4/1969	70
San Antonio	111	9/2000	0	1/1949	113	21	13.35	10/1998	0.7	13.2	1/1985	83	57	9.1	48	7/1979	60
Victoria	111	9/2000	9	12/1989	106	10	9.87	4/1991	0.1	2.1	1/1985	90	63	9.9	99	7/1961	49
Waco	112	8/1969	-5	1/1949	109	33	7.98	12/1997	1.4	7.0	1/1949	84	59	11.1	69	6/1961	59
Wichita Falls	117	6/1980	-8	2/1985	104	64	6.19	12/1980	5.8	9.8	1/1925	81	53	11.6	62	6/1954	60
§Shreveport, LA	109	‡8/2000	3	1/1962	90	35	12.44	7/1933	1.5	11	12/1929	87	61	8.3	63	5/2000	64

*100 mph recorded at 6:15 p.m., Sept. 8, 1900, just before the anemometer blew away. Maximum velocity was estimated to be 120 mph from the northeast between 7:30 p.m. and 8:30 p.m.

†The official Houston station was moved from near downtown to Intercontinental Airport, 12 miles north of the old station.

‡ Also recorded on earlier dates, months or years.

§Shreveport is included because it is near the boundary line and its data can be considered representative of Texas' east border.

**Trace, an amount too small to measure.

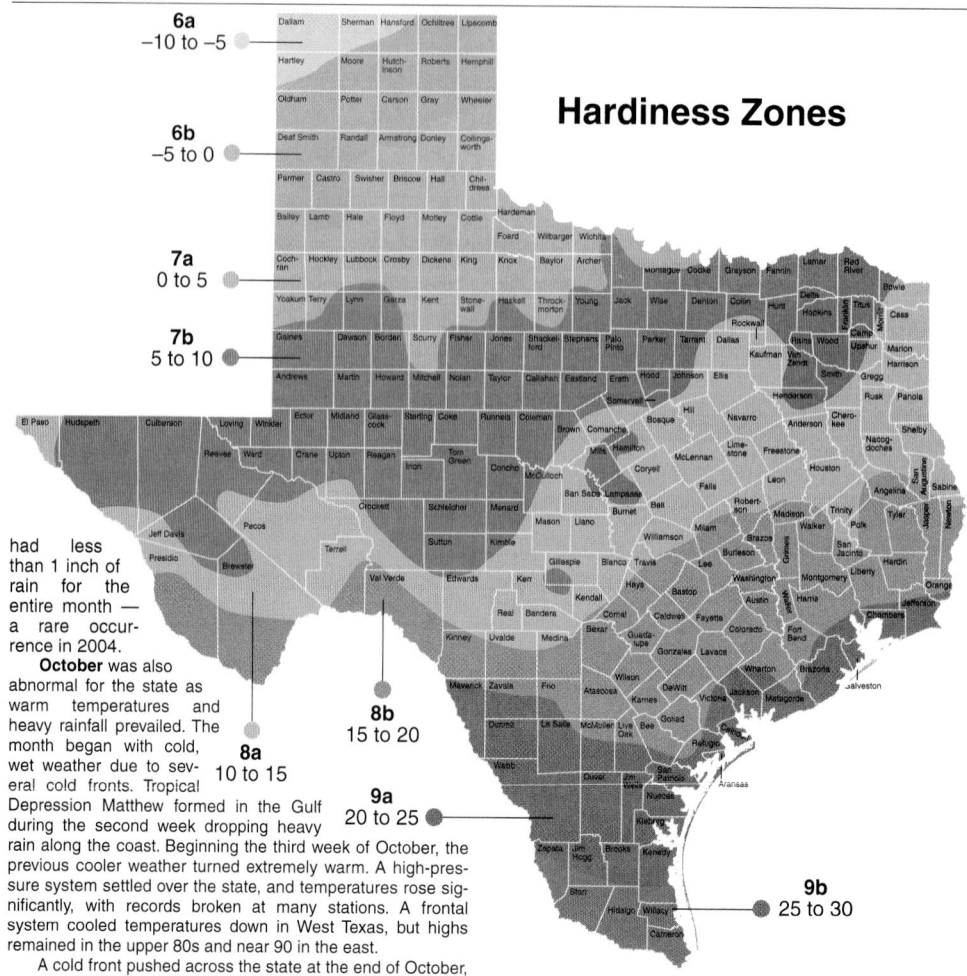

Hardiness Zones

6a −10 to −5

6b −5 to 0

7a 0 to 5

7b 5 to 10

8a 10 to 15

8b 15 to 20

9a 20 to 25

9b 25 to 30

had less than 1 inch of rain for the entire month — a rare occurrence in 2004.

October was also abnormal for the state as warm temperatures and heavy rainfall prevailed. The month began with cold, wet weather due to several cold fronts. Tropical Depression Matthew formed in the Gulf during the second week dropping heavy rain along the coast. Beginning the third week of October, the previous cooler weather turned extremely warm. A high-pressure system settled over the state, and temperatures rose significantly, with records broken at many stations. A frontal system cooled temperatures down in West Texas, but highs remained in the upper 80s and near 90 in the east.

A cold front pushed across the state at the end of October, but stalled in Central Texas, bringing many showers. Every first-order station in the state had above-normal temperatures for October, and several set records: Brownsville, College Station, Corpus Christi, Galveston and Houston all had their warmest Octobers ever. Average monthly temperatures ranged from 1–7 degrees above normal, with the largest deviations in southeast Texas.

November 2004 was one of the wettest Novembers in Texas history. The month began with a cold front crossing the state, causing heavy rain over many stations and snow in the Panhandle. Following the frontal passage, temperatures remained well below normal for a few days. A dry stretch promptly ended during the third week of the month as an upper-level, low-pressure system moved into Texas from northern Mexico. Austin had 5.03 inches of rain in just two days, while San Antonio, Midland, Lubbock, Abilene, Del Rio, San Angelo and Houston all received at least 3 inches during the same period.

A few days later, two frontal systems stalled across the state, leading to several more days of rain for the eastern half of Texas. Victoria received 6.94 inches on the 20th alone. A lot of severe weather was a result of these frontal systems, too, with 55 reports of large hail and 32 reports of tornadoes across the state.

November ended with another cold front that hit the state and lowered temperatures below freezing. Several new and near precipitation records were set for the month: Austin, Del Rio, Lubbock, Midland, San Antonio, Victoria and Wichita Falls all set new monthly precipitation records. Six other stations had near monthly records. Three cities had at least six times their

normal November precipitation: Lubbock (937 percent), Midland (834 percent) and Victoria (611 percent). Every first-order station, except Corpus Christi, received at least 195 percent of their normal November rainfall.

Unlike the rest of 2004, **December** was much drier than normal. Despite some arctic air at the end of the month, a large portion of the state had above-average temperatures. The month began cool and dry until a cold front during the second week of the month, when lows in the western half of Texas dropped to the 20s and 10s. A high-pressure system warmed temperatures over their normals once again, but a large trough brought a mass of arctic air over the state late in the month. High temperatures dropped from the 60s and 70s to the 20s and 30s.

A low-pressure system brought heavy snow to much of the state, giving many people a **white Christmas.** The month ended with another warm up as highs reached near 80 in the south. For the month, only Lubbock and Brownsville were above normal for precipitation. Temperatures were below normal across the entire southern half of the state with the exception of San Antonio. Temperatures in the northern half was well above normal for the month of December.

For 2004, every first-order station received above-normal precipitation. Victoria was the only station to break its record for wettest year ever, but several other stations came close: Abilene (4th wettest year), Amarillo (9th), Austin (3rd), College Station (3rd), Dallas-Fort Worth (5th), Del Rio (4th), Houston (6th), Lubbock (2nd), Midland (6th), San Antonio (6th), Waco (2nd) and Wichita Falls (5th) ☆

Destructive Weather

Source: This list of exceptionally destructive weather in Texas since 1766 was compiled from ESSA-Weather Bureau information.

Sept. 4, 1766: Hurricane. Galveston Bay. A Spanish mission destroyed.

Sept. 12, 1818: Hurricane. Galveston Island. Salt water flowed four feet deep. Only six buildings remained habitable. Of the six vessels and two barges in the harbor, even the two not seriously damaged were reduced to dismasted hulks. **Pirate Jean Lafitte** moved to one hulk so his **Red House** might serve as a hospital.

Aug. 6, 1844: Hurricane. Mouth of Rio Grande. All houses destroyed at the mouth of the river and at **Brazos Santiago,** eight miles north; 70 lives lost.

Sept. 19, 1854: Hurricane. It struck near **Matagorda,** and moved inland, northwestward over **Columbus.** Main impact fell in **Matagorda and Lavaca bays.** Almost all buildings in Matagorda were destroyed. Four lives were lost in town; more lives were lost on the peninsula.

Oct. 3, 1867: Hurricane. This hurricane moved inland **south of Galveston,** but raked the entire Texas coast **from the Rio Grande to the Sabine. Bagdad and Clarksville,** towns at the mouth of the Rio Grande, were destroyed. Much of Galveston was flooded and property damage there was estimated at $1 million.

Sept. 16, 1875: Hurricane. Struck **Indianola,** Calhoun County. Three-fourths of town swept away; 176 lives lost. Flooding from the bay caused nearly all destruction.

Aug. 13, 1880: Hurricane. Center struck **Matamoros, Mexico; lower Texas coast** affected.

Oct. 12–13, 1880: Hurricane. Brownsville. City nearly destroyed, many lives lost.

Aug. 23–24, 1882: Torrential rains caused **flooding** on the **North and South Concho and Bosque rivers** (South Concho reported 45 feet above normal level), destroying **Benficklen,** then county seat of Tom Green County, leaving only the courthouse and jail. More than 50 persons drowned in **Tom Green and Erath counties,** with property damage at $200,000 and 10,000 to 15,000 head of livestock lost.

Aug. 19–21, 1886: Hurricane. Indianola. Every house destroyed or damaged. Indianola was never rebuilt.

Oct. 12, 1886: Hurricane. Sabine, Jefferson County. Hurricane passed over Sabine. The inundation extended 20 miles inland and nearly every house in the vicinity was moved from its foundation; 150 persons were drowned.

April 28, 1893: Tornado. Cisco, Eastland County; 23

Texas Is Tornado Capital

An average of 132 tornadoes touch Texas soil each year. The annual total varies considerably, and certain areas are struck more often than others. Tornadoes occur with greatest frequency in the Red River Valley of North Texas.

Tornadoes may occur in any month and at any hour of the day, but they occur with greatest frequency during the late spring and early summer months, and between the hours of 4 p.m. and 8 p.m. In the period 1959–2004, nearly 63 percent of all Texas tornadoes occurred within the three-month period of April, May and June, with almost one-third of the total tornadoes occurring in May.

More tornadoes have been recorded in Texas than in any other state, which is partly due to the state's size. Between 1959 and 2004, 7,092 funnel clouds reached the ground, thus becoming tornadoes. Texas ranks 11th among the 50 states in the density of tornadoes, with an average of 5.7 tornadoes per 10,000 square miles per year during this period.

The greatest outbreak of tornadoes on record in Texas was associated with Hurricane Beulah in September 1967. Within a five-day period, Sept. 19–23, 115 known tornadoes, all in Texas, were spawned by this great hurricane. Sixty-seven occurred on Sept. 20, a Texas record for a single day.

In addition to Hurricane Beulah's 115 tornadoes, there were another 9 tornadoes in September for a total of 124, which is a Texas record for a single month. The greatest number of tornadoes in Texas in a single year is 232, also in 1967. The second-highest number in a single year is 1995, when 223 tornadoes occurred in Texas. In 1982, 123 tornadoes formed in May, making it the worst outbreak of spring tornadoes in Texas.

The accompanying table, compiled by the National Climatic Data Center, Environmental Data Service and the National Oceanic and Atmospheric Administration, lists tornado occurrences in Texas, by months, for the period 1951–2004.

Number of Tornadoes in Texas, 1959–2004

Source: Office of State Climatologist

Year	Jan.	Feb.	March	April	May	June	July	Aug.	Sept.	Oct.	Nov.	Dec.	Annual
1959	0	0	8	4	32	14	10	3	5	6	0		86
1960	4	1	0	8	29	14	3	4	2	11	1	0	77
1961	0	1	21	15	24	30	9	2	12	0	10	0	124
1962	0	4	12	9	25	56	12	15	7	2	0	1	143
1963	0	0	3	9	19	24	8	4	6	4	5	0	82
1964	0	1	6	22	15	11	9	7	3	1	3	0	78
1965	2	5	3	7	43	24	2	9	4	6	0	3	108
1966	0	4	1	21	22	15	3	8	3	0	0	0	77
1967	0	2	11	17	34	22	10	5	124	2	0	5	232
1968	2	1	3	13	47	21	4	8	5	8	11	16	139
1969	0	1	1	16	65	16	6	7	6	8	1	0	127
1970	1	3	5	23	23	9	5	20	9	20	0	3	121
1971	0	20	10	24	27	33	7	20	7	16	4	23	191
1972	1	0	19	13	43	12	19	13	8	9	7	0	144
1973	14	1	29	25	21	24	4	8	5	3	9	4	147
1974	2	1	8	19	18	26	3	9	6	22	2	0	116
1975	5	2	9	12	50	18	10	3	3	3	1	1	117
1976	1	1	8	53	63	11	16	6	13	4	0	0	176
1977	0	0	3	34	50	4	5	5	12	0	6	4	123
1978	0	0	0	34	65	10	13	6	6	1	2	0	137
1979	1	2	24	33	39	14	12	10	4	15	3	0	157
1980	0	2	7	26	44	21	2	34	10	5	0	2	153
1981	0	7	7	9	71	26	5	20	5	23	3	0	176
1982	0	0	6	27	123	36	4	0	3	0	3	1	203
1983	5	7	24	1	62	35	4	22	5	0	7	14	186
1984	0	13	9	18	19	19	0	4	1	5	2	5	95
1985	0	0	5	41	28	5	3	1	1	3	1	2	90
1986	0	12	4	21	50	24	3	5	4	7	1	0	131
1987	1	1	7	0	54	19	11	3	8	0	16	4	124
1988	0	0	0	11	7	7	6	2	42	4	10	0	89
1989	3	0	5	3	70	63	0	6	3	6	1	0	160
1990	3	3	4	56	62	20	5	2	3	0	0	0	158
1991	20	5	2	39	72	36	1	2	3	8	4	0	192
1992	0	5	13	22	43	66	4	4	4	7	21	0	189
1993	1	4	5	17	39	4	4	0	12	23	8	0	117
1994	0	1	1	48	88	2	1	4	3	9	8	0	165
1995	6	0	13	36	66	75	11	3	2	1	0	10	223
1996	7	1	2	21	33	9	3	8	33	8	4	1	130
1997	0	6	7	31	59	50	2	2	1	16	3	0	177
1998	24	15	4	9	11	6	3	5	3	28	1	0	109
1999	22	0	22	23	70	26	3	8	0	0	0	4	178
2000	0	7	49	33	23	8	3	0	0	10	20	1	154
2001	0	0	4	12	36	12	0	7	15	24	27	5	142
2002	0	0	44	25	61	5	1	4	13	8	0	22	183
2003	0	0	4	31	50	29	6	1	4	12	29	0	166
2004	1	1	27	25	29	34	1	5	0	4	55	2	184
Total	128	150	506	1126	2165	1124	282	350	437	373	311	140	7092

Texas Droughts, 1892–2004

The following tables show the **duration and extent of Texas droughts by climatic division, 1892–2004**. For this purpose, droughts are arbitrarily defined as when the division has less than 75 percent of the 1931–1960 average precipitation. The 1931–1960 average precipitation in inches is shown at the bottom of the table for each division. The short table at bottom right shows the frequency of droughts in each area and the total years of droughts in the area.

Year	High Plains	Low Rolling Plains	North Central	East Texas	Trans-Pecos	Edwards Plateau	South Central	Upper Coast	Southern	Lower Valley
1892	...	...	...	...	68	...	...	73	...	...
1893	...	...	67	70	...	49	56	64	53	59
1894	...	...	...	68	...	...	...	...	...	...
1897	...	...	...	...	...	...	73	...	72	...
1898	...	...	...	...	...	...	...	...	69	51
1901	...	71	70	...	...	60	62	70	44	...
1902	...	...	...	...	...	...	...	...	65	73
1907	...	...	...	...	...	...	...	...	...	65
1909	...	...	72	68	67	74	70	...	...	...
1910	59	59	64	69	43	65	69	74	59	...
1911	...	...	...	...	...	...	...	...	...	70
1916	...	73	...	74	70	...	73	69	...	...
1917	58	50	63	59	44	46	42	50	32	48
1920	...	...	...	...	...	...	...	...	...	71
1921	...	...	...	...	72	...	...	...	...	73
1922	...	...	...	...	68	...	...	...	...	...
1924	...	...	73	73	...	71	...	72	...	...
1925	...	...	72	...	...	...	...	72	...	...
1927	...	...	...	...	...	...	...	74	...	74
1933	72	...	...	...	62	68	...	...	...	...
1934	66	...	...	...	46	69	...	...	...	...
1937	...	...	...	...	...	...	...	...	72	...
1939	...	...	...	...	...	...	69	...	...	72
1943	...	...	72	...	...	...	...	...	...	...
1948	...	...	73	74	62	...	71	67	...	...
1950	...	...	...	...	...	...	68	...	74	64
1951	...	...	...	...	61	53	...	...	...	...
1952	68	66	...	...	73	...	...	...	56	70
1953	69	...	...	...	49	73	...	...	...	...
1954	70	71	68	73	...	50	50	57	71	...
1956	51	57	61	68	44	43	55	62	53	53
1962	...	...	...	...	...	68	...	...	67	65
1963	...	...	63	68	...	65	61	73	...	...
1964	74	...	...	...	69	...	...	...	...	63
1970	65	63	...	...	...	72	...	...	...	...
1988	...	...	...	...	...	67	62	67	68	...
1989	...	...	...	...	...	72	...	...	66	64
1990	...	...	...	...	...	...	...	...	...	73
1994	...	...	...	...	68	...	...	...	...	...
1996	...	...	...	...	...	...	71	...	60	70
1998	...	69	...	...	71	...	...	...	...	...
1999	...	...	73	...	...	...	67	69	69	...
2000	...	...	...	...	74	...	...	...	...	67
2001	...	...	...	...	56	...	...	...	...	...
2002	...	...	...	...	...	...	...	...	...	...
2003	65	71	...	...	...	...	...	...	...	...
2004	...	...	...	...	...	...	...	...	...	...

Normal Annual Rainfall by Region

Listed below is the normal annual rainfall in inches for five 30-year periods in each geographical area. Normals for each area are given in the same order as the divisions which appear in the table above.

Period	Normal Rainfall in Inches									
1931–1960	18.51	22.99	32.93	45.96	12.03	25.91	33.24	46.19	22.33	24.27
1941–1970	18.59	23.18	32.94	45.37	11.57	23.94	33.03	46.43	21.95	23.44
1951–1980	17.73	22.80	32.14	44.65	11.65	23.52	34.03	45.93	22.91	24.73
1961–1990	18.88	23.77	33.99	45.67	13.01	24.00	34.49	47.63	23.47	25.31
1971–2000	19.64	24.51	35.23	48.08	13.19	24.73	36.21	50.31	24.08	25.43

killed, 93 injured; damage $400,000.

May 15, 1896: Tornadoes, Sherman, Grayson County; **Justin,** Denton County; **Gribble Springs,** Cooke County; 76 killed; damage $225,000.

Sept. 12, 1897: Hurricane. Many houses in **Port Arthur** were demolished; 13 killed, damage $150,000.

May 1, 1898: Tornado. Mobeetie, Wheeler County. Four killed, several injured; damage $35,000.

June 27–July 1, 1899: Rainstorm. A storm, centered over the **Brazos River watershed,** precipitated an average of 17 inches over 7,000 square miles. At **Hearne,** the gage overflowed at 24 inches; estimated total rainfall was 30 inches. At **Turnersville,** Coryell County, 33 inches were recorded in three days. This rain caused the **worst Brazos River flood on record.** Between 30 and 35 lives were lost. Property damage was estimated at $9 million.

April 5–8, 1900: Rainstorm. This storm began in two centers, over **Val Verde County** on the Rio Grande, and over **Swisher County** on the High Plains, and converged in the vicinity of **Travis County,** causing disastrous floods in the **Colorado, Brazos and Guadalupe rivers.** McDonald Dam on the Colorado River at Austin crumbled suddenly. A wall of water swept through the city taking at least 23 lives. Damage was estimated at $1,250,000.

Sept. 8–9, 1900: Hurricane. Galveston. The Great Galveston Storm was the **worst natural disaster in U.S. history** in terms of human life. Loss of life at Galveston has been estimated at 6,000 to 8,000, but the exact number has never been exactly determined. The island was completely inundated; not a single structure escaped damage. Most of the loss of life was due to drowning by storm tides that reached 15 feet or more. The anemometer blew away when the wind reached 100 mph at 6:15 p.m. on the 8th. Wind reached an estimated maximum velocity of 120 mph between 7:30 and 8:30 p.m. Property damage has been estimated at $30 to $40 million.

May 18, 1902: Tornado. Goliad. This tornado cut a 250-yard-wide path through town, turning 150 buildings into rubble. Several churches were destroyed, one of which was holding services; all 40 worshippers were either killed or injured. This tornado killed 114, injured 230, and caused an estimated $200,000 in damages.

April 26, 1906: Tornado. Bellevue, Clay County, demolished; considerable damage done at **Stoneburg,** seven miles east; 17 killed, 20 injured; damage $300,000.

May 6, 1907: Tornado. North of Sulphur Springs, Hopkins County; five killed, 19 injured.

May 13, 1908: Tornado. Linden, Cass County. Four killed, seven injured; damage $75,000.

May 22–25, 1908: Rainstorm; unique because it originated on the Pacific Coast. It moved first into **North Texas** and southern Oklahoma and thence to **Central Texas,** precipitating as much as 10 inches. Heaviest floods were in the upper Trinity basin, but flooding was general as far south as the Nueces. Property damage exceeded $5 million and 11

Drought Frequency

This table shows the number of years of drought and the number of separate droughts. For example, the High Plains has had 10 drought years, consisting of five 1-year droughts, one 2-year drought and one 3-year drought, a total of 7 droughts.

Years	High Plains	Low Rolling Plains	North Central	East Texas	Trans-Pecos	Edwards Plateau	South Central	Upper Coast	Southern	Lower Valley
1	5	8	9	6	8	8	13	10	10	14
2	1	1	2	2	4	5	2	2	3	2
3	1	...	...	...	1	...	...	...	...	...
Total Droughts	7	9	11	8	13	13	15	12	13	16
Drght Yrs.	10	10	13	10	20	18	17	14	16	18

lives were lost in the Dallas vicinity.

March 23, 1909: Tornado. Slidell, Wise County; 11 killed, 10 injured; damage $30,000.

May 30, 1909: Tornado. Zephyr, Brown County; 28 killed, many injured; damage $90,000.

July 21, 1909: Hurricane. Velasco, Brazoria County. One-half of town destroyed, 41 lives lost; damage $2,000,000.

Dec. 1–5, 1913: Rainstorm. This caused the **second major Brazos River flood**, and caused more deaths than the storm of 1899. It formed over **Central Texas** and spread both southwest and northeast with precipitation of 15 inches at **San Marcos** and 11 inches at **Kaufman.** Floods caused loss of 177 lives and $8,541,000 damage.

April 20–26, 1915: Rainstorm. Originated over Central Texas and spread into North and East Texas with precipitation up to 17 inches, causing floods in **Trinity, Brazos, Colorado, and Guadalupe rivers.** More than 40 lives lost and $2,330,000 damage.

Aug. 16–19, 1915: Hurricane. Galveston. Peak wind gusts of 120 miles recorded at Galveston; tide ranged 9.5 to 14.3 feet above mean sea level in the city, and up to 16.1 feet near the causeway. Business section flooded with 5 to 6 feet of water. At least 275 lives lost, damage $56 million. A new seawall prevented a repetition of the 1900 disaster.

Aug. 18, 1916: Hurricane. Corpus Christi. Maximum wind speed 100 mph. 20 Lives lost; damage $1,600,000.

Jan. 10–12, 1918: Blizzard. This was the most severe since that of February, 1899; it was accompanied by zero degree temperature in **North Texas** and temperatures from 7° to 12° below freezing along the **lower coast.**

April 9, 1919: Tornado. Leonard, Ector and Ravenna in Fannin County; 20 killed, 45 injured; damage $125,000.

April 9, 1919: Tornado. Henderson, Van Zandt, Wood, Camp, and Red River counties, 42 killed, 150 injured; damage $450,000.

May 7, 1919: Windstorms. Starr, Hidalgo, Willacy and Cameron counties. Violent thunderstorms with high winds, hail and rain occurred between **Rio Grande City** and the coast, killing 10 persons. Damage to property and crops was $500,000. Seven were killed at **Mission.**

Sept. 14, 1919: Hurricane. Near **Corpus Christi.** Center moved inland south of Corpus Christi; tides 16 feet above normal in that area and 8.8 feet above normal at **Galveston.** Extreme wind at Corpus Christi measured at 110 mph; 284 lives lost; damage $20,272,000.

April 13, 1921: Tornado. Melissa, Collin County, and

Petty, Lamar County. Melissa was practically destroyed; 12 killed, 80 injured; damage $500,000.

April 15, 1921: Tornado. Wood, Cass and Bowie counties; 10 killed, 50 injured; damage $85,000.

Sept. 8–10, 1921: Rainstorm. Probably the **greatest rainstorm in Texas history**, it entered Mexico as a hurricane from the Gulf. Torrential rains fell as the storm moved northeasterly across Texas. **Record floods** occurred in **Bexar, Travis, Williamson, Bell and Milam counties**, killing 215 persons, with property losses over $19 million. Five to nine feet of water stood in downtown **San Antonio.** A total of 23.98 inches was measured at the U.S. Weather Bureau station at **Taylor** during a period of 35 hours, with a 24-hour maximum of 23.11 on September 9-10. The **greatest rainfall recorded in United States history during 18 consecutive hours** (measured at an unofficial weather-monitoring site) **fell at Thrall**, Williamson County, 36.40 inches fell on Sept. 9.

April 8, 1922: Tornado. Rowena, Runnels County. Seven killed, 52 injured; damage $55,000.

April 8, 1922: Tornado. Oplin, Callahan County. Five killed, 30 injured; damage $15,000.

April 23–28, 1922: Rainstorm. An exceptional storm entered Texas from the west and moved from the **Panhandle** to **North Central and East Texas.** Rains up to 12.6 inches over Parker, Tarrant and Dallas counties caused severe floods in the Upper Trinity at **Fort Worth**; 11 lives were lost; damage was estimated at $1 million.

May 4, 1922: Tornado. Austin, Travis County; 12 killed, 50 injured; damage $500,000.

May 14, 1923: Tornado. Howard and Mitchell counties; 23 killed, 100 injured; damage $50,000.

April 12, 1927: Tornado. Edwards, Real and Uvalde counties; 74 killed, 205 injured; damage $1,230,000. Most of damage was in **Rocksprings** where 72 deaths occurred and town was practically destroyed.

May 9, 1927: Tornado. Garland; eleven killed; damage $100,000.

May 9, 1927: Tornado. Nevada, Collin County; **Wolfe City**, Hunt County; and **Tigertown**, Lamar County; 28 killed, over 200 injured; damage $900,000.

Jan. 4, 1929: Tornado. Near **Bay City**, Matagorda County. Five killed, 14 injured.

April 24, 1929: Tornado. Slocum, Anderson County; seven killed, 20 injured; damage $200,000.

May 24–31, 1929: Rainstorm. Beginning over **Caldwell County**, a storm spread over much of **Central and Coastal**

Extreme Weather Records in Texas

NOAA Environmental Data Service lists the following recorded extremes of weather in Texas:

Temperature

Lowest - Tulia, February 12, 1899	-23°F
Seminole, February 8, 1933.	-23°F
Highest - Seymour, August 12, 1936.	120°F
Monahans, June 28, 1994	120°F
Coldest Winter.	1898-1899

Snowfall

Greatest seasonal - Romero, 1923-1924	65.0 in.
Greatest monthly - Hale Center, Feb. 1956.	36.0 in.
Greatest single storm - Hale Center, Feb. 2-5, 1956.	33.0 in.
Greatest in 24 Hours - Plainview, Feb. 3-4, 1956	24.0 in.
Maximum depth on ground - Hale Center, Feb. 5, 1956	.33.0 in.

Rainfall

Wettest year - entire state	1941 . . .42.62 in.
Driest year - entire state.	1917 . . .14.30 in.
Greatest annual - Clarksville . .	1873 . .109.38 in.
Least annual - Wink	1956 . . . .1.76 in.
†Greatest in 24 hours - Alvin, July 25-26, 1979	43.00 in.

†This is an unofficial estimate of rainfall that occurred during Tropical Storm Claudette. The greatest 24-hour rainfall ever recorded in Texas at an official observing site occurred at Albany, Shackelford County, on Aug. 4, 1978: 29.05 inches.

Wind Velocity

Highest sustained wind (fastest mile)
*Matagorda - Sept. 11, 1961 . . . . SE, 145 mph
*Port Lavaca - Sept. 11, 1961. . . . . . NE, 145 mph
Highest peak gust (instantaneous velocity)
*Aransas Pass - Aug. 3, 1970 . . . . . SW, 180 mph
*Robstown - Aug. 3, 1970 (est.) . . . WSW, 180 mph

*These velocities occurred during hurricanes. Theoretically, much higher velocities are possible within the vortex of a tor-

nado, but no measurement with an anemometer has ever been made. The U.S. Weather Bureau's experimental Doppler radar equipment, a device which permits direct measurement of the high speeds in a spinning tornado funnel, received its first big test in the Wichita Falls tornado of April 2, 1958. This was the first tornado tracked by the Doppler radar, and for the first time in history, rotating winds up to 280 mph were clocked.

Texas with maximum rainfall of 12.9 inches, causing **floods in Colorado, Guadalupe, Brazos, Trinity, Neches and Sabine rivers**. Much damage at **Houston** from overflow of bayous. Damage estimated at $6 million.

May 6, 1930: Tornado. Bynum, Irene and Mertens in Hill County; **Ennis**, Ellis County; and **Frost**, Navarro County; 41 killed; damage $2,100,000.

May 6, 1930: Tornado. Kenedy and Runge in Karnes County; **Nordheim**, DeWitt County; 36 killed, 34 injured; damage $127,000.

June 30–July 2, 1932: Rainstorm. Torrential rains fell over the upper watersheds of the **Nueces and Guadalupe rivers**, causing destructive floods. Seven persons drowned; property losses exceeded $500,000.

Aug. 13, 1932: Hurricane. Near **Freeport**, Brazoria County. Wind speed at **East Columbia** estimated at 100 mph; 40 lives lost, 200 injured; damage $7,500,000.

March 30, 1933: Tornado. Angelina, Nacogdoches and San Augustine counties; 10 killed, 56 injured; damage $200,000.

April 26, 1933: Tornado. Bowie County near Texarkana. Five killed, 38 injured; damage $14,000.

July 22–25, 1933: Tropical Storm. One of the greatest U.S. storms in area and general rainfall. The storm reached the vicinity of **Freeport** late on July 22 and moved very slowly overland across eastern Texas, July 22-25. The storm center moved into northern Louisiana on the 25th. Rainfall averaged 12.50 inches over an area of about 25,000 square miles. Twenty inches or more fell in a small area of eastern Texas and western Louisiana surrounding Logansport, La. The 4-day total at Logansport was 22.30 inches. Property damage was estimated at $1,114,790.

July 30, 1933: Tornado. Oak Cliff section of Dallas, Dallas County. Five killed, 30 injured; damage $500,000.

Sept. 4–5, 1933: Hurricane. Near **Brownsville**. Center passed inland a short distance north of Brownsville, where an extreme wind of 106 mph was measured before the anemometer blew away. Peak wind gusts were estimated at 120 to 125 mph. 40 known dead, 500 injured; damage $16,903,100. About 90 percent of the citrus crop in the **Lower Rio Grande Valley** was destroyed.

July 25, 1934: Hurricane. Near **Seadrift**, Calhoun County, 19 lives lost, many minor injuries; damage $4.5 million. About 85 percent of damage was in crops.

Sept. 15–18, 1936: Rainstorm. Excessive rains over the **North Concho and Middle Concho rivers** caused a sharp rise in the Concho River, which overflowed **San Angelo**. Much of the business district and 500 homes were flooded. Four persons drowned and property losses estimated at $5 million. Four-day storm rainfall at San Angelo measured 25.19 inches; 11.75 inches fell on the 15th.

June 10, 1938: Tornado. Clyde, Callahan County; 14 killed, 9 injured; damage $85,000.

Sept. 23, 1941: Hurricane. Near **Matagorda**. Center moved inland near Matagorda, and passed over **Houston** about midnight. Extremely high tides along coast in the **Matagorda to Galveston** area. Heaviest property and crop losses were in counties from Matagorda County to the Sabine River. Four lives lost. Damage was $6,503,300.

April 28, 1942: Tornado. Crowell, Foard County; 11 killed, 250 injured; damage $1,500,000.

Aug. 30, 1942: Hurricane. Matagorda Bay. Highest wind estimated 115 mph at **Seadrift**. Tide at **Matagorda**,14.7 feet. Storm moved west-north-westward and finally diminished over the **Edwards Plateau**; eight lives lost, property damage estimated at $11.5 million, and crop damage estimated at $15 million.

May 10, 1943: Tornado. Laird Hill, Rusk County, and **Kilgore**, Gregg County. Four killed, 25 injured; damage $1 million.

July 27, 1943: Hurricane. Near **Galveston**. Center moved inland across **Bolivar Peninsula and Trinity Bay**. A wind gust of 104 mph was recorded at **Texas City**; 19 lives lost; damage estimated at $16,550,000.

Aug. 26–27, 1945: Hurricane. Aransas-San Antonio

Bay area. At **Port O'Connor**, the wind reached 105 mph when the cups were torn from the anemometer. Peak gusts of 135 mph were estimated at **Seadrift, Port O'Connor and Port Lavaca**; three killed, 25 injured; damage $20,133,000.

Jan. 4, 1946: Tornado. Near **Lufkin**, Angelina County and **Nacogdoches**, Nacogdoches County; 13 killed, 250 injured; damage $2,050,000.

Jan. 4, 1946: Tornado. Near **Palestine**, Anderson County; 15 killed, 60 injured; damage $500,000.

May 18, 1946: Tornado. Clay, Montague and Denton counties. Four killed, damage $112,000.

April 9, 1947: Tornado. White Deer, Carson County; **Glazier**, Hemphill County; and **Higgins**, Lipscomb County; 68 killed, 201 injured; damage $1,550,000. Glazier completely destroyed. **One of the largest tornadoes on record.** Width of path, 1 miles at Higgins; length of path, 221 miles across portions of Texas, Oklahoma and Kansas. This tornado also struck Woodward, Okla.

May 3, 1948: Tornado. McKinney, Collin County; three killed, 43 injured; $2 million damage.

May 15, 1949: Tornado. Amarillo and vicinity; six killed, 83 injured. Total damage from tornado, wind and hail, $5,310,000. Total destruction over one-block by three-block area in southern part of city; airport and 45 airplanes damaged; 28 railroad boxcars blown off track.

Sept. 8–10, 1952: Rainstorm. Heavy rains over the **Colorado and Guadalupe River watersheds** in southwestern Texas caused major flooding. From 23 to 26 inches fell between **Kerrville, Blanco and Boerne**. Highest stages ever known occurred in the **Pedernales River**; five lives lost, three injured; 17 homes destroyed, 454 damaged. Property loss several million dollars.

March 13, 1953: Tornado. Jud and O'Brien, Haskell County; and **Knox City**, Knox County; 17 killed, 25 injured; damage $600,000.

May 11, 1953: Tornado. Near **San Angelo**, Tom Green County; eleven killed, 159 injured; damage $3,239,000.

May 11, 1953: Tornado. Waco, McLennan County; 114 killed, 597 injured; damage $41,150,000. **One of two most disastrous tornadoes;** 150 homes destroyed, 900 homes damaged; 185 other buildings destroyed; 500 other buildings damaged.

April 2, 1957: Tornado. Dallas, Dallas County; 10 killed, 200 injured; damage $4 million. Moving through Oak Cliff and West Dallas, it damaged 574 buildings, largely homes.

April–May, 1957: Torrential Rains. Excessive flooding occurred throughout the area **east of the Pecos River to the Sabine River** during the last 10 days of April; 17 lives were lost, and several hundred homes were destroyed. During May, more than 4,000 persons were evacuated from unprotected lowlands on the **West Fork of the Trinity above Fort Worth** and along creeks in Fort Worth. Twenty-nine houses at **Christoval** were damaged or destroyed and 83 houses at **San Angelo** were damaged. Five persons were drowned in floods in **South Central Texas**.

May 15, 1957: Tornado. Silverton, Briscoe County; 21 killed, 80 injured; damage $500,000.

June 27, 1957: Hurricane Audrey. Center crossed the Gulf coast near the Texas-Louisiana line. **Orange** was in the western portion of the eye between 9 and 10 a.m. In Texas, nine lives were lost, 450 persons injured; property damage was $8 million. Damage was extensive in **Jefferson and Orange counties**, with less in **Chambers and Galveston counties**. Maximum wind reported in Texas, 85 m.p.h. at **Sabine Pass**, with gusts to 100 m.p.h.

Oct. 28, 1960: Rainstorm. Rains of 7-10 inches fell in **South Central Texas;** 11 died from drowning in flash floods. In **Austin** about 300 families were driven from their homes. Damage in Austin was estimated at $2.5 million.

Sept. 8–14, 1961: Hurricane Carla. Port O'Connor; maximum wind gust at **Port Lavaca** estimated at 175 mph. Highest tide was 18.5 feet at Port Lavaca. Most damage was to **coastal counties between Corpus Christi and Port Arthur** and inland **Jackson, Harris and Wharton**

counties. In Texas, 34 persons died; seven in a **tornado** that swept across **Galveston Island**; 465 persons were injured. Property and crop damage conservatively estimated at $300 million. The evacuation of an estimated 250,000 persons kept loss of life low. **Hurricane Carla was the largest hurricane of record.**

Sept. 7, 1962: Rainstorm. Fort Worth. Rains fell over the Big Fossil and Denton Creek watersheds ranging up to 11 inches of fall in three hours. Extensive damage from flash flooding occurred in **Richland Hills and Haltom City**.

Sept. 16–20, 1963: Hurricane Cindy. Rains of 15 to 23.5 inches fell in portions of **Jefferson, Newton and Orange counties** when Hurricane Cindy became stationary west of **Port Arthur.** Flooding from the excessive rainfall resulted in total property damage of $11,600,000 and agricultural losses of $500,000.

April 3, 1964: Tornado. Wichita Falls. Seven killed, 111 injured; damage $15 million; 225 homes destroyed, 50 with major damage, and 200 with minor damage. Sixteen other buildings received major damage.

Sept. 21–23, 1964: Rainstorm. Collin, Dallas and Tarrant counties. Rains of more than 12 inches fell during the first eight hours of the 21st. Flash flooding of tributaries of the Trinity River and smaller creeks and streams resulted in two drownings and an estimated $3 million property damage. Flooding of homes occurred in all sections of **McKinney.** In **Fort Worth,** there was considerable damage to residences along Big Fossil and White Rock creeks. Expensive homes in **North Dallas** were heavily damaged.

Jan. 25, 1965: Dust Storm. West Texas. The worst dust storm since February 1956 developed on the **southern High Plains.** Winds, gusting up to 75 mph at **Lubbock,** sent dust billowing to 31,000 feet in the area **from the Texas-New Mexico border eastward to a line from Tulia to Abilene.** Ground visibility was reduced to about 100 yards in many sections. The worst hit was the **Muleshoe, Seminole, Plains, Morton** area on the South Plains. The rain gage at Reese Air Force Base, Lubbock, contained 3 inches of fine sand.

June 2, 1965: Tornado. Hale Center, Hale County. Four killed, 76 injured; damage $8 million.

June 11, 1965: Rainstorm. Sanderson, Terrell County. Torrential rains of up to eight inches in two hours near Sanderson caused a major flash flood that swept through the town. As a result, 26 persons drowned and property losses were estimated at $2,715,000.

April 22–29, 1966: Flooding. Northeast Texas. Twenty to 26 inches of rain fell in portions of Wood, Smith, Morris, Upshur, Gregg, Marion and Harrison counties. Nineteen persons drowned in the rampaging rivers and creeks that swept away bridges, roads and dams, and caused an estimated $12 million damage.

April 28, 1966: Flash flooding. Dallas County. Flash flooding from torrential rains in Dallas County resulted in 14 persons drowned and property losses at $15 million.

Sept. 18–23, 1967: Hurricane Beulah. Near **Brownsville. The third largest hurricane of record,** Hurricane Beulah moved inland near the mouth of the Rio Grande on the 20th. Wind gusts of 136 mph were reported during Beulah's passage. Rains 10 to 20 inches for much of the area **south of San Antonio** resulted in record-breaking floods. An unofficial gaging station at **Falfurrias** registered the highest accumulated rainfall, 36 inches. The resultant stream overflow and surface runoff inundated 1.4 million acres. Beulah spawned 115 tornadoes, all in Texas, the **greatest number of tornadoes on record for any hurricane.** Hurricane Beulah caused 13 deaths and 37 injuries, of which five deaths and 34 injuries were attributed to tornadoes. Property losses were estimated at $100 million and crop losses at $50 million.

April 18, 1970: Tornado. Near **Clarendon,** Donley County. Seventeen killed, 42 injured; damage $2,100,000. Fourteen persons were killed at a resort community at Green Belt Reservoir, 7 miles north of Clarendon.

May 11, 1970: Tornado. Lubbock, Lubbock County.

Twenty-six killed, 500 injured; damage $135 million. Fifteen square miles, almost one-quarter of the city of Lubbock, suffered damage.

Aug. 3–5, 1970: Hurricane Celia. Corpus Christi. Hurricane Celia was a unique but severe storm. Measured in dollars, it was **the costliest in the state's history to that time.** Sustained wind speeds reached 130 mph, but it was great bursts of kinetic energy of short duration that appeared to cause the severe damage. Wind gusts of 161 mph were measured at the **Corpus Christi** National Weather Service Office. At **Aransas Pass,** peak wind gusts were estimated as high as 180 mph, after the wind equipment had been blown away. Celia caused 11 deaths in Texas, at least 466 injuries, and total property and crop damage in Texas estimated at $453,773,000. Hurricane Celia crossed the Texas coastline midway between Corpus Christi and Aransas Pass about 3:30 p.m. CST on Aug. 3. Hardest hit was the metropolitan area of **Corpus Christi,** including **Robstown, Aransas Pass, Port Aransas** and small towns on the north side of Corpus Christi Bay.

Feb. 20–22, 1971: Blizzard. Panhandle. Paralyzing blizzard, worst since March 22–25, 1957, storm transformed Panhandle into one vast snowfield as 6 to 26 inches of snow were whipped by 40 to 60 mph winds into drifts up to 12 feet high. At **Follett,** 3-day snowfall was 26 inches. Three persons killed; property and livestock losses were $3.1 million.

Sept. 9–13, 1971: Hurricane Fern. Coastal Bend. Ten to 26 inches of rain resulted in some of worst flooding since Hurricane Beulah in 1967. Two persons killed; losses were $30,231,000.

May 11–12, 1972: Rainstorm. South Central Texas. Seventeen drowned at **New Braunfels,** one at **McQueeney.** New Braunfels and **Seguin** hardest hit. Property damage $17.5 million.

June 12–13, 1973: Rainstorm. Southeastern Texas. Ten drowned. Over $50 million in property and crop damage. From 10-15 inches of rain recorded.

Nov. 23–24, 1974: Flash Flooding. Central Texas. Over $1 million in property damage. Thirteen people killed, ten in **Travis County.**

Jan. 31–Feb. 1, 1975: Flooding. Nacogdoches County. Widespread heavy rain caused flash flooding here, resulting in three deaths; damage over $5.5 million.

May 23, 1975: Rainstorm. Austin area. Heavy rains, high winds and hail resulted in over $5 million property damage; 40 people injured. Four deaths caused by drowning.

June 15, 1976: Rainstorm. Harris County. Rains in excess of 13 inches caused damage estimated at near $25 million. Eight deaths were storm-related, including three drownings.

Aug. 1–4, 1978: Heavy Rains, Flooding. Edwards Plateau, Low Rolling Plains. Remnants of Tropical Storm Amelia caused some of the worst flooding of this century. As much as 30 inches of rain fell near **Albany** in Shackelford County, where six drownings were reported. In **Bandera, Kerr, Kendall and Gillespie counties,** 27 people drowned and the damage total was at least $50 million.

Dec. 30–31, 1978: Ice Storm. North Central Texas. Possibly the **worst ice storm in 30 years** hit Dallas County particularly hard. Damage estimates reached $14 million, and six deaths were storm-related.

April 10, 1979: The worst single tornado in Texas' history hit Wichita Falls. Earlier on the same day, **several tornadoes** hit farther west. The destruction in Wichita Falls resulted in 42 dead, 1,740 injured, over 3,000 homes destroyed and damage of approximately $400 million. An estimated 20,000 persons were left homeless by this storm. In all, the tornadoes on April 10 killed 53 people, injured 1,812 and caused over $500 million damages.

May 3, 1979: Thunderstorms. Dallas County was hit by a wave of the most destructive thunderstorms in many years; 37 injuries and $5 million in damages resulted.

July 25–26, 1979: Tropical storm Claudette caused over $750 million in property and crop damages, but fortunately only few injuries. Near **Alvin,** an estimated 43 inches of rain fell, a new state record for 24 hours.

Aug. 24, 1979: One of the worst **hailstorms** in **West Texas** in the past 100 years; $200 million in crops, mostly cotton, destroyed.

Sept. 18–20, 1979: Coastal flooding from heavy rain, 18 inches in 24 hours at **Aransas Pass,** and 13 inches at **Rockport.**

Aug. 9–11, 1980: Hurricane Allen hit **South Texas** and left three dead, causing $650 million-$750 million in property and crop damages. Over 250,000 coastal residents had to be evacuated. The worst damage occurred along **Padre Island** and in **Corpus Christi.** Over 20 inches of rain fell in extreme South Texas, and 29 tornadoes occurred; one of the worst hurricane-related outbreaks.

Summer 1980: One of the hottest summers in rhe history of the Lone Star State.

Sept. 5–8, 1980: Hurricane Danielle brought rain and flooding to Southeast and Central Texas. Seventeen inches of rain fell at Port Arthur, and 25 inches near Junction.

May 24–25, 1981: Severe flooding in **Austin** claimed 13 lives, injured about 100 and caused $40 million in damage. Up to 5.5 inches of rain fell in one hour west of the city.

Oct. 11–14, 1981: Record rains in North Central Texas caused by the remains of **Pacific Hurricane Norma.** Over 20 inches fell in some locations.

April 2, 1982: A **tornado outbreak in Northeast Texas.** The most severe tornado struck **Paris;** 10 people were killed, 170 injured and 1,000 left homeless. Over $50 million in damages resulted. A total of 7 tornadoes that day left 11 dead and 174 injured.

May, 1982: Texas recorded **123 tornadoes,** the most ever in May, and one less than the most recorded in any single month in the state. One death and 23 injuries occurred.

Dec. 1982: Heavy snow. El Paso recorded 18.2 inches of snow, the most in any month there.

Aug. 15–21, 1983: Hurricane Alicia was the first hurricane to make landfall in the continental U.S. in three years (Aug. 18), and **one of the costliest in Texas history** ($3 billion). Alicia caused widespread damage to a large section of **Southeast Texas,** including coastal areas near **Galveston** and the entire **Houston** area. Alicia spawned 22 tornadoes, and highest winds were estimated near 130 mph. In all, 18 people in South Texas were killed and 1,800 injured as a result of the tropical storm.

Jan. 12–13, 1985: A **record-breaking snowstorm** struck **West and South Central Texas** with up to 15 inches of snow that fell at many locations **between San Antonio and the Rio Grande.** San Antonio recorded 13.2 inches of snow for Jan. 12 (the greatest in a day) and 13.5 inches for the two-day total. **Eagle Pass** reported 14.5 inches of snow.

June 26, 1986: Hurricane Bonnie made landfall between **High Island and Sabine Pass** around 3:45 a.m. The highest wind measured in the area was a gust to 97 m.p.h., which was recorded at the **Sea Rim State Park.** As much as 13 inches of rain fell in **Ace** in southern Polk County. There were several reports of funnel clouds, but no confirmed tornadoes. While the storm caused no major structural damage, there was widespread minor damage. Numerous injuries were reported.

May 22, 1987: A strong, **multiple-vortex tornado** struck the town of **Saragosa,** Reeves Co.), essentially wiping it off the map. Of the town's 183 inhabitants, 30 were killed and 121 were injured. Eight-five percent of the town's structures were completely destroyed, while total damage topped $1.3 million.

Oct. 15–19, 1994: Extreme amounts of rainfall, up to 28.90 inches over a 4-day period, fell throughout southeastern part of the state. Seventeen lives were lost, most of them victims of flash flooding. Many rivers reached record flood levels. **Houston** was cut off from many other parts of the state, as numerous roads, including Interstate 10, were under water. Damage was estimated to be near $700 million; 26 counties were declared disaster areas.

May 5, 1995: A **thunderstorm** moved across the **Dallas/Fort Worth** area with 70 mph wind gusts and rainfall

rates of almost three inches in 30 minutes (five inches in one hour). Twenty people lost their lives as a result of this storm, 109 people were injured by large hail and, with more than $2 billion in damage, the National Oceanic and Atmospheric Administration dubbed it the **"costliest thunderstorm event in history."**

May 28, 1995: A **supercell thunderstorm** produced extreme winds and giant hail in **San Angelo,** injuring at least 80 people and causing about $120 million in damage. Sixty-one homes were destroyed, and more than 9,000 were slightly damaged. In some areas, hail was six inches deep, with drifts to two feet.

Feb. 21, 1996: Anomalously **high temperatures** were reported over the **entire state,** breaking records in nearly every region of the state. Temperatures near 100°F shattered previous records by as many as 10°F as Texans experienced heat more characteristic of mid-summer than winter.

May 10, 1996: Hail up to five inches in diameter fell in **Howard County,** causing injuries to 48 people and $30 million worth of property damage.

May 27, 1997: A half-mile-wide **F5 tornado** struck **Jarrell,** Williamson Co., leveling the Double Creek subdisivion, claiming 27 lives, injuring 12 others, and causing more than $40 million in damage.

March–May, 1998: According to the Climate Prediction Center, this three-month period ranks as the **seventh driest** for a region including Texas, Oklahoma, Arkansas, Louisiana and Mississippi. May 1998 has been ranked as both the **warmest and the driest May** that this region has ever seen.

Aug. 22–25, 1998: Tropical Storm Charley brought torrential rains and flash floods to the **Hill Country.** Thirteen people lost their lives and more than 200 were injured.

Oct. 17–19, 1998: A massive and devastating flood set all-time records for rainfall and river levels, resulted in the deaths of 25 people, injured more than 2,000 others, and caused more than $500 million damage from the **Hill Country to the counties surrounding San Antonio to the south and east.**

Jan. 22, 1999: Golf ball- and softball-sized **hail** fell in the **Bryan/College Station** area, resulting in $10 million in damage to cars, homes and offices.

May 1999: Numerous severe weather outbreaks caused **damaging winds, large hail, dangerous lightning, and numerous tornadoes.** An F3 tornado moved through **De Kalb's** downtown area and high school on the 4th, injuring 22 people and causing $125 million to the community. On the same day, **two F2 tornadoes** roared through **Kilgore** simultaneously. On the 11th, an **F4 tornado** moved through parts of **Loyal Valley,** taking the life of one and injuring six. The 25th saw storms produce **2.5-inch hail** in **Levelland** and **Amarillo.** The total cost of damages caused by May storms was more than $157 million.

August 1999: Excessive heat throughout the month resulted in 16 fatalities in the **Dallas/Fort Worth** area. The airport reported 26 consecutive days of 100°F or greater temperatures.

January–October 2000: A **severe drought** plagued **most of Texas.** Some regions experienced little to no rain for several months during the summer. Abilene saw no rain for 72 consecutive days, while **Dallas** had **no rain for 84 consecutive days** during the summer. During July, aquifers hit all-time lows, and lakes and streams fell to critical levels. Most regions had to cut back or stop agricultural activities because of the drought, which resulted in $515 million in agricultural loss, according to USDA figures.

March 28, 2000: A supercell over **Fort Worth** produced an **F3 tornado,** which injured 80 people and caused significant damage. Flooding claimed the lives of two people.

May 20, 2000: A **flash flood** in the **Liberty** and **Dayton** area was caused by 18.3 inches of rain's falling in five hours. Up to 80 people had to be rescued from the flood waters; property damage totalled an estimated $10 million.

July 2000: Excessive heat resulted from a high-pressure ridge, particularly from the 12th to the 21st. **Dallas/Fort Worth** airport reported a **10-day average of 103.3°F.**

College Station had **12 consecutive days of 100°F or greater** temperatures. The heat caused 34 deaths in North and Southeast Texas, primarily among the elderly.

Aug. 2, 2000: Lightning struck a tree at Astroworld in Houston injuring 17 teens.

Sept. 5, 2000: Excessive heat resulted in at least eight **all-time high temperature records** around the state, one of which was **Possum Kingdom Lake**, which reached 114°F. This day is being regarded as the **hottest day ever in Texas, considering the state as a whole.**.

Dec. 13 and 24-25, 2000: Two major winter storms blanketed **Northeast Texas** with up to six inches of ice from each storm. Eight inches of snow fell in the **Panhandle**, while areas in North Texas received 12 inches. Thousands of motorists were stranded on Interstate 20 and had to be rescued by the National Guard; 235,000 people lost electric service from the first storm alone. Roads were treacherous, driving was halted in several counties, and the total cost of damages from both storms reached more than $156 million.

Jan. 1–31, 2001: The U.S. Department of Agriculture Farm Service Agency received a **Presidential Disaster Declaration** in December 2000 because of **persistent drought** conditions in **deep Southern Texas;** $125 million in damage was reported in the region.

May 2001: May is typically a month of extreme weather, and May 2001 was no exception, with numerous storms causing excessive damage. **Four-inch hail** caused nearly $150 million in damages in **San Antonio** on the 6th. On the 30th, supercell **thunderstorms** in the **High Plains** region produced winds over 100 mph and golf-ball- sized hail caused more than $186 million in damage. All told, storms caused 36 injuries and more than $358 million in damage to property and agriculture.

June–December 2001: Significant drought-like conditions occurred in Texas from early summer through December. After the yearly drought report was filed, it was determined that the total crop damage across the South Plains region was about $420 million. Consequential losses occurred to crops such as cotton, wheat, grain sorghum and corn.

June 5–10, 2001: Tropical Storm Allison hit the **Houston** area, which dumped large amounts of rain on the city. The storm made landfall on the western end of **Galveston Island** and over the next five days produced record rainfall. These amazing amounts of precipitation led to devastating flooding across southeastern Texas. Some weather stations in the Houston area reported more than 40 inches of rain total and more than 18 inches in a 24-hour period. Twenty-two deaths and $5.2 billion in damage resulted.

July–August 2001: Excessive heat plagued Texas during July and August, which resulted in 17 deaths in the Houston area.

Oct. 12, 2001: An F2 tornado in **Hondo** caused $20 million in damage. The tornado injured 25 people and damaged the Hondo Airport and the National Guard Armory. A large hangar and nearly two dozen aircraft were destroyed at the airport. The armory's roofs and concrete walls were damaged. Nearly 150 homes in Hondo and 50 on its outskirts were damaged, and nearly 100 mobile homes were damaged.

Nov. 15, 2001: Storms caused **flash flooding** and some weak **tornadoes** in the Edwards Plateau, South Central and southern portions of North Central regions. Flash flooding caused 8 deaths and 198 injuries.

March 2002: Several **violent storms** occurred, which produced hail, tornadoes and strong winds. Hail 1-3/4 inches in diameter caused $16 million in damage to **San Angelo** on the 19th, while 30 people where injured on the same day by an **F2 tornado** in **Somerset** that also caused $2 million in damage. For the month, there were three fatalities, 64 injuries and more than $37.5 million in damage.

June 30–July 7, 2002: Excessive rainfall occurred in the **South Central** and **Edwards Plateau** regions, with some areas reporting more than 30 inches of rain. In the South Central region alone nearly $250 million dollars worth of damage was reported from this significant weather event. In central Texas, 29 counties were devastated by the flooding and declared federal disaster areas by President George W. Bush. The total event damage was estimated at more than $2 billion.

Sept. 5–7, 2002: Tropical Storm Fay made landfall along the southeast Texas coast on the 6th. This system produced extremely heavy rainfall, strong damaging wind gusts and tornadoes. Ten to 20 inches of rain fell in eastern **Wharton County. Brazoria County** was hit the hardest from this system with about 1,500 homes flooded. Tropical Storm Fay produced five tornadoes, flooded many areas and caused significant wind damage. Damage of $4.5 million was reported.

Oct. 24, 2002: Severe **thunderstorms** in south Texas and produced heavy rain, causing flooding and two tornadoes in **Corpus Christi.** The most extensive damage occurred across **Del Mar College.** The storm caused one death, 26 injuries and Total storm damages exceeded more then $85 million in damage.

Feb. 24–26, 2003: A severe cold front brought freezing rain, sleet and **snow** to the **North-Central region.** Snow accumulations were as high as **5 inches** resulting in $15 million in damages. Most schools and businesses were closed for this period.

April 8, 2003: A severe thunderstorm caused one of the **most destructive hail events in the history of Brownsville.** Hail exceeded 2.75 inches in diameter and caused $50 million in damages to the city. At least 5 injuries were reported.

July 14–16, 2003: Hurricane Claudette made landfall near Port O'Connor in the late morning hours of the 14th. At landfall, wind speeds were more than 90 mph. The system, which moved westward toward Big Bend and northern Mexico, caused 1 death and 2 injuries, and total damages were estimated at more than **$100 million.**

Sept. 2003: Persistent flooding during the month caused more than $2 million in damages. The remnants of **Tropical Storm Grace** caused flash flooding along the Upper Coast region near **Galveston** early in September, with rainfall estimates in Matagorda County ranging from 6 to 12 inches. During the second half of the month, deep south Texas was hit with a **deluge of rain caused by a tropical wave** combined with approaching cold fronts, and monthly rainfall totals ranged from 7 to 15 inches throughout the deep south.

June 1–9, 2004: Flash flooding due to an upper air disturbance and associated cold front caused damage to more than 1,000 homes through **North-Central Texas.** This was the first of many days in which heavy rains fell throughout the state. Estimated damages were more $7.5 million.

June 21, 2004: Severe weather kicked up just ahead of a frontal boundary causing damage to **Amarillo** and the surrounding area. Eight tornadoes were reported around the Panhandle, and there were many reports of hail, topping out at 4.25 inches in diameter in Potter County. Thousands of homes were damaged, and the total damage was estimated at more than **$150 million.**

July 28–29, 2004: A stationary front lead to **torrential rainfall** in **Dallas and Waco.** Hundreds of homes were damaged by flash flooding, as 24-hour rainfall totals for the two cities approached 5 inches. Outlying areas of the cities reported as much as 7 inches of rain in a 12-hour period on the 29th. Damage estimates topped $20 million.

Sept. 14, 2004: A **lightning strike** during football practice at **Grapeland High School** caused one death and injuries to 40 players and coaches.

Dec. 24–26, 2004: Large portions of **Southeast Texas** saw their **first white Christmas in recorded history.** A cold front past over the state a few days prior to Christmas Eve dropping temperatures below freezing. Another cold front brought snow to the area, and it accumulated Christmas Eve night and into Christmas day. Galveston and Houston recorded 4 inches of snow, while areas even further south, such as **Victoria, had 12 inches.** ☆

Texas Temperature, Freeze, Growing Season and Precipitation Records by County

Data in the table below are from the office of the **Texas State Climatologist**, Texas A&M University, College Station. Because of the small change in averages, data are revised only at intervals of 10 years. Data below are the latest compilations, as of Feb. 1, 2004, and reflect data compiled during 1971–2000. The table shows temperature, freeze, growing season and precipitation for each county in Texas. Data for counties where a National Weather Service Station has not been maintained long enough to establish a reliable mean are interpolated from isoline charts prepared from mean values from stations with long-established records. **Mean maximum temperature for July** is computed from the sum of the daily maxima. **Mean minimum January** is computed from the sum of the daily minima. Weather stations shown in italics do not measure all categories and some data are from the period 1961–1990. An asterisk (*) preceding a record high or low or rainfall extreme denotes a figure that also occurred on an earlier date.

County and Station	Mean Max. July (°F)	Mean Min. Jan. (°F)	Record High (°F)	Yr.	Record Low (°F)	Yr.	Last in Spring	First in Fall	Grow. Days	Jan.	Feb.	Mar.	Apr.	May	June	July	Aug.	Sept.	Oct.	Nov.	Dec.	Annual	Highest Daily Rainfall (In.)	Mo.-Year
Anderson, Palestine	93.9	37.4	114	1954	-4	1930	Mar. 15	Nov. 18	247	3.60	3.34	3.87	3.80	4.51	4.53	2.55	3.23	3.45	4.90	4.44	4.16	46.38	9.10	08-1991
Andrews, Andrews	94.5	30.4	113	1994	-1	1985	Mar. 29	Nov. 10	226	0.48	0.51	0.52	0.85	1.78	2.12	2.25	1.77	2.21	1.43	0.64	0.59	15.15	7.60	07-1914
Angelina, Lufkin	93.5	37.9	*110	2000	-2	1951	Mar. 13	Nov. 15	247	4.45	3.17	3.53	3.13	5.29	4.18	2.60	3.08	4.08	4.13	4.54	4.44	46.62	7.47	10-1994
Aransas, Rockport	90.1	44.9	105	2000	12	1983	Feb. 2	Dec. 20	318	2.40	2.18	2.36	2.07	3.66	3.50	2.43	3.13	5.53	4.23	2.56	1.91	35.96	8.15	09-1979
Archer, Archer City	97.0	26.7	114	1980	*-10	1989	Feb. 28	Nov. 9	225	1.13	1.75	2.05	2.46	4.33	3.46	3.08	2.66	3.11	3.39	1.90	1.75	29.78	7.95	10-1981
Armstrong, Claude	90.5	21.2	*108	1980	-16	1905	Apr. 19	Oct. 20	184	0.51	0.58	1.23	1.60	3.34	3.33	3.08	3.00	2.37	1.91	0.82	0.62	22.39	10.27	05-1982
Atascosa, Poteet	95.9	39.0	111	2000	0	1989	Feb. 25	Dec. 8	279	1.27	1.83	1.54	2.50	4.09	4.06	1.93	2.69	2.90	3.04	1.79	1.65	29.00	8.75	07-1949
Austin, Sealy	94.9	40.7	111	2000	0	1989	Feb. 18	Dec. 8	291	3.14	2.81	2.61	3.22	4.71	3.85	1.93	3.06	4.33	4.44	3.68	2.90	40.68	11.00	08-1945
Bailey, Muleshoe	91.9	20.2	*110	1944	-21	1933	Apr. 17	Oct. 21	186	0.43	0.50	0.64	1.01	2.04	2.49	1.93	3.07	2.34	1.50	0.67	0.59	17.21		
Bandera, Medina	93.9	33.3	109	1980	5	1989	Mar. 22	Nov. 10	233	1.72	1.91	2.27	2.69	4.35	4.29	2.55	2.25	3.66	4.14	2.84	2.28	35.78	9.86	08-1971
Bastrop, Smithville	95.4	44.9	*111	2000	-1	1930	Mar. 4	Nov. 20	260	2.73	2.32	2.56	3.00	5.12	3.66	2.01	2.58	3.56	4.70	3.29	2.84	38.04	16.05	06-1940
Baylor, Seymour	96.5	27.7	120	1936	-14	1947	Mar. 30	Nov. 6	220	1.05	1.56	1.88	1.84	4.13	3.63	1.86	3.02	3.51	2.86	1.48	1.41	27.79	6.20	09-1967
Bee, Beeville	94.6	43.1	111	1939	8	1983	Feb. 14	Dec. 6	294	1.94	1.84	1.90	2.68	3.49	4.19	1.82	2.69	4.30	3.60	2.00	1.83	33.48	10.61	09-1967
Bell, Temple	95.0	34.9	112	1947	*-4	1989	Mar. 3	Nov. 22	264	1.91	2.70	2.65	2.81	4.56	3.71	2.03	2.20	4.00	3.73	3.04	2.68	35.81	9.62	10-1998
Bexar, San Antonio	94.6	38.6	111	2000	0	1949	Feb. 28	Nov. 25	270	1.66	1.75	1.89	2.60	4.72	4.30	2.20	2.57	3.00	3.86	2.58	1.96	32.92	11.26	10-1998
Blanco, Blanco	93.7	34.0	*110	2000	-6	1949	Mar. 20	Nov. 11	235	1.79	2.08	2.63	2.69	4.51	4.18	2.03	2.38	3.26	4.18	2.66	2.37	34.75	17.47	10-1952
Borden, Gail	94.6	29.8	116	1994	-1	1989	Mar. 27	Nov. 8	226	0.58	0.73	0.66	1.20	2.80	2.81	2.35	2.52	2.83	1.77	0.74	0.69	19.68	9.13	10-1960
Bosque, Lake Whitney	96.2	32.7	113	2000	*-3	1989	Mar. 15	Nov. 17	247	1.93	2.39	2.87	3.18	4.29	3.96	2.03	2.37	2.76	3.95	2.67	2.67	35.07	6.22	10-1971
Bowie, Texarkana	93.1	30.7	108	2000	*-6	1989	Mar. 20	Nov. 14	238	3.91	3.80	4.46	4.23	4.97	4.82	3.62	2.41	3.77	4.61	5.69	4.95	51.24	5.45	03-1989
Brazoria, Angleton	91.8	43.7	107	2000	*7	1989	Feb. 15	Dec. 5	290	4.76	3.50	3.76	3.74	5.20	6.44	4.83	4.83	7.49	4.25	4.86	4.17	57.24	14.36	07-1979
Brazos, College Station	95.6	39.8	112	2000	2	1989	Mar. 2	Nov. 29	271	3.32	2.38	2.84	3.20	5.05	3.79	1.92	2.63	3.91	4.22	3.18	3.23	39.67	6.23	05-1983
Brewster, Alpine	88.7	31.3	107	1972	-3	1983	Apr. 8	Nov. 1	207	0.45	0.50	0.34	0.58	1.25	2.18	3.04	2.92	3.23	1.58	0.45	0.67	17.19	3.13	06-1968
Brewster, Chisos Basin	84.2	36.1	103	1973	-3	1989	Mar. 16	Nov. 17	246	0.55	0.69	0.36	0.61	1.60	2.42	3.55	3.72	2.71	1.72	0.66	0.58	19.17	4.29	05-1951
Briscoe, Silverton	90.9	21.6	*109	1994	-9	1963	Apr. 14	Oct. 22	190	0.57	0.78	1.17	1.59	3.22	3.96	1.84	2.76	2.67	1.68	0.90	0.74	22.34	5.25	06-1979
Brooks, Falfurrias	97.0	43.9	115	1998	9	1962	Feb. 6	Dec. 13	311	1.12	1.56	0.86	1.48	2.95	3.75	1.80	2.91	3.84	3.22	1.31	1.08	25.42		
Brown, Brownwood	95.0	29.6	114	2000	-6	1989	Mar. 25	Nov. 11	231	1.28	2.09	2.07	2.45	3.62	3.75	1.78	2.28	2.67	3.01	1.62	1.68	28.32	16.60	06-2000
Burleson, Somerville	96.7	36.4	114	2000	3	1989	Mar. 3	Nov. 23	264	2.93	2.53	2.62	2.92	4.39	3.25	2.04	2.43	3.59	4.33	3.63	3.14	38.50	15.25	10-1994
Burnet, Burnet	93.6	33.3	*114	1917	*-4	1989	Mar. 20	Nov. 12	237	1.61	2.16	2.33	2.48	4.58	4.09	2.06	2.06	3.15	3.46	2.32	2.15	32.43	9.80	09-1936
Caldwell, Luling	95.8	36.9	*110	2000	-3	1949	Mar. 7	Nov. 20	258	2.27	2.20	2.22	3.06	5.44	4.29	1.70	2.32	3.70	4.36	3.00	2.30	36.86	10.53	10-1998
Calhoun, Port O'Connor	88.2	47.9	105	2000	10	1989	Jan. 29	Dec. 31	338	3.07	2.20	1.73	1.55	3.70	2.77	3.05	2.94	4.97	4.45	2.53	1.82	34.78	12.50	07-1976

COUNTY AND STATION	Mean Max. July °F	Mean Min. Jan. °F	Record Highest °F	Year	Record Lowest °F	Year	Last in Spring Mo.	Day	First in Fall Mo.	Day	Growing Season Days	Jan In.	Feb In.	Mar In.	Apr In.	May In.	Jun In.	Jul In.	Aug In.	Sep In.	Oct In.	Nov In.	Dec In.	Annual In.	Highest Daily Rainfall In.	Mo.-Year
Callahan, Putnam	94.9	31.1	110	1964	-8	1989	Mar.	24	Nov.	13	234	1.17	1.55	1.76	1.80	3.13	3.25	1.97	2.02	2.79	3.03	1.64	1.41	25.52	5.00	08-1978
Cameron, Brownsville	92.4	50.5	106	1984	*15	1901	Dec.	25	Jan.	24	>365	1.36	1.18	0.93	1.96	2.48	2.93	1.77	2.99	5.31	3.78	1.75	1.11	27.55	12.09	09-1967
Camp, Pittsburg	94.0	32.0	109		-3		Mar.	21	Nov.	14	238	3.30	3.40	4.40	3.70	4.60	3.90	3.30	3.30	3.30	4.40	4.80	3.90	45.10		
Carson, Panhandle	90.8	19.3	109	1964	*-10	1963	Apr.	18	Oct.	22	186	0.62	0.73	1.43	1.80	3.10	3.54	2.67	2.78	2.21	1.71	0.98	0.64	22.21	8.05	05-1951
Cass, Wright Patman Dam	94.0	31.0	103		8		Mar.	19	Nov.	11	237	3.70	3.60	4.40	4.00	4.50	4.50	3.00	2.60	3.50	4.30	5.30	4.80	48.20		
Castro, Dimmitt	90.1	20.4	111	1983	-9	1986	Apr.	25	Oct.	16	172	0.50	0.51	0.81	0.99	2.76	3.12	2.40	3.06	2.57	1.58	0.71	0.70	19.71	4.38	10-1998
Chambers, Anahuac	91.9	41.7	110	1943	8	1989	Feb.	12	Dec.	9	299	4.84	2.83	3.33	3.56	5.22	5.88	4.59	4.74	6.42	4.06	4.31	4.30	54.08	15.87	08-1945
Cherokee, Rusk	92.8	36.8	110	2000	0	1982	Mar.	10	Nov.	21	255	4.41	3.64	4.12	3.86	4.69	4.34	2.95	2.38	4.01	4.94	4.63	4.53	48.50	10.00	06-2001
Childress, Childress	95.3	26.8	117	1994	*-5	1989	Apr.	1	Nov.	6	218	0.57	0.95	1.41	2.01	3.46	3.51	2.05	2.19	2.51	2.07	1.06	0.86	22.65	5.32	10-1983
Clay, Henrietta	95.0	26.8	*116	1951	-8	1989	Mar.	30	Nov.	5	220	1.53	2.08	2.45	2.71	4.39	3.72	1.74	2.40	3.35	3.35	1.77	2.17	31.66	6.07	06-1959
Cochran, Morton	91.4	23.1	*110	1994	-12	1963	Apr.	14	Nov.	11	193	0.50	0.64	0.64	0.89	1.92	2.52	2.61	2.97	2.51	1.64	0.79	0.62	18.34	4.69	07-1960
Coke, Robert Lee	96.4	29.0	114	2000	*-2	1989	Mar.	26	Nov.	11	230	0.81	1.22	1.05	1.72	3.24	2.90	1.44	2.28	3.46	2.73	1.15	1.00	23.00	8.40	10-1957
Coleman, Coleman	93.7	30.0	114	1943	-5	1930	Mar.	23	Nov.	13	234	1.03	1.75	1.84	2.19	4.11	4.05	1.77	2.58	3.25	3.08	1.57	1.48	28.70	8.55	07-1932
Collin, McKinney	92.7	31.1	118	1936	-7	1930	Mar.	21	Nov.	11	235	2.43	2.91	3.37	3.65	5.68	4.11	2.36	2.16	3.15	4.24	3.71	3.24	41.01	12.10	09-1964
Collingsworth, Wellington	97.9	27.0	113	1994	-6	1989	Apr.	1	Nov.	4	216	0.62	0.62	1.47	2.07	3.88	3.47	2.25	1.85	2.58	2.37	0.89	0.62	22.80	9.50	10-1986
Colorado, Columbus	96.3	36.3	116	2000	*4	1989	Apr.	11	Nov.	16	250	3.61	2.84	2.93	3.57	5.75	5.03	2.64	3.07	3.92	4.16	3.99	3.21	44.72	10.00	06-1973
Comal, New Braunfels	94.7	35.5	112	2000	*2	1989	Mar.	4	Nov.	21	261	1.88	1.98	2.04	2.72	5.01	4.81	1.99	2.32	3.46	4.38	2.71	2.44	35.74	18.35	10-1998
Comanche, Proctor Reservoir	95.5	30.6	113	2000	-8	1989	Mar.	20	Nov.	15	238	1.34	2.02	2.13	2.81	4.75	3.98	1.70	2.22	3.01	3.32	2.07	1.77	31.12	8.37	06-1988
Concho, Paint Rock	97.4	37.4	112	1978	-8	1985	Mar.	31	Nov.	6	219	1.04	1.52	1.35	1.56	3.31	3.77	1.84	2.05	3.55	2.81	1.41	1.29	25.50	8.25	09-1980
Cooke, Gainesville	95.0	28.0	112		-7		Mar.	27	Nov.	8	226	1.80	2.20	3.40	3.20	4.60	3.70	2.00	2.40	4.50	4.60	2.60	1.90	36.90		
Coryell, Gatesville	96.4	33.5	*112	2000	-6	1949	Mar.	24	Nov.	13	234	1.65	2.35	2.57	2.90	4.38	3.66	2.36	2.53	2.87	3.30	2.51	2.35	33.43	8.35	06-1964
Cottle, Paducah	96.8	26.2	118	1994	*-7	1989	Mar.	29	Nov.	5	221	0.82	1.11	1.31	1.92	3.85	3.67	1.72	2.63	2.96	2.06	1.08	0.98	24.11	6.65	06-1991
Crane, Crane	95.3	30.6	115	1994	-8	1985	Mar.	23	Nov.	11	232	0.57	0.78	0.34	0.84	1.86	1.71	1.48	2.02	2.95	1.64	0.68	0.70	15.38	5.55	08-1986
Crockett, Ozona	93.0	27.7	*109	1969	-8	1951	Apr.	1	Nov.	2	215	0.70	0.59	1.06	1.36	2.44	1.94	1.57	2.27	2.92	2.25	0.99	0.67	18.95	5.80	10-1959
Crosby, Crosbyton	92.5	25.3	113	1994	*-10	1930	Apr.	2	Nov.	1	212	0.68	0.96	1.03	1.87	3.05	2.68	2.05	2.30	3.46	1.91	0.95	0.84	22.95	5.78	06-1913
Culberson, Van Horn	91.7	27.8	112	1969	-10	1962	Apr.	4	Nov.	5	215	0.39	0.33	0.16	0.24	0.71	2.27	3.11	2.23	1.56	1.27	0.46	0.53	11.98	7.00	08-1966
Dallam, Dalhart	90.0		*107	1909	-21	1959	Apr.	23	Oct.	16	175	0.52	0.40	1.08	1.35	2.72	2.27	3.11	2.99	1.56	0.71	0.54	0.53	18.57	4.52	08-1985
Dallas, Dallas	96.1	36.4	115	1909	1	1989	Mar.	3	Nov.	25	267	1.89	2.31	3.13	3.46	5.30	3.92	2.43	2.17	2.65	4.65	2.61	2.53	37.05	6.02	03-1977
Dawson, Lamesa	92.9	26.1	114	1994	-12	1933	Apr.	4	Nov.	5	214	0.57	0.77	0.73	0.88	2.35	2.81	2.19	3.00	3.42	1.76	0.82	0.77	19.07	6.24	10-1985
Deaf Smith, Hereford	91.6	21.0	111	1910	-17	1951	Apr.	19	Oct.	19	182	0.50	0.50	0.98	1.02	2.12	2.90	1.84	2.25	2.25	1.80	0.77	0.74	18.65	*5.30	08-1976
Delta, Cooper	94.0	30.0	110		-1		Mar.	25	Nov.	13	233	2.70	3.20	4.10	3.60	5.40	4.00	2.90	2.10	3.90	4.80	4.30	4.00	45.00		
Denton, Denton	94.1	32.0	*113	1954	*-3	1949	Mar.	18	Nov.	16	243	1.94	2.55	2.82	3.30	5.41	4.00	2.53	2.26	3.35	4.81	2.87	2.66	37.79	7.30	05-1982
DeWitt, Cuero	95.1	41.3	113	2000	7	1989	Feb.	28	Nov.	25	270	2.30	1.95	2.32	2.96	4.74	4.51	2.18	2.25	2.25	3.67	2.66	2.23	36.08	12.40	06-1940
Dickens, Spur	95.4	25.5	117	1933	-17	1933	Apr.	2	Nov.	4	215	0.55	0.70	0.84	1.53	3.18	2.68	1.74	2.12	2.17	1.66	0.82	0.69	18.68	4.70	08-1996
Dimmit, Carrizo Springs	98.3	39.6	114	1942	-10	1989	Feb.	14	Dec.	4	292	1.00	0.94	0.89	1.47	2.96	2.78	1.26	2.33	1.95	2.66	1.10	0.87	20.21	8.78	07-1990
Donley, Clarendon	94.7	22.4	117	1936	*-11	1989	Apr.	11	Oct.	25	196	0.64	0.83	1.43	2.25	3.60	3.70	2.37	2.81	2.69	1.78	0.94	0.85	23.89	9.25	05-2001
Duval, Freer	97.3	42.5	116	1998	-6	1971	Feb.	13	Dec.	8	297	1.15	1.31	1.58	1.69	3.63	3.68	1.54	2.25	3.06	2.92	1.54	1.05	25.40	7.85	09-1971
Eastland, Eastland	94.9	26.7	*115	1943	*-6	1973	Mar.	30	Nov.	8	221	1.20	1.73	1.58	2.27	3.72	3.40	1.73	2.29	2.67	2.67	1.72	1.62	27.53	7.00	09-1957
Ector, Penwell	96.0	28.7	116	1994	-12	1985	Mar.	30	Nov.	7	222	0.42	0.58	0.42	0.61	2.11	1.56	1.30	1.46	2.35	1.24	0.63	0.61	13.29	4.53	04-1969

County and Station	July Mean Max (°F)	Jan. Mean Min (°F)	Record High (°F)	Year	Record Low (°F)	Year	Last Freeze in Spring	First Freeze in Fall	Growing Season (Days)	Jan.	Feb.	Mar.	Apr.	May	June	July	Aug.	Sept.	Oct.	Nov.	Dec.	Annual	Highest Daily Rainfall (In.)	Mo.-Year
Edwards, Rocksprings	91.6	34.3	*108	1980	*3	1951	Mar. 18	Nov. 18	243	0.77	1.31	1.36	1.75	3.23	3.07	2.05	2.84	2.44	3.41	1.50	1.03	24.76	9.50	06-1935
Ellis, Waxahachie	96.0	35.0	115	1909	-4	1989	Mar. 14	Nov. 18	248	2.11	2.85	3.21	3.89	4.85	3.51	2.28	2.26	3.16	4.43	3.04	3.22	38.81	10.80	09-1958
El Paso, El Paso	94.5	32.9	114	1994	-8	1962	Mar. 22	Nov. 8	230	0.45	0.39	0.26	0.23	0.38	0.87	1.49	1.75	1.61	0.81	0.42	0.77	9.43	2.26	09-1974
Erath, Stephenville	93.6	30.0	111	1925	-8	1989	Mar. 22	Nov. 13	235	1.31	1.86	2.35	2.53	4.35	3.41	1.47	2.41	2.80	3.28	1.97	1.97	29.71	9.71	05-1956
Falls, Marlin	95.0	37.2	*112	1969	-7	1949	Mar. 10	Nov. 17	251	2.49	2.60	3.30	3.19	5.35	3.55	2.09	1.97	3.08	3.90	3.17	3.30	37.99	11.90	07-1903
Fannin, Bonham	92.6	30.2	115	1936	*-5	1930	Mar. 27	Nov. 8	225	2.39	3.01	3.76	3.41	5.57	4.50	3.45	2.13	3.45	5.40	3.94	3.55	44.56	13.30	07-1903
Fayette, La Grange	95.9	41.4	110	2000	3	1989	Feb. 26	Nov. 23	269	3.05	2.88	2.55	2.99	4.82	4.41	2.25	2.81	3.68	4.47	3.36	3.04	40.31	9.41	06-1940
Fisher, Rotan	94.2	27.2	116	1994	*-5	1989	Mar. 29	Nov. 9	225	0.80	1.35	1.30	1.72	3.68	2.74	1.92	2.76	3.45	2.30	1.13	1.07	24.22	6.85	08-1972
Floyd, Floydada	92.3	23.2	111	1994	-9	1963	Apr. 8	Oct. 30	205	0.45	0.72	0.98	1.58	3.01	3.74	2.00	2.50	2.88	1.62	0.84	0.63	20.95	6.51	09-1942
Foard, Crowell	97.0	24.0	114		-7		Apr. 2	Nov. 7	219	1.00	1.40	1.60	2.10	4.30	3.70	1.70	2.40	3.30	2.40	1.50	1.00	26.40		
Fort Bend, Sugar Land	93.7	41.6	108	2000	*6	1989	Feb. 15	Dec. 10	294	4.06	2.98	3.24	3.48	4.69	5.51	3.30	4.29	5.82	4.03	4.58	3.36	49.34	10.60	06-2001
Franklin, Mount Vernon	92.8	32.2	*108	2000	-1	1989	Mar. 22	Nov. 12	235	2.83	3.41	4.23	3.56	4.71	4.79	3.82	2.19	3.75	4.77	5.10	4.49	47.65	6.10	07-1990
Freestone, Fairfield	95.0	36.4	*110	2000	-2	1989	Mar. 19	Nov. 17	242	2.84	3.29	3.29	3.38	5.04	3.79	2.14	2.56	3.48	4.64	4.16	3.70	42.31	6.75	01-1999
Frio, Pearsall	97.5	37.9	113	2000	*7	1989	Feb. 22	Nov. 25	275	1.30	1.45	1.30	2.15	3.33	3.68	1.58	2.61	2.29	3.20	1.60	1.24	25.73	7.84	08-1946
Gaines, Seminole	94.1	26.7	114	1994	-9	1962	Apr. 2	Nov. 3	215	0.64	0.72	0.61	0.91	2.39	2.45	2.44	2.31	2.73	1.39	0.90	0.71	18.20	5.40	05-1999
Galveston, Galveston	88.7	49.7	102	1999	*14	1989	Jan. 19	Jan. 3	358	3.08	2.61	2.76	2.56	3.70	4.04	3.45	4.22	5.76	3.49	3.64	3.53	43.84	13.63	07-1900
Garza, Post	94.0	27.8	115	1994	*-1	1989	Mar. 30	Nov. 9	223	0.58	0.98	0.76	1.43	3.01	2.83	2.03	2.88	3.07	2.05	0.89	0.78	21.09	6.75	10-1926
Gillespie, Fredericksburg	93.1	36.1	*109	2000	-5	1949	Mar. 18	Nov. 12	238	1.36	1.91	1.86	2.40	4.29	3.97	2.00	2.74	3.07	3.72	2.19	2.14	31.65	8.03	09-1952
Glasscock, Garden City	94.0	26.7	114	1994	-3	1989	Apr. 3	Nov. 3	213	0.73	0.71	0.70	1.14	2.18	1.91	1.86	2.02	2.97	1.66	0.75	0.69	17.32	8.75	07-1945
Goliad, Goliad	95.5	43.3	*112	1998	7	1962	Feb. 25	Nov. 26	273	2.34	2.11	2.00	3.19	4.49	4.96	2.85	3.49	4.56	4.26	2.19	2.14	38.58	9.16	09-1967
Gonzales, Gonzales	93.9	38.7	111	2000	*4	1989	Feb. 26	Dec. 1	277	2.36	2.22	2.22	3.04	5.43	4.24	1.60	2.68	3.20	3.87	2.84	2.46	36.02	16.31	09-1981
Gray, Pampa	92.0	21.9	111	1980	-8	1989	Apr. 13	Oct. 25	195	0.57	0.83	1.50	1.95	3.37	3.52	2.85	2.38	2.29	1.58	1.20	0.70	22.74	3.54	07-1982
Grayson, Sherman	92.7	32.2	113	1936	*-2	1989	Mar. 22	Nov. 14	236	2.11	2.63	3.44	3.49	5.41	4.37	2.34	2.25	4.01	5.15	3.81	3.03	42.04	8.40	08-1920
Gregg, Longview	94.5	33.7	113	1936	-4	1930	Mar. 19	Nov. 15	243	3.79	3.93	4.11	4.19	4.79	5.03	2.83	2.71	3.81	4.34	4.75	4.78	49.06	8.70	03-1989
Grimes, Richards	96.0	40.0	108		4		Mar. 1	Dec. 4	278	4.10	3.00	3.30	3.40	5.20	3.90	2.20	2.60	4.20	4.40	4.10	4.30	44.70		
Guadalupe, New Braunfels	95.0	36.0	110		0		Mar. 6	Nov. 28	267	1.90	2.20	1.80	2.60	5.00	4.10	2.00	2.50	4.10	3.50	2.80	2.00	34.50		
Hale, Plainview	91.0	24.4	111	1994	-8	1933	Apr. 4	Oct. 31	209	0.59	0.63	0.80	1.52	2.91	3.05	2.45	2.38	2.28	1.72	0.84	0.73	19.90	7.00	07-1960
Hall, Memphis	95.7	25.5	*117	1944	-11	1930	Apr. 1	Nov. 4	217	0.57	0.88	1.52	2.04	3.93	3.51	1.88	2.25	2.45	1.77	0.96	0.75	22.51	8.80	06-1960
Hamilton, Hamilton	94.3	33.4	109	1964	-3	1989	Mar. 16	Nov. 15	243	1.64	1.76	2.61	2.72	3.70	3.71	1.53	1.57	2.85	2.90	2.00	1.60	28.59	8.20	10-1959
Hansford, Spearman	95.5	22.4	111	1936	-22	1959	Apr. 16	Oct. 23	189	0.53	0.62	1.52	1.58	2.83	2.97	2.77	2.38	2.08	1.35	1.01	0.66	20.30	5.80	05-1965
Hardeman, Quanah	96.5	24.6	*119	1994	-15	1989	Apr. 4	Nov. 14	211	0.96	1.17	1.65	2.08	3.86	3.73	2.42	2.57	3.43	2.37	1.40	1.12	26.76	8.03	08-1995
Hardin, Evadale	93.0	37.0	102		12		Mar. 31	Nov. 14	246	5.06	3.70	4.20	4.00	5.50	5.50	4.10	4.54	4.50	5.30	5.00	5.10	56.50		
Harris, Houston	93.6	45.2	108	2000	9	1989	Feb. 8	Dec. 20	308	4.25	3.01	3.19	3.46	5.11	6.84	4.36	4.54	5.62	5.26	4.54	3.78	53.96	9.95	10-1949
Harrison, Marshall	92.4	33.4	112	1909	-5	1930	Mar. 20	Nov. 12	236	4.38	4.07	4.33	4.35	5.07	5.23	3.02	2.68	3.89	4.66	4.59	4.95	51.22	8.58	03-1989
Hartley, Channing	90.9	20.0	*108	1981	-9	1979	Apr. 19	Oct. 19	182	0.35	0.45	0.76	1.10	1.88	2.36	2.59	3.50	1.66	1.33	0.61	0.67	17.20	3.80	12-1997
Haskell, Haskell	96.1	28.8	*115	1994	*-6	1989	Mar. 27	Nov. 12	229	0.96	1.47	1.46	1.99	3.32	3.26	1.61	2.74	2.96	2.53	1.26	1.37	24.93	14.29	10-1978
Hays, San Marcos	95.1	38.6	*111	2000	-2	1949	Feb. 28	Nov. 24	268	2.05	2.21	2.09	2.85	5.31	4.84	2.12	2.65	3.46	4.03	3.17	2.41	37.19	15.78	10-1998
Hemphill, Canadian	93.9	18.8	*112	1994	*-14	1942	Apr. 10	Oct. 16	188	0.46	0.71	1.70	1.72	3.75	3.33	2.19	2.36	2.36	1.47	0.94	0.69	21.68	5.15	10-1985

County and Station	TEMPERATURE July Mean Max. (°F)	January Mean Min. (°F)	Record Highest (°F)	Year	Record Lowest (°F)	Year	Avg Freeze — Last in Spring	First in Fall	Growing Season Days	MEAN PRECIPITATION (In.) January	February	March	April	May	June	July	August	September	October	November	December	Annual	EXTREMES Highest Daily Rainfall (In.)	Mo.-Year
Henderson, Athens	93.4	35.2	*109	2000	-6	1985	Mar. 19	Nov. 14	239	2.96	3.37	3.70	3.47	4.82	3.95	1.74	2.43	3.07	4.70	3.94	3.88	42.03	7.19	04-1986
Hidalgo, McAllen	95.5	48.2	109	1999	17	1962	Jan. 05	Jan. 30	>365	1.20	1.37	0.95	1.36	2.51	2.49	1.70	2.31	4.00	2.76	0.95	1.01	22.61	7.81	08-1980
Hill, Hillsboro	95.2	35.2	113	1917	-6	1989	Mar. 19	Nov. 14	240	2.19	2.67	3.21	3.24	4.65	4.07	2.08	2.19	2.92	4.15	2.70	3.08	37.15	11.30	09-1936
Hockley, Levelland	92.7	23.7	115	1994	-16	1963	Apr. 08	Oct. 27	201	0.59	0.63	0.58	1.03	2.35	2.78	2.22	2.87	3.24	1.62	0.85	0.82	19.58	4.23	06-1999
Hood, Cresson	97.0	33.0	110		-6		Mar. 26	Nov. 13	232	1.60	2.20	2.60	2.90	4.70	3.90	1.70	2.40	3.90	2.60	2.30	2.30	33.10		
Hopkins, Sulphur Springs	94.8	31.1	115	1969	-4	1989	Mar. 25	Nov. 12	232	2.88	3.20	4.27	4.34	5.00	4.64	3.22	2.35	3.35	5.21	4.77	4.46	47.69	8.11	07-1994
Houston, Crockett	93.3	35.9	114	1909	*0	1989	Mar. 10	Nov. 18	252	4.00	3.10	3.45	3.87	4.66	4.46	2.84	2.81	4.12	4.22	3.93	4.02	45.48	9.11	06-2001
Howard, Big Spring	93.4	29.6	114	1994	*-5	1985	Mar. 23	Nov. 13	235	0.72	0.81	0.73	1.34	3.05	2.58	1.78	2.38	3.51	1.78	0.77	0.67	20.12	4.84	05-1994
Hudspeth, Sierra Blanca	92.0	25.1	*109	1994	-10	1985	Apr. 18	Oct. 29	193	0.49	0.81	0.26	0.29	0.53	1.11	2.11	2.29	2.19	0.75	0.44	0.66	11.93	3.32	09-1978
Hunt, Greenville	93.3	31.2	116	1936	-4	1930	Mar. 23	Nov. 13	235	2.51	3.16	3.67	3.79	5.47	4.03	2.96	2.18	3.56	4.91	3.98	3.48	43.70	6.95	09-1936
Hutchinson, Borger	92.6	23.4	*108	1998	-12	1951	Apr. 14	Oct. 25	193	0.65	0.69	1.56	1.77	3.08	3.20	2.69	3.16	2.00	1.60	0.88	0.70	21.98	3.79	05-1959
Irion, Funk Ranch	94.4	32.0	108		4		Mar. 27	Nov. 11	229	0.70	1.11	1.00	1.60	2.50	2.50	1.40	1.90	2.10	2.10	1.00	1.00	19.90		
Jack, Jacksboro	94.4	29.7	*113	1980	-7	1989	Mar. 21	Nov. 14	237	1.28	1.79	2.38	2.60	4.96	3.18	2.26	2.15	3.18	3.78	2.05	1.83	31.44	9.60	04-1957
Jackson, Edna	94.0	42.0	105		17		Feb. 19	Dec. 06	290	3.10	2.40	2.00	3.10	5.30	4.60	2.90	2.60	4.90	5.00	3.40	2.80	42.10		
Jasper, Sam Rayburn Dam	94.5	35.2	109	2000	7	1989	Mar. 17	Nov. 14	241	5.94	4.55	5.29	4.51	5.53	5.81	4.24	3.92	3.97	4.84	5.88	6.09	60.57	9.04	03-1999
Jeff Davis, Fort Davis	89.5	32.3	*107	1998	*0	1985	Apr. 09	Nov. 02	206	0.43	0.35	0.34	0.50	1.46	1.79	2.95	2.76	2.97	1.29	0.49	0.53	15.86	5.30	08-1932
Jeff Davis, Mount Locke	84.5	32.4	*104	1994	-10	1962	Apr. 17	Oct. 26	191	0.53	0.49	0.33	0.60	1.73	2.56	3.82	4.02	3.29	1.71	0.56	0.73	20.37	4.13	05-1984
Jefferson, Beaumont	91.6	42.9	108	2000	12	1989	Feb. 14	Dec. 06	295	5.69	3.35	3.75	3.84	5.83	6.58	5.23	4.85	6.10	4.67	4.75	5.25	59.89	12.09	09-1963
Jim Hogg, Hebbronville	97.5	43.8	111	1998	*12	1998	Feb. 08	Dec. 11	307	1.12	1.40	1.14	1.65	3.33	3.13	1.44	2.28	3.68	2.22	1.22	1.10	23.75	9.40	09-1971
Jim Wells, Alice	96.1	44.1	*111	1998	*12	1989	Jan. 29	Dec. 15	320	1.21	1.51	1.34	1.65	3.16	3.41	1.76	2.70	4.52	3.55	1.50	1.21	27.52	12.14	09-1971
Johnson, Cleburne	97.0	34.0	114	1939	-5	1989	Mar. 18	Nov. 18	240	1.90	2.29	3.07	3.53	5.11	3.90	2.18	2.36	2.88	3.92	2.54	2.57	36.25	9.02	05-1989
Jones, Anson	96.3	30.7	114	1994	-12	1989	Mar. 28	Nov. 12	228	1.03	1.51	1.21	1.94	3.20	3.13	2.04	2.94	3.93	2.55	1.22	1.30	26.00	5.60	09-1988
Karnes, Karnes City	95.0	41.0	112	1994	-7		Feb. 24	Dec. 02	281	1.50	1.70	1.50	2.50	3.40	3.70	1.90	2.40	3.40	3.00	1.90	1.50	28.40		
Kaufman, Kaufman	94.6	32.3	113	1936	*-3	1989	Mar. 19	Nov. 14	240	2.74	3.04	3.37	3.06	4.45	3.31	2.12	1.98	2.77	4.81	3.80	3.45	38.90	13.66	08-1908
Kendall, Boerne	91.9	34.3	112	1925	-4	1949	Mar. 20	Nov. 13	238	1.79	2.24	2.57	2.87	4.66	4.77	2.23	3.05	3.61	4.09	3.11	2.37	37.36	9.04	10-1913
Kenedy, Sarita	95.0	45.0	110		14		Feb. 02	Dec. 08	319	1.10	1.80	1.30	1.60	2.70	3.30	1.50	3.40	4.70	3.40	1.90	1.20	27.90		
Kent, Jayton	95.7	24.9	116	1994	-6	1985	Apr. 02	Nov. 06	218	0.91	1.14	1.12	1.73	3.35	3.21	1.59	2.81	3.04	2.17	0.97	0.90	22.94	6.50	06-1991
Kerr, Kerrville	95.0	32.0	110		-7		Apr. 06	Nov. 06	216	2.00	2.10	2.10	2.30	4.20	4.00	2.20	2.30	2.90	3.80	2.60	2.10	32.60		
Kimble, Junction	94.8	29.3	*110	1984	-11	1989	Apr. 02	Nov. 01	212	0.77	1.43	1.42	1.95	3.23	3.10	1.55	2.20	2.28	2.68	1.37	1.26	23.24	6.10	09-1980
King, Guthrie	96.7	23.9	119	1994	-10	1988	Apr. 06	Nov. 04	211	1.03	1.28	1.26	1.79	3.90	3.17	1.94	2.87	3.25	2.38	1.12	1.01	25.00	8.85	07-1986
Kinney, Brackettville	95.5	37.3	*111	2000	*-4	1962	Apr. 05	Nov. 15	255	0.77	1.16	1.10	1.99	2.87	3.18	1.79	2.29	2.77	2.49	1.41	0.97	22.79	6.20	05-1900
Kleberg, Kingsville	95.5	43.4	*111	1994	10	1989	Feb. 10	Dec. 10	303	1.44	1.71	1.24	1.80	3.53	4.02	1.97	3.05	3.98	3.72	1.50	1.07	29.03	6.67	12-1991
Knox, Munday	96.5	28.1	*117	1994	*-9	1989	Mar. 28	Nov. 12	228	1.00	1.54	1.69	1.91	3.85	3.46	1.70	2.68	3.22	2.73	1.38	1.20	26.36	8.00	06-1930
Lamar, Paris	94.3	29.9	115	1936	*-5	1930	Mar. 18	Nov. 14	240	2.63	3.00	4.11	3.56	5.63	4.25	3.89	2.39	4.42	5.04	4.70	4.20	47.82	7.61	06-1928
Lamb, Littlefield	92.0	22.7	*112	1994	-6	1979	Apr. 11	Oct. 25	196	0.55	0.75	0.75	1.11	2.24	3.04	2.44	2.80	2.03	1.52	0.77	0.69	18.69	5.10	06-1969
Lampasas, Lampasas	94.1	30.4	*112	1917	-12	1949	Apr. 11	Nov. 07	219	1.50	2.34	2.31	2.48	4.37	3.49	1.68	2.42	2.61	3.33	2.32	2.23	31.08	6.95	05-1957
La Salle, Fowlerton	98.9	39.1	113	1998	9	1962	Feb. 27	Nov. 26	271	0.93	1.08	1.46	1.84	2.73	2.61	1.53	2.19	2.71	3.15	1.22	1.11	22.56	9.50	10-1986
Lavaca, Hallettsville	94.4	41.8	*111	1980	5	1989	Feb. 25	Nov. 29	277	2.91	2.50	2.46	3.44	5.75	5.02	2.28	2.95	4.49	4.07	3.53	2.83	42.23	11.30	07-1936

COUNTY AND STATION	TEMPERATURE July Mean Max. °F	January Mean Min. °F	Record Highest °F	Year	Record Lowest °F	Year	AVG FREEZE Last in Spring Mo.	Day	First in Fall Mo.	Day	Growing Season Days	MEAN PRECIPITATION January In.	February In.	March In.	April In.	May In.	June In.	July In.	August In.	September In.	October In.	November In.	December In.	Annual In.	EXTREMES Highest Daily Rainfall In.	Mo.-Year
Lee, Lexington	93.6	37.3	111	2000	2	1989	Mar.	1	Nov.	22	265	2.60	2.13	2.54	2.48	4.82	3.78	1.63	2.06	3.26	4.69	3.25	2.78	36.02	10.13	10-1994
Leon, Centerville	94.7	34.3	*111	1954	-3	1949	Mar.	17	Nov.	14	242	3.40	3.18	3.51	3.29	4.77	4.12	2.48	2.62	3.50	4.79	3.82	3.60	43.08	8.50	10-1957
Liberty, Liberty	92.2	40.3	108	1913	7	1989	Feb.	18	Dec.	1	285	4.91	3.74	3.84	4.01	5.80	6.88	4.46	4.34	5.92	5.77	5.84	5.01	60.52	18.50	10-1994
Limestone, Mexia	95.8	33.7	112	1909	-5	1989	Feb.	6	Nov.	20	258	2.44	3.08	3.45	3.14	4.91	3.28	1.99	2.56	4.16	4.29	3.64	3.85	41.40	11.80	09-1932
Lipscomb, Lipscomb	94.2	16.2	114	1978	*-18	1974	Apr.	23	Oct.	11	170	0.54	0.81	1.91	2.00	3.85	2.70	2.30	2.52	1.97	1.46	1.12	0.81	22.57	6.62	05-1951
Live Oak, Choke Canyon Dam	97.0	42.0	109		12		Feb.	20	Dec.	6	289	1.20	1.10	1.80	2.40	2.80	2.70	1.60	1.40	2.10	2.00	1.70	1.20	22.00		
Llano, Llano	96.0	32.3	115	1933	-7	1929	Mar.	18	Nov.	12	238	1.08	1.80	1.90	2.19	3.94	3.40	1.80	2.03	2.14	2.88	2.23	1.90	27.33	12.53	09-1952
Loving, Mentone	96.0	28.0	114		-14		Apr.	3	Nov.	8	222	0.50	0.30	0.30	0.20	1.10	0.90	1.80	1.20	1.20	1.00	0.30	0.30	9.10		
Lubbock, Lubbock	91.9	24.4	114	1994	-17	1933	Apr.	3	Nov.	1	211	0.66	0.71	0.76	1.29	2.31	2.98	2.13	2.36	2.57	1.70	0.71	0.67	18.69	5.70	06-1967
Lynn, Tahoka	92.2	25.1	111	1994	-15	1933	Apr.	4	Nov.	4	213	0.50	0.79	0.71	1.48	2.74	3.22	2.62	2.23	2.65	1.73	0.86	0.79	20.48	8.32	10-1913
Madison, Madisonville	96.0	35.8	112	2000	-2	1949	Apr.	7	Nov.	18	255	3.81	2.83	3.24	3.26	5.06	3.89	2.72	2.95	4.20	4.41	4.01	3.62	44.00	8.00	08-1945
Marion, Jefferson	93.1	31.4	108	2000	-5	1989	Mar.	25	Nov.	6	225	4.13	3.96	4.41	4.07	4.60	4.84	2.89	2.93	4.20	4.64	4.68	4.71	49.26	9.10	04-1921
Martin, Lenorah	94.0	30.0	109		-8		Apr.	5	Nov.	6	215	0.70	0.70	0.70	1.20	2.40	2.50	2.00	1.60	3.10	1.80	0.80	0.70	18.20		
Mason, Mason	94.9	30.0	109	1962	*3	1985	Mar.	26	Nov.	13	227	0.91	1.97	1.74	2.05	3.31	4.00	2.00	2.52	3.00	3.01	2.07	1.37	27.95	7.45	09-1952
Matagorda, Bay City	92.4	40.5	*109	2000	*7	1989	Feb.	11	Dec.	13	306	3.89	2.97	3.00	3.18	4.90	4.68	3.48	3.48	5.61	5.13	3.97	3.33	48.03	8.95	09-1961
Maverick, Eagle Pass	98.1	40.1	*115	1944	*10	1962	Feb.	12	Dec.	5	295	0.80	0.94	0.72	1.75	2.95	3.49	2.03	2.01	2.57	2.33	1.08	0.81	19.36	15.60	06-1936
McCulloch, Brady	94.5	32.3	*110	1980	-2	1989	Mar.	21	Nov.	11	235	1.01	1.68	1.63	1.92	3.60	3.26	2.68	2.57	3.26	2.68	1.73	1.61	27.63	6.51	07-1971
McLennan, Waco	96.7	35.1	112	1969	5	1949	Mar.	13	Nov.	19	250	1.90	2.43	2.48	2.99	4.46	3.08	2.23	1.85	2.88	3.67	2.61	2.76	33.34	7.98	12-1997
McMullen, Tilden	98.7	40.3	119	1910	4	1989	Feb.	21	Dec.	3	284	1.15	1.27	1.33	1.95	3.10	3.37	1.52	2.56	2.80	2.14	1.38	1.19	23.87	6.93	09-1967
Medina, Hondo	95.0	38.0	112		4		Mar.	6	Nov.	24	263	1.30	1.50	1.60	2.70	3.80	3.60	1.40	1.50	2.90	2.90	1.80	1.40	26.30		
Menard, Menard	94.8	30.7	114	1927	-6	1929	Apr.	7	Oct.	29	204	0.97	1.48	1.60	1.72	3.22	3.38	2.14	2.34	2.69	2.57	1.51	1.28	24.90	6.03	09-1936
Midland, Midland	94.3	29.6	116	1994	-11	1985	Mar.	30	Nov.	12	226	0.53	0.58	0.42	0.73	1.79	1.71	1.89	1.77	2.31	1.77	0.65	0.65	14.80	4.75	05-1968
Milam, Cameron	95.7	39.2	114	1917	-7	1930	Mar.	7	Nov.	22	260	2.29	2.53	2.45	2.88	5.01	3.22	1.94	1.95	3.54	3.73	3.12	2.86	35.52	12.45	09-1921
Mills, Goldthwaite	92.0	35.2	110	1964	-7	1989	Mar.	20	Nov.	15	239	1.26	2.10	2.04	2.28	3.85	3.81	1.76	1.95	2.79	3.11	2.05	1.78	28.78	7.20	10-1969
Mitchell, Colorado City	95.9	27.0	115	1907	-11	1947	Mar.	25	Nov.	7	226	0.44	0.89	1.07	1.33	2.49	2.84	1.23	2.29	3.09	2.22	0.90	0.64	19.43	8.65	04-1900
Montague, Bowie	94.7	28.0	115	1980	-11	1989	Mar.	21	Nov.	12	236	1.47	2.13	2.62	2.89	5.04	3.42	1.81	2.27	3.67	4.20	2.18	2.02	33.72	10.25	05-1989
Montgomery, Conroe	94.3	40.3	109	2000	4	1989	Feb.	27	Nov.	25	270	4.21	2.97	2.94	3.85	5.50	4.58	3.22	3.73	4.46	4.70	4.79	4.37	49.32	14.35	10-1994
Moore, Dumas	91.7	20.8	*109	1980	*-18	1980	Apr.	18	Oct.	22	186	0.47	0.58	1.13	1.31	2.74	2.41	2.42	2.47	1.95	1.11	0.66	0.50	17.75	4.10	05-1988
Morris, Daingerfield	95.0	33.7	112	1998	-5	1962	Mar.	3	Nov.	22	263	3.54	3.35	4.64	4.32	4.43	4.24	2.98	2.39	3.29	4.35	4.84	4.39	46.76	7.48	04-1966
Motley, Matador	94.8	27.3	116	1994	0	1989	Apr.	1	Nov.	8	221	0.67	0.90	1.21	1.81	3.16	3.60	2.90	2.41	3.11	2.09	0.99	0.85	22.90	5.30	10-1983
Nacogdoches, Nacogdoches	95.7	36.0	110		-5		Mar.	16	Nov.	23	243	4.40	3.90	4.20	4.10	4.80	4.10	3.10	3.10	3.70	4.00	4.60	4.60	48.40		
Navarro, Corsicana	94.0	34.0	113	1954	7	1947	Mar.	9	Nov.	10	259	2.49	3.08	3.34	3.39	4.95	5.00	2.16	2.37	3.04	4.33	3.33	3.60	39.48	9.96	05-1968
Newton, Toledo Bend Dam	94.5	35.0	107		-11		Mar.	24	Dec.	9	228	5.70	4.40	4.80	4.00	4.90	3.53	3.60	3.40	3.90	4.10	5.00	6.10	54.90		
Nolan, Roscoe	94.0	28.9	113	1994	-17	1989	Mar.	31	Nov.	10	223	1.03	1.18	1.11	1.52	3.04	2.97	2.00	2.59	3.58	2.53	0.99	0.99	23.54	8.28	09-1980
Nueces, Corpus Christi	93.8	46.2	109	2000	13	1989	Feb.	3	Dec.	23	319	1.62	1.84	1.74	2.05	3.48	2.18	2.74	3.54	5.03	3.94	1.74	1.75	32.26	7.92	10-1995
Ochiltree, Perryton	91.4	18.4	111	1981	-11	1988	Apr.	25	Oct.	17	174	0.47	0.62	1.71	1.80	3.33	2.97	2.22	2.22	1.89	1.38	1.09	0.66	20.88	7.11	05-1989
Oldham, Boys Ranch	92.3	20.5	110	1982	10	1983	Apr.	13	Oct.	16	186	0.49	0.28	0.89	1.13	2.47	2.18	2.96	3.20	1.94	1.48	0.66	0.50	18.18	4.50	10-1990
Orange, Orange	91.0	41.0	104		10	1990	Mar.	16	Nov.	11	240	6.00	3.60	3.90	3.60	5.70	6.20	5.30	4.70	5.60	4.60	4.60	5.20	59.00		

Table — Temperature, Average Freeze Dates, Growing Season, Mean Precipitation, and Rainfall Extremes by County and Station. (Mo.–Year = month-year of record; * indicates tie with earlier date.)

County and Station	Mean Max. July (°F)	Mean Min. January (°F)	Record Highest (°F)	Year	Record Lowest (°F)	Year	Last in Spring	First in Fall	Growing Season (Days)	Jan.	Feb.	Mar.	Apr.	May	June	July	Aug.	Sep.	Oct.	Nov.	Dec.	Annual	Highest Daily Rainfall (In.)	(Mo.-Year)
Palo Pinto, Mineral Wells	97.3	33.4	*114	1980	-8	1989	Mar. 23	Nov. 13	233	1.42	1.99	2.69	2.75	4.59	3.25	2.25	2.34	2.80	3.81	2.16	1.74	31.79	6.65	10-1981
Panola, Carthage	93.7	35.9	*109	2000	*1	1989	Mar. 17	Nov. 14	242	4.76	3.88	4.00	4.36	5.05	4.95	3.25	2.92	3.75	4.65	4.93	5.01	51.51	9.25	04-1991
Parker, Weatherford	95.2	29.0	119	1980	*-10	1989	Mar. 29	Nov. 8	223	1.50	2.36	2.79	2.84	4.76	3.93	2.11	2.60	2.85	4.19	2.61	2.16	34.70	7.05	07-1962
Parmer, Friona	89.8	21.7	*108	1990	-15	1963	Apr. 19	Oct. 20	183	0.56	0.53	0.91	1.09	2.19	2.50	2.34	2.89	2.28	1.60	0.80	0.79	18.38	3.90	10-1998
Pecos, Fort Stockton	95.8	31.4	117	1994	-6	1985	Mar. 26	Nov. 12	230	0.50	0.47	0.38	0.72	1.59	1.70	1.24	1.95	2.75	1.45	0.61	0.60	14.06	5.22	10-1986
Polk, Livingston	94.1	35.8	*111	2000	*3	1989	Mar. 17	Nov. 13	241	4.64	3.47	3.89	3.92	5.54	5.20	3.55	3.41	4.73	3.82	4.76	4.92	51.85	10.47	10-1994
Potter, Amarillo	91.0	22.6	*108	1998	-14	1951	Apr. 18	Oct. 20	185	0.63	0.55	1.13	1.33	2.50	3.28	2.83	2.94	1.88	1.50	0.68	0.61	19.71	4.92	06-1984
Presidio, Marfa	88.9	23.9	*106	1994	-2	1972	Apr. 11	Oct. 30	201	0.41	0.47	0.24	0.67	0.66	1.80	2.01	2.70	2.88	1.48	0.39	0.59	15.92	2.93	05-1984
Presidio, Presidio	100.8	31.6	*117	1964	4	1962	Mar. 5	Nov. 20	260	0.31	0.36	0.15	0.38	0.66	1.51	2.33	1.82	1.69	0.99	0.37	0.51	10.76	3.30	04-1979
Rains, Emory	92.4	34.5	110	1964	-5	1989	Mar. 22	Nov. 12	234	3.04	3.34	3.88	3.72	5.31	4.19	2.33	2.23	2.98	4.66	3.89	3.93	43.50	5.65	06-1992
Randall, Canyon	92.6	23.7	*109	1981	-14	1951	Apr. 13	Oct. 22	191	0.46	0.52	0.99	1.08	2.89	2.96	2.39	2.84	1.97	1.78	0.69	0.62	19.19	7.87	08-1968
Reagan, Big Lake	93.4	29.1	110	1998	*1	1989	Apr. 1	Nov. 5	218	0.68	0.92	0.81	1.42	2.39	1.99	1.79	3.07	2.97	1.92	0.88	0.84	18.31	4.85	07-1990
Real, Camp Wood	94.2	33.1	*109	2000	*5	1989	Mar. 22	Nov. 11	233	1.11	1.44	1.55	2.41	3.16	3.68	2.09	3.07	2.87	3.46	1.77	1.38	27.99	8.37	11-2001
Red River, Clarksville	92.2	29.7	115	1936	-7	1930	Mar. 28	Nov. 9	226	2.65	3.17	4.50	4.02	5.43	4.00	1.78	2.07	3.83	4.99	5.43	4.51	47.83	8.30	05-1933
Reeves, Balmorhea	94.7	30.1	112	1939	-9	1933	Mar. 30	Nov. 9	223	0.58	0.56	0.24	0.63	1.45	1.24	1.24	2.29	3.08	1.19	0.54	0.61	14.19	4.13	07-1973
Reeves, Pecos	98.5	28.1	118	1968	-9	1962	Mar. 26	Nov. 7	226	0.47	0.45	0.34	0.47	1.25	1.24	1.35	1.62	2.24	1.10	0.47	0.61	11.61	4.38	05-1992
Refugio, Refugio	94.0	45.0	106		8	1942	Feb. 14	Dec. 15	304	2.50	2.20	1.50	1.90	4.30	4.80	3.30	3.50	7.00	5.20	2.30	1.60	40.10	5.58	10-1985
Roberts, Miami	92.4	20.6	114	1917	*-15	1942	Apr. 15	Oct. 19	186	0.68	0.83	1.74	2.19	3.77	3.26	2.39	2.40	2.38	1.64	1.12	0.90	23.30	7.48	07-1979
Robertson, Franklin	95.1	38.2	112	2000	-1	1989	Mar. 23	Nov. 19	254	3.03	2.86	2.90	3.03	4.81	2.95	2.04	2.60	3.65	4.38	3.26	3.52	39.03		
Rockwall, Rockwall	96.0	33.0	118		-7	1989	Mar. 28	Nov. 14	236	2.10	2.70	3.50	3.60	5.30	3.70	2.30	2.10	3.00	4.60	3.40	3.20	39.40	7.05	05-1946
Runnels, Ballinger	94.3	28.5	116	1907	-6	1949	Mar. 20	Nov. 9	225	0.94	1.32	1.27	1.80	3.38	3.15	1.39	2.40	3.08	2.52	1.31	1.20	23.76	11.05	03-1989
Rusk, Henderson	93.1	33.1	*111	2000	-1	1989	Mar. 21	Nov. 15	239	4.08	3.78	4.00	3.91	4.73	4.87	2.81	2.75	3.71	4.68	4.67	4.23	48.22		
Sabine, Hemphill	93.0	36.0	104		8		Mar. 19	Nov. 12	236	5.50	4.00	5.00	4.20	5.00	5.00	3.80	3.20	3.80	3.90	5.00	6.00	54.40		
San Augustine, Broaddus	93.0	35.0	106		9		Mar. 11	Nov. 19	238	5.30	4.10	4.00	3.40	4.60	4.50	3.30	3.90	4.60	3.60	4.40	5.70	51.10	13.50	06-1973
San Jacinto, Coldspring	93.0	37.5	110	1998	*3	1989	Apr. 1	Nov. 12	255	4.63	3.44	3.61	3.73	5.40	5.93	2.95	3.52	4.45	4.40	4.89	4.82	51.77	12.35	04-1930
San Patricio, Sinton	93.8	44.2	109	2000	10	2000	Feb. 7	Dec. 13	308	1.91	2.02	1.91	1.99	2.50	3.97	2.98	3.16	5.61	4.61	2.04	1.27	35.54	11.20	10-1969
San Saba, San Saba	91.7	33.4	112	1978	-1	1978	Mar. 20	Nov. 11	200	1.09	1.94	1.96	2.13	3.01	3.62	1.87	2.29	2.38	2.82	2.04	1.66	27.72		
Schleicher, Eldorado	95.8	26.7	107		3		Mar. 28	Nov. 20	236	0.70	0.90	0.70	1.70	2.50	1.90	1.60	2.55	3.10	2.10	1.00	0.60	19.00		
Scurry, Snyder	94.6	28.4	115	1936	-11	1985	Apr. 1	Nov. 28	229	0.69	1.03	1.09	1.69	3.06	3.06	2.04	3.04	3.30	3.60	0.91	0.80	22.51	5.26	07-1948
Shackelford, Albany	95.4	34.9	115	1972	-8	1947	Mar. 28	Nov. 1	219	1.01	1.65	1.95	2.34	3.76	3.45	1.91	3.04	3.17	3.00	1.55	1.62	28.45	5.80	07-1953
Shelby, Center	93.9	33.9	112	2000	0	1951	Mar. 20	Nov. 28	222	5.04	4.13	4.21	4.41	5.04	4.81	3.04	3.76	4.20	4.64	4.68	5.05	53.01	9.66	11-1940
Sherman, Stratford	91.1	18.5	*108	1953	*-20	1933	Apr. 26	Oct. 15	171	0.44	0.44	1.21	1.46	2.85	2.26	2.31	2.71	1.71	1.15	0.79	0.56	17.89	5.60	08-1992
Smith, Tyler	94.0	38.0	108		-10	1989	Mar. 7	Nov. 7	259	3.30	3.70	4.00	3.70	3.70	3.70	2.60	3.04	3.30	5.10	4.50	4.80	45.40		
Somervell, Glen Rose	97.3	28.9	115	1984	-15	1989	Apr. 11	Oct. 29	200	1.64	2.28	2.80	2.91	5.20	4.02	2.19	2.18	3.15	3.83	2.24	2.38	34.82	8.48	07-1995
Starr, Rio Grande City	99.1	44.5	116	1998	10	1962	Feb. 9	Dec. 14	309	0.97	1.10	0.74	1.22	2.42	4.02	1.27	1.97	4.68	2.48	0.90	0.92	21.04	12.51	09-1967
Stephens, Breckenridge	96.8	30.9	114	1936	-7	1989	Mar. 29	Nov. 10	226	1.30	1.39	2.05	2.17	3.53	3.12	1.86	2.06	2.93	3.44	1.56	1.63	27.04	15.70	10-1981
Sterling, Sterling City	94.7	27.4	112	1994	-13	1994	Apr. 4	Nov. 3	212	0.85	0.91	0.91	1.43	2.79	2.33	1.40	1.87	3.29	1.84	0.85	0.93	19.40	6.53	07-1948
Stonewall, Aspermont	97.4	27.2	117	1994	-10	1989	Mar. 30	Nov. 8	223	0.90	1.31	1.32	1.65	3.44	2.94	1.32	2.77	3.04	2.35	1.17	1.03	23.24	6.92	04-1930

Weather data — continued (Sutton County through Zavala County)

County and Station	July Mean Max. (°F)	Jan. Mean Min. (°F)	Record Highest (°F)	Year	Record Lowest (°F)	Year	Last in Spring	First in Fall	Growing Season (Days)	Jan.	Feb.	Mar.	Apr.	May	June	July	Aug.	Sep.	Oct.	Nov.	Dec.	Annual	Highest Daily Rainfall (In.)	Mo.-Year
Sutton, Sonora	94.7	27.2	109	1980	−8	1951	Apr. 4	Nov. 3	213	0.84	1.16	1.18	1.57	2.57	2.54	1.93	2.93	3.07	2.53	1.26	0.82	22.40	7.92	09-1976
Swisher, Tulia	91.1	22.2	*110	1994	*−10	1951	Apr. 14	Oct. 24	193	0.59	0.72	1.05	1.31	2.99	3.42	2.32	2.65	2.40	1.63	0.87	0.76	20.71	5.18	06-1985
Tarrant, Benbrook	96.6	31.4	111	1954	−6	1989	Mar. 15	Nov. 17	247	1.70	2.19	2.67	3.17	4.58	3.56	2.29	2.03	2.86	4.14	2.35	2.47	34.01	6.36	10-1991
Taylor, Abilene	94.8	31.8	110	1978	*−7	1989	Mar. 24	Nov. 12	232	0.97	1.13	1.41	1.67	2.83	3.06	1.70	2.63	2.91	2.90	1.30	1.27	23.78	6.50	08-1978
Terrell, Sanderson	91.9	30.5	110	1969	3	1989	Mar. 22	Nov. 10	233	0.39	0.59	0.40	0.86	1.74	2.09	1.52	1.87	2.41	1.75	0.81	0.51	14.94	5.35	06-1965
Terry, Brownfield	92.5	26.1	*111	1994	*−8	1963	Apr. 3	Nov. 2	213	0.54	0.68	0.64	0.95	2.90	3.00	1.80	2.15	2.78	1.50	0.79	0.65	18.89	5.05	10-1983
Throckmorton, Throckmorton	97.0	28.0	114		−11		Mar. 31	Nov. 6	220	1.00	1.50	1.60	2.10	3.30	3.50	2.31	2.60	3.30	2.90	1.50	1.50	26.60	8.06	11-1994
Titus, Mount Pleasant	94.2	29.3	118	1936	−12	1951	Mar. 29	Nov. 5	220	3.27	3.54	4.42	3.77	5.02	4.89	3.75	2.05	3.56	4.74	5.07	4.49	48.57	6.24	09-1980
Tom Green, San Angelo	94.4	31.8	111	1960	−4	1989	Mar. 28	Nov. 13	230	0.82	1.18	0.99	1.60	3.09	2.52	1.10	2.05	2.95	2.57	1.10	0.94	20.91	8.00	06-1941
Travis, Austin	95.0	40.0	112	2000	−2	1949	Feb. 17	Dec. 6	291	1.89	1.99	2.14	2.51	5.03	3.81	1.97	2.31	2.91	3.97	2.68	2.44	33.65	12.10	10-1994
Trinity, Groveton	94.8	37.1	111	2000	1	1989	Mar. 14	Nov. 14	244	4.17	3.21	3.67	3.13	5.11	5.01	3.48	3.25	4.10	4.07	4.49	4.41	48.10	7.88	04-1966
Tyler, Town Bluff Dam	92.1	38.3	109	2000	6	1989	Mar. 9	Nov. 19	255	5.08	4.02	4.56	4.41	5.61	5.74	3.46	3.42	4.17	3.68	5.08	5.56	54.79	9.13	10-1986
Upshur, Gilmer	93.4	31.4	114	1936	*−4	1989	Mar. 29	Nov. 5	220	3.51	3.58	4.38	4.12	4.41	4.13	3.04	2.50	3.84	4.47	4.75	4.35	47.08		
Upton, McCamey	95.6	33.1	*113	1994	−2	1962	Mar. 20	Nov. 12	236	0.47	0.56	0.41	0.93	1.61	1.55	0.94	1.95	2.68	2.06	0.59	0.70	14.45		
Uvalde, Uvalde	96.0	37.0	111		6		Mar. 10	Nov. 21	255	1.00	1.10	1.00	2.00	3.30	3.50	2.02	2.60	2.30	2.40	1.60	1.30	23.30		
Val Verde, Del Rio	96.2	39.7	112	1988	10	1989	Feb. 19	Dec. 1	284	0.57	0.96	0.96	1.71	2.31	2.34	2.02	2.16	2.06	2.00	0.96	0.75	18.80	17.03	08-1998
Van Zandt, Wills Point	93.3	31.4	115	1909	*−2	1989	Mar. 14	Nov. 18	248	3.10	3.22	3.74	3.68	4.74	4.45	2.16	2.26	3.39	4.78	4.23	3.93	43.68		
Victoria, Victoria	93.4	43.6	111	2000	11	1983	Feb. 9	Dec. 11	305	2.44	2.04	2.25	2.97	5.12	4.96	2.90	3.05	5.00	4.26	2.64	2.47	40.10		
Walker, Huntsville	93.8	39.0	108	2000	2	1989	Feb. 23	Nov. 30	279	4.28	3.14	3.47	3.50	5.08	4.66	2.67	3.69	4.73	4.32	4.87	4.10	48.51	7.08	06-1945
Waller, Hempstead	95.0	38.0	107		13		Feb. 28	Dec. 4	283	2.80	2.90	2.10	3.90	4.70	3.60	2.00	2.40	4.60	4.00	3.20	3.00	38.20	9.87	04-1991
Ward, Monahans	98.6	26.5	*118	1994	−9	1962	Apr. 1	Nov. 7	219	0.51	0.57	0.27	0.55	1.80	1.43	1.31	1.65	2.55	1.39	0.53	0.67	13.23	10.21	10-1994
Washington, Brenham	96.7	39.3	113	2000	*−2	1930	Feb. 20	Dec. 5	259	3.41	2.78	2.93	3.39	5.14	4.66	1.93	3.14	4.83	4.48	4.17	3.29	44.15	4.40	09-1980
Webb, Laredo	101.6	43.7	*114	1998	11	1983	Feb. 9	Dec. 5	299	0.76	0.94	0.92	1.55	2.73	2.99	1.79	2.42	2.73	2.72	1.13	0.85	21.53	6.65	07-1981
Wharton, Pierce	94.3	41.8	112	2000	4	1949	Feb. 19	Dec. 6	290	3.42	2.84	2.74	3.18	5.18	4.69	3.10	3.57	5.81	4.61	3.55	3.23	45.92	8.85	11-1943
Wheeler, Shamrock	93.3	22.9	113	1980	−13	1984	Apr. 6	Oct. 27	203	0.56	0.84	1.88	2.19	3.92	3.74	2.17	2.27	2.83	1.92	1.17	0.83	24.32	8.24	06-1995
Wichita, Wichita Falls	97.2	28.9	117	1980	−12	1947	Mar. 28	Nov. 9	225	1.12	1.58	2.27	2.62	3.92	3.69	1.58	2.39	3.19	3.11	1.68	1.68	28.83	6.19	06-1980
Wilbarger, Vernon	97.2	25.7	119	1943	−9	1989	Mar. 30	Nov. 9	223	1.09	1.34	1.98	2.36	4.11	3.82	1.94	3.07	3.54	2.70	1.48	1.12	28.55	14.82	08-1995
Willacy, Raymondville	95.3	47.5	109	1916	*14	1962	Jan. 19	Jan. 1	347	1.36	1.59	1.44	1.53	2.80	3.22	1.91	3.06	5.40	3.17	1.38	1.11	27.97	9.90	09-1975
Williamson, Taylor	95.8	35.8	*112	2000	−5	1949	Mar. 8	Nov. 20	259	2.09	2.38	2.63	2.68	5.19	3.24	1.62	2.09	3.30	3.83	2.95	2.57	35.11	16.00	06-1958
Wilson, Floresville	95.7	38.4	117	1954	5	1985	Mar. 5	Nov. 21	257	1.58	1.60	1.65	2.53	3.69	3.74	1.60	2.54	2.61	2.75	2.24	1.57	27.60	9.25	09-1967
Winkler, Wink	96.1	27.8	117	1994	−14	1962	Apr. 2	Nov. 7	215	0.41	0.48	0.32	0.53	1.34	1.83	1.95	1.29	2.14	1.51	0.55	0.57	12.92	5.64	09-1940
Wise, Bridgeport	98.0	30.5	*115	1980	−8	1989	Mar. 30	Nov. 7	222	1.53	2.06	2.63	2.83	5.53	3.54	2.26	2.01	2.97	4.37	2.28	2.01	34.02	9.07	10-1919
Wood, Mineola	93.1	31.2	110	2000	1	1983	Apr. 1	Nov. 5	219	3.33	3.43	4.05	3.98	4.71	3.99	2.92	2.23	3.67	4.99	4.50	4.08	45.88	6.42	12-1982
Yoakum, Plains	91.7	25.1	*110	1994	*−12	1951	Apr. 5	Oct. 29	206	0.49	0.72	0.60	1.15	2.38	2.55	2.23	2.75	2.67	1.24	0.75	0.77	18.41	6.11	07-1960
Young, Graham	96.6	27.1	117	1936	*−8	1989	Apr. 2	Nov. 6	217	1.16	1.79	2.22	2.45	4.52	3.60	2.17	2.32	3.64	3.79	1.88	1.81	31.35	8.22	10-1981
Zapata, Zapata	98.0	45.4	116	1998	13	1911	Jan. 24	Dec. 25	337	0.70	1.04	0.79	1.39	2.27	2.67	1.55	1.80	3.65	1.85	0.94	0.88	19.53	6.10	04-1966
Zavala, Crystal City	97.1	42.6	115	2000	*11	1989	Feb. 16	Dec. 6	292	0.93	1.08	1.08	1.75	2.41	3.25	1.67	2.03	2.10	2.44	1.12	0.84	20.70	6.83	10-1959

Astronomical Calendar for 2006 and 2007

The subsequent calendars were calculated principally from data on the **U.S. Naval Observatory's Web site** (http://aa.usno.navy.mil/data/), and from its publication, **Astronomical Phenomena** for **2006** and **2007**.

Times listed here are **Central Standard Time**, except for the period from 2:00 a.m. on the first Sunday in April until 2:00 a.m. on the last Sunday in October, when **Daylight Saving Time,** which is one hour later than Central Standard Time, is in effect.

All of Texas is in the Central Time Zone, except El Paso and Hudspeth counties and the northwest corner of Culberson County, which observe **Mountain Time** (see accompanying map). Mountain Time is one hour earlier than Central Time.

All times are calculated for the intersection of 99° 20' west longitude and 31° 08' north latitude, which is about 15 miles northeast of Brady, McCulloch County. This point is the **approximate geographical center of the state.**

To get the time of sunrise or sunset, moonrise or moonset for any point in Texas, apply the following rule: Add four minutes to the time given in this calendar for each degree of longitude that the place lies west of the 99th meridian; subtract four minutes for each degree of longitude the place lies east of the 99th meridian.

At times there will be considerable variation for distances north and south of the line of 31° 08' north latitude, but the rule for calculating it is complicated. The formula given above will get sufficiently close results. An accompanying map shows the intersection for which all times given here are calculated, with some major Texas cities and their longitudes. These make it convenient to calculate time at any given point.

The Naval Observatory's Web site will allow you to determine more exactly the rise and set times of the Sun and the Moon at your location on a given date or for an entire year.

Planetary Configurations and Phenomena

The phenomena and planetary configurations of heavens for 2006 and 2007 are given in the center column of the calendar on pages 137–142. Below is an explanation of the symbols used in those tables:

☉ The Sun	● The Earth	♅ Uranus
☽ The Moon	♂ Mars	♆ Neptune
☿ Mercury	♃ Jupiter	♇ Pluto
♀ Venus	♄ Saturn	

Aspects

♂ This symbol appearing between the symbols for heavenly bodies means that they are "in conjunction," that is, having the same longitude as applies to the sky and appearing near each other.

♂° This symbol means that the two heavenly bodies are in "opposition," or differ by 180 degrees of longitude.

Common Astronomical Terms

★ **Aphelion** — Point at which a planet's orbit is farthest from the sun.

★ **Perihelion** — Point at which a planet's orbit is nearest the sun.

★ **Apogee** — That point of the moon's orbit farthest from the earth.

★ **Perigee** — That point of the moon's orbit nearest the earth.

The Seasons, 2006 and 2007

2006

The seasons of 2006 begin as follows: **Spring,** March 20, 12:26 p.m. (CST); **Summer,** June 21, 7:26 a.m. (CDT); **Fall,** Sept. 22, 11:03 p.m. (CDT); **Winter,** Dec. 21, 6:22 p.m. (CST).

2007

The seasons of 2007 begin as follows: **Spring,** March 20, 6:07 p.m. (CST); **Summer,** June 21, 1:06 p.m. (CDT); **Fall,** Sept. 23, 4:51 a.m. (CDT); **Winter,** Dec. 22, 12:08 a.m. (CST).

Morning and Evening Stars, 2006 and 2007

Morning Stars, 2006
Venus — Jan. 19 – Sept. 19
Mars — Dec. 10 – Dec. 31
Jupiter — Jan. 1 – May 4; Dec. 5 – Dec. 31
Saturn — Jan. 1 – Jan. 27; Aug. 26 – Dec. 31

Evening Stars, 2007
Venus — Jan. 1 – Jan. 8; Dec. 8 – Dec. 31
Mars — Jan. 1– Sept. 7
Jupiter — May 4 – Nov. 9;
Saturn — Jan. 27 – July 20

Morning Stars, 2006
Venus — Aug. 22 – Dec. 31
Mars — Jan. 1 – Dec. 24
Jupiter — Jan. 1 – June 5
Saturn — Jan. 1 – Feb. 10; Sept. 9 – Dec. 31

Evening Stars, 2007
Venus — Jan. 1 – Aug. 13
Mars — Dec. 24 – Dec. 31
Jupiter — June 5 – Dec. 10
Saturn — Feb. 10 – Aug. 4

Eclipses, 2006 and 2007

Eclipses, 2006
There will be three eclipses during 2006, two of the Sun and one of the Moon, as follows:

March 29 — Total eclipse of the sun, visible in Brazil Ghana, Togo, Benin, Nigeria, Niger, northwest Chad, Libya, northwest tip of Egypt, Turkey, northwest Georgia, southwest Russia, Kazakstan, southern tip of Russia, ending in the northern tip of Mongolia.

Sept. 7— Partial eclipse of the moon, visible in parts of Antarctica, Australasia, Asia, Africa, Europe including the British Isles.

Sept. 22 — Annular eclipse of the sun, visible in Guyana, Suriname, French Guiana, south Atlantic Ocean, ending southwest of the Kerguelen Islands.

Eclipses, 2007
There will be four eclipses in 2007, two of the Sun and two of the Moon, as follows:

March 3–4—Total eclipse of the moon, visible in the Arctic, Asia except eastern part, Europe including the British Isles, Africa, South America, and eastern portions of Central and North America.

March 19— Partial eclipse of the sun, visible in most of Alaska, eastern and central Asia except central Japan, and western Russia.

Aug. 28 — Total eclipse of the moon, visible in the Americas except eastern part of South America and northeast parts of North America, the Pacific Ocean, eastern Asia, Australasia and Antarctica.

Sept. 11— Partial eclipse of the sun, visible in parts of Antarctica, South America except northern part, and southwestern Atlantic Ocean.

Major Meteor Showers

These are approximate dates. Listen to local news/weather broadcasts several days beforehand to determine peak observation days and hours. Generally, viewing will be better after 2 a.m. of date listed. (*Meteor shower dates provided by Robert Hawkes, Mt. Allison University, Dept. of Physics, Sackville, New Brunswick, Canada.*)

Meteor Shower	Peak 2006	Peak 2007
Quadrantid	Jan. 4	Jan. 4
Lyrid	April 22–23	April 23
Perseid	Aug. 13	Aug. 13
Orionid	Oct. 22	Oct. 22
Leonid	Nov. 18	Nov. 18
Geminid	Dec. 14	Dec. 15

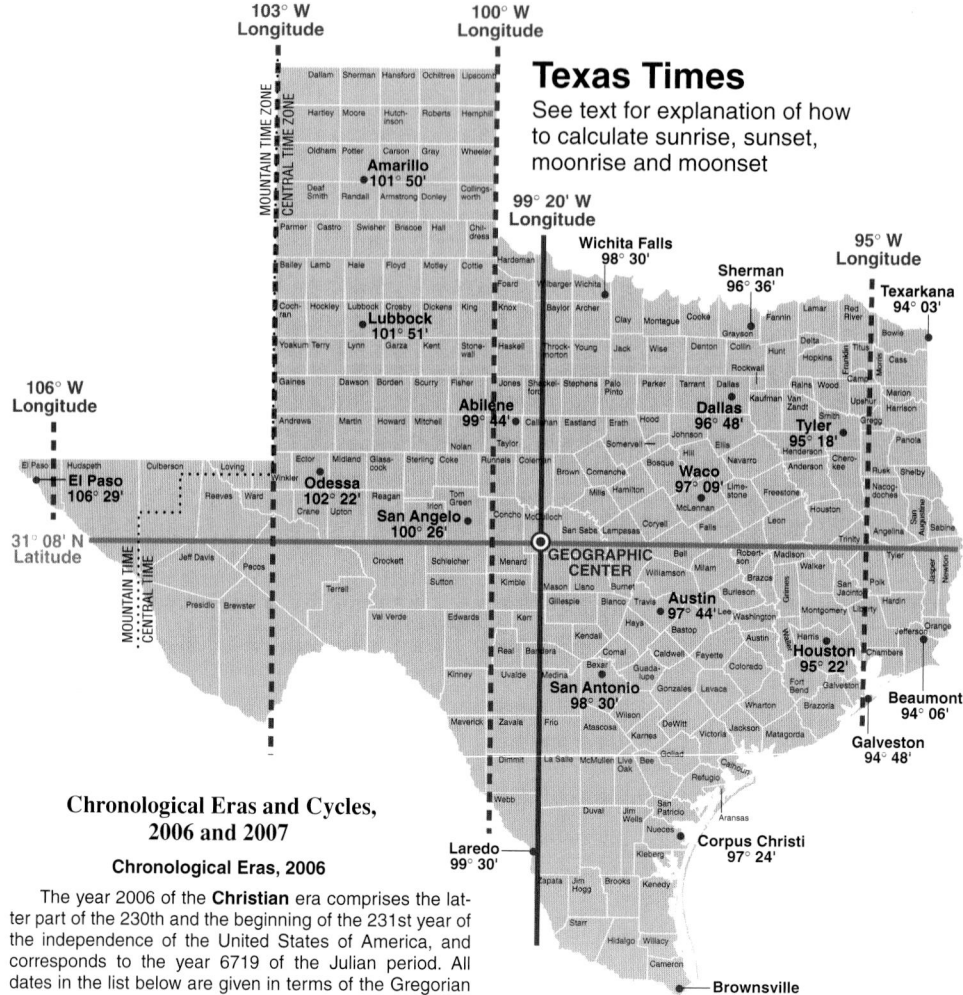

Texas Times

See text for explanation of how to calculate sunrise, sunset, moonrise and moonset

Chronological Eras and Cycles, 2006 and 2007

Chronological Eras, 2006

The year 2006 of the **Christian** era comprises the latter part of the 230th and the beginning of the 231st year of the independence of the United States of America, and corresponds to the year 6719 of the Julian period. All dates in the list below are given in terms of the Gregorian calendar, in which Jan. 14, 2006, corresponds to Jan. 1, 2006, Julian calendar.

Era	Year	Begins
Byzantine	7515	Sept. 14
Jewish (A.M.)*	5767	Sept. 22
Chinese (Bing-xu)	4643	Jan. 29
Roman (A.U.C.)	2759	Jan. 14
Nabonassar	2755	April 22
Japanese	2666	Jan. 1
Grecian (Seleucidae)	2318	Sept. 14 or Oct. 14
Indian (Saka)	1928	March 22
Diocletian	1723	Sept. 11
Islamic (Hegira)*	1427	Jan. 30

*Year begins at sunset.

Chronological Cycles, 2006

Dominical Letter	A	Julian Period	6719
Epact	30	Roman Indiction	14
Golden Number or Lunar Cycle	XII	Solar Cycle	27

Chronological Eras, 2007

The year 2007 of the **Christian** era comprises the latter part of the 231st and the beginning of the 232nd year of the independence of the United States of America, and corresponds to the year 6720 of the Julian period. All dates in the list below are given in terms of the Gregorian calendar, in which Jan. 14, 2007, corresponds to Jan. 1, 2007, of the Julian calendar:

Era	Year	Begins
Byzantine	7516	Sept. 14
Jewish (A.M.)*	5768	Sept. 12
Chinese (Ding-hai)	4644	Feb. 18
Roman (A.U.C.)	2760	Jan. 14
Nabonassar	2756	April 22
Japanese	2667	Jan. 1
Grecian (Seleucidae)	2319	Sept. 14 or Oct. 14
Indian (Saka)	1929	March 22
Diocletian	1724	Sept. 12
Islamic (Hegira)*	1428	Jan. 19

*Year begins at sunset.

Chronological Cycles, 2007

Dominical Letter	G	Julian Period	6720
Epact	11	Roman Indiction	15
Golden Number or Lunar Cycle	XIII	Solar Cycle	28

Calendar for 2006

Times are **Central Standard Time**, except from April 2 to Oct. 29, during which **Daylight Saving Time** is observed. **Boldface times for moonrise and moonset** indicate p.m. Times are figured for the point **99° 10' West and 31° 23' North,** the approximate geographical center of the state. **See page 135 for explanation of how to get the approximate time at any other Texas point.** (**On the Web: http://aa.usno.navy.mil/data/**) Please note: Not all **eclipses** are visible in United States. For visibility, see listing on p. 135.

1st Month — **January 2006** — **31 Days**

Moon's Phases — *First Qtr.,* Jan. 6, 12:56 p.m.; *Full,* Jan. 14, 3:48 a.m.; *Last Qtr.,* Jan. 22, 9:14 a.m.; *New,* Jan. 29, 8:15 a.m.

Day of			Planetary Configurations and Phenomena	*Hour of			
Year	Month	Week		Sunrise	Sunset	Moon-rise	Moon-set
1	1	Su.	♀☌☾; ☾ at perigee	7:36	5:46	9:18	**7:41**
2	2	Mo.	♆☌☾	7:36	5:47	10:03	**8:54**
3	3	Tu.	⛢☌☾	7:36	5:48	10:40	**10:04**
4	4	We.	● at perihelion	7:36	5:48	11:14	**11:11**
5	5	Th.		7:37	5:49	11:44	
6	6	Fr.	1st qtr. ☾	7:37	5:50	**12:14**	12:16
7	7	Sa.		7:37	5:51	**12:45**	1:19
8	8	Su.	♂☌☾	7:37	5:52	**1:18**	2:23
9	9	Mo.		7:37	5:52	**1:55**	3:27
10	10	Tu.		7:37	5:53	**2:38**	4:30
11	11	We.		7:37	5:54	**3:26**	5:32
12	12	Th.		7:37	5:55	**4:20**	6:29
13	13	Fr.	♀ inferior	7:37	5:56	**5:17**	7:21
14	14	Sa.	Full ☾	7:36	5:57	**6:16**	8:05
15	15	Su.	♄☌☾	7:36	5:58	**7:15**	8:43
16	16	Mo.		7:36	5:58	**8:11**	9:16
17	17	Tu.	☾ at apogee	7:36	5:59	**9:06**	9:45
18	18	We.		7:36	6:00	**10:00**	10:11
19	19	Th.		7:35	6:01	**10:54**	10:36
20	20	Fr.		7:35	6:02	**11:48**	11:01
21	21	Sa.		7:35	6:03		11:27
22	22	Su.	Last qtr. ☾	7:34	6:04	12:44	11:55
23	23	Mo.	♃☌☾	7:34	6:05	1:44	**12:27**
24	24	Tu.		7:34	6:06	2:47	**1:06**
25	25	We.		7:33	6:06	3:53	**1:54**
26	26	Th.	☿ superior	7:33	6:07	5:00	**2:51**
27	27	Fr.	♄☍; ♀☌☾	7:32	6:08	6:05	**3:59**
28	28	Sa.		7:32	6:09	7:02	**5:13**
29	29	Su.	New ☾	7:31	6:10	7:52	**6:29**
30	30	Mo.	☾ at perigee	7:31	6:11	8:34	**7:43**
31	31	Tu.	⛢☌☾	7:30	6:12	9:10	**8:54**

2nd Month — **February 2006** — **28 Days**

Moon's Phases — *First Qtr.,* Feb. 5, 12:29 a.m.; *Full,* Feb. 12, 10:44 p.m.; *Last Qtr.,* Feb. 21, 1:17 a.m.; *New,* Feb. 27, 6:31 p.m.;

Day of			Planetary Configurations and Phenomena	*Hour of			
Year	Month	Week		Sunrise	Sunset	Moon-rise	Moon-set
32	1	We.		7:29	6:13	9:43	**10:02**
33	2	Th.		7:29	6:14	10:14	**11:09**
34	3	Fr.	♀ stationary	7:28	6:15	10:45	
35	4	Sa.		7:27	6:15	11:19	12:14
36	5	Su.	1st qtr. ☾; ♂☌☾	7:27	6:16	11:55	1:20
37	6	Mo.	♆☌⊙	7:26	6:17	**12:36**	2:24
38	7	Tu.		7:25	6:18	**1:23**	3:27
39	8	We.		7:24	6:19	**2:15**	4:25
40	9	Th.		7:24	6:20	**3:11**	5:18
41	10	Fr.		7:23	6:21	**4:09**	6:04
42	11	Sa.	♄☌☾	7:22	6:21	**5:07**	6:44
43	12	Su.	Full ☾	7:21	6:22	**6:05**	7:18
44	13	Mo.	☾ at apogee	7:20	6:23	**7:00**	7:48
45	14	Tu.	☿☌⛢	7:19	6:24	**7:55**	8:15
46	15	We.		7:18	6:25	**8:48**	8:40
47	16	Th.		7:18	6:26	**9:42**	9:04
48	17	Fr.	♀ greatest brilliancy	7:17	6:26	**10:37**	9:29
49	18	Sa.		7:16	6:27	**11:34**	9:56
50	19	Su.		7:15	6:28		10:26
51	20	Mo.	♃☌☾	7:14	6:29	12:35	11:02
52	21	Tu.	Last qtr. ☾	7:13	6:30	1:38	11:44
53	22	We.		7:12	6:30	2:43	**12:35**
54	23	Th.	☿ greatest elongation E	7:11	6:31	3:47	**1:36**
55	24	Fr.	♀☌☾	7:09	6:32	4:46	**2:45**
56	25	Sa.		7:08	6:33	5:38	**3:59**
57	26	Su.	♆☌☾	7:07	6:33	6:23	**5:14**
58	27	Mo.	New ☾; ☾ at perigee	7:06	6:34	7:02	**6:28**
59	28	Tu.	☿☌☾	7:05	6:35	7:37	**7:39**

*See text before January calendar for explanation.

3rd Month — **March 2006** — **31 Days**

Moon's Phases — *First Qtr.,* March 6, 2:16 p.m.; *Full,* March 14, 5:35 p.m.; *Last Qtr.,* March 22, 1:10 p.m.; *New,* March 29, 4:15 a.m.

Day of			Planetary Configurations and Phenomena	*Hour of			
Year	Month	Week		Sunrise	Sunset	Moon-rise	Moon-set
60	1	We.	⛢☌⊙	7:04	6:36	8:10	**8:48**
61	2	Th.	☿ stationary	7:03	6:36	8:42	**9:57**
62	3	Fr.		7:02	6:37	9:15	**11:05**
63	4	Sa.	♃ stationary	7:01	6:38	9:52	
64	5	Su.		6:59	6:39	10:32	12:12
65	6	Mo.	1st qtr. ☾; ♂☌☾	6:58	6:39	11:18	1:18
66	7	Tu.		6:57	6:40	**12:09**	2:19
67	8	We.		6:56	6:41	**1:04**	3:15
68	9	Th.		6:55	6:41	**2:02**	4:03
69	10	Fr.	♄☌☾	6:54	6:42	**3:01**	4:45
70	11	Sa.	☿ inferior	6:52	6:43	**3:58**	5:20
71	12	Su.	☾ at apogee	6:51	6:43	**4:55**	5:51
72	13	Mo.		6:50	6:44	**5:49**	6:19
73	14	Tu.	Full ☾; penumbral eclipse	6:49	6:45	**6:43**	6:44
74	15	We.		6:47	6:46	**7:37**	7:09
75	16	Th.		6:46	6:46	**8:32**	7:34
76	17	Fr.		6:45	6:47	**9:29**	8:00
77	18	Sa.		6:44	6:48	**10:28**	8:29
78	19	Su.	♃☌☾	6:42	6:48	**11:30**	9:02
79	20	Mo.	**Spring equinox**	6:41	6:49		9:41
80	21	Tu.		6:40	6:49	12:33	10:28
81	22	We.	Last qtr. ☾	6:39	6:50	1:36	11:24
82	23	Th.		6:37	6:51	2:35	**12:27**
83	24	Fr.	☿ stationary	6:36	6:51	3:28	**1:37**
84	25	Sa.	♀ gr. elong. W; ♀☌☾ ♆☌☾	6:35	6:52	4:15	**2:49**
85	26	Su.	♀☌♆	6:34	6:53	4:55	**4:01**
86	27	Mo.	⛢☌☾; ☿☌☾	6:32	6:53	5:31	**5:13**
87	28	Tu.	☾ at perigee	6:31	6:54	6:04	**6:22**
88	29	We.	New ☾; ♇ stationary	6:30	6:55	6:36	**7:32**
89	30	Th.		6:29	6:55	7:09	**8:42**
90	31	Fr.		6:27	6:56	7:45	**9:52**

4th Month — **April 2006** — **30 Days**

Moon's Phases — *First Qtr.,* April 5, 7:01 a.m.; *Full,* April 13, 11:40 a.m.; *Last Qtr.,* April 20, 10:28 p.m.; *New,* April 27, 2:44 p.m.

Day of			Planetary Configurations and Phenomena	*Hour of			
Year	Month	Week		Sunrise	Sunset	Moon-rise	Moon-set
91	1	Sa.		6:26	6:57	8:24	**11:01**
92	†2	Su.		7:25	7:57	10:09	12:01
93	3	Mo.	♂☌☾	7:24	7:58	11:00	1:06
94	4	Tu.		7:22	7:59	11:55	2:06
95	5	We.	1st qtr. ☾; ♄ stationary	7:21	7:59	**12:54**	2:59
96	6	Th.	♄☌☾	7:20	8:00	**1:53**	3:43
97	7	Fr.		7:19	8:00	**2:51**	4:21
98	8	Sa.	☿ greatest elongation W	7:18	8:01	**3:48**	4:53
99	9	Su.	☾ at apogee	7:16	8:02	**4:43**	5:22
100	10	Mo.		7:15	8:02	**5:37**	5:48
101	11	Tu.		7:14	8:03	**6:31**	6:13
102	12	We.		7:13	8:04	**7:26**	6:37
103	13	Th.	Full ☾	7:12	8:04	**8:22**	7:03
104	14	Fr.		7:11	8:05	**9:21**	7:31
105	15	Sa.	♃☌☾	7:09	8:06	**10:23**	8:03
106	16	Su.		7:08	8:06	**11:26**	8:41
107	17	Mo.		7:07	8:07		9:26
108	18	Tu.	♀☌⛢	7:06	8:08	12:30	10:18
109	19	We.		7:05	8:08	1:30	11:19
110	20	Th.	Last qtr. ☾	7:04	8:09	2:24	**12:26**
111	21	Fr.		7:03	8:10	3:11	**1:35**
112	22	Sa.	♆☌☾	7:02	8:10	3:52	**2:45**
113	23	Su.	⛢☌☾	7:01	8:11	4:28	**3:54**
114	24	Mo.	♀☌☾	7:00	8:12	5:01	**5:02**
115	25	Tu.	☾ at perigee	6:59	8:12	5:33	**6:10**
116	26	We.	☿☌☾	6:58	8:13	6:04	**7:18**
117	27	Th.	New ☾	6:57	8:14	6:38	**8:28**
118	28	Fr.		6:56	8:14	7:16	**9:38**
119	29	Sa.		6:55	8:15	7:59	**10:47**
120	30	Su.		6:54	8:16	8:47	**11:51**

† Daylight Saving Time begins at 2:00 a.m.

Calendar for 2006 (Cont'd.)

5th Month **May 2006** **31 Days**

Moon's Phases — *First Qtr.,* May 5, 12:13 a.m.; *Full,* May 13, 1:51 a.m.; *Last Qtr.,* May 20, 4:20 a.m.; *New,* May 27, 12:26 a.m.

Day of			Planetary Configurations and Phenomena	*Hour of			
Year	Month	Week		Sunrise	Sunset	Moon-rise	Moon-set
121	1	Mo.		6:53	8:16	9:42	
122	2	Tu.	♂ ☌ ☾	6:52	8:17	10:41	12:48
123	3	We.		6:51	8:18	11:41	1:37
124	4	Th.	♄ ☌ ☾; ♃ ☍	6:50	8:18	**12:41**	2:18
125	5	Fr.	1st qtr. ☾	6:49	8:19	**1:39**	2:53
126	6	Sa.		6:48	8:20	**2:34**	3:23
127	7	Su.	☾ at apogee	6:48	8:21	**3:29**	3:50
128	8	Mo.		6:47	8:21	**4:22**	4:15
129	9	Tu.		6:46	8:22	**5:17**	4:40
130	10	We.		6:45	8:23	**6:13**	5:05
131	11	Th.		6:45	8:23	**7:11**	5:33
132	12	Fr.	♃ ☌ ☾	6:44	8:24	**8:13**	6:04
133	13	Sa.	Full ☾	6:43	8:25	**9:17**	6:40
134	14	Su.		6:42	8:25	**10:21**	7:22
135	15	Mo.		6:42	8:26	**11:23**	8:13
136	16	Tu.		6:41	8:27		9:13
137	17	We.		6:41	8:27	12:20	10:18
138	18	Th.	☿ superior	6:40	8:28	1:10	11:27
139	19	Fr.	♆ ☌ ☾	6:39	8:29	1:52	**12:36**
140	20	Sa.	Last qtr. ☾	6:39	8:29	2:29	**1:44**
141	21	Su.	♅ ☌ ☾	6:38	8:30	3:02	**2:50**
142	22	Mo.	☾ at perigee; ♆ stationary	6:38	8:31	3:33	**3:56**
143	23	Tu.		6:37	8:31	4:03	**5:02**
144	24	We.	♀ ☌ ☾	6:37	8:32	4:35	**6:09**
145	25	Th.		6:36	8:32	5:10	**7:18**
146	26	Fr.		6:36	8:33	5:50	**8:27**
147	27	Sa.	New ☾	6:36	8:34	6:36	**9:34**
148	28	Su.		6:35	8:34	7:28	**10:35**
149	29	Mo.		6:35	8:35	8:26	**11:28**
150	30	Tu.	♂ ☌ ☾	6:35	8:35	9:27	
151	31	We.	♄ ☌ ☾	6:34	8:36	10:28	12:13

6th Month **June 2006** **30 Days**

Moon's Phases — *First Qtr.,* June 3, 6:06 p.m.; *Full,* June 11, 1:03 p.m.; *Last Qtr.,* June 18, 9:08 a.m.; *New,* June 25, 11:05 a.m.

Day of			Planetary Configurations and Phenomena	*Hour of			
Year	Month	Week		Sunrise	Sunset	Moon-rise	Moon-set
152	1	Th.		6:34	8:36	11:27	12:50
153	2	Fr.		6:34	8:37	**12:24**	1:23
154	3	Sa.	1st qtr. ☾; ☾ at apogee	6:34	8:38	**1:19**	1:51
155	4	Su.		6:33	8:38	**2:13**	2:17
156	5	Mo.		6:33	8:39	**3:07**	2:41
157	6	Tu.		6:33	8:39	**4:02**	3:06
158	7	We.		6:33	8:40	**4:59**	3:33
159	8	Th.	♃ ☌ ☾	6:33	8:40	**5:59**	4:02
160	9	Fr.		6:33	8:40	**7:02**	4:36
161	10	Sa.		6:33	8:41	**8:07**	5:16
162	11	Su.	Full ☾	6:33	8:41	**9:12**	6:04
163	12	Mo.		6:33	8:42	**10:12**	7:02
164	13	Tu.		6:33	8:42	**11:05**	8:07
165	14	We.		6:33	8:42	**11:51**	9:17
166	15	Th.	♆ ☌ ☾	6:33	8:43		10:28
167	16	Fr.	☾ at perigee; ♇ ☍	6:33	8:43	12:30	11:37
168	17	Sa.	♅ ☌ ☾; ♂ ☌ ♄	6:33	8:43	1:04	**12:44**
169	18	Su.	Last qtr. ☾	6:33	8:44	1:35	**1:49**
170	19	Mo.	♅ stationary	6:34	8:44	2:06	**2:54**
171	20	Tu.	☿ greatest elongation E	6:34	8:44	2:36	**3:59**
172	21	We.	**Summer solstice**	6:34	8:44	3:09	**5:06**
173	22	Th.	♀ ☌ ☾	6:34	8:45	3:47	**6:13**
174	23	Fr.		6:34	8:45	4:29	**7:20**
175	24	Sa.		6:35	8:45	5:18	**8:22**
176	25	Su.	New ☾	6:35	8:45	6:14	**9:18**
177	26	Mo.		6:35	8:45	7:14	**10:06**
178	27	Tu.	☿ ☌ ☾	6:36	8:45	8:15	**10:47**
179	28	We.	♄ ☌ ☾; ♂ ☌ ☾	6:36	8:45	9:15	**11:21**
180	29	Th.		6:36	8:45	10:14	**11:51**
181	30	Fr.		6:37	8:45	11:10	

*See text before January calendar for explanation.

7th Month **July 2006** **31 Days**

Moon's Phases — *First Qtr.,* July 3, 11:37 a.m.; *Full,* July 10, 10:02 p.m.; *Last Qtr.,* July 17, 2:12 p.m.; *New,* July 24, 11:31 p.m.

Day of			Planetary Configurations and Phenomena	*Hour of			
Year	Month	Week		Sunrise	Sunset	Moon-rise	Moon-set
182	1	Sa.	☾ at apogee	6:37	8:45	**12:04**	12:18
183	2	Su.		6:38	8:45	**12:57**	12:43
184	3	Mo.	1st qtr. ☾; ● at aphelion	6:38	8:45	**1:51**	1:07
185	4	Tu.		6:38	8:45	**2:46**	1:32
186	5	We.	♃ ☌ ☾	6:39	8:45	**3:44**	2:00
187	6	Th.	♃ stationary	6:39	8:45	**4:45**	2:31
188	7	Fr.		6:40	8:45	**5:50**	3:08
189	8	Sa.		6:40	8:44	**6:55**	3:53
190	9	Su.		6:41	8:44	**7:58**	4:46
191	10	Mo.	Full ☾	6:41	8:44	**8:55**	5:49
192	11	Tu.		6:42	8:44	**9:45**	6:59
193	12	We.	♆ ☌ ☾	6:42	8:43	**10:27**	8:12
194	13	Th.	☾ at perigee	6:43	8:43	**11:04**	9:24
195	14	Fr.	♅ ☌ ☾	6:43	8:43	**11:37**	10:33
196	15	Sa.		6:44	8:42		11:41
197	16	Su.		6:45	8:42	12:08	**12:47**
198	17	Mo.	Last qtr. ☾	6:45	8:42	12:39	**1:52**
199	18	Tu.	☿ inferior	6:46	8:41	1:11	**2:59**
200	19	We.		6:46	8:41	1:47	**4:05**
201	20	Th.		6:47	8:40	2:27	**5:11**
202	21	Fr.		6:47	8:40	3:13	**6:14**
203	22	Sa.	♀ ☌ ☾	6:48	8:39	4:06	**7:12**
204	23	Su.		6:49	8:39	5:04	**8:02**
205	24	Mo.	New ☾	6:49	8:38	6:04	**8:45**
206	25	Tu.		6:50	8:37	7:05	**9:21**
207	26	We.		6:51	8:37	8:04	**9:52**
208	27	Th.	♂ ☌ ☾	6:51	8:36	9:01	**10:20**
209	28	Fr.	☿ stationary	6:52	8:36	9:56	**10:45**
210	29	Sa.	☾ at apogee	6:52	8:35	10:49	**11:09**
211	30	Su.		6:53	8:34	11:43	**11:34**
212	31	Mo.		6:54	8:33	**12:37**	

8th Month **August 2006** **31 Days**

Moon's Phases — *First Qtr.,* Aug. 2, 3:46 a.m.; *Full,* Aug. 9, 5:54 a.m.; *Last Qtr.,* Aug. 15, 8:51 p.m.; *New,* Aug. 23, 2:10 p.m.; *First Qtr.,* Aug. 31, 5:56 p.m.

Day of			Planetary Configurations and Phenomena	*Hour of			
Year	Month	Week		Sunrise	Sunset	Moon-rise	Moon-set
213	1	Tu.		6:54	8:33	**1:33**	12:00
214	2	We.	1st qtr. ☾; ♃ ☌ ☾	6:55	8:32	**2:31**	12:29
215	3	Th.		6:56	8:31	**3:33**	1:03
216	4	Fr.		6:56	8:30	**4:37**	1:43
217	5	Sa.		6:57	8:29	**5:40**	2:31
218	6	Su.	☿ greatest elongation W	6:57	8:29	**6:40**	3:29
219	7	Mo.	♄ ☌ ☉	6:58	8:28	**7:33**	4:36
220	8	Tu.		6:59	8:27	**8:20**	5:48
221	9	We.	Full ☾; ♆ ☌ ☾	6:59	8:26	**8:59**	7:02
222	10	Th.	☾ at perigee	7:00	8:25	**9:35**	8:14
223	11	Fr.	♆ ☍; ♅ ☌ ☾	7:01	8:24	**10:07**	9:25
224	12	Sa.		7:01	8:23	**10:39**	10:34
225	13	Su.		7:02	8:22	**11:11**	11:42
226	14	Mo.		7:03	8:21	**11:47**	**12:50**
227	15	Tu.	Last qtr. ☾	7:03	8:20		**1:58**
228	16	We.		7:04	8:19	12:26	**3:05**
229	17	Th.		7:04	8:18	1:11	**4:09**
230	18	Fr.		7:05	8:17	2:02	**5:08**
231	19	Sa.		7:06	8:16	2:58	**6:00**
232	20	Su.	☿ ☌ ♄	7:06	8:15	3:57	**6:44**
233	21	Mo.	♀ ☌ ☾	7:07	8:14	4:58	**7:22**
234	22	Tu.		7:07	8:12	5:57	**7:54**
235	23	We.	New ☾	7:08	8:11	6:54	**8:23**
236	24	Th.		7:09	8:10	7:50	**8:48**
237	25	Fr.	♂ ☌ ☾; ☾ at apogee	7:09	8:09	8:43	**9:13**
238	26	Sa.	♀ ☌ ♄	7:10	8:08	9:37	**9:37**
239	27	Su.		7:10	8:07	10:30	**10:03**
240	28	Mo.		7:11	8:05	11:25	**10:30**
241	29	Tu.	♃ ☌ ☾	7:12	8:04	**12:22**	**11:01**
242	30	We.		7:12	8:03	**1:21**	**11:38**
243	31	Th.	1st qtr. ☾	7:13	8:02	**2:23**	

Calendar for 2006 (Cont'd.)

9th Month — **September 2006** — **30 Days**

Moon's Phases — *Full,* Sept. 7, 1:42 p.m.; *Last Qtr.,* Sept. 14, 6:15 a.m.; *New,* Sept. 22, 6:45 a.m.; *First Qtr.,* Sept. 30, 6:04 a.m.

Day of			Planetary Configurations and Phenomena	*Hour of			
Year	Month	Week		Sunrise	Sunset	Moon-rise	Moon-set
244	1	Fr.	☿ superior	7:13	8:01	**3:25**	12:21
245	2	Sa.		7:14	7:59	**4:25**	1:13
246	3	Su.		7:15	7:58	**5:20**	2:15
247	4	Mo.		7:15	7:57	**6:09**	3:23
248	5	Tu.	♇ stationary; ♅ ☍; ♆ ☌ ☾	7:16	7:56	**6:51**	4:35
249	6	We.		7:16	7:54	**7:29**	5:48
250	7	Th.	Full ☾; perigee & eclipse ☾	7:17	7:53	**8:03**	7:00
251	8	Fr.		7:17	7:52	**8:35**	8:12
252	9	Sa.		7:18	7:51	**9:08**	9:22
253	10	Su.		7:19	7:49	**9:43**	10:32
254	11	Mo.		7:19	7:48	**10:22**	11:43
255	12	Tu.		7:20	7:47	**11:06**	**12:53**
256	13	We.		7:20	7:46	**11:56**	**2:00**
257	14	Th.	Last qtr. ☾;	7:21	7:44		**3:02**
258	15	Fr.	☿ ☌ ♂	7:21	7:43	12:52	**3:57**
259	16	Sa.		7:22	7:42	1:51	**4:44**
260	17	Su.		7:23	7:40	2:51	**5:24**
261	18	Mo.	♄ ☌ ☾	7:23	7:39	3:51	**5:57**
262	19	Tu.		7:24	7:38	4:49	**6:26**
263	20	We.		7:24	7:36	5:44	**6:53**
264	21	Th.		7:25	7:35	6:38	**7:18**
265	22	Fr.	New ☾; apogee & eclipse ☾	7:26	7:34	7:32	**7:42**
266	23	Sa.	**Autumnal equinox;** ☿ ☌ ☾	7:26	7:33	8:25	**8:07**
267	24	Su.		7:27	7:31	9:20	**8:33**
268	25	Mo.		7:27	7:30	10:16	**9:03**
269	26	Tu.	♃ ☌ ☾	7:28	7:29	11:14	**9:37**
270	27	We.		7:29	7:27	**12:14**	**10:18**
271	28	Th.		7:29	7:26	**1:15**	**11:06**
272	29	Fr.		7:30	7:25	**2:15**	
273	30	Sa.	1st qtr. ☾	7:30	7:24	**3:10**	12:02

10th Month — **October 2006** — **31 Days**

Moon's Phases — *Full,* Oct. 6, 11:13 p.m.; *Last Qtr.,* Oct. 13, 7:26 p.m; *New,* Oct. 22, 12:14 a.m.; *First Qtr.,* Oct. 29, 3:25 p.m.

Day of			Planetary Configurations and Phenomena	*Hour of			
Year	Month	Week		Sunrise	Sunset	Moon-rise	Moon-set
274	1	Su.		7:31	7:22	**4:00**	1:05
275	2	Mo.		7:32	7:21	**4:43**	2:13
276	3	Tu.	♆ ☌ ☾	7:32	7:20	**5:22**	3:24
277	4	We.	♅ ☌ ☾	7:33	7:19	**5:57**	4:35
278	5	Th.		7:33	7:17	**6:30**	5:45
279	6	Fr.	Full ☾; ☾ at perigee	7:34	7:16	**7:02**	6:56
280	7	Sa.		7:35	7:15	**7:37**	8:07
281	8	Su.		7:35	7:14	**8:15**	9:19
282	9	Mo.		7:36	7:13	**8:58**	10:32
283	10	Tu.		7:37	7:11	**9:47**	11:43
284	11	We.		7:37	7:10	**10:42**	**12:50**
285	12	Th.		7:38	7:09	**11:42**	**1:50**
286	13	Fr.	Last qtr. ☾	7:39	7:08		**2:41**
287	14	Sa.		7:39	7:07	12:43	**3:23**
288	15	Su.		7:40	7:06	1:44	**3:59**
289	16	Mo.	♄ ☌ ☾; ☿ gr. elongation E	7:41	7:04	2:42	**4:29**
290	17	Tu.		7:41	7:03	3:39	**4:57**
291	18	We.		7:42	7:02	4:33	**5:22**
292	19	Th.	☾ at apogee	7:43	7:01	5:27	**5:46**
293	20	Fr.		7:44	7:00	6:20	**6:11**
294	21	Sa.		7:44	6:59	7:14	**6:37**
295	22	Su.	New ☾	7:45	6:58	8:10	**7:06**
296	23	Mo.	♂ ☌ ☉	7:46	6:57	9:08	**7:39**
297	24	Tu.	♃ ☌ ☾; ☿ ☌ ☾	7:47	6:56	10:08	**8:18**
298	25	We.	☿ ☌ ♃	7:47	6:55	11:09	**9:03**
299	26	Th.		7:48	6:54	**12:09**	**9:56**
300	27	Fr.	♀ superior	7:49	6:53	**1:05**	**10:57**
301	28	Sa.	☿ ☌ ♃; ☿ stationary	7:50	6:52	**1:55**	
302	†29	Su.	1st qtr. ☾; ♆ stationary	6:50	5:51	**1:40**	
303	30	Mo.	♆ ☌ ☾	6:51	5:50	**2:18**	12:09
304	31	Tu.		6:52	5:50	**2:53**	1:17

*See text before January calendar for explanation.
† Daylight Saving Time ends at 2:00 a.m.

11th Month — **November 2006** — **30 Days**

Moon's Phases — *Full,* Nov. 5, 6:58 a.m.; *Last Qtr.,* Nov. 12, 11:45 a.m.; *New,* Nov. 20, 4:18 p.m.; *First Qtr.,* Nov. 28, 12:29 a.m.

Day of			Planetary Configurations and Phenomena	*Hour of			
Year	Month	Week		Sunrise	Sunset	Moon-rise	Moon-set
305	1	We.	♅ ☌ ☾	6:53	5:49	**3:25**	2:25
306	2	Th.		6:54	5:48	**3:57**	3:33
307	3	Fr.	☾ at perigee	6:54	5:47	**4:30**	4:42
308	4	Sa.		6:55	5:46	**5:06**	5:52
309	5	Su.	Full ☾	6:56	5:46	**5:46**	7:05
310	6	Mo.		6:57	5:45	**6:33**	8:18
311	7	Tu.		6:58	5:44	**7:27**	9:29
312	8	We.	☿ inferior	6:58	5:43	**8:26**	10:34
313	9	Th.		6:59	5:43	**9:29**	11:31
314	10	Fr.		7:00	5:42	**10:32**	**12:18**
315	11	Sa.		7:01	5:41	**11:33**	**12:57**
316	12	Su.	Last qtr. ☾; ♄ ☌ ☾	7:02	5:41		**1:30**
317	13	Mo.		7:03	5:40	12:31	**1:59**
318	14	Tu.		7:04	5:40	1:26	**2:25**
319	15	We.	☾ at apogee	7:04	5:39	2:20	**2:49**
320	16	Th.		7:05	5:39	3:13	**3:14**
321	17	Fr.	☿ stationary	7:06	5:38	4:07	**3:39**
322	18	Sa.		7:07	5:38	5:02	**4:07**
323	19	Su.	☿ ☌ ☾	7:08	5:37	6:00	**4:39**
324	20	Mo.	New ☾; ♅ stationary	7:09	5:37	7:00	**5:16**
325	21	Tu.	♃ ☌ ☉	7:10	5:37	8:01	**6:00**
326	22	We.		7:10	5:36	9:02	**6:52**
327	23	Th.		7:11	5:36	10:00	**7:51**
328	24	Fr.		7:12	5:36	10:53	**8:55**
329	25	Sa.	☿ greatest elongation W	7:13	5:35	11:39	**10:02**
330	26	Su.	♆ ☌ ☾	7:14	5:35	**12:18**	**11:08**
331	27	Mo.		7:15	5:35	**12:54**	
332	28	Tu.	1st qtr. ☾; ♅ ☌ ☾	7:16	5:35	**1:26**	12:15
333	29	We.		7:16	5:35	**1:56**	1:20
334	30	Th.		7:17	5:35	**2:27**	2:26

12th Month — **December 2006** — **31 Days**

Moon's Phases — *Full,* Dec. 4, 6:25 p.m.; *Last Qtr.,* Dec. 12, 8:32 a.m.; *New,* Dec. 20, 8:01 a.m.; *First Qtr.,* Dec. 27, 8:48 a.m.

Day of			Planetary Configurations and Phenomena	*Hour of			
Year	Month	Week		Sunrise	Sunset	Moon-rise	Moon-set
335	1	Fr.	☾ at perigee	7:18	5:35	**3:00**	3:33
336	2	Sa.		7:19	5:35	**3:37**	4:42
337	3	Su.		7:20	5:35	**4:20**	5:53
338	4	Mo.	Full ☾	7:20	5:35	**5:11**	7:05
339	5	Tu.		7:21	5:35	**6:08**	8:13
340	6	We.	♄ stationary	7:22	5:35	**7:11**	9:15
341	7	Th.		7:23	5:35	**8:15**	10:07
342	8	Fr.		7:23	5:35	**9:18**	10:51
343	9	Sa.	☿ ☌ ♂	7:24	5:35	**10:19**	11:27
344	10	Su.	♄ ☌ ☾; ☿ ☌ ♃	7:25	5:35	**11:16**	11:58
345	11	Mo.	♂ ☌ ♃	7:26	5:36		**12:26**
346	12	Tu.	Last qtr. ☾	7:26	5:36	12:11	**12:51**
347	13	We.	☾ at apogee	7:27	5:36	1:04	**1:15**
348	14	Th.		7:28	5:36	1:57	**1:40**
349	15	Fr.		7:28	5:37	2:52	**2:07**
350	16	Sa.		7:29	5:37	3:48	**2:37**
351	17	Su.		7:30	5:37	4:47	**3:12**
352	18	Mo.	♇ ☌ ☉; ♃ ☌ ☾; ♂ ☌ ☾	7:30	5:38	5:49	**3:54**
353	19	Tu.		7:31	5:38	6:51	**4:43**
354	20	We.	New ☾	7:31	5:39	7:51	**5:41**
355	21	Th.	**Winter solstice**	7:32	5:39	8:47	**6:45**
356	22	Fr.		7:32	5:40	9:36	**7:53**
357	23	Sa.	♆ ☌ ☾	7:33	5:40	10:18	**9:01**
358	24	Su.		7:33	5:41	10:55	**10:08**
359	25	Mo.	♅ ☌ ☾	7:34	5:41	11:28	**11:13**
360	26	Tu.		7:34	5:42	11:59	
361	27	We.	1st qtr. ☾; ☾ at perigee	7:34	5:43	**12:29**	12:18
362	28	Th.		7:35	5:43	**1:00**	1:23
363	29	Fr.		7:35	5:44	**1:35**	2:30
364	30	Sa.		7:35	5:45	**2:14**	3:38
365	31	Su.		7:36	5:45	**3:00**	4:48

*See text before January calendar for explanation.
† Daylight Saving Time ends at 2:00 a.m.

Calendar for 2007

Times are **Central Standard Time**, except from April 1 to Oct. 28, during which **Daylight Saving Time** is observed. **Boldface times for moonrise and moonset** indicate p.m. Times are figured for the point **99° 10' West and 31° 23' North,** the approximate geographical center of the state. **See page 135 for explanation of how to get the approximate time at any other Texas point.** (**On the Web: http://aa.usno.navy.mil/data/**) Please note: Not all **eclipses** are visible in United States. For visibility, see listing on p. 135.

1st Month — January 2007 — 31 Days

Moon's Phases — *Full,* Jan. 3, 7:57 a.m.; *Last Qtr.,* Jan. 11, 6:45 a.m.; *New,* Jan. 18, 10:01 p.m.; *First Qtr.,* Jan. 25, 5:01 p.m.

Day of				*Hour of			
Year	Month	Week	Planetary Configurations and Phenomena	Sunrise	Sunset	Moon-rise	Moon-set
1	1	Mo.		7:36	5:46	**3:53**	5:56
2	2	Tu.		7:36	5:47	**4:53**	7:00
3	3	We.	Full ☾; ● at perihelion	7:36	5:48	**5:57**	7:56
4	4	Th.		7:36	5:48	**7:02**	8:43
5	5	Fr.		7:37	5:49	**8:04**	9:23
6	6	Sa.	♄ ☌ ☾	7:37	5:50	**9:03**	9:56
7	7	Su.	☿ superior	7:37	5:51	**10:00**	10:25
8	8	Mo.		7:37	5:51	**10:54**	10:51
9	9	Tu.		7:37	5:52	**11:48**	11:16
10	10	We.	☾ at apogee	7:37	5:53		11:41
11	11	Th.	Last qtr. ☾	7:37	5:54	12:41	**12:07**
12	12	Fr.		7:37	5:55	1:36	**12:35**
13	13	Sa.		7:37	5:56	2:34	**1:08**
14	14	Su.		7:37	5:56	3:33	**1:46**
15	15	Mo.	♃ ☌ ☾	7:36	5:57	4:35	**2:31**
16	16	Tu.	♂ ☌ ☾	7:36	5:58	5:36	**3:25**
17	17	We.		7:36	5:59	6:35	**4:28**
18	18	Th.	New ☾; ♀ ☌ ♆	7:36	6:00	7:27	**5:35**
19	19	Fr.		7:35	6:01	8:13	**6:45**
20	20	Sa.	♆ ☌ ☾; ♀ ☌ ☾	7:35	6:02	8:53	**7:55**
21	21	Su.		7:35	6:03	9:28	**9:03**
22	22	Mo.	♅ ☌ ☾; ☾ at perigee	7:35	6:04	10:00	**10:10**
23	23	Tu.		7:34	6:04	10:31	**11:16**
24	24	We.		7:34	6:05	11:02	
25	25	Th.	1st qtr. ☾	7:33	6:06	11:36	12:23
26	26	Fr.		7:33	6:07	**12:13**	1:31
27	27	Sa.		7:32	6:08	**12:56**	2:39
28	28	Su.		7:32	6:09	**1:46**	3:47
29	29	Mo.		7:31	6:10	**2:43**	4:51
30	30	Tu.		7:31	6:11	**3:44**	5:48
31	31	We.		7:30	6:12	**4:48**	6:38

2nd Month — February 2007 — 28 Days

Moon's Phases — *Full,* Feb. 1, 11:45 p.m.; *Last Qtr.,* Feb. 10, 3:51 a.m.; *New,* Feb. 17, 10:14 a.m.; *First Qtr.,* Feb. 24, 1:56 a.m.

Day of				*Hour of			
Year	Month	Week	Planetary Configurations and Phenomena	Sunrise	Sunset	Moon-rise	Moon-set
32	1	Th.	Full ☾	7:30	6:13	**5:51**	7:20
33	2	Fr.	♄ ☌ ☾	7:29	6:13	**6:51**	7:55
34	3	Sa.		7:28	6:14	**7:49**	8:25
35	4	Su.		7:28	6:15	**8:44**	8:52
36	5	Mo.		7:27	6:16	**9:38**	9:18
37	6	Tu.		7:26	6:17	**10:32**	9:42
38	7	We.	☾ at apogee; ♀ ☌ ♅	7:25	6:18	**11:26**	10:08
39	8	Th.	♆ ☌ ☉	7:25	6:19		10:35
40	9	Fr.		7:24	6:20	12:22	11:05
41	10	Sa.	Last qtr. ☾; ♄ ☍	7:23	6:20	1:20	11:40
42	11	Su.		7:22	6:21	2:20	**12:21**
43	12	Mo.	♃ ☌ ☾	7:21	6:22	3:20	**1:10**
44	13	Tu.	☿ stationary	7:21	6:23	4:19	**2:08**
45	14	We.	♂ ☌ ☾	7:20	6:24	5:14	**3:12**
46	15	Th.		7:19	6:25	6:03	**4:22**
47	16	Fr.		7:18	6:25	6:46	**5:33**
48	17	Sa.	New. ☾	7:17	6:26	7:23	**6:43**
49	18	Su.		7:16	6:27	7:58	**7:53**
50	19	Mo.	☾ at perigee; ♀ ☌ ☾	7:15	6:28	8:30	**9:02**
51	20	Tu.		7:14	6:29	9:02	**10:11**
52	21	We.		7:13	6:29	9:36	**11:20**
53	22	Th.	☿ inferior	7:12	6:30	10:13	
54	23	Fr.		7:11	6:31	10:54	12:30
55	24	Sa.	1st qtr. ☾	7:10	6:32	11:43	1:39
56	25	Su.		7:09	6:33	**12:37**	2:45
57	26	Mo.		7:08	6:33	**1:37**	3:44
58	27	Tu.		7:07	6:34	**2:39**	4:36
59	28	We.		7:05	6:35	**3:42**	5:19

*See text before January calendar for explanation.

3rd Month — March 2007 — 31 Days

Moon's Phases — *Full,* March 3, 5:17 p.m.; *Last Qtr.,* March 11, 9:54 p.m.; *New,* March 18, 8:43 p.m.; *First Qtr.,* March 25, 12:16 p.m.

Day of				*Hour of			
Year	Month	Week	Planetary Configurations and Phenomena	Sunrise	Sunset	Moon-rise	Moon-set
60	1	Th.	♄ ☌ ☾	7:04	6:36	**4:42**	5:56
61	2	Fr.		7:03	6:36	**5:40**	6:27
62	3	Sa.	Full ☾; eclipse ☾	7:02	6:37	**6:36**	6:55
63	4	Su.		7:01	6:38	**7:30**	7:21
64	5	Mo.	♅ ☌ ☉	7:00	6:38	**8:24**	7:45
65	6	Tu.	☾ at apogee	6:59	6:39	**9:18**	8:10
66	7	We.	☿ stationary	6:57	6:40	**10:13**	8:37
67	8	Th.		6:56	6:41	**11:10**	9:05
68	9	Fr.		6:55	6:41		9:38
69	10	Sa.		6:54	6:42	12:09	10:16
70	11	Su.	Last qtr. ☾; ♃ ☌ ☾	6:53	6:43	1:08	11:01
71	12	Mo.		6:51	6:43	2:06	11:53
72	13	Tu.		6:50	6:44	3:01	**12:53**
73	14	We.		6:49	6:45	3:52	**1:59**
74	15	Th.	♂ ☌ ☾	6:48	6:45	4:36	**3:08**
75	16	Fr.	♆ ☌ ☾; ☿ ☌ ☾	6:46	6:46	5:16	**4:18**
76	17	Sa.		6:45	6:47	5:52	**5:28**
77	18	Su.	New ☾; eclipse ☾	6:44	6:47	6:25	**6:38**
78	19	Mo.	☾ at perigee	6:43	6:48	6:57	**7:48**
79	20	Tu.	**Spring equinox**	6:41	6:49	7:31	**9:00**
80	21	We.	♀ ☌ ☾; ☿ gr. elongation W	6:40	6:49	8:08	**10:13**
81	22	Th.		6:39	6:50	8:49	**11:25**
82	23	Fr.		6:38	6:51	9:37	
83	24	Sa.		6:36	6:51	10:31	12:35
84	25	Su.	1st qtr. ☾; ♂ ☌ ♆	6:35	6:52	11:30	1:38
85	26	Mo.		6:34	6:53	**12:33**	2:33
86	27	Tu.		6:33	6:53	**1:35**	3:19
87	28	We.	♄ ☌ ☾	6:31	6:54	**2:36**	3:58
88	29	Th.		6:30	6:55	**3:35**	4:30
89	30	Fr.		6:29	6:55	**4:31**	4:59
90	31	Sa.	♇ stationary	6:28	6:56	**5:25**	5:25

4th Month — April 2007 — 30 Days

Moon's Phases — *Full,* April 2, 12:15 p.m.; *Last Qtr.,* April 10, 1:04 p.m; *New,* April 17, 6:36 a.m.; *First Qtr.,* April 24, 1:36 a.m.

Day of				*Hour of			
Year	Month	Week	Planetary Configurations and Phenomena	Sunrise	Sunset	Moon-rise	Moon-set
91	†1	Su.	☿ ☌ ♅	7:26	7:56	**7:18**	6:50
92	2	Mo.	Full ☾	7:25	7:57	**8:12**	7:14
93	3	Tu.	☾ at apogee	7:24	7:58	**9:07**	7:40
94	4	We.		7:23	7:58	**10:03**	8:08
95	5	Th.	♃ stationary	7:22	7:59	**11:01**	8:39
96	6	Fr.		7:20	8:00		9:15
97	7	Sa.		7:19	8:00	12:00	9:57
98	8	Su.	♃ ☌ ☾	7:18	8:01	12:58	10:46
99	9	Mo.		7:17	8:02	1:54	11:42
100	10	Tu.	Last qtr. ☾	7:16	8:02	2:44	**12:44**
101	11	We.		7:14	8:03	3:30	**1:49**
102	12	Th.	♆ ☌ ☾	7:13	8:04	4:10	**2:57**
103	13	Fr.	♂ ☌ ☾	7:12	8:04	4:46	**4:04**
104	14	Sa.	♅ ☌ ☾	7:11	8:05	5:19	**5:12**
105	15	Su.		7:10	8:06	5:52	**6:22**
106	16	Mo.	☿ ☌ ☾	7:09	8:06	6:24	**7:33**
107	17	Tu.	New ☾; ☾ at perigee	7:07	8:07	7:00	**8:46**
108	18	We.		7:06	8:08	7:39	**10:01**
109	19	Th.	♄ stationary	7:05	8:08	8:25	**11:15**
110	20	Fr.	♀ ☌ ☾	7:04	8:09	9:18	
111	21	Sa.		7:03	8:10	10:18	12:24
112	22	Su.		7:02	8:10	11:22	1:24
113	23	Mo.		7:01	8:11	**12:26**	2:15
114	24	Tu.	1st qtr. ☾	7:00	8:12	**1:29**	2:57
115	25	We.	♄ ☌ ☾	6:59	8:12	**2:29**	3:32
116	26	Th.		6:58	8:13	**3:26**	4:02
117	27	Fr.		6:57	8:14	**4:20**	4:29
118	28	Sa.	♂ ☌ ♅	6:56	8:14	**5:14**	4:54
119	29	Su.		6:55	8:15	**6:07**	5:19
120	30	Mo.	☾ at apogee	6:54	8:16	**7:01**	5:44

† Daylight Saving Time begins at 2:00 a.m.

Calendar for 2007 (Cont'd.)

5th Month — **May 2007** — **31 Days**

Moon's Phases — *Full,* May 2, 5:09 a.m.; *Last Qtr.,* May 9, 11:27 p.m.; *New,* May 16, 2:27 p.m; *First Qtr.,* May 23, 4:03 p.m.; Full, May 31, 8:04 p.m.

Day of			Planetary Configurations and Phenomena	*Hour of			
Year	Month	Week		Sunrise	Sunset	Moon-rise	Moon-set
121	1	Tu.		6:53	8:16	**7:57**	6:11
122	2	We.	Full ☾; ☿ superior	6:52	8:17	**8:55**	6:41
123	3	Th.		6:51	8:18	**9:54**	7:16
124	4	Fr.		6:50	8:18	**10:52**	7:56
125	5	Sa.	♃ ☌ ☾	6:49	8:19	**11:49**	8:43
126	6	Su.		6:49	8:20		9:37
127	7	Mo.		6:48	8:20	12:41	10:37
128	8	Tu.		6:47	8:21	1:27	11:40
129	9	We.	Last qtr. ☾	6:46	8:22	2:08	**12:45**
130	10	Th.	♆ ☌ ☾	6:45	8:22	2:44	**1:50**
131	11	Fr.		6:45	8:23	3:17	**2:55**
132	12	Sa.	♅ ☌ ☾; ♂ ☌ ☾	6:44	8:24	3:49	**4:01**
133	13	Su.		6:43	8:24	4:20	**5:09**
134	14	Mo.		6:43	8:25	4:53	**6:20**
135	15	Tu.	☾ at perigee	6:42	8:26	5:30	**7:33**
136	16	We.	New ☾	6:41	8:26	6:12	**8:48**
137	17	Th.	☿ ☌ ☾	6:41	8:27	7:02	**10:01**
138	18	Fr.		6:40	8:28	8:00	**11:08**
139	19	Sa.	♀ ☌ ☾	6:39	8:28	9:04	
140	20	Su.		6:39	8:29	10:11	12:05
141	21	Mo.		6:38	8:30	11:16	12:52
142	22	Tu.	♄ ☌ ☾	6:38	8:30	**12:19**	1:30
143	23	We.	1st qtr. ☾	6:37	8:31	**1:18**	2:03
144	24	Th.		6:37	8:32	**2:14**	2:31
145	25	Fr.	♆ stationary	6:37	8:32	**3:08**	2:57
146	26	Sa.		6:36	8:33	**4:01**	3:22
147	27	Su.	☾ at apogee	6:36	8:33	**4:55**	3:47
148	28	Mo.		6:35	8:34	**5:50**	4:13
149	29	Tu.		6:35	8:35	**6:47**	4:43
150	30	We.		6:35	8:35	**7:46**	5:16
151	31	Th.	Full ☾	6:34	8:36	**8:45**	5:55

6th Month — **June 2007** — **30 Days**

Moon's Phases — *Last Qtr.,* June 8, 6:43 a.m.; *New,* June 14, 10:13 p.m., *First Qtr.,* June 22, 8:15 a.m.; *Full,* June 30, 8:49 a.m.

Day of			Planetary Configurations and Phenomena	*Hour of			
Year	Month	Week		Sunrise	Sunset	Moon-rise	Moon-set
152	1	Fr.	♃ ☌ ☾	6:34	8:36	**9:43**	6:40
153	2	Sa.	☿ greatest elongation E	6:34	8:37	**10:37**	7:33
154	3	Su.		6:34	8:37	**11:25**	8:31
155	4	Mo.		6:34	8:38		9:34
156	5	Tu.	♃ ☍	6:33	8:38	12:08	10:38
157	6	We.	♆ ☌ ☾	6:33	8:39	12:45	11:43
158	7	Th.		6:33	8:39	1:18	**12:47**
159	8	Fr.	Last qtr. ☾; ♀ gr. elong. E	6:33	8:40	1:49	**1:51**
160	9	Sa.		6:33	8:40	2:20	**2:55**
161	10	Su.	♂ ☌ ☾	6:33	8:41	2:51	**4:02**
162	11	Mo.		6:33	8:41	3:25	**5:12**
163	12	Tu.	☾ at perigee	6:33	8:42	4:03	**6:25**
164	13	We.		6:33	8:42	4:49	**7:38**
165	14	Th.	New ☾;	6:33	8:42	5:42	**8:47**
166	15	Fr.	☿ stationary	6:33	8:43	6:44	**9:49**
167	16	Sa.	☿ ☌ ☾	6:33	8:43	7:50	**10:41**
168	17	Su.		6:33	8:43	8:58	**11:24**
169	18	Mo.	♀ ☌ ☾	6:33	8:44	10:03	
170	19	Tu.	♇ ☍; ♄ ☌ ☾	6:34	8:44	11:05	12:00
171	20	We.		6:34	8:44	**12:03**	12:31
172	21	Th.	**Summer solstice**	6:34	8:44	**12:59**	12:58
173	22	Fr.	1st qtr. ☾	6:34	8:44	**1:53**	1:24
174	23	Sa.	♅ stationary	6:34	8:45	**2:47**	1:49
175	24	Su.	☾ at apogee	6:35	8:45	**3:42**	2:15
176	25	Mo.		6:35	8:45	**4:38**	2:43
177	26	Tu.		6:35	8:45	**5:36**	3:14
178	27	We.		6:36	8:45	**6:36**	3:51
179	28	Th.	♃ ☌ ☾; ☿ inferior	6:36	8:45	**7:34**	4:34
180	29	Fr.		6:36	8:45	**8:30**	5:25
181	30	Sa.	Full ☾	6:37	8:45	**9:21**	6:22

*See text before January calendar for explanation.

7th Month — **July 2007** — **31 Days**

Moon's Phases — *Last Qtr.,* July 7, 11:54 a.m.; *New,* July 14, 7:04 a.m.; *First Qtr.,* July 22, 1:29 a.m.; *Full,* July 29, 7:48 p.m.

Day of			Planetary Configurations and Phenomena	*Hour of			
Year	Month	Week		Sunrise	Sunset	Moon-rise	Moon-set
182	1	Su.	♀ ☌ ♄	6:37	8:45	**10:06**	7:25
183	2	Mo.		6:37	8:45	**10:46**	8:30
184	3	Tu.	♆ ☌ ☾	6:38	8:45	**11:20**	9:35
185	4	We.		6:38	8:45	**11:52**	10:40
186	5	Th.	♅ ☌ ☾	6:39	8:45		11:44
187	6	Fr.	● at aphelion	6:39	8:45	12:22	**12:48**
188	7	Sa.	Last qtr. ☾	6:40	8:45	12:53	**1:53**
189	8	Su.		6:40	8:44	1:25	**3:01**
190	9	Mo.	♂ ☌ ☾; ☾ at perigee	6:41	8:44	2:00	**4:10**
191	10	Tu.		6:41	8:44	2:42	**5:21**
192	11	We.		6:42	8:44	3:31	**6:31**
193	12	Th.	♀ gr. brilliancy; ☿ ☌ ☾	6:42	8:44	4:28	**7:35**
194	13	Fr.		6:43	8:43	5:32	**8:31**
195	14	Sa.	New ☾	6:43	8:43	6:39	**9:17**
196	15	Su.		6:44	8:43	7:46	**9:56**
197	16	Mo.	♄ ☌ ☾	6:44	8:42	8:50	**10:29**
198	17	Tu.	♀ ☌ ☾	6:45	8:42	9:50	**10:58**
199	18	We.		6:46	8:41	10:48	**11:24**
200	19	Th.		6:46	8:41	11:43	**11:50**
201	20	Fr.	☿ greatest elongation W	6:47	8:40	**12:38**	
202	21	Sa.		6:47	8:40	**1:32**	12:15
203	22	Su.	1st qtr. ☾; ☾ at apogee	6:48	8:39	**2:28**	12:43
204	23	Mo.		6:49	8:39	**3:25**	1:13
205	24	Tu.		6:49	8:38	**4:24**	1:47
206	25	We.	♀ stationary; ♃ ☌ ☾	6:50	8:38	**5:23**	2:27
207	26	Th.		6:50	8:37	**6:20**	3:15
208	27	Fr.		6:51	8:36	**7:13**	4:09
209	28	Sa.		6:52	8:36	**8:01**	5:10
210	29	Su.	Full ☾	6:52	8:35	**8:43**	6:16
211	30	Mo.	♆ ☌ ☾	6:53	8:34	**9:20**	7:23
212	31	Tu.		6:54	8:34	**9:53**	8:29

8th Month — **August 2007** — **31 Days**

Moon's Phases — *Last Qtr.,* Aug. 5, 4:20 p.m.; *New,* Aug. 12, 6:03 p.m.; *First Qtr.,* Aug. 20, 6:54 p.m.; *Full,* Aug. 28, 5:35 a.m.

Day of			Planetary Configurations and Phenomena	*Hour of			
Year	Month	Week		Sunrise	Sunset	Moon-rise	Moon-set
213	1	We.	♅ ☌ ☾	6:54	8:33	**10:25**	9:35
214	2	Th.		6:55	8:32	**10:55**	10:41
215	3	Fr.	☾ at perigee	6:55	8:31	**11:27**	11:46
216	4	Sa.		6:56	8:30		**12:53**
217	5	Su.	Last qtr. ☾	6:57	8:30	12:01	**2:02**
218	6	Mo.	♂ ☌ ☾	6:57	8:29	12:40	**3:12**
219	7	Tu.	♃ stationary	6:58	8:28	1:26	**4:21**
220	8	We.		6:59	8:27	2:19	**5:26**
221	9	Th.		6:59	8:26	3:20	**6:23**
222	10	Fr.		7:00	8:25	4:25	**7:12**
223	11	Sa.		7:00	8:24	5:31	**7:53**
224	12	Su.	New ☾	7:01	8:23	6:36	**8:28**
225	13	Mo.	♆ ☍	7:02	8:22	7:37	**8:58**
226	14	Tu.		7:02	8:21	8:36	**9:25**
227	15	We.	☿ superior	7:03	8:20	9:32	**9:51**
228	16	Th.		7:04	8:19	10:27	**10:17**
229	17	Fr.	♀ inferior	7:04	8:18	11:22	**10:43**
230	18	Sa.	☾ at apogee	7:05	8:17	**12:17**	**11:12**
231	19	Su.		7:05	8:16	**1:14**	**11:44**
232	20	Mo.	1st qtr. ☾	7:06	8:15	**2:12**	
233	21	Tu.	♄ ☌ ☉; ♃ ☌ ☾	7:07	8:14	**3:10**	12:21
234	22	We.		7:07	8:13	**4:07**	1:05
235	23	Th.		7:08	8:12	**5:02**	1:56
236	24	Fr.		7:08	8:10	**5:52**	2:54
237	25	Sa.		7:09	8:09	**6:36**	3:57
238	26	Su.		7:10	8:08	**7:16**	5:03
239	27	Mo.	♆ ☌ ☾	7:10	8:07	**7:51**	6:11
240	28	Tu.	Full ☾; eclipse ☾	7:11	8:06	**8:24**	7:18
241	29	We.	♅ ☌ ☾	7:11	8:05	**8:55**	8:26
242	30	Th.	☾ at perigee	7:12	8:03	**9:27**	9:33
243	31	Fr.		7:13	8:02	**10:01**	10:42

Calendar for 2007 (Cont'd.)

9th Month — September 2007 — 30 Days

Moon's Phases — *Last Qtr.*, Sept. 3, 9:32 p.m.; *New*, Sept. 11, 7:44 a.m., *First Qtr.*, Sept. 19, 11:48 a.m.; *Full*, Sept. 26, 2:45 p.m.

Day of Year	Day of Month	Day of Week	Planetary Configurations and Phenomena	*Hour of Sunrise	*Hour of Sunset	*Hour of Moon-rise	*Hour of Moon-set
244	1	Sa.		7:13	8:01	**10:40**	11:52
245	2	Su.		7:14	8:00	**11:24**	**1:03**
246	3	Mo.	Last qtr. ☾	7:14	7:58		**2:13**
247	4	Tu.	♂ ☌ ☾	7:15	7:57	12:15	**3:20**
248	5	We.		7:16	7:56	1:13	**4:19**
249	6	Th.		7:16	7:55	2:16	**5:10**
250	7	Fr.	♀ & ♇ stationary	7:17	7:54	3:22	**5:53**
251	8	Sa.	♀ ☌ ☾	7:17	7:52	4:26	**6:29**
252	9	Su.	♅ ☍; ♄ ☌ ☾	7:18	7:51	5:28	**7:00**
253	10	Mo.		7:18	7:50	6:27	**7:28**
254	11	Tu.	New ☾; eclipse ☾	7:19	7:48	7:23	**7:54**
255	12	We.		7:20	7:47	8:19	**8:19**
256	13	Th.	☿ ☌ ☾	7:20	7:46	9:13	**8:45**
257	14	Fr.		7:21	7:45	10:08	**9:13**
258	15	Sa.	☾ at apogee	7:21	7:43	11:04	**9:44**
259	16	Su.		7:22	7:42	**12:01**	**10:19**
260	17	Mo.		7:23	7:41	**12:59**	**10:59**
261	18	Tu.	♃ ☌ ☾	7:23	7:39	**1:56**	**11:46**
262	19	We.	1st qtr. ☾	7:24	7:38	**2:51**	
263	20	Th.		7:24	7:37	**3:42**	12:40
264	21	Fr.		7:25	7:36	**4:28**	1:40
265	22	Sa.		7:25	7:34	**5:09**	2:43
266	23	Su.	**Autumnal equinox;** ♆ ☌ ☾	7:26	7:33	**5:45**	3:49
267	24	Mo.		7:27	7:32	**6:19**	4:56
268	25	Tu.	♅ ☌ ☾	7:27	7:30	**6:51**	6:04
269	26	We.	Full ☾	7:28	7:29	**7:24**	7:12
270	27	Th.	☾ at perigee	7:28	7:28	**7:58**	8:21
271	28	Fr.		7:29	7:27	**8:35**	9:33
272	29	Sa.	☿ greatest elongation E	7:30	7:25	**9:19**	10:47
273	30	Su.		7:30	7:24	**10:09**	**12:00**

10th Month — October 2007 — 31 Days

Moon's Phases — *Last Qtr.*, Oct. 3, 5:06 a.m.; *New*, Oct. 11, 12:01 a.m.; *First Qtr.*, Oct. 19, 3:33 a.m.; *Full*, Oct. 25, 11:52 p.m.

Day of Year	Day of Month	Day of Week	Planetary Configurations and Phenomena	*Hour of Sunrise	*Hour of Sunset	*Hour of Moon-rise	*Hour of Moon-set
274	1	Mo.		7:31	7:23	**11:07**	**1:10**
275	2	Tu.	♂ ☌ ☾	7:31	7:21		**2:13**
276	3	We.	Last qtr. ☾	7:32	7:20	12:09	**3:08**
277	4	Th.		7:33	7:19	1:15	**3:53**
278	5	Fr.		7:33	7:18	2:19	**4:30**
279	6	Sa.	♀ ☌ ☾	7:34	7:16	3:21	**5:03**
280	7	Su.	♄ ☌ ☾	7:35	7:15	4:21	**5:31**
281	8	Mo.		7:35	7:14	5:17	**5:57**
282	9	Tu.		7:36	7:13	6:12	**6:23**
283	10	We.		7:37	7:12	7:07	**6:49**
284	11	Th.	New ☾	7:37	7:10	8:02	**7:16**
285	12	Fr.	☿ stationary; ☿ ☌ ☾	7:38	7:09	8:57	**7:45**
286	13	Sa.	☾ at apogee	7:39	7:08	9:54	**8:19**
287	14	Su.		7:39	7:07	10:51	**8:57**
288	15	Mo.	♀ ☌ ♄	7:40	7:06	11:48	**9:42**
289	16	Tu.	♃ ☌ ☾	7:41	7:05	**12:43**	**10:32**
290	17	We.		7:41	7:04	**1:35**	**11:28**
291	18	Th.		7:42	7:03	**2:21**	
292	19	Fr.	1st qtr. ☾	7:43	7:01	**3:03**	12:29
293	20	Sa.	♆ ☌ ☾	7:43	7:00	**3:40**	1:32
294	21	Su.		7:44	6:59	**4:14**	2:36
295	22	Mo.	♅ ☌ ☾	7:45	6:58	**4:46**	3:41
296	23	Tu.	☿ inferior	7:46	6:57	**5:18**	4:48
297	24	We.		7:46	6:56	**5:51**	5:56
298	25	Th.	Full ☾	7:47	6:55	**6:27**	7:06
299	26	Fr.	☾ at perigee	7:48	6:54	**7:08**	8:20
300	27	Sa.		7:49	6:53	**7:57**	9:36
301	†28	Su.	♀ greatest elongation W	6:49	5:52	**7:53**	9:51
302	29	Mo.		6:50	5:52	**8:57**	11:00
303	30	Tu.	♂ ☌ ☾	6:51	5:51	**10:04**	**12:00**
304	31	We.	♆ stationary	6:52	5:50	**11:11**	**12:50**

*See text before January calendar for explanation.

† Daylight Saving Time ends at 2:00 a.m.

11th Month — November 2007 — 30 Days

Moon's Phases — *Last Qtr.*, Nov. 1, 3:18 p.m.; *New*, Nov. 9, 5:03 p.m; *First Qtr.*, Nov. 17, 4:33 p.m.; *Full*, Nov. 24, 8:30 a.m.

Day of Year	Day of Month	Day of Week	Planetary Configurations and Phenomena	*Hour of Sunrise	*Hour of Sunset	*Hour of Moon-rise	*Hour of Moon-set
305	1	Th.	Last qtr. ☾; ☿ stationary	6:53	5:49		**1:31**
306	2	Fr.		6:53	5:48	12:15	**2:05**
307	3	Sa.	♄ ☌ ☾	6:54	5:47	1:15	**2:34**
308	4	Su.		6:55	5:46	2:13	**3:01**
309	5	Mo.	♀ ☌ ☾	6:56	5:46	3:08	**3:27**
310	6	Tu.		6:57	5:45	4:02	**3:52**
311	7	We.		6:57	5:44	4:56	**4:19**
312	8	Th.	☿ ☌ ☾; ☿ gr. elongation W	6:58	5:44	5:51	**4:48**
313	9	Fr.	New ☾; ☾ at apogee	6:59	5:43	6:48	**5:20**
314	10	Sa.		7:00	5:42	7:45	**5:57**
315	11	Su.		7:01	5:42	8:42	**6:40**
316	12	Mo.	♃ ☌ ☾	7:02	5:41	9:38	**7:28**
317	13	Tu.		7:03	5:40	10:31	**8:23**
318	14	We.		7:03	5:40	11:18	**9:21**
319	15	Th.	♂ stationary	7:04	5:39	**12:01**	**10:22**
320	16	Fr.		7:05	5:39	**12:38**	**11:24**
321	17	Sa.	1st qtr. ☾; ♆ ☌ ☾	7:06	5:38	**1:12**	
322	18	Su.		7:07	5:38	**1:43**	12:27
323	19	Mo.	♅ ☌ ☾	7:08	5:37	**2:14**	1:30
324	20	Tu.		7:09	5:37	**2:45**	2:34
325	21	We.		7:09	5:37	**3:18**	3:41
326	22	Th.		7:10	5:36	**3:56**	4:52
327	23	Fr.	☾ at perigee	7:11	5:36	**4:41**	6:06
328	24	Sa.	Full ☾; ♅ stationary	7:12	5:36	**5:34**	7:22
329	25	Su.		7:13	5:36	**6:36**	8:36
330	26	Mo.		7:14	5:35	**7:44**	9:42
331	27	Tu.	♂ ☌ ☾	7:14	5:35	**8:54**	10:39
332	28	We.		7:15	5:35	**10:01**	11:25
333	29	Th.		7:16	5:35	**11:05**	**12:03**
334	30	Fr.		7:17	5:35		**12:35**

12th Month — December 2007 — 31 Days

Moon's Phases — *Last Qtr.*, Dec. 1, 6:44 a.m.; *New*, Dec. 9, 11:40 a.m.; *First Qtr.*, Dec. 17, 4:18 a.m.; *Full*, Dec. 23, 7:16 p.m.; *Last Qtr.*, Dec. 31, 1:51 a.m.

Day of Year	Day of Month	Day of Week	Planetary Configurations and Phenomena	*Hour of Sunrise	*Hour of Sunset	*Hour of Moon-rise	*Hour of Moon-set
335	1	Sa.	Last qtr. ☾; ♄ ☌ ☾	7:18	5:35	12:05	**1:04**
336	2	Su.		7:19	5:35	1:02	**1:30**
337	3	Mo.		7:19	5:35	1:57	**1:56**
338	4	Tu.		7:20	5:35	2:51	**2:22**
339	5	We.	♀ ☌ ☾	7:21	5:35	3:46	**2:50**
340	6	Th.	☾ at apogee	7:22	5:35	4:41	**3:21**
341	7	Fr.		7:23	5:35	5:38	**3:57**
342	8	Sa.		7:23	5:35	6:36	**4:38**
343	9	Su.	New ☾	7:24	5:35	7:33	**5:25**
344	10	Mo.		7:25	5:35	8:27	**6:18**
345	11	Tu.		7:25	5:36	9:16	**7:16**
346	12	We.		7:26	5:36	10:00	**8:17**
347	13	Th.		7:27	5:36	10:39	**9:18**
348	14	Fr.	♆ ☌ ☾	7:28	5:36	11:13	**10:20**
349	15	Sa.		7:28	5:37	11:45	**11:21**
350	16	Su.	♅ ☌ ☾	7:29	5:37	**12:14**	
351	17	Mo.	1st qtr. ☾; ☿ superior	7:29	5:37	**12:44**	12:23
352	18	Tu.	♂ closest approach	7:30	5:38	**1:15**	1:26
353	19	We.		7:31	5:38	**1:49**	2:32
354	20	Th.	♄ stationary; ♇ ☌ ☉	7:31	5:39	**2:29**	3:42
355	21	Fr.		7:32	5:39	**3:17**	4:55
356	22	Sa.	**Winter solstice;** ☾ perigee	7:32	5:40	**4:13**	6:09
357	23	Su.	Full ☾; ♃ ☌ ☉; ♂ ☌ ☾	7:33	5:40	**5:18**	7:19
358	24	Mo.	♂ ☍	7:33	5:41	**6:29**	8:21
359	25	Tu.		7:33	5:41	**7:39**	9:13
360	26	We.		7:34	5:42	**8:47**	9:56
361	27	Th.		7:34	5:43	**9:51**	10:32
362	28	Fr.	♄ ☌ ☾	7:35	5:43	**10:51**	11:03
363	29	Sa.		7:35	5:44	**11:48**	11:31
364	30	Su.		7:35	5:44		11:57
365	31	Mo.	Last qtr. ☾	7:36	5:45	12:43	**12:23**

201-Year Calendar, A.D. 1894–2094, Inclusive

Using this calendar, you can find the day of the week for any day of the month and year for the period 1894–2094, inclusive. To find any day of the week, first look in the table of common years or leap years for the year required. Under the months are figures that refer to the corresponding figures at the heads of the columns of days below. For example, To know on what day of the week March 2 fell in the year 1918, find 1918 in the table of years. In a parallel line under March is Fig. 5, which directs you to Col. 5 in the table of days, in which it will be seen that March 2 fell on Saturday.

Common Years, 1894 to 2094

											Jan.	Feb.	Mar.	Apr.	May	June	July	Aug.	Sept.	Oct.	Nov.	Dec.
1894	1900	...	...	...	...	...	...	...		...												
1906	1917	1923	1934	1945	1951	1962	1973	1979	1990	...	1	4	4	7	2	5	7	3	6	1	4	6
2001	2007	2018	2029	2035	2046	2057	2063	2074	2085	2091												
1895	...	...	...	...	...	...	...	...		...												
1901	1907	1918	1929	1935	1946	1957	1963	1974	1985	1991	2	5	5	1	3	6	1	4	7	2	5	7
2002	2013	2019	2030	2041	2047	2058	2069	2075	2086	2097												
1897	...	...	...	...	...	...	...	...														
1909	1915	1926	1937	1943	1954	1965	1971	1982	1993	1999	5	1	1	4	6	2	4	7	3	5	1	3
2010	2021	2027	2038	2049	2055	2066	2077	2083	2094	2100												
1898	1910	1921	1927	1938	1949	1955	1966	1977	1983	1994	6	2	2	5	7	3	5	1	4	6	2	4
2005	2011	2022	2033	2039	2050	2061	2067	2078	2089	2095												
1899	1905	1911	1922	1933	1939	1950	1961	1967	1978	1989	7	3	3	6	1	4	6	2	5	7	3	5
1995	2006	2017	2023	2034	2045	2051	2062	2073	2079	2090												
1902	1913	1919	1930	1941	1947	1958	1969	1975	1986	1997	3	6	6	2	4	7	2	5	1	3	6	1
2003	2014	2025	2031	2042	2053	2059	2070	2081	2087	2098												
1903	1914	1925	1931	1942	1953	1959	1970	1981	1987	1998	4	7	7	3	5	1	3	6	2	4	7	2
2009	2015	2026	2037	2043	2054	2065	2071	2082	2093	2099												

Leap Years, 1894 to 2094

									Jan. (29)	Feb.	Mar.	Apr.	May	June	July	Aug.	Sept.	Oct.	Nov.	Dec.
...	...	1920	1948	1976	2004	2032	2060	2088	4	7	1	4	6	2	4	7	3	5	1	3
...	...	1924	1952	1980	2008	2036	2064	2092	2	5	6	2	4	7	2	5	1	3	6	1
...	...	1928	1956	1984	2012	2040	2068	2096	7	3	4	7	2	5	7	3	6	1	4	6
...	1904	1932	1960	1988	2016	2044	2072	...	5	1	2	5	7	3	5	1	4	6	2	4
1896	1908	1936	1964	1992	2020	2048	2076	...	3	6	7	3	5	1	3	6	2	4	7	2
...	1912	1940	1968	1996	2024	2052	2080	...	1	4	5	1	3	6	1	4	7	2	5	7
...	1916	1944	1972	2000	2028	2056	2084	...	6	2	3	6	1	4	6	2	5	7	3	5

1		2		3		4		5		6		7	
Mon.	1	Tues.	1	Wed.	1	Thurs.	1	Fri.	1	Sat.	1	SUN.	1
Tues.	2	Wed.	2	Thurs.	2	Fri.	2	Sat.	2	SUN.	2	Mon.	2
Wed.	3	Thurs.	3	Fri.	3	Sat.	3	SUN.	3	Mon.	3	Tues.	3
Thurs.	4	Fri.	4	Sat.	4	SUN.	4	Mon.	4	Tues.	4	Wed.	4
Fri.	5	Sat.	5	SUN.	5	Mon.	5	Tues.	5	Wed.	5	Thurs.	5
Sat.	6	SUN.	6	Mon.	6	Tues.	6	Wed.	6	Thurs.	6	Fri.	6
SUN.	7	Mon.	7	Tues.	7	Wed.	7	Thurs.	7	Fri.	7	Sat.	7
Mon.	8	Tues.	8	Wed.	8	Thurs.	8	Fri.	8	Sat.	8	SUN.	8
Tues.	9	Wed.	9	Thurs.	9	Fri.	9	Sat.	9	SUN.	9	Mon.	9
Wed.	10	Thurs.	10	Fri.	10	Sat.	10	SUN.	10	Mon.	10	Tues.	10
Thurs.	11	Fri.	11	Sat.	11	SUN.	11	Mon.	11	Tues.	11	Wed.	11
Fri.	12	Sat.	12	SUN.	12	Mon.	12	Tues.	12	Wed.	12	Thurs.	12
Sat.	13	SUN.	13	Mon.	13	Tues.	13	Wed.	13	Thurs.	13	Fri.	13
SUN.	14	Mon.	14	Tues.	14	Wed.	14	Thurs.	14	Fri.	14	Sat.	14
Mon.	15	Tues.	15	Wed.	15	Thurs.	15	Fri.	15	Sat.	15	SUN.	15
Tues.	16	Wed.	16	Thurs.	16	Fri.	16	Sat.	16	SUN.	16	Mon.	16
Wed.	17	Thurs.	17	Fri.	17	Sat.	17	SUN.	17	Mon.	17	Tues.	17
Thurs.	18	Fri.	18	Sat.	18	SUN.	18	Mon.	18	Tues.	18	Wed.	18
Fri.	19	Sat.	19	SUN.	19	Mon.	19	Tues.	19	Wed.	19	Thurs.	19
Sat.	20	SUN.	20	Mon.	20	Tues.	20	Wed.	20	Thurs.	20	Fri.	20
SUN.	21	Mon.	21	Tues.	21	Wed.	21	Thurs.	21	Fri.	21	Sat.	21
Mon.	22	Tues.	22	Wed.	22	Thurs.	22	Fri.	22	Sat.	22	SUN.	22
Tues.	23	Wed.	23	Thurs.	23	Fri.	23	Sat.	23	SUN.	23	Mon.	23
Wed.	24	Thurs.	24	Fri.	24	Sat.	24	SUN.	24	Mon.	24	Tues.	24
Thurs.	25	Fri.	25	Sat.	25	SUN.	25	Mon.	25	Tues.	25	Wed.	25
Fri.	26	Sat.	26	SUN.	26	Mon.	26	Tues.	26	Wed.	26	Thurs.	26
Sat.	27	SUN.	27	Mon.	27	Tues.	27	Wed.	27	Thurs.	27	Fri.	27
SUN.	28	Mon.	28	Tues.	28	Wed.	28	Thurs.	28	Fri.	28	Sat.	28
Mon.	29	Tues.	29	Wed.	29	Thurs.	29	Fri.	29	Sat.	29	SUN.	29
Tues.	30	Wed.	30	Thurs.	30	Fri.	30	Sat.	30	SUN.	30	Mon.	30
Wed.	31	Thurs.	31	Fri.	31	Sat.	31	SUN.	31	Mon.	31	Tues.	31

Beginning of the Year

The Athenians began the year in June, the Macedonians in September, the Romans first in March and later in January, the Persians on Aug. 11, and the ancient Mexicans on Feb. 23. The Chinese year, which begins in late January or early February, is similar to the Mohammedan year. Both have 12 months of 29 and 30 days alternating, while in every 19 years, there are seven years that have 13 months. This does not quite fit the planetary movements, hence the Chinese have formed a cycle of 60 years, in which period 22 intercalary (added to the calendar) months occur.

Recreation

Information about recreational opportunities in state and national parks and forests and at U.S. Army Corps of Engineers Lakes, a representative list of festivals and celebrations in individual towns and communities across the state, as well as information on hunting and fishing opportunities and regulations is found in the following pages. Information about hunting, fishing and other recreation on State Wildlife Management Areas and National Wildlife Refuges can be found in the Environment section on pages 110–113. Recreation and special events in each county are also mentioned in the Counties section.

Texas State Parks

Texas' diverse system of state parks offers contrasting attractions — mountains and canyons, arid deserts and lush forests, spring-fed streams, sandy dunes, saltwater surf and fascinating historic sites.

The state park information below was provided by **Texas Parks and Wildlife** (TPW). Additional information and brochures on individual parks are available from the TPW's Austin headquarters, 4200 Smith School Rd., Austin 78744; 1-800-792-1112; **www.tpwd.state.tx.us/park/.**

The TPW's **Central Reservation Center** can take reservations for almost all parks that accept reservations. Exceptions are Indian Lodge, the Texas State Railroad and facilities not operated by the TPW. Call the center during usual business hours at 512-389-8900. The TDD line is 512-389-8915.

The **Texas State Parks Pass**, currently costing $60 per year, waives entrance fees for all members and all passengers in member's vehicle to all state parks when entrance fees are required, as well as other benefits. For further information, contact TPW 512-389-8900.

Texas State Parklands Passport is a windshield decal granting discounted entrance to state parks for Texas residents who are senior citizens or are collecting Social Security disability payments and free entrance for disabled U.S. veterans. Available at state parks with proper identification. Details can be obtained at numbers or addresses above.

The following information is a brief glimpse of what each park has to offer. Refer to the chart on pages 112-113 for a more complete list of available activities and facilities. Entrance fees to state parks range from $1 to $5 per person. There are also fees for tours and some activities. For up-to-date information, call the information number listed above before you go. Road abbreviations used in this list are: IH - interstate highway, US - U.S. Highway, TX - state highway, FM - farm-to-market road, RM - ranch-to-market road, PR - park road.

List of State Parks

Abilene State Park, 16 miles southwest of Abilene on FM 89 and PR 32 in Taylor County, consists of 529.4 acres that were deeded by the City of Abilene in 1933. A part of the **official Texas longhorn herd** and bison are located in the park. Large groves of pecan trees that once shaded bands of Comanches now shade visitors at picnic tables. Activities include camping, hiking, picnicking, nature study, biking, lake swimming and fishing. In addition to **Lake Abilene, Buffalo Gap**, the original Taylor County seat (1878) and one of the early frontier settlements, is nearby. Buffalo Gap was on the **Western**, or **Goodnight-Loving, Trail**, over which pioneer Texas cattlemen drove herds to railheads in Kansas.

Acton State Historic Site is a .01-acre cemetery plot in Hood County where **Davy Crockett's** second wife, Elizabeth, was buried in 1860. It is 4.5 miles east of Granbury on US 377 to FM 167 south, then 2.4 miles south to Acton. Nearby attractions include Cleburne, Dinosaur Valley and Lake Whitney state parks.

Admiral Nimitz Museum State Historic Site (see **National Museum of the Pacific War**).

Atlanta State Park is 1,475 acres located 11 miles northwest of Atlanta on FM 1154 in Cass County; adjacent to **Wright Patman Dam and Reservoir.** Land acquired from the U.S. Army in 1954 by license to 2004 with option to renew to 2054. Camping, biking and hiking in pine forests, as well as water activities, such as boating, fishing, lake swimming. Nearby are historic town of **Jefferson** and **Caddo Lake and Daingerfield** state parks.

Balmorhea State Park is 45.9 acres four miles west of Balmorhea on TX 17 between Balmorhea

The limestone block pavilion at Big Spring State Park in West Texas is one of several park structures erected in the 1930s by the Civilian Conservation Corps. Texas Parks & Wildlife photo.

and Toyahvale in Reeves County. Deeded in 1934-35 by private owners and Reeves Co. Water Imp. Dist. No. 1 and built by the Civilian Conservation Corps (CCC). Swimming pool (1-3/4 acres) fed by artesian **San Solomon Springs;** also provides water to **aquatic refuge** in park. Activities include swimming, picnicking, camping, scuba and skin diving. Motel rooms available at **San Solomon Springs Courts**. Nearby are city of Pecos, **Fort Davis National Historic Site, Davis Mountains State Park** and **McDonald Observatory.**

Barrington Living History Farm is the home of Anson Jones, the last president of the Republic of Texas. He and his family, along with five slaves, built the home in Washington (near Brazoria), and Jones retired there in 1846 after the annexation of Texas as the 28th state of the United States. The farm and its outbuildings function today as an interpretive center where farm life continues much as it did 150 years ago. Activities are guided by entries that Jones made in his daybook while living there. For further information, contact 916-878-2214 or link to Barrington.Farm@tpwd.state.tx.us.

Barton Warnock Environmental Education Center consists of 99.9 acres in Brewster County. Originally built by the Lajitas Foundation in 1982 as the Lajitas Museum Desert Gardens, the TPW purchased it in 1990 and renamed it for Texas botanist Dr. Barton Warnock. The center is also the eastern entrance station to **Big Bend Ranch State Park**. Self-guiding botanical and museum tours. On FM 170 one mile east of Lajitas.

Bastrop State Park is 3,503.7 acres one mile east of

Palo Duro Canyon State Park consists of 16,402 acres 12 miles east of Canyon on TX 217 in Armstrong and Randall counties in the Panhandle. Texas Almanac photo.

Bastrop on TX 21 or from TX 71. The park was acquired by deeds from the City of Bastrop and private owners in 1933-35; additional acreage acquired in 1979. Site of famous **"Lost Pines,"** isolated region of loblolly pine and hardwoods. **Swimming pool, cabins** and **lodge** are among facilities. Fishing at Lake Bastrop, backpacking, picnicking, canoeing, bicycling, hiking. Golf course adjacent to park. **State capitol** at Austin 32 miles away; 13-mile drive through forest leads to **Buescher State Park.**

Battleship Texas State Historic Site (see San Jacinto Battleground State Historic Site and Battleship Texas)

Bentsen-Rio Grande Valley State Park, a scenic park, is along the Rio Grande five miles southwest of Mission off FM 2062 in Hidalgo County. The 760 acres of **subtropical resaca woodlands and brushlands** were acquired from private owners in 1944. Park is excellent base from which to tour **Lower Rio Grande Valley** of Texas and adjacent **Mexico;** most attractions within an hour's drive. Hiking trails provide chance to study unique plants and animals of park. Many birds unique to southern United States found here, including **pauraque, groove-billed ani, green kingfisher, rose-throated becard** and **tropical parula.** Birdwatching tours guided by park naturalists offered daily December –March. Park is one of last natural refuges in Texas for **ocelot** and **jaguarundi.** Trees include **cedar elm, anaqua, ebony** and **Mexican ash.** Camping, hiking, picnicking, boating, fishing also available. Nearby are **Santa Ana National Wildlife Refuge, Falcon State Park** and **Sabal Palm Sanctuary.**

Big Bend Ranch State Park, more than 299,008 acres of **Chihuahuan Desert wilderness** in Brewster and Presidio counties along the Rio Grande, was purchased from private owners in 1988. The purchase more than doubled the size of the state park system, which comprised at that time 220,000 acres. Eastern entrance at Barton Warnock Environmental Education Center one mile east of Lajitas on FM 170; western entrance is at **Fort Leaton State Historical Park** four miles west of Presidio on FM 170. The area includes **extinct volcanoes,** several **waterfalls,** two **mountain ranges,** at least **11 rare species of plants and animals,** and **90 major archaeological sites.** There is little development. Vehicular access limited; wilderness

backpacking, hiking, scenic drive, picnicking, fishing and swimming. There are longhorns in the park, although they are not part of the official **state longhorn herd.**

Big Spring State Park is 382 acres located on FM 700 within the city limits of Big Spring in Howard County. Both city and park were named for a natural spring that was replaced by an artificial one. The park was deeded by the City of Big Spring in 1934 and 1935. Drive to top of **Scenic Mountain** provides panoramic view of surrounding country and look at **prairie dog colony.** The "big spring," nearby in a city park, provided watering place for herds of bison, antelope and wild horses. Used extensively also as campsite for early Indians, explorers and settlers.

Blanco State Park is 104.6 acres along the Blanco River four blocks south of Blanco's town square in Blanco County. The land was deeded by private owners in 1933. Park area was used as campsite by early explorers and settlers. Fishing, camping, swimming, picnicking, boating. **LBJ Ranch** and **LBJ State Historic Site, Pedernales Falls** and **Guadalupe River** state parks are nearby.

Boca Chica State Park is 1,054.92 acres of open beach located at the mouth of the Rio Grande in southeastern Cameron County. Park was acquired in May 1994. From US 77/83 at Olmito, take FM 511 12 miles to TX 4, then 17 miles east to park. Picnicking, wading, swimming, birding, camping, fishing allowed. No facilities provided.

Bonham State Park is a 261-acre park located two miles southeast of Bonham on TX 78, then two miles southeast on FM 271 in Fannin County. It includes a 65-acre lake, **rolling prairies** and **woodlands.** The land was acquired in 1933 from the city of Bonham. Swimming, camping, mountain-bike trail, lighted fishing pier, boating. **Sam Rayburn Memorial Library** in Bonham. **Sam Rayburn Home** and **Valley Lake** nearby.

Brazos Bend State Park in Fort Bend County, seven miles west of Rosharon off FM 1462 on FM 762, approximately 28 miles south of Houston. The 4,897-acre park was purchased from private owners in 1976–77. **George Observatory** in park. **Observation platform** for spotting and photographing the **270 species of birds, 23 species of mammals, and 21 species of reptiles and amphibians, including American alligator,** that frequent the park. Interpretive and educational programs every weekend. Backpacking, camping, hiking, biking, fishing. Creekfield Lake Nature Trail.

Buescher State Park, a scenic area, is 1,016.7 acres 2 miles northwest of Smithville off TX 71 to FM 153 in Bastrop County. Acquired between 1933 and 1936, about one-third deeded by private owner; heirs donated a third; balance from City of Smithville. **El Camino Real** once ran near park, connecting **San Antonio de Béxar** with **Spanish missions in East Texas.** Parkland was part of **Stephen F. Austin's colonial grant.** Some **250 species of birds** can be seen. Camping, fishing, hiking, boating. Scenic park road connects with **Bastrop State Park** through **Lost Pines** area.

Caddo Lake State Park, north of Karnack one mile off TX 43 to FM 2198 in Harrison County, consists of 483.85 acres along **Cypress Bayou,** which runs into Caddo Lake. A scenic area, it was acquired from private owners in 1933. Nearby Karnack is childhood home of Mrs. Lyndon B. Johnson. Close by is old city of **Jefferson,** famous as commercial center of Northeast Texas during last half of 19th century. Caddo Indian legend attributes formation of Caddo Lake to **a huge flood.** Lake originally only natural lake of any size in state; dam added in 1914 for flood control; new dam replaced old one in 1971. **Cypress trees, American lotus** and **lily pads,** as well as **71 species of fish,** predominate in lake. **Nutria, beaver, mink, squirrel, armadillo, alligator** and **turtle** abound. Activities include camping, hiking, swimming, fishing, canoeing. Screened shelters, cabins.

Caddoan Mounds State Historic Site in Cherokee County six miles southwest of Alto on TX 21. Total of 93.8 acres acquired in 1975. Open for day visits only, park offers exhibits and interpretive trails through reconstructed **Caddo dwellings and ceremonial areas,** including two temple mounds, a burial mound and a village area typical of people who lived in region for 500 years beginning about A.D. 800. Closed Tuesday and Wednesday. Nearby are **Jim Hogg State Historic Site, Mission Tejas State Historic Site** and **Texas State Railroad.**

Caprock Canyons State Park, 100 miles southeast of Amarillo and 3.5 miles north of Quitaque off FM 1065 and TX 86 in Briscoe, Floyd and Hall counties, has 15,313 acres. Purchased in 1975. Scenic escarpment's **canyons** provided camping areas for **Indians of Folsom culture** more than 10,000 years ago. **Mesquite** and **cacti** in the **badlands** give way to **tall grasses, cottonwood** and **plum thickets** in the bottomlands. Wildlife includes **aoudad sheep, coyote, bobcat, porcupine** and **fox.** Activities include scenic drive, camping, hiking, mountain-bike riding, horse riding and horse camping. A 64.25-mile trailway (hike, bike and equestrian trail) extends from South Plains to Estelline.

Casa Navarro State Historic Site, on .7 acre at corner of S. Laredo and W. Nueva streets in downtown San Antonio, was acquired by donation from San Antonio Conservation Society Foundation in 1975. Has furnished **Navarro House** three-building complex built about 1848, home of the statesman, rancher and Texas patriot **José Antonio Navarro.** Guided tours; exhibits. Open Wednesday through Sunday.

Cedar Hill State Park, an urban park on 1,826 acres 10 miles southwest of Dallas via US 67 and FM 1382 on **Joe Pool Reservoir,** was acquired by long-term lease from the Corp of Engineers in 1982. Camping mostly in wooded areas. Fishing from two lighted jetties and a perch pond for children. Swimming, boating, bicycling, birdwatching and picnicking. Vegetation includes several sections of **tallgrass prairie.** Penn Farm Agricultural History Center includes reconstructed buildings of the **19th-century Penn Farm** and exhibits; self-guided tours.

Choke Canyon State Park consists of two units, South Shore and Calliham, located on 26,000-acre **Choke Can-**

yon Reservoir. Park acquired in 1981 in a 50-year agreement among Bureau of Reclamation, City of Corpus Christi and Nueces River Authority. Thickets of **mesquite** and **blackbrush acacia** predominate, supporting populations of **javelina, coyote, skunk** and **alligator,** as well as the **crested caracara.** The 385-acre South Shore Unit is located 3.5 miles west of Three Rivers on TX 72 in Live Oak County; the 1,100-acre Calliham Unit is located 12 miles west of Three Rivers, on TX 72, in McMullen County. Both units offer camping, picnicking, boating, fishing, lake swimming, and baseball and volleyball areas. The Calliham Unit also has a hiking trail, wildlife educational center, screened shelters, rentable **gym and kitchen. Sports complex** includes swimming pool and tennis, volleyball, shuffleboard and basketball courts. Across dam from South Shore is North Shore Equestrian and Camping Area; 18 miles of horseback riding trails.

Cleburne State Park is a 528-acre park located 10 miles southwest of Cleburne via US 67 and PR 21 in Johnson County with 116-acre spring-fed lake; acquired from the City of Cleburne and private owners in 1935 and 1936. **Oak, elm, mesquite, cedar** and **redbud** cover white rocky hills. Bluebonnets in spring. Activities include camping, picnicking, hiking, bicycling, canoeing, swimming, boating, fishing. Nearby are **Fossil Rim Wildlife Center** and **dinosaur tracks** in Paluxy River at **Dinosaur Valley State Park.**

Colorado Bend State Park, a 5,328.3-acre facility, is 28 miles west of Lampasas in Lampasas and San Saba counties. Access is from Lampasas to Bend on FM 580 west, then follow signs (access road subject to flooding). Park site was purchased partly in 1984, with balance acquired in 1987. Primitive camping, fishing, swimming, hiking, biking and picnicking; guided tours to Gorman Falls. Rare and endangered species here include **golden-cheeked warbler, black-capped vireo** and **bald eagle.**

Confederate Reunion Grounds State Historic Site, located in Limestone County on the Navasota River, is 77.1 acres in size. Acquired 1983 by deed from Joseph E. Johnston Camp No. 94 CSA. Entrance is 6 miles south of Mexia on TX 14, then 2.5 miles west on FM 2705. **Historic buildings,** two **scenic footbridges** span creek; hiking trail. Nearby are **Fort Parker State Park** and **Old Fort Parker State Historic Site.**

Cooper Lake State Park, comprises 3,026 acres three miles southeast of Cooper in Delta and Hopkins counties acquired in 1991 by 25-year lease from Corps of Engineers. Two units, Doctors Creek and South Sulphur, adjoin 19,300-surface-acre Cooper Lake. Fishing, boating, camping, picnicking, swimming. Screened shelters and cabins. South Sulpher offers equestrian camping and horseback riding trails. Access to Doctors Creek Unit is via TX 24 east from Commerce to Cooper, then east on TX 154 to FM 1529 to park. To South Sulphur Unit, take IH 30 to Exit 122 west of Sulphur Springs to TX 19, then TX 71, then FM 3505.

Copano Bay State Fishing Pier, a 5.9-acre park, is located 5 miles north of Rockport on TX 35 in Aransas County. Acquired by transfer of jurisdiction from state highway department in 1967. Picnicking, saltwater fishing, boating and swimming. Operated by leased concession.

Copper Breaks State Park, 12 miles south of Quanah on TX 6 in Hardeman County, was acquired by purchase from private owner in 1970. Park features rugged scenic beauty on 1,898.8 acres, two lakes, **grass-covered mesas** and juniper breaks. Nearby **medicine mounds** were important ceremonial sites of Comanche Indians. Nearby **Pease River** was site of 1860 battle in which **Cynthia Ann Parker** was recovered from Comanches. State **state longhorn herd** lives at park. Abundant wildlife. Nature, hiking and equestrian trails; natural and historical exhibits; summer programs; horseback riding; camping, equestrian camping.

Daingerfield State Park, off TX 49 and PR 17 southeast of Daingerfield in Morris County, is a 550.9-acre recreational area that includes an 80-surface-acre lake; deeded in 1935 by private owners. This area is center of iron industry in Texas; nearby is Lone Star Steel Co. In spring, **dogwood, redbuds** and **wisteria** bloom; in fall, brilliant foliage of **sweet-gum, oaks** and **maples** contrast with dark green pines. Campsites, lodge and cabins.

Davis Mountains State Park is 2,709 acres in Jeff Davis County, 4 miles northwest of Fort Davis via TX 118 and PR 3. The scenic area was deeded in 1933-1937 by private owners. **First European, Antonio de Espejo,** came to area in 1583. Extremes of altitude produce both **plains grasslands** and **piñon-juniper-oak woodlands. Montezuma quail,** rare in Texas, visit park. Scenic drives, camping and hiking. **Indian Lodge,** built by the Civilian Conservation Corps during the early 1930s, has 39 rooms, restaurant and swimming pool (reservations: 432-426-3254). Four-mile hiking trail leads to **Fort Davis National Historic Site.** Other nearby points of interest include **McDonald Observatory** and 74-mile scenic loop through **Davis Mountains.** Nearby are scenic **Limpia, Madera, Musquiz** and **Keesey** canyons; **Camino del Rio;** ghost town of **Shafter; Big Bend National Park; Big Bend Ranch State Park; Fort Davis National Historic Site;** and **Fort Leaton State Historic Site.**

Devil's River State Natural Area comprises 19,988.6 acres in Val Verde County, 22 miles off US 277, about 65 miles north of Del Rio on graded road. It is an **ecological and archaeological crossroads.** Ecologically, it is in a **transitional area** between the **Edwards Plateau,** the **Trans-Pecos desert** and the **South Texas brush country.** Archaeological studies suggest occupation and/or use by cultures from both east and west. Camping, hiking and mountain biking. Canyon and pictograph-site tours by prearrangement only. Park accessible by reservation only. **Dolan Falls,** owned by The Nature Conservancy of Texas and open only to its members, is nearby.

Devil's Sinkhole State Natural Area, comprising 1,859.7 acres about 6 miles northeast of Rocksprings in Edwards County, is a **vertical cavern.** The sinkhole, discovered by Anglo settlers in 1867, is a registered **National Natural Landmark;** it was purchased in 1985 from private owners. The cavern opening is about 40 by 60 feet, with a vertical drop of about 140 feet. Access by prearranged tour with Devil's Sinkhole Society (830-683-BATS). Bats can be viewed in summer leaving cave at dusk; no access to cave itself. Access to the park is made by contacting **Kickapoo Cavern State Park** to arrange a tour.

Dinosaur Valley State Park, located off US 67 four miles west of Glen Rose in Somervell County, is a 1,524.72-acre scenic park. Land was acquired from private owners in 1968. **Dinosaur tracks** in bed of Paluxy River and two full-scale dinosaur models, originally created for New York World's Fair in 1964-65, on display. Part of state **longhorn herd** is in park. Camping, picnicking, hiking, mountain biking, swimming, fishing.

Eisenhower Birthplace State Historic Site is 6 acres off US 75 at 609 S. Lamar, Denison, Grayson County. The

McKinney Falls State Park is 744 acres just 13 miles south of Austin. The falls are on Onion Creek, the site of Thomas F. McKinney's mid-1800s homestead. Texas Parks & Wildlife photo.

property was acquired in 1958 from the Eisenhower Birthplace Foundation. Restoration of home of Pres. Dwight David "Ike" Eisenhower includes furnishings of period and some personal effects of Gen. Eisenhower. Guided tour; call for schedule. Park open daily, except Christmas Day and New Year's Day; call for hours. Town of Denison established on **Butterfield Overland Mail** Route in 1858.

Eisenhower State Park, 423.1 acres five miles northwest of Denison via US 75 to TX 91N to FM 1310 on the shores of **Lake Texoma** in Grayson County, was acquired by an Army lease in 1954. Named for the **34th U.S. president, Dwight David Eisenhower.** First Anglo settlers came to area in 1835; **Fort Johnson** was established in area in 1840; **Colbert's Ferry** established on Red River in 1853 and operated until 1931. Areas of **tall-grass prairie** exist. Hiking, camping, picnicking, fishing, swimming.

Enchanted Rock State Natural Area is 1,643.5 acres on Big Sandy Creek 18 miles north of Fredericksburg on RM 965 on the line between Gillespie and Llano counties. Acquired in 1978 by The Nature Conservancy of Texas; state acquired from TNCT in 1984. Enchanted Rock is huge **pink granite boulder** rising 425 feet above ground and covering 640 acres. It is **second-largest batholith** (underground rock formation uncovered by erosion) in the United States. Indians believed **ghost fires** flickered at top and were awed by weird creaking and groaning, which geologists say resulted from rock's heating and expanding by day, cooling and contracting at night. Enchanted Rock is a **National Natural Landmark** and is on the **National Register of Historic Places.** Activities include hiking, geological study, camping, **rock climbing** and star gazing.

Fairfield Lake State Park is 1,460 acres adjacent to Lake Fairfield, 6 miles northeast of the city of Fairfield off FM 2570 and FM 3285 in Freestone County. It was leased from Texas Utilities in 1971-72. Surrounding woods offer sanctuary for many species of birds and wildlife. Camping, hiking, backpacking, nature study, water-related activities available. Extensive schedule of tours, seminars and other activities.

Falcon State Park is 572.6 acres located 15 miles north of Roma off US 83 and FM 2098 at southern end of Falcon Reservoir in Starr and Zapata counties. Park leased from International Boundary and Water Commission in 1949. Gently rolling hills covered by **mesquite, huisache, wild olive, ebony, cactus.** Excellent **birding** and **fishing.** Camping and water activities also. Nearby are **Mexico, Fort Ringgold** in Rio Grande City and historic city of **Roma. Bentsen-Rio Grande Valley State**

Parks text continues on page 150.

☆ Texas State Parks ☆

Park/†Type of Park/Special Features	Nearest Town	Day Use Only	Historic Site/Museum	Exhibit/Interpretive Center	Restrooms	Showers	Trailer Dump Stn.	††Camping	Screened Shelters	Cabins	Group Facilities	Nature Trail	Hiking Trail	Picnicking	Boat Ramp	Fishing	Swimming	Water Skiing	Miscellaneous
Abilene SP	BUFFALO GAP				★	★	★	15	★		BG	★		★		☆	★		L
Acton SHS (Grave of Davy Crockett's wife)	GRANBURY	★	★																
Atlanta SP	ATLANTA				★	★	★	14			DG	★	★	★	★	☆	☆	☆	
Balmorhea SP (San Solomon Springs Courts)	BALMORHEA			★	★	★	★	14			DG			★			★		I
Barton Warnock Environmental Education Ctr.	LAJITAS	★		★	★		★				★								
Bastrop SP	BASTROP				★	★	★	10		★	BG	★	★			☆	★		G
Battleship Texas HS (At San Jacinto Battleground)	DEER PARK	★	★	★															
Bentsen-Rio Grande Valley SP	MISSION				★	★		10			BG	★	★	★	★	☆			
Big Bend Ranch SP Complex	PRESIDIO			★	★	★		1			NG	★	★	★		☆	☆		B1, L, E
Big Spring SP	BIG SPRING			★	★			13			BG	★	★	★					
Blanco SP	BLANCO				★	★	★	16	★		DG			★	★	☆	☆		
Boca Chica SP (Open Beach)	BROWNSVILLE							1					☆			☆	☆		
Bonham SP	BONHAM				★	★	★	14			BG	★	★	★	★	☆			B1
Brazos Bend SP (George Observatory)	RICHMOND			★	★	★	★	4	★		BG	★	★	★		★			B1, B2
Buescher SP	SMITHVILLE				★	★	★	14			BG	★	★	★		★	☆		B2
Caddo Lake SP	KARNACK			★	★	★	★	15	★	★	BG	★	★	★	★	★	☆	☆	
Caddoan Mounds SHS	ALTO	★	★	★	★							★							
Caprock Canyons SP and Trailway	QUITAQUE			★	★	★	★	8			BG	★	★	★	★	★	☆		B1, E
Casa Navarro SHS	SAN ANTONIO	★	★	★	★														
Cedar Hill SP	CEDAR HILL				★	★	★	12			DG	★	★	★	★	★	☆	☆	B1
Choke Canyon SP, Calliham Unit	CALLIHAM				★	★	★	10	★		BG	★		★	★	★	☆	☆	
Choke Canyon SP, South Shore Unit	THREE RIVERS				★	★	★	8			DG			★	★	★	☆		B1, E
Cleburne SP	CLEBURNE				★	★	★	16	★		BG	★	★	★	★	★	☆		
Colorado Bend SP (Cave Tours)	BEND				★			1				★	★	★	★	★	☆		B1
Confederate Reunion Grounds SHS	MEXIA	★		★	★			1			BG	★	★			☆			
Cooper Lake SP (Doctors Creek Unit)	COOPER				★	★	★	4	★		DG	★	★	★	★	★	★	☆	
Cooper Lake SP (South Sulphur Unit)	SULPHUR SPRINGS				★	★	★	14	★	★	DG	★	★	★	★	★	★	☆	B1, E
Copano Bay SFP ▲	FULTON				★										★	★			
Copper Breaks SP	QUANAH			★	★	★	★	10			BG	★	★		★	★	☆		B1, E, L
Daingerfield SP	DAINGERFIELD				★	★	★	15		★	BG	★	★	★	★	★	☆		
Davis Mountains SP (Indian Lodge)	FORT DAVIS			★	★	★	★	11			DG	★	★						I, E
Devils River SNA (Use by reservation only)	DEL RIO							1			BG								B1, E
Devil's Sinkhole SNA	ROCKSPRINGS	*(No access to cavern. Tours of SNA by special request only.)*																	
Dinosaur Valley SP (Dinosaur Footprints)	GLEN ROSE			★	★	★	★	12			DG	★	★	★		☆	☆		B1, E, L
Eisenhower SP (Marina)	DENISON				★	★	★	15	★		BG	★	★	★	★	★	☆	☆	B1
Eisenhower Birthplace SHS	DENISON	★	★	★	★						DG								
Enchanted Rock SNA	FREDERICKSBURG			★	★			9			DG	★	★	★					R
Fairfield Lake SP	FAIRFIELD				★	★	★	11			DG	★	★	★	★	★	☆	☆	B1
Falcon SP (Airstrip)	ZAPATA				★	★	★	15	★		BG	★		★	★	☆	☆	☆	B1
Fannin Battleground SHS	GOLIAD	★	★	★	★						DG			★					
Fanthorp Inn SHS	ANDERSON	★	★	★	★														
Fort Boggy SP	CENTERVILLE	★			★						DG	★	★	★	★	☆	☆		
Fort Griffin SHS	ALBANY		★	★	★	★	★	10			BG	★	★	★		☆			L, E
Fort Lancaster SHS	OZONA	★	★	★	★									☆					
Fort Leaton SHS	PRESIDIO	★	★	★	★							★		★					
Fort McKavett SHS	FORT McKAVETT	★	★	★	★							★		★					
Fort Parker SP	MEXIA				★	★	★	14	★		BG	★	★	★	★	☆			B1
Fort Richardson SHS and Lost Creek Res. TW	JACKSBORO		★	★	★	★	★	10	★		DG	★	★	★		★	★		E
Franklin Mountains SP	EL PASO	★			★			6			DG	★	★						B1, E, R
Fulton Mansion SHS	FULTON	★	★	★										★					
Galveston Island SP (Summer Theater)	GALVESTON			★	★	★	★	4	★			★		★		☆	☆		B1
Garner SP	CONCAN				★	★	★	14	★	★	BG	★	★	★		☆	☆		B2
Goliad SHS	GOLIAD		★	★	★	★	★	11	★		DG	★	★	★		★			
Goose Island SP	ROCKPORT				★	★	★	14			BG			★	★	★			
Governor Hogg Shrine SHS	QUITMAN	★	★	★	★						DG	★		★					
Guadalupe River SP/Honey Creek SNA	BOERNE				★	★	★	13				★	★			☆	☆		E
Hill Country SNA	BANDERA							6			NG	★				☆	☆		B1, E
Hueco Tanks SHS (Indian Pictographs)	EL PASO		★	★	★	★	★	14			DG	★	★	★					R
Huntsville SP	HUNTSVILLE			★	★	★	★	14	★		DG	★	★	★	★	★	☆		B1, B2
Inks Lake SP	BURNET				★	★	★	10	★		BG	★	★	★	★	★	☆	☆	G
Jim Hogg SHS	RUSK	★	★	★	★							★		★					
Kerrville-Schreiner SP	KERRVILLE			★	★	★	★	11	★		BG	★	★	★		★	☆		B1
Kickapoo Cavern SP (Use by reservation only)	BRACKETTVILLE				★	★		6			NG	★	★						B1

---

†Types of Parks

SP	State Park	SFP	State Fishing Pier	
SHS	State Historic Site	TW	Trailway	
SNA	State Natural Area			

††Type(s) of Camping

1-Primitive; 2-Walk-in tent; 3-Tent; 4-Water and Electric; 5-Water, Electric, Sewer; 6-1 & 2; 7-1, 2 & 4; 8-1, 2, 3 & 4; 9-1 & 3; 10-1, 3 & 4; 11-1, 3, 4 & 5; 12-1 & 4; 13-2, 3 & 4; 14- 3 & 4; 15-3, 4 & 5; 16-4 & 5; 17-1, 3 & 5.

☆ Texas State Parks ☆

Park/†Type of Park/Special Features	NEAREST TOWN	Day Use Only	Historic Site/Museum	Exhibit/Interpretive Center	Restrooms	Showers	Trailer Dump Stn.	††Camping	Screened Shelters	Cabins	Group Facilities	Nature Trail	Hiking Trail	Picnicking	Boat Ramp	Fishing	Swimming	Water Skiing	Miscellaneous
Lake Arrowhead SP	WICHITA FALLS				★	★	★	10			DG	★	★	★	★	★	☆	☆	E
Lake Bob Sandlin SP	MOUNT PLEASANT				★	★	★	10	★		DG		★	★	★	★	☆	☆	B1
Lake Brownwood SP	BROWNWOOD				★	★	★	15	★	★	BG	★	★	★	★	★	☆	☆	B1
Lake Casa Blanca International SP	LAREDO				★	★	★	14			DG			★	★	☆	☆		B1
Lake Colorado City SP	COLORADO CITY				★	★	★	14		★	BG	★	★	★	★	★	☆	☆	
Lake Corpus Christi SP	MATHIS				★	★	★	15	★		DG			★	★	★	☆	☆	
Lake Houston SP	NEW CANEY				★	★		9			BG	★	★	★		★			B1, E
Lake Livingston SP	LIVINGSTON				★	★	★	15	★		DG	★	★	★	★	★	☆	☆	B1, B2, E
Lake Mineral Wells SP and TW	MINERAL WELLS				★	★	★	10	★		DG	★	★	★	★	★	☆		B1, E, R
Lake Rita Blanca SP	DALHART	★												★					B1, E
Lake Somerville SP and TW, Birch Creek Unit	SOMERVILLE			★	★	★	★	10			BG	★	★	★	★	★	☆	☆	B1, E
Lake Somerville SP and TW, Nails Creek Unit	LEDBETTER			★	★	★	★	10			DG	★	★	★	★	★	☆	☆	B1, E
Lake Tawakoni SP	WILLS POINT				★	★	★	4				★	★	★	☆	☆	☆	☆	
Lake Texana SP	EDNA			★	★	★	★	14			DG	★	★	★	★				B1
Lake Whitney SP (Airstrip)	WHITNEY				★	★	★	15	★		BG	★		★	★	☆	☆	☆	B1
Landmark Inn SHS (Hotel Rooms)	CASTROVILLE		★	★	★						DG	★		★			☆		I
Lipantitlan SHS	SAN PATRICIO	★												★					
Lockhart SP	LOCKHART				★	★		16			BG			★		★			G
Longhorn Cavern SP (Cavern Tours) ▲	BURNET	★	★	★	★							★	★	★					
Lost Maples SNA	VANDERPOOL			★	★	★	★	12				★	★	★			☆	☆	
Lyndon B. Johnson SHS	STONEWALL	★	★	★	★						DG	★		★			☆	★	L
Magoffin Home SHS	EL PASO	★	★	★	★														
Martin Creek Lake SP	TATUM				★	★	★	12	★	★	DG		★	★	★	★	☆	☆	B1
Martin Dies Jr. SP	JASPER				★	★	★	14	★		BG	★	★	★	★	★	☆	☆	B1
Matagorda Island SP (Boat or Air Access Only)	PORT O'CONNOR		★	★	★			★			NG	★	★			☆	☆	☆	
McKinney Falls SP	AUSTIN			★	★	★	★	13	★		BG	★	★	★			☆	☆	B1, B2
Meridian SP	MERIDIAN				★	★	★	13	★		BG	★	★	★	★		☆	☆	
Mission Tejas SHS	WECHES			★	★	★	★	15			BG	★	★	★			☆		
Monahans Sandhills SP	MONAHANS			★	★	★	★	14			DG	★		★					E
Monument Hill/Kreische Brewery SHS	LA GRANGE	★	★	★	★							★		★					
Mother Neff SP	MOODY				★	★	★	10			BG	★	★	★			☆		
Mustang Island SP	PORT ARANSAS				★	★	★	12						★			☆	☆	B1
National Museum of the Pacific War	FREDERICKSBURG	★	★	★	★							★							
Old Fort Parker SP (Managed by City of Groesbeck)	GROESBECK	★	★	★				1											E
Palmetto SP	LULING				★	★	★	15			BC	★	★	★		★	☆		
Palo Duro Canyon SP (Summer Drama: "Texas")	CANYON			★	★	★	★	8		★		★	★	★		★			B1, E, L
Pedernales Falls SP	JOHNSON CITY				★	★	★	9			NG	★	★	★			☆	☆	B1, E
Port Isabel Lighthouse SHS	PORT ISABEL	★	★		★														
Port Lavaca SFP ▲	PORT LAVACA				★									★	★				
Possum Kingdom SP	CADDO				★	★	★	10	★			★	★	★	★	★	☆	☆	
Purtis Creek SP	EUSTACE				★	★	★	10				★	★	★	★	★	☆		P
Ray Roberts Lake SP, Isle du Bois Unit	DENTON				★	★	★	13			DG	★	★	★	★	★	☆	☆	B1, B2, E
Ray Roberts Lake SP, Johnson Unit	DENTON				★	★	★	7			DG	★	★	★	★	★	☆	☆	B1, B2
Rusk/Palestine SP (Texas State RR Terminals)	RUSK/PALESTINE				★	★	★	15			DG	★		★			☆		
Sabine Pass Battleground SHS	SABINE PASS		★	★	★		★	12						★	★	★			
Sam Bell Maxey House SHS	PARIS	★	★	★	★														
San Angelo SP	SAN ANGELO				★	★	★	8		★	BG	★	★	★	★	★	☆	☆	B1, E, L
San Jacinto Battleground SHS (Battleship Texas)	HOUSTON	★	★	★	★						DG	★		★			☆		
Sea Rim SP	PORT ARTHUR			★	★	★	★	10				★		★	★	☆	★		B1
Sebastopol SHS	SEGUIN	★	★	★	★									★					
Seminole Canyon SHS (Indian Pictographs)	LANGTRY		★	★	★	★	★	14				★	★	★					B1
Sheldon Lake SP	HOUSTON	★										★	☆	★	★				
South Llano River SP	JUNCTION			★	★	★	★	10				★	★	★			☆	☆	B1
Starr Family SHS	MARSHALL	★	★	★	★														G
Stephen F. Austin SHS	SAN FELIPE			★	★	★	★	15	★		BG	★	★	★			☆		G
Texas State Railroad SHS (Contact Park for Schedule)	PALESTINE/RUSK	★	★	★	★														
Tyler SP	TYLER				★	★	★	15	★		BG	★	★	★	★	★	☆		B1
Varner-Hogg Plantation SHS (Guided Tours)	WEST COLUMBIA	★	★	★	★							★		★			☆		
Village Creek SP	LUMBERTON				★	★	★	13			BG	★	★	★			☆	☆	B1
Walter Umphrey SP								*(Managed by Jefferson County)*											
Washington-on-the-Brazos SHS (Anson Jones Home)	WASHINGTON	★	★	★	★						DG	★		★					
Wyler Aerial Tramway Franklin Mts. SP	EL PASO	★		★	★														

Facilities

▲ Facilities not operated by Parks & Wildlife.
★ Facilities or services available for activity.
☆ Facilities or services not provided.

Note: Contact individual parks for information on handicap facilities.

Miscellaneous Codes

B1	Mountain Biking	G	Golf
B2	Surfaced Bike Trail	I	Hotel-Type Facilities
BG	Both Day & Night Group Facilities	L	Texas Longhorn Herd
DG	Day-Use Group Facilities	NG	Overnight Group Facilities
E	Equestrian Trails	R	Rock Climbing

Park is 65 miles away.

Fannin Battleground State Historic Site, 9 miles east of Goliad in Goliad County off US 59 to PR 27. The 13.6-acre park site was acquired by the state in 1914; transferred to TPW by legislative enactment in 1965. At this site on March 20, 1836, **Col. J. W. Fannin** surrendered to Mexican **Gen. José Urrea** after **Battle of Coleto;** 342 massacred and 28 escaped near what is now **Goliad State Historic Site.** Near Fannin site is **Gen. Zaragoza's Birthplace** and partially restored **Mission Nuestra Señora del Espíritu Santo de Zúñiga** (see also **Goliad State Historic Site** in this list).

Fanthorp Inn State Historic Site includes a historic double-pen cedar-log dogtrot house and 1.4 acres in Anderson, county seat of Grimes County, on TX 90. Acquired by purchase in 1977 from a Fanthorp descendant and opened to the public in 1987. Inn records report visits from many prominent civic and military leaders, including **Sam Houston, Anson Jones, Ulysses S. Grant** and generals **Robert E. Lee** and **Stonewall Jackson.** Originally built in 1834, it has been restored to its 1850 use as a family home and travelers' hotel. Tours available Friday, Saturday, Sunday. Call TPW for stagecoach-ride schedule. No dining or overnight facilities.

Fort Boggy State Park is 1,847 acres of wooded, rolling hills in Leon County near Boggy Creek, about 4 miles south of Centerville on TX 75. Land donated to TPWD in 1985 by Eileen Crain Sullivan. Area once home to Keechi and Kickapoo tribes. Log fort was built by settlers in 1840s; first settlement north of the Old San Antonio Road and between the Navasota and Trinity rivers. Swimming beach, fishing, picnicking, nature trails for hiking and mountain biking. Fifteen-acre lake open to small craft. Open-air group pavilion overlooking lake can be reserved ($50 per day). Nearby attractions include Rusk/Palestine State Park, Fort Parker State Park, Texas State Railroad, Old Fort Parker. Open Wed.–Sun. for day use only; entrance fee. For reservations, call 512-389-9000.

Fort Griffin State Historic Site is 506.2 acres 15 miles north of Albany off US 283 in Shackelford County. The state was deeded the land by the county in 1935. Portion of **state longhorn herd** resides in park. On bluff overlooking townsite of **Fort Griffin** and **Clear Fork of Brazos River** valley are partially restored ruins of **Old Fort Griffin,** restored bakery, replicas of enlisted men's huts. Fort constructed in 1867, deactivated 1881. Camping, equestrian camping, hiking. Nearby are **Albany** with restored courthouse square, **Abilene and Possum Kingdom State Park.** Albany annually holds **"Fandangle"** musical show in commemoration of frontier times.

Fort Lancaster State Historic Site, 81.6-acres located about 8 miles east of Sheffield on Interstate10 and US 290 in Crockett County. Acquired in 1968 by deed from Crockett County; Henry Meadows donated 41 acres in 1975. **Fort Lancaster** established Aug. 20, 1855, to guard San Antonio-El Paso Road and protect movement of supplies and immigrants from Indian hostilities. Site of part of Camel Corps experiment. Fort abandoned March 19, 1861, after Texas seceded from Union. Exhibits on history, natural history and archaeology; nature trail, picnicking. Open daily; day use only.

Fort Leaton State Historic Site, 4 miles southeast of Presidio in Presidio County on FM 170, was acquired in 1967 from private owners. Consists of 23.4 acres, 5 of which are on site of **pioneer trading post.** In 1848, **Ben Leaton** built fortified adobe trading post known as Fort Leaton near present Presidio. Ben Leaton died in 1851. Guided tours; exhibits trace history, natural history and archaeological history of area. Serves as western entrance to **Big Bend Ranch State Park.** Day use only.

Fort McKavett State Historic Site, 79.5 acres acquired from 1967 through the mid-1970s from Fort McKavett Restoration, Inc., Menard County and private individ-

More Travel Information

Call the **Texas Department of Transportation's** toll-free number: **1-800-888-8TEX** for:
• The **Texas State Travel Guide,** a free 288-page, full-color publication with a wealth of information about attractions, activities, history and historic sites.
• The official **Texas state highway map.**

On the Internet: **www.traveltex.com**

The boardwalk at Galveston Island State Park leads out to the marsh on the park's bay side. Texas Parks & Wildlife photo.

uals, is located 23 miles west of Menard off US 190 and FM 864. Originally called **Camp San Saba,** the fort was built by War Department in 1852 to protect frontier settlers and travelers on Upper El Paso Road from Indians. Camp later renamed for **Capt. Henry McKavett,** killed at Battle of Monterrey, Sept. 21, 1846. A **Buffalo Soldier post.** Fort abandoned March 1859; reoccupied April 1868; abandoned again June 30, 1883. Once called by Gen. Wm. T. Sherman, "the prettiest post in Texas." More than 25 restored buildings, ruins of many others. Interpretive exhibits. Day use only.

Fort Parker State Park includes 1,458.8 acres, including 758.78 land acres and 700-acre lake between Mexia and Groesbeck off TX 14 in Limestone County. Named for the former private fort built near present park in 1836, the site was acquired from private owners and the City of Mexia 1935-1937. Camping, fishing, swimming, canoeing, picnicking. Nearby is **Old Fort Parker Historic Site,** which is operated by the City of Groesbeck.

Fort Richardson State Historic Site, located one-half mile south of Jacksboro off US 281 in Jack County, contains 454 acres. Acquired in 1968 from City of Jacksboro. Fort founded in 1867, northernmost of line of federal forts established after Civil War for protection from Indians; originally named **Fort Jacksboro.** In April 1867, fort was moved to its present location from 20 miles farther south; on Nov. 19, 1867, made permanent post at Jacksboro and named for **Israel Richardson,** who was fatally wounded at Battle of Antietam. Expeditions sent from Fort Richardson arrested Indians responsible for **Warren Wagon Train Massacre** in 1871 and fought Comanches in **Palo Duro Canyon.** Fort abandoned in May 1878. Park contains seven restored buildings and two replicas. Interpretive center, picnicking, camping, fishing; 10-mile trailway.

Franklin Mountains State Park, created by an act of the legislature in 1979 to protect the mountain range as a wilderness preserve and acquired by TPW in 1981, comprises 24,247.56 acres, all within El Paso city limits. **Largest urban park in the nation.** It includes virtually an entire **Chihuahuan Desert mountain range,** with an elevation of 7,192 feet at the summit. The park is habitat for many Chihuahuan Desert plants including **sotol, lechuguilla, ocotillo, cholla** and **barrel cactus,** and such animals as **mule deer, fox** and an occasional **cougar.** Camping, mountain biking, nature study, hiking, picnicking, rock-climbing.

Fulton Mansion State Historic Site is 3.5 miles north of Rockport off TX 35 in Aransas County. The 2.3 acre-property was acquired by purchase from private owner in 1976. Three-story wooden structure, built in 1874-1877, was home of **George W. Fulton,** prominent in South Texas for economic and commercial influence; mansion derives significance from its innovative construction and Victorian design. Call ahead for days and hours of guided tours; open Wednesday–Sunday; 800-792-1112.

Galveston Island State Park, on the west end of Galveston Island on FM 3005, is a 2,013.1-acre site acquired in 1969 from private owners. Camping, birding, nature study, swimming, bicycling and fishing amid **sand dunes and grassland.** Musical productions in **amphitheater** during summer.

Garner State Park is 1,419.8 acres of recreational facilities on US 83 on the Frio River in Uvalde County 9 miles south of Leakey. Named for **John Nance Garner,** U.S. Vice President, 1933-1941, the park was deeded in 1934-36 by private owners. Camping, hiking, picnicking, river recreation, miniature golf, biking, boat rentals. Cabins available. Nearby is **John Nance "Cactus Jack" Garner Museum** in Uvalde. Nearby also are ruins of historic **Mission Nuestra Señora de la Candelaria del Cañon,** founded in 1749; **Camp Sabinal** (a U.S. Cavalry post and later Texas Ranger camp) established 1856; **Fort Inge,** established 1849.

Goliad State Historic Site is 188.3 acres one-fourth mile south of Goliad on US 183 and 77A, along the San Antonio River in Goliad County. The land was deeded to state in 1931 by the City and County of Goliad; transferred to TPW 1949. Nearby are the sites of several battles in the Texas fight for independence from Mexico. The park includes a replica of **Mission Nuestra Señora del Espíritu Santo de Zúñiga,** originally established 1722 and settled at its present site in 1749. Park unit includes **Gen. Ignacio Zaragoza's Birthplace,** which is located near **Presidio la Bahía.** He was Mexican national hero who led troops against French at historic **Battle of Puebla** on May 5, 1862. Park also contains ruins of **Nuestra Señora del Rosario** mission, established 1754, located four miles west of Goliad on US 59. Camping, picnicking, historical exhibits, nature trail. Other nearby points of historical interest: restored **Nuestra Señora de Loreto de la Bahía** presidio, established 1721 and settled on site in 1749; it is located short distance south on US 183. Memorial shaft marking common burial site of **Fannin** and victims of **Goliad massacre** (1836) is near **Presidio la Bahía.** (See also **Fannin Battleground State Historic Site.**)

Goose Island State Park, 321.4 acres 10 miles northeast of Rockport on TX 35 and PR 13 on St. Charles and Aransas bays in Aransas County, was deeded by private owners in 1931-1935 plus an additional seven acres donated in the early 1990s by Sun Oil Co. Located here is "Big Tree" estimated to be a 1,000-year-old **live oak.** Fishing, picnicking and camping, plus excellent birding; no swimming. Rare and endangered **whooping cranes** can be viewed during winter just across St. Charles Bay in **Aransas National Wildlife Refuge.**

Gov. Hogg Shrine State Historic Site is a 26.7-acre tract on TX 37 about six blocks south of the Wood County Courthouse in Quitman. Named for **James Stephen Hogg, first native-born governor of Texas,** the park includes museums housing items that belonged to the Hogg and Stinson families. Seventeen acres deeded by the Wood County Old Settlers Reunion Association in 1946; 4.74 acres gift of Miss Ima Hogg in 1970; 3 acres purchased. **Gov. James Stephen Hogg Memorial Shrine** created in 1941. Three museums: Gov. Hogg's wedding held in **Stinson Home; Honeymoon Cottage; Miss Ima Hogg Museum** houses both park headquarters and display of representative history of entire Northeast Texas area. Operated by City of Quitman.

Guadalupe River State Park comprises 1,938.7 acres on cypress-shaded Guadalupe River in Kendall and Comal counties, 13 miles east of Boerne on TX 46. Acquired by deed from private owners in 1974. Park has four miles of river frontage with several **white-water rapids** and is located in a stretch of **Guadalupe River** noted for canoeing, tubing. Picnicking, camping, hiking, nature study. Trees include **sycamore, elm, basswood, pecan, walnut, persimmon, willow** and **hackberry** (see also **Honey Creek State Natural Area,** below).

Hill Country State Natural Area in Bandera and Medina counties, 9 miles west of Bandera on RM 1077. The 5,369.8-acre site acquired by gift from Merrick Bar-O-Ranch and purchase in 1976. Park is located in typical Texas Hill Country on West Verde Creek and contains several **spring-fed streams.** Primitive and equestrian camping, hiking, horseback riding, mountain biking, fishing. Group lodge.

Honey Creek State Natural Area consists of 2,293.7 acres adjacent to **Guadalupe River State Park** (above); entrance is in the park. Acquired from The Nature Conservancy of Texas in 1985 with an addition from private individual in 1988. Diverse plant life includes **agarita, Texas persimmon** and Ashe juniper in hills, and cedar elm, Spanish oak, pecan, walnut and **Mexican buckeye** in bottomlands. Abundant wildlife includes **ringtail, leopard frog, green kingfisher, golden-cheeked warbler** and **canyon wren.** Schedule varies ; call 830-796-4413for details.

Hueco Tanks State Historic Site, located 32 miles northeast of El Paso in El Paso County on RM 2775 just north of US 62-180, was obtained from the county in 1969, with additional 121 acres purchased in 1970. Featured in this 860.3-acre park are large **natural rock basins** that provided water for archaic hunters, Plains Indians, Butterfield Overland Mail coach horses and passengers, and other travelers in this arid region. In park are **Indian pictographs, old ranch house** and relocated **ruins of stage station. Rock climbing,** picnicking, camping, hiking. Guided tours. Wildlife includes **gray fox, bobcat, prairie falcons, golden eagles.**

Huntsville State Park is 2,083.2-acre recreational area off IH 45 and PR 40 six miles south of Huntsville in Walker County, acquired by deeds from private owners in 1937. Heavily wooded park adjoins **Sam Houston National Forest** and encloses **Lake Raven.** Hiking, camping, fishing, biking, paddle boats, canoeing. At nearby Huntsville are **Sam Houston's old homestead (Steamboat House),** containing some of his personal effects, and **his grave.** Approximately 50 miles away is **Alabama-Coushatta Indian Reservation** in Polk County.

Inks Lake State Park is 1,201 acres of recreational facilities along Inks Lake, 9 miles west of Burnet on the

Canoeists take to the Brazos River in Palo Pinto County near Possum Kingdom State Park. Texas Almanac photo.

Colorado River off TX 29 on PR 4 in Burnet County. Acquired by deeds from the Lower Colorado River Authority and private owners in 1940. Camping, hiking, fishing, swimming, boating, golf. **Deer, turkey** and other wildlife abundant. Nearby are **Longhorn Cavern State Park, LBJ Ranch, LBJ State Historic Site, Pedernales Falls State Park** and **Enchanted Rock State Natural Area. Granite Mountain** quarry at nearby Marble Falls furnished red granite for **Texas state capitol. Buchanan Dam,** largest multi-arch dam in world, located 4 miles from park.

Jim Hogg Historic Site is 178.4 acres of East Texas Pineywoods in Cherokee County, 2 miles east of Rusk off U.S. 84 E. and Fire Tower Road. Memorial to Texas' first native born governor, James Stephen Hogg, 1891–1895. Remnants of 1880s iron ore mining. Scale replica of Hogg birthplace. Picnicking, historical study, nature study, hiking and bird watching. Self-guided and guided museum tours and nature trail tours. Operated by the City of Rusk; 903-683-4850. Area attractions: Caddoan Mounds, Mission Tejas State Historic Sites, Rusk/Palestine State Park, Texas State Railroad, Tyler State Parks and historic Nacogdoches. Day use only; entrance fee.

Kerrville-Schreiner State Park is a 517.2-acre area 3 miles southeast of Kerrville off TX 173 along the Guadalupe River in Kerr County. Land deeded by City of Kerrville in 1934. Trees include **redbud, sumac, buckeye, pecan, mesquite.** Birding, camping, fishing, picknicking, cycling. Near park is site of **Camp Verde,** active 1855–1869, which was a base for an army experiment using **camels** to haul equipment. **Bandera Pass,** 12 miles south of Kerrville, noted gap in chain of mountains through which passed camel caravans, wagon trains, Spanish conquistadors, immigrant trains. In nearby **Fredericksburg** is atmosphere of old country of Germany and famous **Nimitz Hotel** (see **Admiral Nimitz Museum Historic Site).**

Kickapoo Cavern State Park is located about 22 miles north of Brackettville on RM 674 on the Kinney/Edwards county line in the southern Edwards Plateau. The park (6,368.4 acres) contains **15 known caves,** two of which are large enough to be significant: **Kickapoo Cavern,**

about 1/4 mile in length, has impressive formations, and **Green Cave,** slightly shorter, supports a nursery colony of **Brazilian freetail bats** in summer. Birds include rare species such as **black-capped vireo, varied bunting** and **Montezuma quail.** Reptiles and amphibians include **barking frog, mottled rock rattlesnake** and **Texas alligator lizard.** Tours of Kickapoo and observation of bats available only by special arrangement. Group lodge; primitive camping; hiking and mountain-biking trails. Open only by reservation.

Kreische Brewery State Historic Site (see Monument Hill and Kreische Brewery State Historic Sites).

Lake Arrowhead State Park consists of 524 acres in Clay County, about 14 miles south of Wichita Falls on US 281 to FM 1954, then 8 miles to park. Acquired in 1970 from the City of Wichita Falls. **Lake Arrowhead** is a reservoir on the Little Wichita River with 106 miles of shoreline. The land surrounding the lake is generally semiarid, gently rolling prairie, much of which has been invaded by mesquite in recent decades. Fishing, camping, lake swimming, picnicking, horseback-riding area.

Lake Bob Sandlin State Park, on the wooded shoreline of 9,400-acre Lake Bob Sandlin, is located 12 miles southwest of Mount Pleasant off FM 21 in Titus County. Activities in the 639.8-acre park include picnicking, camping, mountain biking, hiking, swimming, fishing and boating. **Oak, hickory, dogwood, redbud, maple** and **pine** produce spectacular fall color. Eagles can sometimes be spotted in winter months.

Lake Brownwood State Park in Brown County is 537.5 acres acquired from Brown County Water Improvement District No. 1 in 1934. Park reached from TX 279 to PR 15, 16 miles northwest of Brownwood on Lake Brownwood near **geographical center of Texas.** Water sports, hiking, camping. Cabins available.

Lake Casa Blanca International State Park, located one mile east of Laredo off US 59 on Loop 20, was formerly operated by the City of Laredo and Webb County and was acquired by TPW in 1990. Park includes 371 acres on Lake Casa Blanca. **Recreation hall** can be reserved. Camping, picnicking, fishing, ball fields, playgrounds, amphitheater, and tennis courts. County-operated golf course nearby.

Lake Colorado City State Park, 500 acres leased for 99 years from a utility company. It is located in Mitchell County 11 miles southwest of Colorado City off IH 20 on FM 2836. Water sports, picnicking, camping, hiking. Part of **state longhorn herd** can be seen in park.

Lake Corpus Christi State Park, a 14,112-acre park in San Patricio, Jim Wells and Live Oak counties. Located 35 miles northwest of Corpus Christi and four miles southwest of Mathis off TX 359 and Park Road 25. Was leased from City of Corpus Christi in 1934. Camping, picnicking, birding, water sports. Nearby are **Padre Island National Seashore; Mustang Island, Choke Canyon, Goliad and Goose Island** state parks; **Aransas National Wildlife Refuge,** and **Fulton Mansion State Historic Site.**

Lake Houston State Park is situated at the confluence of Caney Creek and the East Fork of the San Jacinto River. The 4,919.5-acre site, purchased from Champion Paper Company in 1981, is northeast of Houston in Harris and Montgomery counties. Camping, birding, hiking, biking, horseback riding.

Lake Livingston State Park, in Polk County, about one mile southwest of Livingston on FM 3126 and PR 65, contains 635.5 acres along Lake Livingston. Acquired by deed from private landowners in 1971. Near ghost town of **Swartwout,** steamboat landing on Trinity River in 1830s and 1850s. Camping, picnicking, swimming pool, fishing, mountain biking and stables.

Lake Mineral Wells State Park, located 4 miles east of Mineral Wells on US 180 in Parker County, consists of 3,282.5 acres encompassing Lake Mineral Wells. In 1975, the City of Mineral Wells donated 1,095 land acres and the lake to TPW; the U.S. Government transferred additional land from Fort Wolters army post. Popular for **rock-climbing/rappelling.** Swimming, fishing, boating, camping; **Lake Mineral Wells State Trailway** (hiking, bicycling, equestrian trail).

Lake Somerville State Park, northwest of Brenham in Lee and Burleson counties, was leased from the federal government in 1969. **Birch Creek Unit** (2,365 acres reached from TX 60 and PR 57) and **Nails Creek Unit** (3,155 acres reached from US 290 and FM 180), are connected by a **13-mile trailway system,** with **equestrian and primitive camp sites,** rest benches, shelters and drinking water. Also camping, birding, picnicking, volleyball and water sports. **Somerville Wildlife Management Area,** 3,180 acres is nearby.

Lake Tawakoni State Park is a 376.3-acre park in Hunt County along the shore of its namesake reservoir. It was acquired in 1984 through a 50-year lease agreement with the Sabine River Authority and opened in 2001. Includes a swimming beach, half-mile trail, picnic sites, boat ramp and campsites. A **40-acre tallgrass prairie** will be managed and enhanced in the post-oak woodlands. The park is reached from IH 20 on TX 47 north to FM 2475 about 20 miles past Wills Point.

Lake Texana State Park is 575 acres, 6.5 miles east of Edna on TX 111, half-way between Houston and Corpus Christi in Jackson County, with camping, boating, fishing and picnicking facilities. It was acquired by a 50-year lease agreement with the Bureau of Reclamation in 1977. Good birding in the **oak/pecan woodlands. Alligators** are often found in park coves.

Lake Whitney State Park is 1,280.7 acres along the east shore of Lake Whitney west of Hillsboro via TX 22 and FM 1244 in Hill County. Acquired in 1954 by a Department of the Army lease, effective through 2003. Located near ruins of **Towash,** early Texas settlement inundated by the lake. Towash Village named for chief of Hainai Indians. Park noted for **bluebonnets** in spring. Camping, hiking, birding, picnicking, water activities.

Landmark Inn State Historic Site, 4.7 acres in Castroville, Medina County, about 15 miles west of San Antonio, was acquired through donation by Miss Ruth Lawler in 1974. Castroville, settled in the 1840s by Alsatian farmers, is called **Little Alsace of Texas.** Landmark Inn built about 1844 as residence and store for **Cesar Monod,** mayor of Castroville 1851-1864. Special workshops, tours and events held at inn; grounds may be rented for receptions, family reunions and weddings. **Overnight lodging**; no phones; all rooms air-conditioned and nonsmoking.

Lipantitlan State Historic Site is 5 acres 9 miles east of Orange Grove in Nueces County off Texas 359, FM 624 and FM 70. The property was deeded by private owners in 1937. Fort constructed here in 1833 by Mexican government fell to Texas forces in 1835. Only facilities are picnic tables. **Lake Corpus Christi State Park** is nearby.

Lockhart State Park is 263.7 acres 4 miles south of Lockhart via US 183, FM 20 and PR 10 in Caldwell County. The land was deeded by private owners between 1934 and 1937. Camping, picnicking, hiking, fishing, **9-hole golf course.** After Comanche raid at Linnville, **Battle of Plum Creek** (1840) was fought in area.

Longhorn Cavern State Park, off US 281 and PR 4 about 6 miles west and 6 miles south of Burnet in Burnet County, is 645.62 acres dedicated as a natural landmark in 1971. It was acquired in 1932-1937 from private owners. The cave has been used as a shelter since prehistoric times. Among legends about the cave is that the outlaw **Sam Bass** hid stolen money there. Confederates made gunpowder in the cave during the Civil War. **Nature trail; guided tours** of cave; picnicking, hiking. Cavern operated by concession agreement. **Inks Lake State Park** and **Lyndon B. Johnson Ranch** located nearby.

Lost Maples State Natural Area consists of 2,174.2 scenic acres on the Sabinal River in Bandera and Real counties, 5 miles north of Vanderpool on RM 187. Acquired by purchase from private owners in 1973-1974. Outstanding example of Edwards Plateau flora and fauna, features isolated stand of uncommon **Uvalde bigtooth maple.** Rare **golden-cheeked warbler, black-capped vireo** and **green kingfisher** nest and feed in park. Fall foliage can be spectacular (late Oct. through early Nov.). Hiking trails, camping, fishing, picnicking, birding.

Lyndon B. Johnson State Historic Site, off US 290 in Gillespie County 14 miles west of Johnson City near Stonewall, contains 717.9 acres. Acquired in 1965 with private donations. **Home of Lyndon B. Johnson** located north bank of **Pedernales River** across Ranch Road 1 from park; portion of **official Texas longhorn herd** maintained at park. Wildlife exhibit includes **turkey, deer** and **bison. Living-history demonstrations** at restored **Sauer-Beckmann house.** Reconstruction of **Johnson birthplace** is open to public. Historic structures, swimming pool, tennis courts, baseball field, picnicking. Day use only. Nearby is family cemetery where former president and relatives are buried. In Johnson City is **boyhood home of President Johnson.** (See also **National Parks.**)

Magoffin Home State Historic Site, in El Paso, is a 19-room territorial-style adobe on a 1.5-acre site. Purchased by the state and City of El Paso in 1976, it is operated by TPW. Home was built in 1875 by pioneer El Pasoan **Joseph Magoffin.** Furnished with original family artifacts. Guided tours; call for schedule. Day use only.

Martin Creek Lake State Park, 286.9 acres, is located 4 miles south of Tatum off TX 43 and CR 2183 in Rusk County. It was deeded to the TPW by Texas Utilities in 1976. Water activities; also cabins, camping, picnicking. Roadbed of **Trammel's Trace,** old Indian trail that became major route for settlers moving to Texas from Arkansas, can be seen. **Hardwood and pine** forest shelters abundant wildlife including **swamp rabbits, gophers, nutria** and numerous species of land birds and waterfowl.

Martin Dies Jr. State Park, until 1965 the **Dam B State**

Park, is 705 acres in Jasper and Tyler counties on B. A. Steinhagen Reservoir between Woodville and Jasper via US 190. Land leased for 50 years from Corps of Engineers in 1964. Located at edge of **Big Thicket.** Plant and animal life varied and abundant. Winter **bald eagle census** conducted at nearby Sam Rayburn Reservoir. Camping, hiking, mountain biking, water activities. Wildscape/herb garden. Park is approximately 30 miles from **Alabama and Coushatta Indian Reservation.**

Matagorda Island State Park and Wildlife Management Area is separated from the mainland by San Antonio and Espíritu Santo bays. Matagorda Island is one of the **barrier islands** that border the Gulf and protect the mainland from the great tides and strong wave action of the open ocean. About 43,893 acres of park and WMA are managed by the TPW. The park occupies about 7,325 acres of the total. **La Salle** had a camp on the island in 1684. The first Matagorda Island **lighthouse** was constructed in 1852; the present cast-iron structure was a replacement built in 1873. It is listed on the National Register of Historic Places. Nineteen endangered or threatened species are found here, including **whooping crane, peregrine falcon, brown pelican,** and **Ridley sea turtle.** More than **300 species of birds** use island during spring and fall migrations. Camping, birding, water activities, scheduled tours. Access only by boat; passenger **ferry operates from Port O'Connor** Friday–Sunday.

McKinney Falls State Park is 744.4 acres 13 miles southeast of the state capitol in Austin off US 183. Acquired in 1970 by gift from private owners. Named for Thomas F. McKinney, **one of Stephen F. Austin's first 300 colonists,** who built his home here in the mid-1800s on Onion Creek. Ruins of his homestead can be viewed. Swimming, hiking, biking, camping, picnicking, fishing, guided tours.

Meridian State Park in Bosque County is a 505.4-acre park. The heavily wooded land, on TX 22 three miles southwest of Meridian, was acquired from private owners in 1933-1935. **Texas-Santa Fe expedition** of 1841 passed through Bosque County near present site of park on Bee Creek. **Endangered golden-cheeked warbler** nests here. Camping, picnicking, hiking, fishing, lake swimming, birding, bicycling.

Mission Tejas State Historic Site is a 363.5-acre park in Houston County. Situated 12 miles west of Alto via TX 21 and PR 44, the park was acquired from the Texas Forest Service in 1957. In the park is a replica of **Mission San Francisco de los Tejas,** the first mission in East Texas (1690). It was abandoned, then re-established 1716; abandoned again 1719; re-established again 1721; abandoned for last time in 1730 and moved to San Antonio. Also in park is restored **Rice Family Log Home,** built about 1828. Camping, hiking, fishing, picnicking.

Monahans Sandhills State Park consists of 3,840 acres of sand dunes, some up to 70 feet high, in Ward and Winkler counties 5 miles northeast of Monahans on IH 20 to PR 41. Land leased by state from private foundation until 2056. Dunes used as meeting place by raiding Indians. Camping, hiking, picnicking, **sand-surfing.** Scheduled tours. **Odessa meteor crater** is nearby, as is **Balmorhea State Park.**

Monument Hill State Historic Site and **Kreische Brewery State Historic Site** are operated as one park unit. Monument Hill consists of 40.4 acres one mile south of La Grange on US 77 to Spur Road 92 in Fayette County. Monument and tomb area acquired by state in 1907; additional acreage acquired from the Archbishop of San Antonio in 1956. Brewery and home purchased from private owners in 1977. Monument is dedicated to **Capt. Nicholas Dawson** and his men, who fought at **Salado Creek** in 1842, in Mexican **Gen. Woll's** invasion of Texas, and to the men of the **"black bean lottery"** (1843) of the **Mier Expedition.** Remains were brought to **Monument Hill** for reburial in 1848. Kreische Complex, on 36 acres, is linked to Monument Hill through interpretive trail. **Kreische Brewery State Historic Site** includes Kreische Brewery and stone-and-wood house built between 1850-1855 on Colorado River. One of **first commercial breweries** in state, it closed in 1884. Smokehouse and barn also in complex. Guided tours of brewery and house; call for schedule. Also picknicking, nature study.

Mother Neff State Park was the **first official state park** in Texas. It originated with 6 acres donated by Mrs. I. E. Neff, mother of **Pat M. Neff,** Governor of Texas from 1921 to 1925. Gov. Neff and Frank Smith donated remainder in 1934. The park, located 8 miles west of Moody on FM 107 and TX 236, now contains 259 acres along the Leon River in Coryell County. Heavily wooded. Camping, picnicking, fishing, hiking.

Mustang Island State Park, 3,954 acres on Gulf of Mexico in Nueces County, 14 miles south of Port Aransas on TX 361, was acquired from private owners in 1972. Mustang Island is a barrier island with a complicated ecosystem, dependent upon the sand dune. The foundation plants of the dunes are **sea oats, beach panic grass** and **soilbind morning glory.** Beach camping, picnicking; sun, sand and water activities. Excellent birding. **Padre Island National Seashore** 14 miles south.

National Museum of the Pacific War (formerly **Admiral Nimitz Museum and Historical Center**) is on 7 acres in downtown Fredericksburg. First established as a state agency in 1969 by Texas Legislature; transferred to TPW in 1981. George Bush Gallery opened in 1999. Named for **Adm. Chester W. Nimitz** of World War II fame, it includes the **Pacific War Museum** in the **Nimitz Steamboat Hotel;** the **Japanese Garden of Peace,** donated by the people of Japan; the **History Walk of the Pacific War,** featuring planes, boats and other equipment from World War II; and other special exhibits. Nearby is **Kerrville State Park.**

Old Fort Parker is a 37.5-acre park 4 miles north of Groesbeck on TX 14 in Limestone County. Deeded by private owners in 1936 and originally constructed by the Civilian Conservation Corps (CCC); rebuilt in 1967. Reconstructed fort is pioneer memorial and site of Cynthia Ann Parker abduction on May 19, 1836, by Comanche Indians. Nearby Fort Parker Cemetery has graves of those killed at the Fort in the 1836 raid. Historical study and picnicking. Living History events throughout year. Primitive skills classes/campouts by appointment. Groups welcome. Operated by the City of Groesbeck, 254-729-5253.

Palmetto State Park, a scenic park, is 270.3 acres 8 miles southeast of Luling on US 183 and PR 11 along the San Marcos River in Gonzales County. Land deeded in 1934-1936 by private owners and City of Gonzales. Named for **tropical dwarf palmetto** found there. Diverse plant and animal life; excellent birding. Also picnicking, fishing, hiking, pedal boats, swimming. Nearby **Gonzales** and **Ottine** important in early Texas history. Gonzales settled 1825 as center of **Green DeWitt's colonies.**

Palo Duro Canyon State Park consists of 16,402 acres 12 miles east of Canyon on TX 217 in Armstrong and Randall counties. The land was deeded by private owners in 1933 and is the scene of the annual summer production of the musical drama, "Texas." Spectacular one-million-year-old **scenic canyon** exposes rocks spanning about 200 million years of geological time. **Coronado** may have visited canyon in 1541. Canyon officially discovered by **Capt. R. B. Marcy** in 1852. Scene of decisive battle in 1874 between Comanche and Kiowa Indians and U.S. Army troops under **Gen. Ranald Mackenzie.** Also scene of ranching enterprise started by **Charles Goodnight** in 1876. Part of **state longhorn herd** is kept here. Camping, mountain biking, scenic drives, horseback and hiking trails, horse rentals.

Pedernales Falls State Park, 5,211.7 acres in Blanco County about 9 miles east of Johnson City on FM 2766

The Port Isabel Lighthouse was built in 1852 and is part of a State Historic Site in Cameron County. Texas Almanac photo.

along Pedernales River, was acquired from private owners in 1970. Typical **Edwards Plateau** terrain**,** with **live oaks, deer, turkey** and **stone hills.** Camping, picnicking, hiking, swimming, tubing. Falls main scenic attraction.

Port Isabel Lighthouse State Historic Site consists of 0.9 acre in Port Isabel, Cameron County. Acquired by purchase from private owners in 1950, site includes **lighthouse** constructed in 1852; visitors can climb to top. Park is near sites of Civil War battle of **Palmito Ranch** (1865), and Mexican War battles of **Palo Alto** and **Resaca de la Palma (1846)**. Operated by City of Port Isabel.

Port Lavaca State Fishing Pier, a 10.8-acre recreational area on Lavaca Bay in Calhoun County, was acquired by transfer of authority from state highway department in 1963. The 24-hour, lighted, 3,200-foot-long fishing pier was created from former causeway. **Port Lavaca City Park,** at base of pier, offers a boat ramp and picnicking facilities. Operated by City of Port Lavaca.

Possum Kingdom State Park, west of Mineral Wells via US 180 and PR 33 in Palo Pinto County, is 1,528.7 acres adjacent to **Possum Kingdom Lake**, in **Palo Pinto Mountains** and **Brazos River Valley.** Rugged canyons home to **deer**, other wildlife. Acquired from the Brazos River Authority in 1940. Camping, picnicking, swimming, fishing, boating. Cabins available.

Purtis Creek State Park is 1,582.4 acres in Henderson and Van Zandt counties 3.5 miles north of Eustace on FM 316. Acquired in 1977 from private owners. Fishing, camping, hiking, picnicking, paddle boats and canoes.

Ray Roberts Lake State Park (Isle du Bois Unit), consists of 2,263 acres on the south side of Ray Roberts Lake on FM 455 in Denton County. **Johnson Branch Unit** contains 1,514 acres on north side of lake in Denton and Cooke counties 7 miles east of IH 30 on FM 3002. There are also six satellite parks. Land acquired in 1984 by lease from secretary of Army. Abundant and varied plant and animal life. Fishing, camping, picnicking, swimming, hiking, biking; tours of 19-century farm buildings at Johnson Branch. Includes Lantana Ridge Lodge on the east side of

the lake. It is a full-service lodging facility with restaurant.

Rusk/Palestine State Park, a total of 136 acres, includes Rusk unit, adjacent to **Texas State Railroad Rusk Depot** off US 84 in Cherokee County, and Palestine unit, off US 84 adjacent to **Texas State Railroad Palestine Depot**. Fishing, picnicking, camping, tennis courts, playground. **Train rides** in restored passenger cars (see also **Texas State Railroad State Historic Site).**

Sabine Pass Battleground State Historic Site in Jefferson County 1.5 miles south of Sabine Pass on Dick Dowling Road, contains 57.6 acres acquired from Kountze County Trust in 1972. Lt. **Richard W. Dowling,** with small Confederate force, repelled an attempted 1863 invasion of Texas by Union gunboats. **Monument, World War II ammunition bunkers.** Fishing, picnicking, camping.

Sam Bell Maxey House State Historic Site, at the corner of So. Church and Washington streets in Paris, Lamar County, was donated by City of Paris in 1976. Consists of .4 acre with 1868 Victorian Italianate-style frame house, plus outbuildings. Most of furnishings accumulated by Maxey family. Maxey served in Mexican and Civil wars and was two-term U.S. Senator. House is on the **National Register of Historic Places**. Open for tours Friday through Sunday.

San Angelo State Park, on **O.C. Fisher Reservoir** adjacent to the city of San Angelo in Tom Green County, contains 7,677 acres of land, most of which will remain undeveloped. Leased from U.S. Corps of Engineers in 1995. Access is from US 87 or 67, then FM 2288. Highly diversified plant and animal life. Activities include boating, water activities, hiking, mountain biking, horseback riding, camping, picnicking. Part of **state longhorn herd** in park. Nearby is **Fort Concho**.

San Jacinto Battleground State Historic Site and **Battleship Texas State Historic Site** are located 20 miles east of downtown Houston off TX 225 east to TX 134 to PR 1836 in east Harris County. The park is 1,200 acres with 570-foot-tall monument erected in 1936-1939 in honor of Texans who defeated Mexican **Gen. Antonio**

López de Santa Anna on April 21, 1836, to win Texas' independence from Mexico. The park is original site of Texans' camp acquired in 1883. Subsequent acquisitions made in 1897, 1899 and 1985. Park transferred to TPW in 1965. Park registered as **National Historic Landmark**. Elevator ride to observation tower near top of monument; museum. Monument known as **tallest free-standing concrete structure in the world** at the time it was erected. Interpretive trail around battleground. Adjacent to park is the **U.S.S. Texas**, commissioned in 1914. The battleship, the only survivor of the dreadnought class and the only surviving veteran of two world wars, was donated to people of Texas by U.S. Navy. Ship was moored in the Houston Ship Channel at the **San Jacinto Battleground** on San Jacinto Day, 1948. Extensive repairs were done 1988-1990. Some renovation is on-going, but ship is open for tours. Ship closed Christmas Eve and Christmas Day.

Sea Rim State Park in Jefferson County, 20 miles south of Port Arthur, off TX 87, contains 4,141 acres of marshland and 5.2 miles of **Gulf beach** shoreline, acquired from private owners in 1972. It is prime wintering area for **waterfowl**. Wetlands also shelter such wildlife as river otter, nutria, alligator, mink, muskrat. Camping, fishing, swimming; wildlife observation; nature trail; boating. **Airboat tours of marsh**. Near **McFaddin National Wildlife Refuge**.

Sebastopol State Historic Site at 704 Zorn Street in Seguin, Guadalupe County, was acquired by purchase in 1976 from Seguin Conservation Society; approximately 2.2 acres. Built about 1856 by **Col. Joshua W. Young** of **limecrete**, concrete made from local gravel and lime, the Greek Revival-style house, which was restored to its 1880 appearance by the TPW, is on National Register of Historic Places. Tours available Friday and Sunday. Also of interest in the area is historic **Seguin**, founded 1838.

Seminole Canyon State Historic Site in Val Verde County, 9 miles west of Comstock off US 90, contains 2,172.5 acres; acquired by purchase from private owners 1973-1977. **Fate Bell Shelter** in canyon contains several important **prehistoric Indian pictographs**. Historic interpretive center. Tours of rock-art sites Wednesday-Sunday; also hiking, mountain biking, camping.

Sheldon Lake State Park and Wildlife Management Area, 2,800 acres in Harris County on Garrett Road 20 miles east of Beltway 8. Acquired by purchase in 1952 from the City of Houston. Freshwater marsh habitat. Activities include nature study, birding and fishing. Wildscape gardens of native plants.

South Llano River State Park, 5 miles south of Junction in Kimble County off US 377, is a 524-acre site. Land donated to the TPW by private owner in 1977. Wooded bottomland along the winding South Llano River is **largest and oldest winter roosting site for the Rio Grande turkey** in Central Texas. Roosting area closed to visitors October-March. Other animals include **wood ducks, javelina, fox, beaver, bobcat** and **armadillo**. Camping, picnicking, tubing, swimming and fishing, hiking, mountain biking.

Starr Family State Historic Site, 3.1 acres at 407 W. Travis in Marshall, Harrison County. Greek Revival-style mansion, **Maplecroft**, built 1870-1871, was home to four generations of Starr family, powerful and economically influential Texans. Two other family homes also in park. Acquired by gift in 1976; additional land donated in 1982. Maplecroft is on National Register of Historic Places. Tours Friday–Sunday or by appointment. Special events during year.

Stephen F. Austin State Historic Site is 663.3 acres along the Brazos River in San Felipe, Austin County, named for the **"Father of Texas."** The area was deeded by the San Felipe de Austin Corporation and the San Felipe Park Association in 1940. Site of township of **San Felipe** was seat of government where conventions of 1832 and 1833 and Consultation of 1835 held. These led to **Texas Declaration of Independence**. San Felipe was home of **Stephen F. Austin** and other famous early Texans; home of **Texas' first Anglo newspaper (the Texas Gazette)** founded in 1829; postal system of Texas originated here. Area called **"Cradle of Texas Liberty."** Museum. Camping, picnicking, golf, fishing, hiking.

Texas State Railroad State Historic Site, in Anderson and Cherokee counties between the cities of Palestine and Rusk, adjacent to US 84, contains 499 acres. Acquired by Legislative Act in 1971. Trains run seasonal schedules on 25.5 miles of track. Call for information and reservations: In Texas 1-800-442-8951; outside 903-683-2561. Railroad built by the State of Texas to support the **state-owned iron works** at Rusk. Begun in 1893, and built largely by inmates from the state prison system, the railroad was gradually extended until it reached Palestine in 1909 and established regular rail service between the towns. (See also **Rusk/Palestine State Park**.)

Tyler State Park is 985.5 acres 2 miles north of IH 20 on FM 14 north of Tyler in Smith County. Includes 64-acre lake. The land was deeded by private owners in 1934-1935. Heavily wooded. Camping, hiking, fishing, boating, lake swimming. Nearby Tyler called **rose capital of world, with Tyler Rose Garden and annual Tyler Rose Festival.** Also in Tyler are **Caldwell Children's Zoo** and **Goodman Museum**.

Varner-Hogg Plantation State Historic Site is 66 acres in Brazoria County two miles north of West Columbia on FM 2852. Land originally owned by Martin Varner, a member of Stephen F. Austin's **"Old Three Hundred"** colony; later was home of Texas' governor **James Stephen Hogg**. Property was deeded to the state in 1957 by Miss Ima Hogg, Gov. Hogg's daughter. **First rum distillery** in Texas established in 1829 by Varner. Mansion tours Tuesday through Saturday. Also picnicking, fishing.

Village Creek State Park, comprising 1,004 heavily forested acres, is located in Lumberton, Hardin County, 10 miles north of Beaumont off US 69 and FM 3513. Purchased in 1979 from private owner, the park contains abundant flora and fauna typical of the Big Thicket area. The **200 species of birds** found here include wood ducks, egrets and herons. Activities include fishing, camping, canoeing, swimming, hiking and picnicking. Nearby is the **Big Thicket National Preserve**.

Walter Umphrey State Park is operated by Jefferson County. For RV site reservations, contact SGS Causeway Bait & Tackle, 409-985-4811.

Washington-on-the-Brazos State Historic Site consists of 293.1 acres 7 miles southwest of Navasota in Washington County on TX 105 and FM 1155. Land acquired by deed from private owners in 1916, 1976 and 1996. Park includes the site of the signing on March 2, 1836, of the **Texas Declaration of Independence** from Mexico, as well as the site of the later **signing of the Constitution of the Republic of Texas**. In 1842 and 1845, the land included the **capitol of the Republic**. Daily tours of Barrington, restored **home of Anson Jones, last president of the Republic of Texas. Star of the Republic Museum**. Activities include picnicking and birding.

Wyler Aerial Tramway Franklin Mountains State Park features an aerial cable-car tramway on 195 acres of rugged mountain on east side of Franklin Mountains in El Paso. Purchase tickets at tramway station on McKinley Avenue to ride in Swiss-made gondola to 5,632-foot Ranger Peak. Passengers view cacti, rock formations, wildlife and 7,000 square miles of Texas, New Mexico and Mexico. Accessible ramps and paved grounds at top lead to observation deck with 360-degree view. Check with park for fees and hours; 915-566-6622. Other area attractions include Franklin Mountains State Park, Hueco Tanks State Historic Site and Magoffin Home State Historic Site. ✰

National Parks, Historical Sites, Recreation Areas in Texas

Below are listed the facilities in and the activities that can be enjoyed at the two national parks, a national seashore, a biological preserve, several historic sites, memorials and recreation areas in Texas. They are under supervision of the **U.S. Department of Interior.** On the Web: **www.nps.gov/parks/search.htm**; under "Select State," choose "Texas." In addition, the recreational opportunities in the national forests and national grasslands in Texas, under the jurisdiction of the **U.S. Department of Agriculture,** are listed at the end of the article.

Alibates Flint Quarries National Monument consists of 1,371 acres in Potter County. For more than 10,000 years, **pre-Columbian Indians** dug **agatized limestone** from the quarries to make projectile points, knives, scrapers and other tools. The area is presently undeveloped. You may visit the flint quarries on **guided walking tours** with a park ranger. Tours are at 10:00 a.m. and 2:00 p.m. from Memorial Day to Labor Day. Off-season tours can be arranged by writing to Lake Meredith National Recreation Area, Box 1460, Fritch 79036, or by calling 806-857-3151.

Amistad National Recreation Area is located on the U.S. side of **Amistad Reservoir,** an international reservoir on the Texas-Mexico border. The 57,292-acre park's attractions include **boating, water skiing, swimming, fishing, camping** and archaeological sites. If lake level is normal, visitors can see **4000-year-old prehistoric pictographs** in Panther and Parida caves, which are accessible only by boat. Check with park before visiting. The area is **one of the densest concentrations of Archaic rock art in North America** — more than 300 sites. Commercial campgrounds, motels and restaurants nearby. Marinas located at Diablo East and Rough Canyon. Open year round. NPS Administration, 4121 Hwy. 90 W, Del Rio 78840; 830-775-7491.

Big Bend National Park, established in 1944, has spectacular **mountain and desert scenery** and a variety of **unusual geological structures.** It is the **nation's largest** protected area of **Chihuahuan Desert.** Located in the great bend of the Rio Grande, the 801,000-acre park, which is part of the **international boundary** between the United States and Mexico, was designated a **U.S. Biosphere Reserve** in 1976. **Hiking, birding and float trips** are popular. Numerous campsites are located in park, and the **Chisos Mountain Lodge** has accommodations for approximately 345 guests. Write for reservations to National Park Concessions, Inc., Big Bend National Park, Texas 79834; 915-477-2291; www.chisosmountainslodge.com. Park open year round; facilities most crowded during spring break. PO Box 129, Big Bend National Park 79834; 915-477-2251.

Big Thicket National Preserve, established in 1974, consists of 13 separate units totalling 97,000 acres of diverse flora and fauna, often nicknamed the "**biological crossroads of North America.**" The preserve, which includes parts of seven East Texas counties, has been designated an **"International Biosphere Reserve"** by the United Nations Educational, Scientific and Cultural Organization (UNESCO). The preserve includes **four different ecological systems:** southeastern swamps, eastern forests, central plains and southwestern deserts. The visitor information station is located on FM 420, seven miles north of Kountze; phone 409-951-6725. Open daily from 9 a.m. to 5 p.m. Naturalist activities are available by reservation only; reservations are made through the station. **Nine trails,** ranging in length from one-half mile to 18 miles, visit

The sun sets through "the window" of the Chisos Basin in Big Bend National Park. The 801,000-acre park was established in 1944. File photo.

a variety of forest communities. The two shortest trails are handicapped accessible. Trails are open year round, but flooding may occur after heavy rains. Horses permitted on the **Big Sandy Horse Trail** only. Boating and canoeing are popular on preserve corridor units. Park headquarters are at 3785 Milam, Beaumont 77701; 409-246-2337.

Chamizal National Memorial, established in 1963 and opened to the public in 1973, stands as a monument to Mexican-American friendship and goodwill. The memorial, on 52 acres in El Paso, commemorates the peaceful settlement on Aug. 29, 1963, of a **99-year-old boundary dispute between the United States and Mexico.** Chamizal uses the visual and performing arts as a medium of interchange, helping people better understand not only other cultures but their own, as well. It hosts a variety of programs throughout the year, including: the fall **Chamizal Festival** musical event; the **Siglo de Oro** drama festival (early March); the **Oñate Historical Festival** celebrating the First Thanksgiving (April); and **Music Under the Stars** (Sundays, June-August). The park has a 1.8-mile walking trail and picnic areas. Phone: 915-532-7273.

Fort Davis National Historic Site in Jeff Davis County was a key post in the West Texas defense system, guarding immigrants and tradesmen on the San Antonio-El Paso road from 1854 to 1891. At one time, Fort Davis was manned by black troops, called **"Buffalo Soldiers"** (because of their curly hair) who fought with great distinction in the Indian Wars. **Henry O. Flipper, the first black graduate of West Point,** served at Fort Davis in the early 1880s. The 474-acre historic site is located on the north edge of the town of Fort Davis in the **Davis Mountains,** the second-highest mountain range in the state. The site includes a museum, an auditorium with daily audio-visual programs, restored and refurnished buildings, picnic area and hiking trails. Open year round except Christmas Day. PO Box 1379, Fort Davis 79734; 915-426-3224.

Fort Davis National Historic Site comprises 474 acres that include a museum, restored army barracks, picnic areas and hiking trails. Texas Almanac photo.

Guadalupe Mountains National Park, established in 1972, includes 86,416 acres in Hudspeth and Culberson counties. The Park contains one of the most extensive **fossil reefs** on record. Deep **canyons** cut through this reef and provide a rare opportunity for geological study. Special points of interest are **McKittrick Canyon,** a fragile riparian environment, and **Guadalupe Peak,** the highest in Texas. Camping, hiking on 80 miles of trails, Frijole Ranch Museum, summer amphitheater programs. Orientation, free information and natural history exhibits available at Visitor Center. Open year round. Lodging at Van Horn, Texas, and White's City or Carlsbad, NM. HC 60, Box 400, Salt Flat 79847; 915-828-3251.

Lake Meredith National Recreation Area, 30 miles northeast of Amarillo, centers on a reservoir on the Canadian River, in Moore, Hutchinson and Potter counties. The 50,000-acre recreational area is popular for water-based activities. Boat ramps, picnic areas, unimproved campsites. Commercial lodging and trailer hookups available in nearby towns. Open year round. PO Box 1460, Fritch 79036; 806-857-3151.

Lyndon B. Johnson National Historic Site includes two separate districts 14 miles apart. The **Johnson City District** comprises the **boyhood home of the 36th President of United States** and the **Johnson Settlement,** where his grandparents resided during the late 1800s. The **LBJ Ranch District** can be visited only by taking the National Park Service bus tour starting at the LBJ State Historic Site. The tour includes the reconstructed **LBJ Birthplace,** old school, family cemetery, show barn and a view of the **Texas White House.** Site in Blanco and Gillespie counties was established in 1969, and contains 1,570 acres, 674 of which are federal. Open year round except Thanksgiving, Christmas Day and New Year's Day. No camping on site; commercial campgrounds, motels in area. PO Box 329, Johnson City 78636; 830-868-7128.

Padre Island National Seashore consists of a 67.5-mile stretch of a barrier island along the Gulf Coast; noted for white-sand beaches, excellent fishing and abundant bird and marine life. Contains 133,000 acres in Kleberg, Willacy and Kenedy counties. Open year round. One paved campground (fee charged) located north of Malaquite Beach; unpaved (primitive) campground area south on beach. Five miles of beach are accessible by regular vehicles; 55 miles are accessible only by 4x4 vehicles. Off-road vehicles prohibited. Camping permitted in two designated areas. Commercial lodging available on the island outside the National Seashore boundaries. PO Box 181300, Corpus Christi 78480; 361-949-8068.

Palo Alto Battlefield National Historic Site, Brownsville, preserves the site of the **first major battle in the Mexican-American War.** Fought on May 8, 1846, it is recognized for the innovative use of light or "flying" artillery. Participating in the battle were three future presidents: **General Zachary Taylor and Ulysses S. Grant** on the U.S. side, and **Gen. Mariano Arista** on the Mexican. Historical markers are located at the junction of Farm-to-Market roads 1847 and 511. Access to the 3,400-acre site is currently limited. Exhibits at the park's interim visitor center, at 1623 Central Blvd., Ste. 213 in Brownsville (78520), interpret the battle as well as the causes and consequences of the war. Phone 956-541-2785.

Rio Grande Wild and Scenic River is a 196-mile strip on the U.S. shore of the Rio Grande in the **Chihuahuan Desert,** beginning in Big Bend National Park and continuing downstream to the Terrell-Val Verde County line. There are federal facilities in Big Bend National Park only. Contact Big Bend National Park for more information.

San Antonio Missions National Historic Site preserves four Spanish Colonial Missions — **Concepción, San José, San Juan and Espada** — as well as the Espada dam and aqueduct, which are two of the best-preserved remains in the United States of the **Spanish Colonial irrigation system,** and Rancho de las Cabras, the colonial ranch of Mission Espada. All were crucial elements to Spanish settlement on the Texas frontier. When Franciscan attempts to establish a chain of missions in East Texas in the late 1600s failed, the Spanish Crown ordered three missions transferred to the San Antonio River valley in 1731.

The missions are located within the city limits of **San Antonio,** while **Rancho de las Cabras** is located 25 miles south in Wilson County near **Floresville.** The four missions, which are still in use as active parishes, are open to the public from 9 a.m. to 5 p.m. daily except Thanksgiving, Christmas and New Year's. Public roadways connect the sites; a hike-bike trail is being developed. The visitor center for the mission complex is at San José. For more information, write to 2202 Roosevelt Ave., San Antonio 78210; 210-534-8833 or 210-932-1001 (Visitor Center). ☆

See story, "The Spanish Missions of Texas," beginning on page 16. Visitor information is on page 25.

Recreation in the National Forests

For general information about the National Forests and National Grasslands, see page 103 in the Environment section.

An estimated 3 million people visit the National Forests in Texas for recreation annually. These visitors use established recreation areas primarily for hiking, picnicking, swimming, fishing, camping, boating and nature enjoyment. In the following list of some of these areas, Forest Service Road is abbreviated FSR:

Angelina NF

Bouton Lake, 7 miles southeast of Zavalla off Texas 63 and FSR 303, has a 9-acre natural lake with primitive facilities for camping, picnicking and fishing. Boykin Springs, 11 miles southeast of Zavalla, has a 6-acre lake and facilities for hiking, swimming, picnicking, fishing and camping.

Caney Creek on Sam Rayburn Reservoir, 10 miles southeast of Zavalla off FM 2743, also has an amphitheater. Sandy Creek, 15.5 miles east of Zavalla on Sam Rayburn, offers fishing, sailing and picnicking.

The Sawmill Hiking Trail is 5.5 miles long and winds from Bouton Lake to Boykin Springs Recreation Area.

Davy Crockett NF

Ratcliff Lake, 25 miles west of Lufkin on Texas 7, includes a 45-acre lake and facilities for picnicking, hiking,

Recreational Facilities, Corps of Engineers Lakes, 2004

Source: Southwestern Division, Corps of Engineers, Dallas

Reservoir	Swim Areas	Boat Ramps	Picnic Sites	Camp Sites	Rental Units	Visitor Hours, 2004
Aquilla	0	3	0	0	0	253,418
Bardwell	3	6	47	155	0	701,487
Belton	4	21	268	278	10	13,976,491
Benbrook	2	16	109	186	0	3,519,813
Buffalo Bayou*	0	0	1,111	0	0	8,502,000
Canyon	5	19	284	487	24	2,192,808
Cooper	2	5	106	177	14	5,259,118
Georgetown	1	3	109	224	0	3,542,962
Granger	2	5	129	143	0	1,426,625
Grapevine	1	12	139	161	0	5,535,946
Hords Creek	3	9	15	136	0	2,802,404
Joe Pool	3	7	315	556	0	5,926,051
Lake O' the Pines	7	33	143	492	0	8,340,478
Lavon	3	22	237	264	0	5,281,870
Lewisville	7	25	349	594	0	12,523,989
Navarro Mills	3	6	26	255	0	2,843,314
O.C. Fisher	0	13	75	61	0	843,511
Pat Mayse**	3	9	0	216	0	1,423,421
Proctor	5	7	39	216	0	2,686,182
Ray Roberts	2	11	294	371	30	21,417,506
Sam Rayburn	4	29	40	796	61	12,534,743
Somerville	2	12	150	949	21	19,873,274
Stillhouse Hollow	3	5	75	67	0	3,154,648
Texoma**†	3	25	110	669	370	83,484,524
Town Bluff	2	13	78	370	1	4,879,999
Waco	3	11	149	271	0	2,821,715
Wallisville*	0	2	10	0	0	247,500
Whitney	3	28	42	768	0	3,389,395
Wright Patman	4	22	203	603	0	11,251,658
Totals	**80**	**379**	**4,652**	**9,465**	**531**	**250,636,850**

All above lakes managed by the Fort Worth District, U.S. Army Corps of Engineers, with the following exceptions:
* Includes both Addicks and Barker Dams; managed by Galveston District, USACE.
**Managed by Tulsa District, USACE.
†Figures for facilities on Texas side of lake. Visitation is for entire lake.

swimming, boating, fishing and camping. There is also an amphitheater.

The 20-mile-long 4C National Recreation Trail connects Ratcliff Recreation Area to the Neches Bluff overlook. The Piney Creek Horse Trail, 54 miles long, can be entered approximately 5.5 miles south of Kennard off FSR 514. There are two horse camps along the trail.

Sabine NF

Indian Mounds Recreation Area, accessible via FM 83 3.5 miles east of Hemphill, has camping facilities and a boat-launch ramp. Lakeview, on Toledo Bend Reservoir 20 miles from Pineland, offers camping, hiking, boating and fishing and can be reached via Texas 87, FM 2928 and FSR 120.

Ragtown, 21 miles southeast of Center and accessible by Texas 87 and Texas 139, County Road 3184 and FSR 132, is also on Toledo Bend and has facilities for hiking, camping and boating. Red Hill Lake, 3 miles north of Milam on Texas 87, has facilities for hiking, fishing, swimming, camping and picnicking. Willow Oak Recreation Area, on Toledo Bend 11 miles south of Hemphill off Texas 87, offers fishing, picnicking, camping and boating.

Trail Between the Lakes is 28 miles long from Lakeview Recreation Area on Toledo Bend to U.S. 96 near Sam Rayburn Reservoir.

Sam Houston NF

Cagle Recreation Area is located on the shores of Lake Conroe, 50 miles north of Houston and 5 miles west of I-45 at FM 1375. Cagle offers camping, fishing, hiking, birding and other recreational opportunities in a forested lakeside setting.

Double Lake, 3 miles south of Coldspring on FM 2025, has facilities for picnicking, hiking, camping, swimming and fishing. Stubblefield Lake, 15 miles west-northwest of New Waverly off Texas 1375 on the shores of Lake Conroe, has facilities for camping, hiking, picnicking and fishing.

The Lone Star Hiking Trail, approximately 128 miles long, is located in Sam Houston National Forest in Montgomery, Walker and San Jacinto counties.

Recreation on the National Grasslands

North Texas

Lake Davy Crockett Recreation Area, 12 miles north of Honey Grove on FM 100, has a boat-launch ramp and camping sites on a 450-acre lake.

Coffee Mill Lake Recreation Area has camping and picnicking facilities on a 750-acre lake. This area is 4 miles west of Lake Davy Crockett Recreation Area.

The Caddo Multi-Use Trail system, also 4 miles west of Lake Davy Crockett, offers camping, hiking and horseback riding on 3.5 miles of trails.

Black Creek Lake Recreation Area is 8 miles southeast of Alvord, has camping, picnic facilities and a boat-launch ramp on a 35-acre lake.

Cottonwood Lake, 10 miles north of Decatur, is around 40 acres and offers hiking, boating and fishing.

The Cottonwood-Black Creek Hiking Trail is 4 miles long and connects the two lakes. It is rated moderately difficult. There are nearly 75 miles of multipurpose trails which run in the Cottonwood Lake vicinity.

TADRA Horse Trail, 15 miles north of Decatur, has camping and 35 miles of horse trails. Restrooms and and parking facilities are available.

West Texas

Lake McClellan in Gray County and Lake Marvin, which is part of the Black Kettle National Grassland in Hemphill County, receive more than 28,000 recreation visitors annually. These areas provide camping, picnicking, fishing, birdwatching and boating facilities. Concessionaires operate facilities at Lake McClellan, and a nominal fee is charged for use of the areas. Thompson Grove Picnic Area is 14 miles northeast of Texline.

At the Rita Blanca National Grassland, about 4,500 visitors a year enjoy picnicking and hunting. ☆

National Natural Landmarks in Texas

Nineteen Texas natural areas have been listed on the **National Registry of Natural Landmarks**. The registry was established by the Secretary of the Interior in 1962 to identify and encourage the preservation of geological and ecological features that represent nationally significant examples of the nation's natural heritage.

The registry currently lists a total of 587 national natural landmarks. Texas areas on the list, as of August 2001, and their characteristics, are these (dates of listing in parentheses):

Attwater Prairie Chicken Preserve, Colorado County, 55 miles west of Houston in the national wildlife refuge, is rejuvenated Gulf Coastal Prairie, which is habitat for Attwater's prairie chickens. (April 1968)

Bayside Resaca Area, Cameron County, Laguna Atascosa National Wildlife Refuge, 28 miles north of Brownsville. Excellent example of a resaca, supporting coastal salt-marsh vegetation and rare birds. (Aug. 1980)

Catfish Creek, Anderson County, 20 miles northwest of Palestine, is undisturbed riparian habitat. (June 1983)

Caverns of Sonora, Sutton County, 16 miles southwest of Sonora, has unusual geological formations. (Oct. 1965)

Devil's Sink Hole, Edwards County, 9 miles northeast of Rocksprings, is a deep, bell-shaped, collapsed limestone sink with cave passages extending below the regional water table. (Oct. 1972)

Dinosaur Valley, Somervell County, in Dinosaur Valley State Park, four miles west of Glen Rose, contains fossil footprints exposed in bed of Paluxy River. (Oct. 1968)

Enchanted Rock, Gillespie and Llano counties, 12 miles southwest of Oxford, is a classic batholith, composed of coarse-grained pink granite. (Oct. 1971)

Ezell's Cave, Hays County, within the city limits of San Marcos, houses at least 36 species of cave creatures. (Oct. 1971)

Fort Worth Nature Center and Refuge, Tarrant County, within the Fort Worth city limits. Contains remnants of the Grand Prairie and a portion of the Cross Timbers, with limestone ledges and marshes. Refuge for migratory birds and other wildlife, and home to 11 buffalo raised by the center's staff. Educational programs offered for youth and adults. Self-guided hiking. (Nov. 1980)

Greenwood Canyon, Montague County, along a tributary of Braden Branch, is a rich source of Cretaceous fossils. (May 1975)

High Plains Natural Area, Randall County, Buffalo Lake National Wildlife Refuge, 26 miles southwest of Amarillo, is a grama-buffalo shortgrass area. (Aug. 1980)

Little Blanco River Bluff, Blanco County, comprises an Edwards Plateau limestone-bluff plant community. (May 1982)

Longhorn Cavern, Burnet County, 11 miles southwest of Burnet. Formed at least 450 million years ago, cave contains several unusual geologic features. (Oct. 1971)

Lost Maples State Natural Area, Bandera and Real counties, 61 miles northwest of San Antonio, contains Edwards Plateau fauna and flora, including unusual bigtooth maple. Largest known nesting population of golden-cheeked warbler. (Feb. 1980)

Muleshoe National Wildlife Refuge, Bailey County, 59 miles northwest of Lubbock, contains playa lakes and typical High Plains shortgrass grama grasslands. (Aug. 1980)

Natural Bridge Caverns, Comal County, 16 miles west of new Braunfels, is a multilevel cavern system, with beautiful and unusual geological formations. (Oct. 1971)

Odessa Meteor Crater, Ector County, 10 miles southwest of Odessa, is one of only two known meteor sites in the country. (April 1965)

Palo Duro Canyon State Park, Armstrong and Randall counties, 22 miles south-southwest of Amarillo. Cut by waters of the Red River, it contains cross-sectional views of sedimentary rocks representing four geological periods. (May 1976)

Santa Ana National Wildlife Refuge, Hidalgo County, 7 miles south of Alamo, is a lowland forested area with jungle-like vegetation. It is habitat for more than 300 species of birds and some rare mammals. (Oct. 1966) ☆

Children check out the buffalo that live at the Fort Worth Nature Center and Refuge. The refuge has abundant wildlife and is a home to 213 species of migratory birds. Trails and maps for self-guided hiking are available, and guided hikes also can be scheduled with the center's staff. Family activities and nature classes are offered throughout the year. File photo.

Birding in Texas

World Birding Center

The World Birding Center comprises nine birding education centers and observation sites in the Lower Rio Grande Valley designed to protect wildlife habitat and offer visitors a view of more than 500 species of birds. The center has partnered with the Texas Parks and Wildlife Department, the U.S. Fish and Wildlife Service and nine communities to turn 10,000 acres back into natural areas for birds, butterflies and other wildlife.

This area in Cameron, Hidalgo and Starr counties is a natural migratory path for millions of birds that move between the Americas, but it has been affected by agricultural and urban development and a loss of wildlife habitat. The center wants to reconcile economic development, which will be derived from tourism, with environmental conservation.

The nine WBC sites are situated along the border with Mexico:

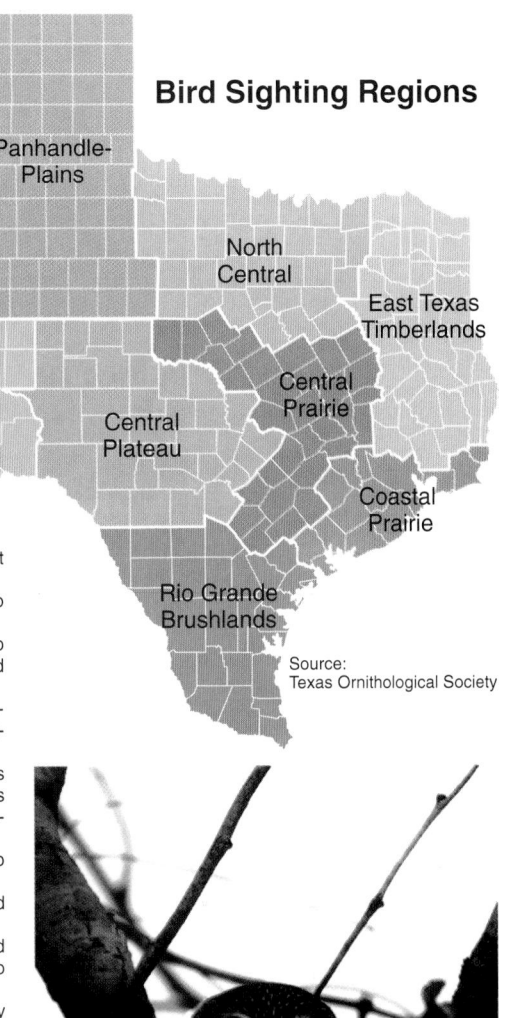

Bird Sighting Regions

Panhandle-Plains

North Central

East Texas Timberlands

Central Prairie

Trans-Pecos

Central Plateau

Coastal Prairie

Rio Grande Brushlands

Source:
Texas Ornithological Society

- **Brownsville** — not yet open; to be constructed at Resaca de la Palma State Park and operated by TPWD.
- **Edinburg** — opened in March 2003 (first WBC site to open); located at Edinburg Scenic Wetlands.
- **Harlingen** — Arroyo Colorado is open daily, sunrise to sunset. Hike and bike trails through urban park area and Harlingen thicket.
- **Hidalgo** — Old Hidalgo Pumphouse is open to the public with historical tours available. Closed Monday and Saturday.
- **McAllen** — Quinta Mazatlan is open for birding groups by reservation or appointment through the McAllen Parks and Recreation Department. Opening set for 2005 season.
- **Mission** — WBC headquarters; located at Bentsen–Rio Grande State Park; open daily; operated by TPWD.
- **Roma** — Roma Bluffs is open to public and prearranged tours; operated by U.S. Fish and Wildlife;
- **South Padre Island** — South Padre Island Birding and Nature Center offers nature trail boardwalk leading to Laguna Madre shore; now open for birding.
- **Weslaco** — Estero Llano Grande State Park is open by appointment and operated by TPWD.

For more information, contact World Birding Center, 2800 S. Bentsen Palm Dr., Mission, TX 78572; 956-584-9156. On the Web: www.worldbirdingcenter.org.

Great Texas Coastal Birding Trail

The Great Texas Coastal Birding Trail winds its way through 43 Texas counties along the entire Texas coast. The trail, completed in April 2000, is divided into upper, central and lower coastal regions. It includes 308 wildlife-viewing sites and such amenities as boardwalks, parking pullouts, kiosks, observation platforms and landscaping to attract native wildlife.

Color-coded maps are available, and signs mark each site. Trail maps contain information about the birds and habitats likely to be found at each site, the best season to visit, and food and lodging.

For information, contact: Nature Tourism Coordinator, Texas Parks and Wildlife, 4200 Smith School Road, Austin, TX 78744; 512-389-4396. On the Web at www.tpwd.state.tx.us/birdingtrails/contact.phtml. ☆

The Pygmy Owl is one of the many bird species that draw birders to the World Birding Center in the Lower Rio Grande Valley and the Great Texas Coastal Birding Trail, which extends along the entire Texas Gulf Coast. File photo.

Freshwater and Saltwater Fish and Fishing

Source: Texas Parks and Wildlife Department

Freshwater Fish and Fishing

In Texas, **247 species of freshwater fish** are found. This includes 78 species that inhabit areas with low salinity and can be found in rivers entering the Gulf of Mexico. Also included in that total are 18 species that are not native, but were introduced into the state.

The estimated **number of freshwater recreational anglers** is 1.84 million, with annual expenditures of $1.49 billion annually. Catch-and-release fishing has emerged on the Texas scene as the conservation theme of anglers who desire continued quality fishing.

The **most popular fish** for recreational fishing are largemouth bass; catfish; crappie; and striped, white and hybrid striped bass.

The **Texas Parks and Wildlife Department** (TPWD) operates field stations, fish hatcheries and research facilities to support the conservation and management of fishery resources.

TPWD has continued its programs of stocking fish in public waters to increase angling opportunities. The hatcheries operated by TPWD raise largemouth and smallmouth bass, as well as catfish, striped and hybrid striped bass and sunfish.

Everardo Garcia, firstmate on an Osprey Fishing Trips outing near South Padre Island, holds one of the day's catch. File photo.

Texas Freshwater Fisheries Center

The Texas Freshwater Fisheries Center in Athens, about 75 miles southeast of Dallas, is an $18 million hatchery, research laboratory, aquarium and educational center, where visitors can learn about the underwater life in Texas' freshwater streams, ponds and lakes.

The 24,000-square-foot hatchery and research facility concentrates on genetic research and the production of 5 to 6 million Florida largemouth bass for restocking Texas reservoirs and rivers.

The interactive Cox Visitors Center includes aquarium displays of fish in their natural environment. Visitors get an "eye-to-eye" view of three authentically designed Texas freshwater habitats: a Hill Country stream, an East Texas pond and a reservoir. A marsh exhibit features live American alligators.

Through touch-screen computer exhibits, visitors can learn more about fish habitats and life cycles and the importance of catch-and-release fishing. Films, seminars and demonstrations are also offered.

A casting pond stocked with rainbow trout in the winter and catfish in the summer provides a place for children to learn how to bait a hook, cast a line and land a fish. A recent addition is the 1.2-mile self-guided wetlands loop trail that explains how land and water create special habitats for plants, birds and other living things. The center also has an active schedule of special programs and events.

The center is a cooperative effort of Texas Parks and Wildlife, the U.S. Fish and Wildlife Service, the City of Athens and private organizations.

The Texas Freshwater Fisheries Center is open Tuesday through Saturday, 9 a.m. to 4 p.m., and Sunday, 1 to 4 p.m. It is closed on Monday. Admission is charged.

The Center is located four-and-a-half miles east of Athens on FM 2495 at Lake Athens. Address: 5550 Flat Creek Road, Athens 75751, or call 903-676-2277.

Saltwater Fish and Fishing

There are about 1 million saltwater anglers in Texas (6 years old and older) who have a $1.328 billion economic impact annually. Catch averaged 2,321,100 fish annually in the 10 years between 1993–2003 for both Texas bays and the Gulf of Mexico off Texas combined.

The most popular **saltwater sport fish** in Texas bays are spotted seatrout, sand seatrout, Atlantic croaker, red drum, southern flounder, black drum, sheepshead and gafftopsail catfish. **Offshore,** some of the fish anglers target are red snapper, king mackerel, dolphin (fish), spotted seatrout, tarpon and yellowfin tuna.

Commercial Fisheries

Total coastwide landings in 2003 were more than 52 million pounds, valued at more than $125 million. Shrimp accounted for 68 percent of the weight and 77 percent of the value of all seafood landed during 2003. The approximately *4,800 licensed saltwater commercial fishermen in Texas in 2003 made an economic impact of more than $529 million. ☆

Commercial Landings, 2003

Finfish	Pounds	Value
Drum, Black	1,676,700	$1,365,100
Flounder	158,500	335,900
Sheepshead	67,600	26,100
Snapper	1,807,100	4,122,700
Other	1,391,900	3,110,200
Total Finfish	**5,101,800**	**$8,960,000**
Shellfish		
Shrimp (Heads On):		
Brown and Pink	24,430,600	$72,979,100
White	8,019,000	21,907,500
Other	714,400	1,340,700
Crabs, Blue	4,811,300	3,157,000
Oyster, Eastern	6,833,400	16,537,700
Other	94,200	143,700
Total Shellfish	**46,902,900**	**$116,065,700**
Grand Total	**52,004,700**	**$125,025,700**

* Deck hands and other crew members no longer need a license to work on commercial boats, so total number of commercial fishermen will vary from previous years.
Source: Trends in Texas Commercial Fishery Landings, 1972–2003, Texas Parks and Wildlife Department Coastal Fisheries Div., Management Data Series, Austin, 2004.

Sea Center Texas

Sea Center Texas is a marine aquarium, fish hatchery and nature center operated by the Texas Parks and Wildlife Department to educate and entertain visitors. The visitor center opened in 1996 and educates through interpretive displays, a "touch tank" and native Texas habitat exhibits depicting a salt marsh, jetty, reef and open Gulf waters. The aquarium features "Gordon," a 300-pound grouper, and sharks. The "Coastal Kids" educational program offers students on field trips hands-on learning activities.

Touted as the **world's largest redfish hatchery,** the facility is one of three marine hatcheries on the Texas coast that produces juvenile red drum and spotted speckled trout for enhancing natural populations in Texas bays. The hatchery has the capability to produce 20 million juvenile fish yearly. It also serves as a testing ground for production of other marine species, such as flounder and tarpon.

A half-acre **youth fishing pond** introduces youngsters to saltwater fishing through scheduled activities. The pond is handicap accessible and stocked with a variety of marine fish.

The center's **wetland area** is part of the Great Texas Coastal Birding Trail, where more than 150 species of birds have been identified. The wetland consists of a one-acre salt marsh and a three-acre freshwater marsh. Damselflies, dragonflies, butterflies and frogs are frequently sited off the boardwalk. A small outdoor pavilion provides a quiet resting place for lunch adjacent to the butterfly and hummingbird gardens.

Sea Center Texas is operated in partnership with The Dow Chemical Company and the Coastal Conservation Association. It is located in Lake Jackson, 50 miles south of Houston off of Texas 288. Admission and parking are free. Open 9 a.m. to 4 p.m. Tuesday through Friday; 10 a.m. to 5 p.m. Saturday, and 1 p.m. to 4 p.m. Sunday. Closed Monday and some holidays. Reservations are required for some group tours, nature tours and hatchery tours. For more information call 979-292-0100. On the web: www.tpwd.state.tx.us/fish. ☆

Hunting and Fishing Licenses

A **hunting license** is required of Texas residents and nonresidents of Texas who hunt any bird or animal. Hunting licenses and stamp endorsements are valid during the period Sept. 1 through the following Aug. 31 of each year, except lifetime licenses and licenses issued for a specific number of days.

A hunting license (except the nonresident special hunting license and non-resident 5-day special hunting license) is valid for taking all legal species of wildlife in Texas including **deer, turkey, javelina, antelope, aoudad (sheep)** and all **small game and migratory game birds.**

A covey of quail rise during a West Texas quail hunt. File photo.

Special licenses and tags are required for taking **alligators**, and a **trapper's license** is required to hunt **fur-bearing animals.**

In addition to a valid hunting license, an Upland Game Bird Stamp Endorsement is required to hunt **turkey, pheasant, quail, lesser prairie chicken** or **chachalaca.** Non-residents who purchase the non-resident spring turkey license are exempt from this stamp endorsement requirement. To hunt any migratory game birds (including **waterfowl, coot, rail, gallinule, snipe, dove, sandhill crane** and **woodcock**), a Migratory Game Bird Stamp Endorsement is required, in addition to a valid hunting license. A valid Federal Duck Stamp and HIP Certification are also required of waterfowl hunters age 16 or older.

All fishing licenses and stamp endorsements are valid only during the period Sept. 1 through Aug. 31, except lifetime licenses and licenses issued for a specific number of days. If you own any valid freshwater fishing package, you will be able to purchase a saltwater stamp, and, if you own any valid saltwater fishing package, you will be able to purchase a freshwater stamp.

Detailed information concerning licenses, stamps, seasons, regulations and related information can be obtained from **Texas Parks and Wildlife, 4200 Smith School Road, Austin 78744; (800) 792-1112 or 512-389-4800.**

On the Web, information from TPW on hunting: www.tpwd.state.tx.us/hunt/hunt.htm;   on   fishing: **www.tpwd.state.tx.us/fish/fish.htm.**

Texas Parks and Wildlife Department reported that for the year ending **August 31, 2003,** there were 1,100,939 paid **hunting-license holders** and 1,662,432 **sport or recreation fishing-license holders.** These licenses, plus stamps, tags or permits, resulted in revenue to the state of $25,966,114 from hunting and $34,137,565 from fishing.

For the year ending **August 31, 2004,** there were 1,102,184 paid **hunting-license holders** and 1,632,101 paid **sport or recreation fishing-license holders.** These licenses, plus stamps, tags or permits, resulted in revenue to the state of $31,463,915 from hunting and $40,201,887 from fishing.

During the 2002–2003 license year, hunters harvested 436,949 **white-tailed deer**; 38,181 **wild turkey** in the fall and 28,953 in the spring; 5,420 **mule deer**; and 17,512 **javelina**. In addition, 201,523 **rabbits**; 325,499 **squirrels**; 4,534,984 **mourning dove**; and 460,384 **bobwhite quail** were harvested.

During the 2003–2004 license year, hunters harvested 436,942 **white-tailed deer**; 38,242 **wild turkey** in the fall and 27,035 in the spring; 4,622 **mule deer**; and 16,025 **javelina**. In addition, 206,509 **rabbits**; 287,366 **squirrels**; 4,296,080 **mourning dove**; and 705,449 **bobwhite quail** were harvested. ☆

Fairs, Festivals and Special Events

Fairs, festivals and other special events provide year-round recreation in Texas. Some are of national interest, while many attract visitors from across the state. In addition to those listed here, the recreational paragraphs in the Counties section list numerous events. Information was furnished by the event sponsors. You can find more events on the Web at: **www.traveltex.com/events_listing.asp**.

Abilene — West Texas Fair & Rodeo; *September;* 1700 Hwy. 36, 79602; www.taylorcountyexpocenter.com.

Albany — Fort Griffin Fandangle; *June;* PO Box 155, 76430-0155; www.fort-griffin fandangle.org.

Alvarado — Pioneers & Old Settlers Reunion; *August* (2nd full week); PO Box 217, 76009-0217.

Amarillo — Tri-State Fair; *September;* PO Box 31087, 79120.

Anderson — Grimes County Fair; *June;* PO Box 435, 77830.

Angleton — Brazoria County Fair; *October;* PO Box 818, 77516; www.bcfa.org.

Aransas Pass — Shrimporee; *June,* 130 W. Goodnight, 78336; www.aransaspass.org.

Arlington — Texas Scottish Festival; *June;* PO Box 511, Clifton, 76634; www.texasscottishfestival.com.

Athens — Old Fiddlers Reunion; *May* (last Fri.); PO Box 1441; 75751-1441.

Austin — Austin Fine Arts Festival; *April;* PO Box 5705, 78763-5705; www.austinfineartsfestival.org.

Bay City — Bay City Rice Festival; *October;* PO Box 867; 77404; www.baycitylions.org.

Bay City — Matagorda County Fair & Livestock Show; *February;* PO Box 1803, 77404; www.matagordacountyfair.com.

Beaumont — South Texas State Fair; *October;* 7250 Wespark Cr., 77705; www.ymbl.org.

Bellville — Austin County Fair; *October;* PO Box 141, 77418; www.austincountyfair.com.

Belton — Belton Rodeo & Celebration; *July;* PO Box 659, 76513; www.seebelton.com.

Big Spring — Howard County Fair; *August;* PO Box 2356, 79720-2356.

Boerne — Boerne Berges Fest; *June;* PO Box 748, 78006; www.boernebergesfest.com.

Boerne — Kendall County Fair; *September;* 7 S. Hwy 46 E., 78006; www.kcfa.org/.

Brackettville — Gunfighter Competition; *July* (Sat., Independence weekend); PO Box 528, 78832; www.alamovillage.com.

Brackettville — Western Horse Races & BBQ; *September* (Labor Day); PO Box 528, 78832; www.alamovillage.com.

Brenham — Washington County Fair; *September;* PO Box 1257, 77834; www.washingtoncofair.com.

Brownsville — Charro Days Fiesta; *February* (last Thurs.); PO Box 3247, 78520; www.charrodaysfiesta.com.

Burton — Burton Cotton Gin Festival; *April;* PO Box 98; 77835-0098; www.cottonginmuseum.org.

Caldwell — Burleson County Fair; *September;* PO Box 634, 77836.

Canyon — "TEXAS Legacies" Outdoor Epic Theatre; *June–August;* 1514 5th Ave., 79015; www.epictexas.com.

Clifton — Norse Smorgasbord; *November;* 152 Cnty. Rd. 4145, 76634.

Clute — Great Texas Mosquito Festival; *July;* PO Box 997, 77531-0997; www.mosquitofestival.com.

John Lee Hicks of Spring Branch rides Indiana Jones in the Bareback Bronc Riding competition at the Mesquite Championship Rodeo. The rodeo takes place each Friday and Saturday from April through September. File photo.

Columbus — Colorado County Fair; *September;* PO Box 506, 78933; www.coloradocountyfair.org.

Conroe — Montgomery County Fair; *March–April;* PO Box 869, 77305-0869; www.mcfa.org.

Corpus Christi — Bayfest; *September–October;* PO Box 1858, 78403-1858; www.bayfesttexas.com.

Corpus Christi – Buc Days; *April–May;* PO Box 30404, 78463; www.bucdays.com.

Corsicana — Derrick Days; *April;* 120 N. 12th St., 75110; www.corsicana.org.

Crowell — Cynthia Ann Parker Festival; *May;* PO Box 452, 79227; www.crowelltex.com/CAP/cappage1.html.

Dalhart — XIT Rodeo & Reunion; *August* (1st full weekend); PO Box 966, 79022.

Dallas — State Fair of Texas; *September–October;* PO Box 150009, 75315-0009; www.bigtex.com.

Decatur — Wise County Old Settlers Reunion; *July* (last full week); PO Box 203, 76234.

De Leon — De Leon Peach & Melon Festival; *August;* PO Box 44, 76444-0044.

Denton — North Texas State Fair & Rodeo; *August;* PO Box 1695, 76202-1695; www.northtexasstatefair.com.

Edna — Jackson County Fair; *October;* PO Box 457, 77957; www.jcyf.org.

Ennis — National Polka Festival; *May;* PO Box 1177, 75120-1237; www.visitennis.org/festivals.html.

Fairfield — Freestone County Fair; *June;* PO Box 196; 75840.

Flatonia — Czhilispiel; *October;* PO Box 610, 78941-0610; www.flatonia-tx.com/czhilispiel.htm.

Wonderland of Lights in Marshall is an East Texas favorite of the Christmas season. File photo.

Fort Worth — Pioneer Days; *September;* 131 E. Exchange Ave., Ste 100B, 76106; www.fortworthstockyards.org.

Fort Worth – Southwestern Expo. & Livestock Show; *January-February;* PO Box 150, 76101; www.fwssr.com.

Fredericksburg — Fredericksburg Food & Wine Fest; *October;* 703 N Llano, 78624; www.fbgfoodandwinefest.com.

Fredericksburg — Night in Old Fredericksburg; *July;* 302 E. Austin, 78624; www.fredericksburg-texas.com.

Fredericksburg — Oktoberfest; *October* (1st weekend); PO Box 222, 78624; www.Oktoberfestinfbg.com.

Freer — Freer Rattlesnake Roundup; *April-May;* PO Box 717, 78357-0717; www.freerrattlesnake.com.

Galveston — Dickens on The Strand; *December;* 502 20th St., 77550-2014; www.dickensonthestrand.org.

Galveston — Galveston Historic Homes Tour; *May;* 502 20th St., 77550-2014; www.galvestonhistory.org.

Gilmer — East Texas Yamboree; *October;* PO Box 854, 75644-0854; www.yamboree.com.

Glen Flora — Wharton County Youth Fair; *April;* PO Box 167, 77443-0167; www.whartoncountyyouthfair.org.

Graham — Art Splash on the Square; *May;* PO Box 1684, 76450; www.art-splash.com.

Graham — Christmas Stroll & Lighted Parade; *December;* PO Box 299, 76450; www.visitgraham.com.

Graham — Red, White & You Parade & Festivities; *July;* PO Box 299; 76450; www.visitgraham.com.

Granbury — Annual July 4th Celebration; *July;* 116 W. Bridge St., 76048; www.granburychamber.com.

Grand Prairie — National Championship Pow-Wow; *September;* 2602 Mayfield Rd, 75052-7299; www.tradersvillage.com.

Greenville — Hunt County Fair; *June;* PO Box 1071, 75401; www.huntcountyfair.com.

Groesbeck — Limestone County Fair; *March-April;* PO Box 965, 76642.

Hallettsville — Hallettsville Kolache Fest; *September;* PO Box 313, 77964-0313; www.hallettsville.com.

Helotes — Helotes Cornyval; *May* (1st weekend); PO Box 376, 78023-0376; www.cornyval.com.

Hempstead — Waller County Fair; *September-October;* PO Box 911, 77445.

Hico — Hico Old Settler Reunion; *July* (last full week); PO Box 93, 76457; www.hico-tx.com.

Hidalgo — BorderFest; March; PO 611 E. Coma; 78557; hidalgotexas.com.

Hondo — Medina County Fair; *September* (3rd weekend); PO Box 4, 78861.

Houston — Harris County Fair; *October;* 1 Abercrombie Dr, 77084-4233; www.hfrc.org.

Houston — Houston International Festival; *April-May;* 1111 Bagby St., Ste. 2550, 77002; www.ifest.org.

Houston —Houston Livestock Show and Rodeo; *March;* PO Box 20070; 77225-0070; www.rodeohouston.com.

Hughes Springs — Wildflower Trails of Texas; *April;* PO Box 805, 75656.

Huntsville — Walker County Fair; *March-April;* PO Box 1817, 77342; www.walkercountyfair.com.

Jefferson — Historical Pilgrimage and Spring Festival; *May;* PO Box 301, 75657-0301; www.theexcelsiorhouse.com.

Johnson City — Blanco County Fair; *August;* PO Box 261, 78636-0261.

Kenedy — Bluebonnet Days; *April;* 205 South 2nd St., 78119-2729.

Kerrville — Kerr County Fair; *October* (4th weekend); PO Box 290842, 78029; www.kerrcountyfair.com.

Kerrville — Kerrville Folk Festival; *May-June;* PO Box 291466; 78029-1466; www.kerrville-music.com.

Kerrville — The Official Texas State Arts & Crafts Fair; *May* (Memorial weekend); PO Box 291527, 78029-1527, www.tacef.org.

Kerrville — Kerrville Wine and Music Festival; *September;* PO Box 291466; 78029-1466; www.kerrville-music.com.

Lamesa — Dawson County Fair; *September;* PO Box 1268, 79331.

Laredo — Border Olympics; *January-March;* PO Box 450037, 78044-0037.

Laredo — Laredo International Fair & Exposition; *March;* PO Box 1770, 78043; www.laredofair.com.

Laredo — Washington's Birthday Celebration; *February;* 1819 E. Hillside Rd., 78041-3383; www.wbca-laredo.com.

Longview — Gregg County Fair & Exposition; *September;* PO Box 1124, 75606; www.greggcountyfair.com.

Lubbock — 4th on Broadway Festival; *July;* PO Box 1643, 79408-0208; www.broadwayfestivals.com.

Lubbock — Lights on Broadway Celebration; *December;* PO Box 1643, 79408-0208; www.broadwayfestivals.com.

Lubbock — Panhandle-South Plains Fair; *September;* PO Box 208, 79408-0208; www.southplainsfair.com.

Lufkin — Texas Forest Festival; *September;* 1615 S. Chestnut St., 75901; www.lufkintexas.org/chamber/forest_fest.htm.

Luling — Luling Watermelon Thump; *June* (last full weekend); PO Box 710, 78648-0710; www.watermelonthump.com.

Marshall — Fire Ant Festival; *October;* PO Box 520, 75671; www.marshalltxchamber.com.

Marshall — Stagecoach Days Festival; *May;* PO Box 520, 75671; www.marshalltxchamber.com.

Marshall — Wonderland of Lights; *November-December;* PO Box 520, 75671; www.marshalltxchamber.com.

Mercedes — Rio Grande Valley Livestock Show; *March;* PO Box 867, 78570-0867; www.rgvlivestockshow.com.

Mesquite — Mesquite Championship Rodeo; *April-Sep-*

tember (each Fri. & Sat.); 1818 Rodeo Dr, 75149-3800; www.mes-quiterodeo.com.

Monahans — Butterfield-Overland Stage Coach and Wagon Festival; *July;* www.monah-ans.org.

Mount Pleasant — Titus County Fair; *September;* PO Box 1232, 75456-1232; www.titus-countyfair.com.

Nacogdoches — Piney Woods Fair; *October;* 3805 NW Stallings Dr., 75961; www.nacexpo.net.

Nederland — Nederland Heritage Festival; *March,* PO Box 1176, 77627-1176; www.ned-erlandhf.org.

New Braunfels — Comal County Fair; *September;* PO Box 310223, 78131-0223; www.comalcounty-fair.org.

New Braunfels — Wurstfest; *November;* PO Box 310309, 78131-0309; www.wurstfest.com.

Louise Prior and Jose Ramon, both of Plano, polka to Brave Combo's music during the Saturday night dance at Westfest, an annual Czechoslovakian cultural festival in West. File photo.

Odessa — Permian Basin Fair & Expo; *September;* 218 W. 46th St., 79764; www.pb-fair.com.

Palestine — Dogwood Trails Festival; *March–April;* PO Box 2828, 75802-2828; www.visitpalestine.com.

Paris — Red River Valley Fair; *August;* 570 E. Center St., 75460-2680; www.rrvfair.org.

Pasadena — Pasadena Livestock Show & Rodeo; *September–October;* 7601 Red Bluff Rd., 77507-1035; www.pasadenarodeo.com.

Plantersville — Texas Renaissance Festival; *October–November* (8 weekends); 21778 FM 1774, 77363-7722; www.texrenfest.com.

Port Arthur — CalOILcade; *October;* PO Box 2336, 77643; www.portarthur.com/cavoilcade.

Port Lavaca — Calhoun County Fair; *October;* PO Box 42, 77979-0042.

Poteet — Poteet Strawberry Festival; *April;* PO Box 227, 78065-0227; www.strawberryfestival.com.

Refugio — Refugio County Fair & Rodeo; *March;* PO Box 88, 78377; www.rcfal.com.

Rio Grande City— Starr County Fair; *March;* PO Box 841, 78582.

Rosenberg — Fort Bend County Fair; *September–October;* PO Box 428, 77471; www.fbcfa.org.

Salado — Salado Scottish Games and Competitions; *November* (2nd weekend); PO Box 36, 76571-0036; www.ctam-salado.org.

San Angelo — San Angelo Stock Show & Rodeo; *February;* 200 W 43rd St., 76903-1675; www.sanangelorodeo.com.

San Antonio — Fiesta San Antonio; *April;* 2611 Broadway St.; 78215-1022; www.fiesta-sa.org.

San Antonio — Texas Folklife Festival; *June;* 801 S. Bowie St., 78205-3296; www.texasfolklifefestival.org.

Sanderson — Cinco de Mayo Celebration; *May* (1st Saturday); PO Box 598, 79848.

Sanderson — Independence Day Celebration; *July;* PO Box 4810, 79848-4810; www.sandersontx.info.

Sanderson — Prickly Pear Pachanga; *October;* PO Box 410, 79848.

Santa Fe — Cowboy Fest; *September;* PO Box 889, 77510-0889; www.galvestoncountyfair.com.

Santa Fe — Galveston County Fair & Rodeo; *April;* PO Box 889, 77510-0889; www.galvestoncountyfair.com.

Seguin — Guadalupe Agricultural & Livestock Fair; *October* (2nd weekend); PO Box 334, 78156; www.guadalu-pecountyfairandrodeo.com.

Shamrock — St. Patrick's Day Celebration; *March;* PO Box 588, 79079-0588.

Stamford — Texas Cowboy Reunion; *July;* PO Box 948, 79553-0928; http://biz.bigcountrytexas.com/tcrrodeo/.

Sulphur Springs — Hopkins County Fall Festival; *September;* PO Box 177, 75483-0177.

Sweetwater — Rattlesnake Roundup; *March* (2nd weekend); PO Box 416, 79556-0416; www.rattlesnakeroundup.com.

Terlingua — Terlingua International Chili Championship; *November* (1st weekend); PO Box 39, 79852; www.chili.org.

Texarkana — Four States Fair; *September;* 3700 E. 50th St., Texarkana AR, 75504; www.fourstatesfair.com.

Tyler — East Texas State Fair; *September;* 2112 W. Front St., 75702-6828; www.etstatefair.com.

Tyler — Texas Rose Festival; *October* (3rd week); PO Box 8224, 75711-8224; www.texasrosefestival.com.

Victoria — Victoria Jaycee's Livestock Show; *February;* PO Box 2255, 77902-2255; victoriajaycees.com/live-stock.htm.

Waco — Brazos River Festival; *April;* 810 S. 4th St., 76706-1036.

Waco — Heart O' Texas Fair & Rodeo; *October;* PO Box 7581, 76714-7581; www.hotfair.com.

Waxahachie — Gingerbread Trail Tour of Homes; *June* (1st full weekend); PO Box 706, 75168; www.-rootsweb.com/~txecm/ginger.htm.

Waxahachie — Scarborough Faire the Renaissance Festival; *April–May;* PO Box 538, 75168-0538; www.scarboroughrenfest.com.

Weatherford — Parker County Peach Festival; *July* (2nd Saturday); 401 Fort Worth St., 76086; www.visitweatherford.com.

West — Westfest; *September* (Labor Day weekend); PO Box 123, 76691; www.westfest.com.

Winnsboro — Autumn Trails Festival; *October;* 201 W. Broadway St., 75494-2608.

Woodville — Tyler County Dogwood Festival; *March–April;* PO Box 2151, 75979-2151; www.woodvilletx.com.

Yorktown — Yorktown's Fiesta En La Calle Festival; *April* (1st Saturday); PO Box 488, 78164-0488; www.yorktowntx.com.

Yorktown — Yorktown's Annual Western Days Celebration; *October* (3rd full weekend); PO Box 488, 78164-0488; www.yorktowntx.com. ☆

Counties of Texas

These pages describe Texas' 254 counties and hundreds of towns. Descriptions are based on reports from chambers of commerce, the Texas Cooperative Extension, federal and state agencies, the *New Handbook of Texas* and other sources. Consult the index for other county information.

County maps are based on those of the Texas Department of Transportation and are copyrighted, 2005, as the entire contents.

Physical Features: Descriptions are from U.S. Geological Survey and local sources.

Economy: From information provided by local chambers of commerce and county extension agents.

History: From Texas statutes, *Fulmore's History and Geography of Texas as Told in County Names*, WPA Historical Records Survey, Texas Centennial Commission Report and the *New Handbook of Texas*.

Ethnicity: Percentages from the 2000 Census of Population, U.S. Bureau of the Census, as compiled by the Texas State Data Center, Texas A&M University. **Anglo** refers to non-Hispanic whites; **Black** refers to non-Hispanic blacks; **Hispanic** refers to Hispanics of all races; **Other** is composed of persons from all other racial groups who are non-Hispanic.

Vital Statistics, 2003: From the Texas Department of Health Annual Report, 2003.

Recreation: From information provided by local chambers of commerce and county extension agents. Attempts were made to note activities unique to the area or that point to ethnic or cultural heritage.

Minerals: From county extension agents.

Agriculture: Condensed from information provided to the *Texas Almanac* by county extension agents in 2004. **Market value** (total cash receipts) of agricultural products sold are from the **2002 Census of Agriculture** of the U.S. Department of Agriculture for that year.

Cities: The county seat, incorporated cities and towns with post offices are listed. Population for incorporated towns are estimates from the State Data Center that were published Jan. 1, 2004. (NA) means a population count is not available. When figures for a small part of a city are given, such as **part [45,155] of Dallas** in Collin County, they are from the 2000 U.S. census because more recent estimates are not available.

Sources of DATA LISTS

Population: The county population estimate as of July 1, 2004, U.S. Census Bureau. The line following gives the percentage of increase or decrease from the 2000 U.S. census count.

Area: Total area in square miles, including water surfaces, as determined in the 2000 U.S. census.

Land Area: The land area in square miles as determined by the Census Bureau in 2000.

Altitude (ft.): Principally from the U.S. Geological Survey. Not all of the surface of Texas has been precisely surveyed for elevation; in some cases data are from the Texas Railroad Commission or the Texas Department of Transportation.

Climate: Provided by the National Oceanic and Atmospheric Administration state climatologist, College Station. Data are revised at 10-year intervals. Listed are the latest compilations, as of Jan. 1, 2003, and pertain to a particular site within the county (usually the county seat). The data include: **Rainfall** (annual in inches); **January** mean minimum temperature; **July** mean maximum temperature.

Workforce/Wages: Prepared by the Texas Workforce Commission, Austin, in cooperation with the Bureau of Labor Statistics of the U.S. Department of Labor. The data are computed from reports by all establishments subject to the Texas Unemployment Compensation Act.

(Agricultural employers are subject to the act if they employ as many as three workers for 20 weeks or pay cash wages of $6,250 in a quarter. Employers who pay $1,000 in wages in a quarter for domestic services are subject also. Still not mandatorily covered are self-employed, unpaid family workers, and those employed by churches and some small nonprofit organizations.)

The **work/wage data include** (state total, lowest county and highest county included here):

Civilian labor force for 2004. Texas, 10,978,591; Loving County, 54; Harris County, 1,910,415.

Unemployed: The average unemployment rate (percentage of workforce) for 2004. Texas, 5.9; Hartley County, 0.8; Presidio County, 19.2.

Total **Wages** paid in the **third quarter**, 2004. Texas, $87,087,119,404; Loving County $333,594; Harris County, $20,531,064,813.

Average Weekly Wage as of the third quarter of 2004. Texas, $719.22; Real County, $330.72; Carson County, $969.86.

Property Values: Appraised gross market value of real and personal property in each county appraisal district in 2003 as reported to the State Property Tax Board.

Retail Sales: Figures for 2003 as reported to the state Comptroller of Public Accounts.

Railroad Abbreviations

AAT	Austin Area Terminal Railroad
AGC	Alamo Gulf Coast Railway Co.
ATK	AMTRAK
ANR	Angelina & Neches River Railroad Co.
ATCX	Austin & Texas Central Railroad
BLR	Blacklands Railroad
BNSF	Burlington Northern Santa Fe Railroad Co.
BOP	Border Pacific Railroad Co.
BRG	Brownsville & Rio Grande Int'l Railroad Co.
CMC	CMC Railroad, Inc.
DART	Trinity Railway Express
DGNO	Dallas, Garland & Northeastern Railroad
FWWR	Fort Worth & Western Railroad/Tarantula
GCSR	Gulf, Colorado & San Saba RailwayCorp.
GRR	Georgetown Railroad Co.
GVSR	Galveston Railroad, L.P.
KCS	Kansas City Southern Railway Co.
KRR	Kiamichi Railroad Company, Inc.
MCSA	Moscow, Camden & San Augustine RR Co.
PCN	Point Comfort & Northern Railway Co.
PNR	Panhandle Northern Railroad Company
PTRA	Port Terminal Railroad Association
PVS	Pecos Valley Southern Railway Co., Inc.
RSS	Rockdale, Sandow & Southern Railroad Co.
RVSC	Rio Valley Switching
SAW	South Plains Switching LTD, Co.
SRN	Sabine River & Northern Railroad Company
SSC	Southern Switching Co. (Lone Star Railroad)
SW	Southwestern Shortline Railroad
TCT	Texas City Terminal Railway Co.
TIBR	Timber Rock Railroad, Inc.
TM	The Texas Mexican Railway Company
TN	Texas & Northern Railway Co.
TNER	Texas Northeastern Railroad
TNMR	Texas & New Mexico Railroad
TNW	Texas North Western Railway Co.
TP	Texas Pacifico Transportation Co.
TSE	Texas South-Eastern Railroad Company
TXGN	Texas, Gonzales & Northern Railway Co.
TXR	Texas Rock Crusher Railway Co.
TSSR	Texas State Railroad
UP	Union Pacific Railroad Company
WTJR	Wichita, Tillman & Jackson Railway Co.
WTLR	West Texas & Lubbock Railroad Co. Inc.

Anderson County

Population	56,117
Change fm 2000	1.8
Area (sq. mi.)	1,077.95
Land Area (sq. mi.)	1,070.79
Altitude (ft.)	198-725
Rainfall (in.)	46.38
Jan. mean min.	37.4
July mean max.	93.9
Civ. Labor	19,912
Unemployed	4.6
Wages	$124,590,386
Av. Weekly Wage	$571.11
Prop. Value	$2,347,736,874
Retail Sales	$3,332,193,155

Physical Features: Forested, hilly East Texas county, slopes to Trinity and Neches rivers; sandy, clay, black soils; pines, hardwoods.

Economy: Manufacturing, distribution, agribusiness, tourism; hunting and fishing leases; prison units.

History: Comanche, Waco, other tribes. Anglo-American settlers arrived in 1830s. Antebellum slaveholding area. County created from Houston County in 1846; named for K.L. Anderson, last vice president of the Republic of Texas.

Race/Ethnicity, 2000: (In percent) Anglo, 63.45; Black, 23.60; Hispanic, 12.17; Other, 0.78.

Vital Statistics, 2003: Births, 610; deaths, 590; marriages, 402; divorces, 295.

Recreation: Fishing, hunting, streams, lakes; dogwood trails; historic sites; railroad park; museum. Tourist information at 1890 depot.

Minerals: Oil and gas.

Agriculture: Cattle, hay, truck vegetables, melons, pecans, peaches. Market value $23.1 million. Timber sold.

PALESTINE (17,358), county seat; clothing, metal, wood products; transportation and agribusiness center; scientific balloon station; historic bakery; library; vocational-technical facilities; hospitals; community college; dulcimer festival in March, hot pepper festival in October.

Other towns include: **Cayuga** (137); **Elkhart** (1,211); **Frankston** (1,202); **Montalba** (110); **Neches** (175); and **Tennessee Colony** (300) site of state prisons.

For explanation of sources, abbreviations and symbols, see p. 167 and foldout map.

Trees provide shade to the cemetery in Andrews. Texas Almanac photo.

Andrews County

Population **12,840**
Change fm 2000 ....-1.3
Area (sq. mi.) 1,500.99
Land Area (sq. mi.) 1,500.64
Altitude (ft.) 2,900-3,500
Rainfall (in.) 15.15
Jan. mean min. 30.4
July mean max. 94.5
Civ. Labor 5,764
Unemployed 3.9
Wages $35,888,136
Av. Weekly Wage $607.26
Prop. Value $1,975,491,370
Retail Sales $84,996,897

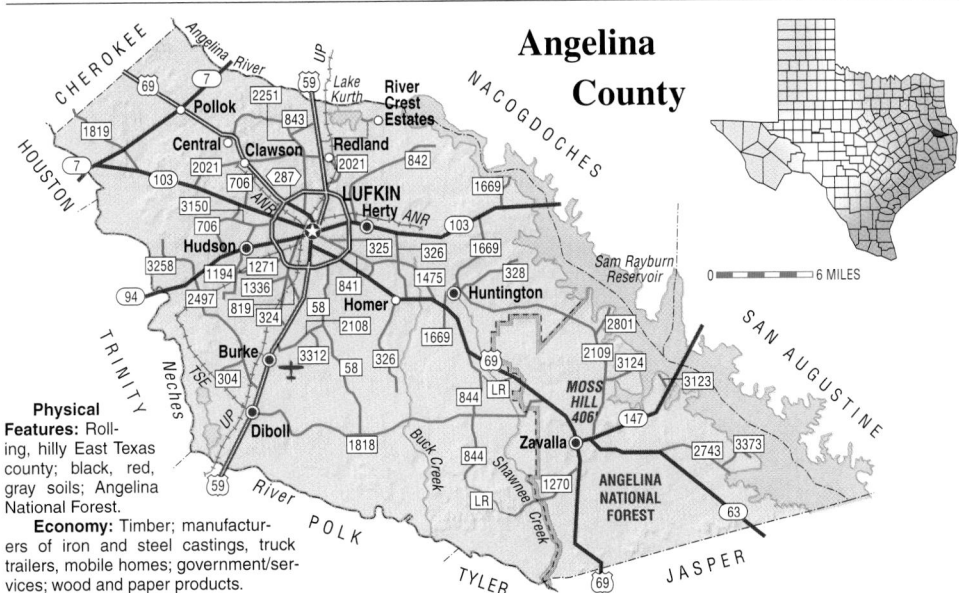

Physical Features:
South Plains, drain to playas; grass, mesquite, shin
oak; red clay, sandy soils.

Economy: Oil; manu-
facturing; govern-
ment/services;
agribusiness.

History: Apache,
Comanche area until
U.S. Army campaigns of
1875. Ranching developed around
1900. Oil boom in 1940s. County created 1876 from Bexar Territory; orga-

nized 1910; named for Texas
Revolutionary soldier Richard
Andrews.

Race/Ethnicity, 2000:
(In percent) Anglo, 57.07;
Black, 1.62; Hispanic, 40.00;
Other, 1.31.

Vital Statistics, 2003: Births,
204; deaths, 108; marriages, 99;
divorces, 56.

Recreation: Prairie dog town;
museum; camper facilities; Fall Fiesta in
September.

Minerals: Oil and gas.

Agriculture: Beef cattle, cotton,
sorghums, grains, corn, hay; significant
irrigation. Market value $8.7 million.

ANDREWS (9,527) county seat;
trade center, amphitheatre, hospital.

Angelina County

**Physical
Features:** Roll-
ing, hilly East Texas
county; black, red,
gray soils; Angelina
National Forest.

Economy: Timber; manufacturers of iron and steel castings, truck
trailers, mobile homes; government/ser-
vices; wood and paper products.

History: Caddoan area. First land
deed to Vicente Micheli 1801. Anglo-
American settlers arrived in 1820s.
County created 1846 from Nacogdo-
ches County; named for legendary
Indian maiden Angelina.

Race/Ethnicity, 2000: (In percent)
Anglo, 69.87; Black, 14.78; Hispanic,
14.35; Other, 1.00.

Vital Statistics, 2003: Births,
1,261; deaths, 797; marriages, 767;
divorces, 482.

Recreation: Sam Rayburn Reservoir; national, state forests, parks; loco-
motive exhibit; Forest Festival, bike ride
in fall.

Minerals: Limited output of natural
gas and oil.

Agriculture: Poultry, beef, landscape horticulture, limited fruits and
vegetables. Market value $18.4 million.
A leading timber-producing county.

LUFKIN (33,235) county seat; man-
ufacturing; Angelina College; hospitals;
U.S., Texas Forest centers; zoo; Expo
Center and Texas Forestry Museum.

Other towns include: **Burke** (317);
Diboll (5,488); **Hudson** (3,928); **Huntington** (2,080); **Pollok** (300); **Zavalla**
(665).

Population **81,492**
Change from 2000 .... 1.7
Area (sq. mi.) 864.45
Land Area (sq. mi.) 801.56
Altitude (ft.) 139-406
Rainfall (in.) 46.62
Jan. mean min. 37.9
July mean max. 93.5
Civ. Labor 38,400
Unemployed 6.9
Wages $264,304,143
Av. Weekly Wage $565.35
Prop. Value $3,604,412,294
Retail Sales $828,452,977

Aransas County

Physical Features: Coastal plains; sandy loam, coastal clays; bays, inlets; mesquites, oaks.

Economy: Tourism, recreational fishing, commercial shrimping; oil refining; agriculture, offshore equipment fabricated; carbon plant.

History: Karankawa, Coahuiltecan area. Settlement by Irish and Mexicans began in 1829. County created 1871 from Refugio County; named for Rio Nuestra Señora de Aranzazu, derived from a Spanish palace.

Race/Ethnicity, 2000: (In percent) Anglo, 74.72; Black, 1.53; Hispanic, 20.32; Other, 3.43.

Vital Statistics, 2003: Births, 266; deaths, 263; marriages, 305; divorces, 105.

Recreation: Fishing, waterfowl hunting; Fulton Mansion; state marine lab; state park; Texas Maritime Museum; bird sanctuaries (a nationally known birding hotspot); Rockport art center.

Minerals: Oil and gas, also oystershell and sand.

Agriculture: Cotton, cow-calf operations. Market value negligible. Fishing; redfish hatchery.

ROCKPORT (8,261) county seat; tourism, commercial, sport fishing; commuting to Corpus Christi and Victoria; retirement residences; Festival of Wines in May.

Fulton (1,648) Oysterfest in March.

Part [867] of **Aransas Pass**.

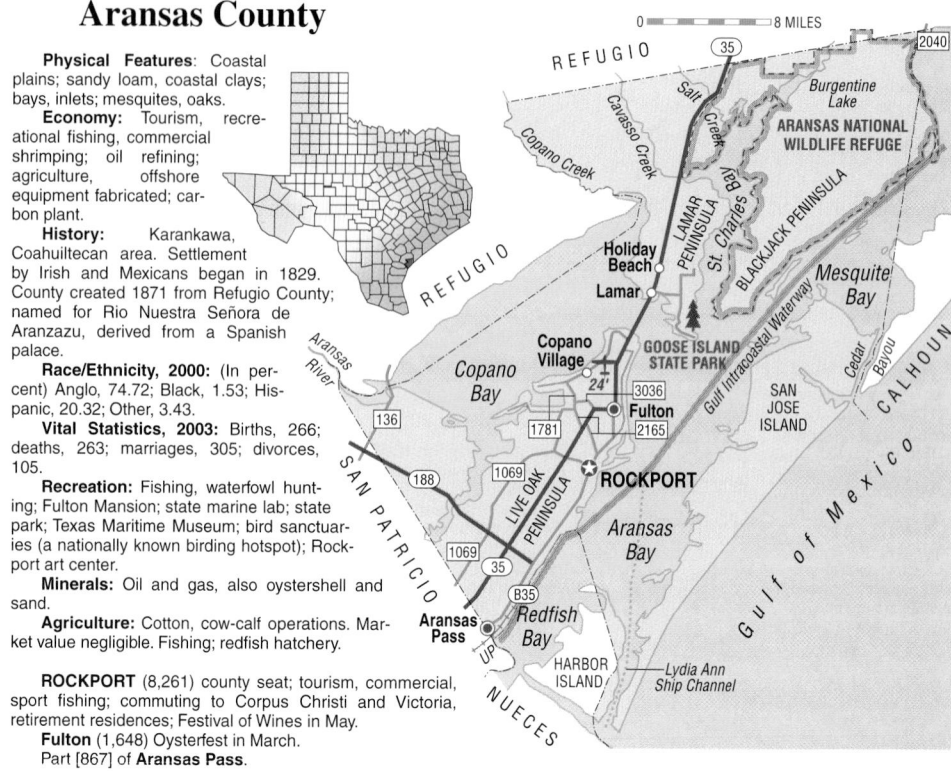

Population **24,041**	Rainfall (in.) 35.96	Wages $33,300,619
Change fm 2000 .... 6.9	Jan. mean min. 44.9	Av. Weekly Wage $444.41
Area (sq. mi.) 527.95	July mean max 90.1	Prop. Value $1,727,485,066
Land Area (sq. mi.) 251.86	Civ. Labor 10,792	Retail Sales $237,919,373
Altitude (ft.) .... sea level-24	Unemployed 8.7	

Sailboats in a Rockport marina, in Aransas County. Texas Almanac photo.

Archer County

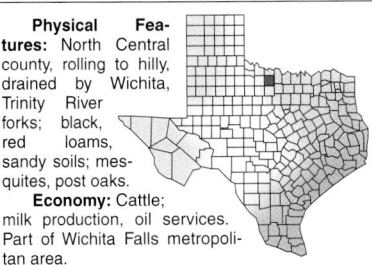

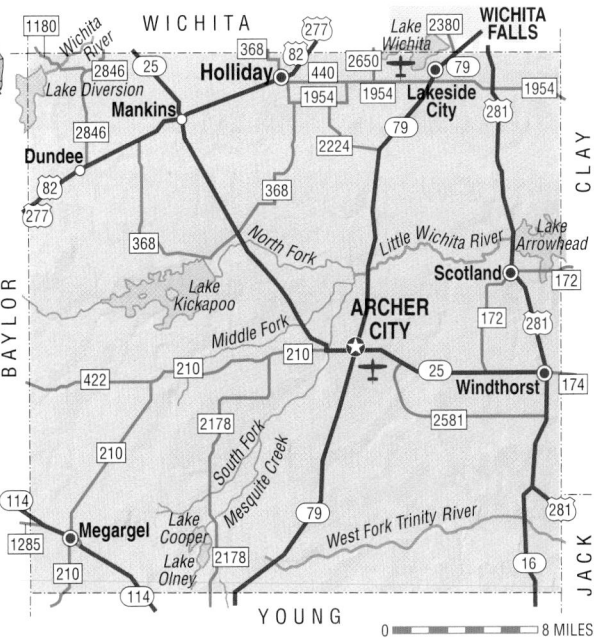

Physical Features: North Central county, rolling to hilly, drained by Wichita, Trinity River forks; black, red loams, sandy soils; mesquites, post oaks.

Economy: Cattle; milk production, oil services. Part of Wichita Falls metropolitan area.

History: Caddo, Comanche, Kiowas and other tribes in area until 1875; Anglo-American settlement developed soon afterward. County created from Fannin Land District, 1858; organized 1880. Named for Dr. B.T. Archer, Republic commissioner to United States.

Race/Ethnicity, 2000: (In percent) Anglo, 94.19; Black, 0.15; Hispanic, 4.87; Other, 0.79.

Vital Statistics, 2003: Births, 116; deaths, 67; marriages, 48; divorces, 38.

Recreation: Lakes; hunting of dove, quail, deer, feral hog, coyote.

Minerals: Oil and natural gas.

Agriculture: Dairy, cow/calf, stocker cattle; swine; poultry; wheat, cotton. Market value $58 million.

ARCHER CITY (1,897) county seat; cattle, oil field service center; museum; book center; some manufacturing.

Other towns include: **Holliday** (1,683) Mayfest in spring; **Lakeside City** (1,028); **Megargel** (257); **Scotland** (468); **Windthorst** (474), biannual German sausage festival (also in Scotland).

Population 9,274	
Change fm 2000 .... 4.7	
Area (sq. mi.) 925.78	
Land Area (sq. mi.) 909.70	

Altitude (ft.) 900-1,286		Unemployed 2.5	
Rainfall (in.) 29.78		Wages $12,809,013	
Jan. mean min. 26.7		Av. Weekly Wage $430.08	
July mean max 97.0		Prop. Value $560,119,129	
Civ. Labor 4,444		Retail Sales $45,101,362	

Armstrong County

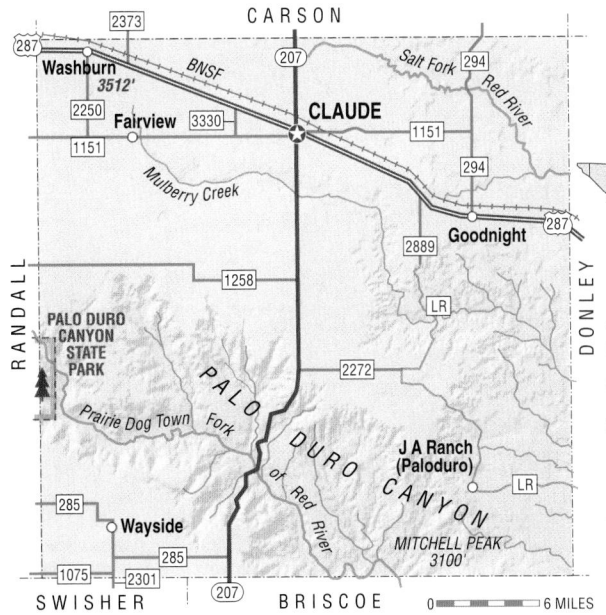

Physical Features: Partly on High Plains, broken by Palo Duro Canyon. Chocolate loam, gray soils.

Economy: Agribusiness, tourism.

History: Apache, then Comanche territory until U.S. Army campaigns of 1874-75. Anglo-Americans began ranching soon afterward. County created from Bexar District, 1876; organized 1890; name honors pioneer Texas family.

Race/Ethnicity, 2000: (In percent) Anglo, 94.00; Black, 0.23; Hispanic, 5.40; Other, 0.37.

Vital Statistics, 2003: Births, 19; deaths, 26; marriages, 18; divorces, 6.

Recreation: Caprock Roundup in July, state park; Goodnight Ranch Home.

Minerals: Sand, gravel.

Agriculture: Stocker cattle, cow-calf operations; wheat, sorghum, cotton and hay; some irrigation. Market value $26.6 million.

CLAUDE (1,272) county seat; farm, ranch supplies; glass company; medical center; Caprock Roundup.

Population 2,163	
Change fm 2000 .... 0.7	
Area (sq. mi.) 913.81	
Land Area (sq. mi.) 913.63	
Altitude (ft.) 2,300-3,512	
Rainfall (in.) 22.39	

Jan. mean min. 21.2		Av. Weekly Wage $467.54	
July mean max 90.5		Prop. Value $178,554,817	
Civ. Labor 1,024		Retail Sales $5,576,765	
Unemployed 2.0			
Wages $2,929,575			

For explanation of sources, abbreviations and symbls, see p. 167 and foldout page.

Atascosa County

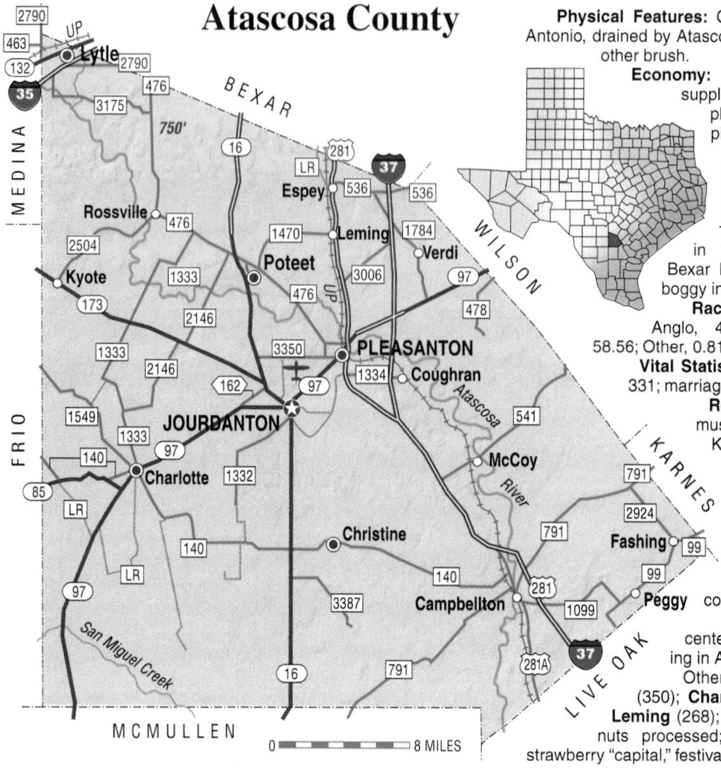

Physical Features: On grassy prairie south of San Antonio, drained by Atascosa River, tributaries; mesquites, other brush.

Economy: Peanut dryer/shellers; oil-well supplies; government/services; coal plant; light manufacturing, shipping.

History: Coahuiltecan Indians; later Apaches, Comanches in area. Families from Mexico established ranches in mid-1700s. Anglo-Americans arrived in 1840s. County created from Bexar District, 1856. Atascosa means boggy in Spanish.

Race/Ethnicity, 2000: (In percent) Anglo, 40.09; Black, 0.54; Hispanic, 58.56; Other, 0.81.

Vital Statistics, 2003: Births, 677; deaths, 331; marriages, 266; divorces, 70.

Recreation: Quail, deer hunting; museum; river park; theater group; Kactus Kick in May.

Minerals: Lignite, oil, gas.

Agriculture: Beef cattle; strawberries, peanuts, corn, milo, watermelons, wheat, winery. 25,000 acres irrigated. Market value $51.8 million.

JOURDANTON (4,059) county seat; hospital.

PLEASANTON (9,023) trading center; hospital; cowboy homecoming in August.

Other towns include: **Campbellton** (350); **Charlotte** (1,764); **Christine** (459); **Leming** (268); **Lytle** (2,535) greenhouse, peanuts processed; **Peggy** (22); **Poteet** (3,533) strawberry "capital," festival in April.

Population	42,696
Change frm 2000	10.5
Area (sq. mi.)	1,235.61
Land Area (sq. mi.)	1,232.12
Altitude (ft.)	200-750
Rainfall (in.)	29.00
Jan. mean min.	39.0
July mean max.	95.9
Civ. Labor	18,363
Unemployed	5.4
Wages	$59,091,980
Av. Weekly Wage	$520.44
Prop. Value	$1,642,558,745
Retail Sales	$324,089,066

'Old Pete,' the national mule memorial in Bailey County, is decorated for Christmas. File photo.

Austin County

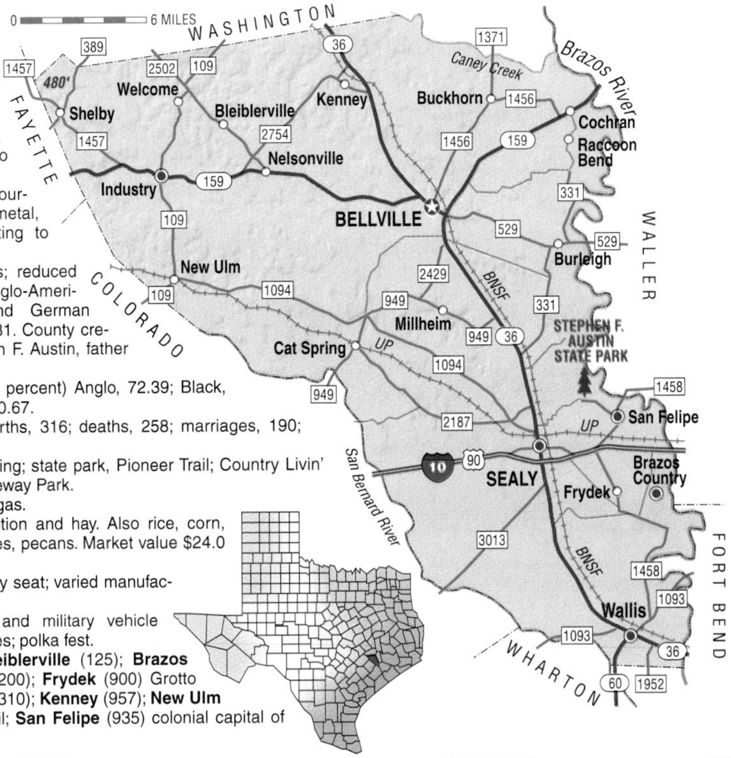

Physical Features: Southeast county; level to hilly, drained by San Bernard, Brazos rivers; black prairie to sandy upland soils.

Economy: Agribusiness; tourism, government/services; metal, other manufacturing; commuting to Houston.

History: Tonkawa Indians; reduced by diseases. Birthplace of Anglo-American colonization, 1821, and German mother colony at Industry, 1831. County created 1837; named for Stephen F. Austin, father of Texas.

Race/Ethnicity, 2000: (In percent) Anglo, 72.39; Black, 10.81; Hispanic, 16.13; Other, 0.67.

Vital Statistics, 2003: Births, 316; deaths, 258; marriages, 190; divorces, 98.

Recreation: Fishing, hunting; state park, Pioneer Trail; Country Livin' festival in May; Lone Star Raceway Park.

Minerals: Oil and natural gas.

Agriculture: Beef production and hay. Also rice, corn, sorghum, nursery crops, grapes, pecans. Market value $24.0 million.

BELLVILLE (3,948) county seat; varied manufacturing; hospital; oil.

SEALY (5,849) oil-field and military vehicle manufacturing, varied industries; polka fest.

Other towns include: **Bleiblerville** (125); **Brazos Country** (283); **Cat Spring** (200); **Frydek** (900) Grotto celebration in April; **Industry** (310); **Kenney** (957); **New Ulm** (974) retail, art festival in April; **San Felipe** (935) colonial capital of Texas; **Wallis** (1,304).

Population **25,800**	
Change fm 2000 ....9.4	
Area (sq. mi.) 656.37	
Land Area (sq. mi.) 652.59	
Altitude (ft.) 96-400	

Rainfall (in.) 40.68	Unemployed 3.7		
Jan. mean min. 40.7	Wages $75,357,719		
July mean max. 94.9	Av. Weekly Wage $648.48		
Civ. Labor 14,131	Prop. Value $2,155,921,058		
	Retail Sales $206,204,233		

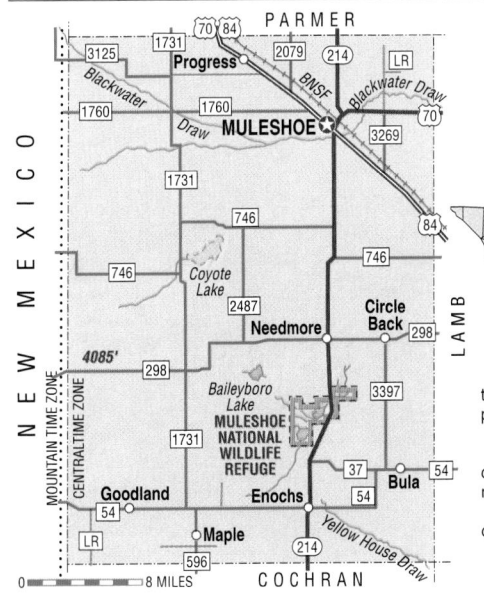

Bailey County

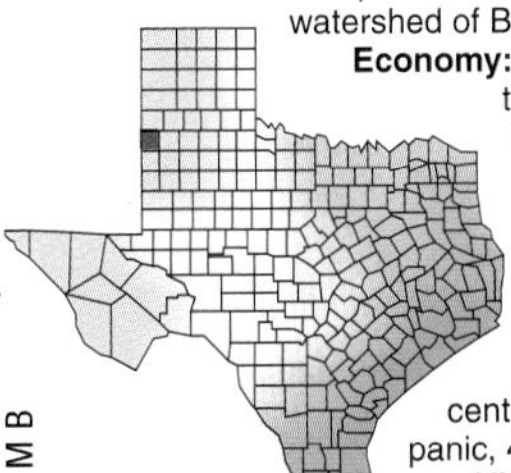

Physical Features: High Plains county, sandy loam soils; mesquite brush; drains to draws forming upper watershed of Brazos River, playas.

Economy: Farm supply manufacturing; electric generating plant; food-processing plants; muffler manufacturing.

History: Settlement began after 1900. County created from Bexar District 1876, organized 1917. Named for Alamo hero Peter J. Bailey.

Race/Ethnicity, 2000: (In percent) Anglo, 50.94; Black, 1.29; Hispanic, 47.30; Other, 0.47.

Vital Statistics, 2003: Births, 123; deaths, 63; marriages, 55; divorces, 17.

Recreation: Muleshoe National Wildlife Refuge; "Old Pete," the national mule memorial; outdoor drama; historical building park; museum; motorcycle rally; pheasant hunting.

Minerals: Insignificant.

Agriculture: Feedlot, dairy cattle; cotton, wheat, sorghum, corn, vegetables; 100,000 acres irrigated. Market value $127.8 million.

MULESHOE (4,425) county seat; agribusiness center; feed-corn milling; hospital; livestock show.

Other towns include: **Enochs** (80); **Maple** (75).

Population **6,662**	
Change fm 2000 .... 1.0	
Area (sq. mi.) 827.38	
Land Area (sq. mi.) 826.69	
Altitude (ft.)........................ 3,700-4,085	

Rainfall (in.) 17.37	Wages $15,423,440		
Jan. mean min. 20.2	Av. Weekly Wage.................. $455.96		
July mean max. 91.9	Prop. Value $341,363,557		
Civ. Labor 3,814	Retail Sales $62,113,932		
Unemployed 5.2			

For explanation of sources, abbreviations and symbols, see p. 167 and foldout page.

Bandera County

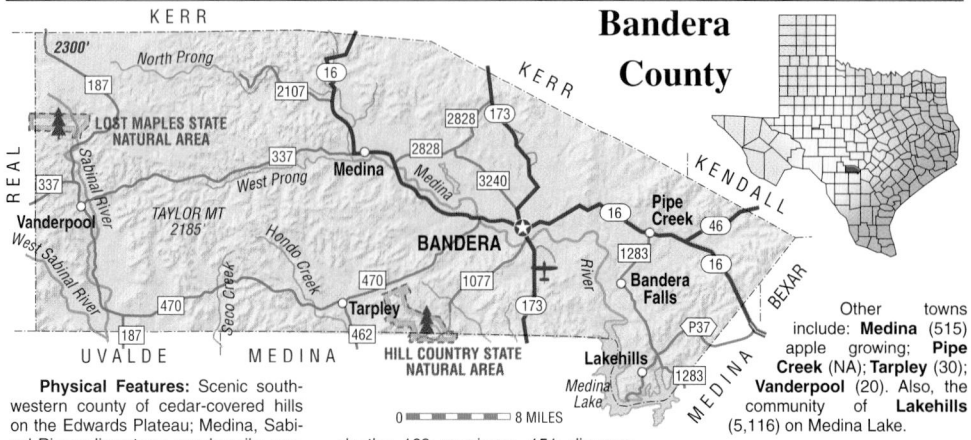

Physical Features: Scenic southwestern county of cedar-covered hills on the Edwards Plateau; Medina, Sabinal Rivers; limestone, sandy soils; species of oaks, walnuts, native cherry and Uvalde maple.

Economy: Tourism, hunting, fishing, ranching supplies, forest products.

History: Apache, then Comanche territory. White settlement began in early 1850s, including Mormons and Poles. County created from Bexar, Uvalde counties, 1856; named for Bandera (flag) Mountains.

Race/Ethnicity, 2000: (In percent) Anglo, 85.03; Black, 0.35; Hispanic, 13.51; Other, 1.11.

Vital Statistics, 2003: Births, 185; deaths, 169; marriages, 151; divorces, 84.

Recreation: RV parks, resort ranches; Lost Maples and Hill Country State Natural Areas; rodeo on Memorial Day weekend; apple festival in July; Medina Lake.

Agriculture: Beef cattle, sheep, goats, horses, apples. Market value $7 million. Hunting and nature tourism important.

BANDERA (1,016) county seat; "cowboy capital of the world"; tourism, ranching, furniture making; Frontier Times Museum.

Other towns include: **Medina** (515) apple growing; **Pipe Creek** (NA); **Tarpley** (30); **Vanderpool** (20). Also, the community of **Lakehills** (5,116) on Medina Lake.

Population	19,754
Change fm 2000	12.0
Area (sq. mi.)	797.54
Land Area (sq. mi.)	791.73
Altitude (ft.)	1,064-2,300
Rainfall (in.)	35.78
Jan. mean min.	33.3
July mean max.	93.9
Civ. Labor	7,971
Unemployed	3.6
Wages	$14,111,124
Av. Weekly Wage	$422.69
Prop. Value	$1,541,256,787
Retail Sales	$83,222,772

Bastrop County

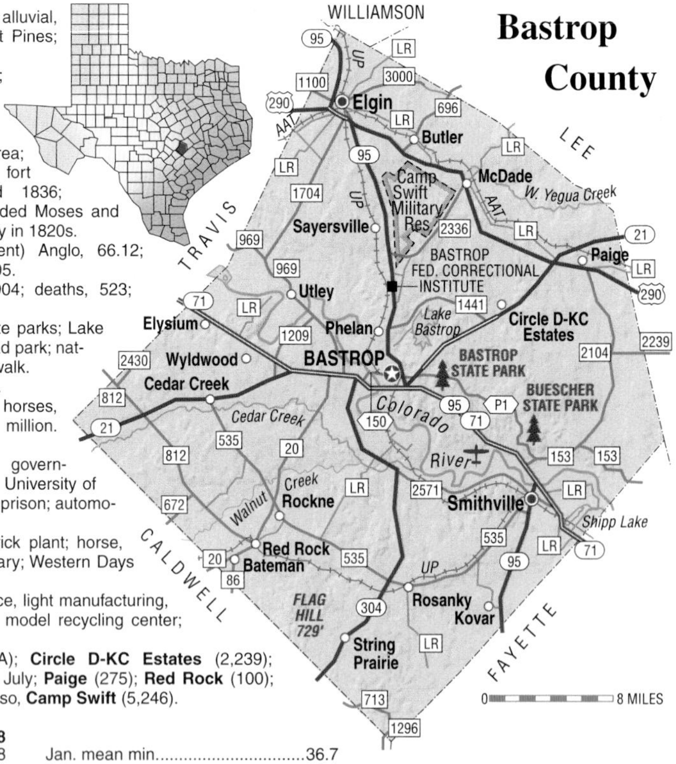

Physical Features: Rolling; alluvial, sandy, loam soils; varied timber, Lost Pines; bisected by Colorado River.

Economy: Government/services; tourism; agribusiness; bio-technology research; computer-related industries; commuters to Austin.

History: Tonkawa Indian area; Comanches also present. Spanish fort established 1804. County created 1836; named for Baron de Bastrop, who aided Moses and Stephen F. Austin in establishing colony in 1820s.

Race/Ethnicity, 2000: (In percent) Anglo, 66.12; Black, 8.85; Hispanic, 23.98; Other, 1.05.

Vital Statistics, 2003: Births, 904; deaths, 523; marriages, 415; divorces, 250.

Recreation: Fishing, hunting; state parks; Lake Bastrop; historic sites; museum; railroad park; natural science center; nature trails, riverwalk.

Minerals: Clay, oil, gas and lignite.

Agriculture: Hay; beef cattle; horses, goats; pecans. Market value $27.8 million. Pine for lumber, oak for firewood.

BASTROP (6,707) county seat; government/services, tourism, medical clinic; University of Texas cancer research center; federal prison; automobile museum; riverwalk.

Elgin (7,128) sausage plants, brick plant; horse, cattle breeding; medical research; library; Western Days in June, Hogeye festival in October.

Smithville (4,281) rail maintenance, light manufacturing, environmental science park; hospital, model recycling center; jamboree on weekend after Easterl.

Other towns: **Cedar Creek** (NA); **Circle D-KC Estates** (2,239); **McDade** (345) watermelon festival in July; **Paige** (275); **Red Rock** (100); **Rosanky** (210); **Wyldwood** (2,573). Also, **Camp Swift** (5,246).

Population		68,608
Change fm 2000		18.8
Area (sq. mi.)		895.92
Land Area (sq. mi.)		888.35
Altitude (ft.)		300-729
Rainfall (in.)		38.04
Jan. mean min.	36.7	
July mean max.	95.4	
Civ. Labor	31,892	
Unemployed	5.2	
Wages	$78,835,138	
Av. Weekly Wage		$532.75
Prop. Value		$4,361,517,196
Retail Sales		$579,151,260

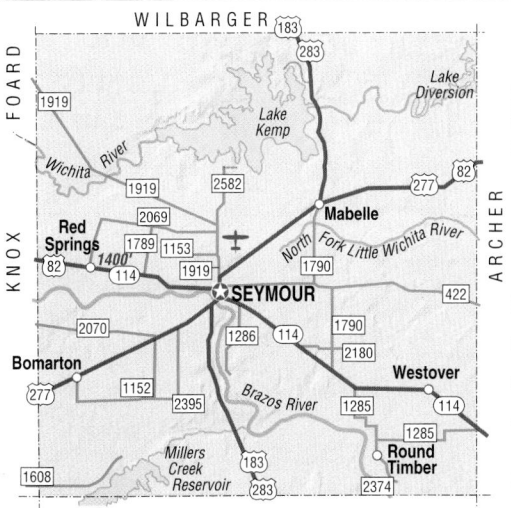

Baylor County

Physical Features: North Central county; level to hilly; drains to Brazos, Wichita rivers; sandy, loam, red soils; grassy, mesquites, cedars.

Economy: Agribusiness; retail/service; health services.

History: Comanches, with Wichitas and other tribes; removed in 1874-75. Anglo-Americans settled in the 1870s. County created from Fannin County 1858; organized 1879. Named for H.W. Baylor, Texas Ranger surgeon.

Race/Ethnicity, 2000: (In percent) Anglo, 86.22; Black, 3.40; Hispanic, 9.33; Other, 1.05.

Vital Statistics, 2003: Births, 52; deaths, 61; marriages, 29; divorces, 17.

Recreation: Lakes; hunting; park, pavilions; settlers reunion, fish day in spring, autumn leaves festival in October.

Minerals: Oil, gas produced.

Agriculture: Cattle, cow-calf operations; wheat, cotton, grain sorghum, hay. Market value $42.6 million.

SEYMOUR (2,873) county seat; agribusiness; hospital; dove hunters' breakfast in September.

Population...................................3,933	Rainfall (in.)................................27.79	
Change fm 2000 .... -3.9	Jan. mean min..................................27.7	Wages $6,354,659
Area (sq. mi.) 901.01	July mean max.............................96.5	Av. Weekly Wage $402,65
Land Area (sq. mi.) 870.77	Civ. Labor 1,814	Prop. Value....................$340,088,275
Altitude (ft.).........................1,053-1,400	Unemployed.....................................4.3	Retail Sales $28,992,403

Bee County

Physical Features: South Coastal Plain, level to rolling; black clay, sandy, loam soils; brushy.

Economy: Agriculture, government/services; hunting leases; oil and gas business.

History: Karankawa, Apache, Pawnee territory. First Spanish land grant, 1789. Irish settlers arrived 1826-29. County created from Karnes, Live Oak, Goliad, Refugio, San Patricio, 1857; organized 1858; named for Gen. Barnard Bee.

Race/Ethnicity, 2000: (In percent) Anglo, 35.53; Black, 9.79; Hispanic, 53.93; Other, 0.75.

Vital Statistics, 2003: Births, 358; deaths, 220; marriages, 173; divorces, 98.

Recreation: Hunting, camping, historical sites, antiques; rodeo/roping events.

Minerals: Oil, gas produced.

Agriculture: Beef cattle, corn, cotton and grain sorghhum. Market value $19.5 million. Hunting leases.

BEEVILLE (13,448) county seat; retail center; prison units, training academy; Costal Bend College; hospital, art museum; Diez y Seis festival in September.

Other towns and places include: **Blue Berry Hill** (962); **Mineral** (65); **Normanna** (126); **Pawnee** (202); **Pettus** (598); **Skidmore** (988); **Tuleta** (285); **Tynan** (301).

Population 33,046	Rainfall (in.) 33.48	
Change fm 2000..........................2.1	Jan. mean min...........................43.1	
Area (sq. mi.)........................880.31	July mean max. 94.6	
Land Area (sq. mi.)...................880.14	Civ. Labor...............................10,725	
Altitude (ft.) 87-500	Unemployed 6.4	
	Wages $51,692,582	
	Av. Weekly Wage.................$498.66	
	Prop. Value...............$1,047,679,490	
	Retail Sales $171,270,077	

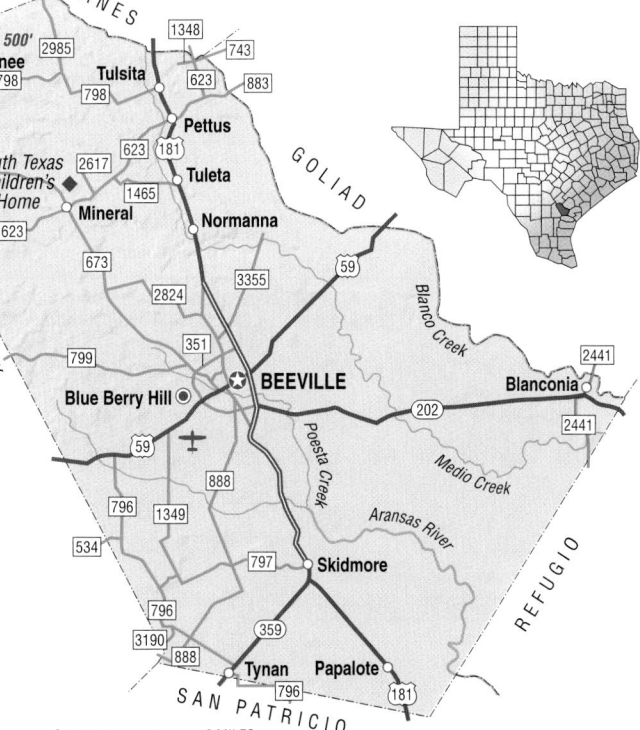

Bell County

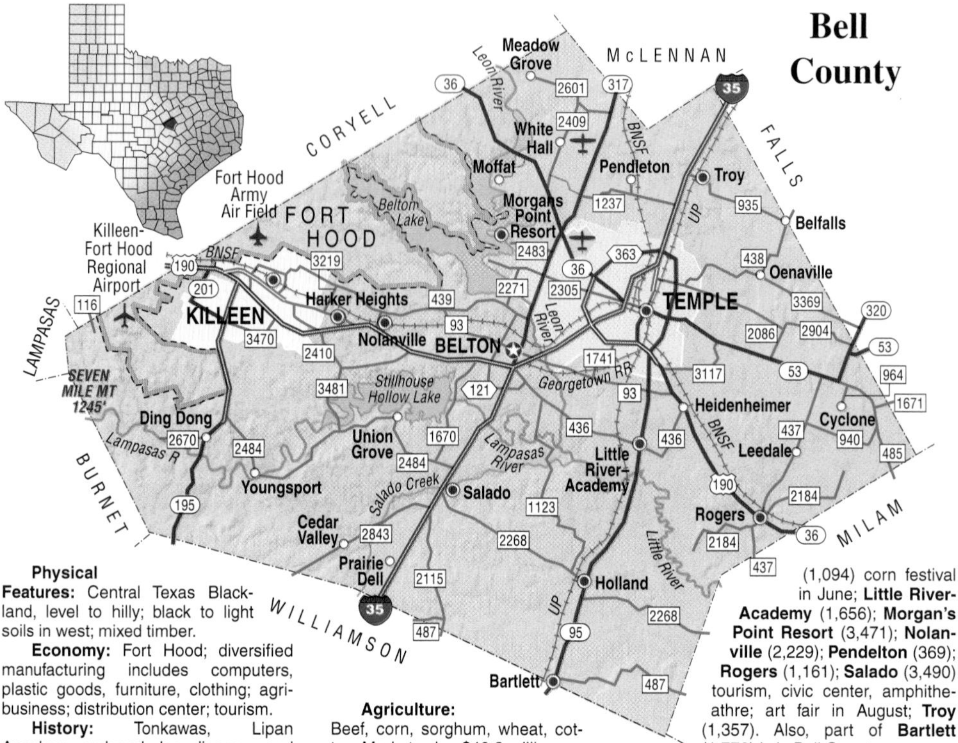

[Map of Bell County showing cities and roads including Meadow Grove, White Hall, Moffat, Pendleton, Troy, Belfalls, Morgans Point Resort, Fort Hood, Fort Hood Army Air Field, Killeen-Fort Hood Regional Airport, Killeen, Harker Heights, Nolanville, Belton, Temple, Oenaville, Heidenheimer, Cyclone, Leedale, Stillhouse Hollow Lake, Ding Dong, Union Grove, Little River-Academy, Rogers, Youngsport, Salado, Cedar Valley, Prairie Dell, Holland, Bartlett; counties McLennan, Coryell, Falls, Milam, Williamson, Lampasas, Burnet]

Physical

Features: Central Texas Blackland, level to hilly; black to light soils in west; mixed timber.

Economy: Fort Hood; diversified manufacturing includes computers, plastic goods, furniture, clothing; agribusiness; distribution center; tourism.

History: Tonkawas, Lipan Apaches; reduced by disease and advancing frontier by 1840s. Comanches raided into 1870s. Settled in 1830s as part of Robertson's colony. A few slaveholders in 1850s. County created from Milam County in 1850; named for Gov. P.H. Bell.

Race/Ethnicity, 2000: (In percent) Anglo, 58.38; Black, 20.93; Hispanic, 16.68; Other, 4.01.

Vital Statistics, 2003: Births, 5,763; deaths, 1,619; marriages, 3,896; divorces, 1,664.

Recreation: Fishing, hunting; lakes; historic sites; exposition center; Salado gathering of Scottish clans in November.

Minerals: Gravel.

Agriculture:
Beef, corn, sorghum, wheat, cotton. Market value $40.8 million.

BELTON (15,244) county seat; University of Mary Hardin-Baylor; manufactures include school and office furniture, roofing felt, athletic equipment; museum, nature center.

KILLEEN (96,858) Fort Hood; colleges; varied manufacturing; medical center; museums, planetarium.

TEMPLE (55,784) Major medical center with two hospitals and VA hospital; diversified industries; rail, wholesale distribution center; retail center; Temple College; Czech museum, early-day tractor, engine show in October.

Other towns include: **Harker Heights** (18,861) Founder's Day in October; **Heidenheimer** (224); **Holland** (1,094) corn festival in June; **Little River-Academy** (1,656); **Morgan's Point Resort** (3,471); **Nolanville** (2,229); **Pendelton** (369); **Rogers** (1,161); **Salado** (3,490) tourism, civic center, amphitheathre; art fair in August; **Troy** (1,357). Also, part of **Bartlett** (1,773) is in Bell County.

Fort Hood has a population of 32,667.

Population	250,324
Change fm 2000	5.2
Area (sq. mi.)	1,087.93
Land Area (sq. mi.)	1,059.72
Altitude (ft.)	400-1,245
Rainfall (in.)	35.81
Jan. mean min.	34.9
July mean max.	95.0
Civ. Labor	102,197
Unemployed	4.5
Wages	$678,096,191
Av. Weekly Wage	$579.05
Prop. Value	$9,558,215,517
Retail Sales	$3,597,647,731

A quiet part of the San Antonio Riverwalk. Texas Almanac photo.

Bexar County

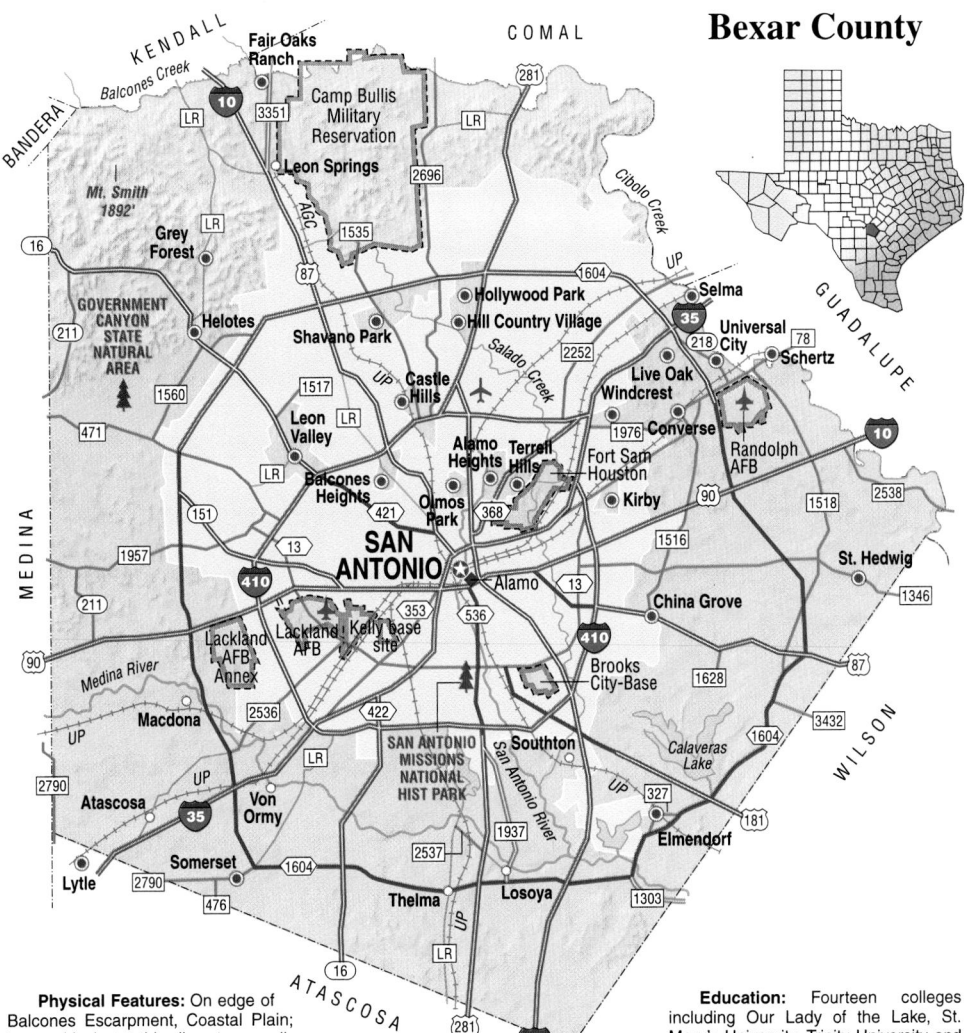

Physical Features: On edge of Balcones Escarpment, Coastal Plain; heavy black to thin limestone soils; spring-fed streams; underground water; mesquite, other brush.

Economy: Government center with large federal payroll, military bases; tourism second-largest industry; developing high-tech industrial park, research center; education center with 14 colleges.

History: Coahuiltecan Indian area; also Lipan Apaches and Tonkawas present. Mission San Antonio de Valero (Alamo) founded in 1718. Canary Islanders arrived in 1731. Anglo-American settlers began arriving in late 1820s. County created 1836 from Spanish municipality named for Duke de Bexar; a colonial capital of Texas.

Race/Ethnicity, 2000: (In percent) Anglo, 36.33; Black, 7.20; Hispanic, 54.35; Other, 2.12.

Vital Statistics, 2003: Births, 24,927; deaths, 10,409; marriages, 12,830; divorces, 5,215.

Recreation: Historic sites include the Alamo, other missions, Casa Navarro, La Villita; Riverwalk; El Mercado (market); Tower of the Americas;

Population	1,493,965
Change fm 2000	7.3
Area (sq. mi.)	1,256.66
Land Area (sq. mi.)	1,246.82
Altitude (ft.)	486-1,892
Rainfall (in.)	32.92
Jan. mean min.	38.6
July mean max.	94.6
Civ. Labor	727,319
Unemployed	5.1
Wages	$5,521,097,031
Av. Weekly Wage	$641.24
Fed. Wages	$347,876,629
Prop. Value	$63,751,774,849
Retail Sales	$18,738,485,426

Brackenridge Park; zoo; Seaworld; symphony orchestra; HemisFair Plaza; Fiesta in April; Institute of Texan Cultures; Folklife Festival in June; parks, museums; hunting, fishing.

Minerals: Gravel, sand, limestone, some oil & gas.

Agriculture: Nursery crops, hay, beef cattle, corn, grain sorghum, small grains, peanuts, vegetables; some irrigation. Market value $80.7 million.

Education: Fourteen colleges including Our Lady of the Lake, St. Mary's University, Trinity University and the University of Texas at San Antonio.

SAN ANTONIO (1,228,512) county seat; Texas' third largest city; varied manufacturing with emphasis on high-tech industries; other products include construction equipment, concrete and dairy products; industrial warehousing.

Other towns include: **Alamo Heights** (7,359); **Balcones Heights** (3,240); **Castle Hills** (4,136); **China Grove** (1,240); **Converse** (12,530); **Elmendorf** (685); **Fair Oaks Ranch** (5,220); **Grey Forest** (416) **Helotes** (5,483); **Hill Country Village** (1,061); **Hollywood Park** (3,231); **Kirby** (8,884); **Leon Valley** (9,949); **Live Oak** (9,876); **Macdona** (297); **Olmos Park** (2,303); **St. Hedwig** (1,931); **Selma** (1,791, parts in Guadalupe and Comal counties); **Shavano Park** (2,745); **Somerset** (1,688); **Terrell Hills** (5,034); **Universal City** (15,317); **Windcrest** (5,108). Part [1,045] of **Schertz** (24,336).

For explanation of sources, abbreviations and symbols, see p. 167 and foldout map.

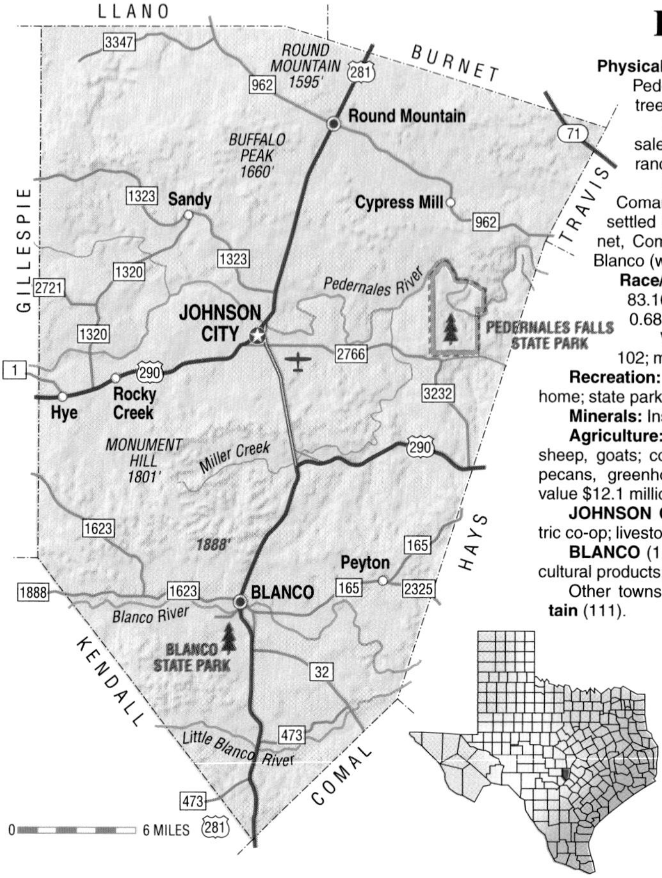

Blanco County

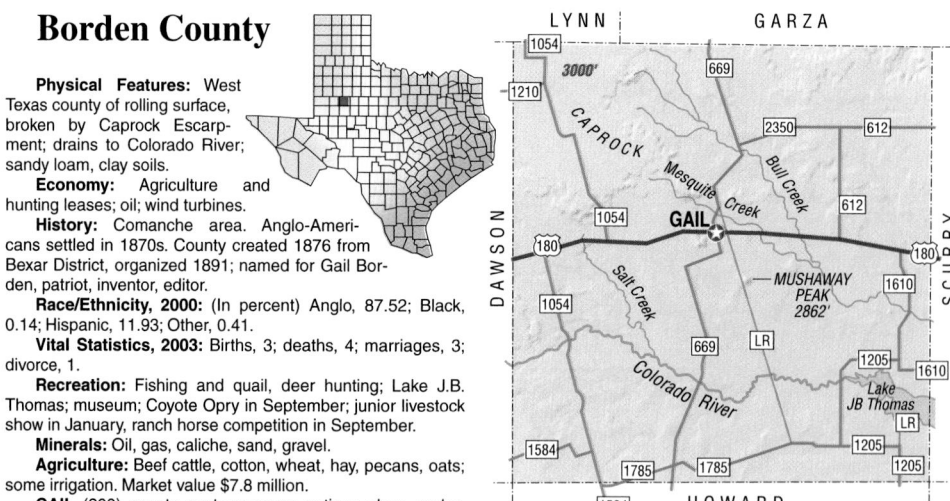

Physical Features: Hill Country county; Blanco, Pedernales rivers; cedars, pecans, other trees.

Economy: Tourism, agribusiness/wholesale nursery, livestock-trailer manufacturing, ranch supplies, hunting/fishing.

History: Lipan Apache area. Comanches present when Anglo-Americans settled in 1850s. County created 1858 from Burnet, Comal, Gillespie, Hays counties; named for Blanco (white) River.

Race/Ethnicity, 2000: (In percent), Anglo, 83.16; Black, 0.84; Hispanic, 15.32; Other, 0.68.

Vital Statistics, 2003: Births, 79; deaths, 102; marriages, 74; divorces, 42.

Recreation: President Lyndon B. Johnson's boyhood home; state parks; hunting, fishing; scenic drives.

Minerals: Insignificant.

Agriculture: Cow-calf operation, stocker cattle; sheep, goats; coastal hay, vegetables, wheat, peaches, pecans, greenhouse nursery; limited irrigation. Market value $12.1 million.

JOHNSON CITY (1,294) county seat; tourism; electric co-op; livestock center.

BLANCO (1,584) tourism; ranch supply center; horticultural products; nature trail; classic car show in May.

Other towns include: **Hye** (105) and **Round Mountain** (111).

Population	9,101
Change fm 2000	8.1
Area (sq. mi.)	713.41
Land Area (sq. mi.)	711.24
Altitude (ft.)	800–1,888
Rainfall (in.)	34.75
Jan. mean min.	34.0
July mean max.	93.7
Civ. Labor	4,222
Unemployed	3.3
Wages	$18,389,123
Av. Weekly Wage	$554.07
Prop. Value	$1,997,729,317
Retail Sales	$46,310,094

Borden County

Physical Features: West Texas county of rolling surface, broken by Caprock Escarpment; drains to Colorado River; sandy loam, clay soils.

Economy: Agriculture and hunting leases; oil; wind turbines.

History: Comanche area. Anglo-Americans settled in 1870s. County created 1876 from Bexar District, organized 1891; named for Gail Borden, patriot, inventor, editor.

Race/Ethnicity, 2000: (In percent) Anglo, 87.52; Black, 0.14; Hispanic, 11.93; Other, 0.41.

Vital Statistics, 2003: Births, 3; deaths, 4; marriages, 3; divorce, 1.

Recreation: Fishing and quail, deer hunting; Lake J.B. Thomas; museum; Coyote Opry in September; junior livestock show in January, ranch horse competition in September.

Minerals: Oil, gas, caliche, sand, gravel.

Agriculture: Beef cattle, cotton, wheat, hay, pecans, oats; some irrigation. Market value $7.8 million.

GAIL (200) county seat; museum; antique shop, ambulance service; "star" construction atop Gail Mountain.

Population	683	Jan. mean min.	29.8	Prop. Value	$360,596,970
Change fm 2000	-6.3	July mean max.	94.6	Retail Sales	$185,193
Area (sq. mi.)	906.04	Civ. Labor	358		
Land Area (sq. mi.)	898.80	Unemployed	3.2		
Altitude (ft.)	2,258–3,000	Wages	$1,081,974		
Rainfall (in.)	19.68	Av. Weekly Wage	$495.41		

For explanation of sources, abbreviations and symbols, see p. 167 and foldout map.

Bosque County

Physical Features: North Central county; hilly, broken by Brazos, Bosque rivers; limestone to alluvial soils; cedars, oaks, mesquites.

Economy: Agribusiness, government/services, tourism, small industries.

History: Tonkawa, Waco and Tawakoni Indians. Settlers from England and Norway arrived in 1850s. County created 1854 from Milam District, McLennan County; named for Bosque (woods) River.

Race/Ethnicity, 2000: (In percent) Anglo, 85.10; Black, 2.02; Hispanic, 12.23; Other, 0.65.

Vital Statistics, 2003: Births, 201; deaths, 257; marriages, 117; divorces, 86.

Recreation: Lake, state park, museum at Clifton, conservatory of fine art; fishing, hunting; scenic routes, Norwegian smorgasbord at Norse in November.

Minerals: Limestone.

Agriculture: Cattle, hunting, wheat and oats, forages, turkeys, feed grains, horses. Market value $38 million.

MERIDIAN (1,522) county seat; distribution center; varied manufacturing.

CLIFTON (3,652) tourism; trade center; light manufacturing; hospital; library.

Other towns include: **Cranfills Gap** (340) Lutefisk dinner in December; **Iredell** (363); **Kopperl** (225); **Laguna Park** (550); **Morgan** (511); **Valley Mills** (1,171); **Walnut Springs** (775).

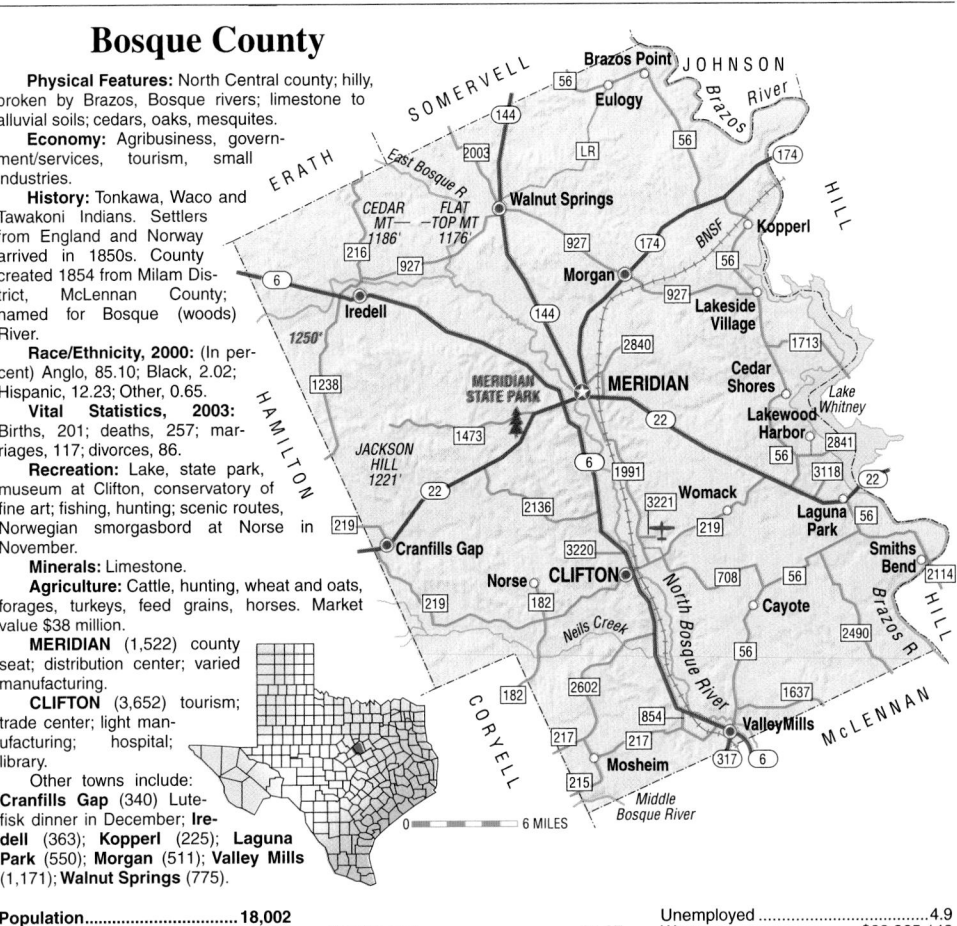

Population	18,002
Change fm 2000	4.6
Area (sq. mi.)	1,002.63
Land Area (sq. mi.)	989.18
Altitude (ft.)	450-1,250

Rainfall (in.)	35.07
Jan. mean min.	32.7
July mean max.	96.2
Civ. Labor	6,815

Unemployed	4.9
Wages	$23,365,142
Av. Weekly Wage	$471.12
Prop. Value	$1,552,893,437
Retail Sales	$76,780,281

Wind generators top the mesa along FM 669 between Gail and Post. Texas Almanac photo.

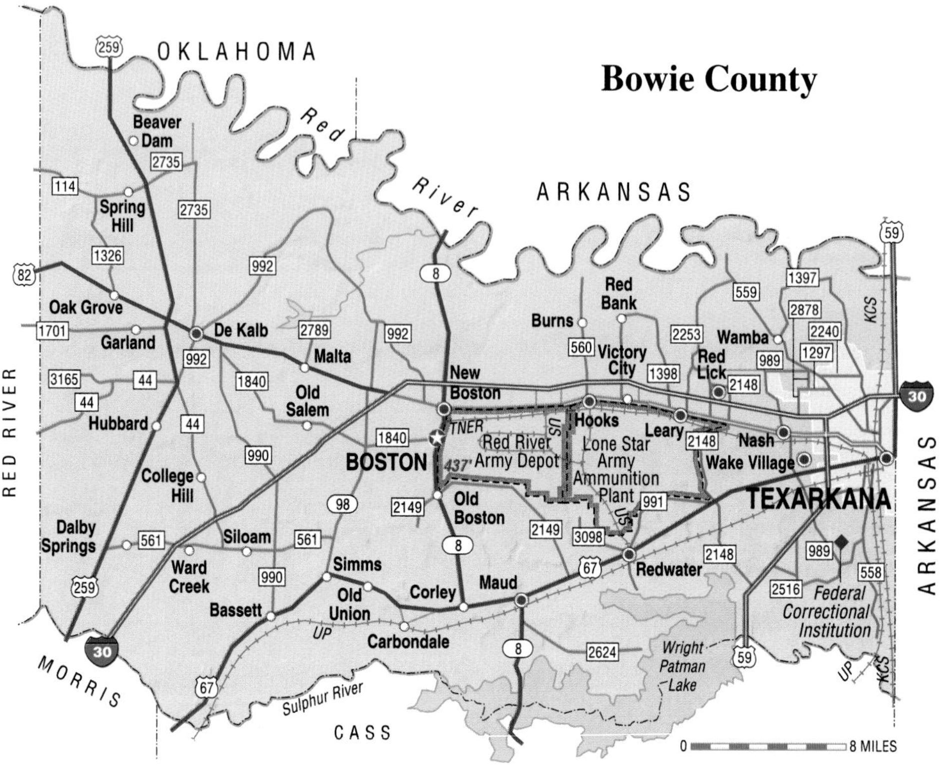

Bowie County

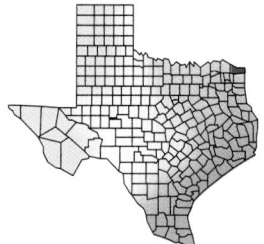

Physical Features: Forested hills at northeast corner of state; clay, sandy, alluvial soils; drained by Red and Sulphur rivers.

Economy: Government/services, lumber mills, manufacturing, agribusiness.

History: Caddo area, abandoned in 1790s after trouble with Osage tribe. Anglo-Americans began arriving 1815-20. County created 1840 from Red River County; named for Alamo hero James Bowie.

Race/Ethnicity, 2000: (In percent) Anglo, 70.83; Black, 23.58; Hispanic, 4.47; Other, 1.12.

Vital Statistics, 2003: Births, 1,123; deaths, 998; marriages, 580; divorces, 431.

Recreation: Lakes, Crystal Springs beach; hunting, fishing, historic sites; Four-States Fair in September, Red Neck Day in July, Octoberfest.

Minerals: Oil, gas, sand, gravel.

Agriculture: Beef cattle, hay, dairy, corn, soybeans, wheat, poultry, pecans, milo, rice, nurseries, truck crops, horses, goats. Market value $37.3 million. Pine timber, hardwoods, pulpwood harvested.

BOSTON (200) county seat (but courthouse now located in New Boston).

TEXARKANA (36,020 in Texas, 26,448 in Arkansas) rubber company, paper manufacturing, distribution; hospitals; tourism; colleges; federal correctional unit; Quadrangle Festival in September, Perot Theatre.

New Boston (4,682) site of county courthouse; steel manufactured; agribusiness; lumber mill; state prison unit; Pioneer Days in August.

Other towns include: **De Kalb** (1,731) agriculture, government/services, commuting to Texarkana, Oktoberfest; **Hooks** (2,896); **Leary** (583); **Maud** (996); **Nash** (2,251); **Red Lick** (867); **Redwater** (893); **Simms** (240); **Wake Village** (5,428).

For explanation of sources, abbreviations and symbols, see p. 167 and foldout map.

Population	90,248
Change fm 2000	1.1
Area (sq. mi.)	922.77
Land Area (sq. mi.)	887.87
Altitude (ft.)	200-437
Rainfall (in.)	51.24
Jan. mean min.	30.7
July mean max.	93.1
Civ. Labor	41,524
Unemployed	5.2
Wages	$292,794,601
Av. Weekly Wage	$576.99
Prop. Value	$3,805,966,845
Retail Sales	$1,097,401,620

Brazoria County

Physical Features: Flat Coastal Plain, coastal soils, drained by Brazos and San Bernard rivers.

Economy: Petroleum and chemical industry; fishing; tourism; agribusiness. Part of Houston metropolitan area.

History: Karankawa area. Part of Austin's "Old Three Hundred" colony of families arriving in early 1820s. County created 1836 from Municipality of Brazoria; name derived from Brazos River.

Race/Ethnicity, 2000: (In percent) Anglo, 66.09; Black, 8.58; Hispanic, 22.78; Other, 2.55.

Vital Statistics, 2003: Births, 4,295; deaths, 1,776; marriages, 1,534; divorces, 1,329.

Recreation: Water sports; fishing, hunting; wildlife refuges, historic sites; state and county parks; replica of the first capitol of the Republic of Texas at West Columbia.

Minerals: Oil, gas, sand, gravel.

Agriculture: Cattle, hay, rice, soybeans, sorghum, nursery, corn, cotton, aquaculture. 20,000 acres of rice irrigated. Market value $47.4 million.

ANGLETON (18,868) county seat; banking, distribution center for oil, chemical, agricultural area; fish-processing plant; hospital.

BRAZOSPORT (58,631) is a community of eight cities; chemical complex; deepwater seaport; commercial fishing; tourism; college; hospital; Brazosport cities include: **Clute** (10,878) mosquito festival in July, **Freeport** (12,995) fishing fiesta in July, **Jones Creek** (2,175), **Lake Jackson** (27,305) museum, sea center, **Oyster Creek** (1,252), **Quintana** (36), **Richwood** (3,199), **Surfside Beach** (791).

ALVIN (22,404) petrochemical processing; agribusiness; rail, trucking; junior college; hospital; Crawfest and Shrimp Boil in April.

PEARLAND (50,504, partly in Harris County) rail, trucking, oilfield, chemical production; commuting to Houston, NASA; community college.

Other towns include: **Bailey's Prairie** (739); **Bonney** (405); **Brazoria** (2,837) library; No-Name Festival in June; **Brookside Village** (2,076).

Also, **Damon** (542); **Danbury** (1,697); **Danciger** (357); **Hillcrest Village** (733); **Holiday Lakes** (1,143); **Iowa Colony** (861); **Liverpool** (419); **Manvel** (3,351); **Old Ocean** (915); **Rosharon** (NA); **Sandy Point** (250); **Sweeny** (3,703) petrochemicals, agriculture, grass farming, hospital, library, Pride Day in May, Levi Jordan Plantation; **West Columbia** (4,297) chemical companies; cattle, rice farming; museum, historic sites, plantation; San Jacinto Festival in April.

Population	271,130
Change fm 2000	12.1
Area (sq. mi.)	1,597.44
Land Area (sq. mi.)	1,386.40
Altitude (ft.)	sea level-146
Rainfall (in.)	57.24
Jan. mean min.	43.7
July mean max.	91.8
Civ. Labor	115,820
Unemployed	8.2
Wages	$680,504,344
Av. Weekly Wage	$693.34
Prop. Value	$18,427,094,300
Retail Sales	$2,320,622,458

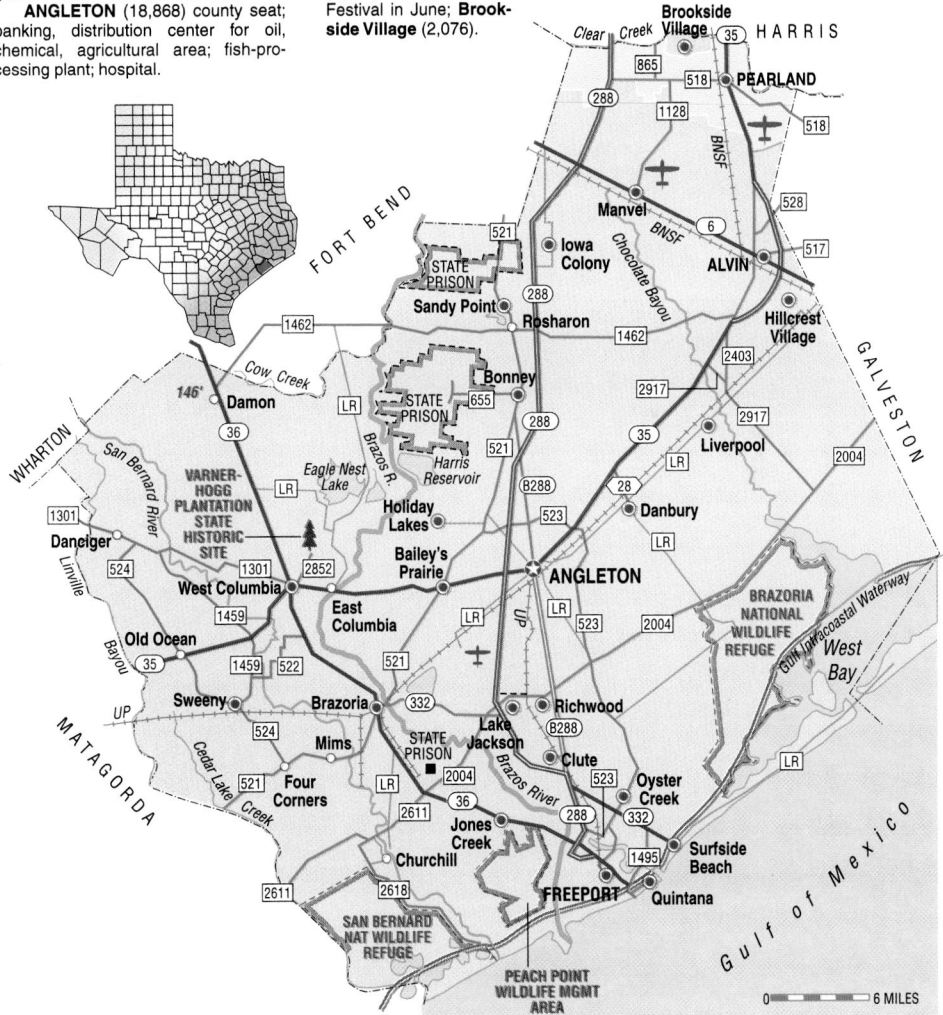

Brazos County

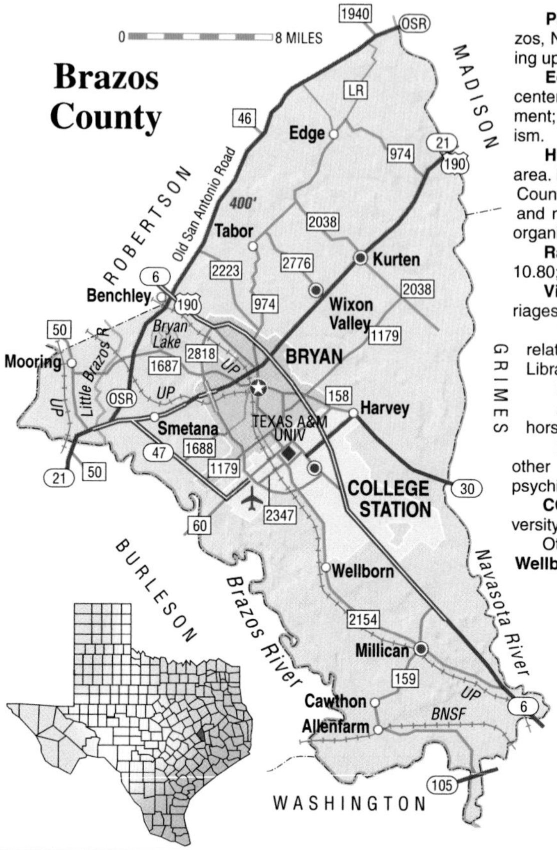

Physical Features: South Central county between Brazos, Navasota rivers; rich bottom soils, sandy, clays on rolling uplands; oak trees.

Economy: Texas A&M University; market and medical center; agribusiness; computers, research and development; government/services; winery; industrial parks; tourism.

History: Bidais and Tonkawas; Comanches hunted in area. Part of Stephen F. Austin's second colony, late 1820s. County created 1841 from Robertson, Washington counties and named Navasota; renamed for Brazos River in 1842, organized 1843.

Race/Ethnicity, 2000: (In percent) Anglo, 66.79; Black, 10.80; Hispanic, 17.88; Other, 4.53.

Vital Statistics, 2003: Births, 2,282; deaths, 843; marriages, 1,398; divorces, 255.

Recreation: Fishing, hunting; raceway; many events related to Texas A&M activities; George Bush Presidential Library and Museum; winery harvest weekends in August.

Minerals: Sand and gravel, lignite, gas, oil.

Agriculture: Cattle, eggs; cotton, hay, corn, sorghum; horses. Market value $47.1 million.

BRYAN (69,146) county seat; defense electronics, other varied manufacturing; agribusiness center; hospital; psychiatric facilities; Blinn College extension.

COLLEGE STATION (73,691) home of Texas A&M University, varied high-tech manufacturing; research; hospitals.

Other towns include: **Kurten** (233); **Millican** (110); **Wellborn** (100); **Wixon Valley** (229).

Population	156,275
Change fm 2000	2.5
Area (sq. mi.)	590.29
Land Area (sq. mi.)	585.78
Altitude (ft.)	197-400
Rainfall (in.)	39.67
Jan. mean min.	39.8
July mean max.	95.6
Civ. Labor	85,195
Unemployed	1.9
Wages	$533,209,124
Av. Weekly Wage	$534.77
Prop. Value	$7,169,567,233
Retail Sales	$1,853,879,939

Elephant and Cathedral Mountains in Brewster County from US 67. Texas Almanac photo.

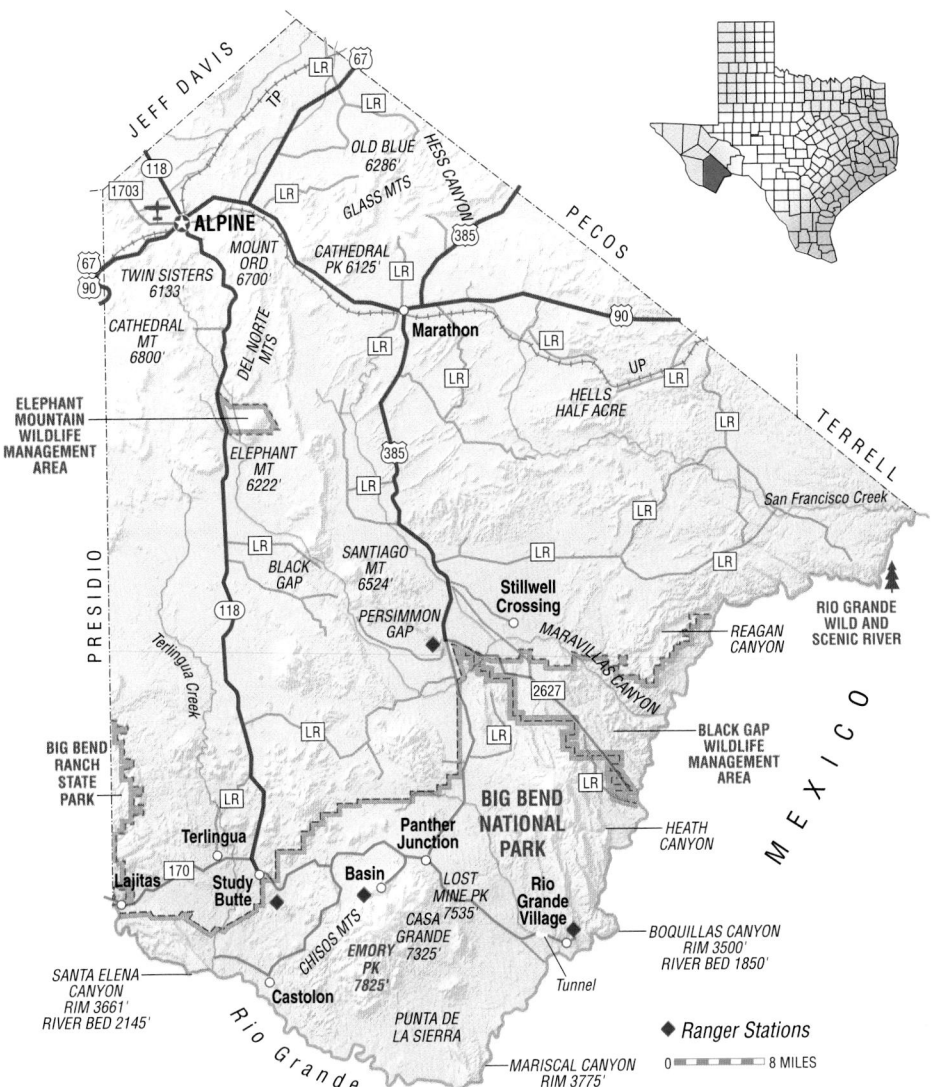

◆ *Ranger Stations*

0 ▬▬▬▬▬ 8 MILES

Brewster County

Physical Features: Largest county, with area slightly less than that of Connecticut plus Rhode Island; mountains, canyons, distinctive geology, plant life, animals.

Economy: Tourism, Sul Ross State University; ranching; government/services; retirement developments; hunting leases.

History: Pueblo culture had begun when Spanish explored in 1500s. Mescalero Apaches in Chisos; Comanches raided in area. Ranching developed in northern part 1880s; Mexican agricultural communites along river. County created 1887 from Presidio County; named for Henry P. Brewster, Republic secretary of war.

Race/Ethnicity, 2000: (In percent) Anglo, 54.08; Black, 1.12; Hispanic, 43.62; Other, 1.18.

Vital Statistics, 2003: Births, 138; deaths, 76; marriages, 67; divorces, 0.

Recreation: Big Bend National Park; Big Bend Ranch State Park; Rio Grande Wild and Scenic River; ghost towns; scenic drives; museum; rockhound areas; November chili cookoff at Terlingua; cavalry post, Barton Warnock Environmental Education Center at Lajitas; hunting.

Minerals: Bentonite.

Agriculture: Beef cattle, pecans, apples, hunting. Market value $5.2 million.

ALPINE (6,237) county seat; ranch trade center; tourism; Sul Ross State University; hospital; varied manufacturing.

Marathon (459) tourism, ranching center, Marathon Basin quilt show in October. Also, **Basin** (22) and **Study Butte-Terlingua** (280).

Population	**9,226**
Change fm 2000	4.1
Area (sq. mi.)	6,192.78
Land Area (sq. mi.)	6,192.61
Altitude (ft.)	1,700-7,825
Rainfall (in.) Alpine	17.19
Rainfall (in.) Big Bend	19.17
Jan. mean min. Alpine	31.3
Jan. mean min. Big Bend	36.1
July mean max. Alpine	88.7
July mean max. Big Bend	84.2
Civ. Labor	6,035
Unemployed	2.5
Wages	$32,291,040
Av. Weekly Wage	$511.62
Prop. Value	$562,631,482
Retail Sales	$76,336,776

For explanation of sources, abbreviations and symbols, see. p. 167 and foldout map.

Briscoe County

Physical Features: Partly on High Plains, broken by Caprock Escarpment, fork of Red River; sandy, loam soils.

Economy: Agribusiness, government/services.

History: Apaches, displaced by Comanches around 1700. Ranchers settled in 1880s. County created from Bexar District, 1876, organized 1892; named for Andrew Briscoe, Republic of Texas soldier.

Race/Ethnicity, 2000: (In percent) Anglo, 74.58; Black, 2.40; Hispanic, 22.74; Other, 0.28.

Vital Statistics, 2003: Births, 14; deaths, 21; marriages, 6; divorces, 2.

Recreation: Hunting, fishing; scenic drives; museum; state park, trailway, Mackenzie Reservoir.

Minerals: Insignificant.

Agriculture: Cotton, cow-calf, stocker cattle, sorghum, wheat, hay. Some 32,000 acres irrigated. Market value $14.6 million.

SILVERTON (847) county seat; agribusiness center; irrigation supplies manufactured; clinics.

Quitaque (428) trade center, agribusiness, nature tourism.

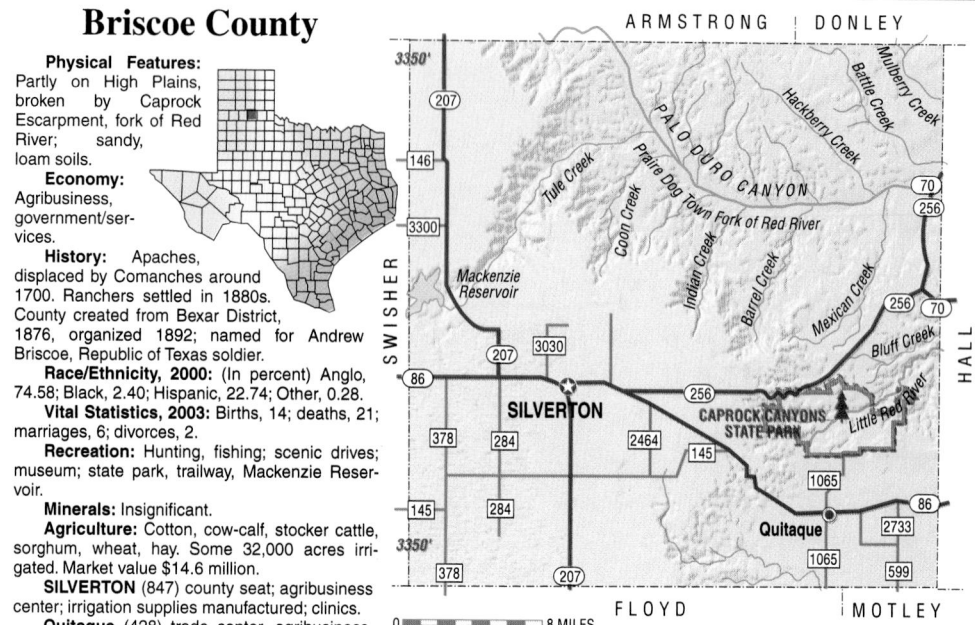

Population	1,716
Change fm 2000	-4.1
Area (sq. mi.)	901.59
Land Area (sq. mi.)	900.25
Altitude (ft.)	2,100-3,350
Rainfall (in.)	22.34
Jan. mean min.	21.6
July mean max.	90.9
Civ. Labor	653
Unemployed	4.3
Wages	$1,771,405
Av. Weekly Wage	$372.30
Prop. Value	$108,960,721
Retail Sales	$6,366,841

Caprock Canyons State Park in Briscoe County. *Texas Almanac photo.*

Brooks County

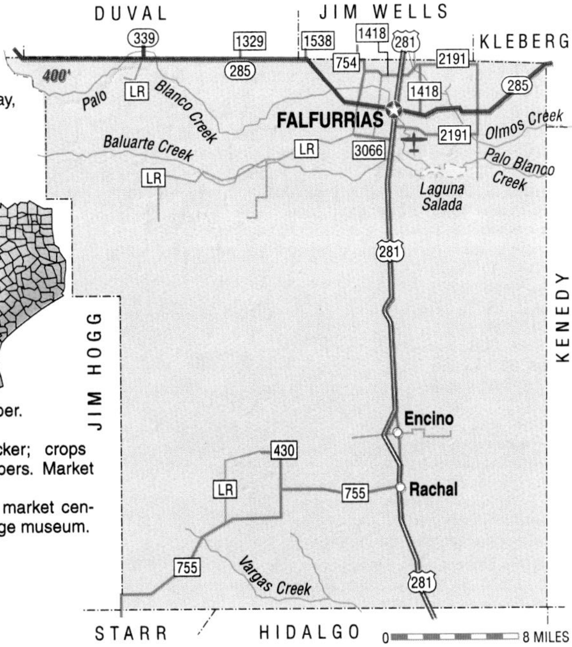

Physical Features: On Rio Grande plain; level to rolling; brushy; light to dark sandy loam soils.

Economy: Oil, gas, cattle, hunting leases, hay, watermelons.

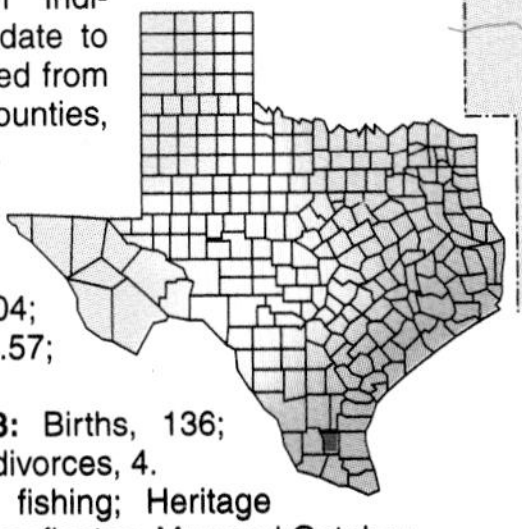

History: Coahuiltecan Indians. Spanish land grants date to around 1800. County created from Hidalgo, Starr, Zapata counties, 1911. Named for J.A. Brooks, Texas Ranger and legislator.

Race/Ethnicity, 2000: (In percent) Anglo, 8.04; Black, 0.06; Hispanic, 91.57; Other, 0.33.

Vital Statistics, 2003: Births, 136; deaths, 82; marriages, 73; divorces, 4.

Recreation: Hunting, fishing; Heritage Museum, Don Pedrito Shrine; fiestas, May and October.

Minerals: Oil, gas production.

Agriculture: Beef cow-calf operations, stocker; crops include hay, squash, watermelons, habanero peppers. Market value $7.6 million.

FALFURRIAS (5,208) county seat; agricultural market center, cattle, watermelons; government/services; heritage museum.

Other towns include: **Encino** (176).

Population	7,753
Change fm 2000	- 2.8
Area (sq. mi.)	943.61
Land Area (sq. mi.)	943.28
Altitude (ft.)	46-400
Rainfall (in.)	25.42
Jan. mean min.	43.9
July mean max.	97.0

Civ. Labor	3,423	Av. Weekly Wage	$442.86
Unemployed	7.8	Prop. Value	$779,174,504
Wages	$14,254,926	Retail Sales	$56,488,466

Brown County

Physical Features: Rolling, hilly; drains to Colorado River; varied soils, timber.

Economy: Manufacturing plants, distribution center; government/services; agribusiness.

History: Apaches; displaced by Comanches who were removed by U.S. Army in 1874-75. Anglo-Americans first settled in mid-1850s. County created 1856 from Comanche, Travis counties, organized in 1857. Named for frontiersman Henry S. Brown.

Race/Ethnicity, 2000: (In percent) Anglo, 79.66; Black, 4.11; Hispanic, 15.38; Other, 0.85.

Vital Statistics, 2003: Births, 477; deaths, 494; marriages, 305; divorces, 77.

Recreation: State park; museum; fishing, hunting.

Minerals: Oil, gas, paving materials, gravel, clays.

Agriculture: Cattle, dairies, poultry, hay, peanuts, pecans, hogs, wheat, goats. Market value $25.7 million.

BROWNWOOD (19,898) county seat; manufacturing, retail trade; distribution center; Howard Payne University, MacArthur Academy of Freedom; state substance abuse treatment center; state 4-H Club center; hospital; bluegrass festival in June.

Early (2,671) varied manufacturing, retail, distribution center; Easter egg hunt.

Other towns include: **Bangs** (1,633); **Blanket** (409); **Brookesmith** (61); **May** (270); **Zephyr** (201). **Lake Brownwood** area has 1,757.

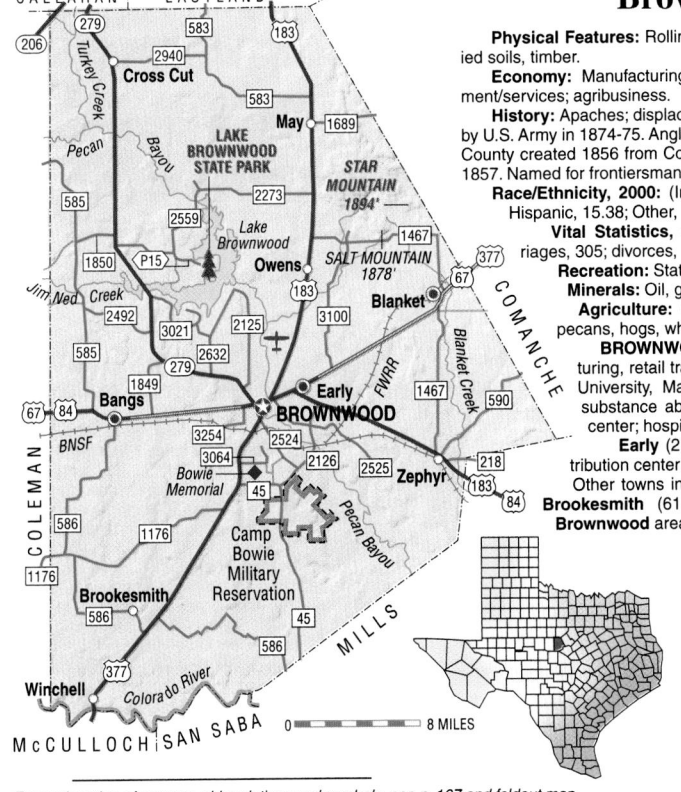

Population	38,183
Change fm 2000	1.4
Area (sq. mi.)	956.94
Land Area (sq. mi.)	943.85
Altitude (ft.)	1,300-1,894
Rainfall (in.)	28.32
Jan. mean min.	29.6
July mean max.	95.0
Civ. Labor	17,397
Unemployed	4.2
Wages	$101,685,800
Av. Weekly Wage	$531.78
Prop. Value	$1,829,308,509
Retail Sales	$416,954,418

For explanation of sources, abbreviations and symbols, see p. 167 and foldout map.

Physical Features: Rolling to hilly; drains to Brazos, Yegua Creek, Somerville Lake; loam and heavy bottom soils; oaks, other trees.

Economy: Oil and gas; tourism; commuters to Texas A&M University; agribusiness.

History: Tonkawas and Caddoes roamed the area. Mexicans and Anglo-Americans settled around fort in 1830. Black freedmen migration increased until 1910. Germans, Czechs, Italians migrated in 1870s-80s. County created 1846 from Milam, Washington counties; named for Edward Burleson, a hero of the Texas Revolution.

Race/Ethnicity, 2000: (In percent) Anglo, 69.68; Black, 15.06; Hispanic, 14.64; Other, 0.62.

Vital Statistics, 2003: Births, 239; deaths, 179; marriages, 82; divorces, 63.

Recreation: Fishing, hunting; lake recreation; historic sites; Czech heritage museum; Kolache Festival in September.

Minerals: Oil, gas, sand, gravel.

Agriculture: Cattle, cotton, corn, hay, sorghum, broiler production, soybeans; some irrigation. Market value $36.2 million.

CALDWELL (3,664) county seat; agribusiness, oil and gas; manufacturing; distribution center; tourism; hospital, civic center, museum.

Somerville (1,704) tourism, railroad center, some manufacturing.

Other towns include: **Chriesman** (30); **Deanville** (130); **Lyons** (360); **Snook** (569) Snookfest in June.

Population	**17,057**
Change fm 2000	3.6
Area (sq. mi.)	677.78
Land Area (sq. mi.)	665.54

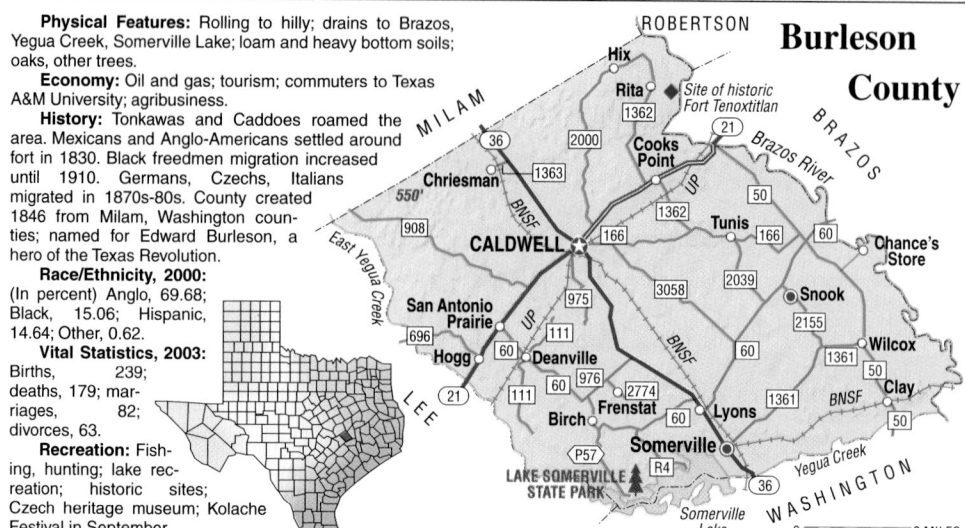

Burleson County

Altitude (ft.)	200-550
Rainfall (in.)	38.50
Jan. mean min.	36.4
July mean max.	96.7
Civ. Labor	8,143
Unemployed	4.9
Wages	$22,832,692
Av. Weekly Wage	$493.22
Prop. Value	$1,112,693,071
Retail Sales	$113,930,828

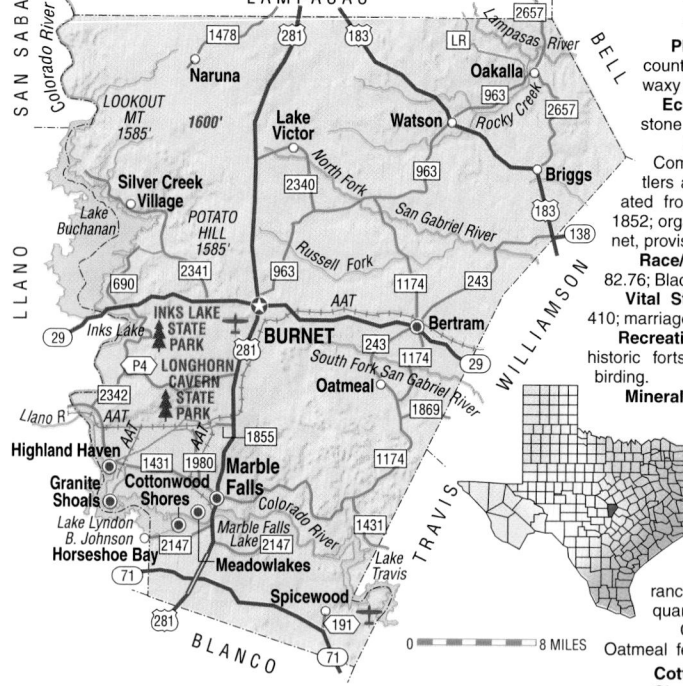

Burnet County

Physical Features: Scenic Hill Country county with lakes; caves; sandy, red, black waxy soils; cedars, other trees.

Economy: Tourism, manufacturing, stone processing, hunting leases.

History: Tonkawas, Lipan Apaches. Comanches raided in area. Frontier settlers arrived in the late 1840s. County created from Bell, Travis, Williamson counties, 1852; organized 1854; named for David G. Burnet, provisional president of the Republic.

Race/Ethnicity, 2000: (In percent) Anglo, 82.76; Black, 1.61; Hispanic, 14.77; Other, 0.86.

Vital Statistics, 2003: Births, 494; deaths, 410; marriages, 318; divorces, 187.

Recreation: Water sports on lakes; sites of historic forts; hunting; state parks; wildflowers; birding.

Minerals: Granite capital of Texas, limestone, graphite.

Agriculture: Beef cattle, goats, hay. Market value $10.3 million.

BURNET (5,338) county seat; tourism; government/services; ranching; varied industries; hospitals; museums; vineyards; Bluebonnet festival at Easter.

Marble Falls (5,508) tourism; ranching; varied manufacturing; stone quarry; August drag boat race.

Other towns include: **Bertram** (1,259) Oatmeal festival on Labor Day; **Briggs** (172); **Cottonwood Shores** (1,000); **Granite Shoals** (2,268); **Highland Haven** (478); **Meadowlakes** (1,559); **Spicewood** (2,000). Also, part of **Horseshoe Bay** (3,514).

Population	**40,286**
Change fm 2000	18.0
Area (sq. mi.)	1,020.96
Land Area (sq. mi.)	996.04
Altitude (ft.)	700-1,600
Rainfall (in.)	32.43
Jan. mean min.	33.3
July mean max.	93.6
Civ. Labor	18,175
Unemployed	4.0
Wages	$82,946,432
Av. Weekly Wage	$561.61
Prop. Value	$3,831,184,447
Retail Sales	$510,935,217

For explanation of sources, abbreviations and symbols, see p. 167 and foldout map.

Caldwell County

Physical Features: Varied soils ranging from black clay to waxy; level, draining to San Marcos River.

Economy: Petroleum, varied manufacturing; government/services; part of Austin metro area, also near San Antonio.

History: Tonkawa area. Part of the DeWitt colony, Anglo-Americans settled in the 1830s. Mexican migration increased after 1890. County created from Bastrop, Gonzales counties, 1848; named for frontiersman Mathew Caldwell.

Race/Ethnicity, 2000: (In percent) Anglo, 50.15; Black, 8.58; Hispanic, 40.44; Other, 0.83.

Vital Statistics, 2003: Births, 516; deaths, 279; marriages, 196; divorces, 153.

Recreation: Fishing; state park; Luling Watermelon Thump in June; Chisholm Trail roundup at Lockhart; museums; nature trails; rodeo.

Minerals: Oil, gas, sand, gravel.

Agriculture: Eggs, beef cattle, broilers; hay, nuseries, cotton. Market value $35.1 million.

LOCKHART (12,880) county seat, petroleum, agribusiness center, tourism; light manufacturing; prison.

Luling (5,478) oil-industry center, oil museum; hospital, barbecue cook-off in April.

Other towns include: **Dale** (500); **Fentress** (291); **Martindale** (1,010); **Maxwell** (500); part of **Mustang Ridge** (929, mostly in Travis County), and **Prairie Lea** (255).

Also, part of **Niederwald** (677), part of **Uhland** (437) and a small part of **San Marcos** (42,102), all mostly in Hays County.

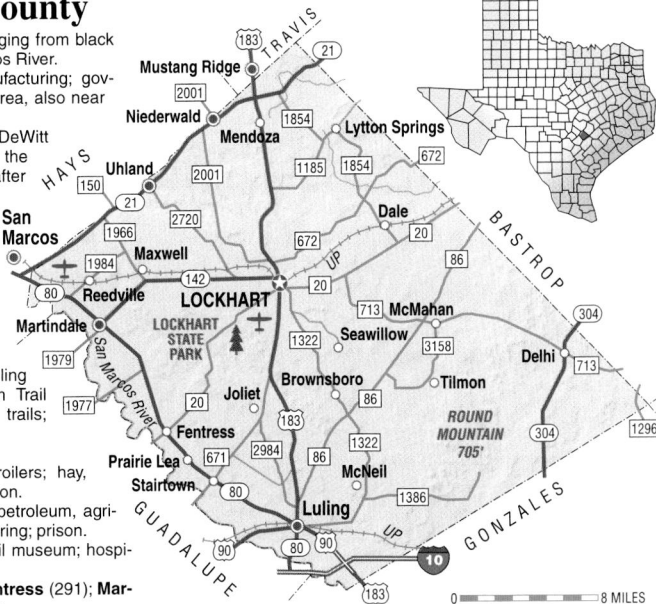

Population	36,498
Change fm 2000	13.4
Area (sq. mi.)	547.41
Land Area (sq. mi.)	545.73
Altitude (ft.)	350-705
Rainfall (in.)	36.86
Jan. mean min.	36.9
July mean max.	95.8
Civ. Labor	16,132
Unemployed	6.2
Wages	$40,487,497
Av. Weekly Wage	$474.90
Prop. Value	$1,689,433,229
Retail Sales	$228,042,959

Calhoun County

Physical Features: Sandy, broken by bays; partly on Matagorda Island.

Economy: Aluminum manufacturing, plastics plant, marine construction, agribusinesses; petroleum; tourism; fish processing.

History: Karankawa area. Empresario Martín De León brought 41 families in 1825. County created from Jackson, Matagorda, Victoria counties, 1846. Named for John C. Calhoun, U.S. statesman.

Race/Ethnicity, 2000: (In percent) Anglo, 52.29; Black, 2.67; Hispanic, 40.92; Other, 3.72.

Vital Statistics, 2003: Births, 306; deaths, 184; marriages, 154; divorces, 54.

Recreation: Beaches, fishing, water sports, duck, goose hunting; historic sites, county park; La Salle Days in April.

Minerals: Oil, gas.

Agriculture: Cotton, cattle, corn, grain sorghum. Market value $18.9 million. Commercial fishing.

PORT LAVACA (12,192) county seat; commercial seafood operations; offshore drilling operations; tourist center; some manufacturing; convention center; hospital.

Other towns include: **Long Mott** (76); **Point Comfort** (748) aluminum, plastic plants, deepwater port; **Port O'Connor** (1,184) tourist center; seafood processing; manufacturing; **Seadrift** (1,386) commercial fishing, processing plants; Bayfront Park; Shrimpfest in June.

Jan. mean min.	47.9
July mean max.	88.2
Civ. Labor	8,557
Unemployed	8.3
Wages	$94,726,501
Av. Weekly Wage	$823,16
Prop. Value	$3,940,235,455
Retail Sales	$177,71,170

Population	20,569	Land Area (sq. mi.)	512.31
Change fm 2000	-0.4	Altitude (ft.)	sea level-50
Area (sq. mi.)	1,032.16	Rainfall (in.)	34.78

Callahan County

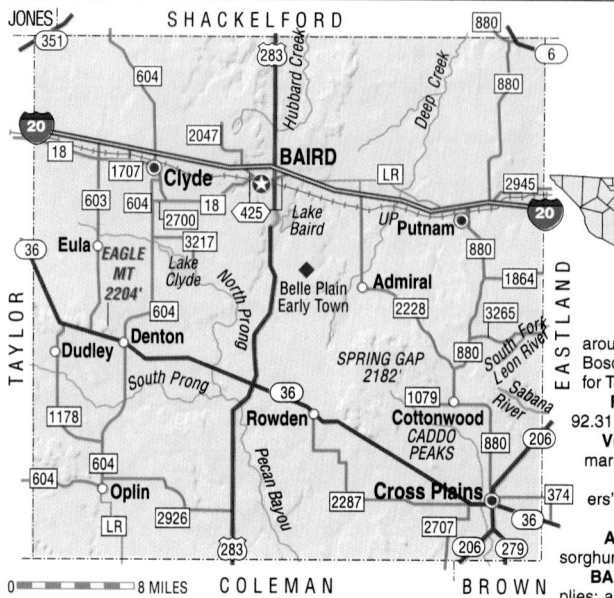

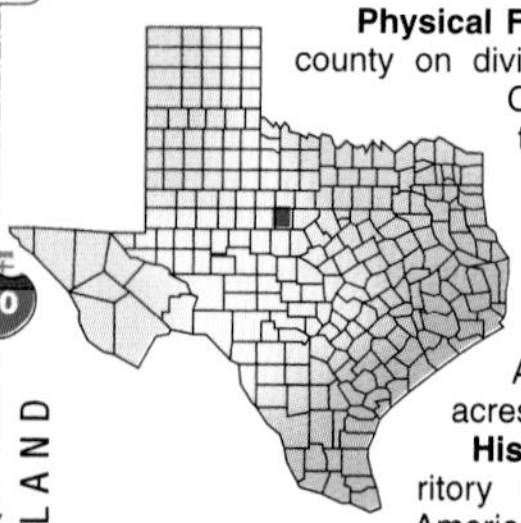

Physical Features: West Texas county on divide between Brazos, Colorado rivers; level to rolling.

Economy: Manufacturing; feed and fertilizer business; many residents commute to Abilene; 200,000 acres in hunting leases.

History: Comanche territory until 1870s. Anglo-American settlement began around 1860. County created 1858 from Bexar, Bosque, Travis counties; organized 1877. Named for Texas Ranger J.H. Callahan.

Race/Ethnicity, 2000: (In percent) Anglo, 92.31; Black, 0.32; Hispanic, 6.29; Other, 1.08.

Vital Statistics, 2003: Births, 147; deaths, 133; marriages, 67; divorces, 85.

Recreation: Hunting; museums; lake; Hunters' Supper at deer season.

Minerals: Oil and gas.

Agriculture: Cattle; wheat, dairy, hay, peanuts, sorghum; goats, horses. Market value $16.9 million.

BAIRD (1,609) county seat; ranching and supplies; antiques shops; some manufacturing, shipping; historic sites.

Clyde (3,621) steel water systems manufacturing; government/services; library; Pecan Festival in October.

Other towns include: **Cross Plains** (1,076) government/services, agriculture, home of creator of Conan the Barbarian; **Putnam** (90).

Population 13,314	July mean max. 94.9
Change fm 2000 .... 3.2	Civ. Labor 6,634
Area (sq. mi.) 901.26	Unemployed 3.5
Land Area (sq. mi.) 898.62	Wages $12,397,065
Altitude (ft.) 1,400-2,204	Av. Weekly Wage $477.29
Rainfall (in.) 25.52	Prop. Value $749,931,697
Jan. mean min. 31.1	Retail Sales $44,286,574

Laguna Madre separates South Padre Island, in the distance, from Port Isabel. Texas Almanac photo.

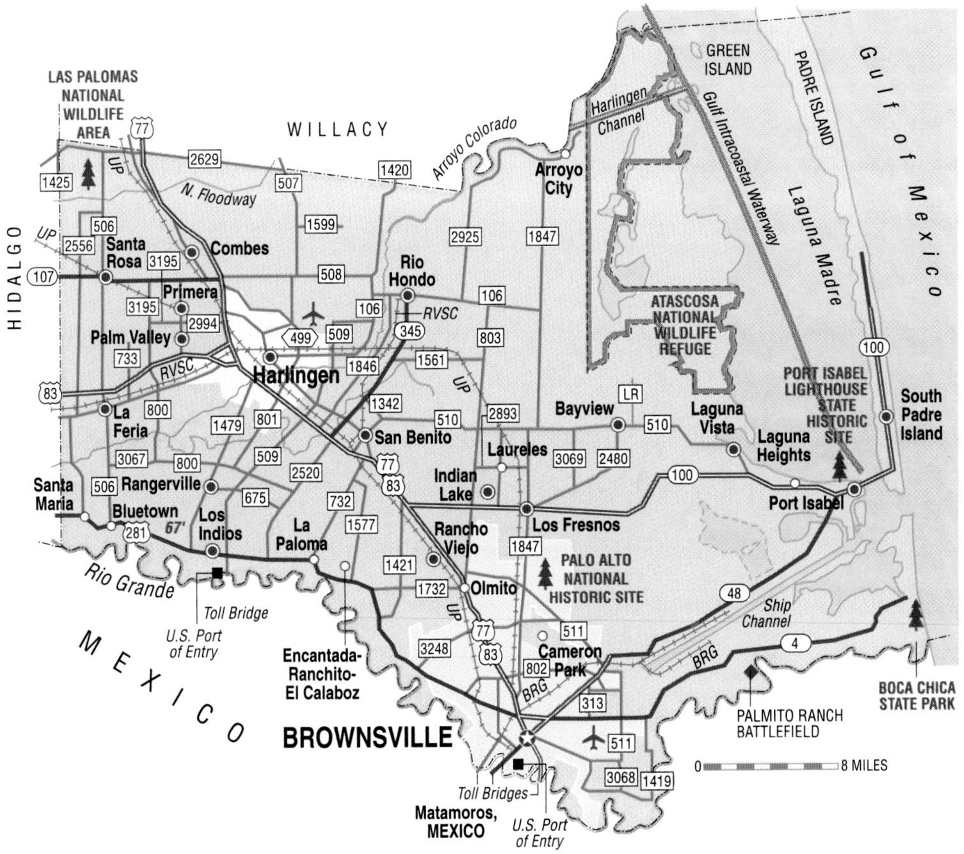

Map Labels

LAS PALOMAS NATIONAL WILDLIFE AREA
WILLACY
GREEN ISLAND
PADRE ISLAND
Gulf of Mexico
N. Floodway
Arroyo Colorado
Harlingen Channel
Gulf Intracoastal Waterway
Laguna Madre
HIDALGO
Santa Rosa
Combes
Rio Hondo
Arroyo City
ATASCOSA NATIONAL WILDLIFE REFUGE
Primera
Palm Valley
RVSC
Harlingen
RVSC
PORT ISABEL LIGHTHOUSE STATE HISTORIC SITE
Laguna Vista
Laguna Heights
South Padre Island
La Feria
San Benito
Bayview
Santa Maria
Bluetown
Los Indios
La Paloma
Rangerville
Indian Lake
Laureles
Los Fresnos
Port Isabel
Rio Grande
Rancho Viejo
Olmito
PALO ALTO NATIONAL HISTORIC SITE
Ship Channel
Toll Bridge
U.S. Port of Entry
Encantada-Ranchito-El Calaboz
Cameron Park
BRG
PALMITO RANCH BATTLEFIELD
BOCA CHICA STATE PARK
MEXICO
BROWNSVILLE
Toll Bridges
Matamoros, MEXICO
U.S. Port of Entry
0 ▭▭▭▭ 8 MILES

Cameron County

Physical Features: Southernmost county in rich Rio Grande Valley soils; flat landscape; semitropical climate.

Economy: Agribusiness; tourism; seafood processing; shipping, manufacturing; government/services.

History: Coahuiltecan Indian area. Spanish land grants date to 1781. County created from Nueces County, 1848; named for Capt. Ewen Cameron of Mier Expedition.

Race/Ethnicity, 2000: (In percent) Anglo, 14.73; Black, 0.30; Hispanic, 84.34; Other, 0.63.

Vital Statistics, 2003: Births, 8,588; deaths, 2,044; marriages, 2,781; divorces, 1,091.

Recreation: South Padre Island: year-round resort; fishing, hunting, water sports; historical sites, Palo Alto visitors center; gateway to Mexico, state parks; wildlife refuge; recreational vehicle center; Birding Festival in February.

Minerals: Natural gas, oil.

Agriculture: Cotton top crop with grain sorghums, vegetables, and sugar cane raised; wholesale nursery plants raised; small feedlot and cow-calf operations; 200,000 acres irrigated, mostly cotton and grain sorghums. Market value $74.6 million.

BROWNSVILLE (161,048) county seat; international trade, varied industries, shipping, tourism; college, hospitals, crippled children health center; Gladys Porter Zoo, historic Fort Brown; University of Texas at Brownsville.

Harlingen (63,404) government/services; hospitals; garment, apparel industries; agribusiness, college; Riofest in April.

San Benito (24,897) varied manufacturing, bottling; tourism; hospital; recreation facilities.

Other towns include: **Bayview** (374); **Bluetown-Iglesia Antigua** (714); **Cameron Park** (6,349); **Combes** (2,739); **Encantada-Ranchito El Calaboz** (2,239); **Indian Lake** (553); **La Feria** (6,844); **Laguna Heights** (2,105); **Laguna Vista** (2,356); **Laureles** (3,426); **Los Fresnos** (5,108); **Los Indios** (1,254); **Olmito** (1,237); **Palm Valley** (1,340).

Also, **Port Isabel** (5,374) tourist center, fishing, Shrimp Cook-Off in November, museums, lighthouse; **Primera** (3,527); **Rancho Viejo** (1,884); **Rangerville** (208); **Rio Hondo** (2,147); **Santa Maria** (914); **Santa Rosa** (3,037); **South Padre Island** (2,612) beaches, tourism, Coast Guard station, Sand Castle Days in October.

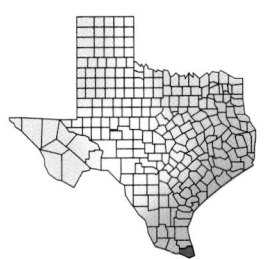

Population	371,825
Change fm 2000	10.9
Area (sq. mi.)	1,276.33
Land Area (sq. mi.)	905.76
Altitude (ft.)	sea level-67
Rainfall (in.)	27.55
Jan. mean min.	50.5
July mean max.	92.4
Civ. Labor	144,268
Unemployed	9.7
Wages	$701,281,979
Av. Weekly Wage	$469.10
Prop. Value	$10,673,809,540
Retail Sales	$3,051,280,549

For explanation of sources, abbreviations and symbols, see p. 167 and foldout map.

Camp County

Physical Features: East Texas county with forested hills; drains to Cypress Creek on north; Lake O' the Pines, Lake Bob Sandlin; third smallest county in Texas.

Economy: Agribusiness, chicken processing; timber industries; light manufacturing; retirement center.

History: Caddo area. Anglo-American settlers arrived in late 1830s. Antebellum slaveholding area. County created from Upshur County 1874; named for jurist J.L. Camp.

Race/Ethnicity, 2000: (In percent) Anglo, 65.45; Black, 19.24; Hispanic, 14.78; Other, 0.53.

Vital Statistics, 2003: Births, 197; deaths, 132; marriages, 93; divorces, 37.

Recreation: Water sports, fishing on lakes; farmstead and airship museum; Chickfest in September, Pittsburg hot links.

Minerals: Oil, gas, clays, coal.

Agriculture: Poultry and products important; beef, dairy cattle, horses; peaches, hay, blueberries, vegetables. Market value $81.7 million. Forestry.

PITTSBURG (4,525) county seat; agribusiness; timber; tourism; food processing; light manufacturing; community college; Prayer Tower.

Other towns include: **Leesburg** (115) and **Rocky Mound** (99).

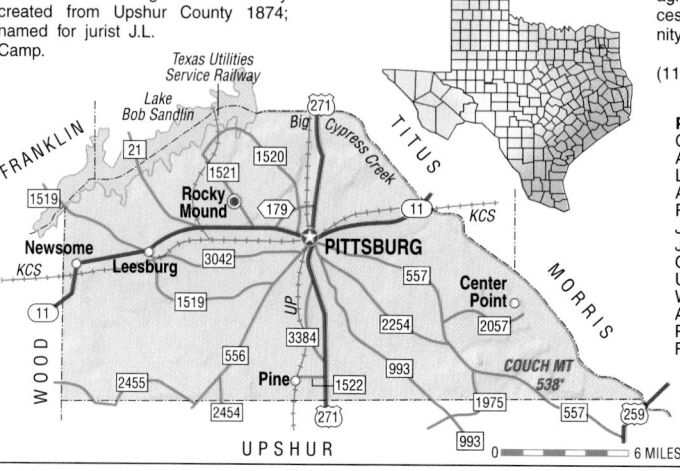

Population	12,011
Change fm 2000	4.0
Area (sq. mi.)	203.20
Land Area (sq. mi.)	197.51
Altitude (ft.)	277-538
Rainfall (in.)	45.10
Jan. mean min.	32.0
July mean max.	94.0
Civ. Labor	5,773
Unemployed	4.7
Wages	$28,673,176
Av. Weekly Wage	$485.18
Prop. Value	$561,151,910
Retail Sales	$116,006,867

Carson County

Physical Features: In center of Panhandle on level, some broken land; loam soils.

Economy: Pantex nuclear weapons assembly/disassembly facility (U.S. Department of Energy), commuting to Amarillo, petrochemical plants; agribusiness.

History: Apaches, displaced by Comanches. Anglo-American ranchers settled in 1880s. German, Polish farmers arrived around 1910. County created from Bexar District, 1876; organized 1888. Named for Republic secretary of state S.P. Carson.

Race/Ethnicity, 2000: (In percent) Anglo, 91.22; Black, 0.81; Hispanic, 7.03; Other, 0.94.

Vital Statistics, 2003: Births, 77; deaths, 62; marriages, 35; divorces, 16.

Recreation: Museum, Square House Barbecue in fall; The Cross at Groom.

Minerals: Oil, gas production.

Agriculture: Cattle, cotton, wheat, sorghum, corn, hay, soybeans. Market value $44.1 million.

PANHANDLE (2,622) county seat; government/services; agribusiness, petroleum center; Veterans Day celebration.

Other towns include: **Groom** (578) Day festival in August, **Skellytown** (585), **White Deer** (1,049) Polish Sausage festival in November.

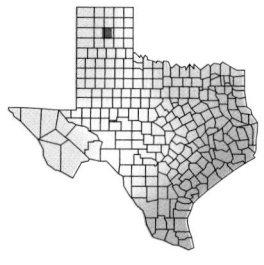

Population	6,478
Change fm 2000	-0.6
Area (sq. mi.)	924.10
Land Area (sq. mi.)	923.19
Altitude (ft.)	3,000-3,573
Rainfall (in.)	22.21
Jan. mean min.	19.3
July mean max.	90.8
Civ. Labor	3,379
Unemployed	2.5
Wages	$59,686,822
Av. Weekly Wage	$969.86
Prop. Value	$784,922,140
Retail Sales	$24,937,069

For explanation of sources, abbreviations and symbols, see p. 167 and foldout map.

Cass County

Physical Features: Forested Northeast county rolling to hilly; drained by Cypress Bayou, Sulphur River.

Economy: Timber, paper industries; varied manufacturing; agribusiness; government/services.

History: Caddoes, displaced by other tribes in 1790s. Anglo-Americans arrived in 1830s. Antebellum slaveholding area. County created 1846 from Bowie County; named for U.S. Sen. Lewis Cass.

Race/Ethnicity, 2000: (In percent) Anglo, 77.89; Black, 19.71; Hispanic, 1.73; Other, 0.67.

Vital Statistics, 2003: Births, 349; deaths, 402; marriages, 220; divorces, 127.

Recreation: Fishing, hunting, water sports; state, county parks; lake, wildflower trails.

Minerals: Oil, iron ore.

Agriculture: Poultry, cattle; nursery; forage; watermelons. Market value $32.3 million. Timber important.

LINDEN (2,220) county seat, timber, agribusiness, tourism; oldest courthouse still in use as courthouse, hospital; Rock and Roll Hall of Fame.

ATLANTA (5,976) Paper and timber industries, government/services, varied manufacturing, hospital, library; Forest Festival in August.

Other towns include: **Avinger** (466); **Bivins** (215); **Bloomburg** (388); **Domino** (58); **Douglassville** (171); **Hughes Springs** (1,870) varied manufacturing, warehousing; trucking school; Pumpkin Glow in October; **Kildare** (104); **Marietta** (115); **McLeod** (600); **Queen City** (1,599).

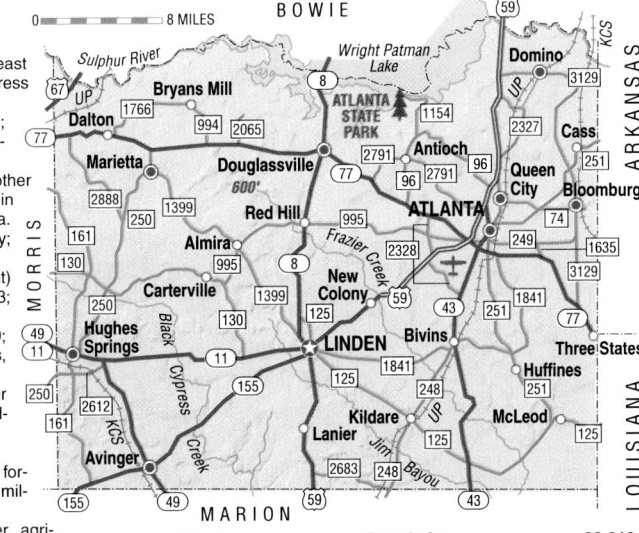

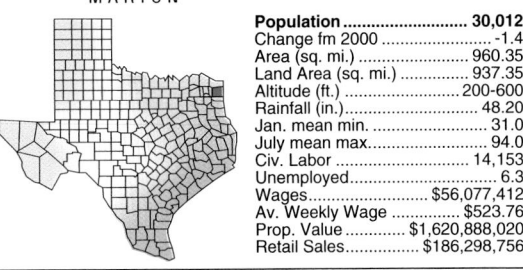

Population	30,012
Change fm 2000	-1.4
Area (sq. mi.)	960.35
Land Area (sq. mi.)	937.35
Altitude (ft.)	200-600
Rainfall (in.)	48.20
Jan. mean min.	31.0
July mean max.	94.0
Civ. Labor	14,153
Unemployed	6.3
Wages	$56,077,412
Av. Weekly Wage	$523.76
Prop. Value	$1,620,888,020
Retail Sales	$186,298,756

Travelers along I-40 are attracted to a giant cross outside Groom in Carson County. Texas Almanac photo.

Castro County

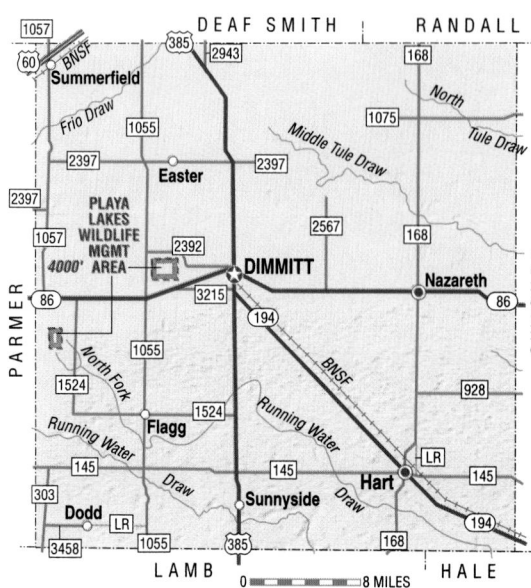

Physical Features: Flat northwest county, drains to creeks, draws and playas; underground water.

Economy: Agribusiness.

History: Apaches, displaced by Comanches in 1720s. Anglo-American ranchers began settling in 1880s. Germans settled after 1900. Mexican migration increased after 1950. County created 1876 from Bexar District, organized 1891. Named for Henri Castro, Texas colonizer.

Race/Ethnicity, 2000: (In percent) Anglo, 45.58; Black, 2.37; Hispanic, 51.65; Other, 0.40.

Vital Statistics, 2003: Births, 128; deaths, 65; marriages, 33; divorces, 16.

Recreation: Pheasant hunting; Harvest Days celebrated in August; Italian POW camp site.

Minerals: Not significant.

Agriculture: Feeder, stocker cattle; corn, cotton, wheat, sheep. Market value $592.6 million; third in state.

DIMMITT (4,162) county seat; agribusiness center; library, geriatric-care facility; Fiestas Patrias in September.

Other towns include: **Hart** (1,115) and **Nazareth** (346).

Population	7,687
Change fm 2000	-7.2
Area (sq. mi.)	899.32
Land Area (sq. mi.)	898.31
Altitude (ft.)	3,600-4,000
Rainfall (in.)	19.71
Jan. mean min.	20.4
July mean max.	90.1
Civ. Labor	3,285
Unemployed	4.8
Wages	$14,266,472
Av. Weekly Wage	$473.43
Prop. Value	$513,909,021
Retail Sales	$61,135,103

Chambers County

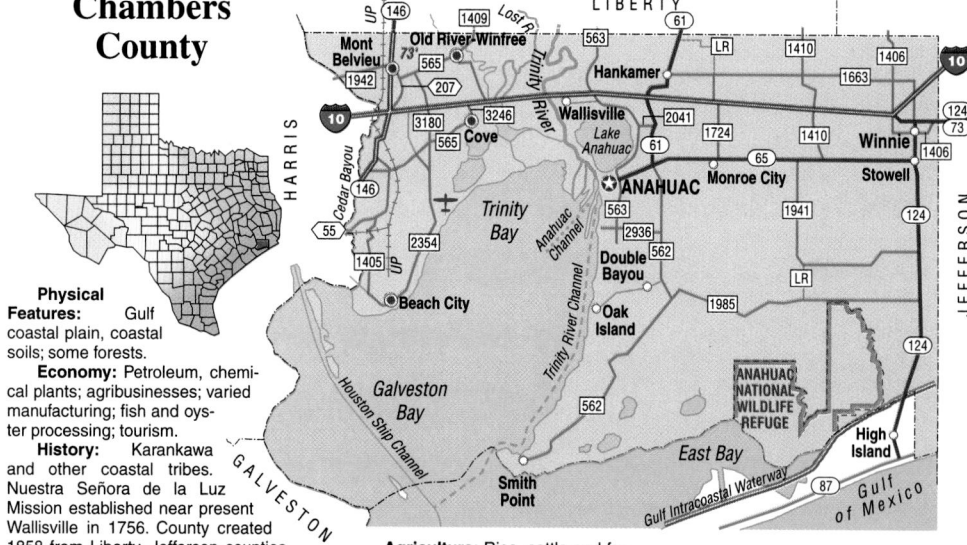

Physical Features: Gulf coastal plain, coastal soils; some forests.

Economy: Petroleum, chemical plants; agribusinesses; varied manufacturing; fish and oyster processing; tourism.

History: Karankawa and other coastal tribes. Nuestra Señora de la Luz Mission established near present Wallisville in 1756. County created 1858 from Liberty, Jefferson counties. Named for Gen. T. J. Chambers, surveyor.

Race/Ethnicity, 2000: (In percent) Anglo, 78.14; Black, 9.88; Hispanic, 10.79; Other, 1.19.

Vital Statistics, 2003: Births, 309; deaths, 201; marriages, 146; divorces, 176.

Recreation: Fishing, hunting; water sports; camping; county parks; wildlife refuge; historic sites; Wallisville Heritage Park; Texas Rice Festival, Texas Gatorfest in September.

Minerals: Oil, gas.

Agriculture: Rice, cattle and forage, soybeans, aquaculture, corn, grain sorghum, sugar cane; significant irrigation. Market value $13.4 million.

ANAHUAC (2,249) county seat; canal connects with Houston Ship Channel; agribusiness; hospital, library.

Winnie (2,983) fertilizer manufacturing; wholesale greenhouse; medical center; depot museum.

Other towns include: **Beach City** (1,787), **Cove** (319), **Hankamer** (226), **Mont Belvieu** (2,532), **Old River-Winfree** (1,485), **Stowell** (1,588) and **Wallisville** (452).

Population	28,227
Change fm 2000	8.4
Area (sq. mi.)	871.99
Land Area (sq. mi.)	599.31
Altitude (ft.)	sea level-73
Rainfall (in.)	54.08
Jan. mean min.	41.7
July mean max.	91.9
Civ. Labor	13,194
Unemployed	5.9
Wages	$68,026,789
Av. Weekly Wage	$723.87
Prop. Value	$4,813,334,700
Retail Sales	$381,149,450

For explanation of sources, abbreviations and symbols, see p. 167 and foldout map.

Mileage between Texas Cities

	Abilene	Amarillo	Austin	Beaumont	Big Bend	Big Spring	Brownsville	Brownwood	Bryan	Childress	Corpus Christi	Dalhart	Dallas	Del Rio	El Paso	Fort Stockton	Fort Worth	Gainesville	Galveston	Houston	Huntsville	Laredo	Longview	Lubbock	Lufkin	McAllen	Odessa	Paris	Pecos	San Angelo	San Antonio	South Padre Island	Texarkana	Tyler	Van Horn	Victoria	Waco
Amarillo	266																																				
Austin	213	478																																			
Beaumont	412	637	238																																		
Big Bend	392	484	462	699																																	
Big Spring	107	222	289	519	281																																
Brownsville	516	765	325	437	636	567																															
Brownwood	77	342	137	350	398	174	471																														
Bryan	253	503	100	158	559	360	382	191																													
Childress	154	116	367	521	483	204	671	231	388																												
Corpus Christi	387	636	192	288	524	438	159	329	237	542																											
Dalhart	343	82	556	719	525	294	842	420	637	197	713																										
Dallas	180	361	192	276	559	287	517	157	165	245	377	443																									
Del Rio	246	450	232	434	253	231	378	231	318	382	268	520	388																								
El Paso	439	418	573	810	329	332	801	493	660	482	691	417	617	424																							
Fort Stockton	250	338	335	572	136	143	563	260	422	347	453	398	416	185	238																						
Fort Worth	150	337	187	301	529	257	512	127	167	222	372	419	30	358	587	385																					
Gainesville	195	309	252	345	584	301	577	185	232	193	437	391	69	416	625	439	65																				
Galveston	398	646	206	78	651	493	374	336	145	531	219	728	288	393	774	536	309	358																			
Houston	348	596	162	86	603	449	352	286	95	480	207	678	238	349	730	492	259	307	50																		
Huntsville	304	528	153	113	602	411	414	241	54	412	269	610	170	369	714	475	191	239	119	69																	
Laredo	373	609	232	396	434	406	199	330	318	528	141	686	424	179	602	364	416	480	341	311	365																
Longview	305	482	256	194	649	412	557	278	177	366	411	564	125	488	742	535	155	178	253	206	151	488															
Lubbock	162	119	368	574	360	104	655	232	415	139	526	196	322	332	344	220	292	290	560	510	466	498	447														
Lufkin	336	529	219	108	675	443	470	274	121	414	325	611	168	439	761	523	199	238	166	119	72	429	87	490													
McAllen	480	728	300	430	578	531	56	423	364	634	152	806	491	322	745	507	486	551	367	345	398	143	541	618	463												
Odessa	167	255	334	567	222	60	609	219	408	263	480	315	347	247	274	83	317	360	538	494	458	422	472	137	491	565											
Paris	281	403	294	292	665	388	615	257	234	287	470	485	103	488	717	516	131	96	342	291	224	527	102	383	184	594	447										
Pecos	240	320	388	625	190	133	616	293	475	337	506	374	420	238	207	53	390	434	589	545	528	417	546	203	565	560	74	521									
San Angelo	89	293	203	436	300	87	481	96	277	225	352	371	252	158	402	164	222	275	407	363	327	321	372	183	360	444	131	352	205								
San Antonio	244	493	79	406	406	295	272	187	165	398	143	570	271	154	548	310	262	326	241	197	217	154	334	382	285	236	336	373	363	209							
South Padre	530	779	339	451	644	251	27	473	396	684	172	856	531	392	815	577	526	591	387	366	428	216	570	668	484	73	622	629	630	495	286						
Texarkana	359	495	340	256	744	466	634	335	261	379	489	576	178	566	795	594	209	188	328	283	235	572	88	475	165	624	525	92	599	430	418	648					
Tyler	277	457	224	192	647	384	526	242	145	342	381	539	97	455	714	500	127	159	247	197	130	456	36	419	84	508	444	101	517	336	302	540	116				
Van Horn	328	401	454	690	199	221	682	378	540	425	571	447	508	304	119	119	478	522	654	610	594	483	633	291	642	626	161	608	88	282	428	696	686	605			
Victoria	334	600	122	209	522	402	230	259	152	489	85	677	292	264	661	423	287	352	154	124	186	187	328	489	242	220	447	385	476	316	114	244	407	296	542		
Waco	183	423	102	242	518	290	427	123	85	307	287	504	91	334	610	372	86	151	230	180	130	334	163	345	157	401	340	194	413	209	181	441	244	128	490	202	
Wichita Falls	141	225	283	412	513	234	608	169	270	109	474	307	136	388	552	376	112	84	421	371	303	490	257	208	304	572	293	178	366	230	336	621	270	232	454	399	198

Counties of Texas

A close-up map of each county is included with each county article on pages 167–336.

Here is a guide to the symbols used on those pages:

Legend to counties

——— Principal road
——— Secondary road
········· Local road
═══════ Divided highway
10 Interstate highway
377 U.S. highway
81 State highway
308 Farm-to-market road
LR Local roads
28 Loop
+++++ Railway
BNSF Railway name
〜〜 River or creek
◯ Lake
◯ Intermittent water source
▬▬▬ Intracoastal Waterway
✪ County seat
◉ Incorporated town
○ Unincorporated town
——— County boundary
P E C O S Name of neighboring county
400' Elevation
880' Highest point in county
✈ Major airport with scheduled jet service
✚ Municipal airport
✦ Military airport
🌲 National park or wildlife management area
▭ Federal land
🌲 State park or wildlife management area
▭ State land
◆ Ranger station
········· Time zone line
▭ Boundary of prison or military installation

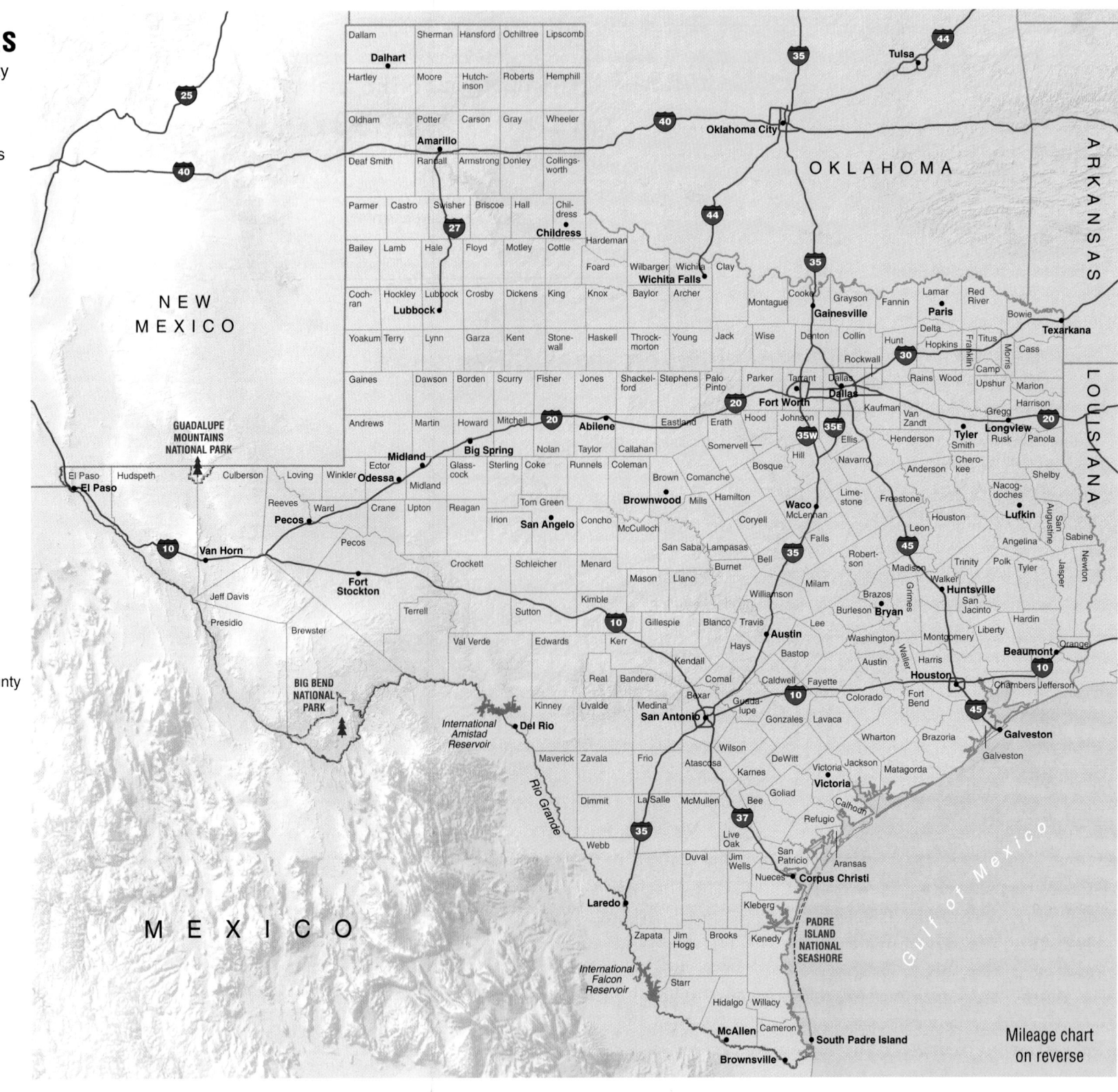

Mileage chart on reverse

Cherokee County

Physical Features: East Texas county; hilly, partly forested; drains to Angelina, Neches rivers; many streams, lakes; sandy, clay soils.

Economy: Nurseries, timber production; government/services; varied manufacturing; agriculture; tourism.

History: Caddo tribes attracted Spanish missionaries around 1720. Cherokees began settling area around 1820, and soon afterward Anglo-Americans began to arrive. Cherokees forced to Indian Territory 1839. Named for Indian tribe; created 1846 from Nacogdoches County.

Race/Ethnicity, 2000: (In percent) Anglo, 69.80; Black, 16.17; Hispanic, 13.24; Other, 0.79.

Vital Statistics, 2003: Births, 744; deaths, 532; marriages, 353; divorces, 177.

Recreation: Water sports; fishing, hunting; historic sites and parks; Texas State Railroad; nature trails through forests; lakes.

Minerals: Gas, oil.

Agriculture: Nurseries; beef cattle; hay; dairies; poultry. Market value $123.2 million. Timber, hunting income significant.

RUSK (5,151) county seat; agribusiness; tourism, state mental hospital; prison unit; Indian Summer festival.

JACKSONVILLE (14,203) varied manufacturing, plastics, agribusiness, tourism, retail center; hospital, junior colleges; Love's Lookout; Tomato Fest in June.

Other towns include: **Alto** (1,207); **Cuney** (146); **Gallatin** (384); **Maydelle** (250); **New Summerfield** (1,055); **Reklaw** (351, partly in Rusk County); **Wells** (757). Part [53] of **Bullard** and part [40] of **Troup**.

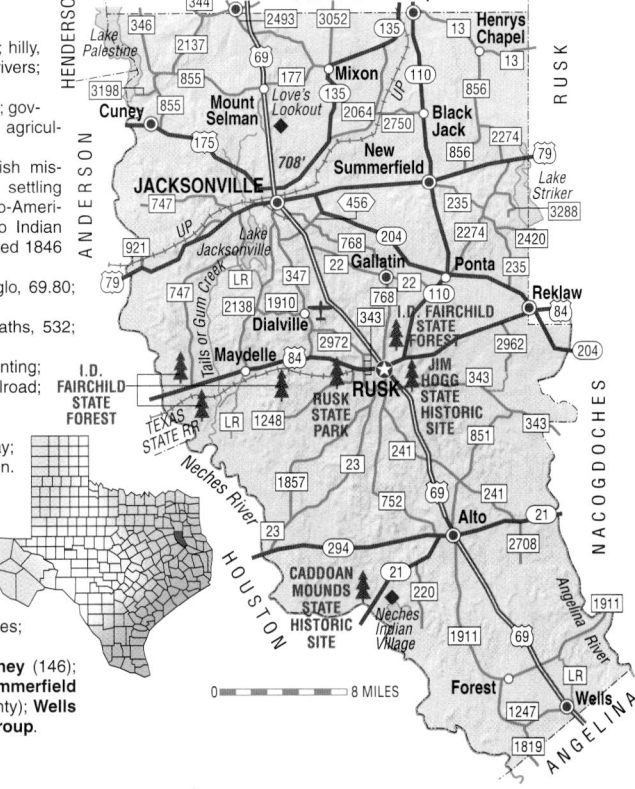

Population	48,091
Change fm 2000	3.1
Area (sq. mi.)	1,061.93
Land Area (sq. mi.)	1,052.22
Altitude (ft.)	200-708
Rainfall (in.)	48.50
Jan. mean min.	36.8
July mean max.	92.8
Civ. Labor	20,314
Unemployed	4.1
Wages	$95,210,735
Av. Weekly Wage	$469.00
Prop. Value	$1,943,753,230
Retail Sales	$361,173,211

Atop one of the mounds at the site of the Neches Indian Village in Cherokee County. Texas Almanac photo.

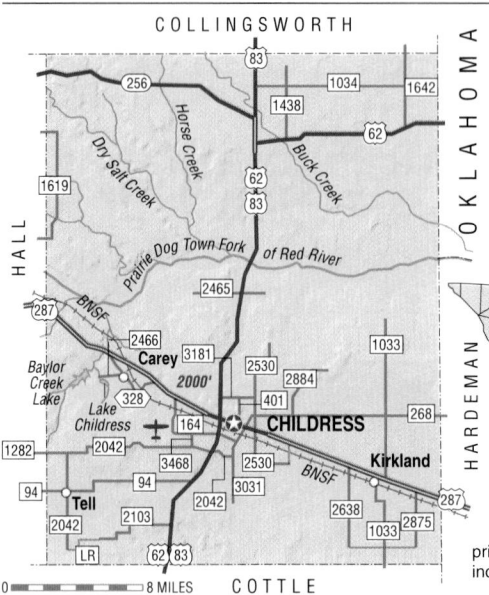

Childress County

Physical Features: Rolling prairie, at corner of Panhandle, draining to fork of Red River; mixed soils.

Economy: Government/services; trade; tourism; agriculture.

History: Apaches, displaced by Comanches. Ranchers arrived around 1880. County created 1876 from Bexar, Young districts; organized 1887; named for author of Texas Declaration of Independence, George C. Childress.

Race/Ethnicity, 2000: (In percent) Anglo, 64.50; Black, 14.30; Hispanic, 20.47; Other, 0.73.

Vital Statistics, 2003: Births, 70; deaths, 66; marriages, 61; divorces, 24.

Recreation: Recreation on lakes and creek, fishing, hunting of deer, turkey, wild hog, quail, dove; parks; county museum.

Agriculture: Cotton, beef cattle, wheat, hay, sorghum, peanuts; 6,000 acres irrigated. Market value $13.6 million. Hunting leases.

CHILDRESS (6,451) county seat; agribusiness, hospital, prison unit; settlers reunion and rodeo in July. Other towns include: **Tell** (15).

Population 7,613	Altitude (ft.) 1,600-2,000	Unemployed 3.2
Change fm 2000 .... -1.0	Rainfall (in.) 22.65	Wages $13,848,931
Area (sq. mi.) 713.61	Jan. mean min. 26.8	Av. Weekly Wage $445.55
Land Area (sq. mi.) 710.34	July mean max. 95.3	Prop. Value.................... $294,234,390
	Civ. Labor 3,229	Retail Sales $69,447,766

Clay County

Physical Features: Hilly, rolling; north central county drains to Red, Trinity rivers, lake; sandy loam, chocolate soils; mesquites, post oaks.

Economy: Oil; agribusiness; varied manufacturing.

History: Wichitas arrived from north-central plains in mid-1700s, followed by Apaches and Comanches. Ranching attempts began in 1850s. County created from Cooke County, 1857; Indians forced disorganization, 1862; reorganized, 1873; named for Henry Clay, U.S. statesman.

Race/Ethnicity, 2000: (In percent) Anglo, 94.81; Black, 0.41; Hispanic, 3.67; Other, 1.11.

Vital Statistics, 2003: Births, 92; deaths, 89; marriages, 89; divorces, 51.

Recreation: Fishing, water sports; state park; pioneer reunion.

Minerals: Oil and gas, stone.

Agriculture: Beef and dairy cattle, horses raised; wheat, cotton, pecan, peaches. Market value $39.2 million. Oaks, cedar, elms sold to nurseries, mesquite cut for firewood.

HENRIETTA (3,395) county seat; agribusiness center; hospital.

Other towns include: **Bellevue** (394), **Bluegrove** (135), **Byers** (515), **Dean** (346), **Jolly** (185), **Petrolia** (780).

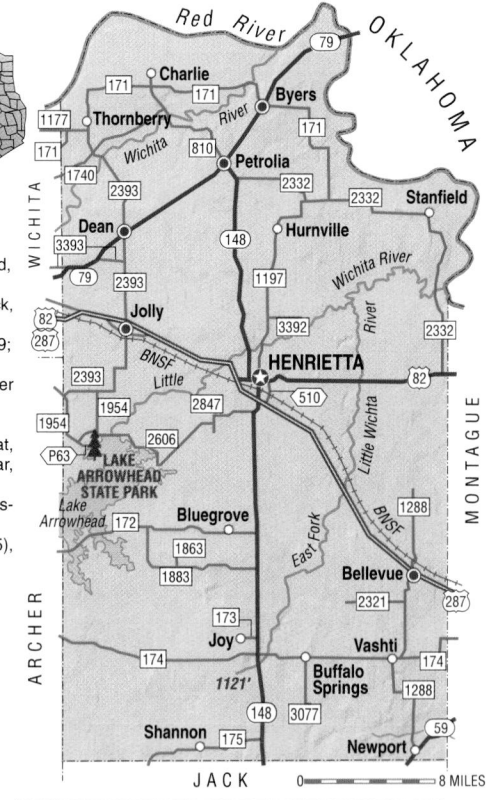

Population 11,231	
Change fm 2000 .... 2.0	
Area (sq. mi.) 1,116.17	
Land Area (sq. mi.) 1,097.82	
Altitude (ft.) 800-1,121	
Rainfall (in.) 31.66	
Jan. mean min. 26.8	
July mean max. 95.0	
Civ. Labor 5,206	
Unemployed 2.7	
Wages $12,490,016	
Av. Weekly Wage $517.38	
Prop. Value..................................... $779,584,579	
Retail Sales $84,507,549	

For explanation of sources, abbreviations and symbols, see p. 167 and foldout map..

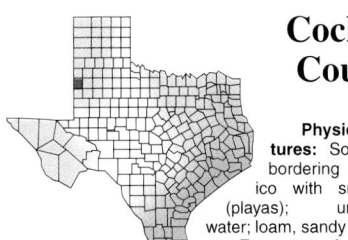

Cochran County

Physical Features: South Plains bordering New Mexico with small lakes (playas); underground water; loam, sandy loam soils.

Economy: Agribusiness, government/services, oil.

History: Hunting area for various Indian tribes. Ranches operated in 1880s but population in 1900 was still only 25. Farming began in 1920s. County created from Bexar, Young districts, 1876; organized 1924; named for Robert Cochran, who died at the Alamo.

Race/Ethnicity 2000: (In percent) Anglo, 50.18; Black, 4.91; Hispanic, 44.13; Other, 0.78.

Vital Statistics, 2003: Births, 54; deaths, 38; marriages, 18; divorces, 8.

Recreation: Rodeo; Last Frontier days in July; museum.

Minerals: Oil, gas.

Agriculture: Cotton, sorghum, wheat, peanuts, sunflowers. Crops 60 percent irrigated. Cattle, swine, sheep. Market value $39.5 million.

MORTON (2,150) county seat; oil, farm center, meat packing; light manufacture; hospital.

Other towns include: **Bledsoe** (126), **Whiteface** (452).

Population	**3,340**
Change fm 2000	-10.5
Area (sq. mi.)	775.31
Land Area (sq. mi.)	775.22
Altitude (ft.)	3,600-4,000

Rainfall (in.)	18.34
Jan. temp. min.	23.1
July temp. max.	91.4
Civ. Labor	1,398
Unemployed	7.6

Wages	$5,772,398
Av. Weekly Wage	$498.91
Prop. Value	$456,134,910
Retail Sales	$25,795,041

Coke County

Physical Features: West Texas prairie, hills, Colorado River valley; sandy loam, red soils; reservoir.

Economy: Oil and gas, government/services, agriculture.

History: From 1700 to 1870s, Comanches roamed the area. Ranches began operating after the Civil War. County created 1889 from Tom Green County; named for Gov. Richard Coke.

Race/Ethnicity, 2000: (In percent) Anglo, 80.18; Black, 1.99; Hispanic, 16.90; Other, 0.93.

Vital Statistics, 2003: Births, 26; deaths, 64; marriages, 12; divorces, 14.

Recreation: Hunting, fishing, Caliche Loop birdwatching trail; lakes; historic sites, Fort Chadbourne, county museum; Ole Coke County Pageant, July 4.

Minerals: Oil, gas.

Agriculture: Beef cattle; sheep and goats; hay, small grains. Market value $12.7 million.

ROBERT LEE (1,136) county seat; government/services, petroleum center, ranching.

Bronte (1,081) ranching, oil.

Other towns include: **Silver** (34) and **Tennyson** (46). Also, a small part of **Blackwell** (355).

Population	**3,715**
Change fm 2000	-3.9
Area (sq. mi.)	927.97
Land Area (sq. mi.)	898.81
Altitude (ft.)	1,700-2,608
Rainfall (in.)	23.00
Jan. mean min.	29.0
July mean max.	96.4
Civ. Labor	1,380
Unemployed	2.7
Wages	$4,614,271
Av. Weekly Wage	$404.26
Prop. Value	$395,655,520
Retail Sales	$22,817,783

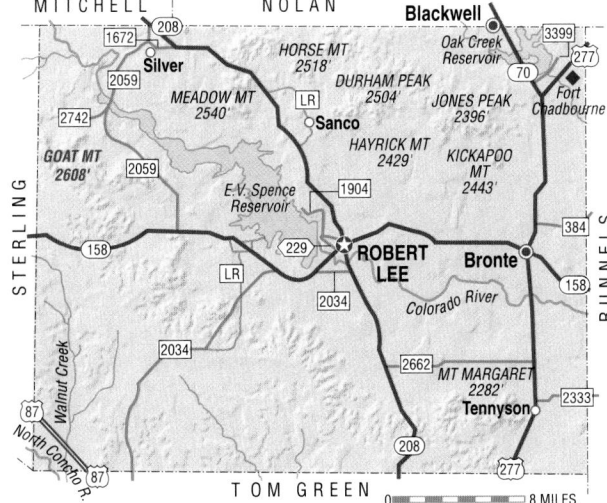

For explanation of sources, abbreviations and symbols, see p. 167 and foldout map.

Coleman County

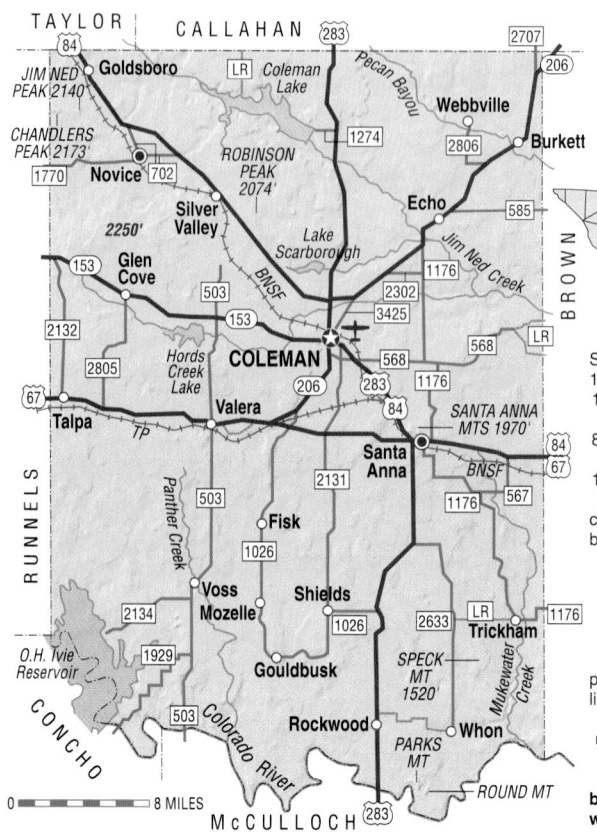

Physical Features: Hilly, rolling; drains to Colorado River, Pecan Bayou; lakes; mesquite, oaks.

Economy: Agribusiness, petroleum, ecotourism; varied manufacturing.

History: Presence of Apaches and Comanches brought military outpost, Camp Colorado, before the Civl War. Settlers arrived after organization. County created 1858 from Brown, Travis counties; organized 1864; named for Houston's aide, R.M. Coleman.

Race/Ethnicity, 2000: (In percent), Anglo, 82.95; Black, 2.35; Hispanic, 13.96; Other, 0.74.

Vital Statistics, 2003: Births, 115; deaths, 169; marriages, 61; divorces, 47.

Recreation: Fishing, hunting; water sports; city park, historic sites; lakes; Santa Anna Peak; bison cook-off in May.

Minerals: Oil, gas, stone, clays.

Agriculture: Cattle, wheat, sheep, hay, grain sorghum, goats, oats, cotton. Market value $15.7 million. Mesquite for firewood and furniture.

COLEMAN (5,121) county seat; agribusiness, petroleum center; varied manufacturing; hospital, library, museum, Fiesta de la Paloma in October.

Santa Anna (1,061) agribusiness; some manufacturing; tourism.

Other towns include: **Burkett** (30), **Goldsboro** (30), **Gouldbusk** (70), **Novice** (142), **Rockwood** (80), **Talpa** (127), and **Valera** (80).

Population **8,738**		
Change fm 2000 ....-5.4	Rainfall (in.) 28.70	Unemployed 6.1
Area (sq. mi.) 1,281.45	Jan. mean min. 30.0	Wages $10,946,089
Land Area (sq. mi.) 1,260.20	July mean max. 93.7	Av. Weekly Wage $401.15
Altitude (ft.) 1,400-2,250	Civ. Labor 2,939	Prop. Value....................$638,242,761
		Retail Sales $56,997,366

Santa Anna Mountains in Coleman County. Texas Almanac photo.

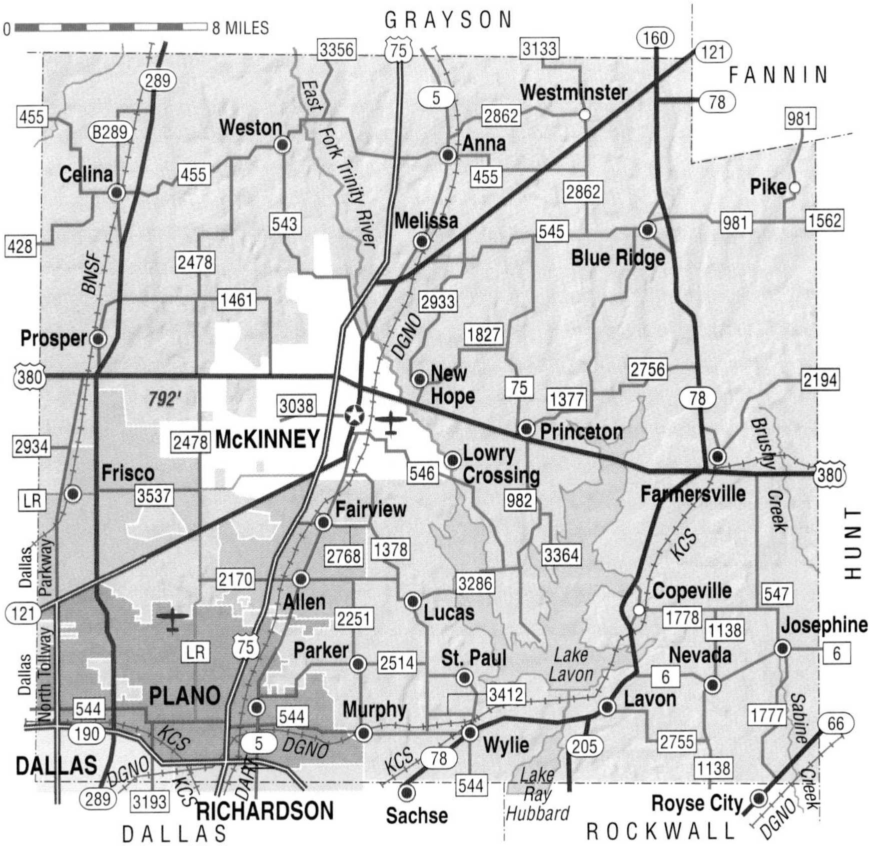

G R A Y S O N

0 ———— 8 MILES

FANNIN

DENTON

Weston

Celina

Prosper

792'

Frisco

McKINNEY

Fairview

Allen

Parker

PLANO

DALLAS

RICHARDSON
DALLAS

Sachse

Westminster

Anna

Melissa

Blue Ridge

Pike

New Hope

Princeton

Lowry Crossing

Farmersville

Lucas

Copeville

Josephine

St. Paul

Nevada

Murphy

Wylie

Lavon

Royse City

Lake Lavon

Lake Ray Hubbard

R O C K W A L L

HUNT

East Fork Trinity River

Collin County

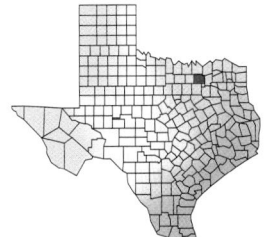

Physical Features: North Texas county with heavy, black clay soil; level to rolling; drains to Trinity, Lake Lavon.

Economy: Government/services; manufacturing plants, retail and wholesale center; many residents work in Dallas.

History: Caddo area until 1850s. Settlers of Peters colony arrived in early 1840s. County created from Fannin County 1846. Named for pioneer settler Collin McKinney.

Race/Ethnicity, 2000: (In percent) Anglo, 77.11; Black, 4.98; Hispanic, 10.27; Other, 7.64.

Vital Statistics, 2003: Births, 10,168; deaths, 2,096; marriages, 4,309; divorces, 2,633.

Recreation: Fishing, water sports; historic sites; old homes restoration, tours; natural science museum; hot-air balloon festival.

Minerals: Stone production.

Agriculture: Greenhouse/nurseries, beef cattle, corn, horses, wheat, grain sorghum, hay. Market value $38.1 million.

McKINNEY (81,462) county seat; agribusiness, trade center; varied industry; hospital, community college; museums.

PLANO (252,368) telecommunications; manufacturing; newspaper printing; medical services, research center; community college; commercial and financial center; hospitals.

Other towns include: **Allen** (61,256) telecommunications, hospital, conservatory, natatorium, historic dam; **Anna** (1,524); **Blue Ridge** (824); **Celina** (2,361) museum, historic town square; **Copeville** (243); **Fairview** (3,747); **Farmersville** (3,081) agriculture, light industries, Audie Murphy Day; **Frisco** (58,927) technical, areospace industry, community college.

Also, **Josephine** (719); **Lavon** (465); **Lowry Crossing** (1,572); **Lucas** (3,559); **Melissa** (1,967); **Murphy** (8,276); **Nevada** (658); **New Hope** (650); **Parker** (1,828); **Princeton** (3,636) manufacturing, marble, government/services; **Prosper** (3,064); **St. Paul** (729); **Westminster** (397); **Weston** (668); **Wylie** (23,029).

Also, part [45,155] of **Dallas**, part [20,873] of **Richardson** and part [1,660] of **Sachse**.

Population	**627,938**
Change fm 2000	27.7
Area (sq. mi.)	885.85
Land Area (sq. mi.)	847.56
Altitude (ft.)	434-792
Rainfall (in.)	41.01
Jan. mean min.	31.1
July mean max.	92.7
Civ. Labor	323,062
Unemployed	4.9
Wages	$2,176,925,026
Av. Weekly Wage	$794.48
Prop. Value	$59,598,546,057
Retail Sales	$8,625,342,138

For explanation of sources, abbreviations and symbols, see p. 167 and foldout map.

Collingsworth County

Physical Features: Panhandle county of rolling, broken terrain, draining to Red River forks; sandy and loam soils.

Economy: Agribusiness.

History: Apaches, displaced by Comanches. Ranchers from England arrived in late 1870s. County created 1876, from Bexar and Young districts, organized 1890. Named for Republic of Texas' first chief justice, James Collinsworth (name misspelled in law).

Race/Ethnicity, 2000: (In percent) Anglo, 72.46; Black, 5.33; Hispanic, 20.43; Other, 1.78.

Vital Statistics, 2003: Births, 29; deaths, 48; marriages, 40; divorces, 12.

Recreation: Deer, quail hunting; children's camp, county museum, peanut festival; pioneer park.

Minerals: Gas, oil production.

Agriculture: Peanuts (second in acreage), cotton; cow-calf operations, stocker cattle; alfalfa, wheat; 22,000 acres irrigated. Market value $34.2 million.

WELLINGTON (2,190) county seat; peanut-processing plants, varied manufacturing; agriculture; hospital, library.

Other towns include: **Dodson** (107), **Quail** (36), **Samnorwood** (40).

Population 3,046
Change fm 2000 .... -5.0

Area (sq. mi.)............................919.44	Civ. Labor 1,733
Land Area (sq. mi.)....................918.80	Unemployed................................. 3.9
Altitude (ft.)....................1,789-2,600	Wages.............................. $5,329,286
Rainfall (in.) 22.80	Av. Weekly Wage $432.89
Jan. mean min...............................27.0	Prop. Value $258,224,930
July mean max. 97.9	Retail Sales..................... $12,210,749

Colorado County

Physical Features: South central county in three soil areas; level to rolling; bisected by Colorado River; oaks.

Economy: Agribusiness; oil-field services and equipment manufacturing, ecotourism; plants process minerals, gravel mining.

History: Karankawa and other tribes. Anglo settlers among Stephen F. Austin's Old Three Hundred families. First German settlers arrived around 1840. Antebellum slaveholding area. County created 1836, organized 1837; named for river.

Race/Ethnicity, 2000: (In percent) Anglo, 65.01; Black, 14.72; Hispanic, 19.74; Other, 0.53.

Vital Statistics, 2003: Births, 256; deaths, 254; marriages, 131; divorces, 77.

Recreation: Hunting, historic sites; prairie chicken refuge; opera house in Columbus, bicycling, canoeing.

Minerals: Gas, oil.

Agriculture: Rice (second in state in acres), cattle, corn, cotton, soybeans, nurseries, hay, poultry, sorghum; significant irrigation for rice. Market value $41.6 million.

COLUMBUS (4,014) county seat; mining, agribusiness center; tourism; oil-field servicing; timber-treating center; hospital; historical sites, homes, walking tour; Live Oak festival in May.

Eagle Lake (3,823) rice drying center, wildflower celebration; goose hunting; hospital.

Weimar (1,920) ranching and rice center, feed mill, light industry, sausage company; hospital, library; "Gedenke" (remember) celebration on Mother's Day; Babe Ruth World Series.

Other towns include: **Altair** (30), **Garwood** (975), **Nada** (165), **Oakland** (80), **Rock Island** (160), **Sheridan** (225).

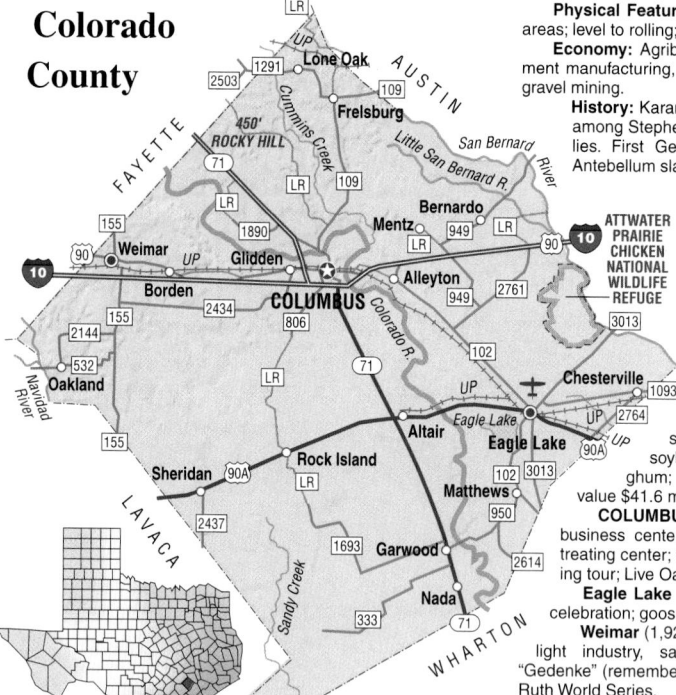

For explanation of sources, abbreviations and symbols, see p. 167 and foldout map.

Population 20,767	July mean max. 96.3
Change fm 2000............................. 1.8	Civ. Labor 8,642
Area (sq. mi.)............................ 973.59	Unemployed................................... 4.4
Land Area (sq. mi.).................... 962.95	Wages............................ $41,220,848
Altitude (ft.)..........................150-450	Av. Weekly Wage.................... $509.13
Rainfall (in.) 44.72	Prop. Value................. $2,025,022,772
Jan. mean min. 36.8	Retail Sales $231,303,857

Comal County

Population.........................91,806
Change fm 2000.....................17.7
Area (sq. mi.)......................574.59
Land Area (sq. mi.)...............561.45
Altitude (ft.)....................600-1,473
Rainfall (in.)..........................35.74
Jan. mean min.........................35.5
July mean max. 94.7
Civ. Labor...........................45,288
Unemployed 4.3
Wages $233,429,709
Av. Weekly Wage..............$548.23
Prop. Value............$8,156,255,830
Retail Sales $3,018,404,953

Physical Features: Scenic Southwest county of hills. Eighty percent above Balcones Escarpment. Spring-fed streams; 2.5-mile-long Comal River, Guadalupe River; Canyon Lake.

Economy: Varied manufacturing; tourism; government/services; agriculture; county in San Antonio metropolitan area.

History: Tonkawa, Waco Indians. A pioneer German settlement 1845. Mexican migration peaked during Mexican Revolution. County created from Bexar, Gonzales, Travis counties and organized in 1846; named for river, a name for Spanish earthenware or metal pan used for cooking tortillas.

Race/Ethnicity, 2000: (In percent) Anglo, 75.46; Black, 1.01; Hispanic, 22.57; Other, 0.96.

Vital Statistics, 2003: Births, 1,220; deaths, 699; marriages, 791; divorces, 297.

Recreation: Fishing, hunting; historic sites, Hummel museum; scenic drives; lake facilities; Prince Solms Park, other county parks; Landa Park

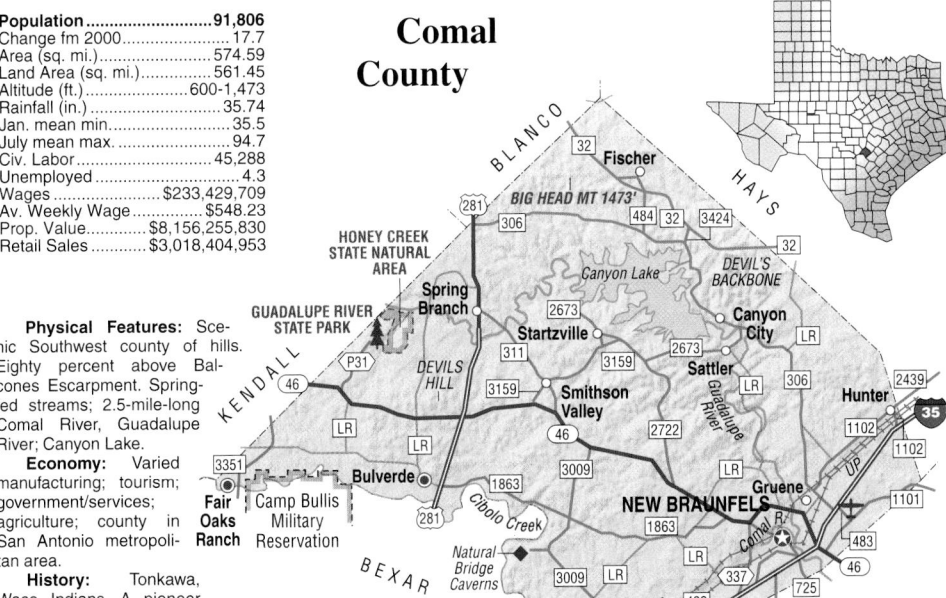

with 76 species of trees; Gruene historic area; caverns; river resorts; river tubing; Schlitterbahn water park; Wurstfest in October-November.

Minerals: Stone, lime, sand and gravel.

Agriculture: Cattle, goats, sheep, hogs, horses; nursery, hay, corn, sorghum, wheat. Market value $5.6 million.

NEW BRAUNFELS (43,680) county seat; manufacturing; retail, distribution; one of the most picturesque

cities in Texas, making it a tourist center; Conservation Plaza; rose garden; hospital; library; mental health and retardation center. **Gruene** is now part of New Braunfels.

Other towns include: **Bulverde** (4,107), **Fischer** (NA), **Garden Ridge** (2,091), **Spring Branch** (NA) and the retirement and recreation community around **Canyon Lake** (17,730).

Also, parts of **Fair Oaks Ranch** (5,220), **Selma** (1,791) and **Schertz** (24,336).

A motorcyclist rides FM 1547 in Collingsworth County. Texas Almanac photo.

Comanche County

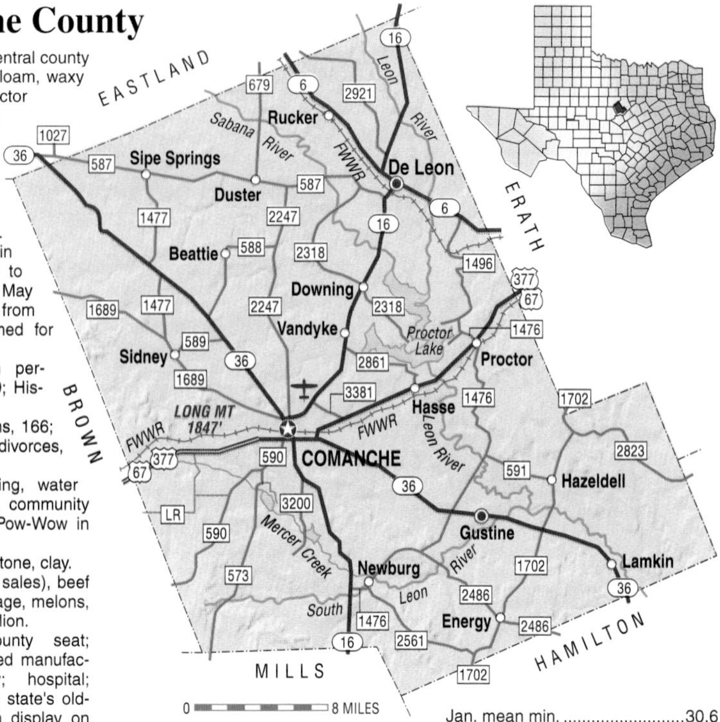

Physical Features: West central county with rolling, hilly terrain; sandy, loam, waxy soils; drains to Leon River, Proctor Lake; pecans, oaks, mesquites, cedars.

Economy: Dairies, other agribusiness; peanut- and pecan-shelling plants; food processing; manufacturing.

History: Comanche area. Anglo-American settlers arrived in 1854 on land granted earlier to Stephen F. Austin and Samuel May Williams. County created 1856 from Bosque, Coryell counties; named for Indian tribe.

Race/Ethnicity, 2000: (In percent) Anglo, 78.10; Black, 0.49; Hispanic, 20.88; Other, 0.53.

Vital Statistics, 2003: Births, 166; deaths, 193; marriages, 100; divorces, 41.

Recreation: Hunting, fishing, water sports, nature tourism; parks, community center, museums; Comanche Pow-Wow in September, rodeo in July.

Minerals: Limited gas, oil, stone, clay.

Agriculture: Dairy (third in sales), beef cattle; hay, peanuts, pecans, silage, melons, wildlife. Market value $102.5 million.

COMANCHE (4,533) county seat; plants process feed, food; varied manufacturing; agribusiness, winery; hospital; Ranger College branch; library; state's oldest courthouse, "Old Cora," on display in town square.

De Leon (2,470) peanuts, pecans; hospital; car museum, Peach and Melon Festival in August.

Other towns include: **Energy** (70), **Gustine** (460), **Proctor** (228) and **Sidney** (148).

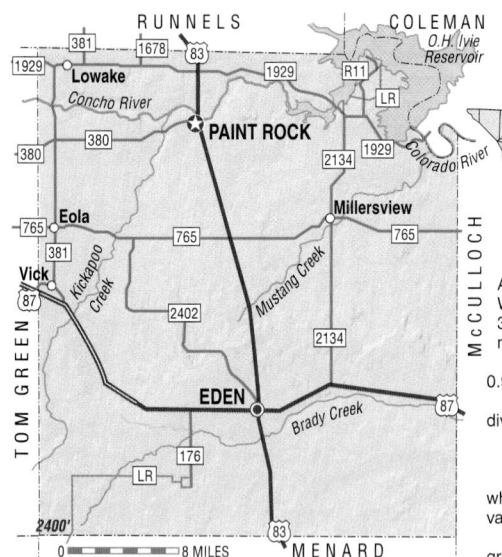

Population	13,616
Change fm 2000	-2.9
Area (sq. mi.)	947.67
Land Area (sq. mi.)	937.69
Altitude (ft.)	1,056-1,847
Rainfall (in.)	31.12
Jan. mean min.	30.6
July mean max.	95.5
Civ. Labor	6,915
Unemployed	3.5
Wages	$21,879,174
Av. Weekly Wage	$454.25
Prop. Value	$924,733,698
Retail Sales	$132,607,942

Concho County

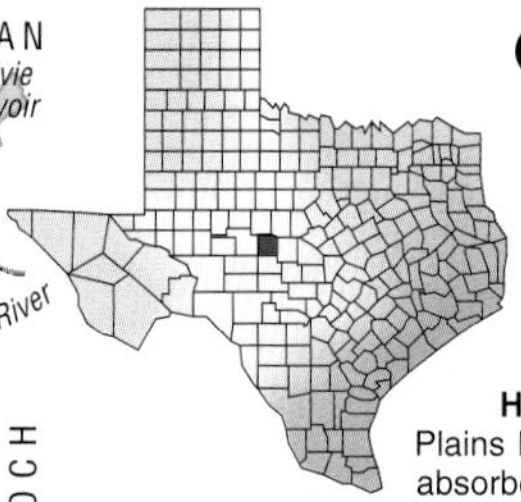

Physical Features: West central county on Edwards Plateau, rough, broken to south; level in north; sandy, loam and dark soils; drains to creeks and Colorado River.

Economy: Agribusinesses.

History: Athabascan-speaking Plains Indians, then Jumanos in 1600s, absorbed by Lipan Apaches 1700s. Comanches raided after 1800. Anglo-Americans began ranching around 1850; farming after the Civil War. Mexican-Americans employed on sheep ranches 1920s-30s. County created from Bexar District, 1858, organized 1879; named for river.

Race/Ethnicity, 2000: (In percent) Anglo, 57.39; Black, 0.98; Hispanic, 41.33; Other, 0.30.

Vital Statistics, 2003: Births, 29; deaths, 28; marriages, 15; divorces, 7.

Recreation: Famed for 1,500 Indian pictographs; reservoir.

Minerals: Oil, gas, stone.

Agriculture: A leading sheep-raising county; cattle, goats; wheat, feed grains; 10,000 acres irrigated for cotton. Market value $14.3 million.

PAINT ROCK (326) county seat; named for Indian pictographs nearby; farming, ranching center.

EDEN (2,563) steel fabrication, detention center; hospital; fall fest.

Other towns include: **Eola** (215), **Lowake** (40) and **Millersview** (80).

Population	3,744
Change fm 2000	-5.6
Area (sq. mi.)	993.69
Land Area (sq. mi.)	991.45
Altitude (ft.)	1,500-2,400
Rainfall (in.)	25.50
Jan. mean min.	31.9
July mean max.	97.4
Civ. Labor	1,484
Unemployed	2.2
Wages	$5,819,609
Av. Weekly Wage	$515.74
Prop. Value	$393,521,700
Retail Sales	$14,645,752

For explanation of sources, abbreviations and symbols, see p. 167 and foldout map.

Cooke County

Physical Features: North central county; drains to Red, Trinity rivers, lakes; sandy, red, loam soils.

Economy: Agribusiness, tourism, varied manufacturing.

History: Frontier between Caddoes and Comanches. Anglo-Americans arrived in late 1840s. Germans settled western part around 1890. County created 1848 from Fannin County; named for Capt. W.G. Cooke of the Texas Revolution.

Race/Ethnicity, 2000: (In percent) Anglo, 85.55; Black, 3.19; Hispanic, 9.97; Other, 1.29.

Vital Statistics, 2003: Births, 517; deaths, 399; marriages, 742; divorces, 159.

Recreation: Water sports; hunting, fishing; zoo; museum; park, Depot Day/car show in October.

Minerals: Oil, sand, gravel.

Agriculture: Beef, horses, wheat, dairy operations, grain sorghum, corn. Market value $46.2 million.

GAINESVILLE (16,160) county seat; tourism, plastics, agribusiness; aircraft, steel fabrication; Victorian homes, walking tours; hospital; community college, juvenile correction unit; Camp Sweeney for diabetic children.

Muenster (1,623) oil, food processing, tourism, varied manufacturing; hospital, Germanfest in April.

Other towns include: **Callisburg** (372), **Era** (150), **Lindsay** (861), **Myra** (150), **Oak Ridge** (254), **Rosston** (75), **Valley View** (771) and the residential community around **Lake Kiowa** (1,783).

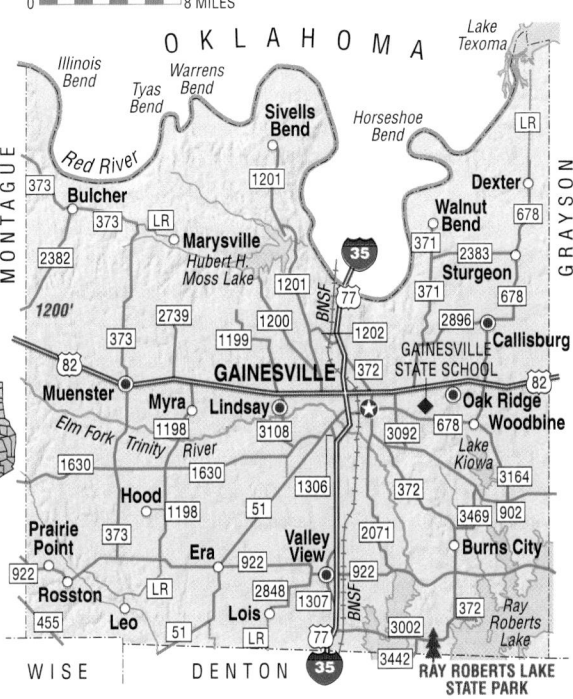

Population....................... 38,626	July mean max. 95.0
Change fm 2000 .... 6.2	Civ. Labor........................ 17,782
Area (sq. mi.) 898.81	Unemployed 4.0
Land Area (sq. mi.) 873.64	Wages $87,637,433
Altitude (ft.) 617-1,200	Av. Weekly Wage........... $541.21
Rainfall (in.)......................... 36.90	Prop. Value........ $2,480,874,702
Jan. mean min. 28.0	Retail Sales $495,915,939

The Concho County Courthouse in Paint Rock. Texas Almanac photo.

Physical Features: Leon Valley in center, remainder rolling, hilly.

Economy: Fort Hood, agribusiness, state prisons, plastics and other manufacturing.

History: Tonkawa area, later various other tribes. Anglo-Americans settled around Fort Gates in late 1840s. Permanent establishment of Fort Hood in 1950 changed cultural geography. County created from Bell County 1854; named for local pioneer James Coryell.

Race/Ethnicity, 2000: (In percent) Anglo, 61.74; Black, 22.30; Hispanic, 12.57; Other, 3.39.

Vital Statistics, 2003: Births, 948; deaths, 313; marriages, 515; divorces, 204.

Recreation: state park; deer, turkey hunting; fishing; nearby lakes and Leon River, bluebonnet area. Historic homes; log jail; Shivaree in June.

Minerals: Rock, sand and gravel production.

Agriculture: Beef cattle, forage, small grains, row crops, sheep and goats. Market value $34.7 million. Hunting leases, timber.

GATESVILLE (15,883) county seat; prisons; varied manufacturing; hospital; refurbished courthouse; museum; branch Central Texas College.

COPPERAS COVE (29,976) business center for Fort Hood; industrial filters, other manufacturing; hospital, library; Central Texas College; Spurfest in September.

Other towns include: **Evant** (372, partly in Hamilton County), **Flat** (210), **Jonesboro** (125), **Mound** (125), **Oglesby** (442), **Purmela** (50), **South Mountain** (405). Part [16,429] of **Fort Hood**.

Coryell County

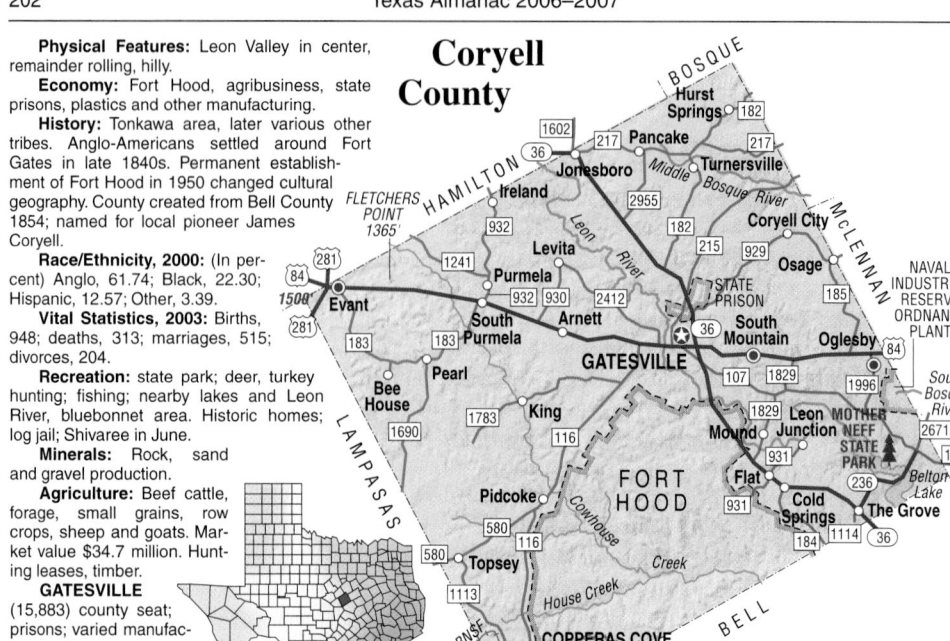

Population 75,074	July mean max. 96.4
Change fm 2000 .... 0.1	Civ. Labor 21,475
Area (sq. mi.) 1,056.73	Unemployed 4.9
Land Area (sq. mi.) 1,051.76	Wages $81,256,692
Altitude (ft.) 600-1,500	Av. Weekly Wage $489.74
Rainfall (in.) 33.43	Prop. Value $2,011,338,872
Jan. mean min. 33.5	Retail Sales $371,489,330

Cottle County

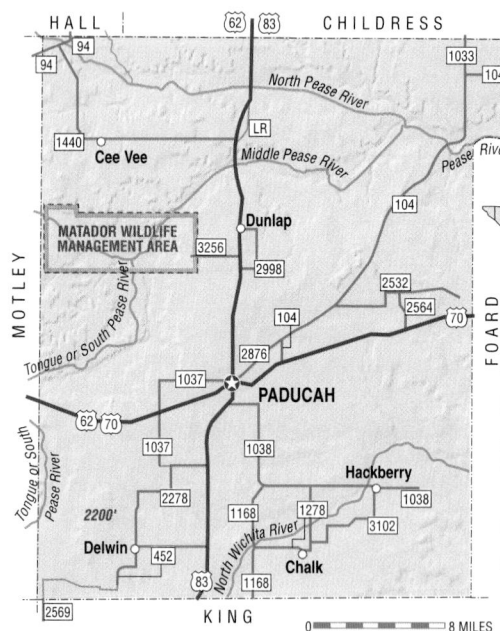

Physical Features: Western county below Caprock, rough in west, level in east; gray, black, sandy and loam soils; drains to Pease River.

Economy: Agribusiness, government/services.

History: Around 1700, Apaches were displaced by Comanches, who in turn were driven out by U.S. Army 1870s. Anglo-American settlers arrived in 1880s. County created 1876 from Fannin County; organized 1892; named for George W. Cottle, Alamo hero.

Race/Ethnicity, 2000: (In percent) Anglo, 71.42; Black, 9.30; Hispanic, 18.91; Other, 0.37.

Vital Statistics, 2003: Births, 21; deaths, 17; marriages, 7; divorces, 4.

Recreation: Hunting of quail, dove, wild hogs, deer; wildlife management area; museum, Fiesta Patria, horse and colt show in April.

Minerals: Oil, natural gas.

Agriculture: Beef cattle, cotton, peanuts, wheat. 3,000 acres irrigated. Market value $13 million.

PADUCAH (1,355) county seat; government/services, library.

Other towns include: **Cee Vee** (45).

Population 1,748	Civ. Labor 908
Change fm 2000 .... -8.2	Unemployed 4.5
Area (sq. mi.) 901.59	Wages $4,016,948
Land Area (sq. mi.) 901.18	Av. Weekly Wage $575.41
Altitude (ft.) 1,600-2,200	Prop. Value $161,999,670
Rainfall (in.) 24.11	Retail Sales $12,715,191
Jan. mean min. 26.2	
July mean max. 96.8	

Crane County

Physical Features: Rolling prairie, Pecos Valley, some hills; sandy, loam soils; Juan Cordona Lake (intermittent).

Economy: Oil and gas; agriculture; government/services.

History: Lipan Apache area. Ranching developed in 1890s. Oil discovered in 1926. County created from Tom Green County 1887, organized 1927; named for Baylor University president W. C. Crane.

Race/Ethnicity, 2000: (In percent) Anglo, 52.42; Black, 2.98; Hispanic, 43.87; Other, 0.73.

Vital Statistics, 2003: Births, 61; deaths, 48; marriages, 32; divorces, 7.

Recreation: Sites of pioneer trails and historic Horsehead Crossing on Pecos River; hunting of mule deer, quail; county stock show in January; camping park.

Minerals: Oil, gas production.

Agriculture: Cattle ranching, goats. Market value $1.3 million.

CRANE (3,219) county seat; oil-well servicing, production; foundry; steel, surfboard manufacturing; hospital.

Population	3,849
Change fm 2000	-3.7
Area (sq. mi.)	785.59
Land Area (sq. mi.)	785.56
Altitude (ft.)	2,300-2,902
Rainfall (in.)	15.38
Jan. mean min.	30.6
July mean max.	95.3
Civ. Labor	1,864
Unemployed	4.1
Wages	$11,858,865
Av. Weekly Wage	$681.27
Prop. Value	$889,990,350
Retail Sales	$21,540,269

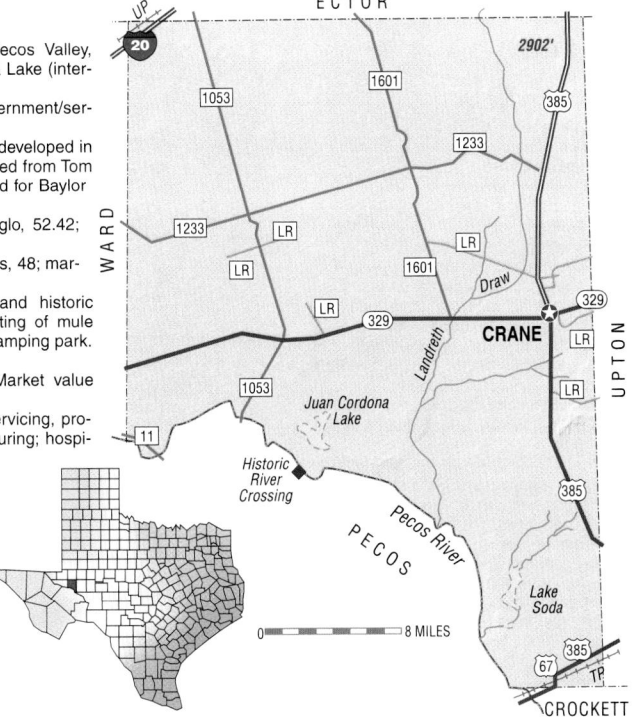

Crockett County

Physical Features: Level to rough, hilly terrain; drains to Pecos River on south; rocky soils.

Economy: Oil and gas, ranching, hunting leases.

History: Apaches and Tonkawas, displaced by Comanches in 1700s. Fort Lancaster established 1855. Ranching developed during 1880s. County created 1875 from Bexar, organized 1891; named for Alamo hero Davy Crockett.

Race/Ethnicity, 2000: (In percent) Anglo, 43.95; Black, 0.59; Hispanic, 54.70; Other, 0.76.

Vital Statistics, 2003: Births, 51; deaths, 33; marriages, 28; divorces, 14.

Recreation: Hunting; historic sites; museum; Davy Crockett statue in park; Deerfest in December; world championship goat roping in June.

Minerals: Oil, gas production.

Agriculture: Sheep, goats; beef cattle. Market value $10.2 million.

OZONA (3,437) county seat; trade center for ranching; hunting leases; tourism.

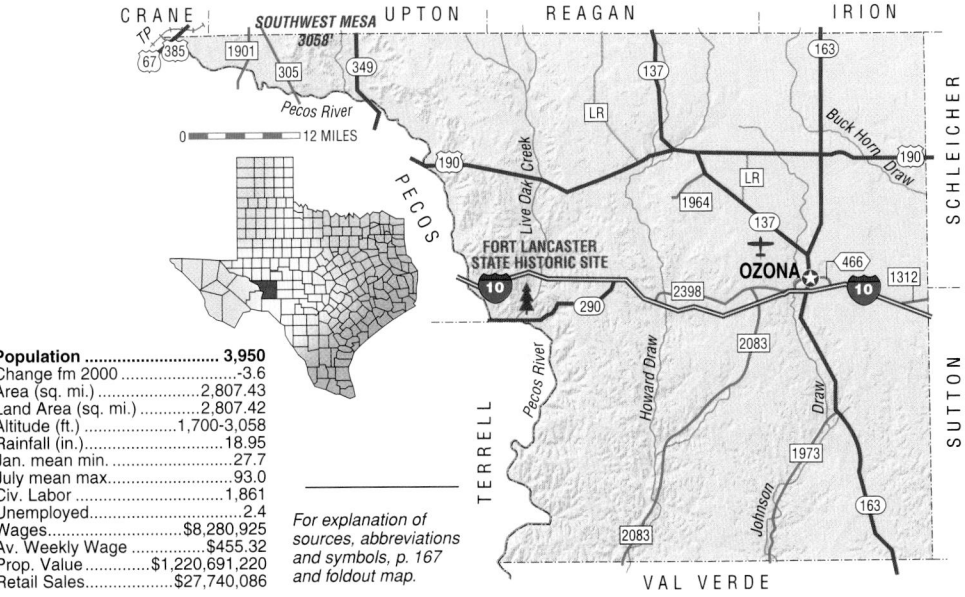

Population	3,950
Change fm 2000	-3.6
Area (sq. mi.)	2,807.43
Land Area (sq. mi.)	2,807.42
Altitude (ft.)	1,700-3,058
Rainfall (in.)	18.95
Jan. mean min.	27.7
July mean max.	93.0
Civ. Labor	1,861
Unemployed	2.4
Wages	$8,280,925
Av. Weekly Wage	$455.32
Prop. Value	$1,220,691,220
Retail Sales	$27,740,086

For explanation of sources, abbreviations and symbols, p. 167 and foldout map.

Crosby County

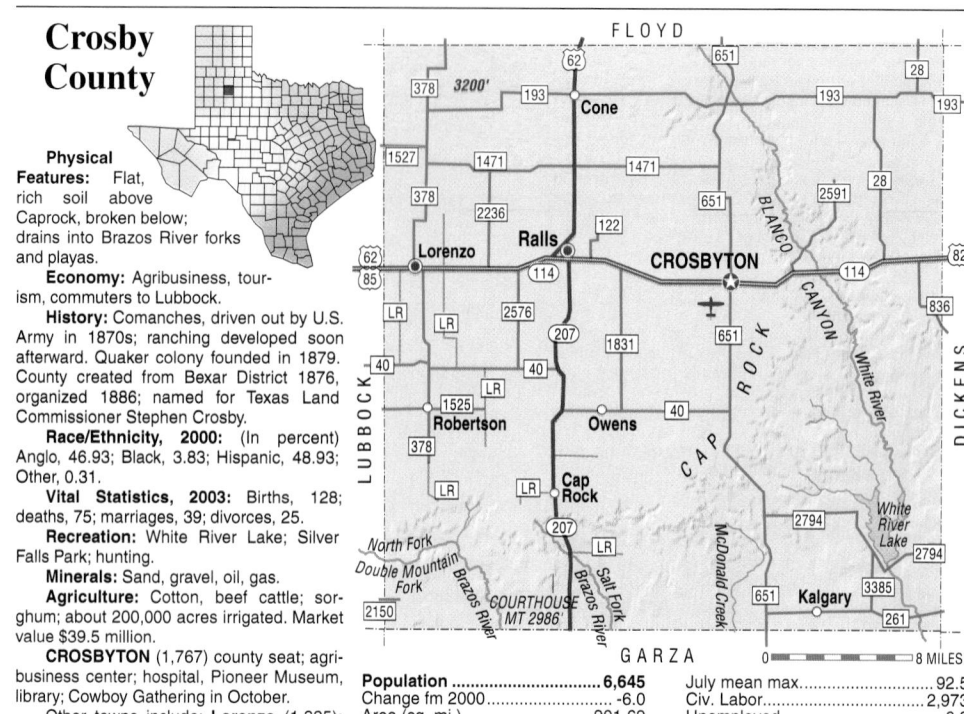

Physical Features: Flat, rich soil above Caprock, broken below; drains into Brazos River forks and playas.

Economy: Agribusiness, tourism, commuters to Lubbock.

History: Comanches, driven out by U.S. Army in 1870s; ranching developed soon afterward. Quaker colony founded in 1879. County created from Bexar District 1876, organized 1886; named for Texas Land Commissioner Stephen Crosby.

Race/Ethnicity, 2000: (In percent) Anglo, 46.93; Black, 3.83; Hispanic, 48.93; Other, 0.31.

Vital Statistics, 2003: Births, 128; deaths, 75; marriages, 39; divorces, 25.

Recreation: White River Lake; Silver Falls Park; hunting.

Minerals: Sand, gravel, oil, gas.

Agriculture: Cotton, beef cattle; sorghum; about 200,000 acres irrigated. Market value $39.5 million.

CROSBYTON (1,767) county seat; agribusiness center; hospital, Pioneer Museum, library; Cowboy Gathering in October.

Other towns include: **Lorenzo** (1,325); **Ralls** (2,142) government/services, agribusiness; museums; Cotton Boll Fest in September.

Population	6,645
Change fm 2000	-6.0
Area (sq. mi.)	901.69
Land Area (sq. mi.)	899.51
Altitude (ft.)	2,300-3,200
Rainfall (in.)	22.95
Jan. mean min.	25.3
July mean max.	92.5
Civ. Labor	2,973
Unemployed	6.2
Wages	$9,281,153
Av. Weekly Wage	$401.76
Prop. Value	$347,867,640
Retail Sales	$66,041,176

White River Lake in Crosby County. Texas Almanac photo.

El Capitan in Culberson County. Texas Almanac photo.

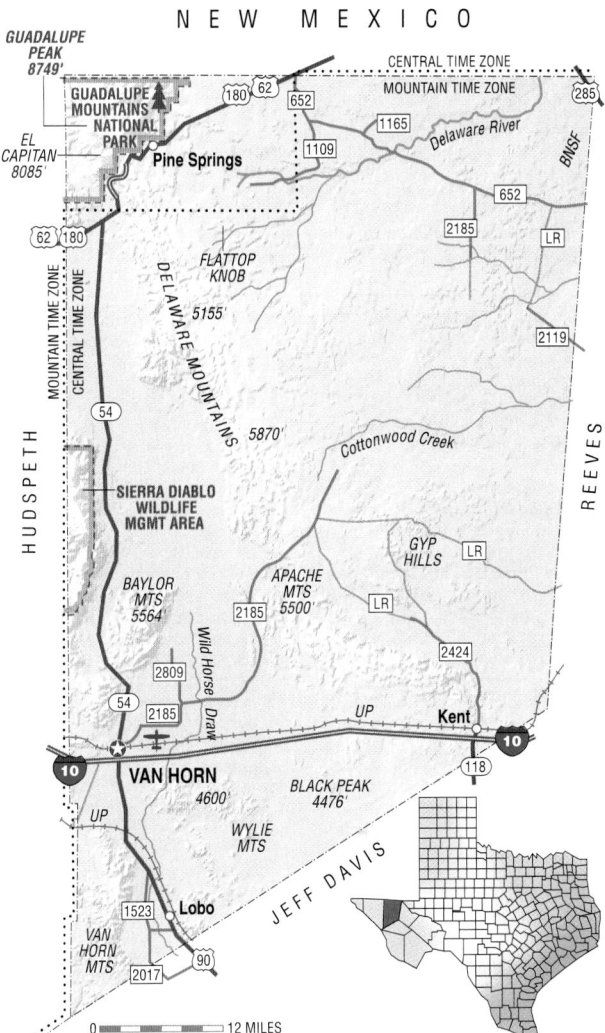

Culberson County

Physical Features: Contains Texas' highest mountain; slopes toward Pecos Valley on east, Diablo Bolson on west; salt lakes; unique vegetation in canyons.

Economy: Tourism; government/services; talc mining, processing; agribusiness.

History: Apaches arrived about 600 years ago. U.S. military frontier after Civil War. Ranching developed after 1880. Mexican migration increased after 1920. County created from El Paso County 1911, organized 1912; named for D.B. Culberson, Texas congressman.

Race/Ethnicity, 2000: (In percent) Anglo, 25.98; Black, 0.64; Hispanic, 72.24; Other, 1.14.

Vital Statistics, 2003: Births, 38; deaths, 17; marriages, 0; divorces, 2.

Recreation: National park; Guadalupe and El Capitan, twin peaks; scenic canyons and mountains; classic car museum; antique saloon bar; frontier days in June, big buck tournament.

Minerals: Sulfur, talc, marble, oil.

Agriculture: Beef cattle; crops include cotton, vegetables, melons, pecans; 4,000 acres in irrigation. Market value $7.5 million.

VAN HORN (2,232) county seat; agribusiness; tourism; rock crushing; government/services.

Other towns: **Kent** (60).

Population	2,727
Change fm 2000	-8.3
Area (sq. mi.)	3,812.71
Land Area (sq. mi.)	3,812.46
Altitude (ft.)	3,000-8,749
Rainfall (in.)	11.98
Jan. mean min.	27.8
July mean max.	91.7
Civ. Labor	1,102
Unemployed	7.5
Wages	$5,268,149
Av. Weekly Wage	$416.06
Prop. Value	$294,385,360
Retail Sales	$68,826,426

For explanation of sources, abbreviations and symbols, see p. 167 and foldout map.

Dallam County

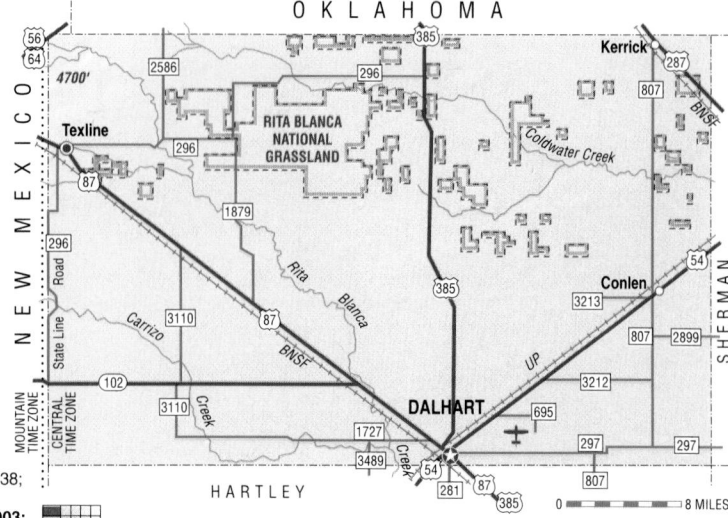

Physical Features: Prairie, broken by creeks; playas; sandy, loam soils; Rita Blanca National Grassland.

Economy: Agribusiness, tourism.

History: Earliest Plains Apaches; displaced by Comanches and Kiowas. Ranching developed in late 19th century. Farming began after 1900. County created from Bexar District, 1876, organized 1891. Named for lawyer-editor James W. Dallam.

Race/Ethnicity, 2000: (In percent) Anglo, 68.95; Black, 1.69; Hispanic, 28.38; Other, 0.98.

Vital Statistics, 2003: Births, 103; deaths, 53; marriages, 83; divorces, 34.

Recreation: Interstate Fair in September; XIT Museum; XIT Rodeo in August; hunting, wildlife; grasslands; La Rita Theater in June-August.

Minerals: Petroleum.

Agriculture: Cattle; hogs (a leader in sales, inventory); a leader in production for grain, (corn, wheat, grain sorghum); sugar beets, potatoes, sunflowers, beans; substantial irrigation. Market value $369.7 million.

DALHART (7,170, partly in Hartley County) county seat; government/services; agribusiness center for parts of Texas, New Mexico, Oklahoma; railroad; grain operations; hospital; prison.

Other towns include: **Kerrick** (35) and **Texline** (520).

Population	6,175
Change fm 2000	-0.8
Area (sq. mi.)	1,505.26
Land Area (sq. mi.)	1,504.69
Altitude (ft.)	3,700-4,700
Rainfall (in.)	18.57
Jan. mean min.	19.0
July mean max.	90.0
Civ. Labor	3,647
Unemployed	2.2
Wages	$22,144,775
Av. Weekly Wage	$521.41
Prop. Value	$701,765,100
Retail Sales	$96,542,805

Physical Features: Mostly flat, heavy blackland soils, sandy clays in west; drains to Trinity River.

Economy: A national center for telecommunications, transportation, electronics manufacturing, data processing, conventions and trade shows; foreign-trade zone located at D/FW International Airport, U.S.

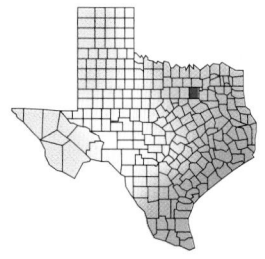

Population	2,294,706
Change fm 2000	3.4
Area (sq. mi.)	908.56
Land Area (sq. mi.)	879.60
Altitude (ft.)	382-870
Rainfall (in.)	37.05
Jan. mean min.	36.4
July mean max.	96.1
Civ. Labor	1,247,568
Unemployed	6.7
Wages	$16,605,578,973
Av. Weekly Wage	$888.34
Prop. Value	$154,267,997,442
Retail Sales	$37,935,355,455

Dallas County

Customs port of entry; government/services.

History: Caddoan area. Anglo-Americans began arriving in 1840. Antebellum slaveholding area. County created 1846 from Nacogdoches, Robertson counties; named for U.S. Vice President George Mifflin Dallas.

Race/Ethnicity, 2000: (In percent) Anglo, 44.99; Black, 20.47; Hispanic, 29.87; Other, 4.67.

Vital Statistics, 2003: Births, 42,297; deaths, 13,834; marriages, 15,705; divorces, 9,335.

Recreation: One of the state's top tourist destinations and one of the nation's most popular convention centers; State Fair, museums, zoo, West End shopping and tourist district, historical sites, including Sixth Floor museum in the old Texas School Book Depository, site of the assassination of President Kennedy.

Other important attractions include the Morton H. Meyerson Symphony Center; performing arts; professional sports; Texas broadcast museum; lakes; theme and amusement parks.

Minerals: Sand, gravel.

Agriculture: Horticultural crops; wheat, hay, corn; horses. Market value $19 million.

Education: Southern Methodist University, University of Dallas, Dallas Baptist University, University of Texas at Dallas, University of Texas Southwestern Medical Center and many other education centers.

DALLAS (1,211,437) county seat; center of state's largest consolidated metropolitan area and second-largest city in Texas; D/FW International Airport is one of the world's busiest; headquarters for the U.S. Army and Air Force Exchange Service; Federal Reserve Bank; a leader in fashions and in computer operations; Infomart, a large computer-sales complex; many hotels in downtown area offer adequate accommodations for most conventions.

Garland (219,070) varied manufacturing, community college branch, hospital, performing arts center.

Irving (194,372) Texas Stadium, home of the Dallas Cowboys; telecommunications; varied light manufacturing, food processing; distribution center; Boy Scout headquarters and museum; North Lake College; hospitals.

Other cities include: **Addison** (14,601) general aviation airport; **Balch Springs** (19,708); part [49,822] of **Carrollton** (118,745 total) residential community, distribution center; **Cedar Hill** (39,095) residential community, Northwood University, Country Day on the Hill in October; **Cockrell Hill** (4,422); **Coppell** (38,909) distribution, varied manufacturing; office center; **DeSoto** (42,792) residential community, light industry and distribution, hospitals.

Also, **Duncanville** (35,362) varied manufacturing, residential community; **Farmers Branch** (27,176) distribution center, varied manufacturing, Brookhaven College, hospital; **Glenn Heights** (8,345, partly in Ellis County); most [99,760] of **Grand Prairie** (141,692 total) wholesale trade, aerospace, entertainment,

Largest U.S. Media Markets

Rank	Homes
1. New York	7.36 million
2. Los Angeles	5.43 million
3. Chicago	3.42 million
4. Philadelphia	2.92 million
5. Boston	2.39 million
6. San Francisco	2.36 million
7. Dallas/Fort Worth	**2.29 million**
8. Washington	2.24 million
9. Atlanta	2.06 million
10. Detroit	1.94 million

Source: Nielsen Media Research, 2004.

plastics; library, Joe Pool Reservoir, Indian pow-wow in September, Lone Star horse-racing track; **Highland Park** (8,504); **Hutchins** (2,773) varied manufacturing; **Lancaster** (27,241) residential, industrial, distri-

bution center, Cedar Valley College, Commemorative Air Force museum, hospital, park, depot, historic town square; Musicfests monthly in spring.

Also, **Mesquite** (128,653) varied industries; hospitals; championship rodeo, rodeo parade in spring; community college, historical parks; most [70,929] of **Richardson** (100,803 total) telecommunications, software development, hospital; Fountain Plaza festival in September; **Rowlett** (52,060) residential, varied manufacturing, government/services, hospital, library, park; Pecan Festival in October; **Sachse** (15,092, partly in Collin County); **Seagoville** (11,100) rural/suburban setting, federal prison; **Sunnyvale** (3,608); **University Park** (22,529); **Wilmer** (3,678).

Part of **Combine** (1,972) and part of **Ovilla** (3,705).

For explanation of sources, abbreviations or symbols, see p. 167 and foldout map.

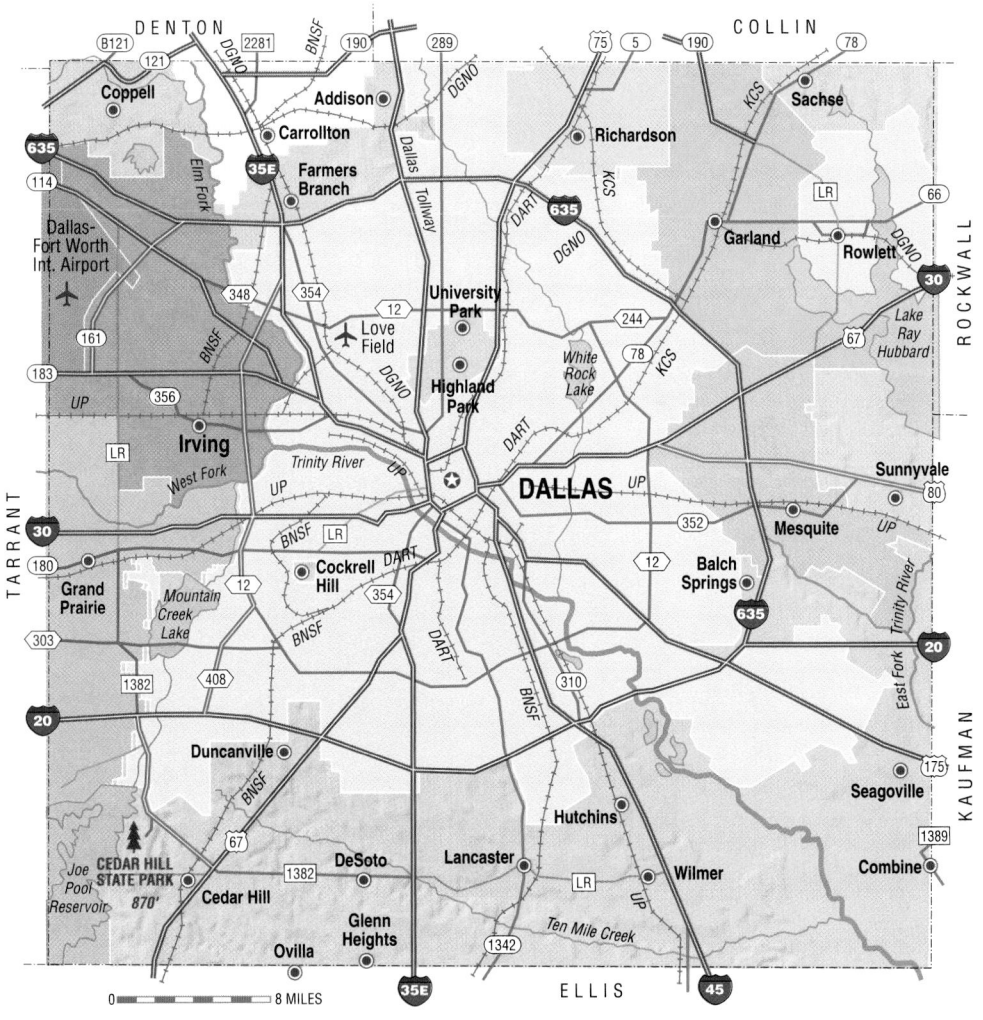

Dawson County

Physical Features: South High Plains county in West Texas, broken on the east; loam and sandy soils.

Economy: Agriculture; farm, gin equipment manufacturing; peanut plant; government/services.

History: Comanche, Kiowa area. Ranching developed in 1880s. Farming began after 1900. Hispanic population increased after 1940. County created from Bexar District, 1876, organized 1905; named for Nicholas M. Dawson, San Jacinto veteran.

Race/Ethnicity, 2000: (In percent) Anglo, 42.65; Black, 8.69; Hispanic, 48.19; Other, 0.47.

Vital Statistics, 2003: Births, 192; deaths, 148; marriages, 56; divorces, 57.

Recreation: Parks; museum; campground; May Fun Fest; July 4 celebration.

Minerals: Oil, natural gas.

Agriculture: A major cotton-producing county; also peanuts, sorghums, watermelons, alfalfa, grapes. 70,000 acres irrigated. Market value $55.4 million.

LAMESA (9,481) county seat; agribusiness; food processing, oil-field services; some manufacturing; computerized cotton-classing office; hospital; campus of Howard College; prison unit.

Other towns include: **Ackerly** (235, partly in Martin County), **Los Ybañez** (32) and **Welch** (95). Also, **O'Donnell** (961, mostly in Lynn County).

Population..........................**14,383**	July mean max......................92.9
Change fm 2000.....................-4.0	Civ. Labor.............................5,580
Area (sq. mi.)....................902.12	Unemployed...........................6.1
Land Area (sq. mi.)............902.06	Wages.....................$27,895,039
Altitude (ft.)................2,600-3,100	Av. Weekly Wage............$449.00
Rainfall (in.).........................19.07	Prop. Value.........$1,037,696,098
Jan. mean min......................26.0	Retail Sales.............$110,257,052

Population 18,510	
Change fm 2000.........................-0.3	
Area (sq. mi.).....................1,498.26	
Land Area (sq. mi.).............1,497.34	
Altitude (ft.)....................3,700-4,400	
Rainfall (in.)...........................18.65	
Jan. mean min...........................21.1	
July mean max..........................91.6	
Civ. Labor.................................6,526	
Unemployed 5.2	
Wages.............................$36,461,830	
Av. Weekly Wage...............$504.91	
Prop. Value................$837,974,349	
Retail Sales................$128,020,805	

For explanation of sources, abbreviations and symbols, see p. 167 and foldout map.

Deaf Smith County

Physical Features: Panhandle High Plains county, partly broken; chocolate and sandy loam soils; drains to Palo Duro and Tierra Blanca creeks.

Economy: Agriculture, varied industries, meat packing, offset printing.

History: Apaches, displaced by Comanches, Kiowas. Ranching developed after U.S. Army drove out Indians 1874-75. Farming began after 1900. Hispanic settlement increased after 1950. County created 1876, from Bexar District; organized 1890. Named for famed scout in Texas Revolution, Erastus (Deaf) Smith.

Race/Ethnicity, 2000: (In percent) Anglo, 40.60; Black, 1.40; Hispanic, 57.40; Other, 0.60.

Vital Statistics, 2003: Births, 351; deaths, 153; marriages, 154; divorces, 50.

Recreation: Museum, tours, POW camp chapel; Cinco de Mayo, Pioneer Days in May.

Minerals: Not significant.

Agriculture: Leading agricultural county, feedlot operations, dairies, cotton, wheat, sorghum, corn; 50 percent irrigated. Market value $841.8 million, first in state.

HEREFORD (14,559) county seat; agribusinesses, food processing; varied manufacturing; trucking; hospital, aquatic center.

Other towns include: **Dawn** (52).

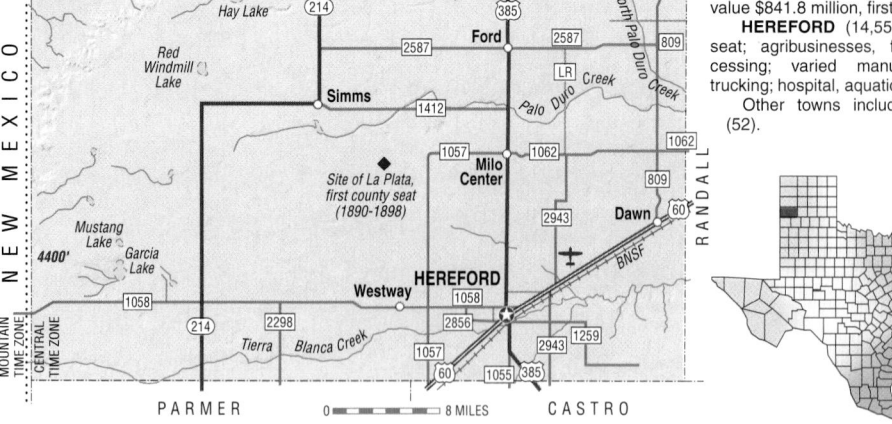

Delta County

Physical Features: Northeast county between two forks of Sulphur River; Cooper Lake (also designated Jim Chapman Lake); black, sandy loam soils.

Economy: Agribusiness; tourism; manufacturing.

History: Caddo area, but disease, other tribes caused displacement around 1790. Anglo-Americans arrived in 1820s. County created from Lamar, Hopkins counties 1870. Greek letter delta origin of name, because of shape of the county.

Race/Ethnicity, 2000: (In percent) Anglo, 87.55; Black, 8.62; Hispanic, 3.10; Other, 0.73.

Vital Statistics, 2003: Births, 73; deaths, 90; marriages, 22; divorces, 13.

Recreation: Fishing, hunting; lakes, state park; Chiggerfest in October.

Minerals: Not significant.

Agriculture: Beef, dairy cattle; crops include hay, soybeans, corn, sorghum, cotton, wheat. Market value $10.7 million.

COOPER (2,171) county seat; industrial park, some manufacturing; agribusiness; museum.

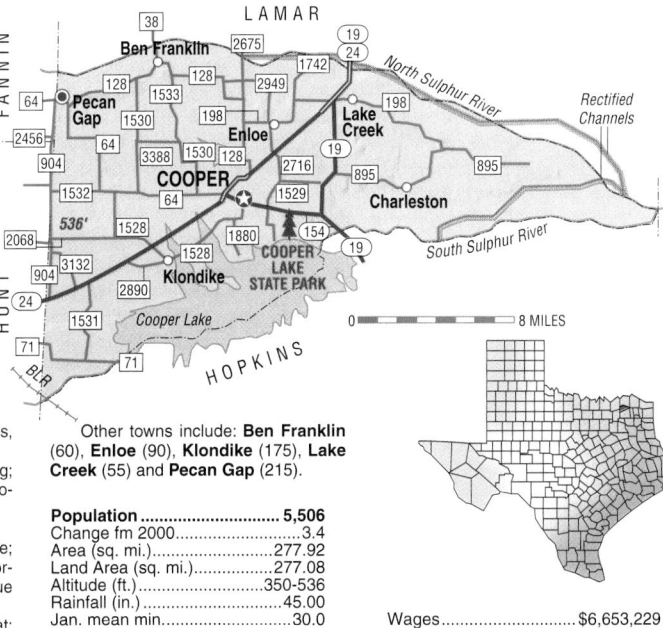

Other towns include: **Ben Franklin** (60), **Enloe** (90), **Klondike** (175), **Lake Creek** (55) and **Pecan Gap** (215).

Population	5,506
Change fm 2000	3.4
Area (sq. mi.)	277.92
Land Area (sq. mi.)	277.08
Altitude (ft.)	350-536
Rainfall (in.)	45.00
Jan. mean min.	30.0
July mean max.	94.0
Civ. Labor	2,748
Unemployed	5.2
Wages	$6,653,229
Av. Weekly Wage	$525.99
Prop. Value	$206,542,556
Retail Sales	$12,566,867

Fishing on Ray Roberts Lake in Denton County. Texas Almanac photo.

Physical Features: North Texas county; partly hilly, draining to Elm Fork of Trinity River, lakes; Blackland and Grand Prairie soils and terrain.

Economy: Varied industries; colleges; horse industry; tourism; government/services; part of Dallas-Fort Worth metropolitan area.

History: Land grant from Texas Congress 1841 for Peters colony. County created out of Fannin County 1846; named for John B. Denton, pioneer Methodist minister.

Race/Ethnicity, 2000: (In percent) Anglo, 76.93; Black, 6.07; Hispanic, 12.15; Other, 4.85.

Vital Statistics, 2003: Births, 8,607; deaths, 1,951; marriages, 3,709; divorces, 2,111.

Recreation: Water sports at Lewisville, Grapevine lakes, seven U.S. Corps of Engineers parks; Ray Roberts lake; universities' cultural, athletic activities, including "Texas Women; A Celebration of History'" exhibit at TWU library; Texas Motor Speedway; State D.A.R. Museum "First Ladies of Texas" collection of gowns and memorabilia; Little Chapel in the Woods; Denton Jazzfest in April.

Minerals: Natural gas.

Education: University of North Texas and Texas Woman's University.

Denton County

Agriculture: Important horse-raising area. Eggs, nurseries, turf, cattle; also, hay, sorghum, wheat, peanuts grown. Market value $49.1 million.

DENTON (93,700) county seat; universities; Denton State School (for the retarded); manufacturers of trucks (Peterbilt), bricks; milling; hospitals; Blues Festival in September, storytelling festival in spring.

LEWISVILLE (90,774) commuting to Dallas and Fort Worth, retail center, electronics and varied industries including missile manufacturing; Lewisville Lake, hospital, library; Celtic Feis & Scottish Highland Games in March.

Flower Mound (60,908) residential community, library, mound of native grasses, bike classic in spring.

Carrollton (118,745, also in Dallas County).

Other towns include: **The Colony** (36,038) on eastern shore of Lewisville Lake, tourism, IBM offices, chili cook-off in June, Las Vegas Night in April.

Also, **Argyle** (2,755); **Aubrey** (1,855) horse farms, training, Death by Chocolate event in November; **Bartonville** (1,280); **Clark** (373); **Copper Canyon** (1,355); **Corinth** (15,918); **Corral**

City (111); **Cross Roads** (691); **Double Oak** (2,761); **Hackberry** (639); **Hebron** (976); **Hickory Creek** (2,643); **Highland Village** (13,923); **Justin** (2,535); **Krugerville** (1,223); **Krum** (2,571); **Lake Dallas** (6,855) light manufacturing, marina.

Also, **Lakewood Village** (378); **Lincoln Park** (582); **Little Elm** (13,369) light manufacturing, lake activities, library, Cinco de Mayo; **Marshall Creek** (516); **Northlake** (1,487); **Oak Point** (2.194); **Pilot Point** (4,124) light manufacturing, agribusinesses, near Lake Ray Roberts, Country Fair on the Square in September; **Ponder** (661); **Roanoke** (3,565); **Sanger** (5,198) lake recreation enterprises; **Shady Shores** (1,766); **Trophy Club** (7,513).

Part [22,273] of **Dallas**, part [3,402] of **Frisco**, part [2,140] of **Plano**. Small part [44] of **Fort Worth**.

Population	530,597
Change fm 2000	22.5
Area (sq. mi.)	957.88
Land Area (sq. mi.)	888.54
Altitude (ft.)	450-950
Rainfall (in.)	37.79
Jan. mean min.	32.0
July mean max.	94.1
Civ. Labor	280,271
Unemployed	4.1
Wages	$1,096,409,842
Av. Weekly Wage	$639.43
Prop. Value	$36,158,602,112
Retail Sales	$5,972,312,510

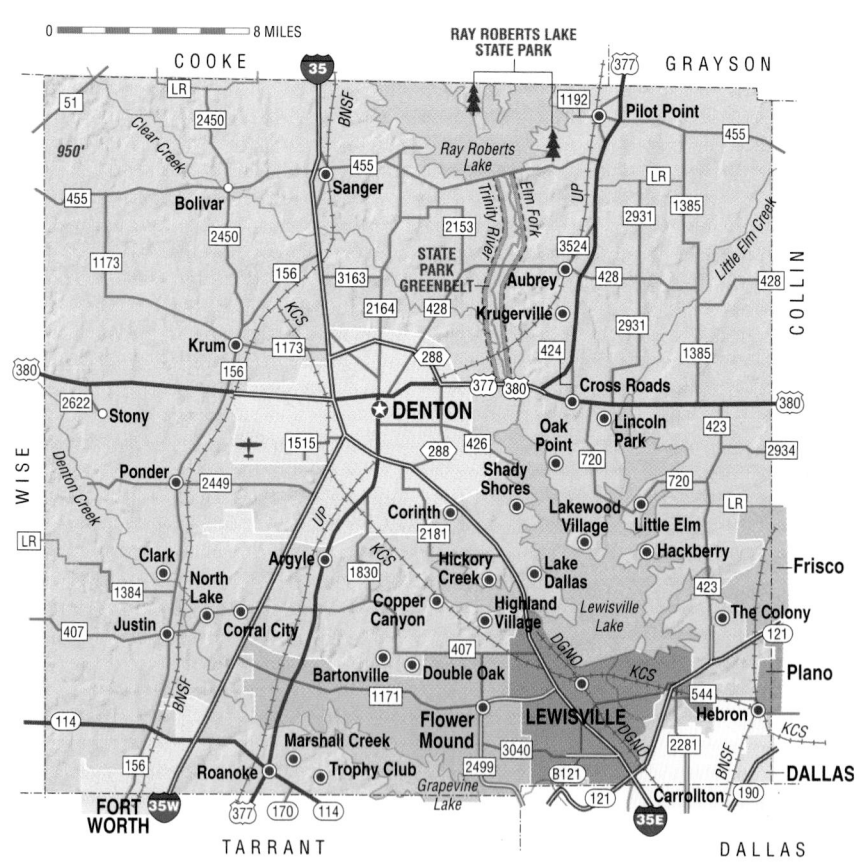

DeWitt County

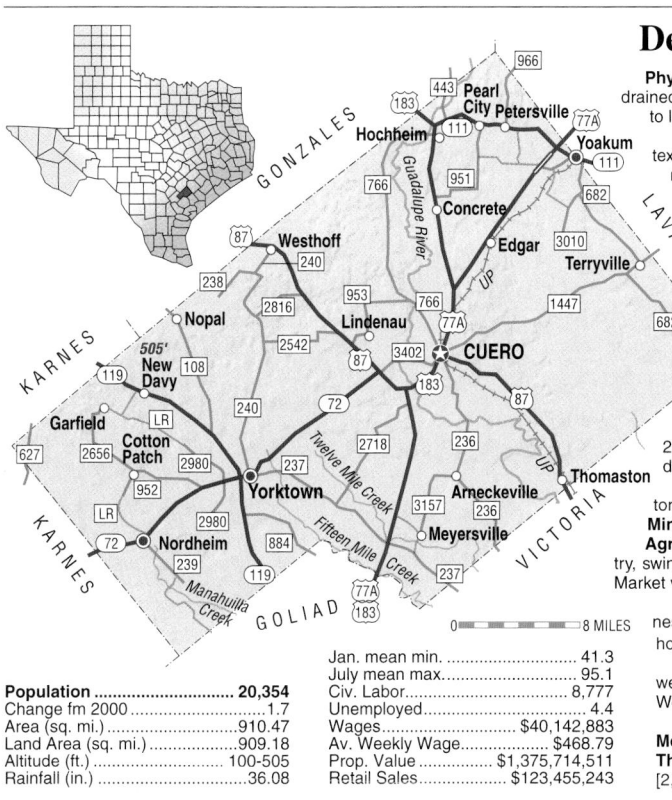

Physical Features: South central county drained by Guadalupe and tributaries; rolling to level; waxy, loam, sandy soils.

Economy: Wood, furniture plants, textile mill; varied manufacturing; agribusinesses; prison unit.

History: Coahuiltecan area, then Karankawas and other tribes, finally the Comanches. Mexican and Anglo-American settlers arrived in 1820s. County created from Gonzales, Goliad, Victoria counties 1846; named for Green DeWitt, colonizer.

Race/Ethnicity, 2000: (In percent) Anglo, 61.22; Black, 10.94; Hispanic, 27.24; Other, 0.60.

Vital Statistics, 2003: Births, 244; deaths, 265; marriages, 119; divorces, 89.

Recreation: Hunting, fishing; historic homes, museums; wildflowers.

Minerals: Oil and natural gas.

Agriculture: Cattle, dairy products, poultry, swine; corn, sorghum, cotton, hay, pecans. Market value $29.5 million.

CUERO (6,839) county seat; agribusiness, leather products; food processing; hospital, Turkeyfest in October.

Yorktown (2,307) agribusiness, oilwell servicing; library, museum, park; Western Days in October.

Other towns include: **Hochheim** (70), **Meyersville** (110), **Nordheim** (324), **Thomaston** (45), **Westhoff** (410). Part [2,137] of **Yoakum** (5,832 total).

Population	20,354
Change fm 2000	1.7
Area (sq. mi.)	910.47
Land Area (sq. mi.)	909.18
Altitude (ft.)	100-505
Rainfall (in.)	36.08
Jan. mean min.	41.3
July mean max.	95.1
Civ. Labor	8,777
Unemployed	4.4
Wages	$40,142,883
Av. Weekly Wage	$468.79
Prop. Value	$1,375,714,511
Retail Sales	$123,455,243

Dickens County

Physical Features: West Texas county; broken land, Caprock in northwest; sandy, chocolate, red soils; drains to Croton, Duck creeks.

Economy: Services/prison unit, agribusiness, hunting leases.

History: Comanches driven out by U.S. Army 1874-75. Ranching and some farming began in late 1880s. County created 1876, from Bexar District; organized 1891; named for Alamo hero who is variously listed as James R. Demkins or Dimpkins and J. Dickens.

Race/Ethnicity, 2000: (In percent) Anglo, 67.67; Black, 8.07; Hispanic, 23.90; Other, 0.36.

Vital Statistics, 2003: Births, 25; deaths, 49; marriages, 15; divorces, 14.

Recreation: Hunting, fishing; Soldiers Mound site, Dickens Springs; downtown Spur.

Agriculture: Cattle, cotton, forages, small grains, horses. Some irrigation. Market value $11.8 million. Hunting leases important.

Minerals: Oil, gas.

DICKENS (328) county seat, market for ranching county.

SPUR (1,030) agribusiness and shipping center, oil and gas, homecoming in October; state prison.

Other towns include: **Afton** (15) and **McAdoo** (75).

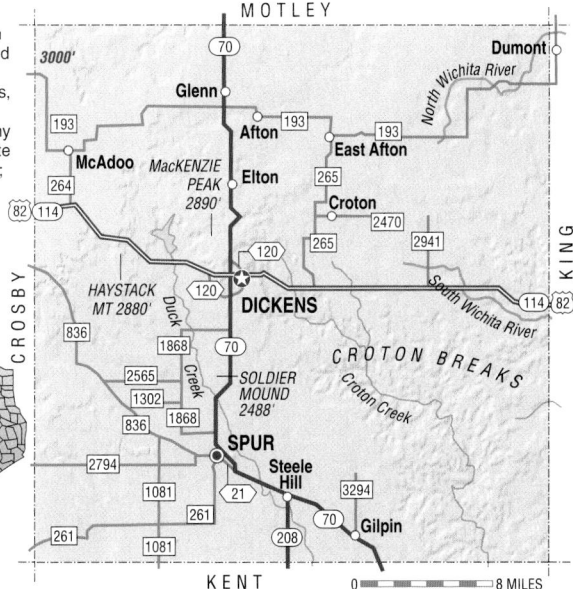

For explanation of sources, abbreviations and symbols, see p. 167 and foldout map.

Population	2,711
Change fm 2000	-1.8
Area (sq. mi.)	905.21
Land Area (sq. mi.)	904.21
Altitude (ft.)	1,800-3,000
Rainfall (in.)	18.68
Jan. mean min.	25.5
July mean max.	95.4
Civ. Labor	822
Unemployed	4.9
Wages	$3,265,192
Av. Weekly Wage	$481.17
Prop. Value	$236,355,560
Retail Sales	$11,39,470

Dimmit County

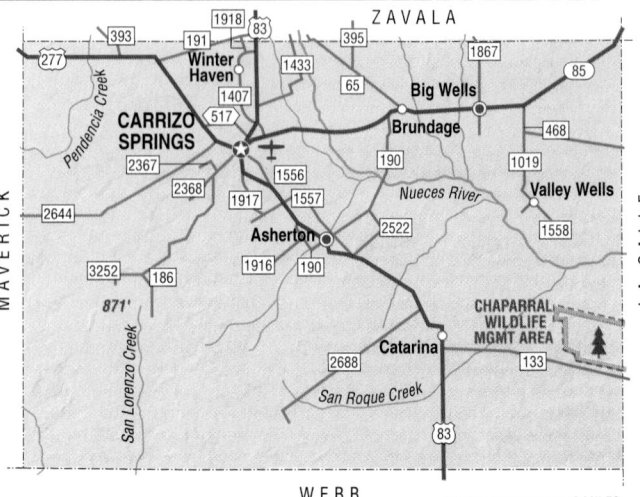

Physical Features: Southwest county; level to rolling; much brush; sandy, loam, red soils; drained by Nueces River.

Economy: Government/services; agribusiness; petroleum products; tourism.

History: Coahuiltecan area, later Comanches. John Townsend, a black man from Nacogdoches, led first attempt at settlement before the Civil War. Texas Rangers forced Indians out in 1877. Mexican migration increased after 1910. County created 1858 from Bexar, Maverick, Uvalde, Webb counties; organized 1880. Named for Philip Dimitt of Texas Revolution; law misspelled name.

Race/Ethnicity, 2000: (In percent) Anglo, 13.39; Black, 0.74; Hispanic, 84.97; Other, 0.90.

Vital Statistics, 2003: Births, 183; deaths, 75; marriages, 57; divorces, 8.

Recreation: Hunting, fishing, campsites, wildlife area; winter haven for tourists.

Minerals: Oil, natural gas.

Agriculture: Onions, pecans, cantaloupes, olives, tomatoes, tangerines; cattle, goats, horses, hay. Market value $27.5 million.

CARRIZO SPRINGS (5,606) county seat; agribusiness center, feedlot, food processing; oil, gas processing; hunting center; hospital; historic Baptist church; Brush Country Day in October.

Other towns include: **Asherton** (1,281), **Big Wells** (759) Cinco de Mayo, and **Catarina** (134) Camino Real festival in April.

Population	10,221
Change fm 2000	-0.3
Area (sq. mi.)	1,334.48
Land Area (sq. mi.)	1,330.91
Altitude (ft.)	400-871
Rainfall (in.)	20.21
Jan. mean min.	39.6
July mean max.	98.3
Civ. Labor	3,969
Unemployed	10.3
Wages	$16,902,542
Av. Weekly Wage	$503.95
Prop. Value	$703,197,343
Retail Sales	$58,757,069

Donley County

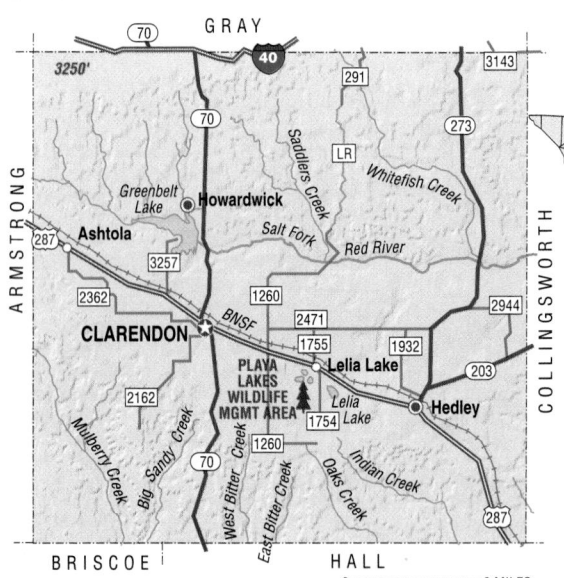

Physical Features: Northwest county bisected by Red River Salt Fork; rolling to level; clay, loam, sandy soils.

Economy: Agribusiness; government/services; tourism.

History: Apaches displaced by Kiowas and Comanches, who were driven out in 1874-75 by U.S. Army. Methodist colony from New York settled in 1878. County created in 1876, organized 1882, out of Bexar District; named for Texas Supreme Court Justice S.P. Donley.

Race/Ethnicity, 2000: (In percent) Anglo, 88.43; Black, 4.36; Hispanic, 6.35; Other, 0.86.

Vital Statistics, 2003: Births, 43; deaths, 38; marriages, 35; divorces, 11.

Recreation: Lake, hunting, fishing, camping, water sports; Col. Goodnight Chuckwagon cook-off in September.

Minerals: Small amount of natural gas.

Agriculture: Cattle top revenue source; cotton, peanuts, alfalfa, wheat, hay, melons; 11,000 acres irrigated. Market value $73.6 million.

CLARENDON (1,934) county seat; junior college; Saints Roost museum; library; agribusiness; tourism; medical center.

Other towns include: **Hedley** (379) cotton festival in October, **Howardwick** (453) and **Lelia Lake** (71).

Population	3,939
Change fm 2000	2.9
Area (sq. mi.)	933.05
Land Area (sq. mi.)	929.77
Altitude (ft.)	2,200-3,250
Rainfall (in.)	23.89
Jan. mean min.	22.4
July mean max.	94.7
Civ. Labor	1,625
Unemployed	3.7
Wages	$5,100,614
Av. Weekly Wage	$417.40
Prop. Value	$278,171,883
Retail Sales	$18,111,746

For explanation of sources, abbreviations and symbols, see p. 167 and foldout map.

Duval County

Physical Features: Southwestern county; level to hilly, brushy in most areas; varied soils.

Economy: Ranching; petroleum; tourism; government/services.

History: Coahuiltecans, displaced by Comanche bands. Mexican settlement began in 1812. County created from Live Oak, Nueces, Starr counties, 1858, organized 1876; named for Burr H. Duval, a victim of Goliad massacre.

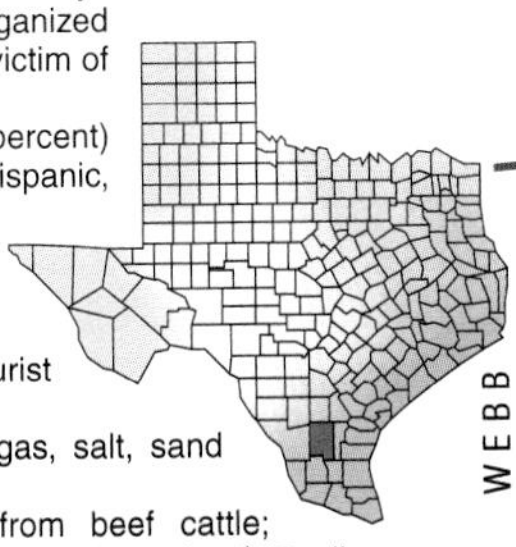

Race/Ethnicity, 2000: (In percent) Anglo, 11.22; Black, 0.44; Hispanic, 87.99; Other, 0.35.

Vital Statistics, 2003: Births, 184; deaths, 136; marriages, 65; divorces, 29.

Recreation: Hunting, tourist crossroads, rattlesnake roundup.

Minerals: Production of oil, gas, salt, sand and gravel.

Agriculture: Most income from beef cattle; grains, cotton, vegetables, hay, dairy. Market value $13 million.

SAN DIEGO (4,596, part [825] in Jim Wells County) county seat; ranching, oil field, tourist center; hospital.

Freer (3,288) oil and gas, construction, ranching; rattlesnake roundup in late April.

Benavides (1,653) serves truck farming area.

Other towns include: **Concepcion** (59) and **Realitos** (197).

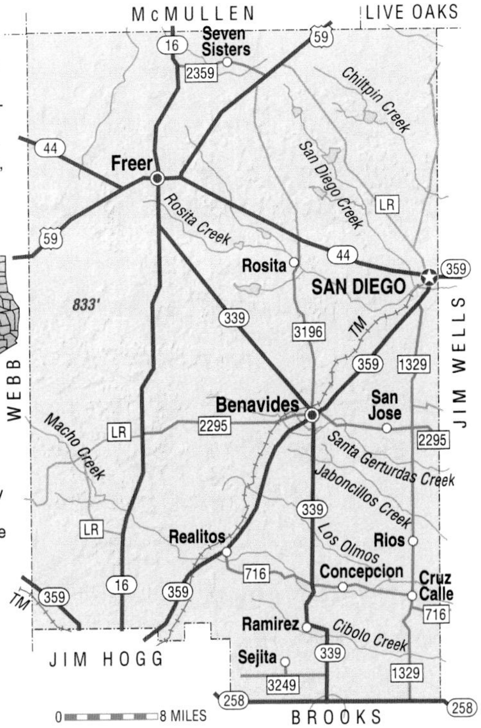

Population	**12,669**
Change fm 2000	-3.4
Area (sq. mi.)	1,795.67
Land Area (sq. mi.)	1,792.71
Altitude (ft.)	150-833
Rainfall (in.)	25.40
Jan. mean min.	42.5
July mean max.	97.3
Civ. Labor	5,065
Unemployed	6.8

Wages	$22,246,005
Av. Weekly Wage	$546.37

Prop. Value	$997,369,589
Retail Sales	$33,129,441

A horse grazes in a field of wildflowers along Texas 359 in Duval County. Texas Almanac photo.

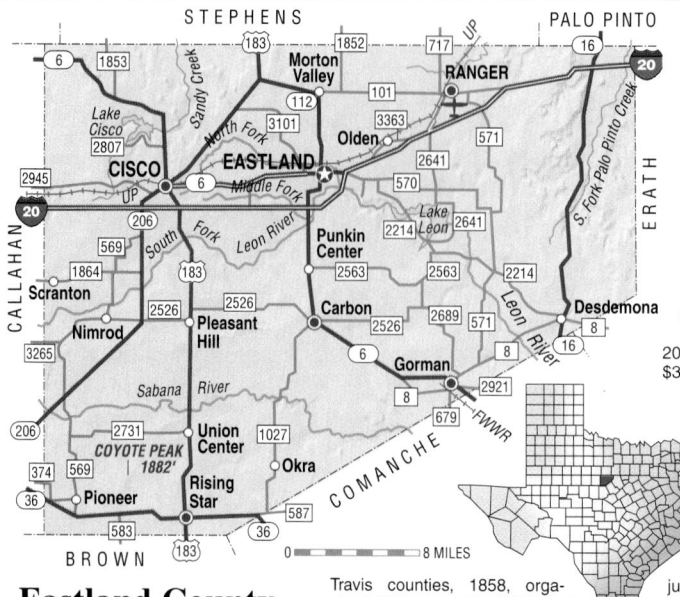

Population	18,379
Change fm 2000	0.4
Area (sq. mi.)	931.90
Land Area (sq. mi.)	926.01
Altitude (ft.)	1,000-1,882
Rainfall (in.)	27.53
Jan. mean min.	26.7
July mean max.	94.9
Civ. Labor	8,568
Unemployed	3.5
Wages	$42,474,097
Av. Weekly Wage	$509.95
Prop. Value	$992,252,360
Retail Sales	$211,807,139

Minerals: Oil, gas, gravel and sand.

Agriculture: Beef cattle, forage. 20,000 acres irrigated. Market value $30.4 million.

EASTLAND (3,796) county seat; tourism; government/services, petroleum industries, varied manufacturing; hospital, library; Old Ripfest in September.

    CISCO (3,746) masonry, government/services, environmental products; Conrad Hilton's first hotel restored, museums; junior college; folklife festival in April.

    RANGER (2,540) oil center, varied manufacturing, junior college, hospital.

    Other towns include: **Carbon** (245) livestock equipment manufacturing; **Desdemona** (180); **Gorman** (1,251) peanut processing, agribusiness, hospital; **Olden** (113), and **Rising Star** (817) cap manufacturing, plant nursery; Octoberfest.

Eastland County

Physical Features: West central county; hilly, rolling; sandy, loam soils; drains to Leon River forks.

Economy: Agribusinesses; education; petroleum industries; varied manufacturing.

History: Plains Indian area. Frank Sánchez among first settlers in 1850s. County created from Bosque, Coryell, Travis counties, 1858, organized 1873; named for W.M. Eastland, Mier Expedition casualty.

Race/Ethnicity, 2000: (In percent) Anglo, 86.26; Black, 2.30; Hispanic, 10.80; Other, 0.64.

Vital Statistics, 2003: Births, 230; deaths, 247; marriages, 129; divorces, 41.

Recreation: Lakes, water sports; fishing, hunting; festivals; historic sites and displays.

Ector County

Physical Features: West Texas county; level to rolling, some sand dunes; meteor crater; desert vegetation.

Economy: Center for Permian Basin oil field operations; plastics.

History: First settlers in late 1880s. Oil boom in 1926. County created from Tom Green County, 1887; organized 1891; named for jurist M.D. Ector.

Race/Ethnicity, 2000: (In percent) Anglo, 51.87; Black, 4.60; Hispanic, 42.36; Other, 1.17.

Vital Statistics, 2003: Births, 2,287; deaths, 1,089; marriages, 993; divorces, 716.

Recreation: Globe Theatre replica; presidential museum; art institute; second-largest U.S. meteor crater.

Minerals: More than 2 billion barrels of oil produced since 1926; gas, cement, stone.

Agriculture: Beef cattle, horses are chief producers; pecans, hay raised; poultry; minor irrigation. Market value $1.9 million.

Education: University of Texas of Permian Basin; Texas Tech University Health Sciences Center; Odessa (junior) College.

ODESSA (93,170, part [1,042] in Midland County) county seat; oil field services, supplies; petrochemical complex; medical, retail center; cultural center; Permian Basin Fair and Expo in September.

    Other towns include: **Gardendale** (1,235), **Goldsmith** (245), **Notrees** (20), **Penwell** (41), and **West Odessa** (18,564).

Population	124,488
Change fm 2000	2.8
Area (sq. mi.)	901.68
Land Area (sq. mi.)	901.06
Altitude (ft.)	2,800-3,300
Rainfall (in.)	13.29
Jan. mean min.	28.7
July mean max.	96.0
Civ. Labor	63,405
Unemployed	5.9
Wages	$399,424,149
Av. Weekly Wage	$603.22
Prop. Value	$5,324,849,820
Retail Sales	$1,600,219,765

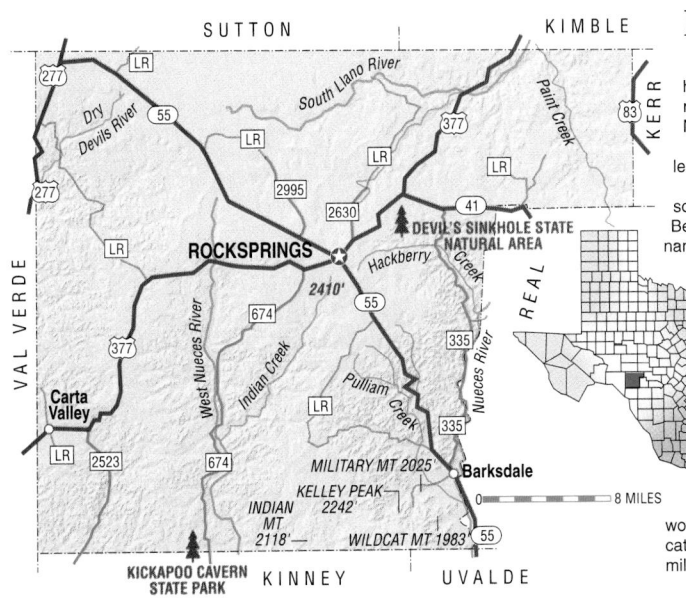

SUTTON
KIMBLE
KERR
REAL
VAL VERDE
KINNEY
UVALDE
277
LR
55
Dry Devils River
South Llano River
377
83
Paint Creek
LR
2995
2630
41
DEVIL'S SINKHOLE STATE NATURAL AREA
ROCKSPRINGS
Hackberry Creek
2410'
674
West Nueces River
Indian Creek
Pulliam Creek
335
Nueces River
Carta Valley
2523
MILITARY MT 2025'
Barksdale
KELLEY PEAK 2242'
INDIAN MT 2118'
WILDCAT MT 1983'
0 8 MILES
KICKAPOO CAVERN STATE PARK

Edwards County

Physical Features: Rolling, hilly; caves; spring-fed streams; rocky, thin soils; drained by Llano, Nueces rivers; varied timber.

Economy: Ranching; hunting leases; tourism; oil, gas production.

History: Apache area. First land sold in 1876. County created from Bexar District, 1858; organized 1883; named for Nacogdoches empresario Hayden Edwards.

Race/Ethnicity, 2000: (In percent) Anglo, 54.25; Black, 0.14; Hispanic, 45.05; Other, 0.56.

Vital Statistics, 2003: Births, 17; deaths, 23; marriages, 18; divorces, 2.

Recreation: Hunting, fishing; scenic drives; state park.

Minerals: Gas.

Agriculture: Center for mohair-wool production; Angora goats, sheep, cattle; some pecans. Market value $7.5 million. Cedar for oil.

Population	**2,013**	July mean max.	91.6
Change fm 2000	-6.9	Civ. Labor	798
Area (sq. mi.)	2,119.95	Unemployed	3.3
Land Area (sq. mi.)	2,119.75	Wages	$2,438,417
Altitude (ft.)	1,507-2,410	Av. Weekly Wage	$427.27
Rainfall (in.)	24.76	Prop. Value	$376,624,519
Jan. mean min.	34.3	Retail Sales	$10,033,767

ROCKSPRINGS (1,261) county seat; ranching, tourism, Top of the World Festival, July 4.

Other towns include: **Barksdale** (100).

For explanation of sources, abbreviations and symbols, see p. 167 and foldout map.

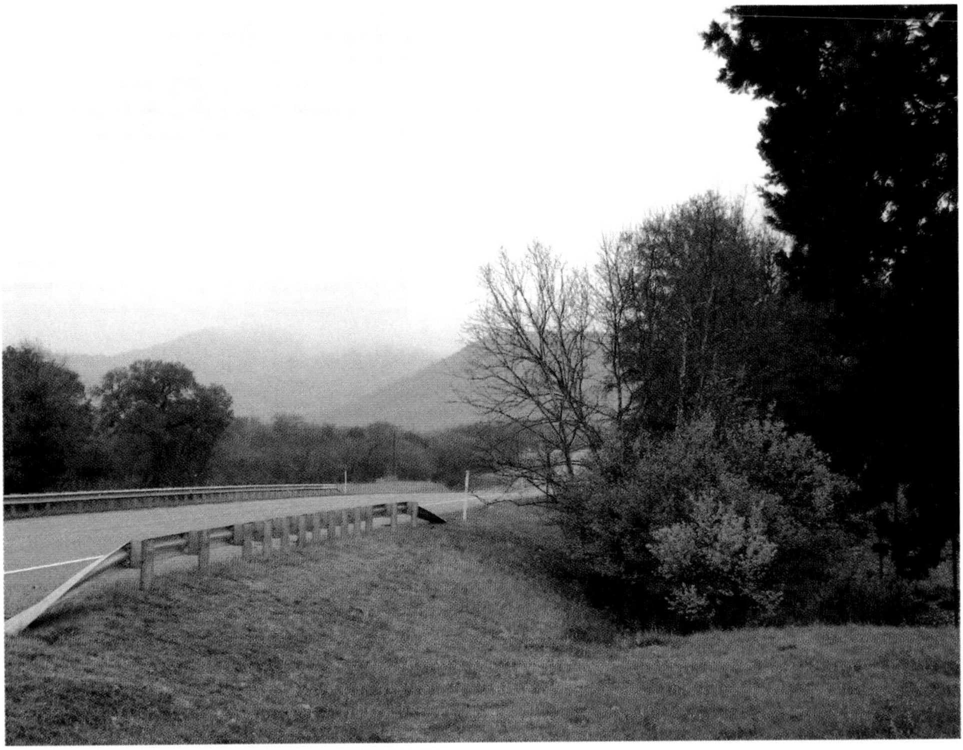

A misty spring day in Edwards County along Texas 55. Texas Almanac photo.

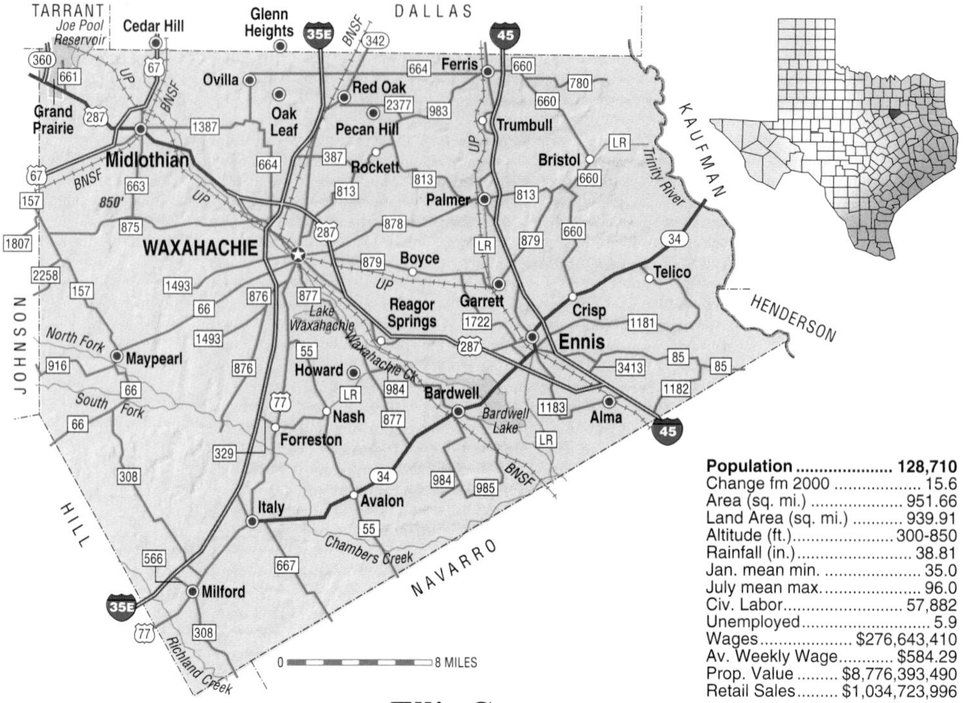

Ellis County

Population **128,710**
Change fm 2000 .... 15.6
Area (sq. mi.) 951.66
Land Area (sq. mi.) 939.91
Altitude (ft.)...................... 300-850
Rainfall (in.)........................ 38.81
Jan. mean min. 35.0
July mean max..................... 96.0
Civ. Labor........................ 57,882
Unemployed........................... 5.9
Wages................... $276,643,410
Av. Weekly Wage........... $584.29
Prop. Value $8,776,393,490
Retail Sales......... $1,034,723,996

Physical Features: North Texas Blackland soils; level to rolling; Chambers Creek, Trinity River.

Economy: Cement, steel production; warehousing and distribution; government/services, agriculture; many residents work in Dallas.

History: Tonkawa area. Part of Peters colony settled in 1843. County created 1849, organized 1850, from Navarro County. Named for Richard Ellis, president of convention that declared Texas' independence.

Race/Ethnicity, 2000: (In percent) Anglo, 71.94; Black, 8.73; Hispanic, 18.42; Other, 0.91.

Vital Statistics, 2003: Births, 1,976; deaths, 885; marriages, 1,031; divorces, 224.

Recreation: Medieval-theme Scarborough Faire; Gingerbread Trail homes tour, fall festival; lakes, fishing, hunting.

Minerals: Cement, gas.

Agriculture: Cattle, nursery crops, hay, cotton, corn, wheat. Market value $43.4 million.

WAXAHACHIE (24,205) county seat; manufacturing; transportation; steel, aluminum; tourism; hospital; colleges; museum; hike and bike trail; Crape Myrtle festival in July.

Ennis (17,635) agribusiness; man-ufacturing; bluebonnet trails, National Polka Festival; tourism; hospital.

Midlothian (10,332) cement plants, steel plant; distribution center; heritage park, cabin; Scarecrow fall festival in October.

Other towns include: **Alma** (322); **Avalon** (400); **Bardwell** (630); **Ferris** (2,301); **Forreston** (400); **Garrett** (488); **Howard** (210); **Italy** (2,142); **Maypearl** (826); **Milford** (728); **Oak Leaf** (1,281); **Ovilla** (3,705); **Palmer** (1,921); **Pecan Hill** (722); and **Red Oak** (5,810) manufacturing, Founders Day in September. Also, **Glenn Heights** (8,345, mostly in Dallas County).

Also, part of **Grand Prairie**.

Mountains along FM 2775 to Hueco Tanks State Historic Site in El Paso County. Texas Almanac photo.

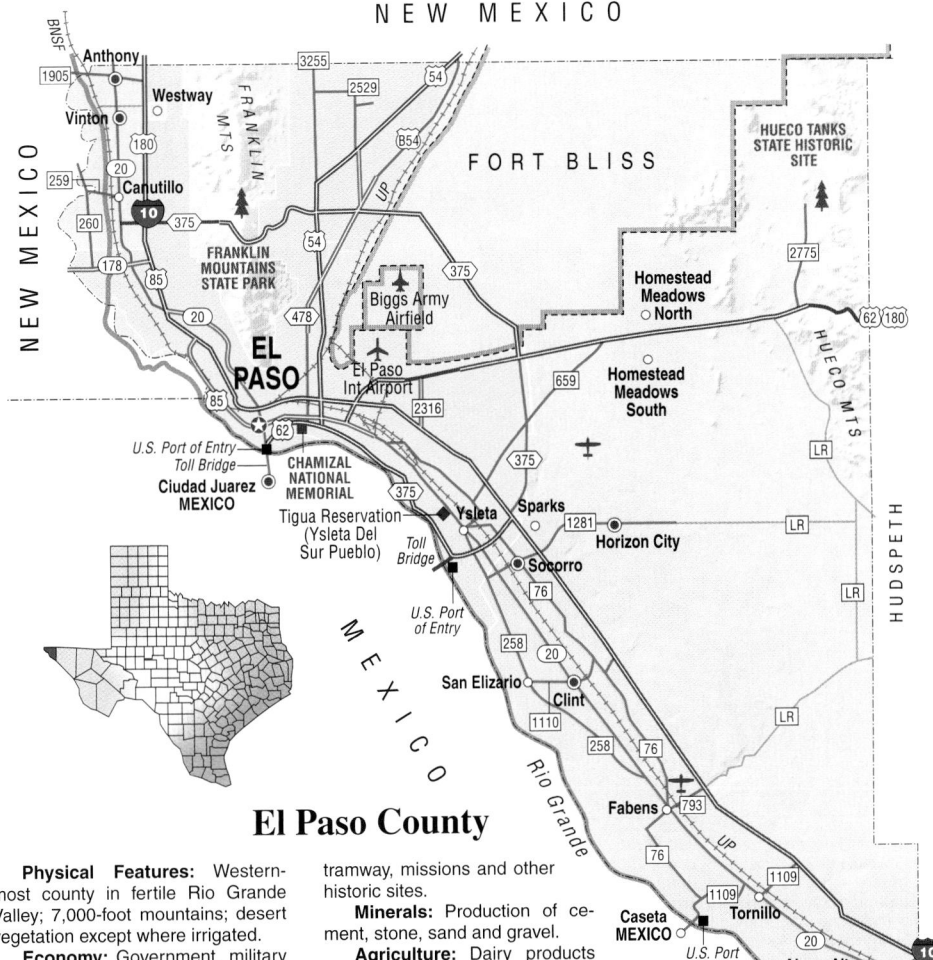

NEW MEXICO

BNSF
Anthony
1905
Westway
Vinton
180
259
Canutillo
260
10
375
178
85
20
FRANKLIN
MOUNTAINS
STATE PARK
EL
PASO
85
62
U.S. Port of Entry
Toll Bridge
Ciudad Juarez
MEXICO
FRANKLIN MTS
3255
2529
54
B54
54
375
478
Biggs Army
Airfield
El Paso
Int Airport
2316
CHAMIZAL
NATIONAL
MEMORIAL
375
Tigua Reservation
(Ysleta Del
Sur Pueblo)
Toll
Bridge
Ysleta
Socorro
76
U.S. Port
of Entry
258
20
San Elizario
Clint
1110
258
76
MEXICO
Rio Grande
FORT BLISS
HUECO TANKS
STATE HISTORIC
SITE
2775
Homestead
Meadows
North
659
Homestead
Meadows
South
375
Sparks
1281
Horizon City
HUECO MTS
LR
LR
LR
LR
LR
HUDSPETH
62 180
Fabens
793
76
UP
1109
1109
Caseta
MEXICO
Tornillo
20
U.S. Port
of Entry
Alamo Alto
10

El Paso County

Physical Features: Westernmost county in fertile Rio Grande Valley; 7,000-foot mountains; desert vegetation except where irrigated.

Economy: Government, military are major economic factors; wholesale, retail distribution center; education; tourism; maquiladora plants, varied manufacturers; ore smelting, refining, cotton, food processing.

History: Various Indian tribes inhabited the valley before Spanish civilization arrived in late 1650s. Agriculture in area dates to at least 100 A.D. Spanish and Tigua and Piro tribes fleeing Santa Fe uprising of 1680 sought refuge at Ysleta and Socorro. County created from Bexar District, 1849; organized 1850; named for historic pass (Paso del Norte), lowest all-weather pass through Rocky Mountains.

Race/Ethnicity, 2000: (In percent) Anglo, 17.41; Black, 2.93; Hispanic, 78.23; Other, 1.43.

Vital Statistics, 2003: Births, 14,201; deaths, 4,362; marriages, 6,232; divorces, 292.

Recreation: Gateway to Mexico; Chamizal Museum; major tourist center; December Sun Carnival with football game; state parks, mountain tramway, missions and other historic sites.

Minerals: Production of cement, stone, sand and gravel.

Agriculture: Dairy products (fourth in sales); cattle; cotton, pecans, onions, forage, peppers also raised; 50,000 acres irrigated, mostly cotton. Market value $67.9 million.

Education: University of Texas at El Paso; UT School of Nursing at El Paso; Texas Tech University Health Sciences Center; El Paso Community College.

EL PASO (588,452) county seat; fifth-largest Texas city, largest U.S. city on Mexican border.

A center for government operations. Federal installations include Fort Bliss, William Beaumont General Hospital, La Tuna federal prison, and headquarters of the U.S. Army Air Defense Command.

Manufactured products include clothing, electronics, auto equipment, plastics; trade and distribution; refining; processing of ore, oil, food, cotton and other farm products.

Hospitals; museums; convention center; theater, symphony orchestra.

For explanation of sources, abbreviations and symbols, see p. 167.

Other towns include:
Anthony (4,117); **Canutillo** (5,257); **Clint** (981); **Fabens** (8,174); **Homestead Meadows North** (4,456); **Homestead Meadows South** (6,758); **Horizon City** (7,757); **Prado Verde** (201); **San Elizario** (11,640); **Socorro** (28,857); **Sparks** (3,151); **Tornillo** (1,624); **Vinton** (2,035); **Westway** (4,043), and **Ysleta** (now within El Paso) settled in 1680, called the oldest town in Texas.

And, **Fort Bliss** (8,724).

Population	713,126
Change fm 2000	4.9
Area (sq. mi.)	1,014.68
Land Area (sq. mi.)	1,013.11
Altitude (ft.)	3,582-7,192
Rainfall (in.)	9.43
Jan. mean min.	32.9
July mean max.	94.5
Civ. Labor	297,724
Unemployed	7.7
Wages	$1,743,246,897
Av. Weekly Wage	$530.47
Prop. Value	$22,241,522,576
Retail Sales	$6,910,246,495

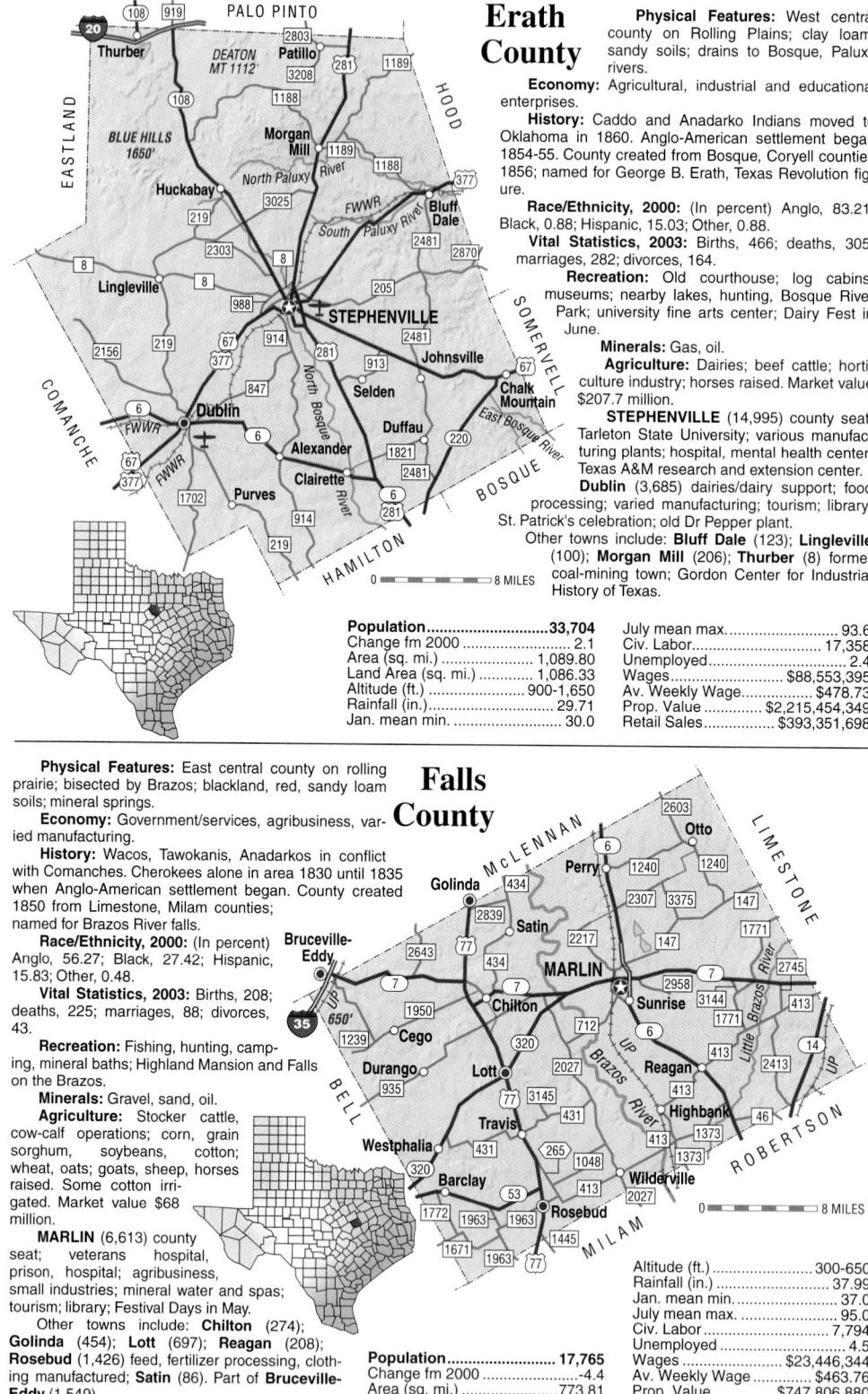

Erath County

Physical Features: West central county on Rolling Plains; clay loam, sandy soils; drains to Bosque, Paluxy rivers.

Economy: Agricultural, industrial and educational enterprises.

History: Caddo and Anadarko Indians moved to Oklahoma in 1860. Anglo-American settlement began 1854-55. County created from Bosque, Coryell counties 1856; named for George B. Erath, Texas Revolution figure.

Race/Ethnicity, 2000: (In percent) Anglo, 83.21; Black, 0.88; Hispanic, 15.03; Other, 0.88.

Vital Statistics, 2003: Births, 466; deaths, 305; marriages, 282; divorces, 164.

Recreation: Old courthouse; log cabins; museums; nearby lakes, hunting, Bosque River Park; university fine arts center; Dairy Fest in June.

Minerals: Gas, oil.

Agriculture: Dairies; beef cattle; horticulture industry; horses raised. Market value $207.7 million.

STEPHENVILLE (14,995) county seat; Tarleton State University; various manufacturing plants; hospital, mental health center; Texas A&M research and extension center.

Dublin (3,685) dairies/dairy support; food processing; varied manufacturing; tourism; library; St. Patrick's celebration; old Dr Pepper plant.

Other towns include: **Bluff Dale** (123); **Lingleville** (100); **Morgan Mill** (206); **Thurber** (8) former coal-mining town; Gordon Center for Industrial History of Texas.

Population............................**33,704**	July mean max...........................93.6
Change fm 2000 ....2.1	Civ. Labor..............................17,358
Area (sq. mi.) 1,089.80	Unemployed..................................2.4
Land Area (sq. mi.) 1,086.33	Wages.........................$88,553,395
Altitude (ft.) 900-1,650	Av. Weekly Wage................$478.73
Rainfall (in.)..............................29.71	Prop. Value $2,215,454,349
Jan. mean min. 30.0	Retail Sales................$393,351,698

Physical Features: East central county on rolling prairie; bisected by Brazos; blackland, red, sandy loam soils; mineral springs.

Economy: Government/services, agribusiness, varied manufacturing.

History: Wacos, Tawokanis, Anadarkos in conflict with Comanches. Cherokees alone in area 1830 until 1835 when Anglo-American settlement began. County created 1850 from Limestone, Milam counties; named for Brazos River falls.

Race/Ethnicity, 2000: (In percent) Anglo, 56.27; Black, 27.42; Hispanic, 15.83; Other, 0.48.

Vital Statistics, 2003: Births, 208; deaths, 225; marriages, 88; divorces, 43.

Recreation: Fishing, hunting, camping, mineral baths; Highland Mansion and Falls on the Brazos.

Minerals: Gravel, sand, oil.

Agriculture: Stocker cattle, cow-calf operations; corn, grain sorghum, soybeans, cotton; wheat, oats; goats, sheep, horses raised. Some cotton irrigated. Market value $68 million.

MARLIN (6,613) county seat; veterans hospital, prison, hospital; agribusiness, small industries; mineral water and spas; tourism; library; Festival Days in May.

Other towns include: **Chilton** (274); **Golinda** (454); **Lott** (697); **Reagan** (208); **Rosebud** (1,426) feed, fertilizer processing, clothing manufactured; **Satin** (86). Part of **Bruceville-Eddy** (1,549).

Falls County

Population............................ 17,765	Altitude (ft.) 300-650
Change fm 2000 ....-4.4	Rainfall (in.) 37.99
Area (sq. mi.) 773.81	Jan. mean min........................37.0
Land Area (sq. mi.) 769.09	July mean max. 95.0
	Civ. Labor 7,794
	Unemployed 4.5
	Wages $23,446,344
	Av. Weekly Wage $463.76
	Prop. Value...............$747,806,880
	Retail Sales $92,412,611

Fannin County

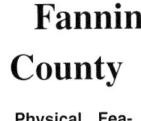

Physical Features: North Texas county of rolling prairie, drained by Red River, Bois d'Arc Creek; mostly blackland soils; national grassland.

Economy: Communications; agriculture; government/services, prisons; petroleum distribution, tourism; varied manufacturing.

History: Caddoes who joined with Cherokees. Anglo-American settlement began in 1836. County created from Red River County, 1837, organized 1838; named for James W. Fannin, a victim of Goliad massacre.

Race/Ethnicity, 2000: (In percent) Anglo, 85.12; Black, 8.12; Hispanic, 5.61; Other, 1.15.

Vital Statistics, 2003: Births, 363; deaths, 419; marriages, 237; divorces, 159.

Recreation: Water activities on lakes; hunting; state park, fossil beds, winery; Sam Rayburn home, memorial library; Bois D'Arc festival in May.

Minerals: Not significant; some sand produced.

Agriculture: Beef cattle, wheat, corn, grain sorghum, hay, horses, pecans. Market value $57.4 million.

BONHAM (10,382) county seat; varied manufacturing; veterans hospital and private hospital; state jail; Sam Rayburn birthday celebration in January.

Other towns include: **Bailey** (223); **Dodd City** (435); **Ector** (626); **Gober** (146); **Honey Grove** (1,772) agribusiness center, varied manufacturing, tourism, historic buildings, library, Davy Crockett Day in October; **Ivanhoe** (110);

Ladonia (690) restored historical downtown, tourism; varied manufacturing, commuters, rodeo; **Leonard** (1,912) varied manufacturing, museum, library; **Randolph** (70); **Ravenna** (221); **Savoy** (841); **Telephone** (210); **Trenton** (666); **Windom** (241).

Also, part of **Pecan Gap** (215).

For explanation of sources, abbreviations and symbols, see p. 167 and foldout map.

Population	32,620
Change fm 2000	4.4
Area (sq. mi.)	899.16
Land Area (sq. mi.)	891.45
Altitude (ft.)	450-800
Rainfall (in.)	44.56
Jan. mean min.	30.2
July mean max.	92.6
Civ. Labor	12,020
Unemployed	6.6
Wages	$53,277,451
Av. Weekly Wage	$578.36
Prop. Value	$1,382,134,480
Retail Sales	$189,866,555

Fall foliage at Bonham State Park in Fannin County. Texas Almanac photo.

Fayette County

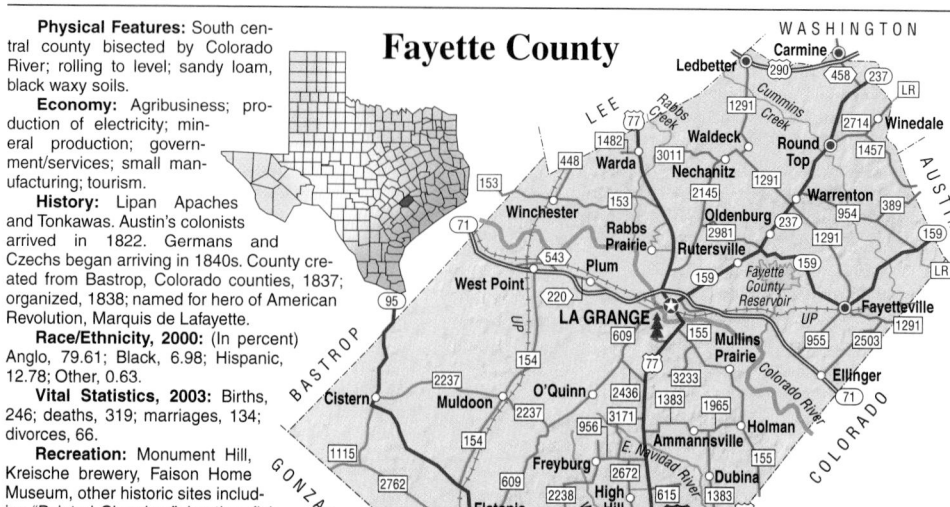

Physical Features: South central county bisected by Colorado River; rolling to level; sandy loam, black waxy soils.

Economy: Agribusiness; production of electricity; mineral production; government/services; small manufacturing; tourism.

History: Lipan Apaches and Tonkawas. Austin's colonists arrived in 1822. Germans and Czechs began arriving in 1840s. County created from Bastrop, Colorado counties, 1837; organized, 1838; named for hero of American Revolution, Marquis de Lafayette.

Race/Ethnicity, 2000: (In percent) Anglo, 79.61; Black, 6.98; Hispanic, 12.78; Other, 0.63.

Vital Statistics, 2003: Births, 246; deaths, 319; marriages, 134; divorces, 66.

Recreation: Monument Hill, Kreische brewery, Faison Home Museum, other historic sites including "Painted Churches"; hunting, fishing, lake; German and Czech ethnic foods; Prazska Pout in August, Octoberfests.

Minerals: Oil, gas, sand, gravel, bentonite clay.

Agriculture: Beef cattle; corn, sorghum, peanuts, hay, pecans. Market value $51.7 million. Firewood sold.

LA GRANGE (4,615) county seat; electric-power generation; varied manufacturing; food processing; retail trade center; tourism; hospital, library, museum, archives; Czech heritage center; Texas Independence Day observance.

Schulenburg (2,808) varied manufacturing; food processing; Bluebonnet Festival.

Round Top (76) music center, International Festival Institute, July-August; museums, tourism, old Bethlehem Lutheran church, and **Winedale** (67), historic restorations including Winedale Inn.

Other towns include: **Carmine** (235); **Ellinger** (386); **Fayetteville** (270); **Flatonia** (1,462) farm market, varied manufacturing, antiques, Czhilispiel in October; **Ledbetter** (83); **Muldoon** (95); **Plum** (145); **Warda** (121); **Warrenton** (186); **West Point** (213), and **Winchester** (232).

Population	22,513
Change fm 2000	3.3
Area (sq. mi.)	959.84
Land Area (sq. mi.)	950.03
Altitude (ft.)	200-590
Rainfall (in.)	40.31
Jan. mean min.	41.4
July mean max.	95.9
Civ. Labor	10,871
Unemployed	2.5
Wages	$58,286,559
Av. Weekly Wage	$537.41
Prop. Value	$2,493,047,863
Retail Sales	$289,571,044

Fisher County

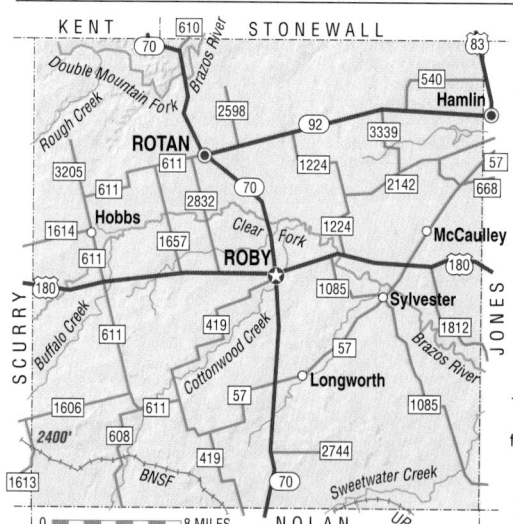

Physical Features: West central county on rolling prairie; mesquite; red, sandy loam soils; drains to forks of Brazos River.

Economy: Agribusiness; electric co-op; gypsum; hunting.

History: Lipan Apaches, disrupted by Comanches and other tribes around 1700. Ranching began in 1876. County created from Bexar District, 1876; organized 1886; named for S.R. Fisher, Republic of Texas secretary of navy.

Race/Ethnicity, 2000: (In percent) Anglo, 75.30; Black, 2.72; Hispanic, 21.36; Other, 0.62.

Vital Statistics, 2003: Births, 32; deaths, 61; marriages, 17; divorces, 13.

Recreation: Quail, dove, turkey hunting; wildlife viewing; fair, rodeo in August.

Minerals: Gypsum, oil.

Agriculture: Cattle, cotton, hay, wheat, sorghum, horses, sheep, goats. Irrigation for cotton and alfalfa. Market value $19 million.

ROBY (661) county seat; agribusiness, cotton gin; hospital between Roby and Rotan.

ROTAN (1,525) gypsum plant; oil mill; agribusinesses.

Other towns include: **McCaulley** (96) and **Sylvester** (79). Part of **Hamlin** (2,136).

Population	4,096
Change fm 2000	-5.7
Area (sq. mi.)	901.74
Land Area (sq. mi.)	901.16
Altitude (ft.)	1,723-2,400
Rainfall (in.)	24.22
Jan. mean min.	27.2
July mean max.	94.2
Civ. Labor	1,867
Unemployed	4.1
Wages	$5,915,622
Av. Weekly Wage	$492.48
Prop. Value	$302,757,969
Retail Sales	$11,174,451

Floyd County

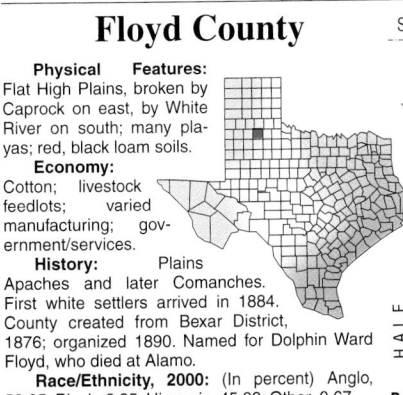

Physical Features: Flat High Plains, broken by Caprock on east, by White River on south; many playas; red, black loam soils.

Economy: Cotton; livestock feedlots; varied manufacturing; government/services.

History: Plains Apaches and later Comanches. First white settlers arrived in 1884. County created from Bexar District, 1876; organized 1890. Named for Dolphin Ward Floyd, who died at Alamo.

Race/Ethnicity, 2000: (In percent) Anglo, 50.05; Black, 3.35; Hispanic, 45.93; Other, 0.67.

Vital Statistics, 2003: Births, 103; deaths, 67; marriages, 40; divorces, 28.

Recreation: Hunting, fishing; Blanco Canyon; Pumpkin Days in October; museum.

Minerals: Not significant.

Agriculture: Cotton, wheat, sorghum; beef cattle, sunflowers; 260,000 acres irrigated. Market value $158.8 million.

FLOYDADA (3,420) county seat; some manufacturing; meat, vegetable processing; distribution center; Old Settlers Reunion; Texas A&M engineering extension.

Lockney (1,917) agriculture center; manufacturing; hospital.

Other towns include: **Aiken** (52), **Dougherty** (91), and **South Plains** (67).

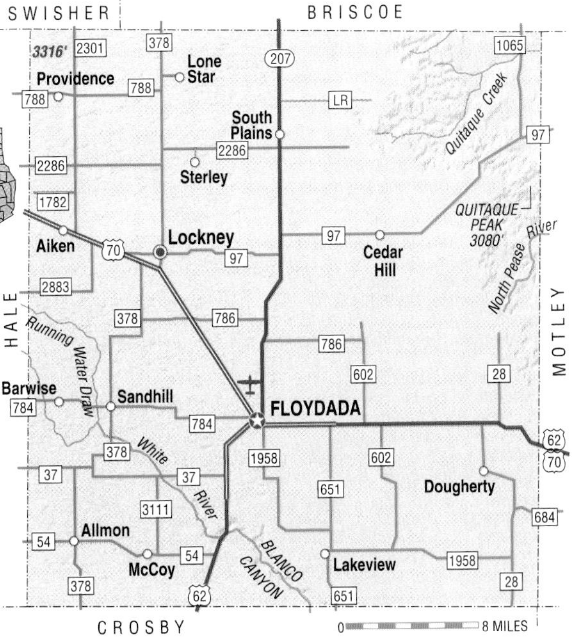

Population.................................. **7,330**
Change fm 2000............................. -5.7

Area (sq. mi.)............................ 992.51
Land Area (sq. mi.)...................... 992.19
Altitude (ft.)....................... 2,574-3,316
Rainfall (in.) 20.95
Jan. mean min.............................. 23.2
July mean max. 92.3
Civ. Labor.................................. 3,008

Unemployed 7.9
Wages $12,006,273
Av. Weekly Wage................... $426.98
Prop. Value.................... $366,909,620
Retail Sales $36,374,437

For explanation of sources, abbreviations and symbols, see p. 167 and foldout map.

At the Caprock Escarpment along FM 97 in northeastern Floyd County. Texas Almanac photo.

Physical Features: Northwest county drains to North Wichita, Pease rivers; sandy, loam soils, rolling surface.

Economy: Agribusiness, clothes manufacturing, government/service.

History: Comanches, Kiowas ranged the area until driven away in 1870s. Ranching began in 1880. County created out of Cottle, Hardeman, King, Knox counties, 1891; named for Maj. Robert L. Foard of Confederate army.

Race/Ethnicity, 2000: (In percent) Anglo, 79.53; Black, 3.39; Hispanic, 16.34; Other, 0.74

Vital Statistics, 2003: Births, 17; deaths, 30; marriages, 0; divorces, 3.

Recreation: Three museums; hunting; wild hog cook-off in November.

Minerals: Natural gas, oil.

Agriculture: Wheat; cow-calf operations, stocker cattle, alfalfa, cotton, sorghum, peanuts, dairies. Market value $9.5 million. Hunting leases important.

CROWELL (1,111) county seat; agriculture/retail center; clothing manufacturing, library.

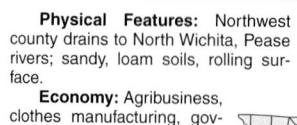

Foard County

Population	1,551
Change fm 2000	-4.4
Area (sq. mi.)	707.69
Land Area (sq. mi.)	706.68
Altitude (ft.)	1,300-1,830
Rainfall (in.)	26.40
Jan. mean min.	24.0
July mean max.	97.0
Civ. Labor	658
Unemployed	5.6
Wages	$1,663,306
Av. Weekly Wage	$368.72
Prop. Value	$122,405,519
Retail Sales	$5,178,716

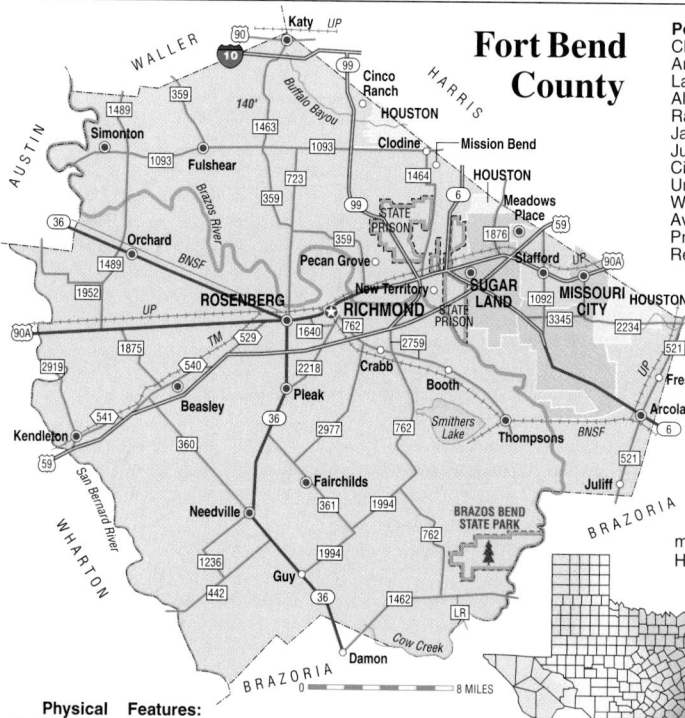

Fort Bend County

Population	442,620
Change fm 2000	24.9
Area (sq. mi.)	886.05
Land Area (sq. mi.)	874.64
Altitude (ft.)	46-140
Rainfall (in.)	49.34
Jan. mean min.	41.6
July mean max.	93.7
Civ. Labor	211,063
Unemployed	5.2
Wages	$959,762,407
Av. Weekly Wage	$721.25
Prop. Value	$27,369,319,235
Retail Sales	$4,049,182,770

Minerals: Oil, gas, sulphur, salt, clays, sand and gravel.

Agriculture: A leading county in nursery crops; cotton, sorghum, hay, soybeans; cattle, horses; irrigation for rice. Market value $49.9 million.

RICHMOND (12,443) county seat; foundry, Richmond State School (for mentally retarded), hospital.

SUGAR LAND (74,079) government/services, prisons; commuting to Houston; hospital; Museum of Southern History.

MISSOURI CITY (63,115, part [5,494] in Harris County).

ROSENBERG (28,190) varied industry; annual Czech festival; Wharton County Junior College campus.

Other towns include: **Arcola** (1,196); **Beasley** (950); **Cinco Ranch** (12,084); **Fairchilds** (746); **Fresno** (7,568); **Fulshear** (905); **Guy** (NA); **Katy** (13,285, mostly in Harris County); **Kendleton** (501); **Meadows Place** (5,403); **Mission Bend** (33,421).

Also, **Needville** (2,996); **New Territory** (15,299); **Orchard** (451); **Pecan Grove** (15,328); **Pleak** (1,068); **Simonton** (807); **Stafford** (18,634, partly in Harris County); **Thompsons** (265).

Also, part [33,384] of **Houston.**

Physical Features: On Gulf Coastal Plain; drained by Brazos, San Bernard rivers; level to rolling; rich alluvial soils.

Economy: Agribusiness, petrochemicals, technology, government/service, retail trade, manufacturing; many residents work in Houston; part of Houston metropolitan area.

History: Karankawas retreated to Mexico by 1850s. Named for river bend where some of Austin's colonists settled 1824. Antebellum plantations made it one of six Texas counties with black majority in 1850. County created 1837 from Austin County; organized 1838.

Race/Ethnicity, 2000: (In percent) Anglo, 47.05; Black, 19.98; Hispanic, 21.12; Other, 11.85.

Vital Statistics, 2003: Births, 5,885; deaths, 1,635; marriages, 2,009; divorces, 1,367.

Recreation: Many historic sites, museums, memorials; George Ranch historical park; state park with George Observatory; fishing, waterfowl hunting.

Franklin County

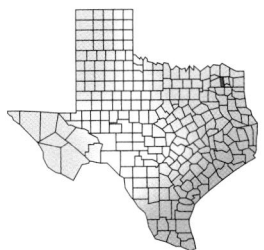

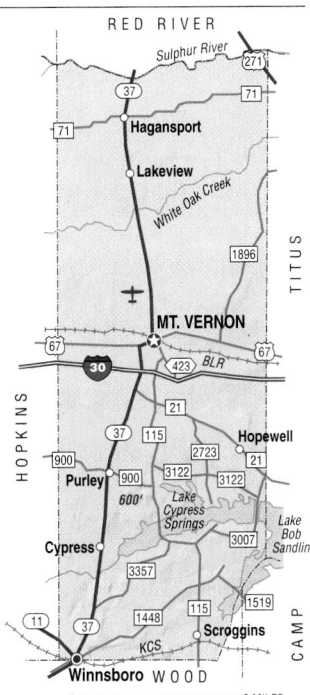

Physical Features: Small Northeast county with many wooded hills; drained by numerous streams; alluvial to sandy clay soils; two lakes.

Economy: Agribusiness; government/services; retirement center; manufacturing; distribution.

History: Caddoes abandoned the area in 1790s because of disease and other tribes. White settlement began in 1830s. County created 1875 from Titus County; named for jurist B.C. Franklin.

Race/Ethnicity, 2000: (In percent) Anglo, 86.40; Black, 3.96; Hispanic, 8.90; Other, 0.74.

Vital Statistics, 2003: Births, 108; deaths, 125; marriages, 74; divorces, 27.

Population	10,066
Change fm 2000	6.4
Area (sq. mi.)	294.77
Land Area (sq. mi.)	285.66
Altitude (ft.)	300-600
Rainfall (in.)	47.65
Jan. mean min.	32.2
July mean max.	92.8
Civ. Labor	4,541
Unemployed	3.6
Wages	$17,677,695
Av. Weekly Wage	$496.10
Prop. Value	$840,205,878
Retail Sales	$61,006,501

Recreation: Fishing, water sports; Countryfest/stew cook-off in October; historic homes; wild hog hunting, horse stables.

Minerals: Lignite, oil and gas.

Agriculture: Dairy and broiler production; beef cattle; hay. Market value $63.9 million. Timber marketed.

MOUNT VERNON (2,316) county seat; distribution center, manufacturing; tourism; antiques; Labor Day rodeo.

Other towns include: **Scroggins** (125), and **Winnsboro** (3,808, mostly in Wood County) commercial center, Autumn Trails.

Freestone County

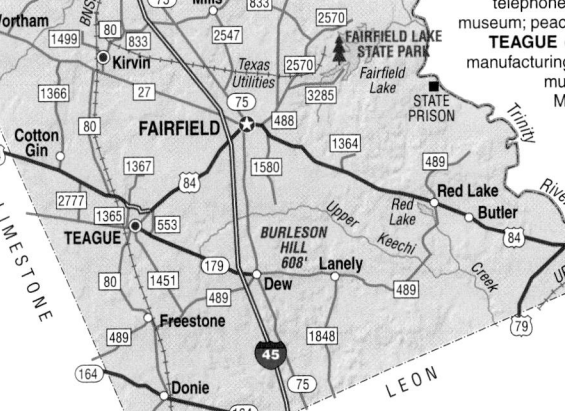

Physical Features: East central county bounded by the Trinity River; rolling Blackland, sandy, loam soils.

Economy: Natural gas, mining, stone quarry; varied manufacturing; agribusinesses; two electricity generating plants, prison, railroad.

History: Caddo and Tawakoni area. David G. Burnet received land grant in 1825. Seven Mexican citizens received grants in 1833. In 1860, more than half population was black. County created 1850 from Limestone County; organized 1851. Named for indigenous stone.

Race/Ethnicity, 2000: (In percent) Anglo, 72.16; Black, 18.98; Hispanic, 8.20; Other, 0.66.

Vital Statistics, 2003: Births, 228; deaths, 217; marriages, 146; divorces, 53.

Recreation: Fishing, hunting; lakes; historic sites; state park; coon hunting championship in September.

Minerals: Natural gas and lignite coal.

Agriculture: Beef cattle and hay; peaches, strawberries, melons, pecans. Market value $32.6 million. Hunting leases. Hardwood, firewood marketed.

FAIRFIELD (3,306) county seat; lignite mining; telephone operations; trade center; hospital; museum; peach festival, July 4 weekend.

TEAGUE (4,885) government/services, prison; varied manufacturing, oil, ranching; library, railroad terminal, museum; Guadalupe celebration in December, M.L. King Jr. celebration in January.

Other towns include: **Donie** (206), **Kirvin** (133), **Streetman** (207), **Wortham** (1,148) agribusiness, blues festival in September; Blind Lemon Jefferson gravesite.

Population	18,597
Change fm 2000	4.1
Area (sq. mi.)	892.13
Land Area (sq. mi.)	877.43
Altitude (ft.)	209-608
Rainfall (in.)	42.31
Jan. mean min.	36.4
July mean max.	95.0
Civ. Labor	8,638
Unemployed	3.7
Wages	$38,560,567
Av. Weekly Wage	$543.36
Prop. Value	$2,978,49,530
Retail Sales	$476,993,404

For explanation of sources, abbreviations and symbols, see p. 167.

Frio County

Physical Features: South Texas county of rolling terrain with much brush; bisected by Frio River; sandy, red sandy loam soils.

Economy: Agribusiness; oil-field services; hunting leases.

History: Coahuiltecans; many taken into San Antonio missions. Comanche hunters kept settlers out until after the Civil War. Mexican citizens recruited for labor after 1900. County created 1858 from Atascosa, Bexar, Uvalde counties, organized in 1871; named for Frio (cold) River.

Race/Ethnicity, 2000: (In percent) Anglo, 20.79; Black, 4.79; Hispanic, 73.76; Other, 0.66.

Vital Statistics, 2003: Births, 236; deaths, 116; marriages, 72; divorces, 72.

Recreation: Hunting; Big Foot Wallace Museum; Winter Garden area; potato festival in May.

Minerals: Oil, natural gas, stone.

Agriculture: Peanuts, potatoes, sorghum, cotton, corn, spinach, cucumbers, watermelons. Market value $71 million. Hunting leases.

PEARSALL (7,107) county seat; agriculture center; oil, gas; food processing, shipping; old jail museum; hospital; Pioneer days in April.

Dilley (3,910) shipping center for melons, peanuts.

Other towns include: **Bigfoot** (301), **Hilltop** (303); **Moore** (639); **North Pearsall** (570) and **West Pearsall** (349).

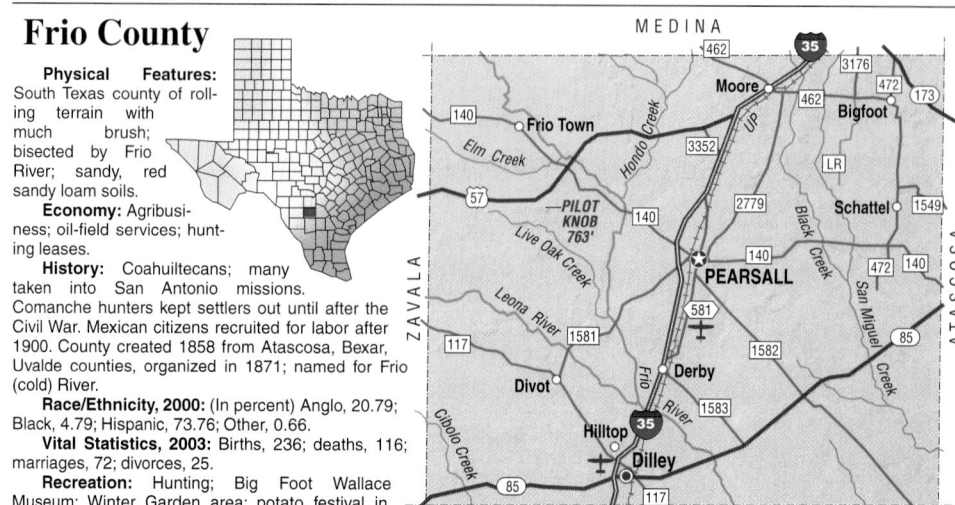

Population	16,386
Change fm 2000	0.8
Area (sq. mi.)	1,134.28
Land Area (sq. mi.)	1,133.02
Altitude (ft.)	400-763
Rainfall (in.)	25.73
Jan. mean min.	37.9
July mean max.	97.5
Civ. Labor	6,146
Unemployed	7.0
Wages	$22,169,147
Av. Weekly Wage	$436.37
Prop. Value	$775,584,470
Retail Sales	$80,463,877

Gaines County

Population	14,563
Change fm 2000	0.7
Area (sq. mi.)	1,502.84
Land Area (sq. mi.)	1,502.35
Altitude (ft.)	3,000-3,625
Rainfall (in.)	18.20
Jan. mean min.	26.7
July mean max.	94.1
Civ. Labor	6,940
Unemployed	4.5
Wages	$31,804,578
Av. Weekly Wage	$496.35
Prop. Value	$2,483,784,502
Retail Sales	$131,314,353

Physical Features: On South Plains, drains to draws; playas; underground water.

Economy: Oil and gas production, cotton and peanut farming.

History: Comanche country until U.S. Army campaigns of 1875. Ranchers arrived in 1880s; farming began around 1900. County created from Bexar District, 1876; organized 1905; named for James Gaines, signer of Texas Declaration of Independence.

Race/Ethnicity, 2000: (In percent) Anglo, 61.48; Black, 2.19; Hispanic, 35.77; Other, 0.56.

Vital Statistics, 2003: Births, 274; deaths, 108; marriages, 120; divorces, 23.

Recreation: Cedar Lake one of largest alkali lakes on Texas plains; Ag and Oil Day in September.

Minerals: One of leading oil-producing counties; gas.

Agriculture: Cotton, peanuts (a leader in acreage), small grains, pecans, vegetables raised; cattle, sheep, hogs; substantial irrigation. Market value $144.6 million.

SEMINOLE (5,866) county seat; oil and gas; market center; hospital; library; county airport.

Seagraves (2,428) market for three-county area; cotton, peanut farming; library, museum; Celebrate Seagraves in July.

Other towns include: **Loop** (315). Also, part of **Denver City** (3,834).

For explanation of sources, abbreviations and symbols, see p.167 and foldout map.

Galveston County

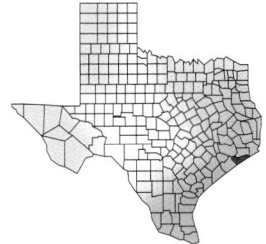

Physical Features: Partly island, partly coastal; flat, artificial drainage; sandy, loam, clay soils; broken by bays.

Economy: Port activities dominate economy; insurance and finance center; petrochemical plants; varied manufacturing; tourism; medical education center; oceanographic research center; ship building; commercial fishing.

History: Karankawa and other tribes roamed the area until 1850. French, Spanish and American settlement began in 1815 and reached 1,000 by 1817. County created from Brazoria County 1838; organized 1839; named for Spanish governor of Louisiana Count Bernardo de Gálvez.

Race/Ethnicity, 2000: (In percent) Anglo, 63.80; Black, 15.54; Hispanic, 17.96; Other, 2.70.

Vital Statistics, 2003: Births, 3,978; deaths, 2,260; marriages, 2,071; divorces, 1,060.

Recreation: One of Texas' most historic cities; popular tourist and convention center; fishing, surfing, boating, sailing and other water sports; state park; historic homes tour in spring, Moody Gardens; Mardi Gras celebration; Rosenberg Library; museums; restored sailing ship, "Elissa," railroad museum; Dickens on the Strand in early December.

Minerals: Production of oil, gas, clays, sand and gravel.

Agriculture: Cattle, aquaculture, nursery crops, rice, hay, horses, soybeans, grain sorghum. Market value $5.7 million.

GALVESTON (57,539) county seat; tourist center; shipyard; other industries; insurance; port container facility; University of Texas Medical Branch; National Maritime Research Center; Texas A&M University at Galveston; Galveston College; hospitals.

League City (53,621) residential community, commuters to Houston.

Texas City (42,441) refining, petrochemical plants; port, rail shipping; College of the Mainland; hospital, library; dike; Cinco de Mayo, Shrimp Boil in August.

Bolivar Peninsula (3,803) includes: **Port Bolivar** (1,200) light-house, free ferry; **Crystal Beach** (787) seafood industry; sport fishing; tourism, Fort Travis Seashore Park, shorebird sanctuary; Crab Festival in May; **Gilchrist** (750) and **High Island** (500).

Other towns include: **Bacliff** (7,359); **Bayou Vista** (1,699); **Clear Lake Shores** (1,247).

Also, **Dickinson** (18,681) manufacturing, commuters; strawberry festival in May; **Friendswood** (32,006, partly [7,800] in Harris County); **Hitchcock** (7,021) residential community, tourism, fishing and shrimping, Good Ole Days in August, WWII blimp base, museum.

Also, **Jamaica Beach** (1,123); **Kemah** (2,486) tourism, boating, commuters, museum, Blessing of Fleet in August; **La Marque** (13,736) refining, greyhound racing, farming; hospital, library; Gulf Coast Grill-off in October; **San Leon** (4,572) **Santa Fe** (10,294); **Tiki Island** (1,105).

Population	271,743
Change fm 2000	8.6
Area (sq. mi.)	872.93
Land Area (sq. mi.)	398.47
Altitude (ft.)	sea level-35
Rainfall (in.)	43.84
Jan. mean min.	49.7
July mean max.	88.7
Civ. Labor	127,856
Unemployed	7.7
Wages	$729,853,094
Av. Weekly Wage	$641.39
Prop. Value	$24,605,695,750
Retail Sales	$2,260,919,818

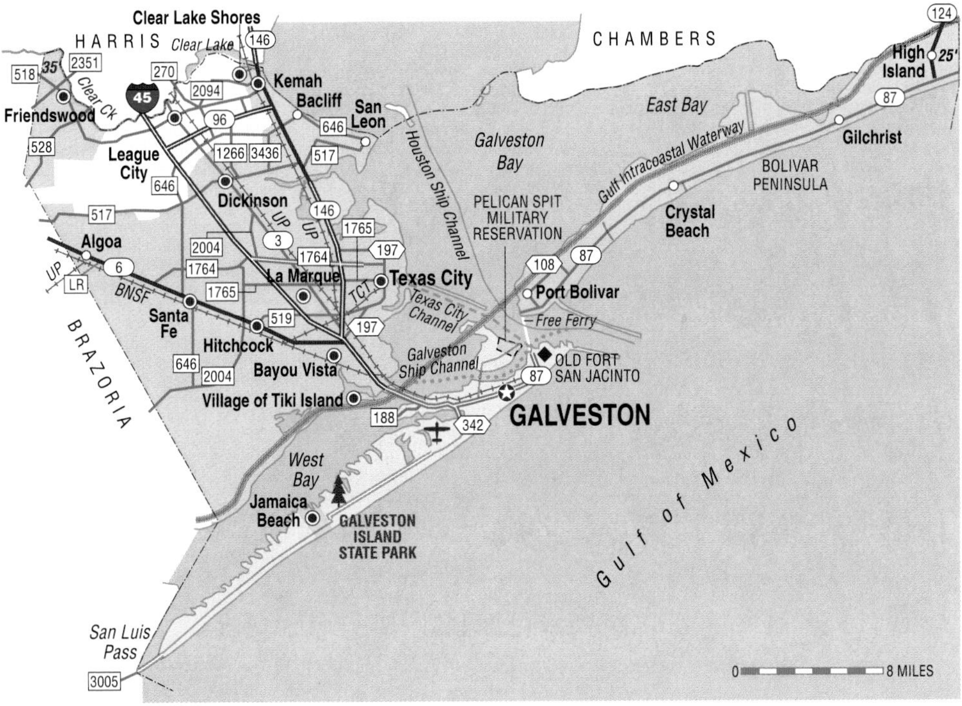

Garza County

Physical Features: On edge of Caprock; rough, broken land, with playas, gullies, canyons, Brazos River forks, lake; sandy, loam, clay soils.

Economy: Agriculture, oil & gas, trade, government/services, hunting leases.

History: Kiowas and Comanches yielded to U.S. Army in 1875. Ranching began in 1870s, farming in the 1890s. C.W. Post, the cereal millionaire, established enterprises in 1906. County created from Bexar District, 1876; organized 1907; named for early Texas family.

Race/Ethnicity, 2000: (In percent) Anglo, 57.44; Black, 4.86; Hispanic, 37.15; Other, 0.55.

Vital Statistics, 2003: Births, 63; deaths, 55; marriages, 43; divorces, 14.

Recreation: Founders Day in September, scenic areas; lake activities; Post-Garza Museum.

Minerals: Oil, gas, sand, gravel.

Agriculture: Cotton, beef cattle, hay; 12,800 acres irrigated. Market value $9.7 million. Hunting leases.

POST (3,909) county seat; founded by C.W. Post; agriculture, tourism, government/services, prisons; Garza Theatre.

Population	5,094
Change fm 2000	4.6
Area (sq. mi.)	896.19
Land Area (sq. mi.)	895.56
Altitude (ft.)	2,176-3,000
Rainfall (in.)	21.29
Jan. mean min.	27.8
July mean max.	94.0
Civ. Labor	2,513
Unemployed	3.9
Wages	$9,992,293
Av. Weekly Wage	$492.09
Prop. Value	$485,885,340
Retail Sales	$27,498,832

Gillespie County

Physical Features: Picturesque Edwards Plateau area with hills, broken by spring-fed streams.

Economy: Agribusiness; tourism; government/services; food processing; hunting leases; small manufacturing; granite for markers.

History: German settlement founded 1846 in heart of Comanche country. County created 1848 from Bexar, Travis counties; named for Texas Ranger Capt. R.A. Gillespie. Birthplace of President Lyndon B. Johnson and Fleet Admiral Chester W. Nimitz.

Race/Ethnicity, 2000: (In percent) Anglo, 83.39; Black, 0.17; Hispanic, 15.90; Other, 0.54.

Vital Statistics, 2003: Births, 229; deaths, 280; marriages, 157; divorces, 65.

Recreation: Among leading deer-hunting areas; fishing; numerous historic sites and tourist attractions include LBJ Ranch, Nimitz Hotel and Pacific war museum; Pioneer Museum Complex, Enchanted Rock.

Population	22,502
Change fm 2000	8.1
Area (sq. mi.)	1,061.48
Land Area (sq. mi.)	1,061.06
Altitude (ft.)	1,400-2,244
Rainfall (in.)	31.65
Jan. mean min.	36.1
July mean max.	93.1
Civ. Labor	10,850
Unemployed	1.9
Wages	$49,036,256
Av. Weekly Wage	$473.10
Prop. Value	$3,140,195,640
Retail Sales	$293,854,138

Minerals: Sand, gravel, gypsum, limestone rock.

Agriculture: Income mostly from beef cattle, turkeys, sheep and goats; a leading peach-producing county; hay; grain sorghum, oats, wheat, grapes also raised. Market value $24 million. Hunting leases.

FREDERICKSBURG (9,651) county seat; agribusiness, tourism, wineries, food processing; museum; tourist attractions; hospital; Easter Fires, Oktoberfest.

Other towns include: **Doss** (100); **Harper** (1,017) ranching, deer hunting; Dachshund Hounds Downs race and Trades Day in October; **Luckenbach** (25); **Stonewall** (499) agribusiness, wineries, tourism, hunting, Peach Jamboree in June, and **Willow City** (22).

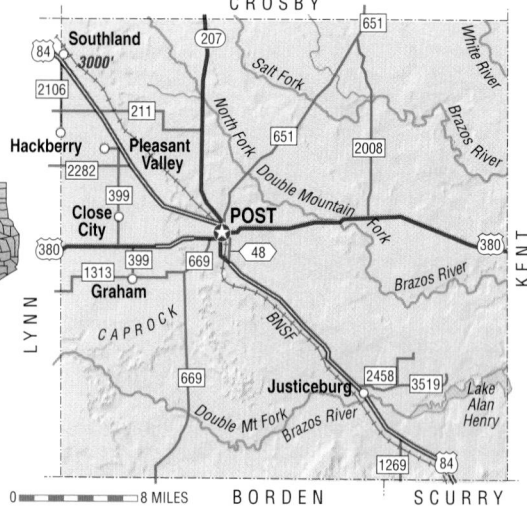

For explanation of sources, abbreviations and symbols, see p. 167 and foldout map.

Glasscock County

Physical Features: Western county on rolling plains, broken by small streams; sandy, loam soils.

Economy: Farming, ranching, hunting leases, oil and gas; quarries.

History: Hunting area for Kickapoos and Lipan Apaches. Anglo-American sheep ranchers and Mexican-American shepherds or *pastores* moved into the area in 1880s. County created 1887, from Tom Green County; organized, 1893; named for Texas pioneer George W. Glasscock.

Race/Ethnicity, 2000: (In percent) Anglo, 69.56; Black, 0.50; Hispanic, 29.87; Other, 0.07.

Vital Statistics, 2003: Births, 15; deaths, 6; marriages, 6; divorces, 0.

Recreation: Hunting of deer, quail, turkey; St. Lawrence Fall Festival.

Minerals: Oil, gas, stone/rock.

Agriculture: Cattle, goats, sheep, hogs raised. Cotton, sorghum, wheat, peanuts, hay. 55,000 acres irrigated. Market value $13.6 million.

GARDEN CITY (293), county seat; serves sparsely settled ranching, oil area.

Population 1,334
Change fm 2000 .... -5.1

Area (sq. mi.)	900.93
Land Area (sq. mi.)	900.75
Altitude (ft.)	2,495-2,727
Rainfall (in.)	17.32
Jan. mean min.	26.7
July mean max.	94.0

Civ. Labor	574
Unemployed	2.9
Wages	$1,997,456
Av. Weekly Wage	$449.27
Prop. Value	$471,162,620
Retail Sales	$2,004,250

Goliad County

Birthplace of Gen. Ignacio Zaragoza, hero of Battle of Puebla (Mexico).

Physical Features: South Texas county; rolling, brushy; bisected by San Antonio River; sandy, loam, alluvial soils.

Economy: Government/services; oil/gas; agriculture, electricity-generating plant.

History: Karankawas, Comanches and other tribes in area in historic period. La Bahía presidio/mission established 1749. County created 1836 from Spanish municipality; organized 1837; name is anagram of (H)idalgo.

Race/Ethnicity, 2000: (In percent) Anglo, 59.75; Black, 4.69; Hispanic, 35.20; Other, 0.36.

Vital Statistics, 2003: Births, 76; deaths, 76; marriages, 34; divorces, 27.

Recreation: Missions, restored Presidio La Bahía, Fannin Battleground; Old Market House museum; lake, fishing, hunting (deer, quail, dove, hogs), camping.

Minerals: Production of oil, gas.

Agriculture: Beef cattle, stocker operations and fed cattle are top revenue producers; corn, grain sorghum, cotton, hay; minor irrigation for pasture. Market value $17 million. Hunting leases.

GOLIAD (2,014) county seat; one of state's oldest towns; oil, gas center; agriculture; tourism; library; Goliad Massacre re-enactment in March; Zaragoza Birthplace State Historic Site, statue.

Other towns include: **Berclair** (253), **Fannin** (359) and **Weesatche** (411).

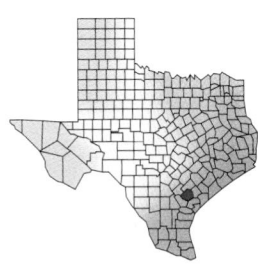

Population 7,104
Change fm 2000 .... 2.5
Area (sq. mi.) 859.35
Land Area (sq. mi.) 853.52
Altitude (ft.) 50-350

Rainfall (in.)	38.58
Jan. mean min.	43.3
July mean max.	95.5
Civ. Labor	2,600

Unemployed	5.5
Wages	$8,019,681
Av. Weekly Wage	$497.10
Prop. Value	$969,441,717
Retail Sales	$32,629,454

Gonzales County

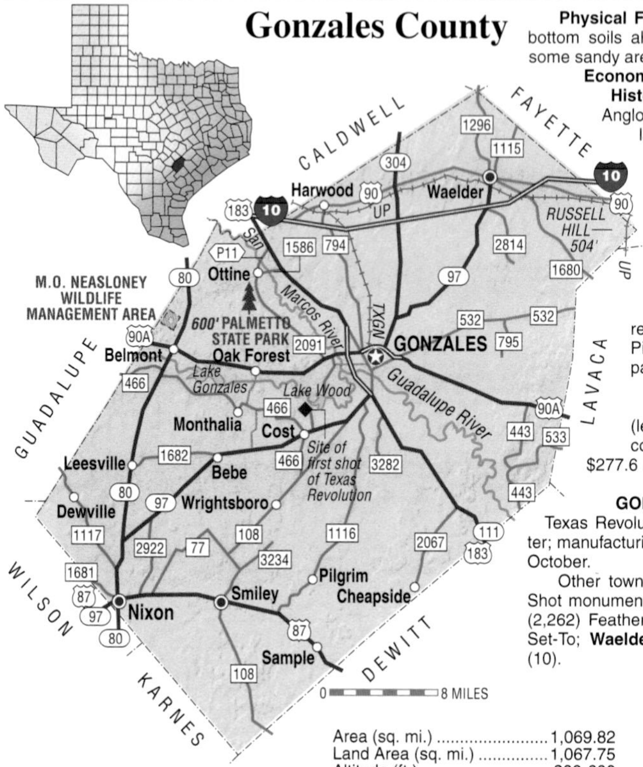

Physical Features: South Texas county; rolling, rich bottom soils along Guadalupe River and its tributaries; some sandy areas; many oaks, pecans.

Economy: Agribusiness, hunting leases.

History: Coahuiltecan area. Among first Anglo-American settlements; the De-Witt colony late 1820s. County created 1836; organized 1837; named for Coahuila y Texas Gov. Rafael Gonzales.

Race/Ethnicity, 2000: (In percent) Anglo, 51.56; Black, 8.15; Hispanic, 39.62; Other, 0.67.

Vital Statistics, 2003: Births, 354; deaths, 181; marriages, 155; divorces, 79.

Recreation: Historic sites, 86 officially recognized homes or historical markers; Pioneer Village Living History Center; state park; museums, Independence Park.

Minerals: Gas, oil, clay, gravel.

Agriculture: Major poultry county (leader in turkeys sold); cattle, hogs; hay, corn, sorghum, pecans. Market value $277.6 million.

GONZALES (7,319) county seat; first shot in Texas Revolution fired here; shipping, processing center; manufacturing; hospital; "Come and Take It" festival in October.

Other towns include: **Belmont** (55); **Cost** (84) First Shot monument; **Harwood** (118); **Leesville** (152); **Nixon** (2,262) Feather Fest; **Ottine** (80); **Smiley** (478) Settlers Set-To; **Waelder** (968) Guacamole Fest; **Wrightsboro** (10).

Population	19,281
Change fm 2000	3.5
Area (sq. mi.)	1,069.82
Land Area (sq. mi.)	1,067.75
Altitude (ft.)	200-600
Rainfall (in.)	36.02
Jan. mean min.	38.7
July mean max.	93.9
Civ. Labor	8,672
Unemployed	4.0
Wages	$39,943,027
Av. Weekly Wage	$501.72
Prop. Value	$1,429,147,890
Retail Sales	$139,327,698

Gray County

Physical Features: Panhandle High Plains, broken by Red River forks, tributaries; sandy loam, waxy soils.

Economy: Petroleum, agriculture, feedlot operations, chemical plant, other manufacturing.

History: Apaches, displaced by Comanches and Kiowas. Ranching began in late 1870s. Farmers arrived around 1900. Oil discovered 1926. County created 1876, from Bexar District; organized 1902; named for Peter W. Gray, member of first Legislature.

Race/Ethnicity, 2000: (In percent) Anglo, 79.61; Black, 6.03; Hispanic, 13.01; Other, 1.35.

Vital Statistics, 2003: Births, 260; deaths, 253; marriages, 155; divorces, 138.

Recreation: Water sports, Lake McClellan and grassland; White Deer Land Museum; barbed-wire museum, Chautauqua on Labor Day.

Minerals: Production of oil, gas.

Agriculture: Cattle, wheat, sorghum, hay, corn, soybeans. Market value $94.9 million.

PAMPA (17,124) county seat; petroleum and agriculture; chemical plant; hospital; college; prison unit.

Other towns include: **Alanreed** (48); **Lefors** (536); **McLean** (793) commercial center for southern part of county.

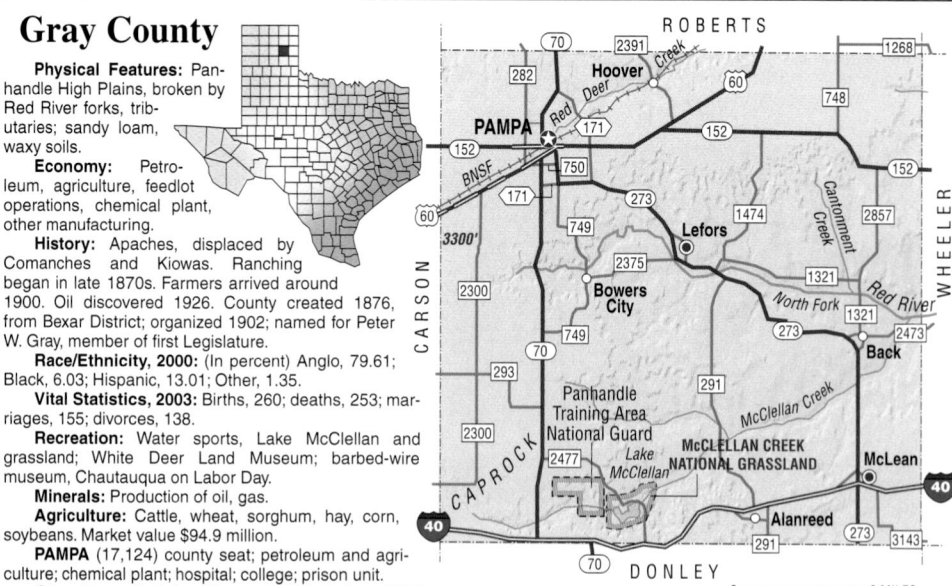

Population	21,409
Change fm 2000	-5.9
Area (sq. mi.)	929.25
Land Area (sq. mi.)	928.28
Altitude (ft.)	2,500-3,300
Rainfall (in.)	22.74
Jan. mean min.	21.9
July mean max.	92.0
Civ. Labor	9,016
Unemployed	4.1
Wages	$62,792,983
Av. Weekly Wage	$630.74
Prop. Value	$1,189,887,570
Retail Sales	$304,437,639

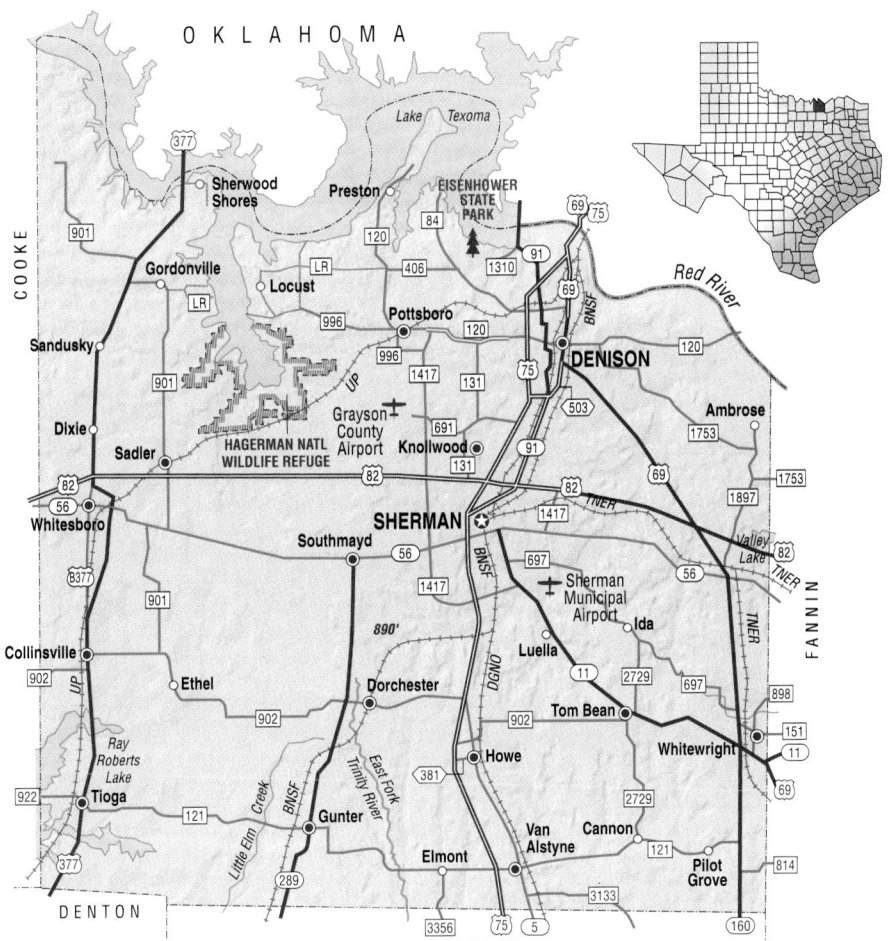

Physical Features: North Texas county; level, some low hills; sandy loam, blackland soils; drains to Red River and tributaries of Trinity River.

Economy: A manufacturing, distribution and trade center for northern Texas and southern Oklahoma; nature tourism; mineral production; prisons.

History: Caddo and Tonkawa area. Preston Bend trading post established 1836-37. Peters colony settlers arrived in 1840s. County created 1846 from Fannin County; named for Republic Atty. Gen. Peter W. Grayson.

Race/Ethnicity, 2000: (In percent) Anglo, 85.10; Black, 6.14; Hispanic, 6.80; Other, 1.96.

Vital Statistics, 2003: Births, 1,581; deaths, 1,198; marriages, 1,196; divorces, 617.

Recreation: Lakes; fishing; pheasant hunting; water sports; state park; cultural activities; wildlife refuge; Pioneer Village; railroad museum.

Minerals: Oil, gas, sand, gravel.

Grayson County

Agriculture: Beef cattle, corn, wheat, hay, sorghum. Market value $41.9 million.

Education: Austin College in Sherman and Grayson County College located between Sherman and Denison.

SHERMAN (36,512) county seat; varied manufacturing; processors, distributors for major companies; Austin College; hospitals.

DENISON (23,300) tourism, hospital, food processing; transportation center; Eisenhower birthplace; Main Street Fall festival.

Other towns include: **Bells** (1,267); **Collinsville** (1,316); **Dorchester** (119); **Gordonville** (165); **Gunter** (1,475); **Howe** (2,673) distribution; varied manufacturing;

museum, Founders' Day in May; **Knollwood** (389); **Pottsboro** (2,024); **Sadler** (446); **Southmayd** (1,060); **Tioga** (833); **Tom Bean** (984); **Van Alstyne** (2,580) window screen, electronics, saddle, tack manufacturing; **Whitesboro** (3,837) agribusiness, tourism, manufacturing, library, Peanut Festival in October; **Whitewright** (1,738) varied manufacturing, government/services.

Population 115,933
Change fm 2000 .... 4.8
Area (sq. mi.) 979.19
Land Area (sq. mi.) 933.51
Altitude (ft.) 500-890
Rainfall (in.) 42.04
Jan. mean min. 32.2
July mean max. 92.7
Civ. Labor 51,697
Unemployed 6.0
Wages $333,857,311
Av. Weekly Wage $610.44
Prop. Value $5,900,081,665
Retail Sales $1,322,001,040

For explanation of sources, abbreviations and symbols, see p. 167 and foldout map.

Population 115,035
Change fm 2000.............................3.3
Area (sq. mi.)..............................276.37
Land Area (sq. mi.)......................274.03
Altitude (ft.) 280-500
Rainfall (in.) 49.06
Jan. mean min................................33.7
July mean max. 94.5
Civ. Labor..................................61,050
Unemployed 5.5
Wages $483,286,291
Av. Weekly Wage....................$572.39
Prop. Value..................$6,570,968,152
Retail Sales $2,053,373,489

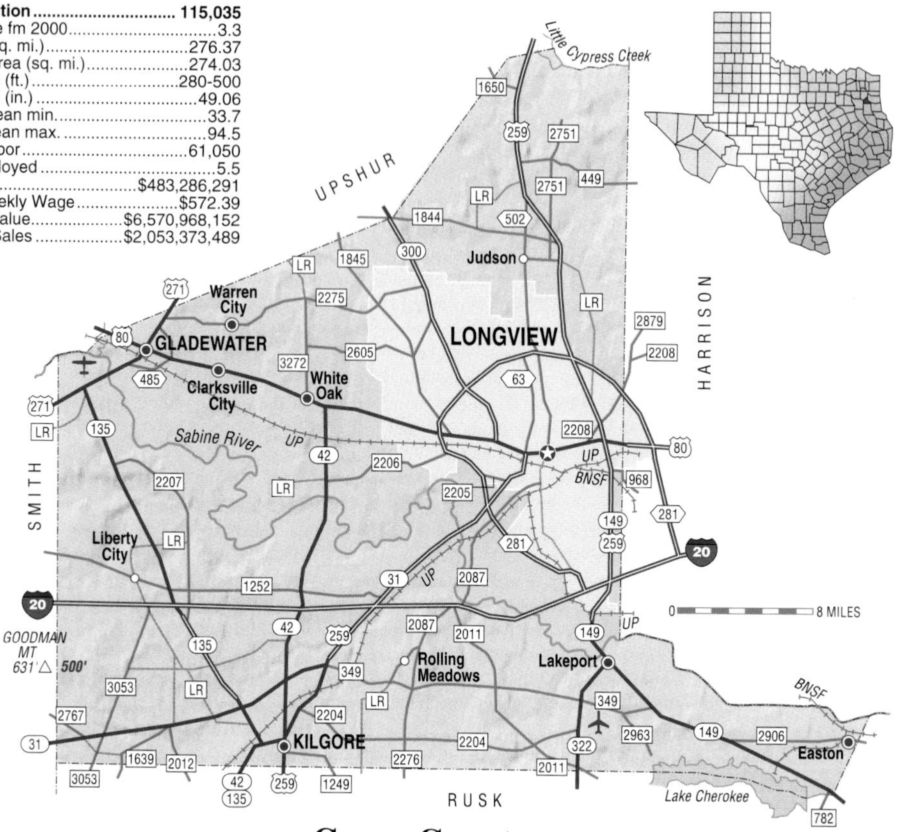

Gregg County

Physical Features: A populous, leading petroleum county, heart of the famed East Texas oil field; bisected by the Sabine River; hilly, timbered; with sandy, clay, alluvial soils.

Economy: Oil but with significant other manufacturing; tourism, conventions; agribusiness and lignite coal production.

History: Caddoes; later Cherokees, who were driven out in 1838 by President Lamar. First land grants issued in 1835 by Republic of Mexico. County created and organized in 1873 from Rusk, Upshur counties; named for Confederate Gen. John Gregg. In U.S. censuses 1880-1910, blacks were more numerous than whites. Oil discovered in 1931.

Race/Ethnicity, 2000: (In percent) Anglo, 69.59; Black, 20.07; Hispanic, 9.14; Other, 1.20.

Vital Statistics, 2003: Births,

1,854; deaths, 1,174; marriages, 1,342; divorces, 410.

Recreation: Water activities on lakes; hunting; varied cultural events; the East Texas Oil Museum, Depot Fest and Loblolly Festival in October.

Minerals: Leading oil-producing county with more than 3 billion barrels produced since 1931; also, sand, gravel and natural gas.

Agriculture: Cattle, horses, hay, nursery crops. Market value $2.4 million. Timber sales.

LONGVIEW (74,904, small part [1,598] in Harrison County) county seat; chemical manufacturing, oil industry, distribution and retail center; hospitals; LeTourneau University, UT-Tyler Longview center; convention center; balloon race in July.

Kilgore (11,508, part [2,580] in

Rusk County), oil center; manufacturing; hospital; Kilgore College (junior college); East Texas Treatment Center; Shakespeare festival in summer.

Gladewater (6,236, part [2,454] in Upshur County) Oil, manufacturing, tourism and antiques center, agriculture; library, airport; Gusher Days in April; daffodil gardens in Febuary-March.

Other towns include: **Clarksville City** (844); **Easton** (562, partly in Rusk County); **Judson** (1,057); **Lakeport** (885); **Liberty City** (1,988) oil, tourism, government/services; Honor America Night in October; **Warren City** (362); **White Oak** (5,799) petroleum, government/services, commuting to Longview; Roughneck Days in April.

For explanation of sources, abbreviations and symbols, see p. 167 and foldout map.

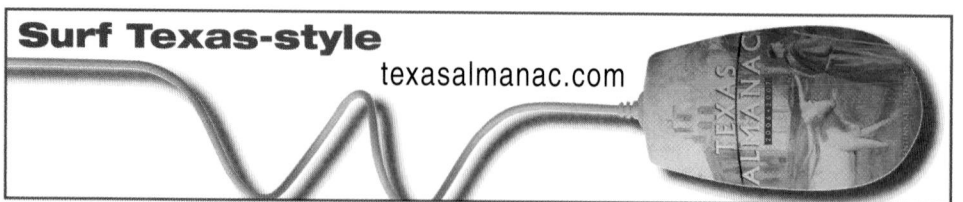

Grimes County

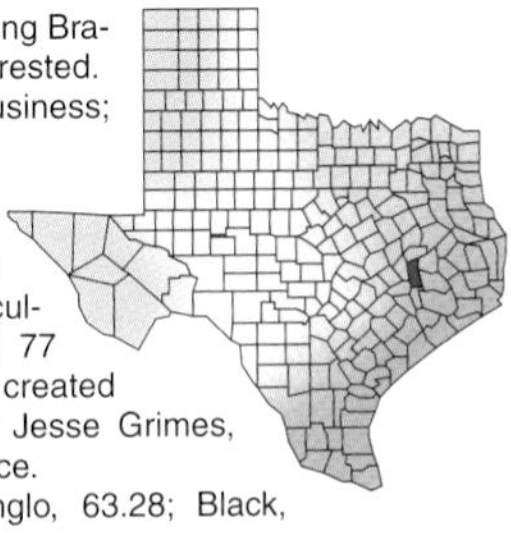

Physical Features: Rich bottom soils along Brazos, Navasota rivers; remainder hilly, partly forested.

Economy: Varied manufacturing; agribusiness; tourism.

History: Bidais (customs similar to the Caddoes) lived peacefully with Anglo-American settlers who arrived in 1820s, but tribe was removed to Indian Territory. Planter agriculture reflected in 1860 census, which listed 77 persons owning 20 or more slaves. County created from Montgomery County 1846; named for Jesse Grimes, who signed Texas Declaration of Independence.

Race/Ethnicity, 2000: (In percent) Anglo, 63.28; Black, 20.02; Hispanic,16.08; Other, 0.62.

Vital Statistics, 2003: Births, 325; deaths, 225; marriages, 142; divorces, 37.

Recreation: Hunting, fishing; Gibbons Creek Reservoir; historic sites; fall Renaissance Festival at Plantersville.

Minerals: Lignite coal, natural gas.

Agriculture: Cattle, forage, horses, poultry; berries, pecans, honey sales significant. Market value $31.8 million. Some timber sold, Christmas tree farms.

ANDERSON (256) county seat; rural center; Fanthorp Inn historic site; Go-Texan weekend in February.

NAVASOTA (7,011) agribusiness center for parts of three counties; varied manufacturing; food, wood processing; hospital; prisons; La Salle statue; Blues Fest in August.

Other towns include: **Bedias** (330); **Iola** (350); **Plantersville** (260); **Richards** (300); **Roans Prairie** (64); **Shiro** (210); **Todd Mission** (166).

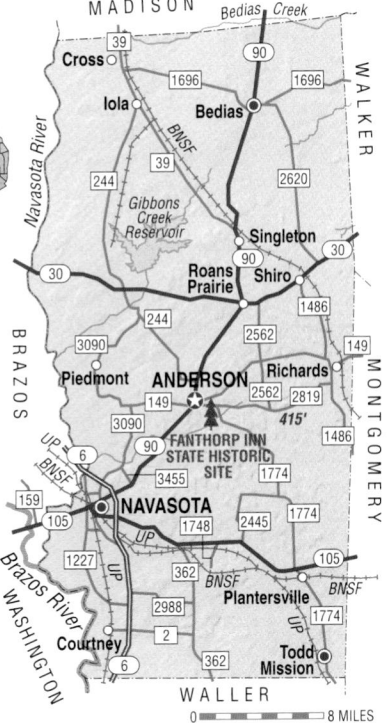

Population **25,241**	July mean max. 96.0
Change fm 2000 .... 7.2	Civ. Labor 8,310
Area (sq. mi.) 801.16	Unemployed 7.0
Land Area (sq. mi.) 793.60	Wages $50,775,333
Altitude (ft.)........................ 150-415	Av. Weekly Wage $631.90
Rainfall (in.).......................... 44.70	Prop. Value...........$1,971,924,849
Jan. mean min. 40.0	Retail Sales $287,055,010

The Fanthorp Inn, an old stagecoach stop in Anderson, dates from the days of the republic. Texas Almanac photo.

Guadalupe County

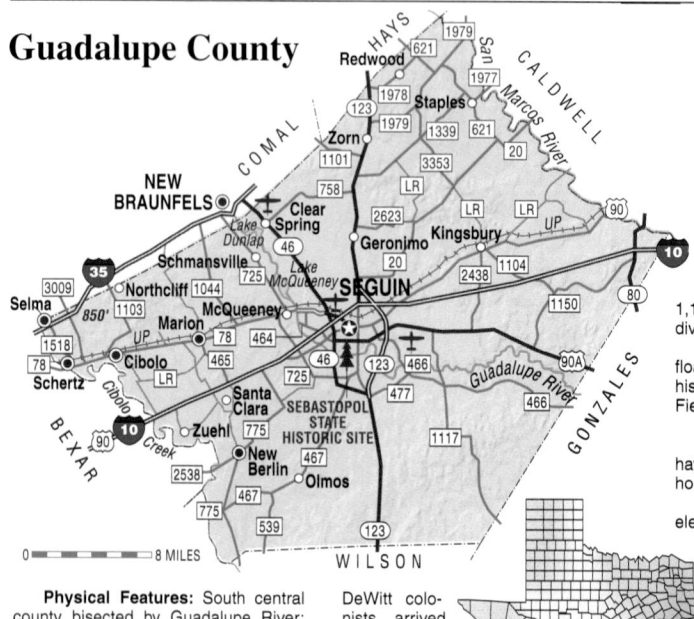

Population	99,620
Change fm 2000	11.9
Area (sq. mi.)	714.17
Land Area (sq. mi.)	711.14
Altitude (ft.)	350-850
Rainfall (in.)	34.50
Jan. mean min.	35.5
July mean max.	94.7
Civ. Labor	50,231
Unemployed	3.7
Wages	$185,199,276
Av. Weekly Wage	$582.16
Prop. Value	$6,372,402,149
Retail Sales	$641,389,059

Vital Statistics, 2003: Births, 1,197; deaths, 712; marriages, 549; divorces, 328.

Recreation: Fishing, hunting, river floating; Sebastopol historic site, other historic sites; river drive, Freedom Fiesta in July, Diez y Seis.

Minerals: Oil, gas, gravel, clays.

Agriculture: Nursery crops, cattle, hay, sorghum, corn, pecans, wheat, hogs. Market value $37.2 million.

SEGUIN (24,532) county seat; electronics, steel, other manufacturing; government/services; hospital, museums; Texas Lutheran University.

Physical Features: South central county bisected by Guadalupe River; level to rolling surface; sandy, loam, blackland soils.

Economy: Varied manufacturing; many residents work in San Antonio; agribusiness, tourism.

History: Karankawas, Comanches, other tribes until 1850s. Spanish land grant in 1806 to José de la Baume.

DeWitt colonists arrived in 1827. County created 1846 from Bexar, Gonzales counties; named for river.

Race/Ethnicity, 2000: (In percent) Anglo, 60.21; Black, 5.10; Hispanic, 33.21; Other, 1.48.

Other towns include: **Cibolo** (4,055), **Geronimo** (652), **Kingsbury** (684), **Marion** (1,171), **McQueeney** (2,729), **New Berlin** (508), **Northcliff** (1,867); **Redwood** (3,859); **Santa Clara** (935); **Schertz** (24,336, parts in Bexar and Comal counties), **Staples** (396).

Also, part [1,166] of **New Braunfels** and part [50] of **Selma**.

Hale County

Physical Features: High Plains; fertile sandy, loam soils; many playas; large underground water supply.

Economy: Agribusiness, food-processing plants, distribution; manufacturing; government/services.

History: Comanche hunters driven out by U.S. Army in 1875. Ranching began in 1880s. First motor-driven irrigation well drilled in 1911. County created from Bexar District, 1876; organized 1888; named for Lt. J.C. Hale, who died at San Jacinto.

Race/Ethnicity, 2000: (In percent), Anglo, 45.54; Black, 5.77; Hispanic, 47.90; Other, 0.79.

Vital Statistics, 2003: Births, 676; deaths, 300; marriages, 281; divorces, 127.

Recreation: Llano Estacado Museum; art gallery, antiques stores; Plainview Cattle Drive in September.

Minerals: Some oil.

Agriculture: Cotton, fed beef, sorghum, dairies, corn, vegetables, wheat. Market value $225.2 million. Irrigation of 448,000 acres.

PLAINVIEW (22,133) county seat; distribution center; food processing, other industries; Wayland Baptist University; hospital, library, mental health center; state prisons.

Hale Center (2,257) farming trade center; food processing plants; wildlife museum, library, parks, murals; car/motorcycle show, July 4.

Abernathy (2,940, part [708] in Lubbock County) government/services, farm supplies, textile plant, gins.

Other towns include: **Cotton Center** (200), **Edmonson** (123), **Petersburg** (1,232), **Seth Ward** (2,014).

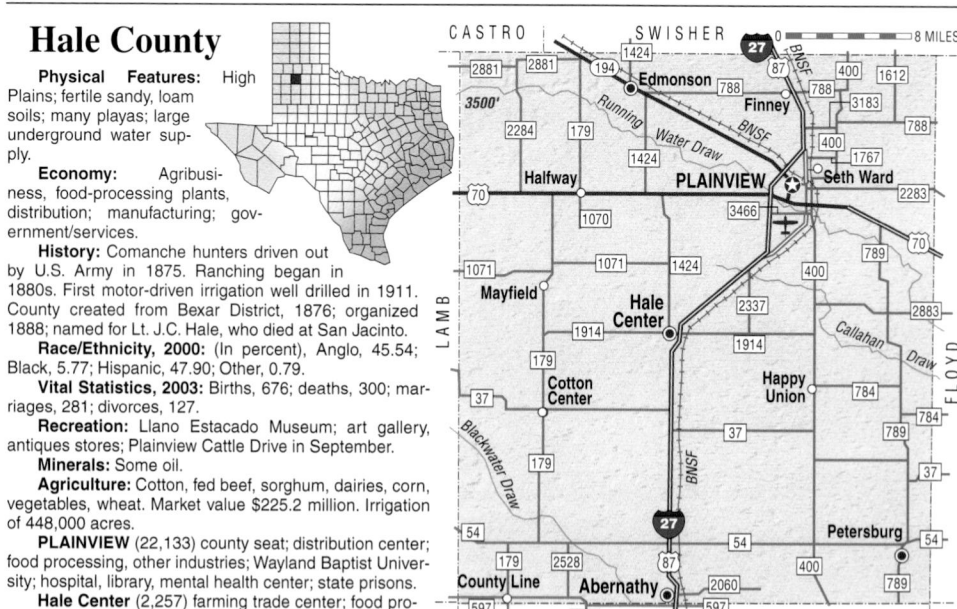

Population	36,029
Change fm 2000	-1.6
Area (sq. mi.)	1,004.77
Land Area (sq. mi.)	1,004.65
Altitude (ft.)	3,315-3,600
Rainfall (in.)	19.90
Jan. mean min.	24.4
July mean max.	91.0
Civ. Labor	16,907
Unemployed	6.1
Wages	$93,149,805
Av. Weekly Wage	$489.94
Prop. Value	$1,588,653,524
Retail Sales	$2,362,644,764

Hall County

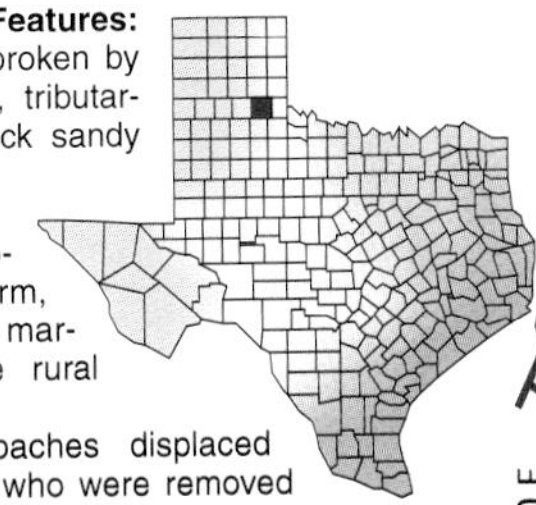

Physical Features: Rolling to hilly, broken by Red River forks, tributaries; red and black sandy loam.

Economy: Grain, cotton processing; farm, ranch supplies, marketing for large rural area.

History: Apaches displaced by Comanches, who were removed to Indian Territory in 1875. Ranching began in 1880s. Farming expanded after 1910. County created 1876 from Bexar, Young districts; organized 1890; named for Republic of Texas secretary of war W.D.C. Hall.

Race/Ethnicity, 2000: (In percent) Anglo, 63.88; Black, 8.12; Hispanic, 27.50; Other, 0.50.

Vital Statistics, 2003: Births, 56; deaths, 60; marriages, 28; divorces, 9.

Recreation: Fishing, hunting of deer, wild hog; Rails to Trails system; museum; Old Settlers reunion in September.

Minerals: Not significant.

Agriculture: Cotton, cattle, peanuts, wheat sorghum. Market value $20.6 million. Hunting leases.

MEMPHIS (2,602) county seat; cotton gins; peanut processing.

Other towns include: **Estelline** (174), **Lakeview** (161), **Turkey** (519) Bob Wills Day in April.

For explanation of sources, abbreviations and symbols, see p. 167 and foldout map.

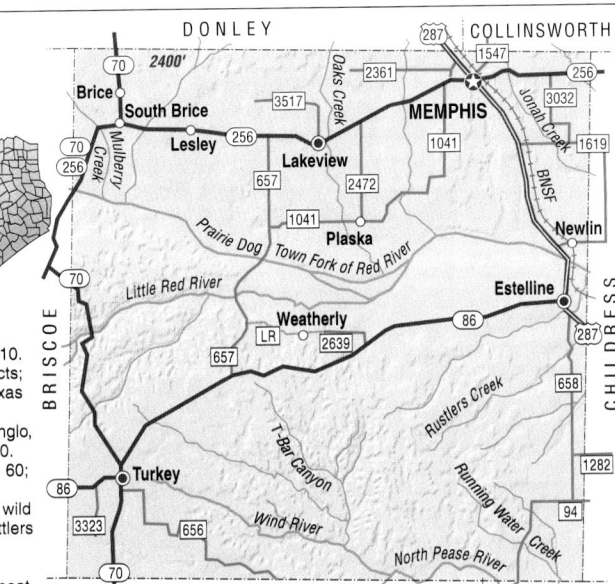

Population	3,735
Change fm 2000	-1.2
Area (sq. mi.)	904.08
Land Area (sq. mi.)	903.09
Altitude (ft.)	1,799-2,400
Rainfall (in.)	22.51
Jan. mean min.	25.5
July mean max.	95.7
Civ. Labor	1,765
Unemployed	4.6
Wages	$5,264,639
Av. Weekly Wage	$392.04
Prop. Value	$257,371,897
Retail Sales	$20,034,154

An old gin in Turkey shelters two mechanical cotton pickers. Texas Almanac photo.

Hamilton County

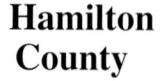

Physical Features: Hilly north central county broken by scenic valleys; loam soils.

Economy: Varied manufacturing; agribusiness; hunting leases; tourism; many residents work outside county.

History: Waco and Tawakoni Indian area. Anglo-American settlers arrived in mid-1850s. County created, organized 1858, from Bosque, Comanche, Lampasas counties; named for South Carolina Gov. James Hamilton, who aided Texas Revolution and Republic.

Race/Ethnicity, 2000: (In percent) Anglo, 91.68; Black, 0.16; Hispanic, 7.41; Other, 0.75.

Vital Statistics, 2003: Births, 99; deaths, 137; marriages, 69; divorces, 44.

Recreation: Deer, quail, duck hunting; dove festival on Labor Day; July arts and crafts show.

Minerals: Limited oil, gas.

Agriculture: Dairies, beef cattle top revenue sources. Hay, wheat, oats, sorghum. Also, pecans, sheep, horses. Market value $41.6 million.

HAMILTON (3,033) county seat; dairies, hunting, antiques shops, historical homes; varied manufacturing; hospital; library.

Hico (1,374) farm center, antiques, Old Settlers Reunion in July.

Other towns include: **Carlton** (75), **Evant** (372, partly in Coryell County), **Jonesboro** (125, partly in Coryell County); **Pottsville** (105).

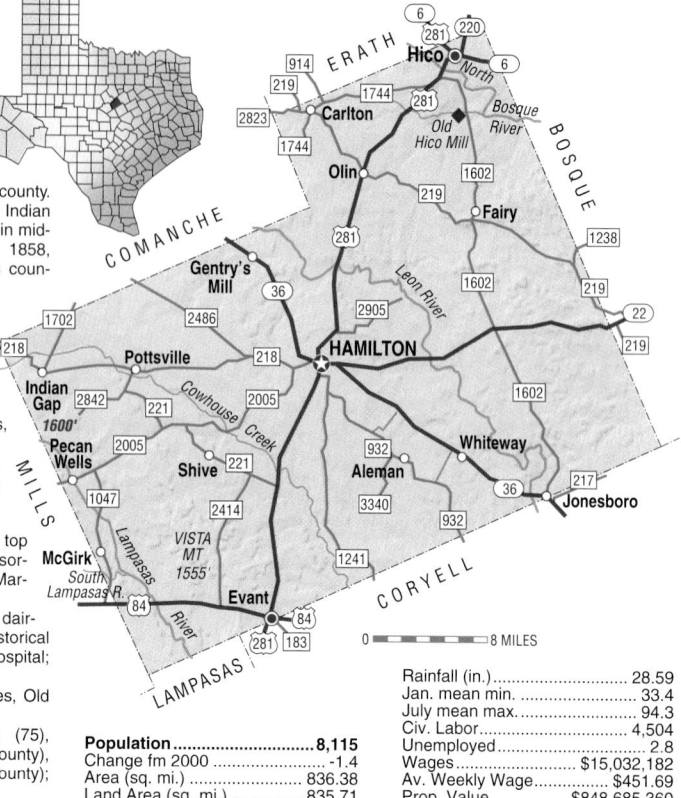

Population	8,115
Change fm 2000	-1.4
Area (sq. mi.)	836.38
Land Area (sq. mi.)	835.71
Altitude (ft.)	900-1,600
Rainfall (in.)	28.59
Jan. mean min.	33.4
July mean max.	94.3
Civ. Labor	4,504
Unemployed	2.8
Wages	$15,032,182
Av. Weekly Wage	$451.69
Prop. Value	$848,685,360
Retail Sales	$62,343,313

Hansford County

Physical Features: High Plains, many playas, creeks, draws; sandy, loam, black soils; underground water.

Economy: Agribusinesses; oil, gas operations.

History: Apaches, pushed out by Comanches around 1700. U.S. Army removed Comanches in 1874-75 and ranching began soon afterward. Farmers, including some from Norway, moved in around 1900. County created 1876, from Bexar, Young districts; organized 1889; named for jurist J.M. Hansford.

Race/Ethnicity, 2000: (In percent) Anglo, 67.64; Black, 0.17; Hispanic, 31.48; Other, 0.71.

Vital Statistics, 2003: Births, 104; deaths, 60; marriages, 47; divorces, 9.

Recreation: Stationmasters House Museum; hunting; lake activities; ecotourism; Heritage Days in June.

Minerals: Production of gas, oil.

Agriculture: Large cattle-feeding operations; corn, wheat, sorghum; hogs. Substantial irrigation. Market value $366.9 million.

SPEARMAN (2,984) county seat; grain marketing, storage center; oil; gas processing; feedlots; hospital, library, windmill collection.

Other towns include: **Gruver** (1,150) farm-ranch market, natural gas production; Fourth of July barbecue; **Morse** (171).

Population	5,207
Change fm 2000	-3.0
Area (sq. mi.)	920.40
Land Area (sq. mi.)	919.80
Altitude (ft.)	2,800-3,360
Rainfall (in.)	20.30
Jan. mean min.	22.4
July mean max.	95.5
Civ. Labor	2,425
Unemployed	2.2
Wages	$12,866,566
Av. Weekly Wage	$525.34
Prop. Value	$675,136,509
Retail Sales	$41,197,166

Hardeman County

Physical Features: Rolling, broken area on divide between Pease, Red rivers' forks; sandy loam soils.

Economy: Mineral production, agribusiness.

History: Apaches, later the semi-sedentary Wichitas and Comanche hunters. Ranching began in late 1870s. Farming expanded after 1900. County created 1858 from Fannin County; re-created 1876, organized 1884; named for pioneer brothers Bailey and T.J. Hardeman.

Race/Ethnicity, 2000: (In percent) Anglo, 79.64; Black, 4.97; Hispanic, 14.50; Other, 0.89.

Vital Statistics, 2003: Births, 57; deaths, 70; marriages, 29; divorces, 21.

Recreation: state park; lake activities; Medicine Mound aborigine gathering site; Quanah Parker monument; old railroad depot.

Minerals: Gypsum, oil.

Agriculture: Cattle, wheat, cotton. Market value $16.8 million. Hunting leases.

QUANAH (2,883) county seat; agribusiness; cotton oil mill; manufacturing; hospital; historical sites; Fall Festival in September.

Other towns include: **Chillicothe** (782) farm market center, hospital.

Population 4,374	Unemployed 4.7
Change fm 2000 .... -7.4	Wages $7,706,867
Area (sq. mi.) 697.00	Av. Weekly Wage $476.94
Land Area (sq. mi.) 695.38	Prop. Value $325,123,300
Altitude (ft.) 1,287-1,749	Retail Sales $20,566,682
Rainfall (in.) 26.76	
Jan. mean min. 24.6	
July mean max. 96.5	
Civ. Labor 1,973	

Hardin County

Physical Features: Southeast county; timbered; many streams; sandy, loam soils; Big Thicket covers much of area.

Economy: Paper manufacturing; wood processing; minerals; food processing; oil, gas; county in Beaumont-Port Arthur-Orange metropolitan area.

History: Lorenzo de Zavala received first land grant in 1829. Anglo-American settlers arrived in 1830. County created 1858 from Jefferson, Liberty counties. Named for Texas Revolutionary leader William Hardin.

Race/Ethnicity, 2000: (In percent) Anglo, 89.93; Black, 6.95; Hispanic, 2.54; Other, 0.58.

Vital Statistics, 2003: Births, 622; deaths, 462; marriages, 454; divorces, 313.

Recreation: Big Thicket with rare plant, animal life; national preserve; Red Cloud Water Park; hunting, fishing; state park.

Minerals: Oil, gas, sand, gravel.

Agriculture: Beef cattle, hay, blueberries and rice; market value negligible. Timber provides most income; more than 85 percent of county forested. Hunting leases.

KOUNTZE (2,094) county seat; government/services, retail center; library, museum; Big Thicket Texian Days in spring.

SILSBEE (6,336) forest products, rail center, oil and gas; library, Ice House

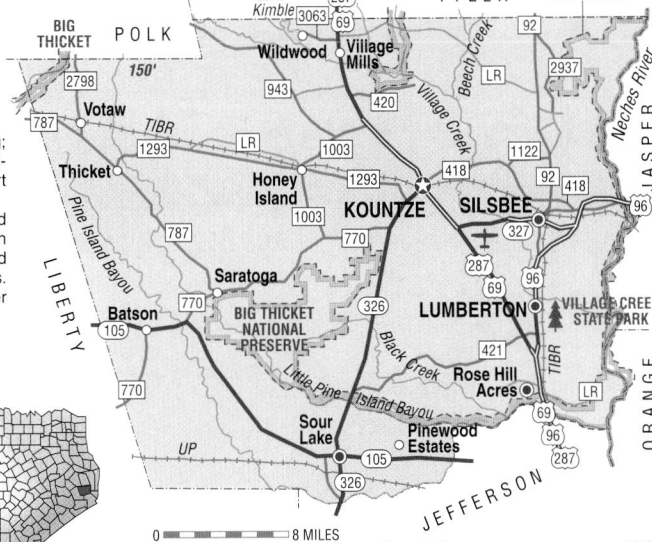

museum; Dulcimer Festival in September.

LUMBERTON (9,366) construction company; government/services; tourism; library, Village Creek Festival in April.

Other towns and places include: **Batson** (140); **Pinewood Estates** (1,671); **Rose Hill Acres** (483); **Saratoga** (1,000) Big Thicket Museum; **Sour Lake** (1,709) oil, lumbering; Old Timer's Day in September; **Thicket** (306); **Village Mills** (1,700); **Votaw** (160).

Population 50,347	
Change fm 2000 .... 4.7	
Area (sq. mi.) 897.37	
Land Area (sq. mi.) 894.33	
Altitude (ft.) 25-150	
Rainfall (in.) 56.50	
Jan. mean min. 37.0	
July mean max. 93.0	
Civ. Labor 23,239	
Unemployed 8.2	
Wages $72,478,380	
Av. Weekly Wage $511.02	
Prop. Value $2,298,706,270	
Retail Sales $416,295,593	

For explanation of sources, abbreviations and symbols, see p. 167 and foldout map.

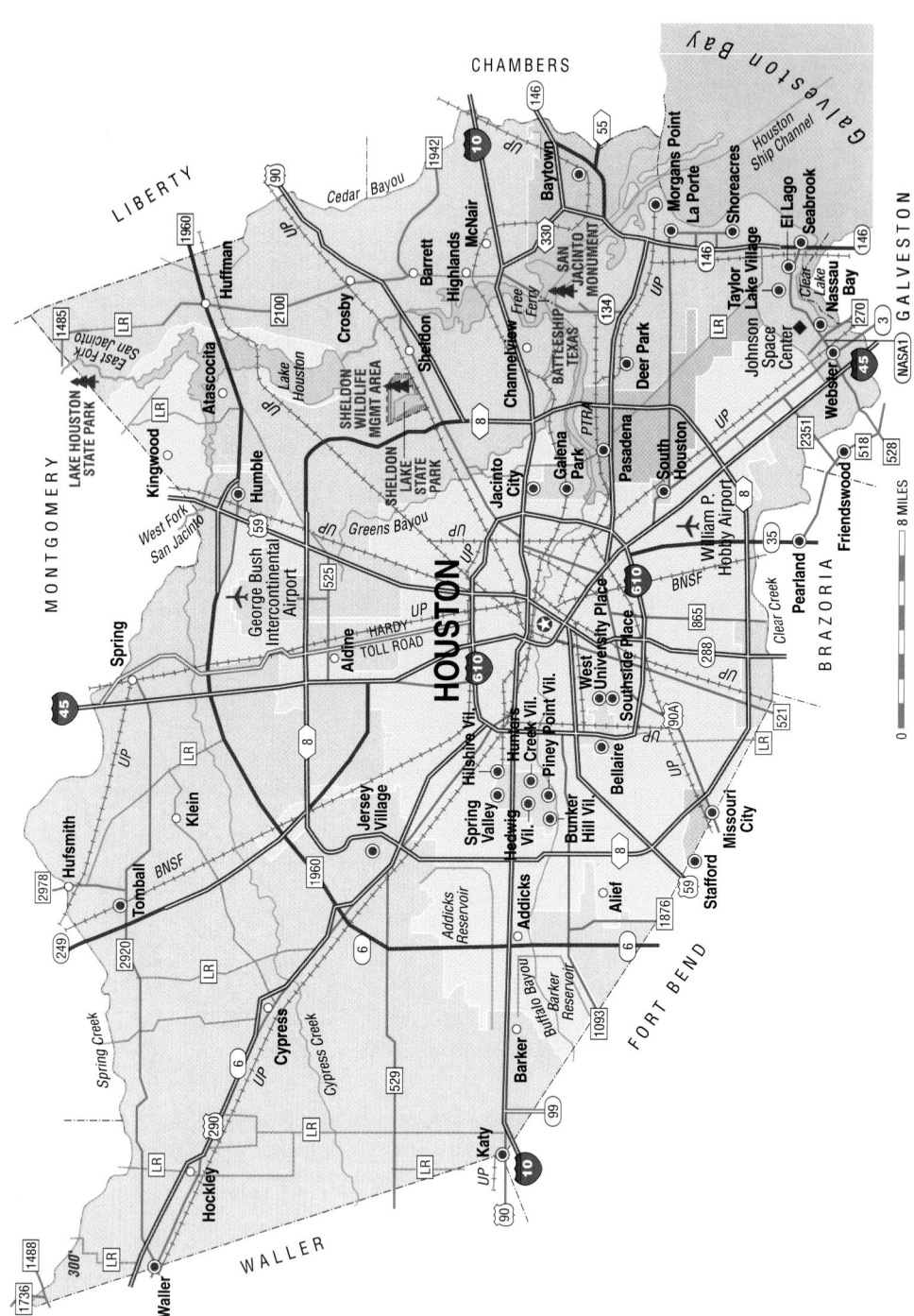

Harris County

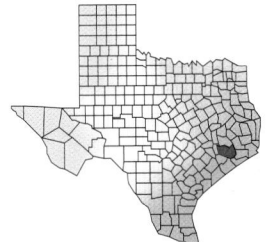

Physical Features: Largest county in eastern half of state; level; typically coastal surface and soils; many bayous, lakes, canals for artificial drainage; partly forested.

Economy: Highly industrialized county with largest population; more than 80 foreign governments maintain offices in Houston; corporate management center; nation's largest concentration of petrochemical plants; largest U.S wheat-exporting port, among top U.S. ports in the value of foreign trade and total tonnage.

Petroleum refining, chemicals, food, fabricated metal products, non-electrical machinery, primary metals, scientific instruments; paper and allied products, printing and publishing; center for energy, space and medical research; center of international business.

History: Orcoquiza villages visited by Spanish authorities in 1746. Pioneer settlers arrived by boat from Louisiana in 1822. Antebellum planters brought black slaves. Mexican migration increased after Mexican Revolution. County created 1836, organized 1837; named for John R. Harris, founder of Harrisburg (now part of Houston) in 1824.

Race/Ethnicity, 2000: (In percent) Anglo, 42.84; Black, 18.53; Hispanic, 32.93; Other, 5.70.

Vital Statistics, 2003: Births, 66,707; deaths, 20,646; marriages, 30,440; divorces, 15,044.

Recreation: Professional baseball, basketball, football; rodeo and livestock show; Jones Hall for the Performing Arts; Nina Vance Alley Theatre; Convention Center; Toyota Center, a 19,000-seat sports and entertainment center; Astroworld and WaterWorld amusement parks, Reliant Stadium and downtown ballpark.

Sam Houston Park, with restored early Houston homes, church, stores; Museum of Fine Arts, Contemporary Arts Museum, Rice Museum; Wortham Theater; Hobby Center for Performing Arts; museum of natural science, planetarium, zoo in Hermann Park.

San Jacinto Battleground, Battleship Texas; Johnson Space Center.

Fishing, boating, other freshwater and saltwater activities.

Minerals: Among leading oil, gas, petrochemical areas; production of petroleum, cement, natural gas, liquids, salt, lime, sulfur, sand and gravel, clays, stone.

Agriculture: Nursery crops, cattle, hay, horses, vegetables, Christmas trees, goats, rice, corn. Market value $52.9 million. Substantial income from forest products.

Education: Houston is a major center of higher education, with more than 140,000 students enrolled in 28 colleges and universities in the county. Among these are Rice University, the University of Houston, Texas Southern University, University of St. Thomas, Houston Baptist University.

Medical schools include University of St. Thomas and Houston Baptist University Schools of Nursing, University of Texas Health Science Center, Baylor College of Medicine, Institute of Religion and Human Development, Texas Chiropractic College, Texas Woman's University-Houston Center.

HOUSTON (2,033,400) county seat; largest Texas city; fourth-largest in nation.

Ranks first in manufacture of petroleum equipment, agricultural chemicals, fertilizers, pesticides, oil and gas pipeline transmission; a leading scientific center; ranks high in manufacture of machinery, fabricated metals; a major distribution, shipping center; engineering and research center; food processing.

Plants make apparel, lumber and wood products; furniture, paper, chemical, petroleum and coal products; publishing center; one of the nation's largest public school systems; prominent corporate center, with more than 200 firms relocating corporate headquarters, divisions or subsidiaries to county since 1970; Go Texan Days in February.

Pasadena (147,236) residential city with large industrial area manufacturing petrochemicals and other petroleum-related products; civic center; San Jacinto College, Texas Chiropractic College; hospitals; historical museum; Strawberry Festival in May.

Baytown (67,659) refining, petrochemical center; Lee College; hospitals; historical homes; youth fair in April.

Bellaire (16,294) residential city with several major office buildings.

The **Clear Lake Area**, which includes **El Lago** (2,974); **Nassau Bay** (4,071); **Seabrook** (10,803); **Taylor Lake Village** (3,666); **Webster** (9,585) tourism, Johnson Space Center, University of Houston-Clear Lake; Bayport Industrial Complex includes Port of Bayport; 12 major marinas; hospitals; Christmas lighted boat parade.

Other towns include: **Aldine** (14,503); **Atascocita** (35,818); **Barrett** (2,803); **Bunker Hill Village** (3,610); **Channelview** (30,295); **Crosby** (1,686); **Deer Park** (28,675) ship-channel industries, Totally Texas celebration in April; **Galena Park** (10,577); **Hedwig Village** (2,244); **Highlands** (7,070); **Hilshire Village** (711); **Hockley** (NA); **Humble** (15,000); **Humble** (15,411) oil-field equipment manufactured, retail center, hospital; **Hunters Creek Village** (4,317); **Jacinto City** (10,290); **Jersey Village** (7,165).

Also, **Katy** (13,285, partly in Fort Bend, Waller counties) oil and gas; government/services, hospitals; rice harvest festival in October; **Klein** (45,000); **La Porte** (33,035) petrochemical industry; Sylvan Beach Festival in April; Galveston Bay; **Morgan's Point** (333); **Piney Point Village** (3,356); **Sheldon** (1,847); **Shoreacres** (1,535); **South Houston** (16,187).

Also, **Southside Place** (1,601); **Spring** (36,501); **Spring Valley** (3,554); **Tomball** (9,955) computers, oil equipment, retail center; antiques; hospital, sports medical center; museum, junior college, parks; Germanfest in March; **West University Place** (14,482).

Parts of **Friendswood, Missouri City, Pearland, Stafford** and **Waller**.

Addicks, Alief and **Kingwood** are now within the city limits of Houston.

Population	**3,644,285**
Change fm 2000	7.2
Area (sq. mi.)	1,777.69
Land Area (sq. mi.)	1,728.83
Altitude (ft.)	sea level-300
Rainfall (in.)	53.96
Jan. mean min.	45.2
July mean max.	93.6
Civ. Labor	1,910,415
Unemployed	6.3
Wages	$20,531,064,813
Av. Weekly Wage	$865.29
Fed. Wages	$344,772,523
Prop. Value	$223,544,107,130
Retail Sales	$50,767,738,579

For explanation of sources, abbreviations and symbols, see p. 167 and foldout map.

Harrison County

Physical Features: East Texas county; hilly, rolling; over half forested; Sabine River; Caddo Lake.

Economy: Oil, gas processing; lumbering; pottery, other varied manufacturing.

History: Agriculturist Caddo Indians whose numbers were reduced by disease. Anglo-Americans arrived in 1830s. In 1850, the county had more slaves than any other in the state. County created 1839 from Shelby County; organized 1842. Named for eloquent advocate of Texas Revolution, Jonas Harrison.

Race/Ethnicity, 2000: (In percent) Anglo, 69.81; Black, 24.13; Hispanic, 5.34; Other, 0.72.

Vital Statistics, 2003: Births, 840; deaths, 572; marriages, 508; divorces, 111.

Recreation: Fishing, other water activities on Caddo and other lakes; hunting; plantation homes, historic sites; Stagecoach Days in May; Old Courthouse Museum; Old World Store; state park, performing arts; Fire Ant festival in October.

Minerals: Oil, gas, lignite coal, clays, sand and gravel.

Agriculture: Cattle, hay. Also, poultry, nursery plants, horses, vegetables, watermelons. Market value $12.3 million. Hunting leases important. Substantial timber industry.

MARSHALL (24,430) county seat;

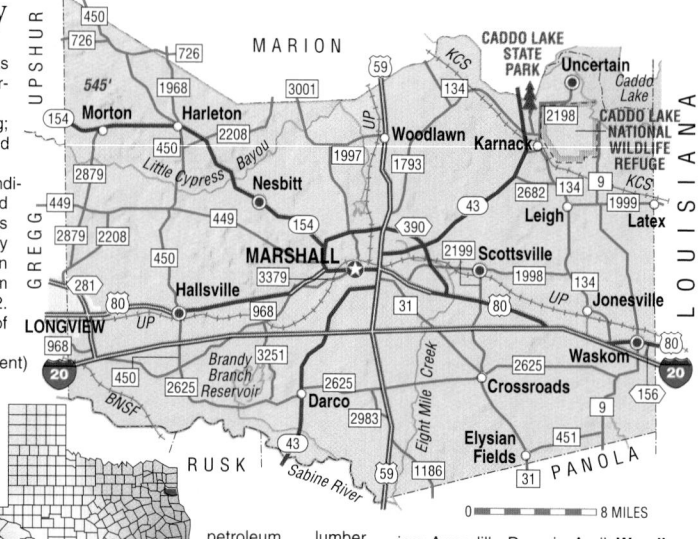

petroleum, lumber processing; varied manufacturing; Wonderland of Lights in December; civic center; historic sites, including Starr Family State Historic Site; hospital; Wiley College; East Texas Baptist University.

Other towns include: **Elysian Fields** (300); **Hallsville** (2,792) Western Days in October, museum; **Harleton** (260); **Jonesville** (28); **Karnack** (775); **Nesbitt** (297); **Scottsville** (267); **Uncertain** (159); **Waskom** (2,086) oil, gas; ranching; Armadillo Daze in April; **Woodlawn** (370). Also, part [1,598] of **Longview**.

Population	62,727
Change fm 2000	1.0
Area (sq. mi.)	915.09
Land Area (sq. mi.)	898.71
Altitude (ft.)	168-545
Rainfall (in.)	51.22
Jan. mean min.	33.4
July mean max.	92.4
Civ. Labor	29,925
Unemployed	5.3
Wages	$183,862,108
Av. Weekly Wage	$651.73
Prop. Value	$4,521,854,888
Retail Sales	$527,500,002

Hartley County

Physical Features: Panhandle High Plains; drains to Canadian River tributaries, playas; sandy, loam, chocolate soils; lake.

Economy: Agriculture, gas production; varied manufacturing.

History: Apaches, pushed out by Comanches around 1700. U.S. Army removed Indians in 1875. *Pastores* (Hispanic sheepmen) in area until 1880s. Cattle ranching began in 1880s. Farming expanded after 1900. County created 1876 from Bexar, Young districts; organized 1891; named for Texas pioneers O.C. and R.K. Hartley.

Race/Ethnicity, 2000: (In percent) Anglo, 77.59; Black, 8.11; Hispanic, 13.69; Other, 0.61.

Vital Statistics, 2003: Births, 106; deaths, 33; marriages, 3; divorces, 12.

Recreation: Rita Blanca Lake activities; ranch museum; local events; XIT Rodeo and Reunion at Dalhart.

Minerals: Sand, gravel, natural gas.

Agriculture: Cattle, corn, wheat, hay, dairy cows, vegetables. 110,000 acres irrigated. Market value $447.3 million. Hunting leases.

CHANNING (333) county seat, Roundup.

DALHART (7,170, mostly in Dallam County), feedlots; feed, meat processing; other industries. Also, **Hartley** (403).

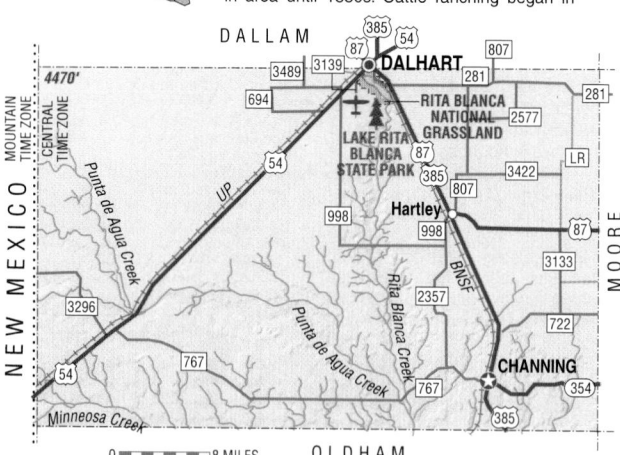

Population	5,423
Change fm 2000	-2.1
Area (sq. mi.)	1,463.20
Land Area (sq. mi.)	1,462.25
Altitude (ft.)	3,400-4,470
Rainfall (in.)	17.20
Jan. mean min.	20.0
July mean max.	90.9
Civ. Labor	3,328
Unemployed	0.8
Wages	$7,046,606
Av. Weekly Wage	$422.81
Prop. Value	$739,975,848
Retail Sales	$17,595,145

Haskell County

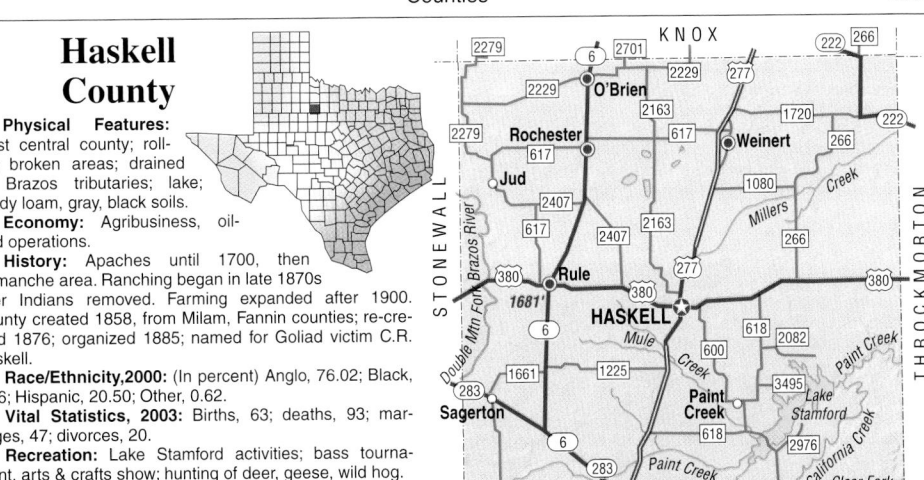

Physical Features: West central county; rolling; broken areas; drained by Brazos tributaries; lake; sandy loam, gray, black soils.

Economy: Agribusiness, oilfield operations.

History: Apaches until 1700, then Comanche area. Ranching began in late 1870s after Indians removed. Farming expanded after 1900. County created 1858, from Milam, Fannin counties; re-created 1876; organized 1885; named for Goliad victim C.R. Haskell.

Race/Ethnicity,2000: (In percent) Anglo, 76.02; Black, 2.86; Hispanic, 20.50; Other, 0.62.

Vital Statistics, 2003: Births, 63; deaths, 93; marriages, 47; divorces, 20.

Recreation: Lake Stamford activities; bass tournament, arts & crafts show; hunting of deer, geese, wild hog.

Minerals: Oil and gas.

Agriculture: Wheat, cotton, peanuts; 28,000 acres irrigated. Beef cattle raised. Market value $40.8 million.

HASKELL (2,870) county seat; farming center; hospital; city park; Wild Horse Prairie Days in June.

Other towns include: **O'Brien** (132), **Rochester** (362), **Rule** (670), **Weinert** (180). Also, **Stamford** (3,514, mostly in Jones County).

Population	5,592
Change fm 2000	-8.2
Area (sq. mi.)	910.25
Land Area (sq. mi.)	902.97
Altitude (ft.)	1,400-1,681
Rainfall (in.)	24.93
Jan. mean min.	28.8

July mean max.	96.1
Civ. Labor	3,006
Unemployed	3.3
Wages	$9,730,084
Av. Weekly Wage	$379.36
Prop. Value	$336,229,360
Retail Sales	$57,599,532

Hays County

Physical Features: Hilly in west, blackland in east; on edge of Balcones Escarpment.

Economy: Education, tourism, retirement area, some manufacturing; part of Austin metropolitan area.

History: Tonkawa area, also Apache and Comanche presence. Spanish authorities attempted first permanent settlement in 1807. Mexican land grants in early 1830s to Juan Martín Veramendi, Juan Vicente Campos and Thomas Jefferson Chambers. County created 1843 from Travis County; named for Capt. Jack Hays, famous Texas Ranger.

Race/Ethnicity, 2000: (In percent) Anglo, 65.26; Black, 3.74; Hispanic, 29.57; Other, 1.43.

Vital Statistics, 2003: Births, 1,638; deaths, 581; marriages, 771; divorces, 338.

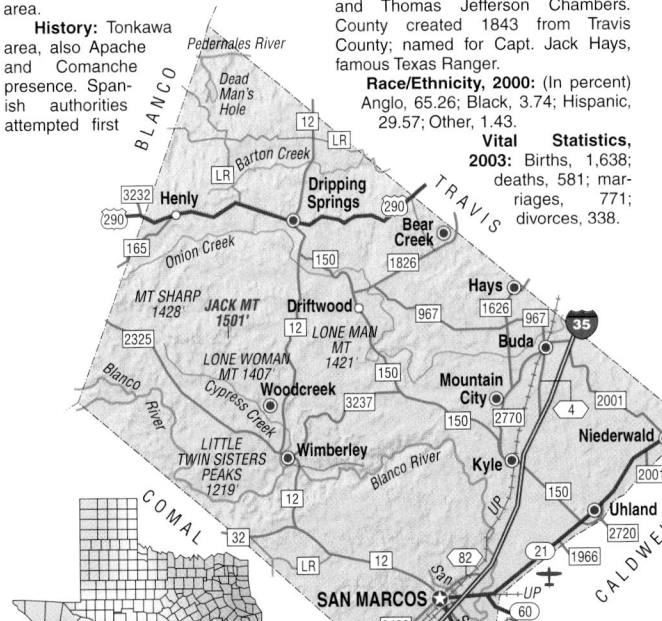

Recreation: Fishing, hunting; college cultural, athletic events; African-American museum, LBJ museum; Cypress Creek and Blanco River resorts, guest ranches, Wonder World park.

Minerals: Sand and gravel, cement produced.

Agriculture: Beef cattle, goats, exotic wildlife; greenhouse nurseries; hay, corn, sorghum, wheat and cotton. Market value $14.6 million.

SAN MARCOS (42,102) county seat; Texas State University, San Marcos Baptist Academy, Gary Job Corps Training Center; government/services; distribution center; outlet centers; hospital, sports medicine, physical therapy center; Scheib Center for mentally handicapped; Cinco de Mayo festival.

Other towns include: **Bear Creek** (388); **Buda** (3,184); **Driftwood** (NA); **Dripping Springs** (1,752); **Hays** (242); **Kyle** (11,870); **Mountain City** (746); **Niederwald** (677, partly in Caldwell County); **Uhland** (437, partly in Caldwell County); **Wimberley** (4,225) tourism, retirement community, artists, concert series; Country Pie Social and Fair in April; **Woodcreek** (1,384).

Population	119,359
Change fm 2000	22.3
Area (sq. mi.)	679.79
Land Area (sq. mi.)	677.87
Altitude (ft.)	550-1,501
Rainfall (in.)	37.19
Jan. mean min.	38.6
July mean max.	95.1
Civ. Labor	57,753
Unemployed	4.7
Wages	$250,579,616
Av. Weekly Wage	$526.26
Prop. Value	$8,236,300,177
Retail Sales	$1,310,620,824

For explanation of sources, abbreviations and symbols, see p. 167.

Hemphill County

Physical Features: Panhandle county; sloping surface, broken by Canadian, Washita rivers; sandy, red, dark soils.

Economy: Oil and gas, agriculture, tourism, government/services.

History: Apaches, who were pushed out by Comanches, Kiowas. Tribes removed to Indian Territory in 1875. Ranching began in late 1870s. Farmers began to arrive after 1900. County created from Bexar, Young districts, 1876; organized 1887; named for Republic of Texas Justice John Hemphill.

Race/Ethnicity, 2000: Anglo, 81.42; Black, 1.55; Hispanic, 15.58; Other, 1.13.

Vital Statistics, 2003: Births, 49; deaths, 22; marriages, 28; divorces, 9.

Recreation: Lake Marvin activities; fall foliage tour; hunting, fishing; Buffalo Wallow Indian Battleground, wildlife management area; 4th of July rodeo.

Minerals: Oil, natural gas, caliche.

Agriculture: Beef cattle top revenue source; crops include wheat, hay, sorghum; some irrigation. Market value $92.5 million. Hunting leases, nature tourism.

CANADIAN (2,267) county seat; oil, gas production; feedlot; hospital.

Population	**3,336**
Change fm 2000	-0.4

Area (sq. mi.)	912.06
Land Area (sq. mi.)	909.68
Altitude (ft.)	2,185-3,000
Rainfall (in.)	21.68
Jan. mean min.	18.8
July mean max.	93.9

Civ. Labor	2,419
Unemployed	2.0
Wages	$12,107,271
Av. Weekly Wage	$506.25
Prop. Value	$973,070,720
Retail Sales	$20,245,759

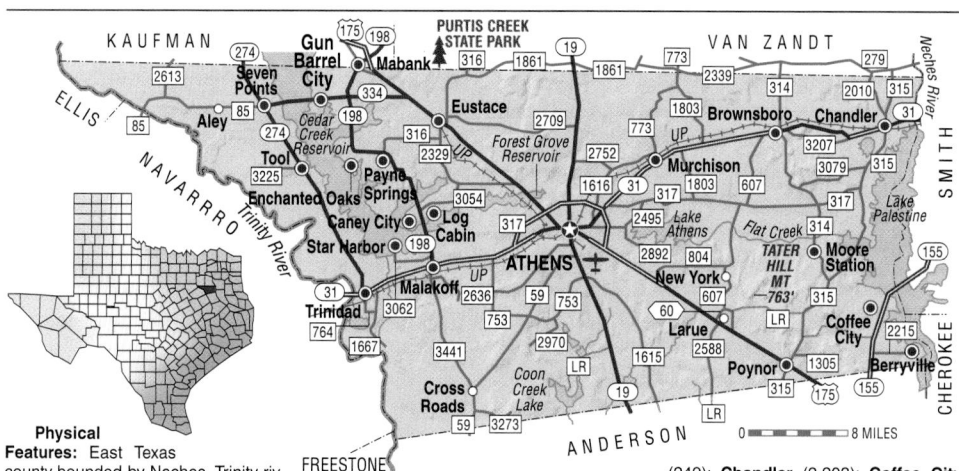

Henderson County

Physical Features: East Texas county bounded by Neches, Trinity rivers; hilly, rolling; one-third forested; sandy, loam, clay soils; commercial timber; Cedar Creek, other lakes.

Economy: Agibusiness, retail trade, varied manufacturing; minerals; recreation; tourism.

History: Caddo area. Cherokee, other tribes migrated into the area in 1819-20 ahead of white settlement. Cherokees forced into Indian Territory in 1839. Anglo-American settlers arrived in 1840s. County created 1846 from Nacogdoches, Houston counties and named for Gov. J. Pinckney Henderson.

Race/Ethnicity, 2000: (In percent) Anglo, 85.49; Black, 6.72; Hispanic, 6.92; Other, 0.87.

Vital Statistics, 2003: Births, 967; deaths, 904; marriages, 598; divorces, 182.

Recreation: Cedar Creek Reservoir, Lake Palestine, and other lakes; Purtis Creek State Park; hunting, fishing, bird-watching; East Texas Arboretum.

Minerals: Oil, gas, clays, lignite, sulfur, sand and gravel.

Agriculture: Nurseries, cattle, hay, horses. Market value $43.2 million. Hunting leases and fishing.

ATHENS (11,976) county seat; agribusiness center; varied manufacturing; tourism; state fish hatchery and museum; hospital, mental health center; Trinity Valley Community College; Texas Fiddlers' Contest in May.

Gun Barrel City (5,457) recreation, retirement, retail center.

Malakoff (2,349) brick factory, varied industry, tourism, library, Cornbread Festival in April.

Other towns include: **Berryville** (911); **Brownsboro** (836); **Caney City** (249); **Chandler** (2,203); **Coffee City** (202); **Enchanted Oaks** (384); **Eustace** (838); **Larue** (250); **Log Cabin** (775); **Moore Station** (194); **Murchison** (626); **Payne Springs** (683); **Poynor** (326); **Seven Points** (1,205) agribusiness, retail trade, recreation, Monte Carlo celebration in November; **Star Harbor** (432); **Tool** (2,334), and **Trinidad** (1,092). Also, **Mabank** (2,477, mostly in Kaufman County).

Population	79,184
Change fm 2000	8.1
Area (sq. mi.)	949.00
Land Area (sq. mi.)	874.24
Altitude (ft.)	256-763
Rainfall (in.)	42.03
Jan. mean min.	35.2
July mean max.	93.4
Civ. Labor	30,355
Unemployed	6.6
Wages	$99,031,245
Av. Weekly Wage	$470.96
Prop. Value	$4,746,510,230
Retail Sales	$644,741,837

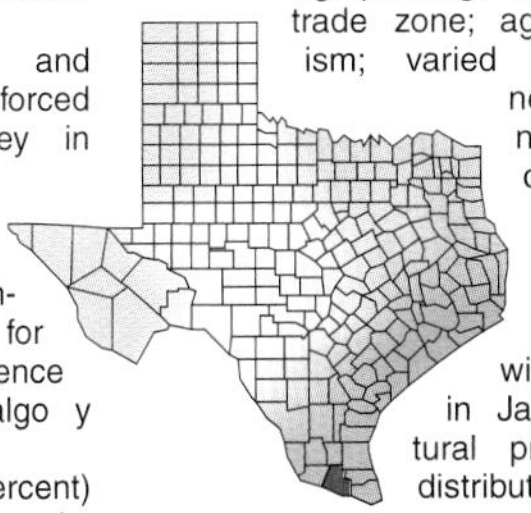

Physical Features: Rich alluvial soils along Rio Grande; sandy, loam soils in north; semitropical vegetation.

Economy: Food processing, shipping; other agribusinesses; tourism; mineral operations.

History: Coahuiltecan and Karankawa area. Comanches forced Apaches southward into valley in 1700s; Comanches arrived in valley in 1800s. Spanish settlement occurred 1750-1800. County created 1852 from Cameron, Starr counties; named for leader of Mexico's independence movement, Father Miguel Hidalgo y Costillo.

Race/Ethnicity, 2000: (In percent) Anglo, 10.59; Black, 0.36; Hispanic, 88.35; Other, 0.70.

Vital Statistics, 2003: Births, 16,233; deaths, 3,083; marriages, 4,735; divorces, 33.

Recreation: Winter resort, retirement area, fishing, hunting; gateway to Mexico; historical sites; Bentsen-Rio Grande Valley State Park; museums; All-Valley Winter Vegetable Show at Pharr.

Minerals: Oil, gas, stone, sand and gravel.

Agriculture: Ninety percent of farm cash receipts from crops, principally from sugar cane, grain, vegetables, citrus; livestock includes cattle; 270,000 acres irrigated. Market value $202.1 million.

EDINBURG (56,845) county seat; vegetable processing, packing; petroleum operations; clothing; tourism; planetarium; the University of Texas-Pan American; hospital; mental health center; museum; Fiesta Hidalgo in February.

Hidalgo County

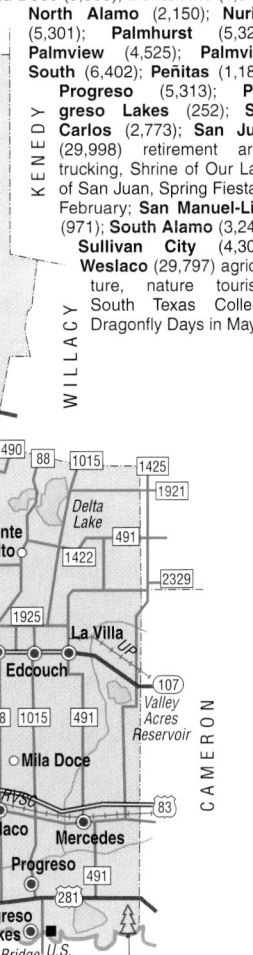

McALLEN (117,650) food processing, packing, shipping; foreign trade zone; agriculture; tourism; varied manufacturing; new air terminal; community college; cancer center.

Mission (56,934) citrus groves, with Citrus Fiesta in January; agricultural processing and distribution; hospital; community college.

Pharr (55,678) agriculture, trading center; trucking; tourism; old clock, juke box museums; folklife festival in February.

Other towns include: **Abram-Perezville** (5,710); **Alamo** (16,689) live steam museum; **Alton** (7,378); **Alton North** (5,290); **Doffing** (4,476); **Donna**

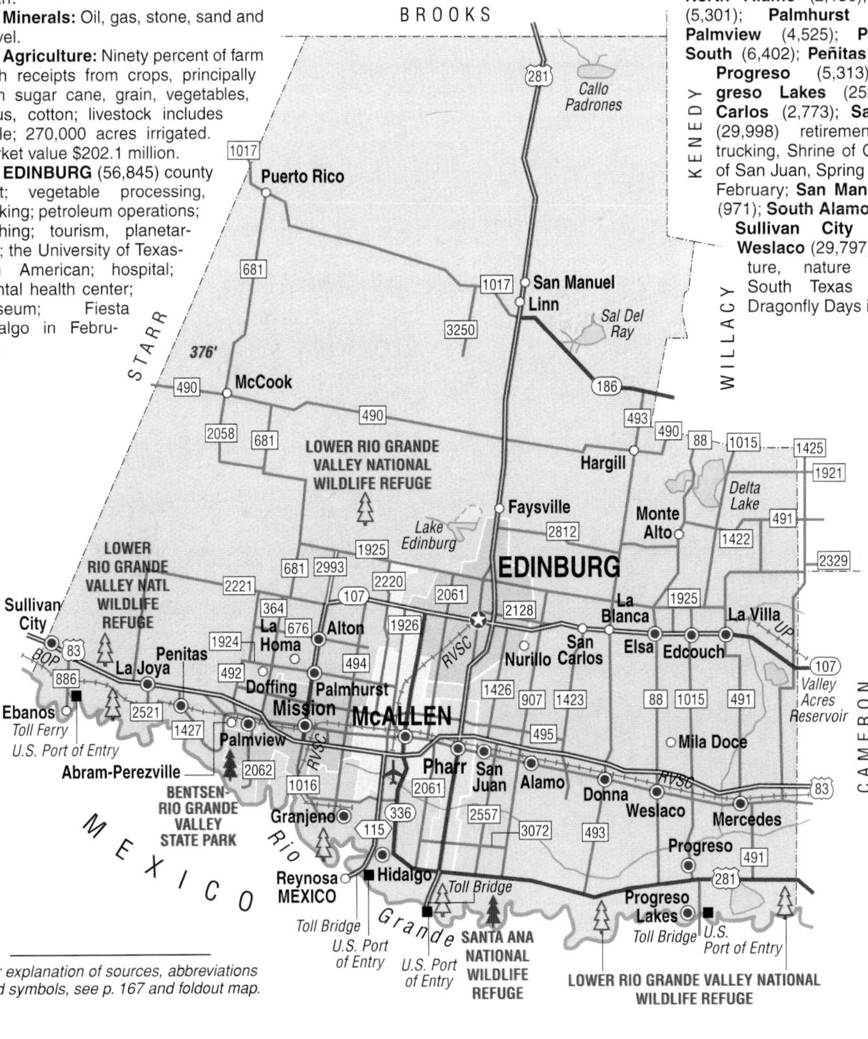

For explanation of sources, abbreviations and symbols, see p. 167 and foldout map.

Population **658,248**
Change fm 2000 .... 15.6
Area (sq. mi.) 1,582.66
Land Area (sq. mi.) 1,569.75
Altitude (ft.) 28-376
Rainfall (in.) 22.61
Jan. mean min. 48.2
July mean max. 95.5
Civ. Labor 236,492
Unemployed 11.8
Wages $1,129,427,797
Av. Weekly Wage $475.08
Prop. Value $18,049,053,524
Retail Sales $5,955,600,460

(15,690) citrus center, varied manufacturing; lamb, sheep show; **Edcouch** (3,926); **Elsa** (5,937); **Granjeno** (325); **Hargill** (1,349); **Hidalgo** (9,074) trade zone, shipping; winter resort, agribusiness, historical sites, library; Borderfest in March; **La Blanca** (2,463); **La Homa** (11,268); **La Joya** (3,938); **Los Ebanos** (407); **La Villa** (1,348).

Also, **Mercedes** (14,355) "boot capital," citrus, vegetable center; food processing; tourism; recreation vehicle show in January, Hispanic Fest July 4; **Mila Doce** (5,305); **Monte Alto** (1,677); **North Alamo** (2,150); **Nurillo** (5,301); **Palmhurst** (5,327); **Palmview** (4,525); **Palmview South** (6,402); **Peñitas** (1,182); **Progreso** (5,313); **Progreso Lakes** (252); **San Carlos** (2,773); **San Juan** (29,998) retirement area, trucking, Shrine of Our Lady of San Juan, Spring Fiesta in February; **San Manuel-Linn** (971); **South Alamo** (3,248); **Sullivan City** (4,307); **Weslaco** (29,797) agriculture, nature tourism, South Texas College; Dragonfly Days in May.

Hill County

Physical Features: North central county; level to rolling; blackland soils, some sandy loams; drains to Brazos; lakes.

Economy: Agribusiness, tourism, varied manufacturing.

History: Waco and Tawakoni area, later Comanches. Believed to be Indian "council spot," a place of safe passage without evidence of raids. Anglo-Americans of the Robertson colony arrived in early 1830s. Fort Graham established in 1849. County created from Navarro County 1853; named for G.W. Hill, Republic of Texas official.

Race/Ethnicity, 2000: (In percent) Anglo, 78.40; Black, 7.51; Hispanic, 13.49; Other, 0.60.

Vital Statistics, 2003: Births, 460; deaths, 433; marriages, 259; divorces, 155.

Recreation: Lake activities; excursion boat on Lake Whitney; Texas Heritage Museum including Confederate and Audie Murphy exhibits, historic structures, rebuilt frontier fort barracks; motorcycle track.

Minerals: Limestone, gas, oil.

Agriculture: Corn, sorghum, cattle, wheat, cotton, dairies. Market value $54 million. Some firewood marketed.

HILLSBORO (8,650) county seat; agribusiness, varied manufacturing, retail, outlet center; tourism, antique malls; Hill College; hospital; Cotton Pickin Fair in September; Cell Block

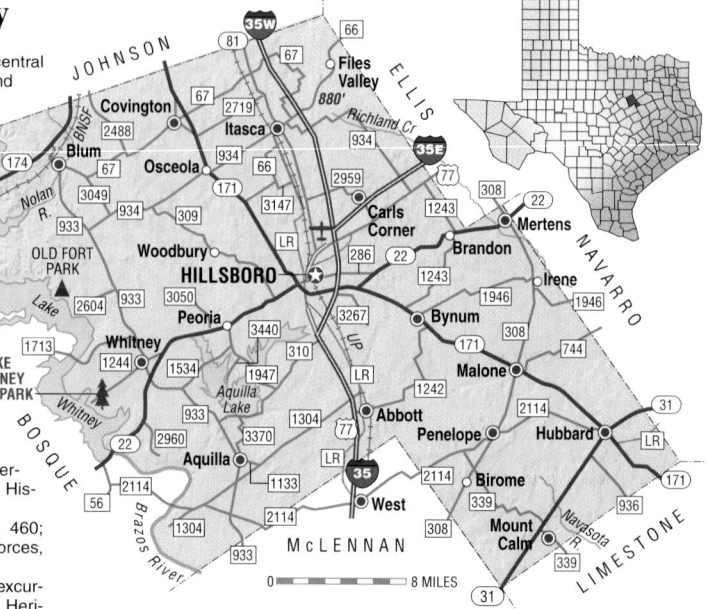

museum, restored courthouse.

Whitney (1,889) tourist center; hospital, varied manufacturing.

Other towns include: **Abbott** (316); **Aquilla** (139); **Blum** (412); **Brandon** (75); **Bynum** (244); **Carl's Corner** (143); **Covington** (305); **Hubbard** (1,622) agriculture, antiques center, museums, Memorial Day celebration; **Irene** (170); **Itasca** (1,546); **Malone** (291); **Mertens** (149); **Mount Calm** (334); **Penelope** (214).

Population	35,157
Change fm 2000	8.8
Area (sq. mi.)	985.65
Land Area (sq. mi.)	962.36
Altitude (ft.)	450-880
Rainfall (in.)	37.15
Jan. mean min.	35.2
July mean max.	95.2
Civ. Labor.	15,008
Unemployed	5.6
Wages	$50,283,419
Av. Weekly Wage	$448.20
Prop. Value	$1,777,104,815
Retail Sales	$370,599,153

Hockley County

Physical Features: West Texas High Plains, numerous playas, drains to Yellow House Draw; loam, sandy loam soils.

Economy: Extensive oil, gas production and services; manufacturing; varied agribusiness.

History: Comanches displaced Apaches in early 1700s. Large ranches of 1880s brought few residents. Homesteaders arrived after 1900. County created 1876, from Bexar, Young districts; organized 1921. Named for Republic of Texas secretary of war Gen. G.W. Hockley.

Race/Ethnicity, 2000: Anglo, 58.37; Black, 3.79; Hispanic, 37.24; Other, 0.60.

Vital Statistics, 2003: Births, 354; deaths, 221; marriages, 130; divorces, 76.

Recreation: Early Settlers' Day in July; Marigolds Arts, Crafts Festival in November.

Minerals: Oil, gas, stone; one of leading oil counties with more than 1 billion barrels produced.

Agriculture: Cotton, grain sorghum; cattle, hogs raised; substantial irrigation. Market value $90.2 million.

LEVELLAND (12,917) county seat; oil, cotton, cattle center; government/services; hospital; South Plains College; Hot Burrito & Bluegrass Music Festival in July.

Other towns include: **Anton** (1,159); **Opdyke West** (191); **Pep** (3); **Ropesville** (518); **Smyer** (480); **Sundown** (1,491); **Whitharral** (158).

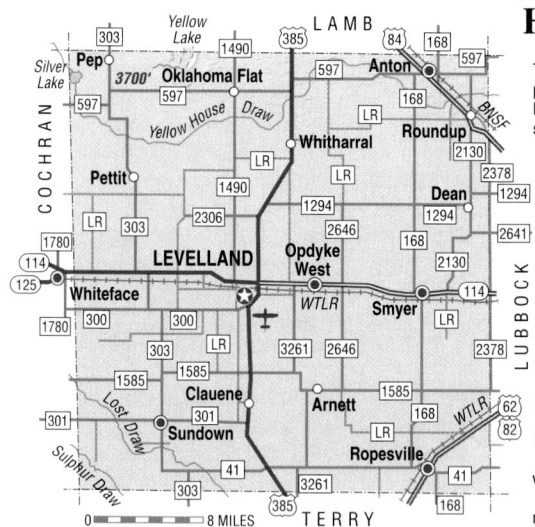

Population	22,781
Change fm 2000	0.3
Area (sq. mi.)	908.55
Land Area (sq. mi.)	908.28
Altitude (ft.)	3,300-3,700
Rainfall (in.)	19.58
Jan. mean min.	23.7
July mean max.	92.7
Civ. Labor.	11,814
Unemployed	3.5
Wages	$54,377,652
Av. Weekly Wage	$519.29
Prop. Value	$2,137,980,324
Retail Sales	$218,192,967

Hood County

Physical Features: Hilly; broken by Paluxy, Brazos rivers; sandy loam soils.

Economy: Tourism; commuting to Fort Worth; nuclear power plant; agriculture.

History: Lipan Apache and Comanche area. Anglo-American settlers arrived in late 1840s. County created 1866 from Johnson and Erath counties; named for Confederate Gen. John B. Hood.

Race/Ethnicity, 2000: (In percent) Anglo, 91.22; Black, 0.36; Hispanic, 7.24; Other, 1.18.

Vital Statistics, 2003: Births, 499; deaths, 449; marriages, 353; divorces, 239.

Recreation: Lakes, fishing, scenic areas; summer theater; Gen. Granbury's Bean & Rib cookoff in March; Acton historic site.

Minerals: Oil, gas, stone.

Agriculture: Hay, turfgrass, beef cattle, nursery crops, pecans, peaches; some irrigation. Market value $21.7 million.

GRANBURY (7,076) county seat; tourism; real estate; power plants; historic downtown area; opera house; hospital; library; Civil War re-enactment in October.

Other towns include: **Acton** (1,129) grave of Elizabeth Crockett, wife of Davy; **Brazos Bend** (300); **Cresson** (2,000); **DeCordova**

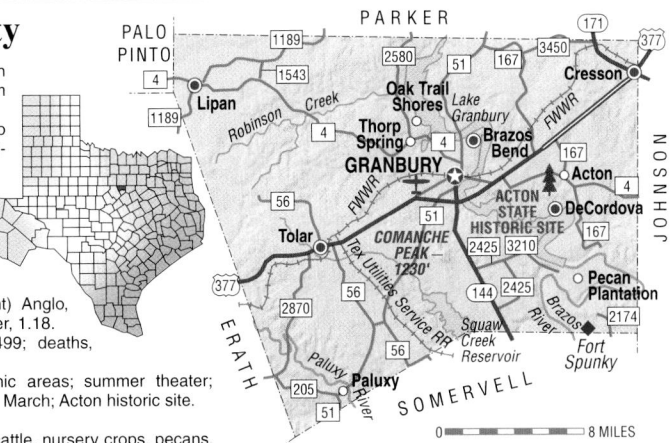

(3,147); **Lipan** (469); **Oak Trail Shores** (2,730); **Paluxy** (76); **Pecan Plantation** (3,690); **Tolar** (640).

Population	46,492
Change fm 2000	13.1
Area (sq. mi.)	436.80
Land Area (sq. mi.)	421.61
Altitude (ft.)	600-1,230
Rainfall (in.)	33.10
Jan. mean min.	33.0
July mean max.	97.0
Civ. Labor	19,156
Unemployed	6.0
Wages	$71,359,852
Av. Weekly Wage	$506.01
Prop. Value	$3,213,315,300
Retail Sales	$419,742,160

Hopkins County

Physical Features: Northeast Texas county of varied timber, including pines; drains north to South Sulphur River; Cooper Lake (also known as Jim Chapman Lake); light, sandy to heavier black soils.

Economy: Agribusiness, feed mills; varied manufacturing.

History: Caddo area, displaced by Cherokees, who in turn were forced out by President Lamar in 1839. First Anglo-American settlement in 1837. County created 1846 from Lamar, Nacogdoches counties; named for pioneer Hopkins family.

Race/Ethnicity, 2000: (In percent) Anglo, 81.74; Black, 8.07; Hispanic, 9.28; Other, 0.91.

Vital Statistics, 2003: Births, 451; deaths, 415; marriages, 311; divorces, 191.

Recreation: Fishing, hunting; lake activities; stew contest in September; dairy museum; dairy festival in June.

Minerals: Lignite coal.

Agriculture: Dairies, beef cattle; forage, horses, poultry. Market value $134.2 million. Firewood and hardwood lumber marketed.

SULPHUR SPRINGS (14,690) county seat; dairy farming; equine center; food processing, distribution; varied manufacturing; tourism; hospital; library, heritage park; music box gallery; civic center.

Other towns include: **Brashear** (280), **Como** (626), **Cumby** (613), **Dike** (170), **Pickton** (300), **Saltillo** (200), **Sulphur Bluff** (280), **Tira** (248).

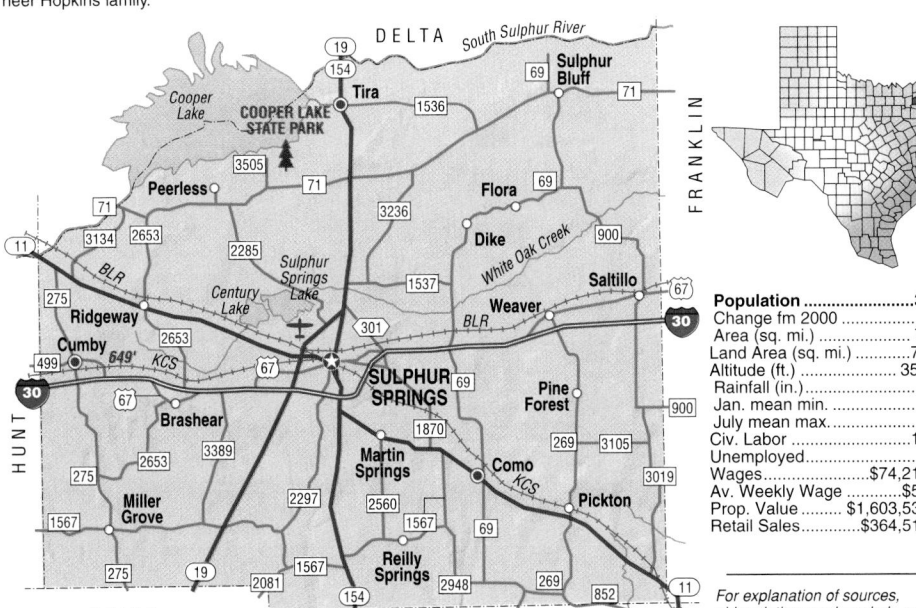

Population	33,201
Change fm 2000	3.9
Area (sq. mi.)	792.74
Land Area (sq. mi.)	782.40
Altitude (ft.)	350-649
Rainfall (in.)	47.69
Jan. mean min.	31.1
July mean max.	94.8
Civ. Labor	14,933
Unemployed	5.0
Wages	$74,216,756
Av. Weekly Wage	$518.20
Prop. Value	$1,603,536,998
Retail Sales	$364,519,197

For explanation of sources, abbreviations and symbols, see p. 167 and foldout map.

Houston County

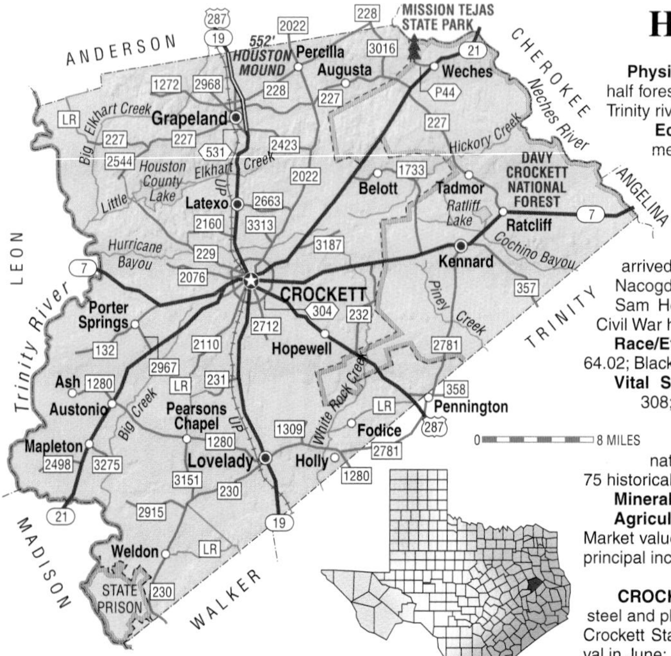

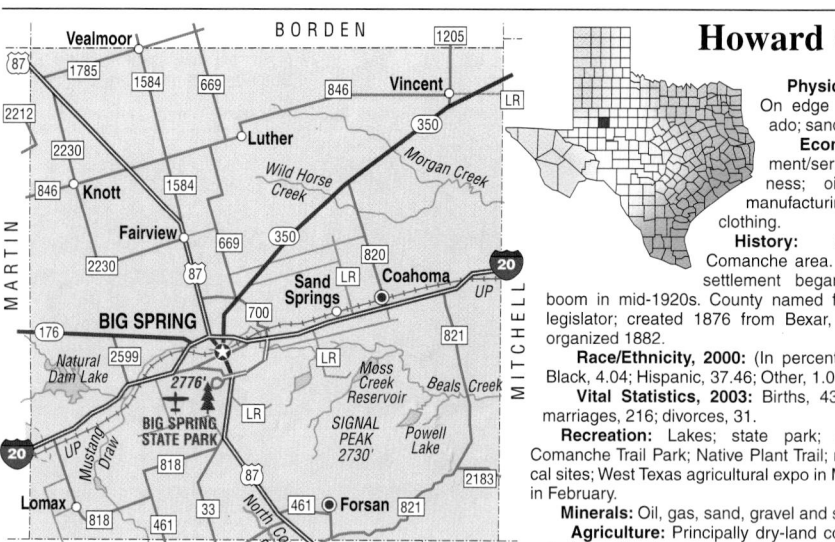

Physical Features: East Texas county over half forested; rolling terrain, draining to Neches, Trinity rivers; commercial timber production.

Economy: Livestock, timber, government/services, manufacturing, tourism.

History: Caddo group attracted mission San Francisco de los Tejas, 1690. Spanish town of Bucareli established in 1774. Both lasted only a few years. Anglo-American settlers arrived in 1820s. County created 1837 from Nacogdoches County by Republic; named for Sam Houston. Cotton plantations before the Civil War had many slaves.

Race/Ethnicity, 2000: (In percent) Anglo, 64.02; Black, 27.97; Hispanic, 7.50; Other, 0.51.

Vital Statistics, 2003: Births, 264; deaths, 308; marriages, 168; divorces, 64.

Recreation: Fishing, hunting; national forest; Mission Tejas State Park; 75 historical markers; Houston County Lake.

Minerals: Oil, gas, sand, gravel.

Agriculture: Cattle, hay, watermelons, cotton. Market value $34.5 million. Hunting leases. Timber principal income source.

CROCKETT (7,127), county seat; timber, steel and plastic products; clothing manufacturing, Crockett State School; historic sites; fiddlers festival in June; African American church tour.

Other towns include: **Grapeland** (1,423) Peanut Festival in October; **Kennard** (303); **Latexo** (270); **Lovelady** (598) Lovefest in February; **Ratcliff** (106).

Population	23,303
Change fm 2000	0.5
Area (sq. mi.)	1,236.83
Land Area (sq. mi.)	1,230.89
Altitude (ft.)	160-552
Rainfall (in.)	45.48
Jan. mean min.	35.9
July mean max.	93.3
Civ. Labor	9,890
Unemployed	4.7
Wages	$60,260,060
Av. Weekly Wage	$624.46
Prop. Value	$1,221,290,570
Retail Sales	$140,396,002

Howard County

Physical Features: On edge of Llano Estacado; sandy loam soils.

Economy: Government/services; agribusiness; oil, gas; varied manufacturing, including clothing.

History: Pawnee and Comanche area. Anglo-American settlement began in 1870. Oil boom in mid-1920s. County named for V.E. Howard, legislator; created 1876 from Bexar, Young districts; organized 1882.

Race/Ethnicity, 2000: (In percent) Anglo, 57.47; Black, 4.04; Hispanic, 37.46; Other, 1.03.

Vital Statistics, 2003: Births, 438; deaths, 349; marriages, 216; divorces, 31.

Recreation: Lakes; state park; campground in Comanche Trail Park; Native Plant Trail; museum; historical sites; West Texas agricultural expo in March; Cranefest in February.

Minerals: Oil, gas, sand, gravel and stone.

Agriculture: Principally dry-land cotton; also, beef, stocker cattle, horses, peanuts, sorghum. Market value $15.1 million.

BIG SPRING (25,458) county seat; agriculture, petrochemicals produced; hospitals, including a state institution and Veterans Administration hospital; federal prison; varied manufacturing; Howard College; railroad plaza.

Other towns include: **Coahoma** (879), **Forsan** (216), **Knott** (200).

Population	32,879
Change fm 2000	-2.2
Area (sq. mi.)	904.19
Land Area (sq. mi.)	902.84
Altitude (ft.)	2,200-2,776
Rainfall (in.)	20.12
Jan. mean min.	29.6
July mean max.	94.3
Civ. Labor	13,928
Unemployed	3.9
Wages	$85,727,442
Av. Weekly Wage	$559.42
Prop. Value	$1,298,918,125
Retail Sales	$290,132,999

The Guadalupe Mountains loom over the irrigated fields outside Dell City. Texas Almanac photo.

Hudspeth County

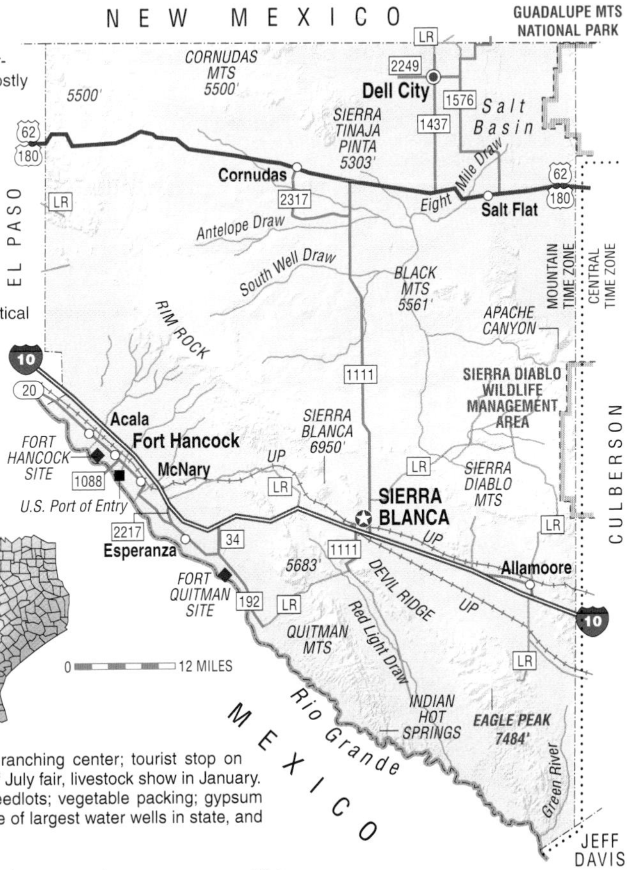

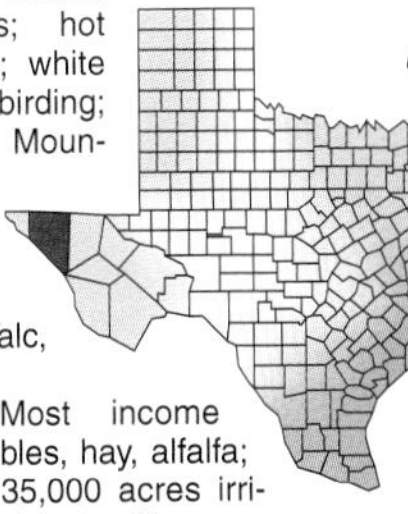

Physical Features: Plateau, basin terrain, draining to salt lakes; Rio Grande; mostly rocky, alkaline, clay soils and sandy loam soils, except alluvial along Rio Grande; desert, mountain vegetation. Fertile agricultural valleys.

Economy: Agribusiness, mining, tourism, hunting leases.

History: Mescalero Apache area. Fort Quitman established in 1858 to protect routes to west. Railroad in 1881 brought Anglo-American settlers. Political turmoil in Mexico (1912-29) brought more settlers from Mexico. County named for Texas political leader Claude B. Hudspeth; created 1917 from El Paso County.

Race/Ethnicity, 2000: (In percent) Anglo, 23.50; Black, 0.21; Hispanic, 75.03; Other, 1.26.

Vital Statistics, 2003: Births, 49; deaths, 16; marriages, 7; divorces, 0.

Recreation: Scenic drives; fort ruins; hot springs; salt basin; white sands; hunting; birding; part of Guadalupe Mountains National Park, containing unique plant life, canyons.

Minerals: Talc, stone, gypsum.

Agriculture: Most income from cotton, vegetables, hay, alfalfa; beef cattle raised; 35,000 acres irrigated. Market value $27.2 million.

SIERRA BLANCA (554) county seat; ranching center; tourist stop on interstate highway; adobe courthouse; 4th of July fair, livestock show in January.

Other towns include: **Dell City** (418) feedlots; vegetable packing; gypsum processing; clinic; trade center; airport; some of largest water wells in state, and **Fort Hancock** (1,795).

Population	3,300
Change fm 2000	-1.3
Area (sq. mi.)	4,571.93
Land Area (sq. mi.)	4,571.00
Altitude (ft.)	3,200-7,484
Rainfall (in.)	11.93

Jan. mean min.	25.1
July mean max.	92.0
Civ. Labor	1,433
Unemployed	5.8
Wages	$5,972,297
Av. Weekly Wage	$574.98

Prop. Value	$339,804,112
Retail Sales	$8,184,367

For explanation of sources, abbreviations and symbols, see p. 167 and foldout map.

Hunt County

Physical Features: North Texas county; level to rolling surface; Sabine, Sulphur rivers; Lake Tawakoni; mostly heavy Blackland soil, some loam, sandy loams.

Economy: Education, varied manufacturing, agribusiness; several Fortune 500 companies in county; many residents employed in Dallas area.

History: Kiowa Indians who left soon after Anglo-American settlers arrived in 1839. County named for Memucan Hunt, Republic secretary of navy; created 1846 from Fannin, Nacogdoches counties.

Race/Ethnicity, 2000: (In percent) Anglo, 80.61; Black, 9.67; Hispanic, 8.31; Other, 1.41.

Vital Statistics, 2003: Births, 1,142; deaths, 764; marriages, 630; divorces, 342.

Recreation: Lake sports; Texas A&M University-Commerce events; museum; Audie Murphy exhibit.

Minerals: Sand and white rock, gas, oil.

Agriculture: Cattle, forage, greenhouse crops, top revenue sources; horses, wheat, oats, cotton, grain sorghum. Market value $28.1 million. Some firewood sold.

GREENVILLE (25,202) county seat; government/services, varied manufacturing, agribusiness; hospital; branch of Paris Junior College; Native American Pow-wow in January; cotton museum.

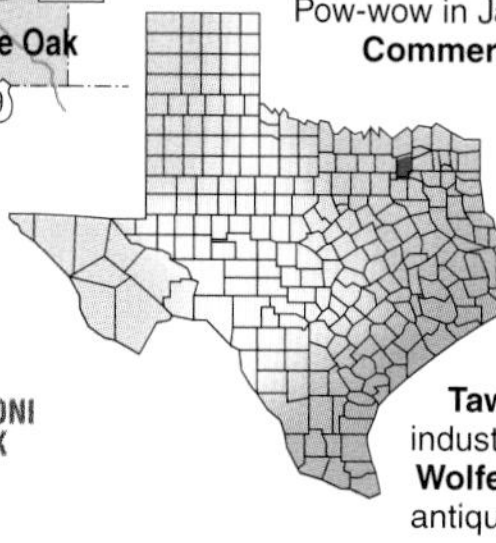

Commerce (8,683) Texas A&M University-Commerce; varied manufacturing; tourism, children's museum; Bois d'Arc Bash in September; hospital.

Other towns include: **Caddo Mills** (1,191); **Campbell** (770); **Celeste** (844); **Hawk Cove** (476); **Lone Oak** (534); **Merit** (215); **Neylandville** (56); **Quinlan** (1,406); **West Tawakoni** (1,561) tourist center, light industry, catfish tournament, Lakefest; **Wolfe City** (1,595) light manufacturing, antiques shops.

Population	81,781
Change fm 2000	6.8
Area (sq. mi.)	882.02
Land Area (sq. mi.)	841.16
Altitude (ft.)	437-692
Rainfall (in.)	43.70
Jan. mean min.	31.2
July mean max.	93.3
Civ. Labor	37,121
Unemployed	6.0
Wages	$194,078,105
Av. Weekly Wage	$601.16
Prop. Value	$3,250,841,318
Retail Sales	$2,778,195,917

Lake Meredith National Recreation Area in Hutchinson County. Texas Almanac photo.

Hutchinson County

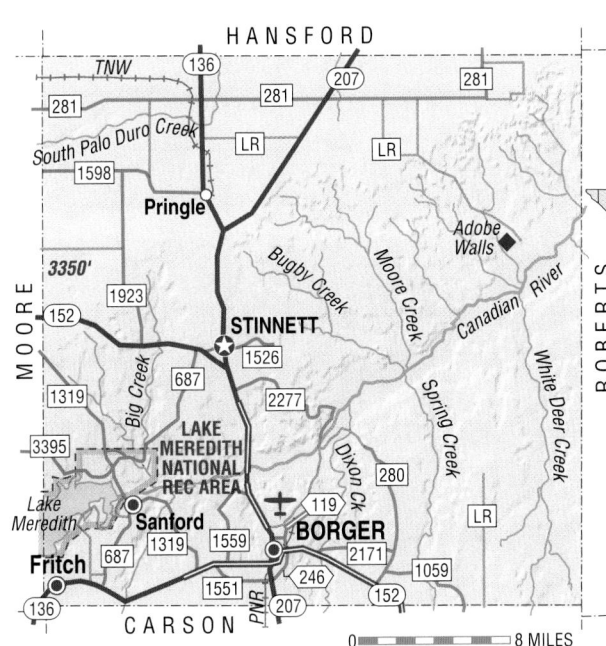

Physical Features: High Plain, broken by Canadian River and tributaries, Lake Meredith; fertile valleys along streams.

Economy: Oil, gas, petrochemicals; agribusiness; varied manufacturing; tourism.

History: Antelope Creek Indian area. Later Comanches were driven out in U.S. cavalry campaigns of 1874-75. Adobe Walls site of two Indian attacks, 1864 and 1874. Ranching began in late 1870s. Oil boom in early 1920s. County created 1876 from Bexar Territory; organized 1901; named for pioneer jurist Anderson Hutchinson.

Race/Ethnicity, 2000: (In percent) Anglo, 81.15; Black, 2.47; Hispanic, 14.70; Other, 1.68.

Vital Statistics, 2003: Births, 308; deaths, 238; marriages, 186; divorces, 131.

Recreation: Lake activities; fishing, camping; Adobe Walls, historic Indian battle site; fish fry in June.

Minerals: Gas, oil, sand, gravel.

Agriculture: Cattle, corn, wheat, grain sorghum; about 45,000 acres irrigated. Market value $29.3 million.

STINNETT (1,843) county seat; petroleum refining; farm center.

BORGER (13,778) petroleum refining, petrochemicals, carbon-black production, oil-field servicing; varied manufacturing; retail center; Frank Phillips College; hospital.

Other cities include: **Fritch** (2,133), **Sanford** (187).

Population 22,617	July mean max........................92.6
Change fm 2000 ....-5.2	Civ. Labor 8,474
Area (sq. mi.)......................894.95	Unemployed...............................6.8
Land Area (sq. mi.)..............887.37	Wages........................$71,545,835
Altitude (ft.) 2,700-3,350	Av. Weekly Wage $711.97
Rainfall (in.) 21.98	Prop. Value $1,772,550,330
Jan. mean min. 23.4	Retail Sales..............$162,606,297

Irion County

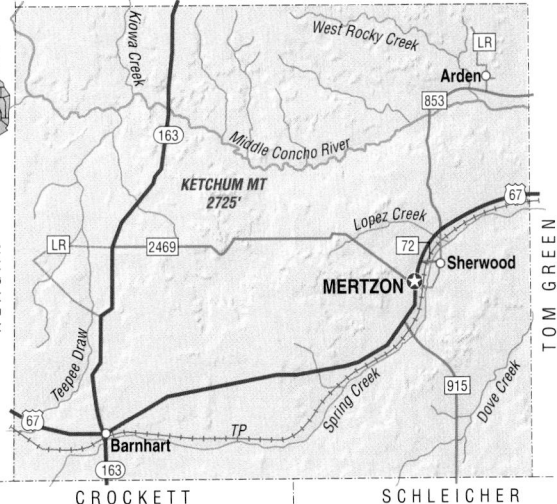

Physical Features: West Texas county with hilly surface, broken by Middle Concho, tributaries; clay, sandy soils.

Economy: Ranching; oil, gas production, wildlife recreation, commuters.

History: Tonkawa Indian area. Anglo-American settlement began in late 1870s. County named for Republic leader R.A. Irion; created 1889 from Tom Green County.

Race/Ethnicity, 2000: (In percent) Anglo, 74.81; Black, 0.23; Hispanic, 24.62; Other, 0.34.

Vital Statistics, 2003: Births 14; deaths, 15; marriages, 5; divorces, 6.

Recreation: Hunting; historic sites, including Dove Creek battlefield and stagecoach stops, old Sherwood courthouse built 1900; hunters appreciation dinner in November.

Minerals: Oil, gas.

Agriculture: Beef cattle, sheep, goats; wheat, cotton, hay. Market value $3.5 million.

MERTZON (837) county seat; farm center; wool warehousing.

Other towns include: **Barnhart** (110).

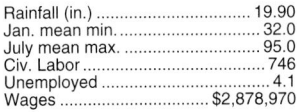

Population..................................1,738	Rainfall (in.) 19.90	Av. Weekly Wage....................$549.53
Change fm 2000 ....-1.9	Jan. mean min..............................32.0	Prop. Value $332,418,750
Area (sq. mi.)........................1,051.59	July mean max. 95.0	Retail Sales........................$2,897,581
Land Area (sq. mi.) 1,051.48	Civ. Labor 746	
Altitude (ft.)........................2,000-2,725	Unemployed 4.1	*For explanation of sources, abbreviations*
	Wages $2,878,970	*and symbols, see p. 167 and foldout map.*

Fort Richardson State Park in Jack County. Texas Almanac photo.

Jack County

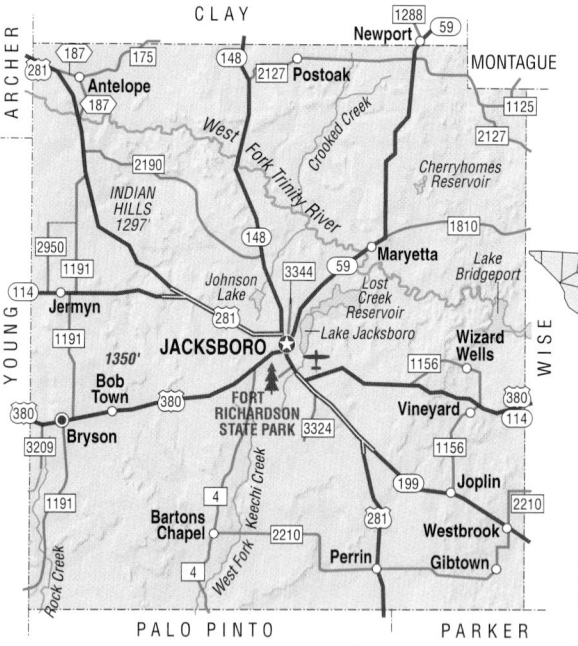

Physical Features: Rolling Cross Timbers, broken by West Fork of the Trinity, other streams; sandy, dark brown, loam soils; lakes.

Economy: Petroleum production, oil-field services, livestock, manufacturing, tourism.

History: Caddo and Comanche borderland. Anglo-American settlers arrived in 1855, part of Peters Colony. County named for brothers P.C. and W.H. Jack, leaders in Texas' independence effort; created 1856 from Cooke County; organized 1857 with Mesquiteville (orginal name of Jacksboro) as county seat.

Race/Ethnicity,2000: (In percent) Anglo, 85.75; Black, 5.50; Hispanic, 7.89; Other, 0.86.

Vital Statistics, 2003: Births, 96; deaths, 96; marriages, 62; divorces, 25.

Recreation: Hunting, wildlife leases; fishing; lake activities; Fort Richardson, museum, other historic sites; Lost Creek Reservoir State Trailway; rattlesnake roundup in March.

Minerals: Oil, gas.

Agriculture: Cattle, hay, wheat, goats, sheep. Market value $15.6 million. Firewood sold.

JACKSBORO (4,532) county seat; agribusiness; manufacturing; tourism; petroleum production and services; hospital; hospice; library; Old Mesquiteville Festival in fall.

Other towns include: **Bryson** (521), **Jermyn** (75), **Perrin** (300).

Population	8,981
Change fm 2000	2.5
Area (sq. mi.)	920.11
Land Area (sq. mi.)	916.61
Altitude (ft.)	836–1,350

Rainfall (in.)	31.44
Jan. mean min.	29.7
July mean max.	94.4
Civ. Labor	4,127
Unemployed	2.5

Wages	$14,127,015
Av. Weekly Wage	$579.88
Prop. Value	$881,087,930
Retail Sales	$36,100,251

Jackson County

Physical Features: South coastal county of prairie and motts of trees; loam, clay, black soils; drains to creek, rivers, bays.

Economy: Petroleum production and operation; metal fabrication and tooling, sheet-metal works, plastics manufacturing; agribusinesses; lake recreation.

History: Karankawa area. Six of Austin's Old Three Hundred families (1820s) settled in area. Lipan Apaches and Kiowas arrived in early 1830s. Mexican municipality, created 1835, became original county the following year; named for U.S. President Andrew Jackson. Oil discovered in 1934.

Race/Ethnicity, 2000: (In percent) Anglo, 66.82; Black, 7.66; Hispanic, 24.68; Other, 0.84.

Vital Statistics, 2003: Births, 210; deaths, 162; marriages, 107; divorces, 50.

Recreation: Hunting, fishing, birding; historic sites; Texana Museum; Lake Texana, Brackenridge Plantation campground, state park; county fair, rodeo in October.

Minerals: Oil and natural gas.

Agriculture: Cotton, cattle, corn, rice; also, sorghums, soybeans; 13,000 acres of rice irrigated. Market value $41.9 million.

EDNA (5,979) county seat; oil, gas; agriculture; tourism; varied manufacturing; hospital, library; Texana Day in April with community bands.

Other towns include: **Francitas** (125), **Ganado** (1,946), **LaSalle** (110), **La Ward** (199), **Lolita** (543), **Vanderbilt** (419).

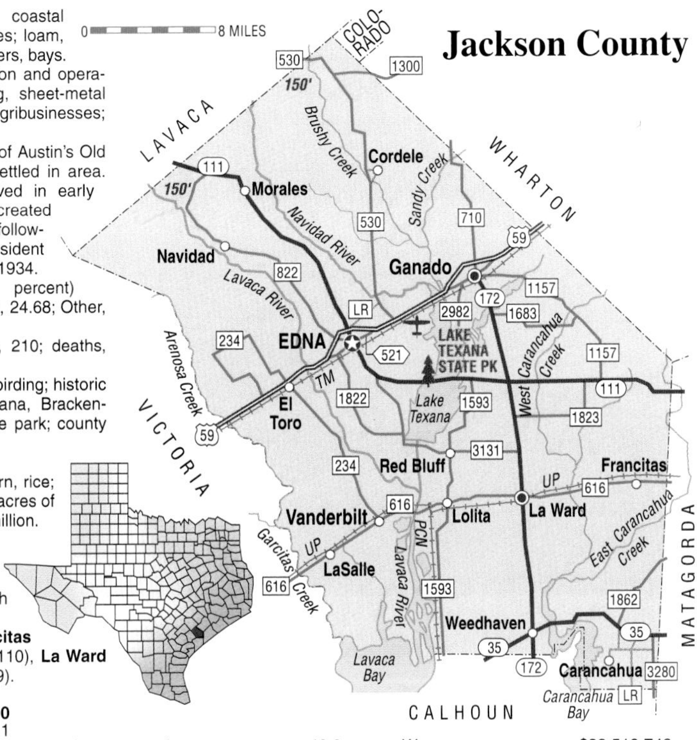

Population............................14,400		
Change fm 2000 .... 0.1		
Area (sq. mi.) 857.03	Jan. mean min. 42.0	Wages $33,519,743
Land Area (sq. mi.) 829.49	July mean max........................ 94.0	Av. Weekly Wage $541.58
Altitude (ft.)................sea level-150	Civ. Labor 7,860	Prop. Value.............$1,284,204,734
Rainfall (in.)............................ 42.10	Unemployed.............................. 4.1	Retail Sales $141,969,108

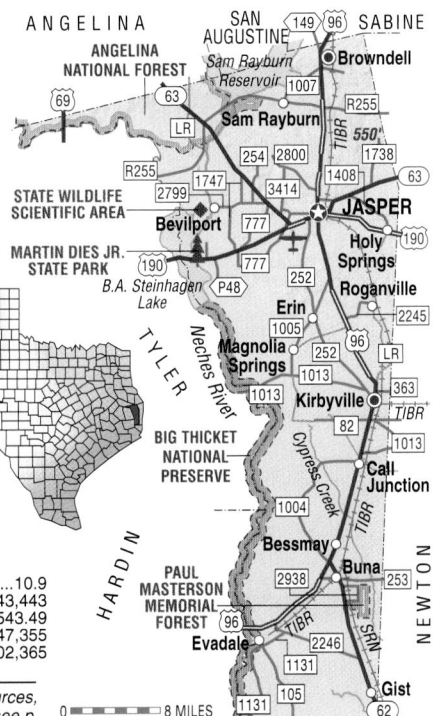

Jasper County

Physical Features: East Texas county; hilly to level; national forests; lakes; Neches River.

Economy: Timber industries; oil; tourism; fishing; aircraft manufacturer; agriculture.

History: Caddo and Atakapa Indian area. Land grants to John R. Bevil and Lorenzo de Zavala in 1829. County created 1836, organized 1837, from Mexican municipality; named for Sgt. William Jasper of American Revolution.

Race/Ethnicity, 2000: (In percent) Anglo, 77.38; Black, 17.94; Hispanic, 3.89; Other, 0.79.

Vital Statistics, 2003: Births, 500; deaths, 399; marriages, 349; divorces, 238.

Recreation: Lake activities; hunting, fishing; state park Big Thicket.

Minerals: Oil, gas produced.

Agriculture: Cattle, hogs, major revenue source; vegetables, fruit, pecans. Market value $4.8 million. Timber is major income producer.

JASPER (8,554) county seat; timber industries; tourism; oil, gas production; hospitals; prison; Azalea Festival in March.

Other towns include: **Browndell** (214); **Buna** (2,315); **Evadale** (1,453); **Kirbyville** (2,087) commuters, government/services; Calaboose museum, Magnolia Festival in April; **Sam Rayburn** (600).

Population 35,609	Unemployed 10.9
Change fm 2000 .... 0.0	Wages $72,943,443
Area (sq. mi.) 969.62	Av. Weekly Wage $543.49
Land Area (sq. mi.) 937.40	Prop. Value..........$2,021,947,355
Altitude (ft.) 25-550	Retail Sales $329,802,365
Rainfall (in.)......................... 60.57	
Jan. mean min. 35.2	
July mean max...................... 94.5	*For explanation of sources,*
Civ. Labor 14,568	*abbreviations and symbols, see p.*
	167 and foldout map.

The McDonald Observatory on Mt. Locke. Texas Almanac photo.

Jeff Davis County

Physical Features: Highest average elevation in Texas; peaks (Mt. Livermore, 8,378 ft.), canyons, plateaus; intermountain wash, clay, loam soils; cedars, oaks in highlands.

Economy: Tourism, ranching, greenhouse/nurseries.

History: Mescalero Apaches in area when Antonio de Espejo explored in 1583. U.S. Army established Fort Davis in 1854 to protect routes to west. Civilian settlers followed, including Manuel Músquiz, a political refugee from Mexico. County named for Jefferson Davis, U.S. war secretary, Confederate president; created 1887 from Presidio County.

Race/Ethnicity, 2000: (In percent) Anglo, 63.20; Black, 0.82; Hispanic, 35.48; Other, 0.50.

Vital Statistics, 2003: Births, 17; deaths, 12; marriages, 4; divorces, 0.

Recreation: Scenic drives including scenic loop along Limpia Creek, Mt. Livermore, Blue Mountain; hunting; Fort Davis National Historic Site (with Restoration Festival on Columbus Day weekend); state park; McDonald Observatory on Mt. Locke; solar power park; Chihuahuan Desert Research Institute.

Minerals: bentonite.

Agriculture: Greenhouse nurseries, beef cattle, apples, grapes. Market value $6.4 million.

FORT DAVIS (1,071), county seat; ranch center; trade, tourism; government/services; library; "Coolest July 4th in Texas".

Other town: **Valentine** (180).

Population	2,253
Change fm 2000	2.1
Area (sq. mi.)	2,264.60
Land Area (sq. mi.)	2,264.43
Altitude (ft.)	3,500-8,378
Rainfall (in.) Fort Davis	15.86
Rainfall (in.) Mt. Locke	20.37
Jan. mean min. Fort Davis	28.4
Jan. mean min. Mt. Locke	32.4
July mean max. Fort Davis	89.5
July mean max. Mt. Locke	84.5
Civ. Labor	1,711
Unemployed	1.3
Wages	$6,338,455
Av. Weekly Wage	$478.48
Prop. Value	$307,114,000
Retail Sales	$8,099,500

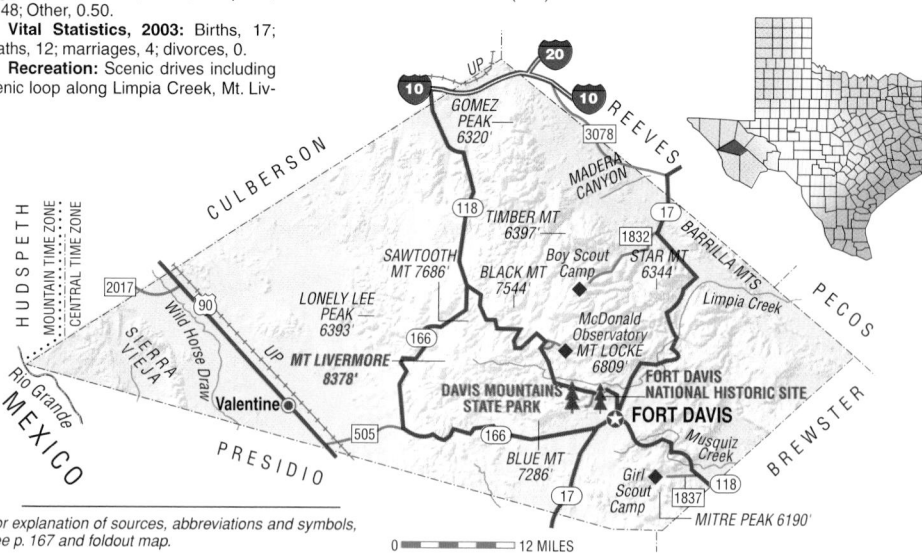

0 ▬▬▬ 12 MILES

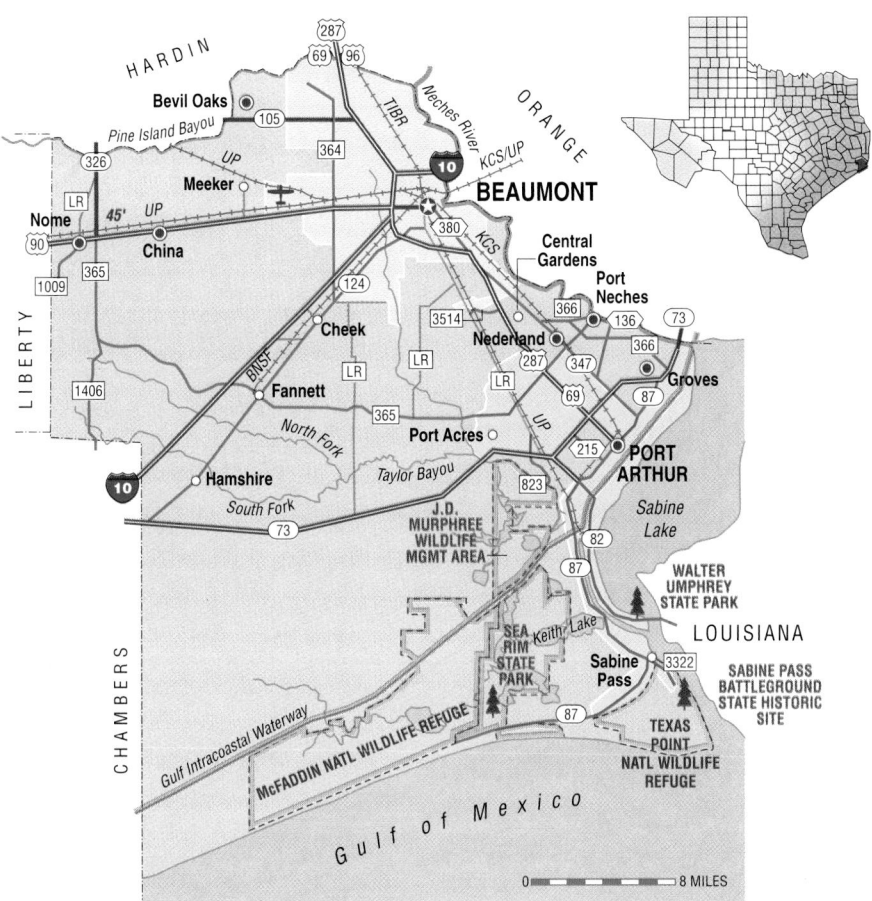

Physical Features: Gulf Coast grassy plain, with timber in northwest; beach sands, sandy loams, black clay soils; drains to Neches River, Gulf of Mexico.

Economy: Government/services; petrochemical, other chemical plants; shipbuilding; steel mill; port activity; oilfield supplies; .

History: Atakapas and Orcoquizas, whose numbers were reduced by epidemics or migration before Anglo-American settlers arrived in 1820s. Cajuns arrived in 1840s; Europeans in 1850s. Antebellum slaveholding area. County created 1836 from Mexican municipality; organized 1837; named for U.S. President Thomas Jefferson.

Race/Ethnicity, 2000: (In percent) Anglo, 52.27; Black, 33.83; Hispanic, 10.53; Other, 3.37.

Vital Statistics, 2003: Births, 3,409; deaths, 2,592; marriages, 2,203; divorces, 1,084.

Recreation: Beaches, fresh and saltwater fishing; duck, goose hunting; water activities; Dick Dowling Monument and Park; Spindletop site, museums; saltwater lake; wildlife refuge; Lamar University events; historic sites; South Texas Fair.

Jefferson County

Minerals: Large producer of oil, gas, sulfur, salt, sand and gravel.
Agriculture: Rice, soybeans; crawfish; beef cattle; hay; considerable rice irrigated. Market value $16.9 million. Timber sales significant.

BEAUMONT (113,473) county seat; government/services; petrochemical production; shipbuilding; port activities; rice milling; Lamar University; hospital; entertainment district; Main Street on the Neches.

Port Arthur (57,341) oil, chemical activities; shrimping and crawfishing; shipping; offshore marine; tourism; hospitals; museum; prison. Asian New Year Tet, Janis Joplin Birthday Bash in January. **Sabine Pass** and **Port Acres** are now within the city limits of Port Arthur.

Other towns include: **Bevil Oaks** (1,273); **Central Gardens** (3,951); **China** (1,061); **Fannett** (1,877); **Groves** (15,371) retail center, some manufacturing, government/services,

tourism; hospital, pecan festival in September; **Hamshire** (759).

Also, **Nederland** (16,729) marine manufacturing; tourism, Windmill and French museums; hospital; Tex Ritter memorial and park, heritage festival (city founded by Dutch immigrants in 1898); **Nome** (496); **Port Neches** (13,088) chemical and synthetic rubber industry, manufacturing, library, riverfront park with La Maison Beausoleil; RiverFest in May.

Population	**248,223**
Change fm 2000	-1.5
Area (sq. mi.)	1,111.26
Land Area (sq. mi.)	903.55
Altitude (ft.)	sea level-45
Rainfall (in.)	59.89
Jan. mean min.	42.9
July mean max.	91.6
Civ. Labor	119,453
Unemployed	8.3
Wages	$1,004,735,468
Av. Weekly Wage	$661.35
Prop. Value	$16,142,827,240
Retail Sales	$2,944,668,281

For explanation of sources, abbreviations and symbols, see p. 167 and foldout map.

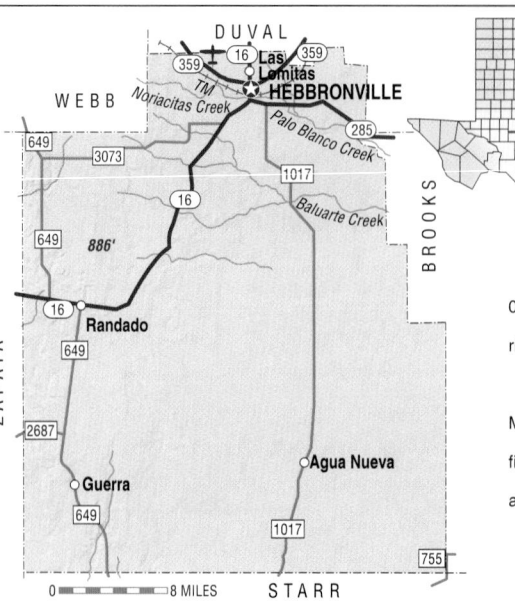

Jim Hogg County

Physical Features: South Texas county on rolling plain, with heavy brush cover; white blow sand and sandy loam; hilly, broken.

Economy: Oil, cattle operations.

History: Coahuiltecan area, then Lipan Apache. Spanish land grant in 1805 to Xavier Vela. County named for Gov. James Stephen Hogg; created, organized 1913 from Brooks, Duval counties.

Race/Ethnicity, 2000: (In percent) Anglo, 9.07; Black, 0.42; Hispanic, 89.98; Other, 0.53.

Vital Statistics, 2003: Births, 73; deaths, 40; marriages, 27; divorces, 0.

Recreation: White-tailed deer and bobwhite hunting.

Minerals: Oil and gas.

Agriculture: Cattle, hay, milk goats; some irrigation. Market value $7 million.

HEBBRONVILLE (4,397) county seat; ranching, oilfield center.

Other towns include: **Guerra** (9), **Las Lomitas** (271) and **South Fork Estates** (45).

Jan. mean min.	43.8
July mean max.	97.5
Civ. Labor	2,327
Unemployed	4.9
Wages	$10,314,238
Av. Weekly Wage	$474.24
Prop. Value	$509,068,391
Retail Sales	$33,382,236

Population	5,062	Land Area (sq. mi.)	1,136.11
Change fm 2000	-4.1	Altitude (ft.)	249-886
Area (sq. mi.)	1,136.16	Rainfall (in.)	23.75

Jim Wells County

Physical Features: South Coastal Plains; level to rolling; sandy to dark soils; grassy with mesquite brush.

Economy: Oil and gas production, agriculture, nature tourism.

History: Coahuiltecans, driven out by Lipan Apaches in 1775. Tomás Sánchez established settlement in 1754. Anglo-American settlement in 1878. County created 1911 from Nueces County; organized 1912; named for developer J.B. Wells Jr.

Race/Ethnicity, 2000: (In percent) Anglo, 23.10; Black, 0.48; Hispanic, 75.71; Other, 0.71.

Vital Statistics, 2003: Births, 577; deaths, 349; marriages, 273; divorces, 29.

Recreation: Hunting; fiestas; Tejano Roots hall of fame; South Texas museum.

Minerals: Oil, gas, caliche.

Agriculture: Cattle, grain sorghum, corn, cotton, dairies, goats, wheat, watermelons, sunflowers, peas, hay. Market value $47.3 million.

ALICE (19,528) county seat; oil-field service center; agribusiness; government/services; Fiesta Bandana (from original name of city) in May; Bee County College extension.

Other towns include: **Alfred-South La Paloma** (453); **Ben Bolt** (1,600); **Orange Grove** (1,338); **Pernitas Point** (281, partly in Live Oak County); **Premont** (2,886) wildflower tour, youth rodeo; **Rancho Alegre** (1,802); **Sandia** (409). Also, a small part of **San Diego** (4,596).

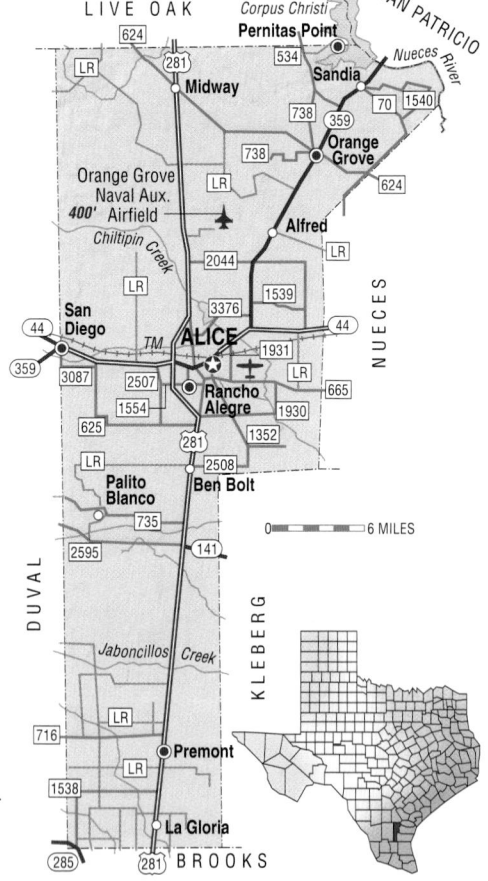

Population	40,807
Change fm 2000	3.8
Area (sq. mi.)	868.22
Land Area (sq. mi.)	864.52
Altitude (ft.)	50-400
Rainfall (in.)	27.52
Jan. mean min.	44.1
July mean max.	96.1
Civ. Labor	19,106
Unemployed	6.9
Wages	$100,762,864
Av. Weekly Wage	$501.58
Prop. Value	$1,313,310,390
Retail Sales	$310,293,555

For explanation for sources, abbreviations and symbols, see p. 167 and foldout map.

Johnson County

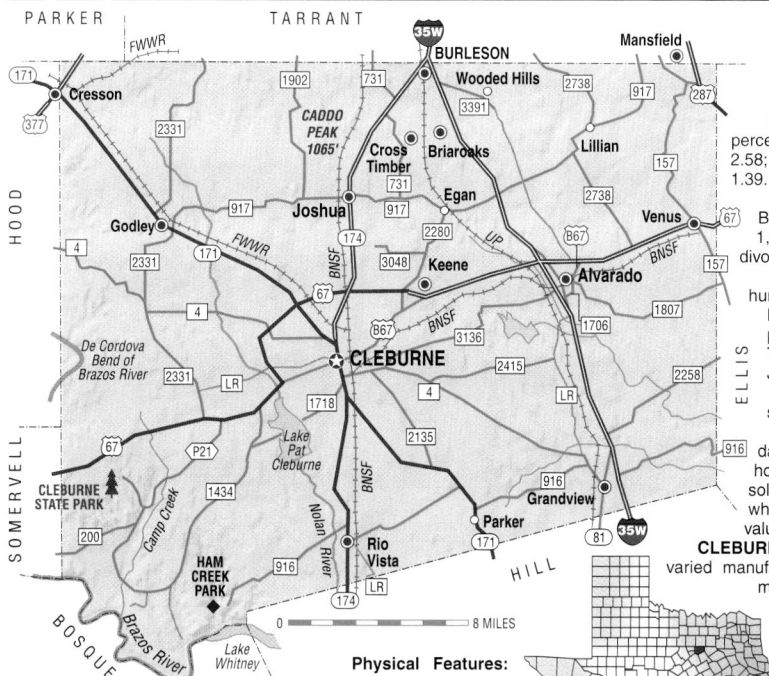

PARKER | TARRANT | Mansfield | BURLESON | Wooded Hills | Cresson | Godley | Joshua | Cross Timber | Briaroaks | Lillian | Egan | Venus | Keene | Alvarado | CLEBURNE | De Cordova Bend of Brazos River | CADDO PEAK 1065' | Grandview | Parker | Rio Vista | Lake Pat Cleburne | CLEBURNE STATE PARK | HAM CREEK PARK | Lake Whitney | HOOD | SOMERVELL | BOSQUE | HILL | ELLIS

0 ▬▬▬▬ 8 MILES

Race/Ethnicity, 2000: (In percent) Anglo, 83.91; Black, 2.58; Hispanic, 12.12; Other, 1.39.

Vital Statistics, 2003: Births, 1,986; deaths, 1,086; marriages, 1,140; divorces, 529.

Recreation: Bird, deer hunting; water activities on Lake Pat Cleburne; state park; museum; Chisholm Trail; Goatneck bike ride in July.

Minerals: Limestone, sand and gravel.

Agriculture: A leading dairy county, cattle, hay, horses (a leader in number sold), cotton, sorghum, wheat, oats, hogs. Market value $43.6 million.

CLEBURNE (28,179) county seat; varied manufacturing; hospital, library, museum; Hill College county campus; Cinco de Mayo.

BURLESON (25,248, part [3,462] in Tarrant County) agriculture, retail center; hospital.

Other towns include: **Alvarado** (3,742) County Pioneer Days; **Briaroaks** (488); **Cresson** (2,000); **Cross Timber** (297); **Godley** (963); **Grandview** (1,464); **Joshua** (4,977) many residents work in Fort Worth; **Keene** (5,721) Southwestern Adventist University; **Lillian** (105); **Rio Vista** (698), and **Venus** (2,006).

Also, part of **Mansfield** (33,707 total, mostly in Tarrant County).

Population	143,418
Change fm 2000	13.1
Area (sq. mi.)	734.46
Land Area (sq. mi.)	729.42
Altitude (ft.)	600-1,065
Rainfall (in.)	36.25
Jan. mean min.	34.0
July mean max.	97.0
Civ. Labor	67,273
Unemployed	6.1
Wages	$240,772,610
Av. Weekly Wage	$547.89
Prop. Value	$6,622,930,860
Retail Sales	$1,437,068,061

Physical Features: North central county drained by tributaries of Trinity, Brazos rivers; lake; hilly, rolling, many soil types.

Economy: Agribusiness; railroad shops; manufacturing; distribution; lake activities; many residents employed in Fort Worth; part of Fort Worth-Arlington metropolitan area.

History: No permanent Indian villages existed in area. Anglo-American settlers arrived in 1840s. County named for Col. M.T. Johnson of Mexican War, Confederacy; created, organized 1854. Formed from McLennan, Hill, Navarro counties.

Scotus College moved to Hebbronville from Mexico in 1926. The Franciscan seminary closed in 1952. Texas Almanac photo.

Jones County

Physical Features: West Texas Rolling Plains; drained by Brazos River fork, tributaries; Lake Fort Phantom Hill.

Economy: Agribusiness; government/services; varied manufacturing.

History: Comanches and other tribes hunted in area. Military presence began in 1851. Ranching established in 1870s. County named for the last president of the Republic, Anson Jones; created 1858 from Bexar, Bosque counties; recreated 1876; organized 1881.

Race/Ethnicity, 2000: (In percent) Anglo, 66.67; Black, 11.53; Hispanic, 20.91; Other, 0.89.

Vital Statistics, 2003: Births, 164; deaths, 191; marriages, 89; divorces, 56.

Recreation: Lake activities, hunting; Fort Phantom Hill site, Cowboys Christmas Ball; Cowboy Reunion on July 4 weekend; old courthouse, opera house, museums, art show.

Minerals: Oil, gas, sand and gravel, stone.

Agriculture: Cotton, wheat, sesame and peanuts; cattle. Some 10,000 acres irrigated for peanuts and hay. Market value $39.2 million.

ANSON (2,489) county seat; farming center; government/services; trailer and ranch furniture manufacturing; hospital; historic buildings; Mesquite Daze festivals in April and October.

STAMFORD (3,514) trade center for three counties.

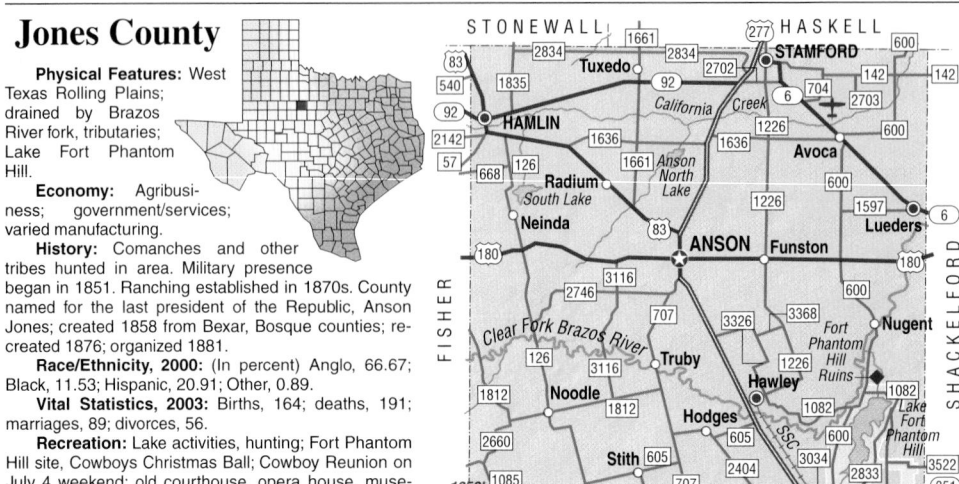

HAMLIN (2,136) trade center for farm and oil, gas area; government/services; feed mills; hospital; historical festival in June.

Other towns include: **Hawley** (637), **Lueders** (284) limestone quarries.

Part [5,488] of **Abilene**.

Population................................ 20,093
Change fm 2000 .... -3.3
Area (sq. mi.) 937.13

Land Area (sq. mi.)	930.99
Altitude (ft.)	1,500-1,950
Rainfall (in.)	26.00
Jan. mean min.	30.7
July mean max.	96.3
Civ. Labor	10,166
Unemployed	2.6
Wages	$29,341,939
Av. Weekly Wage	$484.35
Prop. Value	$616,772,068
Retail Sales	$179,012,730

Karnes County

Physical Features: Sandy loam, dark clay, alluvial soils in rolling terrain; traversed by San Antonio River; mesquite, oak trees.

Economy: Agribusiness; government/services.

History: Coahuiltecan Indian area. Spanish ranching began around 1750. Anglo-Americans arrived in 1840s; Polish in 1850s. County created 1854 from Bexar, Goliad, San Patricio counties; named for Texas Revolutionary figure Henry W. Karnes.

Race/Ethnicity, 2000: (In percent) Anglo, 41.29; Black, 10.53; Hispanic, 47.42; Other, 0.76.

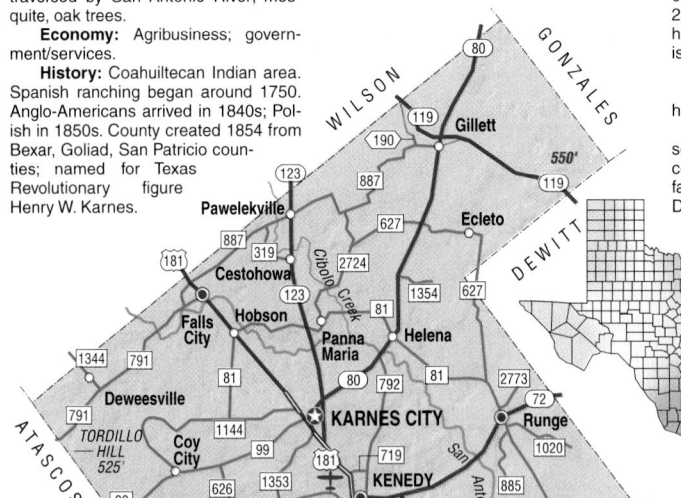

Vital Statistics, 2003: Births, 172; deaths, 144; marriages, 78; divorces, 18.

Recreation: Panna Maria, nation's oldest Polish settlement, founded Dec. 24, 1854; Old Helena restored courthouse, museum; hunting, nature tourism, guest ranches.

Minerals: Oil, gas.

Agriculture: Beef cattle, feed grain, hay, cotton. Market value $18.2 million.

KARNES CITY (3,448) county seat; agribusiness; tourism; processing center; oil-field servicing; varied manufacturing; hospital; library; Lonesome Dove Fest in September.

KENEDY (3,502) farm and oil center, library, dove and quail hunting leases, prison; Bluebonnet Days in April.

Other towns include: **Falls City** (643) ranching, sausage making, library, city park on river; **Gillett** (120); **Hobson** (135); **Panna Maria** (45); **Runge** (1,049) farm center, library.

Population	**15,458**
Change fm 2000	0.1
Area (sq. mi.)	753.58
Land Area (sq. mi.)	750.32
Altitude (ft.)	180-550
Rainfall (in.)	28.40
Jan. mean min.	41.0
July mean max.	95.0
Civ. Labor	5,853
Unemployed	4.8
Wages	$22,423,269
Av. Weekly Wage	$439.23
Prop. Value	$724,291,864
Retail Sales	$102,284,714

Kaufman County

Physical Features: North Blackland prairie, draining to Trinity River, Cedar Creek and Lake.

Economy: varied manufacturing; trade center; government/services; antique center; commuting to Dallas.

History: Caddo and Cherokee Indians; removed by 1840 when Anglo-American settlement began. County created from Henderson County and organized, 1848; named for member of Texas and U.S. congresses D.S. Kaufman.

Race/Ethnicity, 2000: (In percent) Anglo, 76.97; Black, 10.76; Hispanic, 11.11; Other, 1.16.

Vital Statistics, 2003: Births, 1,265; deaths, 742; marriages, 704; divorces, 325.

Recreation: Lake activities; Porter Farm near Terrell is site of origin of U.S.-Texas Agricultural Extension program; antique centers near Forney; historic homes at Terrell.

Minerals: Oil, gas, stone, sand.

Agriculture: Nursery crops; beef cattle, horses, goats, hogs, sheep; wheat, hay, sorghum, oats, cotton, peaches. Market value $30 million.

KAUFMAN (7,512) county seat; varied manufacturing; commuters to Dallas; hospital; Scarecrow Festival in October.

TERRELL (15,640) agribusiness, varied manufacturing; outlet center; private hospital, state hospital; community college, Southwestern Christian College.

Other towns include: **Combine** (1,972, partly in Dallas County); **Cottonwood** (207); **Crandall** (3,132); **Elmo** (90); **Forney** (7,712) important antiques center, light manufacturing, historic homes, Jackrabbit Stampede bike race in September; **Grays Prairie** (361); **Kemp** (1,223); **Lawrence** (279); **Mabank** (2,477, partly in Henderson County) varied manufacturing, tourism, retail trade, Western Week in June; **Oak Grove** (797); **Oak Ridge** (452); **Post Oak Bend** (556); **Rosser** (421); **Scurry** (315); **Talty** (1,188).

For explanation of sources, abbreviations and symbols, see p. 167 and foldout map.

Population	85,377
Change fm 2000	19.7
Area (sq. mi.)	806.81
Land Area (sq. mi.)	786.04
Altitude (ft.)	300-550
Rainfall (in.)	38.90
Jan. mean min.	32.3
July mean max.	94.6
Civ. Labor	36,075
Unemployed	8.0
Wages	$161,453,210
Av. Weekly Wage	$552.17
Prop. Value	$4,764,164,206
Retail Sales	$1,258,293,594

A country road off US 180 west of Anson. Texas Almanac photo.

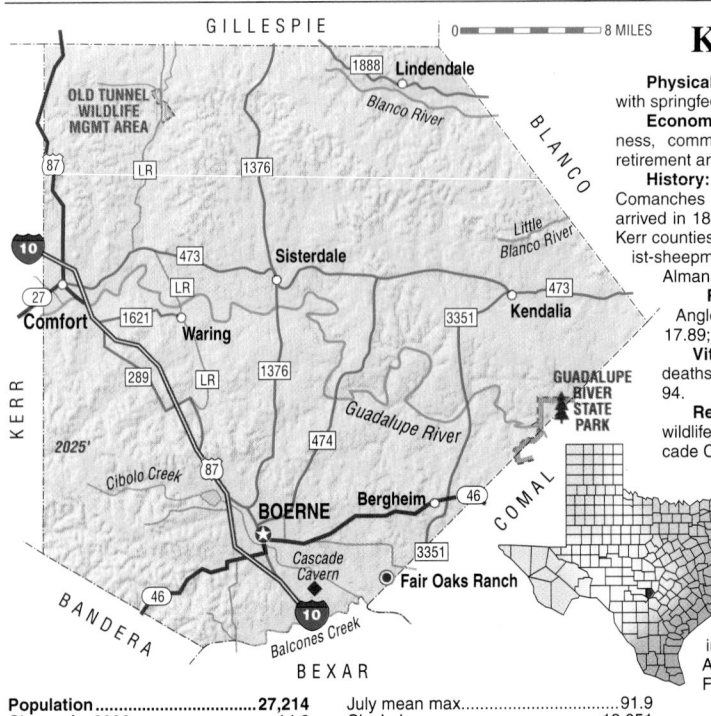

Kendall County

Physical Features: Hill Country, plateau, with springfed streams; caves; scenic drives.

Economy: Government/services, agribusiness, commuters to San Antonio, tourism, retirement area, some manufacturing.

History: Lipan Apaches, Kiowas and Comanches in area when German settlers arrived in 1840s. County created from Blanco, Kerr counties 1862; named for pioneer journalist-sheepman and early contributor to Texas Almanac, George W. Kendall.

Race/Ethnicity, 2000: (In percent) Anglo, 81.06; Black, 0.32; Hispanic, 17.89; Other, 0.73.

Vital Statistics, 2003: Births, 331; deaths, 264; marriages, 333; divorces, 94.

Recreation: Hunting, fishing, exotic wildlife, state park; tourist center; Cascade Cavern; historic sites.

Minerals: Limestone rock, caliche.

Agriculture: Cattle, goats, sheep, hay. Market value $7 million. Cedar posts, firewood sold.

BOERNE (6,745) county seat; tourism, antiques; some manufacturing; ranching; commuting to San Antonio; library; Berges Fest on Father's Day weekend.

Other towns include: **Comfort** (2,556) ranching, tourism, Civil War monument honoring Unionists; **Kendalia** (76); **Sisterdale** (63); **Waring** (73). Part of **Fair Oaks Ranch** (5,220).

Population	27,214
Change fm 2000	14.6
Area (sq. mi.)	663.04
Land Area (sq. mi.)	662.44
Altitude (ft.)	1,000-2,025
Rainfall (in.)	37.36
Jan. mean min.	34.3
July mean max.	91.9
Civ. Labor	19,051
Unemployed	2.4
Wages	$65,756,829
Av. Weekly Wage	$552.69
Prop. Value	$3,894,380,077
Retail Sales	$517,177,177

Kenedy County

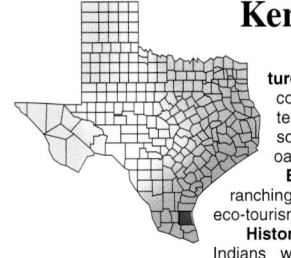

Physical Features: Gulf coastal county; flat, sandy terrain, some loam soils; motts of live oaks.

Economy: Oil, ranching; hunting leases/eco-tourism.

History: Coahuiltecan Indians who assimilated or were driven out by Lipan Apaches. Spanish ranching began in 1790s. Anglo-Americans arrived after Mexican War. Among last counties created, organized 1921, from Cameron, Hidalgo, Willacy counties; named for pioneer steamboat operator and cattleman, Capt. Mifflin Kenedy.

Race/Ethnicity, 2000: (In percent) Anglo, 20.29; Black, 0.00; Hispanic, 78.99; Other, 0.72.

Vital Statistics, 2003: Births, 7; deaths, 1; marriages, 6; divorces, 0.

Recreation: Hunting; fishing; bird watching.

Minerals: Oil, gas.

Agriculture: Beef cattle. Market value $9 million. Hunting leases.

SARITA (250) county seat; cattle-shipping point; ranch headquarters; gas processing; one of state's least populous counties. Also, **Armstrong** (20) and **Norias** (45).

Population	407
Change fm 2000	-1.7
Area (sq. mi.)	1,945.60
Land Area (sq. mi.)	1,456.77
Altitude (ft.)	sea level-118
Rainfall (in.)	27.90
Jan. mean min.	45.0
July mean max.	95.0
Civ. Labor	236
Unemployed	3.1
Wages	$3,042,142
Av. Weekly Wage	$582.12
Prop. Value	$542,097,090
Retail Sales	$49,001

For explanation of sources, abbreviations and symbols, see p. 167 and foldout map.

Kent County

Physical Features: West central county of rolling, broken terrain; lake; drains to Salt and Double Mountain forks of Brazos River; sandy, loam soils.

Economy: Agribusiness, oil-field operations, hunting leases.

History: Comanches driven out by U.S. Army in 1870s. Ranching developed in 1880s. County created 1876 from Bexar, Young territories; organized 1892. Name honors Andrew Kent, one of 32 volunteers from Gonzales who died at the Alamo.

Race/Ethnicity, 2000: (In percent) Anglo, 90.57; Black, 0.23; Hispanic, 9.08; Other, 0.12.

Vital Statistics, 2003: Births, 8; deaths, 6; marriages, 2; divorces, 6.

Recreation: Hunting, fishing; scenic croton breaks and salt flat; wildlife festival in November.

Minerals: Oil, gas.

Agriculture: Cattle, cotton, wheat, sorghum. Market value $5.3 million.

JAYTON (489) county seat; oil-field services; farming center; fun fest in August. Other towns include: **Girard** (50).

Population		744
Change fm 2000		-13.4
Area (sq. mi.)		902.91
Land Area (sq. mi.)		902.33
Altitude (ft.)		1,823-2,830
Rainfall (in.)		22.94
Jan. mean min.		24.9
July mean max.		95.7
Civ. Labor		502
Unemployed		3.4
Wages		$1,963,215
Av. Weekly Wage		$488.73
Prop. Value		$382,059,135
Retail Sales		$12,542,185

Kerr County

Physical Features: Picturesque, hills, spring-fed streams; dams, lakes on Guadalupe River.

Economy: Tourism; medical services; retirement area; agribusiness; manufacturing; hunting leases.

History: Lipan Apaches, Kiowas and Comanches in area. Anglo-American settlers arrived in late 1840s. County created 1856 from Bexar County; named for member of Austin's Colony, James Kerr.

Race/Ethnicity, 2000: (In percent) Anglo, 78.11; Black, 1.78; Hispanic, 19.13; Other, 0.98.

Vital Statistics, 2003: Births, 530; deaths, 622; marriages, 393; divorces, 242.

Recreation: Popular area for tourists, hunters, fishermen; private and youth camps; dude ranches; state park; Point theater; wildlife management area; hatchery; Folk Festival in Kerrville; experimental aircraft fly-in; Cowboy Artists Museum.

Minerals: none.

Agriculture: Cattle, sheep, goats for wool, mohair; meat and breeding goats on increase; crops include hay, pecans. Market value $12 million.

KERRVILLE (21,254) county seat; tourist center; youth camps; agribusiness; aircraft and parts and varied manufacturing; Schreiner University; Kerrville State Hospital; Veterans Administration Medical Center; retirement center; retail trade; state arts, crafts show in May-June; experimental aircraft fly-in during October.

Other towns include: **Camp Verde** (41); **Center Point** (800); **Hunt** (708) youth camps; **Ingram** (1,803) camps, cabins; **Mountain Home** (96).

Population		45,675
Change fm 2000		4.6
Area (sq. mi.)		1,107.66
Land Area (sq. mi.)		1,106.12
Altitude (ft.)		1,450-2,400
Rainfall (in.)		32.60
Jan. mean min.		32.0
July mean max.		92.0
Civ. Labor		19,323
Unemployed		2.7
Wages		$113,620,553
Av. Weekly Wage		$539.91
Prop. Value		$3,179,691,398
Retail Sales		$663,899,001

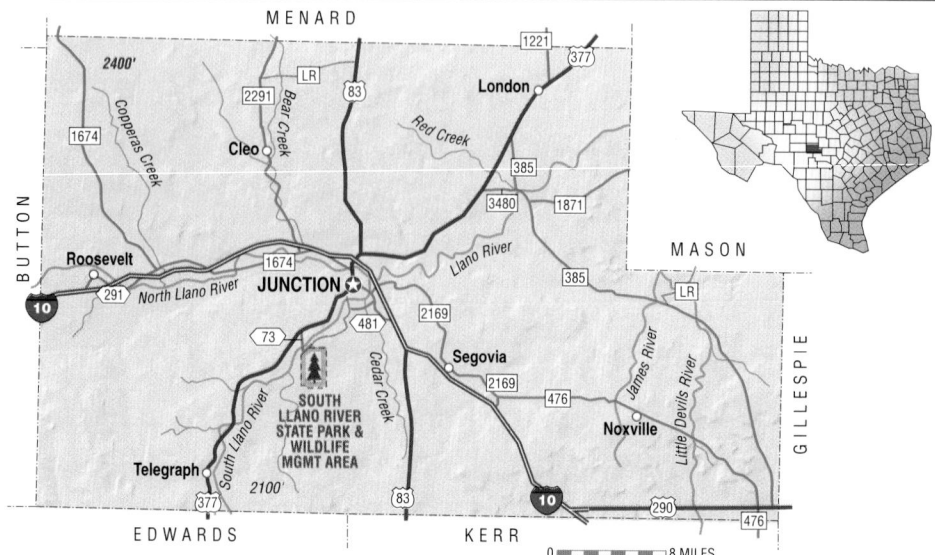

Kimble County

Physical Features: Picturesque southwestern county; rugged, broken by numerous streams; drains to Llano River; sandy, gray, chocolate loam soils.

Economy: Livestock production, market; tourism, cedar oil and wood products sold; metal building materials manufactured.

History: Apache, Kiowas and Comanche stronghold until 1870s. Military outposts protected first Anglo-American settlers in 1850s. County created from Bexar County 1858; organized 1876. Named for George C. Kimble, a Gonzales volunteer who died at the Alamo.

Race/Ethnicity, 2000: (In percent) Anglo, 78.37; Black, 0.09; Hispanic, 20.73; Other, 0.81.

Vital Statistics, 2003: Births, 48; deaths, 53; marriages, 27; divorces, 23.

Recreation: Hunting, fishing in spring-fed streams, nature tourism; among leading deer counties; state park; Kimble Kounty Kow Kick on Labor Day, Wild Game dinner on Thanksgiving Saturday.

Minerals: gravel.

Agriculture: Cattle, meat goats, sheep, Angora goats, pecans. Market value $7.4 million. Hunting leases important. Firewood, cedar sold.

JUNCTION (2,672) county seat; tourism; varied manufacturing; live-stock production; two museums; Texas Tech University center; hospital; library; airport.

Other towns include: **London** (180); **Roosevelt** (14); **Telegraph** (3).

Population	**4,563**
Change fm 2000	2.1
Area (sq. mi.)	1,250.92
Land Area (sq. mi.)	1,250.70
Altitude (ft.)	1,500-2,400
Rainfall (in.)	23.24
Jan. mean min.	29.3
July mean max.	94.8
Civ. Labor	2,324
Unemployed	2.1
Wages	$8,624,287
Av. Weekly Wage	$435.59
Prop. Value	$752,194,250
Retail Sales	$555,834,720

The Telegraph store and community post office. Texas Almanac photo.

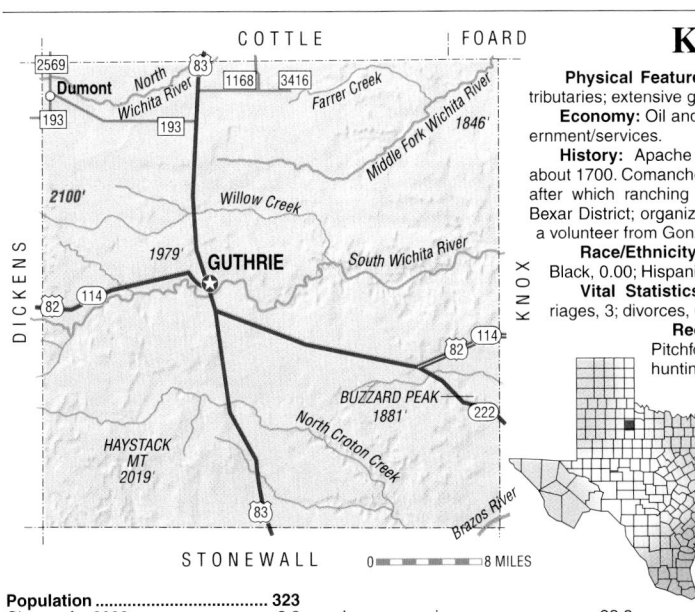

King County

Physical Features: Hilly, broken by Wichita, Brazos tributaries; extensive grassland; dark loam to red soils.

Economy: Oil and gas, ranching, hunting leases, government/services.

History: Apache area until Comanches moved in about 1700. Comanches removed by U.S. Army in 1874-75 after which ranching began. County created 1876 from Bexar District; organized 1891; named for William P. King, a volunteer from Gonzales who died at the Alamo.

Race/Ethnicity, 2000: (In percent) Anglo, 89.33; Black, 0.00; Hispanic, 9.55; Other, 1.12.

Vital Statistics, 2003: Births, 3; deaths, 1; marriages, 3; divorces, 0.

Recreation: Large ranches (6666, Pitchfork, Tongue River) offer tours, visits, hunting; roping and ranch horse competitions.

Minerals: Oil, gas.

Agriculture: Cattle, horses, wheat, hay, cotton. Market value $11.8 million. Hunting leases important.

GUTHRIE (125) county seat; ranch-supply center; government/services; community center complex, library; Thanksgiving community supper.

Population	323
Change fm 2000	-9.3
Area (sq. mi.)	913.33
Land Area (sq. mi.)	912.29
Altitude (ft.)	1,500-2,100
Rainfall (in.)	25.00
Jan. mean min.	23.9
July mean max.	96.7
Civ. Labor	128
Unemployed	1.7
Wages	$2,296,895
Av. Weekly Wage	$703.92
Prop. Value	$243,683,898
Retail Sales	$1,503,587

Kinney County

Physical Features: Hilly, broken by Rio Grande tributaries; Anacacho Mountains; Nueces Canyon.

Economy: Agribusinesses, tourism, government/services, hunting leases.

History: Coahuiltecans, Apaches, Comanches in area. Spanish Franciscans established settlement in late 1700s. English empresarios John Beales and James Grant established English-speaking colony in 1834. Black Seminoles served as army scouts in 1870s. County created from Bexar County 1850; organized 1874; named for H.L. Kinney, founder of Corpus Christi.

Race/Ethnicity, 2000: (In percent) Anglo, 47.79; Black, 1.39; Hispanic, 50.52; Other, 0.30.

Vital Statistics, 2003: Births, 33; deaths, 35; marriages, 23; divorces, 2.

Recreation: Hunting; replica of Alamo; old Fort Clark Springs; state park; Seminole Days.

Minerals: Not significant.

Agriculture: Cattle, meat goats, Angora goats; hay, pecans, wheat, cotton. Market value $4.7 million.

BRACKETTVILLE (1,912) county seat; agriculture, tourism; museum; cowboy cauldron.

Other towns include: **Fort Clark Springs** (1,300); **Spofford** (78).

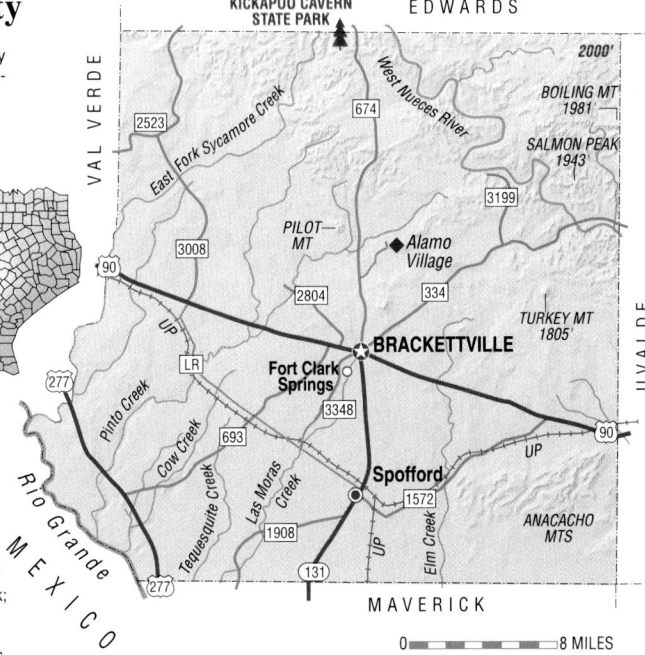

Population	3,337
Change fm 2000	-1.2
Area (sq. mi.)	1,365.31
Land Area (sq. mi.)	1,363.44
Altitude (ft.)	850-2,000
Rainfall (in.)	22.79
Jan. mean min.	37.3
July mean max.	95.5
Civ. Labor	1,288
Unemployed	5.9
Wages	$4,931,267
Av. Weekly Wage	$487.57
Prop. Value	$469,185,349
Retail Sales	$9,112,515

For explanation of sources, abbreviations and symbols, see p. 167 and foldout map.

Kleberg County

Physical Features: Coastal plain, broken by bays; sandy, loam, clay soils; tree motts.

Economy: Oil and gas; Naval air station; chemicals and plastics; agriculture; Texas A&M University-Kingsville.

History: Coahuiltecan and Karankawa area. Spanish land grants date to 1750s. In 1853 Richard King purchased Santa Gertrudis land grant. County created 1913 from Nueces County; named for San Jacinto veteran and rancher Robert Kleberg.

Race/Ethnicity, 2000: (In percent) Anglo, 29.03; Black, 3.59; Hispanic, 65.41; Other, 1.97.

Vital Statistics, 2003: Births, 490; deaths, 196; marriages, 231; divorces, 103.

Recreation: Fishing, hunting, water sports, park on Baffin Bay; wildlife sanctuary; winter bird watching; university events, museum; King Ranch headquarters, tours; La Posada celebration in November.

Minerals: Oil, gas.

Agriculture: Cotton, beef cattle, grain sorghum. Market value $57.8 million. Hunting leases/eco-tourism.

KINGSVILLE (25,836) county seat; government/services; oil, gas; agribusiness; tourism; chemical plant; university, Coastal Bend College branch; hospital; ranching heritage festival in February.

Other towns include: **Riviera** (1,064).

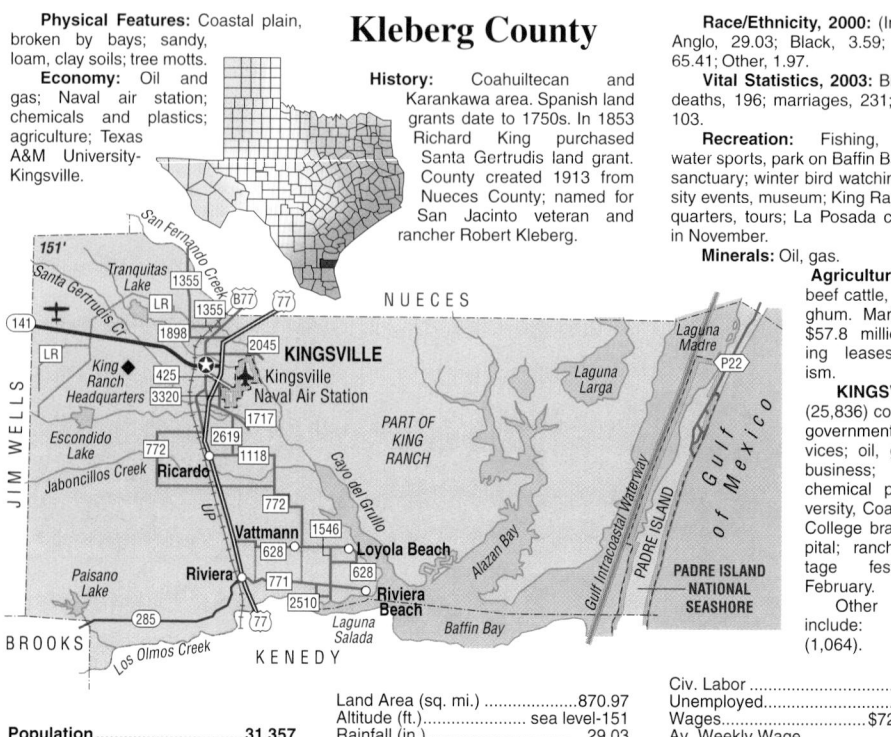

Population	31,357
Change fm 2000	-0.6
Area (sq. mi.)	1,090.29
Land Area (sq. mi.)	870.97
Altitude (ft.)	sea level-151
Rainfall (in.)	29.03
Jan. mean min.	43.4
July mean max.	95.5
Civ. Labor	14,461
Unemployed	5.7
Wages	$72,352,994
Av. Weekly Wage	$490,28
Prop. Value	$1,468,183,583
Retail Sales	$315,362,342

Knox County

Physical Features: Eroded breaks on West Texas Rolling Plains; Brazos, Wichita rivers; sandy, loam soils.

Economy: Oil, agribusiness, government/services.

History: Indian conscripts used during Spanish period to mine copper deposits along the Brazos. Ranching, farming developed in 1880s. German colony settled in 1895. County created from Bexar, Young territories 1858; re-created 1876; organized 1886; named for U.S. Secretary of War Henry Knox.

Race/Ethnicity, 2000: (In percent) Anglo, 67.06; Black, 7.24; Hispanic, 25.09; Other, 0.61.

Vital Statistics, 2003: Births, 52; deaths, 59; marriages, 18; divorces, 8.

Recreation: Lake activities, fishing; hunting; Knox City seedless watermelon festival in July.

Minerals: Oil, gas.

Agriculture: Stocker cattle, cow/calf; wheat, cotton. Cotton irrigated. Market value $46.2 million.

BENJAMIN (247) county seat; ranching, farm center.

MUNDAY (1,477) portable buildings, other manufacturing; Texas A&M Vegetable Research Station; vegetable festival.

KNOX CITY (1,143) agribusiness, petroleum center; USDA Plant Materials Research Center; veterans memorial; hospital.

Other towns include: **Goree** (319); **Rhineland** (120) old church established by German immigrants.

Population	3,893
Change fm 2000	-8.5
Area (sq. mi.)	855.43
Land Area (sq. mi.)	849.00
Altitude (ft.)	1,300-1,700
Rainfall (in.)	26.36
Jan. mean min.	28.1
July mean max.	96.5
Civ. Labor	2,029
Unemployed	4.3
Wages	$9,416,643
Av. Weekly Wage	$556.34
Prop. Value	$259,467,733
Retail Sales	$22,902,076

For explanation of sources, abbreviations and symbols, see p. 167 and foldout map.

Lamar County

Physical Features: North Texas county on divide between Red, Sulphur rivers; soils chiefly blackland, except along Red; pines, hardwoods.

Economy: Varied manufacturing; agribusiness; medical, government/services.

History: Caddo Indian area. First Anglo-American settlers arrived about 1815. County created 1840 from Red River County; organized 1841; named for second president of Republic, Mirabeau B. Lamar.

Race/Ethnicity, 2000: (In percent) Anglo, 81.43; Black, 13.72; Hispanic, 3.33; Other, 1.52.

Vital Statistics, 2003: Births, 637; deaths, 551; marriages, 403; divorces, 347.

Recreation: Lake activities; Gambill goose refuge; hunting, fishing; state park; Sam Bell Maxey Home; State Sen. A.M. Aikin Archives, other museums.

Minerals: Negligible.

Agriculture: Beef, hay, dairy, soybeans, wheat, corn, sorghum, cotton. Market value $39 million.

PARIS (26,256) county seat; varied manufacturing; food processing; government/services; hospital; junior college; Tour de Paris bicycle rally in July; square dance weekend Labor Day.

Other towns include: **Arthur City** (180), **Blossom** (1,423), **Brookston** (130), **Chicota** (150), **Cunningham** (110), **Deport** (690, partly in Red River County), **Pattonville** (180), **Petty** (130), **Powderly** (185), **Reno** (2,934), **Roxton** (714), **Sumner** (95), **Sun Valley** (53), **Toco** (87).

Population 49,710	July mean max........................94.3
Change fm 2000 ....2.5	Civ. Labor 22,160
Area (sq. mi.) 932.47	Unemployed 6.3
Land Area (sq. mi.)............916.81	Wages.....................$138,933,049
Altitude (ft.) 350-650	Av. Weekly Wage $550.43
Rainfall (in.) 47.82	Prop. Value $2,723,311,720
Jan. mean min. 29.9	Retail Sales.............$617,947,399

Lamb County

Physical Features: Rich, red, brown soils on West Texas High Plains; some hills; drains to upper Brazos River tributaries; numerous playas.

Economy: Agribusiness; distribution center; denim textiles.

History: Apaches, displaced by Comanches around 1700. U.S. Army pushed Comanches into Indian Territory in 1875. Ranching began in 1880s; farming after 1900. County created 1876 from Bexar District; organized 1908; named for Lt. G.A. Lamb, who died in battle of San Jacinto.

Race/Ethnicity, 2000: (In percent) Anglo, 51.71; Black, 4.32; Hispanic, 43.46; Other, 0.51.

Vital Statistics, 2003: Births, 237; deaths, 207; marriages, 161; divorces, 74.

Recreation: Pioneer celebration in August; Caprock Soaring glider competition.

Minerals: Oil, stone, gas.

Agriculture: Fed cattle; cotton, corn, wheat, grain sorghum, vegetables, soybeans, hay; sheep. 385,000 acres irrigated. Market value $260.2 million.

LITTLEFIELD (6,490) county seat; tourism; agribusiness; varied manufacturing; hospital, prison.

Olton (2,352) agribusiness, commercial center for northeast part of county; pheasant hunt in winter; Sandhills Celebration in summer.

Other towns include: **Amherst** (811); **Earth** (1,090) farming center, manufacturing, feed lot, supplies; **Fieldton** (20); **Spade** (100); **Springlake** (137); **Sudan** (1,042) farming center, government/services, Homecoming Day in fall.

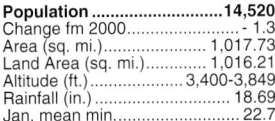

Population 14,520	July mean max. 92.0
Change fm 2000......................- 1.3	Civ. Labor 6,796
Area (sq. mi.)....................1,017.73	Unemployed 6.2
Land Area (sq. mi.)............1,016.21	Wages.......................$32,017,297
Altitude (ft.)....................3,400-3,849	Av. Weekly Wage...............$480.00
Rainfall (in.) 18.69	Prop. Value $1,154,073,111
Jan. mean min.........................22.7	Retail Sales $64,296,114

Lampasas County

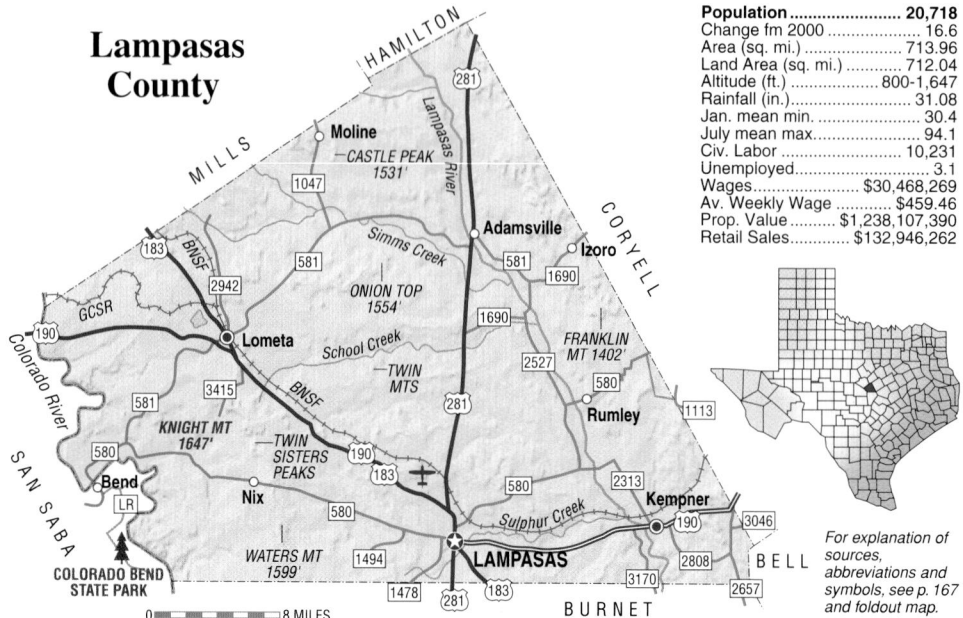

For explanation of sources, abbreviations and symbols, see p. 167 and foldout map.

Population	**20,718**
Change fm 2000	16.6
Area (sq. mi.)	713.96
Land Area (sq. mi.)	712.04
Altitude (ft.)	800-1,647
Rainfall (in.)	31.08
Jan. mean min.	30.4
July mean max.	94.1
Civ. Labor	10,231
Unemployed	3.1
Wages	$30,468,269
Av. Weekly Wage	$459.46
Prop. Value	$1,238,107,390
Retail Sales	$132,946,262

Physical Features: Central Texas on edge of Hill Country; Colorado, Lampasas rivers; cedars, oaks, pecans.

Economy: Many employed at Fort Hood; several industrial plants; tourism; agribusinesses.

History: Mineral springs attracted first Anglo-Americans in 1853. Frontier confrontations between settlers, Comanches continued into 1870s. County created 1856 from Bell, Travis counties. Named for river. Some have speculated that an early expedition named river for city of Lampazos in Mexico.

Race/Ethnicity, 2000: (In percent) Anglo, 80.40; Black, 3.12; Hispanic, 15.07; Other, 1.41.

Vital Statistics, 2003: Births, 209; deaths, 184; marriages, 147; divorces, 96.

Recreation: Scenic drives; state park; deer hunting, fishing in streams.

Minerals: Sand and gravel, building stone.

Agriculture: Beef cattle, hay, sheep, goats; pecans. Market value $13.4 million. Hunting leases, ecotourism.

LAMPASAS (7,579) county seat; varied manufacturing; government/services; ranching, hunting center; historic downtown; hospital; Spring Ho in July.

Other towns include: **Bend** (115, partly in San Saba County); **Izoro** (17); **Kempner** (1,093); **Lometa** (842) market and shipping point; Diamondback Jubilee in March.

The traffic in Los Angeles, La Salle County. Texas Almanac photo.

La Salle County

Physical Features: South Texas county on brushy plain, broken by Nueces, Frio rivers and their tributaries; chocolate, dark gray, sandy loam soils.

Economy: Agribusiness, hunting leases; tourism; government services.

History: Coahuiltecans, squeezed out by migrating Apaches. U.S. military outpost in 1850s; settlers of Mexican descent established nearby village. Anglo-American ranching developed in 1870s. County created from Bexar District 1858; organized 1880; named for Robert Cavelier Sieur de La Salle, French explorer who died in Texas.

Race/Ethnicity, 2000: (In percent) Anglo, 19.15; Black, 3.29; Hispanic, 77.12; Other, 0.44.

Vital Statistics, 2003: Births, 91; deaths, 32; marriages, 25; divorces, 2.

Recreation: Nature trails; Cotulla school where Lyndon B. Johnson taught; wildlife management area; deer, bird, javelina hunting; wild hog cookoff in March; fishing.

Minerals: Oil, gas.

Agriculture: Beef cattle, peanuts, watermelons, grain sorghum. Market value $23.2 million.

COTULLA (3,675) county seat; livestock, state prison; hunting center; Brush Country museum; Cinco de Mayo celebration.

Other towns include: **Encinal** (620), **Fowlerton** (67).

Population	**5,945**
Change fm 2000	1.3
Area (sq. mi.)	1,494.23
Land Area (sq. mi.)	1,488.85
Altitude (ft.)	250-600
Rainfall (in.)	22.56
Jan. mean min.	39.1
July mean max.	98.9
Civ. Labor	2,944
Unemployed	4.6
Wages	$9,270,707
Av. Weekly Wage	$ 556.70
Prop. Value	$487,084,730
Retail Sales	$41,176,164

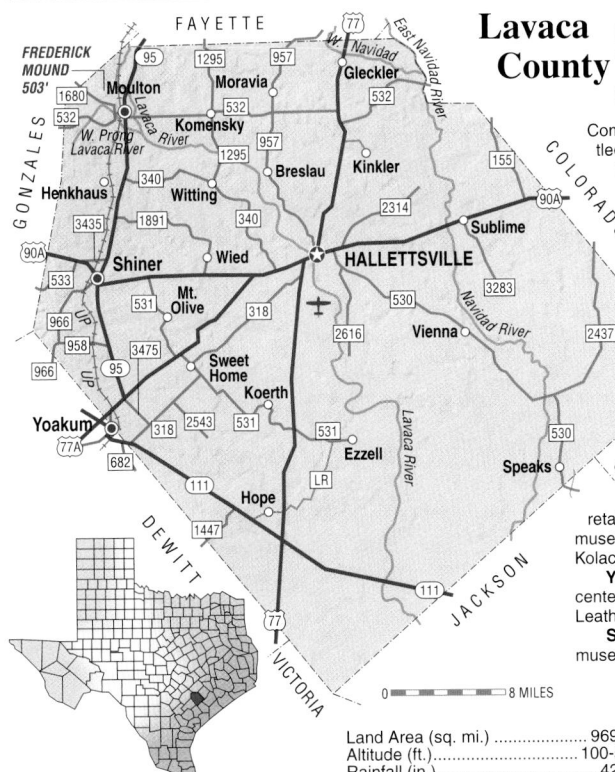

Lavaca County

Physical Features: Southern Coastal Plains county; north rolling; sandy loam, black waxy soils; drains to Lavaca, Navidad rivers.

Economy: Varied manufacturing; oil and gas production; agribusinesses; tourism.

History: Coahuiltecan area; later Comanches until 1850s. Anglo-Americans first settled in 1831. Germans and Czechs arrived 1880-1900. County created 1846 from Colorado, Jackson, Gonzales, Victoria counties. Name is Spanish word for cow, la vaca, from name of river.

Race/Ethnicity, 2000: (In percent) Anglo, 81.37; Black, 6.85; Hispanic, 11.36; Other, 0.42.

Vital Statistics, 2003: Births, 239; deaths, 273; marriages, 138; divorces, 66.

Recreation: Deer, other hunting, fishing; wildflower trails, fiddlers frolic; historic sites, churches.

Minerals: Some oil, gas.

Agriculture: Cattle, forage, poultry, rice, corn, sorghum. Market value $45.7 million. Hunting leases.

HALLETTSVILLE (2,305) county seat; retail center; varied manufacturing; agribusiness; museum, library, hospital; domino, "42" tournaments; Kolache Fest in September.

Yoakum (5,832, partly in DeWitt County); trading center for two counties; hospital; museum; Land of Leather in February.

Shiner (2,050) brewery, varied manufacturing; museum; clinic; Bocktoberfest.

Other towns include: **Moulton** (927) agribusiness, Town & Country Jamboree in July; **Sublime** (75); **Sweet Home** (360).

Population	**18,945**
Change fm 2000	-1.4
Area (sq. mi.)	970.35
Land Area (sq. mi.)	969.90
Altitude (ft.)	100-503
Rainfall (in.)	42.23
Jan. mean min.	41.8
July mean max.	94.4
Civ. Labor	9,498
Unemployed	1.5
Total Wages	$34,190,308
Av. Weekly Wage	$434.28
Prop. Value	$1,780,936,349
Retail Sales	$158,521,525

Lee County

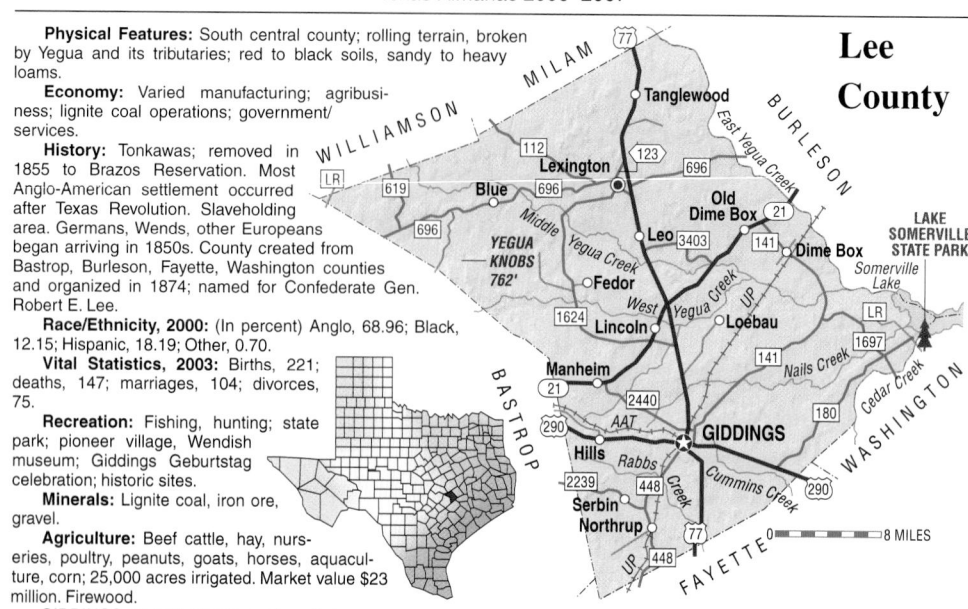

Physical Features: South central county; rolling terrain, broken by Yegua and its tributaries; red to black soils, sandy to heavy loams.

Economy: Varied manufacturing; agribusiness; lignite coal operations; government/services.

History: Tonkawas; removed in 1855 to Brazos Reservation. Most Anglo-American settlement occurred after Texas Revolution. Slaveholding area. Germans, Wends, other Europeans began arriving in 1850s. County created from Bastrop, Burleson, Fayette, Washington counties and organized in 1874; named for Confederate Gen. Robert E. Lee.

Race/Ethnicity, 2000: (In percent) Anglo, 68.96; Black, 12.15; Hispanic, 18.19; Other, 0.70.

Vital Statistics, 2003: Births, 221; deaths, 147; marriages, 104; divorces, 75.

Recreation: Fishing, hunting; state park; pioneer village, Wendish museum; Giddings Geburtstag celebration; historic sites.

Minerals: Lignite coal, iron ore, gravel.

Agriculture: Beef cattle, hay, nurseries, poultry, peanuts, goats, horses, aquaculture, corn; 25,000 acres irrigated. Market value $23 million. Firewood.

GIDDINGS (5,453) county seat; varied manufacturing, food processing; recycling plant; hospital.

Other towns include: **Dime Box** (381); **Lexington** (1,270) livestock-marketing center; **Lincoln** (336); **Serbin** (109) Wendish museum.

Population	16,536
Change fm 2000	5.6
Area (sq. mi.)	634.03
Land Area (sq. mi.)	628.50
Altitude (ft.)	238-762
Rainfall (in.)	36.02
Jan. mean min.	37.3
July mean max.	93.6
Civ. Labor	7,020
Unemployed	3.9
Wages	$36,346,492
Av. Weekly Wage	$537.88
Prop. Value	$1,315,476,043
Retail Sales	$174,840,279

Leon County

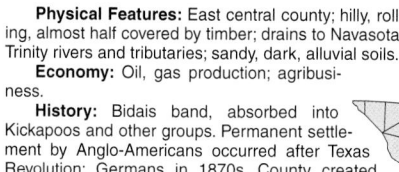

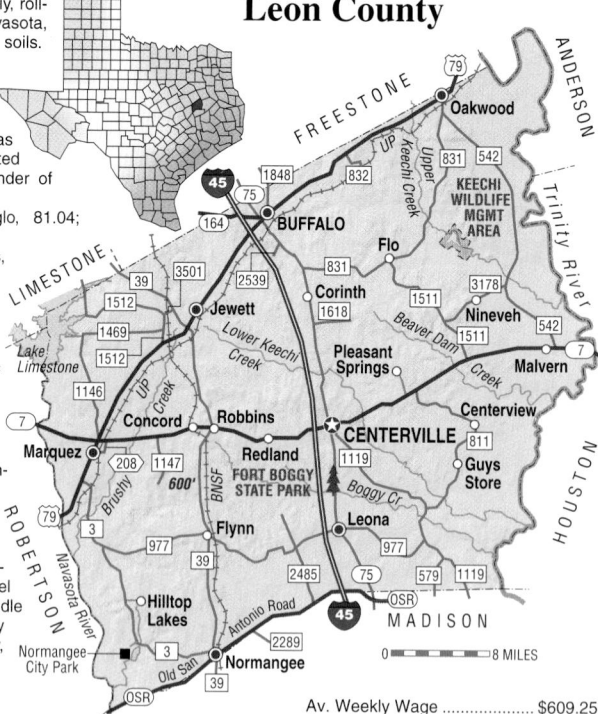

Physical Features: East central county; hilly, rolling, almost half covered by timber; drains to Navasota, Trinity rivers and tributaries; sandy, dark, alluvial soils.

Economy: Oil, gas production; agribusiness.

History: Bidais band, absorbed into Kickapoos and other groups. Permanent settlement by Anglo-Americans occurred after Texas Revolution; Germans in 1870s. County created 1846 from Robertson County; named for founder of Victoria, Martín de León.

Race/Ethnicity, 2000: (In percent) Anglo, 81.04; Black, 10.41; Hispanic, 7.91; Other, 0.64.

Vital Statistics, 2003: Births, 183; deaths, 198; marriages, 87; divorces, 46.

Recreation: Hilltop Lakes resort area; sites of Camino Real, Fort Boggy State Park; deer hunting.

Minerals: Oil, gas, iron ore, lignite.

Agriculture: A leading county in cow-calf production; hogs, poultry raised; hay, watermelons, vegetables, small grains; Christmas trees. Market value $51.3 million. Hardwoods, pine marketed.

CENTERVILLE (924) county seat; farm center; hunting; tourism; oil, gas; timber.

BUFFALO (1,942) farm center; clinic; library; stampede in September.

Other towns include: **Concord** (28); **Flynn** (81); **Hilltop Lakes** (300) resort, retirement center; **Jewett** (934) electricity-generating plant, steel mill, strip mining, civic center; **Leona** (194) candle factory; **Marquez** (214); **Normangee** (765, partly in Madison County) farming, tourism; library, museum, city park; **Oakwood** (500).

Population	16,106
Change fm 2000	5.0
Area (sq. mi.)	1,080.38
Land Area (sq. mi.)	1,072.04
Altitude (ft.)	150-600
Rainfall (in.)	43.08
Jan. mean min.	34.3
July mean max.	94.7
Civ. Labor	6,773
Unemployed	6.0
Wages	$38,666,692
Av. Weekly Wage	$609.25
Prop. Value	$1,641,377,024
Retail Sales	$110,462,571

For explanation of sources, abbreviations and symbols, see p. 167 and foldout map.

Liberty County

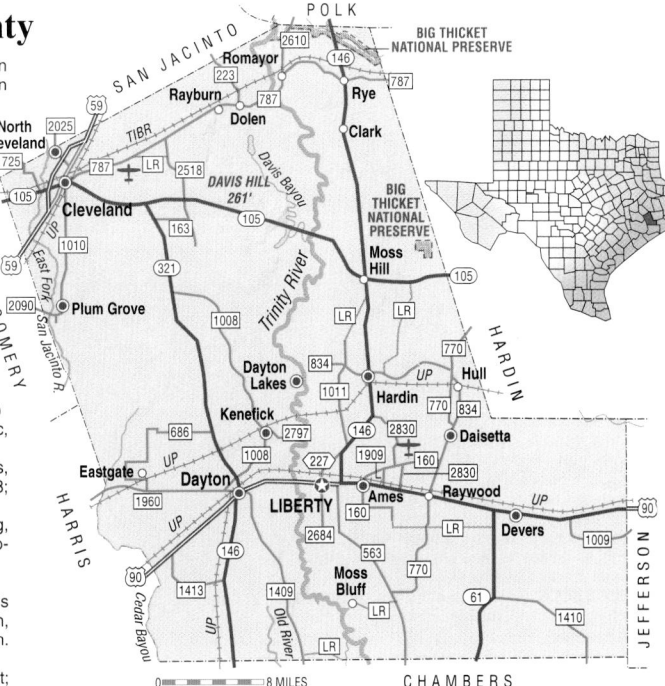

Physical Features: Coastal Plain county east of Houston; 60 percent in pine, hardwood timber; bisected by Trinity River; sandy, loam, black soils; Big Thicket.

Economy: Agribusiness; chemical plants; varied manufacturing; tourism; forest industries; prisons; many residents work in Houston; part of Houston metropolitan area.

History: Karankawa area until 1740s. Spanish established Atascosito settlement in 1756. Settlers from Louisiana began arriving in 1810s. County named for Spanish municipality, Libertad; created 1836, organized 1837.

Race/Ethnicity, 2000: (In percent) Anglo, 75.17; Black, 12.99; Hispanic, 10.92; Other, 0.92.

Vital Statistics, 2003: Births, 1,094; deaths, 701; marriages, 648; divorces, 319.

Recreation: Big Thicket; hunting, fishing; historic sites; Trinity Valley exposition; Liberty Opry.

Minerals: Oil, gas.

Agriculture: Beef cattle; rice is principal crop. Also nursery crops, corn, hay, sorghum. Market value $21 million. Some lumbering.

LIBERTY (8,349) county seat; petroleum-related industry; agribusiness; library; museum; regional historical resource depository; Liberty Bell; hospital; Jubilee in March.

Cleveland (7,754) forest products processed, shipped; tourism; library; museum; hospital.

Dayton (6,296) rice, oil center.

Other towns include: **Ames** (1,099); **Daisetta** (1,053); **Dayton Lakes** (99);

Devers (435); **Hardin** (791); **Hull** (1,800); **Kenefick** (704); **North Cleveland** (268); **Plum Grove** (983); **Raywood** (231); **Romayor** (96); **Rye** (76).

Population	74,821
Change fm 2000	6.7
Area (sq. mi.)	1,176.22
Land Area (sq. mi.)	1,159.68

Altitude (ft.)	23-261
Rainfall (in.)	60.52
Jan. mean min.	40.3
July mean max.	92.2
Civ. Labor	32,381
Unemployed	10.0
Wages	$106,611,883
Av. Weekly Wage	$527.90
Prop. Value	$3,474,769,419
Retail Sales	$612,217,636

A swamp in the Big Thicket National Preserve. File photo.

Limestone County

Physical Features: East central county on divide between Brazos and Trinity rivers; borders Blacklands, level to rolling; drained by Navasota and tributaries.

Economy: Agribusiness; rock quarry, oil and gas.

History: Tawakoni (Tehuacana) and Waco area, later Comanche raiders. First Anglo-Americans arrived in 1833. Antebellum slaveholding area. County created from Robertson County and organized 1846; named for indigenous rock.

Race/Ethnicity, 2000: (In percent) Anglo, 67.20; Black, 19.33; Hispanic, 12.97; Other, 0.50.

Vital Statistics, 2003: Births, 304; deaths, 266; marriages, 219; divorces, 95.

Recreation: Fishing, lake activities; Fort Parker; Confederate Reunion Grounds; historic sites; museum; hunting; Christmas at the Fort.

Minerals: Oil, gas, lignite, crushed rock.

Agriculture: Cow-calf, stocker cattle, hay, corn, cotton, horses, goats, sheep, wheat, ornamental fruit, pecans. Market value $32.8 million.

GROESBECK (4,490) county seat, agribusiness, tourism, hunting, mining, prison, power generating, hospital.

MEXIA (6,712) agribusiness, grocery distribution, state school, hospital.

Other towns include: **Coolidge** (865), **Kosse** (510), **Prairie Hill** (150), **Tehuacana** (312), **Thornton** (540).

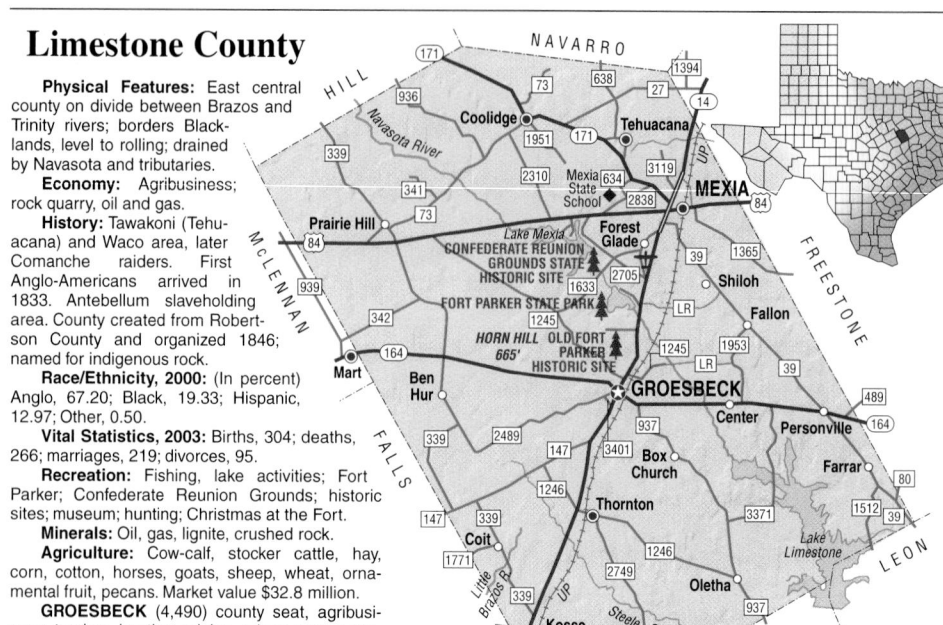

Area (sq. mi.)	933.15	
Land Area (sq. mi.)	908.88	
Altitude (ft.)	363-665	
Rainfall (in.)	41.40	
Jan. mean min.	33.7	
July mean max.	95.8	

Population	22,763
Change fm 2000	3.2

Civ. Labor	10,282
Unemployed	3.9
Wages	$51,940,130
Av. Weekly Wage	$513.81
Prop. Value	$1,579,241,031
Retail Sales	$221,606,505

Lipscomb County

Physical Features: High Plain, broken in east; drains to tributaries of Canadian, Wolf Creek; sandy loam, black soils.

Economy: Oil, gas operations; agribusinesses; government/services.

History: Apaches, later Kiowas and Comanches who were driven into Indian Territory in 1875. Ranching began in late 1870s. County created 1876 from Bexar District; organized 1887; named for A.S. Lipscomb, Republic of Texas leader.

Race/Ethnicity, 2000: (In percent) Anglo, 77.46; Black, 0.46; Hispanic, 20.71; Other, 1.37.

Vital Statistics, 2003: Births, 42; deaths, 36; marriages, 45; divorces, 13.

Recreation: Hunting; Will Rogers Day; Wolf Creek museum.

Minerals: Oil, natural gas.

Agriculture: Cattle; wheat, sorghum, corn; 19,000 acres irrigated. Market value $42.3 million.

LIPSCOMB (44), county seat; livestock center.

Booker (1,341, partly in Ochiltree County) trade center, library.

Other towns include: **Darrouzett** (298) Deutsches Fest, **Follett** (402); **Higgins** (414) library.

Population	3,074
Change fm 2000	0.6
Area (sq. mi.)	932.22
Land Area (sq. mi.)	932.11
Altitude (ft.)	2,300-2,837
Rainfall (in.)	22.57
Jan. mean min.	16.2

July mean max.	94.2
Civ. Labor	1,855
Unemployed	2.2
Wages	$9,335,480
Av. Weekly Wage	$602.44

Prop. Value	$500,235,401
Retail Sales	$10,298,977

Live Oak County

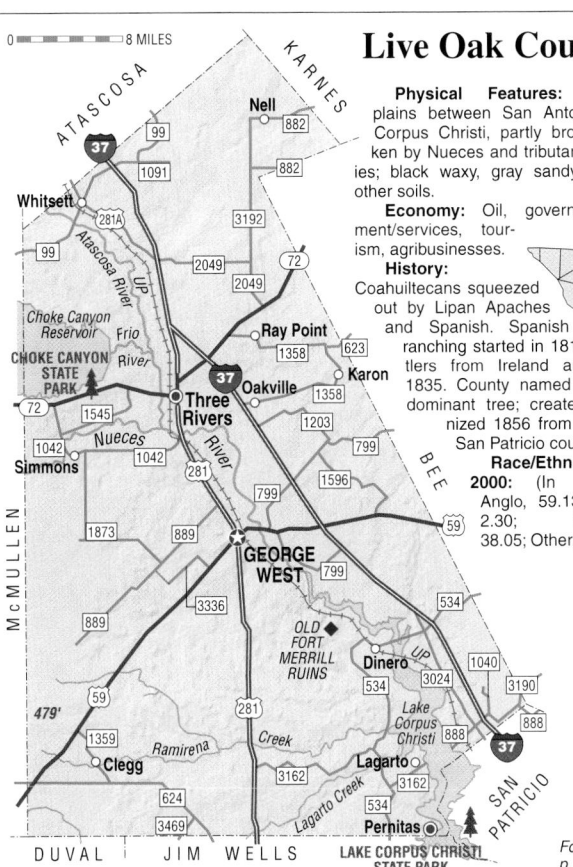

0 ▭▭▭▭ 8 MILES

Physical Features: Brushy plains between San Antonio and Corpus Christi, partly broken by Nueces and tributaries; black waxy, gray sandy, other soils.

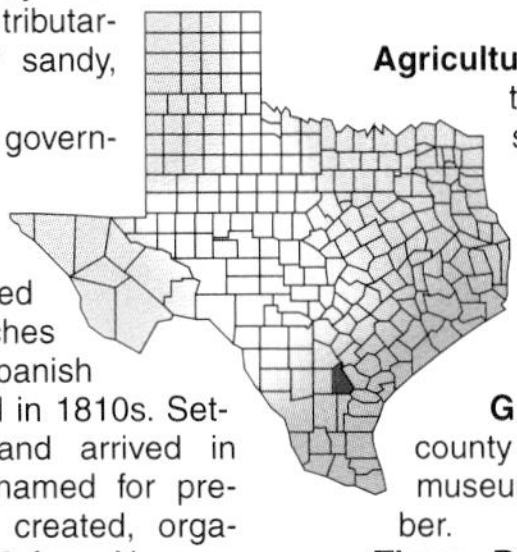

Economy: Oil, government/services, tourism, agribusinesses.

History: Coahuiltecans squeezed out by Lipan Apaches and Spanish. Spanish ranching started in 1810s. Settlers from Ireland arrived in 1835. County named for predominant tree; created, organized 1856 from Nueces, San Patricio counties.

Race/Ethnicity, 2000: (In percent) Anglo, 59.13; Black, 2.30; Hispanic, 38.05; Other, 0.52.

Vital Statistics, 2003: Births, 104; deaths, 88; marriages, 59; divorces, 45.

Recreation: Lakes; water activities; state park; hunting; historic sites.

Minerals: Oil, gas, sand, gravel.

Agriculture: Cow-calf operations; hogs; corn, grain sorghum, cotton; some irrigation for hay, coastal Bermuda pastures. Market value $14 million.

GEORGE WEST (2,556) county seat, oil and gas, museum, Storyfest in November.

Three Rivers (1,845) agribusinesses, refinery, federal prison, tourism, salsa festival in April.

Other towns include: **Dinero** (344); **Lagarto** (735); **Pernitas Point** (281, partly in Jim Wells County), **Whitsett** (200).

Population	11,694
Change fm 2000	-5.0
Area (sq. mi.)	1,078.83
Land Area (sq. mi.)	1,036.30
Altitude (ft.)	94-479
Rainfall (in.)	22.00
Jan. mean min.	42.0
July mean max.	97.0
Civ. Labor	4,562
Unemployed	2.7
Wages	$22,051,797
Av. Weekly Wage	$604.95
Prop. Value	$1,143,482,580
Retail Sales	$92,305,631

For explanation of sources, abbreviations and symbols, see p. 167 and foldout map.

The Lipscomb County Courthouse sits on a large square in a town of only 44 people. Texas Almanac photo.

Llano County

Physical Features: Central county drains to Colorado, Llano rivers; rolling to hilly; Highland lakes.

Economy: Tourism, retirement; ranch trading center; vineyards; granite mined.

History: Tonkawas, later Comanches. Anglo-American and German settlers arrived in 1840s. County name is Spanish for plains; created, organized 1856 from Bexar District, Gillespie County.

Race/Ethnicity, 2000: (In percent) Anglo, 93.74; Black, 0.34; Hispanic, 5.13; Other, 0.79.

Vital Statistics, 2003: Births, 146; deaths, 236; marriages, 112; divorces, 65.

Recreation: Leading deer-hunting county; fishing; lake activities; major tourist area; Enchanted Rock; bluebonnet festival; hang gliding, Hill Country Wine Trail in spring.

Minerals: Granite, vermiculite, llanite.

Agriculture: Beef cattle, sheep, goats. Market value $11.8 million. Deer-hunting, wildlife leases.

LLANO (3,550) county seat; varied manufacturing; hunting center; government/services; hospital; livestock trading; historic district; museum.

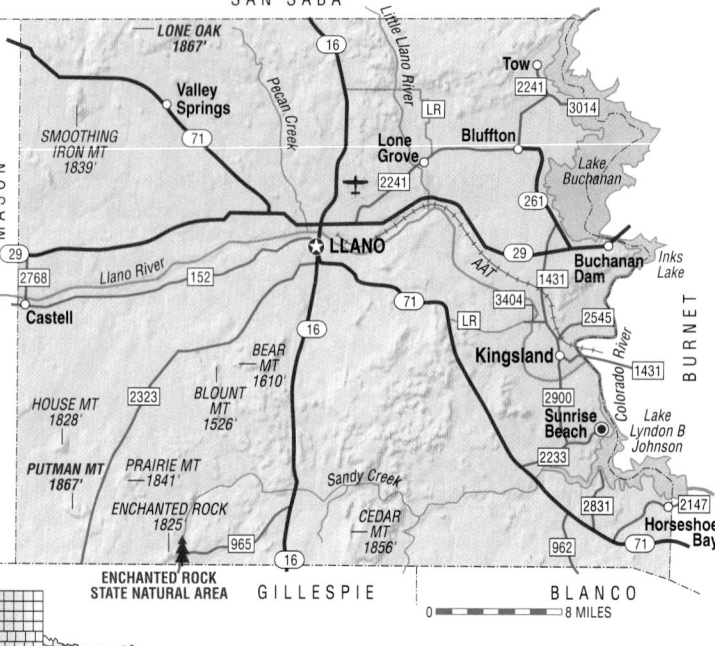

Kingsland (4,954) tourism, retirement community, fishing and water sports; metal fabrication; wood work; library; AquaBoom on July 4.

Other towns include: **Bluffton** (75); **Buchanan Dam** (1,785) hydroelectric industry, tourism; **Castell** (72); **Horseshoe Bay** (3,514, partly in Burnet County); **Sunrise Beach** (756); **Tow** (305); **Valley Spring** (50).

Population	**18,143**
Change fm 2000	6.4
Area (sq. mi.)	966.18
Land Area (sq. mi.)	934.76
Altitude (ft.)	825-1,867
Rainfall (in.)	27.33
Jan. mean min.	32.3
July mean max.	96.0
Civ. Labor	5,942
Unemployed	4.6
Wages	$26,172,447
Av. Weekly Wage	$483.38
Prop. Value	$2,778,521,167
Retail Sales	$115,594,790

Loving County

Physical Features: Western county of dry, rolling prairies; slopes to Pecos River; Red Bluff Reservoir; sandy, loam, clay soils.

Economy: Petroleum operations; cattle.

History: Land developers began operations in late 19th century. Oil discovered in 1925. County created 1887 from Tom Green County; organized 1931, last county organized. Named for Oliver Loving, trail driver. Loving is Texas' least populous county.

Race/Ethnicity, 2000: (In percent) Anglo, 89.55; Black, 0.00; Hispanic, 10.45; Other, 0.00.

Vital Statistics, 2003: Births, 0; deaths, 1; marriages, 5; divorces, 0.

Recreation: NA.

Minerals: Oil, gas.

Agriculture: Some cattle. Market value $523,000.

MENTONE (20) county seat, oilfield supply center; only town.

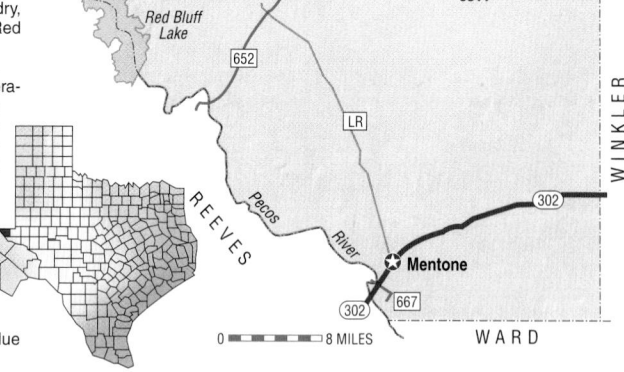

For explanation of sources, abbreviations and symbols, see p. 167 and foldout map.

Population	**52**
Change fm 2000	-22.4
Area (sq. mi.)	676.85
Land Area (sq. mi.)	673.08
Altitude (ft.)	2,685-3,311
Rainfall (in.)	9.10
Jan. mean min.	28.0
July mean max.	96.0
Civ. Labor	54
Unemployed	9.3
Wages	$333,594
Av. Weekly Wage	$570.25
Prop. Value	$185,385,939
Retail Sales	$0

Physical Features: High Plains of West Texas, broken by 1,500 playas, upper Brazos River tributaries; rich soils with underground water.

Economy: Among world's largest cottonseed processing centers; a leading agribusiness center; cattle feedlots; manufacturing; higher education center; medical center; government/services.

History: Evidence of human habitation for 12,000 years. In historic period, Apache Indians, followed by Comanche hunters. Sheep raisers from Midwest arrived in late 1870s. Cotton farms brought in Mexican laborers in 1940s-60s. County named for Col. Tom S. Lubbock, an organizer of Confederate Terry's Rangers; county created 1876 from Bexar District; organized 1891.

Race/Ethnicity, 2000: (In percent) Anglo, 63.06; Black, 7.71; Hispanic, 27.45; Other, 1.78.

Vital Statistics, 2003: Births, 4,064; deaths, 2,048; marriages, 2,016; divorces, 1,142.

Recreation: Lubbock Lake archaeological site; Texas Tech

Lubbock County

events; civic center; Buddy Holly statue, Walk of Fame, festival in September; planetarium; Ranching Heritage Center; Panhandle-South Plains Fair; wine festivals; Buffalo Springs Lake.

Minerals: Oil, gas, stone, sand and gravel.

Agriculture: A leading cotton-producing county. Fed beef, cow-calf operations; poultry, eggs; hogs. Other crops, nursery, grain sorghum, wheat, sunflowers, soybeans, hay, vegetables; more than 230,000 acres irrigated, mostly cotton. Market value $143.6 million.

Education: Texas Tech University with law and medical schools; Lubbock Christian University; South Plains College branch; Wayland Baptist University off-campus center.

LUBBOCK (205,905) county seat; center for large agricultural area; manufacturing includes electronics, earth-moving equipment, food containers, fire-protection equipment, clothing, other products; distribution center for South Plains; feedlots; museum; government/services; hospitals, psychiatric hospital; state school for retarded; wind power center.

Other towns include: **Buffalo Springs** (467); **Idalou** (2,206); **New Deal** (727); **Ransom Canyon** (1,043); **Shallowater** (2,115); **Slaton** (6,323) agribusiness, government/services, varied manufacturing, railroad, Harvey House museum, sausagefest in October; **Wolfforth** (2,705) retail, government/services, harvest festival in September.

Also, part of **Abernathy** (2,940).

Population	**251,018**
Change fm 2000	3.5
Area (sq. mi.)	900.70
Land Area (sq. mi.)	899.49
Altitude (ft.)	2,900-3,402
Rainfall (in.)	18.69
Jan. mean min.	24.4
July mean max.	91.9
Civ. Labor	132,451
Unemployed	3.3
Wages	$849,390,116
Av. Weekly Wage	$553.86
Prop. Value	$10,059,944,128
Retail Sales	$3,529,224,446

Lynn County

Physical Features: South High Plains, broken by Caprock Escarpment, playas, draws; sandy loam, black, gray soils.

Economy: Agribusiness.

History: Apaches, ousted by Comanches who were removed to Indian Territory in 1875. Ranching began in 1880s. Farming developed after 1900. County created 1876 from Bexar District; organized 1903; named for Alamo victim W. Lynn.

Race/Ethnicity,2000: (In percent) Anglo, 51.95; Black, 2.63; Hispanic, 44.63; Other, 0.79.

Vital Statistics, 2003: Births, 103; deaths, 75; marriages, 38; divorces, 23.

Recreation: Pioneer museum in Tahoka; Dan Blocker museum in O'Donnell; sandhill crane migration in winter.

Minerals: Oil, natural gas, stone.

Agriculture: Cotton produces largest income; 77,000 acres irrigated. Market value $48.9 million.

TAHOKA

(2,857) county seat; agribusiness center; cotton compress; some manufacturing; hospital; harvest festival.

O'Donnell (961, partly in Dawson County) commercial center.

Other towns include: **New Home** (339); **Wilson** (520).

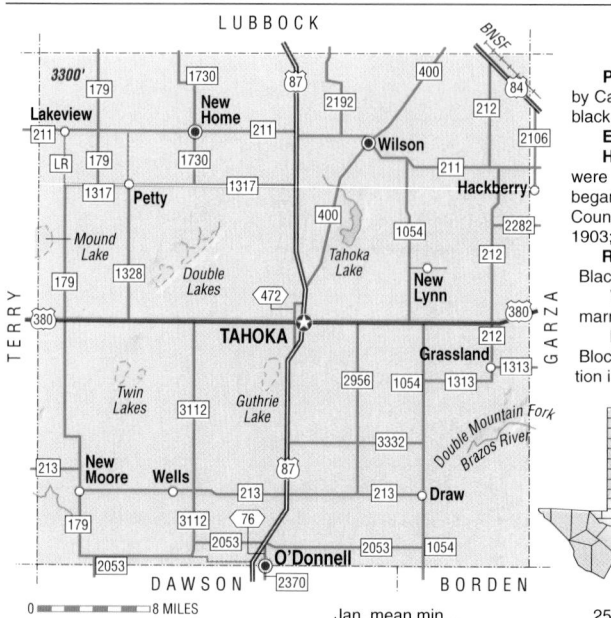

Population	**6,156**
Change fm 2000	-6.0
Area (sq. mi.)	893.46
Land Area (sq. mi.)	891.88
Altitude (ft.)	2,800-3,300
Rainfall (in.)	20.48
Jan. mean min.	25.1
July mean max.	92.2
Civ. Labor	2,792
Unemployed	5.6
Wages	$8,251,240
Av. Weekly Wage	$433.84
Prop. Value	$399,008,128
Retail Sales	$16,117,778

Madison County

Physical Features: East central county; hilly, draining to Trinity, Navasota rivers, Bedias Creek; one-fifth of area timbered; alluvial, loam, sandy soils.

Economy: Prison; government/services; varied manufacturing; agribusinesses; oil production.

History: Caddo and Bidai Indian area; Kickapoos migrated from east. Spanish settlements established in 1774 and 1805. Anglo-Americans arrived in 1829. Census of 1860 showed 30 percent of population was black. County named for U.S. President James Madison; created from Grimes, Leon, Walker counties 1853; organized 1854.

Race/Ethnicity, 2000: (In percent) Anglo, 60.72; Black, 22.76; Hispanic, 15.78; Other, 0.74.

Vital Statistics, 2003: Births, 151; deaths, 144; marriages, 93; divorces, 34.

Recreation: Fishing, hunting; Spanish Bluff where survivors of the Gutiérrez-Magee expedition were executed in 1813; other historic sites.

Minerals: sand, oil.

Agriculture: Nursery crops, cattle, horses, poultry raised; forage for livestock. Market value $60.6 million.

MADISONVILLE (4,280) county seat; farm-trade center; varied manufacturing; hospital, library; Spring Fling in April.

Other towns, **Midway** (291); **Normangee** (765, mostly in Leon County); **North Zulch** (150).

Population	13,203
Change fm 2000	2.0
Area (sq. mi.)	472.44
Land Area (sq. mi.)	469.65
Altitude (ft.)	150-364
Rainfall (in.)	44.00
Jan. mean min.	35.8
July mean max.	96.0
Civ. Labor	4,603
Unemployed	3.5
Wages	$23,180,250
Av. Weekly Wage	$481.01
Prop. Value	$728,406,697
Retail Sales	$153,935,412

For explanation of sources, abbreviations and symbols, see p. 167 and foldout map.

Marion County

Physical Features: Northeastern county; hilly, three-quarters forested with pines, hardwoods; drains to Caddo Lake, Lake O' the Pines, Cypress Bayou.

Economy: Tourism; timber; food processing.

History: Caddoes forced out in 1790s. Kickapoo in area when settlers arrived from Deep South around 1840. Antebellum slaveholding area. County created 1860 from Cass County; named for Gen. Francis Marion of American Revolution.

Race/Ethnicity, 2000: (In percent) Anglo, 72.38; Black, 24.17; Hispanic, 2.40; Other, 1.05.

Vital Statistics, 2003: Births, 101; deaths, 145; marriages, 103; divorces, 47.

Recreation: Lake activities; hunting; Excelsior Hotel; 84 medallions on historic sites including Jay Gould railroad car; museum; Mardi Gras; historical pilgrimage in May, founder's day in October.

Minerals: Iron ore.

Agriculture: Beef cattle, hay, goats. Market value $4.1 million. Forestry is most important industry.

JEFFERSON (2,068) county seat; tourism; board plant; agriculture center; timber; museums, library; historical sites.

Other towns include: **Lodi** (164).

Population	11,115
Change fm 2000	1.6
Area (sq. mi.)	420.36
Land Area (sq. mi.)	381.21
Altitude (ft.)	168-500
Rainfall (in.)	49.26
Jan. mean min.	31.4
July mean max.	93.1
Civ. Labor	3,661
Unemployed	6.0
Wages	$11,013,060
Av. Weekly Wage	$469.60
Prop. Value	$574,315,590
Retail Sales	$65,787,876

Martin County

Physical Features: Western county on South Plains; sandy, loam soils, broken by playas, creeks.

Economy: Petroleum production, agribusiness.

History: Apaches, ousted by Comanches who in turn were forced out by U.S. Army 1875. Farming began in 1881. County created from Bexar District 1876; organized 1884; named for Wylie Martin, senator of Republic of Texas.

Race/Ethnicity, 2000: (In percent) Anglo, 57.37; Black, 1.73; Hispanic, 40.56; Other, 0.34.

Vital Statistics, 2003: Births, 62; deaths, 56; marriages, 39; divorces, 21.

Recreation: Museum, settlers reunion, restored monastery.

Minerals: Oil, gas.

Agriculture: Cotton, milo, wheat; beef cattle, horses, meat goats, sheep raised. Market value $14.1 million.

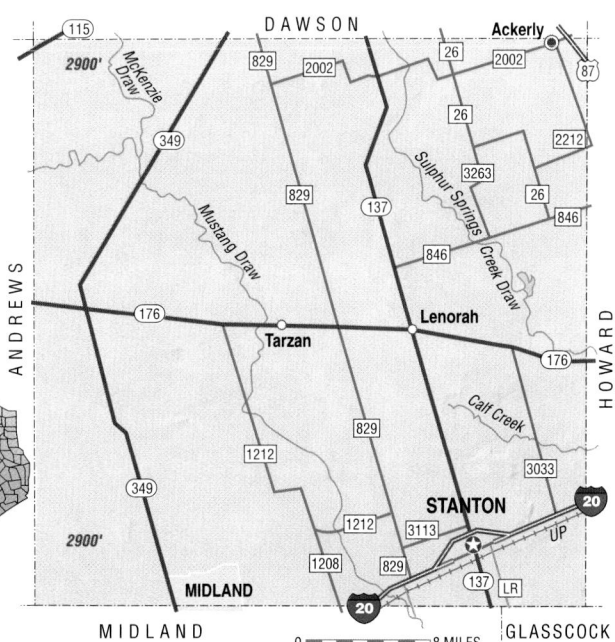

STANTON (2,527) county seat; farm, ranch, oil center; varied manufacturing; electric co-op; communting to Midland, Big Spring; hospital, restored convent, other historic buildings; Old Sorehead trade days three times a year.

Other towns include: **Ackerly** (235, partly in Dawson County); **Lenorah** (83); **Tarzan** (30).

Population	4,448
Change fm 2000	-6.3
Area (sq. mi.)	915.62
Land Area (sq. mi.)	914.78
Altitude (ft.)	2,500-2,900
Rainfall (in.)	18.20
Jan. mean min.	30.0
July mean max.	94.0
Civ. Labor	2,285
Unemployed	4.4
Wages	$9,987,553
Av. Weekly Wage	$590.53
Prop. Value	$701,268,140
Retail Sales	$39,707,604

Mason County

Physical Features: Central county; hilly, draining to Llano and San Saba rivers and their tributaries; limestone, red soils; varied timber.

Economy: Nature tourism, agriculture.

History: Lipan Apaches, driven south by Comanches around 1790. German settlers arrived in mid-1840s, followed by Anglo-Americans. Mexican immigration increased after 1930. County created from Bexar, Gillespie counties 1858; named for Mexican War victim U.S. Army Lt. G.T. Mason.

Race/Ethnicity, 2000: (In percent) Anglo, 78.25; Black, 0.16; Hispanic, 20.95; Other, 0.64.

Vital Statistics, 2003: Births, 37; deaths, 47; marriages, 27; divorces, 18.

Recreation: Outstanding deer, turkey hunting, river fishing; camping; historic homes of stone; Fort Mason, where Robert E. Lee served; wildflower drives in spring.

Minerals: Topaz, sand.

Agriculture: Cattle, sheep, goats, hay, peanuts. Market value $44.8 million. Hunting leases important.

MASON (2,168) county seat; ranching center; camping; tourism; museum; historical district, homes, rock fences built by German settlers; wild game dinner in November.

Other towns include: **Art** (14), **Fredonia** (55), **Pontotoc** (125).

Population	3,844
Change fm 2000	2.8
Area (sq. mi.)	932.18
Land Area (sq. mi.)	932.07
Altitude (ft.)	1,200-2,217
Rainfall (in.)	27.95
Jan. mean min.	30.8
July mean max.	94.9
Civ. Labor	1,708
Unemployed	2.1
Wages	$5,383,297
Av. Weekly Wage	$445.27
Prop. Value	$640,160,980
Retail Sales	$20,245,005

Matagorda County

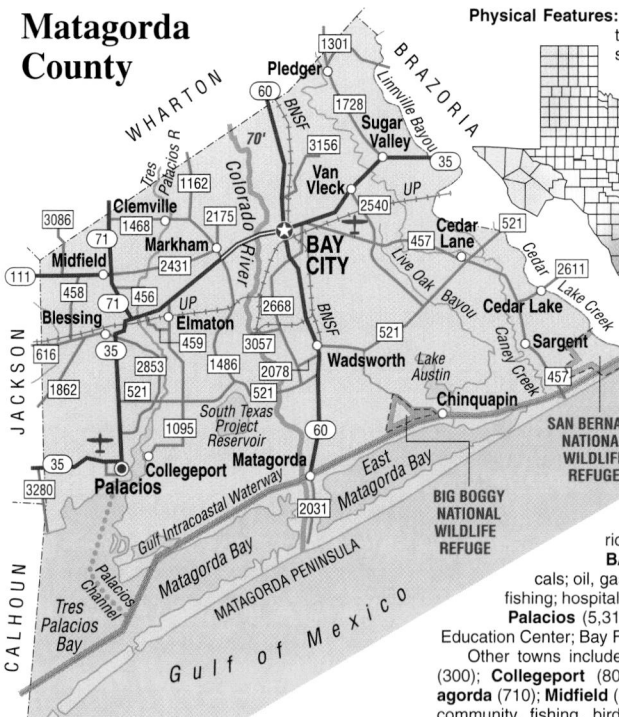

Physical Features: Gulf Coast county; flat, broken by bays; contains part of Matagorda Island; many different soils; drains to Colorado River, creeks, coast.

Economy: Nuclear power plant, petrochemicals, agribusiness.

History: Karankawa Indian area, Tonkawas later. Anglo-Americans arrived in 1822. Mexican immigration increased after 1920. An original county, created 1836 from Spanish municipality, named for canebrake; organized 1837; settled by Austin colonists.

Race/Ethnicity, 2000: (In percent) Anglo, 53.00; Black, 12.84; Hispanic, 31.35; Other, 2.81.

Vital Statistics, 2003: Births, 527; deaths, 393; marriages, 314; divorces, 148.

Recreation: Fishing, water sports, hunting, bird watching; historic sites, museums; rice festival in October.

Minerals: Oil and gas.

Agriculture: Cattle, cotton, rice, sorghum, soybeans; 24,000 acres irrigated for rice. Market value $115.7 million.

BAY CITY (18,572) county seat; petrochemicals; oil, gas processing; nuclear power plant; commercial fishing; hospital.

Palacios (5,312) tourism; seafood industry; hospital; Marine Education Center; Bay Festival Labor Day; public fishing piers.

Other towns include: **Blessing** (853) historic sites; **Cedar Lane** (300); **Collegeport** (80); **Elmaton** (160); **Markham** (1,116); **Matagorda** (710); **Midfield** (305); **Pledger** (265); **Sargent** (900) retirement community, fishing, birding, commercial fishing; **Van Vleck** (1,394); **Wadsworth** (160).

Population	38,092
Change fm 2000	0.4
Area (sq. mi.)	1,612.19
Land Area (sq. mi.)	1,114.46
Altitude (ft.)	sea level-70
Rainfall (in.)	48.03
Jan. mean min.	45.7
July mean max.	92.4
Civ. Labor	14,592
Unemployed	13.4
Wages	$86,936,258
Av. Weekly Wage	$645.19
Prop. Value	$3,207,435,771
Retail Sales	$298,445,758

Maverick County

Physical Features: Southwestern county on Rio Grande; broken, rolling surface, with dense brush; clay, sandy, alluvial soils.

Economy: Oil, government/services, agribusiness, tourism.

History: Coahuiltecan Indian area; later Comanches in area. Spanish ranching began in 1760s. First Anglo-Americans arrived in 1834. County named for Sam A. Maverick, whose name is now a synonym for unbranded cattle; created 1856 from Kinney County; organized 1871.

Race/Ethnicity, 2000: (In percent) Anglo, 3.54; Black, 0.12; Hispanic, 95.01; Other, 1.33.

Vital Statistics, 2003: Births, 1,012; deaths, 250; marriages, 548; divorces, 59.

Recreation: Tourist gateway to Mexico; white-tailed deer, bird hunting; fishing; historic sites, Fort Duncan museum.

Minerals: Oil, gas, sand, gravel.

Agriculture: Cattle feedlots; pecans, vegetables, sorghum, wheat; goats, sheep. Some irrigation from Rio Grande. Market value $34.7 million.

EAGLE PASS (24,667) county seat; government/services; retail center; tourism; hospital; junior college, Sul Ross college campus; entry point to Piedras Negras, Mex., Nacho Festival in Piedras Negras in October.

Other communities include: **Eidson Road** (9,678), **El Indio** (278), **Las Quintas Fronterizas** (2,092), **Rosita North** (3,557); **Rosita South** (2,669); all immediately south of Eagle Pass.

Also, **Elm Creek** (2,013) and **Quemado** (244).

Population	50,436
Change fm 2000	6.6
Area (sq. mi.)	1,291.74
Land Area (sq. mi.)	1,280.08
Altitude (ft.)	600-958
Rainfall (in.)	21.48
Jan. mean min.	40.1
July mean max.	98.1
Civ. Labor	20,484
Unemployed	18.7
Wages	$72,887,107
Av. Weekly Wage	$447.11
Prop. Value	$1,520,807,330
Retail Sales	$445,250,036

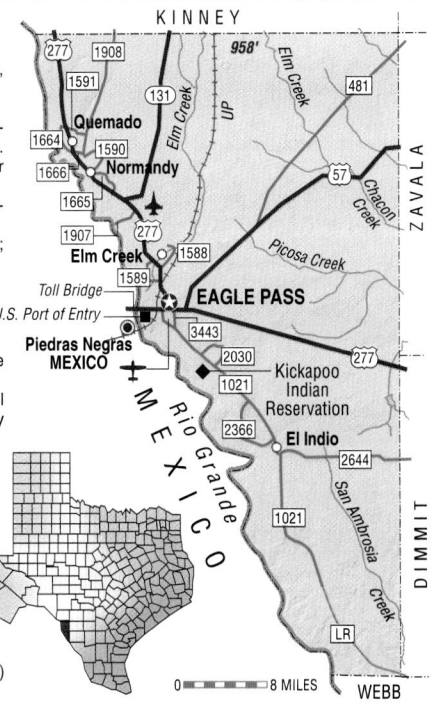

McCulloch County

Physical Features: Central county; hilly and rolling; drains to Colorado, Brady Creek and Lake, San Saba River; black loams to sandy soils.

Economy: Agribusiness; manufacturing; tourism; hunting leases.

History: Apache area. First Anglo-American settlers arrived in late 1850s, but Comanche raids delayed further settlement until 1870s. County created from Bexar District 1856; organized 1876; named for San Jacinto veteran Gen. Ben McCulloch.

Race/Ethnicity, 2000: (In percent) Anglo, 70.93; Black, 1.52; Hispanic, 27.04; Other, 0.51.

Vital Statistics, 2003: Births, 107; deaths, 118; marriages, 80; divorces, 61.

Recreation: Hunting; lake activities; museum; restored Santa Fe depot, goat cookoff on Labor Day; muzzle-loading rifle association state championship; rodeos; golf, tennis tournaments.

Minerals: Sand, gravel, gas and oil.

Agriculture: Beef cattle provide most income; wheat, sheep, goats, hay, cotton, sorghum, hogs, dairy cattle; some irrigation for peanuts. Market value $13 million.

BRADY (5,575) county seat; silica sand, oil-field equipment, ranching, tourism, other manufacturing; hospital; Heart of Texas car show in April, Cinco de Mayo. Other towns: **Doole** (74), **Lohn** (149), **Melvin** (142), **Mercury** (166), **Rochelle** (163) and **Voca** (56).

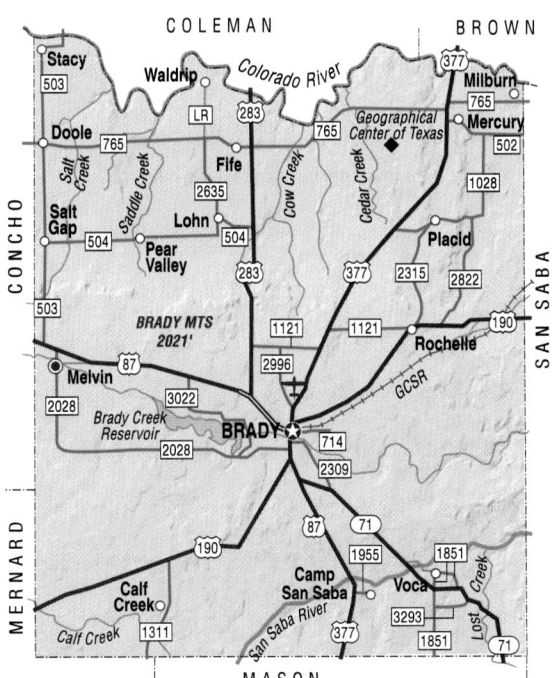

Population	8,108
Change fm 2000	-1.2
Area (sq. mi.)	1,073.35
Land Area (sq. mi.)	1,069.31
Altitude (ft.)	1,300-2,021
Rainfall (in.)	27.63
Jan. mean min.	32.3
July mean max.	94.5
Civ. Labor	4,158
Unemployed	5.2
Wages	$16,247,496
Av. Weekly Wage	$455.97
Prop. Value	$700,335,910
Retail Sales	$103,065,233

For explanation of sources, abbreviations and symbols, see p. 167 and foldout map.

Physical Features: Central Texas county of mostly Blackland prairie, but rolling hills in west; drains to Bosque, Brazos rivers and Lake Waco; heavy, loam, sandy soils.

Economy: A leading distribution, government center for Central Texas; diversified manufacturing; agribusiness; education.

History: Tonkawas, Wichitas and Wacos in area. Anglo-American settlers arrived in 1840s. Indians removed to Brazos reservations in 1854. County created from Milam County in 1850; named for settler, Neil McLennan Sr.

Race/Ethnicity, 2000: (In percent) Anglo, 65.19; Black, 15.33; Hispanic, 17.91; Other, 1.57.

Vital Statistics, 2003: Births, 3,363; deaths, 2,014; marriages, 1,980; divorces, 990.

Recreation: Varied metropolitan activies; Texas Ranger Hall of Fame; Texas Sports Hall of Fame; Dr Pepper Museum; Cameron Park; drag boat races April and May; zoo; historic sites, homes; museums; libraries, art center; symphony; civic theater; Baylor University events; Heart o' Texas Fair.

Minerals: Sand and gravel, limestone, oil, gas.

Agriculture: Poultry, beef cattle, corn, wheat, hay, grain sorghum, soybeans, dairy cattle. Market value $61.1 million.

Education: Baylor University; community college; Texas State Technical College.

WACO (117,464) county seat; varied manufacturing; tourism center, conventions; agribusiness; aerospace firms; hospitals.

Hewitt (12,172) iron works, other manufacturing; hamburger cookoff.

West (2,714) famous for Czech foods; varied manufacturing; Westfest Labor Day weekend.

Other towns include: **Axtell** (300); **Bellmead** (9,341); **Beverly Hills** (2,087); **Bruceville-Eddy** (1,549, partly in Falls County); **China Spring** (1,000);

McLennan County

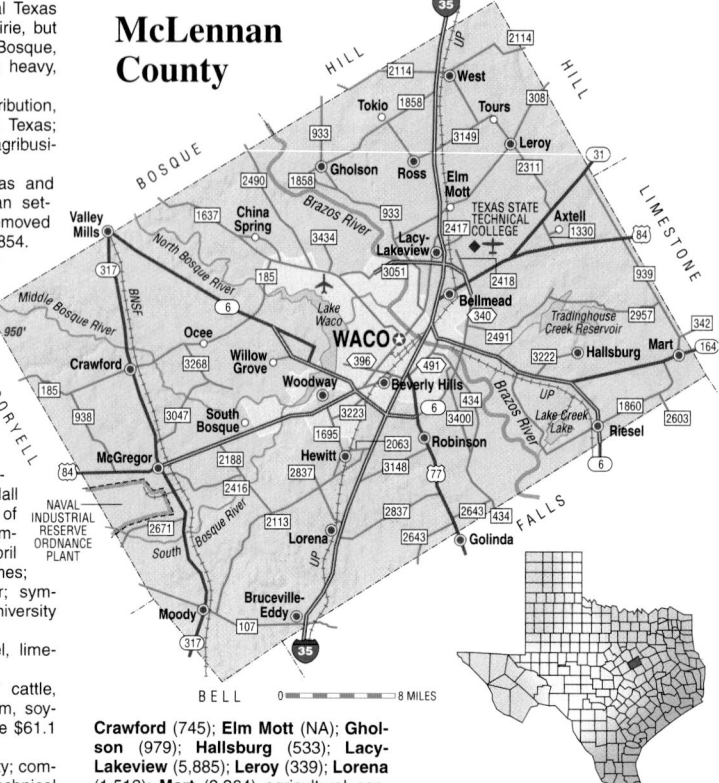

Crawford (745); **Elm Mott** (NA); **Gholson** (979); **Hallsburg** (533); **Lacy-Lakeview** (5,885); **Leroy** (339); **Lorena** (1,512); **Mart** (2,264) agricultural center, some manufacturing, museum, juvenile correction facility; **McGregor** (4,778) agriculture, manufacturing, distribution; private telephone museum; Frontier Founders Day in September; **Moody** (1,411) agriculture, commuting to Waco, Temple; library; Cotton Harvest fest in September; **Riesel** (992); **Robinson** (7,999); **Ross** (238); **Woodway** (8,562).

Part of **Golinda** (454, mostly in Falls County) and part of **Valley Mills** (1,171, mostly in Bosque County).

Population	**222,439**
Change fm 2000	4.2
Area (sq. mi.)	1,060.23
Land Area (sq. mi.)	1,041.88
Altitude (ft.)	350-950
Rainfall (in.)	33.34
Jan. mean min.	35.1
July mean max.	96.7
Civ. Labor	105,870
Unemployed	4.3
Wages	$751,588,547
Av. Weekly Wage	$583.86
Prop. Value	$9,365,219,390
Retail Sales	$2,603,062,854

Oil wells and cattle in McMullen County near Choke Canyon State Park. Texas Almanac photo.

McMullen County

Physical Features: Southern county of brushy plain, sloping to Frio, Nueces rivers and tributaries; saline clay soils.

Economy: Livestock, hunting leases, oil and gas.

History: Coahuiltecans, squeezed out by Lipan Apaches and other tribes. Anglo-American settlers arrived in 1858. Sheep ranching of 1870s attracted Mexican laborers. County created from Atascosa, Bexar, Live Oak counties 1858; organized 1862, reorganized 1877; named for Nueces River pioneer-empresario John McMullen.

Race/Ethnicity, 2000: (In percent) Anglo, 65.44; Black, 1.18; Hispanic, 33.14; Other, 0.24.

Vital Statistics, 2003: Births, 1; deaths, 2; marriages, 9; divorces, 2.

Recreation: Deer hunting; lake activities, state park; Labor Day rodeo; Dogtown Days festival in October.

Minerals: Gas, oil, lignite coal, zeolite-kaline.

Agriculture: Beef cattle, hay, grain sorghum. Market value $6.4 million.

TILDEN (300), county seat; oil, gas, lignite mining; ranch center; government/services.

Other towns include: **Calliham** (100).

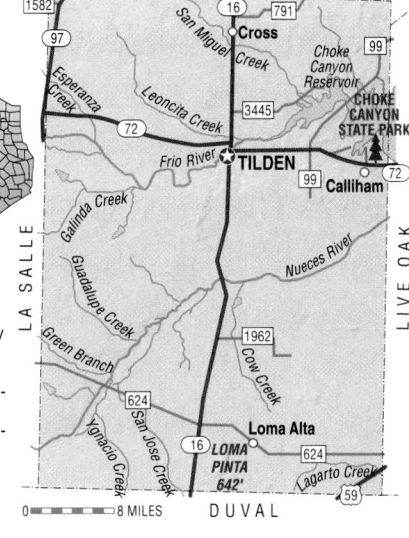

Population	853
Change fm 2000	0.2
Area (sq. mi.)	1,142.60
Land Area (sq. mi.)	1,113.00
Altitude (ft.)	200-642
Rainfall (in.)	23.87
Jan. mean min.	40.1
July mean max.	98.7
Civ. Labor	327
Unemployed	3.3
Wages	$1,999,081
Av. Weekly Wage	$625.10
Prop. Value	$425,282,825
Retail Sales	$3,625,133

Medina County

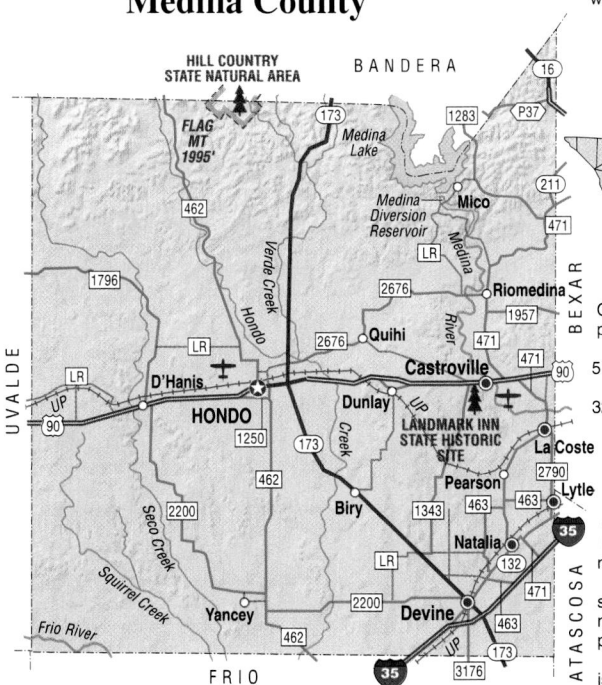

Physical Features: Southwestern county with scenic hills in north; south has fertile valleys, rolling surface; Medina River, Lake.

Economy: Agribusinesses; tourism; varied manufacturing; commuters to San Antonio; government/services.

History: Lipan Apaches and Comanches. Settled by Alsatians led by Henri Castro in 1844. Mexican immigration increased after 1900. County created 1848 from Bexar; named for river, probably for Spanish engineer Pedro Medina.

Race/Ethnicity, 2000: (In percent) Anglo, 51.44; Black, 2.13; Hispanic, 45.47; Other, 0.96.

Vital Statistics, 2003: Births, 552; deaths, 321; marriages, 223; divorces, 105.

Recreation: A leading deer area; scenic drives; camping, fishing; historic buildings, museum; market trail days most months.

Minerals: Oil, gas, clay, sand, gravel.

Agriculture: Most income from cattle; crops include corn, grains, peanuts, hay, vegetables; 40,000 acres irrigated. Market value $60.7 million.

HONDO (8,471) county seat; Air Force screening center; aerospace industry; agribusiness; varied manufacturing; hunting leases; hospital; prisons.

Castroville (2,786) farm, ranch center; tourism; government/services; commuting to San Antonio; Landmark Inn; St. Louis Day celebration in August.

Devine (4,240) commuters to San Antonio, shipping for truck crop-livestock; fall festival in October.

Other towns include: **D'Hanis** (575), **La Coste** (1,337), **Natalia** (1,781), **Riomedina** (60), **Yancey** (209). Also, **Lytle** (2,535, mostly in Atascosa County).

Population	42,269
Change fm 2000	7.5
Area (sq. mi.)	1,334.53
Land Area (sq. mi.)	1,327.76
Altitude (ft.)	635-1,995
Rainfall (in.)	26.30
Jan. mean min.	38.0
July mean max.	95.0
Civ. Labor	16,401
Unemployed	5.2
Wages	$48,211,182
Av. Weekly Wage	$473.03
Prop. Value	$2,088,694,833
Retail Sales	$325,142,703

For explanation of sources, abbreviations and symbols, see p. 167 and foldout map.

Menard County

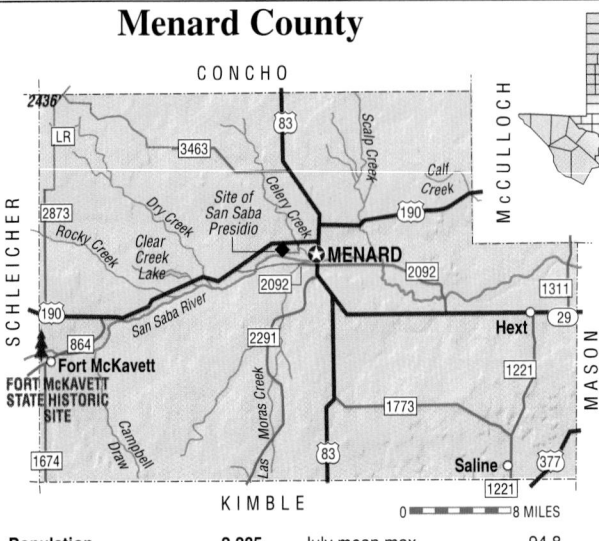

Physical Features: West central county of rolling topography, draining to San Saba River and tributaries; limestone soils.

Economy: Agribusiness; tourism; oil, gas production.

History: Apaches, followed by Comanches in 18th century. Mission Santa Cruz de San Sabá established in 1757. A few Anglo-American and German settlers arrived in 1840s. County created from Bexar County in 1858, organized 1871; named for Galveston's founder, Michel B. Menard.

Race/Ethnicity, 2000: (In percent) Anglo, 66.83; Black, 0.42; Hispanic, 31.69; Other, 1.06.

Vital Statistics, 2003: Births, 17; deaths, 40; marriages, 18; divorces, 3.

Recreation: Hunting, fishing; historic sites, including Spanish presidio, mission, irrigation ditches; U.S. fort; museum; Jim Bowie days in September.

Minerals: Oil, gas.

Agriculture: Sheep, goats, cattle; pecans, wheat, alfalfa, peaches, melons, grapes. Market value $7.4 million.

MENARD (1,657) county seat; ranching center, tourism. Other towns include: **Fort McKavett** (50); **Hext** (75).

Population	2,285
Change fm 2000	-3.2
Area (sq. mi.)	902.25
Land Area (sq. mi.)	901.91
Altitude (ft.)	1,690-2,436
Rainfall (in.)	24.90
Jan. mean min.	30.7
July mean max.	94.8
Civ. Labor	865
Unemployed	5.6
Wages	$2,604,166
Av. Weekly Wage	$395.89
Prop. Value	$446,472,260
Retail Sales	$10,535,835

Midland County

Physical

Features: Flat western county, broken by draws; sandy, loam soils with native grasses.

Economy: Among leading petroleum-producing counties; distribution, administrative center for oil industry; varied manufacturing; government/services.

History: Comanches in area in 19th century. Sheep ranching developed in 1880s. Permian Basin oil boom began in 1920s. County created from Tom Green County 1885; name came from midway location on railroad between El Paso and Fort Worth. Chihuahua Trail and Emigrant Road were pioneer trails that crossed county.

Race/Ethnicity, 2000: (In percent) Anglo, 62.54; Black, 7.05; Hispanic, 29.03; Other, 1.38.

Vital Statistics, 2003: Births, 1,856; deaths, 990; marriages, 905; divorces, 507.

Recreation: Permian Basin Petroleum Museum, Library, Hall of Fame; Museum of Southwest; Commemorative Air Force and Museum; community theater; metropolitan events; homes of Presidents Bush.

Minerals: Oil, natural gas.

Agriculture: Beef cattle, horses, sheep and goats; cotton, hay, pecans; 20,000 acres irrigated. Market value $7.4 million.

MIDLAND (97,048) county seat; petroleum, petrochemical center; varied manufacturing; livestock sale center; hospitals; cultural activities; junior college; Celebration

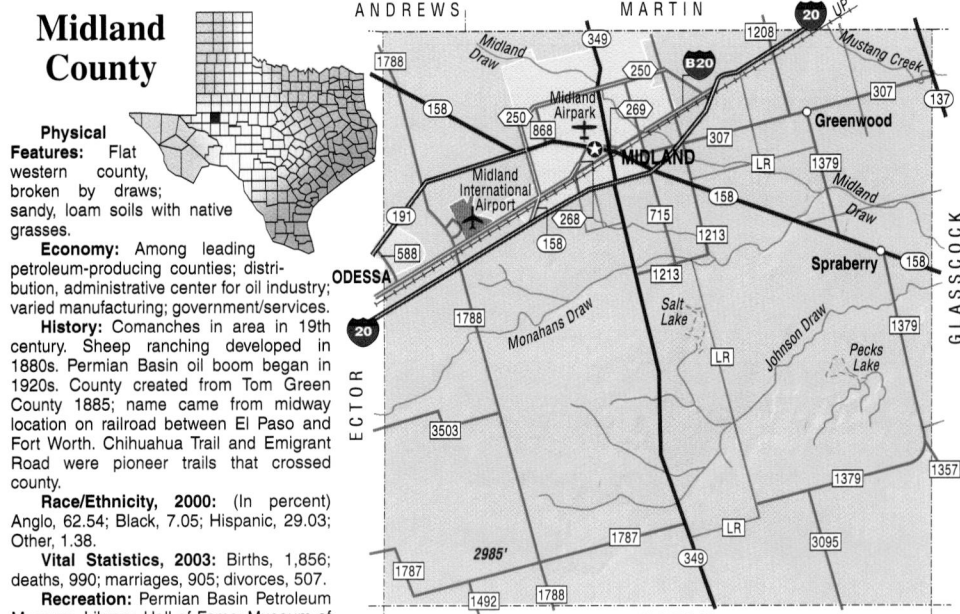

of the Arts in May; polo club, Texas League baseball.

Part [1,042] of **Odessa**.

Population	120,344
Change fm 2000	3.7
Area (sq. mi.)	901.97
Land Area (sq. mi.)	900.25
Altitude (ft.)	2,600-2,985
Rainfall (in.)	14.80
Jan. mean min.	29.6
July mean max.	94.3
Civ. Labor	64,873
Unemployed	3.7
Wages	$466,005,574
Av. Weekly Wage	$643.85
Prop. Value	$5,966,414,251
Retail Sales	$1,653,320,036

For explanation of sources, abbreviations and symbols, see p. 167 and foldout map.

Milam County

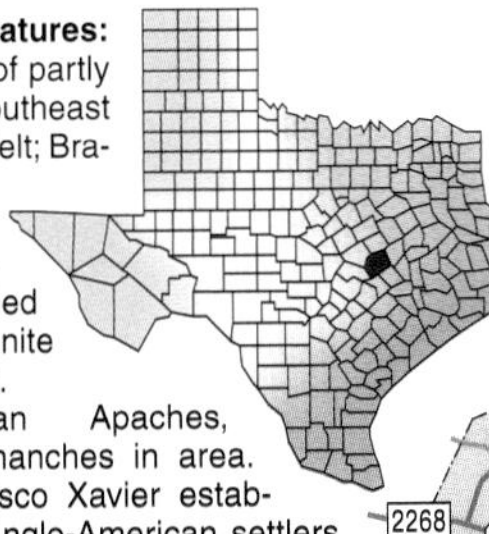

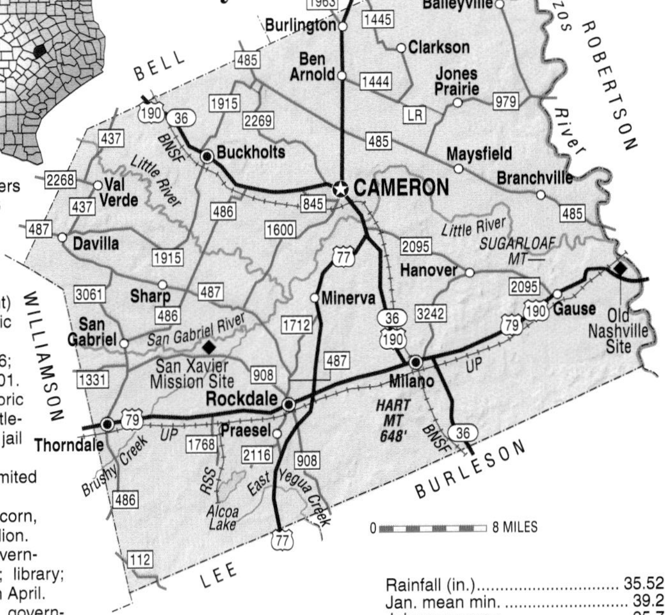

Physical Features:
East central county of partly level Blackland; southeast rolling to Post Oak Belt; Brazos, Little rivers.

Economy:
Aluminum manufacturing; other varied manufacturing; lignite mining; agribusiness.

History: Lipan Apaches, Tonkawas and Comanches in area. Mission San Francisco Xavier established in 1745-48. Anglo-American settlers arrived in 1834. County created 1836 from municipality named for Ben Milam, a leader who died at the battle for San Antonio in December 1835; organized 1837.

Race/Ethnicity, 2000: (In percent) Anglo, 69.64; Black, 11.01; Hispanic 18.63; Other, 0.72.

Vital Statistics, 2003: Births, 366; deaths, 280; marriages, 160; divorces, 101.

Recreation: Fishing, hunting; historic sites include Fort Sullivan, Indian battle-grounds, mission sites; museum in old jail at Cameron.

Minerals: Large lignite deposits; limited oil, natural gas production.

Agriculture: Cattle, poultry, hay, corn, sorghum, cotton. Market value $72.4 million.

CAMERON (5,909) county seat; government/services; manufacturing; hospital; library; restored courthouse; dewberry festival in April.

Rockdale (5,910) aluminum plant, government/services; hospital; juvenile detention center; Culturefest in September.

Other towns include: **Buckholts** (406); **Burlington** (100); **Davilla** (191); **Gause** (425); **Milano** (416); **Thorndale** (1,349) market center.

Population	25,204
Change fm 2000	4.0
Area (sq. mi.)	1,021.67
Land Area (sq. mi.)	1,016.71
Altitude (ft.)	250-648
Rainfall (in.)	35.52
Jan. mean min.	39.2
July mean max.	95.7
Civ. Labor	9,843
Unemployed	5.8
Wages	$49,519,113
Av. Weekly Wage	$587.20
Prop. Value	$1,642,096,538
Retail Sales	$162,680,337

Mills County

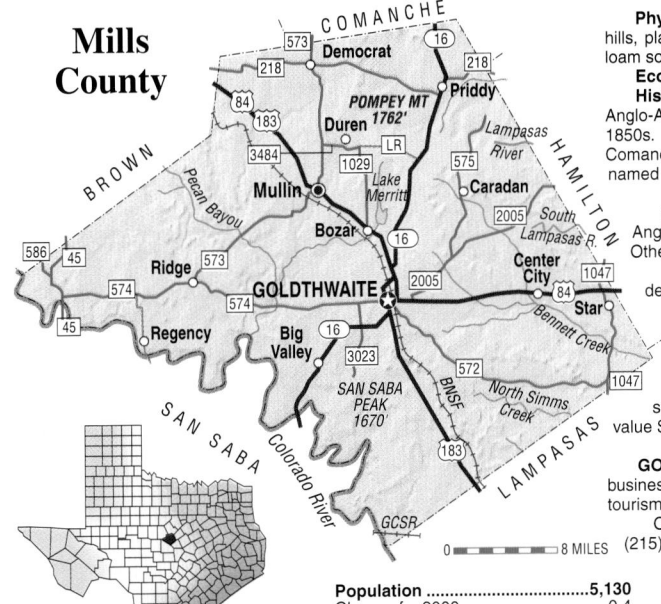

Physical Features: West central county of hills, plateau draining to Colorado River; sandy, loam soils.

Economy: Agribusiness, hunting leases.

History: Apache-Comanche area of conflict. Anglo-Americans and a few Germans settled in 1850s. County created 1887 from Brown, Comanche, Hamilton, Lampasas counties; named for pioneer jurist John T. Mills.

Race/Ethnicity, 2000: (In percent) Anglo, 85.32; Black, 1.30; Hispanic, 13.03; Other, 0.35.

Vital Statistics, 2003: Births, 42; deaths, 78; marriages, 33; divorces, 15.

Recreation: Fishing; deer, dove and turkey hunting; Regency suspension bridge; rangeland recreation.

Minerals: Not significant.

Agriculture: Beef cattle, goats, sheep; some irrigation for pecans. Market value $22 million.

GOLDTHWAITE (1,730) county seat; agribusiness, livestock center; light manufacturing, tourism; barbecue & goat cook-off in April.

Other towns include: **Mullin** (163); **Priddy** (215); **Star** (85).

Population	5,130
Change fm 2000	-0.4
Area (sq. mi.)	749.89
Land Area (sq. mi.)	748.11
Altitude (ft.)	1,200-1,762
Rainfall (in.)	28.78
Jan. mean min.	35.2
July mean max.	92.0
Civ. Labor	2,712
Unemployed	1.8
Wages	$9,973,875
Av. Weekly Wage	$456.14
Prop. Value	$682,773,630
Retail Sales	$55,516,537

For explanation of sources, abbreviations and symbols, see p. 167 and foldout map.

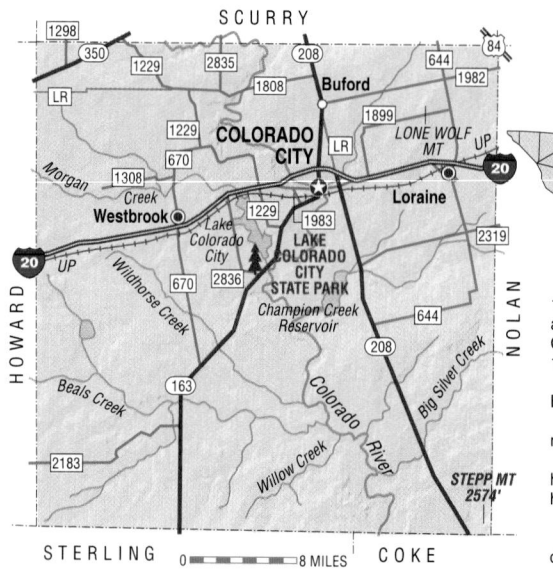

Population 9,402
Change fm 2000 ....-3.1
Area (sq. mi.) 915.90
Land Area (sq. mi.)..................910.04
Altitude (ft.) 2,000-2,574
Rainfall (in.) 19.43
Jan. mean min. 27.0

July mean max. 95.9
Civ. Labor 3,456
Unemployed 4.3
Wages $14,801,058
Av. Weekly Wage..................$499.58
Prop. Value.....................$477,607,203
Retail Sales $38,778,553

Mitchell County

Physical Features: Rolling, draining to Colorado and tributaries; sandy, red, dark soils; Lake Colorado City and Champion Creek Reservoir.

Economy: Government/services; agribusiness, oil, some manufacturing.

History: Jumano Indians in area; Comanches arrived about 1780. Anglo-American settlers arrived in late 1870s after Comanches were forced into Indian Territory. County created 1876 from Bexar District; organized 1881; named for pioneer brothers Asa and Eli Mitchell.

Race/Ethnicity, 2000: (In percent) Anglo, 55.39; Black, 12.79; Hispanic, 31.03; Other, 0.79.

Vital Statistics, 2003: Births, 100; deaths, 128; marriages, 48; divorces, 26.

Recreation: Lake activities; state park; museums, hunting; railhead arts, crafts show, Colorado City playhouse.

Minerals: Oil.

Agriculture: Cotton principal crop, grains also produced. Cattle, sheep, goats, hogs raised. Market value $12.3 million.

COLORADO CITY (4,026) county seat; prisons; varied manufacturing; tourism; electric service center; hospital; bluegrass festival.

Other towns include: **Loraine** (608) and **Westbrook** (185), trade centers.

Montague County

Physical Features: Rolling, draining to tributaries of Trinity, Red rivers; sandy loams, red, black soils; Lake Nocona, Lake Amon G. Carter.

Economy: Agribusiness; oil production; varied manufacturing; government/services.

History: Kiowas and Wichitas who allied with Comanches. Anglo-American settlements developed in 1850s. County created from Cooke County 1857, organized 1858; named for pioneer Daniel Montague.

Race/Ethnicity, 2000: (In percent) Anglo, 93.42; Black, 0.17; Hispanic, 5.41; Other, 1.00.

Vital Statistics, 2003: Births, 256; deaths, 279; marriages, 144; divorces, 60.

Recreation: Lake activities; quail, turkey, deer hunting; scenic drives; museums; historical sites; Chisholm Trail Days in September, Jim Bowie Days in June.

Minerals: Oil, rock, limestone.

Agriculture: Beef, hay, wheat, dairies, pecans, peaches, melons. Market value $31.9 million.

MONTAGUE (400) county seat.

BOWIE (5,609) varied manufacturing, livestock, hospital, library; Second Monday trade day.

NOCONA (3,286) athletic goods, boot manufacturing; hospital; Fun Day each May.

Other towns include: **Forestburg** (50); **Ringgold** (100); **Saint Jo** (999) farm center; Pioneer Days on last weekend in May, saloon; **Sunset** (350).

Population 19,503
Change fm 2000 ....2.0
Area (sq. mi.) 938.44
Land Area (sq. mi.) 930.66

Altitude (ft.).......................... 750-1,318
Rainfall (in.)...................................33.72
Jan. mean min. 28.3
July mean max........................94.7
Civ. Labor...............................7,396

Unemployed 4.7
Wages $25,224,700
Av. Weekly Wage...................$445.24
Prop. Value $1,367,883,212
Retail Sales $144,970,483

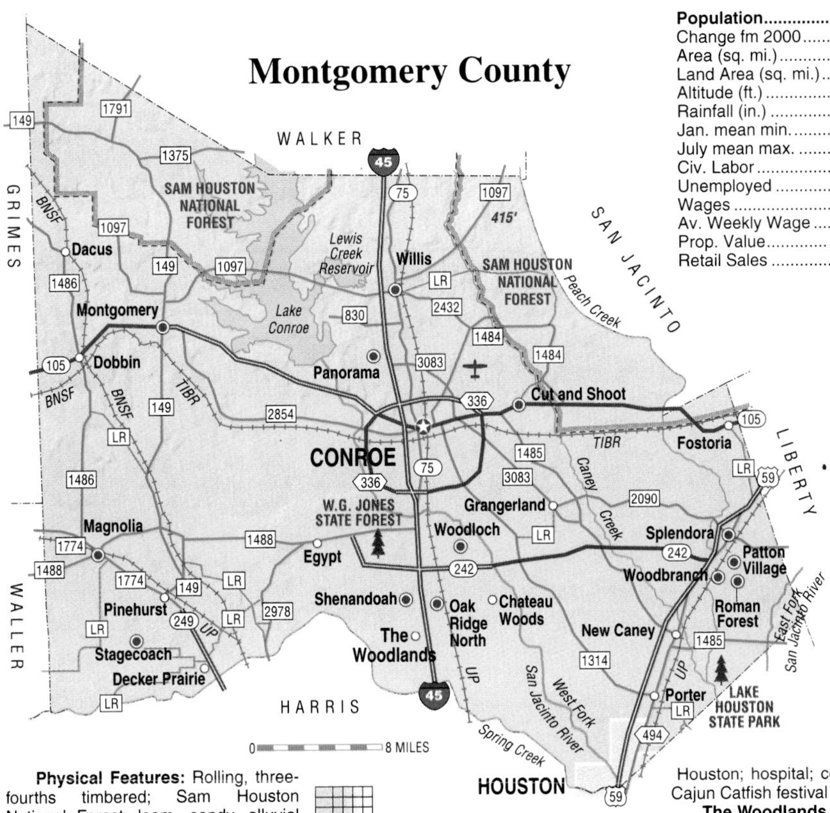

Montgomery County

Population............................**362,382**
Change fm 2000........................ 23.4
Area (sq. mi.)........................ 1,076.81
Land Area (sq. mi.)............... 1,044.03
Altitude (ft.) 50-415
Rainfall (in.) 49.32
Jan. mean min............................ 40.0
July mean max. 94.3
Civ. Labor 162,464
Unemployed 5.0
Wages $785,946,991
Av. Weekly Wage $660.40
Prop. Value............. $20,162,933,712
Retail Sales $3,952,274,225

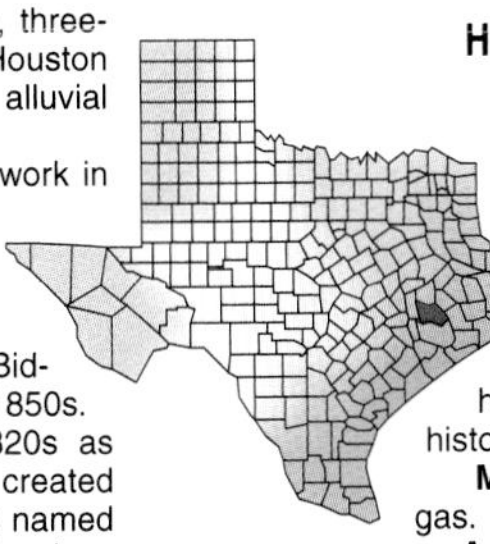

Physical Features: Rolling, three-fourths timbered; Sam Houston National Forest; loam, sandy, alluvial soils.

Economy: Many residents work in Houston; lumber, oil production; government/services; part of Houston metropolitan area.

History: Orcoquisacs and Bidais, removed from area by 1850s. Anglo-Americans arrived in 1820s as part of Austin's colony. County created 1837 from Washington County; named for Richard Montgomery, American Revolution general.

Race/Ethnicity, 2000: (In percent) Anglo, 82.09; Black, 3.57; Hispanic, 12.65; Other, 1.69.

Vital Statistics, 2003: Births, 5,166; deaths, 2,260; marriages, 2,595; divorces, 1,647.

Recreation: Hunting, fishing; Lake Conroe activities; national and state forests; hiking, boating, horseback riding; historic sites.

Minerals: Natural gas.

Agriculture: Greenhouse crops, forage, beef cattle, horses. Also, Christmas trees and blueberries. Market value $20.1 million. Timber is primary industry.

CONROE (42,113) county seat; retail/wholesale center; government/services; manufacturing; commuters to Houston; hospital; community college; Cajun Catfish festival in October.

The Woodlands (61,187) commuters to Houston, research and biotech businesses, hospital, parks; concerts, festivals at Mitchell Pavilion.

Other towns include: **Cut and Shoot** (1,274); **Dobbin** (200); **Grangerland** (NA); **Magnolia** (1,249); **Montgomery** (545) historic buildings, antique stores; **New Caney** (3,500); **Oak Ridge North** (3,312); **Panorama** (2,165); **Patton Village** (1,527); **Pinehurst** (4,747); **Porter** (2,000); **Porter Heights** (1,575); **Roman Forest** (2,401); **Shenandoah** (1,600); **Splendora** (1,419); **Stagecoach** (512); **Willis** (4,678); **Woodbranch** (1,376); **Woodloch** (260).

Also, part [458] of **Houston**.

For explanation of sources, abbreviations and symbols, see p. 167 and foldout map.

The Walden golf course at Lake Conroe. File photo.

Moore County

Physical Features: Northern Panhandle county; flat to rolling, broken by creeks; sandy loams; lake.

Economy: Varied agribusiness, petroleum, natural gas.

History: Comanches, removed to Indian Territory in 1874-75; ranching began soon afterward. Farming developed after 1910. Oil boom in 1920s. County created 1876 from Bexar District; organized 1892; named for Republic of Texas navy commander E.W. Moore.

Race/Ethnicity, 2000: (In percent) Anglo, 50.54; Black, 0.48; Hispanic, 47.50; Other, 1.48.

Vital Statistics, 2003: Births, 459; deaths, 130; marriages, 162; divorces, 104.

Recreation: Lake Meredith activities; pheasant, deer, quail hunting; historical museum; arts center; free overnight RV park; Dogie Days in June.

Minerals: Oil and gas.

Agriculture: Fed beef, corn, wheat, stocker cattle, sorghum, cotton, soybeans, sunflowers. Market value $303.3 million. Irrigation of 162,000 acres.

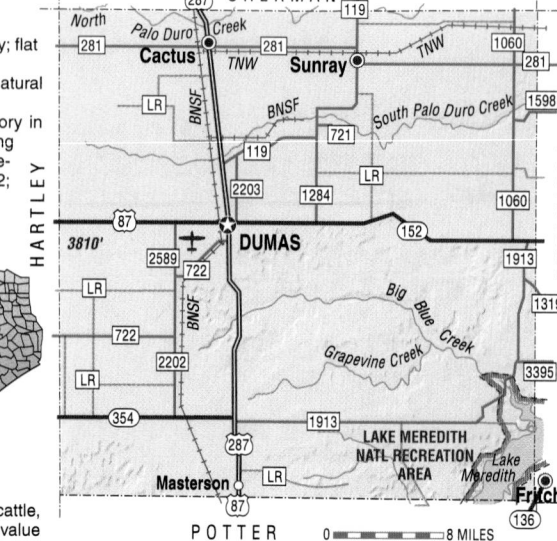

DUMAS (13,809) county seat; tourist, retail trade center; varied agribusiness; hospital, hospice, retirement complex.

Other towns include: **Cactus** (2,732), **Sunray** (1,955). Small part of **Fritch**.

Population	20,333	July mean max.	91.7
Change fm 2000	1.1	Civ. Labor	9,153
Area (sq. mi.)	909.61	Unemployed	3.9
Land Area (sq. mi.)	899.66	Wages	$62,966,491
Altitude (ft.)	2,900-3,810	Av. Weekly Wage	$557.69
Rainfall (in.)	17.75	Prop. Value	$1,785,645,720
Jan. mean min.	20.8	Retail Sales	$122,682,058

Morris County

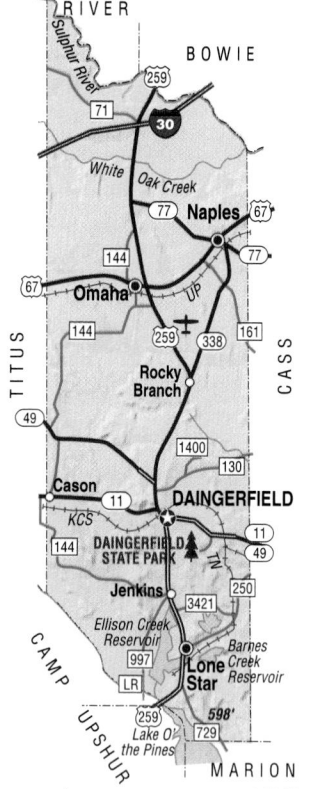

Physical Features: East Texas county of forested hills; drains to streams, lakes.

Economy: Steel manufacturing, agriculture, timber, government/services.

History: Caddo Indians until 1790s. Kickapoo and other tribes in area 1820s-30s. Anglo-American settlement began in mid-1830s. Antebellum slaveholding area. County named for legislator-jurist W.W. Morris; created from Titus County and organized in 1875.

Race/Ethnicity, 2000: (In percent) Anglo, 71.26; Black, 24.26; Hispanic, 3.66; Other, 0.82.

Vital Statistics, 2003: Births, 148; deaths, 187; marriages, 100; divorces, 58.

Recreation: Activities on Lake O' the Pines, small lakes; fishing, hunting; state park.

Minerals: Iron ore.

Agriculture: Beef cattle, broiler production; hay. Market value $20.1 million. Timber industry significant.

DAINGERFIELD (2,404) county seat; varied manufacturing; library, city park; Northeast Texas Community College; Captain Daingerfield Day in October.

Other towns include: **Cason** (173); **Lone Star** (1,604) oil-field equipment manufactured, catfish farming, Starfest in September; **Naples** (1,369) trailer manufacturing, livestock, watermelon festival in July; **Omaha** (987), retail center, government/services, commuters.

Population	13,079
Change fm 2000	0.2
Area (sq. mi.)	258.64
Land Area (sq. mi.)	254.51
Altitude (ft.)	228-598
Rainfall (in.)	46.76
Jan. mean min.	33.7
July mean max.	95.0
Civ. Labor	6,272
Unemployed	7.0
Wages	$38,857,706
Av. Weekly Wage	$706.63
Prop. Value	$959,955,982
Retail Sales	$65,266,928

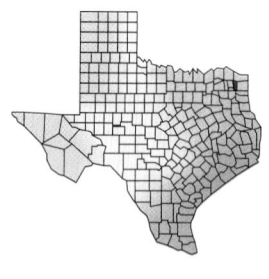

For explanation of sources, abbreviations and symbols, see p. 167 and foldout map.

Motley County

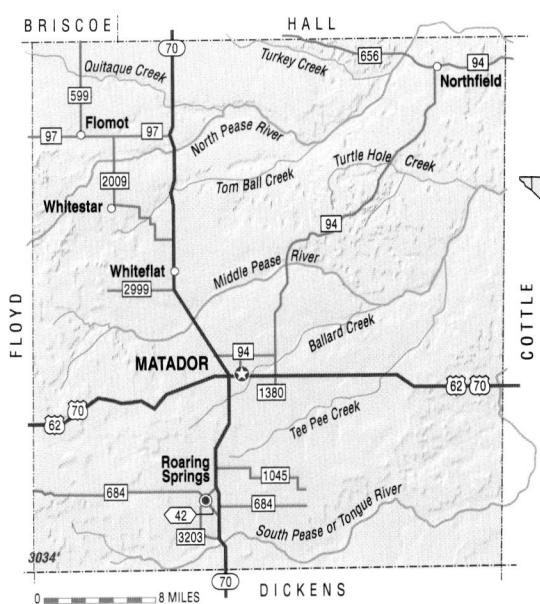

Physical Features: Western county just below Caprock; rough terrain, broken by Pease tributaries; sandy to red clay soils.

Economy: Government/services; ranching; cotton; light manufacturing; hunting.

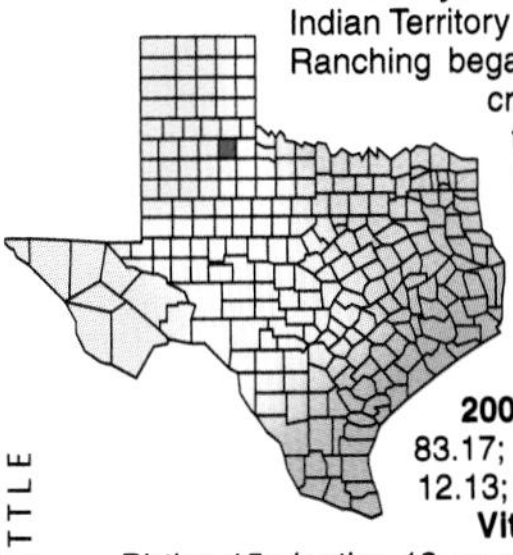

History: Comanches, removed to Indian Territory by U.S. Army in 1874-75. Ranching began in late 1870s. County created out of Bexar District 1876; organized 1891; named for Dr. J.W. Mottley, signer of Texas Declaration of Independence (name misspelled in statute).

Race/Ethnicity, 2000: (In percent) Anglo, 83.17; Black, 4.00; Hispanic, 12.13; Other, 0.70.

Vital Statistics, 2003: Births, 15; deaths, 18; marriages, 10; divorces, 8.

Recreation: Quail, dove, turkey, deer hunting; Matador Ranch headquarters; spring-fed pool at Roaring Springs; camp grounds; settlers reunion in August.

Minerals: Minimal.

Agriculture: Beef cattle, cotton, peanuts, hunting leases. Also vegetables, wheat, hay produced. Extensive irrigation. Market value $9.9 million.

MATADOR (691) county seat; farm trade center; museum; pony express days in June.

Other towns include: **Flomot** (181) and **Roaring Springs** (250).

Population	1,307	Jan. mean min	27.3
Change fm 2000	-8.3	July mean max	94.8
Area (sq. mi.)	989.81	Civ. Labor	668
Land Area (sq. mi.)	989.38	Unemployed	2.9
Altitude (ft.)	1,900-3,034	Wages	$1,806,882
Rainfall (in.)	22.90	Av. Weekly Wage	$386.09

Prop. Value $138,525,736
Retail Sales..........................$8,126,552

For explanation of sources, abbreviations and symbols, see p. 167 and foldout map.

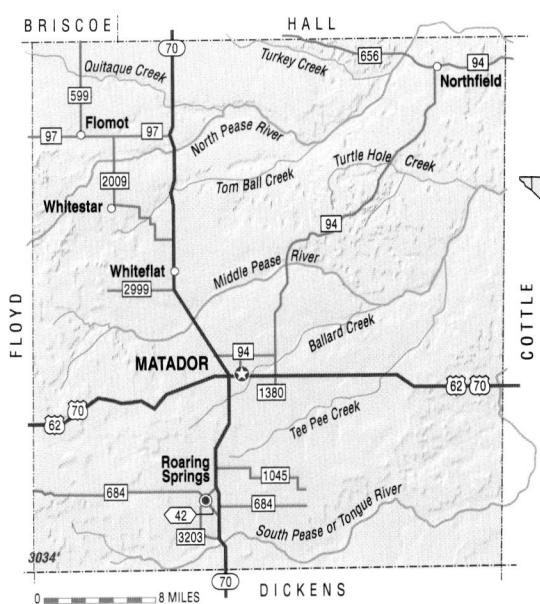

Downtown Matador, a farm trade center and county seat of Motley County. Texas Almanac photo.

Nacogdoches County

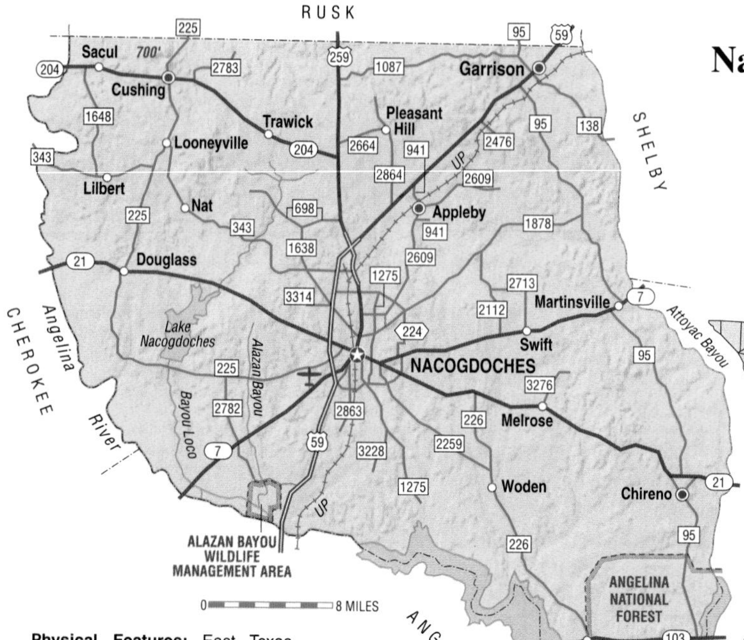

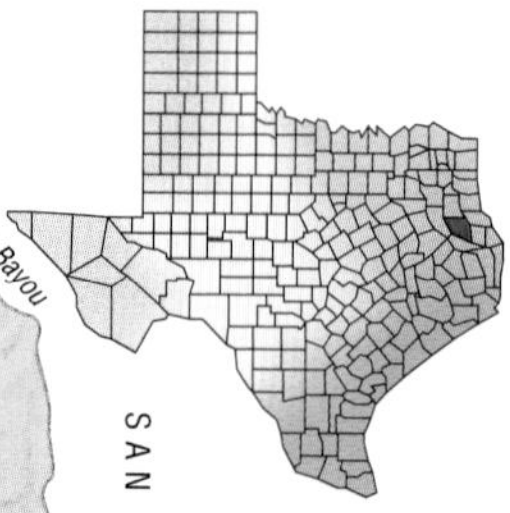

Map labels:

RUSK

225 · Sacul 700' · 204 · 2783 · 259 · 1087 · Garrison · 95 · 59

Cushing

1648 · Trawick · Pleasant Hill · 95 · 138 · SHELBY

343 · Looneyville · 204 · 2664 · 941 · 2476

Lilbert · 2864 · 2609 · UP

225 · Nat · 698 · Appleby · 1878

21 · Douglass · 343 · 1638 · 941 · 2609

3314 · 1275 · 2713 · Martinsville · 7 · Attoyac Bayou

CHEROKEE · Angelina River · Lake Nacogdoches · 3314 · 2112 · Swift · 95

224 · NACOGDOCHES · 3276

Alazan Bayou · 225 · 2782 · Bayou Loco · 2863 · 226 · Melrose · SAN AUGUSTINE

7 · 59 · 3228 · 2259

1275 · Woden · Chireno · 21

ALAZAN BAYOU WILDLIFE MANAGEMENT AREA · 226 · 95

UP

0 — 8 MILES

ANGELINA · ANGELINA NATIONAL FOREST · 103 · Etoile

226 · Sam Rayburn Reservoir

Physical Features: East Texas county on divide between streams; hilly; two-thirds forested; red, gray, sandy soils; Sam Rayburn Reservoir.

Economy: Agribusiness; timber; manufacturing; education; tourism.

History: Caddo tribes, joined by displaced Cherokees in 1820s. Indians moved west of Brazos by 1840. Spanish missions established in 1716. Spanish settlers in mid-1700s. Anglo-Americans arrived in 1820s. Original county of Republic 1836, organized 1837.

Race/Ethnicity, 2000: (In percent) Anglo, 70.83; Black, 16.80; Hispanic, 11.25; Other, 1.12.

Vital Statistics, 2003: Births, 921; deaths, 546; marriages, 550; divorces, 107.

Recreation: Lake, river activities; Stephen F. Austin State University events; Angelina National Forest; historic sites; major tourist attractions include the Old Stone Fort, pioneer homes, museums; Piney Woods Fair, Blueberry Festival in June.

Minerals: First Texas oil found here, 1866; gas, oil, clay, stone.

Agriculture: A leading poultry-producing county; beef cattle raised. Market value $198 million. Substantial timber sold.

Population	**60,249**
Change fm 2000	1.8
Area (sq. mi.)	981.33
Land Area (sq. mi.)	946.77
Altitude (ft.)	164-700
Rainfall (in.)	48.40
Jan. mean min.	36.0
July mean max.	94.0
Civ. Labor	26,893
Unemployed	4.4
Wages	$142,396,296
Av. Weekly Wage	$483.94
Prop. Value	$2,914,041,350
Retail Sales	$642,185,664

NACOGDOCHES (30,468) county seat; varied manufacturing; lumber mills, wood products; trade center; hospitals; Stephen F. Austin State University.

Other towns include: **Appleby** (451), **Chireno** (406), **Cushing** (635), **Douglass** (380), **Etoile** (700), **Garrison** (846), **Martinsville** (350), **Sacul** (150), **Woden** (400).

An autumn day along FM 225 near Cushing. Texas Almanac photo.

Navarro County

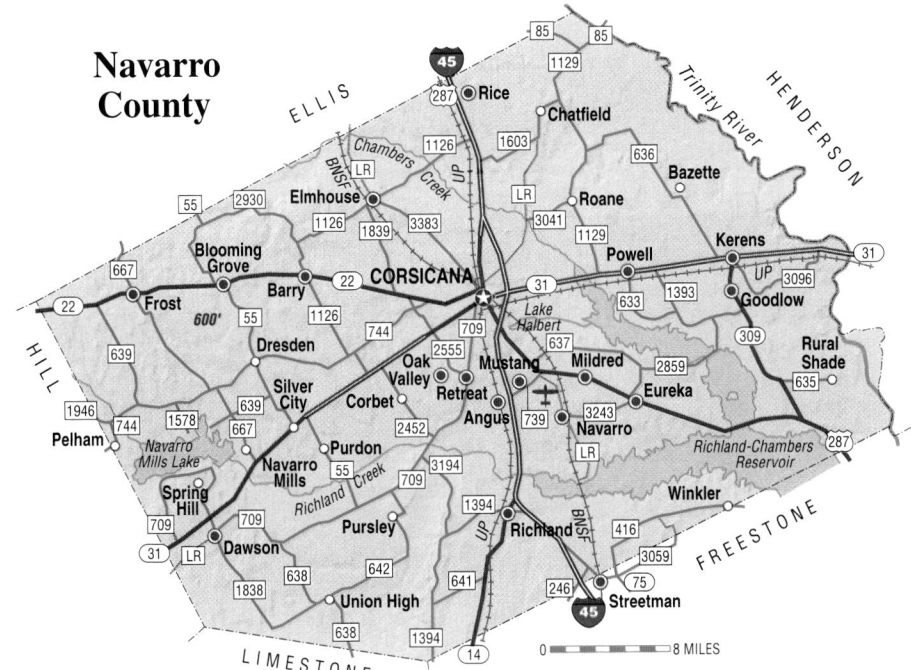

Physical Features: North central county of level Blackland, some rolling; drains to creeks, Trinity River; Navarro Mills Lake, Richland-Chambers Reservoir.

Economy: Diversified manufacturing; agribusinesses; oil-field operations, distribution.

History: Kickapoo and Comanche area. Anglo-Americans settled in late 1830s. Antebellum slave-holding area. County created from Robertson County, organized in 1846; named for Republic of Texas leader José Antonio Navarro.

Race/Ethnicity, 2000: (In percent) Anglo, 66.12; Black, 16.96; Hispanic, 15.76; Other, 1.16.

Vital Statistics, 2003: Births, 704; deaths, 494; marriages, 439; divorces, 223.

Recreation: Lake activities; Pioneer Village; historic buildings; youth exposition, Derrick Days in April.

Minerals: Longest continuous Texas oil flow; more than 200 million barrels produced since 1895; natural gas, sand and gravel also produced.

Agriculture: Beef cattle, cotton, sorghum, corn, wheat, herbs, horses, dairies. Market value $36.5 million.

CORSICANA (26,014) county seat; major distribution center, pecans, candy, fruitcakes; varied manufacturing; agribusiness; hospital; Navarro College; Texas Youth Commission facility.

Other towns include: **Angus** (352); **Barry** (207); **Blooming Grove** (868); **Chatfield** (40); **Dawson** (867); **Em-** house (162); **Eureka** (357); **Frost** (676); **Goodlow** (279).

Also, **Kerens** (1,722) some manufacturing, nature tourism; **Mildred** (407); **Mustang** (54); **Navarro** (196); **Oak Valley** (421); **Powell** (112); **Purdon** (133); **Retreat** (343); **Rice** (867); **Richland** (301).

Population	48,243
Change fm 2000	6.9
Area (sq. mi.)	1,086.17
Land Area (sq. mi.)	1,070.66
Altitude (ft.)	250-600
Rainfall (in.)	39.48
Jan. mean min.	34.0
July mean max.	94.5
Civ. Labor	20,979
Unemployed	6.0
Wages	$101,557,078
Av. Weekly Wage	$491.39
Prop. Value	$2,037,657,373
Retail Sales	$395,266,785

Historic Temple Beth-El in Corsicana is now a civic center. File photo.

For explanation of sources, abbreviations and symbols, see p. 167 and foldout map.

Newton County

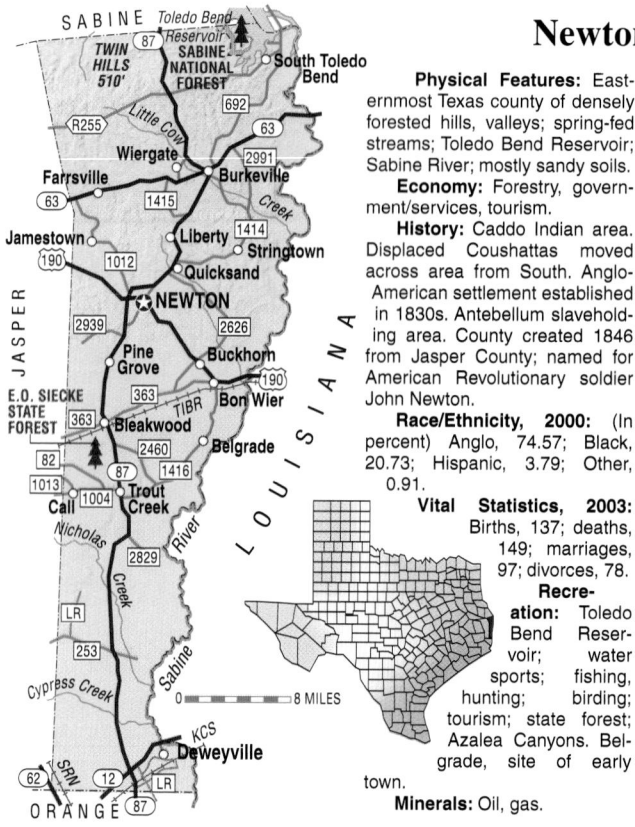

Physical Features: Easternmost Texas county of densely forested hills, valleys; spring-fed streams; Toledo Bend Reservoir; Sabine River; mostly sandy soils.

Economy: Forestry, government/services, tourism.

History: Caddo Indian area. Displaced Coushattas moved across area from South. Anglo-American settlement established in 1830s. Antebellum slaveholding area. County created 1846 from Jasper County; named for American Revolutionary soldier John Newton.

Race/Ethnicity, 2000: (In percent) Anglo, 74.57; Black, 20.73; Hispanic, 3.79; Other, 0.91.

Vital Statistics, 2003: Births, 137; deaths, 149; marriages, 97; divorces, 78.

Recreation: Toledo Bend Reservoir; water sports; fishing, hunting; birding; tourism; state forest; Azalea Canyons. Belgrade, site of early town.

Minerals: Oil, gas.

Agriculture: Cattle, hay, nursery crops, vegetables, goats, hogs. Market value $1.3 million. Hunting leases. Major forestry area.

NEWTON (2,504) county seat; lumber manufacturing; plywood mill; private prison unit; tourist center; genealogical library, museum; Wild Azalea festival in March.

Deweyville (1,126) power plant; commercial center for forestry, farming area.

Other towns include: **Bon Wier** (475); **Burkeville** (515); **Call** (170); **South Toledo Bend** (532); **Wiergate** (461).

Population	14,345
Change fm 2000	-4.8
Area (sq. mi.)	939.51
Land Area (sq. mi.)	932.69
Altitude (ft.)	23-510
Rainfall (in.)	54.90
Jan. mean min.	35.0
July mean max.	94.0
Civ. Labor	5,656
Unemployed	12.9
Wages	$10,841,173
Av. Weekly Wage	$449.08
Prop. Value	$1,082,354,155
Retail Sales	$37,574,502

Nolan County

Physical Features: On divide between Brazos, Colorado watersheds; mostly red sandy loams, some waxy, sandy soils; lakes.

Economy: Varied manufacturing; oil and gas production; ranching;.

History: Anglo-American settlement began in late 1870s. County created from Bexar, Young districts 1876; organized 1881; named for adventurer Philip Nolan, who was killed near Waco.

Race/Ethnicity, 2000: (In percent) Anglo, 66.64; Black, 4.85; Hispanic, 28.04; Other, 0.47.

Vital Statistics, 2003: Births, 221; deaths, 200; marriages, 123; divorces, 71.

Recreation: Lakes; hunting; rattlesnake roundup in March; pioneer museum; Soap Box Derby in June.

Minerals: Oil, gas, sand, gravel.

Agriculture: Cotton is the principal crop; wheat, sorghum also raised. Beef cattle and dairies. Market value $13.4 million. Twenty percent irrigated.

SWEETWATER (10,859) county seat; varied manufacturing, tourism, oil and gas, ranching; hospital; Texas State Technical College.

Other towns include: **Blackwell** (355, partly in Coke County), Oak Creek Reservoir to south; **Maryneal** (61); **Nolan** (47); **Roscoe** (1,312).

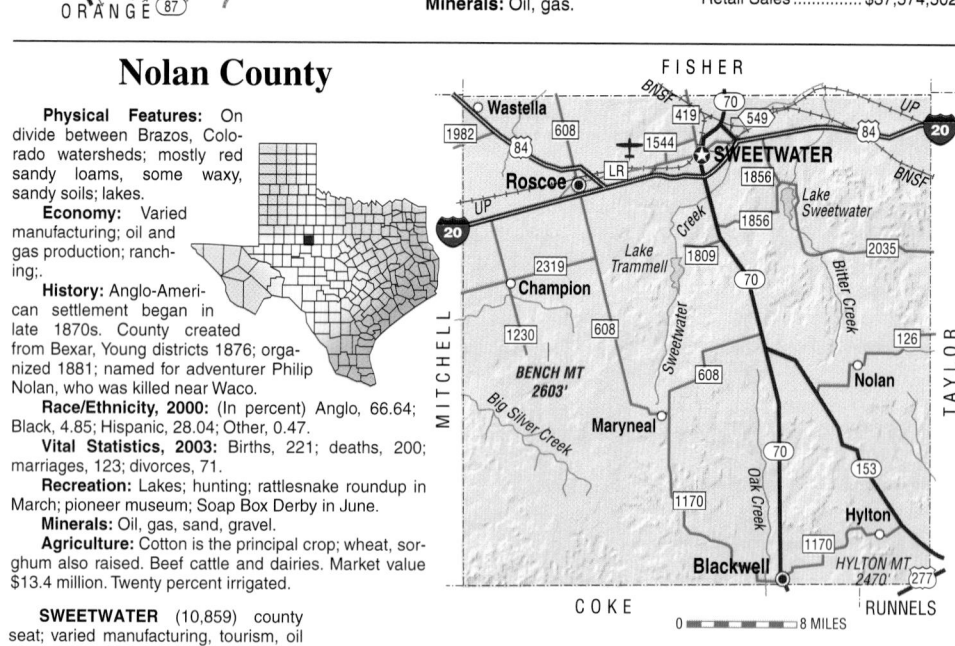

Population	15,129
Change fm 2000	-4.3
Area (sq. mi.)	913.93
Land Area (sq. mi.)	911.98
Altitude (ft.)	1,990-2,603
Rainfall (in.)	23.54
Jan. mean min.	28.9
July mean max.	93.8
Civ. Labor	7,245
Unemployed	4.7
Wages	$36,727,548
Av. Weekly Wage	$486.68
Prop. Value	$933,732,572
Retail Sales	$138,719,490

Nueces County

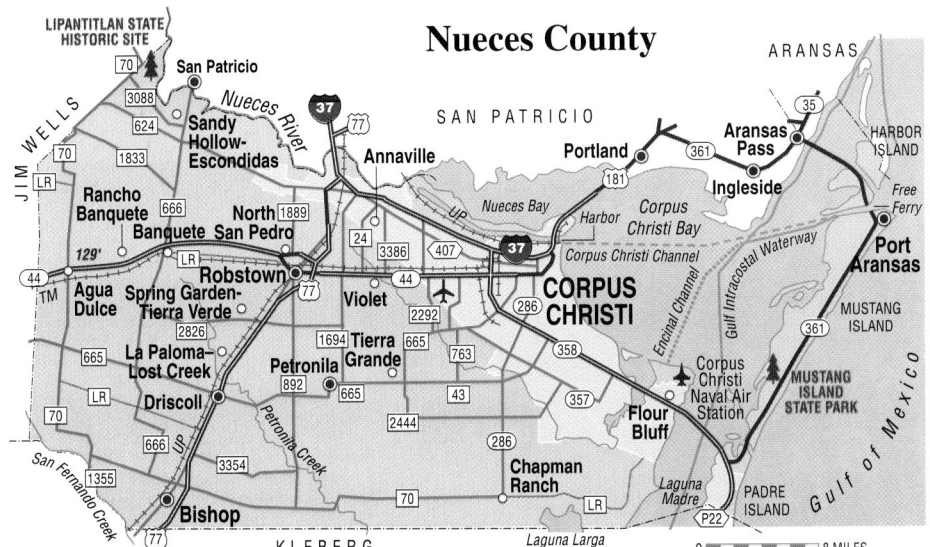

Physical Features: Southern Gulf Coast county; flat, rich soils, broken by bays, Nueces River, Petronila Creek; includes Mustang Island, north tip of Padre Island.

Economy: Diversified economy includes petroleum processing and production; deepwater port facilities; agriculture; tourism; conventions; coastal shipping; manufacturing; military complex.

History: Coahuiltecan, Karankawa and other tribes who succumbed to disease or fled by 1840s. Spanish settlers arrived in 1760s. Settlers from Ireland arrived around 1830. County name is Spanish for nuts; county named for river; created 1846 out of San Patricio County.

Race/Ethnicity, 2000: (In percent) Anglo, 38.32; Black, 4.24; Hispanic, 55.78; Other, 1.66.

Vital Statistics, 2003: Births, 4,908; deaths, 2,534; marriages, 1,266; divorces, 1,483.

Recreation: Major resort area; fishing, water sports, birding; Padre Island National Seashore; Mustang Island State Park; Lipantitlan State Historic Site; Art Museum of South Texas,

Corpus Christi Museum of Science and History; Texas State Aquarium; various metropolitan events; greyhound race track.

Minerals: Sand and gravel, oil and gas.

Agriculture: Grain sorghum (a leader in sales, acreage); cotton, corn, hay, sunflowers, canola, beef cattle. Market value $62.6 million.

CORPUS CHRISTI (278,708) county seat; seaport, naval bases; varied manufacturing; petroleum processing; tourism; hospitals; museums; Army depot; Texas A&M University-Corpus Christi; Del Mar College; Buccaneer Days in late April; replicas of Columbus' ships on display, USS Lexington museum.

Port Aransas (3,549) deepwater port, tourism, Coast Guard base, fishing industry; University of Texas Marine Science Institute; Celebration of Whooping Cranes in Febuary.

Robstown (12,419) market center for oil, farm area; Cottonfest in October; Fiesta Mexicana in March.

Other towns include: **Agua Dulce**

(697); **Banquete** (582); **Bishop** (3,145) petrochemicals, agriculture, pharmaceuticals, plastics; nature trail; Old Tyme Faire in April; **Chapman Ranch** (100); **Driscoll** (818); **La Paloma-Lost Creek** (307); **North San Pedro** (890); **Petronila** (81); **Rancho Banquete** (470); **Sandy Hollow-Escondidas** (407); **Spring Garden-Tierra Verde** (678); **Tierra Grande** (362).

Also, part of **San Patricio** and a small part of **Aransas Pass** on Harbor Island; both cities mostly in San Patricio County.

Flour Bluff and **Annaville** are now part of Corpus Christi.

Population	317,513
Change fm 2000	1.2
Area (sq. mi.)	1,166.42
Land Area (sq. mi.)	835.82
Altitude (ft.)	sea level-129
Rainfall (in.)	32.26
Jan. mean min.	46.2
July mean max.	93.2
Civ. Labor	152,936
Unemployed	6.2
Wages	$1,135,606,322
Av. Weekly Wage	$612.23
Prop. Value	$14,805,470,429
Retail Sales	$3,502,617,616

For explanation of sources, abbreviations and symbols, see p. 167 and foldout map.

The USS Lexington Museum sets next to the Texas State Aquarium in Corpus Christi. Texas Almanac photo.

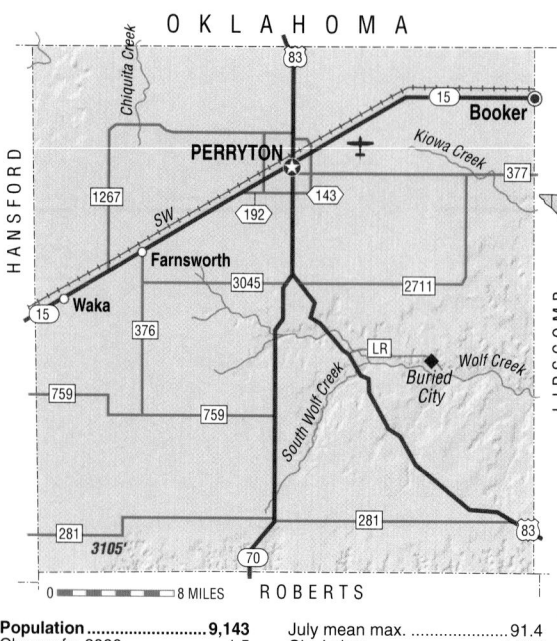

Ochiltree County

Physical Features: Panhandle county bordering Oklahoma; level, broken by creeks; deep loam, clay soils.

Economy: Oil and gas; agribusiness, center of large feedlot and swine operations.

History: Apaches, pushed out by Comanches in late 1700s. Comanches removed to Indian Territory in 1874–75. Ranching developed in 1880s; farming after 1900. County created from Bexar District 1876, organized 1889; named for Republic of Texas leader W.B. Ochiltree.

Race/Ethnicity, 2000: (In percent) Anglo, 66.95; Black, 0.11; Hispanic, 31.79; Other, 1.15.

Vital Statistics, 2003: Births, 168; deaths, 78; marriages, 105; divorces, 49.

Recreation: Wolf Creek park; Wheatheart of the Nation celebration in August; Museum of the Plains; Prehistoric settlement site of "Buried City"; pheasant hunting, also deer and dove.

Minerals: Oil, natural gas, caliche.

Agriculture: Cattle, swine, wheat, soybeans, grain sorghum, corn; 80,000 acres irrigated. Market value $241.9 million.

PERRYTON (7,763) county seat; oil and gas, cattle feeding; grain center; hospital; college; convention center.

Other towns include: **Farnsworth** (130); **Waka** (65). Also, **Booker** (1,341, mostly in Lipscomb County).

Population 9,143	July mean max. 91.4
Change fm 2000 .... 1.5	Civ. Labor 4,885
Area (sq. mi.) 918.07	Unemployed 2.0
Land Area (sq. mi.) 917.56	Wages $30,196,266
Altitude (ft.) 2,642-3,105	Av. Weekly Wage $605.21
Rainfall (in.) 20.88	Prop. Value $677,713,549
Jan. mean min. 18.4	Retail Sales $84,933,007

Oldham County

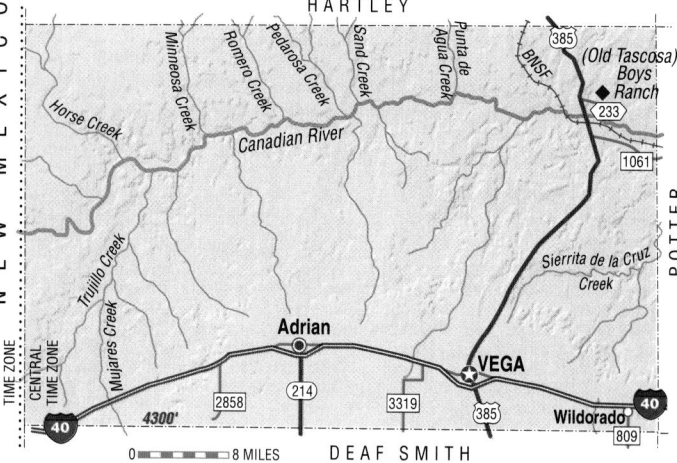

Physical Features: Northwestern Panhandle county; level, broken by Canadian River and tributaries.

Economy: Ranching center.

History: Apaches; followed later by Comanches, Kiowas. U.S. Army removed Indians in 1875. Anglo ranchers and Spanish *pastores* (sheep men) from New Mexico were in area in 1870s. County created 1876 from Bexar District; organized 1880; named for editor-Confederate senator W.S. Oldham.

Race/Ethnicity, 2000: (In percent) Anglo, 85.13; Black, 2.24; Hispanic, 11.03; Other, 1.60.

Vital Statistics, 2003: Births, 23; deaths, 15; marriages, 21; divorces, 5.

Recreation: Old Tascosa with Boot Hill Cemetery nearby, pioneer town;

County Roundup in August; youth cowboy poetry gathering in June; midway point on old Route 66.

Minerals: Sand and gravel, oil, natural gas, stone.

Agriculture: Beef cattle; crops include wheat, grain sorghum. Market value $65.9 million.

VEGA (963) county seat; ranch trade center; museums.

Other towns: **Adrian** (165); **Wildorado** (210). Also, Cal Farley's **Boys Ranch** (470).

Population 2,140	
Change fm 2000 .... -2.1	
Area (sq. mi.) 1,501.42	
Land Area (sq. mi.) 1,500.63	
Altitude (ft.) 3,200-4,300	
Rainfall (in.) 18.18	
Jan. mean min. 20.5	
July mean max. 92.3	
Civ. Labor 1,221	
Unemployed 1.5	
Wages $5,812,283	
Av. Weekly Wage $477.67	
Prop. Value $334,263,626	
Retail Sales $11,205,062	

For explanation of sources, abbreviations and symbols, see p. 167 and foldout map.

Orange County

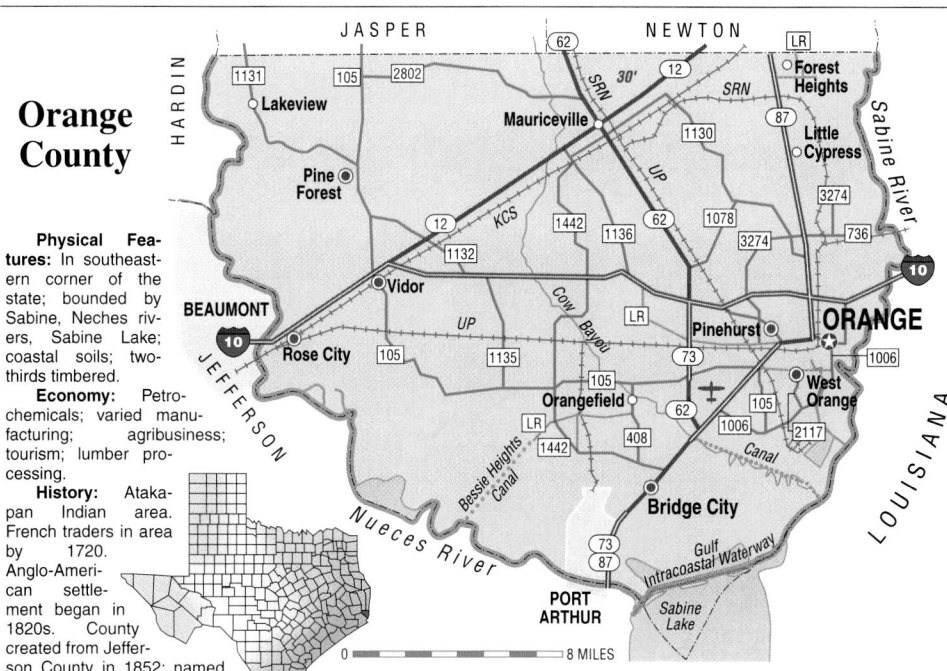

Physical Features: In southeastern corner of the state; bounded by Sabine, Neches rivers, Sabine Lake; coastal soils; two-thirds timbered.

Economy: Petrochemicals; varied manufacturing; agribusiness; tourism; lumber processing.

History: Atakapan Indian area. French traders in area by 1720. Anglo-American settlement began in 1820s. County created from Jefferson County in 1852; named for early orange grove.

Race/Ethnicity, 2000: (In percent) Anglo, 86.54; Black, 8.50; Hispanic, 3.62; Other, 1.34.

Vital Statistics, 2003: Births, 1,114; deaths, 912; marriages, 688; divorces, 363.

Recreation: Fishing, hunting; water sports; birding; county park; museums; historical homes; crawfish and crab festivals in spring.

Minerals: Salt, oil, gas, clays, sand and gravel.

Agriculture: Cattle, hay, Christmas trees and rice are top revenue sources; honey a significant revenue producer; fruits, berries, vegetables. Also, crawfishing. Market value $3.8 million. Hunting leases. Timber important.

ORANGE (18,360) county seat; seaport; petrochemical plants; varied manufacturing; food, timber processing; shipping; hospital, theater, museums; Lamar State College-Orange; Mardi Gras/gumbo festival in February.

Bridge City (8,721) varied manufacturing; ship repair yard; steel fabrication; fish farming; government/services; library; tall bridge and newer suspension bridge over Neches; stop for Monarch butterfly in fall during its migration to Mexico.

Vidor (11,091) steel processing; railroad-car refinishing; library; barbecue festival in April.

Other towns include: **Mauriceville** (2,821); **Orangefield** (725); **Pine Forest** (630); **Pinehurst** (2,231); **Rose City** (499); **West Orange** (3,980).

Population	84,873
Change fm 2000	-0.1
Area (sq. mi.)	379.54
Land Area (sq. mi.)	356.40
Altitude (ft.)	sea level-30
Rainfall (in.)	59.00
Jan. mean min.	41.0
July mean max.	91.0
Civ. Labor	40,935
Unemployed	10.3
Wages	$177,322,149
Av. Weekly Wage	$622.24
Prop. Value	$4,544,228,420
Retail Sales	$682,670,356

The Panhandle landscape at the Ochiltree-Lipscomb county line south of Booker. Texas Almanac photo.

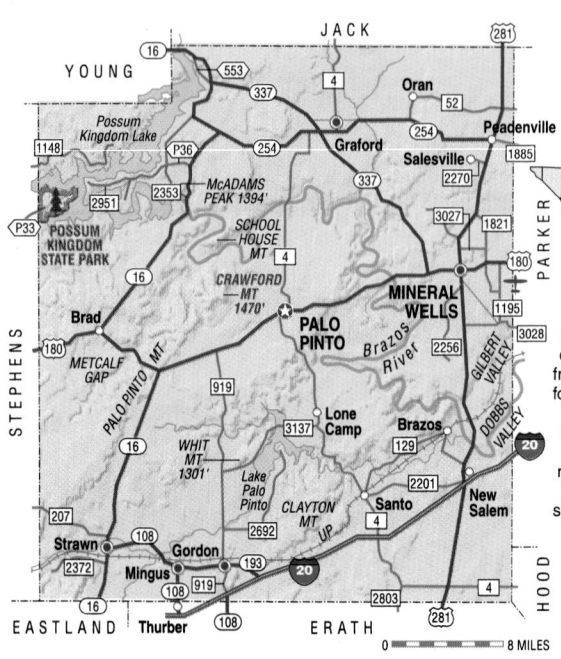

Palo Pinto County

Physical Features: North central county west of Fort Worth; broken, hilly, wooded in parts; Possum Kingdom Lake, Lake Palo Pinto; sandy, gray, black soils.

Economy: Varied manufacturing; tourism; petroleum; agribusiness.

History: Anglo-American ranchers arrived in 1850s. Conflicts between settlers and numerous Indian tribes who had sought refuge on Brazos resulted in Texas Rangers removing Indians in 1856. County created 1856 from Bosque, Navarro counties; organized 1857; named for creek (in Spanish name means painted stick).

Race/Ethnicity, 2000: (In percent) Anglo, 82.77; Black, 2.51; Hispanic, 13.57; Other, 1.15.

Vital Statistics, 2003: Births, 345; deaths, 332; marriages, 235; divorces, 141.

Recreation: Lake activities; hunting, fishing, water sports; state park; Rails to Trails conversion for hiking, biking.

Minerals: Oil, gas, clays.

Agriculture: Cattle, dairy products, nursery crops, hay, wheat. Market value $15.3 million. Cedar fence posts marketed.

PALO PINTO (411) county seat; old settlers reunion; government center.

MINERAL WELLS (17,266, part [2,176] in Parker County) varied manufacturing; tourism; agriculture; hospital, prison; Weatherford College extension; Crazy Water Festival in October; state park east of city in Parker County.

Other towns include: **Gordon** (431); **Graford** (578) retirement and recreation area, Possum Fest in October; **Mingus** (240); **Santo** (445), and **Strawn** (719).

Population	**27,325**
Change fm 2000	1.1
Area (sq. mi.)	985.50
Land Area (sq. mi.)	952.93
Altitude (ft.)	782–1,470
Rainfall (in.)	31.79
Jan. mean min.	33.4
July mean max.	97.3
Civ. Labor	11,783
Unemployed	5.1
Wages	$52,266,670
Av. Weekly Wage	$500.62
Prop. Value	$1,955,314,203
Retail Sales	$253,724,014

Panola County

Physical Features: East Texas county; sixty percent forested, rolling plain; broken by Sabine, Murvaul Creek and Lake, Toledo Bend Reservoir.

Economy: Gas processing; oil-field operation; agribusinesses; food processing.

History: Caddo area. Anglo-American settlement established in 1833. Antebellum slaveholding area. County name is Indian word for cotton; created from Harrison, Shelby counties 1846.

Race/Ethnicity, 2000: (In percent) Anglo, 77.97; Black, 17.85; Hispanic, 3.51; Other, 0.67.

Vital Statistics, 2003: Births, 302; deaths, 237; marriages, 188; divorces, 72.

Recreation: Lake fishing, other water activities; hunting; scenic drives; Jim Reeves memorial, Tex Ritter museum and Texas Country Music Hall of Fame; historic sites, homes.

Minerals: Oil, gas.

Agriculture: Broilers; beef cattle, forages; market value $46.2 million. Timber sales significant.

CARTHAGE (6,634) county seat; petroleum processing; poultry; sawmills; hospital; junior college; Oil & Gas Blast in October.

Other towns include: **Beckville** (740), **Clayton** (79), **DeBerry** (191), **Gary** (315), **Long Branch** (181), **Panola** (296). Also, **Tatum** (1,165, mostly in Rusk County).

Population	**22,865**
Change fm 2000	0.5
Area (sq. mi.)	821.34
Land Area (sq. mi.)	800.92
Altitude (ft.)	172–481
Rainfall (in.)	51.51
Jan. mean min.	33.9
July mean max.	93.7
Civ. Labor	8,637
Unemployed	6.1
Wages	$58,748,281
Av. Weekly Wage	$657.80
Prop. Value	$2,770,975,119
Retail Sales	$182,077,024

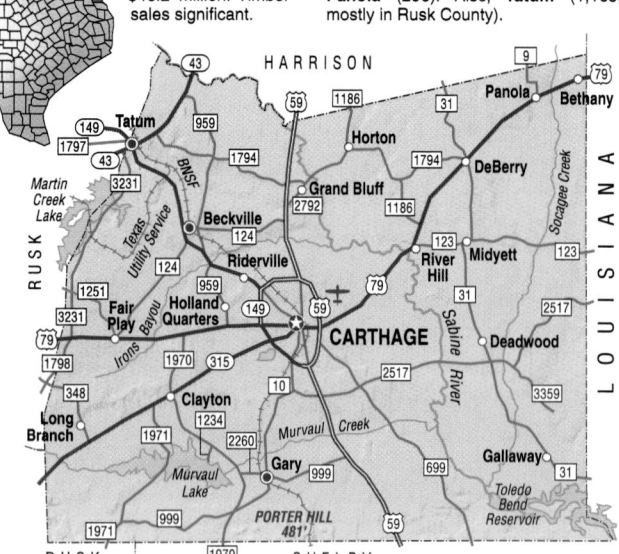

Parker County

Physical Features: Hilly, broken by Brazos, Trinity tributaries, lakes; varied soils.

Economy: Agribusiness; varied manufacturing; government/services; many residents work in Fort Worth; county part of Dallas-Fort Worth-Arlington metropolitan area.

History: Comanche and Kiowa area in late 1840s when Anglo-American settlers arrived. County named for pioneer legislator Isaac Parker; created 1855 from Bosque, Navarro counties.

Race/Ethnicity, 2000: (In percent) Anglo, 90.05; Black, 1.87; Hispanic, 7.02; Other, 1.06.

Vital Statistics, 2003: Births, 1,168; deaths, 750; marriages, 706; divorces, 444.

Recreation: Water sports; state park; nature trails; hunting; Peach Festival in July and frontier days; first Monday trade days monthly.

Minerals: Natural gas, oil, stone, sand and gravel, clays.

Agriculture: Cattle, horticultural plants, hay, horses, dairies, peaches, peanuts, pecans. Market value $47.6 million.

WEATHERFORD (21,515) county seat; agribusiness, retail center; varied manufacturing; government/services; commuting; hospital; Weatherford College; Civil War weekend in September.

Other towns include: **Aledo** (2,198); **Annetta** (1,224), **Annetta North** (517) and **Annetta South** (613); **Cool** (167); **Dennis** (300); **Hudson Oaks** (1,790); **Millsap** (362); **Peaster** (102); **Poolville** (520); **Reno** (2,661); **Sanctuary** (616); **Springtown** (2,369) commuters, government/services, Wild West Festival in September; **Whitt** (38); **Willow Park** (3,089).

Also, part of **Azle** (10,054) and **Briar**, (5,615), both mostly in Tarrant County, and part [2,176] of **Mineral Wells.**

Population 100,336
Change fm 2000 .... 13.4
Area (sq. mi.) 910.09

Land Area (sq. mi.) 903.51
Altitude (ft.) 700-1,275
Rainfall (in.) 34.70
Jan. mean min. 29.0
July mean max. 95.2
Civ. Labor. 45,641
Unemployed 4.6
Wages $137,408,700
Av. Weekly Wage $527.60
Prop. Value $6,097,429,880
Retail Sales $1,149,298,699

Parmer County

Physical Features: Western High Plains, broken by draws, playas; sandy, clay, loam soils.

Economy: Cattle feeding; grain elevators; meat-packing plant; other agribusiness.

History: Apaches, pushed out in late 1700s by Comanches, Kiowas. U.S. Army removed Indians in 1874-75. Anglo-Americans arrived in 1880s. Mexican migration increased after 1950. County named for Republic figure Martin Parmer; created from Bexar District 1876, organized 1907.

Race/Ethnicity, 2000: (In percent) Anglo, 49.17; Black, 1.01; Hispanic, 49.19; Other, 0.63.

Vital Statistics, 2003: Births, 159; deaths, 87; marriages, 56; divorces, 44.

Recreation: Hunting, Border Town Days in July.

Minerals: Not significant.

Agriculture: Among leading counties in total farm income. Beef cattle, dairies; crops include wheat, corn, cotton, grain sorghum, alfalfa; apples and potatoes also raised; 190,000 acres irrigated. Market value $603.9 million, second in state.

FARWELL (1,318) county seat; agribusiness center; grain storage; plants make farm equipment.

FRIONA (3,824) feedlots, grain elevators, meat packing; hospital; museum; Maize Days in September.

Other towns include: **Bovina** (1,873) farm trade center; **Lazbuddie** (248).

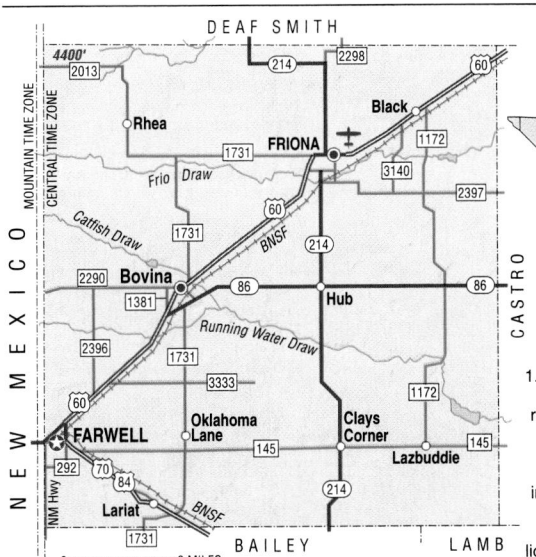

Population 9,933
Change fm 2000 .... -0.8
Area (sq. mi.) 885.17
Land Area (sq. mi.) 881.66
Altitude (ft.) 3,850-4,400
Rainfall (in.) 18.38
Jan. mean min. 21.7
July mean max. 89.8
Civ. Labor. 4,632
Unemployed 3.8
Wages $31,814,561
Av. Weekly Wage $494.20
Prop. Value $562,163,764
Retail Sales $30,142,533

For explanation of sources, abbreviations and symbols, see p. 167 and foldout map.

Pecos County

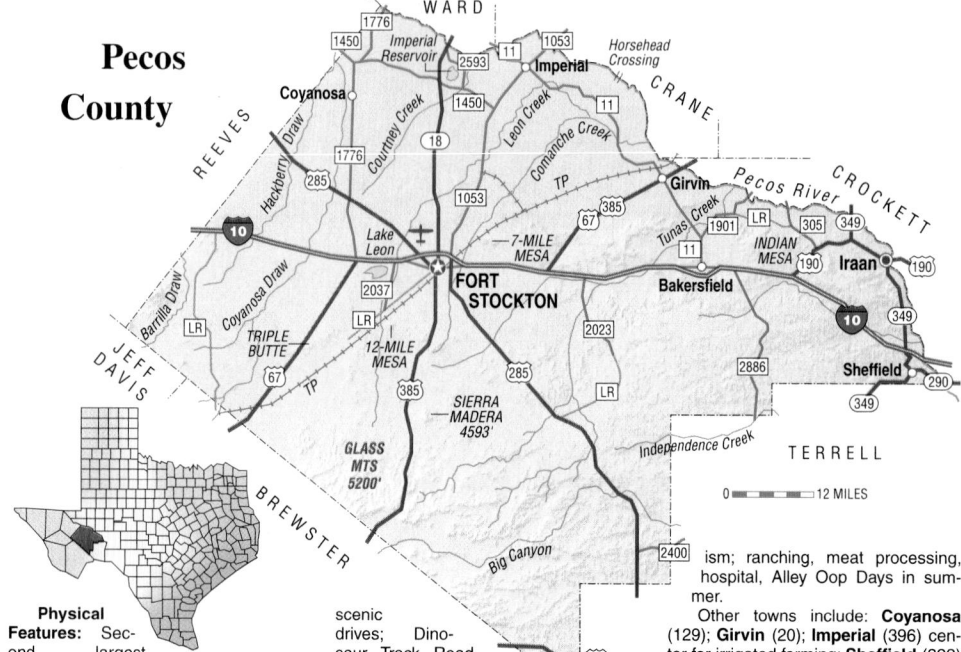

Physical Features:
Second largest county; high, broken plateau in West Texas; draining to Pecos and tributaries; sandy, clay, loam soils.

Economy: Oil, gas; government/ services; agriculture; wind turbines.

History: Comanches in area when military outpost established in 1859. Settlement began after Civil War. Created from Presidio County 1871; organized 1872; named for Pecos River, name origin uncertain.

Race/Ethnicity, 2000: (In percent) Anglo, 33.98; Black, 4.21; Hispanic, 61.05; Other, 0.76.

Vital Statistics, 2003: Births, 241; deaths, 146; marriages, 79; divorces, 30.

Recreation: Old Fort Stockton, Annie Riggs Museum, stagecoach stop; scenic drives; Dinosaur Track Roadside Park; cattle-trail sites; archaeological museum with oil, ranch-heritage collections; Comanche Springs Water Carnival in summer.

Minerals: Natural gas, oil, caliche.

Agriculture: Cotton, vineyards, pecans, alfalfa, cattle, goats, sheep, horses. Market value $38.2 million. Aquaculture firm producing shrimp. Hunting leases.

FORT STOCKTON (7,386) county seat, distribution center for petroleum industry, government/services, agriculture, tourism, varied manufacturing, winery, hospital, historical tours, prison units, spaceport launching small satellites.

Iraan (1,178) oil, gas center, tourism; ranching, meat processing, hospital, Alley Oop Days in summer.

Other towns include: **Coyanosa** (129); **Girvin** (20); **Imperial** (396) center for irrigated farming; **Sheffield** (322) oil, gas center.

Population..............................	**15,949**
Change fm 2000............................	-5.1
Area (sq. mi.).........................	4,764.73
Land Area (sq. mi.).................	4,763.66
Altitude (ft.).......................	2,168-5,200
Rainfall (in.)................................	14.06
Jan. mean min.	31.4
July mean max.	95.8
Civ. Labor	6,684
Unemployed	5.1
Wages	$31,158,235
Av. Weekly Wage	$492.86
Prop. Value.................	$2,177,186,815
Retail Sales	$106,362,703

For explanation of sources, abbreviations and symbols, see p. 167 and foldout map.

Wind turbines on the mesas near Iraan in Pecos County. Texas Almanac photo.

Polk County

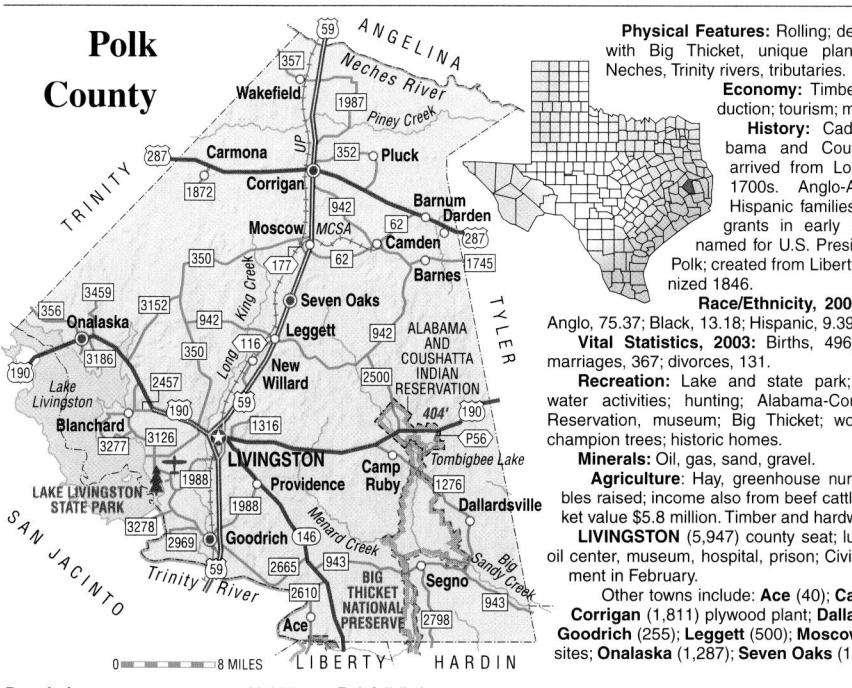

Physical Features: Rolling; densely forested, with Big Thicket, unique plant, animal life; Neches, Trinity rivers, tributaries.

Economy: Timber; lumber production; tourism; manufacturing.

History: Caddo area; Alabama and Coushatta Indians arrived from Louisiana in late 1700s. Anglo-American and Hispanic families received land grants in early 1830s. County named for U.S. President James K. Polk; created from Liberty County, organized 1846.

Race/Ethnicity, 2000: (In percent) Anglo, 75.37; Black, 13.18; Hispanic, 9.39; Other, 2.06.

Vital Statistics, 2003: Births, 496; deaths, 554; marriages, 367; divorces, 131.

Recreation: Lake and state park; fishing, other water activities; hunting; Alabama-Coushatta Indian Reservation, museum; Big Thicket; woodlands trails, champion trees; historic homes.

Minerals: Oil, gas, sand, gravel.

Agriculture: Hay, greenhouse nurseries; vegetables raised; income also from beef cattle, horses. Market value $5.8 million. Timber and hardwood.

LIVINGSTON (5,947) county seat; lumber, tourism, oil center, museum, hospital, prison; Civil War re-enactment in February.

Other towns include: **Ace** (40); **Camden** (1,200); **Corrigan** (1,811) plywood plant; **Dallardsville** (350); **Goodrich** (255); **Leggett** (500); **Moscow** (170) historic sites; **Onalaska** (1,287); **Seven Oaks** (143).

Population 46,397	Rainfall (in.) 51.85	Wages...............................$69,379,777
Change fm 2000 ....12.8	Jan. mean min............................... 35.8	Av. Weekly Wage $520.12
Area (sq. mi.) 1,109.81	July mean max.............................. 94.1	Prop. Value $2,310,203,919
Land Area (sq. mi.) 1,057.26	Civ. Labor.................................. 15,770	Retail Sales....................$365,196,275
Altitude (ft.) 68-404	Unemployed...................................... 5.7	

Potter County

Physical Features: Panhandle county; mostly level, part rolling; broken by Canadian River and tributaries; sandy, sandy loam, chocolate loam, clay soils; Lake Meredith.

Economy: Transportation, distribution hub for large area; manufacturing; agribusinesses; tourism; government/services; petrochemicals; gas processing; .

History: Apaches, pushed out by Comanches in 1700s. Comanches removed to Indian Territory in 1874-75. Ranching began in late 1870s. Oil boom in 1920s. County named for Robert Potter, Republic leader; created 1876 from Bexar District; organized 1887.

Race/Ethnicity, 2000: (In percent) Anglo, 58.49; Black, 10.15; Hispanic, 28.11; Other, 3.25.

Vital Statistics, 2003: Births, 2,200; deaths, 1,185; marriages, 1,676; divorces, 477.

Recreation: Metropolitan activities, events; lake activities; Alibates Flint Quarries National Monument; hunting, fishing; Tri-State Fair in September.

Minerals: Natural gas, oil, helium.

Agriculture: Beef cattle production and processing; wheat, sorghum, cotton. Market value $19.5 million.

AMARILLO (180,380 total, part [73, 794] in Randall County) county seat; hub for northern Panhandle oil and ranching; distribution, marketing center; tourism; varied manufacturing; food processing; hospitals; prison;

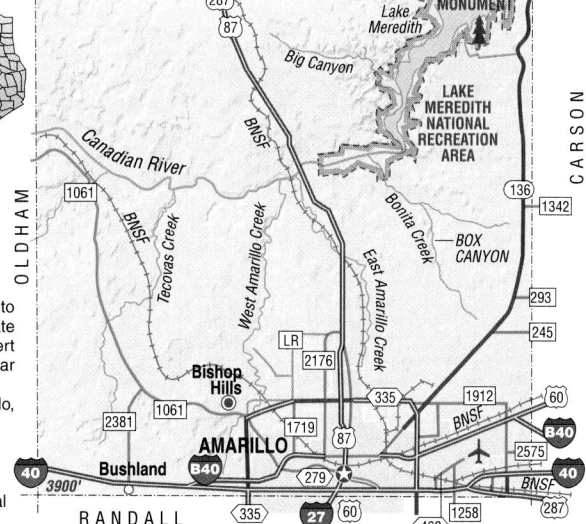

museum; varied cultural, recreational events; junior college, Texas Tech University medical, engineering schools; Texas State Technical College branch; Quarter Horse Heritage Center.

Other towns include: **Bishop Hills** (208) and **Bushland** (1,485).

Population 118,410	Land Area (sq. mi.) 909.24
Change fm 2000 ....4.3	Altitude (ft.) 2,915-3,900
Area (sq. mi.) 921.98	Rainfall (in.)...................................19.71
	Jan. mean min. 22.6
	July mean max..............................91.0
	Civ. Labor 58,492
	Unemployed......................................4.9
	Wages...........................$580,445,572
	Av. Weekly Wage $584.89
	Prop. Value $4,901,101,296
	Retail Sales.................$2,302,594,511

Downtown Marfa and the Presidio County Courthouse. Texas Almanac photo.

Presidio County

Physical Features: Rugged, some of Texas' tallest mountains; scenic drives; clays, loams, sandy loams on uplands; intermountain wash; timber sparse; Capote Falls, state's highest.

Economy: Government/services; ranching; hunting leases; tourism.

History: Presidio area has been cultivated farmland since at least 1200 A.D. Spanish explorers of 1500s encountered villages along Rio Grande. Jumanos, Apaches and Comanches in area when Spanish missions began in 1680s. Anglo-Americans arrived in 1840s. County created 1850 from Bexar District; organized 1875; named for Spanish Presidio del Norte (fort of the north).

Race/Ethnicity, 2000: (In percent) Anglo, 15.03; Black, 0.21; Hispanic, 84.36; Other, 0.40.

Vital Statistics, 2003: Births, 148; deaths, 47; marriages, 72; divorces, 3.

Recreation: Mild climate and scenic surroundings; hunting; scenic drives along Rio Grande, in mountains; ghost towns, mysterious Marfa Lights; Fort D.A. Russell; Big Bend Ranch State Park; hot springs; Cibolo Creek Ranch Resort; Chinati Foundation art festival in fall.

Minerals: Sand, gravel, silver, zeolite.

Agriculture: Cattle, tomatoes, hay, onions, melons. 5,500 acres irrigated near Rio Grande. Market value $51.2 million.

MARFA (2,143) county seat; ranching supply, Border Patrol sector headquarters; tourist center; gateway to mountainous area; Paisano Hotel, headquarters for movie, "Giant"; Old Timers Roping on Memorial Day weekend.

PRESIDIO (4,639) international bridge to Ojinaga, Mex.; gateway to Mexico's West Coast by rail; Fort Leaton historic site; asado cook-off in February.

Other towns include: **Redford** (134); **Shafter** (57) old mining town.

Population	7,639	Jan. mean min. Marfa	23.9	Av. Weekly Wage	$478.32
Change fm 2000	4.6	Jan. mean min. Presidio	34.5	Prop. Value	$308,667,894
Area (sq. mi.)	3,856.26	July mean max. Marfa	88.9	Retail Sales	$36,511,682
Land Area (sq. mi.)	3,855.51	July mean max. Presidio	100.8		
Altitude (ft.)	2,400-7,728	Civ. Labor	3,768		
Rainfall (in.) Marfa	15.79	Unemployed	19.2	*For explanation of sources, abbreviations*	
Rainfall (in.) Presidio	10.76	Wages	$12,355,483	*and symbols, see p. 167 and foldout map.*	

Rains County

Physical Features: Northeastern county; rolling; partly Blackland, sandy loams, sandy soils; Sabine River, Lake Tawakoni.

Economy: Agribusiness, some manufacturing.

History: Caddo area. In 1700s, Tawakoni Indians entered the area. Anglo-Americans arrived in 1840s. County, county seat named for Emory Rains, Republic leader; created 1870 from Hopkins, Hunt and Wood counties; birthplace of National Farmers Union, 1902.

Race/Ethnicity, 2000: (In percent) Anglo, 90.25; Black, 2.98; Hispanic, 5.53; Other, 1.24.

Vital Statistics, 2003: Births, 97; deaths, 104; marriages, 78; divorces, 70.

Recreation: Lake Tawakoni and Lake Fork Reservoir activities; birding, Eagle Fest in January.

Minerals: Gas, oil.

Agriculture: Beef, forages, dairies, vegetables, fruits, nurseries. Market value $11.8 million.

EMORY (1,246) county seat; local trade; tourism; government/services; commuting to Greenville, Dallas; African-American museum.

Other towns include: **East Tawakoni** (907) and **Point** (948), manufacturing, tourism, tamale fest on July 4. Part of **Alba** (439), mostly in Wood County.

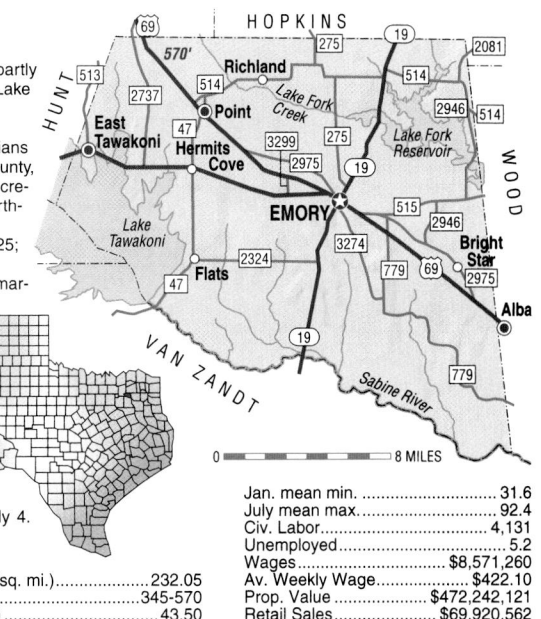

Population	11,066
Change fm 2000	21.1
Area (sq. mi.)	258.87
Land Area (sq. mi.)	232.05
Altitude (ft.)	345-570
Rainfall (in.)	43.50

Jan. mean min.	31.6
July mean max.	92.4
Civ. Labor.	4,131
Unemployed	5.2
Wages	$8,571,260
Av. Weekly Wage	$422.10
Prop. Value	$472,242,121
Retail Sales	$69,920,562

Randall County

Physical Features: Panhandle county; level, but broken by scenic Palo Duro Canyon, Buffalo Lake; silty clay, loam soils.

Economy: Agribusinesses; education; tourism; part of Amarillo metropolitan area.

History: Comanche Indians removed in mid-1870s; ranching began soon afterward. County created 1876 from Bexar District; organized 1889; named for Confederate Gen. Horace Randal (name misspelled in statute).

Race/Ethnicity, 2000: (In percent) Anglo, 86.48; Black, 1.60; Hispanic, 10.27; Other, 1.65.

Vital Statistics, 2003: Births, 1,413; deaths, 829; marriages, 373; divorces, 541.

Recreation: Palo Duro Canyon State Park, with *Texas Legacies* musical drama a tourist attraction each summer; Panhandle-Plains Historical Museum; West Texas A&M University events; aoudad sheep, migratory waterfowl hunting in season; Buffalo Lake National Wildlife Refuge; cowboy breakfasts at ranches.

Minerals: Not significant.

Agriculture: Beef cattle, wheat, sorghum, silage, cotton, dairies, hay. Market value $261.1 million.

CANYON (13,205) county seat; West Texas A&M University; tourism; commuting to Amarillo; ranching; farm center; light manufacturing; gateway to state park.

Other towns include: **Lake Tanglewood** (846); **Palisades** (358); **Timbercreek Canyon** (443); **Umbarger** (327) German sausage festival in November. Part [73,794] of **Amarillo** (180,380 total); also, **Happy** (614, mostly in Swisher County).

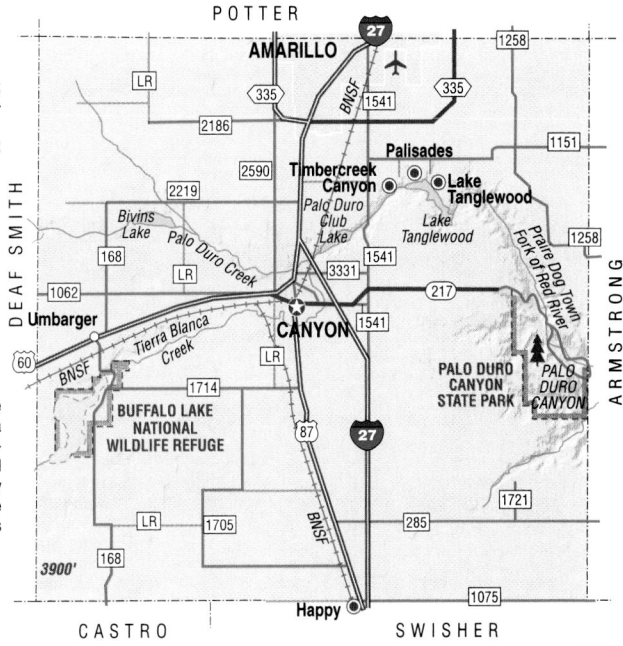

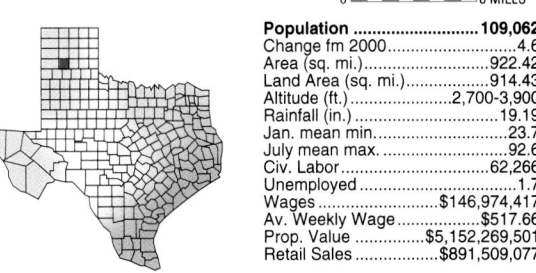

For explanation of sources, abbreviations and symbols, see p. 167 and foldout map.

Population	109,062
Change fm 2000	4.6
Area (sq. mi.)	922.42
Land Area (sq. mi.)	914.43
Altitude (ft.)	2,700-3,900
Rainfall (in.)	19.19
Jan. mean min.	23.7
July mean max.	92.6
Civ. Labor	62,266
Unemployed	1.7
Wages	$146,974,417
Av. Weekly Wage	$517.66
Prop. Value	$5,152,269,501
Retail Sales	$891,509,077

Reagan County

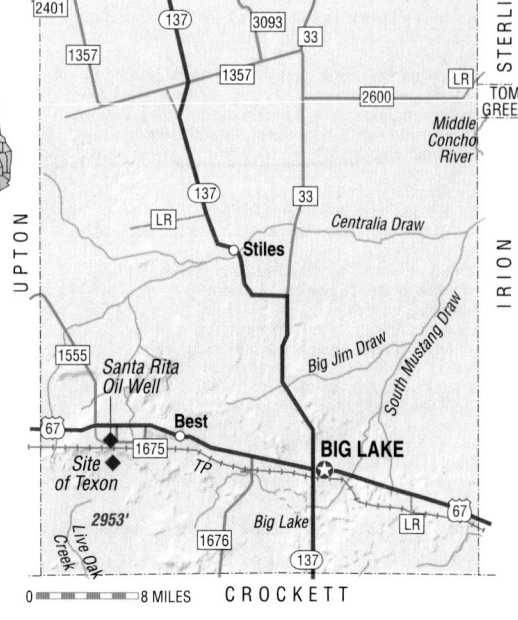

Physical Features: Western county; level to hilly, broken by draws, Big Lake (intermittent); sandy, loam, clay soils.

Economy: Oil production; natural gas; ranching.

History: Comanches in area until mid-1870s. Ranching began in 1880s. Hispanic migration increased after 1950. County named for Sen. John H. Reagan, first chairman, Texas Railroad Commission; county created 1903 from Tom Green County.

Race/Ethnicity, 2000: (In percent) Anglo, 46.84; Black, 3.04; Hispanic, 49.49; Other, 0.63.

Vital Statistics, 2003: Births, 59; deaths, 32; marriages, 14; divorces, 13.

Recreation: Texon reunion; rodeo; site of 1923 discovery well Santa Rita No. 1 on University of Texas land.

Minerals: Gas, oil.

Agriculture: Cotton, cattle, sheep, goats; cotton, grains principal crops; 36,000 acres irrigated. Market value $6.6 million.

BIG LAKE (2,741) county seat; center for oil activities, farming, ranching; hospital; Blue Grass Festival in April.

Population 3,064	Rainfall (in.) 18.79	Wages.................................$8,454,784
Change fm 2000 .... -7.9	Jan. mean min............................... 29.1	Av. Weekly Wage $590.71
Area (sq. mi.) 1,175.98	July mean max. 93.4	Prop. Value $526,285,510
Land Area (sq. mi.) 1,175.30	Civ. Labor 1,577	Retail Sales.......................$18,827,817
Altitude (ft.) 2,400-2,953	Unemployed 2.9	

Real County

Physical Features: Hill Country, spring-fed streams, scenic canyons; Frio, Nueces rivers; cedars, pecans, walnuts, many live oaks.

Economy: Ranching; tourism, government/services; cedar cutting.

History: Tonkawa area; Lipan Apaches arrived in early 1700s; later, Comanche hunters in area. Spanish mission established 1762. Anglo-Americans arrived in 1850s. County created 1913 from Bandera, Edwards, Kerr counties; named for legislator-ranchman Julius Real.

Race/Ethnicity, 2000: (In percent) Anglo, 76.53; Black, 0.23; Hispanic, 22.58; Other, 0.66.

Vital Statistics, 2003: Births, 33; deaths, 48; marriages, 22; divorces, 9.

Recreation: Tourist, hunting center; many deer killed each season; fishing; camping; scenic drives; state natural area.

Minerals: Not significant.

Agriculture: Goats, sheep, beef cattle produce most income. Market value $2.7 million. Cedar posts processed.

LEAKEY (398) county seat; tourism, ranching; museums; July Jubilee.

CAMP WOOD (824) San Lorenzo de la Santa Cruz mission site; museum; settlers reunion in August; a tourist, ranching hub for parts of three counties.

Other towns include: **Rio Frio** (50).

Population....................................2,995		
Change fm 2000.............................-1.8		
Area (sq. mi.)................................ 700.04	July mean max...............................94.2	Prop. Value.....................$392,037,084
Land Area (sq. mi.)..................... 699.91	Civ. Labor 1,288	Retail Sales $12,021,203
Altitude (ft.)...................... 1,450-2,381	Unemployed.....................................2.7	
Rainfall (in.)................................. 27.99	Wages................................$3,031,067	*For explanation of sources, abbreviations*
Jan. mean min................................ 33.1	Av. Weekly Wage $330.72	*and symbols, see p. 167 and foldout map.*

Red River County

Physical Features: On Red-Sulphur rivers' divide; 39 different soil types; half timbered.

Economy: Agribusinesses; lumbering; manufacturing.

History: Caddo Indians abandoned area in 1790s. One of the oldest counties; settlers were moving in from the United States in 1810s. Kickapoo and other tribes arrived in 1820s. Antebellum slaveholding area. County created 1836 as original county of the Republic; organized 1837; named for Red River, its northern boundary.

Race/Ethnicity, 2000: (In percent) Anglo, 76.65; Black, 17.93; Hispanic, 4.67; Other, 0.75.

Vital Statistics, 2003: Births, 153; deaths, 211; marriages, 96; divorces, 95.

Recreation: Historical sites include pioneer homes, birthplace of John Nance Garner; water activities; hunting of deer, turkey, duck, small game.

Minerals: Small oil flow.

Agriculture: Beef cattle, hay, cotton, soybeans, wheat. Market value $30.9 million. Timber sales substantial.

CLARKSVILLE (3,811) county seat; varied manufacturing; hospital; library; century-old courthouse; Historical Society bazaar in October.

Other towns include: **Annona** (283); **Avery** (458); **Bagwell** (150); **Bogata** (1,344); **Detroit** (772) commercial center in west. Part of **Deport** (690).

Population	13,650
Change fm 2000	-4.6
Area (sq. mi.)	1,057.61
Land Area (sq. mi.)	1,050.18
Altitude (ft.)	287-525
Rainfall (in.)	47.83
Jan. mean min.	29.7
July mean max.	92.2
Civ. Labor	5,051
Unemployed	6.9
Wages	$16,487,030
Av. Weekly Wage	$405.70
Prop. Value	$690,343,960
Retail Sales	$55,754,720

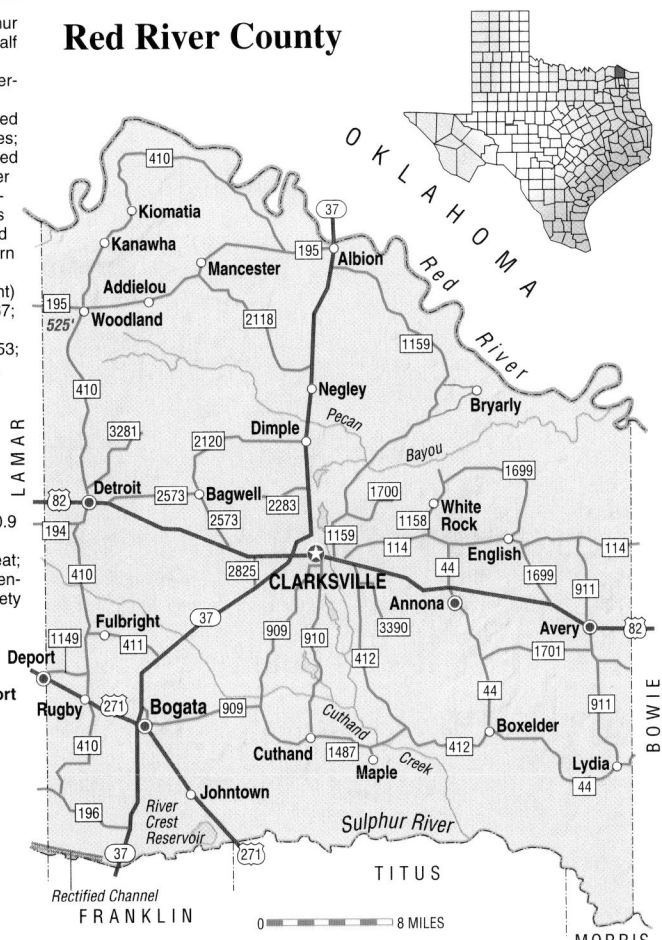

Reagan County's intermittent Big Lake with water, a rare occurrence in recent decades. Texas Almanac photo.

Youngsters enjoy one of the canals that run through Balmorhea. Texas Almanac photo.

Reeves County

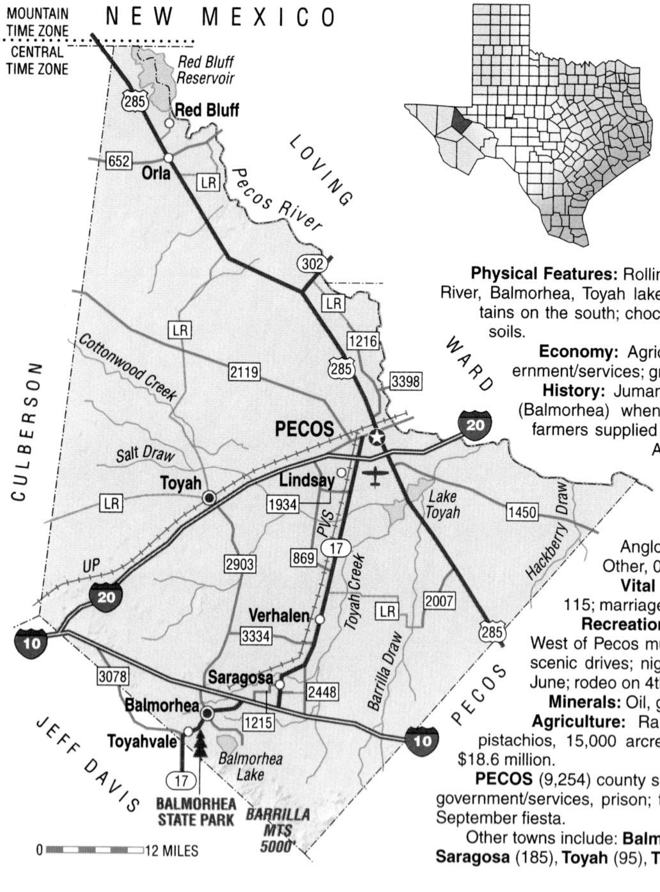

Population	**11,842**
Change fm 2000	-9.9
Area (sq. mi.)	2,641.95
Land Area (sq. mi.)	2,635.88
Altitude (ft.)	2,500-5,000
Rainfall (in.) Pecos	11.61
Rainfall (in.) Balmorhea	14.19
Jan. mean min. Pecos	28.1
Jan. mean min. Balmorhea	30.1
July mean max. Pecos	98.5
July mean max. Balmorhea	94.7
Civ. Labor	5,340
Unemployed	7.4
Wages	$22,132,510
Av. Weekly Wage	$438.34
Prop. Value	$550,264,810
Retail Sales	$84,732,834

Physical Features: Rolling plains, broken by many draws, Pecos River, Balmorhea, Toyah lakes, Red Bluff Reservoir; Barrilla Mountains on the south; chocolate loam, clay, sandy, mountain wash soils.

Economy: Agriculture; tourism; food processing; government/services; gravel.

History: Jumanos were irrigating crops from springs (Balmorhea) when Spanish explored in 1583. Mexican farmers supplied nearby Fort Davis in mid-19th century. Anglo-Americans arrived in 1870s. County created 1883 from Pecos County; organized 1884; named for Confederate Col. George R. Reeves.

Race/Ethnicity, 2000: (In percent) Anglo, 24.01; Black, 1.93; Hispanic, 73.38; Other, 0.68.

Vital Statistics, 2003: Births, 199; deaths, 115; marriages, 66; divorces, 26.

Recreation: Replica of Judge Roy Bean Store, West of Pecos museum; park with javelina, prairie dogs; scenic drives; night in old Pecos, cantaloupe festival in June; rodeo on 4th of July; water activities; state park.

Minerals: Oil, gas, gravel.

Agriculture: Ranching; cotton, cantaloupes, pecans, pistachios, 15,000 arces irrigated; dairy cattle. Market value $18.6 million.

PECOS (9,254) county seat; food processing; produce shipping; government/services, prison; tourism; agribusiness; hospital; 16th of September fiesta.

Other towns include: **Balmorhea** (508), **Lindsay** (397); **Orla** (80), **Saragosa** (185), **Toyah** (95), **Toyahvale** (60).

Refugio County

Physical Features: Coastal plain, broken by streams, bays; sandy, loam, black soils; mesquite, oak, huisache motts.

Economy: Petroleum, petrochemical production, agribusinesses, tourism, commuting to Corpus Christi, Victoria.

History: Karankawa area. Spanish mission, for which the county is named, Our Lady of Refuge, established in 1793. Colonists from Ireland and United States arrived in 1830s. Original county of the Republic created 1836, organized 1837.

Race/Ethnicity, 2000: (In percent) Anglo, 47.78; Black, 6.80; Hispanic, 44.58; Other, 0.84.

Vital Statistics, 2003: Births, 83; deaths, 100; marriages, 52; divorces, 16.

Recreation: Water activities; hunting, fishing; historic sites; chili cook-off in August; wildlife refuge, home of the whooping crane; Festival of Flags in October.

Minerals: Oil, natural gas.

Agriculture: Cotton, beef cattle, sorghum, corn, soybeans, horses. Market value $21.4 million. Hunting leases.

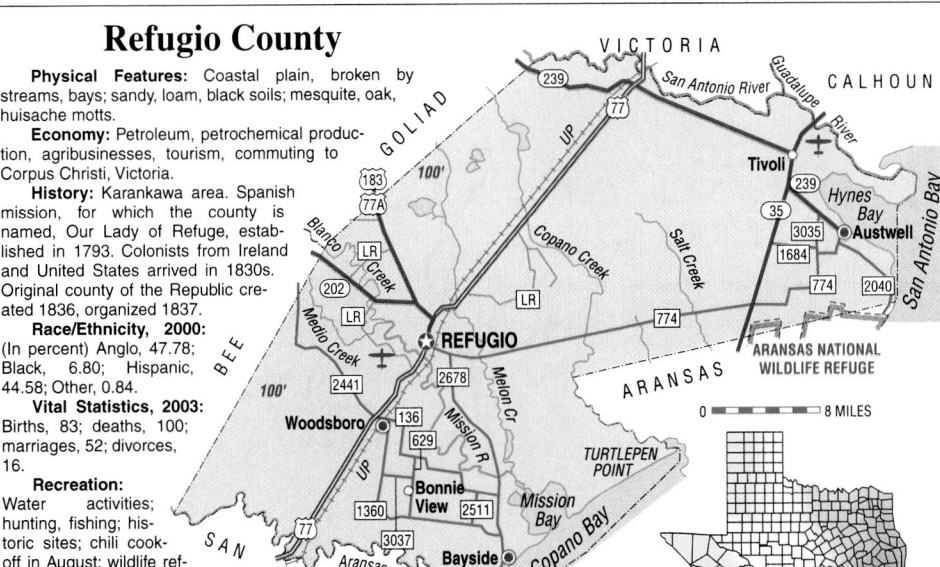

REFUGIO (2,765) county seat; petroleum, agribusiness center; hospital; museum, historic homes.

Other towns include: **Austwell** (178); **Bayside** (333) resorts; **Tivoli** (550); **Woodsboro** (1,603) commercial center.

Population	7,640
Change fm 2000	-2.4
Area (sq. mi.)	818.64
Land Area (sq. mi.)	770.21
Altitude (ft.)	sea level-100
Rainfall (in.)	40.10
Jan. mean min.	45.0

July mean max.	94.0
Civ. Labor	2,702
Unemployed	5.6
Wages	$13,442,284
Av. Weekly Wage	$501.22
Prop. Value	$813,780,370
Retail Sales	$65,523,736

Roberts County

Physical Features: Rolling, broken by Canadian and tributaries; Red Deer Creek; black, sandy loam, alluvial soils.

Economy: Oil-field operations; agribusiness.

History: Apaches; pushed out by Comanches who were removed in 1874-75 by U.S. Army. Ranching began in late 1870s. County created 1876 from Bexar District; organized 1889; named for Texas leaders John S. Roberts and Gov. O.M. Roberts.

Race/Ethnicity, 2000: (In percent) Anglo, 96.39; Black, 0.34; Hispanic, 3.16; Other, 0.11.

Vital Statistics, 2003: Births, 2; deaths, 15; marriages, 5; divorces, 4.

Recreation: National cow-calling contest in June; scenic drives; hunting; museum.

Minerals: Production of gas, oil.

Agriculture: Beef cattle; wheat, sorghum, corn, soybeans, hay; 10,000 acres irrigated. Market value $13.2 million.

MIAMI (539) county seat; ranching, oil center; some manufacturing.

Population	863
Change fm 2000	-2.7
Area (sq. mi.)	924.19
Land Area (sq. mi.)	924.09
Altitude (ft.)	2,400-3,250
Rainfall (in.)	23.30

Jan. mean min.	20.6
July mean max.	92.4
Civ. Labor	410
Unemployed	3.4
Wages	$1,151,644
Av. Weekly Wage	$391.98

Prop. Value	$318,410,565
Retail Sales	$1,616,808

For explanation of sources, abbreviations and symbols, see p. 167 and foldout map.

Physical Features: Rolling in north and east, draining to bottoms along Brazos, Navasota rivers; sandy soils, heavy in bottoms.

Economy: Agribusiness; small manufacturing; power-generating plant.

History: Tawakoni, Waco, Comanche and other tribes. Anglo-Americans arrived in 1820s. Antebellum slaveholding area. County created 1837, organized 1838, subdivided into many others later; named for pioneer Sterling Clack Robertson.

Race/Ethnicity, 2000: (In percent) Anglo, 60.55; Black, 24.11; Hispanic, 14.74; Other, 0.60.

Vital Statistics, 2003: Births, 203; deaths, 186; marriages, 137; divorces, 38.

Recreation: Hunting, fishing; historic sites; historic-homes tour; dogwood trails, wildlife preserves.

Minerals: Gas, oil, lignite coal.

Agriculture: Most revenue from beef cattle, cotton, hay, corn; 20,000 acres of cropland irrigated. Market value $74.7 million.

FRANKLIN (1,478) county seat; farm-trade center, power plants, feed mill, library.

HEARNE (4,460) agribusiness; varied manufacturing; depot museum; music festival in October.

Other towns include: **Bremond** (864) power plant, coal mining, Polish Days in June; **Calvert** (1,390) agriculture, tourism, antiques, Maypole festival, tour of homes; **Mumford** (170); **New Baden** (150); **Wheelock** (225).

Robertson County

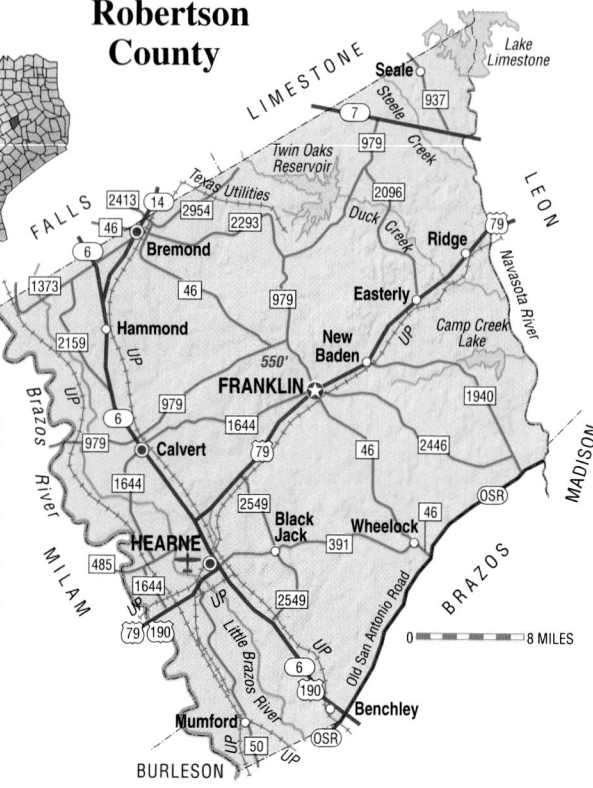

Population 16,136		
Change fm 2000 .... 0.9	Jan. mean min. 38.2	Wages $23,647,718
Area (sq. mi.) 865.67	July mean max. 95.1	Av. Weekly Wage $505.15
Land Area (sq. mi.) 854.56	Civ. Labor 6,748	Prop. Value $1,413,296,350
Altitude (ft.) 250-550	Unemployed........................5.2	Retail Sales $83,381,705
Rainfall (in.) 39.03		

Rockwall County

Physical Features: Rolling prairie, mostly Blackland soil; Lake Ray Hubbard. Texas' smallest county.

Economy: Industrial employment in local plants and in Dallas; in Dallas metropolitan area; residential development around Lake Ray Hubbard.

History: Caddo area. Cherokees arrived in 1820s. Anglo-American settlers arrived in 1840s. County created 1873 from Kaufman; named for wall-like rock formation.

Race/Ethnicity, 2000: (In percent) Anglo, 83.77; Black, 3.32; Hispanic, 11.07; Other, 1.84.

Vital Statistics, 2003: Births, 861; deaths, 329; marriages, 1,350; divorces, 247.

Recreation: Lake activities; proximity to Dallas; unusual rock outcrop.

Minerals: Not significant.

Agriculture: Small grains, cattle, horticulture, horses. Market value $3 million.

ROCKWALL (24,867) county seat; varied manufacturing; hospital; collection car fest in June.

Other towns include: **Fate** (1,240); **Heath** (5,779); **McLendon-Chisholm** (1,035) chili cookoff in October; **Mobile City** (230); **Royse City** (4,313) varied manufacturing, agribusiness, Funfest in April, North Texas Speedway. Part [7,041] of **Rowlett** and a small part [315] of **Wylie**.

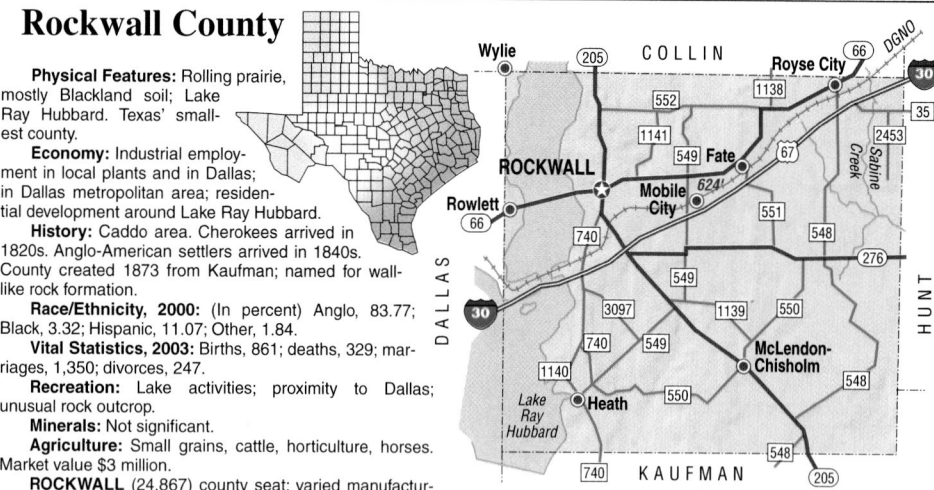

Population 58,260		
Change fm 2000 ....35.2	July mean max..........................96.0	
Area (sq. mi.) 148.70	Civ. Labor............................27,136	
Land Area (sq. mi.) 128.79	Unemployed................................4.9	
Altitude (ft.) 450-624	Wages..........................$117,060,009	
Rainfall (in.)............................39.40	Av. Weekly Wage................$571.47	
Jan. mean min. 33.0	Prop. Value $4,475,247,932	
	Retail Sales................$764,025,677	

Runnels County

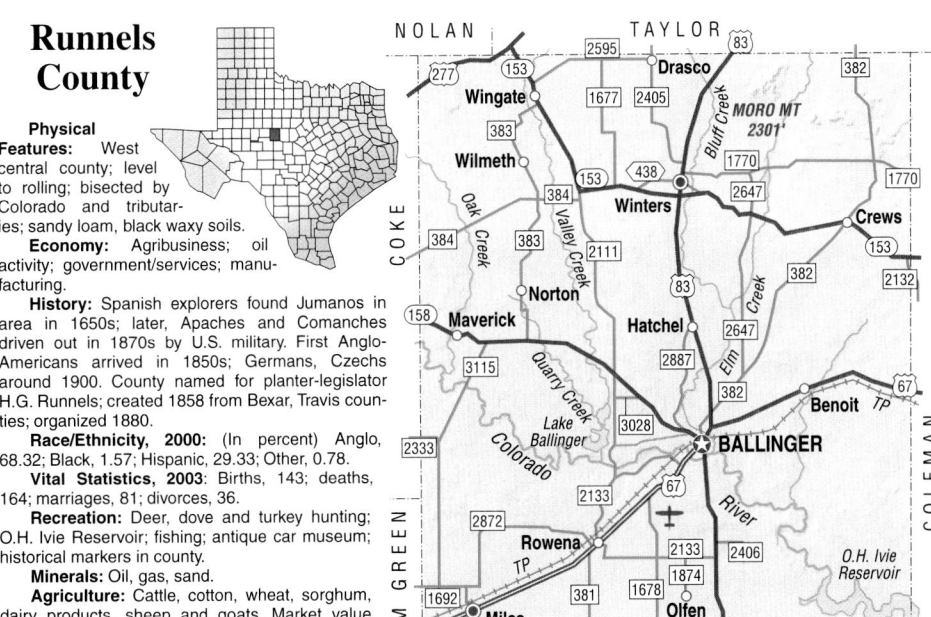

Physical Features: West central county; level to rolling; bisected by Colorado and tributaries; sandy loam, black waxy soils.

Economy: Agribusiness; oil activity; government/services; manufacturing.

History: Spanish explorers found Jumanos in area in 1650s; later, Apaches and Comanches driven out in 1870s by U.S. military. First Anglo-Americans arrived in 1850s; Germans, Czechs around 1900. County named for planter-legislator H.G. Runnels; created 1858 from Bexar, Travis counties; organized 1880.

Race/Ethnicity, 2000: (In percent) Anglo, 68.32; Black, 1.57; Hispanic, 29.33; Other, 0.78.

Vital Statistics, 2003: Births, 143; deaths, 164; marriages, 81; divorces, 36.

Recreation: Deer, dove and turkey hunting; O.H. Ivie Reservoir; fishing; antique car museum; historical markers in county.

Minerals: Oil, gas, sand.

Agriculture: Cattle, cotton, wheat, sorghum, dairy products, sheep and goats. Market value $27.4 million.

BALLINGER (4,104) county seat; varied manufacturing; oil-field services; meat processing; Carnegie Library; hospital; Western Texas College extension; the Cross, 100-ft. tall atop hill south of city; Festival of Ethnic Cultures in April.

Other towns include: **Miles** (819); **Norton** (50); **Rowena** (349); **Wingate** (100); **Winters** (2,783) manufacturing, museum; hospital.

Population	**10,943**
Change fm 2000	-4.8
Area (sq. mi.)	1,057.13
Land Area (sq. mi.)	1,050.73
Altitude (ft.)	1,600-2,301
Rainfall (in.)	23.76
Jan. mean min.	28.5
July mean max	94.3

Civ. Labor	4,083
Unemployed	3.5
Wages	$18,536,115
Av. Weekly Wage	$443.23
Prop. Value	$696,771,530
Retail Sales	$58,665,679

For explanation of sources, abbreviations and symbols, see p. 167 and foldout map.

The cotton fields and farms near Rowena in Runnels County. Texas Almanac photo.

Rusk County

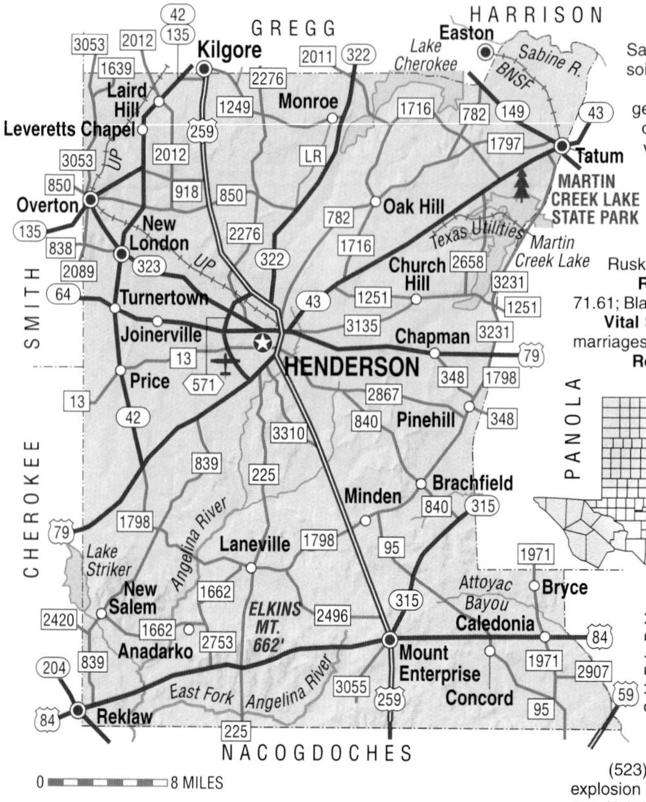

Physical Features: East Texas county on Sabine-Angelina divide; varied deep, sandy soils; over half in pines, hardwoods; lakes.

Economy: Lignite mining, electricity generation, oil and gas, lumbering, brick production, agribusiness, government/services.

History: Caddo area. Cherokees settled in 1820s; removed in 1839. First Anglo-Americans arrived in 1829. Antebellum slaveholding area. County named for Republic, state leader Thomas J. Rusk; created from Nacogdoches County 1843.

Race/Ethnicity, 2000: (In percent) Anglo, 71.61; Black, 19.31; Hispanic, 8.44; Other, 0.64.

Vital Statistics, 2003: Births, 579; deaths, 544; marriages, 353; divorces, 272.

Recreation: Water sports, state park; historic homes, sites; scenic drives; marked site of East Texas Field discovery oil well; syrup festival in November.

Minerals: Oil, natural gas, lignite, clays.

Agriculture: Beef cattle, hay, broilers, nursery plants. Market value $39.3 million. Timber income substantial.

HENDERSON (11,332) county seat; center for agribusiness, oil activities; varied manufacturing; hospital; museum; state jails.

Other towns include: **Joinerville** (140); **Laird Hill** (300); **Laneville** (169); **Minden** (150); **Mount Enterprise** (523); **New London** (983) site of 1937 school explosion that killed 293 students and faculty; **Overton** (2,377, partly in Smith County) oil, lumbering center, petroleum processing, A&M research center, blue grass festival in July, prison unit; **Price** (275); **Tatum** (1,165, partly in Panola County); **Turnertown-Selman City** (271).

Also, part of **Easton** (562, mostly in Gregg County), part of **Reklaw** (351, mostly in Cherokee County) and part [2,580] of **Kilgore** (11,508 total).

Population **47,973**	July mean max. 93.1
Change fm 2000 .... 1.3	Civ. Labor 21,917
Area (sq. mi.) 938.62	Unemployed 4.5
Land Area (sq. mi.) 923.55	Wages $99,631,203
Altitude (ft.) 280-662	Av. Weekly Wage $576.84
Rainfall (in.) 48.22	Prop. Value $3,480,942,350
Jan. mean min. 33.1	Retail Sales $305,601,781

Plant nurseries, such as this one on Texas 42, are an important part of the Rusk County economy. Texas Almanac photo.

Sabine County

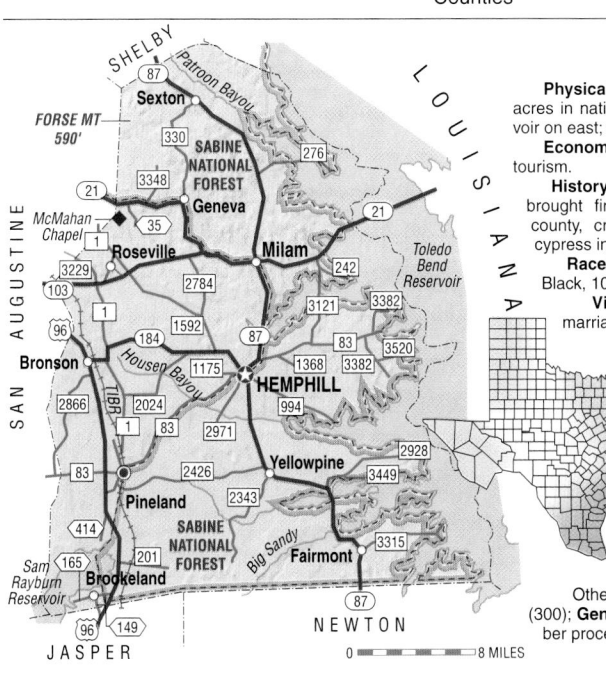

Physical Features: Eighty percent forested; 114,498 acres in national forest; Sabine River, Toledo Bend Reservoir on east; Sam Rayburn Reservoir on southwest.

Economy: Timber industries; government/services; tourism.

History: Caddo area. Spanish land grants in 1790s brought first Spanish and Anglo settlers. An original county, created 1836; organized 1837. Name means cypress in Spanish.

Race/Ethnicity, 2000: (In percent) Anglo, 87.66; Black, 10.11; Hispanic, 1.81; Other, 0.42.

Vital Statistics, 2003: Births, 88; deaths, 152; marriages, 99; divorces, 33.

Recreation: Lake activities; campsites; marinas; McMahan's Chapel, pioneer Protestant church; historic homes; Sabine National Forest; hunting.

Minerals: Glauconite, oil.

Agriculture: Beef cattle; forage, fruit raised. Market value $6.9 million. Significant timber industry.

HEMPHILL (1,087) county seat; timber, livestock center; retail trade; tourism; manufacturing; hospital; jail museum; library; Deerfest in October.

Other towns include: **Bronson** (377); **Brookeland** (300); **Geneva** (200); **Milam** (1,234); **Pineland** (943) timber processing.

Population	10,407
Change fm 2000	-0.6
Area (sq. mi.)	576.61
Land Area (sq. mi.)	490.27
Altitude (ft.)	164-590
Rainfall (in.)	54.40
Jan. mean min.	36.0
July mean max.	93.0
Civ. Labor	3,748
Unemployed	11.4
Wages	$20,594,478
Av. Weekly Wage	$655.71
Prop. Value	$585,033,022
Retail Sales	$50,486,8761

San Augustine County

Physical Features: Hilly East Texas county, 80 percent forested with 66,799 acres in Angelina National Forest, 4,317 in Sabine National Forest; Sam Rayburn Reservoir; varied soils, sandy to black alluvial.

Economy: Lumbering; shipping; varied manufacturing.

History: Presence of Caddoes attracted Spanish mission in 1717. First Anglos and Indians from U.S. southern states arrived around 1800. Antebellum slaveholding area. County created and named for Mexican municipality in 1836; an original county; organized 1837.

Race/Ethnicity, 2000: (In percent) Anglo, 68.13; Black, 27.93; Hispanic, 3.58; Other, 0.36.

Vital Statistics, 2003: Births, 90; deaths, 125; marriages, 88; divorces, 4.

Recreation: Lake activities; pine fest, annual tour of homes in April, sassafras festival in October; many historic homes; tourist facilities in national forests.

Minerals: Small amount of oil.

Agriculture: Poultry, cattle, horses; watermelons, peas, corn, truck crops. Market value $25 million. Timber sales significant.

SAN AUGUSTINE (2,501) county seat; tourism; livestock center; varied manufacturing; Deep East Texas Electric Cooperative; lumbering; hospital; Tour of Homes.

Other towns include: **Broaddus** (182).

Population	8,923
Change fm 2000	-0.3
Area (sq. mi.)	592.21
Land Area (sq. mi.)	527.87
Altitude (ft.)	164-550
Rainfall (in.)	51.10
Jan. mean min.	35.0
July mean max.	93.0
Civ. Labor	3,175
Unemployed	7.0
Wages	$10,225,879
Av. Weekly Wage	$445.67
Prop. Value	$372,127,984
Retail Sales	$57,847,130

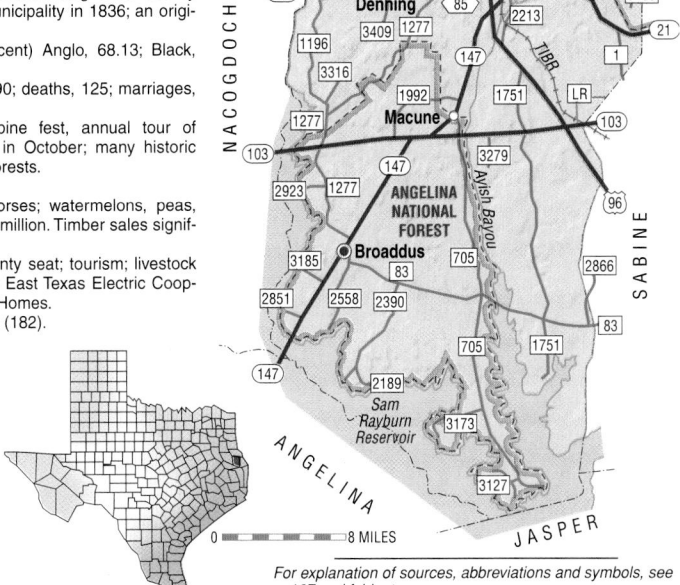

For explanation of sources, abbreviations and symbols, see p. 167 and foldout map.

San Jacinto County

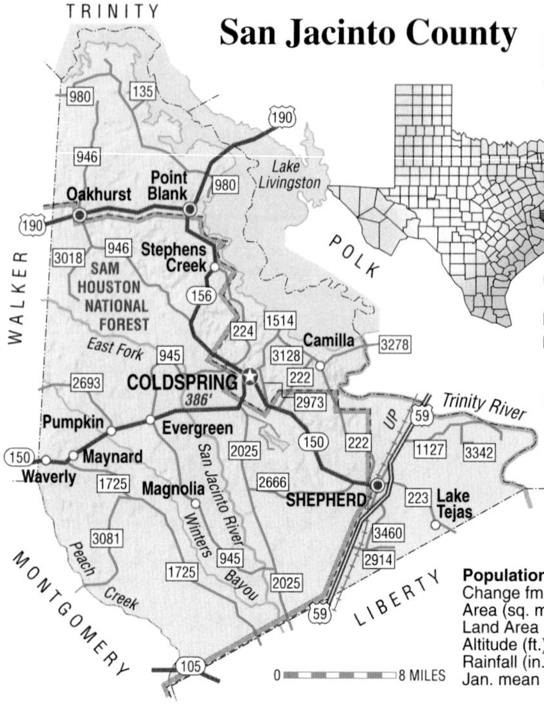

Physical Features: East Texas county north of Houston; rolling hills; 80 percent forested; 58,625 acres in Sam Houston National Forest; Trinity, East Fork San Jacinto rivers.

Economy: Timber and oil.

History: Atakapa Indian area. Anglo-Americans arrived in 1820s. Land grants issued to Mexican families in early 1830s. County created from Liberty, Montgomery, Polk, Walker counties 1869; organized 1870; named for the battle.

Race/Ethnicity, 2000: (In percent) Anglo, 81.60; Black, 12.72; Hispanic, 4.87; Other, 0.81.

Vital Statistics, 2003: Births, 247; deaths, 225; marriages, 155; divorces, 122.

Recreation: Lake activities; hunting; old courthouse and jail are tourist attractions. Approximately 60 percent of county in national forest.

Minerals: Oil, rock, gravel and iron ore.

Agriculture: Beef cattle and forages. Market value $5.5 million. Timber principal product.

COLDSPRING (714) county seat; lumbering; oil; farming center; tourism; historic sites.

SHEPHERD (2,151) lumbering.

Other towns include: **Oakhurst** (228); **Point Blank** (606) logging, agribusiness, construction.

Population 24,678	July mean max. 93.8
Change fm 2000 .... 10.9	Civ. Labor 9,300
Area (sq. mi.) 627.90	Unemployed 5.1
Land Area (sq. mi.) 570.65	Wages $13,190,673
Altitude (ft.) 74-386	Av. Weekly Wage $451.97
Rainfall (in.) 51.77	Prop. Value.... $1,049,513,871
Jan. mean min. 37.5	Retail Sales $61,324,108

San Patricio County

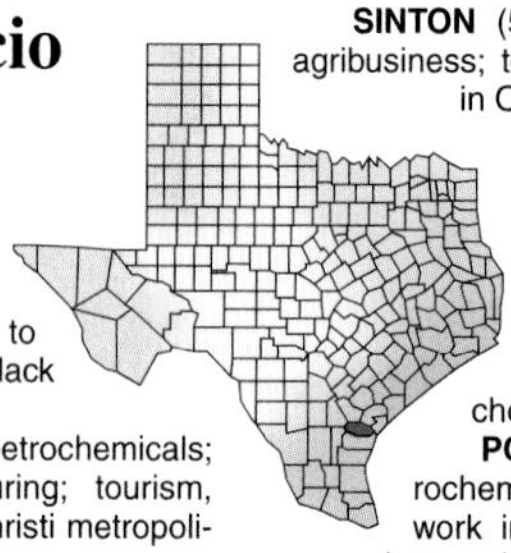

Physical Features: Grassy, coastal prairie draining to Aransas, Nueces rivers and to bays; sandy loam, clay, black loam soils; lake.

Economy: Oil, petrochemicals; agribusiness; manufacturing; tourism; naval base; in Corpus Christi metropolitan area.

History: Karankawa area. Mexican sheep herders in area before colonization. Settled by Irish families in 1830 (name is Spanish for St. Patrick). Created, named for municipality 1836; organized 1837, reorganized 1847.

Race/Ethnicity, 2000: (In percent) Anglo, 46.48; Black, 2.84; Hispanic, 49.42; Other, 1.26.

Vital Statistics, 2003: Births, 1,112; deaths, 530; marriages, 283; divorces, 257.

Recreation: Water activities; hunting; Corpus Christi Bay; state park; Welder Wildlife Foundation and Park; shrimporee; birdwatching.

Minerals: Production of oil, gas, iron ore.

Agriculture: Cotton, grain sorghum, beef cattle, corn. Market value $68.9 million. Fisheries income significant.

SINTON (5,586) county seat; oil, agribusiness; tourism; Go Texan Days in October.

ARANSAS PASS (8,609, parts in Aransas, Nueces counties) deepwater port, shrimping, tourist center; offshore oil-well servicing; aluminum, chemical plants; hospitals.

PORTLAND (15,434) petrochemicals; many residents work in Corpus Christi, naval bases; Indian Point pier; Windfest in April.

Other towns include: **Edroy** (420); **Gregory** (2,234); **Ingleside** (9,563) naval base, chemical and manufacturing plants, ship repair, birding, Round Up Days in May; **Ingleside-on-the-Bay** (680); **Lake City** (533); **Lakeside** (326); **Mathis** (5,143); **Odem** (2,493); **St. Paul** (530); **San Patricio** (314, partly in Nueces County); **Taft** (3,420) manufacturing, processing; drug rehabilitation center; hospital; Christmas parade; **Taft Southwest** (1,643).

Population 68,187	
Change fm 2000 .... 1.6	
Area (sq. mi.) 707.06	
Land Area (sq. mi.) 691.65	
Altitude (ft.) .... sea level-200	
Rainfall (in.) 35.54	
Jan. mean min. 44.2	
July mean max. 91.7	
Civ. Labor 30,394	
Unemployed 8.0	
Wages $127,954,209	
Av. Weekly Wage $605.74	
Prop. Value $3,440,532,922	
Retail Sales $516,855,766	

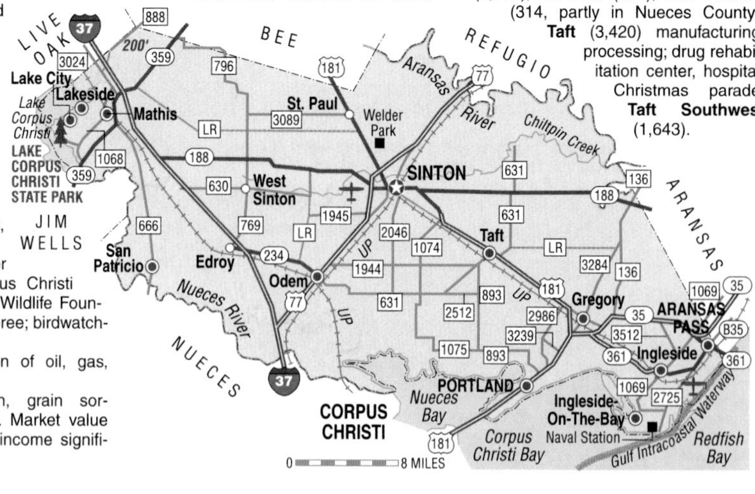

San Saba County

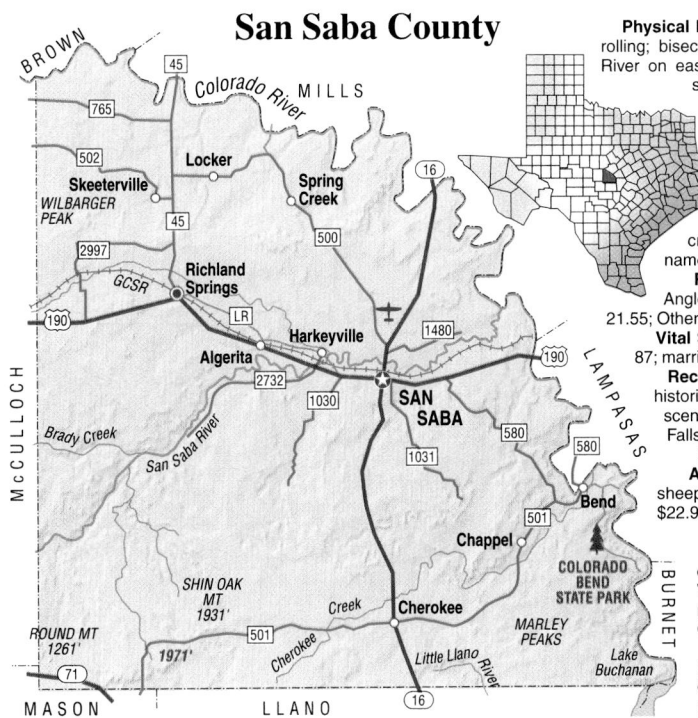

Physical Features: West central county; hilly, rolling; bisected by San Saba River; Colorado River on east; black, gray sandy loam, alluvial soils.

Economy: Government/services; retail pecan industry; tourism, hunting leases.

History: Apaches and Comanches in area when Spanish explored. Anglo-American settlers arrived in 1850s. County created from Bexar District 1856; named for river.

Race/Ethnicity, 2000: (In percent) Anglo, 75.19; Black, 2.63; Hispanic, 21.55; Other, 0.63.

Vital Statistics, 2003: Births, 79; deaths, 87; marriages, 31; divorces, 20.

Recreation: State park; deer hunting; historic sites; log cabin museum; fishing; scenic drives; wildflower trail; Gorman Falls.

Minerals: Limestone, rock quarry.

Agriculture: Cattle, pecans, hay, sheep and goats, wheat. Market value $22.9 million. Hunting, wildlife leases.

SAN SABA (2,593) county seat; claims title "Pecan Capital of the World"; stone processing; varied manufacturing; state prison; Cow Camp cookoff in May.

Other towns include: **Bend** (115, partly in Lampasas County); **Cherokee** (175); **Richland Springs** (343).

Population...............................6,086	
Change fm 2000 ....-1.6	
Area (sq. mi.) 1,138.25	
Land Area (sq. mi.) 1,134.47	
Altitude (ft.)..........................1,100-1,971	
Rainfall (in.) 27.72	
Jan. mean min..............................33.4	
July mean max. 95.8	
Civ. Labor 2,836	
Unemployed 2.6	
Wages...............................$11,185,004	
Av. Weekly Wage....................$445.10	
Fed. Wages............................$193,542	
Prop. Value $757,450,131	
Retail Sales.......................$30,101,862	

Schleicher County

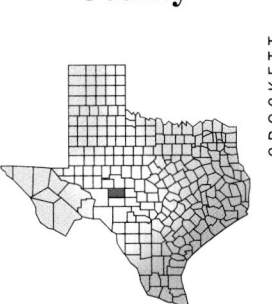

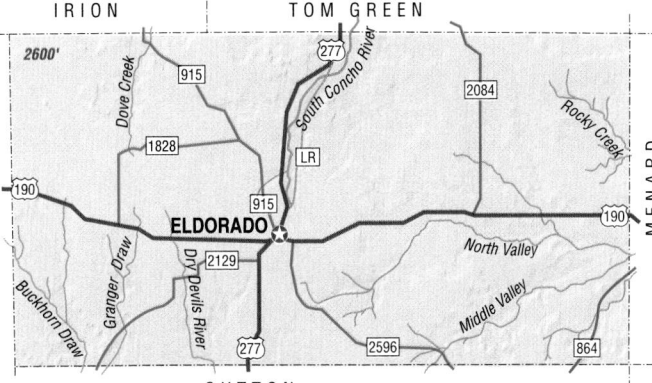

Physical Features: West central county on edge of Edwards Plateau, broken by Devils, Concho, San Saba tributaries; part hilly; black soils.

Economy: Oil, ranching; hunting.

History: Jumanos in area in 1630s. Later, Apaches and Comanches; removed in 1870s. Ranching began in 1870s. Census of 1890 showed third of population from Mexico. County named for Gustav Schleicher, founder of German colony; county created from Crockett County 1887, organized 1901.

Race/Ethnicity, 2000: (In percent) Anglo, 54.59; Black, 1.26; Hispanic, 43.54; Other, 0.61.

Vital Statistics, 2003: Births, 34; deaths, 42; marriages, 17; divorces, 12.

Recreation: Hunting; livestock show in January, youth, open rodeos; mountain bike events; playhouse "Way off Broadway".

Minerals: Oil, natural gas.

Agriculture: Beef cattle, goats, sheep; crops include cotton, milo, hay, small grains. Market value $9.2 million. Hunting leases important.

ELDORADO (1,931) county seat; oil activities; center for livestock, mohair marketing, woolen mill; government/services, medical center.

Population 2,779	
Change fm 2000........................-5.3	
Area (sq. mi.)..................... 1,310.65	
Land Area (sq. mi.)............. 1,310.61	
Altitude (ft.)..................2,100-2,600	
Rainfall (in.) 19.00	
Jan. mean min.......................... 28.0	
July mean max. 93.0	
Civ. Labor.............................. 1,601	
Unemployed 2.1	
Wages $5,213,376	
Av. Weekly Wage $503.17	
Prop. Value...............$414,516,320	
Retail Sales $8,841,237	

For explanation of sources, abbreviations and symbols, see p. 167 and foldout map.

Scurry County

Physical Features: Plains county below Caprock, some hills; drained by Colorado, Brazos tributaries; lake; sandy, loam soils.

Economy: Oil production; government/services; agribusinesses, manufacturing.

History: Apaches; displaced later by Comanches who were relocated to Indian Territory in 1875. Ranching began in late 1870s. County created from Bexar District 1876; organized 1884; named for Confederate Gen. W.R. Scurry.

Race/Ethnicity, 2000: (In percent) Anglo, 65.55; Black, 6.14; Hispanic, 27.77; Other, 0.54.

Vital Statistics, 2003: Births, 245; deaths, 169; marriages, 142; divorces, 76.

Recreation: Lake J.B. Thomas water recreation; Towle Memorial Park; museums, community theater, White Buffalo festival in October.

Minerals: Oil, gas.

Agriculture: Cotton, wheat, cattle, hay. Market value $23 million.

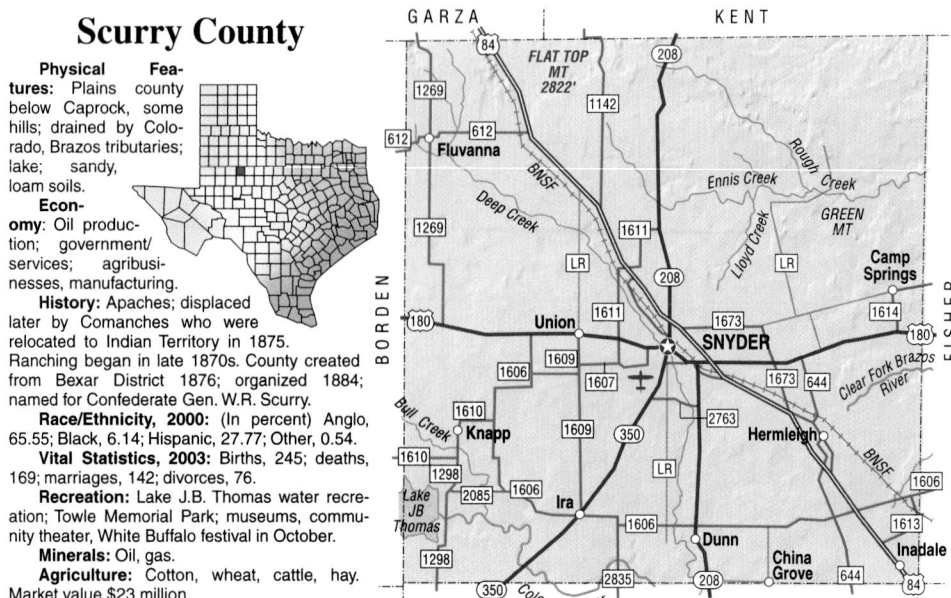

SNYDER (10,681) county seat; textiles, brick plant, cotton, oil center; Western Texas (Jr.) College; hospital; prison; walking trail; Western Swing days in June.

Other towns include: **Dunn** (75); **Fluvanna** (180); **Hermleigh** (369); **Ira** (250).

Population	16,084
Change fm 2000	-1.7
Area (sq. mi.)	907.53
Land Area (sq. mi.)	902.50
Altitude (ft.)	2,000-2,822
Rainfall (in.)	22.51
Jan. mean min.	26.7
July mean max.	94.6
Civ. Labor	7,286
Unemployed	3.6
Wages	$43,920,119
Av. Weekly Wage	$592.92
Prop. Value	$1,154,574,198
Retail Sales	$141,787,180

Shackelford County

Physical Features: Rolling, hilly, drained by tributaries of Brazos; sandy and chocolate loam soils; lake.

Economy: Oil and ranching; some manufacturing; hunting leases.

History: Apaches; driven out by Comanches. First Anglo-American settlers arrived soon after establishment of military outpost in 1850s. County created from Bosque County 1858; organized 1874; named for Dr. Jack Shackelford (sometimes referred to as John), Texas Revolutionary hero.

Race/Ethnicity, 2000: (In percent) Anglo, 91.68; Black, 0.33; Hispanic, 7.60; Other, 0.39.

Vital Statistics, 2003: Births, 25; deaths, 45; marriages, 25; divorces, 12.

Recreation: Fort Griffin State Park, June Fandangle musical about area history; courthouse historical district; hunting, lake, outdoor activities.

Minerals: Oil, natural gas.

Agriculture: Beef cattle, wheat, hay, cotton. Market value $15.1 million. Hunting leases.

ALBANY (1,889) county seat; tourism; oil, agriculture center; quarter-horse breeding; hospital; historical district, Old Jail art center.

Other town: **Moran** (226).

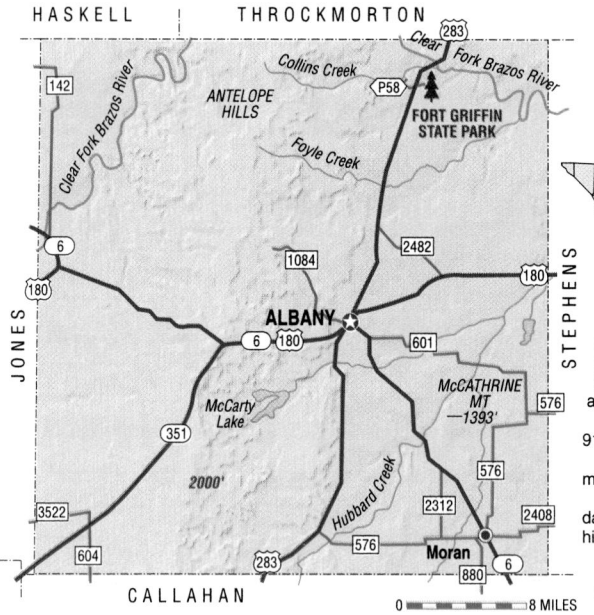

Population	3,232
Change fm 2000	-2.1
Area (sq. mi.)	915.54
Land Area (sq. mi.)	913.95
Altitude (ft.)	1,200-2,000
Rainfall (in.)	28.45
Jan. mean min.	28.4
July mean max.	95.4
Civ. Labor	1,466
Unemployed	1.8
Wages	$6,365,109
Av. Weekly Wage	$452.94
Prop. Value	$399,164,277
Retail Sales	$12,912,898

For explanation of sources, abbreviations and symbols, see p. 167 and foldout map.

Shelby County

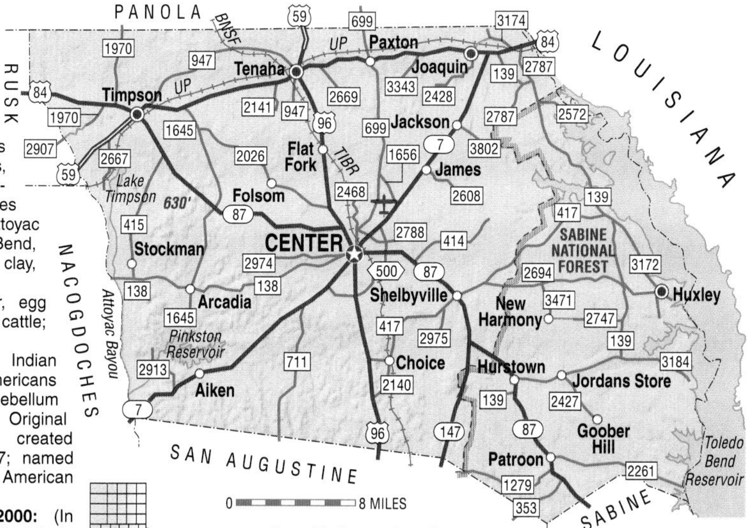

Physical Features: East Texas county; partly hills, much bottomland; well-timbered, 67,762 acres in national forest; Attoyac Bayou and Toledo Bend, other streams; sandy, clay, alluvial soils.

Economy: Broiler, egg production; timber; cattle; tourism.

History: Caddo Indian area. First Anglo-Americans settled in 1810s. Antebellum slaveholding area. Original county of Republic, created 1836; organized 1837; named for Isaac Shelby of American Revolution.

Race/Ethnicity, 2000: (In percent) Anglo, 69.95; Black, 19.53; Hispanic, 9.87; Other, 0.65.

Vital Statistics, 2003: Births, 392; deaths, 314; marriages, 216; divorces, 83.

Recreation: Toledo Bend Reservoir activities; Sabine National Forest; hunting, fishing, camping; historic sites, restored 1885 courthouse.

Minerals: Natural gas, oil.

Agriculture: A leader in broiler and egg production; cattle; hay, vegetables, watermelons. Market value $240.6 million. Timber sales significant.

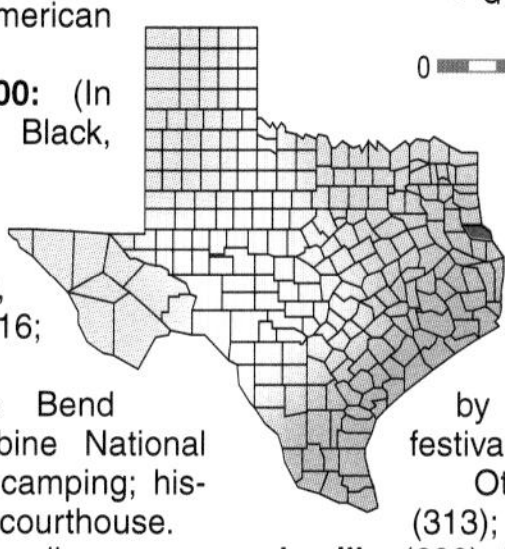

CENTER (5,635) county seat; poultry, lumber processing; tourism; hospital; Shelby College Center; Poultry festival in October.

Other towns: **Huxley** (313); **Joaquin** (930); **Shelbyville** (600); **Tenaha** (1,072); **Timpson** (1,083) livestock, timber, farming, commuters; genealogy library; So-So festival in fall.

Population	26,156
Change fm 2000	3.7
Area (sq. mi.)	834.53
Land Area (sq. mi.)	794.11
Altitude (ft.)	174-630
Rainfall (in.)	53.01
Jan. mean min.	34.9
July mean max.	93.9
Civ. Labor	9,512
Unemployed	6.6
Wages	$46,941,521
Av. Weekly Wage	$491.81
Prop. Value	$1,163,885,658
Retail Sales	$192,155,299

The Shelby County Courthouse in Center, built in 1885. Texas Almanac photo.

Sherman County

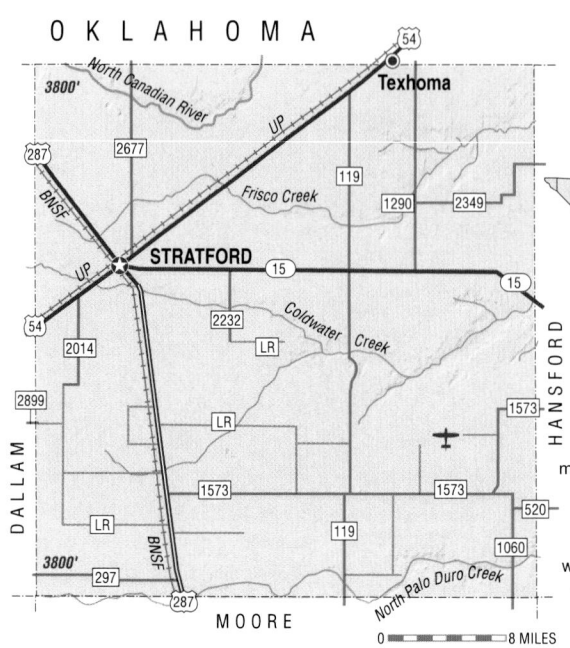

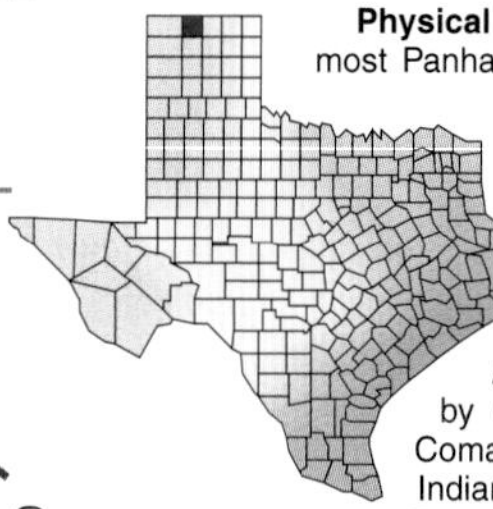

Physical Features: A northern-most Panhandle county; level, broken by creeks, playas; sandy to dark loam soils; underground water.

Economy: Agribusiness, tourism.

History: Apaches; pushed out by Comanches in 1700s. Comanches removed to Indian Territory in 1875. Ranching began around 1880; farming after 1900. County named for Texas Gen. Sidney Sherman; created from Bexar District 1876; organized 1889.

Race/Ethnicity, 2000: (In percent) Anglo, 71.54; Black, 0.50; Hispanic, 27.43; Other, 0.53.

Vital Statistics, 2003: Births, 45; deaths, 36; marriages, 25; divorces, 4.

Recreation: Depot museum; jamboree and ranch rodeo in July; pheasant hunting.

Minerals: Natural gas, oil.

Agriculture: Beef and stocker cattle important; wheat, corn, grain sorghum, alfalfa; swine; 145,000 acres irrigated. Market value $295.1 million.

STRATFORD (2,025) county seat; agribusiness center; government/services; birdseed packaging; VA clinic; German sausage festival in February.

Texhoma (378 in Texas, 985 in Oklahoma) other principal town.

Population	3,095
Change fm 2000	-2.9
Area (sq. mi.)	923.20
Land Area (sq. mi.)	923.03
Altitude (ft.)	3,200-3,800
Rainfall (in.)	17.89

Jan. mean min.	18.5
July mean max.	91.1
Civ. Labor	1,305
Unemployed	1.5

Wages	$5,934,542
Av. Weekly Wage	$505.54
Prop. Value	$598,038,498
Retail Sales	$13,890,926

An early morning pastoral scene in Upshur County in East Texas. Texas Almanac photo.

Smith County

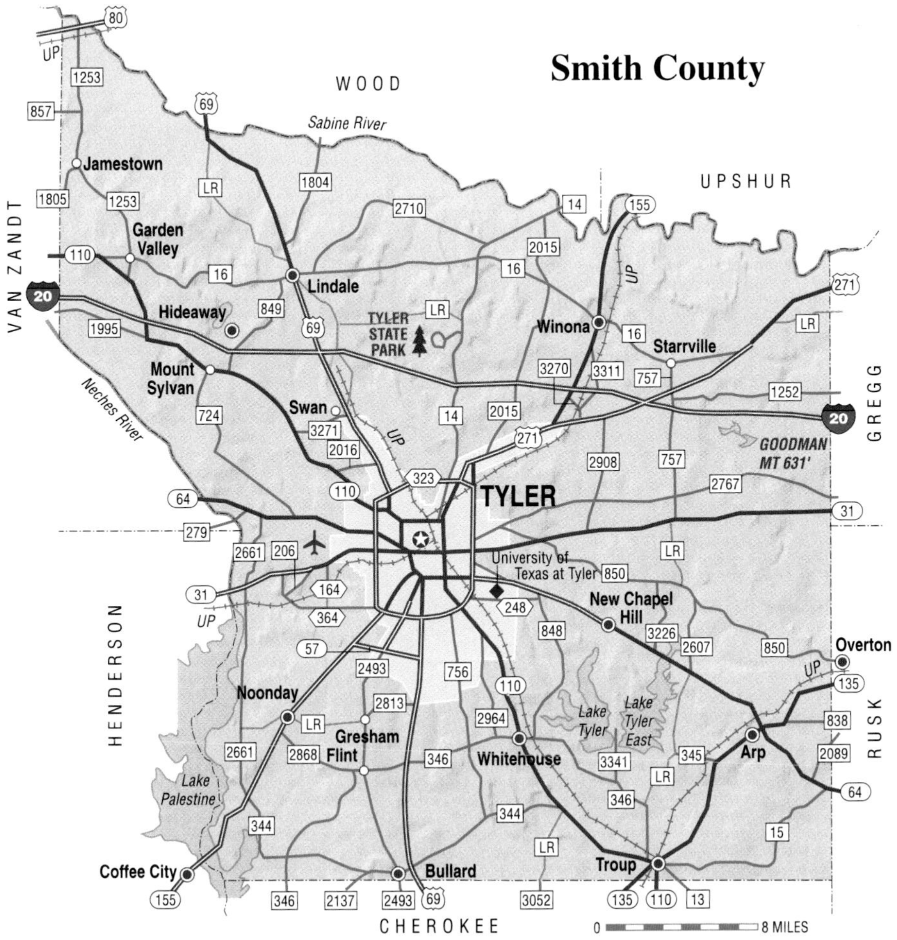

WOOD

Sabine River

VAN ZANDT

UPSHUR

GREGG

HENDERSON

RUSK

CHEROKEE

0 ▬▬▬▬ 8 MILES

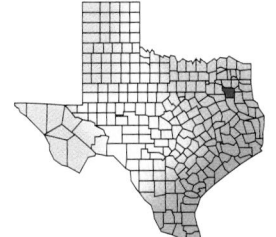

Physical Features: Populous East Texas county of rolling hills, many timbered; Sabine, Neches, other streams; Tyler, Palestine lakes; alluvial, gray, sandy loam, clay soils.

Economy: Medical facilities, education, government/services; agribusiness; petroleum production; manufacturing, distribution center; tourism.

History: Caddoes of area reduced by disease and other tribes in 1790s. Cherokees settled in 1820s; removed in 1839. In late 1820s, first Anglo-American settlers arrived. Antebellum slave-holding area. County named for Texas Revolutionary Gen. James Smith; county created 1846 from Nacogdoches County.

Race/Ethnicity, 2000: (In percent) Anglo, 68.40; Black, 19.24; Hispanic, 11.17; Other, 1.19.

Vital Statistics, 2003: Births, 2,873; deaths, 1,753; marriages, 1,873; divorces, 638.

Recreation: Activities on Palestine, Tyler lakes and others; famed Rose Garden; Texas Rose Festival in October; Azalea Trail; state park; Goodman Museum; Juneteenth celebration, East Texas Fair in Sept./Oct.; Caldwell Zoo; collegiate events.

Minerals: Oil, gas, iron ore, gravel and soils.

Agriculture: Horticultural crops and roses; beef cattle, hay, melons, horses. Market value $63.5 million. Timber sales substantial.

TYLER (90,079) county seat; claims title, "Rose Capital of the Nation"; administrative center for oil production; varied manufacturing; University of Texas at Tyler, Tyler Junior College; Texas College, University of Texas Health Center; hospitals, nursing school.

Other towns include: **Arp** (933) Strawberry Festival in April; **Bullard** (1,357, part in Cherokee County); **Flint** (NA); **Hideaway** (2,712); **Lindale** (3,749) rose distribution, food processing; Country Fest in October, youth rodeo in August; **New Chapel Hill** (578); **Noonday** (536) Sweet Onion festival in June; **Troup** (2,101, part in Cherokee County); **Whitehouse** (6,484) commuters to Tyler, government/services, Yesteryear festival in June; **Winona** (622).

Part of **Overton** (2,377, mostly in Rusk County).

Population	**186,414**
Change fm 2000	6.7
Area (sq. mi.)	949.45
Land Area (sq. mi.)	928.38
Altitude (ft.)	300-631
Rainfall (in.)	45.40
Jan. mean min.	38.0
July mean max.	94.0
Civ. Labor	99,063
Unemployed	4.3
Wages	$728,168,781
Av. Weekly Wage	$649.37
Prop. Value	$10,353,419,353
Retail Sales	$2,558,152,808

For explanation of sources, abbreviations and symbols, see p. 167 and foldout map.

Somervell County

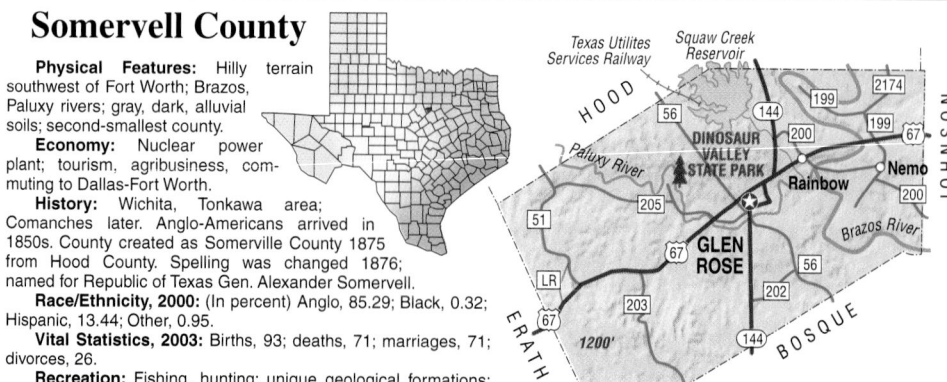

Physical Features: Hilly terrain southwest of Fort Worth; Brazos, Paluxy rivers; gray, dark, alluvial soils; second-smallest county.

Economy: Nuclear power plant; tourism, agribusiness, commuting to Dallas-Fort Worth.

History: Wichita, Tonkawa area; Comanches later. Anglo-Americans arrived in 1850s. County created as Somerville County 1875 from Hood County. Spelling was changed 1876; named for Republic of Texas Gen. Alexander Somervell.

Race/Ethnicity, 2000: (In percent) Anglo, 85.29; Black, 0.32; Hispanic, 13.44; Other, 0.95.

Vital Statistics, 2003: Births, 93; deaths, 71; marriages, 71; divorces, 26.

Recreation: Fishing, hunting; unique geological formations; dinosaur tracks in state park; Glen Rose Big Rocks Park; Fossil Rim Wildlife Center; nature trails, museums; exposition center; Moonshine Festival in October.

Minerals: Sand, gravel, silica.

Agriculture: Cattle, hay, small grains, goats. Market value $2 million.

GLEN ROSE (2,360) county seat; nuclear power plant, tourism, farm trade center; hospital; Hill College branch.

Other towns include: **Nemo** (56); **Rainbow** (121).

Population	7,453
Change fm 2000	9.5
Area (sq. mi.)	191.90
Land Area (sq. mi.)	187.17
Altitude (ft.)	600-1,200
Rainfall (in.)	34.82
Jan. mean min.	28.9

July mean max.	97.3
Civ. Labor	2,079
Unemployed	8.8
Wages	$35,645,557
Av. Weekly Wage	$756.40
Prop. Value	$1,964,501,035
Retail Sales	$48,132,592

Starr County

Physical Features: Rolling, some hills; dense brush; clay, loam, sandy soils, alluvial on Rio Grande; Falcon Reservoir.

Economy: Vegetable packing, shipping, other agribusiness; oil processing; tourism; government/services.

History: Coahuiltecan Indian area. Settlers from Spanish villages that were established in 1749 on south bank began to move across river soon afterward. Fort Ringgold established in 1848. County named for Dr. J.H. Starr, secretary of treasury of the Republic; county created from Nueces 1848.

Race/Ethnicity, 2000: (In percent) Anglo, 2.08; Black, 0.01; Hispanic, 97.54; Other, 0.37.

Vital Statistics, 2003: Births, 1,488; deaths, 294; marriages, 474; divorces, 26.

Recreation: Falcon Reservoir activities; deer, white-wing dove hunting; access to Mexico; historic houses, Lee House at Fort Ringgold; grotto at Rio Grande City; Roma Fest in November.

Minerals: Oil, gas, sand, gravel.

Agriculture: Beef and fed cattle; vegetables, cotton, sorghum; 18,000 acres irrigated for vegetables. Market value $66.7 million.

RIO GRANDE CITY (13,088) county seat; agriculture center; food processing; exports to Mexico; hospital.

ROMA-Los Saenz (10,901) agriculture center; La Purísima Concepcíon Visita.

Other towns include: **Delmita** (50); **Escobares** (1,999); **Falcon Heights** (346); **Fronton** (628); **Garceño** (1,508); **La Casita-Garciasville** (2,353); **La Grulla** (1,232); **La Puerta** (1,719); **La Rosita** (1,810); **Las Lomas** (2,821); **La Victoria** (1,756); **Los Alvarez** (1,507); **Los Villareales** (971); **North Escobares** (1,781); **Salineño** (312); **San Isidro** (277); **Santa Elena** (64).

Population	59,832
Change fm 2000	11.6
Area (sq. mi.)	1,229.28
Land Area (sq. mi.)	1,223.02
Altitude (ft.)	125-531
Rainfall (in.)	21.61
Jan. mean min.	44.5
July mean max.	99.1
Civ. Labor	24,386
Unemployed	17.0
Wages	$58,442,020
Av. Weekly Wage	$380.43
Prop. Value	$1,659,244,580
Retail Sales	$346,561,462

Stephens County

Physical Features: West central county; broken, hilly; Hubbard Creek Reservoir, Possum Kingdom, Daniel lakes; Brazos River; loam, sandy soils.

Economy: Oil, agribusinesses, recreation, some manufacturing.

History: Comanches, Tonkawas in area when Anglo-American settlement began in 1850s. County created as Buchanan 1858 from Bosque; renamed 1861 for Confederate Vice President Alexander H. Stephens; organized 1876.

Race/Ethnicity, 2000: (In percent) Anglo, 81.76; Black, 3.04; Hispanic, 14.66; Other, 0.54.

Vital Statistics, 2003: Births, 131; deaths, 99; marriages, 71; divorces, 42.

Recreation: Lakes activities; hunting; campsites; historical points; Swenson Museum; Sandefer Oil Museum; aviation museum; Fabulous Fifties and car show in September.

Minerals: Oil, natural gas, stone.

Agriculture: Beef cattle, hogs, goats, sheep; wheat, oats, hay, peanuts, grain sorghums, cotton, pecans. Market value $8.8 million.

BRECKENRIDGE (5,813) county seat; oil, agriculture center; oilfield equipment, aircraft parts manufacturing; hospital; prison unit; Texas State Technical College branch, library.

Other towns include: **Caddo** (40) gateway to Possum Kingdom State Park.

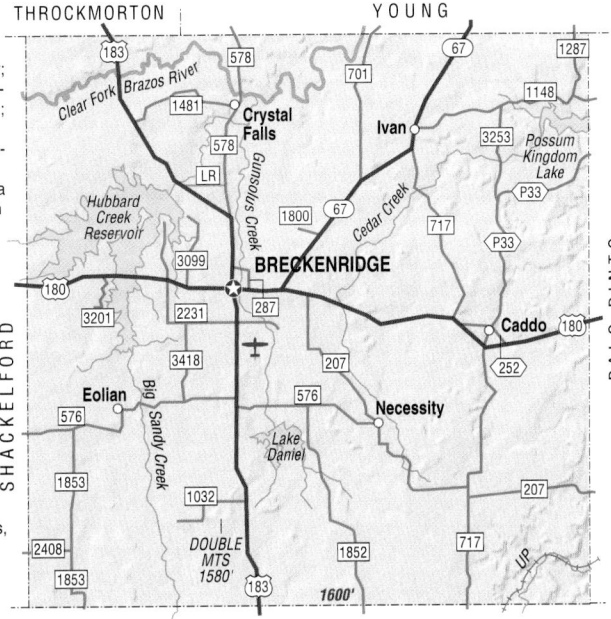

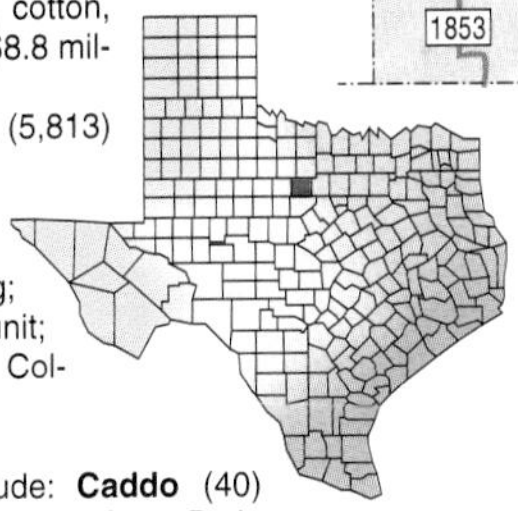

Population **9,523**	July mean max 96.8
Change fm 2000 .... -1.6	Civ. Labor 3,211
Area (sq. mi.) 921.48	Unemployed 3.7
Land Area (sq. mi.) 894.64	Wages $17,858,558
Altitude (ft.) 995-1,600	Av. Weekly Wage $473.05
Rainfall (in.) 27.04	Prop. Value $625,886,440
Jan. mean min 30.9	Retail Sales $69,580,192

For explanation of sources, abbreviations and symbols, see p. 167 and foldout map.

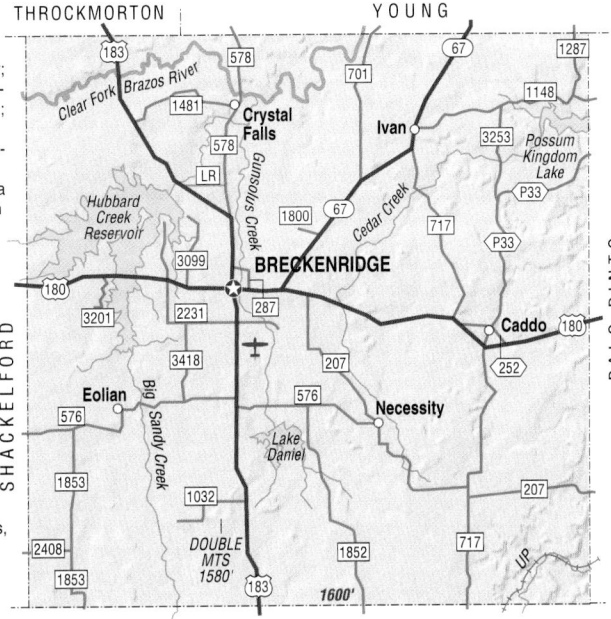

Passengers board the ferry at Los Ebanos in Hidalgo County to cross the Rio Grande into Mexico. Texas Almanac photo.

Sterling County

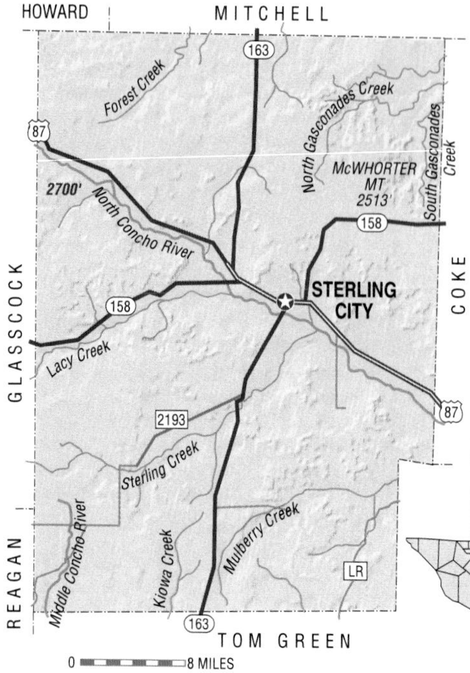

HOWARD | MITCHELL

Forest Creek

163

87

North Gasconades Creek

South Gasconades Creek

2700'

McWHORTER MT 2513'

North Concho River

158

GLASSCOCK

158

Lacy Creek

STERLING CITY

COKE

2193

87

REAGAN

Middle Concho River

Kiowa Creek

Mulberry Creek

Sterling Creek

LR

163

TOM GREEN

0 ▬▬▬▬ 8 MILES

Physical Features: Central prairie, surrounded by hills, broken by Concho River and tributaries; sandy to black soils.

Economy: Ranching; oil and gas; hunting leases.

History: Ranching began in late 1870s after Comanches, Kickapoos and other tribes removed by U.S. Army. County named for buffalo hunter W.S. Sterling; created 1891 from Tom Green County.

Race/Ethnicity, 2000: (In percent) Anglo, 68.63; Black, 0.07; Hispanic, 31.01; Other, 0.29.

Vital Statistics, 2003: Births, 15; deaths, 12; marriages, 5; divorces, 2.

Recreation: Hunting of deer, quail, turkey, dove; hunters appreciation dinner in November; junior livestock show in January.

Minerals: Oil, natural gas.

Agriculture: Beef cattle, meat goats, sheep; wheat, hay; about 1,000 acres irrigated. Market value $5.8 million.

STERLING CITY (1,064) county seat; farm, ranch trade center; oil-field services.

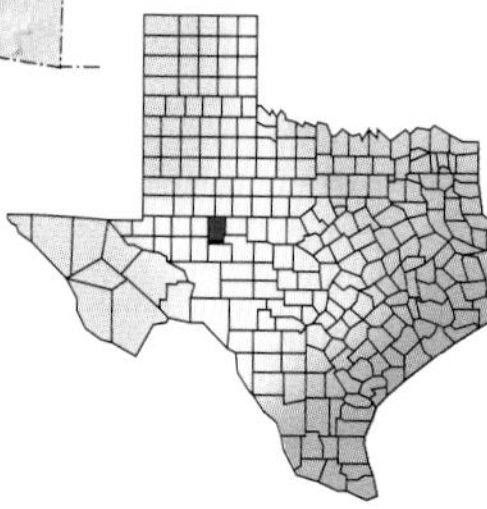

Population	**1,305**
Change fm 2000	-6.3
Area (sq. mi.)	923.49
Land Area (sq. mi.)	923.36
Altitude (ft.)	2,100-2,700
Rainfall (in.)	19.40
Jan. mean min.	27.4
July mean max.	94.7
Civ. Labor	850
Unemployed	3.0
Wages	$3,551,305
Av. Weekly Wage	$491.33
Prop. Value	$361,273,380
Retail Sales	$4,366,315

Stonewall County

Physical Features: Western county on rolling plains below Caprock, bisected by Brazos forks; sandy loam, sandy, other soils; some hills.

Economy: Agribusiness, light fabrication, government/services.

History: Anglo-American ranchers arrived in 1870s after Comanches and other tribes removed by U.S. Army. German farmers settled after 1900. County named for Confederate Gen. T.J. (Stonewall) Jackson; created from Bexar District 1876, organized 1888.

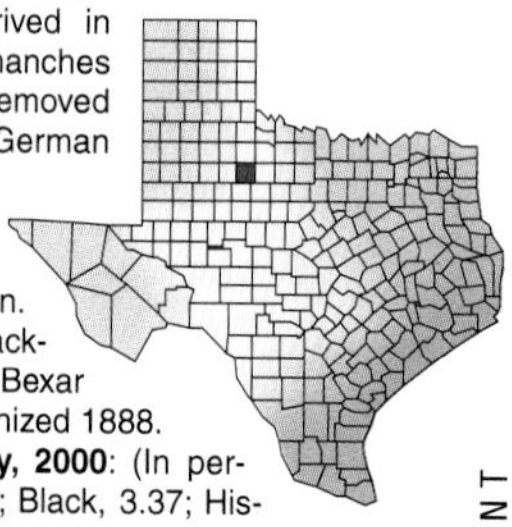

Race/Ethnicity, 2000: (In percent) Anglo, 84.17; Black, 3.37; Hispanic, 11.75; Other, 0.71.

Vital Statistics, 2003: Births, 21; deaths, 29; marriages, 12; divorces, 9.

Recreation: Deer, quail, feral hog, turkey hunting; rodeos in June, September; livestock show.

Minerals: Gypsum, gravel, oil.

Agriculture: Beef cattle, wheat, cotton, peanuts, hay. Also, grain sorghum, meat goats and swine. Market value $9 million.

ASPERMONT (887) county seat; oil field, ranching center; light fabrication; hospital; springfest; livestock show in February.

Other towns include: **Old Glory** (100) farming center.

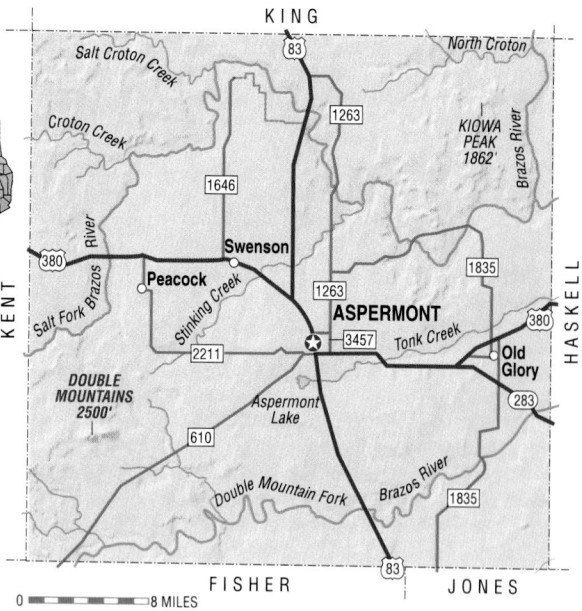

KING

Salt Croton Creek

83

North Croton

Croton Creek

1263

KIOWA PEAK 1862'

Brazos River

1646

KENT

380

River

Salt Fork Brazos

Peacock

Stinking Creek

Swenson

2211

1263

ASPERMONT

3457

Tonk Creek

1835

380

Old Glory

HASKELL

283

DOUBLE MOUNTAINS 2500'

Aspermont Lake

610

Double Mountain Fork

Brazos River

1835

FISHER

83

JONES

0 ▬▬▬▬ 8 MILES

Population		**1,405**
Change fm 2000		-17.0
Area (sq. mi.)		920.23
Land Area (sq. mi.)		918.67
Altitude (ft.)		1,500-2,500
Rainfall (in.)		23.24
Jan. mean min.		27.2
July mean max.		97.4
Civ. Labor		754
Unemployed		3.4
Wages		$3,501,793
Av. Weekly Wage		$449.70
Prop. Value		$163,866,482
Retail Sales		$10,007,801

For explanation of sources, abbreviations and symbols, see p. 167 and foldout map.

Sutton County

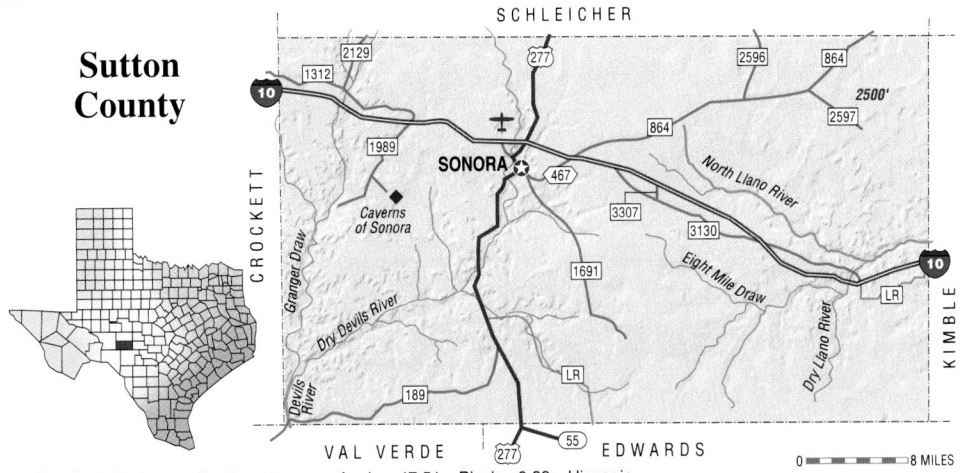

Physical Features: Southwestern county; level in west, rugged terrain in east, broken by tributaries of Devils, Llano rivers; black, red loam soils.

Economy: Oil and gas; agribusiness; hunting; tourism.

History: Lipan Apaches drove out Tonkawas in 1600s. Comanches, military outpost and disease forced Apaches south. Anglo-Americans settled in 1870s. Mexican immigration increased after 1890. County created from Crockett 1887; organized 1890; named for Confederate officer Col. John S. Sutton.

Race/Ethnicity, 2000: (In percent) Anglo, 47.51; Black, 0.29; Hispanic, 51.66; Other, 0.54.

Vital Statistics, 2003: Births, 65; deaths, 41; marriages, 28; divorces, 18.

Recreation: Hunting; Meirs Museum; Caverns of Sonora; goat cookoff; Diez y Seis in September.

Minerals: Oil, natural gas.

Agriculture: Meat goats, sheep, cattle, Angora goats. Exotic wildlife. Wheat and oats raised for grazing, hay; minor irrigation. Market value $6.4 million. Hunting leases important.

SONORA (2,938) county seat; oil; gas production; ranching; tourism; hospital; wool, mohair show in June.

Population	**4,097**
Change fm 2000	0.5
Area (sq. mi.)	1,454.40
Land Area (sq. mi.)	1,453.76
Altitude (ft.)	1,900-2,500
Rainfall (in.)	22.40
Jan. mean min.	27.2
July mean max.	94.7
Civ. Labor	2,302
Unemployed	1.4
Wages	$17,489,414
Av. Weekly Wage	$663.38
Prop. Value	$907,067,781
Retail Sales	$33,271,422

Swisher County

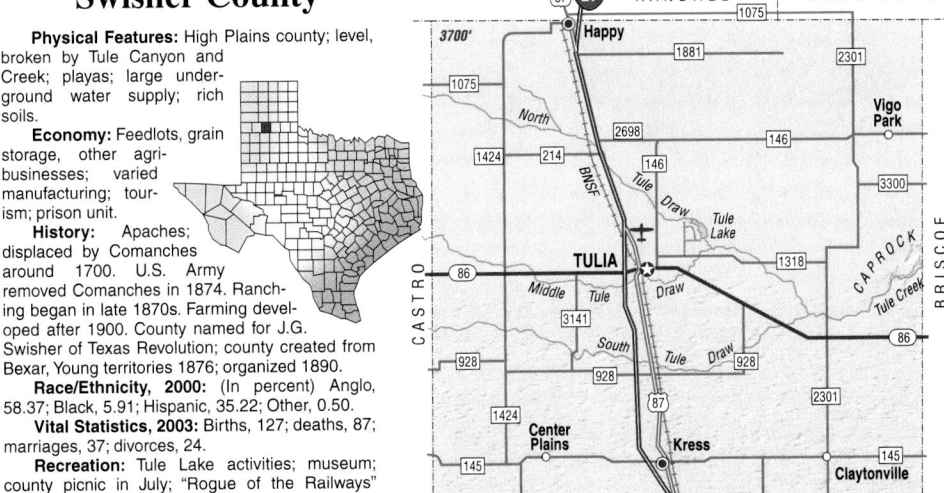

Physical Features: High Plains county; level, broken by Tule Canyon and Creek; playas; large underground water supply; rich soils.

Economy: Feedlots, grain storage, other agribusinesses; varied manufacturing; tourism; prison unit.

History: Apaches; displaced by Comanches around 1700. U.S. Army removed Comanches in 1874. Ranching began in late 1870s. Farming developed after 1900. County named for J.G. Swisher of Texas Revolution; county created from Bexar, Young territories 1876; organized 1890.

Race/Ethnicity, 2000: (In percent) Anglo, 58.37; Black, 5.91; Hispanic, 35.22; Other, 0.50.

Vital Statistics, 2003: Births, 127; deaths, 87; marriages, 37; divorces, 24.

Recreation: Tule Lake activities; museum; county picnic in July; "Rogue of the Railways" melodrama in March.

Minerals: Not significant.

Agriculture: A major agricultural county. Stocker cattle, feed lots. Cotton, corn, wheat, sorghum raised. Some 400,000 acres irrigated. Market value $296.3 million.

TULIA (4,772) county seat; farming center; government/services; food processing; hospital; library; museum; prison; Tule Creek bluegrass festival in July.

Other towns include: **Happy** (614, partly in Randall County); **Kress** (776); **Vigo Park** (36).

Population	**7,854**
Change fm 2000	-6.3
Area (sq. mi.)	900.68
Land Area (sq. mi.)	900.43
Altitude (ft.)	3,100-3,700
Rainfall (in.)	20.71
Jan. mean min.	22.2
July mean max.	91.1
Civ. Labor	3,547
Unemployed	5.3
Wages	$12,519,200
Av. Weekly Wage	$432.04
Prop. Value	$433,425,970
Retail Sales	$35,151,161

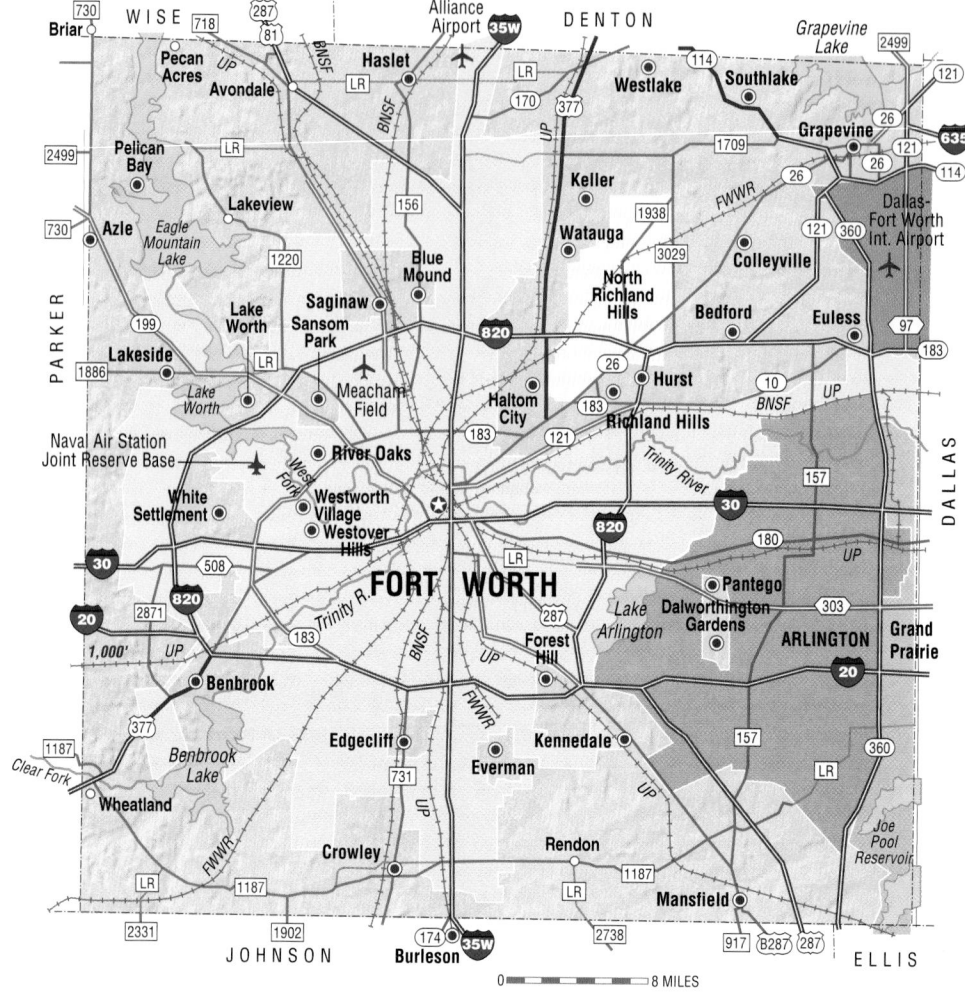

Briar · WISE · 730 · 718 · 287 · 81 · BNSF · Alliance Airport · 35W · DENTON · Grapevine Lake · 2499

Pecan Acres · UP · Haslet · LR · LR · Westlake · Southlake · 114 · 121

Avondale · 170 · 377

2499 · Pelican Bay · LR · Grapevine · 26 · 121 · 635

Lakeview · 156 · Keller · 1709 · 26 · 26 · 114

730 · Azle · Eagle Mountain Lake · 1220 · Watauga · 1938 · FWWR · Dallas-Fort Worth Int. Airport · 121 · 360

Blue Mound · 3029 · Colleyville

Lake Worth · Saginaw · North Richland Hills · Bedford · Euless · 97

PARKER · 199 · Lakeside · 1886 · Sansom Park · 820 · Hurst · 26 · 183 · 10 · UP · 183

Lake Worth · Meacham Field · Haltom City · 183 · 121 · Richland Hills · BNSF

Naval Air Station Joint Reserve Base · River Oaks · West Fork · 183 · Trinity River · 157 · 30 · DALLAS

White Settlement · Westworth Village · Westover Hills · 30 · 820 · 180 · UP

30 · 508 · LR

20 · 2871 · 820 · FORT WORTH · Pantego · Dalworthington Gardens · 303

1,000' · UP · Trinity R. · 183 · BNSF · 287 · Forest Hill · Lake Arlington · ARLINGTON · Grand Prairie · 20

Benbrook · UP

377 · FWWR

1187 · Benbrook Lake · Edgecliff · 731 · Kennedale · Everman · 157 · 360 · LR

Clear Fork · Wheatland · Joe Pool Reservoir

Crowley · Rendon · 1187 · Mansfield · LR

2331 · 1902 · 174 · 35W · Burleson · 2738 · 917 · B287 · 287 · ELLIS

JOHNSON · 0 ━━━━ 8 MILES

Tarrant County

Physical Features: Part Blackland, level to rolling; drains to Trinity; Worth, Grapevine, Eagle Mountain, Benbrook lakes.

Economy: Tourism; planes, helicopters, foods, mobile homes, electronic equipment, chemicals, plastics among products of more than 1,000 factories; large federal expenditure; D/FW International Airport; economy closely associated with Dallas urban area.

History: Caddoes in area. Comanches, other tribes arrived about 1700. Anglo-Americans settled in 1840s. Named for Gen. Edward H. Tarrant, who helped drive Indians from area. County created 1849 from Navarro County; organized 1850.

Race/Ethnicity, 2000: (In percent) Anglo, 62.79; Black, 13.01; Hispanic, 19.73; Other, 4.47.

Vital Statistics, 2003: Births, 27,574; deaths, 9,507; marriages, 12,741; divorces, 7,593.

Recreation: Scott Theatre; Amon G. Carter Museum; Kimbell Art Museum; Modern Art Museum; Museum of Science and History; Casa Manana; Botanic Gardens; Fort Worth Zoo; Log Cabin Village; Six Flags Over Texas at Arlington; Southwestern Exposition, Stock Show; Convention Center; Stockyards Historical District; Texas Rangers major-league baseball at Arlington, other athletic events.

Minerals: Production of cement, sand, gravel, stone, gas.

Agriculture: Hay, beef cattle, wheat, horses, horticulture. Market value $29.1 million. Firewood marketed.

Education: Texas Christian University, University of Texas at Arling-

ton, Texas Wesleyan University, Southwestern Baptist Theological Seminary and several other academic centers including a junior college system (three campuses).

FORT WORTH (592,836) county seat; a major mercantile, commercial and financial center; wholesale trade center for much of West Texas; airplane, helicopter and other plants.

A cultural center with renowned art museums, Bass Performance Hall; many conventions held in downtown center; agribusiness center for wide area with grain-storage and feed-mill operations; adjacent to D/FW International Airport; hospitals.

ARLINGTON (361,717) tourist center with Six Flags Over Texas, the Texas Rangers baseball team, numerous restaurants, retail; educational facilities; industrial and distribution center for automobiles, food products, electronic components, aircraft and parts, rubber and plastic products; hospitals. Scottish Highland games in June.

Other towns include: **Hurst** (37,471); **Euless** (49,848); **Bedford** (48,582) helicopter plant, hospital; **North Richland Hills** (60,455).

Azle (10,054, partly in Parker County) varied industries, Jumpin' Jack Jamboree in September; **Benbrook** (21,496) varied manufacturing; hospitals; **Blue Mound** (2,460); **Briar** (5,615, parts in Wise and Parker counties); **Colleyville** (21,370) major residential development, some retail, manufacturing; **Crowley** (8,676) varied manufacturing, government/services; hospital; **Dalworthington Gardens** (2,352); **Edgecliff** (2,517); **Everman** (5,920); **Forest Hill** (13,447).

Also, **Grapevine** (46,245) varied manufacturing, distribution; near the D/FW International Airport; tourist center; hospital; Grapefest in September; **Haltom City** (40,698) light

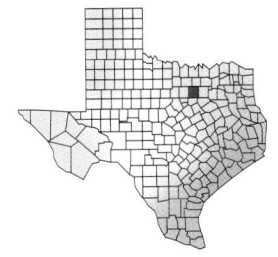

manufacturing, food processing, medical center; library; **Haslet** (1,284); **Keller** (34,467) Bear Creek Park, Wild West Fest.

Also, **Kennedale** (6,462) printing manufacturing; **Lakeside** (1,101); **Lake Worth** (4,689) retail, government/services, Bullfrog festival in April; **Mansfield** (33,707, partly in Johnson County) varied manufacturing; hospital; hometown celebration in September; **Pantego** (2,300); **Pelican Bay** (1,629); **Rendon** (9,391); **Richland Hills** (8,201).

Also, **River Oaks** (7,088); **Saginaw** (15,408) grain milling, manufacturing, distribution; North Texs

Western Days in July; library; **Sansom Park** (4,294); **Southlake** (24,160) technology, financial, retail center, hospital, parks, Oktoberfest; **Watauga** (23,087); **Westlake** (217); **Westover Hills** (658); **Westworth Village** (2,100); **White Settlement** (14,950) near aircraft manufacturing, museums, parks, historical sites; industrial park; White Settlement Day parade in fall.

Also, part [3,462] of **Burleson** (25,248); part [27,621] of **Grand Prairie** (141,692), and part of **Pecan Acres** (2,444).

Population	**1,588,088**
Change fm 2000	9.8
Area (sq. mi.)	897.48
Land Area (sq. mi.)	863.42
Altitude (ft.)	450-1,000
Rainfall (in.)	34.01
Jan. mean min.	31.4
July mean max.	96.6
Civ. Labor	832,073
Unemployed	5.5
Wages	$6,890,006,394
Av. Weekly Wage	$758.41
Prop. Value	$116,803,173,497
Retail Sales	$22,007,761,133

For explanation of sources, abbreviations and symbols, see p. 167 and foldout map.

Lunch at the Kimbell Art Museum in Fort Worth. File photo.

Taylor County

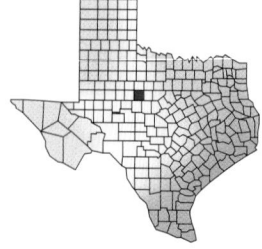

Physical Features: Prairies, with Callahan Divide, draining to Colorado tributaries, Brazos forks; Lakes Abilene, Kirby; mostly loam soils.

Economy: Agribusiness, oil and gas, education, Dyess Air Force Base.

History: Comanches in area about 1700. Anglo-American settlers arrived in 1870s. Named for Alamo heroes Edward, James and George Taylor, brothers; county created from Bexar, Travis counties 1858; organized 1878.

Race/Ethnicity, 2000: (In percent) Anglo, 73.54; Black, 6.95; Hispanic, 17.64; Other, 1.87.

Vital Statistics, 2003: Births, 2,074; deaths, 1,192; marriages, 1,369; divorces, 785.

Recreation: Abilene State Park; lake activities; Nelson Park Zoo; Texas Cowboy Reunion, West Texas Fair in September; Buffalo Gap historical tour and art festival; rodeo, college events.

Minerals: Oil, natural gas.

Agriculture: Beef cattle, small grain, cotton, milo. Market value $55.4 million.

Education: Abilene Christian University, Hardin-Simmons University, McMurry University, Cisco Junior College branch.

ABILENE (114,454, a small part in Jones County) county seat; distribution center; plants make a variety of products; meat, dairy processing; oil-field service center; hospitals; Abilene State School; West Texas Rehabilitation Center; Fort Phantom Hill (in Jones County). **Wylie** is now part of Abilene.

Other communities include: **Buffalo Gap** (464) historic sites; **Impact** (41); **Lawn** (327); **Merkel** (2,609) agribusiness center, clothing manufacturing, oil-field services; **Ovalo** (225); **Potosi** (1,640); **Trent** (297); **Tuscola** (718); **Tye** (1,178).

Population	**125,108**
Change fm 2000	-1.1
Area (sq. mi.)	919.25
Land Area (sq. mi.)	915.63
Altitude (ft.)	1,670-2,500
Rainfall (in.)	23.78
Jan. mean min.	31.8
July mean max.	94.8
Civ. Labor	62,559
Unemployed	3.4
Wages	$361,772,617
Av. Weekly Wage	$519.31
Prop. Value	$5,305,067,914
Retail Sales	$1,682,904,735

For explanation of sources, abbreviations and symbols, see p. 167 and foldout map.

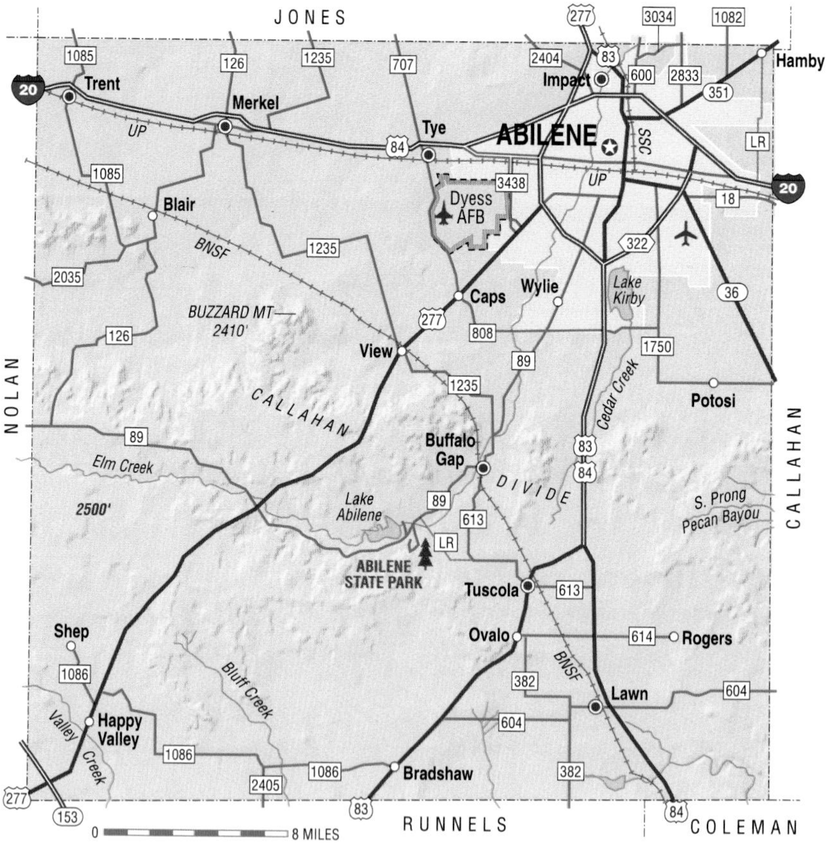

Terrell County

Physical Features: Trans-Pecos southwestern county; semi-mountainous, many canyons; rocky, limestone soils.

Economy: Ranching; oil and natural gas exploration; farm services; tourism, hunting leases.

History: Coahuiltecans, Jumanos and other tribes left many pictographs in area caves. Sheep ranching began in 1880s. Named for Confederate Gen. A.W. Terrell; county created 1905 from Pecos County.

Race/Ethnicity, 2000: (In percent) Anglo, 49.02; Black, 0.00; Hispanic, 48.57; Other, 2.41.

Vital Statistics, 2003: Births, 8; deaths, 14; marriages, 10; divorces, 3.

Recreation: Nature tourism, hunting, especially white-tailed, mule deer, Rio Grande Wild and Scenic River, varied wildlife; Cinco de Mayo, Prickly Pear Pachanga in October.

Minerals: Gas, oil, limestone.

Agriculture: Goats (meat, Angora); sheep (meat, wool); some beef cattle. Market value $3.9 million.

SANDERSON (785) county seat; ranching, petroleum center; government/services. Other town: **Dryden** (13).

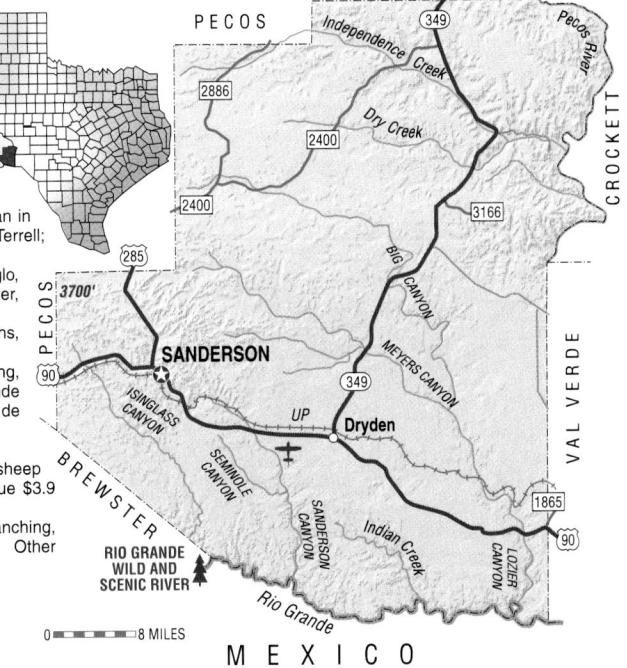

Population	957
Change fm 2000	-11.5
Area (sq. mi.)	2,357.75
Land Area (sq. mi.)	2,357.72
Altitude (ft.)	1,400-3,700
Rainfall (in.)	14.94
Jan. mean min.	30.5
July mean max.	91.9

Civ. Labor	611	Av. Weekly Wage	$583.10
Unemployed	2.5	Prop. Value	$424,058,306
Wages	$2,872,946	Retail Sales	$2,175,151

Terry County

Physical Features: Western county on South Plains, broken by draws, playas; sandy, sandy loam, loam soils.

Economy: Agribusiness, government/services, trade, commuting to Lubbock.

History: Comanches removed in 1870s by U.S. Army. Ranching developed in 1890s; farming after 1900. Oil discovered in 1940. County named for head of famed Texas Ranger troop, Col. B.F. Terry. County created from Bexar District 1876; organized 1904.

Race/Ethnicity, 2000: (In percent) Anglo, 50.32; Black, 5.02; Hispanic, 44.09; Other, 0.57.

Vital Statistics, 2003: Births, 203; deaths, 134; marriages, 89; divorces, 36.

Recreation: Museum; harvest festival in October; Brisket and Bean cook-off in April.

Minerals: Oil, gas, salt mining.

Agriculture: Cotton is principal crop; peanuts, grain sorghum, guar, wheat, melons, cucumbers, sesame. 170,000 acres irrigated. Market value $63.4 million.

BROWNFIELD (9,279) county seat; oil-field services; agribusiness; minerals processed; peanut processing; hospital; prison.

Other towns include: **Meadow** (649); **Tokio** (5); **Wellman** (196).

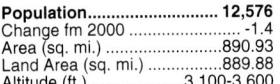

Population	12,576
Change fm 2000	-1.4
Area (sq. mi.)	890.93
Land Area (sq. mi.)	889.88
Altitude (ft.)	3,100-3,600

Rainfall (in.)	18.89	Unemployed	6.5
Jan. mean min.	26.1	Wages	$25,410,209
July mean max.	92.5	Av. Weekly Wage	$520.40
Civ. Labor	5,312	Prop. Value	$634,598,972
		Retail Sales	$105,418,041

Throckmorton County

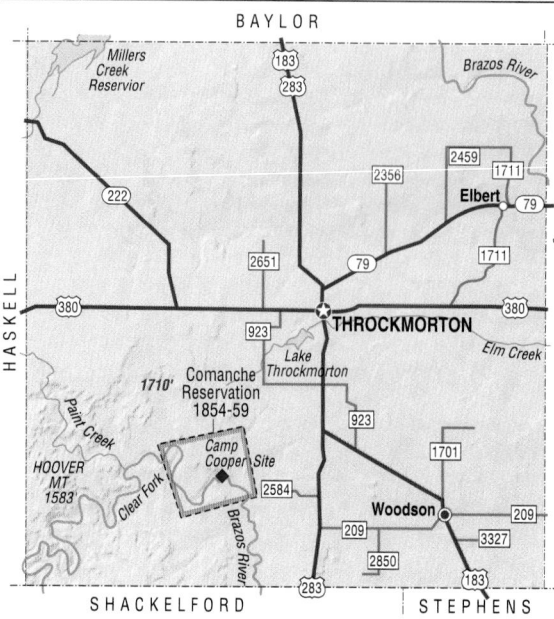

Physical Features: North Central county southwest of Wichita Falls; rolling, between Brazos forks; red to black soils.

Economy: Oil, agribusiness, hunting leases.

History: Site of Comanche Indian Reservation 1854-59. Ranching developed after Civil War. County named for Dr. W.E. Throckmorton, father of Gov. J.W. Throckmorton; county created from Fannin 1858; organized 1879.

Race/Ethnicity, 2000: (In percent) Anglo, 90.11; Black, 0.05; Hispanic, 9.35; Other, 0.49.

Vital Statistics, 2003: Births, 4; deaths, 24; marriages, 5; divorces, 9.

Recreation: Hunting, fishing; historic sites include Camp Cooper, site of former Comanche reservation; restored ranch home, Miller's Creek Reservoir; wild game dinner in January.

Minerals: Natural gas, oil.

Agriculture: Beef cattle, horses, wheat, hay. Market value $16.4 million. Mesquite firewood sold. Hunting leases important.

Population	1,632
Change fm 2000	-11.8
Area (sq. mi.)	915.47
Land Area (sq. mi.)	912.34
Altitude (ft.)	1,140-1,710
Rainfall (in.)	26.60
Jan. mean min.	28.0
July mean max.	97.0
Civ. Labor	838
Unemployed	2.1
Wages	$2,210,801
Av. Weekly Wage	$369.70
Prop. Value	$331,267,770
Retail Sales	$4,930,901

THROCKMORTON (812) county seat; varied manufacturing; oil-field services; hospital.

Other towns include: **Elbert** (49), **Woodson** (259).

Titus County

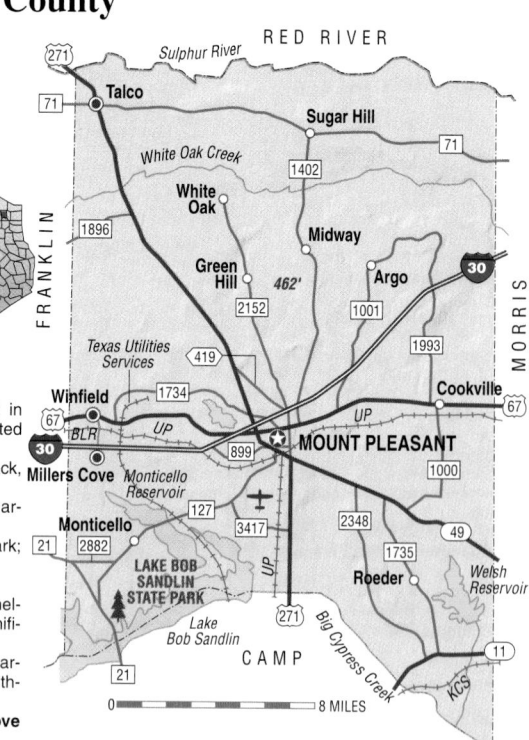

Population	29,224
Change fm 2000	3.9
Area (sq. mi.)	425.69
Land Area (sq. mi.)	410.54
Altitude (ft.)	300-462
Rainfall (in.)	48.57
Jan. mean min.	29.3
July mean max.	94.2
Civ. Labor	14,354
Unemployed	4.3
Wages	$123,674,274
Av. Weekly Wage	$558.30
Prop. Value	$2,428,962,669
Retail Sales	$404,275,893

Physical Features: East Texas county; hilly, timbered; drains to Big Cypress Creek, Sulphur River.

Economy: Agribusinesses; lignite mining and power generation; trailer manufacturing.

History: Caddo area. Cherokees and other tribes settled in 1820s. Anglo-American settlers arrived in 1840s. Named for pioneer settler A.J. Titus; county created from Bowie, Red River counties 1846.

Race/Ethnicity, 2000: (In percent) Anglo, 60.03; Black, 10.72; Hispanic, 28.31; Other, 0.94.

Vital Statistics, 2003: Births, 530; deaths, 244; marriages, 297; divorces, 39.

Recreation: Fishing, hunting; lake activities; state park; rodeo; railroad museum; riverboat; flower gardens.

Minerals: Lignite coal, oil, gas.

Agriculture: Poultry, beef cattle, hay, horses, watermelons, corn. Market value $56.4 million. Timber sales significant.

MOUNT PLEASANT (14,472) county seat; tourism; varied manufacturing; food-processing plants; hospital; Northeast Texas Community College; WranglerFest in October.

Other towns include: **Cookville** (105), **Millers Cove** (129), **Talco** (574), **Winfield** (527).

Tom Green County

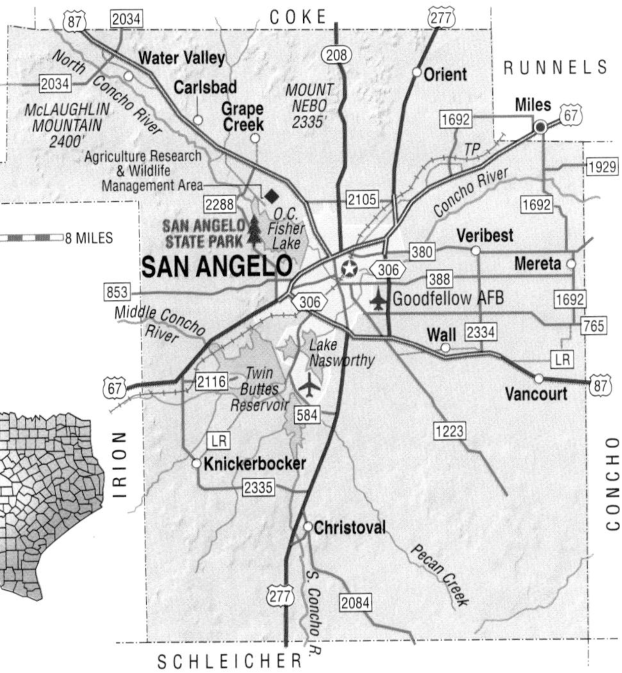

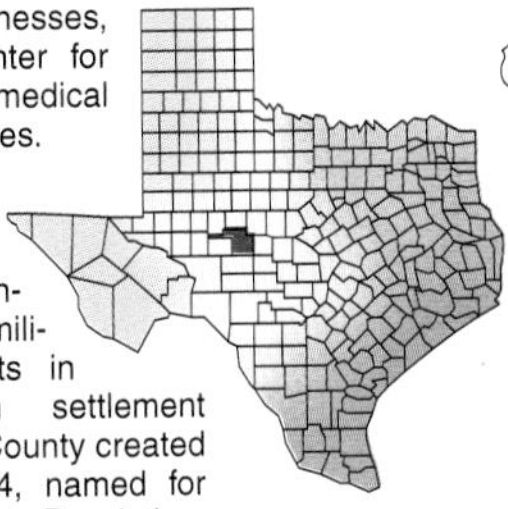

Physical Features: West central county of plains, rolling hills, broken by Concho forks; loams in basin, stony hillsides; lakes.

Economy: "Sheep and Wool Capital"; varied agribusinesses, manufacturing; trade center for area, education center, medical center; government/services.

History: Jumano Indians attracted Spanish missionaries around 1630. Comanches controlled area when U.S. military established outposts in 1850s. Anglo-American settlement occurred after Civil War. County created from Bexar District 1874, named for Gen. Tom Green of Texas Revolution; organized 1875; 12 other counties created from this original area.

Race/Ethnicity, 2000: (In percent) Anglo, 63.65; Black, 4.22; Hispanic, 30.71; Other, 1.42.

Population	103,772
Change fm 2000	-0.2
Area (sq. mi.)	1,540.54
Land Area (sq. mi.)	1,522.10
Altitude (ft.)	1,700-2,600
Rainfall (in.)	20.91
Jan. mean min.	31.8
July mean max.	94.4
Civ. Labor	52,935
Unemployed	3.3
Wages	$300,823,019
Av. Weekly Wage	$540.68
Prop. Value	$3,817,234,373
Retail Sales	$1,255,686,377

Vital Statistics, 2003: Births, 1,626; deaths, 965; marriages, 1,107; divorces, 493.

Recreation: Water sports; hunting; Fort Concho museum; urban, collegiate activities; Christmas at Old Fort Concho; February rodeo; minor league hockey, baseball teams.

Minerals: Oil, natural gas.

Agriculture: Cattle; cotton; a leading sheep-raising county; goats; dairy products. Also, sorghum, wheat, swine, horses. About 30,000 acres irrigated. Market value $97.2 million.

SAN ANGELO (88,170) county seat; government/services, retail center, transportation; airbase; riverwalk; hospitals; Angelo State University, A&M extension center; Museum of Fine Arts.

Other towns include: **Carlsbad** (236); **Christoval** (410); **Grape Creek** (3,070); **Knickerbocker** (94); **Mereta** (131); **Vancourt** (131); **Veribest** (115); **Wall** (329); **Water Valley** (203).

For explanation of sources, abbreviations and symbols, see p. 167 and foldout map.

The South Concho River at Christoval in Tom Green County. Texas Almanac photo.

Travis County

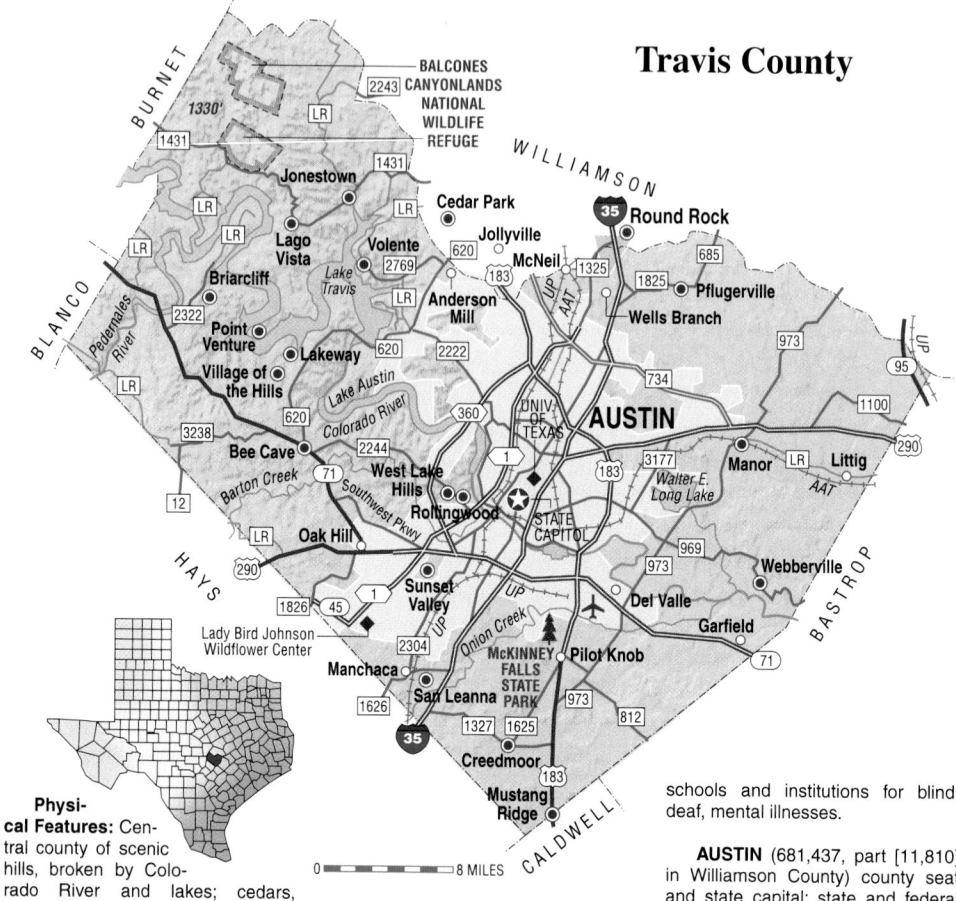

Physical Features: Central county of scenic hills, broken by Colorado River and lakes; cedars, pecans, other trees; diverse soils, mineral deposits.

Economy: Government/services, education, technology, research and industry.

History: Tonkawa and Lipan Apache area; Comanches, Kiowas arrived about 1700. Spanish missions from East Texas temporarily relocated near Barton Springs in 1730 before removing to San Antonio. Anglo-Americans arrived in early 1830s. County created 1840, when Austin became Republic's capital, from Bastrop County; organized 1843; named for Alamo commander Col. William B. Travis; many other counties created from its original area.

Race/Ethnicity, 2000: (In percent) Anglo, 57.28; Black, 9.38; Hispanic, 28.20; Other, 5.14.

Vital Statistics, 2003: Births, 14,531; deaths, 4,085; marriages, 7,298; divorces, 3,010.

Recreation: Colorado River lakes; hunting, fishing; McKinney Falls State Park; Lady Bird Johnson Wildflower Center; South by Southwest film, music festival in March; collegiate, metropolitan, governmental events; official buildings and historic sites; museums; Sixth St. restoration area; scenic drives; many city parks.

Minerals: Production of lime, stone, sand, gravel, oil and gas.

Agriculture: Cattle, nursery crops, hogs; sorghum, corn, cotton, small grains, pecans. Market value $17.1 million.

Education: University of Texas main campus; St. Edward's University, Concordia Lutheran University, Huston-Tillotson College, Austin Community College, Episcopal and Presbyterian seminaries; state schools and institutions for blind, deaf, mental illnesses.

Population	869,868
Change fm 2000	7.1
Area (sq. mi.)	1,022.06
Land Area (sq. mi.)	989.30
Altitude (ft.)	400-1,330
Rainfall (in.)	33.65
Jan. mean min.	40.0
July mean max.	95.0
Civ. Labor	502,342
Unemployed	4.7
Wages	$5,502,307,770
Av. Weekly Wage	$821.61
Prop. Value	$72,235,865,022
Retail Sales	$13,480,226,550

AUSTIN (681,437, part [11,810] in Williamson County) county seat and state capital; state and federal payrolls; IRS center; tourism; Lyndon B. Johnson Library; research, high-tech industries; hospitals, including state institutions; popular retirement area. **Del Valle** is now part of Austin.

Other towns include: **Bee Cave** (868); **Briarcliff** (850); **Creedmoor** (203); **Garfield** (1,666); **Jonestown** (1,744); **Lago Vista** (5,463); **Lakeway** (8,347); **Manchaca** (2,259); **Manor** (1,185); **McNeil** (70); **Mustang Ridge** (929, partly in Caldwell County).

Also, **Pflugerville** (24,662) high-tech industries, agriculture, government/services, Deutchenfest in May; **Point Venture** (470); **Rollingwood** (1,341); **San Leanna** (423); **Sunset Valley** (462); **The Hills** (1,607); **Volente** (450); **Webberville** (530); **Wells Branch** (10,603); **West Lake Hills** (3,023).

Also, part of **Anderson Mill**, part of **Cedar Park**, part of **Jollyville** and part of **Round Rock**, all mostly in Williamson County.

For explanation of sources, abbreviations and symbols, see p. 167 and foldout map.

Trinity County

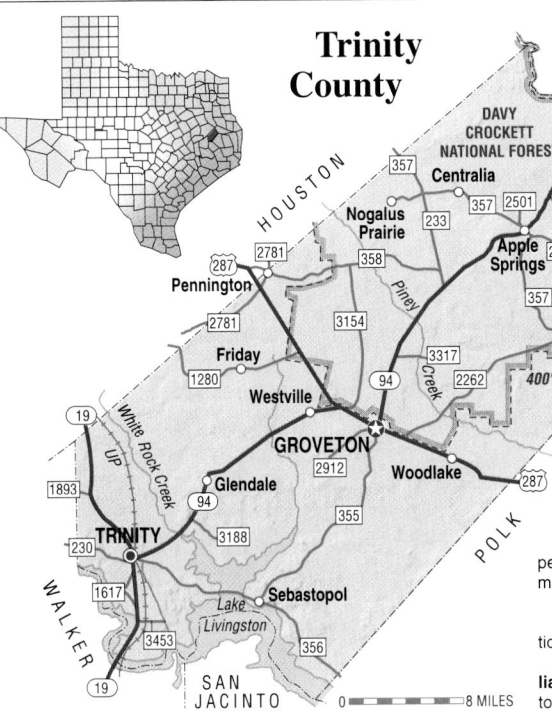

Physical Features: Heavily forested East Texas county of hills, between Neches and Trinity (Lake Livingston) rivers; rich alluvial soils, sandy upland; 67,910 acres in national forest.

Economy: Forestry, cattle, tourism, government/services.

History: Caddoes, reduced by disease in late 1700s. Kickapoo, Alabama, Coushatta in area when Anglo-Americans settled in 1840s. Named for river; county created 1850 out of Houston County.

Race/Ethnicity, 2000: (In percent) Anglo, 82.46; Black, 12.04; Hispanic, 4.85; Other, 0.65.

Vital Statistics, 2003: Births, 151; deaths, 197; marriages, 98; divorces, 32.

Recreation: Lake activities; fishing, hiking, hunting; Davy Crockett National Forest; historic sites; Scottish festival in November.

Minerals: Limited oil, gas, sand and gravel.

Agriculture: Beef cattle. Market value $9 million. Timber sales significant. Hunting leases.

GROVETON (1,087) county seat; lumber center; petroleum processing; varied manufacturing; government/services; museum.

TRINITY (2,724) government/services; steel fabrication; forest-industries center; near Lake Livingston.

Other towns include: **Apple Springs** (185); **Centralia** (53); **Pennington** (67); **Sebastopol** (120) historic town; **Woodlake** (98).

Population **14,345**	Rainfall (in.).................................. 48.10	
Change fm 2000............................4.1	Jan. mean min. 37.1	Wages..............................$12,974,944
Area (sq. mi.)..............................714.00	July mean max.............................. 94.8	Av. Weekly Wage....................$415.17
Land Area (sq. mi.)......................692.84	Civ. Labor 5,170	Prop. Value $696,296,567
Altitude (ft.) 131-400	Unemployed..................................... 6.3	Retail Sales......................$66,163,325

Students learn canoeing on Town Lake in Austin. File photo.

Tyler County

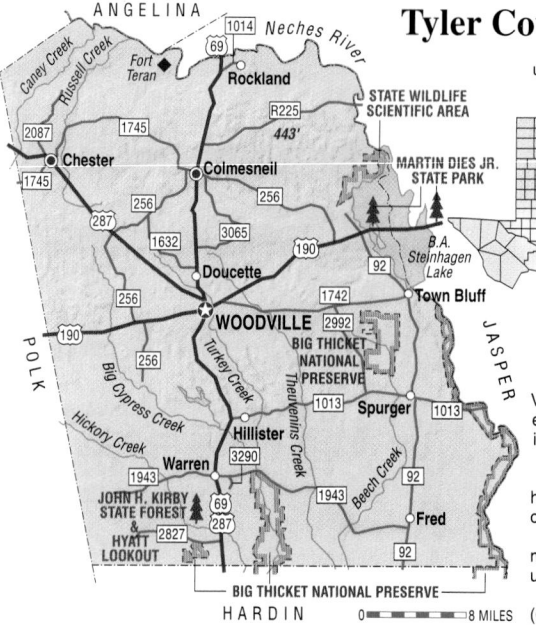

Physical Features: Hilly East Texas county; densely timbered; drains to Neches River; B.A. Steinhagen Lake; Big Thicket is unique plant and animal area.

Economy: Lumbering; government/services, some manufacturing; tourism, hunting leases.

History: Caddoan area. Cherokees, Alabama and Coushatta pushed into area from U.S. South in 1820s. Anglo-Americans settled in 1830s. Named for U.S. President John Tyler; county created 1846 from Liberty County.

Race/Ethnicity, 2000: (In percent) Anglo, 83.49; Black, 12.16; Hispanic, 3.56; Other, 0.79.

Vital Statistics, 2003: Births, 234; deaths, 264; marriages, 148; divorces, 133.

Recreation: Big Thicket National Preserve; Heritage Village; lake activities; Allan Shivers Museum; state forest; historic sites; dogwood festival; rodeo, frontier frolics in September; gospel music fest in June.

Minerals: Oil, natural gas.

Agriculture: Cattle, hay, nursery crops, blueberries, horses. Market value $4.7 million. Timber sales significant.

WOODVILLE (2,394) county seat; lumber, cattle market; varied manufacturing; tourism; hospital; prison unit.

Other towns include: **Chester** (255) **Colmesneil** (639), **Doucette** (160), **Fred** (299), **Hillister** (250), **Spurger** (590), **Warren** (310).

Population 20,806		
Change fm 2000 ....-0.3		
Area (sq. mi.) 935.71	Jan. mean min. 38.3	Wages $26,426,397
Land Area (sq. mi.) 922.90	July mean max. 92.1	Av. Weekly Wage $509.60
Altitude (ft.) 50-443	Civ. Labor.........................8,403	Prop. Value.................$1,004,435,315
Rainfall (in.) 54.79	Unemployed........................7.6	Retail Sales $87,886,666

Upshur County

Physical Features: East Texas county; rolling to hilly, over half forested; drains to Sabine River, Little Cypress Creek, Lake O' the Pines, Lake Gilmer, Lake Gladewater.

Economy: Manufacturing, petroleum products, agribusiness, timber products.

History: Caddoes; reduced by epidemics in 1700s. Cherokees in area in 1820s. Anglo-American settlement in mid-1830s. County created from Harrison, Nacogdoches counties 1846; named for U.S. Secretary of State A.P. Upshur.

Race/Ethnicity, 2000: (In percent) Anglo, 84.82; Black, 10.31; Hispanic, 3.95; Other, 0.92.

Vital Statistics, 2003: Births, 470; deaths, 440; marriages, 278; divorces, 213.

Recreation: Scenic trails; hunting, fishing; Cherokee Rose Festival, Fall Foliage, East Texas Yamboree in October.

Minerals: Oil, gas, sand, gravel.

Agriculture: Poultry (among leading broiler counties), dairies, beef cattle; vegetable crops, hay, peaches raised. Market value $40.8 million. Timber a major product.

GILMER (5,019) county seat; varied manufacturing; timber, ceramics produced; vegetable processing; civic center.

Other towns include: **Big Sandy** (1,318), **Diana** (585); **East Mountain** (585); **Ore City** (1,168); **Union Grove** (345). Part [2,454] of **Gladewater** (6,236).

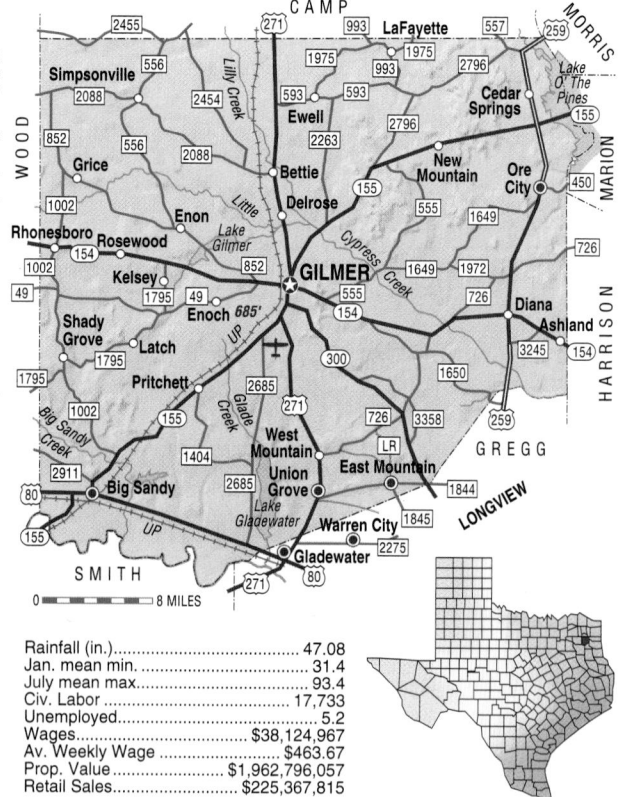

Population 37,397	Rainfall (in.)......................... 47.08	
Change fm 2000 ....6.0	Jan. mean min. 31.4	
Area (sq. mi.) 592.67	July mean max.......................... 93.4	
Land Area (sq. mi.) 587.64	Civ. Labor 17,733	
Altitude (ft.) 228-685	Unemployed............................. 5.2	
	Wages.................................. $38,124,967	
	Av. Weekly Wage $463.67	
	Prop. Value......................... $1,962,796,057	
	Retail Sales......................... $225,367,815	

Upton County

Physical Features: Western county; north flat, south rolling, hilly; limestone, sandy loam soils, drains to creeks.

Economy: Oil, electric power plant, wind turbines, cotton, ranching.

History: Apache and Comanche area until tribes removed by U.S. Army in 1870s. Sheep and cattle ranching developed in 1880s. Oil discovered in 1925. County created in 1887 from Tom Green County; organized 1910; name honors brothers John and William Upton, Confederate colonels.

Race/Ethnicity, 2000: (In percent) Anglo, 54.93; Black, 1.62; Hispanic, 42.57; Other, 0.88.

Vital Statistics, 2003: Births, 44; deaths, 26; marriages, 26; divorces, 17.

Recreation: Historic sites, Mendoza Trail Museum; scenic areas; chili cookoff in October, Christmas bazaar.

Minerals: Oil, natural gas.

Agriculture: Cotton, sheep, goats, beef and feeder cattle, pecans. Extensive irrigation. Market value $4.8 million.

RANKIN (685) county seat, oil, ranching, farming; Barbados cookoff on Memorial Day weekend, All Kid rodeo in June.

McCAMEY (1,675) oil, ranching; hospital; pecan show in November. Other town: **Midkiff** (182).

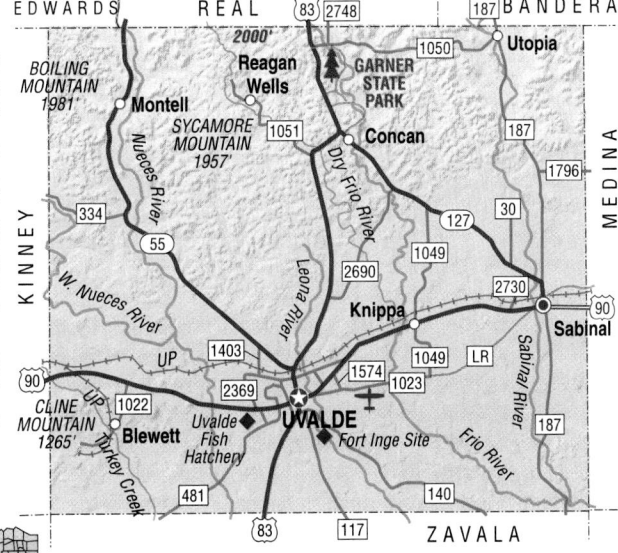

Population **3,147**	
Change fm 2000 .... -7.5	
Area (sq. mi.) 1,241.83	
Land Area (sq. mi.) 1,241.68	
Altitude (ft.) 2,400-3,141	

Rainfall (in.) 14.45	Wages $8,930,871
Jan. mean min. 33.1	Av. Weekly Wage $605.28
July mean max. 95.6	Prop. Value $1,109,686,851
Civ. Labor 1,366	Retail Sales $12,910,962
Unemployed 4.0	

Uvalde County

Physical Features: Edwards Plateau, rolling hills below escarpment; spring-fed Sabinal, Frio, Leona, Nueces rivers; cypress, cedar, other trees; unique maple groves.

Economy: Agribusinesses; hunting leases; light manufacturing; tourism.

History: Spanish mission Nuestra Señora de la Candelaria founded in 1762 for Lipan Apaches near present-day Montell; Comanches harassed mission. U.S. military outpost established in 1849. County created from Bexar 1850; re-created, organized 1856; named for 1778 governor of Coahuila, Juan de Ugalde, with name Anglicized.

Race/Ethnicity, 2000: (In percent) Anglo, 33.08; Black, 0.34; Hispanic, 65.91; Other, 0.67.

Vital Statistics, 2003: Births, 454; deaths, 253; marriages, 161; divorces, 70.

Recreation: Deer, turkey hunting area; Garner State Park; water activities on rivers; John Nance Garner Museum; Uvalde Memorial Park; scenic trails; historic sites; recreational homes.

Minerals: Asphalt, stone, sand and gravel.

Agriculture: Beef cattle, vegetables, corn, cotton, grain sorghum; sheep, goats; hay, wheat. Substantial irrigation. Market value $69 million.

UVALDE (15,404) county seat; vegetable, wool, mohair processing; tourism, opera house; junior college; A&M research center; hospital; Fort Inge Day in April. **Sabinal** (1,599) farm, ranch center; gateway to Frio and Sabinal canyons; tourist, retirement area.

Other towns include: **Concan** (225); **Knippa** (751); **Utopia** (237) resort; **Uvalde Estates** (2,107).

For explanation of sources, abbreviations and symbols, see p. 167 and foldout map.

Population **26,616**	
Change fm 2000 .... 2.7	
Area (sq. mi.) 1,558.60	
Land Area (sq. mi.) 1,556.55	
Altitude (ft.) 699-2,000	
Rainfall (in.) 23.30	
Jan. mean min. 37.0	
July mean max. 96.0	
Civ. Labor 11,541	
Unemployed 8.0	
Wages $53,640,606	
Av. Weekly Wage $423.72	
Prop. Value $1,738,958,355	
Retail Sales $251,683,536	

Val Verde County

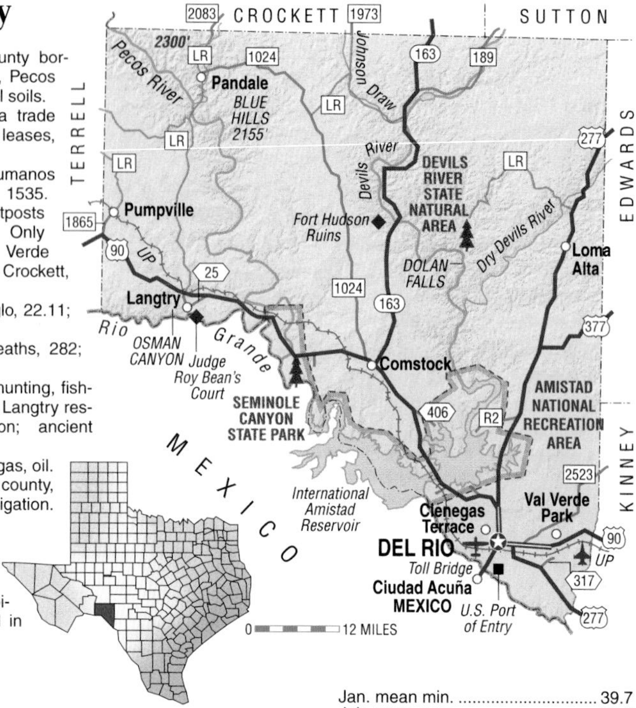

Physical Features: Southwestern county bordering Mexico, rolling, hilly; brushy; Devils, Pecos rivers, Amistad Reservoir; limestone, alluvial soils.

Economy: Agribusiness; tourism; area trade center; large military, Border Patrol; hunting leases, fishing.

History: Apaches, Coahuiltecans, Jumanos present when Spanish explored area 1535. Comanches arrived later. U.S. military outposts established in 1850s to protect settlers. Only county named for Civil War battle; Val Verde means green valley. Created 1885 from Crockett, Kinney, Pecos counties.

Race/Ethnicity, 2000: (In percent) Anglo, 22.11; Black, 1.46; Hispanic, 75.46; Other, 0.97.

Vital Statistics, 2003: Births, 945; deaths, 282; marriages, 394; divorces, 154.

Recreation: Gateway to Mexico; deer hunting, fishing; Amistad lake activities; two state parks; Langtry restoration of Judge Roy Bean's saloon; ancient pictographs; San Felipe Springs; winery.

Minerals: Production sand and gravel, gas, oil.

Agriculture: Major sheep-raising county, Angora goats, cattle, meat goats; minor irrigation. Market value $10.9 million.

DEL RIO (35,400) county seat; tourism and trade with Mexico; government/services, including federal agencies and military; varied manufacturing, winery; hospital; extension colleges; Fiesta de Amistad in October.

Laughlin Air Force Base (2,280).

Other towns and places include: **Cienegas Terrace** (3,008); **Comstock** (375); **Langtry** (30); **Val Verde Park** (2,033).

Population	47,410
Change fm 2000	5.7
Area (sq. mi.)	3,232.40
Land Area (sq. mi.)	3,170.38
Altitude (ft.)	900-2,300
Rainfall (in.)	18.80
Jan. mean min.	39.7
July mean max.	96.2
Civ. Labor	20,125
Unemployed	7.2
Wages	$98,547,224
Av. Weekly Wage	$508.90
Prop. Value	$1,422,823,296
Retail Sales	$455,860,824

A park ranger shows visitors Indian pictographs at Seminole Canyon State Park. File photo.

Van Zandt County

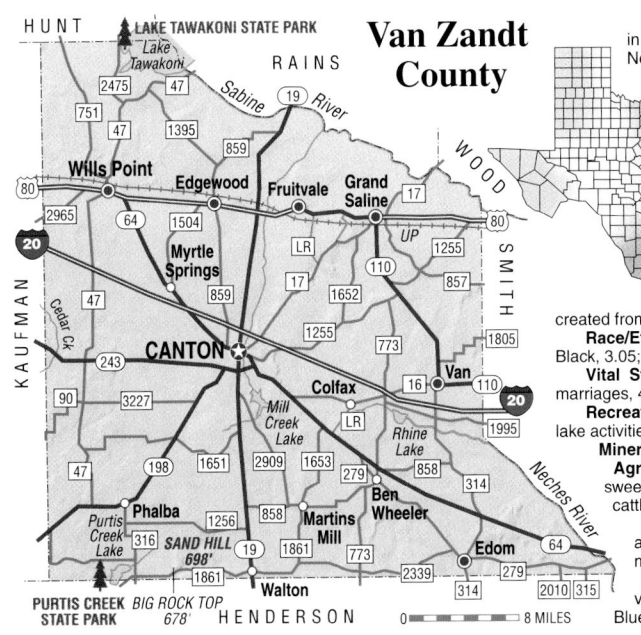

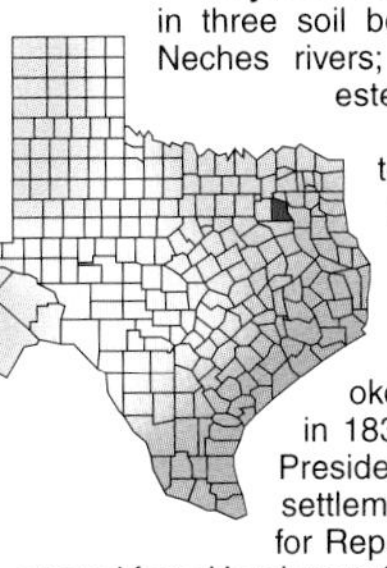

Physical Features: Northeastern county in three soil belts; level to rolling; Sabine, Neches rivers; Lake Tawakoni; partly forested.

Economy: Agribusiness, tourism, oil and gas; light manufacturing; many commute to jobs in Dallas.

History: Caddo tribes, reduced by epidemics before settlers arrived. Cherokees settled in 1820s; removed in 1839 under policies of Republic President Lamar; Anglo-American settlement followed. County named for Republic leader Isaac Van Zandt; created from Henderson County 1848.

Race/Ethnicity, 2000: (In percent) Anglo, 89.57; Black, 3.05; Hispanic, 6.65; Other, 0.73.

Vital Statistics, 2003: Births, 610; deaths, 576; marriages, 419; divorces, 238.

Recreation: Canton First Monday trades days; lake activities; state parks; historic sites.

Minerals: Oil, gas, salt, iron ore, clays.

Agriculture: Nursery crops. A major hay and sweet potato producer, also vegetables. Beef cattle, dairy. Market value $73 million.

CANTON (3,471) county seat; tourism; agribusiness; commuters to Dallas, Tyler; museums; bluegrass festival in June.

Wills Point (3,646) government/services, some manufacturing, retail center, Bluebird festival in April.

Other towns include: **Ben Wheeler** (504); **Edgewood** (1,412) commuters to Dallas; heritage park, antiques; **Edom** (347); **Fruitvale** (425); **Grand Saline** (3,180) salt plant, manufacturing, hospital, salt palace; **Van** (2,497) oil center, hay, cattle; oil festival in October.

Population	51,996
Change fm 2000	8.0
Area (sq. mi.)	859.48
Land Area (sq. mi.)	848.64
Altitude (ft.)	400-698
Rainfall (in.)	43.68
Jan. mean min.	31.4
July mean max.	93.3
Civ. Labor	24,121
Unemployed	4.2
Wages	$58,860,430
Av. Weekly Wage	$460.46
Prop. Value	$2,833,392,100
Retail Sales	$342,023,132

Victoria County

Physical Features: South Central county of rolling prairies, intersected by many streams; sandy loams, clays, alluvial soils.

Economy: Petrochemical plants, government services, oil, manufacturing, agribusiness, tourism.

History: Karankawas, other tribes in area when Spanish explored in 1528. Comanches, Tawakonis arrived later. French Fort St. Louis on Garcitas Creek 1685-87. Spanish ranching developed in 1750s. Anglo-Americans arrived after 1836. An original county, created 1836 from Mexican municipality named for President Guadalupe Victoria of Mexico.

Race/Ethnicity, 2000: (In percent) Anglo, 53.38; Black, 6.33; Hispanic, 39.20; Other, 1.09.

Vital Statistics, 2003: Births, 1,314; deaths, 710; marriages, 707; divorces, 341.

Recreation: Fishing, hunting; saltwater activities; historic homes, sites; riverside park, Coleto Creek Reservoir and park; recreational park; zoo; Czech Heritage Festival in October.

Minerals: Oil, gas, sand, gravel.

Agriculture: Corn, beef cattle, grain sorghums, cotton, rice, soybeans. Market value $29 million.

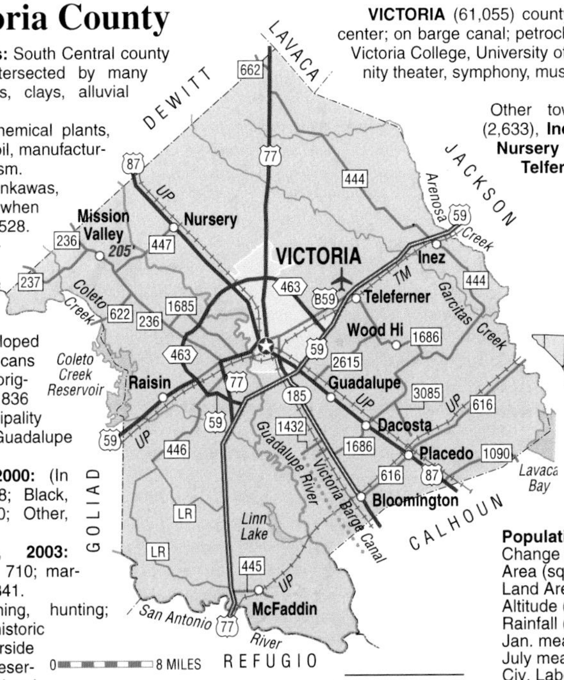

VICTORIA (61,055) county seat; tourism, agribusiness center; on barge canal; petrochemicals; foundry equipment; Victoria College, University of Houston at Victoria; community theater, symphony, museums; hospitals.

Other towns include: **Bloomington** (2,633), **Inez** (1,836), **McFaddin** (175), **Nursery** (260), **Placedo** (760), **Telferner** (700).

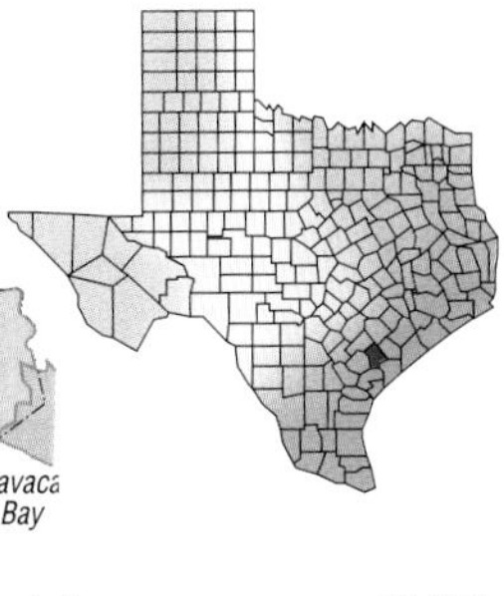

For explanation of sources, abbreviations and symbols, see p. 167 and foldout map.

Population	85,777
Change fm 2000	2.0
Area (sq. mi.)	888.73
Land Area (sq. mi.)	882.50
Altitude (ft.)	sea level-205
Rainfall (in.)	40.10
Jan. mean min.	43.6
July mean max.	93.4
Civ. Labor	46,120
Unemployed	4.4
Wages	$280,386,560
Av. Weekly Wage	$592.89
Prop. Value	$4,053,186,880
Retail Sales	$1,117,636,012

Physical Features: South central county north of Houston of rolling hills; more than 70 percent forested; national forest; San Jacinto, Trinity rivers.

Economy: State employment in prison system, education.

History: Coahuiltecans, Bidais in area when Spanish explored around 1690. Later, area became trading ground for many Indian tribes. Anglo-Americans settled in 1830s. Antebellum slaveholding area. County created 1846 from Montgomery County; first named for U.S. Secretary of Treasury R.J. Walker; renamed 1863 for Texas Ranger Capt. S.H. Walker.

Race/Ethnicity, 2000: (In percent) Anglo, 60.55; Black, 24.04; Hispanic, 14.11; Other, 1.30.

Vital Statistics, 2003: Births, 622; deaths, 428; marriages, 450; divorces, 236.

Recreation: Fishing, hunting; lake activities; Sam Houston Museum, homes, grave; prison museum; other historic sites; state park; Sam Houston National Forest; Cinco de Mayo celebration, Sam Houston folk festival in April.

Minerals: Clays, natural gas, oil, sand and gravel, stone.

Agriculture: Cattle, nursery plants, poultry, cotton, hay. Market value $25.4 million. Timber sales substantial; Christmas trees.

HUNTSVILLE (35,975) county seat; Texas Department of Criminal Justice headquarters, prisons; Sam Houston State University, forest products; museum; varied manufacturing; hospital.

Other towns include: **Dodge** (150), **New Waverly** (924), **Riverside** (453).

Walker County

Population	**62,217**
Change fm 2000	0.7
Area (sq. mi.)	801.44
Land Area (sq. mi.)	787.45
Altitude (ft.)	131-404
Rainfall (in.)	48.51
Jan. mean min.	39.0
July mean max.	93.8
Civ. Labor	23,887
Unemployed	2.8
Wages	$152,286,071
Av. Weekly Wage	$527.67
Prop. Value	$1,824,371,653
Retail Sales	$522,007,637

Balmorhea Lake in Reeves County with the Barrilla and Davis Mountains in the background. Texas Almanac photo.

Waller County

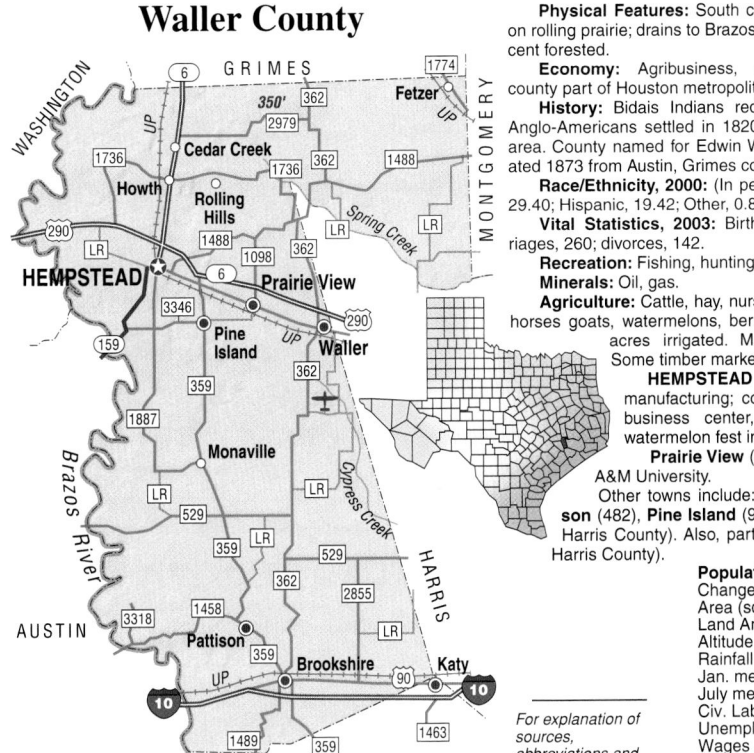

Physical Features: South central county near Houston on rolling prairie; drains to Brazos; alluvial soils; about 20 percent forested.

Economy: Agribusiness, manufacturing, education, county part of Houston metropolitan area; oil.

History: Bidais Indians reduced to about 100 when Anglo-Americans settled in 1820s. Antebellum slaveholding area. County named for Edwin Waller, Republic leader; created 1873 from Austin, Grimes counties.

Race/Ethnicity, 2000: (In percent), Anglo, 50.36; Black, 29.40; Hispanic, 19.42; Other, 0.82.

Vital Statistics, 2003: Births, 503; deaths, 263; marriages, 260; divorces, 142.

Recreation: Fishing, hunting; historic sites; museum.

Minerals: Oil, gas.

Agriculture: Cattle, hay, nurseries, turf grass, rice, corn, horses goats, watermelons, berries and stone fruit. 10,000 acres irrigated. Market value $37.9 million. Some timber marketed.

HEMPSTEAD (5,697) county seat; varied manufacturing; commuting to Houston; agribusiness center, large vegetable market; watermelon fest in July.

Prairie View (4,511) home of Prairie View A&M University.

Other towns include: **Brookshire** (3,683), **Pattison** (482), **Pine Island** (909), **Waller** (2,265, partly in Harris County). Also, part of **Katy** (13,285, mostly in Harris County).

Population	34,757
Change fm 2000	6.4
Area (sq. mi.)	518.49
Land Area (sq. mi.)	513.63
Altitude (ft.)	100-350
Rainfall (in.)	38.20
Jan. mean min.	38.0
July mean max.	95.0
Civ. Labor	15,374
Unemployed	6.4
Wages	$81,039,957
Av. Weekly Wage	$561.76
Prop. Value	$14,318,073,630
Retail Sales	$611,839,547

For explanation of sources, abbreviations and symbols, see p. 167 and foldout map.

Ward County

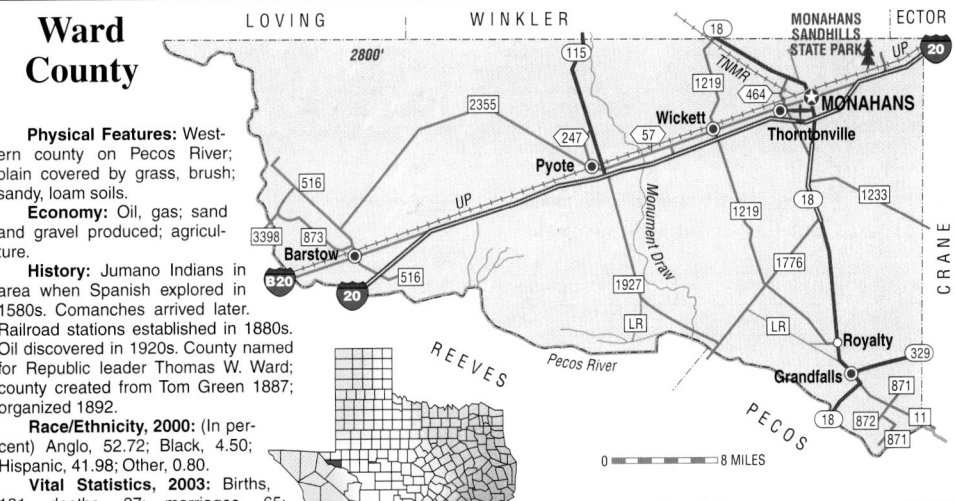

Physical Features: Western county on Pecos River; plain covered by grass, brush; sandy, loam soils.

Economy: Oil, gas; sand and gravel produced; agriculture.

History: Jumano Indians in area when Spanish explored in 1580s. Comanches arrived later. Railroad stations established in 1880s. Oil discovered in 1920s. County named for Republic leader Thomas W. Ward; county created from Tom Green 1887; organized 1892.

Race/Ethnicity, 2000: (In percent) Anglo, 52.72; Black, 4.50; Hispanic, 41.98; Other, 0.80.

Vital Statistics, 2003: Births, 131; deaths, 97; marriages, 65; divorces, 44.

Recreation: Sandhills state park, camel treks; Pyote Rattlesnake museum; Million Barrel museum; county park; stagecoach festival in August.

Minerals: Oil, gas, caliche, sand, gravel.

Agriculture: Beef cattle; cotton, alfalfa, pecans, nursery crops. Goats also raised. Some irrigation for cotton. Market value $1.7 million.

MONAHANS (6,452) county seat; center for oil, gas; sand, gravel; agribusiness; tourism; hospital; fajita festival in May.

Other towns: **Barstow** (381); **Grandfalls** (367); **Pyote** (148) West Texas Children's Home; **Thorntonville** (394); **Wickett** (406).

Population	10,358
Change fm 2000	-5.1
Area (sq. mi.)	835.74
Land Area (sq. mi.)	835.49
Altitude (ft.)	2,400-2,800
Rainfall (in.)	13.23
Jan. mean min.	26.5
July mean max.	98.6
Civ. Labor	3,755
Unemployed	6.1
Wages	$22,907,041
Av. Weekly Wage	$579.06
Prop. Value	$968,338,838
Retail Sales	$61,295,451

Washington County

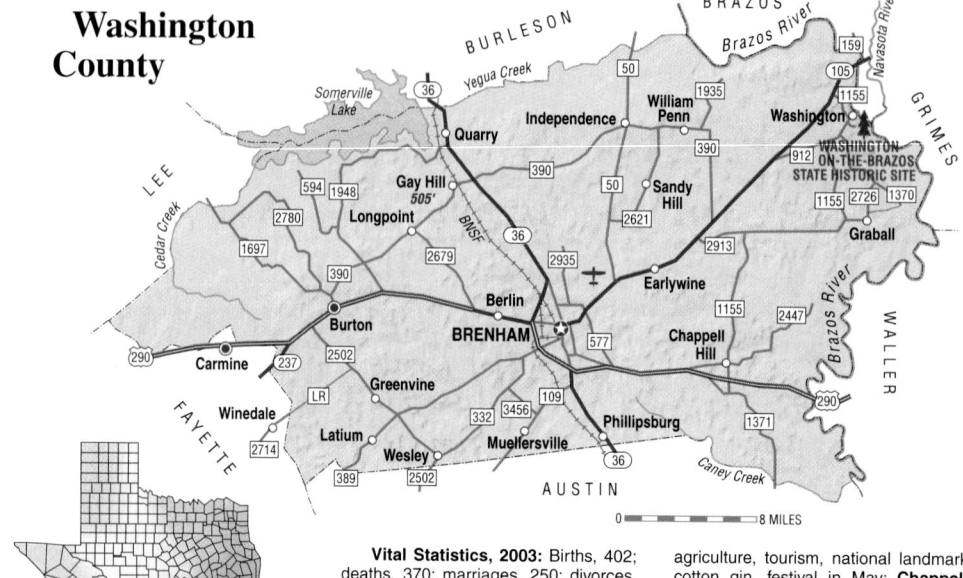

Physical

Features: South central county in Brazos valley; rolling prairie of sandy loam, alluvial soils.

Economy: Agribusinesses, oil, tourism, manufacturing; government/ services.

History: Coahuiltecan tribes and Tonkawas in area when Anglo-American settlers arrived in 1821. Antebellum slaveholding area. Germans arrived around 1870. County named for George Washington; an original county, created 1836, organized 1837.

Race/Ethnicity, 2000: (In percent), Anglo, 71.15; Black, 18.67; Hispanic, 8.71; Other, 1.47.

Vital Statistics, 2003: Births, 402; deaths, 370; marriages, 250; divorces, 82.

Recreation: Many historic sites; Washington-on-the-Brazos; Texas Baptist Historical Museum; Star of Republic Museum; Somerville Lake; fishing, hunting; antique rose nursery, miniature horse farm.

Minerals: Oil, gas and stone.

Agriculture: Beef cattle, poultry, dairy products, hogs, horses; hay, corn, sorghum, cotton, small grains, nursery crops. Market value $36.7 million.

BRENHAM (13,867) county seat; cotton processing; varied manufacturing including ceramics, mattresses, computers, Blue Bell creamery; wholesale distribution center; tourism; hospital; Blinn College, Brenham State School; Maifest.

Other towns include: **Burton** (361)

agriculture, tourism, national landmark cotton gin, festival in May; **Chappell Hill** (600) historic homes; **Washington** (265) site of signing of Texas Declaration of Independence.

Population	**31,248**
Change fm 2000	2.9
Area (sq. mi.)	621.35
Land Area (sq. mi.)	609.22
Altitude (ft.)	150-505
Rainfall (in.)	44.15
Jan. mean min.	39.3
July mean max.	96.7
Civ. Labor	16,320
Unemployed	3.4
Wages	$90,193,557
Av. Weekly Wage	$521.34
Prop. Value	$2,623,347,076
Retail Sales	$343,555,459

For explanation of sources, abbreviations and symbols, see p. 167 and foldout map.

Largest Counties by Population 2004

Rank	County (Major city)	Population
1.	Harris County (Houston)	3,644,285
2.	Dallas County (Dallas)	2,294,706
3.	Tarrant County (Fort Worth)	1,588,088
4.	Bexar County (San Antonio)	1,493,965
5.	Travis County (Austin)	869,868
6.	El Paso County (El Paso)	713,126
7.	Hidalgo County (McAllen)	658,248
8.	Collin County (Plano)	627,938
9.	Denton County (Denton)	530,597
10.	Fort Bend County (Sugar Land)	442,620
11.	Cameron County (Brownsville)	371,825
12.	Montgomery County (Conroe)	362,382
13.	Williamson County (Round Rock)	317,938
14.	Nueces County (Corpus Christi)	317,513
15.	Galveston County (Galveston)	271,743
16.	Brazoria County (Brazosport)	271,130
17.	Lubbock County (Lubbock)	251,018
18.	Bell County (Killeen-Temple)	250,324
19.	Jefferson County (Beaumont)	248,223
20.	McLennan County (Waco)	222,439
21.	Webb County (Laredo)	219,464
22.	Smith County (Tyler)	184,414
23.	Brazos County (Bryan-Coll.Station)	156,275
24.	Johnson County (Cleburne)	143,418
25.	Ellis County (Waxahachie)	128,710
26.	Wichita County (Wichita Falls)	127,321
27.	Taylor County (Abilene)	125,108
28.	Ector County (Odessa)	124,488
29.	Midland County (Midland)	120,344
30.	Hays County (San Marcos)	119,359

Source: Estimates from the U.S. Census Bureau

Webb County

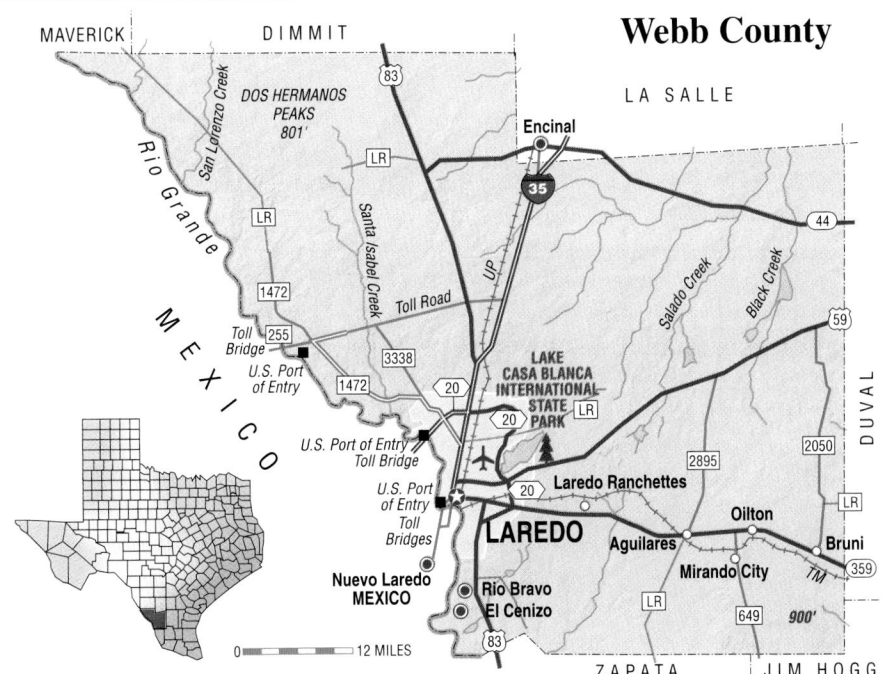

Physical Features: Southwestern county on Rio Grande: rolling, some hills; much brush; sandy, gray soils; alluvial along river.

Economy: International trade, manufacturing, tourism, government/services, natural gas, oil.

History: Coahuiltecan groups squeezed out by Comanches, Apaches and Spanish settlers. Laredo founded in 1755 by Tomás Sánchez. County named for Republic leader James Webb; created 1848 from Nueces and Bexar counties.

Race/Ethnicity, 2000: (In percent) Anglo, 5.02; Black, 0.17; Hispanic, 94.28; Other, 0.53.

Vital Statistics, 2003: Births, 5,921; deaths, 1,026; marriages, 1,757; divorces, 246.

Recreation: Major tourist gateway to Mexico; top hunting, fishing; Lake Casa Blanca park, water recreation; art festival; Washington's Birthday celebration; historic sites; museum; Fort McIntosh.

Minerals: Natural gas, oil, coal.

Agriculture: Onions, melons, nursery crops, cattle, horses, goats. About 4,500 acres irrigated. Market value $23.6 million. Mesquite sold. Hunting leases important.

LAREDO (201,139) county seat; international trade; retail; tourism; manufacturing; meat packing; rail, highway gateway to Mexico; agribusiness; junior college, Texas A&M International University; hospitals; detention centers; "El Grito" on Sept. 15; Jalapeño festival in February.

Other towns and places include: **Bruni** (434); **El Cenizo** (3,750); **Laredo Ranchettes** (1,972); **Mirando City** (517); **Oilton** (329); **Rio Bravo** (5,987).

Population	**219,464**
Change fm 2000	13.6
Area (sq. mi.)	3,375.53
Land Area (sq. mi.)	3,356.83
Altitude (ft.)	300-900
Rainfall (in.)	21.53
Jan. mean min.	43.7
July mean max.	101.6
Civ. Labor	87,621
Unemployed	6.5
Wages	$499,031,653
Av. Weekly Wage	$491.10
Prop. Value	$8,978,517,023
Retail Sales	$2,641,209,213

The campus of Texas A&M International University in Laredo. Texas Almanac photo.

Wharton County

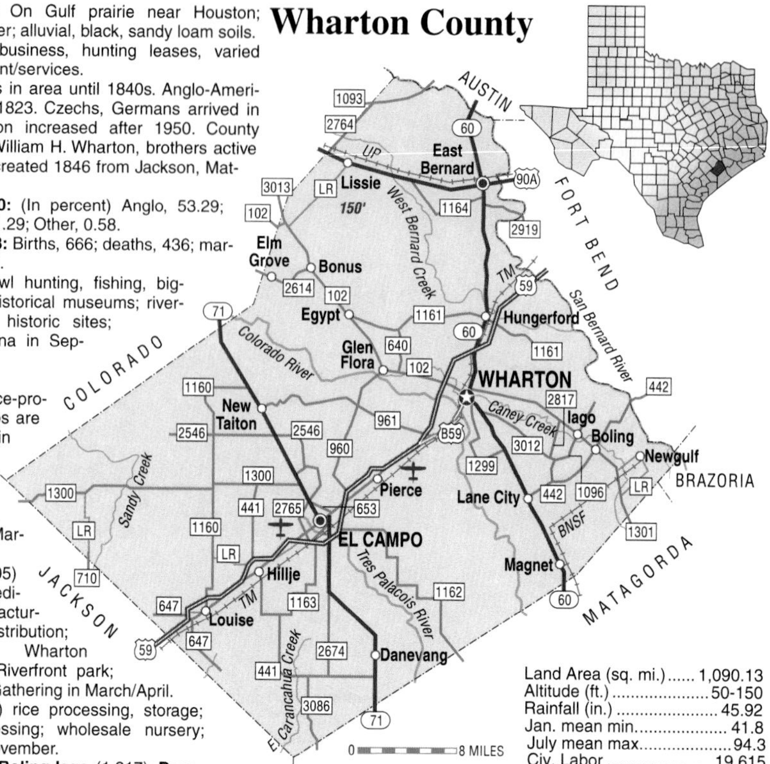

Physical Features: On Gulf prairie near Houston; bisected by Colorado River; alluvial, black, sandy loam soils.

Economy: Oil; agribusiness, hunting leases, varied manufacturing; government/services.

History: Karankawas in area until 1840s. Anglo-American colonists settled in 1823. Czechs, Germans arrived in 1880s. Mexican migration increased after 1950. County named for John A. and William H. Wharton, brothers active in the Texas Revolution; created 1846 from Jackson, Matagorda counties.

Race/Ethnicity, 2000: (In percent) Anglo, 53.29; Black, 14.84; Hispanic, 31.29; Other, 0.58.

Vital Statistics, 2003: Births, 666; deaths, 436; marriages, 300; divorces, 167.

Recreation: Waterfowl hunting, fishing, big-game, birding; art and historical museums; riverfront park in Wharton; historic sites; Fiesta Hispano Americana in September.

Minerals: Oil, gas.

Agriculture: Top rice-producing county; other crops are cotton, milo, corn, grain sorghum, soybeans; about 130,000 acres irrigated, mostly rice. Also, eggs, turfgrass, beef cattle, aquaculture. Market value $146.4 million.

WHARTON (9,405) county seat; regional medical center; plastics manufacturing; agriculture; distribution; government/services; Wharton County Junior College; Riverfront park; Shanghai Days Cowboy Gathering in March/April.

EL CAMPO (11,249) rice processing, storage; plastic, styrofoam processing; wholesale nursery; hospital; Polka Expo in November.

Other towns include: **Boling-Iago** (1,317); **Danevang** (61); **East Bernard** (1,775) agribusiness, varied manufacturing; **Egypt** (26); **Glen Flora** (210); **Hungerford** (658); **Lane City** (111); **Lissie** (72); **Louise** (990); **Pierce** (51).

Land Area (sq. mi.) 1,090.13
Altitude (ft.) 50-150
Rainfall (in.) 45.92
Jan. mean min 41.8
July mean max 94.3
Civ. Labor 19,615
Unemployed 6.1
Wages $99,811,696
Av. Weekly Wage $506.72
Prop. Value $2,137,310,517
Retail Sales $384,778,065

Population 41,594
Change fm 2000 .... 1.0
Area (sq. mi.) 1,094.43

Wheeler County

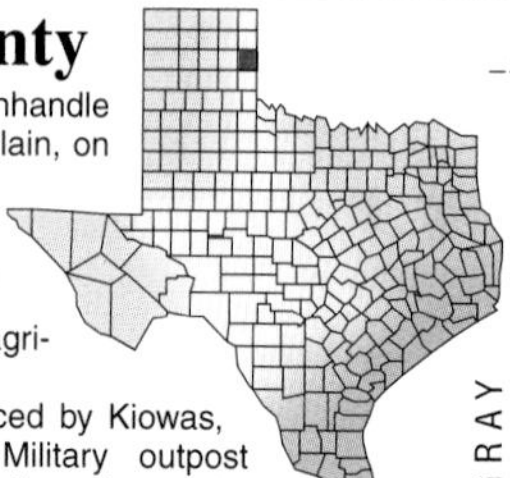

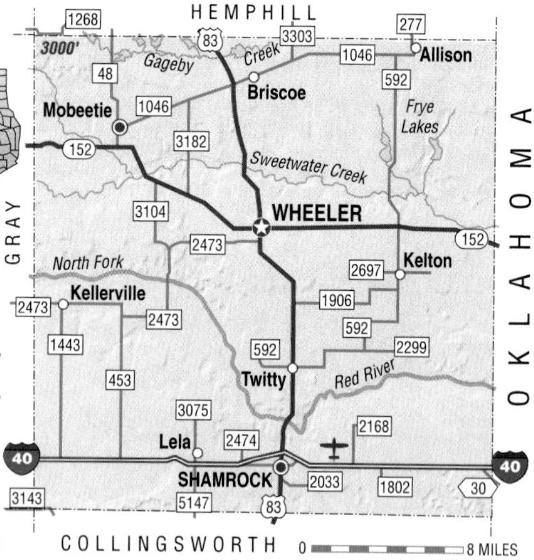

Physical Features: Panhandle county adjoining Oklahoma. Plain, on edge of Caprock; Red River, Sweetwater Creek; some canyons; red sandy loam, black clay soils.

Economy: Oil and gas, agribusinesses, tourism.

History: Apaches, displaced by Kiowas, Comanches around 1700. Military outpost established in 1875 after Indians forced into Oklahoma. Ranching began in late 1870s. Oil boom in 1920s. County named for pioneer jurist R.T. Wheeler; county created from Bexar, Young districts 1876; organized 1879.

Race/Ethnicity, 2000: (In percent) Anglo, 83.55; Black, 2.63; Hispanic, 12.57; Other, 1.25.

Vital Statistics, 2003: Births, 56; deaths, 79; marriages, 180; divorces, 4.

Recreation: Pioneer West museum at Shamrock; historic sites; Old Mobeetie jail, trading post, Fort Elliott; ostrich depot.

Minerals: Oil, natural gas.

Agriculture: Fed beef, cow-calf and stocker cattle, swine, horses; crops include wheat, grain sorghum, cotton. Market value $94 million.

WHEELER (1,250) county seat; agribusiness; petroleum center; tourism; slaughter plant; hospital; library.

SHAMROCK (1,787) tourism; agribusiness; hospital; library; St. Patrick's Day event; old Route 66 sites.

Other towns include: **Allison** (135); **Briscoe** (135); **Mobeetie** (103).

Population 4,787
Change fm 2000 .... -9.4
Area (sq. mi.) 915.34
Land Area (sq. mi.) 914.26
Altitude (ft.) 2,000-3,000
Rainfall (in.) 24.32
Jan. mean min. 22.9
July mean max. 93.3
Civ. Labor 2,552

Unemployed 2.2
Wages $10,106,171
Av. Weekly Wage $425.27
Prop. Value $700,162,708
Retail Sales $33,459,629

For explanation of sources, abbreviations and symbols, see p. 167 and foldout map.

Wichita County

Physical Features: North central county in prairie bordering Oklahoma; drained by Red, Wichita rivers; lakes; sandy, loam soils.

Economy: Retail trade center for large area; air base; government, manufacturing, oil, medical services and agribusiness.

History: Wichitas and other Caddoan tribes in area in 1700s; Comanches, Apaches also present until 1850s. Anglo-American settlement increased after 1870. County named for Indian tribe; created from Young Territory 1858; organized 1882.

Race/Ethnicity, 2000: (In percent) Anglo, 74.34; Black, 10.57; Hispanic, 12.23; Other, 2.86.

Vital Statistics, 2003: Births, 1,851; deaths, 1,260; marriages, 2,681; divorces, 775.

Recreation: Metropolitan events; museums; historic sites; Texas-Oklahoma High School Oil Bowl football game; collegiate activities; water sports on lakes; Fiestas Patrias parade; Ranch Round-up in August.

Minerals: Oil, natural gas, sand, gravel, stone.

Agriculture: Stocker, cow-calf production important; wheat, other small grains; hay; cotton. Seventy-five percent of hay irrigated; 10 percent of wheat/cotton. Market value $15.8 million.

WICHITA FALLS (103,262) county seat; distribution center for large area in

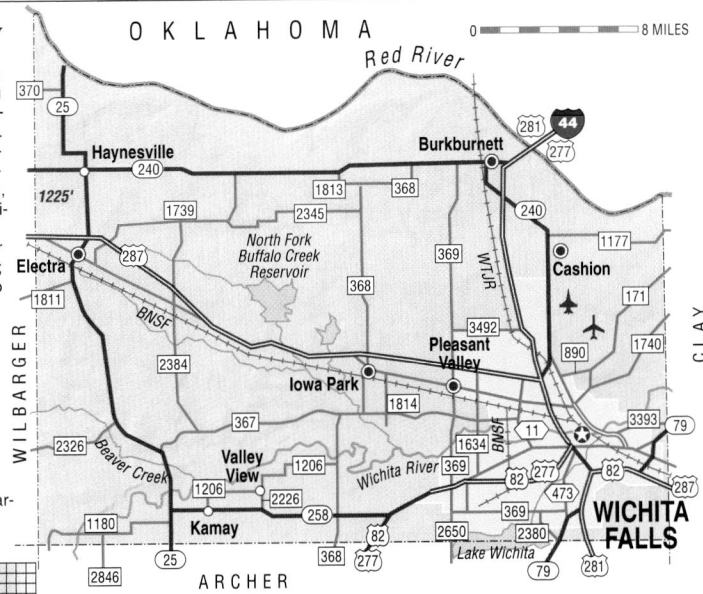

Texas, Oklahoma; government/services; varied manufacturing; oil-field services; hospitals; Midwestern State University, vocational-technical training center; North Texas State Hospital; hiking trails, major bicycle race in August; **Sheppard Air Force Base**.

Other cities include: **Burkburnett** (10,847) some manufacturing; **Cashion** (341); **Electra** (3,091) oil, agriculture, manufacturing, commuters to Wichita Falls; hospital; Goat barbecue in May; **Iowa Park** (6,382) some manufacturing, prison, Whoop-t-do homecoming in September; **Kamay** (640); **Pleasant Valley** (392).

Population	**127,321**
Change fm 2000	-3.3
Area (sq. mi.)	633.01
Land Area (sq. mi.)	627.66
Altitude (ft.)	954-1,225
Rainfall (in.)	28.83
Jan. mean min.	28.9
July mean max.	97.2
Civ. Labor	61,023
Unemployed	3.9
Wages	$384,417,286
Av. Weekly Wage	$539.02
Prop. Value	$5,100,346,842
Retail Sales	$1,460,757,590

The jail at Old Mobeetie in Wheeler County. Texas Almanac photo.

Wilbarger County

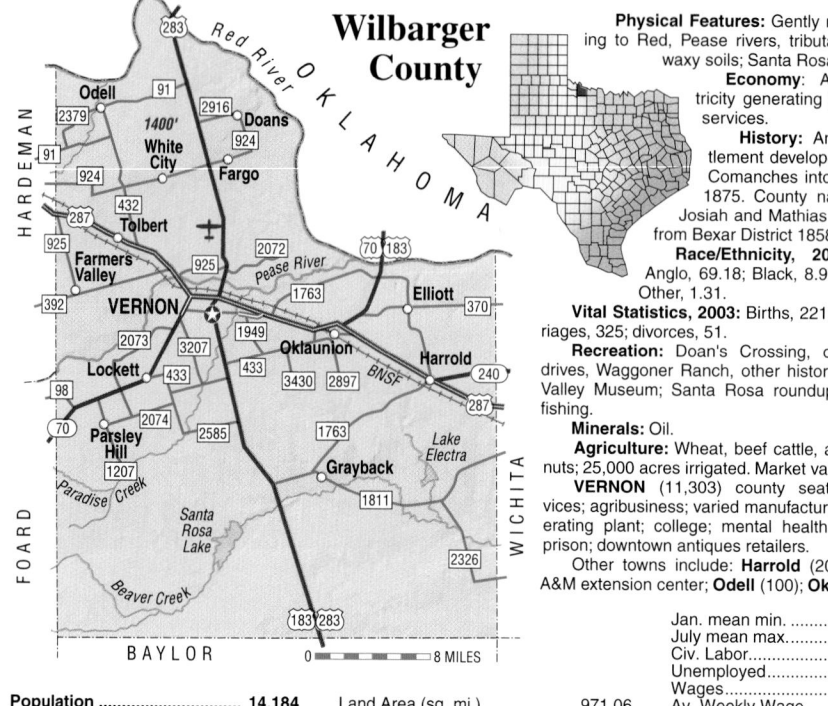

Physical Features: Gently rolling prairie draining to Red, Pease rivers, tributaries; sandy, loam, waxy soils; Santa Rosa Lake.

Economy: Agribusiness, electricity generating plant, government/services.

History: Anglo-American settlement developed after removal of Comanches into Indian Territory in 1875. County named for pioneers Josiah and Mathias Wilbarger; created from Bexar District 1858; organized 1881.

Race/Ethnicity, 2000: (In percent) Anglo, 69.18; Black, 8.97; Hispanic, 20.54; Other, 1.31.

Vital Statistics, 2003: Births, 221; deaths, 205; marriages, 325; divorces, 51.

Recreation: Doan's Crossing, on route of cattle drives, Waggoner Ranch, other historic sites; Red River Valley Museum; Santa Rosa roundup in May; hunting, fishing.

Minerals: Oil.

Agriculture: Wheat, beef cattle, alfalfa, cotton, peanuts; 25,000 acres irrigated. Market value $32.1 million.

VERNON (11,303) county seat; government/services; agribusiness; varied manufacturing; electricity-generating plant; college; mental health center, hospitals; prison; downtown antiques retailers.

Other towns include: **Harrold** (200); **Lockett** (150) A&M extension center; **Odell** (100); **Oklaunion** (138).

Jan. mean min.	25.7
July mean max.	97.2
Civ. Labor	7,405
Unemployed	2.9
Wages	$32,913,434
Av. Weekly Wage	$484.28
Prop. Value	$856,152,970
Retail Sales	$111,385,834

Population	14,184
Change fm 2000	-3.4
Area (sq. mi.)	978.10
Land Area (sq. mi.)	971.06
Altitude (ft.)	1,099-1,400
Rainfall (in.)	28.55

Willacy County

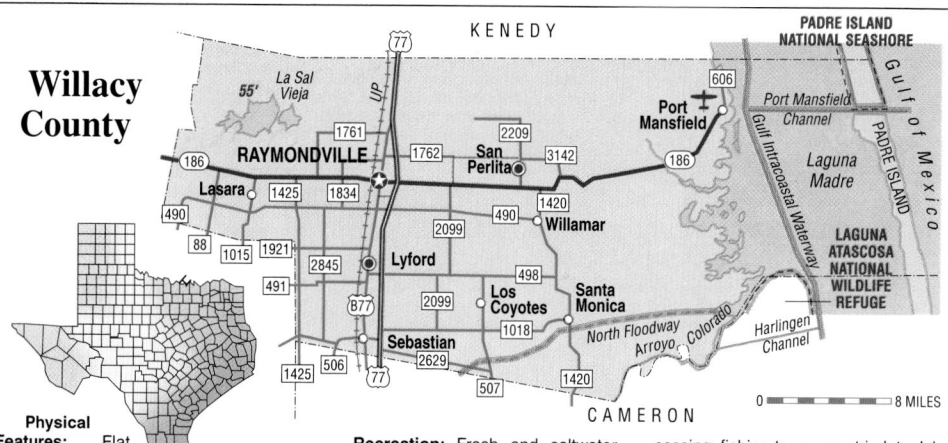

Physical Features: Flat coastal prairie sloping toward Gulf; alluvial, sandy, marshy soils; Padre Island; La Sal Vieja, salt lake; wildlife refuge.

Economy: Agribusiness; oil; government/services.

History: Coahuiltecan area when Spanish explored in 1500s. Spanish ranching began in 1790s. County named for Texas legislator John G. Willacy; created 1911 from Cameron, Hidalgo counties; reorganized 1921.

Race/Ethnicity, 2000: (In percent) Anglo, 11.98; Black, 2.02; Hispanic, 85.69; Other, 0.31.

Vital Statistics, 2003: Births, 393; deaths, 102; marriages, 120; divorces, 9.

Recreation: Fresh and saltwater fishing, hunting of deer, turkey, dove; mild climate attracts many winter tourists; Port Mansfield fishing tournament.

Minerals: Oil, natural gas.

Agriculture: Cotton, sorghum, corn, vegetables, sugar cane; 20 percent of cropland irrigated. Livestock includes cattle, horses, goats, hogs. Market value $18.9 million.

RAYMONDVILLE (9,735) county seat; agribusiness, oil center; food processing, shipping; tourist center; museum; enterprise zone; prison unit; Boot Fest in October.

Other towns include: **Lasara** (1,030); **Lyford** (2,129); **Port Mansfield** (404) popular fishing port; shrimp processing; fishing tournament in late July; **San Perlita** (708); **Sebastian** (1,875).

Population	20,231
Change fm 2000	0.7
Area (sq. mi.)	784.23
Land Area (sq. mi.)	596.68
Altitude (ft.)	sea level-55
Rainfall (in.)	27.97
Jan. mean min.	47.5
July mean max.	95.3
Civ. Labor	6,669
Unemployed	15.2
Wages	$19,790,833
Av. Weekly Wage	$471.61
Prop. Value	$759,097,010
Retail Sales	$65,109,129

For explanation of sources, abbreviations and symbols, see p. 167 and foldout map.

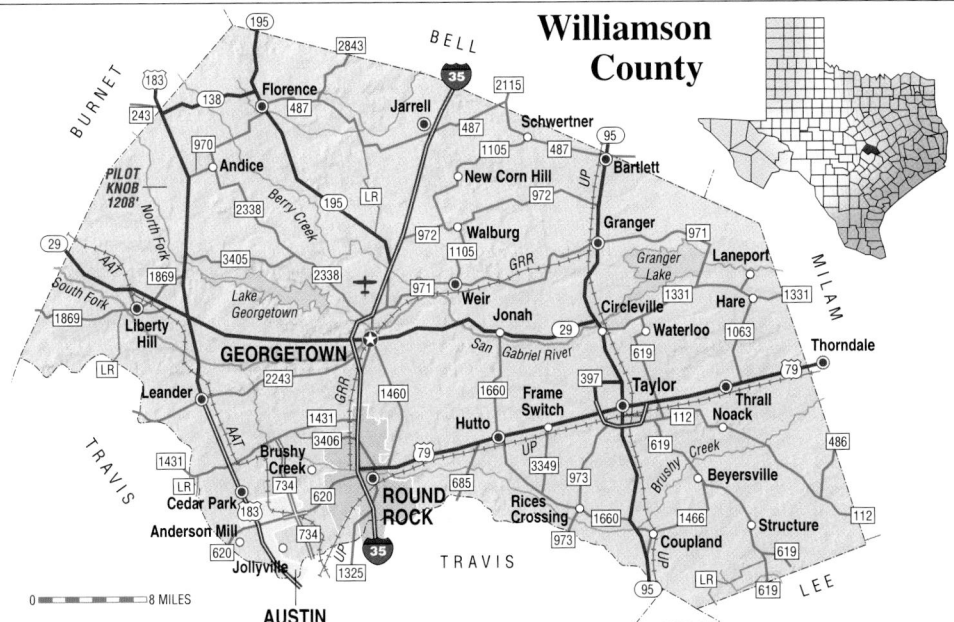

Williamson County

Physical Features: Central county near Austin. Level to rolling; mostly Blackland soil, some loam, sand; drained by San Gabriel River and tributaries.

Economy: Agribusinesses, varied manufacturing, education center, government/services; the county is part of Austin metropolitan area.

History: Tonkawa area; later, other tribes. Comanches raided until 1860s. Anglo-American settlement began in late 1830s. County named for Robert M. Williamson, pioneer leader; created from Milam and organized in 1848.

Race/Ethnicity, 2000: (In percent) Anglo, 74.33; Black, 5.27; Hispanic, 17.20; Other, 3.20.

Vital Statistics, 2003: Births, 5,179; deaths, 1,383; marriages, 1,920; divorces, 1,090.

Recreation: Lake recreation; Inner Space Cavern; historic sites; deer hunting, fishing; Gov. Dan Moody Museum at Taylor; San Gabriel Park; old settlers park; walking tours, rattlesnake sacking, barbecue cookoff, frontier days in summer; Round Rock minor league baseball.

Minerals: Building stone, sand and gravel.

Agriculture: Corn, cattle, grain sorghum, cotton, wheat. Market value $46.4 million.

GEORGETOWN (34,994) county seat; agribusiness, manufacturing, education, tourism, mining; hospital; Southwestern University; Mayfair; Christmas Stroll.

ROUND ROCK (81,265, part [1,076] in Travis County) semiconductor, varied manufacturing; tourism and distribution center; hospital; Texas Baptist Children's Home.

Taylor (13,944) agribusiness, publishing center; varied manufacturing including cottonseed and meat processing; hospital; movie location.

Other towns include: **Andice** (NA); **Bartlett** (1,773, partly in Bell County) cotton, corn production; commuters; prison; first rural electrification in nation in 1933, clinic; library; Friendship Fest in September; **Brushy Creek** (17,965); **Cedar Park** (37,614, partly in Travis County) varied manufacturing, commuting to Austin, steam-engine train; **Coupland** (280); **Florence** (1,175).

Also, **Granger** (1,341); **Hutto** (3,063) agriculture, manufacturing, government/services; commuters to Austin; museum; Olde Tyme Days in October; **Jarrell** (1,400); **Jollyville** (15,391, partly in Travis County); **Leander** (11,987); **Liberty Hill** (1,393) artisans center; **Schwertner** (175); **Thrall** (826); **Walburg** (277); **Weir** (603).

Also, the residential community of **Anderson Mill** (9,051), which extends into Travis County, and part [11,810] of **Austin**.

Population	317,938
Change fm 2000	27.2
Area (sq. mi.)	1,134.74
Land Area (sq. mi.)	1,122.77
Altitude (ft.)	400-1,208
Rainfall (in.)	35.11
Jan. mean min.	35.8
July mean max.	95.3
Civ. Labor	164,835
Unemployed	3.7
Wages	$840,365,299
Av. Weekly Wage	$743.42
Prop. Value	$ 29,645,822,803
Retail Sales	$ 3,795,168,466

The Port Mansfield inlet from Laguna Madre in Willacy County. Texas Almanac photo.

Wilson County

Physical Features: South central county on rolling plains; mostly sandy soils, some heavier; San Antonio River, Cibolo Creek.

Economy: Agribusiness; some residents employed in San Antonio; part of San Antonio metropolitan area.

History: Coahuiltecan Indians in area when Spanish began ranching around 1750. Anglo-American settlers arrived in 1840s. German, Polish settled in 1850s. County created from Bexar, Karnes counties 1860; named for James C. Wilson, member of the Mier Expedition.

Race/Ethnicity, 2000: (In percent) Anglo, 61.51; Black, 1.21; Hispanic, 36.52; Other, 0.76.

Vital Statistics, 2003: Births, 444; deaths, 288; marriages, 233; divorces, 116.

Recreation: Mission ranch ruins, historic homes; Stockdale watermelon festival; Floresville peanut festival in October.

Minerals: Oil, gas, clays.

Agriculture: Cattle, dairy products, hogs, poultry; peanuts, sorghum, corn, small grains, vegetables, watermelons, fruit. Market value $42.7 million.

FLORESVILLE (6,425) county seat; agribusiness center; hospital; veterans home; Heritage Days in spring; annual Pony Express ride.

Other towns include: **La Vernia** (980); **Pandora** (125); **Poth** (1,979) agriculture, commuting to San Antonio; Mayfest; **Stockdale** (1,432) food processing; medical center; recreation facilities; **Sutherland Springs** (362). Part of **Nixon** (2,262, mostly in Gonzales County).

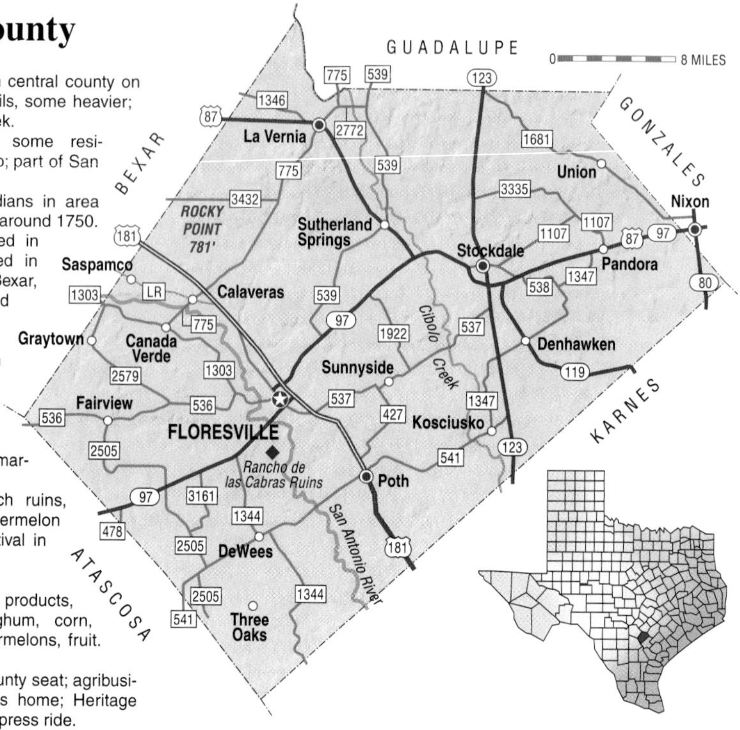

Population	36,726
Change fm 2000	13.3
Area (sq. mi.)	808.57
Land Area (sq. mi.)	806.99
Altitude (ft.)	300-781
Rainfall (in.)	27.60
Jan. mean min.	38.4
July mean max.	95.7
Civ. Labor	17,023
Unemployed	3.7
Wages	$32,976,682
Av. Weekly Wage	$434.96
Prop. Value	$1,884,396,376
Retail Sales	$119,060,367

Visitors prepare to sandboard at Monahans Sandhills State Park, which is in Ward and Winkler counties. File photo.

Winkler County

Physical Features: Western county adjoining New Mexico on plains, partly sandy hills.

Economy: Oil, natural gas; ranching; prison; farming.

History: Apache area until arrival of Comanches in 1700s. Anglo-Americans began ranching in 1880s. Oil discovered 1926. Mexican migration increased after 1960. County named for Confederate Col. C.M. Winkler; created from Tom Green County 1887; organized 1910.

Race/Ethnicity, 2000: (In percent) Anglo, 53.60; Black, 1.87; Hispanic, 44.00; Other, 0.53.

Vital Statistics, 2003: Births, 131; deaths, 69; marriages, 50; divorces, 12.

Recreation: Sandhills Park; museum; zoo; wooden oil derrick; Roy Orbison festival in June at Wink; Wink Sink, large sinkhole.

Minerals: Oil, gas.

Agriculture: Major producer of chip potatoes; meat goats, beef cattle. Market value $1.9 million.

KERMIT (5,264) the county seat, and **Wink** (834) oil, gas, ranching.

Population	6,714
Change fm 2000	-6.4
Area (sq. mi.)	841.24
Land Area (sq. mi.)	841.05
Altitude (ft.)	2,671-3,368
Rainfall (in.)	12.92
Jan. mean min.	27.8
July mean max.	96.1
Civ. Labor	2,949
Unemployed	6.0
Wages	$17,029,199
Av. Weekly Wage	$614.42
Prop. Value	$817,380,969
Retail Sales	$36,179,082

Wise County

Physical Features: North central county of rolling prairie, some oaks; clay, loam, sandy soils; lakes.

Economy: Petroleum; agribusiness; sand and gravel; hunting leases; many residents work in Fort Worth.

History: Caddo Indian groups. Delaware tribe present when Anglo-Americans arrived in 1850s. County created 1856 from Cooke County; named for Virginian, U.S. Sen. Henry A. Wise, who favored annexation of Texas.

Race/Ethnicity, 2000: (In percent) Anglo, 86.88; Black, 1.33; Hispanic, 10.76; Other, 1.03.

Vital Statistics, 2003: Births, 660; deaths, 436; marriages, 433; divorces, 315.

Recreation: Lake activities; hunting; exotic deer preserve; historical sites; Lyndon B. Johnson National Grasslands; Chisholm trail days in June; antique auto swap meet; Butterfield stage days in July; heritage museum, old courthouse.

Minerals: Gas, oil, sand, gravel.

Agriculture: Beef cattle, forages, dairies, horses, wheat, goats. Market value $33.3 million.

DECATUR (5,963) county seat; petroleum center; dairying; cattle marketing; some manufacturing; hospital.

BRIDGEPORT (5,533) trade center for lake resort; oil, gas production; time-share housing; artistic community; manufacturing; prison release facility. Other towns include: **Alvord** (1,102); **Aurora** (934); **Boyd** (1,212); **Briar** (5,615, mostly in Tarrant County); **Chico** (1,008); **Greenwood** (76); **Lake Bridgeport** (393); **Newark** (1,001); **New Fairview** (1,034); **Paradise** (483); **Pecan Acres** (2,444, partly in Tarrant County); **Rhome** (751); **Runaway Bay** (1,188); **Slidell** (175).

For explanation of sources, abbreviations and symbols, see p. 167 and foldout map.

Population	55,539
Change fm 2000	13.8
Area (sq. mi.)	922.77
Land Area (sq. mi.)	904.61
Altitude (ft.)	649-1,180
Rainfall (in.)	34.02
Jan. mean min.	30.5
July mean max.	98.0
Civ. Labor	29,781
Unemployed	3.8
Wages	$108,951,460
Av. Weekly Wage	$574.43
Prop. Value	$4,507,434,772
Retail Sales	$472,646,509

Wood County

Physical Features: Hilly northeastern county almost half forested; sandy to alluvial soils; drained by Sabine and tributaries; many lakes.

Economy: Agribusiness, oil and gas; tourism.

History: Caddo Indians; reduced by disease. Anglo-American settlement developed in 1840s. County created from Van Zandt County 1850; named for Gov. George T. Wood.

Race/Ethnicity, 2000: (In percent) Anglo, 87.23; Black, 6.27; Hispanic, 5.72; Other, 0.78.

Vital Statistics, 2003: Births, 447; deaths, 545; marriages, 303; divorces, 158.

Recreation: Autumn trails; lake activities; hunting, birding; Gov. Hogg shrine and museum; historic sites; scenic drives; Mineola Choo Choo, Chili & Bean Fest in May; railroad heritage days; autumn trails.

Minerals: Natural gas, oil, sand, gravel.

Agriculture: Poultry, dairy, beef cattle, forage, horses. Market value $57.8 million. Timber production. Timber significant.

QUITMAN (2,101) county seat; tourism; food processing; some manufacturing; hospital; Dogwood Fiesta.

MINEOLA (4,768) agribusiness, some manufacturing, railroad center, antiques shops; museum, library.

Winnsboro (3,808, partly in Franklin County) chicken-raising, dairies, distribution; hospital; prison.

Other towns include: **Alba** (439, partly in Rains County); **Golden** (156) Sweet Potato festival; **Hawkins** (1,461) petroleum, water bottling, Jarvis Christian College; oil festival in fall; **Yantis** (357).

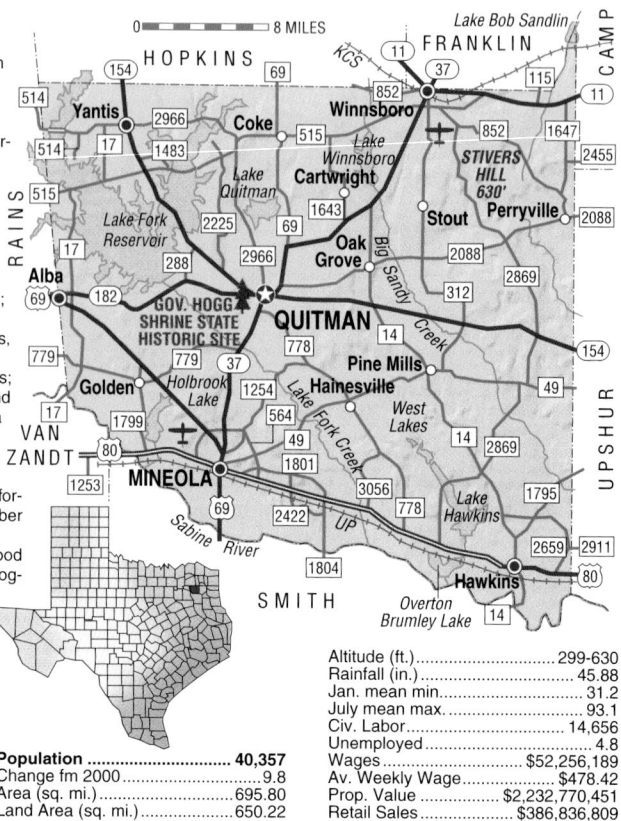

Population	40,357
Change fm 2000	9.8
Area (sq. mi.)	695.80
Land Area (sq. mi.)	650.22

Altitude (ft.)	299-630
Rainfall (in.)	45.88
Jan. mean min.	31.2
July mean max.	93.1
Civ. Labor	14,656
Unemployed	4.8
Wages	$52,256,189
Av. Weekly Wage	$478.42
Prop. Value	$2,232,770,451
Retail Sales	$386,836,809

Yoakum County

Physical Features: Western county is level to rolling; playas, draws; sandy, loam, chocolate soils.

Economy: Oil and gas, cotton, peanuts.

History: Comanche hunting area. Anglo-Americans began ranching in 1890s. Oil discovered 1936. Mexican migration increased in 1950s. County named for Henderson Yoakum, pioneer historian; created from Bexar District 1876; organized 1907.

Race/Ethnicity, 2000: (In percent) Anglo, 52.14; Black, 1.26; Hispanic, 45.93; Other, 0.67.

Vital Statistics, 2003: Births, 131; deaths, 58; marriages, 49; divorces, 29.

Recreation: Tsa Mo Ga Museum at Plains; Roughneck rodeo and farmboy jamboree in May; settlers reunion in August; watermelon roundup on Labor Day weekend.

Minerals: Oil, natural gas.

Agriculture: Cotton, peanuts, watermelons, sorghum, wheat; 100,000 acres irrigated. Cattle, horses, goats raised. Market value $49.9 million.

PLAINS (1,439) county seat; oil, agribusiness center.

DENVER CITY (3,834) center for oil, agriculture activities in two counties; hospital, library.

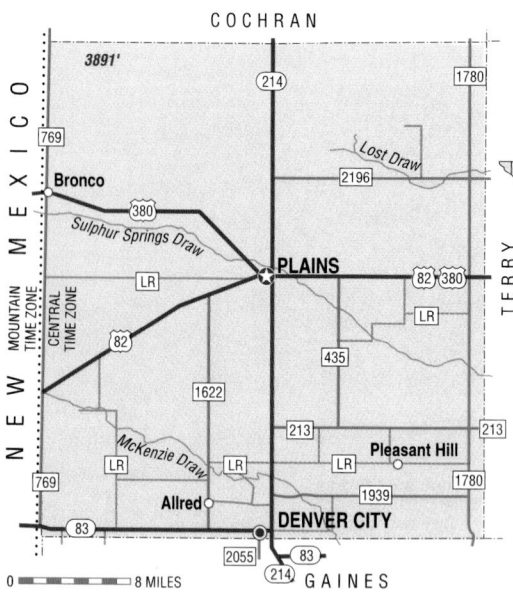

Population	7,348
Change fm 2000	0.4
Area (sq. mi.)	799.76
Land Area (sq. mi.)	799.75
Altitude (ft.)	3,490-3,891
Rainfall (in.)	18.41

Jan. mean min.	25.1
July mean max.	91.7
Civ. Labor	3,042
Unemployed	4.3
Wages	$25,708,450
Av. Weekly Wage	$723.86

Prop. Value	$1,878,075,235
Retail Sales	$46,353,735

Young County

Physical Features: Hilly, broken; drained by Brazos and tributaries; Possum Kingdom Lake, Lake Graham.

Economy: Oil, agribusiness, tourism; hunting leases.

History: U.S. military outpost established 1851. Site of Brazos Indian Reservation 1854-59 with Caddoes, Wacos, other tribes. Anglo-American settlers arrived in 1850s. County named for early Texan, Col. W.C. Young; created 1856 from Bosque, Fannin counties; reorganized 1874.

Race/Ethnicity, 2000: (In percent) Anglo, 87.25; Black, 1.32; Hispanic, 10.62; Other, 0.81.

Vital Statistics, 2003: Births, 239; deaths, 235; marriages, 151; divorces, 114.

Recreation: Lake activities; hunting; Fort Belknap restoration; marker at oak tree in Graham where ranchers formed forerunner of Texas and Southwestern Cattle Raisers Association; vintage auto club tour, antique tractor show in April.

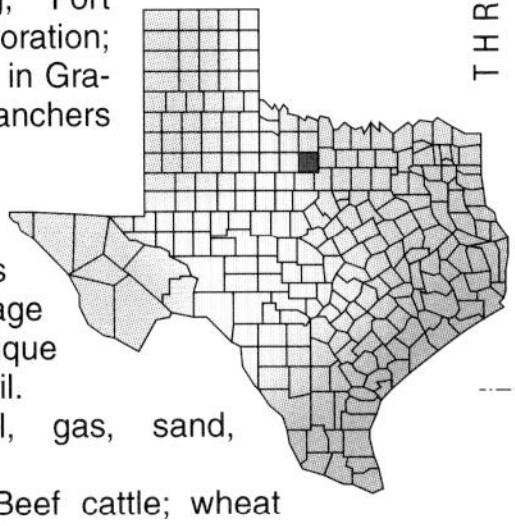

Minerals: Oil, gas, sand, gravel.

Agriculture: Beef cattle; wheat chief crop, also hay, cotton, pecans, nursery plants. Market value $23.9 million.

GRAHAM (8,639) county seat; oil, agribusiness, manufacturing, tourism, hunting; hospital, mental health clinic; celebrity rodeo in fall.

Other towns include: **Loving** (300); **Newcastle** (571); **Olney** (3,370) aluminum, varied manufacturing, hospital; Mayfest; **South Bend** (140).

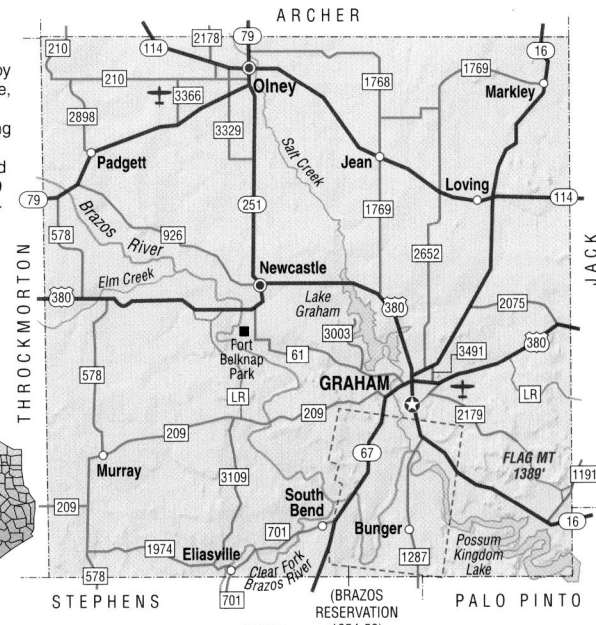

Population	17,938
Change fm 2000	0.0
Area (sq. mi.)	930.84
Land Area (sq. mi.)	922.33
Altitude (ft.)	995-1,389
Rainfall (in.)	31.35
Jan. mean min.	27.1
July mean max.	96.6
Civ. Labor	7,758

Unemployed	4.5
Wages	$41,690,301
Av. Weekly Wage	$518.17
Prop. Value	$947,420,038
Retail Sales	$167,064,614

For explanation of sources, abbreviations and symbols, see p. 167 and foldout map.

The Rio Grande near San Ygnacio in Zapata County. Texas Almanac photo.

Zapata County

Physical Features: Southern county of rolling, brushy topography; broken by tributaries of Rio Grande; Falcon Reservoir.

Economy: Natural gas, oil; ranching, Falcon Reservoir activities, government/services.

History: Coahuiltecan Indians in area when the ranch settlement of Nuestra Señora de los Dolores was established in 1750. Anglo-American migration increased after 1980. County named for Col. Antonio Zapata, pioneer rancher; created 1858 from Starr, Webb counties.

Race/Ethnicity, 2000: (In percent) Anglo, 14.78; Black, 0.18; Hispanic, 84.78; Other, 0.26.

Vital Statistics, 2003: Births, 288; deaths, 88; marriages, 156; divorces, 0.

Recreation: Lake; state park; historic sites; Nuestra Señora de los Dolores Hacienda; winter tourist center; rock hunting; hang gliding encampment in June/July.

Minerals: Natural gas, oil, caliche.

Agriculture: Beef cattle; onions, cantaloupes and melons; goats. Market value $9.8 million. Hunting/wildlife leases.

ZAPATA (5,502) county seat; tourism, agribusiness, oil center; retirement, winter tourist center; clinic; Fajita Cook-off in November.

Other towns and places include: **Falcon** (376); **Lopeño** (166); **Medina** (3,592), and **San Ygnacio** (980) historic buildings, museum.

Population	**13,154**
Change fm 2000	8.0
Area (sq. mi.)	1,058.10
Land Area (sq. mi.)	996.76
Altitude (ft.)	301-800
Rainfall (in.)	19.53
Jan. mean min.	45.4
July mean max.	98.0
Civ. Labor	5,334
Unemployed	6.7
Wages	$21,409,517
Av. Weekly Wage	$514.17
Prop. Value	$1,747,603,541
Retail Sales	$68,455,062

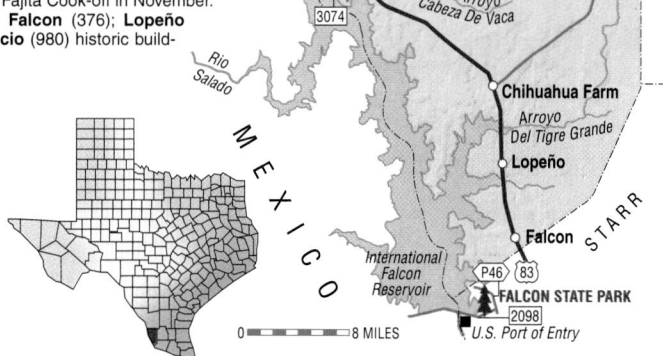

Zavala County

Physical Features: Southwestern county near Mexican border of rolling plains broken by much brush; Nueces, Leona, other streams.

Economy: Agribusiness, food packaging, leading county in Winter Garden truck-farming area; government/services.

History: Coahuiltecan area; Apaches, Comanches arrived later. Ranching developed in late 1860s. County created from Maverick, Uvalde counties 1858; organized 1884; named for Texas Revolutionary leader Lorenzo de Zavala.

Race/Ethnicity, 2000: (In percent) Anglo, 8.15; Black, 0.40; Hispanic, 91.22; Other, 0.23.

Vital Statistics, 2003: Births, 191; deaths, 91; marriages, 40; divorces, 3.

Recreation: Hunting, fishing; spinach festival in November.

Minerals: Oil, natural gas.

Agriculture: Cattle, grains, vegetables, cotton, pecans. About 50,000 acres irrigated. Market value $48.7 million. Hunting leases important.

CRYSTAL CITY (7,063) county seat; agribusiness; food processing; oil-field services; site of Japanese detention center. Home of Popeye statue.

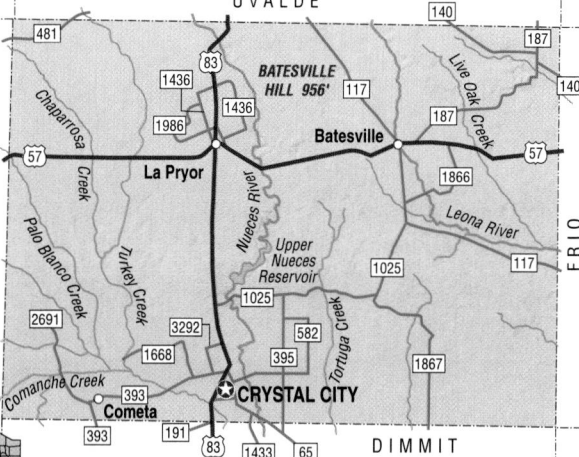

Other towns include: **Batesville** (1,256) and **La Pryor** (1,472).

Population	**11,700**
Change fm 2000	0.9
Area (sq. mi.)	1,301.72
Land Area (sq. mi.)	1,298.48
Altitude (ft.)	540-956
Rainfall (in.)	20.70
Jan. mean min.	42.6
July mean max.	97.1
Civ. Labor	4,880
Unemployed	13.1
Wages	$12,636,370
Av. Weekly Wage	$363.51
Prop. Value	$739,378,851
Retail Sales	$31,598,934

For explanation of sources, abbreviations and symbols, see p. 167 and foldout map.

Texas Population: Growth Exceeds National Rate

By Steve H. Murdock, Md. Nazrul Hoque, and Beverly Pecotte, of the Institute for Demographic and Socioeconomic Research, the University of Texas at San Antonio.

Texas' population is growing and changing rapidly, and such changes may have substantial impacts on the state. Texas' rate of population growth has exceeded that for the nation in every decade since Texas became a state, and its recent population increases have been particularly large.

In the 1990s, Texas was the second-fastest growing state in numerical terms (behind California) and the eighth-fastest growing in percentage terms.

And, in the post-2000 period from April 1, 2000 (the 2000 Census date) to July 1, 2004, it was again the second-fastest growing in numerical terms and was tied with Georgia as the fourth-fastest growing (behind Nevada, Arizona and Florida) in percentage terms.

The size of Texas' population has more than doubled in the past 25 years, increasing from roughly 11.2 million in 1970 to nearly 22.5 million in 2004, and, in the 1990s, its percentage increase of 22.8 percent resulted in a population increase of nearly 3.9 million people.

This 3.9 million is roughly equivalent to having added the number of people who in 1990 lived in the cities of Houston, Dallas, San Antonio, and Corpus Christi combined.

Population increase since 2000 was concentrated in large suburban and central city complexes

This increase was greater than the total population of 24 of the 50 states in 2000 and meant that more than one of every nine persons added to the population of the United States in the 1990s was added in Texas.

In the post-2000 period, population growth has continued with an increase in Texas' population of more than 1.6 million from April 1, 2000, to July 1, 2004. This level of growth, if continued, will mean that Texas' population increase from 2000 to 2010 will likely be between 3.7 and 4.0 million people.

Growth Not Uniform

However, neither the amount nor rate of population change has been uniform across Texas.

Some counties have grown significantly while others have lost population. Growth was particularly pronounced along the Texas-Mexico border where areas such as South Texas and Lower Rio Grande Valley showed growth rates in the 1990s of roughly 40 percent and in the urban complexes of Houston-Galveston, Dallas-Fort Worth, as well as the Austin-to-San Antonio-Corridor where absolute numerical and percentage increases were extensive.

For example, in the Dallas-Fort Worth area the population increased by nearly 1.2 million in the 1990s (greater population growth than occurred in 45 of the 50 states). Population growth was roughly 957,000 in

Counties of Significant Population Change by Percent and Number: 2000 to 2004

Fastest-Growing Counties

Rockwall County.

Fastest-Declining Counties

Loving County.

Rank	Percent	Rank	Number	Rank	Percent	Rank	Number
1. Rockwall	35.2	1. Harris	243,707	1. Loving	-22.4	1. Wichita	-4,343
2. Collin	27.7	2. Tarrant	141,869	2. Stonewall	-17.0	2. Jefferson	-3,828
3. Williamson	27.2	3. Collin	136,164	3. Kent	-13.4	3. Taylor	-1,443
4. Fort Bend	24.9	4. Bexar	101,034	4. Throckmorton	-11.8	4. Gray	-1,335
5. Montgomery	23.4	5. Denton	97,621	5. Terrell	-11.5	5. Reeves	-1,295
6. Denton	22.5	6. Hidalgo	88,785	6. Cochran	-10.5	6. Hutchinson	-1,240
7. Hays	22.3	7. Fort Bend	88,163	7. Reeves	-9.9	7. Pecos	-860
8. Rains	21.1	8. Dallas	75,932	8. Wheeler	-9.4	8. Falls	-811
9. Kaufman	19.7	9. Montgomery	68,614	9. King	-9.3	9. Howard	-748
10. Bastrop	18.8	10. Williamson	67,971	10. Knox	-8.5	10. Newton	-727

Chart shows Rockwall County increased in population by 35.2 percent, while Harris County gained 243,707 people, etc. Source: U.S. Bureau of the Census

the Houston-Galveston area (greater than 40 of the 50 states). And the 748,000 increase in the population of the Austin-San Antonio corridor was more than 31 percent from 1990 to 2000.

At the same time, 68 of Texas' 254 counties, all of which were nonmetropolitan or rural, lost population in the 1990s.

From 2000 to 2003, growth has been even more concentrated in the state's large suburban and central city complexes, with the number of counties with population losses reaching 98, nearly all of these being nonmetropolitan counties.

The characteristics of Texas' population are also changing rapidly, particularly those related to its racial/ethnic and age composition. Although Texas' population in 1980 was roughly two-thirds Anglo, by 2005, Texas' population was approximately 49 percent Anglo, 11 percent African-American, 36 percent Hispanic, and 4 percent members of other racial/ethic groups (primarily Asian).

Similarly, although a relatively young state overall (with the third-youngest median age in 2000), Texas like the rest of the nation has more than 25 percent of its population in the "baby-boom" ages (i.e., 41-59 years of age in 2005) and, as a result, will show increasing numbers of elderly persons in the coming decades.

In fact, these two characteristics are interrelated such that non-Anglo status and youth status, and Anglo and older-age status, tended to be interrelated. Thus, as of 2000, 57 percent of the population under 18 years of age was non-Anglo while 57 percent of the population 18 years of age or older was Anglo.

Projections of Population

Texas' historical pattern of rapid growth is projected to continue. Whereas the U.S. Census Bureau has recently projected that the nation's population will increase by roughly 49 percent by 2050, Texas is projected to grow by at least 71.5 percent for the 40-year period from 2000 to 2040, adding at least 14.9 million people to the state's population over the next 40 years.

Texas will also become increasingly diverse with Anglos coming to account for no more than one-third of the total population by 2040. On the other hand, Hispanics will come to form a majority of the population by no later than 2035 and by 2040 will make up at least 52.6 percent of the total population.

As in the rest of the country, Texas population will

Population change, 1850–2004

Year	Total Population		Percent change	
	Texas	U.S.	Texas	U.S.
1850	212,592	23,191,876	...	...
1860	604,215	31,443,321	184.2	35.6
1870	818,579	39,181,449	35.5	26.6
1880	1,591,749	50,155,783	94.5	26.0
1890	2,235,527	62,947,714	40.4	25.5
1900	3,048,710	75,994,575	36.4	20.7
1910	3,896,542	91,972,266	27.8	21.0
1920	4,663,228	105,710,620	19.7	14.9
1930	5,824,715	122,775,046	24.9	16.1
1940	6,414,824	131,669,275	10.1	7.2
1950	7,711,194	150,697,361	20.2	14.5
1960	9,579,677	179,323,175	24.2	19.0
1970	11,196,730	203,302,031	16.9	13.4
1980	14,229,191	226,545,805	27.1	11.4
1990	16,986,510	248,709,873	19.4	9.8
2000	20,851,820	281,421,906	22.8	13.2
2004	**22,490,022**	**293,655,404**	**7.9**	**4.3**

U.S. Bureau of the Census, compiled by the Texas State Data Center, University of Texas at San Antonio.

age with its median age of 32.3 in 2000 becoming between 38.1 and 38.6 years by 2040. Growth in the population 65 years of age is likely to be twice as rapid as that for the population as a whole.

All racial and ethnic groups will show an aging in their populations and non-Anglos will account for a majority of the net growth in populations in all age groups. However, the impact of non-Anglo populations will be greatest at the youngest ages, where Hispanics in particular are expected to account for nearly all of the net increase.

The rapid growth in the state has strained existing systems and resulted in the need for extensive expansions in services in virtually every major city in Texas.

In slower-growing rural areas the need for service maintenance is high at the same time as the sources of revenue related to population are either declining or relatively stagnant.

Demographic change in Texas may thus substantially challenge Texas in the coming decades. ☆

Percent of Texas Population in 2000 by Ethnicity and Age

Age Group	Anglo	Black	Hispanic	Other	Total
below 18	23.0	31.7	35.8	26.1	**28.2**
18-24	8.8	11.2	13.2	11.2	**10.6**
25-44	30.1	32.1	31.8	37.7	**31.1**
45-64	24.4	17.7	14.0	20.1	**20.2**
65 plus	13.7	7.3	5.2	4.9	**9.9**
Median age of group	38.0	29.6	25.5	31.1	**32.3**
All ages in **2000**	53.1	11.6	32.0	3.3	**100.0**
All ages in **2005**	49.0	11.0	36.0	4.0	**100.0**

Source: Texas State Data Center.

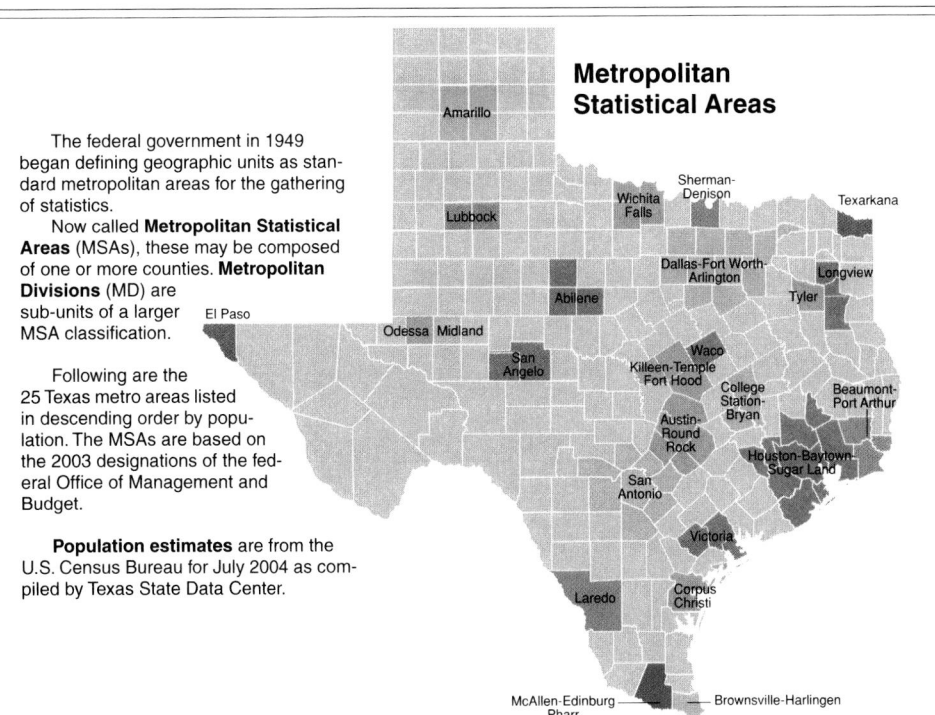

Metropolitan Statistical Areas

The federal government in 1949 began defining geographic units as standard metropolitan areas for the gathering of statistics.

Now called **Metropolitan Statistical Areas** (MSAs), these may be composed of one or more counties. **Metropolitan Divisions** (MD) are sub-units of a larger MSA classification.

Following are the 25 Texas metro areas listed in descending order by population. The MSAs are based on the 2003 designations of the federal Office of Management and Budget.

Population estimates are from the U.S. Census Bureau for July 2004 as compiled by Texas State Data Center.

Metropolitan Statistical Areas	Population estimate	Percent change 2000-2004
1. **Dallas-Fort Worth-Arlington** (Dallas-Plano-Irving MD and Fort Worth-Arlington MD)	5,700,256	10.4
Dallas-Plano-Irving MD (Collin, Dallas, Delta, Denton, Ellis, Hunt, Kaufman, Rockwall counties)		
Fort Worth-Arlington MD (Johnson, Parker,Tarrant, Wise counties)		
2. **Houston-Baytown-Sugar Land** (Austin, Brazoria, Chambers, Fort Bend, Galveston, Harris, Liberty, Montgomery, San Jacinto, Waller counties)	5,180,443	9.9
3. **San Antonio** (Atascosa, Bandera, Bexar, Comal, Guadalupe, Kendall, Medina, Wilson counties)	1,854,050	8.3
4. **Austin-Round Rock** (Bastrop, Caldwell, Hays, Travis, Williamson counties)	1,412,271	13.0
5. **El Paso** (El Paso County)	713,126	4.9
6. **McAllen-Edinburg-Pharr** (Hidalgo County)	658,248	15.6
7. **Corpus Christi** (Aransas, Nueces, San Patricio counties)	409,741	1.6
8. **Beaumont-Port Arthur** (Hardin, Jefferson, Orange counties)	383,443	-0.4
9. **Brownsville-Harlingen** (Cameron County)	371,825	10.9
10. **Killeen-Temple-Fort Hood** (Bell, Coryell, Lampasas counties)	346,116	4.7
11. **Lubbock** (Crosby, Lubbock counties)	257,663	3.2
12. **Amarillo** (Armstrong, Carson, Potter, Randall counties)	236,113	4.2
13. **Waco** (McLennan County)	222,439	4.2
14. **Laredo** (Webb County)	219,464	13.6
15. **Longview** (Gregg, Rusk, Upshur counties)	200,405	3.3
16. **Bryan-College Station** (Brazos, Burleson, Robertson counties)	189,468	2.5
17. **Tyler** (Smith County)	186,414	6.7
18. **Abilene** (Callahan, Jones, Taylor counties)	158,515	-1.1
19. **Wichita Falls** (Archer, Clay, Wichita counties)	147,826	-2.4
20. **Texarkana** (Bowie County, TX, and Miller County, AR)	132,716	2.3
21. **Odessa** (Ector County)	124,488	2.8
22. **Midland** (Midland County)	120,344	3.7
23. **Sherman-Denison** (Grayson County)	115,933	4.8
24. **Victoria** (Calhoun, Goliad, Victoria counties)	113,450	1.6
25. **San Angelo** (Irion, Tom Green counties)	105,510	-0.3

Population 2000 and 2004

Population: Numbers in parentheses are from the 2000 U.S. census. The Census Bureau counts only incorporated cities and a few unincorporated towns called Census Designated Places.

Population **figures at the far right** for those same cities are Texas State Data Center estimates **as of Jan. 1, 2004**. Names of the incorporated cities are in capital letters, e.g., "ABBOTT".

The population figure given for all other towns is an estimate received from local officials through a Texas Almanac survey.

In some cases, when no population estimate could be obtained, these places show "NA" (Not Available) in place of a population figure.

Location: The county in which the town is located follows the name of town. If more than one county is listed, the town is principally in the first-named county, e.g., "ABERNATHY, Hale-Lubbock".

Businesses: The number following the county name indicates the number of business given a credit rating by Dun & Bradstreet as of November 2004. For example, "ABBOTT, Hill, 45" means that Abbott in Hill County had 45 businesses.

In cases where no number was provided by Dun & Bradstreet for incorporated cities, figures from sales tax reports to the state comptroller are used.

Post Offices: Places with post offices, as of Nov. 2004, are marked with an asterisk (*), e.g., "*Ace".

Town, County . . . . Pop. 2004	Town, County . . . . Pop. 2004	Town, County . . . . Pop. 2004
*ABBOTT, Hill, 45, (300) 316	(14,760) 16,689	Altoga, Collin 137
Aberfoyle, Hunt, ... 35	Alamo Alto, El Paso 19	*ALTON, Hidalgo, 89,
*ABERNATHY, Hale-Lubbock, 152,	Alamo Beach, Calhoun. 100	(4,384) 7,378
(2,839). 2,940	ALAMO HEIGHTS, Bexar,	Alton North, Hidalgo, (5,051) . . . 5,290
*ABILENE,Taylor-Jones, 4,680,	(7,319) 7,359	Alum Creek, Bastrop . . . . NA
(115,930). 114,454	*Alanreed, Gray, 3 48	*ALVARADO, Johnson, 495,
Ables Springs, Kaufman . . . . NA	Alazan, Nacogdoches 100	(3,288). 3,742
Abner, Kaufman . . . . NA	*ALBA, Wood-Rains, 133,	*ALVIN, Brazoria, 1,441,
Abram-Perezville, Hidalgo,	(430). 439	(21,413). 22,404
(5,444). 5,710	*ALBANY, Shackelford, 168,	*ALVORD, Wise, 105,
*ACADEMY [Little River-], Bell, 55,	(1,921) 1,889	(1,007). 1,102
(1,645). 1,656	Albert, Gillespie, 2 25	Amargosa [Owl Ranch-], Jim Wells,
Acala, Hudspeth 25	Albion, Red River 50	(527) 510
*Ace, Polk, 3 40	Alderbranch, Anderson 5	*AMARILLO, Potter-Randall,
*ACKERLY, Dawson-Martin, 53,	Aldine, Harris, (13,979) 14,503	8,774, (173,627) 180,380
(245) 235	*ALEDO, Parker, 482,	Ambia, Lamar 16
Acme, Hardeman 14	(1,726) 2,198	Ambrose, Grayson 90
Acton, Hood. 1,129	Aleman, Hamilton 50	Ames, Coryell 10
Acuff, Lubbock 50	Alexander, Erath 40	AMES, Liberty, (1,079). 1,099
Acworth, Red River 52	Aley, Henderson 45	Amherst, Lamar. 125
Adams Gardens, Cameron 200	Alfred-South La Paloma, Jim Wells,	*AMHERST, Lamb, 32, (791) 811
Adams Store, Panola . . . . NA	(451). 453	Amistad [Box Canyon-], Val Verde,
Adamsville, Lampasas 41	Algerita, San Saba 48	(76) 75
Addielou, Red River. 31	Algoa, Galveston 135	Ammannsville, Fayette 137
*ADDISON, Dallas, 2,017,	*ALICE, Jim Wells, 972,	Amphion, Atascosa 26
(14,166). 14,601	(19,010) 19,528	Amsterdam, Brazoria. 193
Addran, Hopkins . . . . NA	Alice Acres, Jim Wells, (491) 493	Anadarko, Rusk 30
Adell, Parker . . . . NA	*Alief, Harris, 26 . . . . . (part of Houston)	*ANAHUAC, Chambers, 179,
*Adkins, Bexar, 225 . . . . NA	Allamoore, Hudspeth 25	(2,210). 2,249
Admiral, Callahan 18	*ALLEN, Collin, 2,533,	*ANDERSON, Grimes, 85,
Adobes, Presidio . . . . NA	(43,554) 61,256	(257) 256
*ADRIAN, Oldham, 23, (159) 165	Allenfarm, Brazos 30	Anderson Mill, Williamson-Travis,
Advance, Parker . . . . NA	Allenhurst, Matagorda 72	(8,953). 9,751
*Afton, Dickens, 8 15	Allen's Chapel, Fannin 41	Ander-Weser-Kilgore, Goliad. 322
Agnes, Parker . . . . NA	Allen's Point, Fannin 76	*Andice, Williamson, 9 . . . . NA
Agua Dulce, El Paso, (738) 772	Allentown, Angelina 110	*ANDREWS Andrews, 426,
*AGUA DULCE, Nueces, 31,	Alleyton, Colorado, 26 165	(9,652). 9,527
(737) 697	*Allison, Wheeler, 9 135	*ANGLETON, Brazoria, 1,014,
Agua Nueva, Jim Hogg 5	Allmon, Floyd 24	(18,130). 18,868
Aguilares, Webb 37	Allred, Yoakum 90	ANGUS, Navarro, 15, (334). 352
*Aiken, Floyd, 2 52	ALMA, Ellis, 7, (302). 322	*ANNA, Collin, 158, (1,225) 1,524
Aiken, Shelby 150	Almira, Cass 30	ANNETTA, Parker, 14, (1,108) . . . 1,224
Aikin Grove, Red River 26	*ALPINE, Brewster, 394,	ANNETTA NORTH, Parker, 7,
Airport City, Bexar 106	(5,786) 6,237	(467) 517
Airport Road Addition, Brooks,	Alsa, Van Zandt 30	ANNETTA SOUTH, Parker, 2,
(132) 132	*Altair, Colorado, 4 30	(555) 613
Airville, Bell 65	*ALTO, Cherokee, 104,	*ANNONA, Red River, 13,
Alabama-Coushatta, Polk, (480) . . 480	(1,190) 1,207	(282) 283
*ALAMO, Hidalgo, 371,	Alto Bonito, Starr, (569). 601	*ANSON, Jones, 141, (2,556) . . . 2,489

CITIES & TOWNS

Town, County	Pop. 2004
Bethel, Henderson	125
Bethel, Runnels	20
Bethlehem, Upshur	75
Bettie, Upshur	110
Beulah, Limestone	12
BEVERLY HILLS, McLennan, 76, (2,113)	2,087
BEVIL OAKS, Jefferson, 10, (1,346)	1,273
Bevilport, Jasper	NA
Beyersville, Williamson	80
Biardstown, Lamar	75
*Bigfoot, Frio, 9, (304)	301
Big Hill, Limestone	9
*BIG LAKE, Reagan, 157, (2,885)	2,741
*BIG SANDY, Upshur, 221, (1,288)	1,318
*BIG SPRING, Howard, 991, (25,233)	25,458
Big Valley, Mills	35
*BIG WELLS, Dimmit, 11, (704)	759
Biloxi, Newton	NA
Birch, Burleson	200
Birome, Hill, 4	30
Birthright, Hopkins	40
Biry, Medina	24
*BISHOP, Nueces, 112, (3,305)	3,145
BISHOP HILLS, Potter, (210)	208
*Bivins, Cass, 21	215
Bixby, Cameron, (356)	365
Black, Parmer, 3	100
Blackfoot, Anderson	33
Black Hill, Atascosa	60
Black Hills, Navarro	80
Black Jack, Cherokee	47
Black Jack, Robertson	45
Blackjack, Smith	NA
Black Oak, Hopkins	NA
*BLACKWELL, Nolan-Coke, 27, (360)	355
Blair, Taylor	25
Blanchard, Polk	200
*BLANCO, Blanco, 270, (1,505)	1,584
Blanconia, Bee	40
Bland Lake, San Augustine	25
*BLANKET, Brown, 31, (402)	409
Blanton, Hill	5
Bleakwood, Newton	300
*Bledsoe, Cochran, 6	126
*Bleiblerville, Austin, 9	125
*Blessing, Matagorda, 51, (861)	853
Blevins, Falls	36
Blewett, Uvalde	10
Blodgett, Titus	60
*BLOOMBURG, Cass, 35, (375)	388
*BLOOMING GROVE, Navarro, 47, (833)	868
*Bloomington, Victoria, 25, (2,562)	2,633
*BLOSSOM, Lamar, 89, (1,439)	1,423
Blue, Lee	75
Blue Berry Hill, Bee, (982)	962
*Bluegrove, Clay, 1	135
BLUE MOUND, Tarrant, 20, (2,388)	2,460
*BLUE RIDGE, Collin, 85, (672)	824
Bluetown-Iglesia Antigua, Cameron, (692)	714
*Bluff Dale, Erath, 40	123

Town, County	Pop. 2004
Bluff Springs, Travis	NA
*Bluffton, Llano, 8	75
*BLUM, Hill, 35, (399)	412
Bluntzer, Nueces	150
Bob Town, Jack	NA
*BOERNE, Kendall, 1,618, (6,178)	6,745
*BOGATA, Red River, 70, (1,396)	1,344
Bois d'Arc, Anderson	10
Bois d'Arc, Rains	10
Bold Springs, Polk	100
Boldtville, Bexar	20
*Boling-Iago, Wharton, 75, (1,271)	1,317
Bolivar, Denton	40
Bolivar Peninsula, Galveston, (3,853)	3,803
Bomarton, Baylor	15
Bon Ami, Jasper	NA
*Bonanza, Hill	NA
Bonanza, Hopkins	26
*BONHAM, Fannin, 505, (9,990)	10,382
Bonita, Montague	25
Bonnerville, Freestone	NA
BONNEY, Brazoria, (384)	405
Bonnie View, Refugio	97
Bonus, Wharton	44
*Bon Wier, Newton, 16	475
*BOOKER, Lipscomb-Ochiltree, 80, (1,315)	1,341
Boonsville, Wise	52
Booth, Fort Bend, 19	NA
Borden, Colorado	60
*BORGER, Hutchinson, 691, (14,302)	13,778
Bosqueville, McLennan	200
Boston, Bowie, 16	200
Botines, Webb, (132)	134
*BOVINA, Parmer, 43, (1,874)	1,873
Bowers, Polk	NA
Bowers City, Gray	26
*BOWIE, Montague, 536, (5,219)	5,609
Bowman, Archer	200
Bowser, San Saba	20
Box Canyon-Amistad, Val Verde, (76)	75
Box Church, Limestone	45
Boxelder, Red River	100
Boxwood, Upshur	20
Boyce, Ellis	125
Boyd, Fannin	40
*BOYD, Wise, 197, (1,099)	1,212
*Boys Ranch, Oldham, 9	470
Bozar, Mills	9
Brachfield, Rusk	40
Bracken, Comal	76
*BRACKETTVILLE, Kinney, 86, (1,876)	1,912
Brad, Palo Pinto	16
Bradford, Anderson	30
Bradshaw, Taylor, 1	61
*BRADY, McCulloch, 359, (5,523)	5,575
Branch, Collin	530
Branchville, Milam	127
*Brandon, Hill, 5	75
*Brashear, Hopkins, 21	280
*BRAZORIA, Brazoria, 356, (2,787)	2,837
Brazos, Palo Pinto	97
BRAZOS BEND, Hood	300
BRAZOS COUNTRY, Austin, 3	283
Brazos Point, Bosque	NA
Brazosport, Brazoria	58,631

Town, County	Pop. 2004
*BRECKENRIDGE, Stephens, 534, (5,868)	5,813
*BREMOND, Robertson, 75, (876)	864
*BRENHAM, Washington, 1,406, (13,507)	13,867
Breslau, Lavaca	65
Briar, Tarrant-Wise-Parker, (5,350)	5,615
BRIARCLIFF, Travis, 13, (895)	850
BRIAROAKS, Johnson, (493)	488
Brice, Hall	20
*BRIDGE CITY, Orange, 319, (8,651)	8,721
*BRIDGEPORT, Wise, 483, (4,309)	5,533
Bridges Chapel, Titus	90
*Briggs, Burnet, 17	172
Bright Star, Rains	592
Brinker, Hopkins	NA
*Briscoe, Wheeler, 13	135
Bristol, Ellis	250
*BROADDUS, San Augustine, 33, (189)	182
Broadway, Lamar	25
Brock, Parker	2,000
Brock Junction, Parker	100
Bronco, Yoakum	30
*Bronson, Sabine, 18	377
*BRONTE, Coke, 53, (1,076)	1,081
*Brookeland, Sabine, 49	300
*Brookesmith, Brown, 8	61
Brooks, Panola	40
Brookshier, Runnels	15
*BROOKSHIRE, Waller, 279, (3,450)	3,683
BROOKSIDE VILLAGE, Brazoria, 20, (1,960)	2,076
*Brookston, Lamar, 23	130
Broom City, Anderson	20
Broome, Panola	21
Brown College, Washington	NA
BROWNDELL, Jasper, 3, (219)	214
*BROWNFIELD, Terry, 468, (9,488)	9,279
Browning, Smith	25
Brownsboro, Caldwell	50
*BROWNSBORO, Henderson, 103, (796)	836
*BROWNSVILLE, Cameron, 3,962, (139,722)	161,048
*BROWNWOOD, Brown, 1,169, (18,813)	19,898
Broyles Chapel, Anderson	40
*BRUCEVILLE-EDDY, McLennan -Falls, 22, (1,490)	1,549
Brumley, Upshur	75
Brundage, Dimmit, (31)	30
*Bruni, Webb, 11, (412)	434
Brushie Prairie, Navarro	35
Brushy Creek, Anderson	50
Brushy Creek, Brazos	NA
Brushy Creek, Williamson, (15,371)	17,965
*BRYAN, Brazos, 3,163, (65,660)	69,146
Bryan Beach, Brazoria	14
Bryans Mill, Cass	150
Bryarly, Red River	5
Bryce, Rusk	15
*BRYSON, Jack, 22, (528)	521
*Buchanan Dam, Llano, 101, (1,688)	1,785
Buchel, DeWitt	45

Town, County . . . . Pop. 2004	Town, County . . . . Pop. 2004	Town, County . . . . Pop. 2004
Buck, Polk . . . . .NA	Burrow, Hunt . . . . NA	Camp Seale, Polk 53
Buckeye, Matagorda 16	*BURTON, Washington, 99,	Camp Springs, Scurry. 10
*BUCKHOLTS, Milam, 35,	(359). .361	Camp Swift, Bastrop, (4,731) . . . 5,246
(387) 406	*Bushland, Potter, 23 1,485	Camp Switch, Gregg 70
Buckhorn, Austin 50	Bustamante, Zapata 15	Campti, Shelby 25
Buckhorn, Newton . . . . .NA	Busterville, Hockley 6	*Camp Verde, Kerr, 5 41
Buckner, Parker . . . . .NA	Butler, Bastrop . . . . NA	*CAMP WOOD, Real, 70,
*BUDA, Hays, 606, (2,404) 3,184	Butler, Freestone. 67	(822). .824
*BUFFALO, Leon, 198,	Butterfield, El Paso, (61). 60	Camp Worth, San Augustine. . . . . . NA
(1,804). 1,942	*BYERS, Clay, 21, (517) 515	Canada Verde, Wilson 23
Buffalo Camp, Brazoria 1,098	*BYNUM, Hill, 16, (225) 244	*CANADIAN, Hemphill, 260,
*BUFFALO GAP, Taylor, 59,	Byrd, Ellis 30	(2,233) 2,267
(463) 464	Byrdtown, Lamar 22	Canary, Leon . . . . NA
Buffalo Mop, Limestone 21		Candelaria, Presidio 55
Buffalo Springs, Clay 45	**C**	CANEY CITY, Henderson, 16,
BUFFALO SPRINGS, Lubbock,	*CACTUS, Moore, 31, (2,538) . . 2,732	(236). .249
(493) 467	*Caddo, Stephens, 13 40	Cannon, Grayson 50
Buford, Mitchell 30	*CADDO MILLS, Hunt, 156,	*CANTON, Van Zandt, 575,
Bula, Bailey, 6 35	(1,149) 1,191	(3,292) 3,471
Bulcher, Cooke. 3	Cade Chapel, Navarro 25	Cantu Addition, Brooks, (217). 221
*BULLARD, Smith-Cherokee,	Cadiz, Bee 15	*Canutillo, El Paso, 271,
282, (1,150) 1,357	Calaveras, Wilson 100	(5,129) 5,257
Bull Run, Newton . . . . .NA	*CALDWELL, Burleson, 410,	Canyon, Lubbock 40
*BULVERDE, Comal, 390,	(3,449) 3,664	*CANYON, Randall, 694,
(3,761). 4,107	Caledonia, Rusk 75	(12,875) 13,205
*Buna, Jasper, 154, (2,269) 2,315	Calf Creek, McCulloch 23	Canyon City, Comal. 100
Buncombe, Panola. 87	Calina, Limestone 10	*Canyon Lake, Comal,
Bunger, Young 40	*Call, Newton, 16 170	(16,870) 17,730
Bunker Hill, Jasper. . . . . .NA	*Calliham, McMullen, 5. 100	Caplen, Galveston 30
BUNKER HILL VILLAGE, Harris,	CALLISBURG, Cooke, (365) 372	Capps Corner, Montague 30
27, (3,654). 3,610	Call Junction, Jasper 50	Cap Rock, Crosby. 6
Bunyan, Erath. 20	*CALVERT, Robertson, 57,	Caps, Taylor 300
*BURKBURNETT, Wichita,	(1,426) 1,390	Caradan, Mills 20
362, (10,927) 10,847	*Camden, Polk, 3 1,200	Carancahua, Jackson 375
BURKE, Angelina, (315). 317	*CAMERON, Milam, 348,	*CARBON, Eastland, 29, (224). 245
*Burkett, Coleman, 19 30	(5,634) 5,909	Carbondale, Bowie 30
*Burkeville, Newton, 38 515	Cameron Park, Cameron,	Carey, Childress, 8 15
Burleigh, Austin 150	(5,961) 6,349	Carl, Travis . . . . NA
*BURLESON, Johnson-Tarrant,	Camilla, San Jacinto 200	Carlisle, Trinity 68
1,848, (20,976) 25,248	Camp Air, Mason 12	Carlos, Grimes 60
*Burlington, Milam, 18 100	*CAMPBELL, Hunt, 77, (734) 770	*Carlsbad, Tom Green, 13 236
*BURNET, Burnet, 577,	*Campbellton, Atascosa, 5. 350	CARL'S CORNER, Hill, 1,
(4,735). 5,338	Camp Creek Lake, Robertson 350	(134). .143
Burns, Bowie 400	Campo Alto, Hidalgo . . . . NA	Carlson, Travis. . . . . NA
Burns City, Cooke 45	Camp Ruby, Polk 35	*Carlton, Hamilton, 14. 75
Burrantown, Houston 70	Camp San Saba, McCulloch 36	*CARMINE, Fayette, 38, (228) 235

Shoppers in downtown Brownsville. Texas Almanac photo.

Town, County	Pop. 2004
Carmona, Polk	50
Caro, Nacogdoches	70
Carricitos, Cameron	147
Carrizo Hill, Dimmit, (548)	545
*CARRIZO SPRINGS, Dimmit, 224, (5,655)	5,606
Carroll, Smith	60
Carroll Springs, Anderson	20
*CARROLLTON, Dallas-Denton, 5,118, (109,576)	118,745
Carson, Fannin	22
Carta Valley, Edwards	12
Carterville, Cass	39
*CARTHAGE, Panola, 606, (6,664)	6,634
Cartwright, Wood	61
Carver, Leon	NA
Casa Piedra, Presidio	21
Cash, Hunt	56
CASHION, Wichita, (346)	341
*Cason, Morris, 4	173
Cass, Cass	100
Cassie, Burnet	496
Cassin, Bexar	NA
*Castell, Llano, 7	72
CASTLE HILLS, Bexar, 223, (4,202)	4,136
Castolon, Brewster	8
*CASTROVILLE, Medina, 259, (2,664)	2,786
*Catarina, Dimmit, 4, (135)	134
*Cat Spring, Austin, 57	200
Cavazos, Cameron	282
Caviness, Lamar	90
Cawthon, Brazos	75
Cayote, Bosque	75
*Cayuga, Anderson, 8	137
Cedar Bayou, Harris	1,555
*Cedar Creek, Bastrop, 236	NA
Cedar Creek, Waller	NA
*CEDAR HILL, Dallas-Ellis, 1,478, (32,093)	39,095
Cedar Hill, Floyd	24
Cedar Lake, Matagorda	160
*Cedar Lane, Matagorda, 6	300
*CEDAR PARK, Williamson-Travis, 1,676, (26,049)	37,614
Cedar Shores, Bosque	170
Cedar Springs, Falls	90
Cedar Springs, Upshur	100
Cedarvale, Kaufman	NA
Cedar Valley, Bell	14
Cedar Valley, Travis	70
*Cee Vee, Cottle, 6	45
Cego, Falls	42
Cele, Travis	NA
*CELESTE, Hunt, 53, (817)	844
*CELINA, Collin, 280, (1,861)	2,361
Center, Limestone	76
*CENTER, Shelby, 535, (5,678)	5,635
Center City, Mills	15
Center Grove, Houston	39
Center Grove, Titus	65
Center Hill, Houston	105
Center Plains, Swisher	20
Center Point, Camp	41
*Center Point, Kerr, 102	800
Center Point, Panola	NA
Center Point, Upshur	50
Centerview, Leon	NA
*CENTERVILLE, Leon, 126, (903)	924
Centerville, Trinity	60
Central, Angelina	200
Central Gardens, Jefferson, (4,106)	3,951
Central High, Cherokee	30
*Centralia, Trinity	53
Cesar Chavez, Hidalgo, (1,469)	1,498
Cestohowa, Karnes	110
Chalk, Cottle, 12	17
Chalk Hill, Rusk	200
Chalk Mountain, Erath	25
Chambersville, Collin	103
Chambliss, Collin	29
Champion, Nolan	8
Champions, Harris	21,250
Chances Store, Burleson	15
*CHANDLER, Henderson, 244, (2,099)	2,203
Chaney, Eastland	35
*Channelview, Harris, 879, (29,685)	30,295
*CHANNING, Hartley, 22, (356)	333
Chapel Hill, Smith	NA
Chapman, Rusk	20
*Chapman Ranch, Nueces, 6	100
Chappel, San Saba	25
*Chappell Hill, Washington, 89	600
Charco, Goliad	96
Charleston, Delta	150
Charlie, Clay	70
*CHARLOTTE, Atascosa, 36, (1,637)	1,764
Chateau Woods, Montgomery	1,087
*Chatfield, Navarro, 9	40
Cheapside, Gonzales	5
Cheek, Jefferson	1,096
Cheneyboro,Navarro	100
*Cherokee, San Saba, 35	175
Cherokee Hill, Smith	NA
Cherry Spring, Gillespie	75
*CHESTER, Tyler, 25, (265)	255
Chesterville, Colorado	50
*CHICO, Wise, 122, (947)	1,008
*Chicota, Lamar, 4	150
Chihuahua, Hidalgo	NA
Chihuahua Farm, Zapata	25
*CHILDRESS, Childress, 287, (6,778)	6,451
*CHILLICOTHE, Hardeman, 40, (798)	782
*Chilton, Falls, 40	274
*CHINA, Jefferson, 44, (1,112)	1,061
CHINA GROVE, Bexar, 24, (1,247)	1,240
China Grove, Scurry	15
*China Spring, McLennan, 171	1,000
Chinati, Presidio	NA
Chinquapin, Matagorda	6
Chinquapin, San Augustine	NA
*CHIRENO, Nacogdoches, 29, (405)	406
CHISHOLM [McLendon-], Rockwall, (914)	1,035
Chita, Trinity	81
Choate, Karnes	20
Chocolate Bayou, Brazoria	60
Choice, Shelby	35
*Chriesman, Burleson	30
*CHRISTINE, Atascosa, 9, (436)	459
*Christoval, Tom Green, 47, (422)	410
Chula Vista-Orason, Cameron, (394)	408
Chula Vista-River Spur, Zavala, (400)	399
Church Hill, Rusk	20
Churchill, Brazoria	NA
*CIBOLO, Guadalupe, 260, (3,035)	4,055
Cienegas Terrace, Val Verde, (2,878)	3,008
Cinco Ranch, Fort Bend-Harris, (11,196)	12,084
Cipres, Hidalgo	20
Circle, Lamb	6
Circleback, Bailey	10
Circle D-KC Estates, Bastrop, (2,010)	2,239
Circleville, Williamson	50
*CISCO, Eastland, 253, (3,851)	3,746
Cistern, Fayette	137
Citrus City, Hidalgo, (941)	992
Citrus Grove, Matagorda	30
Clairemont, Kent	12
Clairette, Erath	55
Clara, Wichita	100
Clardy, Lamar	160
*CLARENDON, Donley, 157, (1,974)	1,934
Clareville, Bee	25
CLARK, Denton, (345)	373
Clark, Liberty	NA
Clarkson, Milam	10
*CLARKSVILLE, Red River, 209, (3,883)	3,811
CLARKSVILLE CITY, Gregg, 15, (806)	844
*CLAUDE, Armstrong, 115, (1,313)	1,272
Clauene, Hockley	10
Clawson, Angelina	195
Clay, Burleson, 2	61
Clays Corner, Parmer	15
*Clayton, Panola, 8	79
Claytonville, Swisher	85
Clear Creek, Burnet	78
CLEAR LAKE SHORES, Galveston, 45, (1,205)	1,247
Clear Spring, Guadalupe	280
*CLEBURNE, Johnson, 1,528, (26,005)	28,179
Clegg, Live Oak	125
Clemons, Waller	NA
Clemville, Matagorda	25
Cleo, Kimble	3
Cleveland, Austin	125
*CLEVELAND, Liberty, 869, (7,605)	7,754
Cliffside, Potter	206
*CLIFTON, Bosque, 344, (3,542)	3,652
Climax, Collin	82
Cline, Uvalde	15
*CLINT, El Paso, 106, (980)	981
Clinton, Hunt	NA
Clodine, Fort Bend	NA
Clopton, Franklin	15
Close City, Garza	94
Cloverleaf, Harris, (23,508)	24,456
*CLUTE, Brazoria, 543, (10,424)	10,878
*CLYDE, Callahan, 251, (3,345)	3,621
*COAHOMA, Howard, 39, (932)	879
Cobb, Kaufman	NA
Coble, Hockley	11
Cochran, Austin	200
COCKRELL HILL, Dallas, 25, (4,443)	4,422
COFFEE CITY, Henderson, 12, (193)	202
Coffeeville, Upshur	50

Town, County . . . . Pop. 2004	Town, County . . . . Pop. 2004	Town, County . . . . Pop. 2004
Cofferville, Lamb 4	788, (29,592) 29,976	Crisp, Ellis 115
Coit, Limestone 25	COPPER CANYON, Denton,	*CROCKETT, Houston, 488,
Coke, Wood 40	17, (1,216) 1,355	(7,141) 7,127
*COLDSPRING, San Jacinto,	Corbet, Navarro 80	*Crosby, Harris, 785,
124, (691) 714	Cordele, Jackson 51	(1,714) 1,686
*COLEMAN, Coleman, 308,	CORINTH, Denton, 289,	*CROSBYTON, Crosby, 100,
(5,127) 5,121	(11,325) 15,918	(1,874) 1,767
Colfax, Van Zandt 44	Corinth, Jones 10	Cross, Grimes 53
Colita, Polk 50	Corinth, Leon . . . . NA	Cross, McMullen 25
College Hill, Bowie 116	Corley, Bowie 35	Cross Cut, Brown 22
College Mound, Kaufman 350	Cornersville, Hopkins . . . . NA	Cross Mountain, Bexar, (1,524) . . 1,564
*Collegeport, Matagorda, 3 80	Cornett, Cass 30	*CROSS PLAINS, Callahan,
*COLLEGE STATION, Brazos,	Cornudas, Hudspeth 19	106, (1,068) 1,076
2,505, (67,890) 73,691	*CORPUS CHRISTI, Nueces,	Crossroads, Cass 60
*COLLEYVILLE, Tarrant, 1,299,	10,653, (277,454) 278,708	Crossroads, Delta 20
(19,636) 21,370	CORRAL CITY, Denton, 2,	CROSS ROADS, Denton, 26,
*COLLINSVILLE, Grayson, 98,	(89) 111	(603) 691
(1,235) 1,316	*CORRIGAN, Polk, 90,	Crossroads, Harrison 100
*COLMESNEIL, Tyler, 50,	(1,721) 1,811	Cross Roads, Henderson 160
(638) 639	*CORSICANA, Navarro,	Crossroads, Hopkins . . . . NA
Colony, Rains 70	1,371, (24,485) 26,014	Cross Roads, Madison 75
*COLORADO CITY, Mitchell,	Coryell City, Coryell 70	Cross Roads, Milam 35
237, (4,281) 4,026	*Cost, Gonzales, 19 84	CROSS TIMBER, Johnson,
Colquitt, Kaufman . . . . NA	Cotton Center, Fannin 5	(277) 297
Coltharp, Houston 40	*Cotton Center, Hale, 20 200	Croton, Dickens 7
Colton, Travis 50	Cottondale, Wise . . . . NA	Crow, Wood 20
Columbia Lakes, Brazoria 646	Cotton Gin, Freestone 28	*CROWELL, Foard, 97,
*COLUMBUS, Colorado, 414,	Cotton Patch, DeWitt 11	(1,141) 1,111
(3,916) 4,014	Cottonwood, Brazos . . . . NA	*CROWLEY, Tarrant, 554,
Comal, Comal 40	Cottonwood, Callahan 65	(7,467) 8,676
*COMANCHE, Comanche, 324,	Cottonwood, Erath 23	Crown, Atascosa 10
(4,482) 4,533	COTTONWOOD, Kaufman,	Cruz Calle, Duval . . . . NA
*COMBES, Cameron, 26,	(181) 207	Cryer Creek, Navarro 15
(2,553) 2,739	Cottonwood, Madison 40	Crystal Beach, Galveston 787
COMBINE, Kaufman-Dallas, 27,	Cottonwood, McLennan 150	*CRYSTAL CITY, Zavala,
(1,788) 1,972	Cottonwood, Somervell 24	166, (7,190) 7,063
Cometa, Zavala 10	COTTONWOOD SHORES, Burnet,	Crystal Falls, Stephens 10
*Comfort, Kendall, 271,	13, (877) 1,000	Crystal Lake, Anderson 20
(2,358) 2,556	*COTULLA, La Salle, 126,	Cuadrilla, El Paso 67
*COMMERCE, Hunt, 321,	(3,614) 3,675	*CUERO, DeWitt, 402,
(7,669) 8,683	Couch, Karnes 10	(6,571) 6,839
*COMO, Hopkins, 54,	Coughran, Atascosa 20	Cuevitas, Hidalgo, (37) 38
(621) 626	County Acres [Falman-],	*CUMBY, Hopkins, 59, (616) 613
*Comstock, Val Verde, 10 375	San Patricio, (289) 290	Cumings, Fort Bend, (683) 756
Comyn, Comanche 30	County Line, Lubbock 15	Cundiff, Jack 45
*Concan, Uvalde, 39 225	County Line, Rains 40	*CUNEY, Cherokee, 7, (145) 146
*Concepcion, Duval, 8, (61) 59	*Coupland, Williamson, 60 280	*Cunningham, Lamar, 5 110
Concord, Cherokee 50	Courtney, Grimes 60	Currie, Navarro 25
Concord, Hunt 30	COVE, Chambers, 4, (323) 319	Curtis, Jasper . . . . NA
*Concord, Leon, 3 28	Cove Springs, Cherokee 40	*CUSHING, Nacogdoches, 62,
Concord, Liberty 26	*COVINGTON, Hill, 39, (282) 305	(637) 635
Concord, Madison 50	Cow Creek, Erath 14	Cusseta, Cass 30
Concord, Rusk 23	Cox, Upshur 30	*CUT AND SHOOT, Montgomery,
Concrete, DeWitt 46	*Coyanosa, Pecos, 6, (138) 129	29, (1,158) 1,274
Cone, Crosby 50	Coy City, Karnes 30	Cuthand, Red River 116
Conlen, Dallam 14	Coyote Acres, Jim Wells, (389) . . . 397	Cyclone, Bell 47
Connor, Madison 20	Crabb, Fort Bend 125	Cypress, Franklin 20
*CONROE, Montgomery,	Crabbs Prairie, Walker 240	*Cypress [-Fairbanks], Harris,
4,516, (36,811) 42,113	Craft, Cherokee 21	2,403 27,000
Content, Bell 25	Crafton, Wise 20	Cypress Creek, Kerr 200
*CONVERSE, Bexar, 561,	*CRANDALL, Kaufman, 145,	Cypress Mill, Blanco, 1 56
(11,508) 12,530	(2,774) 3,132	
Conway, Carson 20	*CRANE, Crane, 127,	**D**
Cooks Point, Burleson 60	(3,191) 3,219	Dacosta, Victoria 89
*Cookville, Titus, 32 105	*CRANFILLS GAP, Bosque, 35,	Dacus, Montgomery 161
COOL, Parker, 7, (162) 167	(335) 340	Daffan, Travis . . . . NA
*COOLIDGE, Limestone, 35,	*CRAWFORD, McLennan, 140,	*DAINGERFIELD, Morris, 177,
(848) 865	(705) 745	(2,517) 2,404
*COOPER, Delta, 138,	Creath, Houston 20	*DAISETTA, Liberty, 18,
(2,150) 2,171	Crecy, Trinity 15	(1,034) 1,053
Cooper, Houston 27	Creechville, Ellis 30	Dalby Springs, Bowie 141
Copano Village, Aransas 210	CREEDMOOR, Travis, 12,	*Dale, Caldwell, 118 500
Copeland, Smith . . . . NA	(211) 203	*DALHART, Dallam-Hartley, 566,
*Copeville, Collin, 10 243	Crescent Heights, Henderson 180	(7,237) 7,170
*COPPELL, Dallas-Denton,	*CRESSON, Hood-Johnson-Parker,	*Dallardsville, Polk, 2 350
1,459, (35,958) 38,909	47 2,000	*DALLAS, Dallas-Collin-Denton,
*COPPERAS COVE, Coryell,	Crews, Runnels 30	59,770, (1,188,580) 1,211,437

Town, County	Pop. 2004
Dalton, Cass	50
DALWORTHINGTON GARDENS, Tarrant, 72, (2,186)	2,352
Dam B (Dogwood Station), Tyler	56
*Damon, Brazoria, 81, (535)	542
*DANBURY, Brazoria, 77, (1,611)	1,697
*Danciger, Brazoria	357
*Danevang, Wharton, 17	61
Daniels, Panola	NA
Danville, Gregg	200
Darby Hill, San Jacinto	50
Darco, Harrison	85
Darden, Polk	320
*DARROUZETT, Lipscomb, 28, (303)	298
Datura, Limestone	2
*Davilla, Milam, 2	191
Davis, Atascosa	8
Davis Prairie, Limestone	17
*Dawn, Deaf Smith, 12	52
*DAWSON, Navarro, 47, (852)	867
*DAYTON, Liberty, 518, (5,709)	6,296
DAYTON LAKES, Liberty, (101)	99
Deadwood, Panola	106
DEAN, Clay, 6, (341)	346
Dean, Hockley	20
*Deanville, Burleson, 11	130
*DeBerry, Panola, 59	191
*DECATUR, Wise, 746, (5,201)	5,963
Decker Prairie, Montgomery	NA
DeCORDOVA, Hood	3,147
*DEER PARK, Harris, 1,057, (28,520)	28,675
*DE KALB, Bowie, 174, (1,769)	1,731
*DE LEON, Comanche, 218, (2,433)	2,470
Delhi, Caldwell	300
Delia, Limestone	20
*DELL CITY, Hudspeth, 37, (413)	418
Del Mar Heights, Cameron, (259)	267
*Delmita, Starr, 2	50
Delray, Panola	40
*DEL RIO, Val Verde, 1,219, (33,867)	35,400
Delrose, Upshur	35
Del Sol-Loma Linda, San Patricio, (726)	728
*Del Valle, Travis, 275,	(part of Austin)
Delwin, Cottle	12
Demi-John Island, Brazoria	18
Democrat, Mills	8
Denhawken, Wilson	46
*DENISON, Grayson, 1,342, (22,773)	23,300
Denman Crossroads, Van Zandt	NA
Denning, San Augustine	361
*Dennis, Parker, 5	300
Denson Springs, Anderson	100
Denton, Callahan	6
*DENTON, Denton, 4,114, (80,537)	93,700
*DENVER CITY, Yoakum, 232, (3,985)	3,834
*DEPORT, Lamar-Red River, 33, (718)	690
Derby, Frio	50
Dermott, Scurry	5
*Desdemona, Eastland, 18	180

Town, County	Pop. 2004
Desert, Collin	35
*DESOTO, Dallas, 1,818, (37,646)	42,792
Dessau, Travis	NA
*DETROIT, Red River, 60, (776)	772
*DEVERS, Liberty, 27, (416)	435
*DEVINE, Medina, 292, (4,140)	4,240
Dew, Freestone	71
DeWees, Wilson	35
Deweesville, Karnes	12
*Deweyville, Newton, 34, (1,190)	1,126
Dewville, Gonzales	15
Dexter, Cooke	12
*D'Hanis, Medina, 32	575
Dial, Fannin	76
Dialville, Cherokee, 1	200
*Diana, Upshur, 76	585
*DIBOLL, Angelina, 170, (5,470)	5,488
Dicey, Parker	NA
*DICKENS, Dickens, 13, (332)	328
*DICKINSON, Galveston, 1,110, (17,093)	18,681
*Dike, Hopkins, 21	170
*DILLEY, Frio, 91, (3,674)	3,910
Dilworth, Gonzales	15
Dilworth, Red River	22
*Dime Box, Lee, 41	381
*DIMMITT, Castro, 273, (4,375)	4,162
Dimple, Red River	60
*Dinero, Live Oak, 3	344
Ding Dong, Bell	301
Direct, Lamar	85
Dirgin, Rusk	50
Divide, Hopkins	NA
Divot, Frio	9
Dixie, Grayson	17
Dixon, Hunt	31
Dixon-Hopewell, Houston	10
Doak Springs, Lee	50
Doans, Wilbarger	20
*Dobbin, Montgomery, 11	200
Dobrowolski, Atascosa	10
Dodd, Castro	12
*DODD CITY, Fannin, 25, (419)	435
*Dodge, Walker, 9	150
*DODSON, Collingsworth, 8, (115)	107
Dodson Prairie, Palo Pinto	18
Doffing, Hidalgo, (4,256)	4,476
Dog Ridge, Bell	215
Dogwood City, Smith	800
Dolen, Liberty	NA
DOMINO, Cass, 5, (52)	58
*Donie, Freestone, 14	206
*DONNA, Hidalgo, 410, (14,768)	15,690
*Doole, McCulloch, 4	74
Doolittle, Hidalgo, (2,358)	2,478
DORCHESTER, Grayson, 4, (109)	119
Dorras, Stonewall	20
Doss, Cass	15
*Doss, Gillespie, 17	100
Dot, Falls	17
Dothan, Eastland	20
Dotson, Panola	40
Double Bayou, Chambers	400
DOUBLE OAK, Denton, 34, (2,179)	2,761
*Doucette, Tyler, 8	160
*Dougherty, Floyd, 4	91

Town, County	Pop. 2004
Dougherty, Rains	342
Douglas, Smith	NA
*Douglass, Nacogdoches, 20	380
*DOUGLASSVILLE, Cass, 11, (175)	171
Downing, Comanche	30
Downsville, McLennan	150
Doyle, Limestone	50
Doyle, San Patricio, (285)	279
Dozier, Collingsworth	4
Drane, Navarro	16
Drasco, Runnels	15
Draw, Lynn	18
Dreka, Shelby	30
Dresden, Navarro	25
Dreyer, Gonzales	20
*Driftwood, Hays, 96	NA
*DRIPPING SPRINGS, Hays, 711, (1,548)	1,752
*DRISCOLL, Nueces, 16, (825)	818
*Dryden, Terrell, 1	13
Dubina, Fayette	272
*DUBLIN, Erath, 334, (3,754)	3,685
Dudley, Callahan	25
Duffau, Erath	76
*DUMAS, Moore, 661, (13,747)	13,809
Dumont, King	19
Dunbar, Rains	40
*DUNCANVILLE, Dallas, 1,802, (36,081)	35,362
Dundee, Archer	12
Dunlap, Cottle	10
Dunlap, Travis	80
Dunlay, Medina, 4	145
*Dunn, Scurry	75
Duplex, Fannin	25
Durango, Falls	54
Duren, Mills	15
Duster, Comanche	25
Dye, Montague	NA
E	
Eagle, Chambers	50
*EAGLE LAKE, Colorado, 190, (3,664)	3,823
Eagle Mountain, Tarrant, (6,599)	6,750
*EAGLE PASS, Maverick, 1,017, (22,413)	24,667
*EARLY, Brown, 118, (2,588)	2,671
Earlywine, Washington	NA
*EARTH, Lamb, 54, (1,109)	1,090
East Afton, Dickens	13
*EAST BERNARD, Wharton, 176, (1,729)	1,775
East Caney, Hopkins	NA
East Columbia, Brazoria	95
East Delta, Delta	60
East Direct, Lamar	48
Easter, Castro	26
Easterly, Robertson	61
Eastgate, Liberty	NA
East Hamilton, Shelby	25
*EASTLAND, Eastland, 341, (3,769)	3,796
EAST MOUNTAIN, Upshur, 6, (580)	585
*EASTON, Gregg-Rusk, 2, (524)	562
East Point, Wood	40
East Sweden, McCulloch	40
EAST TAWAKONI, Rains, 11, (775)	907
East Tempe, Polk	200
Ebenezer, Camp	55

Town, County	Pop. 2004
*Fischer, Comal, 31	NA
Fisk, Coleman	40
Five Points, Ellis	25
Flaccus, Karnes	15
Flagg, Castro	26
*Flat, Coryell, 4	210
Flat Fork, Shelby	10
*FLATONIA, Fayette, 126, (1,377)	1,462
Flat Prairie, Trinity	33
Flats, Rains	646
Flat Top, Stonewall	5
Flatwoods, Eastland	56
*Flint, Smith, 329	NA
Flo, Leon	20
*Flomot, Motley, 11	181
Flora, Hopkins	NA
*FLORENCE, Williamson, 154, (1,054)	1,175
*FLORESVILLE, Wilson, 518, (5,868)	6,425
Florey, Andrews	25
Flowella, Brooks, (134)	133
Flower Hill, Colorado	20
*FLOWER MOUND, Denton, 1,062, (50,702)	60,908
Floyd, Hunt	220
*FLOYDADA, Floyd, 221, (3,676)	3,420
*Fluvanna, Scurry, 18	180
*Flynn, Leon, 9	81
Foard City, Foard	10
Fodice, Houston	49
*FOLLETT, Lipscomb, 48, (412)	402
Folsom, Shelby	30
Ford, Deaf Smith	15
Fords Corner, San Augustine	30
Fordtran, Victoria	18
Forest, Cherokee	85
*Forestburg, Montague, 36	50
Forest Chapel, Lamar	105
Forest Glade, Limestone	340
Forest Grove, Milam	60
Forest Heights, Orange	250
Forest Hill, Lamar	50
FOREST HILL, Tarrant, 182, (12,949)	13,447
Forest Hill, Wood	30
*FORNEY, Kaufman, 679, (5,588)	7,712
*Forreston, Ellis, 9	400
*FORSAN, Howard, 6, (226)	216
Fort Bliss, El Paso, (8,264)	8,724
Fort Clark Springs, Kinney	1,300
*Fort Davis, Jeff Davis, 92, (1,050)	1,071
Fort Griffin, Shackelford	4
*Fort Hancock, Hudspeth, 35, (1,713)	1,795
Fort Hood, Bell-Coryell, 114, (33,711)	32,667
*Fort McKavett, Menard, 11	50
Fort Parker, Limestone	2
Fort Parker State Park, Limestone	30
Fort Spunky, Hood	15
Fort Stanley Creek, Angelina	100
*FORT STOCKTON, Pecos, 383, (7,846)	7,386
*FORT WORTH, Tarrant, 29,703, (534,694)	592,836
Foster, Terry	6
Fostoria, Montgomery	NA
Fouke, Wood	30
Four Corners, Brazoria	NA
Four Corners, Chambers	18

Town, County	Pop. 2004
Four Corners, Fort Bend, (2,954)	3,260
Four Corners, Montgomery	NA
*Fowlerton, La Salle, 3, (62)	67
Frame Switch, Williamson	25
*Francitas, Jackson, 2	125
Frankel City, Andrews	2
Frankell, Stephens	NA
*FRANKLIN, Robertson, 167, (1,470)	1,478
*FRANKSTON, Anderson, 223, (1,209)	1,202
*Fred, Tyler, 14	299
*FREDERICKSBURG, Gillespie, 1,424, (8,911)	9,651
*Fredonia, Mason, 8	55
Freedom, Rains	60
*FREEPORT, Brazoria, 595, (12,708)	12,995
*FREER, Duval, 102, (3,241)	3,288
Freestone, Freestone	35
Freheit, Comal	NA
Frelsburg, Colorado	75
Frenstat, Burleson	50
Fresno, Collingsworth	NA
*Fresno, Fort Bend, 228, (6,603)	7,568
Freyburg, Fayette	148
Friday, Trinity	99
Friendship, Dawson	5
Friendship, Leon	NA
Friendship, Smith	200
Friendship, Upshur	25
Friendship Village, Bowie	200
*FRIENDSWOOD, Galveston-Harris, 1,955, (29,037)	32,006
Frio Town, Frio	9
*FRIONA, Parmer, 190, (3,854)	3,824
*FRISCO, Collin-Denton, 2,561, (33,714)	58,927
*FRITCH, Hutchinson-Moore, 117, (2,235)	2,133
Frog, Kaufman	NA
Front, Panola	NA
Fronton, Starr, (599)	628
*FROST, Navarro, 37, (648)	676
Fruitland, Montague	20
*FRUITVALE, Van Zandt, 30, (418)	425
Frydek, Austin	900
Fulbright, Red River	150
*FULSHEAR, Fort Bend, 145, (716)	905
*FULTON, Aransas, 74, (1,553)	1,648
Funston, Jones	26
Furrh, Panola	40

G

Gadston, Lamar	35
Gafford, Hopkins	NA
*Gail, Borden, 10	200
*GAINESVILLE, Cooke, 1,192, (15,538)	16,160
Galena, Smith	NA
*GALENA PARK, Harris, 188, (10,592)	10,577
Galilee, Smith	150
*GALLATIN, Cherokee, 6, (378)	384
Galloway, Panola	71
*GALVESTON, Galveston, 2,396, (57,247)	57,539
*GANADO, Jackson, 132, (1,915)	1,946
Garceño, Starr, (1,438)	1,508

Town, County	Pop. 2004
Garcias, Starr	200
*Garciasville [La Casita-], Starr, 8, (2,177)	2,353
*Garden City, Glasscock, 83	293
*Gardendale, Ector, 57, (1,197)	1,235
Gardendale, La Salle	40
GARDEN RIDGE, Comal, 37, (1,882)	2,091
Garden Valley, Smith	150
Garfield, DeWitt	16
Garfield, Travis, (1,660)	1,666
Garland, Bowie	125
*GARLAND, Dallas, 7,642, (215,768)	219,070
Garner, Parker	196
Garner State Park, Uvalde	50
GARRETT, Ellis, 4, (448)	488
Garretts Bluff, Lamar	25
*GARRISON, Nacogdoches, 121, (844)	846
*Garwood, Colorado, 65	975
*GARY, Panola, 38, (303)	315
Gastonia, Kaufman	30
*GATESVILLE, Coryell, 554, (15,591)	15,883
*Gause, Milam, 17	425
Gay Hill, Washington	145
Gayle Estates, Brazoria	102
*Geneva, Sabine	200
Geneview, Stonewall	3
Gentry's Mill, Hamilton	20
George's Creek, Somervell	43
*GEORGETOWN, Williamson, 2,374, (28,339)	34,994
*GEORGE WEST, Live Oak, 188, (2,524)	2,556
Georgia, Lamar	55
Germany, Houston	23
*Geronimo, Guadalupe, 14, (619)	652
GHOLSON, McLennan, 10, (922)	979
Gibtown, Jack	NA
*GIDDINGS, Lee, 444, (5,105)	5,453
*Gilchrist, Galveston, 34	750
*Gillett, Karnes, 14	120
Gilliland, Knox	20
*GILMER, Upshur, 619, (4,799)	5,019
Gilpin, Dickens	2
Ginger, Rains	96
*Girard, Kent, 5, (62)	50
Girlstown USA, Cochran	98
*Girvin, Pecos, 1	20
Gist, Jasper	NA
Givens, Lamar	135
*GLADEWATER, Gregg-Upshur, 450, (6,078)	6,236
Glaze City, Gonzales	10
Glazier, Hemphill	48
Glecker, Lavaca	NA
Glen Cove, Coleman	40
Glendale, Trinity	175
Glenfawn, Rusk	100
*Glen Flora, Wharton, 9	210
Glenn, Dickens	4
GLENN HEIGHTS, Dallas-Ellis, 70, (7,224)	8,345
Glenrio, Deaf Smith	5
*GLEN ROSE, Somervell, 277, (2,122)	2,360
Glenwood, Upshur	150
Glidden, Colorado, 3	255
Globe, Lamar	60
Glory, Lamar	30

Town, County . . . . Pop. 2004	Town, County . . . . Pop. 2004	Town, County . . . . Pop. 2004
*Gober, Fannin, 2. 146	(296). 361	(518). 533
*GODLEY, Johnson, 133,	Graytown, Wilson 64	Halls Store, Panola . . . . NA
(879) 963	Greatwood, Fort Bend,	*HALLSVILLE, Harrison, 213,
*Golden, Wood, 25 156	(6,640) 7,289	(2,772). 2,792
Goldfinch, Frio 35	Green, Karnes 35	*HALTOM CITY, Tarrant, 879,
*Goldsboro, Coleman, 2 30	Green Hill, Titus 150	(39,018). 40,698
*GOLDSMITH, Ector, 26, (253) . . . 245	Green Lake, Calhoun 51	Hamby, Taylor 100
*GOLDTHWAITE, Mills, 190,	Greenpond, Hopkins . . . . NA	*HAMILTON, Hamilton, 276,
(1,802). 1,730	Green's Creek, Erath 75	(2,977). 3,033
*GOLIAD, Goliad, 241,	Green Valley Farms, Cameron,	*HAMLIN, Jones-Fisher, 121,
(1,975). 2,014	(720). 747	(2,248). 2,136
GOLINDA, Falls-McLennan, 4,	Greenview, Hopkins . . . . NA	Hammond, Robertson 44
(423) 454	*GREENVILLE, Hunt, 1,406,	Hamon,Gonzales 15
Golly, DeWitt 41	(23,960) 25,202	*Hamshire, Jefferson, 65 759
Gomez, Terry 6	Greenvine, Washington 35	Hancock, Comal . . . . NA
*GONZALES, Gonzales, 512,	Greenwood, Hopkins 35	Hancock, Dawson 30
(7,202). 7,319	Greenwood, Midland 2,000	*Hankamer, Chambers, 12 226
Goober Hill, Shelby 30	Greenwood, Red River 20	Hannibal, Erath . . . . NA
Goodland, Bailey 10	*Greenwood, Wise, 3 76	Hanover, Milam 25
Goodlett, Hardeman 80	*GREGORY, San Patricio, 41,	*HAPPY, Swisher-Randall, 67,
GOODLOW, Navarro, 4, (264). . . . 279	(2,318). 2,234	(647). 614
Good Neighbor, Hopkins . . . . NA	Gresham, Smith . . . . NA	Happy Union, Hale 15
*GORDON, Palo Pinto, 49,	GREY FOREST, Bexar, 6, (418) . . . 416	Happy Valley, Taylor 10
(451) 431	Grice, Upshur 20	Harbin, Erath 21
*Gordonville, Grayson, 67 165	Griffith, Cochran 12	*HARDIN, Liberty, 28, (755) 791
*GOREE, Knox, 12, (321) 319	Grigsby, Shelby 15	Hare, Williamson 60
*GORMAN, Eastland, 81,	Grit, Mason 15	*Hargill, Hidalgo, 10 1,349
(1,236). 1,251	*GROESBECK, Limestone, 233,	*HARKER HEIGHTS, Bell, 316,
Goshen, Walker 250	(4,291) 4,490	(17,308). 18,861
Gossett, Kaufman . . . . NA	*GROOM, Carson, 60, (587) 578	Harkeyville, San Saba 12
Gould, Cherokee 20	*GROVES, Jefferson, 491,	*Harleton, Harrison, 46 260
*Gouldbusk, Coleman, 12 70	(15,733) 15,371	*HARLINGEN, Cameron, 2,466,
Gourdneck, Panola 30	*GROVETON, Trinity, 105,	(57,564). 63,404
Graball, Washington . . . . NA	(1,107) 1,087	Harlow, Hunt . . . . NA
Graceton, Upshur 100	Grow, King 9	Harmon, Lamar 12
*GRAFORD, Palo Pinto, 147,	Gruenau, DeWitt 18	Harmony, Floyd 42
(578) 578	Gruene, Comal,	Harmony, Grimes. 12
Graham, Garza 139	. . . . (part of New Braunfels)	Harmony, Kent 10
*GRAHAM, Young, 842,	Grulla, Starr . . . . (see La Grulla)	Harmony, Nacogdoches 50
(8,716). 8,639	*GRUVER, Hansford, 116,	*Harper, Gillespie, 77,
*GRANBURY, Hood, 2,063,	(1,162) 1,150	(1,006). 1,017
(5,718). 7,076	Guadalupe, Victoria 106	Harpersville, Stephens . . . . NA
Grand Acres, Cameron, (203) 205	Guadalupe Station, Culberson 80	Harris Chapel, Panola 180
Grand Bluff, Panola 97	*Guerra, Jim Hogg, (8) 9	Harrison, McLennan 100
*GRANDFALLS, Ward, 19,	Guion, Taylor 18	*Harrold, Wilbarger, 13 200
(391) 367	Gum Springs, Cass 50	*HART, Castro, 82, (1,198) 1,115
*GRAND PRAIRIE, Dallas-Tarrant,	*GUN BARREL CITY, Henderson,	Hartburg, Newton 275
4,393, (127,427) 141,692	179, (5,145) 5,457	Hart Camp, Lamb 4
*GRAND SALINE, Van Zandt,	Gunsight, Stephens 6	*Hartley, Hartley, 41, (441) 403
266, (3,028). 3,180	*GUNTER, Grayson, 84,	Harvard Switch, Camp 48
Grandview, Dawson. 12	(1,230) 1,475	Harvey, Brazos 310
Grandview, Gray 13	Gus, Burleson 50	Harwell Point, Burnet. 138
*GRANDVIEW, Johnson, 181,	*GUSTINE, Comanche, 31,	*Harwood, Gonzales, 25 118
(1,358). 1,464	(457). 460	*HASKELL, Haskell, 235,
*GRANGER, Williamson, 88,	*Guthrie, King, 14. 125	(3,106). 2,870
(1,299) 1,341	*Guy, Fort Bend, 29 . . . . NA	Haslam, Shelby 100
*Grangerland, Montgomery. . . . . . . NA	Guys Store, Leon . . . . NA	*HASLET, Tarrant, 258,
*GRANITE SHOALS, Burnet,		(1,134). 1,284
36, (2,040). 2,268	**H**	Hasse, Comanche. 50
GRANJENO, Hidalgo, 1, (313) . . . 325	Haciendito, Presidio . . . . NA	Hatchel, Runnels 6
Grape Creek, Tom Green,	Hackberry, Cottle 30	Hatchetville, Hopkins. . . . . NA
(3,138). 3,070	HACKBERRY, Denton, 3, (544). . . 639	Havana, Hidalgo, (452). 472
*GRAPELAND, Houston, 152,	Hackberry, Edwards. 3	HAWK COVE, Hunt, 1, (457) 476
(1,451). 1,423	Hackberry, Garza 5	*HAWKINS, Wood, 205,
*GRAPEVINE, Tarrant, 2,969,	Hackberry, Lavaca . . . . NA	(1,331). 1,461
(42,059). 46,245	Hagansport, Franklin 40	*HAWLEY, Jones, 91, (646). 637
Grassland, Lynn. 40	Hagerville, Houston 70	Hawthorne, Walker 100
Grassyville, Bastrop 50	Hail, Fannin. 30	Haynesville, Wichita 65
Gray, Marion . . . . NA	Hainesville, Wood 74	Haynie Flat, Travis . . . . NA
Grayback, Wilbarger 10	*HALE CENTER, Hale, 115,	HAYS, Hays, 2, (233). 242
GRAYS PRAIRIE, Kaufman, 1,	(2,263) 2,257	Hazeldell, Comanche 12
	Halfway, Hale 58	*HEARNE, Robertson, 230,
	Hall, San Saba 15	(4,690). 4,460
	*HALLETTSVILLE, Lavaca, 370,	HEATH, Rockwall, (4,149) 5,779
	(2,345) 2,305	*Hebbronville, Jim Hogg, 183,
	Hall's Bluff, Houston 67	(4,498). 4,397
	HALLSBURG, McLennan, 4,	HEBRON, Denton, (874) 976

CITIES & TOWNS

Town, County	Pop. 2004
Heckville, Lubbock	NA
*HEDLEY, Donley, 25, (379)	379
HEDWIG VILLAGE, Harris, 176, (2,334)	2,244
Hefner, Knox	3
Hegar, Waller	NA
Heidelberg, Hidalgo, (1,586)	1,644
*Heidenheimer, Bell, 9	224
Helena, Karnes	35
Helmic, Trinity,	86
*HELOTES, Bexar, 566, (4,285)	5,483
*HEMPHILL, Sabine, 197, (1,106)	1,087
*HEMPSTEAD, Waller, 390, (4,691)	5,697
*HENDERSON, Rusk, 878, (11,273)	11,332
Hendricks, Hunt	NA
Henkhaus, Lavaca	NA
Henly, Hays	140
*HENRIETTA, Clay, 249, (3,264)	3,395
Henry's Chapel, Cherokee	75
*HEREFORD, Deaf Smith, 794, (14,597)	14,559
Hermits Cove, Rains	40
*Hermleigh, Scurry, 34, (393)	369
Herty, Angelina	605
Hester, Navarro	35
*HEWITT, McLennan, 435, (11,085)	12,172
*Hext, Menard, 4	75
HICKORY CREEK, Denton, 44, (2,078)	2,643
Hickory Creek, Houston	31
Hickory Creek, Hunt	NA
Hickory Forrest, Guadalupe	445
*HICO, Hamilton, 148, (1,341)	1,374
*HIDALGO, Hidalgo, 381, (7,322)	9,074
Hidden Acres [Lakeshore Gardens-], San Patricio, (720)	707
Hide Away, Brazoria	69
HIDEAWAY, Smith, (2,619)	2,712
Higginbotham, Gaines	NA
*HIGGINS, Lipscomb, 32, (425)	414
High, Lamar	14
Highbank, Falls	68
High Hill, Fayette	176
*High Island, Galveston, 18	500
Highland, Erath	60
Highland, Smith	NA
Highland Bayou, Galveston	1,209
HIGHLAND HAVEN, Burnet, (450)	478
HIGHLAND PARK, Dallas, 225, (8,842)	8,504
*Highlands, Harris, 320, (7,089)	7,070
HIGHLAND VILLAGE, Denton, 202, (12,173)	13,923
Hightower, Liberty	30
HILL COUNTRY VILLAGE, Bexar, 57, (1,028)	1,061
Hillcrest, Colorado	25
HILLCREST VILLAGE, Brazoria, (722)	733
*Hillister, Tyler, 12	250
Hillje, Wharton	51
Hills, Lee	20
*HILLSBORO, Hill, 474, (8,232)	8,650
Hills Prairie, Bastrop	50
Hilltop, Frio, (300)	303

Town, County	Pop. 2004
*Hilltop Lakes, Leon	300
HILSHIRE VILLAGE, Harris, 6, (720)	711
Hinckley, Lamar	40
Hindes, Atascosa	14
Hinkles Ferry, Brazoria	35
Hiram, Kaufman	34
*HITCHCOCK, Galveston, 321, (6,386)	7,021
Hitchland, Hansford	15
Hix, Burleson	35
Hoard, Wood	45
Hobbs, Fisher	32
*Hobson, Karnes, 13	135
*Hochheim, DeWitt	70
*Hockley, Harris, 267	NA
Hodges, Jones	150
Hogansville, Rains	200
Hogg, Burleson	20
Holiday Beach, Aransas	1,000
HOLIDAY LAKES, Brazoria, 5, (1,095)	1,143
*HOLLAND, Bell, 84, (1,102)	1,094
Holland Quarters, Panola	40
*HOLLIDAY, Archer, 73, (1,632)	1,683
Holly, Houston	95
Holly Grove,Polk	20
Holly Springs, Jasper	50
HOLLYWOOD PARK, Bexar, 50, (2,983)	3,231
Holman, Fayette	101
Homer, Angelina	360
Homestead Meadows North, El Paso, (4,232)	4,456
Homestead Meadows South, El Paso, (6,807)	6,758
*HONDO, Medina, 431, (7,897)	8,471
*HONEY GROVE, Fannin, 130, (1,746)	1,772
Honey Island, Hardin	401
Hood, Cooke	13
Hooker Ridge, Rains	250
*HOOKS, Bowie, 139, (2,973)	2,896
Hoover, Gray	5
Hoover, Lamar	20
Hope, Lavaca	45
Hopewell, Franklin	35
Hopewell, Houston	22
Hopewell [Dixon-], Houston	10
Hopewell, Red River	150
HORIZON CITY, El Paso, 59, (5,233)	7,757
Hornsby Bend, Travis	20
Horseshoe Bay, Llano-Burnet, 74, (3,337)	3,514
Hortense, Polk	20
Horton, Delta	40
Horton, Panola	NA
*HOUSTON, Harris-Fort Bend-Montgomery, 113,964, (1,953,631)	2,033,400
HOWARD, Ellis	210
HOWARDWICK, Donley, 4, (437)	453
*HOWE, Grayson, 130, (2,478)	2,673
Howland, Lamar	65
Howth, Waller	65
Hoxie, Williamson	60
Hoyte, Milam	20
Hub, Parmer	25
Hubbard, Bowie	269
*HUBBARD, Hill, 94,	

Town, County	Pop. 2004
(1,586)	1,622
Huber, Shelby	15
Huckabay, Erath	150
HUDSON, Angelina, 31, (3,792)	3,928
Hudson Bend, Travis, (2,369)	2,286
HUDSON OAKS, Parker, 61, (1,637)	1,790
Huffines, Cass	140
*Huffman, Harris, 362	15,000
Hufsmith, Harris	500
*HUGHES SPRINGS, Cass, 141, (1,856)	1,870
*Hull, Liberty, 32	1,800
*HUMBLE, Harris, 5,333, (14,579)	15,411
*Hungerford, Wharton, 30, (645)	658
*Hunt, Kerr, 104	708
Hunter, Comal	30
HUNTERS CREEK VILLAGE, Harris, 42, (4,374)	4,317
*HUNTINGTON, Angelina, 152, (2,068)	2,080
*HUNTSVILLE, Walker, 1,430, (35,078)	35,975
Hurley, Wood	30
Hurlwood, Lubbock	115
Hurnville, Clay	10
*HURST, Tarrant, 2,100, (36,273)	37,471
Hurstown, Shelby	20
Hurst Springs, Coryell	10
*HUTCHINS, Dallas, 137, (2,805)	2,773
*HUTTO, Williamson, 350, (1,250)	3,063
HUXLEY, Shelby, 6, (298)	313
*Hye, Blanco, 6	105
Hylton, Nolan	6

I

Town, County	Pop. 2004
*Iago [Boling-], Wharton, 75, (1,271)	1,317
Ida, Grayson	30
*IDALOU, Lubbock, 121, (2,157)	2,206
Iglesia Antigua [Bluetown-], Cameron, (692)	714
Ike, Ellis	50
Illinois Bend, Montague	40
IMPACT, Taylor, (39)	41
*Imperial, Pecos, 17, (428)	396
Inadale, Scurry	8
Independence, Washington	140
India, Ellis	30
Indian Creek, Smith	300
Indian Gap, Hamilton	35
Indian Hill, Newton	NA
Indian Hills, Hidalgo, (2,036)	2,135
INDIAN LAKE, Cameron, (541)	553
Indianola, Calhoun	200
Indian Rock, Upshur	45
Indian Springs, Polk	250
Indio, Presidio	NA
*INDUSTRY, Austin, 51, (304)	310
*Inez, Victoria, 76, (1,787)	1,836
*INGLESIDE, San Patricio, 206, (9,388)	9,563
INGLESIDE-ON-THE-BAY, San Patricio, (659)	680
*INGRAM, Kerr, 228, (1,740)	1,803
*Iola, Grimes, 72	350
IOWA COLONY, Brazoria, 7, (804)	861
*IOWA PARK, Wichita, 363, (6,431)	6,382

Town, County . . . . Pop. 2004	Town, County . . . . Pop. 2004	Town, County . . . . Pop. 2004

*Ira, Scurry, 26 250
*IRAAN, Pecos, 54,
  (1,238) 1,178
*IREDELL, Bosque, 29,
  (360) 363
Ireland, Coryell 60
*Irene, Hill, 5 170
Ironton, Cherokee 110
*IRVING, Dallas, 7,699,
  (191,615) 194,372
Isla, Sabine 350
Israel, Polk 25
*ITALY, Ellis, 93, (1,993) 2,142
*ITASCA, Hill, 89, (1,503) 1,546
Ivan, Stephens 15
*Ivanhoe, Fannin, 20 110
*Izoro, Lampasas 17

J

*JACINTO CITY, Harris, 171,
  (10,302) 10,290
*JACKSBORO, Jack, 298,
  (4,533) 4,532
Jackson, Shelby 50
Jackson, Smith . . . . NA
Jackson, Van Zandt . . . . NA
*JACKSONVILLE, Cherokee,
  946 (13,868) 14,203
Jacobia, Hunt 60
Jakes Colony, Guadalupe 95
JAMAICA BEACH, Galveston, 27,
  (1,075) 1,123
James, Shelby 75
Jamestown, Newton 70
Jamestown, Smith 75
Jardin, Hunt 22
*JARRELL, Williamson, 98,
  (1,319) 1,400
*JASPER, Jasper, 765,
  (8,247) 8,554
*JAYTON, Kent, 33, (513) 489
Jean, Young 110
Jeddo, Bastrop 75
*JEFFERSON, Marion, 376,
  (2,024) 2,068
Jenkins, Morris 350
Jennings, Lamar 85
*Jermyn, Jack, 6 75
JERSEY VILLAGE, Harris, 147,
  (6,880) 7,165
*JEWETT, Leon, 95,(861) 934
Jiba, Kaufman . . . . NA
*JOAQUIN, Shelby, 55, (925) 930
Joe Lee, Bell 8
*JOHNSON CITY, Blanco, 194,
  (1,191) 1,294
Johnsville, Erath 25
Johntown, Red River 175
*Joinerville, Rusk, 5 140
Joliet, Caldwell 192
JOLLY, Clay, 2, (188) 185
Jollyville, Williamson-Travis,
  (15,813) 15,391
Jonah, Williamson 60
*Jonesboro, Coryell-Hamilton,
  39 125
JONES CREEK, Brazoria, 14,
  (2,130) 2,175
Jones Prairie, Milam 20
JONESTOWN, Travis, 48,
  (1,681) 1,744
*Jonesville, Harrison, 8 28
Joplin, Jack . . . . NA
Joppa, Burnet 84
Jordans Store, Shelby 20
*JOSEPHINE, Collin, 14,
  (594) 719

*JOSHUA, Johnson, 443,
  (4,528) 4,977
Josserand, Trinity 29
Jot-Em-Down, Delta 8
*JOURDANTON, Atascosa, 175,
  (3,732) 4,059
Joy, Clay 110
Juarez [Las Palmas-], Cameron,
  (1,666) 1,707
Jud, Haskell 60
*Judson, Gregg, 7 1,057
Juliff, Fort Bend . . . . NA
Jumbo, Panola . . . . NA
*JUNCTION, Kimble, 223,
  (2,618) 2,672
Justiceburg, Garza, 2 76
*JUSTIN, Denton, 243,
  (1,891) 2,535

K

Kalgary, Crosby 2
*Kamay, Wichita, 10 640
Kamey, Calhoun 25
Kanawha, Red River 90
*Karnack, Harrison, 76 775
*KARNES CITY, Karnes, 144,
  (3,457) 3,448
Karon, Live Oak 25
Katemcy, Mason 80
*KATY, Harris-Waller-Fort Bend,
  5,117, (11,775) 13,285
*KAUFMAN, Kaufman, 555,
  (6,490) 7,512
K-Bar Ranch, Jim Wells, (350) 329
Keechi, Leon 67
*KEENE, Johnson, 130,
  (5,003) 5,721
Keeter, Wise . . . . NA
Keith, Grimes 50
*KELLER, Tarrant, 1,596,
  (27,345) 34,467
Kellers Corner, Cameron 123
Kellerville, Wheeler 50
Kellogg, Hunt . . . . NA
Kellyville, Marion . . . . NA
Kelsey, Upshur 50
Kelton, Wheeler 20
*KEMAH, Galveston, 497,
  (2,330) 2,486
*KEMP, Kaufman, 404,
  (1,133) 1,223
Kemper City, Victoria 16
*KEMPNER, Lampasas, 111,
  (1,004) 1,093
*Kendalia, Kendall, 22 76
*KENDLETON, Fort Bend, 13,
  (466) 501
*KENEDY, Karnes, 179,
  (3,487) 3,502
KENEFICK, Liberty, 8, (667) 704
*KENNARD, Houston, 31,
  (317) 303
*KENNEDALE, Tarrant, 402,
  (5,850) 6,462
*Kenney, Austin, 3 957
Kenser, Hunt . . . . NA
Kensing, Delta 30
*Kent, Culberson, 2 60
Kentucky Town, Grayson 20
*KERENS, Navarro, 105,
  (1,681) 1,722
*KERMIT, Winkler, 198,
  (5,714) 5,264
*Kerrick, Dallam, 8 35
*KERRVILLE, Kerr, 2,162,
  (20,425) 21,254
Kerrville South, Kerr 6,600

Key, Dawson 20
Kiam, Polk . . . . NA
Kicaster, Wilson 100
*Kildare, Cass, 2 104
*KILGORE, Gregg-Rusk, 1,012,
  (11,301) 11,508
*KILLEEN, Bell, 3,012,
  (86,911) 96,858
King, Coryell 30
King Ranch Headquarters,
  Kleberg 191
*Kingsbury, Guadalupe, 61,
  (652) 684
*Kingsland, Llano, 267,
  (4,584) 4,954
Kingston, Hunt 140
*KINGSVILLE, Kleberg, 811,
  (25,575) 25,836
Kingtown, Nacogdoches 300
Kingwood, Harris, 832,
  . . . . (part of Houston)
Kinkler, Lavaca 75
Kiomatia, Red River 50
KIRBY, Bexar, 57, (8,673) 8,884
*KIRBYVILLE, Jasper, 210,
  (2,085) 2,087
Kirk, Limestone 10
Kirkland, Childress, 3 25
Kirtley, Fayette 93
*KIRVIN, Freestone, 8, (122) 133
Kittrell, Walker 126
*Klein, Harris 45,000
Klondike, Dawson 50
*Klondike, Delta, 15 175
Klump, Washington . . . . NA
Knapp, Scurry 10
*Knickerbocker, Tom Green, 4 94
Knight, Polk . . . . NA
*Knippa, Uvalde, 31, (739) 751
Knobbs Springs, Lee 20
KNOLLWOOD, Grayson, 3,
  (375) 389
*Knott, Howard, 15 200
*KNOX CITY, Knox, 74,
  (1,219) 1,143
Koerth, Lavaca 45
Kokomo, Eastland 25
Komensky, Lavaca . . . . NA
Kopernik Shores, Cameron 34
*Kopperl, Bosque, 28 225
Kosciusko, Wilson 390
*KOSSE, Limestone, 33,
  (497) 510
*KOUNTZE, Hardin, 262,
  (2,115) 2,094
Kovar, Bastrop . . . . NA
*KRESS, Swisher, 71, (826) 776
KRUGERVILLE, Denton, 16,
  (903) 1,223
*KRUM, Denton, 227,
  (1,979) 2,571
*KURTEN, Brazos, 8, (227) 233
*KYLE, Hays, 423, (5,314) 11,870
Kyote, Atascosa 34

L

*La Blanca, Hidalgo, 8,
  (2,351) 2,463
La Casa, Stephens . . . . NA
La Casita-Garciasville, Starr, 8,
  (2,177) 2,353
Laceola, Madison 10
Lackland Air Force Base, Bexar,
  (7,123) 7,505
*LA COSTE, Medina, 47,
  (1,255) 1,337
Lacy, Trinity 44

CITIES & TOWNS

Town, County . . . . Pop. 2004	Town, County . . . . Pop. 2004	Town, County . . . . Pop. 2004
LACY-LAKEVIEW, McLennan, 83, (5,764) 5,885	Lakewood Harbor, Bosque . . . . NA	*LAVON, Collin, 46, (387) 465
*LADONIA, Fannin, 36, (667) 690	LAKEWOOD VILLAGE, Denton, (342) 378	Law, Brazos . . . . NA
LaFayette, Upshur 80	*LAKE WORTH, Tarrant, 159, (4,618) 4,689	*LA WARD, Jackson, 14, (200) 199
*LA FERIA, Cameron, 195, (6,115) 6,844	Lamar, Aransas 1,600	*LAWN, Taylor, 22, (353) 327
La Feria North, Cameron, (168) . . . 171	*LA MARQUE, Galveston, 551, (13,682) 13,736	Lawrence, Kaufman 279
Lagarto, Live Oak 735	Lamasco, Fannin 32	*Lazbuddie, Parmer, 22 248
La Gloria, Jim Wells 70	*LAMESA, Dawson, 613, (9,952) 9,481	*LEAGUE CITY, Galveston-Harris, 1,956, (45,444) 53,621
La Gloria, Starr 102	Lamkin, Comanche 87	Leagueville, Henderson 50
Lago, Cameron, (246) 248	*LAMPASAS, Lampasas, 508, (6,786) 7,579	*LEAKEY, Real, 103, (387) 398
*LAGO VISTA, Travis, 185, (4,507) 5,463	Lanark, Cass 30	*LEANDER, Williamson, 1,389, (7,596) 11,987
*LA GRANGE, Fayette, 614, (4,478) 4,615	*LANCASTER, Dallas, 953, (25,894) 27,241	LEARY, Bowie, 12, (555) 583
*LA GRULLA, Starr, 13, (1,211) 1,232	Landrum Station, Cameron 125	*LEDBETTER, Fayette, 22 83
Laguna, Uvalde 20	Lane City, Wharton, 4 111	Leedale, Bell 24
Laguna Heights, Cameron, (1,990) 2,105	Lanely, Freestone 27	*Leesburg, Camp, 37 115
*Laguna Park, Bosque 550	Laneport, Williamson 40	Lee Spring, Smith . . . . NA
Laguna Seca, Hidalgo, (251) 258	*Laneville, Rusk, 28 169	*Leesville, Gonzales, 10 152
Laguna Vista, Burnet 94	*Langtry, Val Verde, 4 30	*LEFORS, Gray, 16, (559) 536
LAGUNA VISTA, Cameron, 28, (1,658) 2,356	Lanier, Cass 80	*Leggett, Polk, 9 500
La Homa, Hidalgo, (10,433) . . . 11,268	Lannius, Fannin 79	Lehman, Cochran 6
*Laird Hill, Rusk, 6 300	Lantana, Cameron 137	Leigh, Harrison 100
La Isla, El Paso 27	La Paloma, Cameron, (354) 356	Lela, Wheeler 135
Lajitas, Brewster 75	La Paloma-Lost Creek, Nueces, (323) 307	*Lelia Lake, Donley, 3 71
*LA JOYA, Hidalgo, 38, (3,303) 3,938	La Parita, Atascosa 48	*Leming, Atascosa, 6 268
La Junta, Parker . . . . NA	*LA PORTE, Harris, 1,252, (31,880) 33,035	*Lenorah, Martin, 17 83
Lake Arrowhead, Clay 250	La Presa, Webb, (508) 543	Lenz, Karnes 20
LAKE BRIDGEPORT, Wise, 5, (372) 393	*La Pryor, Zavala, 25, (1,491) 1,472	Leo, Cooke 20
Lake Brownwood, Brown, (1,694) 1,757	La Puerta, Starr, (1,636) 1,719	Leo, Lee 10
Lake Cisco, Eastland 105	*LAREDO, Webb, 6,369, (176,576) 201,139	*LEONA, Leon, 22, (181) 194
LAKE CITY, San Patricio, (526) 533	Laredo Ranchettes, Webb, (1,845) 1,972	*LEONARD, Fannin, 107, (1,846) 1,912
*Lake Creek, Delta, 10 55	La Reforma, Starr 45	Leona Schroder, Nueces 40
*LAKE DALLAS, Denton, 379, (6,166) 6,855	Larga Vista, Webb, (742) 789	Leonidas, Montgomery . . . . NA
Lake Dunlap, Guadalupe 1,370	Lariat, Parmer 100	Leon Junction, Coryell 50
*Lakehills, Bandera, (4,668) 5,116	La Rosa, Nueces 20	Leon Springs, Bexar . . . . NA
*LAKE JACKSON, Brazoria, 1,084, (26,386) 27,305	La Rosita, Starr, (1,729) 1,810	*LEON VALLEY, Bexar, 374, (9,239) 9,949
Lake Kiowa, Cooke, (1,883) 1,783	*Larue, Henderson, 65 250	*LEROY, McLennan, 7, (335) 339
Lake Leon, Eastland 75	*LaSalle, Jackson, 2 110	Lesley, Hall 25
Lake Nueces, Uvalde 60	Lasana, Cameron, (135) 141	*LEVELLAND, Hockley, 698, (12,866) 12,917
Lake Placid, Guadalupe 574	*Lasara, Willacy, 6, (1,024) 1,030	Leverett's Chapel, Rusk 400
LAKEPORT, Gregg, 21,(861) 885	Las Colonias, Zavala, (283) 276	Levi, McLennan 50
Lakeshore Gardens-Hidden Acres, San Patricio, (720) 707	Las Escobas, Starr 10	Levita, Coryell 70
LAKESIDE, San Patricio, (333) 326	Las Lomas, Starr, (2,684) 2,821	*LEWISVILLE, Denton, 5,687, (77,737) 90,774
LAKESIDE, Tarrant, (1,040) 1,101	Las Lomitas, Jim Hogg, (267) 271	*LEXINGTON, Lee, 107, (1,178) 1,270
LAKESIDE CITY, Archer, 10, (984) 1,028	Las Palmas-Juarez, Cameron, (1,666) 1,707	Liberty, Hopkins . . . . NA
Lakeside Village, Bosque 226	Las Quintas Fronterizas, Maverick, (2,030) 2,092	*LIBERTY, Liberty, 570, (8,033) 8,349
LAKE TANGLEWOOD, Randall, (825) 846	Las Rusias, Cameron 225	Liberty, Lubbock 10
Lake Tejas, San Jacinto 50	Lassater, Marion 48	Liberty, Milam 40
Laketon, Gray 12	Las Yescas, Cameron 221	Liberty, Newton . . . . NA
Lake Victor, Burnet 265	Latch, Upshur 50	Liberty City, Gregg, (1,935) 1,988
Lakeview, Floyd 39	Latex, Harrison 75	Liberty Hill, Houston 73
Lakeview, Franklin 30	*LATEXO, Houston, 4, (272) 270	Liberty Hill, Milam 25
*LAKEVIEW, Hall, 11, (152) 161	La Tina Ranch [Arroyo Gardens-], Cameron, (732) 747	*LIBERTY HILL, Williamson, 368, (1,409) 1,393
Lakeview, Lynn 15	Latium, Washington 30	Lilbert, Nacogdoches 100
Lakeview, Orange 75	Laughlin Air Force Base, Val Verde, (2,225) 2,280	*Lillian, Johnson, 12 105
LAKEVIEW [Lacy-], McLennan, 83, (5,764) 5,885	Laurel, Newton 125	*Lincoln, Lee, 18 336
Lake View, Val Verde, (167) 169	Laureles, Cameron, (3,285) 3,426	LINCOLN PARK, Denton, 6, (517) 582
Lake Water Wheel, San Jacinto 75	Lavender, Limestone 30	*LINDALE, Smith, 637, (2,954) 3,749
*LAKEWAY, Travis, (8,002) 8,347	*LA VERNIA, Wilson, 218, (931) 980	*LINDEN, Cass, 164, (2,256) . . . 2,220
Lakewood, Travis . . . . NA	La Victoria, Starr, (1,683) 1,756	Lindenau, DeWitt 50
	*LA VILLA, Hidalgo, 12, (1,305) 1,348	Lindendale, Kendall 10
		*LINDSAY, Cooke, 31, (788) 861
		Lindsay, Reeves, (394) 397
		*Lingleville, Erath, 6 100
		*Linn [San Manuel-], Hidalgo, 17, (958) 971
		Linn Flat, Nacogdoches 60

Town, County . . . . Pop. 2004	Town, County . . . . Pop. 2004	Town, County . . . . Pop. 2004
Linwood, Cherokee 40	Looneyville, Nacogdoches 50	Macon, Franklin 21
*LIPAN, Hood, 89, (425) 469	*Loop, Gaines, 24. 315	Macune, San Augustine 100
*Lipscomb, Lipscomb, 11, (44) 44	*Lopeno, Zapata, (140) 166	Madero, Hidalgo 720
*Lissie, Wharton, 8. 72	Lopezville, Hidalgo, (4,476) 4,828	*MADISONVILLE, Madison,
Littig, Travis 37	*LORAINE, Mitchell, 21,	353, (4,159) 4,280
Little Cypress, Orange. 1,050	(656). 608	Madras, Red River 61
*LITTLE ELM, Denton, 431,	*LORENA, McLennan, 273,	Magnet, Wharton. 42
(3,646). 13,369	(1,433) 1,512	*MAGNOLIA, Montgomery,
*LITTLEFIELD, Lamb, 318,	*LORENZO, Crosby, 67,	264, (1,111) 1,249
(6,507). 6,490	(1,372) 1,325	Magnolia, San Jacinto. 330
Little Hope, Wood 25	Los Alvarez, Starr, (1,434) 1,507	Magnolia Beach, Calhoun. 250
Little Midland, Burnet. 82	Los Angeles, La Salle. 20	Magnolia Springs, Jasper, 2 80
Little New York, Gonzales 20	Los Angeles Subdivision, Willacy,	Maha, Travis . . . . NA
*LITTLE RIVER-ACADEMY, Bell,	(86). 87	Mahl, Nacogdoches 150
55, (1,645). 1,656	Los Barreras, Starr 75	Mahomet, Burnet. 97
Lively, Kaufman . . . . NA	Los Coyotes, Willacy 4	Majors, Franklin 13
LIVE OAK, Bexar, 182,	*Los Ebanos, Hidalgo, 3,	*MALAKOFF, Henderson, 227,
(9,156). 9,876	(403). 407	(2,257) 2,349
*LIVERPOOL, Brazoria, 28,	Los Escondidos, Burnet. 80	Mallard, Montague 12
(404). 419	*LOS FRESNOS, Cameron,	*MALONE, Hill, 31, (278). 291
*LIVINGSTON, Polk, 953,	212, (4,512) 5,108	Malta, Bowie 297
(5,433). 5,947	*LOS INDIOS, Cameron, 5,	Malvern, Leon . . . . NA
*LLANO, Llano, 315,	(1,149) 1,254	Mambrino, Hood 74
(3,325). 3,550	Losoya, Bexar. 322	*Manchaca, Travis, 206. 2,259
Llano Grande, Hidalgo,	LOS SAENZ [Roma-], Starr,	Manchester, Red River 185
(3,333). 3,427	242, (9,617) 10,901	Mangum, Eastland 15
Lobo, Culberson 40	Lost Creek [La Paloma-],	Manheim, Lee 50
Lochridge, Brazoria . . . . NA	Nueces, (323) 307	Mankin, Henderson 30
Locker, San Saba. 16	Lost Creek, Travis, (4,729) 4,499	Mankins, Archer 10
Lockett, Wilbarger 150	Lost Prairie, Limestone 2	*MANOR, Travis, 346,
Lockettville, Hockley 20	Los Villareales, Starr, (930). 971	(1,204) 1,185
*LOCKHART, Caldwell, 507,	LOS YBANEZ, Dawson, 2, (32) 32	*MANSFIELD, Tarrant-Johnson,
(11,615). 12,880	*LOTT, Falls, 82, (724) 697	1,757, (28,031) 33,707
*LOCKNEY, Floyd, 101,	*Louise, Wharton, 81, (977) 990	*MANVEL, Brazoria, 357,
(2,056). 1,917	Lovelace, Hill 30	(3,046). 3,351
Locust, Grayson 118	*LOVELADY, Houston, 43,	*Maple, Bailey, 4 75
*Lodi, Marion, 4 164	(608). 598	Maple, Red River. 30
Loebau, Lee. 35	*Loving, Young, 15 300	Maple Springs, Titus 25
Logan, Panola 40	*Lowake, Concho, 3 40	Mapleton, Houston 32
LOG CABIN, Henderson, 2,	LOWRY CROSSING, Collin, 7,	*Marathon, Brewster, 45,
(733). 775	(1,229) 1,572	(455). 459
*Lohn, McCulloch, 17 149	Loyal Valley, Mason 52	*MARBLE FALLS, Burnet,
Loire, Wilson 50	Loyola Beach, Kleberg. 195	1,103, (4,959) 5,508
Lois, Cooke 10	*Lozano, Cameron, 1, (324) 328	*MARFA, Presidio, 108,
*Lolita, Jackson, 23, (548). 543	*LUBBOCK, Lubbock, 9,989,	(2,121) 2,143
Loma Alta, McMullen 25	(199,564) 205,905	Margaret, Foard 50
Loma Alta, Val Verde 30	LUCAS, Collin, 46, (2,890) 3,559	Marie, Runnels 10
Loma Linda [Del Sol-], San Patricio,	Luckenbach, Gillespie 25	*MARIETTA, Cass, 18, (112) 115
(726). 728	*LUEDERS, Jones, 17, (300) 284	*MARION, Guadalupe, 145,
Loma Linda East, Jim Wells,	Luella, Grayson 639	(1,099) 1,171
(214) 223	*LUFKIN, Angelina, 2,489,	*Markham, Matagorda, 26,
Lomax, Howard 25	(32,709) 33,235	(1,138) 1,116
*LOMETA, Lampasas, 63,	*LULING, Caldwell, 273,	Markley, Young 50
(782). 842	(5,080). 5,478	Markout, Kaufman 80
*London, Kimble, 9 180	Lull, Hidalgo 999	*MARLIN, Falls, 273,
Lone Camp, Palo Pinto 110	*LUMBERTON, Hardin, 579,	(6,628) 6,613
Lone Cedar, Ellis 18	(8,731). 9,366	Marlow, Milam 45
Lone Elm, Kaufman . . . . NA	Lums Chapel, Lamb. 6	*MARQUEZ, Leon, 56, (220) 214
Lone Grove, Llano 50	Luther, Howard 3	Mars, Van Zandt . . . . NA
Lone Oak, Colorado 50	Lutie, Collingsworth 10	*MARSHALL, Harrison, 1,420,
Lone Oak, Erath. . . . . NA	Lydia, Red River 109	(23,935) 24,430
*LONE OAK, Hunt, 93,	*LYFORD, Willacy, 64,	MARSHALL CREEK, Denton, 2,
(521) 534	(1,973) 2,129	(431) 516
Lone Pine, Houston 81	Lyford South, Willacy, (172) 172	Marshall Ford, Travis . . . . NA
Lone Star, Cherokee 20	Lynn Grove, Grimes 25	Marshall Northeast, Harrison . . . 1,500
Lone Star, Floyd. 42	*Lyons, Burleson, 12 360	Marston, Polk. 25
Lone Star, Lamar 35	*LYTLE, Atascosa-Medina-Bexar,	*MART, McLennan, 111,
*LONE STAR, Morris, 59,	168, (2,383) 2,535	(2,273) 2,264
(1,631). 1,604	Lytton Springs, Caldwell. 500	*MARTINDALE, Caldwell, 61,
*Long Branch, Panola, 9 181		(953). 1,010
Long Hollow, Leon . . . . NA	**M**	Martins Mill, Van Zandt 158
Long Lake, Anderson 15	*MABANK, Kaufman-Henderson,	Martin Springs, Hopkins 200
*Long Mott, Calhoun, 2 76	745, (2,151) 2,477	*Martinsville, Nacogdoches, 5 350
Longpoint, Washington 80	Mabelle, Baylor. 9	Marvin, Lamar 48
*LONGVIEW, Gregg-Harrison,	Mabry, Red River 60	Maryetta, Jack. 7
4,706, (73,344) 74,904	*Macdona, Bexar, 3 297	*Maryneal, Nolan, 4. 61
Longworth, Fisher 47	Macey, Brazos . . . . NA	Marysville, Cooke 12

Town, County	Pop. 2004
*MASON, Mason, 232,	
(2,134)	2,168
Massey Lake, Anderson	30
Masterson, Moore, 3	2
*MATADOR, Motley, 50,	
(740)	691
*Matagorda, Matagorda, 32	710
*MATHIS, San Patricio, 236,	
(5,034)	5,143
Matthews, Colorado	25
*MAUD, Bowie, 58, (1,028)	996
*Mauriceville, Orange, 44,	
(2,743)	2,821
Maverick, Runnels	35
Maxdale, Bell	25
Maxey, Lamar	70
*Maxwell, Caldwell, 47	500
*May, Brown, 36	270
*Maydelle, Cherokee, 10	250
Mayfield, Hale	NA
Mayfield, Hill	25
Mayflower, Newton	100
Mayhill, Denton	150
Maynard, San Jacinto	150
*MAYPEARL, Ellis, 40, (746)	826
Maysfield, Milam	140
*McAdoo, Dickens, 5	75
*McALLEN, Hidalgo, 5,253,	
(106,414)	117,650
*McCAMEY, Upton, 68,	
(1,805)	1,675
*McCaulley, Fisher, 5	96
McClanahan, Falls	42
McCook, Hidalgo	91
McCoy, Atascosa	30
McCoy, Floyd	20
McCoy, Kaufman	20
McCoy, Panola	NA
McCoy, Red River	175
*McDade, Bastrop, 37	345
*McFaddin, Victoria, 1	175
McGirk, Hamilton	9
*McGREGOR, McLennan,	
307, (4,727)	4,778
*McKINNEY, Collin, 3,319,	
(54,369)	81,462
McKinney Acres, Andrews	197
*McLEAN, Gray, 61, (830)	793
McLENDON-CHISHOLM,	
Rockwall, (914)	1,035
*McLeod, Cass, 6	600
McMahan, Caldwell	125
McMillan, San Saba	15
McNair, Harris	2,039
McNary, Hudspeth	250
McNeel, Brazoria	NA
McNeil, Caldwell	200
*McNeil, Travis, 1	70
*McQueeney, Guadalupe, 73,	
(2,527)	2,729
*MEADOW, Terry, 43, (658)	649
Meadow Grove, Bell	20
Meadow Lake, Guadalupe	650
MEADOWLAKES, Burnet,	
(1,293)	1,559
MEADOWS PLACE, Fort Bend,	
55, (4,912)	5,403
Mecca, Madison	48
Medicine Mound, Hardeman	50
Medill, Lamar	50
*Medina, Bandera, 74	515
Medina, Zapata, (2,960)	3,592
Meeker, Jefferson	2,280
Meeks, Bell	6
*MEGARGEL, Archer, 15,	
(248)	257
*MELISSA, Collin, 154,	

Town, County	Pop. 2004
(1,350)	1,967
Melrose, Nacogdoches	400
*MELVIN, McCulloch, 20,	
(155)	142
*MEMPHIS, Hall, 137,	
(2,479)	2,602
*MENARD, Menard, 102,	
(1,653)	1,657
Mendoza, Caldwell	100
Menlow, Hill	12
*Mentone, Loving, 5	20
Mentz, Colorado	100
*MERCEDES, Hidalgo, 380,	
(13,649)	14,355
Mercury, McCulloch	166
*Mereta, Tom Green, 3	131
*MERIDIAN, Bosque, 140,	
(1,491)	1,522
*Merit, Hunt, 13	215
*MERKEL, Taylor, 153,	
(2,637)	2,609
Merle, Burleson	10
Merriman, Eastland	14
*MERTENS, Hill, 4, (146)	149
*MERTZON, Irion, 74, (839)	837
*MESQUITE, Dallas, 4,969,	
(124,523)	128,653
Metcalf Gap, Palo Pinto	6
*MEXIA, Limestone, 443,	
(6,563)	6,712
*Meyersville, DeWitt, 12	110
*MIAMI, Roberts, 51, (588)	539
Mico, Medina	107
Midcity, Lamar	50
Middleton, Leon	26
*Midfield, Matagorda, 12	305
*Midkiff, Upton, 22	182
*MIDLAND, Midland, 5,394,	
(94,996)	97,048
*MIDLOTHIAN, Ellis, 839,	
(7,480)	10,332
Midway, Bell	140
Midway, Dawson	20
Midway, Fannin	7
Midway, Jim Wells	24
Midway, Lavaca	NA
Midway, Limestone	9
*MIDWAY, Madison, 80, (288)	291
Midway, Polk	525
Midway, Red River	40
Midway, Smith	NA
Midway, Titus	110
Midway, Upshur	20
Midway, Van Zandt	31
Midway North, Hidalgo,	
(3,946)	4,122
Midway South, Hidalgo,	
(1,711)	1,782
Midyett, Panola	NA
Mikeska, Live Oak	10
Mila Doce, Hidalgo, (4,907)	5,305
*Milam, Sabine, 19,	
(1,329)	1,234
*MILANO, Milam, 30, (400)	416
Milburn, McCulloch	8
MILDRED, Navarro, (405)	407
*MILES, Runnels, 85, (850)	819
*MILFORD, Ellis, 30, (685)	728
Mill Creek, Washington	40
Miller Grove, Hopkins	115
MILLERS COVE, Titus, 5,	
(120)	129
*Millersview, Concho, 12	80
Millett, La Salle	40
Millheim, Austin	170
*MILLICAN, Brazos, 8, (108)	110
*MILLSAP, Parker, 88, (353)	362

Town, County	Pop. 2004
Milo Center, Deaf Smith	5
Milton, Lamar	50
Mims, Brazoria	NA
Mims Chapel, Marion	NA
*Minden, Rusk, 5	150
*MINEOLA, Wood, 537,	
(4,550)	4,768
*Mineral, Bee	65
*MINERAL WELLS, Palo Pinto-Parker,	
841, (16,946)	17,266
Minerva, Milam, 1	100
Mings Chapel, Upshur	50
*MINGUS, Palo Pinto, 21,	
(246)	240
Minter, Lamar	78
*Mirando City, Webb, 15,	
(493)	517
*MISSION, Hidalgo, 2,080,	
(45,408)	56,934
Mission Bend, Fort Bend-Harris,	
(30,831)	33,421
Mission Valley, Victoria	225
*MISSOURI CITY, Fort Bend-Harris,	
2,680, (52,913)	63,115
Mitchell, Eastland	46
Mixon, Cherokee	50
*MOBEETIE, Wheeler, 15,	
(107)	103
MOBILE CITY, Rockwall, 2,	
(196)	230
Moffat, Bell	1,406
Moffett, Angelina	100
Moline, Lampasas	12
*MONAHANS, Ward, 323,	
(6,821)	6,452
Monaville, Waller	160
Monkstown, Fannin	35
Monroe, Rusk	96
Monroe City, Chambers	11
Mont, Lavaca	30
*Montague, Montague, 35	400
Montague Village, Coryell	1,410
*Montalba, Anderson, 34	110
*MONT BELVIEU, Chambers,	
113, (2,324)	2,532
Monte Alto, Hidalgo,	
(1,611)	1,677
Monte Grande, Cameron	97
Montell, Uvalde	20
*MONTGOMERY, Montgomery,	
167, (489)	545
Monthalia, Gonzales	32
Monticello, Titus	20
*MOODY, McLennan, 141,	
(1,400)	1,411
Moore, Brazos	NA
*Moore, Frio, 14, (644)	639
Moore's Crossing, Travis	25
MOORE STATION, Henderson,	
(184)	194
Mooreville, Falls	96
Mooring, Brazos	80
Morales, Jackson	72
Morales-Sanchez, Zapata, (95)	121
*MORAN, Shackelford, 14,	
(233)	226
Moravia, Lavaca	165
*MORGAN, Bosque, 38, (485)	511
Morgan Creek, Burnet	126
Morgan Farm Area, San Patricio,	
(484)	487
*Morgan Mill, Erath, 8	206
MORGAN'S POINT, Harris,	
(336)	333
MORGAN'S POINT RESORT,	
Bell, (2,989)	3,471
Morning Glory, El Paso, (627)	632

CITIES & TOWNS

Town, County . . . . Pop. 2004	Town, County . . . . Pop. 2004	Town, County . . . . Pop. 2004
*ROBY, Fisher, 44, (673) 661	*ROTAN, Fisher, 104, (1,611) . . . 1,525	*Samnorwood, Collingsworth,
*Rochelle, McCulloch, 37 163	Rough Creek, San Saba 15	4, (39) 40
*ROCHESTER, Haskell, 22,	Round House, Navarro 40	Sample, Gonzales 16
(378) 362	*ROUND MOUNTAIN, Blanco,	*Sam Rayburn, Jasper 600
Rock Bluff, Burnet 90	26, (111) 111	*SAN ANGELO, Tom Green,
Rock Creek, McLennan 25	Round Mountain, Travis 59	3,770, (88,439) 88,170
Rock Creek, Somervell 70	Round Prairie, Navarro 40	*SAN ANTONIO, Bexar,
*ROCKDALE, Milam, 393,	*ROUND ROCK, Williamson-Travis,	42,616, (1,144,646) 1,228,512
(5,439) 5,910	3,637, (61,136) 81,265	San Antonio Prairie, Burleson 20
Rockett, Ellis 300	Round Timber, Baylor 2	*SAN AUGUSTINE, San Augustine,
Rockford, Lamar 30	*ROUND TOP, Fayette, 63, (77) 76	213, (2,475) 2,501
Rockhouse, Austin 100	Roundup, Hockley 20	*SAN BENITO, Cameron, 678,
*Rock Island, Colorado, 5 160	Rowden, Callahan 30	(23,444) 24,897
Rockland, Tyler 98	*Rowena, Runnels, 51 349	San Carlos, Hidalgo, (2,650) 2,773
Rockne, Bastrop 400	*ROWLETT, Dallas-Rockwall,	San Carlos, Starr 10
*ROCKPORT, Aransas, 916,	1,841, (44,503) 52,060	Sanchez [Morales-], Zapata,
(7,385) 8,261	*ROXTON, Lamar, 30, (694) 714	(95) .121
*ROCKSPRINGS, Edwards,	Royalty, Ward 27	Sanco, Coke 15
63, (1,285) 1,261	*ROYSE CITY, Rockwall-Collin,	SANCTUARY, Parker, 11,
*ROCKWALL, Rockwall, 2,051,	437, (2,957) 4,313	(256) .616
(17,976) 24,867	Rucker, Comanche 28	Sandbranch, Dallas 400
*Rockwood, Coleman, 2 80	Rucker's Bridge, Lamar 20	*Sanderson, Terrell, 47, (861) 785
Rocky Branch, Morris 135	Rugby, Red River 24	Sand Flat, Johnson . . . . NA
Rocky Creek, Blanco 20	Ruidosa, Presidio 43	Sand Flat, Leon 32
ROCKY MOUND, Camp, 1,	*RULE, Haskell, 36, (698) 670	Sand Flat, Rains 100
(93) 99	Rumley, Lampasas 8	Sand Flat, Smith 100
Rocky Point, Burnet 152	RUNAWAY BAY, Wise, 13,	Sandhill, Floyd 33
Roddy, Van Zandt . . . . NA	(1,104) 1,188	Sand Hill, Upshur 75
Rodney, Navarro 15	*RUNGE, Karnes, 38,	*Sandia, Jim Wells, 61, (431) 409
Roeder, Titus 110	(1,080) 1,049	*SAN DIEGO, Duval-Jim Wells,
Roganville, Jasper, 1 100	Runn, Hidalgo . . . . NA	88, (4,753) 4,596
*ROGERS, Bell, 79,	Rural Shade, Navarro 30	Sandlin, Stonewall 3
(1,117) 1,161	Rushing, Navarro 10	Sandoval, Williamson 60
Rogers, Taylor 151	*RUSK, Cherokee, 223,	Sand Springs, Howard 1,000
Rolling Hills, Potter 1,000	(5,085) 5,151	Sandusky, Grayson 15
Rolling Hills, Waller . . . . NA	Russell, Leon 27	Sandy, Blanco 25
Rolling Meadows, Gregg 362	Rutersville, Fayette 137	Sandy, Limestone, 1 5
ROLLINGWOOD, Travis, 59,	Ruth Springs, Henderson 120	Sandy Harbor, Llano 85
(1,403) 1,341	*Rye, Liberty, 13 76	Sandy Hill, Washington 50
*ROMA-Los Saenz, Starr, 242,		Sandy Hills, Montgomery . . . . NA
(9,617) 10,901	**S**	Sandy Hollow-Escondidas, Nueces,
Roma Creek, Starr, (610) 640	Sabanno, Eastland 12	(433) 407
ROMAN FOREST, Montgomery,	*SABINAL, Uvalde, 69,	SANDY POINT, Brazoria 250
(1,279) 2,401	(1,586) 1,599	*San Elizario, El Paso, 102,
*Romayor, Liberty, 10 96	*Sabine Pass, Jefferson, 28,	(11,046) 11,640
Romney, Eastland 12	. . . . (part of Port Arthur)	*SAN FELIPE, Austin, 10,
*Roosevelt, Kimble, 3 14	*SACHSE, Dallas-Collin, 206,	(868) 935
Roosevelt, Lubbock 50	(9,751) 15,092	*SANFORD, Hutchinson, 8,
*ROPESVILLE, Hockley, 55,	*Sacul, Nacogdoches, 5 150	(203) 187
(517) 518	*SADLER, Grayson, 40, (404) 446	San Gabriel, Milam 70
Rosalie, Red River 100	Sagerton, Haskell 171	*SANGER, Denton, 443,
*Rosanky, Bastrop, 19 210	*SAGINAW, Tarrant, 159,	(4,534) 5,198
*ROSCOE, Nolan, 80,	(12,374) 15,408	*San Isidro, Starr, 13, (270) 277
(1,378) 1,312	St. Elmo, Freestone . . . . NA	San Jose, Duval 15
*ROSEBUD, Falls, 94,	St. Francis, Potter 30	*SAN JUAN, Hidalgo, 435,
(1,493) 1,426	*ST. HEDWIG, Bexar, 96,	(26,229) 29,998
ROSE CITY, Orange, 19,	(1,875) 1,931	SAN LEANNA, Travis, (384) 423
(519) 499	*SAINT JO, Montague, 64,	*San Leon, Galveston, (4,365) . . 4,572
Rose Hill, Harris 3,500	(977) 999	*San Manuel-Linn, Hidalgo,
Rose Hill, San Jacinto 30	St. John Colony, Caldwell 150	(958) 971
ROSE HILL ACRES, Hardin,	St. Lawrence, Glasscock 35	*SAN MARCOS, Hays-Caldwell,
(480) 483	St. Mary's Colony, Bastrop . . . . . . NA	1,983, (34,733) 42,102
*ROSENBERG, Fort Bend, 1,139,	ST. PAUL, Collin, 19, (630) 729	SAN PATRICIO, San Patricio-Nueces,
(24,043) 28,190	St. Paul, San Patricio, (542) 530	(318) 314
Rosevine, Sabine 50	*SALADO, Bell, 388,	San Pedro, Cameron, (668) 711
Rosewood, Upshur 100	(3,475) 3,490	*SAN PERLITA, Willacy, 4,
*Rosharon, Brazoria, 322 . . . . NA	Salem, Cherokee 20	(680) 708
Rosita, Duval 25	Salem, Grimes 54	San Roman, Starr 5
Rosita North, Maverick,	Salem, Newton 85	*SAN SABA, San Saba, 245,
(3,400) 3,557	Salesville, Palo Pinto 88	(2,637) 2,593
Rosita South, Maverick,	Saline, Menard 70	SANSOM PARK, Tarrant, 55,
(2,574) 2,669	*Salineño, Starr, 2, (304) 312	(4,181) 4,294
*ROSS, McLennan, 9, (228) 238	Salmon, Anderson 20	*SANTA ANNA, Coleman, 75,
*ROSSER, Kaufman, 11,	Salt Flat, Hudspeth, 9 35	(1,081) 1,061
(379) 421	Salt Gap, McCulloch 25	Santa Anna, Starr 20
*Rosston, Cooke, 11 75	*Saltillo, Hopkins, 26 200	Santa Catarina, Starr 15
Rossville, Atascosa 200	Samaria, Navarro 90	Santa Clara, Guadalupe, (889) 935

CITIES & TOWNS

Town, County . . . . Pop. 2004	Town, County . . . . Pop. 2004	Town, County . . . . Pop. 2004
Santa Cruz, Starr, (630) 662	SELMA, Bexar-Guadalupe-Comal,	*Sierra Blanca, Hudspeth, 27,
*Santa Elena, Starr 64	149, (788) 1,791	(533) 554
*SANTA FE, Galveston, 596,	*Selman City [Turnertown-], Rusk,	Siesta Shores, Zapata, (890) 1,042
(9,548) 10,294	12 271	Silas, Shelby 75
*Santa Maria, Cameron, 6,	*SEMINOLE, Gaines, 423,	Siloam, Bowie 50
(846) 914	(5,910) 5,866	*SILSBEE, Hardin, 573,
Santa Monica, Willacy, (78) 77	Sempronius, Austin 25	(6,393) 6,336
*SANTA ROSA, Cameron, 44,	Senior, Bexar . . . . NA	*Silver, Coke, 2 34
(2,833) 3,037	Serbin, Lee 109	Silver City, Milam 25
*Santo, Palo Pinto, 47 445	Serenada, Williamson,	Silver City, Navarro 100
*San Ygnacio, Zapata, 11,	(1,847) 1,832	Silver City, Red River 25
(853) 980	Seth Ward, Hale, (1,926) 2,014	Silver Creek Village, Burnet 300
*Saragosa, Reeves, 3 185	SEVEN OAKS, Polk, 5, (131) 143	Silver Lake, Van Zandt 42
*Saratoga, Hardin, 16 1,000	Seven Pines, Gregg-Upshur 50	Silver Pines, Smith . . . . NA
Sarco, Goliad 78	*SEVEN POINTS, Henderson, 85,	*SILVERTON, Briscoe, 68,
Sardis, Ellis 60	(1,145) 1,205	(771) 847
*Sargent, Matagorda 900	Seven Sisters, Duval 60	Silver Valley, Coleman 20
*Sarita, Kenedy, 4 250	Sexton, Sabine 29	Simmons, Live Oak 65
Saron, Trinity 5	Seymore, Hopkins . . . . NA	*Simms, Bowie, 33 240
Saspamco, Wilson 443	*SEYMOUR, Baylor, 222,	Simms, Deaf Smith 10
*Satin, Falls, 5 86	(2,908) 2,873	*SIMONTON, Fort Bend, 56,
Sattler, Comal 30	Shady Grove, Burnet 114	(718) 807
Saturn, Gonzales 15	Shady Grove, Cherokee 30	Simpsonville, Matagorda 6
Sauney Stand, Washington . . . . . . NA	Shady Grove, Houston 83	Simpsonville, Upshur 100
*SAVOY, Fannin, 56, (850) 841	Shady Grove, Panola . . . . NA	Sims, Brazos . . . . NA
Sayers, Bexar . . . . NA	Shady Grove, Smith 250	Simsboro, Freestone . . . . NA
Sayersville, Bastrop . . . . NA	Shady Grove, Upshur 40	Sinclair City, Smith . . . . NA
Scatter Branch, Hunt . . . . NA	Shady Hollow, Travis, (5,140) . . . 4,927	Singleton, Grimes 47
Scenic Hills, Guadalupe 400	Shady Oaks, Henderson 300	*SINTON, San Patricio, 307,
Scenic Oaks, Bexar,	SHADY SHORES, Denton, 26,	(5,676) 5,586
(3,279) 3,290	(1,461) 1,766	Sipe Springs, Comanche 70
Schattel, Frio 30	Shafter, Presidio 57	*Sisterdale, Kendall, 6 63
*SCHERTZ, Guadalupe-Comal-Bexar,	*SHALLOWATER, Lubbock,	Sivells Bend, Cooke 36
774, (18,694) 24,336	166, (2,086) 2,115	Sixmile, Calhoun 300
Schicke Point, Calhoun 70	*SHAMROCK, Wheeler, 179,	Skeeterville, San Saba 10
School Hill, Erath 22	(2,029) 1,787	*SKELLYTOWN, Carson, 26,
Schroeder, Goliad 347	Shangri La, Burnet 108	(610) 585
*SCHULENBURG, Fayette, 277,	Shankleville, Newton . . . . NA	*Skidmore, Bee, 30, (1,013) 988
(2,699) 2,808	Shannon, Clay 20	Slate Shoals, Lamar 10
Schumansville, Guadalupe 678	Sharp, Milam 52	*SLATON, Lubbock, 269,
Schwab City, Polk 120	SHAVANO PARK, Bexar, 9,	(6,109) 6,323
*Schwertner, Williamson, 5 175	(1,754) 2,745	Slayden, Gonzales 10
Science Hall, Jasper . . . . NA	Shawnee Prairie, Angelina 20	Slide, Lubbock 44
Scissors, Hidalgo, (2,805) 3,017	Shaws Bend, Colorado 100	*Slidell, Wise, 8 175
*SCOTLAND, Archer, 22,	*Sheffield, Pecos, 16 322	Sloan, San Saba 30
(438) 468	Shelby, Austin 300	Slocum, Anderson 250
*SCOTTSVILLE, Harrison, 8,	*Shelbyville, Shelby, 51 600	Smetana, Brazos 80
(263) 267	Sheldon, Harris, (1,831) 1,847	*SMILEY, Gonzales, 29,
Scranton, Eastland 40	SHENANDOAH, Montgomery,	(453) 478
*Scroggins, Franklin, 60 125	106, (1,503) 1,600	Smithland, Marion-Cass 179
*SCURRY, Kaufman, 110 315	Shep, Taylor 60	Smith Point, Chambers 180
*SEABROOK, Harris, 971,	*SHEPHERD, San Jacinto, 137,	Smiths Bend, Bosque . . . . NA
(9,443) 10,803	(2,029) 2,151	Smithson Valley, Comal . . . . NA
*SEADRIFT, Calhoun, 50,	*Sheridan, Colorado, 13 225	*SMITHVILLE, Bastrop, 324,
(1,352) 1,386	*SHERMAN, Grayson, 1,931,	(3,901) 4,281
*SEAGOVILLE, Dallas, 529,	(35,082) 36,512	Smithwick, Burnet 102
(10,823) 11,100	Sherry, Red River 15	*SMYER, Hockley, 25, (480) 480
*SEAGRAVES, Gaines, 87,	Sherwood, Irion 170	Smyrna, Cass 215
(2,334) 2,428	Sherwood Shores, Bell 774	Smyrna, Rains 25
Seale, Robertson 60	Sherwood Shores, Burnet 920	*SNOOK, Burleson, 33,
*SEALY, Austin, 503,	Sherwood Shores, Grayson 1,590	(568) 569
(5,248) 5,849	Shields, Coleman 13	Snow Hill, Collin 23
Seaton, Bell 60	Shiloh, Bastrop . . . . NA	Snow Hill, Upshur 75
Seawillow, Caldwell 100	Shiloh, Leon . . . . NA	Snug Harbor, Brazoria 193
*Sebastian, Willacy, 14,	Shiloh, Limestone 250	*SNYDER, Scurry, 574,
(1,864) 1,875	*SHINER, Lavaca, 191,	(10,783) 10,681
Sebastopol, Trinity 120	(2,070) 2,050	*SOCORRO, El Paso, 202,
Seco Mines, Maverick 692	Shirley, Hopkins . . . . NA	(27,152) 28,857
Security, Montgomery 24	*Shiro, Grimes, 7 210	Soldier Mound, Dickens 10
Sedalia, Collin 24	Shive, Hamilton 60	Solis, Cameron, (545) 567
Segno, Polk 80	SHOREACRES, Harris,	Solms, Comal 40
Segovia, Kimble 12	(1,488) 1,535	*SOMERSET, Bexar, 67,
*SEGUIN, Guadalupe, 1,609,	Short, Shelby 15	(1,550) 1,688
(22,011) 24,532	Shovel Mountain, Burnet 148	*SOMERVILLE, Burleson, 111,
Sejita, Duval 22	*Sidney, Comanche, 26 148	(1,704) 1,704
Selden, Erath 7	Sienna Plantation, Fort Bend,	Sommer's Mill, Bell 27
Selfs, Fannin 30	(1,896) 2,101	*SONORA, Sutton, 227,

Town, County	Pop. 2004
(2,924)	2,938
*SOUR LAKE, Hardin, 188,	
(1,667)	1,709
South Alamo, Hidalgo,	
(3,101)	3,248
*South Bend, Young, 4	140
South Bosque, McLennan	500
South Brice, Hall	10
Southdown, Brazoria	2,427
South Fork Estates, Jim Hogg,	
(47)	45
South Franklin, Franklin	30
*SOUTH HOUSTON, Harris,	
655, (15,833)	16,187
*SOUTHLAKE, Tarrant-Denton,	
920, (21,519)	24,160
Southland, Garza, 2	157
South La Paloma [Alfred-],	
Jim Wells, (451)	453
*SOUTHMAYD, Grayson, 12,	
(992)	1,060
SOUTH MOUNTAIN, Coryell,	
(412)	405
*SOUTH PADRE ISLAND, Cameron,	
351, (2,422)	2,612
*South Plains, Floyd, 3	67
South Point, Cameron,	
(1,118)	1,224
South Purmela, Coryell	10
Southridge Estates, Guadalupe	146
South Shore, Bell	80
SOUTHSIDE PLACE, Harris, 35,	
(1,547)	1,601
South Sulphur, Hunt	60
South Texarkana, Bowie	370
South Toledo Bend, Newton,	
(576)	532
Southton, Bexar	113
*Spade, Lamb, 6, (100)	100
Spanish Fort, Montague	50
Sparenberg, Dawson	20
Sparks, Bell	40
Sparks, El Paso, (2,974)	3,151
Speaks, Lavaca	60
*SPEARMAN, Hansford, 277,	
(3,021)	2,984
Specht Store, Bexar	20
Speegleville, McLennan	111
*Spicewood, Burnet, 428	2,000
Spicewood Springs, Travis	NA
Spider Mountain, Burnet	92
Spiller's Store, Leon	NA
*SPLENDORA, Montgomery,	
270, (1,275)	1,419
SPOFFORD, Kinney, 1, (75)	78
Spraberry, Midland	46
*Spring, Harris, 9,110,	
(36,385)	36,501
*Spring Branch, Comal, 341	NA
Spring Branch, Smith	NA
Spring Creek, Hutchinson	139
Spring Creek, San Saba	20
Springdale, Cass	55
Springfield, Anderson	30
Spring Garden-Tierra Verde,	
Nueces, (693)	678
Spring Hill, Bowie	209
Spring Hill, Navarro	60
Spring Hill, San Jacinto	38
*SPRINGLAKE, Lamb, 45,	
(135)	137
*SPRINGTOWN, Parker, 449,	
(2,062)	2,369
SPRING VALLEY, Harris, 84,	
(3,611)	3,554
Spring Valley, McLennan	400
Spring Valley, Travis	NA

Town, County	Pop. 2004
Sprinkle, Travis	NA
*SPUR, Dickens, 90, (1,088)	1,030
*Spurger, Tyler, 27	590
Stacy, McCulloch	20
Staff, Eastland	65
*STAFFORD, Fort Bend-Harris,	
2,048, (15,681)	18,634
Stag Creek, Comanche	45
STAGECOACH, Montgomery, 5,	
(455)	512
Stairtown, Caldwell	35
Staley, San Jacinto	55
*STAMFORD, Jones-Haskell,	
177, (3,636)	3,514
Stampede, Bell	6
Stamps, Upshur	45
Stanfield, Clay	10
*STANTON, Martin, 152,	
(2,556)	2,527
*Staples, Guadalupe, 10	396
*Star,Mills, 6	85
STAR HARBOR, Henderson, 1,	
(416)	432
Star Route, Cochran	15
Starrville, Smith	75
Startzville, Comal	30
State Line, Culberson	18
Steele Hill, Dickens	4
Steep Creek, San Augustine	NA
Steiner, Bosque	20
Stephens Creek, San Jacinto	385
*STEPHENVILLE, Erath, 965,	
(14,921)	14,995
Sterley, Floyd	31
*STERLING CITY, Sterling, 60,	
(1,081)	1,064
Sterrett, Ellis	30
Stewards Mill, Freestone	22
Stewart, Rusk	15
Stiles, Reagan	4
Stillwell Crossing, Brewster	2
*STINNETT, Hutchinson, 71,	
(1,936)	1,843
Stith, Jones	50
*STOCKDALE, Wilson, 129,	
(1,398)	1,432
Stockholm, Hidalgo	50
Stockman, Shelby	55
Stoneburg, Montague	51
Stone City, Brazos	NA
Stoneham, Grimes	15
Stone Point, Van Zandt	32
*Stonewall, Gillespie, 44,	
(469)	499
Stony, Denton	25
Stout, Wood	86
*Stowell, Chambers, 19,	
(1,572)	1,588
Stranger, Falls	27
*STRATFORD, Sherman, 151,	
(1,991)	2,025
Stratton, DeWitt	25
*STRAWN, Palo Pinto, 51,	
(739)	719
Streeter, Mason, 1	85
*STREETMAN, Freestone,	
70, (203)	207
String Prairie, Bastrop	125
Stringtown, Newton	NA
Structure, Williamson	50
Stuart Place, Cameron	990
Stubblefield, Houston	15
Stubbs, Kaufman	NA
*Study Butte-Terlingua, Brewster,	
36, (267)	280
Sturgeon, Cooke	10
Styx, Kaufman	NA

Town, County	Pop. 2004
*Sublime, Lavaca	75
*SUDAN, Lamb, 89, (1,039)	1,042
Sugar Hill, Titus	150
*SUGAR LAND, Fort Bend, 5,160,	
(63,328)	74,079
Sugar Mill, Brazoria	523
Sugar Valley, Matagorda	47
*SULLIVAN CITY, Hidalgo, 28,	
(3,998)	4,307
*Sulphur Bluff, Hopkins, 8	280
*SULPHUR SPRINGS, Hopkins,	
1,096, (14,551)	14,690
Summerfield, Castro, 6	48
Summerville, Gonzales	40
*Sumner, Lamar, 59	95
*SUNDOWN, Hockley, 50,	
(1,505)	1,491
Sunnyside, Castro	64
Sunnyside, Waller	120
Sunnyside, Wilson	300
SUNNYVALE, Dallas, 127,	
(2,693)	3,608
*SUNRAY, Moore, 89,	
(1,950)	1,955
Sunrise, Falls	845
*SUNRISE BEACH, Llano, 15,	
(704)	756
*SUNSET, Montague, 32,	
(339)	350
Sunset Oaks, Burnet	198
SUNSET VALLEY, Travis, 65,	
(365)	462
SUN VALLEY, Lamar, 4, (51)	53
SURFSIDE BEACH, Brazoria,	
22, (763)	791
*Sutherland Springs, Wilson, 18	362
Swamp City, Gregg	8
Swan, Smith	150
Swearingen, Collingsworth	NA
*SWEENY, Brazoria, 205,	
(3,624)	3,703
Sweet Home, Guadalupe	294
*Sweet Home, Lavaca, 11	360
Sweet Home, Lee	30
Sweet Union, Cherokee	40
*SWEETWATER, Nolan, 566,	
(11,415)	10,859
Swenson, Stonewall	80
Swift, Nacogdoches	210
Swiss Alp, Fayette	17
Sylvan, Lamar	68
*Sylvester, Fisher, 10	79

T

Tabor, Brazos	150
Tadmor, Houston	67
*TAFT, San Patricio, 168,	
(3,396)	3,420
Taft Southwest, San Patricio,	
(1,721)	1,643
*TAHOKA, Lynn, 132,	
(2,910)	2,857
*TALCO, Titus, 45, (570)	574
*Talpa, Coleman, 15	127
TALTY, Kaufman, 1, (1,028)	1,188
Tamina, Montgomery	NA
Tanglewood, Lee	60
Tarkington Prairie, Liberty	NA
*Tarpley, Bandera, 9	30
*Tarzan, Martin, 22	30
Tascosa Hills, Potter	90
*TATUM, Rusk-Panola, 92,	
(1,175)	1,165
*TAYLOR, Williamson, 625,	
(13,575)	13,944
TAYLOR LAKE VILLAGE, Harris,	
27, (3,694)	3,666

Town, County	Pop. 2004
Taylorsville, Caldwell	20
Taylor Town, Lamar	40
Tazewell, Hopkins	NA
*TEAGUE, Freestone, 160, (4,557)	4,885
Teaselville, Smith	150
*TEHUACANA, Limestone, 12, (307)	312
*Telegraph, Kimble, 2	3
*Telephone, Fannin, 22	210
*Telferner, Victoria, 16	700
Telico, Ellis	115
*Tell, Childress, 6	15
*TEMPLE, Bell, 2,488, (54,514)	55,784
*TENAHA, Shelby, 64, (1,046)	1,072
Tenmile, Dawson	30
*Tennessee Colony, Anderson, 29	300
*Tennyson, Coke, 3	46
*Terlingua [Study Butte-], Brewster, 36, (267)	280
*TERRELL, Kaufman, 1,064, (13,606)	15,640
TERRELL HILLS, Bexar, 35, (5,019)	5,034
Terry Chapel, Falls	30
Terryville, DeWitt	40
*TEXARKANA, Bowie, (Miller, Ark.), 2,672, (61,230)	62,468
*TEXAS CITY, Galveston, 1,283, (41,512)	42,441
TEXHOMA, Sherman, (371)	378
*TEXLINE, Dallam, 64, (511)	520
Thalia, Foard	50
*THE COLONY, Denton, 519, (26,531)	36,038
Thedford, Smith	65
The Divide, Kerr	250
The Grove, Coryell	100
THE HILLS, Travis, (1,492)	1,607
Thelma, Bexar	45
Thelma, Limestone	20
Theon, Williamson	30
Thermo, Hopkins	56
*The Woodlands, Montgomery, 857, (55,649)	61,187
*Thicket, Hardin, 5	306
*Thomaston, DeWitt, 3	45
*THOMPSONS, Fort Bend, 4, (236)	265
Thompsonville, Gonzales	30
Thompsonville, Jim Hogg	55
Thornberry, Clay	75
*THORNDALE, Milam, 118, (1,278)	1,349
*THORNTON, Limestone, 29, (525)	540
THORNTONVILLE, Ward, (442)	394
Thorp Spring, Hood	222
*THRALL, Williamson, 32, (710)	826
Three Oaks, Wilson	150
*THREE RIVERS, Live Oak, 115, (1,878)	1,845
Three States, Cass	45
*THROCKMORTON, Throckmorton, 88, (905)	812
Thurber, Erath	8
Tidwell, Hunt	NA
Tierra Bonita, Cameron, (160)	168
Tierra Grande, Nueces, (362)	362
Tierra Verde [Spring Garden-], Nueces, (693)	678

Town, County	Pop. 2004
Tigertown, Lamar	400
TIKI ISLAND VILLAGE, Galveston, 18, (1,016)	1,105
*Tilden, McMullen, 28	300
Tilmon, Caldwell	117
TIMBERCREEK CANYON, Randall, (406)	443
Timberwood, Bexar, (5,889)	6,115
Timesville, Leon	NA
*TIMPSON, Shelby, 110, (1,094)	1,083
Tin Top, Parker	500
*TIOGA, Grayson, 66, (754)	833
TIRA, Hopkins, (248)	248
*Tivoli, Refugio, 25	550
TOCO, Lamar, 2, (89)	87
Todd City, Anderson	10
TODD MISSION, Grimes, 11, (146)	166
Tokio, McLennan	250
*Tokio, Terry, 4	5
*TOLAR, Hood, 95, (504)	640
Tolbert, Wilbarger	15
Tolette, Lamar	40
Tolosa, Kaufman	58
*TOMBALL, Harris, 2,148, (9,089)	9,955
*TOM BEAN, Grayson, 39, (941)	984
Tomlinson Hill, Falls	64
TOOL, Henderson, 21, (2,275)	2,334
Topsey, Coryell	35
*Tornillo, El Paso, 19 ,(1,609)	1,624
Tours, McLennan	100
*Tow, Llano, 37	305
Tower Lake, Wilson	100
Town Bluff, Tyler	429
*TOYAH, Reeves, 4, (100)	95
*Toyahvale, Reeves, 2	60
Tradewinds, San Patricio, (163)	166
Travis, Falls	48
Trawick, Nacogdoches	375
Treasure Island, Guadalupe	172
*TRENT, Taylor, 25, (318)	297
*TRENTON, Fannin, 64, (662)	666
Trickham, Coleman	12
Trimmier, Bell	390
*TRINIDAD, Henderson, 78, (1,091)	1,092
*TRINITY, Trinity, 278, (2,721)	2,724
TROPHY CLUB, Denton, 90, (6,350)	7,513
*TROUP, Smith-Cherokee, 231, (1,949)	2,101
Trout Creek, Newton	NA
*TROY, Bell, 123, (1,378)	1,357
Truby, Jones	26
Trumbull, Ellis	100
Truscott, Knox, 3	50
Tucker, Anderson	304
*Tuleta, Bee, 13, (292)	285
*TULIA, Swisher, 288, (5,117)	4,772
Tulip, Fannin	10
Tulsita, Bee, (20)	19
Tundra, Van Zandt	34
Tunis, Burleson	150
Tupelo, Navarro	NA
*TURKEY, Hall, 31, (494)	519
Turlington, Freestone	27
Turnersville, Coryell	125
Turnersville, Travis	90
*Turnertown-Selman City, Rusk,	

Town, County	Pop. 2004
12	271
Turtle Bayou, Chambers	42
Turtle Cove, Brazoria	50
*TUSCOLA, Taylor, 105, (714)	718
Tuxedo, Jones	42
Twitty, Wheeler	12
*TYE, Taylor, 38, (1,158)	1,178
*TYLER, Smith, 6,324, (83,650)	90,079
*Tynan, Bee, 14, (301)	301
Type, Williamson	40

U

UHLAND, Hays, Caldwell, 8, (386)	437
*Umbarger, Randall, 16	327
UNCERTAIN, Harrison, 8, (150)	159
Union, Brazos	NA
Union, Scurry	20
Union, Terry	8
Union, Wilson	22
Union Center, Eastland	NA
Union Grove, Bell	12
Union Grove, Erath	12
UNION GROVE, Upshur, 4, (346)	345
Union High, Navarro	30
Union Valley, Hunt	25
Unity, Lamar	60
*UNIVERSAL CITY, Bexar, 565, (14,849)	15,317
UNIVERSITY PARK, Dallas, 314, (23,324)	22,529
Upper Meyersville, DeWitt	33
Upshaw, Nacogdoches	400
Upton, Bastrop	25
Urbana, San Jacinto	25
Utley, Bastrop	30
*Utopia, Uvalde, 80, (241)	237
*UVALDE, Uvalde, 759, (14,929)	15,404
Uvalde Estates, Uvalde, (1,972)	2,107

V

Valdasta, Collin	82
*VALENTINE, Jeff Davis, 4, (187)	180
*Valera, Coleman, 6	80
Valley Creek, Fannin	12
Valley Hi, Bexar	3,000
*VALLEY MILLS, Bosque-McLennan, 125, (1,123)	1,171
*Valley Spring, Llano, 8	50
*VALLEY VIEW, Cooke, 166, (737)	771
Valley View, Runnels	10
Valley View, Upshur	75
Valley View, Wichita	210
Valley Wells, Dimmit	21
Val Verde, Milam	25
Val Verde Park, Val Verde, (1,945)	2,033
*VAN, Van Zandt, 172, (2,362)	2,497
*VAN ALSTYNE, Grayson, 237, (2,502)	2,580
Vance, Real	20
*Vancourt, Tom Green, 8	131
Vandalia, Red River	35
*Vanderbilt, Jackson, 10, (411)	419
*Vanderpool, Bandera, 4	20
Vandyke, Comanche	20
*VAN HORN, Culberson, 98, (2,435)	2,232

Town, County	Pop. 2004
*Whitharral, Hockley, 7	158
Whitman, Washington	25
*WHITNEY, Hill, 354, (1,833)	1,889
*Whitsett, Live Oak, 6	200
Whitson, Coryell	50
*Whitt, Parker, 5	38
Whitton, Van Zandt	NA
Whon, Coleman	15
*WICHITA FALLS, Wichita, 4,627, (104,197)	103,262
Wicker, Brazos	NA
*WICKETT, Ward, 16, (455)	406
Wied, Lavaca	65
Wiedeville, Washington	NA
Wieland, Hunt	NA
*Wiergate, Newton, 6	461
Wigginsville, Montgomery	NA
Wilcox, Burleson	39
Wilderville, Falls	45
*Wildorado,Oldham, 30	210
Wild Peach, Brazoria, (2,498)	2,523
Wildwood, Hardin	499
Wilkins, Upshur	75
Willamar, Willacy, (15)	17
William Penn, Washington	100
Williamsburg, Lavaca	65
Williamson Settlement, Orange	175
*WILLIS, Montgomery, 853, (3,985)	4,678
*Willow City, Gillespie, 11	22
Willow Grove, McLennan	100
WILLOW PARK, Parker, (2,849)	3,089

Town, County	Pop. 2004
Willow Springs, Fayette	74
Willow Springs, Rains	50
*WILLS POINT, Van Zandt, 416, (3,496)	3,646
*WILMER, Dallas, 71, (3,393)	3,678
Wilmeth, Runnels	15
Wilson, Falls	42
*WILSON, Lynn, 44, (532)	520
*WIMBERLEY, Hays, 819, (3,797)	4,225
Winchell, Brown	20
*Winchester, Fayette, 6	232
WINDCREST, Bexar, 110, (5,105)	5,108
Windemere, Travis, (6,868)	6,462
*WINDOM, Fannin, 18, (245)	241
*WINDTHORST, Archer, 72, (440)	474
Winedale, Fayette	67
*WINFIELD, Titus, 20, (499)	527
WINFREE [Old River-], Chambers, 10, (1,364)	1,485
*Wingate, Runnels, 17	100
*WINK, Winkler, 21, (919)	834
Winkler, Navarro-Freestone	26
*Winnie, Chambers, 257, (2,914)	2,983
*WINNSBORO, Wood-Franklin, 505 (3,584)	3,808
*WINONA, Smith, 105, (582)	622
Winter Haven, Dimmit	123
*WINTERS, Runnels, 160, (2,880)	2,783
Wise, Van Zandt	29

Town, County	Pop. 2004
Witting, Lavaca	90
WIXON VALLEY, Brazos, 3, (235)	229
Wizard Wells, Jack	69
*Woden, Nacogdoches, 10	400
*WOLFE CITY, Hunt, 95, (1,566)	1,595
*WOLFFORTH, Lubbock, 199, (2,554)	2,705
Womack, Bosque	25
Wonderland Forest, San Jacinto	40
Woodbine, Cooke	250
WOODBRANCH, Montgomery, (1,305)	1,376
Woodbury, Hill	45
WOODCREEK, Hays, 5, (1,274)	1,384
Wooded Hills, Johnson	310
Wood Hi, Victoria	35
*Woodlake, Trinity, 4	98
Woodland, Red River	128
*Woodlawn, Harrison, 8	370
WOODLOCH, Montgomery, (247)	260
Woodridge, Orange	1,000
Woodrow, Lubbock	85
Woods, Panola	65
*WOODSBORO, Refugio, 67, (1,685)	1,603
*WOODSON, Throckmorton, 23, (296)	259
Wood Springs, Smith	200
Woodville, Cherokee	20
*WOODVILLE, Tyler, 326, (2,415)	2,394
Woodward, La Salle	10
WOODWAY, McLennan, 200, (8,733)	8,562
Woosley, Rains	47
*WORTHAM, Freestone, 46, (1,082)	1,148
Worthing, Lavaca	55
Wright City, Smith	172
*Wrightsboro, Gonzales, 2	10
Wyldwood, Bastrop, (2,310)	2,573
*WYLIE, Collin-Rockwall-Dallas, 1,094, (15,132)	23,029
Wynne, Van Zandt	175

Y

Town, County	Pop. 2004
*Yancey, Medina, 16	209
*YANTIS, Wood, 147, (321)	357
Yard, Anderson	18
Yarrellton, Milam	35
Yellowpine, Sabine	97
*YOAKUM, Lavaca-DeWitt, 382, (5,731)	5,832
*YORKTOWN, DeWitt, 205, (2,271)	2,307
Young, Freestone	27
Youngsport, Bell	49
Yowell, Delta-Hunt	30
*Ysleta del Sur Pueblo, El Paso	421
Yznaga, Cameron, (103)	111

Z

Town, County	Pop. 2004
Zabcikville, Bell	76
*Zapata, Zapata, 298, (4,856)	5,502
Zapata Ranch, Willacy, (88)	87
*ZAVALLA, Angelina, 63, (647)	665
*Zephyr, Brown, 27	201
Zimmerscheidt, Colorado	50
Zion Hill, Guadalupe	595
Zipperlandville, Falls	22
Zorn, Guadalupe	287
Zuehl, Guadalupe, (346)	358
Zunkerville, Karnes	15

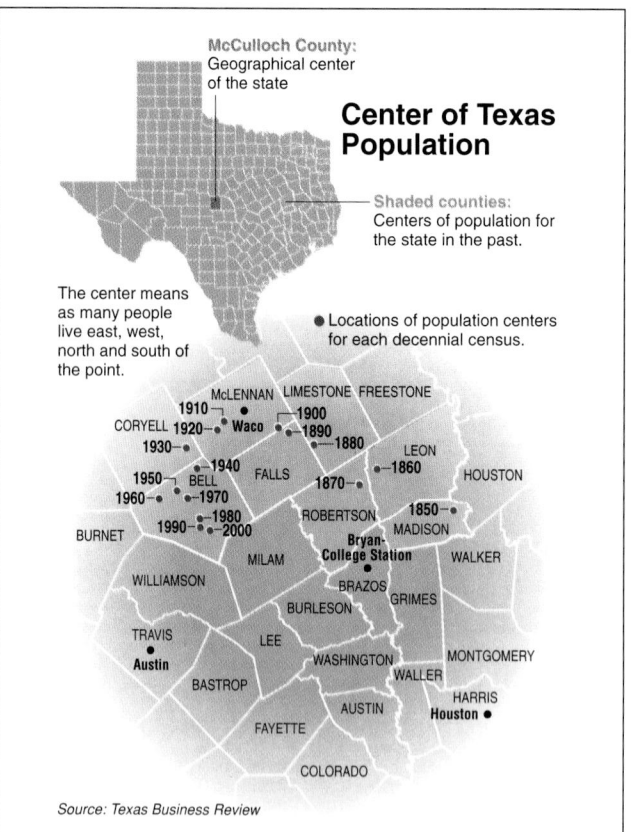

McCulloch County: Geographical center of the state

Center of Texas Population

Shaded counties: Centers of population for the state in the past.

The center means as many people live east, west, north and south of the point.

● Locations of population centers for each decennial census.

Source: Texas Business Review

CITIES & TOWNS

Population History of Texas' Counties from 1850–2000

The population of each county for each United States census beginning with 1850, or the first census after date of organization for counties organized after 1850, is given below.

County	1850	1860	1870	1880	1890	1900	1910	1920	1930	1940	1950	1960	1970	1980	1990	2000
Anderson	2,684	10,398	9,229	17,395	20,923	28,015	29,650	34,318	34,643	37,092	31,875	28,162	27,789	38,381	48,024	55,109
Andrews					24	87	975	350	736	1,277	5,002	13,450	10,372	13,323	14,338	13,004
Angelina	1,165	4,271	3,985	5,239	6,306	13,481	17,705	22,287	27,803	32,201	36,032	39,814	49,349	64,172	69,884	80,130
Aransas				966	1,824	1,716	2,106	2,064	2,219	3,469	4,252	7,006	8,902	14,260	17,892	22,497
Archer				596	2,101	2,508	6,525	5,254	9,684	7,599	6,816	6,110	5,759	7,266	7,973	8,854
Armstrong				31	944	1,205	2,682	2,816	3,329	2,495	2,215	1,966	1,895	1,994	2,021	2,148
Atascosa		1,578	2,915	4,217	6,459	7,143	10,004	12,702	15,654	19,275	20,048	18,828	18,696	25,055	30,533	38,628
Austin	3,841	10,139	15,087	14,429	17,859	20,676	17,699	18,874	18,860	17,384	14,663	13,777	13,831	17,726	19,832	23,590
Bailey [1]						4	312	517	5,186	6,318	7,592	9,090	8,487	8,168	7,064	6,594
Bandera [1]		399	649	2,158	3,795	5,332	4,921	4,001	3,784	4,234	4,410	3,892	4,747	7,084	10,562	17,645
Bastrop	3,099	7,006	12,290	17,215	20,736	26,845	25,344	26,649	23,888	21,610	19,622	16,925	17,297	24,726	38,263	57,733
Baylor				715	2,595	3,052	8,411	7,027	7,418	7,755	6,875	5,893	5,221	4,919	4,385	4,093
Bee		910	1,082	2,298	3,720	7,220	12,090	12,137	15,721	16,481	18,174	23,755	22,737	26,030	25,135	32,359
Bell		4,799	9,771	20,518	33,377	45,535	49,186	46,412	50,030	44,863	73,824	94,097	124,483	157,889	191,088	237,974
Bexar	6,052	14,454	16,043	30,470	49,266	69,422	119,676	202,096	292,533	338,176	500,460	687,151	830,460	988,800	1,185,394	1,392,931
Bexar Dist. [2]			1,077													
Blanco		1,281	1,187	3,583	4,649	4,703	4,311	4,063	3,842	4,264	3,780	3,657	3,567	4,681	5,972	8,418
Borden				35	222	776	1,386	965	1,505	1,396	1,106	1,076	888	859	799	729
Bosque		2,005	4,981	11,217	14,224	17,390	19,013	18,032	15,750	15,761	11,836	10,809	10,966	13,401	15,125	17,204
Bowie		5,052	4,684	10,965	20,267	26,676	34,827	39,472	48,563	50,208	61,966	59,971	67,813	75,301	81,665	89,306
Brazoria	4,841	7,143	7,527	9,774	11,506	14,861	13,299	20,614	23,054	27,069	46,549	76,204	108,312	169,587	191,707	241,767
Brazos	614	2,776	9,205	13,576	16,650	18,859	18,919	21,975	21,835	26,977	38,390	44,895	57,978	93,588	121,862	152,415
Brewster [3]					710	2,356	5,220	4,822	6,624	6,478	7,309	6,434	7,780	7,573	8,681	8,866
Briscoe [5]				12		1,253	2,162	2,948	5,590	4,056	3,528	3,577	2,794	2,579	1,971	1,790
Brooks [49]								4,560	5,901	6,362	9,195	8,609	8,005	8,428	8,204	7,976
Brown [6]		244	544	8,414	11,421	16,019	22,935	21,682	26,382	25,924	28,607	24,728	25,877	33,057	34,371	37,674
Buchanan [7]																
Buchel [8]																
Burleson	1,713	5,683	8,072	9,243	13,001	18,367	18,687	16,855	19,848	18,334	13,000	11,177	9,999	12,313	13,625	16,470
Burnet		2,487	3,688	6,855	10,747	10,528	10,755	9,499	10,355	10,771	10,356	9,265	11,420	17,803	22,677	34,147
Caldwell	1,329	4,481	6,572	11,757	15,769	21,765	24,237	25,160	31,397	24,893	19,350	17,222	21,178	23,637	26,392	32,194
Calhoun	1,110	2,642	3,443	1,739	815	2,395	3,635	4,700	5,385	5,911	9,222	16,592	17,831	19,574	19,053	20,647
Callahan				3,453	5,457	8,768	12,973	11,844	12,785	11,568	9,087	7,929	8,205	10,992	11,859	12,905
Cameron [9] [50]	8,541	6,028	10,999	14,959	14,424	16,095	27,158	36,662	77,540	83,202	125,170	151,098	140,368	209,680	260,120	335,227
Camp				5,951	6,624	9,146	9,551	11,103	10,063	10,285	8,740	7,849	8,005	9,275	9,904	11,549
Carson					356	469	2,127	3,078	7,745	6,624	6,852	7,781	6,358	6,672	6,576	6,516
Cass [10]	4,991	8,411	8,875	16,724	22,554	22,841	27,587	30,041	30,030	33,496	26,732	23,496	24,133	29,430	29,982	30,438
Castro					9	400	1,850	1,948	4,720	4,631	5,417	8,923	10,394	10,556	9,070	8,285
Chambers		1,508	1,503	2,187	2,241	3,046	4,234	4,162	5,710	7,511	7,871	10,379	12,187	18,538	20,088	26,031
Cherokee	6,673	12,098	11,079	16,723	22,975	25,154	29,038	37,633	43,180	43,970	38,694	33,120	32,008	38,127	41,049	46,659
Childress [11]				25	1,175	2,138	9,538	10,933	16,044	12,149	12,123	8,421	6,605	6,950	5,953	7,688
Clay [51]		109		5,045	7,503	9,231	17,043	16,864	14,545	12,524	9,896	8,351	8,079	9,582	10,024	11,006
Cochran						25	65	67	1,963	3,735	5,928	6,417	5,326	4,825	4,377	3,730
Coke [12]					2,059	3,430	6,412	4,557	5,253	4,590	4,045	3,589	3,087	3,196	3,424	3,864
Coleman			347	3,603	6,112	10,077	22,618	18,805	23,669	20,571	15,503	12,458	10,288	10,439	9,710	9,235
Collin	1,950	9,264	14,013	25,983	36,736	50,087	49,021	49,609	46,180	47,190	41,692	41,247	66,920	144,490	264,036	491,675

County	1850	1860	1870	1880	1890	1900	1910	1920	1930	1940	1950	1960	1970	1980	1990	2000
Collingsworth 11				6	357	1,233	5,224	9,154	14,461	10,331	9,139	6,276	4,755	4,648	3,573	3,206
Colorado	2,257	7,885	8,326	16,673	19,512	22,203	18,897	19,013	19,129	17,812	17,576	18,463	17,638	18,823	18,383	20,390
Comal	1,723	4,030	5,283	5,546	6,398	7,008	8,434	8,824	11,984	12,321	16,357	19,844	24,165	36,446	51,832	78,021
Comanche 4		709	1,001	8,608	15,608	23,009	27,186	25,748	18,430	19,245	15,516	11,865	11,898	12,617	13,381	14,026
Concho				800	1,065	1,427	6,654	5,847	7,645	6,192	5,078	3,672	2,937	2,915	3,044	3,966
Cooke	220	3,760	5,315	20,391	24,696	27,494	26,603	25,667	24,136	24,909	22,146	22,560	23,471	27,656	30,777	36,363
Coryell		2,666	4,124	10,924	16,873	21,308	21,703	20,601	19,999	20,226	16,284	23,961	35,311	56,767	64,213	74,978
Cottle				24	240	1,002	4,396	6,901	9,395	7,079	6,099	4,207	3,204	2,947	2,247	1,904
Crane 14					15	51	331	37	2,221	2,841	3,965	4,699	4,172	4,600	4,652	3,996
Crockett 13				127	194	1,591	1,296	1,500	2,590	2,809	3,981	4,209	3,885	4,608	4,078	4,099
Crosby				82	346	788	1,765	6,084	11,023	10,046	9,582	10,347	9,085	8,859	7,304	7,072
Culberson 15								912	1,228	1,653	1,825	2,794	3,429	3,315	3,407	2,975
Dallam					112	146	4,001	4,528	7,830	6,494	7,640	6,302	6,012	6,531	5,461	6,222
Dallas	2,743	8,665	13,314	33,488	67,042	82,726	135,748	210,551	325,691	398,564	614,799	951,527	1,327,321	1,556,549	1,852,810	2,218,899
Dawson 16				24	29	37	2,320	4,309	13,573	15,367	19,113	19,185	16,604	16,184	14,349	14,985
Davis 10																
Deaf Smith				38	179	843	3,942	3,747	5,979	6,056	9,111	13,187	18,999	21,165	19,153	18,561
Delta				5,597	9,117	15,249	14,566	15,887	13,138	12,858	8,964	5,860	4,927	4,839	4,857	5,327
Denton	641	5,031	7,251	18,143	21,289	28,318	31,258	35,355	32,822	33,658	41,365	47,432	75,633	143,126	273,525	432,976
De Witt	1,716	5,108	6,443	10,082	14,307	21,311	23,501	27,971	27,441	24,935	22,973	20,683	18,660	18,903	18,840	20,013
Dickens				28	295	1,151	3,092	5,876	8,601	7,847	7,177	4,963	3,737	3,539	2,571	2,762
Dimmit			109	665	1,049	1,106	3,460	5,296	8,828	8,542	10,654	10,095	9,039	11,367	10,433	10,248
Donley 17				160	1,056	2,756	5,284	8,035	10,262	7,487	6,216	4,449	3,641	4,075	3,696	3,828
Dunn 17																
Duval 17 18			1,083	5,732	7,598	8,483	8,964	8,251	12,191	20,565	15,643	13,398	11,722	12,517	12,918	13,120
Eastland		99	88	4,855	10,373	17,971	23,421	58,505	34,156	30,345	23,942	19,526	18,092	19,480	18,488	18,297
Ector 19					224	381	1,178	760	3,958	15,051	42,102	90,995	91,805	115,374	118,934	121,123
Edwards 20				266	1,970	3,108	3,768	2,283	2,764	2,933	2,908	2,317	2,107	2,033	2,266	2,162
Ellis	989	5,246	7,514	21,294	31,774	50,059	53,629	55,700	53,936	47,733	45,645	43,395	46,638	59,743	85,167	111,360
El Paso 21		4,051	3,671	3,845	15,678	24,886	52,599	101,877	131,597	131,067	194,968	314,070	359,291	479,899	591,610	679,622
Encinal 22		43	427	1,902	2,744											
Erath		2,425	1,801	11,796	21,584	29,966	32,095	28,385	20,804	20,760	18,434	16,236	18,141	22,560	27,991	33,001
Falls		3,614	9,851	16,240	20,706	33,342	35,649	36,217	38,771	35,984	26,724	21,263	17,300	17,946	17,712	18,576
Fannin	3,788	9,217	13,207	25,501	38,709	51,793	44,801	48,186	41,163	41,064	31,253	23,880	22,705	24,285	24,804	31,242
Fayette	3,756	11,604	16,863	27,996	31,481	36,542	29,796	29,965	30,708	29,246	24,176	20,384	17,650	18,832	20,095	21,804
Fisher				136	2,996	2,708	12,596	11,009	13,563	12,932	11,023	7,865	6,344	5,891	4,842	4,344
Floyd				3	529	2,020	4,638	9,758	12,409	10,659	10,535	12,369	11,044	9,834	8,497	7,771
Foard 23						1,568	5,726	4,747	6,315	5,237	4,216	3,125	2,211	2,158	1,794	1,622
Foley 24					25											
Fort Bend	2,533	6,143	7,114	9,380	10,586	16,538	18,168	22,931	29,718	32,963	31,056	40,527	52,314	130,846	225,421	354,452
Franklin				5,280	6,481	8,674	9,331	9,304	8,494	8,378	6,257	5,101	5,291	6,893	7,802	9,458
Freestone		6,881	8,139	14,921	15,987	18,910	20,557	23,264	22,589	21,138	15,696	12,525	11,116	14,830	15,818	17,867
Frio		42	309	2,130	3,112	4,200	8,895	9,286	9,411	9,207	10,357	10,112	11,159	13,785	13,472	16,252
Gaines				8	68	55	1,255	1,018	2,800	8,136	8,909	12,267	11,593	13,150	14,123	14,467
Galveston	4,529	8,229	15,290	24,121	31,476	44,116	44,479	53,150	64,401	81,173	113,066	140,364	169,812	195,940	217,399	250,158
Garza				36	14	185	1,995	4,253	5,586	5,678	6,281	6,611	5,289	5,336	5,143	4,872
Gillespie	1,240	2,736	3,566	5,228	7,056	8,229	9,447	10,015	11,020	10,670	10,520	10,048	10,553	13,532	17,204	20,814
Glasscock 14					208	286	1,143	555	1,263	1,193	1,089	1,118	1,155	1,304	1,447	1,406

County	1850	1860	1870	1880	1890	1900	1910	1920	1930	1940	1950	1960	1970	1980	1990	2000
Goliad	648	3,384	3,628	5,832	5,910	8,310	9,909	9,348	10,093	8,798	6,219	5,429	4,869	5,193	5,980	6,928
Gonzales	1,492	8,059	8,951	14,840	18,016	28,882	28,055	28,438	28,337	26,075	21,164	17,845	16,375	16,883	17,205	18,628
Gray				56	203	480	3,405	4,663	22,090	23,911	24,728	31,535	26,949	26,386	23,967	22,744
Grayson	2,008	8,184	14,387	38,108	53,211	63,661	65,996	74,165	65,843	69,499	70,467	73,043	83,225	89,796	95,021	110,595
Greer [52]					5,336											
Gregg				8,530	9,402	12,343	14,140	16,767	15,778	58,027	61,258	69,436	75,929	99,487	104,948	111,379
Grimes	4,008	10,307	13,218	18,603	21,312	26,106	21,205	23,101	22,642	21,960	15,135	12,709	11,855	13,580	18,828	23,552
Guadalupe	1,511	5,444	7,282	12,202	15,217	21,385	24,913	27,719	28,925	25,596	25,392	29,017	33,554	46,708	64,873	89,023
Hale					721	1,680	7,566	10,104	20,189	18,813	28,211	36,798	34,137	37,592	34,671	36,602
Hall				36	703	1,660	8,279	11,137	16,966	12,117	10,930	7,322	6,015	5,594	3,905	3,782
Hamilton [6]		489	733	6,365	6,313	13,520	15,315	14,676	13,523	13,303	10,660	8,488	7,198	8,297	7,733	8,229
Hansford				18	133	167	935	1,354	3,548	2,783	4,202	6,208	6,351	6,209	5,848	5,369
Hardeman [23]				50	3,904	3,634	11,213	12,487	14,532	11,073	10,212	8,275	6,795	6,368	5,283	4,724
Hardin		1,353	1,460	1,870	3,956	5,049	12,947	15,983	13,936	15,875	19,535	24,629	29,996	40,721	41,320	48,073
Harris	4,668	9,070	17,375	27,985	37,249	63,786	115,693	186,667	359,328	528,961	806,701	1,243,158	1,741,912	2,409,544	2,818,199	3,400,578
Harrison	11,822	15,001	13,241	25,177	26,721	31,878	37,243	43,565	48,937	50,900	47,745	45,594	44,841	52,265	57,483	62,110
Hartley				100	252	377	1,298	1,109	2,185	1,873	1,913	2,171	2,782	3,987	3,634	5,537
Haskell				48	1,665	2,637	16,249	14,193	16,669	14,905	13,736	11,174	8,512	7,725	6,820	6,093
Hays	387	2,126	4,088	7,555	11,352	14,142	15,518	15,920	14,915	15,349	17,840	19,934	27,642	40,594	65,614	97,589
Hemphill [11]				149	519	815	3,170	4,280	4,637	4,170	4,123	3,185	3,084	5,304	3,720	3,351
Henderson	1,237	4,595	6,786	9,735	12,285	19,970	20,131	28,327	30,583	31,822	23,405	21,786	26,466	42,606	58,543	73,277
Hidalgo [25][49]		1,182	2,387	4,347	6,534	6,837	13,728	38,110	77,004	106,059	160,446	180,904	181,535	283,229	383,545	569,463
Hill		3,653	7,453	16,554	27,583	41,355	46,760	43,332	43,036	38,355	31,282	23,650	22,596	25,024	27,146	32,321
Hockley						44	137	137	9,298	12,693	20,407	22,340	20,396	23,230	24,199	22,716
Hood			2,585	6,125	7,614	9,146	10,008	8,759	6,779	6,674	5,287	5,443	6,368	17,714	28,981	41,100
Hopkins	2,623	7,745	12,651	15,461	20,572	27,950	31,038	34,791	29,410	30,264	23,490	18,594	20,710	25,247	28,833	31,960
Houston	2,721	8,058	8,147	16,702	19,360	25,452	29,564	28,601	30,017	31,137	22,825	19,276	17,855	22,299	21,375	23,185
Howard				50	1,210	2,528	8,881	6,962	22,888	20,990	26,722	40,139	37,796	33,142	32,343	33,627
Hudspeth [26]								962	3,728	3,149	4,298	3,343	2,392	2,728	2,915	3,344
Hunt	1,520	6,630	10,291	17,230	31,885	47,295	48,116	50,350	49,016	48,793	42,731	39,399	47,948	55,248	64,343	76,596
Hutchinson				50	58	303	892	721	14,848	19,069	21,580	34,419	24,443	26,304	25,689	23,857
Irion [12]					870	848	1,283	1,610	2,049	1,963	1,590	1,183	1,070	1,386	1,629	1,771
Jack		1,000	694	6,626	9,740	10,224	11,817	9,863	9,046	10,206	7,755	7,418	6,711	7,408	6,981	8,763
Jackson	996	2,612	2,278	2,723	3,281	6,094	6,471	11,244	10,980	11,720	12,916	14,040	12,975	13,352	13,039	14,391
Jasper	1,767	4,037	4,218	5,779	5,592	7,138	14,000	15,569	17,064	17,491	20,049	22,100	24,692	30,781	31,102	35,604
Jeff Davis [27]					1,394	1,150	1,678	1,445	1,800	2,375	2,090	1,582	1,527	1,647	1,946	2,207
Jefferson	1,836	1,995	1,906	3,489	5,857	14,239	38,182	73,120	133,391	145,329	195,083	245,659	244,773	250,938	239,397	252,051
Jim Hogg [28][49]								1,914	4,919	5,449	5,389	5,022	4,654	5,168	5,109	5,281
Jim Wells [29]								6,587	13,456	20,239	27,991	34,548	33,032	36,498	37,679	39,326
Johnson		4,305	4,923	17,911	22,313	33,819	24,460	37,286	33,317	30,384	31,390	34,720	45,769	67,649	97,165	126,811
Jones				546	3,797	7,053	24,299	22,323	24,233	23,378	22,147	19,299	16,106	17,268	16,490	20,785
Karnes		2,171	1,705	3,270	3,637	8,681	14,942	19,049	23,316	23,316	17,139	14,995	13,462	13,593	12,455	15,446
Kaufman	1,047	3,936	6,895	15,448	21,598	33,376	35,323	41,276	40,905	38,308	31,170	29,931	32,392	39,015	52,220	71,313
Kendall			1,536	2,763	3,826	4,103	4,517	4,779	4,970	5,080	5,423	5,889	6,964	10,635	14,589	23,743
Kenedy [30][50]								1,033	701	700	632	884	678	543	460	414
Kent				92	324	899	2,655	3,335	3,851	3,413	2,249	1,727	1,434	1,145	1,010	859
Kerr [31]		634	1,042	2,168	4,462	4,980	5,505	5,842	10,151	11,650	14,022	16,800	19,454	28,780	36,304	43,653
Kimble			72	1,343	2,243	2,503	3,261	3,581	4,119	5,064	4,619	3,943	3,904	4,063	4,122	4,468

County	1850	1860	1870	1880	1890	1900	1910	1920	1930	1940	1950	1960	1970	1980	1990	2000
King	...	61	...	40	173	490	810	655	1,193	1,066	870	640	464	425	354	356
Kinney [32]	...	...	1,204	4,487	3,781	2,447	3,401	3,746	3,980	4,533	2,668	2,452	2,006	2,279	3,119	3,379
Kleberg [29]	...	...	...	...	...	...	...	9,240	12,451	13,344	21,991	30,052	33,166	33,358	30,274	31,549
Knox [23]	...	...	...	77	1,134	2,322	9,625	9,240	11,368	10,090	10,082	7,857	5,972	5,329	4,837	4,253
Lamar	3,978	10,136	15,790	27,193	37,302	48,627	46,544	55,742	48,529	50,425	43,033	34,234	36,062	42,156	43,949	48,499
Lamb	...	...	...	...	4	31	540	1,175	17,452	17,606	20,015	21,896	17,770	18,669	15,072	14,709
Lampasas [6]	...	1,028	1,344	5,421	7,584	8,625	9,532	8,800	8,677	9,167	9,929	9,418	9,323	12,005	13,521	17,762
La Salle	...	...	69	789	2,139	2,303	4,747	4,821	8,228	8,003	7,485	5,972	5,014	5,514	5,254	5,866
Lavaca	1,571	5,945	9,168	13,641	21,887	28,121	26,418	28,964	27,550	25,485	22,159	20,174	17,903	19,004	18,690	19,210
Lee	...	...	...	8,937	11,952	14,595	13,132	14,014	13,390	12,751	10,144	8,949	8,048	10,952	12,854	15,657
Leon	1,946	6,781	6,523	12,817	13,841	18,072	16,563	18,286	19,898	17,733	12,024	9,951	8,738	9,594	12,665	15,335
Liberty	2,522	3,189	4,414	4,999	4,230	8,102	10,686	14,637	19,868	24,541	26,729	31,595	33,014	47,088	52,726	70,154
Limestone	2,608	4,537	8,591	16,246	21,678	32,573	34,621	33,283	39,497	33,781	25,251	20,413	18,100	20,224	20,946	22,051
Lipscomb [11]	...	...	...	69	632	790	2,634	3,684	4,512	3,764	3,658	3,406	3,486	3,766	3,143	3,057
Live Oak	...	593	852	1,994	2,055	2,268	3,442	4,171	8,956	9,799	9,054	7,846	6,697	9,606	9,556	12,309
Llano [14]	...	1,101	1,379	4,962	6,772	7,301	6,520	5,360	5,538	5,996	5,377	5,240	6,979	10,144	11,631	17,044
Loving [14]	...	...	...	...	3	33	249	82	195	285	227	226	164	91	107	67
Lubbock	...	...	...	25	33	293	3,624	11,096	39,104	51,782	101,048	156,271	179,295	211,651	222,636	242,628
Lynn	...	...	...	9	24	17	1,713	4,751	12,372	11,931	11,030	10,914	9,107	8,605	6,758	6,550
Madison	...	2,238	4,061	5,395	8,512	10,432	10,318	11,956	12,227	12,029	7,996	6,749	7,693	10,649	10,931	12,940
Marion	...	3,977	8,562	10,983	10,862	10,754	10,472	10,886	10,371	11,457	10,172	8,049	8,517	10,360	9,984	10,941
Martin	...	...	...	12	264	332	1,549	1,146	5,785	5,556	5,541	5,068	4,774	4,684	4,956	4,746
Mason	...	630	678	2,655	5,180	5,573	5,683	4,824	5,511	5,378	4,945	3,780	3,356	3,683	3,423	3,738
Matagorda	2,124	3,454	3,377	3,940	3,985	6,097	13,594	16,589	17,678	20,066	21,559	25,744	27,913	37,828	36,928	37,957
Maverick	...	726	1,951	2,967	3,698	4,066	5,151	7,418	6,120	10,071	12,292	14,508	18,093	31,398	36,378	47,297
McCulloch	...	...	173	1,533	3,217	3,960	13,405	11,020	13,883	13,208	11,701	8,815	8,571	8,735	8,778	8,205
McLennan	...	6,206	13,500	26,934	39,204	59,772	73,250	82,921	98,682	101,898	130,194	150,091	147,553	170,755	189,123	213,517
McMullen	...	...	230	701	1,038	1,024	1,091	952	1,351	1,374	1,187	1,116	1,095	789	817	851
Medina	909	1,838	2,078	4,492	5,730	7,783	13,415	11,679	13,989	16,106	17,013	18,904	20,249	23,164	27,312	39,304
Menard	...	...	667	1,239	1,215	2,011	2,707	3,162	4,447	4,521	4,175	2,964	2,646	2,346	2,252	2,360
Midland [33]	...	...	...	...	1,033	1,741	3,464	2,449	8,005	11,721	25,785	67,717	65,433	82,636	106,611	116,009
Milam	2,907	5,175	8,984	18,659	24,773	39,666	36,780	38,104	37,915	33,120	23,585	22,263	20,028	22,732	22,946	24,238
Mills [34]	...	...	...	...	5,493	7,851	9,694	9,019	8,293	7,951	5,999	4,467	4,212	4,477	4,531	5,151
Mitchell	...	...	...	117	2,059	2,855	8,956	7,527	14,183	12,477	14,357	11,255	9,073	9,088	8,016	9,698
Montague	...	849	890	11,257	18,863	24,800	25,123	22,200	19,159	20,442	17,070	14,893	15,326	17,410	17,274	19,117
Montgomery	2,384	5,479	6,483	10,154	11,765	17,067	15,679	17,334	14,588	23,055	24,504	26,839	49,479	128,487	182,201	293,768
Moore	...	...	...	...	15	209	561	571	1,555	4,461	13,349	14,773	14,060	16,575	17,865	20,121
Morris	...	...	...	5,032	6,580	8,220	10,439	10,289	10,028	9,810	9,433	12,576	12,310	14,629	13,200	13,048
Motley	...	...	...	24	139	1,257	2,396	4,107	6,812	4,994	3,963	2,870	2,178	1,950	1,532	1,426
Nacogdoches	5,193	8,292	9,614	11,590	15,984	24,663	27,406	28,457	30,290	35,392	30,326	28,046	36,362	46,786	54,753	59,203
Navarro	2,190	5,996	8,879	21,702	26,373	43,374	47,070	50,624	60,507	51,308	39,916	34,423	31,150	35,323	39,926	45,124
Newton	1,689	3,119	2,187	4,350	4,650	7,282	10,850	12,196	12,524	13,700	10,832	10,372	11,657	13,254	13,569	15,072
Nolan	...	...	...	640	1,573	2,611	11,999	10,868	19,323	17,309	19,808	18,963	16,220	17,359	16,594	15,802
Nueces [35]	698	2,906	3,975	7,673	8,093	10,439	21,955	22,807	51,779	92,661	165,471	221,573	237,544	268,215	291,145	313,645
Ochiltree	...	...	...	...	198	267	1,602	2,331	5,224	4,213	6,024	9,380	9,704	9,588	9,128	9,006
Oldham	...	...	...	387	270	349	812	709	1,404	1,385	1,672	1,928	2,258	2,283	2,278	2,185
Orange	...	1,916	1,255	2,938	4,770	5,905	9,528	15,379	15,149	17,382	40,567	60,357	71,170	83,838	80,509	84,966
Palo Pinto	...	1,524	...	5,885	8,320	12,291	19,506	23,431	17,576	18,456	17,154	20,516	28,962	24,062	25,055	27,026

County	1850	1860	1870	1880	1890	1900	1910	1920	1930	1940	1950	1960	1970	1980	1990	2000
Panola	3,871	8,475	10,119	12,219	14,328	21,404	20,424	21,755	24,063	22,513	19,250	16,870	15,894	20,724	22,035	22,756
Parker		4,213	4,186	15,870	21,682	25,823	26,331	23,382	18,759	20,482	24,528	22,880	33,888	44,609	64,785	88,495
Parmer					7	34	1,555	1,699	5,869	5,890	5,787	9,583	10,509	11,038	9,863	10,016
Pecos [36]				1,807	1,326	2,360	2,071	3,857	7,812	8,185	9,939	11,957	13,748	14,618	14,675	16,809
Polk	2,348	8,300	8,707	7,189	10,332	14,447	17,459	16,784	17,555	20,635	16,194	13,861	14,457	24,407	30,687	41,133
Potter				28	849	1,820	12,424	16,710	46,080	54,265	73,366	115,580	90,511	98,637	97,874	113,546
Presidio [37]		580	1,636	2,873	1,698	3,673	5,218	12,202	10,154	10,925	7,354	5,460	4,842	5,188	6,637	7,304
Rains				3,035	3,909	6,127	6,787	8,099	7,114	7,334	4,266	2,993	3,752	4,839	6,715	9,139
Randall [38]				3	187	963	3,312	3,675	7,071	7,185	13,774	33,913	53,885	75,062	89,673	104,312
Reagan [39]							392	377	3,028	1,997	3,127	3,782	3,239	4,135	4,514	3,326
Real [39]								1,461	2,197	2,420	2,479	2,079	2,013	2,469	2,412	3,047
Red River	3,906	8,535	10,653	17,194	21,452	29,893	28,564	35,829	30,923	29,769	21,851	15,682	14,298	16,101	14,317	14,314
Reeves [40]					1,247	1,847	4,392	4,457	6,407	8,006	11,745	17,644	16,526	15,801	15,852	13,137
Refugio	288	1,600	2,324	1,585	1,239	1,641	2,814	4,050	7,691	10,383	10,113	10,975	9,494	9,289	7,976	7,828
Roberts				32	326	620	950	1,469	1,457	1,289	1,031	1,075	967	1,187	1,025	887
Robertson	934	4,997	9,990	22,383	26,506	31,480	27,454	27,933	27,240	25,710	19,908	16,157	14,389	14,653	15,511	16,000
Rockwall				2,984	5,972	8,531	8,072	8,591	7,658	7,051	6,156	5,878	7,046	14,528	25,604	43,080
Runnels				980	3,193	5,379	20,858	17,074	21,821	18,903	16,771	15,016	12,108	11,872	11,294	11,495
Rusk	8,148	15,803	16,916	18,986	18,559	26,099	26,946	31,689	32,484	51,023	42,348	36,421	34,102	41,382	43,735	47,372
Sabine	2,498	2,750	3,256	4,161	4,969	6,394	8,582	12,299	11,998	10,896	8,568	7,302	7,187	8,702	9,586	10,469
San Augustine	3,648	4,094	4,196	5,084	6,688	8,434	11,264	13,737	12,471	11,998	8,837	7,722	7,858	8,785	7,999	8,946
San Jacinto				6,186	7,360	10,277	9,542	9,867	9,711	9,056	7,172	6,153	6,702	11,434	16,372	22,246
San Patricio	200	620	602	1,010	1,312	2,372	7,307	11,386	23,836	28,871	35,842	45,021	47,288	58,013	58,749	67,138
San Saba		913	1,425	5,324	6,641	7,569	11,245	10,045	10,273	11,012	8,666	6,381	5,540	5,693	5,401	6,186
Schleicher [41]					155	515	1,893	1,851	3,166	3,083	2,852	2,791	2,277	2,820	2,990	2,935
Scurry				102	1,415	4,158	10,924	9,003	12,188	11,545	22,779	20,369	15,760	18,192	18,634	16,361
Shackelford		44	455	2,037	2,012	2,461	4,201	4,960	6,695	6,211	5,001	3,990	3,323	3,915	3,316	3,302
Shelby	4,239	5,362	5,732	9,532	14,365	20,452	26,423	27,464	28,627	29,235	23,479	20,479	19,672	23,084	22,034	25,224
Sherman					34	104	1,476	1,473	2,314	2,026	2,443	2,605	3,657	3,174	2,858	3,186
Smith	4,292	13,392	16,532	21,863	28,324	37,370	41,746	46,769	53,123	69,090	74,701	86,350	97,096	128,366	151,309	174,706
Somervell				2,649	3,419	3,498	3,931	3,563	3,016	3,071	2,542	2,577	2,793	4,154	5,360	6,809
Starr [9][49]		2,406	4,154	8,304	10,749	11,469	13,151	11,089	11,409	13,312	13,948	17,137	17,707	27,266	40,518	53,597
Stephens [8]		230	330	4,725	4,926	6,466	7,980	15,403	16,560	12,356	10,597	8,885	8,414	9,926	9,010	9,674
Sterling [42]						1,127	1,493	1,053	1,431	1,404	1,282	1,177	1,056	1,206	1,438	1,393
Stonewall				104	1,024	2,183	5,320	4,086	5,667	5,589	3,679	3,017	2,397	2,406	2,013	1,693
Sutton [41]					658	1,727	1,569	1,598	2,807	3,977	3,746	3,738	3,175	5,130	4,135	4,077
Swisher				4	100	1,227	4,012	4,388	7,343	6,528	8,249	10,607	10,373	9,723	8,133	8,378
Tarrant	664	6,020	5,788	24,671	41,142	52,376	108,572	152,800	197,553	225,521	361,253	538,495	716,317	860,880	1,170,103	1,446,219
Taylor				1,736	6,957	10,499	26,293	24,081	41,023	44,147	63,370	101,078	97,853	110,932	119,655	126,555
Terrell [43]							1,430	1,595	2,660	2,952	3,189	2,600	1,940	1,595	1,410	1,081
Terry					21	48	1,474	2,236	8,883	11,160	13,107	16,286	14,118	14,581	13,218	12,761
Throckmorton [51]		124		711	902	1,750	4,563	3,589	5,253	4,275	3,618	2,767	2,205	2,053	1,880	1,850
Titus	3,636	9,648	11,339	5,959	8,190	12,292	16,422	18,128	16,003	19,228	17,302	16,785	16,702	21,442	24,009	28,118
Tom Green [44]				3,615	5,152	6,804	17,882	15,210	36,033	39,302	58,929	64,630	71,047	84,784	98,458	104,010
Travis	3,138	8,080	13,153	27,028	36,322	47,386	55,620	57,616	77,777	111,053	160,980	212,136	295,516	419,335	576,407	812,280
Trinity		4,392	4,141	4,915	7,648	10,976	12,768	13,623	13,637	13,705	10,040	7,539	7,628	9,450	11,445	13,779
Tyler	1,894	4,525	5,010	5,825	10,877	11,899	10,250	10,415	11,448	11,948	11,292	10,666	12,417	16,223	16,646	20,871
Upshur	3,394	10,645	12,039	10,266	12,695	16,266	19,960	22,472	22,297	26,178	20,822	19,793	20,976	28,595	31,370	35,291

County[14]	1850	1860	1870	1880	1890	1900	1910	1920	1930	1940	1950	1960	1970	1980	1990	2000
Upton[14]	…	…	…	…	52	48	501	253	5,968	4,297	5,307	6,239	4,697	4,619	4,447	3,404
Uvalde	…	506	851	2,541	3,804	4,647	11,233	10,769	12,945	13,246	16,015	16,814	17,348	22,441	23,340	25,926
Val Verde[45]	…	…	…	…	2,874	5,263	8,613	12,706	14,924	15,453	16,635	24,461	27,471	35,910	38,721	44,856
Van Zandt	1,348	3,777	6,494	12,619	16,225	25,481	25,651	30,784	32,315	31,155	22,593	19,091	22,155	31,426	37,944	48,140
Victoria	2,019	4,171	4,860	6,289	8,737	13,678	14,990	18,271	20,048	23,741	31,241	46,475	53,766	68,807	74,361	84,088
Walker	3,964	8,191	9,766	12,024	12,874	15,813	16,061	18,556	18,528	19,868	20,163	21,475	27,680	41,789	50,917	61,758
Waller	…	…	…	9,024	10,888	14,246	12,138	10,292	10,014	10,280	11,961	12,071	14,285	19,798	23,390	32,663
Ward[14]	…	…	…	…	77	1,451	2,389	2,615	4,599	9,575	13,346	14,917	13,019	13,976	13,115	10,909
Washington	5,983	15,215	23,104	27,565	29,161	32,931	25,561	26,624	25,394	25,387	20,542	19,145	18,842	21,998	26,154	30,373
Webb[9,46]	…	1,397	2,615	5,273	14,842	21,851	22,503	29,152	42,128	45,916	56,141	64,791	72,859	99,258	133,239	193,117
Wharton[14]	1,752	3,380	3,426	4,459	7,584	16,942	21,123	24,288	29,681	36,158	36,077	38,152	36,729	40,242	39,955	41,188
Wheeler[11]	…	…	…	512	778	636	5,258	7,397	15,555	12,411	10,317	7,947	6,434	7,137	5,879	5,284
Wichita	…	…	…	433	4,831	5,806	16,094	72,911	74,416	73,604	98,493	123,528	120,563	121,082	122,378	131,664
Wilbarger	…	…	…	126	7,092	5,759	12,000	15,112	24,579	20,474	20,552	17,748	15,355	15,931	15,121	14,676
Willacy[47]	…	…	…	…	…	…	…	…	10,499	13,230	20,920	20,084	15,570	17,495	17,705	20,082
Williamson	1,568	4,529	6,368	15,155	25,909	38,072	42,228	42,934	44,146	41,698	38,853	35,044	37,305	76,521	139,551	249,967
Wilson	…	…	2,556	7,118	10,655	13,961	17,066	17,289	17,606	17,066	14,672	13,267	13,041	16,756	22,650	32,408
Winkler[14]	…	…	…	…	18	60	442	81	6,784	6,141	10,064	13,652	9,640	9,944	8,626	7,173
Wise	…	3,160	1,450	16,601	24,134	27,116	26,450	23,363	19,178	19,074	16,141	17,012	19,687	26,575	34,679	48,793
Wood	…	4,968	6,894	11,212	13,932	21,048	23,417	27,707	24,183	24,360	21,308	17,653	18,589	24,697	29,380	36,752
Yoakum[14]	…	…	…	…	4	26	602	504	1,263	5,354	4,339	8,032	7,344	8,299	8,786	7,322
Young	…	592	135	4,726	5,049	6,540	13,657	13,379	20,128	19,004	16,810	17,254	15,400	19,001	18,126	17,943
Zapata[48,49]	…	1,248	1,488	3,636	3,562	4,760	3,809	2,929	2,867	3,916	4,405	4,393	4,352	6,628	9,279	12,182
Zavala	…	26	138	410	1,097	792	1,889	3,108	10,349	11,603	11,201	12,696	11,370	11,666	12,162	11,600

1 - Part of Bandera taken to form Real in 1913.

2 - Comprised the greater part of West Texas until 1876, when it was divided into counties. It was usually referred to as a part of Bexar County, but there was an old Dawson County existing in 1860 before the creation of the present Dawson County of the South Plains. The older Dawson was west of present Uvalde County. Dawson was listed separately in the United States Census report of 1870, referred to as Bexar Territory and Bexar District.

3 - Organized from part of Presidio in 1887; Buchel and Foley annexed in 1897.

4 - Part of Comanche taken to form part of Mills in 1887.

5 - No population reported for Briscoe County in 1890.

6 - Part taken to form Mills in 1887.

7 - Created from part of Presidio in 1887; annexed to Brewster in 1897.

8 - Name changed from Buchanan to Stephens in 1861.

9 - Cameron, Starr and Webb reported together in 1850; population credited to Cameron.

10 - Name of Cass County changed to Davis in 1861; changed back to Cass in 1871.

11 - Relocation of the 100th meridian (United States Supreme Court decision of March 17, 1930) resulted in the following changes in Texas counties: Part of Harmon County, Okla., acquired by Childress County, Texas; parts of Beckham and Harmon, Okla., acquired by Collingsworth, Texas; parts of Ellis and Roger Mills, Okla., acquired by Hemphill, Texas; part of Ellis, Okla., by Lipscomb, Texas; parts of Beckham and Roger Mills, Okla., by Wheeler, Texas.

12 - Created from parts of Tom Green in 1889.

13 - Parts of Crockett taken to form Schleicher and Sutton in 1887, and part of Val Verde in 1885.

14 - Created from part of Tom Green in 1887.

15 - Culberson created from El Paso in 1911.

16 - There was an old Dawson County existing in 1860 before the creation of the present Dawson County of the South Plains. The older Dawson was west of present Uvalde County.

17 - Formed from part of Duval County in 1913; later disorganized; no census report.

18 - Part of Duval taken to form Jim Hogg in 1913.

19 - Ector formed from part of Tom Green in 1887.

20 - Part of Edwards taken to form part of Real in 1913.

21 - Parts of El Paso taken to form Culberson in 1911 and Hudspeth in 1917.

22 - Annexed to Webb in 1899.

23 - Foard organized from parts of Hardeman and Knox in 1891.

24 - Organized from part of Presidio in 1887; annexed to Brewster 1897.

25 - Parts of Hidalgo taken to form parts of Willacy and Brooks in 1911 and to form new boundaries of Willacy in 1921.

26 - Hudspeth created from El Paso in 1917.

27 - Organized from part of Presidio in 1887.

28 - Jim Hogg created from parts of Duval and Brooks in 1913.

29 - Jim Wells created from parts of Nueces in 1911; Kleberg organized from part of Nueces in 1913.

30 - Kenedy created from part of Willacy in 1921.

31 - Part of Kerr taken to form part of Real in 1913.

32 - Part taken to form part of Val Verde in 1885.

33 - Part taken to form part of Tom Green in 1885.

34 - Created from Brown, Comanche, Hamilton, Lampasas 1887.

35 - Parts of Nueces taken to form Jim Wells in 1911, Kleberg in 1913.

36 - Parts of Pecos taken to form Reeves in 1883, part of Val Verde in 1885 and Crockett and Terrell in 1905.

37 - Parts of Presidio taken to form Buchel, Brewster, Foley and Jeff Davis in 1887.

38 - Reagan created from part of Tom Green in 1903.

39 - Real created from parts of Bandera, Edwards and Kerr in 1913.

40 - Created from part of Pecos in 1883.

41 - Created from part of Crockett in 1887.

42 - Sterling formed from part of Tom Green in 1891.

43 - Terrell created from part of Pecos in 1905.

44 - Parts taken to form Midland in 1885; Crane, Ector, Glasscock, Loving, Upton, Ward and Winkler in 1887; Coke and Irion in 1889; Sterling in 1891; and Reagan in 1903.

45 - Created from parts of Kinney, Crockett and Pecos in 1885.

46 - Encinal annexed in 1899.

47 - Old Willacy created from parts of Cameron and Hidalgo in 1911; name changed to Kenedy in 1921; new Willacy organized from parts of Cameron and Hidalgo in 1921.

48 - Part of Zapata taken to form part of Brooks in 1911.

49 - Brooks created from Hidalgo, Starr, Zapata in 1911; part taken for part of Jim Hogg in 1913.

50 - Part of Cameron taken to form Willacy in 1911; part was taken again in 1921 to form part of new area of Willacy when Kenedy was created from Willacy.

51 - No population for Clay, Palo Pinto or Throckmorton in 1870.

52 - Greer County was organized as Texas civil unit and under Texas administration until 1896, when it was transferred to Oklahoma by decision of the United States Supreme Court.

City Population History, 1850–2000

The table shows, for a selected list of cities, a complete record of population for each decennial year, insofar as such record exists. The official census record is presented below, with a few exceptions. Unofficial figures are given where census figures are unavailable. These, as well as other anomalies, are explained in footnotes.

In recent years, the official census has included not only incorporated towns, but also unincorporated towns that meet certain federal criteria. These are called "Census Designated Places," and some are included in this list. At least one town from each county is listed. Where no figure is given, it means that no census was taken for it. It does not necessarily mean that the town did not exist. Some Texas towns were in existence many years before incorporating.

City, County	1850	1860	1870	1880	1890	1900	1910	1920	1930	1940	1950	1960	1970	1980	1990††	% Change 90-00	2000
Abernathy, Hale									858	847	1,692	2,491	2,625	2,904	2,720	4.38	2,839
Abilene, Taylor					3,194	3,411	9,204	10,274	23,175	26,612	45,570	90,368	89,653	98,315	106,707	8.64	115,930
Addison, Dallas												308	593	5,553	8,783	61.29	14,166
Alamo, Hidalgo									1,018	1,944	3,017	4,121	4,291	5,831	8,210	79.78	14,760
Alamo Heights, Bexar									3,874	5,700	8,000	7,552	6,933	6,252	6,502	12.57	7,319
Albany, Shackelford				129		999		1,469	2,422	2,230	2,255	2,200	1,978	2,450	1,962	-2.09	1,921
Alice, Jim Wells							2,136	1,880	4,239	7,792	16,449	20,861	20,121	20,961	19,788	-3.93	19,010
Allen, Collin												659	1,940	8,314	19,315	125.49	43,554
Alpine, Brewster								931	3,495	3,866	5,261	4,740	5,971	5,465	5,622	2.92	5,786
Alton, Hidalgo														2,732	3,069	42.85	4,384
Alvarado, Johnson					1,543	1,342	1,155		1,210	1,324	1,656	1,907	2,129	2,701	2,918	12.68	3,288
Alvin, Brazoria					261	996	1,453	1,519	1,511	3,087	3,701	5,643	10,671	16,515	19,220	11.41	21,413
Amarillo, Potter					482	1,442	9,957	15,494	43,132	51,686	74,246	137,969	127,010	149,230	157,571	10.19	173,627
Anahuac, Chambers								‡500	‡800	‡1,500	1,282	2,105	1,881	1,840	1,993	10.89	2,210
Andrews, Andrews										611	3,294	11,135	8,625	11,061	10,678	-9.61	9,652
Angleton, Brazoria								1,043	1,229	1,763	3,399	7,312	9,770	13,929	17,140	5.78	18,130
Anson, Jones							1,842	1,425	2,093	2,338	2,708	2,890	2,615	2,831	2,644	-3.33	2,556
Anthony, El Paso												1,082	2,154	2,640	3,328	15.69	3,850
Aransas Pass, San Patricio							1,197	1,569	2,482	4,095	5,396	6,956	5,813	7,173	7,180	13.34	8,138
Archer City, Archer						187	825	689	1,512	1,675	1,895	1,974	1,722	1,862	1,784	3.59	1,848
Arlington, Tarrant					664	1,079	1,794	3,031	3,661	4,240	7,692	44,775	89,723	160,123	261,717	27.22	332,969
Aspermont, Stonewall						205		436	769	1,041	1,060	1,275	1,198	1,357	1,214	-15.90	1,021
Athens, Henderson	*177		†500		1,764	1,301	2,261	3,176	4,342	4,765	5,194	7,086	9,582	10,197	10,982	2.87	11,297
Atlanta, Cass							1,604	1,469	1,685	2,453	3,782	4,076	5,007	6,272	6,118	-6.10	5,745
Austin, Travis	629	3,494	4,428	11,013	14,575	22,258	29,860	34,876	53,120	87,930	132,459	186,545	251,808	345,496	472,020	39.10	656,562
Azle, Tarrant												2,969	4,493	5,822	8,868	8.25	9,600
Balch Springs, Dallas												6,821	10,464	13,746	17,406	11.31	19,375
Balcones Heights, Bexar												950	2,504	2,853	3,022	-0.20	3,016
Ballinger, Runnels					1,390	1,128	3,536	2,767	4,187	4,472	5,302	5,043	4,203	4,207	3,975	6.74	4,243
Bandera, Bandera					372	419		‡700	‡580	‡1,250	‡1,325	‡1,065	891	947	877	9.12	957
Barrett, Harris												2,364	2,750	nc	3,052	-5.90	2,872
Bastrop, Bastrop				1,546	1,634	2,145	1,707	1,828	1,895	1,976	3,176	3,001	3,112	3,789	4,044	32.05	5,340
Bay City, Matagorda							3,156	3,454	4,070	6,594	9,427	11,656	11,733	17,837	18,170	2.74	18,667
**Baytown, Harris											22,983	28,159	43,980	56,923	63,843	4.05	66,430
Beaumont, Jefferson					3,296	9,427	20,640	40,422	57,732	59,061	94,014	119,175	115,919	118,102	114,323	-0.40	113,866
Bedford, Tarrant												2,706	10,049	20,821	43,762	7.75	47,152
Beeville, Bee	*151				‡1,311	‡2,311	3,269	3,062	4,806	6,789	9,348	13,811	13,506	14,574	13,547	-3.09	13,129
Bellaire, Harris									390	1,124	10,173	19,872	19,009	14,950	13,842	12.99	15,642

City, County	1850	1860	1870	1880	1890	1900	1910	1920	1930	1940	1950	1960	1970	1980	1990††	% Change 90-00	2000
Bellmead, McLennan												5,127	7,698	7,569	8,336	10.53	9,214
Bellville, Austin									1,533	1,347	2,112	2,218	2,371	2,860	3,378	12.31	3,794
Belton, Bell	300	305	777	1,797	3,000	3,700	4,164	5,098	3,779	3,572	6,246	8,163	8,696	10,660	12,463	17.33	14,623
Benavides, Duval										3,081	3,016	2,459	2,112	1,978	1,788	-5.70	1,686
Benbrook, Tarrant											617	3,254	8,169	13,579	19,564	3.29	20,208
Benjamin, Knox					107	107		500	485	599		308	308	257	225	17.33	264
Big Lake, Reagan									832	763	2,152	2,668	2,489	3,404	3,672	-21.43	2,885
Big Spring, Howard						‡1,255	4,102	4,273	13,735	12,604	17,286	31,230	28,735	24,804	23,093	9.27	25,233
Bishop, Nueces									953	1,329	2,731	3,722	3,466	3,706	3,337	-0.96	3,305
Boerne, Kendall							886	1,153	1,117	1,271	1,802	2,169	2,432	3,229	4,361	41.66	6,178
Bonham, Fannin	*477			1,880	3,361	5,042	4,844	6,008	5,655	6,349	7,049	7,357	7,698	7,338	6,688	49.37	9,990
Borger, Hutchinson									6,532	10,018	18,059	20,911	14,195	15,837	15,675	-8.76	14,302
Bowie, Montague					1,486	2,600	2,874	3,179	3,131	3,470	4,544	4,566	5,185	5,610	4,990	4.59	5,219
Brackettville, Kinney									1,822	2,653	1,858	1,662	1,539	1,676	1,740	7.82	1,876
Brady, McCulloch				115	560	690	2,669	2,197	3,983	5,002	5,944	5,338	5,557	5,969	5,946	-7.11	5,523
Brazoria, Brazoria											776	1,291	1,681	3,025	2,717	2.58	2,787
Breckenridge, Stephens								1,846	7,569	5,826	6,610	6,273	5,944	6,921	5,665	3.58	5,868
Brenham, Washington			2,221	4,101	5,209	5,968	4,718	5,066	5,974	6,435	6,941	7,740	8,922	10,966	11,952	13.01	13,507
Bridge City, Orange												4,677	8,164	7,667	8,010	8.00	8,651
Bridgeport, Wise					498	900	2,000	1,872	2,464	1,735	2,049	3,218	3,614	3,737	3,581	20.33	4,309
Brownfield, Terry									1,907	4,009	6,161	10,286	9,647	10,387	9,560	-0.75	9,488
Brownsville, Cameron		2,734	4,905	4,938	6,134	6,305	10,517	11,791	22,021	22,083	36,066	48,040	52,522	84,997	107,027	30.55	139,722
Brownwood, Brown				725	2,176	6,965	6,967	8,223	12,789	13,398	20,181	16,974	17,368	19,203	18,387	2.32	18,813
Bryan, Brazos					2,979	3,589	4,132	6,307	7,814	11,842	18,102	27,542	33,719	44,337	55,002	19.38	65,660
Buffalo, Leon				190		310		510	470	737	966	1,108	1,242	1,507	1,555	16.01	1,804
Bunker Hill Village, Harris												2,216	3,977	3,750	3,391	7.76	3,654
Burkburnett, Wichita								5,300	3,281	2,814	4,555	7,621	9,230	10,668	10,145	7.71	10,927
Burleson, Johnson								241	591	573	791	2,345	7,713	11,734	16,113	30.18	20,976
Burnet, Burnet								966	1,055	1,945	2,394	2,214	2,864	3,410	3,423	38.33	4,735
Caldwell, Burleson					1,454	1,003	981	1,689	1,724	2,165	2,109	2,204	2,308	2,953	3,181	8.43	3,449
Calvert, Robertson					1,250	1,535	1,476	2,099	2,103	2,366	2,548	2,073	2,072	1,732	1,536	-7.16	1,426
Cameron, Milam				2,280	2,632	3,322	2,579	4,298	4,565	5,040	5,052	5,640	5,546	5,721	5,635	-0.02	5,634
Canadian, Hemphill					1,608	3,341	3,263	2,187	2,068	2,151	2,700	2,239	2,292	3,491	2,417	-7.61	2,233
Canton, Van Zandt							1,648	583	704	715	881	1,114	2,283	2,845	2,949	11.63	3,292
Canyon, Randall							1,400	1,618	2,821	2,622	4,364	5,864	8,333	10,724	11,365	13.29	12,875
Carrizo Springs, Dimmit								954	2,171	2,494	4,316	5,699	5,374	6,886	5,745	-1.57	5,655
Carrollton, Dallas								573	689	921	1,610	4,242	13,855	40,591	82,169	33.35	109,576
Carthage, Panola								1,366	1,651	2,178	4,750	5,262	5,392	6,447	6,496	2.59	6,664
Castle Hills, Bexar												2,622	5,311	4,773	4,198	0.10	4,202
Cedar Hill, Dallas										476	732	1,848	2,610	6,849	19,988	60.56	32,093
Cedar Park, Williamson														3,474	5,161	404.73	26,049
Center, Shelby							1,684	1,838	2,510	3,010	4,323	4,510	4,989	5,827	4,950	14.71	5,678
Centerville, Leon				223	288	318			388	900	961	836	831	799	812	11.21	903
Channing, Hartley						204		‡475	‡500	‡475	‡300	390	336	304	277	28.52	356
Childress, Childress						692	3,818	5,003	7,163	6,434	7,619	6,399	5,408	5,817	5,055	34.09	6,778
Cisco, Eastland					1,063	1,514	2,410	7,422	6,027	4,868	5,230	4,499	4,160	4,517	3,813	1.00	3,851

City, County	1850	1860	1870	1880	1890	1900	1910	1920	1930	1940	1950	1960	1970	1980	1990††	% Change 90-00	2000
Clarendon, Donley	‡700	*400			1,588	2,069	1,946	2,456	2,756	2,431	2,577	2,172	1,974	2,220	2,067	-4.50	1,974
Clarksville, Red River							2,065	3,386	2,952	4,095	4,353	3,851	3,346	4,917	4,311	-9.93	3,883
Claude, Armstrong					285	310	692	770	1,041	761	820	1,005	992	1,112	1,199	9.51	1,313
Cleburne, Johnson			683	1,855	3,278	7,493	10,364	12,820	11,539	10,558	12,905	15,381	16,015	19,218	22,205	17.11	26,005
Cleveland, Austin									1,422	1,783	5,183	5,838	5,627	5,977	7,124	6.75	7,605
Clifton, Bosque							1,137	1,327	1,367	1,732	1,837	2,335	2,578	3,063	3,195	10.86	3,542
Clute, Brazoria												4,501	6,023	9,577	9,467	10.11	10,424
Clyde, Callahan							495	610	706	800	908	1,116	1,635	2,562	3,002	11.43	3,345
Cockrell Hill, Dallas										1,246	2,207	3,104	3,515	3,262	3,746	18.61	4,443
Coldspring, San Jacinto					439	439		‡500	‡500	‡500	‡500	‡655	‡675	569	538	28.44	691
Coleman, Coleman				‡400	906	1,362	3,046	2,868	6,078	6,054	6,530	6,371	5,608	5,960	5,410	-5.23	5,127
College Station, Brazos										2,184	7,925	11,396	17,676	37,272	52,443	29.45	67,890
Colleyville, Tarrant												1,491	3,368	6,700	12,724	54.32	19,636
Colorado City, Mitchell				‡1,200			1,840	1,766	4,671	5,213	6,774	6,457	5,227	5,405	4,749	-9.85	4,281
Columbus, Colorado				1,959	1,226	2,070	2,756	3,524	2,054	2,422	2,878	3,656	3,342	3,923	3,367	16.31	3,916
Comanche, Comanche				704	810	1,800	2,818	3,842	2,435	3,209	3,840	3,415	3,933	4,075	4,087	9.66	4,482
Commerce, Hunt							1,374	1,858	4,267	4,699	5,889	5,789	9,534	8,136	6,825	12.37	7,669
Conroe, Montgomery									2,457	4,624	7,298	9,192	11,969	18,034	27,675	33.01	36,811
Converse, Bexar													1,383	4,907	8,887	29.49	11,508
Cooper, Delta					629		1,513	2,563	2,023	2,537	2,350	2,213	2,258	2,338	2,153	-0.14	2,150
Coppell, Dallas								509	406	356	1,052	666	1,728	3,826	16,881	113.01	35,958
Copperas Cove, Coryell												4,567	10,818	19,469	24,079	22.90	29,592
Corpus Christi, Nueces		175	2,140	3,257	4,387	4,703	8,222	10,522	27,741	57,301	108,287	167,690	204,525	231,999	257,453	7.77	277,454
Corsicana, Navarro			80	3,373	6,285	9,313	9,749	11,356	15,202	15,232	19,211	20,344	19,972	21,712	22,911	6.87	24,485
Cotulla, La Salle							1,880	1,058	3,175	3,633	4,418	3,960	3,415	3,912	3,694	-2.17	3,614
Crane, Crane										1,420	2,154	3,796	3,427	3,622	3,533	-9.68	3,191
Crockett, Houston	‡600	‡1,500		599	1,445	2,612	3,947	3,061	4,441	4,536	5,932	5,356	6,616	7,405	7,024	1.67	7,141
Crosbyton, Crosby								809	1,250	1,615	1,878	2,650	2,251	2,289	2,026	-7.50	1,874
Crowell, Foard						278	1,341	1,175	1,946	1,817	1,922	1,710	1,399	1,509	1,230	-7.24	1,141
Crowley, Tarrant												583	2,662	5,852	6,974	7.07	7,467
Crystal City, Zavala								800	6,609	6,529	7,198	9,101	8,104	8,334	8,263	-12.99	7,190
Cuero, DeWitt				1,333	2,442	3,422	3,109	3,671	4,672	5,474	7,498	7,338	6,956	7,124	6,700	-1.93	6,571
Daingerfield, Morris										1,032	1,668	3,133	2,630	3,030	2,655	-5.20	2,517
Dalhart, Dallam							2,580	2,676	4,691	4,682	5,918	5,160	5,705	6,854	6,246	15.87	7,237
Dallas, Dallas	*430	‡2,000	‡3,000	10,358	38,067	42,638	92,104	158,976	260,475	294,734	434,462	679,684	844,401	904,078	1,007,618	17.96	1,188,580
Dayton, Liberty									1,207	1,279	1,820	3,367	3,804	4,908	5,042	13.23	5,709
Decatur, Wise				579	1,746	1,562	1,651	2,205	2,037	2,578	2,922	3,563	3,240	4,104	4,245	22.52	5,201
Deer Park, Harris												736	12,773	22,648	27,424	4.00	28,520
Del Rio, Val Verde				50	1,980			10,589	11,693	13,343	14,211	18,612	21,330	30,034	30,705	10.30	33,867
Denison, Grayson				3,975	10,958	11,807	13,632	17,065	13,850	15,581	17,504	22,748	24,923	23,884	21,505	5.90	22,773
Denton, Denton				1,194	2,558	4,187	4,732	7,626	9,587	11,192	21,372	26,844	39,874	48,063	66,270	21.53	80,537
Denver City, Yoakum											1,855	4,302	4,133	4,704	5,156	-24.11	3,985
DeSoto, Dallas											298	1,969	6,617	15,538	30,544	23.25	37,646
Devine, Medina							1,042	995	1,093	1,398	1,672	2,522	3,311	3,756	3,928	5.40	4,140
Diboll, Angelina									1,363		2,391	2,506	3,557	5,227	4,341	26.01	5,470
Dickens, Dickens						176		‡150	‡400	465	416	400	295	409	322	3.11	332

City, County	1850	1860	1870	1880	1890	1900	1910	1920	1930	1940	1950	1960	1970	1980	1990††	% Change 90-00	2000
Dickinson, Galveston									760		2,704	4,715	10,776	7,505	11,692	46.19	17,093
Dilley, Frio									929	1,244	1,809	2,118	2,362	2,575	2,632	39.59	3,674
Dimmitt, Castro									829	943	1,461	2,935	4,327	5,019	4,408	-0.75	4,375
Donna, Hidalgo								1,579	4,103	4,712	7,171	7,522	7,365	9,952	12,652	16.72	14,768
Dublin, Erath					2,025	2,370	2,551	3,229	2,271	2,546	2,761	2,443	2,810	2,723	3,190	17.68	3,754
Dumas, Moore										2,117	6,127	8,477	9,771	12,194	12,871	6.81	13,747
Duncanville, Dallas											841	3,774	14,105	27,781	35,008	3.07	36,081
Eagle Lake, Colorado					769	1,107	1,717	2,017	2,343	2,124	2,787	3,565	3,587	3,921	3,551	3.18	3,664
Eagle Pass, Maverick							3,536	5,765	5,059	6,459	7,276	12,094	15,364	21,407	20,651	8.53	22,413
Eastland, Eastland						596	855	9,368	4,648	3,849	3,626	3,292	3,178	3,747	3,690	2.14	3,769
Edcouch, Hidalgo									914	1,758	2,925	2,814	2,656	3,092	2,878	16.12	3,342
Eden, Concho								593	1,194	1,603	1,978	1,500	1,291	1,294	1,567	63.43	2,561
Edgecliff, Tarrant												339	1,143	2,695	2,715	-6.08	2,550
Edinburg, Hidalgo								1,406	4,821	8,718	12,383	18,706	17,163	24,075	31,091	55.88	48,465
Edna, Jackson								1,766	1,752	2,724	3,855	5,038	5,332	5,650	5,343	10.41	5,899
El Campo, Wharton							1,778	850	2,034	3,906	6,237	7,700	9,332	10,462	10,511	4.13	10,945
Eldorado, Schleicher						112			1,404	1,530	1,653	1,850	1,446	2,061	2,019	-3.37	1,951
Electra, Wichita							640	4,744	6,712	5,588	4,970	4,759	3,895	3,755	3,113	1.77	3,168
Elgin, Bastrop							1,707	1,630	1,823	2,008	3,168	3,511	3,832	4,535	4,846	17.62	5,700
El Lago, Harris													2,308	3,129	3,269	-5.93	3,075
El Paso, El Paso				736	10,338	15,096	39,279	77,560	102,421	96,810	130,485	276,687	322,261	425,259	515,342	9.38	563,662
Elsa, Hidalgo								800	750	1,006	3,179	3,847	4,400	5,061	5,242	5.86	5,549
Emory, Rains					353	426				700	648	570	693	813	963	6.02	1,021
Ennis, Ellis			1,351	2,171	4,919	5,669	7,224	7,069	7,087	7,815	9,347	11,046	12,110	13,869	15.69	16,045
Euless, Tarrant												4,263	19,316	24,002	38,149	20.59	46,005
Everman, Tarrant											451	1,076	4,570	5,387	5,672	2.89	5,836
Fabens, El Paso								1,061	1,623		3,089	1,781	2,074		5,599	43.65	8,043
Fairfield, Freestone										1,047	1,742		3,241	3,505	3,234	-4.33	3,094
Falfurrias, Brooks											6,712	6,515	6,355	6,103	5,788	-8.48	5,297
Farmers Branch, Dallas											915	13,441	27,492	24,863	24,250	13.44	27,508
Floresville, Wilson					913	895	1,398	1,518	1,581	1,708	1,949	2,126	3,707	4,381	5,247	11.84	5,868
Flower Mound, Denton													1,685	4,402	15,527	226.54	50,702
Floydada, Floyd							664	1,384	2,637	2,726	3,210	3,769	4,109	4,193	3,896	-5.65	3,676
Forest Hill, Tarrant											1,519	3,221	8,236	11,684	11,482	12.78	12,949
Fort Davis, Jeff Davis			615	1,162		1,061		‡1,061	‡1,200	‡1,000	‡1,200	850	896	900	‡1,212		1,050
Fort Stockton, Pecos								1,297	2,695	3,294	4,444	6,373	8,283	8,688	8,524	-7.95	7,846
Fort Worth, Tarrant			500	6,663	23,076	26,688	73,312	106,482	163,447	177,662	278,778	356,268	393,476	385,141	447,619	19.45	534,694
Fredericksburg, Gillespie									2,416	3,544	3,854	4,629	5,326	6,412	6,934	28.51	8,911
Freeport, Brazoria								1,798	3,162	2,579	6,012	11,619	11,997	13,444	11,389	11.58	12,708
Freer, Duval										2,346	2,280	2,724	2,804	3,213	3,271	-0.92	3,241
Friendswood, Galveston													5,675	10,719	22,814	27.28	29,037
Friona, Parmer									731	803	1,202	2,048	3,111	3,809	3,688	4.50	3,854
Frisco, Collin							332	733	618	670	736	1,184	1,845	3,420	6,138	449.27	33,714
Gail, Borden						126		‡126	‡175	‡200	‡200	‡200	‡178	‡189	‡202		‡189
Gainesville, Cooke			2,667	6,594	7,874	7,624	8,643	8,915	9,651	11,246	13,083	13,830	14,081	14,256	8.99	15,538
Galena Park, Harris										1,562	7,186	10,852	10,479	9,879	10,033	5.57	10,592

City, County	1850	1860	1870	1880	1890	1900	1910	1920	1930	1940	1950	1960	1970	1980	1990††	% Change 90-00	2000
Galveston, Galveston	4,117	7,307	13,818	22,248	29,084	37,788	36,981	44,255	52,938	60,862	66,568	67,175	61,809	61,902	59,067	-3.08	57,247
Garden City, Glasscock								‡100	‡250	‡250	‡270	‡270	‡286	‡293	‡293		‡293
Garland, Dallas					478	819	804	1,421	1,584	2,233	10,571	38,501	81,437	138,857	180,635	19.45	215,768
Gatesville, Coryell				434	1,375	1,865	1,929	2,499	2,601	3,177	3,856	4,626	4,683	6,260	11,492	35.67	15,591
Georgetown, Williamson	†200		†320	1,354	2,447	2,790	3,096	2,871	3,583	3,682	4,951	5,218	6,395	9,468	14,842	90.94	28,339
George West, Live Oak											1,533	1,878	2,022	2,627	2,586	-2.40	2,524
Giddings, Lee							1,484	1,650	1,835	2,166	2,532	2,821	2,783	3,950	4,093	24.73	5,105
Gilmer, Upshur				624				2,268	1,963	3,138	4,096	4,312	4,196	5,167	4,824	-0.52	4,799
Gladewater, Gregg										4,454	5,305	5,742	5,574	6,548	6,027	0.85	6,078
Glen Rose, Somervell								‡1,000	983	1,050	1,248	1,495	1,554	2,075	1,949	8.88	2,122
Goliad, Goliad	648				400	890	1,261	‡2,500	1,424	1,446	1,580	1,750	1,709	1,990	1,946	1.49	1,975
Gonzales, Gonzales	1,072	1,212		1,581	1,641	4,297	3,139	3,128	3,859	4,722	5,659	5,829	5,854	7,152	6,527	10.34	7,202
**Goose Creek, Harris									5,208	6,929							
Graham, Young					667	878	1,569	2,544	4,981	5,175	6,742	8,505	7,477	9,055	8,986	-3.00	8,716
Granbury, Hood					1,164	1,410	1,336	1,364	996	1,166	1,683	2,227	2,473	3,332	4,045	41.36	5,718
Grand Prairie, Dallas							994	1,263	1,529	1,595	14,594	30,386	50,904	71,462	99,606	27.93	127,427
Grand Saline, Van Zandt							1,065	1,528	1,799	1,641	1,810	2,006	2,257	2,709	2,630	15.13	3,028
Grapevine, Tarrant							681	821	936	1,043	1,824	2,821	7,023	11,801	29,198	44.05	42,059
Greenville, Hunt	*246				4,330	6,860	8,850	12,384	12,407	13,995	14,727	19,087	22,043	22,161	23,071	3.85	23,960
Gregory, San Patricio								1,522	2,059	2,272		1,970	2,246	2,739	2,458	-5.70	2,318
Groesbeck, Limestone					663	1,462	1,454				2,182	2,498	2,396	3,373	3,360	27.71	4,291
Groves, Jefferson												17,304	18,067	17,090	16,744	-6.04	15,733
Guthrie, King								‡101		‡101	‡150	‡210	‡125	‡140	‡160		‡160
Hallettsville, Lavaca					1,011	1,457	1,379	1,444	1,406	1,581	2,000	2,808	2,712	2,865	2,718	-13.72	2,345
Haltom City, Tarrant											5,760	23,133	28,127	29,014	32,856	18.75	39,018
Hamilton, Hamilton							1,548	2,018	2,048	2,716	3,077	3,106	2,760	3,189	2,937	1.36	2,977
Hamlin, Jones							1,978	1,633	2,328	2,406	3,659	3,791	3,325	3,248	2,791	-19.46	2,248
Harker Heights, Bell													4,216	7,345	12,932	33.84	17,308
Harlingen, Cameron								1,784	12,124	13,306	23,229	41,207	33,503	43,543	48,746	18.09	57,564
Haskell, Haskell						‡800	2,346	2,300	2,632	3,051	3,836	4,016	3,655	3,782	3,362	-7.61	3,106
Hearne, Robertson				1,421		2,129	2,353	2,741	2,956	3,511	4,872	5,172	4,982	5,418	5,132	-8.61	4,690
Hebbronville, Jim Hogg								‡3,100			4,302	3,987	4,079	‡4,050	4,465	0.74	4,498
Hedwig Village, Harris												1,182	3,255	2,506	2,616	-10.78	2,334
Hemphill, Sabine						279			731	739	969	913	1,005	1,353	1,182	-6.43	1,106
Hempstead, Waller										1,674	1,395	1,353	1,891	3,456	3,556	31.92	4,691
Henderson, Rusk	*705							2,273	2,932	6,437	6,833	9,666	10,187	11,473	11,139	1.20	11,273
Henrietta, Clay					2,100	1,614	1,750	2,563	2,020	2,391	2,813	3,062	2,897	3,149	2,896	12.71	3,264
Hereford, Deaf Smith								1,696	2,458	2,584	5,207	6,752	13,414	15,853	14,745	-1.00	14,597
Hewitt, McLennan													569	5,247	8,983	23.40	11,085
Highland Park, Dallas								2,321	8,422	10,288	11,405	10,411	10,133	8,909	8,739	1.18	8,842
Highlands, Harris											2,723	4,336	3,462		6,632	6.89	7,089
Highland Village, Denton													516	3,246	7,027	73.23	12,173
Hillsboro, Hill			†313		2,541	5,346	6,115	6,952	7,823	7,799	8,363	7,402	7,224	7,397	7,072	16.40	8,232
Hitchcock, Galveston											1,105	5,216	5,565	6,655	5,868	8.83	6,386
Hollywood Park, Bexar												783	2,299	3,231	2,870	3.94	2,983
Hondo, Medina											4,188	4,992	5,487	6,057	6,018	31.22	7,897

City, County	1850	1860	1870	1880	1890	1900	1910	1920	1930	1940	1950	1960	1970	1980	1990††	% Change 90-00	2000
Hooks, Bowie											2,319	2,048	2,545	2,507	2,684	10.77	2,973
Houston, Harris	2,396	4,845	9,382	16,513	27,557	44,633	78,800	138,276	292,352	384,514	596,163	938,219	1,232,802	1,594,086	1,637,859	19.28	1,953,631
Humble, Harris										1,371	1,388	1,711	3,278	6,729	12,060	20.89	14,579
Huntsville, Walker	*892		†1,600 §	2,536	1,509	2,485	2,072	4,689	5,028	5,108	9,820	11,999	17,610	23,936	27,925	25.62	35,078
Hurst, Tarrant												10,165	27,215	31,420	33,574	8.04	36,273
Hutchins, Dallas											743	1,100	1,755	2,996	2,719	3.16	2,805
Ingleside, San Patricio											1,424	3,022	3,763	5,436	5,696	64.82	9,388
Iowa Park, Wichita							603	2,041	2,009	1,980	2,110	3,295	5,796	6,184	6,072	5.91	6,431
Irving, Dallas								357	731	1,089	2,621	45,985	97,260	109,943	155,037	23.59	191,615
Jacinto City, Harris											6,856	9,547	9,563	8,953	9,343	10.26	10,302
Jacksboro, Jack					751	1,311	1,480	1,373	1,837	2,368	2,951	3,816	3,554	4,000	3,350	35.31	4,533
Jacksonville, Cherokee					970	1,568	2,875	3,723	6,748	7,213	8,607	9,590	9,734	12,264	12,765	8.64	13,868
Jasper, Jasper			†360	†500	‡473			‡750	3,393	3,497	4,403	4,889	6,251	6,959	7,160	15.18	8,247
Jayton, Kent							314		623	770	633	700	703	638	608	-15.63	513
Jefferson, Marion		988	4,190	3,260	3,072	2,850	2,515	2,549	2,329	2,797	3,164	3,082	2,866	2,643	2,199	-7.96	2,024
Jersey Village, Harris												493	765	4,084	4,826	42.56	6,880
Johnson City, Blanco						344		‡400	‡400	†750	645	595	767	872	932	27.79	1,191
Jones Creek, Brazoria													1,763	2,634	2,160	-1.39	2,130
Jourdanton, Atascosa								682	767	950	1,481	1,504	1,271	2,743	3,220	15.90	3,732
Junction, Kimble								787	1,415	2,086	2,471	2,441	2,654	2,593	2,654	-1.36	2,618
Karnes City, Karnes									1,141	1,571	2,588	2,603	2,926	3,296	2,916	18.55	3,457
Katy, Harris											849	1,569	2,923	5,660	8,004	47.11	11,775
Kaufman, Kaufman					1,282	1,378	1,959	2,501	2,279	2,654	2,714	3,087	4,012	4,658	5,251	23.60	6,490
Keene, Johnson												1,532	2,440	3,013	3,944	26.85	5,003
Keller, Tarrant												827	1,474	4,143	13,683	99.85	27,345
Kenedy, Karnes							1,147	2,015	2,610	2,891	4,234	4,301	4,156	3,763	3,763	-7.33	3,487
Kennedale, Tarrant											1,046	1,521	3,076	2,594	4,096	42.75	5,850
Kermit, Winkler										2,584	6,912	10,465	7,884	8,015	6,875	-16.89	5,714
Kerrville, Kerr			†226	156		1,423	1,834	2,353	4,546	5,572	7,691	8,901	12,672	15,276	17,384	17.49	20,425
Kilgore, Gregg										6,708	9,638	10,092	9,495	10,968	11,066	2.12	11,301
Killeen, Bell					285	780	1,265	1,298	1,260	1,263	7,045	23,377	35,507	46,296	63,535	36.79	86,911
Kingsville, Kleberg							1,850	4,770	6,815	7,782	16,898	25,297	28,995	28,808	25,276	1.18	25,575
Kirby, Bexar												680	2,558	6,385	8,326	4.17	8,673
Kountze, Hardin											1,651	1,768	2,173	2,716	2,067	2.32	2,115
Lacy-Lakeview, McLennan												2,272	2,558	2,752	3,617	59.36	5,764
La Feria, Cameron								236	1,594	1,644	2,952	3,047	2,642	3,495	4,360	40.25	6,115
La Grange, Fayette			1,165	1,325	1,044	2,392		1,669	2,354	2,531	2,738	3,623	3,092	3,768	3,951	13.34	4,478
Lake Dallas, Denton											2,897		1,431	3,177	3,656	68.65	6,166
Lake Jackson, Brazoria											2,351	9,651	13,376	19,102	22,771	15.88	26,386
Lakeway, Travis														790	4,044	97.87	8,002
Lake Worth, Tarrant												3,833	4,958	4,394	4,591	0.59	4,618
La Marque, Galveston											7,359	13,969	16,131	15,372	14,120	-3.10	13,682
Lamesa, Dawson								1,188	3,528	6,038	10,704	12,438	11,559	11,790	10,809	-7.93	9,952
Lampasas, Lampasas			†420	653	2,408	2,107	2,119	2,107	2,709	3,426	4,632	5,061	5,922	6,165	6,382	6.33	6,786
Lancaster, Dallas					741	1,045	1,115	1,190	1,133	1,151	1,632	7,501	10,522	14,807	22,117	17.08	25,894
La Porte, Harris						537	678	889	1,280	3,072	4,429	4,512	7,149	14,062	27,923	14.17	31,880
Laredo, Webb		1,256	2,046	3,521	11,319	13,429	14,855	22,710	32,618	39,274	51,910	60,678	69,024	91,449	122,899	43.68	176,576

City, County	1850	1860	1870	1880	1890	1900	1910	1920	1930	1940	1950	1960	1970	1980	1990††	% Change 90-00	2000
League City, Galveston								‡150	‡700	‡550	1,341	2,622	10,818	16,578	30,159	50.68	45,444
Leakey, Real						318					‡550	450	393	468	399	-3.01	387
Leon Valley, Bexar												536	2,487	8,951	9,581	-3.57	9,239
Levelland, Hockley									1,661	3,091	8,264	10,153	11,445	13,809	13,986	-8.01	12,866
Lewisville, Denton									853	873	1,516	3,956	9,264	24,273	46,521	67.10	77,737
Liberty, Liberty						865	980	1,117	2,218	3,087	4,163	6,127	5,591	7,945	7,690	4.46	8,033
Littlefield, Lamb									3,218	3,817	6,540	7,236	6,738	7,409	6,489	0.28	6,507
Live Oak, Bexar		584	458	497									2,779	8,183	10,023	-8.65	9,156
Livingston, Polk								928	1,165	1,851	2,865	3,398	3,965	4,928	5,019	8.25	5,433
Llano, Llano			†500					1,645	2,124	2,658	2,954	2,656	2,608	3,071	2,962	12.26	3,325
Lockhart, Caldwell	*423			718	1,233	2,306	2,945	3,731	4,367	5,018	5,573	6,084	6,489	7,953	9,205	26.18	11,615
Longview, Gregg				1,525	2,034	3,591	5,155	5,713	5,036	13,758	24,502	40,050	46,744	62,762	70,311	4.31	73,344
Lubbock, Lubbock							1,938	4,051	20,520	31,853	71,747	128,691	149,101	173,979	186,206	7.17	199,564
Lufkin, Angelina						1,527	2,749	4,878	7,311	9,567	15,135	17,641	23,049	28,562	30,206	8.29	32,709
Luling, Caldwell					529	1,349	1,404	1,502	5,970	4,437	4,297	4,412	4,719	5,039	4,661	8.99	5,080
Madisonville, Madison					1,792			1,079	1,294	2,095	2,393	2,324	2,881	3,660	3,569	16.53	4,159
Mansfield, Tarrant									635	774	964	1,375	3,658	8,092	15,615	79.51	28,031
Manvel, Brazoria					418	694	627	719					106	3,549	3,733	-18.40	3,046
Marble Falls, Burnet							1,061	639	865	1,021	2,044	2,161	2,209	3,252	4,007	23.76	4,959
Marfa, Presidio									3,909	3,805	3,603	2,799	2,682	2,466	2,424	-12.50	2,121
Marlin, Falls						3,092	3,878	3,553	5,338	6,542	7,099	6,918	6,351	7,099	6,386	3.79	6,628
Marshall, Harrison	‡1,189	‡4,000	1,920	5,624	7,207	7,855	11,452	14,271	16,203	18,410	22,327	23,846	22,937	24,921	23,682	1.07	23,935
Mart, McLennan						‡300	2,939	3,105	2,853	2,856	2,269	2,197	2,183	2,324	2,004	13.42	2,273
Mason, Mason				575		1,137		1,200	1,302	1,500	2,448	1,815	1,806	2,153	2,041	4.56	2,134
Matador, Motley						158		692			1,325	1,217	1,091	1,052	790	-6.33	740
Mathis, San Patricio										1,950	4,050	6,075	5,351	5,667	5,423	-7.17	5,034
McAllen, Hidalgo								5,331	9,074	11,877	20,067	32,728	37,636	67,042	84,021	26.65	106,414
McCamey, Upton									3,446	2,595	3,121	3,375	2,647	2,436	2,493	-27.60	1,805
McGregor, McLennan					774	1,435	1,864	2,081	2,041	2,062	2,669	4,642	4,365	4,513	4,683	0.94	4,727
McKinney, Collin	*523			1,479	2,489	4,342	4,714	6,677	7,307	8,555	10,560	13,763	15,193	16,249	21,283	155.46	54,369
Memphis, Hall							1,936	2,839	4,257	3,869	3,810	3,332	3,227	3,352	2,465	0.57	2,479
Menard, Menard								1,164	1,969	2,375	2,685	1,914	1,740	1,697	1,606	2.93	1,653
Mentone, Loving										‡150	‡110	‡110	‡44	‡50	‡50		‡15
Mercedes, Hidalgo							1,209	3,414	6,608	7,624	10,081	10,943	9,355	11,851	12,694	7.52	13,649
Mertzon, Irion								400	684	869	765	594	513	687	778	7.84	839
Mesquite, Dallas					135	406	687	674	729	1,045	1,696	27,526	55,131	67,053	101,484	22.70	124,523
Mexia, Limestone				1,298	1,674	2,393	2,694	3,482	6,579	6,410	6,627	6,121	5,943	7,094	6,933	-5.34	6,563
Miami, Roberts						286		937	953	713	645	656	611	813	675	-12.89	588
Midland, Midland					297	832	2,192	1,795	5,484	9,352	21,713	62,625	59,463	70,525	89,443	6.21	94,996
Midlothian, Ellis							868	1,298	1,168	1,027	1,177	1,521	2,322	3,219	5,040	48.41	7,480
Mineola, Wood				1,175	1,323	1,725	1,706		3,304	3,223	3,626	3,810	3,926	4,346	4,321	5.30	4,550
Mineral Wells, Palo Pinto					577	2,048	3,950	7,890	5,986	6,303	7,801	11,053	18,411	14,468	14,935	13.47	16,946
Mission, Hidalgo								3,847	5,120	5,982	10,765	14,081	13,043	22,589	28,653	58.48	45,408
Missouri City, Fort Bend												604	4,136	24,533	36,176	46.27	52,913
Monahans, Ward									816	3,944	6,311	8,567	8,333	8,397	8,101	-15.80	6,821
Mont Belvieu, Chambers								‡20	‡600	‡600	‡500	‡500	1,144	1,730	1,323	75.66	2,324

City, County	1850	1860	1870	1880	1890	1900	1910	1920	1930	1940	1950	1960	1970	1980	1990††	% Change 90-00	2000
Morton, Cochran										1,137	2,274	2,731	2,738	2,674	2,597	-13.40	2,249
Mount Pleasant, Titus	*227						3,137	4,099	3,541	4,528	6,342	8,027	9,459	11,003	12,219	13.38	13,935
Mount Vernon, Franklin				311	589	972		1,212	1,222	1,443	1,423	1,338	1,806	2,025	2,219	3.02	2,286
Muleshoe, Bailey									779	1,327	2,477	3,871	4,525	4,842	4,571	-0.90	4,530
Munday, Knox							956	998	1,318	1,545	2,270	1,978	1,726	1,738	1,600	-4.56	1,527
Nacogdoches, Nac.	‡468	*383			1,138	1,827	3,369	3,546	5,687	7,538	12,327	12,674	22,544	27,149	30,872	-3.10	29,914
Nassau Bay, Harris														4,526	4,320	-3.47	4,170
Navasota, Grimes				1,611	2,997	3,857	3,284	5,060	5,128	6,138	5,188	4,937	5,111	5,971	6,296	7.83	6,789
Nederland, Jefferson											3,805	12,036	16,810	16,855	16,192	7.60	17,422
New Boston, Bowie								869	949	1,111	2,688	2,773	4,034	4,628	5,057	-4.92	4,808
New Braunfels, Comal	*1,727	‡3,500	2,261	1,938	1,608	2,097	3,165	3,590	6,242	6,976	12,210	15,631	17,859	22,402	27,334	33.51	36,494
Newton, Newton								‡800	‡1,000	‡1,200	934	1,233	1,529	1,620	1,885	30.45	2,459
Nocona, Montague					381	961	1,338	1,422	2,352	2,605	3,022	3,127	2,871	2,992	2,870	11.43	3,198
North Richland Hills, Tarrant												8,662	16,514	30,592	45,895	21.22	55,635
Odessa, Ector									2,407	9,573	29,495	80,338	78,380	90,027	89,699	1.39	90,943
Olmos Park, Bexar										1,822	2,841	2,457	2,250	2,069	2,161	8.42	2,343
Olney, Young							1,095	1,164	4,138	3,497	3,765	3,872	3,624	4,060	3,519	-3.50	3,396
Orange, Orange					3,173	3,835	5,527	9,212	7,913	7,472	21,174	25,605	24,457	23,628	19,370	-3.75	18,643
Ozona, Crockett											2,885	3,361	2,864	3,766	3,181	8.02	3,436
Paducah, Cottle							1,389	1,335	1,318	2,677	2,952	2,392	2,052	2,216	1,788	-16.22	1,498
Paint Rock, Concho						323		‡750	‡1,000	‡800	‡800	‡810	193	256	227	40.97	320
Palacios, Matagorda							1,350	1,357	2,802	2,288	2,799	3,676	3,642	4,667	4,418	16.64	5,153
Palestine, Anderson	‡2,000			2,997	5,838	8,297	10,482	11,039	11,445	12,144	12,503	13,974	14,525	15,948	18,042	-2.46	17,598
Pampa, Gray										12,895	16,583	24,664	21,726	21,396	19,959	-10.38	17,887
Panhandle, Carson						468	521	638	2,035	978	1,403	1,907	2,141	2,226	2,353	10.03	2,589
Paris, Lamar	*1,003	‡1,500		3,980	8,254	9,358	11,269	15,040	15,649	18,678	21,643	20,977	23,441	25,498	24,799	4.43	25,898
Pasadena, Harris									1,647	3,436	22,483	58,737	89,277	112,560	119,604	18.45	141,674
Pearland, Brazoria													6,444	13,248	18,927	98.87	37,640
Pearsall, Frio							1,799	2,161	2,536	3,164	4,481	4,957	5,545	7,383	6,924	3.37	7,157
Pecos, Reeves					393	639	1,856	1,445	3,304	4,855	8,054	12,728	12,682	12,855	12,069	-21.28	9,501
**Pelly, Harris									3,442	3,712							
Perryton, Ochiltree								‡500	2,824	2,325	4,417	7,903	7,810	7,991	7,619	2.03	7,774
Pflugerville, Travis									‡580	‡500	‡380	‡380	549	745	4,444	267.57	16,335
Pharr, Hidalgo								1,565	3,225	4,784	8,690	14,106	15,829	21,381	32,921	41.73	46,660
Pinehurst, Orange												1,703	2,198	3,055	2,682	-15.21	2,274
Piney Point Village, Harris												1,790	2,548	2,958	3,197	5.72	3,380
Pittsburg, Camp					1,203	1,783	1,916	2,540	2,640	2,916	3,142	3,796	3,844	4,245	4,007	8.49	4,347
Plainview, Hale							2,829	3,989	8,834	8,263	14,044	18,735	19,096	22,187	21,698	2.94	22,336
Plano, Collin					824	1,304	1,258	1,715	1,554	1,582	2,126	3,695	17,872	72,331	127,885	73.62	222,030
Pleasanton, Atascosa								1,036	1,154	2,074	2,913	3,467	5,407	6,346	7,678	7.66	8,266
Port Arthur, Jefferson						900	7,663	22,251	50,902	46,140	57,530	66,676	57,371	61,195	58,551	-1.36	57,755
Port Isabel, Cameron									1,177	1,440	2,372	3,575	3,067	3,769	4,467	8.91	4,865
Portland, San Patricio											1,292	2,538	7,302	12,023	12,224	21.29	14,827
Port Lavaca, Calhoun								1,213	1,367	2,069	5,599	8,864	10,491	10,911	10,886	10.55	12,035
Port Neches, Jefferson									2,327	2,487	5,448	8,696	10,894	13,944	12,908	5.37	13,601
Post, Garza							1,699	1,436	1,668	2,046	3,141	4,663	3,854	3,961	3,768	-1.59	3,708

City, County	1850	1860	1870	1880	1890	1900	1910	1920	1930	1940	1950	1960	1970	1980	1990††	% Change 90-00	2000
Poteet, Atascosa									1,231	2,315	2,487	2,811	3,013	3,086	3,206	3.09	3,305
Prairie View, Waller												2,326	3,589	3,993	4,004	10.14	4,410
Premont, Jim Wells								500		1,080	2,619	3,049	3,282	2,984	2,914	-4.87	2,772
Princeton, Collin									459	564	540	594	1,105	3,408	2,448	42.03	3,477
Quanah, Hardeman					1,477	1,651	3,127	3,691	4,464	3,767	4,589	4,564	3,948	3,890	3,413	-11.46	3,022
Ralls, Crosby								‡500	1,365	1,512	1,771	2,300	1,962	2,422	2,172	3.68	2,252
Ranger, Eastland								16,201	6,208	4,553	3,989	3,313	3,094	3,142	2,803	-7.81	2,584
Raymondville, Willacy									2,050	4,050	9,136	9,385	7,987	9,493	8,880	9.61	9,733
Refugio, Refugio								933	2,019	4,077	4,666	4,944	4,340	3,898	3,158	-6.87	2,941
Richardson, Dallas							773		629	720	1,289	16,810	48,582	72,496	74,840	22.66	91,802
Richland Hills, Tarrant												7,804	8,865	7,977	7,978	1.93	8,132
Richmond, Fort Bend							1,371	1,273	1,432	2,026	2,030	3,668	5,777	9,692	10,042	10.35	11,081
Richwood, Brazoria														2,591	2,732	10.25	3,012
Rio Grande City, Starr		439			1,968				2,283		3,992	5,835	5,676	8,930	10,725	11.17	11,923
River Oaks, Tarrant											7,097	8,444	8,193	6,890	6,580	6.16	6,985
Robert Lee, Coke								‡582	490	662	1,070	975	1,119	1,202	1,276	-8.23	1,171
Robinson, McLennan												2,110	3,807	6,074	7,111	10.32	7,845
Robstown, Nueces								948	4,183	6,780	7,278	10,266	11,217	12,100	12,849	-0.95	12,727
Rockdale, Milam					1,505	2,515	2,073	2,323	2,204	2,136	2,321	4,481	4,655	5,611	5,235	3.90	5,439
Rockport, Aransas					1,069	1,153	1,382	1,545	1,140	1,729	2,266	2,989	3,879	3,686	5,355	37.91	7,385
Rocksprings, Edwards						389		‡600	998	1,339	1,433	1,275	1,221	1,317	1,339	-4.03	1,285
Rockwall, Rockwall					843	1,245	1,136	1,388	1,071	1,318	1,501	2,166	3,121	5,939	10,486	71.43	17,976
Roma-Los Saenz, Starr			479				1,198	1,279	1,941	1,414	1,576	1,496	2,154	3,384	8,059	19.33	9,617
Rosenberg, Fort Bend							1,126	1,000	1,632	3,457	6,210	9,698	12,098	17,995	20,183	19.13	24,043
Rotan, Fisher								900	1,173	2,029	3,163	2,788	2,404	2,284	1,913	-15.79	1,611
Round Rock, Williamson										1,240	1,438	1,878	2,811	11,812	30,923	97.70	61,136
Rowlett, Dallas												1,015	2,579	7,522	23,260	91.33	44,503
Rusk, Cherokee	‡355	*395	‡1,000		1,383	846	1,558	2,348	3,859	5,699	6,598	4,900	4,914	4,681	4,366	16.47	5,085
Saginaw, Tarrant											561	1,001	2,382	5,736	8,551	44.71	12,374
San Angelo, Tom Green							10,321	10,050	25,308	25,802	52,093	58,815	63,884	73,240	84,462	4.71	88,439
San Antonio, Bexar	3,488	8,235	12,256	20,550	37,673	53,321	96,614	161,379	231,542	253,854	408,442	587,718	654,153	785,410	959,295	19.32	1,144,646
San Augustine, San Aug.			920	503	744	261	1,204	1,268	1,247	1,516	2,510	2,584	2,539	2,930	2,337	5.91	2,475
San Benito, Cameron								5,070	10,753	9,501	13,271	16,422	15,176	17,988	20,125	16.49	23,444
Sanderson, Terrell								‡500	‡1,500	‡1,875	‡2,150	‡2,350	‡1,229	‡1,500	1,128	-23.67	861
San Diego, Duval								1,204	1,119	1,000	4,397	4,351	4,490	5,225	4,983	-4.62	4,753
Sanger, Denton					741	112		1,203	1,615		1,170	1,190	1,603	2,574	3,514	29.03	4,534
San Juan, Hidalgo										2,264	3,413	4,371	5,070	7,608	12,561	108.81	26,229
San Marcos, Hays					2,335	2,292	4,071	4,527	5,134	6,006	9,980	12,713	18,860	23,420	28,738	20.86	34,733
San Saba, San Saba					1,232			2,011	2,240	2,927	3,400	2,728	2,555	2,336	2,626	0.42	2,637
Sansom Park, Tarrant											1,611	4,175	4,771	3,921	3,928	6.44	4,181
Santa Fe, Galveston														5,413	8,429	13.28	9,548
Sarita, Kenedy								‡200	‡250	‡200	‡200	‡200	‡196	‡185	‡185		‡250
Schertz, Guadalupe												2,281	4,061	7,262	10,597	76.41	18,694
Seabrook, Harris													3,811	4,670	6,685	41.26	9,443
Seagoville, Dallas									604	760	1,927	3,745	4,390	7,304	8,969	20.67	10,823
Seagraves, Gaines									505	3,225	2,101	2,307	2,440	2,596	2,398	-2.67	2,334

City, County	1850	1860	1870	1880	1890	1900	1910	1920	1930	1940	1950	1960	1970	1980	1990††	% Change 90-00	2000
Sealy, Austin											1,942	2,328	2,685	3,875	4,541	15.57	5,248
Seguin, Guadalupe		*792	†830	1,363	1,716	2,421	3,116	3,631	5,225	7,006	9,733	14,299	15,934	17,854	18,692	17.76	22,011
Seminole, Gaines									2,626	1,761	3,479	5,737	5,007	6,080	6,342	-6.81	5,910
Seymour, Baylor							2,029	2,121	3,780	3,328	3,779	3,789	3,469	3,657	3,185	-8.70	2,908
Shamrock, Wheeler								1,227		3,123	3,322	3,113	2,644	2,834	2,286	-11.24	2,029
Shepherd, San Jacinto						278		‡500	‡450	‡500	‡350	‡1,300	928	1,674	1,812	11.98	2,029
Sherman, Grayson			1,439	6,093	7,335	10,243	12,412	15,031	15,713	17,156	20,150	24,988	29,061	30,413	31,584	11.08	35,082
Sierra Blanca, Hudspeth								‡600	‡500	‡723	‡850	‡850	‡600	‡700	‡700		533
Silsbee, Hardin										2,525	3,179	6,277	7,271	7,684	6,368	0.39	6,393
Silverton, Briscoe								416	873	684	855	1,168	1,026	918	779	-1.03	771
Sinton, San Patricio								1,058	1,852	3,770	4,254	6,008	5,563	6,044	5,549	2.29	5,676
Slaton, Lubbock								1,525	3,876	3,587	5,036	6,568	6,583	6,804	6,078	0.51	6,109
Smithville, Bastrop					616	2,577	3,167	3,204	3,296	3,100	3,379	2,933	2,959	3,470	3,196	22.06	3,901
Snyder, Scurry					500	612	2,514	2,179	3,008	3,815	12,012	13,050	11,171	12,705	12,195	-11.58	10,783
Sonora, Sutton								1,009	1,942	2,528	2,633	2,619	2,149	3,856	2,751	6.29	2,924
South Houston, Harris										982	4,126	7,523	11,527	13,293	14,207	11.45	15,833
Southlake, Denton												1,023	2,031	2,808	7,082	203.85	21,519
Spearman, Hansford									612	1,105	1,852	3,555	3,435	3,413	3,197	-5.51	3,021
Spring Valley, Harris												3,004	3,170	3,353	3,392	6.46	3,611
Spur, Dickens								1,100	1,580	2,136	2,173	2,300	1,747	1,690	1,300	-16.31	1,088
Stafford, Fort Bend												1,485	2,906	4,755	8,395	86.79	15,681
Stamford, Jones							3,902	3,704	4,095	4,810	5,819	5,259	4,558	4,542	3,817	-4.74	3,636
Stanton, Martin								‡600	1,384	1,245	1,594	2,690	2,117	2,314	2,576	-0.78	2,556
Stephenville, Erath					909	1,902	2,561	3,891	3,994	4,768	7,155	7,359	9,277	11,881	13,502	10.51	14,921
Sterling City, Sterling						532		‡532	‡700	‡866	‡800	875	780	915	1,096	-1.37	1,081
Stinnett, Hutchinson										635	1,170	2,695	2,014	2,222	2,166	-10.62	1,936
Stratford, Sherman							520	472	873	877	1,376	1,850	2,139	1,917	1,781	11.79	1,991
Sugar Land, Fort Bend	*441	‡2,500									2,285	2,802	3,318	8,826	33,712	87.85	63,328
Sulphur Springs, Hopkins				1,854	3,033	3,635	5,151	5,558	5,417	6,742	8,991	9,160	10,642	12,804	14,062	3.48	14,551
Sweeny, Brazoria											1,393	3,087	3,191	3,538	3,297	9.92	3,624
Sweetwater, Nolan					614	670	4,176	4,307	10,848	10,367	13,619	13,914	12,020	12,242	11,967	-4.61	11,415
Taft, San Patricio									1,792	2,686	2,978	3,463	3,274	3,686	3,222	5.40	3,396
Tahoka, Lynn								786	1,620	2,129	2,848	3,012	2,956	3,262	2,868	1.46	2,910
Taylor, Williamson					2,584	4,211	5,314	5,965	7,463	7,875	9,071	9,434	9,616	10,619	11,472	18.33	13,575
Taylor Lake Village, Harris													990	3,669	3,352	10.20	3,694
Teague, Freestone							3,288	3,306	3,509	3,157	2,925	2,728	2,867	3,390	3,268	39.44	4,557
Temple, Bell					4,047	7,065	10,993	11,033	15,345	15,344	25,467	30,419	33,431	42,483	46,150	18.12	54,514
Terrell, Kaufman				2,003	2,988	6,330	7,050	8,349	8,795	10,481	11,544	13,803	14,182	13,225	12,490	8.94	13,606
Terrell Hills, Bexar										1,236	2,708	5,572	5,225	4,644	4,592	9.30	5,019
Texarkana, Bowie				1,833	2,852	5,256	9,790	11,480	16,602	17,019	24,753	30,218	30,497	31,271	32,294	7.70	34,782
Texas City, Galveston								2,509	3,534	5,748	16,620	32,065	38,908	41,403	40,822	1.71	41,521
The Colony, Denton														11,586	22,113	19.98	26,531
Throckmorton, Throck.				37	240	506		686	1,135	1,133	1,319	1,260	1,105	1,174	1,036	-12.64	905
Tilden, McMullen								‡250		‡500	‡380	‡380	‡416	‡500	‡500		†450
Tomball, Harris										668	1,065	1,713	2,734	3,996	6,370	42.68	9,089
Trinity, Trinity								1,363	2,036	2,217	2,054	1,787	2,512	2,452	2,648	2.76	2,721

City, County	1850	1860	1870	1880	1890	1900	1910	1920	1930	1940	1950	1960	1970	1980	1990††	% Change 90-00	2000
Tulia, Swisher							1,216	1,189	2,202	2,055	3,222	4,410	5,294	5,033	4,703	8.80	5,117
Tyler, Smith	‡1,024			2,423	6,908	8,069	10,400	12,085	17,113	28,279	38,968	51,230	57,770	70,508	75,450	10.87	83,650
Universal City, Bexar													7,613	10,720	13,057	13.72	14,849
University Park, Dallas									4,200	14,458	24,275	23,202	23,498	22,254	22,259	4.78	23,324
Uvalde, Uvalde					1,265	1,889	3,998	3,885	5,286	6,679	8,674	10,293	10,764	14,178	14,729	1.36	14,929
Van Horn, Culberson										515	1,161	1,953	2,889	2,772	2,930	-16.89	2,435
Vega, Oldham								200	519		619	658	839	900	840	11.43	936
Vernon, Wilbarger					2,857	1,993	3,195	5,142	9,137	9,277	12,651	12,141	11,454	12,695	12,001	-2.84	11,660
Victoria, Victoria	*1,440		2,500		3,046	4,010	3,673	5,957	7,421	11,566	16,126	33,047	41,349	50,695	55,076	10.04	60,603
Vidor, Orange											2,136	4,938	9,738	12,117	10,935	4.62	11,440
Waco, McLennan	*749		3,008	7,295	14,445	20,686	26,425	38,500	52,848	55,982	84,706	97,808	95,326	101,261	103,590	9.78	113,726
Wake Village, Bowie												1,140		3,865	4,761	7.73	5,129
Watauga, Tarrant													3,778	10,284	20,009	9.49	21,908
Waxahachie, Ellis	*175	†1,823		1,354	3,076	4,215	6,205	7,958	8,042	8,655	11,204	12,749	13,452	14,624	17,984	19.14	21,426
Weatherford, Parker				2,046	3,369	4,786	5,074	6,203	4,912	5,924	8,093	9,759	11,750	12,049	14,804	28.34	19,000
Wellington, Collingsworth							576	1,968	3,570	3,308	3,676	3,137	2,884	3,043	2,456	-7.37	2,275
Weslaco, Hidalgo									4,879	6,883	7,514	15,649	15,313	19,331	22,739	18.45	26,935
West Columbia, Brazoria										1,573	2,100	2,947	3,335	4,109	4,372	-2.68	4,255
West Orange, Orange											2,539	4,848	4,820	4,610	4,187	-1.82	4,111
W. University Place, Harris									1,322	9,221	17,074	14,628	13,317	12,010	12,920	9.99	14,211
Westworth Village, Tarrant											529	3,321	4,578	3,651	2,350	-9.62	2,124
Wharton, Wharton							1,505	2,346	2,691	4,386	4,450	5,734	7,881	9,033	9,011	2.51	9,237
White Oak, Gregg												1,250	2,300	4,415	5,136	9.50	5,624
Whitesboro, Grayson					1,170	1,243	1,219	1,810	1,535	1,560	1,854	2,485	2,927	3,197	3,209	17.17	3,760
White Settlement, Tarrant											10,827	11,513	13,449	13,508	15,472	-4.14	14,831
Wichita Falls, Wichita					1,978	2,480	8,200	40,079	43,690	45,112	68,042	101,724	96,265	94,201	96,259	8.25	104,197
Wills Point, Van Zandt					1,025	1,347	1,398	1,811	2,023	1,976	2,030	2,281	2,636	2,631	2,986	17.08	3,496
Windcrest, Bexar												441	3,371	5,332	5,331	-4.24	5,105
Wink, Winkler									3,963	1,945	1,521	1,863	1,023	1,182	1,189	-22.71	919
Winnie, Chambers								‡200	‡370	‡200	325†	‡1,114	‡1,543	‡5,512	2,238	30.21	2,914
Winnsboro, Wood					388	899	1,741	2,184	1,905	2,092	2,512	2,675	3,064	3,458	2,904	23.42	3,584
Winters, Runnels							1,347	1,509	2,423	2,335	2,676	3,266	2,907	3,061	2,905	-0.86	2,880
Woodville, Tyler					239	773	620	945	969	1,521	1,863	1,920	2,662	2,821	2,636	-8.38	2,415
Woodway, McLennan												1,244	4,819	7,091	8,695	0.44	8,733
Wylie, Collin									771	914	1,295	1,804	2,675	3,152	8,716	73.61	15,132
Yoakum, Lavaca					1,745	3,499	4,657	6,184	5,656	4,733	5,231	5,761	5,755	6,148	5,611	2.14	5,731
Yorktown, DeWitt				430	522	846	1,180	1,723	1,882	2,081	2,596	2,527	2,411	2,498	2,207	2.90	2,271
Zapata, Zapata								‡300	‡450	‡500	‡850	‡2,031	‡2,102	‡3,500	7,119	-31.79	4,856

*Census of incorporated towns of Texas taken in 1858 by tax assessors and collectors in each county.

†Federal census of western part of Texas for 1870, as given in Texas Almanac for 1871.

‡An estimate of that date.

**Pelly, Goose Creek and Baytown merged in 1947, and the single community took the name of the latter — Baytown. Baytown was unincorporated prior to this merger and did not show any previous census. However, Pelly and Goose Creek were previously incorporated, hence the census figures for them in 1930 and 1940.

§ Includes Huntsville prison population.

†† After the publication of the original 1990 official Bureau of the Census population count, many places requested an official review of the counts for their areas. The values shown are the revised values provided by the U.S. Bureau of the Census after those reviews. Many of these values are different from the ones published in the 1992-93 Texas Almanac.

Bush Wins Re-election; GOP Solidifies Power in Texas

By Carolyn Barta

Texan George W. Bush won a second term as president in 2004, as Republicans solidified their power in the Lone Star State and in Congress.

As expected, the presidential election was close, but it escaped the drama that marked 2000, when the U.S. Supreme Court determined Bush the victor after 36 days of uncertainty over who won Florida.

Still, 2004 was so tight that a winner could not be projected on election night between the GOP ticket led by Bush and Vice President Dick Cheney and the Democratic ticket of Massachusetts Sen. John Kerry and former North Carolina Sen. John Edwards.

Pivotal Ohio remained too close to call until the day after the election. But Bush by then had won Florida and all but one of the states he carried in 2000. Ohio cinched it. He was re-elected with 286 electoral votes to Kerry's 252.

Unlike 2000, this time Bush also won the popular vote – gaining almost 51 percent in the highest turnout (60.7 percent) since 1968.

President Bush at his ranch in Crawford with Vice President Dick Cheney. File photo.

Bush's 2004 win erased the claim by Democrats that he had been an "accidental president" – a former president's son elected by the Supreme Court. A sea of red Republican states blanketed an Election Day map of the nation. For the second straight election, Democrats were able to paint blue only a handful of states on the West Coast, in New England and in the upper Midwest.

In Texas, the former governor won easily, capturing 4.5 million votes to Kerry's 2.8 million, or 61 percent -- topping the 59 percent he garnered in 2000. The Texas turnout was 56.6 percent of the state's 13 million plus registered voters.

Democrats in Texas, meanwhile, lost their majority status in the state's congressional delegation when Republicans emerged with 21 of the state's 32 seats. For that success, Republicans could credit a bitterly fought redistricting battle in the Texas Legislature, orchestrated from Washington by House Majority Leader Tom DeLay.

The congressional outcome solidified the dominance of the GOP, which already held all statewide elected offices and both legislative chambers in the president's home state. The Texas congressional turnover [see related article] also helped Republicans tighten their grip on Congress and provide more support for the president.

Of 435 House seats, Republicans held 227 before the election and emerged with 231 – the most Republicans had elected in any years since 1946. In the Senate, the GOP majority increased from a scant 51 members to a more comfortable 55. The election left Republicans with their strongest hold on federal government since the 1920s.

DeLay credited Texas with the wider House majority. "God bless Texas," he said. "The Republican Party is a permanent majority for the future of this country."

As for the presidential election, analysts said the continuing war on terrorism along with religious ideals and the "values" debate led a majority of voters to favor the Republican ticket. Many voters did not want to switch commander-in-chief in the middle of the war in Iraq.

The Bush campaign painted Kerry as a flip-flopper who had been on both sides of the Iraqi war issue and who would vacillate on terrorism, even as Kerry tried to use his service in Vietnam to advantage, declaring at the Democratic National Convention that he was "reporting for duty." Controversy during the campaign, however, swirled around his service as a swift boat commander.

For his part, Bush pledged to stand behind Afghanistan and Iraq until their emerging democracies enabled American service men and women to return home. The campaign cast him as a strong, decisive wartime leader determined to battle terrorism,

Exit polls also found Bush more likable and more

in tune with the mainstream on cultural issues. And 11 states passed referendums banning gay marriage, producing turnouts that boosted Bush's margin.

As for his domestic record, Bush touted passage of the No Child Left Behind Act, which demanded increased accountability from the nation's schools. He promised to pursue reforms of Social Security that would allow younger taxpayers to invest in private retirement accounts, and Social Security subsequently became a priority in his second term.

Alberto Gonzales,
Attorney General

Texans continued to have a strong presence on the Potomac. Some who originally went with Bush to Washington left government service, but the president brought others into his second administration.

Senior adviser Karl Rove, the political strategist from Austin who engineered both presidential elections, became deputy chief of staff, a job that would involve him in all White House policy. Bush's communications operation was headed by Texans Dan Bartlett, director, and Scott McClellan, press secretary.

Karen Hughes, former counselor to the president and communications specialist who had returned to Austin with her family, agreed to go back to Washington as undersecretary of state for public diplomacy – to help the U.S. improve its image abroad. Harriet Miers, former deputy chief of staff for policy, moved to legal counsel.

Al Gonzales, the White House counsel who had

Margaret Spellings,
Secretary of Education

been Bush's general counsel as governor, became U.S. attorney general.

Domestic policy adviser Margaret Spellings, who advised Bush on education policy when he was governor, succeeded Texan Rod Paige as education secretary. Mark McClellan, former Food and Drug Administration commissioner, continued as Medicare and Medicaid Administrator.

Bush's diplomatic appointments included Jim Oberwetter, former Hunt Oil officer in Dallas, as ambassador to Saudi Arabia.

Bush continued to maintain a strong presence in Texas, returning frequently for holidays, occasional weekends and August vacations to his ranch in Crawford, where he continued to host world leaders such as Saudi Crown Prince Abdullah and Vicente Fox, president of Mexico.

In his 2004 victory speech, Bush, who grew up in Midland, addressed Texans, saying: "We have known each other the longest, and you started me on this journey. On the open plains of Texas, I first learned the character of our country: sturdy and honest and as hopeful as the break of day."

He promised to return to Texas saying, "Whatever the road that lies ahead, that road will take me home."

Carolyn Barta, a retired staff writer for The Dallas Morning News, *teaches journalism at Southern Methodist University.*

Texas Election Turnout by Voting Age Population

Year	2004	2000	1996	1992	1988	1984	1980	1976	1972
Major Candidates	Bush Kerry	Bush Gore	Clinton Dole	Clinton Bush Perot	Bush Dukakis	Reagan Mondale	Reagan Carter	Carter Ford	Nixon McGovern
Percentage of VAP that voted	**46.1**	**44.3**	**41.0**	**47.6**	**44.3**	**47.6**	**45.6**	**46.1**	**44.9**
Percentage of registered voters that voted	56.6	51.8	53.2	72.9	66.2	68.3	68.4	64.8	89.6

The **voting age population (VAP)** refers to the total number of persons of voting age regardless of citizenship, military status, felonly conviction or mental state. The Bureau of the Census is the source for the VAP estimates.

Since the National Voter Registration Act of 1993, non-voters cannot be removed from registration rolls of a county until two federal elections have been held. So, for instance, if a person moved in December 2000 from one county to another, that person could be counted as a non-voter in the previous county of residence through the general election of November 2004.

These are called "suspense voters" on county rolls and have affected the statistical reports of the percentage of registered voters participating in elections.

In the early 1970s, various election reforms were enacted by the Legislature, including eliminating the requirement for an annual registration and allowing for a continuing voter registration system.

The presidential elections have a larger voter turnout than off-year and state elections. — RP

Sources: Federal Election Commission and the Texas Secretary of State office.

2004 Presidential Election Results by County

Below are the official results by county. Listed are the leading candidates for U.S. president. The total number of votes counted in the presidential race, 7,410,749, was 56.57 percent of the number of regis- tered voters on election day, Nov. 2. The voting age population was 16,071,153. The statewide turnout in the presidential election of 2000 was 51.81 percent. *Source: Texas Secretary of State.*

County	Registered Voters	Turnout %	Total Votes	PRESIDENTIAL RACE					
				BUSH (Republican)	%	KERRY (Democrat)	%	BADNARIK (Libertarian)	NADER (Write-in)
Statewide	**13,098,329**	**56.57**	**7,410,749**	**4,526,917**	**61.08**	**2,832,704**	**38.22**	**38,787**	**9,153**
Anderson	29,612	55.0	16,301	11,525	70.7	4,678	28.7	73	15
Andrews	8,421	53.9	4,536	3,837	84.6	677	14.9	18	1
Angelina	48,109	59.0	28,364	18,932	66.7	9,302	37.8	91	28
Aransas	16,049	57.7	9,268	6,569	70.9	2,640	28.5	41	18
Archer	6,509	68.4	4,451	3,556	79.9	878	19.7	9	7
Armstrong	1,476	68.0	1,004	830	82.7	170	16.9	0	2
Atascosa	24,912	48.6	12,116	7,635	63.0	4,421	36.5	50	7
Austin	17,096	62.6	10,702	8,072	75.4	2,582	24.1	33	9
Bailey	4,071	59.2	2,412	1,882	78.0	525	21.8	3	2
Bandera	13,472	64.9	8,741	6,933	79.3	1,738	19.9	53	13
Bastrop	38,047	61.6	23,441	13,290	56.7	9,794	41.8	274	56
Baylor	2,820	58.2	1,640	1,169	71.3	467	28.5	4	0
Bee	16,513	57.6	9,518	5,428	57.0	4,045	42.5	33	9
Bell	154,459	51.6	79,724	52,135	65.4	27,165	34.1	368	33
Bexar	908,466	52.3	475,314	260,698	54.8	210,976	44.4	2,674	750
Blanco	6,548	70.0	4,584	3,277	71.5	1,267	27.6	30	5
Borden	455	78.9	359	303	84.4	55	15.3	1	0
Bosque	11,495	66.0	7,586	5,737	75.6	1,815	23.9	27	7
Bowie	57,462	58.8	33,760	21,791	64.5	11,880	35.2	66	22
Brazoria	161,485	57.7	93,248	63,662	68.3	28,904	31.0	583	67
Brazos	92,666	58.6	54,309	37,594	69.2	16,128	29.7	461	103
Brewster	6,173	60.9	3,760	1,980	52.7	1,729	46.1	32	9
Briscoe	1,328	61.1	811	620	76.4	191	23.6	0	0
Brooks	6,768	39.5	2,674	845	31.6	1,823	68.2	6	0
Brown	25,703	55.5	14,253	11,640	81.7	2,523	17.7	64	0
Burleson	11,156	60.2	6,721	4,405	65.5	2,276	33.9	29	5
Burnet	24,592	64.0	15,742	11,456	72.8	4,147	26.3	111	15
Caldwell	21,991	52.7	11,587	6,436	55.5	5,052	43.6	78	14
Calhoun	14,454	47.9	6,929	4,348	62.8	2,561	37.0	20	0
Callahan	9,271	61.0	5,654	4,542	80.3	1,073	19.0	26	7
Cameron	162,369	42.1	69,156	34,801	50.3	33,998	49.2	282	62
Camp	7,247	61.3	4,439	2,638	59.4	1,778	40.1	16	7
Carson	4,823	61.0	2,944	2,450	83.2	485	16.5	8	1
Cass	19,034	63.3	12,049	7,383	61.3	4,630	38.4	35	0
Castro	4,738	51.3	2,430	1,794	73.8	631	26.0	4	1
Chambers	20,250	57.5	11,649	8,618	74.0	2,953	25.3	59	15
Cherokee	30,111	52.6	15,839	11,329	71.5	4,439	28.0	58	8
Childress	3,933	54.5	2,144	1,629	76.0	511	23.8	4	0
Clay	7,498	70.5	5,288	3,971	75.1	1,299	24.6	13	5
Cochran	2,147	51.7	1,110	856	77.1	249	22.4	3	1
Coke	2,618	61.5	1,610	1,338	83.1	266	16.5	5	1
Coleman	6,505	58.8	3,826	3,035	79.3	778	20.3	11	2
Collin	369,412	66.4	245,154	174,435	71.2	68,935	28.1	1,424	281
Collingsworth	2,306	60.6	1,398	1,051	75.2	346	24.7	0	1
Colorado	12,985	59.2	7,690	5,488	71.4	2,161	28.10	29	6
Comal	65,739	62.4	41,043	31,574	76.9	9,153	22.30	245	42
Comanche	9,389	56.1	5,268	3,813	72.4	1,431	27.16	21	2
Concho	1,862	64.1	1,193	911	76.4	270	22.63	6	4
Cooke	24,943	60.6	15,107	11,908	78.8	3,142	20.8	46	9
Coryell	38,466	45.8	17,625	12,421	70.5	5,122	29.1	69	13
Cottle	1,355	56.7	768	549	71.5	214	27.9	5	1
Crane	2,705	58.2	1,574	1,314	83.5	254	16.1	5	1
Crockett	2,789	62.0	1,728	1,248	72.2	473	27.4	6	0
Crosby	4,344	52.4	2,275	1,647	72.4	622	27.3	6	0

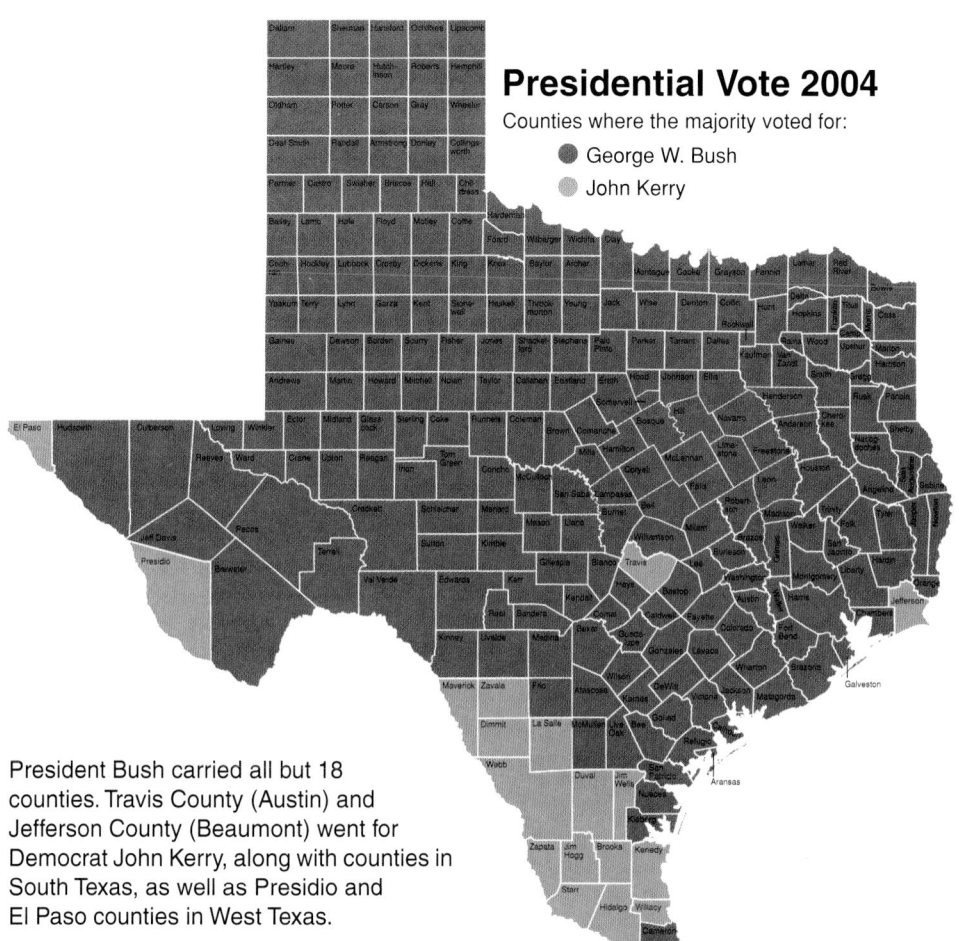

Presidential Vote 2004

Counties where the majority voted for:
- George W. Bush
- John Kerry

President Bush carried all but 18 counties. Travis County (Austin) and Jefferson County (Beaumont) went for Democrat John Kerry, along with counties in South Texas, as well as Presidio and El Paso counties in West Texas.

County	Registered Voters	Turnout %	Total Votes	PRESIDENTIAL RACE					
				BUSH (Republican)	%	KERRY (Democrat)	%	BADNARIK (Libertarian)	NADER (Write-in)
Culberson	2,052	38.4	788	407	51.6	375	47.6	1	3
Dallam	3,330	53.5	1,782	1,473	82.7	305	17.1	3	0
Dallas	1,231,291	55.9	687,709	346,246	50.3	336,641	49.0	3,653	900
Dawson	8,399	54.1	4,545	3,419	75.2	1,114	24.5	11	0
Deaf Smith	9,886	53.5	5,291	4,139	78.2	1,133	21.4	15	4
Delta	3,282	63.4	2,082	1,447	69.5	627	30.11	7	1
Denton	321,700	62.6	201,410	140,891	70.0	59,346	29.5	1,089	73
DeWitt	12,463	54.0	6,732	5,100	75.8	1,610	23.9	15	5
Dickens	1,454	73.1	1,063	815	76.7	245	23.0	3	0
Dimmit	7,848	45.4	3,566	1,188	33.3	2,365	66.3	13	0
Donley	2,670	66.8	1,784	1,429	80.1	349	19.6	5	1
Duval	10,046	40.7	4,091	1,160	28.4	2,916	71.3	15	0
Eastland	10,618	64.6	6,857	5,249	76.5	1,582	23.1	24	1
Ector	69,323	52.4	36,310	27,502	75.7	8,579	23.6	199	23
Edwards	1,567	61.5	963	745	77.4	217	22.5	1	0
Ellis	78,274	59.3	46,444	34,602	74.5	11,640	25.1	135	53
El Paso	371,856	45.6	169,573	73,261	43.2	95,142	56.1	843	263
Erath	20,134	61.0	12,281	9,506	77.4	2,710	22.1	50	11
Falls	10,026	58.9	5,905	3,454	58.5	2,427	41.1	8	6

County	Registered Voters	Turnout %	Total Votes	PRESIDENTIAL RACE					
				BUSH (Republican)	%	KERRY (Democrat)	%	BADNARIK (Libertarian)	NADER (Write-in)
Fannin	18,744	63.8	11,960	7,893	66.0	4,001	33.5	39	12
Fayette	14,433	72.0	10,397	7,527	72.4	2,803	27.0	47	10
Fisher	2,953	65.1	1,923	1,161	60.4	758	39.4	4	0
Floyd	4,440	58.2	2,584	2,032	78.6	545	21.1	6	1
Foard	1,017	57.7	587	347	59.1	235	40.0	4	1
Fort Bend	254,364	64.1	163,169	93,625	57.4	68,722	42.1	590	203
Franklin	6,173	68.3	4,217	3,185	75.5	1,011	24.0	18	3
Freestone	11,506	62.2	7,161	5,057	70.6	2,070	28.9	22	9
Frio	10,225	38.4	3,930	1,991	50.7	1,931	49.1	8	0
Gaines	7,021	59.3	4,164	3,540	85.0	608	14.6	11	3
Galveston	185,911	57.0	105,981	61,290	57.8	43,919	41.4	539	201
Garza	3,002	60.4	1,812	1,480	81.7	326	18.0	5	1
Gillespie	16,486	70.1	11,553	9,297	80.5	2,104	18.2	95	23
Glasscock	758	70.3	533	488	91.6	44	8.3	1	0
Goliad	5,490	63.8	3,501	2,267	64.8	1,219	34.8	11	3
Gonzales	12,483	48.2	6,022	4,291	71.3	1,709	28.4	22	0
Gray	15,060	56.9	8,572	7,260	84.7	1,289	15.0	20	2
Grayson	75,893	58.5	44,423	30,777	69.3	13,452	30.3	168	23
Gregg	76,596	55.4	42,398	29,939	70.6	12,306	29.0	100	38
Grimes	13,577	59.1	8,030	5,263	65.5	2,713	33.8	38	2
Guadalupe	65,640	59.0	38,752	28,208	72.8	10,290	26.6	203	31
Hale	21,593	47.0	10,154	8,025	79.0	2,078	20.5	28	4
Hall	2,289	55.8	1,277	860	67.3	413	32.3	2	2
Hamilton	5,481	68.1	3,730	2,856	76.6	845	22.7	20	3
Hansford	3,285	65.4	2,147	1,903	88.6	240	11.2	4	0
Hardeman	3,023	56.3	1,702	1,214	71.3	480	28.2	3	5
Hardin	33,948	61.0	20,710	15,030	72.6	5,608	27.1	72	0
Harris	1,937,072	55.1	1,067,968	584,723	54.8	475,865	44.6	5,256	1,713
Harrison	43,520	60.3	26,223	16,473	62.8	9,642	36.8	62	32
Hartley	2,888	71.3	2,059	1,736	84.3	315	15.3	5	1
Haskell	4,328	55.8	2,416	1,539	63.7	867	35.9	9	0
Hays	80,858	59.1	47,823	27,021	56.5	20,110	42.1	606	60
Hemphill	2,275	72.2	1,643	1,380	84.0	257	15.6	5	0
Henderson	49,987	57.7	28,849	20,210	70.1	8,505	29.5	110	15
Hidalgo	269,811	42.1	113,683	50,931	44.8	62,369	54.9	347	27
Hill	22,723	57.4	13,053	9,225	70.7	3,751	28.7	59	8
Hockley	14,212	53.3	7,577	6,160	81.3	1,385	18.3	28	4
Hood	32,379	65.8	21,293	16,280	76.5	4,865	22.8	118	21
Hopkins	20,024	60.2	12,062	8,582	71.1	3,443	28.5	25	9
Houston	15,890	55.4	8,806	5,848	66.4	2,921	33.2	26	0
Howard	18,567	54.9	10,201	7,480	73.3	2,663	26.1	55	3
Hudspeth	1,652	53.6	886	577	65.1	302	34.1	7	0
Hunt	50,887	55.4	28,194	20,065	71.5	7,971	28.3	116	31
Hutchinson	17,186	54.5	9,369	7,839	83.7	1,503	16.0	13	11
Irion	1,291	64.1	828	684	82.6	141	17.0	3	0
Jack	5,025	62.2	3,126	2,470	79.0	643	20.6	9	4
Jackson	9,536	53.2	5,077	3,766	74.2	1,296	25.5	10	5
Jasper	21,496	59.9	12,873	8,347	64.8	4,471	34.7	38	13
Jeff Davis	1,823	64.0	1,167	764	65.5	378	32.4	13	8
Jefferson	165,174	55.6	91,866	44,423	48.4	47,066	51.2	336	32
Jim Hogg	4,233	48.8	2,065	712	34.5	1,344	65.0	7	0
Jim Wells	26,473	47.9	12,691	5,817	45.8	6,824	53.8	39	9
Johnson	79,832	59.4	47,422	34,818	73.4	12,325	26.0	182	51
Jones	10,660	55.6	5,931	4,254	71.7	1,658	28.0	18	1
Karnes	8,923	52.4	4,673	3,114	66.6	1,543	33.0	12	4
Kaufman	50,989	59.6	30,366	21,304	70.2	8,947	29.5	104	11
Kendall	20,542	68.5	14,072	11,434	81.3	2,532	18.0	71	20
Kenedy	349	48.4	169	82	48.5	85	50.3	2	0
Kent	776	67.3	522	382	73.2	138	26.4	2	0
Kerr	33,124	64.1	21,246	16,538	77.8	4,557	21.4	111	37
Kimble	2,915	62.3	1,816	1,482	81.6	324	17.8	5	5

County	Registered Voters	Turnout %	Total Votes	PRESIDENTIAL RACE					
				BUSH (Republican)	%	KERRY (Democrat)	%	BADNARIK (Libertarian)	NADER (Write-in)
King	202	77.2	156	137	87.8	18	11.5	1	0
Kinney	2,491	64.2	1,600	1,051	65.7	542	33.9	5	2
Kleberg	19,883	50.2	9,973	5,366	53.8	4,550	45.6	46	11
Knox	2,801	55.4	1,552	1,081	69.7	464	29.9	5	2
Lamar	30,584	57.1	17,470	12,054	69.0	5,338	30.6	53	16
Lamb	9,434	45.3	4,271	3,410	79.8	857	20.1	4	0
Lampasas	11,743	59.8	7,025	5,422	77.2	1,593	22.7	0	8
La Salle	4,416	50.5	2,230	989	44.3	1,229	55.1	11	0
Lavaca	13,999	58.4	8,177	5,974	73.1	2,152	26.3	47	3
Lee	8,779	69.3	6,088	4,160	68.3	1,899	31.2	26	2
Leon	11,100	61.3	6,799	5,023	73.9	1,754	25.8	16	4
Liberty	47,363	45.8	21,691	14,821	68.3	6,780	31.3	76	13
Limestone	14,170	55.2	7,818	5,028	64.3	2,752	35.2	33	5
Lipscomb	1,967	68.0	1,337	1,147	85.8	184	13.8	2	2
Live Oak	7,381	56.9	4,201	3,147	74.9	1,036	24.7	14	3
Llano	13,780	69.4	9,563	7,241	75.7	2,257	23.6	46	13
Loving	108	74.1	80	65	81.3	12	15.0	3	0
Lubbock	162,229	57.4	93,151	70,135	75.3	22,472	24.1	401	118
Lynn	4,295	52.9	2,271	1,776	78.2	490	21.6	5	0
Madison	7,303	56.2	4,101	2,837	69.2	1,235	30.1	22	4
Marion	8,011	54.3	4,348	2,441	56.1	1,884	43.3	16	6
Martin	3,063	59.0	1,807	1,514	83.8	288	15.9	4	0
Mason	2,872	72.3	2,077	1,600	77.0	459	22.1	11	6
Matagorda	21,398	58.5	12,521	8,119	64.8	4,355	34.8	38	6
Maverick	25,041	40.1	10,034	4,025	40.1	5,948	59.3	39	22
McCulloch	5,575	57.8	3,220	2,465	76.6	745	23.1	6	4
McLennan	134,667	58.9	79,254	52,090	65.7	26,760	33.8	267	93
McMullen	688	82.0	564	467	82.8	95	16.8	1	1
Medina	24,428	60.7	14,826	10,389	70.1	4,322	29.6	71	28
Menard	1,846	59.8	1,103	761	69.0	331	30.0	10	0
Midland	71,553	62.7	44,834	36,585	81.6	8,005	17.9	172	52
Milam	14,759	59.5	8,783	5,291	60.2	3,445	39.2	44	2
Mills	3,340	66.8	2,231	1,794	80.4	416	18.6	16	1
Mitchell	5,373	47.6	2,558	1,912	74.7	639	25.0	6	1
Montague	12,939	61.0	7,897	5,910	74.8	1,946	24.6	30	8
Montgomery	214,098	62.6	133,988	104,654	78.1	28,628	21.4	548	113
Moore	10,199	55.2	5,628	4,601	81.8	1,009	17.9	13	1
Morris	8,923	59.2	5,278	2,818	53.4	2,437	46.2	18	1
Motley	928	73.7	684	564	82.5	113	16.5	4	3
Nacogdoches	32,127	66.8	21,466	14,160	66.0	7,152	33.3	104	28
Navarro	28,970	55.3	16,034	10,715	66.8	5,259	32.8	44	13
Newton	9,706	58.7	5,700	3,159	55.4	2,513	44.1	18	8
Nolan	9,909	53.4	5,289	3,722	70.4	1,541	29.1	21	5
Nueces	201,707	51.8	104,560	59,359	56.8	44,439	42.5	446	95
Ochiltree	5,154	61.6	3,177	2,922	92.0	251	7.9	2	2
Oldham	1,523	55.4	843	733	87.0	108	12.8	2	0
Orange	55,446	57.5	31,908	20,292	63.6	11,476	36.0	99	31
Palo Pinto	17,651	56.7	10,014	7,137	71.3	2,816	28.1	43	18
Panola	15,696	63.8	10,007	7,021	70.2	2,958	29.6	25	3
Parker	66,021	62.0	40,957	31,795	77.6	8,966	21.9	154	33
Parmer	5,084	54.5	2,773	2,375	85.6	389	14.0	7	2
Pecos	7,970	55.6	4,428	3,167	71.5	1,242	28.0	18	0
Polk	41,944	49.7	20,846	13,778	66.1	6,964	33.4	93	9
Potter	59,355	49.0	29,056	21,401	73.7	7,489	25.8	104	49
Presidio	5,306	35.6	1,890	715	37.8	1,159	61.3	10	4
Rains	6,576	64.3	4,229	2,998	70.9	1,213	28.7	13	4
Randall	76,399	63.6	48,587	40,520	83.4	7,849	16.2	135	64
Reagan	1,941	58.9	1,143	956	83.6	184	16.1	2	0
Real	2,587	63.6	1,645	1,314	79.9	325	19.8	6	0
Red River	8,468	64.8	5,490	3,379	61.5	2,097	38.2	7	5
Reeves	7,309	46.4	3,395	1,777	52.3	1,600	47.1	12	3

County	Registered Voters	Turnout %	Total Votes	PRESIDENTIAL RACE					
				BUSH (Republican)	%	KERRY (Democrat)	%	BADNARIK (Libertarian)	NADER (Write-in)
Refugio	5,787	59.7	3,455	2,212	64.0	1,232	35.7	9	1
Roberts	725	69.9	507	461	90.9	46	9.0	0	0
Robertson	11,909	57.1	6,795	3,792	55.8	2,979	43.8	22	2
Rockwall	38,126	67.1	25,581	20,120	78.7	5,320	20.8	99	32
Runnels	7,168	56.5	4,049	3,239	80.0	792	19.6	13	4
Rusk	31,680	57.9	18,344	13,390	73.0	4,899	26.7	38	13
Sabine	7,571	61.3	4,639	3,138	67.6	1,476	31.8	14	3
San Augustine	6,740	55.7	3,757	2,235	59.5	1,506	40.1	11	2
San Jacinto	16,115	50.4	8,125	5,394	66.4	2,688	33.1	37	3
San Patricio	47,994	44.4	21,320	13,474	63.2	7,764	36.4	65	13
San Saba	3,732	65.1	2,431	1,894	77.9	529	21.8	7	0
Schleicher	1,900	69.9	1,329	1,012	76.1	312	23.5	4	0
Scurry	10,782	51.7	5,572	4,576	82.1	981	17.6	13	1
Shackelford	2,473	61.7	1,527	1,292	84.6	229	15.0	4	1
Shelby	15,245	60.9	9,279	6,295	67.8	2,951	31.8	26	2
Sherman	1,484	71.8	1,066	942	88.4	124	11.6	0	0
Smith	116,550	63.2	73,664	53,392	72.5	19,970	27.1	290	6
Somervell	5,730	62.0	3,551	2,701	76.1	831	23.4	8	6
Starr	28,268	34.6	9,781	2,552	26.1	7,199	73.6	30	0
Stephens	5,837	60.3	3,519	2,803	79.7	703	20.0	8	5
Sterling	968	63.5	615	544	88.5	71	11.5	0	0
Stonewall	1,191	63.1	752	499	66.4	250	33.2	3	0
Sutton	2,601	55.9	1,453	1,173	80.7	280	19.3	0	0
Swisher	4,690	45.2	2,120	1,487	70.1	626	29.5	2	4
Tarrant	918,656	61.0	560,141	349,462	62.4	207,286	37.0	2,784	477
Taylor	81,647	58.9	48,099	37,197	77.3	10,648	22.1	224	25
Terrell	784	59.8	469	306	65.2	159	33.9	3	1
Terry	7,821	50.8	3,970	3,166	79.7	794	20.0	6	4
Throckmorton	1,221	70.7	863	656	76.0	202	23.4	5	0
Titus	15,477	57.5	8,907	5,709	64.1	3,173	35.6	25	0
Tom Green	65,165	57.4	37,417	28,185	75.3	9,007	24.1	163	48
Travis	584,949	60.2	352,113	147,885	42.0	197,235	56.0	5,075	1,422
Trinity	11,176	55.6	6,213	3,985	64.1	2,204	35.5	20	0
Tyler	13,496	57.4	7,745	5,043	65.0	2,659	34.3	30	10
Upshur	25,293	57.4	14,526	10,232	70.4	4,225	29.1	41	16
Upton	2,143	55.9	1,197	1,009	84.3	185	15.5	0	2
Uvalde	16,391	51.8	8,483	5,148	60.7	3,298	38.9	24	10
Val Verde	26,561	44.4	11,795	6,968	59.1	4,757	40.3	49	15
Van Zandt	33,662	59.0	19,856	14,976	75.4	4,822	24.3	58	0
Victoria	54,738	54.1	29,602	20,875	70.5	8,553	28.9	145	26
Walker	29,886	59.6	17,822	11,710	65.7	5,977	33.5	102	20
Waller	27,923	49.7	13,881	7,679	55.3	6,145	44.3	45	0
Ward	6,655	56.6	3,768	2,856	75.8	901	23.9	7	3
Washington	20,658	63.2	13,063	9,597	73.5	3,389	25.9	52	15
Webb	97,081	42.8	41,556	17,753	42.7	23,654	56.9	122	19
Wharton	25,027	56.1	14,039	9,288	66.2	4,702	33.5	35	10
Wheeler	3,834	62.4	2,394	1,960	81.9	420	17.5	11	3
Wichita	80,463	56.6	45,545	32,472	71.3	12,819	28.1	254	0
Wilbarger	8,548	58.4	4,990	3,685	73.8	1,284	25.7	18	3
Willacy	11,220	44.2	4,962	2,209	44.5	2,734	55.1	19	0
Williamson	200,344	64.0	128,198	83,284	65.0	43,117	33.6	1,436	250
Wilson	23,533	63.3	14,885	10,400	69.9	4,409	29.6	65	6
Winkler	4,143	48.3	2,002	1,604	80.1	391	19.5	6	1
Wise	33,837	59.2	20,031	15,177	75.8	4,783	23.9	71	0
Wood	24,446	69.3	16,929	12,831	75.8	4,034	23.9	54	9
Yoakum	4,637	56.4	2,613	2,228	85.3	376	14.4	7	2
Young	11,774	62.9	7,409	5,874	79.3	1,511	20.4	21	2
Zapata	6,942	41.7	2,898	1,228	42.4	1,662	57.3	6	1
Zavala	8,176	38.1	3,118	777	24.9	2,332	74.8	9	0

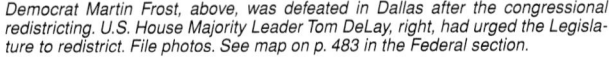

Democrat Martin Frost, above, was defeated in Dallas after the congressional redistricting. U.S. House Majority Leader Tom DeLay, right, had urged the Legislature to redistrict. File photos. See map on p. 483 in the Federal section.

Redistricting Reverberates from Washington to Austin

Democrats lost their last claim to power in the state – a majority in the Texas congressional delegation – after the Legislature produced an extraordinary redistricting re-do in 2003.

The remap had wide reverberations, from Washington to Austin and back to Washington. The impact brought to mind the Energizer bunny: It just kept going and going. For starters, the redistricting drastically changed the partisan makeup of the Texas congressional delegation. Whereas Texas voters sent 17 Democrats and 15 Republicans to Washington in 2002 using federal court-drawn districts, in the 2004 elections the count was 21 Republicans and 11 Democrats under the Legislature's remap.

Four veteran Democratic incumbents who tried to buck the new system went down. Another retired and still another switched parties. While House Majority Leader Tom DeLay (R-Sugar Land) picked up partisan reinforcements in Washington, he also became embroiled in ethics challenges as a result of his redistricting efforts.

Here's what happened. Texas lawmakers failed in 2001 to produce a new map for the state's 32 House seats after census numbers were in, so a federal court crafted a plan that drew two new seats (awarded for population growth) for Republicans but otherwise kept the status quo.

Then, in 2002, Republicans took control of both houses of the Legislature, winning a majority in the House with the help of $1.5 million raised by Texans for a Republican Majority, a political action committee founded by DeLay to help Texas House candidates.

Nicknamed "The Hammer" because of his arm-twisting talents in Congress, DeLay turned his persuasive tactics on the newly minted GOP-heavy statehouse that he had helped to elect. Even though a congressional map was in place, he pressed legislators to redraw it — which they did, producing districts that heavily favored Republicans and targeted white Democratic incumbents.

Democratic legislators staged several walkouts to deny a quorum during 2003 special sessions called by Gov. Rick Perry to address redistricting, moving temporarily to hotels in Oklahoma and New Mexico. When they fled to Oklahoma, DeLay contacted the Federal Aviation Administration to help locate them – an action that raised "serious concerns" later in the House Ethics Committee. The Republican plan finally passed in a special session in October 2003.

The new plan targeted seven Democratic incumbents, putting them in districts with another incumbent, adding Republicans to their districts or giving them thousands of new, unfamiliar constituents. The plan withstood court challenge and was in effect for the 2004 elections.

One of the biggest dominoes to fall was Martin Frost of Dallas, a 25-year House member who had been touted as a future speaker and who previously had lobbied the Legislature to protect Democrat incumbents. Frost switched from his dismantled District 24 to run against Republican Pete Sessions in District 32 and lost.

Charlie Stenholm of Abilene, senior Democrat on the House Agriculture Committee, lost to freshman Republican Randy Neugebauer of Lubbock in the redrawn District 19. Max Sandlin of Marshall and Nick Lampson of Beaumont also lost re-election efforts in Districts 1 and 2. Jim Turner of East Texas retired after the districts were announced, and Ralph Hall of Rockwall switched parties and was re-elected in District 4.

Of five threatened Democrats running for re-election — who together had 82 years of seniority — only Chet Edwards of Waco survived, winning in the Republican-tilting District 17 that contains President Bush's hometown of Crawford.

Among the Republican pickups were five freshmen from Texas: Louie Gohmert, a former state appeals court judge from Tyler; Ted Poe, a state district judge from Houston; Ken Marchant, a state legislator from Coppell; Mike Conaway, a Midland accountant and former energy business partner of George W. Bush; and Mike McCaul of Austin, a former federal prosecutor and deputy Texas attorney general.

DeLay maintained that the redistricting finally gave Texas voters a level playing field in congressional elections. Opponents said the Texas case opened the door to other states to pursue intra-decade redistricting plans when politics changed. In Texas, the redistricting reduced the number of white Texas Democrats in Congress to three by strengthening districts for black and Hispanic candidates. One who lost in the primary was Chris Bell of Houston, a white Democrat who couldn't hold his seat after the Legislature shifted demographics to favor a black candidate. He was replaced by longtime justice of the peace and black leader Al Green in the Beaumont-Galveston District 9.

Bell complained to the House Ethics Committee about DeLay calling in the FAA during redistricting and for golfing with energy executives with an energy bill pending. DeLay was admonished and eventually faced questions in an escalating ethics brouhaha that questioned his ties with lobbyists, overseas travel funded by foreign interests and other matters, creating a political distraction in Washington — all of this stirring up opposition in his home District 22 and threatening his political career.

Delay said he was the victim of a smear campaign by Democrats, and his conservative supporters rallied around him, even as Democrat Lampson said he would run against the congressman in 2006.

As for Bell, who launched the DeLay inquiries, he said he planned to run as a Democrat for governor in 2006. – *Carolyn Barta*

General Election, 2004

Below are the voting returns of the general election held November 2, 2004, for all statewide races and for contested congressional, state senate, courts of appeals and state board of education races. These are official returns as canvassed by the State Canvassing Board. Abbreviations used are (Dem.) Democrat, (Rep.) Republican, (Lib.) Libertarian, (Ind.) Independent and (W-I) Write-In.

PRESIDENT

George W. Bush (Rep.)	4,526,917	61.08%
John F. Kerry (Dem.)	2,832,704	38.22%
Michael Badnarik (Lib.)	38,787	0.52%
Ralph Nader (W-I)	9,153	0.12%
Michael Anthony Peroutka (W-I)	1,626	0.02%
David Keith Cobb	1,014	0.01%
Andrew J. Falk	219	0.00%
John Joseph Kennedy (W-I)	126	0.00%
Walt Brown	111	0.00%
Deborah Elaine Allen	92	0.00%
Total Vote	7,410,749	

U.S. HOUSE OF REPRESENTATIVES
(See map of districts on p. 483)

District 1

Louie Gohmert (Rep.)	157,068	61.47%
Max Sandlin (Dem.)	96,281	37.68%
Dean L. Tucker (Lib.)	2,158	0.84%
Total Vote	255,507	

District 2

Ted Poe (Rep.)	139,951	55.52%
Nick Lampson (Dem.)	108,156	42.91%
Sandra Leigh Saulsbury (Lib.)	3,931	1.55%
Total Vote	252,038	

District 3

Sam Johnson (Rep.)	180,099	85.61%
James Vessels (Dem.)	13,287	6.31%
Paul Jenkins (Ind.)	16,966	8.06%
Total Vote	210,352	

District 4

Ralph Hall (Rep.)	182,866	68.24%
Jim Nickerson (Dem.)	81,585	30.44%
Kevin D. Anderson (Lib.)	3,491	1.30%
Total Vote	267,942	

District 5

Jeb Hensarling (Rep.)	148,816	64.46%
Bill Bernstein (Dem.)	75,911	32.88%
John Gonzalez (Lib.)	6,118	2.65%
Total Vote	230,845	

District 6

Joe Barton (Rep.)	168,767	66.02%
Morris Meyer (Dem.)	83,609	32.70%
Stephen Schrader (Lib.)	3,251	1.27%
Total Vote	255,627	

District 7

John Culberson (Rep.)	175,440	64.11%
John Martinez (Dem.)	91,126	33.30%
Drew Parks (Lib.)	3,372	1.23%
Paul Staton (Ind.)	3,713	1.35%
Total Vote	273,651	

District 8

Kevin Brady (Rep.)	179,599	68.91%
James (Jim) Wright (Dem.)	77,324	29.66%
Paul Hansen (Lib.)	3,705	1.42%
Total Vote	260,628	

District 9

Arlette Molina (Rep.)	42,132	26.57%
Al Green (Dem.)	114,462	72.18%
Stacey Lynn Bourland (Lib.)	1,972	1.24%
Total Vote	158,566	

District 10

Michael T. McCaul (Rep.)	182,113	78.61%
Robert Fritsche (Dem.)	35,569	15.35%
Lorenzo Sadun (W-I)	13,961	6.02%
Total Vote	231,643	

District 11

Mike Conaway (Rep.)	177,291	76.75%
Wayne Raasch (Dem.)	50,339	21.79%
Jeffrey Blunt (Lib.)	3,347	1.44%
Total Vote	230,977	

District 12

Kay Granger (Rep.)	173,222	72.31%
Felix Alvarado (Dem.)	66,316	27.68%
Total Vote	239,538	

District 13

Mac Thornberry (Rep.)	189,448	92.30%
M.J. (Smitty) Smith (Dem.)	15,793	7.69%
Total Vote	205,241	

District 15

Michael D. Thamm (Rep.)	67,917	40.82%
Rubén Hinojosa (Dem.)	96,089	57.76%
William R. Cady (Lib.)	2,352	1.41%
Total Vote	166,358	

District 16

David Brigham (Rep.)	49,972	31.08%
Silvestre Reyes (Dem.)	108,577	67.53%
Brad Clardy (Lib.)	2,224	1.38%
Total Vote	160,773	

District 17

Arlene Wohlgemuth (Rep.)	116,049	47.41%
Chet Edwards (Dem.)	125,309	51.19%
Clyde L. Garland (Lib.)	3,390	1.38%
Total Vote	244,748	

District 18

Sheila Jackson Lee (Dem.)	136,018	88.90%
Brent Sullivan (Lib.)	7,183	4.69%
Tom Bazán (Ind.)	9,787	6.39%
Total Vote	152,988	

District 19

Randy Neugebauer (Rep.)	136,459	58.43%

Charles W. Stenholm (Dem.) . . . . .93,531 . . 40.05%
Richard Peterson (Lib.) . . . . .3,524 . . . 1.50%
 Total Vote 233,514

District 20
Roger Scott (Rep.) . . . . .54,976 . . 31.99%
Charles A. Gonzalez (Dem.) . . . . 112,480 . . 65.46%
Jessie Bouley (Lib.) . . . . .2,377 . . . 1.38%
Michael Idrogo (Ind.) . . . . .1,971 . . . 1.14%
 Total Vote 171,804

District 21
Lamar Smith (Rep.) . . . . 209,774 . . 61.49%
Rhett R. Smith (Dem.) . . . . 121,129 . . 35.50%
Jason Pratt (Lib.) . . . . 10,216 . . . 2.99%
 Total Vote 341,119

District 22
Tom DeLay (Rep.) . . . . 150,386 . . 55.16%
Richard R. Morrison (Dem.) . . . . 112,034 . . 41.09%
Tom Morrison (Lib.) . . . . .4,886 . . . 1.79%
Michael Fjetland (Ind.) . . . . .5,314 . . . 1.94%
 Total Vote 272,620

District 23
Henry Bonilla (Rep.) . . . . 170,716 . . 69.25%
Joe Sullivan (Dem.) . . . . 72,480 . . 29.40%
Nazirite (Comrade) Perez (Lib.) . . . . .3,307 . . . 1.34%
 Total Vote 246,503

District 24
Kenny Marchant (Rep.) . . . . 154,435 . . 63.98%
Gary R. Page (Dem.) . . . . 82,599 . . 34.22%
James H. Lawrence (Lib.) . . . . .4,340 . . . 1.79%
 Total Vote 241,374

District 25
Rebecca Armendariz Klein (Rep.) . . . . .49,252 . . 30.74%
Lloyd Doggett (Dem.) . . . . 108,309 . . 67.60%
James Werner (Lib.) . . . . .2,656 . . . 1.65%
 Total Vote 160,217

District 26
Michael C. Burgess (Rep.) . . . . 180,519 . . 65.75%
Lico Reyes (Dem.) . . . . 89,809 . . 32.71%
James Gholston (Lib.) . . . . .4,211 . . . 1.53%
 Total Vote 274,539

District 27
William (Willie) Vaden (Rep.) . . . . 61,955 . . 34.89%
Solomon P. Ortiz (Dem.) . . . . 112,081 . . 63.13%
Christopher J. Claytor (Lib.) . . . . .3,500 . . . 1.97%
 Total Vote 177,536

District 28
James (Jim) F. Hopson (Rep.) . . . . 69,538 . . 38.59%
Henry Cuellar (Dem.) . . . . 106,323 . . 59.01%
Ken Ashby (Lib.) .4,305 . . . 2.38%
 Total Vote 180,166

District 29
Gene Green (Dem.) . . . . 78,256 . . 94.14%
Clifford L. Messina (Lib.) . . . . .4,868 . . . 5.85%
 Total Vote 83,124

District 30
Eddie Bernice Johnson (Dem.) . . . . 144,513 . . 93.03%
John Davis (Lib.) . . . . 10,821 . . . 6.96%
 Total Vote 155,334

District 31
John R. Carter (Rep.) . . . . 160,247 . . 64.76%
Jon Porter (Dem.) . . . . 80,292 . . 32.45%
Celeste Adams (Lib.) . . . . .6,888 . . . 2.78%
 Total Vote 247,427

District 32
Pete Sessions (Rep.) . . . . 109,859 . . 54.32%
Martin Frost (Dem.) . . . . 89,030 . . 44.02%
Michael David Needleman (Lib.) . . . . .3,347 . . . 1.65%
 Total Vote 202,236

STATE RACES

Railroad Commissioner
Victor G. Carrillo (Rep.) . . . . 3,891,482 . . 55.46%
Bob Scarborough (Dem.) . . . . 2,872,717 . . 40.94%

Anthony Garcia (Lib.) . . . . 252,497 . . . . 3.59%
 Total Vote 7,016,696

Justice, Supreme Court, Place 9
Scott Brister (Rep.) . . . . 4,093,854 . . 59.23%
David Van Os (Dem.) . . . . 2,817,700 . . 40.76%
 Total Vote 6,911,554

Judge, Court of Criminal Appeals, Place 2
Lawrence (Larry) Meyers (Rep.) . . . . . . 4,417,591 . . 83.96%
Quanah Parker (Lib.) . . . . 843,911 . . 16.03%
 Total Vote 5,261,502

Judge, Court of Criminal Appeals, Place 5
Cheryl Johnson (Rep.) . . . . 4,504,264 . . 85.78%
Tom Oxford (Lib.) . . . . 746,476 . . 14.21%
 Total Vote 5,250,740

Judge, Court of Criminal Appeals, Place 6
Michael E. Keasler (Rep.) . . . . 3,990,315 . . 57.85%
J.R. Molina (Dem.) . . . . 2,906,720 . . 42.14%
 Total Vote 6,897,035

STATE SENATE

District 6
Mario Gallegos Jr. (Dem.) . . . . 75,318 . . 91.74%
Tony Depperschmidt (Lib.) . . . . .6,614 . . . 8.05%
Susan Delgado (W-I) . . . . 160 . . . . 0.19%
 Total Vote 82,092

District 10
Kim Brimer (Rep.) . . . . 156,831 . . 59.25%
Andrew B. Hill (Dem.) . . . . 107,853 . . 40.74%
 Total Vote 264,684

District 26
Jim Valdez (Rep.) . . . . 74,070 . . 40.04%
Leticia R. Van de Putte (Dem.) . . . . 105,625 . . 57.09%
Raymundo Aleman (Lib.) . . . . .5,295 . . . 2.86%
 Total Vote 184,990

District 30
Craig L. Estes (Rep.) . . . . 182,057 . . 69.04%
Paul S. Gibbs (Dem.) . . . . 81,614 . . 30.95%
 Total Vote 263,671

District 31
Kel Seliger (Rep.) . . . . 170,299 . . 78.53%
Elaine King Miller (Dem.) . . . . 46,556 . . 21.46%
 Total Vote 216,855

COURTS OF APPEALS
Justice, First District, Place 4
Evelyn Keyes (Rep.) . . . . 780,836 . . 54.03%
Jim Sharp (Dem.) . . . . 664,253 . . 45.96%
 Total Vote 1,445,089

Justice, Third District, Place 4
Bill Green (Rep.) . . . . 361,094 . . 48.19%
Jan Patterson (Dem.) . . . . 389,064 . . 51.80%
 Total Vote 750,968

Justice, Third District, Place 6 (Unexpired term)
Bob Pemberton (Rep.) . . . . 386,274 . . 51.55%
Diane Henson (Dem.) . . . . 362,955 . . 48.44%
 Total Vote 749,229

Justice, Fifth District, Place 12 (Unexpired term)
Amos Mazzant (Rep.) . . . . 555,389 . . 55.00%
David Weiner (Dem.) . . . . 454,344 . . 44.99%
 Total Vote 1,009,733

Justice, Tenth District, Place 3
Felipe Reyna (Rep.) . . . . 190,319 . . 62.87%
Boyd Mangrum (Dem.) . . . . 112,366 . . 37.12%
 Total Vote 302,685

Justice, Thirteenth District, Place 3
Alicia Cuellar (Rep.) . . . . 189,021 . . 47.17%
Linda Yañez (Dem.) . . . . 211,636 . . 52.82%
 Total Vote 400,657

STATE BOARD OF EDUCATION
District 7
David Bradley (Rep.) . . . . 327,771 . . 87.31%
William McNicoll (Lib.) . . . . 47,637 . . 12.68%
 Total Vote 375,408

Gov. Rick Perry makes his State of the State address to the Legislature in January 2005. File photo.

Legislature Fails to Pass School Funding in Regular Session

The 2005 session of the Texas Legislature will likely be remembered for its failure to create a new school finance system, even though it fulfilled its one constitutional mandate — to adopt a budget — and had other successes.

Legislators passed a $139.4 billion biennial appropriations bill that was 19 percent higher than the prior two-year budget, and with considerable more ease, due to more available revenue.

Successful legislation included a revamp of the state workers' compensation system that increased benefits to injured workers and an overhaul of Child Protective Services to reduce excessive case loads that allowed abused children to fall through the cracks – both high priorities of Gov. Rick Perry.

But the major disappointment of the 79th legislative session was the failure of the House and Senate to agree on public school finance reform – a banner issue because a state district judge had ordered the state to fix school funding problems and local districts were crying for property tax relief.

The long-anticipated overhaul would have restructured state taxes to provide an infusion of state funds, reduced local property taxes for homeowners, given teachers their first pay raise in years and authorized other education initiatives.

But the Senate and House passed different versions of the bill and failed to compromise in the waning hours of the 140-day session.

The sticking point came over tax restructuring that would have provided some $3 billion in new money for schools. The House favored a higher sales tax and lower business tax than the Senate, although Republican majorities in both houses were reluctant to increase taxes.

In the final negotiations, the more conservative House members and Speaker Tom Craddick, R-Midland, who was nicknamed the Tominator, held their ground.

Texas was under court order to repair its school financing system that, for more than a decade, had required property-rich districts to share their local taxes with property-poor districts.

Some local districts sued the state, after reaching a limit to their ability to raise taxes at home. Judge John Dietz of Austin had given the Legislature a deadline of Oct. 1, 2005, to fix school funding.

Without action, the Legislature faced the court-imposed cutoff of education spending, the prospect that Perry might call a special session on the issue, or further instructions from the judiciary.

The Texas Supreme Court was scheduled to hear the school finance case in the summer, after the regular session.

At press time, Gov. Perry had called a special session of the Legislature to consider the school finance issue, but no legislation had been approved.

As for the budget, crafting it was easier this time around.

In 2003, reduced sales tax revenues and tougher

economic times forced agencies to slash spending and legislators to cut services to poor children and the elderly to balance a $117.4 billion no-new-taxes budget.

In 2005, legislators were able to restore previous budget cuts to poor children and the elderly — giving additional funds to Adult Protective Services in addition to CPS — but new spending upset some conservative lawmakers and Perry, who threatened vetoes.

The prospect of either U.S. Sen. Kay Bailey Hutchison or Comptroller Carole Keeton Strayhorn running against the governor in the 2006 GOP primary caused him to spend time during the session locking up support from legislators, influential Republican groups and potential financial backers.

The session was the second Legislature this century to be controlled by Republican majorities and presiding officers — Speaker Craddick and Lt. Gov. David Dewhurst in the Senate.

The House had 87 Republicans and 63 Democrats, and the Senate had 19 Republicans and 12 Democrats.

The House tried repeatedly to flex its muscle on social issues.

A much heralded bill that aimed to tone down sexual content in school cheerleading routines drew national attention. The House cheered and waved pompoms when the bill passed to allow the state to monitor cheerleading routines. But the "don't-shake-your-booty" bill failed to pass the Senate and become law.

However, both chambers agreed to send to voters in November 2005 a constitutional amendment that would allow Texas to join 17 other states in constitutionally prohibiting the recognition of gay marriages and civil unions.

Both houses also passed legislation requiring a parent to provide written consent for unmarried girls under 18 to get an abortion. But a House effort to restrict gays from becoming foster parents failed.

Other legislative successes included a bill signed by the governor that would allow only those with serious illnesses to sue companies for asbestos- and silica-related claims.

Gov. Perry also persuaded legislators to put more money into discretionary funds to allow him to attract more jobs to the state.

In other action, the Legislature rejected legalized and taxed video-slot machines, fending off efforts to allow more gambling in the state as a revenue source.

And it failed to pass a law that reflected the 2002 Supreme Court decision banning execution of the mentally retarded.

Finally, the Senate passed but the House declined to act on a proposed constitutional amendment that would require record votes – not just voice votes — on all substantive bills.

Texas is one of 10 states that does not mandate record votes. Various citizen groups and media outlets had pressed for the record-vote requirement. — *Carolyn Barta.*

Members of the 79th Texas Legislature at the swearing-in ceremony January 2005. From left, Republican Tony Goolsby of Dallas and Democrats Pete Gallego of Alpine, Joe Deshotel of Beaumont and Terri Hodge of Dallas. File photo.

Political Party Organizations

DEMOCRATIC State Executive Committee

www.txdemocrats.org

Chair, Charles E. Soechting, 707 Rio Grande, Austin 78701; **Vice Chair**, Gabrielle Hadnot, Houston; **Vice Chair for Finance**, Dennis Speight, Austin; **Secretary**, Ruby Jensen, Houston; **Treasurer**, Miguel Wise, Weslaco; **Parliamentarians**, Ed Cogburn, Houston; Corinne Sabo, San Antonio; and Frank Thompson, Houston; **Sergeant-at-Arms**, Bruce Elfant, Austin.

National Committee members: Norma Fisher-Flores, El Paso; Yvonne Davis, Dallas; Al Edwards, Houston; Jaime A. Gonzalez, McAllen; David Holmes, Austin; Eddie Bernice Johnson, Dallas; Senfronia Thompson, Houston; Sue Lovell, Houston; Betty Richie, Graham; Bob Slagle, Sherman; Oscar Soliz, Corpus Christi, and John Patrick, Friendswood.

District — Member and Hometown

1. Norma Narramore, Winfield; Johnny Weaver, Henderson.
2. Martha Williams, Terrell; Steve Tillery, Garland.
3. Kathleen Hawkins, Buna; Dennis Teal, Livingston.
4. Mary Kirkwood, Beaumont; John Baker, Bridge City.
5. Kay Sweat, Lexington; Bill Holcomb, Crockett.
6. Rose Salas, Houston; Matt Emal, Houston.
7. Joy Demark, Houston; Bill Scruggs, Spring.
8. Nancy G. Machen, Plano; David Griggs, Addison.
9. Christine Asberry, Dallas; Marvin Sutton, Arlington.
10. Amber Anderson, Fort Worth; Marc House,

Arlington.

11. Janet Mayeaux, Seabrook; Karl A. Silverman, League City.

12. Kay Walker, Fort Worth; John Burton, Fort Worth.

13. Jennifer Sanders, Houston; Rodney Griffin, Missouri City.

14. Fran Vincent, Austin; Rich Bailey, Austin.

15. Sheryl Roppolo, Channelview; Michael Harris, Houston.

16. Theresa Daniel, Dallas; Ken Molberg, Dallas.

17. Ella Tyler, Houston; Gary Horton, Galveston.

18. Peggy Miller, Victoria; Phillip A. Ruiz, Lockhart.

19. Jo Ann McCall, San Antonio; Ben Alexander, San Antonio.

20. Victor M. Garza, Edinburg; Latrice Sellers, Corpus Christi.

21. Maria Luisa Martinez, Laredo; Howard C. Berger, Floresville.

22. JoAnn Jenkins, Ovilla; Danny Trull, Waxahachie.

23. Monica Alonzo, Dallas; Lemuel H. Price, Dallas.

24. Kirsten Hancock, Abilene; Bill Perkison, Belton.

25. Zada True-Courage, San Antonio; Bruce Barrick, Austin.

26. Ann Marie Schroeder, San Antonio; Concepcion Elizondo, San Antonio.

27. Remi Garza, San Benito; Irma Pena, Harlingen.

28. Mary Hatfield, Lubbock; Ron Michulka, San Angelo.

29. Lilia Ruiz, El Paso; Michael Apodaca, El Paso.

30. Angela Brewer, Denton; Boyd Richie, Graham.

31. Roberta Hicks, Amarillo; John James, Midland.

Senate Democratic Caucus: Leticia Van de Putte, San Antonio.

House Democratic Caucus: Roberto Alonzo, Dallas.

Texas Young Democrats: Steven Bollinger, Nacogdoches; Elizabeth Macias, El Paso.

County Chairs Assn.: Raymond McNeel, Conroe; Sharon Teal, Livingston.

Texas Democratic Women: Kellie Bailey, Austin; Alieca Hux, Sulphur Springs.

Coalition of Black Democrats: Janice Kinchion, Austin; J.B. Hail, San Angelo.

Non-Urban Caucus: Bill Brannon, Sulphur Springs; Anna Marie Hornsby, Texarkana.

Tejano Democrats: Frank Ortega, Austin; Lenora Sorola-Pohlman, Houston.

Stonewall Democrats: Shannon Bailey, Dallas; Nancy Russell, San Antonio.

Statewide Organizations

Asian American Democrats: www.aadt.org.

Coalition of Black Democrats.

Progressive Populist Caucus: www.texaspopulists.com

Stonewall Democrats: www.stonewalldemocrats.org/texas

Tejano Democrats: www.tejanodemocrats.com.

Texas Democratic Veterans: www.geocities.com/texasdemocraticvets/index.html.

Texas Democratic Women: www.tdw.org.

Texas Young Democrats: www.texasyds.org.

REPUBLICAN State Executive Committee

www.texasgop.org

Chairman, Tina Benkiser, 900 Congress Ave. Ste. 300, Austin 78701; **Vice Chairman,** David Barton; **Secretary,** Loyce McCarter; **Treasurer,** Chris Maska; **General Counsel,** Donna Davidson; **Associate General Counsel**, Dennis Donley; **Parliamentarian**, Burch

Davis; **Finance Chairman**, Susan Howard-Chrane; **Sergeant-at-Arms**, Kenneth Clark; **Chaplain**, Robert Long.

National Committee members: Bill Crocker, Austin; Denise McNamara, Dallas.

District — Member and Hometown

1. Marjorie Chandler, Texarkana; Eric B. Cain, Atlanta.

2. Leah Hubbard, Sachse; John Cook, Terrell.

3. JoAnn McCarty, Athens; James Wiggins, Conroe.

4. Melina Fredricks, Conroe; David Teuscher, Beaumont.

5. Bernice Lewis, College Station; Hal Talton, Round Rock.

6. Larry Bowles, Houston; Linda Gonzales, Galena Park.

7. Sharon Martin, Houston; Clint Moore, Spring.

8. Mandy Tschoepe, Plano; Wayne Tucker, Plano.

9. Timothy Hoy, Dallas; Jane Burch, Arlington.

10. William Ford, Fort Worth; Melba McDow, Arlington.

11. Kathy Haigler, Deer Park; Robin Armstrong, Dickinson.

12. Tom Quinones, Haltom City; Shirley Spellerberg, Corinth.

13. Vickie Clements, Houston; Eugene Pack, Houston.

14. Brian Russell, Austin; Jan Galbraith, Austin.

15. Nelda Eppes, Houston; Josh Flynn, Houston.

16. Daniel Pickens, Garland; Chris Davis, Richardson.

17. Jim Hotze, Bellaire; Terese Raia, Sugar Land.

18. Michael Franks, Wharton; Cress Ann Poston, Sugar Land.

19. Kim Hesley, Pipe Creek; Robert Peden, Hondo.

20. Michael Bergsma, Corpus Christi; Sandra Carraras, McAllen.

21. John Larrison, La Vernia; Dawn Lothringer, Pleasanton.

22. Oneta Leutwyler, Woodway; John Tabor, Waxahachie.

23. Greg Knauer, Duncanville; Marjorie Ford, DeSoto.

24. Sandra Jenkins, Marble Falls; Skipper Wallace, Lampasas.

25. Curt Nelson, San Antonio; Genny Hensz, New Braunfels.

26. Joe Solis, San Antonio; Shirley Thompson, San Antonio.

27. Frank Morris, Harlingen; Karen Ballard, Brownsville.

28. Jane Cansino, Lubbock; Tom Mechler, Claude.

29. Connie Roberts, El Paso; David Thackston, El Paso.

30. Katherine Gear, Mineral Wells; Clyde Siebman, Sherman.

31. Chad Weaver, Midland; Benona Love, Amarillo.

Statewide Auxiliary Organizations

Texas Federation of College Republicans: www.tfcr.net.

Texas Republican County Chairmen's Association: www.trcca.org.

Texas Federation of Republican Women: www.tfrw.org.

Republican National Hispanic Assembly of Texas: mirummell@aol.com.

Texas Federation of Pachyderm Clubs: www.pachyderms.org.

Texas Young Republican Federation: www.tyrf.org. ☆

Texas Primary Elections, 2004

Below are the official returns for the contested races only in the Republican and Democratic Party primaries held March 9, 2004. Included are statewide races and selected district races. The runoffs were held on April 13.

DEMOCRATIC PRIMARY

President

Wesley K. Clark	18,437	2.19%
Randy Crow	6,338	0.75%
Howard Dean	40,035	4.77%
John Edwards	120,413	14.34%
Dick Gephardt	12,160	1.44%
John F. Kerry	563,237	67.11%
Dennis J. Kucinich	15,475	1.84%
Lyndon H. LaRouche Jr.	6,871	0.81%
Joe Lieberman	25,245	3.00%
Al Sharpton	31,020	3.69%
Total Vote	839,231	

U.S. HOUSE OF REPRESENTATIVES
District 4

Jerry D. Ashford Jr.	12,513	34.13%
Jim Nickerson	24,141	65.86%
Total Vote	36,654	

District 9

Chris Bell	8,492	31.29%
Al Green	18,034	66.46%
Beverly A. Spencer	607	2.23%
Total Vote	27,133	

District 22

Richard R. Morrison	7,303	71.43%
Erik Saenz	2,920	28.56%
Total Vote	10,223	

District 23

Joe Sullivan	29,061	63.75%
Virgil W. Yanta	16,523	36.24%
Total Vote	45,584	

District 25

Lloyd Doggett	40,306	64.37%
Leticia Hinojosa	22,305	35.62%
Total Vote	62,611	

District 28

Henry Cuellar	24,651	50.20%
Ciro D. Rodriguez	24,448	49.79%
Total Vote	49,099	

STATE SENATE
District 6

Yolanda Navarro Flores	5,541	46.07%
Mario Gallegos Jr.	6,484	53.92%
Total Vote	12,025	

District 21

Raymond Bruni	17,089	21.34%
Judith Zaffirini	62,960	78.65%
Total Vote	80,049	

District 26

Johnny Rodriguez	3,685	18.05%
Leticia R. Van de Putte	16,723	81.94%
Total Vote	20,408	

Prop. 1 – Privatize Social Security/Medicare

Yes	141,583	16.88%
No	696,814	83.11%
Total Vote	834,397	

Prop. 2 – Prohibit State Mandates that Require Tax Increases

Yes	485,054	58.81%
No	339,681	41.18%
Total Vote	824,735	

REPUBLICAN PRIMARY

President

George W. Bush	635,948	92.48%
Uncommitted	51,667	7.51%
Total Vote	687,615	

U.S. HOUSE OF REPRESENTATIVES
District 1

Wayne Christian	6,854	14.72%
Louis Gohmert	19,421	41.73%

John Graves	13,933	29.94%
Emily Mathews	1,266	2.72%
Larry Thornton	457	0.98%
Lyle Thorstenson	4,604	9.89%
Total Vote	46,535	

District 2

Andrew J. Bolton	246	1.00%
George Fastuca	3,668	15.01%
Mark Henry	2,423	9.92%
Clint Moore	2,868	11.74%
John Nickell	285	1.16%
Ted Poe	14,932	61.14%
Total Vote	24,422	

District 3

Sam Johnson	12,429	84.05%
Brian Rubarts	2,357	15.94%
Total Vote	14,786	

District 4

Ralph Hall	22,484	77.18%
Mike Mosher	3,122	10.71%
Mike Murphy	3,524	12.09%
Total Vote	29,130	

District 7

John Culberson	26,561	92.20%
Sam Texas	2,245	7.79%
Total Vote	28,806	

District 9

A.R. Hassan	1,132	18.96%
Arlette Molina	4,836	81.03%
Total Vote	5,968	

District 10

John Devine	7,096	21.33%
Teresa Doggett Taylor	1,494	4.49%
Pat Elliott	1,245	3.74%
John Kelley	952	2.86%
Michael T. McCaul	7,953	23.91%
Dave Phillips	4,460	13.40%
Ben Streusand	9,364	28.15%
Brad Tashenberg	695	2.08%
Total Vote	33,259	

District 11

Mike Conaway	38,792	74.53%
Bill Lester	13,255	25.46%
Total Vote	52,047	

District 15

Alexander Hamilton	3,795	41.48%
Paul B. Haring	1,954	21.36%
Michael D. Thamm	3,398	37.14%
Total Vote	9,147	

District 16

David Brigham	4,127	53.23%
Bobby Ortiz	3,626	46.76%
Total Vote	7,753	

District 17

Dave McIntyre	10,681	28.19%
Dot Snyder	11,568	30.54%
Arlene Wohlgemuth	15,627	41.25%
Total Vote	37,876	

District 24

Bill Dunn	1,096	8,87%
Kenny Marchant	9,073	73.48%
Cynthia Newman	1,103	8.93%
Terry Waldrum	1,074	8.69%
Total Vote	12,346	

District 25

Regner A. Capener	1,788	32.70%
Rebecca Armendariz Klein	3,679	67.29%
Total Vote	5,467	

District 27

Jesus A. Caquias	2,401	30.07%
William (Willie) Vaden	5,582	69.92%
Total Vote	7,983	

District 28
Chris Bellamy	1,478	14.93%
Francisco (Quico) Canseco	2,115	21.37%
James (Jim) F. Hopson	4,856	49.08%
Gabriel (Gabe) Perales Jr.	1,445	14.60%
Total Vote	9,894	

District 31
Dirk Armbrust	2,868	7.88%
John R. Carter	25,293	69.53%
Wes Riddle	8,215	22.58%
Total Vote	36,376	

STATE OFFICES
Railroad Commissioner
Robert Butler	133,506	23.51%
Victor G. Carrillo	281,660	49.60%
Douglas G. Deffenbaugh	73,039	12.86%
K. Dale Henry	79,630	14.02%
Total Vote	567,835	

Justice, Supreme Court, Place 5
Paul Green	294,935	53.15%
Steven Wayne Smith	259,877	46.84%
Total Vote	554,812	

Judge, Court of Criminal Appeals, Place 2
Guy James Gray	186,193	35.21%
Lawrence (Larry) Meyers	342,527	64.78%
Total Vote	528,720	

Judge, Court of Criminal Appeals, Place 5
Cheryl Johnson	290,197	54.96%
Patricia Noble	237,774	45.03%
Total Vote	527,971	

Judge, Court of Criminal Appeals, Place 6
Michael E. Keasler	298,728	57.82%
Steven M. Porter	217,868	42.17%
Total Vote	516,596	

STATE SENATE
District 31
Bob Barnes	1,850	2.71%
Kirk Edwards	22,486	33.04%
Lee Gibson	391	0.57%
Jesse Quackenbush	407	0.59%
Kel Seliger	41,769	61.38%
Don Sparks	1,140	1.67%
Total Vote	68,043	

COURTS OF APPEALS
Justice, Third District, Place 4
Ernest C. Garcia	38,458	49.50%
Bill Green	39,221	50.49%
Total Vote	77,679	

Justice, Third District, Place 6 (unexpired term)
William C. (Bill) Davidson	35,564	47.62%
Bob Pemberton	39,107	52.37%
Total Vote	74,671	

Justice, Ninth District, Place 2
Ralph K. Harrison	10,280	34.70%
Charles Kreger	19,342	65.29%
Total Vote	29,622	

Justice, Tenth District, Place 3
Lynnan Locke Kendrick	17,242	48.11%
Felipe Reyna	18,591	51.88%
Total Vote	35,833	

Justice, Fourteenth District, Place 9
Eva Guzman	75,683	71.16%
Lloyd Wayne Oliver	30,661	28.83%
Total Vote	106,344	

STATE BOARD OF EDUCATION
District 6
Floy Evans	18,876	44.26%
Terri Leo	23,765	55.73%
Total Vote	42,641	

District 8
Linda Bauer	25,285	41.96%
Barbara Cargill	34,968	58.03%
Total Vote	60,253	

District 14
Gail Lowe	29,125	59.82%
Andrea Williams	19,556	40.17%
Total Vote	48,681	

REPUBLICAN RUNOFF
U.S. House, District 1
Louis Gohmert	16,841	57.16%
John Graves	12,618	42.83%
Total Vote	29,459	

U.S. House, District 10
Michael T. McCaul	15,084	63.14%
Ben Streusand	8,803	36.85%
Total Vote	23,887	

U.S. House, District 15
Alexander Hamilton	1,823	39.17%
Michael D. Thamm	2,830	60.82%
Total Vote	4,653	

U.S. House, District 17
Dot Snyder	13,713	45.09%
Arlene Wohlgemuth	16,694	54.90%
Total Vote	30,407	

U.S. House, District 28
Francisco (Quico) Canseco	1,044	35.63%
James (Jim) F. Hopson	1,886	64.36%
Total Vote	2,930	

Railroad Commissioner
Robert Butler	83,298	37.22%
Victor G. Carrillo	140,471	62.77%
Total Vote	223,769	

Special Elections, 2004–2005

STATE SENATE
District 1
Held Jan. 20, 2004
Kevin Eltife (Republican)	24,919	36.00%
Bill Godsey (Republican)	502	00.72%
Tommy Merritt (Republican)	14,786	21.36%
Paul Sadler (Democrat)	27,339	39.50%
Daryl Ware (Constitution)	480	00.69%
Jerry Yost (Republican)	1,180	01.70%
Total Vote	69,206	

Runoff Held Feb. 17, 2004
District 1
Kevin Eltife (Republican)	46,437	51.86%
Paul Sadler (Democrat)	43,103	48.13%
Total Vote	89,540	

District 31
Held Jan. 20, 2004
Bob Barnes (Republican)	9,478	13.65%
Kirk Edwards (Republican)	14,273	20.56%
Lee Gibson (Republican)	2,429	03.49%
Elaine King Miller (Democrat)	5,738	08.26%
Jesse Quackenbush (Republican)	1,488	02.14%
Kel Seliger (Republican)	24,793	35.71%
Don Sparks	11,216	16.15%
Total Vote	69,415	

Runoff Held Feb. 17, 2004
District 1
Kirk Edwards (Republican)	32,094	43.84%
Kel Seliger (Republican)	41,102	56.15%
Total Vote	73,196	

Texas Vote in Presidential Elections, 1848–2000

Below are the Texas popular vote results for U.S. presidential elections. (Earlier elections listed electors, and often the highest vote recorded by any elector was used as the figure for the presidential candidate.) An asterisk (*) designates the winner of the national election. In the 1860 vote that elected Lincoln president, electors for neither Lincoln nor Stephen Douglas were on the Texas ballot. Texas did not take part in the 1864 and 1868 elections because of the Civil War and Reconstruction.

Election, 1848
Lewis Cass (Democrat) 10,668
*Zachary Taylor (Whig) 4,509
    Total Vote 15,177

Election, 1852
*Franklin Pierce (Democrat) 13,552
Winfield Scott (Whig) 4,995
    Total Vote 18,547

Election, 1856
*James C. Buchanan (Democrat) 31,169
Millard Fillmore (Whig) 15,639
    Total Vote 46,808

Election, 1860
John C Breckinridge (Democrat) 47,548
John Bell (Constitutional Union) 15,438
    Total Vote 62,986

CIVIL WAR and RECONSTRUCTION

Election, 1872
Horace Greeley (Democrat) 66,546
*Ulysses S. Grant (Republican) 47,468
Charles O'Conor (Labor-Reform) 2,580
    Total Vote 116,594

Election, 1876
Samuel J. Tilden (Democrat) 104,755
*Rutherford B. Hayes (Republican) 44,800
    Total Vote 149,555

Election, 1880
Winfield S. Hancock (Democrat) 156,428
*James A. Garfield (Republican) 57,893
    Total Vote 214,321

Election, 1884
*Grover Cleveland (Democrat) 225,309
James G. Blaine (Republican) 93,141
John P. St. John (Prohibitionist) 3,534
Benjamin F. Butler (Greenback) 3,321
    Total Vote 325,305

Election, 1888
Grover Cleveland (Democrat) 234,883
*Benjamin Harrison (Republican) 88,422
Alson J. Streeter (Union Labor) 29,459
Clinton B. Fisk (Prohibitionist) 4,749
    Total Vote 357,513

Election, 1892
*Grover Cleveland (Democrat) 239,148
James B. Weaver (Populist) 99,688
Benjamin Harrison (Republican) 81,144
John Bidwell (Prohibitionist) 2,175
    Total Vote 422,155

Election, 1896
William J. Bryan (Democrat) 234,298
William J. Bryan (Populist) 78,926
*William McKinley (Republican) 167,520

John McA. Palmer (National Democrat) 5,046
Joshua Levering (Prohibitionist) 1,786
    Total Vote 487,576

Election, 1900
William J. Bryan (Democrat) 267,432
*William McKinley (Republican) 130,651
Wharton Barker (Populist) 20,981
John C. Woolley (Prohibitionist) 2,644
Eugene V. Debs (Socialist) 1,846
Joseph F. Malloney (Socialist-Labor) 162
    Total Vote 423,716**

**POLL TAX instituted as requirement for voting, December 1902

Election, 1904
Alton B. Parker (Democrat) 199,799
*Theodore Roosevelt (Republican) 65,823
Thomas E. Watson (Populist) 8,062
Silas C. Swallow (Prohibitionist) 4,292
Eugene V. Debs (Socialist) 2,791
Charles H. Corregan (Socialist-Labor) 421
    Total Vote 281,188**

Election, 1908
William J. Bryan (Democrat) 224,110
*William H. Taft (Republican) 70,458
Eugene V. Debs (Socialist) 7,870
Eugene W. Chafin (Prohibitionist) 1,634
Thomas E. Watson (Populist) 994
August Gillhaus (Socialist-Labor) 176
Thomas L. Hisgen (Independent) 115
    Total Vote 305,357

Election, 1912
*Woodrow Wilson (Democrat) 222,589
Theodore Roosevelt (Progressive) 28,853
William H. Taft (Republican) 26,755
Eugene V. Debs (Socialist) 25,743
Eugene W. Chafin (Prohibitionist) 1,738
Arthur E. Reimer (Socialist-Labor) 442
    Total Vote 306,120

Election, 1916
*Woodrow Wilson (Democrat) 286,514
Charles E. Hughes (Republican) 64,999
Allan L. Benson (Socialist) 18,969
J. Frank Hanly (Prohibitionist) 1,985
    Total Vote 372,467

Election, 1920
James M. Cox (Democrat) 288,767
*Warren G. Harding (Republican) 114,538
James E. Ferguson (American) 47,968
(Black and Tan Republican) 27,247
Eugene V. Debs (Socialist) 8,121
    Total Vote 486,641

Election, 1924
John W. Davis (Democrat) 484,605
*Calvin Coolidge (Republican) 130,023
Robert M. LaFollette (Progressive) 42,881

Total Vote.................657,509

Election, 1928
*Herbert C. Hoover (Republican) 367,036
Alfred E. Smith (Democrat)..................341,032
Norman M. Thomas (Socialist) 722
William Z. Foster (Communist) 209
    Total Vote...................708,999

Election, 1932
*Franklin D. Roosevelt (Democrat) 760,348
Herbert C. Hoover (Republican)..............97,959
Norman M. Thomas (Socialist) 4,450
W.H. Harvey (Liberty)..........................324
William Z. Foster (Communist) 207
(Jacksonian)..................................104
    Total Vote...................863,392

Election, 1936
*Franklin D. Roosevelt (Democrat) 734,485
Alfred M. Landon (Republican)...............103,874
William Lemke (Union) 3,281
Norman M. Thomas (Socialist) 1,075
D. Leigh Colvin (Prohibitionist) 514
Earl R. Browder (Communist)...................253
    Total Vote...................843,482

Election, 1940
*Franklin D. Roosevelt (Democrat) 840,151
Wendell L. Willkie (Republican).............. 199,152
Roger W. Babson (Prohibitionist) 925
Norman M. Thomas (Socialist) 728
Earl R. Browder (Communist)...................212
    Total Vote................. 1,041,168

Election, 1944
*Franklin D. Roosevelt (Democrat) 821,605
Thomas E. Dewey (Republican)............. 191,425
‡(Texas Regulars) 135,439
Claude A. Watson (Prohibitionist)............ 1,017
Norman M. Thomas (Socialist) 594
Gerald L.K. Smith (America First)................251
    Total Vote................. 1,150,331

Election, 1948
*Harry S Truman (Democrat) 750,700
Thomas E. Dewey (Republican)............. 282,240
J. Strom Thurmond (States Rights) 106,909
Henry A. Wallace (Progressive) 3,764
Claude A. Watson (Prohibitionist) 2,758
Norman M. Thomas (Socialist) 874
    Total Vote................. 1,147,245

Election, 1952
*Dwight D. Eisenhower (Republican) 1,102,878
Adlai E. Stevenson (Democrat)............. 969,228
Stuart Hamblen (Prohibitionist) 1,983
Douglas MacArthur (Christian National)...........833
Douglas MacArthur (Constitution) 730
Vincent Hallinan (Progressive) 294
    Total Vote................. 2,075,946

Election, 1956
*Dwight D. Eisenhower (Republican) 1,080,619
Adlai E. Stevenson (Democrat)............. 859,958
T. Coleman Andrews (Constitution) 14,591
    Total Vote................. 1,955,168

Election, 1960
*John F. Kennedy (Democrat)............. 1,167,932
Richard M. Nixon (Republican).............. 1,121,699
Charles L. Sullivan (Constitution) 18,169
Rutherford L. Decker (Prohibitionist)............3,870
    Total Vote................. 2,311,670

Election, 1964**
*Lyndon B. Johnson (Democrat) 1,663,185
Barry Goldwater (Republican)............... 958,566
Joseph B. Lightburn (Conservative) 5,060
    Total Vote.................2,626,811

** First federal election no poll tax required

Election, 1968
Hubert H. Humphrey (Democrat) 1,266,804
*Richard M. Nixon (Republican) 1,227,844
George C. Wallace (American) 584,269
Write-in 489
    Total Vote.................3,079,406

Election, 1972
*Richard M. Nixon (Republican) 2,298,896
George McGovern (Democrat) 1,154,289
Linda Jenness (Socialist) 8,664
John G. Schmitz (American)................. 6,039
Other.. 3,393
    Total Vote................3,471,281

Election, 1976
*Jimmy Carter (Democrat) 2,082,319
Gerald R. Ford (Republican) 1,953,300
Eugene J. McCarthy (Independent) 20,118
Thomas J. Anderson (American).............. 11,442
Peter Camejo (Socialst Worker) 1,723
Write-in Vote 2,982
    Total Vote.................4,071,884

Election, 1980
*Ronald Reagan (Republican) 2,510,705
Jimmy Carter (Democrat) 1,881,147
John Anderson (Independent) 111,613
Ed Clark (Libertarian) 37,643
Write-in Vote 529
    Total Vote................4,541,637

Election, 1984
*Ronald Reagan (Republican) 3,433,428
Walter Mondale (Democrat) 1,949,276
Lyndon Larouche (Independent).............. 14,613
Other..254
    Total Vote.................5,397,571

Election, 1988
*George Bush (Republican) 3,036,829
Michael S. Dukakis (Democrat)............. 2,352,748
Ron Paul (Libertarian)......................30,355
Other.......................................7,478
    Total Vote................5,427,410

Election, 1992
George Bush (Republican) 2,496,071
*Bill Clinton (Democrat)................. 2,281,815
Ross Perot (Independent) 1,354,781
Andre Marrou (Libertarian) 19,699
Other.......................................1,652
    Total Vote.................6,154,018

Election, 1996
Bob Dole (Republican) 2,736,167
*Bill Clinton (Democrat)................. 2,459,683
Ross Perot (Independent) 378,537
Harry Browne (Libertarian) 20,256
Howard Phillips (U.S. Taxpayers) 7,472
Ralph Nader (Write-In) 4,810
John Hagelin (Natural Law) 4,422
Mary Cal Hollis (Write-In) 297
    Total Vote.................5,611,644

Election, 2000

George W. Bush (Republican)	3,799,639
Al Gore (Democrat)	2,433,746
Ralph Nader (Green)	137,994
Harry Browne (Libertarian)	23,160
Pat Buchanan (Independent)	12,394
Howard Phillips (Write-In)	567
James (Jim) Wright (W-I)	74
David McReynolds (W-I)	63
Total Vote	6,407,637

Presidential Primaries in Texas

May 1976
(1976 was the first time presidential primaries were held in the state.)

Republican

Ronald Reagan	278,300
Gerald Ford	139,944
Uncommitted	1,162
Total Vote	419,406

Democratic

Jimmy Carter	736,161
Lloyd Bentsen	343,032
George Wallace	270,798
Fred Harris	31,379
Sargent Shriver	28,520
Ellen McCormack	5,700
Uncommitted	129,478
Total Vote	1,545,068

May 1980

Republican

Ronald Reagan	268,798
George Bush	249,819
Uncommitted	8,152
Total Vote	526,769

Democratic

Jimmy Carter	770,390
Edward M. Kennedy	314,129
Jerry Brown	35,585
Uncommitted	257,250
Total Vote	1,377,354

March 1984

Republican

Ronald Reagan	308,713
Uncommitted	11,126
Total Vote	319,839

Democratic
Democrats held no primary, but voted in precinct caucuses for 169 pledged delegates. With addition of party leaders, the 200-member delegation to the national convention was divided:

Walter Mondale	119
Gary Hart	41
Jesse L. Jackson	35
Uncommitted	5

March 1988

Republican

George Bush	648,178
Pat Robertson	155,449
Bob Dole	140,795
Jack Kemp	50,586
Pete Du Pont	4,245
Alexander M. Haig Jr.	3,140
Uncommitted	12,563
Total Vote	1,014,956

Democratic

Michael S. Dukakis	579,713
Jesse L. Jackson	433,335
Al Gore	357,764
Dick Gephardt	240,158
Gary Hart	82,199

Paul Simon	34,499
Bruce Babbitt	11,618
Lyndon H. LaRouche Jr.	9,013
David E. Duke	8,808
W.A. Williams	6,238
Norbert G. Dennerll Jr.	3,700
Total Vote	1,767,045

March 1992

Republican

George Bush	556,280
Patrick J. Buchanan	190,572
David Duke	20,255
George A. Zimmermann	1,349
Tennie Rogers	754
Uncommitted	27,936
Total Vote	797,146

Democratic

Bill Clinton	972,235
Paul E. Tsongas	285,224
Edmund G. Brown Jr.	118,869
Charles Woods	30,097
Bob Kerrey	20,298
Tom Harkin	19,618
Lyndon H. LaRouche Jr.	12,220
George W. Benns	7,876
Rufus Higginbotham	7,677
Tod Howard Hawks	4,924
J. Louis McAlpine	4,009
Total Vote	1,483,047

March 1996

Republican

Bob Dole	567,164
Patrick J. (Pat) Buchanan	217,974
Steve Forbes	130,938
Alan Keyes	41,746
Lamar Alexander	18,745
Phil Gramm	18,629
Richard G. Lugar	2,266
Susan Ducey	1,093
Mary (France) LeTulle	650
Charles E. Collins	633
Morry Taylor	458
Uncommitted	19,507
Total Vote	1,019,803

Democratic

Bill Clinton	796,041
Fred Hudson	32,232
Heather Harder	28,772
Lyndon H. LaRouche Jr.	28,137
Ted L. Gunderson	15,550
Elvena E. Lloyd-Duffie	10,876
Sal Casamassima	9,648
Total Vote	921,256

March 2000

Republican

George W. Bush	986,416
John McCain	80,082
Alan Keyes	43,518
Steve Forbes	2,865
Gary Bauer	2,189
Orrin G. Hatch	1,324
Charles Bass Urban	793
Uncommitted	9,570
Total Vote	1,126,757

Democratic

All Gore	631,428
Bill Bradley	128,564
Lyndon H. LaRouche Jr.	26,898
Total Vote	786,890

Elections of U.S. Senators from Texas

Below is given a compilation of past U.S. senatorial elections in Texas insofar as information is available to the Texas Almanac. Prior to 1916, U.S. senators were appointed by the Legislature.

1906
Democratic Primary
J.W. Bailey (unopp.)	283,315

1910
Democratic Primary
C.A. Culberson (unopp.)	359,939

1912
Democratic Primary
Morris Sheppard	178,281
Jacob F. Wolters	142,050
Choice B. Randall	40,349
Matthew Zollner	3,868
Total vote	364,548

1916
1st Democratic Primary
Carles A. Culberson	87,421
Robert L. Henry	37,726
O.B. Colquitt	119,598
S.P. Brooks	78,641
T.M. Campbell	65,721
John Davis	9,924
*G.W. Riddle	335
Total vote	399,366

*Had withdrawn

2nd Democratic Primary
Charles A. Culberson	163,182
O.B. Colquitt	94,098
Total Vote	257,280

General Election
Charles A. Culberson (Dem.)	301,905
Alex W. Atcheson (Rep.)	48,775
E.H. Conibear (Proh.)	2,313
T.A. Hickey (Socialist)	18,616
Total Vote	371,609

1918
Democratic Primary
Morris Sheppard (unopp.)	649,876

General Election
Morris Sheppard (Dem.)	155,158
J. Webster Flanagan (Rep.)	22,183
M.A. Smith (Soc.)	1,587
Total vote	178,928

1922
1st Democratic Primary
C.A. Culberson	99,635
Earle B. Mayfield	153,538
Cullen F. Thomas	88,026
James E. Ferguson	127,071
Clarence Ousley	62,451
R.L. Henry	41,567
Sterling P. Strong	1,085
Total vote	573,373

2nd Democratic Primary
Earle B. Mayfield	273,308
James E. Ferguson	228,701
Total vote	502,009

General Election
Earle B. Mayfield (Dem.)	264,260
George E.B. Peddy (Rep.)	130,744
Total vote	395,004

1924
Democratic Primary
Morris Sheppard	440,511
Fred W. Davis	159,663
John F. Maddox	80,070
Total vote	680,244

General Election
Morris Sheppard (Dem.)	579,208
T.M. Kennerly (Rep.)	98,207
Total vote	677,415

1928
1st Democratic Primary
Thomas L. Blanton	126,758
Tom Connally	178,091
Minnie Fisher Cunningham	28,944
Earle B.Mayfield	200,246
Jeff McLemore	9,244
Alvin Owsley	131,755
Total vote	675,038

2nd Democratic Primary
Tom Connally	320,071
Earle B. Mayfield	257,747
Total vote	577,818

General Election
Tom Connally (Dem.)	566,139
T.M. Kennerly (Rep.)	129,910
David Curran (Soc.)	690
John Rust (Communist)	114
Total vote	696,853

1930
Democratic Primary
Morris Sheppard	526,293
C.A. Mitchner	40,130
Robert L. Henry	174,260
Total vote	740,683

Republican Primary
(158 counties reporting)
Doran John Haesly	3,645
*Harve H. Haines	2,568
*C.O. Harris	2,784
Total vote	8,997

*No runoff; candidates withdrew.

General Election
Morris Sheppard (Dem.)	258,929
D.J. Haesly (Rep.)	35,357
Guy. L. Smith (Soc.)	790
W.A. Berry (Com.)	282
Total vote	295,358

1934
Democratic Primary
Joseph W. Bailey	355,963
Tom Connally	567,139
Guy. B. Fisher	41,421
Total vote	964,523

General Election
Tom Connally (Dem.)	439,375
U.S. Goen (Rep.)	12,895
W.B. Starr (Soc.)	1,828
L.C. Keel (Com.)	310
Total vote	454,408

1936
Democratic Primary
Morris Sheppard	616,293
Guy B. Fisher	89,215
Richard C. Bush	37,842
Joseph H. Price	45,919
Joe H. Eagle	136,718
J. Edward Glenn	28,641
Total vote	954,628

General Election
Morris Sheppard (Dem.)	774,975

Carlos G. Watson (Rep.)	59,491
W.B. Starr (Soc.)	958
Gertrude Wilson (Union)	1,836
Total Vote	837,260

1940
Democratic Primary
Tom Connally	923,219
A.P. Belcher	66,962
Guy B. Fisher	98,125
Total vote	1,088,306

General Election
Tom Connally(Dem.)	978,095
George Shannon (Rep.)	59,340
Homer Brooks (Const.)	408
Total vote	1,037,843

1941 Special Election
June 28, 1941
25 Dems., 2 Reps. 1 Ind.
and 1 Communist
W. Lee O'Daniel	175,590
Lyndon B. Johnson	174,279
Gerald C. Mann	140,807
Martin Dies	80,653
*Total vote	571,329

*Above candidates only; votes for others not available.

1942
1st Democratic Primary
James V. Allred	317,501
Dan Moody	178,471
W. Lee O'Daniel	475,541
Floyd E. Ryan	12,213
Total vote	983,726

2nd Democratic Primary
James V. Allred	433,203
W. Lee O'Daniel	451,359
Total vote	884,562

General Election
W.Lee O'Daniel (Dem.)	260,629
Dudley Lawson (Rep.)	12,064
Charles L. Somerville (P.U.P.)	1,934
Total vote	274,627

1946
Democratic Primary
Tom Connally	823,818
Cyclone Davis	74,252
Floyd E. Ryan	85,292
Terrell Sledge	66,947
Laverne Somerville	42,290
Total vote	1,092,599

General Election
Tom Connally (Dem.)	336,931
Murray C. Sells (Rep.)	43,750
Write-in	5
Total vote	380,686

1948
1st Democratic Primary
Otis C. Myers	15,330
F.B. Clark	7,420
Roscoe H. Collier	12,327
Coke R. Stevenson	477,077
Cyclone Davis	10,871
Frank G. Cortez	13,344
Jesse C. Saunders	7,401
George E.B. Peddy	237,195

Lyndon B. Johnson	405,617
Terrell Sledge.	6,692
James F. Alford	9,117
Write-in	1
Total vote	1,202,392

2nd Democratic Primary

Lyndon B. Johnson	494,191
Coke R. Stevenson	494,104
Total vote	988,295

General Election

Lyndon B. Johnson (Dem.).	702,985
Jack Porter (Rep.)	349,665
Sam Morris (Proh.)	8,913
Total vote	1,061,563

1952
1st Democratic Primary

Price Daniel.	940,770
Lindley Beckworth	285,842
E.W. Napier	70,132
Total vote	1,296,744

General Election

Price Daniel (Dem.).	1,425,007
Price Daniel (Rep.)	469,494
Price Daniel (No Party) . .	591
Total vote	1,895,192

1954
1st Democratic Primary

Lyndon B. Johnson	883,264
Dudley T. Dougherty	354,188
Total vote	1,237,452

General Election

Lyndon B. Johnson (Dem.).	538,417
Carlos G. Watson (Rep.) .	95,033
Fred T. Spangler (Const.)	3,025
Total vote	636,475

1957 Special Election

On April 2, Price Daniel had resigned to run for governorship.

Elmer Adams.	2,228
H.J. Antoine Sr.	576
M.T. Banks	2,153
Jacob Bergolofsky	890
Searcy Bracewell.	33,384
John C. Burns Sr.	600
*H.Frank Connally Jr.	514
Frank E. Cortez	1,350
*J.Cal Courtney	879
*R.W. (Waire) Currin	646
Martin Dies	290,803
C.O.Foerster Jr.	776
Curtis Ford.	767
Ralph W. Hammonds. . . .	2,372
James P. Hart	19,739
*Charles W. (Jack) Hill . . .	1,025
Thad Hutcheson	219,591
Walter Scott McNutt.	500
Clyde R. Orms	356
John C. White	11,876
J.Perrin Wills	817
Hugh Wilson	851
Ralph W. Yarborough	364,605
Total vote	957,298

Withdrew, but after ballots printed.

1958
1st Democratic Primary

William A. Blakley	536,073
Ralph W. Yarborough	760,856

Write-in.	4
Total vote	1,296,933

General Election

Ralph W. Yarborough (Dem.)	587,030
Roy Whittenburg (Rep.) . .	185,926
Bard A. Logan (Const.) . .	14,172
Total vote	787,128

1960
1st Democratic Primary

Lyndon B. Johnson	1,407,109
Write-in.	145
Total vote.	1,407,254

General Election

Lyndon B. Johnson (Dem.).	1,306,625
John G. Tower (Rep.)	926,653
Bard A. Logan (Const.) . .	20,506
Total vote	2,253,784

1961 Special Election

On April 4, Lyndon B. Johnson resigned to assume office of Vice President.

John G. Tower	327,308
William A. Blakley	190,818
Jim Wright	171,328
Will Wilson	121,961
Maury Maverick Jr.	104,992
Henry B. Gonzalez	97,659

The remaining 71 candidates were: Dr. G.H. Allen, 849; Jim W. Amos, 527; Dale Baker, 612; Dr. Mali Jean Rauch Barraco, 434; Tom E. Barton, 395; R.G. Becker, 462; Jacob Bergolofsky, 377; Dr.Ted Bisland, 831; G.E. Blewett,474, Lawrence S. Bosworth Jr., 410; Joyce J. Bradshaw, 352; Chester D. Brooks, 711; W.L. Burlison, 1,695; Ronald J. Byers, 175; Joseph M. Carter, 185; George A. Davisson, 897, Mrs. Winnie K. Derrick, 327, Harry R. Diehl, 293, Harvill O. Eaton, 178; Rev. Jonnie Mae Eckman, 342; Paul F. Eix, 317; Ben H. Faber, 363; Dr. H.E. Fanning, 293, Charles Otto Foerster Jr., 133; Harold Franklin, 196; George N. Gallagher Jr., 985; Richard J. Gay,939; Van T. George Jr., 307; Arthur Glover, 1,528; Delbert E. Grandstaff, 2,959; Curtis E. Hill, 389; Willard Park Holland, 669; John N. Hopkins, 490; Mary Hazel Houston, 726; Ben M. Johnson, 681;Guy Johnson, 748; Morgan H. Johnson, 334; C.B. Kennedy, 770; H. Springer Knoblauch, 186; Hugh O. Lea, 651; V.C. Logan, 314; Frank A. Matera, 599, Brown McCallum, 323; James E. McKee, 762; Steve Nemecek, 1,017; George E. Noyes, 174; Floyd Payne, 227; Cecil D. Perkins, 773; W.H. Posey, 592; George Red, 99; Wesley Roberts, 386; D.T. Sampson, 417; Eristus Sams, 4,490; A. Dale Savage, 400; Carl A. Schrade, 283; Albert Roy Smith, 341; Homer Hyrim Stalarow, 735; Frank Stanford, 240; John B. Sypert, 252; Mrs. Martha Tredway, 1,227; S.S. Vela, 241, Bill Whitten, 350; Hoyt G. Wilson, 2,165; Hugh Wilson, 2,997; Marcos Zertuche, 442; Write-ins, 42.

Total vote.	1,058,124

*Runoff Election held May 27

William A. Blakley	437,874
John G. Tower	448,217
Total vote	886,091

Change in state law following 1957 special election required runoff.

1964
1st Democratic Primary

Ralph Yarborough.	905,001
Gordon McLendon	672,573
Write-in.	23

Total vote	1,577,607

1st Republican Primary

George Bush	62,985
Jack Cox.	45,561
Milton V. Davis	6,067
Robert Morris	28,279
Total vote	142,892

2nd Republican Primary

George Bush	49,751
Jack Cox.	30,333
Total vote	80,084

General Election

Ralph Yarborough (Dem.)	1,463,958
George Bush (Rep.)	1,134,337
Jack Carswell (Const.) . . .	5,542
Write-in	19
Total vote	2,603,856

1966
1st Democratic Primary

John R. Willoughby	226,598
Waggoner Carr	899,523
Total vote	1,126,121

General Election

Waggoner Carr (Dem.) . . .	643,855
John G. Tower (Rep.)	842,501
Jas. Barker Holland (Const.)	6,778
Total vote	1,493,134

1970
1st Democratic Primary

Lloyd Bentsen.	814,316
Ralph Yarborough	726,447
Total vote	1,540,763

Republican Primary

George Bush	96,806
Robert Morris	13,659
Total vote	110,465

General Election

Lloyd Bentsen (Dem.). . . .	1,226,568
George Bush (Rep.)	1,071,234
Other.	1,808
Total vote	2,299,610

1972
1st Democratic Primary

Thomas M. Cartlidge	66,240
Barefoot Sanders	787,504
Alfonso Veloz	53,938
Hugh Wilson	125,460
Ralph Yarborough	1,032,606
Total vote	2,065,748

2nd Democratic Primary

Barefoot Sanders	1,008,499
Ralph Yarborough	928,087
Total vote	1,936,586

Republican Primary

John G. Tower (unopp.) . .	107,648

General Election

Barefoot Sanders (Dem.) .	1,511,985
John G. Tower (Rep.)	1,822,877
Flores Amaya (Raza)	63,543
Tom Leonard (Soc.)	14,464
Other.	1,034
Total vote	3,413,903

1976
1st Democratic Primary

Lloyd Bentsen.	970,983
Leon Dugi	19,870
Phil Gramm.	427,597

Hugh Wilson 109,715
Other 1,003
Total vote 1,529,168

Republican Primary
Louis Leman 40,651
Alan Steelman 251,252
Hugh Sweeney 64,404
Total vote 356,307

General Election
Lloyd Bentsen (Dem.) . . . 2,199,956
Alan Steelman (Rep.) . . . 1,636,370
Marjorie P. Gallion (Am.) . 17,355
Pedro Vasques
(Soc. Worker) 20,549
Total vote 3,874,230

1978

1st Democratic Primary
Joe Christie 701,892
Robert Krueger 853,485
Total vote 1,555,377

Republican Primary
John G. Tower 142,202

General Election
Robert Krueger (Dem.) . . 1,139,149
John G. Tower (Rep.) 1,151,376
Luis A. Diaz de Leon
(Raza Unida) 17,869
Miguel Pendas
(Soc. Worker) 4,018
Other 128
Total vote 2,312,540

1982

1st Democratic Primary
Lloyd Bentsen 987,985
Joe Sullivan 276,453
Total vote 1,264,438

Republican Primary
Don I. Richardson 18,616
Jim Collins 152,469
Walter H. Mengden Jr. . . . 91,780
Total vote 262,865

General Election
Jim Collins (Rep.) 1,256,759

Lloyd Bentsen (Dem.) . . . 1,818,223
John E. Ford (Lib.) 23,494
Lineaus H. Lorette
(Const.) 4,564
Darryl Anderson (W-I) . . . 39
Other 88
Total vote 3,103,167

1984

1st Democratic Primary
Lloyd Doggett 456,173
Kent Hance 456,446
Robert Krueger 454,886
Harley Schlanger 14,149
Robert Sullivan 34,733
David Young 47,062
Total vote 1,463,449

2nd Democratic Primary
Lloyd Doggett 491,251
Kent Hance 489,906
Total vote 981,157

Republican Primary
Phil Gramm 246,716
Henry Grover 8,388
Robert Mosbacher 26,279
Ron Paul 55,431
Total vote 336,814

General Election
Lloyd Doggett (Dem.) 2,202,557
Phil Gramm (Rep.) 3,111,348
Other 273
Total vote 5,314,178

1988

Democratic Primary
Lloyd Bentsen 1,365,736
Joe Sullivan 244,805
Total vote 1,610,541

1st Republican Primary
Beau Boulter 228,676
Milton E. Fox 138,031
Wes Gilbreath 275,080
Ned Snead 107,560
Total vote 749,347

2nd Republican Primary
Beau Boulter 111,134
Wes Gilbreath 73,573

Total vote 184,707

General Election
Lloyd Bentsen (Dem.) 3,149,806
Beau Boulter (Rep.) 2,129,228
Other 44,572
Total vote 5,323,606

1990

1st Democratic Primary
Hugh Parmer 766,284
Harley Schlanger 249,445
Total vote 1,015,729

1st Republican Primary
Phil Gramm 687,170

General Election
Phil Gram m(Rep.) 2,302,357
Hugh Parmer (Dem.) 1,429,986
Gary Johnson (Lib.) 89,089
Other 725
Total vote 3,822,157

1993 Special Election
*Held on May 1. Lloyd Bentsen had
resigned to assume post as
U.S. Secretary of Treasury.*
Kay Bailey Hutchison 593,338
Robert Krueger 593,239
Joe Barton 284,137
Jack Fields 277,560
Richard Fisher 165,560

Others: Billy Brown, 2,187; Louis C. Davis,
1,548; Rick Draheim, 5,677; Rose Floyd,
2,301; Jose Angel Gutierrez, 52,103; Lottie
Bolling Hancock, 2,242; Rober Henson,
3,092; Stephen Hopkins, 14,753; Charles
Ben Howell, 3,866; Gene Kelly, 11,331; C.
(Sonny) Payne, 6,782; Don Richardson,
6,209; Chuck Sibley, 2,406; Thomas D.
Spink, 2,281; Herbert Spiro, 4,459; Maco
Stewart, 1,260; James Vallaster, 2,124;
Clymer Wright, 5,111; Lou Zaeske, 2,191.

Total vote 2,045,757

Runoff Election held June 5
Robert Krueger 574,089
Kay Bailey Hutchison 1,183,766
Total vote 1,757,855

*Sen. Ralph Yarborough, above. At right,
Sen. Tom Connally, with Gov. Pat Neff
seated to left. File photos, 1970 and 1951.*

1994

1st Democratic Primary

Michael A. Andrews	159,793
Richard Fisher	388,090
Evelyn K. Lantz	63,523
Jim Mattox	416,503
Total vote	1,027,909

2nd Democratic Primary

Richard Fisher	400,227
Jim Mattox	346,414
Total vote	746,641

1st Republican Primary

James C. Curry	15,625
Roger Henson	14,021
Stephen Hopkins	34,703
Kay Bailey Hutchison	467,975
M. Troy Mata	8,632
Ernest J. Schmidt	8,690
Tom Spink	5,692
Total vote	555,338

General Election

Richard Fisher (Dem.)	1,639,615
Kay Bailey Hutchison (Rep.)	2,604,218
Pierre Blondeau (Lib.)	36,107
Total vote	4,279,940

1996

1st Democratic Primary

John Bryant	267,545
Jim Chapman	239,427
Victor M. Morales	322,218
John Will Odam	61,433
Total vote	890,623

2nd Democratic Primary

John Bryant	235,281
Victor M. Morales	246,614
Total vote	481,895

1st Republican Primary

Phil Gramm	838,339
Henry C. (Hank) Grover	72,400
David Young	75,463
Total vote	986,202

General Election

Phil Gramm (Rep.)	3,027,680
Victor M. Morales (Dem.)	2,428,776
Michael Bird (Lib.)	51,516
John Huff (NLP)	19,469
Total vote	5,527,441

2000

1st Democratic Primary

H. Gerald Bintliff	33,979
Don Clark	139,243
Charles Gandy	140,636
Gene Kelly	220,531
Bobby Wightman	83,643
Total vote	618,032

2nd Democratic Primary

Charles Gandy	101,983
Gene Kelly	143,366
Total vote	245,349

1st Republican Primary

Kay Bailey Hutchison	955,033
Total vote	955,033

General Election

Kay Bailey Hutchison (Rep.)	4,082,091
Gene Kelly (Dem.)	2,030,315
Mary J. Ruwart (Lib.)	72,798
Douglas S. Sandage(Green)	91,448
Total vote	6,276,652

2002

1st Democratic Primary

Ken Bentsen	255,501
Ed Cunningham	22,016
Gene Kelly	44,038
Ron Kirk	316,052
Victor Morales	317,048
Total vote	954,655

2nd Democratic Primary

Ron Kirk	370,878
Victor Morales	249,423
Total vote	620,301

1st Republican Primary

John Cornyn	478,825
Lawrence Cranberg	17,757
Douglas G. Deffenbaugh	43,711
Bruce Rusty Lang	46,907
Dudley F. Mooney	32,202
Total vote	619,302

General Election

John Cornyn (Rep.)	2,497,243
Ron Kirk (Dem.)	1,955,758
Scott Lanier Jameson (Lib.)	35,538
Roy H. Williams (Green)	25,051
James W. (Jim) Wright (W-I)	1,422
Total vote	4,515,012

Elections of Texas Governors, 1845–2002

Following are the results of elections of governors since Texas became a state in 1845. Party primaries, as well as general elections, are included whenever possible, although Republican totals are not available for some elections. Prior to 1857, most candidates ran independently. Party designations are in parentheses; an explanation of abbreviations is on the last page.

1845

J.P. Henderson	7,853
J.B. Miller	1,673
Scattering	52
Total vote	9,578

1847

George T. Wood	7,154
J.B. Miller	5,106
N.H. Darnell	1,276
J.J. Robinson	379
Scattering	852
Total vote	14,767

1849

P.H. Bell	10,319
George T. Wood	8,764
John T. Mills	2,632
Total vote	21,715

1851

P.H. Bell	13,595
M.T. Johnson	5,262
John A. Greer	4,061
B.H. Epperson	2,971
T.J. Chambers	2,320
Scattering	100
Total vote	28,309

1853

E.M. Pease	13,091
W. B. Ochiltree	9,178
George T. Wood	5,983
L.D. Evans	4,677
T.J. Chambers	2,449
John Dancy	315
Total vote	35,693

1855

E.M. Pease	26,336
D.C. Dickson	18,968
M.T. Johnson	809
George T. Wood	226
Total vote	46,339

1857

H.R. Runnels (Dem.)	32,552
Sam Houston	28,628
Total vote	61,180

1859

*Sam Houston	36,227
H.R. Runnels (Dem.)	27,500
Scattering	61
Total vote	63,788

*Ran as independent but received support of Know-Nothing Party.

Edward Clark succeeded Sam Houston on March 16, 1861, shortly after Texas seceded.

1861

F.R. Lubbock	21,854
Edward Clark	21,730
T.J. Chambers	13,759
Total vote	57,343

1863

Pendleton Murrah	17,511
T.J. Chambers	12,455
Scattering	1,070
Total vote	31,036

A.J. Hamilton was named governor under Reconstruction administration June 17, 1865.

1866

J.W. Throckmorton	49,277
E.M. Pease	12,168
Total vote	61,445

E.M. Pease was appointed governor July 30, 1867.

1869

E.J. Davis	39,901
A.J. Hamilton	39,092
Hamilton Stuart	380
Total vote	79,373

1873

Richard Coke (Dem.) ...	85,549
E.J. Davis (Rep.)	42,633
Total vote	128,182

1876

Richard Coke (Dem.) ...	150,581
William Chambers(Rep.)	47,719
Total vote	198,300

Lt. Gov. R.B. Hubbard succeeded Dec. 1, 1876, when Coke became U.S. Senator.

1878

O.M. Roberts (Dem.) ...	158,933
W.H. Hamman (G. B.) ...	55,002
A.B. Norton (Rep.)	23,402
Scattering	99
Total vote	237,436

1880

O.M. Roberts (Dem.) ...	166,101
E.J. Davis (Rep.)	64,382
W.H. Hamman (G.B.) ...	33,721
Total vote	264,204

1882

John Ireland (Dem.)	150,809
G.W. Jones (G.B.)	102,501
J.B. Robertson (I.Dem.)	334
Total vote	253,644

1884

John Ireland (Dem.)	212,234
Geo.W. Jones(G.B.)	88,450
A.B. Norton (Rep.)	25,557
Total vote	326,241

1886

L.S. Ross (Dem.)	228,776
A.M. Cochran (Rep.) ...	65,236
E.L. Dohoney (Prohi.) ...	19,186
Scattering	102
Total vote	313,300

1888

L.S. Ross (Dem.)	250,338
Marion Martin (Ind.Fus.).	98,447
Total vote	348,785

1890

J.S. Hogg (Dem.)	262,432
W. Flanagan (Rep.).....	77,742
E.C. Heath (Prohi.)	2,235
Total vote	342,409

1892

J.S. Hogg (Dem.)	190,486
George Clark (Dem.) ...	133,395
T.L. Nugent (Peo.)	108,483
A.J. Houston (Ref.Rep.) .	1,322
D.M. Prendergast (Prohi.)............	1,605
Scattering	176
Total vote	435,467

1894

C.A. Culberson (Dem.) ..	207,167
T.L. Nugent (Peo.)......	152,731
W.K. Makemson (Rep.)..	54,520
J.B. Schmitz (L.W.Rep.).	5,036
J.M. Dunn (Prohi.)......	2,196
Scattering	1,076
Total vote	422,726

1896

C.A. Culberson (Dem.)	298,528
J.C. Kearby (Peo.)	238,692
Randolph Clark (Prohi.)	1,876
Scattering	682
Total vote	539,778

1898

J.D. Sayers (Dem.)	291,548
Barnett Gibbs (Peo.) ..	114,955
R.P. Bailey (Prohi.).....	2,437
G.H. Royall (Soc. Lab.) .	552
Scattering	62
Total vote	409,554

1900

J.D. Sayers (Dem.)	303,586
R.E. Hanney (Rep.)	112,864
T.J. McMinn (Peo.).....	26,864
G.H. Royall (Soc. Lab.) .	155
Scattering	6,155
Total vote	449,624

1902

S.W.T. Lanham (Dem.) .	219,076
George W. Burkett (Rep.)	65,706
J.M. Mallett (Peo.)	12,387
G.W. Carroll (Prohi.) ...	8,708
Scattering	3,273
Total vote	309,150

1904

S.W.T. Lanham (Dem.) .	206,160
J.G. Lowden (Rep.)	56,865
Pat B. Clark (Peo.).....	9,301
W.D. Jackson (Prohi.) ..	4,509
Frank Leitner (Soc. Lab.)	552
W.H. Mills (Soc. Dem.) .	2,487
Total vote	279,874

1906

The popular vote in the state's first primary in the Democratic party was as follows:

Thomas M. Campbell ..	90,345
M. M. Brooks	70,064
O.B. Colquitt	68,529
Charles K. Bell........	65,168
Total vote	294,106

General Election

T.M. Campbell (Dem.) . .	148,264
C.A. Gray (Rep.)	23,711
J.W. Pearson (Prohi.).. .	5,252
G.C. Edwards (Soc.) ...	2,958
A.S. Dowler (Soc. Lab.) .	260
A.W. Atcheson (Reor. Rep.).............	5,395
Total vote	185,840

1908
Democratic Primary

T.M. Campbell	202,608
R.R. Williams	117,459
Total vote	320,067

General Election

T.M. Campbell (Dem.) . .	218,956
J.N. Simpson (Rep.) ...	73,305
J.C. Rhodes (Soc.)	8,100
W.B. Cook (Soc. Lab.) .	234
E.C. Heath (Prohi.)	148
Total vote	300,743

1910
Democratic Primary

O.B. Colquitt..........	146,526
William Poindexter	79,711
R.V. Davidson.........	53,187
Cone Johnson	76,050
J. Marion Jones	1,906
Total vote..........	357,380

General Election

O.B. Colquitt (Dem.)....	174,596
J.O. Terrell (Rep.)	26,191
Redding Andrews (Soc.).	11,538
A.J. Houston (Prohi.).	6,052
Carl Schmidt (Soc. Lab.).	426
Total vote..........	218,803

1912
Democratic Primary

O.B. Colquitt..........	218,812
William F. Ramsey	177,183
Total vote..........	395,995

General Election

O.B. Colquitt (Dem.)....	234,352
Ed Lasater (Prog.)	15,794
C.W. Johnson (Rep.) ...	23,089
A.J. Houston (Prohi.) ...	2,356
Redding Andrews (Soc.).	25,258
K.E. Choate (Soc. Lab.).	308
Total vote..........	301,157

1914
Democratic Primary

James E. Ferguson	237,062
Thomas H. Ball........	191,558
Total vote..........	428,620

General Election

J.E. Ferguson (Dem.)...	176,599
F.M. Etheridge (Prog.) ..	1,794
John W. Philp (Rep.)....	11,411
E.R. Meitzen (Soc.)	24,977
Total vote..........	214,781

1916
Democratic Primary

James E. Ferguson	240,561
Charles H. Morris	174,611
H.C. Marshall	6,731
Total vote..........	421,903

General Election

J.E. Ferguson (Dem.)...	296,667
R.B. Creager (Rep.)	49,118
E.R. Meitzen (Soc.)	14,580
H.W. Lewis (Prohi.).....	3,200
Total vote..........	363,565

In 1917 Ferguson was removed from office and succeeded by Hobby.

1918
Democratic Primary

W.P. Hobby	461,479
James E. Ferguson	217,012
Total vote..........	678,491

General Election

W.P. Hobby (Dem.)	148,982
Chas. A. Boynton (Rep.).	26,713
Wm.D. Simpson (Soc.)..	1,660
Total vote..........	177,355

1920

In 1918 the primary election law had been amended, requiring a majority for nomination. The **first double primary in the governor's race** was in 1920.

1st Democratic Primary

Pat M. Neff	149,818
Robert E. Thomason . . .	99,002
Joseph W. Bailey	152,340
Ben F. Looney	48,640
Total vote	449,800

2nd Democratic Primary

Pat M. Neff	264,075
Joseph W. Bailey	184,702
Total vote	448,777

General Election

Pat M. Neff (Dem.)	289,188
J.G. Culberson (Rep.) . .	90,217
H. Capers (B. T. Rep.) . .	26,091
T.H. McGregor (Amer.) .	69,380
L.L. Rhodes (Soc.)	6,796
Scattering	59
Total vote	481,731

1922

Democratic Primary

Pat M. Neff	318,000
W. W. King	18,368
Fred S. Rogers	195,941
Harry T. Warner	57,671
Total vote	589,926

General Election

Pat M. Neff (Dem.)	334,199
W.H. Atwell (Rep.)	73,329
Total vote	407,528

1924

1st Democratic Primary

Felix D. Robertson	193,508
George W. Dixon	4,035
W. E. Pope	17,136
Joe Burkett	21,720
Miriam A. Ferguson	146,424
Lynch Davidson	141,208
V.A. Collins	24,864
T.W. Davidson	125,011
Thomas D. Barton	29,217
Total vote	703,123

2nd Democratic Primary

Miriam A. Ferguson	413,751
Felix D. Robertson	316,019
Total vote	729,770

General Election

Miriam A. Ferguson (Dem.)	422,558
George C. Butte (Rep.) .	294,970
Total vote	717,528

1926

1st Democratic Primary

Lynch Davidson	122,449
Miriam A. Ferguson	283,482
Kate M. Johnston	1,029
Dan Moody	409,732
Edith E. Wilmans	1,580
O.F. Zimmerman	2,962
Total vote	821,234

2nd Democratic Primary

Miriam A. Ferguson	270,595

Dan Moody	495,723
Total vote	766,318

Republican Primary
(Party's first statewide.)

H.H. Haines	11,215
E. P. Scott	4,074
Total vote	15,289

General Election

Dan Moody (Dem.)	233,068
H.H. Haines (Rep.)	31,531
M.A. Smith (Soc.)	908
Total vote	265,507

1928

Democratic Party

Wm.E. Hawkins	32,076
Dan Moody	442,080
Louis J. Wardlaw	245,508
Edith E. Wilmans	18,237
Total vote	737,901

General Election,

Dan Moody (Dem.)	582,972
W. H. Holmes (Rep.) . . .	120,504
T. Stedman (Com.)	109
L.L. Rhodes (Soc.)	738
Scattering	2,683
Total vote	707,006

1930

1st Democratic Primary

Miriam A. Ferguson	242,959
Thomas B. Love	87,068
Paul Loven	2,724
Earle B. Mayfield	54,459
Barry Miller	54,652
C.C. Moody	4,382
Frank Putnam	2,365
Clint C. Small	138,934
Ross S. Sterling	170,754
James Young	73,385
C.E. Walker	1,760
Total vote	833,442

2nd Democratic Primary

Ross S. Sterling	473,371
Miriam A. Ferguson	384,402
Total vote	857,773

Republican Primary

George C. Butte	5,001
H.E. Exum	2,773
John F. Grant	1,800
John P. Gaines	203
Total vote	9,777

General Election

Ross S. Sterling (Dem.) .	252,738
Wm.E. Talbot (Rep.) . . .	62,224
Total vote	314,962

1932

1st Democratic Primary

Roger Q. Evans	3,974
Miriam A. Ferguson	402,238
C.A. Frakes	2,338
J. Ed Glenn	2,089
Tom F. Hunter	220,391
Frank Putnam	2,962
Ross S. Sterling	296,383
M.H. Wolfe	32,241
George W. Armstrong . .	5,312
Total vote	967,928

2nd Democratic Primary

Ross S. Sterling	473,846
Miriam A. Ferguson	477,644
Total Vote	951,490

General Election

M.A. Ferguson (Dem.) . .	528,986
Orville Bullington (Rep.) .	317,807
George C. Edwards (Soc.)	1,866
George W. Armstrong (*Jacksonian Dem.) . .	706
Otho L. Heitt (Liberty) . .	101
Philip L. Howe (Com.) . .	72
Total vote	849,538

1934

1st Democratic Primary

C.C. McDonald	206,007
James V. Allred	297,656
Clint C. Small	124,206
Tom F. Hunter	241,339
Edgar Witt	62,208
Edward K. Russell	4,408
Maury Hughes	58,187
Total vote	994,011

2nd Democratic Primary

James V. Allred	497,808
Tom F. Hunter	457,785
Total vote	995,593

Republican Primary

D.E. Waggoner	13,043

General Election

James V. Allred (Dem.) . .	421,422
D.E. Wagonner (Rep.) . .	13,534
George C. Edwards (Soc.)	1,877
Enoch Hardaway (Com.) .	244
Total vote	437,077

1936

Democratic Primary

James V. Allred	553,219
P. Pierce Brooks	33,391
F. W. Fischer	145,877
Tom F. Hunter	239,460
Roy Sanderford	81,170
Total vote	1,053,117

General Election

James V. Allred (Dem.) . .	782,083
C.O. Harris (Rep.)	58,842
Carl Brannin (Soc.)	962
Homer Brooks (Com.) . .	283
Total vote	842,170

1938

Democratic Primary

W. Lee O'Daniel	573,166
Ernest O. Thompson . . .	231,630
William McCraw	152,278
Tom F. Hunter	117,634
S.T. Brogdon	892
Joseph King	773
Clarence E. Farmer	3,869
P.D. Renfro	8,127
Karl A. Crowley	19,153
Clarence R. Miller	667
James A. Ferguson	3,800
Thomas Self	1,405
Marvin P. McCoy	1,491
Total vote	1,114,885

General Election

W. Lee O'Daniel (Dem.) .	473,526
Alexander Boynton (Rep.)	10,940
Earl E. Miller (Soc.)	398
Homer Brooks (Com.). .	424
Total vote	485,288

1940
Democratic Primary

W. Lee O'Daniel	645,646
Ernest O. Thompson . . .	256,923
Harry Hines	119,121
Miriam A. Ferguson. . . .	100,578
Jerry Sadler.	61,396
Arlon B. "Cyclone" Davis Jr.	3,625
R.P. Condron	2,001
Total vote	1,189,290

General Election

W. Lee O'Daniel (Dem.) .	1,019,338
George C. Hopkins (Rep.)	59,885
Ben H. Lauderdale (Com.)	202
Scattering	113
Total vote	1,079,538

1942
Democratic Primary

Hal H. Collins	272,469
Alex M. Ferguson	8,370
Gene S. Porter	4,933
Charles L. Somerville . .	4,853
Coke R. Stevenson	651,218
Hope Wheeler	9,373
Total vote	951,216

General Election

Coke R. Stevenson (Dem.).	280,735
C.K. McDowell (Rep.) . .	9,204
Total vote	289,939

1944
Democratic Primary

Coke R. Stevenson	696,586
Martin Jones	21,379
W. J. Minton	8,537
Alex M. Ferguson.	12,649
Minnie F. Cunningham . .	48,039
Gene S. Porter.	15,243
Edward L. Carey	4,633
William F. Grimes	9,443
Herbert E. Mills	6,640
Write-in votes.	311
Total vote	823,460

General Election

Coke R. Stevenson (Dem.)	1,007,826
B.J. Peasley (Rep.)	100,287
Total vote	1,108,113

1946
1st Democratic Primary

Floyd Brinkley	4,249
William V. Brown	3,902
A.J. Burks	4,881
Chas.B. Hutchison	4,616
Beauford Jester	443,804
Walter Scott McNutt. . . .	4,353
Caso March	20,529
W.J. Minton	2,398
Homer P. Rainey	291,282
Jerry Sadler	103,120
Grover Sellers	162,431
C.R. Shaw	9,764
John Lee Smith	102,941
Reese Turner	4,914
Total vote	1,163,184

2nd Democratic Primary

Beauford H. Jester.	701,018
Homer P. Rainey	335,654
Total vote	1,056,672

General Election

Beauford Jester (Dem.).	345,513
Eugene Nolte Jr. (Rep.) .	33,231
Total vote	378,744

1948
Democratic Primary

Beauford H. Jester	642,025
Sumpter W. Stockton . . .	21,243
Roger Q. Evans	279,602
Charles B. Hutchison . . .	24,441
Holmes A. May	20,538
Caso March	187,658
W.J. Minton.	13,659
Denver S. Whiteley.	16,090
Write-in votes	1
Total vote	1,205,257

General Election

Beauford H. Jester (Dem.).	1,024,160
Alvin H. Lane (Rep.)	177,399
Gerald Overholt (Prohi.).	3,554
Herman Wright (Prog.) . .	3,747
Total vote	1,208,860

In July 1949, Lt. Gove. Allan Shivers succeeded Jester, who died in office.

1950
Democratic Primary

Allan Shivers	829,730
Caso March	195,997
Charles B. Hutchison . . .	16,048
Gene S. Porter	14,728
J.M. Wren	14,138
Benita Louise Marek Lawrence	9,542
Wellington Abbey	6,381
Total vote	1,086,564

General Election

Allan Shivers (Dem.) . .	355,010
Ralph W. Currie (Rep.) .	39,737
Total vote	374,747

1952
Democratic Primary

Allan Shivers	883,861
Ralph W. Yarborough . .	488,345
Allene M. Trayler.	34,186
Total vote	1,356,392

Gov. "Pappy" Lee O'Daniel, above. Right, Gov. James Allred, seated, with Texas Ranger Captain J.W. McCormick. File photo/Allred photo courtesy of Texas Ranger Research Center.

General Election

*Allan Shivers (Dem.) ..	1,375,547
*Allan Shivers (Rep.)...	468,319
Total vote	1,843,866

*Ran on both tickets.

1954
1st Democratic Primary

Allan Shivers........	668,913
Ralph W. Yarborough..	645,994
J.J. Holmes..........	19,591
Arlon B. "Cyclone" Davis.	16,254
Total vote	1,350,752

2nd Democratic Primary

Allan Shivers........	775,088
Ralph W. Yarborough..	683,132
Total vote	1,458,220

General Election

Allan Shivers (Dem.)...	569,533
Tod R. Adams (Rep.)...	66,154
Other...............	1,205
Total vote	636,892

1956
1st Democratic Primary

Price Daniel.........	628,914
J. Evetts Haley	88,772
J.J. Holmes..........	10,165
W. Lee O'Daniel	347,757
Reuben Senterfitt	37,774
Ralph Yarborough	463,416
Write-in	72
Total vote	1,576,870

2nd Democratic Primary

Price Daniel.........	698,001
Ralph Yarborough	694,830
Total vote	1,392,831

General Election

Price Daniel (Dem.)....	1,350,736
William R. Bryant (Rep.)..	261,283
W. Lee O'Daniel (Write-in)	110,234
Other...............	1,838
Total vote	1,724,091

1958
Democratic Primary

Price Daniel.........	799,107
Henry B. Gonzalez	246,969
Joe A. Irwin	33,643
W. Lee O'Daniel	238,767
Write-in	6
Total vote	1,317,492

General Election

Price Daniel (Dem.)....	695,779
Edwin S. Mayer (Rep.).	94,086
Total vote	789,865

1960
Democratic Primary

Jack Cox	619,834
Price Daniel.........	908,992
Write-in	8
Total vote	1,528,834

General Election

Price Daniel (Dem.)....	1,627,698
Wm. M. Steger (Rep.) ..	609,808
Total vote	2,237,506

1962
1st Democratic Primary

John Connally	431,498
Price Daniel..........	248,524
Marshall Formby	139,094
Edwin A. Walker.......	138,387
Will Wilson...........	171,617
Don Yarborough......	317,986
Write-in	9
Total vote	1,447,115

2nd Democratic Primary

John Connally	565,174
Don Yarborough......	538,924
Total vote	1,104,098

Republican Primary

Jack Cox	99,170
Roy Whittenburg	16,136
Total vote	115,306

General Election

John Connally (Dem.) ..	847,038
Jack Cox (Rep.).......	715,025
Jack Carswell (Con.) ...	7,135
Total vote	1,569,198

1964
Democratic Primary

John Connally	1,125,884
Don Yarborough......	471,411
M. T. Banks	22,047
Johnnie Mae Hack-worthe.............	10,955
Total vote	1,630,297

Republican Primary

Jack Crichton.........	128,146

Gov. John Connally

General Election

John Connally (Dem.) ..	1,877,793
Jack Crichton (Rep.) ...	661,675
John C. Williams (Con.) .	5,257
Write-in	28
Total vote	2,544,753

1966
Democratic Primary

John Connally	932,641
Stanley C. Woods	291,651
Johnnie Mae Hack-worthe.............	31,105
Write-in votes.........	3
Total vote	1,255,400

Republican Primary

T. E. Kennerly	49,568

General Election

John Connally (Dem.) ..	1,037,517
T. E. Kennerly (Rep.) ...	368,025
Tommye Gillespie (Con.).	10,454
Bard Logan (Conserv.)..	9,810
Write-ins..............	55
Total vote.........	1,425,861

1968
1st Democratic Primary

Preston Smith	386,875
Pat O'Daniel.........	47,912
John Hill	154,908
Waggoner Carr.......	257,543
Eugene Locke	218,118
Dolph Briscoe........	225,686
Edward L. Whittenburg..	22,957
Don Yarborough.......	421,607
Alfonso Veloz	9,562
Johnnie Mae Hack-worthe.............	5,484
Total vote.........	1,750,652

2nd Democratic Primary

Preston Smith	767,490
Don Yarborough	621,226
Total vote.........	1,388,716

Republican Primary

Paul Eggers	65,501
John Trice..........	28,849
Wallace Sisk.........	10,415
Total vote.........	104,765

General Election

Preston Smith (Dem.) ..	1,662,019
Paul Eggers (Rep.).....	1,254,333
Total vote.........	2,916,352

1970
Democratic Primary

Preston Smith	1,011,300

Republican Primary

Paul Eggers	101,875
Roger Martin	7,146
Total vote..........	109,021

General Election

Preston Smith (Dem.) ..	1,232,506
Paul Eggers (Rep.).....	1,073,831
Other	428
Total vote..........	2,306,765

1972
1st Democratic Primary

Ben Barnes	392,356
Dolph Briscoe........	963,397
Frances Farenthold	612,051
Robert E. Looney......	10,225
William H. Posey	13,727
Preston Smith	190,709
Gordon F. Wills........	10,438
Total vote..........	2,192,903

2nd Democratic Primary

Dolph Briscoe........	1,095,168
Frances Farenthold	884,594
Total vote..........	1,979,762

1st Republican Primary

Albert Fay............	24,329

Henry C. Grover	37,118
John A. Hall Sr.	8,018
J.A. Jenkins.	4,864
Tom McElroy	19,559
David Reagan	20,119
Total vote	114,007

2nd Republican Primary

Albert Fay	19,166
Henry C. Grover	37,842
Total vote	57,008

General Election

Dolph Briscoe (Dem.) . .	1,633,493
Henry C. Grover (Rep.) .	1,533,986
Ramsey Muniz (Raza) .	214,118
Deborah Leonard (Soc.).	24,103
Other	3,891
Total vote	3,409,501

1974
Democratic Primary

Dolph Briscoe	1,025,632
Frances Farenthold . . .	437,287
W.H. Posey	31,498
Steve S. Alexander . . .	26,889
Total vote	1,521,306

Republican Primary

Jim Granberry	53,617
Odell McBrayer	15,484
Total vote	69,101

General Election

Dolph Briscoe (Dem.) . .	1,016,334
Jim Granberry (Rep.) . .	514,725
Ramsey Muniz (Raza) .	93,295
Sherry Smith (Soc.) . . .	8,171
S. W. McDonnell (Am.) .	22,208
Other	251
Total vote	1,654,984

1978
Democratic Primary

Donald R. Beagle	14,791
Dolph Briscoe	753,309
John Hill	932,345
Ray Allen Mayo	20,249
Preston Smith	92,202
Total vote	1,812,896

Republican Primary

William P. Clements Jr. .	115,345
Ray Hutchison.	38,268
Clarence Thompson . . .	4,790
Total vote	158,403

General Election

John Hill (Dem.)	1,166,919
Bill Clements (Rep.} . .	1,183,828
Mario C. Compean (Raza)	14,213
Sara Jean Johnston (Soc.)	4,624
Other .	115
Total vote	2,369,699

1982
Democratic Primary

David L. Young	25,386
Bob Armstrong	262,189
Mark White	592,658
Donald R. Beagle	15,649
Ray Allen Mayo	20,088
*Buddy Temple	402,693
Total vote	1,318,663

*Temple declined to participate in run-off; White declared winner of race.

Republican Primary

William P. Clements Jr. .	246,120
Duke Embs	19,731
Total vote	265,851

General Election

Mark White (Dem.)	1,697,870
William P. Clements Jr. (Rep.).	1,465,937
David Hutzelman (Ind.) .	19,143
Bob Poteet (Con.)	8,065
Other	76
Total vote	3,191,091

1986
Democratic Primary

Sheila Bilyeu	39,370
Andrew C. Briscoe III . .	248,850
A. Don Crowder	120,999
Bobby Locke	58,936
Ron Slover.	38,861
Mark White	589,536
Total vote	1,096,552

Republican Primary

William P. Clements Jr . .	318,808
Kent Hance	108,238
Tom Loeffler.	117,673
Total vote	544,719

General Election

Mark White (Dem.)	1,584,515
William P. Clements Jr.(Rep.).	1,813,779
Theresa Doyle (Lib.). . .	42,496
Other	670
Total vote	3,441,460

1990
1st Democratic Primary

Stanley Adams	16,118
Theresa Hearn-Haynes .	31,395
Earl Holmes.	17,904
Jim Mattox	546,103
Ray Rachal	9,388
Ann W. Richards	580,191
Mark White	288,161
Total vote	1,487,280

2nd Democratic Primary

Jim Mattox	481,739
Ann W. Richards	640,995
Total vote	1,122,734

Republican Primary

Ed Cude.	1,077
Kent Hance	132,142
Tom Luce	115,835
W. N. Otwell	2,310
Royce X. Owens	1,392
Jack Rains.	82,461
Clayton Williams	520,014
Total vote	855,231

General Election

Clayton Williams (Rep.) .	1,826,431
Ann W. Richards (Dem.).	1,925,670
Jeff Daiell (Lib.)	129,128
Write-Ins (19).	11,517
Total vote	3,892,746

1994
Democratic Primary

Gary Espinosa	230,337
Ann W. Richards.	806,607
Total vote	1,036,944

Republican Primary

George W. Bush	520,130
Ray Hollis	37,210
Total vote	557,340

General Election

Ann W. Richards (Dem.)	2,016,928
George W. Bush (Rep.)	2,350,994
Keary Ehlers (Lib.)	28,320
Total vote	4,396,242

1998
Democratic Primary

Garry Mauro.	492,419
Total vote.	492,419

Republican Primary

George W. Bush	576,528
R.C. Crawford.	20,311
Total vote.	596,839

General Election

Garry Mauro (Dem.). . . .	1,165,592
George W. Bush (Rep.)	2,550,831
Lester R. (Les) Turlington Jr. (Lib.)	20,711
Susan Lee Solar (Write-In)	954
Total vote.	4,396,242

In 2000, Lt. Gov. Rick Perry succeeded Bush, who resigned to become president.

2002
Democratic Primary

Bill Lyon	43,011
Dan Morales.	330,873
Tony Sanchez.	609,383
John Worldpeace	20,121
Total vote.	1,003,388

Republican Primary

Rick Perry.	620,463
Total vote.	620,463

General Election

Rick Perry (Rep.)	2,632,591
Tony Sanchez (Dem.). . .	1,819,798
Jeff Daiell (Lib.)	66,720
Rahul Mahajan (Green)	32,187
Elaine Eure Henderson (W-I)	1,715
Earl W. (Bill) O'Neill (W-I)	976
Total vote.	4,553,987

Abbreviations used are:
(Dem.) Democrat,
(Rep.) Republican,
(G.B.) Greenback,
(Lib.) Libertarian,
(Ind.) Independent,
(I. Dem.) Independent Democrat,
(Prohi.) Prohibitionist,
(Ind. Fus.) Independent Fusion,
(Peo.) People's (Populist),
(Ref. Rep.) Reformed Republican,
(L.W. Rep.) Lily White Republican,
(Soc. Lab.) Socialist-Labor,
(Reor. Rep.) Reorganized Republican,
(Soc.) Socialist,
(Prog.) Progressive,
(B.T. Rep.) Black and Tan Republican,
(Amer.) American,
(Com.) Communist,
(Con.) Constitution,
(Conserv.) Conservative,
(Raz.) La Raza Unida.

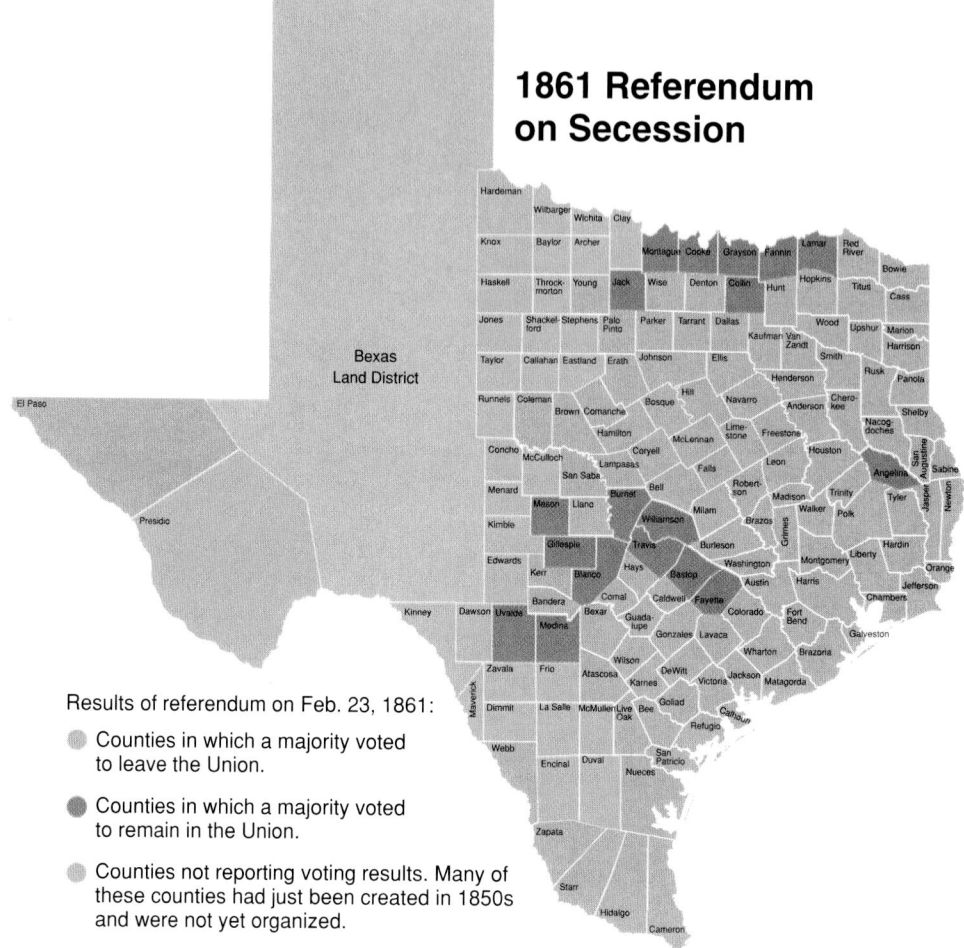

1861 Referendum on Secession

Bexas
Land District

Results of referendum on Feb. 23, 1861:

Counties in which a majority voted
to leave the Union.

Counties in which a majority voted
to remain in the Union.

Counties not reporting voting results. Many of
these counties had just been created in 1850s
and were not yet organized.

Referendum on Ordinance of Secession 1861

More than 75 percent of Texas voters endorsed secession from the United States in the referendum held Feb. 23, 1861.

Of the 122 counties that had been organized at that time, in only 18 of the counties did those who were against secession make up a majority (shaded in the list).

Sources differ slightly on some county returns. The source for the tabulation following is the archives of the Texas State Library, using amended returns when they differ from original reports.

The total vote for secession has been reported in Texas historical sources as 46,153 to 14,747 or 46,129 to 14,797.

Whatever the total number of voters, between 60,825 and 60,950, it was more than 2,000 fewer than the total voting in the presidential election of 1860.

Others sources used:

Secession and the Union in Texas by Walter L. Buenger (one of the alternative count totals presented in the table following).

"The Referendum in Texas on the Ordinance of Secession, February 23, 1861: The Vote," by Joe T. Timmons in the *East Texas Historical Journal,* Fall 1973.

"Secession Movement in Texas," in the *Historical Atlas of Texas* by A. Ray Stephens and William M. Holmes.

The *New Handbook of Texas,* Texas State Historical Association, 1996. — *Robert Plocheck.*

The vote was **for** or **against** the Ordinance of Secession adopted February 1, 1861, by the Secession Convention in Austin.

County	For	Against
Anderson	870	15
Angelina	139	184
Atascosa	145	91
Austin	825	212
Bandera	33	32
Bastrop	305	347
Bee	139	16
Bell	456	198
Bexar	827	709
Blanco	108	192
Bosque	223	79
Bowie	268	15
Brazoria	527	2
Brazos	215	44
Brown	190	0
Burleson	422	84
Burnet	157	248
Caldwell	434	188
Calhoun	276	16
Cameron	600	37
Cass	373	27
Chambers	109	26
Cherokee	1,106	38
Coleman*	25	2
Collin	405	948
Colorado	584	330
Comal	239	86
Comanche	86	4
Cooke	137	221
Coryell	293	55
Dallas	741	237
Denton	331	256
DeWitt	472	49
Ellis	527	172
El Paso	871	2
Erath	185	27
Falls	215	82
Fannin	471	656
Fayette	580	626
Fort Bend	486	0
Freestone	585	3
Galveston	765	33
Gillespie	16	398
Goliad	291	25
Gonzales	802	80
Grayson	463	901
Grimes	907	9
Guadalupe	314	22
Hamilton	78	1
Hardin	167	62
Harris	1,128	163
Harrison	866	44
Hays	166	115
Henderson	397	48
Hidalgo	62	10
Hill	376	63
Hopkins	697	315
Houston	522	38
Hunt	416	339
Jack	14	76
Jackson	147	77
Jasper	318	25
Jefferson	256	15
Johnson	531	31
Karnes	153	1
Kaufman	461	155
Kerr	76	57
Lamar	553	663
Lampasas	85	75
Lavaca	592	36
Leon	534	82
Liberty	422	10
Limestone	525	9
Live Oak	141	9
Llano	150	72
Madison	213	10
Marion	467	0
Mason	1	75
Matagorda	243	8
McLennan	586	191
Medina	140	207
Milam	468	135
Montague	50	86
Montgomery	318	98
Nacogdoches	317	94
Navarro	621	38
Newton	178	3
Nueces	142	42
Orange	142	3
Palo Pinto	107	0
Panola	557	5
Parker	523	61
Polk	567	22
Red River	347	284
Refugio	147	14
Robertson	391	78
Rusk	1,208	135
Sabine	143	18
San Augustine	243	22
San Patricio	56	3
San Saba	113	60
Shelby	333	28
Smith	1,149	50
Starr	180	2
Tarrant	499	132
Titus	411	275
Travis	450	704
Trinity	206	8
Tyler	417	4
Upshur	957	57
Uvalde	16	76
Van Zandt	181	127
Victoria	313	88
Walker	490	61
Washington	1,131	43
Webb	79	0
Wharton	249	2
Williamson	349	480
Wilson	92	21
Wise**	78	76
Wood	451	191
Young	166	31
Zapata	323	0
Total (state archives)	46,179	14,763
From the Buenger book and the New Handbook of Texas	46,153	14,747
All others	46,129	14,697

* Coleman Co. returns are from the militia stationed there.

** The original report for Wise Co. had the figures reversed.

Declaration of Independence of the Republic of Texas

The Declaration of Independence of the Republic of Texas was adopted in general convention at Washington-on-the-Brazos, March 2, 1836.

Richard Ellis, president of the convention, appointed a committee of five to write the declaration for submission to the convention. However, there is much evidence that George C. Childress, one of the members, wrote the document with little or no help from the other members. Childress is therefore generally accepted as the author.

The text of the declaration is followed by the names of the signers of the document. The names are presented here as the signers actually signed the document. Our thanks to the staff of the Texas State Archives for furnishing a photocopy of the signatures.

UNANIMOUS

DECLARATION OF INDEPENDENCE,

BY THE

DELEGATES OF THE PEOPLE OF TEXAS,

IN GENERAL CONVENTION,

AT THE TOWN OF WASHINGTON,

ON THE SECOND DAY OF MARCH, 1836.

When a government has ceased to protect the lives, liberty and property of the people from whom its legitimate powers are derived, and for the advancement of whose happiness it was instituted; and so far from being a guarantee for the enjoyment of those inestimable and inalienable rights, becomes an instrument in the hands of evil rulers for their oppression; when the Federal Republican Constitution of their country, which they have sworn to support, no longer has a substantial existence, and the whole nature of their government has been forcibly changed without their consent, from a restricted federative republic, composed of sovereign states, to a consolidated central military despotism, in which every interest is disregarded but that of the army and the priesthood — both the eternal enemies of civil liberty, and the ever-ready minions of power, and the usual instruments of tyrants; When long after the spirit of the Constitution has departed, moderation is at length, so far lost, by those in power that even the semblance of freedom is removed, and the forms, themselves, of the constitution discontinued; and so far from their petitions and remonstrances being regarded, the agents who bear them are thrown into dungeons; and mercenary armies sent forth to force a new government upon them at the point of the bayonet. When in consequence of such acts of malfeasance and abdication, on the part of the government, anarchy prevails, and civil society is dissolved into its original elements: In such a crisis, the first law of nature, the right of self-preservation — the inherent and inalienable right of the people to appeal to first principles and take their political affairs into their own hands in extreme cases — enjoins it as a right towards themselves and a sacred obligation to their posterity, to abolish such government and create another in its stead, calculated to rescue them from impending dangers, and to secure their future welfare and happiness.

Nations, as well as individuals, are amenable for their acts to the public opinion of mankind. A statement of a part of our grievances is, therefore, submitted to an impartial world, in justification of the hazardous but unavoidable step now taken of severing our political connection with the Mexican people, and assuming an independent attitude among the nations of the earth.

The Mexican government, by its colonization laws, invited and induced the Anglo-American population of Texas to colonize its wilderness under the pledged faith of a written constitution, that they should continue to enjoy that constitutional liberty and republican government to which they had been habituated in the land of their birth, the United States of America. In this expectation they have been cruelly disappointed, inasmuch as the Mexican nation has acquiesced in the late changes made in the government by General Antonio Lopez de Santa Anna, who, having overturned the constitution of his country, now offers us the cruel alternative either to abandon our homes, acquired by so many privations, or submit to the most intolerable of all tyranny, the combined despotism of the sword and the priesthood.

It has sacrificed our welfare to the state of Coahuila, by which our interests have been continually depressed, through a jealous and partial course of legislation carried on at a far distant seat of government, by a hostile majority, in an unknown tongue; and this too, notwithstanding we have petitioned in the humblest terms, for the establishment of a separate state government, and have, in accordance with the provisions of the national constitution, presented the general Congress, a republican constitution which was without just cause contemptuously rejected.

It incarcerated in a dungeon, for a long time, one of our citizens, for no other cause but a zealous endeavor to procure the acceptance of our constitution and the establishment of a state government.

It has failed and refused to secure on a firm basis, the right of trial by jury; that palladium of civil liberty, and only safe guarantee for the life, liberty, and property of the citizen.

It has failed to establish any public system of education, although possessed of almost boundless resources (the public domain) and, although, it is an axiom, in political science, that unless a people are educated and enlightened it is idle to expect the continuance of civil liberty, or the capacity for self-government.

It has suffered the military commandants stationed among us to exercise arbitrary acts of oppression and tyranny; thus trampling upon the most sacred rights of the citizen and rendering the military superior to the civil power.

It has dissolved by force of arms, the state Congress of Coahuila and Texas, and obliged our representatives to fly for their lives from the seat of government; thus depriving us of the fundamental political right of representation.

It has demanded the surrender of a number of our citizens, and ordered military detachments to seize and carry them into the Interior for trial; in contempt of the civil authorities, and in defiance of the laws and constitution.

It has made piratical attacks upon our commerce; by commissioning foreign desperadoes, and authorizing them to seize our vessels, and convey the property of our citizens to far distant ports of confiscation.

It denies us the right of worshipping the Almighty according to the dictates of our own consciences, by the support of a national religion calculated to promote the temporal interests of its human functionaries rather than the glory of the true and living God.

It has demanded us to deliver up our arms; which are essential to our defense, the rightful property of freemen, and formidable only to tyrannical governments.

It has invaded our country, both by sea and by land, with intent to lay waste our territory and drive us from our homes; and has now a large mercenary army advancing to carry on against us a war of extermination.

It has, through its emissaries, incited the merciless savage, with the tomahawk and scalping knife, to massacre the inhabitants of our defenseless frontiers.

It hath been, during the whole time of our connection with it, the contemptible sport and victim of successive military revolutions and hath continually exhibited every characteristic of a weak, corrupt and tyrannical government.

These, and other grievances, were patiently borne by the people of Texas until they reached that point at which forbearance ceases to be a virtue. We then took up arms in defense of the national constitution. We appealed to our Mexican brethren for assistance. Our appeal has been made in vain. Though months have elapsed, no sympathetic response has yet been heard from the Interior. We are, therefore, forced to the melancholy conclusion that the Mexican people have acquiesced in the destruction of their liberty, and the substitution therefor of a military government — that they are unfit to be free and incapable of self-government.

The necessity of self-preservation, therefore, now decrees our eternal political separation.

We, therefore, the delegates, with plenary powers, of the people of Texas, in solemn convention assembled, appealing to a candid world for the necessities of our condition, do hereby resolve and DECLARE *that our political connection with the Mexican nation has forever ended; and that the people of Texas do now constitute a* FREE, SOVEREIGN *and* INDEPENDENT REPUBLIC, *and are fully invested with all the rights and attributes which properly belong to the independent nations; and, conscious of the rectitude of our intentions, we fearlessly and confidently commit the issue to the decision of the Supreme Arbiter of the destinies of nations.*

RICHARD ELLIS, president of the convention and Delegate from Red River.

Charles B Stewart

Tho[s] Barnett
John S.D. Byrom

Fran[co] Ruiz
J. Antonio Navarro
Jesse B. Badgett
W[m] D. Lacey
William Menefee
Jn[o] Fisher
Mathew Caldwell
William Mottley
Lorenzo de Zavala
Stephen H. Everitt
Geo W Smyth

Elijah Stapp
Claiborne West

W[m] B Scates
M.B. Menard
A.B. Hardin
J.W. Bunton
Tho[s] J. Gasley
R. M. Coleman
Sterling C. Robertson
Benj Briggs Goodrich
G.W. Barnett
James G. Swisher
Jesse Grimes
S. Rhoads Fisher
John W. Moore
John W. Bower
Sam[l] A Maverick from Bejar
Sam P. Carson
A. Briscoe
J.B. Woods

Jas Collinsworth
Edwin Waller
Asa Brigham
Geo. C. Childress
Bailey Hardeman
Rob. Potter
Thomas Jefferson Rusk
Chas. S. Taylor
John S. Roberts

Robert Hamilton
Collin McKinney
Albert H Latimer
James Power

Sam Houston
David Thomas

Edw[d] Conrad
Martin Parmer
Edwin O. LeGrand
Stephen W. Blount
Ja[s] Gaines
W[m] Clark, Jr
Sydney O. Penington
W[m] Carrol Crawford
Jn[o] Turner

Test. H.S. Kimble, Secretary

Constitution of Texas

The complete official text of the Constitution of Texas, including the original document, which was adopted on Feb. 15, 1876, plus all amendments approved since that time, is available on the State of Texas Web page at this address: **www.capitol.state.tx.us/txconst/toc.html**. An index at that site points you to the Article and Section of the Constitution that deals with a particular subject.

For election information, upcoming elections, amendment or other election votes and voter registration information, go to: **www.sos.state.tx.us/elections/index.shtml**.

According to the **Legislative Reference Library of Texas:** "The Texas Constitution is one of the longest in the nation and is still growing. As of 2005 (79th Legislature), the Texas Legislature has passed a total of 605 amendments. Of these, 431 have been adopted and 174 have been defeated by Texas voters. Thus, **the Texas Constitution has been amended 431 times since its adoption in 1876.**"

Amendment of the Texas Constitution requires a two-thirds favorable vote by both the Texas House of Representatives and the Texas Senate, followed by a majority vote of approval by voters in a statewide election.

Prior to 1973, amendments to the constitution could not be submitted by a special session of the Legislature. But the constitution was amended in 1972 to allow submission of amendments if the special session was opened to the subject by the governor.

Constitutional amendments are not subject to a gubernatorial veto. Once submitted, voters have the final decision on whether to change the constitution as proposed.

The following table lists the total number of amendments submitted to voters by the Texas Legislature and shows the year in which the Legislature approved them for submission to voters; e.g., the 70th Legislature in 1987 approved 28 bills proposing amendments to be submitted to voters — 25 in 1987 and 3 in 1988.

Constitutional Amendments Submitted to Voters by the Texas Legislature

Year	No.	Year	No.	Year	No.
1879	1	1927	8	1973	9
1881	2	1929	7	1975	12
1883	5	1931	9	1977	15
1887	6	1933	12	1978	1
1889	2	1935	13	1979	12
1891	5	1937	7	1981	10
1893	2	1939	4	1982	3
1895	2	1941	5	1983	19
1897	5	1943	3	1985	17
1899	1	1945	8	1986	1
1901	1	1947	9	1987	28
1903	3	1949	10	1989	21
1905	3	1951	7	1990	1
1907	9	1953	11	1991	15
1909	4	1955	9	1993	18
1911	5	1957	12	1995	14
1913	7	1959	4	1997	15
1915	7	1961	14	1999	17
1917	3	1963	7	2001	20
1919	13	1965	27	2003	22
1921	5	1967	20	**2005**	**9**
1923	2	1969	16		
1925	4	1971	18		

For more information on bills and constitutional amendments, see the Legislative Reference Library of Texas Web site at: **www.lrl.state.tx.us/legis/lrlhome.cfm**.

Amendments, 2003

. The following 22 amendments were submitted to the voters by the 78th Legislature in an election on **Sept. 13, 2003:**

HJR 3 — Concerning civil lawsuits against doctors and health care providers, and other actions, authorizing the legislature to determine limitations on non-economic damages. **Passed:** 751,896 for; 718,547 against.

HJR 16 — Authorize a county, a city or town, or a junior college district to establish an ad valorem tax freeze on residence homesteads of the disabled and of the elderly and their spouses. **Passed:** 1,125,947 for; 264,069 against.

HJR 21 — Prohibiting an increase in the total amount of school district ad valorem taxes that may be imposed on the residence homestead of a disabled person. **Passed:** 1,063,917 for; 304,860 against.

HJR 23 — Permitting refinancing of a home equity loan with a reverse mortgage. **Passed:** 958,293 for; 393,239 against.

HJR 28 — Authorizing the borrowing of money on a short-term basis by a state transportation agency for transportation-related projects, and the issuance of bonds and other public securities secured by the state highway fund. **Passed:** 810,855 for; 517,606 against.

HJR 44 — Permitting a six-person jury in a district court misdemeanor trial. **Passed:** 1,033,199 for; 350,491 against.

HJR 51 — Establishing a two-year period for the redemption of a mineral interest sold for unpaid ad valorem taxes at a tax sale. **Passed:** 830,009 for; 499,696 against.

HJR 54 — Providing that certain benefits in certain public retirement systems may not be reduced or impaired. **Passed:** 964,515 for; 383,710 against.

HJR 55 — Authorizing the legislature to exempt from ad valorem taxation property owned by a religious organization that is leased for use as a school or that is owned with the intent of expanding or constructing a religious facility. **Passed:** 730,127 for; 650,563 against.

HJR 59 — Authorizing the legislature to permit a person to assume an office of a political subdivision without an election if the person is the only candidate to qualify in an election for that office. **Passed:** 720,479 for; 636,863 against.

HJR 61 — Authorizing municipalities to donate surplus fire-fighting equipment or supplies for the benefit of rural volunteer fire departments. **Passed:** 1,284,004 for; 116,677 against.

HJR 62 — Authorizing the legislature to permit a person to take office without an election if the person is the only candidate to qualify in an election for that office. **Passed:** 781,330 for; 604,385 against.

HJR 68 — Authorizing the Veterans' Land Board to make certain payments on revenue bonds and to use assets in certain funds to provide for veterans homes and a constitutional amendment relating to the use of income and appreciation of the permanent school fund. ***Note:*** This bill proposes two different ballot propositions:

> **Prop. 1** — Authorizing the Veterans' Land Board to use assets in certain veterans' land and veterans' housing assistance funds to provide veterans homes for the aged or infirm and to make principal, interest, and bond enhancement payments on revenue bonds. **Passed:** 1,127,888 for; 256,735 against.
>
> **Prop. 9** — Relating to the use of income and appreciation of the permanent school fund. **Passed:** 655,983 for; 648,167 against.

HJR 84 — Providing for the filling of a temporary vacancy in a public office created by the activation for military service of a public officer. **Passed:** 1,069,328 for; 293,083 against.

HJR 85 — Allowing the legislature to authorize and govern the operation of wineries in this state. **Passed:** 851,809 for; 513,053 against.

SJR 19 — Permitting a current or retired faculty member of a public college or university to receive compensation for service on the governing body of a water district. **Passed:** 692,937 for; 631,328 against.

SJR 25 — Authorizing the legislature to exempt certain travel trailers from ad valorem taxation. **Passed:** 846,005 for; 511,507 against.

SJR 30 — Relating to the provision of parks and recreational facilities by certain conservation and reclamation districts. **Passed:** 746,523 for; 576,164 against.

SJR 42 — Authorizing a home equity line of credit, providing for administrative interpretation of home equity lending law, and otherwise relating to the making, refinancing, repayment, and enforcement of home equity loans. **Passed:** 862,009 for; 455,707 against.

SJR 45 — Repealing the authority of the legislature to provide for the creation of rural fire prevention districts. **Passed:** 759,336 for; 533,264 against.

SJR 55 — Authorizing the issuance of general obligation

bonds or notes to provide loans to defense-related communities for economic development projects, including those that enhance military value of military installations. **Passed:** 743,048 for; 563,848 against.

Amendments, 2005

The following 9 amendments were submitted to the voters by the 79th Legislature in an election on **Nov. 8, 2005:**

HJR 6 — Providing that marriage in this state consists only of the union of one man and one woman and prohibiting this state or a political subdivision of this state from creating or recognizing any legal status identical or similar to marriage.

HJR 54 — Creating the Texas rail relocation and improvement fund and authorizing grants of money and issuance of obligations for financing the relocation,rehabilitation, and expansion of rail facilities.

HJR 79 — Authorizing the legislature to provide for a six-year term for a board member of a regional mobility authority.

HJR 80 — Clarifying that certain economic development programs do not constitute a debt.

HJR 87 — Including one additional public member and a constitutional county court judge in the membership of the State Commission on Judicial Conduct.

SJR 7 — Authorizing line-of-credit advances under a reverse mortgage.

SJR 17 — Authorizing the denial of bail to a criminal defendant who violates a condition of the defendant's release pending trial.

SJR 21 — Allowing the legislature to define rates of interest for commercial loans.

SJR 40 — Providing for the clearing of land titles by relinquishing and releasing and state claim to sovereign ownership or title to interest in certain lands in Upshur County and in Smith County. ☆

Joint Resolution for Annexing Texas to the United States

(For an overview of the subject, please see these discussions: The New Handbook of Texas, Texas State Historical Association, Austin, 1996; Vol. 1, pages 192–193. On the Web: **www.tsha.utexas.edu/handbook/online/articles/view/AA/mga2.html**. Also see the Texas State Library and Archives Web site: **www.tsl.state.tx.us/ref/abouttx/annexation/index.html**.)

Resolved

by the Senate and House of Representatives of the United States of America in Congress assembled, That Congress doth consent that the territory properly included within and rightfully belonging to the Republic of Texas, may be erected into a new State to be called the State of Texas, with a republican form of government adopted by the people of said Republic, by deputies in convention assembled, with the consent of existing Government in order that the same may by admitted as one of the States of this Union.

2. And be it further resolved, That the foregoing consent of Congress is given upon the following conditions, to wit: First, said state to be formed, subject to the adjustment by this government of all questions of boundary that may arise with other government, --and the Constitution thereof, with the proper evidence of its adoption by the people of said Republic of Texas, shall be transmitted to the President of the United States, to be laid before Congress for its final action on, or before the first day of January, one thousand eight hundred and forty-six. Second, said state when admitted into the Union, after ceding to the United States all public edifices, fortifications, barracks, ports and harbors, navy and navy yards, docks, magazines and armaments, and all other means pertaining to the public defense, belonging to the said Republic of Texas, shall retain funds, debts, taxes and dues of every kind which may belong to, or be due and owing to the said Republic; and shall also retain all the vacant and unappropriated lands lying within its limits, to be applied to the payment of the debts and liabilities of said Republic of Texas, and the residue of said lands, after discharging said debts and liabilities, to be disposed of as said State may direct; but in no event are said debts and liabilities to become a charge upon the Government of the United States. Third — New States of convenient size not exceeding four in number, in addition to said State of Texas and having sufficient population, may, hereafter by the consent of

said State, be formed out of the territory thereof, which shall be entitled to admission under the provisions of the Federal Constitution; and such states as may be formed out of the territory lying south of thirty-six degrees thirty minutes north latitude, commonly known as the Missouri Compromise Line, shall be admitted into the Union, with or without slavery, as the people of each State, asking admission shall desire; and in such State or States as shall be formed out of said territory, north of said Missouri Compromise Line, slavery, or involuntary servitude (except for crime) shall be prohibited.

3. And be it further resolved, That if the President of the United States shall in his judgment and discretion deem it most advisable, instead of proceeding to submit the foregoing resolution of the Republic of Texas, as an overture on the part of the United States for admission, to negotiate with the Republic; then,

Be it resolved, That a State, to be formed out of the present Republic of Texas, with suitable extent and boundaries, and with two representatives in Congress, until the next appointment of representation, shall be admitted into the Union, by virtue of this act, on an equal footing with the existing States, as soon as the terms and conditions of such admission, and the cession of the remaining Texian territory to the United States shall be agreed upon by the governments of Texas and the United States: And that the sum of one hundred thousand dollars be, and the same is hereby, appropriated to defray the expenses of missions and negotiations, to agree upon the terms of said admission and cession, either by treaty to be submitted to the Senate, or by articles to be submitted to the two houses of Congress, as the President may direct.

Approved, March 1, 1845.

Source: Peters, Richard, ed., The Public Statutes at Large of the United States of America, v.5, pp. 797–798, Boston, Chas. C. Little and Jas. Brown, 1850.

Texas' Chief Governmental Officials

On this and following pages are lists of the principal administrative officials who have served the Republic and State of Texas with dates of their tenures of office. In a few instances there are disputes as to the exact dates of tenures. Dates listed here are those that appear the most authentic.

★ ★ ★ ★ ★ ★ ★

Governors and Presidents
*Spanish Royal Governors

Domingo Terán de los Rios	1691–1692
Gregorio de Salinas Varona	1692–1697
Francisco Cuerbo y Valdés	1698–1702
Mathías de Aguirre	1703–1705
Martín de Alarcón	1705–1708
Simón Padilla y Córdova	1708–1712
Pedro Fermin de Echevers y Subisa	1712–1714
Juan Valdéz	1714–1716
Martín de Alarcón	1716–1719
José de Azlor y Virto de Vera, Marqués de San Miguel de Aguayo	1719–1722
Fernando Pérez de Almazán	1722–1727
Melchor de Mediavilla y Azcona	1727–1731
Juan Antonio Bustillo y Ceballos	1731–1734
Manuel de Sandoval	1734–1736
Carlos Benites Franquis de Lugo	1736–1737
Joseph Fernández de Jáuregui y Urrutia	1737–1737
Prudencio de Orobio y Basterra	1737–1741
Tomás Felipe Winthuisen (or Winthuysen)	1741–1743
Justo Boneo y Morales	1743–1744
Francisco García Larios	1744–1748
Pedro del Barrio Junco y Espriella	1748–1750
Jacinto de Barrios y Jáuregui	1751–1759
Angel de Martos y Navarrete	1759–1767
Hugo Oconór	1767–1770
Juan María Vicencio, Barón de Ripperdá	1770–1778
Domingo Cabello y Robles	1778–1786
Rafael Martínez Pacheco	1787–1790
Manuel Muñoz	1790–1799
Juan Bautista de Elguezábal	1799–1805
Antonio Cordero y Bustamante	1805–1808
Manuel María de Salcedo	1808–1813
Juan Bautista de las Casas (revolutionary gov.)	1811–1811
Cristóbal Domínguez, Benito de Armiñan, Mariano Varela, Juan Ignacio Pérez, Manuel Pardo	1813–1817
Antonio María Martínez	1817–1821

*Some authorities would include Texas under administrations of several earlier Spanish Governors. The late Dr. C.E. Castañeda, Latin-American librarian of The University of Texas and authority on the history of Texas and the Southwest, would include the following four: Francisco de Garay, 1523–26; Pánfilo de Narváez, 1526–28; Nuño de Guzmán, 1528–30; Hernando de Soto, 1538–43.

Governors Under Mexican Rule

The first two Governors under Mexican rule, Trespalacios and García, were of Texas only as Texas was then constituted. Beginning with Gonzáles, 1824, the Governors were for the joint State of Coahuila y Texas.

José Felix Trespalacios	1822–1823
Luciano García	1823–1824
Rafael Gonzáles	1824–1826
Victor Blanco	1826–1827
José María Viesca	1827–1830
Ramón Eca y Músquiz	1830–1831
José María Letona	1831–1832
Ramón Eca y Músquiz	1832–1832
Juan Martín de Veramendi	1832–1833
Juan José de Vidáurri y Villasenor	1833–1834
Juan José Elguezábal	1834–1835
José María Cantú	1835–1835
Agustín M. Viesca	1835–1835
Marciel Borrego	1835–1835
Ramón Eca y Músquiz	1835–1835

Provisional Colonial Governor, Before Independence

Henry Smith (Impeached) 1835

James W. Robinson served as acting Governor just prior to March 2, 1836, after Smith was impeached.

Presidents of the Republic of Texas

David G. Burnet	Mar. 16, 1836–Oct. 22, 1836
(provisional President)	
Sam Houston	Oct. 22, 1836–Dec. 10, 1838
Mirabeau B. Lamar	Dec. 10, 1838–Dec. 13, 1841
Sam Houston	Dec. 13, 1841–Dec. 9, 1844
Anson Jones	Dec. 9, 1844–Feb. 19, 1846

Governors Since Annexation

J. Pinckney Henderson ...... Feb. 19, 1846–Dec. 21, 1847

(Albert C. Horton served as acting Governor while Henderson was away in the Mexican War.)

George T. Wood	Dec. 21, 1847–Dec. 21, 1849
Peter Hansbrough Bell	Dec. 21, 1849–Nov. 23, 1853
J. W. Henderson	Nov. 23, 1853–Dec. 21, 1853
Elisha M. Pease	Dec. 21, 1853–Dec. 21, 1857
Hardin R. Runnels	Dec. 21, 1857–Dec. 21, 1859
Sam Houston (*resigned because of state's secession from the Union*)	Dec. 21, 1859–Mar. 16, 1861
Edward Clark	Mar. 16, 1861–Nov. 7, 1861
Francis R. Lubbock (*resigned to enter Confederate Army*)	Nov. 7, 1861–Nov. 5, 1863
Pendleton Murrah (*administration terminated by fall of Confederacy*)	Nov. 5, 1863–June 17, 1865

Fletcher S. Stockdale (*Lt. Gov. performed some duties of office on Murrah's departure, but is sometimes included in list of Governors. Hamilton's appointment was for immediate succession, as shown by the dates.*)

Andrew J. Hamilton (*Provisional, appointed by President Johnson*)	June 17, 1865–Aug. 9, 1866
James W. Throckmorton	Aug. 9, 1866–Aug. 8, 1867
Elisha M. Pease (*appointed July 30, 1867, under martial law*)	Aug. 8, 1867–Sept. 30, 1869

Interregnum

Pease resigned and vacated office Sept. 30, 1869; no successor was named until Jan. 8, 1870. Some historians extend Pease's term until Jan. 8, 1870, but in reality Texas was without a head of its civil government from Sept. 30, 1869, until Jan. 8, 1870.

Edmund J. Davis (*appointed provisional Governor after being elected*)	Jan. 8, 1870–Jan. 15, 1874
Richard Coke (*resigned to enter United States Senate*)	Jan. 15, 1874–Dec. 1, 1876
Richard B. Hubbard	Dec. 1, 1876–Jan. 21, 1879
Oran M. Roberts	Jan. 21, 1879–Jan. 16, 1883
John Ireland	Jan. 16, 1883–Jan. 18, 1887
Lawrence Sullivan Ross	Jan. 18, 1887–Jan. 20, 1891
James Stephen Hogg	Jan. 20, 1891–Jan. 15, 1895
Charles A. Culberson	Jan. 15, 1895–Jan. 17, 1899
Joseph D. Sayers	Jan. 17, 1899–Jan. 20, 1903
S. W. T. Lanham	Jan. 20, 1903–Jan. 15, 1907
Thos. Mitchell Campbell	Jan. 15, 1907–Jan. 17, 1911
Oscar Branch Colquitt	Jan. 17, 1911–Jan. 19, 1915
James E. Ferguson (*impeached*)	Jan. 19, 1915–Aug. 25, 1917
William Pettus Hobby	Aug. 25, 1917–Jan. 18, 1921
Pat Morris Neff	Jan. 18, 1921–Jan. 20, 1925
Miriam A. Ferguson	Jan. 20, 1925–Jan. 17, 1927

Dan Moody ....Jan. 17, 1927–Jan. 20, 1931
Ross S. Sterling.................Jan. 20, 1931–Jan. 17, 1933
Miriam A. Ferguson ....Jan. 17, 1933–Jan. 15, 1935
James V. Allred ....Jan. 15, 1935–Jan. 17, 1939
W. Lee O'Daniel (*resigned to enter United States
    Senate*)............................. Jan. 17, 1939–Aug. 4, 1941
Coke R. Stevenson.............. Aug. 4, 1941–Jan. 21, 1947
Beauford H. Jester.............. Jan. 21, 1947–July 11, 1949
Allan Shivers (*Lt. Governor succeeded on death of
    Governor Jester. Elected in 1950 and re-elected
    in 1952 and 1954*) .... July 11, 1949–Jan. 15, 1957
Price Daniel ....Jan. 15, 1957–Jan. 15, 1963
John Connally.....................Jan. 15, 1963–Jan. 21, 1969
Preston Smith ....Jan. 21, 1969–Jan. 16, 1973
*Dolph Briscoe....................Jan. 16, 1973–Jan. 16, 1979
**William P. Clements ....Jan. 16, 1979–Jan. 18, 1983
Mark White ....Jan. 18, 1983–Jan. 20, 1987
**William P. Clements ....Jan. 20, 1987–Jan. 15, 1991
Ann W. Richards ....Jan. 15, 1991–Jan. 17, 1995
**George W. Bush...............Jan. 17, 1995–Dec. 21, 2000
**Rick Perry (*Lt. Governor succeeded on inauguration
    of Bush as U.S. President*........Dec. 21, 2000–present

*Effective in 1975, term of office was raised to 4 years,
according to a constitutional amendment approved by Texas
voters in 1972. See introduction to State Government chapter
in this edition for other state officials whose terms were raised
to four years.*
** *Republicans.*

★ ★ ★ ★ ★ ★ ★
Vice Presidents and Lieutenant Governors

Vice Presidents of Republic
Date Elected
Lorenzo de Zavala (*provisional Vice President*)
Mirabeau B. Lamar .... Sept. 5, 1836
David G. Burnet .... Sept. 3, 1838
Edward Burleson .... Sept. 6, 1841
Kenneth L. Anderson .... Sept. 2, 1844

Lieutenant Governors

Albert C. Horton 1846–1847
John A. Greer 1847–1851
J. W. Henderson.. Aug. 4, 1851
D. C. Dickson 1853–1855
H. R. Runnels .... Aug. 6, 1855
F. R. Lubbock .... Aug. 4, 1857
Edward Clark .... Aug. 1, 1859
John M. Crockett...1861–1863
Fletcher S. Stockdale.................................... 1863–1866
George W. Jones 1866
    (*Jones was removed by General Sheridan.*)
J. W. Flanagan..1869
    (*Flanagan was appointed U.S. Senator and was
    never inaugurated as Lt. Gov.*)
R. B. Hubbard 1873–1876
J. D. Sayers 1878–1880
L. J. Storey 1880–1882
Marion Martin 1882–1884
Barnett Gibbs 1884–1886
T. B. Wheeler...1886–1890
George C. Pendleton 1890–1892
M. M. Crane .... Jan. 17, 1893–Jan. 25, 1895
George T. Jester 1895–1898
J. N. Browning...1898–1902
George D. Neal 1902–1906
A. B. Davidson 1906–1912
Will H. Mayes 1912–1914
William Pettus Hobby.....................................1914–1917
W. A. Johnson (*served Hobby's unexpired
    term and until* ....Jan. 1920)
Lynch Davidson 1920–1922
T. W. Davidson 1922–1924
Barry Miller 1924–1931
Edgar E. Witt...1931–1935
Walter Woodul 1935–1939

Coke R. Stevenson....................................1939–1941
John Lee Smith .... Jan. 21, 1947
Allan Shivers ....Jan. 21, 1947–July 11, 1949

(Shivers succeeded to the governorship on death of Governor Beauford H. Jester.)

Ben Ramsey....................................1951–Sept. 18, 1961
(Ben Ramsey resigned to become a member of the State Railroad Commission.)

Preston Smith..1963–1969
Ben Barnes 1969–1973
William P. Hobby Jr. 1973–1991
Robert D. Bullock..1991–1999
Rick Perry 1999–Dec. 21, 2000
*Bill Ratliff ....Dec. 28, 2000–Jan. 21, 2003
David Dewhurst .... Jan. 21, 2003–present

Elected by Senate when Rick Perry succeeded to governorship on election of George W. Bush as U.S. President.

★ ★ ★ ★ ★ ★ ★
Secretaries of State
Republic of Texas

Raines Yearbook for Texas, 1901, gives the following record of Secretaries of State during the era of the Republic of Texas:

Under David G. Burnet — Samuel P. Carson, James Collingsworth and W. H. Jack.

Under Sam Houston (first term) — Stephen F. Austin, 1836. J. Pinckney Henderson and Dr. Robert A. Irion, 1837–38.

Under Mirabeau B. Lamar — Bernard Bee appointed Dec. 16, 1838; James Webb appointed Feb. 6, 1839; D. G. Burnet appointed Acting Secretary of State, May 31, 1839; N. Amory appointed Acting Secretary of State, July 23, 1839; D. G. Burnet appointed Acting Secretary of State, Aug. 5, 1839; Abner S. Lipscomb appointed Secretary of State, Jan. 31, 1840, and resigned Jan. 22, 1841; Joseph Waples appointed Acting Secretary of State, Jan. 23, 1841, and served until Feb. 8, 1841; James S. Mayfield appointed Feb. 8, 1841; Joseph Waples appointed April 30, 1841, and served until May 25, 1841; Samuel A. Roberts appointed May 25, 1841; reappointed Sept. 7, 1841.

Under Sam Houston (second term) — E. Lawrence Stickney, Acting Secretary of State until Anson Jones appointed Dec. 13, 1841. Jones served as Secretary of State throughout this term except during the summer and part of this term of 1842, when Joseph Waples filled the position as Acting Secretary of State.

Under Anson Jones — Ebenezer Allen served from Dec. 10, 1844, until Feb. 5, 1845, when Ashbel Smith became Secretary of State. Allen was again named Acting Secretary of State, March 31, 1845, and later named Secretary of State.

(In addition to the above, documents in the Texas State Archives indicate that Joseph C. Eldredge, Chief Clerk of the State Department during much of the Republic's existence, signed a number of documents in the absence of the officeholder in the capacity of "Acting Secretary of State.")

State Secretaries of State

Charles Mariner.....................Feb. 20, 1846–May 4, 1846
David G. Burnet...................... May 4, 1846–Jan. 1, 1848
Washington D. Miller.................Jan. 1, 1848–Jan. 2, 1850
James Webb........................Jan. 2, 1850–Nov. 14, 1851
Thomas H. Duval................Nov. 14, 1851–Dec. 22, 1853
Edward Clark.......................Dec. 22, 1853–Dec. 1857
T. S. Anderson ....Dec. 1857–Dec. 27, 1859
E. W. Cave ....Dec. 27, 1859–Mar. 16, 1861
Bird Holland............................. Mar. 16, 1861–Nov. 1861
Charles West....................................Nov. 1861–Sept. 1862
Robert J. Townes .... Sept. 1862–May 2, 1865
Charles R. Pryor........................ May 2, 1865–Aug, 1865

James H. Bell....................................Aug. 1865–Aug. 1866
John A. Green ....Aug. 1866–Aug. 1867
D. W. C. Phillips .... Aug. 1867–Jan. 1870
J. P. Newcomb.......................Jan. 1, 1870–Jan. 17, 1874
George Clark ....Jan. 17, 1874–Jan. 27, 1874
A. W. DeBerry .... Jan. 27, 1874–Dec. 1, 1876
Isham G. Searcy ....Dec. 1, 1876–Jan. 23, 1879
J. D. Templeton ....Jan. 23, 1879–Jan. 22, 1881
T. H. Bowman.....................Jan. 22, 1881–Jan. 18, 1883
J. W. Baines ....Jan. 18, 1883–Jan. 21, 1887
John M. Moore.....................Jan. 21, 1887–Jan. 22, 1891
George W. Smith...................Jan. 22, 1891–Jan. 17, 1895
Allison Mayfield.....................Jan. 17, 1895–Jan. 5, 1897
J. W. Madden ....Jan. 5, 1897–Jan. 18, 1899
D. H. Hardy ....Jan. 18, 1899–Jan. 19, 1901
John G. Tod...........................Jan. 19, 1901–Jan., 1903
J. R. Curl .... Jan. 1903–April 1905
O. K. Shannon .... April 1905–Jan. 1907
L. T. Dashiel ....Jan. 1907–Feb. 1908
W. R. Davie ....Feb. 1908–Jan. 1909
W. B. Townsend..........................Jan. 1909–Jan. 1911
C. C. McDonald ....Jan. 1911–Dec. 1912
J. T. Bowman...........................Dec. 1912–Jan. 1913
John L. Wortham ....Jan. 1913–June 1913
F. C. Weinert .... June 1913–Nov. 1914
D. A. Gregg .... Nov. 1914–Jan. 1915
John G. McKay ....Jan. 1915–Dec. 1916
C. J. Bartlett ....Dec. 1916–Nov. 1917
George F. Howard ....Nov. 1917–Nov. 1920
C. D. Mims .... Nov. 1920–Jan. 1921
S. L. Staples ....Jan. 1921–Aug. 1924
J. D. Strickland .... Sept. 1924–Jan. 1, 1925
Henry Hutchings......................Jan. 1, 1925–Jan. 20, 1925
Mrs. Emma G. Meharg.............Jan. 20, 1925–Jan. 1927
Mrs. Jane Y. McCallum....................Jan. 1927–Jan. 1933
W. W. Heath .... Jan. 1933–Jan. 1935
Gerald C. Mann .... Jan. 1935–Aug. 31, 1935
R. B. Stanford ....Aug. 31, 1935–Aug. 25, 1936
B. P. Matocha .... Aug. 25, 1936–Jan. 18, 1937
Edward Clark ....Jan. 18, 1937–Jan. 1939
Tom L. Beauchamp..........................Jan. 1939–Oct. 1939
M. O. Flowers.......................Oct. 26, 1939–Feb. 25, 1941
William J. Lawson.....................Feb. 25, 1941–Jan. 1943
Sidney Latham.............................Jan. 1943–Feb. 1945
Claude Isbell ....Feb. 1945–Jan. 1947
Paul H. Brown ....Jan. 1947–Jan. 19, 1949
Ben Ramsey .... Jan. 19, 1949–Feb. 9, 1950
John Ben Shepperd..............Feb. 9, 1950–April 30, 1952
Jack Ross .... April 30, 1952–Jan. 9, 1953
Howard A. Carney ....Jan. 9, 1953–Apr. 30, 1954
C. E. Fulgham ....May 1, 1954–Feb. 15, 1955
Al Muldrow............................ Feb. 16, 1955–Nov. 1, 1955
Tom Reavley........................ Nov. 1, 1955–Jan. 16, 1957
Zollie Steakley ....Jan. 16, 1957–Jan. 2, 1962
P. Frank Lake ....Jan. 2, 1962–Jan. 15, 1963
Crawford C. Martin...........Jan. 15, 1963–March 12, 1966
John L. Hill.....................March 12, 1966–Jan. 22, 1968
Roy Barrera ....March 7, 1968–Jan. 23, 1969
Martin Dies Jr. .... Jan. 23, 1969–Sept. 1, 1971
Robert D. (Bob) Bullock .... Sept. 1, 1971–Jan. 2, 1973
V. Larry Teaver Jr. ....Jan. 2, 1973–Jan. 19, 1973
Mark W. White Jr. ....Jan. 19, 1973–Oct. 27,1977
Steven C. Oaks....................Oct. 27, 1977–Jan. 16, 1979
George W. Strake Jr..............Jan. 16, 1979–Oct. 6, 1981
David A. Dean .... Oct. 22, 1981–Jan. 18, 1983
John Fainter.........................Jan. 18, 1983–July 31, 1984
Myra A. McDaniel .... Sept. 6, 1984–Jan. 26, 1987
Jack Rains ....Jan. 26, 1987–June 15, 1989
George Bayoud Jr....................June 19, 1989–Jan. 15, 1991
John Hannah Jr. ....Jan. 17, 1991–March 11, 1994
Ronald Kirk........................... April 4, 1994–Jan. 10, 1995
Antonio O. "Tony" Garza Jr.... Jan. 18, 1995–Dec. 2, 1997
Alberto R. Gonzales .... Dec. 2, 1997–Jan. 10, 1999
Elton Bomer........................ Jan. 11, 1999–Dec. 31, 2000
Henry Cuellar ....Jan. 2, 2001–Oct. 5, 2001
Gwyn Shea .... Jan. 2, 2002–Aug. 4, 2003
Geoff Connor......................Sept. 26, 2003–Jan. 1, 2005
J. Roger Williams ....Jan. 1, 2005–present

★ ★ ★ ★ ★ ★ ★

Attorneys General

Of the Republic

David Thomas and
    Peter W. Grayson ....Mar. 2–Oct. 22, 1836
J. Pinckney Henderson, Peter W. Grayson,
    John Birdsall, A. S. Thurston 1836–1838
J. C. Watrous .... Dec. 1838–June 1, 1840
Joseph Webb and F. A. Morris 1840–1841
George W. Terrell, Ebenezer Allen 1841–1844
Ebenezer Allen 1844–1846

*Of the State

Volney E. Howard................. Feb. 21, 1846–May 7, 1846
John W. Harris........................May 7, 1846–Oct. 31, 1849
Henry P. Brewster ....Oct. 31, 1849–Jan. 15, 1850
A. J. Hamilton .... Jan. 15, 1850–Aug. 5, 1850
Ebenezer Allen ....Aug. 5, 1850–Aug. 2, 1852
Thomas J. Jennings ....Aug. 2, 1852–Aug. 4, 1856
James Willie ....Aug. 4, 1856–Aug. 2, 1858
Malcolm D. Graham ....Aug. 2, 1858–Aug. 6, 1860
George M. Flournoy .... Aug. 6, 1860–Jan. 15, 1862
N. G. Shelley .... Feb. 3, 1862–Aug. 1, 1864
B. E. Tarver.......................... Aug. 1, 1864–Dec. 11, 1865
Wm. Alexander ....Dec. 11, 1865–June 25, 1866
W. M. Walton .... June 25, 1866–Aug. 27, 1867
Wm. Alexander ....Aug. 27, 1867–Nov. 5, 1867
Ezekiel B. Turner ....Nov. 5, 1867–July 11, 1870
Wm. Alexander .... July 11, 1870–Jan. 27, 1874
George Clark ....Jan. 27, 1874–Apr. 25, 1876
H. H. Boone ....Apr. 25, 1876–Nov. 5, 1878
George McCormick................. Nov. 5, 1878–Nov. 2, 1880
J. H. McLeary .... Nov. 2, 1880–Nov. 7, 1882
John D. Templeton .... Nov. 7, 1882–Nov. 2, 1886
James S. Hogg .... Nov. 2, 1886–Nov. 4, 1890
C. A. Culberson .... Nov. 4, 1890–Nov. 6, 1894
M. M. Crane .... Nov. 6, 1894–Nov. 8, 1898
Thomas S. Smith .... Nov. 8, 1898–Mar. 15,1901
C. K. Bell .... Mar. 20, 1901–Jan., 1904
R. V. Davidson ....Jan. 1904–Dec. 31, 1909
Jewel P. Lightfoot .... Jan. 1, 1910–Aug. 31, 1912
James D. Walthall .... Sept. 1, 1912–Jan. 1, 1913
B. F. Looney ....Jan. 1, 1913–Jan., 1919
C. M. Cureton ....Jan. 1919–Dec. 1921
W. A. Keeling .... Dec. 1921–Jan. 1925
Dan Moody ....Jan. 1925–Jan. 1927
Claude Pollard ....Jan. 1927–Sept. 1929
R. L. Bobbitt (Apptd.).......................Sept. 1929–Jan. 1931
James V. Allred ....Jan. 1931–Jan. 1935
William McCraw ....Jan. 1935–Jan. 1939
Gerald C. Mann (resigned).............Jan. 1939–Jan. 1944
Grover Sellers ....Jan. 1944–Jan. 1947
Price Daniel ....Jan. 1947–Jan. 1953
John Ben Shepperd....................Jan. 1953–Jan. 1, 1957
Will Wilson ....Jan. 1, 1957–Jan. 15, 1963
Waggoner Carr ....Jan. 15, 1963–Jan. 1, 1967
Crawford C. Martin.................Jan. 1, 1967–Dec. 29, 1972
John Hill...............................Jan. 1, 1973–Jan. 16, 1979
Mark White........................ Jan. 16, 1979–Jan. 18, 1983
Jim Mattox .... Jan. 18, 1983–Jan. 15, 1991
Dan Morales .... Jan. 15, 1991–Jan. 13, 1999
John Cornyn .... Jan. 13, 1999–Dec. 2, 2002
Greg Abbott .... Dec. 2, 2002–present

*The first few Attorneys General held office by appointment
of the Governor. The office was made elective in 1850 by constitutional amendment. Ebenezer Allen was the first elected
Attorney General.

★ ★ ★ ★ ★ ★ ★

Treasurers

Of the Republic

Asa Brigham 1838–1840
James W. Simmons 1840–1841

Asa Brigham...1841–1844
Moses Johnson 1844–1846

Of the State

James H. Raymond ....Feb. 24, 1846–Aug. 2, 1858
*C. H. Randolph ....Aug. 2, 1858–June 1865
*Samuel Harris ....Oct. 2, 1865–June 25, 1866
W. M. Royston......................June 25, 1866–Sept. 1, 1867
John Y. Allen ....Sept. 1, 1867–Jan. 1869
**George W. Honey........................ Jan. 1869–Jan. 1874
**B. Graham (short term) ....beginning May 27, 1872
A. J. Dorn .... Jan. 1874–Jan. 1879
F. R. Lubbock .... Jan. 1879–Jan. 1891
W. B. Wortham .... Jan. 1891–Jan. 1899
John W. Robbins................................ Jan. 1899–Jan. 1907
Sam Sparks....................................... Jan. 1907–Jan. 1912
J. M. Edwards .... Jan. 1912–Jan. 1919
John W. Baker.................................... Jan. 1919–Jan. 1921
G. N. Holton ....July 1921–Nov. 21, 1921
C. V. Terrell.......................Nov. 21, 1921–Aug. 15, 1924
S. L. Staples.........................Aug. 16, 1924–Jan. 15, 1925
W. Gregory Hatcher .... Jan. 16, 1925–Jan. 1, 1931
Charley Lockhart ....Jan. 1, 1931–Oct. 25, 1941
Jesse James......................Oct. 25, 1941–Sept. 29, 1977
Warren G. Harding.................Oct. 7, 1977–Jan. 3, 1983
Ann Richards .... Jan. 3, 1983–Jan. 2, 1991
Kay Bailey Hutchison..................Jan. 2, 1991–June 1993
†Martha Whitehead ....June 1993–Aug. 1996

*Randolph fled to Mexico upon collapse of Confederacy.
No exact date is available for his departure from office or for
Harris' succession to the post. It is believed Harris took office
Oct. 2, 1865.
**Honey was removed from office for a short period in
1872 and B. Graham served in his place.
† The office of Treasurer was eliminated by Constitutional
amendment in an election Nov. 7, 1995, effective the last day
of August 1996.

★ ★ ★ ★ ★ ★ ★

Railroad Commission of Texas

(After the first three names in the following list, each commissioner's name is followed by a surname in parentheses. The
name in parentheses is the name of the commissioner whom
that commissioner succeeded.)

John H. Reagan .... June 10, 1891–Jan. 20, 1903
L. L. Foster .... June 10, 1891–April 30, 1895
W. P. McLean .... June 10, 1891–Nov. 20, 1894
L. J. Storey (McLean) .... Nov. 21, 1894–Mar. 28,1909
N. A. Stedman (Foster) ....May 1, 1895–Jan. 4, 1897
Allison Mayfield (Stedman)....Jan. 5, 1897–Jan. 23, 1923
O. B. Colquitt (Reagan) ....Jan. 21, 1903–Jan. 17, 1911
William D. Williams (Storey)...April 28, 1909–Oct. 1, 1916
John L. Wortham (Colquitt)....Jan. 21, 1911–Jan. 1, 1913
Earle B. Mayfield (Wortham) Jan. 2, 1913–March 1, 1923
Charles Hurdleston (Williams)..... Oct. 10, 1916–Dec. 31,
  1918
Clarence Gilmore (Hurdleston)Jan. 1, 1919–Jan. 1, 1929
N. A. Nabors (A. Mayfield) ..March 1, 1923–Jan. 18, 1925
William Splawn (E. Mayfield)March 1, 1923–Aug. 1, 1924
C. V. Terrell (Splawn) .... Aug. 15, 1924–Jan. 1, 1939
Lon A. Smith (Nabors) ....Jan. 29, 1925–Jan. 1, 1941
Pat M. Neff (Gilmore)................Jan. 1, 1929–Jan. 1, 1933
Ernest O. Thompson (Neff)......Jan. 1, 1933–Jan. 8, 1965
G. A. (Jerry) Sadler (Terrell) ....Jan. 1, 1939–Jan. 1, 1943
Olin Culberson (Smith) ....Jan. 1, 1941–June 22, 1961
Beauford Jester (Sadler)......Jan. 1, 1943–Jan. 21, 1947
William J. Murray Jr. (Jester) Jan. 21, 1947–Apr. 10, 1963
Ben Ramsey (Culberson) ..Sept. 18, 1961–Dec. 31, 1976
Jim C. Langdon (Murray) .... May 28, 1963–Dec. 31, 1977
Byron Tunnell (Thompson) Jan. 11, 1965–Sept. 15, 1973
Mack Wallace (Tunnell).....Sept. 18, 1973–Sept. 22, 1987
Jon Newton (Ramsey) ....Jan. 10, 1977–Jan. 4, 1979
John H. Poerner (Langdon) .. Jan. 2, 1978–Jan. 1, 1981
James E. (Jim) Nugent (Newton) .....Jan. 4, 1979–Jan. 3,
  1995
Buddy Temple (Poerner).......Jan. 2, 1981–March 2, 1986
Clark Jobe (Temple) .... March 3, 1986–Jan. 5, 1987
John Sharp (Jobe)..................Jan. 6, 1987–Jan. 2, 1991
Kent Hance (Wallace)..........Sept. 23, 1987–Jan. 2, 1991

*Robert Krueger (Hance).......Jan. 3, 1991–Jan. 22, 1993
Lena Guerrero (Sharp)........Jan. 23, 1991–Sept. 25, 1992
James Wallace (Guerrero).......Oct. 2, 1992–Jan. 4, 1993
Barry Williamson (Wallace)......Jan. 5, 1993–Jan. 4, 1999
Mary Scott Nabers (Krueger) . Feb. 9, 1993–Dec. 9, 1994
Carole K. Rylander (Nabers) Dec. 10, 1994–Jan. 4, 1999
Charles Matthews (Nugent)............Jan. 3, 1995–present
Michael L. Williams (Rylander) ....Jan. 4, 1999–present
Antonio Garza (Williamson).. Jan. 4, 1999–Nov. 18, 2002
Victor Carrillo (Garza).................. Feb. 19, 2003–present

* Robert Krueger resigned when Gov. Ann Richards
appointed him interim U.S. Senator on the resignation of
Sen.Lloyd Bentsen.

★ ★ ★ ★ ★ ★ ★

Comptroller of Public Accounts

Of the Republic

John H. Money.................... Dec. 30, 1835–Jan. 17, 1836
H. C. Hudson .... Jan. 17, 1836–Oct. 22, 1836
E. M. Pease........................... June 1837–Dec. 1837
F. R. Lubbock ....Dec. 1837–Jan. 1839
Jas. W. Simmons............... Jan. 15, 1839–Sept. 30, 1840
Jas. B. Shaw ....Sept. 30, 1840–Dec. 24, 1841
F. R. Lubbock .... Dec. 24, 1841–Jan. 1, 1842
Jas. B. Shaw .... Jan. 1, 1842–Jan. 1, 1846

Of the State

Jas. B. Shaw .... Feb. 24, 1846–Aug. 2, 1858
Clement R. Johns .... Aug. 2, 1858–Aug. 1, 1864
Willis L. Robards..................Aug. 1, 1864–Oct. 12, 1865
Albert H. Latimer.................Oct. 12, 1865–Mar. 27, 1866
Robert H. Taylor...............Mar. 27, 1866–June 25, 1866
Willis L. Robards................June 25, 1866–Aug. 27, 1867
Morgan C. Hamilton..............Aug. 27, 1867–Jan. 8, 1870
A. Bledsoe .... Jan. 8, 1870–Jan. 20, 1874
Stephen H. Darden ....Jan. 20, 1874–Nov. 2, 1880
W. M. Brown..........................Nov. 2, 1880–Jan. 16, 1883
W. J. Swain .... Jan. 16, 1883–Jan. 18, 1887
John D. McCall.....................Jan. 18, 1887–Jan. 15, 1895
R. W. Finley ....Jan. 15, 1895–Jan. 15, 1901
R. M. Love ....Jan. 15, 1901–Jan. 1903
J. W. Stephen .... Jan. 1903–Jan. 1911
W. P. Lane .... Jan. 1911–Jan. 1915
H. B. Terrell .... Jan. 1915–Jan. 1920
M. L. Wiginton .... Jan. 1920–Jan. 1921
Lon A. Smith .... Jan. 1921–Jan. 1925
S. H. Terrell .... Jan. 1925–Jan. 1931
Geo. H. Sheppard ....Jan., 1931–Jan. 17, 1949
Robert S. Calvert ....Jan. 17, 1949–Jan., 1975
Robert D. (Bob) Bullock .... Jan. 1975–Jan. 3, 1991
John Sharp ....Jan. 3, 1991–Jan. 2, 1999
Carole Keeton Strayhorn ....Jan. 2, 1999–present

★ ★ ★ ★ ★ ★ ★

U.S. Senators from Texas

U.S. Senators were selected by the legislatures of the
states until the U.S. Constitution was amended in 1913 to
require popular elections. In Texas, the first senator chosen by
the voters in a general election was Charles A. Culberson in
1916. Because of political pressures, however, the rules of the
Democratic Party of Texas were changed in 1904 to require
that all candidates for office stand before voters in the primary.
Consequently, Texas' senators faced voters in 1906, 1910 and
1912 before the U.S. Constitution was changed.
Following is the succession of Texas representatives in the
United States Senate since the annexation of Texas to the
Union in 1845:

Houston Succession

Sam Houston.......................... Feb. 21, 1846–Mar. 4, 1859
John Hemphill.........................Mar. 4, 1859–July 11, 1861

Louis T. Wigfall and W. S. Oldham took their seats in the
Confederate Senate, Nov. 16, 1861, and served until the Confederacy collapsed. After that event, the State Legislature on
Aug. 21, 1866, elected David G. Burnet and Oran M. Roberts
to the United States Senate, anticipating immediate readmis-
sion to the Union, but they were not allowed to take their seats.

†Morgan C. Hamilton.............Feb. 22, 1870–Mar. 3, 1877
Richard Coke..........................Mar. 4, 1877–Mar. 3, 1895
Horace Chilton........................Mar. 3, 1895–Mar. 3, 1901
Joseph W. Bailey ....Mar. 3, 1901–Jan. 8, 1913
Rienzi Melville Johnston..........Jan. 8, 1913–Feb. 3, 1913
‡Morris Sheppard (died).........Feb. 13, 1913–Apr. 9, 1941
Andrew J. Houston ....June 2–26, 1941
W. Lee O'Daniel.....................Aug. 4, 1941–Jan. 3, 1949
Lyndon B. Johnson ....Jan. 3, 1949–Jan. 20, 1961
William A. Blakley ....Jan. 20, 1961–June 15, 1961
†John G. Tower..................June 15, 1961–Jan. 21, 1985
†Phil Gramm..........................Jan. 21, 1985–Dec. 2, 2002
†John Cornyn ....Dec. 2, 2002–present

Rusk Succession

Thomas J. Rusk (died)..........Feb 21, 1846–July 29, 1857
J. Pinckney Henderson (died).Nov. 9, 1857–June 4, 1858
Matthias Ward (*appointed*
	interim)..........................Sept. 29, 1858–Dec. 5, 1859
Louis T. Wigfall ....Dec. 5, 1859–March 23, 1861

Succession was broken by the expulsion of Texas Senators following secession of Texas from Union. See note above under "Houston Succession" on Louis T. Wigfall, W. S. Oldham, Burnet and Roberts.

†James W. Flanagan ....Feb. 22, 1870–Mar. 3, 1875
Samuel B. Maxey ....Mar. 3, 1875–Mar. 3, 1887
John H. Reagan (*resigned*) ..Mar. 3, 1887–June 10, 1891
Horace Chilton (*filled vacancy on
	appointment*) ....Dec. 7, 1891–Mar. 30,1892
Roger Q. Mills ....Mar. 30, 1892–Mar. 3, 1899
‡Charles A. Culberson ....Mar. 3, 1899–Mar. 4, 1923
Earle B. Mayfield.....................Mar. 4, 1923–Mar. 4, 1929
Tom Connally...........................Mar. 4, 1929–Jan. 3, 1953
Price Daniel ....Jan. 3, 1953–Jan. 15, 1957
William A. Blakley ....Jan. 15, 1957–Apr. 27, 1957
Ralph W. Yarborough ....Apr. 27, 1957–Jan. 12, 1971
§Lloyd Bentsen....................Jan. 12, 1971–Jan. 20, 1993
Robert Krueger....................Jan. 20, 1993–June 14, 1993
†Kay Bailey Hutchison.................June 14, 1993–present

	† Republicans
	‡ First election to U.S. Senate held in 1916. Prior to that time, senators were appointed by the Legislature.
	§ Resigned from Senate when appointed U.S. Secretary of Treasury by Pres. Bill Clinton.

★ ★ ★ ★ ★ ★ ★

Commissioners of the General Land Office
For the Republic

John P. Borden.....................Aug. 23, 1837–Dec. 12, 1840
H. W. Raglin ....Dec. 12, 1840–Jan. 4, 1841
*Thomas William Ward ....Jan. 4, 1841–Mar. 20, 1848

For the State

George W. Smyth....................Mar. 20, 1848–Aug. 4, 1851
Stephen Crosby.......................Aug. 4, 1851–Mar. 1, 1858
Francis M. White......................Mar. 1, 1858–Mar. 1, 1862
Stephen Crosby.......................Mar. 1, 1862–Sept. 1, 1865
Francis M. White ....Sept. 1, 1865–Aug. 7, 1866
Stephen Crosby ....Aug. 7, 1866–Aug. 27, 1867
Joseph Spence....................Aug. 27, 1867–Jan. 19, 1870
Jacob Kuechler...................Jan. 19, 1870–Jan. 20, 1874
J. J. Groos ....Jan. 20, 1874–June 15, 1878
W. C. Walsh..........................July 30, 1878–Jan. 10, 1887
R. M. Hall ....Jan. 10, 1887–Jan. 16, 1891
W. L. McGaughey ....Jan. 16, 1891–Jan. 26, 1895
A. J. Baker ....Jan. 26, 1895–Jan. 16, 1899
George W. Finger.................. Jan. 16, 1899–May 4, 1899
Charles Rogan ....May 11, 1899–Jan. 10, 1903
John J. Terrell......................Jan. 10, 1903–Jan. 11, 1909
J. T. Robison ....Jan, 1909–Sept. 11, 1929
J. H. Walker ....Sept. 11, 1929–Jan., 1937
William H. McDonald ....Jan 1937–Jan. 1939
Bascom Giles ....Jan. 1939–Jan. 5, 1955
J. Earl Rudder ....Jan. 5, 1955–Feb. 1, 1958
Bill Allcorn..............................Feb. 1, 1958–Jan. 1, 1961
Jerry Sadler ....Jan. 1, 1961–Jan. 1, 1971
Bob Armstrong ....Jan. 1, 1971–Jan. 1, 1983

Garry Mauro ....Jan. 1, 1983–Jan. 7, 1999
David Dewhurst ....Jan. 7, 1999–Jan. 3, 2003
Jerry Patterson ....Jan. 3, 2003–present
	Part of term after annexation.

★ ★ ★ ★ ★ ★ ★
Speaker of the Texas House

The Speaker of the Texas House of Representatives is the presiding officer of the lower chamber of the State Legislature. The official is elected at the beginning of each regular session by a vote of the members of the House.

Speaker, Residence	Year Elected	Legislature
William E. Crump, Bellville	1846	1st
William H. Bourland, Paris	1846	1st
James W. Henderson, Houston	1847	2nd
Charles G. Keenan, Huntsville	1849	3rd
David C. Dickson, Anderson	1851	4th
Hardin R. Runnels, Boston	1853	5th
Hamilton P. Bee, Laredo	1855	6th
William S. Taylor, Larissa	1857	7th
Matt F. Locke, Lafayette	1858	7th
Marion DeKalb Taylor, Jefferson	1859	8th
Constantine W. Buckley, Richmond	1861	9th
Nicholas H. Darnell, Dallas	1861	9th
Constantine W. Buckley, Richmond	1863	9th
Marion DeKalb Taylor, Jefferson	1863	10th
Nathaniel M. Burford, Dallas	1866	11th
Ira H. Evans, Corpus Christi	1870	12th
William H. Sinclair, Galveston	1871	12th
Marion DeKalb Taylor, Jefferson	1873	13th
Guy M. Bryan, Galveston	1874	14th
Thomas R. Bonner, Tyler	1876	15th
John H. Cochran, Dallas	1879	16th
George R. Reeves, Pottsboro	1881	17th
Charles R. Gibson, Waxahachie	1883	18th
Lafayette L. Foster, Groesbeck	1885	19th
George C. Pendleton, Belton	1887	20th
Frank P. Alexander, Greenville	1889	21st
Robert T. Milner, Henderson	1891	22nd
John H. Cochran, Dallas	1893	23rd
Thomas Slater Smith, Hillsboro	1895	24th
L. Travis Dashiell, Jewett	1897	25th
J. S. Sherrill, Greenville	1899	26th
Robert E. Prince, Corsicana	1901	27th
Pat M. Neff, Waco	1903	28th
Francis W. Seabury, Rio Grande City	1905	29th
Thomas B. Love, Lancaster	1907	30th
Austin M. Kennedy, Waco	1909	31st
John W. Marshall, Whitesboro	1909	31st
Sam Rayburn, Bonham	1911	32nd
Chester H. Terrell, San Antonio	1913	33rd
John W. Woods, Rotan	1915	34th
Franklin O. Fuller, Coldspring	1917	35th
R. Ewing Thomason, El Paso	1919	36th
Charles G. Thomas, Lewisville	1921	37th
Richard E. Seagler, Palestine	1923	38th
Lee Satterwhite, Amarillo	1925	39th
Robert L. Bobbitt, Laredo	1927	40th
W. S. Barron, Bryan	1929	41st
Fred H. Minor, Denton	1931	42nd
Coke R. Stevenson, Junction	1933	43rd
"	1935	44th
Robert W. Calvert, Hillsboro	1937	45th
R. Emmett Morse, Houston	1939	46th
Homer L. Leonard, McAllen	1941	47th
Price Daniel, Liberty	1943	48th
Claud H. Gilmer, Rocksprings	1945	49th
William O. Reed, Dallas	1947	50th
Durwood Manford, Smiley	1949	51st
Reuben Senterfitt, San Saba	1951	52nd
"	1953	53rd
Jim T. Lindsey, Texarkana	1955	54th
Waggoner Carr, Lubbock	1957	55th
"	1959	56th
James A. Turman, Gober	1961	57th
Byron M. Tunnell, Tyler	1963	58th
Ben Barnes, DeLeon	1965	59th
"	1967	60th
Gus F. Mutscher, Brenham	1969	61st
"	1971	62nd
Rayford Price, Palestine	1972	62nd
Price Daniel Jr., Liberty	1973	63rd
Bill Clayton, Springlake	1975	64th
"	1977	65th
"	1979	66th
"	1981	67th

Gibson D. Lewis, Fort Worth	1983	68th
"	1985	69th
"	1987	70th
"	1989	71st
"	1991	72nd
James M. (Pete) Laney, Hale Center	1993	73rd
"	1995	74th
"	1997	75th
"	1999	76th
"	2001	77th
Tom Craddick	2003	78th
"	2005	79th

★ ★ ★ ★ ★ ★ ★

Chief Justice of the Supreme Court
Republic of Texas

James Collinsworth	Dec. 16, 1836–July 23, 1838
John Birdsall	Nov. 19–Dec. 12, 1838
Thomas J. Rusk	Dec. 12, 1838–Dec. 5, 1840
John Hemphill	Dec. 5, 1840–Dec. 29, 1845

Under the Constitutions of 1845 and 1861

John Hemphill	Mar. 2, 1846–Oct. 10, 1858
Royall T. Wheeler	Oct. 11, 1858–April 1864
Oran M. Roberts	Nov. 1, 1864–June 30, 1866

Under the Constitution of 1866
(Presidential Reconstruction)

| *George F. Moore | Aug. 16, 1866–Sept. 10, 1867 |

*Removed under Congressional Reconstruction by military authorities who appointed members of the next court.

Under the Constitution of 1866
(Congressional Reconstruction)

| Amos Morrill | Sept. 10, 1867–July 5, 1870 |

Under the Constitution of 1869

Lemuel D. Evans	July 5, 1870–Aug. 31, 1873
Wesley Ogden	Aug. 31, 1873–Jan. 29, 1874
Oran M. Roberts	Jan. 29, 1874–Apr. 18, 1876

Under the Constitution of 1876

Oran M. Roberts	Apr. 18, 1876–Oct. 1, 1878
George F. Moore	Nov. 5, 1878–Nov. 1, 1881
Robert S. Gould	Nov. 1, 1881–Dec. 23, 1882
Asa H. Willie	Dec. 23, 1882–Mar. 3, 1888
John W. Stayton	Mar. 3, 1888–July 5, 1894
Reuben R. Gaines	July 10, 1894–Jan. 5, 1911
Thomas J. Brown	Jan. 7, 1911–May 26, 1915
Nelson Phillips	June 1, 1915–Nov. 16, 1921
C. M. Cureton	Dec. 2, 1921–Apr. 8, 1940
†Hortense Sparks Ward	Jan. 8, 1925–May 23, 1925
W. F. Moore	Apr. 17, 1940–Jan. 1, 1941
James P. Alexander	Jan. 1, 1941–Jan. 1, 1948
J. E. Hickman	Jan. 5, 1948–Jan. 3, 1961
Robert W. Calvert	Jan. 3, 1961–Oct. 4, 1972
Joe R. Greenhill	Oct. 4, 1972–Oct. 25, 1982
Jack Pope	Nov. 29, 1982–Jan. 5, 1985
John L. Hill Jr.	Jan. 5, 1985–Jan. 4, 1988
Thomas R. Phillips	Jan. 4, 1988–Sept. 3 2004
Wallace B. Jefferson	Sept. 14, 2004–present

†Mrs. Ward served as Chief Justice of a special Supreme Court to hear one case in 1925.

Presiding Judges, Court of Appeals (1876–1891)

and Court of Criminal Appeals (1891–present)

Mat D. Ector	May 6, 1876–Oct. 29, 1879
John P. White	Nov. 9, 1879–Apr. 26, 1892
James M. Hurt	May 4, 1892–Dec. 31, 1898
W. L. Davidson	Jan. 2, 1899–June 27, 1913
A. C. Prendergast	June 27, 1913–Dec. 31, 1916
W. L. Davidson	Jan. 1, 1917–Jan. 25, 1921
Wright C. Morrow	Feb. 8, 1921–Oct. 16, 1939
Frank Lee Hawkins	Oct. 16, 1939–Jan. 2, 1951
Harry N. Graves	Jan. 2, 1951–Dec. 31, 1954
W. A. Morrison	Jan. 1, 1955–Jan. 2, 1961
Kenneth K. Woodley	Jan. 3, 1961–Jan. 4, 1965
W. T. McDonald	Jan. 4, 1965–June 25, 1966
W. A. Morrison	June 25, 1966–Jan. 1, 1967
Kenneth K. Woodley	Jan. 1, 1967–Jan. 1, 1971
John F. Onion Jr.	Jan. 1, 1971–Jan. 1, 1989
Michael J. McCormick	Jan. 1, 1989–Jan. 1, 2001
Sharon Keller	Jan. 1, 2001–present

★ ★ ★ ★ ★ ★ ★

Administrators of Public Education
Superintendents of Public Instruction

| Pryor Lea | Nov. 10, 1866–Sept. 12, 1867 |

Edwin M. Wheelock	Sept. 12, 1867–May 6, 1871
Jacob C. DeGress	May 6, 1871–Jan. 20, 1874
O. H. Hollingsworth	Jan. 20, 1874–May 6, 1884
B. M. Baker	May 6, 1884–Jan. 18, 1887
O. H. Cooper	Jan 18, 1887–Sept. 1, 1890
H. C. Pritchett	Sept. 1, 1890–Sept. 15, 1891
J. M. Carlisle	Sept. 15, 1891–Jan. 10, 1899
J. S. Kendall	Jan. 10, 1899–July 2, 1901
Arthur Lefevre	July 2, 1901–Jan. 12, 1905
R. B. Cousins	Jan. 12, 1905–Jan. 1, 1910
F. M. Bralley	Jan. 1, 1910–Sept. 1, 1913
W. F. Doughty	Sept. 1, 1913–Jan. 1, 1919
Annie Webb Blanton	Jan. 1, 1919–Jan. 16, 1923
S. M. N. Marrs	Jan. 16, 1923–April 28, 1932
C. N. Shaver	April 28, 1932–Oct. 1, 1932
L. W. Rogers	Oct. 1, 1932–Jan. 16, 1933
L. A. Woods	Jan. 16, 1933–*1951

State Commissioner of Education

J. W. Edgar	May 31, 1951–June 30, 1974
Marlin L. Brockette	July 1, 1974–Sept. 1, 1979
Alton O. Bowen	Sept. 1, 1979–June 1, 1981
Raymon Bynum	June 1, 1981–Oct. 31, 1984
W. N. Kirby	April 13, 1985–July 1, 1991
Lionel R. Meno	July 1, 1991–March 1, 1995
Michael A. Moses	March 9, 1995–Aug. 18, 1999
Jim Nelson	Aug. 18, 1999–March 25, 2002
Felipe Alanis	March 25, 2002–July 31, 2003
Shirley J. Neeley	Jan. 12, 2004–present

*The office of State Superintendent of Public Instruction was abolished by the Gilmer-Aikin act of 1949 and the office of Commissioner of Education created, appointed by a new State Board of Education elected by the people.

First Ladies of Texas

Martha Evans Gindratt Wood	1847–49
†Bell Administration	1849–53
Lucadia Christiana Niles Pease	1853-57; 1867–69
‡Runnels Administration	1857–59
Margaret Moffette Lea Houston	1859–61
Martha Evans Clark	1861
Adele Barron Lubbock	1861–1863
Susie Ellen Taylor Murrah	1863–1865
Mary Jane Bowen Hamilton	1865–1866
Annie Rattan Throckmorton	1866–1867
Ann Elizabeth Britton Davis	1870–1874
Mary Home Coke	1874–1876
Janie Roberts Hubbard	1876–1879
Frances Wickliff Edwards Roberts	1879–1883
Anne Maria Penn Ireland	1883–1887
Elizabeth Dorothy Tinsley Ross	1887–1891
Sarah Stinson Hogg	1891–1895
Sally Harrison Culberson	1895–1899
Orlene Walton Sayers	1899–1903
Sarah Beona Meng Lanham	1903–1907
Fannie Brunner Campbell	1907–1911
Alice Fuller Murrell Colquitt	1911–1915
§Miriam A. Wallace Ferguson	1915–1917
Willie Cooper Hobby	1917–1921
Myrtle Mainer Neff	1921–1925
Mildred Paxton Moody	1927–1931
Maud Gage Sterling	1931–1933
Jo Betsy Miller Allred	1935–1939
Merle Estella Butcher O'Daniel	1939–1941
**Fay Wright Stevenson	1941–1942
**Edith Will Scott Stevenson	1942–1946
Mabel Buchanan Jester	1946–1949
Marialice Shary Shivers	1949–1957
Jean Houston Baldwin Daniel	1957–1963
Idanell Brill Connally	1963–1969
Ima Mae Smith	1969–1973
Betty Jane Slaughter Briscoe	1973–1979
Rita Crocker Bass Clements	1979–1983
Linda Gale Thompson White	1983–1987
Rita Crocker Bass Clements	1987–1991
Laura Welch Bush	1995–2000
Anita Thigpen Perry	2000–present

†Gov. Peter Hansbrough Bell was not married while in office.
‡Gov. Hardin R. Runnels never married.
**Mrs. Coke R. (Fay Wright) Stevenson, the governor's wife, died in the Governor's Mansion Jan. 3, 1942. His mother, Edith Stevenson, served as Mistress of the Mansion thereafter. ☆

State Government

Texas state government is divided into executive, legislative and judicial branches under the Texas Constitution adopted in 1876. The chief executive is the Governor, whose term is for four years. Other elected state officials with executive responsibilities include the Lieutenant Governor, Attorney General, Comptroller of Public Accounts, Commissioner of the General Land Office and Commissioner of Agriculture. The terms of those officials are also four years. The Secretary of State is appointed by the Governor.

Except for making numerous appointments and calling special sessions of the Legislature, the Governor's powers are limited in comparison with those in most states.

Current state executives "not-to-exceed" salaries are for the 2004–2005 biennium (maximum possible salaries; actual salaries can be lower); salaries for the 2006–2007 biennium were not available from the State Auditor at press time.

Governor: Rick Perry
P.O. Box 12428, Austin 78711
512-463-2000; www.governor.state.tx.us
$115,345

Attorney General: Greg Abbott
P.O. Box 12548, Austin 78711
512-463-2100; www.oag.state.tx.us
$92,217

Land Commissioner: Jerry Patterson
1700 N. Congress, Austin 78701
512-463-5256; www.glo.state.tx.us
$92,217

Lt. Governor: David Dewhurst
P.O. Box 12068, Austin 78711
512-463-0001; www.senate.state.tx.us
For salary, see note* below.

Comptroller of Public Accounts: Carole Keeton Strayhorn
PO Box 13528, Austin 78774
512-463-4000; www.cpa.state.tx.us
$92,217

Commissioner of Agriculture: Susan Combs
P.O. Box 12847, Austin 78711
512-463-7664; www.agr.state.tx.us
$92,217

Secretary of State: J. Roger Williams
P.O. Box 12887, Austin 78711
512-463-5770; www.sos.state.tx.us
$117,516

Salary of Lt. Gov. is same as a Senator when serving as Pres.of the Senate; same as Gov. when serving as Gov.

Ombudsman Office (Citizens' Advocate): Part of the Governor's office, the Ombudsman Office receives citizens's comments and complaints over the toll-free assistance hotline and passes them to government officials and refers citizens to sources of help. **Citizens' Assistance Hotline: 1-800-843-5789.**

Texas Legislature

The Texas Legislature has **181 members: 31 in the Senate** and **150 in the House of Representatives.** Regular sessions convene on the second Tuesday of January in odd-numbered years, but the governor may call special sessions. Article III of the Texas Constitution deals with the legislative branch. On the Web: **www.capitol.state.tx.us.**

The following lists are of members of the **79th Legislature,** which convened for its Regular Session on Jan. 11, 2005, and adjourned on May 30, 2005. A First Called Special Session convened June 21, 2005 and was still in session at press time. The **80th Legislature** is scheduled to convene on Jan. 9, 2007, and adjourn in May 2007.

State Senate

Thirty-one members of the State Senate are elected to **four-year, overlapping terms. Salary:** The salary of all members of the Legislature, both Senators and Representatives, is $7,200 per year and $124 per diem during legislative sessions; mileage allowance at same rate provided by law for state employees. The per diem payment applies during each regular and special session of the Legislature.

Senatorial Districts include one or more whole counties and some counties have more than one Senator.

The **address of Senators** is Texas Senate, P.O. Box 12068, Austin 78711-2068; phone 512-463-0001; Fax: 512-463-0326. On the Web: **www.senate.state.tx.us.**

President of the Senate is Lt. Gov. David Dewhurst; **President Pro Tempore —** Florence Shapiro.; **Secretary of the Senate,** Patsy Spaw; **Sergeant-at-Arms,** Carleton Turner.

Texas State Senators

District, Member, Party-Hometown, Occupation

1. Kevin Eltife, R-Tyler; businessman.
2. Bob Deuell, R-Greenville; family physician.
3. Todd Staples, R-Palestine; small business owner.
4. Tommy Williams, R-The Woodlands; businessman.
5. Steve Ogden, R-Bryan;oil and gas producer.
6. Mario Gallegos Jr., D-Houston; retired firefighter.
7. Jon Lindsay, R-Houston; engineer/consultant.
8. Florence Shapiro, R-Plano; company president.
9. Chris Harris, R-Arlington; attorney.
10. Kim Brimer, R-Fort Worth; businessman.
11. Mike Jackson, R-La Porte; businessman.
12. Jane Nelson, R-Lewisville; businesswoman.
13. Rodney G. Ellis, D-Houston; attorney/businessman.
14. Gonzalo Barrientos, D-Austin; advertising/ public relations.
15. John Whitmire, D-Houston; attorney (**Dean of the Senate**).
16. John J. Carona, R-Dallas; company president.
17. Kyle Janek, R-Houston; anesthesiologist.
18. Kenneth L. Armbrister, D-Victoria; businessman.
19. Frank L. Madla, D-San Antonio; real estate, insurance agent.
20. Juan "Chuy" Hinojosa, D-Mission; attorney.
21. Judith Zaffirini, D-Laredo; communications specialist.
22. Kip Averitt, R-McGregor; small business owner.
23. Royce West, D-Dallas; attorney.
24. Troy Fraser, R-Horseshoe Bay; businessman.
25. Jeff Wentworth, R-San Antonio; attorney, Realtor.
26. Leticia Van de Putte, D-San Antonio; pharmacist.
27. Eddie Lucio Jr., D-Brownsville; advertising executive.
28. Robert L. Duncan, R-Lubbock; attorney.
29. Eliot Shapleigh, D-El Paso; attorney.
30. Craig Estes, R-Wichita Falls; businessman.
31. Kel Seliger, R-Amarillo; businessman.

House of Representatives

This is a list of the 150 members of the House of Representatives in the 79th Legislature. They were elected for two-year terms from the districts shown below. Representatives and senators receive the same salary (see State Senate). The **address of all Representatives** is House of Representatives, P.O. Box 2910, Austin, 78768-2910; phone: 512-463-3000; Fax: 512-463-5896. On the Web: **www.house.state.tx.us/**

Speaker: Tom Craddick (R-Midland). **Speaker Pro Tempore**, Sylvester Turner (D-Houston). **Chief Clerk**, Robert Haney. **Sergeant-at-Arms**, Rod Welsh.

Members of Texas House of Representatives
District, Member, Party-Hometown, Occupation

1. Stephen Frost, D-New Boston, attorney.
2. Dan Flynn, R-Canton; businessman, rancher.
3. Mark Homer, D-Paris; restaurant owner.
4. Betty Brown, R-Athens; rancher.
5. Bryan Hughes, R-Marshall; attorney.
6. Leo Berman, R-Tyler; retired military officer.
7. Tommy Merritt, R-Longview; small business owner.
8. Byron Cook, R-Austin; businessman, rancher.
9. Roy Blake Jr., R-Nacogdoches; insurance agent.
10. Jim Pitts, R-Waxahachie; attorney.
11. Chuck Hopson, D-Jacksonville; pharmacist.
12. Jim McReynolds, D-Lufkin; petroleum landman.
13. Lois Kolkhorst, R-Brenham; business owner/investor.
14. Fred Brown, R-Bryan; car dealer.
15. Rob Eissler, R-Magnolia; executive recruiter.
16. Ruben Hope Jr., R-Conroe; attorney.
17. Robert "Robby" Cook, D-Eagle Lake; farmer.
18. John Otto, R-Dayton; CPA.
19. Mike "Tuffy" Hamilton, R-Mauriceville; restaurateur.
20. Dan Gattis, R-Austin; attorney, rancher.
21. Allan Ritter, D-Nederland; business owner.
22. Joe Deshotel, D-Port Arthur; attorney, contractor.
23. Craig Eiland, D-Texas City; attorney.
24. Larry Taylor, R-League City; insurance agent.
25. Dennis Bonnen, R-Angleton; insurance.
26. Charlie Howard, R-Sugar Land; Realtor, investor, rancher.
27. Dora Olivo, D-Missouri City; attorney.
28. Glenn Hegar Jr., R-Katy; farmer.
29. Glenda Dawson, R-Pearland; speaker facilitator.
30. Geanie Morrison, R-Victoria; state representative.
31. Ryan Guillen, D-San Diego; rancher, businessman.
32. Gene Seaman, R-Corpus Christi; property manager.
33. Vilma Luna, D-Corpus Christi; attorney.
34. Abel Herrero, D-Corpus Christi; attorney.
35. Yvonne Gonzalez Toureilles, D-Austin; attorney.
36. Ismael "Kino" Flores, D-Mission; businessman.
37. Rene Oliveira, D-Brownsville; attorney.
38. Jim Solis, D-Harlingen; attorney, businessman.
39. Armando Martinez, D-Weslaco; firefighter, paramedic.
40. Aaron Pena, D-Edinburg; attorney.
41. Veronica Gonzales, D-McAllen; attorney.
42. Richard Raymond, D-Laredo; consultant.
43. Juan Escobar, D-Kingsville; retired.
44. Edmund Kuempel, R-Seguin; salesman.
45. Patrick Rose, D-Austin; Realtor.
46. Dawnna Dukes, D-Austin; business consultant.
47. Terry Keel, R-Austin; attorney.
48. Todd Baxter, R-Austin; attorney.
49. Elliott Naishtat, D-Austin; attorney.
50. Mark Strama, D-Austin; technology executive.
51. Eddie Rodriguez, D-Austin; state representative.
52. Mike Krusee, R-Austin; business executive.
53. Harvey Hilderbran, R-Kerrville; businessman.
54. Suzanna Gratia Hupp, R-Lampasas; chiropractor, horse breeder.
55. Dianne White Delisi, R-Temple; self-employed.
56. Charles "Doc" Anderson, R-Waco; veterinarian.
57. Jim Dunnam, D-Waco; attorney.
58. Rob Orr, R-Burleson; real estate.
59. Sid Miller, R-Stephenville; rancher, nurseryman.
60. James Keffer, R-Eastland; president, iron company.
61. Phil King, R-Weatherford; attorney.
62. Larry Phillips, R-Sherman; attorney.
63. Mary Denny, R-Flower Mound; businesswoman.
64. Myra Crownover, R-Lake Dallas; real estate, oil.
65. Burt Solomons, R-Carrollton; attorney.
66. Brian McCall, R-Plano; businessman.
67. Jerry Madden, R-Plano; insurance executive.
68. Rick Hardcastle, R-Vernon; rancher, businessman.
69. David Farabee, D-Wichita Falls; insurance agent.
70. Ken Paxton, R-McKinney; attorney.
71. Bob Hunter, R-Abilene; university administrator.
72. Scott Campbell, R-San Angelo; businessman.
73. Carter Casteel, R-New Braunfels; state representative.
74. Pete Gallego, D-Alpine; attorney.
75. Chente Quintanilla, D-El Paso; school administrator.
76. Norma Chavez, D-El Paso; business manager.
77. Paul Moreno, D-El Paso; attorney (**Senior House Member**).
78. Pat Haggerty, R-El Paso; real-estate broker.
79. Joseph Pickett, D-El Paso; real estate.
80. Tracy King, D-Eagle Pass; hearing aid specialist.
81. G.E. "Buddy" West, R-Odessa; retired safety engineer.
82. Tom Craddick, R-Midland; sales representative (**Senior House Member**)
83. Delwin Jones, R-Lubbock; farmer, investor.
84. Carl Isett, R-Lubbock; accountant.
85. James E. "Pete" Laney, D-Hale Center; farmer.
86. John Smithee, R-Amarillo; attorney.
87. David Swinford, R-Amarillo; agricultural consultant.
88. Warren Chisum, R-Pampa; oil & gas producer, rancher.
89. Jodie Laubenberg, R-Rockwall; state representative.
90. Lon Burnam, D-Fort Worth; consultant.
91. Bob Griggs, R-North Richland Hills; consultant.
92. Todd Smith, R-Bedford; attorney.
93. Toby Goodman, R-Arlington; attorney.
94. Kent Grusendorf, R-Arlington; investments.
95. Marc Veasey, D-Fort Worth; nonprofit.
96. William "Bill" Zedler, R-Arlington; consultant.
97. Anna Mowery, R-Fort Worth; state representative.
98. Vicki Truitt, R-Southlake; health-care consultant.
99. Charlie Geren, R-River Oaks; restaurant owner, real estate broker.
100. Terri Hodge, D-Dallas; retired.
101. Elvira Reyna, R-Mesquite; state representative.
102. Tony Goolsby, R-Dallas; insurance.
103. Rafael Anchia, D-Austin; attorney.
104. Roberto Alonzo, D-Dallas; attorney.
105. Linda Harper-Brown R-Irving; CEO.
106. Ray Allen, R-Grand Prairie; businessman.
107. William Keffer, R-Dallas; attorney.
108. Dan Branch, R-Dallas; attorney.
109. Helen Giddings, D-DeSoto; small-business owner.
110. Jesse Jones, D-Dallas; professor.
111. Yvonne Davis, D-Dallas; small-business owner.
112. Fred Hill, R-Richardson; company president.
113. Joe Driver, R-Garland; insurance agent.
114. Will Hartnett, R-Dallas; attorney.
115. Jim Jackson, R-Carrollton; retired county commissioner.
116. Trey Martinez Fischer., D-San Antonio; attorney.
117. David Leibowitz, D-Austin; attorney.
118. Carlos Uresti, D-San Antonio; attorney.
119. Robert Puente, D-San Antonio; attorney.
120. Ruth Jones McClendon, D-San Antonio; business owner.
121. Joe Straus, R-Austin; insurance, investments.
122. Frank Corte Jr., R-San Antonio; real estate, property management.
123. Michael Villarreal, D-San Antonio; reporter.
124. Jose Menendez, D-San Antonio; marketing executive.
125. Joaquin Castro, D-San Antonio; attorney.
126. Peggy Hamric, R-Houston; state representative.
127. Joe Crabb, R-Kingwood; minister, attorney, rancher.
128. Wayne Smith, R-Baytown; civil engineer.
129. John Davis, R-Houston; roofing contractor.
130. Corbin Van Arsdale, R-Houston; attorney.
131. Alma Allen, D-Houston; educator.
132. William Callegari, R-Houston; engineer, investor.
133. Joseph Nixon, R-Austin; attorney.
134. Martha Wong, R-Houston; retired.
135. Gary Elkins, R-Houston; business consultant.
136. Beverly Woolley, R-Houston; small-business owner.
137. Scott Hochberg, D-Houston; software developer.
138. Dwayne Bohac, R-Houston; small-business owner.
139. Sylvester Turner, D-Houston; attorney.
140. Kevin Bailey, D-Houston; college instructor.
141. Senfronia Thompson, D-Houston; attorney.
142. Harold Dutton Jr., D-Houston; attorney.
143. Vacancy due to 5-6-2005 death of Joe Moreno, D-Houston.
144. Robert Talton, R-Pasadena; attorney.
145. Rick Noriega, D-Houston; businessman.
146. Al Edwards, D-Houston; real estate.
147. Garnet Coleman, D-Houston; business consultant.
148. Jessica Farrar, D-Houston; architect.
149. Hubert Vo, D-Austin; Realtor.
150. Debbie Riddle, R-Houston; horse breeder. ☆

Texas State Judiciary

The judiciary of the state consists of 9 members of the State Supreme Court; 9 members of the Court of Criminal Appeals; 80 of the Courts of Appeals; 425 of the State District Courts, including 10 Criminal District Courts; 485 County Court judges; 828 Justices of the Peace; and 1,371 Municipal Courts judges.

In addition to its system of formal courts, the State of Texas has established 14 **Alternative Dispute Resolution Centers**. The centers help ease the caseload of Texas courts by using mediation, arbitration, negotiation and moderated settlement conferences to handle disputes without resorting to more costly, time-consuming court actions. Centers are located in Amarillo, Austin, Beaumont, Bryan, Conroe, Corpus Christi, Dallas, El Paso, Fort Worth, Houston, Lubbock, Richmond, San Antonio and Waco. For the fiscal year ending Aug. 31, 2004, the mediation sections of the centers had closed 19,288 cases and had 4,266 cases pending.

(The list of U.S. District Courts in Texas can be found in the Federal Government section, page 485–486.)

State Higher Courts

The state's higher courts are listed below and are current as of **July 2005.** Notations in parentheses indicate dates of expiration of terms of office. Judges of the Supreme Court, Court of Criminal Appeals and Courts of Appeals are elected to 6-year, overlapping terms. District Court judges are elected to 4-year terms.

The salaries for judges as of July 2005 were as follows: Chief Justice of the Supreme Court and the Presiding Judge of the Court of Criminal Appeals: each $115,000; Justices, $113,000; Chief Justices of the Courts of Appeals, $107,850; justices, $107,350 from the state. A supplemental amount may be paid by counties, not to exceed $15,000 per year, and total salary must be at least $1,000 less than that received by Supreme Court justices. District Court judges receive $101,700 from the state, plus supplemental pay from various subdivisions. Their total salary must be $1,000 less than that received by justices of the Court of Appeals in which the district court is located.

Below is given information on only the Supreme Court, Court of Criminal Appeals and Courts of Appeals. The information was furnished by each court as of July 2005. Elsewhere in this section can be found names of county court judges by counties, names of District Court judges by district number, and the district numbers of the District Court(s) in each county.

Supreme Court

Chief Justice, Wallace B. Jefferson (12-31-06). **Associate Justices:** Scott Brister (12-31-10); Paul W. Green (12-31-10); Nathan L. Hecht (12-31-06); Phil Johnson (12-31-06); David M. Medina (12-31-06); Harriet O'Neill (12-31-10); and J. Dale Wainwright (12-31-08). One vacancy as of press time. **Clerk of Court,** C. Andrew Weber. Location of court, Austin. Web: **www.supreme.courts.state.tx.us**.

Court of Criminal Appeals

Presiding Judge, Sharon Keller (12-31-06). **Judges:** Cathy Cochran (12-31-08); Barbara P. Hervey (12-31-06); Charles R. Holcomb (12-31-06); Cheryl Johnson (12-31-10); Mike Keasler (12-31-10); Lawrence E. Myers (12-31-10); Tom Price (12-31-08); Paul Womack (12-31-08). **State's Attorney,** Matthew Paul. **Clerk of Court,** Troy C. Bennett Jr. Location of court, Austin. Web: **www.cca.courts.state.tx.us**.

Courts of Appeals

These courts have jurisdiction within their respective supreme judicial districts. A constitutional amendment approved in 1978 raised the number of associate justices for Courts of Appeals where needed. Judges are elected from the district for 6-year terms. An amendment adopted in 1980 changed the name of the old Courts of Civil Appeals to the Courts of Appeals and changed the jurisdiction of the courts. Web: **www.courts.state.tx.us/appcourt.asp**

First District — *Houston. Chief Justice, Sherry Radack (12-31-10). **Justices:** Elsa Alcala (12-31-06); Jane Bland (12-31-06); George C. Hanks Jr. (12-31-06); Laura Carter Higley (12-31-08); Terry Jennings (12-31-06); Evelyn Keyes (12-31-10); Sam Nuchia (12-31-08); and Tim G. Taft (12-31-06). **Clerk of Court,** Margie Thompson. Counties in the First District: Austin, Brazoria, Burleson, Chambers, Colorado, Fort Bend, Galveston, Grimes, Harris, Trinity, Walker, Waller, Washington.

Second District — Fort Worth: Chief Justice, John H. Cayce (12-31-06). **Justices:** Lee Ann Dauphinot (12-31-06); Anne L. Gardner (12-31-08); Dixon W. Holman (12-31-08); Terrie Livingston (12-31-08); Bob McCoy (12-31-06); and Sue Walker (12/31/06). **Clerk of Court,** Stephanie Lavake. Counties in Second District: Archer, Clay, Cooke, Denton, Hood, Jack, Montague, Parker, Tarrant, Wichita, Wise, Young.

Third District — Austin: Chief Justice, W. Kenneth Law (12-31-08). **Justices:** Jan P. Patterson (12-31-10); Bob Pemberton (12-31-10); David Puryear (12-31-10); Bea Ann Smith (12-31-06); one vacancy as of press time. **Clerk of Court,** Diane O'Neal. Counties in the Third District: Bastrop, Bell, Blanco, Burnet, Caldwell, Coke, Comal, Concho, Fayette, Hays, Irion, Lampasas, Lee, Llano, McCulloch, Milam, Mills, Runnels, San Saba, Schleicher, Sterling, Tom Green, Travis, Williamson.

Fourth District — San Antonio: Chief Justice, Alma L. Lopez (12-31-06). **Justices:** Karen Anne Angelini (12-31-06); Sarah B. Duncan (12-31-06); Sandee Bryan Marion (12-31-10); Rebecca Simmons (12-31-06); Phylis J. Speedlin (12-31-10); and Catherine M. Stone (12-31-06). **Clerk of Court,** Dan E. Crutchfield. Counties in the Fourth District: Atascosa, Bandera, Bexar, Brooks, Dimmit, Duval, Edwards, Frio, Gillespie, Guadalupe, Jim Hogg, Jim Wells, Karnes, Kendall, Kerr, Kimble, Kinney, La Salle, Mason, Maverick, McMullen, Medina, Menard, Real, Starr, Sutton, Uvalde, Val Verde, Webb, Wilson, Zapata, Zavala.

Fifth District — Dallas: Chief Justice, Linda Thomas (12-31-06). **Justices:** David L. Bridges (12-31-06); Kerry P. FitzGerald, (12-31-08); Molly Meredith Francis (12-31-04); Douglas S. Lang (11-4-03); Elizabeth Lang-Miers (12-31-11); Amos L. Mazzant (12-31-06); Joseph B. Morris (12-31-06); Jim A. Moseley (12-31-06); Michael J. O'Neill (12-31-04); Martin E. Richter (12-31-06); Mark Whittington (12-31-08); Carolyn I. Wright (12-31-08). **Clerk of Court,** Lisa Matz. Counties in the Fifth District: Collin, Dallas, Grayson, Hunt, Kaufman, Rockwall, Van Zandt.

Sixth District — Texarkana: Chief Justice, Josh R. Morris III (12-31-06). **Justices:** Jack Carter (12-31-08) and Donald R. Ross (12-31-06). **Clerk of Court,** Linda Rogers. Counties in the Sixth District: Bowie, Camp, Cass, Delta, Fannin, Franklin, Gregg, Harrison, Hopkins, Hunt, Lamar, Marion, Morris, Panola, Red River, Rusk, Titus, Upshur, Wood.

Seventh District — Amarillo: Chief Justice, Brian P. Quinn (12-31-06). **Justices:** James T. Campbell (12-31-10); Mackey Hancock (12-31-06); and Don H. Reavis (12-31-06). **Clerk of Court,** Peggy Culp. Counties in the Seventh District: Armstrong, Bailey, Briscoe, Carson, Castro, Childress, Cochran, Collingsworth, Cottle, Crosby, Dallam, Deaf Smith, Dickens, Donley, Floyd, Foard, Garza, Gray, Hale, Hall, Hansford, Hardeman, Hartley, Hemphill, Hockley, Hutchinson, Kent, King, Lamb, Lipscomb, Lubbock, Lynn, Moore, Motley, Ochiltree, Oldham, Parmer, Potter,

Randall, Roberts, Sherman, Swisher, Terry, Wheeler, Wilbarger, Yoakum.

Eighth District — El Paso: Chief Justice, Richard Barajas (12-31-08). **Justices:** Ann Crawford McClure (12-31-06); and David Wellington Chew (12-31-06). **Clerk of Court,** Denise Pacheco. Counties in the Eighth District: Andrews, Brewster, Crane, Crockett, Culberson, El Paso, Hudspeth, Jeff Davis, Loving, Pecos, Presidio, Reagan, Reeves, Terrell, Upton, Ward, Winkler.

Ninth District — Beaumont: Chief Justice, Steve McKeithen (12-31-08). **Justices:** David B. Gaultney (12-31-06); Henry Hollis Horton (12-31-06); and Charles Kreger (12-31-10). **Clerk of Court,** Carol Anne Flores. Counties in the Ninth District: Angelina, Hardin, Jasper, Jefferson, Liberty, Montgomery, Newton, Orange, Polk, San Jacinto, Tyler.

Tenth District — Waco: Chief Justice, Thomas W. Gray (12-31-06). **Justices:** Felipe Reyna (12-31-10) and Bill Vance (12-31-08). **Clerk of Court,** Sharri Roessler. Counties in the Tenth District: Bosque, Brazos, Coryell, Ellis, Falls, Freestone, Hamilton, Hill, Johnson, Leon, Limestone, Madison, McLennan, Navarro, Robertson, Somervell.

Eleventh District — Eastland: Chief Justice, William G. Arnot III (12-31-06). **Justices:** Bob Dickenson (12-31-10); Terry McCall (12-31-08); Austin McCloud (12-31-10); and Jim R. Wright (12-31-08). **Clerk of Court,** Sherry Williamson. Counties in the Eleventh District: Baylor, Borden, Brown, Callahan, Coleman, Comanche, Dawson, Eastland, Ector, Erath, Fisher, Gaines, Glasscock, Haskell, Howard, Jones, Knox, Martin, Midland, Mitchell, Nolan, Palo Pinto, Scurry, Shackelford, Stephens, Stonewall, Taylor, Throckmorton.

Twelfth District—Tyler: Chief Justice, Jim Worthen (12-31-08). **Justices:** Diane DeVasto (12-31-10) and Sam Griffith (12-31-06). **Clerk of Court,** Cathy S. Lusk. Counties in the Twelfth District: Anderson, Cherokee, Gregg, Henderson, Hopkins, Houston, Kaufman, Nacogdoches, Panola, Rains, Rusk, Sabine, San Augustine, Shelby, Smith, Upshur, Van Zandt, Wood.

Thirteenth District—Corpus Christi: Chief Justice, Rogelio Valdez (12-31-06). **Justices:** Errlinda Castillo (12-31-06); Dori Contreras Garza (12-31-08); Federico G. Hinojosa Jr. (12-31-06); Nelda V. Rodriguez (12-31-06); and Linda Reyna Yañez (12-31-10). **Clerk of court,** Cathy Wilborn. Counties in the Thirteenth District: Aransas, Bee, Calhoun, Cameron, DeWitt, Goliad, Gonzales, Hidalgo, Jackson, Kenedy, Kleberg, Lavaca, Live Oak, Matagorda, Nueces, Refugio, San Patricio, Victoria, Wharton, Willacy.

Fourteenth District—Houston†: Chief Justice, Adele Hedges (12-31-08). **Justices:** John S. Anderson (12-31-06); Richard H. Edelman (12-31-06); Wanda McKee Fowler (12-31-06); Kem Thompson Frost (12-31-08); Eva M. Guzman (12-31-10); J. Harvey Hudson (12-31-06); Charles W. Seymore (12-31-06); and Leslie Brock Yates (12-31-10). **Clerk of Court,** Ed Wells. Counties in the Fourteenth District: Austin, Brazoria, Burleson, Chambers, Colorado, Fort Bend, Galveston, Grimes, Harris, Trinity, Walker, Waller, Washington.

*The location of the First Court of Appeals was changed from Galveston to Houston by the 55th Legislature, with the provision that all cases originated in Galveston County be tried in that city and with the further provision that any case may, at the discretion of the court, be tried in either city.

†Because of the heavy workload of the Houston area Court of Appeals, the 60th Legislature, in 1967, provided for the establishment of a Fourteenth Appeals Court at Houston.

Administrative Judicial Districts of Texas

There are nine administrative judicial districts in the state for administrative purposes. An active or retired district judge or an active or retired appellate judge with judicial experience in a district court serves as the Presiding Judge upon appointment by the Governor. They receive extra compensation of $5,000 paid by counties in the respective administrative districts.

The Presiding Judge convenes an annual conference of the judges in the administrative district to consult on the state of business in the courts. This conference is empowered to adopt rules for the administration of cases in the district. The Presiding Judge may assign active or retired district judges residing within the administrative district to any of the district courts within the administrative district. The Presiding Judge of one administrative district may request the Presiding Judge of another administrative district to assign a judge from that district to sit in a district court located in the administrative district of the Presiding Judge making the request.

The Chief Justice of the Supreme Court of Texas convenes an annual conference of the nine Presiding Judges to determine the need for assignment of judges and to promote the uniform administration of the assignment of judges. The Chief Justice is empowered to assign judges of one administrative district for service in another whenever such assignments are necessary for the prompt and efficient administration of justice.

First District — John Ovard, Dallas: Anderson, Bowie, Camp, Cass, Cherokee, Collin, Dallas, Delta, Ellis, Fannin, Franklin, Grayson, Gregg, Harrison, Henderson, Hopkins, Houston, Hunt, Kaufman, Lamar, Marion, Morris, Nacogdoches, Panola, Rains, Red River, Rockwall, Rusk, Shelby, Smith, Titus, Upshur, Van Zandt and Wood.

Second District — Olen Underwood, Conroe: Angelina, Bastrop, Brazoria, Brazos, Burleson, Chambers, Fort Bend, Freestone, Galveston, Grimes, Hardin, Harris, Jasper, Jefferson, Lee, Leon, Liberty, Limestone, Madison, Matagorda, Montgomery, Newton, Orange, Polk, Robertson, Sabine, San Augustine, San Jacinto, Trinity, Tyler, Walker, Waller, Washington and Wharton.

Third District — B.B. Schraub, Seguin: Austin, Bell, Blanco, Bosque, Burnet, Caldwell, Colorado, Comal, Comanche, Coryell, Falls, Fayette, Gonzales, Guadalupe, Hamilton, Hays, Hill, Johnson, Lampasas, Lavaca, Llano, McLennan, Mason, Milam, Navarro, San Saba, Travis and Williamson.

Fourth District — David Peeples, San Antonio: Aransas, Atascosa, Bee, Bexar, Calhoun, DeWitt, Dimmit, Frio, Goliad, Jackson, Karnes, LaSalle, Live Oak, Maverick, McMullen, Refugio, San Patricio, Victoria, Webb, Wilson, Zapata and Zavala.

Fifth District — Darrell Hester, Brownsville: Brooks, Cameron, Duval, Hidalgo, Jim Hogg, Jim Wells, Kenedy, Kleberg, Nueces, Starr and Willacy.

Sixth District — Stephen B. Ables, Kerrville: Bandera, Brewster, Crockett, Culberson, Edwards, El Paso, Gillespie, Hudspeth, Jeff Davis, Kendall, Kerr, Kimble, Kinney, Mason, Medina, Pecos, Presidio, Reagan, Real, Sutton, Terrell, Upton, Uvalde and Val Verde.

Seventh District — Dean Rucker, Midland: Andrews, Borden, Brown, Callahan, Coke, Coleman, Concho, Crane, Dawson, Ector, Fisher, Gaines, Garza, Glasscock, Haskell, Howard, Irion, Jones, Kent, Loving, Lynn, Martin, McCulloch, Menard, Midland, Mills, Mitchell, Nolan, Reeves, Runnels, Schleicher, Scurry, Shackelford, Sterling, Stonewall, Taylor, Throckmorton, Tom Green, Ward and Winkler.

Eighth District — Roger Jeffrey "Jeff" Walker, Fort Worth: Archer, Clay, Cooke, Denton, Eastland, Erath, Hood, Jack, Johnson, Montague, Palo Pinto, Parker, Somervell, Stephens, Tarrant, Wichita, Wise and Young.

Ninth District — Kelly G. Moore, Brownfield: Armstrong, Bailey, Baylor, Briscoe, Carson, Castro, Childress, Cochran, Collingsworth, Cottle, Crosby, Dallam, Deaf Smith, Dickens, Donley, Floyd, Foard, Gray, Hale, Hall, Hansford, Hardeman, Hartley, Hemphill, Hockley, Hutchinson, King, Knox, Lamb, Lipscomb, Lubbock, Moore, Motley, Ochiltree, Oldham, Parmer, Potter, Randall, Roberts, Sherman, Swisher, Terry, Wheeler, Wilbarger and Yoakum. ☆

Texas Courts by County

Below are listed the state district court or courts, court of appeals district, administrative judicial district and U.S. judicial district for each county in Texas as of July 2005. For the names of the district court judges, see table by district number on pages 429–430. For the names of other judges in the Texas court system, see listing on pages 425–426.

County	State Dist. Court(s)	Ct. of App'ls Dist.	Adm. Jud. Dist.	U.S. Jud. Dist.
Anderson	3, 87, 349, 369	12	1	E-Tyler
Andrews	109	8	7	W-Midland
Angelina	159, 217	9	2	E-Lufkin
Aransas	36, 156, 343	13	4	S-C.Christi
Archer	97	2	8	N-W. Falls
Armstrong	47	7	9	N-Amarilllo
Atascosa	81, 218	4	4	W-San Ant.
Austin	155	1, 14	3	S-Houston
Bailey	287	7	9	N-Lubbock
Bandera	216	4	6	W-San Ant.
Bastrop	21, 335	3	2	W-Austin
Baylor	50	11	9	N-W. Falls
Bee	36, 156, 343	13	4	S-C.Christi
Bell	27, 146, 169, 264	3	3	W-Waco
Bexar	37, 45, 57, 73, 131, 144, 150, 166, 175, 186, 187, 224, 225, 226, 227, 285, 288, 289, 290, 379, 386, 399, 407,408	4	4	W-San Ant.
Blanco	33	3	3	W-Austin
Borden	132	11	7	N-Lubbock
Bosque	220	10	3	W-Waco
Bowie	5, 102, 202	6	1	E-Texark.
Brazoria	23, 149, 239, 300	1, 14	2	S-Galves.
Brazos	85, 272, 361	1, 10, 14	2	S-Houston
Brewster	394	8	6	W-Pecos
Briscoe	110	7	9	N-Amarilllo
Brooks	79	4	5	S-C.Christi
Brown	35	11	7	N-S. Ang.
Burleson	21, 335	1, 14	2	W-Austin
Burnet	33	3	3	W-Austin
Caldwell	22, 207, 274	3	3	W-Austin
Calhoun	24, 135, 267	13	4	S-Victoria
Callahan	42	11	7	N-Abilene
Cameron	103, 107, 138, 197, 357, 404	13	5	S-Brownsville
Camp	76, 276	6	1	E-Marshall
Carson	100	7	9	N-Amarilllo
Cass	5	6	1	E-Marshall
Castro	64, 242	7	9	N-Amarilllo
Chambers	253, 344	1, 14	2	S-Galves.
Cherokee	2, 369	12	1	E-Tyler
Childress	100	7	9	N-Amarilllo
Clay	97	2	8	N-W. Falls
Cochran	286	7	9	N-Lubbock
Coke	51	3	7	N-S. Ang.
Coleman	42	11	7	N-S. Ang.
Collin	199, 219, 296, 366, 380, 401	5	1	E-Sherman
Collingsworth	100	7	9	N-Amarilllo
Colorado	25, 2nd 25	1, 14	3	S-Houston
Comal	22, 207, 274	3	3	W-San Ant.
Comanche	220	11	3	N-Ft. Worth
Concho	119	3	7	N-S. Ang.
Cooke	235	2	8	E-Sherman
Coryell	52	10	3	W-Waco
Cottle	50	7	9	N-W. Falls
Crane	109	8	7	W-Midland
Crockett	112	8	6	N-S. Ang.
Crosby	72	7	9	N-Lubbock
Culberson	205, 394	8	6	W-Pecos
Dallam	69	7	9	N-Amarilllo
Dallas	14, 44, 68, 95, 101, 116, 134, 160, 162, 191, 192, 193, 194,195, 203, 204, 254, 255, 256, 265, 282, 283, 291, 292, 298, 301, 302, 303, 304, 305, 330, 363, Cr.1, Cr2, Cr.3, Cr.4, Cr.5	5	1	N-Dallas
Dawson	106	11	7	N-Lubbock
Deaf Smith	222	7	9	N-Amarilllo
Delta	8, 62	6	1	E-Paris
Denton	16, 158, 211, 362, 367, 393	2	8	E-Sherman
DeWitt	24, 135, 267	13	4	S-Victoria
Dickens	110	7	9	N-Lubbock
Dimmit	293, 365	4	4	W-San Ant.
Donley	100	7	9	N-Amarilllo
Duval	229	4	5	S-C.Christi
Eastland	91	11	8	N-Abilene
Ector	70, 161, 244, 358	8	7	W-Midland
Edwards	63	4	6	W-Del Rio
Ellis	40, 378	10	1	N-Dallas
El Paso	34, 41, 65, 120, 168, 171, 205, 210, 243, 327, 346, 383, 384, 388, 409	8	6	W-El Paso
Erath	266	11	8	N-Ft. Worth
Falls	82	10	3	W-Waco
Fannin	6, 336	6	1	E-Paris
Fayette	155	3	3	S-Houston
Fisher	32	11	7	N-Abilene
Floyd	110	7	9	N-Lubbock
Foard	46	7	9	N-W. Falls
Fort Bend	240, 268, 328, 387, 400	1, 14	2	S-Houston
Franklin	8, 62	6	1	E-Texark.
Freestone	77, 87	10	2	W-Waco
Frio	81, 218	4	4	W-San Ant.
Gaines	106	8	7	N-Lubbock
Galveston	10, 56, 122, 212, 306, 405	1, 14	2	S-Galves.
Garza	106	7	7	N-Lubbock
Gillespie	216	4	6	W-Austin
Glasscock	118	8	7	N-S. Ang.
Goliad	24, 135, 267	13	4	S-Victoria
Gonzales	25, 2nd 25	13	3	W-San Ant.
Gray	31, 223	7	9	N-Amarilllo
Grayson	15, 59, 336	5	1	E-Sherman
Gregg	124, 188, 307	6, 12	1	E-Tyler
Grimes	12, 278	1, 14	2	S-Houston
Guadalupe	25, 2nd 25, 274	4	3	W-San Ant.
Hale	64, 242	7	9	N-Lubbock
Hall	100	7	9	N-Amarilllo
Hamilton	220	10	3	W-Waco
Hansford	84	7	9	N-Amarilllo
Hardeman	46	7	9	N-W. Falls
Hardin	88, 356	9	2	E-B'mont.
Harris	11, 55, 61, 80, 113, 125, 127, 129, 133, 151, 152, 157, 164, 165, 174, 176, 177, 178, 179, 180, 182, 183, 184, 185, 189, 190, 208, 209, 215, 228, 230, 232, 234, 245, 246, 247, 248, 257, 262, 263, 269, 270, 280, 281, 295, 308, 309, 310, 311, 312, 313, 314, 315, 333, 334, 337, 338, 339, 351	1, 14	2	S-Houston
Harrison	71	6	1	E-Marshall
Hartley	69	7	9	N-Amarilllo
Haskell	39	11	7	N-Abilene
Hays	22, 207, 274	3	3	W-Austin
Hemphill	31	7	9	N-Amarilllo
Henderson	3, 173, 392	12	1	E-Tyler
Hidalgo	92, 93, 139, 206, 275, 332, 370, 389, 398	13	5	S-McAllen
Hill	66	10	3	W-Waco
Hockley	286	7	9	N-Lubbock
Hood	355	2	8	N-Ft. Worth
Hopkins	8, 62	6, 12	1	E-Paris
Houston	3, 349	12	1	E-Lufkin

County	State Dist. Court(s)	Ct. of App'ls Dist.	Adm. Jud. Dist.	U.S. Jud. Dist.
Howard	118	11	7	N-Abilene
Hudspeth	205, 394	8	6	W-Pecos
Hunt	196, 354	5, 6	1	N-Dallas
Hutchinson	84, 316	7	9	N-Amarilllo
Irion	51	3	7	N-S. Ang.
Jack	271	2	8	N-Ft. Worth
Jackson	24, 135, 267	13	4	S-Victoria
Jasper	1, 1A	9	2	E-B'mont.
Jeff Davis	394	8	6	W-Pecos
Jefferson	58, 60, 136, 172, 252, 279, 317, Cr.	9	2	E-B'mont.
Jim Hogg	229	4	5	S-Laredo
Jim Wells	79	4	5	S-C.Christi
Johnson	18, 249	10	3	N-Dallas
Jones	259	11	7	N-Abilene
Karnes	81, 218	4	4	W-San Ant.
Kaufman	86	5, 12	1	N-Dallas
Kendall	216	4	6	W-San Ant.
Kenedy	105	13	5	S-C.Christi
Kent	39	7	7	N-Lubbock
Kerr	198, 216	4	6	W-San Ant.
Kimble	198	4	6	W-Austin
King	50	7	9	N-W. Falls
Kinney	63	4	6	W-Del Rio
Kleberg	105	13	5	S-C.Christi
Knox	50	11	9	N-W. Falls
Lamar	6, 62	6	1	E-Paris
Lamb	154	7	9	N-Lubbock
Lampasas	27	3	3	W-Austin
La Salle	81, 218	4	4	S-Laredo
Lavaca	25, 2nd 25	13	3	S-Victoria
Lee	21, 335	3	2	W-Austin
Leon	12, 87, 278	10	2	W-Waco
Liberty	75, 253	9	2	E-B'mont.
Limestone	77, 87	10	2	W-Waco
Lipscomb	31	7	9	N-Amarilllo
Live Oak	36, 156, 343	13	4	S-C.Christi
Llano	33	3	3	W-Austin
Loving	143	8	7	W-Pecos
Lubbock	72, 99, 137, 140, 237, 364	7	9	N-Lubbock
Lynn	106	7	7	N-Lubbock
Madison	12, 278	10	2	S-Houston
Marion	115, 276	6	1	E-Marshall
Martin	118	8	7	W-Midland
Mason	198	4	6	W-Austin
Matagorda	23, 130	13	2	S-Galves.
Maverick	293, 365	4	4	W-Del Rio
McCulloch	198	3	7	W-Austin
McLennan	19, 54, 74, 170	10	3	W-Waco
McMullen	36, 156, 343	4	4	S-Laredo
Medina	38	4	6	W-San Ant.
Menard	198	4	7	N-S. Ang.
Midland	142, 238, 318, 385	8	7	W-Midland
Milam	20	3	3	W-Waco
Mills	35	3	7	N-S. Ang.
Mitchell	32	11	7	N-Abilene
Montague	97	2	8	N-W. Falls
Montgomery	9, 221, 284, 359, 410	9	2	S-Houston
Moore	69	7	9	N-Amarilllo
Morris	76, 276	6	1	E-Marshall
Motley	110	7	9	N-Lubbock
Nacogdoches	145	12	1	E-Lufkin
Navarro	13	10	3	N-Dallas
Newton	1, 1A	9	2	E-B'mont.
Nolan	32	11	7	N-Abilene
Nueces	28, 94, 105, 117, 148, 214, 319, 347	13	5	S-C.Christi
Ochiltree	84	7	9	N-Amarilllo
Oldham	222	7	9	N-Amarilllo
Orange	128, 163, 260	9	2	E-B'mont.
Palo Pinto	29	11	8	N-Ft. Worth
Panola	123	6, 12	1	E-Tyler
Parker	43	2	8	N-Ft. Worth
Parmer	287	7	9	N-Amarilllo
Pecos	83, 112	8	6	W-Pecos
Polk	258, 411	9	2	E-Lufkin

County	State Dist. Court(s)	Ct. of App'ls Dist.	Adm. Jud. Dist.	U.S. Jud. Dist.
Potter	47, 108, 181, 251, 320	7	9	N-Amarilllo
Presidio	394	8	6	W-Pecos
Rains	8, 354	12	1	E-Tyler
Randall	47, 181, 251	7	9	N-Amarilllo
Reagan	83, 112	8	6	N-S. Ang.
Real	38	4	6	W-San Ant.
Red River	6, 102	6	1	E-Paris
Reeves	143	8	7	W-Pecos
Refugio	24, 135, 267	13	4	S-Victoria
Roberts	31	7	9	N-Amarilllo
Robertson	82	10	2	W-Waco
Rockwall	382	5	1	N-Dallas
Runnels	119	3	7	N-S. Ang.
Rusk	4	6, 12	1	E-Tyler
Sabine	1, 273	12	2	E-Lufkin
San Augustine	1, 273	12	2	E-Lufkin
San Jacinto	258, 411	9	2	S-Houston
San Patricio	36, 156, 343	13	4	S-C.Christi
San Saba	33	3	3	W-Austin
Schleicher	51	3	7	N-S. Ang.
Scurry	132	11	7	N-Lubbock
Shackelford	259	11	7	N-Abilene
Shelby	123, 273	12	1	E-Lufkin
Sherman	69	7	9	N-Amarilllo
Smith	7, 114, 241, 321	12	1	E-Tyler
Somervell	18, 249	10	3	W-Waco
Starr	229, 381	4	5	S-McAllen
Stephens	90	11	8	N-Abilene
Sterling	51	3	7	N-S. Ang.
Stonewall	39	11	7	N-Abilene
Sutton	112	4	6	N-S. Ang.
Swisher	64, 242	7	9	N-Amarilllo
Tarrant	17, 48, 67, 96, 141, 153, 213, 231, 233, 236, 297, 322, 323, 324, 325, 342, 348, 352, 360, 371, 372, 396, Cr.1, Cr.2, Cr.3, Cr.4	2	8	N-Ft. Worth
Taylor	42, 104, 326, 350	11	7	N-Abilene
Terrell	63, 83	8	6	W-Del Rio
Terry	121	7	9	N-Lubbock
Throckmorton	39	11	7	N-Abilene
Titus	76, 276	6	1	E-Texark.
Tom Green	51, 119, 340, 391	3	7	N-S. Ang.
Travis	53, 98, 126, 147, 167, 200, 201, 250, 261, 299, 331, 345, 353, 390, 403	3	3	W-Austin
Trinity	258, 411	1, 14	2	E-Lufkin
Tyler	1A, 88	9	2	E-Lufkin
Upshur	115	6, 12	1	E-Marshall
Upton	83, 112	8	6	W-Midland
Uvalde	38	4	6	W-Del Rio
Val Verde	63, 83	4	6	W-Del Rio
Van Zandt	294	5, 12	1	E-Tyler
Victoria	24, 135, 267, 377	13	4	S-Victoria
Walker	12, 278	1, 14	2	S-Houston
Waller	9, 155	1, 14	2	S-Houston
Ward	143	8	7	W-Pecos
Washington	21, 335	1, 14	2	W-Austin
Webb	49, 111, 341, 406	4	4	S-Laredo
Wharton	23, 329	13	2	S-Houston
Wheeler	31	7	9	N-Amarilllo
Wichita	30, 78, 89	2	8	N-W. Falls
Wilbarger	46	7	9	N-W. Falls
Willacy	103, 107, 138, 197, 357	13	5	S-Browns-ville
Williamson	26, 277, 368, 395	3	3	W-Austin
Wilson	81, 218	4	4	W-San Ant.
Winkler	109	8	7	W-Pecos
Wise	271	2	8	N-Ft. Worth
Wood	402	6, 12	1	E-Tyler
Yoakum	121	7	9	N-Lubbock
Young	90	2	8	N-W. Falls
Zapata	49	4	4	S-Laredo
Zavala	293, 365	4	4	W-Del Rio

District Judges in Texas

Below are the names of all district judges, as of July 2005, in Texas listed in district court order. To determine which judges have jurisdiction in specific counties, refer to the table on pages 427–428.

Source: Texas Judicial System Directory 2005, Office of Court Administration.

Court	Judge
1	Joe Bob Golden
1A	Monte D. Lawlis
2	Dwight L. Phifer
3	James N. Parsons III
4	J. Clay Gossett
5	Ralph K. Burgess
6	Jim D. Lovett
7	Kerry L. Russell
8	Robert E. Newsom
9	Frederick E. Edwards
10	David Edward Garner
11	Mark Davidson
12	William Lee McAdams
13	John Howard Jackson
14	Mary L. Murphy
15	Jim Fallon
16	Carmen Rivera-Worley
17	Fred Wallis Davis
18	John Edward Neill
19	Ralph T. Strother
20	Ed Magre
21	Terry Flenniken
22	Charles R. Ramsay
23	Ben Hardin
24	Joseph Patrick Kelly
25	Dwight E. Peschel
25A	William C. Kirkendall
26	Billy Ray Stubblefield
27	Joe Carroll
28	Nanette Hasette
29	Jerry D. Ray
30	Robert P. Brotherton
31	Steven R. Emmert
32	Glen N. Harrison
33	Guilford L. "Gil" Jones
34	William E. Moody
35	William Stephen Ellis
36	Mike E. Welborn
37	David A. Berchelmann Jr.
38	Mickey Ray Pennington
39	Charles Lewis Chapman
40	Gene Knize
41	Mary Anne Bramblett
42	John Wilson Weeks
43	Don M. Chrestman
44	David D. Kelton
45	Barbara Hanson Nellermoe
46	Tom A. Neely
47	Hal Miner
48	David Lettimore Evans
49	Manuel R. Flores
50	W.H. "Bill" Heatly
51	Barbara Lane Walther
52	Phillip H. Zeigler
53	Scott H. Jenkins
54	George H. Allen
55	Jeffrey V. Brown
56	Lonnie Cox
57	Joe F. Brown
58	James William Mehaffy Jr.
59	Rayburn M. "Rim" Nall Jr.
60	James Gary Sanderson
61	John Donovan
62	Robert Scott McDowell
63	Thomas F. Lee
64	Robert W. Kinkaid Jr.
65	Alfredo Chavez
66	F.B. "Bob" McGregor Jr.
67	Donald Cosby

Court	Judge
68	Charles Stokes
69	Ronald E. Enns
70	Jay Gibson
71	Bonnie Leggat
72	J. Blair Cherry Jr.
73	Andy Mireles
74	Alan M. Mayfield
75	C.T. Hight
76	Jimmy L. White
77	Horace Dickson Black Jr.
78	Roy T. Sparkman
79	Richard Terrell
80	Kent C. Sullivan
81	Donna Rayes
82	Robert Miller Stem
83	Carl Pendergrass
84	William D. Smith
85	J.D. Langley
86	Howard Tygrett
87	Deborah Oakes Evans
88	Earl Stover III
89	Mark Price
90	Stephen O'Neal Crawford
91	Steven R. Herod
92	Horacio Pena Jr.
93	Rodolfo "Rudy" Delgado
94	Jack E. Hunter
95	Karen Johnson
96	Roger Jeffrey "Jeff" Walker
97	Roger E. Towery
98	W. Jeanne Meurer
99	Mackey K. Hancock
100	David M. McCoy
101	Jay Patterson
102	John F. Miller Jr.
103	Menton Murray Jr.
104	Lee Hamilton
105	J. Manuel Banales
106	Carter Tinsley Schildknecht
107	Benjamin Euresti Jr.
108	Abe Lopez
109	James L. Rex
110	John Randy Hollums
111	Raul Vasquez
112	Brock Jones Jr.
113	Patricia Hancock
114	Cynthia Stevens Kent
115	Lauren L. Parish
116	Robert Henry Frost
117	Sandra Watts
118	Robert H. Moore III
119	Garland Benton Woodward
120	Luis Aguilar
121	Kelly Glen Moore
122	John Ellisor
123	Guy William Griffin
124	Alvin G. Khoury
125	John A. Coselli
126	Darlene Byrne
127	Sharolyn P. Wood
128	Patrick A. Clark
129	S. Grant Dorfman
130	Craig Estlinbaum
131	John D. Gabriel Jr.
132	Ernie B. Armstrong
133	Lamar McCorkle
134	Anne Ashby
135	Kemper Stephen Williams
136	Milton Gunn Shuffield
137	Cecil G. Puryear

Court	Judge
138	Robert Garza
139	Bobby Flores
140	Jim Bob Darnell
141	Len Wade
142	George David Gilles
143	Bob Parks
144	Mark Randal Luitjen
145	Campbell Cox II
146	Jack Richard Morris
147	Wilford Flowers
148	Rose Vela
149	Robert E. May
150	Janet P. Littlejohn
151	Caroline E. Baker
152	Kenneth Price Wise
153	Kenneth Charles Curry
154	Felix Klein
155	Dan Raymond Beck
156	Joel B. Johnson
157	Randall W. Wilson
158	Jake Collier
159	Paul E. White
160	Joseph M. Cox
161	Tryon D. Lewis
162	Lorraine Raggio
163	Dennis Powell
164	Martha Hill Jamison
165	Elizabeth Ray
166	Martha B. Tanner
167	Mike F. Lynch
168	Guadalupe Rivera
169	Gordon G. Adams
170	Jim Meyer
171	Bonnie Rangel
172	Donald J. Floyd
173	Willis Daniel Moore
174	George H. Godwin
175	Mary D. Roman
176	James Brian Rains
177	Devon Anderson
178	William T. Harmon
179	J. Michael Wilkinson
180	Debbie Mantooth-Stricklin
181	John B. Board
182	Jeannie S. Barr
183	Joan Huffman
184	Jan Krocker
185	Susan Brown
186	Maria Teresa Herr
187	Raymond C. Angelini
188	David Brabham
189	William R. Burke Jr.
190	Jennifer Walker Elrod
191	Catharina Haynes
192	Merrill L. Hartman
193	David W. Evans
194	Mary E. Miller
195	John Runnels Nelms
196	Joe M. Leonard
197	Migdalia Lopez
198	Emil Karl Prohl
199	Robert T. Dry Jr.
200	Gisela Triana
201	Suzanne Covington
202	Leon F. Pesek Jr.
203	Lana Rolf McDaniel
204	Mark Nancarrow
205	Kathleen H. Olivares
206	Rose Guerra Reyna

Court	Judge
207	Jack Hollis Robison
208	Denise Collins
209	Michael Thomas McSpadden
210	Gonzalo Garcia
211	Lawrence Dee Shipman
212	Susan Criss
213	Robert Keith Gill
214	Jose Longoria
215	Levi James Benton
216	Stephen B. Ables
217	David V. Wilson
218	Stella H. Saxon
219	Curt B. Henderson
220	James Edward Morgan
221	Suzanne Stovall
222	Roland Saul
223	Leland W. Waters
224	O. Rene Diaz
225	John J. Specia Jr.
226	Sid L. Harle
227	Philip A. Kazen Jr.
228	Marc C. Carter
229	Alex W. Gabert
230	Belinda Hill
231	Randy Catterton
232	Mary Lou Keel
233	William W. Harris
234	Mauricio "Reece" Rondon
235	Janelle M. Haverkamp
236	Thomas Wilson Lowe III
237	Sam Medina
238	John Gary Hyde
239	Patrick "Pat" Sebesta
240	Thomas R. Culver III
241	Jack M. Skeen Jr.
242	Edward L. Self
243	David C. Guaderrama
244	William Stacy Trotter
245	Annette Galik
246	Jim York
247	Bonnie Crane Hellums
248	Joan Campbell
249	D. Wayne Bridewell
250	John K. Dietz
251	Pat Pirtle
252	Layne Walker
253	Chap Cain III
254	Jeffrey V. Coen
255	Craig Fowler
256	Brenda Garrett Green
257	Linda Motheral
258	Elizabeth E. Coker
259	Brooks H. Hagler
260	Buddie J. Hahn
261	Lora J. Livingston
262	Mike Anderson
263	Jim Wallace
264	Martha Jane Trudo
265	Keith Dean
266	Donald Richard Jones
267	Juergen "Skipper" Koetter
268	Brady Gifford Elliott
269	John T. Wooldridge
270	Brent Gamble
271	John H. Fostel
272	Richard Davis
273	Charles R. Mitchell
274	Gary L. Steel
275	Juan R. Partida
276	William R. "Bill" Porter
277	Ken Anderson
278	Kenneth H. Keeling
279	Thomas Francis Mulvaney

Court	Judge
280	Tony Lindsay
281	David Jorge Bernal
282	Karen Jane Greene
283	Vickers L. Cunningham Jr.
284	Olen Underwood
285	Michael Peden
286	Harold Phelan
287	Gordon Houston Green
288	Lori C. Massey
289	Carmen Kelsey
290	Sharon MacRae
291	Susan Hawk
292	Henry Wade Jr.
293	Cynthia L. Muniz
294	Teresa Drum
295	Tracy E. Christopher
296	Betty Ann Caton
297	Everett Young
298	Adolph Canales
299	Jon Neil Wisser
300	K. Randall Hufstetler
301	Susan Amanda Rankin
302	Frances A. Harris
303	Dennise Garcia
304	John Sholden
305	Cheryl Lee Shannon
306	Janis L. Yarbrough
307	Robin D. Sage
308	Georgia Dempster
309	Frank Rynd
310	Lisa Millard
311	Doug Warne
312	James D. Squier
313	Pat Shelton
314	John F. Phillips
315	Kent Ellis
316	John La Grone
317	Larry Thorne
318	Dean Rucker
319	Thomas F. Greenwell
320	Don Emerson
321	Carole W. Clark
322	Frank W. Sullivan
323	Jean Hudson Boyd
324	Brian A. Carper
325	Judith G. Wells
326	Aleta Hacker
327	Linda Chew
328	Ronald R. Pope
329	Daniel Richard Sklar
330	Marilea Whatley Lewis
331	Robert A. Perkins
332	Mario E. Ramirez Jr.
333	Joseph James Halbach Jr.
334	Sharon McCally
335	Reva Townslee Corbett
336	Lauri Blake
337	Don R. Stricklin
338	Tommy Brock Thomas Jr.
339	Caprice Cosper
340	Jay Weatherby
341	Elma Salinas Ender
342	Bob McGrath
343	Janna K. Whatley
344	Carroll E. Wilborn Jr.
345	Stephen Yelenosky
346	Angie Juarez Barill
347	Nelva Gonzales-Ramos
348	Dana M. Womack
349	Pamela Fletcher
350	Thomas Wheeler
351	Mark Kent Ellis
352	Bonnie Sudderth
353	Margaret A. Cooper

Court	Judge
354	Richard "Rick" Beacom
355	Ralph H. Walton Jr.
356	Britton Edward Plunk
357	Leonel Alejandro
358	Bill McCoy
359	Kathleen A. Hamilton
360	Debra Lehrmann
361	Steve Lee Smith
362	Bruce McFarling
363	Faith Johnson
364	Bradley S. Underwood
365	Amado Abascal III
366	Nathan E. White Jr.
367	E. Lee Gabriel
368	Alfred Burton "Burt" Carnes
369	Bascom W. Bentley III
370	Noe Gonzalez
371	James R. Wilson
372	Scott Wisch
377	Robert C. Cheshire
378	Roy A. Scoggins Jr.
379	Robert C. "Bert" Richardson
380	Charles F. Sandoval
381	John A. Pope III
382	Brett Hall
383	Mike Herrera
384	Patrick Michael Garcia
385	Robin Malone Darr
386	Laura Lee Parker
387	Robert J. Kern
388	Patricia A. Macias
389	Leticia Lopez
390	Julie Harris Kocurek
391	Thomas J. Gossett
392	Carter William Tarrance
393	Vicki B. Isaacks
394	Kenneth Daly DeHart
395	Michael P. Jergins
396	George W. Gallagher
398	Aida Salinas Flores
399	Juanita A. Vasquez-Gardner
400	Clifford James Vacek
401	Mark Joseph Rusch
402	George Timothy Boswell
403	Brenda P. Kennedy
404	Abel C. Limas
405	Wayne Mallia
406	Oscar "O.J." Hale Jr.
407	Karen Pozza
408	position vacant
409	Sam Medrano
410	K. Michael Mayes
411	Robert Hill Trapp
413	William C. Bosworth
415	Graham Quisenberry
416	John Christopher Oldner
417	Cynthia McCrann Wheless
420	Edwin Allen Klein
421	Todd A. Blomerth
422	B. Michael Chitty

Criminal District Courts

Court	Judge
Dallas 1	Janice Lough Warder
Dallas 2	Don Adams
Dallas 3	Robert Francis
Dallas 4	John Coleman Creuzot
Dallas 5	Manny D. Alvarez
Jefferson	Charles Dana Carver
Tarrant 1	Sharen Wilson
Tarrant 2	Wayne Francis Salvant
Tarrant 3	Elizabeth Berry
Tarrant 4	Mike Thomas

Texas State Agencies

On the following pages is information about several of the many state agencies. The agencies themselves supplied this information to the *Texas Almanac*. The Web address for more information about state agencies, boards and commissions is: **www2.tsl.state.tx.us/trail/agencies.jsp.**

Texas Commission on Environmental Quality

Source: Texas Commission on Environmental Quality; www.tceq.state.tx.us

The Texas Commission on Environmental Quality (TCEQ) is the state's leading environmental agency. Known as the Texas Natural Resource Conservation Commission until September 2002, this agency works to protect Texas' human and natural resources in a manner consistent with sustainable economic development. The goals are clean air, clean water and the safe management of waste, with an emphasis on pollution prevention.

The TCEQ has about 3,000 employees; of those, about 1,000 work in the 16 regional offices. The operating budget for the 2004 fiscal year was $464.4 million, of which 80 percent was generated by fees. The remaining revenues came from federal funds, 10 percent; state general revenue, 6 percent; and other sources, 4 percent.

TCEQ employee Andrew Tachovsky takes soil samples at Barton Creek near Austin. File photo.

One of the TCEQ's major functions is issuing permits and other authorizations for controlling air pollution, the safe operation of water and wastewater utilities, and the management of hazardous and non-hazardous waste. More than 8,000 environmental permit applications are received annually.

The agency promotes voluntary compliance of environmental laws through pollution prevention programs, regulatory workshops, and assistance to businesses and local governments. But when environmental laws are violated, the TCEQ has the authority to levy penalties— as much as $10,000 a day per violation for administrative cases and $25,000 a day per violation in civil judicial cases. In a typical year, the agency investigates more than 70,000 regulated entities for compliance with state and federal laws, and it responds to 5,000 to 6,000 environmental complaints. In 2004, the TCEQ issued 761 administrative orders, which yielded $5.6 million in fines and directed another $2.4 million to supplemental environmental projects benefiting some communities in which the environmental violations occurred.

Air Quality

Texas is home to some of the largest U.S. cities and, therefore, faces air quality challenges that are among the most difficult in the country. The state has a fast-growing population and a large industrial base, especially along the Gulf Coast. The TCEQ has worked with the U.S. Environmental Protection Agency and local municipalities to craft a state implementation plan to bring metropolitan areas into compliance with federal ozone standards. The leading areas of concern are Houston, Dallas-Fort Worth and Beaumont-Port Arthur. Several other metropolitan areas have entered into voluntary compacts to institute programs to reduce emissions.

Water Quality

Surface water bodies in Texas are routinely monitored to determine whether they support their designated uses. The TCEQ coordinates a comprehensive sampling program to collect water quality data. The agency also conducts special studies to determine sources of pollution and the appropriateness of water quality standards. The TCEQ also is responsible for most of the state and federal regulatory programs that protect groundwater and for state and federal storm water permits. It is the primary Texas agency authorized to enforce the federal Safe Drinking Water Act and administers the supervision program for the state's 6,660 public water systems.

Waste Management

Waste management projects at the TCEQ include Superfund projects, pesticide collections and waste tire recycling. In 2004, there were 87 sites in the state and federal Superfund programs. Another major clean-up program focuses on leaking petroleum storage tanks. From 1987 to 2004, more than 19,000 such sites were corrected, and work continues at another 4,400 sites. The TCEQ also permits municipal landfill operations and monitors landfill capacity on a regional basis.

Pollution Prevention

TCEQ offers services to anyone interested in environmental stewardship. Staff members host workshops on recycling and disposal opportunities, and on regulatory and pollution prevention topics. They also offers free on-site technical assistance for regulatory compliance. Contact TCEQ at PO Box 13087, Austin TX 78711; phone: 512-239-1000; www.tceq.state.tx.us. ☆

Texas Historical Commission

Source: Texas Historical Commission; www.thc.state.tx.us

The Texas Historical Commission protects and preserves the state's historic and prehistoric resources. The Texas State Legislature established the Texas State Historical Survey Committee in 1953 to identify important historic sites across the state.

The Texas Legislature changed the agency's name to the Texas Historical Commission in 1973 and increased its mission and its protective powers. Today the agency's concerns include archaeology, architecture, history, economic development, heritage tourism, public administration and urban planning.

Among its many tasks, the commission:

• Provides leadership, training and preservation planning through its Visionaries in Preservation Program for county historical commissions, heritage organizations and museums in Texas' 254 counties;

The Historical Commission's Historic Courthouse Preservation Program helps restore Texas courthouses, such as the Shackelford County Courthouse. This courthouse was built in 1884 and is part of the preservation program. Texas Almanac photo.

• Assists citizens in obtaining historical designations for buildings, cemeteries, sites and other properties important to the state's historic and prehistoric past;

• Works with communities to help protect Texas' diverse architectural heritage, including historic county courthouses and other public buildings;

• Administers the state's historical marker program. There are more than 11,000 historical markers across Texas;

• Assists Texas cities in the revitalization of their historic downtowns through the Texas Main Street Program;

• Promotes travel to historic and cultural sites though its award-winning Texas Heritage Trails Program;

• Works with property owners to save archaeological sites on private land;

• Ensures that archaeological sites are protected when land is developed for highways and other public projects.

Mailing address: PO Box 12276, Austin 78711-2276; phone: 512-463-6100; fax: 512-475-4872; www.thc.state.tx.us. ☆

The Texas Historical Commission's marker program began in 1936 when the Texas Centennial Commission placed hundreds of markers and monuments throughout Texas to commemorate the 100th anniversary of the Texas Revolution. The current program is used to preserve the heritage of Texas by marking historical homes, public buildings, religious congregations, military sites and places where historic events occurred. Texas Almanac photo.

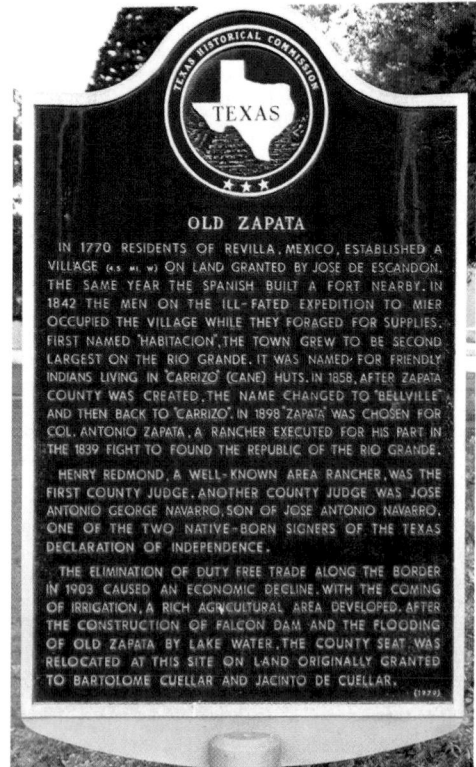

OLD ZAPATA

IN 1770 RESIDENTS OF REVILLA, MEXICO, ESTABLISHED A VILLAGE (4.5 MI. W) ON LAND GRANTED BY JOSE DE ESCANDON. THE SAME YEAR THE SPANISH BUILT A FORT NEARBY. IN 1842 THE MEN ON THE ILL-FATED EXPEDITION TO MIER OCCUPIED THE VILLAGE WHILE THEY FORAGED FOR SUPPLIES. FIRST NAMED "HABITACION", THE TOWN GREW TO BE SECOND LARGEST ON THE RIO GRANDE. IT WAS NAMED FOR FRIENDLY INDIANS LIVING IN "CARRIZO" (CANE) HUTS. IN 1858, AFTER ZAPATA COUNTY WAS CREATED, THE NAME CHANGED TO "BELLVILLE" AND THEN BACK TO "CARRIZO". IN 1899 ZAPATA WAS CHOSEN FOR COL. ANTONIO ZAPATA, A RANCHER EXECUTED FOR HIS PART IN THE 1839 FIGHT TO FOUND THE REPUBLIC OF THE RIO GRANDE.

HENRY REDMOND, A WELL-KNOWN AREA RANCHER, WAS THE FIRST COUNTY JUDGE. ANOTHER COUNTY JUDGE WAS JOSE ANTONIO GEORGE NAVARRO, SON OF JOSE ANTONIO NAVARRO, ONE OF THE TWO NATIVE-BORN SIGNERS OF THE TEXAS DECLARATION OF INDEPENDENCE.

THE ELIMINATION OF DUTY FREE TRADE ALONG THE BORDER IN 1903 CAUSED AN ECONOMIC DECLINE. WITH THE COMING OF IRRIGATION, A RICH AGRICULTURAL AREA DEVELOPED. AFTER THE CONSTRUCTION OF FALCON DAM AND THE FLOODING OF OLD ZAPATA BY LAKE WATER, THE COUNTY SEAT WAS RELOCATED AT THIS SITE ON LAND ORIGINALLY GRANTED TO BARTOLOME CUELLAR AND JACINTO DE CUELLAR.

Texas Department of Aging and Disability Services

Source: Texas Department of Aging and Disability Services; www.dads.state.tx.us

The Texas Department of Aging and Disability Services was established in September 2004 as a result of House Bill 2292 (78th Texas Legislature), which consolidated:

- Mental retardation services and state school programs of the Department of Mental Health and Mental Retardation
- Community care, nursing facility and long-term care regulatory services of the Department of Human Services
- Aging services and programs of the Department on Aging

DADS provides an array of services and supports for older Texans and individuals with physical and cognitive impairments to help them remain as independent as possible.

Services are provided in homes and communities, as well as in institutional settings. Many services require that individuals meet functional and income eligibility requirements.

- Long-term care services and supports for older Texans and individuals who have a physical or cognitive disability are provided through home and community-based programs or in institutions.

Community care services range from meals and attendant care to nursing, therapies, emergency response, adult foster care and assisted living. People who have needs that require more care may receive services in nursing facilities or intermediate care facilities for people with mental retardation.

- Functional eligibility and service levels are determined through the DADS regional offices for both Medicaid and state-funded long-term care programs. Mental retardation services are accessed through the 41 Community Mental Retardation Authorities. The 28 Area Agencies on Aging link older Texans—those age 60 and older—to community services such as congregate meals, care coordination and transportation.
- Regulatory Services provides licensing, certifica-

Budgeted Expenditures

for 2005

The state and federal governments share the costs of most services. Budgeted expenditures for fiscal year 2005 are as follows:

Intake, Access & Eligibility . . .	$104,543,309
Community Care Entitlement . . .	891,695,157
Community Care Waivers	855,979,592
Community Care State	227,294,306
Mental Retardation In-home Services	5,000,000
Program of All-inclusive Care for the Elderly (PACE)	.24,563,542
Nursing Facility and Hospice Payments	1,725,682,581
Intermediate Care Facilities for Persons with Mental Retardation	368,200,427
State Mental Retardation Facilities	385,146,900
Capital Repairs & Renovations	.18,161,214
Licensing, Certification & Outreach	.56,492,358
Indirect Administration	.44,860,414
Total Agency Request	$4,707,619,800

tion and contract enrollment services, as well as financial monitoring and complaint investigation, to ensure that residential facilities, home and community support services agencies, and individuals providing services in facilities or home and community settings comply with state and federal standards.

In addition, Regulatory Services employees ensure that clients receive high-quality services and are protected from abuse, neglect and exploitation. ☆

The Texas Workforce Commission

Source: The Texas Workforce Commission; www.twc.state.tx.us

The Texas Workforce Commission (TWC) is the state government agency charged with overseeing and providing workforce development services to employers and job seekers of Texas.

For employers, TWC offers recruiting, retention, training and retraining, and outplacement services as well as valuable information on labor law and labor market statistics.

For job seekers, TWC offers career development information, job search resources, training programs, and, as appropriate, unemployment benefits. While targeted populations receive intensive assistance to overcome barriers to employment, all Texans can benefit from the services offered by TWC and our network of

workforce partners.

The Texas Workforce Commission is part of a local and state network dedicated to developing the workforce of Texas. The network is composed of the statewide efforts of the commission coupled with planning and service provision on a regional level by 28 local workforce boards. This network gives customers access to local workforce solutions and statewide services in a single location—Texas Workforce Centers.

Primary services of the Texas Workforce Commission and our network partners are funded by federal tax revenue and are generally free to all Texans. Mailing address: 101 E. 15th Street, Rm. 230, Austin 78778; 512-463-2236; www.twc.state.tx.us. ☆

Railroad Commission of Texas

Source: The Railroad Commission of Texas; www.rrc.state.tx.us

The Railroad Commission of Texas has primary regulatory jurisdiction over the oil and natural gas industry, pipeline transporters, the natural gas and hazardous liquid pipeline industry, natural gas utilities, the liquefied petroleum gas (LP-gas) industry, rail industry, and coal and uranium surface mining operations. It also promotes the use of LP-gas as an alternative fuel in Texas through research and education.

The commission exercises its statutory responsibilities under provisions of the Texas Constitution, the Texas Natural Resources Code, the Texas Water Code, the Texas Utilities Code, the Coal and Uranium Surface Mining and Reclamation Acts, the Pipeline Safety Acts, and the Railroad Safety Act.

The commission also has regulatory and enforcement responsibilities under federal law, including the Federal Railroad Safety Act, the Local Rail Freight Assistance Act, the Surface Coal Mining Control and Reclamation Act, the Safe Drinking Water Act, the Pipeline Safety Acts, the Resource Conservation Recovery Act, and the Clean Water Act.

The Railroad Commission was established by the Texas Legislature in 1891 and given jurisdiction over rates and operations of railroads, terminals, wharves and express companies.

In 1917, the legislature declared pipelines to be common carriers and gave the commission regulatory authority over them. It was also given the responsibility to administer conservation laws relating to oil and natural gas production.

During the 1920s, the commission received additional regulatory responsibility over motor carriers and natural gas utility companies. During the 1930s, additional regulations over oil and natural gas production were enacted primarily to conserve natural resources and protect the correlative rights of mineral interest owners.

In the 1950s and 1960s, environmental concerns were addressed by the adoption of additional oil and gas operation regulations, and safety authority over LP-gas products was also delegated to the commission. In the 1970s, the commission assumed authority over coal and uranium surface mining operations, and federal pipeline safety standards were adopted for natural gas pipelines. Throughout the 1980s and 1990s, the commission received additional environmental and safety responsibilities over oil and gas production, natural gas utilities, hazardous liquids pipelines, LP-gas, and surface mining industries. In 1994, the motor carrier industry was deregulated, and the commission's motor carrier responsibilities were transferred to the Texas Department of Transportation.

The Railroad Commission exists to protect the environment, public safety, and the rights of mineral interest owners; to prevent waste of natural resources, and to assure fair and equitable utility rates in those industries over which it has authority.

These functions are carried out through the promulgation of rules, registering organizations, maintaining financial assurance of operators, filings by operators, granting permits and licenses, monitoring performance, inspecting facilities, maintaining records and maps, reviewing variance requests, investigating complaints, emergency response, plugging abandoned wells, cleaning up abandoned sites, public education, research and education on alternative fuels, providing public information, resolving disputes, conducting hearings on disputed matters, and rendering decisions.

Within the U.S. and worldwide energy industry, the Railroad Commission is recognized as a leader in developing workable regulations. While its primary responsibilities are to protect the environment and public safety, it also has taken a balanced approach to maximizing the development of Texas' important energy resources.

Mailing address: PO Box 12967, Austin 78711-2967; phone: 512-463-7288; www.rrc.state.tx.us. ☆

Texas Youth Commission

Source: Texas Youth Commission of Texas; www.tyc.state.tx.us

The Texas Youth Commission provides for the care, custody, rehabilitation, and reestablishment in society of Texas' most chronically delinquent or serious juvenile offenders. Texas judges commit these youth to TYC for mostly felony-level offenses committed when they were at least age 10 and less than age 17. TYC can maintain jurisdiction over these offenders until their 21st birthdays.

TYC operates a system of 13 secure institutions located in: Beaumont, Brownwood, Corsicana, Crockett, Edinburg, Gainesville, Giddings, Marlin, Mart, Pyote, San Saba, Sheffield and Vernon. The nine TYC half-way houses are located in: Austin, Corpus Christi, Dallas, El Paso, Fort Worth, Harlingen, McAllen, Roanoke and San Antonio. The agency also contracts with about 30 private or local government providers for a wide range of services to TYC offenders.

All offenders sent to the Texas Youth Commission start at the Marlin Orientation and Assessment Unit in Falls County, southeast of Temple. During the 50- to 60-day average stay at Marlin, they receive:

• A physical evaluation and survey of medical history
• Educational testing and assessment
• Psychological evaluation

• Social summary
• Introduction to the TYC Resocialization program and to behavioral expectations
• Assessment of needs for specialized treatment

About 80 percent of offenders are assigned to TYC secure correctional facilities, and 20 percent go into facilities and programs operated by contract providers. Halfway houses are used for some youth as transitional assignments after they have completed stays in secure settings.

Youth are assigned minimum lengths of stay based on the crimes committed. TYC youth are required to demonstrate progress in rehabilitation and education programs to earn parole, even if that means they stay months past their minimum lengths of stay.

Some youth are committed to TYC under the Determinate Sentencing law, which provides for sentences of up to 40 years for the most serious crimes. The sentence begins at TYC and, depending on the youth's behavior, he or she can be transferred to the adult prison system (Texas Department of Criminal Justice) to complete the sentence.

Mailing address: PO Box 4260, Austin 78765; phone: 512-424-6130; www.tyc.state.tx.us. ☆

Health and Human Services Commission

Source: Texas Health and Human Services Commission; www.hhs.state.tx.us

The Texas Health and Human Services Commission (HHSC) is the oversight agency for the state's health and human services system. HHSC also administers state and federal programs that provide financial, health and social services to Texans.

In 2003, the 78th Texas Legislature mandated an unprecedented transformation of the state's health and human services system to create an integrated, effective and accessible health and human services enterprise that protects public health and brings high-quality services and support to Texans in need. The transformation blends 12 agencies into five to create a system that is client-centered, efficient in its use of public resources and focused on results and accountability.

The Health and Human Services Commission coordinates administrative functions across the system, determines eligibility for its programs, and administers Medicaid, Children's Health Insurance Program, Temporary Assistance for Needy Families (TANF), food stamps, family violence and disaster assistance, refugee resettlement and special nutrition programs.

The HHSC executive commissioner is Albert Hawkins. The executive commissioner is appointed by the governor and confirmed by the Senate.

The state's health and human services agencies spend nearly $20 billion per year to administer more than 200 programs, employ approximately 46,000 state workers, and operate from more than 1,000 locations.

The new state system includes four new departments, which operate under the oversight of HHSC. The four new departments under HHSC are:

The Department of Family and Protective Services includes the programs previously administered by the Department of Protective and Regulatory Services. DFPS began services Feb. 1, 2004.

The Department of Assistive and Rehabilitative Services combines the programs of the Texas Rehabilitation Commission, Commission for the Blind, Commission for the Deaf and Hard of Hearing, and Interagency Council on Early Childhood Intervention. DARS began services March 1, 2004.

The Department of Aging and Disability Services consolidates mental retardation and state school programs of the Department of Mental Health and Mental Retardation, community care and nursing home services programs of the Department of Human Services, and aging services programs of the Texas Department of Aging. DADS began services Sept. 1, 2004.

The Department of State Health Services includes the programs provided by the Texas Department of Health, the Texas Commission on Alcohol and Drug Abuse and the Health Care Information Council, plus mental-health community services and state hospital programs operated by the Department of Mental Health and Mental Retardation. DSHS began services on Sept. 1, 2004.

Major HHSC Programs at a Glance

The state's **Medicaid** program provides healthcare coverage for one out of every three children in Texas, pays for half of all births and accounts for 27 percent of the state's total budget. In 2004, an average of 2.68 million Texans received healthcare coverage through Medicaid.

The Children's Health Insurance Program (CHIP) is designed for families who earn too much money to qualify for Medicaid health care, yet cannot afford private insurance.

The Temporary Assistance for Needy Families (TANF) program provides basic financial assistance for needy children and the parents or caretakers with whom they live. As a condition of eligibility, caretakers must sign and abide by a personal-responsibility agreement. Time limits for benefits have been set by both state and federal welfare-reform legislation.

A typical TANF family of three (caretaker and two children) can receive a maximum monthly grant of $213. In fiscal year 2004, a monthly average of 255,081 individuals received TANF benefits.

The **Food Stamp program** is a federally funded program that assists low-income families, the elderly and single adults to obtain a nutritionally adequate diet. Those eligible for food stamps include households receiving TANF or federal Supplemental Security Income benefits and non-public assistance households having incomes below 130 percent of the poverty level.

Food stamp and TANF benefits are delivered through the electronic benefit transfer (EBT) system, through which clients access benefits at about 12,000 retail locations statewide with the Lone Star debit card.

In 2004, the monthly average number of recipients (individuals) who received food stamps benefits was 2,266,240. The average monthly food stamp benefit per individual was $81 per month or $213 per household.

Other HHSC programs

The **Family Violence program** educates the public about domestic violence and offers emergency shelter and support services to victims and their children. The program is administered through contracts with family-violence service providers.

The **Disaster Assistance program** processes grant applications for victims of presidentially declared disasters, such as tornados, floods and hurricanes. Victims are eligible for assistance from this state-administered federal program if they do not have insurance and cannot qualify for low-interest loans from the Small Business Administration.

The federally funded **Refugee Resettlement program** provides cash, health care and social services to eligible refugees to help them become self-sufficient as soon as possible after arriving in the United States.

Eight Special Nutrition programs, completely funded by the U.S. Dept. of Agriculture, provide meals to eligible recipients, including elderly or functionally impaired adults and to children and low-income individuals and families.

Information about Medicaid, CHIP and other health and human services programs, including eligibility requirements and how to apply, can be found online at www.hhsc.state.tx.us, www.helpintexas.com or by calling 2-1-1, a toll-free local resource for information on health and human service programs. ☆

The General Land Office

Source: General Land Office of Texas. On the Web: www.glo.state.tx.us

History of the General Land Office

The Texas General Land Office (GLO) is one of the oldest governmental entities in the state, dating back to the Republic of Texas. The first General Land Office was established in 1836 in the Republic's constitution, and the first Texas Congress enacted the provision into law in 1837. The GLO was established to oversee distribution of public lands, register titles, issue patents on land and maintain records of land granted.

In the early years of statehood, beginning in 1845, Texas established the precedent of using its vast public domain for public benefit. The first use was to sell or trade land to eliminate the huge debt remaining from Texas' War for Independence and early years of the Republic.

Texas also gave away land to settlers as homesteads; to veterans as compensation for service; for internal improvements, including building railroads, shipbuilding and improving rivers for navigation; and to build the state Capitol.

The public domain was closed in 1898 when the Texas Supreme Court declared there was no more vacant and unappropriated land in Texas. In 1900, all remaining unappropriated land was set aside by the Texas Legislature to benefit public schools.

Today, 19.9 million acres of land and minerals, owned by the Permanent School Fund, the Permanent University Fund, various other state agencies or the Veterans Land Board, are managed by the General Land Office and the Commissioner of the Texas General Land Office. This includes more than 4 million acres of submerged coastal lands, which consist of bays, inlets and the area from the Texas shoreline to the three-marine-league line (10.36 miles) in the Gulf of Mexico. It is estimated that more than 1 million acres make up the public domain of the state's riverbeds and another 1.7 million acres are excess lands belonging to the Permanent School Fund.

The **Permanent University Fund** holds title to 2.1 million fee acres, and other state agencies or special schools hold title to another 2.3 million acres. The **Permanent School Fund** owns mineral rights alone in almost 7.4 million acres covered under the Relinquishment Act, the Free Royalty Act and the various sales acts, and it has outright ownership to about 747,522 upland acres, mostly west of the Pecos River. The **Veterans Land Board** has liens on more than 557,511 acres of land in active veterans accounts.

The General Land Office handles leases and revenue accounting on all lands dedicated to the Permanent School Fund and on land owned by various state agencies. Jerry Patterson currently serves as the 27th commissioner of the Texas General Land Office.

Veterans Land Board Programs
Veterans Land Program

In 1946, the Texas Legislature created a bond program to aid veterans in purchasing land. Up to $1.5 billion in bonding authority has been authorized over the years in a series of constitutional amendments; as of May 2005, about $1.4 billion of the bonds had been sold to fund loans.

Loans cannot exceed $60,000, and tracts purchased through the program must be at least one acre. To date, more than 120,000 veterans have purchased more than 4.9 million acres of land under the program.

Veterans Housing Assistance Program

The 68th Legislature created the Veterans Housing Assistance Program, which also is funded through bond proceeds. Over the years, Texans have passed constitutional amendments authorizing the sale of up to $2.5 billion in bonds to finance this program. As of May 2005, about $2.2 billion in bonds have been sold to fund housing loans.

Eligible veterans may borrow up to $240,000 toward purchasing a home. The low-interest loans result in reduced monthly payments for veterans. Since the program began operation in January 1984, more than 65,000 Texas veterans have received housing loans worth about $4.56 billion.

Veterans Home Improvement Program

In 1986, the Veterans Land Board implemented the Veterans Home Improvement Program, which is funded through the Veterans Housing Assistance Program. This program allows Texas veterans to borrow up to $25,000 to make substantial home repairs and improvements. Since the program's inception, more than 3,300 veterans have received home improvement loans worth more than $50 million.

All three programs are administered by the Texas Veterans Land Board, which is chaired by the GLO commissioner. The bonded debt for the programs and all administrative costs are financed by veterans who use the programs; there is no cost to Texas taxpayers. Eligible veterans may participate simultaneously in the three loan programs and may apply for additional loans once preceding loans are paid in full.

Texas State Veterans Homes

In 1997, the 75th Legislature approved legislation authorizing the Veterans Land Board to construct and operate Texas State Veterans Homes under a cost-sharing program with the U.S. Department of Veterans Affairs (USDVA) and to issue revenue bonds to obtain the state's necessary share. The homes provide affordable, quality, long-term care for Texas' aging veteran population. The state provides the land and 35 percent of construction costs, and the USDVA provides 65 percent of construction costs. After a search for host communities, construction began on veterans homes in Temple and Floresville in 1998, and the first residents were admitted in December 2000. Since then, veterans homes have opened in Big Spring and Bonham. Additional homes opened in El Paso and McAllen in 2005, and another will open in Amarillo in 2006.

Because the VA subsidizes a significant portion of a veteran's cost to stay in a Texas State Veterans Home, the daily out-of-pocket rates are well below market average and include the cost of medications. As of May 2005, veterans paid $63 to $74 a day for a semi-private room. The average

Distribution of the Public Lands of Texas	
Purpose	**Acres**
Settlers	**68,027,108**
Spain and Mexico	24,583,923
Spanish and Mexican Grants south	
of the Nueces River, recognized by	
Act of Feb. 10, 1852	3,741,241
Headrights	30,360,002
Republic colonies	4,494,806
Preemption land	4,847,136
Military	**9,874,262**
Bounty	5,354,250
Battle donations	1,162,240
Veterans donations	1,377,920
Confederate	1,979,852
Improvements	**37,155,714**
Road	27,716
Navigation	4,261,760
Irrigation	584,000
Ships	17,000
Manufacturing	111,360
Railroads	32,153,878
Education	**52,329,168**
University, public school and eleemos-	
ynary institutions	52,329,168
Total of distributed lands	**167,386,252**

cost for a semi-private room in a private Texas nursing home was about $109 a day in May 2005, which often did not include the cost of medications. Spouses of Texas veterans and Gold Star parents are also eligible for care in Texas State Veterans Homes.

Each home has 120 to 160 beds and provides a broad spectrum of health care services, a comprehensive rehabilitation program, special diets, recreational activities, social services, a library, a meditation room and at least one certified, secured Alzheimer's wing with a secured outdoor courtyard.

Texas State Veterans Cemeteries

In May 2002, Killeen and Mission were chosen as sites for the first two Texas State Veterans Cemeteries. Abilene was selected for the next Texas State Veterans Cemetery, and construction should start in summer 2006.

A typical Texas State Veterans Cemetery will have a covered, open-air structure for committal services, a visitors center, a computer system for locating specific graves or interments, a gateway entrance, a 60-foot flagpole, a paved assembly area for special occasions such as Memorial Day observances, an avenue of flags, a memorial walkway where monuments can be placed, a columbarium for interment of cremated remains and a garden for scattering cremated remains.

The Veterans Land Board owns and operates the cemeteries under USDVA guidelines. The USDVA funds the design and construction of the cemeteries, but the land must be donated.

These cemeteries will complement the four USDVA national cemeteries in Texas, located in San Antonio, Houston, Dallas-Fort Worth and El Paso. There are no known plans for additional national cemeteries in Texas, and about 580,000 of Texas' 1.7 million veterans are 65 or older.

For more information on any of these veterans programs, call 1-800-252-VETS (8387), or visit the Texas Veterans Land Board Web site at www.texasveterans.com.

Voices of Veterans Oral History Program

The Voices of Veterans oral history program seeks to record the stories of Texas veterans and archive the transcripts in the Office of Veterans Records for future researchers and historians. Voices of Veterans represents the first time a state agency has ventured into the field of veterans' oral histories. The program is open to any Texas veteran who has served in the Armed Forces, from World War I to the War on Terror.

Any veteran interested in including his or her story in the Voices of Veterans program should contact the Veterans Land Board at 1-800-252-VETS, or send an e-mail to vlbinfo@glo.state.tx.us. Oral history interviews can be conducted in person at the Veterans Land Board in Austin or by telephone from anywhere in Texas.

Energy Resources

The General Land Office helps fund public education in Texas by maximizing the natural resources from state lands, including oil and gas. Millions of acres of Permanent School Fund land are leased through the GLO to energy firms for oil and gas exploration and production. Royalties and other fees from this production are paid to the GLO, which dedicates the money to the PSF for use in schools around the state.

In the 1990s the GLO also began to accept oil and gas in-kind in lieu of cash royalty payments. Through the In-Kind Gas Program, the agency sells gas at discounted prices to public entities, such as schools and cities. Through the State Power Program, the agency also works with private enterprise to convert in-kind gas into electricity, which is sold to public retail customers, such as school districts, state agencies, state institutions of higher education, and political subdivisions of the state. The value added to the natural gas by converting it into electricity has benefited the PSF, while allowing customers to realize substantial savings through lower electric bills. As of March 2005, this program has enhanced revenues for in-kind volumes sold for electricity by about $29.5 million.

The GLO has expanded into construction of sustainable energy projects, especially wind energy facilities, on PSF lands. The agency pioneered wind power in Texas in the 1990s by leasing PSF land in West Texas for a wind energy facility.

In April 2003, Commissioner Patterson announced his Plan for Sustainable Energy to spur wind power development on state lands. An ongoing wind-mapping project shows prospective wind energy developers the best locations for wind farms. The GLO can reduce easement fees for companies building transmission lines over state lands, which will help reduce the cost of transmission lines and make commercial wind energy more competitive.

Coastal Stewardship

The General Land Office is the steward of the Texas Gulf Coast, serving as the premier state agency for protecting and renourishing the coast and fighting coastal erosion. In 1999, the legislature created the Coastal Erosion Planning and Response Act (CEPRA) and put the GLO in charge of facilitating restoration and preservation of eroding beaches, dunes, wetlands and other bay shorelines along the Texas coast.

The CEPRA program represents the first-ever coastal erosion program in Texas and entails a coordinated effort of state, federal and local project partners to conduct erosion response projects and related studies. As of May 2005, $37.32 million has been appropriated by the legislature and leveraged with project partner monies for construction projects and studies under the CEPRA program. Since its inception, CEPRA has involved 31 project partners working with the GLO on 115 projects and studies spanning 14 coastal counties.

In June 2003, Commissioner Patterson announced the Coastal Texas 2020 program. This long-term, statewide initiative will unite local, state and federal efforts to promote the environmental and economic health of the Texas coast. One goal is to increase the state's share of federal funding to fight rapid coastal erosion.

In 1991, the Oil Spill Prevention and Response Act designated the GLO as the lead state agency for oil spill prevention and response to oil spills that enter, or threaten to enter, coastal waters. In September 2003, the GLO became responsible for all coastal oil spills.

In 1986, the GLO began its Adopt-A-Beach cleanups, held every spring and fall along the Texas coast. Since the program began, more than 328,000 volunteers have removed more than 6,200 tons of trash from Texas beaches. For more information, call the Adopt-A-Beach toll-free number: 1-877-TX COAST (877-892-6278).

Save Texas History

Save Texas History is the historic-document preservation program at the Texas General Land Office. This program seeks private funding to restore the GLO's land records archive, which contains more than 35 million historic documents, including maps, letters, land grants and field notes. Some of the documents carry the signatures of Texas heroes such as William Travis, Stephen F. Austin, Davy Crockett and Jim Bowie. As of February 2005, more than 642 maps and documents had been conserved, 42 were undergoing conservation, and 322 had been fully or partially adopted.

As funding becomes available, selected documents undergo a painstaking restoration process, digital scanning and, finally, safe permanent storage. Once scanned, these maps and documents can be copied and posted on the Internet. To order a copy of one of these historical maps, or to make a contribution to the Save Texas History program, visit www.savetexashistory.org or call 1-800-998-4GLO. ☆

Texas Department of Criminal Justice

On the Web: www.tdcj.state.tx.us

The Texas Board of Criminal Justice (TBCJ) is composed of nine non-salaried members who are appointed by the Governor for staggered six-year terms. Charged with governing the Texas Department of Criminal Justice (TDCJ), the TBCJ develops and implements policies that guide agency operations. The TBCJ also serves as the school board for the Windham School District. For a list of members, see the Boards and Commissions list following this article. Christina Melton Crain was appointed board chairman February 2003.

The TDCJ executive director is appointed by the board and is responsible for the day-to-day administration and operation of the agency. Brad Livingston was appointed the interim TDCJ executive director on Nov. 1, 2004. The TDCJ is composed of the following divisions:

Administrative Review and Risk Management, General Counsel, Community Justice Assistance Division, Correctional Institutions (formerly the State Jail Division, Institutional Division, Private Facilities Division and the Operations Division), Parole, Rehabilitation and Re-entry Programs (formerly Programs and Services), Health Services, Victim Services, Human Resources and the Texas Correctional Office on Offenders with Medical or Mental Illness.

The Community Justice Assistance Division, the Correctional Institutions Division and the Parole Division are most involved in the everyday confinement and supervision of convicted felons. Supervision of probationers is the responsibility of the local community supervision and corrections departments.

The Correctional Institutions Division is responsible for the confinement of adult felony and state jail offenders who are sentenced to incarceration in a secure correctional facility. Institutional facilities house offenders convicted of first, second, or third degree felonies.

The state jail felony classification was created in 1993 and is made up of certain offenses that were previously considered non-violent third degree felonies or Class A misdemeanors. Punishment can be up to two years incarceration in a state jail facility and a fine not to exceed $10,000, with possible community supervision following release from the state jail.

As of April 30, 2005, there were 133,611 Institutional offenders; 14,486 State Jail offenders; 3,211 substance abuse felony punishment offenders, for a total of 151,308 offenders. Approximately 11,300 offenders were housed in privately operated facilities monitored by the CI Division as of April 30, 2005.

The Parole Division processes offenders for release on parole or mandatory supervision and oversees the supervision and rehabilitative services for reintegration into the community. As of April 30, 2005, more than 76,000 adult offenders were under parole or mandatory supervision.

The Community Justice Assistance Division oversees the community supervision and corrections departments that work directly with probationers. As of April 30, 2005, approximately 430,000 felony, misdemeanor and pre-trial probationers were under community supervision.

The Rehabilitation and Re-entry Programs Division is responsible for the centralized management of activities related to offender programs and services that involve two or more divisions.

Victim Services coordinates a central mechanism for victims and the public to participate in the criminal justice process within an environment of integrity, fairness, compassion, and dignity.

The Windham School District and the Continuing Education Program provide appropriate educational programming and services to meet the needs of the eligible offender population in TDCJ.

Inmate Profile

Age/Sex/Ethnicity

92% are male
Average age: 36

38.3% are black
31.8% are white
29.4% are Hispanic

Sentences/Length of Time Served

Average sentence: Prison: 19.5 years; State jail: 1 year
Average part of sentence served:
Prison: 59.8%; State jail: 99.4%
More than 40% of inmates have been in prison before.

Education

Average IQ: 90.7
About 66.6% lack a high school diploma or GED.
Average education achievement score: 7th grade

Correctional Institutions Division

The town listed is the nearest one to the facility, although the unit may actually be in another county. For instance, the Middleton Transfer Unit is in Jones County, but the nearest city is Abilene, which is in Taylor County. Units marked by an asterisk (*) are operated by private companies.

Prisons

Allred, Iowa Park, Wichita Co.; **Beto,** Tennessee Colony, Anderson Co.; **Boyd,** Teague, Freestone Co.; ***Bridgeport,** Bridgeport, Wise Co.; **Briscoe,** Dilley, Frio Co.; **Byrd** (diagnostic intake), Huntsville, Walker Co.; **Central,** Sugar Land, Fort Bend Co.; **Clemens,** Brazoria, Brazoria Co.; **Clements,** Amarillo, Potter Co.; ***Cleveland,** Cleveland, Liberty Co.; **Coffield,** Tennessee Colony, Anderson Co.; **Connally,** Kenedy, Karnes Co.; **Dalhart,** Dalhart, Hartley Co.; **Daniel,** Snyder, Scurry Co.; **Darrington,** Rosharon, Brazoria Co.; ***Diboll,** Diboll, Angelina Co.; **Eastham,** Lovelady, Houston Co.; **Ellis,** Huntsville, Walker Co.; **Estelle,** Huntsville, Walker Co.; ***Estes,** Venus, Johnson Co.; **Ferguson,** Midway, Madison Co.; **Gatesville,** Gatesville, Coryell Co. (Women's Unit); **Goree,** Huntsville, Walker Co.; **Hamilton,** Bryan, Brazos Co.; **Hightower,** Dayton, Liberty Co.; **Hilltop,** Gatesville, Coryell Co.; **Hobby,** Marlin, Falls Co.; **Hodge,** Rusk, Cherokee Co.; **Hospital Galveston,** Galveston, Galveston Co.; **Hughes,** Gatesville, Coryell Co.; **Huntsville,** Huntsville, Walker Co.; **Jester III** and **IV,** Richmond, Fort Bend Co.; **Jordan,** Pampa, Gray Co.; ***Kyle,** Kyle, Hays Co.; **LeBlanc,** Beaumont, Jefferson Co.; **Lewis,** Woodville, Tyler Co.; ***Lockhart,** Lockhart, Caldwell Co.; **Luther,** Navasota, Grimes Co.; **Lynaugh,** Fort Stockton, Pecos Co.; **McConnell,** Beeville, Bee Co.; **Michael,** Tennessee Colony, Anderson Co.; **Montford,** Lubbock, Lubbock Co.; ***B. Moore,** Overton, Rusk Co.; **Mountain View,** Gatesville, Coryell Co.; **Murray,** Gatesville, Coryell Co.; **Neal,** Amarillo, Potter Co.; **Pack,** Navasota, Grimes Co.; **Polunsky,** Livingston, Polk Co.; **Powledge,** Palestine, Anderson Co.; **Ramsey I** and **II,** Rosharon, Brazoria Co.; **Roach,** Childress, Childress Co.; **Robertson,** Abilene, Jones Co.; **Scott,** Angleton, Brazoria Co.; **Segovia,** Edinburg, Hidalgo Co.; **Skyview,** at Rusk State Hospital, Cherokee Co.; **Smith,** Lamesa, Dawson Co.; **Stevenson,** Cuero, DeWitt Co.; **Stiles,** Beaumont, Jefferson Co.; **Telford,** New Boston, Bowie Co.; **C.T. Terrell,** Rosharon, Brazoria Co.; **Torres,** Hondo, Medina Co.; **Vance,** Richmond, Fort Bend Co.; **Wallace,** Colorado City, Mitchell Co.; **Wynne,** Huntsville, Walker Co.; **C. Young,** Dickinson, Galveston Co.

Transfer Units

Cotulla, Cotulla, LaSalle Co.; **Duncan,** Diboll, Angelina Co.; **Fort Stockton,** Fort Stockton, Pecos Co.; **Garza East & West,** Beeville, Bee Co.; **Goodman,** Jasper, Jasper Co.; **Gurney,** Tennessee Colony, Anderson Co.; **Holliday,** Huntsville, Walker Co.; **Middleton,** Abilene, Jones Co.; **C. Moore,** Bonham, Fannin Co.; **Rudd,** Brownfield, Terry Co.; **Tulia,** Tulia, Swisher Co.; **Ware,** Colorado City, Mitchell Co.

State Jails

*Bartlett, Williamson Co.; ***Bradshaw,** Henderson, Rusk Co.; **Cole,** Bonham, Fannin Co.; ***Dawson,** Dallas, Dallas Co.; **Dominguez,** San Antonio, Bexar Co.; **Formby,** Plainview, Hale Co.; **Gist,** Beaumont, Jefferson Co.; **Havins,** Brownwood, Brown Co.; **Henley,** Dayton, Liberty Co.; **Hutchins,** Dallas, Dallas Co.; **Kegans,** Houston, Harris Co.; ***Lindsey,** Jacksboro, Jack Co.; **Lopez,** Edinburg, Hidalgo Co.; **Lychner,** Humble, Harris Co.; **Ney,** Hondo, Medina Co.; **Plane,** Dayton, Liberty Co.; **Sanchez,** El Paso, El Paso Co.; **Travis County,** Austin, Travis Co.; **Wheeler,** Plainview, Hale Co.; ***Williacy County,** Raymondville, Williacy Co.; **Woodman,** Gatesville, Coryell Co.

SAFP Facilities

Glossbrenner, San Diego, Duval Co.; **Halbert,** Burnet, Burnet Co.; **Jester I,** Richmond, Fort Bend Co.; **Johnston,** Winnsboro, Wood Co.; **Sayle,** Breckenridge, Stephens Co. ☆

Texas State Boards and Commissions

Following is a list of appointees to state boards and commissions, as well as names of other state officials, revised to **July 15, 2005.** Information includes, where available, (1) date of creation of agency; (2) whether the position is elective or appointive; (3) length of term; (4) compensation, if any; (5) number of members; (6) names of appointees, their hometowns and the dates of the terminations of their terms. In some instances the dates of expiration of terms have already passed; in such cases, no new appointment had been made by press time, and the official is continuing to fill the position until a successor can be named. Most positions marked "apptv." are appointed by the Governor. Where otherwise, appointing authority is given. Most advisory boards are not listed. Salaries for commissioners and administrators are those that were authorized by the appropriations bill passed by the 78th Legislature for the 2004–2005 biennium (2006–2007 salaries were not available from the State Auditor at press time). They are "not-to-exceed" salaries: maximum authorized salaries for the positions. Actual salaries may be less than those stated here.

Accountancy, Texas State Board of Public – (1945 with 2-yr. terms; reorganized 1959 as 9-member board with 6-yr. overlapping terms; number of members increased to 12 in 1979; increased to 15 in 1989); per diem and expenses: Billy M. Atkinson Jr., Sugar Land (1/31/05); J. Coalter Baker, Austin (1/31/07); Marcela E. Donadio, Houston (1/31/07); Kimberly M. Dryden, Amarillo (1/31/05); David Duree, Midland (1/31/09); April L. Eyeington, College Station (1/31/05); Carlos Madrid Jr., San Antonio (1/31/07); Robert C. Mann, Fort Worth (1/31/05); Orville W. Mills Jr., Sugar Land (1/31/09); Paula Martina Mendoza, Houston (1/31/05); Joseph W. Richardson, Houston (1/31/09); John W. Steinberg, Converse (1/31/07); Edward L. Summers, Austin (1/31/03); Melanie G. Thompson, Canyon Lake (1/31/07); John A. Walton, Dallas (1/31/09). Exec. Dir., William Treacy ($70,000), 333 Guadalupe, Suite 3-900, Austin 78701-3900; (512) 305-7800.

Acupuncture Examiners, Texas State Board of – (1993); apptv.; 2 yrs.; per diem; 9 members: Sheng Ting Chen, Austin (2/1/09); Pedro (Pete) V. Garcia Jr., Lubbock (1/31/03); Everett G. Heinze Jr., Austin (1/31/03); Hoang Xiong Ho, San Antonio (2/1/07); Meng-Sheng Linda Lin, Richardson (1/31/01); Dee Ann Newbold, Austin (1/31/05); Terry Glenn Rascoe, Temple (2/1/07); Claire H. Smith, Dallas (1/31/05).

Ad Valorem Tax Rate, Board to Calculate the – (1907); ex officio; term in other office; 3 members: Governor, State Comptroller of Public Accounts and State Treasurer.

Adjutant General – (1836 by Republic of Texas; present office established 1905); apptv.: Brig Gen. Charles Gary Rodriguez (2/1/07) ($94,832, plus house and utilities), PO Box 5218, Camp Mabry, Austin 78763.

Adjutant General, Assistant for Air – Brig. Gen. Allen Dehnert, PO Box 5218, Camp Mabry, Austin 78763.

Adjutant General, Assistant for Army – Brig. Gen. William W. Goodwin, PO Box 5218, Camp Mabry, Austin 78763.

Administrative Judicial Districts of Texas, Presiding Judges – (Apptv. by Governor); serve terms concurrent with term as District Judge, subject to reappointment if re-elected to bench. No additional compensation. For names of judges, see Administrative Judicial Districts in index.

Aging and Disability Services Board, Department of – (2004); 8 apptv. members: Gilberto Aguirre, San Antonio (2/1/05); Abigail Rios Barrera, San Antonio (2/1/09); Frances Ann (Fran) Brown, Lewisville (2/1/07); Sharon Swift Butterworth, El Paso, (2/1/05); Jean L. Freeman, Galveston (2/1/05); Thomas E. Oliver, Houston, (2/01/07); Teresa D. (Terry) Wilkinson, Midland (2/1/09); David E. Young, Dallas (2/1/07); John H. Winters Human Servc. Complex, 701 W. 51st St., P.O. Box 149030, Austin, TX 78714-9030; (512) 438-3011.

Alcohol and Drug Abuse, Texas Commission on – (1953 as Texas Commission on Alcoholism); abolished by HB 2292 and functions merged into Department of State Health Services in January 2004.

Alcoholic Beverage Commission, Texas – (1935 as Liquor Control Board; name changed 1970); apptv.; 6-yr; per diem and expenses; administrator apptd. by commission; 3 members: Jose Cuevas Jr., Midland, (11/15/09); Gail Madden, Dallas (11/15/05); John T. Steen Jr., San Antonio (11/15/07). Admin., Alan Steen ($91,000), PO Box 13127, Austin 78711-3127; (512) 206-3333.

Angelina and Neches River Authority, Board of Directors – (1935 as Sabine-Neches Conservation Dist.; reorganized 1950 and name changed to Neches River Conservation Dist.; changed to present name in 1977); apptv.; expenses; 6-yr.; 9 members: Karen Elizabeth Barber, Jasper (9/5/09); Dominick B. (Nick) Bruno, Jacksonville (9/5/09); Al Chavira,

Jacksonville (9/5/07); Kenneth R. Darden, Livingston (9/5/09); Joe M. Deason, Lufkin (9/5/07); Julie Dowell, Bullard, (9/5/05); Carl Ray Polk Jr., Lufkin (9/5/05); James E. Raney, Nacogdoches (9/5/05); George S. Vorpahl, Lufkin (9/5/07). Gen. Mgr., Kenneth Reneau, PO Box 387, Lufkin 75902-0387; (936) 632-7795.

Animal Health Commission, Texas – (1893 as Texas Livestock Sanitary Commission; name changed in 1959, membership increased to 9 in 1973; raised to 12 in 1983); apptv.; per diem and expenses; 6-yr.; 12 members: Rita Esther Baca, El Paso (9/6/09); Ron Davenport, Friona (9/6/05); Reta K. Dyess, Jacksonville (9/6/05); William F. Edmiston Jr., Eldorado (9/6/07); Coleman Hudgins Locke, Wharton (9/6/09); Roy Martinez, McAllen (9/6/07); Romulo Rangel Jr., Harlingen (9/6/05); Charles E. Real, Marion (9/6/07); Ralph Simmons, Center (9/6/09); Richard Traylor, Carrizo Springs (9/6/03); Jerry P. Windham, College Station (9/6/07); Jill Bryar Wood, Wimberley (9/6/07);. Exec. Dir., Bob R. Hillman, DVM ($87,500), PO Box 12966, Austin 78711-2966; (512) 719-0700.

Appraiser Licensing and Certification Board, Texas – (1991); 2-yr.; apptd.; per diem on duty; 9 members: Exec. Sec. of Veterans' Land Board (Paul E. Moore) and 8 apptees: Elroy Carson, Lubbock (1/31/06); Malcolm J. Deason, Diboll (1/31/05); William A. Faulk Jr., Brownsville (1/31/05); Larry D. Kokel, Georgetown (1/31/05); Clinton P. Sayers, Austin (1/31/06); Shirley Ward, Alpine (1/31/06); L.W. (Wayne) Mayo, Richardson (1/31/05); Dona S. Scurry, El Paso (2/31/06). Commissioner, Wayne Thorburn, PO Box 12188, Austin 78711-2188; (512) 465-3950.

Architectural Examiners, Texas Board of – (1937 as 3-member board; raised to 6 members in 1951 and to 9 in 1977); apptv.; 6-yr.; per diem and expenses; 9 members: Gordon E. Landreth, Corpus Christi (1/31/07); Rosemary A. Gammon, McKinney (1/31/11); Kyle Garner, Amarillo (1/31/09); Peter L. Pfeiffer, Austin (1/31/09); Alfred Vidaurri Jr., Fort Worth (1/31/09); James S. Walker II, Houston (1/31/11); Janet F. Parnell, Canadian (1/31/07); Diane Steinbrueck, Austin (1/31/07); Peggy Lewene (Lew) Vassberg, Harlingen (1/31/11). Exec. Dir., Cathy L. Hendricks, ($65,000), PO Box 12337, Austin 78711-2337; (512) 305-9000.

Arts, Texas Commission on the – (1965 as Texas Fine Arts Commission; name changed to Texas Commission on the Arts and Humanities and membership increased to 18 in 1971; name changed to present form in 1979); apptv.; 6-yr.; expenses; 18 members: W.C. (Abby) Abernathy Jr., Archer City (8/31/07); Nelson H. Balido, San Antonio (8/31/09); Dorothy E. Caram, Houston (8/31/09); William W. Collins Jr., Fort Worth (8/31/09); Bobbe Crawford, Lubbock (8/31/05); Alphonse A. Dotson, Voca (8/31/07); Susan Howard-Chrane, Boerne (8/31/07); Claudia Ladensohn, San Antonio (8/31/05); Victoria Hodge Lightman, Houston (8/31/07); Laurie G. Lozano, Edinburg (8/31/05); Loren O. McKibbens, Harlingen (8/31/07); Jacoba-Jetske S. Russell, Dallas (8/31/09); George R. Snead, El Paso (8/31/09); Mary H. Teeple, Spicewood (8/31/09); Mildred Anne Witte, Tyler (8/31/07); William P. Wright Jr. Abilene (8/31/05). Exec. Dir., Ricardo Hernandez ($70,000), PO Box 13406, Austin 78711-3406; (512) 463-5535.

Athletic Trainers, Advisory Board of – (1971 as Texas Board of Athletic Trainers; name changed and membership increased to 6 in 1975); expenses; 5 members: T. Ross Bailey, Fort Worth (1/31/05); Lawrence M. Sampleton Jr., Austin (1/31/09); Natalie Steadman, Lubbock (1/31/03); Michael Alan Waters, Diboll (1/31/07); c/o Texas Dept. of

State Health Services, 1100 W. 49th, Austin 78756-3183.

Attorney, State Prosecuting – apptv. by Court of Criminal Appeals: Matthew Paul ($101,700), PO Box 12405, Austin 78711.

Auditor, State – (1929); apptv. by Legislative Audit Committee, a joint Senate-House committee; 2-yr.: John Keel, PO Box 12067, Austin 78711-2067; (512) 936-9500.

Banking Commissioner, State – (1923); apptv. by State Finance Commission; 2-yr.: Randall S. James ($118,427), 2601 N. Lamar Blvd., Austin 78705 (See also Finance Commission of Texas); (512) 475-1300.

Bar of Texas, State – (1939 as administrative arm of Supreme Court); 30 members elected by membership; 3-yr. terms; expenses paid from dues collected from membership. President, president-elect, vice president and immediate past president serve as ex officio members. Interim Exec. Dir., Michelle Hunter, PO Box 12487, Austin 78711; (512) 463-1463.

Barber Examiners, State Board of – (1929 as 3-member board; membership increased in 1975); apptv.; 6-yr.; per diem and expenses; 7 members: Ronald L. Brown, Austin (1/31/07); Mary Lou Daughtrey, Tyler (1/31/05); James Hinton Dickerson, Jr., Lake Jackson (1/31/09); San Juana C. Garza, Mercedes (1/31/07); Terissa Johnson, Sanger (1/31/09); William "Kirk" Kuykendall, Austin (1/31/05); Janice E. Wiggins, Kingsland (1/31/03). Exec. Dir., Glenn Parker ($45,816), 5717 Balcones Dr., Ste. 217, Austin 78731.

Blind and Severely Disabled Persons, Committee on Purchases of Products of – (See **Disabilities, Texas Council on Purchasing from People with**)

Blind, Commission for the – Now the Division for Blind Services withing the Department of Assistive and Rehabilitative Services of the Health and Human Services Commission as of 3/1/04.

Blind and Visually Impaired, Governing Board of Texas School for the – (1979); apptv.; 6-yr.; expenses; 9 members: Janet Ardoyno, Abilene (1/31/07); Jesus H. Bautista, El Paso (1/31/07); Gene Iran Brooks, Austin (1/31/09); Donna Florence Vaden Clopton, Mt. Pleasant (1/31/09); Otilio (Toby) Galindo, San Angelo (1/31/05); Deborah Louder, San Angelo (1/31/05); Frankie D. Swift, Nacogdoches (1/31/07); Mary Sue Welch, Dallas (1/31/05); Jamie Lou Wheeler, Watauga (1/31/09). Superintendent, Dr. Philip H. Hatlen ($84,000), 1100 W. 45th St., Austin 78756; (512) 454-8631.

Board of (Note: In most instances, state boards are alphabetized under key word, as **Accountancy, Texas State Board of Public**.)

Brazos River Authority, Board of Directors – (1929 as Brazos River Conservation and Reclamation Dist.; name changed to present form in 1953); apptv.; 6-yr; expenses; 21 members: Chair: Steve Peña (2/1/05); M.G. Christopher, Granbury (2/1/11); Steve Adams Jr., Granbury (2/1/11); Roberto Bailon, Belton (2/1/09); Suzanne Alderson Baker, Lubbock (2/1/07); Truman Otis Blum, Clifton (2/1/11); Ronald D. Butler II, Stephenville (2/1/07); Mark J. Carrabba, Bryan (2/1/09); Jacqueline Baly Chaumette, Sugar Land (2/1/09); Robert M. Christian, Jewett (2/1/11); Christopher D. DeCluitt, Waco (2/1/11); P.J. Ellison, Brenham (2/1/07); Rodolfo Garcia, Alvin (2/1/03); Wade Compton Gear, Mineral Wells (2/1/09); Fred Lee Hughes, Abilene (2/1/07); Carolyn H. Johnson, Freeport (2/1/11); Roberta Jean Killgore, Somerville (2/1/11); Jere Lawrence, Sweetwater (2/1/09); Martha Stovall Martin, Graford (2/1/07); Billy Wayne Moore, Granbury (2/1/09); John R. Skaggs, Plainview (2/1/07); Salvatore A. Zaccagnino, Caldwell (2/1/07). Gen. Mgr., Phillip J. Ford, P. O. Box 7555, Waco 76714-7555; (254) 761-3100.

Building and Procurement Commission, Texas – apptv.; 6-yr.; 7 members: Chair, Brenda Pejovich, Dallas (1/31/09); Stuart Coleman, Brownwood (1/31/07); James S. Duncan, Houston (1/31/09); Bob Jones, Houston (1/31/07); Victor E. Leal, Amarillo (1/31/09); Mary Ann Newman-Buckley, Houston (1/31/05); Betty Reinbeck, Sealy (1/31/11). Exec. Dir. Cindy Reed ($115,000) PO Box 13047, Austin 78711-3047; (512) 463-6363.

Canadian River Compact Commissioner – (1951); apptv.; salary and expenses; (function is to negotiate with other states respecting waters of the Canadian): Roger S. Cox ($10,767), Amarillo (12/31/03).

Canadian River Municipal Water Authority – 2-yr; 17 members: Glenn Bickel, Plainview (8/31/04); Jerry Carlson, Pampa (7/31/03); James O. Collins, Lubbock (7/31/03); Tom Edmonds, Borger (7/31/04); Larry Hagood, Tahoka (7/31/03); William Hallerberg, Amarillo (7/31/04); Benny Kirksey, Pampa (7/31/04); Pat McCutchin, Levelland (7/31/03); E.R. Moore, O'Donnell (7/31/03); Ray Renner, Lamesa (7/31/03); L.J. Richardson, Brownfield (7/31/03); Robert Rodgers, Lubbock (7/31/04); George Sell, Amarillo (7/31/03); Carl Shamburger, Levelland (7/31/04); Steve Tucker, Slaton (7/31/03); JoAnn Wasicek, Borger (7/31/03); Norman Wright, Plainview (7/31/03). PO Box 9, Sanford 79086-0009; (806) 865-3325.

Cancer Council, Texas – (1985); 6-yr.; expenses; 15 members: James D. Dannenbaum, Houston (2/1/06); Donald C. Spencer, Austin (2/1/06); Karen Heusinkveld, Arlington (2/1/08); F. Diane Barber, Richmond (2/1/06); Karen Bonner, Corpus Christi (2/1/10); Clare Buie Chaney, Dallas (2/1/08); Lloyd K. Croft, Boerne (2/1/08); Sylvia P. Fernandez, San Antonio (2/1/10); Carolyn D. Harvey, Tyler (2/1/06); Rubye H. Henderson, Plainview (2/1/08); Larry Herrera, Temple (2/1/06); Courtney Townsend Jr., Galveston (2/1/04); J. Taylor Wharton, Houston, (2/1/10). Ex officio member, Debra C. Stabeno. Exec. Dir. Sandra Balderrama ($57,691) PO Box 12097, Austin 78711; 512-463-3190.

Central Colorado River Authority (See **Colorado River Authority, Central**.)

Chemist, Office of State – (1911); ex officio, indefinite term: State Chemist, Tim Herrman, P. O. Box 3160, College Station 77841-3160; 979-845-1121.

Childhood Intervention, Interagency Council on Early – Combined into Department of Assistive and Rehabilitative Services of the Health and Human Services Commission as of 3/1/04. Exec. Dir. Mary Beth O'Hanlon.

Chiropractic Examiners, Texas Board of – (1949); apptv.; 6-yr.; expenses; 9 members: Chair Sandra Lee Jensen, Farmers Branch (2/1/07); Robert L. Coburn, West Columbia (2/1/05); Marcia Olivia Daughtrey, Tyler (2/1/09); Paul H. Dickerson, Houston (2/1/05); Narciso Escareño, Brownsville (2/1/07); Serge Francois, Dallas (2/1/05); Scott Edward Isdale, Killeen (2/1/09); Steve Minors, Austin (2/1/07); David Alan Sime, El Paso (2/1/09). Exec. Dir. Sandra D. Smith ($52,000), 333 Guadalupe, Ste. 3-825, Austin 78701; 512-305-6700.

Coastal Water Authority, Board of Directors – (1967 as Coastal Industrial Water Authority, Board of Directors of; name changed in 1985); 7 members — 4 apptd. by mayor of Houston with advice and consent of governing body of Houston; 3 apptd. by Gov.; per diem and expenses; 2-yr.; Gov's. apptees: Dionel E. Aviles (3/31/01); Rick Cloutier (4/1/02); Buster E. French (4/1/00); Darryl L. King (4/1/01); Kurt Metyko (3/31/01); Gary R. Nelson (4/1/01); Dorothy M. Washington (3/31/02). Exec. Dir. Ralph T. Rundle, 1200 Smith St., Ste. 2260, Houston 77002; 713-658-9020.

Colorado River Authority, Central, Board of Directors – (1935); apptv.; 6-yr.; per diem on duty; 9 members: Ann Miller Hargett, Coleman (2/1/01); Alice B. Hemphill, Coleman (2/1/05); John S. Hensley, Santa Anna (2/1/05); Jack B. Horne, Coleman (2/1/03); Nan Knox Markland, Burkett (2/1/01); Ronald W. Owens, Coleman (2/1/01); Ben J. Scott, Coleman (2/1/05); Barbara A. Simmons, Santa Anna (2/1/03). Operations Mgr., Lynn W. Cardinas, PO Box 964, Coleman 76834.

Colorado River Authority, Lower, Board of Directors – (1934 as 9-member board; membership increased in 1951 and 1975); apptv.; 6-yr.; per diem on duty; 15 members: Chair Ray A. Wilkerson, Travis Co. (2/1/07); Vice-Chair G. Hughes Abell, Travis Co. (2/1/07); Secretary, Connie Granberg, Blanco Co. (2/1/07); Kay Morgan Carlton, Fayette Co. (2/1/09); Ida A. Carter, Burnet Co. (2/1/11); Lucy Ortiz Cavazos, Kerr Co. (2/1/09); John C. Dickerson, III, Matagorda Co. (2/1/09); Walter E. Garrett, Wharton Co. (2/1/09); Robert K. Long, Sr., Bastrop Co. (2/1/07); John H. Matthews, Colorado Co. (2/1/05); Woodrow Francis McCasland, Llano Co. (2/1/11); Charles R. Moser, Washington Co. (2/1/07); Clayborne L.

Nettleship, San Saba Co. (2/1/09); Linda Clapp Raun, Wharton Co. (2/1/11); B.R. (Skipper) Wallace, Williamson Co. (2/1/11). Gen. Man., Joseph J. Beal, P. O. Box 220, Austin 78767-0220; 512-473-3200.

Colorado River Authority, Upper, Board of Directors – (1935 as 9-member board; reorganized in 1965); apptv.; 6-yr.; per diem and expenses; indefinite number of members: Chair Fred R. Campbell, Paint Rock (2/1/03); Vice/Chair Jeffie Harmon Roberts, Robert Lee (2/1/05); Secretary, Dorris M. Sonnenberg, Bronte (2/1/01); Treasurer, Hyman Sauer, Eldorado (2/1/05); Board Members: Ray Alderman, Winters (2/1/01); Ralph E. Hoelscher, Miles (2/1/01); Hope Huffman, San Angelo (2/1/03). Ellen Groth, Admin. Asst., 12 Orient, San Angelo 76903; 325-655-0565.

Commissioner of (See keyword, as **Agriculture, Commissioner of.**)

Concho River Water and Soil Conservation Authority, Lower – (1939); 6-yr.; 9 members: Chair Benjamin Orland Sims, Paint Rock (2/1/1997); Joseph Beach, Millersview (2/1/1997); Leroy Beach, Millersview (2/1/1999); Howard Loveless, Eden (2/1/1999); Billy J. Mikeska, Eola (2/1/1999); Eugene R. Rodgers, Eden (2/1/1997); Edwin T. Tickle, Eden (2/1/01); Harvey P. Williams, Eola (2/1/01). Office Address: Rt. 1, PO Box 4, Paint Rock 76866; 325-732-4371.

Consumer Credit Commissioner – Leslie L. Pettijohn ($90, 000), 2601 N. Lamar, Austin 78705-4207.

Cosmetology Commission, Texas – (1935 as 3-member State Board of Hairdressers and Cosmetologists; name changed and membership increased to 6 apptv. and one ex officio in 1971); apptv.; per diem and expenses; 6-yr.; apptv. members: Leif Christiansen, Spring (12/31/07); Heliana L. Kiessling, Friendswood (12/31/03); Philip Lapp, Weatherford (12/31/07); Helen Quiram, Waco (12/31/05); Lucinda Shearer (Cindy) Sandoval, Edinburg (12/31/07); Elida Zapata, Lubbock (12/31/05). Ex officio member, Esther Camacho, Texas Education Agency. Exec. Dir. Antoinette Humphrey ($46,338), PO Box 26700, Austin 78755-0700; 512-380-7600.

Counselors, Texas State Board of Examiners of Professional – (1981); apptv.; 6-yr.; expenses; 9 members: Chair Judith D. Powell, The Woodlands (2/1/05); Ana C. Bergh, Edinburg (2/1/05); Diane J. Boddy, Henrietta (2/1/090); James Castro, San Antonio (2/1/09); Glenda Corley, Pearland (2/1/05); Michelle A. Eggleston, Amarillo (2/1/07); Alma Gloria Leal, Rancho Viejo (2/1/09); J. Helen Perkins, DeSoto (2/1/07); Dan F. Wilkins, Center (2/1/07). Exec. Dir. Bobbe Alexander, 1100 W. 49th, Austin 78756-3183; 512-834-6658.

Court Reporters Certification Board – (1977 as 9-member Texas Reporters Committee; name changed to present form and membership increased to 12 in 1983); apptv. by State Supreme Court; 6-yr.; expenses: Chair Catharina Haynes, Dallas (12/31/06); Attorney members: Olan Boudreaux, San Antonio (12/31/08); Wendy Tolson Ross, San Antonio (12/31/07). Official reporters: Albert Alvarez, Austin (12/31/05); Judy Miller, Fort Worth (12/31/06). Freelance reporter: Paula Richards, Kerrville (12/31/08); one vacancy. Firm representatives: Audree Crutcher, Lubbock (12/31/08); Kim Tindall, San Antonio (12/31/06); Lay members: Sara Dolph, Austin (12/31/05); Michelle Herrera, San Antonio (12/31/07); Ly T. Nguyen, Austin (12/31/08. Director Michele L. Henricks ($52,000), 205 W. 14th St., Ste. 101, Austin 78701; 512-463-1630.

Credit Union Commission – (1949 as 3-member Credit Union Advisory Commission; name changed and membership increased to 6 in 1969; increased to 9 in 1981); apptv.; 6-yr.; expenses; 9 members: Presiding Officer Gary L. Janacek, Temple (2/15/09); Garold R. Base, Plano (2/15/07); Rufino Carbajal Jr., El Paso (2/15/07); Barbara K. Sheffield, Houston (2/15/11); Public members: Floyde Burnside, San Antonio (2/15/05); Thomas Felton Butler, La Porte (2/15/07); Richard A. Glasco Jr. Georgetown (2/15/03); Mary Ann Grant, Houston (2/15/09); Henry E. (Pete) Snow, Texarkana (2/15/11). Commissioner Harold E. Feeney, 914 E. Anderson Ln., Austin 78752-1699; 512-837/9236.

Crime Stoppers Advisory Council – (1981); apptv.; 4-yr.; per diem and expenses; 5 members: Janice C. Gillen, Rosenberg (9/1/04); Juan F. Jorge, Tomball (9/1/04); Tina Alexander Sellers, Lufkin (9/1/04); Dorothy Spinks, Marble

Falls (9/1/05); Brian Thomas, Amarillo (9/1/05).

Criminal Justice, Texas Board of – (1989: assumed duties of former Texas Board of Corrections and Adult Probation Commission; also oversees Board of Pardons and Paroles Division); apptd; 6-yr.; expenses; 9 members: Chair Christina Melton Crain, Dallas (2/1/07); Vice-Chair Don B. Jones, Midland (2/1/05); Secretary William H. (Hank) Moody, Kerrville (2/1/05); Adrian A. Arriaga, McAllen (2/1/07); Mary Bacon, Houston (2/1/05); Oliver J. Bell, Austin (2/1/09); Greg S. Coleman, Austin (2/1/09); Patricia A. Day, Dallas (2/1/03); Pierce Miller, San Angelo (2/1/07). Exec. Dir, Dept. of Criminal Justice: Brad Livingston ($150,000), PO Box 13084, Austin 78711. 512-475-3250.

Deaf, Governing Board of the Texas School for the – (1979); 6-yr.; expenses; 9 members: Charles Estes, Denton (1/31/09); Beatrice M. Burke, Big Spring (1/31/07); Nancy E. Munger, Kyle (1/31/95); Jean Andrews, Beaumont (1/31/05); Walter Camenisch, Austin (1/31/09); Nancy Carrizales, Katy (1/31/07); Kenneth D. Kesterson, Big Spring (1/31/07); Lesa Thomas, Corpus Christi (1/31/05). Superintendent, Claire Bugen ($84,000), 1102 South Congress, Austin 78704; 512-462-5353.

Deaf and Hard of Hearing, Texas Commission for the – – Combined into Department of Assistive and Rehabilitative Services of the Health and Human Services Commission as of 3/1/04.

Dental Examiners, State Board of – (1919 as 6-member board; increased to 9 members in 1971; increased to 12 in 1981; increased to 15 in 1991; sunsetted in 1994; reconstituted with 18 members in 1995); appt.; 6-yr.; per diem while on duty; 18 members: Presiding Officer J. Kevin Irons, Austin (2/1/05); Tammy Lynne Allen, Fort Worth (2/1/07); Oscar X. Garcia, Brownsville (2/1/07); Amy Landess Juba, Amarillo (2/1/05); Martha Lynn Manley Malik, Victoria (2/1/05); Norman Lewis Mason, Austin (2/1/09); Gary W. McDonald, Kingwood (2/1/09); Helen Hayes McKibben, Lubbock (2/1/09); Marti L. Morgan, Fort Worth (2/1/05); Phyllis A. Stine, Midland (2/1/07; George Strunk, Longview (2/1/09); Paul E. Stubbs, Austin (2/1/07); Nathaniel Tippit, Houston (2/1/05); Juan D. Villarreal, Harlingen (2/1/07); Charles Field Wetherbee, Jourdanton (2/1/09). Exec. Dir. Bobby Schmidt ($63,000), 333 Guadalupe, Ste. 3-800, Austin 78701; 512-463-6400.

Depository Board, State – (Abolished May 1997).

Diabetes Council, Texas – (1983; with 5 ex officio and 6 public members serving 2-yr. terms; changed in 1987 to 3 ex officio and 8 public members; changed to present configuration in 1991; term length changed from 4 to 6 years eff. 1997); 6-yr.; 17 members — 5 ex officio; 11 apptv. public members as follows: Chair Lawrence B. Harkless, San Antonio (2/1/07); Public members: Randy Bryon Baker, Mesquite (2/1/09); Belinda Bazan/Lara, San Antonio (2/1/05); Gene Fulton Bell, Lubbock (2/1/03); Victor Hugo Gonzalez, McAllen (2/1/03); Judith L. Haley, Houston (2/1/05); Richard S. (Rick) Hayley, Corpus Christi (2/1/05); Lenore Frances Katz, Dallas (2/1/07); Margaret G. Pacillas, El Paso (2/1/07); Avery Rhodes, Diboll (2/1/09); Jeffrey A. Ross, Bellaire (2/1/07). Director Jan Marie Ozias; c/o Texas Dept. of Health, 1100 W. 49th, Austin 78756; 512-458-7490.

Dietitians, Texas State Board of Examiners of – (1983); apptv.; 6-yr.; per diem and expenses: 9 members: Lucinda Flores, Brownsville (9/1/03); Georgiana S. Gross, San Antonio (9/1/09); Janet S. Hall, Georgetown (9/1/07); Ralph McGahagin, Austin (9/1/05); Amy N. McLeod, Lufkin (9/1/07); Gene Wisakowsky, Dallas (9/1/05); Public members: Carol Davis, Dallas (9/1/05); Linda W. Dickerson, Angleton (9/1/09); Claudia L. Lisle, Amarillo (9/1/07). Texas Dept. of Health, 1100 W. 49th, Austin 78756; 512-834-6601.

Disabilities, Texas Council for Developmental – (1971); apptv.; 6-yr.; 29 members — 8 ex offico: Representatives from Dept. of Mental Health and Mental Retardation, Rehabilitation Commission, Dept. of Health, Dept. of Human Services, Texas Dept. on Aging, Texas Education Agency, Texas Commission for the Blind, Texas Commission for the Deaf; 19 apptv. members: Chair Jan R. Newsom, Dallas (2/1/07); Vice/Chair Richard A. Tisch, Spring (2/1/09). Public members: Raul Acosta, Lubbock (2/1/05); Susan Berkley, Alvin (2/1/07); Kristine Bissmeyer, San Antonio (2/1/05); Melonie S. Caster, Bedford (2/1/09); Brenda K. Coleman/Beattie, Austin (2/1/07); Mary M. Durheim, McAllen (2/1/05); Marcia Dwyer, Plano (2/1/05); Cindy Johnston, Dallas (2/1/07); Diana Kern, Cedar Creek (2/1/09); Amy L. Baxter Ley, Euless (2/1/09); Vickie J. Mitchell, Montgomery (2/1/09); John C. Morris, Austin (2/1/07); Dana S. Perry, Brownwood (2/1/09); Ed Rankin, Dallas (2/1/07); Joe Rivas, Denton (2/1/05); Raul Treviño, Mission (2/1/09); Susan Vardell, Sherman (2/1/07). Exec. Dir. Roger A. Webb, 6201 E. Oltorf, Ste. 600, Austin 78741; 512-437-5432.

Disabilities, Governor's Committee on People with – (1991); 16 members: 4 ex officio: Chmn., TEC; Commissioner, Texas Rehabilitation Comm.; Dir., Texas Commission for the Blind; member, Texas Comm. for the Deaf; 12 members apptd. by governor; 2-year terms: Chair Thomas P. Justis, Granbury (2/1/05); Kara Wilson Anglin, Houston (2/2/05); Douglas F. Grady Jr., Fort Worth (2/1/04); Peter Grojean, San Antonio (2/1/04); Roland Guzman, San Antonio (2/1/05); Anthony G. Jones, Lubbock (2/1/01); Judy Rae Scott, Dallas (2/1/04); Brian D. Shannon, Lubbock (2/1/05); Nancy Shugart, Austin (2/1/04); Kathy S. Strong, Garrison (2/1/04); Shane Whitehurst, Austin (2/1/05); one vacancy. Exec. Dir. Pat Pound, 4900 N. Lamar, Austin 78751-2613; 512-463-5739.

Disabilities, Texas Office for Prevention of Developmental – (1991) 9 members apptd. by governor; 6-year terms: Chair Theresa Mulloy, Stephenville; Vice-Chair J.C. Montgomery Jr., Dallas; Rep. Dwayne Bohac, Houston; Robert L. Carr, Lubbock; Dale Coln, Dallas; Joan Roberts-Scott, Austin; Marian Sokol, San Antonio; Mary S. Tijerina, San Marcos; Rep. Vicki Truitt, Southlake. Exec. Dir. Carolyn Smith, P.O. Box 12668, Austin 78711-2668; 512-206-4544.

Disabilities, Texas Council on Purchasing from People with – (1979 as 10-member Committee on Purchases of Products and Services of Blind and Severely Disabled Persons; name changed and members reduced to 9 in 1995); apptd.; expenses; 6-yr.; 9 members: Chair Margaret (Meg) Pfluger, Lubbock (1/31/05); Board Members: Chuck Brewton, San Antonio (1/31/05); Byron E. Johnson, El Paso (1/31/07); Howard K. Karnes, Dallas (1/31/07); John Luna, Euless (1/31/09); Floyd Glen Self, Jr., Dripping Springs (1/31/09); Wanda White Stovall, Fort Worth (1/31/09); Cathy J. Williams, Austin (1/31/05). Exec. Dir. Kelvin Moore. P.O. Box 13047, Austin 78711/3047; 512-463-3244.

Education, Board of Control for Southern Regional – (1969); apptv.; 4-yr.; 5 members: Gov. ex officio, 4 apptd.: Rep. Dianne White Delisi, Temple (6/30/07); Rep. Kent Grusendorf, Arlington (6/30/08); Shirley J. Neeley, Ed.D. (6/30/06); Sen. Florence Shapiro, Plano (6/30/05); Ex Officio Member, Governor Rick Perry, Austin); President, Mark D. Musick, Southern Regional Education Board, 592 10th St. N.W., Atlanta, GA 30318-5790; 404)-75-9211.

Education, Commissioner of – (1866 as Superintendent of Public Instruction; 1949 changed to present name by Gilmer-Aiken Law); apptv. by State Board of Education; 4-yr.: Shirley J. Neeley ($164,748) (See also Education, State Board of).

Education, State Board of – (1866; re-created 1928 and re-formed by Gilmer-Aikin Act in 1949 to consist of 21 elective members from districts co-extensive with 21 congressional districts at that time; membership increased to 24 with congressional redistricting in 1971, effective 1973; membership increased to 27 with congressional redistricting in 1981, effective 1983; reorganized by special legislative session as 15-member apptv. board in 1984 to become elective board again in 1988; expenses; 4-yr.; 15 members: Chair Geraldine (Tincy) Miller, Dallas, District 12 (2/1/07); Lawrence Allen Jr., Houston, District 4 (1/1/07); Mary Helen Berlanga, Corpus Christi, District 2 (1/1/09); Joe J. Bernal, San Antonio, District 3 (1/1/07); David Bradley, Beaumont, District 7 (1/1/09); Barbara Cargill, The Woodlands, District 8 (1/1/09); Bob Craig, Lubbock, District 15 (1/1/07); Patricia (Pat) Hardy, Fort Worth, District 11 (1/1/09); Mavis B. Knight, Dallas, District 13 (1/1/09); Terri Leo, Spring, District 6 (1/1/09); Gail Lowe, Lampasas, District 14 (1/1/09); Don McLeroy, Bryan, District 9 (1/1/07); Dan Montgomery, Fredericksburg, District 5 (1/1/07);

Rene Nuñez, El Paso, District 1 (1/1/07); Cynthia Thornton, Round Top, District 10 (1/1/07) Executive Assistant, Reneé Jackson. Commissioner of Education, Shirley J. Neeley ($164,748), Texas Education Agency, 1701 N. Congress Ave., Austin 78701-1494.

Educator Certification, State Board for – (1995); apptv.; 6-yr.; expenses; 15 members; 3 non-voting: rep. of Comm. of Education; rep of Comm. of Higher Education; 1 dean of a college of education apptd. by Gov.; 14 voting members apptd. by Gov.: Chair Annette T. Griffin, Carrollton (2/1/05); Vice/Chair Cecilia P. Abbott, Austin (2/1/07); Secretary, Bonny L. Cain, Ed.D., Pearland (2/1/09); Board Members: Glenda Barron, Austin, at will of Comm.); John James Beck, Jr., San Marcos (2/1/05); Patti Lynn Johnson, Canyon Lake (2/1/09); Adele Quintana, Dumas (2/1/07); Cynthia M. Saenz, Austin (2/1/09); Antonio Sanchez, Mission (2/1/05); Robert Scott, Austin, at will of Comm.); John C. Shirley, Dallas (2/1/09); Troy Simmons, Longview (2/1/09); James Windham, Houston (2/1/05); Judie Zinsser, Houston (2/1/07). Exec. Dir. Herman Smith, ($78,000),1701 N. Congress Ave., 5th Fl, Austin 78701/1494; 512-936-8400.

Edwards Aquifer Authority – (1993); elected from single-member districts; 4-yr.; expenses; 15 apptv. members: Chair Doug Miller, Comal County, (12/1/06); Vice-Chair Rafael Zendejas, Bexar Co., (12/1/06); Sec., Levi Jackson III, Bexar Co., (12/1/08); Treas., Hunter Schuehle, Medina Co., (12/1/08); Ken Barnes, Hays Co., (12/1/08); Bailey Barton, Hays Co., (12/1/06); Luana Buckner, Medina Co., (12/1/06); Ramon Chapa, Jr., Comal Co., (12/1/08); Mario H. Cruz, Uvalde Co., (12/1/08); Bruce Gilleland, Uvalde Co., (12/1/06); Rogelio Muñoz, Uvalde Co. (12/1/08); Carol Patterson, Bexar Co., (12/1/06); George Rice, Bexar Co., (12/1/06); Johnny A. Rodriguez, Bexar Co., (12/1/06); Appt. Dir. Clay Binford, (12/1/08); at large, Susan Hughes, Bexar Co., (12/1/08); Appt. Dir. Bob Keith, (12/1/08). Gen. Mgr. Robert J. Potts, ($165,000) 1615 N. St. Mary's St., San Antonio 78215-1415.

Egg Marketing Advisory Board – (Abolished May 1997).

Election Commission, State – (1973); 9 members, ex officio and apptv. as indicated: Chmn. of Democratic State Executive Committee; Chmn. of Republican State Executive Committee; Chief Justice of Supreme Court; Presiding Judge, Court of Criminal Appeals; 2 persons to be named, one a justice of the Court of Appeals apptd. by Chief Justice of Supreme Court, one a District Judge apptd. by presiding judge of Court of Criminal Appeals; 2 county chairmen, one each from Democratic and Republican parties, named by the parties; Secretary of State.

Emergency Communications, Commission on State – (1985 as 17-member Advisory Commission on State Emergency Communications; name changed and membership reduced to 12, 2000); expenses; 12 members: 3 ex offico: exec. directors of Dept. of Health, Public Utilities Comm. and General Services Admin.; 9 public members (6 yr.): 2 apptd. by Lt. Gov.; 2 apptd. by Speaker; 5 apptd. by Gov. Gov's apptees: Presiding Officer, Dorothy Morgan, Brenham (9/1/05); James Beauchamp, Midland (8/31/07); Don Comedy, Haskell (8/30/03); John L. deNoyelles, Tyler (9/1/03); Heberto Gutierrez, San Antonio (9/1/03); Glenn O. Lewis, Fort Worth (9/1/07); James L. O'Neal, Lancaster (9/1/05); Lyn Phillips, Bastrop (9/1/03); H. T. Wright, Lockhart (9/1/07). Exec. Dir. Paul Mallett ($75,000), 333 Guadalupe St., Ste. 2-212, Austin 78701; 512-305-6911.

Emergency Services Personnel Retirement Fund, Texas Statewide – (1977; formerly the Fire Fighters' Relief and Retirement Fund); apptv.; expenses; 6-yr.; 9 members: Chair Francisco R. Torres, Raymondville (9/1/05); Vice-Chair Allen J. Scopel, Rosenburg (9/1/05); Sec., Paul V. Loeffler, Alpine (9/1/07); Oscar Choate, Mineral Wells (9/1/07); Kyle A. Donaldson, Sonora (9/1/09); Graciela G. Flores, Corpus Christi (9/1/09); Rex W. Klesel, Alvin (9/1/09); Maxie L. Patterson, Houston (9/1/09); Robert Weiss, Brenham (9/1/05); Commissioner, Lisa Ivie Miller, PO Box 12577, Austin 78711.

Employment Commission, Texas – (See **Workforce Commission, Texas**)

Engineers, State Board of Registration for Profes-

sional – (1937 as 6-member board; membership increased to 9 in 1981); apptv.; per diem and expenses; 6-yr.; 9 members: Chair James R. Nichols, P.E., Fort Worth (9/26/09); Jose F. Cardenas, P.E., El Paso (9/26/09); C. Roland Haden, Ph.D., P.E., College Station (9/26/07); Govind Nadkarni, P.E., Corpus Christi (9/26/05); Gerry E. Pate, P.E., Houston (9/26/07); Robert M. Sweazy, Ph.D., P.E., Lubbock (9/26/05); Public Members: William Lawrence, Highland Village (9/26/07); Shannon K. McClendon, Dripping Springs (9/26/09); Vicki T. Ravenburg, C.P.A., San Antonio (9/26/05). Exec. Dir., Dale Beebe Farrow ($75,000), 1917 S. IH-35, Austin 78741.

Environmental Quality, Texas Commission on – (1913 as State Board of Water Engineers; name changed in 1962 to Texas Water Commission; reorganized and name again changed in 1965 to Water Rights Commission; reorganized and name changed back to Texas Water Commission in 1977 to perform judicial function for the Texas Dept. of Water Resources; name changed to Texas Natural Resource Conservation Commission in 1993; changed to present form Sept. 1, 2002); apptv.; 6-yr.; 3 members full-time at $107,500–$111,792: Kathleen Hartnett White, Valentine (8/31/07); R.B. (Ralph) Marquez, Texas City (8/31/05); Larry Ross Soward, Austin (8/31/09). Exec. Dir., Glenn Shankle ($132,000), PO Box 13087, Austin 78711.

Ethics Commission, Texas – (1991); apptd.; 4-yr.; 8 members: 2 apptd. by Speaker, 2 apptd. by Lt. Gov, 4 apptd. by Gov.: Chair Wales H. Madden III, Amarillo (11/19/05); Vice-Chair Francisco Hernandez Jr., Fort Worth (11/19/03); Raymond R. (Trip) Davenport III, Dallas (11/19/07); Scott W. Fisher, Bedford (11/19/05); Warren Tom Harrison, Austin (11/19/07); Cullen R. Looney, Edinburg (11/19/07); James David Montagne, Orange (11/19/07); Ralph Wayne, Austin (11/19/05). Exec. Dir., David Allen Reisman ($97,000), 201 E. 14th St., 10th Fl., Austin 78701.

Finance Commission of Texas – (1923 as Banking Commission; reorganized as Finance Commission in 1943 with 9 members; membership increased to 12 in 1983; changed back to 9 members in 1989); apptv.; 6-yr.; per diem and traveling expenses; 9 members: Chair Vernon Bryant, Jr., Aledo (2/1/06); Gary D. Akright, Dallas (2/1/08); Mike Bradford (2/1/06); Hector Delgado, Dallas (2/1/10); Kenneth H. Harris, Austin (2/1/08); Cindy F. Lyons, El Paso (2/1/10); Allan B. Polunsky, San Antonio (2/1/08); John Snider, Center (2/1/06); William James White, Georgetown (2/1/10). Banking Commissioner, Randall S. James , 2601 N. Lamar, Austin 78705, appointee of Finance Commission. (See also Banking Commissioner, State.)

Fire Fighters' Pension Commissioner – (1937); apptv.; 2-yr.: Lisa Ivie Miller, Austin (7/1/07) ($57,000), PO Box 12577, Austin 78711.

Fire Protection, Texas Commission on – (1991; formed by consolidation of Fire Dept. Emergency Board and Commission on Fire Protection Personnel Standards and Education); apptv.; 6-yrs.; expenses; 12 members: Presiding Officer, Kelley M. Stalder, Parker (2/1/03); Commissioners: David Abernathy, Pittsburg (2/1/07); Juan J. Adame, Corpus Christi (2/1/07); Pat Barrett, College Station (2/1/03); Marvin G. Dawson, Brownfield (2/1/07); Mike Jolly, Georgetown (2/1/07); Alonzo Lopez, Jr., Kingsville (2/1/05); Arthur Lee Pertile, III, Waco (2/1/07); Ricardo Saldaña, Mission (2/1/05); Peggy Trahan, South Padre Island (2/1/03); G. Kent Worley, Fort Worth (2/1/03); Carl Wren, Manchaca (2/1/05). Exec. Dir., Gary L. Warren Sr. ($78,000), PO Box 2286, Austin 78768.

Food and Fibers Commission, Texas – (1941 as Cotton Research Committee; name changed in 1971 to Natural Fibers and Food Protein Committee; changed to commission in 1975; changed to present name 1989); 4 members are presidents and chancellor of four major universities (Pres., Texas Woman's University, Denton; Pres., Texas Tech University, Lubbock; Chancellor, Texas A&M University System, College Station; Pres., University of Texas at Austin) serving indefinite terms; and one ex officio member who is director of administrative office in Dallas, apptd. to 2-year term: Exec. Dir., Robert V. Avant Jr., 17360 Coit Rd., Dallas 75252.

Funeral Service Commission, Texas – (1903 as State Board of Embalming; 1935 as State Board of Funeral Directors and Embalmers; 1953 as 6-member board; membership

increased to 9 in 1979; name changed to present form in 1987; membership reduced to 6 in 1999); apptv.; per diem and expenses; 6-yr.; 6 members: Presiding Officer, Harry Whittington, Austin (2/1/07); Laurens B. Fish, III, Austin (2/1/09); Dorothy Grasty, Arlington (2/1/05); Martha Greenlaw, Houston (2/1/07); Janice B. Howard, Missouri City (2/1/07); Martha (Marty) Rhymes, White Oak (2/1/03); Jim Wright, Wheeler (2/1/05). Exec. Dir., O.C. "Chet" Robbins ($45,816), 510 S. Congress, Ste. 206, Austin 78704-1716.

General Services Commission – (1919 as Board of Control; name changed to State Purchasing and General Services Commission in 1979; changed to present form and increased to 6 commissioners in 1991); apptv.; 6-yr.; expenses; 6 members: Tomás Cárdenas Jr., El Paso (1/31/05); James A. Cox Jr., Austin (1/31/05); Gilbert A. Herrera, Houston (1/31/07); Barbara Rusling, Waco (1/31/03); Gene Shull, Tyler (1/31/03). Acting Exec. Dir., Ann Dillon ($115,000), PO Box 13047, Austin 78711-3047.

Geoscientists, Texas Board of Professional – (2001); apptv.; expenses; 6-yr.; 9 members (6 professional geoscientists, 3 public members): William K. Coleman, Cedar Hill (2/1/05); Kelly K. Doe, Friendswood (2/1/09); Shiela B. Hall, Lubbock (2/1/07); Murray H. Milford, Bryan (2/1/07); Edward G. Miller, San Antonio (2/1/05); Rene D. Pena, El Paso (2/1/09); Danny R. Perkins, Houston (2/1/07); Kimberly R. Phillips, Houston (2/1/05); Gordon D. Ware, Corpus Christi (2/1/09). Exec. Dir., Michael D. Hess., P.O. Box 12157, Austin, TX 78711.

Guadalupe River Authority, Upper – (1939); apptv.; 6-yr.; 9 members: Chair Fred R. Campbell, Paint Rock (2/1/03); Vice/Chair Jeffie Harmon Roberts, Robert Lee (2/1/05); Secretary, Dorris M. Sonnenberg, Bronte (2/1/01); Treasurer, Hyman Sauer, Eldorado (2/1/05); Board Members: Ray Alderman, Winters (2/1/01); Ralph E. Hoelscher, Miles (2/1/01); Hope Huffman, San Angelo (2/1/03). Gen. Mgr., Ellen Groth, 125 Lehman Dr., Ste. 100, Kerrville 78028.

Guadalupe-Blanco River Authority – (1935); apptv.; per diem and expenses on duty; 6-yr.; 9 members: Kathleen A. Devine, New Braunfels (2/1/05); Jack R. Gary, San Marcos (2/1/07); Margaret M. Grier, Boerne (2/1/09); Myrna P. McLeroy, Gonzales (2/1/07); Frank J. Pagel, Tivoli (2/1/07); Frederick S. Schlather, Cibolo (2/1/03); John P. Schneider, Jr., Lockhart (2/1/05); Clifton L. Thomas, Jr., Victoria (2/1/09); Stephen F. Wilson, D.V.M., Port Lavaca (2/1/05). Gen. Mgr., William E. West, 933 E. Court St., Seguin 78155.

Gulf Coast Waste Disposal Authority – (1969); apptv.; 2-yr.; per diem and expenses on duty; 9 members: 3 apptv. by Gov., 3 by County Commissioners Courts of counties in district, 3 by Municipalities Waste Disposal Councils of counties in district. Zoe Milian Barinaga, Houston (8/31/03); Ron Crowder, LaMarque (8/31/05); Louis S. (Sam) Dell'Olio, Jr., Galveston (8/31/02); Franklin Jones, Houston (8/31/05); James A. Matthews, Jr., Texas City (8/31/05); Irvin Osborne/Lee, Houston (8/31/04); Mark Schultz, Anahuac (8/31/06); Shirley Seale, Anahuac (8/31/02); Rita Standridge, Beach City (8/31/06). Gen. Mgr., Charles Ganze, 910 Bay Area Blvd., Houston 77058.

Gulf States Marine Fisheries Commission – (1949); apptv.; 3-yr.; 3 members — 2 ex officio: exec. dir., Texas Parks & Wildlife Dept.; one member of House; one apptd. by Gov.: L. Don Perkins, Houston (3/17/02). Exec. Dir., Larry B. Simpson, PO Box 726, Ocean Springs, MS 30564.

Health, Commissioner of – (1879 as State Health Officer; 1955 changed to Commissioner of Health; 1975 changed to Director, Texas Department of Health Resources; 1977 changed to Commissioner, Texas Department of Health; apptv.; 2-yr.: Albert Hawkins ($155,000), 1100 W. 49th, Austin 78756.

Health Coordinating Council, Statewide Rural – (1997); 17 members (6 representatives of care providers; 12 apptd. by Gov.); 6-yr.; Chair Ben G. Raimer, Galveston (8/1/09); Board Members: Joan Wood Biggerstaff, Plano (8/1/05); James A. Endicott, Jr., Harker Heights (8/1/05); Karl Alonzo Floyd, Stafford (8/1/09); Janie Martinez Gonzalez, San Antonio (8/1/09); Elva C. LeBlanc, Galveston (8/1/07); Jimmie Lee Mason, Lubbock (8/1/07); Thalia H. Munoz, Rio Grande City (8/1/09); Richard Madsen Smith,Amarillo (8/1/09); Patricia L.

Starck, Houston (8/1/07); Russell K. Tolman, Fort Worth (8/1/05); David A. Valdez, San Antonio (8/1/07);1100 West 49th St., Austin, TX 78756/3199; 512-458-7261.

Health and Human Services, Texas Commission of – (1991); 9 members apptd.; 4-yr.; Presiding Officer Jerry Kane, Corpus Christi (2/1/09); Kathleen O. Angel, Round Rock (2/1/05); Sharon J. Barnes, Freeport (2/1/07); Maryann Choi, Temple (2/1/05); Manson B. Johnson, Houston (2/1/09); Leon J. Leach, Houston (2/1/07); Ronald Luke, Austin (2/1/07); Gwyn Shea, Irving (2/1/09); Robert A. Valadez, San Antonio (2/1/05). Commissioner Albert Hawkins III ($189,000), (2/1/05). 4900 N. Lamar Blvd., Austin 78751.

Health Services, Texas Department of State – (1975); apptv.; 7 members, 4-yr.; Chair Rodolfo (Rudy) Arredondo, Lubbock (2/1/09); Beverly Barron, Odessa (2/1/07); Jaime A. Davidson, Dallas (2/1/05); Lewis E. Foxhall, Houston (2/1/09); Glenda R. Kane, Corpus Christi (2/1/09); Jeffrey A. Ross, Houston, (2/1/07); James G. (Jim) Springfield, Harlingen (2/1/05). Exec. Dir., Eduardo J. Sanchez, 1100 W. 49th, Austin 78756-3199.

Hearing Instruments, State Committee of Examiners in the Fitting and Dispensing of – (1969); apptv.; 6-yr.; expenses; 9 members: Gordon L. Bisel, Houston (12/31/05); Richard A. Davila II, Lubbock (12/31/09); Kenneth W. Earl, Orange (12/31/07); Ronald J. Ensweiler, Dallas (12/31/07); Sara Ann Garza, Penitas (12/31/09); V. Rosemary Geraci, Lufkin (12/31/09); Jerome Kosoy, Houston (12/31/07); James McCrae, Fredericksburg (12/31/05); Audrey McDonald, Georgetown (12/31/05);. Exec. Dir., Pam K. Kaderka, 4800 N. Lamar, Ste. 150, Austin 78756.

Higher Education Coordinating Board, Texas – (1953 as temporary board; 1955 as permanent 15-member Texas Commission on Higher Education; increased to 18 members in 1965; name changed to present form in 1987); apptv.; 6-yr.; expenses; 18 members: Chair Jerry Farrington, Dallas (8/31/07); Vice Chair Robert W. Shepard, Harlingen (8/31/09); Neal W. Adams, Bedford (8/31/07); Laurie Bricker, Houston (8/31/09); Ricardo G. Cigarroa, Laredo (8/31/05); Paul Foster, El Paso (8/31/09); Cathy Obriotti Green, San Antonio (8/31/05) Gerry Griffin, Hunt (8/31/05); Carey Hobbs, Waco (8/31/05); George Louis McWilliams, Texarkana (8/31/07); Nancy R. Neal, Lubbock (8/31/07); Lorraine Perryman, Odessa (8/31/07); Curtis E. Ransom, Dallas (8/31/07); A.W. (Whit) Riter III, Tyler (8/31/05); Terdema L. Ussery II, Dallas (8/31/050). Commissioner of Higher Education, Raymond A. Paredes, ($150,000) PO Box 12788, Austin 78711; 512-427-6101.

Higher Education Tuition Board, Prepaid – (1995); apptv.; expenses; 6-yr.; 7 members: State Comptroller, 2 apptd. by Lt. Gov., 2 apptd. by Gov. Gov's apptees: Michael D. Gollob, Tyler (2/1/03); Beth Miller Weakley, San Antonio (2/1/05).

Historical Commission, Texas – (1953); apptv.; expenses; 6-yr.; 17 members: Chair John L. Nau III, Houston (2/1/09); Board Members: Thomas E. Alexander, Fredericksburg (2/1/09); Jane C. Barnhill, Brenham (2/1/07); Bob Bowman, Lufkin (2/1/09); Earl P. Broussard, Austin (2/1/11); Diane D. Bumpas, Dallas (2/1/11); Shirley W. Caldwell, Albany (2/1/07); Donna Dean Carter, Austin (2/1/11); Lareatha H. Clay, Dallas (2/1/07); Frank W. Gorman, Jr., El Paso (2/1/07); David A. Gravelle, Dallas (2/1/07); Albert F. (Boo) Haussser, San Antonio (2/1/09); Sara Armstrong (Sarita) Hixon, Houston (2/1/11); Eileen Johnson, Ph.D., Lubbock (2/1/03); Thomas R. Phillips, Houston (2/1/05); Marcus Warren Watson, Plano (2/1/11); Frank D. Yturria, Brownsville (2/1/07); Commissioner Emeritus, T. R. Fehrenbach, San Antonio). Exec. Dir., F. Lawerence Oaks ($85,000), PO Box 12276, Austin 78711; 512-463-6100.

Historical Records Advisory Board, Texas – (1976); apptv.; 3-yr.; 9 members: State Archivist, 6 apptd. by by director and librarian of Texas State Library and Archives Comm.; two members apptd. by Gov. Public members: Martha Doty Freeman, Austin (2/1/02); Richard L. Hooverson, Belton (2/1/06). State Historical Records Coordinator, Chris LaPlante, State Library, PO Box 12927, Austin 78711.

Housing and Community Affairs, Board of Texas Dept. of – (1979 as Texas Housing Agency; merged with Department of Community Affairs and name changed in 1991); apptv.; expenses; 6-yr.; 7 members: Chair Elizabeth M. Anderson, Dallas (1/31/07); Board Members: Shadrick Bogany, Missouri City (1/31/05); Kent C. Conine, Frisco (1/31/09); Vidal Gonzalez, Del Rio (1/31/05); Patrick R. Gordon, El Paso (1/31/09); Norberto Salinas, Mission (1/31/07. Exec. Dir. Edwina Carrington ($112,352), 507 Sabine, Austin 78701.

Housing Corp, Texas State Affordable – Chair Jerry Romero, El Paso (2/1/05); Vice-Chair Thomas A. Leeper, Huntsville (2/1/07); Board Members: Christopher D. DeCluitt, Waco (2/1/09); Jo Van Hovel, Temple (2/1/07); Charles G. Rencher, Sugar Land (2/1/09). Pres. David Long, P.O. Box 12637, Austin, TX 78711/2637; 512-477-3555.

Industrialized Building Code Council, Texas – Martin J. Garza, Seguin (2/01/04); David L Beicher, San Antonio (2/01/03); Joe D. Campos, Dallas (2/01/04); Mark G. Delaney, Tomball (2/01/03); Craig N. Farmer, Lubbock (2/01/04); Rudy V. Gomez, Brownsville (2/01/04); James A. Kingham, Nacogdoches (2/01/04); Michael G. Mount, Burleson (2/01/03); Gary L. Purser, Amarillo (2/01/03); Douglas O. Robinson, Fort Worth (2/01/03); Ravi Shah, Carrollton (2/01/03); Arthur N. Sosa, Corpus Christi (2/01/04). Exec. Dir. William H. Kuntz Jr. 512-463-3173.

Information Resources, Department of – (1981 as Automated Information and Telecommunications Council; name changed in 1990); 6-yr.; expenses; 3 members recommended by Speaker of House, 3 by Lt. Gov.; 3 by Gov.: 9 members: Chair William L. Transier, Houston (2/1/09); Lance K. Bruun, Corpus Christi (2/1/07); Larry Leibrock, Austin (2/1/07); M. Adam Mahmood, Ph.D., El Paso (2/1/07); Phillip (Keith) Morrow, Southlake (2/1/11); Cliff Mountain, Austin (2/1/09); Wllliam Michael Wachel, Dallas (2/1/09); Ex Officio Members: Robert Bray (2/1/07); Brian Rawson (2/1/07); George Rios (2/1/07). Chief Technology Officer, Larry Olson ($120,000), PO Box 13564, Austin 78711.

Insurance, Commissioner of – Mike Geeslin ($163,800), PO Box 149104, Austin 78714.

Interstate Mining Compact Commission – Melvin Hodgkiss, Austin. Exec. Dir.: Gregory Conrad, 459B Carlisle Drv., Herndon, VA 22070.

Interstate Oil and Gas Compact Commission, Texas Rep. – (1935); ex officio or apptv., according to Gov's. choice; per diem and expenses. (Approximately 150 other appointees serve on various committees.) Official representatives for Texas: Victor Carrillo, Michael L. Williams, Barry A. Williamson. Exec. Dir., Christine Hansen, PO Box 53127, Oklahoma City, OK 73152.

Interstate Parole Compact Administrator – (1951); apptv.: Knox Fitzpatrick, Dallas.

Jail Standards, Texas Commission on – (1975); apptv.; 6-yr.; expenses; 9 members: Chair David Gutierrez, Lubbock (2/1/09); Board Members: Albert L. Black, Austin (1/31/11); Stanley D. (Stan) Egger, Abilene (1/31/11); Gonzalo Gallegos, San Antonio (1/31/09); Mark D. Gilliam, Rockport (2/1/09); William C. Morrow, Midland (1/31/07); Evelyn (Kelly) Moyer, Magnolia (1/31/07); Michael M. Seale, M.D., Houston (1/31/05); Charles J. Sebesta, Caldwell (1/31/07). Exec. Dir., Terry Julian ($61,000), PO Box 12985, Austin 78711.

Judicial Conduct, State Commission on – (1965 as 9-member Judicial Qualifications Commission; name changed in 1977 to present form and membership raised to (11); expenses; 6-yr.; 11 members: 5 apptd. by Supreme Court; 2 apptd. by State Bar; 4 apptd. by Gov. as follows: Chair James A. Hall, San Antonio, (11/19/05); Vice-Chair Monica A. Gonzalez, San Antonio, (11/19/03); Secretary, Rex G. Baker, III, Dripping Springs, (11/19/09); Board Members: R.C. Allen, III, Corpus Christi, (11/19/05); Faye Barksdale, Arlington, (11/19/07); Michael R. Fields, Houston, (11/19/09); Gilbert A. Herrera, Houston, (11/19/09); Ronald D. Krist, Houston, (11/19/07); Joseph B. Morris, Dallas, (11/19/07); Kathleen H. Olivares, El Paso, (11/19/05); William A. (Buck) Prewitt, III, Temple, (11/19/09). Exec. Dir., Seana Beckerman Willing ($100,000), PO Box 12265, Austin 78711.

Judicial Council, Texas – (1929 as Texas Civil Judicial Council; name changed in 1975); ex officio terms vary; apptv.; 6-yr. terms; expenses; 19 members, increased to 22 in 1997:

16 ex officio and 6 apptd. from general public. Public members: Jean Birmingham, Marshall (6/30/03); Lance Richard Byrd, Dallas (6/30/07); Joseph Alan Callier, Kingwood (6/30/03); Delia Martínez-Carian, San Antonio (6/30/07); José Luis López, Crystal City (6/30/05); Ann Manning, Lubbock (6/10/05). Exec. Dir., Jerry L. Benedict, PO Box 12066, Austin 78711.

Judicial Districts Board – (1985); 12 ex officio members (term in other office); one apptv. (4 yrs.); ex officio: Chief Justice of Texas Supreme Court; Presiding Judge, Court of Criminal Appeals; Presiding Judge of each of 9 Administrative Judicial Districts; pres. of Texas Judicial Council; apptee: Joseph W. Wolfe, Sherman (12/12/02).

Judicial Districts of Texas, Admin., Presiding Judges of – (See Administrative Judicial Districts, Presiding Judges).

Juneteenth Cultural and Historical Emancipation Commission, Texas – (1997); expenses; 6 yr.; 11 members; 5 ex officio, nonvoting: 2 apptd. by Lt. Gov., 2 apptd. by Speaker of House, and exec. dir. of Texas Historical Comm.; 6 apptd by Gov.: Chair Rep. Al Edwards, Houston); Board Members: Byron E. Miller, San Antonio (2/1/09); Eddie Price Richardson, Lubbock (2/1/05); Stella Wilson Roland, Austin (2/1/05); Willard Stimpson, Dallas (2/1/07); Linda Tarr, Houston (2/1/07).

Juvenile Probation Commission, Texas – (1981); apptv.; 6-yr.; expenses; 9 members — 3 judges of District Courts and 6 private citizens: Chair Cheryl Lee Shannon, Cedar Hill (8/31/09); Vice-Chair Betsy Lake, Houston (8/31/05); Board Members: Jean H. Boyd (2/1/11); Bob Ed Culver, Jr., Canadian (8/31/09); Keith H. Kuttler, College Station (8/31/07); Lyle T. Larson, San Antonio (8/31/05); Roberto I. Lopez, Pasadena (8/31/09); Barbara J. Punch, Missouri City (8/31/07); Carlos Villa, El Paso (8/31/05). Exec. Dir., Vicki Spriggs ($90,000), PO Box 13547, Austin 78711.

Land Board, School – (1939); one ex officio (term in other office); 2 apptd. — one by Atty. Gen. and one by Gov. for 2-yr. term; per diem and expenses; ex officio member: Comm. of General Land Office; appt'd members: Todd F. Barth, Houston (8/29/05); David S. Herrmann, San Antonio (8/29/05).

Land Surveying, Texas Board of Professional – (1979); formed from consolidation of membership of Board of Examiners of Licensed Land Surveyors, est. 1977, and State Board of Registration for Public Surveyors, est. 1955); apptv.; 6-yr.; 10 members — Commissioner of General Land Office serving by statute; 3 members of general public, 2 licensed land surveyors, 4 registered public surveyors, as follows: Chair Douglas Turner, League City (1/31/05); Board Members: Steve Hofer, Midland (1/31/05); Daniel Martinez, Lubbock (1/31/05); Kelly Neumann, San Antonio (1/31/09); A. W. Osborn, Tyler (1/31/07); Stephen Titus (Ty) Runyan, Austin (1/31/09); David G. Smyth, Devine (1/31/07); William C. Wilson, Jr., San Angelo (1/31/09). Exec. Dir., Sandy Smith ($47,000), 7701 N. Lamar, Ste. 400, Austin 78752.

Lands, Board for Lease of University – (1929 as 3-member board; membership increased to 4 in 1985); ex officio; term in other office; 4 members: Commissioner of General Land Office, 2 members of Board of Regents of University of Texas, 1 member Board of Regents of Texas A&M University.

Lavaca-Navidad River Authority, Board of Directors – (1954 as 7-member Jackson County Flood Control District; reorganized as 9-member board in 1959; name changed to present form in 1969); apptv.; 6-yr.; per diem and expenses; 9 members: John Alcus Cotten, Jr., Ganado (5/1/09); Jackie Ann Fowler, Ganado (5/1/09); Sherry Kay Frels, Edna (5/1/07); Basilio R. Jimenez, Edna (5/1/07); Ronald Edwin Kubecka, Palacios (5/1/09); Mike Myers, Edna (5/1/05); John J. Shutt, Edna (5/1/07); Sharla Vee Strauss, La Ward (5/1/05); Willard E. Ulbricht, Edna (5/1/05). Gen. Mgr., Patrick Brzozowski ($110,000) PO Box 429, Edna 77957.

Law Enforcement Officer Standards & Education, Comm. on – (1965); expenses; 14 members; 5 ex officio: Atty. Gen., Directory of Public Safety, Commissioner of Education, Exec. Dir. of Governor's Office Criminal Justice Division, and Commissioner of Higher Education; 9 apptv.

members: Presiding Officer, Daniel J. Smith, Belton (8/30/07); Board Members: Steven M. Byrd, Dallas (8/30/07); Romulo Chavez, Houston (8/30/09); Cathy Ellison, Austin (8/10/07); Charles R. Hall, Midland (8/30/05); William B. Jackson, Arlington (8/30/05); Betty Harper Murphy, Fredericksburg (8/10/09); Joe A. Stivers, Huntsville (8/30/07); Gary M. Swindle, Brownsboro (8/30/09). Exec. Dir., D.C. Jim Dozier ($76,000), 6330 E. Hwy. 290, Ste. 200, Austin 78723.

Law Examiners, Board of – Nine attorneys apptd. by Supreme Court biennially for 2-year terms expiring September 30 of odd-numbered years. Compensation set by Supreme Court not to exceed $20,000 per annum. Exec. Dir., Julia Vaughan, PO Box 13486, Austin 78711.

Law Library Board, State – (1971); ex officio; expenses; 3 members: Chief Justice State Supreme Court, Presiding Judge Court of Criminal Appeals and Atty. General. Dir., Kay Schlueter ($58,000), PO Box 12367, Austin 78711.

Legislative Budget Board – (1949); 10 members; 6 ex officio members: Lt. Gov.; Speaker of House; Chmn., Senate Finance Comm.; Chmn., Senate State Affairs Comm.; Chmn., House Appropriations Comm.; Chmn., House Ways and Means Comm.; plus 4 other members of Legislature. Director, John Keel, PO Box 12666, Austin 78711-2666.

Legislative Council, Texas – (1949); 17 ex officio members — 4 senators named by Lt. Gov.; 9 representatives named by Speaker; Chmn., House Administration Committee; Chmn., Senate Administration Committee; Lt. Gov.; and Speaker. Exec. Dir. Mark Brown, PO Box 12128, Austin 78711.

Legislative Redistricting Board – (1948); 5 ex officio members; term in other office: Lt. Gov., Speaker of House, Atty. Gen., Comptroller and Commissioner of General Land Office.

Librarian, State – (Originally est. in 1839; present office est. 1909); apptv., indefinite term: Robert S. Martin ($65,000), PO Box 12927, Austin 78711.

Library and Archives Commission, Texas State – (1909 as 5-member Library and State Historical Commission; number of members increased to 6 in 1953; name changed to present form in 1979); apptv.; per diem and expenses on duty; 6-yr.; 6 members: Presiding Officer, Sandra Pickett, Liberty (9/28/05); Board Members: Chris A. Brisack, Edinburg (9/28/05); Diana Rae Hester Cox, Canyon (9/28/07); Martha Doty Freeman, Austin (9/28/09); Cruz G. Hernandez, Burleson (9/28/09); Sandra Gunter Holland, Pleasanton (9/28/07); Elizabeth Sanders, Arlington (9/28/05). Dir. and Librarian Peggy D. Rudd ($85,000), PO Box 12927, Austin 78711.

Library, State Legislative Reference – (1909); indefinite term; Director: Dale W. Propp, Box 12488, Austin 78711.

Licensing and Regulation, Texas Department on – (1989); apptv.; 6-yr.; expenses; 6 members: Chair Leopoldo R. Vasquez, III, Houston (2/1/05); Board Members: Frank S. Denton, Conroe (2/1/09); Luann Roberts Morgan, Midland (2/1/09); Fred N. Moses, Plano (2/1/09); Gina Parker, Waco (2/1/07); Bill C. Pittman, Austin (2/1/07); Patricia Stout, San Antonio (2/1/05). Exec. Dir., Willliam H. Kuntz Jr. ($76,000), PO Box 12157, Austin 78711.

Lottery Commission, Texas – (1993); 6-yrs.; apptv.; expenses; 3 members: C. Thomas Clowe Jr., Waco (2/1/05); James A. Cox Jr., Austin (2/1/09); Rolando Olvera, Jr., Dallas (2/1/07). Exec. Dir, (vacancy) ($110,000), PO Box 16630, Austin 78761-6630.

Lower Colorado River Authority – (See **Colorado River Authority, Lower**).

Lower Concho River Water and Soil Conservation Authority – (See **Concho River Water and Soil Conservation, Lower**).

Lower Neches Valley Authority – (See **Neches Valley Authority, Lower**).

Marriage & Family Therapists, Texas State Board of Examiners of – (1991); apptd.; 6 yrs.; per diem and transportation expenses; 9 members: Chair Waymon R. Hinson, Abilene (2/1/07); Joe Ann Clack, Missouri City (2/1/09); Sandra L. DeSobe, Houston (2/1/07); B. W. McClendon, Austin (2/1/07); Asa Wesley Sampson, Sr., Houston (2/1/11); Brenda VanAmburgh, Fort Worth (2/1/05); Jackie Weimer, Plano (2/1/

05); Beverly Walker Womack, Jacksonville (2/1/09). Exec. Dir., Andrew T. Marks, Dept. of Health, 1100 W. 49th St., Austin 78756-3183.

Medical Examiners, Texas State Board of – (1907 as 12-member board, membership raised to 15 in 1981, raised to 18 in 1993); apptv.; 6-yr.; per diem on duty; 18 members: Chair Roberta Kalafut, Abilene (4/13/07); Lee S. Anderson, M.D., Fort Worth (4/13/09); Jose Manuel Benavides, San Antonio (4/14/05); Christine L. Canterbury, Corpus Christi (4/13/07); David Garza, Laredo (4/14/05); Amanullah Khan, M.D., Dallas (4/13/09); Thomas D. Kirksey, Austin (4/13/07); Keith E. Miller, Center (4/13/09); Elvira Pascua/Lim, Lubbock (4/13/07); John W. Pate, El Paso (4/13/07); Larry Price, Temple (4/13/09); Public Members: Patricia Blackwell, Midland (4/13/07); Melinda S. Fredricks, Conroe (1/13/09); Eddie J. Miles, Jr., San Antonio (4/13/07); Annette P. Raggette, Austin (4/13/09); Nancy M. Seliger, Amarillo (4/14/05); Paulette B. Southard, Alice (4/14/05); Timothy J. Turner, Houston (4/13/09). Exec. Dir., Donald Patrick ($85,000), PO Box 149134, Austin 78714-9134.

Medical Physicists, Texas Board of Licensure for Professional – (1991); apptv.; 6-yrs.; 9 members: Presiding Officer, Philip D. Bourland, Ph.D., Temple (2/1/05); Board Members: Shannon D. Cox, M.D., Austin (2/1/03); Walter Grant, Ph.D., Bellaire (2/1/09); Lamk M. Lamki, M.D., Houston (2/1/07); Adrian D. LeBlanc, Ph.D., Houston (2/1/07); Isabel C. Menendez, M.D., Corpus Christi (2/1/03); Rebecca C. Middleton, Ph.D., De Soto (2/1/05); Richard E. Wendt, III, Ph.D., Houston (2/1/07); Public Member, Kumar Krishen, Ph.D., Houston (2/1/05). Exec. Sec., Jeanette Hilsabeck.

Midwestern State University, Board of Regents – (1959); apptv.; 6-yr.; 9 members: Chair Mac Cannedy, Jr., Wichita Falls (2/25/06); Secretary, John C. Bridgman, Wichita Falls (2/25/06); Board Members: Pamela Odom Gough, Graham (2/25/08); Stephen A. Gustafson, Wichita Falls (2/25/10); Patricia A. Haywood, Wichita Falls (6/09/08); Munir A. Lanani, Wichita Falls (2/25/10); Don Ross Malone, Vernon (2/25/08); David Stephens, Plano (2/25/06); Ben F. Wible, Sherman (2/25/10). Pres., Dr. Jesse W. Rogers, 3400 Taft, Wichita Falls 76308.

Military Facilities Commission, Texas – (1935 as 3-member National Guard Armory Board; reorganized as 6-member board in 1981; name changed 1997); 6-yr.; 6 members: Chair Sandra Paret, Dallas (4/30/06); Treasurer, Jorge Perez, McAllen (4/30/05); Public Members: Regino J. Gonzales, Galena Park (4/30/09); Delores Ann Harper, San Antonio (4/30/07); Larry W. Jackson, Temple (4/30/09); Chao/Chiung Lee, Houston (4/30/09); National Guard Member, Michael H. Taylor Major Gen., Lufkin (4/30/07). Exec. Dir. John A. Wells ($57,000), PO Box 5426, Austin 78763.

Municipal Retirement System (See Retirement System, Municipal, Board of Trustees).

National Guard Armory Board, Texas – (see Military Facilities Commission, Texas).

Natural Resource Conservation Commission, Texas (See Environmental Quality, Texas Commission on).

Neches River Municipal Water Authority, Upper – (Est. 1953 as 9-member board; membership changed to 3 in 1959); apptv.; 6-yr.; 3 members: Joe Crutcher, Palestine (2/1/07); Jesse D. Hickman, Palestine (2/1/09); Robert E. McKelvey, Palestine (2/1/05). Gen. Mgr., T.G. Mallory, PO Box 1965, Palestine 75802.

Neches Valley Authority, Lower – (1933); apptv.; per diem and expenses on duty; 6-yr.; 9 members: Lonnie Arrington, Beaumont (7/28/07); Brian Babin, Woodville (7/28/07); Bill Clark, Beaumont (7/28/05); Sue Cleveland, Lumberton (7/28/09); Jimmie Ruth Cooley, Woodville (7/28/09); Kathleen Thea Jackson, Beaumont (7/28/09); Steven M. McReynolds, Groves (7/28/07); Cheryl Olesen, Beaumont (7/28/05); Olan Webb, Silsbee (7/28/05). Gen. Mgr. Robert Stroder, PO Box 5117, Beaumont 77726-5117.

Nueces River Authority Board of Directors – (1953 as Nueces River Conservation and Reclamation District; name changed in 1971); apptv.; 6-yr.; per diem and expenses; 21 members: President, Patty Puig Mueller, Corpus Christi (2/1/07); Vice President, J. R. Schneider, Sr., George West (2/1/

05); Secretary, Roxana P. Tom, Campbellton (2/1/05); Board Members: Steve G. Beever, Pearsall (2/1/05); W. Scott Bledsoe, III, Oakville (2/1/03); Joe M. Cantu, Pipe Creek (2/1/07); William I. Dillard, Uvalde (2/1/07); Robert M. Dullnig, San Antonio (2/1/07); Eddie L. Garcia, Corpus Christi (2/1/07); Ernest R. Garza, Robstown (2/1/05); John William Howell, Portland (2/1/03); Yale Leland Kerby, Uvalde (2/1/11); Lindsey Alfred Koenig, Orange Grove); Dan S. Leyendecker, Corpus Christi (2/1/07); August Linnartz, Jr., Carrizo Springs (2/1/03); James Richard Marmion, III, Carrizo Springs (2/1/11); Rolando B. Pablos, San Antonio (2/1/09); Betty Ann Peden, Hondo (2/1/09); Scott James Petty, Hondo (2/1/07); Thomas M. Reding, Jr., Portland (2/1/03); Fidel R. Rul, Jr., Alice (2/1/11). Exec. Dir., Con Mims, PO Box 349, Uvalde 78802-0349.

Nurse Examiners, State Board of – (1909 as 6-member board; reorganized and membership increased to 9 in 1981); apptv.; per diem and expenses; 6-yr.; 9 members: President, Linda Rounds, Galveston (1/31/11); Vice President, Phyllis Caves Rawley, El Paso (1/31/09); Joyce M. Adams, Houston (1/31/07); George Buchenau, Amarillo (1/31/09); Virginia Milam Campbell, Mesquite (1/31/07); Blanca Rosa (Rosie) Garcia, Corpus Christi (1/31/11); Richard Gibbs, Mesquite (1/31/07); Rachel Gomez., Harlingen (1/31/07); Brenda S. Jackson, San Antonio (1/31/09); Beverly Jean Nutall, Bryan (1/31/11); Public Members: Deborah Hughes Bell, Abilene (1/31/11); Anita Palmer, Olney (2/1/09); Frank Sandoval, Jr., San Antonio (1/31/07). Exec. Dir., Katherine A. Thomas ($62,000), 333 Guadalupe, Suite 3-460, Austin 78701.

Nursing Facility Administrators, Texas Board of – (Abolished effective Sept. 1997; responsibilities transferred to the Texas Department of Human Services.)

Occupational Therapy Examiners, Texas Board of – (1983 as 6-member board; increased to 9 in 1999); apptv.; 6-yr.; per diem and expenses; 9 members: Chair Jean Polichino, Houston (2/1/05); Board Members: Judith E. Brown, Edinburg (2/1/05); Grace L. Butler., Pearland (2/1/05); David G. Cabrales, Dallas (2/1/07); Michael Carreon, El Paso (2/1/09); Dely De Guia Cruz, Houston (2/1/09); Cecilia Fierro, OTR, El Paso (2/1/09); Joseph A. Messmer, Corpus Christi (2/1/07); Clarissa A. Meyers, OTR, McAllen (2/1/07). Exec. Dir., John Maline ($51,198), 333 Guadalupe St., Ste. 2-510, Austin 78701.

Optometry Board, Texas – (1921 as 6-member State Board of Examiners in Optometry; name changed to present form in 1981 and membership increased to 9); apptv.; per diem; 6-yr.; 9 members: Fred Farias, III, McAllen (1/31/07); D. Dixon Golden, Center (1/31/09); Sharon Johnson, Arlington (1/31/07); Mark A. Latta, Amarillo (1/31/05); Randall N. Reichle, Houston (1/31/09); Public Members: Ann Appling Bradford, Midland (1/31/05); Judy M. Eidson, San Antonio (1/31/07); Elsa Silva, El Paso (1/31/09). Exec. Dir., Chris Kloeris ($60,000), 333 Guadalupe St., Ste. 2-420, Austin 78701.

Orthotics and Prosthetics, Texas Board of – (1998); apptv.; compensation and travel expenses; 6-yr.; 6 members: Scott B. Atha, Pflugerville (2/1/03); Erin Elizabeth Berling, Coppell (2/1/07); Wanda Furgason, Brownwood (2/1/05); Richard Michael Neider, Lubbock (2/1/07); Stanley E. Thomas, San Antonio (2/1/03); Lupe M. Young, San Antonio (2/1/05).

Pardons and Paroles, Texas Board of – (1893 as Board of Pardon Advisers; changed in 1936 to Board of Pardons and Paroles with 3 members; membership increased to 6 in 1983; made a division of the Texas Department of Criminal Justice in 1990); apptv.; 6-yr.; (chairman, $85,500; members, $83,200 each); 7 members: Chair Rissie Owens, Huntsville (2/1/09); Jose L. Aliseda, Jr., Beeville (2/1/09); Charles Franklin Aycock, Amarillo (2/1/11); Jackie DeNoyelles, Flint (2/1/09); Linda F. Garcia, Angleton (2/1/07); Juanita M. Gonzalez, Round rock (2/1/09); Elvis Hightower, Georgetown (2/1/07).209 W. 14th St., Ste. 500, Austin 78701.

Parks and Wildlife Commission, Texas – (1963 as 3-member board; membership increased to 6 in 1971; increased to 9 in 1983); apptv.; expenses; 6-yr.; 9 members: Chair Joseph B.C. Fitzsimons, San Antonio (2/1/07); J. Robert Brown, El Paso (2/1/09); T. Dan Friedkin, Houston (2/1/11); Al Henry, Houston (2/1/05); Ned S. Holmes, Houston (2/

1/09); Peter M. Holt, San Antonio (2/1/11); Philip Montgomery, Dallas (2/1/07); John D. Parker, Lufkin (2/1/09); Donato D. Ramos, Laredo (2/1/07). Chairman-Emeritus, Lee Marshall Bass, Fort Worth. Exec. Dir., Robert L. Cook ($115,000), 4200 Smith School Rd., Austin 78744.

Pecos River Compact Commissioner – (1942); apptv.; 6-yr.; expenses: Julian W. Thrasher Jr., Monahans (1/23/05). ($32,247).

Pension Boards – For old age, blind and dependent children's assistance, see Human Services, State Board of. For retirement pay to state and municipal employees and teachers, see proper category under Retirement.

Pension Review Board, State – (1979); apptv.; 6-yr.; 9 members — one senator apptd. by Lt. Gov., one representative apptd. by Speaker, 7 apptd. by Gov. as follows: Chair Frederick E. Rowe, Jr., Dallas (1/31/09); Vice/Chair Rafael A. Cantu, Mission (1/31/05); Board Members: Paul A. Braden, El Paso (1/31/07); Roy Valentine Casanova, Jr., San Antonio (1/31/07); Richard Earl McElreath, Amarillo (1/31/07); Norman W. Parrish, The Woodlands (1/31/07); Rep. Allan B. Ritter, Nederland (1/31/05); Shari O. Shivers, Austin (1/31/09); Sen. John Whitmire, Houston (1/31/09). Exec. Dir., Virginia Smith ($52,000), PO Box 13498, Austin 78711.

Perfusionists, Texas State Board of Examiners of – (1993); apptv.; per diem; 6-yr.; 9 members: Chair Thomas K. Wilkes, Lubbock (2/1/05); Board Members: Debra Sue Douglass, Grapevine (2/1/03); Guadalupe Mendez, San Antonio (2/1/07); Steve A. Raskin, Richmond (2/1/03); Thomas A. Rawles, Plano (2/1/05); Public Members: H. B. Bell, Ed.D., Dallas (2/1/01); Gaye Jackson, Houston (2/1/05); Sheila Tello, Corpus Christi (2/1/09); Physician Member, Scott B. Johnson, M.D., San Antonio (2/1/07). Exec. Sec., Bobbe Alexander.

Pest Control Board, Texas Structural – (1971 as 7-member board, membership raised to 9 in 1979); apptv.; 6-yr.; expenses; 9 members — 3 ex officio: Commissioner of Agriculture; Commissioner of Health; and head of Entomology Dept., Texas A&M University; 6 apptv. members: Chair John Lee Morrison, San Antonio (2/1/07); Board Members: Charles Brown, Bryan (2/1/07); Tomas Cantu, McAllen (2/1/05); Madeline Gamble, Dallas (2/1/05); Brenda Hill, Nacogdoches (2/1/09); Richard M. Rogers, Euless (2/1/09). Exec. Dir., Dale R. Burnett, ($92,000), 1106 Clayton Ln., Ste. 100 LW, Austin 78723-1066.

Pharmacy, Texas State Board of – (1907 as 6-member board; membership increased to 9 in 1981); apptv.; 6-yr.; 9 members: Pres. Oren M. Peacock Jr., Sachse (8/31/05); Vice Pres. Woodrow M. Brimberry, Austin (8/31/07); Treas. Kim A. Caldwell, Plano (8/31/09); Roger W. Anderson, Dr., Houston (8/31/05); Juluette Bartlett-Pack Houston (8/31/07); Rosemary F. Combs, El Paso (8/31/05); Wilson Benjamin Fry, San Benito (8/31/09); Doyle Eugene High, Haskell (8/31/07); Marcelo Laijas, Jr., Floresville (8/31/09). Exec. Dir., Gay Dodson ($70,000), 333 Guadalupe St., Ste. 3-600, Austin 78701.

Physical Therapy and Occupational Therapy Examiners, Executive Council of – (1971); apptv.; 2-yr.; expenses; 5 members: Presiding Officer, L. Suzan Kedron-Lyn, Dallas (2/1/07); Board Members: David Cabrales, Dallas (2/1/05); Sylvia A. Davila, San Antonio (2/1/05); Clarissa A. Meyers, McAllen (2/1/05); Dora Ochoa-Rutledge, San Antonio (2/1/05). Exec. Dir. John Maline, 333 Guadalupe St., Ste. 2-510, Austin 78701.

Physical Therapy and Occupational Therapy Examiners, Texas State Board of – (1971); apptv.; 6-yr.; expenses; 9 members: Chair Sylvia Davila, P.T., San Antonio (1/31/05); Board Members: Karen Gordon, P.T., Port O'Connor (1/31/07); Michael Grady Hines, P.T., Tyler (1/31/05); Manoranjan Mahadeva, The Woodlands (1/31/09); Dora Ochoa/Rutledge, San Antonio (1/31/07); Melinda A. Rodriguez, P.T., San Antonio (1/31/09); George Scott, Lubbock (1/31/07); Joseph J. Spano, P.T., Wharton (1/31/09); Mary Thompson, P.T., Celina (1/31/07). Exec. Dir. John Maline ($51,198), 333 Guadalupe St., Ste. 2-510, Austin 78701.

Plumbing Examiners, State Board of – (1947 as 6-member board; membership increased to 9 in 1981); apptv.; expenses; 6-yr.; Presiding Officer, John Hatchel, Woodway (9/05/07); Board Members: Tammy Betancourt, Houston (9/

05/09); Min Chu, P.E., Houston (9/05/05); Louis A. Cortes, New Braunfels (9/05/07); Robert Franklin Jalnos, San Antonio (9/05/09); Richard Allen Lord, Pasadena (9/05/09); Carol McLemore, La Marque (9/05/05); Robert A. (Al) Tarver, Nederland (9/05/07); Michael Thamm, Cuero (9/05/05). Exec. Dir. Robert L. Maxwell ($62,000), 929 E. 41st, Austin 78751.

Podiatric Medical Examiners, State Board of – (1923 as 6-member State Board of Chiropody Examiners; name changed to State Board of Podiatry Examiners in 1967; made 9-member board in 1981; name changed to present form in 1997); apptv.; 6-yr.; expenses; 9 members: Richard C. Adam, San Antonio (7/10/09); Sandra E. Cuellar, Dallas (7/10/05); Bradford Glass, Midland (7/10/05); Paul Kinberg, Dallas (7/10/09); Donald M. Lynch, Troy (7/10/07); Bruce A. Scudday, El Paso (7/10/07); Public Members: Doris A. Couch, Burleson (7/10/05); Carol Lee Roberts/Baker, Houston (7/10/07); Matthew Washington, Missouri City (7/10/09). Exec. Dir. Jim Zukowski, ($52,000), 333 Guadalupe St., Ste. 2-320, Austin 78701.

Polygraph Examiners Board – (1965); apptv.; 6-yr.; 6 members: Elizabeth P. Bellegarde, El Paso (6/18/07); Edward L. Hendrickson, Katy (6/18/05); Priscilla Jane Kleinpeter, Amarillo (6/18/09); Lawrence D. Mann, Plano (6/18/09); Horacio Ortiz, Corpus Christi (6/18/07); Andy Sheppard, Rowlett (6/18/09); Hugh Douglas Sutton, Lubbock (6/18/05). Exec. Officer, Frank Di Tucci ($40,000), PO Box 4087, Austin 78773.

Preservation Board, State – (1983); 2-yr.; 7 members — 4 ex officio: Gov., Lt. Gov., Speaker and Architect of Capitol; 3 apptv.: one apptd. by Gov., one senator apptd. by Lt. Gov. and one representative apptd. by Speaker. Gov's. apptee: Jocelyn Levi Straus, San Antonio (2/05). Exec. Dir., Gaye Polan ($115,000), PO Box 13286, Austin 78711.

Prison Board, Texas – (See Criminal Justice, Texas Dept. of)

Prison Industry Oversight Authority, Private Sector – (1997); 6-yr.; expenses; 6 ex officio: Senate member, House member, Texas Youth Commission, Department of Criminal Justice, Texas Work Force Commission, employer liaison; 9 apptd. members: Presiding Officer, Kathy L. Flanagan, Houston (2/1/07); Board Members: Lillian Barajas, El Paso (2/1/09); Burnis Brazil, Missouri City (2/1/09); William B. Brod, Granbury (2/1/11); S. Roxanne Carter, Amarillo (2/1/09); Suzanne C. Hart, Ph.D., San Antonio (2/1/11); Brian L. Hatley, El Paso (2/1/07); Raymond G. Henderson, Buda); Jeffery R. LaBroski, Richmond (2/1/07).

Private Security Bureau, Texas – (1969 as Board of Private Investigators and Private Security Agencies; name and makeup of board changed, 1999 to Texas Commission on Private Security; name changed in 2003 by 78th Leg.); apptv.; expenses; 6-yr.; 10 members — 1 ex officio: Dir., Dept. of Public Safety; 7 apptd. members: Chair George B. Craig, Corpus Christi (1/31/05); Secretary, Michael H. Samulin, San Antonio (1/31/07); Board Members: Stella Caldera, Houston (1/31/11); John E. Chism, Irving (1/31/09); Howard H. Johnsen, Dallas (1/31/11); Linda J. Sadler, Lubbock (1/31/07); Harold G. Warren, Austin (1/31/09).

Produce Recovery Fund Board – (1977 as 3-member board; membership increased to 6 in 1981); apptv.; expenses; 6-yr.; 6 members — 2 each from commission merchants, general public and producer representatives. Ralph Diaz, Corpus Christi (1/31/05); Steven Dexter Jones, Lubbock (1/31/01); Ly H. Nguyen, Lake Jackson (1/31/03); Joyce Cook Obst, Alamo (1/31/03); Jay Pack, Dallas (1/31/05); Byron Edward White, Arlington (1/31/01). Admin., Margaret Alvarez, PO Box 12847, Austin 78711.

Psychologists, Texas Board of Examiners of – (1969 as 6-member board; membership increased to 9 in 1981); apptv.; 6-yr.; per diem and expenses; 9 members: Pauline Amos Clansy, Houston, (10/31/07); Gary R. Elkins, Temple, (10/31/09); Arthur E. Hernandez, San Antonio, (10/31/07); Ruben Rendon, Jr., Dallas, (10/31/05); Carl E. Settles, Killeen, (10/31/09); Stephanie Sokolosky, Wichita Falls, (10/31/05); Public Members: Betty Lou (Penny) Angelo, Midland, (10/31/07); Catherine Bernell Estrada, Dallas, (10/31/09); Michael D. Nogueira, Fredericksburg, (10/31/05). Exec. Dir., Sherry L. Lee ($52,000), 333 Guadalupe St., Ste. 2-450, Austin 78701.

Public Finance Authority, Texas – (1984, assumed duties of Texas Building Authority); apptv.; per diem and expenses; 6-yr.; membership increased from 3 to 6 in 1991: Chair R. David Kelly, Dallas (2/1/07); J. Vaughn Brock, Austin (2/1/07); Mark A. Ellis, Houston (2/1/09); Linda McKenna, Harlingen (2/1/11); H.L. (Bert) Mijares, Jr., El Paso (2/1/09); Ruth Schiermeyer, Lubbock (2/1/07); Marcellus A. Taylor, Dallas (2/1/11). Exec. Dir., Kimberly K. Edwards ($95,000), 300 W. 15th St., Ste. 411, Austin 78711.

Public Safety Commission – (1935); apptv.; expenses; 6-yr.; 3 members: James B. Francis Jr., Dallas (12/31/05); Robert B. Holt, Midland (12/31/01); M. Colleen McHugh, Corpus Christi (12/31/03). Dir. of Texas Dept. of Public Safety, Col. Thomas A. Davis ($102,000), PO Box 4087, Austin 78773-0001.

Public Utility Commission – (1975); apptv.; 6-yr., 3 members at $105,000-$107,500: Chair Paul Hudson, Austin (9/1/09); Commissioners: Julie Caruthers Parsley, Austin (9/1/05); Barry Thomas Smitherman, Houston (9/1/07). Exec. Dir., W. Lane Lanford ($92,000), PO Box 13326, Austin 78711-3326.

Racing Commission, Texas – (1986); 6-yr.; per diem and expenses; 8 members — 2 ex officio: Chmn. of Public Safety Commission and Comptroller; 6 apptv.: Chair R. Dyke Rogers, Dalhart (2/1/05); Vice-Chair Michael G. Rutherford, Houston (2/1/07); Board Members: Jesse R. Adams, Helotes (2/1/09); Treva Boyd, Christoval (2/1/05); Gerald Ken Carter, Caldwell (2/1/09); Comer J. Cottrell, Plano (2/1/07); Charles L. Sowell, Houston (2/1/09); Louis E. Sturns, Arlington (2/1/07). Exec. Sec., Paula C. Flowerday ($77,760), PO Box 12080, Austin 78711.

Railroad Commission of Texas – (1891); elective; 6-yr.; 3 members, $92,217 each: Victor Carrillo (12/31/10); Michael L. Williams (12/31/08); Elizabeth Ames Jones (1/1/06). Dir., Ronald Kitchens ($106,381), PO Box 12967, Austin 78711.

Real Estate Commission, Texas – (1949 as 6-member board; membership increased to 9 in 1979); apptv.; per diem and expenses; 6-yr.; 9 members: Chair John Walton, Lubbock (1/31/07); Board Members: James N. Austin, Jr., Fort Worth (1/31/05); Mary Frances Burleson, Aubrey (1/31/09); Louise E. Hull, Victoria (1/31/07); Lawrence D. Jokl, Brownsville (1/31/05); Elizabeth Leal, El Paso (1/31/09); Public Members: Ramon Cantu, Houston (1/31/05); William H. Flores, Sugar Land (1/31/09); Paul H. Jordan, Georgetown (1/31/07). Admin., Wayne Thorburn ($70,000), PO Box 12188, Austin 78711.

Real Estate Research Center – (1971); apptv.; 6-yr.; 10 members — one ex officio: representative of Texas Real Estate Commission; 9 apptv. members: Joseph A. Adame, Corpus Christi (1/31/03); David E. Dalzell, Abilene (1/31/07); Tom H. Gann, Lufkin (1/31/07); Celia Goode/Haddock, College Station (1/31/05); Joe Bob McCartt, Amarillo (1/31/05); Catherine Miller, Fort Worth (1/31/03); Nick Nicholas, Dallas (1/31/05); Jerry L. Schaffner, Dallas (1/31/03); Douglas A. Schwartz, El Paso (1/31/07). Dir., R. Malcolm Richards, Texas A&M, College Station 77843-2115.

Red River Authority, Board of Directors – (1959); apptv.; 6-yr.; per diem and expenses; 9 members: George W. Arrington, Canadian (8/11/01); Nathan J. (Jim) Bell, IV, Paris (8/11/05); Lisa C. Brent, Amarillo (8/11/05); William K. Daniel, Wichita Falls (8/11/03); Carol L. Gunn, Ph.D., Wichita Falls (8/11/03); Janie Matteson, DeKalb (8/11/05); Patricia C. Peale, Lake Kiowa (8/11/01); Cliff A. Skiles, Jr., D.V.M., Hereford (8/11/03); W. F. Smith, Jr., Quanah (8/11/01). Gen. Mgr., Curtis W. Campbell, 900 8th St., Ste. 520, Wichita Falls 76301-6894.

Red River Compact Commissioner – (1949); apptv.; 4-yr.; (Function of commissioner is to negotiate with other states respecting waters of the Red.): William A. Abney ($24,225), El Paso (2/1/05).

Redistricting Board, Legislative – (See Legislative Redistricting Board).

Rehabilitation Commission, Texas – – Combined into Department of Assistive and Rehabilitative Services of the Health and Human Services Commission as of 3/1/04..

Residential Construction Commission, Texas – apptv.; 6-yr.; expenses; 9 members: Chair Patrick Cordero, Midland (2/1/09); Vice/Chair Art Cuevas, Lubbock (2/1/11); Commissioners: Lewis Brown, Spring (2/1/11); Kenneth L. Davis, Weatherford (2/1/09); J. Paulo Flores, Dallas (2/1/11); John R. Krugh, Houston (2/1/09); Glenda C. Mariott, College Station (2/1/07); Scott M. Porter, Kerrville (2/1/07); Mickey R. Redwine, Ben Wheeler (2/1/07). Exec. Dir., Stephen D. Thomas, PO Box 13144, Austin 78711-3144.

Retirement System, Municipal, Board of Trustees – (1947); apptv.; 6-yr.; expenses; 6 members: Connie J. Green, Killeen (2/1/05); Patricia Hernandez, Plainview (2/1/05); Carolyn M. Linér, San Marcos (2/1/07); Rick Menchaca, Midland (2/1/07); H. Frank Simpson, Missouri City (2/1/09); Kathryn M. Usrey, Carrollton (2/1/09). Exec. Dir., Gary W. Anderson, PO Box 149153, Austin 78714-9153.

Retirement System of Texas, Employees – (1949); apptv.; 6-yr.; 6 members — one apptd. by Gov., one by Chief Justice of State Supreme Court and one by Speaker; 3 are employee members of the system serving 6-yr. overlapping terms: Chair Owen Whitworth, Austin (8/31/05); Vice-Chair Carolyn Lewis Gallagher, Austin (8/31/06); Appt'd Mem. Bill Ceverha, Dallas (8/31/08); Elected Members: Don Green, Austin (8/31/07); Yolanda Griego, El Paso (8/31/09); Appointed Member, Milton Hixson, Austin (8/31/04); . Exec. Dir., Ann S. Fuelberg ($175,000), PO Box 13207, Austin 78711-3207; 512-867-7711.

Retirement System, Texas County and District – (1967); apptv.; 6-yr.; 9 members: Chair Robert Eckels, Houston (12/31/07); Vice-Chai Amador E. Reyna, Kountze (12/31/05); Jerry Bigham, Canyo (12/31/09); Martha Gustavsen, Conroe (12/31/05); Daniel R. Haggerty, El Paso (12/31/09); Jan Kennady, New Braunfels (12/31/09); Mitchell E. Liles, Garland (12/31/05); Bridget McDowell, Baird (12/31/07); Robert C. Willis, Livingston (12/31/09). Dir. Gene Glass, PO Box 2034, Austin 78768-2034; 512-328-8889.

Rio Grande Compact Commissioner of Texas – (1929); apptv.; 6-yr.: Joe G. Hanson, El Paso (6/9/07). Box 1917, El Paso 79950-1917 ($41,195).

Risk Management, State Office of – apptv.; 2-yr.; 5 members: Chair Martha Rider, Rosenberg (2/1/07); Vice/Chair Ronald D. Beals, M.D., Tyler (2/1/07); Board Members: Ernest C. Garcia, Austin (2/1/09); Kenneth N. Mitchell, El Paso (2/1/09); Ronald James Walenta, Dallas (2/1/11).

Rural Community Affairs, Office of – apptv.; 6-yr.; 9 members: Chair William M. Jeter, III, Bryan (2/1/07); Board Members: David Alders, Nacogdoches (2/1/09); Nicki Harle, Baird (2/1/07); Carol Harrell, Jefferson (2/1/07); Wallace Klussmann, Fredericksburg (2/1/07); Jim Roberts, Lubbock (2/1/05); Lydia Rangel Saenz, Carrizo Springs (2/1/09); Patrick Wallace, Athens (2/1/05); Michael Waters, Abilene (2/1/11). Exec. Dir. Charles S. (Charlie) Stone.

Rural Community Health System of Texas – (1975); apptv.; 7 members, 4-yr.; Chair Rodolfo (Rudy) Arredondo, Lubbock (2/1/09); Beverly Barron, Odessa (2/1/07); Jaime A. Davidson, Dallas (2/1/05); Lewis E. Foxhall, Houston (2/1/09); Glenda R. Kane, Corpus Christi (2/1/09); Jeffrey A. Ross, Houston (2/1/07); James G. (Jim) Springfield, Harlingen (2/1/05). Exec. Dir., Eduardo J. Sanchez, 1100 W. 49th, Austin 78756-3199.

Sabine River Authority, Board of Directors – (1949); apptv.; per diem and expenses; 6-yr.; 9 members: Claudia J. Abney, Marshall (7/06/05); Don O. Covington, Orange (7/06/05); Sammy D. Dance, Center (7/06/07); Calvin E. Ebner, Deweyville (7/06/05); J. D. Jacobs, Jr., Rockwall (7/06/07); Richard A. Linkenauger, Greenville (7/06/09); Connie Wade, Longview (7/06/09); Constance Moore Ware, Marshall (7/06/09); Clarence Earl Williams, Orange (7/06/07). Gen. Mgr., Jerry Clark, PO Box 579, Orange 77630.

Sabine River Compact Commission – (1953); apptv.; 6-yr.; $8,487 each; 5 members — one member and chmn. apptd. by President of United States without a vote; 2 from Texas and 2 from Louisiana. Texas members: Frank Edward Parker, Center (7/12/01); Gary E. Gagnon, Orange (7/12/07). Box 579, Orange 77630.

San Antonio River Authority – apptv., 6 yr., 12 members: Chair H. B. (Trip) Ruckman, III, Karnes Co. (1/31/09); Vice-Chair Louis E. Rowe, Bexar Co. (1/31/09); Sec. JC Turner, Wilson Co. (1/31/09); Treas., Adair Ramsey Sutherland, Goliad Co. (1/31/07); Terry E. Baiamonte, Goliad Co. (1/31/09); Sara (Sally) Buchanan, Bexar Co. (1/31/05); James (Jim) Johnson, Bexar Co. (1/31/07); Alois (Al) Kollodziej, Jr., Wilson Co. (1/31/07); Gaylon J. Oehlke, Karnes Co. (1/31/05); Roberto G. Rodriguez, Bexar Co. (1/31/07); Nancy Steves, Bexar Co. (1/31/05); Thomas G. Weaver, Bexar Co. (1/31/09). Gen. Mgr., Gregory E. Rothe, PO Box 839980, San Antonio 78283-9980.

San Jacinto River Authority, Board of Directors – (1937); apptv.; expenses while on duty; 6-yr.; 6 members: Linda Koenig, Houston, 10/16/05); R. Gary Montgomery, P.E., The Woodlands, 10/16/07); Mary L. Rummell, Spring, 10/16/09); John H. Stibbs, The Woodlands, 10/16/09); Lloyd B. Tisdale, Conroe, 10/16/07); Joseph V. Turner, Conroe, 10/16/05). Gen. Mgr., James R. Adams, PO Box 329, Conroe 77305.

Savings and Loan Commissioner – Apptv. by State Finance Commission: Danny Payne ($92,676), PO Box 1089, Austin 78767.

School Land Board – (See Land Board, School).

Securities Board, State – (Est. 1957, the outgrowth of several amendments to the Texas Securities Act, originally passed 1913); act is administered by the Securities Commissioner, who is appointed by the board members; expenses; 6-yr.; 3 members: Chair Jack D. Ladd, Midland (1//07); Kenneth W. Anderson, Jr., Dallas (1//05); Beth Ann Blackwood, Dallas (1//07); Bryan K. Brown, Pearland (1//11); William R. Smith, Campbell (1//07). Securities Commissioner, Denise Voigt Crawford ($90,000), PO Box 13167, Austin 78711-3167.

Sex Offender Treatment, Council on – (1997); apptv.; 6-yr.; expenses; 6 members: Chair Walter J. Meyer, III, M.D., RSOTP, Galveston (2/1/07); Board Members: Liles Arnold, L.P.C., RSOTP, Plano (2/1/09); Monica Hernandez, Harlingen (2/1/11); Dr. Glen Allen Kercher, Huntsville (2/1/09); Patricia Rae Lykos (2/1/07); Maria Molett, MA, LPC, RSOTP, Garland (2/1/09); Aaron Paul Pierce, Rockdale (2/1/11). Exec. Dir., Allison Taylor, PO Box 12546, Austin 78711.

Social Worker Examiners, Texas State Board of – (1993); apptd.; 6-yr.; per diem and travel expenses; 9 members: Chair Jeannie McGuire, LBSW, College Station (2/1/07); Board Members: Tim M. Brown, LMSW, Bryan (2/1/07); Julia Dunaway, LCSW, Fort Worth (2/1/07); J. Steven Roberts, LCSW, San Marcos (2/1/05); Jamie B. Ward, LBSW, Boerne (2/1/05); Carrie Yeats, LMSW, Lubbock (2/1/09); Public Members: Holly L. Anawaty, Houston (2/1/07); Lt. Willie McGee, Plainview (2/1/05); Matt Shaheen, Plano (2/1/09). Exec. Dir. Andrew T. Marks.

Soil and Water Conservation Board, Texas State – (1939); elected by members of individual districts; 2 yrs.; 5 members: Guillermo (Memo) Benavides, Laredo (5/06/05); W. T. Crumley, Stephenville (5/06/05); Larry Jacobs, Montgomery (2/1/06); Jerry Nichols, Nacogdoches (5/07/06); Aubrey Russell, Panhandle (5/06/05); Reed Stewart, Sterling City (5/1/06); Joe L. Ward, Telephone (2/1/07). Exec. Dir., Rex Isom ($65,000), PO Box 658, Temple 76503.

Speech-Language Pathology and Audiology, State Board of Examiners for – (1983); apptv.; 6-yr.; per diem and expenses; 9 members: Presiding Officer, Cheryl Lynn Sancibrian, Lubbock (8/31/05); Board Members: Rosario R. Brusniak, Plano (8/31/07); Bertha Moore Campbell, Houston (8/31/05); Deborah L. Carlson, Galveston (8/31/05); Matthew H. Lyon, El Paso (8/31/07); Kerry Ormson, Amarillo (8/31/09); Public Members: Richard J. Caldwell, Houston (8/31/09); Crystal Dawn Perkins, DeSoto (8/31/09); Minnette Son, M.D., San Antonio (8/31/07). Exec. Secy., Sharon Williams, 1100 W. 49th, Austin 78751.

Stephen F. Austin State University, Board of Regents – (1969); apptv.; expenses; 6-yr.; 9 members: Margarita de la Garza/Grahm, M.D., Tyler (1/31/07); Valerie E. Ertz, Dallas (1/31/09); Joe Max Green, Nacogdoches (1/31/09); Kenneth James, Kingwood (1/31/09); Gary Lopez, Dallas (1/31/05); Paul Gifford Pond, Port Neches (1/31/09); Raymond Lyn Stevens, Beaumont (1/31/05); Mike Wilhite, Henderson (1/31/05); Fredrick A. Wulf, Center (1/31/07). Pres. Tito Guerrero III, PO Box 6078, SFA Sta., Nacogdoches 75962.

Sunset Advisory Commission – (1977); 12 members: 5 members of House of Representatives, 5 members of Senate, one public member apptd. by Speaker, one public member apptd. by Lt. Gov.; 4-yr.; expenses. Public members: John Shields, San Antonio (9/1/05); Howard Wolf, Austin (9/1/05). Dir., Joey Longley, PO Box 13066, Austin 78711.

Tax Board, State – (1905); ex officio; term in other office; no compensation; 3 members: Comptroller, Secretary of State and State Treasurer.

Tax Professional Examiners, Board of – (1977 as Board of Tax Assessor Examiners; name changed to present form 1983); apptv.; expenses; 6-yr.; 5 members: Chair Deborah M. Hunt, Austin (3/1/05); Board Members: Michael Amezquita, Harlingen (3/1/05); James E. Childers, Canyon Lake (3/1/07); Linda Hatchel, Woodway (3/1/09); Dorye Kristeen Roe, Robert Lee (3/1/07). Exec. Dir., David E. Montoya ($52,000), 333 Guadalupe, Ste. 2-520 Austin 78701-3942.

Teacher Retirement System – (1937 as 6-member board; membership increased to 9 in 1973); expenses; 6-yr.; 9 members — 2 apptd. by State Board of Education, 3 apptd. by Gov. and 4 TRS members apptd. by Gov. after being nominated by popular ballot of members of the retirement system: Presiding Officer, Jarvis V. Hollingsworth, Missouri City (8/31/07); Board Members: Mary Alice Baker, Ph.D., Beaumont (8/31/05); Terence S. Ellis, New Ulm (8/31/05); James W. Fonteno, Jr., Houston (8/31/07); John Graham, Jr., Fredericksburg (8/31/09); Mark Henry, Ed.D., Galena Park (8/31/09); Greg Poole, Ed.D., Conroe (8/31/07); Dory A. Wiley, Dallas (8/31/09); Linus D. Wright, Dallas (8/31/05). Exec. Dir., Ronnie Jung, 1000 Red River, Austin 78701.

Texas A&M University System Board of Regents – (1875); apptv.; 6-yr.; expenses; 9 members: Phillip David Adams, College Station, (2/1/07); Anne L. Armstrong, Armstrong (2/1/03); Wendy Lee Gramm, College Station (2/1/07); Lester Lowry Mays, San Antonio (2/1/07); Erle Allen Nye, Dallas (2/1/09); Lionel Sosa, San Antonio (2/1/05); R.H. (Steve) Stevens Jr., Houston (2/1/05); John David White, Houston (2/1/09); Susan Rudd Wynn, Benbrook (2/1/05). Chancellor, Dr. Howard D. Graves, College Station 77843-1123.

Texas Southern University, Board of Regents – (1947); expenses; 6-yr.; 9 members: Chair J. Paul Johnson, Fresno (2/1/07); Vice/Chair Regina Giovannini, Houston (2/1/05); Secretary, David Diaz, Corpus Christi (2/1/05); Board Members: Robert E. Childress, Ph.D., Richmond (2/1/09); Earnest Gibson, III, Houston (2/1/05); Belinda M. Griffin, Plano (2/1/09); Harry E. Johnson, Sr., Missouri City (2/1/09); Gerald E. Wilson, Katy (2/1/07); Second Vice/Chair George M. Williams, Houston (2/1/07). Pres., Dr. Priscilla Slade. Exec. Dir. for Board Relations, Karen A. Griffin 3100 Cleburne, Houston 77004.

Texas State Technical College, Board of Regents – (1960 as Board of the Texas State Technical Institute; changed to present name, 1991); apptv.; expenses; 6-yr.; 9 members: Chair C. Connie de la Garza, Harlingen (8/31/07); Vice/Chair Don Elliott, Wharton (8/31/05); Board Members: Nora Castañeda, Harlingen (8/31/09); James Virgil Martin, Sweetwater (8/31/09); Mike Northcutt, Longview (8/31/09); Jerilyn K. Pfeifer, Abilene (8/31/07); Terry W. Preuninger, Royse City (8/31/05); Linda Routh, Corpus Christi (8/31/05); Barbara N. Rusling, China Springs (8/31/09). Chancellor, Dr. Bill Segura, TSTC System, 3801 Campus Dr., Waco 76705; 254-867-4890.

Texas State University System, Board of Regents – (1911 as Board of Regents of State Teachers Colleges; name changed in 1965 to Board of Regents of State Senior Colleges; changed to present form in 1975); apptv.; per diem and expenses; 6-yr.; 9 members: Chair Alan W. Dreeben, San Antonio (2/1/07); Vice/Chair Kent M. Adams, Beaumont (2/1/07); Board Members: Dora G. Alcalá, Del Rio (2/1/09); Patricia D. Dennis, San Antonio (2/1/05); John E. Dudley, Comanche (2/1/09); Dionicio (Don) Flores, El Paso (2/1/05); Bernie C. Francis, Carrollton (2/1/09); James A. Hayley, Texas City (2/1/05); Pollyanna A. Stephens, San Angelo (2/1/07). Chancellor, Dr. Charles R. Matthews, Thomas J. Rusk Bldg., 200 E. 10th Street, Suite 600, Austin, TX 78701; 512-463-1808.

Texas Tech University, Board of Regents – (1923); apptv.; expenses; 6-yr.; 9 members: Larry Keith Anders, Dallas (1/31/11); C. Robert Black, Horseshoe Bay (1/31/07); F. Scott Dueser, Abilene (1/31/09); L. Frederick Francis, El Paso (1/31/07); Mark Griffin, Lubbock (1/31/11); J. Frank Miller, III, Dallas (1/31/09); Daniel T. (Dan) Serna, Arlington (1/31/11); Windy M. Sitton, Lubbock (1/31/09); Bob L. Stafford, M.D., Amarillo (1/31/07). Chancellor, Dr. David R. Smith, P.O. Box 42011, Lubbock 79409.

Texas Woman's University Board of Regents – (1901); apptv.; expenses; 6-yr.; 9 members: Therese B. Bevers M.D., Houston (2/1/07); Harry L. Crumpacker II, Plano (2/1/09); Virginia Chandler Dykes, Dallas (2/1/11); William H. Fleming, III, M.D., Houston (2/1/09); Kenneth L. Ingram, Denton (2/1/07); Tegwin Ann Pulley, Dallas (2/1/09); Lou Halsell Rodenberger, Baird (2/1/11); Sharon Venable, Dallas (2/1/11); Annie F. Williams, Dallas (2/1/07). Chancellor and Pres., Dr. Ann Stuart, PO Box 23925, TWU Sta., Denton 76204-1925.

Transportation Commission, Texas – (1917 as State Highway Commission; merged with Mass Transportation Commission and name changed to State Board of Highways and Public Transportation in 1975; merged with Texas Dept. of Aviation and Texas Motor Vehicle Commission and name changed to present form in 1991); apptv.; 6-yr.; ($15,914); 5 members: Hope Andrade, San Antonio (2/1/07); Ted Houghton, El Paso (2/1/09); John W. Johnson, Houston (2/1/05); Robert Lee Nichols, Jacksonville (2/1/09); Ric Williamson, Weatherford (2/1/07). Exec. Dir., Charles Heald ($155,000), 125 E. 11th St., Austin 78701.

Trinity River Authority, Board of Directors – (1955); apptv.; per diem and expenses; 6-yr.; 24 directors — 3 from Tarrant County, 4 from Dallas County, 2 from area-at-large and one each from 15 other districts: Chair Edd Hargett, Crockett (3/15/03); President, John W. Jenkins, Hankamer (3/15/03); Vice President, Hector Escamilla, Jr., Carrollton (3/15/03); Board Members: Russell B. Arnold, Trinity (3/15/05); Connie H. Arnold, Liberty (3/15/07); Harold L. Barnard, Waxahachie (3/15/05); Leslie C. Browne, Arlington (3/15/03); Karl R. Butler, Dallas (3/15/05); Patricia T. Clapp, Dallas (3/15/07); Michael Cronin, Terrell (3/15/05); Steve Cronin, Shepherd (3/15/05); Vincent Cruz, Jr., Fort Worth (3/15/05); Benny L. Fogleman, Livingston (3/15/03); Sylvia P. Greene, Arlington (3/15/03); Jerry F. House, Sr., D.Min., Leona (3/15/05); Katrina M. Keyes, Dallas (3/15/09); Nancy E. Lavinski, Palestine (3/15/07); Andrew Martinez, Huntsville (3/15/07); Lynn Hardy Neely, Madisonville (3/15/05); Nancy A. Perryman, Athens (3/15/07); AnaLaura Saucedo, Dallas (3/15/07); Louis E. Sturns, Fort Worth (3/15/07); Linda D. Timmerman Ed.D., Streetman (3/15/07); Kim C. Wyatt, Corsicana (3/15/09). Gen. Mgr., Danny F. Vance, PO Box 60, Arlington 76004-0060.

Tuition Board, Prepaid Higher Education – (1996); 6-yr.; 7 members: Comptroller; 4 apptd. by Lt. Gov.; 2 apptd. by Gov.

Uniform State Laws, Commission on – (1941 as 5-member Commissioners to the National Conference on Uniform State Laws; name changed to present form, membership increased to 6 and term of office raised to 6 years in 1977; membership raised to 9 in 2001); apptv.; 6-yr.; 9 members: Levi J. Benton, Houston (9/30/10); Cullen M. Godfrey, Austin (9/30/10); Debra H. Lehrmann, Colleyville (9/30/10); Peter K. Munson, Pottsboro (9/30/08); Marilyn Phelan, Lubbock (9/30/06); Rodney Wayne Satterwhite, Midland (9/30/08); Karen R. Washington, Dallas (9/30/02); Hon. Earl L. Yeakel, III, Austin (9/30/06); Life Member, Patrick Guillot, Dallas).

University of Houston, Board of Regents – (1963); apptv.; expenses; 6-yr.; 9 members: Chair Morgan Dunn O'Connor, Victoria (8/31/05); Vice/Chair Leroy L. Hermes, Houston (8/31/07); Secretary, Raul A. Gonzalez, Austin (8/31/07); Board Members: Morrie K. Abramson, Houston (8/31/05); Michael J. Cemo, Houston (8/31/07); Dennis D. Golden, Carthage (8/31/09); Lynden B. Rose, Houston (8/31/05); Thad (Bo) Smith, Sugar Land (8/31/05); Calvin W. Stephens, Dallas (8/31/09). Chancellor, Dr. Jay Gogue, 3100 Cullen Blvd., Suite 205, Houston 77204-6001; 713-743-3444.

University of North Texas Board of Regents – (1949); apptv.; 6-yr.; expenses; 9 members: Charles Beatty, Waxah-

achie (5/22/05); Marjorie B. Craft, DeSoto (5/22/07); Tom Lazo, Sr., Dallas (5/22/05); Robert A. Nickell, Irving (5/22/09); Burle Pettit, Lubbock (5/22/07); Bobby Ray, Plano (5/22/07); C. Dan Smith, Jr., Plano (5/22/05); Gayle W. Strange, Denton (5/22/09); Rice M. Tilley, Jr., Fort Worth (5/22/09). Chancellor, Dr. Norval F. Pohl, PO Box 311220, Denton 76203.

University of Texas System, Board of Regents – (1881); apptv.; expenses; 6-yr.; 9 members: Chair James R. Huffines, Austin (2/1/09); Vice/Chairs: Rita C. Clements, Dallas (2/1/07); Woody L. Hunt, El Paso (2/1/05); Cyndi Taylor Krier, San Antonio (2/1/07); Board Members: John W. Barnhill, Jr., Brenham (2/1/09); H. Scott Caven, Jr., Houston (2/1/09); Judith L. Craven, M.D., M.P.H., Houston (2/1/07); Robert A. Estrada, Fort Worth (2/1/05); Robert B. Rowling, Dallas (2/1/11); Chancellor, Mark G. Yudof, 201 West Seventh St., Ste. 820, Austin, TX 78701.

Veterans Commission, Texas – (1927 as Veterans State Service Office; reorganized as Veterans Affairs Commission in 1947 with 5 members; membership increased to 6 in 1981; name changed to present form in 1985); apptv.; 6-yr.; per diem while on duty and expenses; 6 members: ames R. Adams Ph.D., Dallas, 12/31/05); Leonardo Barraza, El Paso, 12/31/05); John A. Brieden, III, Brenham, 12/31/07); Hector Farias, Weslaco, 12/31/07); Karen Summerfield Rankin, BGen, USAF (Ret.), San Antonio, 12/31/09). Exec. Dir., James E. Nier ($74,000), PO Box 12277, Austin 78711; 512-463-6564.

Veterans Land Board – (Est. 1949 as 3-member ex officio board; reorganized 1956); 4-yr.; per diem and expenses; 3 members: one ex officio: Comm. of General Land Office; 2 apptd.: Cephus S. Rhodes, El Paso, 12/29/06); M.S. Ussery, Amarillo, 12/29/04). Exec. Sec., Paul E. Moore, P.O. Box 12873, Austin 78701.

Veterinary Medical Examiners, Texas State Board of – (1911; revised 1953; made 9-member board in 1981); apptv.; expenses on duty; 6-yr.; 9 members: Pres, Gary Brantley, Richardson (8/26/05); Vice Pres., Robert L. Lastovica, Fredericksburg (8/26/07); Secy., Gary Wayne Johnsen, El Paso (8/26/07); Bud E. Alldrege, Jr., Sweetwater (8/26/09); Patrick Michael Allen, Lubbock (8/26/09); Dee A. Pederson, Austin (8/26/05); Public Members: Mario A. Escobar, Crystal City (8/26/05); Paul Martinez, Sonora (8/26/09); Dawn Elise Reveley, Cedar Park (8/26/07). Exec. Dir., Ron Allen ($60,000), 333 Guadalupe St., Ste. 2-330, Austin 78701-3998.

Water Development Board, Texas – (1957; legislative function for the Texas Dept. of Water Resources, 1977); apptv.; per diem and expenses; 6-yr.; 6 members: Chair E. G. (Rod) Pittman, Lufkin, 12/31/07); Board Members: Dario Vidal Guerra, Jr., Edinburg, 12/31/07); James Edward Herring, Amarillo, 12/31/09); Jack Hunt, Houston, 12/31/09); Thomas Weir Labatt, III, San Antonio, 12/31/05); William W. Meadows, Fort Worth, 12/31/05). Exec. Admin., J. Kevin Ward ($108,000), PO Box 13231, Austin 78711.

Workers' Compensation Commission, Texas – (1991); 6-yr.; apptv; expenses; 6 members: Mike Hachtman, Chair Houston (2/1/05); William A. Ledbetter, Jr., North Richland Hills (2/1/05); Edward J. Sanchez, Houston (2/1/05); Carolyn J. Walls, San Antonio (2/1/05); Lonnie Watson, Cleburne (2/1/05); Eddie Wilkerson, La Porte (2/1/05). Exec. Dir., Robert L. Shipe ($112,000), 7551 Metro Center Drive, Suite 100, Austin 78744.

Workforce Commission, Texas – (1936 as Texas Employment Commission; name changed 1995); apptv.; $97,000-$99,500; 6-yr.; 3 members: Chair Diane Rath, San Antonio (2/1/07); Ronald G. Congleto, (2/1/11); Ron Lehman, Round Rock (2/1/03). Exec. Dir., Larry Temple ($125,000), 101 E. 15th St., Ste. 618, Austin 78778-0001.

Youth Commission, Texas – (1949 as 9-member board; reorganized 1957 and again in 1975); 6-yr.; per diem on duty; 6 apptv. members: Chair Pete C. Alfaro, Baytown (8/31/07); Vice/Chair Nick Serafy, Jr., Brownsville (8/31/05); Board Members: Donald R. Bethel, Lamesa (8/31/09); Gogi Dickson, San Antonio (8/31/09); Stephen Kurt Fryar, Brownwood (8/31/05); William Mahomes, Jr., Dallas (8/31/09); Patsy Lou Reed Guest, Duncanville (8/31/07). Exec. Dir., Dwight Harris ($118,000), PO Box 4260, Austin 78765. ✩

State Government Income and Expenditures

Taxes are the state government's primary source of income. On this and the following pages are summaries of state income and expenditures, percent change from previous year, tax collections, tax revenue by type of tax, a summary of the state budget for the 2006–2007 biennium, Texas Lottery income and expenditures and the amount of federal payments to state agencies.

State Revenues by Source and Expenditures by Function
Amounts (in Millions) and Percent Change from Previous Year

Revenues by Source	2004	%	2003	%	2002	%	2001	%	2000	%
Tax Collections	$27,913	6.8	$26,127	-0.6	$26,279	-3.5	$27,230	7.7	$25,284	7.1
Federal Income	21,938	4.6	20,976	15.4	18,171	13.4	16,018	8.2	14,799	6.3
Licenses, Fees, Permits, Fines, Penalties	5,546	15.9	4,785	9.6	4,366	2.4	4,265	0.5	4,245	1.5
Interest & Other Investment Income	1,406	-10.7	1,575	-7.2	1,696	-17.6	2,060	9.4	1,883	19.5
Net Lottery Proceeds	1,597	13.6	1,406	1.0	1,392	-0.1	1,393	6.8	1,304	-8.2
Sales of Goods & Services	329	-5.1	347	-36.6	547	34.5	407	13.3	359	9.2
Settlements of Claims	510	-8.0	554	9.9	504	28.6	392	23.4	318	-71.5
Land Income	498	27.8	390	19.9	325	-23.2	423	56.8	270	19.5
Contributions to Employee Benefits	178	11.3	160	12.7	142	11.6	127	9.2	117	16.0
Other Revenues	2,158	8.4	1,991	10.8	1,798	19.2	1,508	19.0	1,267	-14.2
Total Net Revenues	**$62,073**	**6.5**	**$58,310**	**5.6**	**$55,221**	**2.6**	**$53,824**	**8.0**	**$49,846**	**3.9**
Expenditures by Function										
General Government – Total	$2,040	1.8	2,004	7.4	$1,867	-7.3	2,014	15.0	$1,751	5.2
Executive	1,759	3.0	1,709	7.8	1,585	-9.5	1,752	16.4	1,505	3.0
Legislative	112	-7.5	121	6.8	113	3.8	109	12.5	97	0.2
Judicial	169	-3.6	175	4.2	168	10.1	152	2.3	149	0.3
Education	20,734	-0.5	20,834	2.8	20,260	0.8	20,091	5.2	19,105	11.0
Employee Benefits	2,685	-14.7	3,150	31.9	2,389	19.4	2,001	2.0	1,962	9.7
Health and Human Services	22,966	0.4	22,880	13.7	20,123	11.7	18,023	10.3	16,332	1.8
Public Safety and Corrections	3,276	-3.4	3,391	1.8	3,332	5.4	3,162	5.0	3,012	4.6
Transportation	5,248	6.4	4,934	-1.9	5,030	11.2	4,522	1.4	4,459	20.0
Natural Resources/Recreational Services	1,915	38.1	1,387	29.3	1,073	-0.3	1,075	-20.3	1,349	82.3
Regulatory Agencies	310	28.4	242	13.9	212	1.9	208	6.1	196	4.3
Lottery Winnings Paid*	517	25.0	414	-2.1	423	15.4	366	46.8	250	-22.9
Debt Service – Interest	576	-8.1	626	11.0	564	-11.5	637	6.6	598	-24.9
Capital Outlay	452	10.2	410	-11.6	464	-18.6	570	-17.8	693	7.0
Total Net Expenditures	**$60,719**	**0.7**	**$60,270**	**8.1**	**$55,739**	**5.8**	**$52,699**	**6.0**	**$49,708**	

Does not include payments made by retailers. All amounts rounded. Expenditures exclude trust funds. Fiscal years end August 31.

Source: State of Texas 2004 Annual Cash Report, Vol. One, Summary of Financial Information for the year ended August 31, 2004, Comptroller of Public Accounts' Office.

State Tax Collections, 1992–2004

Fiscal Year‡	State Tax Collections	Resident Population*	Per Capita Tax Collections	Taxes as % of Personal Income
1992	$15,848,915,148	17,641,580	$ 898.38	4.8
1993	17,010,737,258	17,989,926	945.57	4.9
1994	18,105,950,592	18,340,852	987.19	4.9
1995	18,858,790,042	18,693,032	1,008.87	4.8
1996	19,762,504,350	18,966,000	1,042.00	4.7
1997	21,187,868,237	19,312,000	1,097.13	4.7
1998	22,634,019,740	20,104,000	1,126.00	4.4
1999	23,614,611,235	20,507,000	1,152.00	4.4
2000	25,283,768,842	20,904,000	1,210.00	4.4
2001	27,230,212,416	21,317,000	1,277.00	4.5
2002	26,279,146,493	21,728,000	1,209.00	4.3
2003	26,126,675,424	22,142,000	1,180.00	4.1
2004	27,913,001,645	22,551,000	1,238.00	4.2

‡ Fiscal years end August 31.
* Revised fiscal year estimates

Sources: Texas Comptroller of Public Accounts, Annual Financial Reports of various years. Population and personal income figures, 1992 to 2001: U.S. Dept. of Commerce (U.S. Census Bureau and Bureau of Economic Analysis), adjusted to Texas fiscal years by Comptroller of Public Accounts. Data for 2002 and 2004 include partial estimates by the Texas Comptroller of Public Accounts.

Tax Revenues, 2003–2004

Below are listed the major taxes and the amounts each contributed to the state in fiscal years 2004 and 2003.

Type of Tax	FY 2004	FY 2003
Sales	$15,417,156,258	$14,277,286,162
Motor Veh. Sales/Rnt*	2,740,287,958	2,693,443,348
Motor Fuels	2,917,706,870	2,838,776,695
Franchise	1,835,013,952	1,716,600,478
Insurance Occupation	1,184,922,211	1,169,061,994
Natural Gas Production	1,392,436,142	1,069,864,123
Cigarette/Tobacco	534,577,125	582,712,236
Alcoholic Beverages	601,839,505	567,796,473
Oil Production	496,111,400	423,587,106
Inheritance	151,131,249	186,844,211
Utility	356,245,152	328,905,408
Hotel/Motel	238,861,664	227,899,404
Other Taxes**	46,712,161	43,897,785
Totals	**$27,913,001,645**	**$26,126,675,424**

*Includes tax on manufactured housing sales and taxes on interstate motor carriers.

Source: State of Texas 2004 Annual Cash Report, Vol. One, Summary of Financial Information for the year ended August 31, 2004, Texas Comptroller of Public Accounts.

State Government Budget Summary, 2006–2007 Biennium

Source: Legislative Budget Board

Article (Govt. Division)	2006-07 Budget (all funds) (in millions)
Art. I, General Government	$ 3,122.0
Art. II, Health and Human Services	49,977.2
Art. III, Education	54,846.7
Art. IV, The Judiciary	456.7
Art. V, Public Safety & Criminal Justice	8,524.6
Art. VI, Natural Resources	2,248.6
Art. VII, Business & Economic Dev.	18,644.3
Art. VIII, Regulatory	539.8
Art. IX, General Provisions	733.9
Art. X, The Legislature	317.3
Total	**$ 139,410.9**

Senate Bill 1 passed by the 79th Legislature totals $139.4 billion from all fund sources for state government operations for the 2006–2007 biennium. These numbers do not include adjustments from Governor's vetoes or supplementary appropriations in other legislation. The appropriations represent an $12.8 billion, or 10.1 percent, increase from the 2004–2005 biennium.

General Revenue funding totals $71.6 billion for the 2006–2007 biennium, an increase of $6.0 bilion, or 9.2 percent, over the 2004–2005 biennial spending level. This includes funds dedicated within the General Revenue Fund. Senate Bill 1 may be obtained on the Legislative Budget Board's Web site: **www.lbb.state.tx.us.** ☆

Texas Lottery

Source: Texas Lottery Commission

The State Lottery Act was passed by the Texas Legislature in July 1991. Texas voters approved a constitutional amendment authorizing a state lottery in an election on Nov. 5, 1991, by a vote of 1,326,154 to 728,994. Sales since the first ticket was sold on May 29, 1992, through May 2005 total more than $38.6 billion. Through the same period, more than $21.8 billion was paid out in prizes.

The Texas Lottery®, the 3rd largest in North America, offers players a wide range of choices, including approximately 80 instant ticket scratch-off games as well as its online games, which feature drawings six days a week.

Approximately 30 percent of all Texas Lottery revenue is transferred to the Foundation School Fund, which supports public education in Texas. Prior to September 1997, lottery revenues were deposited in the state's General Revenue Fund.

Texas Lottery transfers to the state from May 1992 to May 2005 total $12,614,882,635, with $7,361,249,082 going to the Foundation School Fund and $4,956,410,731 to the General Revenue Fund.

Who Plays the Lottery?

The executive director of the Texas Lottery Commission is required to conduct a biennial demographic survey of lottery players to determine the income, age, sex, race, education and frequency of participation of players. The information below is from the survey conducted for the Texas Lottery Commission by the Earl Survey Research Laboratory of Texas Tech University from late November through early December 2004. A total of 1,255 interviews were completed with Texans 18 years of age and older. The report presented to the Texas Lottery Commission included results both with and without "outliers." Outliers are high and low values that fall out of range of typical values, which even in small numbers can have a very strong impact on the final analysis; therefore, the results shown below do not include the outliers.

The percentage of Texans who report purchasing at least one Texas Lottery ticket in 12 months preceding the survey was 47 percent. Eighty percent of those reported playing Lotto Texas™; 59 percent, "scratch off" or instant games; 41 percent, Mega Millions™; 27 percent, Cash Five®; 22 percent, Pick 3® day draw; 12 percent, Pick 3 night draw; and 10 percent, Texas Two Step®.

Age: There is little variation in participation among age groups. Between 39–54 percent of respondents, depending on age group, reported playing a Texas Lottery game in the last year. However, younger players (those 35 and under) report spending more than those in other age categories.

Educational Level: Participation rate in Texas Lottery games is consistent across groups defined by level of education, with no

Texas Lottery Financial Data

Start-up to Dec. 31, 2004

Period	Sales (millions)	Value of Prizes Won (millions)	Retailer Commissions (millions)	Administration (millions)	To State of Texas (millions)
Start-up– FY 1993	$2,448	$1,250	$122	$170	$907
FY 1994	2,760	1,529	138	167	869
FY 1995	3,037	1,689	152	188	927
FY 1996	3,432	1,951	172	217	1,158
FY 1997	3,745	2,152	187	236	1,189
FY 1998	3,090	1,648	155	198	1,157
FY 1999	2,572	1,329	129	169	969
FY 2000	2,657	1,509	133	172	918
FY 2001	2,825	1,643	141	173	865
FY 2002	2,966	1,715	148	167	957
FY 2003	3,131	1,845	157	158	955
FY 2004	3,488	2,069	174	181	1,044

All figures accrued.

group more likely than any other to play. The category that reports spending the most on lottery products per month (those respondents with a high school diploma) spent approximately $67 monthly.

Income Level: Participation in Texas Lottery games is consistent across income categories, with no group more likely than any other to play. The category that reports spending the most on lottery products per month (those respondents with an annual income of $30,000 to $39,000) spent approximately $64 monthly.

Ethnic Background: Hispanic residents are more likely to participate in the Texas Lottery than members of other racial/ethnic groups. White lottery players report spending less per month than non-white players.

Sex: A slightly higher percentage of men than women reported playing Texas Lottery games in the past year, and those male respondents who did play reported outspending women by $48.65 to $41.66 per month. ☆

Federal Revenue by State Agency

Source: Texas Comptroller of Public Accounts, Annual Cash Report for the Year Ended August 31, 2004, Vol. One.

State Agency	2004	2003	2002	2001
Texas Health and Human Services Commission	$10,721,782,083	$10,365,443,434	$8,799,561,287	$7,756,099,712
Texas Department of Health	763,798,877	669,436,838	580,185,493	529,240,689
Department of Human Services	1,071,893,760	1,214,438,981	1,136,811,291	1,161,389,164
Texas Education Agency	3,453,080,099	2,981,494,206	2,585,993,100	2,283,712,720
Texas Department of Transportation	2,776,411,283	2,604,116,090	2,320,038,178	1,808,791,584
Texas Workforce Commission*	885,226,177	894,194,005	927,275,459	782,423,573
Department of Protective and Regulatory Services	280,033,177	282,413,338	267,426,078	209,266,976
Texas Rehabilitation Commission	251,630,297	260,347,382	267,754,770	234,917,087
Texas Department of Housing and Community Affairs	124,820,089	116,476,756	195,173,838	248,344,165
All Other Agencies	1,609,001,691	1,587,325,697	1,090,726,480	1,003,578,840
Total All Agencies	**$21,937,677,532**	**$20,975,686,726**	**$18,170,945,974**	**$16,017,764,510**

Local Governments

Texas has **254 counties**, a number which has not changed since 1931 when Loving County was organized. Loving had a population of 52 according to the 2004 estimate by the State Data Center, compared with 164 in 1970 and a peak of 285 in 1940. It is the **least-populous** county in Texas. In con-

The Houston skyline. Harris County is the most populous county in Texas with more than 3.6 million residents. File photo.

trast, Harris County has **the most residents** in Texas, with a 2004 population estimate of 3,644,285.

Counties range in area from Rockwall's 148.7 square miles to the 6,192.78 square miles in Brewster, which is equal to the combined area of the states of Connecticut and Rhode Island.

The Texas Constitution makes a county a legal subdivision of the state. Each county has a **commissioners court**. It consists of four commissioners, each elected from a commissioner's precinct, and a county judge elected from the entire county. In smaller counties, the county judge retains judicial responsibilities in probate

and insanity cases. **For names of county and district officials, see tables on pages 471–481.**

Twelve hundred and ten **incorporated Texas municipalities** range in size from 32 residents in Los Ybanez to Houston's 2,033,400, according to the State Data Center's 2004 estimate. More than 80 percent of the state's population lives in cities and towns meeting the U.S. Census Bureau definition of urban areas.

Texas had **375 municipalities with more than 5,000 population**, according to State Data Center estimates. Under law, these cities may adopt their own charters by a majority vote. Cities of less than 5,000 may be chartered only under the general law. Some of these cities now show fewer than 5,000 residents, because population has declined since they adopted their home-rule charters. **Home-rule cities are marked in this list by a single-dagger symbol (†) before the name.** ☆

Mayors and City Managers of Texas Cities

The list below was compiled from questionnaires sent out immediately after the municipal elections in May 2005. Included is the name of each city's mayor, as well as the name of the city manager, city administrator, city coordinator or other managing executive of munipalities having that form of government. If a town's mail goes to a post office with a different name, the mailing address is included.

An asterisk (*) before the city name indicates that the Almanac received no response to the questionnaire and that the information on city officials is from the Texas State Directory 2005, 48th edition.

— A —

Abbott .... Robert L. Tufts
Abernathy ... O.C. "Hoppy" Toler
  City Mgr., Mike Cypert
†**Abilene** .... Norm Archibald
  City Mgr., Larry Gilley
***Ackerly** .... Jimmie Schuelke
†**Addison** .... Joe Chow
  City Mgr., Ron Whitehead
Adrian .... Finis Brown
Agua Dulce .... Carl Vajdos
†Alamo** .... Rudy Villarreal
  City Mgr., Luciano Ozuna Jr.
†**Alamo Heights** (6116 Broadway, San Antonio 78209)
  .... Louis Cooper
  City Admin., Susan Rash
Alba .... Orvin Carroll
Albany .... Harold Cox
  City Mgr., Bobby R. Russell
***Aledo** .... Sue Langley
†**Alice** ...... Grace Saenz-Lopez.
  City Mgr., Pete Anaya
†**Allen** .... Stephen Terrell
  City Mgr., Peter H. Vargas
Alma (140 Alma Dr., Ennis

75119) .... Bill Blackmon
†**Alpine** .... Ms. Mickey Clouse
  City Mgr., Karen Philippi
***Alto** .... Dewey A. Simms
  City Admin., Terri Grogan
***Alton** (Box 9004, Mission
  78572) .... Salvador Vela
  City Mgr., Israel Sagredo
Alvarado .... Tom Durington
  City Mgr., Mary Daly
†**Alvin** .... Andy A. Reyes
  City Mgr., Paul Horn
***Alvord** .... Bob Wilson
  City Admin., Ricky Tow
†Amarillo** .... Trent Sisemore
  City Mgr., John Q. Ward
Ames .... John White
Amherst .... Mike Crain
***Anahuac** .... (vacancy)
Anderson .... Gail M. Sowell
†**Andrews** .... Robert Zap
  City Mgr., Glen E. Hackler
†**Angleton** .... L.M. Sebesta Jr.
  City Admin., Michael Stoldt
Angus (6008 S. I-45 W, Corsicana 75110) Eben Dale Stover

Anna .... Kenneth L. Pelham
Annetta (Box 1150, Aledo
  76008) .... Olan Usher
Annetta North (Box 262, Aledo
  76008) .... Kenneth Hall
Annetta South (Box 61, Aledo
  76008) .... Gerhard Kleinschmidt
***Annona** .... George English
†Anson** .... Tom Isbell
  City Mgr., H. Wayne Lisenbee
***Anthony** .... Art Franco
Anton .... Greg Hodges
  City Mgr., Larry G. Conkin
***Appleby** (RR 10, Box 5186,
  Nacogdoches 75961) ..N.F. Burt
***Aquilla** .... Lee Mills
†Aransas Pass**. Juan P. Torres
  City Mgr., Don Taylor
Archer City ....Carl P. Harrelson
Arcola .... Alvin Gipson
***Argyle** ....Richard S. Tucker
  City Admin., Tobin Maples
†**Arlington** .... Robert N. Cluck
  City Mgr., James N. Holgersson
***Arp** .... Vernon L. Bedair
***Asherton** .... Sam Galvan

Aspermont .....John D. Gholson
City Admin., Roger Parker
*†**Athens** .... Jerry G. King
City Mgr., Pam J. Burton
†**Atlanta** ....Kay Phillips
City Mgr., Mike Ahrens
Aubrey ....Tim Leslie
***Aurora** (Box 558, Rhome
76078)...... Martin Steve Derting
†**Austin** .... Will Wynn
City Mgr., Toby Futrell
†**Austwell** ......Dwight Mutschler
Avery ....Bill Trimm
Avinger ....Jane Yarbrough
*†**Azle** ....Linda Arrington
City Mgr., Craig Lemin

— B —

***Bailey** .. John Robert Stephens
***Bailey's Prairie** (Box 71, An-
gleton 77516) .....Randy Taylor
***Baird**.............. Jon E. Hardwick
*†**Balch Springs** James Kelsey
City Mgr., Mark Ewing
Balcones Heights (123 Altgelt
Ave., San Antonio 78201)
.... James Craven
City Admin., Lanny S. Lambert
†**Ballinger**..................Joe Selby
City Mgr., Tommy New
Balmorhea ..Ruben M. Fuentez
Bandera.............. Denise Griffin
City Admin., Gene Foerster
Bangs .... Noble Erler
†**Bardwell** .... P.W. Gentry
Barry....................... John Braly
Barstow .... Angel Abila
***Bartlett** ....Bobby A. Hill
Bartonville........Ron Robertson
Bastrop..................... Tom Scott
City Mgr., Debbie E. Millican
†**Bay City**.........Richard Knapik.
Bayou Vista (2929 Hwy 6, Ste.
100, Hitchcock 77563-2723)
.... William B. Jackson
Bayside .... Billy P. Fricks
†**Baytown** ..... Calvin Mundinger
City Mgr., Gary Jackson
***Bayview** (RR 3 Box 19A, Los
Fresnos 78566)
.... Marc Sundquist
***Beach City** (12723 Tri City
Beach Rd., Baytown 77520)
.......................Guido Persiani
Bear Creek, Village of (6705 W.
Hwy 290, #502-244, Austin
78735) .... Bruce Upham
Beasley .... Frances Smith
*†**Beaumont** ..... Evelyn M. Lord
City Mgr., Kyle Hayes
Beckville...... Gene Mothershed
Bedias ....Mackie Bobo
*†**Bedford** .... R.D. Hurt
City Mgr., Chuck Barnett

Bee Cave (13333 W. Hwy 71,
Austin 78738)
.... Caroline L. Murphy
City Admin., James Fisher
*†**Beeville**..... Kenneth Chesshir
City Mgr., Ford Patton
*†**Bellaire** ....Cynthia Siegel
City Mgr., Bernard M. Sattewhite
Bellevue..............Marvin Bigbie
*†**Bellmead** ....Al Lopez
City Mgr., Scooter Radcliffe
Bells ....Todd Bass
***Bellville** .... Philip B. Harrison
†**Belton** ....Dwayne Digby
City Mgr., Sam A. Listi
***Benavides** .... Cynthia Canales
†**Benbrook** (Box 26569, Fort
Worth 76126).. Jerry B. Dittrich
City Mgr., Cary Conklin
***Benjamin** ....Linda Cox
Berryville (Box 908, Frankston
75763)............James F. Colvin
City Mgr., Sharyn Harrison
***Bertram** .... Robert Ricketson
City Admin., Charles Shell
***Beverly Hills** (3418 Memorial
Dr., Waco 76711)
.... Douglas E. Woodward
***Bevil Oaks** (7390 Sweetgum
Rd., Beaumont 77713)
.... Don Smith
Big Lake ....Jack D. Blakely
City Mgr., Evelyn Ammons
***Big Sandy**...... Lynda Childress
*†**Big Spring**...... Russ McEwen
City Mgr., Gary Fuqua
***Big Wells** .... Gloria V. Flores
***Bishop** .... Geraldine Rypple
***Bishop Hills** (#5 Sheffield Rd.,
Amarillo 79124)
.... Betty Benham
Blackwell ....Ronald Harris
Blanco ....Jim Rodrigue
Blanket ....John H. Jones
Bloomburg ....Jerrell Ritchie
Blooming Grove
.... Gene Hollinsworth
City Mgr., Shelby Thedford
***Blossom** ..... Roger S. Johnson
City Mgr., Tony Chance
Blue Mound (301 Blue Mound
Rd., Fort Worth 76131)
.........................Jace Preston
Blue Ridge.......Dan Standeford
***Blum** ....Elaine Edwards
†**Boerne** .... Patrick Heath
City Mgr., Ronald C. Bowman
Bogata ....Randy G. Kennedy
†**Bonham** .... Roy V. Floyd
City Mgr., Blaine R. Hinds
Bonney (19025 FM 521,
Rosharon 77583)
.... Raymond Cantu
Booker ....Jim Riggs
City Mgr., Don Kerns

†**Borger** .... Jeff Brain
City Mgr., Wanda Klause
Bovina .... Stan Miller
City Mgr., Ernest Terry
†**Bowie** .... Brandon Earp
City Mgr., James Cantwell
Boyd .... Brent Wilson
***Brackettville** .....Joe Garza, Jr.
*†**Brady** .... Jesse McAnally
City Mgr., Merle Taylor
Brazoria...................Ken Corley
City Mgr., Thomas B. Smyser
***Brazos Country** (104 Winding
Creek Ln., Sealy 77474)
.... Charles A. Kalkomey Sr.
†**Breckenridge**. Virgil E. Moore
City Mgr., Gary G. Ernest
***Bremond**............. Ricky Swick
†**Brenham** ......Milton Y. Tate, Jr.
City Mgr., Terry K. Roberts
Briarcliff ......James R. Hamnett
***Briaroaks** (Box 816, Burleson
76097) .... James Dunn
†**Bridge City**.... Bobbie Burgess
City Mgr., Don Fields
Bridgeport .....Donald C. Majka
City Admin., Jeffrey J. Howell
***Broaddus**............. Marion Neill
Bronte .... Martin Lee
***Brookshire**...... Keith A. Woods
Brookside Village
.... Bruce Fundling
***Browndell** (Box 430, Brooke-
land 75931)Edward P. Brooks
†**Brownfield** .... Bobby Brewer
City Mgr., Eldon Jobe
Brownsboro...Ronny K. Harris
†**Brownsville**. Eddie Treviño, Jr.
City Mgr., Charlie Cabler
†**Brownwood**.Bert V. Massey II
City Mgr., Kevin Carruth
Bruceville-Eddy (143 Wilcox
Dr., #A, Eddy 76524)
.... Rick Eaton
City Admin., Jana Garner
†**Bryan**.............. Ernie Wentrcek
City Mgr., Mary Kaye Moore
***Bryson** .... Kennith Boland
***Buckholts** .... Mary Krwawicz
Buda ....John Trube
City Admin., (vacancy)
Buffalo.................. Ken Stevens
Buffalo Gap........David L. Perry
***Buffalo Springs** (RR 10, Box
500, Lubbock 79404)
.............................Rick Lujan
***Bullard** .... Connie Vaughan
Bulverde............... William Cole
City Admin., Phyllis E. Peterson
Bunker Hill Village (11977
Memorial Dr., Houston 77024)
.................William H. Marshall
City Admin., Ruthie P. Sager
†**Burkburnett** ....Bill Vincent
City Mgr., Mike Slye

*Burke (RR 3, Box 315, Diboll 75941) .......................J.L. Bell
†Burleson .... Ken Shetter
City Mgr., Bill Davison
*Burnet .... Dennis Kincheloe
City Mgr., Michael Steele
Burton ....Steve Miller
Byers ....Robert Lawrence
*Bynum ....Jerry Hooker

— C —

*Cactus.................. Luiz Aguilar
City Mgr., Jeffrey G. Jenkins
Caddo Mills.........Buel Bentley
City Admin., Manuel Leal
Caldwell ..... Bernard E. Rychlik
City Admin., William L. Broaddus
Callisburg (59 Campbell St., Whitesboro 76273)
.......Bob Henderson (pro tem)
*Calvert ....Briscoe Cain
†Cameron William C. Meacham
City Mgr., Fred Stephens
Campbell............... Nick Jordan
Camp Wood.................Ben Cox
Canadian............Richard Brock
City Mgr., Beth Briant
Caney City (15241 Barron Rd., Malakoff 75148) ......Joe Barron
*Canton .... William F. Hilliard
City Mgr., Charles R. Fenner
*†Canyon................... Lois Rice
City Mgr., Glen R. Metcalf
*Carbon Shana Davis (pro tem)
*Carl's Corner (RR 3, Box 500, Hillsboro 76645). Carl Cornelius
Carmine.................. Sally Bridie
†Carrizo Springs
.....................Ralph E. Salinas
City Mgr., Mario A. Martinez
†Carrollton ....Becky Miller
City Mgr., Leonard Martin
†Carthage .....Carson C. Joines
City Mgr., Brenda Samford
Cashion (412 Cashion Rd., Wichita Falls 76305)
...............Jerry W. Holmes Sr.
Castle Hills (209 Lemonwood Dr., San Antonio 78213)
........................Marcy Harper
City Mgr., Mike Shands
*Castroville Robert N. Hancock
City Admin., Jack Yates
†Cedar Hill ....Rob Franke
City Mgr., Alan E. Sims
†Cedar Park ....Bob Lemon
City Mgr., Craig Lonon
Celeste .... Pat Jones
Celina .... Corbett Howard
City Admin., Scott Albert
†Center.........John D. Windham
City Mgr., Chad D. Nehring
Centerville.............Billy Walters
*Chandler ....Joye Rains
Channing ....Lary McWright

Charlotte....... Augustine Munoz
Chester .... Elton Lawrence
Chico .... James Robinson
†Childress ....Pat Y. Steed
City Mgr., Jerry Cummins
Chillicothe ....Wallace Clay
China ....Charles Fancey
*China Grove (2456 FM 1516, San Antonio 78263)
.........................Dennis Dunk
*Chireno .... John A. Ragland
*Christine ....Walter W. Stevens
*Cibolo.......... Charles Ruppert
*†Cisco ....Joe Jarvis
Interim City Mgr., Don Henry
Clarendon.............Tex Selvidge
City Admin., Sean Pate
Clark (10109 Clark Air Field Rd., Justin 76247)William D. Merritt
Clarksville .... Ann Rushing
City Mgr., Doug Smith
Clarksville City (Box 1209, Gladewater 75647)
.........................Larry G. Allen
City Mgr., Billy F. Silvertooth Jr.
Claude .... Jim Hubbard
Clear Lake Shores
.... Katherine S. McIntyre
†Cleburne ....Ted Reynolds
City Mgr., Chester Nolen
*†Cleveland
.......Monique McDuffie-Davis
City Mgr., Philip Cook
Clifton .... W. Leon Smith
City Admin., Jerry Golden
Clint .... Dale T. Reinhardt
†Clute ....Jerry Adkins
City Mgr., Barbara Hester
Clyde...............Steve Livingston
City Admin., Tim Atkinson
Coahoma .... Bill Read
*Cockrell Hill (4125 W. Clarendon Dr.,Dallas 75211)
.................Charles P. Slayton
*Coffee City (Box 716, Frankston 75763) ...Michael Warren
Coldspring ....Pat Eversole
†Coleman .... Nick Poldrack
City Mgr., Randy Whiteman
†College Station ......Ron Silvia
City Mgr., Tom Brymer
*†Colleyville ....David Kelly
City Mgr., Bill Lindley
Collinsville ....Brad Kerr
Colmesneil ....Don Baird
City Mgr., Carrie Edwards
†Colorado City ....Jim Baum
City Mgr., Paul Catoe
*Columbus.............Paula Frnka
City Mgr., David K. Stall
Comanche ....Brent Hagood
City Admin., Bill Flannery
Combes ....Silvestre Garcia
City Mgr., Aida Gutierrez

Combine (123 Davis Road, Seagoville 75159)
.... William "Bill" Quinn
†Commerce ....Sheryl Zelhart
City Mgr., Bill Shipp
Como...................Roy G. Darby
†Conroe ....Tommy Metcalf
City Admin., Jerry McGuire
†Converse.............Craig Martin
City Mgr., Samuel R. Hughes
Cool (150 So. FM 113, Millsap 76066) .... Tommy A. Hull
Coolidge ....Bobby Jacobs
Cooper . Thomas Scotty Stegall
*†Coppell .... Douglas N. Stover
City Mgr., James Witt
†Copperas Cove. Bradi D. Diaz
City Mgr., Steven J. Alexander
Copper Canyon (400 Woodland Dr., Lewisville 75077).Sue Tejml
City Admin., Paulette Hartman
†Corinth (2003 S. Corinth St., Denton 76210)
.... Victor J. Burgess
City Mgr., Kenneth Seale
†Corpus Christi. Henry Garrett
City Mgr., George K. Noe
Corral City (14007 Corral City Dr., Argyle 76226)
.... James E. Draper
Corrigan .... Grimes Fortune
City Mgr., Mandy Risinger
†Corsicana..............C.L. Brown
City Mgr., Connie Standridge
Cottonwood (Box 293, Scurry 75158) .... Steve Struck

Cottonwood Shores
.... Sylvia Breem
Cotulla.......Juan R. Dominguez
City Admin., Higinio Martinez Jr.

*Cove (Box 2251, Mont Belvieu 77580.....................Lee Wiley
Covington ....Shirley Erickson

Crandall.................... Joe Baker
City Mgr., Judy Bell
*Crane .... Terry L. Schul
City Admin., Dru Gravens
Cranfills Gap......David D. Witte
Crawford .... David Posten

*Creedmoor (12108 FM 1625, Austin 78747 .....Robert Wilhite
City Admin....Richard Crandal Jr.
Cresson.................John Carroll
†Crockett ....Wayne Mask
City Admin., Ronald Duncan
*Crosbyton..........Joe Hargrove
City Mgr., Jared Miller
Cross Plains ....Ray Purvis
City Admin., Debbie Gosnell
Cross Roads (11700 Hwy 380 E, Aubrey 76227)Harv Kitchens
City Admin., Katherine Ritchie
Cross Timber (Box 2042, Burleson 76097)

.... Wava McCullough
Crowell .... Robert Kincaid
†**Crowley** ....Billy Davis
City Mgr., Truitt Gilbreath
†**Crystal City** ... Raul G. Gomez
City Mgr.,Diana Palacios
*†**Cuero** .... W.L. "Buzz" Edge
City Mgr., Corlis Riedesel
Cumby .... Travis Baxley
***Cuney** ....Oscar Birdow
Cushing.... Don Bruce Richards
City Mgr., Jarry L. Bowers
Cut and Shoot (Box 7364,
Conroe 77306)
.... Alan Lang Thompson

— D —

†**Daingerfield** ..Lou I. Slaughter
City Mgr., Marty Byers
Daisetta ....Edward Lynn Wells
†**Dalhart**............ Kevin Caddell
City Mgr., Greg Duggan
*†**Dallas** .... Laura Miller
City Mgr., Mary K. Suhm
***Dalworthington Gardens**
(2600 Roosevelt Dr., Arlington
76016)................Albert A. Taub
City Admin., Melinda Brittain
Danbury ....Robert Rosier
***Darrouzett**......Billy D. Johnson
***Dawson** ....Paula Sears
*†**Dayton**......Steve E. Stephens
City Mgr., Andy Helms
***Dayton Lakes** (Box 1476,
Dayton 77535)........(vacancy)
***Dean** (6913 State Hwy. 79N,
Wichita Falls 76035)
......................Steve L. Sicking
†**Decatur**...........Joe A. Lambert
City Mgr., Brett Shannon
***De Cordova** (4612 Cimmaron
Tr., Granbury 76049) . Dick Pruitt
†**Deer Park** .... Wayne Riddle
City Mgr., Ronald V. Crabtree
De Kalb......... Paul G. Meadows
City Admin., Elaine Elmora
†**De Leon** .... Jim Adams
Dell City...............Pamela Dean
City Admin., Juanita R. Collier
†**Del Rio**.............Dora G. Alcalá
City Mgr., Rafael Castillo
†**Denison** .... Bill Lindsay
City Mgr., Larry Cruise
†**Denton**...............Euline Brock
City Mgr., Mike Conduff
†**Denver City** .... David Bruton
City Mgr., Stan David
Deport .... Mike Francies
†**DeSoto** ....Michael Hurtt
City Mgr., James Baugh
***Detroit** .... Travis Bronner
Devers .... Edna Johnson
***Devine**............Steve A. Lopez
City Admin., Dora V. Rodriguez

Diboll ....James P. Simms
City Mgr., Lanny Parish
***Dickens** ........R.L. "Bob" Porter
*†**Dickinson** ....Julie Masters
City Admin., Ivan Langford
***Dilley**............ Russell J. Foster
City Admin., Felix Arambula
†**Dimmitt** .... Wayne Collins
City Mgr., David Denman
Dodd City............Jackie Lackey
***Dodson**...........Charles Moraw
***Domino**.........Marvin Campbell
*†**Donna** ....Ricardo Morales
Dorchester....... Alice F. Stewart
Double Oak......... Richard Cook
***Douglassville** Douglass Heath
***Dripping Springs**
.........................Todd Purcell
City Mgr., Michelle Fischer
***Driscoll** ....Rolando Padilla
City Admin., Rachel Saenz
Dublin ..... James "Red" Seigars
City Mgr., David Carrothers
*†**Dumas** .... Rowdy Rhoades
City Mgr., Vince DiPiazza
†**Duncanville** ....David L. Green
City Mgr., Kent Cagle

— E —

***Eagle Lake** ....Mike Morales
City Mgr., Ronald W. Holland
†**Eagle Pass**....... Chad Forester
City Mgr., Jesus M. Olivares
***Early** .... Bob Mangrum
City Admin., Kenneth Thomas
***Earth**......................Mitch Lowe
†**Eastland** .... Mark Pipkin
Int. City Mgr., David Maddox
East Mountain (RR 1, Box 500,
Gilmer 75644) .... Ronnie Hill
City Mgr., Tammy Hazel
***Easton** .... Willis Sammons
East Tawakoni (288 Briggs
Blvd., Point 75472)
.... Gary Vaughan
***Ector**........... Mary Dean Norris
***Edcouch** ....Ramiro Silva
City Admin., Belen Montelongo
Eden.......... Charlie Rodgers, Jr.
Edgecliff Village (1605 Edge-
cliff Rd., Edgecliff 76134)
........................Mary N. King
Edgewood ....Charles Prater
*†**Edinburg** .. Richard H. Garcia
City Admin., Wendy S. Sturgis
***Edmonson** Wendell Edmonson
City Mgr., Franklin Bain
*†**Edna** ....Joe D. Hermes
City Mgr., Kenneth W. Pryor
Edom (150 PR 8279, Ben
Wheeler 75754) ..Barbara Crow
*†**El Campo** ....Randy Collins
City Mgr., John Steelman
El Cenizo .... Raul L. Reyes
***Eldorado** .... John Nikolauk

†**Electra** .... Glen Branch
City Admin., Steve Giesbrent
†**Elgin** ....Eric W. Carlson
City Mgr., Jim D. Dunaway
Elkhart......................Joe Burris
El Lago ....Brad Emel
City Admin., Jill McCammon
Elmendorf ......Thomas P. Hicks
*†**El Paso**.............John F. Cook
City Admin., Joyce A. Wilson
*†**Elsa** .... Tony Barco
City Mgr., Eddy Gonzalez
***Emhouse** (3825 Joe Johnson
Dr., Corsicana 75110)
......................Johnny Pattison
Emory........Cay Frances House
Enchanted Oaks (Box 5019,
Gun Barrel City 75147)
...............Donald G. Warner III
***Encinal**............. Javier Mancha
City Admin., Matt Peter Olivera
†**Ennis** .... Russell R. Thomas
City Mgr., Steve Howerton
***Estelline**............. David Walker
†**Euless** .... Mary Lib Saleh
City Mgr., Joe Hennig
Eureka (1305 FM 2859, Corsi-
cana 75110) ... Barney Thomas
Eustace ....Robert Pickle
City Admin., Drucilla Haynes
***Evant** .... Alma Green
*†**Everman** ......Jim Stephenson
City Mgr., Donna R. Anderson

— F —

Fairchilds (8713 Fairchilds Rd.,
Richmond 77469)
.... Robert Myska
***Fairfield**........................ Roy Hill
City Mgr., Michael R. Gokey
Fair Oaks Ranch Boots Gaubats
Fairview (500 S. Hwy 5,
McKinney 75069)
.... Sim Israeloff
City Mgr., John Godwin
Falfurrias.......J. Wesley Jacobs
Falls City .... Vi Malone
†**Farmers Branch** ..Bob Phelps
City Mgr., Linda Groomer
Farmersville ..... Robbin Lamkin
City Mgr., Alan Hein
Farwell................. Jimmie Mace
Fate .... David Hill
City Mgr., Gerry Boren
***Fayetteville** Ronald Pflughaupt
City Mgr., Billy Wasut
Ferris ....Scott T. Born
City Mgr., Gus Pappas
Flatonia ....Lori Berger
City Mgr., Robert Wood
Florence .... Paul Ward
***Floresville**..Raymond Ramirez
City Mgr., Gary Pelech
†**Flower Mound**.. Jody A. Smith
City Mgr., Van James

*Floydada .... Bobby Gilliland
City Mgr., Gary Brown
*Follett .... Lynn Blau
City Mgr., Robert Williamson
*†Forest Hill (6800 Forest Hill
Dr., Fort Worth 76140)
.... James Gosey
Interim City Mgr., Sam Hill
*†Forney .... Darrell Grooms
City Mgr., Ron Patterson
Forsan .... Roger Hudgins

Fort Stockton ..... Tony Villarreal
City Mgr., Danny Valenzuela
*†Fort Worth .... Mike Moncrief
City Mgr., Charles Boswell
Franklin .... Charles Ellison
Frankston .... James Gouger
City Admin., Laura Griffith
†Fredericksburg Tim Crenwelge
City Mgr., Gary Neffendorf
*†Freeport .... Jim Phillips
City Mgr., Ron P. Bottoms
Freer .... Arnoldo Cantu
*†Friendswood
.... Kimball W. Brizendine
City Mgr., Ronald Cox
Friona .... John C. Taylor
City Mgr., Terri Johnson
†Frisco .... Mike Simpson
City Mgr., George Purefoy
*Fritch .... Kevin Keener
City Mgr., Dottie Williams
Frost .... Ken Reed
Fruitvale .... Danny Gilliam
*Fulshear ...... J. Michael Dinges
Fulton .... Nancy Arispe

— G —

†Gainesville .... Glenn Loch
City Mgr., Mike Land
†Galena Park ..... Robert Barrett
City Admin., John Cooper
Gallatin .... Juanita Cotton
†Galveston .. Lyda Ann Thomas
City Mgr., Steve J. LeBlanc
Ganado .... Fred Rickaway
*Garden Ridge .. Jay Feibelman
City Admin., Nancy Cain
†Garland .... Bob Day
City Mgr., William E. Dollar
*Garrett (208 N. Ferris St.,
Ennis 75119) .... Florinda Smith
Garrison .... Patsy Nugent
*Gary .... Jean L. Heaton
*†Gatesville .... Daren Moore
City Mgr., Brandon Emmons
†Georgetown .... Gary Nelon
City Mgr., Paul Brandenburg
†George West August Caron, Jr.
City Mgr., Benjamin Tanguma
Gholson (1277 Wesley Chapel
Rd., Waco 76705)
.... Larry Binnion
†Giddings .... James R. Arndt
City Mgr., Paul R. Kipp

†Gilmer .... R.D. Cross
City Mgr., Jeff Ellington
†Gladewater .. John Paul Tallent
City Mgr., James J. Stokes
†Glenn Heights ... Alvin DuBois
City Mgr., Fred H. Hays
Glen Rose .... Pam Miller
Godley .... Larry A. Richeson
City Admin., Stephanie Hodges
Goldsmith .... Billy Whittemore
Goldthwaite ..... Mike McMahan
City Mgr., Bobby Rountree
Goliad .... William J. Schaefer
City Admin., Kenneth R. Bays
Golinda (7021 Golinda Dr., Lor-
ena 76685) Anthony J. Wagner III
†Gonzales .... Bobby G. O'Neil
City Mgr., Buddy Drake
*Goodlow (Box 248, Kerens
75144) .... Willie Washington
*Goodrich .... David Armitage
Gordon .... Pat M. Sublett
Goree .... Ray Hudson
*†Gorman .... Robert Ervin
Graford .... Carl S. Walston
City Mgr., Tisha Sanchez
*†Graham .... Wayne Christian
City Mgr., Larry M. Fields
†Granbury .... David Southern
City Mgr., Harold Sandel
Grandfalls .... Leo Bookmiller
City Admin., Roger Mullins
†Grand Prairie
.... Charles Van England
City Mgr., Tom Hart

Grand Saline .... Terry Tolar
Grandview .... Brandon Wright
Granger .... Jerry Lalla
City Admin., Kathleen Vrana
Granite Shoals ...... Pat Crochet

Granjeno (6603 S. FM 494,
Mission 78572) ... Rafael Garza
City Admin., Alfonso Chapa Jr.
*Grapeland .... Dick Bridges
†Grapevine .... William D. Tate
City Mgr., Roger Nelson
*Grayburg (17572 Grayburg Rd,
Sour Lake 77659) ..... J.W. Floyd
Gray's Prairie (Box 116, Scurry
75158) .... Don Murray
Greenville .... Jim Morris
City Mgr., Karen Daly
Gregory .... Fernando P. Gomez
*Grey Forest (18502 Scenic
Loop Rd., Helotes 78023)
.... Ann Mabry
Groesbeck .... Mike McLelland
City Admin., Martha Stanton
Groom .... Joseph L. Homer
†Groves .... Brad P. Bailey
City Mgr., D.E. Sosa
Groveton .... Billy Clemons
Gruver .... Mark K. Irwin
City Mgr., Linda Weller

†Gun Barrel City ..... Paul Eaton
City Mgr., Corrin Magrath
Gunter .... Mark A. Millar
*Gustine .... Adam Stark

— H —

Hackberry (119 Maxwell Rd.,
Ste. B-7, Frisco 75034)
.... Brenda Lewallen
Hale Center ...... Gordon Russell
Hallettsville Warren Grindeland
City Admin., Tom Donnelly
Hallsburg (1115 Wilbanks Dr.,
Waco 76705) .... Mike Glockzin
Hallsville .... T. Bynum Hatley
*†Haltom City .... Calvin White
City Mgr., Tom Muir
*Hamilton .... Roy Rumsey
City Admin., Nathan Davis
Hamlin .... Jack Shields
Happy .... Sara Tirey
Hardin .... Alan Tidwell
*†Harker Heights ..... Ed Mullen
City Mgr., Steve Carpenter
†Harlingen .... Rick Rodriguez
Interim City Mgr., Gabriel
Gonzalez
*Hart .... Stanley Dyer
Haskell .... Ken Lane
City Admin., Sam Watson
Haslet .... Gary Hulsey
*Hawk Cove (Box 670, Quinlan
75474) .... Leetta Goolsby
Hawkins .. Wayne Kirkpatrick Jr.
*Hawley .... Ronnie Woodard
Hays (Box 1285, Buda 78610)
.... Joleen B. Brown
City Admin., Pat Ford
*†Hearne .... Ruben Gomez
City Mgr., Richard Walton
*Heath .... John Ratcliffe
City Mgr., Edward Thatcher
*Hebron (Box 118916,
Carrollton 75010) ... Kelly Clem
Hedley .... Janie Hill
City Mgr., Randy Shaw
Hedwig Village (955 Piney Point
Rd., Houston 77024)
.... Sue V. Speck
City Admin., Beth Staton
Helotes .... Jon Allan
Hemphill .... Robert Hamilton
City Mgr., Donald P. Iles
*Hempstead ... Michael S. Wolfe
City Admin. (vacancy)
†Henderson ...... John W. Fullen
City Mgr., Greg Smith
Henrietta .... Rick Langford
City Admin., Robert Patrick
*†Hereford Robert D. Josserand
City Mgr., Rick L. Hanna
†Hewitt .... Charles D. Turne
City Mgr., Dennis H. Woodard
*Hickory Creek (Box 453,
Lake Dallas 75065) .... Jeff Price

*Hico .... Stan Bundy
*†Hidalgo ..... John David Franz
  City Mgr., Joe Vera III
Hideaway .... Bill Kashouty
Higgins .... Linda Nicholson
  City Mgr., Randy Immel
*Highland Haven ..Roscoe Holt
†Highland Park (4700 Drexel
  Dr., Dallas 75205)
  .... William D. White Jr.
  City Admin., George Patterson
†Highland VillageBill Lawrence
  City Mgr., Mike Leavitt
Hill Country Village (116 Aspen
  Ln., San Antonio 78232)
  .... Kirk W. Francis
  City Admin., David J. Harris
*Hillcrest Village (Box 1172,
  Alvin 77512) .Johnny Villarreal
†Hillsboro .... Will Lowrance
  Acting City Mgr., Betty Harrell
Hilshire Village (8301 West
  View, Houston 77055)
  .... Edward J. Davis
†Hitchcock .... Lee A. Sander
*Holiday Lakes (RR 4, Box 747,
  Angleton 77515)
  .... Charles Rushing
Holland .... Curt Murray
Holliday .... Allen Moore
Hollywood Park Sean Martinez
  City Admin., Drew Traeger
Hondo .... James W. Danner
  City Mgr., Robert T. Herrera
Honey Grove .. Fred Siebenthall
  City Admin., Don Morrison
*Hooks .... Michael W. Babb

*†Horizon City
  .... Raymond Morales
†Houston .... Bill White
*Howardwick (HC 2 Box 2230,
  Clarendon 79226). (vacancy)
Howe .... Michael Jones
  City Admin., Steven McKay
*Hubbard .... Terry Reddell
  City Mgr., William McDonald
Hudson (201 Mount Carmel
  Rd., Lufkin 75904) Robert Smith
City Admin., James M. Freeman
*Hudson Oaks (150 N. Oak-
  ridge Dr., Weatherford 76087)
  .... Gene L. Voyles
  City Admin., L. David Vestal
*Hughes Springs
  .... Reba Simpson
  City Mgr., George K. Fite
*†Humble ... Donald McMannes
  City Mgr., Darrell Boeske
Hunters Creek Village (1 Hunt-
  ers Creek Pl., Houston 77024)
  .... Stephen Reichek
Huntington .... Lamar Tinsley
  City Admin., Robert Walker

†Huntsville .... J. Turner
  City Mgr., Kevin P. Evans
†Hurst .... Richard Ward
  City Mgr., Allan Weegar
Hutchins .... Artis Johnson
Hutto .... Mike Ackerman
  Interim City Mgr., Joni Clarke
Huxley (RR 1, Box 1410, Shel-
  byville 75973) .....Larry Vaughn

— I —
*Idalou .... Linda Turner
  City Admin., Russell Hamilton
Impact (Box 3116, Abilene
  79604).............. Dallas Perkins
*Indian Lake (62 S. Aztec Cove
  Dr., Los Fresnos 78566)
  .... Stanley L. Greeley
Industry .... Alan W. Kuehn
†Ingleside .... Gene Stewart
  City Mgr., Mike Rhea
Ingleside on the Bay (Box B,
  Ingleside 78362)Alfred Robbins
*Ingram .... Monroe Schlabach
*Iowa Colony (12003 Cty. Rd.
  65, Rosharon 77583)
  .... Robert Wall
*Iowa Park .... Randy Catlin
  City Admin., Michael C. Price
*Iraan .... June Heck
Iredell .... Royce P. Heath
†Irving .... Herbert Gears
  City Mgr., Steve McCullough
Italy .... Frank Jackson
  City Admin., Cynthia Olguin
*Itasca .... Brian Kelley
  City Mgr., Mark Gropp

— J —
†Jacinto City ...... Mike Jackson
  City Mgr., Jack Maner
Jacksboro .... Jerry Craft
  City Mgr., Joseph S. Portugal
*†Jacksonville .Kenneth Durrett
  City Mgr., Bill Tackett
Jamaica Beach (Box 5264,
  Galveston 77554)
  .... Victor Pierson
  City Admin., John Brick
Jarrell .... Wayne E. Cavalier
†Jasper .... David G. Barber
  City Mgr., David Douglas
Jayton .... Albert Brown
Jefferson .... Ned Fratangelo
  City Admin., Corby Alexander
†Jersey Village ... Ed Heathcott
  City Mgr., R. Dale Brown
Jewett .... Judi Kirkpatrick
Joaquin .... Steve Hughes
Johnson City .... Rosie Kunkel
Jolly (194 Milton St., Wichita
  Falls 76301) ..... Danny Murphy
Jones Creek (7207 Stephen F.
  Austin Rd., Freeport 77541)
  .... George Mitchell
  City Admin., Linda Shepard

Jonestown ..... James M. Brown
  City Admin., Johnny Sartain
Josephine .... Terry Wagner
†Joshua .... Stan McVey III
  City Mgr., Earl Keaton
*Jourdanton .... Tammy K. Clark
  City Mgr., Daniel G. Nick
Junction .... Alan Herring
  City Mgr., Vivian Saiz
Justin .... Ed Trietsch

— K —
Karnes City .... Don Tymrak
  City Admin., Chad A. Smith
†Katy .... Doyle G. Callender
  City Admin., Johnny Nelson
†Kaufman .... Paula Bacon
  Interim City Mgr., Curtis Snow
†Keene .... Gary Heinrich
  City Admin., James Minor
†Keller ....Julie Tandy
  City Mgr., Lyle H. Dresher
*Kemah .... Greg Collins
  City Admin., Bill Kerber
*Kemp .... Thomas Springer
  City Admin., Melinda Oliver
Kempner .... Gene Isenhour
Kendleton .... Carolyn Jones
*Kenedy .... Randy Garza
  City Admin., Loretta G. Thiele
*Kenefick (3564 FM 1008, Day-
  ton 77535)........ Curtis Schultz
Kennard .... Bill Thomas
†Kennedale .... Jim Norwood
  City Mgr., David Miller
Kerens .... Joe B. Baxter
  City Admin., Cindy Scott
†Kermit .... Ted Westmoreland
  City Mgr., Georgia Vines
†Kerrville .... Stephen Fine
  Interim City Mgr., Don Davis
†Kilgore .... Joe T. Parker
  City Mgr., Jeffrey Howell
*†Killeen ...... Maureen J. Jouett
  Int. City Mgr., Connie J. Green
†Kingsville .... Sam R. Fugate
  City Mgr., Carlos R. Yerena
*†Kirby .... Ray Martin
  City Mgr., Zina Tedford
*Kirbyville .... Giles Horn, Sr.
*Kirvin .... (vacancy)
*Knollwood Village (100 Collins
  Dr., Sherman 75090)
  .... Richard Roelke
Knox City . Charles R. Lankford
  City Mgr., Barbara Rector
*Kosse .... Robert O'Neal
Kountze .... Fred E. Williams
  City Admin., Roderick Hutto
Kress .... Louise Kirk
  City Admin., Kenny Hughes
Krugerville .... Shelby Moore
Krum .... Larry Lamonica
*Kurten (1888 N. FM 2038,
  Bryan 77808 ..Bobby L. Kurten

†**Kyle**................. Mike Gonzalez
City Mgr., Tom Mattis

— L —

*****La Coste** .... Henry Seay
City Admin., Reggie H. Winters
†**Lacy-Lakeview** (Box 154549,
Waco 76715) ......Calvin Hodde
City Mgr., Michael Nicoletti
Ladonia ....Leon Hurse
*****†La Feria**............ Carlos Cantu
City Mgr., Sunny K. Philip
*****Lago Vista**......... Dennis Jones
City Mgr., Bill Angelo
†**La Grange** .... Janet Moerbe
City Mgr., Shawn Raborn
*****La Grulla** .... Alejandro Solis
Laguna Vista (122 Fernandez
St., Port Isabel 78578)
..........................David Privett
City Admin., Alma Deckard
*****La Joya** .. William R. "Billy" Leo
City Mgr., Mike Alaniz
Lake Bridgeport (301 S. Main
St., Bridgeport 76426)
.... Dwayne Slaten
Lake City (Box 177, Mathis
78368) ....Gene Herod
†**Lake Dallas** ..Marjory Johnson
City Mgr., Earl Berner
†**Lake Jackson** Shane W. Pirtle
City Mgr., William P. Yenne
*****Lakeport** .... Ricky L. Shelton
*****Lakeside** (Box 787, Mathis
78368) ..... E.H. "Ed" Gentry, Jr.
Lakeside...........Raymond Beck
City Admin., Donald Seely
Lakeside City (Box 4287,
Wichita Falls 76308)
......................Steve Halloway
City Admin., Don Sheppard
Lake Tanglewood (RR 8, Box
35-15, Amarillo 79118)
.... John Langford
Lakeview .... Kelly Clark
†**Lakeway** .... Steve Swan
City Mgr., Steve Jones
Lakewood Village
.... Frank Jaromin
†**Lake Worth** .... Walter Bowen
City Mgr., Joey Highfill
*****†La Marque**....... Larry E. Crow
City Mgr., Robert Ewart
†**Lamesa**...............John F. Farris
City Mgr., Fred Vera
†**Lampasas** ....Jack Calvert
City Mgr., Michael Talbot
†**Lancaster** .... Joe Tillotson
City Mgr., Jim Landon
†**La Porte**.....Norman L. Malone
City Mgr., Robert T. Herrera
†**Laredo** ......Elizabeth G. Flores
City Mgr., Larry Dovalina
Latexo...........Daphne Hereford
*****La Vernia** ...... D. Bradford Beck

*****La Villa** .... Carlos Perez
City Mgr., Jaime Gutierrez
Lavon ....Jim Albright
City Admin., Mike Jones
*****La Ward** .... Hunter Karl
Lawn .... Johnny B. Hudson
†**League City** ...A. Jeff Harrison
City Admin., Paul I. Davis
*****Leakey** ....Jesse Pendley
*****†Leander** ..... John D. Cowman
City Mgr., Anthony Johnson
Leary (RR 5, Box 435, Texar-
kana 75501). Randal Mansfield
Ledbetter .... (vacancy)
*****Lefors** ......Cindy Stubbs-Scully
*****Leona**............... Travis J. Oden
Leonard ....Bill Yoss
City Admin., George Henderson
*****Leon Valley**............ Chris Riley
City Mgr., Rick Cortes
*****Leroy**............... David Williams

†**Levelland** ...... Hugh L. Bradley
City Mgr., Richard A. Osburn
†**Lewisville**............ Gene Carey
City Mgr., Claude King
Lexington Robert L. Willrich Sr.
†**Liberty**........Bruce E. Halstead
City Mgr., Allen Barnes
Liberty Hill .... Connie Fuller
*****Lincoln Park** (110 Parker
Pkwy., Aubrey 76227)
.... Loretta Ray
City Mgr., Nat Parker III
Lindale ....Bobby McClenny
City Admin., Owen Scott
Linden .... Kenny Hamilton
Lindsay .... Steven Zwinggi
Lipan .... Alford Spencer
*****†Little Elm** .... Doug Cravey
City Mgr., J.C. Hughes
†**Littlefield**...........Bruce A. Peel
City Mgr., Danny Davis
Little River-Academy (Box 521,
Little River 76554)
.... Ronnie W. White
†**Live Oak**Henry O. Edwards Jr.
City Mgr., Joseph W. Painter
*****Liverpool** .... Michael Peters

Livingston . Ben R. Ogletree Jr.
City Mgr., Marilyn Sutton
Llano .... Roger Pinchney
City Mgr., Kenneth Dowell
†**Lockhart** .... James Bertram
City Mgr., Clovia English
*****Lockney** .... Rodger Stapp
City Admin., Ron Hall
Log Cabin .... Gene Bearden
Lometa .... Mike McGarry
*****Lone Oak**.... Harold Slemmons
Lone Star .... Bob McBride
City Mgr., Kathy Kaminski
*****†Longview**........ Murray Moore
City Mgr., Rickey Childers
*****Loraine** .... Ina Vay McAdams

Lorena .... Stacy Loeffler Garvin
City Mgr., John Moran
Lorenzo .... Lester Bownds
City Admin., Dorothy S. Bristow
Los Fresnos.... David Winstead
City Admin., Mark W. Milum
Los Indios .Diamantina Bennett
City Admin., Eluid Garcia
Los Ybañez (1919 CR M, Box
52A, Lamesa 79331)
.......................Mary A. Ybañez
City Mgr., John H. Castillo
Lott .... Cinnie Johnson
Lovelady........ David W. Driskell
*****Lowry Crossing** (1405 S.
Bridgefarmer Rd., McKinney
75069)............... Brett Mayes
*****†Lubbock**....... Marc McDougal
City Mgr., Lou Fox
Lucas (151 Country Club Rd.,
Allen 75002) ...Robert Sanders
City Admin., Joe Gambill
Lueders .... Russell Mullins
†**Lufkin** .... Louis Bronaugh
City Mgr., Paul Parker
*****†Luling**............Mike Hendricks
City Mgr., Pee Wee Drake
*****†Lumberton**..........Don Surratt
City Admin., Norman Reynolds
Lyford ....David Clarida
Lytle............. Horace E. Fincher
City Admin., Josie Campa

— M —

Mabank................ Larry Teague
City Admin., Louann Confer
Madisonville....Scott Singletary
City Mgr., Tom Ginter
*****Magnolia** ....Jimmy Thornton
City Mgr., Roger D. Carlisle
*****Malakoff** ....Pat Isaacson
*****Malone** ....James A. Lucko
Manor .... Jeff Turner
†**Mansfield** ....Mel Neuman
City Mgr., Clayton Chandler
Manvel ....Delores M. Martin
†**Marble Falls**
.................Raymond Whitman
City Mgr., George W. Russell
*****Marfa** ...... Oscar Rice Martinez
City Mgr., Curtis A. Schrader
Marietta ....Susan Brigance
Marion .... Glenn A. Hild
†**Marlin** ...... Norman D. Erskine
City Mgr., Randall E. Holly
Marquez............ Stynette Clary
†**Marshall**................Ed Smith III
City Mgr., Frank Johnson
*****Marshall Creek** (Box 1070,
Roanoke 76262)Stephen White
*****Mart** .... Richard Bryant
*****Martindale**...........Lola Walker
*****Mason** .... Pattie Allen
Matador .... Paul Westbrook
*****†Mathis** .... Vicente Gonzalez
City Admin., Manuel Lara

Maud... John Hershell Robinson
Maypearl ..... Medford E. Marion
*†McAllen .... Leo Montalvo
   City Mgr., Mike R. Perez
McCamey .... Sherry Phillips
   City Mgr., Lou Ann Watson
†McGregor ..... James S. Hering
   City Mgr., Dennis McDuffie
†McKinney .... Bill Whitfield
   City Mgr., Larry Robinson
*McLean .... Bobby Martinez
McLendon-Chisholm (1248 S.
   St. Hwy. 205 Rockwall 75032)
   .... Michael Donegan
Meadow .... Eloisa Cuellar
City Admin., Mary Jane M. Fuller

Meadowlakes .... Gene Staton
   City Mgr., Bobby Minyard
Meadows Place Mark McGrath
Megargel .... Danny Fails
Melissa .... David E. Dorman
   City Admin., Douglas H. Box
Melvin .... Abraham Rodriguez
*Memphis .... Joe Rollo
Menard .... Johnny L. Brown
   City Admin., Sharon L. Key
†Mercedes ....Joel Quintanilla
   City Mgr., Ricardo Garcia
Meridian .... Clark Vandergriff
Merkel .... Derrell Riggan
Mertens .... Linda Maples
Mertzon .... Patsy Kahlig

†Mesquite .... Mike Anderson
   City Mgr., Ted Barron
†Mexia .... Steve Brewer
   City Mgr., Kyle H. McCain
*Miami .... Gene Hodges
†Midland ....Michael J. Canon
   City Mgr., Rick Menchaca
†Midlothian ....Boyce Whatley
   City Mgr., Ron Stephens
Midway ..... Patrick H. Wakefield
Milano .... Billy Barnett
*Mildred (5417 FM 637, Corsi-
   cana 75110) ... Nancy Johnson
Miles .... Ronnie Stringer
   City Mgr., Teresa Scott
Milford .... Claude Wakeland
Miller's Cove (RR 3, Box 491,
   Mt. Pleasant 75455)
   .... Grady Hughes Jr.
*Millican .... (vacancy)
Millsap .... Jamie French
*Mineola .... Toni Border
   City Admin., Dion O. Miller
†Mineral Wells
   .... Clarence F. Holliman
   City Mgr., Lance Howerton
*Mingus .... Milo Moffit
†Mission .... Norberto Salinas
   City Mgr., Isauro Treviño
†Missouri City .... Allen Owen
   City Mgr., Frank Simpson
Mobeetie .... Gordon Estes

*Mobile City (824 Lilac, Rock-
   wall 75087) ..... Wanda Cooper
*†Monahans ..David B. Cutbirth
   City Mgr., David Mills
Mont Belvieu .... Nick Dixon
   City Admin., Bryan Easum
Montgomery .... Edith Moore
   City Admin., Vicky Rudy
Moody .... Mike Alton
   City Admin., Charleen Dowell
*Moore Station (4818 FM 314
   S, LaRue 75770) .. Arthur Earl
Moran .... Marvin Kays
   City Mgr., Cindy Huskey
*Morgan .... Teresa Stacy
Morgan's Point (Box 839, La
   Porte 77572).......Peggy Arisco
   City Admin., Lance Avant
Morgan's Point Resort
   .... Mal Fischer
   City Mgr., Stacy Hitchman
Morton .... Edward Akin
   City Mgr., Brenda Shaw
*Moulton .... Kathy Koranek
*Mountain City (Box 1494,
   Buda 78610) .... Lee Taylor
   City Mgr., Jim Herrmann
Mount Calm ... Jimmy M. Tucker
Mount Enterprise
   .... Harvey Graves
†Mount Pleasant Jerry Boatner
   City Mgr., Courtney Sharp
Mount Vernon.... Kathy Shelton
   City Admin., Jim Blanchard
Muenster.......Henry Weinzapfel
   City Mgr., Stan Endres
†Muleshoe .... Cliff Black
   City Mgr., David Brunson
*Mullin .... Richard Spinks
*Munday .... Robert Bowen
   City Admin., Dwayne Bearden
Murchison .... Larry Everett
Murphy .... David Trudeau
   City Mgr., Craig W. Sherwood
Mustang (Box 325, Corsi-
   cana 75151).... Jackie Bounds
Mustang Ridge (12800 Hwy.
   183 S., Buda 78610)
   .... Alfred Vallejo II

— N —

†Nacogdoches ....Bob Dunn
   City Mgr., Jim Jeffers
Naples .... John Anthony
*Nash .... Henry Slaton
   City Mgr., Elizabeth Lea
†Nassau Bay (1800 NASA Rd.
   1, Houston 77058)
   .... Donald C. Matter
   City Mgr., John Kennedy
*Natalia .... Ruberta C. Vera
   City Mgr., Beth Leonesio
*Navarro (222 S. Harvard Ave.,
   Corsicana 75110) ..Benny Horn
†Navasota....Patricia M. Gruner
   City Mgr., Edward A. Broussard

*Nazareth ....Ralph Brockman
†Nederland R.A. "Dick" Nugent
   City Mgr., André Wimer
*Needville .... Delbert Wendt
*Nesbitt (RR 5, Box 88, Mar-
   shall 75670) ..... James Watson
*Nevada .... Christy Schell
*Newark .... Bill Malone
New Berlin (9180 FM 775, La
   Vernia 78121)....Gilbert Merkle
New Boston .... Johnny Branson
*†New Braunfels...Bruce Boyer
   City Mgr., Charles W. Pinto
Newcastle .... G. Wayne Davis
*New Chapel Hill (14039 Cty.
   Rd. 220, Tyler 75707)
   ....J. T. Pinkerton
New Deal ....Craig Graham
New Fairview (Box 855, Rhome
   76078) ....Jimmy Ray Miller Sr.
   City Mgr., Monica Rodriguez
*New Home .... Steve Lisemby
*New Hope (Box 562, McKinney
   75070) .... Johnny Hamm
New London ....Mollie Ward
   City Admin., Vicki Gerhardt
New Summerfield
   .... Jerry Carlile
*Newton .... Rachel Martin
   City Admin., Donald H. Meek
*New Waverly . Dan Underwood
*Neylandville (2469 Cty. Rd.
   4311, Greenville 75401)
   .... Kathy L. Wilson
Niederwald .. Shirley Whisenant
*Nixon .... Don Chessher
Nocona .... Paul S. Gibbs
   City Mgr., Lynn Henley
Nolanville ....C.W. "Mike" Carter
*Nome .... David Studdert
Noonday (Box 6425, Tyler
   75711) .... Mike Turman
Nordheim .... Paul Baumann
*Normangee .... Tim Taylor
*North Cleveland (Box 1266,
   Cleveland 77327)
   .... Robert Bartlett
Northlake (Box 729, Justin
   76247) .... Michael Savoie
†North Richland Hills
   .... T. Oscar Trevino
   City Mgr., Larry J. Cunningham
*Novice .... Wanda Motley
   — O —
Oak Grove (Box 309, Kaufman
   75142) .... Jerry Holder
*Oakhurst ....Frank AuBuchon
Oak Leaf .... Walter Adams
Oak Point ....Duane E. Olson
   City Mgr., Julie M. Johnston
Oak Ridge (129 Oak Ridge Dr.,
   Gainesville 76240) ..Sara Carter
   City Admin., Darlene Nelson
Oak Ridge (Box 539, Kaufman
   75142) .... Roy W. Perkins

Oak Ridge North (27424 Robinson Rd., Conroe 77385) ....Fred O'Connor
City Admin., Paul Mendes
Oak Valley (2211 Oak Valley, Corsicana 75110)... Bob O'Dell
***Oakwood** .... Teresa Brewer
***O'Brien**...... Charlene Brothers
Odem....... Jessie Rodriguez Sr.
†**Odessa** .... Larry L. Melton
City Mgr., Richard N. Morton
O'Donnell ...... Maurice Jackson
Oglesby ....Kenneth Goodwin
Old River-Winfree (Box 1169, Mont Belvieu 77580) .... Joe Landry
Olmos Park (119 W. El Prado Dr., San Antonio 78212) ....Gerald Dubinski
City Mgr., Barbara Joseph
***†Olney**.....Mary H. Schoonover
Olton..................Johnny Adams
City Mgr., Marvin Tillman
Omaha............. Dwaine Higgins
City Mgr., Debbie LaFollett
Onalaska .... Lew Vail
Opdyke West (Box 1179, Levelland 79336) ..... Wayne Riggins
†**Orange** William Brown Claybar
City Mgr., Sam Kittrell
***Orange Grove**......Seale Brand
City Admin., Perry R. Young
Orchard ....Eugene L. Demny
Ore City ....Glenn Breazeale
Overton ....Robert Young
City Mgr., BJ Potts
***Ovilla**...................... Bill Turner
City Admin., John McDonald
Oyster Creek Richard Merriman

— P —

Paducah .... Howard A. Smith
***Paint Rock** ....Milton Peek
Palacios................John Connor
City Mgr., Charles Winfield
†**Palestine**................George Foss
City Mgr., R Dale Brown
Palisades (115 Brentwood Rd., Amarillo 79118) ......Pat Knight
***Palmer**.................Don Huskins
***Palmhurst** .. Ramiro Rodriguez
City Mgr., Jose E. Garza
Palm Valley (1313 Stuart Place Rd., Harlingen 78552) .... Ray Elledge
Palmview (RR 11, Box 1000, Edinburg 78539) ....Jorge G. García
City Mgr., Johnn V. Alaniz
†**Pampa** .... Lonny Robbins
City Mgr., John Horst
Panhandle ....Dan Looten
City Mgr., Loreu Brand
Panorama (98 Hiwon Dr., Conroe 77304).. Howard L. Kravetz

Pantego ....Dorothy Anderhult
City Mgr., Doug Davis
Paradise... Nathan C. Cleveland
***†Paris** ....Curtis Fendley
City Mgr., Tony N. Williams
Parker (5700 E. Parker Rd., Allen 75002) ......Doug Garber
City Admin., Betty McMenamy
†**Pasadena**......... John Manlove
Pattison .... Larry Sabrsula (pro tem)
***Patton Village** (16940 Main St., Splendora 77372) ...Cecil White
Payne Springs (Box 2, Mabank 75147) ...............J.D. Meredith
†**Pearland** ....Tom Reid
City Mgr., Bill Eisen
†**Pearsall**....... Rolando Segovia
City Mgr., José G. Treviño
***Pecan Gap**......Warner Cheney
Pecan Hill (Box 443, Red Oak 75154) .. Betty J. King (pro tem)
†**Pecos**......................Dot Stafford
City Mgr., Joseph Torres
Pelican Bay (1300 Pelican Cir., Azle 76020)... Marlyn Hawkins
***Penelope** ....Inez Arriola
***Peñitas** ......Servando Ramírez
City Admin., Julian J. Gonzalez
Pernitas Point (HC 1, Box 1440, Sandia 78383) .. Jerry Hedrick
Perryton .... David Hale
City Mgr., David A. Landis
Petersburg..........Ted Matthews
City Mgr., Marie Parr
***Petrolia** ....James Cline
Petronila (RR 3, Box 42, Robstown 78380) William J. Ordner
†**Pflugerville** ..Catherine Callen
City Mgr., David Buesing
†**Pharr**Leopoldo "Polo" Palacios
City Mgr., Fred Sandoval
Pilot Point......... Jerry W. Alford
City Admin., Ryan Kelley
Pine Forest (Box 1004, Vidor 77670)............... Bruce Childs
Pinehurst (3640 Mockingbird, Orange 77630) Jerry D. Hussey
City Admin., C.R. Nash
Pine Island (RR 3, Box 70AF, Hempstead 77445) ....Debra Ferris
***Pineland** ....John O. Booker
***Piney Point Village** (7721 San Felipe, #100 Houston 77063) ....Carol Fox
Pittsburg......... D. H. Abernathy
City Mgr., Ned Muse
Plains..............Shane McKinzie
City Admin., Terry Howard
†**Plainview** ... John C. Anderson
City Mgr., Greg Ingham
***†Plano** ....Pat Evans
City Mgr., Thomas Muehlenbeck

Pleak Village (6621 FM 2218 Rd., Richmond 77469) ....Margie Krenek
***Pleasant Valley** (4006 Hwy 287 E, Iowa Park 76367) ....Raymond Haynes
City Mgr., Jeff Watts
***†Pleasanton** ....Bill Carroll
City Mgr., Kathy Coronado
***Plum Grove** (Box 1358, Splendora 77372)......... T.W. Garrett
Point ....Phillip Kerr
Point Blank .... Lillian Bratton
Point Comfort ... Pam Lambden
Point Venture (549 Venture Blvd. S. Leander 78645) .... William Ratfield
Ponder........... Vivian Cockburn
†**Port Aransas**. Georgia Neblett
City Mgr., Michael Kovacs
†**Port Arthur**...... Oscar G. Ortiz
City Mgr., Steve Fitzgibbons
†**Port Isabel**.......... Pat Marchan
City Mgr., Robert H. García
†**Portland**...............David Krebs
City Mgr., Mike Tanner
†**Port Lavaca**...... Allen Tharling
City Mgr., Gary Broz
†**Port Neches**R. Glenn Johnson
City Mgr., A.R. "Randy" Kimler
Post .... W.G. "Bill" Pool Jr.
Interim City Mgr., Delbert Rudd
Post Oak Bend (Box 758, Kaufman 75142)............Larry Tigert
***Poteet**...............Lino Z. Donato
City Admin., Adolfo Rodriguez
Poth .... Chrystal Eckel
Pottsboro ....Frank Budra
City Mgr., Jerry Guillory
***Powell** ....Dennis Bancroft
Poynor................Dannie Smith
Prairie View ... Frank D. Jackson
Premont .... Mario O. Rodriguez
***Presidio** .... Alcee M. Tavarez
City Admin., Thomas F. Nance
Primera.. John David Osbourne
City Admin., Noe Alaniz
***Princeton** ...Steven Deffibaugh
City Admin. (vacancy)
***Progreso**................Omar Vela
City Admin., Fred Espinosa
Progreso Lakes (Box 760, Progreso 78579)O.D. Emery Jr
Prosper...Charles E. Niswanqer
City Admin., Doug Mouse
***Putnam** ....Roy Petty
***Pyote**..................Glen Garland

— Q —

***†Quanah** ....Chester Ingram
City Admin., Danny Felty
Queen City ...... Bobby Bowman
Quinlan................Sharon Royal
Quintana ....James Nevil

Quitaque .... Clyde Dudley
City Mgr., Maria Cruz Merrell
Quitman .... Larry W. Robertson

— R —

Ralls .... Kelly Wing
City Admin., Jay Rhett Parker
Rancho Viejo .... Ray Downs
City Admin., Cheryl J. Kretz
†Ranger .... Raymond Hart
City Admin., A.J. Ratliff
City Mgr. Mgr., Raymond Hart
*†Rangerville (31850 Ranger-
ville Rd., San Benito 78586)
.... Wayne Halbert
Rankin .... Cora G. McFadden
Ransom Canyon
.... Robert G. Englund
City Admin., Melissa Verett
*Ravenna...........Andy H. Walker
*†Raymondville Joe Alexandre
Red Lick (Box 870, Nash
75569)...........Michael D. Peek
†Red Oak .... Todd B. Little
City Mgr., Ken Pfeifer
Redwater .... Beverly Phares
*Refugio .... Ray Jaso
Reklaw............... Charles Glenn
Reno (Lamar Co.)
.... David Brooks
City Admin., Shannon Barren-
tine
Reno (195 W. Reno Rd., Azle
76020) .... Loyd Bailey
Retreat (125 Ingham Rd., Corsi-
cana 75110) ..Janice Barfknecht
*Rhome .... Mark Lorance
Rice .... Larry Bailey
†Richardson ..... Gary A. Slagel
City Mgr., Bill Keffler
Richland .... Dolores Baldwin
†Richland Hills .. Nelda Stroder
City Mgr., James W. Quin
*Richland Springs
.... Dale McKinnerney
Richmond ...... Hilmar G. Moore
City Mgr., R. Glen Gilmore
Richwood .... Peggy Gartman
*Riesel ....David Guenat, Jr.
City Admin., Bill McLelland
Rio Bravo (1402 Centeno Ln.,
Laredo 78046).. Juan Gonzalez
*Rio Grande City
.... Baldemar Garza
City Admin., Leonardo Olivares
Rio Hondo.... Santiago Saldana
City Admin., José L. Lopez
*Rio Vista ......Russell Green Jr.
*Rising Star.........Earl B. Harris
†River Oaks (4900 River Oaks
Blvd, Fort Worth 76114)
.... Herman Earwood
City Admin., Linda Ryan
*Riverside .... Frank Rich

Roanoke .... Carl Gierisch
City Mgr., Jimmy Stathatos
*Roaring Springs
......................Corky Marshall
City Mgr., Robert Osborn
Robert Lee............ Joe V. White
Robinson .... Bryan Ferguson
City Mgr., Richard Fletcher
*†Robstown .....Rodrigo Ramon
Roby...................... Lance Green
City Mgr., Claude Day
Rochester Marvin Stegemoeller
City Mgr., Gregg Hearn
†Rockdale.. John C. Shoemake
City Mgr., T. Flemming
†Rockport...... Todd W. Pearson
City Mgr., Thomas Blazek
*Rocksprings
..............Charles W. Carson III
†Rockwall ....William R. Cecil
City Mgr., Julie Couch
*Rocky Mound (Box 795, Pitts-
burg 75686) .....Noble T. Smith
Rogers Thomas Carter-Maddux
Rollingwood ..... Hollis Jefferies
City Mgr., Don Ferguson
Roma............... Fernando Pena
City Mgr., Crisanto Salinas
Roman Forest .. Floyd Jackson
*Ropesville ....Alfred Thompson
Roscoe..............Frank S. Porter
City Admin., Jack W. Brown
Rosebud .... Ken Hensel
City Mgr., Megan Henderson
Rose City (370 S. Rose City Dr.,
Vidor 77662) .... David E. Bush
Rose Hill Acres (Box 8285,
Lumberton 77657) .Carl Richard
*†Rosenberg ...Joe M. Gurecky
City Mgr., David E. Neeley
*Ross .... James L. Jaska Sr.
*Rosser .... Albert Davis
Rotan .... Jerry Marshall
City Admin., Harold Sanders
*Round Mountain
.... Alvin Gutierrez
†Round Rock ......Nyle Maxwell
City Mgr., Jim Nuse
Round Top ....Carole Nagel
*†Rowlett .... C. Shane Johnson
Int. City Mgr., George Harris
Roxton .... James Cooper
Royse City ....Jim Mellody
City Admin., Connie Goodwin
Rule...... Malcolm Herttenberger
Runaway Bay Tyce L. Simmons
City Admin., Joe White
*Runge............... Homer Lott Jr.
*†Rusk .... Suzann McCarty
City Mgr., Kevin Bowden

— S —

Sabinal.......... Enrique Alvarado
†Sachse ....Mike Felix
City Mgr., Bill Atkinson

Sadler .... Thomas Filip
†Saginaw........ Frankie Robbins
City Mgr., Nan Stanford
St. Hedwig.......... Mary Jo Dylla
Saint Jo ....Jimmy Dennis Jr.
St. Paul (2505 Butcher's Block,
Wylie 75098) ..Steve Hufstetler
Salado .... Rick Ashe
*†San Angelo. Joseph W. Lown
City Mgr., Dominguez Harold
*†San Antonio .. Edward Garza
Int. City Mgr., Rolando Bono
San Augustine .. Patrick Fussell
City Mgr., James Lyons
†San Benito .. Cesar Gonzalez
City Mgr., Victor Trevino
*Sanctuary (Box 125, Azle
76098) .... Cliff Scallan
San Diego ......Alonzo Lopez Jr.
Sandy Point ....Curt Mowery
*San Elizario ....Raul Diaz
San Felipe .... Bobby Byars
Sanford.................. Gary Moore
*†Sanger ....Tommy Kincaid
City Mgr., Jack Smith
*†San Juan............ San Juanita
.... "Janie" Sanchez
City Mgr., Jorge A. Arcaute
San Leanna (Box 1107, Man-
chaca 78652) . James E. Payne
†San Marcos .....Susan Naruaiz
City Mgr., Dan O'Leary
San Patricio (5617 Main, Mathis
78368) ..... Lonnie Glasscock III
*San Perlita ....Oscar de Luna
*San Saba ....David Parker
City Admin., Joe Ragsdale
Sansom Park (5500 Buchanan
St., Fort Worth 76114)
.... Robert Armstrong
City Admin., Tony White
*Santa Anna .... Jean R. Findley
*Santa Clara (Box 429, Marion
78124) .... David D. Mueller
*†Santa Fe.......... Robert Cheek
City Mgr., Joe Dickson
*Santa Rosa .. Ruben Ochoa Jr.
City Mgr., Javier Mendez
Savoy................ Clete Stogsdill
†Schertz .... Hal Baldwin
City Mgr., Don Taylor
Schulenburg
.............Roger Moellenberndt
City Admin., Ronald Brossman
Scotland ..... Wayne Lindemann
*Scottsville...... Walter Johnson
Scurry............... Robert Stewart
†Seabrook Robin Charles Riley
City Mgr., Robert McDaniel
Seadrift................. Billy F. Ezell
†Seagoville ....George Williams
City Mgr., Denny Wheat
Seagraves ... Patrick L. McAdoo
†Sealy............. Russell L. Koym
City Mgr., John Maresh

†**Seguin** ...... Betty Ann Matthies
City Mgr., Jack Hamlett
Selma .... Jim Parma
City Admin., Ken Roberts
*†**Seminole**.............Mike Carter
City Admin., Tommy Phillips
Seven Oaks (Box 540, Leggett
77350) .... Calvin Cooper
Seven Points....... Gerald Taylor

Seymour........... Dan Craighead
City Admin., Joe Shephard
Shady Shores (Box 362, Lake
Dallas 75065) . Olive Stephens
Shallowater............Moe Dozier
Shamrock....... Wendell Morgan
City Mgr., Johnny Rhodes
***Shavano Park** (99 Saddletree
Rd., San Antonio 78231)
.........................David Marne
City Mgr., Matt Smith
Shenandoah (29811 I-45,
Spring 77381) David J. Vetter Jr.
City Admin., Chip Vansteenberg

Shepherd .... Jerry L. Wade
†**Sherman**.............. Bill Magers
City Mgr., L. Scott Wall
Shiner............ Laura Watzlavick
Shoreacres .. Nancy Edmonson
City Admin., David Stall
†**Silsbee**........Regina Lindsey
City Mgr., Ricky Jorgensen
Silverton........... Lane B. Garvin
City Admin., Jerry Patton
Simonton ...... Paul Sabrsula Jr.
†**Sinton**.............. Pete Gonzales
City Mgr., Ira Knox Jr.
Skellytown .... Red Mills
†**Slaton** ....Laura Lynn Wilson
City Admin., Roger McKinney
Smiley ....Donald Janicek

Smithville ... Renee D. Blaschke
City Mgr., Tex Middlebrook
Smyer ....Mary Beth Sims
***Snook**.............. John W. See III
†**Snyder** .. Francene Allen-Noah
City Mgr., John Gayle
Socorro . Guillermo Gandara Jr.
City Mgr., Lilia Ruiz
Somerset...........Fred Gonzales
City Admin., Linda Wertz
***Somerville** . Tommy Thompson
City Admin., Barbara Pederson
***Sonora** .... Gloria Lopez
City Mgr.(vacancy)
***Sour Lake** ......Bruce Robinson
City Mgr., Larry Saurage
South Houston .... Joe Soto
†**Southlake**.Andy Wambsganss
City Mgr., Shana K. Yelverton
***Southmayd** .... Billy Kerr
***South Mountain** (107 Barton
Ln., Gatesville 76528)
.... Billy Mayhew

***South Padre Island**
.... Bob Pinkerton
City Mgr., Dewey P. Cashwell Jr.
Southside Place (6309 Edloe
St., Houston 77005)
.....................Richard Rothfelder
City Mgr., David Moss
Spearman .... Steve Benton
City Mgr., Edward Hansen
Splendora. Carol Wayne Carley
***Spofford** .............J.B. Herndon
Springlake .... Harlon Watson
Springtown ....Wayne LaCava
City Admin., Bill Funderburk
Spring Valley (1025 Campbell
Rd., Houston 77055)
.................T. Michael Andrews
City Admin., Richard Rocken-
baugh
Spur .... Kenneth Gilcrease
Stafford ....Leonard Scarcella
***Stagecoach** ..... William Berger
†**Stamford** ....Johnny Anders
City Mgr., Jack Harper
Stanton .... Lester Baker
City Admin., Danny Fryar
Star Harbor (Box 949, Malakoff
75148)...... Walter W. Bingham
†**Stephenville**Russell E. Jergins
City Admin., Mark A. Kaiser
Sterling City .... Ray Sparks
***Stinnett** .... Tommy Batson
City Mgr.., James Stroud
***Stockdale** ....Tony Malik
City Mgr., Carl Lambeck
***Stratford** .... David Brown
City Admin., Sean Hardman
Strawn...................... David Day
Streetman ...Dorothy N. Whalen
***Sudan** ....Freddie Maxwell
†**Sugar Land**. David G. Wallace
City Mgr., Allen Bogard
***Sullivan City**....Gumaro Flores
City Mgr., Rolando Gonzalez
†**Sulphur Springs**.. Clay Walker
City Mgr., Mark Maxwell
Sundown .... Jim Winn
City Admin., Brad Stafford
Sunnyvale................Jim Phaup
City Admin., Larry Graves
***Sunray** .... Casey Stone
City Mgr., Greg Smith
***Sunrise Beach Village**
.... Patricia E. Frain
***Sunset** ....Danny Russell
Sunset Valley..Terrence Cowan
***Sun Valley** (RR 2, Box 800,
Paris 75462) .. Maria Z. Wagnon
***Surfside Beach** (1304 Monu-
ment Dr., Freeport 77541)
........................Larry Davison
†**Sweeny** .... Larry G. Piper
City Mgr., H. Timothy Moss
†**Sweetwater** ....David Welch
City Mgr., Edward P. Brown

— T —

***Taft** ....Jerry L. King
City Mgr., Dolores R. Topper
Tahoka................. Mike Mensch
City Admin., Jerry W. Webster
***Talco**............K.M. "Mike" Sloan
***Talty** (Box 565, Forney 75126
.............................Earl Carter
***Tatum** ....Phil Cory
*†**Taylor** .... Donald R. Hill
City Mgr., Frank L. Salvato
Taylor Lake Village
.... Natalie S. O'Neill
Teague.................Earnest Pack
City Admin., Jeff Looney
Tehuacana ......Herman D. East
†**Temple**......William A. Jones III
City Mgr., David A. Blackburn
Tenaha.........George N. Bowers
*†**Terrell**....... Frances Anderson
City Mgr., Gordon C. Pierce
†**Terrell Hills** J. Bradford Camp
City Mgr., (vacancy)
*†**Texarkana** .... James Bramlett
City Mgr., George T. Shackelford
†**Texas City** ... Matthew T. Doyle
***Texhoma** .... Mel Yates
Texline .... Paul Evans
City Mgr., Clark E. Teague
†**The Colony**.......... John Dillard
City Mgr., Dale Cheatham
Thompsons. Freddie Newsome
Thorndale.....Gerald Niemtschk
City Mgr., Keith Kiesling
***Thornton** ....James W. Jackson
City Admin., Beth Johnson
Thorntonville (Box 740, Mona-
hans 79756) ..David L. Mitchell
***Thrall** .... James Dvorak
***Three Rivers** ...Felipe Martinez
City Admin., M.R. Forehand
***Throckmorton** .... Will Carroll
Tiki Island, Village of
.......................Charles Everts
Timbercreek Canyon (101 S.
Timbercreek Dr., Amarillo
79118) ....Elaine Dollar
Timpson .....Douglas McDonald
Tioga .... Stanley Kemp
***Tira** (RR 7, Box 220, Sulphur
Springs 75482)... John Hadley
***Toco** (2103 Chestnut Dr.,
Brookston 75421)
.... John Jason Waller
Todd Mission (390 N. Millcreek
Dr., Plantersville 77363)
......................George Coulam
Tolar....................... Tom Brown
†**Tomball** H.G. "Hap" Harrington
City Mgr., Ben Griffin
***Tom Bean**...........Tom Wilthers
***Tool** .... Scott Confer
Toyah ....Sandra Terry
Trent .... James Wallis
***Trenton**............David Hamrick

Trinidad .... Chris Quinn
    City Admin., Terri R. Newhouse
Trinity ....Lyle Stubbs
Trophy Club .... Nick Sanders
    City Mgr., Donna Welsh
Troup ....John W. Whitsell
    City Admin., Russ Obar
Troy...................Sammy Warren
†**Tulia** .... Boyd W. Vaughn
Turkey............. Pat Carson (Mr.)
    City Mgr., Jerry Landry
Tuscola............. Russell Bartlett
Tye ....Gayland Childers
†**Tyler**.................... Joey Seeber
    City Mgr., Bob Turner

— U —

***Uhland** ....(vacancy)
Uncertain ..... Samuel D. Canup
***Union Grove** (RR 2, Box
196FF, Gladewater 75647)
    .... Randy Simcox
†**Universal City**
    .... Joseph D. Medinger
    City Mgr., Ken Taylor
†**University Park** (3800 Univer-
sity Blvd., Dallas 75205)
    ....James H. Holmes III
    City Mgr., Bob Livingston
*†**Uvalde**..........Josue Garza Jr.
    City Mgr., John H. Harrell

— V —

***Valentine**........ Jesús Calderon
Valley Mills...... Rodney Nichols
***Valley View**..........Carl Kemplin
***Van** ......................E.L. Raulston
    City Admin., Gary McDaniel
***Van Alstyne** .... Willie Boddie
    City Mgr., Wayne Cummings
***Van Horn**.......... Okey D. Lucas
    City Admin., Rebecca Brewster
Vega...........Mark J. Groneman
Venus ....Carolyn Welcher
    City Admin., Jerry Reed
†**Vernon**................. Kelly Couch
    City Mgr., Jim Murray
†**Victoria**............Will Armstrong
    City Mgr., Denny Arnold
†**Vidor**................... Joe Hopkins
    City Mgr., Ricky Jorgensen
***Village of the Hills** (102 Trophy
Dr., Austin 78738)
    ....Virginia W. Jones
    City Admin., Dan Roark
***Vinton** .. Juvencia R. Onfiveros
Volente ....Jan Paul Yenawine

— W —

†**Waco**......... Virginia DuPuy
    City Mgr., Larry D. Groth
***Waelder**....................Roy Tovar
Wake Village ..Mike Huddleston
    City Admin., Bob Long
***Waller**......... Danny Marburger

Wallis .... Tony I. Salazar Jr.
    City Mgr., Flint Little
Walnut Springs Benny Damron
***Warren City** (3004 George
Richey Rd., Gladewater 75647)
    ....Ricky J. Wallace
Waskom .... Jesse Moore
†**Watauga**........... Henry Jeffries
    City Mgr., Kerry Lacy
†**Waxahachie** ..... Jay Barksdale
    City Mgr., Robert W. Sokoll
*†**Weatherford** ..... Joe M. Tison
    City Mgr., George Campbell
*†**Webster** ....Donna Rogers
    City Mgr., Michael W. Jez
***Weimar** .... Bennie Kosler
    City Mgr., Randal W. Jones
***Weinert** .... Julian Estrada
Weir .... Mervin Walker
Wellington ....Gary Brewer
    City Mgr., Jon Sessions
Wellman ....Kent Davis
Wells .... Jim Maddox
†**Weslaco** .... Joe V. Sanchez
    City Mgr., Anthony Covacevich
West ....Russell Willsey
    City Mgr., Ken Kubala
Westbrook ...... Ramiro Fuentes
***West Columbia** ...David Foster
    City Mgr., Roger L. Mumby
Westlake .... Scott Bradley
    City Mgr., Trent Petty
West Lake Hills
    .... Dwight Thompson
    City Admin., Daniel E. Sowada
***Westminster**......... Phil Gophin
    City Mgr., Peter J. Collumb
Weston ....Patti Harrington
*†**West Orange** . Roy McDonald
Westover Hills (5824 Merry-
mount, Fort Worth 76107)
    .... Earle A. Shields Jr.
    City Admin., B.J. Tuttleton
West Tawakoni (1533 E. Hwy
276, Quinlan 75474)
    .... Bill Stausing
    City Admin., Cloy Richards
*†**West University Place**
    .... Burt Ballanfant
    City Mgr., Michael Ross
***Westworth Village** (311 Burton
Hill Rd., Fort Worth 76114)
    .... Andy Fontenot
    City Admin., Lori Bland
†**Wharton** .... Bryce D. Kocian
    City Mgr., Andres Garza Jr.
***Wheeler** ....Wanda Herd
White Deer .... Richard Wuest
    City Admin., Anita Haiduk
WhitefaceVernon Shellenberger
†**Whitehouse**
    .... Suzanne Loudamy
    City Mgr., Ronny Fite
White Oak .... Tim Vaughn
    City Coor., Ralph Weaver

***Whitesboro** .... W.D. Welch
    City Admin., Michael Marter
†**White Settlement**
    ....James O. Ouzts
    City Mgr., Dena Daniel
Whitewright..........Bill Goodson
Whitney .... Gwen Evans
*†**Wichita Falls**
    .... William K. Altman
    City Mgr., James P. Berzina
Wickett ....Harold Ferguson
Willis................. Leonard Reed
    City Admin., James McAlister
***Willow Park** . James Poythress
    City Admin., Claud Arnold
Wills Point........... Roy Caldwell
    City Mgr.,C.C. "Butch" Girdley
Wilmer .... Don Hudson
    City Admin., Thom Lauer
Wilson .... Jackie Bishop
Wimberley ....Stephen Klepfer
    City Admin., Stephen J. Harrison
***Windcrest** ....Jack Leonhardt
    City Admin., Ronnie Cain
Windom .... Billy Joe Roberts
***Windthorst**.... Sue Steinberger
    City Mgr., Donald Frerich
Winfield .... Mel Murphy
Wink .... Betty Lou Dodd
Winnsboro ....Carolyn S. Jones
    City Admin., Ronny Knight
Winona .... Glynn D. Marsh
Winters ....Nelan Bahlman
    City Mgr., Aref Hassan
Wixon Valley (Box 105, Kurten
77862) .... Ruby Andrews
***Wolfe City** .. Richard C. Owens
***Wolfforth** .............L.C. Childers
    City Admin., Frankie Pittman
Woodbranch Village (Box 804,
New Caney 77357)
    ....Sharon Frey
Woodcreek ... Morris Hoggerton
    City Admin., Peg Wolfe
***Woodloch** (Box 1379, Conroe
77305) .... Diane L. Lincoln
***Woodsboro**
    ....George Hernandez
Woodson .... Bobby Mathiews
Woodville ..... Jimmie R. Cooley
    City Admin., Don Shaw
*†**Woodway** ....Donald J. Baker
    City Mgr., Yousry "Yost" Zakhary
Wortham.........Judy Edwards
†**Wylie**....................John Mondy
    City Mgr., Mark Roath

— Y —

Yantis................. Jerry E. Miller
†**Yoakum** ....Anita R. Rodriguez
    City Mgr., Calvin Cook
Yorktown .... Patricia Nelson

— Z —

Zavalla .... Hulon Miller ☆

Texas Main Street Cities
Program Marks 25th Year of Preserving Commercial Districts

Tthe Texas Main Street Program celebrates its 25th anniversary in 2006. Part of the Texas Historical Commission, the Texas Main Street Program, has worked with more than 145 communities across the state to preserve and revitalize their historic commercial districts.

As a result, more than $1 billion in private money has been reinvested in Texas downtowns and neighborhood commercial districts, more than 5,500 new businesses have been established and more than 21,300 jobs have been created.

Each year, the Texas Main Street Program accepts applications for participation in the program. Those cities selected receive technical assistance and training in the areas of design, promotion, economic restructuring and organization.

They also receive comprehensive training for the local downtown manager and volunteers; on-site consultations from an architect, economic development specialist, and interior design and merchandising specialist; strategic planning and work-planning facilitation; and a variety of specialized educational and networking opportunities.

In addition, each new community receives a free three-day assessment, as well as a visit from the Texas First Lady to kick off the new program.

For more information about the Texas Main Street

Program, please visit www.thc.state.tx.us or call 512-463-6092. More information about downtown revitalization can be found through the program's partners: the National Main Street Center at www.mainstreet.org and the Texas Downtown Association at www.texasdowntown.org. ☆

Main Street Cities

2005
La Porte, Harris County
Livingston, Polk County
San Angelo, Tom Green County
Sinton, San Patricio County

2004
Grand Saline, Van Zandt County
McKinney, Collin County
Pecos, Reeves County
Pharr, Hidalgo County

2003
Clarksville, Red River County
Llano, Llano County
Luling, Caldwell County
Van Horn, Culberson County
Winnsboro, Wood and Franklin counties

Texas First Lady Anita Perry, left, kicks off the Texas Main Street Program in San Angelo in Tom Green County. Photo courtesy of the Texas Main Street Program.

Regional Councils of Government

The concept of regional planning and cooperation, fostered by enabling legislation in 1965, has spread across Texas since organization of the **North Central Texas Council of Governments** in 1966.

Regional councils are voluntary associations of local governments that deal with problems and planning needs that cross the boundaries of individual local governments or that require regional attention. These concerns may include criminal justice, emergency communications, job-training programs, solid-waste management, transportation needs, and water-quality management. The councils make recommendations to member governments and may assist in implementing the plans.

The **Texas Association of Regional Councils** is at 1305 San Antonio St., Austin 78701; 512-478-4715; fax: 512-478-1049. Financing is provided by the local governments, the state and the federal government.

The map at right shows the locations of the **24 regional councils**, along with a list of the regional councils, the **counties served** and the **executive director**.

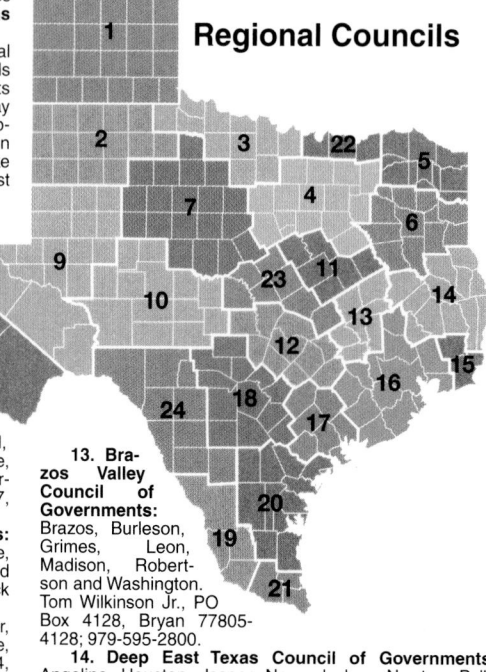

Regional Councils

1. Panhandle Regional Planning Commission: Armstrong, Briscoe, Carson, Castro, Childress, Collingsworth, Dallam, Deaf Smith, Donley, Gray, Hall, Hansford, Hartley, Hemphill, Hutchinson, Lipscomb, Moore, Ochiltree, Oldham, Parmer, Potter, Randall, Roberts, Sherman, Swisher and Wheeler. Gary Pitner, PO Box 9257, Amarillo 79105-9257; 806-372-3381.

2. South Plains Association of Governments: Bailey, Cochran, Crosby, Dickens, Floyd, Garza, Hale, Hockley, King, Lamb, Lubbock, Lynn, Motley, Terry and Yoakum. Jerry D. Casstevens, PO Box 3730, Lubbock 79452-3730; 806-762-8721.

3. Nortex Regional Planning Commission: Archer, Baylor, Clay, Cottle, Foard, Hardeman, Jack, Montague, Wichita, Wilbarger and Young. Dennis Wilde, PO Box 5144, Wichita Falls 76307-5144; 940-322-5281.

4. North Central Texas Council of Governments: Collin, Dallas, Denton, Ellis, Erath, Hood, Hunt, Johnson, Kaufman, Navarro, Palo Pinto, Parker, Rockwall, Somervell, Tarrant and Wise. R. Michael Eastland, PO Box 5888, Arlington 76005-5888; 817-640-3300.

5. Ark-Tex Council of Governments: Bowie, Cass, Delta, Franklin, Hopkins, Lamar, Morris, Red River, Titus and Miller County, Ark. L.D. Williamson, PO Box 5307, Texarkana, Texas 75505-5307; 903-832-8636.

6. East Texas Council of Governments: Anderson, Camp, Cherokee, Gregg, Harrison, Henderson, Marion, Panola, Rains, Rusk, Smith, Upshur, Van Zandt and Wood. Glynn J. Knight, 3800 Stone Rd., Kilgore 75662-6937; 903-984-8641.

7. West Central Texas Council of Governments: Brown, Callahan, Coleman, Comanche, Eastland, Fisher, Haskell, Jones, Kent, Knox, Mitchell, Nolan, Runnels, Scurry, Shackelford, Stephens, Stonewall, Taylor and Throckmorton. Jim Compton, PO Box 3195, Abilene 79601-3195; 325-672-8544.

8. Rio Grande Council of Governments: Brewster, Culberson, El Paso, Hudspeth, Jeff Davis, Presidio and Doña Ana Co., New Mexico. Jake Brisbin Jr., 1100 N. Stanton, Ste. 610, El Paso 79902-4155; 915-533-0998.

9. Permian Basin Regional Planning Commission: Andrews, Borden, Crane, Dawson, Ector, Gaines, Glasscock, Howard, Loving, Martin, Midland, Pecos, Reeves, Terrell, Upton, Ward and Winkler. Gary Gaston, PO Box 60660, Midland 79711-0660; 432-563-1061.

10. Concho Valley Council of Governments: Coke, Concho, Crockett, Irion, Kimble, Mason, McCulloch, Menard, Reagan, Schleicher, Sterling, Sutton and Tom Green. Jeffrey Sutton, Box 60050, San Angelo 76906-0050; 325-944-9666.

11. Heart of Texas Council of Governments: Bosque, Falls, Freestone, Hill, Limestone and McLennan. Kenneth Simons, 300 Franklin Ave., Waco 76701-2244; 254-756-7822.

12. Capital Area Council of Governments: Bastrop, Blanco, Burnet, Caldwell, Fayette, Hays, Lee, Llano, Travis and Williamson. Betty Voights, 2512 S. IH 35 S, Ste. 200, Austin 78704; 512-916-6000.

13. Brazos Valley Council of Governments: Brazos, Burleson, Grimes, Leon, Madison, Robertson and Washington. Tom Wilkinson Jr., PO Box 4128, Bryan 77805-4128; 979-595-2800.

14. Deep East Texas Council of Governments: Angelina, Houston, Jasper, Nacogdoches, Newton, Polk, Sabine, San Augustine, San Jacinto, Shelby, Trinity and Tyler. Walter G. Diggles, 210 Premier Dr., Jasper 75951; 409-384-5704.

15. South East Texas Regional Planning Commission: Hardin, Jefferson and Orange. Chester Jourdan, 2210 Eastex Freeway, Beaumont 77703; 409-899-8444.

16. Houston-Galveston Area Council of Governments: Austin, Brazoria, Chambers, Colorado, Fort Bend, Galveston, Harris, Liberty, Matagorda, Montgomery, Walker, Waller and Wharton. Jack Steele, PO Box 22777, Houston 77227-2777; 713-627-3200.

17. Golden Crescent Regional Planning Commission: Calhoun, DeWitt, Goliad, Gonzales, Jackson, Lavaca and Victoria. Joe Brannan, 568 Big Bend Dr., Victoria 77904; 361-578-1587.

18. Alamo Area Council of Governments: Atascosa, Bandera, Bexar, Comal, Frio, Gillespie, Guadalupe, Karnes, Kendall, Kerr, Medina and Wilson. Al J. Notzon III, 8700 Tesoro Dr., Ste. 700, San Antonio 78217-6228 210-362-5200.

19. South Texas Development Council: Jim Hogg, Starr, Webb and Zapata. Amando Garza Jr., 1002 Vicky Ln, Laredo 78044-2187; 956-722-3995.

20. Coastal Bend Council of Governments: Aransas, Bee, Brooks, Duval, Jim Wells, Kenedy, Kleberg, Live Oak, McMullen, Nueces, Refugio and San Patricio. John P. Buckner, PO Box 9909, Corpus Christi 78469-9909; 361-883-5743.

21. Lower Rio Grande Valley Development Council: Cameron, Hidalgo and Willacy. Kenneth N. Jones Jr., 311 N. 15th, McAllen 78501-4705; 956-682-3481.

22. Texoma Council of Governments: Cooke, Fannin and Grayson. Frances Pelley, 1117 Gallagher Dr., Ste. 100, Sherman 75090; 903-893-2161.

23. Central Texas Council of Governments: Bell, Coryell, Hamilton, Lampasas, Milam, Mills and San Saba. James Reed, PO Box 729, Belton 76513-0729; 254-939-1801.

24. Middle Rio Grande Development Council: Dimmit, Edwards, Kinney, La Salle, Maverick, Real, Uvalde, Val Verde and Zavala. Leodoro Martinez Jr., PO Box 1199, Carrizo Springs 78834-1199; 830-876-3533. ☆

County Courts

Below are listed county courts, including county courts at law, probate courts, juvenile/domestic relations courts, criminal courts and criminal courts of appeals as reported by the county clerks as of July 2005. Other courts with jurisdiction in each county can be found in the list on pages 427–428. Other county and district officials can be found on pages 471–481.

Anderson County Court at Law: Jeff Doran. **Probate Courts:** No. 1, Carey G. McKinney; No. 2, Jeff Doran. **Criminal Court at Law, Domestic Relations & Juvenile Courts:** Jeff Doran.

Austin County Court at Law: Gladys M. Oakley.

Bastrop County Court at Law: Benton Eskew.

Baylor County Probate Court: James D. Coltharp. **Juvenile Court:** W.H. Heatly.

Bee County Criminal Court at Law & Probate Court: Jimmy Martinez. **Juvenile Courts:** Raul Casarez.

Bell County Courts at Law: No. 1, Edward S. Johnson; No. 2, John Barina; No. 3, Gerald Brown.

Bexar County Courts at Law: No. 1, Al Alonso; No. 2, H. Paul Canales; No. 3, David J. Rodriguez; No. 4, Sarah E. Garrahan; No. 5, Timothy F. Johnson; No. 6, Phil Meyer; No. 7, Monica E. Guerrero; No. 8, Karen Crouch; No. 9, Oscar Kazen; No. 10, Irene Rios; No. 11, Jo Ann De Hoyos; No. 12, Michael Mery. **Probate Courts:** No. 1, Polly Jackson Spencer; No. 2, Tom Rickhoff.

Bowie County Court at Law: Jeff Addison. **Probate Court:** James M. Carlow.

Brazoria County Courts at Law & Probate Courts: No. 1, Jerri Lee Mills; No. 2, Marc W. Holder; No. 3, James A. Blackstock.

Brazos County Courts at Law: No. 1, Randy Michel; No. 2, Jim Locke.

Brooks County Criminal Court at Law & Juvenile Court: Joe B. Garcia.

Brown County Court at Law: Frank Griffin.

Burnet County Court at Law: W.R. Savage.

Caldwell County Court at Law: Edward L. Jarrett.

Cameron County Courts at Law: No. 1, Janet Leal; No. 2, Elia Cornejo-Lopez.; No. 3, Daniel Robles.

Carson County Probate Court: Lewis Powers.

Chambers County Probate & Juvenile Courts: Jimmy Sylvia; **Domestic Relations Court:** Carroll E. Wilborn Jr.

Cherokee County Court at Law: Daniel B. Childs.

Coke County Probate Court: Roy Blair. **Juvenile:** Barbara Walther.

Collin County Courts at Law: No. 1, Corinne Mason; No. 2, Jerry Lewis; No. 3, John Barry; No. 4, Raymond Wheless; No. 5, Gregory Brewer. **Probate Court:** Weldon Copeland. **Juvenile Court:** Cynthia Wheless.

Collingsworth County Probate & Juvenile Courts: Jim Forrester.

Colorado County Probate & Juvenile Courts: Al Jamison.

Comal County Court at Law: Brenda Chapman.

Comanche County Probate & Juvenile Courts: James R. Arthur.

Concho County Juvenile Court: Ben Woodward.

Cooke County Court at Law: John Morris.

Coryell County Court at Law: Susan Stephens. **Probate Court:** John Hull.

Culberson County Court at Law, Probate, Juvenile: John Conoly.

Dallam County Probate & Juvenile Courts: David D. Field.

Dallas County Courts at Law: No. 1, Russell Roden; No. 2, John B. Peyton; No. 3, Sally Montgomery; No. 4, Bruce Woody; No. 5, Mark Greenberg. **County Criminal Courts:** No. 1, Daniel Clancy; No. 2, Neil Pask; No. 3, Daniel Wyde; No. 4, Ralph Taite; No. 5, Tom Fuller; No. 6, Phil Barker; No. 7, Elizabeth Crowder; No. 8, Jane Roden; No. 9, Keith Anderson; No. 10, Lisa Fox; No. 11, Dianne Jones. **Probate Courts:** No. 1, Nikki DeShazo; No. 2, Robert E. Price; No. 3, Joe Loving Jr. **County Criminal Courts of Appeals:** No. 1, Kristin Wade; No. 2, Lynn Burson.

Dawson County Probate & Juvenile Courts: Sam Saleh.

Deaf Smith County Juvenile Court: Tom Simons.

Delta County Probate & Criminal Courts: Hugh Charles Whitney.

Denton County Courts at Law: No. 1, Darlene Whitten; No. 2, Margaret Barnes. **Domestic Relations:** Jim Crouch. **Probate Court:** Don Windle. **Juvenile Court:** Darlene Whitten.

DeWitt County Juvenile Court: Ben E. Prause.

Donley County Probate Court: Jack Hall.

Eastland County Probate: Brad Stephenson. **Juvenile Court:** Steven R. Herod.

Ector County Courts at Law: No. 1, J.A. "Jim" Bobo; No. 2, Mark Owens. **Juvenile Court:** J.A. "Jim" Bobo.

Edwards County Probate Court: Nick Gallegos. **Juvenile Court:** Thomas F. Lee.

Ellis County Court at Law: No. 1, Bob Carroll; No. 2, A. Gene Calvert Jr. **Probate:** Bob Carroll. **Juvenile:** A. Gene Calvert Jr.

El Paso County Courts at Law: No. 1, Ricardo Herrera; No. 2, Julie Gonzalez; No. 3, Javier Alvarez; No. 4, Alejandro Gonzalez; No. 5, Carlos Villa; No. 6, M. Sue Kurita; No. 7, Jose Baca. **Probate Court:** Max D. Higgs. **Criminal Court at Law:** No. 1, Alma Trejo; No. 2, Robert Anchondo.

Erath County Court at Law: Bart McDougal. **Domestic Relations Court:** Don Jones.

Fort Bend County Courts at Law: No. 1, Larry Wagenbach; No. 2, Walter McMeans; No. 3, Susan Lowery; No. 4, Sandy Bielstein.

Galveston County Courts at Law: No. 1, Mary Nell Crapitto; No. 2, C.G. Dibrell III; No. 3, Roy Quintanilla. **Probate:** Gladys Burwell.

Grayson County Courts at Law: No. 1, James C. Henderson; No. 2, Carol Siebman. **Juvenile Court:** Rayburn M. Nall Jr.

Gregg County Court at Law: No. 1, Rebecca Simpson; No. 2, Alfonso Charles.

Guadalupe County Court at Law: No. 1, Linda Z. Jones; No. 2,

Frank Follis. **Probate Court:** Linda Z. Jone.

Harris County Courts at Law: No. 1, R. Jack Cagle; No. 2, Gary Michael Block; No. 3, Lynn Bradshaw-Hull; No. 4, Roberta Lloyd. **County Criminal Courts at Law:** No. 1, Reagan Cartright Helm; No. 2, Michael Peters; No. 3, Don Jackson; No. 4, James E. Anderson; No. 5, Margaret Stewart Harrison; No. 6, Larry Standley; No. 7, Pam Derbyshire; No. 8, Jay Karahan; No. 9, Analia Wilkerson; No. 10, Sherman A. Ross; No. 11, Diane Bull; No. 12, Robin Brown; No. 13, Mark Atkinson; No. 14, Mike Fields; No. 15, Jean Spradling Hughes. **Probate Courts:** No. 1, Russell Austin; No. 2, Mike Wood; No. 3, Rory Robert Olsen; No. 4, William C. McCulloch.

Harrison County Court at Law: Jim Ammerman II.

Hays County Courts at Law: No. 1, Howard S. Warner II; No. 2, Linda A. Rodriguez.

Henderson County Courts at Law: No. 1, Matt Livingston; No. 2, Nancy Perryman. **Probate & Juvenile Courts:** David Holstein.

Hidalgo County Courts at Law: No. 1, Rodolfo Gonzalez; No. 2, Jaime Gonzalez. **Probate Court:** Homero Garza.

Hood County Court at Law: Vincent Messina.

Hopkins County Court at Law: Amy M. Smith.

Houston County Court at Law: Sarah Tunnell Clark.

Hunt County Court at Law: Steve Shipp.

Jefferson County Courts at Law: No. 1, Alfred S. Gerson; No. 2, G.R. "Lupe" Flores; No. 3, John Paul Davis. **Domestic Relations Court:** Tom Mulvaney. **Juvenile Court:** Larry Thorne.

Johnson County Courts at Law: No. 1, Robert Mayfield; No. 2, William R. Anderson Jr.

Kaufman County Court at Law & Juvenile Court: Erleigh Norville.

Kerr County Court at Law: Spencer Brown.

Lampasasr County Probate & Juvenile Courts: Joe Carroll.

Liberty County Court at Law: Don Taylor.

Lubbock County Courts at Law: No. 1, Rusty Ladd; No. 2, Drue Farmer; No. 3, Paula Lanehart.

McLennan County Courts at Law: No. 1, Tom Ragland; No. 2, Michael B. Gassaway

Medina County Court at Law: Vivian Torres.

Midland County Courts at Law: No. 1, Al Walvoord; No. 2, Marvin Moore. **Domestic Relations Court:** Dean Rucker.

Montgomery County Courts at Law: No. 1, Dennis Watson; No. 2, Jerry Winfree; No. 3, Mason Marin; No. 4, Mary Ann Turner.

Moore County Court at Law: Delwin McGee.

Nacogdoches County Court at Law: Jack Sinz.

Nolan County Court at Law: Gary Harger.

Nueces County Courts at Law: No. 1, Robert Vargas; No. 2, Lisa Gonzales; No. 3, Marisela Saldaña; No. 4, James E. Klager; No. 5: Carl E. Lewis.

Orange County Court at Law: No. 1, Michael W. Shuff; No 2, Troy Johnson.

Panola County Court at Law: Terry D. Bailey.

Parker County Courts at Law: No. 1, Deborah Dupont; No. 2, Ben Akers.

Polk County Court at Law: Stephen Phillips.

Potter County Courts at Law: No. 1, W.F. "Corky" Roberts; No. 2, Pamela Cook Sirmon.

Randall County Court at Law: James Anderson.

Reeves County Court at Law: Walter M. Holcombe.

Rockwall County Court at Law: David Rakow.

Rusk County Court at Law: Darrell Hyatt.

San Patricio County Court at Law: Richard D. Hatch III.

Smith County Courts at Law: No. 1, Thomas A. Dunn; No. 2, Randall L. Rogers. **Probate:** Becky Dempsey. **Juvenile:** Floyd Getz.

Tarrant County Courts at Law: No. 1, R. Brent Keis; No. 2, Jennifer Rymell; No. 3, Vince Sprinkle. **County Criminal Courts at Law:** No. 1, Sherry Hill; No. 2, Mike Mitchell; No. 3, Billy D. Mills; No. 4, Deborah Nekhom Harris; No. 5, Jamie Cummings; No. 6, Molly Jones; No. 7, Cheril S. Hardy; No. 8, Daryl Coffee; No. 9, Brent A. Carr; No. 10, Phil Sorrels. **Probate Courts:** No. 1, Steve M. King; No. 2, Pat Ferchill.

Taylor County Courts at Law: No. 1, Robert Harper; No. 2, Barbara B. Rollins.

Tom Green County Courts at Law: No. 1, Ben Nolan; No. 2, Penny Roberts.

Travis County Courts at Law: No. 1, J. David Phillips; No. 2, Orlinda Naranjo; No. 3, David Crain; No. 4, Mike Denton; No. 5, Gisela Triana; No. 6, Jan Breland; No. 7, Elizabeth Earle. **Probate Court:** Guy Herman.

Val Verde County Court at Law: Sergio J. Gonzalez.

Victoria County Courts at Law: No. 1, Laura A. Weiser; No. 2, Juan Velasquez III.

Walker County Court at Law: Barbara W. Hale.

Waller County Court at Law: June Jackson.

Washington County Court at Law: Matthew Reue.

Webb County Courts at Law: No. 1, Alvino "Ben" Morales; No. 2, Jesús "Chuy" Garza.

Wichita County Courts at Law: No. 1, Jim Hogan; No. 2, Tom Bacus.

Williamson County Courts at Law: No. 1, Suzanne Brooks; No. 2, Tim Wright; No. 3, Don Higginbothom.

Wise County Court at Law: Melton D. Cude. ☆

County Tax Appraisers

The following list of Chief Appraisers for Texas counties was furnished by the State Property Tax Division of the State Comptroller's office. It includes the mailing address for each appraiser and is current to July 2005.

Anderson—Carson Wages, PO Box 279, Palestine 75802

Andrews—Ron Huckabay, 600 N. Main, Andrews 79714

Angelina—Keith Kraemer, PO Box 2357, Lufkin 75902

Aransas—Jad Smith, 601 S. Church, Rockport 78382

Archer—Kimbra York, PO Box 1141, Archer City 76351

Armstrong—Deborah J. Sherman, Drawer 835, Claude 79019

Atascosa—Edward A. Bridge, PO Box 139, Poteet 78065

Austin—Richard Moring, 906 E. Amelia St., Bellville 77418

Bailey—Kaye Elliott, 302 Main St., Muleshoe 79347

Bandera—Ed Barnes, PO Box 1119, Bandera 78003

Bastrop—Mark Boehnke, Drawer 578, Bastrop 78602

Baylor—Ronnie Hargrove, 211 N. Washington, Seymour 76380

Bee—Bruce Martin, PO Box 1262, Beeville 78104

Bell—Marvin Hahn, PO Box 390, Belton 76513

Bexar—Michael Amezquita, PO Box 830248, San Antonio 78283

Blanco—Hollis Boatright, PO Box 338, Johnson City 78636

Borden—Jill Freeman, PO Box 298, Gail 79738

Bosque—F. Janice Henry, PO Box 393, Meridian 76665

Bowie—Dolores Baird, PO Box 6527, Texarkana 75505

Brazoria—Cheryl Evans, 500 N. Chenango, Angleton 77515

Brazos—Gerald L. Winn, 1673 Briarcrest Dr., A-101, Bryan 77802

Brewster—Betty Jo Rooney, 107 W. Avenue E, #2, Alpine 79830

Briscoe—Pat McWaters, PO Box 728, Silverton 79257

Brooks—Marylou Cantu, Drawer A, Falfurrias 78355

Brown—Doran E. Lemke, 403 Fisk Ave., Brownwood 76801

Burleson—Curtis Doss, PO Box 1000, Caldwell 77836

Burnet—Stan Hemphill, PO Box 908, Burnet 78611

Caldwell—Matthew Allen, PO Box 900, Lockhart 78644

Calhoun—Andrew J. Hahn, PO Box 49, Port Lavaca 77979

Callahan—Bun Barry, 132 W. 4th St., Baird 79504

Cameron—Frutoso Gomez Jr., PO Box 1010, San Benito 78586

Camp—Geraldine Hull, 143 Quitman St., Pittsburg 75686

Carson—Donita Davis, PO Box 970, Panhandle 79068

Cass—Ann Lummus, 502 N. Main St., Linden 75563

Castro—Jerry Heller, 204 S.E. 3rd (Rear), Dimmitt 79027

Chambers—Michael Fregia, PO Box 1520, Anahuac 77514

Cherokee—Lee Flowers, PO Box 494, Rusk 75785

Childress—Anita Manley, 100 Ave. E NW, Childress 79201

Clay—A.G. Reis, PO Box 108, Henrietta 76365

Cochran—H. Loy Kern, 109 S.E. 1st, Morton 79346

Coke—Patsy N. Dunn, PO Box 2, Robert Lee 76945

Coleman—Bill W. Jones, PO Box 914, Coleman 76834

Collin—Jimmie Honea, 2404 Ave. K, Plano 75074

Collingsworth—Ann Wauer, 800 W. Ave., Wellington, Rm. 104 79095

Colorado—William T. Youens, PO Box 10, Columbus 78934

Comal—Lynn E. Rodgers, PO Box 311222, New Braunfels 78131

Comanche—Rhonda Woods, PO Box 6, Comanche 76442

Concho—Terry Farris, PO Box 68, Paint Rock 76866

Cooke—Doug Smithson, 201 N. Dixon St., Gainesville 76240

Coryell—Brett McKibben, 705 Main St., Gatesville 76528

Cottle—Rue Young, PO Box 459, Paducah 79248

Crane—Janet Wilson, 511 W. 8th, Crane 79731

Crockett—Rhonda Shaw, PO Drawer H, Ozona 76943

Crosby—Kathy Harris, PO Box 505, Crosbyton 79322

Culberson—Sally Carrasco, PO Box 550, Van Horn 79855

Dallam—Edward G. Carter, PO Box 579, Dalhart 79022

Dallas—Ken Nolan, 2949 N. Stemmons Fwy., Dallas 75247

Dawson—Tom Anderson, PO Box 797, Lamesa 79331

Deaf Smith—Danny Jones, PO Box 2298, Hereford 79045

Delta—Sarah Pruit, PO Box 47, Cooper 75432

Denton—Joe Rogers, PO Box 2816, Denton 76202

DeWitt—John Haliburton, PO Box 4, Cuero 77954

Dickens—Dexter Clay, PO Box 119, Dickens 79229

Dimmit—Elida Sanchez, 404 W. Peña St., Carrizo Springs 78834

Donley—Paula Lowrie, PO Box 1220, Clarendon 79226

Duval—Ernesto Molina, PO Box 809, San Diego 78384

Eastland—Steve Thomas, PO Box 914, Eastland 76448

Ector—Karen McCord, 1301 E. 8th St., Odessa 79761

Edwards—Jodie Greene, PO Box 858, Rocksprings 78880

Ellis—Kathy Rodrigue, PO Box 878, Waxahachie 75165

El Paso—Cora Viescas, 5801 Trowbridge, El Paso 79925

Erath—Jerry Lee, PO Box 94, Stephenville 76401

Falls—Sharon Scott, PO Box 430, Marlin 76661

Fannin—Mike Shannon, 831 W. State Hwy. 56, Bonham 75418

Fayette—Karen Schubert, PO Box 836, La Grange 78945

Fisher—Jacqueline Martin, PO Box 516, Roby 79543

Floyd—Shelia Faulkenberry, PO Box 249, Floydada 79235

Foard—Jo Ann Vecera, PO Box 419, Crowell 79227

Fort Bend—Glen Whitehead, 2801 B.F. Terry Blvd., Rosenberg 77471

Franklin—John Kirkland, PO Box 720, Mount Vernon 75457

Freestone—Bud Black, 218 N. Mount, Fairfield 75840

Frio—Irma Gonzalez, PO Box 1129, Pearsall 78061

Gaines—Betty Caudle, PO Box 490, Seminole 79360

Galveston—Ken Wright, 600 Gulf Fwy., Texas City 77591

Garza—Shirley A. Smith, PO Drawer F, Post 79356

Gillespie—David Oehler, 101 W. Main St., #11, Fredericksburg 78624

Glasscock—Royce Pruit, PO Box 89, Garden City 79739

Goliad—E.J. Bammert, PO Box 34, Goliad 77963

Gonzales—Glenda Strackbein, PO Box 867, Gonzales 78629

Gray—W. Pat Bagley, PO Box 836, Pampa 79066

Grayson—Larry Ward, 205 N. Travis, Sherman 75090

Gregg—Thomas Hays, 1333 E. Harrison Rd., Longview 75604

Grimes—Bill Sullivan, PO Box 489, Anderson 77830

Guadalupe—Chris Boenig, 3000 N. Austin, Seguin 78155

Hale—Nikki Branscum, PO Box 29, Plainview 79073

Hall—Marlin D. Felts, 512 W. Main St., Memphis 79245

Hamilton—Doyle Roberts, 119 E. Henry St., Hamilton 76531

Hansford—Alice Peddy, 709 W. 7th Ave., Spearman 79081

Hardeman—Twila Butler, PO Box 388, Quanah 79252

Hardin—Amador Reyna, PO Box 670, Kountze 77625

Harris—Jim Robinson, 13013 Northwest Fwy., Houston 77040

Harrison—David Whitmire, PO Box 818, Marshall 75671

Hartley—Mary M. Thompson, PO Box 405, Hartley 79044

Haskell—Kenny Watson, PO Box 467, Haskell 79521

Hays—David G. Valle (interim), 21001 N. IH-35, Kyle 78640

Hemphill—Duane Cox, PO Box 65, Canadian 79014

Henderson—Bill Jackson, PO Box 430, Athens 75751

Hidalgo—Alonzo Vega, PO Box 208, Edinburg 78540

Hill—Mike McKibben, PO Box 416, Hillsboro 76645

Hockley—Greg Kelley, PO Box 1090, Levelland 79336

Hood—Jeff Law, PO Box 819, Granbury 76048

Hopkins—William Sherman, PO Box 753, Sulphur Springs 75483

Houston—Kathryn Keith, PO Box 112, Crockett 75835

Howard—Keith Toomire, PO Box 1151, Big Spring 79721

Hudspeth—Zedoch L. Pridgeon, Box 429, Sierra Blanca 79851

Hunt—Mildred Compton, PO Box 1339, Greenville 75403

Hutchinson—Bill Swink, PO Box 5065, Borger 79008

Irion—Frances Grice, PO Box 980, Mertzon 76941

Jack—Kathy Conner, PO Box 958, Jacksboro 76458

Jackson—Damon D. Moore, 700 N. Wells, Ste. 204, Edna 77957

Jasper—David Luther, PO Box 1300, Jasper 75951

Jeff Davis—Zedoch L. Pridgeon, PO Box 373, Fort Davis 79734

Jefferson—Roland Bieber, PO Box 21337, Beaumont 77720

Jim Hogg—Arnoldo Gonzalez, PO Box 459, Hebbronville 78361

Jim Wells—Sidney Vela, PO Box 607, Alice 78333
Johnson—Jim Hudspeth, 109 N. Main, Cleburne 76033
Jones—Susan Holloway, PO Box 348, Anson 79501

Karnes—Oscar Caballero, 915 S. Panna Maria, Karnes City 78118
Kaufman—Richard L. Mohundro, PO Box 819, Kaufman 75142
Kendall—Leta Schlinke, PO Box 788, Boerne 78006
Kenedy—Bill Fuller, PO Box 701085, San Antonio 78270
Kent—Garth Gregory, PO Box 68, Jayton 79528
Kerr—P.H. "Fourth" Coates IV, PO Box 294387, Kerrville 78029
Kimble—John Dennis, PO Box 307, Junction 76849
King—Sandy Burkett, PO Box 117, Guthrie 79236
Kinney—William F. Haenn, PO Box 1377, Brackettville 78832
Kleberg—Tina Flores, PO Box 1027, Kingsville 78364
Knox—Kim McLemore, PO Box 47, Benjamin 79505

Lamar—Cathy Jackson, PO Box 400, Paris 75461
Lamb—Lesa Kloiber, PO Box 950, Littlefield 79339
Lampasas—Glenda January, Box 175, Lampasas 76550
La Salle—Joe R. Lozano, PO Box O, Cotulla 78014
Lavaca—Diane Munson, PO Box 386, Hallettsville 77964
Lee—Sheri Winn (interim), 218 E. Richmond, Giddings 78942
Leon—Jeff Beshears, PO Box 536, Centerville 75833
Liberty—Alan Conner, PO Box 10016, Liberty 77575
Limestone—Karen Wietzikoski, PO Drawer 831, Groesbeck 76642
Lipscomb—Jerry Reynolds, PO Box 128, Darrouzett 79024
Live Oak—Bob Johanson, PO Box 2370, George West 78022
Llano—Gary Eldridge, 103 E. Sandstone, Llano 78643
Loving—Sherlene Burrows, PO Box 352, Mentone 79754
Lubbock—Dave Kimbrough, PO Box 10542, Lubbock 79408
Lynn—Marquita Scott, PO Box 789, Tahoka 79373

Madison—Larry Krumnow, PO Box 1328, Madisonville 77864
Marion—David Sutton, PO Box 690, Jefferson 75657
Martin—Marsha Graves, PO Box 1349, Stanton 79782
Mason—Ted Smith, PO Box 1119, Mason 76856
Matagorda—Vince Maloney, 2225 Ave. G, Bay City 77414
Maverick—Victor Perry, 2243 Veterans Blvd., Eagle Pass 78852
McCulloch—Orlando Rubio, 306 W. Lockhart, Brady 76825
McLennan—Robert L. Waldrop, PO Box 2297, Waco 76703
McMullen—Jesse Bryan, PO Box 37, Tilden 78072
Medina—James Garcia, 1410 Ave. K, Hondo 78861
Menard—Dianna Miller, PO Box 1008, Menard 76859
Midland—Robert B. Kmiec, PO Box 908002, Midland 79708
Milam—Patricia Moraw, PO Box 769, Cameron 76520
Mills—Doug Stewart, PO Box 565, Goldthwaite 76844
Mitchell—Kaye Cornutt, 2112 Hickory St., Colorado City 79512
Montague—June Deaton, PO Box 121, Montague 76251
Montgomery—Mark Castleschouldt, PO Box 2233, Conroe 77305
Moore—Diane Ball, PO Box 717, Dumas 79029
Morris—Rhonda Hall, PO Box 563, Daingerfield 75638
Motley—Brenda Osborn, PO Box 779, Matador 79244

Nacogdoches—Gary Woods, 216 W. Hospital, Nacogdoches 75961
Navarro—Bill Worthen, PO Box 3118, Corsicana 75151
Newton—Margie Herrin, 109 Court St., Newton 75966
Nolan—Patricia Davis, PO Box 1256, Sweetwater 79556
Nueces—Ollie Grant, 201 N. Chaparral, Corpus Christi 78401

Ochiltree—Terry Symons, 825 S. Main, #100, Perryton 79070
Oldham—Jen Carter, PO Box 310, Vega 79092
Orange—Michael Cedars, PO Box 457, Orange 77631

Palo Pinto—Donna Rhodes, PO Box 250, Palo Pinto 76484
Panola—Loyd Adams, 2 Ball Park Rd., Carthage 75633
Parker—Larry Hammonds, 1108 Santa Fe Dr., Weatherford 76086
Parmer—Ron Procter, PO Box 56, Bovina 79009
Pecos—Sam Calderon Jr., PO Box 237, Fort Stockton 79735
Polk—Carolyn Allen, 114 W. Matthews, Livingston 77351
Potter—Jim Childers, PO Box 7190, Amarillo 79114
Presidio—Irma Salgado, PO Box 879, Marfa 79843

Rains—Carrol Houllis, PO Box 70, Emory 75440

Randall—Jim Childers, PO Box 7190, Amarillo 79114
Reagan—Byron Bitner, PO Box 8, Big Lake 76932
Real—LeAnn Rubio, PO Box 158, Leakey 78873
Red River—Jan Raulston, PO Box 461, Clarksville 75426
Reeves—Carol King-Markman, PO Box 1229, Pecos 79772
Refugio—Bettye Kret, PO Box 156, Refugio 78377
Roberts—DeAnn Williams, PO Box 458, Miami 79059
Robertson—Dan Brewer, PO Box 998, Franklin 77856
Rockwall—Ray Helm, 841 Justin Rd., Rockwall 75087
Runnels—Tylene Gamble, PO Box 524, Ballinger 76821
Rusk—Terry Decker, PO Box 7, Henderson 75653

Sabine—Jim Nethery, PO Box 137, Hemphill 75948
San Augustine—Jamie Doherty, 122 N. Harrison, San Augustine 75972
San Jacinto—Linda Lewis, PO Box 1170, Coldspring 77331
San Patricio—Rufino H. Lozano, PO Box 938, Sinton 78387
San Saba—Henry J. Warren, 423 E. Wallace, San Saba 76877
Schleicher—Scott Sutton, PO Box 936, Eldorado 76936
Scurry—Larry Crooks, 2612 College Ave., Snyder 79549
Shackelford—Teresa Peacock, PO Box 565, Albany 76430
Shelby—Robert Pigg, 724 Shelbyville St., Center 75935
Sherman—Teresa Edmond, PO Box 239, Stratford 79084
Smith—Michael Barnett, 245 South S.E. Loop 323, Tyler 75702
Somervell—Ronnie Babcock, 112 Allen Dr., Glen Rose 76043
Starr—Humberto Saenz Jr., PO Box 137, Rio Grande City 78582
Stephens—Troy Sloan, PO Box 351, Breckenridge 76424
Sterling—Linda Low, PO Box 28, Sterling City 76951
Stonewall—Ozella E. Warner, PO Box 308, Aspermont 79502
Sutton—Rex Ann Friess, 300 E. Oak St., Sonora 76950
Swisher—Cindy McDowell, PO Box 8, Tulia 79088

Tarrant—John Marshall, 2500 Handley-Ederville Rd., Fort Worth 76118
Taylor—Richard Petree, PO Box 1800, Abilene 79604
Terrell—Blain Chriesman, PO Box 747, Sanderson 79848
Terry—Ronny Burran, PO Box 426, Brownfield 79316
Throckmorton—Linda Carrington, Box 788, Throckmorton 76483
Titus—Katrina Perry, PO Box 528, Mount Pleasant 75456
Tom Green—Bill Benson, PO Box 3307, San Angelo 76902
Travis—Art Cory, PO Box 149012, Austin 78714
Trinity—Allen McKinley, PO Box 950, Groveton 75845
Tyler—Travis Chalmers, PO Drawer 9, Woodville 75979

Upshur—Louise Stracener (interim), 105 Diamond Loch, Gilmer 75644
Upton—Sheri Stephens, PO Box 1110, McCamey 79752
Uvalde—Alida Lopez (interim), 209 N. High, Uvalde 78801

Val Verde—Ricardo Martinez, PO Box 420487, Del Rio 78842
Van Zandt—Brenda Barnett, PO Box 926, Canton 75103
Victoria—Albert Molina (interim), 2805 N. Navarro, Ste. 300, Victoria 77901

Walker—Grover Cook, PO Box 1798, Huntsville 77342
Waller—David Piwonka, PO Box 159, Katy 77492
Ward—Arlice Wittie, PO Box 905, Monahans 79756
Washington—Willy Dilworth, PO Box 681, Brenham 77834
Webb—Sergio Delgado, 3302 Clark Blvd., Laredo 78043
Wharton—Larry Holub, 2407 1/2 N. Richmond Rd., Wharton 77488
Wheeler—Jeanine Hawkins, PO Box 1200, Wheeler 79096
Wichita—Eddie Trigg, PO Box 5172, Wichita Falls 76307
Wilbarger—Deborah Echols, PO Box 1519, Vernon 76385
Willacy—Augustin Colchado, Rt. 2, Box 256, Raymondville 78580
Williamson—Bill Carroll, 510 W. 9th St., Georgetown 78726
Wilson—Carlton R. Pape, Box 849, Floresville 78114
Winkler—Connie Carpenter, PO Box 1219, Kermit 79745
Wise—Mickey Hand, 400 E. Business 380, Decatur 76234
Wood—Tracy Nichols, PO Box 1706, Quitman 75783
Yoakum—Saundra Stephens, PO Box 748, Plains 79355
Young—Jerry Patton, PO Box 337, Graham 76450

Zapata—Amada Gonzalez, PO Box 2315, Zapata 78076
Zavala—Alberto Mireles, 323 W. Zavala, Crystal City 78839☆

Wet-Dry Counties

When approved in local-option elections in "wet" precincts of counties, sale of **liquor by the drink** is permitted in Texas. This resulted from adoption of an amendment to the Texas Constitution in 1970 and subsequent legislation, followed by local-option elections.

This amendment marked the first time in 50 years that the sale of liquor by the drink was legal in Texas.

The list below shows the wet-or-dry status of counties in Texas as of August 31, 2003. A dagger (†) indicates counties in which the sale of mixed beverages is legal in all or part of the county (97). An asterisk (*) indicates counties wholly wet (37). All others are dry in part (80).

Texas Liquor Laws

- ● Wet: Liquor by the drink permitted
- ● Wine and beer permitted
- ○ Part of county wet
- ○ Only beer permitted
- ● Dry: No liquor permitted

Counties in Which Distilled Spirits Are Legal (186):

Anderson, †*Aransas, Archer, Atascosa, †*Austin, †Bandera, †*Bastrop, †*Bee, †Bell, †*Bexar, †Blanco, Bosque, †Brazoria, †*Brazos, †*Brewster, Brooks, Brown, Burleson, †Burnet, †Calhoun, Callahan, †*Cameron, †Camp, Carson, Cass, Castro, Chambers, Childress, Clay, Coleman, Collin, †*Colorado, †*Comal, Comanche, Cooke, Coryell, Crane, *Crockett, *Culberson.

Also, Dallam, †Dallas, †Dawson, Deaf Smith, †Denton, †DeWitt, Dickens, †Dimmit, †Donley, †*Duval, Eastland, †Ector, Edwards, Ellis, †*El Paso, †Falls, Fannin, Fayette, †*Fort Bend, Freestone, †Frio, †Galveston, †Garza, †Gillespie, †Goliad, Gonzales, Gray, Grayson, Gregg, †Grimes, †Guadalupe, Hall, Hamilton, Hardin, †Harris, Harrison, Haskell, †Hays, †Henderson, †*Hidalgo, †Hill, †Hockley, Hood, †Howard, †*Hudspeth, Hunt, Hutchinson, Jack, †Jackson, †Jasper, Jeff Davis.

Also †Jefferson, †*Jim Hogg, †Jim Wells, *Karnes, Kaufman, †*Kendall, Kenedy, †Kerr, Kimble, King, †*Kinney, †Kleberg, †Lamar, Lampasas, †La Salle, †Lavaca, †Lee, Leon, Liberty, Live Oak, †Llano, †*Loving, †Lubbock, Marion, †Matagorda, †Maverick, †McCulloch, †McLennan, †Medina, Menard, †Midland, Milam, Mills, Mitchell, Montague, †Montgomery, †*Moore, Nacogdoches, †Navarro, Newton, Nolan, †Nueces.

Also, †Orange, Palo Pinto, Parker, Pecos, †Polk, †Potter, †*Presidio, Rains, †Randall, *Reagan, Red River, †Reeves, Refugio, Robertson, †Rockwall, Runnels, San Augustine, San Jacinto, †San Patricio, San Saba, *Schleicher, Shackelford, Shelby, †*Starr, Stonewall, †*Sutton, †Tarrant, †Taylor, *Terrell, †Titus, †Tom Green, †*Travis, *Trinity, Upshur, *Upton, Uvalde, †Val Verde, †Victoria, †Walker, †Waller, Ward, †*Washington, †*Webb, †Wharton, †Wichita, Wilbarger, †Willacy, †Williamson, †*Wilson, *Winkler, Young, †*Zapata, †Zavala.

Counties in Which Only 4 Percent Beer Is Legal (11):

Baylor, Caldwell, Cherokee, Concho, Hartley, Irion, Mason, McMullen, Oldham, Sabine, Stephens.

Counties in Which 14 Percent or Less (or up to 17 percent, depending on local-option election held) Alcoholic Beverages Are Legal (5):

Glasscock, Johnson, Limestone, Somervell, Wise.

Counties Wholly Dry (52):

Andrews, Angelina, Armstrong, Bailey, Borden, Bowie, Briscoe, Cochran, Coke, Collingsworth, Cottle, Crosby, Delta, Erath, Fisher, Floyd, Foard, Franklin, Gaines, Hale, Hansford, Hardeman, Hemphill, Hopkins, Houston, Jones, Kent, Knox, Lamb, Lynn, Madison, Martin, Morris, Motley, Ochiltree, Panola, Parmer, Real, Roberts, Rusk, Scurry, Sherman, Smith, Sterling, Swisher, Terry, Throckmorton, Tyler, Van Zandt, Wheeler, Wood, Yoakum. ☆

Texas County and District Officials — Table No. 1

County Seats, County Judges, County Clerks, County Attorneys, County Commissioners, County Treasurers, Tax Assessors-Collectors and Sheriffs.

See Table No. 2 on pages following this table for District Clerks, District Attorneys and County Commissioners. Judges in county courts at law, as well as probate courts, juvenile/domestic relations courts, county criminal courts and county criminal courts of appeal, can be found on page 467. The officials listed here are elected by popular vote. An asterisk (*) before a county name marks a county whose county clerk failed to return our questionnaire; the names of officials for those counties are taken from most recent unofficial sources available to us.

County	County Seat	County Judge	County Clerk	County Attorney	County Treasurer	Assessor-Collector	Sheriff
Anderson	Palestine	Carey G. McKinney	Wanda Burke	Douglas E. Lowe	Sharon Peterson	Lynn Palmer	Gregg Taylor
Andrews	Andrews	Richard H. Dolgener	F. Wm. Hoermann	John L. Pool	Office abolished 11-5-1985.	Robin Harper	Sam H. Jones
Angelina	Lufkin	Joe Berry	Jo Ann Chastain	Ed Jones	Lois Warner	Bill Shanklin	Kent Henson
Aransas	Rockport	Glenn D. Guillory	Peggy L. Friebele	James L. Anderson Jr.	Marvine D. Wix	Jeri D. Cox	Mark Gilliam
Archer	Archer City	Paul O. Wylie Jr.	Karren Winter	R.B. "Burk" Morris	Victoria Lear	Teresa K. Martin	Ed Daniels
Armstrong	Claude	Hugh Reed	Joe Reck		Margie Ready	Deborah Sherman	J.R. Walker
Atascosa	Jourdanton	Diana J. Bautista	Laquita Hayden	R. Thomas Franklin	Ray Samson	Barbara Schorsch	Tommy Williams
Austin	Bellville	Carolyn Bilski	Carrie Gregor		Suzanne C. Edwards	Janice Kokemor	R. DeWayne Burger
Bailey	Muleshoe	Marilyn Cox	Sherri Harrison	Carrissa A. Cleavinger	Donna M. Kirk	Berta Combs	Richard Willis
Bandera	Bandera	Richard A. Evans	Candy Wheeler	Kerry K. Schneider	Kay Welch	Mae Vion Meyer	James MacMillan
Bastrop	Bastrop	Ronnie McDonald	Rose Pietsch		Patsy Holmes	Linda Harmon	Richard M. Hernandez
Baylor	Seymour	James D. Coltharp	Clara "Carrie" Coker	Susan Elliott	Kevin Hostas	Jeanette Holub	Bob Elliott
Bee	Beeville	Jimmy Martinez	Mirella Escamilla Davis	Michael J. Knight	Office abolished 11-2-1982.	Andrea W. Gibbud	Carlos Carrizales Jr.
Bell	Belton	Jon H. Burrows	Vada Sutton	Richard J. Miller	Charles Jones	Sharon Long	Dan Smith
Bexar	San Antonio	Nelson W. Wolff	Gerry Rickhoff		Office abolished 11-5-1985.	Sylvia S. Romo	Ralph Lopez
Blanco	Johnson City	Bill Guthrie	Karen Newman	Dean C. Myane	Camille Swift	Hollis Boatright	William R. "Bill" Elsbury
Borden	Gail	Van L. York	Joyce Herridge	Ben Smith	Kenneth P. Bennett	Billy J. Gannaway	Billy J. Gannaway
Bosque	Meridian	Cole Word	Betty Outlaw	David Christian	Randy Pullin	Shana Wallace	Charles E. Jones
Bowie	Boston	James M. Carlow	Velma Moore	Carol Dalby	Pansy Baird	Toni Barron	James Prince
Brazoria	Angleton	John C. Willy	Joyce Hudman	Jeri Yenne	Sharon Reynolds	Ro'vin Garrett	Charles Wagner
Brazos	Bryan	Randy Sims	Karen McQueen	Jim Kuboviak	Kay Hamilton	Gerald L. "Buddy" Winn	Chris Kirk
Brewster	Alpine	Val Clark Beard	Berta Rios Martinez	Steve Houston	Hortencia Ramos	Betty Jo Rooney	Ronny Dodson
Briscoe	Silverton	Wayne Nance	Bena Hester	William P. Smith	Mary Jo Brannon	Betty Ann Stephens	Jeff Fuston
Brooks	Falfurrias	Joe B. Garcia	Frutoso Garza Jr.	David T. Garcia	Gilberto Vela	Balde Lozano	Baldemar Lozano
Brown	Brownwood	E. Ray West III	Margaret Wood	Shane Britton	Judy Stirman	Linda Parker	Bobby Grubbs
Burleson	Caldwell	Mike Sutherland	Anna L. Schielack	Joseph J. Skrivanek	Beth Andrews Bills	Curtis Doss	Dale Stroud
Burnet	Burnet	David Kithil	Janet Parker	Eddie Arredondo	Donna Klaeger	Sherri Frazier	Joe Pollock
Caldwell	Lockhart	H.T. Wright	Nina S. Sells		Lori Rangel-Pompa	Mary Vicky Gonzales	Daniel Law
Calhoun	Port Lavaca	Michael Pfeifer	Anita Fricke		Rhonda McMahan	Gloria Ochoa	Burnard B. Browning
Callahan	Baird	Roger Corn	Jeanie Bohannon	Joel Shane Deel	Dianne Alexander	Tammy T. Walker	Eddie Curtis
Cameron	Brownsville	Gilberto Hinojosa	Joe G. Rivera	Armondo Villalobos	Eddie Gonzalez	Antonio Yzaguirre Jr.	Omar Lucio
Camp	Pittsburg	Preston Combest	Elaine Young	James W. Wallace	Pam Nelson	Gale Burns	Alan D. McCandless
Carson	Panhandle	Lewis Powers	Celeste Bichsel	Scott Sherwood	Jeanie Cunningham	Barbara Cosper	Tam Terry
Cass	Linden	Charles L. McMichael	Jannis Mitchell		Martha Fant Sheridan	Becky Watson	James Troup Estes
Castro	Dimmitt	William F. Sava	Joyce M. Thomas	James R. Horton	Janice Shelton	Billy Hackleman	C.D. Fitzgearld
Chambers	Anahuac	Jimmy Sylvia	Susan E. Rosuto	Cheryl S. Lieck	Carren Sparks	Margie Henry	Joe LaRive
Cherokee	Rusk	Chris Davis	Laverne Lusk	Craig D. Caldwell	Patsy Lassiter	Linda Beard	James E. Campbell
Childress	Childress	Jay Mayden	Zona Prince	Greg Buckley	Jeanie Thomas	Juanell Halford	Darin Smith
Clay	Henrietta	Kenneth Liggett	Kay Hutchison	Eddy Atkins	Debra Alexander	Linda Sellers	Tim King
Cochran	Morton	James St. Clair	Rita Tyson	J.C. Adams Jr.	Doris Sealy	Linda Huckabee	R.W. Stalcup
Coke	Robert Lee	Roy Blair	Mary Grim	Nancy Arthur	Phelan Wrinkle	Gayle Sisemore	Rick Styles
Coleman	Coleman	Jimmie D. Hobbs	JoAnn Hale	Heath A. Hemphill	Kay LeMay	Donna A. Seymore	Robert Wade Turner
Collin	McKinney	Ron Harris	Brenda Taylor		Brenda Taylor	Kenneth Maun	Terry Box
Collingsworth	Wellington	John A. James	Jackie Johnson	G. Keith Davis	Yvonne Brewer	Patsy Barnett	Russell Lee
Colorado	Columbus	Al Jamison	Darlene Hayek	Ken Sparks	Diane Matus	Mary Jane Poenitzsch	R.H. "Curley" Wied
Comal	New Braunfels	Danny Scheel	Joy Streater		Susan Patterson	Sherman Krause	Bob Holder
Comanche	Comanche	James R. Arthur	Ruby Lesley	Charles Williams	Billy Ruth Rust	Gay Horton Green	Jeff Lambert

County	County Seat	County Judge	County Clerk	County Attorney	County Treasurer	Assessor-Collector	Sheriff
Concho	Paint Rock	Allen Amos	Barbara K. Hofman	Bill Campbell	Lisa J. Jost	Richard G. Doane	Richard G. Doane
Cooke	Gainesville	Bill Freeman	Rebecca Lawson	Tanya Davis	Judy Hunter	Billie Jean Knight	Mike Compton
Coryell	Gatesville	John Hull	Barbara Simpson	Brandon Belt	Donna Meadford	Barbara Thompson	Johnny Burks
Cottle	Paducah	John D. Shavor	Beckey J. Tucker	John H. Richards	Kathy Biddy	Rue Young	Kenneth A. Burns
Crane	Crane	Donnie Henderson	Judy Crawford	James McDonald	Cristy Tarin	Rebecca Gonzales	Robert DeLeon
Crockett	Ozona	John R. Jones	Debbi Puckett	William S. Mason	Burl Myers	Rhonda Shaw	Shane Fenton
Crosby	Crosbyton	Joe Heflin	Betty J. Pierce	C. Michael Ward	Debra Riley	Anna Rodriguez	Red Riley
Culberson	Van Horn	John Conoly	Linda McDonald	Stephen L. Mitchell	Norma Hernandez	Amalia Hernandez	Oscar E. Carrillo
Dallam	Dalhart	David D. Field	LuAnn Taylor	Jon King	Wes Ritchey	Kay Howell	Bruce Scott
Dallas	Dallas	Margaret Keliher	Cynthia Figueroa Calhoun	Steven B. Payson	Lisa Hembry	David Childs	Lupe Valdez
Dawson	Lamesa	Sam Saleh	Gloria Vera	Jim English	Gene DeFee	Diane Hogg	Johnny Garcia
Deaf Smith	Hereford	Tom Simons	David Ruland	Michael Bartley	Paula Price	Teresa Garth	Brent Harrison
Delta	Cooper	Hugh Charles Whitney	Jane Jones		Glynana Herin	Brenda "Dawn" Curtis	Mark Bassham
Denton	Denton	Mary Horn	Cynthia Mitchell	Tom Keever	Cindy Yeatts Brown	Steve Mossman	Benny Parkey
DeWitt	Cuero	Ben E. Prause	Elva Petersen	Raymond H. Reese	Peggy Ledbetter	Susie Dreyer	Joe C. "Jode" Zavesky
Dickens	Dickens	Woodie McArthur	Winona Humphreys	David Hazlewood	Sandy Vickrey	Dexter Clay	Ken Brendle
Dimmit	Carrizo Springs	Francisco G. Ponce	Mario Z. Garcia	Daniel M. Gonzalez	Elisa Duran	Esther Z. Perez	Douglas Sample
Donley	Clarendon	Jack Hall	Fay Vargas	Kaye Messer (pro tem)	Rebecca Jackson	Wilma Lindley	Charles "Butch" Blackburn
Duval	San Diego	Edmundo B. Garcia Jr.	Oscar Garcia Jr.	Ricardo O. "Rocky" Carrillo	Lydia P. Molina	Carlos J. Montemayor Jr.	Santiago Barrera Jr.
Eastland	Eastland	Brad Stephenson	Cathy Jentho		Marti Heyser	Sandra Cagle	Wayne Bradford
Ector	Odessa	Jerry D. Caddel	Linda Haney	Cathy Linch	Carolyn Bowen	Barbara Horn	Mark Donaldson
Edwards	Rocksprings	Nick Gallegos	Sarah McNealy	Allen Ray Moody	Lupe Sifuentes-Enriquez	Jodie S. Greene	Don G. Letsinger
Ellis	Waxahachie	Chad Adams	Cindy Polley	Joe F. Grubbs	Ron Langenheder	John Bridges	Ray Stewart
El Paso	El Paso	Dolores Briones	Waldo Alarcon	José R. Rodriguez		Victor A. Flores	Leo Samaniego
Erath	Stephenville	Tab Thompson	Gwinda Jones	Carey S. Fraser	Donna Kelly	Jennifer Carey	Tommy Bryant
Falls	Marlin	Thomas B. Sehon	Frances Braswell	Kathryn J. Gilliam	Sue Ryan	Kate Vande Veegaete	Ben Kirk
Fannin	Bonham	Derrell Hall	Margaret Gilbert	Richard Glaser	Mike Towery	Pamela Sweet Richardson	Kenneth Moore
Fayette	La Grange	Edward F. Janecka	Carolyn Kubos Roberts	Peggy Supak	Office abolished 11-3-87.	Carol Johnson	Keith Korenek
Fisher	Roby	Marshal Bennett	Pat Thomson	Rudy V. Hamric	Marty Williamson	Jonnye Lu Brown	Mickey A. Counts
Floyd	Floydada	William D. Hardin	Marilyn Holcomb	Lex S. Herrington	Elva Martinez	Penny Golightly	Billy R. Gilmore
Foard	Crowell	Charlie Bell	Sherry Weatherred	Daryl Halencak	Esther Kajs	Bobby Bond	Bobby Bond
Fort Bend	Richmond	Robert E. Hebert	Dianne Wilson	Ben W. "Bud" Childers	Clifton Terrell	Patsy Schultz	Milton Wright
Franklin	Mount Vernon	Gerald Hubbell	Betty Crane	Cecil Solomon	Marla Carrell	Marjorie Jaggers	Charles J. "Chuck" White
Freestone	Fairfield	Linda K. Grant	Mary Lynn White	Jack Keith Meredith	Debra Kay Barger	Carolyn J. Varley	Ralph Billings
Frio	Pearsall	Carlos A. Garcia	Angie Tullis	Hector M. Lozano	Anna L. Hernández	Anna Alaniz	Lionel G. Trevino
Gaines	Seminole	Judy House	Vicki Phillips	Sterling Harmon	Lesha Aten	Susan Jones	Jon Key
Galveston	Galveston	James D. Yarbrough	Mary Ann Daigle	Harvey Bazaman	Kevin C. Walsh	Cheryl Johnson	Gean Leonard
Garza	Post	Giles W. Dalby	Jim Plummer	Leslie Acker	Ruth Ann Young	Judy M. Bush	Cliff Laws
Gillespie	Fredericksburg	Mark Stroeher	Mary Lynn Rusche	Tamara Y.S. Keener	Laura Lundquist	Leola Brodbeck	Milton E. Jung
Glasscock	Garden City	Wilburn Bednar	Rebecca Batla	Hardy Wilkerson	Alan Dierschke	Royce Pruit	Royce Pruit
Goliad	Goliad	Harold F. Gleinser	Gail M. Turley	Rob Baiamonte	June Bethke	Anna Breen	Robert de la Garza
Gonzales	Gonzales	David Bird	Lee Riedel	Robert B. Scheske	Sheryl Barborak	Norma Jean DuBose	Glen A. Sachtleben
Gray	Pampa	Richard Peet	Susan Winborne	Joshua Seabourn	Lee Cornelison	Gaye Whitehead	Don Copeland
Grayson	Sherman	Tim McGraw	Wilma Blackshear Bush		Richey Rivers	John Ramsey	Keith Gary
Gregg	Longview	Bill Stoudt	Connie Wade	Jon C. Fultz	Office abolished 1-1-88.	William Kirk Shields	Maxey Cerliano
Grimes	Anderson	James Dixon	David Pasket	Elizabeth Murray-Kolb	Phillis Allen	Connie Perry	Donald Sowell
Guadalupe	Seguin	Donald Schraub	Teresa Kiel	James "Jim" Tirey	Linda Douglass	Tavie Murphy	Arnold Zwicke
Hale	Plainview	Bill Hollars	Diane Williams		Ida Tyler	Kemp Hinch	David B. Mull
Hall	Memphis	Jack Martin	Raye Bailey	John M. Deaver II	Janet Bridges	Pat Floyd	Earnest Neel
Hamilton	Hamilton	Fred Cox	Debbie Rudolph	Andy J. McMullen	Debbie Eoff	Terry Short	W.R. "Randy" Murphree
Hansford	Spearman	Benny Wilson	Kim Vera	John L. Hutchison	Wanda Wagner	Linda Cummings	Gary Evans
Hardeman	Quanah	K.D. McNabb	Linda Walker	Stanley R. Watson	Mary Ann Naylor	Darlene Gamble	Randy L. Akers
Hardin	Kountze	Billy Caraway	Glenda Alston	David Sheffield	Sharon Overstreet	Shirley Stephens	Ed Jay Cain

County	County Seat	County Judge	County Clerk	County Attorney	County Treasurer	Assessor-Collector	Sheriff
Harris	Houston	Robert Eckels	Beverly B. Kaufman	Michael Stafford	Jack Cato	Paul Bettencourt	Tommy Thomas
Harrison	Marshall	Wayne McWhorter	Patsy Cox		Jamie Noland Smith	Betty Wright	Tom McCool
Hartley	Channing	Ronnie Gordon	Diane Thompson	M. Shane Turner	Dinkie Parman	Frank Scott	Franky Scott
Haskell	Haskell	David C. Davis	Rhonda Moeller	Shane Hadaway	Willie Faye Tidrow	Bobbye Collins	David Halliburton
Hays	San Marcos	Jim Powers	Lee Carlisle		Michele Tuttle	Luanne Caraway	Don Montague
Hemphill	Canadian	Bob W. Gober	Charles M. Cole	Ty M. Sparks	Cindy N. Bowen	Debra L. Ford	Gary S. Henderson
Henderson	Athens	David Holstein	Gwen Moffeit	James Owen	Karin Smith	Milburn Chaney	J.R. "Ronny" Brownlow
Hidalgo	Edinburg	Ramon Garcia	Juan D. Salinas III		Norma Garcia	Armando Barrera Jr.	Guadalupe Trevino
Hill	Hillsboro	Kenneth Davis	Ruth Pelham	Mark Pratt	Linda Polley	Marchel Eubank	Brent Button
Hockley	Levelland	Larry Sprowls	Donna K. Stanley	Pat Phelan	Denise Bohannon	Christy Clevenger	David Kinney
Hood	Granbury	Andy Rash	Sally Oubre	Kelton Conner	Kathy Davis	Sandy Tidwell	Gene Mayo
Hopkins	Sulphur Springs	Cletis Millsap	Debbie Shirley	Dusty Hyde Rabe	Betty Bassham	Debbie Pogue Jenkins	Butch Adams
Houston	Crockett	R.C. "Chris" Von Doenhoff	Bridget Lamb	Donna Gordon	Dianne Rhone	Joan Lucas	Darrell E. Bobbitt
Howard	Big Spring	Ben Lockhart	Donna Wright	C.E. "Mike" Thomas III	Teresa Thomas	Kathy A. Sayles	Dale Walker
Hudspeth	Sierra Blanca	Becky Dean Walker	Elizabeth Morales	C.R. "Kit" Bramblett	Jennifer Canaba	L. Kay Scarbrough	Arvin West
Hunt	Greenville	Joe Bobbitt	Linda Brooks	Joel Littlefield	Delores Shelton	Barbara Wiggins	Don Anderson
Hutchinson	Stinnett	Jack L. Worsham	Beverly Turner	Michael D. Milner	Kathy Sargent	Mary Lou Henderson	Guy D. Rowh
Irion	Mertzon	Leon Standard	Reba Criner	Kenneth Greer Jr.	Linda Pierce	Joyce Gray	Jimmy Martin
Jack	Jacksboro	Mitchell G. Davenport	Shelly Clayton	Michael G. Mask	Roger Sharp	Gaye Low	Danny R. Nash
Jackson	Edna	Harrison Stafford II	Kenneth W. McElveen		Mary Horton	Donna Atzenhoffer	Andy Louderback
Jasper	Jasper	Joe Folk	Debbie Newman		Mary Jane Hancock	Bobby Biscamp	Ronnie McBride
Jeff Davis	Fort Davis	George Grubb	Sue Blackley	Bart Medley	Geen Parrott	Tom Roberts	Tom Roberts
Jefferson	Beaumont	Carl R. Griffith Jr.	Carolyn L. Guidry	Tom Rugg	Linda Robinson	Miriam K. Johnson	Mitch Woods
Jim Hogg	Hebbronville	Agapito Molina Jr.	Noemi G. Salinas	Enrique A. Garza	Linda Jo G. Soliz	Marina Vasquez	Erasmo Alarcon
Jim Wells	Alice	L. Arnoldo Saenz	Ruben Sandoval	Jesusa Sánchez-Vera	Becky Dominguez	Lucila Reynolds	Oscar Lopez
Johnson	Cleburne	Roger Harmon	Curtis H. Douglas	Bill Moore	Barbara Robinson	Scott Porter	Bob Alford
Jones	Anson	Dale Spurgin	Julia McCray	Chad Cowan	Irene Hudson	Mary Ann Lovelady	Larry Moore
Karnes	Karnes City	Alger H. Kendall Jr.	Alva Jonas	Rober L. Busselman	Nancy Duckett	Ann Franke	David A. Jalufka
Kaufman	Kaufman	Wayne Gent	Laura Hughes		Johnny Countryman	Richard Murphy	David Byrnes
Kendall	Boerne	Eddie John Vogt	Darlene Herrin	Don Allee	Medana Crow	James A. Hudson Jr.	Roger Duncan
Kenedy	Sarita	J.A. Garcia Jr.	Veronica Vela	Jaime E. Tijerina	Cynthia M. Salinas	Eleuteria S. Gonzalez	Ramiro Medellin Jr.
Kent	Jayton	Jim White	Richard Craig Harrison	Howard Freemyer	Linda McCurry	Brenda Long	William Delmer Scogin
Kerr	Kerrville	Pat Tinley	Jannett Pieper	Melvin Rex Emerson	Barbara Nemec	Paula Rector	W.R. "Rusty" Hierholzer
Kimble	Junction	Delbert R. Roberts	Haydee Torres	Lawrence F. Harrison	Sheila D'Spain	Mike Chapman	Mike Chapman
King	Guthrie	Duane Daniel	Linda Lewis	Marshall Capps	Kay Miller	Sadie Mote	Raymond C. Daniel Jr.
Kinney	Brackettville	Herb Senne	Dora Elia Sandoval	Tully Shahan	Janis Floyd	Martha Pena Padron	Leland Burgess
Kleberg	Kingsville	Pete de la Garza	Leo Alarcon	Alfred Isassi	Rachel S. Alaniz	Melissa T. de la Garza	Ed Mata
Knox	Benjamin	Travis Floyd	Ronnie Verhalen	Bobby D. Burnett	Irma Bell	Linda Parker	Dean Homstad
Lamar	Paris	Maurice Superville	Kathy Marlowe	Gary Young	Shirley Fults	Peggy Noble	B.J. McCoy
Lamb	Littlefield	William A. Thompson Jr.	Bill Johnson	Mark Yarbrough	Janice B. Wells	Linda Charlton	Gary Maddox
Lampasas	Lampasas	Virgil E. Lilley	Connie Hartmann	Larry Allison	Nelda DeRiso	Linda Crawford	Gordon Morris
La Salle	Cotulla	Joel Rodriguez Jr.	Peggy Murray	Elizabeth Martinez	Marissa Mancha	Elida A. Linares	Robbie Thomas
Lavaca	Hallettsville	Ronald L. Leck	Elizabeth A. Kouba	V'Anne Bostick Huser	Lois Henry	Margaret Kallus	Micah C. Harmon
Lee	Giddings	Evan Gonzales	Carol Dismukes	Ted Weems	Melinda Krause	Virginia Jackson	Joe Goodson
Leon	Centerville	Byron Ryder	Carla McEachern	Jim Witt	Audrey Grimes	Louise Wilson	Mike Price
Liberty	Liberty	Lloyd Kirkham	Delia Sellers	A.J. Hartel	Linda Leonard	Mark McClelland	Greg Arthur
Limestone	Groesbeck	Elenor F. Holmes	Sue Lown	Roy DeFriend	Angela Ford	Charlene Black	Dennis D. Wilson
Lipscomb	Lipscomb	Willis Smith	Kim Blau	Randy Phillips	Pat Wyatt	Kathy Fry	James Robertson
Live Oak	George West	Jim Huff	Karen Irving	Gene Chapline	Violet Person	Virginia Horton	Larry R. Busby
Llano	Llano	R.G. Floyd	Bette Sue Hoy	Cheryll Mabray	Diana Cummings	Dexter Sagebiel	Nathan Garrett
Loving	Mentone	Donald C. Creager	Beverly Hanson		Ann Blair	Billy B. Hopper	Billy B. Hopper
Lubbock	Lubbock	Thomas V. Head	Doris Ruff		Sharon Gossett	Barbara Brooks	David Gutierrez
Lynn	Tahoka	H.G. Franklin	Susan Tipton	James Napper	Janet Porterfield	Sherry Pearce	Jerry D. Franklin

County	County Seat	County Judge	County Clerk	County Attorney	County Treasurer	Assessor-Collector	Sheriff
Madison	Madisonville	Cecil N. Neely	Charlotte Barrett	William C. "Bill" Bennett	Judy Weathers	Beverly Plumlee	Dan Douget
Marion	Jefferson	Phil A. Parker	Betty Smith	William Gleason	Dorothy Whatley	Mary Alice Moseley Biggs	Bill McCay
Martin	Stanton	Charles T. Blocker	Susie Hull	James L. McGilvray	H.D. Howard	Kathy Hull	Randy Cozart
Mason	Mason	Jerry Bearden	Beatrice Langehennig	Shain V.H. Chapman	Polly McMillan	Clint Low	Clint Low
Matagorda	Bay City	Greg B. Westmoreland	Gail Denn	Jill Cornelius	Suzanne Kucera	Cristyn Hallmark	James Mitchell
Maverick	Eagle Pass	Jose Aranda	Sara Montemayor	Ricardo Ramos	Manuel Reyes Jr.	Esteban A. Luna	Tomas S. Herrera
McCulloch	Brady	Randy Young	Tina A. Smith	Virginia Treadwell	Donna Robinett	Treva A. Colen	Earl Howell
McLennan	Waco	Jim Lewis	Andy Harwell		Bill Helton	A.F. "Buddy" Skeen	Larry Lynch
McMullen	Tilden	Linda Lee Henry	Dorairene Garza		Donald Haynes Jr.	Angel Bostwick	Bruce Thomas
Medina	Hondo	James Barden	Elva Miranda	Ralph Bernsen	Rita Moos	Loraine Neuman	Gilbert Rodriguez
Menard	Menard	Richard Cordes	Elsie Maserang	Ben Neel	Robert Bean	Angela McCain	Clay Wagner
Midland	Midland	William C. Morrow	Shauna Brown	Russell Malm	Mitzi Wohleking	Kathy Reeves	Gary Painter
Milam	Cameron	Frank Summers	La Verne Soefje	Kerry Spears	Danica Lara	Doug Bryan	Charlie West
Mills	Goldthwaite	Robert E. Lindsey III	Beulah L. "Patty" Roberts	Ken Reynolds Roberts	Patsy E. Miller	Douglas Storey	Douglas Storey
Mitchell	Colorado City	Ray Mayo	Debby Carlock	T.L. Rees Sr.	Ann Hallmark	Faye Lee	Patrick Toombs
Montague	Montague	James O. Kittrell	Valorie Stout	Jeb McNew	Patty Fenoglio	Sydney Nowell	W.E. Bill
Montgomery	Conroe	Alan "Barb" Sadler	Mark Turnbull	David Walker	Martha Gustavsen	J.R. Moore	Tommy Gage
Moore	Dumas	Kari Campbell	Brenda McKanna	Scott Higginbotham	Pam Cox	Nikki McDonald	J.E. "Bo" Dearmond
Morris	Daingerfield	J.C. Jennings	Vicki Camp	J. Stephen Cowan	Nita Beth Traylor	Thelma L. Awtry	Jack. D. Martin
Motley	Matador	Ed. D. Smith	Kate Hurt	Tom Edwards	Eva Barkley	Elaine Hart	Jim Meador
Nacogdoches	Nacogdoches	Sue Kennedy	Carol Wilson	Jefferson Davis	Kay Watkins	Janie Weatherly	Thomas Kerss
Navarro	Corsicana	Alan Bristol	Sherry Dowd		Joe Graves	Peggy Blackwell Moore	Leslie Cotten
Newton	Newton	Truman Dougharty	Mary Cobb	Karen Fuller Pousson		Melissa Burks	Joe A. Walker
Nolan	Sweetwater	Tim Fambrough	Pat McGowan	Lisa Peterson	Gayle Biggerstaff	Fonda Holman	Donnie Rannefeld
Nueces	Corpus Christi	Terry Shamsie	Diana T. Barrera	Laura Garza Jimenez	Office abolished 11-3-87.	Ramiro "Ronnie" Canales	Larry Olivarez Sr.
Ochiltree	Perryton	Kenneth R. Donahue	Jane Hammerbeck	Bruce Roberson	Ginger Hays	Helen Bates	Joe Hataway
Oldham	Vega	Don R. Allred	Becky Groneman	Kent Birdsong	Charlotte Cook	Cynthia Artho	David T. Medlin
Orange	Orange	Carol Thibodeaux	Karen Jo Vance	John Kimbrough	Vergie Moreland	Lynda Gunstream	Mike White
Palo Pinto	Palo Pinto	Mickey D. West	Bobbie Smith	Phil Garrett	Mary M. Motley	Sandra R. Long	Ira Mercer
Panola	Carthage	David L. Anderson	Mickey Dorman	Danny Buck Davidson	Gloria Portman	Jean Whiteside	Jack Ellett
Parker	Weatherford	Mark Riley	Jeane Brunson	John Forrest	Jim Thorp	Larry Lippincott	Larry Fowler
Parmer	Farwell	Bonnie J. Heald	Colleen Stover	Kathryn H. Gurley	Altha Herington	Bobbie Pierson	Randy Geries
Pecos	Fort Stockton	Joe Shuster	Judy Deerfield	Jesse Gonzáles Jr.	Barry McCallister	Santa Acosta	Cliff Harris
Polk	Livingston	John P. Thompson	Barbara Middleton		Nola Reneau	Marion A. "Bid" Smith	Kenneth Hammack
Potter	Amarillo	Arthur Ware	Sue Daniel	Scott Brumley	Leann Jennings	Robert Miller	Mike Shumate
Presidio	Marfa	Jerry C. Agan	Brenda M. Silva		Mario S. Rivera	Norma Arroyo	Danny C. Dominguez
Rains	Emory	Joe Ray Dougherty	Linda Wallace	Robert Vititow	Teresa Northcutt	David Traylor	David Traylor
Randall	Canyon	Ernie Houdashell	Sue Wicker Bartolino		Glenna Canada	Carol Autry	Joel Richardson
Reagan	Big Lake	Larry Isom	Terri Pullig	J. Russell Ash	Nancy Ratliff	Sue Turner	Kirk Pullig
Real	Leakey	W.B. Sansom Jr.	Bella A. Rubio	Garry A. Merritt	Kathy Brooks	Donna Brice	James Brice
Red River	Clarksville	Powell W. Peek	Lorie Moose	Val Varley	Glenda Garrison	Leslie Nix	Jerry Conway
Reeves	Pecos	Jimmy B. Galindo	Dianne O. Florez	Luis U. Carrasco	Linda Clark	Elfida Zuniga	Arnulfo "Andy" Gomez
Refugio	Refugio	Roger Fagan	Ruby Garcia	Robert P. McGuill	Louise Null Adudell	Veronica Rocha	Earl Petropoulos
Roberts	Miami	Vernon H. Cook	Donna L. Goodman	Leslie Breeding	Billie Lunsford	DeAnn Williams	Dana Miller
Robertson	Franklin	Fred Elliott	Kathryn N. Brimhall	John C. Paschall	Jacqueline Vann	Carol Bielamowicz	Gerald Yezak
Rockwall	Rockwall	Bill Bell	Paulette Burks		Shereé Jones	Kathryn Feldpausch	Harold Eavenson
Runnels	Ballinger	Marilyn Egan	Elesa Ocker	Stuart Holden	Margarette Smith	Robin Burgess	William Baird
Rusk	Henderson	Sandra Hodges	Joyce Lewis	Micheal E. Jimerson	Nora Rousseau	Matt B. Johnson	Glen Deason
Sabine	Hemphill	Jack Leath	Janice McDaniel	Robert G. Neal Jr.	Tricia Jacks	Tammy Reeves	Thomas Maddox
San Augustine	San Augustine	Wayne Holt	Diana Kovar	Heather Land Watts	Carol W. Vaughn	Regina A. Barthol	John M. Cartwright
San Jacinto	Coldspring	Fritz Faulkner	Charlene Vann		Charlene Everitt	Barbara Shelly	Lacy Rogers
San Patricio	Sinton	Terry Simpson	Gracie Alaniz-Gonzales	David Aken	Courtenay Dugat	Dalia Sanchez	Leroy Moody
San Saba	San Saba	Byron Theodosis	Kim Wells	David M. Williams	Gayla Hawkins	John L. Wells	John L. Wells

County	County Seat	County Judge	County Clerk	County Attorney	County Treasurer	Assessor-Collector	Sheriff
Scheicher	Eldorado	Johnny F. Griffin	Peggy Williams	Raymond C. Loomis Jr.	Karen Henderson	Jeanne Snelson	David Doran
Scurry	Snyder	Rod Waller	Joan Bunch	Michael Hartman	Nelda Colvin	Jana Young	Darrin Jackson
Shackelford	Albany	Ross Montgomery	Cheri Hawkins	Colton P. Johnson	Sherry Enloe	Richard Wagman	Richard Wagman
Shelby	Center	Floyd A. Watson	Allison Harbison	Gary W. Rholes	Carolyn Golden	Janie Graves	Newton Johnson Jr.
Sherman	Stratford	Kim Crippen	Mary Lou Albert	Kimberly Allen	Doris Parson	Valerie McAlister	Jack Haile
Smith	Tyler	Becky Dempsey	Judy Carnes	John Cornelius	Joyce Smith	Gary Barber	J.B. Smith
Somervell	Glen Rose	Walter Maynard	Candace Garrett	Ronald Hankins	Barbara Hudson	Darlene Chambers	Greg Doyle
Starr	Rio Grande City	Eloy Vera	Dennis D. Gonzalez	Victor Canales	David Porras	Carmen A. Peña	Reymundo Guerra
Stephens	Breckenridge	Gary L. Fuller	Helen Haddock	Gary Trammel	Nancy Clary	Terry Sullivan	James D. "Jim" Reeves
Sterling	Sterling City	Robert L. Browne	Diane A. Browne	Bill Stroman	Wanda Foster	Joy Manning	Don Howard
Stonewall	Aspermont	Bobby McGough	Belinda Page	Kristen Fouts	Linda Messick	Jim Ward	Bill Mullen
Sutton	Sonora	Carla Garner	Veronica E. Hernandez	David W. Wallace	Joyce H. Chalk	Deedie McIntire	Joe Fincher
Swisher	Tulia	Harold Keeter	Brenda Hudson	J. Michael Criswell	Tricia Speed	Brenda Gunnels	Larry P. Stewart
Tarrant	Fort Worth	Tom Vandergriff	Suzanne Henderson		Office abolished 4-2-83.	Betsy Price	Dee Anderson
Taylor	Abilene	George A. Newman	Janice Lyons		Lesa Crosswhite	Lavena Cheek	Jack Dieken
Terrell	Sanderson	Leo Smith	Martha Allen	Marsha Monroe	Lynda Helmers	Clint McDonald	Clint McDonald
Terry	Brownfield	Douglas Ryburn	Ann Willis	Ramon Gallegos	Bobbye Jo Floyd	Redelle Martin	Jerry L. Johnson
Throckmorton	Throckmorton	Trey Carrington	Mary Walraven	Shane Hadaway	Brenda Rankin	John Riley	John Riley
Titus	Mt. Pleasant	Danny Pat Crooks	Sherry Jo Mars	Tim Taylor	Debby Rhea	Judy Cook	Arvel Shepard
Tom Green	San Angelo	Michael D. Brown	Elizabeth McGill	Chris Taylor	Dianna Spieker	Cindy Jetton	Joe Hunt
Travis	Austin	Samuel T. Biscoe	Dana DeBeauvoir	David Escamilla	Dolores Ortega-Carter	Nelda Wells Spears	Greg Hamilton
Trinity	Groveton	Mark Evans	Diane McCrory	Joe W. Bell	Jo Bitner-Bartee	Kathy McCarty	Jimmy Smith
Tyler	Woodville	Jerome Owens	Donece Gregory		Joyce Moore	Lynette Cruse	Jessie Wolf
Upshur	Gilmer	Dean Fowler	Robin Rodenberg	Mike Fetter	Myra Harris	Mike Smith	Anthony Betterton
Upton	Rankin	Vikki Bradley	Phyllis Stephens	Melanie Spratt-Anderson	Nancy Poage	Dan Brown	Dan Brown
Uvalde	Uvalde	William R. Mitchell	Lucille C. Hutcherson	John P. Dodson	Joni Deorsam	Margarita "Maggie" Del Toro	Terry L. Crawford
Val Verde	Del Rio	Manuel "Mike" L. Fernandez	Maria Elena Cardenas	Ana Markowski Smith	Morris Taylor	Beatriz I. "Bea" Munoz	A. D'Wayne Jernigan
Van Zandt	Canton	Rhita Koches	Elizabeth Everitt		Judy Peoples	Vicki Looney	R.P. "Pat" Burnett Jr.
Victoria	Victoria	Donald R. Pozzi	Val D. Huvar		Cathy Bailey	Rena Scherer	T. Michael O'Connor
Walker	Huntsville	R.D. "Danny" Pierce	James D. Patton		Barbara McGilberry	Tom Cauthen	Clint McRae
Waller	Hempstead	Owen Ralston	Cheryl Peters	Kevin Acker	Susan Winfree	Ellen C. Shelburne	Randy Smith
Ward	Monahans	Sam G. Massey	Natrell Cain	Julie Renken	Teresa Perry	Dolores Fine	Mikel Strickland
Washington	Brenham	Dorothy Morgan	Beth A. Rothermel	J. Homero Ramirez	Norman Draehn	Candy Arth	J.W. Jankowski
Webb	Laredo	Louis H. Bruni	Margie Ramirez Ibarra	G.W. "Trey" Maffett	Delia Perales	Patricia Barrera	Rick Flores
Wharton	Wharton	John W. Murrie	Sandra K. Sanders	Misty Walker	Donna Kocurek	Patrick L. Kubala	Jess Howell
Wheeler	Wheeler	Jerry Dan Hefley	Margaret Dorman		Jauna Benefield	Scott Porter	Joel Finsterwald
Wichita	Wichita Falls	Woodrow "Woody" Gossom	Lori Bohannon	Michael Baskerville	R.J. "Bob" Hampton	Lou Murdock	Tom Callahan
Wilbarger	Vernon	Gary Streit	Frances McGee	Juan Angel Guerra	Joann Carter	Chris Quisenberry	David Quisenberry
Willacy	Raymondville	Simon Salinas	Terry Flores		Arturo "Tuttie" Gomez	LaQuita Garza	Larry G. Spence
Williamson	Georgetown	John Doerfler	Nancy E. Rister	Jana Duty	Vivian Wood	Deborah Hunt	James R. Wilson
Wilson	Floresville	Marvin Quinney	Eva S. Martinez	Russell H. Wilson	Carolyn Orth	Anna D. Gonzales	Joe D. Tackitt Jr.
Winkler	Kermit	Bonnie Leck	Shethelia Reed	Thomas Cameron	Tabby Curtis Gilbert	Patti Franks	Robert Roberts
Wise	Decatur	Richard R. Chase	Sherry Parker	Greg Lowery	Katherine Canova	Monte Shaw	David Walker
Wood	Quitman	Royce McCoy	Brenda Taylor		Bryan Jeanes	Tommie Bradshaw	Dwaine Daugherty
Yoakum	Plains	Dallas Brewer	Deborah L. Rushing	Richard Clark	Barbara Wright	Jan Parrish	Don Corzine
Young	Graham	Stanley H. Peavy III	Shirley Choate	Boyd L. Richie	Charlotte Farmer	Nanacy Thomas	Bryan Walls
Zapata	Zapata	David Morales	Consuelo R. Villarreal	José Antonio Lopez	Romeo Salinas	Rosalva D. Guerra	Sigifredo Gonzalez Jr.
Zavala	Crystal City	Joe Luna	Oralia G. Treviño	Eduardo Serna	Susie Perez	Florinda Perez	Eusevio Salinas

Texas County and District Officials — Table No. 2

District Clerks, District Attorneys and County Commissioners

See Table No. 1 on preceding pages for County Seats, County Judges, County Clerks, County Treasurers, Tax Assessors-Collectors and Sheriffs. An asterisk (*) before a county name marks a county whose county clerk failed to return our questionnaire; the names of officials for those counties are taken from most recent unofficial sources available to us.

† If more than one District Attorney is listed for a county, the district court number is noted in parentheses after each attorney's name. If no District Attorney is listed, the County Attorney, whose name can be found in Table No. 1, assumes the duties of that office.

County	District Clerk	District Attorney†	Comm. Precinct 1	Comm. Precinct 2	Comm. Precinct 3	Comm. Precinct 4
Anderson	Janice Staples	Douglas E. Lowe	Joe W. Chaffin	Darrell Emanuel	Ronny Smith	Randy Watkins
Andrews	Cynthia Jones	John L. Pool	Barney Fowler	Brad Young	Hiram Hubert	Paul Williams
Angelina	Reba Squyres	Clyde Herrington	Rick Harrison	Kenneth Timmons	Robert Louis Loggins	Lynn George
Aransas	Pam Heard	Patrick Flanigan	Oscar Piña	Floyd Clark	Danny Adams	Howard Murph
Archer	Jane Ham	Tim Cole	Richard Shelley	Darin Wolf	Pat Martin III	Darryl Lightfoot
Armstrong	Joe Reck	Randall Sims	John Britten	Mike Baker	Tom Ferris	Todd Cagle
Atascosa	Jerome T. Brite	Rene Pena	David Caballero	Leslie Mikolajczyk Sr.	Freddie Ogden	Weldon P. Cude
Austin	Marie Myers	Travis J. Koehn	David Ottmer	Wilbert Frank Jr.	Randy Reichardt	David Hubenak
Bailey	Elaine Parker	Johnny Actkinson	Floyd J. "Butch" Vandiver	C. E. Grant Jr.	Joey Kindle	Juan Chavez
Bandera	Tammy Kneuper	E. Bruce Curry	H. Bruce Eliker	Ronald Basinger	Richard Keese	Doug King
Bastrop	Cathy Smith	Bryan Goertz	David Goertz	Clara Beckett	John Klaus	Lee Dildy
Baylor	Clara "Carrie" Coker	David Hajek	Don Matus	Jerry Ermis	Charles R. Morris	Eric Hostas
Bee	Sandra Clark	Martha Warren	Carlos Salazar Jr.	Susan C. Stasny	Eloy Rodriguez	Ronnie Olivares
Bell	Sheila Norman	Henry L. Garza	Richard Cortese	Tim Brown	Eddy Lange	John Fisher
Bexar	Margaret G. Montemayor	Susan D. Reed	Sergio "Chico" Rodriguez	Paul Elizondo	Lyle T. Larson	Tommy Adkisson
Blanco	Debby Elsbury	Sam Oatman	Floyd Cooley	James Sultemeier	Robert A. "Bob" Mauck	Paul Granberg
Borden	Joyce Herridge	Danna W. Cooley	Monte Smith	Randy L. Adcock	Ernest Reyes	Joe T. Belew
Bosque	Sandra L. Woosley	B.J. Shepherd	Kent Harbison	Durwood Koonsman	Jerry Smith	Jimmy Schmidt
Bowie	Billie Fox	Bobby Lockhart	Jack Stone	John Addington	Kelly Blackburn	Carl Teel
Brazoria	Jerry Deere	Jeri Yenne	Donald "Dude" Payne	James D. Clawson	Jack Harris	Larry L. Stanley
Brazos	Marc Hamlin	Bill Turner	Lloyd Wassermann	Duane Peters	Kenny Mallard	Carey Cauley Jr.
Brewster	Jo Ann Salgado	Frank Brown	Asa Stone	J.W. Pattillo	Ruben Ortega	Matilde Pallanez
Briscoe	Bena Hester	Becky McPherson	Terry Grimland	Danny Maynard	Larry Comer	Gary Weaks
Brooks	Noe Guerra	Joe Frank Garza	Gloria Garza	Ramon Navarro Jr.	Jose Garcia	Mae Saenz
Brown	Jan Brown	Michael Brandon Murray	Steve Adams	Adron Beck	Richard Gist	David Carroll
Burleson	Doris H. Brewer	Renee Mueller	Frank L. Kristof	Donnie Hej	David Hildebrand	John B. Landolt Jr.
Burnet	Dana DeBerry	Sam Oatman	Bille Neve	Russell Graeter	Ronny Hibler	James Oakley
Caldwell	Emma Jean Schulle	F.C. Schneider	Tom D. Bonn	Charles Bullock	Neto Madrigal	Joe Ivan Roland
Calhoun	Pamela Martin-Hartgrove	Dan W. Heard	Roger C. Galvan	Michael Balajka	Neil E. Fritsch	Kenneth W. Finster
Callahan	Sharon Owens		Harold Hicks	Bryan Farmer	Tommy Holland	Doris Grider
Cameron	Aurora de la Garza	Armando Villalobos	Pedro "Pete" Benavides	John Wood	David Garza	Edna Tamayo
Camp	Mariann Groves	Charles Bailey	Bart Townsend	Larry Shelton	Norman Townsend	Bobby Barrett
Carson	Celeste Bichsel	Stuart Messer	Mike Britten	Kenneth Ware	Jerry Strawn	Kevin Howell
Cass	Becky Wilbanks	Randal Lee	Kenneth L. Pate	Danny Joe Shaddix	Paul Cothren	Max Bain
Castro	Joyce M. Thomas	James R. Horton	Tom McLain	Larry Gonzales	W.A. Baldridge	Dan Schmucker
Chambers	Bobby Scherer	Michael R. Little	Mark Huddleston	Judy Edmonds	W.E. " Buddy" Irby	W.O. "Bill" Wallace
Cherokee	Marlys Mason	Elmer C. Beckworth Jr.	Mary Gregg	Kevin Pierce	Moody Glass Jr.	Billy McCutcheon
Childress	Zona Prince	Stuart Messer	Denzil Ray	Dan Imhof	Lyall Foster	Don Ray Crook
Clay	Dan Slagle	Tim Cole	Lindy Choate	Johnny Gee	Wilson Scaling	Brice Jackson

County	District Clerk	District Attorney†	Comm. Precinct 1	Comm. Precinct 2	Comm. Precinct 3	Comm. Precinct 4
Cochran	Rita Tyson	Gary Goff	Gerald Ramsey	J.B. Allen	Stacey Dunn	Jimmy Mullinax
Coke	Mary Grim	Stephen Lupton	Gene Montgomery	Bill Wheat	Gaylon Pitcock	George Snapp
Coleman	JoDean Chapman	Joe Lee Rose	Jimmie R. Porter	Billy Don McCrary	Michael L. Barker	Alan Davis
Collin	Hannah Kunkle	John R. Roach	Phyllis Cole	Jerry Hoagland	Joe Jaynes	Jack Hatchell
Collingsworth	Jackie Johnson	Stuart Messer	Dan Langford	Zeb Roberson	Eddie Orr	Pat Glenn
Colorado	Harvey Vornsand	Ken Sparks	Doug Wessels	Herbert Helmcamp	Tommy Hahn	Darrell Gertson
Comal	Katherine "Kathy" Faulkner	Dib Waldrip	Jack Dawson	Jay Millikin	Gregory Parker	Jan Kennady
Comanche	Brenda Dickey	B.J. Shepard	Garry Steele	Chris Biggs	Bobby Schuman	Clyde Brinson
Concho	Barbara K. Hoffman	George E. McCrea	R.M. "Hoss" Kingston	Ralph Willberg	Ernest R. Gomez	Aaron B. Browning Jr.
Cooke	Patricia Payne	Cindy Stormer	Gary Hollowell	Bill Cox	Al Smith	Virgil Hess
Coryell	Jaice Gray	David Castillio	Jack Wall	Cliff Price	Don Jones	Kyle Pruitt
Cottle	Beckey J. Tucker	David W. Hajek	Jim Sweeney	Hazel Biddy	Manuel Cruz Jr.	Gus Timmons
Crane	Judy Crawford	Mike Fostel	Jack Damron	Lewis Overton	Domingo Escobedo	Mickey Hurst
Crockett	Debbi Puckett	Laurie K. English	Frank Tambuga	Pleas Childress	Freddie Nicks	Rudy Martinez
Crosby	Karla Isbell	C. Michael Ward	Gary Jordan	Frank Mullins	Larry Wampler	Billy Bob Wright
Culberson	Linda McDonald	Jaime Esparza	Cornelio Garibay	Manuel Molinar	John Jones	Israel Navarrette
Dallam	LuAnn Taylor	David Green	Glenn Reagan	Oscar Przilas	Don Bowers	Carl French
Dallas	Jim Hamlin	Bill Hill Jr.	Maureen Dickey	Mike Cantrell	John Wiley Price	Kenneth Mayfield
Dawson	Carolyn Turner	Ricky Smith	Jerry Beaty	Tino Morales	Troy Howard	Foy O'Brien
Deaf Smith	Jean Schumacher Coody	Jim English	Pat Smith	Jerry Roberts	Troy Don Moore	Jerry O'Connor
Delta	Jane Jones	Martin Braddy	B.V. Templeton	David Max Moody	Wayne Poole	Ted Carrington
Denton	Sherri Adelstein	Bruce Isaacks	Cynthia White	Sandy Jacobs	Bobbie J. Mitchell	Jim Carter
DeWitt	Tabeth Gardner	Michael Sheppard	Curtis Afflerbach	Joe Machalec	Gilbert Pargmann	Alfred Rangnow
Dickens	Winona Humphreys	Becky McPherson	Don Condron	Billy George Drennan	Doc Edwards	Duane "Slim" Durham
Dimmit	Alicia Lopez-Martinez	Roberto Serna	Larry Speer	Johnny Gloria	Jose P. Martinez	Rodrigo Jaime
Donley	Fay Vargas	Stuart Messer	Ernest Johnston	Don Hall	Andy Wheatly	Bob Trout
Duval	Richard M. Barton	Heriberto Silva	Alejo C. Garcia	Rene M. Perez	Nestor Garza Jr.	Gilberto Uribe Jr.
Eastland	Karen Moore	Russ Thomason	Wayne Honea	Norman Christian	Bill Underwood	Reggie Pittman
Ector	Janis Morgan	John W. Smith	Freddie Gardner	Greg Simmons	Barbara Graff	Bob Bryant
Edwards	Sarah McNealy	Fred Hernandez	Robert Pena	F.O. Burleson	James E. Epperson Jr.	Chisholm Erwin Parks
Ellis	Billie Ann Fuller	Joe F. Grubbs	Dennis Robinson	Larry Jones	Heath Sims	Ron Brown
El Paso	Gilbert Sanchez	Jaime E. Esparza	Barbara Perez	Betti Flores	Miguel A. Teran	Daniel R. Haggerty
Erath	Wanda Pringle	John Terrill	Jerry Martin	Lynn Tidwell	Doug Eberhart	Randy Lowe
Falls	Larry Hoelscher	Kathryn J. Gilliam	Tom Zander	Robert Paul Sr.	Nelson Coker	Bernhard Neumann
Fannin	Rochelle Turner		Ronnie Rhudy	Stan Barker	Dewayne Strickland	Pat Hilliard
Fayette	Virginia Wied		Johns Saunders	Gary Weishuhn	James Kubecka	Tom Muras
Fisher	Tammy Haley	Mark Edwards	Gordon Pippin	Rodney Tankersley	Earnest Ragan	Gene Terry
Floyd	Barbara Edwards	Becky McPherson	Ray Nell Bearden	Lennie Gilroy	Craig Gilly	Jon Jones
Foard	Sherry Weatherred	Dan Mike Bird	Rick Hammonds	Rockne Wisdom	Larry Wright	Edward Crosby
Fort Bend	Glory Hopkins	John Healey	Tom Stavinoha	Grady Prestage	Andy Meyers	James Patterson
Franklin	Barbara Keith Campbell	Martin Braddy	Danny Chitsey	Bobby Elbert	Deryl Carr	Sam Young
Freestone	Janet Chappell	Jack Keith Meredith	Luke Ward Sr.	Craig Oakes	Stanley Gregory	Clyde E. Ridge Jr.
Frio	Ramona Rodriguez	Rene M. Peña	Jesus G. Salinas	Richard Muzquiz	Ruben Maldonado	Jose Flores
Gaines	Virginia Stewart	Ricky Smith	Danny Yocom	Craig Belt	Blair Tharp	Charlie Lopez
Galveston	Latonia Wilson	Kurt Sistrunk	Patrick Doyle	Eddie Janek	Stephen Holmes	Kenneth Clark

County	District Clerk	District Attorney†	Comm. Precinct 1	Comm. Precinct 2	Comm. Precinct 3	Comm. Precinct 4
Garza	Jim Plummer	Ricky B. Smith	Gary McDaniel	Mason McClellan	John Valdez	Mike Sanchez
Gillespie	Barbara Meyer	E. Bruce Curry	Curtis Cameron	William A. Roeder	Calvin Ransleben	John E. Thompson Jr.
Glasscock	Rebecca Batla	Hardy Wilkerson	Jimmy Strube	Mark Halfmann	Marck Schafer	Michael Hoch
Goliad	Gail M. Turley	Michael Sheppard	Arturo Rojas	Jerry Rodriguez	Jim Kreneck	Ted Long
Gonzales	Sandra Baker	Vicki Pattillo	Kenneth O. "Dell" Whiddon	James "Jim" Kelso	Kevin T. LaFleur	Otis "Bud" Wuest
Gray	Gay Honderich	Richard Roach	Joe Wheeley	Gary Willoughby	Gerald Wright	James Hefley
Grayson	Cyndi Spencer	Joe Brown	Johnny Waldrip	David Whitlock	Jackie Crisp	Gene Short
Gregg	Barbara Duncan	William M. Jennings	Charles Davis	Darryl Primo	Bob Barbee	Dan Craig
Grimes	Wayne Rucker	Tuck Moody McLain	John Bertling	Bill Pendley	Julian Melchor Jr.	Pam Finke
Guadalupe	James Behrendt	Vicki Pattillo	Roger Baenziger	Cesareo Guadarrama	Jim O. Wolverton	Judy Cope
Hale	Carla Cannon	Wally Hatch	Neal Burnett	Mario Martinez	Gary Koelder	Benny Cantwell
Hall	Raye Bailey	Stuart Messer	Milton Beasley	Terry Lindsey	Buddy Logsdon	James Fuston
Hamilton	Leoma Larance	B.J. Shepherd	Jim Boatwright	Mike Lewis	Jon Bonner	Dickie Clary
Hansford	Kim Vera	Clay Ballman	Ira G. "Butch" Reed	Joe T. Venneman	Tim Stedje	Danny Henson
Hardeman	Linda Walker	Dan Mike Bird	Johnny Akers	Rodger Tabor	C.L. "Clois" Wall	Rodney Foster
Hardin	Vicki Johnson	Henry A. Coe III	Bob Burgess	Patricia McGallion	Ken Pelt	Bobby Franklin
Harris	Charles Bacarisse	Chuck Rosenthal	El Franco Lee	Sylvia Garcia	Steve Radack	Jerry Eversole
Harrison	Sherry Griffis	Joe Black	Jerry Lomax	Emma Bennett	James Greer	Jeff Thompson
Hartley	Diane Thompson	David Green	David Vincent	Andy Michael	John Newsom	Butch Owens
Haskell	Penny Anderson	Mike Fouts	Johnny Scoggins	Tiffen Mayfield	Kenny Thompson	Bobby Smith
Hays	Cecelia Adair	Michael Wenk	Debbie Ingalsbe	Susie Carter	Will Conley	Russ Molenaar
Hemphill	Charles M. Cole	Richard J. "Rick" Roach	Joe Schaef	Ed Culver	John Ramp	Lynard Schafer
Henderson	Becky Hanks	Donna Bennett	Joe D. Hall	Wade McKinney	Ronny Lawrence	Jerry West
Hidalgo	Omar Guerrero	Rene A. Guerra	Sylvia Handy	Hector "Tito" Palacios	Joe M. Flores	Oscar L. Garza Jr.
Hill	Charlotte Barr	Dan V. Dent	Bob Atwell	James W. Buzbee	Sam McClendon	John Erwin
Hockley	Dennis Price	Gary Goff	Marvin "Smitty" Smith	Larry Carter	J.L. "Whitey" Barnett	Billy Thetford
Hood	Tonna Hitt	Rob Christian	Mike Sumpson	Charles Baskett	Leonard Heathington	Larry Shafer
Hopkins	Patricia Dorner	Martin Braddy	Beth B. Wisenbaker	Burke Bullock	Don Patterson	Danny Evans
Houston	Pam Pugh	David Cervantes	Jerry McLeod	Willie Kitchen	Pat Perry	Kennon Kellum
Howard	Colleen Barton	Hardy Wilkerson	Emma Puga Brown	Jerry Kilgore	W.B. "Bill" Crooker	Gary Simer
Hudspeth	Elizabeth Morales	Jaime Esparza	Wayne West	Curtis Carr	Jim Ed Miller	James Kiehne
Hunt	Stacey Landrum	Duncan Thomas	Kenneth Thornton	Ralph Green	Phillip Martin	Jim Latham
Hutchinson	Joan Carder	Clay L. Ballman	RD Cornelison	Jerry Hefner	S.T. "Red" Isbell Jr.	Eddie Whittington
Irion	Reba Criner	Stephen Lupton	Michael Dolan	Eva McCutchen	John Nanny	Barbara Searcy
Jack	Tracie Pippin	Jana Jones	Joe Paul Nichols	Jerry M. Adams	James L. Cozart	Milton R. "Sonny" Pruitt
Jackson	Sharon Whitley	Bobby Bell	Wayne Hunt	Wayne Bubela	Johnny E. Belicek	Larry Deyton
Jasper	Linda Ryall	Ted Walker	Charles Shofner Jr.	Rodney Barger	Willie Stark	Mack Rose
Jeff Davis	Sue Blackley	Frank Brown	Larry Francell	Diane Lacy	Curtis Evans	William Gearhart
Jefferson	Lolita Ramos	Tom Maness	Eddie Arnold	Mark L. Domingue	Waymon D. Hallmark	Everette "Bo" Alfred
Jim Hogg	Noemi G. Salinas	Heriberto Silva	Antonio Flores	Joe R. Stacy	Zaragoza Ramirez	Juan Lino Ramirez
Jim Wells	R. David Guerrero	Joe Frank Garza	Zenaida Sanchez	Lawrence Cornelius	Oswald Alanis	Javier N. Garcia
Johnson	David Lloyd	Dale Hanna	R.C. McFall	John Matthews	Mark Carpenter	Troy Thompson
Jones	Nona Carter	Billy John Edwards	James Clawson	Mike Polk	Jimmy "Buz" Wylie	Steve Lollar
Karnes	Patricia Brysch	Rene Pena	Darrel Blaschke	Jeffrey Wiatrek	James Rosales	Isidro D. Rossett Jr.
Kaufman	Sandra Featherston	Ed Walton	Jerry Rowden	Ken Leonard	Kenneth Schoen	Jim Deller

County	District Clerk	District Attorney†	Comm. Precinct 1	Comm. Precinct 2	Comm. Precinct 3	Comm. Precinct 4
Kendall	Shirley R. Stehling	E. Bruce Curry	Anne Reissig	Gene Miertschin	Darrel L. Lux	Russell C. Busby
Kenedy	Veronica Vela	Carlos Valdez	Leonard May	Roberto Salazar Jr.	Tobin Armstrong	Gus A. Puente
Kent	Richard Craig Harrison	Mike Fouts	Roy W. Chisum	Don Long	Tommy Stanaland	Robert Graham
Kerr	Linda Uecker	E. Bruce Curry	H.A. Baldwin	William Williams	Jonatha A. Letz	Dave Nicholson
Kimble	Haydee Torres	Ronald L. Sutton	Vicente Menchaca	Charles McGuire	Jim Watson	Tooter Schulze
King	Linda Lewis	David Hajek	Stephen Brady	Larry Rush	Bob Tidmore	Darwood Marshall
Kinney	Dora Elia Sandoval	Fred Hernandez	Marvin Davis	Joe Montalvo	Nat Terrazas	Pat Melancon
Kleberg	Martha L. Soliz	Carlos Valdez	David Rosse	Joe Hinojosa	Roy Cantu	Romeo L. Lomas
Knox	Ronnie Verhalen	David Hajek	Weldon Skiles	Jerry Parker	Jimmy Urbanczyk	Johnny Birkenfeld
Lamar	Marvin Ann Patterson	Gary Young	Mike Blackburn	Carl Steffey	Rodney Pollard	Jackie Wheeler
Lamb	Celia A. Kuykendall	Mark Yarbrough	Rodney Smith	Thurman Lewis	Emil Macha	Jimmy Young
Lampasas	Terri Cox	Larry Allison	Robert L. Vincent Jr.	Alex Wittenburg	Lowell B. Ivey	Jack B. Cox
La Salle	Peggy Murray	René M. Peña	Chris Hinojosa III	Roberto F. Aldaco	Jose Jimenez	Domingo B. Martinez
Lavaca	Calvin J. Albrecht	Vicki Pattillo	Charles A. Netardus	Mark H. Zimmerman	David Wagner	Dennis W. Kocian
Lee	Adeline Melcher	Ted Weems	Maurice Pits Jr.	Douglas Hartfield	O.B. "Butch" Johnson	Thomas Kovar
Leon	Diane Davis	Whitney Smith	Joey Sullivan	David Ferguson	Ray Gaskin	Dean Player
Liberty	Melody Gilmore	Mike Little	Todd Fontenot	Lee Groce	Melvin Hunt	Norman Brown
Limestone	Peggy Hill		John McCarver	Billy Waldrop	Morris Beaver	Don C. Ford
Lipscomb	Kim Blau	Richard Roach	Juan Cantu	Stanley Born	Scotty Schilling	Gene Ashpaugh
Live Oak	Lois Shannon	Martha Warner	Richard Lee	Barbara Kopplin	Jim Bassett	Emilio Garza
Llano	Debbie Honig	Sam Oatman	Wayne Brascom	Henry Parker	Duane Stueven	Leon Tucker
Loving	Beverly Hanson	Randall Reynolds	Harlan Hopper	Joe Renteria	Skeet Jones	Royce Creager
Lubbock	Barbara Sucsy	William Sowder	Bill McCay	James Kitten	Ysidro Gutierrez	Patti Jones
Lynn	Sandra Laws	Rickey Smith	Don Morton	Mike Braddock	Don Blair	J.T. Miller
Madison	Joyce Batson	William C. "Bill" Bennett	Roland Standley	Don Farris	Tommy Cornelius	J.T. Andrus
Marion	Janie McCay	William Gleason	Bob Higgins	Sam Smith	C.E. "Cecil" Bourne	Charlie Treadwell
Martin	Susie Hull	Hardy L. Wilkerson	Jesus Garza	Valentino Sotelo	Bobby Kelly	David Pribyla
Mason	Beatrice Langehennig	Ronald L. Sutton	Wayne Hofmann	John D. Fleming	Stanley Toeppich	Eldon Kothmann
Matagorda	Becky Denn	Steven E. Reis	Daniel Pustka	George Deshotels	James Gibson	Percy Carroll
Maverick	Irene Rodriguez	Roberto Serna	Eliaz Maldonado	Rudy Heredia	David Saucedo	Cesar Flores
McCulloch	Mackye Johnson	Ron Sutton	Joe Johnson	Jerry Bratton	Nelson Solsbery	Brent C. Deeds
McLennan	Karen Matkin	John Segrest	Wendall Crunk	Lester Gibson	Joe A. Mashek	Ray Meadows
McMullen	Dorairene Garza	Martha Warner	Tim Teal	Rodney Swaim Jr.	Paul Koonce	Maximo Quintanilla Jr.
Medina	Eva Soto	Tony Hackebeil	Christine Mitchell	Beverly Keller	Arturo Barrientes	Kelly Carroll
Menard	Elsie Maserang	Ronald Sutton	Boyd Murchison	Sam Brownlee	Pete Crothers	Bill Royal
Midland	Vivian Wood	Al Schorre	Jimmy Smith	Mike Bradford	Juluis Brooks	Randy Prude
Milam	Betty Robertson	Kerry Spears	Clifford Whiteley	Kenneth Hollas	C. Dale Jaecks	Burke Bauerschlag
Mills	Beulah L. "Patty" Roberts	Michael Murray	John Mann	Carroll Bunting	Billy L. Hobbs	Farrel Thorne
Mitchell	Sharon Hammond	Glen Harrison	Jimmy Rees	Carl Guelker	Larry Johnson	Billy H. Preston
Montague	Lesia Darden	Tim Cole	Dickey J. Cox	Jerry Clement	Glenn Seay	Tommie Sappington
Montgomery	Barbara Adamick	Mike McDougal	Mike Meador	Craig Doyal	Ed Chance	Ed Rinehart
Moore	Diane Hoefling	David Green	A. Gordon Clark	Bobby Barker	Milton Pax	Lynn Cartrite
Morris	Gwen Oney	J. Stephen Cowan	Hubert L. Mitchell Jr.	Dearl Quarles	J.P. Cobb	Gary Camp
Motley	Kate Hurt	Becky McPherson	Ronnie Davis	Donnie Turner	Franklin Jameson	Russell Alexander
Nacogdoches	Donna Phillips	Stephanie Stephens	Tom Bush	Reggie Cotton	Charles Simmons	Tom Strickland

County	District Clerk	District Attorney†	Comm. Precinct 1	Comm. Precinct 2	Comm. Precinct 3	Comm. Precinct 4
Navarro	Marilyn Greer	Steve Keathley	Kit Herrington	Olin Nickelberry	William Baldwin	John Paul Ross
Newton	Bree Allen	A.W. Davis Jr.	William "Bill" Filler	Thomas Gill	Prentiss Hopson	Charles Brinson
Nolan	Vera Hollman	Mark Edwards	Randall Smith	Leslie Bond	Tommy White	Tony Lara
Nueces	Patsy Perez	Carlos Valdez	Peggy Banales	Betty Jean Longoria	Oscar O. Ortiz	H.C. "Chuck" Cazalas
Ochiltree	Shawn Bogard		Duane Pshigoda	Doug Barnes	James W. Clark	Larry Hardy
Oldham	Becky Groneman	Kent Birdsong	Quincy Taylor	Donnie Knox	Roger Morris	Billy Don Brown
Orange	Vickie Edgerly	John Kimbrough	James Stringer	Owen Burton	John DuBose	Beamon Minton
Palo Pinto	Janie Glover	Tim Ford	Ted Ray	Robert Murray	George Nowak	Raymond Procter
Panola	Sandra King	Danny Buck Davidson	Ronnie LaGrone	Douglas M. Cotton	Hermon Reed Jr.	Dale LaGrone
Parker	Elvera Johnson	Don Schnebly	Danny Choate	Joe Brinkley	John Roth	Jim Webster
Parmer	Sandra Warren	Johnny Actkinson	Kirk Frye	Tom Ware	Michael Haseloff	Elvis Powell
Pecos	Lisa Villarreal	Frank Brown (83rd) Laurie English (112th)	George Riggs	Oscar Gonzalez	J.H. "Jay" Kent	Paul Valenzuela
Polk	Kathy E. Clifton	John S. Holleman	Robert C. "Bob" Willis	Bobby Smith	James J. "Buddy" Purvis	Tommy Overstreet
Potter	Caroline Woodburn	Randall Sims	Lacy Borger	Manuel "Perez" Villasenor	Joe Kirkwood	Iris S. Lawrence
Presidio	Brenda M. Silva	Frank Brown	Felipe Cordero	Eloy Aranda	Carlos Armendariz	Danny Watts
Rains	Deborah Traylor		Herschel Bullard	Evelyn Malone	Gary Mike Bishop	Rodney Smith
Randall	Jo Carter	James Farren	Robert "Bob" Karrh	George "Skip" Huskey	Gene Parker	Buddy DeFord
Reagan	Terri Pullig	Laurie English	Jessie Barrera	Ron Galloway	Mikel Jones	Thomas Strube
Real	Bella A. Rubio	Tony Hackebeil	Manuel Rubio	Clayton Crider	Castulo San Miguel	Joe W. Connell Sr.
Red River	Janice Gentry		Rufus Ward Jr.	M.D. Whittle	Elmer Caton	Josef Hausler
Reeves	Patricia Tarin	Randall "Randy" Reynolds	Rojelio "Roy" Alvarado	Norman Hill	Saul Herrera	Gilberto "Hivi" M. Rayos
Refugio	Ruby Garcia	Michael A. Sheppard	Rindle Wilson	Janis Gillespie	Gary Bourland	John Reyna
Roberts	Donna L. Goodman	Richard J. Roach	William H. Clark	Ken Gill	Kelly Flowers	James F. Duvall Jr.
Robertson	Cornelia Starkey	John C. Paschall	John Anderson	Jim Davis	Keith Nickelson	Marie Abraham
Rockwall	Kay McDaniel	Galen Ray Sumrow	Jerry Wimpee	Scott Self	Bruce Beaty	David Magness
Runnels	Tammy Burleson	George McCrea	Robert Moore	Freddie Grohman	James T. Self	Richard W. Strube
Rusk	Jean Hodges	Micheal E. Jimerson	W.D. "Bill" Hale	Jerry Weaver	Freddy Swann	Kimble Harris
Sabine	Tanya Walker	John Fisher	Keith C. Clark	Lynn Smith	Doyle Dickerson	Fayne Warner
San Augustine	Jean Steptoe	John Fisher	Tommy Hunter	Edward Wilson	Dale Mixon	B.R. Bryan
San Jacinto	Marilyn Nettles	Mark Price	Michael Griffith	Royce Wells	David Brandon Sr.	Joe Johnson
San Patricio	Carmen Garza	Patrick L. Flanigan	Nina G. Trevino	Fred P. Nardini	Pedro G. Rodriguez	Jim Price Jr.
San Saba	Kim Wells	Sam Oatman	Otis Judkins	Rickey Lusty	Wayland Perry	Roger McGehee
Schleicher	Peggy Williams	Stephen Lupton	Johnny F. Mayo Jr.	William Garth Clark	Kirk Griffin	Matthews Brown
Scurry	Trina Rodgers	Dana Cooley	Terry Williams	Jerry House	Howard Limmer	Chloanne Lindsey
Shackelford	Cheri Hawkins	Billy John Edwards	Danny Peacock	Greg Simpson	Jimmy T. Brooks	Stan West
Shelby	Lori Oliver	Lynda K. Russell	Donnie Borders	Jimmy Lout	Travis Rodgers	Kevin Foster
Sherman	Mary Lou Albert	David Green	Steve Pemberton	Randy Williams	David Hass	Tommy Asher
Smith	Lois Rogers	Matt Bingham	JoAnn Fleming	Don Pinkerton	Bobby Van Ness	JoAnn Hampton
Somervell	Candace Garrett	Dale Hanna	Zach Cummings	Dennis Ramsay	Lloyd Wirt	James Barnard
Starr	Juan Erasmo Saenz	Heriberto Silva	Jaime Alvarez	Raul Pena Jr.	Elroy Garza	Abel N. Gonzalez
Stephens	Shirley Parker	Steve Bristow	Jerry Toland	D.C. "Button" Sikes	Joe F. High	Rickie Carr
Sterling	Diane A. Browne	Stephen Lupton	Billy Joe Blair	Russell Noletubby	Deborah H. Horwood	Skeete Foster
Stonewall	Belinda Page	Michael Fouts	W.D. Ellison	Kenny Spitzer	Billy Kirk Meador	Gary Myers
Sutton	Veronica E. Hernandez	Laurie English	Miguel "Mike" Villanueva	John Wade	Milton Cavaness	Belia Castaneda

County	District Clerk	District Attorney†	Comm. Precinct 1	Comm. Precinct 2	Comm. Precinct 3	Comm. Precinct 4
Swisher	Brenda Hudson	Wally Hatch	Lloyd Rahlfs	Joe Bob Thompson	Harvey N. Foster	Tim Reed
Tarrant	Tom Wilder	Tim Curry	Roy Brooks	Marti VanRavenswaay	Glen Whitley	J.D. Johnson
Taylor	Patricia Henderson	James Eidson	Jack Turner	Nowlin Cox	Stan Egger	Chuck Statler
Terrell	Martha Allen	Fred Hernandez	Yolanda G. Lopez	Santiago Flores	Charles Stegall	Kenn Norris
Terry	Paige Lindsey		Eddie Ryburn	Dale Andrews	Don Robertson	Jessie Hartman
Throckmorton	Mary Walraven	Mike Fouts	Casey Wells	Jimmy Glenn	Carlton Sullivan	Wilton Cantrell
Titus	Debra Bowen	Charles Bailey	Bob Fitch	Mike Fields	Phillip Hinton	Thomas Hockaday
Tom Green	Sheri Woodfin	Stephen R. Lupton (51st) George McCrea (119th)	Ralph Hoelscher	Karl Bookter	Steve Floyd	Richard S. Easingwood Jr.
Travis	Amalia Rodriguez-Mendoza	Ronnie Earle	Ron Davis	Karen Sonleitner	Gerald Daugherty	Margaret Gómez
Trinity	Cheryl Cartwright	Joe Ned Dean	Grover Worsham	Bill Burton	Cecil Webb	Travis Forrest
Tyler	Melissie Evans	Joe R. Smith	Martin Nash	James Hughes	Joe Marshall	Jack Walston
Upshur	Carolyn Bullock		James Criteden	Buddy Ferguson	Lloyd Crabtree	Gary Drennen
Upton	Phyllis Stephens	Laurie English	Brent Wrinkle	Tommy Owens	W.M. "Willie" Martinez	Leon Patrick
Uvalde	Lydia Steele	Anton "Tony" Hackabeil	Randy Scheide	Mariano Pargas Jr.	Jerry W. Bates	Jesse R. Moreno
Val Verde	Martha Mitchell	Fred Hernandez	Ramiro V. Ramon	Rogelio "Roy" H. Musquiz	Robert Beau Nettleton	Jesus E."Cheo" Ortiz
Van Zandt	Karen Wilson	Leslie Poynter Dixon	Ricky LaPrade	David Risner	Kelles Miller	Ron Carroll
Victoria	Cathy Stuart	M.P. "Dexter" Eaves	Chris F. Rivera	Jerry Nobles	Gary E. Burns	Wayne Dierlam
Walker	Robyn Flowers	David P. Weeks	B.J. Gaines	Robert E. Autery	James "Buddy" Reynolds	Tim Paulsel
Waller	Patricia Spadachene	Bill Parham	W.M. "Bill" Eplen	Frank Pokluda	Milton Whiting	Louis Canales
Ward	Patricia Oyerbides	Randy Reynolds	Julian Florez	Kathy Fausett	Dexter Nichols	Eddie Nelms
Washington	Vicki Lehmann	Renee Mueller	Zeb Hackmann	Robert Mikeska	Kirk Hanath	Joy Fuchs
Webb	Manuel Gutierrez	Jose Rubio	Frank Sciaraffa	Judith G. Gutierrez	Gerardo "Jerry" Garza	David R. Cortez
Wharton	Denice K. Malota	Josh McCown	Mickey Reynolds	D.C. "Chris" King	Philip Miller	James "Jimmy" Kainer
Wheeler	Sherri Jones	Richard "Rick" Roach	Daryl Snelgrooes	Tom Puryear	Hubert Moore	Robbie Robinson
Wichita	Dorsey Trapp	Barry Macha	Joe Miller	Pat Norris	Gordon Griffith	William "Bill" Presson
Wilbarger	Brenda Peterson	Dan Mike Bird	Richard Jacobs	Freddie Streit	Rodney Johnston	Lenville Morris
Willacy	Gilbert Lozano	Juan Angel Guerra	Abiel Cantu	Noe T. Loya	Emilio Vera	Aurelio Guerra
Williamson	Bonnie Wolbrueck	John Bradley	Lisa Birkman	Greg Boatright	Tom McDaniel	Frankie Limmer
Wilson	Shirley D. Polasek	René M. Peña	Albert Gamez	Leonard Rotter	Robert "Bobby" H. Lynn	Wayne H. Stroud
Winkler	Sherry Terry	Michael L. Fostel	Tommy R. Smith	Robbie Wolf	Randy Neal	Jose G. Dominguez
Wise	Christi Fuqua	Jana Jones	Robert Rankin	Kevin Burns	Mikel Richardson	Terry Ross
Wood	Jenica Turner	Marcus D. Taylor	Roy Don Shipp	Jerry Gaskill	Roger Pace	Jerry Galloway
Yoakum	Vicki Blundell	Richard Clark	Woody Lindsey	Ben Coston	Ty Earl Powell	Jack Cobb
Young	Carolyn Collins	Stephen Bristow	John L. Hawkins	John C. Bullock	R.L. Spivey	David Yoder
Zapata	Consuelo R. Villarreal	Joe M. Rubio	Jose Emilio Vela	Angel Garza	Joseph Rathmell	Norberto Garza
Zavala	Rachel Ramirez	Roberto Serna	Alfredo Sanchez	Miguel Acosta	David López	Matthew McHazlett

Texans in Congress

Besides the two members of the U.S. Senate allocated to each state, Texas is allocated 32 members in the U.S. House of Representatives. The term of office for members of the House is two years; the terms of all members will expire on Jan. 1, 2007. Senators serve six-year terms. Sen. Kay Bailey Hutchison's term will end in 2007. Sen. John Cornyn's term will end in 2009.

Addresses and phone numbers of the lawmakers' Washington and district offices are below, as well as the committees on which they serve. Washington **zip codes** are **20515** for members of the House and **20510** for senators. The telephone **area code** for Washington is **202**. On the Internet, House members can be reached through **www.house.gov/writerep**. In 2005, members of Congress received a salary of $162,100. Members in leadership positions received $180,100.

U.S. Senate

CORNYN, John. Republican (Home: Austin); Washington Office: 517 HSOB, Washington, D.C. 20510; (202) 224-2934, Fax 228-2856. Website, cornyn.senate.gov.

Texas Offices: 221 W. 6th Ste. 1530, **Austin** 78701, (512) 469-6034; 5005 LBJ Ste. 1150, **Dallas** 75244, (972) 239-1310; 222 E. Van Buren Ste. 404, **Harlingen** 78550, (956) 423-0162; 5300 Memorial Dr. Ste. 980, **Houston** 77007, (713) 572-3337; 3405 22nd Ste. 203, **Lubbock** 79410, (806) 472-7533; 600 Navarro Ste. 210, **San Antonio** 78205, (210) 224-7485; 100 E. Ferguson Ste. 1004, **Tyler** 75702, (903) 593-0905.

Committees: Armed Services, Budget, Judiciary, Small Business and Entrepreneurship, Joint Economic Committee.

HUTCHISON, Kay Bailey. Republican (Home: Dallas); Washington Office: 284 RSOB, Washington, D.C. 20510; (202) 224-5922, Fax 224-0776. Website, hutchison.senate.gov.

Texas Offices: 961 Federal Bldg., 300 E. 8th St., **Austin** 78701, (512) 916-5834; 500 Chestnut Ste. 1570, **Abilene** 79602, (325) 676-2839; 10440 N. Central Expy. Ste. 1160, **Dallas** 75231, (214) 361-3500; 222 E. Van Buren Ste. 404, **Harlingen** 78550, (956) 425-2253; 1919 Smith Ste. 800, **Houston** 77002, (713) 653-3456; 145 Duncan Dr. Ste. 120, **San Antonio** 78226, (210) 340-2885.

Committees: Appropriations; Commerce, Science and Transportation; Rules and Administration; Veterans Affairs.

U.S. House of Representatives

BARTON, Joe, R-Ennis, District 6; Washington Office: 2109 RHOB; (202) 225-2002. Fax 225-3052; **District Offices**: 6001 West I-20 Ste. 200, Arlington 76017, (817) 543-1000; 2106A W. Ennis Ave., Ennis 75119, (817) 543-1000. **Committee**: Energy and Commerce (chairman).

BONILLA, Henry, R-San Antonio, District 23; Washington Office: 2458 RHOB; (202) 225-4511, Fax 225-2237; **District Offices**: 11120 Wurzbach Ste. 300, San Antonio 78230, (210) 697-9055; 1300 Matamoros Ste. 113B, Laredo 78040, (956) 726-4682; 111 E. Broadway Ste. 101, Del Rio 78840, (830) 774-6547; 107 W. Ave. E No.14, Alpine 79830, (432) 837-1313. **Committee**: Appropriations.

BRADY, Kevin, R-The Woodlands, District 8; Washington Office: 428 CHOB; (202) 225-4901, Fax 225-5524. **District Office**: 200 River Pointe Ste. 304, Conroe 77304, (936) 441-5700. **Committee**: Ways and Means, Joint Economic.

BURGESS, Michael, R-Flower Mound, District

26; **Washington Office**: 1721 LHOB; (202) 225-7772. **District Office**: 1660 S. Stemmons Fwy. Ste. 230, Lewisville 75067, (972) 434-9700. **Committee**: Energy and Commerce.

CARTER, John R. R-Round Rock, District 31; Washington Office: 408 CHOB; (202) 225-3864. **District Offices**: 1717 N. I-35 Ste. 303, Round Rock 78664 (512) 246-1600; 116 S. East, Belton 76513, (254) 933-1392. **Committee**: Appropriations.

CONAWAY, K. Michael, R-Midland, District 11; Washington Office: 511 CHOB; (202) 225-3605. **District Offices:** 6 Desta Dr. Ste. 2000, Midland 79705, (432) 687-2390; 33 Twohig Ste. 307, San Angelo 76903, (325) 659-4010. **Committees**: Agriculture, Armed Services, Budget.

CUELLAR, Henry, D-Laredo, District 28; Washington office: 1404 LHOB; (202) 225-1640, Fax 225-1641. **District Offices**: 1149 E. Commerce Ste. 210, San Antonio, (210) 271-2851; 111 E. San Antonio Ste. 205, San Marcos 78666, (512) 392-2364; 1300 Matamoros Ste. 210, Laredo 78040, (956) 725-0639. **Committees**: Agriculture, Budget.

CULBERSON, John Abney, R-Houston, District 7; Washington Office: 1728 LHOB; (202) 225-2571, Fax 225-4381; **District Office**: 10000 Memorial Dr. Ste. 620, Houston 77024, (713) 682-8828. **Committee**: Appropriations.

DeLAY, Tom, R-Sugar Land, District 22; Washington Office: 242 CHOB; (202) 225-5951, Fax 225-5241; **District Offices**: 10701 Corporate Dr. Ste. 118, Stafford 77477, (281) 240-3700; 711 W. Bay Area Blvd. Ste. 410, Webster 77598, (281) 557-8855. **House Majority Leader**.

DOGGETT, Lloyd, D-Austin, District 25; Washington Office: 201 CHOB; (202) 225-4865; **District Offices**: 300 E. 8th Ste. 763, Austin 78701, (512) 916-5921; McAllen (956) 687-5921. **Committee**: Ways and Means.

EDWARDS, Chet, D-Waco, District 17; Washington Office: 2264 RHOB; (202) 225-6105, Fax 225-0350; **District Offices**: 600 Austin Ave. Ste. 29, Waco 76701, (254) 752-9600; 115 S. Main Ste. 202, Cleburne 76033, (817) 645-4743; 111 University Dr. Ste. 216, College Station 77840, (979) 691-8787. **Committees**: Appropriations, Budget.

GOHMERT, Louie, R-Tyler, District 1; Washington Office: 508 CHOB; (202) 225-3035, Fax 225-5866; **District Office**: 1121 ESE Loop 323 Ste. 206, Tyler 75701, (903) 561-6349. **Committees**: Judiciary, Resources, Small Business.

GONZALEZ, Charlie A., D-San Antonio, District 20; Washington Office: 327 CHOB; (202) 225-3236, Fax 225-1915; **District Office**: 124-B Federal Building,

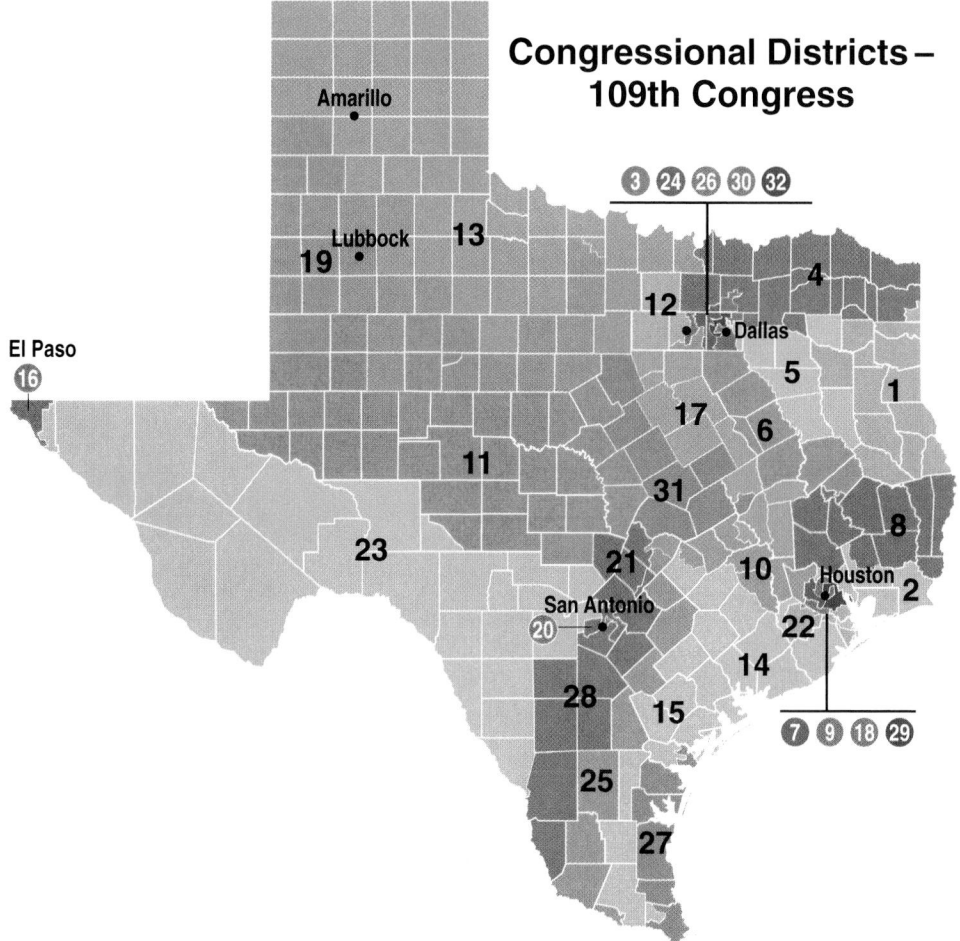

Congressional Districts – 109th Congress

727 East Durango, B-124 Federal Building, San Antonio 78206, (210) 472-6195. **Committee**: Energy and Commerce.

GRANGER, Kay, R-Fort Worth, District 12; Washington Office: 435 CHOB; (202) 225-5071, Fax 225-5683; **District Office**: 1701 River Run Rd. Ste. 407, Fort Worth 76107, (817) 338-0909. **Committee**: Appropriations.

GREEN, Al, D-Houston, District 9; Washington Office: 1529 LHOB; (202) 225-7508; **District Office:** 7707 Fannin Ste. 203, Houston 77054, (713) 383-9234. **Committees:** Financial Services, Science.

GREEN, Gene, D-Houston, District 29; Washington Office: 2335 RHOB; (202) 225-1688, Fax 225-9903; **District Offices**: 256 N. Sam Houston Pkwy. E. Ste. 29, Houston 77060, (281) 999-5879; 11811 I-10 East Ste. 430, Houston 77029, (713) 330-0761. **Committees**: Energy and Commerce, Standards of Official Conduct.

HALL, Ralph M., R-Rockwall, District 4; Washington Office: 2405 RHOB; (202) 225-6673, Fax 225-3332; **District Offices**: 104 N. San Jacinto, Rockwall 75087, (972) 771-9118; 101 E. Pecan, Sherman 75090, (903) 892-1112; 700 James Bowie Dr., New Boston 75570, (903) 628-8309. **Committees**: Energy and

Commerce, Science.

HENSARLING, Jeb, R-Dallas, District 5; Washington Office: 132 CHOB; (202) 225-3484, Fax 226-4888. **District Offices**: 6510 Abrams Rd. Ste. 243, Dallas 75231, (214) 349-9996; 100 E. Corsicana Ste. 208, Athens 77571, (903) 675-8288. **Committee**: Budget, Financial Services.

HINOJOSA, Rubén, D-Mercedes, District 15; Washington Office: 2463 RHOB; (202) 225-2531, Fax 225-5688; **District Offices**: 311 N. 15th St., McAllen 78501, (956) 682-5545; 107 S. St. Mary's St., Beeville 78102, (361) 358-8400. **Committees**: Education and the Workforce, Financial Services.

JACKSON LEE, Sheila, D-Houston, District 18; Washington Office: 2435 RHOB; (202) 225-3816, Fax 225-3317; **District Offices**: 1919 Smith Ste. 1180, Houston 77002, (713) 655-0050; 420 W. 19th St., Houston 77008, (713) 861-4070; 6719 W. Montgomery Ste. 204, Houston 77091. **Committees**: Homeland Security, Judiciary, Science.

JOHNSON, Eddie Bernice, D-Dallas, District 30; Washington Office: 1511 LHOB; (202) 225-8885, Fax 225-1477; **District Offices**: 3102 Maple Ave. Ste. 600, Dallas 75201, (214) 922-8885; 8344 East R.L. Thornton Ste. 222, Dallas 75228, (214) 324-0080. **Commit-**

tees: Science, Transportation and Infrastructure.

JOHNSON, Sam, R-Plano, District 3; Washington Office: 1211 LHOB; (202) 225-4201, Fax 225-1485; **District Office**: 2929 N. Central Expressway, Ste. 240, Richardson 75080, (972) 470-0892. **Committees**: Education and the Workforce, Ways and Means.

MARCHANT, Kenny, R-Coppell, District 24; Washington Office: 501 CHOB; (202) 225-6605, Fax 225-0074. **District Office**: 9901 E. Valley Ranch Parkway Ste. 3035, Irving 75063, (972) 556-0162. **Committees**: Education and the Workforce, Government Reform, Transportation and Infrastructure.

McCAUL, Michael, R-Austin, District 10; Washington Office: 415 CHOB; (202) 225-2401, Fax 225-5955. **District Offices:** 300 E. 8th St., Austin 78701, (512) 473-2357; 990 Village Sq. Ste. B, Tomball 77375. **Committees**: Homeland Security, International Relations, Science.

NEUGEBAUER, Randy, R-Lubbock, District 19; Washington Office: 429 CHOB; (202) 225-4005, Fax 225-9615. **District Offices:** 500 Chestnut Rm. 819, Abilene 79602, (325) 675-9779; 1510 Scurry, Big Spring 79720, (432) 264-7592; 1205 Texas Ave. Ste. 810, Lubbock 79401, (806) 763-1611. **Committees:** Agriculture, Financial Services.

ORTIZ, Solomon P., D-Corpus Christi, District 27; Washington Office: 2470 RHOB; (202) 225-7742, Fax 226-1134; **District Offices**: 3649 Leopard Ste. 510, Corpus Christi 78408, (361) 883-5868; 1805 Ruben Torres B-27, Brownsville 78526, (956) 541-1242. **Committees**: Armed Services, Resources.

PAUL, Ron, R-Surfside, District 14; Washington Office: 203 CHOB; (202) 225-2831. **District Offices**: 200 W. Second Ste. 210, Freeport 77541, (979) 230-0000; 312 S. Main Ste. 228, Victoria 77901, (361) 576-1231. **Committees**: Financial Services, International Relations, Joint Economic.

POE, Ted, R-Humble, District 2; Washington Office: 1605 LHOB; (202) 225-6565, Fax 225-5547. **District Offices:** 2615 Calder Ste. 100, Beaumont 77702, (409) 212-1997; 20202 U.S. Hwy 59 N. Ste. 105, Humble 77338, (281) 446-0242. **Committees**: International Relations, Small Business, Transportation and Infrastructure.

REYES, Silvestre, D-El Paso, District 16; Washington Office: 2433 RHOB; (202) 225-4831, Fax 225-2016; **District Office**: 310 N. Mesa Ste. 400, El Paso 79901, (915) 534-4400. **Committees**: Armed Services, Intelligence, Veterans' Affairs.

SESSIONS, Pete, R-Dallas, District 32; Washington Office: 1514 LHOB; (202) 225-2231, Fax 225-5878; **District Office**: 12750 Merit Dr. Ste. 1434, Dallas 75251, (972) 392-0505. **Committees**: Budget, Rules.

SMITH, Lamar S., R-San Antonio, District 21; Washington Office: 2184 RHOB; (202) 225-4236, Fax 225-8628; **District Offices:** 1100 NE Loop 410 Ste. 640, San Antonio 78209, (210) 821-5024; 5608 Parkcrest Dr. Ste 260, Austin 78731, (512) 402-9743. **Committees**: Homeland Security, Judiciary, Science, Standards of Official Conduct.

THORNBERRY, William M. (Mac), R-Clarendon, District 13; Washington Office: 2457 RHOB; (202) 225-3706, Fax 225-3486; **District Offices**: 905 S. Fillmore Ste. 520, Amarillo 79101, (806) 371-8844; 4245 Kemp Ste. 506, Wichita Falls 76308, (940) 692-1700. **Committees**: Armed Services, Intelligence. ☆

Medal of Freedom Honors Tommy Franks

The nation's highest civil honor was awarded to retired Gen. Tommy Franks in 2004.

The Army general received the Presidential Medal of Freedom from President George W. Bush at the White House on Dec. 14, 2004.

Born June 17, 1945, Franks was raised in Midland. He enlisted in the Army in 1965 after two years at the University of Texas at Austin. In 1967, he was commissioned as second lieutenant upon completion of officer candidate school and served in Vietnam. In 1971, he received a degree in business administration from the University of Texas at Arlington.

He served in the first Gulf War and later rose to command the American forces that invaded Afghanistan and Iraq.

The president, at the White House ceremony, called Franks a liberator, praising him for "your courage, your leadership and your lifetime of service in the cause of freedom and security."

Franks went to the same

Gen. Tommy Franks. File photo.

high school in Midland as Laura Bush, but did not know the president, who was also raised in Midland.

The two other architects of the Iraq invasion and reconstruction that were honored by the president in 2004 were George Tenet, former CIA director, and L. Paul Bremer, who had served as occupation administrator.

President Harry Truman established the Medal of Freedom in 1945 to recognize civilians who had contributed to the efforts in World War II.

In 1963, President John F. Kennedy reintroduced the medal as an honor for distinguished civilian service in peacetime.

Other Texans who received the honor in the past include Barbara Jordan, Lloyd Bentsen, Lady Bird Johnson, J. Frank Dobie, James Farmer, Dr. Michael DeBakey, Van Cliburn and Willie Velásquez.

Also, several astronauts serving in Houston have been honored, as well as national figures who spent part of their lives in Texas, including author James Michener and artist Georgia O'Keeffe. ☆

Federal Courts in Texas

Source: The following list of U.S. appeals and district court judges and officials was compiled from reports of the clerks of the individual courts and from court Websites.

Texas is divided into four federal judicial districts, each of which comprises several divisions. Appeal from all Texas federal courts is to the **U.S. Court of Appeals Fifth Circuit,** New Orleans.

U.S. Court of Appeals Fifth Circuit

The Fifth Circuit is composed of Louisiana, Mississippi and Texas. Sessions are held in each of the states at least once a year and may be scheduled at any location having adequate facilities. U.S. circuit judges are appointed for life and received a salary of $171,800 in 2005.
Circuit Judges — Chief Judge, Carolyn Dineen King, Houston. **Senior Judges:** Thomas M. Reavley and Will Garword, Austin. **Judges:** Fortunato P. Benavides and Priscilla R. Owen, Austin; Patrick E. Higginbotham, Dallas; Edith H. Jones, Jerry E. Smith and Harold R. DeMoss Jr., Houston; Rhesa H. Barksdale and E. Grady Jolly, Jackson, Miss.; W. Eugene Davis, Lafayette, La.; Jacques L. Wiener Jr., James L. Dennis and Edith Brown Clement, New Orleans; Emilio M. Garza and Edward C. Prado, San Antonio; Carl E. Stewart, Shreveport, La. **Circuit Executive:** Gregory A. Nussel, New Orleans.

U.S. District Courts

U.S. district judges are appointed for life and received a salary in 2005 of $162,100.

Northern Texas District
www.txnd.uscourts.gov
District Judges — Chief Judge, A. Joe Fish, Dallas. **Senior Judges:** Barefoot Sanders, Dallas; Eldon B. Mahon, Fort Worth; Robert B. Maloney, Dallas; Jerry Buchmeyer, Dallas. **Judges:** Mary Lou Robinson, Amarillo; Sidney A. Fitzwater, Jorge A. Solis, Sam A. Lindsay, David C. Godbey, Ed Kinkeade, Jane J. Boyle, Dallas; John H. McBryde, Terry R. Means, Fort Worth; Sam R. Cummings, Lubbock. **Clerk of District Court:** Karen Mitchell, Dallas. **U.S. Attorney:** Richard Roper, Dallas. **U.S. Marshal:** Randy Ely, Dallas. **Bankruptcy Judges:** Harlan D. Hale, Barbara J. Houser and Steve Felsenthal, Dallas; D. Michael Lynn, Fort Worth; Robert Jones, Lubbock. Court is in continuous session in each division of the Northern Texas District.

Following are the different divisions of the Northern District and the counties in each division:
Abilene Division
Callahan, Eastland, Fisher, Haskell, Howard, Jones, Mitchell, Nolan, Shackelford, Stephens, Stonewall, Taylor and Throckmorton. **Magistrate:** Phillip R. Lane, Abilene. **Deputy-in-charge:** Marsha Elliott.
Amarillo Division
Armstrong, Briscoe, Carson, Castro, Childress, Collingsworth, Dallam, Deaf Smith, Donley, Gray, Hall, Hansford, Hartley, Hemphill, Hutchinson, Lipscomb, Moore, Ochiltree, Oldham, Parmer, Potter, Randall, Roberts, Sherman, Swisher and Wheeler. **Magistrate:** Clinton E. Averitte, Amarillo. **Deputy-in-charge:** Lynn Sherman.

Dallas Division
Dallas, Ellis, Hunt, Johnson, Kaufman, Navarro and Rockwall. **Magistrates:** William F. Sanderson Jr., Jeff Kaplan, Paul Stickney and Irma C. Ramirez, Dallas.
Fort Worth Division
Comanche, Erath, Hood, Jack, Palo Pinto, Parker, Tarrant and Wise. **Magistrate:** Charles Bleil, Fort Worth. **Deputy-in-charge:** Pam Murphy.
Lubbock Division
Bailey, Borden, Cochran, Crosby, Dawson, Dickens, Floyd, Gaines, Garza, Hale, Hockley, Kent, Lamb, Lubbock, Lynn, Motley, Scurry, Terry and Yoakum. **U.S. District Judge:** Sam R. Cummings, Lubbock. **Magistrate:** Nancy M. Koenig, Lubbock. **Deputy-in-charge:** Kristy Weinheimer.
San Angelo Division
Brown, Coke, Coleman, Concho, Crockett, Glasscock, Irion, Menard, Mills, Reagan, Runnels, Schleicher, Sterling, Sutton and Tom Green. **Deputy-in-charge:** Beverly Roper.
Wichita Falls Division
Archer, Baylor, Clay, Cottle, Foard, Hardeman, King, Knox, Montague, Wichita, Wilbarger and Young. **Magistrate:** R. Kerry Roach, Wichita Falls. **Deputy-in-charge:** Allison Terry.

Western Texas District
www.txwd.uscourts.gov
District Judges — Chief Judge, Walter S. Smith Jr., Waco. **Senior Judges:** Harry Lee Hudspeth, William Wayne Justice and James R. Nowlin, Austin. **Judges:** Xavier Rodriguez, Orlando Garcia, Fred Biery and W. Royal Furgeson Jr., San Antonio; Kathleen Cardone, Frank J. Montalvo, Philip R. Martinez and David Briones, El Paso; Sam Sparks and Lee Yeakel, Austin; Alia M. Ludlum, Del Rio; Robert A. Junell, Midland. **Clerk of District Court:** William G. Putnicki, San Antonio. **Chief Deputy Clerk:** Michael J. Simon. **U.S. Attorney:** Johnny Sutton, San Antonio. **U.S. Marshal:** Lafayette Collins, San Antonio. **Bankruptcy Judges:** Larry E. Kelly and Frank P. Monroe, Austin; Lief M. Clark and Ronald B. King, San Antonio.

Following are the different divisions of the Western District, and the counties in each division.
Austin Division
Bastrop, Blanco, Burleson, Burnet, Caldwell, Gillespie, Hays, Kimble, Lampasas, Lee, Llano, Mason, McCulloch, San Saba, Travis, Washington and Williamson. **Magistrates:** Andrew W. Austin and Robert Pitman, Austin. **Divisional Office Manager:** Elizabeth Saunders. **Bankruptcy Court Deputy-in-charge:** Cynthia Gutierrez.
Del Rio Division
Edwards, Kinney, Maverick, Terrell, Uvalde, Val Verde and Zavala. **Magistrate:** Dennis Green and Victor Roberto Garcia, Del Rio. **Divisional Office Manager:** Rebecca Moore, temporary supervisor.
El Paso Division
El Paso County only. **Magistrates:** Norbert J. Garney, Michael S. McDonald and Richard P. Mesa, El Paso. **Divisional Office Manager:** Richard Delgado. **Bankruptcy Court Deputy-in-charge:** Mark Vargas.

Midland-Odessa Division

Andrews, Crane, Ector, Martin, Midland and Upton. Court for the Midland-Odessa Division is held at Midland, but may, at the discretion of the court, be held in Odessa. **Magistrate:** L. Stuart Platt and Stephen Capelle, Midland. **District Court Divisional Office Manager:** Laura Gonzales, Midland. **Bankruptcy Court Deputy-in-charge:** Christy L. Carouth.

Pecos Division

Brewster, Culberson, Hudspeth, Jeff Davis, Loving, Pecos, Presidio, Reeves, Ward and Winkler. **Magistrate:** Durwood Edwards, Pecos/Alpine. **Divisional Office Manager:** Karen J. White.

San Antonio Division

Atascosa, Bandera, Bexar, Comal, Dimmit, Frio, Gonzales, Guadalupe, Karnes, Kendall, Kerr, Medina, Real and Wilson. **Magistrates:** Pamela A. Mathy, John W. Primomo and Nancy Stein Nowak, San Antonio. **Clerk of Bankruptcy Court:** George D. Prentice, San Antonio. **Divisional Office Manager:** Michael F. Oakes.

Waco Division

Bell, Bosque, Coryell, Falls, Freestone, Hamilton, Hill, Leon, Limestone, McLennan, Milam, Robertson and Somervell. **Magistrate:** Jeffrey C. Manske Jr., Waco. **Divisional Office Manager:** Mark G. Borchardt. **Bankruptcy Court Deputy-in-charge:** Bridget Hardage.

Eastern Texas District

www.txed.uscourts.gov

District Judges — Chief Judge, Thad Heartfield, Beaumont. **Judges:** Howell Cobb, Ron Clark and Marcia A. Crone, Beaumont; William M. Steger, Michael H. Schneider and Leonard Davis, Tyler; T. John Ward, Marshall; Paul N. Brown and Richard A. Schell, Sherman; David J. Folsom, Texarkana.

Clerk of District Court: David J. Maland, Tyler. **U.S. Attorney:** Matt Orwig, Beaumont. **U.S. Marshal:** John Moore, Tyler. **Bankruptcy Judges:** William Parker, Tyler, and Brenda T. Roades, Plano.

Following are the divisions of the Eastern District and the counties in each division:

Beaumont Division

Hardin, Jasper, Jefferson, Liberty, Newton, Orange. **Magistrates:** Earl Hines and Wendell Radford. **Chief Deputy:** Johnette Cartwright.

Lufkin Division

Angelina, Houston, Nacogdoches, Polk, Sabine, San Augustine, Shelby, Trinity, Tyler. **Deputy-in-charge:** Kathy Riley.

Marshall Division

Camp, Cass, Harrison, Marion, Morris, Upshur. **Deputy-in-charge:** Peggy Anderson.

Paris Division

Delta, Fannin, Hopkins, Lamar and Red River. **Deputy-in-charge:** Patricia Davidson.

Sherman Division

Collin, Cooke, Denton and Grayson. **Magistrate:** Don Bush. **Deputy-in-charge:** Sandra Southerland.

Texarkana Division

Bowie, Franklin and Titus. **Magistrate:** Caroline M. Craven. **Deputy-in-charge:** Rhonda Lafitte.

Tyler Division

Anderson, Cherokee, Gregg, Henderson, Panola, Rains, Rusk, Smith, Van Zandt and Wood. **Magistrates:** Henry W. McKee and Judith Guthrie, Tyler. **Chief Deputy:** Jeanne Henderson.

Southern Texas District

www.txs.uscourts.gov

District Judges — Chief Judge, Hayden W. Head Jr., Corpus Christi. **Senior Judges:** Filemon B. Vela, Brownsville, and David Hittner, Houston. **Judges:** Nancy F. Atlas, Kenneth M. Hoyt, Sim Lake, Lynn N. Hughes, Melinda Harmon, Vanessa D. Gilmore, Ewing Werlein Jr., and Lee H. Rosenthal, Houston; Janis Graham Jack, Corpus Christi; Samuel B. Kent, Galveston; Hilda G. Tagle and Andrew S. Hanen, Brownsville; Ricardo H. Hinojosa and Randy Crane, McAllen; George P. Kazen, Keith P. Ellison and Micaela Alvarez, Laredo; John D. Rainey, Victoria.

Clerk of Court: Michael N. Milby, Houston. **U. S. Attorney:** Michael T. Shelby, Houston. **U.S. Marshal:** Ruben Montzon, Houston. **Bankruptcy Judges:** Chief, Karen K. Brown, Houston; Jeff Bohm, Marvin Isgur and Wesley W. Steen, Houston; Richard S. Schmidt, Corpus Christi; Letitia Z. Clark, Galveston.

Following are the different divisions of the Southern District and the counties in each division:

Brownsville Division

Cameron and Willacy. **Magistrates:** John Wm. Black, Felix Recio. **Deputy-in-charge:** Juan Barbosa.

Corpus Christi Division

Aransas, Bee, Brooks, Duval, Jim Wells, Kenedy, Kleberg, Live Oak, Nueces and San Patricio. **Magistrate:** B. Janice Ellington and Jane Cooper-Hill. **Deputy-in-charge:** Monica Seaman.

Galveston Division

Brazoria, Chambers, Galveston and Matagorda. **Magistrate:** John R. Froeschner. **Deputy-in-charge:** Marrianne Gore.

Houston Division

Austin, Brazos, Colorado, Fayette, Fort Bend, Grimes, Harris, Madison, Montgomery, San Jacinto, Walker, Waller and Wharton. **Magistrates:** Calvin Botley, Frances H. Stacy, Nancy Johnson, Marcia A. Crone, Mary Milloy and Stephen W. Smith. **Clerk:** Michael N. Milby.

Laredo Division

Jim Hogg, La Salle, McMullen, Webb and Zapata. **Magistrates:** Adriana Arce-Flores, Marcel C. Notzon. **Deputy-in-charge:** Rosie Rodriguez.

McAllen Division

Hidalgo and Starr. **Magistrate:** Dorina Ramos. **Deputy-in-charge:** Eddie Leandro.

Victoria Division

Calhoun, DeWitt, Goliad, Jackson, Lavaca, Refugio and Victoria. **Magistrates:** B. Janice Ellington and Jane Cooper-Hill. **Deputy-in-charge:** Joyce Richards. ☆

Federal Funds to Texas by County, 2003

Texas received **$140,450,968,456** in 2003 from the federal government. Below, the distribution of funds is shown by county. The first figure after the county name represents total **direct expenditures to the county** for fiscal year 2003. The second and third figures are that part of the total that went directly for individuals, either in **retirement** payments, such as Social Security, or **other** direct payments, principally Medicare. In the last column are direct payments **other than to individuals**, principally agricultural programs such as crop insurance. *For a more complete explanation, see end of chart.

Source: Consolidated Federal Funds Report 2003, U.S. Commerce Dept.

COUNTY	TOTAL	For INDIVIDUALS		other direct (ag., etc.)
		retirement	other	
(Thousand dollars 000)				
Anderson	$ 262,451	$ 118,797	$ 66,367	$ 523
Andrews	54,542	26,143	14,053	4,116
Angelina	409,139	188,989	107,579	1,342
Aransas	122,248	69,543	25,789	771
Archer	57,843	29,270	7,060	4,436
Armstrong	22,388	5,574	2,624	3,392
Atascosa	179,314	79,748	34,493	14,002
Austin	657,798	56,702	29,309	1,828
Bailey	51,956	13,613	10,528	17,245
Bandera	82,883	59,122	12,643	405
Bastrop	247,334	123,165	41,996	651
Baylor	33,063	13,837	8,758	2,709
Bee	155,882	57,479	42,009	5,161
Bell	3,556,404	650,148	172,120	4,489
Bexar	12,747,556	3,798,631	1,493,321	23,887
Blanco	67,744	42,914	16,637	101
Borden	6,998	736	620	1,869
Bosque	97,627	54,036	23,630	1,005
Bowie	719,485	271,993	122,187	3,604
Brazoria	750,619	407,066	175,671	24,548
Brazos	1,826,878	198,217	104,919	2,736
Brewster	60,973	21,667	11,780	282
Briscoe	23,561	5,256	3,910	8,724
Brooks	67,848	17,321	13,050	671
Brown	228,214	101,259	62,353	3,047
Burleson	91,053	43,244	18,532	2,480
Burnet	165,314	106,683	30,704	322
Caldwell	147,274	65,741	34,520	1,415
Calhoun	111,300	44,600	19,249	6,234
Callahan	70,385	36,632	14,974	1,728
Cameron	1,655,349	495,098	345,738	19,974
Camp	79,331	35,463	19,054	552
Carson	46,010	15,175	8,013	6,900
Cass	203,837	96,941	46,994	496
Castro	59,591	13,397	8,910	26,331
Chambers	146,182	34,480	24,117	6,666
Cherokee	223,932	97,926	62,461	892
Childress	47,805	15,977	9,658	5,671
Clay	52,580	25,084	11,375	2,297
Cochran	38,394	7,786	5,361	19,705
Coke	20,805	10,276	4,891	1,012
Coleman	76,684	30,735	22,972	1,412
Collin	1,398,153	563,081	160,146	3,339
Collingsworth	49,684	8,611	6,285	20,908
Colorado	125,945	50,313	27,507	13,001
Comal	374,311	241,088	65,726	4,311
Comanche	99,705	38,416	25,478	14,939
Concho	23,176	8,842	5,183	3,813
Cooke	163,750	82,749	43,854	1,575
Coryell	216,738	126,100	34,077	1,063
Cottle	26,668	5,779	3,508	4,010

COUNTY	TOTAL	For INDIVIDUALS		other direct (ag., etc.)
		retirement	other	
(Thousand dollars 000)				
Crane	14,631	7,328	5,166	44
Crockett	18,037	8,172	3,173	890
Crosby	67,391	14,688	15,256	25,808
Culberson	14,172	4,221	3,709	818
Dallam	49,709	17,568	9,098	18,122
Dallas	11,483,718	3,275,707	1,809,521	27,589
Dawson	124,291	28,390	29,555	32,655
Deaf Smith	108,711	31,471	19,463	31,009
Delta	37,779	14,577	9,165	1,419
Denton	1,154,034	447,638	177,654	3,017
DeWitt	114,523	44,581	30,086	1,331
Dickens	24,473	7,195	8,518	3,514
Dimmit	74,891	17,004	14,279	644
Donley	31,645	11,743	6,999	3,573
Duval	110,213	27,417	25,867	2,070
Eastland	140,011	57,750	37,954	8,399
Ector	500,918	226,094	140,456	387
Edwards	18,727	6,402	7,386	501
Ellis	407,883	206,649	97,127	5,567
El Paso	4,317,608	1,303,389	695,778	14,483
Erath	172,008	74,022	43,173	11,844
Falls	119,328	45,278	25,464	3,675
Fannin	204,984	84,768	41,411	5,644
Fayette	140,131	66,147	34,123	1,566
Fisher	37,853	12,010	7,875	8,042
Floyd	84,326	15,687	11,871	38,731
Foard	16,591	5,468	3,126	2,604
Fort Bend	724,793	369,732	111,130	54,467
Franklin	50,970	23,605	11,658	983
Freestone	90,931	42,996	17,856	157
Frio	94,022	23,867	16,444	19,089
Gaines	137,514	20,944	15,707	85,570
Galveston	1,642,408	522,165	283,481	9,061
Garza	49,834	9,789	9,199	3,137
Gillespie	122,527	79,978	27,261	1,981
Glasscock	18,346	1,891	720	7,743
Goliad	39,781	16,752	9,232	1,375
Gonzales	139,272	50,315	24,190	1,770
Gray	125,551	59,247	42,617	3,272
Grayson	561,352	302,606	140,244	4,025
Gregg	593,902	298,303	151,318	483
Grimes	113,730	47,744	24,072	277
Guadalupe	417,609	265,206	63,651	5,502
Hale	241,614	68,398	51,191	54,768
Hall	40,234	10,717	7,671	11,207
Hamilton	50,272	22,693	16,349	995
Hansford	40,009	11,682	5,759	17,587
Hardeman	40,086	13,722	8,391	2,693
Hardin	219,556	113,319	58,940	878
Harris	18,719,109	4,628,363	2,796,997	63,600
Harrison	317,344	127,361	67,488	226
Hartley	15,495	2,701	959	10,843
Haskell	55,849	18,636	11,620	11,151

COUNTY	TOTAL	For INDIVIDUALS		other direct (ag., etc.)
		retirement	other	
(Thousand dollars 000)				
Hays	413,502	170,764	66,580	1,189
Hemphill	14,235	6,843	4,123	641
Henderson	300,402	155,053	80,781	520
Hidalgo	2,608,320	702,286	567,541	42,846
Hill	205,475	94,013	46,292	6,344
Hockley	146,755	43,130	37,212	27,636
Hood	211,532	146,851	41,744	833
Hopkins	168,097	75,732	40,391	7,073
Houston	160,414	64,169	36,256	1,327
Howard	268,822	86,128	54,303	8,904
Hudspeth	34,406	4,983	2,863	1,996
Hunt	1,000,282	177,654	94,686	2,099
Hutchinson	115,916	57,450	30,281	3,043
Irion	7,747	3,981	1,782	299
Jack	33,642	17,416	9,715	206
Jackson	86,526	30,428	21,231	15,009
Jasper	206,107	86,061	55,819	307
Jeff Davis	13,229	6,172	1,981	101
Jefferson	1,678,136	565,509	413,777	22,485
Jim Hogg	42,226	9,843	9,880	183
Jim Wells	237,802	79,815	60,919	4,303
Johnson	465,160	269,118	110,265	1,875
Jones	101,405	42,065	24,857	10,878
Karnes	99,288	31,931	21,734	2,240
Kaufman	377,970	202,939	99,570	822
Kendall	146,741	95,083	21,090	505
Kenedy	2,192	640	340	2
Kent	12,158	2,935	1,480	1,819
Kerr	316,556	189,213	62,504	183
Kimble	26,998	12,581	5,880	147
King	2,185	423	214	945
Kinney	26,574	12,801	5,399	659
Kleberg	374,051	59,561	43,991	6,894
Knox	36,061	11,481	8,690	5,645
Lamar	301,515	130,899	64,787	5,113
Lamb	127,581	32,866	24,846	45,559
Lampasas	108,444	69,255	23,954	191
La Salle	46,769	10,979	7,524	1,779
Lavaca	142,693	62,164	35,097	1,619
Lee	59,772	31,121	13,640	1,396
Leon	121,027	55,506	25,569	152
Liberty	329,976	147,665	97,649	10,077
Limestone	135,293	58,145	29,097	1,426
Lipscomb	16,923	6,972	3,680	2,460
Live Oak	83,495	20,774	12,982	2,768
Llano	108,528	71,075	25,678	315
Loving	649	279	13	2
Lubbock	1,216,364	468,401	318,237	33,413
Lynn	67,094	13,265	10,175	15,586
Madison	51,985	24,869	12,203	142
Marion	75,394	28,847	13,057	133
Martin	39,074	8,208	5,759	12,647
Mason	29,742	11,971	5,730	5,816
Matagorda	206,981	78,993	39,043	19,163
Maverick	242,217	66,539	53,276	769
McCulloch	58,293	24,113	15,060	2,977
McLennan	1,236,159	523,503	239,970	7,689
McMullen	3,677	1,918	598	208
Medina	169,554	89,860	33,948	3,697
Menard	16,735	7,292	4,432	399
Midland	427,562	213,941	107,715	4,379
Milam	139,510	64,607	26,220	3,814

COUNTY	TOTAL	For INDIVIDUALS		other direct (ag., etc.)
		retirement	other	
(Thousand dollars 000)				
Mills	31,737	15,263	8,879	401
Mitchell	52,725	19,275	12,674	5,846
Montague	114,923	62,875	29,944	820
Montgomery	945,685	530,914	223,442	5,623
Moore	65,923	30,923	13,044	9,513
Morris	87,730	43,617	21,506	866
Motley	14,498	4,660	2,916	4,120
Nacogdoches	315,505	122,309	78,194	9,141
Navarro	250,341	108,829	59,727	3,440
Newton	84,221	31,736	18,039	134
Nolan	95,516	41,035	27,188	4,345
Nueces	2,139,083	683,956	365,451	19,918
Ochiltree	42,927	15,243	7,589	10,132
Oldham	26,818	5,360	2,220	3,752
Orange	444,540	204,121	121,740	6,446
Palo Pinto	151,614	69,074	35,652	500
Panola	122,178	54,541	31,425	187
Parker	323,560	191,432	62,571	1,307
Parmer	71,744	17,290	9,087	36,043
Pecos	59,070	23,000	12,540	2,445
Polk	344,496	223,241	71,579	784
Potter	1,239,934	382,664	152,415	1,571
Presidio	47,720	14,810	7,050	240
Rains	42,133	25,488	8,985	395
Randall	159,763	62,653	52,528	7,921
Reagan	15,850	5,130	2,727	3,783
Real	24,793	11,609	4,556	69
Red River	121,630	41,788	25,046	3,272
Reeves	68,613	23,166	15,098	2,663
Refugio	53,945	20,428	12,910	5,783
Roberts	5,474	1,980	1,034	833
Robertson	111,297	40,848	21,025	3,353
Rockwall	186,961	77,504	22,508	590
Runnels	72,911	30,556	17,137	6,850
Rusk	213,845	94,698	53,734	481
Sabine	93,123	47,878	23,715	119
S. Augustine	66,901	26,954	15,154	164
San Jacinto	118,763	48,170	24,318	37
San Patricio	461,206	141,938	76,962	15,670
San Saba	49,524	15,086	10,777	1,174
Schleicher	16,551	6,828	3,706	1,934
Scurry	92,993	37,844	22,758	5,058
Shackelford	19,746	10,092	4,969	613
Shelby	176,782	65,403	40,229	168
Sherman	25,047	5,606	3,256	14,316
Smith	921,687	431,159	208,569	965
Somervell	26,609	14,248	6,535	514
Starr	238,225	61,313	51,281	6,056
Stephens	49,234	22,690	15,146	404
Sterling	6,588	2,291	1,484	196
Stonewall	13,681	5,113	2,949	3,212
Sutton	17,499	7,385	3,536	1,100
Swisher	66,585	19,044	10,970	25,796
Tarrant	15,523,699	2,408,515	1,102,721	18,247
Taylor	926,273	322,649	135,732	5,184
Terrell	8,213	3,543	1,399	202
Terry	114,072	27,005	20,964	38,404
Throckmorton	13,515	5,432	2,996	2,384
Titus	130,704	54,345	36,964	232
Tom Green	670,673	259,197	104,705	10,943
Travis	7,399,351	1,504,705	482,654	23,672
Trinity	101,611	48,166	26,985	99

COUNTY	TOTAL	For INDIVIDUALS		other direct (ag., etc.)	COUNTY	TOTAL	For INDIVIDUALS		other direct (ag., etc.)
		retirement	other				retirement	other	
		(Thousand dollars 000)					(Thousand dollars 000)		
Tyler	110,086	56,275	31,579	209	Wheeler	39,064	15,465	12,379	4,547
Upshur	184,348	98,941	44,133	959	Wichita	1,185,326	369,850	140,790	4,418
Upton	21,746	7,394	5,044	1,612	Wilbarger	91,875	34,850	27,376	5,523
Uvalde	139,632	50,678	34,305	4,318	Willacy	136,745	29,935	24,190	14,975
Val Verde	385,829	91,507	33,356	1,220	Williamson	1,309,283	392,409	94,967	8,800
Van Zandt	271,633	164,289	64,619	1,623	Wilson	137,229	73,911	22,548	8,214
Victoria	380,999	172,083	91,699	7,115	Winkler	32,675	15,191	11,453	68
Walker	212,687	93,262	51,309	562	Wise	168,901	91,117	32,604	1,641
Waller	149,353	47,088	37,623	5,293	Wood	222,618	125,580	54,103	1,969
Ward	51,903	24,706	13,058	350	Yoakum	57,668	13,704	7,559	25,746
Washington	165,749	74,209	38,118	726	Young	111,884	51,134	28,285	2,343
Webb	896,234	227,973	170,535	2,506	Zapata	56,973	17,590	17,093	263
Wharton	249,941	89,936	56,671	32,508	Zavala	66,974	17,316	15,247	2,167

*Total federal government expenditures include: grants, salaries and wages (Postal Service, Dept. of Defense, etc.), procurement contract awards, direct payments for individuals, and other direct payments other than for individuals, such as some agriculture programs.

Retirement and disability programs include federal employee retirement and disability benefits, Social Security payments of all types, and veterans benefit payments.

Other direct payments for individuals include Medicare, excess earned income tax credits, food stamps, unemployment compensation benefit payments and lower income housing assistance, but not salaries and wages.

Other direct payments other than for individuals include crop insurance, wool and mohair loss assistance program, conservation reserve program, production flexibility payments for contract commodies and postal service funds other than salaries and procurements.

Source: Consolidated Federal Funds Report, Fiscal Year 2003, U.S. Department of Commerce, Bureau of the Census.

U.S. Tax Collections in Texas

(1,000 of dollars)
This information was furnished by the Internal Revenue Service.

*Fiscal Year	Individual Income and Employment Taxes	Corporation Income Taxes	Estate Taxes	Gift Taxes	Excise Taxes	TOTAL U.S. Taxes Collected in Texas
2003	$ 116,353,959	$ 11,487,059	$ 958,791	$ 147,351	$ 12,987,394	$ 141,934,554
2002	117,685,965	13,702,495	1,287,937	109,064	13,654,721	146,440,182
2001	127,738,858	17,598,181	1,242,130	248,892	14,350,268	161,178,329
2000	116,094,820	20,310,672	1,176,278	269,109	14,732,513	152,583,349
1999	104,408,504	13,098,033	968,736	446,168	16,729,589	135,651,029
1998	94,404,751	14,526,238	1,300,104	247,989	11,877,230	122,356,312
1997	90,222,786	13,875,653	933,616	159,111	12,185,271	117,376,440
1996	76,863,689	12,393,992	733,282	158,237	10,418,847	101,079,028
1995	69,706,333	10,677,881	869,528	152,683	11,135,857	92,342,282
1994	63,916,496	9,698,069	624,354	347,900	9,528,449	84,086,676
1993	59,962,756	7,211,968	618,469	111,896	7,552,247	75,457,335
1992	57,367,765	6,338,621	598,918	121,164	7,558,642	71,985,109
1991	55,520,001	8,761,621	588,298	87,739	6,647,312	71,604,791
1990	52,795,489	6,983,762	521,811	196,003	5,694,006	66,191,071
1989	50,855,904	8,675,006	458,106	96,699	5,766,594	66,052,309
1988	45,080,428	6,058,172	444,349	39,137	5,957,085	57,579,171
1987	43,165,241	4,124,164	443,947	27,342	3,908,826	51,669,519
1986	44,090,929	4,808,703	493,405	35,355	4,169,857	53,598,248
1985	41,497,114	5,637,148	528,106	41,560	6,058,110	53,762,038
1984	37,416,203	4,750,079	494,431	19,844	5,553,491	48,234,047
1983	35,856,192	4,496,084	506,680	39,936	5,610,894	46,511,726
1982	36,072,975	6,574,940	624,559	6,789	6,880,102	50,159,365
1981	31,692,219	7,526,687	526,420	31,473	8,623,799	48,400,598
1980	25,707,514	7,232,486	453,830	23,722	4,122,538	37,540,089
1979	22,754,959	5,011,334	397,810	18,267	1,680,118	29,862,488
1978	17,876,628	5,128,609	337,883	19,189	1,757,045	25,119,354
1977	16,318,652	4,135,046	422,984	182,623	1,324,989	22,384,294
1976	11,908,546	2,736,374	350,326	48,804	1,320,496	16,364,546
1975	11,512,883	2,882,776	269,185	44,425	1,338,713	16,047,982

*Fiscal Year	Individual Income and Employment Taxes	Corporation Income Taxes	Estate Taxes	Gift Taxes	Excise Taxes	TOTAL U.S. Taxes Collected in Texas
1974	9,884,442	1,989,710	259,306	43,109	1,338,656	13,515,223
1973	8,353,841	1,614,204	240,470	53,329	1,511,754	11,773,598
1972	7,125,930	1,485,559	288,674	24,792	1,478,340	10,403,295
1971	6,277,877	1,229,479	179,694	31,817	1,056,540	8,775,407
1970	6,096,961	1,184,342	135,694	20,667	843,724	8,281,389
1969	5,444,372	1,180,047	158,028	23,024	810,061	7,615,532
1968	4,721,316	935,302	138,102	24,878	821,576	6,707,952
1967	3,616,869	1,133,126	124,052	20,764	691,156	5,651,336
1966	3,063,000	847,000	130,000	17,000	717,000	4,774,000
1965	2,705,318	786,916	115,733	15,771	710,940	4,334,678
1964	2,745,342	716,288	93,497	14,773	670,309	4,240,209
1963	2,582,821	654,888	83,013	12,840	638,525	3,972,087
1962	2,361,614	675,035	101,263	13,095	444,279	3,595,287
1961	2,131,707	622,076	80,001	9,550	266,714	3,110,047
1960	2,059,075	622,822	70,578	10,583	209,653	2,972,712
1959	1,868,515	545,334	63,138	7,205	198,285	2,682,478
1958	1,786,686	625,267	68,379	10,672	206,307	2,697,309
1957	1,696,288	615,527	55,592	7,918	192,413	2,567,739

Beginning in 1976, the fiscal year ending date was changed to Sept. 30, from June 30.

Major Military Installations

Below are listed the major military installations in Texas in 2005. Data are taken from the U.S. Department of Defense and other sources. "Civilian" refers to Department of Defense personnel, "other" refers to employees such as contractor personnel.

U.S. ARMY

Fort Bliss

Location: Northeast El Paso (est. 1849).
Address: Fort Bliss, Texas 79916
Main phone number: (915) 568-2121
Personnel: 10,587 active-duty plus trainees; 2,202 civilians; 2,816 other.
Major units: Army Air Defense Artillery School; 32nd Air and Missile Defense Command; 6th, 11th, 31st, 35th and 108th Air Defense Artillery Brigades; 204th Military Intelligence Battalion, 76th Military Police Battalion; Biggs Army Airfield (est. 1916, originally called Bliss Field).

Fort Hood

Location: In Killeen (est. 1942).
Address: Fort Hood, Texas 76544
Main phone number: (254) 287-2131
Personnel: 37,269 active-duty; 3,327 civilians; 3,537 other.
Major units: 1st Cavalry Div.; 4th Infantry Div.; Headquarters Command III Corps; NCO Academy; 13th Corps Support Group; 13th Finance Group; 3rd Personnel Group; 3rd Signal Brigade; 89th Military Police Brigade; 504th Military Intelligence Brigade; 21st Cavalry Brigade (Air Combat); Dental Activity and Medical Support Activity; Army Operational Test Command.

Fort Sam Houston

Location: In San Antonio (est. 1878).
Address: Fort Sam Houston, Texas 78234
Main phone number: (210) 221-1211
Personnel: 9,946 active-duty; 3,784 civilians; 2,504 other.
Major units: Fifth U.S. Army; U.S. Army South; Brooke Army Medical Center; Institute of Surgical Research; Army Medical Command; Army Medical Dept. Center and School; 5th Recruiting Brigade; 12th Brigade, Western Region (ROTC); Camp Bullis (est. 1917), training area.

Red River Army Depot

Location: 18 miles west of Texarkana (est. 1941).
Address: Red River Army Depot, Texarkana 75507
Main phone number: (903) 334-2141
Personnel: 54 active-duty; 1,713 civilians; 942 other.
Major unit: Defense Distribution Center; U.S. Army Tank-automotive and Armaments Command.

U.S. AIR FORCE

Brooks City-Base

Location: In San Antonio (est. 1917).
Address: Brooks City-Base, San Antonio 78235
Main phone number: (210) 536-1110
Personnel: 1,218 active-duty; 1,176 civilians.
Major units: 311th Human Systems Wing, 311th Mission Support Group; School of Aerospace Medicine; Air Force Institute for Occupational Health; 68th Information Operations Squadron; 710th Intelligence Flight.

Dyess AFB

Location: On west side of Abilene (est. 1942 as Tye Army Airfield, closed at end of World War II, re-established in 1956).
Address: Dyess AFB, Texas 79607
Main phone number: (915) 696-0212
Personnel: 5,546 active-duty; 347 civilians.
Major units: 7th Bomb Wing (Air Combat Command); 317th Airlift Group.

Army troops at Fort Hood meet near their barracks. File photo.

Goodfellow AFB

Location: On south side of San Angelo (est. 1940).

Address: Goodfellow AFB, San Angelo 76908

Main phone number: (915) 654-3231

Personnel: 1,553 active-duty, approximately 1,200 trainees; 536 civilians.

Major units: 17th Training Wing; 344th Military Intelligence Battalion.

Lackland AFB

Location: Eight miles southwest of San Antonio (est. 1942 when separated from Kelly Field).

Address: Lackland AFB, Texas 78236

Main phone number: (210) 671-1110

Personnel: 14,125 active-duty; 4,251 civilians.

Major units: 37th Training Wing; Defense Language Institute English Language Center, Inter-American Air Forces Academy; Kelly Field Annex (was Kelly AFB, est. 1916, closed 2001).

Laughlin AFB

Location: Six miles east of Del Rio (est. 1942).

Address: Laughlin AFB, Texas 78843

Main phone number: (830) 298-3511

Personnel: 1,024 active-duty; 899 civilians.

Major units: 47th Flying Training Wing.

Randolph AFB

Location: In San Antonio (est. 1930).

Address: Randolph AFB, Texas 78150

Main phone number: (210) 652-1110

Personnel: 4,100 active-duty; 4,713 civilians.

Major units: 12th Flying Training Wing; Air Education and Training Command; Air Force Military Personnel Center; Air Force Recruiting Service; Air Force Management Engineering Agency; USAF Instrument Flight Center.

Sheppard AFB

Location: Four miles north of Wichita Falls (est. 1941).

Address: Sheppard AFB, Texas 76311

Main phone number: (940) 676-2511

Personnel: 3,529 active-duty; 1,361 civilians.

Major units: 82nd Training Wing; 80th Flying Training Wing.

U.S. NAVY

Naval Air Station Corpus Christi

Location: 10 miles southeast of Corpus Christi in the Flour Bluff area (est. 1941).

Address: NAS Corpus Christi, 11001 D St., Corpus Christi 78419

Main phone number: (361) 961-2811

Personnel: 1,930 active-duty; 492 civilians.

Major units: Headquarters, Naval Air Training Command; Training Air Wing Four; Commander of Mine Warfare Command; Coast Guard Air Group; Corpus Christi Army Depot (est. 1961).

Naval Air Station-Joint Reserve Base
(Carswell Field)
Location: westside Fort Worth (est. 1994) [Carswell, est. 1942 as Fort Worth Army Air Field, closed 1993].

Address: NAS-JRB, 1215 Depot Ave., Fort Worth 76127

Main phone number: (817) 782-5000

Personnel: 3,969 active-duty; 234 civilians.

Major units: Fighter Squadron 201, Marine Air Group 41; 14th Marines; Fleet Support Squadron 59; Army Reserve; Coast Guard Reserve; and Texas Air Guard; 301st Fighter Wing; 607th Military Police Battal.

Naval Station Ingleside
Location: In Ingleside (est. 1990).

Address: 1455 Ticonderoga Rd., #W123, Ingleside 78362

Main phone number: (361) 776-4200

Personnel: 2,388 active-duty; 173 civilians.

Major units: Mine Warfare Force; 14 mine countermeasure-class vessels; 10 hunter-class vessels; Mine Countermeasures Command.

Naval Air Station Kingsville
Location: In Kingsville (est. 1942).

Address: NAS Kingsville, Texas 78363

Main phone number: (361) 516-6136

Personnel: 437 active-duty; 183 civilians.

Major units: Training Air Wing II; Naval Auxiliary Landing Field Orange Grove, and McMullen Target Range, Escondido Ranch.

TEXAS MILITARY FORCES
Camp Mabry
Location: 2210 W. 35th St. in Austin. Just west of MoPac Blvd.

Address: Box 5218, Austin, Texas 78763

Main phone number: (512) 465-5101

Website: www.agd.state.tx.us

Personnel: Various offices employ 800.

Adjutant General of Texas: Maj. General Charles G. Rodriguez.

Major units: 36th Infantry Division, Headquarters; 71th Troop Command; Texas National Guard Academy; the U.S. Property and Fiscal Office; the Texas National Guard Armory Board. **Texas Military Forces Museum,** open Wednesday-Sunday, 10 a.m. - 4 p.m.

Tracing their history to early frontier days, the Texas Military Forces are organized into the Army and Air National Guard, the Texas State Guard and the Adjutant General's Department.

When not in active federal service, Camp Mabry, in northwest Austin, is the main storage maintenance and administrative headquarters.

Camp Mabry was established in the early 1890s as a summer encampment of the Texas Volunteer Guard, a forerunner of the Texas National Guard. The name, Camp Mabry, honors Woodford Haywood Mabry, adjutant general of Texas from 1891-98.

The Texas State Guard, an all-volunteer backup force, was originally created by the Texas Legislature in 1941. It became an active element of the state military forces in 1965 with a mission of reinforcing the National Guard in state emergencies, and of replacing National Guard units called into federal service. The Texas State Guard, which has a membership of approximately 1,450 personnel, also participates in local emergencies.

When the forces were reorganized following World War II, the Texas Air National Guard was added. Texas Air National Guard units serve as augmentation units to major Air Force commands, including the Air Defense Command, the tactical Air Command and the Strategic Air Command. Approximately 3,100 men and women made up the Air Guard in 2004.

The Army National Guard is available for either national or state emergencies and has been used extensively during hurricanes, tornadoes and floods. There are more than 180 units in Texas, with a total Army Guard membership of 16,500 in 2004, with some 5,000 serving on active duty, mostly in Iraq.

The governor of Texas is commander-in-chief of the Texas National and State Guards. This command function is exercised through the adjutant general appointed by the governor and approved by both federal and state legislative authority.

The adjutant general is the active administrative head of the Texas National Guard, and head of the Adjutant General's Department, a state agency, working in conjunction with the National Guard Bureau, a federal agency.

When called into active federal service, National Guard units come within the chain of command of the Army and Air Force units. ☆

Medal of Honor

Texas-born Sgt. 1st Class Paul Ray Smith became the Iraq war's first recipient of the Medal of Honor, which was awarded posthumously in April 2005.

Smith was accorded the nation's highest recognition for valor for protecting his comrades before he was killed in the battle for Baghdad in April 2003.

Smith was born in El Paso in 1969, but moved with his family to Florida when he was nine.

He enlisted in the Army in 1989 and had served in the Persian Gulf War, Bosnia-Herzegovina and Kosovo, as well as Iraq.

President Bush delivered the medal to Smith's widow and two children at the White House. ☆

Sgt. Paul Smith. U.S. Army photo.

State Cultural Agencies Assist the Arts

Source: Principally, the Texas Commission on the Arts, along with other state cultural agencies.

Culture in Texas, as in any market, is a mixture of activity generated by both the commercial and the non-profit sectors.

The commercial sector encompasses Texas-based profit-making businesses including commercial recording artists, nightclubs, record companies, private galleries, assorted boutiques that carry fine art collectibles and private dance and music halls.

Texas also has extensive cultural resources offered by nonprofit organizations that are engaged in charitable, educational and/or humanitarian activities.

The Texas Legislature has authorized five state agencies to administer cultural services and funds for the public good. The agencies are:

Texas Commission on the Arts, Box 13406, Austin (78711); **Texas Film Commission**, Box 13246, Austin (78711); **Texas Historical Commission**, Box 12276, Austin (78711); **Texas State Library and Archives Commission**, Box 12927, Austin (78711); and the **State Preservation Board**, Box 13286, Austin (78711).

Although not a state agency, another organization that provides cultural services to the citizens of Texas is **Humanities Texas** (formerly the Texas Council for the Humanities), 3809A South 2nd, Austin 78704.

The **Texas Commission on the Arts** was established in 1965 to develop a receptive climate for the arts through the conservation and advancement of Texas' rich and diverse arts and cultural industries.

The Texas Commission on the Arts' three primary goals are: 1) provide grants for the arts and cultural industries in Texas; 2) promote widespread attendance at arts and cultural performances and exhibitions in Texas and 3) secure necessary resources from public and private sector sources.

The arts commission is responsible for several initiatives, including:
• Arts education – It implements programs that serve the curricular and training needs of the state's school districts, private schools and home schools.
• Technology – It operates a full service network for the arts on the Internet providing a one-stop location for the arts and cultural industry of Texas to conduct business electronically.
• Marketing and public relations – It utilizes marketing and fundraising expertise to generate funds for agency operations and increase visibility of the arts in Texas.
• Texas Cultural Endowment Fund – It seeks continued legislative and private sector support for the fund.
• "State of the Arts" specialty license plate - It markets the specialty license plate program in an effort to earn the dollars necessary to conduct business.
• Texas Music Project - It works closely with the project and all other project partners to market the "Don't Mess with Texas Music" CD series and secure funding for music education programs.
• Cultural tourism – The commission is a partner in the development and promotion of Texas as a tourism destination.

Additional information on programs and services is available on the Texas Commission on the Arts' Website at www.arts.state.tx.us or by calling (800) 252-9415 or (512) 463-5535. ☆

Texas Performing Arts Organizations

Below are links, listed by city, to Web pages of Texas performing arts organizations — theatre, dance and music.

Abilene
Paramount Theatre
www.paramount-abilene.org/
Addison
Water Tower Theatre
www.watertowertheatre.org/
Alamo Heights
Texas Photographic Society
www.texasphoto.org/
Amarillo
Amarillo Symphony
www.amarillosymphony.org/
Lone Star Ballet
www.lonestarballet.org
Arlington
Theatre Arlington
www.theatrearlington.org/
Austin
Austin Shakespeare Festival
www.austinshakespeare.org/
Austin Symphony
www.austinsymphony.org/
Ballet Austin
www.balletaustin.org/
Gilbert & Sullivan Society of Austin

The Dallas Symphony Orchestra at Meyerson Center in Dallas. File photo.

www.gilbertsullivan.org
Austin Theatre Alliance (Paramount Theatre and State Theatre)
www.austintheatrealliance.org
Sharir+Bustamante Danceworks
www.sbdanceworks.org/company.html
Zachary Scott Theatre
www.zachscott.com/

Canyon
Texas Legacies, Musical Drama
www.epictexas.com/

Carrollton
Texas Chamber Orchestra
wwoww.com/csm/

College Station/Bryan
Arts Council of Brazos Valley
www.acbv.org/index2.html
Brazos Valley Chorale
www.bvchorale.org/

Conroe
Crighton Players
www.crightonplayers.org/main.htm

Corpus Christi
Corpus Christi Ballet
www.corpuschristiballet.com/flash.html
Harbor Playhouse
www.harborplayhouse.com/

Dallas
Dallas Opera
www.dallasopera.org/
Dallas Puppet Theater
www.puppetry.org/
Dallas Summer Musicals
www.dallassummermusicals.org/
Dallas Symphony
www.dallassymphony.com/
Dallas Theater Center
www.dallastheatercenter.org/
Dallas Wind Symphony
www.dws.org/
Junior Players
www.juniorplayers.org/
Pegasus Theatre
www.pegasustheatre.org/
Pocket Sandwich Theatre
www.dallas.net/~pst/
Shakespeare Festival of Dallas
www.shakespearedallas.org/
Teatro Dallas
web2.airmail.net/teatro/
Theatre Three
www.theatre3dallas.com
TITAS (Texas International Theatrical Arts Society)
www.titas.org/
Turtle Creek Chorale
www.turtlecreek.org/
Undermain Theatre
www.undermain.com/aboutus.html

Del Rio
The Upstagers
www.upstagers.org

Denton
Campus Theatre
campustheatre.com/

El Paso
El Paso Playhouse
www.elpasoplayhouse.org/
El Paso Symphony Orchestra

www.epso.org

Fort Worth
Allied Theatre Group (Stage West and Fort Worth Shakespeare Festival)
www.alliedtheatre.org
Casa Manana
www.casamanana.org/
Circle Theatre
www.circletheatre.com/
Contemporary Dance/Fort Worth
www.cdfw.org/
Fort Worth Classic Guitar Society
www.guitarsociety.org/
Fort Worth Symphony
www.fwsymphony.org
Texas Ballet Theater
www.texasballettheater.org

Fredericksburg
Fredericksburg Theater Company
www.fredericksburgtheater.org/

Frisco
Frisco Community Theatre
www.FriscoCommunityTheatre.com

Galveston
Galveston Symphony Orchestra
www.galvestonsymphony.org

Granbury
Granbury Opera House
www.granburyoperahouse.org

Grand Prairie
Grand Prairie Arts Council
www.artsgp.com/

Houston
Alley Theatre
www.alleytheatre.com/
Clear Lake Symphony
www.clearlakesymphony.org/
Gilbert and Sullivan Society of Houston
www.gilbertandsullivan.net/
Houston Ballet
www.houstonballet.org/
Houston Grand Opera
www.houstongrandopera.com/
Houston Symphony
www.houstonsymphony.org/
Masquerade Theatre
masqueradetheatre.com/
Stages Repertory Theatre
www.stagestheatre.com/
Stages Theatre Company (children's)
www.stagestheatre.org/
Theatre Under the Stars
www.TUTS.com/

Ingram
Point Theater (Hill Country Arts Foundation)
www.hcaf.com/

Irving
Irving Community Theater
www.irvingtheatre.org/
New Philharmonic Orchestra of Irving
home.earthlink.net/~youngj1/npoi.htm

Kilgore
Texas Shakespeare Festival
www.texasshakespeare.com/

Killeen
Vive les Arts

www.vlatheatre.com/vlahome.html

Lockhart
Baker Theater
www.lockhart.net/lockhartcommunitytheater/

Lubbock
Lubbock Arts Alliance
www.lubbockarts.org/

Mesquite
Mesquite Symphony Orchestra
members.aol.com/TchrfromOz/mso.html

Midland
Midland-Odessa Symphony & Chorale
www.mosc.org

Odessa
Globe of the Great Southwest
www.GlobeSW.org/

Orange
Lutcher Theatre for the Performing Arts
www.lutcher.org/

Pasadena
Pasadena Little Theatre
web.wt.net/~plth/

Round Rock
Sam Bass Community Theatre
www.SamBassTheatre.com

Round Top
Festival-Institute at Round Top (James Dick Foundation)
festivalhill.org/

San Antonio
Arts San Antonio
www.ArtsSanAntonio.com
Carver Cultural Center
www.thecarver.org
Guadalupe Cultural Arts Center
www.guadalupeculturalarts.org/
Majestic Theatre
www.themajestic.com/theatre.htm
San Antonio Symphony
www.sasymphony.org/
San Pedro Playhouse
members.tripod.com/~San_Pedro_Playhouse/index.html
Southwest School of Art & Craft
www.swschool.org

Stephenville
Cross Timbers Fine Arts Council
www.our-town.com/ctfac/

Texarkana
Perot Theatre
www.trahc.org/SERIES.aspx

The Woodlands
The Woodlands Symphony Orchestra
www.woodlands-symphony.org/

Tyler
East Texas Symphony Orchestra
www.etso.org/
Tyler Civic Ballet
www.tylercivicballet.com

Victoria
Victoria Ballet Theatre
www.victoriaballet.org/

Texas
Texas Nonprofit Theatres
geocities.com/texastheatres/ ☆

Texas Museums of Art, Science, History

Listed below, by city, are links to the Web pages of Texas museums of art and history. Where required some have indication of the area of emphasis of the exhibits.

An exhibit at the African American Museum at Fair Park in Dallas. File photo.

Abilene
Grace Museum (Art, History)
www.thegracemuseum.org
National Center for Children's
Illustrated Literature
www.nccil.org

Addison
Cavanaugh Flight Museum
www.cavanaughflightmuseum.com/

Albany
Old Jail Art Center
www.oldjailartcenter.org

Alpine
Museum of the Big Bend (History)
www.sulross.edu/~museum/

Amarillo
American Quarter Horse Heritage
Center & Museum
www.aqha.com/foundation/
museum/
Don Harrington Discovery Center
(Science, Children's)
www.dhdc.org/

Angleton
Brazoria County Historical Museum
www.bchm.org/

Arlington
Legends of the Game Baseball
Museum
www.rangers.mlb.com/NASApp/
mlb/tex/ballpark/
tex_ballpark_museum.jsp

Austin
Austin Children's Museum
www.austinkids.org/
Austin Museum of Art
www.amoa.org/
Bob Bullock Texas State History
Museum
www.thestoryoftexas.com/
index.shtm
Capitol Visitors Center (Historical)
www.tspb.state.tx.us/CVC/home/
home.html
Elisabet Ney Museum (Art)
www.ci.austin.tx.us/elisabetney/
French Legation Museum (History)
www.frenchlegationmuseum.org/
Harry Ransom Humanities Research
Center (History, Literature)
www.hrc.utexas.edu/
Jack S. Blanton Museum of Art
www.blantonmuseum.org/
Jourdan-Bachman Pioneer Farm
www.heritagesocietyaustin.org/
pioneerfarm.html
Lady Bird Johnson Wildflower Center
www.wildflower.org/
Lyndon B. Johnson Library
www.lbjlib.utexas.edu/

Mexic-Arte Museum (Art)
www.mexic-artemuseum.org/
O. Henry Museum (History)
www.ci.austin.tx.us/parks/
ohenry.htm
Texas Memorial Museum (History,
Natural History)
www.tmm.utexas.edu/
Texas Music Museum
www.texasmusicmuseum.org
Umlauf Sculpture Garden & Museum
www.umlaufsculpture.org
Wild Basin Wilderness Preserve
www.wildbasin.org/

Beaumont
Art Museum of Southeast Texas
www.amset.org/
Edison Museum (Science)
www.edisonmuseum.org/
McFaddin-Ward House (History)
www.mcfaddin-ward.org/
Spindletop/Gladys City Boomtown
Museum (History)
www.spindletop.org/
Texas Energy Museum (History)
www.texasenergymuseum.org

Big Spring
Heritage of Big Spring
www.bigspringmuseum.com/

Bonham
Sam Rayburn Library/Museum
www.cah.utexas.edu/divisions/
Rayburn.html

Brownwood
Brown County Museum of History
www.browncountyhistory.org/
bcmoh.html

Bryan
Brazos Valley Museum of Natural
History
bvmuseum.myriad.net/

Buffalo Gap
Buffalo Gap Historic Village
www.mcwhiney.org/buffgap/
bghome.html

Burton
Burton Cotton Gin and Museum
(Historical)
www.cottonginmuseum.org/

Canyon
Panhandle-Plains Historical Museum
www.panhandleplains.org

Carthage
Texas Country Music Hall of Fame
& Tex Ritter Museum
www.carthagetexas.com/tcmhof/
index.htm

Clarendon
Saints' Roost Museum (Historical)
www.saintsroose.org

College Station
George Bush Presidential Library
bushlibrary.tamu.edu/
J. Wayne Stark University Center
Galleries
stark.tamu.edu/
Virtual Museum of Nautical
Archaeology
ina.tamu.edu/vm.htm

Conroe
Heritage Museum of Montgomery
County
www.heritagemuseum.us/

Corpus Christi
Art Museum of South Texas
www.stia.org/
Asian Cultures Museum
www.geocities.com/asiancm/
Corpus Christi Museum of Science
and History
cctexas.com/?fuseaction
=main.view&page=200
U.S.S. Lexington Museum
www.usslexington.com/

Cotulla
Brush Country Historical Museum
historicdistrict.com/museum/

Dalhart
XIT Museum (Historical)
www.xitmuseum.com/

Dallas
African American Museum
www.aamdallas.org
Age of Steam Railroad Museum
www.dallasrailwaymuseum.com
American Museum of Miniature Arts
(Doll Houses)
minimuseum.org/
Biblical Arts Center

www.biblicalarts.org/
Dallas Historical Society (Fair Park)
www.dallashistory.org/
Dallas Museum of Art
www.dm-art.org/
Dallas Museum of Natural History
www.dallasdino.org/
Frontiers of Flight Museum
flightmuseum.com/
International Museum of Cultures
www.internationalmuseumof
cultures.org/
Meadows Museum (Art)
www.meadowsmuseum
dallas.org/index_main.htm
Old City Park(History)
www.oldcitypark.org/
The Science Place
www.scienceplace.org/
The Sixth Floor Museum (History)
www.jfk.org/

Del Rio
Whitehead Memorial Museum
(History)
whitehead-museum.com

Denison
Red River Railroad Museum
www.denisontx.com/railroad/
museum.htm

Denton
Courthouse-on-the-Square Museum
(Historical)
www.co.denton.tx.us/dept/
hcm.htm
University of North Texas
Art Galleries
www.art.unt.edu/gallery/
Denton County Historical Museum
www.dentoncountyhistorical
museum.com

Edgewood
Edgewood Heritage Park and
Historical Village
www.vzinet.com/heritage/

Edinburg
Museum of South Texas History
www.mosthistory.org/

El Campo
El Campo Museum of
Natural History
www.elcampomuseum.com/

El Paso
El Paso Museum of Art
www.elpasoartmuseum.org/

Emory
A.C. McMillan African American
Museum
geocities.com/acmmuseum/

Fort Davis
Chihuahuan Desert Research
Institute and Visitor Center
www.cdri.org/

Fort Worth
Amon Carter Museum (Art)
www.cartermuseum.org/
Cattle Raisers Museum
www.cattleraisersmuseum.org/
Fort Worth Museum of Science
and History
www.fwmuseum.org/
Kimbell Art Museum
www.kimbellart.org/
Log Cabin Village

www.logcabinvillage.org
Modern Art Museum of Fort Worth
www.mamfw.org/
National Cowgirl Museum
and Hall of Fame
www.cowgirl.net/
Sid Richardson Collection
of Western Art
www.sidrmuseum.org/

Fredericksburg
Gillespie County Historical Society
www.pioneermuseum.com/
National Museum of the Pacific War
www.nimitz-museum.org/

Galveston
Lone Star Flight Museum
www.lsfm.org
Texas Seaport Museum and Tallship
"Elissa"
www.tsm-elissa.org/

Gilmer
Flight of the Phoenix Aviation
Museum
www.flightofthephoenix.org/

Greenville
American Cotton Museum
www.cottonmuseum.com/

Henderson
The Depot Museum (Historical)
www.depotmuseum.com/

Houston
Blaffer Gallery, University of Houston
www.hfac.uh.edu/blaffer/
Children's Museum of Houston
www.cmhouston.org/
Contemporary Arts Museum
www.camh.org/
Houston Center for Photography
www.hcponline.org/
Houston Fire Museum (History)
www.houstonfiremuseum.org/
Houston Museum of Natural Science
www.hmns.org/
Lawndale Art Center
www.lawndaleartcenter.org/
The Menil Collection (Art)
www.menil.org/
Museum of Fine Arts
mfah.org/
Museum of Health and
Medical Science
www.mhms.org/
Museum of Printing History
www.printingmuseum.org/
Offshore Energy Center/Ocean Star
(Science, Industry)
www.oceanstaroec.com/
Rice University Art Gallery
www.ricegallery.org/
San Jacinto Museum of History
http://www.sanjacinto
-museum.org/
Sarah Campbell Blaffer Foundation
(Art)
www.rice.edu/projects/Blaffer/
Space Center Houston
www.spacecenter.org/

Huntsville
Sam Houston Memorial Museum
www.shsu.edu/~smm_www/

Kerrville
Museum of Western Art
www.caamuseum.com/

Kilgore
East Texas Oil Museum
www.easttexasoilmuseum.com/

Lake Jackson
Lake Jackson Historical Museum
www.lakejacksonmuseum.org/

La Porte
San Jacinto Monument and Museum
www.sanjacinto-museum.org/

Laredo
Laredo Center for the Arts
www.laredoartcenter.org/

League City
West Bay Common School
Children's Museum (Historical)
www.oneroomschoolhouse.org/

Longview
Longview Museum of Fine Arts
www.lmfa.org/

Lubbock
Buddy Holly Center (Historical)
www.buddyhollycenter.org/
Museum of Texas Tech University
(Art, Humanities, Science)
www.depts.ttu.edu/museumttu/
National Ranching Heritage Center
www.depts.ttu.edu/ranchhc/
home.htm
Science Spectrum
www.sciencespectrum.com/

Lufkin
Texas Forestry Museum
www.texasforestry.org/

Marfa
The Chinati Foundation (Art)
www.chinati.org/

Marshall
Harrison County Historical Museum
txgenes.com/TXHarrison/
NewHome.htm
Michelson Museum of Art
www.michelsonmuseum.org/

McAllen
McAllen International Museum
(Art, Science)
www.mcallenmuseum.org

McKinney
Heard Natural Science Museum
www.heardmuseum.org/

Midland
American Airpower Heritage
Museum and Commerative
Air Force
www.airpowermuseum.org/
Museum of the Southwest
(Art, Science, Children's)
www.museumsw.org/
Petroleum Museum
www.petroleummuseum.org/

Mobeetie
Old Mobeetie Texas Association
www.mobeetie.com/

New Braunfels
New Braunfels Sophienburg
Museum (History)
www.nbtx.com/sophienburg/

Odessa
Ellen Noel Art Museum
www.noelartmuseum.org/

Orange
Stark Museum of Art
www.starkmuseum.org/

Panhandle
Carson County Square House
Museum
www.squarehousemuseum.org/
Plano
Heritage Farmstead Museum
www.heritagefarmstead.org/
JCPenney Museum
www.jcpenney.net/company/
history/archive2.htm
Port Arthur
Museum of the Gulf Coast
(Historical)
museum.lamarpa.edu/
Port Lavaca
Calhoun County Museum (Historical)
www.calhouncountymuseum.
org/
Richmond
George Ranch Historical Park
www.georgeranch.org/
Rockport
Texas Maritime Museum
www.texasmaritimemuseum.org/
Round Top/Winedale
Henkel Square (History)
www.texaspioneerarts.org/
henkel_square.html
Winedale Historical Center
www.cah.utexas.edu/divisions/
Winedale.html
San Angelo
San Angelo Museum of Fine Arts
and Children's Art Museum
www.samfa.org/
San Antonio
The Alamo
www.thealamo.org/
Hertzberg Circus Collection/Museum
www.sat.lib.tx.us/Hertzberg/
hzmain.html
Institute of Texan Cultures
www.texancultures.utsa.edu/
public/index.htm
Magic Lantern Castle
Museum (History)
www.magiclanterns.org/
McNay Art Museum
www.mcnayart.org/
San Antonio Art League Museum
www.saalm.org/
San Antonio Museum of Art
www.sa-museum.org/
Witte Museum (Science, Historical)
www.wittemuseum.org/
Wooden Nickel Historical Museum
www.wooden-nickel.net/
San Marcos
Southwestern Writers Collection and
Wittliff Gallery of Southwestern
& Mexican Photography
www.library.txstate.edu/swwc/
Sarita
Kenedy Ranch Museum of
South Texas
www.kenedymuseum.org/
Sherman
Red River Historical Museum
hosting.texoma.net/rrhms/
Sulphur Springs
Southwest Dairy Center/Museum
www.southwestdairyfarmers.
com/

Teague
The B-RI Railroad Museum
www.therailroadmuseum.com/
Temple
Railroad and Heritage Museum
www.rrdepot.org/
railroadmuseum.htm
Texarkana
Museum of Regional History
www.texarkanamuseums.org/
texarkana_historical_museum.
htm
The Woodlands
Woodlands Science and Art Center
www.woodsac.org/
Tyler
Discovery Science Place
www.discoveryscienceplace.
com/
Smith County Historical Museum
www.smithcountyhistory.org/
Museum.htm
Tyler Museum of Art
www.tylermuseum.org
Vernon
Red River Valley Museum
(History, Art)
www.rrvm.org/

Victoria
Museum of the Coastal Bend
(Historical)
www.museumofthecoastalbend.
org/
Waco
Dr Pepper Museum (Historical)
www.drpeppermuseum.com/
Mayborn Museum Complex
(including Strecker Museum)
(History, Science)
www.baylor.edu/mayborn/
Texas Ranger Hall of Fame/ Museum
www.texasranger.org/
Texas Sports Hall of Fame
www.tshof.org/
Washington
Star of the Republic Museum
(Historical)
www.starmuseum.org/
White Settlement
White Settlement Historical Museum
www.wsmuseum.com/
Wichita Falls
Kell House Museum (History)
www.wichitaheritage.org/
kellhouse.html
Museum of North Texas History
www.wichitamuseum.org/ ☆

A display of an archaeological dig draws interests at the Panhandle-Plains Historical Museum in Canyon. Photo courtesy of the museum.

Film and Television Work in Texas

Source: Texas Film Commission

Film production in Texas is a long-standing and vital part of Texas' economy, bringing thousands of jobs and hundreds of millions of dollars into the state.

Texas is one of the nation's top filmmaking states, after California and New York.

More than 1,000 projects have been made in Texas since 1910, including **Wings**, the first film to win an Academy Award for Best Picture, which was made in San Antonio in 1927.

Texas' attractions to filmmakers are its diverse locations, abundant sunshine and moderate winter weather and a variety of support services experienced at dealing with the special needs of filmmaking.

The economic benefits of hosting on-location filming are clear. Over the past decade, more than $2 billion has been spent in Texas.

Besides salaries paid to locally hired technicians and actors, as well as fees paid to location owners, the production companies do business with hotels, car rental agencies, lumberyards, restaurants, fabric stores, grocery stores, utilities, office furniture suppliers, gas stations, dry cleaners, security services, florists and more.

And it is not just feature films that use Texas. All types of projects come to Texas, such as television specials, commercials, corporate films and videos.

The production crew in Shafter working on the set of The Three Burials of Melquiades Estrada. The movie was shot at various West Texas locations in 2004. Texas Almanac photo.

Many projects made in Texas originate in California studios, but Texas is also the home of many independent filmmakers who make films outside the studio system.

Some films and television shows made in Texas have become icons. **Giant**, John Wayne's **The Alamo**, and the long-running TV series **Dallas** all made their mark on the world's perception of Texas and continue to draw tourists to their film locations.

The Texas Film Commission, a division of the Office of the Governor, markets to Hollywood Texas' locations, support services and workforce. The commission's free services include location research, employment referrals, red-tape cutting, and information on laws, weather, travel and other topics affecting filmmakers.

The online *Texas Production Manual* includes more than 1,200 individuals and businesses serving every facet of the film industry. ☆

Film/TV Projects in Texas

Year	All projects	Feature films	Budgets (in millions)
2004	55	25	$ 214.8
2003	46	19	230.2
2002	59	23	84.8
2001	55	34	203.8
2000	51	35	231.6
1999	33	22	143.7
1998	49	39	206.6
1997	56	24	172.8
1996	58	35	254.7
1995	59	30	$ 290.3

Source: Texas Film Commission

Film Commissions

In addition to the offices below, many other Texas cities have employees who specialize in assisting filmmakers.

The **Texas Film Commission** (www.governor.state.tx.us/film) can provide information on local contacts for most Texas cities and counties:

Amarillo Film Office
1000 S, Polk
Amarillo 79101
(806) 374-1497
jutta@amarillo-cvb.org
visitamarillotx.com

Austin Film Office
301 Congress Ave.
Austin 78701
(800) 926-2282
gbond@austintexas.org
austintexas.org

Brownsville Border Film Commission
P.O. Box 911, City Hall
Brownsville 78520
(956) 548-6176
peter@cob.us
filmbrownsville.com

Dallas Film Commission
325 N. St. Paul Ste. 700
Dallas 75201
(214) 571-1050
info@filmdfw.com
filmdfw.com

El Paso Film Commission
One Civic Center Plaza
El Paso 79901
(800) 351-6024
sgaines@elpasocvb.com
elpasocvb.com

Houston Film Commission
901 Bagby Ste. 100
Houston 77002

(800) 365-7575
rferguson@ghcvb.org
filmhouston.texaswebhost.com

San Antonio Film Commission
203 S. St. Mary's, 2nd Floor
San Antonio 78205
(800) 447-3372
filmsa@filmsanantonio.com
filmsanantonio.com

South Padre Island Film Commission
7355 Padre Blvd
South Padre Island 78597
(800) 657-2373
maryk@sopadre.com
sopadre.com

Texas Panhandle Film Commission
P.O. Box 3293, Amarillo 79116
(806) 679-1116
info@txpanhandlefilm.com
txpanhandlefilm.com

Texas Medal of the Arts Awards

Source: Texas Commission on the Arts

The Third Texas Medals of the Arts were presented to artists and arts patrons in April 2005.

The awards are administered by the Texas Cultural Trust Council.

The council was established to raise money and awareness for the Texas Cultural Trust Fund, which was created by the Legislature in 1993 to support cultural arts in Texas (www.txculturaltrust.org).

The medals, awarded every two years, were first presented in 2001.

A concurrent proclamation by the state Senate and House of Representatives honors the recepients, and the governor presents the awards in Austin.

The **2005** recepients were:

A **Lifetime Acheivement Award** was presented to singer Vikki Carr of El Paso. She has won three Grammy Awards and released 59 best-selling recordings.

Television/theater: Phylicia Rashad of Houston, actress on *The Cosby Show* and winner of a Tony Award for her leading role in *A Raisin in the Sun*.

Music: singer/songwriter Lyle Lovett of Klein.

Dance: Ben Stevenson of Houston and Fort Worth, helped turn Houston Ballet into an internationally acclaimed company.

Literary arts: Naomi Shihab Nye of San Antonio, poet, essayist and writer of novels and short stories for teens.

Visual arts: Jose Cisneros of El Paso, artist and illustrator of Spanish colonial period in Southwest.

Theater: Robert Wilson of Waco, known for experimental theater pieces.

Arts education: Ginger Head-Gearheart of Fort Worth, advocate of arts education in public schools.

Individual arts patron: Joe R. and Teresa Lozano Long of Austin, philanthropists.

Foundation arts patron: Nasher Foundation of Dallas.

2003

A **Lifetime Achievement Award** was presented to writer John Graves of Glen Rose, author of *Goodbye to A River*.

Media-film/television acting: Fess Parker of Fort Worth, star of *Davy Crockett* and *Daniel Boone*.

Music: country singer Charley Pride of Dallas.

Dance: choreographer, singer, director, dancer Tommy Tune of Wichita Falls and Houston.

Theater: Enid Holm of Odessa, actress and former executive director of Texas Non-profit Theatres.

Phylicia Rashad, left, and Vikki Carr, above, were among the Texans honored April 2005. File photos.

Lyle Lovett, right, was honored for his music. File photo.

Literary arts: novelist Sandra Cisneros of San Antonio.

Visual arts: sculptor Glenna Goodacre of Dallas.

Folk arts: Tejano singer Lydia Mendoza of San Antonio.

Architecture: State Capitol Preservation Project of Austin, headed by Dealey Herndon.

Arts education: theater teacher Marca Lee Bircher of Dallas.

Individual arts patron: philanthropist Nancy B. Hamon of Dallas.

Corporate arts patron: Exxon/Mobil based in Irving.

Foundation arts patron: Houston Endownment Inc.

2001

Lifetime Achievement: Van Cliburn of Fort Worth, cited as "acclaimed concert pianist and mentor."

Film: actor Tommy Lee Jones of San Saba.

Music: singer-songwriter Willie Nelson of Austin.

Dance: Debbie Allen of Houston, choreographer, director, actress and composer.

Theater: *Texas* musical-drama producer Neil Hess of Amarillo.

Literary arts: playwright Horton Foote of Wharton.

Visual arts: muralist John Biggers of Houston.

Folk arts: musician brothers Santiago Jimenez Jr. and Flaco Jimenez of San Antonio.

Architecture: restoration architect Wayne Bell of Austin.

Arts education: theater arts director Gilberto Zepeda Jr. of Pharr.

Individual arts patron: philanthropist Jack Blanton of Houston.

Corporate arts patron: SBC Communications Inc. of San Antonio.

Foundation arts patron: Meadows Foundation of Dallas. ☆

Texas Institute of Letters Awards

Each year since 1939, the **Texas Institute of Letters** (www.wtamu.edu/til/) has honored outstanding literature and journalism that is either by Texans or about Texas subjects. Awards have been made for fiction, nonfiction, Southwest history, general information, magazine and newspaper journalism, children's books, translation, poetry and book design. The awards of recent years are listed below:

Writer/Designer: Title

2004

Steven Mintz: *Huck's Raft*
Laurie Lynn Drummond: *Anything You Say Can and Will Be Held Against You*
Bret Anthony Johnston: *Corpus Christi*
William Wenthe: *Not Till We Are Lost*
Andres Resendez: *Changing National Identities at the Frontier: Texas and New Mexico, 1800–1850*
Philip Boehm: translator of *Death in Danzig* by Stefan Chwin
Mike Nichols: *Balaam Gimble's Gumption*
Ben Fountain: "Bouki and the Cocaine"
Zanto Peabody: "The Search for Eddie Peabody" in the *Houston Chronicle*
DJ Stout and Julie Savasky: *Maps of the Imagination*
Lawrence Wright: "The Kingdom of Silence" in the *New Yorker*
Diane Stanley: *Jack and the Beanstalk*
Susan Abraham and Denise Gonzales: *Cecilia's Year*
Lon Tinkle Award (for career): T.R. Fehrenbach

2003

Betty Lou Phillips: *Emily Goes Wild*
Brian Yansky: *My Road Trip to the Pretty Girl Capital of the Word*
D.J. Stout and Julie Savasky: *The Texas Cowboy Kitchen*
Steve Barthelme: "Claire"
Dick J. Reavis: articles on homelessness in the *San Antonio Express-News*
Jan Reid: "End of the River" in *Texas Monthly*
John Blair: *The Green Girls*
Jennifer Grotz: *Cusp*
Lynn Hoggard: translator of *Nelida* by Marie D'Agoult
B.H. Fairchild: *Early Occult Memory Systems of the Lower Midwest*
Jack Jackson: *Almonte's Texas*, translated by John Wheat
Don Graham: *Kings of Texas*
Robert Ford: *The Student Conductor*
Joseph Skibell: *The English Disease*
Lon Tinkle Award (for career): Bud Shrake

2002

Kathi Appelt: *Where, Where Is Swamp Bear?*
Carolee Dean: *Comfort*
Juan Rulfo: *Pedro Paramo*
Ben Fountain III: "Near-Extinct Birds of the Central Cordillera"
Mark Lisheron and Bill Bishop: "Cities of Ideas" in the *Austin American-Statesman*
Lawrence Wright: "The Man Behind Bin Laden" in the *New Yorker*
Dan Rifenburgh: *Advent*
Reginald Gibbons: *It's Time*
Kinky Friedman: *Meanwhile Back at the Ranch*
Michael Gagarin: *Antiphon the Athenian: Oratory, Law, and Justice in the Age of the Sophists*
Ray Gonzalez: *The Underground Heart: A Return to a Hidden Landscape*
Lisa Schamess: *Borrowed Light*
Rick Bass: *Hermit's Story*
Lon Tinkle Award: Shelby Hearon

2001

Carmen Bredeson: *Animals that Migrate*
Lori Aurelia Williams: *When Kambia Elaine Flew from Neptune*
Vicki Trego Hill: *Folktales of the Zapatista Revolution*
Tom McNeely: "Tickle Torture"
Mike Tolson, James Kimberly, Steve Brewer, Allan Turner: "A Deadly Distinction" in the *Houston Chronicle*
Larry L. King: "The Book on Willie Morris" in *Texas Monthly*
Ted Genoways: *Bullroarer*
Susan Wood: *Asunder*
Wendy Barker and Saranindranath Tagore: *Final Poems* by Rabindranath Tagore
Marco Perela: *Adventures of a No Name Actor*
Betje Klier: *Pavie in the Borderlands*
Larry McMurtry: *Sacagawea's Nickname: Essays on the American West*
Katherine Tannery: *Carousel of Progress*
Sarah Bird: *The Yokota Officers Club*
Lon Tinkle Award: William H. Goetzmann

2000

Rosa Shand: *The Gravity of Sunlight*
Laura Wilson: *Hutterites of Montana*
Richard V. Francaviglia: *The Cast Iron Forest*
Corey Marks: *Renunciation*
Edward Snow: *The Duino Elegies* by Rainer Maria Rilke
Glen Pourciau: "Deep Wilderness"
Pamela Colloff: "Sins of the Father"
Joe Holley: "The Hill Country: Loving It to Death"
Anne Coyle: *Crookwood*
Molly Ivins and Lou DuBose: *Shrub*
Bradley Hutchinson: *Willard Clark: Printer and Printmaker*
D.J. Stout and Julie Savasky: *John Graves and the Making of Goodbye to a River*
Lon Tinkle Award: Leon Hale

1999

Rick DeMarinis: *New and Selected Stories*
Robert Draper: *Hadrian's Walls*
Ann Rowe Seaman: *Swaggart: The Unauthorized Biography of an American Evangelist*
J.Gilberto Quezada: *Border Boss: Manuel B. Bravo and Zapata County*
Walt McDonald: "Whatever the Wind Delivers"
Jenny Lind Porter: *Verses on Death by Helinand of Froidmont*
Tracy Daugherty: *Comfort Me With Apples*
Steven and Rick Barthelme: "Good Losers"
James Hoggard: "Greetings from Cuba"
Benjamin Alire Saenz: *Grandma Fina and Her Wonderful Umbrellas/La Abuelita Fina y Sus Sombrillas Maravillosas*
Neil Barrett Jr.: *Interstate Dreams*
Margerie Adkins West: *Angels on High: Marton Varo's Limestone Angels on Bass Performance Hall*
Peter Brown: *On the Plains*
Lon Tinkle Award: Walt McDonald

1998

C.W. Smith: *Understanding Women*
Susan Choi: *The Foreign Student*
William C. Davis: *Three Roads to the Alamo: The Lives and Fortunes of David Crockett, James Bowie, and William Barret Travis*
Don Carleton: *A Breed So Rare: The Life of J.R. Parten, Liberal Texas Oil Man, 1896-1992*
B.H. Fairchild: "The Art of the Lathe"
Marian Schwartz: *The Ladies from St. Petersburg: Three Novellas*
James Hoggard: *Poems from Cuba: Alone Against the Sea*
Jane Roberts Wood: "My Mother Had a Maid"
Rick Bass: "Into the Fire"
Patrick Beach: "The Struggle for the Soul of Kreuz Market"
Bryan Woolley: "A Legend Runs Through It"
Pat Mora: *The Big Sky*
Lon Tinkle Award: Robert Flynn

Bud Shrake, 2003 honoree. File photo.

1997

Lisa Sandlin: *A Message to the Nurse of Dreams*
Joseph Skibell: *A Blessing on the Moon*
Tara Holley with Joe Holley: *My Mother's Keeper: A Daughter's Memoir of Growing up in the Shadow of Schizophrenia*
John Miller Morris: *El Llano Estacado*
Bruce Bond: "Radiography"
Debbie Nathan and Willavaldo Delgadillo: *The Moon Will Forever Be a Distant Love*
Clifford Hudder: "Misplacement"
Skip Hollandsworth: "The Curse of Romeo and Juliet"
Michael Leahy: "Oswald: A Brother's Burden"
Jerry Herring: *Charles Schorre*
David Timmons: *The Wild and Vivid Land*
Naomi Shihab Nye: *Habibi*
Lon Tinkle Award: Rolando Hinojosa-Smith

1996

Sandra Scofield: *A Chance to See Egypt*
Nolan Porterfield: *Last Cavalier: The Life and Times of John A Lomax*
Kathleen Cambor: *The Book of Mercy*
Rick Bass: *The Book of Yaak*
Isabel Nathaniel: "The Dominion of Light'"
Daniel Stern: "The Passion According to St. John by J.S. Bach"
Debbie Nathan: "The Death of Jane Roe"
Mike Tolson: "When Hope Dies"
D.J. Stout: *Heaven of Animals*
Thomas Taylor and Barbara Whitehead: *Trading in Santa Fe*
J.A. Benner: *Uncle Comanche*
Lon Tinkle Award: Cormac McCarthy

1995

Paul Scott Malone: *In an Arid Land: Thirteen Stories of Texas*
Mary Karr: *The Liars' Club: A Memoir*
Jewel Mogan: *Beyond Telling*
Ben Huseman: *Wild River, Timeless Canyon*
Paul Christensen: "Water"
Rick Bass: "The Fires Next Time'
Mike Tolson: "Race to the Future"
Dick Gerdes: *The Fourth World* (trans.)
Ellen McKie: *Codex Telleriano-Remensis*
Diane Stevens: *Liza's Blue Moon*
Lon Tinkle Award: William Humphrey

1994

Reginald Gibbons: *Sweetbitter*
Lawrence Wright: *Remembering Satan*
Ron Tyler: *Prints of the West*
Pattiann Rogers: *Firekeeper*
Donley Watt: *Can You Get There From Here?*
William J. Cobb: "White Circles"
Mimi Swartz: "Promised Land"
Dr. Bertie Acker: *Iphigenia* (trans.)
Florence George Graves: "The Other Woman"
W. Thomas Taylor: *The War Between the United States and Mexico*
Barbara Elmore: *Breathing Room*
Lon Tinkle Award: Américo Paredes

1993

Dagoberto Gilb: *The Magic of Blood*
Howard Swindle: *Deliberate Indifference*
William H. Goetzmann: *Sam Chamberlain's Mexican War: The San Jacinto Museum Paintings*
Jack Myers: *Blindsided*
Lee Merrill Byrd: *My Sister Disappears*
Dagoberto Gilb: "Nancy Flores"
Elizabeth Franklin: "The Quest of a Projects Kid"
Denise Gamino: "The Lost Children"
W. Thomas Taylor: *Audubon's Great National Work: The Royal Octavo Edition of The Birds of America*
Dee Stuart: *The Astonishing Armadillo*
Lon Tinkle Award: Horton Foote

1992

Cormac McCarthy: *All the Pretty Horses*
David Weber: *The Spanish Frontier in North America*
Joel Barna: *The See-Through Years: Creation and Destruction in Texas Architecture*
Susan Wood: *Campo Santo*
Christopher Middleton and Letitia Garza-Falcon: *The Andalusian Poems* (trans.)
William Cobb: "The Atmosphere of Venus"
Dudley Althaus: "The New Awakening: Breaking the Chain of Conquest in Latin America"
Dudley Althaus: *Prayers, Death and Angels: A Day in Baidoa*

Sherry Garland: *Song of the Buffalo Boy*
D. J. Stout: *Mojo*
Lon Tinkle Award: Vassar Miller

1991

Sarah Bird: *The Mommy Club*
Max Oelschlaeger: *The Idea of Wilderness*
Robert S. Weddle: *The French Thorn*
Andrew Hudgins: *The Never-Ending*
Lee Merrill Byrd: "Major Six Pockets"
Lawrence Wright: "The Sensual Christian"
Mike Cochran: "Profile of Pinkie Roden"
Charlotte Baker Montgomery: *The Trail North*
W. Thomas Taylor: *Self-Portrait With Birds*
Lon Tinkle Award: Margaret Cousins

1990

Lionel G. Garcia: *Hardscrub*
Virginia Stem Owens: *If You Do Love Old Men*
Nicolas Kanellos: *A History of Hispanic Theatre in the United States: Origins to 1940*
Daryl Jones: *Someone Going Home Late*
Frances M. Lopez-Morillas: *Behind the Curtains* (trans.)
Rick Bass: "The Legend of the Pig-Eye"
Bryan Woolley: "A Family Nightmare"
Scott McCartney: "S & Ls on Main Street"
Zinita Fowler: *The Last Innocent Summer*
Lon Tinkle Award: Marshall Terry

1989

James Magnuson: *Ghost Dancing*
Ernestine Sewell Linck and Joyce Gibson Roach: *Eats: A Folk History of Texas Foods*
Randolph B. Campbell: *An Empire for Slavery: The Peculiar Institution in Texas*
Pattiann Rogers: *Splitting and Binding*
James Hoggard: "The Scapegoat"
Lance Bertelsen: "San Pietro and the 'Art' of War"
Ilo Hiller: *Introducing Birds to Young Naturalists*
George Lennox: *Epitaphs for the Living: Words and Images in the Time of AIDS*
Lon Tinkle Award: John Edward Weems

1988

William Hauptman: *Good Rockin' Tonight*
William Hauptman: "Moon Walking"
Lawrence Wright: *In the New World: Growing Up with America, 1960-1984*
Emily Fourmy Cutrer: *The Art of the Woman: The Life and Work of Elisabet Ney*
William Olsen: *The Hand of God and a Few Bright Flowers*
Evan Moore: "Cult of Terror"
Ronnie Dugger: "Voting by Computer"
David Price: *The Song of Things Begun*
Lon Tinkle Award: C. L. Sonnichsen

1987

Beverly Lowry: *The Perfect Sonya*
Kenneth B. Ragsdale: *The Year America Discovered Texas: Centennial '36*
David Montejano: *Anglos and Mexicans in the Making of Texas 1836-1986*
Walter McDonald: *The Flying Dutchman*
Steve Barthelme: "Zorro"
Mike Cochran: "Texas Fugitives"
Robert Sherrill: "Can Miami Save Itself?"
Ruby C. Tolliver: *Muddy Banks*
Walter Horton: "Texas Wildflower Portraits"
Lon Tinkle Award: A. C. Greene

1986

William H. and William N. Goetzmann: *The West of the Imagination*
Rosalind Wright: *Veracruz*
Alfred W. Crosby: *Ecological Imperialism: The Biological Expansion of Europe, 900-1900*
Gail Galloway Adams: "Inside Dope"
Edward Hirsch: *Wild Gratitude*
Brenda Bell: "Life After Death"
George Lenox and Omega Clay: *The Panoramic Photography of Eugene O. Goldbeck*
Lon Tinkle Award: Elmer Kelton

1985

Elizabeth W. and Robert A. Fernea: *The Arab World: Personal Encounters*
Larry McMurtry: Lonesome Dove
Darwin Payne: *Owen Wister: Chronicler of the West*
Reginald Gibbons: "Mr. Walsh's Mare"
Paula G. Paul: *Sarah, Sissy Weed and the Ships of the Desert*
C. W. Smith: "Uncle Dad"

Andrew Hudgins: *Saints and Strangers*
Walter McDonald: *Witching on Hardscrabble*
Doug Swanson: Woodrow Wilson High School (Dallas) series
Walter Horton: *Dallas Architecture, 1936-1986*
Lon Tinkle Award: Don Barthelme.

1984

Max Apple: *Free Agents*
Celia Morris Eckhardt: *Fanny Wright*
John Bloom and Jim Atkinson: *Evidence of Love*
William Roger Louis: *The British Empire in the Middle East, 1945-1951*
Rosemary Catacalos: *Again for the First Time*
Beverly Lowry: "So Far from the Road, So Long Until Morning"
Judith Alter: *Luke and the Van Zandt County War*
Jeff Unger: *Huck at 100*
John Davidson: "The Man Who Dreamed Luckenbach"

Drew Jubera: "To Find a Mockingbird"
George Lenox: *The Other Texas Frontier*
Lon Tinkle Award: Larry McMurtry

1983

Joe Coomer: *The Decatur Road*
Michael Mewshaw: *Short Circuit*
Lawrence C. Kelly: *The Assault on Assimilation*
Albert Goldbarth: *Original Light: New and Selected Poems, 1973-1983*
Bryan Woolley: "Where Texas Meets the Sea"
Jack Kent: *Silly Goose*
Tim Zigal: "Curios"
Barbara and Fred Whitehead: *Clem Maverick*
Lon Tinkle Award: William Owens

Special Citation: The *Texas Almanac* ☆

National Arts Medal Honors Texans, TV Music Showcase

The 2003 National Medal of Arts honored actor Tommy Tune, singer George Strait and the long-running TV show *Austin City Limits*.

In 2004, opera composer Carlisle Floyd was honored with the award.

Floyd is co-founder of the Houston Opera Studio and long-time professor at the University of Houston. The medal citation honoring him called him "the most important American composer and librettist in our nation's history." His works include *Susannah* (1955), *Of Mice and Men* (1970), and *Cold Sassy Tree* (2000).

In the 2003 award presentation, George Strait was cited for being "one of the all-time most successful recording artists since his debut album, *Strait Country*, in 1981."

The singer, the top traditionalist on the country scene, has released more than 30 albums including *Pure Country* and *For the Last Time: George Strait Live from the Astrodome*.

Strait, who was born in Poteet and grew up in Pearsall, has received scores of music awards and is a member of the Texas Cowboy Hall of Fame.

Tommy Tune, the 6-foot-6 tap dancer and musical director, has received nine Tony Awards. He started on Broadway in 1965 winning his first Tony in 1973 in *Seesaw*. Tune, from Wichita Falls and Houston, has previously received the Texas Medal of Arts for dance.

The 2004 Austin City Limits Music Festival. File photo.

Carlisle Floyd.

George Strait.

Tommy Tune.

In Houston, the Tommy Tune Award recognizes excellence in high school musical theater.

Austin City Limits was recognized for showcasing "an array of American music including blues, bluegrass, rock, folk, country, Latin, traditional, and contemporary." It was also cited for its "unique commitment to presenting both established and diverse emerging artists and for its stylistically seamless format."

The concert series, produced at KLRU-TV in Austin, has been on the air since 1976.

In 1998, *Austin City Limits* won a W.C. Handy "Keeping the Blues Alive" Award for Visual Broadcast presented by the Blues Foundation.

The Medal of Arts was established by Congress in 1984 to honor those who make outstanding contributions to the arts.

Each year, the National Endowment for the Arts seeks nominations from across the country. The president selects the recipients.

Previous Texas recipients include Lydia Mendoza, Tejano recording star since the 1920s. ☆

Poets Laureate of Texas

Since 2001, a committee of seven members appointed by the governor, lt. governor, and speaker of the House selects the poet laureate, state artist and state musician based on recommendations from the Texas Commission on the Arts. Earlier, the Legislature made the nominations.

Sources: Texas State Library and Archives; Texas Commission on the Arts; Dallas Morning News.

1932-34	Judd Mortimer Lewis, Houston
1934-36	Aline T. Michaelis, Austin
1936-39	Grace Noll Crowell, Dallas
1939-41	Lexie Dean Robertson, Rising Star
1941-43	Nancy Richey Ranson, Dallas
1943-45	Dollilee Davis Smith, Cleburne
1945-47	DavidRiley Russell, Dallas
1947-49	Aline B. Carter, San Antonio
1949-51	Carlos Ashley, Llano
1951-53	Arthur M. Sampley, Denton
1953-55	Mildred Lindsey Raiborn, San Angelo Dee Walker, Texas City, alternate
1955-57	Pierre Bernard Hill, Hunt
1957-59	Margaret Royalty Edwards, Waco
1959-61	J.V. Chandler, Kingsville Edna Coe Majors, Colorado City, alternate
1961	Lorena Simon, Port Arthur
1962	Marvin Davis Winsett, Dallas
1963	Gwendolyn Bennett Pappas, Houston Vassar Miller, Houston, alternate
1964-65	Jenny Lind Porter, Austin Edith Rayzor Canant, Texas City, alternate
1966	Bessie Maas Rowe, Port Arthur Grace Marie Scott, Abilene, alternate
1967	William E. Bard, Dallas Bessie Maas Rowe, Port Arthur, alternate
1968	Kathryn Henry Harris, Waco Sybil Leonard Armes, El Paso, alternate
1969-70	Anne B. Marely, Austin Rose Davidson Speer, Brady, alternate
1970-71	Mrs. Robby K. Mitchell, McKinney Faye Carr Adams, Dallas, alternate
1971-72	Terry Fontenot, Port Arthur Faye Carr Adams, Dallas, alternate
1972-73	Mrs. Clark Gresham, Burkburnett Marion McDaniel, Sidney, alternate
1973-74	Violette Newton, Beaumont Stella Woodall, San Antonio, alternate
1974-75	Lila Todd O'Neil, Port Arthur C.W. Miller, San Antonio, alternate
1975-76	Ethel Osborn Hill, Port Arthur Gene Shuford, Denton, alternate
1976-77	Florice Stripling Jeffers, Burkburnett Vera L. Eckert, San Angelo, alternate
1977-78	Ruth Carruth, Vernon Joy Gresham Hagstrom, Burkburnett, alternate
1978-79	Patsy Stodghill, Dallas Dorothy B. Elfstroman, Galveston, alternate
1979-80	Dorothy B. Elfstroman, Galveston Ruth Carruth, Vernon, alternate
1980-81	Weems S. Dykes, McCamey Mildred Crabree Speer, Amarillo, alternate
1981-82	*none designated*

Red Steagall, 2006 Poet Laureate. File photo.

1982-83	William D. Barney, Fort Worth Vassar Miller, Houston, alternate
1983-87	*none designated*
1987-88	Ruth E. Reuther, Wichita Falls
1988-89	Vassar Miller, Houston
1989-93	*none designated*
1993-94	Mildred Baass, Victoria
1994-99	*none designated*
2000	James Hoggard, Wichita Falls
2001	Walter McDonald, Lubbock
2002	*none designated*
2003	Jack Myers, Mesquite
2004	Cleatus Rattan, Cisco
2005	Alan Brikelbach, Plano
2006	Red Steagall, Fort Worth

State Musicians of Texas

2003	James Dick, Round Top
2004	Ray Benson, Austin
2005	Johnny Gimble, Tyler
2006	Billy Joe Shaver, Waco

Billy Joe Shaver, State Musician for 2006. File photo.

State Artists of Texas

1971-72	Joe Ruiz Grandee, Arlington
1972-73	Melvin C. Warren, Clifton
1973-74	Ronald Thomason, Weatherford A.C. Gentry Jr., Tyler, alternate
1974-75	Joe Rader Roberts, Dripping Springs Bette Lou Voorhis, Austin, alternate
1975-76	Jack White, New Braunfels
July 4, 1975 -July 4, 1976	Robert Summers, Glen Rose Bicentennial Artist
1976-77	James Boren, Clifton Kenneth Wyatt, Lubbock, alternate
1977-78	Edward "Buck" Schiwetz, DeWitt County Renne Hughes, Tarrant County, alternate
1978-79	Jack Cowan, Rockport Gary Henry, Palo Pinto County, alternate Joyce Tally, Caldwell County, alternate
1979-80	Dalhart Windberg, Travis County Grant Lathe, Canyon Lake, alternate
1980-81	Harry Ahysen, Huntsville Jim Reno, Simonton, alternate
1981-82	Jerry Newman, Beaumont Raul Guiterrez, San Antonio, alternate
1982-83	Dr. James H. Johnson, Bryan Armando Hinojosa, Laredo, alternate
1983-84	Raul Gutierrez, San Antonio James Eddleman, Lubbock, alternate
1984-85	Covelle Jones, Lubbock Ragan Gennusa, Austin, alternate
1986-87	Chuck DeHaan, Graford
1987-88	Neil Caldwell, Angleton Rey Gaytan, Austin, alternate
1988-89	George Hallmark, Walnut Springs Tony Eubanks, Grapevine, alternate

	Two-dimensional	Three-dimensional
1990-91	Mondel Rogers, Sweetwater	Ron Wells, Cleveland
1991-92	Woodrow Foster, Center	Kent Ullberg, Corpus Christi
	Harold Phenix, Houston, alternate	Mark Clapham, Conroe, alternate
1993-94	Roy Lee Ward	James Eddleman, Lubbock

Sculptor James Surl, 2006 State Artist. File photo.

1994-95	Frederick Carter, El Paso	Garland A. Weeks, Wichita Falls
1998-99	Carl Rice Embrey, San Antonio	Edd Hayes, Humble
2000-02	*none designated*	
2003	Ralph White, Austin	Dixie Friend Gay, Houston
2004	Sam Caldwell, Houston	David Hickman, Dallas
2005	Kathy Vargas, San Antonio	Sharon Kopriva, Houston
2006	George Boutwell, Bosque	James Surls, Athens

2005 Gold Medalist Alexander Kobrin, left, is congratulated by Van Cliburn. File photo.

Van Cliburn Piano Competition

The Van Cliburn International Piano Competition was initiated in 1962 by music teachers and community leaders in Fort Worth. The event is held every four years. It commemorates Van Cliburn's victory in the Tchaikovsky International Piano Competition in Moscow in 1958.

Gold medalists receive cash prizes, tour engagements and free management for two years.

Past gold medalists are as follows:

1962	Ralph Votapek, USA
1966	Radu Lupu, Romania
1969	Christina Ortiz, Brazil
1973	Vladimir Viardo, USSR
1977	Steven De Groote, South Africa
1981	André-Michel Schub, USA
1985	José Feghali, Brazil
1989	Alexei Sultanov, USSR
1993	Simone Pedroni, Italy
1997	Jon Nakamatsu, USA
2001	Olga Kern, Russia, and Stanislav Ioudenitch of Uzbekistan
2005	Alexander Kobrin, Russia

Lebanese-Syrian Texans: From Peddlers to Professionals

The U.S. Census Bureau estimated* in 2000 that there were 29,518 Texans of Lebanese and Syrian ancestry. Although their numbers may be small in comparison to the state's population, the Lebanese-Syrian impact on the culture has been profound.

Names of well-known Lebanese- and Syrian-Texans appear in many fields. They include medicine (Dr. Michael DeBakey, the heart surgeon); business (the Haggar and Farah families, clothing manufacturers); and law and politics (the Kazens of Laredo and the Jamails of Houston). And in the arts there is actor F. Murry Abraham of El Paso who won an Academy Award in 1985 for his role in the movie "Amadeus."

Their influence can be seen across the state from Houston, where the Antone family has a food import business and where names like Halbouty and Haddad are big in oil, to El Paso, home of the Azar Nut Company.

Beginnings

Lebanese and Syrian families began coming to Texas around 1880 from what were then Middle Eastern provinces within the Ottoman Turkish Empire. But the first Arabic-speaking individuals from that region already had arrived in Texas in 1856 as camel tenders.

Hadji Ali was a young man from Syria who, along with a few Turks and Greeks, arrived in May 1856 in Indianola with a shipload of camels. The camels, part of an experiment by the U.S. Army, were used for a few years before the Civil War as pack animals in caravans that linked the military forts on the western frontier.

Hadji Ali, a Muslim convert, was the son of a Syrian father and Greek mother. He was called "Hi Jolly" by the soldiers, and by that name became an American folk figure. After the job with the Army ended, he mined for gold and silver in the desert Southwest, using camels as part of his work. He died in 1902 in Arizona.

Elias, another Syrian who worked in the Army camel experiment, moved on to Sonora, Mexico. Elias' son, Plutarco Elias Calles, became president of Mexico in 1928.

The first Syrian family to visit Texas was that of Professor Joseph Arbeely, who came in 1878 after having served as president of the Patriarchal Syrian Orthodox College in Damascus. He taught Arabic to American missionaries. Two of his sons remained in Austin until 1881.

About that same year, Cater Joseph Cater, a teacher at the Presbyterian school in Roumieh, Lebanon, began sending his children to Austin. In Austin, the family name was changed to Joseph. The oldest son eventually opened a confectionary and other sons opened retail stores there.

By 1910, there were 1,125 immigrants in Texas "from Turkey in Asia," as the U.S. Census Bureau referred to the Ottoman Empire. Another 466 persons had parents born there. The vast majority of them were from the provinces then called Mount Lebanon and Greater Syria. However, most of the immigrants did not arrive directly, but instead worked briefly in other states before settling in Texas.

Ethnic History

Almost all of the early immigrants were Christians: Antiochian Orthodox, Maronite Catholic and Greek Catholic (called Melkites), all of whom trace their roots to the Church of Antioch of the first century. There were also some Protestants, mostly members of the Presbyterian Church, which had established schools in Lebanon. After 1945, some of the immigrants from Lebanon and Syria were Muslims who were fleeing the unsettled situation in the Middle East. However, today the majority of Texans from these two Arabic-speaking countries remains Christian.

In the 19th century, Christians in the Muslim-ruled empire were tolerated but had to pay extra taxes and faced some professional restrictions. Also in the latter 19th century, there was unease in Lebanon following the "troubles of 1860," a conflict between the Druze and Maronites that resulted in the deaths of thousands of Christians.

The Maronite Christians are unique to Lebanon. The name comes from a priest named Maron who died in 410. After conflicts within the Church of Antioch, his

The Dallas Lebanese Folk Dancers perform at Our Lady of Lebanon Maronite Catholic Church festival. File photo.

followers took refuge on Mount Lebanon. Because of their isolation, these Maronites were unknown to the West until the Crusaders encountered them in the 12th century. Today, the Maronite Catholics are in union with the pope but maintain their own liturgy and hierarchy.

Communities

Many of the Maronite Catholic Lebanese who came to Texas assimilated into the Roman Catholic parishes because none of their own clergy was here. Only in the late 20th century did Maronite parishes become established in the urban areas of Dallas, Houston, Austin and El Paso. The exception was the creation in 1925 of St. George Maronite Church in San Antonio.

The Antiochian Orthodox (sometimes called Syrian Orthodox), on the other hand, began to establish churches in Texas much earlier. Galveston's Sts. Constantine and Helen Church was founded in 1895 mainly by Serbians and Greeks, but it also had a few Syrians among the parishioners. The first Antiochian Orthodox church, St. Michael's, was formed in Beaumont in 1907. Other Antiochian Orthodox churches followed in Austin, Houston, Corpus Christi and El Paso.

In smaller Texas cities, some of the immigrants joined Episcopalian, Methodist or other Protestant churches.

Professions

Although the Christian identity within a Muslim empire was one catalyst for emigration to the West, the principal reason was the lack of economic opportunity in the old societies.

The Middle East's central location had contributed to a tradition of trade, dating back to the time of the Phoenicians. Thus, many of the first Lebanese and Syrians in Texas began making their livelihood here as itinerant peddlers and traversed the state from Canadian in the Panhandle to Del Rio on the Rio Grande and Tyler in East Texas.

These enterprising and adaptable merchants, who have also been described as clannish, soon had relatives joining them to create the first Lebanese and Syrian communities within Texas cities. The second and third generations then began moving into the fields of law, education and oil exploration.

Social Clubs and Festivals

The close-knit communities, mostly in urban areas, began to form social and benevolent organizations. The Jamails of Houston, the largest clan, formed the United Jamail Club in 1890, which in turn became part of the Southern Federation of Syrian Lebanese Clubs.

The Southern Federation was founded in 1931 and held its first convention in Beaumont in 1932. Besides serving to tie together all the various clubs in each city, the federation began to help the most recent immigrants from Syria and Lebanon and to provide scholarships to young people of the ethnic community.

Since the 1960s, it also has been contributing to the Center for Middle Eastern Studies at the University of Texas at Austin.

Other ethnic organizations include the Cedars of Lebanon Clubs in Austin, Waco and Tyler, and various women's clubs throughout the state.

Also, the clubs provided a way to celebrate and to preserve the traditional food, dances and customs of the Syrians and Lebanese. Most of the clubs have annual gatherings called sahrias where delicacies are served, including Arabic bread, tahini (a paste made of sesame seeds), baklava pastries, and kibbe, a kind of meatloaf.

The traditional circle dance, dabke, is also part of the festivities. Music is provided by small bands made up of a lute, called an oud, a hand drum, or derbukki, and the tambourine.

These same customs of music, dance and food are celebrated with other Texans at annual festivals put on by community churches. They include:

Austin — St. Elias Orthodox Church, Mediterranean Festival, second weekend of October.

San Antonio — St. George Maronite Church, Magic Is the Night, September.

Lewisville — Our Lady of Lebanon Maronite Church, Lebanese Food Festival, first weekend in October.

Houston — St. George Antiochian Orthodox Church, Mediterranean Festival, September.

El Paso — St. George Antiochian Orthodox Church, Middle East Feast, May.

San Antonio — The Texas Folklife Festival, held in June, includes Lebanese and Syrian food, music and dances.— *Robert Plocheck*

The estimates of ethnic groups are determined by the U.S. Census Bureau based on the census long-form sent to 1 in 6 households. Respondents may list a primary and secondary ancestry.

Sources

The Syrian and Lebanese Texans, The University of Texas Institute of Texan Cultures at San Antonio, 1974.

Country of Origin, 1910, U.S. Census Bureau, Department of Commerce.

New Handbook of Texas, Texas State Historical Association, 1996, various: "Lebanese-Syrians" by James Patrick McGuire; "Nahim Abraham" by H. Allen Anderson; "Clothing Manufacture" by Dorothy D. DeMoss; "Farah, Incorporated" by Myrna Zanetell; "Camels" by Chris Emmett and Odie B. Faulk; "Folk Festivals" by Beverly J. Stoeltje.

Antiochian Orthodox Christian Archdiocese of North America, online.

Affiliated Clubs and Syrian Lebanese Americans, Southern Federation of Syrian Lebanese American Clubs, online.

Haggar Hall, University of Notre Dame, online.

Middle Eastern, Mallouf Boot Shop, and Texas Folklife Festival, Texas Culture, Office of Governor, Economic Development and Tourism, online.

Prominent Lebanese Americans, American Middle-Eastern Association founded by Lebanese Internet Developers, online.

** "The Arab Population, 2000" and "Ancestry, 1990," U.S. Census Bureau, Department of Commerce, online.

Texas, Arab American Institute Foundation, online.

The Arab Americans, Middle East Policy Council, online.

Arab American National Museum, Arab Community Center for Economic and Social Services, online.

"Museum Gives Arab-Americans Long-Overdue Recognition," *Houston Chronicle*, online.

Our Lady of Lebanon Maronite Catholic Church, Lewisville, online.

St. George Maronite Catholic Church, San Antonio, online.

St. George Antiochian Orthodox Church, Houston, online.

Our Lady of the Cedars Maronite Catholic Church, Houston, online.

Our Lady's Maronite Catholic Church, Austin, online.

St. Anthony of the Desert Mission (Lebanese), El Paso, online.

St. Elias Antiochian Orthodox Church, Austin, online.

**The U.S. Census Bureau notes "the lack of consensus about the definition of an Arab ethnic category" but uses the designation "with ancestries originating from Arabic-speaking countries." The bureau adds in its report "The Arab Population, 2000"; "It is important to note, however, that some people from these countries may not consider themselves to be Arab."

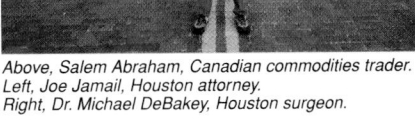

Above, Salem Abraham, Canadian commodities trader.
Left, Joe Jamail, Houston attorney.
Right, Dr. Michael DeBakey, Houston surgeon.

LEBANESE-SYRIANS IN TEXAS

1910   1,511 total — 1,125 from "Turkey in Asia" plus 466 whose parents were born there.

2000   29,518 total — 23,652 Lebanese, 5,866 Syrian

Early arrivals and professions

1856   **Hadji Ali** arrived as camel tender at Indianola as part of a military experiment with caravans. Syrian Orthodox native, but raised Muslim.

1878   **Arbeely** family in Austin. The father, Joseph, was a professor of Arabic to missionaries. Two of the sons, Abraham, a physician, and Khaleel, a pharmacist, worked in Austin for several years.

1881   **Cater Joseph Cater** (changed family name to Joseph) in Austin. In 1891, other family members arrived. Retailing.

1889   Monsour **Bashara** in Waco, then moved to Beaumont. Nephews in Houston oil. Monsour later in Wichita Falls oil.

1890   **Jamails** in Houston. Family includes Jim (Najeeb), the grocer, and Joe Jr., attorney.

1891   **Kazens** in Laredo. Three brothers Abraham Sr., Anthony and Joe came in the 1880s and peddled dry goods in South Texas before settling in Laredo. Also, San Marcos and Benavides. In legal, public service and business fields.

1895   **Semaans** in San Antonio. Retailers, attorneys.

1896   **Nami** in Cuero, then San Antonio. Retailers, attorneys.

1897   **Kadane** in Denison. Oil, dry goods. In Dallas in 1910, making butter, cheese, margarine.

1900   **Azar** in El Paso and San Antonio. Brothers Elias and Shibley established a confectionary and added the pecan shelling business in 1919. Nuts, pecans. Descendants in business and public service.

1902   **Halbouty** in Beaumont, then Houston. Thomas and wife Sodia. Children entered teaching, insurance, and medicine. Son Michel T., a geologist, made fortune in oil.

1904   **Lotief** in Tyler. Cecil peddled merchandise and opened confectionary. In 1929 moved west near Abilene. He was the first Texas Lebanese legislator (1932) representing Callahan and Eastland counties.

1907   **Antone** in Columbus, Port Arthur, then Houston. Import foods.

1907   **Malooly** in El Paso. Realtor, investor, furniture.

1908   **Haddad** in Tyler. Mecca Café, real estate, oil.

1909   **Curry** in San Antonio. Food processing, attorneys, judges.

1910   **Mafrige** (cousin to Nami, above) in Cuero, then Houston. Zachary operated a hotel and dry goods store.

1910   **Halaby** in Dallas. Rugs, art. Son Najeeb Jr., born 1915, attended Dallas schools. Najeeb Jr. headed Pan American World Airways and the Federal Aviation Administration. His daughter, Lisa Najeeb Halaby, married King Hussein of Jordan and became Queen Noor.

1913   **Abraham** to Canadian, Panhandle. Real estate, oil, legislature

1913   **Malouf** to Canadian (Abraham relatives). Dry goods, also in Dallas. Clan includes Schadeds of Tyler, Salems of Sudan.

1920   **Farah** of El Paso. Mansour had operated a dry goods store in Las Cruces, N.M., beginning in 1905, with his brother Andrew. Moved to El Paso and slowly built the Farah Company, which manufactured shirts, pants.

1920   **Haggar** of Dallas. Lebanese-born J.M. arrived from Oklahoma and started clothing business with used sewing machines. Family build Haggar slacks into a national brand.

1948   Dr. Michael **DeBakey**. Raised in Lake Charles, La., he came to head surgery at Baylor University College of Medicine and worked at Methodist Hosptial in Houston. ☆

Public Libraries in Texas

The following information was furnished by Margaret Whitehead of the Library Development Division of the Texas State Library, Austin.

Texas public libraries continue to strive to meet the education and information needs of Texans by providing library services of high quality with oftentimes limited resources. Each year, services provided by public libraries to the citizens of Texas increase, with more visits to public libraries and higher attendance in library programs.

The challenges facing the public libraries in Texas are many and varied. The costs for providing electronic and online sources, in addition to traditional library services, are growing faster than library budgets.

Urban libraries are trying to serve growing populations, while libraries in rural areas are trying to serve remote populations and provide distance learning where possible.

National rankings of public libraries are published by the National Center for Education Statistics. This report may be found at http://nces.ed.gov/pubsearch/pubsinfo.asp?pubid=2005356. When comparing Texas statistics to those nationally, Texas continues to rank below most of the other states in most categories, with the exception of reference transactions (Texas ranks 15th) and public-use Internet terminals (it ranks 5th.)

Complete statistical information on public libraries is available on the Texas State Library's Web page at: http://www.tsl.state.tx.us/ld/pubs/pls/index.html.

The following table lists, by city, Texas public libraries and some branches with addresses and phone numbers. Many of these have established homepages on the Internet. To visit your local library's Web page, call the library for the Web address or find a list of libraries with addresses at http://www.tsl.state.tx.us/texshare/pl/texlibs.html.

CITY	LIBRARY	MAILING ADDRESS	ZIP	PHONE
Abernathy	Abernathy Public	PO Box 686	79311 0686	806 298-4138
Abilene	Abilene Public	202 Cedar St	79601 5793	325 676-6328
Alamo	Lalo Arcaute Public	502 E Duranta St	78516 2317	956 787-6160
Albany	Shackelford County	PO Box 445	76430 0445	325 762-2672
Aledo	East Parker County	PO Box 275	76008 0275	817 441-6545
Alice	Alice Public	401 E 3rd St	78332 4798	361 664-9506
Allen	Allen Public	2 Allen Civic Plaza	75013 2559	972 727-0190
Alpine	Alpine Public	203 N 7th St	79830 4615	432 837-2621
Alvarado	Alvarado Public	104 W College St	76009 4319	817 783-7323
Alvin	Alvin	105 S Gordon St	77511 2332	281 388-4300
Alvord	Alvord Public	PO Box 323	76225 0323	940 427-2842
Amarillo	Amarillo Public	PO Box 2171	79105 2171	806 378-3050
Anahuac	Chambers County System	PO Box 520	77514 0520	409 267-8263
Andrews	Andrews County	109 NW 1st St	79714 6301	432 523-9819
Angleton	Brazoria County System	111 E Locust Bldg A 29	77515 4641	979 864-1505
Angleton	Angleton	401 E Cedar St	77515 4652	979 864-1517
Anson	Anson Public	1137 12th St	79501 4306	325 823-2711
Aransas Pass	Ed & Hazel Richmond Public	110 N Lamont St	78336 3698	361 758-2350
Archer City	Archer Public	PO Box 957	76351 0957	940 574-4954
Arlington	Arlington Public System	101 E Abram St	76010 1183	817 459-6900
Aspermont	Stonewall County	PO Box H	79502 0907	940 989-2730
Athens	Henderson County Murchison	121 S Prairieville St	75751 2595	903 677-7295
Atlanta	Atlanta Public	101 W Hiram St	75551 2509	903 796-2112
Aubrey	Aubrey Area	109 S Main St	76227 9164	940 365-9162
Austin	Austin Public	PO Box 2287	78768 2287	512 974-7300
Austin/Wells Branch	Wells Branch Community	15001 Wells Port Dr	78728	512 989-3188
Azle	Azle Public	609 SE Parkway St	76020 3695	817 444-7114
Baird	Callahan County	100 W 4th B1	79504 5305	325 854-1718
Balch Springs	Balch Springs Public	4301 Pioneer Rd	75180 4001	972 557-6096
Ballinger	Carnegie	204 N 8th St	76821 4706	915 365-3616
Bandera	Bandera County	PO Box 1568	78003 1568	830 796-4213
Barstow	Barstow	PO Box 74	79719 0074	915 445-5205
Bartlett	Teinert Memorial Public	PO Box 12	76511 0012	254 527-3208
Bastrop	Bastrop Public	PO Box 670	78602 0670	512 321-5441
Bay City	Bay City Public	1100 7th St	77414 4915	979 245-6931
Baytown	Sterling Municipal	Wilbanks Ave	77520 4258	281 420-7147
Beaumont	Beaumont Public System	PO Box 3827	77704 3827	409 838-6606
Beaumont	Jefferson County	7933 Viterbo Rd Ste 7	77705 9295	409 727-2735
Bedford	Bedford Public	1805 L Don Dodson Dr	76021 1897	817 952-2330
Beeville	Joe Barnhart Bee County	110 W Corpus Christi	78102 5604	361 362-4901
Beeville	Westside Branch	P O Box 760	78104 0760	361 358-6520
Bellaire	Bellaire City	5111 Jessamine St	77401 4498	713 662-8160
Bellville	Bellville Public	12 W Palm St	77418 1446	979 865-3731
Belton	Lena Armstrong Public	PO Box 120	76513 0120	254 933-5832
Benavides	Duval County/Benavides Branch	PO Box Drawer R	78341	361 256-4646
Benbrook	Benbrook Public	1065 Mercedes St	76126 2742	817 249-6632
Bertram	Bertram Free	PO Box 243	78605 0243	512 355-2113

CITY	LIBRARY	MAILING ADDRESS	ZIP	PHONE
Big Lake	Reagan County	300 Courthouse Sq	76932 4515	325 884-2854
Big Spring	Howard County	500 S Main St	79720 2729	432 264-2260
Bishop	Bishop Branch	115 S Ash Ave	78343 2658	361 584-2222
Blanco	Blanco	1118 N Main St	78606 4838	830 833-4280
Blessing	Blessing	PO Box 210	77419 0210	361 588-7717
Blue Mound/Fort Worth	Blue Mound Community	1600 Bell Ave	76131 1002	817 232-4095
Boerne	Boerne Public	210 N Main St	78006 2036	830 249-3053
Bonham	Bonham Public	305 E 5th St	75418 4002	903 583-3128
Booker	Booker School/Public	PO Box 288	79005 0288	806 658-9323
Borger	Hutchinson County	625 N Weatherly St	79007 3621	806 273-0126
Bowie	Bowie Public	301 W Walnut St	76230 4828	940 872-2681
Boyd	Boyd Public	PO Box 1238	76023 1238	940 433-5580
Brackettville	Kinney County Public	PO Box 975	78832 0975	830 563-2884
Brady	F.M. (Buck) Richards Memorial	1106 S Blackburn St	76825 6222	325 597-2617
Brazoria	Brazoria	620 S Brooks St	77422 9022	979 798-2372
Breckenridge	Breckenridge Public	209 N Breckenridge Ave	76424 3503	254 559-5505
Bremond	Bremond Public	PO Box 132	76629 0132	254 746-7752
Brenham	Nancy Carol Roberts Memorial	100 W Academy St	77833 3107	979 277-1271
Bridge City	Bridge City Public	101 Parkside Dr	77611 2442	409 735-4242
Bridgeport	Bridgeport Public	2159 10th St	76426 2071	940 683-4412
Brookshire	Waller County/Brookshire-Pattison	3815 6th St	77423	281 375-5550
Brownfield	Kendrick Memorial	301 W Tate St	79316 4329	806 637-3848
Brownsville	Brownsville Public	2600 Central Blvd	78520 8824	956 548-1055
Brownwood	Brownwood Public	600 Carnegie St	76801 7097	325 646-0155
Bryan	Bryan-College Station Public	201 E 26th St	77803 5356	979 209-5611
Buchanan Dam	Lakeshore Branch	7346 Ranch Road 261	78609 4490	325 379-1174
Buda	Buda Public	PO Box 608	78610 0608	512 295-5899
Buffalo	Buffalo Public	PO Drawer 1290	75831 1290	903 322-4146
Bullard	Bullard Community	PO Box 368	75757 0368	903 894-6125
Bulverde	Bulverde / Spring Branch	20475 Hwy 46 W Ste 340	78070 6147	830 438-3666
Buna	Buna Public	PO Box 1571	77612 1571	409 994-5501
Burkburnett	Burkburnett	215 E 4th St	76354 3446	940 569-2991
Burleson	Burleson Public	248 SW Johnson Ave	76028 4765	817 447-5431
Burnet	Burnet County System	100 E Washington St	78611 3114	512 715-5229
Cactus	Cactus Branch	PO Box 99	79013	806 966-3706
Caldwell	Harrie P. Woodson Memorial	704 W Highway 21	77836 1198	979 567-4111
Cameron	Cameron Public	304 E 3rd St	76520 3350	254 697-2401
Camp Wood	Camp Wood Public	PO Box 138	78833 0138	830 597-3208
Canadian	Hemphill County	500 Main St	79014 2702	806 323-5282
Canton	Van Zandt County	317 1st Monday Ln	75103 1052	903 567-4276
Canyon	Canyon Area	1501 3rd Ave	79015 2828	806 655-5015
Canyon Lake	Tye Preston Memorial	1321 Highway 2673	78133 4565	830 964-3744
Carrizo Springs	Dimmit County Public	200 N 9th St	78834 3741	830 876-5788
Carrollton	Carrollton Public	1700 Keller Springs Rd	75006 2900	972 466-3360
Carthage	Sammy Brown	522 W College St	75633 1408	903 693-6741
Castroville	Castroville Public	802 London St	78009 4032	830 931-4095
Cedar Hill	Zula Bryant Wylie	225 Cedar St	75104 2655	972 291-7323
Cedar Park	Cedar Park Public	550 Discovery Blvd	78613 2200	512 259-5353
Celina	Celina Community	710 E Pecan St	75009 6070	972 382-3750
Center	Fannie Brown Booth Memorial	619 Tenaha St	75935 3553	936 598-5522
Centerville	Elmer P. & Jewel Ward Memorial	PO Box 567	75833 0567	903 536-7261
Chandler	Henderson County East	PO Box 301	75758 0301	903 849-4122
Charlotte	Charlotte Public	PO Box 757	78011 0757	830 277-1212
Chico	Chico Public	PO Box 707	76431 0707	940 644-2330
Childress	Childress Public	117 Avenue B NE	79201 4509	940 937-8421
Cisco	Cisco Public	600 Avenue G	76437 3039	254 442-1020
Clarendon	Burton Memorial	PO Box 783	79226 0783	806 874-3685
Clarksville	Red River County Public	PO Box 508	75426 0508	903 427-3991
Claude	Claude Public	PO Box 109	79019	806 226-7881
Cleburne	Cleburne Public	PO Box 677	76033 0657	817 645-0936
Cleveland	Austin Memorial	220 S Bonham Ave	77327 4591	281 592-3920
Clifton	Nellie Pederson Civic	PO Box 231	76634 0231	254 675-6495
Clint/El Paso	Clint ISD/Public	14521 Horizon Blvd	79928 8564	915 851-2302
Clute	Clute	215 N Shanks St	77531 4122	979 265-4582
Clyde	Clyde Public	PO Box 1779	79510 1779	325 893-5315
Cockrell Hill/Dallas	Cockrell Hill Public	4125 W Clarendon	75211 4919	214 330-9935
Coldspring	Coldspring Area Public	PO Box 1756	77331 1756	936 653-3104
Coleman	Coleman Public	402 Commercial Ave	76834 4202	325 625-3043

CITY	LIBRARY	MAILING ADDRESS	ZIP	PHONE
College Station	College Station Public	1818 Harvey Mitchell Pkwy S	77840 4297	979 764-3416
Colleyville	Colleyville Pulic	110 Main Street	76034	817 503-1153
Colorado City	Mitchell County Public	340 Oak St	79512 6213	325 728-3968
Columbus	Nesbitt Memorial	529 Washington St	78934 2326	979 732-3392
Comanche	Comanche Public	PO Box 777	76442 0777	325 356-2122
Comfort	Comfort Public	PO Box 536	78013 0536	830 995-2398
Commerce	Commerce Public	PO Box 308	75429 0308	903 886-6858
Conroe	Montgomery County Memorial	104 I 45 N	77301 2720	936 788-8377
Converse	Converse Area Public	601 S Seguin Rd	78109 2003	210 659-4160
Cooper	Delta County Public	300 W Dallas Ave	75432 1632	903 395-4575
Coppell	William T. Cozby Public	177 N Heartz Rd	75019 2121	972 304-3661
Copperas Cove	Copperas Cove Public	501 S Main St	76522 2241	254 547-3826
Corpus Christi	Corpus Christi Public	805 Comanche St	78401 2798	361 880-7070
Corrigan	Mickey Reily Public	604 S Mathews St	75939 2645	936 398-4156
Corsicana	Corsicana Public	100 N 12th St	75110 5205	903 654-4810
Cotulla	Alexander Memorial	201 S Center St	78014 2255	830 879-2601
Crandall	Crandall-Combine Community	PO Box 128	75114 0128	972 427-8170
Crane	Crane County	701 S Alford St	79731 2521	432 558-1142
Crockett	J.H. Wootters Crockett Public	709 E Houston Ave	75835 2124	936 544-3089
Crosby	Crosby Branch	135 Hare Rd	77532 8895	281 328-3535
Crosbyton	Crosby County	114 W Aspen St	79322 2502	806 675-2673
Cross Plains	Cross Plains Public	PO Box 333	76443 0333	254 725-7722
Crowell	Foard County	PO Box 317	79227 0317	940 684-1250
Crowley	Crowley Public	PO Box 747	76036 0747	817 297-6707
Crystal City	Crystal City Memorial	101 E Dimmit St	78839 3505	830 372-0036
Cuero	Cuero Public	207 E Main St	77954 3098	361 275-2864
Cypress	Northwest Branch	11355 Regency Green Dr	77429 4705	281 890-2665
Daingerfield	Daingerfield Public	207 Jefferson St	75638 1713	903 645-2823
Dalhart	Dallam-Hartley County	420 Denrock Ave	79022 2628	806 244-2761
Dallas	Dallas Public	1515 Young St	75201 5499	214 670-1400
Dallas	Lancaster-Kiest Branch	3039 S Lancaster Rd	75216 4498	214 670-1952
Danbury	Danbury	1720 N Main St	77534	979 922-1905
Dayton	Jones Public	307 W Houston St	77535 2537	936 258-7060
De Leon	DeLeon City County	125 E Reynosa St	76444 1842	254 893-2417
De Soto	DeSoto Public	211 E Pleasant Run Rd Ste C	75115 3939	972 230-9658
Decatur	Decatur Public	1700 S FM 51	76234 3613	940 627-5512
Deer Park	Deer Park Public	3009 Center St	77536 5099	281 478-7208
Del Rio	Val Verde County	300 Spring St	78840 5199	830 774-7595
Dell City	Grace Grebing Public/School	PO Box 37	79837 0037	915 964-2468
Denison	Denison Public	300 W Gandy St	75020 3153	903 465-1797
Denton	Denton Public	3020 N Locust St	76209 7600	940 349-8752
Denver City	Yoakum County/Cecil Bickley	205 W 4th St	79323 3113	806 592-2754
Devine	Driscoll Public	202 E Hondo Ave	78016 3342	830 663-2993
Deweyville	Deweyville	PO Box 801	77614 0801	409 746-0222
Diboll	T.L.L. Temple Memorial	300 Park St	75941 1633	936 829-5497
Dickinson	Mares Memorial	4324 Highway 3	77539 6801	281 534-3812
Dilley	Dilley Public	PO Box 230	78017 0230	830 965-1951
Dime Box	Black Bridge	PO Box 157	77853 0157	979 884-0124
Dimmitt	Rhoads Memorial	103 SW 2nd St	79027 2501	806 647-3532
Donna	Donna Public	301 S Main St	78537 3288	956 464-2221
Dripping Springs	Dripping Springs Community	PO Box 279	78620 0279	512 858-7825
Dublin	Dublin Public	206 W Blackjack St	76446 2204	254 445-4141
Dumas	Killgore Memorial	124 S Bliss Ave	79029 3804	806 935-4941
Duncanville	Duncanville Public	201 James Collins Blvd	75116 4818	972 780-5050
Eagle Lake	Eula & David Wintermann	101 N Walnut Ave	77434 2326	979 234-5411
Eagle Pass	Eagle Pass Public	589 E Main St	78852 4518	830 773-2516
Earth	Springlake-Earth Community	PO Box 259	79031 0259	806 257-3357
East Bernard	East Bernard Branch	746 Clubside Drive	77435	979 335-6142
Eastland	Centennial Memorial	210 S Lamar St	76448 2794	254 629-2281
Eden	Eden Public	PO Box 896	76837 0896	325 869-7761
Edinburg	Edinburg Public	401 E Cano St	78539 4596	956 383-6246
Edna	Jackson County Memorial	411 N Wells St	77957 2734	361 782-2162
El Campo	El Campo Branch	200 W Church St	77437 3316	979 543-2362
El Paso	El Paso Public	501 N Oregon St	79901 1103	915 543-5401
Eldorado	Schleicher County Public	PO Box 611	76936 0611	325 853-3767
Electra	Electra Public	401 N Waggoner St	76360 2134	940 495-2208
Elgin	Elgin Public	404 N Main St	78621 2625	512 281-5678
Elsa	Elsa Public	PO Box 1447	78543 1447	956 262-3061
Emory	Rains County Public	PO Box 189	75440 0189	903 473-2221

CITY	LIBRARY	MAILING ADDRESS	ZIP	PHONE
Ennis	Ennis Public	501 W Ennis Ave	75119 3803	972 875-5360
Euless	Euless Public	201 N Ector Dr	76039 3595	817 685-1679
Everman	Everman Public	212 N Race St	76140 3297	817 551-0726
Fabens	El Paso County	PO Box 788	79838 0788	915 764-3635
Fairfield	Fairfield	350 W Main St	75840 3028	903 389-3574
Falfurrias	Ed Rachal Memorial	203 S Calixto Mora Ave	78355 4321	361 325-2144
Falls City	Falls City Public	PO Box 220	78113 0220	830 254-3361
Farmers Branch	Farmers Branch Manske Public	13613 Webb Chapel Rd	75234 3799	972 247-2511
Farmersville	Charles J. Rike Memorial	PO Box 352	75442 0352	972 782-6681
Ferris	Ferris Public	514 S Mabel St	75125 3028	972 544-3696
Florence	Florence Public	PO Box 430	76527 0430	254 793-2672
Floresville	Sam Fore Jr./ Wilson County Public	1 Lane	78114 2239	830 393-7361
Flower Mound	Flower Mound Public	3030 Broadmoor Ln	75022 2703	972 874-6200
Floydada	Floyd County	111 S Wall St	79235 2811	806 983-4922
Forney	Ellen Brooks West Memorial	800 FM 741	75126 3913	972 564-7027
Fort Davis	Jeff Davis County	PO Box 1054	79734 1054	432 426-3802
Fort Hancock	Fort Hancock ISD/Public	PO Box 98	79839 0098	915 769-3811
Fort Stockton	Fort Stockton Public	500 North Water	79735 5634	432 336-3374
Fort Worth	Fort Worth Public	500 W 3rd St	76102 7333	817 871-7706
Franklin	Robertson County	PO Box 1027	77856 1027	979 828-4331
Frankston	Frankston Depot	PO Box 639	75763 0639	903 876-4463
Fredericksburg	Pioneer Memorial	115 W Main St	78624 3751	830 997-6513
Freeport	Freeport	410 Brazosport Blvd	77541	979 233-3622
Freer	Duval County/Freer Branch	PO Box 1203	78357 1203	361 394-5350
Friendswood	Friendswood Public	416 S Friendswood Dr	77546 3906	281 482-7135
Friona	Friona Public	109 W 7th St	79035 2548	806 250-3200
Frisco	Frisco Public	8750 McKinney Rd	75034 3000	972 335-5510
Fritch	Hutchinson County/Fritch	PO Box 430	79036 0430	806 857-0000
Fulshear	Bob Lutts Fulshear/Simonton Branch	8100 FM 359 S	77441 0907	281 346-1432
Gainesville	Cooke County	200 S Weaver St	76240 4790	940 665-2401
Galena Park	Galena Park Branch	1500 Keene St	77547 2400	713 450-0982
Galveston	Rosenberg	2310 Sealy Ave	77550 2296	409 763-8854
Garland	Nicholson Memorial System	625 Austin St	75040 6365	972 205-2543
Gatesville	Gatesville Public	111 N 8th Street	76528 1432	254 865-5367
George West	Live Oak County	402 Houston St	78022	361 449-1124
Georgetown	Georgetown Public	808 Martin Luther King Jr	78626 5527	512 930-3551
Giddings	Giddings Public	276 N Orange St	78942 3317	979 542-2716
Gilmer	Upshur County	702 W Tyler St	75644 2198	903 843-5001
Gladewater	Lee Public	312 W Pacific Ave	75647 2135	903 845-2640
Glen Rose	Somervell County	108 Allen Dr	76043 4526	254 897-4582
Goldthwaite	Jennie Trent Dew	PO Box 101	76844 0101	325 648-2447
Goliad	Goliad County	PO Box 1025	77963 1025	361 645-2291
Gonzales	Gonzales Public	PO Box 220	78629	830 672-6215
Gorman	Charlie Garrett Memorial	PO Box 219	76454 0219	254 734-3301
Graham	Graham	910 Cherry St	76450 3547	940 549-0600
Granbury	Hood County Public	222 N Travis St	76048 2164	817 573-3569
Grand Prairie	Grand Prairie Memorial	901 Conover Dr	75051 1590	972 237-5700
Grand Saline	Grand Saline Public	201 E Pacific St	75140 1934	903 962-5516
Grandfalls	Grandfalls	PO Box 186	79742 0186	915 547-2861
Grandview	Grandview Public	PO Box 694	76050 0694	817 866-3965
Grapevine	Grapevine Public	1201 Municipal Way	76051 7657	817 410-3400
Greenville	W. Walworth Harrison Public	1 Lou Finney Blvd	75401 5988	903 457-2992
Groesbeck	Maffett Memorial	601 W Yeagua St	76642 1658	254 729-3667
Groom	Groom Branch	PO Box 308	79039 0308	806 249-0000
Groves	Groves Public	5600 W Washington St	77619 3629	409 962-6281
Groveton	Groveton Public	PO Box 399	75845 0399	936 642-2483
Gruver	Gruver City	PO Box 701	79040 0701	806 733-2191
Guthrie	Guthrie CSD/ King County	PO Box 70	79236 0070	806 596-4466
Hale Center	Hale Center Public	PO Box 214	79041 0214	806 839-2055
Hallettsville	Friench Simpson Memorial	705 E 4th St	77964 2828	361 798-3243
Haltom City	Haltom City Public	PO Box 14277	76117 0277	817 222-7790
Hamilton	Hamilton Public	201 N Pecan St	76531 1926	254 386-3474
Harker Heights	Harker Heights Public	100 E Beeline Ln	76548 1285	254 699-5008
Harlingen	Harlingen Public	410 76 Dr	78550 5072	956 430-6650
Haskell	Haskell County	412 N 1st St	79521 5706	940 864-2747
Hawkins	Allen Memorial Public	PO Box 329	75765 0329	903 769-2241
Hearne	Smith-Welch Memorial	114 W 4th St	77859 2506	979 279-5191
Hebbronville	Jim Hogg County Public	210 N Smith Ave	78361 2899	361 527-3421

CITY	LIBRARY	MAILING ADDRESS	ZIP	PHONE
Hemphill	J.R. Huffman Public	Rt 5 Box 2140	75948 9695	409 787-4829
Hempstead	Waller County	2331 11th St	77445 6799	979 826-7658
Henderson	Rusk County System	106 E Main St	75652 3117	903 657-8557
Henrietta	Edwards Public	210 W Gilbert St	76365 2816	940 538-4791
Hereford	Deaf Smith County	211 E 4th St	79045 5521	806 364-1206
Hewitt	Hewitt Community	100 Zuni Dr	76643 3008	254 666-2442
Hidalgo	Hidalgo Public	710 E Texano Dr	78557 4104	956 843-2093
Higgins	Higgins Public	PO Box 250	79046 0250	806 852-2214
Highland Park	Highland Park	4700 Drexel Dr	75205 3198	214 559-9400
Highlands	Stratford Branch	509 Stratford St	77562 2547	281 426-3521
Hillsboro	Hillsboro City	118 S Waco St	76645 7708	254 582-7385
Hitchcock	Genevieve Miller Hitchcock Public	8005 Barry Ave	77563 3238	409 986-7814
Holland	B.J. Hill	PO Box 217	76534 0217	254 657-0175
Hondo	Hondo Public	1011 19th St	78861 2431	830 426-5333
Honey Grove	Bertha Voyer Memorial	PO Box 47	75446 0047	903 378-2206
Hooks	Hooks Public	PO Box 1540	75561	903 547-3365
Houston	Harris County Public	8080 El Rio St	77054 4195	713 749-9000
Houston	Houston Public	500 McKinney St	77002 2534	832 393-1300
Howe	Howe Community	315 S Collins Fwy	75459 4592	903 532-5519
Humble	Octavia Fields Branch	1503 S Houston Ave	77338 4304	281 446-3377
Huntington	McMullen Memorial	PO Box 849	75949 0849	936 876-4516
Huntsville	Huntsville Public	1216 14th St	77340 4507	936 291-5470
Hurst	Hurst Public	901 Precinct Line Rd	76053 4997	817 788-7300
Hutchins	Hutchins-Atwell Public	PO Box 888	75141 0888	972 225-4711
Idalou	Idalou Public	PO Box 1277	79329 1277	806 892-2114
Imperial	Imperial Public	PO Box 307	79743 0307	915 536-2236
Industry	West End	PO Box 179	78944 0179	979 357-4434
Ingleside	Ingleside Public	PO Drawer 400	78362 0400	361 776-5355
Iowa Park	Tom Burnett Memorial	400 W Alameda St	76367 1616	940 592-4981
Iraan	Iraan Public	PO Box 638	79744 0638	432 639-2235
Irving	Irving Public	PO Box 152288	75015 2288	972 721-2628
Jacksboro	Gladys Johnson Ritchie Public	626 W College St	76458 1655	940 567-2240
Jacksonville	Jacksonville Public	502 S Jackson St	75766 2415	903 586-7664
Jasper	Jasper Public	175 E Water St	75951 4438	409 384-3791
Jayton	Kent County	PO Box 28	79528 0028	806 237-3287
Jefferson	Jefferson Carnegie	301 W Lafayette St	75657 2209	903 665-8911
Johnson City	Johnson City	PO Box 332	78636 0332	830 868-4469
Jonestown	Jonestown Community	18649 FM 1431 Ste 10A	78645 3413	512 267-7511
Joshua	Joshua School & Public	907 S Broadway St	76058 3155	817 202-8324
Jourdanton	Jourdanton Community	1101 Campbell Ave	78026 3507	830 769-3087
Junction	Kimble County	208 N 10th St	76849 4604	325 446-2342
Justin	Justin Community	PO Box 877	76247 0877	940 648-3649
Karnes City	Karnes City Public	302 S Panna Maria Ave	78118 3240	830 780-2539
Katy	Katy Branch	5414 Franz Rd	77493 1717	281 391-3509
Kaufman	Kaufman County	3790 S Houston St	75142 3714	972 932-6222
Keller	Keller Public	640 Johnson Rd	76248 4136	817 431-9011
Kendalia	Kendalia Public	PO Box 399	78027 0399	830 336-2002
Kenedy	Kenedy Public	303 W Main St	78119 2795	830 583-3313
Kennedale	Kennedale	PO Box 430	76060 0430	817 478-7876
Kermit	Winkler County	307 S Poplar St	79745 4315	432 586-3841
Kerrville	Butt-Holdsworth Memorial	505 Water St	78028 5316	830 257-8422
Kilgore	Kilgore Public	301 N Henderson Blvd	75662 2799	903 984-1529
Killeen	Killeen City System	205 E Church St	76541 4898	254 501-8994
Kingsland	Kingsland Branch	125 W Polk St	78639 5908	325 388-3170
Kingsville	Robert J. Kleberg Public	220 N 4th St	78363 4410	361 592-6381
Kingwood	Kingwood Branch	4102 Rustic Woods Dr	77345 1350	281 360-6804
Kirbyville	Kirbyville Public	PO Box 567	75956 0567	409 423-4653
Kountze	Kountze Public	800 Redwood St	77625 8966	409 246-2826
Krum	Krum Public	PO Box 780	76249 0780	940 482-3455
Kyle	Kyle Community	PO Box 366	78640 0366	512 268-7411
La Feria	Bailey H. Dunlap Memorial	PO Box 5804	75559 2580	956 797-1242
La Grange	Fayette Public	855 S Jefferson St	78945 3230	979 968-3765
La Joya	La Joya Municipal	PO Box H City Hall	78560	956 581-4533
La Marque	La Marque Public	1011 Bayou Rd	77568 4195	409 938-9270
La Porte	La Porte Branch	600 S Broadway	77571 5498	281 471-4022
Lago Vista	Lago Vista Community	5803 Thunderbird Ste 40	78645 5851	512 267-3868
Laguna Vista	Laguna Vista Public	1300 Palm Blvd	78578	956 943-7155
Lake Dallas	Lake Cities	PO Box 775	75065 0775	940 497-3566
Lake Jackson	Lake Jackson	250 Circle Way St	77566 5203	979 415-2590

CITY	LIBRARY	MAILING ADDRESS	ZIP	PHONE
Lake Travis/Austin	Lake Travis Community	3322 Ranch Road 620 S	78738 6804	512 533-6131
Lake Worth	Mary Lou Reddick Public	3801 Adam Grubb Dr	76135 3509	817 237-9681
Lakehills	Lakehills Area	7200 FM 1283	78063 6083	830 612-2777
Lamesa	Dawson County Public	PO Box 1264	79331 1264	806 872-6502
Lampasas	Lampasas Public	201 S Main St	76550 2843	512 556-3251
Lancaster	Lancaster Veterans Memorial	1600 Veterans Memorial Pkwy	75134 3270	972 227-1550
Laredo	Laredo Public	1120 E Calton Rd	78041 7328	956 795-2400
League City	Helen Hall	100 W Walker St	77573 3899	281 554-1111
Leakey	Real County Public	PO Box 488	78873 0488	830 232-5199
Leander	Leander Public	PO Box 410	78646 0410	512 259-5259
Leon Valley	Leon Valley Public	6425 Evers Rd	78238 1453	210 684-0720
Leonard	Leonard Public	PO Box 1188	75452 1188	903 587-2391
Levelland	Hockley County Memorial	802 Houston St Ste 108	79336 3705	806 894-6750
Lewisville	Lewisville Public	PO Box 299002	75029 9002	972 219-3566
Liberty	Liberty Municipal	1710 Sam Houston Ave	77575 4796	936 336-8901
Liberty Hill	Liberty Hill Public	PO Box 1072	78642 1072	512 515-7723
Lindale	Lindale	PO Box 1535	75771 1535	903 882-1900
Little Elm	Little Elm Public	100 W Eldorado Pkwy	75068	214 975-0435
Littlefield	Lamb County	232 Phelps Ave	79339 3428	806 385-5223
Livingston	Murphy Memorial	601 W Church St	77351 3199	936 327-4252
Llano	Llano County System	102 E Haynie St	78643 2072	325 247-5248
Lockhart	Dr. Eugene Clark	PO Box 209	78644 0209	512 398-3223
Lockney	Floyd County Branch	PO Box 249	79241 0249	806 652-3561
Lone Oak	Lone Oak Area Public	PO Box 501	75453 0501	903 662-4565
Longview	Longview Public	222 W Cotton St	75601 6348	903 237-1350
Lorenzo	Lorenzo	PO Box 426	79343 0426	806 634-5639
Los Fresnos	Ethel L. Whipple Memorial	402 W Ocean Blvd	78566 3650	956 233-5330
Louise	Louise Branch	PO Box 36	77455 0036	979 648-2018
Lubbock	Lubbock Public	1306 9th St	79401 2798	806 775-2824
Lufkin	Kurth Memorial	706 S Raguet St	75904 3922	936 630-0561
Luling	J B Nickells Memorial	215 S Pecan Ave	78648 2607	830 875-2813
Lumberton	Lumberton Public	130 E Chance Rd	77657 7763	409 755-7400
Lytle	Lytle Public	PO Box 831	78052 0831	830 772-3142
Mabank	Tri-County	PO Box 1770	75147 1770	903 887-9622
Madisonville	Madison County	605 S May St	77864 2561	936 348-6118
Magnolia	Malcolm Purvis–Magnolia	510 Melton St	77354 8551	281 259-8324
Malakoff	Red Waller Community	PO Box 1177	75148 1177	903 489-1818
Mansfield	Mansfield Public	104 S Wisteria St	76063 2424	817 473-4391
Manvel	Manvel	7104 Masters Rd	77578 0157	281 489-7596
Marathon	Marathon Public	PO Box 177	79842 0177	915 386-4136
Marble Falls	Marble Falls Public	101 Main St	78654 5722	830 693-3023
Marfa	Marfa Public	PO Box U	79843 0609	432 729-4631
Marion	Marion Community	PO Box 619	78124 0619	830 914-2803
Marlin	Marlin Public	301 Winter St	76661 2865	254 883-6602
Marshall	Marshall Public	300 S Alamo Blvd	75670 4273	903 935-4465
Mart	Nancy Nail Memorial	124 S Pearl St	76664 1425	254 876-2465
Mason	Mason County /Eckert Memorial	PO Box 1785	76856 1785	325 347-5446
Matador	Motley County	PO Box 557	79244 0557	806 347-2717
Matagorda	Matagorda Branch	800 Fisher St	77457	979 863-7925
Mathis	Mathis Public	103 Lamar St	78368 2441	361 547-6201
Maud	Maud Public	PO Box 100	75567 0100	903 585-5255
McAllen	McAllen Memorial	601 N Main St	78501 4666	956 688-3300
McCamey	Upton County Public	PO Box 1377	79752 1377	432 652-8718
McGregor	McGinley Memorial Public	317 S Main St	76657 1608	254 840-3732
McKinney	McKinney Memorial Public	101 E Hunt St	75069 3807	972 547-7323
McLean	Lovett Memorial	PO Box 8	79057	806 779-2851
Medina	Medina Community	PO Box 300	78055 0300	830 589-2825
Melissa	Melissa Public	1713 Cooper St	75454 9542	972 837-4540
Memphis	Memphis Public	303 S 8th St	79245 3211	806 259-2062
Menard	Menard Public	PO Box 404	76859 0404	325 396-2717
Mercedes	Mercedes Memorial	434 S Ohio St	78570 3196	956 565-2317
Meridian	Meridian Public	PO Box 679	76665 0679	254 435-9100
Merkel	Merkel Public	100 Kent St	79536 3612	325 928-5054
Mertzon	Irion County	PO Box 766	76941 0766	325 835-2704
Mesquite	Mesquite Public	300 W Grubb Dr	75149 3492	972 216-6220
Mexia	Gibbs Memorial	305 E Rusk St	76667 2398	254 562-3231
Midkiff	Midkiff Public	PO Box 160	79755 0160	915 535-2311
Midland	Midland County Public	301 W Missouri Ave	79701 5108	432 688-4320
Midlothian	A.H. Meadows	921 S 9th St	76065 3636	972 775-3417

CITY	LIBRARY	MAILING ADDRESS	ZIP	PHONE
Mineola	Mineola Memorial	301 N Pacific St	75773 1799	903 569-2767
Mineral Wells	Boyce Ditto Public	2300 SE Martin Luther King Jr	76067 5763	940 328-7880
Mission	Speer Memorial	801 E 12th St	78572 4493	956 580-8750
Missouri City	Missouri City Branch	1530 Texas Pkwy	77489 2170	281 499-4100
Monahans	Ward County	409 S Dwight St	79756 4609	432 943-3332
Mont Belvieu	West Chambers County Branch	PO Box 1289	77580 1289	281 576-2243
Montgomery	West Branch	19380 Highway 105 W Ste K	77356 1984	936 788-8314
Moody	Moody Community	PO Box 57	76557 0057	254 853-2004
Morton	Cochran County Love Memorial	318 S Main St	79346 3006	806 266-5051
Mount Calm	Mount Calm Public	PO Box 84	76673 0084	254 993-2761
Mount Pleasant	Mount Pleasant Public	213 N Madison Ave	75455 3944	903 575-4180
Mount Vernon	Franklin County	PO Box 579	75457 0579	903 537-4916
Mount Enterprise	Morrow Branch	PO Box 360	75681 0360	903 822-3532
Muenster	Muenster Public	PO Box 707	76252 0707	940 759-4291
Muleshoe	Muleshoe Area Public	322 W 2nd St	79347 3633	806 272-4707
Munday	Munday City–County	PO Box 268	76371 0268	940 422-4877
Nacogdoches	Nacogdoches Public	1112 North St	75961 4482	936 559-2970
Naples	Naples Public	PO Box 705	75568 0705	903 897-2964
Navasota	Navasota Public	1411 E Washington Ave	77868 3240	936 825-6744
Nederland	Marion & Ed Hughes Public	2712 Nederland Ave	77627 7015	409 722-1255
Needville	Albert George Branch	9230 Gene St	77461 8313	979 973-4270
New Boston	New Boston Public	127 N Ellis St	75570 2905	903 628-5414
New Braunfels	New Braunfels Public	700 E Common St	78130 4273	830 608-2150
New Caney	RB Tullis	21130 US Hwy 59 No. K	77357 8290	281 577-8968
New Waverly	New Waverly Public	200 Gibbs St Ste 1	77358 9743	936 344-2198
Newark	Newark Public	PO Box 1219	76071 1219	817 489-2224
Newton	Newton County Public	212 High St	75966 3216	409 379-8300
Nixon	Aphne Pattillo Nixon Public	401 N Nixon Ave	78140 2709	830 582-1913
Nocona	Nocona Public	10 Cooke St	76255 2148	940 825-6373
Noonday/Tyler	Noonday Community	16662 CR 196	75703 7112	903 939-0540
North Richland Hills	North Richland Hills Public	6720 NE Loop 820	76180 7901	817 427-6800
Odem	Odem Public	PO Box 636	78370 0636	361 368-7388
Odessa	Ector County	321 W 5th St	79761 5066	432 332-0633
Olney	Olney Community	PO Box 67	76374 0067	940 564-5513
Olton	Olton Area	PO Box 675	79064 0000	806 285-7772
Onalaska	Onalaska Public	PO Box 880	77360 0888	936 646-2665
Orange	Orange Public	220 N 5th St	77630 5705	409 883-1086
Orange Grove	Orange Grove School/Public	PO Box 534	78372 0534	361 384-0000
Overton	McMillan Memorial	302 E South St	75684 1818	903 834-6318
Ozona	Crockett County Public	PO Box 3030	76943 3030	325 392-3565
Paducah	Bicentennial City-County	PO Box AD	79248 1197	806 492-2006
Paint Rock	Harry Benge Crozier Memorial	PO Box 173	76866 0173	325 732-4320
Palacios	Palacios	326 Main St	77465 5499	361 972-3234
Palestine	Palestine Public	1101 N Cedar St	75801 7607	903 729-8087
Pampa	Lovett Memorial	PO Box 342	79066 0342	806 669-5780
Panhandle	Carson County Public	PO Box 339	79068 0339	806 537-3742
Paris	Paris Public	326 S Main St	75460 5825	903 785-8531
Pasadena	Pasadena Public	1201 Jeff Ginn Memorial Dr	77506 4895	713 477-0276
Pearland	Pearland	3522 Liberty Dr	77581 5415	281 485-4876
Pearsall	Pearsall Public	200 E Trinity St	78061 3351	830 334-2496
Pecos	Reeves County	505 S Park St	79772 3735	432 445-5340
Perryton	Perry Memorial	22 SE 5th Ave	79070 3112	806 435-5801
Petersburg	Petersburg Public	PO Box 65	79250 0065	806 667-3657
Pflugerville	Pflugerville Community	102 10th St	78660 3968	512 251-9185
Pharr	Pharr Memorial	121 E Cherokee	78577	956 787-3966
Pilot Point	Pilot Point Community	PO Box 969	76258 0969	940 686-5004
Pineland	Arthur Temple Sr. Memorial	PO Box 847	75968 0847	409 584-2546
Pittsburg	Pittsburg-Camp County Public	613 Quitman St	75686 1035	903 856-3302
Plains	Yoakum County	PO Box 419	79355 0419	806 456-8725
Plainview	Unger Memorial	825 Austin St	79072 7235	806 296-1148
Plano	Plano Public System	2501 Coit Rd	75075 3712	972 769-4269
Pleasanton	Pleasanton Public	321 N Main St	78064 3554	830 569-3622
Point Comfort	Point Comfort Branch	PO Box 382	77978 0382	361 987-2954
Ponder	Betty Foster Public	PO Box 582	76259 0582	940 479-2683
Port Aransas	William R. 'Bill' Ellis Memorial	700 W Avenue A	78373 4128	361 749-4116
Port Arthur	Port Arthur Public	4615 9th Ave	77642 5799	409 985-8838
Port Isabel	Port Isabel Public	213 N Yturria St	78578 4602	956 943-1822
Port Lavaca	Calhoun County Public	200 W Mahan St	77979 3368	361 552-7323
Port Neches	Effie & Wilton Hebert Public	2025 Merriman St	77651 3797	409 722-4554

CITY	LIBRARY	MAILING ADDRESS	ZIP	PHONE
Port O'Connor	Port O'Connor Branch	PO Box 424	77982 0424	361 983-4365
Portland	Bell/Whittington Public	2400 Memorial Pkwy	78374 3208	361 777-0921
Post	Post Public	105 E Main St	79356 3229	806 495-2149
Poteet	Poteet Public	PO Box 380	78065 0380	830 742-8917
Pottsboro	Pottsboro Area Public	PO Box 477	75076 0477	903 786-8274
Prairie Lea	Tri-Community	PO Box 44	78661 0044	512 488-2164
Premont	Premont Public	PO Box 829	78375 0829	361 348-0000
Presidio	City of Presidio	PO Box 2440	79845 2440	432 229-3317
Princeton	Princeton Community	321 Panther Pkwy	75407 9099	972 736-3741
Prosper	Prosper Community	PO Box 490	75078 0490	972 346-2455
Quanah	Thompson Sawyer Public	403 W 3rd St	79252 3825	940 663-2654
Quemado	Quemado Public	PO Box 210	78877 0210	830 757-1313
Quitaque	Caprock Public	PO Box 487	79255 0487	806 455-1225
Quitman	Quitman Public	PO Box 1677	75783 1677	903 763-4191
Ralls	Ralls	PO Box 601	79357 0601	806 253-2755
Ranger	Ranger City	400 W Main St	76470 1295	254 647-1880
Rankin	Rankin Public	PO Box 6	79778 0006	432 693-2881
Raymondville	Reber Memorial	193 N 4th St	78580 1994	956 689-2930
Refugio	Dennis M. O'Connor Public	815 S Commerce St	78377 3107	361 526-2608
Rhome	Rhome Public	PO Box 427	76078 0427	817 636-2767
Richardson	Richardson Public	900 Civic Center Dr	75080 5298	972 744-4350
Richland Hills	Richland Hills Public	6724 Rena Dr	76118 6273	817 299-1860
Richmond	Fort Bend County	1001 Golfview Dr	77469 5199	281 342-4455
Rio Hondo	Rio Hondo Public	PO Box 389	78583 0389	956 748-3322
River Oaks	River Oaks Public	4900 River Oaks Blvd	76114 3007	817 624-7344
Roanoke	Roanoke Public	308 S Walnut St	76262 6626	817 491-2691
Robert Lee	Coke County	PO Box 637	76945 0637	915 453-2495
Robstown	Nueces County Public	710 E Main Ave Ste 2	78380 3198	361 767-5228
Roby	Roby	PO Box 387	79543 0387	915 776-1132
Rockdale	Lucy Hill Patterson Memorial	201 Ackerman St	76567 2901	512 446-3410
Rockport	Aransas County Public	701 E Mimosa St	78382 4150	361 790-0153
Rocksprings	Claud H. Gilmer Memorial	PO Box 157	78880 0157	830 683-8130
Rockwall	Rockwall County	105 S 1st St	75087 3649	972 882-0340
Rosebud	D. Brown Memorial	PO Box 657	76570 0657	254 583-2328
Rotan	Rotan Public	404 E Sammy Baugh Ave	79546 3820	325 735-3362
Round Rock	Round Rock Public	216 E Main Ave	78664 5245	512 218-7010
Round Top	Round Top	PO Box 245	78954 0245	979 249-2700
Rowlett	Rowlett Public	PO Box 1017	75030 1017	972 412-6161
Royse City	Royse City	124 S Arch St	75189	972 635-2772
Runge	Runge Public	PO Box 37	78151 0037	830 239-4192
Rusk	Singletary Memorial	207 E 6th St	75785 1103	903 683-5916
Sabinal	Sabinal Public	PO Box 245	78881 0245	830 988-2911
Sabine Pass	Sabine Pass Branch	PO Box 546	77655 0546	409 972-2944
Sachse	Sachse Public	5560 S Hwy 78	75048 3763	972 530-8966
Saginaw	John Ed Keeter Public	PO Box 79070	76179 0070	817 232-2100
Salado	Salado Public	PO Box 1178	76571 1178	254 947-9191
San Angelo	Tom Green County System	113 W Beauregard Ave	76903 5834	325 655-7321
San Antonio	San Antonio Public	600 Soledad St	78205 1200	210 207-2500
San Augustine	San Augustine Public	413 E Columbia St	75972 2111	936 275-5367
San Benito	San Benito Public	101 W Rose St	78586 5169	956 361-3860
San Diego	Duval County/San Diego Public	PO Box 1062	78384 1062	361 279-8201
San Juan	San Juan Public	1010 S Standard Ave	78589 2511	956 702-0926
San Marcos	San Marcos Public	625 E Hopkins St	78666 6313	512 393-8200
San Saba	Rylander Memorial	103 S Live Oak St	76877 4799	325 372-3079
San Ygnacio	Zapata County Branch	PO Box 219	78076 0219	956 766-0000
Sanderson	Terrell County Public	PO Box 250	79848 0250	915 345-2294
Sanger	Sanger Public	PO Box 1729	76266 1729	940 458-3257
Santa Anna	Santa Anna	606 Wallis Ave	76878 2031	325 348-3395
Santa Fe	Mae S. Bruce	PO Box 950	77510 0950	409 925-5540
Sargent	Sargent Branch	8146 Highway 457	77414 8954	979 245-3032
Schertz	Schertz Public	608 Schertz Pkwy	78154 1911	210 658-6011
Schulenburg	Schulenburg Public	700 Bohlmann Ave	78956 1316	979 743-3345
Seabrook	Evelyn Meador Branch	2400 N Meyer Rd	77586 2964	281 474-9142
Seadrift	Seadrift Branch	PO Box 567	77983 0567	361 785-4241
Seagoville	Seagoville Public	702 N Highway 175	75159 1774	972 287-7720
Seagraves	Gaines County Branch	PO Box 366	79359 0366	806 546-3053
Sealy	Virgil & Josephine Gordon Memorial	917 N Circle Dr	77474 3333	979 885-7469
Seguin	Seguin–Guadalupe County Public	707 E College St	78155 3217	830 401-2422
Seminole	Gaines County	704 Hobbs Hwy	79360 3402	432 758-4007

CITY	LIBRARY	MAILING ADDRESS	ZIP	PHONE
Seven Points	Cedar Creek Lake	PO Box 43711	75143 0711	903 432-4185
Seymour	Baylor County	101 S Washington St	76380 2558	940 889-2007
Shamrock	Shamrock Public	712 N Main St	79079 2038	806 256-3921
Shepherd	Shepherd Public	30 N Liberty St	77371 2460	936 628-3515
Sheridan	Sheridan Memorial	PO Box 274	77475 0274	979 234-3280
Sherman	Sherman Public	421 N Travis St	75090 5975	903 892-7240
Shiner	Shiner Public	PO Box 1602	77984 1602	361 594-3044
Silsbee	Silsbee Public	Santa Fe Park	77656 4000	409 385-4831
Silverton	Silverton Public	PO Box 69	79257 0069	806 823-2339
Sinton	Sinton Public	100 N Pirate Blvd	78387 2912	361 364-4545
Skellytown	Skellytown Branch	PO Box 92	79080 0092	806 848-0000
Slaton	Slaton City	200 W Lynn St	79364 4136	806 828-2008
Smithville	Smithville Public	507 Main St	78957 1430	512 237-2707
Snyder	Scurry County	1916 23rd St	79549 1910	325 573-5572
Sonora	Sutton County	306 E Mulberry St	76950 2603	325 387-2111
Sour Lake	Alma M. Carpenter Public	PO Box 536	77659 0536	409 287-3592
South Houston	South Houston Branch	607 Avenue A	77587 3659	713 941-2385
Southlake	Southlake Public	1400 Main St Ste 130	76092 7628	817 481-5718
Spearman	Hansford County	122 Main St	79081 2064	806 659-2231
Spring	Barbara Bush Branch	6817Cypresswood Dr	77379 7705	281 376-4610
Spring Branch	Bulverde / Spring Branch	20475 Hwy 46 W Ste 340	78070 6147	830 438-3666
Springtown	Springtown Public	PO Box 428	76082 0428	817 523-5862
Spur	Dickens County Spur Public	PO Box 282	79370 0282	806 271-3714
Stafford	Mamie George Branch	320 Dulles Ave	77477 4799	281 491-8086
Stamford	Stamford Carnegie	600 E McHarg St	79553 4310	325 773-2532
Stanton	Martin County	PO Box 1187	79782 1187	432 756-2472
Stephenville	Stephenville Public	174 N Columbia St	76401 3421	254 918-1240
Sterling City	Sterling County Public	PO Box 1130	76951 1130	325 378-2212
Stinnett	Hutchinson County / Stinnett	PO Box 478	79083 0478	806 878-4013
Stratford	Sherman County Public	PO Box 46	79084 0046	806 366-2200
Sugar Land	Sugar Land Branch	550 Eldridge	77478 2823	281 277-8934
Sulphur Springs	Sulphur Springs Public	611 Davis St N	75482 2621	903 885-4926
Sundown	Sundown Branch	PO Box 600	79372 0600	806 266-3131
Sunnyvale	Sunnyvale Public	402 Tower Pl	75182 9278	972 226-4491
Sunray	Britain Memorial	PO Box 180	79086 0180	806 948-5501
Sweeny	Sweeny	205 W Ashley Wilson Rd	77480 1023	979 548-2567
Sweetwater	County–City	206 Elm St	79556 4524	325 235-4978
Taft	Taft Public	PO Box 416	78390 0416	361 528-3512
Tahoka	City County	PO Box 1018	79373 1018	806 561-4050
Tatum	Tatum Public	PO Box 1087	75691 1087	903 947-2211
Taylor	Taylor Public	400 Porter St	76574 3600	512 352-3434
Teague	Teague Public	400 Main St	75860 1641	254 739-3311
Temple	Temple Public	100 W Adams Ave	76501 7658	254 298-5556
Terrell	Terrell Public	301 N Rockwall St	75160 2618	972 551-6663
Texarkana	Texarkana Public	600 W 3rd St	75501 5054	903 794-2149
Texas City	Moore Memorial Public	1701 9th Ave N	77590 5496	409 643-5979
Texline	Texline Public	PO Box 356	79087 0356	806 362-4849
The Colony	The Colony Public	6800 Main St	75056 1133	972 625-1900
The Woodlands	South Regional	2101 Lake Robbins Dr	77380 1152	281 298-9110
Three Rivers	Live Oak County Branch	102 E Leroy	78071	361 786-3031
Throckmorton	Depot Public	PO Box 6	76483 0006	940 849-3076
Tivoli	Tivoli Public	211 Oleander St	77990	361 286-0145
Tomball	Tomball Branch	30555 Tomball Pkwy	77375 4096	832 559-4200
Tornillo	Tornillo Media Center	PO Box 170	79853 0170	915 764-2040
Trinity	Blanche K. Werner Public	PO Box 1168	75862 1168	936 594-2087
Troup	Cameron–J. Jarvis Troup Municipal	PO Box 721	75789 0721	903 842-3101
Tulia	Swisher County	127 SW 2nd St	79088 2747	806 995-3447
Turkey	Turkey Public	PO Box 415	79261 0415	806 423-1033
Tyler	Tyler Public	201 S College Ave	75702 7381	903 593-7323
Universal City	Universal City Public	100 Northview Dr	78148 4150	210 659-7048
University Park/Dallas	University Park Public	6517 Hillcrest Ste 110	75205 1857	214 363-9095
Utopia	Utopia Memorial	PO Box 677	78884 0677	830 966-3448
Uvalde	El Progreso Memorial	129 W Nopal St	78801 5284	830 278-2017
Valley Mills	Valley Mills Public	PO Box 25	76689 0025	254 932-5616
Van Alstyne	Van Alstyne Public	PO Box 629	75495 0629	903 482-5991
Van Horn	Van Horn City County	PO Box 129	79855 0129	432 283-2855
Vega	Oldham County Public	PO Box 640	79092 0640	806 267-2635
Venus	Hall High School and Community	PO Box 364	76084 0364	972 366-8353

CITY	LIBRARY	MAILING ADDRESS	ZIP	PHONE
Vernon	Carnegie City–County	2810 Wilbarger St	76384 4597	940 552-2462
Victoria	Victoria Public	302 N Main St	77901 6592	361 572-2704
Vidor	Vidor Public	440 E Bolivar	77662 5098	409 769-7148
Village Mills	Wildwood Civic	PO Box 774	77663 0774	409 834-2924
Waco	Waco-McLennan County	1717 Austin Ave	76701 1794	254 750-5941
Waelder	Waelder Public	PO Box 428	78959 0428	830 788-7167
Wallis	Austin County System	PO Box 519	77485 0519	979 478-6813
Waskom	Waskom Public	PO Box 1187	75692 1187	903 687-3041
Watauga	Watauga Public	7109 Whitley Rd	76148 2024	817 514-5855
Waxahachie	Nicholas P. Sims	515 W Main St	75165 3235	972 937-2671
Weatherford	Weatherford Public	1014 Charles St	76086 5098	817 598-4150
Weimar	Weimar Public	1 Jackson Sq	78962 2019	979 725-6608
Wellington	Collingsworth Public	711 15th St	79095 3600	806 447-2116
Weslaco	Weslaco Public	525 S Kansas Ave	78596 6215	956 968-4533
West	West Public	PO Box 513	76691 0513	254 826-3070
West Columbia	West Columbia Branch	518 E Brazos	77486 2944	979 345-3394
West Lake Hills/Austin	Westbank Community	1309 Westbank Dr	78746 6565	512 314-3580
West Tawakoni	Tawakoni Area Public	340 W Highway 276	75474 2644	903 447-3445
Wharton	Wharton County	1920 N Fulton St	77488 2845	979 532-8080
Wheeler	Wheeler Public	PO Box 676	79096 0676	806 826-5977
White Deer	White Deer Branch	PO Box 85	79097 0085	806 884-0000
White Oak	White Oak School Community	200 S White Oak Rd	75693 1520	903 291-2052
White Settlement	White Settlement Public	8215 White Settlement Rd	76108 1604	817 367-0166
Whitehouse	Whitehouse Community	107 Bascom Rd	75791 3230	903 839-2949
Whitesboro	Whitesboro Public	308 W Main St	76273 1639	903 564-5432
Whitewright	Whitewright Public	PO Box 984	75491 0984	903 364-2955
Whitney	Lake Whitney Public	PO Box 2050	76692 2050	254 694-4639
Wichita Falls	Wichita Falls Public	600 11th St	76301 4604	940 767-0868
Willis	RF Meador Branch	709 W Montgomery St	77378 8682	936 856-4411
Wills Point	Wills Point High School/Wingo Public	1800 W South Commerce	75169 2378	903 873-2371
Wilmer	Gilliam Memorial Public	205 E Belt Line Rd	75172 1127	972 441-3713
Wimberley	Wimberley Village	PO Box 1240	78676 1240	512 847-2188
Wink	Wink Branch	PO Box 457	79789 0457	915 527-0000
Winnie	Juanita Hargraves Memorial Branch	PO Box 597	77665 0597	409 296-8245
Winnsboro	Gilbreath Memorial	916 N Main St	75494 2120	903 342-6866
Winters	Winters Public	120 N Main St	79567 5108	325 754-4251
Wolfe City	Wolfe City Public	PO Box 109	75496 0109	903 496-7311
Wolfforth	City of Wolfforth	PO Box 36	79382 0036	806 866-9280
Woodville	Allan Shivers & Museum	302 N Charlton St	75979 4806	409 283-3709
Wylie	Rita & Truett Smith Public	800 Thomas St	75098 3872	972 442-7566
Yoakum	Carl & Mary Welhausen	810 Front St	77995 3058	361 293-5001
Yorktown	Yorktown Public	PO Box 308	78164 0308	316 564-3232
Zapata	Zapata County Public	2806 STOP 28-A	78076 2836	956 765-5351

The San Antonio Central Library, called Enchilada Red. Texas Almanac photo.

Holidays, Anniversaries and Festivals, 2006 and 2007

Below are listed the principal federal and state government holidays; Christian, Jewish and Islamic holidays and festivals; and special recognition days for 2006 and 2007. Technically, the United States does not observe national holidays. Each state has jurisdiction over its holidays, which are usually designated by its legislature. This list was compiled partially from *Astronomical Phenomena 2006* and *2007*, published by the U.S. Naval Observatory, and from the Texas Government Code. See the footnotes for explanations of the symbols.

2006

†§New Year's Day	Sun., Jan. 1
Epiphany	Fri., Jan. 6
‡Sam Rayburn Day	Fri., Jan. 6
†§Martin Luther King, Jr., Day	Mon., Jan. 16
†*Confederate Heroes Day	Thurs., Jan. 19
†§**Presidents' Day	Mon., Feb. 20
§§Islamic New Year	Tues., Jan. 31
Ash Wednesday	Wed., March 1
†Texas Independence Day	Thurs., March 2
‡Sam Houston Day	Thurs., March 2
‡Texas Flag Day	Thurs., March 2
Primary Election Day	Tues., March 7
†César Chávez Day	Fri., March 31
Palm Sunday	Sun., April 9
‡Former Prisoners of War Recognition Day	Sun., April 9
¶Passover (Pesach), first day of	Thurs., April 13
†§Good Friday	Fri., April 14
Easter Day	Sun., April 16
†San Jacinto Day	Fri., April 21
Mother's Day	Sun., May 14
Armed Forces Day	Sat., May 20
Ascension Day	Thurs., May 25
†§Memorial Day	Mon., May 29
¶Shavuot (Feast of Weeks)	Fri., June 2
Whit Sunday — Pentecost	Sun., June 4
Trinity Sunday	Sun., June 11
Flag Day (U.S.)	Wed., June 14
Father's Day	Sun., June 18
†Emancipation Day in Texas (Juneteenth)	Mon., June 19
†§Independence Day	Tues., July 4
†Lyndon Baines Johnson Day	Sun., Aug. 27
†§Labor Day	Mon., Sept. 4
Grandparents Day	Sun., Sept. 10
¶Rosh Hashanah (Jewish New Year)	Sat., Sept. 23
§§Ramadan, first day of	Sun., Sept. 24
¶Yom Kippur (Day of Atonement)	Mon., Oct. 2
¶Sukkot (Tabernacles), first day of	Sat., Oct. 7
§‡Columbus Day	Mon., Oct. 9
Halloween	Tues., Oct. 31
‡Father of Texas (Stephen F. Austin) Day	Fri., Nov. 3
†General Election Day	Tues., Nov. 7
†§Veterans Day	Sat., Nov. 11
†§††Thanksgiving Day	Thurs., Nov. 23
First Sunday in Advent	Sun., Dec. 3
¶Hanukkah, first day of	Sat., Dec. 16
†§Christmas Day	Mon., Dec. 25

2007

†§New Year's Day	Mon., Jan. 1
Epiphany	Sat., Jan. 6
‡Sam Rayburn Day	Sat., Jan. 6
†§Martin Luther King, Jr., Day	Mon., Jan. 15
†*Confederate Heroes Day	Fri., Jan. 19
§§Islamic New Year	Sat., Jan. 20
†§**Presidents' Day	Mon., Feb. 19
Ash Wednesday	Wed., Feb. 21
†Texas Independence Day	Fri., March 2
‡Sam Houston Day	Fri., March 2
‡Texas Flag Day	Fri., March 2
†César Chávez Day	Sat., March 31
Palm Sunday	Sun., April 1
¶Passover (Pesach), first day of	Tues., April 3
†§Good Friday	Fri., April 6
Easter Day	Sun., April 8
‡Former Prisoners of War Recognition Day	Sun., April 9
†San Jacinto Day	Sat., April 21
Mother's Day	Sun., May 13
Ascension Day	Thurs., May 17
Armed Forces Day	Sat., May 19
¶Shavuot (Feast of Weeks)	Wed., May 23
Whit Sunday — Pentecost	Sun., May 27
†§Memorial Day	Mon., May 28
Trinity Sunday	Sun., June 3
Flag Day (U.S.)	Thurs., June 14
Father's Day	Sun., June 17
†Emancipation Day in Texas (Juneteenth)	Mon., June 19
†§Independence Day	Wed., July 4
†Lyndon Baines Johnson Day	Mon., Aug. 27
†§Labor Day	Mon., Sept. 3
Grandparents Day	Sun., Sept. 9
§§Ramadan, first day of	Thurs., Sept. 13
¶Rosh Hashanah (Jewish New Year)	Thurs., Sept. 13
¶Yom Kippur (Day of Atonement)	Sat., Sept. 22
¶Sukkot (Tabernacles), first day of	Thurs., Sept. 27
§‡Columbus Day	Mon., Oct. 8
Halloween	Wed., Oct. 31
‡Father of Texas (Stephen F. Austin) Day	Sat., Nov. 3
†§Veterans Day	Sun., Nov. 11
†§††Thanksgiving Day	Thurs., Nov. 22
First Sunday in Advent	Sun., Dec. 2
¶Hanukkah, first day of	Wed., Dec. 5
†§Christmas Day	Tues., Dec. 25

¶ §§ In these tables, the **Jewish** (¶) and **Islamic** (§§) holidays are tabular, which means they begin at sunset on the previous evening.

† **State holiday in Texas.** For state employees, the Friday after Thanksgiving Day, Dec. 24 and Dec. 26 are also holidays. Optional holidays are César Chávez Day, Good Friday, Rosh Hashanah and Yom Kippur. Partial-staffing holidays are Confederate Heroes Day, Texas Independence Day, San Jacinto Day, Emancipation Day in Texas and Lyndon Baines Johnson Day. State offices will be open on optional holidays and partial-staffing holidays.

‡ **State Recognition Days,** designated by the Texas Legislature. In addition, the legislature has designated the week of May 22–26 as International Trade Awareness Week.

§ **Federal** legal public holiday.

*Confederate Heroes Day combines the birthdays of Robert E. Lee (Jan. 19) and Jefferson Davis (June 3).

**Presidents' Day combines the birthdays of George Washington (Feb. 22) and Abraham Lincoln (Feb. 12).

†† Between 1939 and 1957, Texas observed Thanksgiving Day on the last Thursday in November. As a result, in all Novembers having five Thursdays, Texas celebrated national Thanksgiving on the fourth Thursday and Texas Thanksgiving on the fifth Thursday. In 1957, Texas changed the state observance to coincide in all years with the national holiday. ☆

Church Affiliation Change: 1990 to 2000

Texas remains one of the nation's more "churched" states, even though a smaller portion of Texans is affiliated with a church than ten years ago.

Texas ranks 18th among the states in percentage of the population belonging to a denomination. According to *Churches and Church Membership in the United States 2000*, at least 55.5 percent of Texans are adherents to a religion.

The survey, from the Glenmary Research Center in Nashville, is the only U.S. survey to report church membership at the state and county level. It relies on reports from the different denominations for membership numbers.

But in 2000, the African-American churches did not participate in the study. This probably leaves out more than one million church-going Texans.

In 1990, when the survey was last done, it was estimated that there were 815,000 black Baptists in Texas. A conservative estimate of the membership in black Pentecostal churches in 2000 would be about 300,000. And, an estimate for black Methodists in Texas would be approximately 200,000.

Adjusting for those additions, then the percentage of Texans that are members of a religion would be closer to 61.7 percent. Although that is higher than the 55.5 percent figure compiled from the reporting churches, still, it would be down from 67.1 percent ten years ago, indicating a move away from church membership.

This decrease occurred while many indicators have been showing that Americans are more interested in their spiritual lives than at any time in recent decades. Churches reported an increase of 1.5 million members while the total population of Texas increased by 4 million from 1990 to 2000. During the same period, the number of Texans not attached to a religion rose by 2.5 million.

Thus, according to the *Texas Almanac* analysis from a variety of sources, there are 7.9 million persons in the state who are not claimed by a church and about 13 million who are church members. (The U.S. census counted 20,851,820 persons in Texas in 2000.)

From the 2000 church survey, diversity among religious believers can be seen in the congregations of Muslims, Hindus, Buddhists and other non-Christian faiths. In 1990, these groups were not surveyed, so increases cannot be determined.

The estimate of Jewish Texans, 128,000, is from the congregations in the state. The number increased by 20,000 from 1990.

During the decade, the number of Catholics increased by almost 800,000, the greatest numerical gain among the churches. However, the percentage of Texans who are Catholic remained at 21 percent.

The largest faith group, the Baptists, increased by

Mentone Community Church, Loving County. *Texas Almanac photo.*

Texas' ranking among states

According to *Churches and Church Membership in the United States 2000*, Texas ranks:

- First in number of Evangelical Protestants, with 5,083,087. California, ranked second, has less than half as many with 2,432,285.
- Second, behind Pennsylvania, in number of Mainline Protestants at 1,705,394.
- Third in number of Catholics, behind California and New York.
- Third in number of Buddhist congregations.
- Fifth in number of Muslims.
- Fifth in number of Hindu congregations.
- Sixth in number of Mormons.
- Tenth in number of Jews.

314,761 members, a rate less than the statewide population increase. Thus in 2000, Baptists made up 21.8 percent of the population, down from 24.9 percent in 1990.

The trend in the state's two largest denominations, Roman Catholic and Southern Baptist, which together make up over 40 percent of the population, was especially noticeable in the four largest metropolitan areas. More than half of all Texans live in these areas.

In the eight-county Houston metro area, the percentage of Catholics rose from 17.3 percent to 18.2 percent, while the percentage of Southern Baptists went down slightly from 14.9 percent to 14.8.

In the five-county Austin metro area, the percentage of Catholics increased from 13.6 percent to 18.4 percent. The percentage of Southern Baptists decreased from 13.5 percent to 10.2 percent.

In the four-county San Antonio metro area, the percentage of Catholics increased from 36.0 to 38.8, while the percentage of Southern Baptists decreased from 10.4 to 8.8.

The 12-county Dallas-Forth Worth metro area is the only one of the four where the number of Southern Baptists, 855,680, is higher than Catholics, 808,167. But, here also, the percentage of Southern Baptists declined from 19.0 to 16.4, while the percentage of

Catholics rose from 9.0 in 1990 to 15.5 in 2000.

As noted, while these shifts in religious make-up were occurring, the number of persons not affiliated with a religious group was increasing.

In Houston in 1990, the percentage of the population not counted as church members was 43.1. In 2000, that had risen to 50.1 percent.

In Austin, the figure increased from 52.4 percent to 55.3 percent.

In San Antonio, the percentage of non-adherents to a religion was 36.2 in 1990. In 2000, it had risen slightly to 37.0 percent.

In the Dallas-Fort Worth area, it increased from 43.6 percent in 1990, to 47.7 percent in 2000.

These trends reflect what was happening in the nation at large, where the percentage of the population not affiliated with a church rose from 44.9 to 55.1.

The Southern Baptists and Catholics also were the largest religious groups in the nation. And the percentage of Catholics remained about the same, 21.5 in 1990 and 22.0 in 2000, while the percentage of the total population that was Southern Baptist declined from 13.8 to 7.1.

The Glenmary study is a combined effort of the Catholic research center and the Church of the Nazarene, a Protestant denomination with headquarters in Kansas City, Mo..

The study distinguishes between members, which it defines as adult members only, and adherents, which includes adults and children. **All figures for members used by the *Texas Almanac* refer to children and adults**.

Sources

Churches and Church Membership in the United States 2000, Glenmary Research Center, Nashville, Tenn., 2002.

National Council of Churches of Christ in the USA, New York, *Yearbook of American and Canadian Churches*, annual.

New Handbook of Texas, 1996, various: "Christian Methodist Episcopal Church," by Charles E. Tatum; "African-American Churches," "African Methodist Episcopal Church," and "African Methodist Episcopal Zion Church," by William E. Montgomery; "Religion," by John W. Storey. — *Robert Plocheck*

Numbers of Members by Denomination

Religious Groups in Texas	1990	Change	2000
Baha'i			**10,777**
Baptist	**4,223,157**	**+ 314,761**	**4,537,918**
American Baptist Association			61,272
American Baptist Churches in the USA	12,905	- 5,848	7,057
Baptist General Conference	278	+ 62	340
Baptist Missionary Association of America	125,323	- 2,125	123,198
Conservative Baptist Association of America (1 congregation)			
Free Will Baptist, National Association of, Inc.	4,936	- 2,114	2,822
Interstate & Foreign Landmark Missionary Baptists Association	76	+ 17	93
Landmark Baptist, Indep. Assns. & Unaffil. Churches			964
National Primitive Baptist Convention, USA			4,463
North American Baptist Conference	1,634	- 65	1,569
Primitive Baptists Associations	2,544		
Primitive Baptist Church — Old Line (118 congregations)			NR
Progressive Primitive Baptists			197
Reformed Baptist Churches (10 congregations)			
Regular Baptist Churches, General Association of			684
Seventh Day Baptist General Conference	242		
Southern Baptist Convention	3,259,395	+ 260,064	3,519,459
Southwide Baptist Fellowship (13 congregations)			
Two-Seed-in-the-Spirit Predestinarian Baptists	53	- 24	29
*(Black Baptists Estimate)**	*(815,771)**	—	*(815,771)**
Buddhism (88 congregations)			**NR**
Catholic Church	**3,574,728**	**+ 794,241**	**4,368,969**
(Independent) Christian Churches & Churches of Christ	**33,766**	**+ 9,836**	**43,602**
Churches of Christ	**380,948**	**- 3,684**	**377,264**
(Disciples of Christ) Christian Church	**105,495**	**+ 5,793**	**111,288**
Episcopal	**169,227**	**+ 8,683**	**177,910**
Episcopal Church, The	169,112	+ 8,798	177,910
Reformed Episcopal Church	115		
Hindu (34 congregations)			**NR**
Holiness	**61,487**	**+ 25,052**	**86,539**
Christian & Missionary Alliance, The	3,082	+ 776	3,858
Church of God (Anderson, Ind.)	5,854	- 1,185	4,669
Free Methodist Church of North America	886	- 12	874
Nazarene, Church of the	45,097	+ 5,431	50,528
Salvation Army	5,676	+ 19,394	25,070
Wesleyan Church, The	892	+648	1,540
Independent Non-Charismatic Churches	**132,292**	**+ 12,957**	**145,249**

Religious Groups in Texas	1990	Change	2000
Jain (6 congregations)			NR
Jewish, estimate	107,980	+ 20,020	128,000
Lutheran	294,524	+ 6,994	301,518
Church of the Lutheran Brethren of America	71		
Church of the Lutheran Confession	144		
Evangelical Lutheran Church in America	155,276	- 257	155,019
Evangelical Lutheran Synod	146		
Free Lutheran Congregations, The Association of	144	+ 224	368
Lutheran Church—Missouri Synod, The	134,280	+ 5,826	140,106
Wisconsin Evangelical Lutheran Synod	4,463	+ 1,562	6,025
Mennonite/Amish	2,608	+ 2,011	4,619
Amish, Old Order	400	- 376	24
Amish, other			68
Beachy Amish Mennonite Churches	70	+ 57	127
Church of God in Christ (Mennonite)	522	+ 327	849
Conservative Mennonite Conference			191
Evangelical Bible Churches, Fellowship of (was Ev. Menn. Bre.)	20		
Eastern Pennsylvania Mennonite Church	39	+ 26	65
Mennonite Brethren Churches, U.S. Conference of	329	+ 96	425
Mennonite, other			1,655
Mennonite Church USA	1,228	- 13	1,215
Methodist	1,202,991	+ 16,542	1,219,533
African Methodist Episcopal Zion	2,191	—	(2,191)*
(African Methodist Episcopal estimate)*(300 congregations)	(150,000)*	—	(150,000)*
(Christian Methodist Episcopal estimate)*	(45,000)*	—	(45,000)*
Evangelical Methodist Church	1,482		
United Methodist Church, The	1,004,318	+ 18,024	1,022,342
(Mormons) Church of Jesus Christ of Latter-day Saints	111,276	+ 44,175	155,451
Muslim, estimate			114,999
Orthodox	2,082	+ 20,673	22,755
Antiochian Orthodox of North America			4,642
Armenian Apostolic Church/Cilicia			80
Armenian Apostolic Church/Etchmiadzin			1,275
Assyrian Apostolic Church	282		
Coptic Orthodox Church (8 congregations)			NR
Greek Orthodox Archdiocese of America			9,444
Greek Orthodox Archdiocese of Vasiloupulis			135
Malankara Archdiocese/Syrian Orthodox Church in North Amer.			825
Malankara Orthodox Syrian Church, American Diocese of the			2,675
Orthodox Church in America (Romanian Diocese)			413
Orthodox Church in America (Territorial Dioceses)			2,096
Russian Orthodox Church Outside of Russia (4 congregations)			NR
Serbian Orthodox Church in the USA			1,110
Serbian Orthodox Ch./New Gracanica Metropolitanate (1 cong)			NR
Syrian Orthodox Church of Antioch	1,800	- 1,740	60
Pentecostal/Charismatic	682,769	+ 80,301	763,070
Assemblies of God	202,082	+ 26,016	228,098
Pentecostal Church of God	12,296	- 704	11,592
Pentecostal Holiness Church, International	5,517	+ 4,748	10,265
Church of God (Cleveland, Tenn.)	27,828	+ 10,431	38,259
Church of God of Prophecy	2,918	- 12	2,906
(Church of God in Christ estimate)*(268 congregations)	(300,000)*	—	(300,000)*
International Church of the Foursquare Gospel	4,278	+ 8,223	12,501
Independent Charismatic Churches	127,850	+ 31,599	159,449
Presbyterian	217,277	- 12,473	204,804
Associate Reformed Presbyterian Church			28
Cumberland Presbyterian Church	10,373	- 1,951	8,422
Evangelical Presbyterian Church	490	+ 959	1,449
Orthodox Presbyterian Church, The			644
Presbyterian Church (USA)	200,969	- 20,654	180,315
Presbyterian Church in America	5,445	+ 8,501	13,946
(Quakers) Friends	2,548	- 1,474	1,074
Seventh-day Adventists	41,470	+ 4,798	46,268
Sikh (13 congregations)			NR
Tao (1 congregation)			NR
United Church of Christ	20,950	- 4,363	16,587

Religious Groups in Texas	1990	Change	2000
Zoroastrian (3 congregations)			NR
OTHERS (less than 12,000 reported)			
Advent Christian Church	221		
Apostolic Christian Churches of America	13	+ 14	27
Brethren In Christ Church	73		
Calvary Chapel Fellowship Church (19 congregations)			NR
Christ Catholic Church	3		
Christian (Plymouth) Brethren	6,766		
Christian Reformed Church	866	+ 1,070	1,936
Church of Christ, Scientist (93 congregations)			NR
Church of God General Conference, Abrahamic Faith	93	- 38	55
Church of God (Seventh Day) Denver, Col., The	1,743		
Church of the Brethren	302	- 18	284
Community of Christ			2,817
Congregational Christian Churches, National Association of	721		
Congregational Christian Churches (Not part of CCC body)	23		
Conservative Congregational Christian Conference	104	- 79	25
Evangelical Covenant Church, The			1,022
Evangelical Free Church of America, The	5,463	+ 4,257	9,720
Independent Fundamental Churches of America (4 cong.)			NR
International Churches of Christ			4,041
International Council of Community Churches			1,152
Metropolitan Community Churches, Universal Fellowship of			5,570
Missionary Church USA			403
Open Bible Standard Churches, Inc. (2 congregations)			NR
Reformed Church in America	1,592	+ 448	2,040
Unitarian Universalist Association	5,843	+ 1,029	6,872
Vineyard USA			11,637
Statewide Totals	**11,391,401**	**+ 1,483,617**	**12,875,018**
Unclaimed (not counted as adherent to religion)	5,460,358	+ 2,516,444	7,976,802

Compiled principally from Glenmary Research Center, also other sources. NR, not reported. *Almanac estimates.

One of the Painted Churches of Texas, St. Mary's Catholic Church in Plantersville. Texas Almanac photo.

Death, Birth Rates Continue Trends in Texas Statistics

Source: Texas Department of State Health Services.

Heart disease and cancer remained the major causes of death in 2003, the latest year for which statistics are available from the Bureau of Vital Statistics, Texas Department of Health.

Heart disease accounted for 27.0 percent of the 154,501 deaths. Cancer accounted for 21.9 percent of the deaths during the year. These two diseases have been the leading causes of death in Texas and the nation since 1950.

Cerebrovascular diseases (strokes), accidents and pulmonary (chronic lower respiratory) diseases ranked third, fourth and fifth, respectively.

Together, these five leading causes of death represented 65.9 percent of all deaths in 2003.

While the number of babies born to Texas mothers continued to increase in 2003 (377,374), the state's birth rate was at an all-time low of 17.1 per 1,000 population. In 1961, that figure was 24.8. *(See accompanying chart comparing other state and world birth rates.)*

Although there has been a general decrease since 1990 in the number of abortions, there was a slight increase in 2001 as well as 1995 and 1996.

Abortions were induced in 17 percent of the state's reported pregnancies in 2002, continuing a gradual decline from 22 percent in 1990.

Health Care and Deaths in Texas Counties

County	Patient Care 2004		Total Deaths			Leading Causes of Death by County, 2003										Misc., 2003	
	Physicians	Hospital Beds	1999	2001	2003	Heart Disease	Cancer	Cerebrovascular	Accidents	Pulmonary	Diabetes	Pneumonia	Alzheimer's	Kidney Disease	Suicides	Pregnancy Rate*	Abortions
Statewide Total	40,785	58,467	146,649	152,526	154,501	41,654	33,782	10,286	8,341	7,548	5,663	3,603	4,012	2,671	2,355	92.9	76,019*
Anderson	86	148	601	573	590	116	179	41	28	21	17	16	17	11	9	84.0	77
Andrews	14	44	119	99	108	32	24	5	5	16	2	1	0	2	2	79.8	13
Angelina	143	365	779	806	797	239	174	81	36	34	17	17	13	10	11	82.6	111
Aransas	16	0	287	262	263	58	72	25	14	16	9	6	4	7	0	80.7	51
Archer	1	0	75	66	67	19	17	5	2	4	2	0	1	2	0	70.7	7
Armstrong	0	0	31	19	26	8	3	2	0	1	0	1	0	1	0	62.3	5
Atascosa	31	47	303	314	331	75	71	36	20	11	20	4	13	3	5	86.9	79
Austin	8	26	244	285	258	80	53	21	18	10	12	9	6	2	5	75.7	56
Bailey	6	25	60	56	63	10	13	3	7	3	0	4	1	4	1	108.7	12
Bandera	5	0	146	160	169	41	46	8	12	11	2	4	2	2	10	60.5	26
Bastrop	31	36	371	451	523	130	120	25	44	28	20	10	18	11	12	76.2	137
Baylor	4	44	67	79	61	21	17	2	0	3	0	1	1	0	0	92.2	6
Bee	23	63	204	246	220	67	38	10	12	8	10	9	6	8	6	79.3	68
Bell	745	761	1,463	1,540	1,619	452	366	94	87	86	60	30	59	27	27	116.1	1,023
Bexar	3,803	4,297	10,108	9,995	10,409	2,814	2,217	721	517	425	517	201	264	198	146	96.9	7,246
Blanco	4	0	79	111	102	26	18	9	9	4	1	4	3	4	1	64.7	22
Borden	0	0	6	4	4	1	1	0	1	0	0	0	0	0	0	38.8	2
Bosque	12	40	255	276	257	73	46	25	12	20	12	16	4	4	6	72.3	22
Bowie	245	634	910	984	998	280	216	79	49	37	38	24	35	10	16	65.9	33
Brazoria	183	234	1,540	1,692	1,776	415	442	114	97	91	70	42	60	38	32	86.8	460
Brazos	340	414	678	748	843	228	176	82	47	41	42	21	29	7	8	60.8	531
Brewster	9	29	69	81	76	18	11	5	5	7	6	2	2	3	0	79.5	15
Briscoe	0	0	23	21	21	5	3	1	2	3	2	0	0	1	0	85.3	10
Brooks	3	0	101	71	82	26	11	8	5	2	8	2	8	1	3	99.3	17
Brown	68	169	464	451	494	119	103	55	20	39	16	6	7	8	1	69.7	29
Burleson	6	25	141	144	179	57	37	13	7	4	6	3	10	4	3	83.7	40
Burnet	47	26	350	411	410	118	82	23	30	24	12	10	15	5	7	81.0	65
Caldwell	13	61	279	283	279	64	63	18	14	9	19	5	8	3	5	80.2	85
Calhoun	17	49	176	169	184	38	43	6	13	9	10	8	6	7	3	82.8	29
Callahan	2	0	147	143	133	44	33	11	6	6	9	1	1	1	1	64.4	12
Cameron	486	1,063	1,747	1,996	2,044	581	423	101	81	67	151	66	35	53	17	116.1	770
Camp	14	42	145	132	132	39	27	13	11	10	2	3	1	1	3	92.2	15
Carson	0	0	67	62	62	20	11	4	3	5	2	2	1	0	1	70.5	8
Cass	14	84	382	380	402	118	72	38	18	22	14	18	5	6	3	64.4	8
Castro	3	41	63	71	65	10	16	2	11	3	2	2	4	1	0	92.0	10
Chambers	5	39	176	192	201	52	37	11	22	15	4	5	2	6	4	57.4	34

County	Patient Care 2004		Total Deaths			Leading Causes of Death by County, 2003										Misc., 2003	
	Physicians	Hospital Beds	1999	2001	2003	Heart Disease	Cancer	Cerebrovascular	Accidents	Pulmonary	Diabetes	Pneumonia	Alzheimer's	Kidney Disease	Suicides	Pregnancy Rate*	Abortions
Cherokee	76	76	557	542	532	145	105	54	36	25	24	11	10	7	12	87.8	44
Childress	9	38	87	88	66	14	20	7	3	1	4	1	1	0	1	71.7	9
Clay	3	25	108	91	89	25	19	7	7	5	2	4	3	0	0	48.5	12
Cochran	0	9	41	45	38	9	13	1	3	3	1	1	0	0	0	73.0	1
Coke	2	0	64	63	64	16	10	5	5	7	2	1	4	0	0	49.3	5
Coleman	4	46	163	145	169	35	34	12	7	6	10	13	9	0	0	81.0	8
Collin	971	1,083	1,654	1,945	2,096	489	507	124	140	102	51	50	80	33	41	84.1	1,593
Collingswth	1	16	49	53	48	15	8	4	2	1	4	3	1	1	0	59.5	2
Colorado	28	99	277	290	254	71	59	19	14	13	11	7	13	3	2	70.4	22
Comal	122	132	653	668	699	172	165	43	32	32	26	14	28	15	9	75.1	199
Comanche	15	33	212	203	193	43	42	20	8	13	11	3	7	9	2	75.1	21
Concho	2	16	32	39	28	8	3	5	1	1	2	2	1	0	0	71.1	2
Cooke	25	70	380	383	399	116	95	33	21	16	11	12	12	8	6	78.4	49
Coryell	22	138	326	329	313	86	70	9	17	14	11	9	7	3	6	55.9	164
Cottle	0	0	29	25	17	6	2	2	1	1	1	0	0	0	0	91.8	6
Crane	1	25	38	28	48	10	8	4	3	3	1	1	6	2	0	81.3	3
Crockett	1	0	50	33	33	7	8	1	1	3	1	0	0	0	2	83.9	10
Crosby	2	25	85	75	75	29	10	5	3	1	2	1	3	1	0	108.2	16
Culberson	1	12	22	21	17	1	8	2	0	1	1	0	0	0	0	70.2	0
Dallam	6	0	63	40	53	14	8	8	5	3	2	0	1	2	0	85.7	6
Dallas	6,086	6,599	13,518	14,063	13,834	3,748	3,058	911	703	602	343	272	426	227	217	102.0	11,784
Dawson	7	38	146	157	148	34	31	9	7	10	10	2	6	2	1	86.8	15
Deaf Smith	12	35	164	158	153	36	24	10	14	10	7	5	12	3	1	99.1	16
Delta	1	0	83	59	90	20	19	6	3	7	4	5	4	3	0	78.1	7
Denton	602	640	1,662	1,805	1,951	461	410	121	131	126	72	45	57	21	42	74.5	1,394
DeWitt	14	60	259	253	265	72	62	20	16	8	12	7	11	4	3	77.5	24
Dickens	1	0	37	44	49	16	10	2	3	1	3	3	1	1	0	67.0	0
Dimmit	6	35	98	92	75	15	12	11	4	3	2	2	1	4	1	96.2	12
Donley	1	0	66	55	38	11	7	3	0	6	2	2	0	1	0	72.9	7
Duval	2	0	79	137	136	37	25	7	4	4	14	3	2	7	2	84.4	31
Eastland	13	40	319	312	247	72	48	23	12	12	9	9	5	4	4	78.9	21
Ector	211	549	954	965	1,089	285	232	55	60	100	42	40	36	8	10	95.4	275
Edwards	1	0	16	15	23	5	9	0	0	3	1	0	0	0	0	52.2	1
Ellis	94	95	860	936	885	268	191	58	34	53	33	25	33	4	11	81.9	236
El Paso	950	1,831	3,930	4,035	4,362	1,072	1,021	231	225	185	263	49	112	73	46	102.1	2,257
Erath	44	75	310	338	305	88	61	22	18	16	3	8	15	4	4	70.0	80
Falls	6	36	247	242	225	79	43	8	6	9	3	11	4	6	3	58.1	36
Fannin	26	39	411	411	419	121	84	25	15	23	17	16	10	5	5	71.7	34
Fayette	27	40	299	317	319	122	50	24	16	13	6	18	14	6	3	67.9	18
Fisher	3	9	52	59	61	18	18	4	0	2	4	1	2	1	1	49.4	3
Floyd	6	25	88	95	67	19	15	2	6	2	5	3	4	2	0	80.0	9
Foard	0	0	24	15	30	15	2	8	0	0	2	0	0	0	0	73.4	2
Fort Bend	408	423	1,380	1,533	1,635	425	396	105	79	50	59	29	41	36	37	74.6	909
Franklin	7	30	108	110	125	46	24	18	3	4	1	4	2	2	0	78.1	21
Freestone	10	44	179	209	217	63	47	14	10	8	6	10	2	7	1	83.3	36
Frio	9	40	123	128	116	33	22	9	3	5	13	2	1	1	1	95.4	43
Gaines	6	37	87	81	108	31	22	8	11	5	5	1	6	1	1	91.0	12
Galveston	727	992	2,087	2,183	2,260	572	556	135	106	96	73	37	58	32	28	83.6	751
Garza	0	0	51	57	55	16	9	5	5	4	1	3	0	0	1	84.8	10
Gillespie	65	77	276	266	280	60	60	21	17	17	7	8	6	1	5	80.4	36
Glasscock	0	0	5	4	6	1	1	1	1	0	0	0	0	0	0	59.3	0
Goliad	1	0	57	62	76	18	17	3	5	3	1	3	4	2	1	66.9	10
Gonzales	14	34	221	213	181	44	42	14	14	7	10	5	4	5	0	106.0	40
Gray	22	91	282	283	253	65	45	11	16	22	14	8	17	5	3	73.3	15
Grayson	225	508	1,257	1,280	1,198	412	253	66	58	65	30	56	38	19	13	77.6	212
Gregg	296	620	1,162	1,213	1,174	298	253	83	66	72	50	20	27	14	21	83.7	112

County	Patient Care 2004		Total Deaths			Leading Causes of Death by County, 2003										Misc., 2003	
	Physicians	Hospital Beds	1999	2001	2003	Heart Disease	Cancer	Cerebrovascular	Accidents	Pulmonary	Diabetes	Pneumonia	Alzheimer's	Kidney Disease	Suicides	Pregnancy Rate*	Abortions
Grimes	13	25	240	254	225	67	45	16	15	12	7	4	4	3	7	81.2	38
Guadalupe	65	97	609	616	712	197	173	44	39	27	20	13	17	15	9	66.3	186
Hale	33	36	287	310	300	75	66	28	22	12	10	4	8	6	1	98.7	43
Hall	1	0	69	58	60	20	15	1	5	3	1	3	1	1	1	86.6	1
Hamilton	9	24	145	143	137	44	26	6	8	9	2	6	2	7	2	79.8	7
Hansford	2	20	57	56	60	18	6	4	5	3	0	2	2	2	1	107.6	4
Hardeman	5	44	81	61	70	15	17	7	1	3	6	1	2	3	2	75.4	5
Hardin	16	0	484	465	462	133	90	19	34	42	20	22	7	8	4	71.7	101
Harris	8,908	11,560	19,204	20,652	20,646	5,486	4,601	1,423	1,148	770	647	412	399	431	348	100.4	17,233
Harrison	55	122	611	641	572	167	118	54	35	33	18	7	7	8	7	65.8	21
Hartley	0	21	44	35	33	12	8	1	0	3	0	0	0	1	0	149.3	3
Haskell	2	25	80	85	93	32	27	5	3	5	4	0	2	0	2	70.1	5
Hays	146	113	490	542	581	101	132	34	45	25	26	17	40	4	11	65.7	340
Hemphill	3	19	46	36	22	8	1	5	1	2	1	1	0	0	0	86.8	1
Henderson	59	117	861	932	904	245	243	79	42	126	20	18	19	5	17	80.0	123
Hidalgo	712	1,494	2,675	2,985	3,083	913	593	161	170	112	165	86	36	48	34	122.1	1,419
Hill	24	102	438	430	433	116	96	40	16	28	12	10	4	5	8	84.9	64
Hockley	15	39	215	202	221	53	47	19	10	21	6	7	8	1	2	86.0	54
Hood	45	34	456	496	449	89	126	32	27	33	12	2	25	8	7	70.5	53
Hopkins	33	44	368	357	415	103	109	31	22	21	12	11	10	9	5	76.4	27
Houston	16	54	308	321	308	83	64	24	17	17	16	19	6	6	4	81.0	43
Howard	49	122	356	383	349	94	64	16	15	25	12	7	12	4	6	82.5	34
Hudspeth	0	0	18	16	16	4	0	1	2	1	3	2	0	1	0	71.1	3
Hunt	69	162	764	716	764	211	146	66	45	41	24	27	22	14	10	76.3	157
Hutchinson	19	52	259	283	238	61	47	19	11	27	12	6	5	1	4	76.8	25
Irion	1	0	8	11	15	5	3	1	1	2	1	1	0	0	0	49.4	3
Jack	5	17	87	95	96	31	23	8	6	9	5	1	3	2	0	75.5	11
Jackson	6	17	164	138	162	51	40	11	6	4	3	2	4	6	1	84.7	31
Jasper	35	76	395	353	399	99	103	38	25	23	13	8	10	8	5	85.3	92
Jeff Davis	1	0	24	24	12	5	4	0	0	1	0	0	0	0	1	67.2	9
Jefferson	553	1,323	2,505	2,571	2,592	804	551	182	109	120	90	59	77	57	32	80.2	617
Jim Hogg	2	0	37	61	40	13	12	1	2	1	6	0	1	3	0	84.2	12
Jim Wells	36	211	330	353	349	121	54	22	25	14	22	7	6	10	3	83.7	111
Johnson	106	121	987	1,042	1,086	231	239	101	47	69	28	11	23	15	16	74.7	252
Jones	5	79	214	250	191	52	43	14	10	11	5	9	7	1	5	62.3	19
Karnes	4	30	159	175	144	37	30	13	5	10	6	8	2	4	2	82.3	17
Kaufman	82	198	625	711	742	197	161	45	47	38	22	17	29	11	15	82.8	177
Kendall	29	0	210	243	264	80	57	12	20	14	9	6	12	1	3	76.2	52
Kenedy	0	0	3	19	1	0	0	0	0	0	0	0	0	0	0	118.4	2
Kent	0	0	12	17	6	2	2	0	1	0	0	0	0	0	0	68.7	1
Kerr	137	114	598	629	622	143	150	39	27	36	22	20	34	12	6	83.0	83
Kimble	4	15	55	76	53	23	13	1	4	2	0	1	1	0	1	83.0	11
King	0	0	1	3	1	0	0	0	0	0	0	0	0	0	0	72.5	2
Kinney	1	0	35	42	35	7	10	1	0	1	2	0	0	0	0	74.8	5
Kleberg	18	100	216	273	196	58	53	9	6	10	11	3	1	4	4	81.8	104
Knox	2	14	70	73	59	16	13	4	1	4	2	2	0	3	0	75.8	1
Lamar	104	266	601	572	551	165	115	28	24	27	17	23	12	14	13	70.4	57
Lamb	6	38	177	169	207	55	48	15	13	6	6	6	2	5	3	87.8	11
Lampasas	11	25	150	193	184	54	42	9	16	10	7	3	2	3	0	62.1	32
La Salle	3	0	54	50	32	12	4	4	1	0	3	1	0	0	0	99.0	15
Lavaca	20	64	249	273	273	91	54	24	12	15	9	8	9	6	1	77.4	16
Lee	3	0	177	132	147	39	38	9	15	6	5	5	4	1	4	72.2	17
Leon	3	0	211	212	198	58	44	15	13	12	5	8	2	2	1	76.0	23
Liberty	56	136	651	702	701	204	153	35	67	35	14	25	10	13	15	68.3	76
Limestone	19	75	320	291	266	81	47	20	17	11	11	19	10	6	1	89.5	45
Lipscomb	0	0	31	30	36	10	8	3	3	4	0	1	1	0	1	80.9	0

County	Patient Care 2004		Total Deaths			Leading Causes of Death by County, 2003										Misc., 2003	
	Physicians	Hospital Beds	1999	2001	2003	Heart Disease	Cancer	Cerebrovascular	Accidents	Pulmonary	Diabetes	Pneumonia	Alzheimer's	Kidney Disease	Suicides	Pregnancy Rate*	Abortions
Live Oak	2	0	116	96	88	32	24	4	7	5	2	0	4	1	0	58.9	12
Llano	16	30	249	259	236	50	54	9	6	23	9	13	13	5	0	70.8	13
Loving	0	0	1	0	1	0	0	0	0	0	0	0	0	0	0	*	2
Lubbock	791	1,479	1,985	1,961	2,048	532	391	119	110	132	97	86	40	49	27	79.0	652
Lynn	3	24	72	55	75	18	9	11	5	7	6	3	2	4	1	85.3	5
Madison	7	25	127	142	144	44	29	7	11	7	7	11	2	2	1	89.0	22
Marion	5	0	135	152	145	47	37	12	2	10	4	1	1	0	4	57.9	3
Martin	3	20	43	52	56	16	9	3	1	4	1	6	0	3	0	70.6	5
Mason	1	0	59	57	47	12	14	2	3	4	4	0	1	0	0	66.9	0
Matagorda	39	84	357	367	393	124	91	18	13	16	13	17	4	7	6	75.3	46
Maverick	32	73	275	266	250	69	49	12	9	10	18	4	1	6	3	98.6	57
McCulloch	6	25	145	119	118	38	25	12	5	9	3	0	4	1	1	81.0	7
McLennan	413	436	2,023	1,951	2,014	502	458	134	79	83	80	58	52	40	18	79.7	639
McMullen	0	0	7	3	2	1	1	0	0	0	0	0	0	0	0	29.9	4
Medina	15	25	275	313	321	76	68	12	17	13	17	6	5	5	4	78.3	84
Menard	1	0	42	32	40	16	7	2	1	2	0	2	1	0	0	48.6	2
Midland	181	392	839	922	990	250	210	44	46	83	31	77	27	8	19	82.5	232
Milam	9	59	301	306	280	66	65	32	8	17	5	6	14	2	5	89.0	41
Mills	3	0	72	95	78	23	17	8	2	5	6	2	1	1	1	57.3	3
Mitchell	4	25	106	100	128	38	27	7	5	9	1	3	2	1	3	89.0	14
Montague	14	77	326	278	279	78	48	25	25	13	9	5	9	3	7	78.6	11
Montgomery	444	805	1,946	2,104	2,260	608	540	113	176	110	78	46	51	37	59	78.5	523
Moore	17	60	121	132	130	33	33	12	10	8	4	3	1	2	0	111.5	18
Morris	5	0	155	190	187	63	30	7	14	14	13	3	6	5	2	70.1	15
Motley	1	0	23	19	18	7	5	0	1	2	1	0	0	0	0	95.5	4
Nacogdoches	127	287	517	515	546	150	119	31	34	47	23	8	19	10	7	69.7	102
Navarro	52	144	536	539	494	139	98	43	19	30	18	8	25	2	6	82.3	84
Newton	7	0	150	142	149	59	29	9	8	6	3	2	4	2	2	53.0	9
Nolan	15	54	204	179	200	48	43	11	8	23	8	8	3	3	1	80.5	17
Nueces	770	1,583	2,428	2,524	2,534	592	580	175	127	124	147	48	67	39	29	89.2	1,259
Ochiltree	6	45	78	70	78	26	13	5	6	5	5	1	4	1	1	95.4	5
Oldham	0	0	23	22	15	5	3	0	0	2	0	1	1	0	2	61.9	2
Orange	42	126	832	911	912	291	171	47	71	63	29	17	20	13	15	73.5	148
Palo Pinto	25	48	314	399	332	112	76	26	13	29	7	4	3	3	2	74.1	27
Panola	15	37	255	251	237	71	48	14	21	24	9	7	3	0	3	72.2	11
Parker	63	78	739	741	750	187	165	56	46	62	16	20	19	15	14	69.3	197
Parmer	3	25	79	85	87	24	21	6	6	4	0	1	2	4	2	82.0	6
Pecos	9	36	120	128	146	39	22	11	11	11	6	3	7	0	1	77.5	19
Polk	29	35	486	530	554	176	123	27	34	29	5	12	11	8	4	73.1	27
Potter	452	927	1,201	1,199	1,185	301	245	67	60	106	26	30	36	12	17	94.7	187
Presidio	1	0	53	27	47	15	6	4	0	5	4	1	1	0	1	94.5	4
Rains	3	0	118	112	104	29	35	7	5	3	4	0	2	1	3	59.5	12
Randall	76	4	692	716	829	184	195	55	46	66	17	20	28	14	18	65.7	188
Reagan	2	14	26	21	32	11	5	4	2	2	0	0	1	0	2	97.0	5
Real	2	0	49	40	48	13	9	4	3	3	0	3	5	0	0	71.9	2
Red River	7	36	210	224	211	79	44	18	13	12	7	10	2	3	1	64.4	13
Reeves	11	44	115	100	115	28	26	5	9	6	6	10	1	4	1	91.5	15
Refugio	2	20	95	90	10	28	19	6	5	4	6	3	2	1	0	67.6	10
Roberts	0	0	8	2	15	3	5	1	0	2	0	0	1	0	1	13.2	0
Robertson	5	0	220	209	186	60	42	7	14	14	5	4	2	3	1	77.0	25
Rockwall	51	84	249	302	329	113	63	22	14	22	7	11	6	3	8	83.2	109
Runnels	5	37	134	137	164	60	38	4	8	10	9	6	3	1	2	78.7	16
Rusk	29	76	550	542	544	161	117	41	37	28	13	14	17	7	7	71.4	34
Sabine	2	29	180	178	152	47	29	17	9	13	4	2	0	0	3	60.8	7
S. Augustine	4	18	145	109	125	37	31	6	5	4	4	8	4	1	2	62.0	5
San Jacinto	3	0	214	213	225	56	51	8	20	10	8	6	5	4	4	65.1	14

County	Patient Care 2004		Total Deaths			Leading Causes of Death by County, 2003										Misc., 2003	
	Physicians	Hospital Beds	1999	2001	2003	Heart Disease	Cancer	Cerebrovascular	Accidents	Pulmonary	Diabetes	Pneumonia	Alzheimer's	Kidney Disease	Suicides	Pregnancy Rate*	Abortions
SanPatricio	29	64	558	533	530	130	129	30	40	19	32	6	19	8	5	87.6	148
San Saba	2	0	63	97	87	34	17	6	3	4	0	1	2	3	0	92.2	10
Schleicher	2	14	31	30	42	14	5	6	3	0	3	2	1	0	1	66.9	3
Scurry	12	73	192	178	169	41	31	10	8	8	7	5	7	1	1	97.5	33
Shackelford	2	0	41	34	45	14	14	3	0	1	4	0	1	1	0	50.9	2
Shelby	13	46	332	295	314	110	58	21	15	16	13	4	5	3	7	82.2	6
Sherman	2	0	20	30	36	8	8	1	3	2	0	1	3	0	0	107.7	23
Smith	644	1,039	1,638	1,819	1,753	514	396	94	91	80	61	44	51	21	40	84.2	350
Somervell	8	16	66	81	71	19	14	6	1	4	3	3	6	0	3	69.3	10
Starr	23	49	229	272	294	92	49	11	21	14	17	6	6	5	3	120.7	81
Stephens	9	33	118	112	99	29	23	10	6	6	2	2	0	1	3	82.4	6
Sterling	0	0	12	12	12	2	5	1	0	0	0	0	0	0	0	56.5	2
Stonewall	1	12	34	30	29	6	10	2	2	0	0	1	1	1	0	82.7	1
Sutton	2	12	41	25	41	10	11	2	4	0	1	1	0	3	2	103.0	13
Swisher	3	20	80	76	87	19	20	9	10	7	4	3	3	1	2	99.5	9
Tarrant	2,868	3,864	9,282	9,679	9,507	2,572	2,055	702	454	482	302	170	258	148	166	94.8	6,399
Taylor	277	554	1,213	1,176	1,192	321	260	98	62	59	35	30	40	11	15	79.2	189
Terrell	0	0	20	4	14	6	2	2	1	1	0	0	0	0	0	222.9	29
Terry	7	42	136	120	134	48	20	9	11	6	6	3	7	4	1	97.6	17
Throckmortn	1	14	25	25	24	6	5	8	2	1	0	2	1	0	1	22.1	2
Titus	49	142	280	287	244	84	52	11	16	12	8	5	6	11	7	96.5	42
Tom Green	220	417	992	1,014	965	288	191	63	41	39	47	23	13	17	19	79.8	196
Travis	2,212	2,004	3,871	4,002	4,085	906	899	277	268	181	126	66	97	87	92	87.1	4,141
Trinity	5	22	215	195	197	60	59	6	8	12	6	3	3	1	2	72.5	21
Tyler	6	25	236	253	264	83	61	12	11	23	2	7	5	3	5	100.1	122
Upshur	15	37	370	413	440	136	104	28	21	23	18	11	8	2	5	68.3	19
Upton	3	19	30	45	26	11	8	1	2	1	1	0	0	1	0	68.3	0
Uvalde	22	54	203	256	253	60	55	14	19	6	11	8	2	8	2	96.8	64
Val Verde	46	79	326	315	282	85	56	13	12	9	10	9	6	5	5	103.5	78
Van Zandt	18	24	594	589	576	189	118	46	35	29	17	29	12	11	8	73.6	57
Victoria	206	652	680	698	710	196	128	49	44	30	37	12	32	10	9	81.2	158
Walker	64	127	444	419	428	101	84	26	21	22	16	12	14	12	9	60.5	146
Waller	6	0	218	239	263	76	63	18	14	6	11	5	7	6	2	67.7	84
Ward	5	49	114	83	97	28	23	7	3	9	3	2	5	3	0	67.6	4
Washington	35	60	320	340	370	101	77	26	19	13	6	15	8	7	2	75.9	61
Webb	202	500	856	1,016	1,026	280	193	55	51	26	55	17	9	21	20	129.6	631
Wharton	62	158	410	424	436	125	100	19	34	15	18	14	11	11	7	84.7	54
Wheeler	6	41	87	99	79	23	14	6	3	2	6	1	7	1	1	74.1	6
Wichita	288	533	1,300	1,298	1,260	326	264	102	54	87	55	24	34	16	16	77.9	266
Wilbarger	20	47	171	178	205	67	43	27	10	6	7	3	5	0	2	87.2	22
Willacy	8	0	116	102	102	28	19	7	6	7	3	3	1	6	0	106.3	44
Williamson	298	267	1,134	1,159	1,383	325	319	91	83	75	36	46	47	16	23	87.2	768
Wilson	14	31	254	242	288	90	54	17	13	16	9	14	11	4	3	72.0	74
Winkler	1	15	87	77	69	18	15	1	6	8	0	5	0	2	2	103.1	9
Wise	39	85	411	395	436	136	89	28	29	33	16	12	9	7	3	64.5	42
Wood	36	74	493	525	545	153	127	36	39	23	18	16	6	6	11	77.4	44
Yoakum	5	21	60	51	58	17	12	1	1	3	5	0	3	1	2	91.8	4
Young	16	62	269	257	235	45	52	11	21	25	10	4	10	2	3	80.4	17
Zapata	5	0	94	89	88	22	16	4	4	4	7	3	0	2	0	109.9	22
Zavala	7	0	99	102	91	29	15	4	3	5	4	2	2	3		92.2	18

Sources: Texas Department of Health: Vital Statistics, 2003 (by county of residence) and **Center for Health Statistics,** December 2004. **Texas State Board of Medical Examiners**, January 2005.
Physicians - All practicing licensed M.D.s and D.O.s.
Hospital Beds - Staffed Beds (2003), not including U.S. military and veteran's hospitals.
Definition of categories of death: Cerebrovascular - pertaining to the blood vessels of the brain; Pulmonary - bronchitis, emphysema, asthma; Kidney Disease - nephritis, nephrosis.
*Pregnancy Rate figured per 1,000 women age 15-44.
*Abortion total statewide includes abortions performed in Texas plus abortions obtained outside the state by Texas residents.

Comparison of Vital Statistics

The most current data available, with selected states; those bordering Texas and other large states. **Lowest and highest with number in bold.**

State/ Country	BIRTH rate*	DEATH rate*	LIFE expect- ancy
Texas	17.1	7.3	76.8
Alaska	15.4	**4.7**	-
Arkansas	13.8	10.5	-
California	15.1	6.7	-
Florida	12.3	10.0	-
Georgia	15.6	7.6	-
Illinois	14.3	8.4	-
Louisiana	14.5	9.4	-
Massachusetts	12.5	8.9	-
Michigan	12.9	8.7	-
New Mexico	15.0	7.7	-
New York	13.1	8.3	-
Ohio	13.0	9.6	-
Oklahoma	14.4	10.2	-
Utah	**21.2**	5.6	-
Vermont	**10.4**	8.5	-
West Virginia	11.5	**11.7**	-
United States	13.9	8.5	77.1
Afghanistan	**47.5**	21.5	42.0
Brazil	17.7	6.1	71.1
Canada	11.0	7.6	79.8
China	13.0	6.9	71.6
Congo	45.1	14.9	48.9
Egypt	24.4	5.4	70.4
France	12.5	9.1	79.3
Germany	**8.6**	10.3	78.4
India	23.3	8.5	63.6
Iraq	33.7	5.8	67.8
Italy	9.2	10.1	79.4
Japan	9.6	8.6	**80.9**
Mexico	21.9	4.7	74.7
Mozambique	36.9	**23.0**	**38.2**
Nigeria	38.8	13.8	51.0
Pakistan	32.0	8.9	62.2
Philippines	26.3	5.6	69.3
Poland	10.5	10.0	73.9
Russia	9.4	15.3	66.1
Saudi Arabia	29.9	**2.7**	75.0
South Africa	18.9	18.4	46.6
Spain	10.1	9.5	79.2
Ukraine	9.9	16.4	66.5
United Kingdom	11.0	10.2	78.2
World	20.2	8.9	64.1

*Rates are number during 1 year per 1,000 persons.

Sources: Statistical Abstract of the United States, 2004-2005; CIA World Factbook, 2004; Texas Vital Statistics Annual Report 2003. Statistics are from 2002-2004.

Life Expectancy for Texans by Group

	All	Whites	Blacks	Hispanics
Total population	76.82	77.34	71.76	78.06
Males	74.07	74.54	68.55	75.02
Females	79.59	79.88	74.72	80.81

Source: Texas Department of State Health Services, 2002.

Texas Births by Race/Ethnicity and Sex

	2003	2000	1990	1980
All Races	377,374	363,325	316,257	273,433
All Male	192,581	185,591	161,522	139,999
All Female	184,793	177,734	154,735	133,434
White Total	138,464	142,553	150,461	151,725
White Male	70,783	72,972	77,134	78,086
White Female	67,681	69,581	73,327	73,639
Black Total	41,700	41,180	43,342	38,544
Black Male	21,174	21,128	21,951	19,501
Black Female	20,526	20,052	21,391	19,043
Hispanic Total	182,528	166,440	115,576	79,324
Hispanic Male	92,991	84,750	58,846	40,475
Hispanic Female	89,537	81,690	56,730	38,849
Other* Total	14,682	13,152	6,687	3,840
Other Male	7,633	6,741	3,591	1,937
Other Female	7,049	6,411	3,287	1,903

*Other includes births of unknown race/ethnicity.
Source: Texas Department of State Health Services, 2003.

Persons Without Health Insurance by State, 2002

Comparison with states bordering Texas, over large states, highest and lowest percentage of coverage (in bold).

State	Total covered (1,000)	Total not covered Number (1,000)	Total not covered Percent	Children not covered Number (1,000)	Children not covered Percent
Texas	15,973	5,556	**25.8**	1,352	**22.4**
Arkansas	2,252	440	16.3	67	10.0
California	28,761	6,398	18.2	1,352	14.0
Florida	13,586	2,843	17.3	563	14.5
Georgia	7,072	1,354	16.1	279	12.3
Illinois	10,737	1,767	14.1	373	11.3
Louisiana	3,627	820	18.4	140	11.9
Mass.	5,827	644	9.9	88	5.9
Michigan	8,752	1,158	11.7	175	6.9
Minnesota	4,657	397	**7.9**	72	5.8
New Mexico	1,452	388	21.1	73	14.5
New York	16,241	3,042	15.8	641	9.9
Ohio	9,938	1,344	11.9	239	8.2
Oklahoma	2,876	601	17.3	102	11.6
Wisconsin	4,938	538	9.8	63	**4.6**
U.S. total	242,360	43,574	15.2	8,531	11.6

Source: U.S. Census Bureau.

Community Hospitals in Texas

Source: The Texas Hospital Association

As the population increases and technological advances continue, this field of essential services is greatly expanding in Texas. Houston, Dallas and other Texas cities are internationally known for their medical centers.

However, many small communities in the state have no hospital or access to professional medical care.

As the population ages, access to health care becomes a greater concern for many Texans, as evidenced by coverage of health-care issues in the Texas media.

Of the 520 reporting hospitals in Texas in 2003, 414 were considered community hospitals.

A community hospital is defined as either a nonfederal, short-term general hospital or a special hospital whose facilities and services are available to the public.

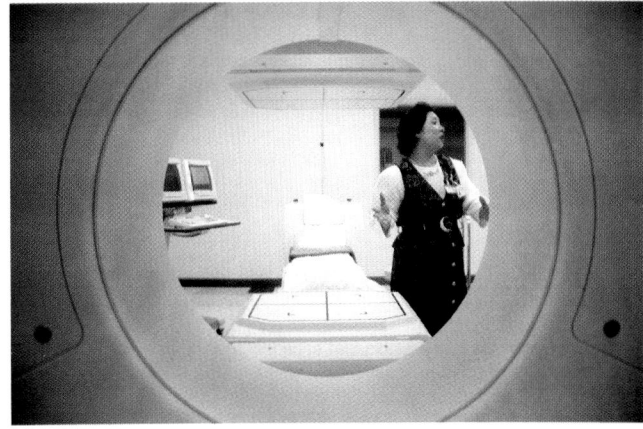

A technologist explains use of a nuclear medicine camera at Medical Center of Arlington. File photo

A hospital may include a nursing home-type unit and still be classified as short-term, provided that the majority of its patients are admitted to units where the average length-of-stay is less than 30 days.

These 414 hospitals employed 309,388 full-time equivalent people (FTEs) with a payroll, including benefits, of more than $14.99 billion. These hospitals contained approximately 57,400 beds. One of every 12 community hospitals in the country is located in Texas.

The average length-of-stay was 5.2 days in 2003, compared to 6.8 days in 1975. This was more than half a day less than the U.S. average of 5.7 days.

The average cost per adjusted admission in Texas was $7,553 or $1,482 per day. This was 3.13 percent less than the U.S. average of $7,797.

There were 2,550,314 admissions in Texas, which accounted for 13,296,596 inpatient days.

There were 32,695,035 outpatient visits in 2003, of which 8,315,483 were emergency room visits.

Of the FTEs working in community hospitals within Texas, there were 78,652 registered nurses and 15,942 licensed vocational nurses. ☆

U.S. Hosptials: By the Numbers

ITEM	1980	1990	1995	2000	2002
Hospitals	6,965	6,649	6,291	5,810	5,794
Beds (000)	1,365	1,213	1,081	984	976
Daily census of patients (000)	1,060	844	710	650	662
Personnel (000)	3,492	4,063	4,273	4,554	4,610
Outpatient visits (millions)	263.0	368.2	483.2	592.7	640.5
Emergency (millions)	82.0	92.8	99.9	106.9	114.2

Source: Statistical Abstract of the United States 2004—2005, from Hospital Statistics.

U.S. Hospital Care: Source of Payments

Source of payment	1990	1995	2000	2002
Hospital care, total ($ billions)	$ 253.9	$ 343.6	$ 413.2	$ 486.5
Out-of-pocket payments	11.2	10.5	12.7	14.7
Third-party payments	242.7	333.1	400.5	471.8
Private health insurance	97.1	111.7	137.5	165.0
Federal Government	102.7	166.4	194.2	229.9
State/Local Government	32.4	40.2	48.6	56.5
Physician and clinical services, total ($ billions)	157.5	220.5	290.3	339.5
Out-of-pocket payments	30.4	26.2	32.1	34.3
Third-party payments	127.1	194.3	258.2	305.3
Private health insurance	67.7	107.0	140.9	166.9
Federal Government	38.7	56.4	79.7	94.7
State/Local Government	9.4	13.3	16.4	20.1

Source: Statistical Abstract of the United States: 2004—2005, from U.S. Centers for Medicare and Medicaid Services.

State Institutions for Mental Health Services

Source: Texas Department of State Health Services.

Mental health services are provided to more than 218,000 Texans each year. The institutions employ about 20,000 people, and operate on an annual appropriation of $2.4 billion.

On September 1, 2004, the Texas Department of State Health Services (DSHS) was created, bringing together:

— the mental health services of the Texas Department of Mental Health and Mental Retardation (MHMR),

— the Commission on Alcohol and Drug Abuse,

— the Texas Department of Health, and

— the Texas Health Care Information Council.

With the consolidation of the four agencies, DSHS now includes treatment and prevention for mental illness and substance abuse in its public health framework. The focus is on improving the health of all Texans. The Web address is: **www.dshs.state.tx.us**

Adult Mental Health Services

The Texas Department of State Health Services contracts with 39 Community Mental Health Centers and NorthSTAR to deliver mental health services in communities across Texas.

NorthSTAR is a Medicaid managed care plan that serves seven counties in the Dallas Medicaid service region.

Today, community mental health centers, also referred to as Local Mental Health Authorities (LMHAs) provide services to a specific geographic area of the state, called the local service area.

Children's Mental Health Services

The local mental health authority provides services that help children access needed resources and services.

For children with intensive needs, the local mental health authority/community mental health center provides service coordination to help the child access needed medical, social, educational and other appropriate services that will help the child achieve an acceptable quality of life and community participation.

Following is a list of hospitals and centers, the year each was founded and the number of patients served in the most recent year statistics were available.

Hospitals for Persons with Mental Illness

Austin State Hospital — Austin; 1857; 3,323 patients.
Big Spring State Hospital — Big Spring; 1937; 1,250 patients.
El Paso Psychiatric Center — El Paso; 1974; 164 customers.
Kerrville State Hospital — Kerrville; 1950; 681 patients.
Rusk State Hospital — Rusk; 1919; 2,034 patients.
San Antonio State Hospital — San Antonio; 1892; 2,703 patients.
Terrell State Hospital — Terrell; 1885; 2,327 patients.
North Texas State Hospital at Vernon — 1969; 2,933 patients*.
North Texas State Hospital at Wichita Falls — 1922; *combined census.
Rio Grande State Center — Harlingen; 1962; 1,086 customers.
Waco Center for Youth — Waco; 1979; 217 patients.

Community Mental Health Centers

Abilene — Betty Hardwick MHMR Center; 1971; 1,515.
Amarillo — Texas Panhandle MHMR; 1968; 3,217.
Austin — Austin-Travis County MHMR Center; 1967; 7,046.
Beaumont — Spindletop MHMR Services; 1967; 5,072.
Big Spring — West Texas Centers for MHMR; 1997; 3,043.
Brownwood — Center for Life Resources; 1969; 840.
Bryan-College Station — MHMR Authority of Brazos Valley; 1972; 1,845.
Cleburne — Johnson-Ellis-Navarro County MHMR Center; 1985; 1,195.
Conroe — Tri-County MHMR Services; 1983; 2,708.
Corpus Christi — Nueces County MHMR Community Center; 1970; 3,264.
Dallas — Dallas MetroCare; 1967; (included in Dallas NorthSTAR).
Dallas — NorthSTAR; 1999; 31,537.
Denton — Denton County MHMR Center; 1987; 2,392.
Edinburg — Tropical Texas Center for MHMR; 1967; 5,420.
El Paso — Community Center; 1968; 6,521.
Fort Worth — MHMR of Tarrant County; 1969; 9,607.
Galveston — Gulf Coast Center; 1969; 3,080.
Houston — MHMR Authority of Harris County; 1965; 21,197.
Jacksonville — Anderson-Cherokee Community Enrichment Services; 1995; 1,691.
Kerrville — Hill Country Community MHMR; 1997; 3,539.
Laredo — Border Region MHMR Community Center; 1969; 2,458.
Longview — Sabine Valley Center; 1970; 2,877.
Lubbock — Lubbock Regional MHMR Center; 1969; 3,244.
Lufkin — Burke Center; 1975; 2,251.
Lytle — Camino Real Community MHMR Center; 1996; 1,783.
McKinney — LifePath Systems; 1986; (with Dallas NorthSTAR).
Midland/Odessa — Permian Basin Community Centers for MHMR; 1969; 2,556.
Plainview — Central Plains Center for MHMR; 1969; 899.
Portland — Coastal Plains Community MHMR; 1996; 3,098.
Rosenberg — Texana MHMR Center; 1996; 3,268.
Round Rock — Bluebonnet Trails Community MHMR Center; 1997; 6,175.
San Angelo — MHMR Services for the Concho Valley; 1969; 891.
San Antonio — The Center for Health Care Services; 1966; 9,052.
San Marcos — Hill Country Community MHMR; (see Kerrville).
Sherman — MHMR Services of Texoma; 1974; 1,110.
Stephenville — Pecan Valley MHMR Region; 1977; 1,816.
Temple — Central Counties Center for MHMR Services; 1967; 2,559.
Terrell — Lakes Regional MHMR Center; 1996; 1,858.
Texarkana — Northeast Texas MHMR Center; 1974; 906.
Tyler — Andrews Center; 1970; 2,255.
Victoria — Gulf Bend MHMR Center; 1970; 1,304.
Waco — Heart of Texas Region MHMR Center; 1969; 2,588.
Wichita Falls — Helen Farabee Regional Centers; 1969; 4,230. ☆

Texans in National Academy of the Sciences

Source: National Academy of Sciences

The National Academy of Sciences is a private organization of scientists and engineers dedicated to the furtherance of science and its use for the general welfare. A total of 67 scientists affiliated with Texas institutions have been named members.

Established by congressional acts of incorporation, which were signed by Abraham Lincoln in 1863, the academy acts as official adviser to the federal government in matters of science or technology.

Selected to the academy in 2004 were: **Alan M. Lambowitz**, professor of molecular biology and director of the Institute for Cellular and Molecular Biology at the University of Texas at Austin. Also, **Xiaodong Wang**, George L. MacGregor Distinguished Chair in Biomedical Science at the Univserity of Texas Southwestern Medical Center in Dallas. Also, **Huda Y. Zoghi**, professor in the departments of pediatrics, neurology, neuroscience, and molecular and human genetics at the Baylor College of Medicine in Houston.

Added in 2003 were **Stephen J. Elledge**, professor of biochemistry and molecular genetics at Baylor College of Medicine in Houston, and **Masashi Yanagisawa**, professor of molecular genetics at the University of Texas Southwestern Medical Center, Dallas.

Election to the academy is one of the highest honors that can be accorded a U.S. scientist.

As of May 3, 2005, the number of active members was 1,976. In addition, 360 scientists with citizenship outside the United States are nonvoting foreign associates. In 1970, D.H.R. Barton from Texas A&M University, and, in 1997, Johann Deisenhofer of the University of Texas Southwestern Medical Center at Dallas, were elected as foreign associates.

In 1948, Karl Folkers of the University of Texas at Austin became the first Texan elected to the science academy. ☆

Academy Member	Affiliation*	Yr. Elected
Perry L. Adkisson	A&M	1979
Abram Amsel	UT-Austin	1992
Neal R. Amundson	U of H	1992
Charles J. Arntzen	A&M	1983
David H. Auston	Rice	1991
Allen J. Bard	UT-Austin	1982
Brian J.L. Berry	UT-Dallas	1975
Lewis R. Binford	SMU	2001
Norman E. Borlaug	A&M	1968
Michael S. Brown	UTSWMC	1980
Karl W. Butzer	UT-Austin	1996
Luis A. Caffarelli	UT-Austin	1991
C. Thomas Caskey	Baylor Med.	1993
Joseph W. Chamberlain	Rice	1965
C.W. Chu	U of H	1989
F. Albert Cotton	A&M	1967
Robert F. Curl	Rice	1997
Gerard H. de Vaucouleurs†	UT-Austin	1986

Academy Member	Affiliation*	Yr. Elected
Bryce DeWitt†	UT-Austin	1990
Stephen J. Elledge	Baylor Med.	2003
Ronald W. Estabrook	UTSWMC	1979
Karl Folkers†	UT-Austin	1948
Marye Anne Fox	UT-Austin	1994
David L. Garbers	UTSWMC	1993
Quentin H. Gibson	Rice	1982
Alfred G. Gilman	UTSWMC	1985
Joseph L. Goldstein	UTSWMC	1980
William E. Gordon	Rice	1968
Verne E. Grant	UT-Austin	1968
Norman Hackerman	Welch	1971
A. James Hudspeth	UTSWMC	1991
James L. Kinsey	Rice	1991
Ernst Knobil†	UTHSC-Houston	1986
Jay K. Kochi	U of H	1982
Alan M. Lambowitz	UT-Austin	2004
Alan G. MacDiarmid	UT-Dallas	2002
John L. Margrave†	Rice	1974
S.M. McCann	UTSWMC	1983
Steven L. McKnight	UTSWMC	1992
Ferid Murad	UTHSC-Houston	1997
Jack Myers	UT-Austin	1975
Eric N. Olson	UTSWMC	2000
Bert W. O'Malley	Baylor Med.	1992
Kenneth L. Pike†	SIL	1985
Lester J. Reed	UT-Austin	1973
Marlan O. Scully	A&M	2001
Richard E. Smalley	Rice	1990
Esmond E. Snell†	UT-Austin	1955
Richard C. Starr†	UT-Austin	1976
Thomas Südhof	UTSWMC	2002
Max D. Summers	A&M	1989
Harry L. Swinney	UT-Austin	1992
John T. Tate	UT-Austin	1969
Karen K. Uhlenbeck	UT-Austin	1986
Jonathan W. Uhr	UTSWMC	1984
Roger H. Unger	UTSWMC	1986
Ellen S. Vitetta	UTSWMC	1994
Salih J. Wakil	Baylor Med.	1990
Xiaodong Wang	UTSWMC	2004
Steven Weinberg	UT-Austin	1972
D. Fred Wendorf	SMU	1987
Jean D. Wilson	UTSWMC	1983
James E. Womack	A&M	1999
Masahi Yanagisawa	UTSWMC	2003
Huda Y. Zoghbi	Baylor Med.	2004

†Deceased
Source: National Academy of Sciences

* A&M - Texas A&M University
UT-Austin - The University of Texas at Austin
U of H - University of Houston
UT-Dallas - The University of Texas at Dallas
UTSWMC - The University of Texas Southwestern Medical Center at Dallas
Baylor Med. - Baylor College of Medicine
Rice - Rice University
Welch - Robert A. Welch Foundation
UTHSC - Houston - The University of Texas Health Science Center at Houston
SIL - Summer Institute of Linguistics
SMU - Southern Methodist University

Crime in Texas — 2004

Source: Texas Department of Public Safety, Austin

The **total number of major crimes** committed in Texas in 2004 decreased by 0.5 percent compared to 2003. In addition, the **2004 crime rate** — the number of crimes per 100,000 population — decreased 2.2 percent from 2003. In 2004, there were 5,032 crimes per 100,000 people.

The **violent crime rate** decreased 2.1 percent from 2003 to 2004. While the number of murders in 2004 was down 4 percent from 2003, the number of rapes increased by 5.2 percent over 2003.

The **nonviolent, or property, crime rate** decreased 2.2 percent from 2003 to 2004. The **value of property stolen** during the commission of index crimes in 2004 was more than $1.7 billion. The **value of stolen property recovered** by Texas law-enforcement agencies in 2004 was more than $633 million.

The total number of arrests in Texas increased 6 percent in 2004 over 2003. The number of juvenile arrests increased 6.1 percent, while adult arrests increased 6.0 percent. There were 1.12 million arrests in 2004 and 1.06 million arrests in 2003.

The crime rate is tabulated on seven major offenses designated Index Crimes by the Federal Bureau of Investigation's **Uniform Crime Reporting program**. These seven categories include four violent offenses (murder, rape, robbery and aggravated assault) and three nonviolent crimes (burglary, larceny-theft and motor-vehicle theft). In Texas, these figures are collected by the Texas Department of Public Safety for the national UCR program. In 2004, 1,007 Texas law enforcement agencies participated in the Texas UCR program, representing 99.6 percent of the population. Data are estimated for non-reporting agencies.

Arson

In 2004, reported arson offenses decreased 12.2 percent from 2003. Property damage from arson was reported at more than $91 million in 2004. There were 6,711 arsons in 2004, a drop from 7,645 arsons in 2003.

Family Violence in Texas in 2004

Family violence decreased by about 1 percent in 2004 from 2003. In 2004, there were 182,087 reported incidents of family violence committed against 195,042 victims by 190,865 offenders. In 2003, there were 185,299 incidents

of family violence reported committed against 199,444 victims by 195,354 offenders. In 50.7 percent of the 2004 incidents, the relationship of victim to offender was marital. Of the total number of these victims, 21.7 percent were wives and 16.7 percent were common-law wives.

Of the remaining offenses, 16 percent involved parents against children or children against parents; and 33.3 involved other family/household relationships, such as grandparents or grandchildren, siblings, step-siblings, roommates or in-laws. The 77th Legislature amended the Texas Family Code to also include violence that occurs in a "dating relationship."

There are six general categories of family violence: assault, homicide, kidnapping/abduction, robbery, forcible sex offenses and nonforcible sex offenses. Assaults (including aggravated, simple and intimidation) accounted for 97.3 percent of all family violence in 2004.

Investigation of reports of domestic violence can be hazardous to police officers. During 2004, 505 Texas law officers were assaulted while investigating such reports.

Hate Crimes in Texas in 2004

There were 285 reported incidents of hate crime in Texas in 2004. This is a decrease of 3.4 percent from the 295 incidents in 2003. These crimes involved 317 victims, 314 offenders, resulting in a total of 302 offenses.

These crimes were motivated by race (50%), ethnicity/national origin (19.2%), sexual orientation (17.6%), religion (12.6%) and disability (0.6%).

Hate crimes, as defined by the Texas Hate Crimes Act, are crimes motivated by prejudice and hatred. The federal Hate Crimes Statistics Act defines hate crimes as those that manifest evidence of prejudice based on race, religion, sexual orientation, ethnicity or disability. The Texas Hate Crimes Act directs all law enforcement agencies in Texas to report bias offenses to the DPS.

Law Enforcement Deaths, Injuries

In 2004, three Texas law enforcement officers were killed in the line of duty because of criminal activity, and 11 officers were killed in duty-related accidents.

There were 4,899 officers assaulted during 2004 compared to 5,036 in 2003. This represents a decrease of 2.7 percent. ☆

Texas Crime History 1984–2004

Year	Murder	Rape	Robbery	Aggra-vated Assault	Burglary	Larceny-Theft	Motor Vehicle Theft	Rate per 100,000 Population
1984	2,091	7,340	28,537	42,764	266,032	529,469	87,781	6,029.2
1985	2,124	8,367	31,693	47,868	289,913	596,130	99,561	6,570.9
1986	2,255	8,605	40,018	59,002	341,560	664,832	119,095	7,408.2
1987	1,960	8,068	38,049	57,903	355,732	711,739	123,378	7,724.3
1988	2,021	8,122	39,307	60,084	362,099	739,784	134,271	8,019.6
1989	2,029	7,953	37,910	63,978	342,360	741,642	150,974	7,926.8
1990	2,388	8,746	44,316	73,860	314,346	730,926	154,387	7,823.7
1991	2,651	9,265	49,698	84,104	312,719	734,177	163,837	7,818.6
1992	2,240	9,368	44,582	86,067	268,864	689,515	145,039	7,055.1
1993	2,149	9,923	40,464	84,892	233,944	664,738	124,822	6,438.5
1994	2,023	9,101	37,639	81,079	214,698	624,048	110,772	5,873.1
1995	1,694	8,526	33,666	80,377	202,637	632,523	104,939	5,684.5
1996	1,476	8,374	32,796	80,572	204,335	659,397	104,928	5,708.3
1997	1,328	8,007	30,513	77,239	200,966	645,174	101,687	5,478.2
1998	1,343	7,914	28,672	73,648	194,872	606,805	96,614	5,110.7
1999	1,218	7,629	29,424	74,165	190,347	614,478	91,992	5,035.2
2000	1,236	7,821	30,186	73,987	188,205	634,575	92,878	4,952.4
2001	1,331	8,191	35,330	77,221	204,240	669,587	102,838	5,152.3
2002	1,305	8,541	37,599	78,713	212,702	690,028	102,943	5,196.7
2003	1,417	7,986	37,000	75,706	219,733	697,790	98,174	5,144.1
2004	1,360	8,401	35,811	75,983	220,079	696,220	93,844	5,032.0

Source: Texas Department of Public Safety, Austin, and the Federal Bureau of Investigation, Washington. Population figures used to determine crime rate per 100,000 population based on U.S. Bureau of Census. The population figure used in determining the crime rate for 2004 in Texas was 22,490,022.

Crime Profile of Texas Counties for 2004

County	Agencies	Commissioned Personnel †	Murder	Rape	Robbery	Assault	Burglary	Larceny-Theft	Auto Theft	Total Index Crimes (see page 532 for definition)	Crime Rate per 100,000
Anderson	3	68	2	5	21	113	410	813	92	1,456	2,613.5
Andrews	2	27	2	13	1	30	89	281	10	426	3,255.9
Angelina	5	148	3	47	63	424	855	1,860	191	3,443	4,183.8
Aransas	2	42	3	5	12	102	404	1,073	48	1,647	7,174.6
Archer	2	10	0	2	0	6	43	36	14	101	1,081.0
Armstrong	1	3	0	0	0	4	8	20	2	34	1,626.0
Atascosa	5	60	8	14	5	42	279	611	50	1,009	2,350.0
Austin	4	53	0	9	5	87	197	341	44	683	2,680.7
Bailey	2	12	0	0	0	13	37	118	13	181	2,672.8
Bandera	1	27	0	5	1	28	110	275	22	441	2,241.8
Bastrop	4	89	1	9	11	180	678	1,282	131	2,292	3,356.7
Baylor	2	10	0	0	1	9	32	66	1	109	2,742.1
Bee	2	38	0	6	4	55	216	488	33	802	2,432.1
Bell	13	553	20	109	232	785	3,043	6,693	482	11,364	4,477.5
Bexar	28	2,944	104	755	2,277	5,484	17,063	69,271	6,182	101,136	6,760.0
Blanco	3	17	0	1	0	5	60	129	6	201	2,244.1
Borden	1	2	0	0	0	0	6	3	0	9	1,298.7
Bosque ‡	4	20	0	3	1	35	93	75	9	216	1,200.3
Bowie	7	162	5	39	85	463	854	2,707	232	4,385	4,807.8
Brazoria	20	455	6	100	102	360	1,860	4,555	343	7,326	2,712.4
Brazos	4	325	0	107	128	706	1,653	6,512	340	9,446	5,812.4
Brewster	3	27	0	2	1	19	50	121	3	196	2,084.7
Briscoe	1	2	0	0	0	0	8	8	5	21	1,241.9
Brooks	2	20	0	0	1	13	106	156	1	277	3,528.7
Brown	4	67	3	16	11	83	378	1,507	76	2,074	5,353.2
Burleson	3	27	5	3	4	26	85	101	14	238	1,381.6
Burnet	7	93	0	6	4	70	241	601	62	984	2,325.4
Caldwell	4	71	0	11	9	109	211	692	35	1,067	3,023.3
Calhoun	4	46	3	6	6	47	197	427	39	725	3,485.9
Callahan	3	14	4	0	1	19	51	61	14	150	1,125.3
Cameron	16	628	7	126	301	1,290	3,737	15,376	905	21,742	5,889.1
Camp	2	18	0	10	2	20	100	195	19	346	2,894.7
Carson	2	9	0	0	0	9	11	15	1	36	544.1
Cass	5	36	2	18	6	42	176	446	42	732	2,400.1
Castro	3	17	0	1	1	21	61	154	13	251	3,124.6
Chambers	2	47	2	3	10	48	270	480	58	871	3,499.0
Cherokee ‡	6	70	1	27	21	158	440	937	99	1,683	3,487.9
Childress	2	14	0	2	1	14	55	82	6	160	2,080.6
Clay	1	10	0	3	2	10	79	124	14	232	2,036.0
Cochran	1	7	0	0	0	3	10	51	7	71	2,002.8
Coke	1	5	0	0	0	4	7	4	1	16	422.4
Coleman	3	17	0	1	2	8	103	131	8	253	2,835.1
Collin	13	762	12	146	212	719	3,051	11,790	958	16,888	3,108.3
Collingsworth	1	5	0	0	0	3	31	15	0	49	1,594.0
Colorado	4	42	1	5	2	46	100	253	25	432	2,058.1
Comal	2	189	1	42	19	202	675	2,499	118	3,556	3,923.1
Comanche	3	20	0	9	0	18	104	186	16	333	2,418.7
Concho	2	8	0	0	0	5	8	10	3	26	677.6
Cooke ‡	4	61	1	3	24	45	408	1,137	114	1,732	4,483.1
Coryell	3	75	0	27	21	110	362	978	49	1,547	2,017.8
Cottle	2	3	0	0	0	1	8	2	2	13	729.9
Crane	2	13	1	0	0	17	25	65	3	111	2,810.1
Crockett	1	12	0	1	1	5	22	42	1	72	1,800.0
Crosby	2	8	0	4	2	10	28	32	6	82	1,196.2
Culberson	1	8	0	0	0	2	2	4	3	11	392.0
Dallam	2	18	0	2	1	30	61	143	7	244	2,758.6
Dallas	36	5,531	295	858	8,669	10,398	34,124	94,204	22,151	170,699	6,741.0
Dawson	2	22	0	1	3	37	115	240	14	410	2,819.0
Deaf Smith	2	32	0	4	3	72	141	433	18	671	3,583.6
Delta	1	9	0	0	1	10	72	112	6	201	3,626.2
Denton ‡	19	679	10	120	192	511	1,954	9,027	863	12,677	3,034.7
DeWitt	3	26	0	7	5	48	127	322	15	524	2,865.9
Dickens	2	4	0	1	0	0	8	5	0	14	509.1
Dimmit	1	12	0	0	3	42	85	194	31	355	3,376.1
Donley	1	5	0	0	1	13	27	27	4	72	1,826.5
Duval	3	29	1	2	0	52	103	164	10	332	2,421.4
Eastland	6	31	1	3	3	15	142	366	23	553	2,972.0
Ector	4	279	3	19	95	528	1,156	3,963	292	6,056	4,810.4
Edwards	1	4	0	0	0	7	25	15	6	53	2,566.6

County	Agencies	Commissioned Personnel †	Murder	Rape	Robbery	Assault	Burglary	Larceny-Theft	Auto Theft	Total Index Crimes (see page 532 for definition)	Crime Rate per 100,000
Ellis	8	204	3	36	45	212	917	2,746	273	4,232	3,521.8
El Paso	10	1,503	17	229	606	2,780	2,720	18,833	2,071	27,256	3,799.9
Erath	4	75	2	27	9	40	196	711	32	1,017	2,997.3
Falls	3	31	2	1	6	47	93	159	30	338	1,861.4
Fannin	2	37	1	14	7	77	178	444	36	757	2,306.7
Fayette	3	28	0	2	1	14	60	153	10	240	1,055.1
Fisher	1	5	0	0	1	7	18	40	2	68	1,614.4
Floyd	3	13	0	4	2	7	70	89	5	177	2,337.9
Foard	2	4	0	0	0	4	14	5	0	23	1,467.8
Fort Bend ‡	11	676	16	148	363	785	2,162	6,043	627	10,144	2,578.2
Franklin	1	8	1	1	0	6	37	50	4	99	1,064.2
Freestone	4	33	2	5	0	26	89	112	31	265	1,400.9
Frio	3	27	1	0	8	43	128	226	10	416	2,503.0
Gaines	3	24	0	1	0	6	30	130	7	174	1,185.2
Galveston	15	719	15	179	321	877	2,712	7,312	851	12,267	4,376.2
Garza	1	7	1	1	0	1	11	61	6	81	1,589.8
Gillespie	2	45	0	2	0	13	60	302	9	386	1,708.0
Glasscock	1	3	0	0	0	0	0	0	0	0	0.0
Goliad	1	11	1	0	2	2	15	18	0	38	525.2
Gonzales	3	39	3	2	7	96	98	365	7	578	2,982.9
Gray	2	38	0	8	7	70	233	638	38	994	4,547.7
Grayson	11	195	7	20	55	249	991	2,951	200	4,473	3,820.2
Gregg	5	269	7	73	186	700	1,469	5,054	524	8,013	6,531.5
Grimes	2	42	2	1	13	42	203	428	36	725	2,856.4
Guadalupe	5	162	1	40	27	195	653	2,012	111	3,039	3,087.4
Hale	4	66	1	5	18	52	408	1,387	42	1,913	5,143.4
Hall	2	8	0	0	1	7	22	14	7	51	1,308.7
Hamilton	2	12	2	2	0	10	44	51	5	114	1,381.1
Hansford	3	8	0	0	0	3	7	30	4	44	830.5
Hardeman	3	8	0	2	0	9	29	76	5	121	2,680.0
Hardin	5	77	1	2	12	65	247	691	75	1,093	2,165.7
Harris ‡	39	9,130	351	1,472	12,572	17,786	40,622	115,020	27,953	215,776	5,859.3
Harrison	3	97	5	18	42	223	805	1,410	154	2,657	4,278.3
Hartley	1	4	0	2	0	0	19	11	1	33	1,236.9
Haskell	2	6	0	0	0	16	34	58	2	110	1,899.2
Hays	4	228	1	28	40	155	512	2,057	194	2,987	2,563.2
Hemphill	1	8	0	0	1	6	18	21	4	50	1,475.4
Henderson	9	129	5	13	23	352	750	1,406	237	2,786	3,545.7
Hidalgo ‡	21	1,052	30	196	662	2,432	6,774	27,237	2,388	39,719	6,146.4
Hill	5	59	1	4	14	45	258	652	52	1,026	2,929.5
Hockley	4	40	1	4	2	65	150	383	11	616	2,656.3
Hood	3	56	1	2	3	60	288	917	74	1,345	2,936.5
Hopkins	2	55	2	7	6	70	228	485	50	848	2,551.9
Houston	3	35	1	6	8	44	126	347	27	559	2,379.0
Howard	2	56	1	18	11	51	434	591	42	1,148	3,437.0
Hudspeth	1	16	0	0	0	5	21	19	2	47	1,447.5
Hunt	8	125	9	10	72	266	1,100	2,546	357	4,360	5,292.2
Hutchinson ‡	3	34	0	11	8	42	187	749	44	1,041	4,459.2
Irion	1	4	0	0	0	5	11	8	2	26	1,468.1
Jack	2	21	0	0	0	6	23	54	6	89	978.1
Jackson	3	22	0	6	2	16	56	166	8	254	1,753.4
Jasper	3	38	1	13	7	112	242	604	30	1,009	2,794.6
Jeff Davis	1	2	0	1	0	2	5	5	1	14	615.7
Jefferson	7	554	14	109	479	883	3,223	9,676	906	15,290	6,048.7
Jim Hogg	1	20	0	0	1	6	21	58	1	87	1,703.2
Jim Wells	4	78	2	24	8	353	737	1,829	95	3,048	7,569.7
Johnson	7	209	1	41	45	367	1,231	3,341	357	5,383	3,733.8
Jones	5	25	2	6	0	34	119	120	8	289	1,954.4
Karnes	3	19	1	0	0	15	48	58	3	125	804.7
Kaufman	5	128	5	50	56	416	1,073	1,999	309	3,908	4,691.8
Kendall	2	54	1	5	2	27	74	290	18	417	1,616.5
Kenedy	1	11	0	0	2	0	0	0	0	2	481.9
Kent	1	2	0	0	0	2	9	2	0	13	1,660.3
Kerr	3	102	0	10	13	71	247	928	43	1,312	2,847.7
Kimble	2	16	0	0	1	20	32	127	3	183	3,968.8
King	1	2	0	0	0	0	0	0	0	0	0.0
Kinney	1	7	0	0	0	0	0	1	1	2	59.4
Kleberg	3	84	0	15	12	174	483	1,370	32	2,086	6,552.7
Knox	3	7	0	2	0	8	25	44	9	88	2,203.3
Lamar	4	91	6	91	41	267	577	2,304	93	3,379	6,718.4
Lamb	4	34	0	6	0	47	123	231	15	422	2,835.4

County	Agencies	Commissioned Personnel †	Murder	Rape	Robbery	Assault	Burglary	Larceny-Theft	Auto Theft	Total Index Crimes (see page 532 for definition)	Crime Rate per 100,000
Lampasas	2	37	0	8	4	20	53	300	8	393	2,012.9
La Salle	1	12	0	2	0	15	39	56	11	123	2,077.7
Lavaca	3	27	0	1	0	10	66	206	6	289	1,341.9
Lee	3	26	0	4	3	38	89	214	23	371	2,207.3
Leon	1	21	0	3	1	52	75	96	12	239	1,467.5
Liberty	4	88	8	18	29	200	587	1,356	190	2,388	3,168.7
Limestone	4	46	3	12	17	48	205	662	49	996	4,330.2
Lipscomb	1	5	0	0	0	3	6	4	3	16	508.9
Live Oak	2	17	0	0	0	5	32	77	6	120	991.6
Llano ‡	3	31	1	8	0	15	125	205	11	365	2,357.6
Loving	1	2	0	0	0	1	1	0	0	2	3,174.6
Lubbock	9	511	19	113	325	1,871	3,076	10,731	802	16,937	6,669.8
Lynn	3	11	0	2	0	6	30	69	4	111	1,735.7
Madison	2	16	1	4	4	30	112	228	24	403	3,091.4
Marion	2	19	0	9	3	21	145	147	27	352	3,139.2
Martin	2	8	0	1	0	1	25	17	0	44	940.8
Mason	1	6	0	0	0	8	16	27	1	52	1,354.2
Matagorda	4	92	4	6	32	162	365	1,182	63	1,814	4,659.3
Maverick	2	102	0	2	16	143	362	1,165	48	1,736	3,402.5
McCulloch	2	14	0	1	2	16	43	145	10	217	2,702.7
McLennan	17	506	19	87	287	849	2,977	9,005	764	13,988	6,258.7
McMullen	1	2	0	0	0	0	6	1	0	7	792.8
Medina	4	47	3	22	14	63	259	537	40	938	2,238.7
Menard	1	5	0	0	0	12	9	16	1	38	1,587.3
Midland	3	251	2	26	49	180	503	1,388	65	2,213	1,852.3
Milam	4	35	2	9	6	54	177	456	35	739	2,895.2
Mills	1	5	0	0	0	2	13	11	0	26	507.5
Mitchell	2	12	0	0	1	8	38	124	7	178	1,879.2
Montague ‡	4	27	2	12	4	17	158	420	51	664	3,363.4
Montgomery	8	476	10	89	219	993	2,388	7,075	739	11,513	3,290.9
Moore	2	38	0	11	5	51	93	395	23	578	2,809.4
Morris ‡	4	23	0	3	2	22	84	152	17	280	2,091.4
Motley	1	3	0	0	0	0	0	0	3	3	226.2
Nacogdoches	3	138	1	13	34	154	554	1,308	99	2,163	3,570.2
Navarro	2	104	4	14	26	55	532	1,327	103	2,061	4,282.5
Newton	1	9	0	2	1	13	73	76	7	172	1,137.6
Nolan	3	34	0	4	2	23	150	207	18	404	2,629.5
Nueces	7	585	26	235	557	1,370	4,480	16,274	1,120	24,062	7,510.4
Ochiltree	2	17	0	1	0	22	31	138	7	199	2,178.0
Oldham	1	5	1	6	0	3	13	16	1	40	1,822.3
Orange	7	151	2	37	75	363	944	1,876	243	3,540	4,125.5
Palo Pinto	2	46	1	13	15	43	318	842	69	1,301	4,335.1
Panola	2	41	0	2	5	69	117	359	52	604	2,652.8
Parker	5	133	1	14	24	87	652	1,442	161	2,381	2,503.3
Parmer	4	14	0	2	5	20	51	71	11	160	1,590.1
Pecos	2	31	1	1	0	12	122	201	9	346	2,121.7
Polk	4	74	5	20	13	72	371	650	82	1,213	2,632.1
Potter	4	408	11	76	378	975	2,374	8,460	951	13,225	6,732.7
Presidio	3	15	0	0	0	9	19	40	4	72	932.8
Rains	1	9	0	2	0	8	75	110	16	211	1,911.4
Randall	3	97	1	10	4	62	150	415	41	683	2,133.6
Reagan	1	10	0	0	0	2	4	15	1	22	708.5
Real	1	3	1	0	0	2	14	9	0	26	846.6
Red River	3	21	0	4	1	32	111	123	11	282	2,008.0
Reeves	2	35	0	0	0	13	73	220	6	312	2,507.2
Refugio	2	19	0	1	1	25	46	57	10	140	1,805.8
Roberts	1	4	0	0	0	1	7	16	0	24	2,877.7
Robertson	4	32	0	8	9	89	143	213	20	482	2,994.2
Rockwall	4	101	0	8	15	83	282	741	95	1,224	2,586.4
Runnels	3	17	0	0	3	20	86	179	10	298	2,686.1
Rusk	4	82	4	38	14	271	359	1,085	119	1,890	4,127.0
Sabine	3	13	1	0	1	3	116	129	10	260	2,463.8
San Augustine	2	11	0	2	2	33	93	109	15	254	2,802.6
San Jacinto	1	14	3	1	6	31	173	223	52	489	2,010.8
San Patricio	9	127	2	22	25	123	656	1,620	96	2,544	3,617.5
San Saba	2	8	1	0	0	6	33	33	5	78	1,267.3
Schleicher	1	4	0	0	0	2	5	17	0	24	838.3
Scurry	2	25	0	0	1	3	42	97	205	20	368	2,250.6
Shackelford	1	4	0	0	0	0	6	9	2	17	505.8
Shelby	2	26	0	4	8	62	191	334	40	639	2,428.1
Sherman	2	7	0	0	0	2	19	25	1	47	1,463.7

County	Agencies	Commissioned Personnel †	Murder	Rape	Robbery	Assault	Burglary	Larceny-Theft	Auto Theft	Total Index Crimes (see page 532 for definition)	Crime Rate per 100,000
Smith ‡	11	365	9	97	167	608	1,847	5,106	440	8,274	4,422.8
Somervell	1	19	0	1	0	6	81	64	6	158	2,119.7
Starr	3	77	4	8	22	125	385	682	175	1,401	2,388.9
Stephens	2	17	0	1	0	7	60	73	5	146	1,519.6
Sterling	1	3	0	0	0	0	3	0	0	3	219.8
Stonewall	1	2	0	0	0	0	3	3	1	7	475.5
Sutton	2	9	0	1	1	6	8	31	2	49	1,172.5
Swisher	3	14	0	0	1	26	48	99	7	181	2,220.9
Tarrant	38	3,685	77	677	2,416	4,184	16,580	58,774	6,871	89,579	5,761.9
Taylor	6	257	6	58	181	275	1,841	4,092	297	6,750	5,072.3
Terrell	1	5	0	0	0	7	9	6	0	22	293.2
Terry	2	25	0	3	4	29	73	162	23	294	2,321.9
Throckmorton	1	2	0	0	0	0	5	23	0	28	1,622.2
Titus	2	51	2	7	21	84	213	660	57	1,044	3,589.7
Tom Green	3	218	1	90	60	293	1,164	4,782	253	6,643	6,310.6
Travis	14	2,277	31	374	1,454	2,196	8,272	36,674	2,953	51,954	5,884.9
Trinity	2	17	0	1	7	25	116	142	34	325	2,258.7
Tyler	2	27	1	4	3	24	87	102	10	231	1,100.1
Upshur ‡	5	56	4	4	6	67	279	612	61	1,033	2,949.5
Upton	1	9	0	0	0	1	5	25	2	33	1,029.3
Uvalde	3	45	1	1	7	75	407	785	44	1,320	4,846.3
Val Verde	2	105	1	1	9	57	339	881	79	1,367	2,887.0
Van Zandt ‡	6	65	4	2	15	130	468	725	167	1,511	2,933.1
Victoria	2	193	7	38	97	323	1,061	3,684	223	5,433	6,257.1
Walker	2	75	3	18	33	218	436	1,275	101	2,084	3,303.7
Waller	6	79	3	6	7	75	372	741	112	1,316	3,803.1
Ward	2	26	0	3	2	26	43	133	4	211	2,016.1
Washington	2	55	1	17	10	86	239	529	39	921	2,926.6
Webb	5	604	19	55	229	854	2,195	10,524	1,061	14,937	6,877.0
Wharton	3	86	0	12	29	141	493	992	91	1,758	4,202.2
Wheeler	2	7	0	1	2	9	35	21	7	75	1,533.7
Wichita	6	252	9	78	220	939	2,020	5,795	613	9,674	7,360.7
Wilbarger	2	29	0	2	8	56	112	418	30	626	4,442.6
Willacy	3	31	0	3	3	111	289	538	21	965	4,723.0
Williamson	11	459	3	85	55	352	1,022	3,988	255	5,760	1,939.9
Wilson	3	50	0	5	2	83	177	350	18	635	1,772.0
Winkler	3	21	1	2	1	7	30	45	6	92	1,334.5
Wise	4	81	0	14	2	156	326	790	47	1,335	2,410.6
Wood	5	56	0	0	0	30	309	432	12	785	1,928.0
Yoakum	2	17	0	0	1	13	12	70	3	99	1,343.1
Young	3	37	0	5	0	19	93	316	24	457	2,510.7
Zapata	1	37	0	3	2	49	243	169	36	502	3,825.6
Zavala	2	21	0	0	0	20	61	170	14	265	2,248.0

County population figures used for calculation of crime rate are the U.S. Census Bureau revised figures for 2004.

† *The commissioned officers listed here are those employed by sheriffs' offices and police departments of municipalities; universities, colleges and public-school districts; transit systems; park departments; and medical facilities. The Texas Department of Public Safety also has 3,407 commissioned personnel stationed statewide.*

‡ *County in which one or more law-enforcement agencies did not report data for 2004 to the DPS. The number of commissioned officers listed for this county does not include those employed by nonreporting agencies. The numbers of index crimes for the county includes estimates for nonreporting agencies to enable the DPS to provide comparable data for 2004.*

Crime Rates by State, 2003

(Index Crimes per 100,000 population*)

1.	Arizona	6,145
2.	Hawaii	5,508
3.	South Carolina	5,271
4.	Florida	5,182
5.	**Texas**	**5,148**
6.	Washington	5,102
7.	Oregon	5,078
8.	Tennessee	5,067
9.	Louisiana	4,996
10.	Nevada	4,902
11.	Oklahoma	4,812
12.	New Mexico	4,789
13.	North Carolina	4,733
14.	Georgia	4,709
15.	Maryland	4,505
16.	Missouri	4,488

Source: Federal Bureau of Investigation.
*Based on Census Bureau estimated resident population as of July 1, 2002.

Texas Public Schools

Source: Texas Education Agency; www.tea.state.tx.us

Public school **enrollment in Texas reached a peak of 4,400,644 in 2004–2005,** according to the Texas Education Agency. That is an increase of almost 400,000 students over the last four years; enrollment was 4,059,619 in 2000–2001.

The **seven largest districts** (listed in descending order by average daily attendance) are: Houston, Dallas, Austin, Fort Worth, Cypress-Fairbanks (Harris Co.), Northside (Bexar Co.) and El Paso.

In Texas, there are **1,037 independent and common school districts** and **190 charter districts.** Independent school districts are administered by an elected board of trustees and deal directly with the Texas Education Agency. Common districts are supervised by elected county school superintendents and county trustees. Charter schools are discussed later in this article.

Dolores Huerta (seated at table) signs school textbook covers printed with her portrait at the dedication of the Dolores Huerta Elementary School in the Fort Worth Independent School District. Huerta, co-founder of the United Farm Workers, a labor leader and a social activist, drew a large crowd at the 2004 event. Texas Almanac photo.

Enrollment and Expenditures per Student

School Year	Enrollment	Spending per student
2003–2004	4,311,502	$7,708
2002–2003	4,239,911	7,088
2001–2002	4,146,653	6,913
2000–2001	4,059,619	6,638
1999–2000	3,991,783	6,354
1998–1999	3,945,367	5,853
1997–1998	3,900,488	5,597
1996–1997	3,628,975	5,282
1995–1996	3,740,260	5,358
1994–1995	3,670,196	5,057
1993–1994	3,601,839	4,898

Graduates and Dropouts

School Year	Graduates	*Dropouts
2002–2003	238,109	15,117
2001–2002	225,167	16,622
2000–2001	215,316	17,563
1999–2000	212,925	23,457
1998–1999	203,393	27,592
1997–1998	197,186	27,550
1996–1997	181,794	26,901
1995–1996	171,844	29,207
1994–1995	169,085	29,518
1993–1994	163,191	40,211
1992–1993	161,399	43,402

*Grades 9–12.

Brief History of Public Education

Public education was one of the primary goals of the early settlers of Texas, who listed the failure to provide education as one of their grievances in the Texas Declaration of Independence from Mexico.

As early as 1838, President Mirabeau B. Lamar's message to the Republic of Texas Congress advocated setting aside public domain for public schools. His interest caused him to be called the "Father of Education in Texas." In 1839 Congress designated three leagues of land to support public schools for each Texas county and 50 leagues for a state university. In 1840 each county was allocated one more league of land.

The Republic, however, did not establish a public school system or a university. After being admitted into the Union, the 1845 Texas State Constitution advocated public education, instructing the Legislature to designate at least 10 percent of the tax revenue for schools. Further delay occurred until Gov. Elisha M. Pease, on Jan. 31, 1854, signed the bill setting up the Texas public school system.

The public school system was made possible by setting aside $2 million out of $10 million Texas received for relinquishing its claim to land north and west of its present boundaries in the Compromise of 1850 (see map on page 57).

During 1854, legislation provided for state apportionment of funds based upon an annual census. Also, railroads receiving grants were required to survey alternate sections to be set aside for public-school financing. The first school census that year showed 65,463 students; state fund apportionment was 62 cents per student.

When adopted in 1876, the present Texas Constitution provided: "All funds, lands and other property heretofore set apart and appropriated for the support of public schools; all the alternate sections of land reserved by the state of grants heretofore made or that may hereafter be made to railroads, or other corporations, of any nature whatsoever; one half of the public domain of the state, and all sums of money that may come to the state from the

Texas School Personnel & Salaries

Year/ Personnel Type	Personnel (Full-Time Equivalent)*	Average Total Salaries†
2003–2004 Personnel	**573,411**	**$34,326**
Teachers	289,188	41,768
Campus Administrators	15,543	61,284
Central Administrators	5,672	75,397
Support Staff*	44,995	48,856
Total Professionals	*355,397*	*44,056*
Educational Aides	58,413	15,757
Auxiliary Staff	159,600	19,456
2002–2003 Personnel	**571,118**	**$34,021**
Teachers	288,386	41,479
Campus Administrators	15,562	60,581
Central Administrators	5,756	73,369
Support Staff*	42,975	48,720
Total Professionals	*352,679*	*43,725*
Educational Aides	58,626	15,851
Auxiliary Staff	159,812	19,270

*Support staff includes supervisors, counselors, educational diagnosticians, librarians, nurses/physicians, therapists and psychologists.

†Supplements for non-teaching duties and career-ladder supplements are not included in this figure.

The UIL Current Events and Issues team from Grand Prairie High School included, from left, Miguel Chavez, teacher-sponsor Johnathan Head, Michael Morgan and Justin Strauch. For Academic and Athletic UIL results from 1999–2000 through 2004–2005, **see pages 548–554.** File photo.

sale of any portion of the same shall constitute a perpetual public school fund."

More than 52 million acres of the Texas public domain were allotted for school purposes. **(See table, Distribution of the Public Lands of Texas on page 436.)**

The Constitution also provided for one-fourth of occupation taxes and a poll tax of one dollar for school support and made provisions for local taxation. No provision was made for direct ad valorem taxation for maintenance of an available school fund, but a maximum 20-cent state ad valorem school tax was adopted in 1883 and raised to 35 cents in connection with provision of free textbooks in the amendment of 1918.

In 1949, the Gilmer-Aikin Laws reorganized the state system of public schools by making sweeping changes in administration and financing. The Texas Education Agency, headed by the governor-appointed Commissioner of Education, administers the public-school system. The policy-making body for public education is the 15-member State Board of Education, which is elected from separate districts for overlapping four-year terms. Current membership of the board may be found in the State Government section of this Almanac.

Recent Changes in Public Education

Members of the 68th Legislature passed a historic education-reform bill in the summer of 1984. House Bill 72 came in response to growing concern over deteriorating literacy among Texas' schoolchildren over two decades, reflected in students' scores on standardized tests.

Provisions of HB 72 raised teachers' salaries, but tied those raises to teacher performance. It

Permanent School Fund

The Texas public school system was established and the permanent fund set up by the Fifth Legislature, Jan. 31, 1854.

Year	Total Investment Fund*	Total Income Earned by P.S.F.
1854	$ 2,000,000.00	. . .
1880	3,542,126.00	. . .
1900	9,102,872.75	$ 783,142.08
1910	16,752,406.93	1,970,526.52
1920	25,698,281.74	2,888,555.44
1930	38,718,106.35	2,769,547.05
1940	68,299,081.91	3,331,874.12
1950	161,179,979.24	3,985,973.60
1960	425,821,600.53	12,594,000.28
1970	842,217,721.05	34,762,955.32
1980	2,464,579,397.00	163000,000.00
1985	5,095,802,979.00	417,080,383.00
1988	6,493,070,622.00	572,665,253.00
1989	6,873,610,771.00	614,786,823.00
1990	7,328,172,096.00	674,634,994.00
1991	10,227,777,535.00	661,744,804.00
1992	10,944,944,872.00	704,993,826.00
1993	11,822,465,497.00	714,021,754.00
1994	11,330,590,652.00	716,972,115.00
1995	12,273,168,900.00	737,008,244.00
1996	12,995,820,070.00	739,996,574.00
1997	15,496,646,496.00	692,678,412.00
1998	16,296,199,389.00	690,802,024.00
1999	19,615,730,341.00	661,892,466.00
2000	22,275,586,452.00	698,487,305.00
2001	19,021,750,040.00	794,284,231.00
2002	17,047,245,212.00	764,554,567.00
2003	18,037,320,374.00	896,810,915.00
2004	19,261,799,285.00	54,922,310.00

*For years before 1991, includes cash, bonds at par and stocks at book value. For years beginning with 1991, includes cash, bonds and stocks at fair value.

PSF Apportionment, 1854–2004

The first apportionment by Texas to public schools was for school year 1854–1855

Years	Amount of P.S.F. Distributed to Schools
1854–55	$ 40,587
1880–81	679,317
1900–01	3,002,820
1910–11	5,931,287
1920–21	18,431,716
1930–31	27,342,473
1940–41	34,580,475
1950–51	93,996,600
1960–61	164,188,461
1970–71	287,159,758
1980–81	3,042,476
1985–86	807,680,617
1988–89	882,999,623
1989–90	917,608,395
1990–91	700,276,846
1991–92	739,200,044
1992–93	739,494,967
1993–94	737,677,545
1994–95	737,008,244
1995–96	739,996,574
1996–97	692,678,412
1997–98	690,802,024
1998–99	661,892,466
1999–00	698,487,305
2000–01	794,284,231
2001–02	764,554,567
2002–03	896,810,915
2003–04	879,981,965

Source: Texas Education Agency.

also introduced more stringent teacher certification and initiated competency testing for teachers.

Academic achievement was set as a priority in public education with stricter attendance rules; adoption of a no-pass, no-play rule prohibiting students who were failing courses from participating in sports and other extracurricular activities for a six-week period; and national norm-referenced testing throughout all grades to assure parents of individual schools' performance through a common frame of reference. No-pass, no-play now requires only a three-week suspension for a failing course grade, during which time the student can continue to practice, but not participate in competition.

Graduates listen to the National Anthem during the Flower Mound High School commencement in May 2005. During the 2004–2005 school year, public school enrollment reached a peak of 4,400,644 students. File photo

The 74th Legislature passed the Public Schools Reform Act of 1995, which increased local control of public schools by limiting the Texas Education Agency to recommending and reporting on educational goals; overseeing charter schools; managing the permanent, foundation and available school funds; administering an accountability system; creating and implementing the student testing program; recommending educator appraisal and counselor evaluation instruments; and developing plans for special, bilingual, compensatory, gifted and talented, vocational and technology education.

Texas students, beginning with the Class of 1987, have been required to pass an exit-level exam, along with their courses, in order to receive a diploma from a Texas public high school. Beginning with the Class of 2005, Texas students must pass the exit-level Texas Assessment of Knowledge and Skills (TAKS) to meet this graduation requirement. TAKS, which is the most rigorous graduation test ever given to Texas students, covers English language arts, mathematics, science and social studies.

To give Texas residents a sense of how schools are performing, the state has issued ratings for its public school districts and campuses since 1993. The new system is based on state test scores and high school completion rates.

A teacher also may remove a disruptive student from class and, subject to review by a campus committee, veto the student's return to class. The district must provide alternative education for students removed from class. A student must be placed in alternative education for assault, selling drugs or alcohol, substance abuse or public lewdness. A student must be expelled and referred to the appropriate court for serious offenses, such as murder or aggravated assault.

Actions of the 79th Texas Legislature

Affecting Public Schools

During the 79th Legislative session, lawmakers again wrestled with the issue of providing equitable and adequate funding for the public schools after a state district declared the existing school finance system, in place since 1993, unconstitutional. Efforts to pass a finance bill failed during the regular session. Gov. Rick Perry then vetoed all funding for the public schools and ordered lawmakers back to Austin. The Legislature was meeting in special session at press time.

Lawmakers during the regular session agreed to move the duties of the State Board of Educator Certification, which certifies Texas teachers, into the Texas Education Agency, essentially eliminating the 10-year-old SBEC. Responding to concerns about the health of the state's children, they passed legislation requiring school districts to develop a treatment and management plan for each student with diabetes.

They also required the state to add personal financial literacy education to one or more courses required for high school graduation.

In reaction to revelations that some student athletes were using performance-enhancing drugs, lawmakers passed a bill that requires the University Interscholastic League to adopt rules related to steroid use and/or abuse. The UIL is to develop an educational program on the topic aimed at student athletes.

Charter Schools

Charter-school legislation in Texas provides for three types of charter schools: the home-rule school district charter, the campus or campus-program charter and the open-enrollment charter.

As of July 2005, no district has expressed official interest in home-rule charter status, because of its complex developmental procedures. Houston, Dallas, Nacogdoches, San Antonio and Spring Branch school districts have created campus charter schools, which are overseen by each school district's board of trustees.

Open-enrollment charter schools are public schools released from some Texas education laws and regulations. These schools are granted by the State Board of Education (SBOE). This charter contract is typically granted for 5 to 10 years and can be revoked if the school violates its charter.

As of July 2005, a total of 237 open-enrollment charter schools have been chartered. As of the summer of 2005, 201 charters are open and educating about 66,000 students. Many charter schools have focused their efforts on educating young people who are at risk of dropping out of school or who have dropped out and then returned to school. ☆

Brief History of Higher Education in Texas

While there were earlier efforts toward higher education, the first permanent institutions established were church-supported schools:

• *Rutersville University*, established in 1840 by Methodist minister Martin Ruter in Fayette County, predecessor of *Southwestern University*, Georgetown, established in 1843;

• *Baylor University,* now at Waco, but established in 1845 at Independence, Washington County, by the Texas Union Baptist Association; and

• *Austin College*, now at Sherman, but founded in 1849 at Huntsville by the Brazos Presbytery of the Old School Presbyterian Church.

Other historic Texas schools of collegiate rank included: *Larissa College*, 1848, at Larissa, Cherokee County; *McKenzie College*, 1841, Clarksville; *Chappell Hill Male and Female Institute*, 1850, Chappell Hill; *Soule University*, 1855, Chappell Hill; *Johnson Institute*, 1852, Driftwood, Hays County; *Nacogdoches University*, 1845, Nacogdoches; *Salado College*, 1859, Salado, Bell County. *Add-Ran College*, established at Thorp Spring, Hood County, in 1873, was the predecessor of present *Texas Christian University*, Fort Worth.

Texas A&M and University of Texas

The *Agricultural and Mechanical College of Texas* (now *Texas A&M University*), authorized by the Legislature in 1871, opened its doors in 1876 to become the first publicly supported institution of higher education. In 1881, Texans established the *University of Texas* in Austin, with a medical branch in Galveston. The Austin institution opened Sept. 15, 1883, the Galveston school in 1891.

First College for Women

In 1901, the 27th Legislature established the *Girls Industrial College*, which began classes at its campus in Denton in 1903. A campaign to establish a state industrial college for women was led by the State Grange and Patrons of Husbandry.

A bill was signed into law on April 6, 1901, creating the college. It was charged with a dual mission, which continues to guide the university today — to provide a liberal education and to prepare young women with a specialized education "for the practical industries of the age." In 1905 the name of the college was changed to the *College of Industrial Arts*; in 1934, it was changed to *Texas State College for Women*. Since 1957 the name of the institution, which is now the largest university principally for women in the United States, has been the *Texas Woman's University.*

Historic, Primarily Black Colleges

A number of Texas schools were established primarily for blacks, although collegiate racial integration is now complete in the state. The black-oriented institutions include state-supported *Prairie View A&M University* (originally established as *Alta Vista Agricultural College* in 1876), Prairie View; *Texas Southern University*, Houston; and privately supported *Huston-Tillotson College*, Austin; *Jarvis Christian College*, Hawkins; *Wiley College*, Marshall; *Paul Quinn College*, originally located in Waco, now in Dallas; and *Texas College*, Tyler.

Predominantly black colleges that are important in the history of higher education in Texas, but which have ceased operations, include *Bishop College*, established in Marshall in 1881, then moved to Dallas; *Mary Allen College*, established in Crockett in 1886; and *Butler College*, originally named the *Texas Baptist Academy,* in 1905 in Tyler. ☆

Recent Developments in Texas Higher Education

Source: Texas Higher Education Coordinating Board; *www.thecb.state.tx.us/*

State Appropriations

For the 2006–2007 biennium, beginning Sept. 1, 2005, and ending Aug. 31, 2007, general revenue appropriations to higher education were $18,007,200,000, which represented a 6.3 percent ($1,068,700,000) increase from the $16,938,600,000 appropriated for the previous biennium (Sept. 1, 2003, through Aug. 31, 2005).

Enrollment

Enrollment in Texas public and independent, or private, colleges and universities in fall 2004 totaled 1,173,109 students, an increase of 33,194, or 2.9 percent, from fall 2003.

Enrollment in the 35 public universities increased by 9,306 students, or 2 percent, to 482,124 students. Twenty-eight universities reported enrollment increases, while seven reported decreases.

The state's public community college districts and Lamar State Colleges, which offer two-year degree programs, reported fall 2004 enrollments totaling 545,989 students, an increase of 20,572, or 3.9 percent, over fall 2003.

The public Texas State Technical College System, which also offers two-year degree programs, reported fall 2004 enrollments totaling 11,384 students, an increase of 796 students, or 7.5 percent, over fall 2003.

Enrollments for fall 2004 at the state's 37 independent senior colleges and universities increased to 115,155 students, up 1,658 students, or 1.5 percent, from fall 2003. The state's two independent junior colleges reported 697 students in fall 2004, a decrease of 63 students, or down 8.3 percent from the previous fall.

Public medical, dental, nursing, and allied health institutions of higher education reported enrollments totaling 15,089 students in fall 2004, up 846, or 5.9 percent, from fall 2003.

Enrollment at independent health-related institutions totaled 2,671 students, up 79 students, or 3 percent from the previous fall.

Closing the Gaps plan

Closing the Gaps by 2015, the state's higher education plan, was adopted in 2000. It establishes goals to "close the gaps"—both within Texas and in comparison with other states—in student participation, student success, educational excellence and research by 2015.

The plan's first goal calls for enrolling by 2015 an additional 300,000 academically prepared students in Texas higher education; this is above the 200,000 students already expected, based on past trends.

The second goal calls for the state to increase by 50 percent the number of degrees and other higher education academic credentials awarded by 2015.

The third goal challenges the state to substantially increase the number of nationally recognized programs and services at colleges and universities in our state.

The fourth goal aims at increasing federal science and research funding to Texas higher education institutions by 50 percent.

The Texas Higher Education Coordinating Board continually monitors the latest available data to determine if these goals remain appropriate for the state.

Distinctive architecture is a prominent feature of the University of Texas at El Paso campus. Higher education enrollment across the state totalled 1,173,109 students in fall 2004, an increase of 33,194 over fall 2003. Texas Almanac photo.

To support the plan, the Legislature in recent years has increased funding for financial aid programs to help students pay college costs, strengthened the curriculum for public school students, and established a statewide higher education awareness and motivational campaign (see College for Texans campaign web site: http://www.thecb.state.tx.us/SAMC/index.cfm).

Closing the Gaps progress

Closing the Gaps progress reports are produced annually by the Texas Higher Education Coordinating Board to measure the state's advances toward interim targets that are established at five-year intervals for most of the plan's four goals.

The most recent report, published in 2004, measures progress in 2003 toward targets established for 2005:

Progress toward the "Participation" target: Led by significant increases in the number of white and African-American students between 2000 and 2003, Texas has already achieved an overall statewide higher education enrollment target established for 2005. However, those achievements were tempered by further analysis indicating that enrollment growth among Hispanics—the state's largest and fastest growing minority group—was not yet on track to meet the 2005 target for that group. Hispanic enrollment growth averaged 18,188 more students annually over the first three years of the plan. An average annual increase of 23,520 Hispanic students was needed to meet the 2005 target for that group.

Statewide enrollment totaled 1,176,937 students in 2003, or 105 percent of the target for 2005. As part of that total, the state enrolled 132,211 African-American students (101 percent of its 2005 enrollment target for that group), 626,201 white students (268 percent of the target for that group), and 291,959 Hispanic students (53 percent of the target for that group).

The report also noted that the percentage of high school graduates who immediately enter college remains relatively unchanged over recent years, suggesting that the enrollment increases are driven primarily by increased student persistence rates. Factors contributing to increased persistence rates include the Legislature's continuing support for financial aid, which has allowed many students to continue their studies instead of dropping out

of college; decisions by many more high school students to take college-preparatory courses; and economic conditions that could have led more people to enroll or remain in college until employment opportunities increased.

The college-going rate for recent high school graduates is expected to increase as a result of the state's College for Texans campaign, which is helping more students and their parents learn how to prepare for college academically and financially.

Progress toward the "Success: target: By 2003, the state had achieved 90 percent of the overall statewide 2005 target for certificates, associate's degrees, and bachelor's degrees awarded. Further analysis, however, indicates that the state had only achieved 49 percent of the target for bachelor's degrees, compared to 200 percent of the target for associate's degrees.

In addition, the number of certificates and degrees awarded to African-American students in 2003 surpassed the 2005 target for that group, while the number of those awards to Hispanics was on track to meet its target.

The number of doctoral degrees awarded, however, was slightly lower in 2003 than in 2000.

Progress toward the "Excellence" target: By 2003, Texas public and independent higher education institutions were home to about 100 programs identified among the "Top 10" in various categories ranked by U.S. News & World Report magazine. Some Texas institutions consistently appear in other national ranking systems, as well. Achieving excellence requires diligent and sustained effort over many years, and additional progress toward the state's excellence target is difficult to measure only a few years into the 15-year life of the Closing the Gaps plan.

Progress toward the "Research" target: Federal obligations for science and engineering at Texas higher education institutions in Fiscal Year 2003 totaled $1.3 billion, well above the $1 billion target for 2007 (the research goal has an interim target established for 2007 rather than 2005).

Texas ranked fifth among the states in federal obligations for science and engineering research, up from sixth in 2000 but down from third in 2002.

For more information about Closing the Gaps by 2015, see the Texas Higher Education Coordinating Board's web site: www.thecb.state.tx.us. ☆

Universities and Colleges

Source: Texas Higher Education Coordinating Board and institutions. In some cases, dates of establishment differ from those given in the preceding discussion because schools use the date when authorization was given, rather than actual date of first classwork. For explanation of type of institution and other symbols, see notes at end of table. **www.thecb.state.tx.us**

Name of Institution; Location; (Type* - Ownership, if private sectarian institution); Date of Founding; President (unless otherwise noted)	Number of Faculty†	Fall Term 2004	Summer Session 2004	Extension or Continuing Ed.
Abilene Christian University—Abilene; (3 - Church of Christ); 1906 (as Childers Classical Institute; became **Abilene Christian College** by 1914; became university in 1976); Dr. Royce Money,	347	4,786	1,042	
ALAMO COMMUNITY COLLEGE DISTRICT (9) — Dr. J. Terence Kelly, chancellor				
‡ **Northwest Vista College** — San Antonio; (7); 1995; Dr. Jacqueline Claunch	298	8,703	2,817	285
‡ **Palo Alto College**—San Antonio; (7); 1985; Dr. Ana M. "Cha" Guzmán	433	7,988	4,157	597
‡ **St. Philip's College**—San Antonio; (7); 1898; Dr. Angie S. Runnels	200	10,422	3,758	8,323
San Antonio College—San Antonio; (7); 1925; Dr. Robert E. Zeigler	1,124	36,029	10,724	1,776
Alvin Community College—Alvin; (7); 1949; Dr. A. Rodney Allbright	92	4,079	4,043	2,387
Amarillo College—Amarillo; (7); 1929; Dr. Steven W. Jones	448	10,701	3,917	11,051
Amberton University—Garland; (3); 1971 (as **Amber University**; name changed in spring 2001); Dr. Douglas W. Warner	65	1,704	1,600	NA
Angelina College—Lufkin; (7); 1968; Dr. Larry Phillips	110	4,940	2,613	2,574
Angelo State University—San Angelo (See **Texas State University System**)				
‡**Arlington Baptist College**—Arlington; (3 - Baptist); 1939 (as **Bible Baptist Seminary**; changed to present name in 1965); Dr. David Bryant	26	224	70	6
Austin College—Sherman; (3 - Presbyterian USA); 1849; Dr. Oscar C. Page	350	1,366	**	**
Austin Community College—Austin; (7); 1972; Dr. Robert Aguero	1,290	30,955	21,883	NA
Austin Presbyterian Theological Seminary—Austin; Presbyterian; 3-yr; 1902 (successor to **Austin School of Theology**, est. 1884); Theodore J. Wardlaw	23	310	54	75
Baptist Missionary Association Theological Seminary—Jacksonville; Baptist Missionary, 3-yr.; 1955; Dr. Charley Holmes	13	98	42	46
‡ **Baylor College of Medicine**—Houston; (5 - Baptist until 1969); 1903 (Dallas; moved to Houston, 1943); Peter Traber, M.D.	**	1,287	**	**
‡ **Baylor University**—Waco; (3 - So. Baptist); 1845 (at Independence; merged with Waco University in 1887 and moved to Waco); Bill Underwood (interim)	777	13,799	5,851	**
Bee County College—Beeville (see **Coastal Bend College**)				
Blinn College—Brenham; (7); 1883 (as academy; jr. college, 1927); Dr. Donald E. Voelter	524	14,000	6,900	1,564
Brazosport College—Lake Jackson; (7); 1967; Dr. Millicent M. Valek	155	3,503	2,490	9,252
Brookhaven College—Farmers Branch (See **Dallas County Community College District**)				
Cedar Valley College—Lancaster (See **Dallas County Community College District**)				
Central Texas College District—Killeen; (7); 1965; Dr. James R. Anderson, chancellor	870	11,270	3,065	1,317
Cisco Junior College—Cisco; (7); 1909 (as private institution; became state school in 1939); Dr. John Muller	163	3,580	757	92
Clarendon College—Clarendon; (7); 1898 (as church school; became state school in 1927); Dr. W. Myles Shelton	69	1,013	452	6
‡ **Coastal Bend College**—Beeville; (7); (1966 as **Bee Co. College**, name changed in 1999); Dr. John Brockman	99	3,821	2,266	588
‡ **College of the Mainland**—Texas City; (7); 1967; Dr. Homer M. Hayes	89	3,961	2,949	**
‡ **College of St. Thomas More**—Fort Worth; (3-Roman Catholic); 1981 (as **St. Thomas More Inst.**; became college 1989; accredited as 2-year college 1994); Dr. Dean M. Cassella, Provost	14	76	4	NA
‡ **Collin County Community College**—McKinney; (7); 1985; Dr. Cary A. Israel	975	17,702	8,351	2,003
Concordia University—Austin; (3 - Mo. Lutheran); 1926 (as **Concordia Lutheran College**; name changed in 1995); Dr. Tom Cedel	150	1,200	400	100
Cooke County College—Gainesville (See **North Central Texas College**)				
Corpus Christi State University—Dallas—(See **Texas A&M University–Corpus Christi** listing under **Texas A&M University System**)				
‡ **Dallas Baptist University**—Dallas; (3 - Southern Baptist).; 1891 (as **Northwest Texas Bible College**; name changed to Decatur Baptist College in 1897; moved to Dallas, name changed to Dallas Baptist College in 1965; became university in 1985); Dr. Gary Cook	344	4,714	2,305	NA
Dallas Christian College—Dallas; (3 - Christian); 1950; Dr. Dustin D. Rubeck	75	366	71	NA
DALLAS COUNTY COMMUNITY COLLEGE DISTRICT (9) — Dr. Jesus "Jess" Carreon, chancellor				
Brookhaven College—Farmers Branch; (7); 1978; Dr. Alice W. Villadsen	533	10,123	6,813	4,366
Cedar Valley College—Lancaster; (7); 1977; Dr. Jennifer Wimbish	182	4,345	2,652	1,858
Eastfield College—Mesquite; (7); 1970; Dr. Rodger Pool	509	11,705	9,081	2,895
El Centro College—Dallas; (7); 1966; Dr. Wright Lassiter	372	6,015	1,937	5,127
Mountain View College—Dallas; (7); 1970; Dr. Monique Amerman	382	6,598	3,786	2,631
North Lake College—Irving; (7); 1977; Dr. Herlina M. Glassock	550	8,382	3,844	4,148
Richland College—Dallas; (7); 1972; Dr. Stephen K. Mittelstet	903	14,128	16,946§	8,200

Name of Institution; Location; (Type* - Ownership, if private sectarian institution); Date of Founding; President (unless otherwise noted)	Number of Faculty†	Enrollment Fall Term 2004	Summer Session 2004	Extension or Continuing Ed.
Dallas Theological Seminary—Dallas; private, graduate; 1924 (as **Evangelical Theological College**; name changed in 1936); Dr. Mark L. Bailey	73	1,877	1,020	472
Del Mar College—Corpus Christi; (7); 1935; Dr. Carlos A. Garcia	739	11,345	7,388	10,111
Eastfield College—Mesquite (See **Dallas County Community College District**)				
East Texas Baptist University—Marshall; (3 - Baptist); 1913 (as **College of Marshall**; became **East Texas Baptist Coll.**, 1944; became university in 1984); Dr. Bob E. Riley . .	112	1,412	NA	NA
East Texas State University (see **Texas A&M University-Commerce** in **Texas A&M System** listing)				
East Texas State University at Texarkana (see **Texas A&M University-Texarkana** in **Texas A&M System** listing)				
El Centro College—Dallas (See **Dallas County Community College District**)				
# El Paso Community College District—El Paso; (7); 1969; three campuses: **Rio Grande, TransMountain** and **Valle Verde**; Dr. Richard Rhodes	1,200	26,435	**	**
Episcopal Theological Seminary of the Southwest—Austin; Episcopal; Graduate-level; 1952; Very Rev. Dr. Titus L. Presler	32	127	NA	NA
‡ Frank Phillips College—Borger; (7); 1948; Dr. Herbert J. Swender.	111	1,398	563§	NA
Galveston College—Galveston; (7); 1967; Dr. Elva Concha LeBlanc	73	2,360	1,606	250
Grayson County College—Denison; (7); 1963; Dr. Alan Scheibmeir	175	4,000	1,560	3,000††
Hardin-Simmons University—Abilene; (3 - So. Baptist); 1891 (as **Simmons College**; became **Simmons University**, 1925; present name since, 1934); Dr. W. Craig Turner . . .	179	2,392	1,142	0
‡ Hill College—Hillsboro; (7); 1923 (as **Hillsboro Junior College**; name changed, 1962); Dr. William R. Auvenshine	66	3,173	724	404
Houston Baptist University—Houston; (3 - Baptist); 1960; Dr. E.D. Hodo	181	1,818	1,242	NA
HOUSTON COMMUNITY COLLEGE SYSTEM—Houston; (9); 1971; **Bruce H. Leslie, chancellor**. System consists of following colleges (president):	3,010	54,758	39,875	1,366
Central College — (Dr. Patricia Williamson) Northeast College — (Dr. Margaret Forde) Northwest College— (Dr. Zachary Hodges) Southeast College — (Dr. Diane Castillo) Southwest College— (Dr. Sue Cox)				
# Howard College—Big Spring; (7); 1945; (includes **SouthWest Collegiate Institute for the Deaf**, Ron Brasel, Provost); Dr. Cheryl T. Sparks	119	2,876	1,339	2,992
Howard Payne University—Brownwood; (3 - Baptist); 1889; Dr. Lanny Hall	140	1,319	357	NA
Huston-Tillotson College—Austin; (3 - Methodist/Church of Christ); 1875 (**Tillotson College**, 1875, **Samuel Huston College**, 1876; merged 1952); Dr. Larry L. Earvin	37	685	133	0
International Bible College—San Antonio; (3); 1944; Rev. David W. Cook	16	120	NA	NA
Jacksonville College—Jacksonville; (8 - Missionary Baptist); 1899; Dr. Edwin Crank	25	301	153	NA
‡ Jarvis Christian College—Hawkins; (3); 1912; Dr. Sebetha Jenkins	**	538	**	**
Kilgore College—Kilgore; (7); 1935; Dr. William M. Holda	139	4,968		4,968
Kingwood College—Kingwood (See **North Harris Montgomery Community College Dist.**)				
Lamar University and all branches (see **Texas State University System**)				
‡ Laredo Community College—Laredo; (7); 1946; Dr. Ramon H. Dovalina	337	9,030	4,480	3,545
‡ Lee College—Baytown; (7); 1934; Dr. Martha Ellis	364	5,854	4,615	2,616
‡ LeTourneau University—Longview; (3); 1946 (as **LeTourneau Technical Institute**; became 4-yr. college in 1961); Dr. Alvin O. Austin	62	3,758	2,174	25
‡ Lon Morris College—Jacksonville; (8 - Methodist); 1854 (as **Danville Academy**; changed in 1873 to **Alexander Inst.**; present name, 1923); Dr. Clifford M. Lee	**	437	NA	NA
Lubbock Christian University—Lubbock; (3 - Church of Christ); 1957; Dr. L. Ken Jones . .	155	1,974	1,032	NA
McLennan Community College—Waco; (7); 1965; Dr. Dennis Michaelis	351	7,562	7,516	2,911
‡ McMurry University—Abilene; (3 - Methodist); 1923; Dr. John H. Russell	104	1,386	612	NA
‡ Midland College—Midland; (7); 1972; Dr. David E. Daniel	**	5,535	**	**
Midwestern State University—Wichita Falls; (2); 1922; Dr. Jesse W. Rogers	429	6,343	4,938	2,584
Montgomery College—Conroe (See **North Harris Montgomery Community College Dist.**)				
Mountain View College—Dallas (See **Dallas County Community College District**)				
‡ Navarro College—Corsicana; (7); 1946; Dr. Richard Sanchez	325	6,029	1,562	1,488
‡ North Central Texas College—Gainesville; (7); 1924 (as **Gainesville Jr. College**; **Cooke County College**, 1960; present name, 1994); Dr. Ronnie Glasscock . .	256	6,458	2,609	1,316
Northeast Texas Community College—Mount Pleasant; (7); 1984; Dr. Charles B. Florio .	135	2,474	1,678	2,533
NORTH HARRIS MONTGOMERY COMMUNITY COLLEGE DISTRICT (9)— **Dr. John E. Pickelman, chancellor**. Includes these colleges, location (president)	2,040	42,500	22,196	14,000
Cy-Fair College — (Dr. Diane Troyer)	444	8,727	4,420	2,178
Kingwood College — Kingwood (Dr. Linda Stegall)	350	6,421	3,082	1,953
Montgomery College — Conroe (Dr. Thomas Butler)	300	7,219	3,300	5,000
North Harris College — Houston (Dr. David Sam)		10,114		
Tomball College — Tomball (Dr. Raymond H. Hawkins)	**	7,406	4,637	**
North Lake College—Irving (See **Dallas County Community College District**)				

Name of Institution; Location; (Type* - Ownership, if private sectarian institution); Date of Founding; President (unless otherwise noted)	Number of Faculty†	Fall Term 2004	Summer Session 2004	Extension or Continuing Ed.
Northwest Vista College (see **Alamo Community College District**)				
Northwood University—Cedar Hill; private; 1966; Dr. Kevin Fegan	57	1,135	524	0
Oblate School of Theology—San Antonio; Rom. Catholic, 4-yr.; 1903 (formerly **DeMazenod Scholasticate**); Rev. Warren Brown, O.M.I.	24	133	126	273
Odessa College—Odessa; (7); 1946; Dr. Vance Gipson	287	4,578	2,503§	3,915
Our Lady of the Lake University of San Antonio—San Antonio; (3 - Catholic); 1895 (as acad. for girls; sr. college, 1911; university, in 1975); Dr. Tessa Martinez Pollock	296	3,025	589	13
Palo Alto College—San Antonio (See **Alamo Community College District**)				
Panola College—Carthage; (7); 1947 (as **Panola Junior College**; name changed, 1988); Dr. Gregory S. Powell	60	1,780	1,046	303
Paris Junior College—Paris; (7); 1924; Dr. Pamela Anglin	215	4,209	2,150	2,246
Paul Quinn College—Dallas; (3-AME Church); 1872 (Waco; Dallas, 1990); Dr. Dwight Fennell	146	954	170	472
Prairie View A&M University—Prairie View (See **Texas A&M University System**)				
Ranger College—Ranger; (7); 1926; Dr. Joe Mills	65	916	617	125
Rice University (William Marsh)—Houston; (3); chartered 1891, opened 1912 (as **Rice Institute**; name changed in 1960); Dr. David Leebron	662	4,973	2,019	3,532
Richland College—Dallas (See **Dallas County Community College District**)				
St. Edward's University—Austin; (3 - Roman Catholic); 1885; Dr. George E. Martin	410	4,651	**	282
St. Mary's University—San Antonio; (3 - Catholic); 1852; Dr. Charles Cotrell	327	4,110	1,828	65
St. Philip's College—San Antonio (See **Alamo Community College District**)				
Sam Houston State University—Huntsville (See **Texas State University System**)				
San Antonio College—San Antonio (See **Alamo Community College District**)				
SAN JACINTO COLLEGE DISTRICT (9) — Dr. Bill Lindemann Includes these campuses, location (president):	1,122	23,441	16,381	22,50
Central, Pasadena — (Dr. Monte Blue)		11,540	8,470	10,000
North, Houston — (Dr. Charles Grant)	250	5,497	4,540	784
‡South, Houston — (Dr. Linda Watkins)				
Schreiner University—Kerrville; (3 - Presbyterian); 1923; Dr. Charles Timothy Summerlin	73	842	120	0
Southern Methodist University—Dallas; (3 - Methodist); 1911; Dr. R. Gerald Turner	528	10,901	4,029	NA
South Plains College—Levelland; (7); 1957; Dr. Gary D. McDaniel	289	9,561	2,500	**
South Texas College of Law—Houston; private, 3-yr.; 1923; James J. Alfiui, Dean and Pres.	100	1,200	499	NA
South Texas Community College—McAllen; (7); NA; Dr. Shirley A. Reed	296	17,132	5,479	1,000††
Southwest Collegiate Institute for the Deaf — Big Spring (See **Howard College**)				
‡ Southwest Texas Junior College—Uvalde; (7); 1946; Dr. Ismael Sosa	**	5,202	**	**
Southwest Texas State University—San Marcos (see **Texas State University–San Marcos** under **Texas State University System**)				
Southwestern Adventist University—Keene; (3 - Seventh-Day Adventist); 1893 (as **Keene Industrial Acad.**; named **Southwestern Jr. College** in 1916; changed to **Southwestern Union College** in 1963, then to **Southwestern Adventist College** in 1980; became university in 1996); Dr. Don Sahly	75	894	260	289
Southwestern Assemblies of God University—Waxahachie; (3 - Assemblies of God); 1927 (in Enid, Okla., as **Southwestern Bible School**; moved to Fort Worth and merged with **South Central Bible Institute** in 1941; moved to Waxahachie as **Southwestern Bible Institute** in 1943; changed to **Southwestern Assemblies of God College**,1963; university since 1996); Dr. Kermit S. Bridges	96	1,702	**	NA
Southwestern Baptist Theological Seminary—Fort Worth; Southern Baptist, 4-yr.; 1908; Dr. Kenneth Hemphill	91	3,005	1,179	26
Southwestern Christian College—Terrell; (3 - Church of Christ); 1948 (as **Southern Bible Inst.** in Fort Worth; moved to Terrell, changed name to present, 1950); Dr. Jack Evans Sr.	18	241	NA	NA
Southwestern University—Georgetown; (3 - Methodist); 1840 (**Southwestern University** was a merger of **Rutersville** (1840), **Wesleyan** (1846) and **McKenzie** (1841) colleges and **Soule University** (1855). First named **Texas University**; chartered under present name in 1875); Dr. Jake B. Schrum	150	1,277	NA	NA
Stephen F. Austin State University—Nacogdoches; (2); 1921; Dr. Tito Guerrero III	667	11,287	9,415	NA
Sul Ross State University—Alpine (See **Texas State University System**)				
Sul Ross State University-Rio Grande College—Uvalde (See **Texas State University System**)				
Tarleton State University—Stephenville (See **Texas A&M University System**)				
TARRANT COUNTY COLLEGE DISTRICT—Fort Worth; (7); 1965 (as Tarrant County Junior College; name changed 1999); Dr. Leonardo de la Garza, chancellor; four campuses (location, campus president):	2,369	34,586	17,832	7,709
Northeast (Hurst, Dr. Larry Darlage)	412	10,975	7,130	5,553
Northwest (Fort Worth, Dr. Michael Saenz)	261	5,259	2,987	8,597
‡South (Fort Worth, Dr. Ernest Thomas)				
‡Southeast (Arlington, Dr. Judith Carrier)				
Temple College—Temple; (7); 1926; Dr. Marc A. Nigliazzo	215	4,068	1,628	712

Name of Institution; Location; (Type* - Ownership, if private sectarian institution); Date of Founding; President (unless otherwise noted)	Number of Faculty†	Enrollment		
		Fall Term 2004	Summer Session 2004	Extension or Continuing Ed.
Texarkana College—Texarkana; (7); 1927; Dr. Frank Coleman	110	4,216	1,841	10,300
Texas A&I University—Kingsville (See **Texas A&M University-Kingsville** listing under **Texas A&M University System**)				
TEXAS A&M UNIVERSITY SYSTEM (1) —Dr. Robert D. McTeer, chancellor				
Prairie View A&M University—Prairie View; (2); 1876 (as **Alta Vista Agricultural College**; changed to **Prairie View State Normal Institute** in 1879; later **Prairie View Normal and Industrial College**; in 1947 changed to **Prairie View A&M College** as branch of **Texas A&M University System**; present name since 1973); Dr. George C. Wright	467	8,350	3,389	NA
‡ Tarleton State University—Stephenville; (2); 1899 (as **John Tarleton College**; taken over by state in 1917 as **John Tarleton Agricultural College**; changed 1949 to **Tarleton State College**; present name since 1973; includes campus in Killeen); Dr. Dennis McCabe	453	9,021	4,865	NA
Texas A&M International University-Laredo; (2); 1970 (as **Laredo State University**; name changed to present form 1993); Dr. Ray M Keck	266	4,272	3,755	NA
Texas A&M University—College Station; (2); 1876 (as **Agricultural and Mechanical College of Texas**; present name since 1963; includes **College of Veterinary Medicine** and **College of Medicine** at College Station); Dr. Robert M. Gates	2,527	46,111	19,087	3,196
Texas A&M University - Commerce—Commerce; (2); 1889 (as **East Texas Normal College**; renamed **East Texas State Teachers College** in 1923; "Teachers" dropped, 1957; university status conferred and named changed to **East Texas State University**, 1965; transferred to Texas A&M system 1995; includes **ETSU Metroplex Commuter Facility**, Mesquite); Dr. Keith D. McFarland	330	8,566	4,834	152
‡ Texas A&M University-Corpus Christi —Corpus Christi; (2); 1973 (as upper-level **Corpus Christi State Univ.**; present name since 1993; 4-year in 1994); Dr. Flavius Killebrew ...	513	8,234	4,387	NA
‡ Texas A&M University at Galveston—Galveston; (2); 1962 (as **Texas Maritime Academy**; changed to **Moody College of Marine Sciences and Maritime Resources** and became 4-yr. college in 1971); Dr. William C. Hearn	135	1,636	521	1,210
Texas A&M University-Kingsville—Kingsville; (2); 1925 (as **South Texas Teachers College**; name changed to **Texas College of Arts and Industries** in 1929; to **Texas A&I University**, 1967; made part of **Univ. of South Texas System** in 1977; entered A&M system in 1993); Dr. Rumaldo Z. Juárez	454	7,126	6,591	NA
Texas A&M University System Health Science Center —(Includes **Baylor College of Dentistry, College of Medicine, Graduate School of Biomedical Sciences, Institute of Biosciences and Technology, School of Rural Public Health,** and **HSC Satellite** locations)				
Texas A&M University - Texarkana—Texarkana; (2 - upper-level); 1971 (as **East Texas State University at Texarkana**, transferred to Texas A&M system and name changed, 1995); Dr. Stephen R. Hensley	101	1,540	901	NA
West Texas A&M University—Canyon; (2); 1910 (as **West Texas State Normal College**; became **West Texas State Teachers College** in 1923; **West Texas State College**, 1949; changed to **West Texas State Univ.**, 1949; present name, 1993); Dr. Russell C. Long ...	293	7,314	4,212	2,220
Texas Baptist Institute-Seminary—Henderson; (3 - Calvary Baptist); 1948; Dr. Ray O. Brooks	12	50	NA	40
Texas Christian University—Fort Worth; (3 - Disciples of Christ); 1873 (as **Add- Ran College** at Thorp Spring; name changed to **Add-Ran Christian Univ.** 1890; moved to Waco 1895; present name, 1902; moved to Fort Worth 1910); Dr. Victor J. Boschini Jr.	442	8,632	2,606	1,497
Texas College—Tyler; (3 - C.M.E.); 1894; Dr. Billy C. Hawkins	42	757	109	0
Texas College of Osteopathic Medicine—Fort Worth (See **University of North Texas Health Science Center at Fort Worth**)				
‡ Texas Lutheran University—Seguin; (3 - Lutheran); 1891 (in Brenham as **Evangelical Lutheran College**; moved to Seguin, 1912 and renamed **Lutheran College of Seguin**; renamed **Texas Lutheran College**, 1932; changed to university, 1996); Dr. Jon N. Moline	125	1,414	230	142
‡ Texas Southern University—Houston; (2); 1926 (as **Houston Colored Junior Coll.**; upper level added, name changed to **Houston College for Negroes** in mid-1930s; became **Texas State University for Negroes**, 1947; present name, 1951); Dr. Priscilla Slade	**	12,199	2,674	500
Texas Southmost College—Brownsville (see **The University of Texas at Brownsville** under **University of Texas System** listing)				
‡ TEXAS STATE TECHNICAL COLLEGE SYSTEM (6) — Dr. Willaim Segura, chancellor. Includes extension centers in Abilene, Breckenridge and Brownwood, and the colleges listed below (location, president):	**	11,253	**	**
Texas State Technical College-Harlingen (Dr. J. Gilbert Leal)	**	4,350	**	**
Texas State Technical College-Marshall (Dr. J. Gary Hendricks)	46	687	393	246
Texas State Technical College- Waco (established as James Connally Technical Institute; name changed in 1969), (Dr. Elton E. Stuckly)	280	4,491	2,602	88
Texas State Technical College-West Texas—Sweetwater (Dr. Homer Taylor)	123	1,725	1,208	1,990
TEXAS STATE UNIVERSITY SYSTEM (1)—Dr. Charles R. Matthews, chancellor				
Angelo State University—San Angelo; (2); 1928; Dr. E. James Hindman	337	6,137	3,807	896
Lamar University—Beaumont; (2); 1923 (as **South Park Junior Coll.**; name changed to **Lamar Coll.**, 1932; name changed to **Lamar State Coll. of Technology**, 1951; present name, 1971; transferred from **Lamar Univ. System**, 1995); Dr. James M. Simmons	525	10,804	5,828	277

Name of Institution; Location; (Type* - Ownership, if private sectarian institution); Date of Founding; President (unless otherwise noted)	Number of Faculty†	Enrollment		Extension or Continuing Ed.
		Fall Term 2004	Summer Session 2004	
Lamar State College - Orange—Orange; (10); 1969 (transferred from **Lamar University System**, Sept. 1995; name changed to State College, 2000); Dr. J. Michael Shahan	97	2,047	977	275
Lamar State College - Port Arthur—Port Arthur; (10); 1909 (as **Port Arthur College**; became part of **Lamar Univ.** in 1975; part of TSU system, 1995; name changed to State College, 2000); Dr. W. Sam Monroe	130	2,916	2,268	225
Lamar Institute of Technology—Beaumont; (10); (part of TSU system, 1995); Dr. Robert D. Krienke	125	2,600	800	900
Sam Houston State University—Huntsville; (2); 1879; Dr. James F. Gaertner	704	14,371	5,290	660
Sul Ross State University—Alpine; (2); 1917 (as **Sul Ross State Normal Coll.**; changed to **Sul Ross State Teachers Coll.**, 1923; to **Sul Ross State Coll.**, 1949; present name since 1969) Dr. R. Vic Morgan	148	1,937	1,024	NA
Sul Ross State University-Rio Grande College—Uvalde, Eagle Pass and Del Rio (2 - upper level); 1973 (name changed from **Sul Ross State University, Uvalde Center** 1995) Dr. Joel Vela, vice president; Dr. Frank Abbott, dean.	48	907	700	0
Texas State University–San Marcos—San Marcos; (2); 1903 (as **Southwest Texas Normal School**; changed1918 to **Southwest Texas State Normal College**, in 1923 to **Southwest Texas State Teachers College**, in 1959 to **Southwest Texas State College**, in 1969 to **Southwest Texas State University**, and to present form in 2003); Dr. Denise M. Trauth	1,128	27,000	8,658	**
TEXAS TECH UNIVERSITY (1) —David R. Smith, chancellor				
Texas Tech University—Lubbock; (2); 1923 (as **Texas Technological College**; present name since 1969); Dr. Jon Whitmore	1,437	28,483	9,156	2,137
Texas Tech University Health Sciences Center—Lubbock; (4); 1972; Roy Wilson, M.D. ...	596	2,272	**	NA
Texas Wesleyan University—Fort Worth; (3 - United Methodist); 1891 (as college; present name since 1989); Dr. Harold G. Jeffcoat	140	2,607	951	NA
Texas Woman's University—Denton; (2); 1901 (as **Coll. of Industrial Arts**; name changed to **Texas State Coll. for Women**, 1934; present name, 1957); Dr. Ann Stuart, Chancellor and President...	800	10,737	7,287	3,597
Tomball College—Tomball (See **North Harris Montgomery Community College Dist.**)				
Trinity University—San Antonio; (3 - Presbyterian); 1869 (at Tehuacana; moved to Waxahachie, 1902; to San Antonio, 1942); Dr. John R. Brazil	235	2,718	390	NA
Trinity Valley Community College—Athens; also campus at Terrell; (7); 1946 (originally **Henderson County Junior College**); Dr. Ronald C. Baugh	124	6,456	2,500	1,400
Tyler Junior College—Tyler; (7); 1926; Dr. William R. Crowe	485	9.617	4,000	9,000
University of Central Texas—Killeen (see **Texas A&M University System, Tarleton State University Systems Center/Central Texas**)				
University of Dallas—Irving; (3 - Catholic); 1956; Dr. Frank Lazarus	121	3,005	1,500	300
UNIVERSITY OF HOUSTON SYSTEM (1) — Dr. Jay Gogue, chancellor				
‡ **University of Houston**—Houston; (2); 1927; Dr. Jay Gogue	3,036	35,100	NA	NA
University of Houston-Clear Lake—Houston; (2 - upper level and grad.); 1974; Dr. William A. Staples...	501	7,785	4,423	NA
University of Houston-Downtown—Houston; (2); 1948 (as **South Texas College**; became part of **University of Houston** in 1974) ; Dr. Max Castillo......................	550	11,974	4,838	1,712
‡ **University of Houston-Victoria**—Victoria; (2 - upper-level); 1973; Tim Hudson	108	2,183	1,955	NA
University of the Incarnate Word—San Antonio; (3 - Catholic); 1881 (as **Incarnate Word College**; name changed 1996); Dr. Louis J. Agnese Jr.	147	4,800	**	NA
University of Mary Hardin-Baylor—Belton; (3 - So. Baptist); 1845; Dr. Jerry G. Bawcom ..	127	2,706	726	NA
University of North Texas—Denton; (2); 1890 (as **North Texas Normal College**; name changed 1923 to **North Texas State Teachers Coll.**; in 1949 to **North Texas State Coll.**; became university, 1961; present name since 1988); Dr. Norval F. Pohl	1,992	31,155	25,159	506
University of North Texas Health Science Center at Fort Worth—Fort Worth; (4);1966 (as private college; came under direction of **North Texas State University** in 1975; present name since 1993); Dr. Ronald R. Blanck, D.O.	222	1,021	777	2,400
‡ **University of St. Thomas**—Houston; (3); 1947; Rev. J. Michael Miller, CSB	190	3,648	**	NA
UNIVERSITY OF TEXAS SYSTEM (1) — Mark G. Yudof, chancellor				
University of Texas at Arlington, The—Arlington; (2); 1895 (as **Arlington Coll.**; became state inst. in 1917 and renamed **Grubbs Vocational Coll.**; 1923 became **North Texas Agricultural and Mechanical Coll.**; became **Arlington State Coll.**, 1949; present name since 1967); Dr. James Spaniolo	1,081	25,297	12,310	3,374
University of Texas at Austin, The—Austin; (2); 1883; Dr. Larry R. Faulkner	2,137	50,403	**	**
University of Texas at Brownsville, The (2 - upper-level); 1973 (as branch of **Pan American Coll.**; changed to **Univ. of Texas-Pan American - Brownsville**; present name, 1991) and **Texas Southmost College** (7); 1926 (as **Brownsville Jr. Coll.**; name changed, 1949) — Brownsville; Dr. Juliet V. Garcia	506	9,204	5,396	1,395
University of Texas at Dallas, The—Richardson; (2); 1961 (as **Graduate Research Center of the Southwest**; changed to **Southwest Center for Advanced Studies** in 1967; joined U.T. System and present name, 1969; full undergraduate program, 1975); David Daniel..	**	14,113	**	NA

Name of Institution; Location; (Type* - Ownership, if private sectarian institution); Date of Founding; President (unless otherwise noted)	Number of Faculty†	Enrollment		Extension or Continuing Ed.
		Fall Term 2004	Summer Session 2004	
University of Texas at El Paso, The—El Paso; (2); 1913 (as **Texas Coll. of Mines and Metallurgy**; changed to **Texas Western Coll.** of U.T., 1949; present name, 1967); Dr. Diana S. Natalicio	945	18,918	8,000	2,857
University of Texas-Pan American, The—Edinburg; (2); 1927 (as **Edinburg Junior Coll.**; changed to **Pan American College** and made 4-yr., 1952; became **Pan American University** in 1971; present name since 1991); Dr. Blandina Cardenas	772	17,030	10,353	NA
‡ University of Texas of the Permian Basin, The—Odessa; (2); 1969 (as 2-yr. upper- level institution; expanded to 4-yr., Sept. 1991); Dr. W. David Watts	158	3,347	1,185	NA
‡ University of Texas at San Antonio—San Antonio; (2); 1969; Dr. Ricardo Romo	**	26,175	10,530	512
University of Texas at Tyler—Tyler; (2 - upper-level); 1971 (as **Tyler State Coll.**; became **Texas Eastern University**, 1975; joined U.T. System, 1979); Dr. Rodney H. Mabry	324	5,342	2,232	NA
‡ University of Texas Health Science Center at Tyler (4) — **Dr. Kirk A. Calhoun, M.D.** Established 1949 as East Texas Tuberculosis Sanatorium; renamed Easts Texas Chest Hospital, 1971; joined UT system and gained present name in 1977). Primary emphasis is on pulmonary and heart disease	125	75	NA	NA
University of Texas Health Science Center at Houston (4) — **Dr. James T. Willerson** Established 1972; consists of following divisions (year of founding): **Dental Branch** (1905); **Graduate School of Biomedical Sciences** (1963); **Medical School** (1970); **School of Allied Health Sciences** (1973); **School of Nursing** (1972); **School of Public Health** (1967); **Division of Continuing Education** (1958).	1,224	3,399	1,961	25,559
‡ University of Texas Health Science Center at San Antonio (4) — **Dr. Francisco G. Cigarroa, M.D.** Established 1968; consists of following divisions (year of founding): **Dental School** (1970); **Graduate School of Biomedical Sciences** (1970); **Health Science Center** (1972); **Medical School** (1959 as **South Texas Medical School** of UT; present name, 1966); **School of Allied Health Sciences** (1969); **School of Nursing** (1969).	1,400	2,845	NA	NA
University of Texas M.D. Anderson Cancer Center — **Dr. John Mendelsohn, M.D.**	1,050	70	NA	2,252
‡ University of Texas Medical Branch at Galveston (4) — **Dr. John D. Stobo** Established 1891; consists of following divisions (year of founding): **Graduate School of Biomedical Sciences** (1952); **Medical School** (1891); **School of Allied Health Sciences** (1968); **School of Nursing** (1890).	1,984	2,149	1,481	NA
University of Texas Southwestern Medical Center at Dallas (4) — **Dr. Kern Wildenthal, M.D.** Established 1943 (as private institution; became **Southwestern Medical Coll.** of UT 1948; became **UT Southwestern Medical School at Dallas**, 1967; made part of **UT Health Science Center at Dallas**, 1972); consists of following divisions (year of founding): **Graduate School of Biomedical Sciences** (1947); **School of Allied Health Sciences** (1968); **Southwestern Medical School** (1943).	1,902	1,768	NA	NA
‡ Vernon Regional Junior College—Vernon; (7); 1970; Dr. Steve Thomas	71	2,691	1,224	2,245
Victoria College, The —Victoria; (7); 1925; Dr. Jimmy Goodson	110	4,036	2,046	924
Wayland Baptist University—Plainview; (3 -Southern Baptist); 1910; Dr. Wallace Davis Jr., Chancellor; Dr. Paul W. Ames, President	482	6,185	4,673	NA
Weatherford College—Weatherford; (7); 1869 (as branch of **Southwestern Univ.**; 1922, became denominational junior college; became muni. jr. college, 1949); Dr. Don Huff . . .	173	3,166	1,904	1,834
‡ Western Texas College—Snyder; (7); 1969; Dr. Gregory Williams	72	1,698	1,099	876
‡ Wharton County Junior College—Wharton; (7); 1946; Betty A. McCrohan	413	6,106	2,612	740
‡ Wiley College—Marshall; (3 - Methodist); 1873; Dr. Haywood L. Strickland	62	775	**	100

Key to Table Symbols

*Type: (1) Public University System
(2) Public University
(3) Independent Senior College or University
(4) Public Medical School or Health Science Center
(5) Independent Medical or Dental School

(6) Public Technical College System
(7) Public Community College
(8) Independent Junior College
(9) Public Community College System
(10) Public Lower-Level Institution

NA - Not applicable

† Unless otherwise noted, faculty count includes professors, associate professors, adjunct professors, instructors and tutors, both full and part-time, but does not include voluntary instructors.

‡ No reply received to questionnaire. Name of president and number of students enrolled in fall 2004 was obtained from the institutions Web site or the Texas Higher Education Coordinating Board Web site: www.thecb.state.tx.us/DataAndStatistics/institutions.htm.

\# Includes faculty and enrollment at all branches or divisions.

§ Includes all students in two summer sessions.

¶ Full-time faculty only.

** Information not supplied by institution.

†† Approximate count.

§§ Latest figures available from institution's Web page were for 2002–2003 school year.

§§§ Enrollment in online courses only.

¶¶ Number of students in extension courses or continuing education for all of fiscal year 2002.

University Interscholastic League Winning Schools for the School Years 1999–2000 to 2004–2005

Winners in the academic, music and the arts categories are listed first, then winners in sports categories. Winners in earlier years can be found in the *Texas Almanac 2000—2001*. If years are missing in certain categories, that competition did not take place in those years. If there is a dash (—) in the box, there was no competition in that conference in that category for that year.

Academics

Year	Conference A	Conference AA	Conference AAA	Conference AAAA	Conference AAAAA
Overall State Meet Academic Champions					
1999–00	Valley View	Salado	Bridgeport	Friendswood	Klein
2000–01	Lindsay	Salado	Bridgeport	Southlake Carroll	Klein
2001–02	Muenster	Salado	Seminole	Southlake Carroll	Klein
2002–03	Lindsay	Salado	Bridgeport	Longview Pine Tree	Klein
2003–04	Lindsay	Argyle	Lindale	Friendswood	Katy Taylor
2004–05	Lindsay	Salado	Lindale	Azle	College Station A&M
Accounting					
1999–00	Lazbuddie	Rosebud-Lott	Hamshire-Fannett	Lockhart	Abilene
2000–01	Lazbuddie	Rosebud-Lott	Cameron Yoe	Paris North Lamar	Abilene
2001–02	Trenton	Rosebud-Lott	Giddings	Snyder	Fort Bend Dulles
2002–03	Trenton	Rosebud-Lott	Cameron Yoe	Brownwood	Southlake Carroll
2003–04	Lazbuddie	Caddo Mills	Hamshire-Fannett	Brownwood	Southlake Carroll
2004–05	Trenton	Rosebud-Lott	Dalhart	Brownwood	Keller
Accounting Team Event					
1999–00	Lazbuddie	Rosebud-Lott	Dalhart	Sulphur Springs	Abilene
2000–01	Lazbuddie	Rosebud-Lott	Cameron Yoe	Snyder	Abilene
2001–02	Trenton	Rosebud-Lott	Giddings	Snyder	Laredo United
2002–03	Trenton	Rosebud-Lott	Cameron Yoe	Brownwood	Southlake Carroll
2003–04	Trenton	Rosebud-Lott	Hamshire-Fannett	Cleburne	Southlake Carroll
2004–05	Trenton	Rosebud-Lott	Dalhart	Brownwood	Keller
Calculator Applications					
1999–00	Valley View	Plains	Bridgeport	Fredericksburg	McAllen
2000–01	Nazareth	Elkhart	Bridgeport	Pharr-San Juan-Alamo	Sugar Land Elkins
2001–02	Nazareth	Elkhart	Bridgeport	Pharr-San Juan-Alamo	San Antonio Southwest
2002–03	Plains	Elkhart	Bridgeport	Pharr-San Juan-Alamo	McAllen
2003–04	San Isidro	Valley View	Bridgeport	Pharr-San Juan-Alamo	McAllen Memorial
2004–05	San Isidro	Argyle	Bridgeport	Azle	La Joya
Calculator Applications Team Event					
1999–00	Valley View	Hamilton	Bridgeport	Fredericksburg	McAllen
2000–01	Nazareth	Elkhart	Bridgeport	Pharr-San Juan-Alamo	Klein
2001–02	Nazareth	Elkhart	Bridgeport	Longview Pine Tree	San Antonio Southwest
2002–03	Plains	Elkhart	Bridgeport	Longview Pine Tree	San Antonio Southwest
2003–04	Henrietta Midway	Argyle	Bridgeport	Pharr-San Juan-Alamo	San Antonio Southwest
2004–05	Plains	Argyle	Bridgeport	Longview Pine Tree	Lubbock
Computer Applications					
1999–00	Garden City	Keene	Giddings	Friendswood	College Station A&M
2000–01	Granger	Edgewood	Midland Greenwood	Friendswood	College Station A&M
2001–02	Lazbuddie	Edgewood	Giddings	Friendswood	Pasadena Dobie
2002–03	Rocksprings	Rosebud-Lott	Pearsall	Harlingen South	San Antonio Clark
2003–04	Lazbuddie	Wall	Hamshire-Fannett	Friendswood	Klein
2004–05	Loop	Mt. Pleasant Chap. Hill	Llano	Sherman	College Station A&M
Computer Science					
1999–00	Muenster	Seymour	Sour Lake Hardin-Jefferson	Austin Lake Travis	Lewisville Marcus
2000–01	Muenster	Ozona	Monahans	Austin Lake Travis	Dallas Science & Eng.
2001–02	Muenster	Seymour	Sour Lake Hardin-Jefferson	Austin Johnson	Lewisville Flower Mound
2002–03	Barksdale Nuece Can.	Seymour	Sour Lake Hardin-Jefferson	Denton Ryan	Plano East
2003–04	Barksdale Nuece Can.	Geronimo Navarro	Lindale	Austin Lake Travis	Dallas Gifted & Talented
2004–05	Barksdale Nuece Can.	Salado	Needville	Waller	Tomball
Computer Science Team					
1999–00	Muenster	Seymour	Stafford	Cedar Hill	Dallas Science & Eng.
2000–01	Muenster	Ozona	Monahans	Southlake Carroll	Dallas Science & Eng.
2001–02	Muenster	Seymour	Center	Southlake Carroll	Katy Taylor
2002–03	Perrin-Whitt	Ozona	Lindale	Austin-Johnson	Southlake Carroll
2003–04	Ivanhoe Rayburn	Ozona	Lindale	Waller	Katy Taylor
2004–05	Plains	Mt. Pleasant Chap. Hill	Gonzales	Waller	Katy Taylor
Number Sense					
1999–00	Muenster	Elkhart	Bridgeport	Pharr-San Juan-Alamo	Spring Westfield
2000–01	Muenster	Elkhart	Seminole	Pharr-San Juan-Alamo	Edinburg North

Year	Conference A	Conference AA	Conference AAA	Conference AAAA	Conference AAAAA
2001–02	Muenster	Salado	Falfurrias	Cor. Christi Flour Bluff	Klein
2002–03	Tenaha	Salado	Bridgeport	Phar-San Juan-Alamo	Edinburg North
2003–04	San Isidro	Salado	Bridgeport	Wichita Falls Hirschi	Pearland
2004–05	Lindsay	Argyle	Bridgeport	Castroville Medina Val.	Pearland

Team Number Sense

Year	Conference A	Conference AA	Conference AAA	Conference AAAA	Conference AAAAA
1999–00	Valley View	Salado	Bridgeport	Azle	Klein
2000–01	Muenster	Salado	Bridgeport	Cor. Christi Flour Bluff	Edinburg North
2001–02	Muenster	Salado	Bridgeport	Cor. Christi Flour Bluff	Edinburg North
2002–03	Muenster	Salado	Bridgeport	Azle	Edinburg North
2003–04	Lindsay	Salado	Bridgeport	Castroville Medina Val.	Pearland
2004–05	Lindsay	Argyle	Bridgeport	Castroville Medina Val.	La Joya

MathematicsL

Year	Conference A	Conference AA	Conference AAA	Conference AAAA	Conference AAAAA
1999–00	Valley View	Yorktown	Liberty	Pharr-San Juan-Alamo	College Station A&M
2000–01	Abbott	Valley View	Seminole	Pharr-San Juan-Alamo	Klein
2001–02	Muenster	Elkhart	Seminole	Pharr-San Juan-Alamo	Klein
2002–03	Tenaha	Elkhart	Bridgeport	Longview Pine Tree	Spring Westfield
2003–04	San Isidro	Argyle	Bridgeport	Mission Sharyland	Katy Taylor
2004–05	San Isidro	Argyle	Bridgeport	Azle	Sugar Land Dulles

Mathematics Team Event

Year	Conference A	Conference AA	Conference AAA	Conference AAAA	Conference AAAAA
1999–00	Valley View	Elkhart	Bridgeport	Cor. Christi Flour Bluff	Klein
2000–01	Abbott	Valley View	Bridgeport	Mission Sharyland	Klein
2001–02	Muenster	Elkhart	Bridgeport	Longview Pine Tree	Klein
2002–03	Plains	Elkhart	Liberty	Cor. Christi Flour Bluff	Klein
2003–04	D'Hanis	Argyle	Bridgeport	Cor. Christi Flour Bluff	Lubbock
2004–05	Lindsay	Argyle	Bridgeport	Cor. Christi Flour Bluff	Sugar Land Dulles

Science

Year	Conference A	Conference AA	Conference AAA	Conference AAAA	Conference AAAAA
1999–00	Water Valley	Salado	La Feria	Gregory-Portland	Houston Bellaire
2000–01	Lenorah Grady	Stinnett West Texas	Seminole	Kingsville King	Arlington Lamar
2001–02	High Island	Pattonville Prairiland	Seminole	Cedar Park	Humble
2002–03	Port Aransas	Argyle	Wimberley	Wh. Settlement Brewer	Clute Brazoswood
2003–04	Avery	Argyle	Ballinger	Friendswood	Klein
2004–05	Port Aransas	Argyle	Seminole	Friendswood	Sugar Land Clements

Science Team Event

Year	Conference A	Conference AA	Conference AAA	Conference AAAA	Conference AAAAA
1999–00	Hedley	Stinnett West Texas	Bridgeport	Gregory-Portland	Houston Bellaire
2000–01	Lenorah Grady	Seymour	Bridgeport	Carthage	Arlington Lamar
2001–02	Sudan	Argyle	Seminole	Fredericksburg	S. Texas Science Acad.
2002–03	Port Aransas	Lago Vista	Wimberley	Jacksonville	Fort Bend Hightower
2003–04	Vega	Argyle	Ballinger	Wichita Falls	Katy Taylor
2004–05	Kingsville Academy	Argyle	Wimberley	Friendswood	Sugar Land Clements

Social Studies

Year	Conference A	Conference AA	Conference AAA	Conference AAAA	Conference AAAAA
2004–05	Comstock	Gainesville Callisburg	Wylie	El Paso	Katy Taylor

Social Studies Team Event

Year	Conference A	Conference AA	Conference AAA	Conference AAAA	Conference AAAAA
2004–05	Lindsay	Sadler S&S	Atlanta	Joshua	Katy Taylor

Current Issues & Events

Year	Conference A	Conference AA	Conference AAA	Conference AAAA	Conference AAAAA
1999–00	Crosbyton	Sadler S&S	Vernon	Cor. Christi Flour Bluff	Katy Taylor
2000–01	Lindsay	Celina	Cotulla	Sulphur Springs	College Station A&M
2001–02	Lindsay	Stamford	Atlanta	Southlake Carroll	Pflugerville
2002–03	San Isidro	Sadler S&S	Forney	Cor. Christi Flour Bluff	College Station A&M
2003–04	Ben Wheeler M'rtin's Mill	Schulenburg	Jourdanton	Castroville Medina Val.	Corpus Christi Ray
2004–05	Apple Springs	Gainesville Callisburg	Wylie	El Paso	Corpus Christi Ray

Current Issues & Events Team

Year	Conference A	Conference AA	Conference AAA	Conference AAAA	Conference AAAAA
1999–00	Crosbyton	Sadler S&S	Teague	Cor. Christi Flour Bluff	College Station A&M
2000–01	Lindsay	Sadler S&S	Abilene Wylie	Cor. Christi Flour Bluff	Edinburg Economedes
2001–02	Lindsay	Sadler S&S	Atlanta	Sulphur Springs	College Station A&M
2002–03	Lindsay	Sadler S&S	Jourdanton	Cor. Christi Flour Bluff	College Station A&M
2003–04	Ben Wheeler M'rtin's Mill	Sadler S&S	Jourdanton	Castroville Medina Val.	Austin Westlake
2004–05	Apple Springs	Sadler S&S	Wylie	Castroville Medina Val.	College Station A&M

Literary Criticism

Year	Conference A	Conference AA	Conference AAA	Conference AAAA	Conference AAAAA
1999–00	Valley View	Lindsay	Atlanta	Brenham	San Antonio Clark
2000–01	Menard	Weimar	Barbers Hill	Mission Sharyland	Klein
2001–02	Santa Anna	Hale Center	Lytle	Friendswood	Corpus Christi Moody
2002–03	Ben Wheeler M'rtin's Mill	Hale Center	Lytle	Dripping Springs	Del Rio
2003–04	Ben Wheeler M'rtin's Mill	Sadler S&S	Canton	Dickinson	Arlington Lamar
2004–05	Lindsay	Salado	Liberty	Aledo	S.Texas Bs. Ed. & Tech.

Literary Criticism Team Event

Year	Conference A	Conference AA	Conference AAA	Conference AAAA	Conference AAAAA
1999–00	Ben Wheeler M'rtin's Mill	Salado	Atlanta	Grapevine	Midland Lee
2000–01	Menard	Hale Center	Atlanta	Stephenville	San Antonio Clark
2001–02	Lindsay	Idalou	Atlanta	Friendswood	Plano East
2002–03	Lindsay	Sadler S&S	Lytle	Stephenville	San Antonio Clark
2003–04	Ben Wheeler M'rtin's Mill	Weimar	Abilene Wylie	Friendswood	San Antonio Clark
2004–05	Ben Wheeler M'rtin's Mill	Salado	Liberty	Aledo	Irving MacArthur

Year	Conference A	Conference AA	Conference AAA	Conference AAAA	Conference AAAAA
Poetry Interpretation					
1999–00	Rice	Jewett Leon	Bishop	Denton Ryan	Houston Nimitz
2000–01	Rocksprings	Jewett Leon	White Oak	Denton Ryan	Rosenberg Terry
2001–02	Kingsville Academy	Holliday	Bishop	Denton Ryan	San Antonio Churchill
2002–03	Rice	Lago Vista	Bishop	Denton Ryan	Amarillo
2003–04	Rice	Salado	Clyde	Gregory-Portland	San Antonio Churchill
2004–05	Rice	Holliday	Giddings	Gregory-Portland	Amarillo Tascosa
Prose Interpretation					
1999–00	Barksdale Nueces Can.	Olney	Tulia	Bay City	Austin Westlake
2000–01	Guthrie	Jewett Leon	Brownfield	Burkburnett	Spring
2001–02	Bruni	Gunter	Gatesville	Athens	Houston Yates
2002–03	Roby	Premont	Canton	Rosenberg Lamar	San Antonio MacArthur
2003–04	Lindsay	Holliday	Van	Athens	Katy Taylor
2004–05	Rice	Premont	Zapata	Bay City	Harlingen South
Ready Writing					
1999–00	Wells	Lexington	Atlanta	Grapevine	Houston Memorial
2000–01	Gruver	Stockdale	Abilene Wylie	Rosenberg Lamar	Odessa
2001–02	Menard	Hale Center	Breckenridge	Austin Johnson	Garland Naaman Forest
2002–03	Paducah	Alpine	Royse City	SA Alamo Heights	Conroe The Woodlands
2003–04	Lazbuddie	Argyle	Barber's Hill	Rosenberg Lamar	Grand Prairie
2004–05	Port Aransas	Salado	Bridge City	Wylie	Conroe The Woodlands
Informative Speaking					
1999–00	Menard	Holliday	Sealy	Friendswood	Alief Hastings
2000–01	Sul. Springs N. Hopkins	Holliday	Abilene Wylie	Friendswood	Plano
2001–02	Sul. Springs N. Hopkins	Holliday	La Vernia	Richmond Foster	Alief Hastings
2002–03	Ranger	Holliday	Bishop	Richmond Foster	Deer Park
2003–04	Ranger	Jewett Leon	Lindale	Rosenberg Lamar	Plano East
2004–05	Gorman	Holliday	Lindale	Friendswood	Katy Taylor
Persuasive Speaking					
1999–00	Muenster	Holliday	Bishop	Kerrville Tivy	Lewisville
2000–01	Gail Borden	Idalou	Muleshoe	Paris North Lamar	Lewisville
2001–02	Follett	Holliday	Bishop	Bay City	Alief Hastings
2002–03	Ropesville Ropes	Gainesville Callisburg	Bishop	Rosenberg Lamar	Humble
2003–04	Gail Borden	Aubrey	Jourdanton	Corpus Christi Calallen	Humble Kingwood
2004–05	Gail Borden	Aubrey	Lindale	Frisco	Southlake Carroll
Speech					
2001–02	Kingsville Academy	Holliday	Bishop	Denton Ryan	Alief Hastings
2002–03	Lindsay & Follett (tie)	Quitman	Bishop	Rosenberg Lamar	Bryan
2003–04	Gail Borden	Aubrey	Lindale	Rosenberg Lamar	Humble Kingwood
2004–05	Lindsay	Holliday	Lindale	Bay City	San Antonio Churchill
Lincoln-Douglas Debate					
1999–00	Springlake-Earth	Lago Vista	Lindale	Sherman	Alief Hastings
2000–01	Kingsville Academy	Shelbyville	Wimberley	El Paso Burges	Georgetown
2001–02	Kingsville Academy	Forsan	Royse City	Andrews	Alief Hastings
2002–03	Terlingua Big Bend	Quitman	Royse City	Hereford	Austin
2003–04	Dawson	Blanco	Lindale	Harlingen South	Plano East
2004–05	Menard	Blanco	Van	Big Spring	San Antonio Churchill
Cross Examination Team Debate					
1999–00	Springlake-Earth	Blanco	White Oak	Hewitt Midway	Odessa
2000–01	Whitharral	Shelbyville	Muleshoe	Dallas Highland Park	Round Rock
2001–02	Christoval	Gunter	Royse City	Crosby	Houston Jersey Village
2002–03	Gail Borden	Gainesville Callisburg	Carthage	Mission Sharyland	College Station A&M
2003–04	Gail Borden	Gainesville Callisburg	Lindale	Conroe Caney Creek	Galveston Ball
2004–05	Gail Borden	Blanco	Lindale	Conroe Caney Creek	Plano
Spelling & Vocabulary					
1999–00	Wink	East Bernard	Falfurrias	Friendswood	Humble Kingwood
2000–01	Wink	Eldorado	Bridge City	Big Spring	Arlington Lamar
2001–02	Bloomburg	Troup	Lytle	Livingston	Houston Cypress Fairbanks
2002–03	Abbott	Yorktown	Perryton	Bastrop	Arlington Lamar
2003–04	Irion County	Grandview	Abilene Wylie	Bastrop	San Antonio MacArthur
2004–05	Lindsay	Tuscola Jim Ned	Wylie	Dayton	Bastrop
Spelling & Vocabulary Team Event					
1999–00	Wink	Post	Teague	Bridge City	Arlington Lamar
2000–01	Bartlett	Groveton	Bridge City	Mission Sharyland	Humble Kingwood
2001–02	Lindsay	Yorktown	Lytle	Friendswood	Mansfield
2002–03	Muenster	Yorktown	Atlanta	Friendswood	Arlington Lamar
2003–04	Yantis	Salado	Lytle	Canyon Randall	Arlington Lamar
2004–05	Lindsay	Salado	Liberty	Dayton	Bastrop

Year	Conference A	Conference AA	Conference AAA	Conference AAAA	Conference AAAAA
			Journalism Team		
2001–02	Miles	Clarendon	Glen Rose	Hillcrest	San Antonio Holmes
2002–03	Claude	Bangs	Lindale	Sulphur Springs	Pflugerville
2003–04	Moulton	San Antonio Cole	Lindale	Big Spring	McKinney
2004–05	Moulton	Corsicana Mildred	Lindale	Azle	Flower Mound Marcus
			Editorial Writing		
1999–00	Agua Dulce	Karnes City	Lake Dallas	Lampasas	Houston Cypress Falls
2000–01	Lindsay	San Antonio Cole	Lindale	C. Christi Tuloso-Midway	Conroe The Woodlands
2001–02	Afton Patton Springs	Clarendon	Huffman Hargrave	SA Alamo Heights	Mansfield
2002–03	Utopia	Big Sandy Harmony	Ballinger	Burkburnett	Pflugerville
2003–04	Itasca	George West	Lindale	Alief Kerr	McKinney
2004–05	Clarendon	Hamilton	Mount Vernon	Azle	San Antonio Clark
			Feature Writing		
1999–00	Paducah	Winters	Odem	Dallas Highland Park	Houston Stratford
2000–01	Claude	Stamford	Devine	Burleson	Lewisville Marcus
2001–02	Kingsville Academy	Winnie East Chambers	Glen Rose	Dallas Highland Park	Katy Cinco Ranch
2002–03	Gail Borden	Hawkins	Huffman Hargrave	Sulphur Springs	Abilene
2003–04	Utopia	San Antonio Cole	Lindale	Corpus Christi Calallen	Amarillo
2004–05	Moulton	Corsicana Mildred	Lindale	Austin Connally	Mansfield
			Headline Writing		
1999–00	Elkhart Slocum	Plains	Lytle	Fredericksburg	Waco
2000–01	Paducah	Plains	Ballinger	Plainview	San Antonio Southwest
2001–02	Lindsay	Idalou	Mount Vernon	Pflugerville Connally	Del Rio
2002–03	Port Anansas	Bangs	Forney	Sulphur Springs	Del Rio
2003–04	Nazareth	Forsan	Paris North Lamar	Sulphur Springs	Houston Nimitz
2004–05	Moulton	Crawford	Cuero	Azle	Bellaire
			News Writing		
1999–00	Savoy	Rosebud-Lott	Lake Dallas	Wichita Falls Rider	San Antonio Holmes
2000–01	Groom	Honey Grove	Springtown	Dallas Highland Park	McKinney
2001–02	Nazareth	Clarendon	New Boston	Port Neches-Groves	Pasadena Dobie
2002–03	Clarendon	Rosebud-Lott	Texarkana Pleasant Grove	Azle	Plano
2003–04	Moulton	San Antonio Cole	Lindale	Mission	Houston Cypress Fairbanks
2004–05	Axtell	Argyle	Lindale	Vidor	Flower Mound Marcus

Publications

Year	Yearbooks	Newspapers
1999–00	Canyon Randall, Pflugerville, Duncanville, McKinney	Mansfield, DeSoto, Dallas Hillcrest, Austin Anderson, Duncanville, Austin Westlake
2000–01	Duncanville, Abilene, Cypress Falls, Burges	DeSoto, Hillcrest, Highland Park, Duncanville, Austin Westlake, Burges
2001–02	Duncanville; Abilene Cypress Falls, Burges, White Oak	DeSoto, Highland Park, Duncanville, Liberty-Eylau
2002–03	Duncanville, Cypress Falls, White Oak	Marcus, DeSoto, Duncanville, Burges
2003–04	Duncanville, Cypress Falls, White Oak, McKinney	DeSoto, Highland Park, Austin Johnson, Austin Westlake, Duncanville
2004–05	Burges, Connally, Duncanville, McKinney, Pleasant Grove, Spring Hill, Trinity	Burges, Connally, DeSoto, Duncanville, Highland Park, Marcus, St. Mark's School of Texas

Note: *Before the 1991–92 school year, the UIL named only one top yearbook and one top newspaper each year. Beginning with the 1991-92 school year, awards were presented to all yearbooks and newspapers judged to be worthy of the honors, which were divided into gold, silver and bronze categories. Only the gold-award winners are listed here.*

Year	Conference A	Conference AA	Conference AAA	Conference AAAA	Conference AAAAA
			Music and Theatre		
			One-Act Play		
1999–00	Roscoe Highland	New Diana	Mount Vernon	Kerrville Tivy	Conroe The Woodlands
2000–01	Follett	Comfort	Wimberley	Southlake Carroll	Carrollton Creekview
2001–02	Yantis	Rogers	Van	Gregory-Portland	Galveston
2002–03	Lindsay	Omaha Paul Pewitt	Barber's Hill	Bay City	Kingwood
2003–04	Lindsay	New Diana	Mount Vernon	Friendswood	Houston Bellaire
2004–05	Lindsay	Rogers	Van	Longview Pine Tree	Arlington
			State Marching Band Contest		
1999–00	Jayton	Holliday	—	Coppell	—
2000–01	—	—	Hidalgo	—	Bell
2001–02	Overton	Holliday	—	Cedar Park	—
2002–03	—	—	Canton	—	Duncanville
2003–04	Sundown (tie) Throckmorton (tie)	Argyle	—	Richland	—
2004–05	—	—	Canton	—	Hurst Bell

Athletics

Year	Conference A	Conference AA	Conference AAA	Conference AAAA	Conference AAAAA
Baseball					
1999–00	Evadale	Weimar	China Spring	Corpus Christi Calallen	Conroe The Woodlands
2000–01	Bremond	Weimar	La Grange	Ft. Worth Western Hills	Midland
2001–02	Shiner	Celina	Sinton	Southlake Carroll	Fort Bend Elkins
2002–03	Colmesneil	Weimar	Lorena	Hewitt Midway	Fort Bend Elkins
2003–04	Shiner	Nacog. Central Heights	LaGrange	Boerne	Corpus Christi Moody
2004–05	Thorndale	Woodville	Carthage	Corpus Christi Calallen	Humble Kingwood
Basketball, Boys					
1999–00	Brookeland	Peaster	Waco LaVega	Denton Ryan	Sugar Land Willowridge
2000–01	Evadale	Ponder	Mexia	Beaumont Ozen	Sugar Land Willowridge
2001–02	Brock	Little River Academy	Gainesville	Dallas Lincoln	San Antonio Jay
2002–03	Nazareth	Brock	Everman	Fort Worth Dunbar	De Soto
2003–04	Normangee	Shallowater	Kountze	Houston Jones	Houston Milby
2004–05	I: Morton II: Lipan	Kountze	Van	Dallas South Oak Cliff	Humble Kingwood
Basketball, Girls					
1999–00	Nazareth	Farwell	Winnsboro	Canyon	Mansfield
2000–01	Nazareth	Nacog. Central Heights	Winnsboro	Plainview	Mansfield
2001–02	Brock	Buffalo	Llano	Plainview	Mansfield
2002–03	Priddy	Brock	Canyon	Plainview	Duncanville
2003–04	Archer City	Shallowater	Canyon	Dallas Lincoln	Westfield
2004–05	I: Seagraves II: Nazareth	Brock	Canyon	Fort Worth Dunbar	Arlington Bowie
Cross Country, Boys					
1999–00	Trenton	Premont	Luling	Fabens	Conroe The Woodlands
2000–01	Snook	Premont	Canton	Lockhart	Conroe The Woodlands
2001–02	Iraan	Premont	Decatur	C. Christi Tuloso-Midway	Humble Kingwood
2002–03	Iraan	Premont	Pharr Valley View	Wolfforth Frenship	Humble Kingwood
2003–04	Iraan	Krum	Elgin	Boerne	Conroe The Woodlands
2004–05	Plains	Ozona	Bridge City	Boerne	Conroe The Woodlands
Cross Country, Girls					
1999–00	Alvord	Crawford	Decatur	Dallas Highland Park	Lewisville Marcus
2000–01	Miles	Celina	Llano	Southlake Carroll	Lewisville Marcus
2001–02	Miles	Krum	Ballinger	Dallas Highland Park	Humble Kingwood
2002–03	Iraan	Krum	Celina	Dallas Highland Park	Humble Kingwood
2003–04	Sul. Springs N. Hopkins	Tuscola Jim Ned	Canyon	El Paso Del Valle	Cedar Park
2004–05	Sul. Springs N. Hopkins	Holliday	Canyon	Dallas Highland Park	Humble Kingwood

Year	6-man	A	AA	AAA	AAAA	AAAAA
Football						
1999–00	Gordon	Bartlett	I: Mart II: Celina	I: Liberty-Eylau II: Commerce	I: Texas City II: Stephenville	I: Midland Lee II: Garland
2000–01	Panther Creek	Stratford	I: Sonora II: Celina	I: Gatesville II: La Grange	I: Bay City II: Ennis	I: Midland Lee II: Katy
2001–02	Whitharral	Burkeville	I: Blanco II: Celina	I: Everman II: Commerce	I: Denton Ryan II: Ennis	I: Mesquite II: Lufkin
2002–03	Calvert	Petrolia	I: Corrigan Camden II: Rosebud-Lott	I: Everman II: Bandera	I: Texarkana Texas II:Denton Ryan	I: Judson II: Southlake Carroll
2003–04	Strawn	Windthorst	I: San Augustine II: Garrison	I: Gainesville II: Atlanta	I: North Crowley II: La Marque	I: North Shore II: Katy
2004–05	Richland Springs	Shiner	I: Boyd II: Crawford	I: Abilene Wylie II: Gilmer	I: Ennis II: Kilgore	I: Tyler Lee II: Southlake Carroll

Year	Conference A	Conference AA	Conference AAA	Conference AAAA	Conference AAAAA
Golf, Boys					
1999–00	Wheeler	Olney	Sour Lake Hardin-Jefferson	Dallas Highland Park	Lubbock Coronado
2000–01	Brock	San Saba	Longview Spring Hill	Palestine	Austin Westlake
2001–02	Throckmorton	Memphis	Perryton	Dallas Highland Park	Conroe The Woodlands
2002–03	Memphis	Three Rivers	Snyder	Dallas Highland Park	Fort Bend Elkins
2003–04	Iraan	Three Rivers	Slaton	Dallas Highland Park	Southlake Carroll
2004–05	Iraan	Jacksboro	Palestine	Dallas Highland Park	Conroe The Woodlands
Golf, Girls					
1999–00	Baird	Hamilton	Breckenridge	Dallas Highland Park	San Antonio Churchill
2000–01	Baird	Hamilton	Fort Stockton	Montgomery	Conroe The Woodlands
2001–02	Baird	Salado	Bridgeport	Montgomery	Conroe The Woodlands
2002–03	Throckmorton	Salado	Snyder	Montgomery	Conroe The Woodlands
2003–04	Baird	Lago Vista	Yoakum	Montgomery	Victoria Memorial
2004–05	Baird	Refugio	Snyder	Montgomery	Allen

Year	Conference A	Conference AA	Conference AAA	Conference AAAA	Conference AAAAA
Softball					
1999–00	—	Troy	Kennedale	Weatherford	Freeport Brazoswood
2000–01	Shiner	Archer City	Sanger	Spr. Brch. Smithson Val.	Coppell
2001–02	Shiner	Weimar	Splendora	Frisco	Bryan
2002–03	Flatonia	Weimar	Kirbyville	Crowley	Keller
2003–04	Windthorst	Danbury	Lindale	Crowley	Fort Bend Elkins
2004–05	Windthorst	Elysian Fields	La Grange	Brenham	Keller
Team Tennis					
1999–00				SA Alamo Heights	Abilene
2000–01				SA Alamo Heights	El Paso Coronado
2001–02				Dallas Highland Park	Plano West
2002–03				SA Alamo Heights	Katy Taylor
2003–04				Dallas Highland Park	Lubbock Coronado
2004–05				Dallas Highland Park	Plano West
Tennis, Boys Singles					
1999–00	Mertzon Irion County	Port Aransas	Vernon	New Braunfels Canyon	Amarillo Tascosa
2000–01	Rotan	Spearman	Fort Stockton	Cor. Christi Flour Bluff	College Station A&M
2001–02	Rotan	Wall	Abilene Wylie	New Braunfels	North Garland
2002–03	Rotan	San Antonio Cole	Kaufman	SA Alamo Heights	Plano West
2003–04	Rotan	Wall	Clyde	Conroe Oak Ridge	San Antonio Marshall
2004–05	Nazareth	Franklin	Clyde	SA Alamo Heights	Amarillo Tascosa
Tennis, Boys Doubles					
1999–00	Menard	Mason	Abilene Wylie	Wichita Falls	Sugar Land Kempner
2000–01	Mertzon Irion County	Thorndale	Lindale	Conroe Oak Ridge	Katy Taylor
2001–02	Knox City	Spearman	Lindale	SA Alamo Heights	Katy Taylor
2002–03	Knox City	Spearman	Canyon	SA Alamo Heights	El Paso Coronado
2003–04	Miami	San Saba	Lindale	Richardson Pearce	Tomball
2004–05	Miami	Mason	Levelland	Wichita Falls	Richardson Pearce
Tennis, Girls Singles					
1999–00	Leakey	San Antonio Cole	West	Fredericksburg	Duncanville
2000–01	Gruver	San Antonio Cole	Crandall	New Braunfels	Houston Memorial
2001–02	San Antonio Stacey	San Saba	Crandall	Fredericksburg	Houston Jersey Village
2002–03	San Antonio Stacey	Spearman	Crandall	Dallas Highland Park	Houston Jersey Village
2003–04	San Antonio Stacey	Comfort	Crandall	Dallas Highland Park	Lewisville Marcus
2004–05	San Antonio Stacey	Comfort	Abilene Wylie	Whitehouse	Lewisville Marcus
Tennis, Girls Doubles					
1999–00	Anton	Thrall	Lindale	Wichita Falls	Lubbock Coronado
2000–01	White Deer	Eldorado	Gladewater	Richardson Pearce	El Paso Coronado
2001–02	Sabinal	Eldorado	Abilene Wylie	Dallas Highland Park	College Station A&M
2002–03	Clarendon	Mason	Lindale	Dallas Highland Park	El Paso Coronado
2003–04	Clarendon	Mason	Abilene Wylie	Wichita Falls Rider	Arlington Bowie
2004–05	Nazareth	Mason	Abilene Wylie	Dallas Highland Park	Arlington Bowie
Track & Field, Boys					
1999–00	Karnack	Refugio	Hearne	Houston Forest Brook	Duncanville
2000–01	Iraan & Trent (tie)	Refugio	Abilene Wylie	Houston Forest Brook	Abilene
2001–02	Mertzon Irion County	Junction	Atlanta	Fort Worth Wyatt	Dallas Carter
2002–03	Mertzon Irion County	Corrigan-Camden	Atlanta	Lancaster	Arlington Bowie
2003–04	Mertzon Irion County	Alto	Atlanta	Lancaster	Katy Cinco Ranch
2004–05	Lindsay	Lexington	Cuero	Crowley	Katy Cinco Ranch
Track & Field, Girls					
1999–00	Karnack	Spearman	Luling	Austin Reagan	Houston Westbury
2000–01	Karnack	Cisco	Everman	Lancaster	Houston Lamar
2001–02	Shamrock	Cisco	Wilmer Hutchins	Lancaster	Dallas Skyline
2002–03	Shamrock	Alto	Celina	Lancaster	Alief Elsik
2003–04	Granger	Crane	Kennedale	Lancaster	Dallas Skyline
2004–05	Hamlin	Alto	Canyon	Lancaster	Dallas Skyline
Volleyball					
1999–00	Windthorst	Hutto	Wimberley	Hereford	Round Rock Westwood
2000–01	Windthorst	Jewitt Leon	Caldwell	New Braunfels	Houston Cypress Falls
2001–02	Windthorst	Pattonville Prairiland	Wimberley	Hereford	Amarillo
2002–03	Windthorst	Jewett Leon	Wimberley	Red Oak	Austin Westlake
2003–04	Round Top-Carmine	Wallis Brazos	Wimberley	Stephenville	San Antonio Clark
2004–05	Windthorst	Poth	Monahans	Lewisville Hebron	Austin Westlake

	Soccer			
	Girls		**Boys**	
Year	AAAA	AAAAA	AAAA	AAAAA
1999–00	Dallas Highland Park	Plano West	Wichita Falls Rider	Plano
2000–01	Friendswood	Plano West	Southlake Carroll	San Antonio Churchill
2001–02	Dallas Highland Park	Plano West	Hewitt Midway	San Antonio Reagan
2002–03	Denton	Klein	Red Oak	San Antonio Churchill

Soccer			
Girls		**Boys**	
Year	**AAAA**	**AAAAA**	**AAAA**	**AAAAA**

Year	**AAAA**	**AAAAA**	**AAAA**	**AAAAA**
2003–04	Denton	Carrollton Creekview	Brownsville Lopez	Coppell
2004–05	McKinney	Lewisville Marcus	El Paso Del Valle	Klein

Swimming & Diving			
Year	**Girls**		**Boys**	
	AAAA	**AAAAA**	**AAAA**	**AAAAA**
1999–00	Austin Johnson	San Antonio Reagan	Dallas Highland Park	San Antonio Churchill
2000–01	Dallas Highland Park	Katy Taylor	Dallas Highland Park	Katy Taylor
2001–02	Dallas Highland Park	San Antonio Reagan	Southlake Carroll	Humble Kingwood
2002–03	Dallas Highland Park	Austin Bowie	Texarkana Texas	Katy Taylor
2003–04	Dallas Highland Park	Humble Kingwood	Richardson Pearce	Conroe The Woodlands
2004–05	Dallas Highland Park	San Antonio Churchill	Frisco	Humble Kingwood

Wrestling, Boys	
1999–00	**Team:** Dallas Highland Park; **Weight Class 103:** El Paso Eastwood; **112:** El Paso Ysleta; **119:** Grapevine; **125:** Canyon Randall; **130:** Lewisville Marcus; **135:** Austin Bowie; **140:** Plano East; **145:** Boys Ranch; **152:** Arlington Lamar; **160:** Katy; **171:** Colleyville Heritage; **180:** El Paso Franklin; **189:** El Paso Eastwood; **215:** San Antonio Roosevelt; **275:** Grapevine
2000–01	**Team:** Rockwall; **Weight Class 103:** Katy Taylor; **112:** El Paso Eastwood; **119:** El Paso Eastwood; **125:** Canyon Randall; **130:** Bryan; **135:** El Paso Hanks; **140:** Amarillo Caprock; **145:** Austin Westlake; **152:** Canyon Randall; **160:** Colleyville Heritage; **171:** Dumas; **180:** Rockwall; **189:** Amarillo River Road; **215:** Arlington Martin; **275:** Conroe Oak Ridge
2001–02	**Team:** Rockwall; **Weight Class 103:** El Paso Hanks; **112:** Euless Trinity; **119:** Arlington Houston; **125:** El Paso Ysleta; **130:** Dallas Highland Park; **135:** Euless Trinity; **140:** Lewisville Hebron; **145:** Carrollton Smith; **152:** Austin Westlake; **160:** Canyon Randall; **171:** Amarillo Tascosa; **180:** San Antonio Churchill; **189:** Rockwall; **215:** Amarillo; **275:** San Antonio Churchill
2002–03	**Team:** Dallas Highland Park; **Weight Class 103:** El Paso Hanks; **112:** Katy Taylor; **119:** Euless Trinity; **125:** Conroe The Woodlands; **130:** Euless Trinity; **135:** Conroe The Woodlands; **140:** Azle; **145:** Arlington Lamar; **152:** Lewisville Hebron; **160:** Rockwall; **171:** Katy; **180:** Katy Cinco Ranch; **189:** Rockwall; **215:** El Paso Riverside; **275:** Amarillo
2003–04	**Team:** Arlington Martin; **Weight Class 103:** Katy Cinco Ranch; **112:** Arlington Martin; **119:** Borger; **125:** Dallas Highland Park; **130:** Canyon Randall; **135:** Arlington Martin; **140:** Dallas Jesuit; **145:** Colleyville Heritage; **152:** Arlington Lamar; **160:** Coppell; **171:** Dallas Highland Park; **180:** Katy Cinco Ranch; **189:** Katy; **215:** Houston Westside; **275:** Arlington Martin
2004–05	**Team:** Dallas Highland Park; **Weight Class 103:** Amarillo Caprock; **112:** Plano East; **119:** Klein Oak; **125:** Colleyville Heritage; **130:** Dallas Highland Park; **135:** El Paso Hanks; **140:** Arlington Martin; **145:** Katy Cinco Ranch; **152:** Arlington; **160:** Dumas; **171:** San Antonio MacArthur; **180:** Dallas Highland Park; **189:** Conroe The Woodlands; **215:** Katy; **275:** Rockwall

Wrestling, Girls	
1999–00	**Team:** Amarillo Caprock; **Weight Class 95:** Amarillo Palo Duro; **102:** Arlington Bowie; **110:** Klein Oak; **119:** Amarillo Caprock; **128:** Arlington Houston; **138:** Katy; **148:** Amarillo Caprock; **165:** Arlington; **185:** Waller; **215:** Amarillo Caprock
2000–01	**Team:** Amarillo Caprock; **Weight Class 95:** Amarillo Palo Duro; **102:** El Paso Hanks; **110:** Hereford; **119:** Amarillo Palo Duro; **128:** El Paso Hanks; **138:** Amarillo Tascosa; **148:** Amarillo Palo Duro; **165:** Amarillo Palo Duro; **185:** Amarillo Palo Duro; **215:** Amarillo Palo Duro
2001–02	**Team:** Amarillo Tascosa; **Weight Class 95:** Amarillo Palo Duro; **102:** El Paso Hanks; **110:** Austin Lanier; **119:** El Paso Hanks; **128:** Katy; **138:** Amarillo Tascosa; **148:** Amarillo Tascosa; **165:** Killeen Ellison; **185:** Killeen Ellison; **215:** Herefordr
2002–03	**Team:** Dallas Highland Park; **Weight Class 95:** Amarillo Palo Duro; **102:** Amarillo Tascosa; **110:** Arlington Lamar; **119:** El Paso Hanks; **128:** Pflugerville; **138:** Hurst Bell; **148:** Amarillo Palo Duro; **165:** San Antonio Lee; **185:** Killeen Ellison; **215:** San Antonio Lee
2003–04	**Team:** Amarillo Caprock; **Weight Class 95:** Katy; **102:** Katy Taylor; **110:** South Grand Prairie; **119:** Amarillo Palo Duro; **128:** Hereford; **138:** Katy; **148:** Amarillo Palo Duro; **165:** El Paso Eastwood; **185:** Amarillo Palo Duro; **215:** Waller
2004–05	**Team:** Amarillo Caprock; **Weight Class 95:** Amarillo Caprock; **102:** El Paso Hanks; **110:** Amarillo Tascosa; **119:** Katy Cinco Ranch; **128:** Amarillo Caprock; **138:** Amarillo; **148:** Klein; **165:** El Paso Eastwood; **185:** Richardson Lake Highlands; **215:** Killeen Shoemaker

Jourdan Norman (above, center) of the 4A championship Lewisville Hebron High School volleyball team. Carthage High School baseball players celebrates their 3A state championship. File photos.

Belo Covers the Nation

Belo, a Dallas-based media company, has been a part of Texas history since the days of the Republic. The oldest continuously operating business in Texas, Belo had its origins in Galveston with the one-page *The Daily News,* which was first published in April 1842.

Today, Belo is one of the nation's largest media companies with a diversified group of market-leading broadcasting, publishing, cable and interactive media assets. A Fortune 1000 company with approximately 7,600 employees and $1.5 billion in annual revenues, Belo has news and information operations in some of the most desirable markets in Texas, the Northwest, the Southwest, Rhode Island and the Mid-Atlantic. Belo's media outlets reach more than 30 million viewers, readers and online users each week.

The company owns 19 television stations that reach almost 14 percent of U.S. television households, manages one television station under a local marketing agreement, owns or operates seven cable news channels and publishes four daily newspapers: *The Dallas Morning News,* which publishes the *Texas Almanac; The Providence Journal* in Providence, R.I.; *The Press-Enterprise* in Riverside, Calif.; and the *Denton Record-Chronicle* in Denton, Texas. Belo operates more than 30 Web sites associated with its operating companies. The company also produces specialty publications, including *Quick* and *al dia* in Dallas/Fort Worth; and *the d, El D* and *La Prensa* in Riverside.

The Early Days

The Daily News in Galveston was established in 1842, three years before the Republic of Texas achieved statehood. The newspaper was printed on equipment owned by Massachusetts native Samuel Bangs, along with his brother-in-law and The Daily News publisher, George H. French. In June 1843, Bangs leased the printing equipment to Wilbur F. Cherry and Michael Cronican; Cherry soon acquired sole ownership of The News.

Another Massachusetts émigré, Willard Richardson, became editor of the paper in 1844 and its sole owner in 1845. He campaigned editorially for annexation, fiscal responsibility and railroads. In 1857, Richardson conceived and founded the Texas Almanac, which he hoped would help attract settlers to the new state. Eight years later, he hired Alfred Horatio Belo, a former Confederate colonel from North Carolina, as bookkeeper. Belo was made a full partner in the growing company after only three months. The company eventually was named for him.

In 1874, George Bannerman Dealey, a 15-year-old English emigrant, was hired as an office boy. Working tirelessly, he made his way from office boy to business manager and then to publisher of *The Dallas Morning News.* It was Dealey who chose the then-small settlement of Dallas as the site for a sister paper. Dealey and other members of the Galveston newspaper's staff relocated to Dallas, and the company prospered and grew.

Belo Was a Radio Broadcasting Pioneer

On June 26, 1922, Belo began operating a 50-watt radio station, WFAA-AM, which was the first network station in the state. The company sold this radio property in 1987.

The Newspaper Group

The Dallas Morning News began publication on Oct. 1, 1885, with a circulation of 5,000 subscribers. After being in operation only two months, *The Dallas Morning News* acquired its first competitor, the *Dallas Herald* (not to be confused with the *Dallas Times Herald* that closed in December 1991). Rather than compete with each other for subscribers, the two newspapers combined, keeping the name *The Dallas Morning News.*

In 1906, on the 21st anniversary of *The Dallas Morning News,* Dealey gave a speech from which emerged the company's motto: "Build the news upon the rock of truth and righteousness. Conduct it always upon the lines of fairness and integrity. Acknowledge the right of the people to get from the newspaper both sides of every important question." Today these words are carved in a 3-story-high space above the entrance to *The Dallas Morning News.* The News building, a long-standing dream of Dealey's, was completed in 1949, three years after his death.

While Belo has become one of the nation's largest, most diversified media companies, *The Dallas Morning News* remains the flagship newspaper of the company's publishing business.

In 1997, Belo purchased *The Press-Enterprise,* a daily newspaper serving Riverside County and the inland Southern California area. The *Press-Enterprise* also publishes *La Prensa,* the area's top-rated Spanish language newspaper, and *The Business Press.* Also in 1997, through the acquisition of The Providence Journal Company, Belo acquired *The Providence Journal,* the leading newspaper in Rhode Island and southeastern Massachusetts, and Rhode Island Monthly Communications, Inc., the state's only full-service publisher of magazines and specialty publications. Founded in 1829, The Providence Journal is America's oldest major daily general circulation newspaper in continuous publication.

In 1999, Belo acquired the Denton Publishing Company, whose assets included the *Denton Record-Chronicle,* a daily newspaper serving Denton County and surrounding areas in North Texas.

In 2003, Belo expanded its portfolio of specialized publications to serve young adults, affluent populations and the fast-growing Hispanic market with the launch of *Quick* and *al dia* in Dallas, and *the d* and *El D* in Riverside.

At the end of 2004, Belo's major newspapers had a combined readership of 2.1 million daily customers and more than 2.8 million on Sunday.

The Television Group and Cable Operations

Belo entered the television broadcasting business in 1950 with the acquisition of its flagship station, ABC affiliate WFAA-TV in Dallas/Fort Worth. In 1983, in the nation's largest broadcast acquisition to date, Belo acquired KHOU-TV (CBS) in Houston; KXTV (ABC) in Sacramento/Stockton/Modesto, Calif.; WVEC-TV (ABC) in Hampton/Norfolk, Va.; and KOTV (CBS) in Tulsa, Okla. In June 1994, Belo acquired WWL-TV (CBS) in New Orleans, La., and in Sept. 1994, the company acquired KIRO-TV in Seattle/Tacoma, Wash. Belo's acquisition of The Providence Journal Company in 1997 is the largest transaction to date in the company's history. The acquisition included five NBC affiliates (KING-TV in Seattle/Tacoma, Wash.; KGW-TV in Portland, Ore.; WCNC-TV in Charlotte, N.C.; KHNL-TV in Honolulu, Hawaii; and KTVB in Boise, Idaho); one ABC affiliate (WHAS-TV in Louisville, Ky.); one CBS affiliate (KREM-TV in Spokane, Wash.); two FOX affiliates (KASA-TV in Albuquerque/Santa Fe, and KMSB-TV in Tucson); and NorthWest Cable News (NWCN) in Seattle/Tacoma.

Belo also assumed the management of four television stations through local marketing agreements and became the managing general partner of The Television Food Network, a cable channel in New York, N.Y.

In connection with the acquisition of The Providence Journal Company, Belo agreed to exchange KIRO-TV for a station in another market to comply with Federal Communications Commission regulations, which prohibited a company from owning multiple television stations in a single market. The agreement resulted in Belo's June 1997 acquisition of KMOV-TV (CBS) in St. Louis, Mo.

In early 1997, the company opened its Capital Bureau in Washington, D.C., which houses Washington-based journalists representing the company's 17 network-affiliated television stations as well as *The Dallas Morning News* and *The Providence Journal.*

In February 1997, Belo began operating Local News on Cable in Hampton/Norfolk, Va., through a partnership with Cox Communications and *The Virginian-Ledger,* which also leveraged WVEC-TV's local news programming and marketing strengths.

In December 1997, Belo exchanged its interest in the Television Food Network for KENS-TV (CBS) and KENS-AM in San Antonio.

Belo's WFAA-TV made television history in February 1998 by becoming the first VHF station in the country to transmit a digital signal on a permanent basis.

Belo expanded its cable operations in October 1998 with the addition of NewsWatch on Channel 15 through another partnership with Cox Communications, which extended the company's presence in New Orleans.

On Jan. 1, 1999, Belo launched Texas Cable News (TXCN), the first 24-hour regional cable news channel in Texas. On June 1, 1999, Belo exchanged KXTV (ABC) in Sacramento/Stockton/Modesto for KVUE-TV (ABC) in Austin. By the end of 1999, the combined reach of Belo's Texas television stations reached 67 percent of all television households in Texas.

In November 1999, Belo acquired KTVK (Ind.) in Phoenix along with the rights to operate KASW-TV, the Phoenix WB affiliate; a 50-percent interest in the Arizona News Channel; and azfamily.com, Arizona's leading Web publishing and design services firm. Belo also divested KHNL and KASA.

In March 2000, Belo acquired two television stations that it had previously operated under local marketing agreements, KONG-TV (Ind.) in Seattle/Tacoma and KASW-TV in Phoenix, creating the company's first two duopoly markets. Belo began operating KBEJ-TV (UPN) in San Antonio under a local marketing agreement in August 2000. Together with Cox Communications, Belo launched ¡Mas! Arizona, the Southwest's first Spanish-language cable news, information and sports channel in Phoenix, in October 2000.

Belo divested KOTV, its Tulsa station, in December 2000. In October 2001, Belo acquired KSKN-TV, the WB/UPN affiliate in Spokane, Wash., which the company had operated under a local marketing agreement, creating the company's third duopoly market. In a similar move in March 2002, Belo acquired KTTU-TV, the UPN affiliate in Tucson, which also had been operated through a local marketing agreement, creating Belo's fourth duopoly market.

Between June 2002 and April 2003, Belo formed a joint venture with Time Warner that launched 24-hour cable news channels in Houston, San Antonio and Charlotte to augment its network-affiliated local television stations, KHOU-TV, KENS-TV and WCNC-TV. In October 2003, the company launched the 24/7 News Channel to complement its KTVB operation in Boise. In July 2004, as marketplace needs shifted, Belo discontinued its joint venture relationship with Time Warner in Houston, San Antonio and Charlotte. In November 2004, Belo identified new opportunities in Dallas/Fort Worth and formed a strategic alliance to provide sales, advertising, operations and programming support to KFWD-TV.

Belo sold its only remaining radio station, KENS-AM in San Antonio, in March 2003.

By January 2005, Belo's Television Group reached almost 14 percent of all U.S. television households.

In July 2005, Belo announced plans to purchase WUPL-TV, the UPN affiliate in New Orleans, creating the company's fifth duopoly market with WWL-TV.

Interactive Media

Belo Interactive, Inc., was established in 1999 to manage the Web sites affiliated with Belo's newspapers, television stations and cable news operations. In January 2005, the operations of the company's more than 30 Web sites were integrated into their related media operating companies, with centralized product development, sales and marketing, news content and technology support provided by Belo's interactive media group.

By the first quarter 2005, Belo's network of news and information Web sites reached more than 6.5 million registered customers, and averaged more than 5.7 million unique visitors and more than 131 million page views each month.

Belo Officers

Officers of Belo are Robert W. Decherd, chairman of the board, president and chief executive officer; John L. (Jack) Sander, president/media operations; Dunia A. Shive, executive vice president; James M. Moroney III, publisher and chief executive officer of The Dallas Morning News; Dennis A. Williamson, senior corporate vice president/chief financial officer; Guy H. Kerr, senior vice president/law and government and secretary; Marian Spitzberg, senior vice president/human resources;

Donald F. (Skip) Cass Jr., senior vice president; Richard J. Keilty, senior vice president; David T. Lougee, senior vice president; and Lee Salzberger, senior vice president/administration; Robert W. Barner, vice president/management development; Daniel J. Blizzard, vice president/operations; Russell F. Coleman, vice president/general counsel and assistant secretary;

David M. Duitch, vice president/Capital Bureau; Carey P. Hendrickson, vice president/investor relations & corporate communications; John P. Irvin, vice president/facilities planning; Wesley A. Jackson, vice president/interactive media; Doretha F. (DeDe) Lea, vice president/government affairs; Brenda C. Maddox, vice president/treasurer & tax and assistant secretary; J. William Mosley, vice president/financial planning & analysis; and Caren Shiozaki, vice president/chief information officer. Amy Meadows is vice president and executive director of The Belo Foundation.

The Dallas Morning News

Officers of The Dallas Morning News are James M. Moroney III, publisher and chief executive officer; Robert W. Mong Jr., editor; Evelyn Miller, executive vice president; Gilbert Bailon, publisher and editor/al dia; Laura Gordon, senior vice president/marketing, and publisher/Quick; John Walsh, senior vice president/circulation; Steven Weaver, senior vice president/advertising;

Jim Berry, vice president/financial planning and analysis; Cynthia Carr, vice president/advertising marketing; Tom Caywood, vice president/classified advertising; Bill May, vice president/production; Scott Messer, vice president/controller; George Rodrigue, vice president/managing editor; Lorie Schrader, vice president/information technology; Darryl Thornton, vice president/human resources; and Keven Ann Willey, vice president/editorial page editor.

The Providence Journal

Officers of The Providence Journal are Howard G. Sutton, chairman of the board, publisher, president and chief executive officer; Mark T. Ryan, executive vice president/general manager; John Palumbo, president and publisher/Rhode Island Monthly; Paul Farrell, senior vice president/advertising; Sandra J. Radcliffe, senior vice president/finance; Joel P. Rawson, senior vice president and executive editor; Maura Brodeur, vice president/advertising; Michael J. Dooley, vice president/circulation; Debra Hill, vice president/publishing technology; Wayne Pelland, vice president/operations; and Robert Whitcomb, vice president and editorial page editor.

The Press-Enterprise

Officers of The Press-Enterprise include Ronald J. Redfern, publisher and chief executive officer; Sue Barry, vice president/advertising; Maria De Varenne, vice president/news and editor; Steve Favero, vice president/operations; Ed Lasak, vice president/finance and information technology; and Kathy Michalak, vice president/circulation.

The Denton Record-Chronicle

Officers of the Denton Record-Chronicle include Bill Patterson, publisher and chief executive officer and Barry Boesch, executive editor.

The Television Group

Officers of Belo's Television Group include John L. (Jack) Sander, president/media operations; Dunia A. Shive, executive vice president; Donald F. "Skip" Cass, senior vice president; Richard J. Keilty, senior vice president; and David T. Lougee, senior vice president.

Officers of Belo's television stations include Kathy Clements, president and general manager, WFAA-TV; David F. Muscari, vice president/strategic alliances, WFAA-TV; Mike Devlin, vice president and station manager, WFAA-TV, and manager, Texas Cable News;

Peter Diaz, president and general manager, KHOU-TV; Ray Heacox, president and general manager, KING-TV, KONG-TV and NorthWest Cable News; Jay Cascio, vice president/programming and creative services, KING-TV; Mark A. Higgins, president and general manager, KTVK; Jamie T. Aitken, vice president and general manager, KASW-TV;

Allan R. Cohen, president and general manager, KMOV-TV; R. Paul Fry, president and general manager, KGW-TV; Stuart B. Powell, president and general manager, WCNC-TV; Robert G. McGann, president and general manager, KENS-TV; Mario A. Hewitt, president and general manager, WVEC-TV; Bud Brown, president and general manager, WWL-TV; Robert A. Klingle, president and general manager, WHAS-TV;

Patti C. Smith, president and general manager, KVUE-TV; Laurence D. "Nick" Nicholson, vice president and general manager, KMSB-TV and KTTU-TV; Deborah "DJ" Wilson, president and general manager, KREM-TV and KSKN-TV; and Douglas Armstrong, president and general manager, KTVB. ☆

Belo Corp. Directors

Robert W. Decherd

Robert W. Decherd has served as a director of Belo since March 1976. He has been Belo's chairman and chief executive officer since January 1987. Decherd became president of Belo in January 1994, and previously served as president from January 1985 through December 1986. From January 1984 through December 1986, he served as chief operating officer. Decherd is a member of the board of directors, lead director, and chairman of the Executive Committee of Kimberly-Clark Corporation. He also serves on the Advisory Council for Harvard University's Center for Ethics and the Professions, and is a member of the Media Security and Reliability Council, which is part of President Bush's Homeland Security initiative.

Henry P. Becton Jr.

Henry P. Becton, Jr. has served as a director of Belo since May 1997. He has been president of WGBH Educational Foundation, a public broadcasting organization, since 1984 and served as its general manager from 1978 until 1999. He is the lead director of Becton Dickinson and Company and is a trustee or director of 18 Scudder Fund investment companies or trusts advised by Deutsche Asset Management. Becton served as a director of The Providence Journal Company from 1992 to 1997. Becton is a trustee of the Boston Museum of Science and is a member of the boards of directors of Public Radio International and America's Public Television Stations.

Louis E. Caldera

Louis E. Caldera has served as a director of Belo since July 2001. Caldera has served as president of the University of New Mexico since August 2003. He served as vice chancellor for university advancement at The California State University from June 2001 to June 2003. Caldera was Secretary of the Army in the Clinton Administration from July 1998 until January 2001. He previously served as managing director and chief operating officer for the Corporation for National and Community Service, a federal grant-making agency, from September 1997 to June 1998. Caldera also serves on the boards of directors of IndyMac Bancorp, Inc.,

and Southwest Airlines Co.

France A. Córdova, Ph.D.

France A. Córdova, Ph.D., has served as a director of Belo since May 2003. She has been chancellor of the University of California Riverside since July 2002. From August 1996 to July 2002, she was vice chancellor for research and professor of physics at University of California Santa Barbara. She served as chief scientist of National Aeronautics and Space Administration (NASA) from 1993 to 1996. Córdova is a member of the board of directors of Edison International and its subsidiary, Southern California Edison. She currently serves on advisory committees for the National Academy of Sciences and NASA.

Judith L. Craven, M.D., M.P.H.

Judith L. Craven, M.D., M.P.H., has served as a director of Belo since December 1992. She is a member of the board of regents of The University of Texas System and serves on the boards of directors of SYSCO Corporation, Luby's, Inc., Sun America Mutual Funds, and Variable Annuity Life Insurance Company of America. From July 1992 until her retirement in October 1998, Craven served as president of the United Way of the Texas Gulf Coast. From 1983 to 1992, she was dean of the School of Allied Health Sciences of the University of Texas Health Science Center at Houston, and from 1987 to 1992 was vice president of multicultural affairs for the University of Texas Health Science Center.

Roger A. Enrico

Roger A. Enrico has been a director of Belo since July 1995. Enrico is chairman of the board of DreamWorks Animation SKG, a developer and producer of computer-generated animated feature films. He is the former chairman and chief executive officer of PepsiCo, Inc., having served as chief executive officer from April 1996 until May 2001, chairman of the board from November 1996 to May 2001, and vice chairman from May 2001 until April 2002. Enrico joined PepsiCo in 1971 and held numerous other senior positions. Enrico is a member of the boards of directors of Target Corporation, Electronic Data Systems Corporation, The National Geographic Society, The Dallas Center for the Performing Arts, and The Eisenhower Fellowships.

Dealey D. Herndon

Dealey D. Herndon has served as a director of Belo since May 1986. She has been president of Herndon, Stauch & Associates, a project and construction manage-ment firm, since Septem-ber 1995. From January 2001 to October 2001, she also served as director of appointments for Texas Governor Rick Perry. From 1991 to September 1995, she was executive director of the State Pres-ervation Board of the State of Texas and man-aged the Texas Capitol Restoration in that capac-ity. Herndon is trustee emeritus of the National

Trust for Historic Preservation in Washington, D.C., and serves on the board of the Texas State History Museum Foundation.

Laurence E. Hirsch

Laurence E. Hirsch has served as a director of Belo since August 1999. He is the chairman of Eagle Materials Inc., a construction prod-ucts company, a position he has held since July 1999. He is also the Chairman of Highlander Partners, L.P., a private equity firm. Hirsch is the former chairman and chief executive officer of Centex Corporation, one of the nation's largest homebuilders. He was chief executive officer of Centex from July 1988 through March 2004 and chairman of the board from July 1991 through

March 2004. Hirsch serves as an advisory director of Heidelberger Cement AG and also is a trustee of the Univer-sity of Pennsylvania.

Wayne R. Sanders

Wayne R. Sanders has served as a director of Belo since May 2003. Sanders is the former chairman and chief execu-tive officer of Kimberly-Clark Corporation. He served as president and chief executive officer of Kimberly-Clark from 1991 until September 2002 and as chairman of the board from 1992 until February 2003. Sanders joined Kimberly-Clark in 1975 and held other senior positions prior to 1991. He also serves on the board of directors of Texas Instruments Incor-porated. Sanders is vice chairman of the board of

Marquette University and serves as national trustee and governor of the Boys and Girls Clubs of America.

William T. Solomon

William T. Solomon has served as a director of Belo since April 1983. He is chairman of the board of Austin Industries, Inc., a general construction com-pany, a position he has held since 1987. Solomon was chairman and chief executive officer from 1987 to March 2001 and, prior to 1987, president and chief executive officer of Austin Indus-tries. He also serves on the boards of the Hoblit-zelle Foundation and the Southwestern Medical Foundation.

M. Anne Szostak

M. Anne Szostak has served as a director of Belo since October 2004. From Feb-ruary 1998 until her retirement in June 2004, Szostak served as execu-tive vice president of FleetBoston Financial, a diversified financial ser-vices company. She also served as director of Human Resources and Diversity of Fleet from February 1998 until June 2004. During her 31-year career with Fleet, she held several executive positions, including chairman and chief exec-utive officer of Fleet

Bank-Rhode Island from 2001 to 2003. Szostak is a director of Spherion Corporation and Tupperware Corporation. She chairs the board of governors of Boys and Girls Clubs of America and is a member of the boards of directors of Women & Infants Hospital in Providence, Women & Infants Hospital Foundation, and the Institute for Contemporary Art in Boston.

Lloyd D. Ward

Lloyd D.Ward has served as a director of Belo since July 2001. Ward has been chairman of BodyBlocks Nutrition Systems, Inc., a manufac-turer of snack food and beverages, since April 2003. He served as chief executive officer and sec-retary general of the United States Olympic Committee, positions he held from October 2001 until March 2003. Ward was chairman and chief executive officer of May-

tag Corporation from August 1999 to November 2000, pres-ident and chief operating officer of Maytag from 1998 to August 1999, and executive vice president of Maytag from 1996 to 1998.

J. McDonald Williams

J. McDonald Williams has served as a director of Belo since April 1985. Williams served as chairman of Trammell Crow Company, a real estate services firm, from August 1994 until May 2002, when he was named chairman emeritus. From 1991 until July 1994, He was president and chief executive officer of Trammell Crow, and from 1977 to December 1990, he was managing partner of Trammell Crow. In addition to his continued service as a director of Trammell Crow, Williams also serves on the boards of directors of Tenet Healthcare Corporation, the Children's Medical Center Dallas Associates, Children's Medical Center Foundation, Abilene Christian University, the Hoblitzelle Foundation, Southern Methodist University's Perkins School of Theology, and the Dallas Foundation. ☆

Texas Newspapers, Radio and Television Stations

In the list of print and broadcast media below, frequency of publication of newspapers is indicated after the names by the following codes: (D), daily; (S), semiweekly; (TW), triweekly; (BW), biweekly; (SM), semimonthly; (M), monthly; all others are weeklies. "DT" following the call letters of a TV station indicates digital transmission. The radio and television stations are those with valid operating licenses as of July 2005. Not included are those with only construction permits or with applications pending. Sources: Newspapers: 2005 Texas Newspaper Directory, Texas Press Association, Austin; Broadcast Media: Federal Communications Commission Web site: http://svartifoss2.fcc.gov/prod/cdbs/pubacc/prod/cdbs_pa.htm.

Abernathy—Newspaper: Abernathy Weekly Review.
Abilene—Newspaper: Abilene Reporter-News (D). **Radio-AM:** KSLI,1280 kHz; KWKC, 1340; KYYW, 1470; KZQQ, 1560. **Radio-FM:** KGNZ, 88.1 MHz; KACU, 89.7; KAGT, 90.5; KAQD, 91.3; KULL, 92.5; KHYS, 100.7; KEAN, 105.1; KKHR, 106.3; KEYJ, 107.9. **TV:** KRBC-Ch. 9; KXVA-Ch. 15; KTAB-Ch. 32.
Alamo—Radio-FM: KJAV, 104.9 MHz.
Alamo Heights—Radio-AM: KDRY, 1100 kHz.
Albany—Newspaper: Albany News.
Aledo—Newspaper: The Community News.
Alice—Newspaper: Alice Echo-News-Journal (D). **Radio-AM:** KOPY, 1070 kHz. **Radio-FM:** KOPY, 92.1 MHz; KNDA, 102.9.
Allen—Newspaper: The Allen American (S). **Radio-FM:** KESN, 103.3 MHz.
Alpine—Newspaper: Alpine Avalanche. **Radio-AM:** KVLF, 1240 kHz. **Radio-FM:** KALP, 92.7 MHz.
Alvarado—Newspapers: Alvarado Post; Alvarado Star.
Alvin—Newspaper: Alvin Sun. **Radio-AM:** KTEK, 1110 kHz. **Radio-FM:** KACC, 89.7 MHz. **TV:** KFTH-Ch. 67.
Alvord—Newspaper: Alvord Gazette.
Amarillo—Newspapers: Globe-News (D). **Radio-AM:** KGNC, 710 kHz; KIXZ, 940; KTNZ, 1010; KZIP, 1310; KDJW, 1360; KPUR, 1440. **Radio-FM:** KJRT, 88.3 MHz; KXLV, 89.1; KACV, 89.9; KAVW, 90.7; KXRI, 91.9; KQIZ, 93.1; KMXJ, 94.1; KMML, 96.9; KGNC, 97.9; KPRF, 98.7; KBZD, 99.7; KXGL, 100.9; KATP, 101.9; KRGN, 103.1; KJJP, 105.7. **TV:** KACV-Ch. 2; KAMR-Ch. 4; KVII-Ch. 7; KACV-DT-Ch. 8; KFDA-DT-Ch. 9; KFDA-Ch. 10; KCIT-Ch. 14.
Anahuac—Newspaper: The Progress.
Andrews—Newspaper: Andrews County News (S). **Radio-AM:** KACT, 1360 kHz. **Radio-FM:** KACT, 105.5 MHz.
Angleton—Newspaper: The Bulletin.
Anna—Newspaper: The Anna/Melissa Tribune.
Anson—Newspapers: Western Observer. **Radio-FM:** KTLT, 98.1 MHz.
Aransas Pass—Newspaper: Aransas Pass Progress; The Coastal Bend Herald.
Archer City—Newspaper: Archer County News; The Archer Advocate.
Arlington—Radio-FM: KLTY, 94.9 MHz. **TV:** KPXD-DT-Ch. 42; KPXD-Ch. 68.
Aspermont—Newspaper: Stonewall County Courier.
Athens—Newspaper: Athens Daily Review (D). **Radio-AM:** KLVQ, 1410 kHz.
Atlanta—Newspaper: Atlanta Citizens Journal (S). **Radio-AM:** KPYN, 900 kHz; KALT, 1610. **Radio-FM:** KNRB, 100.1 MHz.
Aubrey—Newspaper: The Town Charter.
Austin—Newspapers: Austin American-Statesman (D); Austin Business Journal; Austin Chronicle; Austin Monthly (M); Daily Texan (D); Lake Travis View; Texas Observer

(BW); Texas Weekly; West Austin News; Westlake Picayune. **Radio-AM:** KLBJ, 590 kHz; KVET, 1300; KFON, 1490. **Radio-FM:** KAZI, 88.7 MHz; KMFA, 89.5; KUT, 90.5; KVRX, 91.7; KLBJ, 93.7; KKMJ, 95.5; KVET, 98.1; KASE, 100.7; KPEZ, 102.3. **TV:** KTBC-Ch. 7; KLRU-Ch. 18; KLRU-DT-Ch. 22; KVUE-Ch. 24; KXAN-Ch. 36; KEYE-Ch. 42; KEYE-DT-Ch. 43; KNVA-Ch. 54.
Azle—Newspaper: Azle News. **Radio-FM:** KTCY,101.7 MHz.

Baird—Newspapers: Baird Banner; Callahan Co. Star. **Radio-FM:** KORQ, 95.1 MHz.
Balch Springs—Radio-AM: KSKY, 660 kHz.
Ballinger—Newspaper: Ballinger Ledger. **Radio-AM:** KRUN, 1400 kHz. **Radio-FM:** KKCN, 103.1 MHz.
Bandera—Newspapers: The Bandera Bulletin. **Radio-FM:** KEEP, 103.1 MHz.
Bartlett —Newspaper: Tribune-Progress.
Bastrop—Newspaper: Bastrop Advertiser (S) **Radio-FM:** KHIB, 88.5 MHz; KGSR, 107.1.
Bay City—Newspaper: The Bay City Tribune (S). **Radio-FM:** KXGJ, 101.7 MHz; KMKS, 102.5.
Baytown—Newspaper: Baytown Sun (D). **Radio-AM:** KWWJ, 1360 kHz. **TV:** KAZH-Ch. 57.
Beaumont—Newspaper: Beaumont Enterprise (D). **Radio-AM:** KLVI, 560 kHz; KZZB, 990; KRCM, 1380; KIKR, 1450. **Radio-FM:** KTXB, 89.7 MHz; KVLU, 91.3; KQXY, 94.1; KYKR, 95.1; KIOL, 97.5; KTCX, 102.5; KQQK, 107.9. **TV:** KFDM-Ch. 6; KBMT-Ch. 12; KFDM-DT-Ch. 21; KITU-Ch. 34.
Beeville—Newspaper: Beeville Bee-Picayune (S). **Radio-AM:** KIBL, 1490 kHz. **Radio-FM:** KVFM, 91.3 MHz; KTKO, 105.7; KRXB, 107.1.
Bellaire—Radio-AM: KILE, 1560 kHz.
Bells—Radio - FM: KMKT, 93.1 MHz.
Bellville—Newspaper: Bellville Times. **Radio-FM:** KNUZ, 1090 kHz.
Belton—Newspaper: The Belton Journal. **Radio-AM:** KTON, 940 kHz. **Radio-FM:** KOOC, 106.3 MHz. **TV:** KNCT-Ch. 46.
Benbrook—Newspaper: Benbrook Star. **Radio-FM:** KDXX, 107.1 MHz.
Big Lake—Newspaper: Big Lake Wildcat. **Radio-FM:** KPDB, 98.3 MHz; KWTR, 104.1
Big Sandy—Newspaper: Big Sandy-Hawkins Journal. **Radio-FM:** KTAA, 90.7 MHz.
Big Spring—Newspaper: Big Spring Herald (D). **Radio-AM:** KBYG, 1400; KBST, 1490. **Radio-FM:** KBCX, 91.5 MHz; KBTS, 94.3 MHz; KBST, 95.7. **TV:** KWAB-Ch. 4.
Bishop—Newspaper: Kingsville Record and Bishop News. **Radio-FM:** KFLZ, 106.9 MHz.
Blanco—Newspaper: Blanco County News.
Bloomington—Radio-FM: KLUB, 106.9 MHz.
Blossom—Newspaper: Blossom Times.
Boerne—Newspapers: Boerne Star & Hill Country Recorder (S). **Radio-AM:** KBRN, 1500 kHz.

Bogata—Newspaper: Bogata News.
Bonham—Newspaper: Bonham Journal. **Radio-AM:** KFYN, 1420 kHz. **Radio-FM:** KFYZ, 98.3 MHz.
Booker—Newspaper: Booker News.
Borger—Newspaper: Borger News-Herald (D). **Radio-AM:** KQTY, 1490 kHz. **Radio-FM:** KASV, 88.7 MHz; KAXH, 91.5; KQFX, 104.3; KQTY, 106.7.
Bowie—Newspaper: Bowie News (S). **Radio-AM:** KNTX, 1410 kHz.
Brackettville—Newspaper: The Brackett News.
Brady—Newspaper: Brady Standard-Herald (S). **Radio-AM:** KNEL, 1490 kHz. **Radio-FM:** KNEL, 95.3 MHz.
Breckenridge—Newspaper: Breckenridge American (S). **Radio-AM:** KROO, 1430 kHz. **Radio-FM:** KLXK, 93.5 MHz.
Bremond—Newspaper: Bremond Press.
Brenham—Newspaper: Brenham Banner-Press (D). **Radio-AM:** KWHI, 1280 kHz. **Radio-FM:** KULF, 94.1 MHz; KTTX, 106.1.
Bridgeport—Newspaper: Bridgeport Index. **Radio-FM:** KBOC, 98.3 MHz.
Brookshire—Newspaper: The Times Tribune. **Radio-AM:** KCHN, 1050 kHz.
Brownfield—Newspaper: Brownfield News (S). **Radio-AM:** KKUB, 1300 kHz. **Radio-FM:** KPBB, 88.5 MHz; KLZK, 104.3.
Brownsboro—Newspaper: Brownsboro and Chandler Statesman.
Brownsville—Newspaper: The Brownsville Herald (D). **Radio-AM:** KYNS, 1700 kHz. **Radio-FM:** KBNR, 88.3 MHz; KKPS, 99.5; KTEX, 100.3. **TV:** KVEO-Ch. 23.
Brownwood—Newspaper: Brownwood Bulletin (D). **Radio-AM:** KXYL, 1240 kHz; KBWD, 1380. **Radio-FM:** KPBE, 89.3 MHz; KBUB, 90.3; KHPU, 91.7; KXYL, 96.9; KPSM, 99.3; KOXE, 101.3.
Bryan—Newspaper: Bryan-College Station Eagle (D). **Radio-AM:** KTAM, 1240 kHz; KAGC, 1510. **Radio-FM:** KORA, 98.3 MHz; KNFX, 99.5; KKYS, 104.7. **TV:** KBTX-Ch. 3; KYLE-Ch. 28.
Buda—Newspaper: The Free Press. **Radio-FM:** KROX, 101.5 MHz.
Buffalo—Newspapers: Buffalo Express; Buffalo Press.
Bullard—Newspaper: Bullard Weekly News; The Banner.
Buna—Newspaper: The Buna Beacon.
Burkburnett—Newspaper: Burkburnett Informer Star. **Radio-FM:** KYYI, 104.7 MHz.
Burleson—Newspaper: Burleson Star (S). **Radio-AM:** KTFW, 1460 kHz.
Burnet—Newspapers: Burnet Bulletin; Citizens Gazette. **Radio-AM:** KRHC, 1340 kHz. **Radio-FM:** KBEY, 92.5 MHz; KHLB, 106.9.
Bushland—Radio-FM: KTXP, 91.5 MHz.

Caldwell—Newspaper: Burleson County Tribune. **Radio-FM:** KLTR, 107.3 MHz.
Callisburg—Radio-FM: KPFC, 91.9 MHz.
Calvert—Newspaper: Calvert Tribune.
Cameron—Newspaper: The Cameron Herald. **Radio-AM:** KMIL, 1330 kHz. **Radio-FM:** KNVR, 94.3 MHz; KXCS, 103.9 MHz.
Campbell—Radio-FM: KRVA, 107.1 MHz.
Camp Wood—Radio-FM: KAYG, 99.1 MHz.
Canadian—Newspaper: Canadian Record.
Canton—Newspapers: Canton Herald; Van Zandt News. **Radio-AM:** KVCI, 1510 kHz.
Canyon—Newspaper: The Canyon News (S). **Radio-AM:** KZRK, 1550 kHz. **Radio-FM:** KWTS, 91.1 MHz; KPUR, 107.1; KZRK, 107.9.
Canyon Lake—Newspaper: Times Guardian.
Carrizo Springs—Newspaper: Carrizo Springs Javelin. **Radio-AM:** KBEN, 1450 kHz. **Radio-FM:** KCZO, 92.1 MHz.
Carrollton—Radio AM: KJON, 850 kHz.
Carthage—Newspaper: Panola Watchman (S). **Radio-AM:** KGAS, 1590 kHz. **Radio-FM:** KTUX, 98.9 MHz; KGAS, 104.3.
Castroville—Newspaper: Castroville News Bulletin.
Cedar Hill—Newspapers: Cedar Hill Today.
Cedar Park—Newspapers: Hill Country News Weekender. **Radio-FM:** KDHT, 93.3 MHz.
Celina—Newspaper: Celina Record.
Center—Newspaper: The Light & Champion (S). **Radio-AM:** KDET, 930 kHz. **Radio-FM:** KQBB, 100.5 MHz.
Centerville—Newspaper: Centerville News. **Radio-FM:** KTCJ, 105.9 MHz.

Chico—Newspaper: Chico Texan.
Childress—Newspaper: The Childress Index (TW). **Radio-AM:** KCTX, 1510 kHz. **Radio-FM:** KCTX, 96.1 MHz.
Cisco—Newspaper: Cisco Press (S).
Clarendon—Newspaper: Clarendon Enterprise. **Radio-FM:** KEFH, 99.3 MHz.
Clarksville—Newspaper: Clarksville Times. **Radio-AM:** KCAR, 1350 kHz. **Radio-FM:** KGAP, 98.5 MHz.
Claude—Newspaper: The Claude News. **Radio-FM:** KARX, 95.7 MHz.
Clear Lake—Newspaper: The Citizen.
Cleburne—Newspaper: Cleburne Times-Review (D). **Radio-AM:** KCLE, 1140 kHz.
Cleveland—Newspaper: Cleveland Advocate. **Radio-FM:** KTHT, 97.1 MHz.
Clifton—Newspaper: Clifton Record. **Radio-FM:** KWOW, 104.1 MHz.
Clute—Newspaper: The Facts (D).
Clyde—Newspaper: Clyde Journal.
Cockrell Hill—Radio-AM: KRVA, 1600 kHz.
Coleman—Newspaper: Chronicle & Democrat-Voice (S). **Radio-AM:** KSTA, 1000 kHz. **Radio-FM:** KXCT, 102.3 MHz.
College Station—Newspaper: The Battalion (D). **Radio-AM:** KZNE, 1150 kHz, WTAW, 1620. **Radio-FM:** KEOS, 89.1 MHz; KAMU, 90.9; KNDE, 95.1. **TV:** KAMU-DT-Ch. 12; KAMU-Ch. 15.
Colorado City—Newspaper: Colorado City Record. **Radio-AM:** KVMC, 1320 kHz. **Radio-FM:** KAUM, 107.1 MHz.
Columbus—Newspapers: The Banner Press Newspaper; Colorado County Citizen. **Radio-FM:** KULM, 98.3 MHz.
Comanche—Newspaper: Comanche Chief. **Radio-AM:** KCOM, 1550 kHz. **Radio-FM:** KYOX, 94.3 MHz.
Comfort—Newspaper: The Comfort News. **Radio-FM:** KCOR, 95.1 MHz.
Commerce—Newspaper: Commerce Journal. **Radio-FM:** KETR, 88.9 MHz.
Conroe—Newspaper: The Courier (D). **Radio-AM:** KJOJ, 880 kHz; KYOK, 1140. **Radio-FM:** KAFR, 88.3 MHz; KHPT, 106.9. **TV:** KPXB-DT-Ch. 5; KTBU-DT-Ch. 42; KPXB-Ch. 49; KTBU-CH. 55.
Cooper—Newspaper: Cooper Review.
Coppell—Newspaper: Citizens' Advocate.
Copperas Cove—Newspaper: Copperas Cove Leader-Press (S). **Radio-FM:** KSSM, 103.1 MHz.
Corpus Christi—Newspapers: Caller-Times (D); Coastal Bend Legal & Business News (D); South Texas Catholic (BW). **Radio-AM:** KCTA, 1030 kHz; KCCT, 1150; KSIX, 1230; KKTX, 1360; KUNO, 1400; KEYS, 1440. **Radio-FM:** KKLM, 88.7 MHz; KEDT, 90.3; KBNJ, 91.7; KMXR, 93.9; KBSO, 94.7; KZFM, 95.5; KLTG, 96.5; KRYS, 99.1. **TV:** KIII-Ch. 3; KRIS-Ch. 6; KZTV-Ch. 10; KEDT-Ch. 16; KORO-Ch. 28.
Corrigan—Newspaper: Corrigan Times.
Corsicana—Newspaper: Corsicana Daily Sun (D). **Radio-AM:** KAND, 1340 kHz.
Crane—Newspaper: Crane News. **Radio-AM:** KXOI, 810 kHz. **Radio FM:** KMML, 101.3 MHz.
Creedmoor—Radio AM: KZNX, 1530 kHz.
Crockett—Newspaper: Houston Co. Courier (S). **Radio-AM:** KIVY, 1290 kHz. **Radio-FM:** KCKT, 88.5 MHz; KIVY, 92.7; KBHT, 93.5.
Crosbyton—Newspaper: Crosby Co. Reporter-Examiner; Crosbyton Review.
Cross Plains—Newspaper: Cross Plains Review.
Crowell—Newspaper: Foard Co. News.
Crowley—Newspaper: Crowley Star.
Crystal Beach—Radio FM: KSTB, 101.5 MHz; KPTI, 105.3.
Crystal City—Newspaper: Zavala County Sentinel. **Radio-FM:** KHER, 94.3 MHz.
Cuero—Newspaper: Cuero Record. **Radio-FM:** KNGT, 97.7 MHz.
Cypress—Radio-AM: KYND, 1520 kHz.

Daingerfield—Newspaper: The Bee. **Radio-AM:** KNGR, 1560 kHz.
Dalhart—Newspaper: Dalhart Daily Texan (D). **Radio-AM:** KXIT, 1240 kHz. **Radio-FM:** KXIT, 96.3 MHz.
Dallas—Newspapers: The Dallas Morning News (D); Al Día; Dallas Business Journal; Daily Campus; Daily Com-

mercial Record (D); Dallas Examiner; Oak Cliff Tribune; Park Cities News; Park Cities People; Texas Jewish Post; Texas Lawyer; The White Rocker. **Radio-AM:** KLIF, 570 kHz; KGGR, 1040; KRLD, 1080; KFXR, 1190; KTCK, 1310; KHCK, 1480. **Radio-FM:** KNON, 89.3 HMz; KERA, 90.1; KCBI, 90.9; KVTT, 91.7; KZPS, 92.5; KBFB, 97.9; KLUV, 98.7; KJKK, 100.3; WRR, 101.1; KDMX, 102.9; KKDA, 104.5; KLLI, 105.3. **TV:** KDFW-Ch. 4; WFAA-Ch. 8; WFAA-DT-Ch. 9; KERA-Ch. 13; KERA-DT-Ch. 14; KDFI-Ch. 27; KDAF-Ch. 33; KDFW-DT-Ch. 35; KXTX-Ch. 39; KXTX-DT-Ch. 40; KDTX-Ch. 58.
Decatur—Newspaper: Wise County Messenger (S). **Radio-FM:** KDKR, 91.3 MHz; KRNB, 105.7. **TV:** KMPX-Ch. 29.
Deer Park—Newspaper: Deer Park Progress.
De Kalb—Newspaper: De Kalb News (S).
De Leon—Newspapers: De Leon Free Press.
Dell City—Newspaper: Hudspeth County Herald.
Del Mar Hills—Radio-AM: KVOZ, 890 kHz.
Del Rio—Newspaper: Del Rio News-Herald (D). **Radio-AM:** KTJK, 1230 kHz; KWMC, 1490. **Radio-FM:** KDLK, 94.1 MHz; KTDR, 96.3. **TV:** KTRG-Ch. 10.
Del Valle—Radio-AM: KIXL, 970 kHz.
Denison—Newspapers: Herald Democrat (D). **Radio-AM:** KYNG, 950 kHz.
Denton—Newspaper: Denton Record-Chronicle (D). **Radio-FM:** KNTU, 88.1 MHz; KFZO, 99.1; KHKS, 106.1. **TV:** KDTN-Ch. 2; KDTN-DT-Ch. 43.
Denver City—Newspaper: Denver City Press.
Deport—Newspaper: Deport Times.
DeSoto—Newspapers: Focus Daily News (D); DeSoto Today.
Detroit—Newspaper: Detroit Weekly.
Devine—Newspaper: Devine News. **Radio-FM:** KHTY, 92.5 MHz.
Diboll—Newspaper: The Free Press. **Radio-AM:** KSML, 1260 kHz. **Radio-FM:** KAFX, 95.5 MHz.
Dilley—Radio-FM: KLMO, 98.9 MHz.
Dimmitt—Newspaper: Castro County News. **Radio-AM:** KDHN, 1470 kHz. **Radio-FM:** KNNK, 100.5 MHz.
Doss—Radio FM: KGLF, 88.1 MHz.
Dripping Springs—Newspapers: Dripping Springs Century News; The News-Dispatch.
Dublin—Newspaper: Dublin Citizen.
Dumas—Newspapers: Moore County News-Press (S). **Radio-AM:** KDDD, 800 kHz. **Radio-FM:** KDDD, 95.3 MHz.
Duncanville—Newspaper: Duncanville Today.

Eagle Lake—Newspaper: Eagle Lake Headlight.
Eagle Pass—Newspapers: The News Gram; Eagle Pass News-Guide. **Radio-AM:** KEPS, 1270 kHz. **Radio-FM:** KEPI, 88.7 MHz; KEPX, 89.5; KINL, 92.7. **TV:** KVAW-Ch. 16.
East Bernard—Newspaper: East Bernard Express (S).
Eastland—Newspaper: Eastland Telegram (S). **Radio-AM:** KEAS, 1590 kHz. **Radio-FM:** KATX, 97.7 MHz.
Eden—Newspaper: The Eden Echo.
Edgewood—Newspaper: Edgewood Enterprise.
Edinburg—Newspaper: Edinburg Daily Review (D). **Radio-AM:** KSAH, 720 kHz. **Radio-FM:** KOIR, 88.5 MHz; KBFM, 104.1; KVLY, 107.9.
Edna—Newspaper: Jackson Co. Herald-Tribune. **Radio-AM:** KTMR, 1130 kHz. **Radio-FM:** KGUL, 96.1 MHz.
El Campo—Newspaper: El Campo Leader-News (S). **Radio-AM:** KULP, 1390 kHz. **Radio-FM:** KIOX, 96.9 MHz.
Eldorado—Newspaper: Eldorado Success.
Electra—Newspaper: Electra Star-News. **Radio-FM:** KOLI, 94.9 MHz.
Elgin—Newspaper: Elgin Courier. **Radio-FM:** KKLB, 92.5 MHz.
El Paso—Newspapers: El Paso Times (D). **Radio-AM:** KROD, 600 kHz; KTSM, 690; KAMA, 750; KBNA, 920; KXPL, 1060; KSVE, 1150; KVIV, 1340; KHEY, 1380; KELP, 1590; KHRO, 1650. **Radio-FM:** KTEP, 88.5 MHz; KXCR; 89.5; KVER, 91.1; KOFX, 92.3; KSII, 93.1; KINT, 93.9; KYSE, 94.7; KLAQ, 95.5; KHEY, 96.3; KBNA, 97.5; KTSM, 99.9; KPRR, 102.1. **TV:** KDBC-Ch. 4; KVIA-Ch. 7; KTSM-Ch. 9; KCOS-Ch. 13; KFOX-Ch. 14; KINT-Ch. 26; KSCE-Ch. 38; KTFN-Ch. 65.
Emory—Newspaper: Rains Co. Leader.
Ennis—Newspaper: Ennis Daily News (D).
Everman—Newspaper: South Tarrant Star.

Fabens—Radio-FM: KPAS, 103.1 MHz.
Fairfield—Newspapers: Freestone County Times; The

Fairfield Recorder. Radio-FM: KNES, 99.1 MHz.
Falfurrias—Newspaper: Falfurrias Facts. **Radio-AM:** KLDS, 1260 kHz. **Radio-FM:** KDFM, 103.3 MHz; KPSO, 106.3.
Fannett—Radio FM: KZFT, 90.5 MHz.
Farmersville—Newspaper: Farmersville Times. **Radio-FM:** KXEZ, 92.1 MHz.
Farwell—Newspaper: State Line Tribune. **Radio-AM:** KIJN, 1060 kHz. **Radio-FM:** KIJN, 92.3 MHz; KICA, 98.3. **TV:** KPTF-Ch. 18.
Ferris—Newspaper: Ellis County Press. **Radio-AM:** KDFT, 540 kHz.
Flatonia—Newspaper: The Flatonia Argus.
Floresville—Newspapers: Floresville Chronicle-Journal; Wilson County News. **Radio-FM:** KWCB, 89.7 MHz; KTFM, 94.1.
Flower Mound—Radio-FM: KTYS, 96.7 MHz.
Floydada—Newspaper: Floyd Co. Hesperian-Beacon. **Radio-AM:** KFLP, 900 kHz. **Radio-FM:** KFLP, 106.1 MHz.
Follett—Newspaper: The Golden Spread.
Forney—Newspaper: Forney Messenger.
Fort Davis—Newspaper: Jeff Davis Co. Mt. Dispatch.
Fort Stockton—Newspaper: Fort Stockton Pioneer. **Radio-AM:** KFST, 860 kHz. **Radio-FM:** KFST, 94.3 MHz.
Fort Worth - Newspapers: Fort Worth Business Press; Commercial Recorder (D); Fort Worth Star-Telegram (D); Fort Worth Weekley; NW Tarrant Co. Times-Record; Weekly Livestock Reporter. **Radio-AM:** WBAP, 820 kHz; KFJZ, 870; KHVN, 970; KFLC, 1270; KKGM, 1630. **Radio-FM:** KTCU, 88.7 MHz; KLNO, 94.1; KSCS, 96.3; KEGL, 97.1; KPLX, 99.5; KDGE, 102.1; KOAI, 107.5. **TV:** KXAS-Ch. 5; KTVT-Ch. 11; KTXA-DT-Ch. 18; KTVT-DT-Ch. 19; KTXA-Ch. 21; KXAS-DT-Ch. 41; KFWD-DT-Ch. 51; KFWD-Ch. 52.
Franklin—Newspapers: Franklin Advocate; Franklin News Weekly. **Radio FM:** KZTR, 101.9 MHz.
Frankston—Newspaper: The Frankston Citizen. **Radio-AM:** KTXV, 890 kHz. **Radio-FM:** KOYE, 96.7 MHz.
Fredericksburg—Newspaper: Standard/Radio Post. **Radio-AM:** KNAF, 910 kHz. **Radio-FM:** KNAF, 105.7 MHz. **TV:** KBEJ-Ch. 2.
Freeport—Radio-AM: KBRZ, 1460 kHz. **Radio-FM:** KJOJ, 103.3 MHz.
Freer—Newspaper: Freer Press. **Radio-FM:** KBRA, 95.9 MHz.
Friendswood—Newspapers: Friendswood Journal; Friendswood Reporter News.
Friona—Newspaper: Friona Star. **Radio FM:** KGRW, 94.7 MHz.
Frisco—Newspaper: Frisco Enterprise. **Radio-AM:** KXEB, 910 kHz.
Fritch—Newspaper: The Eagle Press.

Gail—Newspaper: Borden Star.
Gainesville—Newspaper: Gainesville Daily Register (D). **Radio-AM:** KGAF, 1580 kHz. **Radio-FM:** KSOC, 94.5 MHz.
Galveston—Newspaper: Galveston Co. Daily News (D). **Radio-AM:** KHCB, 1400 kHz; KGBC, 1540. **Radio-FM:** KOVE, 105.5 MHz. **TV:** KLTJ-Ch. 22; KTMD-Ch. 47; KTMD-DT-Ch. 48.
Ganado—Radio-FM: KZAM, 104.7 MHz.
Gardendale—Radio-FM: KFZX, 102.1 MHz.
Garland—Radio-AM: KAAM, 770 kHz. **TV:** KUVN-Ch. 23; KUVN-DT-Ch. 24.
Garrison—Newspaper: Garrison In The News.
Gatesville—Newspaper: Gatesville Messenger and Star Forum (S). **Radio-FM:** KVLZ, 98.3 MHz.
Georgetown—Newspapers: Sunday Sun; Williamson Co. Sun. **Radio-FM:** KHFI, 96.7 MHz; KINV, 107.7.
Giddings—Newspapers: Giddings Times & News. **Radio-FM:** KANJ, 91.5 MHz.
Gilmer—Newspaper: Gilmer Mirror (S). **Radio-AM:** KOFY, 1060 kHz. **Radio-FM:** KFRO, 95.3 MHz.
Gladewater—Newspaper: Gladewater Mirror. **Radio-AM:** KEES, 1430 kHz.
Glen Rose—Newspaper: Glen Rose Reporter. **Radio-FM:** KTFW, 92.1 MHz.
Goldthwaite—Newspaper: Goldthwaite Eagle.
Goliad—Newspaper: The Texan Express. **Radio FM:** KHMC, 95.9 MHz.
Gonzales—Newspaper: Gonzales Inquirer (S). **Radio-AM:** KCTI, 1450 kHz. **Radio-FM:** KQQT, 106.3 MHz.
Gorman—Newspaper: Gorman Progress.
Graford—Newspaper: Lake Country Sun.

Graham—Newspaper: The Graham Leader (S). **Radio-AM:** KSWA, 1330 kHz. **Radio-FM:** KWKQ, 94.7 MHz.
Granbury—Newspaper: Hood Co. News (TW). **Radio-AM:** KPIR, 1420 kHz. **Radio-FM:** KDXT, 106.7 MHz.
Grand Prairie—Radio-AM: KKDA, 730 kHz.
Grand Saline—Newspaper: Grand Saline Sun.
Grandview—Newspaper: Grandview Tribune.
Grapeland—Newspaper: Grapeland Messenger.
Greenville—Newspaper: Herald-Banner (D). **Radio-AM:** KGVL,1400 kHz. **Radio-FM:** KIKT, 93.5 MHz. **TV:** KTAQ-DT-Ch. 46; KTAQ-Ch. 47.
Greenwood—Newspaper: Greenwood Ranger.
Gregory—Radio-FM: KPUS, 104.5 MHz.
Groesbeck—Newspaper: Groesbeck Journal.
Groom—Newspaper: Groom/McLean News.
Groves—Radio-FM: KCOL, 92.5 MHz.
Groveton—Newspaper: Groveton News.
Gun Barrel City—Newspaper: Cedar Creek Pilot.

Hale Center—Newspaper: Hale Center American.
Hallettsville—Newspaper: Hallettsville Tribune-Herald. **Radio-AM:** KHLT, 1520 kHz. **Radio-FM:** KTXM, 99.9 MHz.
Haltom City—Radio FM: KDBN, 93.3 MHz.
Hamilton—Newspaper: Hamilton Herald-News. **Radio-AM:** KCLW, 900 kHz.
Hamlin—Newspaper: Hamlin Herald. **Radio-FM:** KCDD, 103.7 MHz.
Harker Heights—Radio-FM: KUSJ, 105.5 MHz.
Harlingen—Newspaper: Valley Morning Star (D). **Radio-AM:** KGBT, 1530 kHz. **Radio-FM:** KMBH, 88.9 MHz; KFRQ, 94.5; KBTQ, 96.1. **TV:** KGBT-Ch. 4; KGBT-DT-Ch. 31; KMBH-DT-Ch. 38; KLUJ-Ch. 44; KMBH-Ch. 60.
Hart—Newspaper: Hart Beat.
Haskell—Newspaper: Haskell Free Press. **Radio-FM:** KVRP, 97.1 MHz.
Hawkins—Newspaper: Big Sandy-Hawkins Journal.
Hearne—Newspaper: Hearne Democrat. Radio-FM: KVJM, 103.1 MHz.
Hebbronville—Newspapers: Hebbronville View; Jim Hogg Co. Enterprise. **Radio-FM:** KAZF, 91.9 MHz; KEKO, 101.7.
Helotes—Radio-FM: KONO, 101.1 MHz.
Hemphill—Newspaper: The Sabine Co. Reporter. **Radio-AM:** KPBL, 1240 kHz. **Radio-FM:** KTHP, 103.9 Mhz.
Hempstead—Newspaper: Waller County News-Citizen. **Radio-FM:** KEZB, 105.3 MHz.
Henderson—Newspaper: Henderson Daily News (D). **Radio-AM:** KWRD, 1470 kHz.
Henrietta—Newspaper: Clay County Leader.
Hereford—Newspaper: Hereford Brand (D). **Radio-AM:** KPAN, 860 kHz. **Radio-FM:** KJNZ, 103.5 MHz; KPAN, 106.3.
Hewitt—Newspaper: Hometown News.
Hico—Newspaper: Hico News Review.
Highland Park—Radio-AM: KBIS, 1150 kHz. **Radio-FM:** KVIL, 103.7 MHz.
Highlands—Newspaper: Highlands Star/Crosby Courier.
Highland Village—Radio-FM: KWRD, 100.7 Mhz.
Hillsboro—Newspaper: Hillsboro Reporter (S). **Radio-AM:** KHBR, 1560 kHz. **Radio-FM:** KBRQ, 102.5 MHz.
Hondo—Newspaper: Hondo Anvil Herald. **Radio-AM:** KCWM, 1460 kHz. **Radio-FM:** Kmfr, 105.9 MHz.
Honey Grove - Newspaper: Weekly Gazette.
Hooks —Radio-FM: KPWW, 95.9 MHz.
Hornsby—Radio FM: KOOP, 91.7 MHz.
Houston—Newspapers: Houston Business Journal; Houston Chronicle (D); Daily Court Review (D); Houston Forward Times; Houston Informer & Texas Freeman; Jewish Herald-Voice; Texas Catholic Herald (SM). **Radio-AM:** KILT, 610 kHz; KTRH, 740; KBME, 790; KEYH, 850; KPRC, 950; KLAT, 1010; KNTH, 1070; KQUE, 1230; KXYZ, 1320; KCOH, 1430; KMIC, 1590. **Radio-FM:** KUHF, 88.7 MHz; KPFT, 90.1; KTSU, 90.9; KTRU, 91.7; KKRW, 93.7; KTBZ, 94.5; KHJZ, 95.7; KHMX, 96.5; KBXX, 97.9; KODA, 99.1; KILT, 100.3; KLOL, 101.1; KMJQ, 102.1; KLTN, 102.9; KRBE, 104.1; KHCB, 105.7. **TV:** KPRC-Ch. 2; KUHT-Ch. 8; KUHT-DT-Ch. 9; KHOU-Ch. 11; KTRK-Ch. 13; KETH-CH. 14; KTXH-DT-Ch. 19; KTXH-Ch. 20; KRIV-Ch. 26; KRIV-DT-Ch. 27; KHOU-DT-Ch 31; KTRK-DT-Ch. 32; KPRC-DT-Ch. 35; KPRC-DT-Ch. 35; KHWB-DT-Ch. 38; KHWB-Ch. 39; KZJL-Ch. 61.
Howe—Newspaper: Texoma Enterprise. **Radio-FM:** KHYI, 95.3 MHz.
Hubbard—Newspaper: Hubbard City News.

Hudson—Radio-FM: KLSN, 96.3 MHz.
Humble—Radio-AM: KGOL, 1180 kHz. **Radio-FM:** KSBJ, 89.3 MHz.
Huntington—Radio-FM: KSML, 101.9 MHz.
Huntsville—Newspaper: Huntsville Item (D).**Radio-AM:** KHCH, 1400 kHz; KHVL, 1490. **Radio-FM:** KSHU, 90.5 MHz; KUST, 99.7; KSAM, 101.7.
Hurst—Radio-AM: KMNY, 1360 kHz.
Hutto—Radio-FM: KQJZ, 92.1 MHz.

Idalou—Newspaper: Idalou Beacon. **Radio-FM:** KRBL, 105.7 MHz.
Ingleside—Newspaper: Ingleside Index. **Radio FM:** KRPX, 107.3 MHz.
Ingram—Radio-FM: KTXI, 90.1 MHz.
Iowa Park—Newspaper: Iowa Park Leader.
Iraan—Newspaper: Iraan News.
Irving—TV: KSTR-DT-Ch. 48; KSTR-Ch. 49.
Italy—Newspaper: Italy News-Herald.

Jacksboro—Newspapers: Jacksboro Gazette-News; Jack County Herald.
Jacksonville—Newspaper: Jacksonville Daily Progress (D). **Radio-AM:** KEBE, 1400 kHz. **Radio-FM:** KBJS, 90.3 MHz; KLJT, 102.3; KOOI, 106.5. **TV:** KETK-Ch. 56.
Jasper—Newspaper: The Jasper Newsboy. **Radio-AM:** KCOX, 1350 kHz. **Radio-FM:** KTXJ, 102.7 MHz; KJAS, 107.3.
Jefferson—Newspaper: Jefferson Jimplecute. **Radio-FM:** KJTX, 104.5 MHz.
Jewett—Newspaper: Jewett Messenger.
Johnson City—Newspaper: Johnson City Record-Courier. **Radio-FM:** KFAN, 107.9 MHz.
Joshua—Newspaper: Joshua Star.
Jourdanton—Radio-FM: KLEY, 95.7 Mhz.
Junction—Newspaper: Junction Eagle. **Radio-AM:** KMBL, 1450 kHz. **Radio-FM:** KOOK, 93.5 MHz.

Karnes City—Newspaper: The Countywide. **Radio-AM:** KAML, 990 kHz.
Katy—Newspaper: Katy Times (S). **TV:** KNWS-Ch. 51.
Kaufman—Newspaper: Kaufman Herald.
Keene—Newspaper: Keene Star. **Radio-FM:** KJCR; 88.3 MHz.
Kenedy—Radio-AM: KAML, 990 kHz. **Radio-FM:** KTNR, 92.1 MHz.
Kerens—Newspaper: Kerens Tribune. **Radio-FM:** KRVF, 106.9 MHz.
Kermit—Newspaper: Winkler Co. News. **Radio-AM:** KERB, 600 kHz. **Radio-FM:** KERB, 106.3 MHz.
Kerrville—Newspapers: Kerrville Daily Times (D); The Mountain Sun. **Radio-AM:** KERV, 1230 kHz. **Radio-FM:** KKER, 88.7 MHz; KHKV, 91.1; KRNH, 92.3; KRVL, 94.3. **TV:** KRRT-Ch. 35.
Kilgore—Newspaper: Kilgore News Herald (D). **Radio-AM:** KBGE, 1240 kHz. **Radio-FM:** KTPB, 88.7 Mhz; KKTX, 96.1.
Killeen—Newspaper: Killeen Daily Herald (D). **Radio-AM:** KRMY, 1050 kHz. **Radio-FM:** KNCT, 91.3 MHz; KIIZ, 92.3. **TV:** KAKW-Ch. 62.
Kingsville—Newspaper: Kingsville Record and Bishop News (S). **Radio-AM:** KINE, 1330 kHz. **Radio-FM:** KTAI, 91.1 MHz; KKBA, 92.7; KFTX, 97.5.
Kirbyville—Newspaper: Kirbyville Banner.
Knox City—Newspaper: Knox Co. News.
Kress—Newspaper: Kress Chronicle.
Krum—Radio-FM: KNOR, 93.7 MHz.

La Feria—Newspapers: La Feria News.
La Grange—Newspaper: Fayette County Record (S). **Radio-AM:** KVLG, 1570 kHz. **Radio-FM:** KBUK, 104.9 MHz.
Lake Dallas—Newspaper: The Lake Cities Sun. **TV:** KLDT-Ch. 55.
Lake Jackson—Radio-FM: KYBJ, 91.1 MHz; KLDE, 107.5.
Lamesa—Newspaper: Lamesa Press Reporter (S). **Radio-AM:** KPET, 690 kHz. **Radio-FM:** KBKN, 91.3 MHz; KTXC, 104.7.
Lampasas—Newspaper: Lampasas Dispatch Record (S). **Radio-AM:** KCYL, 1450 kHz.
Lancaster—Newspaper: Lancaster Today.
La Porte—Newspaper: Bayshore Sun (S).
Laredo—Newspaper: Laredo Morning Times (D). **Radio-AM:** KLAR, 1300 kHz; KLNT, 1490. **Radio-FM:** KHOY,

88.1 MHz; KBNL, 89.9; KJBZ, 92.7; KQUR, 94.9; KRRG, 98.1; KNEX, 106.1. **TV:** KGNS-Ch. 8; KVTV-Ch. 13; KLDO-Ch. 27.
La Vernia—Newspaper: La Vernia News.
Leakey—Newspaper: Real American Newspaper. **Radio-FM:** KBLT, 104.3 MHz.
Leander—Radio-FM: KHHL, 98.9 MHz.
Leonard—Newspaper: Leonard Graphic.
Levelland—Newspaper: Levelland and Hockley Co. News-Press (S). **Radio-AM:** KLVT, 1230 kHz. **Radio-FM:** KLVT, 105.3 MHz.
Lewisville—Radio-FM: KESS, 107.9 MHz.
Lexington—Newspaper: Lexington Leader.
Liberty—Newspaper: Liberty Vindicator (S). **Radio-FM:** KSHN, 99.9 MHz.
Liberty Hill—Newspaper: The Liberty Hill Independent.
Lindale—Newspapers: Lindale News & Times.
Linden—Newspaper: Cass County Sun.
Little Elm—Newspaper: The Little Elm Journal.
Littlefield—Newspaper: Lamb Co. Leader-News (S). **Radio-AM:** KZZN, 1490 kHz. **Radio-FM:** KAIQ, 95.5 MHz.
Livingston—Newspaper: Polk Co. Enterprise (S). **Radio-AM:** KETX, 1440 kHz. **Radio-FM:** KETX, 92.3 MHz.
Llano—Newspaper: Llano News. **Radio-FM:** KQBT, 96.3 MHz; KITY, 102.9. **TV:** KXAM-Ch. 14.
Lockhart—Newspaper: Lockhart Post-Register. **Radio-AM:** KFIT, 1060 kHz.
Lometa—Radio-FM: KACQ, 101.9 MHz.
Longview—Newspaper: Longview News-Journal (D). **Radio-AM:** KFRO, 1370 kHz. **Radio-FM** KYKX, 105.7 MHz. **TV:** KFXK-Ch. 51; KCEB-Ch. 54.
Lorenzo—Radio-FM: KKCL, 98.1 MHz.
Los Ybañez—Radio-FM: KYMI, 98.5 MHz.
Lubbock—Newspaper: Lubbock Avalanche-Journal (D). **Radio-AM:** KRFE, 580 kHz; KFYO, 790; KJTV, 950; KKAM, 1340; KLFB, 1420; KBZO, 1460; KDAV, 1590. **Radio-FM:** KTXT, 88.1 MHz; KOHM, 89.1; KAMY, 90.1; KKLU, 90.9; KXTQ, 93.7; KFMX, 94.5; KLLL, 96.3; KQBR, 99.5; KONE, 101.1; KZII, 102.5; KEJS, 106.5. **TV:** KTXT-Ch. 5; KCBD-DT-Ch. 9; KCBD-Ch. 11; KLBK-Ch. 13; KPTB-Ch. 16; KAMC-Ch. 28; KJTV- Ch. 34; KTXT-DT-Ch. 39.
Lufkin—Newspaper: Lufkin Daily News (D). **Radio-AM:** KRBA, 1340 kHz. **Radio-FM:** KLDN, 88.9 Mhz; KSWP, 90.9; KAVX, 91.9. KYBI, 100.1; KYKS, 105.1. **TV:** KTRE-Ch. 9.
Luling—Newspaper: Luling Newsboy and Signal. **Radio-FM:** KAMX, 94.7 MHz.
Lytle—Newspapers: Leader News; Medina Valley Times. **Radio-FM:** KZLV, 91.3 MHz.

Mabank—Newspaper: The Monitor (S).
Madisonville—Newspaper: Madisonville Meteor. **Radio-AM:** KMVL, 1220 kHz. **Radio-FM:** KAGG, 96.1 MHz; KMVL, 100.5.
Malakoff—Newspaper: Malakoff News. **Radio-FM:** KCKL, 95.9 MHz.
Manor—Radio-AM: KELG, 1440 kHz.
Mansfield—Newspaper: Mansfield News-Mirror (S).
Marble Falls—Newspapers: Marble Falls Highlander (S); The River Cities Tribune. **Radio-FM:** KBMD, 88.5 MHz; KXXS, 104.9 MHz.
Marfa—Newspaper: The Big Bend Sentinel.
Marion—Radio-AM: KBIB, 1000 kHz.
Markham—Radio-FM: KZRC, 92.5 Mhz.
Marlin—Newspaper: The Marlin Democrat. **Radio-FM:** KLRK, 92.9 MHz.
Marshall—Newspapers: Marshall News Messenger (D); Lone Star Eagle. **Radio-AM:** KCUL, 1410 kHz; KMHT, 1450. **Radio-FM:** KBWC, 91.1 MHz; KCUL, 92.3; KMHT, 103.9.
Mart—Newspaper: Mart Messenger.
Mason—Newspaper: Mason County News. **Radio-FM:** KOTY, 95.7 MHz.
Matador—Newspaper: Motley County Tribune.
Mathis—Newspaper: Mathis News.
McAllen—Newspaper: The Monitor (D). **Radio-AM:** KRIO, 910 kHz. **Radio-FM:** KHID, 88.1 MHz; KVMV, 96.9; KGBT, 98.5. **TV:** KNVO-Ch. 48.
McCamey—Newspaper: McCamey News. **Radio-FM:** KPBM, 95.3 MHz.
McCook—Radio-FM: KCAS, 91.5 Mhz.
McGregor—Newspaper: McGregor Mirror and Crawford Sun.

McKinney—Newspaper: McKinney Courier-Gazette (D). **Radio-FM:** KNTU, 88.1 MHz.
Melissa—Newspaper: The Anna/Melissa Tribune.
Memphis—Newspaper: Memphis Democrat. **Radio-FM:** KLSR, 105.3 MHz.
Menard—Newspaper: Menard News and Messenger.
Mercedes—Newspaper: Mercedes Enterprise. **Radio-FM:** KHKZ, 106.3 MHz.
Meridian—Newspaper: Bosque Co. News.
Merkel—Newspaper: Merkel Mail. **Radio-AM:** KMXO, 1500 kHz. **Radio-FM:** KHXS, 102.7 MHz.
Mesquite—Radio-FM: KEOM, 88.5 MHz.
Mexia—Newspaper: Mexia Daily News (D). **Radio-AM:** KRQX, 1590 kHz. **Radio-FM:** KYCX, 104.9 MHz.
Miami—Newspaper: Miami Chief.
Midland—Newspaper: Midland Reporter-Telegram (D). **Radio-AM:** KCRS, 550 kHz; KWEL, 1070; KJBC, 1150; KMND, 1510. **Radio-FM:** KNFM, 92.3 MHz; KBAT, 93.3; KQRX, 95.1; KCRS, 103.3; KCHX, 106.7. **TV:** KMID-Ch. 2; KUPB-Ch. 18.
Midlothian—Newspapers: Midlothian Mirror; Midlothian Today.
Miles—Newspaper: Miles Messenger.
Mineola—Newspaper: Mineola Monitor. **Radio-FM:** KMOO, 99.9 MHz.
Mineral Wells—Newspaper: Mineral Wells Index (D). **Radio-AM:** KJSA, 1120 kHz. **Radio-FM:** KFWR, 95.9 MHz.
Mirando City—Radio-FM: KBDR, 100.5 MHz.
Mission—Newspaper: Progress-Times. **Radio-AM:** KIRT, 1580 kHz. **Radio-FM:** KQXX, 105.5 MHz.
Missouri City—Radio-FM: KPTY, 104.9 MHz.
Monahans—Newspaper: The Monahans News (S). **Radio-AM:** KLBO, 1330 kHz. **Radio-FM:** KGEE, 99.9 MHz.
Moody—Newspaper: The Courier.
Morton—Newspaper: Morton Tribune.
Moulton—Newspaper: Moulton Eagle.
Mount Pleasant—Newspaper: Daily Tribune (D). **Radio-AM:** KIMP, 960 kHz.
Mount Vernon—Newspaper: Mount Vernon Optic-Herald.
Muenster—Newspaper: Muenster Enterprise. **Radio-FM:** KZZA, 106.7 MHz.
Muleshoe—Newspaper: Muleshoe Journal. **Radio-AM:** KMUL, 1380 kHz. **Radio-FM:** KMUL, 103.1 MHz.
Munday—Newspaper: The Munday Courier.

Nacogdoches—Newspaper: Nacogdoches Daily Sentinel (D). **Radio-AM:** KSFA, 860 kHz. **Radio-FM:** KSAU, 90.1 MHz; KJCS, 103.3; KTBQ, 107.7. **TV:** KYTX-Ch. 19.
Naples—Newspaper: The Monitor.
Navasota—Newspaper: The Navasota Examiner. **Radio-AM:** KWBC, 1550 kHz. **Radio-FM:** KHTZ, 92.5 MHz.
Nederland—Radio-AM: KQHN, 1510 kHz.
Needville—Newspaper: The Gulf Coast Tribune.
New Boston—Newspaper: Bowie County Citizen Tribune (S). **Radio-AM:** KNBO, 1530 kHz. **Radio-FM:** KEWL, 95.1 MHz; KZRB, 103.5.
New Braunfels—Newspaper: Herald-Zeitung (D). **Radio-AM:** KGNB, 1420 kHz. **Radio-FM:** KNBT, 92.1 MHz.
Newton—Newspaper: Newton Co. News.
New Ulm—Newspaper: New Ulm Enterprise. **Radio-FM:** KNRG, 92.3 MHz.
Nixon—Newspaper: Cow Country Courier.
Nocona—Newspaper: Nocona News.
Nolanville—Radio FM: KLFX, 107.3 MHz.
Normangee—Newspaper: Normangee Star.

Odem—Newspaper: Odem-Edroy Times. **Radio-FM:** KLHB, 98.3 MHz.
Odessa—Newspaper: Odessa American (D). **Radio-AM:** KFLB, 920 kHz; KOZA, 1230; KRIL, 1410. **Radio-FM:** KBMM, 89.5 MHz; KFLB, 90.5 MHz; KOCV, 91.3; KMRK, 96.1; KMCM, 96.9; KODM, 97.9; KHKX, 99.1; KQLM, 107.9. **TV:** KOSA-Ch. 7; KWES-Ch. 9; KPEJ-Ch. 24; KPXK-Ch. 30; KOCV-Ch. 36; KMLM-Ch. 42.
O'Donnell—Newspaper: O'Donnell Index-Press.
Olney—Newspaper: The Olney Enterprise.
Olton—Newspaper: Olton Enterprise.
Orange—Newspaper: Orange Leader (D). **Radio-AM:** KOGT, 1600 kHz. **Radio-FM:** KKMY, 104.5 MHz; KIOC, 106.1.
Ore City—Radio-FM: KAZE, 106.9 Mhz.
Overton—Newspaper: Overton Press. **Radio-FM:** KPXI, 100.7 Mhz.

Ozona—Newspaper: Ozona Stockman. **Radio-FM:** KYXX, 94.3 MHz.

Paducah—Newspaper: Paducah Post.
Paint Rock—Newspaper: Concho Herald.
Palacios—Newspaper: Palacios Beacon. Radio-FM: KROY, 99.7 MHz.
Palestine—Newspaper: Palestine Herald Press (D). **Radio-AM:** KNET, 1450 kHz. **Radio-FM:** KYFP, 89.1 MHz; KYYK, 98.3.
Pampa—Newspaper: Pampa News (D). **Radio-AM:** KGRO, 1230 kHz. **Radio-FM:** KAVO, 90.9 MHz; KOMX, 100.3.
Panhandle—Newspaper: Panhandle Herald.
Paris—Newspaper: Paris News (D). **Radio-AM:** KPJC, 1250 kHz; KPLT, 1490. **Radio-FM:** KHCP, 89.3 MHz; KOYN, 93.9; KBUS, 101.9; KPLT, 107.7.
Pasadena—Newspaper: Pasadena Citizen (D). **Radio-AM:** KIKK, 650 kHz; KLVL, 1480. **Radio-FM:** KFTG, 88.1 MHz; KKBQ, 92.9.
Pearland—Newspapers: Pearland Journal; Pearland Reporter News.
Pearsall—Newspaper: Frio-Nueces Current. **Radio-AM:** KVWG, 1280 kHz. **Radio-FM:** KVWG, 95.3 MHz; KRIO, 104.1.
Pecan Grove—Radio-AM: KREH, 900 kHz.
Pecos—Newspaper: Pecos Enterprise (S). **Radio-AM:** KIUN, 1400 kHz. **Radio-FM:** KKLY, 97.3 MHz; KPTX, 98.3.
Perryton—Newspaper: Perryton Herald (S). **Radio-AM:** KEYE, 1400 kHz. **Radio-FM:** KEYE, 96.1 MHz.
Petersburg—Newspaper: Petersburg Post.
Pflugerville—Newspaper: Pflugerville Pflag. **Radio-AM:** KOKE, 1600 kHz.
Pharr—Newspaper: Advance News Journal. **Radio-AM:** KVJY, 840 kHz.
Pilot Point—Newspaper: Pilot Point Post-Signal. **Radio-FM:** KZMP, 104.9 MHz.
Pittsburg—Newspaper: Pittsburg Gazette. **Radio-FM:** KSCN, 96.9; KKXI, 91.7 MHz; KDVE, 103.1.
Plains—Newspaper: Cowboy Country News. **Radio-FM:** KPHS, 90.3 MHz.
Plainview—Newspaper: Plainview Daily Herald (D). **Radio-AM:** KVOP, 1090 kHz; KREW, 1400. **Radio-FM:** KPMB, 88.5 MHz; KBAH, 90.5; KWLD, 91.5; KSTQ, 97.3; KRIA, 103.9; KKYN, 106.9.
Plano—Newspaper: Plano Star Courier (D). **Radio AM:** KMKI, 620 kHz.
Pleasanton—Newspaper: Pleasanton Express. **Radio-AM:** KFNI, 1380 kHz.
Point Comfort—Radio-FM: KAJI, 94.1 MHz.
Port Aransas—Newspaper: Port Aransas South Jetty.
Port Arthur—Newspaper: Port Arthur News (D). **Radio-AM:** KDEI, 1250 kHz; KOLE, 1340. **Radio-FM:** KQBU, 93.3 MHz; KTJM, 98.5. **TV:** KBTV-Ch. 4.
Port Isabel—Newspaper: Port Isabel/South Padre Press (S). **Radio-FM:** KNVO, 101.1 MHz.
Portland—Newspaper: Portland News. **Radio-FM:** KSGR, 91.1 MHz; KMJR, 105.5.
Port Lavaca—Newspaper: Port Lavaca Wave (S). **Radio-FM:** KITE, 93.3 MHz.
Port Neches—Radio-AM: KUHD, 1150 kHz.
Post—Newspaper: Post Dispatch. **Radio-FM:** KPOS, 107.3 MHz.
Pottsboro—Newspaper: Pottsboro Press.
Prairie View—Radio-FM: KPVU, 91.3 MHz.
Premont—Radio-FM: KMFM, 100.7 MHz.
Presidio—Newspaper: The International Presidio Paper.
Princeton—Newspaper: Princeton Herald.

Quanah—Newspaper: Quanah Tribune-Chief (S). **Radio-AM:** KVDL, 1150 kHz. **Radio-FM:** KIXC, 100.9 MHz.
Quinlan—Newspaper: The Tawakoni News.
Quitaque—Newspaper: Valley Tribune.
Quitman—Newspaper: Wood Co. Democrat.

Ralls—Newspaper: Crosby County Reporter-Examiner. **Radio-AM:** KCLR, 1530 kHz.
Ranger—Newspaper: Ranger Times (S).
Rankin—Newspaper: Rankin News.
Raymondville—Newspaper: Chronicle/Willacy Co. News. **Radio-AM:** KSOX, 1240 kHz. **Radio-FM:** KBUC, 102.1 MHz; KBIC, 105.7.
Red Oak—Newspapers: Ellis Co. Chronicle (S).
Refugio—Newspaper: Refugio Co. Press. **Radio-FM:**

KTKY, 106.1 MHz.
Richmond—Newspaper (see **Rosenberg**).
Riesel—Newspaper: Riesel Rustler.
Rio Grande City—Newspaper: Rio Grande Herald. **Radio-FM:** KQBO, 103.1 MHz. **TV:** KTLM-Ch. 40.
Rising Star—Newspaper: Rising Star.
Robert Lee—Newspaper: Observer/Enterprise.
Robinson—Radio-FM: KDOS, 107.9 MHz.
Robstown—Newspaper: Nueces Co. Record-Star. **Radio-AM:** KROB, 1510 kHz. **Radio-FM:** KLUX, 89.5 MHz; KSAB, 99.9; KMIQ, 104.9.
Rochester—Newspaper: Twin Cities News.
Rockdale—Newspaper: Rockdale Reporter. **Radio-FM:** KRXT, 98.5 MHz.
Rockport—Newspapers: Rockport Pilot (S); The Coastal Bend Herald. **Radio-FM:** KKPN, 102.3 MHz.
Rocksprings—Newspaper: Texas Mohair Weekly.
Rockwall—Newspaper: Rockwall County News.
Rollingwood—Radio-AM: KJCE, 1370 kHz.
Roma—Newspaper: South Texas Reporter. **Radio-FM:** KBMI, 97.7 MHz.
Rosebud—Newspaper: Rosebud News.
Rosenberg—Newspaper: Rosenberg Herald-Coaster (D). **Radio-AM:** KRTX, 980 kHz. **TV:** KXLN-Ch. 45; KXLN-DT-Ch. 46.
Rotan—Newspaper: Rotan Advance-Star-Record.
Round Rock—Newspaper: Round Rock Leader (TW). **Radio-FM:** KNLE, 88.1 MHz; KFMK, 105.9.
Rowena—Newspaper: Rowena Press.
Rowlett—Newspaper: The Rowlett Lakeshore Times.
Rudolph—Radio-FM: KTER, 90.7 MHz.
Rusk—Newspaper: Cherokeean/Herald. **Radio-AM:** KTLU, 1580 kHz. **Radio-FM:** KWRW, 97.7 Mhz.

Saint Jo—Newspaper: Saint Jo Tribune.
San Angelo—Newspaper: San Angelo Standard-Times (D). **Radio-AM:** KGKL, 960 kHz; KKSA, 1260; KCRN, 1340. **Radio-FM:** KUTX, 90.1 MHz; KDCD, 92.9; KCRN, 93.9; KIXY, 94.7; KGKL, 97.5; KELI, 98.7; KYZZ, 100.1; KWFR, 101.9; KMDX, 106.1; KSJT, 107.5. **TV:** KSAN-Ch. 3; KIDY-Ch. 6; KLST-Ch. 8.
San Antonio—Newspapers: San Antonio Business Journal; Commercial Recorder (D); Express-News (D); North San Antonio Times; Today's Catholic. **Radio-AM:** KTSA, 550 kHz; KSLR, 630; KKYX, 680; KTKR, 760; KONO, 860; KRDY, 1160; WOAI, 1200; KZDC, 1250; KAHL, 1310; KCOR, 1350; KCHL, 1480; KEDA, 1540. **Radio-FM:** KPAC, 88.3 MHz; KSTX, 89.1; KSYM, 90.1; KYFS, 90.9; KRTU, 91.7; KROM, 92.9; KXXM, 96.1; KAJA, 97.3; KISS, 99.5; KCYY, 100.3; KQXT, 101.9; KSRX, 102.7; KZEP, 104.5; KXTN, 107.5. **TV:** WOAI-Ch. 4; KENS-Ch. 5; KLRN-DT-Ch. 8; KLRN-Ch. 9; KSAT-Ch. 12; KHCE-Ch. 23; KABB-Ch. 29; KVDA-DT-Ch. 38; KWEX-DT-Ch. 39; KWEX-Ch. 41; KSAT-DT-Ch. 48; WOAI-DT-Ch. 58; KVDA-Ch. 60.
San Augustine—Newspaper: San Augustine Tribune. **Radio-FM:** KQSI, 92.5 MHz.
San Benito—Newspaper: San Benito News (S).
San Diego—Newspaper: Duval County Picture (S). **Radio-FM:** KUKA, 105.9 MHz.
Sanger—Newspaper: Sanger Courier. **Radio-FM:** KVRK, 89.7 MHz; KTDK, 104.1.
San Juan—Radio-AM: KUBR, 1210 kHz.
San Marcos—Newspaper: San Marcos Daily Record (D). **Radio-AM:** KUOL, 1470 kHz. **Radio-FM:** KTSW, 89.9 MHz; KBPA, 103.5.
San Saba—Newspaper: San Saba News & Star. **Radio-AM:** KBAL, 1410 kHz. **Radio-FM:** KBAL, 106.1 MHz.
Santa Fe—Radio-FM: KJIC, 90.5 MHz.
Schertz—Radio-FM: KBBT, 98.5 MHz.
Schulenburg—Newspaper: Schulenburg Sticker.
Seabrook—Radio-FM: KROI, 92.1 MHz.
Seadrift—Radio-FM: KMAT, 105.1 MHz.
Seagoville—Newspaper: Suburbia News.
Seagraves—Newspaper: Tri-Country Tribune.
Sealy—Newspaper: The Sealy News (S).
Seguin—Newspaper: Seguin Gazette-Enterprise (D). **Radio-AM:** KWED, 1580 kHz. **Radio-FM:** KSMG, 105.3 MHz.
Seminole—Newspaper: Seminole Sentinel (S). **Radio-AM:** KIKZ, 1250 kHz. **Radio-FM:** KSEM, 106.3 MHz.
Seymour—Newspaper: Baylor Co. Banner. **Radio-AM:** KSEY, 1230 kHz. **Radio-FM:** KSEY, 94.3 MHz.
Shamrock—Newspaper: County Star-News. **Radio-FM:** KBKH, 92.9 MHz.

Shepherd—Newspaper: San Jacinto News-Times.
Sherman—Newspaper: Herald Democrat (D). **Radio-AM:** KXEB, 910 kHz; KJIM, 1500; KTBK, 1700. **TV:** KXII-Ch. 12; KXII-DT-Ch. 20.
Shiner—Newspaper: The Shiner Gazette.
Silsbee—Newspaper: Silsbee Bee. **Radio-AM:** KSET, 1300 kHz. **Radio-FM:** KAYD, 101.7 MHz.
Silverton—Newspaper: Briscoe Co. News.
Sinton—Newspaper: San Patricio Co. News. **Radio-AM:** KDAE, 1590 kHz. **Radio-FM:** KNCN, 101.3 MHz; KOUL, 103.7.
Slaton—Newspaper: Slaton Slatonite. **Radio-FM:** KJAK, 92.7 MHz.
Smithville—Newspaper: Smithville Times.
Snyder—Newspaper: Snyder Daily News (D). **Radio-AM:** KSNY, 1450 kHz. **Radio-FM:** KLYD, 98.9 MHz; KSNY, 101.5. **TV:** KPCB-Ch. 17.
Somerset—Radio-AM: KSJL, 810 kHz.
Sonora—Newspaper: Devil's River News. **Radio-AM:** KHOS, 980 kHz. **Radio-FM:** KHOS, 92.1 MHz.
South Padre Island—Radio-FM: KESO, 92.7 MHz; KZSP, 95.3.
Spearman—Newspaper: Hansford Co. Reporter-Statesman. **Radio-FM:** KTOT, 89.5 MHz; KRDF, 98.3.
Springtown—Newspaper: Springtown Epigraph. **Radio-FM:** KSQX, 89.1 MHz.
Spur—Newspaper: Texas Spur.
Stamford—Newspaper: Stamford American. **Radio-AM:** KVRP, 1400 kHz. **Radio-FM:** KJTZ, 106.9 Mhz.
Stanton—Newspaper: Martin Co. Messenger. **Radio-FM:** KKJW, 105.9 MHz.
Stephenville—Newspaper: Stephenville Empire-Tribune (D). **Radio-AM:** KSTV, 1510 kHz. **Radio-FM:** KQXS, 89.1 MHz; KCUB, 98.3.
Sterling City—Radio-FM: KCSE, 96.5 MHz.
Stratford—Newspaper: Stratford Star.
Sudan—Newspaper: Sudan Beacon-News.
Sugar Land—Newspaper: The Fort Bend Mirror.
Sulphur Springs—Newspaper: News-Telegram (D). **Radio-AM:** KSST, 1230 kHz. **Radio-FM:** KSCH, 95.9 MHz.
Sweetwater—Newspaper: Sweetwater Reporter (D). **Radio-AM:** KXOX, 1240 kHz. **Radio-FM:** KXOX, 96.7 MHz. **TV:** KTXS-Ch. 12.

Taft - Newspaper: Taft Tribune.
Tahoka—Newspaper: Lynn Co. News. **Radio-FM:** KMMX, 100.3 MHz; KAMZ, 103.5.
Talco—Newspaper: Talco Times.
Tatum—Newspaper: Trammel Trace Tribune. **Radio-FM:** KXAL, 100.3 MHz.
Taylor—Newspaper: Taylor Daily Press (D). **Radio-AM:** KWNX, 1260 kHz. **Radio FM:** KXBT, 104.3 MHz.
Teague—Newspaper: Teague Chronicle.
Temple—Newspaper: Temple Daily Telegram (D). **Radio-AM:** KTEM, 1400 kHz. **Radio-FM:** KVLT, 88.5 MHz; KBDE, 89.9; KLTD, 101.7 MHz. **TV:** KCEN-Ch. 6; KCEN-DT-Ch. 9.
Terrell—Newspaper: Terrell Tribune (D). **Radio-AM:** KPYK, 1570 kHz.
Terrell Hills—Radio-AM: KLUP, 930 kHz. **Radio-FM:** KELZ, 106.7 MHz.
Texarkana—Newspaper: Texarkana Gazette (D). **Radio-AM:** KCMC, 740 kHz; KTFS, 940; KEWL, 1400. **Radio-FM:** KTXK, 91.5 MHz; KTAL, 98.1; KKYR, 102.5. **TV:** KTAL-Ch. 6.
Texas City—Radio-AM: KYST, 920 kHz.
Thorndale—Newspaper: Thorndale Champion.
Three Rivers—Newspaper: The Progress. **Radio-FM:** KEMA, 94.5 MHz.
Throckmorton—Newspaper: Throckmorton Tribune.
Timpson—Newspaper: Timpson & Tenaha News.
Tomball—Radio-AM: KSEV, 700 kHz.
Trenton—Newspaper: Trenton Tribune.
Trinity—Newspaper: Trinity Standard.
Tulia—Newspaper: Tulia Herald. **Radio-AM:** KTUE, 1260 kHz. **Radio-FM:** KBTE, 104.9 Mhz.
Tye—Radio-FM: KBCY, 99.7 MHz.
Tyler—Newspapers: Tyler Morning Telegraph (D); Catholic East Texas (SM). **Radio-AM:** KTBB, 600 kHz; KZEY, 690; KGLD, 1330; KYZS, 1490. **Radio-FM:** KVNE, 89.5 MHz; KGLY, 91.3; KDOK, 92.1; KTYL, 93.1; KNUE, 101.5; KKUS, 104.1. **TV:** KLTV-Ch. 7.

Universal City—Radio-AM: KSAH, 720 kHz.
University Park—Radio-AM: KTNO, 1440 kHz; KZMP, 1540.
Uvalde—Newspaper: Uvalde Leader-News (S). **Radio-AM:** KVOU, 1400 kHz. **Radio-FM:** KBNU, 93.9 MHz; KUVA, 102.3; KVOU, 104.9. **TV:** KPXL-Ch. 26.

Valley Mills—Newspaper: Valley Mills Progress.
Van—Newspaper: Van Banner.
Van Alstyne—Newspaper: Van Alstyne Leader.
Van Horn—Newspaper: Van Horn Advocate.
Vega—Newspaper: Vega Enterprise.
Vernon—Newspaper: Vernon Daily Record (D). **Radio-AM:** KVWC, 1490 kHz. **Radio-FM:** KVWC, 103.1 MHz.
Victoria—Newspaper: Victoria Advocate (D). **Radio-AM:** KVWC, 1340 kHz; KNAL, 1410. **Radio-FM:** KAYK, 88.5 MHz; KXBJ, 89.3; KVRT, 90.7; KQVT, 92.3; KVIC, 95.1; KTXN, 98.7; KEPG, 100.9; KIXS, 107.9. **TV:** KVCT-Ch. 19; KAVU-Ch. 25.
Vidor—Newspaper: Vidor Vidorian.

Waco—Newspapers: The Waco Citizen (S); Waco Tribune-Herald (D). **Radio-AM:** KBBW, 1010 kHz; KWTX, 1230; KQRL, 1580; KRZX, 1660. **Radio-FM:** KBCT, 94.5 MHz; KBGO, 95.7; KWTX, 97.5; WACO, 99.9; KWBU, 103.3. **TV:** KWTX-Ch. 10; KXXV-Ch. 25; KWBU-Ch. 34; KWKT-Ch. 44.
Wake Village—Radio-FM: KHTA, 92.5 Mhz.
Wallis—Newspaper: Wallis News-Review.
Waxahachie—Newspaper: Waxahachie Daily Light (D). **Radio-AM:** KBEC, 1390 kHz.
Weatherford—Newspaper: Weatherford Democrat (D). **Radio-AM:** KZEE, 1220 kHz. **Radio-FM:** KMQX, 88.5 MHz; KYQX, 89.5.
Weimar—Newspaper: Weimar Mercury.
Wells—Radio-FM: KVLL, 94.7 MHz.
Wellington—Newspaper: Wellington Leader.
Weslaco—Radio-AM: KRGE, 1290 kHz. **TV:** KRGV-Ch. 5; KRGV-DT-Ch. 13.
West—Newspaper: West News.
West Lake Hills—Radio-AM: KTXZ, 1560 kHz.
West Odessa—Radio-FM: KLVW, 88.7 MHz.
Wharton—Newspaper: Wharton Journal-Spectator (S). **Radio-AM:** KANI, 1500 kHz.
Wheeler—Newspaper: The Wheeler Times. **Radio-FM:** KPDR, 90.5 MHz.
Whitehouse—Newspaper: Tri Co. Leader. **Radio-FM:** KISX, 107.3 MHz.
White Oak—Newspaper: White Oak Independent. **Radio-FM:** KLBL, 99.3 MHz.
Whitesboro—Newspaper: Whitesboro News-Record. **Radio-FM:** KMAD, 102.5 MHz.
Whitewright—Newspaper: Whitewright Sun.
Whitney—Newspaper: Lake Whitney Views (M).
Wichita Falls—Newspaper: Times Record News (D). **Radio-AM:** KFCD, 990 kHz; KWFS, 1290. **Radio-FM:** KMCU, 88.7 MHz; KMOC, 89.5; KTEO, 90.5; KNIN, 92.9; KLUR, 99.9; KWFS, 102.3; KQXC, 103.9; KBZS, 106.3. **TV:** KFDX-Ch. 3; KAUZ-Ch. 6; KJTL-Ch. 18.
Willis—Radio FM: KVST, 103.7 MHz.
Wills Point—Newspaper: Wills Point Chronicle.
Wimberley—Newspaper: Wimberley View (S).
Winfield—Radio-FM: KALK, 97.7 MHz.
Winnie—Newspaper: The Hometown Press. **Radio FM:** KKHT, 100.7 MHz.
Winnsboro—Newspapers: Winnsboro News. **Radio-FM:** KWNS, 104.7 MHz.
Winona—Radio-FM: KBLZ, 102.7 MHz.
Winters—Newspaper: Winters Enterprise. **Radio-FM:** KNCE, 96.1 MHz.
Wolfe City—Newspaper: Wolfe City Mirror.
Wolfforth—TV: KUPT-Ch. 22.
Woodville—Newspaper: Tyler Co. Booster. **Radio-AM:** KWUD, 1490 kHz.
Wylie—Newspaper: The Wylie News.

Yoakum—Newspaper: Yoakum Herald-Times. **Radio-FM:** KYKM, 92.5 MHz.
Yorktown—Newspaper: Yorktown News-View.

Zapata—Newspaper: Zapata Co. News. **Radio-FM:** KBAW, 93.5 MHz. ☆

Texas Economy: A Cautious Rebound

Source: State of Texas Annual Cash Report 2004, Comptroller of Public Accounts.

The Texas economy is finally rebounding after the sharp decline, paralleling the national downturn, that began during 2001. Statewide nonfarm employment added 116,600 nonfarm jobs during fiscal 2004. This represented a year-to-year employment growth of 1.2 percent from August 2003 to August 2004.

As statewide jobs have increased, the jobless rate has slowly declined. The statewide unemployment rate fell from 6.8 percent at the beginning of fiscal 2004 to 5.7 percent as the fiscal year came to a close, although it remained considerably above its low point of 3.8 percent in December 2000.

PRODUCTS

Although Texas industrial output is growing, strong productivity gains (increases in output per hour of work) continue to put a damper on manufacturing job growth, both in Texas and in the nation.

Manufacturing

Texas manufacturers were producing more with fewer workers, fueled by steady advances in information technology and processing. During fiscal 2004, the real, inflation-adjusted gross state product in Texas manufacturing rose about two and a half percentage points, even though employment in manufacturing declined by 8,100 jobs.

According to the Texas Workforce Commission, both the durable and nondurable manufacturing goods industries lost jobs, with the largest percentage drops in paper manufacturing (down 1,800 jobs, or 7.6 percent); printing and related support manufacturing (down 2,000 jobs, or 5.3 percent), and electrical equipment, appliances, and electrical components (down 1,200 jobs, or 6.7 percent).

Not all manufacturing sectors lost jobs, however. The one that added the most was petroleum refining (up 1,000 jobs, or 4.3 percent), which was boosted by strong demand for gasoline and other refined products. Other industries that added employment were fabricated metals (600 jobs, or 0.6 percent), primary metals (400 jobs, or 1.6 percent) and furniture manufacturing (400 jobs, or 1.3 percent).

Also on the economic bright side, fiscal 2004 saw a re-emergence of growth in the high technology sectors. While computer and electronic products experienced double-digit job losses in fiscal 2003, this sector added jobs, albeit slowly, increasing by 1,200 jobs (1.1 percent) statewide from August 2003 to August 2004.

The state's total loss in manufacturing employment, at -0.9 percent for the year, was marginally worse than manufacturing employment nationwide, which registered a modest 0.1 percent increase. Texas' manufacturing industries are more concentrated than nationally in petrochemicals and the machinery assembly industries, which remained weak throughout the year.

Oil and Gas

The segments of the oil and gas industry that have most benefited from higher fuel prices are oil and gas drilling and other support activities. The state's oil and gas extraction sector actually lost jobs during fiscal 2004 (down 700 jobs, or –1.1 percent), given that oil and gas production within the state's borders are declining nearly 5 percent per year.

Texas, serving as a headquarters site—and with four times the national concentration of oil and gas as a percentage of the economy—saw the net addition of 1,300 natural resources and mining jobs (up 0.9 percent) in fiscal 2004.

Construction

The Texas construction industry continued a relentless climb in fiscal 2004, taking advantage of residential mortgage rates that remained favorable through the year. Again residential, rather than commercial, construction led to the total increase of 5,200 construction jobs (1.0 percent) in Texas during fiscal 2004.

Statewide, building construction (combining both residential and nonresidential) added 1,800 jobs (up 1.3 percent) in fiscal 2004, with heavy and civil engineering construction also growing at about the same rate (1.2 percent). Housing sales had another up year, at 12 percent above their level a year ago, giving impetus to housing starts, which reached a 20-year high. The level of housing starts in fiscal 2004 matched numbers not seen since the state's 1983-1984 real estate boom.

SERVICES

Service-providing jobs now account for 83.2 percent of all Texas nonfarm jobs, up from 80.7 percent ten years ago.

Education and Health

Education and health services accounted for about one-third of the state's total nonfarm employment

Workers grout in stones in a residential subdivision in Southlake. File photo.

growth during fiscal 2004. Drawing primarily from the growth in physician's offices and outpatient health care, as well as home health and ambulatory health services, education and health services added 37,300 jobs during the fiscal year.

The health care and social assistance sector alone now employs more than one million Texans, with more people employed in this sector than in manufacturing, and nearly as many as in retail trade. Based on job growth, the ambulatory health care services sector was the fastest growing sub-industry over the past year, adding 21,400 jobs, for a 5.0 percent increase .

The educational services component, which includes private schools, universities, training schools and other private educational instruction, grew more slowly (at 1.4 percent) and accounted for only 1,700 of the jobs added in the industry.

Trade, Transportation, Utilities

The trade, transportation, and utilities industry is the state's largest employment sector, with 1.95 million Texas jobs. In fiscal 2004, it turned around two years of job losses and substantially outperformed its last growth year, fiscal 2001, which registered a 0.2 percent increase.

Growing 1.7 percent during fiscal 2004, trade, transportation, and utilities exceeded all but education and health services in the number of new jobs, with an increase of 32,600 workers for the year. Retail trade accounted for 13,900 of these jobs, spread across a broad range of retailing sectors. During the fiscal year, the wholesale trade sector added 8,300 jobs, or 1.8 percent, patterning closely the retail trade sector.

Transportation and warehousing enjoyed moderate growth of 1.9 percent during the fiscal year, partly as airline employment overcame the significant losses seen over the last three fiscal years.

The utilities sector, traditionally the most stable part of the trade, transportation, and utilities industry, was the slowest growing segment of the industry. Even this sector lost employment in fiscal 2003, but it added 300 jobs statewide during fiscal 2004, for an employment increase of 0.6 percent.

Information Industry

The sole service-providing industry to end fiscal 2004 with fewer jobs than it began was the information industry, although some components of the industry have turned the corner to eke out growth.

Overall, the industry lost 3,700 jobs statewide (-1.6 percent). The main component to suffer, telecommunications, was responsible for these losses and then some. Telecommunications alone lost 5,500 jobs, with an additional 700 jobs lost in printing and publishing. The remaining sectors of the information industry actually netted a positive 2,500 jobs.

The bulk of Texas telecommunications employment is in wired and wireless cellular providers of telephone services, although there is also substantial employment in paging services, satellite and cable providers, and telecommunications reselling services.

Information is actually a conglomerate of several industries, some old-economy (such as printing, publishing, data processing, television broadcasting, and wired telephone services) and some newer economy (cellular telephone providers, Internet providers, DSL,

Shoppers at the Broadway Mall in Tyler. File photo.

and software services).

Parts of the newer information economy have not yet recovered from the one-two punch of high technology-related overcapacity and the collapse of stock values in 2000 and 2001. The last few years have been difficult for publishers of newspapers and magazines not only in Texas but nationwide.

Internet service providers and Web search portals saw some renewed job gains statewide. Alternative electronic media, which can be updated more immediately, are now clearly pressuring the printing segment of the industry. Publishing lost 1.4 percent of its Texas employment over the past year.

Finance

Like information, the state's financial activities industry was boosted by a relatively healthy year in one area and stifled by weakness in another. Banking and credit intermediation services tacked on 4,900 jobs during the year (up 2.3 percent), taking advantage of healthy mortgage and refinancing activity, growing fee income, and mostly favorable lending spreads.

The real estate and leasing services sector experienced another positive year for residential housing sales, but losses in nonresidential real estate and leasing services exceeded the gains on the residential side. Overall, real estate lost 1,400 jobs (-1.3 percent) and rental and leasing services lost 700 jobs (-1.2 percent).

Professional and Business

Texas' professional and business services industry lost 1.5 percent of its jobs in fiscal 2001, 2.9 percent in fiscal 2002, and 2.0 percent in fiscal 2003, so it was a welcome change to see this industry add 25,700 jobs in fiscal 2004, chalking up job growth of 2.5 percent.

All segments of the professional and business services industry experienced net job gains in fiscal 2004, with the largest percentage increase (3.2 percent) in the management of companies sector, and the largest number of net jobs (13,400) in administrative, support, and waste services. Most of this growth was in temporary help jobs.

Restaurants and Hospitality

Unlike professional and business services, the leisure and hospitality industry continued to grow over the last three years, and restaurants provided the momentum underlying most of this growth.

Growing even faster over the past year, restaurants and bars, including caterers, added 17,600 jobs from August 2003 to August 2004, for a fiscal 2004 job increase of 2.6 percent. Losses in hotel and motel employment, as well as small declines in arts, sports, museum, and zoo employment were more than counterbalanced by gains in eating and drinking places, bars, amusement parks, and recreation/fitness centers. Overall, leisure and hospitality services added 19,500 jobs for a 2.3 percent gain during the year.

Government

Government employment rose slightly during fiscal 2004, but once again, it was entirely due to growth in the local government sector, particularly in public schools. Due to cutbacks and a tendency toward shifting more governmental responsibilities away from the federal government, federal civilian employment in Texas and the nation fell, dropping in Texas by 4,200

jobs, or 2.3 percent.

State government, operating under deeper budget constraints, also lost jobs, as state government gave up a net 3,200 jobs, or 1.0 percent over the past year.

The local government sector, boosted by school district hiring, added more than 10,000 jobs, or 1.0 percent. Overall, civilian government employment tacked on a net of 2,800 jobs, 0.2 percent growth between August 2003 and August 2004.

Consequently, of the total 116,600 jobs added to the state during fiscal 2004, nearly 98 percent (113,800 new jobs) was in the private sector. ☆

Gross State Product Rankings, 2003

	Millions of dollars	Percent of U.S. total
UNITED STATES	$ 10,911,103*	100.0
California	1,446,430	13.3
New York	821,667	7.5
Texas	**813,112**	**7.5**
Florida	550,005	5.0
Illinois	499,466	4.6
Pennsylvania	449,947	4.1

*Prototype estimates of the U.S. Bureau of Economic Analysis.

Texas Gross State Product, 1995-2003, By Industry (in millions)

Industry	1995	1996	1997	1998	1999	2000	2001	2002*	2003*
Agriculture	$ 7,347	$ 7,175	$ 8,331	$ 8,197	$ 9,410	$ 9,585	$ 9,575	$ 10,520	$ 11,024
%change	(4.7)	(2.7)	16.1	(1.6)	14.8	1.9	(0.1)	9.9	4.8
Mining	33,470	41,543	44,289	35,601	33,081	45,499	47,890	45,728	52,256
%change	5.1	24.1	6.6	(19.6)	(7.1)	37.5	5.3	(4.5)	14.3
Construction	21,945	24,433	25,498	29,262	33,133	36,295	37,846	40,130	41,124
%change	7.9	11.3	4.4	14.8	13.2	9.5	4.3	6.0	2.5
Manufacturing	78,902	81,214	90,363	94,199	93,853	95,935	93,754	90,821	92,201
%change	7.4	2.9	11.3	4.2	(0.4)	2.2	(2.3)	(3.1)	1.5
Transportation and Utilities	56,945	61,452	65,662	70,595	75,547	82,999	83,010	85,676	89,222
%change	5.8	7.9	6.9	7.5	7.0	9.9	0.0	3.2	4.1
Wholesale and Retail Trade	85,130	91,281	100,803	110,401	119,002	128,695	131,723	134,648	138,549
%change	6.0	7.2	10.4	9.5	7.8	8.1	2.4	2.2	2.9
Finance, Insurance and Real Estate	72,892	77,744	89,235	95,857	102,165	111,458	118,235	120,253	123,915
%change	7.2	6.7	14.8	7.4	6.6	9.1	6.1	1.7	3.0
Services	94,537	103,160	115,542	125,615	136,668	146,172	156,410	160,572	165,078
%change	8.2	9.1	12.0	8.7	8.8	7.0	7.0	2.7	2.8
Local, State and Federal Government	62,687	65,178	68,898	71,679	75,948	81,633	85,431	88,886	92,797
%change	4.8	4.0	5.7	4.0	6.0	7.5	4.7	4.0	4.4
TOTAL**	$ 513,882	$ 553,180	$ 608,621	$ 641,406	$ 678,807	$ 738,271	$ 763,874	$ 777,234	$ 806,166
%change	6.5	7.6	10.0	5.4	5.8	8.8	3.5	1.7	3.7
Total (in 1996 $)	$ 527,685	$ 553,180	$ 597,889	$ 631,688	$ 660,534	$ 688,473	$ 698,547	$ 701,760	$ 717,458
% change	4.6	4.8	8.1	5.7	4.6	4.2	1.5	0.5	2.2

*2002 and 2003 numbers are estimated from incomplete data. **Totals may not add due to rounding.
Source: Texas Comptroller of Public Accounts and U.S. Bureau of Economic Analysis. Texas 2003 Comprehensive Annual Financial Report.

Economies in Largest Metropolitan Areas

Source: Annual Cash Report 2004, State Comptroller of Public Accounts.

The economy of the **AUSTIN** metropolitan area* was one of the fastest growing in the nation during the 1990s when the area experienced strong job gains and posted low unemployment rates. In 2001, the metro area's rapid economic expansion slowed with the high tech downturn and the U.S. recession.

By August 2003, the metro area's unemployment rate stood at 5.7 percent, but in August 2004, after Austin-San Marcos again began to see job growth, the unemployment rate dipped to 4.3 percent. The Austin metro area's unemployment rate was the lowest of the six largest metropolitan areas in the state in 2004.

A positive sign for the Texas economy is that all of the major metro areas gained jobs between 2003 and 2004. The Austin-San Marcos metro area increase of 4,800 jobs was a small gain of 0.7 percent. Job losses in

Austin-San Marcos during the period occurred in information services, down 700 jobs; professional business services, down 1,500 jobs; federal government, down 600 jobs; and state government, down 100 jobs.

Government accounted for 22.3 percent of the Austin-San Marcos metro workforce. The largest job gains between August 2003 and August 2004 were in the local government sector (1,500 jobs), a 2.3 percent increase.

Professional business services accounted for 12.7 percent of the metro area's workforce and posted the largest number of job losses, finishing the year in August 2004 with 1,500 fewer jobs. This job loss represents a drop of 1.7 percent between August 2003 and August 2004.

Sales subject to tax in the Austin-San Marcos area rose from $15.6 billion in 2002 to $16 billion in 2003, an increase of 2.3 percent. During the first quarter of 2004, sales subject to tax in the Austin-San Marcos metro area climbed 4.6 percent from the same period in 2003 to $3.8 billion.

Single family building permits issued increased 68.4 percent during the twelve months ending August 2004, totaling 12,700 compared to the 7,500 recorded a year earlier. The average value of the dwellings built fell to $124,300 in August 2004, down 3.6 percent from $129,000 a year earlier.

The top employers in Austin in 2004 (outside of state government), according to the Greater Austin Chamber of Commerce, are the University of Texas at Austin (20,300 employees), Dell Computer Corporation (16,000 employees), the City of Austin (11,800 employees), the Austin Independent School District (10,400 employees) and Seton Health Care (7,200 employees).

Rounding out the top ten are Motorola (6,600 employees), IBM Corporation (6,300 employees), the H-E-B Grocery Company (6,200 employees), the IRS (5,000) and Austin Community College (4,600 employees).

After slipping in recent years, **DALLAS** was ranked 18th by *Business 2.0* magazine's survey of the hottest job markets in the U.S. in early 2004. Total non-farm employment expanded 0.6 percent, to 1,908,800 from 1,897,300, in the same period.

The unemployment rate fell to 5.8 percent in August 2004 from 7.1 percent in August 2003, placing the Dallas metro area's unemployment rate third highest of the six largest metro areas in Texas behind Houston (6.0 percent) and El Paso (7.2 percent).

Comparing Dallas metro area employment totals between August 2003 and August 2004, the area gained 20,900 jobs in seven sectors and lost 9,400 in four sectors. The information services sector lost 3,300 jobs, professional and business services shed 3,000 jobs, construction employment dipped by 2,100 and other services lost 1,000 jobs.

Between August 2003 and August 2004, a handful of major Dallas metro area employers continued to trim their payrolls. According to the Texas A&M Real Estate

South Congress Avenue with the State Capitol in the background. File photo.

(*The metropolitan statistical area definitions used in this report do not reflect revised geographic designations and definitions provided by the U.S. Office of Management and Budget [June 6, 2003]).

Center, Southwest Airlines eliminated almost 500 jobs in early 2004. Also in 2004, The Management and Training Corporation laid off 400, and The American General Life Companies, The Andrew Corporation, and Americo Services, Inc. each dismissed another 200. Texas Instruments (TI) research, design, and manufacturing employed 9,300 in August 2004, a reduction of 1 percent from the 10,300 employees on TI's payroll in August 2003.

Health services' employment stayed level at Parkland Memorial Hospital (7,400), Baylor University Medical Center (7,400) and University of Texas Southwest Medical Center (6,500).

The largest job gains from August 2003 to August 2004 occurred in government, which added 8,500 jobs. The education and health services sector added 6,900 jobs, and the leisure and hospitality sector added 3,000 jobs, an increase of 1.8 percent.

The headquarters of 17 Fortune 500 companies call Dallas home. These include Affiliated Computer Services, Brinker International, Centex, Dean Foods, Southwest Airlines, and Texas Instruments.

According to Texas A&M University's Real Estate Center, the Dallas metro area issued 16.9 percent more single-family building permits (29,800) during the twelve months ending in August 2004 than in the same measure for August 2003.

In addition, the price of the average Dallas metro area single-family home of $171,400 in August 2004 was down 0.6 percent from the August 2003 average value of $172,400.

Located close to New Mexico along the Texas-Mexico border, the **EL PASO** metro area, with its sister city Juarez, Mexico, represent the largest population center on an international border in the world, with 2.2 million people.

The strong dollar and a slow U.S. recovery battered El Paso's international economy from 2002 through 2003. In its current transition from a goods-producing economy to a service economy, El Paso's financial outlook should improve given its low taxes, abundance of labor, and moderate wage rates.

As of August 2004, El Paso's unemployment rate was 7.2 percent, almost three full percentage points lower than the 10.1 percent reached in August 2003. El Paso lost 1,300 jobs in three sectors from August 2003 to August 2004.

The manufacturing sector declined 3.8 percent (down 1,000 jobs); other services contracted 2.5 percent, (down 200 jobs); and the information sector slipped 1.8 percent, (down 100 jobs).

More than offsetting these losses, the El Paso metro area added 5,300 jobs to its economy in government, education and health services, professional and business services, leisure and hospitality, financial activities, and construction.

Government jobs expanded by 2,500 jobs, or 4.2 percent; education and health services grew by 1,100 jobs, or 3.9 percent; and professional and business services added 800 jobs, up 3.3 percent.

The largest employer in the El Paso area is the Fort Bliss Army Air Defense Artillery Training Center. A study by the University of Texas at El Paso's Institute for Policy and Economic Development noted that about one of every six dollars in El Paso's economy comes from the military, with around $1.7 billion area sales tied to spending by Fort Bliss military personnel and staff.

According to Texas A&M University's Real Estate Center, El Paso's largest five private employers include the Sierra Providence Health Network (3,800), Wal-Mart (3,700), the Las Palmas and Del Sol Regional Healthcare System (2,200), the Echo-star Satellite Corporation call center (2,000) and MCI/GC telemarketing services (1,700). El Paso's largest public employers are the El Paso Independent School District (ISD), the City of El Paso, the Socorro ISD, and the Ysleta ISD.

According to the Greater El Paso Chamber of Commerce, Fortune 500 companies operating in the El Paso region include Boeing, Eureka, General Electric, Hoover, and Leviton.

El Paso apparel manufacturer VF Jeanswear (maker of Lee and Wrangler jeans) is shifting the majority of its operations to Mexico to reduce manufacturing costs. As with cutbacks by apparel manufacturers nationwide, the company has been incrementally reducing its workforce in El Paso, leaving only 400 in El Paso.

Automotive vehicles and components, and electronic parts and equipment dominate El Paso's cross-border trade activity with its sister city Juarez, Mexico. Between 2002 and 2003, the previously depressed maquiladora sector in northern Mexico and the negative impacts from the U.S. economic downturn contributed to reductions in cross-border pedestrian, rail, truck, and car traffic.

El Paso issued 29.9 percent fewer single-family building permits (3,200) during the 12 months ending in August 2004 than in the pervious 12 months. Between August 2003 and August 2004, the metro area's single-family home average value climbed 6.2 percent, to $63,500 from $59,800.

Economic growth is on the upswing in the **FORT WORTH - ARLINGTON** metro area. The unemployment rate in Fort Worth-Arlington dropped from 6.5 percent in August 2003 to 5.4 percent in August 2004.

Total employment in the metro area increased by more than 3,900 jobs between August 2003 and August 2004. The employment sectors posting the highest employment gains were government, which increased 3.3 percent, or 3,500 jobs, and professional business services, which increased by 2.7 percent, or 2,200 jobs.

Despite the growth in total employment, many sectors saw employment declines. The most significant decline was in the construction sector, which lost 2,200 jobs, or 5.1 percent. No other employment sector experienced declines of more than 1.2 percent.

Though manufacturing declined 1.1 percent between August 2003 and August 2004, it remains an important employment sector in the metro area. In August 2004, it contributed 95,000 jobs, or 12.2 percent of the workforce.

Single-family building permits have increased each year since 1998. In the twelve months ending in August 2004, they totaled more than 15,000 units, a 9.2 percent gain from the previous year.

The average value of new dwellings in the MSA was $141,400 in August 2004, up 6.3 percent from $133,000 in August 2003.

Arlington was awarded the 2004 Community Economic Development Award from the Texas Economic Development Council for cities with populations above 100,000. The honor came for helping to retain the local General Motors Arlington assembly plant.

The City of Arlington, the Arlington Chamber of Commerce, and local GM officials worked together to show local support for awarding the next generation of SUVs to the Arlington facility. This local support was a critical element to GM Arlington's business case and the subsequent retention of the GM plant.

The top private employers, according to the Fort-Worth Chamber of Commerce, include American Airlines, Inc. (28,500 employees), Lockheed Martin Tactical Aircraft Systems (16,800 employees), Bell Helicopter – Textron, Inc. (6,000 employees), Radio Shack Corporation (4,300 employees), and Harris Methodist Hospital (3,800).

The **HOUSTON** metropolitan area had an unemployment rate of 6.0 percent in August 2004, lower than the 7.0 percent unemployment rate seen in August 2003. Houston's unemployment rate is the second highest of the state's six major metropolitan areas, behind El Paso's 7.2 percent.

Employment in the Houston metro area increased from August 2003 through August 2004 by more than 24,500 jobs, despite one of the largest business bankruptcies in U.S. and Texas history.

As with the other large metro areas in Texas, Houston's employment gains and losses varied by sector. The largest sector of Houston's economy is trade, transportation and utilities, which accounts for 21 percent of Houston employment, or 441,200 jobs, followed by government with 14.2 percent or 300,000 jobs, and professional business services with 13.9 percent or 294,200 jobs.

The largest job increases occurred in education and health services, up by 9,600 jobs (4.1 percent increase). The lowest job growth came in the trade, transportation and utilities sector, which added only 1,700 jobs (a 0.4 percent gain). Houston's largest job losses came in manufacturing, which fell by 2,100 jobs or 1.1 percent.

According to the Real Estate Center at Texas A&M University, new residential building permits in Houston continue to increase as they have for more than a decade.

New residential building permits issued during the 12 months ending in August 2004 were up 13.1 percent in the Houston metro area, to 37,500, with an average new-home value of $125,600, up 3.2 percent over August 2003.

Houston is home to the Texas Medical Center, the largest medical center in the world, with more than 61,000 employees working in its facilities, serving 5.1 million patients in 2001 and delivering an economic punch of $13.5 billion to the area.

The Port of Houston ranked first among U.S. ports in volume of foreign waterborne commerce. The port ranked sixth largest in the world in total tonnage, handling 190 million tons of cargo in 2003.

Houston is a major corporate center, ranking third among U.S. metro areas in the number of corporate headquarters of Fortune 500 companies.

As the headquarters of 20 Fortune 500 companies in 2004, Houston is universally acknowledged as the nation's energy capital, with more than 5,000 energy-related forms.

The city is a focal point for international trade and banking, a major health care center and one of the nation's largest consumer markets. In addition, the Houston metro area was ranked by the ACCRA Cost of Living Index as having the lowest cost of living and least expensive housing among 25 metro areas with populations of more than 2 million.

Houston's five largest private employers, according to the *Houston Business Journal*, are Administaff (18,200), Continental Airlines (16,000), Memorial Hermann Healthcare System (15,000), M.D. Anderson Cancer Center (13,350), and Halliburton (13,000).

The **SAN ANTONIO** metro area employment forecast is one of the brightest on the U.S. horizon. According to a survey of 16,000 public and private employers in 470 markets coast-to-coast, San Antonio's metro area ranked in the top 10 in 2004. San Antonio also ranked fourth in Inc. magazine's list of "Top Cities to Do Business in America" (March 2004) due to its low cost of living, population growth, diversified economy, and strong military presence.

San Antonio's higher education facilities, strategic location near the border with Mexico, bilingual working population, transportation infrastructure, thriving aerospace, and tourism industries make the area a magnet for businesses and capital investment.

Eight employment sectors witnessed job gains between August 2003 and August 2004. The strongest growth occurred in the professional and business services sector, which added 2,700 jobs, and the education and health services sector, which increased by 2,000 jobs.

In the same period, low mortgage rates stimulated homebuilding and helped create 1,500 jobs in the construction sector. The leisure and hospitality industry added 1,400 jobs; the financial, insurance, and real estate services sector gained 1,000 jobs; and the trade, transportation and utilities industry added 900 jobs. Other services and government generated more than 800 jobs each to the Alamo City's economy.

Only two San Antonio employment industry sectors experienced job losses between 2003 and 2004. Metro area manufacturing lost 900 jobs and the information sector cut 100 jobs. Mining employment was essentially unchanged.

San Antonio's five largest private employers in 2004 ranked by total number of employees are USAA (15,000), H-E-B Grocery Company with 44 stores and 14,500 employees, Methodist Healthcare System (7,200), SBC (6,700) and Administaff, Inc. (4,300).

The metro area's top five largest public employers, measured by employee totals, are Fort Sam Houston (17,500), Kelly USA (12,200 civilian and government), Lackland Air Force Base (10,700), The City of San Antonio (9,800), and Northside Independent School District (8,800).

Sales subject to sales tax in the metro area reached $3.9 billion during the first quarter of 2004, an increase of 6.2 percent above the $3.7 billion for the same quarter of 2003. ☆

Personal Income and Per Capita Income by County, 2003

Below are listed data for 2003 for personal income and per capita income by county. Total income is reported in millions of dollars. The middle column indicates the percent of change in total income from 2002 to 2003.

In the far right column is the county's rank in the state for per capita income. Loving County, a unique case — with a population of less than 60, leads in per capita income with $72,063. Sherman County, at the top of the Panhandle, is second with $43,314.

The lowest per capita income is in Starr County, along the Rio Grande, at $10,805.

Source: Bureau of Economic Analysis, U.S. Department of Commerce.

County	Total Income ($ mil)	% change 02/03	Per capita income	Rank
United States	$9,151,694	3.2	$ 31,472	-
Metropolitan	7,973,539	3.1	33,038	-
Nonmetro	1,178,155	3.9	23,827	-
Texas	$ 642,630	3.0	$ 29,074	-
Metropolitan	577,243	2.9	30,141	-
Nonmetro	65,387	3.6	22,149	-
Anderson	$ 1,052	2.5	$ 18,779	223
Andrews	292	6.8	22,762	138
Angelina	2,073	3.7	25,576	67
Aransas	601	4.6	25,394	70
Archer	249	2.3	27,167	45
Armstrong	57	14.0	27,144	46
Atascosa	825	3.3	19,770	209
Austin	693	2.8	27,493	41
Bailey	149	1.2	22,498	149
Bandera	483	3.1	24,905	81
Bastrop	1,450	3.2	21,692	169
Baylor	86	8.6	21,911	162
Bee	521	4.0	15,695	247
Bell	6,581	6.1	26,412	57
Bexar	40,801	3.9	27,810	37
Blanco	244	2.0	27,473	42
Borden	18	18.9	26,651	55
Bosque	397	1.6	22,310	153
Bowie	2,202	2.9	24,540	88
Brazoria	7,377	2.6	27,985	34
Brazos	3,373	4.3	21,741	166
Brewster	217	2.9	23,440	113
Briscoe	36	3.6	21,626	171
Brooks	128	3.3	16,573	234
Brown	812	2.7	21,376	177
Burleson	375	4.1	22,116	159
Burnet	1,013	5.0	26,099	62
Caldwell	717	2.9	20,175	202
Calhoun	457	2.9	22,351	152
Callahan	290	2.0	22,145	158
Cameron	5,910	4.6	16,308	241
Camp	315	1.4	26,725	54
Carson	162	-0.3	24,829	82
Cass	668	2.9	22,234	156
Castro	334	48.6	42,430	3
Chambers	785	3.1	28,470	30
Cherokee	1,160	2.8	24,341	90
Childress	128	3.4	16,747	233
Clay	273	2.3	24,088	98
Cochran	80	-0.8	23,034	128

County	Total Income ($ mil)	% change 02/03	Per capita income	Rank
Coke	72	-2.8	19,023	218
Coleman	183	-0.2	20,875	186
Collin	23,857	2.9	39,941	4
Collingsworth	88	13.5	28,636	26
Colorado	502	3.5	24,243	94
Comal	2,588	5.0	29,486	20
Comanche	318	-0.2	23,477	111
Concho	63	2.6	16,529	236
Cooke	973	4.2	25,560	68
Coryell	1,539	5.9	20,389	197
Cottle	49	4.0	27,814	36
Crane	78	3.0	20,241	200
Crockett	71	-0.9	18,122	229
Crosby	170	6.4	25,215	75
Culberson	43	-3.1	15,522	248
Dallam	175	4.0	28,615	27
Dallas	83,551	1.5	36,617	6
Dawson	291	6.2	20,042	205
Deaf Smith	428	1.6	23,286	122
Delta	108	2.8	20,091	204
Denton	16,259	3.2	31,841	16
DeWitt	432	3.1	21,399	175
Dickens	44	1.1	16,250	243
Dimmit	168	5.9	16,333	240
Donley	88	-0.5	22,466	150
Duval	233	3.1	18,330	226
Eastland	430	0.3	23,504	110
Ector	2,789	3.7	22,665	144
Edwards	39	2.6	19,338	215
Ellis	3,355	3.1	26,881	51
El Paso	14,667	4.3	20,875	186
Erath	779	-1.5	23,332	119
Falls	346	3.3	19,304	216
Fannin	669	3.4	20,683	191
Fayette	631	1.4	28,200	32
Fisher	96	6.0	23,033	129
Floyd	187	6.1	24,973	80
Foard	36	5.2	23,440	113
Fort Bend	13,812	4.0	32,887	14
Franklin	256	0.3	25,944	63
Freestone	369	4.9	19,903	207
Frio	270	1.9	16,532	235
Gaines	339	9.1	23,506	109
Galveston	8,206	3.2	30,762	18
Garza	102	5.7	20,197	201
Gillespie	609	3.1	27,424	43
Glasscock	34	23.7	25,526	69
Goliad	155	2.8	21,737	167
Gonzales	476	1.3	25,014	79

County	Total Income ($ mil)	% change 02/03	Per capita income	Rank	County	Total Income ($ mil)	% change 02/03	Per capita income	Rank
Gray	580	3.3	26,765	53	Lipscomb	87	8.2	27,963	35
Grayson	2,694	2.7	23,424	115	Live Oak	224	7.5	18,905	219
Gregg	3,321	4.0	29,092	22	Llano	427	3.3	23,622	106
Grimes	468	3.1	18,712	224	Loving	5	7.8	72,063	1
Guadalupe	2,454	5.6	25,302	74	Lubbock	6,271	2.7	25,081	78
Hale	813	3.7	22,848	136	Lynn	158	21.7	25,386	71
Hall	73	6.2	19,392	214	Madison	278	1.4	21,322	178
Hamilton	193	0.6	23,763	104	Marion	203	3.4	18,242	227
Hansford	178	7.3	34,080	11	Martin	107	18.3	23,513	107
Hardeman	104	2.4	23,313	120	Mason	84	3.1	22,303	154
Hardin	1,228	5.6	24,753	83	Matagorda	818	1.3	21,377	176
Harris	130,478	2.4	36,314	7	Maverick	637	6.3	12,774	253
Harrison	1,497	4.9	24,053	99	McCulloch	192	5.9	24,140	96
Hartley	164	12.0	29,735	19	McLennan	5,271	2.9	24,007	100
Haskell	137	9.1	23,940	101	McMullen	24	1.2	27,519	40
Hays	2,705	4.1	23,341	118	Medina	879	4.8	21,147	183
Hemphill	123	9.8	37,096	5	Menard	43	-1.0	18,436	225
Henderson	1,797	2.3	23,218	124	Midland	3,991	3.4	33,578	12
Hidalgo	9,648	6.5	15,184	249	Milam	539	1.1	21,546	173
Hill	745	2.2	21,616	172	Mills	115	1.7	22,728	139
Hockley	518	4.5	22,687	141	Mitchell	154	6.8	16,270	242
Hood	1,290	2.1	28,503	29	Montague	447	3.8	22,983	132
Hopkins	751	2.8	22,987	131	Montgomery	11,052	3.9	32,068	15
Houston	536	3.0	23,121	127	Moore	481	5.3	23,835	102
Howard	722	3.7	21,925	161	Morris	306	2.7	23,145	125
Hudspeth	54	0.0	16,482	237	Motley	27	0.8	20,647	192
Hunt	1,958	5.3	24,318	91	Nacogdoches	1,254	1.2	21,057	184
Hutchinson	608	8.1	26,554	56	Navarro	1,017	2.5	21,463	174
Irion	41	-3.2	23,303	121	Newton	258	3.7	17,360	231
Jack	174	1.0	19,453	211	Nolan	329	2.1	21,683	170
Jackson	321	2.8	22,394	151	Nueces	8,307	4.0	26,368	59
Jasper	779	3.6	21,873	163	Ochiltree	258	9.3	28,814	23
Jeff Davis	45	-4.8	20,154	203	Oldham	49	-1.2	22,661	145
Jefferson	6,743	4.8	27,108	47	Orange	2,144	4.5	25,362	72
Jim Hogg	107	5.7	21,259	179	Palo Pinto	640	1.9	23,409	116
Jim Wells	856	7.0	21,149	182	Panola	524	3.4	22,906	133
Johnson	3,453	2.8	24,728	84	Parker	2,715	2.5	27,782	38
Jones	368	4.8	18,214	228	Parmer	240	4.3	24,264	92
Karnes	249	3.1	16,234	244	Pecos	255	3.9	15,955	245
Kaufman	2,031	3.8	24,720	85	Polk	1,146	2.6	25,174	76
Kendall	871	5.6	33,056	13	Potter	2,836	3.7	24,110	97
Kenedy	12	4.7	28,792	24	Presidio	110	3.1	14,465	250
Kent	19	3.9	23,755	105	Rains	205	4.0	18,896	220
Kerr	1,321	3.5	29,250	21	Randall	2,879	3.4	26,835	52
Kimble	85	0.0	18,889	222	Reagan	61	9.6	19,928	206
King	8	4.6	25,090	77	Real	59	0.0	19,414	213
Kinney	65	2.0	19,419	212	Red River	272	2.2	19,796	208
Kleberg	660	6.7	21,157	181	Reeves	200	-4.9	16,372	239
Knox	88	8.4	22,275	155	Refugio	200	5.7	26,411	58
Lamar	1,118	2.7	22,562	148	Roberts	21	-0.2	25,623	66
Lamb	311	3.3	21,190	180	Robertson	364	5.8	22,778	137
Lampasas	453	5.0	23,446	112	Rockwall	1,868	4.7	34,135	10
La Salle	94	3.4	15,917	246	Runnels	223	2.0	20,362	199
Lavaca	468	4.1	24,656	86	Rusk	1,082	3.2	22,698	140
Lee	379	2.6	23,017	130	Sabine	232	2.2	22,222	157
Leon	366	1.4	22,850	135	San Augustine	183	1.0	20,603	193
Liberty	1,731	2.9	23,358	117	San Jacinto	492	3.1	20,589	194
Limestone	490	4.4	21,737	167	San Patricio	1,530	5.1	22,669	143

County	Total Income ($ mil)	% change 02/03	Per capita income	Rank	County	Total Income ($ mil)	% change 02/03	Per capita income	Rank
San Saba	127	3.4	21,005	185	Upton	70	4.0	21,824	164
Schleicher	54	1.9	19,210	217	Uvalde	540	4.0	20,381	198
Scurry	361	-1.7	22,575	147	Val Verde	883	5.8	18,894	221
Shackelford	86	-0.5	26,260	60	Van Zandt	1,251	1.8	24,604	87
Shelby	587	2.3	22,640	146	Victoria	2,307	0.8	27,015	49
Sherman	137	10.7	43,316	2	Walker	1,112	1.7	17,839	230
Smith	5,229	3.6	28,441	31	Waller	804	3.9	23,244	123
Somervell	189	2.3	25,808	65	Ward	214	2.0	20,727	190
Starr	627	7.7	10,805	254	Washington	891	2.4	28,747	25
Stephens	209	0.0	21,933	160	Webb	3,629	5.5	17,060	232
Sterling	26	-7.4	19,506	210	Wharton	1,000	1.6	24,197	95
Stonewall	40	-2.3	27,238	44	Wheeler	166	17.4	34,441	8
Sutton	92	0.7	22,686	142	Wichita	3,529	3.6	27,527	39
Swisher	228	11.9	28,611	28	Wilbarger	344	1.5	24,247	93
Tarrant	48,347	1.9	31,054	17	Willacy	329	9.8	16,397	238
Taylor	3,262	3.5	26,120	61	Williamson	8,567	6.2	28,178	33
Terrell	27	-8.0	27,007	50	Wilson	831	3.3	23,512	108
Terry	298	8.0	23,782	103	Winkler	141	4.9	20,814	188
Throckmorton	45	1.3	27,078	48	Wise	1,246	3.1	22,898	134
Titus	665	4.8	23,126	126	Wood	820	3.8	20,804	189
Tom Green	2,685	3.2	25,851	64	Yoakum	178	8.7	24,514	89
Travis	29,425	1.9	34,439	9	Young	455	2.8	25,322	73
Trinity	292	3.2	20,538	195	Zapata	179	5.5	13,847	251
Tyler	423	4.5	20,521	196	Zavala	155	10.0	13,304	252
Upshur	807	3.4	21,810	165					

Cost of Living Index for Metro Areas

The comparison standard of all values is for the **United States set at 100**. Data are for the third quarter of 2004. The overall composite is excluding taxes. The column at the far right refers to miscellaneous goods and services.

Metro area	Overall	Groceries	Housing	Utilities	Transport	Health	Goods/ Services
Abilene	87.7	84.7	79.0	88.7	96.8	85.2	93.9
Amarillo	86.8	87.2	83.6	90.9	89.2	88.0	87.7
Austin/Round Rock	94.1	77.8	86.5	88.3	100.2	97.5	106.0
Beaumont/Port Arthur	89.1	94.6	74.8	105.7	102.3	89.3	91.5
Brownsville/Harlingen	87.0	74.7	78.1	87.7	102.4	105.7	93.1
Corpus Christi	85.4	75.9	75.5	102.0	88.7	87.4	92.1
Dallas	93.9	97.1	80.0	98.6	106.4	97.4	99.7
Del Rio	88.4	80.7	66.7	139.2	95.2	99.6	93.9
El Paso	90.6	103.2	80.3	98.9	93.7	103.0	90.3
Fort Worth	92.4	99.8	79.6	100.6	97.3	99.7	96.4
Houston	90.3	86.1	75.9	100.3	100.8	104.3	97.2
Killeen/Temple	84.8	79.9	74.1	94.9	90.5	85.4	91.5
Laredo	83.8	80.3	81.8	81.3	94.9	98.3	82.8
Longview	88.9	85.5	82.9	75.6	92.7	97.6	96.9
Lubbock	87.1	86.5	78.3	81.3	84.8	105.8	94.8
McAllen/Pharr/Edinburg	85.8	80.8	72.6	93.9	90.2	84.9	95.7
Midland	85.4	82.9	75.0	79.8	97.6	96.8	92.2
Odessa	87.7	89.4	78.6	78.9	97.0	99.2	93.3
San Angelo	88.3	86.7	75.8	88.0	95.8	92.3	97.3
San Antonio	95.2	82.7	96.9	75.9	98.4	104.2	101.4
Sherman/Denison	90.7	89.1	77.9	103.9	94.1	103.2	96.5
Texarkana	92.5	95.9	85.7	85.8	91.1	92.9	99.1
Tyler	92.2	86.5	85.4	100.2	92.7	108.8	96.2
Victoria	86.5	77.5	76.9	91.4	89.5	104.2	94.0
Waco	94.7	93.5	85.1	106.3	90.5	91.2	101.8
Wichita Falls	91.0	104.5	79.8	83.0	97.8	94.0	95.4

Source: The Institute for Policy and Economic Development, the University of Texas at El Paso.

Employment in Texas by Industry

Source: Texas Workforce Commission. Additional information available at Web site: www.twc.state.tx.us.

Nonfarm employment in Texas increased to 9,443,600 in January 2005, up from 9,304,200 in January 2004.

The following table shows Texas Workforce Commission estimates of the nonagricultural labor force by industry for January 2004 and 2005. The final column shows the percent change in the number employed.

(in thousands 000)

Industry	2005	2004	Chng.
GOODS PRODUCING	1,570.4	1,566,5	0.2
Mining	151.9	149.3	3.0
Oil & Gas Extraction	63.4	63.6	-0.3
Support Activities	78.5	73.9	6.2
Construction	532.6	534.4	-0.3
Manufacturing	884.0	882.8	0.1
Durable Goods	558.8	550.9	1.4
Wood Products	26.7	25.9	3.1
Furniture/Fixtures	30.3	30.5	-0.7
Primary Metals	25.2	24.0	5.0
Fabricated Metal Industries	108.3	104.4	3.7
Machinery	77.1	75.9	1.6
Computers/Electronics	111.9	111.8	0.1
Electric/Appliance	17.4	17.9	-2.8
Transportation Equipment	84.2	84.0	0.2
Misc. Manufacturing	34.1	33.9	0.6
Non-Durable Goods	325.2	331.9	-2.0
Food	91.8	91.0	0.9
Beverage/Tobacco	10.3	10.4	-1.0
Paper	21.8	23.2	-6.0
Printing	36.2	37.4	-3.2
Petroleum/Coal Products	23.6	24.2	-2.5
Chemicals	72.3	74.9	-3.5
Rubber/Plastics	44.7	44.2	1.1
SERVICE PROVIDING	7,873.2	7,737.7	1.8
Trade/Transportation/Utilities	1,945.4	1,915.0	1.6
Wholesale Trade	462.8	455.0	1.7
Merchants/Durable Goods	266.6	259.3	2.8
Merchants/Non-Durable Goods	152.3	151.7	0.4
Retail Trade	1,086.6	1,069.5	1.6
Building/Garden Supplies	83.4	78.7	6.0
General Merchandise	236.8	228.9	3.5
Food/Beverage Stores	191.3	189.2	1.1
Motor Vehicle/Parts Dealers	148.6	148.7	-0.1
Clothing/Accessories Stores	100.4	99.7	0.7
Furniture	42.3	40.5	4.4
Electronics/Appliances	43.5	41.4	5.1
Gasoline Stations	66.9	67.6	-1.0
Sporting Goods/Books/Music	35.9	37.0	-3.0
Misc. Store Retailers	61.0	61.3	-0.5
Nonstore Retailers	19.7	20.1	-2.0
Transportation/Utilities	396.0	390.5	1.4
Utilities	47.0	47.8	-1.7
Transportation	349.0	342.7	1.8
Air	65.1	65.4	-0.5
Rail	16.8	16.1	4.3
Trucking	100.2	99.5	0.7
Pipeline	11.8	12.7	-7.1
Support Activities	61.1	58.8	3.9
Couriers/Messengers	35.8	35.4	1.1
Warehousing/Storage	37.3	33.7	10.7
Information	225.6	227.6	-0.9
Publishing	49.6	49.3	0.6
Telecommunications	93.8	97.2	-3.5
Internet Providers/Data	35.3	35.9	-1.7
Financial Activities	596.0	586.5	1.6
Finance/Insurance	426.9	419.8	1.7
Credit Intermediation	219.6	213.7	2.8
Securities/Investments	38.4	37.6	2.1
Insurance Carriers	158.2	159.1	-0.6
Real Estate/Rental	169.1	166.7	1.4
Real Estate	110.2	108.9	1.2
Rental/Leasing	58.9	56.0	1.8
Professional Services	1,076.8	1,053.1	2.3
Professional/Scientific/Tech	464.5	462.1	0.5
Management/Enterprises	49.2	47.9	2.7
Administration/Support	563.1	543.1	3.7
Education/Health	1,151.9	1,124.8	2.4
Educational	134.8	131.8	2.3
Health Care	1,017.1	993.0	2.4
Ambulatory	443.5	426.5	4.0
Hospitals	257.7	256.2	0.6
Residential Care	146.8	145.9	0.6
Social Assistance	169.1	164.4	2.9
Leisure/Hospitality	859.0	839.3	2.3
Accommodations	88.7	87.1	1.8
Food/Drinking Places	678.1	665.5	1.9
Amusements/Recreation	64.7	60.6	6.8
Other Services	356.5	351.2	1.5
Repair/Maintenance	101.4	101.2	0.2
Personal/Laundry	94.2	91.8	2.6
Religious/Civic	160.9	158.2	1.7
Total Government	1,662.0	1,640.2	1.3
Federal	181.9	179.2	1.5
State	338.6	333.1	1.7
Local	1,141.5	1,127.9	1.2

Average Hours and Earnings

The following table shows the **average weekly earnings, hours worked per week** and **average hourly wage** in Texas for selected industries in March 2005. Figures are provided by the Texas Workforce Commission.

Industry	Earnings	Hours	Wage
NATURAL RESOURCES	$657.58	42.7	$15.40
Oil/Gas Extraction	591.62	30.2	19.59
Support Activities	713.00	46.0	15.50
MANUFACTURING	553.82	39.7	13.95
Durable Goods	568.43	42.2	13.47
Lumber/Wood Products	401.71	38.7	10.38
Primary Metal	651.79	44.4	14.68
Fabricated Metal Products	604.15	45.7	13.22
Structural Metals	465.25	41.1	11.32
Machinery	541.51	41.4	13.08
Agriculture/Mining	569.38	41.5	13.72
Semiconductor/Electronic	557.15	34.8	16.01
Transportation Equipment	719.71	41.1	16.32
Furniture	411.84	42.9	9.60
Non-Durable Goods	533.16	36.0	14.81
Food Manufacturing	476.14	38.9	12.24
Printing	482.76	36.0	13.41
Chemicals	858.26	43.5	19.73
Plastics/Rubber	467.50	34.4	13.59
TRADE, TRANSPORT., UTILITIES	448.02	34.2	13.10
Wholesale	619.37	39.3	15.76
Electronic/Electical Goods	596.70	45.9	13.00
Motor Vehicle/Parts	615.25	35.4	17.38
Machinery/Supplies	518.20	37.2	13.93
Grocery	555.01	40.9	13.57
Chemical Products	634.92	40.7	15.60
Retail	343.11	30.8	11.14
Automotive Dealers	619.74	33.0	18.78
Building/Garden Supply	359.05	32.7	10.98
Clothing Stores	267.53	26.7	10.02
Food/Beverage	293.88	31.0	9.48
Grocery Stores	271.15	29.0	9.35
Furniture	363.05	28.1	12.95
Electronics/Appliances	485.60	29.7	16.35
Gasoline Stations	291.93	37.0	7.89
Sporting Goods	173.74	23.8	7.30
Office Supplies	291.79	30.3	9.63
Newpapers/Periodicals	467.28	35.4	13.20
Telecommunications	643.59	39.9	16.13
Internet Service Providers	556.12	38.7	14.37
Finance, Depository Insts.	497.62	42.1	11.82

Selected Metro Areas

	Earnings	Hours	Wage
DALLAS-FORT WORTH			
Manufacturing	$ 596.52	39.4	$ 15.14
Durable Goods	666.25	40.1	16.25
Non-Durable Goods	466.82	36.3	12.86
HOUSTON			
Manufacturing	725.92	41.6	17.45
Durable Goods	617.95	42.5	14.54
Non-Durable	873.04	40.4	21.61
SAN ANTONIO			
Manufacturing	413.88	38.5	10.75
Durable Goods	443.39	41.4	10.71
Non-Durable Goods	381.24	35.3	10.80

Top 100 Banks in Texas by Asset Size

Source: Texas Department of Banking, Dec. 31, 2004
Abbreviations: NA, not available; N.A., National Association.

	Name	City	Class	Assets	Loans
				(in thousands 000)	
1	JP Morgan Chase Bank	New York, N.Y.	National	$ 55,646,000	NA
2	Bank of America	Charlotte, N.C.	National	36,393,000	NA
3	Wells Fargo Bank	San Francisco, Calif.	National	22,746,000	NA
4	Treasury Bank	Alexandria, Va.	National	15,245,000	NA
5	Frost National Bank	San Antonio	National	9,998,202	$ 5,114,877
6	International Bank of Commerce	Laredo	State	8,394,373	4,419,130
7	Southwest Bank of Texas, N.A.	Houston	National	7,495,446	4,575,312
8	Compass Bank	Birmingham, Ala.	State	7,032,000	NA
9	Texas State Bank	McAllen	State	5,829,193	3,750,519
10	Comerica Bank	Detroit, Mich.	State	3,549,000	NA
11	Hibernia National Bank	New Orleans, La.	National	3,398,000	NA
12	Sterling Bank	Houston	State	3,346,734	2,338,096
13	Bank of Texas, N.A.	Dallas	National	2,955,213	1,606,133
14	Laredo National Bank	Laredo	National	2,877,712	1,606,591
15	Prosperity Bank	El Campo	State	2,692,610	1,035,513
16	Texas Capital Bank, N.A.	Dallas	National	2,612,495	1,564,578
17	First National Bank	Edinburg	National	2,563,464	1,325,014
18	Plains Capital Bank	Lubbock	State	2,426,358	1,765,222
19	South Trust Bank	Birmingham, Ala.	State	1,966,000	NA
20	American State Bank	Lubbock	State	1,801,367	641,511
21	Regions Bank	Birmingham, Ala.	State	1,789,000	NA
22	Southside Bank	Tyler	State	1,618,734	623,877
23	Amarillo National Bank	Amarillo	National	1,605,726	1,027,193
24	Woodforest National Bank	Houston	National	1,578,790	985,332
25	Broadway National Bank	San Antonio	National	1,540,084	568,828
26	TexasBank	Weatherford	State	1,519,218	1,159,052
27	State National Bank	Lubbock	National	1,350,572	937,784
28	TIB The Independent Bankersbank	Dallas	State	1,316,535	575,996
29	American National Bank of Texas	Terrell	National	1,167,623	610,921
30	Southern National Bank of Texas	Sugar Land	National	1,129,322	598,717
31	Lone Star National Bank	Pharr	National	1,089,207	680,086
32	Northern Trust Bank of Texas, N.A.	Dallas	National	1,012,166	878,824
33	Summit Bank, N.A.	Fort Worth	National	988,710	702,619
34	Legacy Bank	Plano	State	939,401	620,781
35	Inwood National Bank	Dallas	National	936,858	696,615
36	Inter National Bank	McAllen	National	921,395	517,559
37	MetroBank, N.A.	Houston	National	916,067	592,745
38	Moody National Bank	Galveston	National	908,961	234,162
39	North Dallas Bank & Trust Co.	Dallas	State	896,884	298,087
40	State Bank	La Grange	State	886,304	500,232
41	Extraco Banks, N.A.	Temple	National	880,013	534,686
42	City Bank	Lubbock	State	868,206	706,762
43	First Victoria National Bank	Victoria	National	840,763	577,376
44	American Bank of Texas	Sherman	State	810,178	579,372
45	International Bank of Commerce	Brownsville	State	772,457	234,427
46	First Financial Bank, N.A.	Abilene	National	762,941	341,145
47	Century Bank, N.A.	New Boston	National	689,703	478,763
48	Austin Bank, N.A.	Jacksonville	National	676,358	531,016
49	South Texas National Bank	Laredo	National	641,374	292,826
50	American Bank, N.A.	Corpus Christi	National	626,046	449,394
51	First State Bank Central Texas	Temple	State	619,362	440,885
52	Citizens 1st Bank	Tyler	State	614,458	189,855
53	Texas Bank and Trust Co.	Longview	State	613,327	449,534
54	Bank of the West	El Paso	State	598,573	310,629
55	Citizens National Bank	Henderson	National	592,393	258,410
56	Republic National Bank	Houston	National	573,004	402,492
57	First Community Bank, N.A.	Houston	National	569,632	402,228
58	Town North Bank, N.A.	Dallas	National	569,142	294,611
59	Jefferson State Bank	San Antonio	State	559,794	317,645
60	Guaranty Bond Bank	Mount Pleasant	State	541,039	375,585

	Name	City	Class	Assets	Loans
				(in thousands 000)	
61	Bancorp South Bank	Tupelo, Miss.	State	539,000	NA
62	First Bank & Trust East Texas	Diboll	State	536,280	312,713
63	Western National Bank	Odessa	National	523,463	342,108
64	Security State Bank and Trust	Fredericksburg	State	522,910	382,488
65	US Trust Company	Greenwich, Conn.	National	513,000	NA
66	First National Bank Texas	Killeen	National	505,795	224,026
67	Union Planters Bank	Memphis, Tenn.	National	473,000	NA
68	American Bank of Commerce	Wolfforth	State	472,546	360,626
69	Colonial Bank	Montgomery, Ala.	National	472,000	NA
70	FirstBank Southwest, N.A.	Amarillo	National	451,617	269,446
71	Whitney National Bank	New Orleans, La.	National	451,000	NA
72	Alliance Bank	Sulphur Springs	State	418,475	255,498
73	Commerce Bank	Laredo	State	415,462	128,226
74	Central National Bank	Waco	National	414,043	288,609
75	Lubbock National Bank	Lubbock	National	410,412	269,540
76	Independent Bank	McKinney	State	404,077	282,519
77	Citizens National Bank	Waxahachie	National	399,521	331,442
78	North Houston Bank	Houston	State	397,202	344,420
79	First National Bank	Bryan	National	393,501	254,741
80	First State Bank	Uvalde	State	387,029	171,171
81	Herring National Bank	Vernon	National	387,012	292,814
82	Horizon Capital Bank	Webster	State	380,030	297,489
83	First United Bank	Dimmitt	State	378,830	250,649
84	Falcon International Bank	Laredo	State	359,918	265,508
85	Happy State Bank	Happy	State	357,154	215,899
86	West Texas National Bank	Midland	National	352,315	204,185
87	Security State Bank	Pearsall	State	344,909	58,375
88	National Bank	Gatesville	National	343,916	213,523
89	Community Bank	Granbury	State	340,290	238,857
90	Texas First National Bank	Houston	National	338,240	217,842
91	United Central Bank	Garland	State	326,910	260,177
92	First Bank	Creve Coeur, Mo.	State	317,000	NA
93	Worth National Bank	Lake Worth	National	316,953	224,222
94	Community National Bank	Midland	National	315,668	178,510
95	Legend Bank, N.A.	Bowie	National	315,301	199,460
96	International Bank of Commerce	Zapata	State	314,130	103,157
97	San Angelo National Bank	San Angelo	National	312,829	114,937
98	Omnibank, N.A.	Houston	National	306,580	277,687
99	Alamo Bank of Texas	Alamo	State	293,045	208,764
100	Northstar Bank of Texas	Denton	State	292,716	218,728

Deposits and Assets of Insured Commercial Banks by County

Source: Federal Reserve Bank of Dallas as of Dec. 31, 2004.

in thousands of dollars (000)

COUNTY	Banks	Deposits	Assets
Anderson	3	$ 251,590	$ 278,806
Andrews	2	194,090	212,581
Angelina	2	605,017	674,364
Armstrong	1	74,303	84,094
Atascosa	3	163,385	194,401
Austin	4	505,040	587,875
Bailey	2	127,084	144,979
Bandera	1	26,418	29,747
Bastrop	2	290,975	337,665
Baylor	2	70,996	81,775
Bee	2	152,713	173,559
Bell	7	2,004,305	2,404,465
Bexar	8	10,472,486	12,516,387
Blanco	3	222,385	248,111
Bosque	3	183,679	203,011

COUNTY	Banks	Deposits	Assets
Bowie	3	801,317	960,434
Brazoria	6	595,081	695,774
Brazos	2	342,579	407,446
Briscoe	1	31,891	36,974
Brooks	3	102,751	114,799
Brown	2	258,738	302,613
Burleson	2	215,789	238,045
Burnet	3	364,390	425,888
Caldwell	2	144,954	165,362
Calhoun	2	130,011	156,154
Callahan	3	247,189	283,519
Cameron	4	620,816	972,269
Camp	1	181,094	241,216
Carson	1	24,077	26,091
Cass	4	188,078	221,090
Castro	1	319,447	378,830
Chambers	3	140,684	160,121

Total bank assets in Dallas County were $13.6 billion, down from $44.1 billion in 2000. In Bexar County (San Antonio), assets were $12.5 billion, down from $31 billion, and, in Harris County (Houston), assets were $18.5 billion, up from $13.6 billion.

Besides the major metropolitan areas, two counties on the border had assets over $10 billion, Webb County (Laredo) and Hidalgo County (McAllen).

No independent banks were reported in 30 counties: Aransas, Archer, Borden, Brewster, Cochran, Falls, Gaines, Garza, Glasscock, Hardin, Hartley, Hays, Hudspeth, Kendall, Kenedy, King, Kinney, Lipscomb, Loving, Marion, Maverick, Moore, Oldham, Randall, Reagan, San Augustine, Somervell, Upton, Willacy and Winkler.

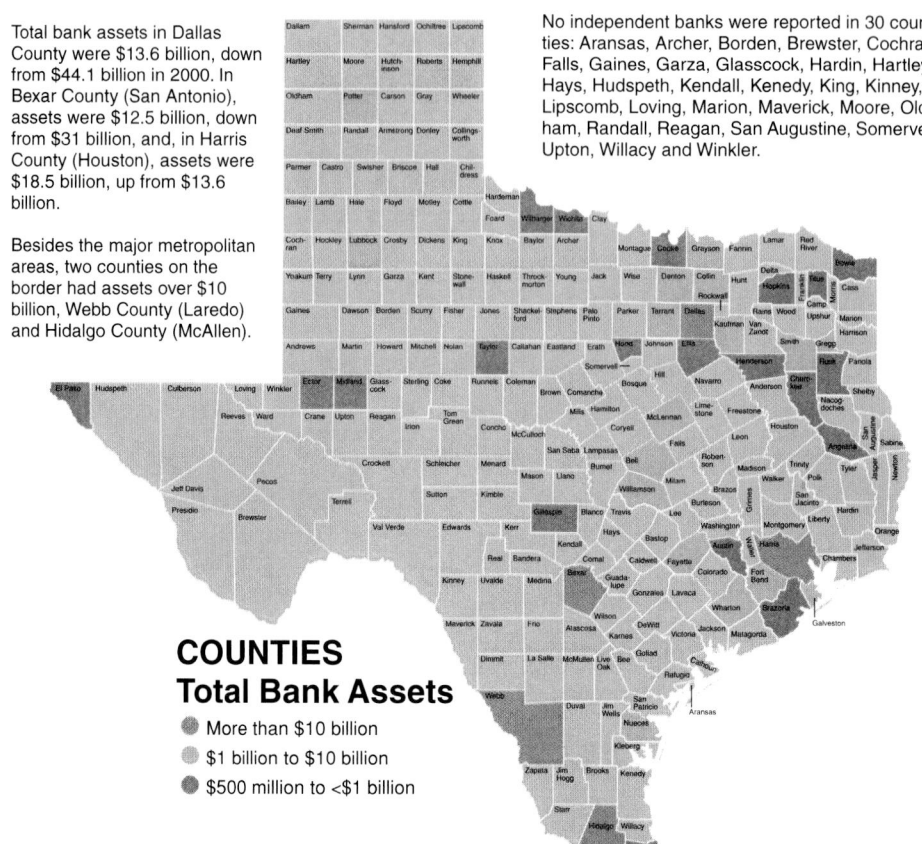

COUNTIES
Total Bank Assets

- More than $10 billion
- $1 billion to $10 billion
- $500 million to <$1 billion

COUNTY	Banks	Deposits	Assets
Cherokee	2	665,622	743,217
Childress	1	52,688	59,873
Clay	1	58,606	66,244
Coke	2	48,093	61,673
Coleman	3	104,895	130,337
Collin	9	1,706,716	1,987,055
Collingsworth	2	145,451	159,003
Colorado	4	284,571	337,416
Comal	1	137,695	159,356
Comanche	2	159,845	184,528
Concho	2	86,941	98,215
Cooke	3	482,876	578,847
Coryell	3	341,268	376,767
Cottle	1	41,727	47,263
Crockett	2	270,812	316,722
Crosby	2	130,476	148,067
Culberson	1	20,604	25,168
Dallam	1	47,525	51,552
Dallas	38	9,952,370	13,649,010
Dawson	2	249,159	284,506
Deaf Smith	2	149,842	172,542
Delta	3	45,962	52,971
Denton	8	977,216	1,086,131
DeWitt	2	180,964	209,310
Dickens	1	26,898	29,123

COUNTY	Banks	Deposits	Assets
Dimmit	1	31,547	37,100
Donley	1	$ 26,989	$ 33,700
Duval	2	72,239	80,098
Eastland	2	90,652	102,869
Ector	4	731,980	943,341
Edwards	1	37,880	42,785
Ellis	6	581,352	644,711
El Paso	3	743,818	854,543
Erath	4	414,907	466,113
Fannin	5	247,984	299,130
Fayette	6	1,004,998	1,250,213
Fisher	1	33,994	39,115
Floyd	1	68,404	79,108
Foard	1	18,933	21,864
Fort Bend	1	886,536	1,129,322
Franklin	1	88,753	111,893
Freestone	2	151,572	173,325
Frio	2	186,330	393,302
Galveston	6	1,461,859	1,638,359
Gillespie	1	429,616	522,910
Goliad	1	39,545	42,503
Gonzales	2	234,912	258,449
Gray	1	10,888	12,357
Grayson	6	1,030,132	1,160,690
Gregg	7	1,008,425	1,172,918

COUNTY	Banks	Deposits	Assets
Grimes	3	180,914	206,214
Guadalupe	4	391,548	480,306
Hale	2	192,763	261,991
Hall	2	70,084	79,621
Hamilton	2	56,466	62,062
Hansford	3	157,673	180,294
Hardeman	3	78,984	90,658
Harris	30	13,997,719	18,511,973
Harrison	2	76,033	90,065
Haskell	1	52,628	58,514
Hemphill	2	144,187	159,097
Henderson	3	464,421	526,945
Hidalgo	10	9,340,457	11,167,345
Hill	3	122,733	148,322
Hockley	2	83,805	92,079
Hood	4	783,209	866,738
Hopkins	2	554,850	661,649
Houston	5	264,521	318,521
Howard	2	246,408	279,367
Hunt	1	31,920	35,125
Hutchinson	1	33,032	38,267
Irion	1	124,179	139,127
Jack	2	208,310	225,191
Jackson	1	40,687	43,825
Jasper	1	164,879	188,340
Jeff Davis	1	46,561	50,793
Jefferson	1	99,157	124,569
Jim Hogg	2	124,616	147,905
Jim Wells	1	117,176	155,236
Johnson	3	377,741	425,000
Jones	2	109,644	127,666
Karnes	3	179,426	203,177
Kaufman	2	1,004,316	1,215,387
Kent	1	34,197	36,625
Kerr	2	268,526	289,520
Kimble	2	64,565	73,470
Kleberg	1	$ 157,357	$ 187,836
Knox	1	60,671	65,935
Lamar	4	361,432	434,733
Lamb	3	111,787	132,225
Lampasas	1	82,825	95,619
La Salle	1	27,516	31,304
Lavaca	2	209,944	244,348
Lee	1	74,475	102,443
Leon	4	213,655	243,906
Libery	3	248,589	303,114
Limestone	3	187,878	206,826
Live Oak	2	160,009	181,637
LLano	2	151,765	170,008
Lubbock	11	6,499,985	7,897,402
Lynn	2	80,901	92,397
McCulloch	2	132,420	150,913
McLennan	10	1,478,832	1,685,273
McMullen	1	31,023	34,224
Madison	1	144,068	237,508
Martin	1	50,706	59,361
Mason	2	67,702	87,187
Matagorda	1	38,078	42,550
Medina	7	357,738	402,383

COUNTY	Banks	Deposits	Assets
Menard	2	43,641	49,306
Midland	3	713,836	798,103
Milam	3	364,714	412,893
Mills	1	120,904	136,188
Mitchell	2	70,768	81,976
Montague	2	314,004	348,515
Montgomery	2	268,240	305,098
Morris	3	156,925	183,699
Motley	1	10,862	12,206
Nacogdoches	1	$ 253,343	$ 288,555
Navarro	5	228,786	272,764
Newton	1	94,183	110,014
Nolan	3	212,801	243,854
Nueces	5	1,022,973	1,129,760
Ochiltree	1	63,012	71,831
Orange	1	76,409	83,505
Palo Pinto	4	253,761	286,298
Panola	2	302,340	365,182
Parker	3	358,712	398,170
Parmer	2	147,266	175,571
Pecos	3	132,834	150,558
Polk	3	391,231	462,863
Potter	3	1,737,232	2,092,447
Presidio	2	57,057	63,990
Rains	1	68,922	77,561
Real	1	28,136	31,687
Red River	1	17,647	19,810
Reeves	1	87,239	98,414
Refugio	2	74,983	87,604
Roberts	1	23,594	25,940
Robertson	1	168,030	189,891
Rockwall	1	36,748	40,587
Runnels	4	140,204	156,688
Rusk	3	687,373	775,181
Sabine	1	46,066	52,602
San Jacinto	2	79,977	87,462
San Patricio	2	104,768	116,322
San Saba	1	38,397	45,066
Schleicher	1	36,399	42,624
Scurry	2	183,559	202,007
Shackelford	1	209,072	237,225
Shelby	3	$ 271,645	$ 304,199
Sherman	1	126,681	141,266
Smith	5	1,519,128	2,582,670
Starr	1	52,002	60,832
Stephens	1	55,983	64,357
Sterling	1	32,347	39,017
Stonewall	1	21,679	32,382
Sutton	1	117,662	129,542
Swisher	2	319,418	383,185
Tarrant	24	3,940,945	4,595,922
Taylor	3	742,915	837,751
Terrell	1	15,607	23,620
Terry	1	98,096	117,285
Throckmorton	1	19,368	21,491
Titus	2	501,310	615,525
Tom Green	2	396,599	464,872
Travis	3	137,832	160,108
Trinity	3	81,523	92,401

COUNTY	Banks	Deposits	Assets
Tyler	1	89,469	113,582
Upshur	3	328,674	371,962
Uvalde	2	365,051	421,311
Val Verde	1	12,794	15,205
Van Zandt	5	$ 233,029	$ 264,455
Victoria	1	727,182	840,763
Walker	2	293,991	326,860
Waller	1	61,571	69,919
Ward	1	179,223	199,874
Washington	4	230,256	275,469
Webb	5	9,182,601	12,688,839
Wharton	5	2,775,623	3,192,749
Wheeler	1	41,272	43,529

COUNTY	Banks	Deposits	Assets
Wichita	5	653,278	739,700
Wilbarger	3	491,337	603,286
Williamson	10	915,915	1,023,927
Wilson	1	23,271	27,865
Wise	3	223,594	252,563
Wood	4	291,360	349,418
Yoakum	1	16,707	19,135
Young	5	310,021	363,257
Zapata	2	278,292	385,926
Zavala	1	51,961	61,000
Total 2004	639	$ 122,928,270	$ 151,461,211

Texas Bank Resources and Deposits—1905-2004

On Dec. 31, 2004, Texas had a total of 639 national and state banks, the lowest number since 1906. In 1986, the number of independent banks in the state peaked at 1,972. In 2004, the total assets were $151.4 billion. The peak for total assets was in 1997 with $235 billion.

Source: Federal Reserve Bank of Dallas.

Date	National Banks			State Banks			Combined Total		
	No. Banks	Assets (add 000)	Deposits (add 000)	No. Banks	Assets (add 000)	Deposits (add 000)	No. Banks	Assets (add 000)	Deposits (add 000)
Sept. 30, 1905	440	$ 189,484	$ 101,285	29	$ 4,341	$ 2,213	469	$ 193,825	$ 103,498
Oct. 31, 1906	483	221,574	116,331	136	19,322	13,585	619	240,896	129,916
Dec. 3, 1907	521	261,724	141,803	309	34,734	20,478	830	296,458	162,281
Nov. 27, 1908	535	243,240	115,843	340	40,981	27,014	875	284,221	142,857
Dec. 31, 1909	523	273,473	139,024	515	72,947	51,472	1,038	346,420	190,496
Nov. 10, 1910	516	293,245	145,249	621	88,103	59,766	1,137	381,348	205,015
Dec. 5, 1911	513	313,685	156,083	688	98,814	63,708	1,201	412,499	219,791
Nov. 26, 1912	515	352,796	179,736	744	138,856	101,258	1,259	491,652	280,994
Oct. 21, 1913	517	359,732	183,623	832	151,620	101,081	1,349	511,352	284,704
Dec. 31, 1914	533	377,516	216,953	849	129,053	73,965	1,382	506,569	290,648
Dec. 31, 1915	534	418,094	273,509	831	149,773	101,483	1,365	567,867	374,992
Dec. 27, 1916	530	567,809	430,302	836	206,396	160,416	1,366	774,205	590,718
Dec. 31, 1917	539	679,316	531,066	874	268,382	215,906	1,413	947,698	746,972
Dec. 31, 1918	543	631,978	431,612	884	259,881	191,500	1,427	891,859	623,112
Dec. 31, 1919	552	965,855	777,942	948	405,130	336,018	1,500	1,370,985	1,113,960
Dec. 29, 1920	556	780,246	564,135	1,031	391,127	280,429	1,587	1,171,373	844,564
Dec. 31, 1921	551	691,087	501,493	1,004	334,907	237,848	1,555	1,025,994	739,341
Dec. 29, 1922	557	823,254	634,408	970	338,693	262,478	1,527	1,161,947	896,886
Sept. 14, 1923	569	860,173	648,954	950	376,775	306,372	1,519	1,236,948	955,326
Dec. 31, 1924	572	999,981	820,676	933	391,040	322,392	1,505	1,391,021	1,143,068
Dec. 31, 1925	656	1,020,124	832,425	834	336,966	268,586	1,490	1,357,090	1,101,011
Dec. 31, 1926	656	1,020,113	820,778	782	290,554	228,741	1,438	1,310,667	1,049,519
Dec. 31, 1927	643	1,134,595	938,129	748	328,574	267,559	1,391	1,463,168	1,205,688
Dec. 31, 1928	632	1,230,469	1,017,168	713	334,870	276,875	1,345	1,565,339	1,294,043
Dec. 31, 1929	609	1,124,369	897,538	699	332,534	264,013	1,308	1,456,903	1,161,551
Dec. 31, 1930	560	1,028,420	826,723	655	299,012	231,909	1,215	1,327,432	1,058,632
Dec. 31, 1931	508	865,910	677,307	594	235,681	172,806	1,102	1,101,591	850,113
Dec. 31, 1932	483	822,857	625,586	540	208,142	148,070	1,023	1,030,999	773,653
Dec. 30, 1933	445	900,810	733,810	489	185,476	132,389	934	1,086,286	866,199
Dec. 31, 1934	456	1,063,453	892,264	460	197,969	148,333	916	1,261,422	1,040,597
Dec. 31, 1935	454	1,145,488	1,099,172	442	205,729	162,926	896	1,351,217	1,172,098
June 30, 1936	456	1,192,845	1,054,284	426	228,877	169,652	882	1,421,722	1,223,936
Dec. 31, 1937	453	1,343,076	1,194,463	415	217,355	177,514	868	1,560,431	1,371,977
Sept. 28, 1938	449	1,359,719	1,206,882	406	217,944	170,286	855	1,577,663	1,377,168
Dec. 31, 1939	445	1,565,108	1,409,821	395	235,467	201,620	840	1,800,575	1,611,441
Dec. 31, 1940	446	1,695,662	1,534,702	393	227,866	179,027	839	1,923,528	1,713,729
Dec. 31, 1941	444	1,975,022	1,805,773	391	312,861	269,505	835	2,287,883	2,075,278
Dec. 31, 1942	439	2,696,768	2,525,299	391	417,058	353,109	830	3,113,826	2,878,408
Dec. 31, 1943	439	3,281,853	3,099,964	391	574,463	536,327	830	3,856,316	3,636,291

Date	National Banks			State Banks			Combined Total		
	No. Banks	Assets (add 000)	Deposits (add 000)	No. Banks	Assets (add 000)	Deposits (add 000)	No. Banks	Assets (add 000)	Deposits (add 000)
Dec. 31, 1944	436	4,092,473	3,891,999	398	780,910	738,779	834	4,873,383	4,630,778
Dec. 31, 1945	434	5,166,434	4,934,773	409	998,355	952,258	843	6,164,789	5,887,031
Dec. 31, 1946	434	4,883,558	4,609,538	418	1,019,369	964,938	852	5,902,927	5,574,476
Dec. 31, 1947	437	5,334,309	5,039,963	436	1,149,887	1,087,347	873	6,484,196	6,127,310
Dec. 31, 1948	437	5,507,823	5,191,334	444	1,208,884	1,137,259	881	6,716,707	6,328,593
Dec. 31, 1949	440	5,797,407	5,454,118	446	1,283,139	1,203,244	886	7,080,546	6,657,362
Dec. 31, 1950	442	6,467,275	6,076,006	449	1,427,680	1,338,540	891	7,894,955	7,414,546
Dec. 31, 1951	443	6,951,836	6,501,307	453	1,571,823	1,473,569	896	8,523,659	7,974,876
Dec. 31, 1952	444	7,388,030	6,882,623	457	1,742,270	1,631,757	901	9,130,300	8,514,380
Dec. 31, 1953	443	7,751,667	7,211,162	460	1,813,034	1,696,297	903	9,564,701	8,907,459
Dec. 31, 1954	441	8,295,686	7,698,690	465	1,981,483	1,851,724	906	10,277,169	9,550,414
Dec. 31, 1955	446	8,640,239	7,983,681	472	2,087,066	1,941,706	918	10,727,305	9,925,387
Dec. 31, 1956	452	8,986,456	8,241,159	480	2,231,497	2,067,927	932	11,217,953	10,309,086
Dec. 31, 1957	457	8,975,321	8,170,271	486	2,349,935	2,169,898	943	11,325,256	10,340,169
Dec. 31, 1958	458	9,887,737	9,049,580	499	2,662,270	2,449,474	957	12,550,007	11,499,054
Dec. 31, 1959	466	10,011,949	9,033,495	511	2,813,006	2,581,404	977	12,824,955	11,614,899
Dec. 31, 1960	468	10,520,690	9,560,668	532	2,997,609	2,735,726	1,000	13,518,299	12,296,394
Dec. 30, 1961	473	11,466,767	10,426,812	538	3,297,588	3,009,499	1,011	14,764,355	13,436,311
Dec. 28, 1962	486	12,070,803	10,712,253	551	3,646,404	3,307,714	1,037	15,717,207	14,019,967
Dec. 30, 1963	519	12,682,674	11,193,194	570	4,021,033	3,637,559	1,089	16,703,707	14,830,753
Dec. 31, 1964	539	14,015,957	12,539,142	581	4,495,074	4,099,543	1,120	18,511,031	16,638,685
Dec. 31, 1965	545	14,944,319	13,315,367	585	4,966,947	4,530,675	1,130	19,911,266	17,846,042
Dec. 31, 1966	546	15,647,346	13,864,727	591	5,332,385	4,859,906	1,137	20,979,731	18,724,633
Dec. 31, 1967	542	17,201,752	15,253,496	597	6,112,900	5,574,735	1,139	23,314,652	20,828,231
Dec. 31, 1968	535	19,395,045	16,963,003	609	7,107,310	6,489,357	1,144	26,502,355	23,452,360
Dec. 31, 1969	529	19,937,396	16,687,720	637	7,931,966	7,069,822	1,166	27,869,362	23,757,542
Dec. 31, 1970	530	22,087,890	18,384,922	653	8,907,039	7,958,133	1,183	30,994,929	26,343,055
Dec. 31, 1971	530	25,137,269	20,820,519	677	10,273,200	9,179,451	1,207	35,410,469	29,999,970
Dec. 31, 1972	538	29,106,654	23,892,660	700	12,101,749	10,804,827	1,238	41,208,403	34,697,487
Dec. 31, 1973	550	32,791,219	26,156,659	716	14,092,134	12,417,693	1,266	46,883,353	38,574,352
Dec. 31, 1974	569	35,079,218	28,772,284	744	15,654,983	13,758,147	1,313	50,734,201	42,530,431
Dec. 31, 1975	584	39,138,322	31,631,199	752	17,740,669	15,650,933	1,336	56,878,991	47,282,132
Dec. 31, 1976	596	43,534,570	35,164,285	761	19,846,695	17,835,078	1,357	63,381,265	52,999,363
Dec. 31, 1977	604	49,091,503	39,828,475	773	22,668,498	20,447,012	1,377	71,760,001	60,275,487
Dec. 31,1978	609	56,489,274	44,749,491	786	25,987,616	23,190,869	1,395	82,476,890	67,940,360
Dec. 31,1979	615	65,190,891	50,754,782	807	30,408,232	26,975,854	1,422	95,599,123	77,730,636
Dec. 31,1980	641	75,540,334	58,378,669	825	35,186,113	31,055,648	1,466	110,726,447	89,434,317
Dec. 31, 1981	694	91,811,510	68,750,678	829	42,071,043	36,611,555	1,523	133,882,553	105,362,233
Dec. 31, 1982	758	104,580,333	78,424,478	841	48,336,463	41,940,277	1,599	152,916,796	120,364,755
Dec. 31, 1983	880	126,914,841	98,104,893	848	55,008,329	47,653,797	1,728	181,923,170	145,758,690
Dec. 31, 1984	999	137,565,365	105,862,656	855	60,361,504	52,855,584	1,854	197,926,869	158,718,240
Dec. 31, 1985	1,058	144,674,908	111,903,178	878	64,349,869	56,392,634	1,936	209,024,777	168,295,812
Dec. 31, 1986	1,077	141,397,037	106,973,189	895	65,989,944	57,739,091	1,972	207,386,981	164,712,280
Dec. 31, 1987	953	135,690,678	103,930,262	812	54,361,514	47,283,855	1,765	190,052,192	151,214,117
Dec. 31, 1988	802	130,310,243	106,740,461	690	40,791,310	36,655,253	1,492	171,101,553	143,395,714
Dec. 31, 1989	687	133,163,016	104,091,836	626	40,893,848	36,652,675	1,313	174,056,864	140,744,511
Dec. 31, 1990	605	125,808,263	103,573,445	578	45,021,304	40,116,662	1,183	170,829,567	143,690,107
Dec. 31, 1991	579	123,022,314	106,153,441	546	46,279,752	41,315,420	1,125	169,302,066	147,468,861
Dec. 31, 1992	562	135,507,244	112,468,203	529	40,088,963	35,767,858	1,091	175,596,207	148,236,061
Dec. 31, 1993	502	139,409,250	111,993,205	510	44,566,815	39,190,373	1,012	183,976,065	151,183,578
Dec. 31, 1994	481	140,374,540	111,881,041	502	47,769,694	41,522,943	983	188,144,234	153,403,984
Dec. 31, 1995	456	152,750,093	112,557,468	479	49,967,946	42,728,454	935	202,718,039	155,285,922
Dec. 31, 1996	432	152,299,695	122,242,990	445	52,868,263	45,970,674	877	205,167,958	168,213,664
Dec. 31, 1997	417	180,252,942	145,588,677	421	54,845,186	46,202,808	838	235,098,128	191,791485
Dec. 31, 1998	402	128,609,813	106,704,893	395	50,966,996	42,277,367	797	179,576,809	148,982,260
Dec. 31, 1999	380	128,878,607	99,383,776	373	52,266,148	42,579,986	753	181,144,755	141,963,762
Dec. 31, 2000	358	112,793,856	88,591,657	351	53,561,550	43,835,525	709	166,355,406	132,427,182
Dec. 31, 2001	342	85,625,768	72,812,548	344	59,047,520	47,843,799	686	144,673,288	120,656,347
Dec. 31, 2002	332	95,308,420	79,183,418	337	62,093,220	49,715,186	669	157,401,640	128,898,604
Dec. 31, 2003	316	75,003,613	62,567,943	337	61,448,617	49,790,333	653	136,452,230	112,358,276
Dec. 31, 2004	311	$ 82,333,800	$ 67,977,669	328	$ 69,127,411	$ 54,950,601	639	$151,461,211	$122,928,270

Texas State Banks

Consolidated Statement, Foreign and Domestic Offices, as of Dec. 31, 2004

Source: Federal Reserve Bank of Dallas

Number of Banks	311
In thousands of dollars (000)	
Assets	
Cash and balances due from banks:	
Non-interest-bearing balances and currency and coin	$ 2,385,054
Interest-bearing balances	678,818
Held-to-maturity securities	4,923,221
Available-for sale securities	15,347,573
Federal funds sold in domestic offices	1,908,929
Securities purchases under agreements to resell	0
Loans and lease financing receivables:	
Loans and leases held for sale	389,193
Loans and leases, net of unearned income	39,617,110
Less: allowance for loan and lease losses	513,658
Loans and leases, net	39,103,452
Trading Assets	37,047
Premises and fixed assets	1,519,582
Other real estate owned	84,096
Investments in unconsolidated subsidiaries and associated companies	6,659
Customers liability on acceptances outstanding	1,447
Intangible assets:	
Goodwill	848,060
Other intangible assets	176,464
Other assets	1,717,822
Total Assets	**$ 69,127,411**
Liabilities	
Deposits:	
In domestic offices	$ 54,950,601
Non-interest-bearing	12,492,045
Interest-bearing	42,458,555
In foreign offices, edge & agreement subsidiaries and IBF's	122,865
Non-interest-bearing	0
Interest-bearing	122,865
Federal funds purchased and securities sold under agreements to repurchase:	
in domestic offices	903,744
securities sold under agreement to repurchase	1,001,786
Trading Liabilities	0
Other borrowed money (mortgages/leases)	4,824,409
Banks' liability on acceptances executed and outstanding	1,447
Subordinated notes and debentures	48,386
Other liabilities	422,118
Total Liabilities	**$ 62,275,355**
Minority interest in consolidated subsidiaries	1,064
Equity Capital	
Perpetual preferred stock	525
Common stock	458,735
Surplus (exclude surplus related to preferred stock)	3,799,057
Retained earnings	2,587,711
Accumulated other comprehensive income	6,696
Other equity capital components	-1,733
Total Equity Capital	**$ 6,850,991**
Total liabilities, minority interest and equity capital	**$ 69,127,411**

Texas National Banks

Consolidated Statement, Foreign and Domestic Offices, as of Dec. 31, 2004

Source: Federal Reserve Bank of Dallas

Number of Banks	328
In thousands of dollars (000)	
Assets	
Cash and balances due from banks:	
Non-interest-bearing balances and currency and coin	$ 3,357,266
Interest-bearing balances	835,398
Held-to-maturity securities	2,335,877
Available-for sale securities	19,925,134
Federal funds sold in domestic offices	3,704,168
Securities purchases under agreements to resell	363,525
Loans and lease financing receivables:	
Loans and leases held for sale	548,071
Loans and leases, net of unearned income	46,951,792
Less: allowance for loan and lease losses	612,610
Loans and leases, net	46,339,182
Trading Assets	92,753
Premises and fixed assets	1,749,208
Other real estate owned	93,704
Investments in unconsolidated subsidiaries and associated companies	19,607
Customers liability on acceptances outstanding	12,604
Intangible assets:	
Goodwill	777,010
Other intangible assets	155,817
Other assets	2,024,481
Total Assets	**$ 82,333,800**
Liabilities	
Deposits:	
In domestic offices	$ 67,977,669
Non-interest-bearing	17,069,338
Interest-bearing	50,908,333
In foreign offices, edge & agreement subsidiaries and IBF's	764,766
Non-interest-bearing	0
Interest-bearing	764,766
Federal funds purchased and securities sold under agreements to repurchase:	
in domestic offices	583,305
securities sold under agreement to repurchase	1,889,229
Trading Liabilities	4,124
Other borrowed money (mortgages/leases)	2,485,241
Banks' liability on acceptances executed and outstanding	12,604
Subordinated notes and debentures	150,000
Other liabilities	496,173
Total Liabilities	**$74,363,106**
Minority interest in consolidated subsidiaries	4,982
Equity Capital	
Perpetual preferred stock	910
Common stock	509,892
Surplus (exclude surplus related to preferred stock)	3,302,897
Retained earnings	4,199,434
Accumulated other comprehensive income	-44,581
Other equity capital components	-2,840
Total Equity Capital	**$ 7,965,712**
Total liabilities, minority interest and equity capital	**$ 82,333,800**

Texas Credit Unions

Source: Texas Credit Union League and the National Credit Union Administration.

There are **640** credit unions in Texas, and 7,126,831 credit union members. As of June 2005, share (savings) accounts stood at $40.5 billion, and loans amounted to $31.6 billion.

Nationally, there are approximately 10,000 credit unions with $628 billion in assets. They serve some 84 million people.

Credit unions are chartered at federal and state lev-els. The **National Credit Union Administration** (NCUA) is the regulatory agency for the federal chartered credit unions in Texas. The **Texas Credit Union Department**, Austin, is the regulatory agency for the state-chartered credit unions.

The **Texas Credit Union League** has been the state association for federal and state chartered credit unions since October 1934. The league's address is 4455 LBJ Freeway Ste. 909, Farmers Branch 75244-5998.

They also can be reached at (469) 385-6400, Fax 385-6505 or (800) 442-5762. Their Web site address is www.tcul.coop. ☆

Savings and Loan Associations in Texas

For the purpose of this table, this section includes all thrifts that are not also classified as banks under federal law: that is, it includes federal savings and loan associations, federal savings banks and state-chartered savings and loan associations. *Source: Texas Savings and Loan Department.*

Year ending	Number of Institutions	Total Assets	*Mortgage Loans	†Cash	†Investment Securities	Deposits	FHLB/ Borrowed Money	‡Net Worth
					in thousands of dollars (000)			
Dec. 31, 2004	20	$ 51,000,806	$ 40,740,030	$ 6,648,858	. . .	$ 26,526,138	$ 12,786,086	$ 3,647,046
Dec. 31, 2003	21	45,941,356	16,840,610	17,362,664	. . .	23,954,623	10,725,209	3,130,442
Dec. 31, 2002	24	43,940,058	31,604,285	4,900,880	. . .	23,264,510	11,662,118	3,189,629
Dec. 31, 2001	24	42,716,060	35,823,258	9,542,688	. . .	22,182,152	15,531,159	3,608,222
Dec. 31, 2000	25	55,709,391	43,515,610	1,512,444	. . .	28,914,234	17,093,369	4,449,097
Dec. 31, 1999	25	45,508,256	40,283,186	2,615,072	. . .	26,369,005	14,790,241	3,802,977
Dec. 31, 1998	30	40,021,239	35,419,110	5,236,596	. . .	21,693,469	15,224,654	3,101,795
Dec. 31, 1997	32	40,284,148	33,451,365	4,556,626	. . .	21,854,620	15,190,014	3,089,458
Dec. 31, 1996	37	54,427,896	27,514,639	5,112,995	. . .	28,053,292	20,210,616	4,345,257
Dec. 31, 1995	45	52,292,519	27,509,933	5,971,364	. . .	28,635,799	15,837,632	3,827,249
Dec. 31, 1994	50	50,014,102	24,148,760	6,790,416	. . .	29,394,433	15,973,056	3,447,110
Dec. 31, 1993	62	42,983,595	14,784,215	10,769,889	. . .	25,503,656	13,356,018	2,968,840
Dec. 31, 1992	64	47,565,516	14,137,191	14,527,573	. . .	33,299,278	10,490,144	2,917,881
Dec. 31, 1991	80	53,500,091	15,417,895	11,422,071	. . .	41,985,117	8,189,800	2,257,329
Dec. 31, 1990§	131	72,041,456	27,475,664	20,569,770	. . .	56,994,387	17,738,041	-4,566,656
Conservatorship	51	14,952,402	6,397,466	2,188,820	. . .	16,581,525	4,304,033	-6,637,882
Privately Owned	80	57,089,054	21,078,198	18,380,950	. . .	40,412,862	13,434,008	2,071,226
Dec. 31, 1989§	196	90,606,100	37,793,043	21,218,130	. . .	70,823,464	27,158,238	-9,356,209
Conservatorship	81	22,159,752	11,793,445	2,605,080	. . .	25,381,494	7,103,657	-10,866,213
Privately Owned	115	68,446,348	25,999,598	18,613,050	. . .	45,441,970	20,054,581	1,510,004
Dec. 31, 1988	204	110,499,276	50,920,006	26,181,917	. . .	83,950,314	28,381,573	-4,088,355
Dec. 31, 1987	279	99,613,666	56,884,564	12,559,154	. . .	85,324,796	19,235,506	-6,677,338
Dec. 31, 1986	281	96,919,775	61,489,463	9,989,918	. . .	80,429,758	14,528,311	109,807
Dec. 31, 1985	273	91,798,890	60,866,666	10,426,464	. . .	72,806,067	13,194,147	3,903,611
Dec. 31, 1980	318	34,954,129	27,717,383	3,066,791	. . .	28,439,210	3,187,638	1,711,201
Dec. 31, 1975	303	16,540,181	13,367,569	167,385	$ 1,000,095	13,876,780	919,404	914,502
Dec. 31, 1970	271	7,706,639	6,450,730	122,420	509,482	6,335,582	559,953	531,733
Dec. 31, 1965	267	5,351,064	4,534,073	228,994	230,628	4,631,999	286,497	333,948
Dec. 31, 1960	233	$ 2,508,872	$ 2,083,066	$ 110,028	$ 157,154	$ 2,238,080	$ 48,834	$ 166,927

Texas Savings Banks

The savings bank charter was approved by the Legislature in 1993 and the first savings bank was chartered in 1994. Savings banks operate similarly to savings and loans associations in that they are housing-oriented lenders. Under federal law a savings bank is categorized as a commercial bank and not a thrift. Therefore savings-bank information is also reported with state and national-bank information. *Source: Texas Savings and Loan Department.*

Year ending	Number of Institutions	Total Assets	*Mortgage Loans	†Cash	†Investment Securities	Deposits	FHLB/ Borrowed Money	‡Net Worth
					in thousands of dollars (000)			
Dec. 31, 2004	22	$ 12,981,650	$ 6,035,081	$ 1,654,978	. . .	$ 8,377,409	$ 3,000,318	$1,482,078
Dec. 31, 2003	23	17,780,413	8,396,606	3,380,565	. . .	11,901,441	3,315,544	2,422,317
Dec. 31, 2002	24	15,445,211	7,028,139	3,147,381	. . .	10,009,861	3,422,600	1,910,660
Dec. 31, 2001	25	11,956,074	5,845,605	1,305,731	. . .	8,742,372	1,850,076	1,270,273
Dec. 31, 2000	25	11,315,961	9,613,164	514,818	. . .	8,644,826	1,455,497	1,059,638
Dec. 31, 1999	28	13,474,299	8,870,291	4,101,480	. . .	7,330,776	4,822,372	1,188,852
Dec. 31, 1998	23	12,843,828	7,806,738	193,992	. . .	7,299,636	4,477,546	1,067,977
Dec. 31, 1997	17	7,952,703	6,125,467	892,556	. . .	5,608,429	1,615,311	745,515
Dec. 31, 1996	15	7,872,238	6,227,811	856,970	. . .	5,329,919	1,930,378	611,941
Dec. 31, 1995	13	7,348,647	5,644,591	1,106,557	. . .	4,603,026	2,225,793	519,827
Dec. 31, 1994	8	$ 6,347,505	$ 2,825,012	$ 3,139,573	. . .	$ 3,227,886	$ 2,628,847	$ 352,363

* Beginning in 1982, net of loans in process.
† Beginning in 1979, cash and investment securities data combined.
‡ Net worth includes permanent stock and paid-in surplus general reserves, surplus and undivided profits.
§ In 1989 and 1990, the Office of Thrift Supervision, U.S. Department of the Treasury, separated data on savings and loans (thrifts) into two categories: those under the supervision of the Office of Thrift Supervision (Conservatorship Thrifts) and those still under private management (Privately Owned).

Insurance in Texas

Source: 2004 Annual Report, Texas Department of Insurance

The **Texas Department of Insurance** reported that on Aug. 31, 2004, there were **2,727** firms licensed to handle insurance business in Texas, down from 2,778 in 2000. The total includes **789** Texas firms and **1,938** out-of-state companies.

The former **Robertson Law**, enacted in 1907 and repealed in 1963, encouraged the establishment of many Texas insurance firms. It required life insurance companies operating in the state to invest in Texas three-fourths of all reserves held for payment of policies written in the state. Many out-of-state firms withdrew from Texas. Later many companies re-entered Texas and the law was liberalized and then repealed.

Until 1993, the State Board of Insurance adminis-

tered legislation relating to the insurance. This agency was established in 1957, following discovery of irregularities in some firms. It succeeded two previous regulatory groups, established in 1913 and changed in 1927.

Under terms of sunset legislation passed by the 73rd Legislature in the spring of 1993, most of the board's authority transferred on Sept. 1, 1993, to the **Commissioner of Insurance** appointed by the governor for a two-year term in each odd-numbered year and confirmed by the Texas Senate.

The new law permitted the board to continue its authority over the area of rates, policy forms and related matters until Aug. 31, 1994. On Nov. 18, 1993, however, the board voted unanimously to turn over full authority to the commissioner as of Dec. 16, 1993.

Companies in Texas

The following table shows the number and kinds of insurance companies licensed in Texas on Aug. 31, 2004:

Type of Insurance	Texas	Out-of-State	Total
Stock Life	121	493	614
Mutual Life	3	41	44
Stipulated Premium Life	36	0	36
Non-profit Life	0	1	1
Stock Fire	2	6	8
Stock Fire and Casualty	98	976	774
Mutual Fire and Casualty	5	53	58
Stock Casualty	9	127	136
Mexican Casualty	0	10	10
Lloyds	71	0	71
Reciprocal Exchanges	10	15	25
Fraternal Benefit Societies	9	26	35
Titles	4	25	29
Non-profit Legal Services	3	0	3
Health Maintenance	48	2	50
Risk Retention Groups	1	0	1
Multiple Employers Welfare Arrang.	7	0	7
Joint Underwriting Associations	3	3	6
Third Party Administrators	278	458	736
Workers' Comp. Self	1	0	1
Continuing Care Retirement Communities	19	2	21
Total	**728**	**1,936**	**2,666**
Statewide Mutual Assessment	1	0	1
Local Mutual Aid Associations	3	0	3
Burial Associations	2	0	2
Exempt Associations	10	0	10
Non-profit Hospital Service	4	0	4
County Mutual Fire	24	0	24
Farm Mutual Fire	17	0	17
Total	**61**	**0**	**61**
Grand Total	**789**	**1,938**	**2,727**

Premium Income and Losses Paid, 2003

(Texas business only)	Texas Companies	Out-of-State Companies
Legal Reserve Life Insurance Companies		
Life premiums	$ 733,335,324	$ 6,483,577,574
Claims & benefits paid	1,503,316,177	14,441,915,203
Accident & health premiums	694,205,758	11,313,060,604
Accident & health loss paid	522,433,063	8,200,105,824
Mutual Fire & Casualty Companies		
Premiums	$ 959,302,648	$ 3,486,117,176
Losses	283,797,803	2,569,296,568
Lloyds Insurance		
Premiums	$ 4,775,827,953	. . .
Losses	2,929,246,770	. . .
Reciprocal Insurance Companies		
Premiums	$ 806,084,362	$ 712,934,857
Losses	430,980,709	504,515,129
Fraternal Benefit Societies		
No. Life Certificates issued	9,515	19,446
Amount issued 2003	$ 192,057,948	$ 1,529,389,319
Considerations from members:		
Life	89,888,010	294,776,776
Accident & Health	0	25,967,384
Benefits paid to members:		
Life	33,709,373	190,385,996
Accident & Health	0	12,783,987
Amount of insurance in force	2,410,070,386	16,912,759,906
Title Guaranty Companies		
Premiums	$ 443,695,652	$ 1,082,561,684
Paid Losses	6,286,012	27,753,153
Stock Fire, Stock Casualty, and Stock Fire & Casualty Companies		
Premiums	$ 1,744,569,124	$11,015,948,975
Losses	1,207,440,99	6,610,023,126

Top Health Maintenance Insurers, 2003

Company	% of market
1. Aetna Health	13.25
2. Southwest Texas HMO	13.01
3. Pacificare of Texas	10.57
4. Humana Health	9.75
5. Amerigroup Texas	8.63
6. Cigna Healthcare	6.36
7. Scott and White	5.76
8. United Healthcare	5.30

Top Homeowner Insurers, 2003

Company	% of market
1. State Farm Lloyds	29.57
2. Allstate Texas Lloyds	15.85
3. Farmers Insurance Exchange	5.49

Construction Industry

The following information was furnished by Liz Moucka, editor of the Texas Contractor, *from official sources.*

Although office, manufacturing, and warehousing construction fell into a slump after the turn of the century, infrastructure construction remained strong and has grown, thanks in great part to new housing developments that continue to spring up by the dozens in sub-

urbs around Texas' major metropolitan areas.

In addition to streets and utilities that must be installed prior to development, new neighborhoods act as magnets for school and light commercial construction.

Adding to the increased dollar volume are skyrocketing steel, cement and fuel prices.

Comparison of Construction Awards by Years, 1960-2004

Year	Total Awards	Year	Total Awards	Year	Total Awards
2004	$ 13,014,672,068	1989	$ 4,176,355,929	1974	$ 2,396,488,520
2003	12,897,933,353	1988	3,562,336,666	1973	1,926,778,365
2002	7,297,909,363	1987	4,607,051,270	1972	1,650,897,233
2001	6,067,377,351	1986	4,636,310,266	1971	1,751,331,262
2000	5,232,788,835	1985	4,806,998,065	1970	1,458,708,492
1999	4,941,352,362	1984	3,424,721,025	1969	1,477,125,397
1998	4,951,275,224	1983	4,074,910,947	1968	1,363,629,304
1997	5,088,017,435	1982	3,453,784,388	1967	1,316,872,998
1996	4,383,336,574	1981	3,700,112,809	1966	1,421,312,029
1995	4,771,332,413	1980	3,543,117,615	1965	1,254,638,051
1994	4,396,199,988	1979	3,353,243,234	1964	1,351,656,302
1993	5,394,342,718	1978	2,684,743,190	1963	1,154,624,634
1992	4,747,666,912	1977	2,270,788,842	1962	1,132,607,006
1991	3,926,799,801	1976	1,966,553,804	1961	988,848,239
1990	3,922,781,630	1975	1,737,036,682	1960	1,047,943,630

Approved Texas Construction, 2005

Federal:	
General Services Administration	$ 7,300,000
Federal Aviation Administration	102,250,000
Department of Veterans Affairs	13,450,000
NASA	3,800,000
Department of Defense	373,400,000
Rural Utilities Service	103,000,000
U.S. Department of Agriculture	123,000,000
Department of Energy	7,400,000
Natural Res. Conserv. Service	6,100,000
Department of Justice	1,600,000
Department of the Interior	1,075,000
Federal Highway Administration	2,423,027,000
Total Federal	**$ 3,165,402,000**
State:	
Texas Dept. of Transportation	$ 3,420,000,000
State Agencies	205,235,000
State Colleges and Universities	1,060,250,000
Total State	**$ 4,685,485,000**
Water Projects:	
Corps of Engineers	$ 93,200,000
Bureau of Reclamation	405,000
River Authorities	910,500,000
Clean Water StateRevolvingFund	463,300,000
Drinking WaterState Revolving Fund	92,700,000
Total Water Projects	**$ 1,560,105,000**
Cities:	
Schools	$ 304,530,000
New Streets, Bridges	921,413,000
Street Maintenance	316,030,200
Waterworks, Sewers	2,190,900,000
City Buildings	465,511,500
Total Cities	**$ 4,198,384,700**
Counties:	
New Roads	$ 413,060,000
Road Maintenance	533,850,300
Machinery Purchases	51,900,000
County Buildings	114,369,000
Total Counties	**$ 1,113,179,300**
Grand Total	**$14,722,556,000**

Analysis of Awards

The following table classifies awards in Texas for the year 2004, as compared with 2003.

Category	2004		2003	
	No.	Amount	No.	Amount
Civil Engineering Awards	2,612	$ 9,192,449,587	2,634	$ 9,500,819,326
Non-Residential Awards	1,212	3,822,222,481	1,034	3,397,114,027
Total	**3,824**	**$ 13,014,672,068**	**3,668**	**$ 12,897,933,353**

CIVIL ENGINEERING AWARDS

Type of Project	2004		2003	
	No.	Amount	No.	Amount
Highways, Streets, Airports	1,743	$ 5,391,290,036	1,726	$ 5,310,267,000
Waterworks, Sewers, etc.	580	2,747,709,551	632	3,477,862,500
Irrigation, Drainage, etc.	289	1,053,450,000	276	712,689,826
Total	**2,612**	**$ 9,192,449,587**	**2,186**	**$ 9,500,819,326**

NON-RESIDENTIAL CONSTRUCTION AWARDS

Type of Project	2004		2003	
	No.	Amount	No.	Amount
Educational Bldgs	314	$ 1,719,640,210	305	$ 1,567,350,225
Churches, Theaters, etc.	56	54,116,000	54	52,328,400
Hospitals, Hotels, Motels	82	842,423,140	73	780,645,000
Public Bldgs	212	609,590,093	195	562,455,540
Commercial/ Industrial	548	596,453,038	407	434,334,862
Total	**1,212**	**$3,822,222,481**	**1,034**	**$ 3,397,114,027**

Foreign Trade Zones in Texas

Source: The International Trade Reporter, *copyright 1979 by the Bureau of National Affairs, Inc., Washington, D.C.*

Foreign-trade-zone status endows a domestic site with certain customs privileges, causing it to be considered outside customs territory and therefore available for activities that might otherwise be carried on overseas.

Operated as public utilities for qualified corporations, the zones are established under grants of authority from the Foreign-Trade Zones board, which is chaired by the U.S. Secretary of Commerce.

Zone facilities are available for operations involving storage, repacking, inspection, exhibition, assembly, manufacturing and other processing.

A foreign trade zone is especially suitable for export processing or manufacturing operations when foreign components or materials with a high U.S. duty are needed to make the end product competitive in markets abroad.

Additional information on the zones is available from each zone manager; from U.S. customs offices; from the executive secretary of the Foreign-Trade Zones Board, Dept. of Commerce, Washington, D.C., or from the nearest Dept. of Commerce district office.

Source: U.S. Department of Commerce

There were 29 Foreign Trade Zones in Texas as of January 2005.

Amarillo, FTZ 252
City of Amarillo
600 S. Tyler Ste. 1503
Amarillo 79101

Austin, FTZ 183
FTZ of Central Texas Inc.
101 E. Old Settlement Rd., Ste. 200
Round Rock 78664

Beaumont, FTZ 115
Port Arthur, FTZ 116
Orange, FTZ 117
FTZ of Southeast Texas Inc.
P.O. Drawer 2297
Beaumont 77704

Brownsville, FTZ 62
Brownsville Navigation District
1000 Foust Road
Brownsville 78521

Calhoun/Victoria Counties FTZ 155
Calhoun-Victoria FTZ Inc.
P.O. Drawer 397
Point Comfort 77978

Corpus Christi, FTZ 122
Port of Corpus Christi Authority
P.O. Box 1541
Corpus Christi 78403

Dallas/Ft.Worth, FTZ 39
D/FW International Airport Board
P.O. Drawer 619428
D/FW Airport 75261

Dallas/Fort Worth, FTZ 168
FTZ Operating Company of Texas
P.O. Box 742916
Dallas 75374

Eagle Pass, FTZ 96
Maverick County Development Corp.
P.O. Box 3693
Eagle Pass 78853

Edinburg, FTZ 251
City of Edinburg
P.O. Box 1079
Edinburg 78540

Ellis County, FTZ 113
Trade Zone Operations Inc.
1500 N. Service Road, Highway 67
Midlothian 76065

El Paso, FTZ 68
City of El Paso
5B Butterfield Trail Blvd.
El Paso 79906

El Paso, FTZ 150
Westport Economic Dev. Corp.
4401 N. Mesa, Ste. 201
El Paso 79982

Fort Worth, FTZ 196
Alliance Corridor Inc.
13600 Heritage Pkwy., Ste. 200
Fort Worth 76177

Freeport, FTZ 149
Brazos River Harbor Navigation Dist.
Box 615
Freeport 77542

Galveston, FTZ 36
Port of Galveston
P.O. Box 328
Galveston 77553

Gregg County, FTZ 234
Gregg County
Route 3 Hwy 322
Longview 75603

Harris County, FTZ 84
Port of Houston Authority
111 East Loop North
Houston 77029

Laredo, FTZ 94
Laredo International Airport
5210 Bob Bullock Loop
Laredo 78041

Liberty County, FTZ 171
Liberty Co. Economic Development
Corp.
P.O. Box 857
Liberty 77575

McAllen, FTZ 12
McAllen Economic Development
Corp.
6401 South 33rd Street
McAllen 78501

Midland, FTZ 165
City of Midland
c/o Midland International Airport
P.O. Box 60305
Midland 79711

Orange (see Beaumont)

Port Arthur (see Beaumont)

San Antonio, FTZ 80
City of San Antonio
P.O. Box 839966
San Antonio 78283

Starr County, FTZ 95
Starr County Industrial Foundation
P.O. Box 502
Rio Grande City 78582

Texas City, FTZ 199
Texas City Harbor FTZ Corp.
P.O. Box 2608
Texas City 77592

Waco, FTZ 246
City of Waco
c/o Greater Waco Chamber
of Commerce
900 Washington Ave., Ste. 501
Waco 76701

Weslaco, FTZ 156
City of Weslaco
500 South Kansas
Weslaco 78596

Foreign Consulates in Texas

In the list below, these abbreviations appear after of the city: (CG) Consulate General; (C) Consulate; (VC) Vice Consulate. The letter "H" before the designation indicates honorary status. Compiled from "Foreign Consular Offices in the United States," U.S. Dept. of State, Spring/Summer 2004, and recent Internet sources.

Albania: Houston (HC); 526 Kingwood Dr., Ste. 401, Kingwood, 77339. (281) 548,4740.

Angola: Houston (CG); 3040 Post Oak Blvd., Ste. 780, 77056. (713) 212-3840.

Argentina: Houston (CG); 3050 Post Oak Blvd., Ste. 1625, 77056. (713) 871-8935.

Australia: Houston (HC); 4623 Feagan St., 77007. (713) 782-6009.

Austria: Houston (HCG); 1717 Bissonet St., Ste 306, 77005. (713) 526-0127.

Bangladesh: Houston (HCG); 35 N. Wynden Dr., 77056. (713) 621-8462.

Barbados: Houston (HC); 25226 Sandi Lane, Katy, 77494. (281) 392-9794.

Belgium: Houston (HCG); 2009 Lubbock St., 77019. (713) 426-3933.
Fort Worth (HC); 6201 South Fwy., 76134. (817) 551-8389.
San Antonio (HC); 105 S. St. Mary's St., 78205. (210) 271-8820.

Belize: Houston (HCG); 7101 Breen, 77086. (713) 999-4484.
Dallas (HC); 1315 19th St., Ste. 2A, Plano, 75074. (972) 579-0070.

Bolivia: Houston (HCG); 800 Wilcrest, Ste. 100, 77042 (713) 977-2344.
Dallas (HC); 1881 Sylvan Ave., Ste. 110, 75208. (214) 571-6131.

Botswana: Houston (HC); 4615 Post Oak Pl. Ste.104, 77027. (713) 622-1900.

Brazil: Houston (CG); 1233 W. Loop S., Ste. 1150, 77027. (713) 961-3063.

Cameroon: Houston (HC); 2711 Weslayan, 77027. (713) 499-3502.

Canada: Dallas (CG); 750 N. Saint Paul, Ste. 1700, 75201. (214) 922-9806.
Houston (C); 5847 San Felipe St., Ste. 1700, 77057. (713) 821-1440.

Chile: Houston (CG):1360 Post Oak Blvd., Ste. 1330, 77056; (713) 963-9066.
Dallas (HC); 3500 Oak Lawn, Apt. 200, 75219. (214) 528-2731.

China: Houston (CG); 3417 Montrose, Ste. 700, 77006. (713) 524-0780.

Colombia: Houston (CG); 5851 San Felipe, Ste. 300, 77057; (713) 527-8919.

Costa Rica: Houston (CG); 3000 Wilcrest, Ste. 112, 77042. (713) 266-0484.
Austin (C); 1730 E. Oltorf, Unit 320, 78741. (512) 445-0023.
Dallas (C); 7777 Forrest Lane, Ste. B-445, 75230. (972) 566-7020.
San Antonio (CG); 6836 San Pedro, Ste. 206-B, 78216. (210) 824-8474.

Cyprus: Houston (HCG); 320 S. 66th St., 77011. (713) 928-2264.

Czech Republic: Dallas (HC); 7979 Inwood Rd., 75209. (214) 351-2074.
Houston (HC); 4544 Post Oak Pl., Ste. 378, 77027. (713) 629-6963.

Denmark: Dallas (HC); 2100 McKinney Ave., Ste. 700, 75201. (214) 661-8399.
Houston (HC); 4545 Post Oak Place, Ste. 347, 77027. (713) 622-9018.

Dominican Republic: Houston (C); 3300 S. Gessner, Ste. 113, 77024. (713) 266-0165.

Ecuador: Houston (CG); 4200 Westheimer, Ste. 218, 77027. (713) 622-1787.
Dallas (HC); 7510 Acorn Lane, Frisco, 75034. (972) 712-9107.

Egypt: Houston (CG); 3 Post Oak Central, 1990 Post

Oak Blvd., Ste. 2180, 77056. (713) 961-4915.

El Salvador: Dallas (CG); 1555 W. Mockingbird Lane, Ste. 216, 75235.
Houston (CG); 6420 Hillcroft, Ste. 100, 77081. (713) 270-6239.

Ethiopia: Houston (HC); 9301 Southwest Freeway, Ste. 250, 77074. (713) 271-7567.

Finland: Dallas (HC); 1445 Ross Ave., Ste. 3200, 75202. (214) 855-4715.
Houston (HC); 14 Greenway Plaza, Ste. 22R, 77046. (713) 552-1722.

France: Houston (CG); 777 N. Post Oak Blvd. Ste. 600, 77056. (713) 572-2799.
Austin (HC); 515 Congress Ave, 78701. (512) 480-5605.
Dallas (HC); 6370 LBJ Freeway, Ste. 272, 75240. (972) 789-9305.
San Antonio (HC); Route 1, 78109. Box 229, 78109. (210) 659-3101.

Georgia: Houston (HC); 3040 Post Oak Blvd., Ste. 700, 77056. (281) 633-3500.

Germany: Houston (CG); 1330 Post Oak Blvd., Ste. 1850, 77056. (713) 627-7770.
Corpus Christi (HC); 615 N. Upper Broadway, Ste.630,78477. (361) 884-7766.
Dallas (HC); 4265 Kellway, Addison, 75001. (972) 239-0788.
San Antonio (HC); 310 S. St. Mary's, 78205. (210) 226-1788.

Ghana: Houston (HC); 3434 Locke Lane, 77027. (713) 960-8806.

Greece: Houston (CG); 520 Post Oak Blvd., Ste. 310, 77027. (713) 840-7522.

Guatemala: Houston (CG); 3013 Fountain View, Ste 210, 77057. (713) 953-9531.
San Antonio (HC); 4840 Whirlwind, 78217.

Guyana: Houston (HC); 1810 Woodland Park Dr., 77077. (713) 497-4466.

Haiti: Houston (HC); 3535 Sage Rd., 77027.

Honduras: Houston (CG); 4151 Southwest Fwy., Ste. 700, 77027. (713) 622-4572.

Hungary: Houston (HC); 2800 Post Oak Blvd., Ste. 5230, 77056. (713) 529-2727.

Iceland: Dallas (HC); 17910 Windflower, Apt. 2201, 75252. (214) 540-9135.
Houston (HC); 2348 W. Settler's Way, The Woodlands, 77380. (713) 367-2777.

India: Houston (CG); 1990 Post Oak Blvd., Ste 600, 77056. (713) 626-2148.

Indonesia: Houston (CG); 10900 Richmond Ave., 77042.

Ireland: Houston (HC); 2630 Sutton Ct., 77027. (713) 961-8115.

Israel: Houston (CG); 24 Greenway Plz., Ste. 1500, 77046. (713) 627-3780.

Ivory Coast: Houston (HCG); 412 Hawthorne, 77006. (713) 529-4928.

Italy: Houston (CG); 1300 Post Oak Blvd., Ste. 660, 77056. (713) 850-7520.
Dallas (HC); 6255 W. Northwest Hwy., Apt. 304, 75225. (214) 368-4113.

Jamaica: Houston (HC); 7737 Southwest Fwy., Suite 580, 77074. (713) 541-3333.
Dallas (HC); 3068 Forrest, 75234. (972) 396-7969.

Japan: Houston (CG);1000 Louisiana, Ste. 2300, 77002. (713) 652-2977.
Dallas (HCG); 5819 Edinburgh St., 75252. (972) 713-8683.

Jordan: Houston (HC); 723 Main St., Ste. 408, 77002. (713) 224-2911.

Korea: Houston (CG); 1990 Post Oak Blvd., Ste. 1250, 77056. (713) 961-0186.

Dallas (HC); 13111 N. Central Expy., 75243. (214) 454-1112.

Kyrgyzstan: Houston (HCG); 2302 Greens Ct., Richmond, 77469. (281) 920-1841.

Latvia: Houston (HC); 5847 San Felipe, Ste. 3400, 77057. (713) 785-0807.

Lebanon: Houston (HC); 1701 Hermann Dr., Ste. 1305, (713) 526-1141.

Lesotho: Austin (HC); 7400 Valburn Dr., 78731.

Luxembourg: Fort Worth (HC); 48 Valley Ridge Rd, 76107. (817) 738-8600.

Malaysia: Houston (HC); 600 Travis St., Ste. 1600, 77002. (713) 227-8008.

Malta: Houston (HCG); 1221 Lamar, Ste. 1313, 77010. (713) 654-7900.

Dallas (HC); PO Box 830688, SM-24, Richardson, 75083. (972) 883-4785.

Mexico: Austin (CG); 800 Brazos St. Ste. 330, 78701.
Brownsville (C); 724 E. Elizabeth, 78520. (956) 542-4431.
Corpus Christi (C); 800 N. Shoreline, Ste. 410, 78401.
Dallas (CG); 8855 N. Stemmons Fwy, 75247. (214) 522-9740.
Del Rio (C); 2398 Spur 239, 78840. (830) 774-5031.
Eagle Pass (C); 140 Adams St., 78852. (830) 773-9255.
El Paso (CG); 910 E. San Antonio St., 79901. (915) 533-3644.
Fort Worth (HC); 813 W. Magnolia Ave., 76104, 76104. (817) 870-2270.
Houston (CG); 4507 San Jacinto St., 77004. (713) 271-6800. **Tourism Office:** 2707 N. Loop, Ste. 450, 77008.
Laredo (CG); 1612 Farragut St., 78040. (956) 723-6369.
McAllen (C); 600 S. Broadway, 78501. (956) 686-0243.
Midland (C); 511 W. Ohio St., Ste. 121, 79701.
Presidio (C); 6717 Kelley Addition 1 Hwy, 79845. (915) 229-2788.
San Antonio (CG); 127 Navarro St., 78205. (210) 227-9145. **Commercial Affairs Office**: 203 S. Saint Mary's St., Ste. 450, 78213.

Monaco: Dallas (HC); 8350 N. Central Expressway, Ste. 1900, 75206. (214) 234-4124.

Mongolia: Houston (HCAgent); 1221 Lamar, Ste. 1201, 77010. (713) 759-1922.

Netherlands: Houston (CG); 2200 Post Oak Blvd., Ste. 610, 77056. (713) 622-8000.

New Zealand: Houston (HC); 246 Warrenton Dr., 77024. (713) 973-8680.

Nicaragua: Houston (CG); 8989 Westheimer, Ste. 103, 77063. (713) 789-2762.

Norway: Houston (CG); 2777 Allen Parkway, Ste. 1185, 77019. (713) 521-2900.
Dallas (HC); 5500 Caruth Haven Lane, 75225. (214) 750-4222.

Panama: Houston (CG); 24 Greenway Plaza, Ste. 1307, 77046. (713) 622-4451.

Peru: Houston (CG); 5177 Richmond Ave., Ste. 695, 77056. (713) 355-9571.

Philippines: Houston (HCG); 8 Greenway Plaza, Ste. 930, 77046. (713) 877-6700.

Poland: Houston (HC); 35 Harbor View, Sugar Land, 77479. (281) 565-1507.

Portugal: Houston (HC); 4544 Post Oak Place, Ste. 350, 77027. (713) 759-1188.

Qatar: Houston (CG); 1990 Post Oak Blvd, Ste. 810, 77056. (713) 355-8221.

Romania: Dallas (HC); 220 Ross Ave., Ste. 2200, 75201. (214) 740-8608.
Houston (HC); 4265 San Felipe, Ste. 220, 77027. (713) 629-1551.

Russia: Houston (CG); 2500 McCue St., 77056. (713) 840-9757.

Saint Kitts/Nevis: Dallas (HC); 6336 Greenville Ave., 75206.

Saudi Arabia: Houston (CG); 5718 Westheimer, Ste. 1500, 77057. (713) 785-5577.

Slovenia: Houston (HC); 2925 Briarpark, 7 Floor, 77042. (713) 430-7350.

Spain: Houston (CG); 1800 Bering Dr., Ste. 660, 77057. (713) 783-6200.
Corpus Christi (HC); 7517 Yorkshire Blvd., 78413 (361) 994-7517.
Dallas (HC); 5499 Glen Lakes Dr., Ste. 209, 75231. (214) 373-1200.
El Paso (HC); 420 Golden Springs Dr., 79912. (915) 534-0677.
San Antonio (HC); 8350 Delphian, 78148.

Sweden: Houston (HC); 2909 Hillcroft, Ste. 515, 77057. (713) 953-1417.
Dallas: (HC); 100 Cresent Ct., Ste. 880, 75201, (214) 220-9910.

Switzerland: Houston (CG); 1200 Smith St., Ste. 1040, 77002. (713) 650-0000.
Dallas (HC); 2651 N. Harwood, Ste. 455, 75201. (214) 965-1025.

Syria: Houston (HCG); 5433 Westheimer Rd., Ste. 1020, 77056. (713) 622-8860.

Thailand: Houston (HCG); 600 Travis St., Ste. 2800, 77002. (713) 229-8733.
Dallas (HCG); 1717 Main St., Ste. 4100, 75201.
El Paso (HCG); 4401 N. Mesa, Ste. 204, 79902. (915) 533-5757.

Trinidad/Tobago: Houston (HC); 1330 Post Oak Blvd., 77056. (713) 840-1100.

Tunisia: Dallas (HC); 4227 N. Capistrano Dr., 75287. (972) 267-4191.

Turkey: Houston (CG); 1990 Post Oak Central, Ste.1300, 77056. (713) 622-5849.

Ukraine: Houston (HC); 2934 Fairway Dr., Sugar Land, 77478. (281) 242-2842.

United Kingdom: Houston (CG); 1000 Louisiana St., Ste. 1900, 77002. (713) 659-6270.
Dallas (C); 2911 Turtle Creek, Ste. 940, 75219. (214) 637-3600.

Venezuela : Houston (CG); 2925 Briarpark Dr., Ste. 900, 77027. (713) 961-5141. ☆

A container ship moves through the Houston Ship Channel in Galveston Bay. File photo.

Tonnage Handled by Texas Ports, 1994–2003

Table below gives consolidated tonnage (**x1,000**) handled by Texas ports. All figures are in short tons (2,000 lbs.). Note that " - " indicates no commerce was reported, "0" means tonnage reported was less than 500 tons. *Source: Corps of Engineers, U.S. Army*

Port	2003	2002	2001	2000	1999	1998	1997	1996	1995	1994
Beaumont	87,541	85,911	79,131	76,894	69,406	60,052	48,665	35,705	20,937	21,201
Brownsville	3,731	4,739	4,100	3,268	2,487	2,799	2,284	2,401	2,656	3,396
Corpus Christi	77,216	71,939	77,576	81,164	78,003	86,140	86,806	80,436	70,218	76,060
Freeport	30,537	27,164	30,143	28,966	28,076	29,014	26,281	24,571	19,662	17,450
Galveston	7,545	9,136	9,038	10,402	10,336	11,049	10,126	11,641	10,465	10,257
Houston	190,923	177,561	185,050	186,567	158,828	169,070	165,456	148,183	135,231	143,663
Matagorda Chl. (Port Lavaca)	11,673	9,590	9,086	10,552	9,078	8,040	9,429	9,151	9,237	7,380
Port Arthur	27,170	22,676	22,802	20,524	18,308	29,557	37,318	37,158	49,800	45,586
Sabine Pass	894	1,214	1,203	910	949	1,200	725	135	231	296
Texas City	61,338	55,233	62,270	58,109	49,503	49,477	56,646	56,394	50,403	44,351
Victoria Chl.	4,750	4,734	4,733	5,104	5,522	5,298	5,000	4,351	4,624	4,567
Anahuac	-	-	-	-	-	-	-	0	-	0
Aransas Pass	127	207	15	6	169	48	91	39	181	45
Arroyo Colorado (Harlingen)	964	898	1,132	837	940	992	928	964	994	1,016
Port Isabel	1			5	7	30	88	114	130	206
Cedar Bayou	972	965	871	1,002	955	666	435	404	473	321
Chocolate Byu.	3,338	2,932	3,411	3,488	3,329	4,048	3,983	3,845	3,480	3,757
Clear Creek	-	-	-	-	11	-	-	0	-	5
Colorado River	435	361	390	445	388	503	570	622	576	639
Dickinson	994	813	929	904	954	1,073	669	625	657	556
Double Bayou	0	-	-	0	-	0	0	0	-	0
Harbor Island (Port Aransas)	9	62	105	151	143	40	38	44	209	64
Liberty Chl.	18	9	-	-	-	18	-	39	-	-
Orange	825	764	798	681	873	756	691	616	693	686
Palacios	-	0	-	-	0	-	-	0	-	-
Port Mansfield	-	-	-	-	1	3	8	8	20	10
Rockport	-	1	-	-	2	-	-	1	-	3
San Bernard Rr.	878	662	613	633	666	565	578	565	653	724
Other Ports	0	0	0	0	0	0	0	0	0	0
TOTAL*	473,941	442,251	454,765	452,991	406,166	427,296	422,592	385,585	371,021	373,668

*Totals exclude duplication.

Foreign/Domestic Commerce: Breakdown for 2003

Data below represent inbound and outbound tonnage for major Texas ports in **2003**. Note that "-" means no tonnage was reported. *Does not include Canadian. *Source: U.S. Army Corps of Engineers*
(**All figures in short tons** x1,000)

Port	Foreign*		Domestic				Local
			Coastwise		Internal		
	Imports	Exports	Receipts	Shipments	Receipts	Shipments	
Beaumont	61,936	5,306	491	2,241	5,972	8,642	1,408
Brownsville	1,817	449	-	58	1,276	81	-
Corpus Christi	44,640	7,482	1,041	7,589	3,858	8,630	2,703
Freeport	22,648	2,230	805	1,953	1,706	451	9
Galveston	1,065	2,723	8	1,672	1,330	642	105
Houston	89,353	35,772	2,901	7,791	25,055	15,963	12,320
Matagorda Chl. (Port Lavaca)	6,451	1,507	575	187	456	2,409	20
Port Arthur	14,251	3,677	202	2,375	2,672	3,393	61
Sabine Pass	-	-	-	-	53	841	-
Texas City	39,824	3,154	365	4,940	5,383	6,880	378
Victoria	-	-	-	-	1,166	3,584	-

Gulf Intracoastal Waterway by Commodity (Texas portion)

(**All figures in short tons** x1,000) *Source: U.S. Army Corps of Engineers*

	2003	2002	2001	2000	1999	1998	1997
Total	68,517	63,300	65,097	66,440	61,563	63,105	65,112
Coal	168	75	105	121	136	71	126
Petroleum products	36,057	34,662	36,393	34,816	30,886	32,763	33,816
Chemicals	22,024	20,314	20,002	21,382	20,540	20,723	21,958
Raw materials	6,208	4,713	4,780	5,822	5,535	4,979	4,860
Manufactured goods	2,208	1,536	1,969	2,301	1,872	1,826	2,171
Food, farm products	643	957	900	960	789	736	759

U.S. ports ranked by tonnage 2003
(x1,000)

1. S. Louisiana. . . 198,825
2. **Houston** 190,923
3. New York 145,889
4. **Beaumont**. 87,541
5. New Orleans . . . 83,847
6. Huntington, WV . . 77,641
7. **Corpus Christi** . 77,225*
8. Long Beach. . . . 69,195
9. **Texas City**. 61,338
10. Baton Rouge . . 61,264

*includes Harbor Island

States ranked by tonnage 2003
(x1,000)

1. **Texas** 473,941
2. Louisiana 469,461
3. California 193,378
4. Florida 131,570
5. Ohio 113,743
6. Illinois. 113,314
7. New Jersey . . . 111,661
8. Washington . . . 106,489
9. Pennsylvania . . 104,404
10. New York 99,406

Texas Transportation System

Texas is a leader among the states in a number of transportation indicators, including total road and street mileage, total railroad mileage and total number of airports. Texas ranks second behind California in motor-vehicle registrations.

The Texas transportation system includes 300,000 miles of streets, highways and interstate roads, more than 10,000 miles of railroad line, and approximately 1,800 airports and landing strips. Texans operate more than 18 million motor vehicles, and the state has more than 48,000 pilots.

The transportation industry is a major employer in Texas. Texas Workforce Commission indicates that transportation employs some 345,000 Texans. The largest group, almost 100,000, is employed in trucking. Air transportation involves more than 56,000 workers.

The largest state agency involved, the **Texas Department of Transportation**, is responsible for highway construction and maintenance, motor vehicle titles and registration, general aviation, public transportation, commercial trucking, automobile dealer licensing and the state's official Tourist Welcome Centers. The **Railroad Commission** has intrastate authority over railroad safety, truck lines, buses and pipelines.

Vehicles, Highway Miles, Construction, Maintenance, 2004

The following mileage, maintenance and construction figures refer only to roads that are maintained by the state: Interstates, U.S. highways, state highways, farm-to-market roads and some loops around urban areas. Not included are city- or county-maintained streets and roads. A lane mile is one lane for one mile; i.e., one mile of four-lane highway equals four lane miles. Source: Texas Dept. of Transportation.

County	Vehicles Registered	Lane Miles of Highways	Vehicle Miles Driven Daily	State/Contracted Maintenance Expenditures	State Contruction Expenditures	Vehicle Registration Fees	County Net Receipts	State Net Receipts
Anderson	43,716	966	1,210,047	$ 5,231,479	$ 6,055,245	$ 2,628,039	$ 1,016,013	$ 1,612,026
Andrews	12,599	542	401,876	3,621,108	50,869	790,972	430,918	360,054
Angelina	76,222	926	2,043,881	6,152,849	8,637,930	5,346,090	1,702,963	3,643,127
Aransas	20,821	192	445,624	810,259	8,844,386	1,216,586	523,586	693,000
Archer	9,852	530	350,364	2,502,334	2,891,434	586,325	446,584	139,741
Armstrong	2,685	378	316,085	1,744,320	112,351	157,892	154,132	3,761
Atascosa	31,728	1,011	1,329,595	4,822,348	3,741,665	1,886,257	814,700	1,071,558
Austin	30,585	607	1,198,432	3,348,016	6,904,580	1,976,643	792,263	1,184,380
Bailey	6,169	490	224,437	1,690,156	2,917,200	425,193	371,352	53,841
Bandera	20,541	393	379,805	2,089,279	362,536	1,137,829	599,340	538,489
Bastrop	58,427	790	1,796,507	2,433,212	16,555,384	3,515,292	1,437,348	2,077,945
Baylor	4,205	437	168,705	1,568,279	1,099,621	262,524	243,397	19,127
Bee	19,570	640	647,656	2,744,481	6,903,903	1,157,917	632,065	525,852
Bell	217,037	1,471	5,836,335	13,088,817	39,380,298	13,856,207	4,941,559	8,914,648
Bexar	1,170,227	3,107	24,182,963	32,717,922	215,457,286	77,873,547	25,032,780	52,840,767
Blanco	11,191	462	507,994	1,425,070	124,223	731,137	398,981	332,157
Borden	993	344	53,431	1,332,901	1,655,136	43,149	42,115	1,034
Bosque	18,543	695	555,978	5,225,284	679,300	1,053,380	594,361	459,019
Bowie	83,338	1,181	2,750,724	7,588,607	12,332,340	5,115,612	1,833,824	3,281,789
Brazoria	236,214	1,240	4,192,092	6,778,880	42,369,823	13,682,872	3,361,625	10,321,247
Brazos	121,423	831	3,064,901	3,727,301	35,714,311	7,975,508	2,699,802	5,275,705
Brewster	8,184	591	250,367	2,845,358	6,119,617	496,064	340,668	155,397
Briscoe	1,966	326	59,862	1,624,032	15,428	125,858	122,371	3,487
Brooks	5,680	310	527,649	3,337,105	787,728	335,526	245,979	89,547
Brown	38,131	756	770,260	4,790,672	4,354,798	2,281,679	1,002,158	1,279,521
Burleson	18,283	504	716,831	3,860,333	3,064,048	1,103,197	626,471	476,726
Burnet	43,126	793	1,189,125	2,485,317	3,189,284	2,618,183	1,134,746	1,483,437
Caldwell	28,042	604	839,923	3,060,445	2,696,302	1,694,680	738,389	956,291
Calhoun	20,884	382	446,446	2,320,839	2,890,164	1,215,680	612,889	602,791
Callahan	15,439	750	824,715	4,117,647	4,727,440	911,292	604,039	307,253
Cameron	213,887	1,628	5,441,058	10,610,799	94,562,064	13,784,281	4,167,014	9,617,267
Camp	13,947	271	303,003	1,498,565	6,457,102	1,343,092	517,336	825,756
Carson	6,522	776	662,370	4,120,984	3,132,304	374,848	323,091	51,756
Cass	30,388	986	1,013,696	4,789,141	6,387,505	1,765,552	798,688	966,864
Castro	7,175	533	266,757	1,406,521	4,993,793	552,049	435,966	116,084
Chambers	31,066	747	2,167,812	3,522,643	21,375,802	1,941,924	760,694	1,181,231
Cherokee	39,458	1,133	1,208,029	6,066,975	12,780,173	2,331,943	979,845	1,352,098
Childress	5,877	477	364,931	7,361,663	3,836,035	340,952	315,571	25,382
Clay	12,963	793	814,089	2,596,319	5,785,080	752,112	590,963	161,149
Cochran	2,978	469	95,562	1,062,572	0	197,911	192,634	5,276
Coke	4,275	357	185,761	1,665,723	234,578	234,586	228,098	6,488
Coleman	9,957	754	344,788	2,717,316	3,986,775	563,390	453,126	110,264
Collin	504,194	1,444	6,909,284	8,871,384	54,559,524	32,338,151	10,961,601	21,376,550
Collingsworth	3,109	446	104,518	1,551,232	757,818	185,231	179,770	5,461
Colorado	23,541	759	1,434,605	4,054,724	2,196,952	1,535,576	735,386	800,190
Comal	94,317	652	2,911,813	4,817,933	24,086,079	6,416,106	2,299,912	4,116,194
Comanche	15,162	738	473,420	2,379,427	2,454,579	923,762	593,573	330,190

Northbound traffic lines up at the contruction area on I-45 south of Corsicana. File photo.

County	Vehicles Registered	Lane Miles of Highways	Vehicle Miles Driven Daily	State/ Contracted Maintenance Expenditures	State Contruction Expenditures	Vehicle Registration Fees	County Net Receipts	State Net Receipts
Concho	3,092	441	240,199	$ 2,623,947	$ 423,214	$ 162,390	$ 157,883	$ 4,507
Cooke	38,967	849	1,482,324	3,477,223	5,943,324	2,449,204	954,221	1,494,983
Coryell	41,931	684	1,041,993	3,102,164	3,046,272	2,433,702	991,155	1,442,548
Cottle	1,817	391	76,465	1,106,059	12,780,684	98,310	95,282	3,028
Crane	4,248	318	175,008	927,300	1,017,832	264,762	189,002	75,760
Crockett	4,142	790	432,156	2,180,646	1,117,229	232,312	226,564	5,749
Crosby	5,796	569	196,648	2,254,383	393,845	346,400	322,121	24,279
Culberson	1,917	749	618,262	2,721,188.88	4,291,879	125,012	121,714	3,298
Dallam	5,629	609	349,667	1,349,199	5,317,344	456,240	383,297	72,943
Dallas	1,806,870	3,280	36,488,106	41,903,626	314,385,395	121,763,703	37,252,174	84,511,530
Dawson	11,424	713	385,059	2,018,017	113,841	768,369	567,318	201,051
Deaf Smith	16,781	603	363,570	2,186,151	4,081,320	1,339,099	640,965	698,134
Delta	6,232	342	191,878	2,079,362	446,706	358,372	294,792	63,580
Denton	405,106	1,423	8,235,815	9,237,422	118,353,611	25,687,711	7,643,348	18,044,363
DeWitt	18,547	641	450,589	2,007,084	9,373,306	1,062,693	613,487	449,206
Dickens	2,783	469	96,546	1,504,207	385,568	134,465	131,086	3,379
Dimmit	7,263	507	307,192	3,332,124	3,435,719	462,592	339,381	123,211
Donley	3,582	455	492,932	3,317,682	1,547,927	205,461	199,013	6,449
Duval	10,183	630	427,435	2,103,759	2,351,779	816,422	452,856	363,566
Eastland	20,916	1,023	1,039,739	3,452,898	7,044,458	1,346,426	729,992	616,434
Ector	112,802	957	1,606,694	6,398,482	13,876,392	7,838,267	2,600,620	5,237,647
Edwards	2,385	499	76,492	1,932,936	1,082,967	126,076	122,754	3,322
Ellis	125,833	1,494	4,187,143	13,991,989	64,809,920	8,367,218	2,214,554	6,152,664
El Paso	498,868	1,572	8,999,430	10,026,087	121,221,994	32,410,518	9,356,959	23,053,559
Erath	32,283	822	1,048,992	5,709,046	7,805,590	1,958,127	877,243	1,080,884
Falls	14,846	706	708,512	5,045,490	11,471,419	862,075	557,794	304,281
Fannin	34,714	991	766,097	3,458,330	4,384,170	2,012,204	983,127	1,029,077
Fayette	27,844	1,034	1,398,822	3,469,946	5,506,074	1,636,905	787,798	849,107
Fisher	4,282	555	141,595	2,640,176	975,108	233,021	226,092	6,928
Floyd	7,018	670	188,601	2,525,808	902,826	431,565	384,348	47,217
Foard	1,561	299	57,484	1,304,136	420,853	88,381	85,907	2,474
Fort Bend	310,980	1,072	5,615,586	6,882,650	77,490,219	20,294,732	5,704,506	14,590,226
Franklin	9,691	336	425,719	2,087,747	3,787,345	548,906	401,887	147,019
Freestone	20,452	807	1,588,466	4,673,858	8,394,817	1,192,870	722,567	470,303
Frio	10,286	758	853,715	2,602,304	1,058,747	679,661	490,655	189,006
Gaines	13,427	668	442,271	2,494,784	375,196	816,768	422,039	394,729
Galveston	222,049	1,056	4,469,833	9,346,854	68,930,802	13,559,823	3,975,638	9,584,185
Garza	4,362	460	407,255	2,861,474	16,857,982	266,032	218,802	47,230
Gillespie	24,881	689	651,653	2,625,408	1,291,662	1,451,250	724,109	727,141
Glasscock	2,111	274	150,848	859,030	5,988,488	168,277	149,931	18,346

County	Vehicles Registered	Lane Miles of Highways	Vehicle Miles Driven Daily	State/ Contracted Maintenance Expenditures	State Contruction Expenditures	Vehicle Registration Fees	County Net Receipts	State Net Receipts
Goliad	6,897	501	347,569	$ 2,687,127	$ 1,749,161	$ 353,558	$ 299,585	$ 53,973
Gonzales	18,755	878	1,052,624	2,826,001	6,080,993	1,200,477	622,106	578,371
Gray	23,195	773	672,788	3,129,779	1,268,065	1,481,546	744,131	737,415
Grayson	115,571	1,182	3,108,502	7,622,541	31,877,706	7,119,384	2,370,317	4,749,067
Gregg	115,734	781	2,588,951	5,373,002	13,337,476	7,988,102	2,657,497	5,330,605
Grimes	23,701	611	854,236	3,839,649	5,245,003	1,387,082	693,425	693,657
Guadalupe	90,806	902	2,615,645	5,095,388	14,558,186	5,649,511	1,838,721	3,810,790
Hale	28,487	1,056	800,525	3,512,776	1,234,637	1,814,715	794,174	1,020,542
Hall	3,122	458	214,046	1,546,781	907,054	196,464	191,118	5,346
Hamilton	9,397	580	339,186	2,690,958	702,350	552,335	445,283	107,053
Hansford	5,928	525	124,449	2,057,706	642,090	389,108	339,894	49,214
Hardeman	4,270	466	345,781	2,184,766	6,165,409	254,378	246,362	8,016
Hardin	51,220	573	1,289,433	6,397,763	11,875,360	3,063,897	1,294,198	1,769,699
Harris	2,824,370	4,740	57,393,352	43,100,024	660,680,756	194,082,189	62,190,124	131,892,066
Harrison	59,390	1,185	2,602,105	5,519,646	5,796,387	3,609,786	1,298,683	2,311,104
Hartley	5,148	540	298,295	2,075,629	133,276	411,091	317,632	93,459
Haskell	7,016	647	208,864	2,494,037	3,464,498	410,680	375,470	35,210
Hays	95,196	667	3,317,066	4,064,837	20,398,561	6,060,357	2,076,867	3,983,490
Hemphill	4,814	386	157,289	1,957,745	2,381,504	310,036	259,314	50,722
Henderson	76,528	972	1,705,807	5,684,227	18,557,152	4,529,630	1,402,431	3,127,200
Hidalgo	367,651	2,069	9,367,435	13,573,399	98,043,014	25,832,689	7,546,721	18,285,968
Hill	35,030	1,078	2,175,988	7,115,890	16,943,326	2,122,371	890,768	1,231,603
Hockley	20,328	752	570,698	2,409,675	267,720	1,386,495	664,538	721,956
Hodd	51,561	387	919,651	2,511,094	3,211,732	3,091,526	1,230,979	1,860,547
Hopkins	34,069	956	1,420,284	5,376,881	6,864,506	2,186,132	894,933	1,291,199
Houston	21,012	845	573,389	3,334,185	6,619,009	1,248,122	654,059	594,064
Howard	26,049	856	866,053	3,167,869	1,329,225	1,632,335	774,642	857,693
Hudspeth	2,704	824	1,139,912	2,226,425	19,614,958	136,280	132,304	3,976
Hunt	81,265	1,273	2,621,846	9,675,415	8,732,373	4,751,698	1,703,296	3,048,402
Hutchinson	25,249	478	337,322	2,403,020	3,415,729	1,514,712	557,059	957,654
Irion	2,857	247	111,504	1,062,252	1,404,073	199,044	160,852	38,192
Jack	9,298	575	336,613	2,947,683	1,084,403	632,441	452,051	180,390
Jackson	14,057	637	873,708	6,306,628	1,284,298	842,739	547,101	295,638
Jasper	35,871	738	1,182,943	6,512,046	17,744,547	2,052,299	750,357	1,301,942
Jeff Davis	2,636	469	170,383	918,008	513,639	191,370	146,762	44,607
Jefferson	204,034	1,144	4,894,241	15,884,850	23,885,819	13,251,547	4,176,279	9,075,268
Jim Hogg	4,668	288	189,613	1,047,922	906,383	314,590	253,763	60,827
Jim Wells	32,640	715	1,221,501	5,077,235	1,623,172	2,338,708	981,420	1,357,288
Johnson	129,465	947	2,876,412	5,993,385	12,311,783	8,285,812	2,347,205	5,938,607
Jones	15,728	1,012	495,098	4,294,106	4,916,306	1,002,130	662,697	339,434
Karnes	10,838	695	390,447	3,512,473	3,076,655	624,984	487,463	137,520
Kaufman	82,967	1,196	3,578,596	9,284,833	23,757,199	4,965,646	1,924,237	3,041,408
Kendall	39,367	444	851,108	1,493,268	272,181	2,410,646	1,295,369	1,115,277
Kenedy	680	188	455,252	688,271	165,119	33,184	32,373	810
Kent	1,484	325	46,008	1,460,103	2,837,011	67,803	65,807	1,996
Kerr	48,256	712	1,042,820	4,050,360	4,720,612	2,859,049	1,131,158	1,727,892
Kimble	5,521	687	448,662	5,628,169	6,341,597	308,430	268,059	40,371
King	499	199	73,840	965,035	205,265	33,130	32,530	600
Kinney	2,811	407	168,084	1,010,852	486,385	167,391	138,565	28,826
Kleberg	24,822	368	774,237	1,699,701	17,389,101	1,548,637	739,535	809,102
Knox	4,056	439	136,140	1,308,445	2,838,613	282,052	264,341	17,711
Lamar	48,146	985	1,198,529	6,562,964	6,931,166	2,983,919	1,141,573	1,842,345
Lamb	12,910	805	458,845	1,848,198	1,897	834,976	554,819	280,157
Lampasas	20,512	489	521,694	1,997,115	3,880,220	1,225,401	758,933	466,468
La Salle	4,490	649	551,528	3,053,529	6,317,552	460,351	327,802	132,548
Lavaca	22,242	641	513,170	2,333,380	6,324,486	1,319,906	668,770	651,136
Lee	18,965	531	631,023	2,196,256	1,963,203	1,235,843	645,723	590,121
Leon	17,651	834	1,377,941	3,470,515	7,477,143	1,077,182	557,876	519,306
Liberty	65,378	816	1,890,971	8,700,900	6,166,415	4,312,122	1,382,325	2,929,797
Limestone	21,997	769	718,063	4,009,989	4,328,618	1,309,035	677,196	631,838
Lipscomb	3,186	411	79,174	1,016,065	61,332	235,504	229,789	5,714
Live Oak	11,479	995	1,175,233	4,480,816	11,495,947	731,181	547,936	183,245
Llano	20,868	500	447,428	2,243,314	1,873,588	1,209,716	646,620	563,096
Loving	261	67	13,262	702,450	0	15,518	15,312	205
Lubbock	208,351	1,705	3,470,515	7,450,257	63,233,034	13,843,098	4,763,173	9,079,925
Lynn	5,608	711	333,520	3,074,303	2,953,166	326,391	304,892	21,499
Madison	13,904	572	839,692	5,295,958	5,295,958	818,128	630,376	187,752
Marion	10,309	323	315,815	1,883,233	1,889,252	562,919	426,476	136,443

U.S. 67 heading north from Presidio to Marfa. Texas Almanac photo.

County	Vehicles Registered	Lane Miles of Highways	Vehicle Miles Driven Daily	State/ Contracted Maintenance Expenditures	State Contruction Expenditures	Vehicle Registration Fees	County Net Receipts	State Net Receipts
Martin	5,173	574	365,668	$ 3,278,493	$ 2,832,081	$ 280,232	$ 272,506	$ 7,727
Mason	4,494	423	157,226	1,367,408	12,727	237,863	219,257	18,606
Matagorda	33,486	680	798,784	2,963,800	6,080,476	2,035,140	871,167	1,163,973
Maverick	28,293	488	681,086	2,278,050	4,013,037	1,889,398	709,230	1,180,168
McCulloch	9,203	608	296,394	2,365,323	68,704	527,087	428,415	98,672
McLennan	182,713	1,634	5,512,868	12,832,178	58,411,020	12,273,390	3,587,705	8,685,686
McMullen	2,240	317	119,806	2,182,796	63,158	229,186	178,336	50,849
Medina	38,765	763	1,153,393	4,823,591	4,465,916	2,327,107	1,061,946	1,265,161
Menard	2,620	346	138,797	639,288	462,367	130,786	127,123	3,664
Midland	120,039	1,011	1,825,612	4,542,688	12,298,779	8,661,970	2,519,659	6,142,311
Milam	24,737	689	876,163	4,273,324	2,947,843	1,417,796	691,577	726,219
Mills	6,506	449	250,317	2,078,707	571,661	352,587	333,288	19,299
Mitchell	6,290	663	512,395	3,192,779	4,578,457	349,439	306,698	42,741
Montague	21,979	850	729,656	3,666,696	2,110,206	1,365,905	684,483	681,423
Montgomery	302,377	1,206	7,229,669	8,549,377	37,643,363	19,135,953	5,364,986	13,770,967
Moore	18,405	467	474,548	2,113,061	11,119,978	1,316,324	587,005	729,319
Morris	13,003	371	487,289	3,055,680	3,207,362	760,777	455,831	304,946
Motley	1,598	331	64,809	1,014,130	549,261	91,041	88,436	2,606
Nacogdoches	49,630	952	1,661,185	5,326,708	11,762,537	2,966,659	1,210,285	1,756,374
Navarro	42,901	1,192	1,829,781	6,866,958	29,595,678	2,637,566	1,050,771	1,586,795
Newton	12,790	547	439,458	3,871,869	12,407,149	672,681	456,138	216,543
Nolan	14,063	695	831,478	3,293,250	3,681,038	890,195	581,402	308,793
Nueces	251,297	1,450	5,515,663	13,180,021	73,316,197	16,419,238	5,125,484	11,293,753
Ochiltree	10,529	428	204,758	1,594,431	4,052,962	747,734	529,648	218,086
Oldham	2,347	473	696,837	1,921,049	13,246,374	161,415	151,672	9,742
Orange	75,947	600	2,399,335	5,190,746	50,342,191	4,487,745	1,410,410	3,077,335
Palo Pinto	29,567	829	852,931	5,954,943	13,960,748	1,805,801	748,695	1,057,105
Panola	24,465	778	1,008,864	4,754,001	14,085,906	1,338,514	516,371	822,143
Parker	104,881	872	2,734,181	4,481,827	8,437,233	6,437,073	2,291,479	4,145,594
Parmer	9,423	611	384,835	1,329,408	4,629,377	656,810	487,479	169,331
Pecos	12,715	1,662	820,440	7,374,126	2,911,222	813,826	525,223	288,603
Polk	54,489	857	1,607,825	4,636,094	12,405,367	4,001,091	1,340,739	2,660,353
Potter	96,666	891	2,556,425	11,633,874	16,083,668	6,534,427	2,043,205	4,491,221
Presidio	6,508	545	195,225	4,407,959	8,855	408,153	299,796	108,357
Rains	12,742	268	305,502	1,748,893	341,0367	645,861	420,135	225,726
Randall	108,582	901	1,216,159	3,605,144	9,566,424	6,942,931	2,478,722	4,464,208

County	Vehicles Registered	Lane Miles of Highways	Vehicle Miles Driven Daily	State/ Contracted Maintenance Expenditures	State Contruction Expenditures	Vehicle Registration Fees	County Net Receipts	State Net Receipts
Reagan	3,367	320	109,849	1,054,678	4,777,302	233,503	202,263	31,240
Real	3,577	297	85,001	$ 1,545,781	$ 3,922,388	$ 215,799	$ 184,799	$ 31,000
Red River	13,719	748	432,912	3,209,572	10,377,811	746,370	523,296	223,074
Reeves	8,443	1,184	708,714	9,545,563	11,827,994	464,308	383,894	80,413
Refugio	6,970	464	748,260	3,528,177	1,504,140	429,065	324,467	104,598
Roberts	1,092	241	70,664	912,431	46,963	56,128	54,816	1,312
Robertson	15,424	625	825,091	5,443,664	3,730,099	885,712	574,930	310,782
Rockwall	52,993	331	1,505,362	1,646,221	4,563,255	3,434,353	1,103,123	2,331,231
Runnels	12,006	741	345,879	2,310,908	1,989,731	784,512	543,920	240,593
Rusk	45,772	1,166	1,303,430	5,619,285	7,434,748	2,813,147	1,066,905	1,746,243
Sabine	10,994	474	316,650	3,000,049	2,517,377	636,059	446,627	189,432
San Augustine	8,524	532	280,980	2,813,804	1,056,823	508,924	394,421	114,503
San Jacinto	21,098	510	722,956	4,659,575	10,146,707	1,379,880	625,580	754,301
San Patricio	56,424	937	2,008,393	4,276,029	20,555,615	3,562,097	1,249,314	2,312,783
San Sabe	7,017	437	160,284	2,145,197	659,367	421,101	377,953	43,148
Schleicher	3,329	362	141,918	556,057	977,416	201,080	184,934	16,145
Scurry	17,584	680	550,703	2,579,156	8,204,316	1,340,324	657,126	683,198
Shackelford	3,736	353	183,187	1,906,864	1,287,653	241,312	211,218	30,094
Shelby	23,691	859	755,053	4,940,470	13,371,155	1,670,222	783,952	886,270
Sherman	2,781	429	267,569	1,831,685	32,584	176,072	171,241	4,831
Smith	183,891	1,583	4,961,373	9,714,012	37,497,239	11,440,246	3,831,521	7,608,725
Somervell	7,782	190	245,465	1,277,002	762,704	407,059	279,849	127,210
Starr	33,065	473	1,038,113	2,740,835	5,559,629	2,115,116	871,259	1,243,857
Stephens	9,796	561	246,710	2,324,035	1,909,248	593,526	436,536	156,990
Sterling	1,729	265	163,929	1,378,130	3,605,135	76,386	74,427	1,959
Stonewall	1,949	329	85,998	1,384,496	773,240	125,081	122,603	2,477
Sutton	5,739	592	438,587	2,016,869	2,806,683	459,536	320,622	138,913
Swisher	5,996	806	413,151	1,781,448	796	375,997	338,248	37,749
Tarrant	1,326,899	3,130	27,532,884	30,115,195	130,710,616	88,219,736	26,780,928	61,438,808
Taylor	115,885	1,195	2,076,161	7,418,732	18,748,409	7,600,897	2,617,956	4,982,941
Terrell	1,110	353	141,012	1,192,034	1,852	55,306	53,756	1,550
Terry	11,187	630	413,173	1,392,581	930,813	766,955	562,767	204,187
Throckmorton	1,926	341	69,814	2,064,726	146,245	100,533	98,131	2,402
Titus	30,032	541	1,049,911	5,373,134	6,198,206	1,772,843	855,522	917,320
Tom Green	97,461	976	1,402,126	3,455,749	21,107,111	6,124,658	2,161,593	3,963,066
Travis	695,533	1,774	15,534,573	16,194,434	309,322,189	45,296,593	14,754,797	30,541,796
Trinity	13,161	429	320,958	2,227,146	9,357,928	789,361	498,677	290,683
Tyler	18,540	518	559,318	3,348,379	385,701	1,046,976	591,194	455,783
Upshur	35,059	782	965,206	3,304,232	8,701,028	2,014,679	841,506	1,173,173
Upton	3,241	392	145,478	922,192	6,124,978	195,605	161,906	33,700
Uvalde	21,649	729	695,791	3,730,043	1,387,177	1,447,989	626,495	821,494
Val Verde	37,623	712	479,824	2,620,781	7,247,110	2,358,397	968,841	1,389,555
Van Zandt	55,732	1,166	2,098,778	6,589,782	3,751,070	3,197,579	1,140,111	2,057,468
Victoria	81,739	762	1,910,926	6,216,715	32,752,526	5,237,048	1,834,242	3,402,805
Walker	41,333	791	2,143,801	5,719,945	6,310,696	2,506,585	1,074,866	1,431,719
Waller	41,924	584	1,616,972	5,809,245	6,011,126	2,558,294	1,531,552	1,026,742
Ward	9,998	668	485,476	3,663,802	8,446,230	592,496	314,469	278,027
Washington	34,713	657	1,168,730	4,632,899	2,473,217	2,263,063	923,071	1,339,992
Webb	122,950	1,053	2,452,100	9,677,229	53,637,123	9,620,082	2,962,964	6,657,118
Wharton	40,978	884	1,573,960	6,472,864	7,572,331	2,873,985	1,001,757	1,872,228
Wheeler	5,844	672	586,669	2,135,739	1,521,398	314,707	299,143	15,564
Wichita	111,607	1,117	2,056,203	7,736,479	18,403,899	6,973,008	2,414,405	4,558,603
Wilbarger	13,212	736	651,005	3,205,032	7,736,220	783,724	554,915	228,809
Willacy	12,570	479	461,138	2,051,479	6,573,621	833,287	570,669	262,618
Williamson	262,911	1,454	5,799,377	6,760,637	314,518,997	17,076,760	5,851,360	11,225,401
Wilson	32,658	745	786,009	3,146,244	3,670,202	1,864,916	805,636	1,059,280
Winkler	6,220	294	134,840	1,829,079	21,009	410,551	289,711	120,841
Wise	64,593	852	2,238,095	4,932,855	17,443,718	4,326,466	1,419,433	2,907,033
Wood	44,995	894	887,235	4,580,975	3,613,172	2,603,642	1,022,768	1,580,875
Yoakum	8,204	431	220,495	1,115,077	6,578	576,862	456,227	120,635
Young	20,613	707	338,578	4,712,568	2,402,955	1,302,558	644,069	658,489
Zapata	8,571	250	400,236	1,791,834	3,957,273	606,807	311,788	295,018
Zavala	6,855	542	294,858	3,939,142	3,690,253	447,199	318,345	128,855
TOTAL:	18,453,290	189,745	449,486,854	$ 1,122,090,877	$ 4,449,810,426	$1,205,421,191	$421,798,524	$ 783,622,667
State collect.						56,307,443		56,307,443
Exempt reg.	420,829							
Special veh.	75,380							
Grand Total	18,949,499					$1,261,728,633	$421,798,524	$ 839,930,109

Motor Vehicle Accidents, Losses

Year	Number Killed	†Number Injured	Accidents by Kinds				‡Vehicle Miles Traveled		Economic Loss (000,000)
			Fatal	†Injury	†Non-Injury	†Total	*Number (000,000)	Deaths per 100 mil miles	
1960	2,254	127,980	1,842	71,100	239,300	312,242	46,353	4.9	$ 350
1961	2,314	132,570	1,899	73,650	248,600	324,149	47,937	4.8	356
1962	2,421	144,943	2,002	80,524	277,680	360,206	49,883	4.9	388
1963	2,729	161,543	2,251	89,746	307,920	399,917	52,325	5.2	433
1964	3,006	182,081	2,486	101,156	351,120	454,762	55,677	5.4	487
1965	3,028	186,062	2,460	103,368	365,160	470,988	*52,163	5.8	498
1966	3,406	208,310	2,784	115,728	406,460	524,972	55,261	6.2	557
1967	3,367	205,308	2,778	114,060	768,430	885,268	58,124	5.8	793
1968	3,481	216,972	2,902	120,540	816,830	940,272	62,794	5.5	837
1969	3,551	223,000	2,913	124,000	850,000	976,913	67,742	5.2	955
1970	3,560	223,000	2,965	124,000	886,000	1,012,965	‡68,031	5.2	1,042
1971	3,594	224,000	2,993	124,000	890,000	1,016,993	70,709	5.1	1,045
1972	3,688	128,158	3,099	83,607	346,292	432,998	76,690	4.8	1,035
1973	3,692	132,635	3,074	87,631	373,521	464,226	80,615	4.6	1,035
1974	3,046	123,611	2,626	83,341	348,227	434,194	78,290	3.9	1,095
1975	3,429	138,962	2,945	92,510	373,141	468,596	84,575	4.1	1,440
1976	3,230	145,282	2,780	96,348	380,075	479,203	91,279	3.5	1,485
1977	3,698	161,635	3,230	106,923	393,848	504,001	96,998	3.8	1,960
1978	¶3,980	178,228	3,468	117,998	**304,830	**426,296	102,624	3.9	2,430
1979	4,229	184,550	3,685	122,793	322,336	448,814	101,909	4.1	2,580
1980	4,424	185,964	3,863	123,577	305,500	432,940	103,255	4.3	3,010
1981	4,701	206,196	4,137	136,396	317,484	458,017	111,036	4.2	3,430
1982	4,271	204,666	3,752	135,859	312,159	451,770	††124,910	3.4	3,375
1983	3,823	208,157	¶3,328	137,695	302,876	443,899	129,309	3.0	3,440
1984	3,913	220,720	3,466	145,543	293,285	442,294	137,280	2.9	§3,795
1985	3,682	231,009	3,270	151,657	300,531	452,188	143,500	2.6	3,755
1986	3,568	234,120	3,121	154,514	298,079	452,593	150,474	2.4	3,782
1987	3,261	226,895	2,881	146,913	246,175	395,969	151,221	2.2	3,913
1988	3,395	238,845	3,004	152,004	237,703	392,711	152,819	2.2	4,515
1989	3,361	243,030	2,926	153,356	233,967	390,249	159,679	2.1	4,873
1990	3,243	262,576	2,882	162,424	216,140	381,446	163,103	2.0	4,994
1991	3,079	263,430	2,690	161,470	207,288	371,448	162,780	1.9	5,604
1992	3,057	282,025	2,690	170,513	209,152	382,355	162,769	1.9	6,725
1993	3,037	298,891	2,690	178,194	209,533	390,417	167,988	1.8	§11,784
1994	3,142	326,837	2,710	192,014	219,890	414,614	172,976	1.8	12,505
1995	3,172	334,259	2,790	196,093	152,190	351,073	183,103	1.7	§ 13,005
1996	3,738	350,397	3,247	204,635	90,261	298,143	187,064	2.0	7,766
1997	3,508	347,881	3,079	205,595	97,315	305,989	194,665	1.8	7,662
1998	3,576	338,661	3,160	202,223	102,732	308,115	201,989	1.8	8,780
1999	3,519	339,448	3,106	203,220	105,375	311,701	213,847	1.6	8,729
2000	3,775	341,097	3,247	205,569	110,174	318,990	210,340	1.8	9,163
2001	3,739	340,554	3,319	207,043	113,596	323,958	216,276	1.7	$ 9,348

*Vehicle miles traveled since 1964 were estimated on the basis of new data furnished by U.S. Bureau of Public Roads through National Safety Council.

† In August 1967, amended estimating formula received from National Safety Council. Starting 1972, actual reported injuries are listed rather than estimates.

‡ Vehicle miles traveled estimated by Texas Highway Department starting with 1970. Method of calculation varies from that used for prior years.

§ Economic loss formula changed. Last changed in July 1995, when only property damage accidents having at least one vehicle towed due to damages is tabulated.

¶ Change in counting fatalities. In 1978, counted when injury results in death within 90 days of accident. In 1983, counted when injury results in death within 30 days.

**Total accidents and non-injury accidents for 1978 and after cannot be compared with years prior to 1978 due to changes in reporting laws.

†† Method of calculating vehicle miles traveled revised 1982 by Texas Department of Transportation. The 1981 mileage adjusted for comparison purposes.

Source: Analysis Section, Accident Records Bureau of the **Texas Department of Public Safety**, Austin.

Accidents by road class

2001	Miles of road	Accidents
City/Town	78,671	124,884
Interstate	3,233	46,831
U.S./State	28,275	93,777
Farm-Market	40,991	34,974
County	142,357	21,431
Other*	7,624	2,061
Total	301,141	323,958

*Toll roads, frontage roads and park roads.

Texas Department of Public Safety.

Drivers' Licenses

In 2004, the Texas Department of Public Safety issued 5,760,405 driver's licenses and identification cards, including renewals.

The following list shows the number of licensed drivers by year for Texas and for all the states. Sources are the Texas Department of Public Safety and the Federal Highway Administration.

Year	Texas licensed drivers	Total U.S. licensed drivers
2004	**15,562,484**	NA
2003	15,091,776	196,165,666
2002	14,639,132	194,295,633
2001	14,303,799	191,275,719
2000	14,024,305	190,625,023
1999	13,718,319	187,170,420
1998	13,419,288	184,980,177
1997	12,833,603	182,709,204
1996	12,568,265	179,539,340
1995	12,369,243	176,628,482
1994	12,109,960	175,403,465
1993	11,876,268	173,149,313
1992	11,437,571	173,125,396
1991	11,293,184	168,995,076
1990	11,136,694	167,015,250
1989	11,103,511	165,555,295
1988	11,080,702	162,853,255
1987	11,153,472	161,818,461
1986	11,129,193	159,487,000
1985	10,809,078	156,868,277
1984	10,855,549	155,423,709
1983	11,406,433	154,389,178
1982	10,154,386	150,233,659
1981	9,673,885	147,075,169
1980	9,287,286	145,295,036
1975	7,509,497	129,790,666
1970	6,380,057	111,542,787
1965	5,413,887	98,502,152
1960	4,352,168	87,252,563
1955	3,874,834	74,685,949
1950	2,687,349	59,322,278

— The driving age in Texas changed in 1967 from 14 to 16 years of age with driver's education.

— The first photos appeared on Texas driver's licenses in 1967.

Texas Department of Public Safety.

Railroads in Texas

All data in the charts below are for the year 2003, the latest available. Included are reports for tons of freight transported by rail, the number of carloads moved within the state and comparison to the totals in the United States. A complete list of railroads operating in Texas is at the beginning of the Counties section on page 167.

Texas Freight Railroads	Miles Operated
Union Pacific Railroad Co.	6,408
Burlington Northern/Santa Fe Rwy. Co.	4,645
Kansas City Southern Railway Co.	379
Class I (total of three above)	11,432
Regional (2)	937
Local (19)	686
Switching & Terminal (20)	994
Total	**14,049**
TOTAL exluding trackage rights*	**10,354**

*Trackage rights – track provided by another railroad.
The numbers in parentheses represent the number
of railroads in each category.
Source: Association of American Railroads.

Class I Railroads Nationwide	
Number of Railroads	**7**
Miles of road excluding trackage*	99,126
Locomotives in service	20,774
Freight cars in service	467,063
Carloads originated (millions)	28.87
Intermodal units (millions)	9.78
Tons orginated (billions)	1.799
Operating Statistics	
Freight revenue per ton-mile	2.283 cents
Average tons per carload	62.3
Average tons per train	3,024
Average length of haul (miles)	862.4

Source: Association of American Railroads.

State Rank	Miles of rail	State Rank	Carloads	State Rank	Freight tons carried
1. Texas	**10,354**	1. Illinois	10,958,376	1. Illinois	500,564,073
2. Illinois	7,292	**2. Texas**	**8,315,683**	2. Wyoming	457,262,838
3. California	5,733	3. Missouri	7,437,435	3. Nebraska	439,092,321
4. Ohio	5,230	4. Indiana	6,385,066	4. Missouri	385,159,465
5. Pennsylvania	5,085	5. Ohio	6,376,699	**5. Texas**	**335,757,329**
6. Kansas	5,103	6. California	6,100,530	6. Kansas	312,047,655
7. Georgia	4,707	7. Kansas	5,680,419	7. Ohio	305,916,309
8. Minnesota	4,631	8. New Mexico	5,527,050	8. Indiana	289,772,670
9. Indiana	4,237	9. Iowa	5,519,565	9. Iowa	284,394,262
10. Missouri	4,089	10. Arizona	5,255,492	10. Kentucky	278,719,883

Source: Association of American Railroads.

A railroad spur in southeast Collin County. File photo.

Freight Traffic in Texas 2003

Tons originated		%		Tons terminated		%
Chemicals	36,409,891	33%		Coal	56,035,751	33%
Nonmetallic Minerals	26,237,218	24%		Nonmetallic Minerals	35,223,201	18%
Petroleum	7,875,063	7%		Farm Products	22,370,338	12%
Mixed Freight	7,390,516	7%		Chemicals	18,893,787	10%
Stone/Glass Products	5,012,852	5%		Food Products	11,476,192	6%
All other	26,122,535	24%		All other	48,999,412	25%
Total	**109,048,075**			**Total**	**192,998,681**	

Source: Association of American Railroads.

Texas Freight Rail at Record Levels

By Suzanne Marta

Freight rail in Texas, like the rest of the nation, is booming, fueled by a recovering economy that increasingly relies on global manufacturers.

Nationally, 2004 was a record-breaking year for rail shipments. U.S. carloads jumped 2.9 percent over 2003, and intermodal loadings were up 10.4 percent, according to preliminary statistics collected by the Association of American Railroads.

In 2004, railroad companies experienced record levels of demand that resulted in network congestion, but also historic changes in the way the industry does business. In Texas and other states with major rail routes, congestion came early in 2004, as shipping demand significantly exceeded forecasts.

U.S. Surface Transportation Board chairman Roger Nober, in an unprecedented move, called for railroad companies to file action plans, describing how they would manage the surge in business.

Part of the surge stemmed from an ongoing movement to send more goods through intermodal transportation, especially for transcontinental trips. After goods are unloaded from cargo ships, they are put onto rail cars for the long-haul portion of their journey. Once in the destination's region, the goods are shifted to trucks to handle the rest of the journey.

In 2003, intermodal shipments nationally exceeded shipments of traditional rail freight such as coal or grain for the first time. Even with that growth, the volume of freight carried by rail is dwarfed by trucks, which command some 70 percent of the market.

For shippers, rail congestion was just one headache. A nationwide shortage of drivers also made it more difficult — and expensive — to secure truck transportation. Record fuel prices have also added pressure to rail and truck shippers and operators.

The quicker-than-expected economic growth in late 2003 and early 2004 left several major rail companies scrambling to add both employees and equipment. Key problem areas included the Sunset route between Los Angeles and El Paso, and choke-points in Houston and South Texas.

Texas' rail congestion in 2004 was not nearly as bad as the gridlock situation shippers faced following Union Pacific's merger with Southern Pacific in 1997; however, it did cause costly operational headaches for many companies.

Some chemical companies based in Houston — where some of the state's worst congestion occurred — reported temporary shutdowns because needed materials had not arrived in time. Routine trips across Houston that once took two days were stretching to a week. The congestion woes were exacerbated because some shippers leased additional empty rail cars — translating to even more cars clogging rail lines. Shippers typically own their rail cars, but complained that schedules were so far behind that the cars weren't being returned on time for reloading.

Shippers opted to shift some in-route products off the rail and onto trucks to meet deadlines. Such shifts were also costly because it typically takes four trucks to carry what one rail car can hold.

To cope with congestion, rail companies sought to simplify operations by eliminating some small shippers. The railroads also built longer trains to eke out more capacity.

Texas aggregate shippers served by Union Pacific also faced a 30 percent cut in rail car capacity, as the railroad sought to unclog its lines. The effort resulted in higher volumes being moved, because they weren't stuck in traffic jams.

Other developments in Texas' rail business include growing business to Mexico, where total U.S. trade by rail reached $31 billion in 2004. Union Pacific commands the most connections with the Mexican railway system, dominating cross-border traffic near Laredo.

Fort Worth-based Burlington Northern Santa Fe Corp. has sought to build traffic near El Paso, to capture high value intermodal shipments traveling between the U.S. and Mexico.

And in 2005, the South Orient Railroad launched service across the U.S.-Mexico border at Presidio, in hopes of offering yet another alternative to shippers. The South Orient hadn't offered regular service for more than six years. Grupo Mexico's U.S. subsidiary Texas Pacifico Transportation paid $3.5 million in 2001 to lease the South Orient from the state of Texas for 50 years, along with annual lease fees.

Grupo Mexico, which also owns Mexico railroad Ferromex, planned to invest in rehabilitation work on the line, whose poor condition required trains to reduce their speed 10 mph in many sections.

Suzanne Marta is a business writer for the Dallas Morning News.

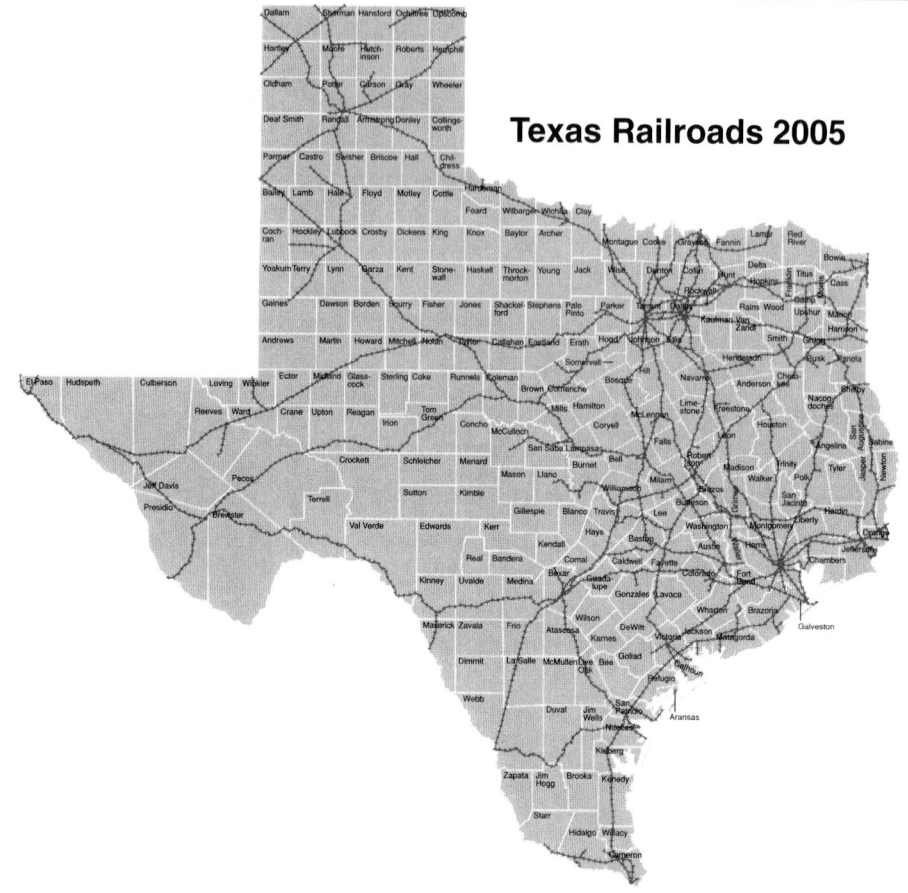

Texas Railroads 2005

Amtrak Passengers On/Off at Texas Stations

City	2004	2003	2002	2001	2000	1999	1998	1997	1996	1995	1994	1993
Alpine	1,661	1,796	1,474	2,141	2,380	2,281	1,884	1,934	2,373	2,417	2,668	2,767
Austin	20,934	18,646	14,801	18,374	17,276	11,516	11,173	8,185	10,783	10,440	12,116	18,954
Beaumont	1,519	1,708	1,543	2,233	2,375	2,529	2,008	2,237	2,495	2,572	2,330	2,772
Cleburne	1,614	1,531	1,359	1,494	1,429	814	618	519	699	655	758	1,649
College Sta.-Bryan	—	—	—	—	—	—	—	—	—	2,346	3,300	9,447
Corsicana										507	783	1,766
Dallas	33,409	31,981	26,580	33,287	32,649	24,197	24,526	19,815	25,851	34,197	40,991	69,823
Del Rio	1,140	1,135	931	1,123	1,639	1,624	1,103	1,134	1,213	1,369	1,532	1,221
El Paso	9,222	10,165	8,253	11,657	12,858	13,591	13,054	10,918	14,027	17,580	20,528	22,860
Fort Worth	73,080	64,247	57,554	66,654	70,796	46,166	10,278	8,878	11,005	9,972	11,424	20,156
Gainesville	10,240	8,981	10,844	14,096	15,764	9,574	—	—	—	—	—	—
Houston	16,177	19,661	13,776	16,544	17,336	16,038	15,391	16,663	16,005	29,158	32,314	48,638
Longview	23,692	20,720	16,039	16,610	13,305	13,585	12,666	11,525	12,439	8,459	7,142	10,679
Marshall	5,076	3,696	2,982	3,594	2,709	2,897	2,233	2,448	3,100	3,989	4,656	7,052
McGregor	2,444	1,776	1,967	2,010	2,220	1,366	1,349	1,324	1,469	1,243	1,435	3,134
Mineola	3,923	2,308	2,212	2,455	2,981	1,855	1,527	1,500	1,836	—	—	—
San Antonio	46,759	44,682	34,880	42,955	45,254	35,234	42,384	47,289	34,144	33,584	35,544	50,525
Sanderson	148	194	145	212	274	417	163	205	274	326	366	317
San Marcos	2,847	2,646	1,984	2,123	1,654	892	828	684	835	860	1,152	1,933
Taylor	3,248	2,590	1,633	2,155	1,597	820	958	815	1,727	1,406	1,495	3,009
Temple	10,431	8,006	6,273	7,115	6,482	3,982	3,730	2,846	3,038	2,972	3,371	7,684
Texarkana	NA	NA	4,326	5,466	5,732	4,507	4,555	4,536	4,173	4,914	5,689	7,821
Totals	267,568	246,469	209,556	253,666	262,709	193,885	150,428	143,455	147,486	168,966	189,594	292,207

Source: Amtrak (National Railroad Passenger Corporation), 2005.

Jets line up at Austin Bergstrom International Airport. File photo.

Aviation in Texas: Important Economic Factor

Source: Texas Transportation Institute

Air transportation is a vital and vigorous part of the Texas economy, and Texans are major users of air transportation. The state's airport system ranks as one of the busiest and largest in the nation.

The economic impact of general aviation in Texas includes total employment of 56,554 jobs, a total payroll of $1,872,675,700 and total economic output of $5,896,626,900. The state's 48,777 active pilots represent 7.8 percent of the nation's pilots.

The State of Texas has long been committed to providing air transportation to the public. In 1945, the Texas Aeronautics Commission (TAC) was created and directed by the legislature to foster and assist in the development of aeronautics within the state, and to encourage the establishment of airports and air navigational facilities.

The commission's first annual report of Dec. 31, 1946, stated that Texas had 592 designated airports and 7,756 civilian aircraft.

In 1989, the TAC became the Texas Department of Aviation (TDA). And, on Sept. 1, 1991, when the Texas Department of Transportation (TxDOT) was created, the TDA became the Aviation Division within the department.

The primary responsibilities of the Aviation Division include providing engineering and technical services for planning, constructing, and maintaining aeronautical facilities in the state. It is also responsible for long-range aviation facility development planning (statewide system of airports), and applying for, receiving and disbursing federal funds.

In 2003, Texas' commercial service airports with scheduled passenger service enplaned more than 60 million passengers; scheduled carriers served 27 Texas airports in 24 cities. More than 91 percent of the state's population lived within 50 miles of an airport with scheduled air passenger service.

Dallas/Fort Worth International, Dallas Love Field, Houston George Bush Intercontinental, and Houston's William P. Hobby together accounted for 80 percent of these enplanements.

Texas leads the nation in the number of landing facilities with more than 1,857, followed by California with 939.

One of TxDOT's goals is to develop a statewide system of airports that will provide adequate air access to the population and economic centers of the state.

In the Texas Aeronautical System Plan, TxDOT has identified 300 airports that are needed to meet the forecast aviation demand and to maximize access by aircraft to the state's population, business, and agricultural and mineral resource centers. Of these 300 airports, 27 are commercial service airports, 23 are reliever airports, and 250 are general aviation airports.

Commercial service airports provide scheduled passenger service. The reliever airports provide alternative landing facilities in the metropolitan areas separate from the commercial service airports, and, together with the transport airports, provide access for business and executive turbine-powered aircraft.

The general and basic utility airports provide access for single- and multi-engine, piston-powered aircraft to smaller communities in the state.

TxDOT is charged by the legislature with planning, programming, and imple-

Top U.S. Airports
Ranked by passengers arriving and departing, 2003

Rank	Airport	(000)
1	Atlanta	79,087
2	Chicago (O'Hare)	69,354
3	Los Angeles (LAX)	54,969
4	**Dallas-Fort Worth**	**53,243**
5	Denver	37,462
6	Phoenix	37,409
7	Las Vegas	36,266
8	**Houston (Bush)**	**34,120**
9	Minneapolis-St. Paul	33,196
10	Detroit	32,679
11	JFK (New York)	31,713
12	Miami	29,596
13	Newark	29,585
14	San Francisco	29,297
15	Orlando	27,316

Source: Airports Council International

menting improvement projects at the general aviation airports. In carrying out these responsibilities, TxDOT channels Airport Improvement Program (AIP) funds provided by the Federal Aviation Administration (FAA) for all general aviation airports in Texas.

Since 1993, TxDOT has participated in the FAA's state block grant demonstration program. Under this program, TxDOT assumes most of the FAA's responsibility for the administration of the AIP funds for general aviation airports.

The Aviation Facilities Development Program (AFDP) oversees planning and research, assists with engineering and technical services, and provides financial assistance through state grants and loans to public bodies operating airports for the purpose of establishing, enlarging or repairing airports, airstrips or navigational facilities.

The 78th Legislature appropriated funds to TxDOT who subsequently allocated a portion of those funds to the Aviation Division. TxDOT allocated approximately $16 million annually for the 2004-2005 biennium to the Aviation Division to help implement and administer the AFDP.

Scheduled passenger traffic (air carrier and commuters) continued to decline from 2001 to 2003 following the trend since 2000. Scheduled passenger enplanements in Texas decreased by nearly 5 million or 8 percent over the period.

Twenty-three airports saw their enplanements decrease as only Houston's Ellington Field, San Antonio International Airport, Longview's East Texas Regional Airport, and San Angelo's Mathis Field saw increases.

Fourteen airports endured double-digit declines with Beaumont, El Paso, and Victoria seeing their enplanements plummet 43 percent, 25 percent, and 25 percent, respectively.

Since 1999, enplanements are down more than 9 percent or more than 6 million passengers. This decline is widely believed to be the result of a series of events.

These include the prolonged recovery of the air transportation industry following the Sept. 11, 2001, terrorist attacks, the domestic economic downturn and its lingering recovery, volatile international conditions, and other specific factors related to the airline industry including overcapacity, profitability, and sensitivity to oil prices.

These trends do appear to be reversing as passenger enplanements at Texas' commercial service airports increased by approximately 9 percent through the first half of 2004.

General aviation continues to be an important part of both the aviation industry and the national economy. According to industry data, the state of general aviation is stable. The past three years, however, have been difficult.

Passenger Enplanements by Airport

Source: Texas Department of Transportation, Division of Aviation. Calendar year data.

Airport	1995	1997	1999	2001	Percent change*	2003
Abilene	69,555	52,864	52,714	62,628	-10	56,083
Amarillo	454,536	450,432	434,110	423,297	-9	384,521
Austin	2,658,039	2,948,701	3,298,729	3,661,702	-7	3,411,373
Beaumont	108,520	112,456	99,343	73,989	-43	42,476
Brownsville	—	81,439	70,866	70,854	-13	61,973
Brownwood**	2,015	—	1,717	2,090	-3	2,035
College Station	85,331	93,331	94,414	86,115	-20	68,838
Corpus Christi	511,841	471,914	474,027	421,752	-12	371,038
D/FW International	27,013,761	28,152,220	29,965,777	27,741,848	-12	24,391,440
Dallas/Love	3,355,238	3,413,519	3,409,920	3,350,234	-17	2,785,554
El Paso	1,835,162	1,634,578	1,664,890	1,942,543	-25	1,466,432
Harlingen	489,082	461,619	469,214	438,565	-11	391,103
Houston/Bush Int'cont.	10,165,671	13,212,686	16,447,012	17,361,526	-2	16,987,868
Houston/ Hobby	4,111,175	3,949,236	4,422,032	4,318,209	-10	3,901,871
Houston/Ellington	NA	50,503	49,776	32,064	31	42,114
Killeen	59,126	84,963	89,131	96,572	-3	94,026
Laredo	59,948	67,664	89,524	74,911	-2	73,637
Longview	33,761	26,779	30,092	29,738	2	30,269
Lubbock	602,680	592,101	570,452	535,366	-4	514,250
McAllen	313,082	313,506	325,861	298,298	-5	284,567
Midland	566,904	527,760	487,533	450,127	-12	394,367
San Angelo	52,674	41,404	41,639	47,682	2	48,856
San Antonio	3,058,274	3,343,818	3,522,946	3,448,484	22	4,223,110
Texarkana	45,242	36,367	43,527	33,034	-13	28,615
Tyler	78,524	69,639	77,795	63,834	-6	60,284
Victoria	19,517	21,656	20,962	16,356	-25	12,256
Waco	55,824	58,742	56,147	60,135	-6	56,459
Wichita Falls	59,275	53,942	55,754	47,533	-14	41,045
Total	**57,751,285**	**60,329,687**	**66,365,904**	**65,189,486**	**-8**	**60,226,460**

*Percent change from 2001 to 2003. **Not a commercial scheduled airport.

Following years of growth and more recently strong declines, the most recent data show the industry to be recovering and growing again. The peak for total worldwide shipments and billings of general aviation aircraft occurred in 2000 and 2001, respectively.

Since 2001, general aviation manufacturers have seen declines in both shipments and billings.

Worldwide billings for general aviation aircraft have dropped from $13.87 billion in 2001 to $9.99 billion in 2003, a decline of nearly 28 percent. In the same period, worldwide shipments have dropped from 2,994 aircraft to 2,686, a decline of more than 10 percent.

The same is true for billings and shipments of U.S. manufactured general aviation aircraft. In 2001, billings and shipments were $8.64 billion and 2,632 aircraft. In 2003, they were $6.43 billion and 2,137 aircraft. This is a decline in billings and shipments of approximately 26 percent and 19 percent, respectively, from 2001 to 2003.

For U.S. manufacturers, the decline was led by the drop in turbine aircraft shipments. The sector which had seen rapid growth in the late 1990s saw a decrease of more than 39 percent, which included decreases in shipments of both turbojet and turboprop aircraft of nearly 36 percent and 47 percent, respectively.

Piston-powered aircraft shipments also declined, but not nearly as much. Overall, they declined by 8 percent.

Leading U.S. Routes, 2003

Rank, Route	Passengers
1. New York to-from Fort Lauderdale	3.51 million
2. New York to-from Orlando	2.91 million
3. New York to-from Chicago	2.69 million
4. New York to-from Atlanta	2.27 million
5. New York to-from Los Angeles	2.20 million
14. **Dallas/Fort Worth** to-from **Houston**	1.48 million
23. New York to-from **Dallas/Fort Worth**	1.21 million

Leading U.S. Airlines, 2003

Rank	Airline	Passengers (000)	Planes
1	**American**	88,151	743
2	Delta	84,076	523
3	**Southwest**	74,719	387
4	United	66,018	528
5	Northwest	51,865	431
6	US Airways	41,250	277
7	**Continental**	38,474	358
8	America West	20,031	140

Source: Air Transport Assoc. of America. (**Texas-based in boldface.**)

General aviation aircraft billings followed the same course with across the board declines. Turbine aircraft saw the largest decrease with a 27 percent drop from 2001. The bulk (93 percent) of billings in the turbine sector comes from turbojet aircraft.

Turbojets saw a decline of more than 26 percent from 2001 to 2003 while turboprops saw a decline of nearly 45 percent over the same period. Piston-powered aircraft, which account for approximately 7 percent of total billings, saw a decline of more than 6 percent over the same period. The business jet sector was clearly the hardest hit.

However, as seen with airport enplanements in the state, the general aviation manufacturers are poised for a recovery. Data from the first three quarters of 2004 show solid increases over 2003.

Worldwide shipments over this period are up nearly 8 percent with billings up nearly 20 percent. ☆

Texas Air History

Source: FAA

Airline passenger traffic enplaned in Texas by scheduled carriers.

Fiscal Year*	Scheduled Enplanements
1950	1,169,051
1955	2,434,814
1960	3,113,582
1965	5,757,689
1970	10,256,691
1975	13,182,957
1980	26,282,723
1985	40,719,223
1986	41,413,294
1987	43,449,267
1988	45,342,155
1989	47,735,102
1990	49,317,619
1991	49,192,106
1992	51,740,699
1993	52,437,367
1994	54,416,477
1995	57,166,515
1996	58,183,838
1997	60,156,456
1998	61,712,342
1999	62,558,165
2000	65,109,179
2001	63,531,007
2002	57,733,384

*1950-1965 figures are for calendar years.

Passengers check in at DFW Airport. File photo.

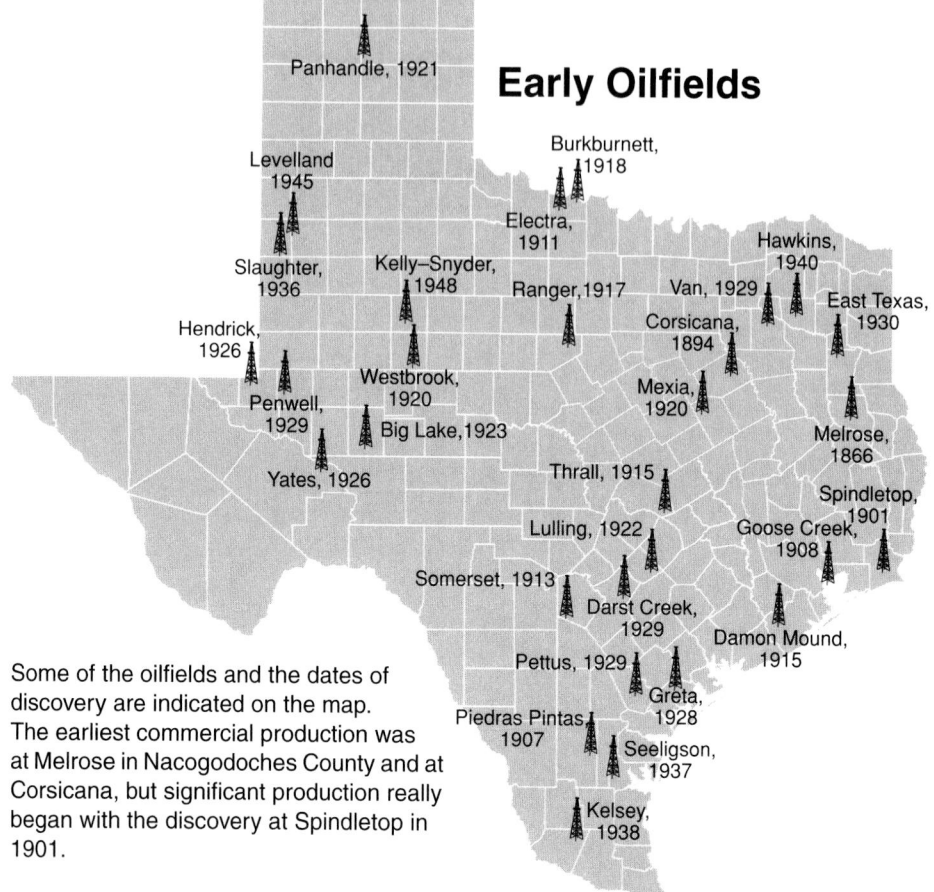

Early Oilfields

Panhandle, 1921

Levelland 1945

Burkburnett, 1918

Slaughter, 1936

Kelly–Snyder, 1948

Electra, 1911

Hawkins, 1940

Hendrick, 1926

Ranger, 1917

Van, 1929

East Texas, 1930

Corsicana, 1894

Penwell, 1929

Westbrook, 1920

Mexia, 1920

Big Lake, 1923

Yates, 1926

Thrall, 1915

Melrose, 1866

Spindletop, 1901

Lulling, 1922

Goose Creek, 1908

Somerset, 1913

Darst Creek, 1929

Damon Mound, 1915

Pettus, 1929

Piedras Pintas, 1907

Greta, 1928

Seeligson, 1937

Kelsey, 1938

Some of the oilfields and the dates of discovery are indicated on the map. The earliest commercial production was at Melrose in Nacogodoches County and at Corsicana, but significant production really began with the discovery at Spindletop in 1901.

History of Oil Discoveries in Texas

Oil and natural gas are the most valuable minerals produced in Texas, contributing 18 percent of the oil production in the United States in 2001, and 30 percent of the gas production in the nation in 2001, the latest figures available.

Oil and gas have been produced from most areas of Texas and from rocks of all geologic eras except the Precambrian.

All of the major sedimentary basins of Texas have produced some oil or gas.

The well-known Permian Basin of West Texas has yielded large quantities of oil since the Big Lake discovery in 1923, although there was a smaller discovery in the Westbrook field in Mitchell County three years earlier.

The 1923 discovery, **Santa Rita No. 1** in Reagan County, was on University of Texas land, and it and Texas A&M University both have benefitted from the royalties.

Although large quantities of petroleum have been produced from rocks of Permian age, production in the area also occurs from older Paleozoic rocks.

Production from rocks of Paleozoic age occurs pri-

marily from North Central Texas westward to New Mexico and southwestward to the Rio Grande, but there is also significant Paleozoic production in North Texas.

Mesozoic rocks are the primary hydrocarbon reservoirs of the East Texas Basin and the area south and east of the Balcones Fault Zone. Cenozoic sandstones are the main reservoirs along the Gulf Coast and offshore state waters.

Earliest Oil

Indians found oil seeping from the soils of Texas long before the first Europeans arrived. They told explorers that the fluid had medicinal values. The first record of Europeans using crude oil, however, was the caulking of boats in 1543 by survivors of the DeSoto expedition near Sabine Pass.

Melrose, in Nacogdoches County, was the site in 1866 of the first drilled well to produce oil in Texas. The driller was Lyne T. Barret.

Barret used an auger, fastened to a pipe and rotated by a cogwheel driven by a steam engine — a basic principle of rotary drilling that has been used since, although with much improvement.

In 1867 Amory (Emory) Starr and Peyton F. Edwards brought in a well at Oil Springs, in the same area.

Other wells followed and **Nacogdoches County** was the site of Texas' first commercial oil field, pipeline and effort to refine crude. Several thousand barrels of oil were produced there during these years.

First refinery, 1899

Other oil was found in crudely dug wells in Bexar County in 1889 and in Hardin County in 1893. The three small wells in Hardin County led to the creation of two small refineries in 1896 and 1898.

But it was not until June 9, 1894, that Texas had a major discovery. This occurred in the drilling of a water well for the city of **Corsicana**. Oil caused that well to be abandoned, but a company formed in 1895 drilled several producing oil wells.

The first well-equipped refinery in Texas was built in 1898, and this plant, which shipped its first production in 1899, usually is called the state's **first refinery,** despite the earlier efforts. Discovery of the Powell Field, also near Corsicana, followed in 1900.

Spindletop, 1901

Jan. 10, 1901, is the most famous date in Texas petroleum history. This is the date that the great gusher erupted in the oil well being drilled at Spindletop, near Beaumont, by a mining engineer, Capt. A. F. Lucas.

Thousands of barrels of oil flowed before the well could be capped. This was the first salt dome oil discovery.

Spindletop created a sensation throughout the world, and encouraged exploration and drilling in Texas that has continued since.

Texas oil production increased from 836,039 barrels in 1900 to 4,393,658 in 1901; and in 1902 Spindletop alone produced 17,421,000 barrels, or 94 percent of the state's production. Prices dropped to 3 cents a barrel, an all-time low.

Offshore, 1908

The first offshore drilling was in shallow northern Galveston Bay, where the **Goose Creek** Field was discovered in 1908. Several dry holes followed and the field was abandoned. But a gusher in 1916 created the real boom there.

A water-well drilling outfit on the W. T. Waggoner Ranch in Wichita County hit oil, bringing in the **Electra** Field in 1911.

Salt dome oilfields followed at Damon Mound in 1915, Barbers Hill in 1916, and Blue Ridge in 1919.

In 1917 came the discovery of the **Ranger** Field in Eastland County. The **Burkburnett** Field in Wichita County was discovered in 1919.

About this time, oil discoveries brought a short era of swindling, with oil stock promotion and selling on a nationwide scale. It ended after a series of trials in federal courts.

The **Mexia** Field in Limestone County was discovered in 1920, and the second Powell Field in Navarro County in 1924.

Another great area really developed in 1921 in the **Panhandle,** a field with sensational oil and gas discoveries in Hutchinson and contiguous counties and the booming of Borger.

The **Luling** Field was opened in 1922, and 1925 saw the comeback of Spindletop with a production larger than that of the original field.

In 1925 **Howard County** was opened for production. **Hendricks** in Winkler County opened in 1926 and **Raccoon Bend**, Austin County, opened in 1927. **Sugar Land** was the most important Texas oil development in 1928.

The **Darst Creek** Field was opened in 1929. In the same year, new records of productive sand thickness were set for the industry at **Van**, Van Zandt County. **Pettus** was another contribution of 1929 in Bee County.

East Texas Field

The **East Texas** field, biggest of them all, was discovered near Turnertown and Joinerville, Rusk County, by veteran wildcatter C. M. (Dad) Joiner, in October 1930. The success of this well — drilled on land condemned many times by geologists of the major companies — was followed by the biggest leasing campaign in history.

The field soon was extended to Kilgore, Longview and northward. The East Texas field brought overproduction and a rapid sinking of the price. Private attempts were made to prorate production, but without much success.

On Aug. 17, 1931, Gov. Ross S. Sterling ordered the National Guard into the field, which he placed under martial law. This drastic action was taken after the Texas Railroad Commission had been enjoined from enforcing production restrictions.

After the complete shutdown, the Texas Legislature enacted legal **proration,** the system of regulation still utilized.

West Texas

The most significant subsequent oil discoveries in Texas were those in West Texas. In 1936, oil was discovered west of Lubbock in the Duggan Field in Cochran County.

Originally it was thought to be one of two fields, it and the adjacent **Slaughter** Field, but in 1940 the Railroad Commission ruled that the two produced from one reservoir, called Slaughter. The prolific **Levelland** Field, in Cochran and Hockley counties, was discovered in 1945.

A discovery well in **Scurry** County on Nov. 21, 1948, was the first of several major developments in that region. Many of the leading Texas counties in minerals value are in that section.

Austin Chalk

The **Giddings** Field on the Austin Chalk in Lee, Fayette and Burleson counties had significant drilling in the 1970s that continued into the 1980s. ☆

Chronological Listing of Major Oilfield Discoveries

The following list gives the name of the field, county and discovery date. Sources include Texas Mid-Continent Oil and Gas Association from records of the U.S. Bureau of Mines; the Oil and Gas Journal; previous Texas Almanacs, the New Handbook of Texas, and the Energy Information Administration of the U.S. Department of Energy.

Corsicana, Navarro, 1894;
Powell, Navarro, 1900;
Spindletop, Jefferson, 1901;
Sour Lake, Hardin, 1902;
Batson-Old, Hardin, 1903;
Humble, Harris, 1905;
Mission, Bexar, 1907;
Piedras Pintas, Duval, 1907;
Goose Creek, Harris, 1908;
Panhandle Osborne, Wheeler, 1910;
Archer County, 1911;
Electra, Wichita, 1911;
Burk, Wichita, 1912;
Iowa Park, Wichita, 1913;
Orange, Orange, 1913;
Somerset, Bexar, 1913
Damon Mound, Brazoria, 1915;
Thrall, Williamson, 1915;
Wilbarger County, 1915;
Barbers Hill, Chambers, 1916;
Stephens County Regular, 1916;
Ranger, Eastland, 1917;
Young County, 1917;
Burkburnett Townsite, Wichita, 1918;
Desdemona, Eastland, 1918;
Hull, Liberty, 1918;
West Columbia, Brazoria, 1918;
Blue Ridge, Fort Bend, 1919;
KMA (Kemp-Munger-Allen), Wichita, 1919;
Mexia, Limestone-Freestone, 1920;
Refugio, Refugio, 1920;
Westbrook, Mitchell, 1920;
Panhandle, Carson-Collingsworth-Gray-Hutchinson-Moore-Potter-Wheeler, 1921;
Currie, Navarro, 1921;
Mirando City, Webb, 1921;
Pierce Junction, Harris, 1921;
Thompsons, Fort Bend, 1921;
Aviators, Webb, 1922;
High Island, Galveston-Chambers, 1922;
Luling-Branyon, Caldwell-Guadalupe, 1922;
Big Lake, Reagan, 1923;
Cooke County, 1924;
Richland, Navarro, 1924;
Wortham, Freestone, 1924;
Boling, Wharton, 1925;
Howard-Glasscock, Howard, 1925;
Lytton Springs, Caldwell, 1925;
McCamey, Upton, 1925;
Hendrick, Winkler, 1926;
Iatan East, Howard, 1926;
McElroy, Crane, 1926;
Yates, Pecos, 1926;
Raccoon Bend, Austin, 1927;
Waddell, Crane, 1927;
Agua Dulce-Stratton, Nueces, 1928;

Greta, Refugio, 1928;
Kermit, Winkler, 1928;
Salt Flat, Caldwell, 1928;
Sugarland, Fort Bend, 1928;
Darst Creek, Guadalupe, 1929;
Penwell, Ector, 1929;
Pettus, Bee, 1929;
Van, Van Zandt, 1929;
Cowden North, Ector, 1930;
East Texas, Cherokee-Gregg-Rusk-Smith-Upshur, 1930;
Fuhrman-Mascho, Andrews, 1930;
Sand Hills, Crane, 1930;
Conroe, Montgomery, 1931;
Manvel, Brazoria, 1931;
Tomball, Harris, 1933;
Dickinson, Galveston, 1934;
Hastings East, Brazoria, 1934;
Means, Andrews, 1934;
Old Ocean, Brazoria, 1934;
Tom O'Connor, Refugio, 1934;
Anahuac, Chambers, 1935;
Goldsmith, Ector, 1935;
Keystone, Winkler, 1935;
Plymouth, San Patricio, 1935;
Withers, Wharton, 1936;
Pearsall, Frio, 1936;
Seminole, Gaines, 1936;
Slaughter, Cochran-Hockley, 1936;
Talco, Titus-Franklin, 1936;
Wasson, Gaines, 1936;
Webster, Harris, 1936;
Jordan, Crane-Ector, 1937;

Seeligson, Jim Wells-Kleberg, 1937;
Dune, Crane, 1938;
Kelsey, Brooks-Jim Hogg-Starr, 1938;
Walnut Bend, Cooke, 1938;
West Ranch, Jackson, 1938;
Diamond M, Scurry, 1940;
Hawkins, Wood, 1940;
Fullerton, Andrews, 1941;
Oyster Bayou, Chambers, 1941;
Tijerina-Canales-Blucher, Jim Wells-Kleberg, 1941;
Quitman, Wood, 1942;
Welch, Dawson, 1942;
Russell, Gaines, 1943;
Anton-Irish, Hale-Lamb-Lubbock, 1944;
Mabee, Andrews-Martin, 1944;
Midland Farms, Andrews, 1944;
TXL Devonian, Ector, 1944;
Block 31, Crane, 1945;
Borregos, Kleberg, 1945;
Dollarhide, Andrews, 1945;
Levelland, Cochran-Hockley, 1945;
Andector, Ector, 1946;
Kelly-Snyder, Scurry, 1948;
Cogdell Area, Scurry, 1949;
Pegasus, Upton-Midland, 1949;
Spraberry Trend, Glasscock-Midland, 1949;
Prentice, Yoakum, 1950;
Salt Creek, Kent, 1950;
Dora Roberts, Midland, 1954. ☆

The Santa Rita No. 1, discovered in Reagan County in 1923. Texas Almanac photo.

Petroleum Production and Income in Texas

Year	Crude Oil & Condensate			Natural Gas		
	Production (thousand barrels)	Value (add 000)	Average Price per Barrel	Production (million cubic feet)	Value (add 000)	Average Price (cents per MCF)
1915	24,943	$ 13,027	$ 0.52	13,324	$ 2,594	19.5
1925	144,648	262,270	1.81	134,872	7,040	5.2
1935	392,666	367,820	0.94	642,366	13,233	2.1
1945	754,710	914,410	1.21	1,711,401	44,839	2.6
1955	1,053,297	2,989,330	2.84	4,730,798	378,464	8.0
1965	1,000,749	2,962,119	2.96	6,636,555	858,396	12.9
1966	1,057,706	3,141,387	2.97	6,953,790	903,993	13.0
1967	1,119,962	3,375,565	3.01	7,188,900	948,935	13.2
1968	1,133,380	3,450,707	3.04	7,495,414	1,011,881	13.5
1969	1,151,775	3,696,328	3.21	7,853,199	1,075,888	13.7
1970	1,249,697	4,104,005	3.28	8,357,716	1,203,511	14.4
1971	1,222,926	4,261,775	3.48	8,550,705	1,376,664	16.1
1972	1,301,685	4,536,077	3.48	8,657,840	1,419,886	16.4
1973	1,294,671	5,157,623	3.98	8,513,850	1,735,221	20.4
1974	1,262,126	8,773,003	6.95	8,170,798	2,541,118	31.1
1975	1,221,929	9,336,570	7.64	7,485,764	3,885,112	51.9
1976	1,189,523	10,217,702	8.59	7,191,859	5,163,755	71.8
1977	1,137,880	9,986,002	8.78	7,051,027	6,367,077	90.3
1978	1,074,050	9,980,333	9.29	6,548,184	6,515,443	99.5
1979	1,018,094	12,715,994	12.49	7,174,623	8,509,103	118.6
1980	977,436	21,259,233	21.75	7,115,889	10,673,834	150.0
1981	945,132	32,692,116	34.59	7,050,207	12,598,712	178.7
1982	923,868	29,074,126	31.47	6,497,678	13,567,151	208.5
1983	876,205	22,947,814	26.19	5,643,183	14,672,275	260.0
1984	874,079	25,138,520	28.76	5,864,224	13,487,715	230.0
1985	860,300	23,159,286	26.92	5,805,098	12,665,114	218.0
1986	813,620	11,976,488	14.72	5,663,491	8,778,410	155.0
1987	754,213	13,221,345	17.53	5,516,224	7,612,389	138.0
1988	727,928	10,729,660	14.74	5,702,643	7,983,700	140.0
1989	679,575	12,123,624	17.84	5,595,190	8,113,026	145.0
1990	672,081	15,047,902	22.39	5,520,915	8,281,372	150.0
1991	672,810	12,836,080	19.05	5,509,990	7,713,986	140.0
1992	642,059	11,820,306	18.41	5,436,408	8,643,888	159.0
1993	572,600	9,288,800	16.22	4,062,500	7,365,800	181.0
1994	533,900	7,977,500	14.94	3,842,500	6,220,300	162.0
1995	503,200	8,177,700	16.25	3,690,000	5,305,200	143.0
1996	478,100	9,560,800	20.00	3,458,100	6,945,000	200.0
1997	464,900	8,516,800	18.32	3,672,300	8,134,200	221.5
1998	440,600	5,472,400	12.42	3,557,900	6,362,900	178.8
1999	337,100	5,855,800	17.37	3,321,600	6,789,700	204.4
2000	348,900	10,037,300	28.77	3,552,000	12,837,600	361.4
2001	325,500	7,770,500	23.87	3,732,700	13,708,700	367.3
2002	335,600	8,150,400	24.29	3,476,800	9,840,800	283.0
2003	331,600	$9,733,000	$ 29.35	3,594,400	$16,122,700	448.6

MCF (thousand cubic feet).

Sources: Data since 1993 are from the state comptroller. Previously from the Texas Railroad Commission, Texas Mid-Continent Oil & Gas Association and, beginning in 1979, data are from Department of Energy.

DOE figures do not include gas that is vented or flared or used for pressure maintenance and repressuring, but do include non-hydrocarbon gases.

Oil well pumping unit sits next to the First Baptist Church in Van, in Van Zandt County. Texas Almanac photo.

Average Annual Drilling Counts 1982-2004

Source: Texas Railroad Commission

Year	Rotary rigs active*		Permits†	Texas wells completed		Wells drilled**
	Texas	U.S.	Texas	Oil	Gas	Texas
1982	994	3,117	41,224	16,296	6,273	27,648
1983	796	2,232	45,550	15,941	5,027	26,882
1984	850	2,428	37,507	18,716	5,489	30,898
1985	680	1,980	30,878	16,543	4,605	27,124
1986	313	964	15,894	10,373	3,304	18,707
1987	293	1,090	15,297	7,327	2,542	13,121
1988	280	936	13,493	6,441	2,665	12,261
1989	264	871	12,756	4,914	2,760	10,054
1990	348	1,009	14,033	5,593	2,894	11,231
1991	315	860	12,494	6,025	2,755	11,295
1992	251	721	12,089	5,031	2,537	9,498
1993	264	754	11,612	4,646	3,295	9,969
1994	274	775	11,030	3,962	3,553	9,299
1995	251	723	11,244	4,334	3,778	9,785
1996	283	779	12,669	4,061	4,060	9,747
1997	358	945	13,933	4,482	4,594	10,778
1998	303	827	9,385	4,509	4,907	11,057
1999	226	622	8,430	2,049	3,566	6,658
2000	343	918	12,021	3,111	4,580	8,854
2001	462	1,156	12,227	3,082	5,787	10,005
2002	338	830	9,716	3,268	5,474	9,877
2003	449	1,032	12,664	3,111	6,336	10,420
2004	506	1,192	14,700	3,446	7,118	10,564

*Source for rig count: Baker Hughes Inc. This is an annual average from monthly reports.

†Totals shown for 1988 and after are number of drilling permits issued; data for previous years were total drilling applications received.
**Wells drilled are oil and gas well completions and dry holes drilled.

Texas Oil Production History

The table shows the year of oil or gas discovery in each county, oil production in 2003 and 2004 and total oil production from date of discovery to Jan. 1, 2005. The 19 counties omitted have not produced oil.

The table has been compiled by the *Texas Almanac* from information provided in past years by the Texas Mid-Continent Oil & Gas Assoc. Since 1970, production figures have been compiled from records of the Railroad Commission of Texas. In prior years, U.S. Bureau of Mines and State Comptroller reports were the basis of these compilations. The figures in the final column are cumulative of all previously published figures. The change in sources, due to different techniques, may create some discrepancies in year-to-year comparisons among counties.

County	Year of Discovery	Production in Barrels* 2003	Production in Barrels* 2004	Total Production to Jan. 1, 2005
Anderson	1928	1,027,237	918,936	299,707,245
Andrews	1929	24,279,753	23,233,003	2,783,911,447
Angelina	1936	9,295	8,170	870,198
Aransas	1936	429,503	270,422	85,217,610
Archer	1911	1,259,985	1,106,737	494,072,274
Atascosa	1917	703,278	765,458	149,778,538
Austin	1915	324,678	318,767	114,769,634
Bandera	1995	2,176	1,495	21,831
Bastrop	1913	128,436	118,323	16,543,675
Baylor	1924	129,739	124,546	57,990,102
Bee	1929	677,357	588,027	107,761,821
Bell	1980	0	0	446
Bexar	1889	121,231	132,646	35,835,075
Borden	1949	4,558,279	4,530,348	405,593,743
Bowie	1944	129,388	109,121	6,405,421
Brazoria	1902	2,719,492	2,549,261	1,270,790,962
Brazos	1942	2,394,186	2,214,816	137,027,692
Brewster	1969	0	0	56
Briscoe	1982	0	0	3,554
Brooks	1935	1,484,111	1,280,360	169,075,429
Brown	1917	112,087	113,621	53,259,568
Burleson	1938	2,806,135	2,449,581	192,213,840
Caldwell	1922	963,806	901,836	281,352,954
Calhoun	1935	636,588	593,989	103,913,124
Callahan	1923	210,548	186,384	85,925,832
Cameron	1944	780	1,471	466,157
Camp	1940	320,236	253,804	28,968,483
Carson	1921	355,553	345,918	179,852,233
Cass	1936	339,828	347,828	114,129,324
Chambers	1916	1,781,786	1,732,360	907,859,827
Cherokee	1926	287,733	291,564	70,710,888
Childress	1961	30,418	43,723	1,582,553
Clay	1917	794,041	742,144	204,088,003
Cochran	1936	4,051,251	3,827,565	503,034,125
Coke	1942	471,736	471,960	223,231,158
Coleman	1902	330,924	301,121	94,687,781
Collin	1963	0	0	53,000
Collingsworth	1936	2,596	2,483	1,237,935
Colorado	1932	444,200	420,476	41,221,056
Comanche	1918	17,057	12,194	5,957,594
Concho	1940	625,689	506,514	25,948,824
Cooke	1924	1,666,162	1,608,729	388,560,201
Coryell	1964	0	0	1,100
Cottle	1955	101,041	101,769	4,544,121
Crane	1926	10,047,177	10,154,341	1,742,795,087
Crockett	1925	3,712,518	3,897,057	361,863,500
Crosby	1955	593,240	555,634	24,473,015
Culberson	1953	130,489	134,926	24,754,067
Dallas	1986	0	0	231
Dawson	1934	5,262,019	4,866,523	379,794,917
Delta	1984	0	0	65,089
Denton	1937	668,968	744,979	5,696,331
DeWitt	1930	170,116	336,706	66,454,753
Dickens	1953	1,607,398	1,660,624	17,167,369
Dimmit	1943	729,659	589,627	105,348,756

County	Year of Discovery	Production in Barrels* 2003	Production in Barrels* 2004	Total Production to Jan. 1, 2005
Duval	1905	1,301,545	1,365,275	585,742,696
Eastland	1917	297,164	292,802	156,401,544
Ector	1926	20,330,426	19,964,838	3,089,706,584
Edwards	1946	3,474	4,599	528,686
Ellis	1953	201	152	839,880
Erath	1917	4,810	4,223	2,084,835
Falls	1937	5,511	4,266	847,846
Fannin	1980	0	0	13,281
Fayette	1943	2,576,472	2,179,725	151,003,151
Fisher	1928	737,823	637,193	248,366,557
Floyd	1952	1,646	1,000	155,007
Foard	1929	143,307	134,761	24,071,029
Fort Bend	1919	3,277,449	2,906,424	689,309,940
Franklin	1936	463,219	462,712	176,830,482
Freestone	1916	315,226	294,408	44,889,337
Frio	1934	593,735	620,189	145,829,486
Gaines	1935	30,481,427	29,630,915	2,173,908,952
Galveston	1922	2,123,967	1,688,781	452,937,590
Garza	1926	4,757,543	4,291,075	334,732,515
Glasscock	1925	4,341,224	3,999,408	265,952,636
Goliad	1930	638,054	700,015	82,542,084
Gonzales	1902	282,873	219,318	43,603,970
Gray	1925	1,495,730	1,368,975	672,307,787
Grayson	1930	1,309,382	1,323,298	255,420,303
Gregg	1931	3,333,731	3,001,180	3,285,627,108
Grimes	1952	186,877	266,960	18,220,020
Guadalupe	1922	1,003,158	1,013,249	203,553,119
Hale	1946	3,490,243	2,974,554	176,565,482
Hamilton	1938	1,978	839	150,546
Hansford	1937	204,703	190,583	39,045,882
Hardeman	1944	2,257,068	2,044,694	82,027,274
Hardin	1893	1,896,583	1,945,588	437,858,292
Harris	1905	2,174,688	1,875,635	1,374,009,392
Harrison	1928	887,965	870,664	88,982,056
Hartley	1937	270,292	230,489	7,349,147
Haskell	1929	417,064	398,755	116,573,953
Hays	1956	0	0	296
Hemphill	1955	782,524	1,091,101	37,062,243
Henderson	1934	843,334	728,936	177,265,508
Hidalgo	1934	3,613,838	2,777,037	110,100,308
Hill	1929	253	55	75,393
Hockley	1937	21,694,470	20,534,492	1,632,173,974
Hood	1958	232	321	113,235
Hopkins	1936	419,548	408,047	89,457,991
Houston	1934	684,717	669,506	56,522,738
Howard	1925	7,097,041	6,315,372	811,901,455
Hunt	1942	15	0	2,024,660
Hutchinson	1923	910,229	874,712	530,501,534
Irion	1928	1,637,207	1,484,869	100,768,844
Jack	1923	749,892	706,009	203,811,409
Jackson	1934	1,098,686	1,030,166	681,128,930
Jasper	1928	643,798	732,671	34,846,879
Jeff Davis	1980	0	0	20,866
Jefferson	1901	1,673,538	1,933,383	534,599,480
Jim Hogg	1921	403,109	297,916	112,153,008

Counties
of Large Production

Leading counties through a century of oil production have been in the Permian Basin of West Texas, the East Texas Field and on the Coastal Plains near Houston (Harris County). Counties not shaded have produced less that 250 million barrels. Of Texas' 254 counties, 19 have not produced oil and are omitted from the list below.

- ● More than 1 billion
- ● 500 million to <1 billion
- ● 250 million to <500 million

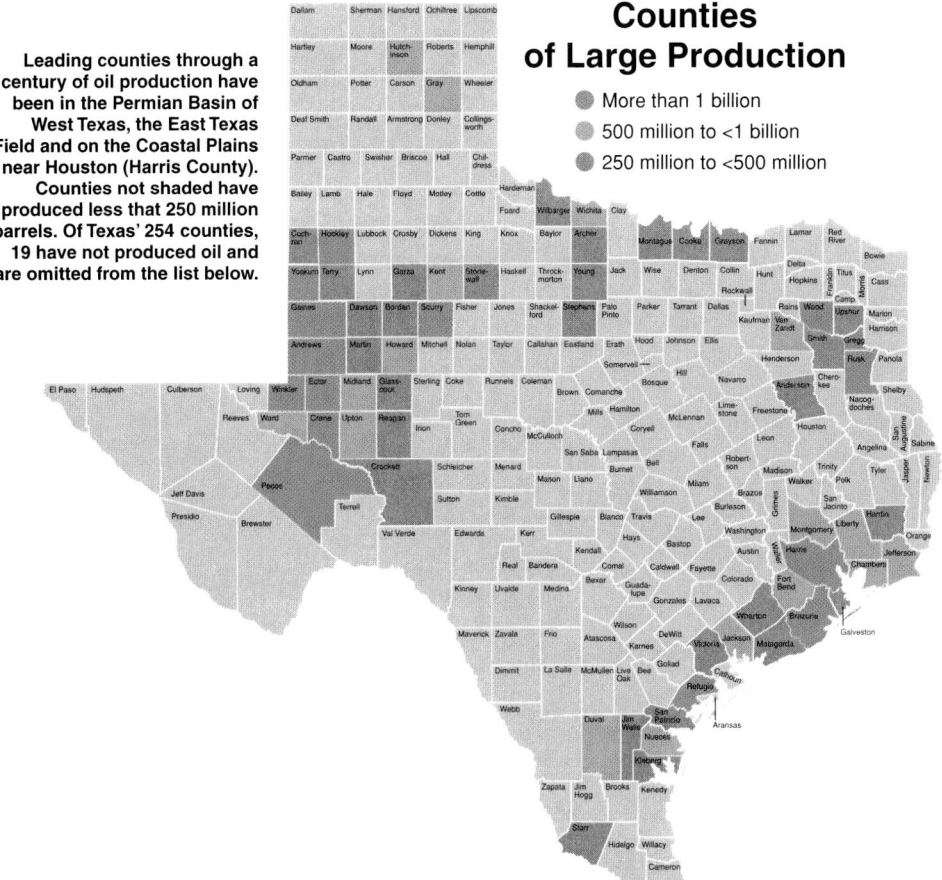

County	Year of Discovery	Production in Barrels* 2003	Production in Barrels* 2004	Total Production to Jan. 1, 2005
Jim Wells	1931	220,450	195,999	462,560,723
Johnson	1962	0	5,540	199,540
Jones	1926	724,704	745,729	220,345,838
Karnes	1930	379,040	363,773	108,228,299
Kaufman	1948	55,579	60,950	24,596,705
Kenedy	1947	502,392	356,309	39,040,143
Kent	1946	6,619,113	6,057,040	569,277,197
Kerr	1982	106	646	77,907
Kimble	1939	703	547	97,450
King	1943	2,618,930	2,226,609	176,388,813
Kinney	1960	0	0	402
Kleberg	1919	1,806,604	708,348	336,320,467
Knox	1946	309,494	273,940	62,123,812
Lamb	1945	1,696,535	1,393,747	37,567,146
Lampasas	1985	0	0	111
La Salle	1940	279,943	263,253	27,526,826
Lavaca	1941	721,889	590,024	30,805,165
Lee	1939	1,694,097	1,521,755	133,853,281
Leon	1936	840,799	896,423	62,573,364
Liberty	1904	3,158,277	3,799,855	529,396,655
Limestone	1920	163,552	164,563	119,406,143
Lipscomb	1956	429,724	448,167	59,654,376
Live Oak	1930	587,062	555,736	83,650,473
Llano	1978	0	0	647
Loving	1921	1,080,437	1,003,372	110,306,695

County	Year of Discovery	Production in Barrels* 2003	Production in Barrels* 2004	Total Production to Jan. 1, 2005
Lubbock	1941	1,617,381	1,604,909	68,089,579
Lynn	1950	178,763	152,115	19,103,799
Madison	1946	388,874	415,691	32,985,267
Marion	1910	187,258	181,304	55,597,674
Martin	1945	4,659,602	4,796,227	308,546,191
Matagorda	1901	1,950,740	1,248,714	279,982,827
Maverick	1929	1,420,979	1,047,159	51,298,601
McCulloch	1938	145,727	125,210	1,813,230
McLennan	1902	1,693	1,767	335,907
McMullen	1922	1,133,880	1,233,131	103,777,777
Medina	1901	83,176	82,240	10,744,502
Menard	1946	160,580	135,799	7,307,198
Midland	1945	11,099,970	11,099,482	618,291,788
Milam	1921	623,676	565,850	20,670,316
Mills	1982	0	0	28,122
Mitchell	1920	2,744,724	2,971,582	224,512,072
Montague	1919	1,480,260	1,512,440	290,366,434
Montgomery	1931	1,112,197	1,046,268	775,123,441
Moore	1926	245,609	246,457	29,813,521
Morris	2004	0	2,154	2,154
Motley	1957	60,860	59,268	10,978,188
Nacogdoches	1866	132,703	180,493	3,816,402
Navarro	1894	378,592	316,129	218,357,721
Newton	1937	660,126	706,556	63,097,015
Nolan	1939	1,500,811	1,387,111	197,903,657

County	Year of Discovery	Production in Barrels*		Total Production to Jan. 1, 2005
		2003	2004	
Nueces	1930	1,963,767	1,474,373	562,045,176
Ochiltree	1951	920,646	875,292	160,012,711
Oldham	1957	109,907	87,808	13,803,240
Orange	1913	1,046,839	1,046,114	157,638,380
Palo Pinto	1902	271,188	421,943	23,603,894
Panola	1917	1,788,508	1,952,819	92,220,935
Parker	1942	15,951	40,298	2,912,394
Parmer	1963	0	0	144,000
Pecos	1926	9,542,389	9,758,843	1,754,059,142
Polk	1930	1,325,707	1,280,689	124,328,817
Potter	1925	138,208	150,429	9,807,078
Presidio	1980	0	0	4,377
Rains	1955	0	0	148,896
Reagan	1923	5,1919,486	5,002,436	503,132,321
Real	2003	6,864	9,292	16,156
Red River	1951	256,644	224,732	7,791,684
Reeves	1939	789,446	749,564	77,845,628
Refugio	1920	4,649,014	5,335,708	1,319,317,029
Roberts	1945	562,497	519,263	46,900,995
Robertson	1944	1,330,358	1,295,431	25,984,999
Runnels	1927	530,358	443,664	147,080,840
Rusk	1930	2,933,928	2,823,149	1,828,535,077
Sabine	1981	12,636	8,046	4,901,791
San Augustine	1947	12,399	10,657	2,469,569
San Jacinto	1940	231,867	262,986	25,950,544
San Patricio	1930	1,018,213	1,662,315	485,076,804
San Saba	1982	0	0	32,362
Schleicher	1934	523,356	451,700	87,801,081
Scurry	1923	11,479,564	14,491,506	2,032,634,636
Shackelford	1910	855,237	792,437	182,163,651
Shelby	1917	175,146	212,344	2,964,178
Sherman	1938	129,563	114,415	9,286,483
Smith	1931	1,547,948	1,569,256	264,421,700
Somervell	1978	0	0	141
Starr	1929	3,146,441	2,306,457	294,560,032
Stephens	1916	2,282,996	2,323,132	338,435,078
Sterling	1947	1,056,687	1,048,678	88,001,091
Stonewall	1938	1,326,705	1,193,631	262,265,174
Sutton	1948	87,078	73,888	7,744,839
Swisher	1981	0	0	6
Tarrant	1969	2,115	3,331	6,162
Taylor	1929	574,988	552,109	144,338,236
Terrell	1952	298,062	252,865	8,789,845
Terry	1940	4,699,591	4,372,928	438,303,224
Throckmorton	1925	1,041,810	912,177	220,858,120
Titus	1936	473,915	507,332	211,214,411
Tom Green	1940	420,424	420,945	92,176,086
Travis	1934	856	866	751,959
Trinity	1946	59,801	78,311	853,462
Tyler	1937	1,074,462	1,426,050	42,250,695
Upshur	1931	659,941	656,650	287,268,076
Upton	1925	8,690,477	8,576,627	827,595,699
Uvalde	1950	0	0	1,814
Val Verde	1935	1,802	888	139,235
Van Zandt	1929	1,184,038	1,014,890	550,659,088
Victoria	1931	814,401	922,031	252,939,959
Walker	1934	7,807	6,866	520,936
Waller	1934	1,505,822	1,501,256	27,752,794
Ward	1928	4,816,378	4,542,371	756,897,566
Washington	1915	862,583	768,400	31,162,254
Webb	1921	1,618,042	1,483,843	160,374,486
Wharton	1925	2,322,594	2,055,012	342,766,363
Wheeler	1910	529,989	764,715	100,738,226
Wichita	1910	2,113,405	2,130,744	827,590,641
Wilbarger	1915	594,951	620,369	263,414,033
Willacy	1936	620,333	742,574	113,350,604
Williamson	1915	7,794	7,799	9,543,330
Wilson	1941	337,252	279,694	48,828,041
Winkler	1926	4,371,862	3,723,141	1,073,796,157
Wise	1942	973,897	931,699	100,594,525
Wood	1940	5,280,931	4,616,489	1,199,801,565
Yoakum	1936	24,753,573	25,181,917	2,063,377,676
Young	1917	1,428,694	1,343,940	308,713,521
Zapata	1919	543,809	257,091	47,779,811
Zavala	1937	348,773	567,897	46,287,137

*Total includes condensate production.
Source: Railroad Commission, 2003-04 production reports.

Oil and Gas Production by County, 2004

In 2004 in Texas, the total natural gas production was 4,893,348,699 thousand cubic feet (MCF) and total crude oil production was 349,326,081 barrels (BBL). Total condensate was 38,380,813 BBL. Total casinghead was 926,264,654 MCF. Counties not listed in the chart below had no production in 2004.

Source: Texas Railroad Commission.
BBL refers to barrels and MCF to thousand cubic feet.

County	Oil BBL	Casinghead MCF	Gas Well Gas MCF	Conden-sate BBL
Anderson	842,809	6,175,969	7,140,581	76,127
Andrews	23,230,204	33,723,693	1,669,622	2,799
Angelina	5,711	9,462	860,732	2,459
Aransas	73,632	477,894	7,888,921	196,790
Archer	1,106,737	514,728	0	0
Atascosa	751,612	251,169	6,001,540	13,846
Austin	157,308	63,074	14,600,084	161,459
Bandera	1,495	0	0	0
Bastrop	103,591	206,227	230,043	14,732
Baylor	124,546	248	0	0
Bee	349,225	473,018	32,537,611	238,802
Bexar	132,646	292	20	0
Borden	4,530,348	2,549,214	91	0
Bowie	100,305	72,416	280,858	8,816
Brazoria	1,710,149	1,631,235	44,831,552	839,112
Brazos	2,107,740	5,895,093	6,807,187	107,076
Brooks	200,157	550,206	86,761,261	1,080,203
Brown	111,303	387,623	1,237,325	2,318
Burleson	2,378,171	11,755,009	3,003,263	71,410
Caldwell	901,686	498,340	16,089	150
Calhoun	462,861	701,652	9,446,198	131,128
Callahan	183,152	293,824	663,266	3,232
Cameron	761	296	273,368	710
Camp	253,792	12	811,514	12
Carson	345,918	2,389,630	20,821,130	0
Cass	322,654	498,709	3,566,821	25,174
Chambers	1,102,436	2,466,587	23,892,480	629,924

County	Oil BBL	Casinghead MCF	Gas Well Gas MCF	Condensate BBL	County	Oil BBL	Casinghead MCF	Gas Well Gas MCF	Condensate BBL
Cherokee	199,929	312,660	13,822,614	91,635	Hidalgo	47,811	133,563	234,486,550	2,729,226
Childress	43,723	225	0	0	Hill	55	0	0	0
Clay	731,187	695,012	258,589	10,957	Hockley	20,532,449	49,690,291	128,518	2,043
Cochran	3,826,273	3,533,604	272,618	1,292	Hood	0	0	771,787	321
Coke	468,931	2,270,024	793,412	3,029	Hopkins	400,877	246,405	1,163,996	7,170
Coleman	298,136	645,979	1,317,282	2,985	Houston	639,076	239,422	3,625,830	30,430
Collingswth	2,127	37,528	1,380,927	356	Howard	6,307,825	6,262,551	1,096,142	7,547
Colorado	226,369	1,043,618	20,588,278	194,107	Hutchinson	869,737	5,504,310	10,305,668	4,975
Comanche	10,469	94,394	645,951	1,725	Irion	1,460,931	6,827,044	2,939,110	23,938
Concho	491,934	1,210,424	550,205	14,580	Jack	607,556	3,332,813	12,131,871	98,453
Cooke	1,607,138	598,563	142,227	1,591	Jackson	826,043	4,826,811	20,928,565	204,123
Coryell	0	0	0	0	Jasper	301,825	1,251,063	11,160,962	430,846
Cottle	62,345	38,351	4,621,391	39,424	Jefferson	700,850	916,755	29,206,120	1,232,533
Crane	10,081,595	51,352,399	11,690,763	72,746	Jim Hogg	56,447	129,589	27,891,857	241,469
Crockett	3,671,522	5,198,129	105,404,309	225,535	Jim Wells	150,188	463,214	8,904,693	45,811
Crosby	555,634	71,413	0	0	Johnson	0	0	12,226,206	5,540
Culberson	129,406	156,024	728,902	5,520	Jones	744,789	470,429	23,820	940
Dawson	4,866,523	5,530,987	0	0	Karnes	263,797	781,865	8,527,920	99,976
DeWitt	86,633	80,977	16,322,074	250,073	Kaufman	60,950	11,954	0	0
Denton	36,040	182,133	138,207,337	708,939	Kenedy	118,245	277,046	66,023,029	238,064
Dickens	1,660,624	121,513	0	0	Kent	6,057,040	10,145,206	0	0
Dimmit	562,523	859,730	2,717,597	27,104	Kerr	646	0	0	0
Donley	0	0	17,526	0	Kimble	543	0	494,941	4
Duval	1,052,184	413,815	72,169,865	313,091	King	2,204,507	162,362	2,046,978	22,102
Eastland	271,135	1,058,668	3,792,012	21,667	Kleberg	49,726	137,467	33,859,808	658,622
Ector	19,956,133	31,844,947	18,590,357	8,705	Knox	273,940	1,434	0	0
Edwards	2,303	24	16,662,884	2,296	Lamb	1,393,747	159,788	0	0
Ellis	152	0	0	0	La Salle	126,235	126,120	12,169,596	137,018
Erath	2,729	16,674	1,946,401	1,494	Lavaca	145,013	551,552	83,673,031	445,011
Falls	4,266	67	101	0	Lee	1,472,946	10,886,667	2,882,621	48,809
Fayette	1,806,607	13,162,139	15,431,953	373,118	Leon	831,505	1,563,875	21,749,843	64,918
Fisher	635,762	967,441	67,481	1,431	Liberty	1,457,922	2,979,357	56,399,482	2,341,933
Floyd	1,000	0	0	0	Limestone	100,923	1,860	58,008,447	63,640
Foard	134,761	2,423	1,224,167	0	Lipscomb	304,383	3,451,644	36,283,355	143,784
Fort Bend	1,933,476	2,019,915	47,944,863	972,948	Live Oak	323,577	305,449	23,320,425	232,159
Franklin	406,785	118,308	3,629,922	55,927	Loving	993,743	2,772,652	27,119,262	9,629
Freestone	75,474	85,247	263,851,056	218,934	Lubbock	1,604,909	56,934	0	0
Frio	618,977	378,831	805,503	1,212	Lynn	152,115	46,069	0	0
Gaines	29,627,231	47,649,831	12,723,424	3,684	Madison	384,280	519,137	8,683,569	31,411
Galveston	813,269	2,073,743	18,467,476	875,512	Marion	128,158	455,236	4,735,632	53,146
Garza	4,291,075	908,464	0	0	Martin	4,795,758	10,853,307	51,806	469
Glasscock	3,979,657	12,362,299	1,876,793	19,751	Matagorda	611,294	1,486,691	25,729,936	637,420
Goliad	248,271	473,601	43,651,684	451,744	Maverick	1,017,265	93,690	4,664,700	29,894
Gonzales	206,265	94,148	1,368,043	13,053	McCulloch	125,210	15,798	41,053	0
Gray	1,361,042	3,583,959	11,625,238	7,933	McLennan	1,767	36	0	0
Grayson	1,311,332	3,647,322	2,320,308	11,966	McMullen	972,882	3,553,263	44,698,707	260,249
Gregg	2,816,303	2,818,493	57,982,077	184,887	Medina	82,240	336	0	0
Grimes	198,775	697,943	21,337,795	68,185	Menard	135,799	32,459	19,978	0
Guadalupe	1,012,889	94,362	11,047	360	Midland	10,741,649	36,126,552	18,869,275	357,833
Hale	2,974,554	95,283	0	0	Milam	565,638	339,840	25,708	212
Hamilton	294	0	157,576	545	Mills	0	0	16,382	0
Hansford	161,574	701,309	27,992,164	29,009	Mitchell	2,971,582	436,107	0	0
Hardeman	2,040,840	552,440	107,416	3,854	Montague	1,506,485	1,849,249	292,212	5,955
Hardin	1,319,466	1,353,436	11,176,605	626,122	Montgomery	861,405	1,864,940	12,615,888	184,863
Harris	1,405,326	1,473,316	33,535,465	470,309	Moore	245,564	2,799,195	45,947,133	893
Harrison	463,868	2,754,864	59,392,335	406,796	Morris	2,154	0	0	0
Hartlety	230,489	180	2,514,309	0	Motley	59,268	84	0	0
Haskell	398,755	59,586	227	0	Nacogdches	3,567	44,970	45,005,119	176,926
Hemphill	180,652	2,258,420	89,855,720	910,449	Navarro	310,588	43,425	430,343	5,541
Henderson	694,021	17,810,920	17,825,930	34,915	Newton	611,795	2,235,495	1,116,689	94,761

County	Oil BBL	Casinghead MCF	Gas Well Gas MCF	Condensate BBL
Nolan	1,385,194	1,668,830	483,391	1,917
Nueces	549,844	2,492,224	65,176,179	924,529
Ochiltree	795,703	2,898,227	22,271,484	79,589
Oldham	87,808	732	198,271	0
Orange	371,296	621,650	17,669,231	674,818
Palo Pinto	385,678	1,641,580	12,444,524	36,265
Panola	423,565	3,541,079	244,308,296	1,529,254
Parker	5,821	28,993	10,267,360	34,477
Pecos	9,557,075	42,431,203	143,363,299	201,768
Polk	587,118	582,774	33,380,803	693,571
Potter	150,036	540,681	18,881,431	393
Rains	0	0	5,849,519	0
Reagan	4,961,090	24,841,181	2,167,860	41,346
Real	9,292	3,306	96,878	0
Red River	224,732	3,477	0	0
Reeves	707,206	1,903,588	27,833,789	42,358
Refugio	5,313,750	19,206,226	16,097,047	21,958
Roberts	378,287	4,830,947	24,672,033	140,976
Robertson	1,242,293	759,029	71,256,092	53,138
Runnels	442,464	1,231,949	226,677	1,200
Rusk	2,564,564	1,620,624	75,642,595	258,585
Sabine	8,046	41,836	0	0
S.Augustine	10,547	0	37,308	110
San Jacinto	48,817	126,146	6,605,715	214,169
San Patricio	463,897	1,063,026	25,484,920	1,198,418
Schleicher	411,508	1,307,221	8,794,046	40,192
Scurry	14,491,506	111,260,071	0	0
Shackelford	781,662	1,003,324	2,690,222	10,775
Shelby	50,662	595,977	37,090,070	161,682
Sherman	111,766	198,317	23,300,702	2,649
Smith	1,318,132	2,341,949	36,198,599	251,124
Somervell	0	0	12,443	0
Starr	571,252	1,634,969	140,278,247	1,735,205
Stephens	2,289,819	3,174,653	9,736,985	33,313
Sterling	949,135	10,390,508	7,391,622	99,543
Stonewall	1,193,631	561,586	0	0

County	Oil BBL	Casinghead MCF	Gas Well Gas MCF	Condensate BBL
Sutton	12,699	24,236	63,286,205	61,189
Tarrant	0	0	71,348,635	3,331
Taylor	551,737	181,926	52,097	372
Terrell	29,877	996,852	61,685,901	222,988
Terry	4,372,928	1,664,142	379,635	0
Throckmrton	910,858	1,408,974	308,210	1,319
Titus	507,332	2,414	0	0
Tom Green	411,501	1,949,207	1,057,504	9,444
Travis	866	12	0	0
Trinity	77,812	176,535	38,581	499
Tyler	800,019	3,304,898	5,065,164	626,031
Upshur	153,381	61,992	53,309,846	503,269
Upton	7,646,874	27,337,571	37,019,975	929,753
Uvalde	0	0	725	0
Val Verde	142	583	17,740,050	746
Van Zandt	1,003,714	1,582,940	7,959,418	11,176
Victoria	690,040	733,693	23,859,338	231,991
Walker	2,948	39,523	1,376,696	3,918
Waller	1,436,827	197,675	6,852,751	64,429
Ward	4,399,975	11,835,467	43,736,468	142,396
Washington	602,197	3,859,013	25,965,878	166,203
Webb	153,648	190,332	236,180,010	1,330,195
Wharton	1,216,701	683,932	55,224,344	838,311
Wheeler	343,423	874,853	35,318,950	421,292
Wichita	2,130,744	201,577	0	0
Wilbarger	620,369	27,217	6,630	0
Willacy	554,830	577,981	22,926,967	187,744
Williamson	7,799	0	0	0
Wilson	279,694	22,676	2,405	0
Winkler	3,556,407	13,557,277	29,711,865	166,734
Wise	344,851	5,465,039	173,836,959	586,848
Wood	4,581,992	6,604,144	9,578,670	34,497
Yoakum	25,181,917	120,843,920	2,023,632	0
Young	1,329,467	2,071,584	1,617,641	14,473
Zapata	34,502	40,620	296,265,484	222,589
Zavala	566,569	268,073	1,274,321	1,328

A refinery perches on a hillside at Borger in the Panhandle. Texas Almanac photo.

Receipts by Texas from Tidelands

The Republic of Texas had proclaimed its Gulf boundaries as three marine leagues, recognized by international law as traditional national boundaries. These boundaries were never seriously questioned when Texas joined the Union in 1845. But, in 1930 a congressional resolution authorized the U.S. Attorney General to file suit to establish offshore lands as properties of the federal government. Congress returned the disputed lands to Texas in 1953, and the U.S. Supreme Court confirmed Texas' ownership in 1960. In 1978, the federal government also granted states a "fair and equitable" share of the revenues from offshore leases within three miles of the states' outermost boundary. The states did not receive any such revenue until April 1986.

The following table shows receipts from tidelands in the Gulf of Mexico by the Texas General Land Office to Aug. 31, 2004. It does not include revenue from bays and other submerged area owned by Texas. Source: General Land Office

From	To	Total	Bonus	Rental	Royalty	Lease
6-09-1922	9-28-1945	$ 924,363.81	$ 814,055.70	$ 61,973.75	$ 48,334.36	...
9-29-1945	6-23-1947	296,400.30	272,700.00	7,680.00	16,020.30	...
6-24-1947	6-05-1950	7,695,552.22	7,231,755.48	377,355.00	86,441.74	...
6-06-1950	5-22-1953	55,095.04	—	9,176.00	45,919.04	...
5-23-1953	6-30-1958	54,264,553.11	49,788,639.03	3,852,726.98	623,187.10	...
7-01-1958	8-31-1959	771,064.75	—	143,857.00	627,207.75	...
9-01-1959	8-31-1960	983,335.32	257,900.00	98,226.00	627,209.32	...
9-01-1960	8-31-1961	3,890,800.15	3,228,639.51	68,578.00	593,582.64	...
9-01-1961	8-31-1962	1,121,925.09	297,129.88	127,105.00	697,690.21	...
9-01-1962	8-31-1963	3,575,888.64	2,617,057.14	177,174.91	781,656.59	...
9-01-1963	8-31-1964	3,656,236.75	2,435,244.36	525,315.00	695,677.39	...
9-01-1964	8-31-1965	54,654,576.96	53,114,943.63	755,050.12	784,583.21	...
9-01-1965	8-31-1966	22,148,825.44	18,223,357.84	3,163,475.00	761,992.60	...
9-01-1966	8-31-1967	8,469,680.86	3,641,414.96	3,711,092.65	1,117,173.25	...
9-01-1967	8-31-1968	6,305,851.00	1,251,852.50	2,683,732.50	2,370,266.00	...
9-01-1968	8-31-1969	6,372,268.28	1,838,118.33	1,491,592.50	3,042,557.45	...
9-01-1969	8-31-1970	10,311,030.48	5,994,666.32	618,362.50	3,698,001.66	...
9-01-1970	8-31-1971	9,969,629.17	4,326,120.11	726,294.15	4,917,214.91	...
9-01-1971	8-31-1972	7,558,327.21	1,360,212.64	963,367.60	5,234,746.97	...
9-01-1972	8-31-1973	9,267,975.68	3,701,737.30	920,121.60	4,646,116.78	...
9-01-1973	8-31-1974	41,717,670.04	32,981,619.28	1,065,516.60	7,670,534.16	...
9-01-1974	8-31-1975	27,321,536.62	5,319,762.85	2,935,295.60	19,066,478.17	...
9-01-1975	8-31-1976	38,747,074.09	6,197,853.00	3,222,535.84	29,326,685.25	...
9-01-1976	8-31-1977	84,196,228.27	41,343,114.81	2,404,988.80	40,448,124.66	...
9-01-1977	8-31-1978	118,266,812.05	49,807,750.45	4,775,509.92	63,683,551.68	...
9-01-1978	8-31-1979	100,410,268.68	34,578,340.94	7,318,748.40	58,513,179.34	...
9-01-1979	8-31-1980	200,263,803.03	34,733,270.02	10,293,153.80	155,237,379.21	...
9-01-1980	8-31-1981	219,126,876.54	37,467,196.97	13,100,484.25	168,559,195.32	...
9-01-1981	8-31-1982	250,824,581.69	27,529,516.33	14,214,478.97	209,080,586.39	...
9-01-1982	8-31-1983	165,197,734.83	10,180,696.40	12,007,476.70	143,009,561.73	...
9-01-1983	8-31-1984	152,755,934.29	32,864,122.19	8,573,996.87	111,317,815.23	...
9-01-1984	8-31-1985	140,568,090.79	32,652,027.75	6,837,603.70	101,073,959.34	...
9-01-1985	8-31-1986	516,503,771.05	6,365,426.23	4,241,892.75	78,289,592.27	$ 427,606,859.83
9-01-1986	8-31-1987	60,066,571.05	4,186,561.63	1,933,752.50	44,691,907.22	9,254,349.70
9-01-1987	8-31-1988	56,875,069.22	14,195,274.28	1,817,058.90	28,068,202.53	12,794,533.51
9-01-1988	8-31-1989	61,793,380.04	12,995,892.74	1,290,984.37	35,160,568.40	12,345,934.53
9-01-1989	8-31-1990	68,701,751.51	7,708,449.54	1,289,849.87	40,331,537.06	19,371,915.04
9-01-1990	8-31-1991	90,885,856.99	3,791,832.77	1,345,711.07	70,023,601.01	15,724,712.14
9-01-1991	8-31-1992	51,154,511.34	4,450,850.00	1,123,585.54	26,776,191.35	18,803,884.45
9-01-1992	8-31-1993	60,287,712.60	3,394,230.00	904,359.58	34,853,679.68	21,135,443.34
9-01-1993	8-31-1994	57,825,043.59	3,570,657.60	694,029.30	32,244,987.95	21,315,368.74
9-01-1994	8-31-1995	62,143,227.78	8,824,722.93	674,479.79	34,691,023.35	17,951,001.71
9-01-1995	8-31-1996	68,166,645.51	13,919,246.80	1,102,591.39	32,681,315.73	20,463,491.59
9-01-1996	8-31-1997	90,614,935.93	22,007,378.46	1,319,614.78	41,605,792.50	25,682,150.19
9-01-1997	8-31-1998	104,016,006.75	36,946,312.49	2,070,802.90	38,760,320.91	26,238,570.45
9-01-1998	8-31-1999	53,565,810.30	5,402,171.00	2,471,128.47	23,346,515.93	22,345,994.90
9-01-1999	8-31-2000	55,465,763.99	3,487,564.80	2,171,636.35	24,314,241.99	25,492,320.85
9-01-2000	8-31-2001	68,226,347.58	9,963,608.68	1,830,378.11	23,244,034.74	33,188,326.05
9-01-2001	8-31-2002	30,910,283.91	9,286,015.20	1,545,583.01	13,369,771.56	6,708,914.14
9-01-2002	8-31-2003	50,881,515.90	15,152,092.40	1,071,377.60	19,648,641.39	15,009,404.51
9-01-2003	8-31-2004	54,379,791.20	14,448,555.70	1,094,201.41	25,199,635.21	13,637,398.88
Total		**$ 3,414,147,587.45**	**$ 706,145,758.97**	**$ 137,227,063.40**	**$ 1,805,74,190.53**	**$ 765,070,574.55**
Inside three-mile line		$ 479,995,300.95	$ 166,125,871.21	$ 36,722,986.33	$ 277,146,443.41	0
Between three-mile and three marine-league line		$ 2,166,256,346.37	$ 537,367,803.37	$ 100,330,795.88	$ 1,528,557,747.12	0
Outside three marine-league line		$ 767,895,940.13	$ 2,652,084.39	$ 173,281.19	0	$ 765,070,574.55

Offshore Production History — Oil and Gas

The cumulative offshore natural gas production as of Jan. 1, 2005, was **2,796,383,897** thousand cubic feet (MCF). The cumulative offshore oil production was **37,721,686** barrels.

Production in Recent Years

YEAR	Crude Oil BBL	Casing-head MCF	Gas Well Gas MCF	Conden-sate BBL
1993	1,685,177	1,370,634	86,264,924	275,945
1994	1,367,850	1,068,230	87,315,422	303,451
1995	1,108,868	807,468	64,295,758	223,103
1996	908,743	724,651	68,159,547	212,048
1997	765,283	698,488	76,974,574	328,025
1998	586,999	611,882	60,080,329	233,044
1999	433,958	382,566	48,816,099	132,827
2000	539,489	336,891	44,086,157	220,236
2001	516,677	370,317	53,535,529	475,389
2002	1,144,389	2,404,329	54,990,950	405,607
2003	760,824	1,370,696	52,662,329	409,416
2004	403,324	314,797	43,073,787	356,045

Source: Texas Railroad Commission.

2004 Production by Area

Offshore Area	Crude Oil BBL	Casing-head MCF	Gas Well Gas MCF	Conden-sate BBL
Brazos-LB	0	0	1,823,492	3,896
Brazos-SB	0	0	3,892,514	3,203
Galveston-LB	0	0	5,588,107	27,899
Galveston-SB	0	0	294,483	1,099
High Island-LB	60,351	98,249	1,593,535	5,505
High Island-SB	111,838	57,637	87,173	0
Matagrda Island-LB	167,406	3,078	16,743,848	82,912
Matagrda Island-SB	0	0	2,907,275	35,199
Mustang Island-LB	3,664	26,748	4,767,899	31,161
Mustang Island-SB	60,065	128,985	4,439,890	135,707
N. Padre Island-LB	0	0	935,571	29,464
S. Padre Island-LB	0	0	0	0
Sabine Pass	0	0	0	0
All Offshore	**403,324**	**314,797**	**43,073,787**	**356,045**

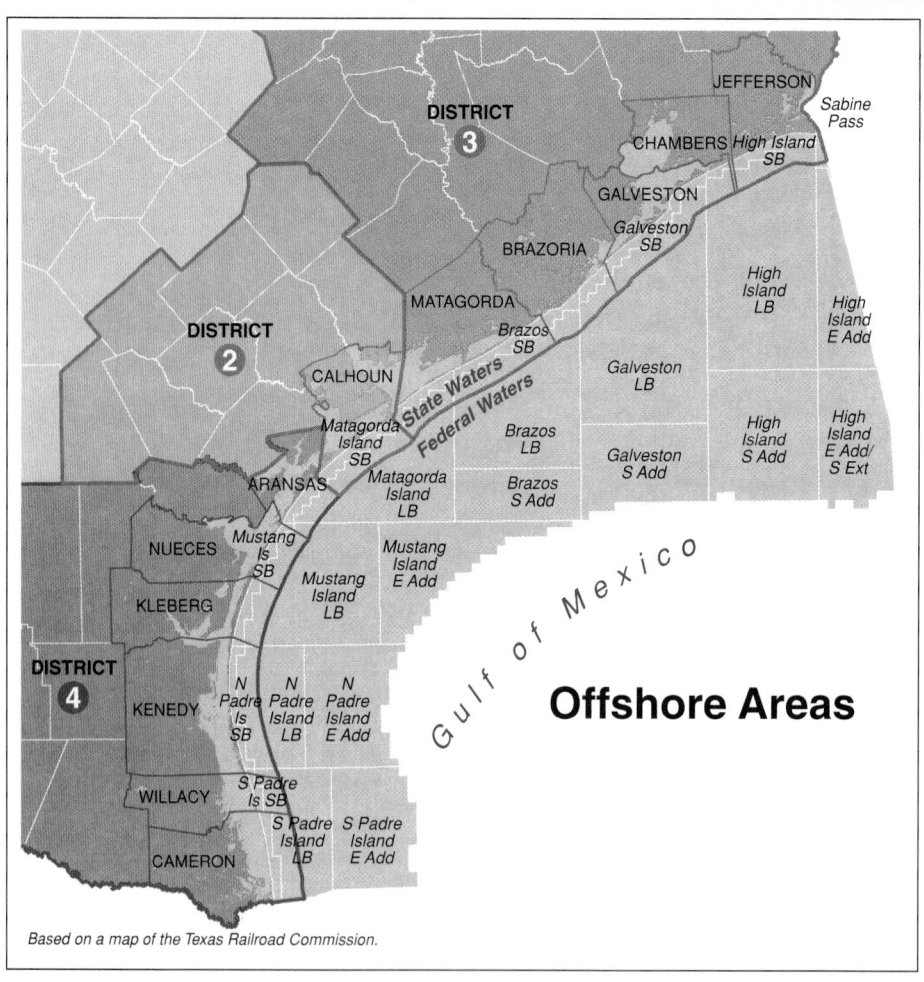

Based on a map of the Texas Railroad Commission.

Nonfuel Mineral Production and Value,
2001, 2002 and 2003

Source: U.S. Geological Survey and the Texas Bureau of Economic Geology.
*(Production measured by mine shipments, sales or marketable production, including consumption by producers. Production and value data given in **thousand metric tons** and **thousand dollars**, unless otherwise specified.)*

Mineral	2001		2002		2003*	
	Production	Value	Production	Value	Production	Value
Cement:						
Masonry	291	$ 32,700*	294	$36,000*	300	$ 33,000*
Portland.	10,400	745,000*	10,500	740,000*	10,600	753,000*
Clays:						
Common	2,120	8,750	2,160	21,200	2,160	21,200
Fuller's earth	29	2,270	W	W	W	W
Kaolin	W	W	39	8,420	39	8,420
Gemstones	NA	12	NA	12	NA	12
Gypsum, crude.	W	W	2,060	13,400	2,090	13,300
Helium, crude (million cubic meters)	9	9,320	W	W	W	W
Lime.	1,610	108,000	1,530	98,400	1,580	104,000
Salt.	9,370	104,000	9,100	103,000	8,470	99,300
Sand and gravel:						
Construction	82,900	405,000	82,600	413,000	78,000	394,000
Industrial	1,850	70,000	1,670	62,200	1,750	45,700
Stone:						
Crushed.	126,000	606,000	113,000	543,000	104,000	504,000
Dimension	86	12,600	65	12,200	79	13,300
Talc, crude	234	4,070	W	W	W	W
Zeolites	W	NA	W	NA	W	NA
‡Combined value	§	35,100	§	40,900	§	37,900
††Total Texas Values.	§	$2,140,000	§	$2,090,000	§	$2,030,000

Nonpetroleum Minerals

The nonpetroleum minerals that occur in Texas constitute a long list. Some are currently mined; some may have a potential for future development; some are minor occurrences only. Although overshadowed by the petroleum, natural gas and natural gas liquids that are produced in the state, many of the non-petroleum minerals are, nonetheless, important to the economy. In 1999, they were valued at an estimated $2.05 billion. Texas is annually **among the nation's leading states in value of nonpetroleum mineral production.** In 2000, **Texas ranked fifth nationally** in total mineral output.

The **Bureau of Economic Geology,** which functions as the state geological survey of Texas, revised the following information about nonpetroleum minerals for this edition of the Texas Almanac. Publications of the Bureau, on file in many libraries, contain more detailed information. Among the items available is the Bureau map, "Mineral Resources of Texas," showing locations of resource access of many nonpetroleum minerals.

A catalog of Bureau publications is also available free on request from the Bureau Publications Sales, University Station, Box X, Austin, TX 78713-7508; 512-471-1534. On the Web: **www.beg.utexas.edu/.**

Texas' nonpetroleum minerals are as follows:

ALUMINUM — No aluminum ores are mined in Texas, but three Texas plants process aluminum materials in one or more ways. Plants in San Patricio and Calhoun counties produce **aluminum oxide (alumina)** from imported raw ore **(bauxite)**, and a plant in Milam County reduces the oxide to aluminum.

ASBESTOS — Small occurrences of amphibole-type asbestos have been found in the state. In West Texas, **richterite**, a white, long-fibered amphibole, is associated with some of the **talc deposits** northwest of **Allamoore** in Hudspeth County. Another type, **tremolite**, has been

found in the **Llano Uplift** of Central Texas where it is associated with **serpentinite** in eastern Gillespie and western Blanco County. No asbestos is mined in Texas.

ASPHALT (Native) — Asphalt-bearing Cretaceous limestones crop out in Burnet, Kinney, Pecos, Reeves, Uvalde and other counties. The most significant deposit is in southwestern Uvalde County where asphalt occurs naturally in the pore spaces of the Anacacho Limestone. The material is quarried and used extensively as **road-paving material.** Asphalt-bearing sandstones occur in Anderson, Angelina, Cooke, Jasper, Maverick, Montague, Nacogdoches, Uvalde, Zavala and other counties.

BARITE — Deposits of a heavy, nonmetallic mineral, barite (barium sulphate), have been found in many localities, including Baylor, Brown, Brewster, Culberson, Gillespie, Howard, Hudspeth, Jeff Davis, Kinney, Llano, Live Oak, Taylor, Val Verde and Webb counties. During the 1960s, there was small, intermittent production in the **Seven Heart Gap** area of the **Apache Mountains** in Culberson County, where barite was mined from open pits. Most of the deposits are known to be relatively small, but the Webb County deposit has not been evaluated. Grinding plants, which prepare barite imported outside of Texas for use chiefly as a **weighting agent** in well-drilling muds and as a **filler**, are located in Brownsville, Corpus Christi, El Paso, Galena Park, Galveston, and Houston.

BASALT (TRAP ROCK) — Masses of basalt — a hard, dark-colored, fine-grained igneous rock — crop out in Kinney, Travis, Uvalde and several other counties along the **Balcones Fault Zone**, and also in the Trans-Pecos area of West Texas. Basalt is quarried near Knippa in Uvalde County for use as **road-building material, railroad ballast and other aggregate.**

BENTONITE (see **CLAYS**).

BERYLLIUM — Occurrences of beryllium minerals at

several Trans-Pecos localities have been recognized for several years.

BRINE (see also **SALT, SODIUM SULPHATE**) — Many wells in Texas produce brine by solution mining of subsurface salt deposits, mostly in West Texas counties such as Andrews, Crane, Ector, Loving, Midland, Pecos, Reeves, Ward and others. These wells in the Permian Basin dissolve salt from the **Salado Formation,** an enormous salt deposit that extends in the subsurface from north of the Big Bend northward to Kansas, has an east-west width of 150 to 200 miles, and may have several hundred feet of net salt thickness. The majority of the brine is used in the **petroleum industry**, but it also is used in **water softening, the chemical industry** and other uses. Three Gulf Coast counties, Fort Bend, Duval and Jefferson, have brine stations that produce from **salt domes**.

The Texas Industries cement plant in Midlothian, Ellis County, is the second largest producer of concrete in the United States and the largest in Texas. File photo.

BUILDING STONE (DIMENSION STONE) — **Granite** and **limestone** currently are quarried for use as dimension stone. The granite quarries are located in Burnet, Gillespie, Llano and Mason counties; the limestone quarries are in Shackelford and Williamson counties. Past production of limestone for use as dimension stone has been reported in Burnet, Gillespie, Jones, Tarrant, Travis and several other counties. There has also been production of **sandstone** in various counties for use as dimension stone.

CEMENT MATERIALS — Cement is currently manufactured in Bexar, Comal, Dallas, Ector, Ellis, Hays, McLennan, Nolan and Potter counties. Many of these plants utilize Cretaceous limestones and shales or clays as raw materials for the cement. On the Texas High Plains, a cement plant near Amarillo uses impure **caliche** as the chief raw material. **Iron oxide**, also a constituent of cement, is available from the iron ore deposits of East Texas and from smelter slag. **Gypsum**, added to the cement as a retarder, is found chiefly in North Central Texas, Central Texas and the Trans-Pecos area.

CHROMIUM — Chromite-bearing rock has been found in several small deposits around the margin of the Coal Creek **serpentinite** mass in northeastern Gillespie County and northwestern Blanco County. Exploration has not revealed significant deposits.

CLAYS — Texas has an abundance and variety of ceramic and non-ceramic clays and is one of the country's leading producers of clay products.

Almost any kind of clay, ranging from common clay used to make ordinary brick and tile to clays suitable for manufacture of specialty whitewares, can be used for ceramic purposes. **Fire clay** suitable for use as **refractories** occurs chiefly in East and North Central Texas; **ball clay**, a high-quality plastic ceramic clay, is found locally in East Texas.

Ceramic clay suitable for quality structural clay products such as **structural building brick, paving brick and drain tile** is especially abundant in East and North Central Texas. Common clay suitable for use in the manufacture of cement and ordinary brick is found in most counties of the state. Many of the Texas clays will expand or bloat upon rapid firing and are suitable for the manufacture of lightweight aggregate, which is used mainly in concrete blocks and highway surfacing.

Nonceramic clays are utilized without firing. They are used primarily as **bleaching and absorbent clays, fillers, coaters, additives, bonding clays, drilling muds, catalysts** and potentially as sources of alumina. Most of the nonceramic clays in Texas are **bentonites and fuller's earth**. These occur extensively in the Coastal Plain and locally in the High Plains and Big Bend areas. **Kaolin clays** in parts of East Texas are potential sources of such nonceramic products as **paper coaters and fillers, rubber fillers and drilling agents**. Relatively high in alumina, these clays also are a potential source of metallic aluminum.

COAL (see also LIGNITE) — **Bituminous coal**, which occurs in North Central, South and West Texas, was a significant energy source in Texas prior to the large-scale development of oil and gas. During the period from 1895 to 1943, Texas mines produced more than 25 million tons of coal. The mines were inactive for many years, but the renewed interest in coal as a major energy source prompted a revaluation of Texas' coal deposits. In the late 1970s, bituminous coal production resumed in the state on a limited scale when mines were opened in Coleman, Erath and Webb counties.

Much of the state's bituminous coal occurs in North Central Texas. Deposits are found there in Pennsylvanian rocks within a large area that includes Coleman, Eastland, Erath, Jack, McCulloch, Montague, Palo Pinto, Parker, Throckmorton, Wise, Young and other counties. Before the general availability of oil and gas, underground coal mines near **Thurber, Bridgeport, Newcastle, Strawn** and other points annually produced significant coal tonnages. Preliminary evaluations indicate substantial amounts of coal may remain in the North Central Texas area. The coal seams there are generally no more than 30 inches thick and are commonly covered by well-consolidated overburden. Ash and sulphur content are high. Beginning in 1979, two bituminous coal mine operations in North Central Texas — one in southern Coleman County and one in northwestern Erath County — produced coal to be used as fuel by the cement industry. Neither mine is currently operating.

In South Texas, bituminous coal occurs in the Eagle Pass district of Maverick County, and bituminous **cannel coal** is present in the **Santo Tomas district** of Webb County. The Eagle Pass area was a leading coal-producing district in Texas during the late 1800s and early 1900s. The bituminous coal in that area, which occurs in the Upper Cretaceous Olmos Formation, has a high ash content and a moderate moisture and sulfur content. According to reports, Maverick County coal beds range from four to seven feet thick.

The **cannel coals** of western Webb County occur near the Rio Grande in middle Eocene strata. They were mined for more than 50 years and used primarily as a boiler fuel. Mining ceased from 1939 until 1978, when a surface mine was opened 30 miles northwest of Laredo to produce cannel coal for use as fuel in the cement industry and for export. An additional mine has since been opened in that county. Tests show that the coals of the Webb County Santo Tomas district have a high hydrogen content and yield significant amounts of gas and oil when distilled. They also have a high sulfur content. A potential use might be as a source of various petrochemical products.

Coal deposits in the Trans-Pecos country of West Texas include those in the Cretaceous rocks of the Terlingua area of Brewster County, the Eagle Spring area of Hudspeth County and the **San Carlos** area of Presidio County. The coal deposits in these areas are believed to have relatively little potential for development as a fuel. They have been sold in the past as a soil amendment (see **LEONARDITE**).

COPPER — Copper minerals have been found in the **Trans-Pecos** area of West Texas, in the **Llano Uplift** area of Central Texas and in redbed deposits of North Texas. No copper has been mined in Texas during recent years, and the total copper produced in the state has been relatively small. Past attempts to mine the North Texas and Llano Uplift copper deposits resulted in small shipments, but practically all the copper production in the state has been from the **Van Horn-Allamoore** district of Culberson and Hudspeth Counties in the Trans-Pecos area. Chief output was from the **Hazel copper-silver mine** of Culberson County that yielded over 1 million pounds of copper during 1891–1947. Copper ores and concentrates from outside of Texas are processed at **smelters** in El Paso and Amarillo.

CRUSHED STONE — Texas is among the leading states in the production of crushed stone. Most production consists of **limestone**; other kinds of crushed stone produced in the state include **basalt (trap rock), dolomite, granite, marble, rhyolite, sandstone and serpentinite**. Large tonnages of crushed stone are used as **aggregate** in concrete, as **road material** and in the manufacture of cement and lime. Some is used as **riprap, terrazzo, roofing chips, filter material, fillers** and for other purposes.

DIATOMITE (DIATOMACEOUS EARTH) — Diatomite is a very lightweight siliceous material consisting of the remains of microscopic aquatic plants (diatoms). It is used chiefly as a **filter and filler**; other uses are for **thermal insulation**, as an **abrasive**, as an **insecticide carrier** and as a **lightweight aggregate**, and for other purposes. The diatomite was deposited in shallow freshwater lakes that were present in the High Plains during portions of the Pliocene and Pleistocene epochs. Deposits have been found in Armstrong, Crosby, Dickens, Ector, Hartley and Lamb counties. No diatomite is mined in Texas.

DOLOMITE ROCK — Dolomite rock, which consists largely of the mineral dolomite (calcium-magnesium carbonate), commonly is associated with limestone in Texas. Areas in which dolomite rock occurs include Central Texas, the Callahan Divide and parts of the Edwards Plateau, High Plains and West Texas. Some of the principal deposits of dolomite rock are found in Bell, Brown, Burnet, Comanche, Edwards, El Paso, Gillespie, Lampasas, Mills, Nolan, Taylor and Williamson counties. Dolomite rock can be used as crushed stone (although much of Texas dolomite is soft and not a good aggregate material), in the manufacture of lime and as a source of **magnesium**.

FELDSPAR — Large crystals and crystal fragments of feldspar minerals occur in the Precambrian pegmatite rocks that crop out in the **Llano Uplift** area of Central Texas — including Blanco, Burnet, Gillespie, Llano and Mason counties — and in the **Van Horn area** of Culberson and Hudspeth Counties in West Texas. Feldspar has been mined in Llano County for use as **roofing granules** and as a **ceramic material**. Feldspar is currently mined in Burnet County for use as an aggregate.

FLUORSPAR — The mineral fluorite (calcium fluoride), which is known commercially as fluorspar, occurs in both Central and West Texas. In Central Texas, the deposits that have been found in Burnet, Gillespie and Mason counties are not considered adequate to sustain mining operations. In West Texas, deposits have been found in Brewster, El Paso, Hudspeth, Jeff Davis and Presidio counties. Fluorspar has been mined in the **Christmas Mountains** of Brewster County and processed in Marathon. Former West Texas mining activity in the **Eagle Mountains** district of Hudspeth County resulted in the production of approximately 15,000 short tons of fluorspar during the peak years of 1942-1950. No production has been reported in Hudspeth County since that period. Imported fluorspar is processed in Brownsville, Eagle Pass, El Paso and Houston. Fluorspar is used in the **steel, chemical, aluminum, magnesium, ceramics and glass industries** and for various other purposes.

FULLER'S EARTH (see **CLAY**).

GOLD — No major deposits of gold are known in Texas. Small amounts have been found in the **Llano Uplift** region of Central Texas and in West Texas; minor occurrences have been reported on the **Edwards Plateau** and the **Gulf Coastal Plain** of Texas. Nearly all of the gold produced in the state came as a by-product of silver and lead mining at **Presidio mine**, near **Shafter**, in Presidio County. Additional small quantities were produced as a by-product of copper mining in Culberson County and from residual soils developed from gold-bearing quartz stringers in metamorphic rocks in Llano County. No gold mining has been reported in Texas since 1952. Total **gold production** in the state, 1889-1952, amounted to more than 8,419 troy ounces according to U.S. Bureau of Mines figures. Most of the production — at least 73 percent and probably more — came from the Presidio mine.

GRANITE — Granites in shades of red and gray and related intrusive igneous rocks occur in the **Llano Uplift** of Central Texas and in the **Trans-Pecos** country of West Texas. Deposits are found in Blanco, Brewster, Burnet, El Paso, Gillespie, Hudspeth, Llano, McCulloch, Mason, Presidio and other counties. Quarries in Burnet, Gillespie, Llano and Mason counties produce Precambrian granite for a variety of uses as **dimension stone and crushed stone**.

GRAPHITE — Graphite, a soft, dark-gray mineral, is a form of very high-grade carbon. It occurs in Precambrian schist rocks of the **Llano Uplift** of Central Texas, notably in Burnet and Llano counties. Crystalline-flake graphite ore formerly was mined from open pits in the **Clear Creek area** of western Burnet County and processed at a plant near the mine. The mill now occasionally grinds imported material. Uses of natural crystalline graphite are **refractories, steel production, pencil leads, lubricants, foundry facings and crucibles** and for other purposes.

GRINDING PEBBLES (ABRASIVE STONES) — Flint pebbles, suitable for use in **tube-mill grinding**, are found in the **Gulf Coastal Plain** where they occur in gravel deposits along rivers and in upland areas. Grinding pebbles are produced from **Frio River terrace** deposits near the McMullen-Live Oak county line, but the area is now part of the Choke Canyon Reservoir area.

GYPSUM — Gypsum is widely distributed in Texas. Chief deposits are bedded gypsum in the area east of the **High Plains**, in the **Trans-Pecos** country and in **Central Texas**. It also occurs in **salt-dome caprocks** of the Gulf Coast. The massive, granular variety known as rock gypsum is the kind most commonly used by industry. Other varieties include **alabaster, satin spar and selenite.**

Gypsum is one of the important industrial minerals in Texas. Bedded gypsum is produced from surface mines in Culberson, Fisher, Gillespie, Hardeman, Hudspeth, Kimble, Nolan and Stonewall counties. Gypsum was formerly mined at **Gyp Hill salt dome** in Brooks County and at **Hockley salt dome** in Harris County. Most of the gypsum is calcined and used in the manufacture of **gypsum wallboard, plaster, joint compounds** and other construction products. Crude gypsum is used chiefly as a **retarder in portland cement** and as a **soil conditioner.**

HELIUM — Helium is a very light, nonflammable, chemically inert gas. The **U.S. Interior Department has ended its helium operation** near Masterson in the Panhandle. The storage facility at **Cliffside gas field** near Amarillo and the 425-mile pipeline system will remain in operation until the government sells its remaining unrefined, crude helium. Helium is used in **cryogenics, welding, pressurizing and purging, leak detection, synthetic breathing mixtures** and for other purposes.

IRON — Iron oxide **(limonite, goethite and hematite)** and iron carbonate **(siderite)** deposits occur widely in East Texas, notably in Cass, Cherokee, Marion and Morris counties, and also in Anderson, Camp, Harrison, Henderson, Nacogdoches, Smith, Upshur and other counties. **Magnetite (magnetic, black iron oxide)** occurs in Central Texas, including a deposit at **Iron Mountain** in Llano County. Hematite occurs in the **Trans-Pecos** area and in the **Llano Uplift** of Central Texas. The extensive deposits of **glauconite** (a complex silicate containing iron) that occur in East Texas and the hematitic and goethitic Cambrian sandstone that crops out in the northwestern Llano Uplift region are potential sources of low-grade iron ore.

Limonite and other East Texas iron ores are mined from open pits in Cherokee and Henderson counties for use in the preparation of **portland cement,** as a **weighting agent in well-drilling fluids,** as an **animal feed supplement** and for other purposes. East Texas iron ores also were mined in the past for use in the iron-steel industry.

KAOLIN (see **CLAY**).

LEAD AND ZINC — The lead mineral **galena (lead sulfide)** commonly is associated with zinc and silver. It formerly was produced as a by-product of West Texas silver mining, chiefly from the **Presidio mine at Shafter** in Presidio County, although lesser amounts were obtained at several other mines and prospects. Deposits of galena also are known to occur in Blanco, Brewster, Burnet, Gillespie and Hudspeth counties.

Zinc, primarily from the mineral **sphalerite (zinc sulphide)**, was produced chiefly from the **Bonanza** and **Alice Ray** mines in the **Quitman Mountains** of Hudspeth County. In addition, small production was reported from several other areas, including the **Chinati** and **Montezuma mines** of Presidio County and the **Buck Prospect** in the **Apache Mountains** of Culberson County. Zinc mineralization also occurs in association with the lead deposits in Cambrian rocks of Central Texas.

LEONARDITE — Deposits of weathered (oxidized) low-Btu value bituminous coals, generally referred to as "leonardite," occur in Brewster County. The name leonardite is used for a mixture of chemical compounds that is high in humic acids. In the past, material from these deposits was sold as **soil conditioner.** Other uses of leonardite include **modification of viscosity of drill flu-**ids and as **sorbants in water-treatment.**

LIGHTWEIGHT AGGREGATE (see **CLAY, DIATOMITE, PERLITE, VERMICULITE**).

LIGNITE — Lignite, a low-rank coal, is found in belts of Tertiary Eocene strata that extend across the Texas Gulf Coastal Plain from the Rio Grande in South Texas to the Arkansas and Louisiana borders in East Texas. The largest resources and best grades (approximately 6,500 BTU/pound) of lignite occur in the Wilcox Group of strata north of the Colorado River in East and Central Texas.

The near-surface lignite resources, occurring at depths of less than 200 feet in seams of three feet or thicker, are estimated at 23 billion short tons. **Recoverable reserves of strippable lignite** — those that can be economically mined under current conditions of price and technology — are estimated to be 9 billion to 11 billion short tons.

Additional lignite resources of the Texas Gulf Coastal Plain occur as deep-basin deposits. Deep-basin resources, those that occur at depths of 200 to 2,000 feet in seams of five feet or thicker, are comparable in magnitude to near-surface resources. The deep-basin lignites are a potential energy resource that conceivably could be utilized by *in situ* (in place) recovery methods such as underground gasification.

As with bituminous coal, lignite production was significant prior to the general availability of oil and gas. Remnants of old underground mines are common throughout the area of lignite occurrence. Large reserves of strippable lignite have again attracted the attention of energy suppliers, and Texas is now the nation's **5th leading producer of coal**, 99 percent of it lignite. Eleven large strip mines are now producing lignite that is burned for **mine-mouth electric-power generation,** and additional mines are planned. One of the currently operating mines is located in Milam and Lee counties, where part of the electric power is used for **alumina reduction.** Other mines are in Atascosa, Bastrop, Franklin, Freestone, Grimes, Harrison, Hopkins, Leon, McMullen, Panola, Robertson, Rusk and Titus counties. New permit applications have been submitted to the Railroad Commission of Texas for Freestone, Lee, Leon and Robertson counties.

LIME MATERIAL — **Limestones**, which are abundant in some areas of Texas, are heated to produce lime (calcium oxide) at a number of plants in the state. High-magnesium limestone and dolomite are used to prepare lime at a plant in Burnet County. Other lime plants are located in Bexar, Bosque, Comal, Hill, Johnson and Travis counties. Lime production captive to the kiln's operator occurs in several Texas counties. Lime is used in **soil stabilization, water purification, paper and pulp manufacture, metallurgy, sugar refining, agriculture, construction, removal of sulfur from stack gases** and for many other purposes.

LIMESTONE (see also **BUILDING STONE**) — Texas is one of the nation's leading producers of limestone, which is quarried in more than 60 counties. Limestone occurs in nearly all areas of the state with the exception of most of the Gulf Coastal Plain and High Plains. Although some of the limestone is quarried for use as **dimension stone,** most of the output is crushed for uses such as **bulk building materials (crushed stone, road base, concrete aggregate), chemical raw materials, fillers or extenders, lime and portland cement raw materials, agricultural limestone and removal of sulfur from stack gases.**

MAGNESITE — Small deposits of magnesite (natural magnesium carbonate) have been found in Precambrian rocks in Llano and Mason counties of Central Texas. At one time there was small-scale mining of magnesite in the area; some of the material was used as **agricultural stone** and as **terrazzo chips**. Magnesite also can be cal-

Texas is one of the leading U.S. producers of limestone, which is quarried in more than 60 counties. Although most of the output is crushed for uses such as bulk building materials, some is used for decorative purposes. Eliseo Garcia works on a limestone architectural frieze for the Arcadia Park Elementary School in Dallas. File photo.

cined to form **magnesia**, which is used in **metallurgical furnace refractories** and other products.

MAGNESIUM — On the Texas Gulf Coast in Brazoria County, magnesium chloride is **extracted from sea water** at a plant in Freeport and used to produce **magnesium compounds and magnesium metal**. During World War II, high-magnesium Ellenburger dolomite rock from Burnet County was used as magnesium ore at a plant near Austin.

MANGANESE — Deposits of manganese minerals, such as **braunite, hollandite and pyrolusite**, have been found in several areas, including Jeff Davis, Llano, Mason, Presidio and Val Verde counties. Known deposits are not large. Small shipments have been made from Jeff Davis, Mason and Val Verde counties, but no manganese mining has been reported in Texas since 1954.

MARBLE — Metamorphic and sedimentary marbles suitable for **monument and building stone** are found in the **Llano Uplift** and nearby areas of Central Texas and the **Trans-Pecos** area of West Texas. Gray, white, black, greenish black, light green, brown and cream-colored marbles occur in Central Texas in Burnet, Gillespie, Llano and Mason counties. West Texas metamorphic marbles include the bluish-white and the black marbles found southwest of Alpine in Brewster County and the white marble from **Marble Canyon** north of Van Horn in Culberson County. Marble can be used as **dimension stone, terrazzo and roofing aggregate** and for other purposes.

MERCURY (QUICKSILVER) — Mercury minerals, chiefly **cinnabar**, occur in the **Terlingua district** and nearby districts of southern Brewster and southeastern Presidio counties. Mining began there about 1894, and from 1905 to 1935, Texas was one of the nation's leading producers of quicksilver. Following World War II, a sharp drop in demand and price, along with depletion of developed ore reserves, caused abandonment of all the Texas mercury mines.

With a rise in the price, sporadic mining took place between 1951-1960. In 1965, when the price of mercury moved to a record high, renewed interest in the Texas mercury districts resulted in the reopening of several mines and the discovery of new ore reserves. By April 1972, however, the price had declined and the mines have reported no production since 1973.

MICA — Large crystals of flexible, transparent mica minerals in igneous pegmatite rocks and mica flakes in metamorphic schist rocks are found in the **Llano area** of Central Texas and the **Van Horn area** of West Texas. Most Central Texas deposits do not meet specifications for sheet mica, and although several attempts have been made to produce West Texas sheet mica in Culberson and Hudspeth counties, sustained production has not been achieved. A mica quarry operated for a short time in the early 1980s in the Van Horn Mountains of Culberson and Hudspeth counties to mine mica schist for use as an **additive in rotary drilling fluids**.

MOLYBDENUM — Small occurrences of molybdenite have been found in Burnet and Llano counties, and **wulfenite**, another molybdenum mineral, has been noted in rocks in the **Quitman Mountains** of Hudspeth County. Molybdenum minerals also occur at **Cave Peak** north of Van Horn in Culberson County, in the **Altuda Mountain area** of northwestern Brewster County and in association with uranium ores of the Gulf Coastal Plain.

PEAT — This spongy organic substance forms in bogs from plant remains. It has been found in the **Gulf Coastal Plain** in several localities including Gonzales, Guadalupe, Lee, Milam, Polk and San Jacinto counties. There has been intermittent, small-scale production of some of the peat for use as a **soil conditioner**.

PERLITE — Perlite, a glassy igneous rock, expands to a lightweight, porous mass when heated. It can be used as a **lightweight aggregate, filter aid, horticultural aggregate** and for other purposes. Perlite occurs in Presidio County, where it has been mined in the **Pinto Canyon area** north of the **Chinati Mountains**. No perlite is currently mined in Texas, but perlite mined outside of Texas is expanded at plants in Bexar, Dallas, El Paso, Guadalupe, Harris and Nolan counties.

PHOSPHATE — Rock phosphate is present in Paleozoic rocks in several areas of Brewster and Presidio counties in West Texas and in Central Texas, but the known deposits are not large. In Northeast Texas, sedimentary rock phosphate occurs in thin conglomeratic lenses in Upper Cretaceous and Tertiary rock units; possibly some of these low-grade phosphorites could be processed on a small scale for local use as a **fertilizer**. Imported phosphate rock is processed at a plant in Brownsville.

POTASH — The potassium mineral **polyhalite** is widely distributed in the subsurface Permian Basin of West Texas and has been found in many wells in that area. During 1927-1931, the federal government drilled a series of potash-test wells in Crane, Crockett, Ector, Glasscock, Loving, Reagan, Upton and Winkler counties. In addition to polyhalite, which was found in all of the counties, these wells revealed the presence of the potassium minerals **carnallite and sylvite** in Loving County and carnallite in Winkler County. The known Texas potash deposits are not as rich as those in the New Mexico portion of the Permian Basin and have not been developed.

PUMICITE (VOLCANIC ASH) — Deposits of volcanic ash occur in Brazos, Fayette, Gonzales, Karnes, Polk, Starr and other counties of the Texas Coastal Plain. Deposits also have been found in the Trans-Pecos area, High Plains and in several counties east of the High Plains. Volcanic ash is used to prepare **pozzolan cement, cleansing and scouring compounds and soaps and sweeping compounds**; as a **carrier for insecticides**, and for other purposes. It has been mined in Dickens, Lynn, Scurry, Starr and other counties.

QUICKSILVER (see **MERCURY**).

RARE-EARTH ELEMENTS AND METALS — The term, "rare-earth elements," is commonly applied to elements of the **lanthanide** group (atomic numbers 57 through 71) plus **yttrium**. Yttrium, atomic number 39 and not a member of the lanthanide group, is included as a rare-earth element because it has similar properties to members of that group and usually occurs in nature with them. The metals **thorium and scandium** are sometimes termed "rare metals" because their occurence is often associated with the rare-earth elements.

The majority of rare-earth elements are consumed as **catalysts** in petroleum cracking and other chemical industries. Rare earths are widely used in the **glass industry for tableware, specialty glasses, optics and fiber optics**. Cerium oxide has growing use as a **polishing compound** for glass, gem stones, cathode-ray tube faceplates, and other polishing. Rare earths are alloyed with various metals to produce materials used in the **aeronautic, space and electronics** industries. Addition of rare-earth elements may improve resistance to metal fatigue at high temperatures, reduce potential for corrosion, and selectively increase conductivity and magnetism of the metal.

Various members of this group, including **thorium**, have anomalous concentrations in the **rhyolitic and related igneous rocks** of the **Quitman Mountains** and the **Sierra Blanca area** of Trans-Pecos.

SALT (SODIUM CHLORIDE) (see also **BRINES**) — Salt resources of Texas are virtually inexhaustible. Enormous deposits occur in the subsurface **Permian Basin** of West Texas and in the **salt domes of the Gulf Coastal Plain**. Salt also is found in the alkali **playa lakes** of the High Plains, the **alkali flats or salt lakes in the Salt Basin** of Culberson and Hudspeth counties and along some of the bays and lagoons of the South Texas **Gulf Coast**.

Texas is one of the leading salt-producing states. **Rock salt** is obtained from underground mines in **salt domes at Grand Saline** in Van Zandt County. Approximately one-third of the salt produced in the state is from rock salt; most of the salt is produced by solution mining as brines from wells drilled into the underground salt deposits.

SAND, INDUSTRIAL — Sands used for special purposes, due to **high silica content** or to unique physical properties, command higher prices than common sand. Industrial sands in Texas occur mainly in the **Central Gulf Coastal Plain** and in **North Central Texas**. They include **abrasive, blast, chemical, engine, filtration, foundry, glass, hydraulic-fracturing (propant), molding and pottery sands**. Recent production of industrial sands has been from Atascosa, Colorado, Hardin, Harris, Liberty, Limestone, McCulloch, Newton, Smith, Somervell and Upshur counties.

SAND AND GRAVEL (CONSTRUCTION) — Sand and gravel are among the most extensively utilized resources in Texas. Principal occurrence is along the major streams and in stream terraces. Sand and gravel are important **bulk construction materials, used as railroad ballast, base materials** and for other purposes.

SANDSTONE — Sandstones of a variety of colors and textures are widely distributed in a number of geologic formations in Texas. Some of the sandstones have been quarried for use as **dimension stone** in El Paso, Parker, Terrell, Ward and other counties. **Crushed sandstone** is produced in Freestone, Gaines, Jasper, McMullen, Motley and other counties for use as **road-building material, terrazzo stone and aggregate**.

SERPENTINITE — Several masses of serpentinite, which formed from the alteration of basic igneous rocks, are associated with other Precambrian metamorphic rocks of the **Llano Uplift**. The largest deposit is the **Coal Creek serpentinite mass** in northern Blanco and Gillespie counties from which **terrazzo chips** have been produced. Other deposits are present in Gillespie and Llano counties. (The features that are associated with surface and subsurface Cretaceous rocks in several counties in or near the **Balcones Fault Zone** and that are commonly known as "**serpentine plugs**" are not serpentine at all, but are altered igneous volcanic necks and pipes and mounds of altered volcanic ash — **palagonite** — that accumulated around the former **submarine volcanic pipes**.)

SHELL — Oyster shells and other shells in shallow coastal waters and in deposits along the **Texas Gulf Coast** have been produced in the past chiefly by dredging. They were used to a limited extent as raw material in the **manufacture of cement, as concrete aggregate and road base**, and for other purposes. No shell has been produced in Texas since 1981.

SILVER — During the period 1885-1952, the production of silver in Texas, as reported by the U.S. Bureau of Mines, totaled about **33 million troy ounces**. For about 70 years, silver was the most consistently produced metal in Texas, although always in moderate quantities. All of the production came from the **Trans-Pecos country** of West Texas, where the silver was mined in Brewster County (**Altuda Mountain**), Culberson and Hudspeth counties (**Van Horn Mountains and Van Horn-Allamoore district**), Hudspeth County (**Quitman Mountains and Eagle Mountains**) and Presidio County (**Chinati Mountains area, Loma Plata mine and Shafter district**).

Chief producer was the **Presidio mine in the Shafter**

district, which began operations in the late 1800s, and, through September 1942, produced more than 30 million ounces of silver — more than 92 percent of Texas' total silver production. Water in the lower mine levels, lean ores and low price of silver resulted in the closing of the mine in 1942. Another important silver producer was the **Hazel copper-silver mine** in the **Van Horn-Allamoore district** in Culberson County, which accounted for more than 2 million ounces.

An increase in the price of silver in the late 1970s stimulated prospecting for new reserves, and exploration began near the old **Presidio mine**, near the old **Plata Verde mine** in the Van Horn Mountains district, at the **Bonanza mine** in the **Quitman Mountains** district and at the old **Hazel mine**. A decline in the price of silver in the early 1980s, however, resulted in reduction of exploration and mine development in the region. There is no current exploration in these areas.

SOAPSTONE (see **TALC AND SOAPSTONE**).

SODIUM SULFATE (SALT CAKE) — Sodium sulfate minerals occur in salt beds and brines of the alkali **playa lakes** of the High Plains in West Texas. In some lakes, the sodium sulfate minerals are present in deposits a few feet beneath the lakebeds. Sodium sulfate also is found in underground brines in the Permian Basin. Current production is from brines and dry salt beds at alkali lakes in Gaines and Terry counties. Past production was reported in Lynn and Ward counties. Sodium sulfate is used chiefly by the **detergent and paper and pulp industries**. Other uses are in the **preparation of glass and other products**.

STONE (see **BUILDING STONE** and **CRUSHED STONE**).

STRONTIUM — Deposits of the mineral **celestite (strontium sulfate)** have been found in a number of places, including localities in Brown, Coke, Comanche, Fisher, Lampasas, Mills, Nolan, Real, Taylor, Travis and Williamson counties. Most of the occurrences are very minor, and no strontium is currently produced in the state.

SULFUR — Texas is **one of the world's principal sulfur-producing areas**. The sulfur is mined from deposits of native sulfur, and it is extracted from sour (sulfur-bearing) natural gas and petroleum. **Recovered sulfur** is a growing industry and accounted for approximately 60 percent of all 1987 sulfur production in the United States, but only approximately 40 percent of Texas production. Native sulfur is found in large deposits in the caprock of some of the **salt domes** along the Texas Gulf Coast and in some of the surface and subsurface Permian strata of West Texas, notably in Culberson and Pecos counties.

Native sulfur obtained from the underground deposits is known as **Frasch sulfur**, so-called because of Herman Frasch, the chemist who devised the method of drilling wells into the deposits, melting the sulfur with super-heated water and forcing the molten sulfur to the surface. Most of the production now goes to the users in molten form.

Frasch sulfur is produced from only one Gulf Coast salt dome in Wharton County and from West Texas underground Permian strata in Culberson County. Operations at several Gulf Coast domes have been closed in recent years. During the 1940s, acidic sulfur earth was produced in the **Rustler Springs district** in Culberson County for use as a **fertilizer and soil conditioner**. Sulfur is recovered from sour natural gas and petroleum at plants in numerous Texas counties.

Sulfur is used in the preparation of **fertilizers and organic and inorganic chemicals, in petroleum refining** and for many other purposes.

TALC AND SOAPSTONE — Deposits of talc are found in the Precambrian metamorphic rocks of the **Allamoore area** of eastern Hudspeth and western Cul-berson counties. Soapstone, containing talc, occurs in the Precambrian metamorphic rocks of the **Llano Uplift** area, notably in Blanco, Gillespie and Llano counties. Current production is from surface mines in the **Allamoore area**. Talc is used in **ceramic, roofing, paint, paper, plastic, synthetic rubber** and other products.

TIN — Tin minerals have been found in El Paso and Mason counties. Small quantities were produced during the early 1900s in the Franklin Mountains north of El Paso. **Cassiterite (tin dioxide)** occurrences in Mason County are believed to be very minor. The **only tin smelter in the United States**, built at **Texas City** by the federal government during World War II and later sold to a private company, processes tin concentrates from ores mined outside of Texas, tin residues and secondary tin-bearing materials.

TITANIUM — The titanium mineral **rutile** has been found in small amounts at the **Mueller prospect** in Jeff Davis County. Another titanium mineral, **ilmenite**, occurs in sandstones in Burleson, Fayette, Lee, Starr and several other counties. Deposits that would be considered commercial under present conditions have not been found.

TRAP ROCK (see **BASALT**).

TUNGSTEN — The tungsten mineral **scheelite** has been found in small deposits in Gillespie and Llano counties and in the **Quitman Mountains** in Hudspeth County. Small deposits of other tungsten minerals have been prospected in the **Cave Peak area** north of Van Horn in Culberson County.

URANIUM — Uranium deposits were discovered in the **Texas Coastal Plain** in 1954 when abnormal radioactivity was detected in the Karnes County area. A number of uranium deposits have since been discovered within a belt of strata extending more than 250 miles from the middle Coastal Plain southwestward to the Rio Grande.

Various uranium minerals also have been found in other areas of Texas, including the **Trans-Pecos**, the **Llano Uplift** and the **High Plains**. With the exception of small shipments from the High Plains during the 1950s, all the uranium production in Texas has been from the Coastal Plain. Uranium has been obtained from surface mines extending from northern Live Oak County, southeastern Atascosa County, across northern Karnes County and into southern Gonzales County.

All mines are now reclaimed. Until recently, uranium was produced by in-situ leaching, brought to the surface through wells, and stripped from the solution at several Coastal Plain recovery operations. There has been no uranium production in Texas since 2000 because of decreased prices and demand.

VERMICULITE — Vermiculite, a mica-like mineral that expands when heated, occurs in Burnet, Gillespie, Llano, Mason and other counties in the **Llano region**. It has been produced at a surface mine in Llano County. Vermiculite, mined outside of Texas, is exfoliated (expanded) at plants in Dallas, Houston and San Antonio. Exfoliated vermiculite is used for **lightweight concrete aggregate, horticulture, insulation** and other purposes.

VOLCANIC ASH (see **PUMICITE**).

ZEOLITES — The zeolite minerals **clinoptilolite** and **analcime** occur in Tertiary lavas and tuffs in Brewster, Jeff Davis and Presidio counties, in West Texas. Clinoptilolite also is found associated with Tertiary tuffs in the southern Texas Coastal Plain, including deposits in Karnes, McMullen and Webb counties, and currently is produced in McMullen County. Zeolites, sometimes called "molecular sieves," can be used in **ion-exchange processes to reduce pollution**, as a catalyst in **oil cracking**, in obtaining **high-purity oxygen and nitrogen** from air, in **water purification** and for many other purposes.

ZINC (see **LEAD AND ZINC**). ☆

Electric Utilities: Rising Power Bills

By Sudeep Reddy

Despite the promise of lower electricity rates from deregulation, most Texas consumers continued to face rising power bills through 2005.

But lawmakers and regulators held firm to the mission put forth when the state restructured the electricity industry with its landmark legislation in 1999. Over time, they say, consumers would benefit from competitive forces in the industry.

Large business customers had gained the most from those forces after three full years of competition for retail electricity service. In March 2005, about two-thirds of large commercial customers were purchasing power from a company other than their incumbent provider, according to the Electric Reliability Council of Texas, the state's power grid operator.

Residential and small-business customers, however, were slower to change providers.

Non-incumbent providers served about 22 percent of the roughly 5 million residential customers eligible to switch. Competing providers served about 27 percent of small-business electricity meters, but those customers represented about 70 percent of the electricity load for that category because companies with larger power bills had switched more than others.

By April 2005, 91 companies were authorized by the Texas Public Utility Commission to sell electricity in Texas. More than 50 were actively serving customers, according to the PUC.

Residential customers could choose from 10 to 13 providers – including their former monopoly – depending on their location. Most competitors offered lower rates than the former monopoly, but some providers charged more in order to offer clean-electricity plans or other benefits.

The ultimate promise of competition – lowering prices for consumers – wasn't realized for most residential customers.

The former monopolies continued to raise their rates, citing higher wholesale power costs as a result of the skyrocketing price of natural gas, which fuels most of the state's power plants. Average natural gas prices more than doubled in the three years of electric competition.

The residential rates of the state's largest provider, TXU Energy, shot up 46 percent between January 2002 and May 2005. A customer in TXU's original service territory of North Texas who used an average of 1,000 kilowatt-hours of electricity a month would have paid about $121 a month for electricity in June 2005, up from almost $83 a month three years earlier. TXU

Power lines deliver electricity from the Comanche Peak nuclear plant in Somervell County. File photo.

served about 2 million residential customers in North Texas through spring 2005.

Other former monopolies – Reliant Energy, CPL Retail Energy, WTU Retail Energy, and First Choice Power – also delivered similar price increases to customers in their original territories. Outside their home zones, however, the providers often charged less by operating as competing providers against the incumbents.

During a five-year transition to competition that ends in 2007, regulators must approve residential rate increases by the former monopolies.

Consumer groups criticized the rate increases for causing hardship for customers who weren't interested in switching. In areas of the state that aren't open to competition but still served by investor-owned utilities, rates over the previous three years had increased by less than 20 percent.

Critics have alleged that the formula used for rate increases is unfair, and that it was set higher than necessary to force consumers to switch to a competitor. The formula allows rate changes by the incumbent providers twice a year based on an increase in natural gas prices.

Other electricity sources – such as coal and nuclear plants – are not factored into the formula for rate increases. Also, the former monopolies are not required to lower their rates if gas prices fall, though they would be vulnerable to losing customers to competitors. In 2004, about half of the

Consumer Switching in Texas

Type Service	March 2005	March 2004	March 2003
Percent served by non-incumbent provider			
Residential	22	15	8
Small commercial	27	18	12
Large commercial	64	55	49
Source: Electric Reliabilbity Council of Texas			

state's electricity was generated from gas-fired power plants, according to the PUC. Almost 40 percent was from coal and lignite plants, and nuclear plants generated about 11 percent. Wind and other sources generated the remaining small fraction.

Rising prices were only part of the growing pains Texas faced in its path toward deregulation.

From 2003 to 2005, the PUC was forced to investigate claims that some electric companies were manipulating the wholesale power market operated by ERCOT, the grid operator.

The collapse of Enron Corp. in late 2001, and the allegations of market manipulation that shook the West Coast, reverberated nationwide in the years that followed.

In Texas, some companies claimed that energy traders used Enron-style tactics to raise prices in the wholesale electricity market to benefit their companies' power plants. The allegations have led to investigations by the PUC and probes into whether some companies have too much market power that allows them to influence prices.

The adequacy of the state's power supplies also started to gain greater scrutiny in 2005. While California's power crisis in 2000 and 2001 was due in part to a shortage of power plants, Texas officials had taken pride in the state's surplus. In 2003, Texas had about 40 percent more power available than necessary when demand peaked on the hottest summer day.

But the retirement and mothballing of older and less efficient gas-fired power plants sent that cushion falling quickly. Under an ERCOT calculation released in June 2005, the state was projected to have a surplus cushion of about 16.9 percent for the year. The peak electricity demand was projected at 60,475 megawatts, near the record 60,095 megawatts recorded in August 2003.

If mothballed plants are not returned to service, the cushion of excess capacity was projected to fall to 12.6 percent in 2006 and 11.1 percent in 2007, below ERCOT's minimum requirement of 12.5 percent. But state officials expressed confidence that companies would build new power plants as the market received the signal of rising wholesale power prices.

Leading into the 2005 legislative session, much of the attention focused on how lawmakers would reform ERCOT's organizational structure after revelations of a contracting scandal the previous year. Six former ERCOT workers – including a senior executive and top security officials – were indicted in January 2005 for what the Texas attorney general called an "elaborate organized crime scheme" inside the nonprofit organization, which is funded by electricity consumers.

The workers allegedly used a network of shell companies to bill the organization $2 million for security and computer-contracting services, even though much of the work was not performed.

ERCOT, which controls the flow of power around the state and directs key pieces of the $27 billion deregulated power market, faced several outside audits that identified holes in the organization's business practices. During the session, lawmakers passed measures to increase PUC oversight of the grid operator and include more independent directors on its board.

The Legislature largely sidestepped measures to address rising power prices, including a bill to allow city governments to automatically pool their residents and negotiate lower prices on their behalf.

Even with rising power costs, a budget committee voted to redirect money from the System Benefit Fund, which provided a 10 percent discount on electricity bills for low-income Texans. The fund, which collects money from fees on consumers, had supported the discount for more than 380,000 households through March 2005.

In one of the few electricity bills that survived during the session, lawmakers approved a measure to limit the ability of electricity providers to use credit scores in setting rates and offering service.

Overall, legislators – along with regulators and power providers – have strongly supported competition, saying that consumers can save money if they switched providers. They also cite improving customer service and other benefits – such as development of cleaner power plants and renewable energy sources – as signs that deregulation is working.

In January 2007, the market is expected to face a larger test when price caps come off the residential rates of former monopolies. At that point, all companies – incumbents and competitors alike – will be allowed to raise or lower their prices without the approval of state regulators.

Consumer groups say that would lead to even larger price increases, while companies say it could spark more competitive activity along with better products and services for customers.

Sudeep Reddy is a staff writer of The Dallas Morning News.

Electric Cooperatives

Source: The Texas Electric Cooperatives

Electric cooperatives are nonprofit, consumer-owned utilities providing electric service primarily in rural areas. Rates and services are regulated by the Public Utility Commission of Texas.

The nation's first electric cooperative was established in 1935 in Bartlett. It and others were organized when investor-owned utilities neglected or refused to serve farms and rural communities. By 1940, there were 567 cooperatives in 46 states.

In 2005, 930 electric co-ops serve 35 million people throughout the nation.

Texas was home to **64** electric-distribution cooperatives and **11** generation and transmission cooperatives (G&Ts) — which are owned by local distribution cooperatives — serving nearly **3** million member-customers in **231** of the 254 counties.

Three of the G&Ts generate power while the others represent their member distribution systems in wholesale power supply arrangements. The systems operate more than **260,000** miles of line.

Under the 1999 Texas legislation for deregulation of the electric utililties, cooperatives as well as municipally owned utilities have the option to enter the competitve market or not.

Each elected co-op board of directors will decide on their direction and options for expansion. ☆

Telecommunications Technology Changes, Jobs Decline

By Terry Maxon

The telecommunications industry continued a slow recovery from its deep plummet at the start of the decade, but the drain of jobs did not end for many companies or for the state. Many other telecom companies remained far below their employment numbers of 1999 and 2000 before the telecom and Internet bubbles burst.

Statewide, more than 135,000 people held telecommunications jobs at the end of 2000; by December 2004, that had dropped under 95,000, down 30 percent.

Both the traditional telephone companies and wireless providers (cellular companies) have seen a continuous decline in jobs during the 2001-2004 period, but the traditional firms have been hit the hardest. Total employment dropped 1 percent for the wireless companies between 2003 and 2004, compared to 6 percent for the old-line telephone companies.

The rapid growth of cellular telephone service has offset a steady decline in the number of Texans with local phone lines – good news for cellular companies, not so good for traditional telephone companies without a wireless product to sell.

In 1999, Texas boasted 13.2 million local lines, compared to 5.8 million cellphone subscribers. By mid 2004, the number of local lines had dropped to 12.5 million, but cellphone subscribers increased to 12.1 million. By 2005, the number of cellphone subscribers in Texas was expected to exceed the number of traditional telephone lines.

The advent of telephone service over the Internet, known as Voice over Internet Protocol (VoIP), opened the door for many competitors to traditional telephone companies. In some cases, the telephone companies and cable operators offered VoIP service. However, many other firms provided VoIP service without owning the high-speed broadband lines that carried the voice calls.

The cable industry won a major victory in June 2005 when the U.S. Supreme Court ruled that cable companies don't have to provide access to their lines to other firms that want to sell Internet access.

As the industry continued to change, the eyes of some major players turned to marriage. Assuming regulators agree, four of the industry's biggest companies – all with significant employment in Texas – were expected to shrink to two.

SBC Communications Inc. struck a deal in early 2005 to acquire AT&T Corp., and Verizon Communications Inc. won a bidding war to buy MCI Corp.

After weeks of talks, executives of SBC & AT&T announced the acquisition on Jan. 31, 2005. San Anto-

nio-based SBC, spun off from AT&T more than two decades earlier, was expected to finalize the combination in late 2005 or early 2006.

SBC, the state's largest telecom company, steadily shed employees in the first half of the decade, declining from 220,090 at the first of 2000 to 162,700 at the end of 2004.

SBC will grow from its successful bid to buy AT&T Corp., its one-time parent, for nearly $16 billion. Even so, SBC was eliminating thousands of additional positions, some as a result of the merger.

SBC wanted to acquire AT&T's extensive system of long-distance lines and networks, both in the United States and internationally, and the large business customers that AT&T had signed up.

Similarly, Verizon won a battle in May 2005 to buy MCI Corp. for about $8.5 billion, even though its bid wound up $1.3 billion less than the offer from Qwest Communications International Inc.

MCI, which was founded in 1963, became the first company allowed to compete against AT&T on long-distance service, and its fight against AT&T helped bring about the breakup of the AT&T empire.

In 1997, WorldCom Inc. bought MCI, but went bankrupt in 2002 and became embroiled in a scandal over falsified accounting. When the reorganized company emerged from bankruptcy in April 2004, it took the less-sullied name of MCI.

The AT&T and MCI transactions were coming at a time in which most major telecommunications companies had seen their long-distance business and local telephone revenues decline steadily.

AT&T revenues for long-distance calls dropped from $12.4 billion in 2002 to $9.5 billion, or 23 percent, in 2004. Similarly, MCI saw its long distance revenues fall 62 percent, from $6.5 billion in 2002 to $2.5 billion in 2004.

The decrease in long distance revenues was blamed on two factors. One, rates continued falling as long-distance service became more of a commodity. Second, the regional Bell operating companies like SBC and Verizon, were freed to sell long distance service in markets where they also provided local telephone service. They took immediate advantage of their new powers.

At the end of 2002, for example, SBC had only 7.4 million long-distance lines in service. In 2004, that number jumped more than 244 percent, to 20.9 million. Verizon increased its numbers from 7.4 million in 2002 to 17.7 million in 2004, a 139 percent increase.

The second half of the decade promises to be a tough battle between the traditional telephone compa-

Texas Telephone/Telecommunication Statistics

Service	2004	2003	2002	2001	2000	1999
Local phone lines	12,459,719	12,717,073	12,949,056	13,531,474	13,657,444	13,188,047
former monopolies	10,139,446	10,451,045	10,766,127	11,365,441	11,892,768	12,601,936
competitors	2,320,273	2,266,028	2,182,929	2,166,033	1,764,676	586,111
Wireless subscribers	12,091,134	10,776,234	9,650,715	8,294,338	6,705,423	5,792,453
Broadband lines	2,246,862	1,610,935	1,050,511	646,839	276,087	152,518

Source: Federal Communications Commission.

nies and the cable companies for customers in Texas and nationwide.

The new catchphrase was the "triple play" – the selling of voice, Internet service and television packages to customers.

SBC is deploying its "Project Lightspeed," a $4 billion project to build a fiber-optics network to at least 50 percent of its customers by the end of 2007. Project Lightspeed will extend lines generally to within 3,000 feet of customers' home, with traditional copper wire spanning the last section.

Verizon, with its "FiOs" service, has taken a more ambitious and expensive approach. It is building the fiber-optic network all the way to the home, seeking to transmit data faster and provide more capacity for data and video services than a combination fiber/copper setup.

At the same time, Comcast Corp., Time Warner Cable and other traditional cable companies began offering telephone services to go along with their video and data subscriptions.

During the regular session of the 79th Legislature in 2005, the telephone companies fought an ultimately unsuccessful battle for the right to raise basic telephone rates and to secure statewide franchises for telephone service.

The telcos, led by SBC and Verizon, wanted to bypass the time-consuming process of asking each city for the right to provide video service, the route that cable companies by and large had to follow over the previous 30 years. Cable companies, backed by cities concerned about losing revenues and some say about what goes inside their borders, opposed the effort.

The proposal sparked a tremendously vigorous and expensive lobbying effort by all sides, and efforts continued to rewrite the state's telecommunications laws.

Nowhere has the competition been fiercer than for the right to sell broadband service to consumers. By 2005, price-cutting became the norm as both telephone companies and cable companies sought to woo or hold onto customers.

In 1999, companies had only 152,518 broadband lines installed. By mid 2004, that had increased to over 2.2 million. Cable companies provided the majority of those lines, 1.2 million.

On the cellular side, Cingular Wireless and AT&T Wireless closed their merger in October 2004, and the AT&T Wireless brand disappeared inside Cingular.

The combination made Cingular the largest wireless company with more than 50 million customers in the first quarter of 2005, bypassing Verizon Wireless and its 45.5 million customers.

The No.3 and 4 competitors, Sprint Corp. and Nextel Communications Inc., in December 2004 agreed to merge and were awaiting approval from regulators. The two plan to use Sprint as the overall brand, with Nextel as a product brand.

Terry Maxon is a staff writer of The Dallas Morning News.

Top 5 Gas Distribution Utilities, 2002

UTILITY	Customers	Sales (MMcf)*
TXU Gas Company	1,452, 000	146,892
Centerpoint Energy Entex	1,339,000	124,971
San Antonio Public Service	306,000	60,638
Atmos Energy	288,000	41,354
Texas Gas Service	538,000	35,380

Note: These utilities represent 95 percent of all distribution sales in Texas. *MMcf: Million cubic feet. Source: Texas Railroad Comm.

Top 5 Gas Transmission Utilities, 2002

UTILITY	Volume (MMcf)	Average Rate ($/Mcf)*
EPGT Texas Pipeline	1,519,669	0.067
Tejas Gas Pipeline	581,393	0.070
TXU Lone Star Pipeline	425,104	0.122
Oasis Pipe Line TX	335,739	0.072
Oneok Westex Transmission	255,190	0.094

Note: These utilities transport 51 percent of all gas in Texas. *$/Mcf: Dollars per thousand cubic feet. Railroad Commission.

Gas Utilities

Source: Gas Services Division, Texas Railroad Commission

Approximately **202** investor-owned gas companies in Texas are classified as gas utilities and come under the regulatory jurisdiction of the Railroad Commission of Texas. Approximately **122** of these companies reported gas operating revenue of $10.5 billion in 2002, with operating expenses of $**9.8** billion.

In 2002, fixed investment for distribution facilities in Texas was $3.5 billion and for transmission facilities, $**4.5** billion. Investment in Texas plants in service totaled $**10.3** billion. There were **32** investor-owned and **84** municipally owned distribution systems in operation in 2002 serving **1,050** Texas cities.

The **eight** largest distribution systems - six private and two municipal - served 97 percent of all residential customers. In 2002, there were approximately **3.8** million residential customers, **314,903** small commercial and industrial users, **8,159** large industrial customers and **14,229** other gas utility customers. The breakdown of distribution sales to these customers was: **56** Mcf (thousand cubic feet) per residential customer, **463** Mcf per commercial customer, **8,691** per industrial customer, and **1,554** Mcf for customers in the "other" category. Distribution sales amounted to **450.6** billion cubic feet in 2002.

In addition to industrial sales made by distribution companies, transmission companies reported pipeline-to-industry sales of **2.2** trillion cubic feet and revenue from these sales of $**7.4** billion.

In 2002, the average annual residential gas bill in the United States was $**612**. The average annual bill in Texas for the same year was $**402**, down $**94** from the previous year. The State of Texas collected $**5.7** million in gas utility taxes from gas utilities in fiscal year 2003.

Texas had a total of **157,748** miles of natural gas pipelines in operation in 2002, including **7,842** miles of field and gathering lines, **52,792** miles of transmission lines and **97,114** miles of distribution lines. ☆

Agriculture in Texas

Information was provided by Texas Cooperative Extension specialists, Texas Agricultural Statistics Service, U.S. Department of Agriculture and U.S. Department of Commerce. Carl G. Anderson, professor and extension specialist–emeritus of Texas A&M University, coordinated the information. All references are to Texas unless otherwise specified.

Agribusiness, which is the combined phases of food and fiber production, processing, transporting and marketing, is a leading Texas industry. Most of this article focuses on the production phase that occurs on farms and ranches.

Agriculture is one of the most important industries in Texas. Many businesses, financial institutions and individuals are involved in providing supplies, credit and services to farmers and ranchers and in processing and marketing agricultural commodities.

Including all of its agribusiness phases, agriculture added about $36 billion to the economic activity of the state in 2004. The estimated value of farm assets in Texas — the land, buildings, livestock, machinery, crops, inventory on farms, household goods and farm financial assets — totaled approximately $113 billion at the beginning of 2003.

Texas agriculture is a strong industry. Receipts from farm and ranch marketings in 2004 were estimated at $16.0 billion, compared with $14.9 billion in 2003.

The potential for further growth is favorable. With the increasing demand for food and fiber throughout the

Farming and ranching contributed about $16 billion to the Texas economy in 2004. File photo.

world, and because of the importance of agricultural exports to the trade balance of the United States, agriculture in Texas is destined to play an even greater role in the future.

Major efforts of research and educational programs by the Texas A&M University System are directed toward developing the state's agricultural industry to its fullest potential. The goal is to capitalize on natural advantages that agriculture has in Texas because of the relatively warm climate, productive soils, and availability of excellent export and transportation facilities.

Texas Farms

The number and nature of farms have changed over time. The number of farms in Texas has decreased from 420,000 in 1940 to 229,000 in 2004, with an average size of 568 acres. Average value per farm of all farm assets, including land and buildings, has increased from $20,100 in 1950 to $491,516 in 2004. The number of small farms is increasing, although part-time farmers operate them.

Balance Sheet of Texas Farms and Ranches
Jan. 1, 1994–2003

Table below shows the financial status of Texas farms and ranches as of Jan. 1 of the years 1994–2003.

(All amounts are given in millions of dollars.)

Item	1994	1995	1996	1997	1998	1999	2000	2001	2002	2003
ASSETS:										
Physical Assets:										
Real estate	$60,931	$62,927	$64,314	$68,842	$70,277	$72,303	$78,041	$82,632	$86,075	$90,861
Non-real estate:										
*Livestock and poultry	8,703	6,417	6,403	8,060	7,242	8,003	8,567	8,513	8,597	8,513
†Machinery and motor vehicles	5,997	6,114	6,217	6,383	6,490	6,522	6,574	6,852	7,013	7,190
‡Crops stored on and off farms	641	741	839	1,028	1,146	1,100	795	651	797	728
Purchased Inputs	194	124	159	178	183	146	178	153	205	205
***Financial assets:**	3,958	4,055	4,006	3,960	4,095	4,217	4,383	4,696	4,794	5,024
Total Assets.	80,424	80,377	81,937	88,450	89,433	92,290	98,539	103,497	107,480	112,521
LIABILITIES:										
††Real estate debt	4,070	4,233	4,439	4,835	5,020	5,355	5,584	5,934	6,465	6,769
‡‡Non-real estate debt:										
Excluding CCC loans	5,390	5,464	5,596	5,777	5,896	5,849	6,386	6,542	6,534	6,517
Total Liabilities	9,461	9,697	10,035	10,612	10,916	11,204	11,970	12,476	13,000	13,286
Owners' equities	70,963	70,681	71,903	77,838	78,517	81,086	86,569	91,021	94,480	99,234
TOTAL CLAIMS	$80,424	$80,377	$81,937	$88,450	$89,433	$92,290	$98,539	$103,497	$107,480	$112,521

*Excludes horses, mules and broilers.
†Includes only farm share value for trucks and autos.
‡All non-CCC crops held on farms plus value above loan rate for crops held under CCC.
†† Includes Farm Credit System, Farm Service Agency, commercial banks, life insurance companies, individuals and others, and CCC storage and drying loans.
‡‡ Includes Farm Credit System, Farm Service Agency, commercial banks and individual and others.
** As of 1987, investments in Co-ops and Other Financial reported as Financial.
Source: "Farm Business Economic Report," Farm Business Balance Sheet, USDA/ERS, as of Nov. 18, 2004.

Mechanization of farming continues as new and larger machines replace manpower. Even though machinery price tags are high relative to times past, machines are technologically advanced and efficient. Tractors, mechanical harvesters and numerous cropping machines have virtually eliminated menial tasks that for many years were traditional to farming.

Revolutionary agricultural chemicals have appeared along with improved plants and animals and methods of handling them. Many of the natural hazards of farming and ranching

Livestock and livestock products accounted for 67.2 percent of the $15.34 billion cash receipts from farm marketings in 2003. Crops accounted for the remaining 32.8 percent. File photo.

have been reduced by better use of weather information, machinery and other improvements; however, rising costs, including energy costs, and labor availability are a major concern for farmers and ranchers.

Changes in Texas agriculture in the last 50 years include:

1. More detailed record keeping that assists in management and marketing decisions

2. More restrictions on choice or inputs/practices

3. Precision agriculture will take on new dimensions through the use of satellites, computers and other high-tech tools to help producers manage inputs, such as seed, fertilizers, pesticides and water.

Farms have become fewer, larger, more specialized, and much more expensive to own and operate, but they are also far more productive. The number of small farms operated by part-time farmers is increasing. Land ownership is becoming more of a lifestyle used mostly for recreational purposes. Non-farm landowners are increasing.

Irrigation has become an important factor in crop production; see page 627.

Crops and livestock have made major changes in production areas, such as in the concentration of cotton on the High Plains and livestock increases in Central and Eastern Texas.

Pest and disease control methods have greatly improved. Herbicides are relied upon for weed control.

Ranchers and farmers are better educated and informed, more science- and business-oriented. Today, agriculture operates in a global, high-tech, consumer-driven environment.

Livestock and poultry efficiency have greatly increased because of feedlot finishing, commercial broiler production, artificial insemination, improved pastures and brush control,

reduced feed requirements, along with other changes. Biotechnology and genetic engineering promise new breakthroughs in reaching even higher levels of productivity.

Horticultural plant and nursery businesses have expanded. Improved wildlife management has increased

Texas Crop Production 2004

Crop	Harvested Acres (000)	Yield Per Acre	Unit	Total Production (000)	Value (000)
Beans, dry edible	17.5	800	lb.	140	3,080
Corn, grain	1,680	139	bu.	233,520	595,476
Corn, silage	110	23.0	ton	2,530	—
Cotton, American-Pima	20.5	890	lb.	38	14,556
Cotton, upland	5,350	694	lb.	7,740	1,582,675
Cottonseed	—	—	ton	2,939	305,656
Grapefruit *	—	—	box	5,700	22,710
Hay	5,350	2.3	ton	12,295	833,580
Oats	160	40	bu.	6,400	12,160
Oranges†	—	—	box	1,650	7,085
Peaches	—	—	lb.	19,800	15,097
Peanuts	235	3,300	lb.	775,500	156,651
Pecans	—	—	lb.	40,000	61,800
Potatoes	20.1	320	cwt.	6,429	54,554
Rice	218	6,740	lb.	14,690	120,458
Sorghum, grain	2,050	3,472	lb.	71,176	288,263
Sorghum, silage	80	17	ton	1,360	—
Soybeans	270	32	bu.	8,640	50,544
Sugar cane	44	39.9	ton	1,757	—
Sunflowers	38	1,474	lb.	56,000	7,920
Sweet potatoes	3.3	140	cwt.	462	8,316
Vegetables, commercial:					
Fresh market ‡	74.6	—	cwt.	17,878	341,915
Processing §	18.9	—	cwt.	2,331	24,337
Wheat, winter	3,500	31	bu.	108,500	363,475
Total of Listed Crops	**24,589.9**	**—**	**—**	**—**	**$5,703,888**

Grapefruit, 80-lb. box reflects 2003–2004 crop year. † Oranges, 85-lb. box, reflects 2003–2004 crop year. ‡ Includes processing total for dual-usage crops (asparagus, broccoli and cauliflower). Total Texas fresh-market vegetables include bell peppers, cabbage, cantaloupes, carrots, cauliflower, celery, cucumbers, honeydew melons, onions, spinach, sweet corn, tomatoes and watermelons. § Total Texas processing vegetables include carrots, cucumbers, snap beans, spinach and tomatoes.
Source: "Texas Ag Facts Annual Summary," TASS/USDA, 5/12/2005.

deer, turkey and other wildlife populations. The use of land for recreation and ecotourism is growing.

Cooperation among farmers in marketing, promotion and other fields has increased.

Agricultural producers have become increasingly dependent on off-the-farm services to supply production inputs, such as feeds, chemicals, credit and other essentials.

Agribusiness

Texas farmers and ranchers have developed considerable dependence on agribusiness. With many producers specializing in the production of certain crops and livestock, they look beyond the farm and ranch for supplies and services. On the input side, they rely on suppliers of production needs and services, and, on the output side, they need assemblers, processors and distributors. The impact of production agriculture and related businesses on the Texas economy is about $36 billion annually.

Since 1940, the proportion of Texans whose liveli-

hoods are linked to agriculture has vastly changed. In 1940, about 23 percent were producers on farms and ranches, and about 17 percent were suppliers or were engaged in assembly, processing and distribution of agricultural products. The agribusiness alignment in 2004 was less than 2 percent on farms and ranches, with about 15 percent of the labor force providing production or marketing supplies and services, and retailing food and fiber products.

Cash Receipts

Farm and ranch cash receipts in 2003 totaled $15.342 billion. Realized gross farm income totaled $19.632 billion, including estimates of $1.666 billion for government payments, $1.032 billion of non-cash income, and $1.592 billion of other farm-related income. With farm production expenses of $13.693 billion, net farm income totaled $5.939 billion. The value of inventory adjustment was –$184.5 million.

Farm and Ranch Assets

Farm and ranch assets totaled $112.5 billion in 2003. This was up from the 2002 level of $107.5 billion. Value of real estate increased almost 5.3 percent to $90.9 billion in 2003. Liabilities totaled $13.3 billion, up slightly from $13.0 billion in 2002.

Percent of Income from Products

Livestock and livestock products accounted for 67.2 percent of the $15.34 billion cash receipts from farm marketings in 2003. Crops accounted for the remaining 32.8 percent. Receipts from livestock have trended up largely because of increased feeding operations and reduced crop acreage associated with farm programs and low prices. However, these relationships change because of variations in commodity prices and volume of marketings.

Meat animals (cattle, hogs and sheep) accounted for 52.1 percent of total cash receipts received by Texas farmers and ranchers in 2003. Most of these receipts were from cattle and calf sales. Dairy products made up 4.8 percent of receipts; poultry and eggs, 9.1 percent; and miscellaneous livestock, 1.3 percent.

Cotton and cottonseed accounted for 8.7 percent of total receipts; feed crops, 6.9 percent; food grains, 2.2 percent; vegetables, 3.8 percent; greenhouse and nursery products, 8.6 percent; oil crops, 1.2 percent; fruits and nuts, 0.7 percent; and other crops, 0.6 percent.

Texas Rank Among States

Measured by cash receipts for farm and ranch marketings, Texas ranked second in 2003 among the states. California ranked first and Iowa third.

Texas normally leads all other states in the number of farms and ranches, the amount of farm and ranch land, cattle slaughtered, cattle on feed, calf births, sheep and lambs, goats, cash receipts from livestock marketings, cattle and calves, beef cows, wool production, mohair production, and exports of fats, oils, and greases. The state also usually leads in production of cotton.

Texas Agricultural Exports

The value of Texas' share of agricultural exports in fiscal year 2003 was $3.428 billion. Cotton accounted for $802.8 million of the exports; feed grains and products, $316.2 million; wheat and products, $245.6 million; fats, oil, and greases, $85.3 million; rice, $66.9 million; cottonseed and products, $30.9 million; hides

*Realized Gross Income and Net Income from Farming, Texas, 1980–2003

Year	**Realized Gross Farm Income	Farm Production Expenses	Net Change In Farm Inventories	***Total Net Farm Income	***Total Net Income Per Farm
	— Million Dollars —				Dollars
1980	9,611.4	9,154.6	–542.5	456.8	2,330.6
1981	11,545.7	9,643.1	699.9	1,902.6	9,756.9
1982	11,404.5	10,016.2	–127.8	1,388.3	7,156.2
1983	11,318.1	9,796.5	–590.7	1,521.6	7,843.3
1984	11,692.6	10,285.7	186.1	1,406.9	7,252.1
1985	11,375.3	9,882.4	–9.0	1,492.9	7,775.5
1986	10,450.1	9,341.3	–349.0	1,108.8	5,835.8
1987	12,296.6	10,185.0	563.2	2,111.5	11,231.4
1988	12,842.8	10,816.8	–128.4	2,026.0	10,552.1
1989	12,843.1	10,703.7	–798.6	2,139.4	11,027.8
1990	14,463.2	11,412.4	343.9	3,050.8	15,565.3
1991	14,393.4	11,551.4	150.0	2,842.0	14,426.4
1992	14,392.5	10,994.9	464.1	3,397.6	17,159.6
1993	15,758.5	11,612.1	197.0	4,146.4	20,732.0
1994	15,450.5	11,593.4	107.7	3,857.1	17,532.0
1995	15,709.7	12,984.4	243.7	2,725.3	12,276.0
1996	15,076.8	12,552.9	–290.1	2,524.0	11,268.0
1997	16,515.8	13,240.5	709.2	3,275.3	14,557.0
1998	15,552.3	12,556.1	–817.1	2,996.2	13,258.0
1999	17,453.0	12,452.9	196.0	5,000.1	22,027.0
2000	16,542.5	12,674.0	–50.2	3,867.5	17,113.0
2001	17,554.5	13,061.3	112.8	4,493.2	19,794.0
2002	16,610.6	11,364.3	458.8	5,206.3	22,810.0
2003	19,632.1	13,692.9	–184.5	5,939.2	25,935.0

*Details for items may not add to totals because of rounding. Series revised, September 1981.

**Cash receipts from farm marketings, government payments, value of home consumption and gross rental value of farm dwellings.

***Farm income of farm operators.

†A positive value of inventory change represents current-year production not sold by Dec. 31. A negative value is an offset to production from prior years included in current-year sales.

§Starting in 1977, farms with production of $1,000 or more used to figure income.

Source: "Economic Indicators of the Farm Sector, State Financial Summary, 1985," 1987," 1989," 1993," USDA/ERS; "Farm Business Economics Report", August 1996; "Texas Agricultural Statistics Service, 2004."

and skins, $282.9 million; live animals and meat, excluding chickens, $756.1 million; fruits, $40.7 million; peanuts and products, $36.7 million; soybeans and products, $17.3 million; vegetables, $68.0 million; poultry and products, $109.1 million; dairy products, $32.7 million; and miscellaneous and other products, $536.6 million.

In 2002, Texas' exports of $2.881 billion of farm and ranch products compares with $2.893 billion in 2001 and $3.111 billion in 2000.

Hunting

The management of wildlife as an economic enterprise through hunting leases makes a significant contribution to the economy of many counties. Leasing the right of ingress on a farm or ranch for the purpose of hunting is the service marketed. After the leasing, the consumer — the hunter — goes onto the land to seek the harvest of the wildlife commodity. Hunting lease income to farmers and ranchers in 2004 was estimated at $431 million.

The demand for hunting opportunities is growing while the land capable of producing wildlife for hunting is decreasing. As a result, farmers and ranchers are placing more emphasis on wildlife management practices to help meet requests for hunting leases.

Irrigation

Agricultural irrigation in Texas peaked in 1974 at 8.6 million acres. Over the next 20 years, irrigation declined because of many factors, including poor farm economics, falling water tables and conversion to more efficient technologies. In the 1990s, irrigation stabilized at 6.4 million acres. This puts Texas third in the nation, behind California and Nebraska.

Although some irrigation is practiced in nearly all of the state's 254 counties, about 50 percent of the total irrigated acreage is on the High Plains of Texas. Other concentrated areas of irrigation are the Gulf Coast rice producing area, the Lower Rio Grande Valley, the Winter Garden area of South Texas, the Trans-Pecos area of West Texas, and the peanut producing area of North-Central Texas, primarily around Erath, Eastland and Comanche counties. The largest growth in irrigation is occurring in the Coastal Bend area.

Sprinkler irrigation is used on about 63 percent of the total irrigated acreage, with surface irrigation methods, primarily furrow and surge methods, being used on the remaining irrigated area. Texas farmers lead the nation in the adoption of efficient irrigation technologies, particularly LEPA (low energy precision application) and LESA (low elevation spray application) center pivot systems, both of which were developed by Texas A&M.

The use of drip irrigation is increasing, with current acreage estimated to be 150,000 acres. Drip irrigation is routinely used on vegetables and tree crops, such as citrus, pecans and peaches. Some drip irrigation of cotton and forages is used in West Texas. Farmers continue to experiment with drip irrigation, but the high costs are limiting its widespread use.

Agricultural irrigation uses about 64 percent of all freshwater in the state, and landscape irrigation accounts for about 40 percent of total municipal water use. To meet future water demand for our rapidly growing cities

Export Shares of Commodities

Commodity*	2000	2001	2002	2003	2003 % of U.S. Total
	(Figures in Millions of Dollars)				
Rice	74.9	64.8	51.0	66.9	6.55
Cotton...........	521.2	464.3	425.6	802.8	29.44
Fats, oils & greases	64.6	48.6	68.4	85.3	15.84
Hides & skins	227.0	303.0	280.4	282.9	15.96
Meats other than poultry	820.4	743.5	696.4	756.1	11.66
Feed grains	321.9	313.5	261.1	316.2	4.70
Poultry products	108.8	127.0	121.4	109.1	5.18
Fruits	52.8	39.4	44.9	40.7	1.15
Vegetables	59.2	56.4	74.2	68.0	1.45
Wheat & flour	225.3	143.1	250.4	245.6	4.61
Soybeans & prod...	25.7	17.3	14.8	17.3	0.21
Cottonseed & prod.	28.4	21.5	22.6	30.9	30.03
Peanuts	58.6	35.7	67.5	36.7	19.55
Tree nuts	13.8	8.8	13.7	18.5	1.24
Dairy products	24.0	28.9	24.5	32.7	3.16
†All other	484.2	476.7	464.4	518.1	5.67
Total...........	**3,110.8**	**2,892.5**	**2,881.3**	**3,427.8**	**6.10**

Totals may not add because of rounding.
*Commodity and related preparations.
† Mainly confectionary, nursery and greenhouse, essential oils, sunflower-seed oil, beverages, and other miscellaneous animal and vegetable products.
Source: Foreign Agricultural Trade of the United States, various issues, March/April, 1994, 1995, and April/May/June, 1998; www.ers.usda.gov for 2003 data. USDA/ERS.

About 6.4 million acres in Texas is irrigated for agriculture, putting Texas third in the nation, behind California and Nebraska. About 50 percent of the total irrigated acreage is on the High Plains. Atmos Energy technicians check a natural gas meter used to drive irrigation pumps on a West Texas cotton and sorghum farm. Photo courtesy of Atmos Energy.

and industries, several regions of Texas are looking at water transfers from agriculture. In recent years, major water transfer projects have been proposed, including transferring water from the Texas High Plains to the Dallas-Fort Worth Metroplex, from the Colorado River to San Antonio, and from the Brazos Valley to several cities. The potential economic, political and environmental benefits and consequences of such transfers are currently under investigation. Water utilities in San Antonio have water transfer programs with irrigators in the Edwards Aquifer region. The effects of such transfers on farm and rural economies are uncertain.

In about 20 percent of the irrigated areas, water is delivered to farms by irrigation and water districts through canals and pipelines. Many of these delivery networks are aging, are in poor condition and have high seepage losses. Some federal funds have been obtained to help cover the costs of rehabilitating districts along the Rio Grande River, including about $9 million from the U.S. Congress under Public Law 106, which was passed in 2000, and $26 million from the North American Development Bank.

About 80 percent of the state's irrigated acreage is supplied with water pumped from wells. Surface water sources supply the remaining area. Declining groundwater levels in several of the major aquifers is a serious problem, particularly in the Ogallala Aquifer in the Texas High Plains and the southern portion of the Carrizo-Wilcox formation (see Major Aquifers of Texas map, page 82). As the water level declines, well yields decrease and pumping costs increase.

Irrigation is an important factor in the productivity of Texas agriculture. The value of crop production from irrigated acreage is 50 to 60 percent of the total value of all crop production, although only about 30 percent of the state's total harvested cropland acreage is irrigated.

Principal Crops

In most recent years, the value of crop production in Texas was less than 40 percent of the total value of the state's agricultural output. Cash receipts from farm sales of crops have been reduced somewhat because some grain and roughage is fed to livestock on farms where it is grown. Drought and low prices have also reduced receipts in recent years.

Receipts from all Texas crops totaled $5.03 billion in 2003, $4.51 billion in 2002, and $4.15 billion in 2001.

Cotton, corn, grain sorghum and wheat account for a large part of the total crop receipts. In 2003, cotton contributed about 23.0 percent of the crop total; corn, 6.5 percent; grain sorghum, 6.5 percent; and wheat, 5.1 percent. Hay, cottonseed, vegetables, peanuts, rice, and soybeans are other important cash crops.

Barley

Texas barley acreage and production falls far below that of wheat and oats. Barley is usually harvested from 10,000 of the 15,000 acres planted, with total production value of less than $500,000. Estimated production data was discontinued in 2000.

Corn

Interest in corn production throughout the state has increased since the 1970s as yields improved with new varieties. Once the principal grain crop, corn acreage declined as plantings of grain sorghum increased. Only

500,000 acres were harvested annually until the mid-1970s when development of new hybrids occurred.

Harvested acreage was 1.68 million in 2004; 1.65 million in 2003; and 1.79 million in 2002. Yields for those years were 139, 118 and 113 bushels per acre, respectively.

Most of the acreage and yield increase has occurred in Central and South Texas. In 2004, corn ranked fourth in value among the state's crops. It was valued at $595.48 million in 2004; $504.27 million in 2003; and $528.55 million in 2002. The grain is largely used for livestock feed, but other important uses are in food products.

The leading counties in production for 2003 were Dallam, Hartley, Sherman, Castro and Moore.

Cotton

Cotton has been a major crop in Texas for more than a century. Since 1880, Texas has led all states in cotton production in most years, and today the annual Texas cotton harvest amounts to approximately one-fourth of total production in the United States. The annual cotton crop has averaged 4.71 million bales since 1990.

Value of Cotton and Cottonseed 1900–2004

Crop Year	Upland Cotton		Cottonseed	
	Production (Bales)	Value	Production (Tons)	Value
	(All Figures in Thousands)			
1900	3,438	$157,306	1,531	$20,898
1910	3,047	210,260	1,356	31,050
1920	4,345	376,080	1,934	41,350
1930	4,037	194,080	1,798	40,820
1940	3,234	162,140	1,318	31,852
1950	2,946	574,689	1,232	111,989
1960	4,346	612,224	1,821	75,207
1970	3,191	314,913	1,242	68,310
*1980	3,320	1,091,616	1,361	161,959
1981	5,645	1,259,964	2,438	207,230
1982	2,700	664,848	1,122	90,882
1983	2,380	677,443	1,002	162,324
1984	3,680	927,360	1,563	157,863
1985	3,910	968,429	1,634	102,156
1986	2,535	560,945	1,053	82,118
1987	4,635	1,325,981	1,915	157,971
1988	5,215	1,291,651	2,131	238,672
1989	2,870	812,784	1,189	141,491
1990	4,965	1,506,182	1,943	225,388
1991	4,710	1,211,789	1,903	134,162
1992	3,265	769,495	1,346	145,368
1993	5,095	1,308,396	2,147	255,493
1994	4,915	1,642,003	2,111	215,322
1995	4,460	1,597,037	1,828	201,080
1996	4,345	1,368,154	1,784	230,136
1997	5,140	1,482,787	1,983	226,062
1998	3,600	969,408	1,558	204,098
1999	5,050	993,840	1,987	160,947
2000	3,940	868,061	1,589	162,078
2001	4,260	580,723	1,724	159,470
2002	5,040	967,680	1,855	191,065
2003	4,330	1,199,237	1,616	202,000
2004	7,740	1,582,675	2,939	306,656

*Beginning in 1971, the basis for cotton prices was changed from 500-pound gross weight to 480-pound net weight bale. To compute comparable prices for previous years, multiply price times 1.04167.

Source: "Texas Agricultural Facts," Annual Summary, February 2005, and "Texas Ag Statistics," Texas Agricultural Statistics Service, Austin, various years.

Since 1880, Texas has led all states in cotton production in most years, and today harvests about one-fourth of total U.s. production. Bobby Britton, above, manages the Staton Co-op Gin in Slaton. File photo.

Total value of Upland and Pima lint cotton produced in Texas in 2004 was $1.597 billion. Cottonseed value in 2004 was $305.6 million, making the total value of Texas cotton around $1.903 billion.

Upland cotton was harvested from 5.35 million acres in 2004, and American-Pima cotton from 20,500 acres, for a total of 5.371 million acres. Yield for upland cotton in 2004 was 694 pounds per harvested acre, with American-Pima cotton yielding 890 pounds per acre. In 2003. total cotton acreage harvested was 4.35 million, with a yield of 478 pounds per acre for upland cotton and 1,056 pounds per acre for American-Pima. Total cotton production amounted to 7.778 million bales in 2004 and 4.374 million in 2003. Counties leading in production of upland cotton in 2003 included Gaines, Nueces, San Patricio, Lynn, Dawson and Hale.

Cotton is the raw material for processing operations at gins, oil mills, compresses and a small number of textile mills in Texas. Less than 10 percent of the raw cotton produced is processed within the state.

Cotton in Texas is machine harvested. Field storage of harvested seed cotton is gaining in popularity as gins decline in number. Much of the Texas cotton crop is exported. China, Japan, South Korea and Mexico are major buyers. With the continuing development of fiber spinning technology and the improved quality of Texas cotton, more utilization of cotton by mills within the state may develop in the future. Spinning techniques can efficiently produce high-quality yarn from relatively strong, short or longer staple upland cotton with fine mature fiber.

The first high-volume instrument cotton-classing office in the nation was opened at Lamesa in 1980.

Flaxseed

Earliest flax planting was at Victoria in 1900. Since the first planting, Texas flax acreage has fluctuated depending on market, winterkill and drought. Flax acreage has dropped in recent years and estimates were discontinued in 1980.

Forest Products

For information on Texas forest products, turn to the section titled "Texas Forest Resources," page 97.

Grain Sorghum

Grain sorghum in 2004 ranked eighth in dollar value among Texas crops. Much of the grain is exported, as well as being used in livestock and poultry feed throughout the state.

Total production of grain sorghum in 2004 was 71.17 million hundredweight (cwt), with a 3,472 pound per acre yield. With an average price of $4.05 per cwt., the total value reached $288.26 million. In 2003, 2.85 million acres of grain sorghum were harvested, yielding an average of 3,024 pounds per acre for a total production of 86.18 million cwt. It was valued at $4.13 per cwt., for a total value of $355.94 million. In 2002, 2.40 million acres were harvested with an average of 2,856 pounds per acre, or 68.54 million cwt. The season's price was $4.18 per cwt., for a total value of $304.42 million.

Although grown to some extent in all counties where crops are important, the largest concentrations are in the High Plains, Rolling Plains, Blackland Prairie, Coastal Bend and Lower Rio Grande Valley areas. Counties leading in production in 2003 were Nueces, Hidalgo, Cameron, Willacy, San Patricio and Hale. Research to develop high-yielding hybrids resistant to diseases and insect damage continues.

Hay, Silage and Other Forage Crops

A large proportion of Texas' agricultural land is devoted to forage crop production. This acreage produces forage needs and provides essentially the total feed requirements for most of the state's large domestic livestock population, as well as game animals.

About 86.1 million acres of native rangeland, which are primarily in the western half of Texas, provide grazing for beef cattle, sheep, goats, horses and game animals. An additional 20 million acres are devoted to introducing forage species. Of this total, approximately 16 million acres have been established for improved perennial grasses and legumes, which are harvested by grazing animals. The average annual acreage of crops grown for hay, silage and other forms of machine-harvested forage is increasing with the estimated value in excess of $900 million.

Hay accounts for a large amount of this production with some corn and sorghum silage being produced. The most important hay crops are annual and perennial grasses and alfalfa. Production in 2004 totaled 12.29 million tons of hay from 5.35 million harvested acres at a yield of 2.30 tons per acre. Value of hay was $833.58 million, or $74 per ton. In 2003, 12.38 million tons of hay was produced from 5.24 million harvested acres at a yield of 2.36 tons per acre. The value in 2003 was $844.21 million, or $74 per ton. In 2002, the production of hay was 13.41 million tons from 5.45 million harvested acres with a value of $930.4 million, or $77 per ton, at a yield of 2.46 tons per acre.

Alfalfa hay production in 2004 totaled 855,000 tons with 150,000 acres harvested and a yield of 5.7 tons per acre. At a value of $132 per ton, the total value was $112.86 million. In 2003, 658,000 tons of alfalfa hay was harvested from 140,000 acres at a yield of 4.7 tons per acre. Value was $99.36 million, or $151 per ton. Alfalfa hay was harvested from 150,000 acres in 2002, producing an average of 4.6 tons per acre for total production of 690,000 tons valued at $98.8 million.

An additional sizable acreage of annual forage crops is grazed, as well as much of the small grain acreage. Alfalfa, sweet corn, vetch, arrowleaf clover, grasses and other forage plants also provide income as seed crops.

Horticultural Specialty Crops

The trend to increase production of horticulture specialty crops continues to rise as transportation costs on long-distance hauling rise. This has resulted in a marked increase in the production of container-grown plants within the state. This increase is noted especially in the production of bedding plants, foliage plants, sod and woody landscape plants.

Plant rental services have become a multi-million dollar business. This relatively new service charges a fee to provide plants and maintenance for office buildings, shopping malls, public buildings and homes. The response has been good as evidenced by the growth of companies providing these services.

The interest in plants for interior landscapes is not confined to a specific age group and both retail nurseries and florist shops report that people of all ages are buying plants, from the elderly in retirement homes to high school and college students in dormitory rooms and apartments.

Texas Cooperative Extension specialists estimated cash receipts from horticultural specialty crops in Texas to be around $1.6 billion in 2004. Ranking counties in

Production of horticultural specialty crops continues to rise, and the Texas Cooperative Extension Service estimates cash receipts from these crops in Texas to be around $1.6 billion in 2004. Texas Almanac photo.

specialty crops are Harris, Dallas, Rusk, Fort Bend, Cherokee and Smith. Texans are creating colorful and green surroundings by improving their landscape plantings.

Oats

Oats are grown extensively in Texas for winter pasture, hay, silage and greenchop feeding, and some acreage is harvested for grain.

Of the 680,000 acres planted in oats in 2004, 160,000 acres were harvested. The average yield was 40 bushels per acre. Production totaled 6.4 million bushels with a value of $12.16 million. In 2003, 625,000 acres were planted. From that, 140,000 acres were harvested, with an average yield of 45 bushels per acre and a total production of 6.3 million bushels. Average price per bushel was $2.20, and total production value was $13.86 million.

Texas farmers planted 750,000 acres of oats in 2002. They harvested 160,000 acres that averaged 44 bushels per acre for a total production of 7.0 million bushels. Average price was $1.72 per bushel with an estimated value of $12.11 million. Most of the acreage was used for grazing.

Almost all oat grain produced in Texas is utilized as feed for livestock within the state. A small acreage is grown exclusively for planting seed.

Leading oat grain producing counties in 2003 were Hamilton, McLennan, Coryell, Medina and Uvalde.

Peanuts

Peanuts are grown on more than 300,000 acres in Texas. Well over three-fourths of the crop annually produced is on acreage that is irrigated. Texas ranked second nationally in production of peanuts in 2004. Among Texas crops, peanuts rank ninth

in value.

Until 1973, essentially all of the Texas acreage was planted in the Spanish type, which was favored because of its earlier maturity and better drought tolerance. The

Cash Receipts for Commodities, 1999–2003

Commodity *	1999	2000	2001	2002	2003	% of 2003
	(All values in thousands of dollars)					
All Commodities:	13,032,757	12,968,996	13,496,157	12,593,645	15,341,961	100.00
Livestock & products	8,483,847	9,159,600	9,345,177	8,088,537	10,311,441	67.21
Crops, fruits & others	4,548,910	3,809,396	4,150,980	4,505,108	5,030,520	32.79
Livestock & Products						
Cattle & calves	6,124,290	6,815,081	6,812,228	5,862,734	7,872,092	51.31
Broilers	883,227	880,498	1,058,616	893,327	1,031,590	6.72
Milk	839,400	766,346	803,588	680,604	729,430	4.75
Eggs	240,509	256,903	267,077	273,312	310,007	2.02
Hogs	70,456	113,497	103,510	65,974	64,705	0.42
Sheep and lambs	56,488	38,274	40,175	44,766	50,428	0.33
Wool	3,898	3,678	3,122	4,046	5,040	0.03
Mohair	9,384	10,088	3,775	3,110	2,586	0.02
† Other livestock	256,195	275,235	253,086	260,664	245,563	1.60
Crops:						
Cotton lint	1,205,274	428,435	577,627	770,596	1,156,685	7.54
Hay	178,364	280,671	295,209	436,646	396,556	2.58
Corm	414,197	439,530	308,158	285,814	326,312	2.13
Sorghum grain	254,206	295,067	270,608	305,172	324,588	2.12
Wheat	241,528	185,775	270,756	225,665	257,972	1.68
Cottonseed	149,999	145,536	140,668	164,704	182,506	1.19
Onions	93,788	96,342	106,386	122,871	158,712	1.03
Peanuts	190,921	171,831	202,473	157,976	149,040	0.97
Rice	115,404	78,762	78,691	55,363	81,948	0.53
Watermelons	29,611	21,840	32,400	56,610	67,760	0.44
Cantaloupes	56,743	42,412	69,720	80,798	63,444	0.41
Potatoes	44,423	50,985	52,358	56,031	59,196	0.39
Cabbage	41,290	52,480	66,011	39,917	53,869	0.35
Sugar cane for sugar	26,962	52,597	56,702	52,480	52,480	0.34
Soybeans	31,058	38,752	30,500	31,361	32,664	0.21
Cucumbers	22,396	19,688	28,178	35,050	24,231	0.16
Honeydew melons	17,111	14,131	13,608	16,357	19,437	0.13
Carrots	32,259	15,684	26,934	12,305	14,295	0.09
Peppers, chile	NA	11,963	16,965	11,000	13,703	0.09
Spinach	11,344	12,239	11,796	12,988	10,246	0.07
Sweet potatoes	4,337	4,469	5,958	8,983	9,214	0.06
Beans, dry	6,812	5,473	5,274	6,315	8,335	0.05
Tomatoes, fresh	6,086	C	6,480	7,680	7,605	0.05
Sunflowers	5,670	5,866	8,431	8,040	7,425	0.05
Peppers, green	6,224	9,048	11,083	7,520	5,670	0.04
Corn, sweet	7,785	8,011	7,020	4,968	5,377	0.04
Oats	1,305	1,375	2,725	8,753	4,888	0.03
Barley	322	235	582	486	336	0.00
‡ Other crops	105,244	123,431	105,678	104,569	108,017	0.70
Fruits & Nuts:						
Pecans	68,000	34,600	50,000	33,400	63,840	0.42
Grapefruit	39,472	29,633	21,256	20,568	18,364	0.12
Oranges	3,936	6,054	7,867	7,195	5,936	0.04
Peaches	6,820	10,034	14,820	6,840	4,891	0.03
Grapes	NA	NA	8,370	4,004	5,220	0.03
Other fruits & nuts	7,930	13,215	4,176	4,813	4,978	0.03
Other Farm Income:						
Greenhouse/nursery	1,122,089	1,103,232	1,235,512	1,341,270	1,324,780	8.64

*Commodities are listed in order of importance for 2003 by crop items and by livestock items.
†For 2000–2003, includes milkfat, turkey eggs, equine, goats, goat milk, honey, catfish, and other poultry and livestock. For 1999, includes milkfat, turkey eggs, goats, goat milk, honey, catfish, and other poultry and livestock. ‡For 1999–2000, includes peppers, chile, greens, okra, miscellaneous vegetables, and field crops. For 2001–2003, includes miscellaneous vegetables and field crops. For 2001, includes miscellaneous vegetables, field crops, fruit and nuts. NA, not available; C, confidential.
Source: 2003 Texas Agricultural Statistics, USDA/Texas Agricultural Statistics Service, September 2004; various issues of Texas Agricultural Statistics and Texas Agricultural Cash Receipts and Price Statistics, USDA/TASS.

Charles McQuinney stacks bags of freshly cleaned grain at Porter Farm, a demonstration farm in Terrell that is both a Texas and a National Historical Landmark. (At left, in background, is farm owner John Porter.) The farm was established in 1903. File photo.

Spanish variety is also preferred for some uses because of its distinctive flavor. The Florunner variety, a runner market type, is now planted on a sizable amount of acreage where soil moisture is favorable. The variety is later maturing but better yielding than Spanish varieties under good-growing conditions. Florunner peanuts have acceptable quality to compete with the Spanish variety in most products.

In 2004, peanut production totaled 775.5 million pounds from 235,000 harvested acres, yielding 3,300 pounds per acre. At 20.2 cents per pound, the value of the crop was estimated at $156.65 million. In 2003, peanut production amounted to 810 million pounds from 275,000 acres planted and 270,000 acres harvested. Average yield was 3,000 pounds per acre and average price was 19.5 cents per pound for a total value of $157.95 million. Production in 2002 amounted to 868 million pounds of peanuts from 315,000 acres planted and 280,000 acres harvested, or an average of 3,100 pounds per harvested acre With a value of 18.2 cents per pound, total value was $157.98 million.

Leading counties in peanut production in 2003 included Gaines, Terry, Collingsworth, Yoakum, Frio, Dawson and Cochran.

Rice

Rice, which is grown in about 20 counties on the Coastal Prairie of Texas, ranked third in value among Texas crops for a number of years. However, in recent years, cotton, grain sorghum, wheat, corn, peanuts and hay have outranked rice.

Farms are highly mechanized, producing rice through irrigation and using airplanes for much of the planting, fertilizing, and application of insecticides and herbicides.

Texas farmers grow long- and medium-grain rice only. The Texas rice industry, which has grown from 110 acres in 1850 to a high of 642,000 acres in 1954, has been marked by significant yield increases and improved varieties. Record production was in 1981, with 27.23 million hundredweights harvested. Highest yield was 7,100 pounds per acre in 2002.

Several different types of rice-milling procedures are used today. The simplest and oldest method produces a product known as regular milled white rice, the most prevalent on the market.

During this process, rice grains are subjected to additional cleaning to remove chaff, dust and foreign seed, and then husks are removed from the grains. This results in a product that is the whole unpolished grain of rice with only the outer hull and a small amount of bran removed. This product is called brown rice and is sometimes sold without further treatment, other than grading. It has a delightful nutlike flavor and a slightly chewy texture.

When additional layers of the bran are removed, the rice becomes white in color and begins to appear as it is often recognized at retail level. The removal of the bran layer from the grain is performed in a number of steps using two or three types of machines. After the bran is removed, the product is ready for classification as to size. Rice is more valuable if the grains are not broken. In many cases, additional vitamins are added to the grains to produce what is called "enriched rice."

Another process may be used in rice milling to produce a product called parboiled rice. In this process, the rice is subjected to a combination of steam and pressure prior to milling. This process gelatinizes the starch in the grain, which helps retain much of the natural vitamin and mineral content. After cooking, parboiled rice tends to be fluffy, more separate and plump.

Still another type of rice is precooked rice, which is actually milled rice that, after milling, has been cooked. Then the moisture is removed through a dehydration process. Precooked rice cooks quickly because it needs merely to have the moisture restored.

The United States produces only a small part of the world's total rice production, but it is one of the leading exporters. American rice is popular abroad and is exported to more than 100 foreign countries.

Rice production in 2004 totaled 14.69 million cwt. from 218,000 harvested acres, with a yield of 6,740 pounds per acre. The crop value totaled $120.45 million. Rice production in 2003 was 11.88 million cwt. from 180,000 harvested acres, yielding 6,600 pounds per acre. Total value in 2003 was $87.31 million. Rice production was 14.62 million cwt. in 2002 from 206,000 harvested acres, yielding 7,100 pounds per acre. Production in 2002 was valued at $60.80 million. Counties leading in production in 2003 included Wharton, Colorado, Matagorda, Jackson, Brazoria and Jefferson.

Rye

Rye is grown mainly on the northern and southern High Plains, the northern Low Plains, the Cross Timbers, the Blacklands and in East Texas. Minor acreages are seeded in South-Central Texas, the Edwards Plateau and the Upper Coast. Rye is grown primarily as a cover crop and for grazing during the fall, winter and early spring. Estimated production data was discontinued in 1999.

Soybeans

Soybean production is largely in the areas of the Upper Coast, irrigated High Plains and Red River Valley of Northeast Texas. Soybeans are adapted to the same general soil climate conditions as corn, cotton or grain sorghum, provided moisture, disease and insects are not limiting factors. The major counties in soybean production in 2003 were Lamar, Lamb, Ochiltree, Victoria, Fannin, Hale and Dallas.

In low-rainfall areas, yields have been too low or inconsistent for profitable production under dryland conditions. Soybeans's need for moisture in late summer minimizes economic crop possibilities in the Blacklands and Rolling Plains. In the Blacklands, cotton root rot seriously hinders soybean production. Limited moisture at critical growth stages may occasionally prevent economical yields, even in high-rainfall areas of Northeast Texas and the Coastal Prairies.

Because of day length sensitivity, soybeans should be planted in Texas during the long days of May and June to obtain sufficient vegetative growth for optimum yields. Varieties planted during this period usually cease vegetative development and initiate reproductive processes during the hot, usually dry months of July and August. When moisture is insufficient during the blooming and fruiting period, yields are drastically reduced. In most areas of Texas, July and August rainfall is insufficient to permit economical dryland production. The risk of dryland soybean production in the Coastal Prairies and Northeast Texas is considerably less when compared to other dryland areas because moisture is available more often during the critical fruiting period.

The 2004 soybean crop totaled 8.64 million bushels

and was valued at $50.54 million, or $5.85 per bushel. Of the 290,000 acres planted, 270,000 were harvested with an average yield of 32 bushels per acre. In 2003, the Texas soybean crop averaged 29 bushels per acre from 185,000 acres harvested. Total production of 5.36 million bushels was valued at $37.55 million, or $7 per bushel. In 2002, the Texas soybean crop averaged 28 bushels per acre from 205,000 acres harvested. Total production of 5.74 million bushels was valued at $29.27 million, or $5.10 per bushel.

Sugarcane

Sugarcane is grown from seed cane planted in late summer or fall. It is harvested 12 months later and milled to produce raw sugar and molasses. Raw sugar requires additional refining before it is in final form and can be offered to consumers.

The sugarcane grinding mill operated at Santa Rosa, Cameron County, is considered one of the most modern mills in the United States. Texas sugarcane producing counties are Hidalgo, Cameron and Willacy.

At a yield of 39.9 tons per acre, sugarcane production in 2004 totaled 1.76 million tons from 44,000 harvested acres. In 2003, 43,000 acres were harvested with a yield of 39.7 tons per acre and a total production of 1.71 million tons; total value was $51.38 million, or $30.10 per ton. In 2002, 44,500 acres were harvested, from which 1.73 million tons of sugarcane were milled. The yield averaged 38.9 tons per acre. The price averaged $30.30 per ton for a total value of $52.48 million.

Sunflowers

Sunflowers constitute one of the most important annual oilseed crops in the world. The cultivated types, which are thought to be descendants of the common wild sunflower native to Texas, have been successfully grown in several countries including Russia, Argentina, Romania, Bulgaria, Uruguay, Western Canada and portions of the northern United States. Extensive trial plantings conducted in the Cotton Belt states since 1968 showed sunflowers have considerable potential as an oilseed crop in much of this area, including Texas. This crop exhibits good cold and drought tolerance, is adapted to a wide range of soil and climate conditions, and tolerates higher levels of hail, wind and sand abrasion than other crops normally grown in the state.

In 2004, sunflower production totaled 56 million pounds and was harvested from 38,000 acres at a yield of 1,474 pounds per acre. With an average price of $14.20 per cwt., the crop was valued at $7.92 million. In 2003, 56,000 of the 59,000 acres planted to sunflowers were harvested with an average yield of 1,257 pounds per acre. Total production of 70.4 million pounds was valued at $10.13 million, or $14.40 per cwt.

In 2002, of 35,000 acres planted to sunflowers, 29,000 acres were harvested, yielding 862 pounds per acre for a total yield of 25 million pounds valued at $3.94 million, or $14.50 per cwt. The leading counties in production in 2003 were Moore, Bailey, Lamb, Dallam, Lubbock and Hartley.

Reasons for growing sunflowers include the need for an additional cash crop with low water and plant nutrient requirements, the development of sunflower hybrids, and interest by food processors in Texas sunflower oil, which has a high oleic acid content. Commercial users have found many advantages in this high oleic oil, including excellent cooking stability, particularly for use as a deep-frying medium for potato chips, corn chips and similar products.

Sunflower meal is a high-quality protein source free of nutritional toxins that can be included in rations for swine, poultry and ruminants. The hulls constitute a source of roughage, which can also be included in livestock rations.

Wheat

Wheat for grain is one of the state's most valuable cash crops. In 2004, wheat was exceeded in value only by cotton, hay and corn. Wheat pastures also provide considerable winter forage for cattle that is reflected in value of livestock produced.

Texas wheat production totaled 108.5 million bushels in 2004, and yield averaged 31.0 bushels per acre. Planted acreage totaled 6.3 million acres, and 3.5 million acres were harvested. With an average price of $3.35 per bushel, the 2004 wheat value totaled $363.47 million. In 2003, Texas wheat growers planted 6.6 million acres and harvested 3.4 million acres. The 2003 yield was 28.0 bushels per acre; total production was 96.6 million bushels at $3.06 per bushel, with a total value of $295.6 million.

Texas wheat growers planted 6.4 million acres in 2002 and harvested grain from 2.7 million acres. The yield was 29.0 bushels per acre for a total production of 78.3 million bushels valued at $236.47 million.

Leading wheat-producing counties, based on production in 2003, were Sherman, Castro, Dallam, Ochiltree, Wilbarger and Parmer. The leading counties, based on acreage planted in 2003 were Deaf Smith, Hansford, Parmer, Ochiltree, Sherman and Knox.

Wheat was first grown commercially in Texas near Sherman in about 1833. The acreage expanded greatly in North-Central Texas after 1850 because of rapid settlement of the state and introduction of the well-adapted Mediterranean strain of wheat. A major family flour industry was developed around Fort Worth, Dallas and Sherman between 1875 and 1900. Today, around half of the state's wheat acreage is planted on the High Plains and about a third of this is irrigated. Most of the Texas wheat acreage is of the hard red winter class. Because of the development of varieties with improved disease resistance and the use of wheat for winter pasture, there has been a sizable expansion of acreage in Central and South Texas.

Most all wheat harvested for grain is used in some phase of the milling industry. The better-quality hard red winter wheat is used in the production of commercial bakery flour. Lower grades and varieties of soft red winter wheat are used in family flours. By-products of milled wheat are used for feed.

Vegetable Crops

Some market vegetables are produced in almost all Texas counties, but most of the commercial crop comes from about 200 counties. Hidalgo County is the leading county in vegetable acres harvested, followed by Parmer and Uvalde counties. Other leading producing counties are Hale, Frio, Yoakum, Zavala, Hudspeth and Gaines.

Texas is one of the five leading states in the production of fresh market vegetables. Nationally in 2004, Texas ranked fifth in production, exceeded by California, Florida, Arizona and Georgia, and fifth in value of fresh-market vegetables. Texas had 3.7 percent of the U.S. production and 3.5 percent of the value of fresh-market vegetables produced. Onions were the number-one cash crop, with watermelons second. Other vegetables leading in value of production for 2004 were cabbage, cantaloupes, carrots, chili pepper (all peppers, excluding bell pepper), and cucumbers.

In 2004, total vegetable production of 20.21 million cwt. was valued at $366.25 million from 93,500 acres harvested. In 2003, Texas growers harvested total commercial vegetable crops valued at $460.21 million from 103,300 acres with a production of 22.27 million cwt. In 2002, Texas growers harvested 22.8 million cwt. of commercial vegetable crops from 105,100 acres, valued at $468.1 million.

Bell Peppers

Bell pepper production in 2004 was 80,000 cwt. from 500 harvested acres with a yield of 160 cwt. per acre. It was valued at $3.98 million. In 2003, 175,000 cwt. were harvested from 700 acres, at a yield of 250 cwt. per acre and a value of $5.67 million. Bell peppers in 2002 were harvested from 1,000 acres and valued at $7,520,000. Production was 160,000 cwt. with a yield of 160 cwt. per acre.

Broccoli

Broccoli is primarily a South Texas crop and is produced on 800 to 900 harvested acres. Estimated production data was discontinued in 2000.

Cabbage

In 2004, 8,300 acres of cabbage were harvested, which yielded total production of 3.24 million cwt. and a value of $60.21 million. Yield was 390 cwt. per acre. In 2003, 7,700 acres of cabbage were harvested yielding total production of 2.54 million cwt., or 330 cwt. per

Texas Vegetable Production 2004

Crop	Harvested Acres (000)	Yield Per Acre, Cwt.	Production (000) Cwt.	Value (000)
Bell Peppers	500	160	80	3,984
Cabbage	8,200	390	3,237	60,208
Cantaloupes	7,500	160	1,200	26,760
Carrots	2,100	335	704	18,304
Chile Peppers	4,100	40	165	12,788
Cucumbers	1,500	350	525	11,025
Honeydew Melons	1,300	260	338	8,822
Onions, Spring	12,500	310	3,875	87,575
Onions, Summer	2,800	370	1,036	24,968
Spinach	2,000	125	250	9,625
Squash	1,500	100	150	7,080
Sweet Corn	1,900	80	152	2,736
Tomatoes	1,100	105	116	7,540
Watermelons	27,500	220	6,050	60,500
Total Fresh Market*	**74,600**	**—**	**17,878**	**341,915**
Processed†	18,900	—	2,331	24,337
Total Vegetables	**93,500**	**—**	**20,209**	**366,252**

Numbers may not add due to rounding.
* Includes some quantities of processed vegetables.
†Carrots, cucumbers and spinach.
Chile peppers are defined as all peppers except bell peppers.
Estimates include both fresh and dried products.
Source: "Texas Ag Facts," Texas Agricultural Statistics Service/ USDA, February 2005.

acre, valued at $53.87 million. The 7,700 acres of cabbage harvested in Texas in 2002 brought a value of $39.92 million. At a yield of 320 cwt. per acre, total production was 2.46 million cwt.

Cantaloupe and Honeydew Melons

Cantaloupe production in 2004 totaled 1.2 million cwt. from 7,500 harvested acres; it was valued at $26.76 million at a yield of 160 cwt. per acre. In 2003, cantaloupes were harvested from 8,500 acres for total production of 2.04 million cwt. They were valued at $63.44 million and yielded 240 cwt. per acre. Of the 9,500 harvested acres in 2002, 2.56 million cwt. cantaloupes were produced at a yield of 270 cwt. per acre and were valued at $80.8 million.

Honeydew production in 2004 totaled 338,000 cwt. and was valued at $8.82 million at a yield of 260 cwt. per acre. In 2003, 570,000 cwt. of honeydew melons were harvested from 1,700 acres for a total value of $19.43 million, yielding 335 cwt. per acre. In 2002, honeydew melons valued at $16.36 million were harvested on 1,700 acres, producing a yield of 340 cwt. per acre and a total production of 578,000 cwt.

Carrots

Carrot production in 2004 totaled 704,000 cwt. from 2,100 harvested acres at a yield of 335 cwt. per acre. Production was valued at $18.30 million. In 2003, carrots were harvested from 2,100 acres with a value of $12.67 million. At a yield of 290 cwt. per acre, 2003 production was 609,000 cwt. Carrot production in 2002 was valued at $10.56 million from 2,400 acres harvested. Production was 480,000 cwt. at a yield of 200 cwt. per acre.

The winter carrot production from South Texas accounts for about three-fourths of total production during the winter season.

Cucumbers

In 2004, 1,500 acres of cucumbers were harvested. Production totaled 525,000 cwt., or 350 cwt. per acre, and was valued at $11.02 million. In 2003, 1,400 acres of cucumbers were harvested with a value of $6.76 million. Production was 322,000 cwt., or 230 cwt. per acre. At a yield of 250 cwt. per acre, the 450,000 cwt. cucumber crop during 2002 was harvested from 1,800 acres and valued at $11.07 million.

Onions

Onion production in 2004 totaled 4.91 million cwt. from 15,300 harvested acres and was valued at $112.54 million; yield was 321 cwt. per acre. In 2003, 4.52 million cwt. of onions were harvested from 13,500 acres, at

In 2004, 1,100 acres of tomatoes were harvested with a value of $7.54 million. Increases in greenhouse production allows Texas tomatoes to be marketed year-round. File photo.

a yield of 335 cwt. per acre, and valued at $158.71 million. In 2002, a total of 5.70 million cwt. of onions were produced from 17,800 harvested acres, at 321 cwt. per acre, and valued at $122.87 million.

Potatoes

In 2004, all potatoes (except sweet potatoes) were harvested from 20,100 acres with production of 6.43 million cwt., or 320 cwt. per acre. Total value was $54.55 million. In 2003, potatoes were harvested from 20,900 acres with production of 6.53 million cwt., or 312 cwt. per acre, and valued at $68.17 million. This compares with 20,300 acres harvested in 2002 with a value of $57.46 million, production of 5.36 million cwt. and a yield of 264 cwt. per acre.

Spinach

Spinach production is primarily concentrated in the Winter Garden area of South Texas.

The 2004 production value of spinach was estimated at $9.62 million. Production of 250,000 cwt. was harvested from 2,000 acres with a yield of 125 cwt. per acre. In 2003, 1,700 acres were harvested with a value of $7.81 million. At a yield of 120 cwt. per acre, production was 204,000 cwt. In 2002, the 2,200 acres harvested produced 242,000 cwt. at a yield of 110 cwt. per acre and a value of $11.13 million.

Sweet Corn

In 2004, 152,000 cwt. of sweet corn was harvested from 1,900 acres. Value of production was estimated at $2.74 million with a yield of 80 cwt. per acre. In 2003, 261,000 cwt. of sweet corn was produced from 2,900 harvested acres at a yield of 90 cwt. per acre and a value of $5.38 million. In 2002, sweet corn was harvested from 3,000 acres and valued at $4.97 million. Production was 240,000 cwt. at a yield of 80 cwt. per acre.

Sweet Potatoes

Sweet potatoes were harvested from 3,300 acres in 2004; with a yield of 140 cwt. per acre, production totaled 462,000 cwt. for a value of $8.32 million. Sweet potatoes in 2003 produced 448,000 cwt. from 3,200 harvested acres with a value of $8.51 million. Yield was 140 cwt. per acre. This compares with 450,000 cwt. produced in 2002 at a yield of 180 cwt. per acre from 2,500 harvested acres. Total value in 2002 was $7.56 million.

Tomatoes

Commercial tomatoes from Texas are marketed throughout the year partly as a result of recent increases in greenhouse production during the winter.

In 2004, 1,100 harvested acres of tomatoes at a yield of 105 cwt. per acre produced 116,000 cwt. of tomatoes

The Texas peach crop totaled 19.8 million pounds in 2004 for a value of $15.1 million. At Marburger Orchard in Fredericksburg, customer Elizabeth Borden of Plano picks her own peaches. File photo.

with a value of $7.54 million. In 2003, 1,300 acres of tomatoes were harvested, producing 169,000 cwt. at a yield of 130 cwt. per acre and a value of $7.6 million. The tomato crop in 2002 was valued at $7.68 million from 1,200 harvested acres. Tomato production was 240,000 cwt. at a yield of 200 cwt. per acre.

Watermelons

Watermelon production in 2004 was 6.05 million cwt., or 220 cwt. per acre, from 27,500 acres with a value of $60.5 million. In 2003, 7.7 million cwt. of watermelons were harvested from 35,000 acres at a yield of 220 cwt. per acre. Total production was valued at $67.76 million. Watermelon production in 2002 was 6.6 million cwt. from 37,000 acres, with a value of $56.61 million and a yield of 180 cwt. per acre.

Vegetables for Processing

In 2004, 2.33 million cwt. of cucumbers, carrots and spinach for processing were harvested from 18,900 acres and valued at $24.34 million. In 2003, 20,700 acres were harvested and valued at $27.07 million with a production of 2.68 million cwt. In 2002, 23,400 acres were harvested and valued at $32.96 million, producing 2.95 million cwt.

Fruits and Nuts

Texas is noted for producing a wide variety of fruits. The pecan is the only commercial nut crop in the state. The pecan is native to most of the state's river valleys and is the Texas state tree. Citrus is produced in the three southernmost counties in the Lower Rio Grande Valley, although some new orchards have been planted. Peaches represent the next most important Texas fruit crop, and there also is a considerable amount of interest in growing apples.

Apples

Small acreages of apples, usually marketed in the state, are grown in a number of counties. The leading counties in production are Montague and Gillespie. Other counties which have apples include Callahan, Collingsworth, Clay, Cass, Donley, Eastland, Hudspeth, Jeff Davis, Lampasas, Parker, San Saba and Young. The crop is harvested and marketed from July to October.

A considerable number of apple trees have been planted in the Hill Country. Most of the trees are new varieties of Red and Golden Delicious types on semi-dwarfing rootstocks. Trees are established in high-density plantings of 100 to 200 trees per acre. Most of the apples are sold at roadside stands or go to nearby markets.

Apricots

Not a commercial crop, apricots are grown chiefly in Comanche, Denton, Wilbarger, Parker and Collingsworth counties. Other counties reporting apricots include Martin, Clay, Young, Lampasas, Gillespie, Anderson, Erath, Wichita and Eastland.

Avocados

Avocados grow on small acreage in the Lower Rio Grande Valley. Interest in this crop is increasing, and production is expected to expand. Lulu is the principal variety.

Blackberries

Smith County is a blackberry center, and the Tyler-Lindale area have processed the crop since 1890. Other counties with blackberry acreage include Wood, Van Zandt and Henderson. The Brazos blackberry is grown as a local market or "pick-your-own" fruit in many sections of Texas. Dewberries grow wild in Central and East Texas and are gathered for home use and local sale in May and June.

Citrus

Texas ranks with Florida, California and Arizona as leading states in the production of citrus. Most of the Texas production is in Cameron, Hidalgo and Willacy counties of the Lower Rio Grande Valley. In 2003–2004, grapefruit production was estimated at 5.7 million boxes. At $3.98 per box, value of production was $22.71 million. Grapefruit production in 2002–2003 was 5.65 million boxes at $3.45 per box for a total value of $19.48 million. Production in 2001–2002 was 5.9 million boxes at $3.91 per box with a value of $23.04 million.

Production of oranges in 2003–2004 was 1.65 million boxes. At $4.29 per box, total value was $7.08 million. In 2002–2003, production was 1.57 million boxes at $4.26 per box for a total value of $6.69 million. In 2001–2002, production was 1.74 million boxes at $4.64 per box for a value of $8.07 million.

Peaches

Primary production areas are East Texas, the Hill Country and the West Cross Timbers. Production varies substantially because of adverse weather conditions. Low-chilling varieties for early marketings are being grown in Atascosa, Frio, Webb, Karnes and Duval counties.

The Texas peach crop totaled 19.8 million pounds in 2004 for a value of $15.1 million, or 76 cents per pound. In 2003, production was 6.7 million pounds, with a value of $4.89 million, or 73 cents per pound. In 2002, production was 11.4 million pounds, which was valued at $6.84 million, or 60 cents per pound.

The demand for high-quality Texas peaches greatly exceeds the supply. Texas ranked 19th nationally in peach production in 2003. Leading Texas counties in production are Gillespie, Parker, Montague, Comanche, Limestone and Eastland.

Pears

Well adapted for home and small orchard production, the pear is not commercially significant in Texas. Comanche, Parker, Lampasas, Cooke, McCulloch and Eastland counties lead in trees. Usually the fruit goes for home consumption or to nearby market.

Pecans

The pecan, the state tree, is one of the most widely distributed trees in Texas. It is native to more than 150 counties and is grown commercially in about 30 additional counties. The pecan is also widely used as a dual-purpose yard tree. The commercial plantings of pecans have accelerated in Central and West Texas, and many new orchards are irrigated. Many new pecan plantings are being established under trickle-irrigation systems.

In 2004, pecan production totaled only 40 million pounds and was valued at $61.8 million or $1.55 per pound. In 2003, 70 million pounds were produced, and total value was estimated at $68.53 million with prices averaging 97.9 cents per pound. The 2002 crop totaled 40 million pounds valued at $33.4 million, or 83.5 cents per pound. In 2001, the pecan crop totaled 75 million pounds valued at $50 million, or 66.7 cents per pound.

Nationally in 2003, Texas ranked second behind Georgia in pecan production. Leading Texas counties in pecan production are Hood, El Paso, Pecos, San Saba, Mills, Comanche, Wharton and Gonzales.

Plums

Plum production is scattered over a wide area of the state with the heaviest production in East and Central Texas. The leading counties in production are Smith, Gillespie and Knox. Most of the crop goes to nearby markets or to processors.

Strawberries

Atascosa County is the leading commercial area, although strawberries are grown for local markets in Wood, Van Zandt and Smith counties in East Texas. The most concentrated production occurs in the Poteet area south of San Antonio.

Livestock and Their Products

Livestock and their products accounted for about 67.2 percent of the agricultural cash receipts in Texas in 2003. The state ranks first nationally in all cattle, beef cattle, cattle on feed, sheep and lambs, wool, goats and mohair.

Meat animals normally account for about 77.5 percent of cash receipts from marketings of livestock and their products. Sales of livestock and products in 2003 totaled $10.31 billion, up from $8.09 billion in 2002.

Cattle and calves dominate livestock production in Texas, contributing more than 76 percent of cash receipts from livestock and products each year. The Jan. 1, 2005, inventory of all cattle and calves in Texas totaled 13.8 million head, valued at $10.76 billion, compared to 13.9 million as of Jan. 1, 2004, valued at $9.73 billion.

On Jan. 1, 2005, the sheep and lamb inventory stood at 1.07 million head, valued at $112.35 million, compared with 1.1 million head as of Jan. 1, 2004, valued at $105.6 million. The numbers of sheep and lambs has fallen over the decades. In 1973, sheep and lambs numbered 3.21 million, and in 1943, a high of 10.83 million sheep and lambs was reported. Sheep and lamb production fell from 148.29 million pounds in 1973 to 51.63 million pounds on Jan. 1, 2005.

Wool production in 2004 was 5.6 million pounds, valued at $5.71 million, and in 2003, production was 5.6 million pounds, valued at $5.04 million. This is a steep drop from the 1973 figures of 26.35 million pounds of wool, valued at $23.19 million. The price of wool per pound was $1.02 in 2004, 90 cents in 2003 and 88 cents in 1973.

Lamb prices averaged $110.00 per cwt. as of Jan. 1, 2005, $97.10 per cwt. in 2004 and $75.90 per cwt. in 2003. The average price of sheep was $43.40 per cwt. as of Jan. 1, 2005, $39.60 in 2004 and $35.30 in 2002.

Mohair production in Texas has dropped from a 1965 high of 31.58 million pounds to 1.62 million pounds in 2004. Production in 2004 was valued at $3.4 million, or $2.10 per pound. In 2003, production was 1.68 million pounds, valued at $2.86 million, or $1.70 per pound. Mohair production in 2002 was 1.94 million pounds, valued at $3.11 million, or $1.60 per pound.

Beef Cattle

Raising beef cattle is the most extensive agricultural operation in Texas. In 2003, 51.3 percent of total cash receipts from farm and ranch marketings—$7.87 million of $15.34 million—came from cattle and calves, compared with $5.86 million of $12.59 million in 2002 (46.6 percent) and $6.81 million of $13.5 million in 2001 (50.5 percent).Nearly all of the 254 counties in Texas derive more revenue from cattle than from any other agricultural commodity, and those that don't usually rank cattle second in importance.

Within the boundaries of Texas are 14 percent of all cattle in the United States, as are 16 percent of the beef breeding cows and 13 percent of the calf crop, as of the Jan. 1, 2005, inventory.

The number of all cattle in Texas on Jan. 1, 2005, totaled 13.8 million, compared with 13.9 million on Jan. 1, 2004, and 14 million in 2003. Calves born on Texas farms and ranches in 2004 totaled 5 million, compared with 5.1 million in 2003 and 5 million in 2002.

Sale of cattle and calves at approximately 155 livestock auctions inspected by the Texas Animal Health Commission totaled 4.64 million head in 2004; 5.14 million head in 2003; and 4.84 million in 2002. The number of cattle and calves shipped into Texas totaled 3.32 million head as of Jan. 1, 2005, 3.67 million head in 2004 and 3.26 million head in 2003.

Livestock Industries

A large portion of Texas livestock is sold through local auction markets. In 2003, the Texas Animal Health Commission reported 155 livestock auctions. Auctions in 2004 sold 4.64 million head of cattle and calves, 73,000 hogs and 1.14 million sheep and goats. This compares with 2003 totals of 5.14 million cattle and calves, 87,000 hogs and 1,246,000 sheep and goats. Figures for 2002 were 4.84 million cattle and calves, 69,000 hogs 1.61 million sheep and goats.

During 2004, the commission reported 1.26 million cattle and calves shipped from Texas to other states and 2.34 million shipped into Texas. This compares with 1.26 million shipped out and 2.83 million shipped in during 2003, and 1.05 million shipped out and 2.81 million shipped in during 2002. (Figures exclude cattle shipped direct to slaughter where no health certificates are required.)

Texas shipped out 107,396 sheep and lambs in 2004 and shipped in 56,994, compared with 164,052 shipped out and 105,558 shipped in during 2003. In 2002, 472,815 sheep and lambs were shipped out and 127,300 were shipped in.

Feedlot Production

Feedlot production of livestock, mainly cattle, is a major industry in Texas. Annual fed cattle marketings totaled 5.68 million for 1,000-and-over feedlot capacity (head) in 2004. Texas lots marketed a total of 5.97 million head of grain-fed cattle in 2003, compared with 5.98 million in 2002 and 6.03 million in 2001. In recent years, more cattle have been fed in Texas than any other state.

In 2004, there were 131 feedlots in Texas with a capacity of 1,000 animals or more. This compared with 134 in 2003, 136 in 2002, and 138 in 2001.

Federally inspected slaughter plants in Texas num-

Texas Cattle Marketed by Size of Feedlots, , 1965–2004

Year	Feedlot Capacity (head)						Total
	Under 1,000	1,000– 1,999	2000– 3,999	4,000– 7,999	8,000– 15,999	16,000 & Over	
	Cattle Marketed — 1,000 head —						
1965	104	108	205	324	107	246	1,094
1970	98	53	112	281	727	1,867	3,138
1975	50	22	51	134	485	2,325	3,067
1976	60	33	62	170	583	3,039	3,947
1977	146	22	38	206	604	3,211	4,277
1978	80	20	50	242	697	3,826	4,915
1979	54	19	46	227	556	3,543	4,445
1980	51	18	47	226	533	3,285	4,160
1981	50	20	50	220	510	3,110	3,960
1982	55	20	60	210	540	3,190	4,075
1983	100	20	80	130	490	3,580	4,400
1984	60	20	180	150	540	4,140	5,090
1985	70	10	20	170	620	4,140	5,030
1986	90	10	40	180	550	4,390	5,260
1987	90	20	35	170	625	4,375	5,255
1988	30	15	35	185	650	4,120	5,035
1989	40	15	40	165	675	3,810	4,745
1990	35	24	56	180	605	3,940	4,840
1991	35	25	45	225	500	4,250	5,080
1992	50	10	25	140	505	4,065	4,795
1993	30	20	70	160	640	4,370	5,290
1994	14	13	55	173	725	4,680	5,660
1995	12	24	43	166	630	4,665	5,540
1996	NA	17	43	180	460	4,800	5,500
1997	NA	17	48	250	485	5,000	5,800
1998	NA	10	20	140	420	5,470	6,060
1999	NA	10	20	140	385	5,510	6,065
2000	NA	8	17	125	470	5,570	6,190
2001	NA	8	22	90	450	5,460	6,030
2002	NA	10	15	85	390	5,480	5,980
2003	NA	10	15	75	420	5,450	5,970
2004	NA	20	20	485	485	5,180	5,685

Number of feedlots with 1,000 head or more capacity is number of lots operating any time during the year. Number under 1,000 head capacity and total number of all feedlots is number at end of year. Source: "Texas Agricultural Facts, 1997," Texas Agricultural Statistics Service, September 1998. Numbers for 1986–1992, "1993 Texas Livestock Statistics," Bulletin 252, August 1994. "Cattle on Feed" annual summary, USDA/NASS, February 2005.

bered 41 in 2004. This compares with 44 in 2003 and 43 in 2002. In 2004, the number of cattle slaughtered in Texas totaled 6.15 million cattle, 319,200 hogs, 261,400 sheep and 11,000 calves. This compares with 2003 figures of 6.46 million cattle, 321,700 hogs, 357,700 sheep and 20,200 calves. Figures for 2002 total 6.43 million cattle, 338,300 hogs, 289,700 sheep and 17,200 calves.

Feeding of cattle in commercial feedlots is a major economic development that has stimulated the establishment and expansion of beef slaughtering plants. Most of this development is in the northern High Plains area of northwest Texas. This area alone accounts for around 82 percent of the cattle fed in the state as of Jan. 1, 2004.

Total feedlot marketings represented about 25 percent of total U.S. fed cattle marketings in 2004. Large amounts of capital are required for feedlot operations. This has forced many lots to become custom feeding facilities.

Feedlots are concentrated on the High Plains largely because of extensive supplies of corn, sorghum and other feed. Beef breeding herds have increased most in East Texas, where grazing is abundant.

There were 1,700 farm operations in Texas reporting milk cows in 2004. Dwayne Richardson and his family have been dairy farming in Collin County for more than 50 years. Their dairy is one of only four still operating in the county. File photo.

Dairying

Most of the state's dairy industry is located east of the line from Wichita Falls to Brownwood and from San Antonio to Corpus Christi. As of the Jan. 1, 2004, inventory, leading counties in milk production are Erath, Hopkins, Comanche, Lamb, Archer and El Paso, which combine to produce 53 percent of the milk in Texas. Erath County produces 22 percent of the total.

All the milk sold by Texas dairy farmers is marketed under the terms of Federal Marketing Orders. Most Texas dairymen are members of one of four marketing cooperatives. Associate Milk Producers, Inc., is the largest, representing the majority of the state's producers.

Texas dairy farmers received an average price for milk of $16.30 per hundred pounds in 2004, $13.00 in 2003 and $12.90 in 2002. A total of 5.986 billion pounds of milk was sold to plants and dealers in 2004, bringing in cash receipts from milk to dairy farmers of $975.72 million. This compares with 5.611 billion pounds sold in 2003 that brought in $729.43 million in cash receipts. In 2002, Texas dairymen sold 5.276 billion pounds of milk, which brought in cash receipts of $680.6 million.

The annual average number of milk cows in Texas was 318,000 head as of the Jan. 1, 2005, inventory. This compares with 317,000 head as of Jan. 1, 2004, and 320,000 as of Jan. 1, 2003. Average production per cow in the state has increased steadily over the past several decades. The average production per cow was 18,837 pounds in 2004, 17,649 pounds in 2003 and 16,719 pounds in 2002. Total milk production in Texas was 6.01 billion pounds in 2004, 5.63 billion pounds in 2003 and 5.30 billion pounds in 2002.

There were 1,700 operations reporting milk cows in Texas in 2004, 1,800 in 2003 and 1,900 in 2002.

Dairy Manufacturing

The major dairy products manufactured in Texas include condensed, evaporated and dry milk; creamery butter; and cheese. However, data are not available because of the small number of manufacturing plants producing these products.

Frozen Desserts

Production of frozen desserts in Texas totaled 95.94 million gallons in 2004, 95.76 million gallons in 2003and 115.93 million in 2002. Ice cream production in Texas in 2004 amounted to 53.28 million gallons, compared to 52.33 million gallons in 2003 and 61.88 million gallons in 2002. Ice cream mix produced in Texas totaled 28.08 million gallons in 2004; 28.17 million gallons in 2003 and 30.28 million gallons in 2002. Milk sherbet mix in Texas totaled 518,000 gallons in 2004, 440,000 gallons in 2003 and 1,107,000 gallons in 2002. Milk sherbet production in 2004 totaled 830,000 gallons, which compares with 699,000 gallons in 2003and 1,752,000 gallons in 2002.

Goats and Mohair

Goats in Texas numbered 1.25 million as of Jan. 1, 2005. This compares with 1.2 million on Jan. 1, 2004, and 1.2 million on Jan. 1, 2003. They had a value of $136.25 million, or $109 per head, in 2005; $115.2 million, or $96 per head, in 2004; and $110.4 million, or $92 per head, in 2003.

The goat herd largely consists of Angora goats for mohair production. Angora goats totaled 210,000 as of Jan. 1, 2005; 220,000 as of Jan. 1, 2004; and 240,000 as of Jan. 1, 2003. Spanish goats and others numbered 1.04 million as of Jan. 1, 2005; 980,000 as of Jan. 1, 2004; and 960,000 as of Jan. 1, 2003.

Milk from Alpine and Nubian dairy goats is used for the organic products produced by Pure Luck Farm and Dairy in Dripping Springs. File photo.

Goats and Mohair 1900–2005

Year	Goats		Mohair	
	*Number	Farm Value	Produc-tion (lbs)	Value
1900	627,000	$924,000	961,000	$268,000
1910	1,135,000	2,514,000	1,998,000	468,000
1920	1,753,000	9,967,000	6,786,000	1,816,000
1930	2,965,000	14,528,000	14,800,000	4,995,000
1940	3,300,000	10,560,000	18,250,000	9,308,000
1950	2,295,000	13,082,000	12,643,000	9,735,000
1960	3,339,000	29,383,000	23,750,000	21,375,000
1970	2,572,000	19,033,000	17,985,000	7,032,000
1980	1,400,000	64,400,000	8,800,000	30,800,000
1981	1,380,000	53,130,000	10,100,000	35,350,000
1982	1,410,000	57,810,000	10,000,000	25,500,000
1983	1,420,000	53,250,000	10,600,000	42,930,000
1984	1,450,000	82,215,000	10,600,000	48,160,000
1985	1,590,000	76,797,000	13,300,000	45,885,000
1986	1,770,000	70,977,000	16,000,000	40,160,000
1987	1,780,000	82,592,000	16,200,000	42,606,000
1988	1,800,000	108,180,000	15,400,000	29,876,000
1989	1,850,000	100,270,000	15,400,000	24,794,000
1990	1,900,000	93,100,000	14,500,000	13,775,000
1991	1,830,000	73,200,000	14,800,000	19,388,000
1992	2,000,000	84,000,000	14,200,000	12,354,000
1993	1,960,000	84,280,000	13,490,000	11,197,000
1994	1,960,000	74,480,000	11,680,000	30,602,000
1995	1,850,000	81,400,000	11,319,000	20,940,000
1996	1,900,000	89,300,000	7,490,000	14,606,000
1997	1,650,000	70,950,000	6,384,000	14,556,000
1998	1,400,000	71,400,000	4,650,000	12,044,000
1999	1,350,000	71,550,000	2,550,000	9,384,000
2000	1,300,000	74,100,000	2,346,000	10,088,000
2001	1,400,000	105,000,000	1,716,000	3,775,000
2002	1,250,000	106,250,000	1,944,000	3,110,400
2003	1,200,000	110,400,000	1,680,000	2,856,000
2004	1,200,000	115,200,000	1,620,000	3,402,000
2005	1,250,000	136,250,000	NA	NA

*Goat number includes all goats, not just Angora goats.
NA = not available.
Source: "1985 Texas Livestock, Dairy and Poultry Statistics," USDA Bulletin 235, June 1986. "Texas Agricultural Facts," Crop and Livestock Reporting Service, various years; "1993 Texas Livestock Statistics," Texas Agricultural Statistics Service, Bulletin 252, August 1994. "Texas Agricultural Statistics, 2003," September 2004.

Mohair production during 2004 totaled 1.62 million pounds. This compares with 1.68 million in 2003 and 1.94 million pounds in 2002. Average price per pound in 2004 was $2.10 from 210,000 goats clipped for a total value of $3.4 million. In 2003, producers received $1.70 per pound from 210,000 goats clipped for a total value of $2.86 million. In 2002, producers received $1.60 per pound from 240,000 goats clipped for a total value of $3.11 million.

Nearly half of the world's mohair and 84 percent of the U.S. clip are produced in Texas. The leading Texas counties in Angora goats are Edwards, Sutton, Val Verde, Uvalde, Kinney, Gillespie, Mills, Kendall, Mason and Kimble.

Horses

Nationally, Texas ranks as one of the leading states in horse numbers and is the headquarters for many national horse organizations. The largest single breed registry in America, the American Quarter Horse Association, has its headquarters in Amarillo. The National Cutting Horse Association and the American Paint Horse Association are both located in Fort Worth. In addition to these national associations, Texas also has active state associations that include Palominos, Arabians, Thoroughbreds, Appaloosa and Ponies.

Horses are still used to support the state's giant beef cattle and sheep industries. However, the largest horse numbers within the state are near urban and suburban areas where they are used mostly for recreational activities, such as horse shows, trail rides, play days, rodeos, polo and horse racing. Residential subdivisions have been developed within the state to provide facilities for urban and suburban horse owners.

Poultry and Eggs

Poultry and eggs annually contribute about 9 percent to the average yearly cash receipts of Texas farmers. In 2004, Texas ranked sixth among the states in broilers produced, seventh in eggs, and seventh in hens.

In 2004, cash receipts to Texas producers from the production of poultry and eggs totaled $1.790 billion. This compares with $1.404 billion in 2003 and $1.223 billion in 2002.

Value of production from eggs was $306.39 million in 2004. This compares with $310.01 million in 2003 and $273.31 million in 2002. Eggs produced in 2004 totaled 4.83 billion, compared with 4.75 billion in 2003 and 4.774 billion in 2002. The average price received per dozen in 2004 was 76.2 cents, compared with 78.4 cents in 2003 and 68.7 cents in 2002.

Broiler production in 2004 totaled 620.7 million birds, compared with 601.5 million in 2003 and 588.1 million in 2002. Value of production from broilers totaled $1.425 billion in 2004, $1.032 billion in 2003 and $893.33 million in 2002. Price per pound averaged 45 cents in 2004, 35 cents in 2003 and 31 cents in 2002.

Sheep and Wool

Sheep and lambs in Texas numbered 1.07 million head as of Jan. 1, 2005, compared to 1.1 million as of Jan. 1, 2004, and 1.04 million as of Jan. 1, 2003. All sheep were valued at $112.35 million, or $105 per head, on Jan. 1, 2005; compared with $105.6 million, or $96 per head, as of Jan. 1, 2004; and $82.16 million, or $79 per head as of Jan. 1, 2003.

Breeding ewes 1 year old and older numbered 650,000 as of Jan. 1, 2005; 675,000 as of Jan. 1, 2004; and 660,000 as of Jan. 1, 2003. Replacement lambs less than 1 year old totaled 145,000 head as of Jan. 1, 2005; 120,000 as of Jan 1, 2004; and 120,000 as of Jan. 1, 2003. Sheep operations in Texas were estimated to be 7,000 as of Jan. 1, 2005; 7,000 as of Jan. 1, 2004; and 7,000 as of Jan. 1, 2003.

Texas wool production in 2004 was 5.6 million pounds from 810,000 sheep. Value totaled $5.71 million, or $1.02 per pound. This compares with 2003 figures of 5.6 million pounds of wool from 800,000 sheep that was valued at $5.04 million, or 90 cents per pound; and 2002 figures of 5.95 million pounds from 850,000 sheep valued at $4.05 million, or 68 cents per pound.

Most sheep and lambs in Texas are concentrated in the Edwards Plateau area of West-Central Texas and nearby counties. As of Jan. 1, 2004, the 10 leading counties were Val Verde, Crockett, Tom Green, Pecos, Concho, Schleicher, Gillespie, Edwards, Menard and Sutton.

Sheep production is largely dual in purpose and is conducted for both wool and lamb production.

San Angelo long has been the largest sheep and wool market in the nation and the center for wool and mohair warehouses, scouring plants and slaughterhouses.

Swine

Texas had 980,000 head of swine on hand as of Dec. 1, 2004, only 1.6 percent of the U.S. swine herd. Swine producers in the state usually produce about one-fifth of the pork consumed by the state's population, which is about 1.36 million head marketed annually.

Although the number of farms producing hogs has steadily decreased, the size of production units has increased substantially, which points to a favorable potential for increased production.

In 2004, 1.43 million head of hogs were marketed in Texas, producing 202.06 million pounds of pork valued at $44.90 per 100 pounds, or $90.73 million. In 2003, 1.23 million head of hogs were marketed, producing 197.88 million pounds of pork valued at $33.60 per 100 pounds, or $66.49 million. Comparable figures for 2002 were 1.36 million head of hogs marketed, producing 224.44 million pounds of pork valued at $28.70 per 100 pounds, or $64.41 million. ☆

Texas Sheep and Wool Production 1850–2005

Year	Sheep		Wool	
	*Number	Value	Production (lbs)	Value
1850	100,530	N A	131,917	N A
1860	753,363	N A	1,493,363	N A
1870	1,223,000	$2,079,000	N A	N A
1880	6,024,000	12,048,000	N A	N A
1890	4,752,000	7,128,000	N A	N A
1900	2,416,000	4,590,000	9,630,000	N A
1910	1,909,000	5,536,000	8,943,000	$1,699,170
1920	3,360,000	33,600,000	22,813,000	5,019,000
1930	6,304,000	44,758,000	48,262,000	10,135,000
1940	10,069,000	49,413,000	79,900,000	23,171,000
1950	6,756,000	103,877,000	51,480,000	32,947,000
1960	5,938,000	85,801,000	51,980,000	21,832,000
1970	3,708,000	73,602,000	30,784,000	11,082,000
1980	2,400,000	138,000,000	18,300,000	17,751,000
1981	2,360,000	116,820,000	20,500,000	24,600,000
1982	2,400,000	100,800,000	19,300,000	16,212,000
1983	2,225,000	86,775,000	18,600,000	15,438,000
1984	1,970,000	76,830,000	17,500,000	16,100,000
1985	1,930,000	110,975,000	16,200,000	13,284,000
1986	1,850,000	107,300,000	16,400,000	13,284,000
1987	2,050,000	133,250,000	16,400,000	19,844,000
1988	2,040,000	155,040,000	18,200,000	35,854,000
1989	1,870,000	133,445,000	18,000,000	27,180,000
1990	2,090,000	133,760,000	17,400,000	19,662,000
1991	2,000,000	108,000,000	16,700,000	13,861,000
1992	2,140,000	111,280,000	17,600,000	16,896,000
1993	2,040,000	118,320,000	17,000,000	11,050,000
1994	1,895,000	106,120,000	14,840,000	15,582,000
1995	1,700,000	100,300,000	13,468,000	15,488,000
1996	1,650,000	108,900,000	9,900,000	8,316,000
1997	1,400,000	100,800,000	10,950,000	11,607,000
1998	1,530,000	122,400,000	9,230,000	5,815,000
1999	1,350,000	95,850,000	7,956,000	3,898,000
2000	1,200,000	94,800,000	7,506,000	3,678,000
2001	1,150,000	92,000,000	6,003,000	3,122,000
2002	1,130,000	88,140,000	5,950,000	4,046,000
2003	1,040,000	82,160,000	5,600,000	5,040,000
2004	1,100,000	105,600,000	5,600,000	5,712,000
2005	1,070,000	112,350,000	NA	NA

NA = not available.
Source: "1985 Texas Livestock, Dairy and Poultry Statistics," USDA Bulletin 235, June 1986. "Texas Agricultural Facts," Annual Summary, Crop and Livestock Reporting Service, various years; "1993 Texas Livestock Statistics," Texas Agricultural Statistics Service, Bulletin 252, August 1994. "Texas Agricultural Statistics, 2003," September 2004.

Hog Production 1960–2004

Year	Production (1,000 Pounds)	Avg. Market Wt. (Pounds)	Avg. Price Per Cwt. (Dollars)	Gross Income (1,000 Dollars)
1960	288,844	228	$14.70	$44,634
1970	385,502	241	22.50	75,288
1980	315,827	259	35.90	111,700
1981	264,693	256	41.70	121,054
1982	205,656	256	49.60	112,726
1983	209,621	256	45.20	95,343
1984	189,620	262	45.50	95,657
1985	168,950	266	43.40	72,512
1986	176,660	269	47.30	82,885
1987	216,834	NA	50.60	103,983
1988	236,658	NA	41.30	100,029
1989	224,229	NA	39.90	93,178
1990	196,225	NA	48.20	92,222
1991	207,023	NA	45.10	97,398
1992	217,554	NA	36.40	79,436
1993	221,130	NA	39.90	90,561
1994	224,397	NA	35.10	78,394
1995	221,323	NA	35.50	81,509
1996	203,761	NA	45.90	93,526
1997	224,131	NA	47.40	106,238
1998	270,977	NA	30.70	83,190
1999	274,572	NA	27.50	71,604
2000	328,732	NA	36.60	115,105
2001	260,875	NA	39.10	105,217
2002	223,441	NA	28.70	67,255
2003	197,876	NA	33.60	67,998
2004	202,064	NA	44.90	90,468

Source: "1985 Texas Livestock, Dairy and Poultry Statistics," USDA, Bulletin 235, June 1986, pp. 32, 46; 1991 "Texas Livestock Statistics"; USDA, "Meat Animals—Prod., Dips., & Income," April 1996–2005; "1993 Texas Livestock Statistics," Bulletin 252, Texas Agricultural Statistics Service, August 1994; "Texas Agricultural Facts, 2003," September 2004; "Texas Ag Facts," various years.

The Green Place in Mills County was founded by E.H. "Hink" and Alice M. Green (seated at far right). They are shown here with nine of their children. The farm has stayed in the Green family for more than 100 years and is listed on the Family Land Heritage Registry. Since the Family Land Heritage Program began in 1974, the Texas Department of Agriculture has recognized more than 4,020 farms and ranches in 226 Texas counties. Photo courtesy of Family Land Heritage Program.

Family Land Heritage Program

Texas Land Registry Has Honored 4,020 Historic Farms and Ranches

Every year, the Texas Department of Agriculture's Family Land Heritage Program recognizes farms and ranches that have been kept in continuous agricultural production by the same family for 100 years or more.

Since the program began in 1974, TDA has honored more than 4,020 farms and ranches from 226 Texas counties. The program chronicles the unique history of these counties, the settlement of Texas, the state's agricultural production and the contributions of Texas families to agriculture — the state's second largest industry. The Family Land Heritage Program also traces the immigration from Germany, Czechoslovakia, Italy, Mexico, Spain, France and other areas as families came to stake their claim in the Lone Star State.

A ceremony is held each year to recognize the families who own the farms and ranches accepted into the program. Families receive a certificate of honor at the ceremony, and the farm and ranch's agricultural history is documented in the Family Land Heritage Registry, which is published annually.

To date, 226 of Texas' 254 counties have properties in the program, with Gaines, Hartley, Lynn and Midland counties joining the honor roll in 2005. Fayette County has the most Family Land Heritage honorees with 124 properties; Houston County is next with 84 properties; Austin and Gillespie counties are tied with 82 properties each; DeWitt County has 80 properties and Medina County has 78 properties.

In 2000, TDA began recognizing 150- and 200-year old farms and ranches. As of 2004, five ranches have been honored for 200 years of family agricultural operation and 53 properties for 150 years.

The oldest recognized property in Texas is the Noriecitas Ranch in Jim Hogg County. In 1740, Simon de Hinojosa came to Texas and began working a 25,000-acre land grant he received from the King of Spain. He raised cattle, horses and goats and was an Indian fighter along the frontier. The land has passed through five generations, and today his great-great-great-great-grandchildren own and

operate the land, which was honored in 1976 for 100 years of continuous operation and in 2001 for 200 years. The four other properties recognized for 200 years include the Agua Nueva Ranch in Jim Hogg County, established in 1779 and recognized in 1994 for 100 years and in 2001 for 200 years; and the El Sauz Ranch, Los Chapotes Ranch and San Antonio Ranch "La Mahada Ranch" were all established in 1767 in Starr County and recognized in 2000 for 200 years.

The first Family Land Heritage ceremony was held in 1974 at the Pan American Livestock Arena at the State Fair of Texas in Dallas. Despite record autumn rainstorms, more than 560 properties from 120 counties were honored that day. Today, the ceremony is held every March in Austin. This historic program is more important than ever as family farms and ranches continue to face new challenges.

The Family Land Heritage Program celebrated its 30th anniversary on March 18, 2005, and 142 farms and ranches from 89 counties were honored. Twenty farms and ranches were honored for reaching their 150-year milestone, the largest number of properties since this recognition began in 2000. The 4,000th property also was recognized.

For a farm or ranch to be eligible for the Family Land Heritage honor and listing in the registry, it must meet the following requirements:

• The same family must have maintained the land in continuous agricultural production for 100 years or more. "Family" can include relatives by blood, marriage or adoption.

• The land must fit the old U.S. Census definition of a farm: 10 acres or more with agricultural sales of $50 or more a year; or if less than 10 acres, sales of at least $250 a year.

• Owners must actively manage the daily operation of the farm or ranch, and they must reside in Texas.

• If all the land has ever been rented or leased to someone outside of the family, it will not qualify for the program. However, it still is eligible if the family retained 10 acres or more for agricultural production with sales of at least $50 annually.

Texas Pronunciation Guide

Texas' rich cultural diversity is reflected nowhere better than in the names of places. Standard pronunciation is used in many cases, but purely colloquial pronunciation often is used, too.

In the late 1940s, George Mitchel Stokes, a graduate student at Baylor University, developed a list of pronunciations of 2,300 place names across the state.

Stokes earned his doctorate and eventually served as director of the speech division in the Communications Studies Department at Baylor University. He retired in 1983.

In the following list based on Stokes' longer list, pronunciation is by respelling and diacritical marking. Respelling is employed as follows: "ah" as in the exclamation, ah, or the "o" in tot; "ee" as in meet; "oo" as in moot; "yoo" as in use; "ow" as in cow; "oi" as in oil; "uh" as in mud.

Note that ah, uh and the apostrophe(') are used for varying degrees of neutral vowel sounds, the apostrophe being used where the vowel is barely sounded. Diacritical markings are used as follows: bāle, băd, lĕt, rīse, rĭll, ōak, brōōd, fŏŏt.

The stressed syllable is capitalized. Secondary stress is indicated by an underline as in Atascosa—ăt uhs KŌ suh.

A

Agua Dulce—ah wuh DŌŌL sĭ
Agua Nueva—ah wuh nyŏŏ Ā vuh
Algoa—ăl GŌ uh
Alief—Ā leef
Altair—awl TĂR
Alta Loma—ăl tuh LŌ muh
Alto—ĂL tō
Altoga—ăl TŌ guh
Alvarado—ăl vuh RĀ dō
Alvord—ĂL vord
Amarillo—ăm uh RĬL ŏ
Anahuac—ĂN uh wăk
Andice—ĂN dĭs
Angelina—ăn juh LEE nuh
Anna—ĂN uh
Annona—ă NŌ nuh
Anton—ĂNT n
Aquilla—uh KWĬL uh
Aransas—uh RĂN zuhs
Aransas Pass—uh răn zuhs PĂS
Arbala—ahr BĀ luh
Arcadia—ahr KĀ dĭ uh
Arcola—ahr KŌ luh
Argo—AHR gō
Arneckeville—AHR nĭ kĭ vĭl
Arp—ahrp
Artesia Wells—ahr tee zh' WĔLZ
Aspermont—ĂS per mahnt
Atascosa—ăt uhs KŌ suh
Attoyac—AT uh yăk
Austin—AWS t'n
Austonio—aws TŌ nĭ ŏ
Austwell—AWS wĕl
Avalon—ĂV uhl n
Avinger—Ă vĭn jer
Avoca—uh VŌ kuh
Axtell—ĂKS t'l
Azle—Ā z'l

B

Ballinger—BĂL ĭn jer
Balmorhea—băl muh RĀ
Bandera—băn DĔR uh
Banquete—băn KĔ tĭ
Bastrop—BĂS trahp
Beasley—BEEZ lĭ
Beaukiss—bō KĬS
Beaumont—BŌ mahnt

Bebe—bee bee
Bedias—BEE dīs
Belcherville—BĔL cher vĭl
Bellevue—BĔL vyŏŏ
Benavides—bĕn uh VEE d's
Ben Hur—bĕn HER
Berclair—ber KLĂR
Bessmay—bĕs MĀ
Bettie—BĔT ĭ
Bexar—BA är
Biardstown—BĂRDZ t'n
Birome—bī RŌM
Blanco—BLĂNG kō
Boerne—BER nĭ
Bogata—buh GŌ duh
Bolivar—BAH lĭ ver
Bomarton—BŌ mer t'n
Bonham—BAH n'm
Bonita—bō NEE tuh
Bonney—BAH nĭ
Bon Wier—bahn WEER
Borger—BŌR ger
Bosque—BAHS kĭ
Boston—BAWS t'n
Bovina—bō VEE nuh
Bowie—BŌŌ Ĭ
Boyce—bawis
Brashear—bruh SHĬR
Brazoria—bruh ZŌ rĭ uh
Brazos—BRĂZ uhs
Breckenridge—BRĔK uhn rĭj
Bremond—bree MAHND
Brenham—BRĔ n'm
Brewster—BRŌŌ ster
Briscoe—BRĬS kō
Britton—BRĬT n
Broaddus—BRAW d's
Bronte—brahnt
Brundage—BRUHN dĭj
Bruni—BRŌŌ nĭ
Buchanan Dam—buhk hăn uhn DĂM
Buda—BYŎŎ duh
Buena Vista—bwă nuh VEES tuh
Buffalo—BUHF uh lō
Bula—BYŎŎ luh
Bullard—BŌŌL erd
Bulverde—bŏŏl VER dĭ
Buna—BYŎŎ nuh
Burkburnett—berk ber NET

Burkett—BER kĭt
Burleson—BER luh s'n
Burnet—BER nĕt
Bustamante—buhs tuh MAHN tĭ

C

Caddo Mills—kă dō MĬLZ
Calallen—kăl ĂL ĭn
Calaveras—kăl uh VĔR's
Camilla—kuh MEEL yuh
Candelaria—kăn duh LĔ rĭ uh
Canton—KĂNT n
Caradan—KĂR uh dăn
Carlisle—KAHR lĭl
Carlsbad—KAHR uhlz bad
Carmine—kahr MEEN
Carmona—kahr MŌ nuh
Caro—KAH rō
Carrizo Springs—kuh ree zuh SPRĬNGZ
Carrollton—KĂR 'l t'n
Carthage—KAHR thĭj
Cason—KĀ s'n
Castell—kăs TĔL
Castroville—KĂS tro vĭl
Catarina—kăt uh REE nuh
Cayuga—kā YŎŎ guh
Cedar Bayou—see der BĪ ō
Cee Vee—see VEE
Celeste—suh LĔST
Celina—suh LĬ nuh
Centralia—sĕn TRĂL yuh
Charco—CHAHR kō
Cherokee—CHĔR uh kee
Chico—CHEE kō
Chicota—chĭ KŌ tuh
Childress—CHĬL drĕs
Chillicothe—chĭl ĭ KAH thĭ
Chireno—sh' REE nō
Chisholm—CHĬZ uhm
Chita—CHEE tuh
Chocolate Bayou—chah kuh lĭt BĪ ō
Chriesman—KRĬS m'n
Christoval—krĭs TŌ v'l
Cibolo—SEE bō lō
Cisco—SĬS kō
Clarendon—KLĂR ĭn d'n
Cleburne—KLEE bern
Clodine—klaw DEEN

Clute—klōōt
Coahoma—kuh HŌ muh
Cockrell Hill—kahk ruhl HĬL
Colfax—KAHL făks
College Station—<u>kah</u> lĭj STĀ sh'n
Colmesneil—KŌL m's neel
Colorado—<u>kahl</u> uh RAH dō
Colorado City—kah luh <u>rā</u> duh SĬT ĭ
Columbus—kuh LUHM b's
Comal—KŌ măl
Comanche—kuh MĂN chĭ
Combes—kōmz
Comfort—KUHM fert
Como—KŌ mō
Concan—KAHN kăn
Concepcion—kuhn sep sĭ ŌN
Concho—KAHN chō
Concrete—kahn KREET
Cone—kōn
Conlen—KAHN lĭn
Conroe—KAHN rō
Cooper—KŌŌ per
Coppell—kuhp PĔL or kuh PĔL
Copperas Cove—kahp ruhs KŌV
Corbett—KAWR bĭt
Cordele—kawr DĔL
Corinth—KAH rĭnth
Corpus Christi—<u>kawr</u> p's KRĬS tĭ
Corrigan—KAWR uh g'n
Corsicana—<u>kawr</u> sĭ KĂN uh
Coryell—kō rĭ ĔL
Cottle—KAH t'l
Cotulla—kuh TŌŌ luh
Coupland—KŌP l'n
Cresson—KRĔ s'n
Crockett—KRAH kĭt
Crowell—KRŌ uhl
Crowley—KROW li
Cuero—KWĔR o
Culberson—KUHL ber s'n
Cumby—KUHM bĭ
Cuney—KYŌŌ nĭ
Currie—KER rĭ
Cuthand—KUHT hănd

D

Dacosta—duh KAHS tuh
Dacus—DĂ k's
Daingerfield—DĀN jer feeld
Daisetta—dā ZĔT uh
Danciger—DĂN sĭ ger
Danevang—DĂN uh văng
Darrouzett—dăr uh ZĔT
Davilla—duh VĬL uh
Deaf Smith—děf SMĬTH
De Berry—duh BĚ rĭ
Decatur—<u>dee</u> KĂT er
De Kalb—dĭ KĂB
De Leon—da lee AHN
Del Rio—děl REE o
Delvalle—děl VĂ lĭ
Denhawken—DĬN haw kĭn
Denton—DĔNT n
Deport—dĭ PŌRT
Derby—DER bĭ
Desdemona—<u>děz</u> dĭ MŌ nuh
DeSoto—dĭ SŌ tuh
Detroit—dee TROIT
Devers—DĚ vers

Devine—duh VĬN
DeWitt—dĭ WĬT
D'Hanis—duh HĂ nĭs
Dialville—DĬ uhl vil
Diboll—DĬ bawl
Dilley—DĬL i
Dimmit—DĬM ĭt
Dinero—dĭ NĚ rō
Direct—duh RĔKT
Dobrowolski—<u>dah</u> bruh WAHL skĭ
Donie—DŌ nĭ
Dorchester—dawr CHĚS ter
Doucette—DŌŌ sět
Dougherty—DAHR tĭ
Dozier—DŌ zher
Dryden—DRĬD n
Duffau—DUHF ō
Dumas—DŌŌ m's
Dumont—DYŌŌ mahnt
Durango—duh RĂNG go
Duval—DŌŌ vawl

E

East Bernard—<u>eest</u> ber NAHRD
Edcouch—ĕd KOWCH
Eddy—E di
El Campo—ĕl KĂM pō
Eldorado—<u>ĕl</u> duh RĂ duh
Electra—ĭ LĔK truh
Elgin—ĔL gĭn
El Indio—ĕl ĬN dĭ ō
Ellinger—ĔL ĭn jer
Elmendorf—ĔLM 'n dawrf
Elm Mott—ĕl MAHT
Elmo—ĔL mō
Eloise—ĔL o <u>eez</u>
El Paso—ĕl PĂS ō
Encinal—ĕn suh NAHL
Encino—ĕn SEE nō
Engle—ĔN g'l
Enloe—ĔN lō
Ennis—ĔN ĭs
Enochs—EE nuhks
Eola—ee Ō luh
Era—EE ruh
Erath—EE răth
Esperanza—<u>ĕs</u> per RĂN zuh
Estelline—ĔS tuh leen
Etoile—ĭ TOIL
Etter—ĔT er
Eula—YŌŌ luh
Euless—YŌŌ lis
Eureka—yōō REE kuh
Eustace—YŌŌS t's
Evant—EE vănt
Everman—Ĕ ver m'n

F

Fabens—FĀ b'nz
Falfurrias—făl FYŌŌ rĭ uhs
Fannett—fă NĔT
Fannin—FĂN ĭn
Fargo—FAHR gō
Farrar—FĂR uh
Farwell—FAHR w'l
Fashing—FĂ shĭng
Fayette—fă ĔT
Fayetteville—FĂ uht vĭl
Flatonia—flă TŌN yuh

Flomot—FLŌ maht
Florence—FLAH ruhns
Floresville—FLŌRZ vil
Florey—FLŌ ri
Floydada—floi DĂ duh
Fluvanna—<u>flōō</u> VĂN uh
Fodice—FŌ dĭs
Follett—fah LĔT
Fordtran—förd TRĂN
Forney—FAWR nĭ
Forsan—FŌR săn
Fort Chadbourne—<u>fört</u> CHĂD bern
Fort Worth—fört WERTH
Fowlerton—FOW ler t'n
Francitas—frăn SEE t's
Fredericksburg—FRĔD er rĭks berg
Fredonia—<u>free</u> DŌN yuh
Freer—FREE er
Frelsburg—FRĔLZ berg
Frio—FREE ō
Friona—free O nuh
Frisco—FRĬS ko
Frydek—FRĪ děk
Fulshear—FUHL sher

G

Gallatin—GĂL uh t'n
Galveston—GĂL věs t'n
Ganado—guh NĂ dō
Garceno—gahr SĂ nō
Garciasville—gahr SEE uhs vĭl
Garza—GAHR zuh
Gause—gawz
Geneva—juh NEE vuh
Geronimo—<u>juh</u> RAH nĭ mō
Giddings—GĬD ĭngz
Gillespie—guh LĚS pĭ
Gillett—juh LĔT
Gilliland—GĬL ĭ l'nd
Gilmer—GĬL mer
Ginger—JĬN jer
Girard—juh RAHRD
Girvin—GER vĭn
Glazier—GLĀ zher
Glidden—GLĬD n
Gober—GŌ ber
Godley—GAHD lĭ
Goldthwaite—GŌLTH wāt
Goliad—GŌ lĭ ăd
Golindo—gō LĬN duh
Gonzales—<u>guhn</u> ZAH l's
Goree—GŌ ree
Gouldbusk—GŌŌLD buhsk
Grand Saline—grăn suh LEEN
Granger—GRĂN jer
Greenville—GREEN v'l
Groesbeck—GRŌZ běk
Gruene—green
Grulla—GRŌŌL yuh
Gruver—GRŌŌ ver
Guadalupe—<u>gwah</u> duh LŌŌ pĭ
Guerra—GWĔ ruh
Gustine—GUHS <u>teen</u>
Guthrie—GUHTH rĭ

H

Hallettsville—HĂL ĕts vĭl
Hamshire—HĂM sher
Hankamer—HĂN kăm er

Hardeman—HAHR duh m'n
Harleton—HAHR uhl t'n
Harlingen—HAHR lĭn juhn
Haskell—HĂS k'l
Haslam—HĂZ l'm
Haslet—HĂS lĕt
Hasse—HĂ sĭ
Hatchell—HĂ ch'l
Hearne—hern
Heath—heeth
Hebbronville—HĔB r'n vĭl
Heidenheimer—HĪD n hīmer
Helena—HĔL uh nuh
Helotes—hĕl Ō tĭs
Hempstead—HĔM stĕd
Hermleigh—HER muh lee
Hico—HĪ kō
Hidalgo—hĭ DĂL gō
Hillister—HĬL ĭs ter
Hindes—hīndz
Hochheim—HŌ hīm
Hondo—HAHN dō
Houston—HYŌŌS t'n or YŌŌS t'n
Hubbard—HUH berd
Huckabay—HUHK uh bĭ
Hudspeth—HUHD sp'th
Humble—HUHM b'l
Hungerford—HUHNG ger ferd
Hutto—HUH tō
Hye—hī
Hylton—HĬL t'n

I

Iago—ī Ā gō
Idalou—Ī duh lōō
Inadale—Ī nuh dāl
Iola—ī Ō luh
Iraan—ī ruh ĂN
Iredell—Ī ruh dĕl
Irion—ĪR i uhn
Italy—ĬT uh lĭ
Itasca—ī TĂS kuh
Ivan—Ī v'n
Ivanhoe—Ī v'n hō

J

Jardin—JAHRD n
Jarrell—JĂR uhl
Jeddo—JĔ dō
Jermyn—JER m'n
Jewett—JŌŌ ĭt
Jiba—HEE buh
Joaquin—waw KEEN
Jolly—JAH lĭ
Jollyville—JAH lĭ vĭl
Jonah—JŌ nuh
Joshua—JAH sh' wa
Jourdanton—JERD n t'n
Juliff—JŌŌ lĭf
Juno—JŌŌ nō

K

Kalgary—KĂL gĕ rĭ
Kamay—KĂ ĭm ā
Kanawha—KAHN uh wah
Karnack—KAHR năk
Katemcy—kuh TĔM sĭ
Kaufman—KAWF m'n
Keechi—KEE chĭ

Keene—keen
Kemah—KEE muh
Kendalia—kĔn DĀL yuh
Kennard—kuh NAHRD
Kerens—KER 'nz
Kerr—ker
Kerrville—KER vĭl
Kilgore—KĬL gōr
Killeen—kuh LEEN
Kleberg—KLĀ berg
Knickerbocker—NĬK uh bah ker
Knippa—kuh NĬP uh
Kosciusko—kuh SHŌŌS kō
Kosse—KAH sĭ
Kountze—kōōntz
Kress—kres
Krum—kruhm
Kurten—KER t'n
Kyle—kīl

L

La Blanca—lah BLAHN kuh
La Coste—luh KAWST
Ladonia—luh DŌN yuh
LaFayette—lah fĭ ĔT
Laferia—luh FĔ rĭ uh
Lagarto—luh GAHR tō
La Gloria—lah GLŌ rĭ uh
La Grange—luh GRĀNJ
Laguna—luh GŌŌ nuh
Laird Hill—lărd HĬL
La Joya—luh HŌ yuh
Lamarque—luh MAHRK
Lamasco—luh MĂS kō
Lamesa—luh MEE suh
Lamkin—LĂM kĭn
Lampasas—lăm PĂ s's
Lancaster—LĂNG k's ter
Langtry—LĂNG trĭ
Lanier—luh NĬR
La Paloma—lah puh LŌ muh
La Porte—luh PŌRT
La Pryor—luh PRĬ er
Laredo—luh RĂ dō
Lariat—LĂ ri uht
La Rue—luh RŌŌ
La Salle—luh SĂL
Lasara—luh SĔ ruh
Lassater—LĂ sĭ ter
Latexo—luh TĔKS ō
Lavaca—luh VĂ kuh
La Vernia—luh VER nĭ uh
La Villa—lah VĬL uh
Lavon—luh VAHN
La Ward—luh WAWRD
Lazbuddie—LĂZ buh dĭ
Leakey—LĀ kĭ
Leander—lee ĂN der
Leary—LĬ er ĭ
Lefors—lĭ FŌRZ
Leggett—LĔ gĭt
Leigh—lee
Lela—LEE luh
Lelia Lake—leel yuh LĀK
Leming—LĔ mĭng
Lenorah—lĕ NŌ ruh
Leon—lee AHN
Leona—lee Ō nuh
Leroy—LEE roi

Levelland—LĔ v'l lănd
Levita—luh VĪ tuh
Lewisville—LŌŌ ĭs vĭl
Lindenau—lĭn duh NOW
Lipan—lĭ PĂN
Lipscomb—LĬPS k'm
Lissie—LĬ sĭ
Llano—LĂ nō
Lockney—LAHK nĭ
Lodi—LŌ dĭ
Lohn—lahn
Lolita—lō LEE tuh
Loma Alto—lō muh ĂL tō
Lometa—lō MEE tuh
London—LUHN d'n
Long Mott—lawng MAHT
Lopeno—lō PEE nō
Loraine—lō RĂN
Lorena—lō REE nuh
Los Angeles—laws AN juh l's
Los Ebanos—lōs ĔB uh nōs
Los Fresnos—lōs FRĔZ nōs
Los Indios—lōs ĬN dĭ ōs
Losoya—luh SAW yuh
Lubbock—LUH buhk or LUH b'k
Lueders—LŌŌ derz
Luella—lōō ĔL uh
Lufkin—LUHF kĭn
Luling—LŌŌ lĭng
Lund—luhnd
Lutie—LŌŌ tĭ

M

McAdoo—MĂK uh dōō
McCamey—muh KĂ mĭ
McCaulley—muh KAW lĭ
McCulloch—muh KUH luhk
McLean—muh KLĂN
McLennan—muh LĔN uhn
McLeod—măk LOWD
McQueeney—muh KWEE nĭ
Mabank—MĂ băngk
Macune—muh KŌŌN
Magnolia—măg NŌL yuh
Malakoff—MĂL uh kawf
Malone—muh LŌN
Malta—MAWL tuh
Manchaca—MĂN shăk
Manheim—MĂN hīm
Manor—MĂ ner
Manvel—MĂN v'l
Marathon—MĂR uh th'n
Marfa—MAHR fuh
Marquez—mahr KĂ
Maryneal—mă rĭ NEEL
Matador—MĂT uh dōr
Matagorda—măt uh GAWR duh
Mathis—MĂ thĭs
Maud—mawd
Mauriceville—maw REES vĭl
Maverick—MĂV rĭk
Maydell—MĂ dĕl
Maypearl—mā PERL
Medill—mĕ DĬL
Medina—muh DEE nuh
Megargel—muh GAHR g'l
Menard—muh NAHRD
Mendoza—mĕn DŌ zuh
Mentone—mĕn TON

Mercedes—mer SĂ deez
Mereta—muh RĔT uh
Meridian—muh RĬ dĭ uhn
Merkel—MER k'l
Mertens—mer TĔNZ
Mertzon—MERTS n
Mesquite—muhs KEET
Mexia—muh HĂ uh
Miami—mĭ ĂM ĭ
Mico—MEE kō
Midland—MĬD l'nd
Midlothian—mĭd LŌ thĭ n
Milam—MĬ l'm
Milano—mĭ LĂ nō
Millett—MĬL ĭt
Millheim—MĬL hīm
Millican—MĬL uh kuhn
Millsap—MĬL săp
Minden—MĬN d'n
Mineola—mĭn ĭ Ō luh
Minerva—mĭ NER vuh
Mingus—MĬNG guhs
Minter—MĬNT er
Mirando City—mĭ răn duh SĬT ĭ
Missouri City—muh zōōr uh SĬT ĭ
Mitchell—MĬ ch'l
Mobeetie—mō BEE tĭ
Moline—mō LEEN
Monahans—MAH nuh hănz
Montague—mahn TĂG
Montalba—mahnt ĂL buh
Mont Belvieu—mahnt BĔL vyōō
Montell—mahn TĔL
Montgomery—mahnt GUHM er ĭ
Monthalia—mahn THĂL yuh
Moody—MŌŌ dĭ
Moore—mor
Morales—muh RAH lĕs
Moran—mō RĂN
Moscow—MAHS kow
Mosheim—MŌ shīm
Moss Bluff—maws BLUHF
Motley—MAHT lĭ
Moulton—MŌL t'n
Muenster—MYŌŌNS ter
Muldoon—muhl DŌŌN
Muleshoe—MYŌŌL shōō
Munday—MUHN dĭ
Murchison—MER kuh s'n
Mykawa—mĭ KAH wuh
Myra—MĬ ruh

N

Nacogdoches—năk uh DŌ chĭs
Nada—NĂ duh
Natalia—nuh TĂL yuh
Navarro—nuh VĂ rō
Navasota—năv uh SŌ tuh
Neches—NĂ chĭs
Nederland—NEE der l'nd
Neuville—NYŌŌ v'l
Nevada—nuh VĂ duh
Newark—NŌŌ erk
New Baden—nyōō BĂD n
New Braunfels—nyōō BROWN fĕlz
New Caney—nyōō KĂ nĭ
New Ulm—nyōō UHLM
New Waverly—nyōō WĂ ver lĭ
New Willard—nyōō WĬL erd

Nimrod—NĬM rahd
Nineveh—NĬN uh vuh
Nocona—nō KŌ nuh
Nopal—NŌ păl
Nordheim—NAWRD hīm
Normangee—NAWR m'n jee
Normanna—nawr MĂN uh
North Zulch—nawrth ZŌŌLCH
Nueces—nyōō Ă sĭs

O

Oakalla—ō KĂL uh
Ochiltree—AH k'l tree
Odell—ō DĔL
Odem—Ō d'm
Odessa—ō DĔS uh
Oenaville—ō EEN uh v'l
Oglesby—Ō g'lz bĭ
Oilton—OIL t'n
Oklaunion—ōk luh YŌŌN y'n
Olivia—ō LĬV ĭ uh
Olmito—awl MEE tuh
Olmos Park—ahl m's PAHRK
Olney—AHL ni
Olton—ŌL t'n
Omaha—Ō muh haw
Omen—Ō mĭn
Onalaska—uhn uh LĂS kuh
Oplin—AHP lĭn
Osceola—ō sĭ Ō luh
Otey—Ō tĭ
Ottine—ah TEEN
Ovalo—ō VĂL uh
Ozona—ō ZŌ nuh

P

Paducah—puh DYŌŌ kuh
Palacios—puh LĂ sh's
Palestine—PAL uhs teen
Palito Blanco—p' lee to BLAHNG kō
Palo Pinto—pă lō PĬN tō
Paluxy—puh LUHK sĭ
Panna Maria—păn uh muh REE uh
Papalote—pah puh LŌ tĭ
Paris—PĂ rĭs
Pasadena—păs uh DEE nuh
Patroon—puh TRŌŌN
Pawnee—paw NEE
Pearland—PĂR länd
Pearsall—PEER sawl
Peaster—PEES ter
Pecos—PĂ k's
Penelope—puh NĔL uh pĭ
Penitas—puh NEE t's
Peoria—pee Ō rĭ uh
Percilla—per SĬL uh
Petrolia—puh TRŌL yuh
Petteway—PĔT uh wă
Pettit—PĔT ĭt
Pettus—PĔT uhs
Pflugerville—FLŌŌ ger vĭl
Pharr—fahr
Phelps—fĕlps
Pidcoke—PĬD kōk
Placedo—PLĂS ĭ dō
Plano—PLĂ nō
Plaska—PLĂS kuh
Plateau—plă TŌ
Pledger—PLĔ jer

Plum—pluhm
Ponta—pahn TĂ
Pontotoc—PAHNT uh tahk
Port Aransas—pōrt uh RĂN zuhs
Port Bolivar—pōrt BAH lĭ ver
Port Isabel—pōrt ĬZ uh bĕl
Port Lavaca—pōrt luh VĂ kuh
Port Neches—pōrt NĂ chĬs
Posey—PŌ zĭ
Poteet—pō TEET
Poth—pōth
Potosi—puh TŌ sĭ
Poynor—POI ner
Prairie Lea—prĕr ĭ LEE
Premont—PREE mahnt
Presidio—pruh SĬ dĭ ō
Priddy—PRĬ dĭ
Primera—pree MĔ ruh
Pritchett—PRĬ chĭt
Progreso—prō GRĔ sō
Purdon—PERD n
Purley—PER lĭ
Purmela—per MEE luh
Pyote—PĬ ōt

Q

Quanah—KWAH nuh
Quemado—kuh MAH dō
Quihi—KWEE hee
Quintana—kwĭn TAH nuh
Quitaque—KĬT uh kwa
Quitman—KWĬT m'n

R

Ratcliff—RĂT klĭf
Ravenna—rĭ VĔN uh
Reagan—RĂ g'n
Real—REE awl
Realitos—ree uh LEE t's
Refugio—rĕ FYŌŌ rĭ ō
Reklaw—RĔK law
Reno—REE nō
Ricardo—rĭ KAHR dō
Riesel—REE s'l
Ringgold—RĬNG gōld
Rio Frio—ree ō FREE ō
Rio Grande City—ree ō grahn dĭ SĬT ĭ
Rio Hondo—ree ō HAHN dō
Riomedina—ree ō muh DEE nuh
Rios—REE ōs
Rio Vista—ree ō VĬS tuh
Riviera—ruh VĬR uh
Roane—rōn
Roanoke—RŌN ōk
Roans Prairie—rōnz PRĔR Ĭ
Roby—RŌ bĭ
Rochelle—rō SHĔL
Roganville—RŌ g'n vĭl
Roma—RŌ muh
Romayor—rō MĂ er
Roosevelt—RŌŌ suh v'lt
Rosanky—rō ZĂNG kĭ
Rosenberg—RŌZ n berg
Rosenthal—RŌZ uhn thawl
Rosharon—rō SHĔ r'n
Rosita—rō SEE tuh
Rosser—RAW ser
Roswell—RAHZ w'l
Rotan—rō TĂN

Rowena—rō EE nuh
Rowlett—ROW lĭt
Royse City—roi SĪT ĭ
Rugby—RUHG bĭ
Ruidosa—<u>ree</u> uh DŌ suh
Runge—RUHNG ĭ
Rutersville—RŌŌ ter vĭl
Rye—rī

S

Sabinal—SĂB uh năl
Sabine—suh BEEN
Sachse—SĂK sĭ
Sacul—SĂ k'l
Salado—suh LĂ dō
Salesville—SĂLZ vĭl
Salineno—suh LEEN yō
Salmon—SĂL m'n
Saltillo—săl TĬL ō
Samfordyce—săm FOR dis
Samnorwood—săm NAWR wŏŏd
San Angelo—<u>săn</u> ĂN juh lō
San Antonio—<u>săn</u> ăn TŌ nĭ ō
San Augustine—<u>săn</u> AW g's teen
San Benito—săn buh NEE tuh
Sandia—săn DEE uh
San Diego—<u>săn</u> dĭ Ā gō
San Felipe—<u>săn</u> fuh LEEP
San Gabriel—săn GĂ brĭ uhl
San Jacinto—<u>săn</u> juh SĬN tuh
San Juan—săn WAHN
San Marcos—<u>săn</u> MAHR k's
San Patricio—<u>săn</u> puh TRĬSH ĭ ō
San Perlita—<u>săn</u> per LEE tuh
San Saba—<u>săn</u> SĂ buh
Santa Anna—<u>săn</u> tuh ĂN uh
Santa Elena—săn tuh LEE nuh
Santa Maria—<u>săn</u> tuh muh REE uh
Santa Rosa—<u>săn</u> tuh RŌ suh
Santo—SĂN tō
San Ygnacio—<u>săn</u> ĭg NAH sĭ ō
Saragosa—<u>sĕ</u> ruh GŌ suh
Saratoga—<u>sĕ</u> ruh TŌ guh
Sargent—SAHR juhnt
Sarita—suh REE tuh
Saspamco—suh SPĂM kō
Savoy—suh VOI
Schattel—SHĂT uhl
Schertz—sherts
Schleicher—SHLĪ ker
Schroeder—SHRĀ der
Schulenburg—SHŌŌ lĭn berg
Schwertner—SWERT ner
Scyene—sĭ EEN
Segno—SĔG nō
Segovia—<u>sĭ</u> GŌ vĭ uh
Seguin—sĭ GEEN
Seminole—SĔM uh nōl
Shafter—SHĂF ter
Shiro—SHĪ rō
Shive—shĭv
Sierra Blanca—sĭer ruh BLĂNG kuh
Siloam—suh LŌM
Silsbee—SĬLZ bĭ
Simonton—SĪ m'n t'n
Sinton—SĬNT n
Sipe Springs—SEEP sprĭngz
Sivells Bend—<u>sĭ</u> v'lz BĔND
Slaton—SLĂT n

Slidell—slĭ DĔL
Slocum—SLŌ k'm
Smyer—SMĪ er
Somervell—SUH mer vĕl
Somerville—SUH mer vĭl
Sonora—suh NŌ ruh
South Bosque—sowth BAHS kĭ
Southmayd—sowth MĀD
Splendora—splĕn DŌ ruh
Spofford—SPAH ferd
Spurger—SPER ger
Sterley—STER lĭ
Stiles—stīlz
Stinnett—stĭ NĔT
Stoneham—STŌN uhm
Stout—stowt
Stowell—STO w'l
Study Butte—styōō dĭ BYŌŌT
Sublime—s'b LĬM
Sudan—SŌŌ dăn
Sunray—SUHN rā
Swan—swahn
Sweeny—SWEE nĭ

T

Tahoka—tuh HŌ kuh
Talco—TĂL kō
Talpa—TĂL puh
Tankersley—TĂNG kers lĭ
Tarzan—TAHR z'n
Tascosa—tăs KŌ suh
Tatum—TĂ t'm
Tavener—TĂV uh ner
Tehuacana—<u>tuh</u> WAW kuh nuh
Telferner—TĔLF ner
Tenaha—TĔN uh haw
Terlingua—TER lĭng guh
Texarkana—tĕks ahr KĂN uh
Texhoma—tĕks Ō muh
Texline—TĔKS līn
Texon—tĕks AHN
Thalia—THĂL yuh
Tioga—tī Ō guh
Tivoli—tĭ VŌ luh
Tokio—TŌ kĭ ō
Tolosa—tuh LŌ suh
Tornillo—tawr NEE yō
Tow—tow
Toyah—TOI yuh
Toyahvale—TOI yuh văl
Trinidad—TRĬN uh dăd
Troup—trŏŏp
Truby—TRŌŌ bĭ
Trumbull—TRUHM b'l
Truscott—TRUHS k't
Tuleta—tōō LEE tuh
Tulia—TŌŌL yuh
Tulsita—tuhl SEE tuh
Tundra—TUHN druh
Tunis—TŌŌ nĭs
Tuscola—tuhs KŌ luh
Tuxedo—TUHKS ĭ dō

U

Uhland—YŌŌ l'nd
Umbarger—UHM bahr ger
Urbana—<u>er</u> BĀ nuh
Utley—YŌŌT lĭ
Utopia—yōō TŌ pĭ uh

Uvalde—yōō VĂL dĭ

V

Valdasta—văl DĂS tuh
Valera—vuh LĬ ruh
Van Alstyne—văn AWLZ <u>teen</u>
Vashti—VĂSH tī
Vega—VĀ guh
Velasco—vuh LĂS kō
Veribest—VĔR ĭ bĕst
Victoria—vĭk TŌ rĭ uh
Vidor—VĪ der
Vienna—<u>vee</u> ĔN uh
Vinegarone—<u>vĭn</u> er guh RŌN
Voca—VŌ kuh
Von Ormy—vahn AHR mĭ
Votaw—VŌ taw

W

Waco—WĀ kō
Waelder—WĔL der
Waka—WAH kuh
Waldeck—WAWL dĕk
Waller—WAW ler
Wallis—WAH lĭs
Warda—WAWR duh
Waskom—WAHS k'm
Wastella—wahs TĔL uh
Watauga—wuh TAW guh
Waxahachie—<u>wawks</u> uh HĂ chĭ
Weches—WEE chĭz
Weesatche—WEE săch
Weimar—WĪ mer
Weinert—WĪ nert
Weir—weer
Weser—WEE zer
Weslaco—WĔS luh kō
Westhoff—WĔS tawf
Westphalia—<u>wĕst</u> FĂL yuh
Whitharral—HWĬT här uhl
Whitsett—HWĬT sĭt
Whitson—HWĬT s'n
Whitt—hwĭt
Whon—hwahn
Wichita—WĬCH ĭ taw
Wiergate—WEER gāt
Wilbarger—WĬL bahr ger
Wildorado—wĭl duh RĂ dō
Willacy—WĬL uh sĭ
Wimberley—WĬM ber lĭ
Windthorst—WĬN thr'st
Wingate—WĬN gāt
Winona—wĭ NŌ nuh
Woden—WŌD n
Wolfforth—WŌŌL forth
Woodbine—WŌŌD bīn
Wylie—WĪ lĭ

Y

Yancey—YĂN sĭ
Yantis—YĂN tĭs
Yoakum—YŌ k'm
Ysleta—ĭs LĔT uh

Z

Zapata—zuh PAH tuh
Zavalla—zuh VĂL uh
Zephyr—ZĔF er
Zuehl—ZEE uhl ☆

Obituaries: August 2003-June 2005

Abbott, "Dimebag" Darrell, 38; one of heavy-metal's top guitarists, gained fame in 1990s with group Pantera; Dalworthington Gardens resident was shot to death, along with four others, Dec. 8, 2004, while performing in Columbus, Ohio.

Abraham, Elias, 90; businessman who was the last of the 12 brothers and sisters who immigrated from Syria to start the Abraham dynasty in El Paso; July 17, 2004.

Adair, Paul N. "Red," 89; oilfield firefighter for 50 years; immortalized by John Wayne in the movie, *The Hellfighters,* based on his life; in Houston, Aug. 7, 2004.

Agnich, Fred J., 91; business executive and legislator who in 1970 was the first Republican elected countywide in Dallas since Reconstruction; served in Legislature until 1988 where he was a member of the Dirty Thirty, a reform-minded coalition; Oct. 28, 2004.

Anderson, M.J. "Andy," 96; one of Austin's first black real estate agents, political science professor at Huston-Tillotson College and political power broker; was national director for minority affairs for Lyndon Johnson's presidential campaign; Oct. 10, 2004.

Armstrong, Garner Ted, 73; evangelist known for radio program *World Tomorrow;* founded Church of God International in 1978 after his father, Herbert W. Armstrong, excommunicated him from the Worldwide Church of God; in Tyler, Sept. 15, 2003.

Azpiazu, José, 100; priest who founded the popular San Juan del Valle shrine in the Lower Rio Grande Valley in 1954; in San Antonio, July 29, 2004.

Baker, Edith, 78; founding member of the American Women in Radio and Television in Houston; credited with helping Tejano music onto the airwaves iin 1980s; in Houston, Nov. 1, 2003.

Barnett, Etta Moten, 102; Weimar native played romantic roles in movies in the 1930s when most black actresses were relegated to roles as maids; was featured in the show-stopping "Carioca" number in *Flying Down to Rio;* named one of Texas' 100 most influential women of the 20th century by the state's Women's Chamber of Commerce in 1999; Jan. 2, 2004.

Belden, Joe, 90; polling pioneer who in 1940 founded the Texas Poll, the first statewide opinion survey in the country and a model for others that followed; born José Belden to Mexican parents in Eagle Pass; worked in Austin and Dallas; June 16, 2005.

Bellows, George Ferris, 80; head of the family construction firm that built the San Jacinto Momument and other Houston landmarks, such as the Alley Theatre, the Wortham Center and the Tenneco Building; on the board of the Texas Medical Center and Texas Children's Hospital since 1967; May 30, 2005.

Bright, H.R. "Bum," 84; owner of Dallas Cowboys 1984-89; Dallas businessman; longtime member of the Texas A&M University Board of Regents; Dec. 11, 2004.

Brooks, Donald Arthur, 83; the first black doctor in Texas to be board certified in surgery in 1957; became chief of surgery at St. Joseph Hospital in Fort Worth; March 5, 2005.

Bumgardner, Max, 81; Wichita Falls native was University of Texas co-captain in 1947 when he caught passes from Bobby Layne; coach at Angelo State University 1950-68; on football staff at Texas A&M until 1978; April 12, 2005.

Burns, Robert, 60; University of Texas drama graduate who did special effects for several movies, best known as art director for the horror classic *Texas Chainsaw Massacre;* in Seguin, June 4, 2004..

Bynum, Raymond T. "Prof," 96; orginator of Texas' first high school marching band during halftime at an Abilene High School football game in 1926; Aug. 1, 2003.

Canales, Laura, 50; Kingsville native was once known as the Queen of Tejano music, paved the way for other female Tejano singers; in Corpus Christi, April 16, 2005, from complications from gall bladder surgery.

Carr, Waggoner, 95; former Texas attorney general 1963–67, House speaker and legislator from Lubbock; in Austin, Feb. 25, 2004.

Carruthers, Jacob H. Jr., 73; raised in Houston, one of six blacks to break the color barrier at the University of Texas School of Law in 1950; went on to teach at Northeastern Illinois University, considered at expert in African history; Jan. 11, 2004.

Casey, Albert V., 84; former CEO of American Airlines who decided to move the company headquarters to Fort Worth in 1979, bringing thousands of jobs to the area; in Dallas, July 10, 2004.

Clinton, Sam Houston, 81; Waco native was former Texas Court of Criminal Appeals judge; among his clients when he was a defense attorney were Madalyn Murray O'Hair and Jack Ruby; Oct. 5, 2004.

Cooper, Gordon Jr., 77; one of the original Mercury 7 astronauts working at NASA in Houston and the last American to fly solo in space; Oct. 4, 2004.

Crenshaw, Roberta, 90; Austin philanthropist and civic activist who was the catalyst for the Town Lake greenbelt and the founding of the Austin Parks and Recreation Department; Feb. 8, 2005.

Dealey, Doris Carolyn Russell, 85; Dallas civic figure and widow of former Belo Corp. CEO Joe M. Dealey; Jan. 19, 2005.

DeCicco, Frank, 81; Houston real estate visionary who founded Re/Max of Texas, specializing in selling residential properties; Dec. 18, 2004.

De La Rosa, Tony, 72, Sarita native, accordionist and bandleader was one of the first to amplify conjunto music and use drums; in Corpus Christi, June 2, 2004.

Diaz, Alfonso Gonzales, 65; handcraft bootmaker recruited from Mexico by San Antonio bootmaker Sam Lucchese where he worked for 23 years; his customers included Lyndon Johnson and John Wayne; Aug. 16, 2003.

Evangelist Garner Ted Armstrong, above. Right, Gov. Preston Smith. File photos.

Tejano innovator Isidro Lopez.

Actress Etta Moten Barnett, with Harry Belafonte.

Jockey Bill Shoemaker.

Distin, Vivian Liberto, 71; San Antonio-born first wife of Johnny Cash and mother of singer Rosanne Cash; it was during their 13-year marriage that Cash pledged to remain faithful in "I Walk the Line"; May 24, 2005.

Dyer, A.R. "Happy," 96; Odessa civic leader who helped found the Permian Basin International Oil Show; charter member of the Odessa Chuck Wagon Gang; Feb. 28, 2005.

Ellis, George T., 70; son of Lebanese immigrants, earned law degree from University of Texas in 1959, served on the state 14th Court of Appeals 1989–92; in Houston, Sept. 21, 2003.

Faget, Maxime, 83; chief architect of NASA's Mercury capsule and contributor to the design of other spacecraft; in Houston, Oct. 9, 2004.

Fallon, Frank, 73; veteran broadcaster was "Voice of the Baylor Bears" where he announced football and basketball games for 43 years; in Waco, April 30, 2004.

Gabler, Mel, 89; conservative critic of school textbooks who testified before state regulators regularly for 40 years; in Longview, Dec. 19, 2004.

Ganter, Donald B., 65; co-founder in 1974 of the well-known Aggie bar, the Dixie Chicken, as well as other restaurants in College Station; in Abilene, Nov. 23, 2004.

Garza, Reynaldo, 89; son of Mexican immigrants was appointed a federal judge by President Kennedy in 1961; appointed to 5th U.S. Circuit Court of Appeals by President Carter; in Brownsville, Sept. 14, 2004.

Gemberling, Robert Perry, 82; FBI special agent who coordinated the Dallas investigation of the Kennedy assassination and supervised the Lee Harvey Oswald investigation in 1963; in Dallas, Dec. 4 , 2004.

Goldthwaite, Aniela, 91; top female golfer of the 1930s–40s; won

Texas Women's Open four times; in Fort Worth, Dec. 24, 2003.

Graves, Howard, 64; Roaring Springs native and career military officer; was former superintendent of West Point; chancellor of Texas A&M University system 1999–2003; in Fort Worth, Sept. 13, 2003.

Haggar, Edmond R. "Ed," 88; clothier who as president launched to national prominence the family business, which was founded by his father, a Lebanese immigrant; credited with coining the term "slacks;" in Dallas, Sept. 29, 2004.

Halbouty, Michel T., 95; famed wildcatter who made millions in the oil business; Beaumont native was son of Lebanese immigrants; in Houston, Nov. 6, 2004.

Hannah, John H., 64; federal judge in the Eastern District of Texas; raised in Diboll; served in Legislature where he was member of the Dirty Thirty; Dec. 4, 2003.

Harding, Warren G., 84; Princeton native rode presidential name to 33 years as Dallas County treasurer and state treasurer, retiring in 1983; April 2, 2005.

Hargis, Billy James, 79; Texarkana-born evangelist who founded in 1950 the anti-communist Christian Crusade; Nov. 27, 2004.

Harris, Ruth R., 84; longtime employee of The Dallas Morning News; worked on Texas Almanac from 1941 to 1986 where she was associate editor; Aug. 13, 2004.

Harrison, Ivan Elton "Sonny," 85; Naples native was an amateur radio operator who built the first Carterfone, the precursor to the computer modem; in Wimberley, April 22, 2005.

Herrera, Johnny, 73; Lower Valley native was Tejano songwriter of the 1940s–50s; his songs included "La Tracalera" covered by Selena; Sept. 10, 2003.

Herring, Charles F. Sr., 89; Waco native was former federal prosecutor and state senator 1956–73 from Central Texas; in Austin, Jan.

15, 2004.

Hopps, Walter, 72; founding director of Houston's Menil Collection; also served as curator of 20th century art for the Smithsonian Institution; lived in Houston and Los Angeles; March 20, 2005.

Hovis, Larry, 67; actor best known as Sgt. Carter on Hogan's Heros; lecturer in theater at Texas State University–San Marcos since 1990; Sept. 9, 2003.

Jackson, Gordon Dealey, 85; next-to-last surviving grandson of G.B. Dealey, who was co-founder of The Dallas Morning News; worked in water resource management; Nov. 26, 2004.

Jamail, Jeffrey G. "Jeff," 52; known as the face of Jamail's grocery, which was Houston's premier purveyor of fine food; his grandfather Najeeb "Jim" Jamail, a Lebanese immigrant, began the grocery business in 1907; May 23, 2004, from a heart attack.

Jennings, James, 71; stadium voice of the Dallas Cowboys for 22 years until 1989; also announced at the Mesquite rodeo; served three terms on the Dallas school board in the 1970s; Dec. 2, 2004.

Johnson, James L. "Rocky," 77; Vernon native was CEO of GTE Corp. in 1991 when he brought the domestic headquarters of the company (now Verizon) to North Texas; in Irving, Nov. 18, 2004.

Jurow, Martin, 92; a Dallas resident since 1971, he was a vital force on Broadway and in Hollywood; produced classics including Breakfast at Tiffany's; in Dallas, Feb. 12, 2004.

Kilby, Jack St. Clair, 81; the Nobel laureate and longtime engineer at Texas Instruments whose 1958 invention of the integrated circuit made possible the microprocessor and ushered in the electroics age; in Dallas, June 20, 2005.

Korioth, Tony, 71; legislator from Sherman brought successful "one man, one vote" lawsuit in the 1960s, which challenged districting that concentrated power in rural areas; in Austin, May 29, 2004.

Leddy, James, 66; legendary Abilene bootmaker whose exotic leathers of snake and ostrich drew many famed customers from George Jones to Jane Seymour; Sept. 30, 2003.

LeDoux, Chris, 56; country singer-songwriter; raised in Austin, former rodeo champion had hit duet, "Whatcha Gonna Do With a Cowboy," with Garth Brooks in 1992; March 9, 2005, from cancer.

Lee, Amy Freeman, 89; painter, author, art critic and art patron in San Antonio; headed board of trustees at the University of the Incarnate Word 1973–1990; July 20, 2004.

Lezar, Harold J. "Tex" Jr., 55; member of the staffs of Presidents Nixon and Reagan, assistant to William F. Buckley; ran unsuccessfuly for lieutenant govenor in 1994; Jan. 5, 2004, of a heart attack at his Dallas home.

Ling, James J., 81; pioneer of the modern-day conglomerate, tycoon of LTV Corp., which helped propel Dallas into world financial spotlight in 1960s; Dec. 17, 2004.

Look, G.D. Sonny, 84; legendary Houston restaurateur whose Sir-Loin House and Inn were noted steak houses from 1959-1991; active supporer of Houston rodeo; in Houston, Dec. 29, 2003.

Lopez, Isidro, 75; saxophonist and singer from Alice who combined conjunto with Orquesta to forge Tejano music in 1940s–60s; half Apache, his nickname was "El Indio"; in Corpus Christi, Aug. 16, 2004.

Love, Jim, 77; Houston sculptor born in Amarillo; highly visible works include *Portable Trojan Bear* in Houston's Hermann Park; May 10, 2005.

Lyle, John Emmett, 93; former legislator and congressman from Corpus Christi during the 1940s–50s; Nov. 11, 2003.

MacEoin, Gary, 94; San Antonio resident and writer known internationally for his reporting on Latin America and the Roman Catholic Church; U.N. representative for the International Catholic Press Union 1954–63; July 9, 2003.

Marsh, Estelle Fariss, 90; Amarillo philanthropist who married Stanley Marsh Jr. in 1936; active in city's charities; in Amarillo, Sept. 15, 2003.

Martinez, Matt, 86; owner of Austin's popular El Rancho restaurant, which he opened in 1952; was Texas Golden Gloves boxing champion in 1937; in Austin, Nov. 27, 2003.

Mayes, Charlotte, 56; Dallas political leader; served four terms on the city council; of leukemia, Feb. 25, 2004.

McCall, David B. Jr., 79; called Mr. Plano, he helped transform a small farm community into a massive suburb; served as mayor in 1950s; Feb. 17, 2004.

McKnight, Felix R., 93; considered by many the dean of Dallas newspaper journalism, held key management positions at *The Dallas Morning News* and the *Dallas Times Herald*; Feb. 7, 2004.

Miller, Ann, 81; Chireno native became the glamorous tapdancer in Hollywood's golden age of musicals; performed on Broadway in *Sugar Babies* in 1979; from 1958–61 was married to Dallas oilman William Moss; Jan. 22, 2004.

Mitchan, Junior, 72; Corpus Christi native was bass player and vocalist with pioneers of western swing, Bob Wills and Adolph Hofner; Jan. 3, 2005.

Moreno, Joe, 40; legislator from Houston killed in auto crash near La Grange; Democrat had been state representative since 1998; May 6, 2005.

Morgan, Grant B., 83; started Big Tex Western Wear in San Antonio, which was later joined by branches in Houston, Austin and San Marcos; Dec. 8, 2004.

Morton, Azie Taylor, 67; only African-American to serve as U.S. treasurer 1977–1980; civil rights activist in Austin in 1960s; in Bastrop, Dec. 7, 2003.

Mueller, Marge, 69; called "Sheriff," for three decades she served beer and kept order in Luckenbach; in Fredericksburg, July 25, 2004.

Oates, Johnny, 58; baseball manager who guided Texas Rangers to three play-off berths; Dec. 24, 2004, from a brain tumor.

Onstead, Robert, 73; Houston businessman raised in Ennis, co-founder and longtime president of Randalls Food Markets, which grew to 114 stores in the late 1990s; Aug. 4, 2004.

Palmer, Lester E., 94; former Austin city council member and mayor who in the 1960s pushed construction of MoPac Boulevard, Loop 1, a major city thoroughfare; in Austin, Sept. 21, 2003.

Pennington, Mel, 69; a fixture on Austin television and radio beginning in 1965 as sportscaster and talk show host; in Austin, Aug. 4, 2003.

Peterson, Ray, 65; Denton-born singer was billed as "the Golden Voice of Rock 'n' Roll; had hits "Tell Laura I Love Her"; and "The Wonder of You" in 1950s–60s; Jan. 25, 2005.

Petty, Opal, 86; raised in Goldthwaite, she won landmark case against the state in 1989 for being wrongly confined in mental institu-

Left, oilfield firefigher Red Adair.

Above, country singer-songwriter Chris LeDoux.

Right, dancer and Chireno native Ann Miller cuts up with Debbie Reynolds.

File photos.

tions for 51 years; lived out the last 19 years of her life with her nephew's family in Christoval, March 10, 2005.

Pickle, J.J. "Jake," 91; represented Central Texas in Congress for 31 years, retiring in 1995; Roscoe native grew up in Big Spring; was young protégé of Lyndon Johnson; in Austin, June 18, 2005.

Pinkston, David "Pappy Dave Stone," 90; Post native launched KDAV in 1953 in Lubbock, one of the first full-time country music stations; employed Waylon Jennings as a disc jockey; Feb. 18, 2004.

Price, Robert D. "Bob," 76; Pampa rancher was former state senator; represented part of the Panhandle in Congress from 1966–74; Aug. 24, 2004.

Proffitt, Tony, 61; political strategist and adviser to Bob Bullock, Bill Clements and Jake Pickle; Liberty Hill resident also worked on the Jimmy Carter presidential campaign in 1976; Oct. 17, 2004.

Reeves, Connie, 101; Eagle Pass native, cowgirl who taught more than 30,000 girls to ride horses at Camp Waldemar near Hunt; retired at 80 but continued to teach at the camp; in San Antonio, Aug. 17, 2003, two weeks after a fall from her horse.

Richter, Walter H., 86; Marble Falls native served in the state Senate 1963–65 and on several state boards; in Austin, Sept. 8, 2003.

Riddle, Ned, 81; former *Dallas Morning News* artist who drew the syndicated cartoon *Mr. Tweedy*; in Dallas, Oct. 13, 2003.

Roddy, Rod, 66; Fort Worth native who was the voice of television's *The Price is Right*, where he invited contestants to "Come on down!"; worked in radio in Dallas-Fort Worth before going to Hollywood; Oct. 27, 2003.

Roegelein, William Jr., 82; San Antonio businessman who lead the family processed-meat business, founded in 1905, which became one of the largest in the state; Jan. 24, 2004.

Rogers, N.J. "Nate," 87; optometrist who in the 1930s co-founded Texas State Optical in Beaumont along with three brothers; served on the Texas Optometry Board; Dec. 11, 2003.

Rudder, Margaret, 87; called the First Lady of Texas A&M; Sonora native was wife of the university's best-known president, Gen. James Earl Rudder, who served from 1959–70; in Bryan, March 3, 2004.

Runyon, Marvin, 79; raised in Dallas; U.S. postmaster general 1992–98; chairman of TVA under President Reagan; executive for Ford Motors and Nissan; May 3, 2004.

Rush, E.F. "Frank," 89; beginning in 1971, developed Sandy Lake Amusement Park in Carrollton, which became a regional institution known to band students in five states for its competitions; Jan. 5, 2005.

Scoggins, Jerry, 93; Mount Pleasant native who sang the theme song "The Ballad of Jed Clampett" for *The Beverly Hillbillies*; got his start in Dallas radio in the 1930s; Dec. 7, 2004.

Sears, Barbra Pace, 71; secretary to Martin Luther King Jr. at the Southern Christian Leadership Conference; later served as urban planner and community affairs manager for Fort Worth; March 5, 2005.

Semos, Chris, 68; served 16 years in the Legislature and 12 years as a Dallas County commissioner; active in the Dallas Greek community; June 14, 2004.

Seybold, William D., 89; physician who with Dr. Marvin Kelsey founded in 1951 a Houston clinic as the first multi-specialty physician group; Kelsey-Seybold now has 21 clinics; in Dallas, July 19, 2004.

Shoemaker, Bill, 72; Fabens native whose 41-year career as a jockey included winning four Kentucky Derbies; worked on his grandfather's ranch near Abilene before moving to Los Angeles; Oct. 12, 2003.

Simmons, William F. "Bill," 80; longtime keyboard player for the Light Crust Doughboys; veteran Western swing musician won a Grammy Award in 2003; in Irving, Jan 24, 2005.

Smith, Preston, 91; Texas governor 1969–73 known for his focus on higher education and work for Texas Tech University; plain-spoken son of poor tenant farmer who went on to own movie theaters in West Texas; created the Texas Film Commission; was in the Legislature beginning in 1944; served three terms as lieutenant governor 1962-68; in Lubbock, Oct. 18, 2003.

Smothers, Clay, 69; black conservative legislator who switched parties twice in the 1970s; ran unsuccessfully for Congress as a Republican in 1980; in Fort Worth, June 11, 2004.

Sullivan, Niki, 66; raised in Lubbock; played guitar with Buddy Holly and the Crickets during their climb to stardom in 1957; April 6, 2004.

Supple, Jerome, 67; president of Texas State University–San Marcos 1989-2002, where he increased admission standards, research funding and the university endowment; Jan. 16, 2004.

Tillman, Floyd, 88; raised in Post, began playing guitar with Adolph Hofner; went on to write crossover county-to-pop hits such as " Slipping Around" and "It Makes No Difference Now"; at his Houston area home, Aug. 22, 2003.

Tinsley, Jack, 69; guided the *Fort Worth Star-Telegram* to two Pulitzer Prizes as executive editor, retiring in 2000; started as reporter there in 1959; in Fort Worth, Oct. 12, 2004.

Vandiver, Frank E., 79; military historian who served as president of Texas A&M University 1981–88; also was president of the University of North Texas 1979–81 and acting president of Rice University 1968–70; in College Station, Jan. 7, 2005.

Vela, Filemon, 68; federal judge since 1980; was member of South Texas family with roots to mid-1700s; in Harlingen, April 13, 2004.

Wacker, Jim, 66; colorful former football coach at Texas Christian University and Southwest Texas State University; in San Marcos, Aug. 26, 2003.

Wenglein, George Herman, 88; CEO and chairman of Luby's Cafeterias 1972-88 when company made Forbes list of 200 Best Small Companies; in San Antonio, April 12, 2005.

Williams, Helen White, 81; Manor native was, along with her husband Eugene, longtime personal assistant in the Lyndon Johnson household beginning in 1950 and until President Johnson left the White House in 1969; Johnson, in his memoirs, wrote that his discovery of what the Williamses faced every time they drove back to Texas was an awakening to the indignity of discrimination against blacks; Feb. 25, 2005.

Willingham, Noble, 72; Mineola native was character actor best-known for role as lawman C.D. Parker on th long-running *Walker, Texas Ranger* series; ran unsuccessfully for Congress from East Texas in 2000; Jan. 17, 2004.

Wilson, Glen Parten Jr., 82; aeronautical engineer who helped create NASA; Waco native earlier was assistant to then Sen. Lyndon Johnson; in Fort Worth, Jan. 8, 2005.

Wood, Gordon, 89; second-winningest coach in Texas high school football history, mostly in Brownwood where he won seven titles; Dec. 17, 2003.

Zale, Stanley, 71; executive in the family jewelry business, civic leader was founder of the Autistic Society of Dallas and president of the Northeast Texas Chapter of the Cystic Fibrosis Foundation; Jan. 17, 2004. ☆

2004.

Advertisers' Index

General Index

Page numbers in *italics* refer to photographs, illustrations and maps. **Bold face** page numbers indicate major discussions of the topic. For cities and towns not listed in the index, see lists of towns on pp. 340–364 and pp. 453–464. Also see the "Cities and Towns" tabbed section.

For CITIES and TOWNS not listed in the index, see complete list of towns on pages 340–364.

For CITIES and TOWNS not listed in the index, see complete list of towns on pages 340–364.

For CITIES and TOWNS not listed in the index, see complete list of towns on pages 340–364.

For CITIES and TOWNS not listed in the index, see complete list of towns on pages 340–364.

For CITIES and TOWNS not listed in the index, see complete list of towns on pages 340–364.

For CITIES and TOWNS not listed in the index, see complete list of towns on pages 340–364.

For CITIES and TOWNS not listed in the index, see complete list of towns on pages 340–364.

For CITIES and TOWNS not listed in the index, see complete list of towns on pages 340–364.

For CITIES and TOWNS not listed in the index, see complete list of towns on pages 340–364.

For CITIES and TOWNS not listed in the index, see complete list of towns on pages 340–364.

For CITIES and TOWNS not listed in the index, see complete list of towns on pages 340–364.

For CITIES and TOWNS not listed in the index, see complete list of towns on pages 340–364.

For CITIES and TOWNS not listed in the index, see complete list of towns on pages 340–364.

For CITIES and TOWNS not listed in the index, see complete list of towns on pages 340–364.

For CITIES and TOWNS not listed in the index, see complete list of towns on pages 340–364.

For CITIES and TOWNS not listed in the index, see complete list of towns on pages 340–364.

For CITIES and TOWNS not listed in the index, see complete list of towns on pages 340–364.

For CITIES and TOWNS not listed in the index, see complete list of towns on pages 340–364.

For **CITIES and TOWNS** not listed in the index, see complete list of towns on pages 340–364.